C4

BENSON and HEDGES Golfer's Handbook 1987

Eighty-fourth year of publication

Editor Laurence Viney
Associate Editor Bernard Gallacher

MACMILLAN
PRESS

This edition published 1987 by
MACMILLAN PRESS LIMITED
4 Little Essex Street London WC2R 3LF
and Basingstoke

British Library Cataloguing in Publication Data

Benson and Hedges golfer's handbook.——1987–
1. Golf——Periodicals
796.352'05 GV961

ISBN 0-333-41726-7
ISBN 0-333-41727-5 Pbk

Note

Whilst every care has been taken in compiling the information contained in this book, the Publishers, Editors and Sponsors accept no responsibility for any errors or omissions.

Correspondence

Letters on editorial matters should be addressed to:

The Editor, Benson & Hedges Golfer's Handbook
Macmillan Press Limited
4 Little Essex Street
London WC2R 3LF

Enquiries about despatch, invoicing and commercial matters should be addressed to:

Customer Services Department
Macmillan Press Limited
Houndmills
Basingstoke
Hampshire RG21 2XS

Advertising

Enquiries about advertising space in this book should be addressed to:
Communications Management International
Chiltern House
120 Eskdale Avenue
Chesham
Buckinghamshire HP5 3BD

Illustrations for Centenary Clubs reproduced by kind permission of the Clubs; illustrations for *With the BBC at the Open* reproduced with the permission of the BBC

Consultant editor Klaus Boehm

Designed by Bruce Porteous

Maps by Pete Ferris (colour), Hilary Evans (black and white)

Typeset by Bell and Bain Limited, Glasgow

Printed and bound in Great Britain by The Bath Press Ltd, Bath

Contents

The Burberry Look

Photographed at The Royal Blackheath Golf Club.

The additions to the Burberry range of new golf accessories. Red golfbags and hold-alls trimmed with the New Navy Blue Check. Featuring skirts and trousers, sports shirts, knitwear, and golfing shoes for men and women. For further information contact: The Wholesale Showroom, Burberrys Limited, 165 Regent Street, London W1R 8AS. Telephone: 01-734 5929.

'Burberry' and 'Burberrys' and the device of an Equestrian Knight in armour are the registered trade marks of Burberrys Limited, London. The New Navy Check D110/8 is a registered design of Burberrys Limited in the U.K. (No: 513563) and other major countries.

Foreword

In recent years, the changes in presenting information in the *Golfer's Handbook* have been favourably received by readers. The vast amount of information available meai constantly balancing leaving something out against including new material to produce a book that is not too large to handle easily. The aim is to give all the information required readily to hand, whether for Club Secretary, Golf Administrator or average golfer. For instance, if the results of all open competitions and tournaments which might merit inclusion are added the number of pages would be greatly increased. As it is no competition played under handicap is listed, with three small exceptions.

A privilege that is much appreciated by the *Golfer's Handbook* is the permission from the Royal and Ancient General Committee to publish the *Rules of Golf* and to include for the first time this year, the *Statement of Functions*. A short account of how the Club came to be the Governing Body of the game is also included to show clearly the Club's world-wide responsibilities to the game.

1986 was a year to remember, especially for Greg Norman, Jack Nicklaus, Seve Ballesteros and Bob Tway, to name only a few. But it may be that they, like many others, are unaware of the best performance by British golfers. In August at Prairie Dunes, Kansas, the success of the Curtis Cup Team captained by Diane Bailey, must rate as the outstanding result of 1986. It was the first victory ever by a British team against the United States on their home ground; the decisive 13-5 to Great Britain and Ireland was the most remarkable result for Britain since 1970 when Tony Jacklin won the US Open Championship at Chaska, Minnesota. Michael Williams reports this event in Part I.

It is a pity that match-play, which some consider old-fashioned, has less TV appeal than stroke-play, although it is encouraging that this year the BBC will cover the Walker Cup at Sunningdale in May. While playing a medal round is a good discipline for Club golfers to improve their skill, the cut and thrust of a match can be more enjoyable.

Similarly some regret the demise of foursomes in Club games in favour of the 4-ball. Often those who decry the alternate shot game have rarely played it and are unaware of how enjoyable it can be. They feel they must play their own ball to ensure full value for their round or they are nervous of letting the partner down. For enjoyment, and incidentally a much faster round, foursomes are worth a try especially on cold winter mornings. In contrast to the disappearance of men's foursomes at many clubs (a few still positively discourage 4-balls), the Sunday afternoon mixed-foursome is enjoyed by many couples at clubs all over the country.

The Club golfer with his week-end round is in a world far apart from the professional player who, from April to November, has a weekly crack at the European tour prizes which are likely to total about £7,000,000 in 1987. Some query whether the drive, flair and efficiency of Ken Schofield and his team of European tour managers will be matched by the dedication of some of his tournament players. The all-exempt provision and annual Qualifying School at La Manga help to sort out those with the ability and strength of mind required for the constant play and travel which touring demands. But having qualified, is there sufficient dedication to improve standards if one can earn over £30,000 by finishing about 40th in the Order of Merit Table? Yet the vast gap between the tour leaders and their less successful colleagues means those at the lower end who may not be sponsored, will be struggling to make ends meet as well as to finish among the top 125 in the Order of Merit to guarantee their place for the following year. It can be fine at the top, but so depressing at the other end of the Table.

Television has been a great service to golf with the BBC presentations acknowledged as the World's best. What goes on behind the scenes for our enjoyment is well described by Bruce Critchley in Part I. Unfortunately, it is probably TV which has unwittingly introduced that unruly element among spectators, whose attitude and behaviour can spoil the enjoyment of the majority. Greg Norman had good reason to criticise openly the partisan attitude of a small part of the Wentworth crowd who applauded when he missed putts or bunkered an approach. Much can be learnt from the players themselves in the way defeat is accepted, with admirable self-control whatever their feelings may be. But most golf crowds are orderly and the volunteer stewards, by raising a small board inscribed with *Quiet Please* nearly always produce the required effect immediately which will last until the stoke has been played.

Another new feature covers those Clubs, some 16 in all, which are celebrating their centenaries in 1987. (Pages 36–45 contain an illustration and short description of each Club.) A few clubs, including one in Scotland are much older; witness the Crail Golfing Society and the Glasgow Club at Killermont which have achieved 200 years in 1986 and 1987 respectively.

The Editor and Publishers congratulate each of these Clubs, and as they celebrate their centenaries in their own way we wish them a thriving future and look forward to more clubs achieving this.

Laurence Viney
Berkhamsted, January 1987

The Televised Tournaments 1987

The twelve Tournaments listed below will be shown on television. All but the Carrolls Irish and Bell's Scottish Opens will be on the BBC, the other two being respectively on Irish and Scottish Television. Maps of nine courses, designed to help viewers follow the play, are shown in this section.

On the maps, holes have been treated individually to give as clear a pictorial representation as possible; this means, however, that each hole is not necessarily to scale with its neighbours. Rather than following the actual north–south layout of the courses, most holes are represented as they will appear to the viewer—in other words, as if seen from high-up behind the tee.

Users should also note that at Woburn the holes on the course have been re-numbered as shown and that at Walton Heath the Championship course is an amalgamation of holes on the Old and New courses.

Date	Tournament	Course
7–10 May	Epson Grand Prix of Europe	St Pierre, Chepstow
22–25 May	Whyte & McKay PGA Championship	Wentworth, Surrey
27–28 May	Walker Cup	Sunningdale
4–7 June	Dunhill British Masters	Woburn, Bedfordshire
2–5 July	Carrolls Irish Open	Portmarnock, Co. Dublin
8–11 July	Bell's Scottish Open	Gleneagles, Perthshire
16–19 July	Open Championship	Muirfield, East Lothian
13–16 August	Benson & Hedges International	Fulford, York
10–13 Sept	Panasonic European Open	Walton Heath, Surrey
24–27 Sept	Ryder Cup	Muirfield Village, Ohio, USA
1–4 Oct	Dunhill Cup	St Andrews, Fife
15–18 Oct	Suntory World Match-Play	Wentworth, Surrey

St Pierre Course

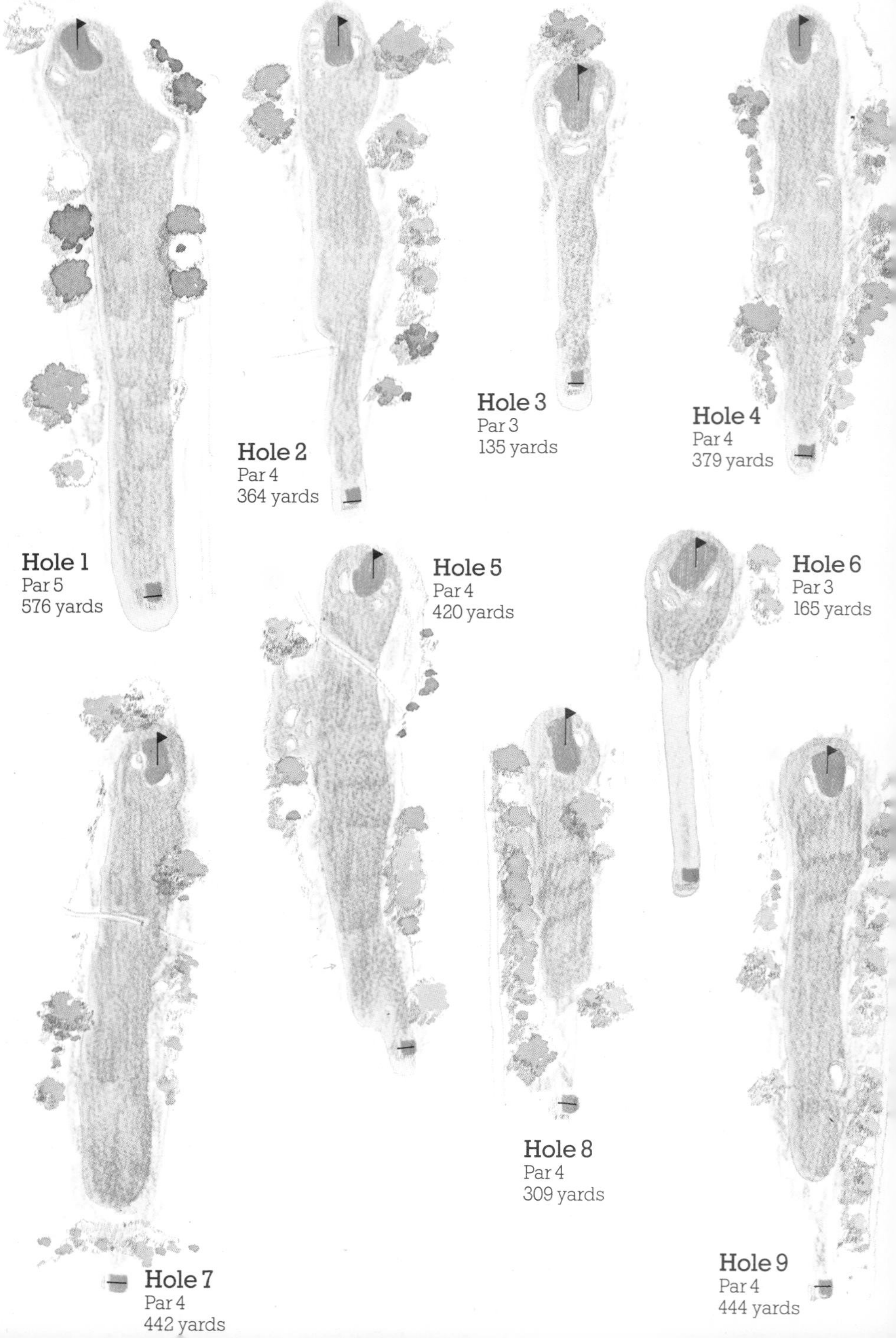

Hole 1
Par 5
576 yards

Hole 2
Par 4
364 yards

Hole 3
Par 3
135 yards

Hole 4
Par 4
379 yards

Hole 5
Par 4
420 yards

Hole 6
Par 3
165 yards

Hole 7
Par 4
442 yards

Hole 8
Par 4
309 yards

Hole 9
Par 4
444 yards

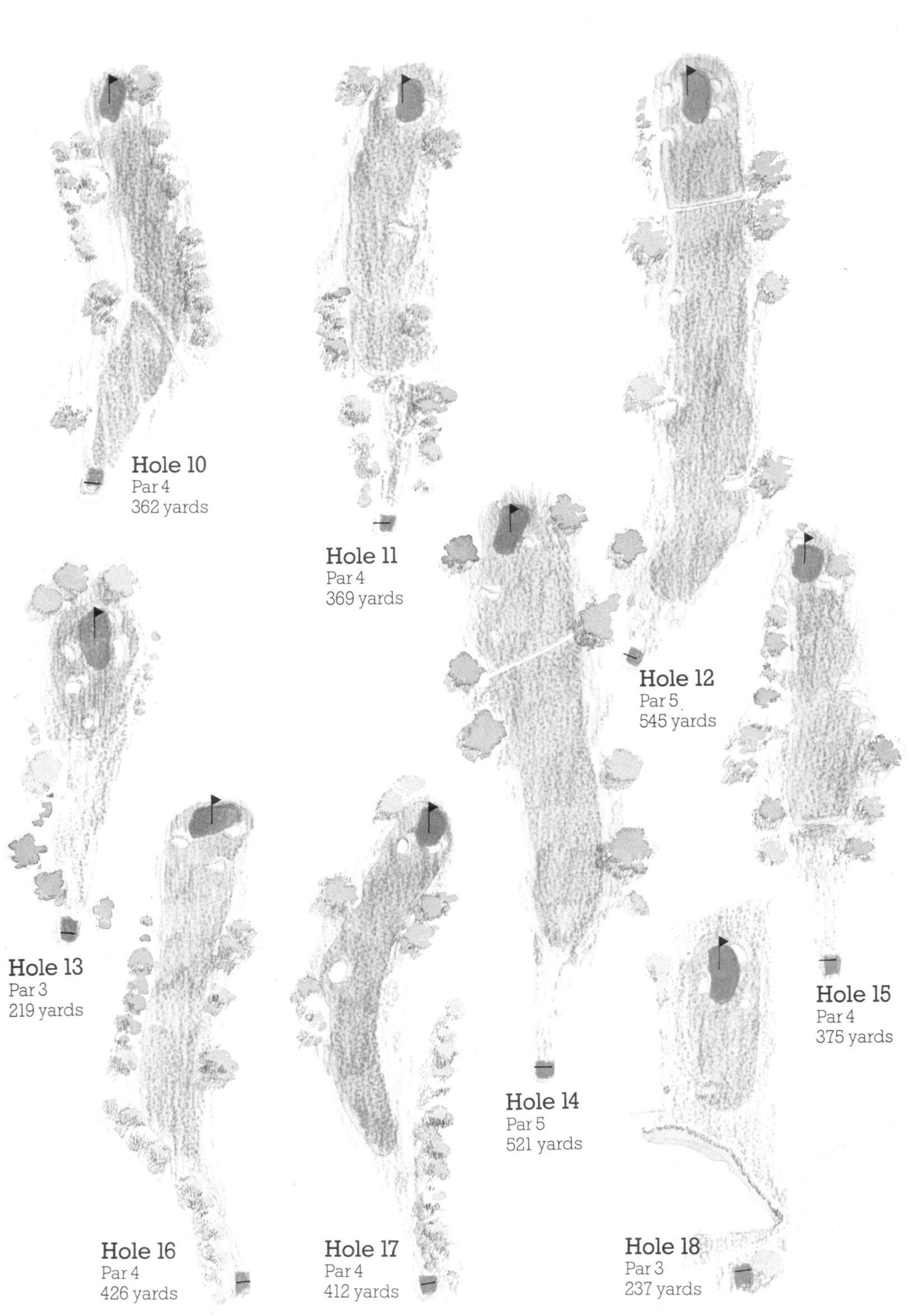
Hole 10
Par 4
362 yards
Hole 11
Par 4
369 yards
Hole 12
Par 5
545 yards
Hole 13
Par 3
219 yards
Hole 14
Par 5
521 yards
Hole 15
Par 4
375 yards
Hole 16
Par 4
426 yards
Hole 17
Par 4
412 yards
Hole 18
Par 3
237 yards

Golfing Hotel Compendium

This year the Golfing Hotel Compendium *has been enlarged, and is now established as a major source of information for golfers wishing to find the most comfortable place to stay at or close to some of the finest golf courses in the country. This section has been compiled from the premier hotels of the British Isles which include golf among their major attractions.*

If a reader wishes to especially recommend an establishment which is not currently listed in this edition of the Benson and Hedges Golfer's Handbook *the editors will be happy to be advised.*

England: South-west

Beaufort Hotel

Torrs Park, Ilfracombe, Devon EX34 8AYX. *Tel* (0271) 65483

Ilfracombe's foremost golfing hotel. Special rates for golfers, superb food, rooms and facilities. Lively bar. Parties welcome. *(See advertisement page 63 for further details.)*

Bel Alp House

Country Hotel, Haytor, Nr Bovey Tracey, South Devon. *Tel* (03646) 217

Small elegant country house in most spectacular setting providing a remarkable standard of food, comfort and hospitality. Close to many excellent South Devon golf courses.

Budock Vean Golf and Country House Hotel

Mawnan Smith, Falmouth, Cornwall TR11 5LG. *Tel* (0326) 250288

Challenging 9-hole (18 tee) private golf course set in sub-tropical grounds; free to guests. Excellent amenities, luxurious surroundings, top quality service and cuisine. *(See advertisement page 25 for further details.)*

Culloden House Hotel

Fosketh Hill, Westward Ho!, Devon EX39 1JA. *Tel* (02372) 79421

Only golfers stay at Culloden. Special 'packages' available March–October. 6 courses on the itinerary. Championship courses–Champion Holidays!

The Dormy Hotel and Leisure Club

New Road, Ferndown, Dorset BH22 8ES. *Tel* (0202) 872121

De Vere **** Hotel, adjacent to Ferndown golf course, offering sporting and leisure activities combined with a high standard of accommodation and cuisine. *(See advertisement page 21 for further details.)*

Gloucester Hotel and Country Club

Robinswood Hill, Gloucester. *Tel* (0452) 25653

Extensive golfing facilities include 18-hole par 70 course, floodlit driving range, 9-hole par 3 pitch and putt. Other leisure facilities. Luxury accommodation, excellent cuisine. *(See advertisement page 62 for further details.)*

Lee Bay Hotel

Lee, Nr Ilfracombe, North Devon EX34 8LP. *Tel* (0271) 63503

One of the west country's leading sporting hotels where all the sportsman's needs, as well as wives and families, are professionally catered for. *(See advertisement page 29 for details.)*

Wentworth Golf Club West Course

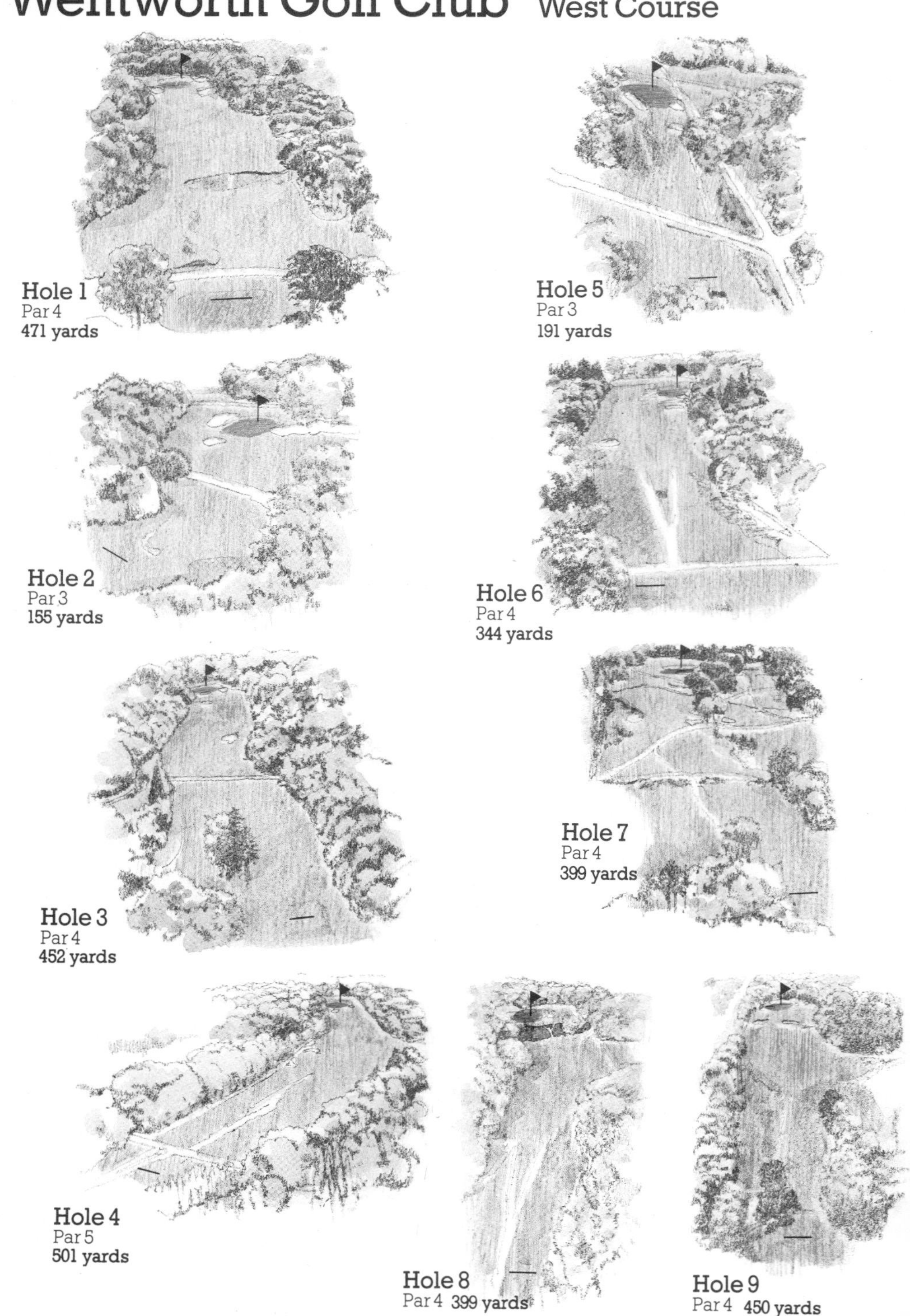

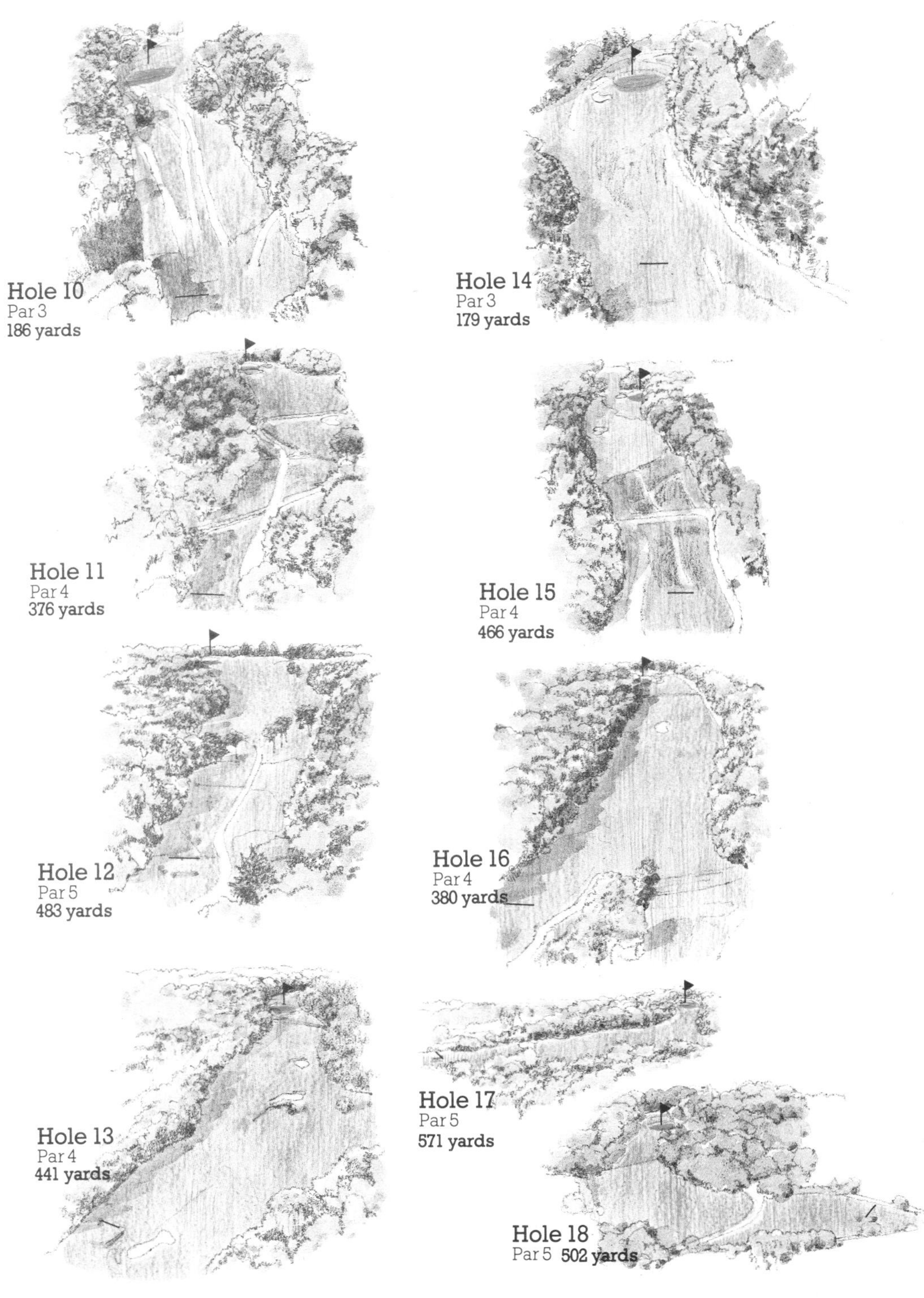
Hole 10
Par 3
186 yards
Hole 14
Par 3
179 yards
Hole 11
Par 4
376 yards
Hole 15
Par 4
466 yards
Hole 12
Par 5
483 yards
Hole 16
Par 4
380 yards
Hole 13
Par 4
441 yards
Hole 17
Par 5
571 yards
Hole 18
Par 5 502 yards

Owlpen Manor
Owlpen, Dursley, Gloucester GL11 5BZ. *Tel* (0453) 860261 *Tx* 43690
Nine special self-catering cottages in medieval Cotswold hamlet. Historic listed buildings sleep 2–10 with first class hotel comfort. Take-away wine/food. Six superb courses within 20 minutes.

St Mellion Hotel
St Mellion Golf and Country Club, St Mellion, Saltash, Cornwall PL12 6SD. *Tel* (0579) 50101
Modern Hotel situated next to the St Mellion complex—24 rooms—AA and RAC ***. Two golf courses (The Nicklaus and The Old), tennis, indoor swimming pool, squash and badminton courts.

Whitsand Bay Hotel Golf and Country Club
Portwrinkle (BH), By Torpoint, Cornwall PL11 3BU. *Tel* (0503) 30276
18-hole seaside course in dramatic setting. Nationally-known teaching professional. Four other courses nearby. Indoor heated pools, leisure complex, sauna, solarium. Golf competitions. Societies welcomed.

England: South-east

Ashdown Forest Hotel
Chapel Lane, Forest Row, East Sussex. *Tel* Forest Row 4866
With its own 18-hole golf course, this hotel is ideal for Golf Breaks and Society Days. Superb cuisine, warm and friendly welcome. Resident proprietors.

Bedford Arms Thistle Hotel
Chenies, Nr Rickmansworth, Hertfordshire WD3 6EQ. *Tel* (09278) 3301
Easily accessible West M40, North M1 standing on M25. Country house offering 10 deluxe bedrooms with all comfort. Egon Ronay recommended special rate at weekends. *(See advertisement page 29 for further details.)*

Cambridgeshire Moat House
Bar Hill, Cambridge CB3 8EU. *Tel* (0954) 80555
Free golf and other sports facilities available to residents of this first class hotel and sports complex 5 miles from Cambridge. Resident Pro G Huggett, sports shop, tuition, special rates available, 18-hole course. Golf Societies welcome.

Evergreens Hotel
Romsey Road, Lyndhurst, New Forest, Hampshire SO43 7AR. *Tel* (042128) 2175
Owner operated Hotel. Austrian Chef proprietor, super food, very friendly. In the heart of the New Forest golfing country. See you at the 19th. *(See advertisement page 62 for further details.)*

Links Country Park Hotel
West Runton, Cromer, Norfolk NR27 9QH. *Tel* West Runton 691
A late Victorian Hotel recently modernised, own 9-hole golf course opening Winter 1986/7 indoor heated pool, sauna, solarium. 600 yards from Safe Sandy Beach. *(See advertisement page 874 for further details.)*

Selsdon Park Hotel
Addington Road, Sanderstead, Croydon, Surrey CR2 8YA. *Tel* 01-657 8811
Traditional country house set in 200 acres of parkland with 18-hole championship course and residents' exclusive tropical leisure complex. *(See advertisement page 873 for details.)*

Westwood Country Hotel
Wirksey Hill Top, Oxford OX1 5BG. *Tel* (0865) 735408
Frilford Heath, North Oxford and Southfield Golf Courses are within 5 miles of the Hotel other amenities close by are squash, tennis and sailing. ETB 4 crowns.

England: Midlands

The Belfry
Wishaw, North Warwickshire B76 9PR. *Tel* (0675) 70301
Set in 370 acres of parkland, the championship Brabazon course, venue of the 1985 and 1989 Ryder Cup, par 73, and easier Derby course, par 70. Green Fees Derby Weekday £8 Weekend £10 and Brabazon Weekday £15 and Weekend £17. **** Hotel on site.

The Cedars Hotel
Cedar Road, Loughborough, Leicestershire LE11 2AB. *Tel* (0509) 214459
37 bedrooms with *en suite* facilities. Colour TV, radio, telephones. Outdoor heated swimming pool, sauna and solarium. 6 golf courses within easy reach. RAC and AA***

Moortown Golf Club

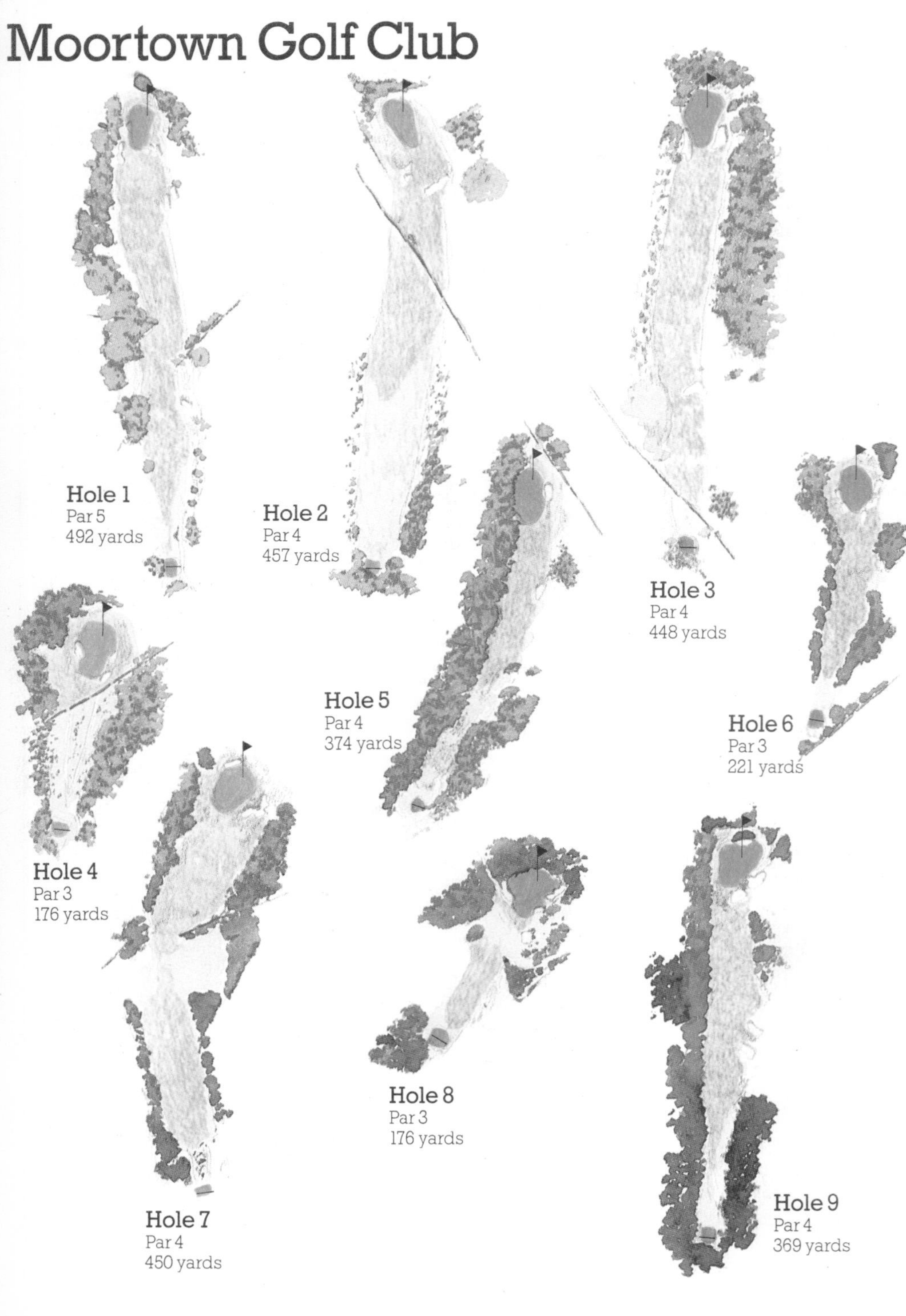

Hole 1
Par 5
492 yards
Hole 2
Par 4
457 yards
Hole 3
Par 4
448 yards
Hole 4
Par 3
176 yards
Hole 5
Par 4
374 yards
Hole 6
Par 3
221 yards
Hole 7
Par 4
450 yards
Hole 8
Par 3
176 yards
Hole 9
Par 4
369 yards

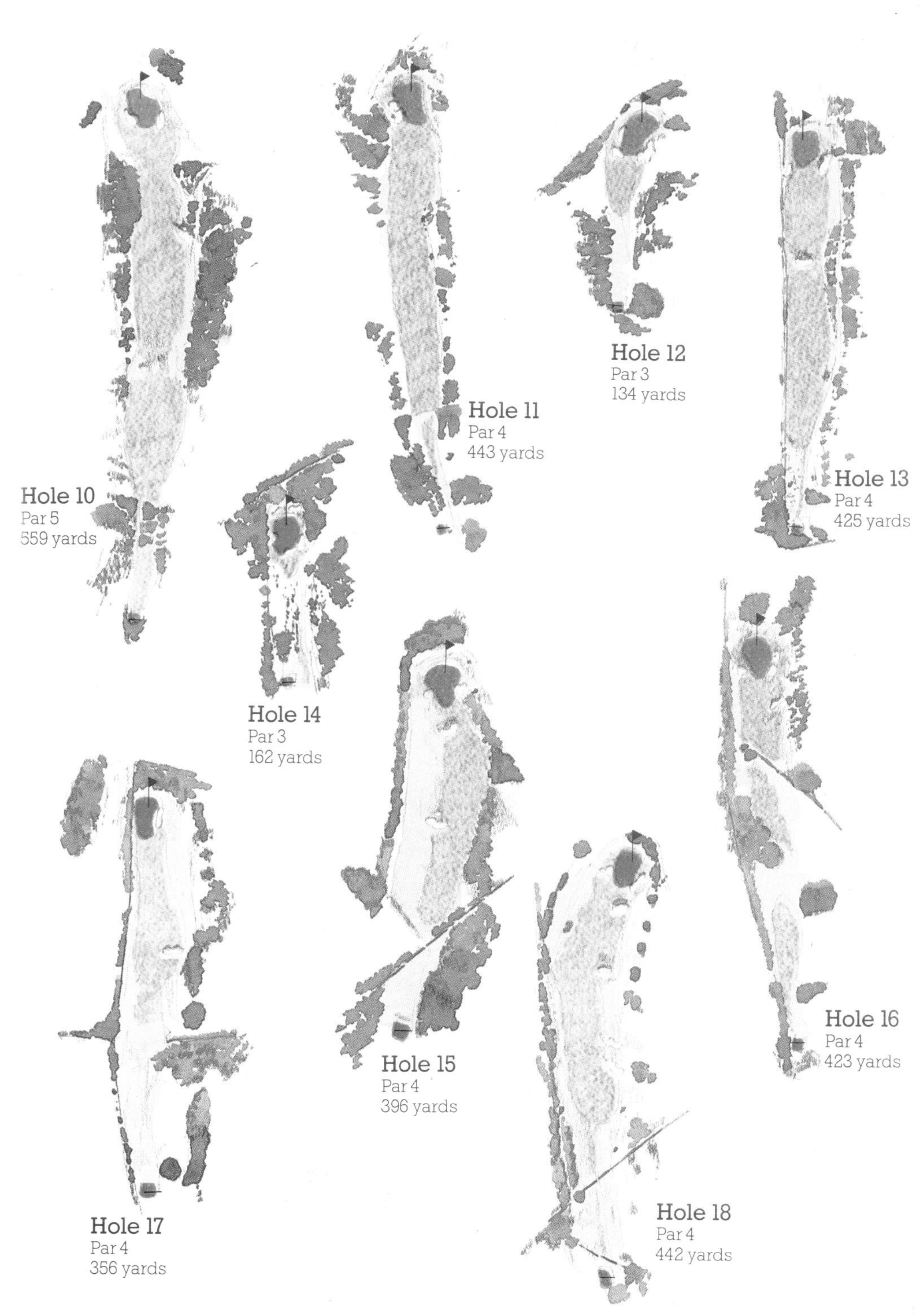
Hole 10
Par 5
559 yards
Hole 11
Par 4
443 yards
Hole 12
Par 3
134 yards
Hole 13
Par 4
425 yards
Hole 14
Par 3
162 yards
Hole 15
Par 4
396 yards
Hole 16
Par 4
423 yards
Hole 17
Par 4
356 yards
Hole 18
Par 4
442 yards

Dower House Hotel

The Manor Estate, Woodhall Spa, Lincolnshire. *Tel* (0526) 52588

Situated adjacent to the golf course. Ideal for individual golfers and small parties. The hotel is under the personal management of the proprietors.

Hawkstone Park Hotel

Weston-under-Redcastle, Shrewsbury, Shropshire SY4 5UY. *Tel* (093924) 611

Two superb 18-hole courses: the Hawkstone, one of the most picturesque inland courses, and the newer, more open, Weston Course. *(See advertisement page 874 for further details.)*

North Shore Hotel

North Shore Road, Skegness, Lincolnshire PE25 1DN. *Tel* (0754) 3298

The hotel is the 19th and is on the golf course, so we are the natural choice for the golfer who likes good food, friendly service and value for money.

Patshull Park Hotel

Pattingham, Shropshire WV6 7NR. *Tel* (0902) 700100

Own 18-hole course laid out in exquisite grounds of former Earl of Dartmouth estate providing enjoyable golf in idyllic lakeside setting with beautiful trees. *(See advertisement page 874 for further details.)*

Peterborough Moat House

Thorpe Wood, Peterborough PE3 6SG. *Tel* (0733) 260000

Hotel adjacent to golf course. 100 luxury bedrooms, all bathrooms *en suite*, colour TV, etc. Special weekend rates. Ring Peterborough (0733) 260000 for brochure.

Tewkesbury Park Hotel Golf and Country Club

Lincoln Green Lane, Tewkesbury, Gloucester GL20 7DN. *Tel* (0684) 295405

This 80-bedroom hotel with modern facilities, surrounded by an 18-hole course combined squash, heated pool, sauna and whirlpool.

Titchwell Manor Hotel

Titchwell, Kings Lynn, Norfolk PE31 8BB. *Tel* (0485) 210221

Charming family owned country house Hotel noted for fine local food and comfort. Within easy reach of Brancaster, Hunstanton, Kings Lynn, Sherringham and Cromer golf courses.

Welcombe Hotel and Golf Course

Warwick Road, Stratford-upon-Avon, Warwickshire CV37 0NR. *Tel* (0789) 295252

A 4-star Jacobean style mansion set within its own 6,202 yards golf course and 150 acres of parkland. Special packages available on request.

England: North

The Dormy House

Royal Lytham & St Anne's Golf Club, Links Gate, Lytham St Anne's, Lancashire FY8 3LQ. *Tel* St Anne's 724206

Ideal for small parties wishing to play the championship course. Accommodation for men only. Apply to the secretary. *(See advertisement page 21 for further details.)*

George Washington Hotel

Stone Cellar Road, Washington, Tyne and Wear NE37 1PH. *Tel* (091) 4172626

Everything for the golfer, championship course, floodlit driving range and professional. Accommodation offers every comfort. Other facilities snooker, squash and leisure club.

Golden Lion Hotel

Market Square, Ley Burn, North Yorkshire. *Tel* (0969) 22161

Set in heart of Yorkshire Dales. Easy reach of 6 good courses, a friendly coaching house. With traditional food £25.50 Dinner, bed and Breakfast. Green fees.

The Golf Hotel

Criffel Street, Silloth-on-Solway, Carlisle, Cumbria CA5 4AB. *Tel* (0965) 31438

Specialists in golfing holidays, 100 yards from popular course. Close to Lake District. 23 rooms all *en suite*. Excellent food. Brochure and details on request.

Leasowe Castle Hotel

Moreton, Wirral. *Tel* (0511606) 9191

All bedrooms have bath/shower, colour TV, trouser press, hairdryer. There are 12 golf courses in the area. Special golf-break tariff. Sea fishing. *(See advertisement page 25 for further details.)*

Metropole Hotel

3 Portland Street, Southport, Merseyside PR8 1LL. *Tel* (0704) 36836

Situated within 5 minutes of Royal Birkdale. Fully licensed, private facilities, special golf terms. Golfing proprietors can assist with golf bookings. Colour brochure.

The Schooner Hotel

Northumberland Street, Alnmouth, Northumberland NE66 2RS. *Tel* (0665) 830216

Warm, friendly old seaside village hotel. Rooms *en suite* for 40 in great comfort. Excellent food, 2 golf courses within walking distance. *(See advertisement page 62 for further details.)*

Woburn Golf and Country Club

Duke's Course

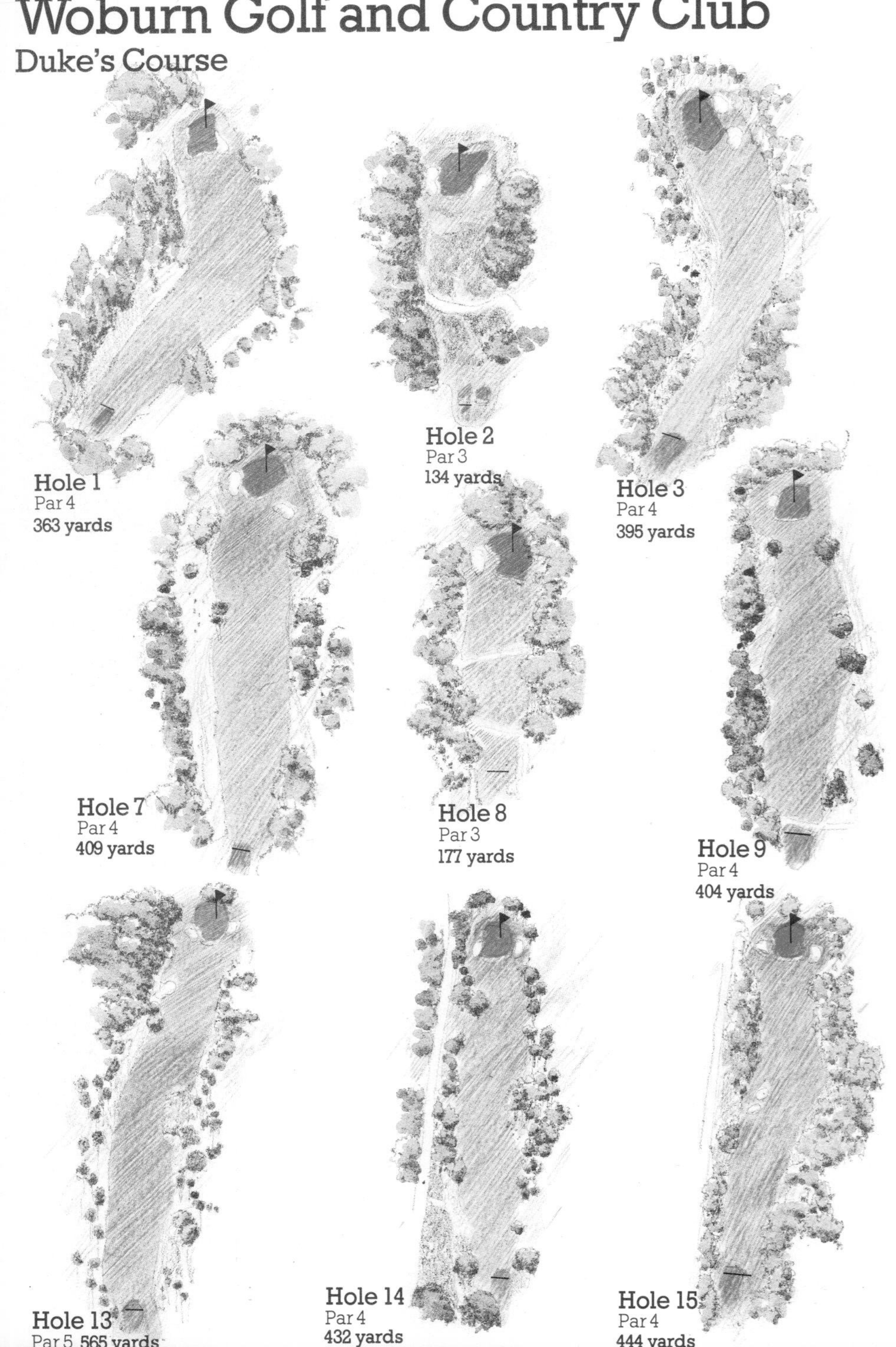

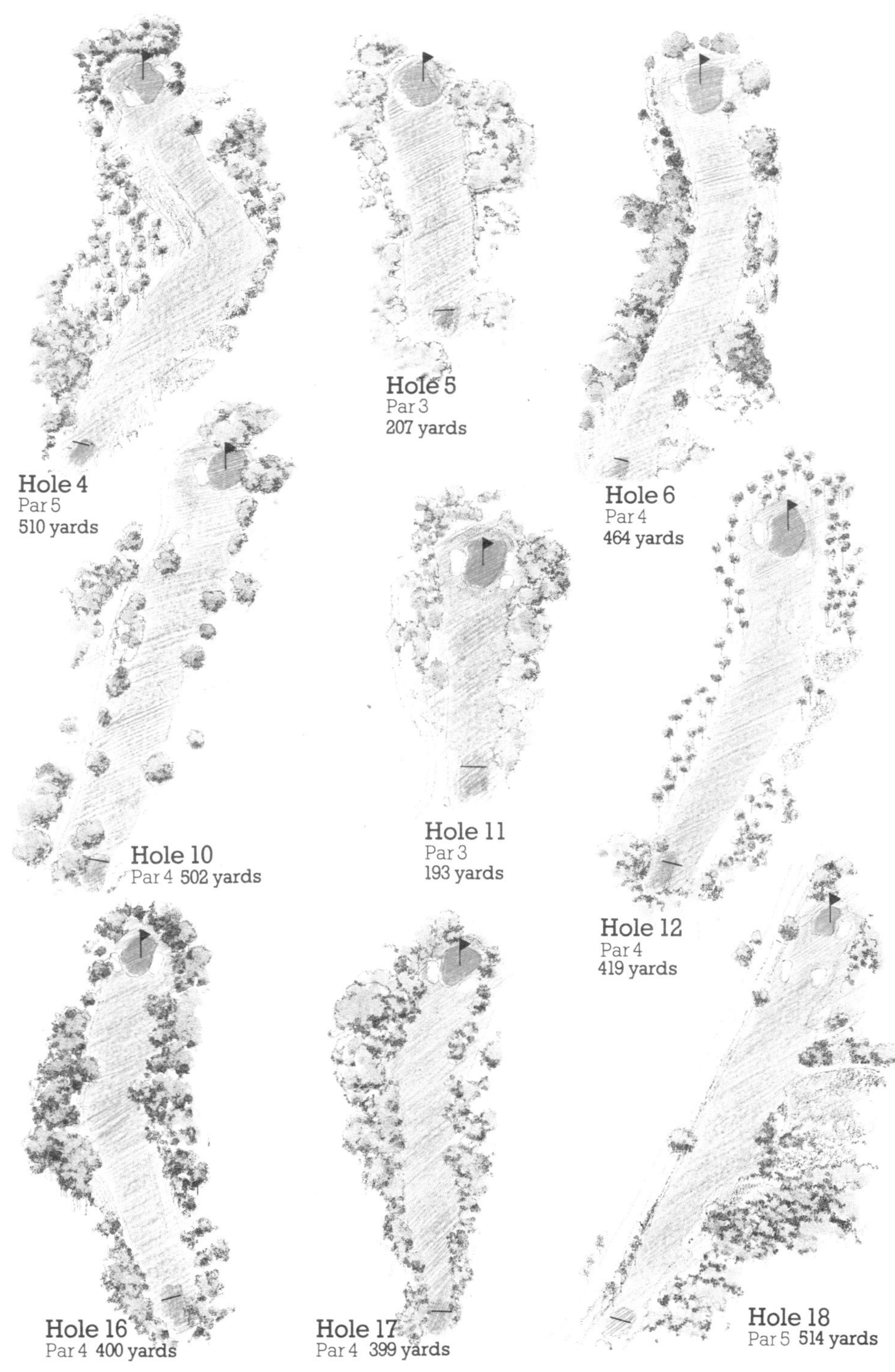
Hole 4
Par 5
510 yards
Hole 5
Par 3
207 yards
Hole 6
Par 4
464 yards
Hole 10
Par 4 502 yards
Hole 11
Par 3
193 yards
Hole 12
Par 4
419 yards
Hole 16
Par 4 400 yards
Hole 17
Par 4 399 yards
Hole 18
Par 5 514 yards

Sunningdale Hotel
Lucker Road, Bamburgh, Northumbria.
***Tel* (06684) 334**
Comfortable hotel, only one mile from Northumbria's most beautiful golf course; eight other courses within easy reach. Reduced terms for golfers in early and late season.

Isle of Man

Castletown Golf Links Hotel
Castletown, Isle of Man. *Tel* (0624) 822201
Unique setting with sea on three sides of this famous championship links of 6,731 yards. Inclusive packages available at own 3-star 60-bedroom hotel.

Wales

Nythfa House Hotel
Brecon, Powys LD3 7NG. *Tel* (0874) 4287
RAC 2-star country house hotel. Cradoc course 2 miles, Town course 1 mile. 18 bedrooms *en suite*, colour televisions, sauna, squash, 9-hole putting course. *(See advertisement page 63 for further details.)*

Trefeddian Hotel
Aberdovey, Gwynedd, Wales LL35 0SB.
***Tel* (065 472) 213**
3-star hotel with 46 rooms, all with *en suite* bathroom. Overlooks golf links and sea. Golfers Tariff and brochure sent on request.

Hotel Mariners
Mariners Square, Haverfordwest, Pembrokeshire SA61 2DU. *Tel* (0437) 3353
Situated in quiet town centre, 29 rooms with colour TV, the majority with *en suite* bathroom. Fully licensed with bar lunches and dinner. Special weekend rates.

The Mill at Glynhir
Llandybid, Nr Ammanford, Dyfed SA18 2TE.
***Tel* (0269) 850672**
FREE golf to residents. Overlooking Glynhir golf course. Indoor swimming pool. Special bargain breaks all year round. All rooms *en suite*, TV, radio etc. Excellent food. *(See advertisement page 62 for further details.)*

Deganwy Castle Hotel
Station Road, Gwynedd LL31 9DA.
***Tel* (0492) 83555**
Superbly located beside the Conwy river. Adjacent to 3 championship golf clubs. Warm friendly bars, excellent food, rooms with bath, car park.

Hotel 70°
Penmaenhead, Old Colwyn, Colwyn Bay, Clwyd. *Tel* (0492) 516555
Luxury modern hotel situated on the cliff tops with breathtaking views. Each bedroom has every modern facility. Superb award-winning restaurant. *(See advertisement page 21 for further details.)*

Noddfa Hotel
Lower Road, Harlech, North Wales LL46 2UB. *Tel* (0766) 780043
Family run small hotel close to Harlech Castle. Opposite the Royal St David's Golf Club. Reduced green fees and free archery lessons.

Scotland

Ardlochan Hotel
Maidens, Culzean, Nr Maybole, Ayrshire KA19 8LA. *Tel* (06556) 254
5 courses within 25 miles. Turnberry 2 miles, sea front adjoining country park. Central heating, TV, tea maker. 6 rooms, 4 rooms *en suite*. Lounge bar. Chalet for hire. Touring caravans.

The Bein Inn Hotel
Glenfarg, Perthshire PH2 9PY.
***Tel* (057 73) 216**
Excellent facilities in beautiful surroundings 8 miles from Perth and within 30 minutes of Carnoustie, Gleneagles, St Andrews, Downfield and Ladybank. *(See advertisement page 25 for further details)*.

Columba House Hotel
Manse Road, Kingussie, Inverness-shire PH21 1JH. *Tel* (05402) 402
A welcoming family-run small country house hotel. Licensed. AA listed. Golfing arranged at six beautiful courses nearby. Small parties catered for. Groups rates. B&B £11/D, B&B £21 Contact: Ian Shearer, Columba House Hotel, Kingussie, PH21 1JF. *Tel* (05402) 402.

Dornoch Castle
Dornoch, Sutherland IV25 3SE.
***Tel* (0862) 810216**
Formerly a Bishop's palace, the hotel has 20 bedrooms. The panelled cocktail bar, elegant lounge and Bishop's Room restaurant overlooking historic Dornoch Cathedral. An INTER hotel. AA RAC STB Commended 3 crowns.

Fort Lodge Hotel
2 Citadel Place, Ayr KA7 1JN Scotland.
***Tel* (0292) 265232**
Situated between Turnberry and Royal Troon. This privately owned hotel on the 'Golf Coast' is ideal for small parties and individuals, all rooms *en suite*, colour TV. Discounts for groups.

Gleneagles Kings Course

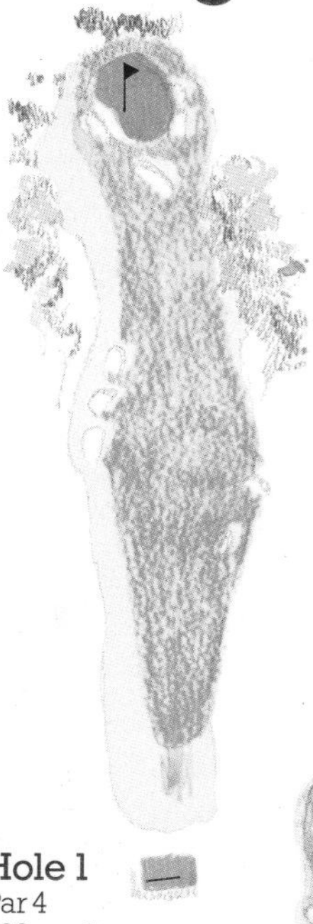

Hole 1
Par 4
362 yards

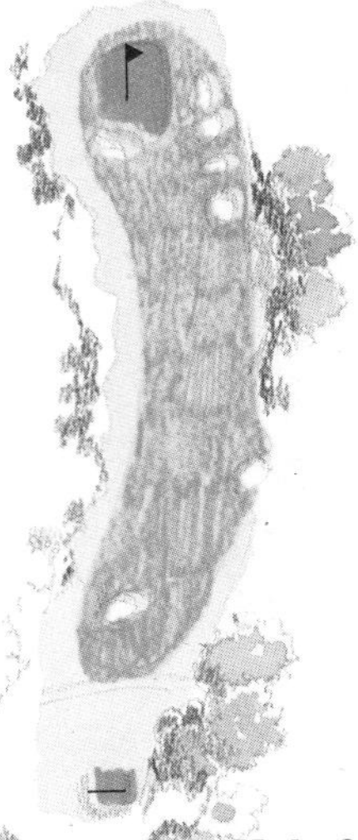

Hole 2
Par 4
405 yards

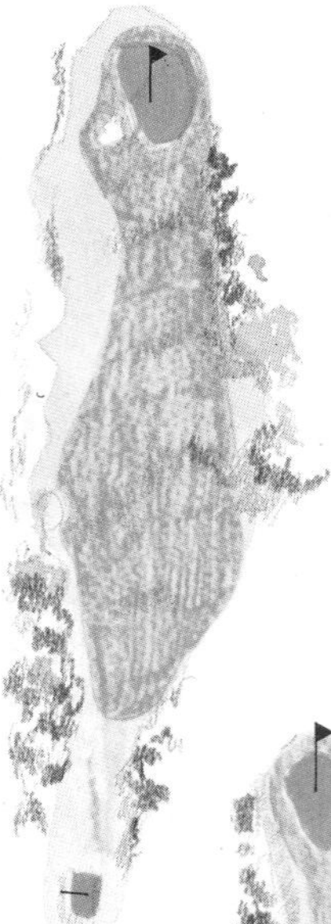

Hole 3
Par 4
377 yards

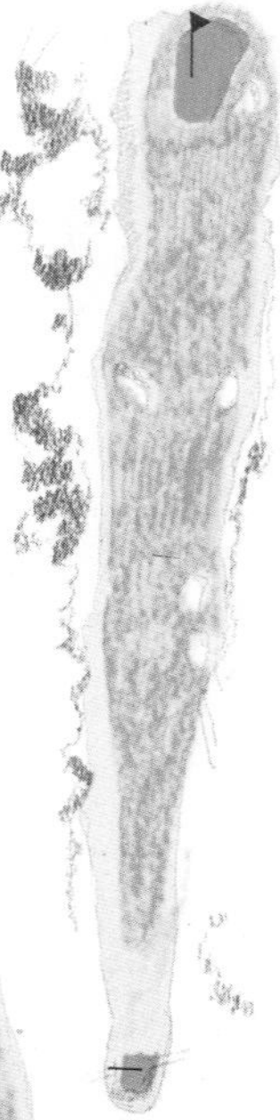

Hole 4
Par 4
465 yards

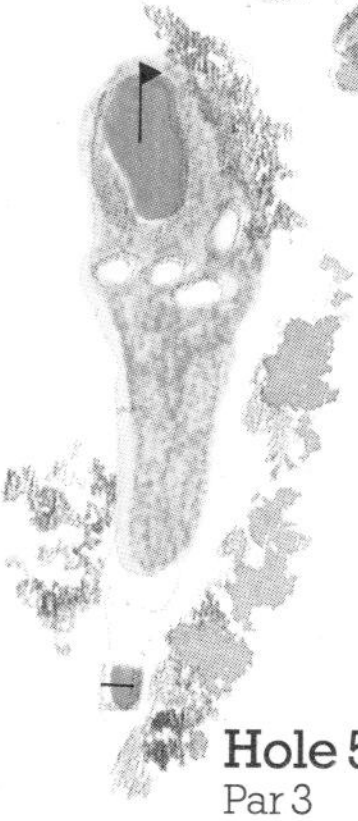

Hole 5
Par 3
160 yards

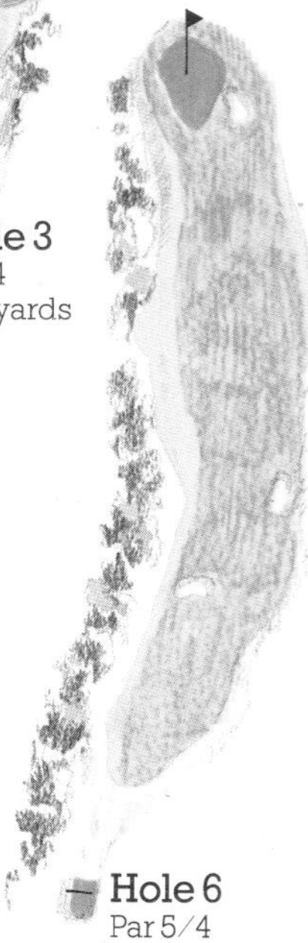

Hole 6
Par 5/4
476 yards

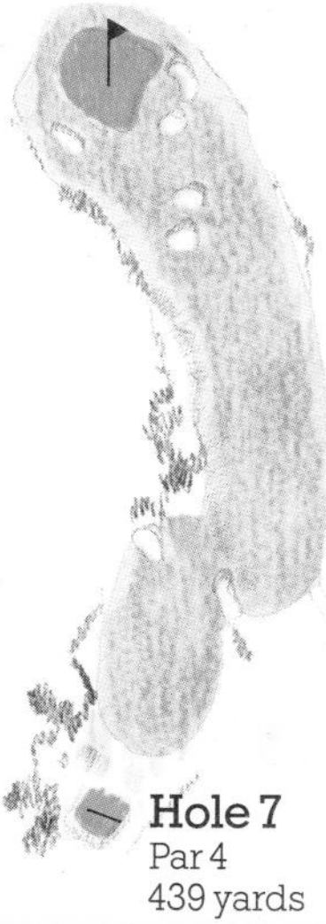

Hole 7
Par 4
439 yards

Hole 8
Par 3
158 yards

Hole 9
Par 4
351 yards

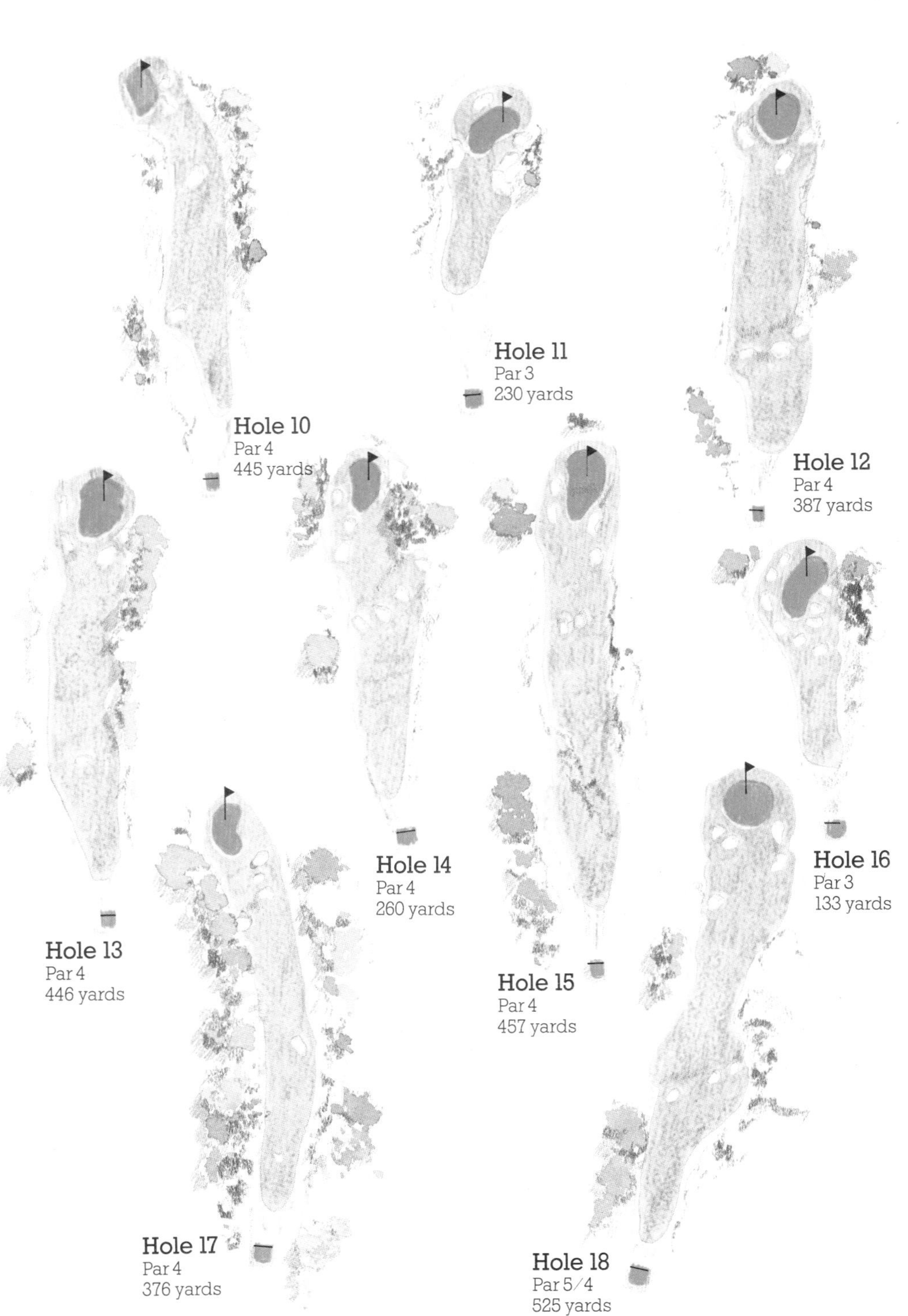
Hole 10
Par 4
445 yards
Hole 11
Par 3
230 yards
Hole 12
Par 4
387 yards
Hole 13
Par 4
446 yards
Hole 14
Par 4
260 yards
Hole 15
Par 4
457 yards
Hole 16
Par 3
133 yards
Hole 17
Par 4
376 yards
Hole 18
Par 5/4
525 yards

Glencoe Hotel
8 Links Parade, Carnoustie, Angus DD7 7JF. *Tel* (0241) 53273
Directly opposite 1st tee of the championship course. 11 bedrooms, majority with private bathroom, all with colour TV and direct-dial telephone. 2-star AA and RAC.

Gleneagles Hotel
Auchterarder, Perthshire PH3 1NF. *Tel* (07646) 2231
In addition to four championship golf courses, Gleneagles boasts an indoor sports and leisure complex, tennis courts, the Gleneagles Jackie Stewart Shooting School and of course the luxury of Scotland's first and foremost 5-star hotel.

The Glenesk Hotel
High Street, Edzell, Tayside. *Tel* (03564) 319
Family-run 3-star hotel adjoins 18-hole golf course, 25 bedrooms all with modern facilities. Within easy reach of St Andrews, Carnoustie and other courses.

Golf Links Hotel
Golspie, Sutherland KW10 6TT. *Tel* (04083) 3408
STB 3 crown Hotel with *en suite* bedrooms, good restaurant. Package deals with full board, green fees on Royal Dornoch, Golspie and Bruno courses.

Kirroughtree Hotel
Newton Stewart, Galloway DG8 6AN. *Tel* (0671) 2141
Unlimited free golf at 2 courses, including a championship course. Also 18-hole putting course in grounds of this luxurious country house hotel. Finest cuisine provided by our Master Chef. Please send for details. AA *** RAC, AA Rosette & HBL. *(See advertisement page 17 for further details.)*

Letham Grange
Colliston, By Arbroath DD11 4RL. *Tel* (024189) 373
20-bedroom Victorian mansion, with 18-hole championship standard golf course, first class facilities, set in the heartland of golf. Company/Society golf breaks welcome.

Lockerbie House Country Hotel
Lockerbie, Dumfries and Galloway DG11 2RG. *Tel* (05762) 2610
Situated 25 miles north of Carlisle. AA and RAC *** Free golf Monday to Friday at Lockerbie and Moffat. A delightful country mansion. *(See advertisement page 17 for further details.)*

Lundin Links Hotel
Lundin Links, Fife. *Tel* (0333) 320207
Tudor-style hotel 15 minutes drive from St Andrews. Surrounded by top golf courses. Superb food and hospitality by Campbell and Helen MacIntyre. *(See advertisement page 25 for further details.)*

Marine Hotel
Cromwell Road, North Berwick. *Tel* (0620) 2406
Golfers in North Berwick have a choice of 14 splendid courses, and the superb Marine Hotel overlooks the famous West Links. *(See advertisement page 29 for further details.)*

The Old Course Golf and Country Club
St Andrews, Fife KY16 9SP. *Tel* (0334) 74371
A luxury modern hotel overlooking the famous Road Hole of the Old Course, with the highest standards of cuisine, service and recreational facilities.

The Park Hotel
John Street, Montrose, Angus DD10 8RJ. *Tel* (0674) 73415 *Tx* 76367
A short distance from Montrose Medal Course. Privately-owned hotel, 59 bedrooms all with colour TV and most with private bathrooms. Golfing breaks from £66.00. *(See advertisement page 63 for further details.)*

Rosemount Golf Hotel
Golf Course Road, Blairgowrie, Perthshire PH10 6LJ. *Tel* (0250) 2604
Rosemount close by, Gleneagles, Carnoustie, etc within easy reach. 12 *en suite* rooms plus self-catering chalets in lovely grounds. Or try shooting, fishing, walking or skiing nearby.

The Rusacks Hotel
Pilmour Links, St Andrews KY16 9JQ Fife, Scotland. *Tel* (0334) 74321
Famous golfing 4-star hotel overlooking 18th green. Champions Bar and Clubhouse provide full facilities for individuals and parties. Day and residential packages. All day bar and catering.

St Andrews Golf Hotel
St Andrews, Fife KY16 9AS. *Tel* (0334) 72611
Most comfortable, traditional, Scottish Hotel (all bedrooms *en suite*). Fine restaurant. Extensive cellar. On the seafront 200 yards from 'Old Course'. Let us arrange your Golf in Scotland.

Sun Court
19 Crosbie Road, Troon, Ayrshire. *Tel* (0292) 312727
Overlooking Royal Troon and the sea. Excellent restaurant, 4 squash courts, lawn tennis and real tennis. Special rates for golf groups.

Turnberry Hotel and Golf Courses
Turnberry, Ayrshire KA26 9LT. *Tel* (0655) 31000
Situated overlooking Scotland's South West Ayrshire coast. Within its 360 acres are a luxury hotel, golf and leisure resort with few equals in the world.

Muirfield Championship Tees

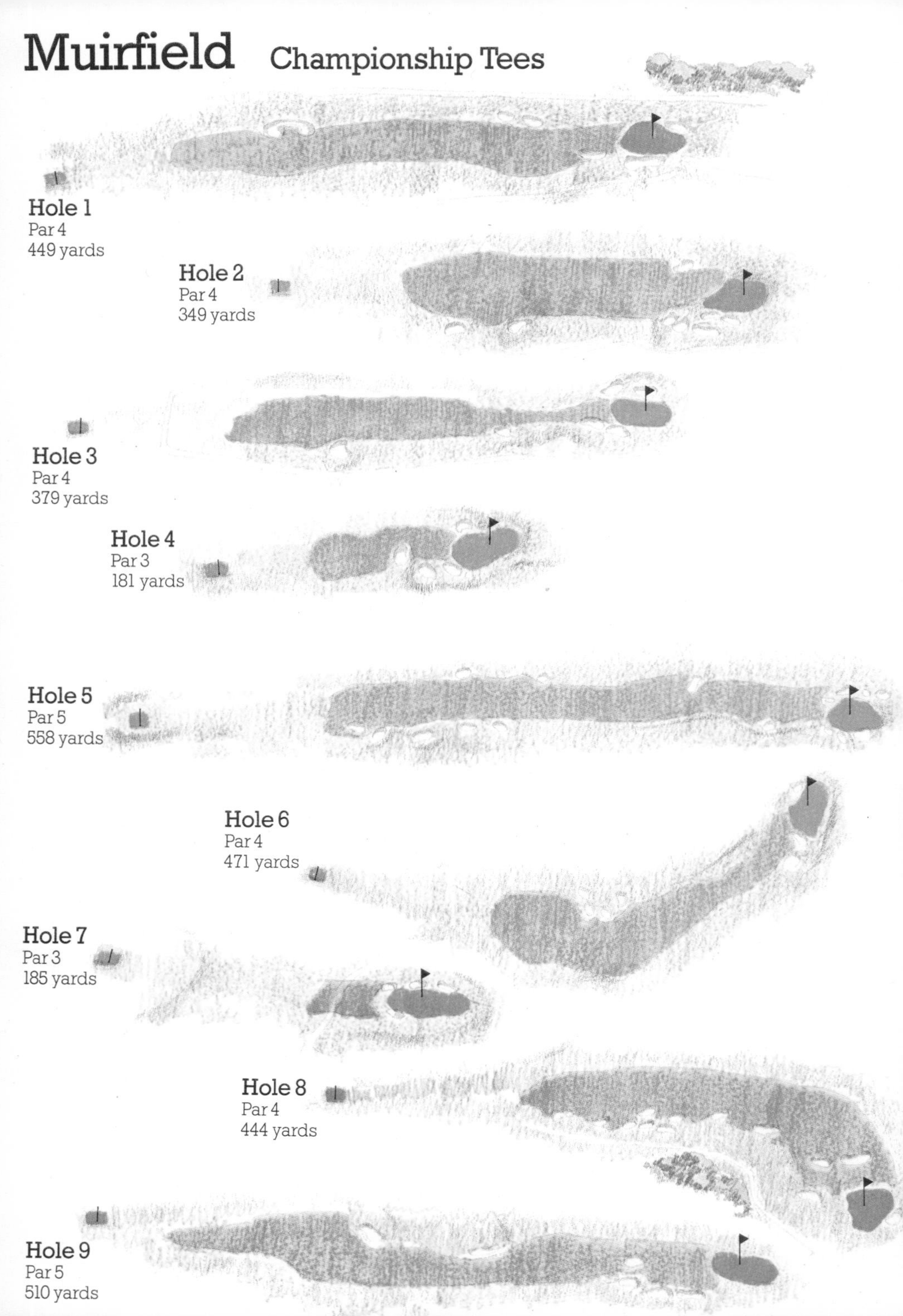

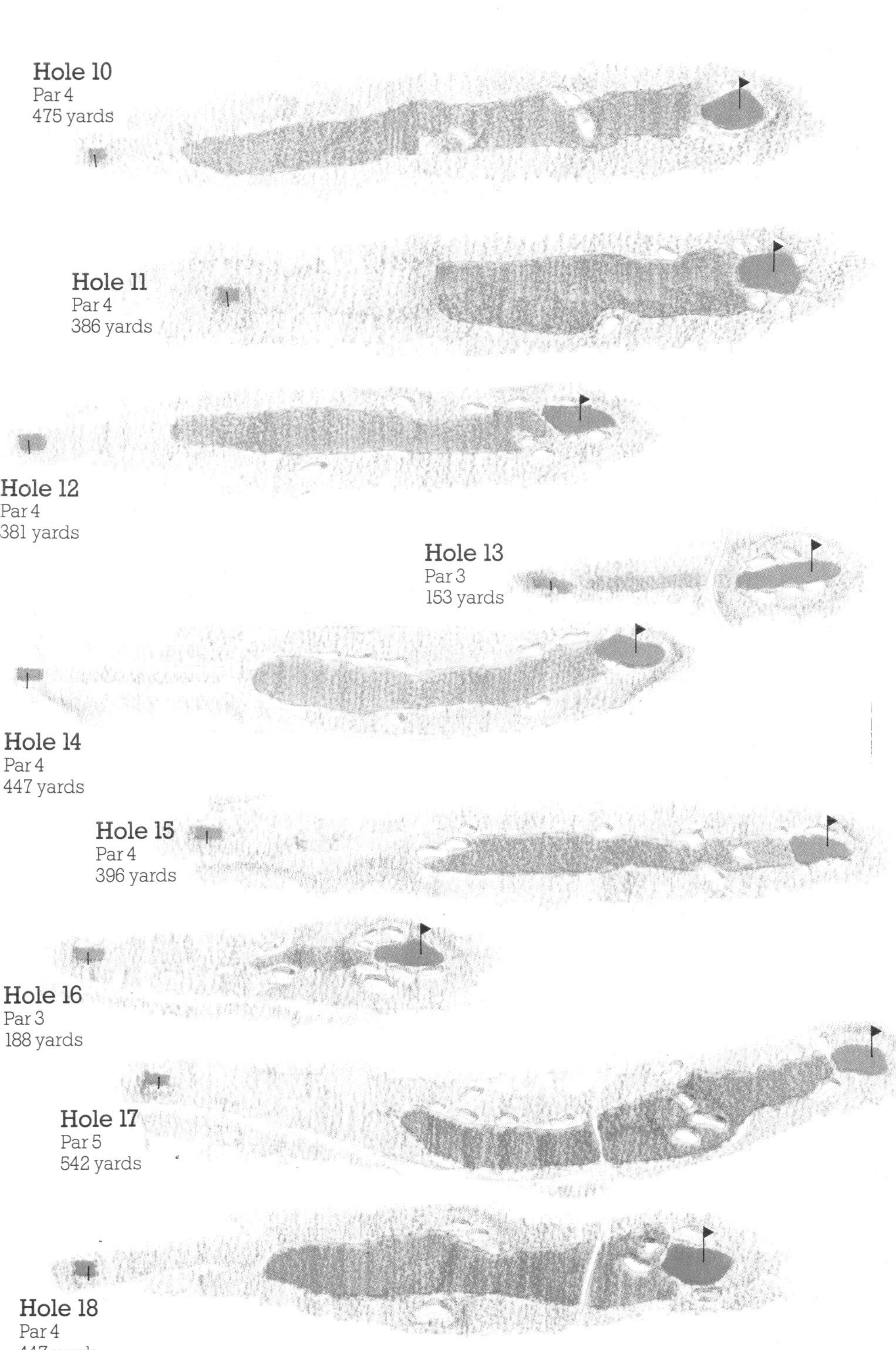
Hole 10
Par 4
475 yards
Hole 11
Par 4
386 yards
Hole 12
Par 4
381 yards
Hole 13
Par 3
153 yards
Hole 14
Par 4
447 yards
Hole 15
Par 4
396 yards
Hole 16
Par 3
188 yards
Hole 17
Par 5
542 yards
Hole 18
Par 4
447 yards

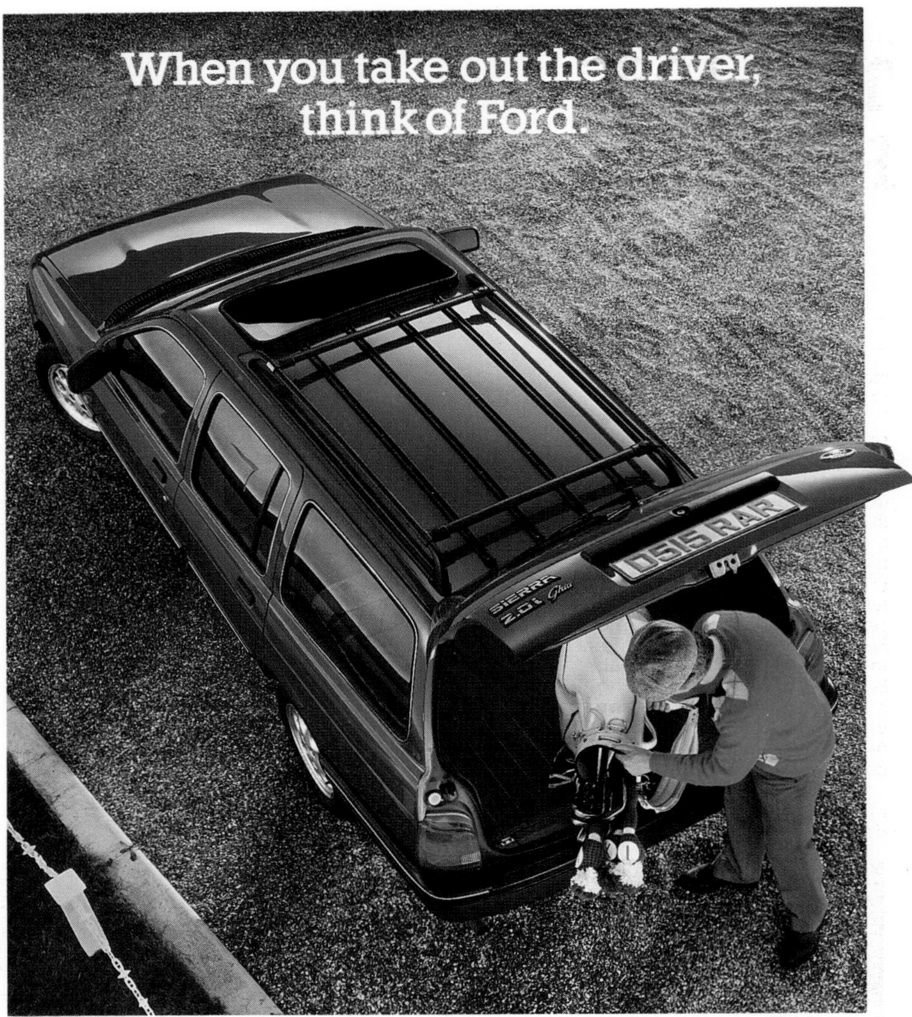
When you take out the driver,
think of Ford.
SIERRA
2.0i Ghia
D515 RAR

Golf, like every other sport, draws its future strength from the young people entering the game. And that is the main reason why Ford continue to raise money for the Golf Foundation through the Ford Amateur Golf Tournament – £108,000 over the last four years.

Ford are also pleased with their sponsorship of the increasingly competitive Ford Ladies Classic, with its £30,000 prize money. They will also be supplying Courtesy Cars at this year's Open Championship.

So you can see that whether it's giving young players a helping hand or established players a lift home, Ford are involved in golf at all levels.

Ford

The 1987 Season with Ford

For 1987, Ford Motor Company continues its support of golf with a variety of events covering the whole spectrum of the game.

We kick-off the season with our largest programme, the Ford Amateur Golf Tournament. Now into its twenty-first year, the tournament proves to be more and more popular each year. From April to July this year, some 1200 golf clubs around the country will be holding a preliminary round of the tournament, sponsored by their local Ford dealer. August sees us holding four national trials to find the twelve representatives from England, Ireland, Scotland and Wales to go forward and play in the Home Internationals Final at the Belfry. As shown below, England, captained by Tommy Horton, were last year's victorious winning team after 3 days of fierce battle against the three other countries.

We will be donating one of our Fiesta models for this year's Golf Foundation prize draw. We are very proud to say that this draw, which is linked to the Ford Amateur Golf Tournament, has so far raised over £108,000 for the Golf Foundation and the development of junior golf.

The Ford Ladies Golf Classic, which is the first tournament on the WPGA calendar of events, will again be held at Woburn Golf and Country Club from 29 April to 2 May. The women's professional circuit has grown considerably over the past few years and for 1987 the total prize money is over a million pounds. Come along and see the girls play at the Ford Classic—rest assured you will see some very competitive play.

Finally, you will see us at the 116th Open Championship at Muirfield as the official courtesy car supplier to the Royal and Ancient. A fleet of our latest models will be in operation transporting the world's top players to and from the golf course.

Victorious England team from 1986 Ford Amateur Golf Tournament.

Fulford Golf Club, York

Hole 1
Par 4
416 yards

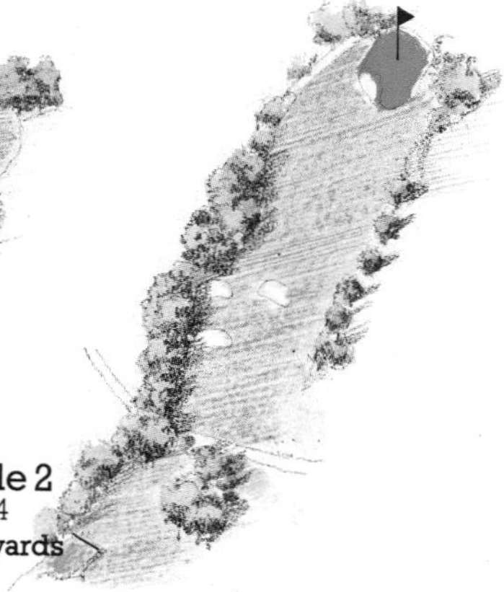

Hole 2
Par 4
444 yards

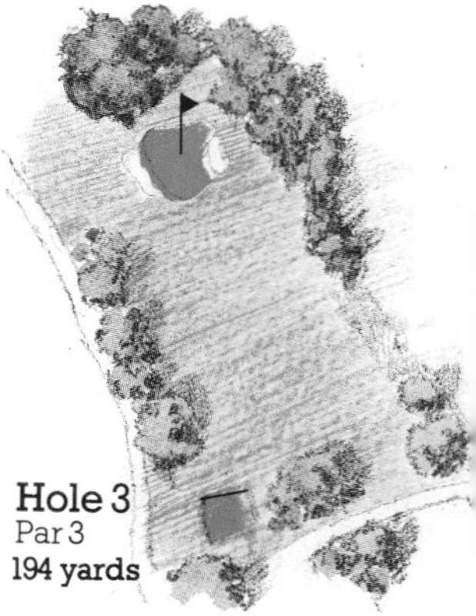

Hole 3
Par 3
194 yards

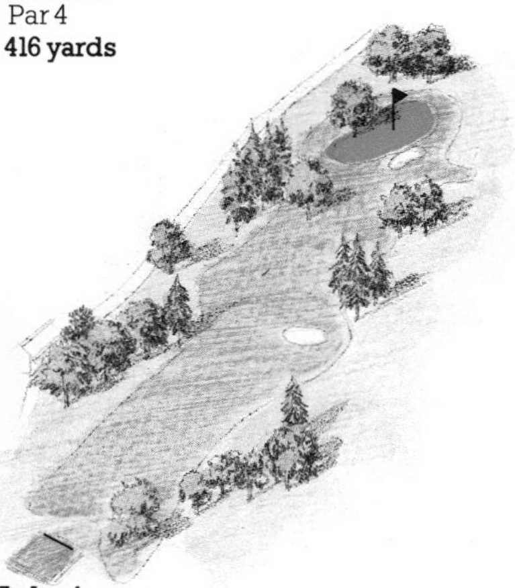

Hole 4
Par 4
458 yards

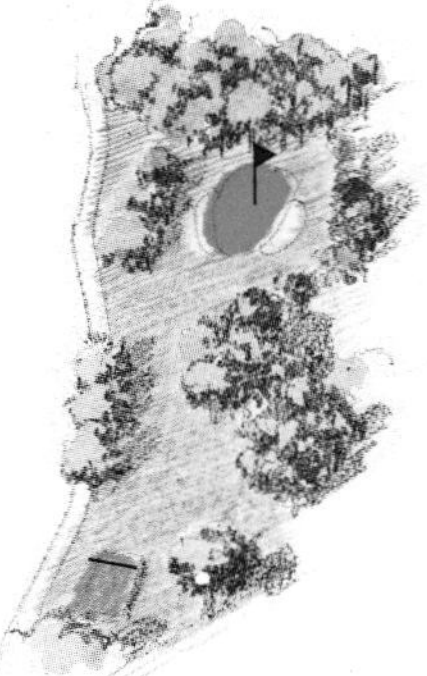

Hole 5
Par 3
165 yards

Hole 6
Par 5
545 yards

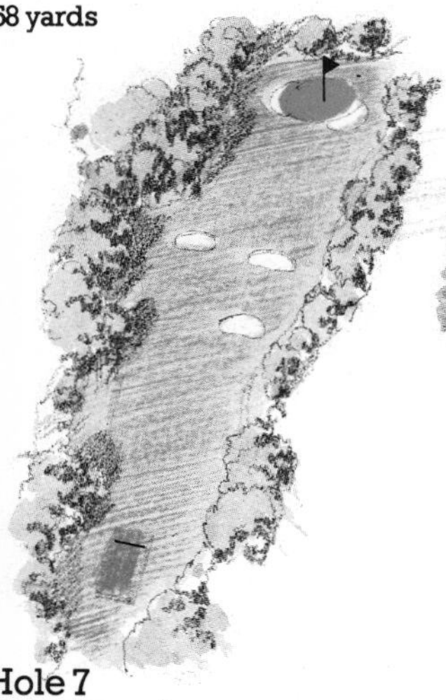

Hole 7
Par 4 **415 yards**

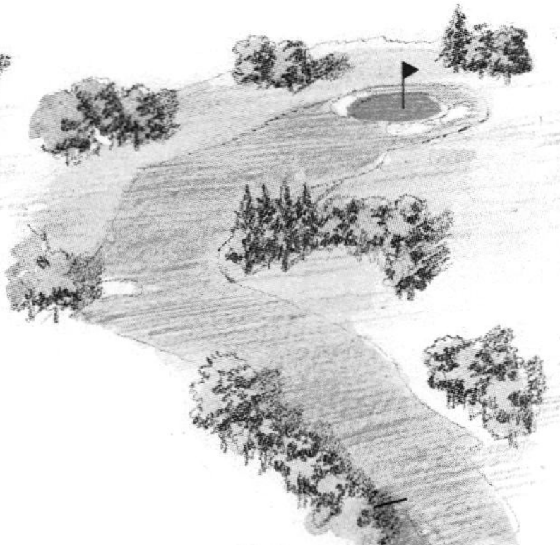

Hole 8
Par 4
375 yards

Hole 9
Par 5 **486 yards**

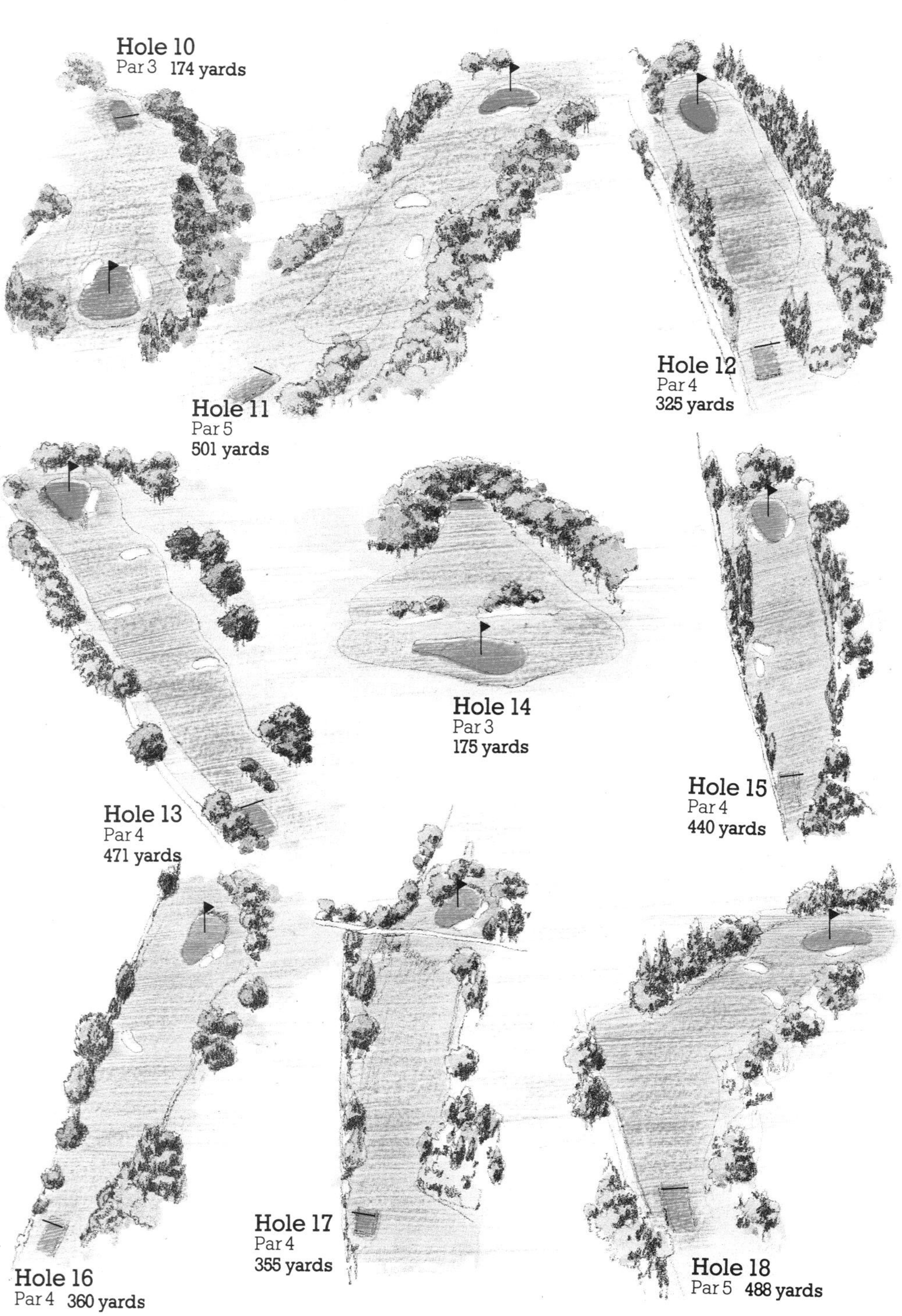
Hole 10
Par 3 174 yards
Hole 11
Par 5
501 yards
Hole 12
Par 4
325 yards
Hole 13
Par 4
471 yards
Hole 14
Par 3
175 yards
Hole 15
Par 4
440 yards
Hole 16
Par 4 360 yards
Hole 17
Par 4
355 yards
Hole 18
Par 5 488 yards

British Clubs Celebrating their Centenaries in 1987

The Editor and Publishers of the *Golfer's Handbook* are pleased to note the centenaries of 16 Clubs in the UK, and especially that the Glasgow Club is now 200 years old. The result of the remarkable growth of the game in the last quarter of the 19th century, some of these still play the same or an altered course, while others have been forced to move through urban developments.

We congratulate all these clubs which still flourish in spite of the vicissitudes of time, and wish each all the best for the future.

Glasgow Golf Club

Founded 1787

Kirk Session records of 1589 refer to golf in Glasgow but it was not until 1787 that the first Club in the West of Scotland was formed. There were 22 members listed in the Directory and they shared Glasgow Green with Fairs, Reviewings, Drillings and Camps not to mention grazing herds of cows. From 1794–1809 the club lapsed due to volunteering, early members appeared eager for the fray. There was a further period of suspended animation from 1835–70 resulting from profound changes in social and industrial conditions.

In 1870 the reconstituted Club played at Queens Park before moving to Alexandra Park four years later. In 1880 the Club first staged the Tennant Cup, the oldest Amateur Strokeplay Competition in the world. In 1885 the Club had 18 holes for the first time, and in 1888 the October meeting had 133 competitors, thought to be the greatest number in the history of any club at that time. An additional course was sought resulting in the acquisition of Gailes, a links course, on the Ayrshire coast which was opened on 19th May 1892.

Following complaints in the correspondence columns about conflicting interests of Alexandra Park users, the Club moved to Blackhill where the first ball was struck on 6th April 1895. By then the list of Glasgow Golf Club Captains included 4 Lord Provosts, 4 magistrates, 2 councillors, 4 clergymen and 5 doctors. Provan Gas Works put an end to Blackhill as a suitable Course and in 1904 the Club moved to Killermont, Bearsden, its present home.

Killermont was opened by Sir John Ure Primrose, Lord Provost of Glasgow on 21st May 1904, driving off with silver cleek and Haskell ball. The course was laid out by Old Tom Morris of St Andrews. The Club survived World War I although the War Department Land Agency requisitioned Gailes Clubhouse and Killermont was under similar threat.

Other significant dates in the history of the club are:

1920 Decision to make Lord Provosts of Glasgow Honorary Members
1922 Club admitted to the Scottish Golf Union
1931 British Boys at Killermont
1933 Prince of Wales, later Edward VIII, played over Killermont
1942 Gailes Club house again requisitioned
1947 Scottish Amateur played over the Course
1957 Swallow Penfold Tournament at Killermont
1962 Clubhouse placed on list of buildings of historical interest (Preservation Order of 1971)

Gailes has been used as a final qualifying Course on three occasions in recent years when The Open was being held at Royal Troon and Turnberry. Glasgow Golf Club hosts the Scottish Seniors Open Amateur Strokeplay Championship at Killermont every alternate year.

Killermont—Parkland Course 5968 yds/5456 metres

Gailes—Links Course 6447 yds/5896 metres

Total membership 1,100
Captain 1986: JB Halley
Secretary: WD Robertson
Professional: J Steven

England

Buxton and High Peak

In the heart of the Peak District of Derbyshire, the course has meadowland turf in a moorland setting with fine views of the surrounding hills. With the A6 road running alongside, members and visitors appreciate the well-kept condition of the course of nearly 6000 yards, par 69, which presents a challenge to all golfers. The membership of 600 is well-known for its hospitality and the Clubhouse for its friendly atmosphere with a warm welcome to all.

Captain 1987: Mike Whalley
Hon Secretary: Brian Webb
Professional: RM Head

Cleveland

Yorkshire's oldest Club plays on the County's only links course. It is close to Redcar's town centre and has a stiff SSS of 72. Being so near to the sea and although in the north of the country, only rarely does snow prevent play, few if any days being missed each year. The Clubhouse is large

Walton Heath Championship Course

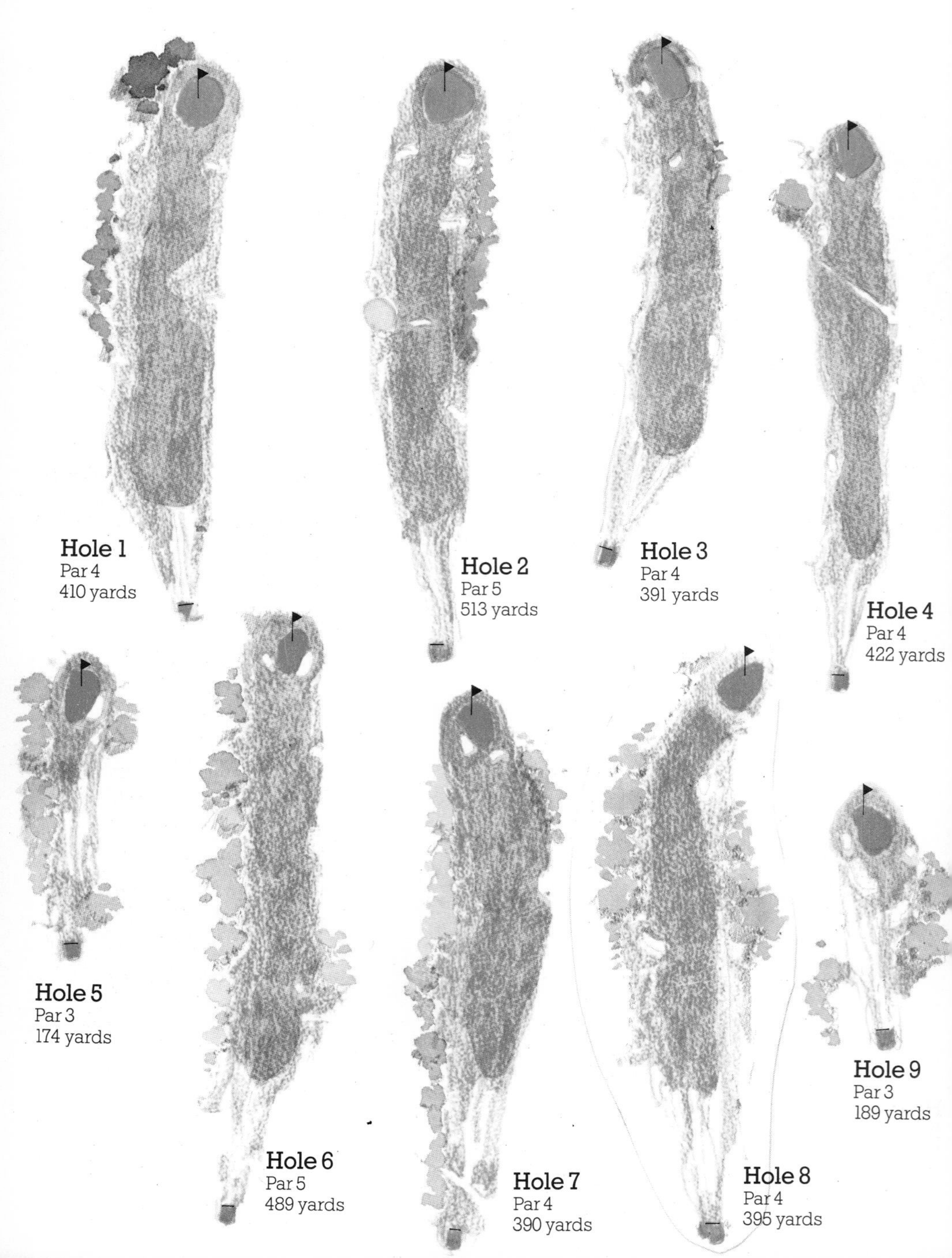

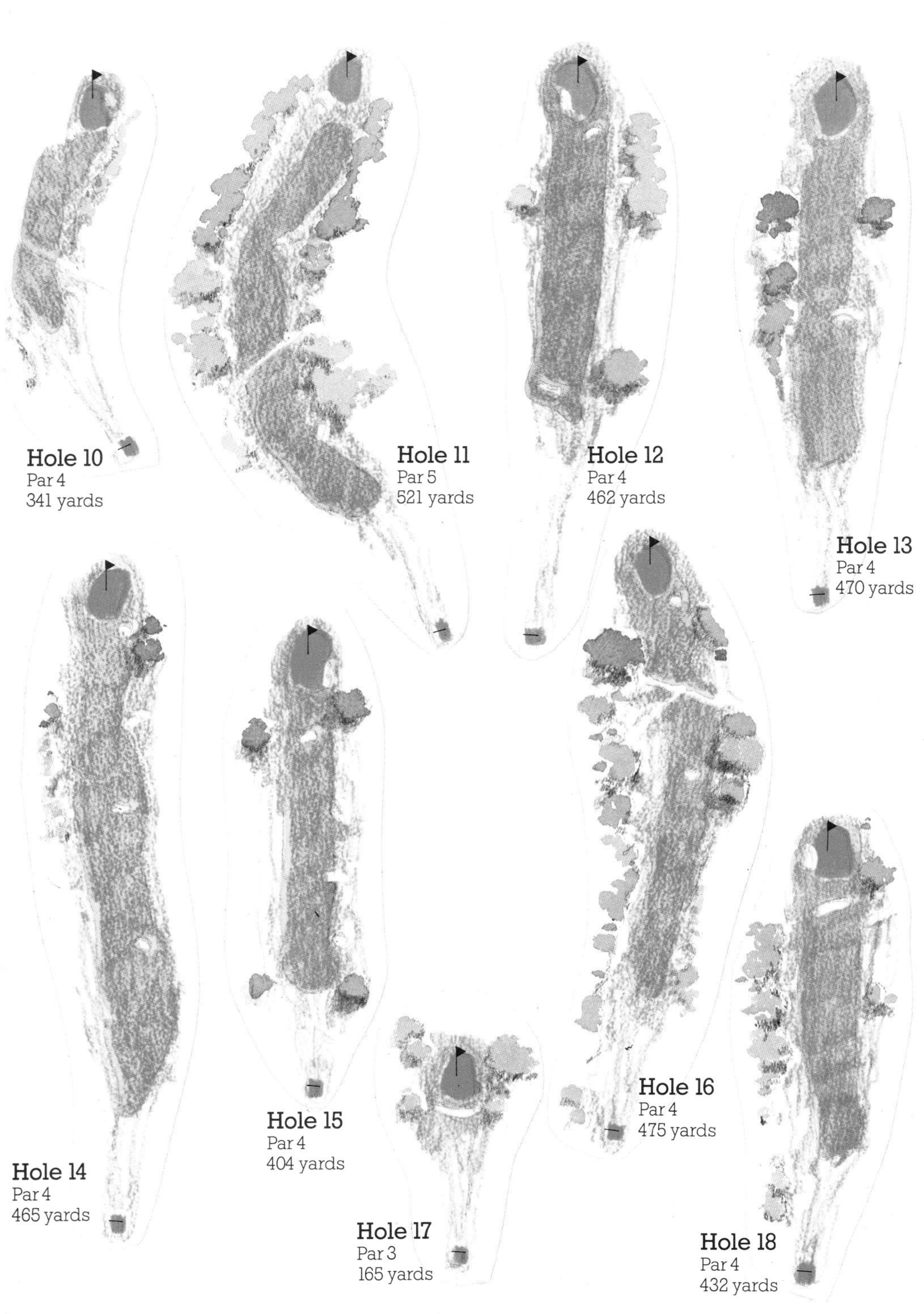
Hole 10
Par 4
341 yards
Hole 11
Par 5
521 yards
Hole 12
Par 4
462 yards
Hole 13
Par 4
470 yards
Hole 14
Par 4
465 yards
Hole 15
Par 4
404 yards
Hole 16
Par 4
475 yards
Hole 17
Par 3
165 yards
Hole 18
Par 4
432 yards

and comfortable with splendid facilities for members and visitors.

Joint Captains 1987: Dr JK Mackay and S Nixon
Secretary: GAE Toon
Professional: Bruce Whipham

Coventry

Celebrating its Centenary this year the Club is one of the most successful in the Midlands and is a well-kept course at Finham Park, to where it moved in 1911. It now has a smart new Clubhouse, opened by Henry Longhurst in 1974. The first course was at Whitley Common, north of the city with holes laid out by Peter Paxton of the nearby Malvern Club. Jack Burns who had won the Open at St Andrews in 1888 from the Warwick Club was later professional at Coventry in the 1890s. Colonel Hugh Rotherham, an earlier member, was the first man to think of having a recognised number of strokes for a hole which he termed the 'ground score'. This standard soon came to be termed 'bogey', meaning the par for a hole today. The term 'bogey', meaning one over par, is a post World War II importation from the USA. Membership is now 750, the course 6613. With SSS of 72.

Captain 1987: Cyril R Corke
Secretary: MSH Tott
Professional: P Wheeler

Durham City

The first inland course in County Durham was at Pinkerknowle with the founding of the Durham City Club in 1887. Pinkerknowle remained the home of the Club until 1928. The first course was 6 holes only, with a further 3 added in 1894, giving a length of 2200 yards with a bogey of 39. The Club moved in 1928 to an 18-hole layout at Mount Oswal until the shift to its present location at Littleburn Farm in 1974. This meadowland course of 6117 yards, SSS 69, was designed by Chris Stanton, the current course Chairman. Membership is now 750 including thriving Junior, Ladies and Senior sections.

Captain 1987: AS Parkin
Hon Secretary: JT Ross
Professional: S Corbally

Notts

A fine inland test of golf, the Notts Club at Hollinwell moved to its present location on the edge of Sherwood Forest in 1900. The moorland course of 7200 yards, SSS 74, was designed by Willie Park jr on part of Newstead Abbey land, one time home of Byron. Tom Williamson, the Club's former respected professional was appointed on a three months trial in 1896 and stayed for 52 years. He played in more than 40 Opens and in his time designed over 30 courses and remodelled many others. Golf writers give Hollinwell the accolade of one of the best inland courses in the land.

Captain 1987: AT Slade
Secretary: JR Walker
Professional: Brian Waites

Redhill and Reigate

The course has always been on Earlswood Common, the lay-out having been altered several times over the years, often in the Club's first half-century with James Braid as adviser. The Club had been founded by a local man, Charles Hall, who worked in London and started playing with a few City friends on experimental greens on the south-east corner of the Common. In 1891 a limited membership was charged, 5 guineas entrance fee and 3 guineas subscription, an average rate at the time. Members were encouraged to wear red coats with brown collars. In 1889 the London & South Coast Railway offered fare concessions for golfers from London to Earlswood station which adjoined the Clubhouse. The Club moved to its present premises in 1978, where a thriving and happy membership continues to enjoy the game.

Captain 1987: Douglas Anderson
Secretary: Roger Whitson
Professional: Barry Davis

Royal Ascot

Although founded in 1887, the layout of the present course, which is within the Ascot race course, was to the design of JH Taylor a few years later. The Club's title was granted by Queen Victoria, her son, the Prince of Wales, later King Edward VII, was a Patron and member. The course, which is short but attractive, has been altered over the years due to the expansion of the race track and the new lawn in front of the Main Stand. With the extension and updating of the Clubhouse, membership is now over 600.

Captain 1987: Alan Brabiner
Secretary: RJ Young
Professional: C Dell

Royal Eastbourne

Permission to use the 'Royal' title was granted the same year as the Club was founded. The Dukes of Devonshire, whose Compton Place seat adjoins the course, have always been President of the Club, which has had a Prime Minister, AJ Balfour (Captain in 1897), and two Amateur Champions, Horace Hutchinson in 1886 and 1887 and Cyril Tolley 1920 and 1929, as members. The original 9 holes were extended to 18 in 1894, with further alterations in 1904 when the present Clubhouse was built, 1912 and 1954. Most of the original 9 holes are still in use without significant changes. An independent Royal Eastbourne Ladies Golf Club existed from 1889 to 1937 playing on what is now the inner 9 hole course. The Ladies section of the main club was formed in 1933. The Club has had only 8 Professionals in 100 years of whom CW (Cyril) Thomson served from 1922 to 1973.

Captain 1987: WH Perkins
Secretary: HW Scallon OBE
Professional: Richard Wooler

Royal St George's

This famous Club and course has staged 11 Open and 11 Amateur Championships since 1892, when it was the venue for the 8th Amateur Championship, followed by the first Open in England in 1894. For many years this fine links course, one of the sternest tests of golf in Great Britain, has

St Andrews Old Course

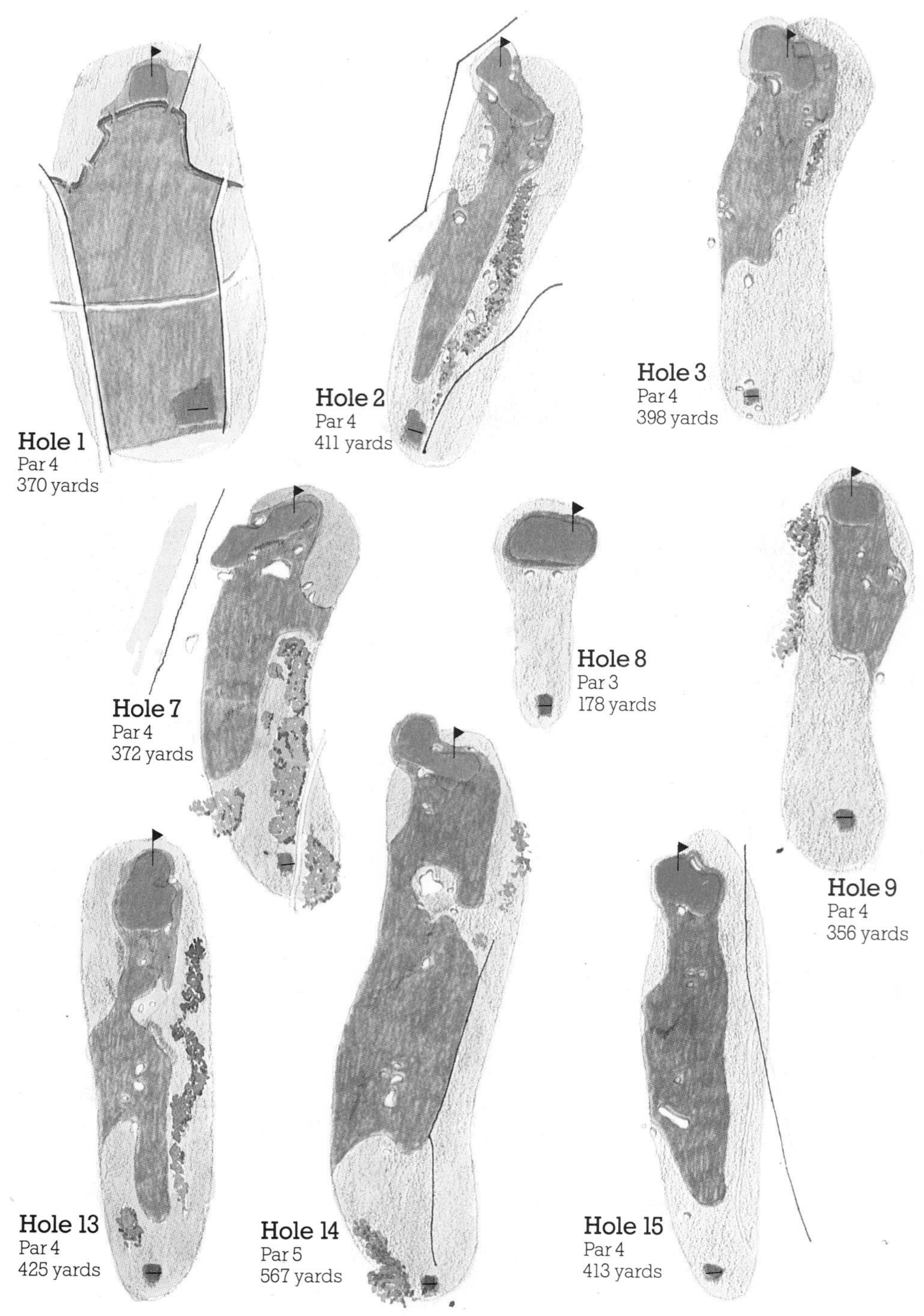

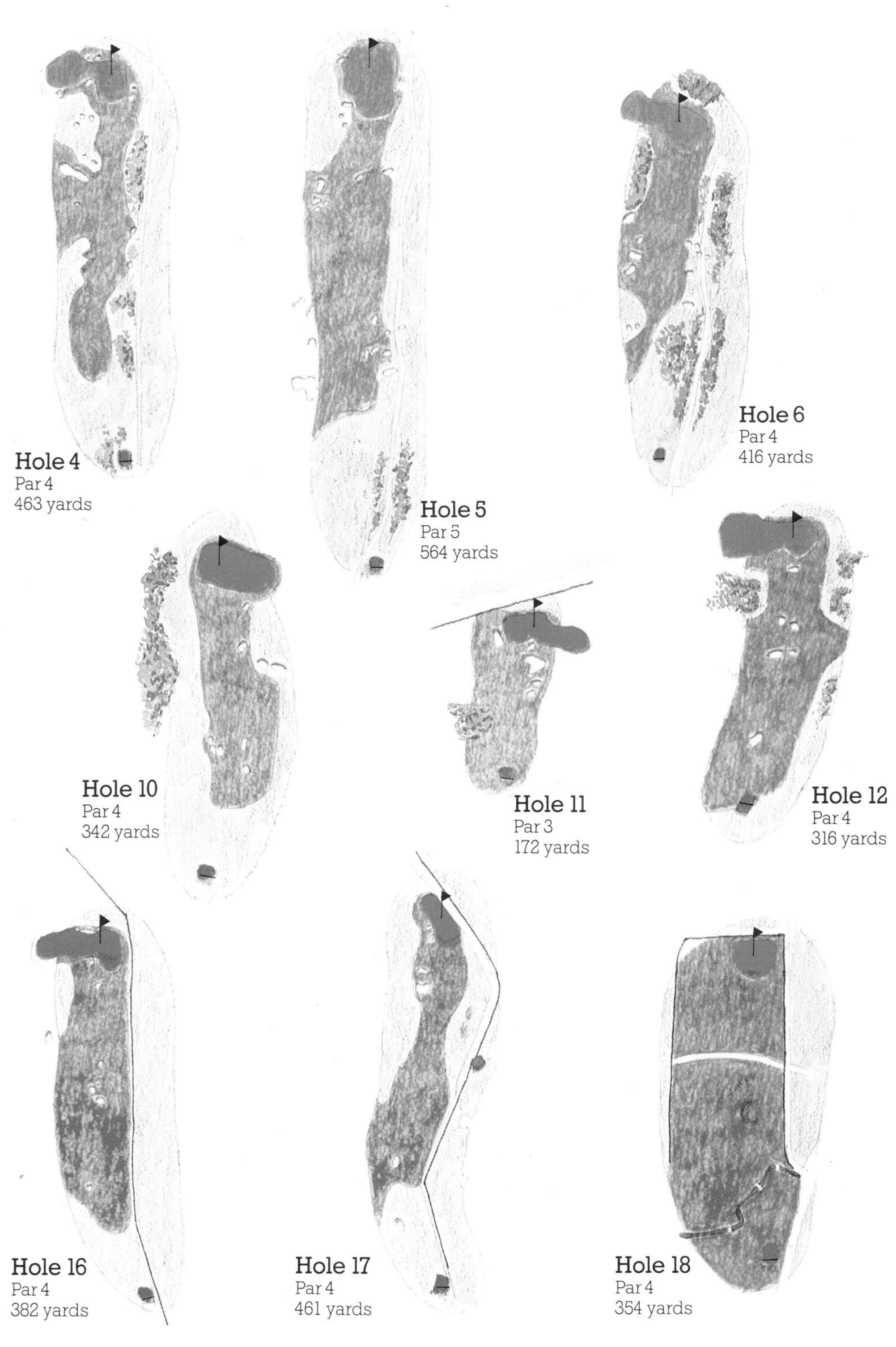
Hole 4
Par 4
463 yards
Hole 5
Par 5
564 yards
Hole 6
Par 4
416 yards
Hole 10
Par 4
342 yards
Hole 11
Par 3
172 yards
Hole 12
Par 4
316 yards
Hole 16
Par 4
382 yards
Hole 17
Par 4
461 yards
Hole 18
Par 4
354 yards

been the scene of many other international tournaments and matches. It was the home club of several past amateur champions. The St George's Champion Grand Challenge Cup, a tournament open to top-class amateurs, first won by John Ball in 1888, has many other distinguished players who have won it, including Harold Hilton, Freddie Tait, Francis Ouimet, Roger Wethered and, in 1957, Jack Nicklaus.

Captain 1987: PJS Lumsden
Secretary: Captain RJ Hitchen RN
Professional: Cyril Whiting

Seaford

The Club began with 12 holes at Seaford Head. In 1907 it moved to its present site at East Blatchington above Seaford, high up on the Downs, with a full 18 holes designed by JH Taylor. It was good downland turf and has been the venue for numerous Sussex Men's and Ladies' Championships. The Clubhouse was extended 1956/7 to include a Dormy House which has been a feature of the Club ever since, many guests coming year after year. Membership is now over 800.

Captain 1987: TH Brewster
Secretary: MB Hichisson
Professional: PT Brown

Scotland

Dunfermline

The Club has had four courses in its time of which little is known of the first. Early on it moved to Ferryhills, North Queensferry at the Fife end of the Forth Bridge, to a site with turf above rock, which was much in demand. Extensive quarrying forced a further move to Torryburn in 1927, where James Braid designed a testing course. The large Clubhouse was in a poor state needing constant repairs. In 1952 the Club moved again to Pitfirrane, where it now owns a 16th century mansion which has been modernised and extended. The course has 18 holes, par 70, which is not easy to achieve. Membership is 670. One of the original 1887 members, R Lockhart, emigrated to New York and was a founder member of the first Club in the USA, the St Andrews Club of Yonkers.

President 1987: Douglas M Ferguson
Hon Secretary: JA Gillies
Professional: D Symington

Irvine

Irvine is termed a links course although it is not next to the sea. It was re-designed by James Braid many years ago. Membership is 450 and 130 Ladies section and 30 Juniors. It claims to be the only Club in Scotland with 3 Scottish Champions as members, Hammy McInally, Jimmy Walker and Jack Cannon.

Captain 1987: Wm Cowan
Secretary: A MacPherson
Professional: D Williamson

Kelso

Kelso, as with another centenary club Royal Ascot, has its 18 holes within the racecourse, one mile outside the town. Its first course was in the grounds of Floors Castle, the seat of the Dukes of Roxburghe, moving in 1913 to its present site, then with 9 holes only. Extended in the 1920s, it became 18 holes in 1980, with a new Clubhouse opened the following year.

Captain 1987: Alan H McGhee
Secretary: Andrew Walker

Kinghorn

Founded as a Club in 1887, 9 holes of the course were laid out by Tom Morris Sr that year, the great man confirming his opinion that the site chosen was 'admirably adapted for the purpose of playing golf'. In 1905 the course was extended to 18 holes through the purchase of additional land. The course is short at 5245 yards, SSS 67, but the challenge Tom Morris considered would 'test the skill of the player' remains. The Club thrives on a small membership with many visitors.

Captain 1987: David Gordon
Secretary: Donald Mackenzie

Nairn

Originally laid out by Andrew Simpson, greenkeeper at Aberdeen, and remodelled two years later by Tom Morris Sr. Some time afterwards the holes were much improved by James Braid. They follow the traditional old links plan of holes going straight out and back along a narrow strip of land. There are magnificant views of the Moray Firth which have been enjoyed by players in many Amateur and Professional Championships played at Nairn over the years. The course has been included in a list of the 40 top courses in Britain. Current membership is 850.

Captain 1987: James R Asher
Secretary: D Patrick
Professional: Robin Fyfe

Week beginning	Major Championships	PGA European Tour	WPGA Tour
JAN 4			
11			
18			
25			
FEB 1			
8			
15			
22			
MAR 1			
8			
15		**Moroccan Open** Mar 19-20 Rabat	
22			
29		**Dunhill Cup Qualif** Apr 2-5 Rome	

UK & Ireland Men's Amateur

Berkhamsted Trophy
Mar 14
Berkhamsted

W of Ireland Open Chpshp
Mar 17-21
Co Sligo

Duncan Putter
Mar 28-29
Southerndown

Cent England Open Men's 4s
Apr 3-5
Woodhall Spa

UK & Ireland Women's Amateur

Roehampton Gold Scratch Cup
Mar 13
Roehampton

Avia Watches 4s
Mar 17-19
The Berkshire

London 4s
Mar 31-Apr 2
Harewood Downs

USPGA Tour

Mony Tnmt of Champions
Jan 7-10
La Costa CC, Carlsbad

Bob Hope Chrysler Classic
Jan 14-18
La Quinta, Calif

Phoenix Open
Jan 22-25
TPC at Scottsdale, Ariz

AT&T Pebble Beach Pro-Am
Jan 29-Feb 1
Pebble Beach, Calif

Hawaiian Open
Feb 5-8
Waialae CC, Honolulu

Shearson Lehman Bros-Andy Williams Open
Feb 12-15
Torrey Pines GC, Calif

Los Angeles Open
Feb 19-22
Riviera CC, Pacific Palisades

Doral Ryder Open
Feb 26-Mar 1
Doral CC, Miami, Fla

Honda Classic
Mar 5-8
TPC at Eagle Trace, Coral Springs

Hertz Bay Hill Classic
Mar 12-15
Bay Hill Club & Lodge Orlando, Fla

USF&G Classic
Mar 19-22
Lakewood CC, New Orleans

Tnmt Players Chpshp
Mar 26-29
TPC at Sawgrass, Fla

Greater Greensboro Open
Apr 2-5
Forest Oaks CC, NC

Abbreviations used:

Cent	=	Central
Champ	=	Champion
Chpshp	=	Championship
Euro	=	European
4s	=	Foursomes
Intl	=	International
MP	=	Matchplay
Qualif	=	Qualifying
R	=	Royal
Regl	=	Regional
Scand	=	Scandinavian
SP	=	Strokeplay
T	=	Team
Tnmt	=	Tournament

Week beginning	Major Championships	PGA European Tour	WPGA Tour
APR 5			
12	**The Masters** Apr 9-12 Augusta, Ga	**Jersey Open** Apr 9-12 La Moye	
19		**Suze Open** Apr 16-19 Cannes Mougins	
26		**CEPSA Madrid Open** Apr 23-26 Puerta de Hierro	
MAY 3		**Italian Open** Apr 30-May 2 Monticello, Como	**Ford Ladies' Classic** Apr 29-May 2 Woburn
10		**Epson Grand Prix** May 7-10 St Pierre, Chepstow	
17		**Peugeot Spanish Open** May 14-17 Las Brisas, Malaga	**French Open** May 14-17 *Tba*
24		**Whyte & Mackay PGA Chpshp** May 22-25 Wentworth	**British Olivetti Tnmt** May 20-23 Moor Hall
31		**London Standard 4 Stars Natl Pro-Celebrity** May 28-31 Moor Park	**Ulster VW Classic** May 27-30 Belvoir Park
JUN 7		**Dunhill British Masters** June 4-7 Woburn	**McEwan's Wirral Classic** June 3-6 Caldy
14		**Peugeot French Open** June 11-14 *Tba*	**Belgian Ladies' Open** June 11-14 R Waterloo
21	**US Open** June 18-21 Olympia, San Francisco	*Tba* June 18-21	**Volmac Ladies' Open** June 18-21 The Hague
28		**Carrolls Irish Open** July 2-5 Portmarnock **Johnnie Walker Monte Carlo Open** June 24-27 Mont Agel	**Hennessy Cognac Ladies' Cup** July 2-5 St Germain **Portuguese Ladies' Open** June 25-28 Vale do Lobo

UK & Ireland Men's Amateur

Halford-Hewitt Cup
Apr 9-12
R Cinque Ports & R St Georges

Peter McEvoy Trophy
Apr 15-16
Copt Heath

Hampshire Hog
Apr 19
North Hants

Selborne Salver
Apr 18
Blackmoor

Scottish Boys' Chpshp
Apr 13-18
Dunbar

W of England SP
Apr 26-27
Tba

Wimborne Cup
May 2
Parkstone

Pines Trophy
May 10
Hillside, Lancs

Lytham Trophy
May 2-3
R Lytham & St Anne's

Welsh SP
May 9-10
Llandudno (Maesdu)

Scotland *v* France
May 16-17
Chantilly

England *v* Spain
May 10-11
Fulford

Lagonda Trophy
May 20-21
Camberley Heath

Brabazon Trophy
May 15-17
Ganton

Tillman Trophy
May 22-24
Woodhall Spa

Scottish Boys' T Chpshp
May 24
Baberton

Walker Cup
May 27-28
Sunningdale

Rosebery Cup
May 23
Ashridge

The Amateur Chpshp
June 1-6
Prestwick & Prestwick St Nicholas

E of Ireland Open
May 30-June 1
Co Louth

Irish Seniors' Open
June 11-12
Castleroy

English Open Seniors'
June 4-6
Fleet, North Hants

Berkshire Trophy
June 13-14
The Berkshire, Ascot

Scottish Open SP
June 13-14
Lundin Links & Ladybank

Scottish Youths' Open SP
June 20-21
Irvine Bogside & Irvine

Euro Men's Team
June 24-28
Murhof, Austria

SW Counties Week
June 15-20
Burnham & Berrow

Midland Open
June 26-27
Little Aston & Sutton Coldfield

Scottish Seniors' Open SP
July 1-2
Glasgow Killer

Scottish Youths *v* Irish Youths
July 3
Killarney

Irish Youths' Open
July 4-5
Killarney

UK & Ireland Women's Amateur

Midland 4s
Apr 7
Whittington Barracks

Northern 4s
Apr 7-10
Dunham Forest

Mothers' and Daughters' Open 4s
Apr 11
Royal Mid-Surrey

Vilmourin Trophy
Apr 16-20
St Cloud, Paris

Helen Holm Trophy
Apr 25-26
Royal Troon & Troon Portland

W of Scotland
May 1-3
Lanark

SE Counties Week
May 11-15
Royal Cinque Ports

Welsh Chpshp
May 21-23
Aberdovey

Scottish Chpshp
May 19-23
Nairn

English Chpshp
May 19-23
Alwoodley, W Yorks

Wentworth Scratch Trophy
May 29
Wentworth

St Rule Trophy
May 30
St Andrews

Astor Salver
June 3
The Berkshire

Critchley Salver
June 5
Sunningdale

Cotswold Hills Gold Vase
June 6
Cotswold Hills

British Open MP Chpshp
June 9-13
Royal St Davids

European Chpshp
June 22-25
Belgium

Welsh Open SP
June 27-28
Newport

USPGA Tour

The Masters
April 9-12
Augusta, Ga

Deposit Guaranty Classic
Apr 9-12
Hattiesburg CC, Mo

Sea Pines Heritage Classic
Apr 16-19
Harbor Town, SC

Houston Open
Apr 23-26
TPC at Woodlands

Panasonic Las Vegas Invitational
Apr 29-May 3
Las Vegas, CC, Nev

Byron Nelson Classic
May 7-10
Las Colinas Sports Club, Irving

Colonial National Invitl
May 14-17
Colonial CC, Tex

Georgia-Pacific Atlanta Classic
May 21-24
Atlanta CC, Ga

Memorial Tnmt
May 28-31
Muirfield Village GC, Ohio

Kemper Open
June 4-7
TPC at Avenel, Md

Manufacturers' Hanover Westchester Classic
June 11-14
Westchester

The US Open
June 18-21
Olympic GC, San Francisco

Provident Classic
June 18-21
Valleybrook G&CC, Tenn

Canon Sammy Davis Jnr Greater Hartford Open
June 25-28
TPC of Connecticut

Canadian Open
July 2-5
Glen Abbey

Week beginning	Major Championships	PGA European Tour		WPGA Tour		
JUL 5		**The Open Chpshp Regl Qualif** July 6-7 Glenbervie, Haggs Castle, Hankley Common, Langle Park, Lindrick, Little Aston, Ormskirk, Porters Park	**Open Chpshp Final Qualif** July 12-13 Gullane, Longniddry, Luffness, North Berwick			
12				**European Open** July 9-12 *Tba*		
19	**The Open** July 16-19 Muirfield		**116th Open Chpshp** July 16-19 Muirfield			
26		**KLM Dutch Open** July 23-26 Hilversum				**Bloor Homes' Eastleigh Classic** July 22-25 Fleming Park
AUG 2			**Scand Enterprise Open** July 30-Aug 2 Ullna, Sweden	**British Open** July 30-Aug 2 *Tba*		
9	**USPGA** Aug 6-9 PGA National, Palm Beach Gardens, Fla	**PLM Open** Aug 6-9 Ljunghusens, Malmö			**BMW German Open** Aug 6-9 Hamburg	
16			**Benson & Hedges Intl** Aug 13-16 Fulford, York			**Borlänge Open** Aug 13-16 Borlänge, Sweden
23		**Lawrence Batley Intl** Aug 20-23 Birkdale		**Kristianstad Open** Aug 20-23 Kristianstad, Sweden		
30			**Lufthansa German Open** Aug 27-30 Frankfurt		**Euro Masters** Aug 27-30 Boras, Sweden	
SEP 6		**EBEL Euro Masters – Swiss Open** Sept 3-6 Crans-sur-Sierre				**Bowring Scottish Ladies' Open** Sept 3-6 *Tba*
13			**Panasonic Euro Open** Sept 10-13 Walton Heath	**Italian Ladies' Open** Sept 10-13 Croara, Piacenza		
20		*Tba* Sept 17-20				
27		**Dunhill Cup** Oct 1-14 St Andrews	**Ryder Cup** Sept 24-27 Muirfield Village, Ohio		**Laing Ladies' Classic** Oct 23-26 Stoke Poges	

UK & Ireland Men's Amateur

Euro Boys' T Chpshp
July 7-11
Chantilly, France

N of Ireland Open
July 11-15
Royal Portrush

Gold Cross
July 12
Royal St Davids

Scottish Boys' Open SP
July 14-15
Lanark

Welsh Boys' Chpshp
July 21-24
Monmouthshire

Carris Trophy
July 22-23
Moor Park

Frame Trophy
July 23-25
Worplesdon

The English Chpshp
July 27-Aug 1
Frilford Heath

The Scottish Chpshp
July 27-Aug 1
Nairn

The Welsh Chpshp
July 25-Aug 1
Royal Porthcawl

British Seniors'
Aug 5-7
R Cinque Ports

N of England Open Youths'
Aug 5-7
Middlesborough

Scotland *v* Germany
Aug 7
Leven

British Youths' Chpshp & Intls
Aug 18-22
Hollinwell

Irish Boys' Close
Aug 27-28
Warrenpoint, Co Down

West Midlands Open
Aug 30
Sandwell Park

English Champ Club Tnmt
Sept 4-5
Finham Park

Home Intls
Sept 9-11
Lahinch

County Presidents & IMS Tnmt
Sept 19
Wollaton Park, Notts

English County Champs Tnmt
Sept 20
Sherwood Forest, Notts

Welsh Seniors' Chpshp
Sept 23-24
Aberdovey

Open Mixed 4s
Sept 25-27
Worplesdon

Central Eng Mixed 4s
Oct 1-4
Woodhall Spa

English County Finals
Sept 25-27
Northumberland

UK & Ireland Women's Amateur

Scottish Girls' Chpshp
July 15-17
Stirling

Euro Team Chpshp
July 8-12
Turnberry

English County Finals
July 15-17
Copt Heath

Bridget Jackson Bowl
July 21
Handsworth

Northern Girls' Chpshp
July 23
Seaton Carew

SW Girls' Chpshp
July 23
Launceston

Welsh Girls' Chpshp
July 26-30
Cardiff

Scottish Girls' Open SP
Aug 4-5
Douglas Park

English Girls' Chpshp
Aug 4-7
Sandy Lodge & Aldenham

Girls' Home Intls
Aug 11-12
Barnham Broom

British Girls' Open Chpshp
Aug 13-14
Barnham Broom

English SP
Aug 12-14
Northumberland

English Intermediate Chpshp
Aug 19-20
Sheringham

British Open SP
Aug 26-28
Purdis Hill

Home Intls
Sept 16-18
Ashburnham

Vagliano Trophy
Sept 25-26
The Berkshire

British Senior Chpshp
Oct 6-7
Copt Heath

USPGA Tour

Anheuser-Busch Golf Classic
July 9-12
Kingsmil GC, Williamsburg

Hardee's Classic
July 16-19
Oakwood CC, Ill

Buick Open
July 23-26
Warwick Hills G&CC
Grand Blanc, Mich

Federal Express St Jude Classic
July 30-Aug 2
Colonial CC, Tenn

USPGA Chpshp
Aug 6-9
PGA National, Palm Beach Gardens, Fla

The International
Aug 12-16
Castle Pines GC, Castle Rock, Colo

Western Open
Aug 20-23
Butler National GC, Oak Brook, Ill

NEC World Series of Golf
Aug 27-30
Firestone CC, Akron, Ohio

BC Open
Sept 3-6
En-Joie CC, Endicott, NY

Bank of Boston Classic
Sept 10-13
Pleasant Valley CC, Sutton

Greater Milwaukee Open
Sept 17-20
Tuckaway CC, Franklin, Wis

Ryder Cup
Sept 24-27
Muirfield Village, Ohio

Southwest Classic
Sept 24-27
Fairway Oaks, Abilene, Tex

Week beginning	Major Championships	PGA European Tour	WPGA Tour
OCT 4		**German Masters** Oct 8-11 Stuttgart	
11		**Equity and Law Challenge** Oct 12-13 Royal Mid-Surrey	
18		**Suntory World Matchplay** Oct 15-18 Wentworth	**James Capel Guernsey Open** Oct 1-4 Royal Guernsey, CI
25		**Barcelona Open** Oct 22-25 El Prat	
NOV 1		**Portuguese Open** Oct 29-Nov 1 *Tba*	
8		**Nissan Cup** Nov 5-8 Tokyo, Japan	
15			
22			
29			
DEC 6			
13			
20			
27			

UK & Ireland Men's Amateur

UK & Ireland Women's Amateur

Mixed Open 4s
Sept 25-27
Worplesdon

Ladies' Commonwealth Tnmt
Oct 23-24
New Zealand

USPGA Tour

Southern Open
Oct 1-4
Green Island CC, Columbus, Ga

Pensacola Open
Oct 8-11
Perdido Bay CC, Pensacola, Fla

Walt Disney World/ Oldsmobile Classic
Oct 15-18
Lake Buena Vista, Fla

Tallahassee Open
Oct 22-25
Killearn G&CC, Fla

Tucson Open
Oct 22-25
TPC at Star Pass, Ariz

Nabisco Chpshp
Oct 29-Nov 1
Oak Hills CC, Tex

Nissan Cup World Chpshp
Nov 5-8
Japan

Isuzu Kapalua Intl
Nov 12-15
The Bay Course, Maui

Skins Game
Nov 28-29
TPC at PGA West, Calif

JC Penney Classic
Dec 3-6
Bardmoor CC, Largo, Fla

Chrysler Team Chpshp
Dec 10-13
Boca Raton, Fla

Buyer's Guide to Good Golfing and Golf Course Maintenance

The immense value of a simple, compact but informative guide to manufacturers and organisations offering services to golf clubs and individual golfers has not gone unnoticed, and the editors are pleased to include the **Buyer's Guide to Good Golfing** *for the first time in the 1987 edition.*

This useful addition to the **Benson and Hedges Golfer's Handbook** *should prove to be especially valuable to golf club officials.*

Club Management and Training Courses

Club Management Services
50 Town Street, Duffield, Derby DE6 4GG. *Tel* (0332) 840075
Provision of training courses in Golf Club Management. Existing correspondence courses for Secretary/Managers and Stewards. Management consultancy service for Golf Clubs.

Club Ties

Macaseta
George St Mills, Macclesfield, Cheshire SK11 6HT. *Tel* (0625) 23078/22411
Club ties from the weaving specialist, friendly advice, free artwork, also headsquares, scarves, sweaters, sweat-shirts, T-shirts and badges.

Event Organisers

Tryangle Management International Ltd
2nd Floor, 6 Church Street, Altrincham, Cheshire WA14 4DW. *Tel* 061-941 5747
If golf is your game, Tryangles aim is making the most of events you host. Specialists in Pro-Ams, Company Days and Clinics incorporating WPGA Players.

Golf Cars and Trolleys

F & L Smout & Sons Ltd
Station Works, Woods Lane, Cradley Heath, West Midlands B64 7AH. *Tel* Cradley Heath 69508
Manufacturers and distributors of the Fordham range of golf trolleys. Bag stands and ball retrievers.

Froe Cars Ltd
Unit 2, Avongorge Industrial Centre, Portview Road, Bristol BS11 9LQ. *Tel* (0272) 821934
Importers and distributors of one of America's top selling golf buggies in 4-stroke petrol or quiet electric motor.

Mitsui Machinery Sales (UK) Ltd
Oakcroft Road, Chessington, Surrey KT9 1SA. *Tel* 01-397 5111
Suppliers of top selling Yamaha golf car. Available through national network of distributors. Various schemes include lease purchase or seasonal hire contracts to Clubs.

Powa Kaddy International Ltd
Sittingbourne Industrial Park, Sittingbourne, Kent ME10 3JH. *Tel* (0795) 73555
Manufacturers and distributors worldwide of electronic self-propelled golf trolleys. Powakaddy is totally maintenance free and is enjoyed by over 40,000 golfers around the world.

Quality Golf Clothing

Burberrys of London
29/53 Chatham Place, London E9 6LP. *Tel* 01-985 3344
A comprehensive range of golf bags and holdalls, in five colour ways with matching golf umbrellas, head covers, shoes, etc. Also available, a comprehensive collection of golf clothing for men and women.

Lady Golf
405 Kingston Road, Ewell, Epsom, Surrey KT19 0BT. *Tel* 01-393 8731
Ladies Only! Clothing and equipment—comprehensive ranges for summer and winter. (Branches at Ewell, Surrey and Amersham, Bucks.)

RC Redman (Pro Quip) Ltd
Wisloe Road, Cambridge, Gloucestershire GL2 7AF. *Tel* **(0453) 89707**
Manufacturers of the world's leading waterproof golf suit. Pro Quip suits incorporate a GORETEX membrane, making them 100% waterproof and breatheable—guaranteed for two years.

Golf Course Architects

British Association of Golf Course Architects
Hon Secretary, 5 Oxford Street, Woodstock, Oxford OX7 1TQ. *Tel* **(0993) 811976**
Professional Association of qualified golf course Architects officially recognised by the R&A and English Golf Union.

Golf Development International (Joan F Dudok Van Heel)
4 Beukenlaan, 1640 St Genesius-Rode, Belgium. *Tel* **(02) 3585518/3583387**
Architecture, design and construction—supervision of golf courses. Consultancy on golf course and club management. Feasibility studies—promoting and developing the game of golf.

Hamilton Stutt & Co
12 Bingham Avenue, Poole, Dorset BH14 8NE. J Hamilton Stutt. *Tel* **(0202) 708406**
Founder member of the British Association of Golf Course Architects.

Donald Harradine Golf Course Architect
CH-6987 Caslano, Switzerland. *Tel* **091 71 17 61**
Planning and construction of golf courses and playing fields.

Harradine Ltd
CH-6300 ZUG, Untermuhlenweg 7, Switzerland. *Tel* **(042) 319966**
Design and/or construction of golf courses including all related landscaping, buildings and adjacent sports facilities.

Hawtree & Son
5 Oxford Street, Woodstock, Oxford OX7 1TQ. *Tel* **(0993) 811976**
Hawtree & Son celebrates 75 years of architectural service throughout the world. Three generations of Hawtrees have built 200 new golf courses and made alterations to 600 existing courses.

John Jacobs Golf Associates Ltd
68a High Street, Walkern, Stevenage, Herts SG2 7PG. *Tel* **(0438) 86438**
Golf course architects/consultants with a vast knowledge and understanding of public and private sector golf. Leaders in the golf centre design and development field.

Dr ING Pier Luigi Mancinelli (AGW EAGCA)
21 Via Achille Papa, 00195 Roma, Italy. *Tel* **06-311764**
Design golf complexes, club houses, urban planning. Complete assistance with construction, landscaping and water systems.

TJA McAuley
38 Moira Drive, Bangor BT20 4RW, Ireland. *Tel* **(0247) 465953** *Tx* **74195**
Golf course design, environmental impact appraisal, civil and structural engineering, water resources.

Golf Course Maintenance

J Gibbs Ltd
Stanwell Road, Bedfont, Feltham, Middlesex TW14 8ND. *Tel* **01-890 5071**
For service–get on to GIBBS: Tractor and machinery sales, parts and service specialists for the grass maintenance of golf courses, playing fields and estates.

Golf Landscapes Ltd
Ashwells Road, Bentley, Brentwood, Essex CM15 9SR. *Tel* **(0277) 73720**
The country's leading specialists in golf course, construction, drainage and irrigation working throughout Europe, with leading international golf course architects.

P & E
New Road Warehouse, Princes Riseborough, Bucks HP17 0JN. *Tel* **(084 44) 4122/3**
Supply of professional and domestic horticultural machinery including Yanmar and Wheel House tractors, Greens Gang and Cylinder mower systems, Oravely grass machinery, Blues Brushcutters, etc.

Rigby Taylor Ltd
Sports Turf Specialists, Garside Street, Bolton BL1 4AE. *Tel* **(0204) 394888**
Suppliers of high quality turf care products, straight and slow release fertilizers. Total and selective weedkillers, fungicides, grass seed and all ancillary golfers' items.

Golf Club Manufacturers

Dunlop Golf Division
PO Box 8, Normanton, West Yorkshire WF6 1YX. *Tel* **(0924) 896868**
Manufacturers of golf balls (Maxfli DDH 500, Dunlop 65i) and golf clubs under the Maxfli and Dunlop brands. A wide range of bags, gloves, umbrellas and accessories are available.

John Letters of Scotland
Old Bridge Golf Works, Earl Haig Road, Hillington, Glasgow G52 4JU. ***Tel*** **041-882 9923**
Established in 1918, traditional makers of high quality clubs including the Master Model range, PGA European Tour Model, Leading Lady, Golden Goose and Barker putters.

Prosimmon Golf (UK) Pty Ltd
21 Monkspath Business Park, Highlands Road, Shirley, Solihull, West Midlands B90 4NZ. ***Tel*** **021-744 9551**
Manufacturers of golf clubs, seven models, men's, ladies' right-hand, left-hand, individual clubs and customising available. Also golf bags, holdalls, shirts, sweaters, rainwear, gloves and accessories.

Ram Golf UK
Bell Lane, Uckfield, East Sussex TN22 1QL. ***Tel*** **(0825) 61266**
Manufacturers and wholesalers of the Ram range of golf clubs, balls, bags and leisurewear, including the Tour Grind, Laser, Axial and Accubar models.

Slazenger Golf Division
PO Box 8, Normanton, West Yorkshire WF6 1YX. ***Tel*** **(0924) 896868**
Slazenger manufacture a complete range of golfing equipment. Golf balls include B51 XTC Tour Wound and B51 XD+ Two Piece. Clubs include the forged Supremo and the new cavity back Seve XTC. Gloves, bags and umbrellas complete the range.

Swilken Golf Company Ltd
Tom Stewart Lane, St Andrews, Fife, Scotland. ***Tel*** **(0334) 72266**
Manufacturers of golf clubs and putters, sole distributor of Dexter golf shoes and Bridgestone golf balls.

Taylor Made (Great Britain) Ltd
Annecy House, Gastons Wood, Reading Road, Basingstoke, Hants RG24 0TW. ***Tel*** **(0256) 479797**
Distributors of Metalwoods, TDF Irons, TDA Putters. Taylor Made is the number one used driver on the USPGA Tour. No. 1 Fairway wood on the European Tour.

Golf Ball Manufacturers

Dunlop Golf Division
PO Box 8, Normanton, West Yorkshire WF6 1YX. ***Tel*** **(0924) 896868**
Manufacturers of golf balls (Maxfli DDH 500, Dunlop 65i) and golf clubs under the Maxfli and Dunlop brands. A wide range of bags, gloves, umbrellas and accessories are available.

Kamatari (UK) Ltd
Unit 20, Forbury Industrial Park, Kenavon Drive, Reading RG1 3HS. ***Tel*** **(0734) 508616**
The world's largest manufacturer and distributor of golf gloves with a wide range of gloves. Also the most advanced technical golf ball manufacturer and distributor.

Ram Golf UK
Bell Lane, Uckfield, East Sussex TN22 1QL. ***Tel*** **(0825) 61266**
Manufacturers and wholesalers of the Ram range of golf clubs, balls, bags and leisurewear, including the Tour Grind, Laser, Axial and Accubar models.

Slazenger Golf Division
PO Box 8, Normanton, West Yorkshire WF6 1YX. ***Tel*** **(0924) 896868**
Slazenger manufacture a complete range of golfing equipment. Golf balls include B51 XTC Tour Wound and B51 XD+ Two Piece. Clubs include the forged Supremo and the new cavity back Seve XTC. Gloves, bags and umbrellas complete the range.

Swilken Golf Company Ltd
Tom Stewart Lane, St Andrews, Fife, Scotland. ***Tel*** **(0334) 72266**
Manufacturers of golf clubs and putters. Sole distributor of Dexter golf shoes and Bridgestone golf balls.

General Accessories

Dunlop Golf Division
PO Box 8, Normanton, West Yorkshire WF6 1YX. ***Tel*** **(0924) 896868**
Manufacturers of golf balls (Maxfli DDH 500, Dunlop 65i) and gold clubs under the Maxfli and Dunlop brands. A wide range of bags, gloves, umbrellas and accessories are available.

Kamatari (UK) Ltd
Unit 20, Forbury Industrial Park, Kenavon Drive, Reading RG1 3HS. ***Tel*** **(0734) 508616**
The world's largest manufacturer and distributor of golf gloves with a wide range of gloves. Also the most advanced technical golf ball manufacturer and distributor.

Prosimmon Golf (UK) Pty Ltd
21 Monkspath Business Park, Highlands Road, Shirley, Solihull, West Midlands B90 4NZ. ***Tel*** **021-744 9551**
Manufacturers of golf clubs, seven models, men's, ladies' right-hand, left-hand, individual clubs and customising available. Also golf bags, holdalls, shirts, sweaters, rainwear, gloves and accessories.

Ram Golf UK
Bell Lane, Uckfield, East Sussex TN22 1QL. *Tel* (0825) 61266
Manufacturers and wholesalers of the Ram range of golf clubs, balls, bags and leisurewear, including the Tour Grind, Laser, Axial and Accubar models.

Shoobag Company
2215 Coventry Road, Sheldon, Birmingham B26 3EH. *Tel* 021-742 0721
The Shoobag company manufacture and personalise shoe bags for golfers and for the individual, but mainly for companies sponsoring events, Captains' days out or pro-ams. The ideal giveaway.

Slazenger Golf Division
PO Box 8, Normanton, West Yorkshire WF6 1YX. *Tel* (0924) 896868
Slazenger manufacture a complete range of golfing equipment. Golf balls include B51 XTC Tour Wound and B51 XD+ Two Piece. Clubs include the forged Supremo and the new cavity back Seve XTC. Gloves, bags and umbrellas complete the range.

Swilken Golf Company Ltd
Tom Stewart Lane, St Andrews, Fife, Scotland. *Tel* (0334) 72266
Manufacturers of golf clubs and putters. Sole Distributor of Dexter golf shoes and Bridgestone golf balls.

Golf Club Grips

Avon Industrial Polymers Ltd
Bath Road, Melksham, Wiltshire SN12 8AA. *Tel* (0225) 707666 *Tx* 44142
Avon's range of pioneering golf grip designs includes the Chamois, Charger Pro-cushion and Pro-Select grips, suitable for all skill levels from the high handicap player to the professional.

Golf Holidays

Arrow Holidays
Alban Row, 27–31 Verulam Road, St Albans, Herts. *Tel* (0727) 66200
Summer programme, we concentrate on villa and apartments. Write: Sun and Sports—mainly golf.

Jet Golf Holidays
Prospect House, East Cliff, Preston, Lancashire PR1 3JE. *Tel* (0772) 28222
Europe's major golf Tour operator offers exciting golf holidays to Costa del Sol, Algarve, Villamartin, Tenerife, Lisbon, Las Palmas, Almeria, Majorca. Phone (0772) 28222 for further details.

La Manga Club
c/o Silver City House, 62 Brompton Road, London SW3 1BW. *Tel* 01-225 0411
The most prestigious golf resort in Southern Spain. Two championship golf courses. Seve Ballesteros is the Touring Professional. Winter HQ of the PGA European Tour.

Golf Practice Equipment

Golf Aids of Reading
470 Reading Road, Winnersh, Wokingham, Berkshire RG11 5ET. *Tel* (0836) 240509
Manufacturers of probably the finest range of golf practice nets in Europe. Exclusive green polyethylene netting also sold by the roll for multi-purpose uses.

PN Structures Ltd
Piccadilly, 5 Vigo Street, London W1X 1AH. *Tel* 01-734 2578 *Tx* 884 392
Suppliers and installers of low-maintenance synthetic golf greens fully guaranteed and developed to the latest state of the art. Also suppliers of golf mats for practice ranges.

Irrigation Equipment and Installation

Sportsground Irrigation Co
Hereward Lodge, Paget Road, Lubenham, Market Harborough, Leics LE16 9TC. *Tel* (0858) 63153
Irrigation engineers, specializing in golf course equipment and installations. Annual service contracts offered on any system.

Watermation Ltd
Monument Way East, Woking, Surrey GU21 5LY. *Tel* (04862) 70303
Manufacturers and installers of top quality golf course irrigation equipment, including computer controllers (TW1 and TW2) and pop-up sprinklers (GN range) made from brass and bronze with rubber covers.

Publishers and Booksellers

Grant Books
Victoria Square, Droitwich, Worcester. *Tel* (0905) 778155
Booksellers and publishers of golf books. Trade and retail sales. Publishers of golf club histories and limited edition golf books. *A Golf Book Centre*.

Specialist Sports Matting

Nuway Manufacturing Co Ltd
Colport, Telford, Shropshire TF8 7HX. *Tel* (0952) 680400
Nuway Longlife Golf mats—for protecting heavily played teeing areas during the winter. Tuf-F-tuff—matting for sports complexes where studded/spiked footwear presents a problem.

Benson and Hedges Sports Photographers' Awards 1986

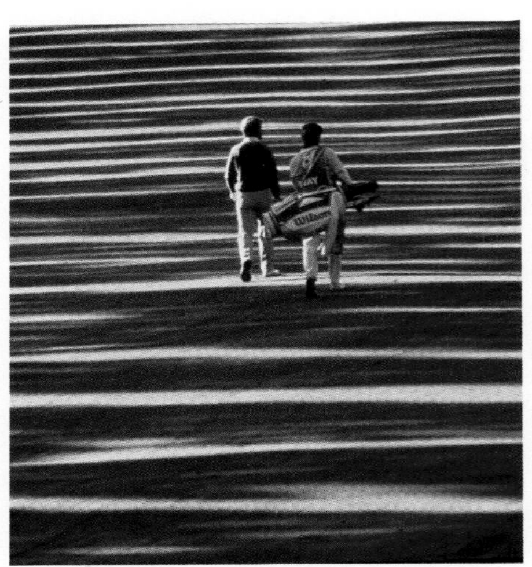

Norman Lomax's winning photograph. Paul Way and his caddie during the Benson and Hedges International at Fulford in August 1986.

Norman Lomax, a freelance photographer from Brixton Hill, South London, was the winner in the golf category of the Benson and Hedges Sports Photographers' Awards for 1986.

The Awards, formed earlier this year, are a union of the previously successful Benson and Hedges Cricket Year and Golfer's Handbook Professional Photographers' Awards. The new competition comprises three Award categories: Golf, Cricket and Portfolio, and entrants are asked to submit photographs of a high standard, both technically and visually.

Norman's winning entry captures Paul Way and his caddie during the Benson and Hedges International at Fulford in August 1986. Originally commissioned by *Sportsweek*, this evocative photograph won Norman one of the three top prizes – a Gold Trophy and £500.

Tommy Hindley, a freelance photographer from Great Amwell, Hertfordshire, won a Highly Commended Award of £100 for his photograph of Nick Faldo chipping out of a bunker in the European Open, Sunningdale, in September 1986.

Simon Bruty, an Allsport photographer from Winchester also received a Highly Commended Award for his shot of Lanny Wadkins at St Andrews, September 1986.

A special award was presented to Mathew Harris, a freelance photographer from Tring, for an individual photograph included in his portfolio entry of six golf pictures. Entitled *Aussie Rodger Snaps Back* it features Rodger Davis posing with an imaginary camera at the Four Stars Tournament, Moor Park, in June 1986.

The Cricket Award was won by Adrian Murrell of Allsport Photographic who lives in Long Ditton, Surrey. Patrick Eagar, a freelance photographer from Kew Gardens, Surrey, won the Award for the best Portfolio entry.

The expert judging panel for the Awards included Peter Alliss, TV and radio golf commentator; Michael Cranmer, Picture Editor, *Sunday Times*; golfer Bernard Gallacher, Associate Editor of the *Benson and Hedges Golfer's Handbook* and Gerry Cranham, Sports Photographer. They were set the task of selecting the most outstanding photographs of the season. Sally Jones, Sports Presenter of BBC TV's *Breakfast Time*, presented the Awards at a reception held at The Savoy, London, at the end of last year.

Sally Jones, BBC TV Breakfast Time *Sports Reporter presents Photographers' Awards. Pictured from left to right are Mathew Harris, Sally Jones, Norman Lomax, Cliff Jameson of Benson and Hedges, Tommy Hindley and Simon Bruty.*

Part I
1986 Season

Golfer of the Year

The Champion with his wife, Laura, and children Morgan Leigh and Gregory.

The selection panel did not take long to choose the Benson & Hedges Golfer of the Year for 1986. After a few other candidates had been eliminated for a variety of reasons, Greg Norman of Australia was adjudged the winner.

The Norman Invasion

Greg Norman has been a familiar figure on the European tour since he first came here in 1977 at the age of 22 and won the Martini Tournament at Blairgowrie. It was then that the appellation *the Norman Conquest* was originated by the Tournament Press Officer, George Simms, who, with a flash of sharp-eyed inspiration, noted that Norman was 10 under after 66 holes. He promptly recorded that moment on the leader board with his camera.

Over the years he has often been seen, with his bright fair hair shining in the sunlight, patrolling the fairways with an air of determination, looking a likely winner all the time; but contrary to expectations he never won a major championship. Many successes had come his way, including two at each of the World Match-Plays at Wentworth and the Australian Open, one at each of the Canadian, French and New Zealand Opens and many other victories on the US, European, Australian and Japanese tours.

It has taken Greg a long time to prove to his many supporters that he could win a Major. When he finally broke through at Turnberry, he did it in style by 5 shots, the widest margin since Johnny Miller won at Birkdale in 1976. Some had doubted whether he possessed the steel to avoid the wayward shot at the crucial stage in the last round of a Championship. Earlier in the year at the Masters in Augusta, he had thrown away a winning lead at the last hole losing by a stroke to Nicklaus's amazing charge. Two months later in the US Open at Shinnecock Hills he again led into the final round and was unable to clinch the title. However, his record of leading in the last round at each of the four Major Championships is unlikely to be equalled for a long time.

Photograph taken by George Simms

Martini Tournament 1977 at Blairgowrie. Norman 10 under after 66 holes!

The First Major

The critical round at Turnberry was the second when he returned a marvellous 63, which equalled the course record and was the lowest round in any Open. His 74 in the third, when bad weather meant that no-one broke 70, kept him in front by one stroke from Tommy Nakajima, the best of the Japanese professionals. Nakajima, playing with Greg, scuppered his chances in the opening holes of that final round. Thereafter it was a triumphal march for the title. The further Greg went, the more he looked the ultimate winner and this time he sailed home comfortably with all his pursuers trailing.

There was no question of relaxing after Turnberry. Three weeks later he looked a likely winner in the USPGA at Inverness, Ohio. In a head-to-head encounter in the last round with Bob Tway, the most improved player on the US tour in 1986, he did not play one loose shot, but was beaten by Tway holing out from a bunker beside the 18th green. In September he returned to the UK to play in three events. By now he was playing with tremendous confidence. First he won the European Open at Sunningdale at the first hole of a play-off with Ken Brown. He moved on to St Andrews to lead the Australian team of three to a win in the Dunhill Nations Cup for the second successive year, and the next week collected the Suntory World Match-play title at Wentworth for the third time, beating Jack Nicklaus by one hole in the semi-final and then Sandy Lyle by 2 and 1.

After so much success it is hardly surprising that he has become the first man to win over $1,000,000 in a year on the world golf circuit. The last occasion an overseas player was the leading money-winner on the US tour was Gary Player in 1961. Greg's total was $653,296. In the UK he amassed £274,363 in four weeks, which included a special bonus of £50,000 for winning both the Open and the European Open.

A Golden Future

Throughout his year he is keenly supported by his wife, Laura, and sometimes his young children, Morgan Leigh and Gregory, are also seen enjoying their father's play. The family now live for most of the year in Florida where Greg returns to snatch the occasional days of leisure which his arduous schedule allows. At 31, he is moving towards his peak and we can expect more Championships to come his way. Tom Watson won five Opens in nine years between 1975 and 1983, most of them in his thirties. There is still plenty of opportunity for more sparkling golf to come from Greg Norman and one has the feeling we shall see his name at the top of the leader board for a few years yet.

The Open Championship

Michael Williams

© Peter Dazeley Photography

Greg Norman holding the most coveted trophy in Golf.

A Major for Norman—at last

The question mark that had long stood against the name of Greg Norman when the golfing stakes are at their highest, was at last erased in the Open Championship at Turnberry when the tall, dashing Australian finally won the major title that had hitherto eluded him. He did it, moreover, in style, taking the lead in the second round and only briefly being under threat again before he won by five strokes from Gordon J. Brand, of England, who in turn was one ahead of the German, Bernhard Langer, and the Welshman, Ian Woosnam.

This was undoubtedly the peak of a record-breaking year by Norman. He subsequently became the second overseas player, Gary Player being the first, to head the American money list, the first golfer to earn more than one million dollars in prize money worldwide and the first to have gone into the last round of each of the four major championships in the lead. In the wake of all this he also, late in the season, won six consecutive tournaments, three in Britain and three in Australia.

Therefore, at 31, Norman at last realised his full potential. It may well be that in years to come he will always look back at Turnberry as the place where the tide turned. The nerves that had previously betrayed him were still there but this time they were controlled.

This tell-tale flaw in Norman's make-up was evident earlier in the year when, in the Masters at Augusta National, he had needed a birdie three at the last hole to beat Jack Nicklaus. Instead he took five and lost by a stroke. Then, in the United States Open at Shinnecock Hills, he wasted a three-stroke lead after 12 holes of the third round, sliding away on the last day to an anonymous 11th place.

An outstanding round

Even those who believed that Norman was much too good a player for this sort of thing to last for ever were beginning to have their doubts. Norman answered them at Turnberry not in the end by steady consistency (two 74s in his four rounds was indication of that) but by one flash of total brilliance. That has always been his style and it came on the second day when he equalled the championship record with a 63. Yet the measure of that particular round was that it should have been a 62, could have been a 61 and might conceivably have been a 60.

What it also did was put into perspective the severe criticism that had been voiced about the manner in which the course had been set up. During the early days of practice not a breath of wind had filled the sails of the yachts on the Firth of Clyde and one was put in mind of the glorious weather that had attended the last Open at Turnberry in 1977, when Tom Watson and Jack Nicklaus so outplayed everyone else that the rest of the field might as well have gone home. Watson set a record of 268 for the four rounds, Nicklaus finished a stroke behind him but only Hubert Green otherwise beat the par of 280 and then only by a stroke.

Variable weather

This was something that tended to be forgotten and when, on the eve of the 1986 Championship, the weather broke, Turnberry became an entirely different kettle of fish. Some players did not even bother to go out for their final practice rounds while those that did found themselves hitting one irons when previously they had been using wedges. Already narrow fairways looked even narrower, particularly when the driving area was at an angle and the rough was so thick that Raymond Floyd, who a few weeks earlier had won the American Open, speculated that a player could injure himself.

On reflection the Royal and Ancient admitted that perhaps they had overdone the severity here and there, notably at the first, where some players were hitting as little as a five iron for safety, and at the ninth, where the domed fairway proved to be too elusive. Weeks before, Deane Beman, the US Tour commissioner who was briefly abandoning his desk job for a late fling on the golf course, had predicted that no one would beat par at Turnberry. He was dead right. Norman was level par when he won with rounds of 74, 63, 74 and 69.

Though the wind was not as fierce on the opening day of the championship as it had been 24 hours earlier, it was still grey and miserable enough to stop anyone scoring in the 60s. Woosnam alone matched the par of 70 and he led by a stroke from Nick Faldo, the elder Brand, Robert Lee and Anders Forsbrand, of Sweden. While nearly everyone was shedding strokes left, right and centre down the inward half, Woosnam played the last nine holes in 31 and he even had a birdie three at the 14th, which most found to be out of reach in two strokes.

© Peter Dazeley Photography

Ian Woosnam, Welsh Ryder Cup star, finished 4th ahead of all British players except Gordon J. Brand.

© Peter Dazeley Photography

Gordon J. Brand (England), the senior Brand, was second by a stroke from Langer and Woosnam, but still five behind the winner.

Norman had a 74, which left him sharing 16th place but when the sun peeped through again on the Friday afternoon and the wind dropped, so the Australian moved into a majestic stride that carried him into a lead he was never to lose. Out in 32, three under par, he started for home with two more birdies, almost knocked the flag out of the hole for another at the 14th, holed for another three at the 16th and was seven under.

So nearly a 60

All manner of possibilities now loomed for the 17th, though a par five, was within easy reach of two strokes to these chaps and a 62 therefore seemed inevitable. The whole course seemed to hold its breath and when Norman hit a five iron second to 12 feet, the calculations were that if he sank that putt and then finished with a birdie three, he would be round in 60!

Norman was of course only too well aware of what he was about and he admitted later that he could hardly see the hole for excitement as he putted for an eagle on the 17th. He missed it, settled for a birdie and now needed a four at the last for his 62 and the championship record. Sadly even that eluded him as he took three putts, striking his first just too far past to hole the one back. So a 63 it was after all but, much more important, he was in the lead by two strokes from Brand. Faldo and Tommy Nakajima (67) shared third place.

After reasonable weather during the

morning of the third round, there was a sharp deterioration after lunch, which was the last thing the leaders wanted. Only Ho Ming Chung, of Taiwan, succeeded in breaking 70 while Norman, lashed by driving rain, could do no better than a 74. It was good enough to keep him in front but he lost ground to Nakajima who, with some remarkable salvage work around the greens, managed to get round in 71 despite a six at the 16th, where he was in Wilson's burn with his approach.

© Peter Dazeley Photography

Tommy Nakajima (Japan), lying second going into the last round, driving at the famous 9th hole. He threw away his chance early, leaving Norman to romp home.

No win for Japan

Nevertheless there was the distinct possibility of a Japanese golfer at last winning a major championship as the final day dawned to fast clearing skies. Just a stroke separated Norman and Nakajima, Brand and Woosnam being three behind and Gary Koch, of the United States, Jose-Maria Canizares (Spain) and Faldo all six strokes adrift.

The previous evening in the Turnberry Hotel, Nicklaus had advised Norman to think about the pressure of his grip, believing this to be one of the first essentials. Any number of other players also wished the Australian well, clearly believing that it was about time he broke through. His task was quickly made much easier by an untypical mistake from Nakajima.

At the first hole the Japanese missed the green with his approach, though not seriously. He chipped back to six feet or so, which seemed good enough but then, of all things, not only missed his first putt but his second as well. Six. Immediately therefore Norman was three strokes clear of the field.

Victory by five strokes

There was a slight hint of uncertainty with a dropped shot at the fifth and then a pulled drive into the rough at the seventh. But Norman's caddie saw the symptoms in a marginally quickening swing and promptly slowed his man down by telling him to walk at the pace he, the caddie, would dictate. Norman never faltered again and came triumphantly home well clear of the senior Brand, whose eagle three at the 17th for second place capped the week of his life.

Norman is the first Australian to have won the Open Championship since Peter Thomson took the last of his five titles at Royal Birkdale in 1965, and his five-stroke margin was one of the biggest in post-war years. Only Johnny Miller, at Royal Birkdale in 1976, and Arnold Palmer, at Royal Troon in 1982, have won by more: six strokes in each case.

With the BBC at the Open

Bruce Critchley

The great all came
The Open Championship is one of the peaks in the British sporting Summer. Along with Wimbledon, Henley, Ascot and Lords, it helps shape the summer months for the sports enthusiast.

Each year the world's great sportsmen and women visit our shores during June and July. Significantly, they come here without the added lure of appearance money, something that is increasingly rare in the huge cash factory that sport has become around the world. This says much for the esteem in which our major sporting contests are held.

Millions would love to visit these events but a shortage of space and personal resources prohibit it. Thanks to the BBC you can have a ringside seat, and all you need to do is to tune in at the appropriate moment. For the BBC, however, life is not quite so simple. For them the Open Championship starts in October of the previous year. When the golfers tee off at Muirfield in July this year, the BBC will have been planning the coverage for more than 9 months.

© Peter Dazeley Photography

Part of the rear view of the Scanner, the nerve centre of any outside broadcast.

Complexity of TV coverage
Televising any golf tournament is difficult, but the Open is perhaps the most complex sporting broadcast of them all. Compared with football or cricket, golf has 18 *pitches* and up to 30 games going on at any one time. Not only does the BBC have to show the sporting action, but also portray visually the difficulties facing the golfers at each hole and indeed on each shot. To achieve this, there will be some 40 camera rostrums from which it is possible to follow the flight of the ball on every shot. Add to that a commando unit of 6 mobile cameras showing the line of the meanest putt and the agonised expression of the golfer having just missed it, and you begin to realise the sort of facilities which go to make the BBC the best broadcaster of golf in the world.

Obviously, this needs not only careful planning, but a lot of equipment as well. By the time play starts in the Open there will be nearly 50 vehicles of one sort or another in the television compound, some 60 miles of cable draped around the course and more than 250 personnel on site associated with the production. Not only is the BBC resourcing itself, but it also has to provide facilities for other golfing nations, particularly the United States and Japan.

With a lot of neurotic equipment to keep going, there has to be an army of engineers to deal with any misbehaving mechanicals. Since this equipment requires more power than the national grid in that part of the world can provide, the BBC also has to bring its own.

Space at a premium
Muirfield occupies perhaps the smallest piece of ground of any championship course and is not blessed with wide open spaces or even a second course on which to spread the massive paraphernalia that is part of today's Open Championship. What

space there is outside the course is taken over by the tented village and the BBC has to squeeze itself into a tiny corral in the middle of the course. That exercise alone needs the mind of a Rubik cube genius.

Meticulous as the planning will be, flexibility must also be built in. However, no one was prepared for what happened in 1984 when the Open was due to be played at St Andrews. The Old Course can be played backwards, from the 1st tee to 17th green etc., and in fact there is an annual competition played just that way. Imagine the producer's reaction when he received a telex saying that because of the number of people expected to come and watch that year, grandstands would be easier to position if the course was played backwards and that was what the Championship Committee was planning to do. The date? April 1st!

The nerve centre of any outside broadcast is the scanner, a huge control room on wheels, with sides which expand when on site. This unique vehicle moves from event to event and has a top speed of only 23 mph. In summer, so tight is the schedule that often a team of drivers is needed to get it from one place to the next on time.

High technical skills

Without great human skills all these wonderful toys would be useless. The scanner is the home of the production team and it's here that they make the whole box of tricks come to life. Sitting opposite a bank of maybe 30 monitors, they have in front of them a control panel that would do credit to the flight deck of Concorde. From here they mastermind the day's coverage.

The executive producer is the man in overall charge. He decides which matches to follow and the pace and shape of the programme. The director interprets this policy and selects which cameras and shots are to be used, with half-a-dozen others carrying out the instructions. Finally there is the chief engineer, responsible for ensuring that everything works. Answerable to him and sitting in cubby holes at either end of the main area, are skilled technicians monitoring the quality of sound and vision. To an outsider, the whole operation must seem like grown-ups playing space-invaders.

© Peter Dazeley Photography

The Director's choice. He needs a spare set of eyes and not in the back of his head!

Cameras and cameramen

Although there are 40 fixed camera positions covering the whole course, the facilities can only handle 20 cameras at any one time. This is no problem on the first two days when only the closing holes are covered. However, on days 3 and 4, when all 18 holes are covered, this means moving cameras from their positions on the opening holes to others on the back nine while play is in progress. The cameras have to be man-handled off their rostrums, put on the back of landrovers and ferried through the golf and the galleries, an exercise not dissimilar to the car chase in the *Italian Job*.

Golf, unlike most other summer sports continues in any weather. While the play goes on the cameras must follow it. (Spare a thought this year for the cameramen perched on their rostrums should the weather be foul.) Only thunder and lightening brings play to a halt as it's not much fun with all that metal around.

Television viewers not only expect to see every shot but to hear them as well. This means sound men, carrying their grey caterpillar booms, have to get as close as possible to the action. Having done that, their only crime is to get into the picture, and they soon hear about it if they do.

Pitfalls for commentators

There is the equipment, the vision and the sound. Some would say that is enough, but there are commentators as well. A source of irritation or a fund of knowledge? Take your pick. The leader of the pack is, of course, Peter Alliss, a sort of sporting Terry Wogan. He handles the prime moments, such as the leaders going out and, of course, the last groups coming up the 18th, *the final scenes* as Henry Longhurst used to call them.

But Alliss cannot handle it all. With over 30 hours of coverage over the 4 days, even his cosy line of chat might begin to pall. In fact, there are 4 or 5 *ball by ball* commentators working in rota with 2 on at any one time. The producer decides who's doing what and no one argues. One does the odds and the other the evens.

With the exception of Clive Clark, who roams the fairways whatever the weather, all commentary is done from a box usually

The Commentary Box and Studio with Henry Cotton, Alex Hay and Peter Alliss are ready to commentate, with Harry Carpenter in vision.

overlooking some part of the 18th hole. Although all can see out of the window, monitors show the picture you see at home and commentary is laid over that. Early in a commentator's career he learns that the camera can tell a very different story to the one he sees through the window.

To a casual visitor, the box would appear to be a haven of peace and quiet, an ordered existence. Were he able to don a set of headphones, he would soon realise that reality was different. The *cans* as they are known, are the link with the scanner. Through them comes the cocktail party background of the production in full swing.

What the viewer does not see

The producer and director can speak to all concerned with the broadcast. Although both would deny it, they frequently do so at the same time. In moments of crisis the decibels rise in accordance with the severity of the situation. Out of all this the commentator must pick what is relevant to him.

The days are long and tension is often high. Like an airline pilot, the commentator sometimes has to keep the calm flow going, while chaos momentarily reigns. But a great team spirit and a universal sense of humour usually sorts things out.

The commentator has available a vast range of information. Scoring sheets record the performance of every player at every hole. There is a computer linked to the scoring system evaluating all data and providing a mass of statistics. A daily scavenge around the locker room and the press tent provides a few tasty morsels with which to fill the rare pauses in play.

Muirfield is the site for the 1987 Open, the time when all the planning comes to fruition. The BBC will prove once again that it has no peer in major sport presentation. The cast will gather for the performance, but the makeup will have been going on for months. The Open is the event by which golf on television is judged and no effort is spared to see that it succeeds.

PGA European Tour Review of the Year

Colin Callander

Seve Ballesteros, winner of six tournaments, with the Dunlop Masters Trophy.

Ballesteros Europe's star

On the face of things there is no doubt who was the star of European golf in 1986. Seve Ballesteros won six times and accumulated a total of £242,208 in official earnings. Such was his superiority that his lead at the top of the Epson Order of Merit was in excess of £100,000.

Ballesteros had started the year in turmoil. His father had died and he had been suspended for the year from the US PGA Tour. Five near misses in-a-row were not designed to improve his mood, especially as one of those was in The Masters, a tournament he felt he should have won. Nevertheless, once he had won five tournaments in the space of eight weeks during the months of June and July there was never a doubt that he would win the race for the Order of Merit for the fourth time in his career, but for the first time since 1978. His unique tie in the Lancôme Trophy late in the season was, in a sense, incidental as was the fact that during his glorious season he became the first man to win £1 million in career earnings on the PGA European Tour. Perhaps his only regrets were his failure to add to his list of Majors and the fact that his tally of six wins in Europe was one short of the record for most wins in a season set by Australia's Norman von Nida in 1947 and later equalled by Belgium's Flory van Donck in 1953.

Nevertheless, Ballesteros wasn't the only hero during a year in which the total prize money available on the Tour rose to a record £5.4 million. José-Maria Olazabal was one of seven first-time winners, the others being David Feherty, Ove Sellberg, John Morgan, Mark Mouland, Greg Turner and Peter Senior. He shattered all the records for a first year pro. In his baptismal season he was second on the Order of Merit with £136,775, which was three times more than a first year pro had ever won before. He became the first *rookie* since Gordon Brand Jr in 1982 to win two tournaments on Tour and his 50-under par total for 72 rounds and his stroke average of 70.62 were also both records for a first year man.

Norman the World No 1

Then there was Greg Norman who in 1986 was indisputably the No 1 golfer in the world. He led the US PGA money list, the first foreigner to do so for 25 years, and spent most of his time on that Tour. But he also made his mark in Europe. The blond Australian entered only four tournaments on the European Tour in 1986 but won them all. The Open was his first success and when he added the European Open he won a £50,000 bonus for the double. Not content with that he was also Captain of the Australian side which successfully defended the Dunhill Cup and he then won the Suntory World Match-Play Championship for the third time in his career.

Those were the main successes but there were disappointments too. Sandy Lyle won the Greensboro Open in the States but failed to win a tournament in Europe for the

Greg Norman, Open Champion, European and World leading money winner, after winning the European Open at Sunningdale.

first time in eight seasons. The '85 Open Champion dropped to 24th on the Order of Merit and a similar fate befell Sam Torrance who also did not win a tournament. All the same, neither of them were short of a bob or two which was something that couldn't be said for England's Paul Way. Way, a hero of the last two Ryder Cups, slumped to 125th on the Order of Merit and in the process won a mere £5,260. It was a tragic year for the 23-year-old who, during the season before, had won the PGA Championship and a total of £63,097.

Spring Continental Championships
Way's problems started at the Suze Open at Cannes Mougin in France, the first event on the 1986 Tour. He missed the cut there and so was on the sidelines when South Africa's John Bland lifted the trophy with Ballesteros in second place. It was Bland's second win in Europe but his first since the Benson & Hedges in 1983. It was also to be his last for the year, but he went on to win a total of £58,306 which was much more than he had ever won before.

Ballesteros also finished runner-up in the Cepsa Madrid Open, won by Howard Clark, and he could do no better than fourth at Isola Di Albarella where the Italian Open was held. That event was a personal triumph for Ireland's David Feherty who defeated his compatriot, Ronan Rafferty, in a play-off. It was Feherty's first ever victory on Tour but he was to go on to another win in the inaugural Bell's Scottish Open later in the season.

After Feherty's win in Italy the Tour moved to the British Isles for the new Epson Grand Prix Match-Play Championship and again, there was a first-time winner. Both Seve Ballesteros and Bernhard Langer had declined to attend so in their absence Sandy Lyle and Howard Clark had started as tournament favourites. It wasn't to be. Lyle lost in a third place play-off to Sweden's Anders Forsbrand and in the final Forsbrand's friend and compatriot, Ove Sellberg, beat Clark by 3 and 2.

It was a surprise result and the first-ever win by a Swede on the Tour, but the following week Clark bounced back into the winner's circle with a victory in the Peugeot Spanish Open. At that stage the Yorkshireman had opened a considerable gap at the top of the Order of Merit but he wasn't to win again. In the end he dropped to third place but had the not inconsiderable consolation of winning £121,902 in official earnings.

Back to Britain
Australia's Rodger Davis had missed the first four events of the year in Europe but arrived in time to finish eighth in Spain. The following week he did even better defeating Ireland's Des Smyth in a sudden-death play-off for the Whyte & Mackay PGA Championship. It was Davis' first win in Europe for five years but by the end of the season he had gone on to earn a total of £180,000 in official and unofficial earnings. That sum easily eclipsed the total he had earned in nine previous European campaigns.

Australian Rodger Davis, Whyte & Mackay PGA Champion at Wentworth, had his best year and played his part in Australia's Dunhill Cup victory.

The next two tournaments belonged to Spain. Antonio Garrido, himself without a win for four years, won the London Standard Four Stars National Pro-Celebrity tournament and then Seve Ballesteros triumphed at the Dunhill British Masters. That was the start of an incredible run for Ballesteros. He missed the Jersey Open, won by John Morgan, but then captured the Carrolls Irish Open, the Johnnie Walker

Monte Carlo Open and the Peugeot French Open in successive weeks. He didn't compete in the Car Care Plan International, won by another first-timer Mark Mouland, slipped to 6th in The Open, but then won the KLM Dutch Open at Noordwijkse as well. That was enough to guarantee him the top spot on the Order of Merit. Such had been his form that up to and including the Dutch Open he was 87 under par for ten tournaments. He was to finish the year at 127 under par to shatter his own existing cumulative record of 87 under, set last year.

Ballesteros was entitled to a rest and he didn't compete again until the Lufthansa German Open a month or so later. In the interim there turned out to be a surprise or two in store. Greg Turner from New Zealand won the Scandinavian Enterprise Open after a play-off against America's Craig Stadler and the new PLM Open title also went Down Under this time in the hands of Peter Senior. Both were first-time winners in Europe and Senior's victory was all the more surprising because he had spent most of the year struggling on the US Tour where he'd won a mere $2,500. The Queenslander faced a $1,200 fine from the US authorities for missing more than the five tournaments allowed under their rules, but it was a sum he could well afford after winning more than £40,000 during his trip to Europe.

There also turned out to be a surprise at the Benson & Hedges International at Fulford if only because the winner, Mark James, had never won a European Tour title in his native country before. Since turning pro in 1975, the year after he captured the English Amateur title, James had won twice in Ireland, once in Wales and Scotland apiece and three times on the Continent but he had never triumphed in an individual event in England. At Fulford he missed a putt to clinch the title on the 72nd hole but edged out America's Lee Trevino and South Africa's Hugh Baiocchi with a birdie at the first extra hole.

© Peter Dazeley Photography

Mark James, Benson & Hedges winner at Fulford, had his first Tour win since 1983.

There was also a sudden-death play-off needed the following week at the Bell's Scottish Open at Haggs Castle after David Feherty, Christy O'Connor and Ian Baker-Finch had all tied with a four round total of 14-under par at 270. Feherty had suffered a lean spell after the first European win of his career in Italy but he put that behind him in Glasgow in a tournament that had last been contested thirteen years before when Australia's Graham Marsh won at St Andrews.

In 1987, Bell's will have increased their prize fund to around £200,000 and the tournament has been re-scheduled for Gleneagles, just before The Open in an effort to improve the standard of the field. One of those whom the sponsors want to attract is Bernhard Langer who missed the event in 1986 in order to practice for the Lufthansa German Open. It turned out to be the right decision, as the German won his native title for the fourth time in six years. Ballesteros was in the field at Hubbelrath GC but he could only finish in a tie for tenth place as Langer, in front of his own fans, pipped Rodger Davis on the fifth hole of a marathon play-off.

Brand's £1000,000 without a win

At that stage in the season José-Maria Olazabal had become the centre of considerable media attention. The 20-year-old from San Sebastian had been second once and fourth twice earlier in the year so it was not a surprise when he captured his first Tour title at the Ebel European Masters Swiss Open. The Spaniard closed with a six-under par 66 to win the title three ahead of Anders Forsbrand and five ahead of Ian Baker-Finch and Gordon J. Brand, the last of whom won more than £100,000 during the season without a single win.

Brand's biggest cheque for the year came when he finished second behind Greg Norman in the Open Championship at Turnberry. He won £50,000 there, more than he'd collected in a single season before, but that was peanuts compared to the earnings of the Open Champion himself. Norman had won £70,000 at The Open and in the space of three tournaments in the autumn he added a further £204,204. First he won the £35,000 first prize at the European Open at Sunningdale plus a bonus of £50,000 for winning both of Europe's top two titles. He missed the Lawrence Batley International at The Belfry, which was won by Ian Woosnam, but returned to lead his country to victory in the Dunhill Cup and the following week to capture his third Suntory World Match-Play title in six years. The latter two victories were worth a total of £119,204 and he was to continue his winning sequence with a further three wins in a row in Australia.

© Peter Dazeley Photography

José-Maria Olazabal (Spain) after an outstanding Amateur career, finished second in the Order of Merit in his rookie professional year, a remarkable effort.

Olazabal's remarkable debut

The Suntory was the final Tour event within the UK but it wasn't the last on the schedule. From Wentworth, and a tournament marred by Norman's contention that the crowd had been the worst-behaved he'd ever encountered, the Tour moved to the Real Club de Golf El Prat in Barcelona where José-Maria Olazabal notched his second win of the year, this time from a field which included Seve Ballesteros. It was predictable that Olazabal would win the Henry Cotton *Rookie of the Year* Award as the season drew to a close. The award was first given in 1960, during which time it has gone to Tony Jacklin, Peter Oosterhuis and Sandy Lyle among others. But none of them had made such an impact as Olazabal had during his first year.

Olazabal was invited to the next event, the Lancôme Trophy in Paris, but there he had to be content with a share of sixth place. It was an incredible tournament which for the first time in the history of the European Tour failed to produce an outright winner. Bernhard Langer and Seve Ballesteros were level after the regulation 72 holes and it was still the same after bad light halted the proceedings after four extra holes. Due to prior commitments neither could return the following day so the tournament was declared a tie. Ballesteros was awarded his sixth title of the season, Langer his second, and both men departed with an equal share of the £54,544 available for first and second places.

During the season thus far there had been a mere sixteen different winners in 27 events but that number was raised by one when in the final tournament of the season Mark McNulty captured the Quinta do Lago Portuguese Open. It was a title which, for much of the time, seemed destined to go to Sandy Lyle but he slipped in the final round and found himself relegated to a share of fifth place behind McNulty, Ian Mosey, John Bland and José-Maria Canizares. It was McNulty's sixth title of the year worldwide but his first in Europe since 1980 and it raised his earnings for the year in Europe to over £100,000.

© Peter Dazeley Photography

Mark McNulty, one of several South Africans regularly supporting the Tour, rose 60 places in the Order of Merit, winning the Portuguese Open.

Prize Money Record

In fact, McNulty's exact earnings for the year were £101,327 but that was good enough only for sixth place on the Order of Merit. Such has been the growth in European prize money that no fewer than 23 men won in excess of £50,000 and a total of 88 won more than £10,000. In 1987 it might well be that the top 100 all earn a five figure sum because, just as the 1986 season drew to a close, it was announced that the total prize money for 1987 had leapt to a new record of £6.5 million.

This was announced just as six of Europe's top golfers – Ballesteros declined an invitation on health grounds – travelled to Japan to compete in the annual Nissan Cup. After starting well with wins in the preliminary rounds against Japan, Australasia and the United States, the European side, with Bernhard Langer as its Captain and featuring Sandy Lyle, Nick Faldo, Howard Clark, Gordon J. Brand and Ian Woosnam, lost in the final to the home side.

It was a result which summed up the season. It had been a season with much to praise but which never quite reached the heights of 1985 when Europe won the Ryder Cup for the first time since 1957 and a Briton won The Open.

Safari Tour, 1986

Nigerian Open
at Ikoyi Club Lagos

Name	Score	Prize £
G Brand	70-67-65-70-272	16581
M Mackenzie	70-70-70-70-280	11051
N Hansen	67-75-73-68-283	5140
G Smith	70-75-69-69-283	5140
P Kent	68-70-71-74-283	5140
P Carrigill	72-72-70-71-285	2780
A Murray	70-70-74-71-285	2780
D Jones	74-72-66-73-285	2780
J Omoruah	69-71-70-75-285	2780

Ivory Coast Open
at President GC Yamoussoukro

Name	Score	Prize £
G Brand	71-67-66-69-273	9737
B Marchbank	68-67-68-72-275	6484
A Murray	72-67-70-67-276	3661
B Longmuir	72-67-68-72-279	2921
G Cullen	73-68-66-73-280	2473
J Morgan	72-71-70-68-281	1640
J Higgins	73-74-70-64-281	1640
P Cowen	73-71-67-70-281	1640
S Bennett	70-70-69-72-281	1640

555 Kenya Open
at Muthaiga GC Nairobi

Name	Score	Prize £
I Woosnam	70-64-67-72-273	9455
B Longmuir	68-70-69-66-273	6304
(I Woosnam won play-off)		
J-M Canizares	68-66-72-70-276	3552
J-M Olazabal	73-70-66-68-277	2626
G Brand Jr	69-70-68-70-277	2626
G Cullen	69-73-72-64-278	1471
G Brand	70-69-71-68-278	1471
B Mitchell	72-68-69-69-278	1471
P Kent	70-71-66-71-278	1471
B Gallacher	68-71-68-71-278	1471

Zimbabwe Open
at Chapman GC Harare

Name	Score	Prize £
S Bennett	68-69-71-69–277	9096
S Reese	69-72-66-72–279	6061
S Bishop	69-73-71-67–280	3074
R Rafferty	73-70-69-68–280	3074
K Waters	69-70-71-71–281	2312
B McColl	70-70-71-71–282	1910
S Stephen	70-73-72-68–283	1328
R Drummond	74-69-68-72–283	1328
P Brown	71-71-67-74–283	1328
G Ralph	72-69-72-70–283	1328

Zambia Open
at Lusaka GC Zambia

Name	Score	Prize £
G Cullen	70-69-75-69–283	9160
E Darcy	73-68-73-69–283	6110
(G Cullen won play-off)		
B Longmuir	71-73-69-71–284	3220
G Brand	72-74-66-72–284	3220
I Woosnam	71-67-74-73–285	2600
P Thomas	70-68-76-72–286	2050
B McColl	77-71-67-71–286	2050
G Ralph	71-73-69-74–287	1250
J Morgan	72-73-69-73–287	1250
T Horton	74-69-74-70–287	1250
G Brand Jr	71-69-76-71–287	1250

Safari Tour Money List 1986

Pos	Name	Total Prize Money £
1	Gordon Brand (Eng)	31538
2	Garry Cullen (Eng)	14322
3	Bill Longmuir (Scot)	13662
4	Malcolm Mackinezie (Eng)	12764
5	Ian Woosnam (Wal)	12055
6	Stephen Bennett (Eng)	11733
7	Brian Marchbank (Scot)	8915
8	Paul Kent (Eng)	7842
9	Stuart Reese (NZ)	7134
10	Andrew Murray (Eng)	7116
11	Neil Hansen (Eng)	6811
12	Eamonn Darcy (Ire)	6110
13	Gary Smith(Eng)	5793
14	Bill McColl (Scot)	5097
15	Paul Carrigill (Eng)	4926
16	John Morgan (Eng)	4878
17	Keith Waters (Eng)	4731
18	Joe Higgins (Eng)	4616
19	Glenn Ralph (Eng)	4519
20	Paul Thomas (Wal)	4405
21	David Jones (N Ire)	4051
22	Gordon Brand Jr (Scot)	3876
23	Ronan Rafferty (N Ire)	3865
24	David Llewellyn (Wal)	3681
25	Simon Bishop (Eng)	3555
26	Jose-Maria Canizares (Sp)	3552
27	Grant Turner (Eng)	3465
28	Jose-Maria Olazabal (Sp)	3438
29	Mark Roe (Eng)	3427
30	David Ray (Eng)	3418
31	Peter Cowen (Eng)	3264
32	Tommy Horton (Eng)	3237
33	Bobby Mitchell (Eng)	3146
34	Carl Mason (Eng)	3087

European Tour Results, 1986

Suze Open
at Cannes Mougins France

Name	Score	Prize £
J Bland	68-71-70-67-276	17003
S Ballesteros	70-69-68-73-280	11326
N Hansen	73-68-69-72-282	6391
D Smyth	70-71-70-72-283	5102
M Pinero	74-71-73-66-284	3947
I Woosnam	70-72-69-73-284	3947
M Mouland	75-73-67-70-285	2806
G Brand Jr	74-70-70-71-285	2806
H Clark	75-71-72-68-286	2065
A Forsbrand	72-76-67-71-286	2065
M Roe	70-74-70-72-286	2065

Cepsa Madrid Open
at Real Club de Puerta de Hierro Madrid

Name	Score	Prize £
H Clark	70-68-67-69-274	20000
S Ballesteros	69-67-69-70-275	13320
I Woosnam	69-69-70-71-279	7520
J-M Olazabal	72-68-71-69-280	6000
O Sellberg	67-70-72-72-281	5080
B Waites	71-69-69-73-282	3370
R Rafferty	70-70-71-71-282	3370
R Drummond	71-73-71-67-282	3370
G Ralph	73-71-68-70-282	3370
G Brand Jr	69-70-71-73-283	2160
S Torrance	70-71-73-69-283	2160
M King	70-67-73-73-283	2160
A Chandler	73-70-70-70-283	2160

Italian Open
at Isola di Albarella

Name	Score	Prize £
D Feherty	69-67-66-68-270	16587
R Rafferty	69-69-68-64-270	11048
(D Feherty won play-off)		
A Chandler	72-69-65-66-272	6236
E Darcy	73-67-69-64-273	4595
S Ballesteros	70-67-65-71-273	4595
J Slaughter	67-72-71-64-274	2634
M Harwood	68-70-68-68-274	2634
R Lee	72-66-71-65-274	2634
M James	65-71-67-71-274	2634
A Sowa	67-69-68-70-274	2634

Epson Grand Prix of Europe Match-Play Championship

at St Pierre Chepstow Gwent

First round:

S Lyle (Scot) beat C O'Connor Jr (Ire) 1 hole
R Davis (Aus) beat I Baker-Finch (Aus) 5 and 4
P Parkin (Wal) beat J O'Leary (Ire) 3 and 2
E Darcy (Ire) beat P Way (Eng) 5 and 3
R Chapman (Eng) beat M Pinero (Sp) at 20th
D Feherty (N Ire) beat D Smyth (Ire) 4 and 2
B Gallacher (Scot) beat M McLean (Eng) 2 and 1
H Clark (Eng) beat J Rivero (Sp) at 20th
S Bennett (Eng) beat S Torrance (Scot) 1 hole
O Sellberg (Swe) beat N Faldo (Eng) 1 hole
DJ Russell (Eng) beat G Brand (Eng) 2 and 1
R Rafferty (N Ire) beat J-M Canizares (Sp) 1 hole
G Brand Jr (Scot) beat R Hartmann (USA) 5 and 4
R Lee (Eng) beat M James (Eng) 1 hole
A Forsbrand (Swe) beat C Mason (Eng) 2 and 1
I Woosnam (Wal) beat H Baiocchi (SA) at 21st
(Losers won £1350)

Second round:

S Lyle beat R Davis 2 and 1
P Parkin beat E Darcy 1 hole
D Feherty beat R Chapman 3 and 1
H Clark beat B Gallacher 2 and 1
O Sellberg beat S Bennett 2 and 1
DJ Russell beat R Rafferty 1 hole
G Brand Jr beat R Lee 4 and 3
A Forsbrand beat I Woosnam 2 and 1
(Losers won £2850)

Quarter finals:

S Lyle beat P Parkin 2 and 1
H Clark beat D Feherty 1 hole
O Sellberg beat DJ Russell at 19th
A Forsbrand beat G Brand Jr 1 hole
(Losers won £5000)

Semi-finals:

H Clark beat S Lyle 1 hole
O Sellberg beat A Forsbrand 3 and 2

Play-off for 3rd and 4th place:

A Forsbrand beat S Lyle 3 and 2
(Forsbrand won £11250 and Lyle won £8850)

Final:

O Sellberg beat H Clark 3 and 2
(Sellberg won £25000 and Clark won £17500)

Car Care Plan International

at Moortown Leeds

Name	Score	Prize £
M Mouland	72-71-65-64–272	18330
A Forsbrand	69-70-68-66–273	12210
S Torrance	68-72-67-67–274	6890
V Somers	70-67-69-69–275	5500
J-M Canizares	69-68-70-69–276	4660
C Mason	70-71-67-69–277	3300
J Quiros	68-71-73-65–277	3300
H Baiocchi	72-70-69-66–277	3300
D Edwards	69-71-69-69–278	2073
M James	69-72-67-70–278	2073
M Clayton	70-71-67-70–278	2073
L Stephen	65-67-76-70–278	2073
V Fernandez	70-68-72-68–278	2073

French Open

at La Boulie Paris

Name	Score	Prize £
S Ballesteros	65-66-69-69–269	20181
V Fernandez	69-65-69-68–271	13454
B Langer	71-65-68-68–272	7584
N Faldo	66-70-68-70–274	6056
R Hartmann	71-69-67-68–275	4686
A Saavedra	71-68-66-70–275	4686
R Stewart	68-66-77-65–276	3122
M Roe	70-68-70-68–276	3122
R Lee	68-70-66-72–276	3122
W Westner	69-69-72-72–277	2422
M Mouland	71-68-71-68–278	2056
I Baker-Finch	71-69-67-71–278	2056
G Levenson	71-64-71-72–278	2056
O Moore	71-70-68-69–278	2056

The London Standard Four Stars National Pro-Celebrity

At Moor Park GC Herts

Name	Score	Prize £
A Garrido	69-67-71-68–275	21660
R Rafferty	71-67-68-70–276	11290
J-M Olazabal	68-68-72-68–276	11290
M Clayton	69-72-67-69–277	6500
H Baiocchi	71-65-74-69–279	5510
M McNulty	70-70-71-69–280	4225
P Parkin	73-68-69-70–280	4225
B Marchbank	70-72-69-70–281	2788
H Clark	71-69-74-67–281	2788
T Johnstone	72-72-69-68–281	2788
I Woosnam	68-71-74-68–281	2788

Whyte & Mackay PGA Championship

at Wentworth

Name	Score	Prize £
R Davis	73-70-68-70–281	34990
D Smyth	70-72-71-68–281	23310
(R Davis won play-off)		
N Faldo	68-74-74-68–284	13150
S Torrance	74-71-71-69–285	9700
P Walton	71-72-77-65–285	9700
G Brand	74-74-70-68–286	6825
G Taylor	71-71-74-70–286	6825
M McLean	72-71-73-71–287	4716
I Woosnam	74-70-72-71–287	4716
S Lyle	69-78-72-68–287	4716

Jersey Open
at La Moye Jersey

Name	Score	Prize £
J Morgan	65-68-71-71–275	13330
P Fowler	65-71-70-69–275	8890
(J Morgan won play-off)		
H Clark	68-68-75-66–277	4500
G Brand Jr	62-70-75-70–277	4500
I Mosey	72-70-69-67–278	2866
R Davis	64-73-69-72–278	2866
H Baiocchi	72-64-69-73–278	2866
B Marchbank	73-68-69-69–279	2000
N Hansen	67-70-74-69–280	1700
C Moody	69-70-72-69–280	1700
C Mason	68-71-72-70–281	1440
A Stubbs	70-68-70-73–281	1440

Dunhill Masters'
at Woburn G & CC Milton Keynes

Name	Score	Prize £
S Ballesteros	67-68-70-70–275	33333
G Brand Jr	70-71-69-67–277	21117
B Langer	68-68-72-70–278	10690
R Lee	69-65-73-71–278	10690
B Marchbank	73-70-68-70–281	6810
C O'Connor Jr	68-73-69-71–281	6810
R Hartman	66-72-70-73–281	6810
A Chandler	72-70-69-71–282	4750
S Torrance	70-73-68-72–283	3728
N Faldo	73-71-72-68–283	3728
M McNulty	71-70-73-69–283	3728
J Rivero	70-73-74-66–283	3728

PLM Open
at Falsterbö Malmo Sweden

Name	Score	Prize £
P Senior	69-72-64-68–273	19512
M Lanner	73-70-65-67–275	12995
O Sellberg	76-66-68-66–276	7336
T Armour III	70-68-70-69–277	5853
M Persson	71-70-71-66–278	3873
GJ Brand	69-70-70-69–278	3873
DA Russell	71-65-70-72–278	3873
G Turner	68-66-72-72–278	3873
E Darcy	76-70-65-68–279	2367
R Stewart	74-68-69-68–279	2367
R Rafferty	72-68-73-66–279	2367

Johnnie Walker Monte Carlo Open

at Mont Angel

Name	Score	Prize £
S Ballesteros	66-71-64-64–265	26365
M McNulty	68-69-63-67–267	17561
J Bland	66-68-65-69–268	7515
A Garrido	67-66-65-70–268	7515
M McLean	67-64-67-70–268	7515
P Senior	66-67-66-69–268	7515
G Cali	70-67-63-69–269	3850
J Rivero	68-68-66-67–269	3850
M Martin	72-63-66-68–269	3850
S Elkington	67-66-66-70–269	3850
R Commans	66-63-67-74–270	2819
F Allem	71-67-66-66–270	2819
G Brand	73-66-65-67–271	2508
J-M Canizares	71-67-70-63–271	2508

Bell's Scottish Open

at Haggs Castle

Name	Score	Prize £
D Feherty	69-68-66-67–270	21660
C O'Connor Jr	67-66-69-68–270	11290
I Baker-Finch	66-66-66-72–270	11290
R Drummond	71-71-65-65–272	6500
H Baiocchi	68-68-67-70–273	5510
P Thomas	72-66-68-68–274	4550
S Lyle	70-69-66-71–276	3575
B Waites	67-69-72-68–276	3575
M Roe	73-68-71-65–277	2752
G Brand Jr	69-70-71-67–277	2752

Scandinavian Enterprise Open

at Ullna GC Stockholm

Name	Score	Prize £
G Turner	69-62-69-70–270	25536
C Stadler	66-66-66-72–270	17030
I Baker-Finch	65-67-71-71–274	9578
J Rivero	70-67-67-72–276	7088
R Rafferty	67-66-68-75–276	7088
H Clark	72-70-66-70–278	5363
M James	66-71-71-72–280	4597
O Sellberg	71-72-72-66–281	3065
R Stewart	71-70-71-69–281	3065
M Lanner	69-73-70-69–281	3065
M Clayton	71-71-69-70–281	3065
T Gale	70-67-72-72–281	3065
R Davis	73-65-71-72–281	3065

Lawrence Batley International
at The Belfry

Name	Score	Prize £
I Woosnam	71-71-66-69–277	21660
K Brown	73-70-72-69–284	11290
J-M Canizares	70-72-71-71–284	11290
M Allen	70-72-72-72–286	4742
R Drummond	76-67-70-73–286	4742
N Hansen	73-71-71-71–286	4742
J Hawkes	69-71-73-73–286	4742
J Rivero	70-71-70-75–286	4742
A Forsbrand	75-68-70-74–287	2905
S Bennett	71-71-73-73–288	2286
C O'Connor Jr	75-72-73-68–288	2286
M Pinero	73-72-71-72–288	2286
G Powers	72-72-72-72–288	2286
R Stelten	71-69-74-74–288	2286

Open Championship
at Turnberry Ayrshire

Name	Score	Prize £
G Norman	74-63-74-69–280	70000
G Brand	71-68-75-71–285	50000
B Langer	72-70-76-68–286	35000
I Woosnam	70-74-70-72–286	35000
N Faldo	71-70-76-70–287	25000
S Ballesteros	76-75-73-64–288	22000
G Koch	73-72-72-71–288	22000
F Zoeller	75-73-72-69–289	17333
B Marchbank	78-70-72-69–289	17333
T Nakajima	74-67-71-77–289	17333
C O'Connor Jr	75-71-75-69–290	14000
D Graham	75-73-70-72–290	14000
J-M Canizares	76-68-73-73–290	14000
C Strange	79-69-74-69–291	11500
A Bean	74-73-73-71–291	11500

KLM Dutch Open
at Noordwijk

Name	Score	Prize £
S Ballesteros	69-63-71-68–271	23330
J Rivero	72-66-69-72–279	15550
V Fernandez	68-69-71-72–280	7880
P Parkin	71-74-73-72–280	7880
I Baker-Finch	72-66-71-72–281	4336
G Brand Jr	71-67-69-74–281	4336
B Marchbank	73-66-72-70–281	4336
M Pinero	70-66-71-74–281	4336
D Smyth	75-63-73-70–281	4336
G Marsh	72-66-75-69–282	2800
M Allen	70-64-74-75–283	2440
G Turner	74-66-72-71–283	2440
I Woosnam	73-64-76-70–283	2440

Carrolls Irish Open
at Port Marnock Co Dublin Eire

Name	Score	Prize £
S Ballesteros	68-75-68-74–285	31699
M McNulty	74-72-71-70–287	16515
R Davis	74-73-71-69–287	16515
W Riley	67-78-71-74–290	8080
J-M Olazabal	68-78-73-71–290	8080
H Clark	74-75-70-71–290	8080
R Lee	66-79-73-73–291	4406
G Turner	71-76-72-72–291	4406
G Brand	71-78-72-70–291	4406
R Chapman	72-79-70-70–291	4406
D Jones	74-73-73-71–291	4406

Benson & Hedges International Open
at Fulford York

Name	Score	Prize £
M James	65-70-69-70–274	30000
H Baiocchi	66-70-70-68–274	15650
L Trevino	66-67-73-68–274	15650
G Brand Jr	65-67-72-71–275	9000
M McNulty	68-69-72-67–276	6466
J O'Leary	66-69-72-69–276	6466
I Woosnam	71-68-70-67–276	6466
C O'Connor Jr	72-65-72-68–277	4130
J Olazabal	67-71-67-72–277	4130
R Lee	68-69-71-70–278	3400
J Canizares	68-72-68-70–278	3400
N Faldo	71-70-71-67–279	3100

Lufthansa German Open
at Hubbelrath Düsseldorf

Name	Score	Prize £
B Langer	75-65-66-67–273	27446
D Davis	68-72-68-64–273	18286
(B Langer won play-off)		
M McNulty	67-72-69-72–275	9275
S Lyle	70-71-68-66–275	9275
M Mouland	68-73-66-69–276	6375
I Woosnam	74-68-68-66–276	6375
I Baker-Finch	68-68-70-72–278	4250
G Brand Jr	71-71-66-70–278	4250
D Smyth	73-67-70-68–278	4250
P Baker	67-70-70-72–279	3053
I Mosey	72-67-70-70–279	3053
S Ballesteros	69-69-73-68–279	3053

Ebel European Masters Swiss Open
at Crans-sur-Sierre Switzerland

Name	Score	Prize £
J-M Olazabal	64-66-66-66–262	43846
A Forsbrand	69-68-63-65–265	29230
GJ Brand	68-65-63-71–267	14817
I Baker-Finch	70-63-65-69–267	14817
R Rafferty	64-66-68-70–268	10182
H Baiocchi	65-68-68-67–268	10182
M McNulty	69-66-68-66–269	6097
J-M Canizares	71-68-69-61–269	6097
S Torrance	66-70-69-64–269	6097
T Armour III	71-69-64-65–269	6097
C Stadler	67-67-65-70–269	6097

Panasonic European Open
at Sunningdale Berkshire

Name	Score	Prize £
G Norman	67-67-69-66–269	35000
K Brown	67-67-68-67–269	23310
(G Norman won play-off)		
B Langer	69-68-66-68–271	13150
S Ballesteros	64-72-72-65–273	8916
N Faldo	62-72-71-68–273	8916
J-M Olazabal	68-67-72-66–273	8916
R Davis	71-67-69-67–274	5775
P Fowler	65-68-73-68–274	5775
J Bland	68-72-67-68–275	4253
B Gallacher	65-68-73-69–275	4253
M Martin	67-73-67-68–275	4253

Sanyo Open
at Real Club de Golf El Prat Barcelona

Name	Score	Prize £
J-M Olazabal	69-68-69-67–273	29150
H Clark	72-68-69-67–276	19440
I Mosey	73-67-68-69–277	10950
S Ballesteros	67-67-73-71–278	7433
O Sellberg	70-71-65-72–278	7433
I Woosnam	71-68-69-70–278	7433
J Anglada	67-74-67-71–279	4056
G Brand Jr	69-70-68-72–279	4056
E Darcy	71-70-70-68–279	4056
A Oldcorn	73-67-71-68–279	4056
R Rafferty	69-71-70-69–279	4056

Suntory World Match Play Championship
at Wentworth

First Round

R Davis (Aus) beat N Price (Zim) 2 and 1
S Lyle (Scot) beat H Clark (Eng) 1 hole
J-M Olazabal (Sp) beat L Wadkins (USA) 2 and 1
J Ozaki (Jap) beat B Crenshaw (USA) 7 and 6
(each loser received £7500)

Second round

R Davis (Aus) beat S Ballesteros (Sp) 7 and 6
S Lyle (Scot) beat T Nakajima (Jap) at 38th
J Nicklaus (USA) beat J-M Olazabal (Sp) 5 and 4
G Norman (Aus) beat J Ozaki (Jap) 4 and 2
(each loser received £10000)

Semi-finals

S Lyle (Scot) beat R Davis (Aus) 2 and 1
G Norman (Aus) beat J Nicklaus (USA) 1 hole

3rd & 4th place play-off

J Nicklaus (USA) beat R Davis (Aus) 2 and 1
(Winner received £20000, runner-up £15000)

Final

G Norman (Aus) beat S Lyle (Scot) 2 and 1
(Winner received £50000, runner-up £25000)

Lancôme Trophy
at St Nom la Breteche

Name	Score	Prize £
S Ballesteros	67-69-68-70–274	27272
B Langer	73-66-66-69–274	27272
(Ballesteros and Langer shared trophy)		
D Smyth	72-69-68-66–275	12834
S Torrance	71-64-74-67–276	9625
S Lyle	70-66-70-70–276	9625
J Bland	72-71-68-66–277	5811
GJ Brand	69-69-68-71–277	5811
J-M Olazabal	71-69-66-71–277	5811
C Strange	69-67-70-72–278	4705
H Baiocchi	69-70-73-67–279	4278

Dunhill Nations Cup
at Old Course St Andrews

First Round

Wales			New Zealand		
M Mouland	69	1	G Turner	77	0
I Woosnam	66	1	F Nobilo	71	0
P Parkin	69	1	B Charles	73	0
		3			0

Japan			South Korea		
T Nakajima	68	1	Y-S Choi	78	0
T Ozaki	71	1	S-H Choi	79	0
N Ozaki	67	1	H-S Cho	74	0
		3			0

Canada			Sweden		
D Barr	69	1	M Lanner	74	0
R Zokol	75	0	O Sellberg	72	1
D Halldorson	69	1	A Forsbrand	71	0
		2			1

USA			Zambia		
R Floyd	72	1	P Sinyana	81	0
M O'Meara	70	1	S Mwanza	83	0
L Wadkins	70	1	P Tembo	79	0
		3			0

Scotland			Indonesia		
S Torrance	69	1	S Sumarno	76	0
G Brand Jr	71	1	M Naasim	83	0
S Lyle	69	1	E Tachyana	83	0
		3			0

Argentina			England		
V Fernandez	67	1	H Clark	70	0
A Sowa	69	1	GJ Brand	70	0
A Saavedra	72	0	N Faldo	69	1
		2			1

Australia			Italy		
R Davis	65	1	C Rocca	70	0
G Norman	67	1	G Cali	77	0
D Graham	68	1	B Dassu	79	0
		3			0

Ireland			Spain		
R Rafferty	67	1	S Ballesteros	74	0
D Feherty	73	0	J Rivero	71	1
D Smyth	71	1	J-M Olazabal	73	0
		2			1

Each of the losing players in the first round received £5190

Dunhill Nations Cup
continued

Quarter-Finals

USA			Canada		
M O'Meara	74	1	R Zokol	76	0
L Wadkins	68	0	D Barr	66	1
R Floyd	68	1	D Halldorson	70	0
		2			1

Japan			Argentina		
T Nakajima	67	1	V Fernandez	68	0
N Ozaki	69	1	A Sowa	71	0
T Ozaki	72	0	A Saavedra	69	1
		2			1

Australia			Wales		
R Davis	71	1	M Mouland	73	0
G Norman	67	1	I Woosnam	71	0
D Graham	68	1	P Parkin	69	0
		3			0

Scotland			Ireland		
G Brand Jr	68	1	R Rafferty	70	0
S Torrance	70	1	D Smyth	72	0
S Lyle	70	1	D Feherty	72	0
		3			0

Each of the 12 losers in the quarter-finals received £10380

Semi-Finals

Japan			USA		
T Ozaki	77	0	M O'Meara	70	1
N Ozaki	69	1	L Wadkins	74	0
T Nakajima	69	1	R Floyd	76	0
		2			1

Australia			Scotland		
R Davis	72	1	G Brand Jr	74	0
D Graham	70	0	S Lyle	68	1
G Norman	70	1	S Torrance	72	0
		2			1

Play-off for 3rd and 4th place

Scotland			USA		
G Brand Jr	75	1	M O'Meara	78	0
S Torrance	78	0	R Floyd	73	1
S Lyle	73	1	L Wadkins	78	0
		2			1

The Scottish players received £25374 each; the USA players received £18454

Final

Australia			Japan		
R Davis	76	1	T Ozaki	81	0
D Graham	81	1	N Ozaki	82	0
G Norman	73	1	T Nakajima	76	0
		3			0

The Australian players received £69204 each; the Japanese players received £34602

Peugeot Spanish Open
at La Morealja Madrid

Name	Score
H Clark	66-71-66-67–272
I Baker-Finch	69-68-68-68–273
S Ballesteros	74-66-68-68–276
R Lee	72-70-65-71–278
R Drummond	68-72-72-68–280
M Pinero	73-69-70-68–280
J Rivero	72-68-67-74–281
I Mosey	74-70-68-70–282
R Davis	75-71-72-64–282
P Parkin	72-70-71-70–283
M McNulty	73-71-68-71–283

Portuguese Open
at Quinta do Lago Algarve

Name	Score	Prize £
M McNulty	66-69-69-66–270	16660
I Mosey	69-69-69-67–274	11100
J Bland	67-66-71-72–276	5630
J-M Canizares	68-70-72-66–276	5630
A Forsbrand	72-66-71-68–277	3580
T Johnstone	69-71-66-71–277	3580
S Lyle	66-67-71-73–277	2246
GJ Brand	68-70-72-69–279	2246
R Chapman	73-71-69-66–279	2246
J Higgins	72-67-68-72–279	2246

Nissan World Cup
at Tokyo Japan

Day 1	European Tour beat Japan	7–5
	Australia/New Zealand beat USA	7–5
Day 2	European Tour beat USA	8–4
	Japan beat Australia/New Zealand	7–5
Day 3	European Tour beat Australia/New Zealand	7–5
	Japan beat USA	7–5
Final	Japan beat European Tour	8–4
	Australia/New Zealand beat USA	11–1

Team Prize Money

Japan	$300000	Australia/New Zealand	$120000
European Tour	$180000	USA	$90000

Individual leaders with Prize Money

Pos	Name	Score	Prize $
1	T Nakajima (Japan)	270	25000
2	B Langer (Germany)	272	18000
3	N Ozaki (Japan)	274	13000
4T	I Baker-Finch (Aus/NZ)	275	9000
	B Tway (USA)		9000
6T	G Norman (Aus/NZ)	276	6500
	K Susuki (Japan)		6500
8T	S Lyle (Europe)	278	4333
	H Sutton (USA)		4333
	J Mahaffey (USA)		4333

PGA European Tour Final Statistics

PGA European Tour Prize Money, 1986

	Official Money	No of OM Events	Average OM Prize Fund	'Approved' Money	Total
	£		£	£	£
1979	1,102,220 (76.43%)	23	48,439	340,000 (23.57%)	1,442,220
1980	1,304,830 (76.22%)	22	59,310	407,100 (23.78%)	1,711,930
1981	1,442,555 (74.85%)	22	65,570	363,925 (20.15%)	1,806,480
1982	1,885,975 (82.07%)	26	72,537	412,060 (17.93%)	2,298,035
1983	2,410,931 (85.72%)	27	89,293	401,405 (14.28%)	2,812,336
1984	2,908,879 (85.49%)	26	111,880	493,886 (14.51%)	3,402,765
1985	3,460,726 (72.71%)	26	133,109	1,298,864 (27.29%)	4,759,590
1986	4,333,178 (76.55%)	26	166,661	1,327,300 (23.45%)	5,660,478

Details of 1986 Prize Money

	£		£
Total Official Prize Money	4,320,322		
+Prize Money beyond 65th place	12,856		4,333,178
'Approved' Prize Money			
	£	£	
Suntory World Match-Play Championship		180,000	
Dunhill Nations Cup: European Pre-qualifying	68,493		
Finals	692,041	760,534	
Satellite Tournaments: Jack Mulcahy	21,909		
Rolex	21,476		
Associate Members Cup	7,365		
Future Masters Cup	8,903	59,653	
Open Pre-qualifying: Regional	5,858		
Finals	6,501	12,359	
Pro-Ams: with Tournaments	119,597		
One-day Official	142,900		
Guiness Pro-Am	30,020	292,517	
Non OM Prize Money			
Lancôme Trophy		22,237	1,327,300
			5,660,478

PGA Final Statistics, 1986

(Provided by Philips Business Systems)

Driving Distance

		Yards
1	P Senior	272
2	S Ballesteros	270
	I Woosnam	270
4	P Thomas	269
	G Turner	269
6	P Parkin	268
7	S Torrance	267
8	A Forsbrand	266
9	C Moody	264
10	B Lane	263
11	H Clark	262
	M Mackenzie	262
13	N Faldo	261
	R Drummond	261
	B Marchbank	261
	B Malley	261
17	R Davis	260
	D Cooper	260
	G Turner	260
	M Mouland	260

Greens in Regulation

		%
1	S Torrance	72
	J Bland	72
3	J-M Canizares	70
	C O'Connor Jr	70
	R Davis	70
	G Brand	70
	T Webber	70
8	H Clark	69
	D Smyth	69
	E Darcy	69
	J-M Olazabal	69
12	S Ballesteros	68
	O Sellberg	68
	V Fernandez	68
	R Drummond	68
	M Roe	68
17	G Brand Jr	67
	D Feherty	67
	R Rafferty	67
	I Baker-Finch	67
	A Chandler	67

Fairways Hit

		%
1	J Bland	80
2	T Webber	77
3	V Somers	76
4	D Smyth	74
5	I Baker-Finch	73
	M McLean	73
	R Hartmann	73
	A Garrido	73
	K Waters	73
10	O Sellberg	72
	M McNulty	72
12	S Torrance	71
	J Pinero	71
	J Rivero	71
	H Baiocchi	71
	C Mason	71
	M Mouland	71
18	R Lee	70
19	J-M Canizares	69
	E Darcy	69
	S Bennett	69
	B Waites	69
	M Martin	69
	J Heggarty	69

Putts Per Round

		%
1	M Mouland	28.53
2	N Faldo	28.57
3	P Senior	28.68
4	M Roe	28.88
5	C Mason	28.95
6	M McNulty	29.00
	N Hansen	29.00
8	I Woosnam	29.05
9	A Forsbrand	29.06
10	P Parkin	29.11
11	S Ballesteros	29.12
12	I Baker-Finch	29.16
	G Turner	29.16
14	J O'Leary	29.21
15	M Pinero	29.28
	C Moody	29.28
17	O Sellberg	29.33
18	B Smith	29.35
19	R Hartmann	29.42
20	D Williams	29.43

Sand Saves

		%
1	N Faldo	81
2	J Rivero	66
3	S Ballesteros	65
4	P Senior	64
5	R Hartmann	63
6	R Johnstone	62
7	S Bennett	61
8	R Davis	59
	M Martin	59
10	C O'Connor Jr	58
11	J O'Leary	57
	M Roe	57
13	R Rafferty	56
	O Sellberg	56
	M Mackenzie	56
	R Boxall	56
	B Malley	56
18	M Pinero	55
19	I Mosey	54
	M McNulty	54
	J-M Olazabál	54
	G Turner	54

The 1986 Epson Order of Merit

1986 Official Money List

Those who have played 7, or more, OM Tournaments

Pos	Name (1985 position)	Country	Tourns Played	Rounds Played	Stroke Average	+or− Par	Official Prize Money £
1	**Severiano Ballesteros** (3)	Sp	14	56	68.95	−127	242,208.70
2	**Jose-Maria Olazabal** (−)	Sp	19	72	70.69	− 50	136,775.03
3	**Howard Clark** (6)	Eng	19	70	70.84	− 53	121,902.82
4	**Ian Woosnam** (4)	Wal	20	70	71.17	− 28	111,798.79
5	**Gordon J Brand** (23)	Eng	22	80	71.05	− 16	106,314.17
6	**Mark McNulty** (66)	SA	19	76	70.32	− 68	101,327.38
7	**Rodger Davis** (19)	Aus	15	52	70.77	− 26	95,428.78
8	**Anders Forsbrand** (34)	Swe	21	69	71.41	− 5	84,706.12
9	**Ronan Rafferty** (17)	N Ire	25	92	70.96	− 44	80,335.98
10	**Gordon Brand Jr** (9)	Scot	25	88	71.01	− 33	78,639.43
11	**Ian Baker-Finch** (18)	Aus	17	62	70.45	− 56	76,304.36
12	**Des Smyth** (16)	Ire	22	74	71.19	− 14	68,905.93
13	**Hugh Baiocchi** (21)	SA	19	70	70.76	− 39	66,243.35
14	**Jose-Maria Canizares** (8)	Sp	20	72	70.89	− 28	66,225.27
15	**Nick Faldo** (42)	Eng	12	40	70.92	− 7	65,418.62
16	**Ove Sellberg** (30)	Swe	19	64	71.20	− 7	64,175.55
17	**Sam Torrance** (5)	Scot	23	86	71.05	− 38	63,341.17
18	**David Feherty** (15)	N Ire	24	75	72.31	+ 67	62,569.32
19	**John Bland** (37)	SA	18	70	70.79	− 37	58,306.20
20	**Mark James** (14)	Eng	22	76	72.17	+ 51	57,822.20
21	**Robert Lee** (27)	Eng	26	89	71.60	+ 4	55,173.97
22	**Christy O'Connor Jr** (12)	Ire	20	64	71.52	+ 9	53,433.60
23	**Jose Rivero** (13)	Sp	20	66	71.44	+ 7	50,210.11
24	**Sandy Lyle** (1)	Scot	14	50	70.46	− 45	48,639.47
25	**Greg Turner** (−)	NZ	15	52	71.65	+ 20	47,652.47
26	**Vicente Fernandez** (39)	Arg	17	64	71.19	− 4	46,894.08
27	**Antonio Garrido** (45)	Sp	17	61	71.67	+ 12	45,510.53
28	**Brian Marchbank** (80)	Scot	23	74	71.84	+ 38	45,132.53
29	**Ian Mosey** (55)	Eng	21	70	72.14	+ 46	42,975.07
30	**Mark Mouland** (71)	Wal	25	80	72.16	+ 67	42,148.78
31	**Peter Senior** (79)	Aus	11	42	70.88	− 3	40,359.57
32	**Manuel Pinero** (7)	Sp	18	58	71.55	+ 8	39,437.59
33	**Philip Parkin** (32)	Wal	19	61	72.20	+ 52	35,905.74
34	**Ross Drummond** (48)	Scot	21	72	72.01	+ 47	35,438.52
35	**John Morgan** (58)	Eng	23	80	72.31	+ 73	33,568.60
36	**Carl Mason** (22)	Eng	22	74	71.84	+ 24	30,224.56
37	**Eamonn Darcy** (20)	Ire	21	69	72.14	+ 54	29,424.06
38	**Roger Chapman** (28)	Eng	24	71	71.99	+ 53	26,941.40
39	**Mark Roe** (104)	Eng	22	69	71.52	+ 17	26,601.90
40	**Rick Hartmann** (35)	USA	18	56	71.52	+ 11	26,079.39
41	**Michael McLean** (26)	Eng	24	73	72.48	+ 77	25,048.14
42	**Miguel Martin** (69)	Sp	21	74	71.80	+ 37	24,441.38
43	**Mats Lanner** (81)	Swe	18	52	72.48	+ 59	24,387.02
44	**Andrew Chandler** (106)	Eng	21	66	72.61	+ 94	23,935.88
45	**Neil Hansen** (78)	Eng	23	70	72.34	+ 74	23,504.50
46	**Tony Johnstone** (41)	Zim	20	68	71.99	+ 51	23,434.30
47	**Vaughan Somers** (91)	Aus	16	56	72.12	+ 47	23,054.70
48	**Peter Fowler** (52)	Aus	17	52	73.02	+ 91	22,062.39
49	**Stephen Bennett** (33)	Eng	24	78	72.35	+ 83	20,538.72
50	**Tommy Armour III** (−)	USA	7	28	70.79	− 10	20,512.08
51	**Mike Clayton** (62)	Aus	19	56	72.64	+ 74	20,023.98
52	**John O'Leary** (25)	Ire	21	60	72.23	+ 46	19,783.17
53	**Philip Walton** (84)	Ire	20	62	73.18	+119	19,335.33
54	**Paul Thomas** (96)	Wal	21	70	72.54	+ 78	18,051.09
55	**Bernard Gallacher** (31)	Scot	18	53	72.23	+ 42	18,050.53
56	**Jeff Hawkes** (43)	SA	14	48	72.29	+ 50	17,893.07

Pos	Name (1985 position)	Country	Tourns Played	Rounds Played	Stroke Average	+or− Par	Official Prize Money £
57	**Grant Turner** (64)	Eng	24	78	72.24	+ 71	17,773.42
58	**David Williams** (77)	Eng	24	78	72.58	+ 93	17,222.31
59	**Derrick Cooper** (54)	Eng	23	77	72.96	+116	16,924.17
60	**Chris Moody** (51)	Eng	21	63	72.33	+ 63	15,889.41
61	**Brian Waites** (60)	Eng	15	46	72.35	+ 34	15,667.69
62	**Ray Stewart** (–)	Can	16	46	71.83	+ 32	15,582.09
63	**Magnus Persson** (50)	Swe	18	52	72.00	+ 26	15,361.21
64	**Ron Commans** (–)	USA	13	44	72.70	+ 65	14,575.02
65	**Wayne Riley** (47)	Aus	19	55	72.96	+ 87	14,515.15
66	**Warren Humphreys** (38)	Eng	23	72	72.47	+ 80	13,889.19
67	**Malcolm Mackenzie** (76)	Eng	22	72	73.03	+120	13,776.88
68	**Tony Charnley** (89)	Eng	21	74	72.88	+105	13,297.71
69	**Adan Sowa** (–)	Arg	16	50	73.16	+ 94	13,048.54
70	**David Llewellyn** (36)	Wal	21	68	72.49	+ 85	12,999.01
71	**Barry Lane** (–)	Eng	21	64	72.64	+ 81	12,928.09
72	**Jimmy Heggarty** (97)	N Ire	17	55	73.31	+106	12,854.04
73	**Gavin Levenson** (44)	SA	19	56	72.20	+ 79	12,585.56
74	**Keith Waters** (92)	Eng	23	70	73.11	+120	12,421.55
75	**Ronald Stelten** (–)	USA	18	54	72.31	+ 55	12,293.96
76	**Bill Longmuir** (67)	Scot	22	58	73.79	+144	11,725.71
77	**Bob E Smith** (103)	USA	16	48	72.19	+ 49	11,448.63
78	**David A Russell** (98)	Eng	20	57	72.88	+102	11,410.61
79	**Armando Saavedra** (–)	Arg	13	38	71.82	+ 23	11,183.73
80	**Ossie Moore** (53)	Aus	9	34	71.44	+ 17	11,161.41
81	**Gerry Taylor** (119)	Aus	10	30	72.63	+ 45	10,928.43
82	**Andrew Oldcorn** (107)	Eng	16	46	73.26	+ 88	10,549.12
83	**David J Russell** (24)	Eng	19	49	74.06	+123	10,480.08
84	**Edward Webber** (–)	Zim	16	52	72.29	+ 59	10,480.03
85	**Philip Harrison** (127)	Eng	20	58	72.67	+ 85	10,447.50
86	**Richard Boxall** (121)	Eng	21	59	73.66	+134	10,293.38
87	**David Jones** (90)	N Ire	14	44	73.02	+ 75	10,172.68
88	**Manuel Calero** (56)	Sp	16	50	72.52	+ 62	10,013.83
89	**Frank Nobilo** (–)	NZ	11	38	72.74	+ 62	9,874.82
90	**Denis Durnian** (100)	Eng	11	40	72.03	+ 25	9,694.77
91	**Michael Allen** (–)	USA	6	18	71.33	PAR	9,413.67
92	**Andrew Murray** (113)	Eng	22	60	73.85	+149	9,162.51
93	**Mike Harwood** (–)	Aus	14	40	72.78	+ 69	8,783.17
94	**Martin Poxon** (61)	Eng	20	62	73.45	+130	8,555.91
95	**Glenn Ralph** (83)	Eng	14	41	73.80	+110	8,346.25
96	**Peter Teravainen** (72)	USA	22	59	73.59	+138	8,013.69
97	**Emmanuel Dussart** (–)	Fr	19	56	72.54	+ 70	7,915.10
98	**Art Russell** (68)	USA	17	46	73.17	+ 92	7,577.77
99	**Giuseppe Cali** (–)	It	9	26	71.92	+ 24	7,503.00
100	**Wayne Westner** (85)	SA	17	46	73.61	+ 98	7,386.76
101	**Tom Lamore** (–)	USA	17	50	73.38	+117	7,307.57
102	**Paul Curry** (–)	Eng	17	47	72.70	+ 53	7,279.23
103	**Jerry Anderson** (57)	Can	17	40	73.72	+ 99	7,217.34
104	**Bill McColl** (63)	Scot	21	51	73.86	+115	7,178.42
105	**Juan Anglada** (115)	Sp	13	34	72.91	+ 63	7,173.47
106	**Bill Malley** (–)	USA	19	58	73.38	+116	7,110.80
107	**Neil Coles** (86)	Eng	9	30	72.57	+ 39	6,865.21
108	**Mark Wiltshire** (–)	SA	19	60	73.75	+139	6,722.86
109	**John Slaughter** (–)	USA	19	50	73.10	+ 95	6,539.16
110	**Emilio Rodriguez** (74)	Sp	16	42	73.24	+ 82	6,522.67
111	**Mariano Aparicio** (–)	Sp	10	30	72.60	+ 28	6,440.89
112	**Michel Tapia** (75)	Fr	16	48	73.00	+ 72	6,259.54
113	**Lyndsay Stephen** (120)	Aus	14	32	72.19	+ 40	6,180.18
114	**Dillard Pruitt** (–)	USA	17	43	72.60	+ 72	6,150.30
115	**Nathaniel Crosby** (87)	USA	21	54	73.44	+108	6,125.39
116	**Simon Bishop** (49)	Eng	21	56	73.80	+141	6,059.75
117	**Lee Jones** (–)	Eng	20	52	73.48	+111	6,029.91
118*	**Steve Elkington** (–)	Aus	8	22	72.00	+ 28	6,017.80
119	**Maurice Bembridge** (101)	Eng	19	52	73.96	+146	5,960.32
120*	**Peter Baker** (–)	Eng	10	26	72.50	+ 27	5,959.52
121	**David Ray** (114)	Eng	22	57	73.46	+119	5,904.47
122	**Santiago Luna** (128)	Sp	21	54	73.63	+120	5,762.91
123	**Jaime Gonzalez** (59)	Bra	22	59	74.22	+171	5,761.95
124	**Noel Ratcliffe** (108)	Aus	19	52	73.35	+106	5,555.40
125	**Paul Way** (10)	Eng	20	44	74.73	+141	5,260.00
126	**Eddie Polland** (73)	Ire	17	47	74.00	+124	5,248.27
127	**Bruce Zabriski** (110)	USA	9	28	72.68	+ 43	5,246.38

***non-member**

European Tour 1987

All exempt categories

1 Winners of the PGA Championship, the Open Championship and Order of Merit in the last 10 years.

2 Winners of the Tournament Players' Championship in the last 5 years.

3 Winners of the European Open in the last 5 years.

4 Winners of the European Masters Tournaments for 6 years, commencing 1983.

5 **Tournament Winners:** Winners of PGA European Tour events for three years. 1984 winners exempt for 1986 and 1987: 1985 winners exempt for 1986, 1987 and 1988.

6 Members of the last-named European Ryder Cup Team.

7 The top 40 from the 1986 Career Money List.

8 10 Sponsors' Invitations.

9 **National/Regional Orders of Merit**

(a) For full field Continental Tournaments and the Carrolls Irish Open: Players from the top 20 of the relative National Order of Merit.

(b) For regular PGA European Tour competitions in the British Isles: Players from the top 5 of the relative PGA Region.

10 Past winners of the tournament in question.

11 The top 127 from the 1986 Epson Order of Merit.

12 **Qualifying School:** The top 50 from the 1986 PGA European Tour Qualifying School.

13 Players finishing between 128 and 158 (inclusive) on the 1986 Epson Order of Merit.

14 Players finishing between 51st and 80th place in the 1986 PGA European Tour Qualifying School.

15 Past champions and Ryder Cup players.

General: Regular Fields
For regular full-field PGA European Tour competitions, starting fields will be 144.

1987 All Exempt Tour

Category 1

Winners PGA

	Eligible 1st Jan	*Expires* 31st Dec	
Rodger Davis *(Aus)*	1987	1996	
Paul Way *(Eng)*	1986	1995	
Howard Clark *(Eng)*	1985	1994	
Tony Jacklin *(Eng)*	1983	1992	
Vicente Fernandez *(Arg)*	1980	1989	
Manuel Pinero *(Sp)*	1978	1987	

Winners Open

Greg Norman *(Aus)*	1987	1996	
Sandy Lyle *(Scot)*	1986	1995	
Tom Watson *(USA)*	1984	1993	
Bill Rogers *(USA)*	1982	1991	
Jack Nicklaus *(USA)*	1979	1988	

Winners' Order of Merit

Severiano Ballesteros *(Sp)*	1987	1996	
Bernhard Langer *(W Ger)*	1985	1994	
Nick Faldo *(Eng)*	1984	1993	No in category 14

Category 2

Winners TPC

Ian Woosnam *(Wal)*	1987	1991	
Jaime Gonzalez *(Bra)*	1985	1989	No in category 2

Category 3

Winners European Open

Gordon Brand Jr *(Scot)*	1985	1989	
Isao Aoki *(Jap)*	1984	1988	No in category 2

Category 4

Winners European Masters

José-Maria Olazabal *(Sp)*	1987	1991	
Craig Stadler *(USA)*	1986	1990	
Jerry Anderson *(Can)*	1985	1989	No in category 3

Category 5

Tournament Winners

Stephen Bennett *(Eng)*	1986	1988
David J Russell *(Eng)*	1986	1988
Mark James *(Eng)*	1987	1989
Ken Brown *(Scot)*	1986	1988
Lee Trevino *(USA)*	1986	1988
Graham Marsh *(Aus)*	1986	1988
Sam Torrance *(Scot)*	1986	1988
Ian Baker-Finch *(Aus)*	1986	1988
Nick Price *(Zim)*	1986	1988
Robert Lee *(Eng)*	1986	1988
Warren Humphreys *(Eng)*	1986	1988
Bernard Gallacher *(Scot)*	1985	1987
Mike Clayton *(Aus)*	1985	1987
Ian Mosey *(Eng)*	1985	1987
Jose Rivero *(Sp)*	1985	1987
Wayne Grady *(Aus)*	1985	1987
David Frost *(SA)*	1985	1987
Tony Johnstone *(Zim)*	1985	1987
David Feherty *(N Ire)*	1987	1989
Ove Sellberg *(Swe)*	1987	1989
Antonio Garrido *(Sp)*	1987	1989
John Morgan *(Eng)*	1987	1989
Mark Mouland *(Wal)*	1987	1989

1986 All Exempt Tour
continued

	Eligible	*Expires*	
	1st Jan	31st Dec	
Peter Senior *(Aus)*	1987	1989	
Greg Turner *(NZ)*	1987	1989	
Mark McNulty *(SA)*	1987	1989	
John Bland *(SA)*	1987	1989	No in category 27

Category 6
European Ryder Cup Team

Jose-Maria Canizares *(Sp)*	1987		No in category 1

Category 7
Top 40 Career Money List

Hugh Baiocchi *(SA)*	1987	1987	
Neil Coles *(Eng)*	1987	1987	
Graham Marsh *(Aus)*	1987	1987	
Des Smyth *(Ire)*	1987	1987	
Eamonn Darcy *(Ire)*	1987	1987	
Brian Barnes *(Scot)*	1987	1987	
Brian Waites *(Eng)*	1987	1987	
Bob Charles *(NZ)*	1987	1987	
Christy O'Connor Jr *(Ire)*	1987	1987	
Carl Mason *(Eng)*	1987	1987	
John O'Leary *(Ire)*	1987	1987	
Ronan Rafferty *(N Ire)*	1987	1987	
Tommy Horton *(Eng)*	1987	1987	
Eddie Polland *(Ire)*	1987	1987	
Michael King *(Eng)*	1987	1987	
Gary Player *(SA)*	1987	1987	No in category 16

Category 8
10 Sponsors' Invitations

No in category 10

Category 9
National/Regional Orders of Merit

(a) For full field Continental and the Carrolls Irish Open: players from the top 20 of the relative National Order of Merit.

(b) For regular PGA European Tour competitions in the British Isles: players from the top 5 of the relative PGA Region.

No in category 20/5

Category 10
Past winners of the tournament in question

Category 11
Top 127 members from the 1986 Epson Order of Merit

	Eligible	*Expires*	*Ranking in Category*
	1st Jan	31st Dec	
Anders Forsbrand *(Swe)*	1987	1987	8
Brian Marchbank *(Scot)*	1987	1987	28
Philip Parkin *(Wal)*	1987	1987	33
Ross Drummond *(Scot)*	1987	1987	34
Roger Chapman *(Eng)*	1987	1987	38
Mark Roe *(Eng)*	1987	1987	39
Rick Hartmann *(USA)*	1987	1987	40
Michael McLean *(Eng)*	1987	1987	41
Miguel Martin *(Sp)*	1987	1987	42
Mats Lanner *(Swe)*	1987	1987	43
Andrew Chandler *(Eng)*	1987	1987	44
Neil Hansen *(Eng)*	1987	1987	45
Vaughan Somers *(Aus)*	1987	1987	47
Peter Fowler *(Aus)*	1987	1987	48
Tommy Armour III *(USA)*	1987	1987	50
Philip Walton *(Ire)*	1987	1987	53

1986 All Exempt Tour
continued

	Eligible	Expires	Ranking in Category
	1st Jan	31st Dec	
Paul Thomas *(Wal)*	1987	1987	54
Jeff Hawkes *(SA)*	1987	1987	56
Grant Turner *(Eng)*	1987	1987	57
David Williams *(Eng)*	1987	1987	58
Derrick Cooper *(Eng)*	1987	1987	59
Chris Moody *(Eng)*	1987	1987	60
Ray Stewart *(Can)*	1987	1987	62
Magnus Persson *(Swe)*	1987	1987	63
Ron Commans *(USA)*	1987	1987	64
Wayne Riley *(Aus)*	1987	1987	65
Malcolm Mackenzie *(Eng)*	1987	1987	67
Tony Charnley *(Eng)*	1987	1987	68
Adan Sowa *(Arg)*	1987	1987	69
David Llewellyn *(Wal)*	1987	1987	70
Barry Lane *(Eng)*	1987	1987	71
Jimmy Heggarty *(N Ire)*	1987	1987	72
Gavin Levenson *(SA)*	1987	1987	73
Keith Waters *(Eng)*	1987	1987	74
Ronald Stelten *(USA)*	1987	1987	75
Bill Longmuir *(Scot)*	1987	1987	76
Bob E Smith *(USA)*	1987	1987	77
David A Russell *(Eng)*	1987	1987	78
Armando Saavedra *(Arg)*	1987	1987	79
Ossie Moore *(Aus)*	1987	1987	80
Gerry Taylor *(Aus)*	1987	1987	81
Andrew Oldcorn *(Eng)*	1987	1987	82
Edward Webber *(Zim)*	1987	1987	84
Philip Harrison *(Eng)*	1987	1987	85
Richard Boxall *(Eng)*	1987	1987	86
David Jones *(N Ire)*	1987	1987	87
Manuel Calero *(Sp)*	1987	1987	88
Frank Nobilo *(NZ)*	1987	1987	89
Denis Durnian *(Eng)*	1987	1987	90
Michael Allen *(USA)*	1987	1987	91
Andrew Murray *(Eng)*	1987	1987	92
Mike Harwood *(Aus)*	1987	1987	93
Martin Poxon *(Eng)*	1987	1987	94
Glenn Ralph *(Eng)*	1987	1987	95
Peter Teravainen *(USA)*	1987	1987	96
Emmanuel Dussart *(Fr)*	1987	1987	97
Art Russell *(USA)*	1987	1987	98
Guiseppe Cali *(It)*	1987	1987	99
Wayne Westner *(SA)*	1987	1987	100
Tom Lamore *(USA)*	1987	1987	101
Paul Curry *(Eng)*	1987	1987	102
Bill McColl *(Scot)*	1987	1987	104
Juan Anglada *(Sp)*	1987	1987	105
Bill Malley *(USA)*	1987	1987	106
Mark Wiltshire *(SA)*	1987	1987	108
John Slaughter *(USA)*	1987	1987	109
Emilio Rodriguez *(Sp)*	1987	1987	110
Mariano Aparicio *(Sp)*	1987	1987	111
Michel Tapia *(Fr)*	1987	1987	112
Lyndsay Stephen *(Aus)*	1987	1987	113
Dillard Pruitt *(USA)*	1987	1987	114
Nathaniel Crosby *(USA)*	1987	1987	115
Simon Bishop *(Eng)*	1987	1987	116
Lee Jones *(Eng)*	1987	1987	117
***Steve Elkington** *(USA)*	1987	1987	118
Maurice Bembridge *(Eng)*	1987	1987	119
***Peter Baker** *(Eng)*	1987	1987	120
David Ray *(Eng)*	1987	1987	121
Santiago Luna *(Sp)*	1987	1987	122
Noel Ratcliffe *(Aus)*	1987	1987	124
Bruce Zabriski *(USA)*	1987	1987	127

*Denotes non-member in 1985

No in category 81

Category 12
Top 50 from the 1986 Qualifying School

	Eligible	Expires	Ranking in Category
	1st Jan	31st Dec	
Wayne Smith *(Aus)*	1987	1987	1
Justin Hobday *(SA)*	1987	1987	2
***Steen Tinning** *(Den)*	1987	1987	3
Magnus Sunesson *(Swe)*	1987	1987	4
Andrew Sherborne *(Eng)*	1987	1987	5

1986 All Exempt Tour
continued

	Eligible	*Expires*	*Ranking in Category*
	1st Jan	31st Dec	
John Clifford *(Aus)*	1987	1987	6
Willie Milne *(Scot)*	1987	1987	7
Andrew Stubbs *(Eng)*	1987	1987	8
Lee Fickling *(Eng)*	1987	1987	9
James Spence *(Eng)*	1987	1987	10
Brad Bell *(USA)*	1987	1987	11
Wesley Adcock *(USA)*	1987	1987	12
Ian Young *(Scot)*	1987	1987	13
Manuel Moreno *(Sp)*	1987	1987	14
Andrea Canessa *(It)*	1987	1987	15
Ross McFarlane *(Eng)*	1987	1987	16
Alfonso Pinero *(Sp)*	1987	1987	17
Michael Few *(Eng)*	1987	1987	18
Kelly Clair *(USA)*	1987	1987	19
Dana Banke *(USA)*	1987	1987	20
Don Klenk *(USA)*	1987	1987	21
Sandy Stephen *(Scot)*	1987	1987	22
Costantino Rocca *(It)*	1987	1987	23
Chris Platts *(Eng)*	1987	1987	24
Peter Van Der Riet *(SA)*	1987	1987	25
Gregory Aune *(USA)*	1987	1987	26
Robert Stephens *(Aus)*	1987	1987	27
Rafael Navarro *(Bra)*	1987	1987	28
Juan Pinero *(Sp)*	1987	1987	29
***David Gilford** *(Eng)*	1987	1987	30
Mark Davis *(Eng)*	1987	1987	31
Jose Davila *(Sp)*	1987	1987	32
Neal Briggs *(Eng)*	1987	1987	33
Neil Burke *(Eng)*	1987	1987	34
Jesus Lopez *(Sp)*	1987	1987	35
Wilhelm Winsnes *(SA)*	1987	1987	36
Peter Carsbo *(Swe)*	1987	1987	37
Nicholas Mitchell *(Eng)*	1987	1987	38
David James *(Scot)*	1987	1987	39
Adam Hunter *(Scot)*	1987	1987	40
Ignacio De Leon *(Mex)*	1987	1987	41
Heinz-Peter Thül *(W Ger)*	1987	1987	42
Jeremy Bennett *(Eng)*	1987	1987	43
Bryan Norton *(USA)*	1987	1987	44
Peter Allan *(Eng)*	1987	1987	45
Per-Arne Brostedt *(Swe)*	1987	1987	46
Joe Higgins *(Eng)*	1987	1987	47
Brian Evans *(Eng)*	1987	1987	48
Richard Fish *(Eng)*	1987	1987	49
Todd Meena *(USA)*	1987	1987	50

*Denotes affiliated member in 1986 — No in category 50

Category 13
128–153 1986 Epson Order of Merit

Juan Quiros *(Sp)*	1987	1987	128
Peter Harrison *(Eng)*	1987	1987	131
Jeff Hall *(Eng)*	1987	1987	132
Luis Carbonetti *(Arg)*	1987	1987	133
Paul Hoad *(Eng)*	1987	1987	134
Mark Johnson *(Eng)*	1987	1987	138
Jack Ferenz *(USA)*	1987	1987	139
Roger Gunn *(USA)*	1987	1987	140
Paul Carrigill *(Eng)*	1987	1987	142
***Gary Weir** *(Scot)*	1987	1987	144
Baldovino Dassu *(It)*	1987	1987	145
Ewen Murray *(Scot)*	1987	1987	146
Steve Cipa *(Eng)*	1987	1987	148
Anthony Stevens *(Eng)*	1987	1987	150
Jay Townsend *(USA)*	1987	1987	152

*Denotes affiliated member in 1986 — No in category 15

1986 All Exempt Tour
continued

Category 14
51–113 from the 1986 Qualifying School

	Eligible 1st Jan	*Expires* 31st Dec	*Ranking in Category*
Oliver Eckstein *(W Ger)*	1987	1987	51
Peter Barber *(Eng)*	1987	1987	52
Donald MacMillan Jr *(USA)*	1987	1987	54
James White *(Scot)*	1987	1987	55
David Blakeman *(Eng)*	1987	1987	56
David Wills *(Eng)*	1987	1987	58
Robert Michael *(USA)*	1987	1987	59
***Mikael Högberg** *(Swe)*	1987	1987	60
Simon Townend *(Eng)*	1987	1987	61
Murray Supple *(Eng)*	1987	1987	62
Alan Evans *(Wal)*	1987	1987	63
Donald Stirling *(Eng)*	1987	1987	64
Glyn Davies *(Wal)*	1987	1987	65
Paul Kent *(Eng)*	1987	1987	66
Silvio Grappasonni *(It)*	1987	1987	67
Steve Martin *(Scot)*	1987	1987	68
Colin Gillies *(Scot)*	1987	1987	69
Stuart Smith *(Eng)*	1987	1987	70
Colin Brooks *(Scot)*	1987	1987	71
Jeff Pinsent *(Eng)*	1987	1987	72
Mike Miller *(Scot)*	1987	1987	74
Johan Tumba *(Swe)*	1987	1987	75
Mark Tomlinson *(Eng)*	1987	1987	76
Robert Green *(Eng)*	1987	1987	77
Gary Broadbent *(Eng)*	1987	1987	78
Yvon Houssin *(Fr)*	1987	1987	79
John Brennand *(Eng)*	1987	1987	80
Steven Thompson *(Eng)*	1987	1987	81
Chip Drury *(USA)*	1987	1987	82
Frederic Regard *(Fr)*	1987	1987	83
Jim Rutledge *(Can)*	1987	1987	84
Frederick Dupré *(USA)*	1987	1987	85
Ian Higby *(Eng)*	1987	1987	86
Mark Sharman *(Eng)*	1987	1987	87
Erin McGrew *(USA)*	1987	1987	88
Rene Michelsen *(Den)*	1987	1987	89
Antonio Postiglione *(W Ger)*	1987	1987	90
Craig Laurence *(Eng)*	1987	1987	91
Robin Mann *(Eng)*	1987	1987	92
David Whelan *(Eng)*	1987	1987	93
George Serhan *(Aus)*	1987	1987	95
Tim Planchin *(Fr)*	1987	1987	96
Mats Hallberg *(Swe)*	1987	1987	97
Robert Joyce *(Eng)*	1987	1987	98
Robert Richardson *(SA)*	1987	1987	99
Cai Nilsson *(Swe)*	1987	1987	100
Evan Schiller *(USA)*	1987	1987	101
Nigel Burch *(Eng)*	1987	1987	102
Hendrick Buhrmann *(SA)*	1987	1987	103
Jose Cabo *(Sp)*	1987	1987	104
Garry Harvey *(Scot)*	1987	1987	105
Peter Jones *(Aus)*	1987	1987	106
Richard Adams *(Eng)*	1987	1987	107
John Vingoe *(Eng)*	1987	1987	108
Nick Haynes *(Eng)*	1987	1987	109
John Woof *(Eng)*	1987	1987	110
Tim Huyton *(Eng)*	1987	1987	111
David Webb *(Eng)*	1987	1987	113

*Denotes affiliated member in 1986

No in category 58

Category 15

Past Champions/Ryder Cup Players

Francisco Abreu *(Sp)*
Peter Alliss *(Eng)*
A Angelini *(It)*
Brian Bamford *(Eng)*
Harry Bannerman *(Scot)*
Valentin Barrios *(Sp)*
Jaime Benito *(Sp)*
Roberto Bernardini *(It)*
Ken Bousfield *(Eng)*
Hugh Boyle *(Ire)*
Peter Butler *(Eng)*
Manuel Cabrera *(Sp)*
Alex Caygill *(Eng)*
Clive Clark *(Eng)*
John Cockin *(Swe)*
Tony Coop *(Eng)*
Peter Dawson *(Eng)*
Max Faulkner *(Eng)*
Angel Gallardo *(Sp)*
Jean Garaialde *(Fr)*
John Garner *(Eng)*
German Garrido *(Sp)*
Malcolm Gregson *(Eng)*
Tony Grubb *(Eng)*
Liam Higgins *(Ire)*
Jimmy Hitchcock *(Eng)*
Guy Hunt *(Eng)*
Brian Huggett *(Wal)*
Bernard Hunt *(Eng)*
Jimmy Kinsella *(Ire)*
Bill Large *(Eng)*
Doug McClelland *(Eng)*
Paddy McGuirk *(Ire)*
Jimmy Martin *(Ire)*
Angel Miguel *(Sp)*
Sebastian Miguel *(Sp)*
Ralph Moffitt *(Eng)*
Hedley Muscroft *(Eng)*
John Panton *(Scot)*
Lionel Platts *(Eng)*
Manuel Ramos *(Sp)*
Doug Sewell *(Eng)*
Paddy Skerritt *(Ire)*
Ramon Sota *(Sp)*
Arnold Stickley *(Eng)*
David Talbot *(Eng)*
David Thomas *(Wal)*
Philippe Toussaint *(Bel)*
Peter Townsend *(Eng)*
Ross Whitehead *(Eng)*
George Will *(Scot)*
Norman Wood *Scot)*

No in category 52

Breakdown of nationalities of those eligible for membership

Category	England	USA	Australia	Scotland	Spain	South Africa	Argentina	Sweden	Wales	Ireland	Italy	N Ireland	Canada	France	New Zealand	W Germany	Zimbabwe	Brazil	Denmark	Japan	Mexico	Totsl
1	4	3	2	1	2		1									1						14
2									1									1				2
3				1																1		2
4		1			1								1									3
5	7	1	4	3	2	3		1	1			1			1		2					26
7	6		1	1	1	2				5		1			1							18
11	27	15	8	4	6	4	2	3	3	1	1	2	1	2	1		1					81
12	17	8	3	5	5	3		3			2					1		1	1		1	50
13	7	3		2	1		1				1											15
14	13	2		5				2	2		1			1		1						27
	81	33	18	22	18	12	4	9	7	6	5	4	2	3	3	3	3	2	1	1	1	238

Summary

Argentina	4
Australia	18
Brazil	2
Canada	2
Denmark	1
England	81
France	3
Ireland	6
Italy	5
Japan	1
Mexico	1
New Zealand	3
N Ireland	4
Scotland	22
Spain	18
South Africa	12
Sweden	9
USA	33
Wales	7
W Germany	3
Zimbabwe	3

Women's Professional Golf

Elizabeth Price

Laura Davies, big hitting winner of the Ring and Brymer Order of Merit in her first full professional year.

Laura Davies's outstanding year

The 1986 season on the Professional tour was marked by 4 events.

In the purely playing sphere the dramatic winning of the Ring and Brymer Order of Merit by Laura Davies for the second year running was exciting. The appointment of Mickey Walker as the Senior Professional at the Warren Golf Club at the end of the year was a new step for the women and the resignation of Colin Snape, the WPGA executive director sees the Association moving on to a new era. But one of the innovations which may have a vast impact in the future is the possible introduction of pre-qualifying.

Laura Davies, who was top of the Order of Merit in her Rookey year had a spectacular finish to the 1986 season snatching top spot for the second time running when she won the last two tournaments of the season. She is the first British player to win the Open Championship since Amateur Janet Melville in 1978. At that time the tournament was in the throes of evolving from an amateur tournament in which professionals could play to the LGU-run open it now is, with R & A backing and prize money to warrant American professionals entering. There were few professionals playing then and the WPGA was only formed the following year.

Miss Davies started the season quietly and there was no sign of the excitement which was to develop at the end of the year when she came from behind to beat Liselotte Neumann by just £500 to repeat her 1st place of the previous year.

Muriel Thomson came off the starting blocks quickly, taking the first tournament of the season, the Ford Classic. She had won the last tournament played in the UK the previous year and had obviously wintered well. In 1985 she finished 4th overall and was looking to win the Order of Merit title for the third time having won in 1980 and 1983. She has never been out of the top ten on the money list and as the year progressed she was doing well.

When Kelly Leadbetter from the US took the £9,000 cheque for winning the Hennessy Cognac tournament Miss Thomson was relegated to 2nd place but regained the premier spot after 6 events at which time Miss Neumann and Miss Davies were lying 5th and 7th respectively.

Young Swede's success

It was not until Liselotte won the German Open, the 12th event on the tour that Miss Thomson was knocked out of the leading spot and the young Swede took over. Still Miss Davies had not made a significant move and was in 6th place, £9,000 behind the Swede. Miss Neumann continued to head Miss Davies as the tour moved through Sweden and back to Scotland, and although the English girl moved up to 4th place Miss Neumann was still in the lead and the gap between the two was nearly £13,000.

The Swede, 3 years younger than the 23-year-old Miss Davies must have felt that second place Gillian Stewart was her main threat and even she was £11,000 behind. Miss Stewart had reached her elevated position with consistently high finishes and her final placing was 4th, with Australian Corrine Dibnah, having won two tournaments in the year, in 3rd position.

The Swede, Liselotte Neumann, led the Order of Merit pack for most of the year, only to lose it to Laura Davies in the last tournament.

Then Miss Davies won the Greater Manchester Tournament to jump to second place and £10,000 behind with only 4 events to play. Time was running out. Not only did she win the Tournament but her score of 20 under par was a new record for the tour. It was not the increase in winnings that gave her a boost, it was the extra confidence that such a performance produced. Two weeks later she recorded her greatest win The British Ladies' Open.

The holder Betsy King, who was the LPGA Player of the Year in 1984, and one of the leading money winners on the American circuit, never really found her form and it was left to Marta Figueras-Dotti the Spanish player on the American tour to lead the LPGA players' challenge. Miss Dotti had won the British Open Championship as an amateur in 1982.

Great length and improved putting

It was the power of Miss Davies that saw her through to win by 4 shots from Miss Dotti who shared second place with Peggy Conley, an American who regularly plays on the WPGA tour. This boosted the English girl's earnings by £9,000.

In this tournament the highest placed amateur was the Welsh Curtis Cup star Vicki Thomas, who finished in 5th place ahead of Miss King. Miss Neumann was 7th and took £2,000 so that Miss Davies gained £7,000 on her and was now just over £3,000 short. The scene was set for the grand finale at La Manga.

Miss Davies had to win and Miss Neumann had to finish worse than 7th for the English girl to take the £5,000 Ring and Brymer Award. Miss Davies won in style and the Swedish girl failed so that she was overtaken at the post.

Miss Davies had won 3 of the last 5 events which must be a record in itself. She could continue to do well. Her prodigious length alone gives her an enormous advantage but lately she has learnt the finer art of the short game and her iron shots are much more accurate. Where she used to complain of bad putting she now copes very well but she admits this is still the part of her game which needs more practice.

One of the highlights of her year was her 11th place finish in the American Open and it has understandably given her a taste for the American circuit. Wisely she thinks she will not go there for another year but will try for her American card in August when Trish Johnson will join her.

Pre-qualifying

Obviously there will be many new intakes in the coming year and the established players will be tested. The WPGA Executive Committee voted for pre-qualifying to be introduced in 1987, a move that should improve the quality of the tournaments. It would only come into effect if there was an entry of over 80, and the number on the tour has increased to such an extent that this is a figure which is likely at some of the more popular venues.

It is possible that pre-qualifying would give some amateurs a reason to think twice before letting the glamour of the tour colour their judgement. Only the first 40 on this year's Order of Merit plus other categories such as past winners of tournaments will be exempt.

The players voted against the idea saying that some of the original members, without whom the professional circuit would never have materialised, would be at risk and they felt this would be a pity. Pre-qualifying must come but perhaps it will not be brought in just yet.

Snape's surprise resignation

The resignation of Colin Snape came as a surprise. Mr Snape has been responsible for the continual growth not only of the tour but the increase of the prize money which in 1987 should be over £1 million. It will be difficult to find a replacement.

One of the founder members of the WPGA, Mickey Walker took another pioneering step, being appointed Senior Professional at the Warren Golf Club. Miss Walker after an amateur career full of success went on to be one of the first British players to turn professional and play on the American circuit. She came home when the WPGA tour was mooted and has been Chairman of the Association. Now she is breaking new ground although she is not strictly speaking first in the field. Mary Holway was a club professional for some years.

WPGA Tour, 1986

Ford Ladies' Classic
at Woburn G&CC Milton Keynes Buckinghamshire

Name	Score	Prize £
M Thomson	73-74-70-73–290	4500
A Nicholas	70-73-71-77–291	3075
V Marvin	73-71-75-74–293	2250
J Brown	76-71-74-73–294	1830
P Nilsson	81-68-70-76–295	1470
M Walker	75-71-80-70–296	1155
L Neumann	73-72-79-72–296	1155

Ulster Volkswagen Classic
at Belvoir Park GC Belfast

Name	Score	Prize £
B Huke	74-70-69–213	3000
P Conley	74-71-69–214	2050
S Van Wyk	72-76-70–218	1132
M Thomson	76-69-73–218	1132
D Hermida	73-71-74–218	1132
D Reid	71-72-75–218	1132

Hennessy Cognac Ladies' Cup
at Chantilly Paris

Name	Score	Prize £
K Leadbetter	73-71-73-76–293	9000
K Lunn	76-72-71-75–294	6150
J Connachan	75-74-74-72–295	4500
K Douglas	76-77-72-72–297	3030
B Lunsford	77-75-72-73–297	3030
M Thomson	76-74-73-74–297	3030
A Nicholas	75-75-71-77–298	1980
L Neumann	74-79-74-71–298	1980
*M de Taya	78-72-73-75–298	—

*Denotes amateur

British Olivetti Tournament
at Moor Hall GC Sutton Coldfield

Name	Score	Prize £
D Reid	73-71-70-71–285	3000
L Davies	73-70-69-73–285	2050
(D Reid won play-off)		
A Nicholas	79-74-69-68–290	1500
M Thomson	77-76-68-72–293	1220
C Dibnah	75-73-72-74–294	980
P Gonzalez	83-70-71-71–295	770
K Espinasse	72-73-74-76–295	770

Portuguese Ladies' Open
at Vilamoura

Name	Score	Prize £
C Panton	74-69-71-72–286	3750
K Leadbetter	74-73-71-68–286	2217
G Stewart	73-74-69-70–286	2217
(C Panton won play-off)		
B New	77-74-70-67–288	1525
C Dibnah	79-70-71-71–291	1225
L Neumann	72-72-73-75–292	1035
M Wennersten	77-76-73-67–293	822
E Glass	74-77-71-71–293	822

British Midland Ladies' Irish Open
at City of Derry GC Co Londonderry

Name	Score	Prize £
M Thomson	71-72-75-72–290	3750
L Neumann	76-73-72-75–296	2560
R Comstock	74-77-73-73–297	1525
L Davies	74-73-76-75–298	1275
K Lunn	79-72-74-75–300	976
D Heinicke	74-73-77-76–300	976
D Reid	78-73-72-77–300	976
M Burton	75-74-72-79–300	976

McEwans Wirral Classic
at Caldy GC Wirral Cheshire

Name	Score	Prize £
L Davies	72-71-70-72–285	3000
D Reid	71-72-75-70–288	1590
B New	69-76-72-71–288	1590
P Grice-Whittaker	73-75-68-72–288	1590
A Sheard	76-74-67-72–289	980
G Stewart	73-72-75-71–291	770
D Dowling	76-71-73-71–291	770

Bowring Scottish Women's Open

at Dalmahoy Edinburgh

Name	Score	Prize £
M Marshall	71-72-69-71–283	4500
L Davies	70-75-72-73–290	3075
S Strudwick	70-74-76-71–291	1572
B New	72-75-72-72–291	1572
L Neumann	73-72-72-74–291	1572
P Conley	72-74-71-74–291	1572
D Reid	75-72-70-74–291	1572

Belgian Ladies' Open

at Royal Waterloo GC

Name	Score	Prize £
P Grice-Whittaker	70-65-72-68–275	7500
G Stewart	73-69-75-67–284	5125
P Gonzalez	71-73-74-67–285	3400
L Neumann	71-72-70-72–285	3400
A Nicholas	67-75-73-71–286	2450
D Dowling	72-71-71-73–287	1925
K Leadbetter	70-67-76-74–287	1925
M Thomson	75-74-70-69–288	1341
L Davis	79-69-69-71–288	1341
D Hermida	69-72-73-74–288	1341

Bloor Homes Eastleigh Classic

at Fleming Park GC Eastleigh Hampshire

Name	Score	Prize £
D Dowling	62-65-63-64–254	3000
A Nicholas	64-66-63-67–260	2050
K Lunn	63-69-67-63–262	1500
K Douglas	72-65-62-66–265	935
D Reid	68-68-62-67–265	935
S Young	65-67-65-68–265	935
J Smith	65-67-65-68–265	935
B Huke	70-70-65-61–266	536
S Strudwick	65-67-70-64–266	536
E Glass	66-66-66-68–266	536

Trusthouse Forte Ladies' Classic

at Cologne W Germany

Name	Score	Prize £
C Dibnah	75-69-67-69–280	6000
G Stewart	75-68-69-70–282	4100
K Leadbetter	71-74-71-67–283	2466
L Neumann	67-70-75-71–283	2466
D Dowling	74-67-71-71–283	2466
L Davies	72-73-68-71–284	1540
J Connachan	72-73-67-72–284	1540
K Douglas	67-75-74-69–285	1073
P Grice-Whittaker	71-73-70-71–285	1073
D Reid	70-70-73-72–285	1073

Mitsubishi Colt Cars Jersey Open
at Royal Jersey CI

Name	Score	Prize £
K Douglas	71-67-71-69–278	3000
P Conley	70-71-72-71–284	2050
C Dibnah	70-70-76-69–285	1500
G Stewart	74-70-70-72–286	1100
F Dassu	76-65-72-73–286	1100
S Van Wyk	75-66-79-67–287	670
B New	74-75-67-71–287	670
C Panton	75-69-72-71–287	670
D Dowling	73-76-65-73–287	670

Kristianstad Open
at Kristianstad GC Sweden

Name	Score	Prize £
C Dibnah	75-72-71-70–288	6000
L Neumann	75-71-71-72–289	4100
D Dowling	76-71-75-68–290	2467
M Thomson	76-73-70-71–290	2467
B Huke	70-72-75-73–290	2467

Borlange Open
at Borlange Golf Club Sweden

Name	Score	Prize £
K Lunn	70-71-71–212	6000
L Neumann	72-71-71–214	3550
P Conley	72-71-71–214	3550
M Wennersten	74-73-69–216	2440
L Davies	71-76-70–217	1960

Dutch Ladies' Open
at Hilversum

Name	Score	Prize £
J Forrest	72-74-66-70–282	6750
L Neumann	73-73-70-71–287	4612
D Chudzinski	73-72-75-68–288	3375
C Panton	72-70-75-72–289	2475
G Stewart	72-69-76-72–289	2475
K Douglas	70-74-75-71–290	1732
M Thomson	74-73-73-70–290	1732
K Espinasse	71-75-71-74–291	1372
P Grice-Whittaker	75-69-74-74–292	1072

BMW Ladies' German Open
at Oching Munich W Germany

Name	Score	Prize £
L Neumann	71-72-72-67–282	6750
A Nicholas	73-73-68-70–284	4612
P Conley	73-73-69-70–285	3060
G Stewart	75-67-71-72–285	3060
D Dowling	77-71-69-70–287	2205
L Davies	68-78-74-68–288	1867
M Wennersten	79-71-69-70–289	1597
D Reid	70-74-72-74–290	1372
B Lunsford	72-74-74-71–291	1124
K Lunn	74-73-72-72–291	1124

Greater Manchester Open
at Haigh Hill Wigan Lancashire

Name	Score	Prize £
L Davies	63-70-67-68–268	3000
P Whittaker	69-68-67-67–271	2050
D Reid	69-67-71-71–278	1500
A Sheard	74-64-68-73–279	1220
E Glass	68-70-71-71–280	980
K Douglas	72-70-69-70–281	830
M Burton	68-70-73-71–282	660
R Comstock	69-72-69-72–282	660

Laing Ladies' Classic
at Stoke Poges Berks

Name	Score	Prize £
D Dowling	69-66-69-70–274	3750
C Dibnah	71-65-70-69–275	2560
D Reid	72-69-66-69–276	1875
B Huke	66-70-70-73–279	1525
G Stewart	71-70-71-69–281	1130
R Comstock	71-70-71-69–281	1130

Ladies' British Open

at Birkdale Southport Lancashire

Name	Score	Prize £
L Davies	71-73-69-70–283	9000
P Conley	70-69-71-77–287	5050
M Figueras-Dotti	68-72-74-73–287	5050
B New	69-77-76-66–288	3600
*V Thomas	75-73-71-70–289	—
B King	73-71-72-74–290	2900
D Dowling	70-70-75-76–291	2600
L Neumann	71-73-74-74–292	2250
D Massey	76-71-72-74–293	2000
P Grice-Whittaker	75-74-75-70–294	1800
*C Duffy	73-73-73-75–294	—

*Denotes amateur

Spanish Open

at La Manga Spain

Name	Score	Prize £
L Davies	72-72-68-74–286	3750
C Dibnah	70-76-74-70–290	2560
D Reid	72-71-74-74–291	1875
P Grice-Whittaker	72-76-73-72–293	1261
A Sheard	72-76-73-72–293	1261
S Strudwick	69-69-79-76–293	1261

WPGA Order of Merit, 1986

1986 WPGA Money List

Pos	Name	Official Money $	No of Events
1 (1)	**Laura Davies**	37500	19
2 (12)	**Liselotte Neumann** (Sweden)	37006	17
3 (13)	**Corinne Dibnah** (Australia)	26969	19
4 (8)	**Gillian Stewart**	26395	17
5 (5)	**Debbie Dowling**	25495	20
6 (21)	**Peggy Conley** (USA)	25229	18
7 (4)	**Muriel Thomson**	24960	19
8 (6)	**Dale Reid**	23892	20
9 (14)	**Penny Grice-Whittaker**	22654	19
10 (15)	**Alison Nicholas**	21585	18
11 (19)	**Karen Lunn** (Australia)	19440	19
12 (7)	**Kitrina Douglas**	17292	19
13 (42)	**Kelly Leadbetter** (USA)	16939	6
14 (9)	**Catherine Panton**	16180	15
15 (3)	**Beverly Huke**	15611	19
16 (28)	**Beverley New**	15421	18
17 (22)	**Jane Forrest**	14914	17
18 (2)	**Jane Connachan**	14676	17
19 (10)	**Marie Wennersten** (Sweden)	10146	17
20 (60)	**Rica Comstock** (USA)	10017	20
21 (40)	**Suzanne Strudwick**	9746	19
22 (27)	**Alison Sheard** (South Africa)	9725	18
23 (—)	**Meredith Marshall** (USA)	9577	18
24 (37)	**Elizabeth Glass** (Zimbabwe)	8881	20
25 (32)	**Brenda Lunsford** (USA)	8699	19
26 (18)	**Vanessa Marvin**	8154	20
27 (—)	**Patricia Gonzalez** (Colombia)	7570	18
28 (16)	**Julie Brown**	6906	18
29 (—)	**Karine Espinasse** (France)	6725	19
30 (23)	**Diana Heinicke** (USA)	6297	19
31 (11)	**Maxine Burton**	5926	19
32 (—)	**Maureen Garner**	5594	16
33 (53)	**Nicola McCormack**	5273	18
34 (17)	**Federica Dassu** (Italy)	5206	19
35 (50)	**Sonja Van Wyk** (South Africa)	5122	18
36 (65)	**Diana Chudzinski** (W Germany)	5065	7
37 (20)	**Sapphire Young**	4834	17
38 (31)	**Christine Sharp**	4587	16

Position in 1985 in brackets.
Nationality is British unless otherwise stated.

The Amateurs

Raymond Jacobs

© Peter Dazeley Photography

Ronnie Shade, a great Amateur in the 1960s, won the Scottish Championship 5 years in succession.

The two episodes in 1986 which illustrated most vividly, if also poignantly and paradoxically, the changing face of amateur golf in these islands were the untimely death of Ronnie Shade and the headlong, some thought headstrong, flight of leading players to become professionals. Shade may well turn out to have been the last of a breed, encompassing such contemporaries of his as Michael Bonallack and Joe Carr, whose careers as amateurs also extended for about as many years as the months the best of more recent generations seem to last before they succumb to the seductive tune they hear from the Pied Piper of Professionalism.

The innocent bystanders, who also included those entrusted with the selection of teams for Scotland and England, and, when coupled with those of Wales and Ireland, the British Isles were lucky not to be knocked down in the rush. Before the English championship was over Peter Baker, Mark Davis and David Gilford had indicated their intentions to turn professional. Not to be upstaged and scarcely had a month elapsed since his victory in the Scottish championship than Colin Brooks crossed over, accompanied by Angus Moir, his predecessor by two years, and David James, runner-up for the title in 1985. Steven McKenna, the unranked winner of the Lytham Trophy, was another to take the plunge.

The Amateur Status – New Rule

Their strike was pre-emptive of the changes announced by the Royal and Ancient Club to the rules governing amateur status. Realistic as these unquestionably were, they were assessed sceptically by some as cosmetic and by others as being another wordly example of having subtly moved the goalposts without having gone to the trouble of radically changing the game. But it was never less than doubtful that these amendments would do anything to give pause to those whose reach might exceed their grasp, but whose ambition would not be diverted by the harsh facts of the humble life led by the generality of tournament professionals. On the other hand, a free society entitles everyone to the opportunity to make their own mistakes.

Ronnie Shade's fine record

Ironically, Shade made his miscalculation, later self-admitted, by not turning professional soon enough. He did so at the comparatively advanced age of 30, by which time he had won the Scottish title for five successive years, a record surely unlikely to be broken now, three English Stroke-play Championships and one Scottish, been runner-up in the Amateur Championship, represented Scotland for eight years and Britain four times each in the Walker Cup Match and Eisenhower Trophy Tournament. Shade's christian names of Ronald David Bell Mitchell came aptly to describe the nature of his game, the initials becoming the acronym for Right

Down the Bloody Middle. To say that his like will never be seen again is simply to acknowledge the irreversibly changed direction amateur golf has taken.

It was, of course, ironic, too, that Shade, amidst all his achievements, should never win the British title. David Curry of Prudhoe did, however, and with a vengeance, by 11 and 9 over Geoff Birtwell, a former member of the Royal Lytham and St Annes Club, whose centenary year the championship helped to celebrate. The victory of Curry, a semi-finalist two years before, was by far the greatest margin since Lawson Little's demolition of James Wallace, another local hero, by 14 and 13 at Prestwick in 1934. None who were persuaded to research the fact more extensively could discover a club other than Prudhoe, in the north-east of England, to provide the winner of both the British Amateur and Boys' championships, Neville Dunn having captured the latter title 35 years before, also at Prestwick.

National champions

The outcome of the four national championships was in distinctive character. Having waited for 60 years to produce the winner of the English title, in Roger Winchester in 1985, Devon, a county comprising only 26 clubs, provided his successor, Jonathan Langmead. Brook's victim in the Scottish Championship was Alan Thomson, who had also been the beaten finalist five years before. They both were established players, in contrast to the Welsh finalists. Neither Christopher Rees, the winner, nor Bradley Knight, the runner-up, were seeds, further evidence of the expanding force of Welsh golf despite limited resources both of the personnel and financial sort. But Irish players, not for the first time and probably not for the last, took the eye particularly.

Leslie Walker became the first golfer from the Republic of Ireland for 50 years, since Jimmy Bruen no less, to win the British Boys' Championship, but his compatriot, John McHenry, made an even greater impact, negatively and positively. Having been reported by his partners for his undisciplined conduct during the East of Ireland Championship, McHenry, aged 22 and the product of the American college system, became a reformed character and carried almost all before him. Apart from stroke-play success at Waterford and Mullingar, McHenry added the Irish Close Championship to his victory in the South of Ireland event, the first double achievement of its kind for 37 years. It was not surprising, then, that McHenry should be involved in further accomplishment, albeit of a quite different kind.

The experienced and successful Peter McEvoy, whose surprising omission from the 1987 Walker Cup Team many think is a Selector's aberration.

© Peter Dazeley Photography

Home Internationals and other titles

McHenry was able to boast that, in Ireland's match against England in the Home Internationals at Harlech, he inflicted on Peter McEvoy, who was making his 100th appearance, only his third defeat in 51 singles games for his country. But as it happened, neither of the countries won the series, that distinction belonged to Scotland. Significantly or not, in terms of equalising the amateur forces among the four participants, Scotland gained the relatively rare feat of defeating the three other sides to capture the mythical Triple Crown only 12 months after having been left holding the equally fictitious Wooden Spoon. Subsequently, McEvoy and Curry of England, Colin Montgomerie of Scotland, and Garth McGimpsey of Ireland, made up the composite Eisenhower Trophy side.

It was possibly another sign of the times, reflected also in the widening spread of achievement among the professionals, that of that quartet Curry alone won a national title. Hospitable to a fault, Britain allowed two of its more prestigious titles to emigrate, the English Stroke-play Championship to South Africa with Richard Kaplan, and the Scottish Youths' Championship to Sweden with Adam Mednick. On the other hand, Kenny Walker kept the Scottish Stroke-play title in the host country's keeping, as did Gilford, who won the British Youths' Championship at

Carnoustie by no fewer than eight strokes, the same margin as Mednick's. One player, however, went some way towards reducing the need for British blushes.

Tait's consistency

Alan Tait, who in the spring had won the Scottish Boys' Championship at Dunbar, in the late summer at Aberdeen resumed his successful activities by winning first the Doug Sanders European title and then the corresponding World Championship. On the King's Links, whose par is 71, Tait had successive rounds of 71, 69, 65, 68, 74, 71, 67 and 75. As if that were not enough, Tait became the first Scottish player to win the Bell's Junior PGA Championship, which he did by five strokes with rounds of 74, 76 and 77 over the testing King's Course at Gleneagles Hotel. Since these 11 scores were produced over a period of only 11 days Tait was entitled to claim a rare sustaining of quality over a highly concentrated spell, supportive confirmation, if that were really needed, of the advantage – the necessity, even – of full-time golf for the amateur, however young.

Success and failure

Success also accompanied British golf into team events. Britain and Ireland beat the Continent of Europe by 14½ to 9½ at Halmstad, Sweden, to retain the St Andrews Trophy, and England again won the European Boys' Team title, beating Sweden 4–3 in the final at Turin. In the final of an inaugural Six-nations Youths' Tournament at Serdana, Scotland beat the host country, Spain, by 4–3 in the final. In the first of these contests, the Continent's cause was not helped when Anders Haglund, winner of the first European Amateur Championship, went down with chickenpox and was withdrawn on medical advice two minutes before he was to tee-off in the opening foursomes game. The season finished, however, on a decidedly less positive note.

In the 15th World Amateur Team Championship at Caracas, Britain and Ireland struggled into 12th place, the four-man side finishing all of 42 strokes behind Canada, the winners over the United States by three strokes. The realisation was strengthened that for the Walker Cup to join the Ryder Cup and Curtis Cup on this side of the Atlantic would require perhaps even greater measures of ability, character, encouragement and luck. The omission of McEvoy and McGimpsey from the side for Sunningdale was totally unexpected, but the optimist could not help reflecting, however, that the American superiority once taken for granted had in Venezuela received another rebuff; with a round to play they were in the lead by three strokes.

Women's Amateur Golf

Elizabeth Price

A great year

What a wonderful year 1986 proved to be for women's amateur golf in these islands.

Having won the Curtis Cup only twice since its inauguration in 1932 and then only on home soil, Diane Bailey took her team to Prairie Dunes in the US where they delivered a drubbing by 13 to 5 to the young collegiate team selected by the Americans to oppose them under the captaincy of Judy Bell. Even acknowledging the suspicion that the Americans could have found a stronger side *it was a glorious victory*.

Mrs Bailey who had also captained the team 2 years ago at Muirfield where we lost by the slender margin of the last putt in the deciding match was convinced we could and would win. She was a captain who left nothing to chance and looked after her team's health as well as their games, going so far as to find an answer to fatigue and dehydration in the heat that was to be encountered. It was a fitting climax to the year when Mrs Bailey and her team were presented with the Avia Woman Golfer of the Year Award.

© Peter Dazeley Photography

Trish Johnson, 1985 English Match and Stroke-play Champion, won 4 points in the Curtis Cup and remains an amateur – but for how long?

The Americans had selected a little known team mainly composed of college players, while Great Britain and Ireland included three players with more experience in their little fingers than the entire opposition.

Another pointer to a possible first was that Karen Davies, at University in the US, had won 4 tournaments and played for the US collegiate team against Japan in Tokyo winning all her matches and being named *most valuable player*. If Karen was the American's *most valuable player* and yet now one of our champions surely we should have an advantage. The young Welsh girl returned to the US in the British Team to play her erstwhile colleagues, winning the leading foursomes with Trish Johnson and halving her two singles.

At the end of the year the World Team Championship was played in Caracas and the team of Jill Thornhill, Trish Johnson and Claire Hourihane began in fine form leading after the first day. Over the next 3 rounds they slipped back finishing in 4th place behind Spain, France and the US.

Youth to the fore

Jill Thornhill and Trish Johnson played outstandingly in both these events, Miss Johnson winning all her matches in America and finishing 3rd Individual in Venezuela, while Mrs Thornhill scored $3\frac{1}{2}$ points in the Curtis Cup.

However, it is to the juniors we must look and the result of the Junior European Team Championship, this year played in Hamburg, must have thrilled the selectors. In this event the four home countries each send a team. There are qualifying rounds and then the Matchplay stages are played in flights.

The order of qualifying was England 1st, Wales 2nd and Scotland 3rd from an entry of 14 countries. Ireland might also have qualified high but for the fact that two of their team were disqualified, one for playing a wrong ball and not correcting the error before driving at the next hole, and the other for signing an incorrect score. These infringements put the team out of the competition though they were allowed to play on and take last place.

The final was between England and Scotland where England prevailed by 7 to 0. Wales came in 7th place. Miss Johnson was again the outstanding player. She and Karen Davies, who was the top Welsh player, returned record breaking 68s in the qualifying rounds.

New Zealand's first win

For some years now, players from Australia and New Zealand have been coming to play in the British Amateur Matchplay Championship and 1986 was no exception. One rather hoped, in Curtis Cup Year, that home players would make more impact and there would be a victory for one of the team, but the fact was far from the wish. None even reached the semi-final and it was left to Caroline Pierce to carry the flag through to that stage.

Marnie McGuire, 17 years old, from New Zealand beat the Australian International Louise Briers to become the youngest winner of the title this century and the first New Zealander ever. Miss McGuire came here as runner-up in the New Zealand Girl's Championship but her accuracy and putting took her through the week to become the British Champion.

Claire Hourihane wins Stroke-play

The British Stroke-play title went to Claire Hourihane from Ireland who having started the year quietly and gained in confidence as the year went on. The tournament was played at the end of August and the Irish girl was involved in a play-off with Miss Johnson. It was her first British title although she has been Irish Champion three times. Later still she confirmed her good form by breaking the record for the North Hants course when she won the Hampshire Rose.

The Welsh Open Amateur Stroke-play Championship was won by Helen Wadsworth from Prince's. Miss Wadsworth is another product of the American University system and is proving herself in many of the one day events. This was her first senior title.

Evergreen Pru Riddiford, 62, won the British Senior title for the second time. Mrs Riddiford seems to go from strength to strength and as well as winning once before she has been runner-up three times.

Susan Shapcott's two titles

The British Girl's title went overseas with Italian Stephanie Crosse beating Sarah

© Peter Dazeley Photography

Vicky Thomas, Welsh Champion for the fifth time in 8 years, raises morale, and enjoys the game and respect of her opponents.

Bennett from Colchester in the final. Miss Bennett had beaten Susan Shapcott the holder, who in the previous two weeks had won the English Girls' Championship and the English Women's Stroke-play titles.

Miss Shapcott, a quiet yet determined competitor, must be in line for the highest honours in amateur golf. It seems unlikely that she will go over to the paid ranks at least for a few years. At present she puts her education first, and because of exams she missed the British Match-play Championship, a fact which might well have kept her out of the Curtis Cup side. Even so she continues to make her mark on the amateur scene with the English Girls' title, the English Senior Stroke-play Championship and many high finishes including runner-up in the English Match-play. Despite wearing spectacles Miss Shapcott revels in bad weather and we had plenty of that. Had the Bristol Girl been chosen for the Curtis Cup she could not have won her one senior title as the English Stroke-play was played when the team was away, a bad clashing of dates which surely should be rectified. After all, dates for major internationals are published well in advance.

Jill and Belle – the ageless winners

1986 seems to have been the year when the *oldies* have tried and, in many cases, succeeded in slapping down the new entrants.

Jill Thornhill, at 43, took the English Title to add to her 1983 British Championship. In the finals she beat Miss Shapcott as she had in Spain earlier in the year. The Scottish was won by Belle Robertson, now 50 and eligible for the Seniors' Championship, while Vicki Thomas, who won the Welsh

© Peter Dazeley Photography

Claire Hourihane, ex-Irish Champion and Curtis Cup player, won the British Stroke-play title at Blairgowrie in a play-off with Trish Johnson.

title for the 5th time, and Therese O'Reily, the Irish winner, are both 32.

The Avia Watches Foursomes Championship is the first tournament of the year which does all it can to encourage young players, yet this went to Belle Robertson and Mary McKenna who continued their successful partnership in the Curtis Cup.

Home Internationals

Iteland won the Home International Matches at Whittington Barracks. After being tipped as favourites they made their task much harder when, on the first day, they lost to Wales. The shock of this defeat stirred them into life and they came back to beat both Scotland and England.

England again won the Junior Home Internationals but this tournament really emphasised the rising of the Welsh Players. At one time the Principality could only hope that one of their players would gain International honours, now quite a few are emerging. The latest is Julie Foster, 17, who beat each of the Junior Champions from England, Ireland and Scotland.

Opportunities in the USA

Perhaps the Americans are coaching our future teams. So many of our young hopefuls, men and women, are gaining scholarships to American Universities, where they play intensive golf in a lovely climate. The facilities are so much better than at home. The belief that the European player is as good as his or her American counterpart, but does not have the opportunity of continuous golf, is beginning to be proved. With Karen Davies, Helen Wadsworth and Caroline Pierce, all in America it looks as though the American coaching is doing us good.

But what of the future? There must be some more young players who see the professional circuit as their ultimate goal and quite a few may defect this winter. Already 20-year-old Miss Johnson has let it be known that she intends to play in the Ford Classic, the opening tournament of the professional season, as a professional, and she will try for her American players card in August with the LPGA Tour as her goal. With the money to be won increasing every year, who can blame those who think they are good enough for having a go?

Curtis Cup

Michael Williams

Courtesy of Mr Bailey

Mrs Diane Bailey, the inspired Captain who gave her all in leading the first ever British and Irish team, amateur or professional, to beat the US on its home ground.

Historic victory

Great Britain and Ireland's defeat of the United States in the Curtis Cup at Prairie Dunes, Kansas, ranks not only as the performance of 1986 but also as one of the finest achievements in the whole history of British golf. The statistics alone show the size of the mountain scaled by these eight players under the shrewd guidance and inspirational leadership of their captain, Diane Bailey.

This was the 24th match between the two countries and of the preceding 23, America had won 20, drawn one and lost only two. Both of those British victories had come in the fifties, both at home, at Muirfield in 1952 and then at Prince's four years later. They had also tied at Brae Burn in 1958 but that was the only occasion on which they had ever come close to winning in America, more often than not receiving some quite demoralising defeats.

The various Curtis Cup teams were nevertheless in good company. In the Walker Cup, which goes back longest of all, to 1922, and in the Ryder Cup (1927) American supremacy was just as great. Britain's amateurs had brief moments of glory in 1938 and 1971, each time at St Andrews, and once, in 1965, at Baltimore they too managed a tie in America. The professionals on the other hand have been defeated every time they have gone to the States, their four victories having been in 1929, 1933, 1957 and then in 1985 by which time their forces had been strengthened by the inclusion of players from the continent.

Inspired captaincy

This was therefore the first time that a visiting British team had ever won in America, which was startling enough. That they also achieved it by the overwhelming margin of 13–5 still boggles the imagination. However, in Mrs Bailey, herself a former Curtis Cup player, they found a captain very much in the mould of Tony Jacklin who, a year earlier, had captained Europe to that memorable Ryder Cup victory at The Belfry. While Jacklin had seen the glimmer of light in a narrow defeat in the 1983 PGA National in Florida, so Mrs Bailey drew her inspiration from a similarly close result, $8\frac{1}{2}$–$9\frac{1}{2}$, at Muirfield in 1984. She was absolutely convinced that Britain could and indeed would win at Prairie Dunes and her belief was such that by the time her team arrived in the torrid heat of Kansas in August, they believed it too.

Mrs Bailey's attention to detail included consultation with the medical advisers to the England football team, which had experienced similar extreme heat in the World Cup in Mexico. They recommended drinking Isostar, which replaces lost minerals, and wearing wet towels around the neck. Mrs Bailey also insisted that the team used golf carts in their early acclimatisation, building up their strength by degrees in time for the match itself. She also studied past results and brought a whole new approach to foursomes play, at which the British record was nothing like as good as it ought to have been.

Her instruction was for each player to play her own game and not to confuse matters with unnecessary consultation with her partner, which as likely as not would leave her in two minds. An even closer analysis of past results revealed that a score of two over par would lead to more wins than losses. She also stressed the importance of starting quickly and playing the first hole well. Four years earlier in Denver the repeated loss of the first hole had sent Britain spinning to one of their worst defeats by $14\frac{1}{2}$–$3\frac{1}{2}$.

Inexperienced US team

The whole approach to the match was therefore much more businesslike and Judy Bell, the American captain, noticed it immediately. *They really have come here to win*, she said to herself and the first seed of uncertainty was planted in the American camp. Nor did it help that not one of Miss Bell's team, picked very early in the year on the results of the previous season, had played in the Curtis Cup before. This lack of experience was almost certainly an important factor.

Looking back now, several months later, the abiding impression remains of how fast the British team came out of the starting gate. From the moment Patricia Johnson, who won all her four games, struck the opening tee shot straight and true while Dottie Pepper Mochrie followed with a smothered drive that could not have travelled more than 130 yards, the boot was on the British foot.

Behind them Jill Thornhill very nearly pitched her second shot straight into the hole and with all three British pairs getting their par fours they were all at once one up.

Veteran Belle Robertson, Scottish Champion for the 7th time in 22 years, holed vital putts at critical moments.

Indeed in the nine games, three foursomes and six singles, on that opening day, Britain did not once lose the first hole, winning it five times and halving the other four.

The first four holes at Prairie Dunes which, with its yucca plant, wild plum thickets and knee-high grasses, is quite British in character, form something of a loop and it was even more significant that Britain came out of it ahead in seven games on the first day and down only once. The Americans were immediately rattled and contributed to their defeat with some extraordinary errors as they gave away holes by building stances in bunkers, hitting the ball out of turn and inadvertently out of ignorance improving the lie. This was where the lack of experience came in.

Without, in any way, wishing to detract from the British performance this was the most inept American team I have seen, reflecting indeed the whole country's decline in global terms. They were aware of the Ryder Cup having been lost the previous year; they were aware of all the successes of Severiano Ballesteros, Bernhard Langer and Sandy Lyle in the major championships and in certain ways it all prompted self doubt.

Indeed it was not until nearly seven o'clock on a first day protracted by an early morning storm and then another in mid-afternoon that they won their first point,

Jill Thornhill, a latecomer to the top echelons of Women's Amateur Golf, who played so well in winning 3 points for the side.

Kandid Kessler defeating Vicki Thomas. But by then Britain were leading 6–0 and they were able to go to bed exultantly $6\frac{1}{2}$–$2\frac{1}{2}$ ahead.

(For detailed results see pages 730–7).

Britain storms home

Nor was that the end of it for the following morning Britain were soon in even greater control, quickly three up in all three foursomes and in with a genuine chance of wrapping the whole match up by lunch time. It did not quite happen, for in the end Patricia Johnson and Karen Davies had to work very hard to beat Donna Ammaccapane and Dottie Mochrie, securing a win only when they matched an American birdie at the 18th.

Behind them Belle Robertson and Mary McKenna, having been three up after five holes, became one down after 11 to Kim Gardner and Kathy McCarthy and got a half only when Mrs Robertson, at 50 the oldest golfer ever to have appeared in the match, holed with nerves of steel across the 18th green for the second time in two days.

However, with a lead now of 9–3, Britain needed only half a point from the second series of singles and it was Miss Johnson, their star player (though Mrs Thornhill ran her close), who got it very appropriately with her very best golf. She was three under par when she beat Miss McCarthy, who came into the match with the reputation of having the best potential since JoAnne Carner, by five and three. There were not too many dry eyes around at that moment.

USPGA Tour Results, 1986

Bob Hope Chrysler Classic
at Bermuda Dunes CC Indian Wells CC La Quinta CC and Eldorado CC

Name	Score	Prize $
D Hammond	69-64-68-68-66–335	108000
J Cook	68-67-65-69-66–335	64800
(D Hammond won play-off)		
J Mudd	72-65-63-68-69–337	40800
H Sutton	65-70-69-65-69–338	28800
C Stadler	67-65-69-70-68–339	21900
P Stewart	72-67-71-64-65–339	21900
G Koch	67-68-68-68-68–339	21900

Phoenix Open
at Phoenix CC Arizona

Name	Score	Prize $
H Sutton	64-64-68-71–267	90000
T Sills	68-68-65-68–269	44000
C Peete	64-69-68-68–269	44000
D Forsman	70-68-66-66–270	24000
D Pooley	74-61-67-69–271	19000
G Norman	64-71-66-70–271	19000
L Mize	64-71-68-70–273	14041
J Sindelar	69-64-69-71–273	14041
J Mahaffey	67-65-70-71–273	14041
A Bean	66-69-68-70–273	14041
R Black	66-66-69-72–273	14041
B Langer	69-68-67-69–273	14041

Los Angeles Open
at Riviera CC California

Name	Score	Prize $
D Tewell	69-72-66-63–270	81000
C Rose	73-70-66-68–277	48600
W Wood	72-69-67-70–278	30600
J Delsing	66-74-71-68–279	19800
J Gallagher Jr	71-71-68-69–279	19800
L Wadkins	71-70-67-72–280	14568
C Pavin	74-68-69-69–280	14568
A Cerda	74-67-69-70–280	14568
B Jaeckel	73-70-67-70–280	14568

AT & T Pebble Beach National Pro-Am
at Pebble Beach Cypress Point and Spyglass Hill California

Name	Score	Prize $
F Zoeller	69-66-70–205	108000
P Stewart	71-79-70–210	64800
M Wiebe	70-69-72–211	31200
T Watson	71-67-73–211	31200
T Sills	72-68-71–211	31200
D Pohl	71-70-72–213	19425
M Pfeil	73-67-73–213	19425
K Brown	74-73-66–213	19425
B Eastwood	70-70-73–213	19425

Hawaiian Open
at Waialae CC Honolulu

Name	Score	Prize $
C Pavin	67-67-72-66–272	90000
P Azinger	70-65-69-70–274	54000
B Langer	67-74-67-68–276	29000
T Watson	68-69-66-73–276	29000
D Ogrin	66-70-74-67–277	18250
A Dillard	69-71-69-68–277	18250
H Green	71-68-68-70–277	18250
J Mudd	71-69-66-72–278	15500

Shearson Lehman Brothers–Andy Williams San Diego Open
at Torrey Pines GC La Jolla California

Name	Score	Prize $
B Tway	67-68-69–204	81000
B Langer	70-66-68–204	48600
(B Tway won play-off)		
M Hulbert	69-69-67–205	23400
M Lye	70-66-69–205	23400
P Azinger	67-69-69–205	23400
G Koch	70-69-67–206	15075
L Rinker	66-72-68–206	15075
G Hallberg	70-69-67–206	15075

Doral Eastern Open
at Doral CC Miami Florida

Name	Score	Prize $
A Bean	71-68-68-69–276	90000
H Green	70-70-64-72–276	54000
(A Bean won play-off)		
M O'Meara	70-67-74-66–277	29000
T Kite	66-67-73-71–277	29000
M O'Grady	73-67-69-70–279	19000
M Sullivan	71-69-69-70–279	19000
T Purtzer	66-71-73-70–280	16750
B Wadkins	72-69-69-71–281	13500
M Calcavecchia	65-72-72-72–281	13500
E Fiori	68-68-74-71–281	13500
D Frost	69-70-73-69–281	13500
B Kratzert	72-70-69-70–281	13500

Honda Classic
at Eagle Trace Coral Springs Florida

Name	Score	Prize $
K Knox	66-71-80-70–287	90000
J Mudd	70-72-75-71–288	33000
C Rose	70-73-72-73–288	33000
J Mahaffey	74-70-76-68–288	33000
A Bean	69-69-77-73–288	33000
B Jaeckel	76-70-74-69–289	18000
T Purtzer	71-71-80-68–290	16750
P Stewart	69-74-73-75–291	15000
M Reid	69-78-72-72–291	15000

Bay Hill Classic
at Bay Hill C & L Orlando Florida

Name	Score	Prize $
D Forsman	68-67-67–202	90000
R Floyd	68-69-66–203	44000
M Hulbert	70-69-64–203	44000
W Levi	70-67-67–204	24000
C Strange	70-70-65–205	19000
D Pohl	68-70-67–205	19000
B Langer	72-66-68–206	15583
C Pavin	69-70-67–206	15583
M Wiebe	70-70-66–206	15583

USF&G Classic
at Lakewood CC New Orleans Louisana

Name	Score	Prize $
C Peete	68-67-66-68–269	90000
P McGowan	69-69-68-68–274	54000
G Ladehoff	75-68-64-70–277	24000
T Sieckmann	73-70-67-67–277	24000
D Tewell	71-69-69-68–277	24000
N Faldo	68-72-68-69–277	24000
D Pooley	71-71-70-69–281	14550
T Watson	71-74-66-70–281	14550
D Mast	72-64-71-74–281	14550
D Barr	73-72-67-69–281	14550
B. Israelson	73-65-74-69–281	14550

Panasonic-Las Vegas Invitational
at Las Vegas Desert Inn and Spanish Trail Nevada

Name	Score	Prize $
G Norman	73-63-68-64-65–333	207000
D Pohl	68-70-67-66-69–340	124200
L Nelson	67-69-67-69-69–341	66700
S Pate	67-73-69-65-67–341	66700
D Pooley	70-70-67-68-67–342	43700
A Bean	70-69-66-79-78–342	43700
B Tway	70-71-63-68-71–343	35843
G Morgan	67-67-70-71-68–343	35843
J Cook	66-68-70-71-68–343	35483

Tournament Players' Championship
at Tournament Players' Club Sawgrass Florida

Name	Score	Prize $
J Mahaffey	69-70-65-71–275	162000
L Mize	66-68-66-76–276	97200
T Simpson	72-70-66-72–280	61200
J Thorpe	69-68-74-70–281	37200
B Upper	71-65-73-72–281	37200
T Kite	69-69-71-72–281	37200
H Sutton	71-72-68-71–282	28050
J Cook	71-73-70-68–282	28050
J Haas	73-68-73-68–282	28050

Greater Greensboro Open

at Forest Oaks CC Greensboro North Carolina

Name	Score	Prize $
S Lyle	68-64-73-70–275	90000
A Bean	68-70-72-67–277	54000
L Thompson	66-72-72-69–279	29000
I Aoki	73-71-69-66–279	29000
L Wadkins	75-68-68-69–280	20000
T Purtzer	68-72-68-73–281	15125
C Stadler	69-69-71-72–281	15125
P Stewart	70-70-74-67–281	15125
C Beck	72-69-71-69–281	15125
D Edwards	67-72-74-68–281	15125
D Frost	69-72-68-72–281	15125
W Wood	71-72-68-71–282	11500

The US Masters

at Augusta National GC Augusta Georgia

Name	Score	Prize $
J Nicklaus	74-71-69-65–279	144000
T Kite	70-74-68-68–280	70400
G Norman	70-72-68-70–280	70400
S Ballesteros	71-68-72-70–281	38400
N Price	79-69-63-71–282	32000
T Watson	70-74-68-71–283	27800
J Haas	76-69-71-67–283	27800
P Stewart	75-71-69-69–284	23200
B Tway	70-73-71-70–284	23200
T Nakajima	70-71-71-72–284	23200

Sea Pines Heritage Classic

at Harbour Town GC Hilton Head Island South Carolina

Name	Score	Prize $
F Zoeller	68-68-69-71–276	81000
R Maltbie	67-72-69-69–277	33600
G Norman	70-68-69-70–277	33600
C Beck	70-67-70-70–277	33600
J Haas	71-70-66-71–278	18000
R Floyd	69-72-72-66–279	15075
K Green	71-70-71-67–279	15075
T Kite	70-72-70-67–279	15075

Houston Open
at The TCP of Texas

Name	Score	Prize $
C Strange	72-68-68-66–274	90000
C Peete	65-70-70-69–274	54000
T Watson	69-68-68-71–276	34000
B Lietzke	68-72-71-68–279	20666
D Edwards	73-71-66-69–279	20666
J Haas	68-70-67-74–279	20666
D Tewell	71-70-71-68–280	16125
P Stewart	69-73-71-67–280	16125

Mony Tournament of Champions
at La Costa CC Carlsbad California

Name	Score	Prize $
C Peete	68-67-64-68–267	90000
M O'Meara	70-65-67-71–273	57000
P Blackmar	74-68-66-69–277	37000
D Edwards	70-69-69-71–279	25000
B Langer	69-69-71-70–279	25000
*S Verplank	72-67-68-72–279	—
H Sutton	71-77-66-67–281	19166
J Thorpe	70-68-71-72–281	19166
T Simpson	72-73-66-70–281	19166

Byron Nelson Golf Classic
at Las Colinas SC Irving Texas

Name	Score	Prize $
A Bean	66-68-67-68–269	108000
M Wiebe	69-66-68-67–270	64800
B Wadkins	68-69-66-70–273	40800
C Stadler	69-69-65-71–274	23625
P Stewart	70-66-67-71–274	23625
G Sauers	71-68-66-69–274	23625
M Hayes	64-72-68-70–274	23625

Colonial National Invitation
at Colonial CC Fort Worth Texas

Name	Score	Prize $
D Pohl	68-69-68–205	108000
P Stewart	72-67-66–205	64800
(D Pohl won play-off)		
B Rogers	67-71-69–207	31200
T Watson	75-68-64–207	31200
B Langer	70-70-67–207	31200
M Sullivan	70-69-69–208	20100
G Sauers	66-72-70–208	20100
D Frost	70-71-67–208	20100

Memorial Tournament
at Muirfield Village GC Dublin Ohio

Name	Score	Prize $
H Sutton	68-69-66-68–271	100000
D Pooley	69-67-70-69–275	60000
J Miller	70-69-69-68–276	32225
M O'Meara	68-75-67-66–276	32225
J Mahaffey	68-71-69-69–277	21110
J Nicklaus	66-70-72-69–277	21110
S Simpson	70-72-68-68–278	17313
P Stewart	72-69-69-68–278	17313
C Beck	71-66-70-71–278	17313

Kemper Open
at Congressional CC Bethesda Maryland

Name	Score	Prize $
G Norman	72-69-70-66–277	90000
L Mize	67-71-70-69–277	54000
(G Norman won play-off)		
M Reid	68-70-71-70–279	29000
J Cook	72-68-71-67–279	29000
B Wadkins	70-71-73-66–280	20000
C Strange	73-67-71-71–282	18000
B Gilder	73-71-73-66–283	15583
C Beck	74-70-68-71–283	15583
B Gardner	72-70-71-70–283	15583

Manufacturers Hanover Westchester Classic
at Westchester CC Harrison New York

Name	Score	Prize $
B Tway	73-63-69-67–272	108000
W Wood	71-63-73-66–273	64800
S Simpson	71-67-70-67–275	34800
G Morgan	69-69-70-67–275	34800
M Reid	68-69-68-72–277	24000
A Magee	72-67-71-70–280	20850
M Wiebe	68-71-73-68–280	20850
T Watson	72-70-70-69–281	16800
B Upper	68-66-74-73–281	16800
D Tewell	70-66-74-71–281	16800
J Haas	65-73-73-70–281	16800

US Open Championship
at Shinnecock Hills Long Island New York

Name	Score	Prize $
R Floyd	75-68-70-66–279	115000
L Wadkins	74-70-72-65–281	47646
C Beck	75-73-68-65–281	47646
L Trevino	74-68-69-71–282	26269
H Sutton	75-70-66-71–282	26269
P Stewart	76-68-69-70–283	19009
B Crenshaw	76-69-69-69–283	19009
B Tway	70-73-69-72–284	14500
B Langer	74-70-70-70–284	14500
J Nicklaus	77-72-67-68–284	14500
M McCumber	74-71-68-71–284	14500

Georgia-Pacific Atlanta Classic
at Atlanta CC Marietta Georgia

Name	Score	Prize $
B Tway	68-66-71-64–269	90000
H Sutton	66-68-67-70–271	54000
S Hoch	67-66-70-70–273	24000
G Norman	71-72-66-64–273	24000
W Wood	67-68-70-68–273	24000
M O'Meara	67-67-70-69–273	24000
G Koch	72-63-72-67–274	16750
T Purtzer	69-69-66-71–275	15500

St Jude Federal Express Classic
at Colonial CC Cordova Tennessee

Name	Score	Prize $
M Hulbert	71-72-68-69–280	109064
J Sindelar	71-71-71-68–281	65438
P Stewart	71-70-71-70–282	41202
L Nelson	76-70-67-70–283	29084
L Mize	73-70-68-73–284	23024
G Koch	73-69-69-73–284	23024

Canadian Open
at Glen Abbey GC Oakville Ontario

Name	Score	Prize $
B Murphy	71-70-66-71–280	108000
G Norman	72-76-62-73–283	64800
A Bean	69-69-74-72–284	31200
D Love III	72-68-70-74–284	31200
M Donald	69-73-69-73–284	31200
C Rose	69-76-70-70–285	20100
B Claar	73-73-69-70–285	20100
M O'Grady	73-68-69-75–285	20100

Anheuser-Busch Golf Classic

at Kingsmill GC Williamsburg Virginia

Name	Score	Prize $
F Zoeller	70-68-72-64–274	90000
J Mudd	65-70-72-69–276	54000
J Sindelar	70-68-72-67–277	34000
S Hoch	68-69-74-67–278	22000
M O'Grady	69-72-70-67–278	22000
C Rose	69-71-70-69–279	16187
TC Chen	71-70-70-68–279	16187
R Fehr	71-67-72-69–279	16187
D Frost	68-71-72-68–279	16187

Hardee's Golf Classic

Oakwood CC Coal Valley Illinois

Name	Score	Prize $
M Wiebe	69-65-66-68–268	72000
C Byrum	64-70-64-71–269	43200
P Lindsey	73-66-66-66–271	27200
B Glasson	72-68-66-66–272	19200
B Lohr	63-71-69-70–273	14600
C Peete	68-67-72-66–273	14600
M Hatalsky	72-68-65-68–273	14600
B Upper	71-70-65-68–274	11200
G Archer	69-67-68-70–274	11200
M Brooks	67-70-66-71–274	11200
R Cochran	66-67-70-71–274	11200

Canon Sammy Davis Jr-Greater Hartford Open

at TPC of Connecticut Cromwell Connecticut

Name	Score	Prize $
M O'Grady	71-69-67-62–269	126000
R Maltbie	66-67-70-66–269	75600
(M O'Grady won play-off)		
M O'Meara	69-72-64-67–272	36400
P Azinger	67-70-66-69–272	36400
S Hoch	71-66-68-67–272	36400
C Strange	71-69-65-68–273	23450
T Watson	65-67-70-71–273	23450
T Simpson	64-66-74-69–273	23450

Western Open
at Butler National GC Oak Brook Illinois

Name	Score	Prize $
T Kite	70-75-73-68–286	90000
N Price	71-71-73-71–286	37333
F Couples	70-68-73-75–286	37333
D Frost	74-66-71-75–286	37333
(T Kite won play-off)		
G Norman	71-74-72-70–287	16950
B Wadkins	69-69-74-75–287	16950
L Thompson	71-73-69-74–287	16950
D Mast	69-73-72-73–287	16950
B Lietzke	74-70-73-70–287	16950

PGA Championship
at The Inverness Club Toledo Ohio

Name	Score	Prize $
B Tway	72-70-64-70–276	140000
G Norman	65-68-69-76–278	80000
P Jacobsen	68-70-70-71–279	60000
DA Weibring	71-72-68-69–280	42865
B Lietzke	69-71-70-71–281	32500
P Stewart	70-67-72-72–281	32500
M Hulbert	69-68-74-71–282	20833
J Thorpe	71-67-73-71–282	20833
D Graham	75-69-71-67–282	20833

The International
at Castle Pines GC Castle Rock Colorado

Name	Prize $
K Green	180000
B Langer	113000
J Sindelar	63000
JC Snead	63000
N Price	45000
H Twitty	41000
B Lietzke	37250
K Knox	37250
A Dillard	34000
T Kite	31000
D Hammond	31000
TC Chen	28000

Tallahassee Open
at Killearn CC Florida

Name	Score	Prize $
M Hayes	68-67-68-70	36000
R Cochran	66-72-66-70	21600
D Briggs	67-69-70-69	10400
J Gallagher	73-69-68-65	10400
T Sieckmann	68-70-71-66	10400

Buick Open
at Warwick Hills G & CC Grand Blanc Michigan

Name	Score	Prize $
B Crenshaw	69-67-66-68–270	90000
J Snead	67-70-68-66–271	44000
D Tewell	70-68-67-66–271	44000
E Fiori	66-69-70-67–272	24000
B Wadkins	69-66-70-68–273	19000
D Love III	65-67-70-71–273	19000
G Sauers	69-67-67-71–274	16125
S Pate	70-67-65-72–274	16125

NEC World Series of Golf
at Firestone CC Akron Ohio

Name	Score	Prize $
D Pohl	69-66-71-71–277	126000
L Wadkins	68-68-70-72–278	75600
B Cole	74-67-68-70–279	47600
J Mahaffey	71-66-72-71–280	33600
A Bean	72-74-69-66–281	24550
R Davis	72-69-69-71–281	24550
D Hammond	66-68-73-74–281	24550
T Simpson	71-73-72-65–281	24550

BC Open
at Pleasant Valley Little Rock Arkansas

Name	Score	Prize $
R Fehr	65-66-67-69–267	72000
L Mize	64-67-70-68–269	43200
H Twitty	69-68-68-66–271	27200
B Wadkins	66-68-73-65–272	19200
C Peete	71-67-70-66–274	15200
B Glasson	66-70-71-67–274	15200
J Renner	72-68-67-68–275	12900
J Haas	70-69-69-67–275	12900

Bank of Boston Classic
at Pleasant Valley CC Sutton Massachusetts

Name	Score	Prize $
G Sauers	70-71-64-69–274	81000
B McCallister	72-68-67-67–274	48600
(G Sauers won play-off)		
C Byrum	71-68-69-68–276	30600
J Renner	73-70-68-66–277	19800
W Levi	68-71-70-68–277	19800
P Azinger	71-71-69-67–278	16200
C Strange	73-65-68-73–279	14512
M Calcavecchia	70-69-68-72–279	14512
L Rinker	68-74-66-73–281	13050

Greater Milwaukee Open
at Tuckaway CC Franklin Wisconsin

Name	Score	Prize $
C Pavin	66-72-67-67–272	72000
D Barr	69-64-69-70–272	43200
(C Pavin won play-off)		
D Frost	69-66-68-70–273	27200
T Purtzer	66-71-68-69–274	16533
R Maltbie	72-68-67-67–274	16533
B Gardner	69-68-67-70–274	16533
J Sindelar	70-67-67-71–275	12900
R Black	68-69-68-70–275	12900

Southwest Golf Classic
at Fairway Oaks G & RC Abilene Texes

Name	Score	Prize $
M Calcavecchia	68-70-66-71–275	72000
T Byrum	68-74-67-69–278	43200
C Stadler	72-72-72-63–279	20800
DA Weibring	66-76-68-69–279	20800
M Hatalsky	66-74-71-68–279	20800
R Black	69-74-69-69–281	14400
J Maggert	68-73-70-71–282	13400
C Pavin	70-74-69-70–283	11600
D Tewell	69-74-69-71–283	11600
B Crenshaw	73-72-71-67–283	11600

Vantage Championship
at Oak Hills CC San Antonio Texas

Name	Score	Prize $
B Crenshaw	65-67-64–196	180000
P Stewart	67-65-65–197	108000
R Black	68-66-67–201	48000
P Blackmar	66-67-68–201	48000
B Clampett	67-68-66–201	48000
E Gonzalez	68-67-66–201	48000

Southern Open
at Green Island CC Columbus Georgia

Name	Score	Prize $
F Wadsworth	67-67-68-67–269	63000
T Simpson	68-67-70-66–271	23100
J Thorpe	65-71-64-71–271	23100
G Archer	69-66-67-69–271	23100
J Cook	70-71-65-76–271	23100
J Renner	70-69-65-68–272	11725
J Sindelar	70-70-67-65–272	11725
P Stewart	66-67-68-71–272	11725

Walt Disney World Golf Classic
at Lake Buena Vista

Name	Score	Prize $
R Floyd	68-66-70-71–275	90000
M Sullivan	65-69-70-71–275	44000
L Hinkle	67-69-68-71–275	44000
(R Floyd won play-off)		
P McGowan	69-70-69-68–276	20666
P Stewart	65-66-71-74–276	20666
G Koch	66-73-68-69–276	20666
A North	71-69-69-69–278	16125
P Blackmar	67-73-68-70–278	16125
B Murphy	68-72-69-70–279	14500

Pensacola Open
at Perdido Bay CC Pensacola Florida

Name	Score	Prize $
E Gonzalez	65-63–128	40500
J Sindelar	67-62–129	24300
L Thompson	66-65–131	15300
M Hulbert	68-65–133	9900
K Knox	66-67–133	9900

Seiko-Tucson Match-Play Championship
at Randolph Park Mun GC Tucson Arizona

First round:

J Thorpe beat B Crenshaw 65-67
T Simpson beat L Clements 66-67
P Blackmar beat D Barr 65-69
D Pooley beat T Purtzer 69-70
K Green beat S Pate 69-70
D Edwards beat M Calcavecchia 67-69
S Simpson beat G Koch 66-73
L Wadkins beat J Colbert 70-71

Quarter-finals:

J Thorpe beat T Simpson 69-71
K Green beat D Edwards 70-71
P Blackmar beat D Pooley 71-75
S Simpson beat L Wadkins 65-68

Semi-finals:

J Thorpe beat P Blackmar 68-71
S Simpson beat K Green 69-70

Final:

J Thorpe beat S Simpson 67-71

USLPGA Tour Results, 1986

Mazda Classic
at Stonebridge G & CC Deerfield Beach Florida

Name	Score	Prize $
V Skinner	74-69-68-69–280	30000
S Palmer	70-69-72-70–281	18500
B Pearson	71-70-71-71–283	12000
H Stacy	70-70-71-72–283	12000
B Thomas	72-70-66-76–284	8500
P Sheehan	75-70-66-74–285	7000
P Bradley	72-71-71-72–286	5900
J Dickinson	68-74-70-76–288	5200

Elizabeth Arden Classic
at Turnberry Isle CC Miami Florida

Name	Score	Prize $
A Okamoto	69-67-73-71–280	30000
M Spencer-Devlin	69-71-72-69–281	18500
D Massey	68-72-71-72–283	13500
L Young	73-71-71-70–285	7420
P Bradley	70-74-71-70–285	7420
L Garbacz	75-67-71-72–285	7420
H Stacy	72-68-72-73–285	7420
B Daniel	70-69-71-75–285	7420
S Quinlan	75-66-75-70–286	4234
B King	74-68-73-71–286	4233
J Inkster	70-71-72-73–286	4233

Sarasota Classic
at Bent Tree G & RC Sarasota Florida

Name	Score	Prize $
P Sheehan	68-69-71-71–279	30000
P Bradley	73-70-70-69–282	16000
J Inkster	74-72-64-72–282	16000
S Farwig	70-68-72-73–283	10500
B Daniel	71-75-68-70–284	7134
B Pearson	73-70-71-70–284	7133
L Garbacz	74-68-72-70–284	7133
A Benz	74-68-71-73–286	5200
H Farr	77-69-69-72–287	4050
J Geddes	75-66-72-74–287	4050
L Young	73-70-69-75–287	4050
B Thomas	71-70-70-76–287	4050

Circle K Tucson Open

at Randolph Park GC Tucson Arizona

Name	Score	Prize $
P Pulz	72-71-69-64–276	30000
B King	73-71-70-66–280	18500
J Britz	70-69-72-70–281	10834
M Blackwelder	70-69-69-73–281	10833
P Bradley	65-68-72-76–281	10833
V Fergon	75-74-68-65–282	7000
A Alcott	73-69-69-72–283	5900

Standard Register/Samaritan Turquoise Classic

at Arizona Biltmore Phoenix Arizona

Name	Score	Prize $
MB Zimmerman	68-69-70-71–278	37500
D Caponi	74-67-69-69–279	20000
C Kratzert	74-69-66-70–279	20000
B King	73-69-70-69–281	13125
V Fergon	74-68-73-67–282	9688
A Ritzman	71-74-69-68–282	9687
D Richard	72-76-70-65–283	6250
P Bradley	69-73-72-69–283	6250
J Britz	74-68-70-71–283	6250
A Alcot	69-70-72-72–283	6250

Uniden LPGA Invitational

at Mesa Verde CC Costa Mesa California

Name	Score	Prize $
MB Zimmerman	70-70-70-71–281	49500
P Bradley	72-70-71-69–282	26400
L Baugh	68-70-68-76–282	26400
V Skinner	69-74-70-70–283	17325
C Kratzert	70-72-76-67–285	12788
J Stephenson	69-72-74-72–287	7343
P Sheehan	68-73-70-76–287	7342

Kemper Women's Open

at Princeville Makai Kauai

Name	Score	Prize $
J Inkster	72-64-70-70–276	45000
A Alcott	70-69-69-69–277	27750
C Johnson	69-66-73-70–278	18000
M Bozarth	67-70-69-72–278	18000
J-A Carner	70-70-73-66–279	12750
B King	70-68-72-71–281	10500
P Sheehan	71-71-72-68–282	7900
S Galbraith	73-70-68-71–282	7900
J Stephenson	71-70-70-71–282	7900
M Blackwelder	71-70-73-69–283	6000
K Postlewait	68-70-75-70–283	6000

GNA/Glendale Classic
at Oakmont CC Glendale California

Name	Score	Prize $
C Johnson	75-70-67–212	37500
J Geddes	72-71-71–214	23125
J Inkster	73-72-71–216	16875
A Alcott	71-74-72–217	11875
L Rinker	72-69-76–217	11875
S Palmer	73-75-70–218	7125
H Stacy	73-75-70–218	7125
A Finney	75-71-72–218	7125
L Hunt	74-70-74–218	7125

Nabisco Dinah Shore Invitational
at Mission Hills CC Rancho Mirage California

Name	Score	Prize $
P Bradley	68-72-69-71–280	75000
V Skinner	71-72-70-69–282	40000
MB Zimmerman	70-73-72-70–285	25000
B King	70-71-74-72–287	17385
J Stephenson	71-72-76-69–288	12980
J Geddes	75-73-70-70–288	12980
J Inkster	69-71-72-76–288	12980

Kyocera Inamori Classic
at Bernardo Heights CC San Diego California

Name	Score	Prize $
P Sheehan	69-71-68-70–278	30000
P Bradley	69-68-74-68–279	18500
J Carner	72-70-71-70–283	12000
J Stephenson	71-72-69-71–283	12000
M Figueras-Dotti	71-72-74-68–285	6650
J Geddes	73-71-72-69–285	6650
V Skinner	69-75-72-69–285	6650
D Richard	70-71-71-73–285	6650

S&H Classic
at Pasadena Yacht & CC St Petersburg Florida

Name	Score	Prize $
P Bradley	69-67-71-65–272	30000
J Coles	68-69-67-69–273	18500
J Crafter	68-69-73-69–279	13500
B King	71-71-71-67–280	7975
C Kratzert	67-72-72-69–280	7975
J Stephenson	70-70-70-70–280	7975
B Barrett	74-70-65-71–280	7975

United Virginia Bank Classic

at Sleepy Hole CC Portsmouth Virginia

Name	Score	Prize $
M Spencer-Devlin	76-69-69–214	37500
B Thomas	74-71-70–215	17709
J Rosenthal	72-73-70–215	17708
D Massey	75-69-71–215	17708
P Sheehan	77-70-69–216	7396
L Howe	73-72-71–216	7396
D Richard	69-76-71–216	7396
A Benz	73-71-72–216	7396
K Whitworth	72-72-72–216	7396
B Lauer	69-73-74–216	7395

Chrysler-Plymouth Classic

at Fairmount CC Chatham New Jersey

Name	Score	Prize $
B Pearson	71-70-71–212	30000
D Richard	73-69-71–213	16000
B King	67-72-74–213	16000
J Dickinson	73-71-70–214	9500
D Coe	70-70-74–214	9500
C Morse	69-74-72–215	7000
S Quinlan	73-74-69–216	5000
P Hammel	72-73-71–216	5000
S Palmer	71-74-71–216	5000
J Anderson	69-73-74–216	5000

Corning Classic

at Corning CC Corning New York

Name	Score	Prize $
L Rinker	72-70-70-66–278	37500
P Bradley	70-70-69-72–281	20000
B Daniel	67-70-70-74–281	20000
L Hunt	76-72-69-65–282	11875
L Howe	72-71-72-67–282	11875
MB Zimmerman	72-74-68-70–284	7542
A Okamoto	72-70-71-71–284	7542
C Hill	73-65-73-73–284	7541

LPGA Championship

at Mason Ohio

Name	Score	Prize $
P Bradley	67-72-70-68–277	45000
P Sheehan	72-70-69-67–278	27750
J Inkster	70-72-68-69–279	18000
A Okamoto	66-70-69-74–279	18000
M Spencer-Devlin	72-67-74-68–281	12750
C Mackey	70-70-68-74–282	10500
M Blackwelder	71-71-71-70–283	8850
P Pulz	71-71-70-72–284	7800

McDonald's Championship
at White Manor CC Malvern Pennsylvania

Name	Score	Prize $
J Inkster	68-67-69-77–281	67500
MB Zimmerman	70-69-73-72–284	41625
A Alcott	70-72-73-70–285	30375
B Pearson	78-72-68-69–287	19500
B Lauer	70-73-73-71–287	19500
O-H Ku	73-70-71-73–287	19500
P Sheehan	70-71-74-73–288	12488
J Dickinson	72-74-68-74–288	12487
A Okamoto	73-71-73-72–289	10013

Rochester International
at Locust Hill CC Pittsford New York

Name	Score	Prize $
J Dickinson	74-69-68-70–281	38250
P Bradley	72-73-69-68–282	23587
C Johnson	75-72-70-66–283	17212
J Stephenson	73-71-68-72–284	13387
L Baugh	72-72-72-69–285	10837
M Figueras-Dotti	71-74-70-71–286	8224
V Skinner	71-74-66-75–286	8223

Mayflower Classic
at The CC of Indianapolis Indiana

Name	Score	Prize $
S Palmer	68-68-72-72–280	52500
J Stephenson	68-71-69-72–280	28000
C Johnson	72-70-70-68–280	28000
(S Palmer won play-off)		
J Rosenthal	73-71-71-67–282	18375
B Lauer	73-69-71-70–283	13563
J Dickinson	72-69-71-71–283	13562
K Whitworth	73-68-72-71–284	10325

Lady Keystone Open
at Hershey CC Hershey Pennsylvania

Name	Score	Prize $
J Inkster	70-70-70–210	37500
C Hill	72-68-70–210	20000
D Massey	72-66-72–210	20000
(J Inkster won play-off)		
J Crafter	73-69-69–211	10834
L Young	70-71-70–211	10833
S Turner	69-70-72–211	10833

Mazda Hall of Fame Championship

at Sweetwater CC Sugar Land Texas

Name	Score	Prize $
A Alcott	70-70-72-72–284	45000
L Howe	69-73-74-68–284	27750
(A Alcott won play-off)		
A Benz	67-71-75-73–286	20250
L Garbacz	74-73-73-67–287	15750
M Berteotti	73-74-74-68–289	11620
J Coles	75-70-73-71–289	11620
V Fergon	72-72-73-73–290	8850

US Women's Open Championship

at NCR GC Ohio

Name	Score	Prize $
J Geddes	74-74-70-69–287	50000
S Little	73-72-72-70–287	25000
(J Geddes won play-off)		
A Okamoto	76-69-69-74–288	16534
B King	72-71-70-75–288	16534
P Bradley	76-71-74-69–290	9196
J Rosenthal	72-76-71-71–290	9196
A Alcott	75-69-74-72–290	9196
J Dickinson	72-71-74-73–290	9196
C Morse	75-71-75-70–291	6801
D Richard	76-69-72-74–291	6801

Boston Five Classic

at Sheraton Tara CC Denver Massachusetts

Name	Score	Prize $
J Geddes	71-70-72-68–281	41250
D Richard	70-68-73-71–282	25437
O-H Ku	68-68-76-71–283	16500
P Bradley	71-66-74-72–283	16499
C Hill	71-69-71-74–285	10656
V Skinner	73-66-72-74–285	10656
M Spencer-Devlin	76-72-68-70–286	8112

Du Maurier Classic
at Board of Trade Toronto Ontario

Name	Score	Prize $
P Bradley	73-70-67-66–276	52500
A Okamoto	73-70-69-64–276	32375
(P Bradley won play-off)		
N Scranton	70-64-78-69–281	21000
B King	72-67-71-71–281	21000
C Morse	70-73-68-71–282	13563
C Johnson	67-68-74-73–282	13562
R Jones	72-72-71-68–283	10325
S Turner	71-71-73-69–284	8225
A Alcott	75-72-68-69–284	8225
P Rizzo	74-69-70-71–284	8225

Atlantic City Classic
at Seaview New Jersey

Name	Score	Prize $
J Inkster	67-71-71–209	33750
P Rizzo	70-68-74–212	20812
J Dickinson	69-72-72–213	15187
M Figueras-Dotti	73-69-72–214	11812
B Daniel	70-71-74–215	9562
B Solomon	72-73-71–216	7875
P Pulz	68-78-70–217	6244
L Rinker	71-69-77–217	6243

Henredon Classic
at Willow Creek GC High Point North Carolina

Name	Score	Prize $
B King	70-67-70-70–277	34500
J Carner	69-69-70-69–277	21275
(B King won play-off)		
N Lopez	71-69-70-69–279	13800
R Walton	68-69-68-74–279	13800
C Kratzert	71-69-72-68–280	9775
K Whitworth	71-72-68-70–281	7418
D Massey	70-71-67-73–281	7417

Nestlé World Championship of Women's Golf
at Pine Isle Resort Burford Georgia

Name	Score	Prize $
P Bradley	72-72-72-63–279	78000
N Lopez	73-66-73-69–281	34800
B King	69-68-71-73–281	34800
C Johnson	69-74-68-71–282	19000
J Geddes	73-67-71-73–284	14400
P Sheehan	67-72-76-70–285	9000
MB Zimmerman	71-73-66-75–285	9000
A Alcott	73-69-72-73–287	6200

Mastercard International Pro-Am

at Knollwood CC Ridgeway CC and Westchester Hills CC New York

Name	Score	Prize $
C Mackey	71-70-65-70–276	30000
J Rosenthal	76-70-73-71–290	16000
C Johnson	76-72-70-72–290	16000
L Howe	76-72-73-70–291	10500
L Adams	78-73-72-69–292	7134
M Berteotti	72-74-74-72–292	7133
K Young	72-74-73-73–292	7133

LPGA National Pro-Am

at Lone Tree CC and Meridian CC Denver Colorado

Name	Score	Prize $
A Alcott	72-69-72-70–283	45000
P Bradley	71-75-67-71–284	24000
C Johnson	70-70-72-72–284	24000
D Massey	68-73-70-74–285	15750
AM Palli	70-76-70-70–286	12750
V Fergon	72-74-72-69–287	9675
P Hammel	70-74-73-70–287	9675
L Adams	70-74-75-69–288	6718
J Rosenthal	71-75-72-70–288	6718
J Stephenson	75-72-70-71–288	6718
M Blackwelder	72-73-71-72–288	6718

Mazda Japan Classic

at Osaka Japan

Name	Score	Prize $
Ai Yu Tu	68-69-76–213	45000
B Pearson	71-72-70–213	21250
C Kratzert	68-74-71–213	21250
M Zimmerman	74-71-68–213	21250
J Geddes	72-73-69–214	9975
C Higuchi	71-74-69–214	9975
D Massey	72-72-70–214	9975
S Palmer	69-71-74–214	9975

(Ai-Yu Tu won play-off at 4th extra hole)

Rail Charity Classic

at Rail GC Springfield Illinois

Name	Score	Prize $
B King	70-72-63–205	30000
A Ritzman	68-68-69–205	16000
C Kratzert	65-70-70–205	16000
J Dickinson	67-72-67–206	10500
K Postlewait	67-72-68–207	7750
L Peterson	70-65-72–207	7750
M Nause	70-72-66–208	5900

Cellular One Ping Championship

at Columbia-Edgewater CC Portland Oregon

Name	Score	Prize $
A Okamoto	70-71-66–207	30000
C Walker	72-68-73–213	16000
N Lopez	70-70-73–213	16000
J Crafter	74-71-69–214	9500
D Eggeling	71-71-72–214	9500
M Murphy	74-70-71–215	6450
MJ Smith	66-73-76–215	6450
H Stacy	75-69-72–216	4480
B Pearson	69-74-73–216	4480
J Stephenson	70-72-74–216	4480
M Figueras-Dotti	70-72-74–216	4480

Safeco Classic

at Meridian Valley CC Seattle Washington

Name	Score	Prize $
J Dickinson	71-73-63-67–274	30000
H Stacy	68-73-68-69–278	18500
J Stephenson	69-67-71-73–280	14000
K Monaghan	67-72-71-72–282	9500
B Daniel	71-67-70-74–282	9500
B King	69-71-76-68–284	5550
B Pearson	72-69-72-71–284	5550

Konica San José Classic

at Almaden G & CC San José California

Name	Score	Prize $
P Sheehan	71-70-71–212	41250
B King	72-71-69–212	19479
A Alcott	72-68-72–212	19479
A Okamoto	69-71-72–212	19478
(P Sheehan won play-off)		
J Dickinson	76-69-68–213	10656
J Geddes	69-74-70–213	10656
L Rinker	71-74-69–214	8112
M Figueras-Dotti	73-72-70–215	6463
C Walker	74-71-70–215	6462
N Ledbetter	73-69-73–215	6462

USLPGA Money Winners

Place	Name	Official Money $
1	Pat Bradley	492021
2	Betsy King	290195
3	Julie Inkster	285969
4	Amy Alcott	244410
5	Jane Geddes	221225
6	Mary Beth Zimmerman	221072
7	Patty Sheehan	214281
8	Chris Johnson	200648
9	Ayako Okamoto	198362
10	Judy Dickinson	195834
11	Val Skinner	165243
12	Jan Stephenson	165238
13	Becky Pearson	155244
14	Sandra Palmer	148422
15	Debbie Massey	122495
16	Laurie Rinker	111756
17	Cathy Kratzert	107638
18	Jodi Rosenthal	106523
19	Hollis Stacy	104286
20	Muffin Spencer-Devlin	104034
21	Beth Daniel	103547
22	Deb Richard	98451
23	Patti Rizzo	88936
24	Lauren Howe	86951
25	Alice Ritzman	84443
26	Jo Anne Carner	82802
27	Mindy Moore	82406
28	Jane Crafter	79431
29	Ok-Hee Ku	79327
30	Penny Pulz	77652

Top 100 US Money Winners, 1986

1	Greg Norman	$653296	35	Nick Price	225373	69	Larry Nelson	124338
2	Bob Tway	652780	36	Scott Hoch	222077	70	Dave Barr	122181
3	Payne Stewart	535389	37	Tom Purtzer	218280	71	David Edwards	122079
4	Andy Bean	491938	38	Tony Sills	216881	72	Bill Glasson	121516
5	Dan Pohl	463630	39	Chip Beck	215140	73	Hubert Green	120051
6	Hal Sutton	429434	40	Roger Maltbie	213206	74	Mark Hayes	117837
7	Tom Kite	394164	41	Scott Simpson	202223	75	Brian Claar	117355
8	Ben Crenshaw	388169	42	Gene Sauers	199044	76	Fred Couples	116065
9	Ray Floyd	380508	43	Phil Blackmar	191228	77	Davis Love III	113245
10	Bernhard Langer	379800	44	Clarence Rose	189387	78	Peter Jacobsen	112964
11	John Mahaffey	378172	45	Jay Haas	189204	79	Lennie Clements	112642
12	Calvin Peete	374953	46	David Frost	187944	80	Mark McCumber	110442
13	Fuzzy Zoeller	358115	47	Bruze Lietzke	183761	81	Jim Colbert	109517
14	Joey Sindelar	341231	48	Jodie Mudd	182812	82	Mike Donald	108772
15	Jim Thorpe	326087	49	Bob Murphy	182673	83	Morris Hatalsky	105543
16	Ken Green	317835	50	Gary Koch	180693	84	Gil Morgan	98770
17	Larry Mize	314051	51	Steve Pate	176100	85	Bob Gilder	98181
18	Doug Tewell	310285	52	Willie Wood	172629	86	Lon Hinkle	97610
19	Corey Pavin	304558	53	Craig Stadler	170076	87	Bobby Clampett	97178
20	Tom Watson	278338	54	Dan Forsman	169445	88	David Graham	95109
21	Mike Hulbert	276687	55	DA Weibring	167602	89	Brett Upper	94918
22	Don Pooley	268274	56	Ronnie Black	166761	90	Brad Faxon	92716
23	Lanny Wadkins	264931	57	Howard Twitty	156119	91	Buddy Gardner	92006
24	Kenny Knox	261608	58	Mark Calcavecchia	155012	92	Russ Cochran	89817
25	Mark Wiebe	260180	59	Wayne Levi	154777	93	Tom Byrum	89739
26	Mac O'Grady	256344	60	Jeff Sulman	154129	94	Blaine McCallister	88732
27	John Cook	255126	61	Rick Fehr	151162	95	Bobby Cole	88472
28	Donnie Hammond	254987	62	Mike Sullivan	150407	96	Charles Bolling	88328
29	Paul Azinger	254019	63	JC Snead	147882	97	TC Chen	86590
30	Mark O'Meara	252827	64	Sandy Lyle	143415	98	Lee Trevino	86315
31	Tim Simpson	240911	65	Pat McGowan	137665	99	Bob Lohr	85949
32	Curtis Strange	237700	66	Mike Reid	135143	100	Jack Renner	84028
33	Bobby Wadkins	226079	67	Danny Edwards	126139			
34	Jack Nicklaus	226015	68	Ernie Gonzalez	124548			

The leader of the final money-winners' table receives the Arnold Palmer Award – a bronze casting of Palmer, inaugurated in 1981.

USPGA Tour Official Statistics

Scoring Leaders

1	S Hoch	70.08
2	B Langer	70.19
3	G Norman	70.22
4	P Stewart	70.36
5	B Tway	70.45
6	C Peete	70.51
7	A Bean	70.56
8	R Floyd	70.66
9	L Mize	70.70
10	T Purtzer	70.72

Driving Distance

1	D Love III	285.7
2	G Twiggs	283.9
3	J McComish	281.4
4	F Couples	279.9
5	B Glasson	278.4
6	J Sindelar	277.7
7	G Norman	277.5
8	M O'Grady	277.3
9	S Jones	276.4
10	L Hinkle	275.8

Driving Accuracy

1	C Peete	0.817
2	M Reid	0.811
3	D Edwards	0.756
4	B Lietzke	0.750
5	J Renner	0.749
6	L Mize	0.742
7	T Kite	0.741
8	P Jacobsen	0.738
9	H Sutton	0.737

Greens in Regulation

1	J Mahaffey	0.720
2	C Peete	0.711
3	T Purtzer	0.706
4	A Bean	0.701
5	T Sills	0.693
6	S Hoch	0.692
7	L Mize	0.685
8	T Kite	0.683

Putting Leaders

1	G Norman	1.736
2	R Floyd	1.758
3	R Fehr	1.761
4T	B Tway	1.764
	B Langer	1.764
6T	L Wadkins	1.766
	H Sutton	1.766
8T	F Zoeller	1.767
	J Renner	1.767

Par Breakers

1	G Norman	0.248
2	A Bean	0.220
3	P Stewart	0.213
4	T Purtzer	0.211
5	M O'Grady	0.210
6T	H Sutton	0.209
	C Stadler	0.209
8T	B Tway	0.207
	F Zoeller	0.207
10	R Floyd	0.206

Eagle Leaders

1	J Sindelar	16
2T	R Wrenn	12
	G Norman	12
	M McCumber	12
5	J Gallagher Jr	11
6T	C Rose	10
	J Adams	10
	D Halldorson	10

Birdie Leaders

1	J Sindelar	415
2	B Tway	402
3	T Purtzer	375
4	A Bean	371
5	B Wadkins	369
6	M Hulbert	363
7	C Bolling	360
8	P Stewart	358
9	G Sauers	356
10	H Sutton	352

Sand-Saves

1	P Azinger	0.638
2	M Brooks	0.615
3	M Hatalsky	0.604
4	D Stockton	0.603
5T	P Stewart	0.601
	P McGowan	0.601
7	C Beck	0.600
8	M Nicolette	0.596
9	K Knox	0.595
10	G Norman	0.590

Awards

Golf Writers' Association Trophy

Awarded to the man or woman who, in the opinion of Golf Writers, has done most for golf during the year

1951 Max Faulkner
1952 Miss Elizabeth Price
1953 JB Carr
1954 Mrs Roy Smith (Miss Frances Stephens)
1955 Ladies' Golf Union's Touring Team
1956 JC Beharrell
1957 DJ Rees
1958 Harry Bradshaw
1959 Eric Brown
1960 Sir Stuart Goodwin (sponsor of international golf)
1961 Commdr RCT Roe (ex-hon secretary, PGA)
1962 Mrs Marley Spearman, British Ladies' Champion 1961-1962
1963 MSR Lunt, Amateur Champion, 1963
1964 Great Britain and Ireland Team, winners of Eisenhower Trophy–JB Carr (non-playing Captain), MG Bonallack, MSR Lunt, RDBM Shade, R Foster
1965 Gerald Micklem, golf administrator, President, English Golf Union
1966 RDBM Shade, Scottish Amateur Champion for fourth successive year; Eisenhower Trophy, Best individual score, 1966; runner-up Amateur Championship, 1966
1967 John Panton
1968 Michael Bonallack
1969 Tony Jacklin
1970 Tony Jacklin
1971 British Walker Cup Team–MF Bonallack, R Carr, R Foster, CW Green, W Humphreys, JS Macdonald, G Macgregor, GC Marks, DM Marsh, HB Stuart
1972 Miss Michelle Walker
1973 PA Oosterhuis
1974 PA Oosterhuis
1975 Golf Foundation
1976 Great Britain and Ireland Team, winners of Eisenhower Trophy–Sandy Saddler (non-playing captain), John Davies, Ian Hutcheon, Mike Kelley, Steve Martin
1977 C O'Connor
1978 Peter McEvoy
1979 S Ballesteros
1980 Sandy Lyle
1981 B Langer
1982 G Brand jnr
1983 N Faldo
1984 S Ballesteros
1985 European Ryder Cup Team
1986 Great Britain and Ireland Curtis Cup Team

Harry Vardon Trophy

Currently awarded to the PGA member heading the order of merit at the end of the season

1937 CA Whitcombe
1938 TH Cotton
1939 RA Whitcombe
1940-45 *In abeyance*
1946 AD Locke
1947 NG Von Nida
1948 CH Ward
1949 CH Ward
1950 AD Locke
1951 J Panton
1952 H Weetman
1953 F van Donck
1954 AD Locke
1955 DJ Rees
1956 H Weetman
1957 EC Brown
1958 BJ Hunt
1959 DJ Rees
1960 BJ Hunt
1961 C O'Connor
1962 C O'Connor
1963 NC Coles
1964 P Alliss
1965 BJ Hunt
1966 P Alliss
1967 ME Gregson
1968 BGC Huggett
1969 B Gallacher
1970 NC Coles
1971 PA Oosterhuis
1972 PA Oosterhuis
1973 PA Oosterhuis
1974 PA Osterhuis
1975 Dale Hayes
1976 S Ballesteros
1977 S Ballesteros
1978 S Ballesteros
1979 AWB Lyle
1980 AWB Lyle
1981 B Langer
1982 G Norman
1983 N Faldo
1984 B Langer
1985 AWB Lyle
1986 S Ballesteros

Rookie of the Year

1960 T Goodwin
1961 A Caygill
1962 No Award
1963 A Jacklin
1964 No Award
1966 R Liddle
1967 No Award
1968 B Gallacher
1969 P Oosterhuis
1970 S Brown
1971 D Llewellyn
1972 S Torrance
1973 P Elson
1974 C Mason
1975 No Award
1976 M James
1978 AWB Lyle
1979 MJ Miller
1980 P Hoad
1981 J Bennett
1982 G Brand Jnr
1983 G Turner
1984 AP Parkin
1985 P Thomas
1986 J-M Olazabal

Avia Watches' Woman Golfer of the Year

1982 Jane Connachan
1983 Jill Thornhill
1984 Gillian Stewart
Claire Waite
1985 Belle Robertson
1986 Great Britain and Ireland Curtis Cup Team

Benson and Hedges Golfer's Handbook Golfer of the Year

1983 Tom Watson
1984 Lee Trevino
1985 Sandy Lyle
1986 Greg Norman

Byron Nelson Award

Awarded for most victories on USPGA Tour

Year	Winner
1955	Cary Middlecoff
1956	Ted Kroll
1957	Arnold Palmer
1958	Ken Venturi
1959	Gene Littler
1960	Arnold Palmer
1961	Arnold Palmer
1962	Arnold Palmer
1963	Arnold Palmer
1964	Jack Nicklaus
1965	Jack Nicklaus
1966	Billy Casper
1967	Jack Nicklaus
1968	Billy Casper
1969	Dave Hill
1970	Billy Casper
1971	Lee Trevino
1972	Jack Nicklaus
1973	Jack Nicklaus
1974	Johnny Miller
1975	Jack Nicklaus
1976	Ben Crenshaw
1977	Tom Watson
1978	Tom Watson
1979	Tom Watson
1980	Tom Watson
1981	Bruce Lietzke
	Ray Floyd
	B Rogers
1982	Calvin Peete
	Craig Stadler
1983	Seve Ballesteros
	Hal Sutton
	Fuzzy Zoeller
	Lanny Wadkins
	Calvin Peete
	Gil Morgan
	Mark McCumber
	Jim Colbert
1984	Denis Watson
	Tom Watson
1985	Curtis Strange
	Lanny Wadkins
1986	Bob Tway

The US Vardon Trophy

The award is made to the member of the USPGA with the lowest scoring average over the calendar year.

Year	Winner
1948	Ben Hogan
1949	Sam Snead
1950	Sam Snead
1951	Lloyd Mangrum
1952	Jack Burke
1953	Lloyd Mangrum
1954	EJ Harrison
1955	Sam Snead
1956	Cary Middlecoff
1957	Dow Finsterwald
1958	Bob Rosburg
1959	Art Wall
1960	Billy Casper
1961	Arnold Palmer
1962	Arnold Palmer
1963	Billy Casper
1964	Arnold Palmer
1965	Billy Casper
1966	Billy Casper
1967	Arnold Palmer
1968	Billy Casper
1969	Dave Hill
1970	Lee Trevino
1971	Lee Trevino
1972	Lee Trevino
1973	Bruce Crampton
1974	Lee Trevino
1975	Bruce Crampton
1976	Don January
1977	Tom Watson
1978	Tom Watson
1979	Tom Watson
1980	Lee Trevino
1981	Tom Kite
1982	Tom Kite
1983	Ray Floyd
1984	Calvin Peete
1985	Don Pooley
1986	Scott Hoch

US Rookie of the Year

Awarded by Golf Digest

Year	Winner
1957	Ken Venturi
1958	Bob Goalby
1959	Joe Campbell
1960	Mason Rudolph
1961	Jacky Cupit
1962	Jack Nicklaus
1963	Ray Floyd
1964	RH Sikes
1965	Homero Blancas
1966	John Schlee
1967	Lee Trevino
1968	Bob Murphy
1969	Grier Jones
1970	Ted Hayes
1971	Hubert Green
1972	Lanny Wadkins
1973	Tom Kite
1974	Ben Crenshaw
1975	Roger Moger Maltbie
1976	J Pate
1977	G Marsh
1978	Pat McGowan
1979	John Fought
1980	Gary Hallberg
1981	M O'Meara
1982	Hal Sutton
1983	Nick Price
1984	Corey Pavin
1985	Phil Blackmar
1986	Brian Claar

Bobby Jones Award

Awarded by USGA for distinguished sportsmanship in golf

Year	Winner
1955	Francis Ouimet
1956	Bill Campbell
1957	Babe Zaharias
1958	Margaret Curtis
1959	Findlay Douglas
1960	Charles Evans Jun
1961	Joe Carr
1962	Horton-Smith
1963	Patty Berg
1964	Charles Coe
1965	Mrs Edwin Vare
1966	Gary Player
1967	Richard Tufts
1968	Robert Dickson
1969	Gerald Micklem
1970	Roberto De Vicenzo
1971	Arnold Palmer
1972	Michael Bonallack
1973	Gene Littler
1974	Byron Nelson
1975	Jack Nicklaus
1976	Ben Hogan
1977	Joseph C Dey
1978	Bob Hope and
	Bing Crosby
1979	Tom Kite
1980	Charles Yates
1981	Mrs JoAnne Carner
1982	WJ Patton
1983	Mrs Maureen Garrett
1984	J Sigel
1985	Fuzzy Zoeller
1986	Tom Watson

USPGA Player of the Year Award

The award is made on the basis of points gained by winning the major events (30 points), the TPC and World Series (20), tour events (10), and additional points for final Top 10 positions in the Money List and Scoring Averages.

Year	Winner
1948	Ben Hogan
1949	Sam Snead
1950	Ben Hogan
1951	Ben Hogan
1952	Julius Boros
1953	Ben Hogan
1954	Ed Furgol
1955	Doug Ford
1956	Jack Burke
1957	Dick Mayer
1958	Dow Finsterwald
1959	Art Wall
1960	Arnold Palmer
1961	Jerry Barner
1962	Arnold Palmer
1963	Julius Boros
1964	Ken Venturi
1965	Dave Marr
1966	Billy Casper
1967	Jack Nicklaus
1968	*Not awarded*
1969	Orville Moody
1970	Billy Casper
1971	Lee Trevino
1972	Jack Nicklaus
1973	Jack Nicklaus
1974	Johnny Miller
1975	Jack Nicklaus
1976	Jack Nicklaus
1977	Tom Watson
1978	Tom Watson
1979	Tom Watson
1980	Tom Watson
1981	Bill Rogers
1982	Tom Watson
1983	Hal Sutton
1984	Tom Watson
1985	Lanny Wadkins
1986	Bob Tway

Arnold Palmer Award

Awarded to the USPGA leading money-winner

Year	Winner
1981	Tom Kite
1982	Craig Stadler
1983	Hal Sutton
1984	Tom Watson
1985	Curtis Strange
1986	Greg Norman

Part II
Golf History

The Origin of Golf

David Hamilton

Beginnings

The game of golf was not a sudden invention; it evolved and matured out of many other stick-and-ball games played in medieval Europe. France had its game of *chole* and England had a stick-and-ball game called 'cambuca'. Only two games, however, are serious contenders as the forerunner of the modern game of golf. The first was *colf* (or *koffe*), popular in the Low Countries, and the second was the game already known as 'golf' (or 'gouff' or 'gollfe' in the random, phonetic spelling of the day), which is persistently mentioned in Scottish records from medieval times onwards.

Dutch *colf*

The Dutch *colf* was popular and appears frequently in early Dutch records–of which many more have survived than the few scrappy Scottish documents of the same period–from 1300 onwards. A major study by Steven van Hengel, *Early Golf* (privately published in 1982), has at last described the game from original documents. A single iron-headed club, which had considerable loft, was used. It seems to have been mostly a town game, played towards a target such as a door, and may have been popular with children. The game became a nuisance in the towns, but only occasionally did regulations successfully move it out into the open fields nearby, where it may have been played into a hole in the ground. The Dutch towns where *colf* was popular were inland and, without adjacent coastal links, it could not be played very successfully outside the towns. When the canals were frozen, a form might be played using a post, or even a hole, in the ice as the target.

In Scotland, early records are less well preserved, and portrait and landscape painting did not exist. Nevertheless, sufficient is known about the early game of 'golf' to suggest that until about 1650 it may have resembled *colf*, as many records show that it was played in the churchyard or street. Scotland and the Low Countries were closely linked by trade, and hence there are good reasons why the games should have been similar.

Move to links

But by 1650 another version of the Scottish golf can be seen emerging as the dominant form, changing it to resemble the modern game. At this time it moved out of the towns on to the hard links – land beside the east-coast towns and ports, where in winter (and early golf was a winter game) a game of skill developed, combining lengthy shots with accuracy as the hole was neared. Wooden-headed clubs, which could be expensive, were now the kind most in use and even in the Low Countries were known as 'Scotch cleeks'. In Scotland an iron club was reserved for bunkers or ruts. The target in this long game was a hole in the ground.

REGULUS,

Baculus, Pila calvaria, *a goulf ball*. Fovea, *a goat*. Percute pilam baculo. Nimis curtâsti hunc missum, *this is too short a stroke*. Pila tua devia est, procul excussisti pilam, *that is a good stroak*. Statumina pilam arena, *Teaz your ball on the sand*. Statumen, *the teaz*. Frustra es, *that is a miss*. Vel irritus hic conatus est, percute pilam sensim, *give the ball but a little chap*. Apposité *that is very well*. Immissa est pila in fossam, *the ball is goated*. Quomodo eam hinc elidam? Cedo baculum ferreum, *let see the bunkard club*. Jam iterum frustra es, *this is the second miss*. Tertia quarta, &c. Bene tibi cessit hic ictus, *that is well stricken*. Malè tibi cessit hic ictus. Huc rectà pilam dirige. Dirige rectà versus foramen, *strike directly upon the hole*. Percute pilam sursum versus, *strike up the hill*. Percute deorsum versus, *strike down the hill*. An prætereiapsa est foramen. Factum quod volui, *I would not wish a better stroak*. Immissa est in paludem, *it is in the mire*. Rectè evolavit, *it hath flowen directly on*. Baculi caput, *the head of the club*. Baculi caulis, *the shaft of the club*. Baculi manubrium, *the handle where the wippen is*. Baculi filum, *the wippen*.

The earliest description of the Scottish game of golf, taken from a Latin grammar for schools, Aberdeen 1632. It mentions bunkers, iron clubs, holes and sand used for teeing up. (Courtesy of Aberdeen University Library.)

Why should the game have been different in Scotland from that played elsewhere in Europe and why should it have changed in this way? Perhaps the interest of the aristocracy and the Stuart monarchs was important, since they took up golf seriously; they could afford to buy the expensive equipment. For this reason golf appeared in London after the Union of the Crowns, when James VI of Scotland ascended the throne of Great Britain as James I. In Scotland too, the east-coast ports, notably Leith near Edinburgh, had links, whereas the Low Countries' *colf*-playing towns were inland, with wet, heavy land in winter.

There is no evidence that the Dutch game evolved along the same lines as its Scottish counterpart, and indeed *colf* disappeared about 1700, probably eliminated by the growth of the towns and the congestion of their streets. Ball-and-stick games in Holland developed in a different way to give *kolf*, an indoor game played over a short, formal court. It seems reasonable to conclude that, in the absence of other evidence, golf as we now know it evolved in Scotland, but perhaps later than was once supposed.

The first Clubs

In the late 1600s, golf was popular in Scotland along the east coast and two centres in particular were of interest. St Andrews had keen aristocratic student golfers, whose fathers were among those who played at Leith. Numerous diaries and local records show the popularity of Leith, and it was not surprising that here the world's first Golf Club was founded – the Honourable Company of Edinburgh Golfers. There were many golfing cliques in Leith and the club's foundation was probably a response to the fading fortunes of the town, in decline after the Union of the Parliaments. Already the Leith races were popular and a trophy had been given by the Town Council. The new Company of Golfers was also provided with a trophy – a silver club – and though this did not herald any sudden change in the game, it did mean that rules had to be drawn up for the new competition – the first rules of golf.

Other Clubs were founded in the seventeenth century, imitating the Leith golfers, and, as Scottish attitudes relaxed in an increasingly sociable century, these Clubs became known for their heavy drinking and hearty eating. They seem to have had little turnover of members, who were often bound together for reasons other than golf – often military or masonic. The Clubs played a valuable role in supporting the early club- and ballmakers, and were vigilant in protecting the rights of the townspeople to use the links for recreation. Many records show that golf was still popular with the tradespeople of the towns, who were not members of the Golf Clubs. Whether these poorer golfers played with the expensive equipment used by the rich or with a cheaper club and ball is not certain.

Temporary cessation

The early 1800s saw a crisis in the Scottish game. Industrialization brought rapid expansion to the towns without regard for amenities, and public links such as those at Leith, Aberdeen, Glasgow and Leven were throttled. Some Clubs, like the Honourable Company of Edinburgh Golfers and the Glasgow Club, ceased to exist for a spell and others dispersed to new, quieter areas, such as Musselburgh. The game itself appeared to be less popular.

The Trophy for the Gentlemen Golfers of Edinburgh (later the Honourable Company) on display.

The game takes off

But in the year 1848 a revolution in the game occurred. The appearance of the new gutty ball, made out of malleable gutta-percha, produced a cheap, durable alternative to the short-lived featherie or the wooden ball of the common game. Less dramatic but of similar significance was the change from the brittle woods to tough hickory for club shafts. To the older men who earned their living by club- and ball-making, like Allan Robertson, it seemed that their trade was in danger, but others, like 'old' Tom Morris, realized that the new equipment might help spread the game. In this belief they were correct beyond any reasonable expectation. The new well-off middle class produced by the growth of industry flocked to Scotland for their holidays using the expanding rail network. St Andrews and North Berwick were favourite places and there the visitors imitated the games of the old leisured class. Their wives and families also learned the game on these Scottish holidays, and women's golf was born at St Andrews.

Celebrities such as AJ Balfour, then Secretary of State for Ireland, were keen players and helped its popularity further.

Back home, in England and elsewhere, they drew up plans for courses, for which they hired Scottish help. From Scotland poured a stream of designers and professionals, like Willie Dunn and, later, Donald Ross. The Carnoustie Club (drawn from the artisans of the town) produced a remarkable number of emigrés who could be found playing golf and tending the courses all over North America.

English and US expansion

Blackheath claimed great antiquity, dating back to the Stuart kings. The first English Club of the modern era, however, was perhaps the Old Manchester Club (1818), though the first of the continuous modern era was the Royal North Devon (1864) at Westward Ho!, a Club which had the distinction of raising JH Taylor who became the first professional to beat the Scots at their own game. In Ireland, Royal Belfast (1881) was the first golf club to be formed, and in Europe, Pau (1856) led the way. Britain's expanding Empire spread golf around the world. In Britain, a new burst of Club foundation occurred, reaching its peak in the 1890s. The number of Clubs rose from less than 100 in 1875 to 1300 in 1900. Golf had been played in a small way in America before the foundation of the St Andrews Golf Club of Yonkers in 1888, but the Club's pioneers had met with ridicule. This Club's course was primitive, but by 1895 came America's first open championship links, at Newport, Rhode Island–although as late as 1899 leading British professionals like Harry Vardon met little opposition on tours in America.

'Old' and 'young' Tom Morris.

Early competitive play

Competitive golf dates from the inter-Club matches of the early nineteenth century, the first of which was recorded in 1818 when two of the Edinburgh Clubs playing over Bruntisfield Links, the Burgess Golfing Society and the Bruntisfield Links Club, competed against each other. In 1857 the Prestwick Club organized a successful inter-Club tournament, and in 1860 they arranged an event for professional golfers, which later became known as the Open Championship. They may have wished to show the skills of the invited professionals, particularly their own man, Tom Morris, whom they had hired as a ball- and clubmaker, and who looked after the Prestwick links – the first such salaried post for a golfer. Sadly, Allan Robertson did not live to play in the competition, though the year previously he was the first to have broken 80 in a round over the Old Course. The Open was unusual in being a stroke-play competition, as the early inter-Club tournaments were match play.

New horizons

Golf prospered and by the time of Willie Park's success the small number of professional golfers could hope for larger stakes in challenge matches and the rewards of occasional tournaments. Park was perhaps the first to capitalize on his fame in the modern way as a golf consultant and by publicizing his own branded clubs, notably an infallible putter, and by using mass production, advertising and postal sales he was highly successful. At St Andrews the first golf club manufacturing firm that had not been set up by a professional golfer appeared–the Forgan's firm, which survived for almost a century.

Scottish professional dominance ended in 1894 when an English-born professional, JH Taylor, won the Open. The rise of American golf was signalled when WJ Travis won the British Amateur Championship in 1904.

Though a home-bred player, JJ McDermott, had won the US Open in 1911, it was Francis Ouimet's win in 1913 that caught the popular imagination. Another feature of the growing dominance of America was the appearance of the Haskell ball in 1902, quickly capturing the market. Club design changed to suit the new ball: heads became deeper and the scarehead design changed to the socket joint.

From George M Colville Five Open Champions and the Musselburgh Golf Story, *Musselburgh 1980.*

THE MAN WHO CAN PUTT IS A MATCH FOR ANYBODY.

If you want to putt well, use

Park's SPECIAL PUTTING-CLEEK (Patented) Price 7/6 each

AS USED BY

MR H. H. HILTON,

WINNER OF THE

OPEN CHAMPIONSHIP, 1897.

Mr Hilton writes in the "Sporting Chronicle" on 19th July 1898, as follows:

"If Willie Park, jun. did not succeed in winning the Open Championship, he at least had the satisfaction of knowing that the man who did succeed in beating him accomplished the feat with one of the Musselburgh man's patent putters; and the extraordinary run of success attained in the series of open tournaments was probably more due to his deadly execution with this club than to any other department of his game. It is needless to go farther than to say that the winner used one of Park's patent putters, as, in truth, the first three to finish all used what I have heard termed 'that wry-neck abortion of Park's.' Wry-necked or not, there can be no shadow of doubt as to the popularity of this very putter. It has outlived the prejudice which patent tools are more or less subject to contract at first, and it is in general use from one end of the kingdom to the other. I have frequently been asked what advantage it enjoys compared with the ordinary straight-faced putter. I am afraid I have always had to plead ignorance on this point, and have referred the inquirer to the patentee for information, while I have attributed my personal liking for the putter to a mere matter of fancy. The first time I tried it I was eminently successful with the implement, and although I am a great believer in an occasional change of clubs, I always find that eventually I fall back on the original 'Park' putter. Whether the fact that the face is set back behind the perpendicular of the shaft gives a better sight of the ball I cannot say, but I know that it imbues me with a feeling of confidence when playing an approach putt."

Beware of Imitations.

See that every Cleek is stamped "PARK'S SPECIAL."

WM. PARK & SON, GOLF CLUB MAKERS, Musselburgh.

CHAMPION GOLFERS,

1860, 1863, 1866, 1875, 1887, 1889.

BRANCHES AT—115 CANNON STREET, LONDON; 6 SOUTH ST ANDREW STREET, EDINBURGH; and 118 WEST 23rd STREET, NEW YORK.

From George M Colville Five Open Champions and the Musselburgh Golf Story, *Musselburgh 1980.*

Improved status

Professionals' status remained low until the end of the century and they were usually called by their second names only. Even Open Champions had to tee the ball up for their amateur partners in exhibition matches, and even James Braid never entered Walton Heath clubhouse by the front door. JH Taylor organized the professionals in Britain, promoting their image until they became national figures even outside the narrow world of sport. Their new-found popularity was marked by an increasing number of tournaments, notably the sponsorship by the *News of the World* of the first tournament of the modern era. The changing status of professionals in Britain was pioneered and continued by Henry Cotton, who, on being appointed to Ashridge GC in 1937, made the bold stipulation that he be made an honorary member of the Club. The modern professional had arrived.

Today golf is played world-wide, and is perhaps the most popular participant outdoor sport in the world. The government of the game still bears out its Scottish origins – the Royal and Ancient Golf Club of St Andrews shares with the United States Golf Association the regulation of all golf. And only in Scotland is it still universally the game of the ordinary people.

Evolution of the Rules of Golf

J Stewart Lawson

The late Henry Longhurst always maintained that perfectly adequate rules for the game of golf could be written on the back of a score card. When challenged to show how this could be done, Henry produced a set of ten Rules, the key one reading: *The game shall be played in the traditional manner....* Sadly, Henry was never pressed to say to which of the many different traditions he was referring. Should we, for example, be following the Leith system (*At Holling, you are to play your Ball honestly for the Hole, and not to play upon your Adversary's Ball, not lying in your way to the Hole*–The Gentlemen Golfers, 1744) or the Brunonian system (*It shall be deemed fair to play a ball against the adversary's ball, provided the player does not touch the adversary's ball with his club*–Edinburgh Burgess Golfing Society, 1814)?

No doubt there are many traditionalists who will shake their heads mournfully over the 1984 version of the Rules of Golf. Not only are the playing rules presented in an entirely new and, it is hoped, more logical order, but several important changes of principle and procedure have also been made. What many people forget, however, is that from the very outset the rules of the game have been organic: they have grown and proliferated; they have changed their form and shape many times; and, by discarding provisions as they became outmoded, they have supported Darwin's theory of the survival of the fittest. Nevertheless, through all phases of this evolution, the organism's backbone has remained unaffected: the game of golf still *consists in playing a ball from the* teeing ground *into the hole by a* stroke *or successive strokes in accordance with the Rules*–Rule 1-1.

Early rules

Golf in Scotland had managed to survive three centuries without any apparent need for written rules when, in 1744, the Gentlemen Golfers at Leith drew up thirteen Articles & Laws in Playing at Golf, the occasion being the first competition for the City of Edinburgh's Silver Club and the Gentlemen Golfers apprehending that entrants from other parts of the country might not be familiar with the Leith tradition. As other golfing societies were formed in the ensuing years, each drew up its own rules of play, but the leadership of the Gentlemen Golfers, later to become The Honourable Company of Edinburgh Golfers, was generally acknowledged. From the 1830s onwards, however, due to a temporary eclipse of the Honourable Company, this leadership gradually passed to the Society of St Andrews Golfers, which in 1834 had been granted the title of Royal and Ancient Golf Club of St Andrews. This shift of influence to the Royal and Ancient is illustrated by the fact that, whereas in 1810 the first 15 Rules of the Glasgow Golf Club were, with one minor difference, word for word the same as those of the Honourable Company, in 1851 the newly formed Prestwick Golf Club decided to adopt the St Andrews Rules of Play.

The last quarter of the 19th century saw a tremendous expansion of golf both at home and overseas, and there was a growing demand for a uniform code of rules. It was natural, in these circumstances, that the leading clubs should invite the Royal and Ancient to assume this responsibility, and the first Rules of Golf Committee was appointed in 1897. The United States Golf Association had been organized in 1894, and these two bodies, the Royal and Ancient and the USGA, now became the game's two governing authorities, responsible for the formulation of rules and for their interpretation. During the first half of the present century, the Royal and Ancient and the USGA shared the same basic code of rules, but each body issued its own interpretative Decisions, and many differences arose, particularly in the area of the game's equipment: the Royal and Ancient's banning of the centre-shafted putter after WJ Travis had won the British Amateur with a Schenectady; the eventual, and still extant, disagreement over the minimum size of the golf ball; and the legalization of steel shafts by the USGA some years before the Royal and Ancient followed suit. Interpretation of the playing rules also differed, and the USGA, without the same long tradition of match play, had no qualms about abolishing the stymie.

Royal and Ancient–USGA co-operation

By 1950 there was a grave danger of the Royal and Ancient and the USGA drifting farther apart, but conferences held in 1951, which representatives from Canada and Australia also attended, resulted in the formulation of a uniform code; apart from a couple of minor lapses and the continuing difference over the size of the ball, that uniformity has been maintained ever since. Arrangements were also made in 1951 for the Royal and Ancient and the USGA to meet periodically to review the Rules, and these meetings now take place every four years; on the Royal and Ancient's part, only after detailed consultation with the 65 Golfing Unions and Associations affiliated to it. It would have been anomalous, however, to have uniform rules if they were not being interpreted in the same way. A comprehensive analysis of Royal and Ancient and USGA Decisions carried out a few years ago revealed several important differences of interpretation, and a Joint Decisions Committee was therefore appointed to establish uniformity in this area as well as in the Rules themselves. So successful has this new venture been that in 1984 the Royal and Ancient and the USGA have jointly published a book of uniform Decisions on the Rules of Golf, and the two bodies are also co-operating in the production of a film about the Rules.

One alteration in the 1984 Rules may have startled more than traditionalists: the change in the manner in which a ball is to be dropped. In future, the player *shall stand erect, hold the ball at shoulder height and arm's length and drop it* (Rule 20-2a) and there is no requirement that he must face the hole when doing so. The chief reason for this change was that the spot where the ball first strikes the ground when dropped is important (see Rule 20-2c), but under the old Rule how was the player-standing erect, facing the hole and dropping the ball over his shoulder-to identify that spot with any certainty? The change is certainly a major one, and the traditionalists might claim that the old Rule embodied a procedure hallowed by nearly two and a half centuries of usage. But would they be right?

Ways of dropping the ball

Article 8 of the 1744 code at Leith required a player whose ball was lost to *drop another Ball*, but it did not say in what manner this should be done. In 1754 at St Andrews the player was at liberty to take his ball out of *water, or any watery filth, and throw it behind the hazard six yards at least.* The Edinburgh Burgess Golfing Society varied not only the manner of dropping but even the identity of the dropper: in 1773 the ball was to be dropped by *the opposite party*, i.e. the opponent; in 1776 it was to be thrown over his head by the player; in 1807 the player was to drop it over his shoulder; and in 1839 the *right* shoulder was specified. Facing the hole when dropping was first introduced by the Honourable Company in 1809, but the method of dropping varied again: *the player shall ... fronting the hole to which he is playing, drop the ball over the back of his head.* Finally, in 1829 and 1834 the Musselburgh Golf Club required that the ball be dropped by *a cady.* Which of these several variations on the dropping theme would the traditionalists accept as Henry Longhurst's *traditional manner*?

The first written Rules of Golf were no more than 14 years old when it was thought necessary to amend them, but it was clear that the Gentlemen Golfers in 1758 believed that they had now got the wording absolutely right and that no further change would be required. Did not their Captain, Thomas Boswall, preface the amendment with these bold words, *That in all time Coming the Law shall be ...*? Successive generations of legislators have been equally sanguine in believing that they have produced a perfect set of rules, and the Royal and Ancient and the USGA doubtless hope that the 1984 code has closed all loopholes and provided for all eventualities. Is evolution now complete? Has the definitive tradition at last been established? Only time will tell.

Editor's note: J Stewart Lawson was Chairman of The Rules of Golf Committee 1973–77 and Captain of the Royal and Ancient Golf Club, St Andrews, 1979–80.

Golf Terminology

Bogey–origin of the term

The term was first used in 1891. Hugh Rotherham, Coventry, suggested what was termed the *ground score* of the Coventry course. The scheme propounded by Rotherham was taken up by the Great Yarmouth Club hon secretary, Dr T Browne, who inaugurated matches for Great Yarmouth on the lines indicated. About this time the popular music hall ditty, *Hush, hush, here comes the Bogey man*, was on almost everyone's lips, and it must have been uppermost in the mind of Major C Wellman one day when he exclaimed to Dr Browne: *This ground score player of yours is a regular 'Bogey man'*. So the expression *bogey* was at once adopted at Great Yarmouth. Dr Browne introduced *Bogey* to the United Services Club *as a quiet, modest and retiring gentleman, uniformly steady, but never over brilliant*. He was heartily welcomed, and the hon secretary, Captain Vidal, was so impressed with the personality of the newest member that he suggested it was but fitting he should hold service rank, so he was given the position of *Colonel*, which he still retains. The Royal and Ancient did not recognize the term until 1910, when the Rules of Golf Committee framed special rules for bogey competitions. It is now almost in disuse in its original sense since the general adoption of the standard scratch score and the assignment of par to each hole. However in the 1960s it came back into golfing parlance through its American use denoting one over par for any hole.

Golf terms

Birdie, Eagle and **Albatross** are words coined in America to represent, respectively, holes done in one below par, two below par and three below par. The word *birdie* is attributed to AH Smith, who, in 1903, when playing at Atlantic City, holed out for a 1-under par at one hole and exclaimed *that was a bird of a shot.*

Twosome is not a golf term. If one man plays against another, the match is a **Single**. In stroke play, two players competing together are a **Couple**.

Threesome designates a match in which one player plays against two playing alternate strokes with one ball, such a match being rare. The word does not mean three players each playing against the other; that is a **Three-ball Match.**

Foursome covers two players playing alternate strokes with one ball against two others playing one ball in match play or against the field in stroke play. There has been a tendency to use the word to cover a four-ball match, and so the term **Scotch Foursome** has been used in some cases to distinguish between the two.

Medal Play has crept into golf language as a synonym for **Stroke Play**. *Stroke play* is the correct term, according to the Rules and tradition.

Dormie is when a player, or his side, is as many holes up as there are holes remaining to play. A match consists of 18 holes or 36 holes. If extra holes are to be played to obtain a winning result, then the term *dormie* does not apply.

The Championships of Great Britain

History of the Open Championship

The Open Championship was initiated by Prestwick Golf Club in 1860 and was played there until 1870. The Club presented the Championship Belt which was to be held for a year by the winner and which would become the absolute property of any player who won three years in succession. The competition consisted of three rounds of the 12 holes Prestwick then had, to be played on one day. The Open did not become a four round contest until 1892. There were few entrants in the early years and nearly all were professionals, who were sometimes also greenkeepers and clubmakers, with a few amateurs.

Young Tom Morris won the Belt outright in 1870. There was no contest the following year, but in 1872 Prestwick, the Royal and Ancient and the Honourable Company, who were still playing at Musselburgh, subscribed to provide the present trophy, which was not to be won outright. Since then only three winners would have so earned it: Jamie Anderson and Bob Ferguson during the following ten years and Peter Thomson since in 1954-56. The Championship was to be held on the courses of the three subscribing Clubs in turn. Young Tom won the first for the new cup in 1872 at St Andrews, but died tragically young in 1875.

The three courses continued to be used until 1892 when it was first played at Muirfield to where the Honourable Company had moved. That year was also the first in which the Championship became a 72-hole contest over two days. In 1890, at Prestwick, John Ball had become the first amateur to win. Only two others have followed his success, Harold Hilton in 1892 and 1897, and Bobby Jones in 1926, 1927 and 1930. Roger Wethered tied with Jock Hutchison at St Andrews in 1920, but lost the play-off; if he had not incurred a penalty stroke through treading on his ball in the third round, he may well have won.

The Triumvirate

The year 1894 saw the first occasion the Open was played in England at Sandwich and the first English professional to win, JH Taylor. He won again the next year and for fifth time in 1913. Harry Vardon and James Baird were the two others of the *great triumvirate* who together won sixteen Opens between 1894 and 1914. Taylor's five wins were spread over twenty years and Vardon's six over nineteen. Braid's wins were concentrated into ten years from 1901 to 1910, all of them in Scotland. Vardon won three times at Prestwick but never at St Andrews where Taylor and Braid both won twice. Only Taylor managed a win at Hoylake. No other player won more than once during their supremacy. The winning scores at the time were very high by today's standards, for although the courses were marginally shorter, the equipment and clothing were primitive compared with those in use now. At Sandwich Taylor's score was 326, or 38 over an average of 4s. His 304 at Hoylake in 1913 was played in appalling weather, wearing a tweed jacket, cap and boots, and using wooden shafts and leather grips. He had no protective clothing or umbrella and won by 8 strokes from Ted Ray. The last winning total over 300 was Hagen's 301 at Hoylake in 1924.

Better Standards

That improved equipment has defeated the greater length and heavier rough of today's Championship courses is suggested by comparing the average winning scores for decades of this century:

Decade	*Average winning score*	*Decade*	*Average winning score*
1905-14	302	1956-65	280
1920-29	295	1966-75	280
1930-39	289	1976-85	277
1946-55	284		

Of the 115 Opens held so far, twenty Scots have won, seventeen Americans, fourteen English, three Australians, two South Africans and one each from France, Ireland, New Zealand, Argentina and Spain. The Scots have won thirty-nine times but only twice since Braid in 1910 (Duncan in 1920 and Lyle in 1985), the USA thirty times, England twenty-six, Australia and South Africa seven times each, Spain twice and each of the others once each. Since the triumvirate's day ended, the only Englishman to win more than once has been Henry Cotton with three victories. The Americans have won thirty out of the last sixty-two Opens played.

It will be seen that certain nationalities tend to dominate for a decade or so; the Scots until 1893, then the English until 1914, the USA in the 1920s and until 1933 when the English had a short resuscitation. The Commonwealth were to the fore from 1949 to 1965 (Locke, Thomson, Nagle and Charles) with the Americans coming back again to win in 13 out of 18 years between 1966 and 1983. Equally dominating in their periods were Hagen and Jones in the twenties, Cotton in the thirties, Locke and Thomson the fifties, and thereafter Palmer, Nicklaus, Player, Trevino, Watson and Ballasteros.

Open Courses

Only fourteen courses have accommodated the Open. Prestwick, discarded after 1925 as unsuitable for large crowds, still leads with twenty-four occasions, twenty of them before 1900. St Andrews follows with twenty-three. The second group comprises Muirfield with twelve, Sandwich eleven and Hoylake with ten. Hoylake's last Open was in 1967; that it is not used now is due not to any lack of quality of the course but to lack of space. Deal appeared in 1909 and 1920, and was due again in 1948 but the sea broke across the course, and Sandwich came in for the last time until 1981. Troon and Lytham St Annes each held an Open between the wars, Carnoustie two and Princes, Sandwich, when Sarazen won in 1932, one; this course, which was used as a tank training ground during the second war, has not been asked again. In 1951, Portrush, the only Irish course to stage an Open, also provided the only English winner between Cotton and Jacklin in Max Faulkner. Birkdale and Turnberry are firmly established in the rota which appears to have settled at four Scottish courses, St Andrews, Muirfield, Troon and Turnberry (this will be five if, hopefully, Carnoustie reappears), and three in England, Lytham St Annes, Birkdale and Sandwich.

Traditionally the Open is only played on Links courses. While there may yet be new venues by the sea capable of being stretched and groomed to be worthy of holding an Open, the many other considerations to be weighed, such as an adequate road system to carry vast crowds and nearly as many acres as the course covers to accommodate the tented village and services, it is not easy to see where the Championship Committee will turn. It is possible, even likely, in this present age that a links course of repute with the necessary acreage round it will be developed by a consortium that will bid for an Open and succeed.

Qualifying

How does one qualify to play in an Open? Since qualifying was first introduced in 1914, there have been numerous changes. Regional qualifying was tried for a year in 1926. At one of the courses used, Sunningdale, Bobby Jones (and even he had to qualify) played what many consider the classic round of golf: a 66, all 4s and 3s, never over par, 8 birdies, 33 putts and 33 other shots.

Until 1963 all competitors, even the holder, had to play two qualifying rounds on the Open course on the Monday and Tuesday of the Open week. The qualifiers then had one round on Wednesday, one on Thursday and the leading group of between 40 and 60 players finished with two rounds on Friday. In 1963 certain exemptions from qualifying were introduced. The two rounds on the Friday were dropped in 1966 in favour of one round each on Friday and Saturday; not until 1980 was the first round played on Thursday and the last on Sunday. As the entry continued to increase, in 1970 nearby courses were used for qualifying and in 1977 regional qualifying was re-introduced in up to four areas in the previous week with final qualifying on nearby courses later.

There have been surprisingly few ties involving a play-off, only eleven in 115 Championships. The first should have been in 1876 involving David Strath and Bob Martin. However, Strath took umbrage over a complaint against him and refused to play again, Martin being declared the winner. Until 1963 ties were decided over 36 holes; the last two, between Nicklaus and Sanders at St Andrews in 1971 and Watson and Newton at Carnoustie in 1975, were played over 18. Two years ago it was decided that in the event of a tie, the winner would be found immediately by a play-off over specified holes, followed by sudden death if necessary.

Prize Money

In 1863 the total prize money was £10, its distribution among the fourteen entrants, six of whom were amateurs, is unknown. A year later it had risen by over 50% to £16, with the winner taking £6. By 1986 the total prize fund had risen to £634,000, of which Greg Norman received £70,000. All 75 qualifiers for the last day received £1500 or more. Additionally winners of the qualifying rounds won smaller amounts. Until about 1955, the winner's and leaders' rewards were very modest; even in 1939 the cheque for the first man was £100 out of a total of £500. With some justification the prestige of winning the Open then was adjudged to be of much more value than any monetary award. The growth since the 1950s has been astonishing and is evidence that, while it is still a tremendous asset for any man to have won the Open, the authorities have recognised that it will not maintain its leading place without substantial reward.

The rapid advance of the Open to the major spectacle it has become is due to a combination of factors. Not least of these is the TV presentation of the BBC, acknowledged as the world's best in golf, the interest and enthusiasm of thousands of spectators keen to watch on the spot rather than on the box, and the Royal and Ancient's promotion of this world fair of golf that it has become. Behind it all has been the foresight of successive Championship Committees and, in the late 1960s and 1970s, the masterly spreading of the gospel by Keith Mackenzie, Secretary of the R&A in 1966-82, that is so ably continued by his successor, Michael Bonallack.

The detailed list of Open Winners can be found on pages 562–83.

The Editor

The Amateur Championship

Early History

Golf has always been a competitive game and club medals have been keenly contested since the nineteenth century. Many of the leading amateurs were members of several clubs and, aided by an excellent railway system, they competed against each other at such venues as St Andrews, Prestwick, Hoylake and Musselburgh. An embryonic *open amateur competition* was held in the late 1850s (the first being won by Robert Chambers, the publisher, in 1858), but there seems to have been little enthusiasm for such an event and it died around the time of the first Open Championship (1860). The best amateurs began to enter the Open from 1861. By the 1870s, there was renewed interest in organising a tournament for amateurs only but nothing happened, probably because no one club took a strong enough lead. A proposal in 1877 to the membership of the R&A that it sponsor a sort of Amateur Championship (involving club members and others nominated by members) was defeated.

It fell to the Hoylake golfers to set in motion the championship we now know as *The Amateur*. In 1884 the Secretary of Royal Liverpool, Thomas Potter, proposed that an event – open to all amateurs – should be organised. This original intention was not carried out until 1886 and so the winner of 1885 (AF Macfie) triumphed over a strong, but limited, field drawn from certain clubs. The clubs which were responsible for the running of the championship until the R&A took over in 1920 – and who made contributions for the purchase of the trophy – were:

Royal and Ancient
Royal Burgess Golfing Society of Edinburgh
Royal Liverpool
Royal St George's
Royal Albert, Montrose
Royal North Devon
Royal Aberdeen
Royal Blackheath
Royal Wimbledon
Royal Dublin
Alnmouth
North Berwick, New Club
Panmure, Dundee
Prestwick
Bruntsfield Links Golfing Society, Edinburgh
Dalhousie
Gullane
Formby
Honourable Company of Edinburgh Golfers
Innerleven
King James VI, Perth
Kilspindie
Luffness
Tantallon
Troon
West Lancashire

The first championship was not without its teething troubles. The format which was adopted allowed both golfers to proceed to the next round if their match was halved, so the first championship had three semi-finalists – and Macfie got a bye into the final. From 1886, the usual format was adopted.

More serious than the problem of an idiosyncratic draw, however, was the question of amateur status, raised for the first time in 1886.

The committee had to decide if it should accept the entries of John Ball III and Douglas Rolland. As a 15-year-old, Ball had finished fourth in the 1878 Open at Prestwick and on the advice of Jack Morris he accepted the prize money of 10s (50p). Rolland, a stonemason, had accepted second prize in the 1884 Open. Rolland's entry to the Amateur was refused while Ball's was accepted. Ball went on to win the championship a record eight times and the Open Championship of 1890.

The Format

After such a difficult start, the format of 18-hole matches with a 36-hole final remained until 1956. This arrangement made for many closely fought matches, as shown in 1930, the year of RT Jones' Grand Slam triumph. Jones' only victory in the event came in the right year and it is worth pointing out that, in making his way to the final, he won in the fourth round at the 19th (by laying a stymie) against Cyril Tolley, the holder, and his victories in the sixth round and in the semi-final were by the narrowest of margins. In addition, the fact that the draw was not seeded sometimes meant early meetings between top golfers; for example, in 1926 the visiting American Walker Cup Team members, von Elm and Ouimet, met in the second round and von Elm went on to meet Jesse Sweetser in the third. As a result of such events, there was some pressure for the introduction of seeding the draw but it was not until 1958 that the practice was officially adopted. In the fifties and sixties there were other changes in format in an attempt to satisfy large numbers of golfers who wished to play and to ensure a worthy winner.

The popularity of the championship has posed difficulties for the R&A. The mathematically ideal number of entrants to be fitted into a convenient format is 256. In 1950, 324 entered the championship causing golf to be played on the Old Course for 14 hours a day. In order to restrict the numbers turning up to the championship proper, an experiment in regional qualifying was held in 1958 (again a St Andrews year) and 488 players with handicaps of 5 and under played 36 holes of stroke play on 14 courses. This system was quickly replaced and in 1961 the handicap limit was lowered (to 3) and a balloting-out of higher handicaps was introduced so that 256 were left to play for the trophy. This method was followed until 1983 with the introduction of 36 holes of stroke play to find 64 players for match play, from which to find the eventual winner.

There was also pressure for the introduction of 36-hole matches. As early as 1922 the R & A's championship committee canvassed the opinion of the 252 men who played that year. Nineteen of these voted in favour of 36-hole matches, seven for district qualification, fifty-two voted for a stroke play qualification followed by 18-hole matches and the others who replied wanted no change to the system. In 1956 and 1957 the last 3 rounds were played over 36 holes, in 1958 and 1959 the semi-final and final were over 36 holes and then the old format returned.

There is constant pressure on the organisers to find a format to satisfy the needs of large numbers of home and foreign players, to take into account differences in national handicapping systems, to preserve the atmosphere of the championship, to maintain match play as a central feature of top-level amateur golf and even to take into account the vagaries of the weather. The task is almost impossible and it is unlikely that the championship will continue in its present form for all time.

The Winners

Any man who wins the Amateur is a considerable golfer but attention should be paid to certain outstanding champions. John Ball of Royal Liverpool won the title eight times between 1888 and 1912. It is interesting to note that he never successfully defended his title. Michael Bonallack triumphed five times between 1961 and 1970, including an incredible hat-trick of final victories in which he successively beat Joe Carr and Bill Hyndman twice.

Several golfers have successfully defended their title: Horace Hutchinson, Harold Hilton, Lawson Little, Peter McEvoy and Philip Parkin, while others have won twice or more – Johnny Laidlay, Freddie Tait, Bob Maxwell, Cyril Tolley, Edward Holderness, Frank Stranahan, Joe Carr and Trevor Homer.

The oldest man to win was the Hon Michael Scott, at the age of 54 in 1933. The youngest winners – John Beharrell and Bobby Cole – were both 18 years and 1 month old. Cole's victory over Ronnie Shade was achieved over 18 holes – play being affected by poor visibility. The first overseas winner was Walter Travis who won in 1904 – one consequence of his victory was the banning of the use of centre-shafted putters. The first continental winner was the Frenchman, Philippe Ploujoux, who won in 1981. A visiting Walker Cup team always makes for an exciting championship and from fifteen visits to Great Britain the title has crossed the Atlantic twelve times. Indeed, on six occasions the final was an all-American affair.

No doubt there have been hundreds of thrilling matches played in the championship but few can have been as pulsating as the 1899 final at Prestwick where Johnny Ball beat Freddie Tait at the 37th hole. The victory must have been a sweet one for Ball, since Tait, the hero of Scotland, had won the previous year over Ball's home links of Hoylake. Tait was killed the following year in the Boer War. *The great battle* as Jones described his 4th round tie against Tolley in 1930 rivals the Ball-Tait final for tense excitement and for sheer brilliance of scoring Michael Bonallack's 1st round in the final of 1968 must take pride of place.

The Amateur Championship was 100 years old in 1985 and in essence it has changed remarkably little. How will the Championship react to changes such as the increasing popularity of the game at home and abroad, the lure of the professional ranks with its dependence on stroke play and the increasing commercialisation of all sport? There is every reason to believe that it will continue to stand for all that is great in golf.

David Christie

How Grows the Professional Tour

George Simms

When Gordon J Brand received the Tooting Bec Trophy at the end of 1986 – he got it for the lowest score in the Open Championship (68) by a PGA member resident in Great Britain and Ireland – he had some history in his hands to contemplate. Eighty-five years previously, when the Professional Golfers' Association was born, that same silver trophy, presented by the Tooting Bec Golf Club and contested on their own South London course, went to the winner of what was the Association's very first tournament. With it went prize money of £15 – something else that Brand could contemplate in a year when his own tournament winnings at home and abroad approached ten thousand times that figure!

Early Purses

Not that all tournament purses at that time were £15, for records have it that a Machrie tournament in 1901 was the first to have a winner's prize of £100 and that JH Taylor got it for beating James Braid in the final. It was JH who won the PGA's first tournament, receiving a first prize of £5 from the £15 kitty for his rounds of 76-73 which put him three shots ahead of his nearest challengers in a field of 46. That particular competition was contested until 1922, and two years later the Tooting Bec trophy was accorded its present association with the Open Championship.

Comparisons between the spending power of Taylor's £5 in 1901 and its 1986 equivalent are pointless. It suffices to say that it would have been a pretty good weekly wage in the years immediately preceding World War II, and therefore more so prior to the 1914-18 conflict of Taylor's era. When one considers, however, that PGA tournaments subsequent to the Tooting Bec had prize money of around only £20, and that the *News of the World* PGA Match-play Championship, inaugurated in 1903 with a prize fund of £200 was practically front page news, it cannot help but make the mind boggle at the rewards of the present time.

In 1987 the PGA European Tour will have something like £6 million to dispense among its successful members seeking to increase their lifestyles, not least Severiano Ballesteros who passed through the magic million mark in August with his victory in the KLM Dutch Open. It took him a mere ten years. On the way to the bank, however, a little reflection by the game's professors on the foundations of today's millions and the rewards that went to their forebears, might not come amiss.

The Role of Sponsorship

Undoubtedly the 1903 PGA Match-play Championship was the cornerstone. Under the *News of the World* sponsorship it ran unbroken, apart from the war years, until 1969, thereafter enjoying other sponsors – Benson and Hedges among them – until ceasing in 1979. It was to the delight of many of us that the Epson computer giant, in sponsoring the PGA European Tour's Order of Merit, undertook as well to restore match-play golf to the calendar. James Braid won the first of these Championships, played at Walton Heath, Surrey, beating Ted Ray in the final and receiving £100 for doing so.

By the middle of the 1920s, some half-a-dozen official PGA tournaments were producing over £5000 in prize money. A decade later, when Cotton, the Whitcombes, Padgham, Burton, Rees and others had stepped into the limelight previously occupied by the PGA's founding fathers Braid, Taylor and Vardon, sponsorship took a marked upturn. No small reason for this was Cotton's victory in the Open Championship at Sandwich in 1934 which ended a 10-year home drought.

Commander Charles Roe came into the PGA's secretarial chair in that year, in the cramped and almost Dickensian offices they occupied in Ethelburga House in London's Bishopsgate. He was to hold sway until 1962, an authoritarian figure from the quarter-deck who knew what he wanted for his members and more often than not got it – particularly in the matter of tournaments for them to play in.

These were not the days of the world-travelling tournament-playing superstar of today, but mostly the club professional taking a break from the shop to which he had to get back sharply come Saturday morning in time for the club competition and the workshop. Principal sponsorship support of golf prior to and immediately after the Second World War came from the golf trade and the national and provincial press. Earlier, in 1921, the *Daily Mail* and the *Glasgow Herald* had sponsored tournaments with prize funds of 1000 guineas, and when in 1936 the *Daily Mail* returned to the golf scene its £2000 tournament that year was record prize money. Among regular sponsors were the *News Chronicle*, the *Daily Telegraph*, *Daily Sketch*, *Yorkshire Evening News*, Dunlop, Penfold, and Silver King.

When tournament golf resumed in 1946, total prize money topped £25,000, and remained around that figure for a decade – to the frequently-expressed dissatisfaction of the pros. But there were landmarks. The Penfold-Bournemouth Festival of Britain event in 1951 had a largest-ever £3000 prize fund, and the Swallow-Penfold in 1955 had the first £1000 winner's cheque which went to a grateful Christy O'Connor. By 1960, however, total prize money had climbed to around £50,000, and went to £60,000 in 1961, and £80,000 in 1962.

By now Palmer, Player, and Nicklaus were commanding world attention, and in the spin-off the British scene began to prosper. Sponsorship reached out into the consumer market, with the tobacco and drinks trade prominent, and prize money levels moved through the £200,000 barrier in the late sixties, aided by the four-year Alcan Golf of the Year Series with its £20,000 or so first prize which for the first two years of 1967 and 1968 went to America's Gay Brewer. In 1970 the John Player Classic outpaid everyone with its world record £25,000 winner's cheque; again Christy O'Connor was grateful to one and all.

That same year an important decision had been taken acknowledging the long-standing French Open Championship as an official event on the PGA Tour. It had been a recognised *PS*, as it were, to the Open Championship for many a year.

Influence of the PGA

Holding the PGA Secretarial reins by then was Major John Bywaters with the almost impossible task of overseeing the tournament scene, the lot of the club professional, the training of assistants, entry into the profession, and the administration of his own headquarters. Delegation became essential, and so it was that in 1971 John Jacobs, a player of quality and a coach of distinction, was appointed the PGA's Tournament Director-General with the responsibility of re-fashioning a circuit that was in danger of standing still. Here was another landmark, and one that was to lead directly to the highly-regarded position that the PGA European Tour, and its administration, holds in world golf today.

The disappearance of the Alcan series and the John Player event after 1970, saw a slump in prize money overall. Jacobs crossed his fingers, took a deep breath, and decreed that henceforth there would be a minimum level of prize money of £8000 for tournaments in a week when the PGA couldn't guarantee the field to the sponsor, and £15,000 in such special weeks when Tony Jacklin and Peter Oosterhuis would be available. Jacklin in particular, having won the British and US Opens, was the ace in the hole. All sponsors hoped for him in their field.

The immediate effect of the Jacobs dictum was to lose the Agfa-Gavaert, the Daks and the Classic International tournaments! Nonetheless, with the long-established Italian, Spanish, German and Swiss Opens having joined the French Open in the Tour Calendar in 1971 – all with the encouragement of Order of Merit points not previously enjoyed – the European pattern began to shape. Holland joined the Official Tour in 1972 and the Madrid Open was also given official blessing. Portugal came in from the cold a year later.

Gradually Jacobs *raised the ante*, laying down minimum prize funds of £15,000 for Continental championships, and by 1974 the tournament circuit was playing for around £600,000. In 1971, when Jacobs had first taken over, the figure had been £250,000-plus, and he had said, *What we so badly need is two or three* international *British figures in order to take advantage of the money which is no doubt available for sponsored golf.* How right he was, as the coming years were to prove.

Tournament Players' Division

In 1974 a strong case was being made for the introduction of a Tournament Players' Division, and it was formally voted into being at the PGA's annual meeting at the end of that year. It appointed Ken Schofield as Secretary, now its Executive Director. With a strong Tournament Committee under the chairman, Neil Coles, and with the continued guidance for a while of Jacobs, the infant TPD grew into the current PGA European Tour.

In a dozen years, prize money has grown from £600,000 to £6 million. It went through the first million barrier in 1977, two million in 1982, three million in 1984, and has climbed, as the accompanying graph shows, by a million pounds a year ever since.

PGA European Tour: Prize Money Growth 1976–1986

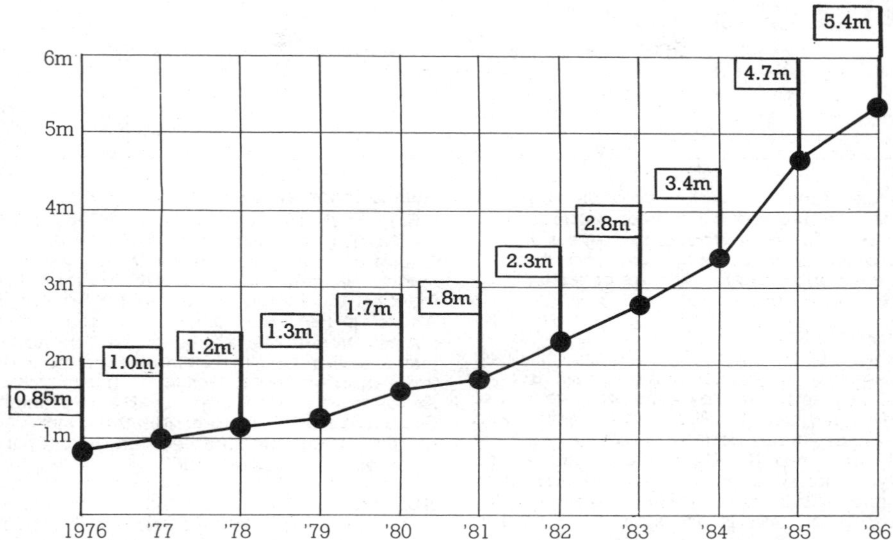

Cheques for £25,000, £35,000 and more, are becoming the norm for a tournament winner.

Nor must one forget the unsponsored Open Championship which is, of course, entirely under the aegis of the Royal and Ancient Golf Club. Taking 1975, the year of the birth of the PGA European Tour, as a comparison, prize money in the Open has risen from £75,000 to over £600,000 in 1986. In 1975 Tom Watson's reward for winning at Carnoustie was £7500. Greg Norman got £70,000 for his victory last year at Turnberry, virtually a ten-fold increase in 10 years.

The Future

The impact made by Ballesteros, Langer, Lyle and other European Tour golfers of world class – such as Jacobs had yearned for years earlier – has been a major attraction for sponsorship money. BBC Television, which for a while in the late sixties and early seventies *went cool* on the sluggish domestic Tour, now has a contract with the Tour dating from 1979 and renewed into 1989.

The introduction of the PGA Qualifying School in 1976, and the birth of the All-Exempt Tour in 1985, disposing as it did of irksome and often heart-breaking pre-qualifying days, have all combined to establish the most enviable and prosperous of sporting organisations. A successful defence of the Ryder Cup at Jack Nicklaus's Muirfield Village course in Ohio later this year can do the PGA European Tour's upward growth no harm whatsoever!

From the £15 purse of Tooting Bec's 1901 tournament to what heights yet?

Famous Players of the Past

In making the difficult choice of the names to be included, effort has been made to acknowledge the outstanding players and personalities of each successive era from the early pioneers to the stars of recent times.

Anderson, Jamie

Born 1842, died 1912. Winner of three consecutive Open Championships (1877-78-79). Born at St Andrews, he was the son of *Old Daw*, a St Andrews caddie and character. Jamie began golf when 10 years old, and rapidly developed into a fine player, noted for straight hitting and good putting. Anderson's method was to play steadily and on one occasion at St Andrews he remarked that he had played 90 consecutive holes without a bad shot or one stroke made otherwise than he had intended. He was for a period professional to Ardeer Club, but returned to St Andrews to follow his vocation of playing professional.

Anderson, Willie

Born in Scotland, 1878, died 1910. One of the Scottish emigrants to America, his flat swing won him the US Open in 1901, 1903, 1904 and 1905. He shares the record of four Open titles with Jones, Hogan and Nicklaus, and remains the only man to win three in a row.

Armour, Thomas D

Born Edinburgh, 1896. Died 1968. Open Champion, 1931. US Open Champion 1927. USPGA 1930. He had a distinguished amateur career – including the French Open Amateur and tied first place in the Canadian Open. He had the unique distinction of playing in 1921 for Britain against the US as an amateur and in 1925 as a professional for the US against Britain in the unofficial international matches that preceded the inception of the Walker Cup and Ryder Cup events. When he came to the end of his tournament career he quickly gained an outstanding reputation as a coach, and books he wrote on the technique of the game were best-sellers.

Auchterlonie, William

Born St Andrews in 1872, died 1963. Won the Open title at Prestwick at the age of 21 with a set of seven clubs which he had made himself and shortly afterwards founded the famous club-making firm in St Andrews. He never played with more than his seven clubs and was a great believer that a golfer had to be master of the half, three-quarter and full shots with each club. As professional to the Royal and Ancient Golf Club from 1935 to his death he saw one of his ambitions fulfilled–the Centenary Open at St Andrews in 1960.

Ball, John

One of the greatest amateur golfers of all time. Born at Hoylake, 24th December, 1862, his father owned the Royal Hotel, Hoylake, prior to the formation of the golf links and when there was a small racecourse on the land later formed into the Royal Liverpool Links. The links became John Ball's playground. In 1878, when fifteen years old, he competed in the Open Championship, finished fourth, eight strokes behind the winner and ahead of many famous Scottish professionals of that time. Between 1888 and 1912 he won the Amateur Championship eight times. In 1890 he was the first amateur to win the Open Championship. He played for England against Scotland continuously from 1902 to 1911, captaining the side each year. He was Amateur Champion in 1899 when war with South Africa broke out and Ball served in that campaign with the Cheshire Yeomanry and did not compete in the Championships of 1900-01-02. In the First World War he served in the Home Forces. He played in his last Amateur Championship in 1921, the year of the first American invasion, and he reached the fifth round although in his fifty-eighth year. Modest and retiring, he rarely spoke about his golf. On the morning of his last round in the Championship he remarked to a friend in the clubhouse, *If only a storm of wind and rain would sweep across the links from the Welsh hills I feel I could beat all of them once again.* But it was a week of torrid heat and he failed. He retired to his farm in

North Wales, where he died in December 1940.

Barton, Miss Pamela

Born London, 4th March, 1917. Died 13th November, 1943. At the age of twenty-two when the Second World War broke out, Miss Pamela Barton had already achieved great fame in the golfing world. She won the Ladies' Championship, 1936-39, runner-up, 1934-35, the American Ladies' Championship, 1936 and the French Ladies' Championship, 1934. In 1936, at the age of nineteen, she held both the British and American Ladies' Championships, the first person to do so since 1909. Miss Barton played for England in the home internationals in 1935-36-37-38-39; for Great Britain *v* United States in 1934-36; *v* France, 1934-36-37-38-39. She was a member of the Ladies' Golf Union teams which toured Canada and America, 1934, and Australia and New Zealand in 1935. Of a charming and cheerful disposition, Miss Barton, who became a Flight-Officer in the WAAF, was killed in a plane crash at an RAF airfield in Kent.

Braid, James

Born Elie, Fife, 6th February, 1870. Died London, 27th November, 1950. One of the greatest figures in golf of all times, James Braid, with Harry Vardon and JH Taylor, made up the Triumvirate which dominated British professional golf for twenty years before the First World War. He was the first person to win the Open Championship five times. This record was later equalled by Taylor and beaten by Vardon. Braid's achievements were remarkable for the short time in which they were accomplished. In ten years he won five times and was second on three occasions. His victories were in 1901, 1905, 1906, 1908, 1910. He won the Match Play Tournament four times, 1903-5-7-11, a record which was unequalled till 1950, and the French Open Championship in 1910. He played for Scotland *v* England in 1903-4-5-6-7-9-10-12 and for Great Britain against America, 1921. A joiner by trade, Braid played as an amateur in Fife and Edinburgh and in 1893 went to London and worked as a club maker. Taylor and Vardon were well established in the golfing world before Braid turned professional in 1896 and he quickly came into prominence by finishing level with Taylor, who by that time had been Champion twice, in a challenge match. In a historic international foursomes, Braid partnered by Alex Herd lost to Vardon and Taylor in a match for £400 over four courses. A tall powerful player who lashed the ball with *divine* fury, he was famous for his imperturbability; no matter how the game was progressing he always appeared outwardly calm and it was this serenity of temperament which assisted him to his Championship victories on two occasions. A man of few words, it was once said that *Nobody could be as wise as James Braid looked.* One of the founder members of the Professional Golfers' Association, Braid did much to elevate the status of the professional golfer. Braid made a major contribution to golf architecture; Gleneagles, Rosemount, Carnoustie and Dalmahoy all bear his stamp. He was admired and respected by all who knew him, as much for his modest and kindly nature as for his prowess as a golfer. He was professional at Romford for eight years and at Walton Heath for forty-five, and was for twenty-five years an honorary member of the latter club, becoming one of its directors. He was made an honorary member of the Royal and Ancient Golf Club in the last years of his life and had the distinction of being the only honorary member of the Parliamentary Golfing Society.

Campbell, Miss Dorothy Iona

Born Edinburgh, 1883. Died in America, 1946. Won British Ladies' Championship, 1909-11; Scottish Ladies' Championship, 1905-6-8; American Ladies' Championship, 1909-10; Canadian Ladies' Championship, 1910-11-12. One of only two women golfers to win the British, American and Canadian Championships, the other being Marlene Stewart (Mrs M Stewart Streit). Played for Scotland in international matches and for British Ladies *v* American Ladies.

Campbell, Willie

A native of Musselburgh, Willie Campbell never shirked a match anywhere or with anybody, and it was only on rare occasions that he did not win. He was a tall, strapping fellow and was regarded as one of the finest match players of the time, fearless and courageous. In 1887 Campbell was professional at Prestwick, and in the Open Championship of that year he seemed destined to win but took eight strokes with three holes left. He joined the outflow of Scots professionals to the USA in 1891 where he died at the age of 33.

Compston, Archie Edward Wones

Born Penn, Wolverhampton, 14th January, 1893, died September, 1962. One of the outstanding personalities of British golf in the years between the two world wars who fought hard to resist the developing dominance of the American invasion. He played in three Ryder Cup matches–in 1927, 1929 and 1931. In a 72 hole Challenge match he beat Hagen by 18 and 17 in 1928 at Moor

Park and in the Open which followed he finished third to Hagen. He tied for second place in the Open of 1925.

Darwin, Bernard

One of the most respected and widely known personalities in the game died soon after his 85th birthday in 1961. As a graceful and authoritative writer on golf and golfers he had no equal. He knew intimately every player and every course of note throughout the world, and his phenomenal memory, fluent pen and gentle humour established him as the top historian of the game over many years. In 1937 he was awarded the CBE for his services to literature which included journalism, books of children's stories and other sports besides golf. He was captain of the Royal and Ancient Club in 1934-35, and played internationally for England from 1902 until 1924 and in the first Walker Cup match (1922). He had travelled to the US to report the match for *The Times* and had been called in to play and captain the side when Robert Harris fell ill. During his playing career he won many amateur titles and trophies. He was a grandson of Charles Darwin.

The Dolemans

Four brothers, natives of Musselburgh, who were associated with golf for seventy years. John, born 1826, died at Musselburgh 1918; AH, born 1836, died at Blackpool 1914; William born 1838, died at Glasgow 1918, and Frank born Musselburgh 1848, died Edinburgh, 1929. William was the best player. He was first amateur in the Open Championship in 1865-68, 1870 and 1872. He played in nearly every Amateur Championship up to 1911, and at Hoylake in 1910, when 73 years of age, he won his tie in the first round. AH was one of the pioneers of golf in England, and founder of golf at Lytham and St Annes. John, the eldest, introduced golf to Nottingham. In 1908 he took part in an octogenarian foursome, which was continued annually until 1914. Frank was a club maker and for many years he carried on a golf club making business at the ancient Wright's Houses, Bruntsfield Links, Edinburgh.

Duncan, George

Died on 15th January, 1964, aged 80. He is the last Scottish-born winner of the Open title domiciled in Britain. He won the title in 1920 and his victory was achieved after two opening rounds of 80 which left him 13 strokes behind the leader. Two years later, at Sandwich, he finished second to Hagen after one of the most exciting finishes up to that time. Hagen had finished and was already being hailed as the winner when Duncan, a very late starter, reached the 18th hole needing a 4 to tie. He failed but his round was notable as the only one under 70 in that Open and the first to break 70 in the Open since 1904. Prior to the first war, Duncan was a prominent challenger to the established Triumvirate and would probably have achieved greater fame but for the war years during which he would have been at his prime. One of the fastest players of all time, he wasted no time especially on the greens and his book *Golf at a Gallop* was appropriately titled.

The Dunns

The twin brothers Dunn, born at Musselburgh in 1821, were prominent in golf between 1840 and 1860. In 1849, old Willie Dunn and Jamie Dunn played their great match against Allan Robertson and old Tom Morris. Willie Dunn became custodian in the Blackheath Links until 1864, and he then returned to Leith, and later to North Berwick, where he died at the age of 59. Willie Dunn was celebrated for the peculiar grace of his style and, as the longest driver of his day, he was a doughty match fighter, and one of his famous games was with Allan Robertson in 1843, when he played the St Andrews champion 20 rounds, and lost by 2 rounds and 1 to play. Another famous match was in 1852, when, partnered by Sir Robert Hay, he played Allan Robertson and Old Tom. Jamie Dunn, his twin brother, was also a fine player. Willie's son went to America, and won the first Championship of America in 1894. He was among the first to experiment with the idea of steel shafts. About 1900 he inserted thin steel rods in split cane and lancewood shafts. He invented a coneshaped paper tee, the forerunner of the wooden tee and was a pioneer of indoor golf schools. He died in London in 1952.

Ferguson, Bob

Born Musselburgh, 1848. Died 1915. Started to caddie on Musselburgh when aged 8. In 1866, when 18, he won the first prize in the Leith Tournament, in which all the great professionals of the day took part. The late Sir Charles Tennant put up the money for young Ferguson, who, in 1868 and 1869, beat Tom Morris six times. In 1875, at Hoylake, with young Tom Morris representing Scotland in a foursome, he beat Bob Kirk, Blackheath, and John Allan, Westward Ho! representing England. He won the Open Championship in 1880, 1881, and 1882. In 1883 he tied with Willie Fernie, losing the 36-hole play-off by one stroke. After this Championship he became ill with typhoid, and was never able to reproduce his great form. He became the custodian of the Musselburgh links, taught the young and was widely respected in the community.

Fernie, Willie

Born St Andrews 1851; died Troon, June 1924. In 1880 he went to Dumfries as greenkeeper. In 1882 he was second to Bob Ferguson in the Open Championship and after a tie with the same player he won the Open Championship in 1883 at Musselburgh after a 36-hole play-off. He became professional to Felixstowe and Ardeer and in 1887 to Troon, and was there as professional until February 1924. He was a very stylish player and in great demand as a teacher. He played in many important stake matches, the two biggest being against Andrew Kirkaldy over Troon, Prestwick and St Andrews which he won by 4 and 3, and against Willie Park over Musselburgh and Troon which he lost by 13 and 12. He played for Scotland against England in 1904.

Hagen, Walter C

Born Rochester, New York, 21st December, 1892. Died October, 1969. The first of the great golfers with star quality. People flocked to see him as much because he was a *character* as for his outstanding skill and many achievements. He did not want to be a millionaire, but merely to live like one, and this he did in dramatic style as when he used a hired Rolls-Royce as a changing room at the Open because professionals were not admitted to the clubhouse, and when he gave the whole of his first prize in the Open to his caddie. He also pioneered stylish dressing on the course. As a player he had great mastery of the recovery shot, nerves of steel beneath his debonair exterior and a fine putting touch. His best achievement was probably his four consecutive wins in the USPGA championship when the event was decided by matchplay over 36 holes. He won the US Open in 1914 and 1919 and the Open in 1922-24-28-29 and represented the US against Britain on seven occasions. His world tours with Kirkwood, his extrovert approach and the entertainment he provided on and off the course were the forerunners of the spectacular development of golf as a spectator sport. In spite of his being a contemporary of the immortal Bobby Jones, his personality was such that he was never overshadowed.

Herd, Alexander (Sandy)

Born at St Andrews in 1868, died London, 18th February, 1944. His life in the forefront of the game was more prolonged than his contemporaries of the Victorian era, and when he took part in his last Open at St Andrews in 1939 he was 71 and his appearances in the Championship covered a span of 54 years. A brilliant shot player, success often eluded him as he was prone to leave his putts short and to indecision. On his first appearance in the Open, at the age of 17, he possessed only four clubs and although he was frequently in contention it was not until 1902 that he won the Championship. He was the first player to win the Open using a rubber-cored ball. In 1920 at Deal and again the following year at St Andrews he was joint leader in the Open after three rounds. In 1926, aged 58, he won the PGA match-play tournament at Royal Mid-Surrey in a 36-hole final, having played five rounds in the previous three days to reach it. Those three achievements in his fifties are convincing proof of the longevity of his game. His life in golf brought him into competition with all the great Victorians – Taylor, Vardon, Kirkaldy, Braid and Park – and continued through the Jones and Hagen era up to the days of Locke, Cotton, Rees and Sarazen and others who, over 100 years after Herd's birth, were still playing Open Championship golf.

Hilton, Harold Horsfall

Born at West Kirby, a few miles from Hoylake, 12th January, 1869. Died 5th March, 1942. He was one of the most scientific of golfers. He learned his game at Royal Liverpool, where he won success in Boys' Competitions. In 1892, the year the Open Championship was extended to 72 holes, he won, and again in 1897. He won the Amateur Championship and the Irish Open Championship four times each, the St George's Cup twice, the American Amateur Championship once and became the first player, and the only Britisher, to hold both the US and British Amateur titles at the same time. He was small, 5 feet 7 inches, but immensely powerful in build. Hilton made a major contribution to golf literature as the first editor of *Golf Monthly*.

Hunter, Charles

Born Prestwick, 1836; died Prestwick, 24th January, 1921. A caddie and club maker under old Tom Morris at Prestwick, he was for three years professional at the Blackheath Club, London, and succeeded old Tom as the Prestwick Club professional in 1864. He played in the first Open Championship at Prestwick in 1860, and he was a conspicuous figure at every championship and tournament held at Prestwick, acting as starter and in charge of the house flag up till the time of his death. He did not take much part in professional competitions, preferring to attend to his club making and his members. In fact, during one championship round, while playing a niblick shot, he received word that the Lord Ailsa wished him to come at once and pick him out a set of clubs. He put his niblick back in his bag, pocketed his ball and returned to his workshop. In 1919 he was presented with his portrait in oils by the Prestwick Club, and a replica hangs in the Club. At the Open Championship of 1914 at Prestwick, he was the recipient of a presentation from his brother professionals. As a man of fine integrity, his friendship was valued by all golfers of his time.

Hutchinson, Horatio Gordon

Born London, 16th May, 1859, died in London, 28th July, 1932; an eminent golfer from the early eighties until 1907. He was a stylish and attractive player. Won the Amateur Championship in 1886 and 1887, runner-up 1885 (the first year of the Championship), and he was in the final in 1903. He was a semi-finalist in 1896, 1901, and 1904. He represented England *v* Scotland 1902-3-4-6-7, and was chosen in 1905 but illness prevented him taking his place. His career in the front rank of the game extended over twenty years. He was a voluminous and pleasant writer on golf and out-door life. He was the first Englishman to captain the Royal and Ancient. In other years he was also Captain of Royal Liverpool, Royal St George's and President of Royal North Devon.

Jones, Robert Tyre

Born Atlanta, Georgia, USA, 17th March 1902. Died 18th December, 1971 after many years of a crippling spinal disease. By the time he retired from competitive golf in 1930 at the age of 28, Jones had established himself as one of the greatest golfers of all time, if not the greatest. He represented America in the Walker Cup from its inauguration in 1922 until 1930 and played in the match against Great Britain in 1921. His victories included the US Open in 1923-26-29-30 (tied in 1925 and 1928 but lost the play-off; second in 1922 and 1924); US Amateur 1924-25-27-28-30 (runner-up in 1919 and 1926); Open Championship 1926-27-30; Amateur Championship 1930. In 1930, Jones reached a pinnacle which will probably never be equalled when he achieved the Grand Slam–winning in one year the Open and Amateur Championships of America and Britain. He then retired from championship golf. His stylish swing was the subject of admiration wherever he went–full, flowing, smooth, graceful and rhythmical. Yet he was of such a nervous disposition that he was frequently physically sick and unable to eat during a championship. During his championship winning years, Jones was also a keen scholar and gained first-class honours degrees in law, English literature and mechanical engineering at three different universities. He finally settled on a legal career with his own practice in Atlanta. It was there that he and his friend Clifford Roberts conceived and developed the idea of the great Augusta National course and the Masters tournament, now a fitting memorial to the *Master Golfer* himself. In recognition of his great skill and courage, and the esteem in which he was held in Britain and St Andrews, he was made an honorary member of the Royal and Ancient in 1956 and two years later, when in St Andrews as captain of the US team in the inaugural competition for the Eisenhower Trophy, he was given the Freedom of the Burgh of St Andrews. As a final tribute, a memorial service was held for him in St Andrews. The 10th hole of the Old Course, St Andrews (previously nameless) is now called after him.

Kirkaldy, Andrew

Born Denhead, near St Andrews, 18th March, 1860. Died St Andrews, 16th April, 1934. A rugged type of the old school of Scottish professionals, he was the last survivor of that race. After army service in Egypt and India he was appointed professional at Winchester. He had no liking for the steady sedate life of an English professional and after six weeks returned to his native St Andrews, where he lived the rest of his days acting as a playing professional until he was appointed professional to the Royal and Ancient Golf Club. He was a man of powerful physique. He was a beautiful golfer to watch, particularly his iron shots. In the Open Championship, 1889, he tied with Willie Park at Musselburgh, but lost on the replay. He played in many money matches and the most notable was in 1895. JH Taylor had won the Open Championship in 1894, the first English professional to do so, and prior to the Open Championship, at St Andrews in 1895, the young English champion challenged the world for £50 a-side. Kirkaldy accepted and won by a hole. Candid, outspoken, sometimes uncouth, Kirkaldy in his old age was respected by princes and peers.

Laidlay, John Ernest

Born in East Lothian in 1860, Johnny Laidlay played high-quality golf for fifty years – a testimony to his technique and temperament. In all, he won more than 130 medals. At a time when golf was booming and the opposition tough, he won the Amateur Championship twice (1889, 1891) was runner-up three times and beaten semi-finalist three times. He was second in the 1893 Open Championship when his characteristically good putting failed. He played for Scotland every year from 1902 until 1911, when he was fifty-one. The longevity of his very individual swing was perhaps due to his early golfing experiences at Musselburgh where he saw Young Tom Morris, knew Willie Park well and played a lot with Bob Ferguson (including a famous round by moonlight). His contribution to the game was the overlapping grip – known erroneously as the Vardon grip. Laidlay played cricket for Scotland (vs Yorkshire – taking 6 wickets for 18 runs); he was a pioneer of wildlife photography and carved beautiful furniture. He died at Sunningdale in 1940.

Leitch, Miss Charlotte Cecilia Pitcairn (Cecil)

Born Silloth, Cumbria, 13th April, 1891. Died London, 16th September, 1977. Although Cecil Leitch had reached the semi-final of the British Ladies' Championship in 1908 at the age of 17 and had won the French Ladies' Championship in 1912, it was in 1914 that she really established herself as Britain's dominant woman golfer when she won the English Ladies', the French Ladies' and the British Ladies'. She retained each of these titles when they were next held after World War I (the English in 1919 and the British and French in 1920) and who can say how many times she might have won them in the intervening years. In all she won the French Ladies' in 1912-14-20-21-24, the English Ladies' in 1914-19, the British Ladies' in 1914-20-21-26 and the Canadian Ladies' in 1921. Her total of four victories in the British Ladies' has never been bettered and has been equalled only by her great rival Joyce Wethered, against whom in the 1920s she had many memorable matches. Miss Leitch was an outspoken person who occasionally battled with the golfing authorities. Her strong attacking play mirrored her personality. Aged 19, in 1910 she accepted the challenge from Harold Hilton, at his peak, to take on any woman golfer over 72 holes giving half a stroke (a stroke at every second hole). Miss Leitch won this famous challenge match by 2 and 1 and later also beat John Ball, eight times Amateur Champion. Right to the end of her life, Cecil Leitch took an active interest in golf, attending major events whenever possible.

Little, W Lawson, Jun

Born Newport, RI, 23rd June, 1910, died February, 1968. As an amateur he established two records in that he won both the Amateur and American Amateur Championships in 1934 and again in 1935. In the final of the 1934 Amateur he won by the margin of 14 and 13 and for the 23 holes played he was ten under 4's. He turned professional in 1936 and won the Canadian Open in the same year and in 1940, won the US Open after a play-off.

Longhurst, Henry

Died 22nd July, 1978, aged 69. After leaving Cambridge University, he acquired a job as a golf writer in which he could indulge his love of the game and be paid for it. He never ceased to be amazed at his own good fortune. His regular weekly article in the *Sunday Times* became compulsory reading for the golfing cognoscenti. From writing he became involved in radio and, later, television, through which he became world famous as a commentator. Television was the perfect medium for his talents. His humour, easy manner, gifted observation and perception, mellow voice, calm delivery and economy of word were all perfectly suited to a slow-moving sport, and from his vast knowledge and understanding of the game, he was always able to fill in any gaps in the action with an apt story or two. Longhurst also wrote several amusing books about different periods of his life, including a brief spell as an MP. He was awarded the CBE for his services to golf and was one of only a handful of people to be made an honorary member of the Royal and Ancient Golf Club. His own golf was good enough to have won the German Open Amateur in 1936 and to be runner-up in the French Open Amateur in 1937.

Massy, Arnaud

Born Biarritz in 1877, died 1958. Was the first overseas player to win the Open in 1907 from Taylor, Vardon and Braid; tied with Vardon in 1911 and lost play-off, conceding on the 35th hole.

Mitchell, Abe

Born East Grinstead, 1887, died 1947. *The finest player who never won an Open Championship* was the tribute paid by JH Taylor. He finished in the first 6 five times in the Open and was 3 times winner of the Match Play Championship. Along with Duncan and later Compston, he was one of the few British hopes against the American invasion of the twenties.

The Morrisses

Old Tom Morris and his son, young Tom Morris, played a prominent part in golf in the period from 1850 to 1875. The father was born at St Andrews on 16th June, 1821. At the age of eighteen, he was apprenticed to Allan Robertson in the ball-making trade. When Morris was thirty years of age, Colonel Fairlie of Coodham took him to Prestwick, and he remained there until 1865, when he returned to St Andrews and became greenkeeper to the Royal and Ancient Golf Club, a position he held until 1904. Young Tom was born at St Andrews in 1851, and early exhibited remarkable powers as a golfer. At the age of sixteen he won the Open Professional Tournament at Montrose against the best players in the country, and he won the Championship Belt outright by scoring three successive victories in 1868-9-70. The Championship lapsed for a year, but when it was resumed in 1872, young Tom scored his fourth successive victory. There is no doubt that young Tom was the finest golfer of his time, but the tragic death of his wife, while he was engaged playing with his father in a great golf match at North Berwick against the brothers Willie and Mungo Park, had a most depressing effect on him, and he only survived his wife by a few months. Near the finish of this match, a telegram reached North Berwick intimating that, following her confinement, young Tom's wife was dangerously ill. The telegram was held over by Provost Brodie and not handed to young Tom until the end of the match. The yacht of John Lewis, an Edinburgh golfer, was put at the service of the Morrises but before the party embarked, a second telegram brought the sad news to young Tom that his wife had died. It was a mournful party that made the voyage across the Forth to St Andrews. The brilliant young golfer never recovered from the shock, and he died on Christmas Day of the same year, 1875, at the age of twenty-four. There was a second son, JOF Morris, who played in professional tournaments, but, although a fine golfer, he never approached the brilliant execution of his elder brother. Old Tom competed in every Open Golf Championship up to and including 1896, which, curiously, was the year Harry Vardon scored his first victory in the Open Championship. Old Tom died at St Andrews in 1908. He was respected throughout the golfing world for his honest, sturdy qualities. His portrait hangs in the Royal and Ancient Clubhouse, and the home green at St Andrews is named in his memory. A monument, with a sculptured figure of Young Tom, in golfing pose, was erected by public subscription in St Andrews Cathedral Churchyard and a smaller memorial stone was placed on the grave when Old Tom died.

Ouimet, Francis D

Born Brookline, Mass, 1893, died 1967. Described as the player who started the golf boom in the US when as a young amateur he tied with Vardon and Ray for the 1913 US Open and then won the play-off. In an illustrious career he won the US Amateur twice and was a member of every Walker Cup team from 1922 to 1934 and was non-playing Captain from then until 1949. The first non-British national, to be elected Captain of the Royal and Ancient Golf Club in 1951. He was prominent in golf legislation and administration in America and a committee member of the USGA for many years.

The Parks

Brothers Willie and Mungo Park of Musselburgh are famous in the annals of golf for the numerous money matches they played. Willie had the distinction of winning the very first Open Championship in 1860 and repeated his victory in 1863, 1866 and 1875. For twenty years Willie had a standing challenge in *Bell's Life*, London, to play any man in the world for £100 a side. Willie took part in numerous matches against Tom Morris for very large stakes and in the last of these at Musselburgh in 1882, the match came to an abrupt end when Park was 2 up with 6 to play. The referee stopped play because spectators were interfering with the balls. Morris and the referee retired to Foreman's public house. Park sent a message saying if Morris did not come out and finish the match he would play the remaining holes alone and claim the stakes. This he did. Mungo followed in his brother's footsteps by winning the Open Championship in 1874. He was for many years greenkeeper and professional at Alnmouth. Willie's son, Willie Jun, kept up the golfing tradition of the family by winning the Open in 1887 and 1889. He designed many golf courses in Europe and America, sometimes in conjunction with property development as at Sunningdale, and was the pioneer of the modern ideas of golf course construction. Like his forebears he took part in many private challenge matches, the one against Harry Vardon at North Berwick in 1899 being watched by the greatest crowd ever for that time and for many years afterwards. Willie Jun died in 1925 aged 61. The third generation of this golfing family sustained a prominent golf association through Miss Doris Park (Mrs Aylmer Porter), daughter of Willie Jun, who had a distinguished record in ladies' international and championship golf.

Philp, Hugh

The master craftsman among the half-dozen club makers located in St Andrews in the early days of the nineteenth century. He was especially skilled in making a wooden putter with a long head of pear shaped design. He is believed to have made not many more than one hundred putters. The wooden putter was for centuries a favoured club at St Andrews for long approach putting. The creations of Hugh Philp are highly prized by golf club collectors. After his death in 1856 his business was carried on by Robert Forgan.

Ray, Edward

Born Jersey in 1877, died 1943. His early days coincided with the famous Triumvirate and it was not until 1912 that he won the Open and was runner-up the following year to Taylor. He was again runner-up in 1925 at the age of 48. In 1913 he tied for the US Open with Ouimet and Vardon, but lost the play-off. After the war he returned to America and won the US Open title in 1920 and was the last British player to hold the title until Tony Jacklin, in 1970. He and Vardon were the only British players to win both the US Open and the Open until they were joined by Jacklin. Noted for his long driving and powers of recovery, he was invariably to be seen playing with a pipe clenched between his teeth.

Rees, David James

One of Britain's outstanding golfers from the 1930s to the 1960s. He played in nine Ryder Cup matches between 1937 and 1961, and was also non-playing captain in 1967. In 1957, he captained the only British PGA team to win the Ryder Cup since 1933. He was three times a runner-up in the Open Championship and once third, and won the PGA Match-Play Championship four times, and the Dunlop Masters twice, in addition to numerous other tournament successes in Britain, on the Continent of Europe, and in Australasia. At the age of 60, in 1973, he finished third in the Martini Tournament. He was made an honorary member of the Royal and Ancient GC in 1976. Born in March, 1913, he died in November, 1983.

Robertson, Allan

Born St Andrews, 1815, died 1858. According to tradition, he was never beaten in an individual stake match on level terms. A short, thick-set man, he had a beautiful well-timed swing, and several golfers who could recall Robertson, and who saw Harry Vardon at his best, were of the opinion that there was considerable similarity in the elegance and grace of the two players. Tom Morris, senior, worked in Allan Robertson's shop, where the principal trade was making feather balls. A disagreement occurred between Robertson and Morris on the advent of the gutta ball, because Old Tom decided to play with the invention, and Allan considered the gutta might damage his trade in featheries. Allan, through agents, endeavoured to buy up all gutta balls in order to protect his industry of feather balls. Allan Robertson and Tom Morris never seem to have come together in any single match for large stakes, but it is recorded that they never lost a foursome in which they were partners.

Sayers, Bernard

Born Leith, 1857, died at North Berwick, 9th March, 1924. Of very small stature, one of the smallest professionals, and light of build, he nevertheless took a leading position in the game for over forty years with his outstanding skill and rigid physical training. He engaged in numerous stake matches and played for Scotland against England in every match from 1903 to 1913, except 1911. He played in every Open Championship from 1880 to 1923. Of a bright and sunny disposition, he contributed much to the merriment of championship and professional gatherings. He taught princes and nobles to play the game, was presented to King Edward, and received a presentation from King George, when Duke of York.

Smith, Mrs Frances (*née* Bunty Stephens)

Died July 1978, aged 53. Dominated post war women's golf by winning the British Ladies' Championship in 1949 and 1954 (runner-up 1951-52), the English Ladies' in 1948-54-55 (runner-up 1959) and the French Ladies' in 1949. She represented Great Britain in the Curtis Cup on six consecutive occasions from 1950 to 1960. A pronounced pause at the top of her swing made her style most distinctive. She was awarded the OBE for her services to golf and was president of the English Ladies' Golf Association at the time of her death.

Smith, Horton

Died October, 1963, aged 55. Came to notice first from Joplin, Missouri, when 20 years old, and brilliantly embarked on the professional circuit in the winter of 1929 when he won all but one of the open tournaments in which he played. He was promoted to that year's Ryder Cup team and also played in 1933 and 1935. He won the first US Masters Tournament in 1934 and again in 1936 as well as more than thirty other major events. On his 21st birthday he won the French Open. He was President of the American PGA, 1952-54 and received two national distinctions: the Ben Hogan Award for overcoming illness or injury, and the Bobby Jones Award for distinguished sportsmanship in golf. The day after the Ryder Cup match which he attended in Atlanta in 1963 he collapsed and died in a Detroit hospital.

Smith, Macdonald

Born at Carnoustie in 1890 and died at Los Angeles in 1949. Was one of the great golfers who never won the Open Championship, in which he consistently finished in a high place, coming second in 1930 and 1932, third in 1923 and 1924, fourth in 1925 and 1934 and fifth in 1931. He went to America before he was twenty. In the Open Championship at Prestwick in 1925 he entered the last round with a lead of five strokes over the field, but a wildly enthusiastic Scottish crowd of 20,000 engulfed and overwhelmed him. The sequel of these unruly scenes was the introduction of gate money the following year and the dropping of Prestwick from the rota for the Open.

Tait, Frederick Guthrie

Freddie Tait was born at 17 Drummond Place, Edinburgh (his father PG Tait was a Professor in Edinburgh University), on 11th January, 1870. He was killed in the South African War at Koodoosberg Drift, 7th February, 1900. He joined the Royal and Ancient in 1890, and on 5th August that year he beat all previous amateur records for St Andrews by holing the course in 77, and in 1894 he reduced the record to 72. He was first amateur in the Open Championship in 1894 (Sandwich), 1896 (Muirfield), 1899 (Sandwich). He was third in 1896 and 1897. He won the Amateur Championship in 1896 at Sandwich, beating in successive rounds GC Broadwood, Charles Hutchings, JE Laidlay, John Ball, Horace Hutchinson, and HH Hilton, the strongest amateurs of the day. He repeated his victory in 1898 at Hoylake, and in 1899 he fought and lost at the 37th the historic final with John Ball at Prestwick. There is a Freddie Tait Cup given annually to the best amateur in the South African Open Championship. This cup was purchased from the surplus of the fund collected during the visit of the British amateur golfers to South Africa in 1928.

Taylor, John Henry

Last survivor of the famous Triumvirate – Taylor, Braid and Vardon – died at his Devonshire home in February, 1963, within a month of his 92nd birthday. He was born at Northam, North Devon, 19th March, 1871, and had been professional at Burnham, Winchester and Royal Mid-Surrey. JH won the Open Championship five times – in 1894-95-1900-09-13 – and also tied with Harry Vardon in 1896, but lost the replay. He was runner-up also in 1904-05-06-14. His brilliant career included the French and German Open Championships and he was second in the US Open in 1900. Among the many honours he received were honorary membership of the Royal and Ancient Golf Club in 1949. He was regarded as the pioneer of British professionalism and helped to start the Professional Golfers' Association. He did much to raise the whole status of the professional and, in the words of Bernard Darwin, *turned a feckless company into a self-respecting and respected body of men.* On his retirement in 1957 the Royal North Devon Golf Club paid him their greatest compliment by electing him President.

Tolley, Cyril James Hastings

Born in 1896, Tolley was a dominant figure in amateur golf in the inter-war period. He won the first of two Amateur Championships in 1920 while still a student at Oxford and continued to win championships and represent England and Britain until 1938. Among other titles he won the Welsh Open (1921 and 1923) and remains the only amateur to have won the French Open (1924 and 1929). A powerful hitter with a delicate touch, Tolley was a crowd pleaser. He is remembered as much for a match he lost as much as for some of his victories. Having won the Amateur Championship in 1929, Tolley was a favourite to win at St Andrews in 1930. The draw was unseeded and he met Bobby Jones in the fourth round. A huge crowd turned out to watch an extremely exciting match which Jones won on the 19th with a stymie. The rest is history. Tolley was elected Captain of the R and A in 1948. He died in 1978.

Travis, Walter J

Born in Australia in 1862, died in New York 1925. Travis was the first overseas golfer to win the British Amateur, at Sandwich in 1904. He won the title using a centre-shafted putter, which was subsequently banned for many years. He won the US Amateur Championship in 1900, having taken up the game four years previously at the age of 35. He repeated his victory in 1901 and 1903 and was a semi-finalist five times between 1898 and 1914, winning also the stroke competition six times between 1900 and 1908. The *Old Man* as he was known is reckoned to have been one of the finest judges of distance who ever played golf.

Vardon, Harry

Born Grouville, Jersey, died at South Herts on 20th March, 1937. Created a record by winning the Open Championship six times, his wins being in 1896, 1898, 1899, 1903, 1911 and 1914. He also won the American Open in 1900 and tied in 1913, subsequently losing the play-off. He had a serious illness in 1903 and it was said that he never quite regained his former dominance, particularly on the putting green. That he was the foremost golfer of his time cannot be disputed and he innovated the modern upright swing and popularised the over-lapping grip invented by JE Laidlay. Had it not been for ill-health and the intervention of World War I, his outstanding records both in the UK and America would almost certainly have been added to in later years. But in any event his profound influence on the game lives on. More than 100 years after his birth his achievements are still the standard of comparison with the latter day giants of the game.

Wethered, Roger H

Born 3rd January, 1899, in Malden, Surrey and died in 1983, aged 84. He was one of the outstanding amateurs of the period between the two world wars, winning the Amateur Championship in 1923, and being runner-up in 1928 and 1930. He won the President's Putter of the Oxford and Cambridge GS five times (once a tie) between 1926 and 1936, played against the United States six times between 1921 and 1934, and for England against Scotland every year from 1922 to 1930. He was captain of the Royal and Ancient in 1946. But he will probably be best remembered for the fact that he tied with Jock Hutchison, a Scot who had settled in the United States, for first place in the 1921 Open Championship at St Andrews, having incurred a penalty stroke in the course of the event by inadvertently stepping backwards and treading on his ball, while Hutchison, in the first round, had had a hole in one. Wethered was reluctant to stay on for the 36-hole play-off the following day because of a cricket engagement in England, but was persuaded to do so, only to be beaten by nine strokes, 150 to 159. No British amateur has come so close to winning the Open Championship since.

Wood, Craig Ralph

Born Lake Placid, New York, 18th November, 1901. Died 1968. Visited Great Britain for first time in 1933, and tied for Open Championship with Denny Shute, but lost on replay. Won American Open Championship, 1941; US Masters' Tournament, 1941; Canadian Open Championship, 1942; runner-up American PGA Championship, 1934. In 1936 second in USPGA Championship. A member of the American Ryder Cup team, 1931-33-35, and US Australian team, 1937. In 1939 tied for US Open, but lost on replay.

Zaharias, Mrs George (Mildred *Babe* Didrikson)

Born at Port Arthur, Texas, USA, in June 1915, and died of cancer at Galveston in September 1956. In the 1932 Olympic Games she established three world records for women: 80 metres hurdles, javelin, and high jump. On giving up athletics she took up golf and won the Texas Women's Open in 1940-45-46; Western Open, 1940-44-45-50; US National Women's Amateur, 1946. In 1947 won the Ladies' Championship, being the first American to do so. In August 1947 she turned professional and went on to win the US National Women's Open, 1948-50. In winning the Tampa Open, 1951, she set up a then women's world record aggregate of 288 for 72 holes. She was voted Woman Athlete of the year 1932-45-46-47-50, and in 1949 was voted Greatest Female Athlete of the Half-Century. First woman to hold the post of head professional to a golf club. The *Babe* was a courageous and fighting character who left her mark in the world of sport.

Part III
The Government of the Game

Introduction

The Editor and Publishers of the* Golfer's Handbook *are grateful to the General Committee of the Royal and Ancient Club for its agreement to reproduce the* Statement of Functions of the Club. *A brief history of how the Royal and Ancient came to be the Governing Body of the Game has been added, followed by a description of the important work of the Championship Committee, especially in its responsibility for the Open.

The Royal and Ancient Golf Club

In Britain it is not unusual for the Governing Body of a Sport to have its origins in a private club, which later comes to be recognised as the authority through which the game is administered. The Royal and Ancient Golf Club of St Andrews is a prime example and enjoys a similar status to the Marylebone Cricket Club. With the world-wide spread of golf and cricket this century, both have emerged as the international body to which most other countries look for rulings and guidance.

The Royal and Ancient Club's records date back to 1754 when the Society of St Andrews Golfers adopted the rules which had been formulated in 1744 by the Gentlemen Golfers of Leith, later to become the Honourable Company of Edinburgh Golfers, the older Club located across the Forth at Muirfield.

When in 1834 King William IV granted the St Andrews Gentlemen Golfers the right and privilege of using the title *Royal and Ancient*, the Honourable Company had temporarily lost cohesion and the R&A gradually acquired the status of the premier club. During the latter half of the Victorian age, in the 1880s and 1890s when, following the spread of the railway system, many new clubs were founded, they looked to the R&A for leadership and advice.

With the appointment of the first Rules of Golf Committee in 1897, the R&A became recognised as the Governing Authority in all countries except the United States and Mexico where the United States Golf Association controls the game. Golf federations of many countries are affiliated to the R&A. This is made clear in the *Statement of Functions* of the R&A, reproduced with the permission of the General Committee. The work of the Championship Committee is expanded in a note below, with particular reference to the Open Championship.

The success of the Open in recent years, both as a spectacle and financially, has meant that the R&A can now support fully the development of the game, while remaining the guardian of its traditions. Its encouragement of young players, especially through the Boys and Youths Championships and the Golf Foundation, has helped produce the higher standards of play and younger champions now so apparent to all followers of the game.

Statement of Functions of the Royal and Ancient Golf Club throughout the world

With the developing interest in golf and the increasing complexity of the administration of the game, the Royal and Ancient Golf Club feels that a statement of its activities in this field would be of interest.

The functions for which the Club is responsible fall into three clearly defined categories. First, functions of an international nature, secondly functions of a national nature, and finally, the running of a Club with wide national and international Membership.

International Functions

In 1897 the Royal and Ancient became the Governing Authority on the Rules of Golf at the suggestion of the leading Golf Clubs in the United Kingdom at the time. Since then an ever increasing number of countries have sought affiliation to it, until today they number over 60, including several other Unions or Associations (eg the Ladies' Golf Union, European Golf Association, South American Golf Federation and Asia-Pacific Golf Confederation).

The Club in its negotiations with the United States Golf Association on matters pertaining to the Rules of Golf is not merely representing Great Britain and Ireland, but these many countries as well.

In 1919, when it took over the running of the Open and Amateur Championships, the Royal and Ancient became responsible for the Rules of Amateur Status and in matters pertaining thereto likewise represents these many countries.

The Royal and Ancient also supplies one of the two Joint Chairmen of the World Amateur Golf Council which is responsible for the organisation of all World Amateur Team Championships.

There is close liaison at all times with the Professional Golfers' Association and the PGA European Tour.

National Functions

Prior to the First World War, a group of Clubs had been responsible for the running of the Open and Amateur Championships. In 1919 a meeting of these Clubs confirmed that the Royal and Ancient should be the Governing Authority for the game and agreed it should assume responsibility for the two Championships.

The decision that the Royal and Ancient should be the Governing Authority was endorsed at a Meeting of the English, Scottish, Irish and Welsh Unions in 1924, at which Meeting what is now the Council of National Golf Unions was formed with the object amongst others of directing the system of Standard Scratch Scores and Handicaps.

In 1948 the Royal and Ancient took over the Boys and in 1963 the Youths Championship from the private interests which had previously run them; this was done at the request of the individuals concerned. In 1969 the Royal and Ancient itself inaugurated the British Seniors Amateur Championship.

In addition to the organisation of five Championships, the Royal and Ancient is also responsible for the selection of Teams to represent Great Britain & Ireland in the Walker Cup, the Eisenhower Trophy, the St Andrews Trophy, and other International Tournaments. It is responsible for the organisation of such events when they are held in Great Britain and Ireland.

Club Functions

The Membership of the Club is limited to a total of 1,800, of which 1,050 may be resident in Great Britain and Ireland and 750 elsewhere: this Overseas Membership is spread over countries throughout the world.

The Membership both at home and abroad is representative and includes many who have given and are giving great services to golf in this country and abroad to many different Unions and Associations. This permits broad and effective representation on all the Club Committees concerned with international and national functions.

Exercise of International Functions

1. Rules of Golf

(a) Committee:

The Rules of Golf Committee exists for the purpose of reviewing the Rules of Golf from time to time and of making decisions on their interpretation and publishing these decisions where necessary.

The Committee consists of twelve Members elected by the Club, of whom three retire each year and are not eligible for re-election for one year, except in the case of the Chairman and Deputy Chairman, and of up to twelve additional persons invited annually to join the Committee from Golf Authorities at home and abroad.

At present the bodies represented are:

Council of National Golf Unions
United States Golf Association
European Golf Association
Australian Golf Union
New Zealand Golf Association
Royal Canadian Golf Association
South African Golf Union
Asia-Pacific Golf Confederation
South American Golf Federation
Japan Golf Association

(b) Revision of the Rules of Golf:
As the only other Governing Authority for the Rules of Golf is the USGA, the R&A works closely with this body when amendments to the Rules are under consideration for the purpose of maintaining uniformity in the Rules and their interpretation. Every four years a Conference takes place with the USGA for the purpose of deciding on the changes to be made. The Rules were last amended in January 1984 when a complete reorganisation and some simplification took place and the next revision will be held in 1987 with a view to introducing any agreed amendments in 1988. Although the Conference takes place quadrennially, the Rules are under constant review and investigations as to possible improvements start not long after a revision has taken place, so that ample time can be given to consult with interested parties.

Two years after a revision has taken place an important meeting is held with the USGA in the United States at the time of the Walker Cup to discuss progress and to start clearing the ground for the next Conference.

(c) Decisions:
The Rules of Golf Committee has a Decisions Sub-Committee which answers queries from Clubs and from all the Unions and Associations affiliated to the R&A. Those Decisions which seem to establish important or interesting points of interpretation are available in the form of a loose-leaf Decisions Service published jointly by the R&A and the USGA and issued world-wide. The number of subscribers to this Service is about 3,500 and is increasing steadily as golf expands.

2. Implements and Ball

The Committee consists of four Members elected by the Club, one Member of the Rules of Golf Committee and one Member of the Championship Committee, together with Consultant Members invited by the Committee to advise on technical matters. One of the elected Members retires each year but the Chairman may be re-elected immediately for the sake of continuity.

The Committee works in close co-operation with the USGA I&B Committee in interpreting the Rules and Appendices relating to the control of the form and make of golf clubs and the specifications of the golf ball to ensure that the game and established golf courses are not harmed by technical developments.

3. Rules of Amateur Status

(a) Committee:
The Committee consists of five Members, of which four are elected by the Club and one provided by the Council of National Golf Unions. There are also Advisory Members to the Committee, representing the same Golfing Authorities as on the Rules of Golf Committee.

(b) Revision of Rules of Amateur Status:
A procedure, similar to that for the Rules of Golf, is adopted for revision of the Rules of Amateur Status and no policy changes are made without full consultation with all the affiliated Unions, the USGA and the PGA.

(c) Decisions:
The work of the Committee consists of (a) dealing with Applications for reinstatement to Amateur Status, (b) answering inquiries about the nature of prizes, conditions for Tournaments, etc, arising out of the increased impact of commercial sponsors on Amateur golf and the issue of guidelines and Decisions, (c) answering queries from individuals regarding their own position under the Rules and (d) controlling Scholarships and other Grants-in-aid.

Exercise of National Functions

Championship Committee

The Championship Committee is responsible for the control of the five Championships and of the International Matches and Tournaments mentioned above.

The Committee consists of twelve elected Members elected by the Club, of whom three retire annually and are not eligible for re-election for one year. Two additional Members may also be invited to join the Committee annually together with two Business Members co-opted for four years.

For the organisation of any particular event, others may be co-opted, if required.

The work of this Committee has greatly increased in recent years, as is clearly evident from the staging of the Open Championship, for which prizes in 1984 amounted to £450,000. At the same time, more substantial reserve funds have been built up to ensure the continuance of the Open Championship as a premier world event.

The Committee makes annual donations to a number of golfing bodies, especially those concerned with the training and development of junior golf and for research on greenkeeping matters.

Selection Committee

The Selection Committee consists of a Chairman, who is a Member of the Club, and other Members, who need not be Members of the Club, appointed by the General Committee. These other Members have for some years now been representative of each of the four Home Unions. Normally they hold their appointments for four years.

Exercise of Club Functions

The domestic affairs of the Club are run by Committees which it is not necessary to describe in this statement.

It is appropriate, however, to mention that the Club does not own a Golf Course. It is, nevertheless, much concerned with the maintenance and improvements of all four Golf Courses in St Andrews. These Courses are controlled by the St Andrews Links Trust and are run by the Links Management Committee. Three of the Trustees and four Members of the Management Committee are appointed by the Club and equal numbers are appointed by the North-East Fife District Council. The Chairman of the Trust is appointed by the Secretary of State for Scotland and the current MP is also a Trustee. The Club contributes an annually negotiated sum to the Trust in return for Members' playing privileges.

Finance

International Functions:

After taking into account income derived from subscriptions to the Rules of Golf Decisions Service and the sale of official Rules publications, the net expenses of the Rules of Golf, Rules of Amateur Status and Rules for Implements and Ball are borne by External Activities.

National Functions:

Income and expenditure of all Championships run by the R&A and the expenses of Teams representing Great Britain & Ireland are accounted for in separate divisions of one Account.

Surpluses of all income over expenditure in the External Activities Account are held in reserve to ensure the continuance of the running of the various events at a high standard.

The Royal and Ancient Golf Club as a private Members' Club does not in any way benefit from the External Activities Account.

General Committee

Responsibility for directing and co-ordinating the three functions of the R&A – as a private club, as a governing authority for golf and as the body responsible for organising and running the championships and international matches – rests with the Club's General Committee, which controls all matters of policy. The Committee consists of sixteen R&A Members, eight of whom are elected by the Club; the other eight *ex-officio* members are the Captain and Chairmen of the Finance, Membership, House, Green, Rules of Golf, Championship and Amateur Status Committees.

The execution of the decisions of the Club Committees and of the decisions taken by the Members at Business Meetings is in the hands of the Secretary of the R&A, who is assisted by several senior officers and the appropriate infrastructure of secretaries and clerical staff.

Contacts with Affiliated Golfing Authorities

The R&A endeavours to consult with all those Golfing Authorities concerned whenever an issue of importance arises. This covers, in particular, matters relating to Rules of Golf, Rules of Amateur Status, and the Championships.

Meetings are held when appropriate with representatives of Golfing Authorities in Great Britain & Ireland and the European Golf Association. Consultations with other Golfing Authorities abroad are regularly conducted by correspondence.

In January 1970, a Conference attended by Golfing Unions and Associations in this country and representatives of the European Golf Association was held under the auspices of the R&A to discuss all matters of mutual interest, and in particular to establish the best means of communication in the future between the Unions and Associations concerned. This was followed by a similar Conference at Chantilly, Paris in 1976.

In May 1980 the first ever International Golf Conference was held in St Andrews at which 33 countries affiliated to the R&A were represented and to which the USGA, PGA and other golfing bodies in this country sent observers. Owing to the great success of this Conference the R&A has agreed to organise a similar one every four years starting in 1985.

The R&A is represented at Meetings of the World Amateur Golf Council and the Council of National Golf Unions and on the CCPR.

January 1985 (revised)

MF Bonallack OBE
Secretary
Royal and Ancient Golf Club
of St Andrews
Fife KY16 9JD

Rules of Golf

As Approved by
The Royal and Ancient Golf Club
of St. Andrews, Scotland
and the
United States Golf Association

25th EDITION
EFFECTIVE 1st APRIL 1984

The Championship Committee

Until 1919 the Open and Amateur Championships of Great Britain were organised by a group of leading Clubs in Scotland and England. The Club where the Championship was to be played was charged with running it for that year. In 1919, the Royal and Ancient, by then the recognised governing authority of the game, was invited to take over the responsibility for both Championships and ever since its Championship Committee has controlled both. Once the course on which a Championship is to be played has been decided, usually several years ahead, the Committee works closely with the Club concerned.

The Amateur, which is nearly as old as the Open, may have lost some of its public appeal with the growth of Professional golf and the defection of so many able young amateurs to its lucrative tour. Sadly too, match-play has not so much interest for today's spectators and virtually none for TV. However, the Amateur Championship is still considered the most prestigious event in the amateur game and is always played on one of the best courses.

The Championship Committee today

controls several more events besides the two oldest Championships. The Boys, started privately in 1921, and the Youths, in 1954, both now come under its wing, as does the Seniors which was inaugurated by the R&A in 1969. In addition, the biennial amateur matches against the United States and the Rest of Europe for the Walker Cup and the St Andrews Trophies respectively, are run by the Committee when played in Great Britain, as also are Boys' and Youths' Internationals against the Rest of Europe. The R&A Selection Committee chooses the team for all these amateur matches, as well as the team which competes for the Eisenhower Trophy, the World Amateur Team Championship. This was first played at St Andrews in 1958 and has since been held every two years in different parts of the world.

The remarkable development of the Open to the great occasion it is today has meant heavily increased responsibilities for the Championship Committee. TV and the media have given it an audience in millions compared with the few thousand interested in the past. The R&A's determination to match the growing interest with a new attitude and astute promotion has given the event the kudos and following it now enjoys. The last 20 years has seen the winner's cheque grow from £1200 to £70,000, the total prize money from £15,000 to £632,000, with the attendance nearly five times greater at close on 200,000. The financial success of the Open has provided considerable sums of money for the development of junior golf.

The R&A works closely with the Club of the course where the Championship is to be played, whose members take on many of the essential duties necessary if it is to run smoothly. These include spectator control where local Clubs take charge of a hole each, usually providing three-hour shifts of up to 16 members at a time. This can involve as many as 800 men daily. Local volunteer stewards also cover such diverse duties as course controllers, supervision of litter collection and spectator stand control. Security, courtesy transport, car park supervision and public catering, to name a few of the mass of services necessary, are provided under contract by companies expert in these fields. Close liaison with the area police authority is vital. Facilities for the Press, Television and the vast tented village, each involving several hundred people, occupy large areas and are a major limiting factor when considering possible venues for future championships.

Important for both competitors and spectators and appreciated by both is the radio network which provides up-to-the-minute scores and positions of the leading players which appear very quickly on the leader boards erected at strategic points round the course. The system developed over many years is as quick, informative and accurate as any in existence.

The Committee consists of thirteen Royal and Ancient members, who devote much time to their tasks. It has a full-time secretary who, together with the Secretary of the Club and some of his staff, is involved in the planning of the Open and other events throughout the year. Members of the Committee work long hours during Open week. From first light at about 5 am, when the Head Greenkeeper and a nominated member of the Committee tour the course deciding the pin positions on each green for the day, to dusk when the last competitor comes in, all are occupied, mostly out on the course at selected points, in two-way radio contact with the centre, ready to give a ruling when required. In the final rounds the leading players are accompanied by a member of the committee for the whole round.

The many stands erected around the course, providing seats for sometimes 18,000 spectators, often quite close to greens, make for special problems. A loose shot which ends under a stand will probably mean the ball may be dropped without penalty in an area nearby, which has been pre-designated by the committee; his shot should be of equal difficulty as it would have been if the stand had not been there. In these cases often an official decision is required.

At the end of every round each competitor's card must be immediately checked and recorded following which, in the case of a leader, he will meet the press in the interview room.

It is the Championship Committee too which decides if any round has to be halted, postponed or cancelled due to storm and tempest. Such decisions, so difficult with so many factors, consequent on a postponement, to be considered, have been eased a little with improved weather forecasting and continuous contact with the local weather bureau.

It will be seen that the work of the Committee is never ending with the myriad of tasks necessary to ensure the even flow to a Championship. The success of the Open is due to sound planning, moving with the times and the expertise of the R&A staff which is the executive arm of the Committee. The Open may be the Championship with which all are familiar; however, it must be remembered that the many other events under the R&A's control also require planning and organisation. The work for these events goes on largely unnoticed, but must not be forgotten.

Rules of Golf Committee

The Rules of Golf Committee shall consist of twelve Members of the Club to be elected by the Club, and additional Members not exceeding ten in number (who need not be Members of the Club) from Golf Authorities at home and abroad invited annually to join the Committee by the twelve Members elected by the Club. Such Invited Members shall, irrespective of the date of their invitation to become Members of the Rules of Golf Committee, remain so only until the date of the first Autumn Business Meeting occurring after their being invited to become Members but may again be invited thereafter. During their term of office such Invited Members (if not Members of the Club) shall be admitted as Temporary Members of the Club.

The Rules of Golf are the subject of quadrennial review by the R&A and the USGA in order to maintain uniformity and keep abreast of changing conditions.

Queries on the Rules may only be referred to the Rules of Golf Committee through the Secretary of the Club or the Association responsible for the competition. Many queries have to be returned unanswered because they have been sent direct to the Committee by individuals.

Rules of Golf Committee 1986/87

WFJ Bryce ***(Chairman)***
AC Caithness ***(Deputy Chairman)***
PJW Greenhough
HM Campbell
JS Scrivener
DI Pepper
GR Bristowe
PMG Unsworth
WJ Uzielli
Dr DM Marsh
RT Robinson

Additional Members

D Currie (CONGU)
JL Dupont (EGA)
H Stahlberg (EGA)
EJH Yong (Asia Pacific Golf Confederation)
GL Miles (Australian Golf Union)
JX Robert (Canada)
T Kawata (Japan Golf Association)
TM Gault (New Zealand Golf Association)
HL Whitefield (South African Golf Union)
JV Garasino (South American Golf Federation)
CG Spaeth (USGA)

CONTENTS

Other Forms of Play

Administration

Foreword
to the 1984 Edition of the Rules of Golf

The Royal and Ancient Golf Club of St. Andrews and the United States Golf Association have adopted the accompanying new Rules of Golf which will become effective on 1st April 1984.

The new Rules represent the first comprehensive revision of the Rules of Golf since international uniformity (other than the specifications of the ball) was achieved in 1952. The revision is based on a proposal submitted to golfing bodies around the world in 1981 for which strong support was received. In revising the Rules, the R. & A. and the USGA attempted, where feasible, to simplify them as well. The principal substantive changes are summarised on pages 187 and 188. The R. & A. and the USGA believe that the new Rules will be easier to learn and apply.

In order to achieve uniformity of interpretation of the Rules, the R. & A. and the USGA are combining their two Decisions services into a single completely rewritten Decisions service which will be available for worldwide reference in early 1984.

The R. & A. and the USGA, in consultation with other golfing bodies, will continue their close liaison in all matters concerning the Rules and their interpretation.

D.L. Hayes
Chairman
Rules of Golf Committee
Royal and Ancient Golf Club of St. Andrews

William J. Williams, Jr.
Chairman
Rules of Golf Committee
United States Golf Association

CHANGES
Principal Changes introduced in 1984 Code

Definitions
The Definitions have been placed in unnumbered alphabetical order. Some Definitions are also repeated at the beginning of their relevant Rule.
In the Rules themselves, defined terms which may be important to the application of a Rule are underlined the first time they appear.

Rules
The sequence of the Rules has been rearranged and incorporates certain Decisions made under the Rules.

4-1. Form and Make of Clubs
Previously, flat sides were allowed on all grips. In the new Rules, the grips for all clubs, except putters, are required to be generally circular in cross-section. Flat sides will continue to be allowed in putter grips.

5-3. Ball Unfit for Play
Player shall additionally give his opponent, marker or fellow-competitor an opportunity to examine the ball.

6-2b. Handicap – Stroke Play (handicap competition)
Handicap to be recorded on the competitor's score card before it is returned to the Committee.

6-3. Time of Starting
The penalty of disqualification for late starting has been retained. However, a Note has been added to provide that a Committee may, in the conditions of a competition, modify the penalty for being up to five minutes late to loss of the first hole to be played in match play or two strokes in stroke play.

7. Practice
Amended to limit practice between holes to putts or chips on or near the putting green of the hole last played, any practice putting green or the next teeing ground. Such practice strokes must not be played from a hazard.
The prohibition against practice on a competition course before a stroke play round has been expanded to prohibit also the testing of the surface of any putting green on the course before such a round.

8-1. Advice
A Note has been added permitting the Committee in charge of a team competition to allow each team to receive advice from one person such as a team captain or coach. However, this will not be permissible if an individual competition is being held concurrently with the team competition.

10. Order of Play
In all forms of match play, a player may require his opponent to replay a stroke played out of turn. Previously, in the case of three-ball and four-ball matches, a player could not require an opponent to replay a stroke played out of turn from through the green or in a hazard.
There is no penalty in stroke play for playing out of turn from the teeing ground or elsewhere unless competitors have agreed to play out of turn for the purpose of giving one of them an advantage. Previously, there was a penalty for deliberately playing out of turn from the teeing ground.

12-1. Searching for Ball
There is no penalty if a ball lying in casual water, ground under repair or a burrowing animal hole is accidentally moved during search. Previously, the player was exempt from penalty only if his ball was moved in probing for it.

12-2. Identifying Ball
Player shall additionally give his opponent, marker or fellow-competitor an opportunity to observe the lifting and replacement.

14-3. Artificial Devices and Unusual Equipment
Redrafted to include unusual equipment and to apply only during a stipulated round.

18-2. Ball at Rest Moved by Player, etc.
Ball moved without authority and not replaced. In stroke play penalty modified to two strokes.

18-5. Ball at Rest Moved – By Another Ball
In all forms of play, if a player's ball at rest is moved by another ball, the moved ball must be replaced and the other ball played as it lies. There is no penalty except that in stroke play, if both balls lay on the putting green prior to the stroke, the player of the stroke will continue to be subject to a penalty of two strokes. Previously, in singles match play, if a player's ball at rest was moved by his opponent's ball, the player had the option of playing his ball as it lay or replacing it.

20-1. Lifting
Before lifting a ball anywhere on the course which is required to be replaced, its position must be marked.

20-2a. Dropping – By Whom and How
In dropping a ball under a Rule, the player

is required to stand erect, hold the ball at shoulder height and arm's length and drop it. There is no restriction on the direction the player faces. If the dropped ball touches the player or his equipment before or after it strikes the ground, the ball must be re-dropped without penalty.

20-3b. Lie of Ball to Be Placed or Replaced Altered
Previously, if the lie of a ball to be placed or replaced was altered, the ball had to be placed in the nearest lie within *two* club-lengths which was most similar to that which it originally occupied. *Two* club-lengths have been reduced to *one* club-length and, in a bunker, the original lie has to be recreated as nearly as possible and the ball placed in that lie.

22. Ball Interfering with or Assisting Play
In all forms of play, an opponent or fellow-competitor is permitted to lift his ball if he considers that it might assist any other player or have any other ball lifted if he considers that it might interfere with his play or assist the play of any other player. Formerly, in singles and foursome match play, if the player considered an opponent's ball might assist him, the player could require his opponent to leave his ball there.

24-2. Immovable Obstructions
If a ball lies in a water hazard, the player is no longer entitled to relief without penalty if his swing or stance is interfered with by an immovable obstruction. On the other hand, if an immovable obstruction on a putting green, such as a sprinkler head, intervenes between a ball on the putting green and the hole, relief is permitted.

24-2b and 25-1b
Exceptions have been added to the Rules relating to relief from immovable obstructions, casual water, ground under repair and burrowing animal holes to provide there is no relief if (a) it is clearly unreasonable for the player to play a stroke because of interference by any other condition or (b) interference would occur only through use of an unnecessarily abnormal stance, swing or direction of play.

25-1. Casual Water, Ground Under Repair and Certain Damage to Course
If a ball lies in a water hazard, the player is no longer entitled to relief without penalty from a hole made by a burrowing animal, reptile or bird which interferes with his swing or stance.

26-2. Ball Played Within Water Hazard
Incorporates a new provision permitting a player who has played from within a water hazard and failed to cross any margin of the hazard, or is out of bounds, lost or unplayable, a further option under additional penalty to play his next stroke as nearly as possible at the spot from which the last stroke from outside the hazard was played.

29. Threesomes and Foursomes
Amended to allow partners in both match play and stroke play to change the order of teeing off from round to round.

30 and 31. Four-Ball Competitition
In four-ball match play and stroke play one partner may represent the side for all or any part of a match or round. The absent player/competitor may join his match partner between the play of any two holes, but not during the play of a hole.

31-4. Four-Ball Stroke Play
The gross scores to count must be individually identifiable on the score card.

The Rules of Golf

Section I Etiquette

Courtesy on the Course

Consideration for Other Players

The player who has the honour should be allowed to play before his opponent or fellow-competitor tees his ball.

No one should move, talk or stand close to or directly behind the ball or the hole when a player is addressing the ball or making a stroke.

In the interest of all, players should play without delay.

No player should play until the players in front are out of range.

Players searching for a ball should signal the players behind them to pass as soon as it becomes apparent that the ball will not easily be found. They should not search for five minutes before doing so. They should not continue play until the players following them have passed and are out of range.

When the play of a hole has been completed, players should immediately leave the putting green.

Priority on the Course

In the absence of special rules, two-ball matches should have precedence over and be entitled to pass any three- or four-ball match.

A single player has no standing and should give way to a match of any kind.

Any match playing a whole round is entitled to pass a match playing a shorter round.

If a match fails to keep its place on the course and loses more than one clear hole on the players in front, it should allow the match following to pass.

Care of the Course

Holes in Bunkers

Before leaving a bunker, a player should carefully fill up and smooth over all holes and footprints made by him.

Etiquette

Replace Divots; Repair Ball-Marks and Damage by Spikes

Through the green, a player should ensure that any turf cut or displaced by him is replaced at once and pressed down and that any damage to the putting green made by a ball is carefully repaired. Damage to the putting green caused by golf shoe spikes should be repaired on *completion of the hole*.

Damage to Greens—Flagsticks, Bags, etc.

Players should ensure that, when putting down bags or the flagstick, no damage is done to the putting green and that neither they nor their caddies damage the hole by standing close to it, in handling the flagstick or in removing the ball from the hole. The flagstick should be properly replaced in the hole before the players leave the putting green. Players should not damage the putting green by leaning on their putters, particularly when removing the ball from the hole.

Golf Carts

Local notices regulating the movement of golf carts should be strictly observed.

Damage Through Practice Swings

In taking practice swings, players should avoid causing damage to the course, particularly the tees, by removing divots.

Section II Definitions

Addressing the Ball

A player has "addressed the ball" when he has taken his stance and has also grounded his club, except that in a hazard a player has addressed the ball when he has taken his stance.

Advice

"Advice" is any counsel or suggestion which could influence a player in determining his play, the choice of a club or the method of making a stroke.

Information on the Rules or on matters of public information, such as the position of hazards or the flagstick on the putting green, is not advice.

Ball Deemed to Move

See "Move or Moved".

Ball Holed

See "Holed".

Ball Lost

See "Lost Ball".

Ball in Play

A ball is "in play" as soon as the player has made a stroke on the teeing ground. It remains in play until holed out, except when it is out of bounds, lost or lifted, or another ball has been substituted under an applicable Rule; a ball so substituted becomes the ball in play.

Bunker
A "bunker" is a hazard consisting of a prepared area of ground, often a hollow, from which turf or soil has been removed and replaced with sand or the like. Grass-covered ground bordering or within a bunker is not part of the bunker.

Caddie
A "caddie" is one who carries or handles a player's clubs during play and otherwise assists him in accordance with the Rules.

When one caddie is employed by more than one player, he is always deemed to be the caddie of the player whose ball is involved, and equipment carried by him is deemed to be that player's equipment, except when the caddie acts upon specific directions of another player, in which case he is considered to be that other player's caddie.

Casual Water
"Casual water" is any temporary accumulation of water on the course which is visible before or after the player takes his stance and is not in a water hazard. Snow and ice are either casual water or loose impediments, at the option of the player. Dew is not casual water.

Committee
The "Committee" is the committee in charge of the competition or, if the matter does not arise in a competition, the committee in charge of the course.

Competitor
A "competitor" is a player in a stroke competition. A "fellow-competitor" is any person with whom the competitor plays. Neither is partner of the other.

In stroke play foursome and four-ball competititions, where the context so admits, the word "competitor" or "fellow-competitor" shall be held to include his partner.

Course
The "course" is the whole area within which play is permitted (see Rule 33-2).

Equipment
"Equipment" is anything used, worn or carried by or for the player except any ball he has played and any small object, such as a coin or a tee, when used to mark the position of a ball or the extent of an area in which a ball is to be dropped. Equipment includes a golf cart, whether or not motorised. If such a cart is shared by more than one player, its status under the Rules is the same as that of a caddie employed by more than one player. See "Caddie"

Fellow-Competitor
See "Competitor".

Flagstick
The "flagstick" is a movable straight indicator, with or without bunting or other material attached, centred in the hole to show its position. It shall be circular in cross-section.

Forecaddie
A "forecaddie" is one who is employed by the Committee to indicate to players the position of balls on the course, and is an outside agency.

Ground Under Repair
"Ground under repair" is any portion of the course so marked by order of the Committee or so declared by its authorised representative. It includes material piled for removal and a hole made by a greenkeeper, even if not so marked. Stakes and lines defining ground under repair are in such ground.

Note 1: Grass cuttings and other material left on the course which have been abandoned and are not intended to be removed are not ground under repair unless so marked.

Note 2: The Committee may make a Local Rule prohibiting play from ground under repair.

Hazards
A "hazard" is any bunker or water hazard.

Hole
The "hole" shall be $4\frac{1}{4}$ inches (108 mm) in diameter and at least 4 inches (100 mm) deep. If a lining is used, it shall be sunk at least 1 inch (25 mm) below the putting green surface unless the nature of the soil makes it impracticable to do so; its outer diameter shall not exceed $4\frac{1}{4}$ inches (108 mm)

Holed
A ball is "holed" when it is at rest within the circumference of the hole and all of it is below the level of the lip of the hole.

Honour
The side entitled to play first from the teeing ground is said to have the "honour".

Lateral Water Hazard
A "lateral water hazard" is a water hazard or that part of a water hazard so situated that it is not possible or is deemed

by the Committee to be impracticable to drop a ball behind the water hazard and keep the spot at which the ball last crossed the margin of the water hazard between the player and the hole.

That part of a water hazard to be played as a lateral water hazard should be distinctively marked.

Note: Lateral water hazards should be defined by red stakes or lines.

Loose Impediments

"Loose impediments" are natural objects such as stones, leaves, twigs, branches and the like, dung, worms and insects and casts or heaps made by them, provided they are not fixed or growing, are not solidly embedded and do not adhere to the ball.

Sand and loose soil are loose impediments on the putting green, but not elsewhere.

Snow and ice are either casual water or loose impediments, at the option of the player.

Dew is not a loose impediment.

Lost Ball

A ball is "lost" if:

a. It is not found or identified as his by the player within five minutes after the player's side or his or their caddies have begun to search for it; or

b. The player has put another ball into play under the Rules, even though he may not have searched for the original ball; or

c. The player has played any stroke with a provisional ball from the place where the original ball is likely to be or from a point nearer the hole than that place, whereupon the provisional ball becomes the ball in play.

Time spent in playing a wrong ball is not counted in the five-minute period allowed for search.

Marker

A "marker" is one who is appointed by the Committee to record a competitor's score in stroke play. He may be a fellow-competitor. He is not a referee.

A marker should not lift a ball or mark its position unless authorised to do so by the competitor and, unless he is a fellow-competitor, should not attend the flagstick or stand at the hole or mark its position.

Matches

See "Sides and Matches".

Move or Moved

A ball is deemed to have "moved" if it leaves its position and comes to rest in any other place.

Observer

An "observer" is one who is appointed by the Committee to assist a referee to decide questions of fact and to report to him any breach of a Rule. An observer should not attend the flagstick, stand at or mark the position of the hole, or lift the ball or mark its position.

Obstructions

An "obstruction" is anything artificial, including the artificial surfaces and sides of roads and paths, except:

a. Objects defining out of bounds, such as walls, fences, stakes and railings;

b. Any part of an immovable artificial object which is out of bounds; and

c. Any construction declared by the Committee to be an integral part of the course.

Out of Bounds

"Out of bounds" is ground on which play is prohibited.

When out of bounds is defined by reference to stakes or a fence or as being beyond stakes or a fence, the out of bounds line is determined by the nearest inside points of the stakes or fence posts at ground level excluding angled supports.

When out of bounds is defined by a line on the ground, the line itself is out of bounds.

The out of bounds line is deemed to extend vertically upwards and downwards.

A ball is out of bounds when all of it lies out of bounds.

A player may stand out of bounds to play a ball lying within bounds.

Outside Agency

An "outside agency" is any agency not part of the match or, in stroke play, not part of a competitor's side, and includes a referee, a marker, an observer or a forecaddie. Neither wind nor water is an outside agency.

Partner

A "partner" is a player associated with another player on the same side.

In a threesome, foursome or a four-ball match where the context so admits, the word "player" shall be held to include his partner.

Penalty Stroke

A "penalty stroke" is one added to the score of a player or side under certain Rules. In a threesome or foursome, penalty strokes do not affect the order of play.

Provisional Ball

A "provisional ball" is a ball played under Rule 27-2 for a ball which may be lost outside a water hazard or may be out of bounds. It ceases to be a provisional ball when the Rule provides either that the player continue play with it as the ball in play or that it be abandoned.

Putting Green
The "putting green" is all ground of the hole being played which is specially prepared for putting or otherwise defined as such by the Committee. A ball is on the putting green when any part of it touches the putting green.

Referee
A "referee" is one who is appointed by the Committee to accompany players to decide questions of fact and apply the Rules of Golf. He shall act on any breach of a Rule which he observes or is reported to him.

A referee should not attend the flagstick, stand at or mark the position of the hole, or lift the ball or mark its position.

Rub of the Green
A "rub of the green" occurs when a ball in motion is accidentally deflected or stopped by any outside agency (see Rule 19-1).

Rule
The term "Rule" includes Local Rules made by the Committee under Rule 33-8a.

Sides and Matches
Side: A player, or two or more players who are partners.

Single: A match in which one plays against another.

Threesome: A match in which one plays against two, and each side plays one ball.

Foursome: A match in which two play against two, and each side plays one ball.

Three-ball: A match in which three play against one another, each playing his own ball.

Best ball: A match in which one plays against the better ball of two or the best ball of three players.

Four-ball: A match in which two play their better ball against the better ball of two other players.

Stance
Taking the "stance" consists in a player placing his feet in position for and preparatory to making a stroke.

Stipulated Round
The "stipulated round" consists of playing the holes of the course in their correct sequence unless otherwise authorised by the Committee. The number of holes in a stipulated round is 18 unless a smaller number is authorised by the Committee. As to extension of stipulated round in match play, see Rule 2-4.

Stroke
A "stroke" is the forward movement of the club made with the intention of fairly striking at and moving the ball.

Teeing Ground
The "teeing ground" is the starting place for the hole to be played. It is a rectangular area two club-lengths in depth, the front and the sides of which are defined by the outside limits of two tee-markers. A ball is outside the teeing ground when all of it lies outside the teeing ground.

Through the Green
"Through the green" is the whole area of the course except.

a. The teeing ground and putting green of the hole being played; and

b. All hazards on the course.

Water Hazard
A "water hazard" is any sea, lake, pond, river, ditch, surface drainage ditch or other open water course (whether or not containing water) and anything of a similar nature.

All ground or water within the margin of a water hazard is part of the water hazard. The margin of a water hazard is deemed to extend vertically upwards. Stakes and lines defining the margins of water hazards are in the hazards.

Note: Water hazards (other than lateral water hazards) should be defined by yellow stakes or lines.

Wrong Ball
A "wrong ball" is any ball other than:

a. The ball in play,

b. A provisional ball or

c. In stroke play, a second ball played under Rule 3-3 or Rule 20-7b.

R.1/2

Section III
The Rules of Play

THE GAME

Rule 1. The Game

1-1. General
The Game of Golf consists in playing a ball from the teeing ground into the hole by a stroke or successive strokes in accordance with the Rules.

PENALTY FOR BREACH OF RULE 1-1:
Match play – Loss of hole; Stroke play – Disqualification.

1-2. Exerting Influence on Ball

No player or caddie shall take any action to influence the position or the movement of a ball except in accordance with the Rules.

PENALTY FOR BREACH OF RULE 1-2:
Match play – Loss of hole; Stroke play – Two strokes.

Note: In the case of a serious breach of Rule 1-2, the Committee may impose a penalty of disqualification.

1-3. Agreement to Waive Rules

Players shall not agree to exclude the operation of any Rule or to waive any penalty incurred.

PENALTY FOR BREACH OF RULE 1-3:
Match play – Disqualification of both sides; Stroke play – Disqualification of competitors concerned.

1-4. Points Not Covered by Rules

If any point in dispute is not covered by the Rules, the decision shall be made in accordance with equity.

Rule 2. Match Play

2-1. Winner of Hole

In match play the game is played by holes.

Except as otherwise provided in the Rules, a hole is won by the side which holes its ball in the fewer strokes. In a handicap match the lower net score wins the hole.

2-2. Halved Hole

A hole is halved if each side holes out in the same number of strokes.

When a player has holed out and his opponent has been left with a stroke for the half, if the player thereafter incurs a penalty, the hole is halved.

2-3. Reckoning of Holes

The reckoning of holes is kept by the terms: so many "holes up" or "all square", and so many "to play".

A side is "dormie" when it is as many holes up as there are holes remaining to be played.

2-4. Winner of Match

A match (which consists of a stipulated round, unless otherwise decreed by the Committee) is won by the side which is leading by a number of holes greater than the number of holes remaining to be played.

A side may concede a match at any time prior to the conclusion of the match.

The Committee may, for the purpose of settling a tie, extend the stipulated round to as many holes as are required for a match to be won.

2-5. Claims

In match play, if a doubt or dispute arises between the players and no duly authorised representative of the Committee is available within a reasonable time, the players shall continue the match without delay. Any claim, if it is to be considered by the Committee, must be made before any player in the match plays from the next teeing ground or, in the case of the last hole of the match, before all players in the match leave the putting green.

No later claim shall be considered unless it is based on facts previously unknown to the player making the claim and the player making the claim had been given wrong information (Rules 6-2a and 9) by an opponent. In any case, no later claim shall be considered after the result of the match has been officially announced, unless the Committee is satisfied that the opponent knew he was giving wrong information.

2-6. General Penalty

The penalty for a breach of a Rule in match play is loss of hole except when otherwise provided.

Rule 3. Stroke Play

3-1. Winner

The competitor who plays the stipulated round or rounds in the fewest strokes is the winner.

3-2. Failure to Hole Out

If a competitor fails to hole out at any hole before he has played a stroke from the next teeing ground or, in the case of the last hole of the round, before he has left the putting green, *he shall be disqualified.*

3-3. Doubt as to Procedure

In stroke play only, when during play of a hole a competitor is doubtful of his rights or procedure, he may, without penalty, play a second ball. After the doubtful situation has arisen and before taking further action, he should announce to his marker his decision to proceed under this Rule and which ball he will score with if the Rules permit.

On completing the round, the competitor shall report the facts immediately to the Committee; if he fails to do so, *he shall be disqualified.* If the Rules allow the procedure selected in advance by the competitor, the score with the ball selected shall be his score for the hole. If the competitor fails to announce in advance his procedure or selection, the ball with the higher score shall count if the Rules allow the procedure adopted for such ball.

Note: A second ball played under Rule 3-3 is not a provisional ball under Rule 27-2.

3-4. Refusal to Comply with a Rule
If a competitor refuses to comply with a Rule affecting the rights of another competitor, *he shall be disqualified*.

3-5. General Penalty
The penalty for a breach of a Rule in stroke play is two strokes except when otherwise provided.

CLUBS AND THE BALL

The Royal and Ancient Golf Club of St. Andrews and the United States Golf Association reserve the right to change the Rules and make and change the interpretations relating to clubs, balls and other implements at any time.

Rule 4. Clubs

If a manufacturer is in doubt as to whether a club which he proposes to manufacture conforms with Rule 4 and Appendix II, he should submit a sample to the Royal and Ancient Golf Club of St. Andrews for a ruling, such sample to become its property for reference purposes.

A player in doubt as to the conformity of a club should consult the Royal and Ancient Golf Club of St. Andrews.

4-1. Form and Make of Clubs
A club is an implement designed to be used for striking the ball.

A putter is a club designed primarily for use on the putting green.

The player's clubs shall conform with the provisions of this Rule and with the specifications and interpretations set forth in Appendix II.

a. General
The club shall be composed of a shaft and a head. All parts of the club shall be fixed so that the club is one unit. The club shall not be designed to be adjustable except for weight. The club shall not be substantially different from the traditional and customary form and make.

b. Shaft
The shaft shall be generally straight, with the same bending and twisting properties in any direction, and shall be attached to the clubhead at the heel either directly or through a single plain neck or socket. A putter shaft may be attached to any point in the head.

c. Grip
The grip consists of that part of the shaft designed to be held by the player and any material added to it for the purpose of obtaining a firm hold. The grip shall be substantially straight and plain in form and shall not be moulded for any part of the hands.

d. Clubhead
The length of the clubhead, from heel to toe, shall be greater than the breadth from face to back. The clubhead shall be generally plain in shape.

The clubhead shall have only one face designed for striking the ball, except that a putter may have two such faces if the loft of each is substantially the same and does not exceed ten degrees.

e. Club Face
The face shall not have any degree of concavity and, in relation to the ball, shall be hard and rigid. It shall be generally smooth except for such markings as are permitted by Appendix II. If the basic structural material of the head and face of a club, other than a putter, is metal, no inset or attachment is permitted.

f. Wear
A club which conforms to Rule 4-1 when new is deemed to conform after wear through normal use. Any part of a club which has been purposely altered is regarded as new and must conform, in the altered state, to the Rules.

g. Damage
A club which ceases to conform to Rule 4-1 because of damage sustained in the normal course of play may be used in its damaged state, but only for the remainder of the stipulated round during which such damage was sustained. A club which ceases to conform because of damage sustained other than in the normal course of play shall not be used unless it is repaired so as to conform to Rule 4-1.

4-2. Playing Characteristics Not to be Changed
During a stipulated round, the playing characteristics of a club shall not be purposely changed, except that damage occurring during such round may be repaired, provided play is not unduly delayed. Damage which occurred prior to the round may be repaired, provided the playing characteristics are not changed.

4-3. Foreign Material
No foreign material shall be applied to the club face for the purpose of influencing the movement of the ball.

PENALTY FOR BREACH OF RULE 4-1, -2 or -3:
Disqualification

4-4. Maximum of Fourteen Clubs

a. Selection and Replacement of Clubs
The player shall start a stipulated round with not more than fourteen clubs. He is limited to the clubs thus selected for that round except that, without unduly delaying

play, he may:

(i) if he started with fewer than fourteen, add as many as will bring his total to that number; and

(ii) replace, with any club, a club which becomes unfit for play in the normal course of play.

The addition or replacement of a club or clubs may not be made by borrowing from any other person playing on the course.

b. Partners May Share Clubs

Partners may share clubs, provided that the total number of clubs carried by the partners so sharing does not exceed fourteen.

PENALTY FOR BREACH OF RULE 4-4a or b, REGARDLESS OF NUMBER OF EXCESS CLUBS CARRIED:

Match play—At the conclusion of the hole at which the breach is discovered, the state of the match shall be adjusted by deducting one hole for each hole at which a breach occurred. Maximum deduction per round: two holes.

Stroke play—Two strokes for each hole at which any breach occurred; maximum penalty per round: four strokes.

Bogey and par competitions—Penalties as in match play.

Stableford competitions—see Rule 32-1b.

c. Excess Club Declared Out of Play

Any club carried or used in breach of this Rule shall be declared out of play by the player immediately upon discovery that a breach has occurred and thereafter shall not be used by the player during the round *under penalty of disqualification.*

Rule 5. The Ball

5-1. General

The ball the player uses shall conform to specifications set forth in Appendix III on maximum weight, minimum size, spherical symmetry and initial velocity when tested under specified conditions.

Note 1: The Rules of the United States Golf Association specify a larger minimum size and also an Overall Distance Standard.

In international team competitions, the size of the ball shall not be less than 1.620 inches (41.15mm) and the Overall Distance Standard shall not apply.

Note 2: In laying down the conditions under which a competition is to be played (Rule 33-1), the Committee may stipulate that the ball to be used shall be of certain specifications, provided these specifications are within the limits prescribed by Appendix III, and that it be of a size, brand and marking as detailed on the current List of Conforming Golf Balls issued by the Royal and Ancient Golf Club of St. Andrews.

5-2. Foreign Material Prohibited

No foreign material shall be applied to a ball for the purpose of changing its playing characteristics.

PENALTY FOR BREACH OF RULE 5-1 or 5-2: *Disqualification.*

5-3. Ball Unfit for Play

A ball is unfit for play if it is visibly cut or out of shape or so cracked, pierced or otherwise damaged as to interfere with its true flight or true roll or its normal behaviour when struck. A ball is not unfit for play solely because mud or other materials adhere to it, its surface is scratched or its paint is damaged or discoloured.

If a player has reason to believe his ball has become unfit for play during play of the hole being played, he may during the play of such hole lift his ball without penalty to determine whether it is unfit, provided he announces his intention in advance to his opponent in match play or his marker or a fellow-competitor in stroke play and gives his opponent, marker or fellow-competitor an opportunity to examine the ball. If he lifts the ball without announcing his intention in advance or giving his opponent, marker or fellow-competitor in stroke play and gives his opponent, marker or fellow-competitor an opportunity to examine the ball, *he shall incur a penalty of one stroke.*

If it is determined that the ball has become unfit for play during play of the hole being played, the player may substitute another ball, placing it on the spot where the original ball lay. Otherwise, the original ball shall be related.

If a ball breaks into pieces as a result of a stroke, the stroke shall be replayed without penalty (see Rule 20-5).

*PENALTY FOR BREACH OF RULE 5-3:
Match play—Loss of hole; Stroke play—Two strokes.

*If a player incurs the general penalty for breach of Rule 5-3, no additional penalty under the Rule shall be applied.

Note 1: The ball may not be cleaned to determine whether it is unfit for play – see Rule 21.

Note 2: If the opponent, marker or fellow-competitor wishes to dispute a claim of unfitness, he must do so before the player plays another ball.

PLAYER'S RESPONSIBILITIES

Rule 6. The player

Definition

A "marker" is one who is appointed by the Committee to record a competitor's score in stroke play. He may be a fellow-competitor. He is not a referee.

A marker should not lift a ball or mark its

position unless authorised to do so by the competitor and, unless he is a fellow-competitor, should not attend the flagstick or stand at the hole or mark its position.

6-1. Conditions of Competition

The player is responsible for knowing the conditions under which the competition is to be played (Rule 33-1).

6-2. Handicap

a. Match Play

Before starting a match in a handicap competition, the player shall declare to his opponent the handicap to which he is entitled under the conditions of the competition. If a player declares and begins the match with a higher handicap which would affect the number of strokes given or received, *he shall be disqualified*; otherwise, the player shall play off the declared handicap.

b. Stroke Play

In any round of a handicap competition, the competitor shall ensure that the handicap to which he is entitled under the conditions of the competition is recorded on his score card before it is returned to the Committee. If no handicap is recorded on his score card before it is returned, or if the recorded handicap is higher than that to which he is entitled and this affects the number of strokes received, *he shall be disqualified* from that round of the handicap competition; otherwise, the score shall stand.

Note: It is the player's responsibility to know the holes at which handicap strokes are to be given or received.

6-3. Time of Starting and Groups

a. Time of Starting

The player shall start at the time laid down by the Committee.

b. Groups

In stroke play, the competitor shall remain throughout the round in the group arranged by the Committee unless the Committee authorises or ratifies a change.

PENALTY FOR BREACH OF RULE 6-3:
Disqualification.
(Best-ball and four-ball play – see Rules 30-3a and 31-2.)

Note: The Committee may provide in the conditions of a competition (Rule 33-1) that, in the absence of circumstances which warrant waiving the penalty of disqualification as provided in Rule 33-7, if the player arrives at his starting point, ready to play, within five minutes of his starting time, the penalty for failure to start on time is *loss of the first hole to be played in match play or two strokes in stroke play* instead of disqualification.

6-4. Caddie

The player may have only one caddie at any one time, *under penalty of disqualification.*

For any breach of a Rule by his caddie, the player incurs the relative penalty.

6-5. Ball

The responsibility for playing the proper ball rests with the player. Each player should put an identification mark on his ball.

6-6. Scoring in Stroke Play

a. Recording Scores

After each hole the marker should check the score with the competitor. On completion of the round the marker shall sign the card and hand it to the competitor; if more than one marker record the scores, each shall sign for the part for which he is responsible.

b. Checking Scores

The competitor shall check his score for each hole, settle any doubtful points with the Committee, ensure that the marker has signed the card, countersign the card himself and return it to the Committee as soon as possible. The competitor is responsible for the correctness of the score recorded for each hole.

PENALTY FOR BREACH OF RULE 6-6b:
Disqualification.

Note: As to the Committee's responsibility to add the scores and apply the recorded handicap, see Rule 33-5.

c. No Alteration of Scores

No alteration may be made on a card after the competitor has returned it to the Committee.

If the competitor returns a score for any hole lower than actually taken, *he shall be disqualified.* If he returns a score for any hole higher than actually taken, the score as returned shall stand.

Note: In four-ball stroke play, see also Rule 31-4 and -7a.

6-7. Undue Delay

The player shall play without undue delay. Between completion of a hole and playing from the next teeing ground, the player shall not unduly delay play.

PENALTY FOR BREACH OF RULE 6-7:
Match play—Loss of hole; Stroke play—Two strokes.
For repeated offence—Disqualification.

If the player unduly delays play between holes, he is delaying the play of the next hole and the penalty applies to that hole.

6-8. Discontinuance of Play

a. When Permitted

The player shall not discontinue play unless:

(i) the Committee has suspended play;
(ii) he believes there is danger from lightning;
(iii) he is seeking a decision from the Committee on a doubtful or disputed point (see Rules 2-5 and 34-3); or
(iv) there is some other good reason such as sudden illness.

Bad weather is not of itself a good reason for discontinuing play.

If the player discontinues play without specific permission from the Committee, he shall report to the Committee as soon as practicable. If he does so and the Committee considers his reason satisfactory, the player incurs no penalty. Otherwise, *the player shall be disqualified.*

Exception in match play: Players discontinuing match play by agreement are not subject to disqualification unless by so doing the competition is delayed.

Note: Leaving the course does not of itself constitute discontinuance of play.

b. Procedure

When play is discontinued in accordance with the Rules, it should, if feasible, be discontinued after the completion of the play of a hole. If this is not feasible, the player should lift his ball. The ball may be cleaned when so lifted. If a ball has been so lifted, the player shall, when play is resumed, place a ball on the spot from which the original ball was lifted.

PENALTY FOR BREACH OF RULE 6-8b:
Match play—Loss of hole; Stroke play—Two strokes.

Rule 7. Practice

7-1. Before or Between Rounds

a. Match Play

On any day of a match play competition, a player may practise on the competition course before a round.

b. Stroke Play

On any day of a stroke competition or play-off, a competitor shall not practise on the competition course or test the surface of any putting green on the course before a round or play-off. When two or more rounds of a stroke competition are to be played over consecutive days, practice between those rounds on any competition course remaining to be played is prohibited.

Exception: Practice putting or chipping on or near the first teeing ground before starting a round or play-off is permitted.

PENALTY FOR BREACH OF RULE 7-1b:
Disqualification.

Note: The Committee may in the conditions of a competition (Rule 33-1) prohibit practice on the competition course on any day of a match play competition or permit practice on the competition course or part of the course (Rule 33-2c) on any day of or between rounds of a stroke competition.

7-2. During Round

A player shall not play a practice stroke either during the play of a hole or between the play of two holes except that, between the play of two holes, the player may practise putting or chipping on or near the putting green of the hole last played, any practice putting green or the teeing ground of the next hole to be played in the round, provided such practice stroke is not played from a hazard and does not unduly delay play (Rule 6-7).

Exception: When play has been suspended by the Committee, a player may, prior to resumption of play, practise (a) as provided in this Rule, (b) anywhere other than on the competition course and (c) as otherwise permitted by the Committee.

PENALTY FOR BREACH OF RULE 7-2:
Match play—Loss of hole; Stroke play—Two strokes.

In the event of a breach between the play of two holes, the penalty applies to the next hole.

Note 1: A practice swing is not a practice stroke and may be taken at any place, provided the player does not breach the Rules.

Note 2: The Committee may prohibit practice on or near the putting green of the hole last played.

Rule 8. Advice; Indicating Line of Play

Definition

"Advice" is any counsel or suggestion which could influence a player in determining his play, the choice of a club or the method of making a stroke.

Information on the Rules or on matters of public information, such as the position of hazards or the flagstick on the putting green, is not advice.

8-1. Advice

Except as provided in Rule 8-2, a player may give advice to, or ask for advice from, only his partner or either of their caddies.

Note: In a team competition without concurrent individual competition, the Committee may in the conditions of the competition (Rule 33-1) permit each team to appoint one person, e.g., team captain or coach, who may give advice to members of that team. Such person shall be identified to the Committee prior to the start of the competition.

8-2. Indicating Line of Play

a. Other Than on Putting Green

Except on the putting green, a player may have the line of play indicated to him by anyone, but no one shall stand on or close to the line while the stroke is being played. Any mark placed during the play of a hole by the player or with his knowledge to indicate the line shall be removed before the stroke is played.

Exception: Flagstick attended or held up – Rule 17-1.

b. On the Putting Green

When the player's ball is on the putting green, the player's caddie, his partner or his partner's caddie may, before the stroke is played, point out a line for putting, but in so doing the putting green shall not be touched in front of, to the side of, or behind the hole. No mark shall be placed anywhere on the putting green to indicate a line for putting.

PENALTY FOR BREACH OF RULE:
Match play—Loss of hole; Stroke play—Two strokes.

Rule 9. Information as to Strokes Taken

9-1. General

The number of strokes a player has taken shall include any penalty strokes incurred.

9-2. Match Play

A player who has incurred a penalty shall inform his opponent as soon as practicable. If he fails to do so, he shall be deemed to have given wrong information, even though he was not aware that he had incurred a penalty.

An opponent is entitled to ascertain from the player, during the play of a hole, the number of strokes he has taken and, after play of a hole, the number of strokes taken on the hole just completed.

If during the play of a hole the player gives or is deemed to give wrong information as to the number of strokes taken, he shall incur no penalty if he corrects the mistake before his opponent has played his next stroke. If after play of a hole the player gives or is deemed to give wrong information as to the number of strokes taken on the hole just completed, he shall incur no penalty if he corrects his mistake before any player plays from the next teeing ground or, in the case of the last hole of the match, before all players leave the putting green. If the player fails so to correct the wrong information, *he shall lose the hole*.

9-3. Stroke Play

A competitor who has incurred a penalty should inform his marker as soon as practicable.

ORDER OF PLAY

Rule 10. Order of Play

10-1. Match Play

a. Teeing Ground

The side entitled to play first from the teeing ground is said to have the "honour".

The side which shall have the honour at the first teeing ground shall be determined by the order of the draw. In the absence of a draw, the honour should be decided by lot.

The side which wins a hole shall take the honour at the next teeing ground. If a hole has been halved, the side which had the honour at the previous teeing ground shall retain it.

b. Other Than on Teeing Ground

When the balls are in play, the ball farther from the hole shall be played first. If the balls are equidistant from the hole, the ball to be played first should be decided by lot.

Exception: Rule 30-3c (best-ball and four-ball match play).

c. Playing Out of Turn

If a player plays when his opponent should have played, the opponent may immediately require the player to abandon the ball so played and, without penalty, play a ball in correct order (see Rule 20-5).

10-2. Stroke Play

a. Teeing Ground

The competitor entitled to play first from the teeing ground is said to have the "honour".

The competitor who shall have the honour at the first teeing ground shall be determined by the order of the draw. In the absence of a draw, the honour should be decided by lot.

The competitor with the lowest score at a hole shall take the honour at the next teeing ground. The competitor with the second lowest score shall play next and so on. If two or more competitors have the same score at a hole, they shall play from the next teeing ground in the same order as at the previous teeing ground.

b. Other Than on Teeing Ground

When the balls are in play, the ball farthest from the hole shall be played first. If two or more balls are equidistant from the hole, the ball to be played first should be decided by lot.

Exceptions: Rules 22 (ball interfering with or assisting play) and 31-5 (four-ball stroke play).

c. Playing Out of Turn

If a competitor plays out of turn, no penalty shall be incurred and the ball shall be played as it lies. If, however, the Committee determines that competitors have agreed to play in an order other than that set forth in Clauses 2a and 2b of this Rule to give one of them an advantage, *they shall be disqualified.*

(Incorrect order of play in threesomes and foursomes stroke play – see Rule 29-3.)

10-3. Provisional Ball or Second Ball from Teeing Ground

If a player plays a provisional ball or a second ball from a teeing ground, he should do so after his opponent or fellow-competitor has played his first stroke. If a player plays a provisional ball or a second ball out of turn, Clauses 1c and 2c of this Rule shall apply.

10-4. Ball Moved in Measuring

If a ball is moved in measuring to determine which ball is farther from the hole, no penalty is incurred and the ball shall be replaced.

TEEING GROUND

Rule 11. Teeing Ground

Definition

The "teeing ground" is the starting place for the hole to be played. It is a rectangular area two club-lengths in depth, the front and the sides of which are defined by the outside limits of two tee-markers. A ball is outside the teeing ground when all of it lies outside the teeing ground.

11-1. Teeing

In teeing, the ball may be placed on the ground, on an irregularity of surface created by the player on the ground or on a tee, sand or other substance in order to raise it off the ground.

A player may stand outside the teeing ground to play a ball within it.

When the first stroke with any ball (including a provisional ball) is played from the teeing ground, the tee-markers are immovable obstructions (see Rule 24-2).

11-2. Ball Falling Off Tee

If a ball, when not in play, falls off a tee or is knocked off a tee by the player in addressing it, it may be re-teed without penalty, but if a stroke is made at the ball in these circumstances, whether the ball is moving or not, the stroke shall be counted but no penalty shall be incurred.

11-3. Playing Outside Teeing Ground

a. Match Play

If a player, when starting a hole, plays a ball from outside the teeing ground, the opponent may immediately require the player to replay the stroke from within the teeing ground, without penalty.

b. Stroke Play

If a competitor, when starting a hole, plays a ball from outside the teeing ground, *he shall be penalised two strokes* and shall then play a ball from within the teeing ground. Strokes played by a competitor from outside the teeing ground do not count in his score. If the competitor fails to rectify his mistake before making a stroke on the next teeing ground or, in the case of the last hole of the round, before leaving the putting green, *he shall be disqualified.*

PLAYING THE BALL

Rule 12. Searching for and Identifying Ball

Definitions

A "hazard" is any bunker or water hazard.

A "bunker" is a hazard consisting of a prepared area of ground, often a hollow, from which turf or soil has been removed and replaced with sand or the like. Grass-covered ground bordering or within a bunker is not part of the bunker.

A "water hazard" is any sea, lake, pond, river, ditch, surface drainage ditch or other open water course (whether or not containing water) and anything of a similar nature.

All ground or water within the margin of a water hazard is part of the water hazard. The margin of a water hazard is deemed to extend vertically upwards. Stakes and lines defining the margins of water hazards are in the hazards.

12-1. Searching for Ball; Seeing Ball

If a ball lies in long grass, rushes, bushes, whins, heather or the like, only so much thereof may be touched as will enable the player to find and identify his ball, except that nothing shall be done which improves its lie, the area of his intended swing or his line of play.

A player is not necessarily entitled to see his ball when playing a stroke.

In a hazard, if the ball is covered by loose impediments or sand, the player may remove only as much thereof as will enable him to see a part of the ball. If the ball is moved in such removal, no penalty is incurred and the ball shall be replaced. As to removal of loose impediments outside a hazard, see Rule 23.

If a ball lying in casual water, ground under repair or a hole, cast or runway made by a burrowing animal, a reptile or a bird is accidentally moved during search, no penalty is incurred; the ball shall be replaced, unless the player elects to proceed under Rule 25-1b.

If a ball is believed to be lying in water in a water hazard, the player may probe for it with a club or otherwise. If the ball is moved in so doing, no penalty shall be incurred; the ball shall be replaced, unless the player elects to proceed under Rule 26-1.

PENALTY FOR BREACH OF RULE 12-1:
Match play—Loss of hole; Stroke play—Two strokes.

12-2. Identifying Ball

The responsibility for playing the proper ball rests with the player. Each player should put an identification mark on his ball.

Except in a hazard, the player may, without penalty, lift a ball he believes to be his own for the purpose of identification and clean it to the extent necessary for identification. If the ball is the player's ball, he shall replace it on the spot from which it was lifted. Before the player lifts the ball, he shall announce his intention to his opponent in match play or his marker or a fellow-competitor in stroke play and give his opponent, marker or fellow-competitor an opportunity to observe the lifting and replacement. If he lifts the ball without announcing his intention in advance or giving his opponent, marker or fellow-competitor an opportunity to observe, or if he lifts his ball for identification in a hazard, *he shall incur a penalty of one stroke* and the ball shall be replaced.

If a player who is required to replace a ball fails to do so, *he shall incur the penalty* for a breach of Rule 20-3a, but no additional penalty under Rule 12-2 shall be applied.

Rule 13. Ball Played As It Lies; Lie, Area of Intended Swing and Line of Play; Stance

Definitions

A "hazard" is any bunker or water hazard.

A "bunker" is a hazard consisting of a prepared area of ground, often a hollow, from which turf or soil has been removed and replaced with sand or the like. Grass-covered ground bordering or within a bunker is not part of the bunker.

A "water hazard" is any sea, lake, pond, river, ditch, surface drainage ditch or other open water course (whether or not containing water) and anything of a similar nature.

All ground or water within the margin of a water hazard is part of the water hazard. The margin of a water hazard is deemed to extend vertically upwards. Stakes and lines defining the margins of water hazards are in the hazards.

13-1. Ball Played As It Lies

The ball shall be played as it lies, except as otherwise provided in the Rules. (Ball at rest moved – Rule 18.)

13-2. Improving Lie, Area of Intended Swing or Line of Play

Except as provided in the Rules, a player shall not improve or allow to be improved:
the position or lie of his ball,
the area of his intended swing or
his line of play
by any of the following actions:
moving, bending or breaking anything growing or fixed (including objects defining out of bounds) or
removing or pressing down sand, loose soil, replaced divots, other cut turf placed in position or other irregularities of surface
except as follows:
as may occur in fairly taking his stance, in making a stroke or the backward movement of his club for a stroke.
on the teeing ground in creating or eliminating irregularities of surface, or
on the putting green in removing sand and loose soil as provided in Rule 16-1a or in repairing damage as provided in Rule 16-1c.

The club may be grounded only lightly and shall not be pressed on the ground.

Exception: Ball lying in or touching hazard – Rule 13-4.

13-3. Building Stance

A player is entitled to place his feet firmly in taking his stance, but he shall not build a stance.

13-4. Ball Lying in or Touching Hazard

Except as provided in the Rules, before making a stroke at a ball which lies in or touches a hazard (whether a bunker or a water hazard), the player shall not:

a. Test the condition of the hazard or any similar hazard,
b. Touch the ground in the hazard or water in the water hazard with a club or otherwise, or
c. Touch or move a loose impediment lying in or touching the hazard.

Exceptions:

1. At address or in the backward movement for the stroke, the club may touch any obstruction or any grass, bush, tree or other growing thing.

2. The player may place his clubs in a hazard, provided nothing is done which may constitute testing the soil or improving the lie of the ball.

3. The player after playing the stroke, or his caddie at any time without the authority of the player, may smooth sand or soil in the hazard, provided that, if the ball still lies in the hazard, nothing is done which

improves the lie of the ball or assists the player in his subsequent play of the hole.

PENALTY FOR BREACH OF RULE:
Match play—Loss of hole; Stroke play—Two strokes.
(Searching for ball – Rule 12-1.)

Rule 14. Striking the Ball

Definition

A "stroke" is the forward movement of the club made with the intention of fairly striking at and moving the ball.

14-1. Ball to be Fairly Struck At

The ball shall be fairly struck at with the head of the club and must not be pushed, scraped or spooned.

14-2. Assistance

In making a stroke, a player shall not accept physical assistance or protection from the elements.

PENALTY FOR BREACH OF RULE 14-1 or -2;
Match play—Loss of hole; Stroke play—Two strokes.

14-3. Artificial Devices and Unusual Equipment

Except as provided in the Rules, during a stipulated round the player shall not use any artificial device or unusual equipment:

a. For the purpose of gauging or measuring distance or conditions which might affect his play; or

b. Which might assist him in gripping the club, in making a stroke or in his play, except that plain gloves may be worn, resin, tape or gauze may be applied to the grip (provided such application does not render the grip non-conforming under Rule 4-1c) and a towel or handkerchief may be wrapped around the grip.

PENALTY FOR BREACH OF RULE 14-3:
Disqualification.

14-4. Striking the Ball More than Once

If a player's club strikes the ball more than once in the course of a stroke, the player shall count the stroke and *add a penalty stroke*, making two strokes in all.

14-5. Playing Moving Ball

A player shall not play while his ball is moving.

Exceptions:

Ball falling off tee—Rule 11-2.
Striking the ball more than once—Rule 14-4.
Ball moving in water—Rule 14-6.

When the ball begins to move only after the player has begun the stroke or the backward movement of his club for the stroke, he shall incur no penalty under this Rule for playing a moving ball, but he is not exempt from any penalty incurred under the following Rules:

Ball at rest moved by player—Rule 18-2a.
Ball at rest moving after address—Rule 18-2b.
Ball at rest moving after loose impediment touched—Rule 18-2c.

14-6. Ball Moving in Water

When a ball is moving in water in a water hazard, the player may, without penalty, make a stroke, but he must not delay making his stroke in order to allow the wind or current to improve the position of the ball. A ball moving in water in a water hazard may be lifted if the player elects to invoke Rule 26.

PENALTY FOR BREACH OF RULE 14-5 or -6:
Match play—Loss of hole; Stroke play—Two strokes.

Rule 15. Playing a Wrong Ball

Definition

A "wrong ball" is any ball other than:
a. The ball in play,
b. A provisional ball or
c. In stroke play, a second ball played under Rule 3-3 or Rule 20-7b.

15-1. General

A player must hole out with the ball played from the teeing ground unless a Rule permits him to substitute another ball.

15-2. Match Play

If a player plays a stroke with a wrong ball except in a hazard, *he shall lose the hole*.

If a player plays any strokes in a hazard with a wrong ball, there is no penalty. Strokes played in a hazard with a wrong ball do not count in the player's score.

If the player and opponent exchange balls during the play of a hole, the first to play the wrong ball other than from a hazard shall lose the hole; when this cannot be determined, the hole shall be played out with the balls exchanged.

15-3. Stroke Play

If a competitor plays a stroke with a wrong ball except in a hazard, *he shall add two penalty strokes to his score* and shall then play the correct ball.

If a competitor plays any strokes in a hazard with a wrong ball, there is no penalty.

Strokes played with a wrong ball do not count in a competitor's score.

If a competitor holes out with a wrong ball, but has not made a stroke on the next teeing ground or, in the case of the last hole of the round, has not left the putting green, he may rectify his mistake by playing the correct ball, subject to the prescribed penalty. *The competitor shall be disqualified* if he does not so rectify his mistake.

Note: For procedure to be followed by owner of wrong ball, see Rule 18-1.

THE PUTTING GREEN

Rule 16. The Putting Green

Definitions

The "putting green" is all ground of the hole being played which is specially prepared for putting or otherwise defined as such by the Committee. A ball is on the putting green when any part of it touches the putting green.

A ball is "holed" when it is at rest within the circumference of the hole and all of it is below the level of the lip of the hole.

16-1. General

a. Touching Line of Putt

The line of putt must not be touched except:

(i) the player may move sand, loose soil and other loose impediments by picking them up or by brushing them aside with his hand or a club without pressing anything down;
(ii) in addressing the ball, the player may place the club in front of the ball without pressing anything down;
(iii) in measuring – Rule 10-4;
(iv) in lifting the ball – Rule 16-1b;
(v) in repairing old hole plugs or ball marks – Rule 16-1c; and
(vi) in removing movable objects – Rule 24-1.

(Indicating line for putting on putting green—Rule 8-2b.)

b. Lifting Ball

A ball on the putting green may be lifted and, if desired, cleaned. A ball so lifted shall be replaced on the spot from which it was lifted.

c. Repair of Hole Plugs and Ball Marks

The player may repair an old hole plug or damage to the putting green caused by the impact of a ball, whether or not the player's ball lies on the putting green. If the ball is moved in the process of such repair, it shall be replaced, without penalty.

d. Testing Surface

During the play of a hole, a player shall not test the surface of the putting green by rolling a ball or roughening or scraping the surface.

e. Standing Astride or on Line of Putt

The player shall not make a stroke on the putting green from a stance astride, or with either foot touching, the line of the putt or an extension of that line behind the ball. For the purpose of this Clause only, the line of putt does not extend beyond the hole.

f. Position of Caddie or Partner

While making the stroke, the player shall not allow his caddie, his partner or his partner's caddie to position himself on or close to an extension of the line of putt behind the ball.

g. Other Ball to Be at Rest

A player shall not play a stroke or touch his ball in play while another ball is in motion after a stroke on the putting green.

h. Ball Overhanging Hole

When any part of the ball overhangs the edge of the hole, the player is allowed enough time to reach the hole without unreasonable delay and an additional ten seconds to determine whether the ball is at rest. If by then the ball has not fallen into the hole, it is deemed to be at rest.

PENALTY FOR BREACH OF RULE 16-1:
Match play—Loss of hole; Stroke play—Two strokes.

16-2. Conceding Opponent's Next Stroke

When the opponent's ball is at rest or is deemed to be at rest, the player may concede the opponent to have holed out with his next stroke and the ball may be removed by either side with a club or otherwise.

Rule 17. The Flagstick

17-1. Flagstick Attended, Removed or Held Up

Before and during the stroke, the player may have the flagstick attended, removed or held up to indicate the position of the hole. This may be done only on the authority of the player before he plays his stroke.

If the flagstick is attended or removed by an opponent, a fellow-competitor or the caddie of either with the player's knowledge and no objection is made, the player shall be deemed to have authorised it. If a player or a caddie attends or removes the flagstick or stands near the hole while a stroke is being played, he shall be deemed to attend the flagstick until the ball comes to rest.

If the flagstick is not attended before the stroke is played, it shall not be attended or removed while the ball is in motion.

17-2. Unauthorised Attendance

a. Match Play

In match play, an opponent or his caddie shall not attend or remove the flagstick without the player's knowledge or authority.

b. Stroke Play

In stroke play, if a fellow-competitor or his caddie attends or removes the flagstick without the competitor's knowledge or authority while the competitor is making a stroke or his ball is in motion, *the fellow-competitor shall incure the penalty* for breach of this Rule. In such circumstances, if the competitor's ball strikes the flagstick or the person attending it, the competitor incurs no penalty and the ball shall be played as it lies, except that, if the stroke was played from the putting green, the stroke shall be replayed.

PENALTY FOR BREACH OF RULE 17-1 or -2: *Match play—Loss of hole; Stroke play—Two strokes.*

17-3. Ball Striking Flagstick or Attendant

The player's ball shall not strike:

a. The flagstick when attended or removed by the player, his partner or either of their caddies, or by another person with the player's knowledge or authority; or

b. The player's caddie, his partner or his partner's caddie when attending the flagstick, or another person attending the flagstick with the player's knowledge or authority, or equipment carried by any such person; or

c. The flagstick in the hole, unattended, when the ball has been played from the putting green.

PENALTY FOR BREACH OF RULE 17-3: *Match play—Loss of hole; Stroke play—Two strokes, and the ball shall be played as it lies.*

17-4. Ball Resting Against Flagstick

If the ball rests against the flagstick when it is in the hole, the player or someone authorised by him may move or remove the flagstick and if the ball falls into the hole, the player shall be deemed to have holed out at his last stroke; otherwise the ball, if moved, shall be placed on the lip of the hole, without penalty.

BALL MOVED, DEFLECTED OR STOPPED

Rule 18. Ball at Rest Moved

Definitions

A ball is deemed to have "moved" if it leaves its position and comes to rest in any other place.

An "outside agency" is any agency not part of the match or, in stroke play, not part of a competitor's side, and includes a referee, a marker, an observer or a forecaddie. Neither wind nor water is an outside agency.

"Equipment" is anything used, worn or carried by or for the player except any ball he has played and any small object, such as a coin or a tee, when used to mark the position of a ball or the extent of an area in which a ball is to be dropped. Equipment includes a golf cart, whether or not motorised. If such a cart is shared by more than one player, its status under the Rules is the same as that of a caddie employed by more than one player. See "Caddie".

A player has "addressed the ball" when he has taken his stance and has also grounded his club, except that in a hazard a player has addressed the ball when he has taken his stance.

Taking the "stance" consists in a player placing his feet in position for and preparatory to making a stroke.

18-1. By Outside Agency

If a ball at rest is moved by an outside agency, the player shall incur no penalty and the ball shall be replaced before the player plays another stroke. If the ball moved is not immediately recoverable, another ball may be substituted.

(Player's ball at rest moved by another ball – see Rule 18-5.)

18-2. By Player, Partner, Caddie or Equipment

a. General

When a player's ball is in play, if:

(i) the player, his partner or either of their caddies lifts or moves it, touches it purposely (except with a club in the act of addressing it) or causes it to move except as permitted by a Rule, or

(ii) equipment of the player or his partner causes the ball to move,

the player shall incur a penalty stroke. The ball shall be replaced unless the movement of the ball occurs after the player has begun his swing and he does not discontinue his swing.

Under the Rules no penalty is incurred if a player accidentally causes his ball to move in the following circumstances:

In measuring to determine which ball farther from hole – Rule 10-4

In searching for covered ball in hazard or for ball in casual water, ground under repair, etc. – Rule 12-1

In the process of repairing hole plug or ball mark – Rule 16-1c

In the process of removing loose impediment on putting green – Rule 18-2c

In the process of lifting ball under a Rule – Rule 20-1

In the process of placing or replacing ball under a Rule – Rule 20-3a

In complying with Rule 22 relating to lifting ball interfering with or assisting play

In removal of movable obstruction – Rule 24-1.

b. Ball Moving After Address

If a ball in play moves after the player has addressed it other than as a result of a stroke, he shall be deemed to have moved the ball and *shall incur a penalty stroke*, and the ball shall be played as it lies.

c. Ball Moving After Loose Impediment Touched

Through the green, if the ball moves after any loose impediment lying within a club-length of it has been touched by the player, his partner or either of their caddies and before the player has addressed it, the player shall be deemed to have moved the ball and *shall incur a penalty stroke*. The player shall replace the ball unless the movement of the ball occurs after he has begun his swing and he does not discontinue his swing.

On the putting green, if the ball moves in the process of removing any loose impediment, it shall be replaced without penalty.

18-3. By Opponent, Caddie or Equipment in Match Play

a. During Search

If, during search for a player's ball, it is moved by an opponent, his caddie or his equipment, no penalty is incurred and the player shall replace the ball.

b. Other Than During Search

If, other than during search for a ball, the ball is touched or moved by an opponent, his caddie or his equipment, except as otherwise provided in the Rules, *the opponent shall incur a penalty stroke*. The player shall replace the ball.

(Ball moved in measuring to determine which ball farther from the hole—Rule 10-4.)

(Playing a wrong ball—Rule 15-2.)

(Ball moved in complying with Rule 22 relating to lifting ball interfering with or assisting play.)

18-4. By Fellow-Competitor, Caddie or Equipment in Stroke Play

If a competitor's ball is moved by a fellow-competitor, his caddie or his equipment, no penalty is incurred. The competitor shall replace his ball.

(Playing a wrong ball—Rule 15-3.)

18-5. By Another Ball

If a player's ball at rest is moved by another ball, the player's ball shall be replaced.

*PENALTY FOR BREACH OF RULE:
Match play—Loss of hole; Stroke play—Two strokes.

**If a player who is required to replace a ball fails to do so, he shall incur the general penalty for breach of Rule 18 but no additional penalty under Rule 18 shall be applied.*

Note: If it is impossible to determine the spot on which a ball is to be placed, see Rule 20-3c.

Rule 19. Ball in Motion Deflected or Stopped

Definitions

An "outside agency" is any agency not part of the match or, in stroke play, not part of a competitor's side, and includes a referee, a marker, an observer or a forecaddie. Neither wind nor water is an outside agency.

"Equipment" is anything used, worn or carried by or for the player except any ball he has played and any small object, such as a coin or a tee, when used to mark the position of a ball or the extent of an area in which a ball is to be dropped. Equipment includes a golf cart, whether or not motorised. If such a cart is shared by more than one player, its status under the Rules is the same as that of a caddie employed by more than one player. See "Caddie".

19-1. By Outside Agency

If a ball in motion is accidentally deflected or stopped by any outside agency, it is a rub of the green, no penalty is incurred and the ball shall be played as it lies except:

a. If a ball in motion after a stroke other than on the putting green comes to rest in or on any moving or animate outside agency, the player shall, through the green or in a hazard, drop the ball, or on the putting green place the ball, as near as possible to the spot where the outside agency was when the ball came to rest in or on it, and

b. If a ball in motion after a stroke on the putting green is deflected or stopped by, or comes to rest in or on, any moving or animate outside agency, the stroke shall be cancelled and the ball shall be replaced.

If the ball is not immediately recoverable, another ball may be substituted.

(Player's ball deflected or stopped by another ball at rest – see Rule 19-5.)

Note: If the referee or the Committee determines that a ball has been deliberately deflected or stopped by an outside agency, including a fellow-competitor or his caddie, further procedure should be prescribed in equity under Rule 1-4.

19-2. By Player, Partner, Caddie or Equipment

a. Match Play

If a player's ball is deflected or stopped by himself, his partner or either of their caddies or equipment, *he shall lose the hole.*

b. Stroke Play

If a competitor's ball is deflected or stopped by himself, his partner or either of their caddies or equipment, *the competitor shall incur a penalty of two strokes.* The ball shall be played as it lies, except when it comes to rest in or on the competitor's, his partner's or either of their caddies' clothes or equipment, in which case the competitor shall, through the green or in a hazard, drop the ball, or on the putting green place the ball, as near as possible to where the article was when the ball came to rest in or on it.

Exception: Dropped Ball – see Rule 20-2a.

19-3. By Opponent, Caddie or Equipment in Match Play

a. Purposely

If a player's ball is purposely deflected or stopped by an opponent, his caddie or his equipment, *the opponent shall lose the hole.*

Note: In the case of a serious breach of Rule 19-3a, the Committee may impose a penalty of disqualification.

b. Accidentally

If a player's ball is accidentally deflected or stopped by an opponent, his caddie or his equipment, no penalty is incurred. The player may play the ball as it lies or, before another stroke is played by either side, cancel the stroke and replay the stroke (see Rule 20-5). If the ball has come to rest in or on the opponent's or his caddie's clothes or equipment, the player may through the green or in a hazard drop the ball, or on the putting green place the ball, as near as possible to where the article was when the ball came to rest in or on it.

Exception: Ball striking person attending flagstick—Rule 17-3b.

19-4. By Fellow-Competitor, Caddie or Equipment in Stroke Play

See Rule 19-1 regarding ball deflected by outside agency.

19-5. By a Ball at Rest

If a player's ball in motion is deflected or stopped by a ball at rest, the player shall play his ball as it lies. In stroke play, if both balls lay on the putting green prior to the stroke, *the player incurs a penalty of two strokes.* Otherwise, no penalty is incurred.

PENALTY FOR BREACH OF RULE:
Match play—Loss of hole; Stroke play—Two strokes.

RELIEF SITUATIONS AND PROCEDURE

Rule 20. Lifting, Dropping and Placing: Playing from Wrong Place

20-1. Lifting

A ball to be lifted under the Rules may be lifted by the player, his partner or another person authorised by the player. In any such case, the player shall be responsible for any breach of the Rules.

The position of the ball shall be marked before it is lifted under a Rule which requires it to be replaced. If it is not marked, the player *shall incur a penalty of one stroke* and the ball shall be replaced. If it is not replaced, *the player shall incur the general penalty* for breach of this Rule but no additional penalty under Rule 20-1 shall be applied.

If a ball is accidentally moved in the process of lifting it under a Rule, no penalty shall be incurred and the ball shall be replaced.

Note: The position of a lifted ball should be marked, if feasible, by placing a ball-marker or other small object immediately behind the ball. If the ball-marker interferes with the play, stance or stroke of another player, it should be placed one or more clubhead-lengths to one side.

20-2. Dropping and Re-dropping

a. By Whom and How

A ball to be dropped under the Rules shall be dropped by the player himself. He shall stand erect, hold the ball at shoulder height and arm's length and drop it. If a ball is dropped by any other person or in any other manner and the error is not corrected as provided in Rule 20-6, *the player shall incur a penalty stroke.*

If the ball touches the player, his partner, either of their caddies or their equipment before or after it strikes the ground, the ball shall be redropped, without penalty.

(Taking action to influence position or movement of ball – Rule 1-2.)

b. Where to Drop

When a ball is to be dropped, it shall be dropped as near as possible to the spot where the ball lay, but not nearer the hole, except when a Rule permits it to be dropped elsewhere. If a ball is to be dropped in a hazard, the ball shall be dropped in and come to rest in that hazard.

c. When to Re-drop

A dropped ball shall be re-dropped without penalty if it:

(i) rolls into a hazard;
(ii) rolls out of a hazard;
(iii) rolls onto a putting green;
(iv) rolls out of bounds;
(v) rolls back into the condition from which relief was taken under Rule

24-2 (immovable obstruction) or Rule 25 (abnormal ground conditions and wrong putting green);

(vi) rolls and comes to rest more than two club-lengths from where it first struck the ground; or

(vii) rolls and comes to rest nearer the hole than is permitted by the Rules.

If the ball again rolls into such position, it shall be placed as near as possible to the spot where it first struck the ground when re-dropped.

20-3. Placing and Replacing

a. By Whom and Where

A ball to be placed under the Rules shall be placed by the player or his partner. A ball to be replaced shall be replaced by the player, his partner or the person who lifted or moved it on the spot where the ball lay. In any such case, the player shall be responsible for any breach of the Rules.

If a ball is accidentally moved in the process of placing or replacing it under a Rule, no penalty shall be incurred and the ball shall be replaced.

b. Lie of Ball to Be Placed or Replaced Altered

Except in a bunker, if the original lie of a ball to be placed or replaced has been altered, the ball shall be placed in the nearest lie most similar to that which it originally occupied, not more than one club-length from the original lie and not nearer the hole. In a bunker, the original lie shall be recreated as nearly as possible and the ball shall be placed in that lie.

c. Spot Not Determinable

If it is impossible to determine the spot where the ball is to be placed, the ball shall through the green or in a hazard be dropped, or on the putting green be placed, as near as possible to the place where it lay but not nearer the hole.

d. Ball Fails to Remain on Spot

If a ball when placed fails to remain on the spot on which it was placed, it shall be replaced without penalty. If it still fails to remain on that spot, it shall be placed at the nearest spot not nearer the hole where it can be placed at rest.

PENALTY FOR BREACH OF RULE 20-1, -2 or -3;
Match play—Loss of hole; Stroke play—Two strokes.

20-4. Ball in Play When Dropped or Placed

A ball dropped or placed under a Rule governing the particular case is in play.

20-5. Playing Next Stroke from Where Previous Stroke Played

When, under the Rules, a player elects or is required to play his next stroke from where a previous stroke was played, he shall proceed as follows: If the stroke is to be played from the teeing ground, the ball to be played shall be played from anywhere within the teeing ground and may be teed; if the stroke is to be played from through the green or a hazard, it shall be dropped; if the stroke is to be played on the putting green, it shall be placed.

PENALTY FOR BREACH OF RULE 20-5:
Match play—Loss of hole; Stroke play—Two strokes.

20-6. Lifting Ball Wrongly Dropped or Placed

A ball dropped or placed in a wrong place or otherwise not in accordance with the Rules but not played may be lifted, without penalty, and the player shall then proceed correctly.

In match play, if, before the opponent plays his next stroke, the player fails to inform him that the ball has been lifted, *the player shall lose the hole.*

20-7. Playing from Wrong Place

For a ball played outside teeing ground, see Rule 11-3.

a. Match Play

If a player plays a stroke with a ball which has been dropped or placed under an applicable Rule but in a wrong place, *he shall lose the hole.*

b. Stroke Play

If a competitor plays a stroke with a ball which has been (i) dropped or placed under an applicable Rule but in a wrong place or (ii) moved and not replaced in a case where the Rules require replacement, *he shall incur the penalty prescribed by the relevant Rule* and play out the hole with the ball. If a serious breach of the relevant Rule is involved, *the competitor shall be disqualified*, unless the breach has been rectified as provided in the next paragraph.

If a serious breach may be involved and the competitor has not made a stroke on the next teeing ground or, in the case of the last hole of the round, has not left the putting green, the competitor may rectify any such serious breach by *adding two penalty strokes to his score*, dropping or placing a second ball in accordance with the Rules and playing out the hole. The competitor should play out the hole with both balls. On completion of the round the competitor shall report the facts immediately to the Committee; if he fails to do so, *he shall be disqualified.* The Committee shall determine whether a serious breach of the Rule was involved and, accordingly, whether the score with the second ball shall count.

Note: Penalty strokes incurred by playing

the ball ruled not to count and strokes subsequently taken with that ball shall be disregarded.

Rule 21. Cleaning Ball

A ball may be cleaned when lifted as follows:

Upon suspension of play in accordance with Rule 6-8b;
For identification under Rule 12-2, but the ball may be cleaned only to the extent necessary for identification;
On the putting green under Rule 16-1b;
For relief from an obstruction under Rule 24-1b or -2b;
For relief from abnormal ground conditions or wrong putting green under Rules 25-1b, -2 and -3;
For relief from a water hazard under Rule 26;
For relief for an unplayable ball under Rule 28; or
Under a Local Rule permitting cleaning the ball.

If the player cleans his ball during the play of a hole except as permitted under this Rule, *he shall incur a penalty of one stroke* and the ball, if lifted, shall be replaced.

If a player who is required to replace a ball fails to do so, *he shall incur the penalty* for breach of Rule 20-3a, but no additional penalty under Rule 21 shall be applied.

Rule 22. Ball Interfering with or Assisting Play

Any player may:

a. Lift his ball if he considers that it might assist any other player or

b. Have any other ball lifted if he considers that it might interfere with his play or assist the play of any other player, but this may not be done while another ball is in motion. In stroke play, a player required to lift his ball may play first rather than lift. A ball lifted under this Rule shall be replaced.

If a ball is accidentally moved in complying with this Rule, no penalty is incurred and the ball shall be replaced.

PENALTY FOR BREACH OF RULE:
Match play—Loss of hole; Stroke play—Two strokes.

Rule 23. Loose Impediments

Definition

"Loose impediments" are natural objects such as stones, leaves, twigs, branches and the like, dung, worms and insects and casts or heaps made by them, provided they are not fixed or growing, are not solidly embedded and do not adhere to the ball.

Sand and loose soil are loose impediments on the putting green but not elsewhere.

Snow and ice are either casual water or loose impediments, at the option of the player.

Dew is not a loose impediment.

23-1. Relief

Except when both the loose impediment and the ball lie in or touch a hazard, any loose impediment may be removed without penalty. If the ball moves, see Rule 18-2c.

When a player's ball is in motion, a loose impediment on his line of play shall not be removed.

PENALTY FOR BREACH OF RULE:
Match play—Loss of hole; Stroke play—Two strokes.

(Searching for ball in hazard—Rule 12-1.)
(Touching line of putt—Rule 16-1a.)

Rule 24. Obstructions

Definition

An "obstruction" is anything artificial, including the artificial surfaces and sides of roads and paths, except:

a. Objects defining out of bounds, such as walls, fences, stakes and railings;

b. Any part of an immovable artificial object which is out of bounds; and

c. Any construction declared by the Committee to be an integral part of the course.

24-1. Movable Obstruction

A player may obtain relief from a movable obstruction as follows:

a. If the ball does not lie in or on the obstruction, the obstruction may be removed; if the ball moves, no penalty is incurred and the ball shall be replaced.

b. If the ball lies in or on the obstruction, the ball may be lifted, without penalty, and the obstruction removed. The ball shall through the green or in a hazard be dropped, or on the putting green be placed, as near as possible to the spot directly under the place where the ball lay in or on the obstruction, but not nearer the hole.

The ball may be cleaned when lifted for relief under Rule 24-1b.

When a ball is in motion, an obstruction on the player's line of play other than an attended flagstick and equipment of the players shall not be removed.

24-2. Immovable Obstruction

a. Interference

Interference by an immovable obstruction occurs when a ball lies in or on the obstruction, or so close to the obstruction that the obstruction interferes with the player's stance or the area of his intended swing. If the player's ball lies on the putting green, interference also occurs if an immovable obstruction on the putting green intervenes on his line of putt. Otherwise, intervention on the line of play is not, of itself, interference under this Rule.

b. Relief

Except when the ball lies in or touches a water hazard or a lateral water hazard, a player may obtain relief from interference by an immovable obstruction, without penalty, as follows:

(i) **Through the Green:** If the ball lies through the green, the point on the course nearest to where the ball lies shall be determined (without crossing over, through or under the obstruction) which (a) is not nearer the hole, (b) avoids interference (as defined) and (c) is not in a hazard or on a putting green. The player shall lift the ball and drop it within one club-length of the point thus determined on ground which fulfils (a), (b) and (c) above.

Note: The prohibition against crossing over, through or under the obstruction does not apply to the artificial surfaces and sides of roads and paths or when the ball lies in or on the obstruction.

(ii) **In a Bunker:** If the ball lies in or touches a bunker, the player shall lift and drop the ball in accordance with Clause (i) above, except that the ball must be dropped in the bunker.

(iii) **On the Putting Green:** If the ball lies on the putting green, the player shall lift the ball and place it in the nearest position to where it lay which affords relief from interference, but not nearer the hole nor in a hazard.

The ball may be cleaned when lifted for relief under Rule 24-2b.

(Ball rolling back into condition from which relief taken – see Rule 20-2c(v).)

Exception: A player may not obtain relief under Rule 24-2b if (a) it is clearly unreasonable for him to play a stroke because of interference by anything other than an immovable obstruction or (b) interference by an immovable obstruction would occur only through use of an unnecessarily abnormal stance, swing or direction of play.

Note: If a ball lies in or touches a water hazard (including a lateral water hazard), the player is not entitled to relief without penalty from interference by an immovable obstruction. The player shall play the ball as it lies or proceed under Rule 26-1.

PENALTY FOR BREACH OF RULE:
Match play—Loss of hole; Stroke play—Two strokes.

Rule 25. Abnormal Ground Conditions and Wrong Putting Green

Definitions

"Casual water" is any temporary accumulation of water on the course which is visible before or after the player takes his stance and is not in a water hazard. Snow and ice are either casual water or loose impediments, at the option of the player. Dew is not casual water.

"Ground under repair" is any portion of the course so marked by order of the Committee or so declared by its authorised representative. It includes material piled for removal and a hole made by a greenkeeper, even if not so marked. Stakes and lines defining ground under repair are in such ground.

Note 1: Grass cuttings and other material left on the course which have been abandoned and are not intended to be removed are not ground under repair unless so marked.

Note 2: The Committee may make a Local Rule prohibiting play from ground under repair.

25-1. Casual Water, Ground Under Repair and Certain Damage to Course

a. Interference

Interference by casual water, ground under repair or a hole, cast or runway made by a burrowing animal, a reptile or a bird occurs when a ball lies in or touches any of these conditions or when the condition interferes with the player's stance or the area of his intended swing.

If the player's ball lies on the putting green, interference also occurs if such condition on the putting green intervenes on his line of putt.

If interference exists, the player may either play the ball as it lies (unless prohibited by Local Rule) or take relief as provided in Clause b.

b. Relief

If the player elects to take relief, he shall proceed as follows:

(i) **Through the Green:** If the ball lies through the green, the point on the course nearest to where the ball lies shall be determined which (a) is not nearer the hole, (b) avoids interference by the condition, and (c) is not in a hazard or on a putting green. The player shall lift the ball and drop it without penalty within one club-length of the point thus determined on ground which fulfils (a), (b) and (c) above.

(ii) **In a Hazard:** If the ball lies in or touches a hazard, the player shall lift and drop the ball either:
(a) Without penalty, in the hazard, as near as possible to the spot where the ball lay, but not nearer the hole, on ground which affords maximum available relief from the condition;
or
(b) *Under penalty of one stroke*, outside the hazard, keeping the spot where the ball lay directly between himself and the hole.

Exception: If a ball lies in or touches a water hazard (including a lateral water hazard), the player is not entitled to relief without penalty from a hole, cast or runway made by a burrowing animal, a reptile or a bird. The player shall play the ball as it lies or proceed under Rule 26-1.

(iii) **On the Putting Green:** If the ball lies on the putting green, the player shall lift the ball and place it without penalty in the nearest position to where it lay which affords maximum available relief from the condition, but not nearer the hole nor in a hazard.

The ball may be cleaned when lifted under Rule 25-1b.

(Ball rolling back into condition from which relief taken – see Rule 20-2c(v).)

Exception: A player may not obtain relief under Rule 25-1b if (a) it is clearly unreasonable for him to play a stroke because of interference by anything other than a condition covered by Rule 25-1a or (b) interference by such a condition would occur only through use of an unnecessarily abnormal stance, swing or direction of play.

c. Ball Lost Under Condition Covered by Rule 25-1

It is a question of fact whether a ball lost after having been struck toward a condition covered by Rule 25-1 is lost under such condition. In order to treat the ball as lost under such condition, there must be reasonable evidence to that effect. In the absence of such evidence, the ball must be treated as a lost ball and Rule 27 applies.

(i) **Outside a Hazard** – If a ball is lost outside a hazard under a condition covered by Rule 25-1, the player may take relief as follows: the point on the course nearest to where the ball last crossed the margin of the area shall be determined which (a) is not nearer the hole than where the ball last crossed the margin, (b) avoids interference by the condition and (c) is not in a hazard or on a putting green. He shall drop a ball without penalty within one club-length of the point thus determined on ground which fulfils (a), (b) and (c) above.

(ii) **In a Hazard** – If a ball is lost in a hazard under a condition covered by Rule 25-1, the player may drop a ball either;
(a) Without penalty, in the hazard, as near as possible to the point at which the ball last crossed the margin of the area, but not nearer the hole, on ground which affords maximum available relief from the condition;
or
(b) *Under penalty of one stroke*, outside the hazard, keeping the spot at which the ball last crossed the margin of the hazard directly between himself and the hole.

Exception: If a ball lies in a water hazard (including a lateral water hazard), the player is not entitled to relief without penalty for a ball lost in a hole, cast or runway made by a burrowing animal, a reptile or a bird. The player shall proceed under Rule 26-1.

25-2. Embedded Ball

A ball embedded in its own pitch-mark in any closely mown area through the green may be lifted, cleaned and dropped, without penalty, as near as possible to the spot where it lay but not nearer the hole. "Closely mown area" means any area of the course, including paths through the rough, cut to fairway height or less.

25-3. Wrong Putting Green

If a ball lies on a putting green other than that of the hole being played, the point on the course nearest to where the ball lies shall be determined which (a) is not nearer the hole and (b) is not in a hazard or on a putting green. The player shall lift the ball and drop it without penalty within one club-length of the point thus determined on ground which fulfils (a) and (b) above. The ball may be cleaned when so lifted.

Note: Unless otherwise prescribed by the Committee, the term "a putting green other than that of the hole being played" includes a practice putting green or pitching green on the course.

PENALTY FOR BREACH OF RULE:
Match play—Loss of hole; Stroke play—Two strokes.

Rule 26. Water Hazards (Including Lateral Water Hazards)

Definitions

A "water hazard" is any sea, lake, pond, river, ditch, surface drainage ditch or other open water course (whether or not containing water) and anything of a similar nature.

All ground or water within the margin of a water hazard is part of the water hazard. The margin of a water hazard is deemed to extend vertically upwards. Stakes and lines defining the margins of water hazards are in the hazards.

Note: Water hazards (other than lateral water hazards) should be defined by yellow stakes or lines.

A "lateral water hazard" is a water hazard or that part of a water hazard so situated that it is not possible or is deemed by the Committee to be impracticable to drop a ball behind the water hazard and keep the spot at which the ball last crossed the margin of the water hazard between the player and the hole.

That part of a water hazard to be played as a lateral water hazard should be distinctively marked.

Note: Lateral water hazards should be defined by red stakes or lines.

26-1. Ball in Water Hazard

It is a question of fact whether a ball lost after having been struck toward a water hazard is lost inside or outside the hazard. In order to treat the ball as lost in the hazard, there must be reasonable evidence that the ball lodged therein. In the absence of such evidence, the ball must be treated as a lost ball and Rule 27 applies.

If a ball lies in, touches or is lost in a water hazard (whether the ball lies in water or not), the player may *under penalty of one stroke:*

a. Play his next stroke as nearly as possible at the spot from which the original ball was last played or moved by him (see Rule 20-5);

or

b. Drop a ball behind the water hazard, keeping the point at which the original ball last crossed the margin of the water hazard directly between himself and the hole, with no limit to how far behind the water hazard the ball may be dropped;

or

c. *As additional options available only if the ball lies or is lost in a lateral water hazard,* drop a ball outside the water hazard within two club-lengths of (i) the point where the original ball last crossed the margin of the water hazard or (ii) a point on the opposite margin of the water hazard equidistant from the hole. The ball must be dropped and come to rest not nearer the hole than the point where the original ball last crossed the margin of the water hazard.

The ball may be cleaned when lifted under this Rule.

26-2. Ball Played Within Water Hazard

a. Ball Remains in Hazard

If a ball played from within a water hazard has not crossed any margin of the hazard, the player may:

(i) proceed under Rule 26-1; or
(ii) *under penalty of one stroke*, play his next stroke as nearly as possible at the spot from which the last stroke from outside the hazard was played (see Rule 20-5).

b. Ball Lost or Unplayable Outside Hazard or Out of Bounds

If a ball played from within a water hazard is lost or declared unplayable outside the hazard or is out of bounds, the player, after taking a stroke-and-distance penalty under Rule 27-1 or 28a, may:

(i) play a ball as nearly as possible at the spot from which the original ball was last played by him (see Rule 20-5); or
(ii) under the penalty prescribed therein, proceed under Rule 26-1b or, as additional options in the case of a lateral water hazard, under Rule 26-1c, using as the reference point the point where the ball last crossed the margin of the hazard before it came to rest in the hazard; or
(iii) *under penalty of one stroke*, play his next stroke as nearly as possible at the spot from which the last stroke from outside the hazard was played (see Rule 20-5).

PENALTY FOR BREACH OF RULE:
Match play—Loss of hole; Stroke play—Two strokes.

Rule 27. Ball Lost or Out of Bounds; Provisional Ball

If the original ball is lost under a condition covered by Rule 25-1 (casual water, ground under repair and certain damage to the course), the player may proceed under that Rule. If the original ball is lost in a water hazard, the player shall proceed under Rule 26.

Such Rules may not be used unless there is reasonable evidence that the ball is lost under a condition covered by Rule 25-1 or in a water hazard.

Definitions

A ball is "lost" if:

a. It is not found or identified as his by the player within five minutes after the player's side or his or their caddies have begun to search for it; or

b. The player has put another ball into play under the Rules, even though he may not have searched for the original ball; or

c. The player has played any stroke with a provisional ball from the place where the original ball is likely to be or from a point nearer the hole than that place, whereupon the provisional ball becomes the ball in play.

Time spent in playing a wrong ball is not counted in the five-minute period allowed for search.

"Out of bounds" is ground on which play is prohibited.

When out of bounds is defined by reference to stakes or a fence, or as being beyond stakes or a fence, the out of bounds line is determined by the nearest inside points of the stakes or fence posts at ground level excluding angled supports.

When out of bounds is defined by a line on the ground, the line itself is out of bounds.

The out of bounds line is deemed to extend vertically upwards and downwards.

A ball is out of bounds when all of it lies out of bounds.

A player may stand out of bounds to play a ball lying within bounds.

A "provisional ball" is a ball played under Rule 27-2 for a ball which may be lost outside a water hazard or may be out of bounds. It ceases to be a provisional ball when the Rule provides either that the player continue play with it as the ball in play or that it be abandoned.

27-1. Ball Lost or Out of Bounds

If a ball is lost outside a water hazard or is out of bounds, the player shall play a ball, *under penalty of one stroke*, as nearly as possible at the spot from which the original ball was last played or moved by him (see Rule 20-5).

27-2. Provisional Ball

a. Procedure

If a ball may be lost outside a water hazard or may be out of bounds, to save time the player may play another ball provisionally as nearly as possible at the spot from which the original ball was played (see Rule 20-5). The player shall inform his opponent in match play or his marker or a fellow competitor in stroke play that he intends to play a provisional ball, and he shall play it before he or his partner goes forward to search for the original ball. If he fails to do so and plays another ball, such ball is not a provisional ball and becomes the ball in play *under penalty of stroke and distance* (Rule 27-1); the original ball is deemed to be lost.

b. When Provisional Ball Becomes Ball in Play

The player may play a provisional ball until he reaches the place where the original ball is likely to be. If he plays a stroke with the provisional ball from the place where the original ball is likely to be or from a point nearer the hole than that place, the original ball is deemed to be lost and the provisional ball becomes the ball in play under *penalty of stroke and distance* (Rule 27-1).

If the original ball is lost outside a water hazard or is out of bounds, the provisional ball becomes the ball in play, *under penalty of stroke and distance* (Rule 27-1).

c. When Provisional Ball to Be Abandoned

If the original ball is neither lost outside a water hazard nor out of bounds, the player shall abandon the provisional ball and continue play with the original ball. If he fails to do so, any further strokes played with the provisional ball shall constitute playing a wrong ball and the provisions of Rule 15 shall apply.

Note: If the original ball lies in a water hazard, the player shall play the ball as it lies or proceed under Rule 26. If it is lost in a water hazard or unplayable, the player shall proceed under Rule 26 or 28, whichever is applicable.

PENALTY FOR BREACH OF RULE:
Match play—Loss of hole; Stroke play—Two strokes.

Rule 28. Ball Unplayable

At any place on the course except in a water hazard a player may declare his ball unplayable. The player is the sole judge as to whether his ball is unplayable.

If the player deems his ball to be unplayable, he shall, *under penalty of one stroke*:

a. Play his next stroke as nearly as possible at the spot from which the original ball was last played or moved by him (see Rule 20-5);

or

b. Drop a ball within two club-lengths of the spot where the ball lay, but not nearer the hole;

or

c. Drop a ball behind the spot where the ball lay, keeping that spot directly between himself and the hole, with no limit to how far behind that spot the ball may be dropped.

If the unplayable ball lies in a bunker and the player elects to proceed under Clause b or c, a ball must be dropped in the bunker.

The ball may be cleaned when lifted under this Rule.

PENALTY FOR BREACH OF RULE:
Match play—Loss of hole; Stroke play—Two strokes.

OTHER FORMS OF PLAY

Rule 29. Threesomes and Foursomes

Definitions

Threesome: A match in which one plays against two, and each side plays one ball.

Foursome: A match in which two play against two, and each side plays one ball.

29-1. General

In a threesome or a foursome, during any stipulated round the partners shall play alternately from the teeing grounds and alternately during the play of each hole. Penalty strokes do not affect the order of play.

29-2. Match Play

If a player plays when his partner should have played, *his side shall lose the hole.*

29-3. Stroke Play

If the partners play a stroke or strokes in incorrect order, such stroke or strokes shall be cancelled and *the side shall be penalised two strokes.* A ball shall then be put in play as nearly as possible at the spot from which the side first played in incorrect order (see Rule 20-5) before a stroke has been played from the next teeing ground or, in the case of the last hole of the round, before the side has left the putting green. If this is not done, *the side shall be disqualified.*

Rule 30. Three-Ball, Best-Ball and Four-Ball Match Play

30-1. Rules of Golf Apply

The Rules of Golf, so far as they are not at variance with the following special Rules, shall apply to three-ball, best-ball and four-ball matches.

30-2. Three-Ball Match Play

In a three-ball match, each player is playing two distinct matches.

a. Ball at Rest Moved by an Opponent

Except as otherwise provided in the Rules, if the player's ball is touched or moved by an opponent, his caddie or equipment other than during search, Rule 18-3b applies. *That opponent shall incur a penalty stroke in his match with the player,* but not in his match with the other opponent.

b. Ball Deflected or Stopped by an Opponent Accidentally

If a player's ball is accidentally deflected or stopped by an opponent, his caddie or equipment, no penalty shall be incurred. In his match with that opponent the player may play the ball as it lies or, before another stroke is played by either side, he may cancel the stroke and replay the stroke (see Rule 20-5). In his match with the other opponent, the occurrence shall be treated as a rub of the green and the hole shall be played out with the original ball.

Exception: Ball striking person attending flagstick – Rule 17-3b.

(Ball purposely deflected or stopped by opponent – Rule 19-3a.)

30-3. Best-Ball and Four-Ball Match Play

a. Representation of Side

A side may be represented by one partner for all or any part of a match; all partners need not be present. An absent partner may join a match between holes, but not during play of a hole.

b. Maximum of Fourteen Clubs

The side shall be penalised for a breach of Rule 4-4 by any partner.

c. Order of Play

Balls belonging to the same side may be played in the order the side considers best.

d. Wrong Ball

If a player plays a stroke with a wrong ball except in a hazard, *he shall be disqualified for that hole,* but his partner incurs no penalty even if the wrong ball belongs to him. The owner of the ball shall replace it on the spot from which it was played, without penalty. If the ball is not immediately recoverable, another ball may be substituted.

e. Disqualification of Side

(i) *A side shall be disqualified* for a breach of any of the following by any partner:

Rule 1-3 –	Agreement to Waive Rules.
Rule 4-1, -2 or -3 –	Clubs.
Rule 5 –	The ball.
Rule 6-2a –	Handicap (playing off higher handicap).
Rule 6-4 –	Caddie.
Rule 6-7 –	Undue Delay (repeated offence).
Rule 14-3 –	Artificial Devices and Unusual Equipment.

(ii) *A side shall be disqualified* for a breach of any of the following by all partners:

Rule 6-3 –	Time of Starting and Groups.
Rule 6-8 –	Discontinuance of Play.

f. Effect of Other Penalties
If a player's breach of a Rule assists his partner's play or adversely affects an opponent's play, *the partner incurs the relative penalty in addition to any penalty incurred by the player.*
In all other cases where a player incurs a penalty for breach of a Rule, the penalty shall not apply to his partner. Where the penalty is stated to be loss of hole, the effect shall be to disqualify the player for that hole.

g. Another Form of Match Played Concurrently
In a best-ball or four-ball match when another form of match is played concurrently, the above special Rules shall apply.

Rule 31. Four-Ball Stroke Play

In four-ball stroke play two competitors play as partners, each playing his own ball. The lower score of the partners is the score for the hole. If one partner fails to complete the play of a hole, there is no penalty.

31-1. Rules of Golf Apply
The Rules of Golf, so far as they are not at variance with the following special Rules, shall apply to four-ball stroke play.

31-2. Representation of Side
A side may be represented by either partner for all or any part of a stipulated round; both partners need not be present. An absent competitor may join his partner between holes, but not during play of a hole.

31-3. Maximum of Fourteen Clubs
The side shall be penalised for a breach of Rule 4-4 by either partner.

31-4. Scoring
The marker is required to record for each hole only the gross score of whichever partner's score is to count. The gross scores to count must be individually identifiable; otherwise *the side shall be disqualified.* Only one of the partners need be responsible for complying with Rule 6-6a and b.
(Wrong score – Rule 31-7a.)

31-5. Order of Play
Balls belonging to the same side may be played in the order the side considers best.

31-6. Wrong Ball
If a competitor plays a stroke with a wrong ball except in a hazard, *he shall add two penalty strokes to his score for the hole* and shall then play the correct ball. His partner incurs no penalty even if the wrong ball belongs to him.

The owner of the ball shall replace it on the spot from which it was played, without penalty. If the ball is not immediately recoverable, another ball may be substituted.

31-7. Disqualification Penalties

a. Breach by One Partner *A side shall be disqualified from the competition* for a breach of any of the following by either partner:

Rule 1-3 – Agreement to Waive Rules.
Rule 3-4 – Refusal to Comply with Rule.
Rule 4-1, -2 or -3 – Clubs.
Rule 5 – The Ball.
Rule 6-2b – Handicap (playing off higher handicap; failure to record handicap).
Rule 6-4 – Caddie.
Rule 6-6b – Checking Scores.
Rule 6-6c – No Alteration of Scores, i.e. when the recorded lower score of the partners is lower than actually played. If the recorded lower score of the partners is higher than actually played, it must stand as returned.
Rule 6-7 – Undue Delay (repeated offence).
Rule 7-1 – Practice Before or Between Rounds.
Rule 14-3 – Artificial Devices and Unusual Equipment.
Rule 31-4 – Gross Scores to count Not Individually Identifiable.

b. Breach by Both Partners
A side shall be disqualified for a breach of any of the following by both partners:
Rule 6-3 – Time of Starting and Groups.
Rule 6-8 – Discontinuance of Play.
At the same hole, of a Rule or Rules, the penalty for which is disqualification either from the competition or for a hole.

c. For the Hole Only
In all other cases where a breach of a Rule would entail disqualification, *the competitor shall be disqualified only for the hole at which the breach occurred.*

31-8. Effect of Other Penalties
If a competitor's breach of a Rule assists his partner's play, *the partner incurs the relative penalty in addition to any penalty incurred by the competitor.*
In all other cases where a competitor incurs a penalty for breach of a Rule, the penalty shall not apply to his partner.

Rule 32. Bogey, Par and Stableford Competitions

32-1. Conditions

Bogey, par and Stableford competitions are forms of stroke competition in which play is against a fixed score at each hole. The Rules for stroke play, so far as they are not at variance with the following special Rules, apply.

a. Bogey and Par Competitions

The reckoning for bogey and par competitions is made as in match play. Any hole for which a competitor makes no return shall be regarded as a loss. The winner is the competitor who is most successful in the aggregate of holes.

The marker is responsible for marking only the gross number of strokes for each hole where the competitor makes a net score equal to or less than the fixed score.

Note: Maximum of 14 Clubs – Penalties as in match play – see Rule 4-4.

b. Stableford Competitions

The reckoning in Stableford competitions is made by points awarded in relation to a fixed score at each hole as follows:

Hole Played in	Points
More than one over fixed score	0
One over fixed score	1
Fixed score	2
One under fixed score	3
Two under fixed score	4
Three under fixed score	5

The winner is the competitor who scores the highest number of points.

The marker shall be responsible for marking only the gross number of strokes at each hole where the competitor's net score earns one or more points.

Note: Maximum of 14 Clubs (Rule 4-4) – Penalties applied as follows: From total points scored for the round, deduction of two points for each hole at which any breach occurred; maximum deduction per round: four points.

32-2. Disqualification Penalties

a. From the Competition

A competitor shall be disqualified from the competition for a breach of any of the following:

Rule 1-3 – Agreement to Waive Rules.
Rule 3-4 – Refusal to Comply with Rule.
Rule 4-1, -2 or -3 – Clubs.
Rule 5 – The Ball.
Rule 6-2b – Handicap (playing off higher handicap; failure to record handicap).
Rule 6-3 – Time of Starting and Groups.
Rule 6-4 – Caddie.
Rule 6-6b – Checking Scores.
Rule 6-6c – No alteration of scores, except that the competitor shall not be disqualified when a breach of this Rule does not affect the result of the hole.
Rule 6-7 – Undue Delay (repeated offence).
Rule 6-8 – Discontinuance of Play.
Rule 7-1 – Practice Before or Between Rounds.
Rule 14-3 – Artificial Devices and Unusual Equipment.

b. For a Hole

In all other cases where a breach of a Rule would entail disqualification, *the competitor shall be disqualified only for the hole at which the breach occurred.*

ADMINISTRATION

Rule 33. The Committee

33-1. Conditions

The Committee shall lay down the conditions under which a competition is to be played.

Certain special rules governing stroke play are so substantially different from those governing match play that combining the two forms of play is not practicable and is not permitted. The results of matches played and the scores returned in these circumstances shall not be accepted.

In stroke play the Committee may limit a referee's duties.

33-2. The Course

a. Defining Bounds and Margins

The Committee shall define accurately:

(i) the course and out of bounds,
(ii) the margins of water hazards and lateral water hazards,
(iii) ground under repair, and
(iv) obstructions and integral parts of the course.

b. New Holes

New holes should be made on the day on which a stroke competition begins and at such other times as the Committee considers necessary, provided all competitors in a single round play with each hole cut in the same position.

Exception: When it is impossible for a damaged hole to be repaired so that it conforms with the Definition, the Committee may make a new hole in a nearby similar position.

c. Practice Ground

Where there is no practice ground available outside the area of a competition course, the Committee should lay down the area on which players may practise on any day of a competition, if it is practicable to do so. On any day of a stroke competition, the Committee should not normally permit practice on or to a putting green or from a hazard of the competition course.

d. Course Unplayable

If the Committee or its authorised representative considers that for any reason the course is not in a playable condition or that there are circumstances which render the proper playing of the game impossible, it may, in match play or stroke play, order a temporary suspension of play or, in stroke play, declare play null and void and cancel all scores for the round in question. When play has been temporarily suspended, it shall be resumed from where it was discontinued, even though resumption occurs on a subsequent day. When a round is cancelled, all penalties incurred in that round are cancelled.

(Procedure in discontinuing play – Rule 6-8.)

33-3. Times of Starting and Groups

The Committee shall lay down the times of starting and, in stroke play, arrange the groups in which competitors shall play.

When a match play competition is played over an extended period, the Committee shall lay down the limit of time within which each round shall be completed. When players are allowed to arrange the date of their match within these limits, the Committee should announce that the match must be played at a stated time on the last day of the period unless the players agree to a prior date.

33-4. Handicap Stroke Table

The Committee shall publish a table indicating the order of holes at which handicap strokes are to be given or received.

33-5. Score Card

In stroke play, the Committee shall issue for each competitor a score card containing the date and the competitor's name.

The Committee is responsible for the addition of scores and application of the handicap recorded on the card.

In four-ball stroke play, the Committee is responsible for recording the better ball score for each hole, the addition and the application of the handicaps recorded on the card.

33-6. Decision of Ties

The Committee shall announce the manner, day and time for the decision of a halved match or of a tie, whether played on level terms or under handicap.

A halved match shall not be decided by stroke play. A tie in stroke play shall not be decided by a match.

33-7. Modification of Penalty

The Committee has no power to waive a Rule of Golf. A penalty of disqualification, however, may, in exceptional individual cases, be waived or be modified or be imposed if the Committee considers such action warranted.

33-8. Local Rules

a. Policy

The Committee may make and publish Local Rules for abnormal conditions if they are consistent with the policy of the Governing Authority for the country concerned as set forth in Appendix I to these Rules.

b. Waiving Penalty

A penalty imposed by a Rule of Golf shall not be waived by a Local Rule.

Rule 34. Disputes and Decisions

34-1. Claims and Penalties

a. Match Play

In match play if a claim is lodged with the Committee under Rule 2-5, a decision should be given as soon as possible so that the state of the match may, if necessary, be adjusted.

If a claim is not made within the time limit provided by Rule 2-5, it shall not be considered unless it is based on facts previously unknown to the player making the claim and the player making the claim had been given wrong information (Rules 6-2a and 9) by an opponent. In any case, no later claim shall be considered after the result of the match has been officially announced, unless the Committee is satisfied that the opponent knew he was giving wrong information.

b. Stroke Play

No penalty shall be imposed after the competition is closed unless the Committee is satisfied that the competitor has knowingly returned a score for any hole lower than actually taken (Rule 6-6c); no penalty shall be rescinded after the competition is closed. A competition is deemed to have closed when the result of the competition is officially announced or, in stroke play qualifying followed by match play, when the player has teed off in his first match.

34-2. Referee's Decision

If a referee has been appointed by the Committee, his decision shall be final.

34-3. Committee's Decision

In the absence of a referee, the players shall refer any dispute to the Committee, whose decision shall be final.

If the Committee cannot come to a decision, it shall refer the dispute to the Rules of Golf Committee of the Royal and Ancient Golf Club of St. Andrews, whose decision shall be final.

If the point in doubt or dispute has not been referred to the Rules of Golf Committee, the player or players have the right to refer an agreed statement through the Secretary of the Club to the Rules of Golf Committee for an opinion as to the correctness of the decision given. The reply will be sent to the Secretary of the Club or Clubs concerned.

If play is conducted other than in accordance with the Rules of Golf, the Rules of Golf Committee will not give a decision on any question.

APPENDIX I

LOCAL RULES (RULE 33-8) AND CONDITIONS OF THE COMPETITION (RULE 33-1)

Part A Local Rules

1. The Committee may make and publish Local Rules (for Specimen Local Rules see Part B) for such abnormal conditions as:

a. Obstructions

Stipulating the limits of obstructions and the extent of relief if the application of Rule 24 is impracticable or inequitable.

Clarifying the status of objects which may be obstructions (Rule 24).

Declaring any construction to be an integral part of the course and, accordingly, not an obstruction, e.g., artificial surfaces and sides of roads and paths.

Providing relief from fixed sprinkler heads within two club-lengths of the putting green.

(Tournament Local Rules for Temporary Obstructions are available from the Royal and Ancient Golf Club of St. Andrews.)

b. Stones in Bunkers

Allowing the removal of stones in bunkers by declaring them movable obstructions.

c. Areas Requiring Preservation

Declaring such areas "ground under repair" and prohibiting play thereon.

d. Unusual Damage to the Course or Accumulation of Leaves (or the Like)

Declaring such areas "ground under repair" (Rule 25).

Note: Relief from an accumulation of leaves, etc. which is seasonal must be temporary and the Local Rule withdrawn as soon as possible.

e. Extreme Wetness, Mud, Poor Conditions and Protection of Course

(i) **Lifting an Embedded Ball, Cleaning**
Where the ground is unusually soft, the Committee may, by Local Rule, allow the lifting of a ball which is embedded in its own pitch-mark in an area "through the green" which is not "closely mown" (Rule 25-2) if it is satisfied that the proper playing of the game would otherwise be prevented. The Local Rule shall be for that day only or for a short period, and if practicable shall be confined to specified areas. The Committee shall withdraw the Local Rule as soon as conditions warrant and should not print it on the score card.

In similarly adverse conditions, the Committee may, by temporary Local Rule, permit the cleaning of a ball "through the green".

(ii) **"Preferred Lies" and "Winter Rules"**
Adverse conditions, including the poor condition of the course or the existence of mud, are sometimes so general, particularly during winter months, that the Committee may decide to grant relief by Local Rule either to protect the course or to promote fair and pleasant play. Such Local Rule shall be withdrawn as soon as conditions warrant.

f. Other Local Conditions which Interfere with the Proper Playing of the Game

If this necessitates modification of a Rule of Golf the approval of the Governing Authority must be obtained.

g. Dropping Zones

Where it is not feasible or practicable to proceed in conformity with Rule 24-2b (Immovable Obstruction), Rule 26 (Water Hazards including Lateral Water Hazards) or Rule 28 (Ball Unplayable) the Committee may establish special zones in which balls may or shall be dropped when relief is taken.

h. Provisional Ball for Ball in Water Hazard

Subject to the approval of the Governing Authority, the Committee may permit play of a provisional ball for a ball which may be in a water hazard of such character that it would be impracticable to determine whether the ball is in the hazard or to do so would unduly delay play. In such case, if a provisional ball is played and the original ball is in the water hazard, the player may play the original ball as it lies or continue the provisional ball in play, but he may not proceed under Rule 26-1.

2. Practice

The Committee may make regulations governing Practice under Rules 7 and 33-2c.

3. Priority on the Course

The Committee may make regulations governing Priority on the Course (see Etiquette).

Conditions of the Competition

4. Specifications of the Ball

See Note 2 to Rule 5-1.

5. Time of Starting

See Note to Rule 6-3a.

6. Advice in Team Competitions

See Note to Rule 8-1.

Part B Specimen Local Rules

Within the policy set out in Part A of this Appendix the Committee may adopt a Specimen Local Rule by referring, on a score card or notice board, to the examples given below. However Specimen Local Rules 4 or 5 should not be printed or referred to on a score card as they are both of limited duration.

1. Fixed Sprinkler Heads

All fixed sprinkler heads are immovable obstructions and relief from interference by them may be obtained under Rule 24-2. In addition, if such an obstruction on or within two club-lengths of the putting green of the hole being played intervenes on the line of play between the ball and the hole, the player may obtain relief, without penalty, as follows:

If the ball lies off the putting green but not in a hazard and is within two club-lengths of the intervening obstruction, it may be lifted, cleaned and dropped at the nearest point to where the ball lay which (a) is not nearer the hole, (b) avoids such intervention and (c) is not in a hazard or on a putting green.

PENALTY FOR BREACH OF LOCAL RULE: *Match play—Loss of hole; Stroke play—Two strokes.*

2. Stones in Bunkers

Stones in bunkers are movable obstructions. Rule 24-1 applies.

3. Areas Requiring Preservation

In any area of "ground under repair" from which play is prohibited, the player shall not play his ball from, or take his stance in, such ground. He must take relief under Rule 25-1b.

PENALTY FOR BREACH OF LOCAL RULE: *Match play—Loss of hole; Stroke play—Two strokes.*

4. Lifting an Embedded Ball

(Specify the area if practicable)..... through the green, a ball embedded in its own pitch-mark in ground other than sand may be lifted, cleaned and dropped, without penalty, as near as possible to the spot where it lay but not nearer the hole.

PENALTY FOR BREACH OF LOCAL RULE: *Match play—Loss of hole; Stroke play—Two strokes.*

5. "Preferred Lies" and "Winter Rules"

A ball lying on any "closely mown area" through the green may, without penalty, be moved or may be lifted, cleaned and placed within six inches of where it originally lay, but not nearer the hole. After t' ball has been so moved or placed, it is in play, and if it moves after the player has addressed it, the *penalty shall be one stroke* – see Rule 18-2b.

PENALTY FOR BREACH OF LOCAL RULE: *Match play—Loss of hole; Stroke play—Two strokes.*

APPENDICES II and III

Any design in a club or ball which is not covered by Rules 4 and 5 and Appendices II and III, or which might significantly change the nature of the game, will be ruled on by the Royal and Ancient Golf Club of St. Andrews and the United States Golf Association.

Note: Equipment approved for use or marketed prior to January 1st, 1984 which conformed to the Rules in effect in 1983 but does not conform to the 1984 Rules may be used until December 31st, 1989; thereafter all equipment must conform to the current Rules.

APPENDIX II

Design of Clubs

Rule 4-1 prescribes general regulations for the design of clubs. The following paragraphs provide some detailed specifications and clarify how Rule 4-1 is interpreted.

4-1b. Shaft

Generally Straight. The shaft must be straight from the top of the grip to a point not more than 5 inches (127 mm) above the sole, measured along the axis of the shaft and the neck or socket.

Bending and Twisting Properties. The shaft must be so designed and manufactured that at any point along its length:

(i) it bends in such a way that the deflection is the same regardless of how the shaft is rotated about its longitudinal axis; and
(ii) it twists the same amount in both directions.

Attachment to Clubhead. The neck or socket must not be more than 5 inches (127 mm) in length, measured from the top of the neck or socket to the sole along its axis. The shaft and the neck or socket must remain in line with the heel, or with a point to the right or left of the heel, when the club is viewed in the address position. The distance between the axis of the shaft or the neck or socket and the back of the heel must not exceed 0.625 inches (16 mm).

Exception for Putters: The shaft or neck or socket of a putter may be fixed at any point in the head and need not remain in line with the heel. The axis of the shaft from

CLUBS

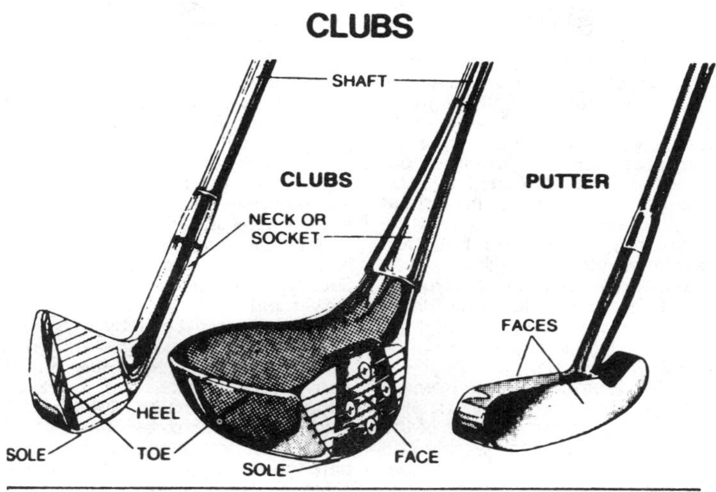

GRIPS

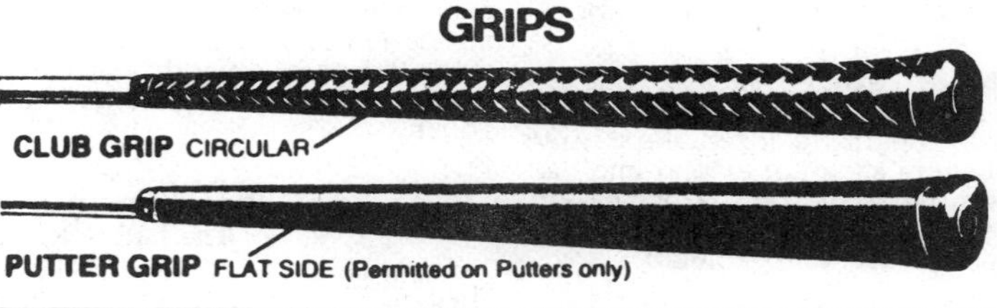

GROOVES

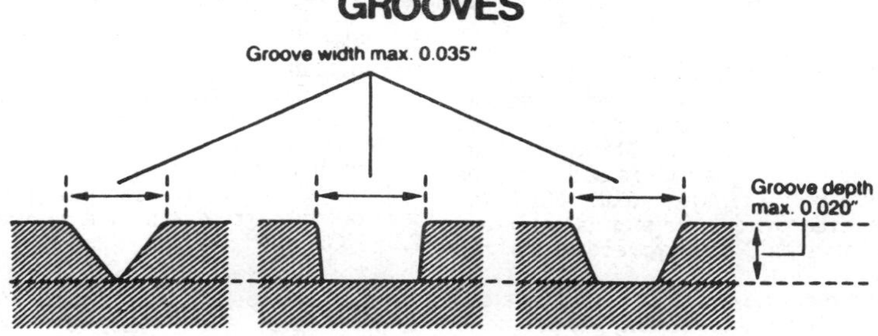

EXAMPLES OF PERMISSIBLE GROOVE CROSS SECTIONS

the top to a point not more than 5 inches (127 mm) above the sole must diverge from the vertical in the toe-heel plane by at least 10 degrees in relation to the horizontal line determining length of head under Appendix II, Clubhead.

4-1c. Grip

(i) For clubs other than putters, the grip must be generally circular in cross-section, except that a continuous, straight, slightly raised rib may be incorporated along the full length of the grip.

(ii) A putter grip may have a non-circular cross-section, provided the cross-section has no concavity and remains generally similar throughout the length of the grip.

(iii) The grip may be tapered but must not have any bulge or waist.

(iv) The axis of the grip must coincide with the axis of the shaft except for a putter.

4-1d. Clubhead

Dimensions. The length and the breadth of a clubhead are measured on horizontal lines between the vertical projections of the extremities when the clubhead is soled in its normal address position. If the heel extremity is not clearly defined, it is deemed to be 0.625 inches (16 mm) above the sole.

Plain in Shape. Features such as fins or holes are not permitted, but certain exceptions may be made for putters. Any furrows or runners shall not extend into the face. Windows, holes or transparencies for the purpose of aiding the player in positioning himself are not permitted.

4-1e. Club Face

Hardness and Rigidity. The club face must not be designed and manufactured to have the effect at impact of a spring which would unduly influence the movement of the ball.

Markings. Except for specified markings, the surface roughness must not exceed that of decorative sandblasting. Markings must not have sharp edges or raised lips, as determined by a finger test. Markings within the area where impact is intended (the "impact area") are governed by the following:

(i) **Grooves.** A series of straight grooves with diverging sides and a symmetrical cross-section may be used (see diagram). The width of grooves must be generally consistent and not exceed 0.035 inches (0.9 mm) along their length. The distance between edges of adjacent grooves must not be less than three times the width of a groove, and not less than 0.075 inches (1.9 mm). The depth of a groove must not exceed 0.020 inches (0.5 mm).

(ii) **Punch Marks.** Punch marks may be used. The area of any such mark must not exceed 0.0044 square inches (2.8 sq. mm). A mark must not be closer to an adjacent mark than 0.168 inches (4.3 mm) measured from centre to centre. The depth of a punch mark must not exceed 0.040 inches (1.0 mm). If punch marks are used in combination with grooves, a punch mark may not be closer to a groove than 0.168 inches (4.3 mm), measured from centre to centre.

Decorative Markings. The centre of the impact area may be indicated by a design within the boundary of a square whose sides are 0.375 inches (9.5 mm) in length. Such a design must not unduly influence the movement of the ball. Markings outside the impact area must not be greater than 0.040 inches (1.00 mm) in depth and width.

Non-metallic Club Face Markings. The above specifications for markings do not apply to non-metallic clubs with loft angles less than 24 degrees, but markings which could unduly influence the movement of the ball are prohibited. Non-metallic clubs with a loft or face angle exceeding 24 degrees may have grooves of maximum width 0.04 inches (1.0 mm) and maximum depth of $1\frac{1}{2}$ times the groove width, but must otherwise conform to the markings specifications above.

APPENDIX III

The Ball

a. Weight

The weight of the ball shall not be greater than 1.620 ounces avoirdupois (45.93 gm).

b. Size

The diameter of the ball shall be not less than 1.620 inches (41.15 mm). This specification will be satisfied if, under its own weight, a ball falls through a 1.620 inches diameter ring gauge in fewer than 25 out of 100 randomly selected positions, the test being carried out at a temperature of 23±1°C.

Note: The Rules of the United States Golf Association specify a minimum diameter of 1.680 inches (42.67 mm) and apply an Overall Distance Standard.

c. Spherical Symmetry

The ball shall be designed and manufactured to perform in general as if it were spherically symmetrical.

As outlined in procedures on file at the Royal and Ancient Golf Club of St. Andrews and the United States Golf Association, differences in peak angle of trajectory, carry and time of flight will be measured when 40 balls of the same types are launched, spinning 20 about one axis and 20 about another axis.

These tests will be performed using apparatus approved by the Royal and Ancient Golf Club of St. Andrews and the United States Golf Association. If in two successive tests differences in the same two or more measurements are statistically significant at the 5% level of significance and exceed the limits set forth below, the ball type will not conform to the symmetry specification.

Measurement	Maximum Absolute Difference of the means
Peak angle of trajectory	0.9 grid units (approx. 0.4 degrees)
Carry distance	2.5 yards
Flight time	0.16 seconds

Note: Methods of determining whether a ball performs as if it were generally spherically symmetrical may be subject to change as instrumentation becomes available to measure other properties accurately, such as the aerodynamic coefficient of lift, coefficient of drag and moment of inertia.

d. Initial Velocity

The velocity of the ball shall not be greater than 250 feet (76.2 m) per second when measured on apparatus approved by the Royal and Ancient Golf Club of St. Andrews and the United States Golf Association. A maximum tolerance of 2% will be allowed. The temperature of the ball when tested shall be 23 ± 1°C.

HANDICAPS

The Rules of Golf do not legislate for the allocation and adjustment of handicaps or their playing differentials. Such matters are within the jurisdiction and control of the National Union concerned and queries should be directed accordingly.

DECISIONS ON THE RULES OF GOLF

Published by the Royal and Ancient Golf Club of St. Andrews and the United States Golf Association

The Rules of Golf were revised by the two Governing Authorities of the Game and came into force in 1984. *Decisions on the Rules* are issued regularly to all subscribers to the service. This reference book is considered a vital aid to all Competitions Organisers and Club Committees. Details of the cost of the Service can be obtained from the Secretary of the Rules of Golf Committee at the Royal and Ancient Club, St. Andrews.

Help in the Interpretation of the Rules of Golf, published in 1984, is also obtainable from the Royal and Ancient Club, price £3.00 (incl. p & p). Subscribers to the Decisions Service receive a complimentary copy.

RULES OF AMATEUR STATUS

(Effective from 1st August 1987)

as approved by the Royal and Ancient Golf Club of St. Andrews

Definitions

An Amateur Golfer
An Amateur Golfer is one who plays the game as a non-remunerative or non-profit-making sport.

The Governing Body
The Governing Body of golf for the Rules of Amateur Status in any country is the National Union of the country concerned except in Great Britain and Ireland where the Governing Body is the Royal and Ancient Golf Club of St. Andrews.

Any person who considers that any action he is proposing to take might endanger his Amateur Status should submit particulars to the Committee for consideration.

RULE 1

Forfeiture of Amateur Status at any age

The following are examples of acts which are contrary to the Definition of an Amateur Golfer and cause forfeiture of Amateur Status:

1. Professionalism.
a. Receiving payment or compensation for serving as a Professional golfer or a teaching or playing assistant to a Professional golfer.
b. Taking any action for the purpose of becoming a Professional golfer except applying unsuccessfully for the position of a teaching or playing assistant of a Professional golfer.
Note 1. Such actions include filing application to a school or competition conducted to qualify persons to play as Professionals in tournaments; receiving services from or entering into an agreement, written or oral, with a sponsor or Professional agent; agreement to accept payment or compensation for allowing one's name or likeness as a skilled golfer to be used for any commercial purpose; and holding or retaining membership in any organisation of Professional golfers.
Note 2. Receiving payment or compensation as a shop assistant is not itself a breach of the Rules, provided duties do not include playing or giving instruction.

2. Playing for Prize Money. Playing for prize money or its equivalent in a match, tournament or exhibition.

3. Instruction. Receiving payment or compensation for giving instruction in playing golf, either orally, in writing, by pictures or by other demonstrations, to either individuals or groups.
Exceptions:
1. Golf instruction may be given by an employee of an educational institution or system to students of the institution or system and by camp counsellors to those in their charge, provided that the total time devoted to golf instruction during a year comprises less than 50 percent of the time spent during the year in the performance of all duties as such employee or counsellor.
2. Payment or compensation may be accepted for instruction in writing, provided one's ability or reputation as a golfer was not a major factor in his employment or in the commission or sale of his work.

4. Prizes and Testimonials
(a) Acceptance of a prize or prize voucher of retail value exceeding as follows;

	In GB&I	*Elsewhere*
For an event of more than 2 rounds	£170	$400 US or the equivalent
For an event of 2 rounds or less	£110	$260 US or the equivalent

or such lesser figure, if any, as may be decided by the Governing Body of golf in any country, or
(b) Acceptance of a testimonial in Great Britain and Ireland of retail value exceeding £170, elsewhere of retail value exceeding $400 US or the equivalent, or such lesser figure as may be decided by the Governing Body of golf in any country, or
(c) For a junior golfer, of such age as may be determined by the Governing Body of golf in any country, taking part in an event limited exclusively to juniors, acceptance of a prize or prize voucher in Great Britain and Ireland of retail value exceeding £50; elsewhere of retail value exceeding $120 US or the equivalent, or such lesser figure, if any, as may be decided by the Governing Body of golf in any country, or
(d) Conversion of a prize or prize voucher into money, or
(e) Accepting a gratuity in connection with a golfing event.

Exceptions:
1. Prizes of only symbolic value, provided that their symbolic nature is distinguished by distinctive permanent marking.

2. More than one testimonial award may be accepted from different donors even though their total retail value exceeds £170 or $400 U.S., provided they are not presented so as to evade such value limit for a single award.

Note 1. Events covered. The limits referred to in Clauses (a) or (c) above apply to total prize or prize vouchers received by any one person for any event or series of events in any one tournament or exhibition, including hole-in-one or other events in which golf skill is a factor.

Note 2. "Retail value" is the price at which merchandise is available to anyone at a retail source, and the onus of proving the value of a particular prize rests with the donor.

Note 3. Purpose of prize vouchers. A prize voucher may be issued and redeemed only by the Committee in charge of a competition for the purchase of goods from a Professional's shop or other retail source, which may be specified by the Committee. It may not be used for such items as travel or hotel expenses, a bar bill, or a Club Subscription.

Note 4. Maximum Value of Prizes in any event for individuals. It is recommended that the total value of scratch or each division of handicap prizes should not exceed twice the maximum retail value of prize permitted in Rule 1-4(a) and (c) in an 18-hole competition, three times in a 36-hole competition, four times in a 54-hole competition and five times in a 72-hole competition.

Note 5. Testimonial Awards. Such awards relate to notable performances or contributions to golf as distinguished from tournament prizes.

5. Lending Name or Likeness. Because of golf skill or golf reputation receiving or contracting to receive payment, compensation or personal benefit, directly or indirectly, for allowing one's name or likeness to be used in any way for the advertisement or sale of anything, whether or not used in or appertaining to golf except as a golf author or broadcaster as permitted by Rule 1-7.

Note: A player may accept equipment from anyone dealing in such equipment provided no advertising is involved.

6. Personal Appearance. Because of golf skill or golf reputation, receiving payment or compensation, directly or indirectly, for a personal appearance.

Exception:

Actual expenses in connection with personal appearances may be paid or reimbursed provided no golf competition or exhibition is involved.

7. Broadcasting and Writing. Because of golf skill or golf reputation, receiving payment or compensation, directly or indirectly, for broadcasting concerning golf, a gold event or golf events, writing golf articles or books, or allowing one's name to be advertised or published as the author of golf articles or books of which he is not actually the author.

Exceptions:

1. Broadcasting or writing as part of one's primary occupation or career, provided instruction in playing golf is not included (Rule 1-3).

2. Part-time broadcasting or writing, provided (a) the player is actually the author of the commentary, articles or books, (b) instruction in playing golf is not included and (c) the payment or compensation does not have the purpose or effect, directly or indirectly, of financing participation in a golf competition or golf competitions.

8. Expenses. Accepting expenses, in money or otherwise, from any source to engage in a golf competition or exhibition.

Exceptions:

A player may receive expenses, not exceeding the actual expenses incurred, as follows:

1. From a member of the family or legal guardian;

or

2. As a player in a golf competition or exhibition limited exclusively to players who have not reached their 18th birthday;

or

3. As a representative of his Country, County, Club or similar body in team competitions or team training camps at home or abroad, or as a representative of his Country taking part in a National Championship abroad immediately preceding or following directly upon an international team competition, where such expenses are paid by the body he represents, or by the body controlling golf in the territory he is visiting;

or

4. As an individual nominated by a National or County Union or Club to engage in an event at home or abroad provided that:

(a) The player nominated has not reached such age as may be determined by the Governing Body of Golf in the country from which the nomination is made.

(b) The expenses shall be paid only by the National Union or County Union responsible in the area from which the nomination is made and shall be limited to twenty competitive days in any one calendar year. The expenses are deemed to include reasonable travelling time and practice days in connection with the twenty competitive days.

(c) Where the event is to take place abroad, the approval of the National Union of the country in which the event is to be staged and, if the nominating body is not the National Union of the country from which the nomination is made, the approval of the National Union shall first be obtained by the nominating body.

(d) Where the event is to take place at home, and where the nomination is made by a County Union or Club, the approval of the National Union or the County Union in the area in which the event is to be staged shall first be obtained.

(*Note:* The term "County Union" covers any Province, State or equivalent Union or Association);

or

5. As a player invited for reasons unrelated to golf skill, e.g. celebrities, business associates, etc., to take part in golfing events;

or

6. As a player in an exhibition in aid of a recognised Charity provided the exhibition is not run in connection with another golfing event.

7. As a player in a handicap individual or handicap team sponsored golfing event where expenses are paid by the sponsor on behalf of the player to take part in the event provided the event has been approved as follows:

(a) where the event is to take place at home the approval of the Governing Body (see Definition) shall first be obtained in advance by the sponsor, and

(b) where the event is to take place both at home and abroad the approval of the two or more Governing Bodies shall first be obtained in advance by the sponsor. The application for this approval should be sent to the Governing Body of golf in the country where the competition commences.

(c) where the event is to take place abroad the approval of two or more Governing Bodies shall first be obtained by the sponsor. The application for this approval should be sent to the Governing Body of golf of the country whose players shall be taking part in the event abroad.

(*Note 1:* Business Expenses. It is permissible to play in a golf competition while on a business trip with expenses paid provided that the golf part of the expenses is borne personally and is not charged to business. Further, the business involved must be actual and substantial, and not merely a subterfuge for legitimising expenses when the primary purpose is a golf competition).

(*Note 2:* Private Transport. Acceptance of private transport furnished or arranged for by a tournament sponsor, directly or indirectly, as an inducement for a player to engage in a golf competition or exhibition shall be considered accepting expenses under Rule 1-8).

9. Scholarships. Because of golf skill or golf reputation, accepting the benefits of a scholarship or grant-in-aid other than one whose terms and conditions have been approved by the Amateur Status Committee of the Royal and Ancient Golf Club of St. Andrews.

10. Membership. Because of golf skill accepting membership in a Golf Club without full payment for the class of membership for the purpose of playing for that Club.

11. Conduct Detrimental to Golf. Any conduct, including activities in connection with golf gambling, which is considered detrimental to the best interests of the game.

RULE 2

Procedure for Enforcement and Reinstatement

1. Decision on a Breach. Whenever information of a possible breach of the Definition of an Amateur Golfer by a player claiming to be an Amateur shall come to the attention of the appropriate Committee of the Governing Body, the Committee, after such investigation as it may deem desirable, shall decide whether a breach has occurred. Each case shall be considered on its merits. The decision of the Committee shall be final.

2. Enforcement. Upon a decision that a player has acted contrary to the Definition of an Amateur Golfer, the Committee may declare the Amateur Status of the player forfeited or require the player to refrain or desist from specified actions as a condition of retaining his Amateur Status.

The Committee shall use its best endeavours to ensure that the player is notified and may notify any interested golf association of any action taken under this paragraph.

3. Reinstatement. The Committee shall have sole power to reinstate a player to Amateur Status or to deny reinstatement. Each application for reinstatement shall be decided on its merits. In considering an application for reinstatement, the Committee shall normally be guided by the following principles:

a. Awaiting Reinstatement.
The professional holds an advantage over the amateur by reason of having devoted himself to the game as his profession; other persons infringing the Rules of Amateur Status also obtain advantages not available to the amateur. They do not necessarily lose such advantage merely by deciding to cease infringing the Rules. Therefore, an applicant for reinstatement to Amateur Status shall undergo a period awaiting reinstatement as prescribed by the Committee.
The period awaiting reinstatement shall start from the date of the player's last breach of the Definition of an Amateur Golfer unless the Committee decides that it shall start from the date when the player's last breach became known to the Committee.

b. Period Awaiting Reinstatement.
The period awaiting reinstatement shall normally be related to the period the player was in breach. However, no applicant shall normally be eligible for reinstatement until he has conducted himself in accordance with the Definition of an Amateur Golfer for a period of at least two consecutive years. The Committee, however, reserves the right to extend or to shorten such a period. A longer period will normally be required of applicants who have been in breach more than five years. Players of national prominence who have been in breach for more than five years shall not normally be eligible for reinstatement.

c. One Reinstatement
A player shall not normally be reinstated more than once.

d. Status While Awaiting Reinstatement.
During the period awaiting reinstatement an applicant for reinstatement shall conform with the Definition of an Amateur Golfer.
He shall not be eligible to enter competitions as an Amateur. He may, however, enter competitions, and win a prize, solely among members of a Club of which he is a member, subject to the approval of the Club; but he may not represent such Club against other Clubs.

Forms of Application for Countries under the jurisdiction of the Royal and Ancient Golf Club

(a) Each application for reinstatement shall be submitted on the approved form to the County Union where the applicant wishes to play as an Amateur. Such Union shall, after making all necessary enquiries, forward it through the National Union (and in the case of lady applicants, the Ladies Golf Union) and the appropriate Professional Golfers' Association, with comments endorsed thereon, to the Governing Body of golf in that country. Forms of application for reinstatement may be obtained from the Royal and Ancient Golf Club or from the National or County Unions. The application shall include such information as the Royal and Ancient Golf Club may require from time to time and it shall be signed and certified by the applicant.
(b) Any application made in countries under the jurisdiction of the Royal and Ancient Golf Club of St. Andrews which the Governing Body of golf in that country considers to be doubtful or not to be covered by the above regulations may be submitted to the Royal and Ancient Golf Club of St. Andrews whose decision shall be final.

R. & A. POLICY ON GAMBLING

The Definition of an Amateur Golfer provides than an Amateur golfer is one who plays the game as a non-remunerative or non-profit-making sport. When gambling motives are introduced evils can arise to threaten the integrity of both the game and the individual players.
The R&A does not object to participation in wagering among individual golfers or teams of golfers when participation in the wagering is limited to the players, the players may only wager on themselves or their teams, the sole source of all money won by players is advanced by the players and the primary purpose is the playing of the game for enjoyment.
The distinction between playing for prize money and gambling is essential to the validity of the Rules of Amateur Status. The following constitute golf wagering and not playing for prize money:
1. Participation in wagering among individual golfers.
2. Participation in wagering among teams.
Organised Amateur events open to the general golfing public and designed and promoted to create cash prizes are not approved by the R&A. Golfers participating in such events without irrevocably waiving their right to cash prizes are deemed by the R&A to be playing for prize money.
The R&A is opposed to and urges Unions and Clubs, and all other sponsors of golf competitions to prohibit types of gambling such as: Calcuttas, auction sweepstakes and any other forms of gambling organised for general participation or permitting

participants to bet on someone other than themselves or their teams.

Attention is drawn to Rule 1-11 relating to conduct detrimental to the game, under which players can forfeit their Amateur Status. It is the Club which, by permitting competitions where excessive gambling is involved, or illegal prizes are offered, bears the responsibility for which the individual is penalised and Unions have the power to invoke severe sanctions against a Club or individual for consistently ignoring this policy.

INDEX

The Standard Scratch Score and Handicapping Scheme 1983

Revised 1st January 1986

(This scheme does not apply to ladies' clubs under the jurisdiction of the Ladies' Golf Union)

Published and administered by the Council of National Golf Unions and adopted by the Unions affiliated to the European Golf Association

Foreword

The Standard Scratch Score and Handicapping Scheme was prepared by the British Golf Unions' Joint Advisory Council in 1925 at the request of the Royal and Ancient Golf Club of St Andrews and has been in operation throughout Great Britain and Ireland since 1st March, 1926.

The Scheme incorporated in this book introduces a new concept in handicapping based on the system presently used by the Australian Golf Union. The Council of National Golf Unions acknowledges the assistance received from that Union and its officials in formulating the Scheme, which takes account of all scores returned by players under Medal Play conditions.

No change has been made in the present method of fixing the Standard Scratch Scores of courses but, on the principle that uniformity and equity in handicapping can be more effectively achieved if there is uniformity and equity in the fixing of Standard Scratch Scores, the Council of National Golf Unions will, as a further step, be investigating methods which would ensure closer alignment of Standard Scratch Scores throughout Great Britain and Ireland.

In view of the radically changed method of handicapping, its introduction cannot be regarded as a further revision of the existing Scheme and, for that reason, the Council of National Golf Unions has decided that the Scheme to be introduced on the 1st January 1983, will be known as the Standard Scratch Score and Handicapping Scheme 1983.

Since its introduction on 1st January 1983 amendments have been made to the Scheme. The amendments recognise that handicaps generally rose more quickly than was originally anticipated and stem from the Council's policy of keeping the effects of the Scheme's requirements constantly under review. The principal changes are (a) the introduction of a *Winter Period* (Definition Q), (b) limit of 0.1 to the increase of a player's *Exact Handicap* in all *Categories*, and (c) the establishment of a *Buffer Zone* (Definition R). These caused additions to Definitions and amendments to clauses throughout the Scheme all of which, with other minor alterations are referred to on the following page.

Principal Changes Incorporated since 1st January 1983

(a) Modification of Definition G (2).
(b) Addition of Definitions Q and R.
(c) Addition of sub clause 9.(7).
(d) Addition of sub clauses 12.(5)(i) and 12.(5)(j).
(e) Modification of sub clause 13.(8).
(f) Modification of sub clause 15.(2).
(g) Modification of sub clauses 16.(1), 16.(2), 16.(3), 16.(6), 16.(8) and 16.(11).
(h) Modification of sub clause 17.(3).
(i) A complete revision of clause 19.
(j) The deletion of clause 20.
(k) The modification of Appendices A and B.
(l) The addition of Appendix D.

Part One
Definitions

Definition
A. Union.
B. Area Authority.
C. Home Club.
D. Affiliated Club.
E. Handicapping Authority.

F. Handicap Committee.
G. Handicaps.
H. Categories of Handicap.
I. Measured Course.
J. Distance Point.
K. Medal Tee.
L. Medal Play Conditions.
M. Qualifying Competition.
N. Qualifying Score.
O. Aggregate Fourball Competition.
P. Nett Differential.
Q. Winter Period.
R. Buffer Zone.

Definitions

(Throughout the scheme whenever a word or expression is used which is defined within the following definitions the word or expression is printed in italics.)

A–Union

A *Union* is any national organisation in control of amateur golf in any country.

B–Area Authority

An *Area Authority* is any authority appointed by a *Union* to act on behalf of that *Union* for the purposes of the Scheme within a specified area.

C–Affiliated Club

An *Affiliated Club* is a club affiliated to a *Union* or *Area Authority* which pays to the *Union* and *Area Authority* a specified annual per capita fee in respect of each eligible member.

D–Home Club

A player's *Home Club* is an *Affiliated Club* of which the player is a member. If the player is a member of more than one *Affiliated Club* he shall nominate one as his *Home Club*.

E–Handicapping Authority

The *Handicapping Authority* for a player is his *Home Club* subject to the overall jurisdiction of the *Union*.

F–Handicap Committee

The *Handicap Committee* is the body appointed by an *Affiliated Club* to administer the Scheme within the club.

G–Handicaps

(1) *Exact Handicap*–a player's *Exact Handicap* is his handicap calculated in accordance with the provisions of the Scheme to one decimal place.

(2) *Playing Handicap*–a player's *Playing Handicap* is his *Exact Handicap* calculated to the nearest whole number (0.5 is rounded upwards).

H–Categories of Handicap

Handicaps are divided into the following *Categories:*
Category 1: Handicaps of 5 or less.
Category 2: Handicaps of 6 to 12 inclusive.
Category 3: Handicaps of 13 to 20 inclusive.
Category 4: Handicaps of 21 to 28 inclusive.

I–Measured Course

Any course played over by an *Affiliated Club* the measured length of which has been certified in accordance with the requirements of clause 2.

J–Distance Point

The *Distance Point* is the position of a permanent marker indicating the point from which the length of a hole is measured.

K–Medal Tee

A *Medal Tee* is a rectangular area the front of which shall not be more than 10 yards (9 metres) in front of the relevant *Distance Point* and the rear of which shall not be less than 2 yards (2 metres) behind the *Distance Point*. (NOTE: Special rules apply when the length of a *Measured Course* has been temporarily reduced by more ,than 100 yards (91 metres)–see clause 7(b)).

L–Medal Play Conditions

Medal Play Conditions prevail during stroke, par and Stableford competitions played with full handicap allowance over 18 holes under the Rules of Golf from *Medal Tees*. *Medal Play Conditions* shall not prevail unless the length of the course played varies by no more than 100 yards (91 metres) from the length of the *Measured Course*. (NOTE: Special rules apply when the length of a *Measured Course* has been temporarily reduced by more than 100 yards (91 metres)–see clause 7(b)).

M–Qualifying Competition

A *Qualifying Competition* is any competition in which *Medal Play Conditions* prevail subject to the restrictions and limitations contained in the Scheme or imposed by *Unions*.

N–Qualifying Score

A *Qualifying Score* is any score including a *no return* returned in a *Qualifying Competition*.

O–Aggregate Fourball Competition

An *Aggregate Fourball Competition* is a *Qualifying Competition* in which the completed scores at each hole of a team of not more than two amateur players are aggregated.

P–Nett Differential

The *Nett Differential* is the difference (+ or −) between the nett score returned by a player in a *Qualifying Competition* and the Standard Scratch Score.

Q–Winter Period

The *Winter Period* is a period of four consecutive calendar months between the months of December and April inclusive to be stipulated by *Unions* during which the *Exact Handicap* of a player who returns a score in a *Qualifying Competition* above his *Playing Handicap* shall not be increased.

R–Buffer Zone

The *Buffer Zone* is a zone which applies only to scores returned by players in *Qualifying Competitions* with *Nett Differentials* of +1 and +2 (one or two strokes above *Playing Handicaps*).

Table of Provisional Standard Scratch Scores

Standard length of course	Lengths included in standard length		Provisional Standard Scratch Score
Yards	*Yards*	*Metres*	
7100	7001-7200	6402-6584	74
6900	6801-7000	6219-6401	73
6700	6601-6800	6036-6218	72
6500	6401-6600	5853-6035	71
6300	6201-6400	5670-5852	70
6100	5951-6200	5442-5669	69
5800	5701-5950	5213-5441	68
5500	5451-5700	4984-5212	67
5300	5201-5450	4756-4983	66
5100	5001-5200	4573-4755	65
4900	4801-5000	4390-4572	64
4700	4601-4800	4207-4389	63
4500	4401-4600	4024-4206	62
4300	4201-4400	3841-4023	61
4100	4001-4200	3659-3840	60

1 yard = 0.91440 metre
1 metre = 1.09361 yards

Part Two

The Golf Course and the Standard Scratch Score

Clause

1. The Standard Scratch Score.
2. Course measurement.
3. Alterations to courses.
4. Tees.
5. Par.
6. Preferred lies.
7. Permitted adjustments to a *Measured Course*.

1. The Standard Scratch Score

1.(1) The Standard Scratch Score is the score which a scratch player is expected to return over a *Measured Course*. In the case of a nine-hole course it represents two rounds.

1.(2) The allocation of Standard Scratch Scores shall be the responsibility of the *Union*.

1.(3) The table above will provide a guide to officials in making their assessments.

1.(4) In assessing the Standard Scratch Score of a course, officials will take as the starting point the provisional Standard Scratch Score from the Table. They will then consider the following points:

(a) The terrain and general layout of the course.
(b) Normal ground conditions–Is run average, above average, or below average?
(c) Sizes of greens and whether watered or unwatered.
(d) Hazards–Are greens well guarded or open?
(e) Width of fairways, the effect of trees and nature of rough.
(f) Nearness of *out of bounds* to fairways and greens.
(g) Average weather conditions throughout the playing year. Is the course exposed and subject to high winds for most of the year? Is it sheltered from the full effects of adverse weather?
(h) The distance by which the length of the course varies from the standard length shown in column one of the Table.

1.(5) Having considered all these points officials will fix the Standard Scratch Score of the course by:

(a) Confirming the Provisional Standard Scratch Score as the Standard Scratch Score.
(b) Adding a stroke or strokes to the provisional Standard Scratch Score.

(c) Deducting a stroke or strokes from the Provisional Standard Scratch Score.

1.(6) The Standard Scratch Score so fixed will have taken into account the playing difficulty of the course or lack of it, and average weather conditions throughout the year and, once fixed, will remain constant.

1.(7) At the discretion of a *Union* courses of less than 4001 yards may be allocated such Standard Scratch Score as the *Union* shall determine.

2. Course Measurement

Measurement shall be by plan or projection along the horizontal plane from the *Distance Point* on the *Medal Tee* to the centre of the green of each hole.

In the case of a dog-leg hole, measurement shall be along the centre line of the fairway to the axis and then to the centre of the green. Measurement shall be carried out by a qualified surveyor, or someone competent and experienced in the handling of surveying instruments, who shall grant a certificate showing details of the length of the hole and the total playing length of the course. Subsequent alterations to the length of the course will require a certificate only for the altered hole or holes which shall be measured in the manner prescribed above.

3. Alterations to Courses

When alterations have been carried out to a course increasing or decreasing its length, the club shall submit a *Form of Application* through its *Area Authority* to the *Union*. In the case of a new course, a *Form of Application* shall be submitted by the club through its *Area Authority* to the *Union* who will fix the Standard Scratch Score. The *Union* is responsible for all Standard Scratch Scores in that country.

4. Tees

All clubs with the necessary facilities should have back and forward *Medal Tees* with a yardage measurement from each tee and a separate Standard Scratch Score as measured from back and forward *Medal Tees* permanently marked.

To facilitate the use of the correct tees, tee boxes or other objects in use to mark the teeing ground, the Royal and Ancient Golf Club of St Andrews recommends that they shall be painted as follows:

Ladies' Standard *Medal Tees*	Red
Men's Forward *Medal Tees*	Yellow
*Ladies' Back Tees	Black
Men's Back *Medal Tees*	White

**Not adopted by the Ladies' Golf Union.*

When a National Championship is being played over a course the tee markers may be coloured Blue.

5. Par

The Standard Scratch Score must not be allocated amongst the individual holes, but should be printed as a total on the card. The par figure for each hole should be printed alongside each hole on the card. Par for each hole is fixed as follows:

Par	*Yards*	*Metres*
3	Holes of 250 yards and under	Holes of 228 metres and under
4	Holes from 251 to 475 yards inclusive	Holes from 229 to 434 metres inclusive
5	Holes of 476 yards and over	Holes of 435 metres and over

The total of the Par figures for each hole of a course will not necessarily coincide with the Standard Scratch Score of that course. Par should be used for Stableford and similar competitions.

6. Preferred Lies

When preferred lies are in operation the following points shall be taken into consideration:

Medal Play Conditions will apply notwithstanding the application of a Local Rule for preferred lies as a result of adverse conditions especially during the winter. For this purpose the winter period shall be from 1st November to 30th April. Preferred lies may be used during that period but are not mandatory upon clubs during any part thereof. The Local Rule may apply to specified holes only. Outside the winter period *Medal Play Conditions* will not apply if preferred lies are in operation unless the consent of the *Union* or *Area Authority* has been first obtained.

The Royal and Ancient Golf Club Rules of Golf Committee recommends that a Local Rule be made, worded as follows:

A ball lying through the green may be lifted and cleaned without penalty and placed within 6 inches of where it originally lay, but not nearer the hole and so as to preserve as nearly as possible the stance required to play from the original lie. After the ball has been so placed, it is in play.

If however, a Club Committee considers that the term 'through the green' ***(Definition 35)*** *gives too much latitude, and if it is satisfied that the area in which it wishes to apply the Local Rule is clearly defined by the term 'fairway',* *the Rules of Golf Committee would have no objection to the use of the term 'fairway' in the Local Rule, notwithstanding that it is neither defined nor used in the Rules of Golf (Decision 65/20/248) under Local Rules.*

It is recommended that clubs use the term *fairway* in their Local Rule which must be posted on the Club Notice Board together with the club's definition of *fairway*.

7. Permitted Adjustments to a Measured Course

Whilst each *Affiliated Club* must endeavour to maintain the length of its *Measured Course* at all times *Medal Play Conditions* nevertheless prevail when the length of a course has been reduced in the following circumstances:

(a) When, to allow movement of the playing position on the *Medal Tee* or the use of a temporary green, the length of the course being played has been reduced by not more than 100 yards (91 metres) from the length of the *Measured Course*. The tee positions used must nevertheless be within the area defined by Definition K. (NOTE: The maximum movement forward on any *Medal Tee* must not exceed 10 yards (9 metres)–See Definition K.)

(b) When, to allow work to proceed on course alterations, or for reasons other than weather conditions, it is necessary to reduce the playing length of the *Measured Course* by between 100 and 300 yards (91 and 274 metres). In these circumstances, the club shall reduce the Standard Scratch Score of the *Measured Course* temporarily by 1 stroke and report to the *Union*, or to such other body nominated by the *Union*, the reduction in the Standard Scratch Score, and the reason for it. The club must also notify the *Union* or other body when the course has been restored to its measured length and the official Standard Scratch Score reinstated.

Part Three
Handicapping

8. Introduction

8.(1) The Council of National Golf Unions Standard Scratch Score and Handicapping Scheme has been revised to achieve a uniformity and equity in handicapping throughout Great Britain and Ireland and member countries of the European Golf Association adopting the Scheme. The nature of the game of golf, with its varying playing conditions, makes handicapping a relatively inexact operation. Nevertheless if the same principles are sensibly and universally applied by *Handicap Committees*, a high degree of uniformity in handicapping can be achieved. It is therefore of paramount importance that all parties to the Scheme fulfil their obligation to it and these are set out below.

8.(2) Handicapping within the Scheme is delegated to *Affiliated Clubs* subject to the overall jurisdiction of the *Union*.

9. Rights and Obligations of the Union

The *Union*:

9.(1) Shall have overall jurisdiction for the administration of the Scheme.

9.(2) May delegate any part of that jurisdiction to an *Area Authority*.

9.(3) Shall ratify all *Playing Handicaps* reduced to scratch or below immediately after the reduction.

9.(4) Shall have the right to obtain information upon handicaps from *Affiliated Clubs* at any time.

9.(5) Shall establish within the *Union* conditions, restrictions and limitations to be imposed in respect of competitions deemed to be *Qualifying Competitions*.

9.(6) Shall settle any dispute referred to it. Its decision shall be final.

9.(7) Shall stipulate the four consecutive months which shall be the *Winter Period* in the Country over which it exercises jurisdiction. The *Winter Period* need not be the same four months throughout a Country.

10. Rights and Obligations of the Area Authority

The *Area Authority* shall:

10.(1) Administer the responsibilities delegated to it by the *Union*.

10.(2) Have the right to obtain information upon handicaps from *Affiliated Clubs* at any time.

11. Rights and Obligations of the Affiliated Club

The *Affiliated Club* shall:

11.(1) Act as the *Handicapping Authority* for all members for whom it is the *Home Club* subject to the overall jurisdiction of the *Union*.
11.(2) Ensure that the Scheme is properly applied in the club.
11.(3) Ensure that all handicaps are calculated in accordance with the Scheme.
11.(4) Appoint a *Handicap Committee* to perform the obligations set out in clause 12 below.

12. Rights and Obligations of the Handicap Committee

The *Handicap Committee* shall:

12.(1) Maintain a list in which the names of competitors must be entered prior to competing in a *Qualifying Competition* at the club.
12.(2) Ensure, so far as possible, that all cards taken out in *Qualifying Competitions* are returned to the committee including incomplete cards.
12.(3) Post on the club's notice board all changes of members' *Playing Handicaps* immediately they are made.
12.(4) Ensure that a record of members' current *Playing Handicaps* is available in a prominent position in the club house.
12.(5) When the club is a player's *Home Club:*
(a) Maintain on his behalf a handicap record sheet which shall include the information shown in Appendix A.
(b) Ensure his scores are recorded immediately after completion of each *Qualifying Competition* at the *Home Club* or the reporting of a *Qualifying Score* returned elsewhere.
(c) Keep his *Exact Handicap* up to date at all times.
(d) Notify the *Union* and *Area Authority* immediately the committee reduces a member's *Playing Handicap* to scratch or below and obtain ratification from the *Union* or, if so delegated, from the *Area Authority*. (NOTE: The reduction is effective before ratification.)
(e) Exercise the power to suspend handicaps contained in clause 17.
(f) When a member changes his *Home Club* send to the new *Home Club* a copy of the player's current handicap record sheet.
(g) Be empowered, if the committee considers that weather conditions during the play of any round of a *Qualifying Competition* were such as to render the proper playing of the game extremely difficult, to declare that that round shall not count as a *Qualifying Score*. The declaration shall be made in exceptional circumstances only and may be made at any time during the playing of the round or immediately thereafter. A player who returns a score below his *Playing Handicap* in such circumstances shall nevertheless report that score to his *Home Club* and it will be recorded in his handicap record sheet as a *Qualifying Score*. (NOTE: This power shall be exercised by *Unions, Area Authorities* and other organisations approved by a *Union* in respect of *Qualifying Competitions* organised by them.)
(h) Specify the conditions which apply when a player wishes to obtain a handicap under the provisions of clause 15.
(i) Exercise the powers to adjust players' handicaps contained in clause 19.
(j) As required by sub clause 19.(5) advise players of changes made to their handicaps under the provisions of clause 19.

13. Rights and Obligations of the Player

The player shall:

13.(1) Have one handicap only which shall be allotted and adjusted by his *Home Club*. That handicap shall apply elsewhere including other clubs of which the player is a member.
13.(2) If he is a member of more than one *Affiliated Club* select one as his *Home Club* and notify that club and the others of his choice.
13.(3) Not change his *Home Club* except by giving advance notice of the change which can take effect only at the end of a calendar year unless he has ceased to be a member of his *Home Club* or both clubs agree to the change taking place at an earlier date.
13.(4) Report to his *Home Club* the names of all other *Affiliated Clubs* of which he is, becomes, or ceases to be, a member and report to all other *Affiliated Clubs* of which he is a member:
(a) The name of his *Home Club* and any changes of his *Home Club* and
(b) Alterations to his *Playing Handicap* made by his *Home Club*.
13.(5) Ensure that before competing in a *Qualifying Competition* his entry has been inserted in the competition entry list.
13.(6) Ensure that all competition cards in *Qualifying Competitions*, whether or not complete, are returned to the organising committee.
13.(7) Report to his *Home Club* immediately all *Qualifying Scores* (including no returns) returned away from his *Home Club* advising the *Home Club* of the date of the *Qualifying*

Competition, the venue and the Standard Scratch Score together with the following:
(a) After a stroke play *Qualifying Competition* the gross score returned.
(b) After a Stableford *Qualifying Competition* the par of the course and the number of points scored.
(c) After a par *Qualifying Competition* the par of the course and the score versus par.
(NOTE: Players are reminded that failure to report scores returned away from their *Home Clubs* (including no returns) is likely to lead to the suspension of offending players' handicaps under the provisions of clause 17.
13.(8) Prior to playing in any competition at a club other than his *Home Club* ensure that any appropriate reductions to his *Playing Handicap* have been made or alternatively comply with the obligations set out in clause 16.(11) by either reducing his *Playing Handicap* for that competition only or informing the committee organising the competition of scores returned which may justify a reduction of his handicap.

14. Qualifying Scores

14.(1) The only scores to be recorded on a player's handicap record sheet are:
(a) *Qualifying Scores* as defined.
(b) Scores returned below his *Playing Handicap* in any abandoned round of a *Qualifying Competition* or in any round of a *Qualifying Competition* when that round has been declared by the committee under the provision of clause 12.(5)(g) not to be a *Qualifying Score*.
(c) Correct scores in a *Qualifying Competition* which are disqualified for any reason.
(d) Scores returned in a *Qualifying Competition* played over 18 holes on a course reduced in length under the provisions of clause 7.
(e) Scores returned in a *Qualifying Competition* played over a *Measured Course* when local rules are in operation for preferred lies (as permitted by clause 6) or for any other purpose provided the rules are authorised by Appendix 1 of the Rules of Golf or have been approved by the Rules of Golf Committee of the Royal and Ancient Golf Club of St Andrews.
(f) The individual scores and no returns returned by players in *Aggregate Fourball Competitions*. NOTE: The competition must be a *Qualifying Competition*.
NOTE: *Qualifying Scores* returned in Stableford and par competitions shall be converted into *Nett Differentials* by using the tables in Appendix C.
14.(2) The following returns shall not be accepted as *Qualifying Scores* in any circumstances:
(a) Scores returned in any better ball fourball competition.
(b) Scores returned in competitions over less than 18 holes.
(c) Scores returned in any competition which is not played in accordance with the Rules of Golf and authorised Local Rules.
(d) Scores returned in *running medals*. A running medal is an extended competition in which the player has the option of selecting the day or days on which he shall compete and/or how many returns he shall make. A competition extended over two or more days solely to accommodate the number of players entered is not a running medal.
(e) Subject to clause 14.(1)(b) scores returned in any round of a *Qualifying Competition* declared by the committee not to be *Qualifying Scores* under the provisions of clause 12.(5)(g).
(f) Any competition other than an *Aggregate Fourball Competition* in which competitors play in partnership with another competitor.
(g) Stableford and par competitions played with less than full handicap allowance.

15. Allotment of Handicaps

15.(1) The maximum handicap is 28. (Maximum *Exact Handicap* 28.0.)
15.(2) A handicap can be allotted only to an amateur member of an *Affiliated Club*.
15.(3) To obtain a handicap a player shall submit three cards preferably marked over a *Measured Course* which shall be adjusted by the *Handicap Committee* so that any score of more than 2 over par at any hole shall be amended to 2 over par. After these adjustments have been made, the three cards shall be averaged and the player allotted an *Exact Handicap* equivalent to the number of strokes by which the average differs from the Standard Scratch Score and rounded to the nearest whole number. The *Handicap Committee* may allot a player an initial whole number *Exact Handicap* less than the average if it has reason to consider that a lower handicap is more appropriate to the player's ability. When a player fails to return cards justifying an *Exact Handicap* of 28 he may, at the discretion of the *Handicap Committee*, be given an *Exact Handicap* of 28. The player's *Playing Handicap* shall equal the *Exact Handicap* allotted.
15.(4) A player without a handicap shall not be allotted a *Category 1 Handicap* without the written authority of the *Union*, or *Area Authority* if so delegated.

16. Alteration of Handicaps

16.(1) Definition 1 divides handicaps into the following four *Categories*:
Category 1: Handicaps of 5 or less.

Category 2: Handicaps of 6 to 12 inclusive.
Category 3: Handicaps of 13 to 20 inclusive.
Category 4: Handicaps of 21 to 28 inclusive.

16.(2) If a player plays to his *Playing Handicap* or returns a score within the *Buffer Zone* (i.e. one or two strokes above his *Playing Handicap*) his *Exact Handicap* is not changed.

16.(3) Subject to the provisions of sub clause 12.(5)(g) if a player at any time other than in the *Winter Period* returns a score with a *Nett Differential* of +3 or more (three strokes or more above his *Playing Handicap*) or records a *no return* his *Exact Handicap* is increased by 0.1 (not by an amount determined by the extent to which he was above his *Playing Handicap*). Scores returned and *no returns* recorded by a player in the *Winter Period* do not increase his *Exact Handicap*.

16.(4) If a player plays below his *Playing Handicap* his *Exact Handicap* is reduced by an amount per stroke that he was below his *Playing Handicap*, the amount per stroke being determined by his *Handicap Category*.

16.(5) The recording of scores shall be kept by *Nett Differential* i.e. the difference (+ or −) between the player's nett score and the Standard Scratch Score. The date, *Nett Differential, Exact Handicap* and *Playing Handicap* must be recorded on the player's handicap record sheet.

16.(6) *Exact Handicaps* shall be adjusted as follows, with reference to the handicap adjustment tables, Appendix B:

		If Nett Differential is:	
Category	**Playing Handicap**	**Above Buffer Zone add *only***	**Below SSS subtract for *each* stroke below**
1	Up to 5	0.1	0.1
2	6 to 12	0.1	0.2
3	13 to 20	0.1	0.3
4	21 to 28	0.1	0.4

For example:

If a player on 11.2 returns a score with a *Nett Differential* of 4 his *Exact Handicap* becomes 11.3. If he then returns a score with a *Nett Differential* of −7 his *Exact Handicap* is reduced by 7 times 0.2=1.4, i.e. to an *Exact Handicap* of 9.9 and his *Playing Handicap* is 10 which is immediately his new handicap.

16.(7) When a player's handicap is to be reduced so that it goes from a higher *Category* to a lower *Category*, it shall be reduced at the rate appropriate to the higher *Category* only so far as brings his *Playing Handicap* into the lower *Category* and the balance of the reduction shall be at the rate appropriate to the lower *Category*.

For example:

It a player on 21.2 returns a score with a *Nett Differential* of −6, i.e. 6 strokes below his *Playing Handicap* of 21, his handicap is reduced as follows:

21.2−(2 times 0.4) (i.e. −0.8)=20.4
20.4−(4 times 0.3) (i.e. −1.2)=19.2.

16.(8) A player whose *Exact Handicap* contains 0.5 or over shall be given the next higher handicap, e.g. 12.5 exact would be 13 *Playing Handicap*. This applies when handicaps are to be increased or reduced.

NOTE: *Exact Handicap* −0.5 rounded upwards is *Playing Handicap* scratch and not plus one.

16.(9) Reductions shall be made on the day the score becomes known to the *Home Club*.

16.(10) Increases shall be made at the end of each calendar month or at such more frequent intervals as the *Home Club* may decide.

16.(11) If, for any reason, a player is unable to report to his *Home Club* a *Qualifying Score* or *Scores* below his *Playing Handicap* or has been unable to ascertain, after reporting such scores, whether or not his *Playing Handicap* has been reduced, he shall then, before competing in a further competition at a club other than his *Home Club*, either;

(a) For that competition only, make such reduction to his *Playing Handicap* as shall be appropriate under the Scheme, or

(b) Report to the committee organising the competition the relevant score or scores returned below his *Playing Handicap*. The committee may, for that competition only, reduce the player's *Playing Handicap*.

NOTE: Increases to *Playing Handicaps* may not be made under the provisions of this sub clause.

16.(12) The procedure for the restoration of handicaps which have been lost is contained in clause 18.

17. Suspension, Lapsing and Loss of Handicaps

17.(1) The *Handicap Committee*, or other body appointed by the *Home Club* for the purposes of this clause, shall suspend the handicap of any player who in its opinion has constantly or blatantly failed to comply with his obligations under the Scheme. The player must be notified of the period of suspension and of any other conditions imposed. No player's handicap shall be suspended without first affording him the opportunity of appearing before the committee or other body.

17.(2) If a player is suspended from

membership of his *Home Club* his handicap shall lapse automatically until his membership is reinstated.

17.(3) A player's handicap is lost immediately he ceases to be a member of an *Affiliated Club* or loses his amateur status.

17.(4) Whilst a player's handicap is suspended, lapsed or has been lost he shall not enter or compete in any competition which requires a competitor to be the holder of a handicap for either entering or competing in the competition.

18. Restoration of Handicaps

18.(1) A player who has lost his handicap for any reason other than suspension or lapsing may obtain a new handicap by complying with the requirements of clause 15. When allotting him a handicap the *Handicap Committee* will give due consideration to the handicap he last held. A *Category 1 Handicap* shall not be allotted without the written approval of the *Union*, or *Area Authority* if so delegated.

18.(2) The lapsed handicap of a player suspended from membership of his *Home Club* shall be reinstated when his membership is restored and shall be the same as the handicap he held when his membership was suspended.

19. Powers of the Handicap Committee Relating to General Play

19.(1) Whenever the *Handicap Committee* of a player's *Home Club* considers that a player's *Exact Handicap* is too high and does not reflect his current playing ability the *Handicap Committee* must, subject to the provisions of sub clause (3) of this clause, reduce his *Exact Handicap* to the figure it considers appropriate.

19.(2) Whenever the *Handicap Committee* of a player's *Home Club* considers that a player's *Exact Handicap* is too low and does not reflect his current playing ability the *Handicap Committee* must, subject to the provisions of sub clause (3) of this clause, recommend to the *Union*, or *Area Authority* if so delegated, that his *Exact Handicap* should be increased to the figure it considers appropriate.

19.(3) When the *Handicap Committee* has decided that the *Exact Handicap* of a player should be reduced to less than 5.5 or that the *Exact Handicap* of a player should be increased the *Handicap Committee* must refer the matter to the *Union*, or *Area Authority* if so delegated, with its recommended adjustment. The *Union* or *Area Authority* shall then authorise the recommended variation, reject the recommendation or refer the matter back to the *Handicap Committee* for further consideration. The *Union* or *Area Authority* shall be supplied with all the information upon which the recommendation is based and with any further information required.

19.(4) When deciding whether to effect or recommend an adjustment of handicap the *Handicap Committee* of the player's *Home Club* shall consider all available information regarding the player's golfing ability.

It shall consider in particular:

(a) The frequency of *Qualifying Scores* recently returned by the player to and below his *Playing Handicap*.

(b) The player's achievements in match play, fourball better ball competitions and other non-qualifying events.

(c) *Qualifying Scores* returned by the player in stroke play competitions which are adversely affected by one or more particularly bad holes. It may prove helpful to take into account the number of points the player would have scored if these *Qualifying Scores* had been in stableford competitions played with full handicap allowance.

19.(5) The *Handicap Committee* shall advise a player of any change of handicap under this clause and the change will become effective when the player becomes aware of the adjustment.

19.(6) The *Handicap Committee* or other body organising a competition at a Club which is not the player's *Home Club* may if it considers his handicap is too high because of scores reported pursuant to sub clause 16.(11)(b) or for any other reason reduce that handicap. Any reduction made under this sub clause shall apply only to the competition for which it is made.

19.(7) Decisions made by a *Handicap Committee*, *Union* or *Area Authority* under this clause shall be final.

NOTES

1. In the interests of equitable handicapping it is essential that all *Handicap Committees* keep the handicaps of the members for whom they act as the *Home Club* under review and that adjustments of handicaps are considered as soon as it comes to the committee's notice that a player's handicap may no longer correctly reflect his current general golfing ability.

2. The *Handicap Committee* should consider dealing more severely with a player whose general standard of play is known to be improving than it should with a player who it is believed has returned scores below his general ability but whose general playing ability is not considered to be improving.

Appendix A

Handicap Record Sheet

Name ______________________________

Home Club ______________________________

Other Clubs ______________________________

____

Date	Nett differential	Handicap		Date	Nett differential	Handicap		
		Exact	Playing			Exact	Playing	
May 1	B/F	21.0	21	June 30	B/F	19.4	19	
6	2	21.0	21	July				
7	4	21.1	21	8	7	19.5	19	
20	N/R	21.2	21	9	6	19.6	19	
21	−6	19.2	19	29	8	19.7	19	*Note 2*
June				30	3	19.8	20	
4	1	19.2	19	Aug				
5	4	19.3	19	6	2	19.8	20	
25	7	19.4	19	7	−6	18.0	18	
26	2	19.4	19	20	0	18.0	18	
				21	7	18.1	18	

Notes to Appendix A

1. The sheet above shows the *Playing Handicaps* when increases are made on the last day of each calendar month.
2. If increases had been made immediately the *Playing Handicap* would have been increased to 20 on the 8th July and the *Nett Differentials* of 6, 8 and 3 respectively on the 9th, 29th and 30th July would each have been reduced by 0.1. Thus, with the operation of the *Buffer Zone*, the *Exact Handicap* would have remained at 19.7 on 31st July and been 0.1 less than those shown thereafter.
3. *Nett Differential* is the difference (+ or −) between the Nett Score returned by a player in a *Qualifying Competition* and the Standard Scratch Score.
4. Scores returned on courses other than that of the player's *Home Club* should be distinguished by marking the *Nett Differential* thus: □.
5. Reductions of handicaps are effected immediately.
6. Increases of handicaps shall be made at the end of each calendar month or at such more frequent intervals as the *Home Club* may decide.

Appendix B

Table of Handicap Adjustments

Nett differentials	−1	−2	−3	−4	−5	−6	−7	−8	−9	−10	−11	−12	Over Buffer Zone
Exact handicaps Up to 5.4	-0.1	-0.2	-0.3	-0.4	-0.5	-0.6	-0.7	-0.8	-0.9	-1.0	-1.1	-1.2	0.1
5.5– 5.6	-0.2	-0.3	-0.4	-0.5	-0.6	-0.7	-0.8	-0.9	-1.0	-1.1	-1.2	-1.3	0.1
5.7– 5.8	-0.2	-0.4	-0.5	-0.6	-0.7	-0.8	-0.9	-1.0	-1.1	-1.2	-1.3	-1.4	0.1
5.9– 6.0	-0.2	-0.4	-0.6	-0.7	-0.8	-0.9	-1.0	-1.1	-1.2	-1.3	-1.4	-1.5	0.1
6.1– 6.2	-0.2	-0.4	-0.6	-0.8	-0.9	-1.0	-1.1	-1.2	-1.3	-1.4	-1.5	-1.6	0.1
6.3– 6.4	-0.2	-0.4	-0.6	-0.8	-1.0	-1.1	-1.2	-1.3	-1.4	-1.5	-1.6	-1.7	0.1
6.5– 6.6	-0.2	-0.4	-0.6	-0.8	-1.0	-1.2	-1.3	-1.4	-1.5	-1.6	-1.7	-1.8	0.1
6.7– 6.8	-0.2	-0.4	-0.6	-0.8	-1.0	-1.2	-1.4	-1.5	-1.6	-1.7	-1.8	-1.9	0.1
6.9– 7.0	-0.2	-0.4	-0.6	-0.8	-1.0	-1.2	-1.4	-1.6	-1.7	-1.8	-1.9	-2.0	0.1
7.1– 7.2	-0.2	-0.4	-0.6	-0.8	-1.0	-1.2	-1.4	-1.6	-1.8	-1.9	-2.0	-2.1	0.1
7.3– 7.4	-0.2	-0.4	-0.6	-0.8	-1.0	-1.2	-1.4	-1.6	-1.8	-2.0	-2.1	-2.2	0.1
7.5– 7.6	-0.2	-0.4	-0.6	-0.8	-1.0	-1.2	-1.4	-1.6	-1.8	-2.0	-2.2	-2.3	0.1
7.7–12.4	-0.2	-0.4	-0.6	-0.8	-1.0	-1.2	-1.4	-1.6	-1.8	-2.0	-2.2	-2.4	0.1
12.5–12.7	-0.3	-0.5	-0.7	-0.9	-1.1	-1.3	-1.5	-1.7	-1.9	-2.1	-2.3	-2.5	0.1
12.8–13.0	-0.3	-0.6	-0.8	-1.0	-1.2	-1.4	-1.6	-1.8	-2.0	-2.2	-2.4	-2.6	0.1
13.1–13.3	-0.3	-0.6	-0.9	-1.1	-1.3	-1.5	-1.7	-1.9	-2.1	-2.3	-2.5	-2.7	0.1
13.4–13.6	-0.3	-0.6	-0.9	-1.2	-1.4	-1.6	-1.8	-2.0	-2.2	-2.4	-2.6	-2.8	0.1
13.7–13.9	-0.3	-0.6	-0.9	-1.2	-1.5	-1.7	-1.9	-2.1	-2.3	-2.5	-2.7	-2.9	0.1
14.0–14.2	-0.3	-0.6	-0.9	-1.2	-1.5	-1.8	-2.0	-2.2	-2.4	-2.6	-2.8	-3.0	0.1
14.3–14.5	-0.3	-0.6	-0.9	-1.2	-1.5	-1.8	-2.1	-2.3	-2.5	-2.7	-2.9	-3.1	0.1
14.6–14.8	-0.3	-0.6	-0.9	-1.2	-1.5	-1.8	-2.1	-2.4	-2.6	-2.8	-3.0	-3.2	0.1
14.9–15.1	-0.3	-0.6	-0.9	-1.2	-1.5	-1.8	-2.1	-2.4	-2.7	-2.9	-3.1	-3.3	0.1
15.2–15.4	-0.3	-0.6	-0.9	-1.2	-1.5	-1.8	-2.1	-2.4	-2.7	-3.0	-3.2	-3.4	0.1
15.5–15.7	-0.3	-0.6	-0.9	-1.2	-1.5	-1.8	-2.1	-2.4	-2.7	-3.0	-3.3	-3.5	0.1
15.8–20.4	-0.3	-0.6	-0.9	-1.2	-1.5	-1.8	-2.1	-2.4	-2.7	-3.0	-3.3	-3.6	0.1
20.5–20.8	-0.4	-0.7	-1.0	-1.3	-1.6	-1.9	-2.2	-2.5	-2.8	-3.1	-3.4	-3.7	0.1
20.9–21.2	-0.4	-0.8	-1.1	-1.4	-1.7	-2.0	-2.3	-2.6	-2.9	-3.2	-3.5	-3.8	0.1
21.3–21.6	-0.4	-0.8	-1.2	-1.5	-1.8	-2.1	-2.4	-2.7	-3.0	-3.3	-3.6	-3.8	0.1
21.7–22.0	-0.4	-0.8	-1.2	-1.6	-1.9	-2.2	-2.5	-2.8	-3.1	-3.4	-3.7	-4.0	0.1
22.1–22.4	-0.4	-0.8	-1.2	-1.6	-2.0	-2.3	-2.6	-2.9	-3.2	-3.5	-3.8	-4.1	0.1
22.5–22.8	-0.4	-0.8	-1.2	-1.6	-2.0	-2.4	-2.7	-3.0	-3.3	-3.6	-3.9	-4.2	0.1
22.9–23.2	-0.4	-0.8	-1.2	-1.6	-2.0	-2.4	-2.8	-3.1	-3.4	-3.7	-4.0	-4.3	0.1
23.3–23.6	-0.4	-0.8	-1.2	-1.6	-2.0	-2.4	-2.8	-3.2	-3.5	-3.8	-4.1	-4.4	0.1
23.7–24.0	-0.4	-0.8	-1.2	-1.6	-2.0	-2.4	-2.8	-3.2	-3.6	-3.9	-4.2	-4.5	0.1
24.1–24.4	-0.4	-0.8	-1.2	-1.6	-2.0	-2.4	-2.8	-3.2	-3.6	-4.0	-4.3	-4.6	0.1
24.5–24.8	-0.4	-0.8	-1.2	-1.6	-2.0	-2.4	-2.8	-3.2	-3.6	-4.0	-4.4	-4.7	0.1
24.9–28.0	-0.4	-0.8	-1.2	-1.6	-2.0	-2.4	-2.8	-3.2	-3.6	-4.0	-4.4	-4.8	0.1

Appendix C

Table for converting Par and Stableford scores to nett differentials (Note: The table is based on full handicap allowance)

Scores versus PAR	**4 down**	**3 down**	**2 down**	**1 down**	**All square**	**1 up**	**2 up**	**3 up**	**4 up**	**5 up**	**6 up**	**7 up**	**8 up**	**9 up**
Stableford points scored	32	33	34	35	36	37	38	39	40	41	42	43	44	45
Par 4 less than SSS	0	-1	-2	-3	-4	-5	-6	-7	-8	-9	-10	-11	-12	-13
Par 3 less than SSS	+1	0	-1	-2	-3	-4	-5	-6	-7	-8	-9	-10	-11	-12
Par 2 less than SSS	+2	+1	0	-1	-2	-3	-4	-5	-6	-7	-8	-9	-10	-11
Par 1 less than SSS	+3	+2	+1	0	-1	-2	-3	-4	-5	-6	-7	-8	-9	-10
Par equal to SSS	+4	+3	+2	+1	0	-1	-2	-3	-4	-5	-6	-7	-8	-9
Par 1 more than SSS	+5	+4	+3	+2	+1	0	-1	-2	-3	-4	-5	-6	-7	-8
Par 2 more than SSS	+6	+5	+4	+3	+2	+1	0	-1	-2	-3	-4	-5	-6	-7
Par 3 more than SSS	+7	+6	+5	+4	+3	+2	+1	0	-1	-2	-3	-4	-5	-6
Par 4 more than SSS	+8	+7	+6	+5	+4	+3	+2	+1	0	-1	-2	-3	-4	-5
Par 5 more than SSS	+9	+8	+7	+6	+5	+4	+3	+3	+1	0	-1	-2	-3	-4
Par 6 more than SSS	+10	+9	+8	+7	+6	+5	+4	+3	+2	+1	0	-1	-2	-3
Par 7 more than SSS	+11	+10	+9	+8	+7	+6	+5	+4	+3	+2	+1	0	-1	-2
Par 8 more than SSS	+12	+11	+10	+9	+8	+7	+6	+5	+4	+3	+2	+1	0	-1
Par 9 more than SSS	+13	+12	+11	+10	+9	+8	+7	+6	+5	+4	+3	+2	+1	0

Examples:

(a) 3 up on a par 72 course with an SSS of 70. Par is 2 more than SSS so Nett Differential = −1.

(b) 37 Stableford points on a course with Par 68 and SSS 69. Par is 1 less than SSS so Nett Differential = −2.

Appendix D

Decisions

1. **Non-counting Scores** – Clause 12.(5)(g)

(a) A decision may be made at any time during the playing of the round in question or after completion of the round.

(b) The decision must be based on the weather conditions prevailing and the committee's view of their effect on the playing difficulty of the course.

(c) If the committee has doubts or the decision seems borderline, no decision should be made until all scores have been returned. The scores will then assist the committee to reach a decision e.g. if no competitor has played to or below his handicap *that is a clear* indication that conditions have made the playing of the game extremely difficult.

(d) If the conditions of the course are such that they alone make scoring extremely difficult the competition should be stated to be non-qualifying from the outset.

(e) A *non-counting* decision made on one day of an 18-hole *Qualifying Competition*, which is played over more than one day purely to accommodate the number of entries, will apply to all scores returned in that *Qualifying Competition*.

NOTE: In a 36-hole *Qualifying Competition* played on one day the *non-counting* decision may apply to one round only. Similarly in a 72-hole *Qualifying Competition* played over two or more days the decision may be made in respect of one or more rounds only on any day, the decision having no effect on the remaining rounds of the competition.

2. **Running Medals** – Clause 14.(2)(d)

(a) Any competition which can be described as a Running Medal is not a *Qualifying Competition*.
(b) The following are defined as Running Medals:

(i) An 18-hole competition extended over two or more days for any reason other than to accommodate the number of players entered.
(ii) An 18-hole competition played on one day or over several days in which players are allowed to return more than one score.

NOTE: If from a series of any number of scores special prizes are awarded for the best eclectic score or the best nett or gross aggregate of a prescribed number of scores, the individual scores in the series would not be regarded as constituting a *running medal* provided each score is returned under *Medal Play Conditions* in a *Qualifying Competition,* as defined in the Scheme, and not returned solely for the purpose of the eclectic, nett or gross aggregate awards.

3. **Qualifying Scores**

(a) If a club with a large number of *Qualifying Competitions* in the calendar year wishes to deprive certain of the competitions of their status as *Qualifying Competitions* it may do so provided competitors are so advised before play commences.

(b) It would be outside the spirit of the Handicapping Scheme to declare that all Club Medal Competitions during a specified period would not be regarded as *Qualifying Competitions,* although played under full *Medal Play Conditions*.
(c) In both (a) and (b) above it would be more appropriate to play unofficial *Medal Competitions* under conditions which would not give them the status of *Qualifying Competitions*.

NOTE: A declaration that a competition is not a *Qualifying Competition* disqualifies all scores returned in that competition for handicapping purposes. Thus a player returning a score below his handicap will not have his handicap reduced.

(d) A competition will not lose the status of *Qualifying Competition* when played under conditions when, because of work proceeding or ground conditions in the area, pegging-up has been made obligatory by the club on a restricted area of the course, provided the playing of *Qualifying Competitions* under such conditions has the prior approval of the *Union* or *Area Authority*.

4. **Upwards adjustment of Handicaps**

(a) Clubs may elect to adjust handicaps upwards at the end of each calendar month or at shorter intervals, including immediate adjustment after completion of each *Qualifying Competition* at the Club.

(b) There could be slight differences in *Exact Handicaps* produced by each method when comparison is made at the end of a calendar month.
(c) The procedure for recording *Nett Differentials* set out in the Scheme should be adhered to whatever method is used.
(d) There is no objection to clubs electing to adjust handicaps upwards at the end of each calendar month, or at more frequent intervals, taking steps to adjust and record *Exact* and *Playing Handicaps* so that at the end of each month they correspond with those derived by adjusting handicaps after the playing of each *Qualifying Competition*.

5. **Limitation of Handicaps**

Clubs have inquired whether they may impose a limit of handicap to some of their competitions e.g. insist that a 24 handicap player competes from a handicap of 18. This is permitted by Rule of Golf 33-1. However, when recording the players' scores for handicapping purposes, adjustments must be made to ensure that the *Nett Differential* is recorded from his current *Playing Handicap* i.e. in the example quoted 24 instead of 18.

This is comparatively simple for *Medal Competition,* but is impractical for Stableford and Par competitions as it is unlikely for example that a player would record a score at a hole where a stroke allowance of one from an 18 handicap gave him no points, whereas from a handicap of 24 with a stroke allowance of two at that particular hole he might have registered one point.

6. **Incomplete Cards and No Returns**

(a) All cards must be returned, whether complete or not.
(b) It is expected that every player who enters for an 18-hole *Qualifying Competition* intends to complete the round.
(c) Since an Incomplete Card and a No Return have the effect of increasing a player's handicap, the club would be

justified in refusing to accept a card or record a *N.R.* when the player has walked in after playing only a few holes if it has reason to suppose that a genuine effort was not made to complete the 18 holes.

(d) Cards should not be issued to players when there is obviously insufficient light for them to complete the round.

(e) Sympathetic consideration should be given to players who have had to discontinue play because of injury to themselves or their markers or because of their, or their markers, being taken ill on the course.

(f) Clauses 17 and 19 of the Scheme gives clubs the discretion to deal with players who persistently submit Incomplete Cards or make No Returns if they consider they are attempting to *build a handicap*.

7. **Reduction of Handicaps during a competition**

Where the conditions of a competition do not provide otherwise the handicap of a player applying at the beginning of a competition shall apply throughout that competition. This provision shall apply to a competition in which supplementary prizes are awarded for the best scores returned in an individual round or in combinations of individual rounds of the competition. The provisions shall not apply in circumstances where the winner is the player returning the lowest aggregate score in two or more separate competitions. Where a player's handicap has been reduced during the course of a competition in which the original handicap continues to apply the player shall nevertheless play from his reduced handicap in all other competitions commencing after the handicap reduction.

8. **Overseas Scores**

Scores returned in tournaments organised by the European Golf Association are *Qualifying Scores* for handicapping purposes and must be returned to the Home Club pursuant to Clause 13.(7). Other scores returned in overseas tournaments may be returned and used, if considered appropriate, under the terms of Clause 19.

Stationery

Enquiries regarding storage binders and handicap record sheets suitable for use in connection with the Standard Scratch Score and Handicapping Scheme 1983 to be directed to Hon. Secretary of the Council of National Golf Unions: A. Thirlwell, Formby Golf Club, Formby, Liverpool L37 1LQ.

Forms of application for:

An alteration to the Basic Standard Scratch Score.

An addition for course value to the Provisional Standard Scratch Score.

The above forms may be obtained from the Secretaries of:

(a) County Golf Unions or District Committees.
(b) Area Authorities.
(c) National Golf Unions.
(d) Council of National Golf Unions.

Application of Handicaps

Stroke Index

Each club should draw up a list, called the Stroke Index, giving the order of holes at which any handicap strokes awarded should be taken. This order should be printed on the club's score card. The general principle for fixing the order of the Stroke Index is that the hole at which it is most difficult to achieve par should be Stroke Index 1, the next most difficult, Stroke Index 2 and so on until the easiest which should be Stroke Index 18.

However, certain other factors should be taken into consideration. Stroke Index 1 should not be one of the very early or very late holes on the course. The reason is that if a game were to finish all square and go on to the 19th and subsequent holes to determine the winner, the person in receipt of only one stroke would have an unfair advantage if he were to receive it at the 19th or 20th. Similarly, if Stroke Index 1 were a hole at the very end of the round, then the person in receipt of only one stroke might never be able to use it as the game might well be over by then. In general, therefore, Stroke Index 1 should not be at holes 1, 2, 17 or 18.

The other important factor to be taken into account in fixing the order of Stroke Index is that the strokes should be fairly evenly spread out over the 18 holes. If Stroke Index 1 is in the first 9 holes, Stroke Index 2 should be in the second 9 holes and so on. For example, if a person were to receive, say, four strokes, it would not be fair if he received them all in the early holes or all in the late holes.

Competition Formats and Handicap Allowances

Note 1: ***In all calculations of handicap allowances, fractions under ½ are ignored and those of ½ or over are rounded up to the next higher figure.***

Note 2: ***Handicap allowances shown are recommendations only. They are not Rules of Golf. The allowance to be used is at the discretion of the committee who should stipulate that allowance in the conditions of the competition.***

Competitions take two basic forms–match play or stroke play. In match play two players or sides compete against each other on a hole by hole basis. In stroke play a player or side competes against the whole field on his score over the whole round or rounds.

Single

Format

One player competes directly against one other player. It applies only to match play.

Handicap Allowance

The player with the higher handicap of the two receives strokes amounting to ¾ of the difference between the two players' handicaps. These strokes are taken at the holes indicated by the Stroke Index.

Foursome

Format

Two players form a side and hit alternate shots with one ball. The two players drive alternately from successive tees. Can be used for both match play and stroke play.

Handicap Allowance

Match play: The two players on each side add their handicaps together. The couple with the higher combined handicaps receive strokes amounting to ⅜ of the difference between the combined handicaps of the two sides. These strokes are taken at the holes indicated by the Stroke Index.

Stroke play: The two players forming a side add their handicaps together and divide by 2. This figure is deducted from the side's gross score.

Mixed Foursome

Format

Same as Foursome except that each side must consist of a man and a woman.

Handicap Allowance

Same as Foursome.

Four-Ball Better-Ball

Format

Two players form a side, each playing his own ball throughout. The better score of the partners is the score of the side. Can be used for both match play and stroke play.

Handicap Allowance

Match play: The three players with the highest handicaps of the four each receive strokes amounting to ¾ of the difference between their own handicaps and that of the lowest handicap of the four. These strokes are taken at the holes indicated by the Stroke Index. *Example:* A–16; B–12; C–20; D–8. Player A would receive $(16-8)\times\frac{3}{4}=6$ strokes; B would receive $(12-8)\times\frac{3}{4}=3$ strokes; C would receive $(20-8)\times\frac{3}{4}=9$ strokes; D would receive 0 strokes.

Stroke play: $\frac{3}{4}$ of each player's full handicap is allocated at the holes according to the Stroke Index and the stroke or strokes deducted at these holes.

Four-Ball Aggregate

Format

Two players form a side, each playing his own ball throughout. The combined score of the two partners is the score for the side. Can be used for both match play and stroke play.

Handicap Allowance

Match play: Same as Four-ball Better-ball.
Stroke play: Same as Four-ball Better-ball.

Greensome

Format

Two players form a side and both drive off each tee. Either ball may be selected to continue the hole and subsequent shots are played alternately until the hole is completed. *Example:* If player A's drive is selected at any hole, B must play the second shot at that hole, A the third shot and so on alternately until the ball is holed and vice versa if player B's drive is selected. Can be used for both match play and stroke play.

Handicap Allowance

Match play: Multiply the lower handicap of the two partners by .6 and the higher handicap by .4 and add the two figures together to give the full greensome handicap of the side. The couple with the higher greensome handicap receive strokes amounting to $\frac{3}{4}$ of the difference between the greensome handicaps of the two sides. These strokes are taken at the holes indicated by the Stroke Index. *Example:* A–2; B–10; C–8; D–12. AB *v* CD: Side AB full greensome handicap=$(2\times.6)+(10\times.4)=5.2$. Side CD full greensome handicap= $(8\times.6)+(12\times.4)=9.6$. Side CD receives stroke amounting to $\frac{3}{4}$ of the difference between the two couples, i.e. $(9.6-5.2)\times\frac{3}{4}=3$ strokes.

Stroke play: The two players forming a side deduct their full greensome handicap (as calculated above) from their gross score.

Bogey/Par

Format

Each player or side plays against the bogey (or par) for each hole, counting a win if he holes out in less than the bogey (or par) for the hole, a half if he equals it and a loss if he holes out in more. The aggregate of wins, losses and halves is taken to give a final score of so many holes up (or down as the case may be) to bogey (or par). Suitable for stroke play only.

Handicap Allowance

Each player receives strokes amounting to $\frac{3}{4}$ of his full handicap. In the case of foursomes, each side receives strokes amounting to $\frac{3}{8}$ of the combined handicaps of the partners. In all cases these strokes are allocated at the holes according to the Stroke Index and the stroke or strokes deducted at these holes.

Stableford

Format

The Stableford system of scoring was invented in 1931 by Dr Frank Stableford of the Wallasey and Royal Liverpool Golf Clubs and the first competition was played on 16th May, 1932 at Wallasey GC. Each player or side plays against the par for each hole and receives points according to how he scores in relation to par. The scoring system is as follows: 2 or more over par–0 points; 1 over par–1 point; par–2 points; 1 under par–3 points; 2 under par–4 points; 3 under par–5 points and so on. The number of points gained at each of the 18 holes is added together to give a total points score. Suitable for stroke play only.

Handicap Allowance

$\frac{7}{8}$ of full handicap.

Eclectic

Format

Competitors play two or more rounds choosing their better or best score at each hole to make up their eclectic score. Suitable for stroke play only.

Handicap Allowance

If played over two rounds, each competitor deducts five-sixths of his full handicap from his eclectic score for the two rounds. If played over three rounds, deduct four-fifths of his handicap from his eclectic score. If played over four rounds deduct $\frac{3}{4}$, five rounds, $\frac{2}{3}$, and six or more rounds, $\frac{1}{2}$.

Round Robin

Format

This is a form of league where each competitor or side plays every other competitor or side in the league. Suitable for match play only and can be used for singles, foursomes, four-ball better-ball, four-ball aggregate or greensomes, with the appropriate handicap allowance applying according to the type of competition.

Mixed Events

In competitions where men and women compete on an equal footing, the women's handicaps should be increased by the difference between the men's and ladies' Standard Scratch Scores if the women play from the ladies' tees. If the women play from the men's tees, their handicaps should be increased by the difference between the two Standard Scratch Scores plus an equitable figure (somewhere between 2 and 6) to take account of the distance between the men's and ladies' tees, one stroke being added for every 200 yards of difference over the 18 holes.

This adjustment does not apply where each side must consist of a man and woman; it only applies where women are in direct competition with men or where a side may consist of any combination of men and women, i.e. two men, two women or one man and one woman.

Bisques

Instead of receiving strokes to be taken at holes according to the Stroke Index, in match play friendly games, a number of bisques can be agreed upon instead. A bisque is a stroke which may be used at any hole the recipient decides upon after the completion of the hole. Because bisques can be used more advantageously than strokes, which may be of no value at certain holes, a lesser number of bisques than handicap strokes allowance is usually agreed upon. A player may use any number of bisques from his quota at any hole but he must announce whether he is using any of them before any stroke is played from the next tee. The bisque form of handicapping is not used in official competitions. It is suitable only for singles or foursomes, not for four-ball games.

Callaway Handicapping

It frequently occurs in social competitions such as an office or business association outing that many of the competitors do not have official handicaps. In such cases the best solution is to use the Callaway handicapping system, so called after the name of its inventor, as it is simple to use yet has proved equitable.

Competitors complete their round marking in their gross figures at every hole and their handicaps are awarded and deducted at the end of the 18 holes using the following table:

Competitor's gross score	Handicap deduction
par or less	none
1 over par-75	½ worst hole
76-80	worst hole
81-85	worst hole plus ½ next worst
86-90	two worst holes
91-95	two worst holes plus ½ next
96-100	three worst holes
101-105	three worst holes plus ½ next
106-110	four worst holes
111-115	four worst holes plus ½ next
116-120	five worst holes
121-125	five worst holes plus ½ next
126-130	six worst holes

Note 1: ***Worst hole equals highest score at any hole regardless of the par of the hole except that the maximum score allowed for any one hole is twice the par of the hole.***
Note 2: ***The 17th and 18th holes are not allowed to be deducted.***
Example. Competitor scores 104. From the table he should deduct as his handicap the total of his three worst (i.e. highest) individual scores plus half of his fourth worst hole. If he scored one 9, one 8 and several 7s he would therefore deduct a total of 27½ from his gross score of 104 to give a nett score of 76½.

Draws for Match Play Competitions

Cold Draw

When the number of entries is not a whole power of 2, i.e. 4, 8, 16, 32, 64 etc, a number of first round byes are necessary. Subtract the number of entries from the nearest of these numbers above the number of entries to give the number of byes. *Example:* (a) 28 entries–subtracting from 32 gives 4 first round byes; (b) 33 entries–subtracting from 64 gives 31 first round byes.

All names (or numbers representing names) are put in a hat and the requisite number of byes drawn out singly and placed in pairs in the second round of the draw, alternately at the top and bottom, i.e. the first two names go at the top of the draw, the next two at the bottom and so on until all the byes have been drawn. If there is an odd number of byes, the last drawn is bracketed to play against the winner of either the first or last first round match. Having drawn all the byes, the remaining names are then drawn and placed in pairs in the first round in the order drawn in the middle of the draw.

Automatic Draw

When a stroke play qualifying round(s) is used to determine the qualifiers for the ensuing match play, the automatic draw is used, based on the qualifying position of each qualifier, i.e. the leading qualifier is number 1 in the draw, the second qualifier is number 2 and so on.

The following table gives the automatic draw for up to 64 qualifiers. Use the first column for 64 qualifiers, the second column for 32 qualifiers, and so on.

1	1	1	1	1	1
64					
33	32				
32					
17	17	16			
48					
49	16				
16					
9	9	9	8		
56					
41	24				
24					
25	25	8			
40					
57	8				
8					
5	5	5	5	4	
60					
37	28				
28					
21	21	12			
44					
53	12				
12					
13	13	13	4		
52					
45	20				
20					
29	29	4			
36					
61	4				
4					
3	3	3	3	3	2
62					
35	30				
30					
19	19	14			
46					
51	14				
14					
11	11	11	6		
54					
43	22				
22					
27	27	6			
38					
59	6				
6					
7	7	7	7	2	
58					
39	26				
26					
23	23	10			
42					
55	10				
10					
15	15	15	2		
50					
47	18				
18					
31	31	2			
34					
63	2				
2					

The LGU System of Handicapping

Effective 1 February 1985

CONTENTS

Section I Summary of Principal Changes Introduced in the 1985 Edition

1. The Regulations have been rearranged.
2. Definitions have been added.
3. Gaining a handicap–a marker may mark for one player only.
4. In the event of the LGU teeing ground having been moved beyond the permitted limit of ten yards from the LGU permanent mark, scores cannot count for handicap nor for LGU Competitions unless a special Scratch Score has been allotted by the National Organisation.
5. Handicap 18* has been abolished except where the * denotes a handicap limited at Revision by the Table of Permitted Increases. A player remains on 19 until the average of four scores is 18½ or less over SS.
6. Handicap 6–4; a new category, handicap 6–4, has been introduced, requiring six scores, all returned in competition on courses with a Scratch Score of not less than 70, to average 6⅓ or less over SS.
7. Handicap categories have been designated A, B, C, D, E, as follows:
   A=plus to 3
   B=4 to 6
   C=7 to 18
   D=19 to 29
   E=30 to 36*
8. Handicaps 3 and under: the handicap is the average of the best *ten* differentials, all returned in competition on courses with a SS of not less than 70, only six of which may

be a Home Course. Scores from at least two other courses must be included.

9. Senior Veterans' and Disabled Persons' handicaps have been abolished, but clubs may continue to award unofficial handicaps to such members. The former basis for calculation is suggested as a guide, but an SS for the nine holes used will not be allotted by the National Organisation.

10. To retain a handicap a player in Category B must return six scores annually and in Category A ten scores annually, except when increasing from A to B or from B to C, when the number is six or four, respectively.

11. Consideration will be given by the National Organisation to all applications for increase in handicap after illness or disablement, whether or not the handicap has lapsed.

12. Clubs are no longer permitted to except Running Competitions from the regulation governing immediate reduction of handicap.

Note: Suggestions for alterations or additions to the Handicapping System must be received by the General Administrator, Ladies' Golf Union, before 1 July in order to be considered for adoption in the following year.

Section II Definitions

Throughout the text defined terms are printed as underlined capitals when used for the first time.

Committee

The term *Committee* is deemed to refer to the Committee of the Ladies' Section. The term *Club Committee* refers to the Committee in charge of the course. Where the management of the club and/or course is entirely in the hands of the Ladies' Committee the term *Club Committee* shall be deemed to refer to such.

Completed Scores

A score is deemed completed for handicap purposes when a gross score has been entered on the card for each hole and the card has been checked and signed by both marker and player. The card should also show the player's name and the date.

Differential

The differential is the difference between the gross score and the Scratch Score of the course on which it is returned.

The average differential is the sum of the differentials divided by their number.

Extra Day Scores

An Extra Day Score is one which is not returned in competition.

Handicap Advisers

Handicap Advisers and their Deputies are persons appointed by the National Organisations to assist HANDICAP SECRETARIES in dealing with problems and exceptional cases, and to keep records of all players with handicaps under 4.

Handicap Secretary

A player's Handicap Secretary is the Handicap Secretary of her HOME CLUB. The Handicap Secretary of an INDIVIDUAL MEMBER of the LGU or of a NATIONAL ORGANISATION is the Secretary, respectively, of the LGU or of the National Organisation. The Handicap Secretary of a visitor from overseas, unless she joins an affiliated club as an annual member, is the Secretary, LGU.

Home Club

The Home Club is the club which a member of more than one club has chosen to be that where her handicap records shall be maintained and of which the Handicap Secretary shall be her Handicap Secretary.

Home Course

A Home Course is any course situated at and associated with a player's Home Club.

Individual Members

a. of the LGU: Players temporarily resident overseas are entitled to apply for individual membership of the LGU.

b. of the National Organisations: Players unable to become annual playing members of an affiliated club may apply to their National Organisation for individual membership.

Lapsed Handicaps

A handicap has lapsed if four scores have not been returned in an LGU year by Category C, D and E players, six scores by Category B players (unless increasing to Category C) and ten scores by Category A players (unless increasing to Category B).

LGU Tees and Teeing Grounds

The LGU tees, indicated by a permanent mark on the right-hand side of the tee, are those from which the SCRATCH SCORE has been fixed. The actual teeing ground in play (see Rules of Golf Definition) is indicated by *red* tee markers which, for the convenience of the greenkeeper, may be moved in any direction from the permanent mark provided the hole is not altered in length by more than ten yards.

Note: In the event of the teeing ground having been accidentally or otherwise moved beyond the permitted limit the score cannot count for handicap or for LGU Competitions unless a special Scratch Score has been allotted.

Live Score

A live score is one which has been returned (in accordance with Regulation IV.4) in the current LGU year (1 February to 31 January) or in the preceding LGU year.

National Organisation

The National Organisations are: the English Ladies' Golf Association, the Irish Ladies' Golf Union, the Scottish Ladies' Golfing Association and the Welsh Ladies' Golf Union. In the case of overseas affiliated clubs for *National Organisation* read *LGU*.

Scratch Score

The Scratch Score of a course is the score expected of a Scratch player in normal Spring and Autumn conditions of wind and weather.

Section III Introduction

1. Basis of the System

The chief features of the LGU System of Handicapping are: that all handicaps shall be fixed on the basis of the LGU SCRATCH SCORE; that handicaps shall be assessed on actual scores returned and not on general form; and that the player's handicap shall be the same in every club.

2. Overseas Unions and Clubs

Overseas affiliated Unions and Clubs shall be permitted to make such adjustments to these regulations as may be deemed by their Executive Committee to be necessary on account of climatic or other conditions peculiar to the territory administered by them, so long as these adjustments do not depart from the fundamental principles of the LGU System of Handicapping as stated in the paragraph above or contravene the Rules of Golf as laid down by the Royal and Ancient Golf Club of St Andrews. The LGU must be informed as and when such adjustments are made.

3. Queries

Queries on LGU Regulations or the Rules of Golf should be submitted in accordance with the following procedures:

a. Committees of Affiliated Clubs should submit queries to their NATIONAL ORGANISATION.

b. Members of Affiliated Clubs may submit queries to their National Organisation and must have their statements signed as read on behalf of the Ladies' Committee. If there is any difference of opinion the Committee or opposing party should submit their own statement in writing.

c. Secretaries of Affiliated Clubs should refer queries on handicaps to their HANDICAP SECRETARY.

d. Handicap Secretaries of Affiliated Clubs should refer queries to their HANDICAP ADVISER or National Organisation, in that order.

e. Overseas Unions and Clubs. In the case of clubs affiliated to an affiliated Ladies' Golf Union outside Great Britain and Ireland or directly affiliated to the LGU, queries should be submitted to the LGU. Statements should be signed as read on behalf of such Union or Club Committee.

Correspondence of this nature sent to the LGU and the National Organisations is filed for reference and cannot be returned.

Section IV The Player's Responsibilities and Rights

1. General

Playing off the Correct Handicap. It is the player's responsibility to know and to apply the Handicapping Regulations and to play off the correct handicap at all times. She should be able to produce a current Handicap Certificate when required to do so. In case of doubt or disagreement between the player and her Handicap Secretary as to what is the player's correct handicap, she should play from the lower until an official decision can be obtained from the Handicap Adviser or the National Organisation.

Handicap Reduction. Any reduction in handicap is automatic and comes into force immediately, *except*

i. in the event of a tie in a competition, where this is resolved by a replay or a play-off; *and*
ii. in a 36-, 54- or 72-hole competition played within eight days.

Playing away from Home. A player must notify her Handicap Secretary of any score (which might affect her handicap) returned by her on any course other than at her HOME CLUB.

2. Eligibility to Hold an LGU Handicap

An LGU handicap may be obtained and held by an amateur lady golfer who is *either*

a. an annual playing member, including a country, junior or life member (whether honorary or paying) of a club affiliated to the LGU either directly or through its National Organisation; *or*

b. an individual member of either the LGU or one of the four National Organisations; *or*

c. a temporary member of an affiliated club, provided her membership is to last for a period of not less than twelve months.

Note. Should membership cease or expire the player's LGU handicap is no longer valid, but her scores remain LIVE if returned before such cessation or expiry.

3. How to Gain an LGU Handicap

Four scores must be returned on the course or courses of an LGU affiliated club or clubs, the Scratch Score of which must be not less than 60. Play must be in twos (threes and fours are not acceptable), no more than one player per marker, and must be in accordance with Regulations IV.4 (a), (b), (c), (d) and (e).

4. Scores Acceptable for LGU Handicap

To be acceptable for handicap:

a. Scores must be returned in accordance with the Rules of Golf as approved by the Royal and Ancient Golf Club of St Andrews and with the Club's Local Rules and By-Laws, which must not contravene any R. & A. Rule or LGU Regulation. The gross score must be entered for every hole.

b. Scores must be returned on the course of an LGU affiliated club with an LGU Scratch Score of not less than 60 for players with a handicap of 36*–7 and of not less than 70 for players with a handicap of less than 7. Play must be from LGU tees. Scores returned on a course of which the player is not a member must be countersigned by an official of the local ladies' committee, who should certify that the Scratch Score is correctly stated. Completed cards should either be returned in person by the player to her Handicap Secretary without delay or left in the card box of the club visited, together with the name and address of the home club and the cost of postage.

Note. Scores returned on non-affiliated courses overseas (see lists on pages 92–100 of the Lady Golfer's Handbook) *may* count for handicap at the discretion of the LGU. Such cards, duly countersigned by a local official as showing the correct Scratch Score and accompanied by relevant information about local conditions, type of soil, terrain, course difficulty, etc., should be forwarded to the Secretary, Ladies' Golf Union, 12 The Links, St Andrews, Fife, KY16 9JB, with a stamped, addressed envelope to the Handicap Secretary of the player's Home Club.

c. Scores must be marked by an annual playing member of a recognised golf club, who has or has had a handicap. A marker should not mark the card of more than one player.

d. A score must be that of the first round of the day on any one course, except in the case of a competition consisting of 36 holes played on one day, when both scores shall count.

e. Scores may be returned when the following conditions apply:

i. Winter Conditions. Where, for the preservation of the course, the Club Committee has made a Local Rule that the ball may be teed or placed without penalty through the green.

ii. Summer Conditions. a. Where, for the preservation of the course, the Club Committee has made a Local Rule that the ball may be placed without penalty through the green; and **b.** where, for the preservation of the course, the Club Committee has made a Local Rule that tee pegs must be used through the green and a deduction from the Scratch Score of two strokes where more than nine holes are affected, and of one stroke where nine or fewer holes are affected, has been made by the Ladies' Committee (and notified to the area Scratch Score Committee member).

iii. The Green. Where, for the preservation of the green, a temporary hole (see Rules of Golf – Definition) is off but adjacent to the green, provided this does not alter the length of the hole by more than ten yards.

Note: LGU TEES. Where, for the preservation of the course, the teeing ground has been moved beyond the permitted ten yards, scores may count for handicap only if a special Scratch Score has been allotted by the National Organisation.

f. All scores returned in Stroke Competitions, even if declared null and void, count for LGU handicap purposes, subject to Regulations IV.4 (a) to (e) above and provided competitors play from LGU TEES (see Definition and Note) and the SS of the course is not less than 60 (or not less than 70 for players with handicaps less than 7). Scores may be returned in twos, threes or fours, as arranged by the Committee.

Note. The exception to this is in a competition where the best-ball or better-ball score (see Rules of Golf Definitions) is to count.

g. EXTRA DAY SCORES must be returned in accordance with Regulations IV.4 (a) to (e) and should normally be marked in twos, but at the discretion of the Committee may be marked in threes, in which case a notice to this effect must be posted on the Notice Board (but see Regulation IV.3 for gaining a first handicap). Extra Day Scores marked in fours are NOT acceptable.

h. Gross scores returned in a competition from which a player has been disqualified under Rule of Golf 6–2b on her nett score shall count for handicap.

5. Calculation of an LGU Handicap

Handicaps are divided into five categories: Silver Division – A, B, C – and Bronze Division – D and E. Handicaps are calculated as follows, on the basis of live scores returned in accordance with Regulation IV.4 above:

Note 1. For handicaps 36*–7 scores must be returned on courses with a Scratch Score of not less than 60, and for handicaps 6 and under scores must be returned on courses with a Scratch Score of not less than 70.

Note 2. In all calculations above Scratch ½, two-thirds and three-quarters count as 1 and one-third, one-quarter count as 0. In all calculations below Scratch fractions of ½ and less count as 0, fractions greater than ½ count as 1.

a. *Bronze Division*

(i) **Category E, 36–30.** The handicap is the difference between the player's best live score and the Scratch Score of the course on which it was played, i.e. the handicap is her best DIFFERENTIAL. If the differential is more than 36 the handicap is 36* (*Example E*[1]). If the differential is 36–30 then that is the handicap (*Example E*[2]). If the best differential is less than 30 the handicap is 30 until the average of the *two* best differentials is less than 29½ (*Example E*[3]).

EXAMPLES:

E^1 Best gross score	117	SS 72	Differential	45
				Handicap 36*
E^2 Best gross score	102	SS 69	Differential	33
				Handicap 33
E^3 Best gross scores	101	SS 74	Differential	27
	106	SS 70	Previous best differential	36
			Average differential	31½
				Handicap 30

(ii) **Category D, 29–19.** The handicap is the average of the two best differentials (*Examples D*[1], *D*[2]), but if the average is less than 18½ the handicap is 19 until the average of the *four* best differentials is less than 18½ (*Example D*[3]).

EXAMPLES:

D^1 Gross score	99	SS 73	Best differential	26
Gross score	104	SS 73	Previous best differential	31
			Average differential	28½
				Handicap 29
D^2 Gross score	95	SS 71	Best differential	24
Gross score	98	SS 70	Previous best differential	28
			Average differential	26
				Handicap 26

D^3 Gross scores	SS	Best differentials		
87	72	15		
92	72	20	Average 17½ but ...	**Handicap 19**
96	73	23		
94	71	23		
Average diff (of four)		20¼		**Handicap 19**

b. *Silver Division*

(i) **Category C, 18–7.** The handicap is the average of the four best differentials (*Example C*[1]), but if this average is less than 6½ the handicap is 7 until the conditions for Category B are fulfilled (*Example C*[2]).

EXAMPLES:

C^1 Best differentials

10		
11		
13		
17	Average 12¾	**Handicap 13**

C^2 EDS=Extra Day Scores; CS=Competition Scores, SS not less than 70.

Best differentials

3 (EDS)		
5 (CS)		
6 (EDS)		
7 (CS)	Average 5¼ but ...	**Handicap 7**
8 (CS)		
9 (CS)		
10 (CS)		
9 (CS)		

Average differential of six Comp scores = 8 **Handicap 7**

(ii) **Category B, 6–4.** The handicap is the average of the six best differentials of scores returned in competition on courses with a Scratch Score of not less than 70 (*Example B*[1]), but if this average is less than 3½ the handicap is 4 until the conditions for Category A are fulfilled (*Example B*[2]).

EXAMPLES:

B^1 Best differentials from competition scores on courses with a SS of not less than 70:

7		
5		
5		
6		
4		
4	Average differential 5⅙	**Handicap 5**

B^2 Best differentials from competition scores on courses with a SS of not less than 70: H1, H2=Home Courses, A1, A2 etc.=Away Courses.

3 (H1)		
5 (H2)		
4 (H1)		
2 (H1)		
2 (H1)		
3 (A1)	Average differential 3⅙ but...	**Handicap 4**
6 (A1)		
7 (A2)		
6 (H2)		
8 (A1)	Average differential 4.6	**Handicap 4**

(iii) **Category A, 3 and under.** To obtain a handicap of 3 or under a player must return at least ten scores in competition, on courses with a Scratch Score of not less than 70. Only six of these scores may be from a Home Course, and the remaining four must be from at least two different Away courses. The handicap is the average of the ten best differentials so obtained (*Examples A^1 and A^2*).

EXAMPLES: (Abbreviations as in B^2)

A^1 Best differentials from competition scores on courses with a SS of not less than 70:

0 (H)
+1 (H)
+1 (H)
0 (H)
3 (H)
0 (H)
1 (A1)
0 (A1)
1 (A2)
3 (A2) Average differential 0.6

Handicap 1

A^2 Best differentials from competition scores on courses with a SS of not less than 70:

+1 (H)
+1 (H)
+2 (H)
1 (A1)
+2 (H)
+1 (A2)
0 (H)
+1 (H)
2 (A3)
0 (A1) Average differential +0.5

Handicap Scratch (+0.5=0)

6. Annual Revision of Handicaps and Lapsed Handicaps

a. General

On 31 January each year all handicaps shall be recalculated on the basis of scores returned during the preceding twelve months and in accordance with the Regulations in force during that period. Any increase in handicap resulting from such recalculation shall be limited by the Table of Permitted Increases (Table I) for Revised Handicaps set out below. At no other time during the year may a player's handicap be increased (except in accordance with Regulation IV.7 (b) or (c)).

TABLE I – TABLE OF PERMITTED INCREASES FOR REVISED HANDICAPS

Handicaps plus to 6 may go up 1 stroke.
Handicaps 7 to 34 may go up 2 strokes.
Handicap 35 may go up 1 stroke.

A handicap limited by the Table of Permitted Increases for Revised Handicaps shall be marked with an asterisk until the calculation on live scores results in a handicap equal to or less than that held.

b. Minimum Number of Scores to be Returned

Handicap Categories E, D, C. To retain a handicap players with handicaps 36*–7 must have returned at least four scores.

Handicap Category B. To retain a handicap players with handicaps 6–4 must have returned at least six scores. If six scores have been returned but the other conditions for this category have not been fulfilled, the handicap shall be that held prior to Revision and shall be marked with a $^{\phi}$ until the appropriate scores have been returned and the calculation results in a handicap equal to or less than that held prior to Revision.

Exception: If players with handicap 6 prior to Revision have returned at least four (not necessarily all in competition and on courses with a SS of 70 or more) and the average of the best four is 6½ or more, the handicap shall be retained and shall be calculated in accordance with Regulations governing handicaps 7–18 and the Table of Permitted Increases (Table I) for Revised Handicaps.

Handicap Category A. To retain a handicap players with handicaps 3 and under must have returned at least ten scores. If ten scores have been returned in competition on a course or courses with a SS of not less than 70, the handicap may be increased by one stroke if the scores average 0.5 or more above the handicap held prior to Revision. It shall be marked with a $^{\phi}$ if the necessary scores on "away" courses are not included. If ten scores have been returned but not all in competition and on a course or courses with a SS of 70 or more, the handicap shall be that held prior to Revision and shall be marked with a $^{\phi}$ until all the necessary conditions have been fulfilled and the calculation results in a handicap equal to or less than that held prior to Revision.

Exception: If players with handicap 3 prior to Revision have returned at least six scores in competition on a course or courses with a SS of not less than 70, and the average of the best six is 3½ or more, the handicap shall be retained and shall be calculated in accordance with Regulations governing handicaps 4–6 and the Table of Permitted Increases (Table I) for Revised Handicaps.

c. Lapsed Handicaps

A handicap lapses if a player has not returned the minimum number of scores necessary to retain a handicap (see **b.** above). When a player's handicap has lapsed she does not have a valid handicap until the conditions have been fulfilled to regain it (see **d.** below).

d. To Regain a Handicap which has Lapsed

Handicap Categories E, D, C. To regain a handicap which has lapsed players with handicaps 36*–7 must return the number of

Extra Day Scores necessary to increase the number of *live* scores to four. The handicap shall then be calculated in accordance with Regulations, but it shall be limited by the Table of Permitted Increases (Table II) for Lapsed Handicaps set out below and must be confirmed, before use, by the player's Handicap Secretary.

Handicap Category B. To regain a handicap which has lapsed players with handicaps 6–4 must return the necessary Extra Day Scores on courses with a Scratch Score of not less than 70 to increase the number of *live* scores to six. The handicap shall then be calculated in accordance with Regulations (except that the scores need not be returned in competition), but it shall be limited by the Table of Permitted Increases (Table II) for Lapsed Handicaps set out below and must be confirmed, before use, by the player's Handicap Secretary. Until scores returned fulfil all the conditions necessary for this Category of player, the handicap shall be marked with a ɸ.

Handicap Category A. To regain a handicap which has lapsed players with handicaps under 4 must return the necessary Extra Day Scores on courses with a Scratch Score of not less than 70 to increase the number of *live* scores to ten.

The handicap shall then be calculated in accordance with Regulations (except that the scores need not be returned in competition), but it shall be limited by the Table of Permitted Increases (Table II) for Lapsed Handicaps set out below and must be confirmed, before use, by the player's Handicap Secretary. Until scores returned fulfil all the conditions necessary for this Category of player, the handicap shall be marked with a ɸ.

Transition to a Higher Category. The number of scores required to regain a handicap by players in Categories A or B should be determined after taking into account the scores returned and the Table (II) of Permitted Increases for Lapsed Handicaps. For instance, a player previously in Category A, after a lapse of several years may require only six scores, and similarly a player previously in Category B may require only four, if the former handicap category is not maintained or bettered by the scores returned.

TABLE II – TABLE OF PERMITTED INCREASES FOR LAPSED HANDICAPS

(i) If lapsed for less than one year the handicap shall be limited to one stroke higher than that last held.

(ii) If lapsed for more than one year but less than two years the handicap shall be limited to two strokes higher than that last held.

(iii) For each year in excess of two the handicap may be increased by a further stroke.

EXAMPLES:

	Handicap Lapsed	*Necessary EDS Returned*	*Max Inc over Previous H'cap*
(i)	January 31 1981	1981–82 (LGU year)	1 stroke (less than one year)
(ii)		1982–83 (LGU year)	2 strokes (one-two years)
(iii)		1983–84 (LGU year)	3 strokes (two+one year)
		1984–85 (LGU year)	4 strokes (two+two years)
		1985–86 (LGU year)	5 strokes (two+three years) and so on

A handicap limited by the Table of Permitted Increases for Lapsed Handicaps shall be marked with an asterisk.

7. Special Categories of Handicap

a. Juniors. An LGU Junior handicap (limit 45) may be obtained and held by any girl who is a junior, i.e. who has not reached her twelfth birthday on 1 January, by returning two scores over nine specified holes. Any nine holes on the course may be chosen to make up the round, at the discretion of the club, and a special SS for those holes must be obtained from the National Organisation. Each score returned, and the special SS for the nine holes, shall be doubled in order to arrive at the number of strokes above SS. Handicaps will be reduced in accordance with Regulations (one card 45–30, etc.). Juniors may hold a standard LGU handicap but may not hold both.

To retain a Junior LGU handicap two scores over nine holes must be returned annually.

An LGU Junior handicap shall be acceptable for all junior competitions, and these Regulations shall apply to all players with Junior handicaps. Handicap Certificates for LGU Junior handicaps will be issued by the Handicap Secretary and *the date and year when the player will attain her twelfth birthday must be entered on the Handicap Certificate.*

b. Former Professional Golfers. On reinstatement as an amateur a player who has been a professional golfer must apply for a handicap to the Secretary, LGU. The Executive Council shall, at their discretion, allot a handicap of not more than Scratch on the basis of live scores returned during the player's period of probation in accordance with the Regulations for Extra Day Scores and those governing handicaps of 3 and under.

For the first two years after reinstatement the player's Handicap Secretary must submit all scores returned twice yearly on 1 January and 1 July to the Secretary, LGU, 12

The Links, St Andrews, Fife, KY16 9JB. Handicaps will be reviewed by the Executive Council and revised at their discretion.

c. After Serious Illness and Disablement. A person wishing to regain a handicap or have her handicap reassessed after serious illness or disablement may apply through her Club Committee to the National Organisation with all relevant details, including a minimum of four live scores returned, so that consideration may be given to the circumstances and the player may obtain a realistic handicap. Handicaps shall be adjusted in accordance with Regulations.

d. Individual Members and Visitors from Overseas. The handicaps of individual members of the LGU or of the National Organisations shall be managed by the Secretary of the LGU or of the appropriate National Organisation. All scores returned must be countersigned by the Handicap Secretary of the club at which they were returned and forwarded to the appropriate Secretary, who will act as Handicap Secretary for these players.

Handicaps of visitors from overseas who are not annual playing members of an affiliated club in Great Britain or Ireland shall be managed by the Secretary of the LGU, to whom scores should be forwarded after countersignature as above.

8. Membership of More than One Club

a. A member belonging to more than one affiliated club must inform the Ladies' Secretary and Handicap Secretary of each club of the names of other affiliated clubs to which she belongs and also of any scores (together with the Scratch Score) which may affect her handicap.

b. Handicap Secretary. If a player is a member of more than one club she must decide which club she wishes to be her Home Club for handicap purposes and notify the Ladies' Secretary of that club accordingly. A player's Handicap Secretary shall be the Handicap Secretary of her Home Club.

c. A member changing her Home Club must take her LGU4 sheet and her Handicap Certificate to the Handicap Secretary of her new Home Club.

d. A member joining an additional club must inform the Ladies' Secretary and the Handicap Secretary of such club of her existing or lapsed handicap, and of the scores, with relative dates, on which it was gained, and also the names of all clubs of which she is or has been a member.

e. A member shall play on the same handicap at all clubs.

For details of the following, please refer to the Lady Golfer's Handbook:

Scratch Scores
LGU Tees and Teeing Grounds in Play
Starting Places
Handicap Records and Certificates
LGU Silver and Bronze Medal Competitions
LGU Gold and Silver Medal Competitions
LGU Challenge Bowl Competitions
Coronation Foursomes Competition
LGU Pendant Competition
Australian Spoons Competitions

INDEX

Governing Bodies

Home Unions

Golfing Union of Ireland

The Golfing Union of Ireland, founded in 1891, embraces 262 Clubs. Its objects are:

(1) Securing the federation of the various Clubs.
(2) Arranging Amateur Championships, Inter-Provincial and Inter-Club Competitions, and International Matches.
(3) Securing a uniform standard of handicapping.
(4) Providing for advice and assistance to affiliated Clubs in all matters appertaining to Golf, and generally to promote the game in every way in which this can be better done by the Union than by individual Clubs.

Its functions include the holding of the *Close* Championship for Amateur Golfers and Tournaments for Team Matches.

Its organisation consists of Provincial Councils in each of the four Provinces elected by the Clubs in the Province–each province electing a limited number of delegates to the Central Council which meets annually.

Secretary: Ivan ER Dickson, Glencar House, 81 Eglinton Road, Donnybrook, Dublin 4. Tel: Dublin 694111.

Welsh Golfing Union

The Welsh Golfing Union was founded in 1895 and is the second oldest of the four National Unions. Unlike the other Unions it is an association of Golf Clubs and Golfing Organisations. The present membership is 118. For the purpose of electing the Executive Council, Wales and Gwent are divided into ten districts which between them return 22 members.

The objects of the Union are:

(a) To take any steps which may be deemed necessary to further the interests of the game in Wales and Gwent.
(b) To hold a Championship Meeting or Meetings each year.
(c) To encourage, financially and/or otherwise, Inter-Club, Inter-County, and International Matches, and such other events as may be authorised by the Council.
(d) To assist in setting up and maintaining a uniform system of Handicapping.
(e) To assist in the maintenance of the Sports Turf Research Institute.
(f) To co-operate with the Royal and Ancient Golf Club of St Andrews through the medium of the Council of National Golf Unions.

Note: The union recognises the Royal and Ancient Golf Club of St Andrews as the ruling authority.

Secretary: JW Treharne, 2 Isfryn, Burry Port, Dyfed SA16 0BY. Tel: Burry Port (05546) 2595.

The Scottish Golf Union

The Scottish Golf Union was founded in 1920 and embraces 660 clubs. Subject to the stipulation and declaration that the Union recognises the Royal and Ancient Golf Club of St Andrews as the Ruling Authority in the game of golf, the objects of the Union are:

(a) To foster and maintain a high standard of Amateur Golf in Scotland and to administer and organise and generally act as the governing body of amateur golf in Scotland.
(b) To institute and thereafter carry through annually a Scottish Amateur Championship, a Scottish Open Amateur Stroke Play Championship and other such competitions and matches as they consider appropriate.
(c) To administer and apply the rules of the Standard Scratch Score and Handicapping Scheme as approved by the Council of National Golf Unions from time to time.
(d) To deal with other matters of general or local interest to amateur golfers in Scotland.

The Union's organisation consists of Area Committees covering the whole of Scotland. There are 16 Areas, each having its own

Association or Committee elected by the Clubs in that particular area and each Area Association or Committee elects one delegate to serve on the Executive of the Union.

Secretary: JW Hume, The Cottage, 181A Whitehouse Road, Barnton, Edinburgh EH4 6BY. Tel: 031-339 7546.

The English Golf Union

The English Golf Union was founded in 1924 and embraces 34 County Unions with over 1,300 affiliated clubs, 22 clubs overseas, and over 130 Golfing Societies and Associations. Its objects are:

(1) To further the interests of Amateur Golf in England.
(2) To assist in maintaining a uniform system of handicapping.
(3) To arrange an English Championship; an English Stroke Play Championship; an English County Championship, International and other Matches and Competitions.
(4) To co-operate with the Royal and Ancient Golf Club of St Andrews and the Council of National Golf Unions.
(5) To co-operate with other National Golf Unions and Associations in such manner as may be decided.

Secretary: K Wright, 1–3 Upper King Street, Leicester LE1 6XF. Tel: (0533) 553042.

The Council of National Golf Unions

At a meeting of Representatives of Golf Unions and Associations in Great Britain and Ireland, called at the special request of the Scottish Golf Union, and held in York, on 14th February, 1924, resolutions were adopted from which the Council of National Golf Unions was constituted.

The Council holds an Annual Meeting in March, and such other meetings as may be necessary. Two representatives are elected from each national Home Union–England, Scotland, Ireland and Wales–and hold office until the next Annual meeting when they are eligible for re-election.

The principal function of the Council, as laid down by the York Conference, was to formulate a system of Standard Scratch Scores and Handicapping, and to co-operate with the Royal and Ancient Championship Committee in matters coming under their jurisdiction. The responsibilities undertaken by the Council at the instance of the Royal and Ancient Golf Club or the National Unions are as follows:

1. The Standard Scratch Score and Handicapping Scheme, formulated in March, 1926, approved by the Royal and Ancient, and last revised in 1983.
2. The nomination of four members on the Board of Management of The Sports Turf Research Institute, with an experimental station at St Ives, Bingley, Yorkshire.
3. The management of the Annual Amateur International Matches between the four countries–England, Scotland, Ireland and Wales.

Hon. Sec.: Alan Thirlwell, Formby GC, Golf Road, Formby, Liverpool L37 1LQ. Tel: Formby 72164.

United States Golf Association

The USGA is the national governing body of golf. Its single most important goal is preserving the integrity and values of the game.

Formed on 22nd December, 1894, a year when two clubs proclaimed different US Amateur Champions, representatives of five clubs met at a dinner at the Calumet Club in New York City. They created a central governing body to establish uniform rules, to conduct national championships and to nurture the virtues of sportsmanship in golf.

The names of the standing committees give an idea of what the USGA does:

Rules of Golf, Championship, Amateur Status and Conduct, Implements and Ball, Handicap, Women's, Sectional Affairs, Green Section, Public Links, Women's Public Links, Junior Championship, Girls' Junior, Senior Championship, Senior Women's Championship, Bob Jones Award, Museum, Green Section Award, Finance, Public Information, Membership, Regional Association, Associates, Intercollegiate Relations, Mid-Amateur Championship, International Team Selection, Development, Turfgrass Research, Nominating.

The USGA, as the governing body of the sport in the United States, makes and interprets the Rules of Golf in co-operation with the Royal & Ancient Golf Club of St Andrews, Scotland; developed and maintains the national system of handicapping; controls the standards of the ball and the implements of the game; works in turfgrass and turf management; and, generally speaking, preserves and promotes the game.

The Professional Golfers' Association

The Professional Golfers' Association was founded in 1901 to promote interest in the game of golf, to protect and advance the mutual and trade interests of its members, to arrange and hold meetings and tournaments periodically for members, to institute and operate a benevolent fund for the relief of deserving members, to assist members to obtain employment and to effect any other objects of a like nature as may be determined from time to time by the Association.

Membership Regulations

There shall be nine classes of membership:

Class A– Members engaged as the nominated professional at a PGA Training Establishment in Great Britain and Ireland
Class B– Members engaged by Class A and Class G members to work at PGA Establishments in Great Britain and Ireland
Class C– Tournament playing members
Class D– Associate Members
Class E– Special Members
Class F– Members of the Women's Professional Golf Association
Class G– Members engaged as the nominated professional at PGA Establishments with limited facilities in Great Britain and Ireland
Class H– Overseas members
H.L.M.– Honorary Life Membership

The Management of the Association is under the overall direction and control of a board of management. The Association is divided into six Regions each of which employs a full-time secretary and runs tournaments for the benefit of members within its Region.

The Association is responsible for arranging and obtaining sponsorship of the Club Professionals' Championship, PGA Cup matches, Seniors' Championship, Under-23 Match Play Championship and other National Championships.

Anyone who intends to become a club professional must serve a minimum of three years in registration and qualify at the PGA Training School before election as a full member.

The Women's Professional Golf Association is a division of the Association. The WPGA is responsible on behalf of the Association for the overall control, supervision and promotion of all professional golf tournaments for women at which members of the WPGA compete.

For further information apply to the appropriate organisation.

The Professional Golfers' Association: Apollo House, The Belfry, Sutton Coldfield, West Midlands B76 9PT. Tel: Curdworth (0675) 70333.

Women's Professional Golf Association: PGA Apollo House, The Belfry, Sutton Coldfield, West Midlands B76 9PT. Tel: (0675) 70333.

PGA European Tour

To be eligible to become a member of the PGA European Tour a player must possess certain minimum standards which shall be determined by the Tournament Committee. In 1976 a Qualifying School for potential new members was introduced to be held annually. The leading players are awarded cards allowing them to compete in all PGA European Tour tournaments.

In 1985 the PGA European Tour became ALL EXEMPT with no more Monday pre-qualifying. Full details can be obtained from the Wentworth Headquarters: Ken Schofield, Executive Director, PGA European Tour, Wentworth Club, Wentworth Drive, Virginia Water, Surrey GU25 4LS. Tel: (09904) 2881.

Government of the Amateur and Open Golf Championship

In December 1919 on the invitation of the clubs who had hitherto controlled the Amateur and Open Golf Championships, the Royal and Ancient took over the government of those events. These two championships are controlled by a committee appointed by the Royal and Ancient Golf Club of St Andrews. The Committee shall be called the Royal and Ancient Golf Club Championship Committee and shall consist of twelve members (who shall be members of the Club) to be elected by the Club, and additional members not exceeding two (who shall not necessarily be members of the Club) from Golf Authorities both at home and abroad, who shall be invited annually to join the Committee by the twelve members elected by the Club. Such invited members shall, irrespective of the date of their invitation to become members of the Committee, remain members only until the date of the first Autumn Meeting occurring after the date of their invitation to become members. During their term of office, such invited members (who are not already members of the Club), shall be admitted as honorary temporary members of the Club. Two Business Members, who shall be members of the Club, shall be co-opted on the nomination of the Chairman of the Championship Committee after consultation with the Chairman of the General Committee.

Secretary: MF Bonallack OBE, Royal and Ancient Golf Club, St Andrews. Telegrams *Ancient St Andrews.* Tel: 0334 72112/3. Telex 76348.

LGU

The Ladies' Golf Union was founded in 1893 with the following objects:

(1) To promote the interests of the game of Golf.

(2) To obtain a uniformity of the rules of the game by establishing a representative legislative authority.
(3) To establish a uniform system of handicapping.
(4) To act as a tribunal and court of reference on points of uncertainty.
(5) To arrange the Annual Championship Competition and obtain the funds necessary for that purpose.

Ninety years on only the language has changed, the present Constitution defining the objects as:

(1) To uphold the rules of the game, to advance and safeguard the interests of women's golf and to decide all doubtful and disputed points in connection therewith.
(2) To maintain, regulate and enforce the LGU system of handicapping.
(3) To employ the funds of the Union in such a manner as shall be deemed best for the interests of women's golf, with power to borrow or raise money to use for the same purpose.
(4) To maintain and regulate International Events, Championships and Competitions held under the LGU regulations and to promote the interests of Great Britain and Ireland in Ladies International Golf.
(5) To make, maintain and publish such regulations as may be considered necessary for the above purposes.

The constituents of the LGU are:

Home Countries. The English Ladies' Golf Association (founded 1952), the Irish Ladies' Golf Union (founded 1893), the Scottish Ladies' Golfing Association (founded 1904), the Welsh Ladies' Golf Union (founded 1904), plus ladies' societies, girls' schools and ladies' clubs affiliated to these organisations.

Overseas. Affiliated ladies' golfing unions and golf clubs in the Commonwealth and any other overseas ladies' golfing organisation affiliated to the LGU.

Individual lady members of clubs within the above categories are regarded as *members of the LGU.*

The Rules of the Game and of Amateur Status, which the LGU is bound to uphold, are those published by the Royal and Ancient Golf Club of St Andrews.

In endeavouring to fulfil its responsibilities towards advancing and safeguarding women's golf, the LGU maintains contact with other golfing organisations – the Royal and Ancient Golf Club of St Andrews, the Council of National Golf Unions, the Golf Foundation, the Central Council of Physical Recreation, the Sports Council, the Women's Professional Golf Association and the Women's Committee of the United States Golf Association. This contact ensures that the LGU is informed of developments and projected developments and has an opportunity to comment upon and to influence the future of the game for women.

Either directly or through its constituent national organisations the LGU advises and is the ultimate authority on doubts or disputes which may arise in connection with the handicapping system and regulations governing competitions played under LGU conditions.

The handicapping system, together with the system for assessment of Scratch Scores, is formulated and published by the LGU. The handicapping system undergoes detailed revision and is republished every four years, in the year following the revision of the Rules of Golf. Handicap Certificates are provided by the LGU and distributed through the national organisations and appointed club officials to every member of every affiliated club which has fulfilled the requisite conditions for obtaining an LGU handicap. No other form of certificate is recognised as evidence of an LGU handicap.

The funds of the LGU are administered by the Hon. Treasurer on the authority of the Executive Council, and the accounts are submitted annually for adoption in General Meeting.

All ladies' British Open Championships and the Home International matches, at both senior and junior level, are organised annually by the LGU. International events involving a British or a combined British and Irish team are organised and controlled by the LGU when held in this country and the LGU acts as the co-ordinating body for the Commonwealth Tournament in whichever of the four participating countries it is held, four-yearly, by rotation. The LGU selects and trains the teams, provides the uniforms and pays all the expenses of participation, whether held in this country or overseas. The LGU also maintains and regulates certain competitions played under handicap, such as Medal Competitions, Coronation Foursomes, Challenge Bowls, Australian Spoons and the LGU Pendant Competition.

The day-to-day administration of certain of the LGU responsibilities in the home countries is undertaken by the national organisations, such as that concerned with handicapping regulations, Scratch Scores, and the organisation of Challenge Bowls and Australian Spoons Competitions.

Membership subscriptions to the LGU are assessed on a per capita basis of the club membership. To save unnecessary expense and duplication of administrative work in the home countries LGU subscriptions are collected by the national organisations along with their own, and transmitted in bulk to the LGU.

Policy is determined and control over all the LGU's activities is exercised by an Executive Council of eight members – two each elected by the English, Irish, Scottish and Welsh national organisations. The Chairman is elected annually by the Councillors and may hold office for one year only, during which term her place on the Council is taken by her Deputy and she has no vote other than a casting vote. The President and the Hon. Treasurer of the Union also attend and take part in Council meetings but with no vote. The Council meets five times a year.

The Annual General Meeting is held in January. The formal business includes presentation of the Report of the Executive Council for the previous year and of the Accounts for the last completed financial year, the election or re-election of President, Vice-Presidents, Hon. Treasurer and Auditors, and a report of the election of Councillors and their Deputies for the ensuing year and of the European Technical Committee representative. Voting is on the following basis: Executive Council, one each (8); members in the four home countries, one per national organisation (4) and in addition one per 100 affiliated clubs or part thereof (at present 22); one per overseas Commonwealth Union with a membership of 50 or more clubs (at present 3), and one per 100 individually affiliated clubs (1).

The Lady Golfer's Handbook is published annually by the LGU and is distributed free to all affiliated clubs and organisations and to appointed Handicap Advisers. It is also available for sale to anyone interested. It contains the regulations for handicapping and Scratch Score assessment, for British Championships and international matches (with results for the past twenty years) and for LGU competitions, and sets out the Rules of the Union. It also lists every affiliated organisation, with names and addresses of officials, and every affiliated club, with Scratch Score, county of affiliation, number of members, and other useful information.

Miscellaneous Rulings

Limitation of the Golf Ball

At the Autumn Business Meeting, 1920, of the Royal and Ancient Club the following resolution was adopted:

On and after 1st May, 1921, the weight of the ball shall not be greater than 1.62 ounces avoirdupois, and the size not less than 1.62 inches in diameter. The Rules of Golf Committee and the Executive Committee of the United States Golf Association will take whatever steps they think necessary to limit the powers of the ball with regard to distance, should any ball of greater power be introduced.

The United States Golf Association intimated, May, 1929, that they had resolved to adopt *an easier and pleasanter ball for the average golfer,* and from 1st January, 1931, to 31st December, 1932, the standards of specification of the ball in competitions under their jurisdiction was not less than 1.68 inches in diameter, and not greater than 1.55 ounces in weight. In January, 1932, another alteration was made in the specification of the ball, the weight being increased to 1.62 and the size remaining the same, viz, not less than 1.68.

The Royal Canadian Golf Association adopted the USGA specification as from 1st January, 1948. The effect of this difference between the legislation of the Royal and Ancient, the Royal Canadian Golf Association, and the USGA is that golfers competing in the United States and Canada must use a ball that is larger, but no heavier, than the ball which is legal in other parts of the world.

In May, 1951, a special committee was set up by the Royal and Ancient Golf Club and the United States Golf Association to discuss the desirability of uniformity in the Rules of Golf and the form and make of clubs and balls. The committee recommended that both sizes of ball (1.62 inches and 1.68 inches in diameter both having the same weight, 1.62 ounces) be legal in all countries. At their autumn meeting the United States Golfers' Association rejected this proposal but agreed that in international team competition in the United States, the size of the ball be not less than 1.62 inches in diameter.

The matter of a uniform ball world-wide was investigated by a special committee from the R & A and the USGA but was dropped in 1974 when the two bodies could not reach agreement.

A maximum initial velocity standard of not greater than 250 feet per second on special apparatus was introduced by the R & A in 1976.

The R & A issues lists of conforming golf balls annually.

Limitation of Number of Clubs

At the Business Meeting of the Royal and Ancient Golf Club, May, 1937, the Rules of Golf Committee submitted a recommendation that on and after 1st January, 1938, the preamble to the Rules of Golf shall read: *The game of golf consists of a ball being played from a teeing ground to a hole by successive strokes with clubs (not exceeding fourteen in number) and balls made in conformity with the directions laid down in the clause on 'Form and make of golf clubs and balls'.* The recommendation was not approved by the members.

In September, 1938, at the Business Meeting of the Royal and Ancient, a similar recommendation was approved by the members, and the limitation of the number of clubs to fourteen became operative as from 1st May, 1939.

The United States Golf Association decided to limit the number of clubs to fourteen as from 1st January, 1938.

Steel-Shafted Clubs

The Royal and Ancient Golf Club authorised steel shafts, November, 1929, in the following announcement: *The Rules of Golf Committee have decided that steel shafts, as approved by the Rules of Golf Committee are declared to conform with the requirements of the clause in the Rules of Golf on the form and make of golf clubs.*

Laminated Shafts

The Rules of Golf Committee on 5th December, 1932, announced that clubs with laminated shafts built entirely of wood are permissible.

Recognised Golf Clubs

The Rules of Golf Committee, in answering a query, gave the opinion that a recognised Golf Club is one which has regularly appointed office-bearers.

The English Golf Union decided that a recognised Golf Club for the purpose of competitive golf in England is a golf club affiliated to the English Golf Union through its County Union, or where there is no County Union direct to the English Golf Union as an Associate Member.

Championship Conditions

Men

The Amateur Championship

The Championship, until 1982, was decided entirely by match play over 18 holes except for the final which was over 36 holes. Since 1983 the Championship has comprised two stroke-play rounds of 18 holes each from which the top 64 scores over the 36 holes qualify for the match-play stages. Matches are over 18 holes except for the final which is over 36 holes.

Full particulars of conditions of entry and method of play can be obtained from the Secretary, Championship Committee, Royal and Ancient Golf Club, St Andrews, Fife.

The Seniors' Open Amateur

The Championship consists of 18 holes on each of two days, the lowest 50 scores over the 36 holes and any tying for 50th place then playing a further 18 holes the following day.

Conditions for entry include:

Entrants must have attained the age of 55 years prior to the first day on which the Championship is played.

Entries are limited to 250 competitors, the higher handicaps being balloted out if necessary.

Full particulars of conditions of entry and method of play can be obtained from the Secretary, Championship Committee, Royal and Ancient Golf Club, St Andrews, Fife.

National Championships

The English, Scottish, Irish and Welsh Amateur Championships are played by holes, each match consisting of one round of 18 holes except the final which is contested over 36 holes.

Full particulars of conditions of entry and method of play can be obtained from the secretaries of the respective national Unions.

English Open Amateur Stroke Play Championship

The Championship consists of one round of 18 holes on each of two days after which the leading 45 and those tying for 45th place play a further two rounds. The remainder are eliminated.

Conditions for entry include:

Entrants must have a handicap not exceeding three.

Where the entries exceed 130, an 18-hole qualifying round is held the day before the Championship. Certain players are exempt from qualifying.

Full particulars of conditions of entry and method of play can be obtained from the Secretary, English Golf Union.

Youths

British Youths' Open Amateur Championship

The Championship consists of 18 holes on each of two days, the lowest 40 scores over the 36 holes and any tying for 40th place then playing a further 36 holes the following day.

Conditions of entry include:

Entrants must be under 21 years of age on the last day on which the Championship is played.

Entries are limited to 150 competitors, the higher handicaps being balloted out if necessary.

Full particulars of conditions of entry and method of play can be obtained from the Secretary, Championship Committee, Royal and Ancient Golf Club, St Andrews, Fife.

Boys

Boys' Amateur Championship

The Championship is played by match play, each match consisting of one round of 18 holes except for the final which is over 36 holes.

Conditions of entry include:

Entrants must be under 18 years of age on the last day on which the Championship is played.

Entries are limited to 192 competitors, the higher handicaps being balloted out if necessary.

Full particulars of conditions of entry and method of play can be obtained from the Secretary, Championship Committee, Royal and Ancient Golf Club, St Andrews, Fife.

Ladies

Ladies' British Open Amateur Championship

The Championship consists of one 18 hole qualifying round on each of two days. If entries exceed 110 there will be 64 qualifiers for matchplay. If entries number 110 or less, 32 will qualify for matchplay. Handicap limit is 4.

Ladies' British Open Amateur Stroke Play Championship

The Championship consists of 72 holes stroke play; 18 holes are played on each of two days after which the first 32 and all ties for 32nd place qualify for a further 36 holes on the third day. Handicap limit is 4.

Ladies' British Open Championship

The Championship consists of 72 holes stroke play. 18 holes are played on each of four days, the field being reduced after the first 36 holes and again after 54 holes.

Entries accepted from lady amateurs with a handicap not exceeding scratch and from lady professionals.

Full particulars of conditions of entry and method of play for all three Championships can be obtained from the General Administrator, LGU, 12 The Links, St Andrews, Fife.

National Championships

Conditions of entry and method of play for the English, Scottish, Welsh and Irish Ladies' Close Championships can be obtained from the secretaries of the respective associations.

Other championships organised by the respective national associations, from whom full particulars can be obtained, include English Ladies', Intermediate, English Ladies' Stroke-Play, Scottish Girls' Open Amateur Stroke Play (under 21) and Welsh Ladies' Open Amateur Stroke Play.

Girls

Girls' British Open Amateur Championship

The Championship consists of two 18-hole qualifying rounds, followed by match-play in two flights each of sixteen players.

Conditions of entry include:

Entrants must be under 18 years of age on the last day of the British Girls' Championship.

Competitors are required to hold a certified LGU international handicap not exceeding 15, or to be members of their National Junior Team for the current year.

Full particulars of conditions of entry and method of play can be obtained from the General Administrator, LGU, 12 The Links, St Andrews, Fife.

National Championships

The English, Scottish, Irish and Welsh Girls' Close Championships are open to all girls of relevant nationality and appropriate age which may vary from country to country. A handicap limit may be set by some countries.

Full particulars of conditions of entry and method of play can be obtained via the secretaries of the respective associations.

International Match Conditions

Men–Amateur

Walker Cup–Great Britain and Ireland *v* United States

Deed of Gift to United States Golf Association

International Challenge Trophy

Mr GH Walker of the United States presented a Cup for international competition to be known as *The United States Golf Association International Challenge Trophy*, popularly described as *The Walker Cup*.

The Cup shall be played for by teams of amateur golfers selected from Clubs under the jurisdiction of the United States Golf Association on the one side and from England, Scotland, Wales, Northern Ireland and Eire on the other.

The International Walker Cup Match shall be held every two years in the United States of America and Great Britain alternately.

The teams shall consist of not more than ten players and a captain.

The contest consists of 4 foursomes and 8 singles matches over 18 holes on each of two days.

Eisenhower Trophy (Formerly World Cup)

Founded in 1958 in recognition of the need for an official team championship for amateurs. Each country enters a team of four players who play stroke play over 72 holes, the total of the three best individual scores to be counted each day. (One score to be discarded.) The winner to be the team with the lowest aggregate for the 72 holes. The first event was played at St Andrews in 1958 and the trophy has been played for every second year.

European Team Championship

Founded in 1959 by the European Golf Association for competition among member countries of the Association. The Championship is held biennially and played in rotation round the countries which are grouped in four geographical zones.

Each team consists of six players who play two qualifying rounds of 18 holes, the five best scores of each round constituting the team aggregate. Flights for match play are then arranged according to qualifying round rankings. For the match play, teams consist of five players, playing two foursomes in the morning and five singles in the afternoon.

A similar championship is held every year for junior teams.

Home Internationals (Raymond Trophy)

The first official International Match recorded was in 1903 at Muirfield between England and Scotland when singles only were played.

In 1932 International Week was inaugurated under the auspices of the British Golf Unions' Joint Advisory Council with the full approval of the four National Golf Unions. The Council of National Golf Unions is now responsible for running the matches.

Teams of 11 players from England, Scotland, Ireland and Wales engage in matches consisting of 5 foursomes and 10 singles over 18 holes, the foursomes being in the morning and the singles in the afternoon. Each team plays every other team.

The eligibility of players to play for their country shall be their eligibility to play in the Amateur Championship of their country.

Men–Professional

Ryder Cup

This Cup was presented by Mr Samuel Ryder, St Albans, England (who died 2nd January, 1936), for competition between a team of British professionals and a team of American professionals. The trophy was first competed for in 1927. In 1929 the original conditions were varied to confine the British team to British-born professionals resident in Great Britain, and the American team to American-born professionals resident in the United States, in the year of the match. In 1977 the British team was extended to include European players. The matches are played biennially, in alternate continents, in accordance with the conditions as agreed between the respectives PGAs.

World Cup (formerly Canada Cup)

Founded in America in 1953 as an International Team event for professional golfers with the intention of spreading international goodwill.

Each country is represented by two players, the best team score over 72 holes being the winners of the World cup and the best individual score the International Trophy. It is played annually.

Ladies

Great Britain and Ireland v United States

(Curtis Cup)

For a trophy presented by the late Misses Margaret and Harriot Curtis of Boston, USA, for biennial competition between teams from the United States of America and Great Britain and Ireland.

The match is sponsored jointly by the United States Golf Association and the Ladies' Golf Union who may select teams of not more than 8 players.

The match consists of 3 foursomes and 6 singles of 18 holes on each of two days, the foursomes being played each morning.

Great Britain and Ireland v Continent of Europe

(Vagliano Trophy)

For a trophy presented to the Comité des Dames de la Fédération Française de Golf and the Ladies' Golf Union by Monsieur AA Vagliano, originally for annual competition between teams of women amateur golfers from France and Great Britain and Ireland but, since 1959, by mutual agreement, for competition between teams from the Continent of Europe and Great Britain and Ireland.

The match is played biennially, alternately in Great Britain and Ireland and on the Continent of Europe, with teams of not more than 9 players plus a non-playing captain.

The match consists of 4 foursomes and 8 singles, of 18 holes on each of two days. The foursomes are played each morning.

Women's World Amateur Team Championship

(Espirito Santo Trophy)

For the Espirito Santo Trophy presented by Mrs Ricardo Santo of Portugal for biennial competition between teams of not more than three women amateur golfers who represent a national association affiliated to the World Amateur Golf Council. First competed for in 1964.

The tournament consists of 72 holes stroke play, 18 holes on each of four days, the two best scores in each round each day constituting the team aggregate.

Commonwealth Tournament

(Lady Astor Trophy)

For a trophy presented by the late Viscountess Astor CH, and the Ladies' Golf Union for competition once in every four years between teams of women amateur golfers from Commonwealth countries.

The inaugural Commonwealth Tournament was played at St Andrews in 1959 between teams from Australia, Canada, New Zealand, South Africa and Great Britain and was won by the British team. The tournament is played in rotation in the competing countries, for the present Great Britain, Australia, Canada, and New Zealand, each country being entitled to nominate 6 players including a playing or non-playing captain.

Each team plays every other team and each team match consists of 2 foursomes and 4 singles over 18 holes. The foursomes are played in the morning and the singles in the afternoon.

European Ladies' Amateur Team Championship

The championship is held biennially between teams of amateur women golfers from the European countries. Each team consists of not more than six players who play two qualifying rounds, the five best scores in each round constituting the team aggregate. The match play draw is made in flights according to the position in the qualifying rounds. The match play consists of two foursomes and five singles on each of three days.

A similar championship is held in alternate years for junior ladies' teams, under 22 years of age.

Home Internationals

Teams from England, Scotland, Ireland and Wales compete annually for a trophy presented to the LGU by the late Mr TH Miller. The qualifications for a player being eligible to play for her country are the same as those laid down by each country for its Close Championship.

Each team plays each other team. The matches consist of 6 singles and 3 foursomes, each of 18 holes. Each country may nominate teams of not more than 8 players.

Youths

England *v* Scotland

The International Match between England and Scotland is played either one or two days before the Youths' Championship begins, depending on the location of the match between Great Britain and Ireland *v* Continent of Europe.

Great Britain and Ireland *v* Continent of Europe

The International Match between Great Britain and Europe is played the day before the Youths' Championship begins. On alternate years, the match is played on the Continent. On this occasion the match is held the day before the start of the Youths' Championship.

Boys

England *v* Scotland; Wales *v* Ireland

The International Matches between England and Scotland (10 players a side) and Wales and Ireland (10 players a side) are played on the Thursday preceding the Boys' Championship. The following day the winners of these two matches play against each other, as do the losers. To be eligible to play in these matches a boy must qualify by age to be eligible to play in the Boys' Championship.

Great Britain and Ireland *v* Continent of Europe

The International Match between Great Britain and Ireland and the Continent of Europe is played on the Saturday preceding the Boys' Championship.

Girls

Home Internationals

Teams from England, Scotland, Ireland and Wales compete annually for the Stroyan Cup. The qualifications for a player for the Girls' International Matches shall be the same as those laid down by each country for its Girls' Close Championship except that a player shall be under 18 years on the last day of the British Girls' Championship of that year.

Each team, consisting of not more than 8 players, plays each other team, a draw taking place to decide the order of play between the teams. The matches consist of 7 singles, each of 18 holes.

Golf Associations

The Golf Foundation

During the last decade, the growth of golf throughout Britain has scaled new heights with each passing year as more and more people become smitten with its addictive qualities. It was Tony Jacklin who initially sparked this explosion of interest with his victories in the Open Championship and the United States Open some 17 years ago and further fuel has been added by the emergence of Spain's Severiano Ballesteros as one of the most exciting players the game has ever seen. The exploits of the world's leading professionals are now regularly beamed into millions of homes via television and so people who would never have dreamed of taking an interest in the game have been fascinated and eventually drawn into finding out for themselves its magnetic qualities.

Many of these people are youngsters–girls and boys who witness the achievements of today's stars and feel that they too would like to experience the allure and charm of golf with dreams, perhaps, of emulating some of the modern day heroes and heroines. In a great many cases, these dreams are frustrated at the outset. If the parents of a child do not play golf then all the questions the child may have about starting golf can go unanswered. He or she may enquire about the game from school teachers but unless one of them is a golfer, it is unlikely that this approach will bear any fruit so the seeds of interest are soon stifled and the child turns to other games which are included in the school curriculum.

It is this gap in the education of young, potential golfers that The Golf Foundation fills. Founded in 1952, The Golf Foundation's original motives of promoting the development of junior golf throughout the country still hold good today and in the space of 35 years, thousands of junior golfers have benefited from its work. From this number have emerged some famous names such as Bernard Gallacher, Brian Barnes, Peter Oosterhuis, Michelle Walker and more recently Paul Way, Michael McLean and Ronan Rafferty all of whom received instruction and assistance under The Golf Foundation Coaching Scheme.

This scheme forms the basis of the Foundation's work whereby it subsidises instruction by qualified members of the Professional Golfer's Association (PGA) to students of schools, universities and other places of higher education and to junior members of golf clubs who are in full-time education. This enables schools who do not have golf as part of their sports' programme to take advantage of giving their pupils an introduction to the game and a solid grounding in its techniques.

But the work of the Golf Foundation does not begin and end there; the Foundation realised that young people's initial interest in the game must be sustained. Thus, over the years it has expanded its field of operations to cover the development of a junior golfer right through to the adult ranks. This area includes the awarding of vouchers for individual tuition for promising girls and boys; the sponsoring of Open Coaching Centres during school holidays; the encouragement of school competitive golf and assisting the formation of National and County Schools' Golf Associations; the operation of a film and visual aids service; the organisation and sponsorship of the Schools' Team Championship; the promotion of an Eclectic Competition for club juniors; the operation of a Merit Award Scheme whereby juniors can have their progress measured and rewarded and the sponsorship of an Under-15 Championship for Boys and Girls.

The Foundation also makes an annual award to the boy or girl showing the most improvement as a result of Golf Foundation tuition and in 1983 this award was won by a 17-year-old boy who is deaf and has limited speech–proof, if any were needed, of the therapeutic powers of the game and evidence of the particular interest the Golf Foundation takes in handicapped young people.

The implementation of these activities and the running of the coaching scheme costs a great deal of money and the Golf Foundation relies heavily on club golfers for a large part of its income. Organisations within the game and companies also assist in providing funds so that its work can continue and expand.

At present, the future of British golf looks bright but in order to maintain that progress, more and more youngsters must be given the opportunity to learn about and play golf. As one old scribe once wrote, *it is a game at which you may exhaust yourself but never your subject,* and it is a game that teaches self-discipline, good manners, sportsmanship and an appreciation of other people's qualities. It is *the game of a lifetime* for it can be played by people of all ages. The Golf Foundation hopes that you too, once you have experienced the pleasures of golf, will find it a lasting source of enjoyment.

For details about the Golf Foundation's work, please apply to: The Director, The Golf Foundation, 78 Third Avenue, Bush Hill Park, Enfield, Middlesex EN1 1BX. (Tel: 01-367 4404).

The National Association of Public Golf Courses

(Affiliated to English Golf Union)

Hon Secretary: JHH Burdett, 948 Castle Lane East, Bournemouth BH7 6SP. ***Tel*** Christchurch (0202) 483017.

1927 saw the foundation of the Association by the late FG Hawtree (Golf Course Architect) and the late JH Taylor (five times Open Champion). They were both farsighted enough to see the need for cohesion between *Private* golf, *Public* golf and the Local Councils. Up to the outbreak of World War II the Association struggled on, sustained by a small amount of very welcome financial support from the News of the World. This enabled the *unofficial* Championship to be staged.

After the War, the Association was revitalised and the Championship was recognised by the National Union–and so from a shaky start of 240 qualifiers–there are now some 3500 Public Course golfers trying to qualify, from a total estimated membership of 50,000. The success and importance of the *Public Courses Championship of England* prompted the commencement of the Championship for Ladies and then the Championship for Juniors–which share equal importance. Soon after the establishment of Individual Championships there came the introduction of various Club Team events, and these have now progressed to National Level with a vast following from the Clubs in membership. Thus the Association now organises some 14 National events each year for the total membership.

Some years ago it was realised that the Local Councils (Course Management Authorities) could not enjoy official recognition and membership of the County Unions or National Unions except through the Association, this has now been remedied and many CMA are full subscribing members of the Association, and many others permit the *Courtesy of the Course* for all our National & Zonal Tournaments. Advice is offered to CMA–when requested–on such matters as Course Construction, Club formation and integration, establishment of Standard Scratch Score and Par Values, and many other topics concerned with the management of the game of golf.

Some overseas organisations and Councils have already sought our advice and help in recent years, when forming their own Courses, Clubs and Associations.

The Constitutional aims have not changed over the years, and the Association is proud to have maintained these Aims through the activities provided by the National Executive of the Association. The aims are:

1. To unite the Clubs formed on Public Courses in England and Wales, and their Course Managements, in the furtherance of the interests of Amateur Golf.
2. To promote Annual Public Courses Championships and such other matches, competitions and Tournaments as shall be authorised by the Executive of the Association.
3. To afford direct representation of Public Course Interests in the National Union.

The total organisation of the Association is wholly voluntary and honorary, from the President down through Vice-Presidents, Chairmen, Secretary, Treasurer and Zone Secretaries. It is quite fantastic for an unpaid Organisation to cover such an exacting *field* of work, but most gratifying to all of us of the National Executive who have secured the steady progress of recent years.

The Association of Golf Club Secretaries

Membership is 1500, consisting of Secretaries and retired Secretaries of Clubs largely situated in Great Britain but also from 200 Clubs in other parts of the World. The Association offers from the Headquarters at Bakewell, Derbyshire advice on all aspects of Golf Club Management, together with a training course for new and intending Golf Club Secretaries. Apart from national events, including a Conference, the Association organises golfing and business meetings for its members at regional level. There are twelve regions within the British Isles.

Secretary: John Crowther, Victoria Mill, Buxton Road, Bakewell, Derbyshire DE4 1DA. ***Tel*** 062-981 4314.

Association of Golf Writers

Secretary: Renton Laidlaw, 5 Cheniston Court, Ridgemount Rd, Sunningdale, Berks.

The Sports Turf Research Institute

(Bingley, West Yorkshire).

The Institute is officially recognised as the national centre for sports and amenity turf. Non-commercial and non-profit making, its affairs are administered by a Board of Management whose members are nominated by the sport controlling bodies in membership of the Institute. Golf is represented by nominees of the Royal and Ancient Golf Club of St. Andrews, four individual National Golf Unions, and the Councils of National Golf Unions.

The institute has as its object the raising of the standard of turf used for all sports. Much valuable data is accumulated from the research activities and is incorporated in the advice given to subscribing clubs and organisations.

For further information as to subscriptions and visiting fees, etc., write tc: ***The Secretary,*** The Sports Turf Research Institute, Bingley, West Yorks BD16 1AU. ***Tel*** Bradford 565131.

The British Association of Golf Course Architects

Objects of the Association:

To encourage the highest standards of Golf Course Design and Construction.

To have the fullest regard to the best interests of Members' Clients.

To maintain a Register of Members fully qualified by training and experience in the design and construction of Golf Courses.

To promote the interests of its members and the game of golf.

To support research and development in golf course Design, Construction and Maintainance.

To enable members to meet together, share knowledge and experience, and discuss matters affecting their work.

To follow the best accepted principles of golf course architecture and modern design requirements with the object of providing the maximum enjoyment of the game for all standards of players.

Hon Secretary: Martin Hawtree, 5 Oxford Street, Woodstock, Oxford OX7 1TQ. Tel: 0993-811976.

The British Association of Golf Course Constructors

Objects: To promote the development of the golf course construction industry, to promote the adoption of policies which will ensure a high quality of workmanship and working practices, to collect and disseminate information of value regarding the construction of golf courses to other members of the association, to members of the allied industries and to the public at large, to promote the training and education of personnel within the industry and to maintain agreed standards of golf course construction by adherence to contractual procedures and codes of practice.

All enquiries to M Haughtree, British Association of Golf Course Constructors, Miller House, Corporation Street, Rugby. ***Tel*** 0788 77191 ext. 384.

British Golf Greenkeepers' Association

The objects are to advance golf greenkeeping, to assist and encourage the proficiency of members, arrange lectures, and maintain a benevolent fund. The Association magazine, *Golf Greenkeeping and Course Maintenance,* is issued monthly and sent free to all members. ***Hon Secretary and Treasurer***: Walter Heeles, 7 Tentergate Close, Knaresborough, North Yorkshire HG5 9BJ. ***Tel*** (0423) 863851.

English and International Golf Greenkeepers' Association

The EIGGA was formed in January 1983. Its aims are to raise the status of Golf Greenkeepers and their profession, and to provide them with the personal and professional benefits which they require. The official magazine of the Association is *Greenkeeper,* which is sent free to all members.

General Administrator: Danielle Jones, National Headquarters, 2 Golf Cottage, Bucklesham Road, Ipswich IP3 8UG, Suffolk. ***Tel*** 0473 711810.

Scottish and International Golf Greenkeepers' Association

To advance the status of golf greenkeepers and to educate the members by way of lectures, discussions, seminars; to arrange golf competitions and functions of like nature; to assist the colleges involved in the training of apprentice greenkeepers and to assist golf clubs to our mutual benefit and to collaborate with the greenkeeper training committee, and to promote golf greenkeeping. *General Secretary:* JD McKean, 82 Dumbreck Road, Glasgow G41 9DW. Tel: 041-427 4242.

International Greenkeepers' Association

Object: Improvement of members by arranging lectures and courses of instruction in different parts of Europe. ***Secretary***: Mrs B Harradine, Via Golf, CH 6987 Caslano, Switzerland.

National Golf Clubs' Advisory Association

The National Golf Clubs' Advisory Association was founded in 1922. The objects are to protect the interests of Golf Clubs in general and to give legal advice and direction, under the opinion of Counsel, on the administrative and legal responsibilities of Golf Clubs. In cases taken to the Courts for decisions on any points which in the opinion of the Executive Committee involve principles affecting the general interests of affiliated clubs financial assistance may sometimes be given. ***Secretary***: John Crowther, Victoria Mill, Buxton Road, Bakewell, Derbyshire DE14 1DA. ***Tel*** 062981 3844.

European Golf Association

Association Européenne de Golf

At a meeting held at Luxembourg, 20th November, 1937, this Association was formed.

Membership shall be restricted to European National Amateur Golf Associations or Unions. The Association shall concern itself solely with matters of an international character. The Association shall have as its prime objects:

(a) To encourage the international development of golf and strengthen the bonds of friendship existing between the national organisations and to encourage the formation of new ones.
(b) To co-ordinate the dates of the Open and Amateur Championships of its members.
(c) To arrange when such have been decided upon, European Team Championships and Matches of international character.
(d) To decide and publish the Calendar dates of the Open and Amateur Championships and Matches.

Hon Secretary: Neil S Hotchkin, 69 Avenue Victor Hugo, 75783 Paris 16, France. ***Tel*** (33) 1.45.00.82.61.

Addresses of British and Overseas Golfing Organisations

United Kingdom

National

Amateur Golf Championship
Sec, MF Bonallack, OBE, Royal and Ancient Golf Club, St Andrews.

Artisan Golfers' Association
Hon Sec, A. Everett, 51 Rose Hill, Park West, Sutton, Surrey. ***Tel*** 01-644 7037.

Association of Golf Club Secretaries
Sec, J. Crowther, Victoria Mill, Buxton Road, Bakewell, Derbyshire DE4 1DA. ***Tel*** 062 981 4314.

Boys' Amateur Golf Championship
Sec, MF Bonallack, OBE Royal and Ancient Golf Club, St Andrews.

British Association of Golf Course Architects
Hon Sec & Treas, MG Hawtree, 5 Oxford Street, Woodstock, Oxford OX7 1TQ. ***Tel*** (0993) 811976.

British Association of Golf Course Constructors
Mr H Swan, Little Dukes, The Street, Roxwell, Essex CM1 4PE. ***Tel*** (0245) 48640.

British Golf Greenkeepers' Association
Hon Sec, Walter Heeles, 7 Tentergate Close, Knaresborough, N. Yorkshire HG5 9BJ. ***Tel*** (0423) 863851.

British Left-Handed Golfers' Society
Hon Sec, AC Kirkland, Squirrel Cottage, Mereheath Lane, Knutsford, Cheshire. ***Tel*** (0565) 4671.

Council of National Golf Unions
Hon Sec, Alan Thirlwell, Formby GC, Golf Road, Formby, Liverpool L37 1LQ. ***Tel*** Formby 72164.

English Golf Union
Sec, K Wright, 1–3 Upper King Street, Leicester LE1 6XF. ***Tel*** (0533) 553042.

Midland Group *Sec,* RJW Baldwin, Chantry Cottage, Friar Street, Droitwich, Worcs. WR9 8EQ. ***Tel*** (0905) 778560.

Northern Group *Hon Sec,* JE Hiles, 16 Evesham Road, Lytham St Annes, Lancs. FY8 1HE. ***Tel*** St Annes 728767.

South Eastern Group *Hon Sec,* MA Hobson, 22 Wye Court, Malvern Way, Ealing, London W13 8EA. ***Tel*** 01-997 7466.

South Western Group *Sec,* JT Lumley, Hartland, Potterne, Devizes, Wilts. ***Tel*** (0380) 3935.

English Ladies' Golf Association
Sec, Miss GC Hickson, PO Box 14, 52 Boroughgate, Otley, West Yorkshire LS21 1QW. ***Tel*** Otley (0943) 464010.

Northern Division *Hon Sec,* Mrs D Vaux, Methley 3 Belle Vue Crescent, Filey, North Yorkshire YO14 9AD. ***Tel*** Scarborough (0723) 513213.

Midlands Division *Hon Sec,* Mrs W Earnshaw, 260 Widney Lane, Solihull, West Midlands B91 3JY. ***Tel*** 021-705 4285.

South-Eastern Division *Hon Sec,* Mrs E Block, 71 Parkanaur Avenue, Thorpe Bay, Essex SS1 3JA. ***Tel*** (0702) 588336.

South-Western Division *Hon Sec,* Mrs VJ Wilde, Tyrock, West Hill, Wraxall, Bristol. ***Tel*** Nailsea (0272) 853912.

English Schools' Golf Association
Hon Sec, R Snell, 20 Dykenook Close, Whickham, Newcastle-upon-Tyne. ***Tel*** (091) 488 3538.

Golf Club Stewards' Association
Sec, G Shaw, 50 The Park, St Albans, Herts. ***Tel*** St Albans (0727) 57334.

Chairman, A Reay, Robin Hood Golf Club, St Bernard's Road, Solihull, Birmingham. ***Tel*** 021-706 0159.

Special Events, DJ Lithgow, Great Barr Golf Club, Chapel Lane, Great Barr, Birmingham B43 7BA. ***Tel*** 021-357 1232.

Regional Secretaries

South Roger Gregory, Southwick Park Golf Club. ***Tel*** (0705) 370683.

Midlands Carol Reay, Robin Hood Golf Club. ***Tel*** 021-706 0159.

North East J Armstrong, Hexham Golf Club. ***Tel*** (0434) 602057.

Yorkshire K Millington, Whitby Golf Club. ***Tel*** Whitby (0947) 601632/602768.

Wales & West Peter Blackmore, Stinchcombe Hill Golf Club. ***Tel*** (0453) 2015.

Golf Foundation

78 Third Avenue, Bush Hill Park, Enfield, Middx. EN1 1BX. ***Tel*** 01-367 4404.

Sectional Secretaries:

Cleveland Mr B Burnell, 2 Clarence Road, Eaglescliffe, Stockton, Cleveland.

Devon and Cornwall Mr W Pile, 33 Knowle Drive, Exwick, Exeter, Devon.

East Midland Mr RW Willars, 27 Condor Close, Broughton Astley, Leics. LE9 6RR.

Mid Anglia Mr L Wakrell, 26 Loxley Road, Berkhamsted, Herts. HP4 3PS.

Midland Mr D Keen, 31 Rothley Close, Radbrook Green, Shrewsbury, Shropshire.

Northern Mr D Hannam, 12 Moorfield Avenue, Menston, Nr Ilkley, W Yorks.

North East Mr JF Richardson, 20 Aston Way, Clevering Park, Whickham, Tyne & Wear.

North West Mr S Arrowsmith, 12 Fernbank, Hartwood Estate, Chorley, Lancs.

Sheffield Mr F Barratt, 46 Lister Avenue, Sheffield S12 3FP.

South West Mr P Worster, 14 Manor Close, Cirencester, Glos.

South Coast Mr N Butler, 25 Malin Close, Stubbington, Fareham, Hampshire PO14 3RD.

Wales Mr PJ Swain, 6 Lock Street, Newport, Gwent.

Golf Society of Great Britain

Gleneagles, Maddox Park, Little Bookham, Surrey KT23 3BW. ***Tel*** 0372-54260.

Hill Samuel School Foursomes

Competition Hon Sec, GR Scott, Yew Tree Cottage, 93 Wells Road, Malvern, Worcs. WR14 4PB. ***Tel*** Malvern 65605.

Hole in One Golf Society

Sec, EW Parker, 1 Vigilant Way, Gravesend, Kent. ***Tel*** Gravesend (0474) 534298.

Ladies' Golf Union

General Administrator, Mrs Alison White, 12 The Links, St Andrews, Fife KY16 9JB. ***Tel*** St Andrews (0334) 75811.

The Society of One-Armed Golfers

Hon Sec, Don Reid, 11 Coldwell Lane, Felling, Tyne and Wear NE10 9EX. ***Tel*** 091-4694742.

The Professional Golfers' Association

Executive Director, Colin Snape. PGA Headquarters, Apollo House, The Belfry, Sutton Coldfield, West Midlands, B76 9PT. ***Tel*** Curdworth (0675) 70333. ***General Secretary,*** ML Hully, PGA Headquarters

PGA European Tour

Executive Director, KD Schofield, PGA European Tour, The Wentworth Club, Wentworth Drive, Virginia Water, Surrey GU25 4LS. ***Tel*** 09904 2921.

Women's Professional Golf Association

National Headquarters, Apollo House, The Belfry, Sutton Coldfield, West Midlands B76 9PT. ***Tel*** 0675 70333.

Midland Region *Sec,* Lawrence Thornton, PGA National Headquarters, Apollo House, The Belfry, Sutton Coldfield, West Midlands B76 9PT. ***Tel*** 0675 70333.

North Region *Sec,* Norman Fletcher, ***Tel*** 02572 73823.

West Region *Sec,* Bill Morton, Exeter Golf and Country Club, Topham Road, Countess Wear, Exeter EX2 7AE. ***Tel*** 0392 877657.

South Region *Sec,* Chris Gotla, Tyrells Wood GC, Leatherhead, Surrey KT22 8QP. ***Tel*** 0372 370111.

Irish Region *Sec,* Brian Campbell, 26 Rosetta Avenue, Belfast BT7 3HG. ***Tel*** 0232 641815.

Scottish Region *Sec,* Sandy Jones, Glenbervie Golf Club, Stirling Road, Larbert FK5 4SL. ***Tel*** 0324 562451.

Public Schools' Old Boys' Golf Association

Jt Secs, P de Pinna, Bruins, Wythwood, Haywards Heath, West Sussex, ***Tel*** Haywards Heath 454883 and JBM Urry, Dormers, 232 Dickens Heath Road, Shirley, Solihull, West Midlands. ***Tel*** (home) 0564 823114, (office) 021-772 5754.

Public Schools' Golfing Society

Hon Sec, PH Kenyon, Hyde's, Winderton, Nr Banbury, Oxfordshire OX15 5JF. ***Tel*** Brailes 229.

Seniors' Championship

Sec, MF Bonallack, OBE, Royal and Ancient Golf Club, St Andrews.

Senior Golfers' Society
Sec, Brigadier D Ross CBE, Milland Farmhouse, Liphook, Hants GU30 7JP. ***Tel*** Milland 200.

Women's Professional Golf Association
see PGA.

Youths' Amateur Golf Championship
Sec, MF Bonallack, OBE, Royal and Ancient Golf Club, St Andrews.

England

Bedfordshire County Golf Union
Hon Sec, G Keeling, Fordwych, 2 Phillpotts Avenue, Bedford. ***Tel*** Bedford 63222 (Bus); 55564 (Home).

Bedfordshire Ladies' County Golf Association
Hon Sec, Mrs D Macleod, 1 Warwick Close, Raunds, Northamptonshire. ***Tel*** Wellingborough (0933) 625000.

Berks, Bucks and Oxon Union of Golf Clubs
Sec, RMF Fenning, The Lodge, Commonwood, Chipperfield, Herts. WD4 9BA. ***Tel*** Kings Langley (09277) 63156 (Home). (09277) 65319 (Office).

Berkshire Ladies' County Golf Association
Hon Sec, Mrs BE Baird, 11 Lynton Green, College Road, Maidenhead. ***Tel*** Maidenhead 21462.

Buckinghamshire Ladies' County Golf Association
Hon Sec, Mrs N Williams, 15 Furze View, Chorleywood, Herts. ***Tel*** Chorleywood 3253.

Cambridgeshire Area Golf Union
Sec, RAC Blows, *Rydalcroft,* 2a Dukes Meadow, Stapleford, Cambs CB2 5BH. ***Tel*** Cambridge (0223) 842062.

Cambs. and Hunts. Ladies' County Golf Association
Hon Sec, Mrs A Guy, 19 Greenfield Close, Stapleford, Cambs. CB2 5BF. ***Tel*** (0223) 843267.

Channel Islands Ladies' GA
Sec, Mrs JMT Willis, Oakebirch, Park Estate, St Brelade, Jersey CI.

Cheshire County Ladies' Golf Assocation
Hon Sec, Miss J Watson, 10 Tolland Lane, Hale, Altrincham, Cheshire WA15 0LD.

Cheshire PGA
Tournament Director, Keith Brain, The Virgate, Abbey Way Hartford, Northwich, Cheshire CW8 1LY.

Cheshire Union of Golf Clubs
Hon Sec, BC Jones, 4 Curzon Mews, Wilmslow, Cheshire SK9 5JN. ***Tel*** (0625) 520894.

Cornwall Golf Union
Hon Sec, JG Rowe, 8 Lydcott Crescent, Cornwall PL13 1QG. ***Tel*** Widegates (05034) 492.

Cornwall Ladies' County Golf Association
Hon Sec, Mrs A Eddy, Penmester, Hain Walk, St Ives, Cornwall. ***Tel*** Penzance 795392.

Cumbria Ladies' County Golf Association
Hon Sec, Mrs M Angus, 17 Inglewood Crescent, Morton West, Carlisle. ***Tel*** Carlisle 20593.

Cumbria Union of Golf Clubs
Hon Sec, WJ Ward, 16 Sand Croft, Fell Lane, Penrith, Cumbria CA11 8BB. ***Tel*** Penrith 62522.

Derbyshire Alliance
Hon Sec, R Reid, c/o Buxton & High Peak GC, Fairfield, Buxton, Derbyshire. ***Tel*** Buxton (0298) 3112.

Derbyshire Ladies' County Golf Association
Hon Sec, Mrs J Nix, Chevin Close, 58 Broadway, Duffield. ***Tel*** Derby 841703.

Derbyshire Union of Golf Clubs
Hon Sec, CF Ibbotson, 67 Portland Close, Mickleover, Derby DE3 5BR. ***Tel*** Derby (0332) 512465.

Devon County Golf Union
Hon Sec, J Marshall, *Appledowne,* Keyberry Park, Newton Abbot, Devon TQ12 1DF. ***Tel*** Newton Abbott (0626) 52999.

Devon County Ladies' Golf Association
Hon Sec, Mrs Lorna Shaw, 10 Heath Rise, Heath Road, Brixham, Devon TQ5 9BG. ***Tel*** (08045) 2898.

Devon Professional Golfers' Alliance
Hon Sec, Michael J Dunk, Sunhaven, 2 Landscore Close, Crediton, Devon. ***Tel*** Crediton (03632) 3145.

Dorset County Golf Union
Hon Sec, Lt Col MD Hutchins, 38 Carlton Road, Bournemouth BH1 3TG. ***Tel*** (0202) 290821.

Dorset Ladies' County Golf Association
Mrs P Norrie, 38 Chine Walk, West Parley, Wimbourne, Dorset BH22 8PU. *Tel* (0202) 883629.

Durham County Golf Union
Hon Sec, WP Murray, Highnam Lodge, Park Mews, Hartlepool, Cleveland TS26 0DX. *Tel* (0429) 273185.

Durham County Ladies' Golf Association
Sec, Mrs CF Anderson, 107 Harlsey Road, Stockton-on-Tees.

East Anglian PGA
Hon Sec, John Carter, Hunstanton GC, Hunstanton, Norfolk. *Tel* 04853-2751.

Essex County Amateur Golf Union
Hon Sec, LF Wood, Timberley, 93 Eastwood Old Road, Leigh-on-Sea, Essex SS9 4RS. *Tel* Southend-on-Sea 523758.

Essex Ladies' County Golf Association
Hon Sec, Mrs A Chisholm, 38a High Road, Hockley, Essex. *Tel* Southend-on-Sea 203228.

Essex Professional Golfers' Union
Sec, John Turner, 93 Beehive Lane, Ilford, Essex. *Tel* 01-554 4208 (Home).

Gloucestershire and Somerset Professional Golfers' Association
Sec, Bob Newton, Henbury GC, Westbury-on-Trym, Bristol BS10 7QB. *Tel* Bristol (0272) 502121.

Gloucestershire Golf Union
Hon Sec, RF Crisp, 2 Hartley Close, Sandy Lane, Charlton Kings, Cheltenham. *Tel* (0242) 514024.

Gloucester Ladies' County Golf Association
Hon Sec, Mrs JM Graham, 3 The Alders, Manor Park, Frenchay, Bristol. *Tel* Bristol 567440.

Hampshire Ladies' County Golf Association
Hon Sec, Mrs E Buckley, 182 Bassett Green Road, Southampton SO2 3LW.

Hampshire, Isle of Wight and Channel Islands Golf Union
Hon Sec/Treas, JLS McCracken, *Glyngarth*, Tower Road, Hindhead, Surrey GU26 6SL. *Tel* Hindhead (STD 042-873) 4090.

Hampshire Professional Golfers' Association
Hon Sec, Jack V Wells, Orchard Cottage, Old Romsey Road, Cadnam, Southampton SO4 2NP. *Tel* Southampton 812252.

Herts County Professional Golfers' Alliance
Hon Sec, RA Gurney, 1 Field Lane, Letchworth, Herts SG6 3LF
Tel (0462) 682256.

Hertfordshire County Ladies' Golf Association
Hon Sec, Mrs EM Copley, 22 The Avenue, Radlett, Herts *Tel* Radlett 6330.

Hertfordshire Golf Union
Hon Sec, WA de Podesta, 2 The Heath, Radlett, Herts WD7 7DF. *Tel* Radlett 7184.

Isle of Man Golf Union
Hon Sec, JT Pugh, 17 Close Quane, Peel, Isle of Man. *Tel* 0624 842052.

Isle of Wight Ladies' Golf Association
Hon Sec, Mrs F Harrison, 47 Palmers Road, Wootton, Isle of Wight.

Kent County Golf Union
Hon Sec, HF Darkins, Flat 7, Charing Court, 32 Shortlands Road, Bromley, Kent BR2 0XX. *Tel* 01-464 0345.

Kent County Ladies' Golf Association
Hon Sec, Mrs D Hall-Thompson, Colleton House, North Road, Hythe, Kent. *Tel* Hythe 66285.

Kent Professional Golfers' Union
Sec, E Impett, 20 The Grove, Barnham, Kent. *Tel* (0227) 831655.

Lancashire Ladies' County Golf Association
Hon Sec, Mrs L Wilson, 22 Gorse Hey Court, Queens Drive, Liverpool L13 0DF. *Tel* 051-220 2394.

Lancashire Union of Golf Clubs
Sec, N Hardman, Caleb Garth, 52 Bryning Lane, Wrea Green, Nr Preston, Lancs PR4 2NL. *Tel* Kirkham 685555.

Leicestershire and Rutland Ladies' County Golf Association
Hon Sec, Mrs EK Eastabrook, 8 The Woodlands, Market Harborough, Leicestershire. *Tel* Market Harborough (0858) 63117.

Leicestershire and Rutland Golf Union
Hon Sec, GH Upward, 187 Leicester Road, Groby, Leicester. *Tel* 0533-873675 (Home). 0533 871313 (Bus).

Leicestershire Professional Golfers' Association
Hon Sec, R Larratt, Glen Gorse GC, Glen Road, Oadby, Leics LE2 4RF. *Tel* Leicester (0533) 713748.

Lincolnshire Ladies' County Association
Hon Sec, Mrs G Newcombe, 7 Chapman Street, Market Rasen. ***Tel*** Market Rasen (0673) 842287.

Lincolnshire Professional Golfers' Association
Sec, MD Smith, 10 Highfield Drive, Kirton, Lindsey, South Humberside. ***Tel*** (0652) 648658.

Lincolnshire Union of Golf Clubs
Hon Sec, TJ Hale *Dapselah*, Allenby Cres., Fotherby, Nr Louth LN11 0UJ. ***Tel*** Louth 604298.

Manchester and District Golf Alliance
Hon Sec, JGF Brain, 18 Riverside, Leftwich, Northwich, Cheshire. ***Tel*** 0606 41441.

Middlesex County Golf Union
Hon Sec, PSV Cooke, 36 Grants Close, Mill Hill, London NW7 1DD. ***Tel*** 01-349 0414 (Home).

Middlesex Ladies' County Golf Association
Hon Sec, Mrs C Hume, 62 Church Crescent, London N3 1BJ.

Midland Golf Union
Hon Sec, RJW Baldwin, Chantry Cottage, Friar Street, Droitwich, Worcs WR9 8EQ. ***Tel*** (Home) 0905 778560, (Bus) 0905 774344.

Norfolk County Golf Union
Hon Sec/Treas, RJ Trower, 246 Unthank Road, Norwich NR2 2AH. ***Tel*** Norwich 53332 (Home). Norwich 625854 (Office).

Norfolk Ladies' County Association
Hon Sec, Mrs VM Munro, 17 Taylor Avenue, Cringleford, Norfolk NR4 6XY. ***Tel*** Norwich 56049.

Norfolk PGA
Sec, M Garrett, Sheringham GC, Sheringham, Norfolk. ***Tel*** (0263) 823488.

North East and North West PGA
Hon Sec, KW Reddall, 87 Parkside, Greenways, Spennymoor, Co Durham DL16 6SA.

Northamptonshire Golf Union
Joint Hon Secs, AF Stevens and TCA Knight, c/o 75 Queens Park Parade, Northampton. ***Tel*** Northampton (0604) 715038 (Home); 21455 (Bus).

Northamptonshire Ladies' County Golf Association
Hon Sec, Mrs E Coker, 534 Wellingborough Road, Northampton NN3 3HZ. ***Tel*** Northampton (0604) 409298.

Northamptonshire PGA
Hon Sec, TJ Giles, Kingsthorpe GC, Northampton. ***Tel*** Northampton (0604) 719602.

Northumberland Ladies' County Golf Association
Hon Sec, Mrs FK Marshall, 15 Magdalene Fields, Warkworth, Morpeth, Northumberland NE65 0UF. ***Tel*** Alnwick (0665) 711621.

Northumberland Union of Golf Clubs
Hon Sec, WE Procter, 5 Oakhurst Drive, Kenton Park, Gosforth, Newcastle-upon-Tyne 3. ***Tel*** 091-2854981 (Home); 091-2745310 (Bus).

Nottinghamshire County Ladies' Golf Association
Hon Sec, Mrs B Jackson, Cranmer Lodge, Kinoulton, Notts, NA12 3EL. ***Tel*** Kinoulton 81201.

Nottinghamshire PGA
Sec, RW Futer, 52 Barden Road, Mapperley, Nottingham NG3 5QD. ***Tel*** 269635.

Nottinghamshire Union of Golf Clubs
Hon Sec, DB Ash, 32 Compton Road, Sherwood, Nottingham N25 2NJ. ***Tel*** (0602) 621918.

Oxfordshire Ladies' County Golf Association
Hon Sec, Miss BM Nicklin, 532 Banbury Road, Oxford OX2 8EG. ***Tel*** Oxford 58300.

Shropshire and Herefordshire Union of Golf Clubs
Hon Sec, JR Davies, 23 Poplar Crescent, Bayston Hill, Shrewsbury. ***Tel*** Bayston Hill 2655.

Shropshire Ladies' County Golf Association
Hon Sec, Mrs O Higgs, 122 Fieldhouse Drive, Muxton, Telford, Salop. ***Tel*** Telford (0952) 4522.

Somerset Golf Union
Hon Sec, CJE Betty, 11 Middleway Court, Middleway, Taunton TA1 3QJ. ***Tel*** 0823-72842.

Somerset Ladies' County Golf Association
Hon Sec, Mrs P Harker, 83 Milford Avenue, Wick, Nr Bristol BS15 5PP. ***Tel*** Abson 3087.

South-Western Counties Golf Association
Hon Sec/Treas, JT Lumley, Hartland, Potterne, Devizes, Wilts. SN10 5PA. ***Tel*** Devizes (0380) 3935.

Staffordshire Ladies' County Golf Association
Hon Sec, Mrs DB Banks, 11 Westhill, Finchfield, Wolverhampton WV3 9HL. *Tel* 753279.

Staffordshire and Shropshire Union of Professional Golfers
Sec, E Griffiths, 22 Wynn Road, Penn, Wolverhampton. *Tel* W'ton 332180 (Home);

Staffordshire Union of Golf Clubs
Hon Sec, A Smith, 19 Broadway, Walsall, W Mids WS1 3EX. *Tel* Walsall 24988 (Home); Willenhall 65454 (Bus).

Suffolk County Golf Union
Hon Sec, JJ Kerrison, Heath View, Purdis Avenue, Ipswich IP3 8UE. *Tel* Ipswich 74753.

Suffolk Ladies' County Golf Association
Hon Sec, Mrs R Stutely, The Cottage, Great Finborough, Stowmarket, Suffolk IP14 3AE. *Tel* Stowmarket 612888.

Suffolk PGA
Sec, Nigel Whyte, Bungay GC, Bungay, Suffolk. *Tel* (0986) 2337 (Club); (0986) 2555 (Home).

Surrey County Golf Union
Sec, GE Hewan, Newquay, Nursery Close, Horsell, Woking GU21 4UQ. *Tel* Woking 62597.

Surrey Ladies' County Golf Association
Hon Sec, Mrs P Lloyd, The Pheasantry, Tandridge GC, Oxted. *Tel* Oxted (08833) 2072.

Surrey PGA
Director, R Crawford, 48 Hyde Road, Sanderstead, Surrey. *Tel* 01-657 6748.

Sussex County Golf Union
Sec, RP George *Calhame,* Hawkhurst Road, Sedlescombe, East Sussex TN33 0QS. *Tel* Sedlescombe 284.

Sussex County Ladies' Golf Association
Sec, RP George *Calhame,* Hawkhurst Road, Seaford, E Sussex. *Tel* (0323) 894871.

Sussex Professional Golfers' Union
Sec, C Pluck, 96 Cranston Avenue, Bexhill-on-Sea, Sussex. *Tel* (0424) 221298 (Home); (0424) 214121 (Bus).

Tees-side and District Union of Golf Clubs
Hon Sec, F. Simpson, 27 Marton Drive, Billingham, Cleveland *Tel* Stockton 555374.

Warwickshire Ladies' County Golf Association
Hon Sec, Mrs J Plant, 57 White House Green, Solihull B91 1SP. *Tel* (021) 705 8062.

Warwickshire Professional Golfers' Association
Sec, GL Taylor, Labrook Park GC, Poolhead Lane, Wood-End, Tamworth-in-Arden, Solihull B94 5ED. *Tel* 056-44 2581.

Warwickshire Union of Golf Clubs
Hon Sec, JBM Urry, Dormers, 232 Dickens Heath Road, Shirley, Solihull B90 1QQ. *Tel* (Home) 056482-3114; (Office) 021-772 5754.

Wiltshire County Golf Union
Hon Sec/Treas, RF Buthlay, 10 Priory Park, Bradford-on-Avon, Wilts. BA15 1QU. *Tel* (02216) 6401.

Wiltshire Ladies' County Golf Association
Hon Sec, Mrs Joan Jackson, Willow Lee, 1 Boscombe Village, Salisbury. *Tel* Idmiston (0980) 610315.

Wiltshire PGA
L Ross, Professional, Marlborough GC, The Common, Marlborough, Wilts. *Tel* (0672) 52493.

Worcestershire Association of Professional Golfers
Sec, Chris Thompson, Droitwich GC, Ford Lane, Droitwich WR9 0BH, Worcestershire. *Tel* (0905) 770207.

Worcestershire County Ladies' Golf Association
Hon Sec, Mrs SR Rutter, 173 Alcester Road, Moseley, Birmingham B13 8JR. *Tel* 021-449 0266.

Worcestershire Union of Golf Clubs
Hon Sec, WR Painter, 10 Gainsborough Mews, Kidderminster, Worcs DY11 6PZ. *Tel* Kidderminster 2295/3109.

Yorkshire Ladies' County Golf Association
Hon Sec, Mrs M Clarke, 35 West End Rise, Horsforth, Nr Leeds. *Tel* Horsforth 583960.

Yorkshire Professional Golfers' Association
Hon Sec, David Bulmer, Temple Newsam GC, Halton, Leeds 15. *Tel* Leeds (0532) 647362/641464.

Yorkshire Union of Golf Clubs
Hon Sec, Alan Cowman, 50 Bingley Road, Bradford, West Yorkshire BD9 6HH. *Tel* (0274) 42661.

Ireland

Irish Golf Union
Sec, Ivan ER Dickson, Glencar House, 81 Eglington Road, Donnybrook, Dublin 4. *Tel* Dublin 694111.

Ulster Branch *Sec,* Alf Collis, 58A High Street, Holywood, Co Down BT18 9AE. *Tel* 08487 3708.

Leinster Branch *Sec,* Ken Haughton, 1 Clonskeagh Square, Clonskeagh Road, Dublin 14. *Tel* Dublin 696977.

Munster Branch *Hon Sec,* Richard Barry, Sunville, Dromsligo, Mallow, Co Cork. *Tel* Co Cork (Office) Mallow 21117/21123; (Home) Mallow 22760.

Connacht Branch *Hon Sec,* D Howley, Rosses Point, Co Sligo. *Tel* (Office) Sligo 62211; (Home) Sligo 77154.

Irish Ladies' Golf Union

Sec, Miss MP Turvey, 1 Clonskeagh Square, Clonskeagh Road, Dublin 14. *Tel* 01 696244.

Northern District *Hon Sec,* E Watson, 14D Adelaide Park, Belfast BT9 6FX. *Tel* Belfast 682152.

Southern District *Hon Sec,* Mrs N Flynn, 11 Barnstead Drive, Church Road, Blackrock, Cork. *Tel* (021) 291698.

Eastern District *Hon Sec,* Mrs R Kenny, 2a The Rise, Glasnevin, Dublin 9. *Tel* Dublin 372915.

Western District *Hon Sec,* Mrs A Bradshaw, Dooney Rock, Cleveragh Drive, Sligo. *Tel* (071) 77178.

Midland District *Hon Sec,* Mrs B Jordan, 6 Glena Terrace, Spawell Road, Wexford. *Tel* Wexford 22865.

Scotland

Aberdeen Ladies' County Golf Association

Hon Sec, Mrs J Middleton, Crochdane, Aulton Road, Cruden Bay. *Tel* 077-981 812315.

Angus Ladies' County Golf Association

Hon Sec, Miss M Napier, 377 King Street, Broughty Ferry, Dundee. *Tel* Dundee (0382) 78203.

Ayrshire Ladies' County Golf Association

Hon Sec, Mrs A McMillan, 8 Station Road, Prestwick.

Border Counties' Golf Association

Hon Sec, Mrs E Wanless, Fullarton, Darnick, Melrose. *Tel* Melrose (089 682) 2962.

Dumfriesshire and Galloway Lady Golfers' Association

Hon Sec, Miss MJ Greig, Strathdon, 10 Nelson Street, Dumfries. *Tel* (0387) 54429.

Dumfriesshire Ladies' County Golf Association

Hon Sec, Miss MJ Greig, Strathdon, 10 Nelson Street, Dumfries. *Tel* (0387) 54429.

Dunbartonshire and Argyll Ladies' County Association

Hon Sec, Mrs AG Pairman, 19 Hutchison Drive, Bearsden G61 2JT. *Tel* 041-942 0451.

East Lothian Ladies' County Association

Hon Sec, Mrs IG Campbell, Glenlair, Main Street, Gullane. *Tel* (0620) 842534.

Fife County Ladies' Golf Association

Hon Sec, Mrs CH Matheson, Greyfriars, Greyfriars Garden, St Andrews. *Tel* St Andrews (0334) 72639.

Galloway Ladies' County Golf Association

Hon Sec, Mrs W Lyon, Mossdene, Lewis Street, Stranraer.

Lanarkshire Ladies' County Golf Association

Hon Sec, Mrs GE Duncanson, 75 Kenmure Gardens, Bishopbriggs, Glasgow G64 2BZ.

Midlothian County Ladies' Golf Association

Hon Sec, Mrs EB Kemp, 84 Redford Loan, Edinburgh EH13 0AT. *Tel* 031-441 1800.

Northern Counties' Ladies Golf Association

Hon Sec, Mrs AF Blackwood, Airlie, 6 Deveron Terrace, Banff AB4 1BB. *Tel* 02612 2284.

Perth and Kinross Ladies' County Golf Association

Hon Sec, Mrs RG Morris, *Moorlands,* Burrelton, Blairgowrie PH13 9NY. *Tel* 082 87204.

Renfrewshire Ladies' County Golf Association

Hon Sec, Miss SC Goudie, 25 Florence Drive, Giffnock, Glasgow G46 6UN. *Tel* 041-638 4971.

Scottish and International Golf Greenkeepers' Association

Gen Sec, JD McKean, 82 Dumbreck Road, Glasgow G41 9DW. *Tel* 041-427 4242.

District Branches:

Ayrshire *Hon Sec,* J Paton, 1 North Road, West Kilbride, Ayrshire. *Tel* (0294) 823210.

East *Hon Sec,* W Blair, 13 Redhall Avenue, Edinburgh. *Tel* 031-443 3214.

West *Hon Sec,* A McDougall, 67 Hilton, Cowie, Stirlingshire.

North and Midland *Hon Sec,* I Hamilton, 58 Whitecraig Road, Newburgh, Fife. *Tel* Newburgh (0337) 40727.

Central *Hon Sec,* J Crawford, 1 Katrine Drive, Crossford, Dunfermline. *Tel* 0383-1737753.

Scottish Golf Union

Sec, JW Hume, The Cottage, 181a Whitehouse Road, Barnton, Edinburgh EH4 6BY. *Tel* 031-339 7546.

Area Associations:

Angus G Hardie, Conachan, 4 Cliffburn Road, Arbroath, Angus. *Tel* Arbroath (0241) 73018 (Home); 722861 (Bus).

Argyll and Bute J Forgreive, 9 Dalintart Drive, Oban. *Tel* (0631) 65298 (Home); 0631 63626 (Bus).

Ayrshire RL Crawford, 14 Maxwell Gardens, Hurlford, Kilmarnock, Ayrshire. *Tel* (0563) 31932 (Home); (0563) 21190 (Bus).

Borders NJ Scott, Brackendale, Craig Brown Avenue, Selkirk. *Tel* (0750) 21623 (Home); (0750) 20506 (Bus).

Clackmannanshire H Hunter, 27 Newton Crescent, Dunblane, Perthshire. *Tel* Dunblane (0786) 822805.

Dunbartonshire RW Jenkins, Dunedin, 14 Hawthorn Avenue, Lenzie G66 4RA. *Tel* 041-776 1148.

Fife BR Wright, 2 West Fergus Place, Kirkcaldy, Fife KY1 1WR. *Tel* (0592) 263304 (Home); (0592) 206605 (Bus).

Glasgow GO McInnes, 50 Hamilton Avenue, Glasgow. *Tel* 041-427 3156 (Home); 041-226 4471 (Bus).

Lanarkshire JT Durrant, 30 Woodlands Crescent, Bothwell, Glasgow. *Tel* Bothwell (0698) 852331.

Lothians IR Graham, 29 Morningside Grove, Edinburgh EH10 5PX. *Tel* 031-447 3281.

North JP Ford, Timbertop, Croy, Inverness IV1 2PH. *Tel* 06678-363.

North-East DJ Miller, 25 Albyn Place, Aberdeen AB1 1YL. *Tel* (0224) 589345 (Bus); 0224 732168 (Home).

Perth and Kinross JS Miller, 7 Moredun Terrace, Craigie, Perth. *Tel* (0738) 26204 (Home); (0738) 39911 (Bus).

Renfrewshire JI McCosh, Muirfield, 20 Williamson Place, Johnstone, Renfrewshire. *Tel* (0505) 27974 (Home).

South JM Dickie, *Cairnsmore*, 46 Barrashead, Lochmaben, Lockerbie, Dumfriesshire DG11 1RP. *Tel* Lochmaben (03013) 713 (Home); Lockerbie (05762) 2746 (Bus).

Stirlingshire RM McLaren, Yarrow, Touch Road, Cambusbarron, Stirling. *Tel* Stirling (0786) 72347 (Home); Stirling (0786) 73141 (Bus).

Scottish Golfers' Alliance

Sec/Treas, Mrs Margaret Caldwell, 5 Deveron Avenue, Giffnock, Glasgow G46 6NH.

Scottish Ladies' Golfing Association

Sec, Mrs Judy Cox, 5 Brownhills House, St Andrews, Fife KY16 8PL. *Tel* (0334) 76849.

Scottish Ladies' Golfing Association–County Golf

Hon Sec, Miss MJ Greig, Strathdon, Nelson Street, Dumfries. *Tel* (0387) 54429.

Scottish Schools' Golf Association

Hon Sec, JB MacLeod, Leith Academy, Duke Street, Edinburgh. *Tel* 031-554 0606.

Stirling and Clackmannan County Ladies' Golf Association

Hon Sec, Mrs HM Hudson, 14 Drummond Place, Stirling FK8 2JE. *Tel* Stirling 72033.

West of Scotland Girls' Golfing Association

Hon Sec, Mrs PI McKay, 7 Gardenside Avenue, Uddingston, Glasgow G71 7BU.

Wales

Anglesey Golf Union

Hon Sec, GP Jones, 20 Gwelfor Estate, Cemaes Bay, Anglesey. *Tel* Cemaes Bay 710755.

Caernarvonshire and Anglesey Ladies' County Golf Association

Hon Sec, Mrs BR Williams, Deunant, Llangefni LL7 7YP. *Tel* Llangefni (0248) 722338.

Caernarvonshire and District Golfing Union

Hon Sec, R Eric Jones, 23 Bryn Rhos, Rhosbodrual, Caernarfon, Gwynedd. *Tel* 3486.

Denbighshire Golfing Union

Hon Sec, J. Johnson, 15 Ffordd Elfed, Wrexham, Clwyd.

Denbighshire Ladies' County Golf Association

Hon Sec, Mrs GM Scott, Bellendean, Llanbedr. DC, Ruthin, Clwyd. *Tel* Ruthin 2989.

Dyfed Golfing Union

Hon Sec, J Gottwaltz, Diamond Villa, Cosheston, Pembroke Dock.

Flintshire Golfing Union
Hon Sec, H Griffith, Cornist Lodge, Cornist Park, Flint, Clwyd. ***Tel*** Flint (03526) 2186.

Flintshire Ladies' Golf Association
Hon Sec, Mrs CM Scott, *Newlyn,* 46 Park Avenue, Hawarden, Deeside, Clwyd CH5 3HZ. ***Tel*** Hawarden 534397.

Glamorgan County Golf Union
Hon Sec, John Banfill, 332 North Road, Cardiff. ***Tel*** Cardiff 628493.

Glamorgan Ladies' County Golf Association
Mrs S Williams, 19 Trem-y-Don, Barry, South Glamorgan. ***Tel*** Barry 734865.

Gwent Golf Union
Sec, J Huckin, 33 South Avenue, Griffthstown, Pontypool, Gwent. ***Tel*** 55802.

Monmouthshire Ladies' County Golf Association
Hon Sec, Mrs M Menzies, 35 Park View Gardens, Bassales, Gwent NP1 GJ2. ***Tel*** Newport (0633) 891843.

North Wales Counties Golf Association
Hon Sec, GP Jones, 20 Gwelfor Estate, Cemaes Bay, Anglesey LL67 0NL. ***Tel*** Cemaes Bay 710755.

North Wales Golfing Union
Hon Sec, RD Rogers, 52 Blackbrook Avenue, Upperdale, Hawarden, near Chester.

North Wales Junior Golf Association
Hon Sec, T Evans, 35 Parc Sychnant, Conwy, Gwynedd. ***Tel*** Conwy 6270.

North Wales Professional Golfers' Alliance
Hon Sec, P Lees, Conway GC, Conway, Gwynedd. ***Tel*** 049263-3225.

South Wales Professional Golfers' Association
Hon Sec, A Palmer, Aberdare GC, Aberdare, Mid-Glam. ***Tel*** Aberdare (0685) 878735.

Welsh Golfing Union
Sec, JW Treharne, 2 Isfryn, Burry Port, Dyfed. ***Tel*** (05546) 2595.

Welsh Ladies' Golf Union
Hon Sec, Miss P Roberts, Ysgoldy Gynt, Llanhennock, Newport, Gwent NP6 1LT. ***Tel*** 0633-420642.

Overseas

America: USA & Canada

American Ladies' Professional Golf Association
Commissioner, John D Laupheimer, 1250 Shoreline Drive, Suite 200, Sugarland, Texas, 77478, USA. ***Tel*** 713 980 5742.

American Professional Golfers' Association
Executive Director, Mark H Cox, Box 12458, 100 Avenue of the Champions, Palm Beach Gardens, Florida 33410.

Canadian Ladies' Golf Association
Executive Director, Les Whamond, 333 River Road, Ottawa, Ontario, K1L 8H9, Canada. ***Tel*** (613) 746 5564.

Canadian Professional Golfers' Association
General Manager, Robert H Noble, 59 Berkeley Street, Toronto M5A 2W5, Canada. ***Tel*** (4216) 368-6104.

Canadian (Royal) Golf Association
Golf House, RR no 2, Oakville, Ontario L6J 4Z3, Canada.

Provincial Golf Associations
British Columbia *Sec/Treas,* RE Maze, Room 322, 1675 West 8th Ave, Vancouver, BC V6J 1V2.

Alberta *Manager,* ER Wood, 200-H Haddon Road, Calgary, Alberta T2V 2Y6.

Saskatchewan *Ex Director,* WF Macrae, 2205 Victoria Avenue, Regina, Saskatchewan S4P 0S4.

Manitoba *Ex Director,* DI Macdonald, 1700 Ellice Ave, Winnipeg, Manitoba R3H 0B1.

Ontario *Exec/Dir,* WJ Williams, 400 Esna Park Drive, Unit 11, Markham, Ontario L3R 1H5.

Quebec *Ex Director,* CH Gribbin, 3300 Cavendish Blvd, Suite 250, Montreal, Quebec H4B 2M8.

New Brunswick *Sec/Treas,* EA Trites, 3 Sunset Lane, St John, New Brunswick E2H 1C8.

Nova Scotia *Sec/Treas,* W MacDonald, 14 Limardo Drive, Dartmouth, Nova Scotia B3A 3X4.

Newfoundland–Labrador *Sec,* CR Cook, PO Box 5361, St Johns, Newfoundland.

Prince Edward Island *Sec/Treas,* David Kassner, PO Box 51, Charlottetown, PEI C1A 7K2.

Golf Course Association
111 East Wacker Drive, Chicago, Illinois 60601, USA. *Tel* (312) 644-6610.

International Golf Association
Room 746, Lincoln Building, 60 E 42nd Street, New York 10165.

TPA Tour
(USA), ***Commissioner,*** Deane R Beman, Sawgrass, Ponte Verde Beach, Florida 32082; USA.

United States Golf Association
Senior Executive Director, Frank Hannigan, USGA Golf House, Liberty Corner Road, Far Hills, New Jersey 07931. *Tel* 201-234-2300.

United States Seniors' Golf Association
Suite, 1306, 60 E 42nd Street, New York 10017.

Central America

Bahamas Golf Federation
Sec, Calvin Cooper, PO Box F.3774, Free Port, Grand Bahama, Bahamas.

Barbados Golf Association
Sec, TM Hanton, c/o Sandy Lane GC, St James, Barbados.

Bermuda Golf Association
Sec-Treas, Mrs Eric N Parker, PO Box 433, Hamilton 5, Bermuda. *Tel* 809 298 1367.

Jamaica Golf Association
Constant Spring Golf Club, Constant Spring, Kingston 8, Jamaica.

Mexican Golf Association
Cincinnati, No. 40-104, Mexico 18, DF.

Trinidad and Tobago Golf Association
Texaco Trinidad Inc, Point-a-Pierre, Trinidad, West Indies.

South America

Asociacion Argentina de Golf
Gen Manager, JT Salorio; ***Hon Sec,*** Ignacio JR Soba Rojo, Corrientes 538, Piso 11, 1043 Buenos Aires.

Argentine Professional Golfers' Association
Calle Libertad No. 956 (Local No. 22), Buenos Aires.

Asuncion Golf Union
Casilla de Correo 302, Asuncion, Paraguay.

Bolivian Golf Federation (Federación Boliviana de Golf)
Sec, Raul Zabalaga, Casilia de Correo 6130, La Paz, Bolivia.

Brazilian Golf Confederation
(Confederacão Brasileira de Golf), ***Administrative Director,*** SS Marvin, Rua 7 de Abril, 282-S/84-01044, São Paulo, Brazil

Chilean Golf Federation
Casilla 13307, Correo 21, Santiago, Chile.

Colombian Golf Union (Federación Colombiana de Golf)
Sec, Louis Restrepo, Carrer 7A, 72-64 of Int 26 Apartado 90985, Bogota, Colombia.

Ecuador Golf Federation (Asociación Equatoriana de Golf)
Casilia 521, Guayaquil, Ecuador.

Guyana Golf Union
c/o Demerara Bauxite Co, Limited, Mackenzie, Guyana.

Paraguay Golf Association
Asuncion GC, Casilla de Correo 302, Asuncion, Paraguay.

Peru Golf Federation (Federación Peruana de Golf)
Sec, HB Sanchez, Casilla 5637, Lima, Peru.

South American Golf Federation
Hon Sec, E Anchordoqui, Guipuzcoa 486-P7, Montevideo, Uruguay.

Uruguay Golf Association (Asociación Uruguaya de Golf)
Sec, Jorge Brignoni, Casilia de Correo 1484, Montevideo.

Venezuela Golf Federation
Unidad Comercial, *La Florida,* Local 5, Avenida Avila, La Florida, Caracas 1050, Venezuela.

Asia and Far East

Asia-Pacific Golf Confederation
Sec Gen, EJH Yong, c/o The Royal Selangor Golf Club, PO Box 1051, Kuala Lumpur.

Asia Professional Golf Circuit
Tournament Co-ordinator, Mrs LE Kim Hall, 1710 Star House, 3 Salisbury Road, Kowloon, Hong Kong. *Tel* 3-679927. *Telex* 75561 M1K HX.

Ceylon Golf Union
2 Gower Street, Colombo 5, Sri Lanka.

China (Republic of) Golf Association
Charles C Chang, ***Sec Gen,*** 71, Lane 369, Tanhua S Road, Taipei, Taiwan (106), Rep of China. *Tel* 711 3046, 711 7482.

Hong Kong Golf Association
President, Michael J Steele, ***Hon Sec,*** PO Box 98677, Tsim Sha Tsui, Kowloon, Hong Kong.

Hong Kong Professional Golfers' Association
Hon Sec, AR Hamilton, PO Box 690, Hong Kong. *Telex* HX73751; *Tel* 5-222111.

Indian Golf Union
Hon Sec, Raj Bir Singh, Tata Centre (3rd Floor), 43 Chowringhee Road, Calcutta 700071.

Indonesian Golf Association
Soebroto Koesmardjo,c/o Bank Bumi Daya, Jln Imam Bonjol 61-PO Box 106, Jakarta Pusat.

Japan Golf Association
Exec Dir, Toshizo Takeuchi, 606-6th Floor, Palace Building, Marunouchi, Chiyoda-ku, Tokyo, Japan. ***Tel*** (03) 215 0003.

Japan Ladies' Professional Golfers' Association
Kuranae Kogyo Kaikan 7F, Shinbasi 2-19-10, Minato-ku, Tokyo. ***Tel*** 03-571-0928.

Japan Professional Golf Association
Shineido Building 5F, 1-5-14 Shinbashi, Minato-ku, Tokyo. ***Tel*** 03-504-3300.

Korean Golf Association
Sec General, Room 1B, 13th Floor, Manhattan Bldg, 36-2, Yeo-Eui-Do-Dowg, Yeong Deung Po-Ku, Seoul, Korea. ***Tel*** 783-4748/783-4749.

Malaysian Golf Association
Hon Sec, TK Kee, 12A Persiaran Ampang, 55000 Kuala Lumpur, Malaysia.

New Guinea Papua Territory Amateur Golf Association
Sec, Jack Page, PO Box 382, Lae, TPNG.

Pakistan Golf Federation
Hon Sec, Hashim Khan, PO Box 845, Rawalpindi, Pakistan.

Papua New Guinea Ladies' Golf Association
Mrs Mavis Harvey, PO Box 1256, Port Moresby. ***Tel*** 214745.

Republic of the Philippines Golf Association
209 Administration Building, Rizal Memorial Sports Complex, Vito Cruz, Manila, Philippines.

Singapore Golf Association
Hon Sec, Gerald Loong, Singapore Golf Association, 4 Battery Rd, #12-00 Bank of China Building, Singapore 0104.

Sri Lanka Ladies' Golf Union
c/o Royal Colombo Golf Club, PO Box 309, Colombo, Sri Lanka.

Sri Lanka Golf Union
2 Gower Street, Colombo 5, Sri Lanka.

Thailand Golf Association
Hon. Sec, T Ansusinha, c/o Dusit Golf Club, Bangkok, Thailand.

Australasia

Australian Golf Union
Sec, CA Phillips, 3 Bowen Crescent, 9th Floor, Melbourne 3004, Victoria. ***Telex*** AA 38149.

Members of the Union:

Victoria *Sec,* TS Duguid, Victorian Golf Association, PO Box 187, Elsternwick, Victoria 3185.

New South Wales *Sec,* B Scott, New South Wales Golf Association, 17-19 Brisbane Street, Darlinghurst, NSW 2010.

Tasmanian Golf Council, *Sec,* A Rollins, GPO Box 940K, Hobart 7001. ***Tel*** (002) 348315.

Queensland *Sec,* W Kennedy, Queensland Golf Union, PO Box 260, Mt Gravatt, Queensland 4122, Australia.

Western Australia *Sec,* G Fitzhardinge, Western Australian Golf Association Inc, 57 Labouchere Road, South Perth 6151, WA.

South Australia *Sec,* MH Hall, South Australia Golf Association, 249 Henley Beach Road, Torvensville, South Australia 5031.

Australian Ladies' Golf Union
Executive Director, Mrs KD Brown, 22 McKay Road, Rowville 3178, Victoria, Australia. ***Tel*** (03) 763 6919.

Members of the Union:

Victoria *Sec,* Miss K Mahlook, 589 Malvern Road, Toorak, 3142, Victoria.

New South Wales *Sec,* Miss Wendy V Weil, 17 Brisbane Street, Darlinghurst, NSW 2010. ***Tel*** 264 7327.

Queensland *Sec,* Mrs M Barnett, PO Box 83, Chermside, 4032, Queensland. ***Tel*** 221 6677.

Western Australia *Sec,* Mrs M Cutter, Suite 1-4, Stratham House, 49 Melville Parade, South Perth. ***Tel*** 368 2618.

South Australia *Sec,* Mrs GA Small, 13 Pitcairn Ave, Urrbrae, 5064. ***Tel*** 79 3200.

Tasmania *Sec,* Mrs IP Allen, 45 Balmoral Road, Kingston Beach, 7151. ***Tel*** 29 5120.

Australian Professional Golfers' Association
Sec, DN Johnson, 113 Queen Street, North Strathfield, New South Wales, 2137.

New Zealand Golf Association (Inc)
Dominion Sports House, Mercer Street, Wellington, PO Box11842. ***Tel*** 845-408. ***Telegrams*** *Enzedgolf.*

New Zealand Professional Golfers' Association
Sec, Sqn Ldr AR Bleakley, PO Box 21-482, Auckland 8. *Tel* Auckland 836 4703.

New Zealand Ladies' Golf Union
Mrs A Rogers, PO Box 446, Waipukurau, Hawkes Bay, New Zealand.

Africa (south of Sahara)

Botswana Golf Union
Hon Sec, Robert Stewart, PO Box 1033, Gaborone, Botswana. *Tel* 53989 (Home).

Ghana Golf Association
Sec, Kwasi E Chinbush, PO Box 888, Tema.

Kenya Golf Union
PO Box 49609, Nairobi. *Tel* Nairobi 720074.

Kenya Ladies' Golf Union
PO Box 45615, Nairobi, Kenya.

Malawi Golf Union
PO Box 1198, Blantyre, Malawi.

Malawi Ladies' Golf Union
PO Box 5319, Limbe, Malawi.

Nigerian Golf Union
PO Box 423, Lagos, Nigeria.

Sierra Leone Golf Federation
Pres, JS Baird, PO Box 575, Freetown, Sierra Leone.

South African Golf Union
Sec, JM Kellie, PO Box 1537, Cape Town 8000. *Cablegram address: Sagolfunion, Cape Town. Tel* 467585 (Bus.) 653617 (Home).

Provincial Unions:
Border Golf Union *Hon Sec,* Mrs S Boniface, Box 1773, East London 5200, CP.

Eastern Province Golf Union *Hon Sec,* CAL Fowles, PO Box 146, Port Elizabeth 6000, CP.

Karoo Golf Association *Hon Sec,* Mrs CL Hobson, PO Box 71, Middleburg 5900, CP.

OFS & Northern Cape Golf Union *Hon Sec,* S Daly, PO Box 799, Welkom 9460, OFS.

Natal Golf Union *Sec,* RT Runge, PO Box 1939, Durban 4000, Natal.

South-West Africa Golf Union *Hon. Sec,* E Barbour, PO Box 2989, Windhoek 9000.

Transvaal Golf Union *Sec,* RC Witte, PO Box 391661, Bramley 2018, Transvaal.

Western Province Golf Union *Sec* BW Myles, Box 153, Howard Place, 7450, CP.

South African Ladies' Golf Union
Sec, Mrs E Cutler, PO Box 135, Vereeniging, Transvaal, South Africa.

South African Professional Golfers' Association
c/o Wanderers Golf Club, PO Box 55253, Northlands, Johannesburg 2116.

Swaziland Golf Union
A Rutt, PO Box 1739, Mbabane, Swaziland.

Tanzania Golf Union
Hon Sec, R Virjee, Tanzania Golf Union, c/o Dar es Salaam Gymkhana Club, PO Box 286, Dar es Salaam, Tanzania.

Uganda Golf Union
Sec, PO Box 2574, Kampala, Uganda. Kampala, Uganda.

Zaire Golf Federation
Pres, Tshilombo Mwin Tshitol, BP 1648, Lubumbashi, Zaire. *Tel* 2269.

Zambian Golf Union
Hon Sec/Treas, OT Phillips, PO Box 1986, Lusaka, Zambia.

Zambia Ladies' Golf Union
Sec, Mrs C Howell, PO Box 32150, Lusaka, Zambia. *Tel* Lusaka 251668.

Zimbabwe Golf Association
Sec, B de Kock, PO Box 3327, Harare, Zimbabwe.

Zimbabwe Ladies' Golf Union
PO Box 3814, Harare, Zimbabwe.

Europe

Austrian Golf Federation
Sec, G Jungk, (Osterreichischer Golf-Verband), Haus des Sports, Prinz Eugen-Strasse 12, A-1040 Wien, Austria. *Tel* 010 43 222 653245; *Telex* 133132.

Belgian Royal Federation of Golf
Sec, Roger Duys, Route de la Marche 19, B-1328-Ohain. *Tel* 010 32(2) 633 2496.

Czechoslovak Golf Federation
Sec, H Goldscheider, Na Porici, 12, 11530 Praha 1. *Tel* 010 42 (2)249451; *Telex* 122650.

Danish Golf Union (Dansk Golf Union)
Sec, Jens Thomasen, Bredgade 56, DK-1260 Copenhagen, Denmark. *Tel* 010 45 (1)131221.

European Golf Association
Hon Sec, Neil S Hotchkin, 69 Avenue Victor Hugo, 75783 Paris. *Tel* (33) 1500 8261. *Telex* 614 406 FF Golf

Amateur Technical Committee: ***Hon Sec,*** JL Dupont, 51 Av Victor Hugo, 93300 Aubervilliers. ***Tel*** (33) 1 833 49 49.

Finnish Golf Union (Finlands Golfforbund)
Hon Sec, J Huhtanen, Topeliuksenkatu 41a, 00250 Helsinki 25. ***Tel*** 010 358 (90) 47 371; ***Telex*** 121797.

French Golf Federation (Federation Française de Golf)
Hon Sec, J Labatut, 69 Avenue Victor Hugo, 75116 Paris, Cedex 16. ***Tel*** 010 33 (1)450062 20; ***Telex*** 614 406 FF Golf.

French Professional Golfers' Association
69 Avenue Victor Hugo, 75116 Paris 16, France. ***Tel*** 500-43-72.

German Golf Association (Deutscher Golf Verband)
Hon Sec, H Bremer, Dr F Billion, 6200 Wiesbaden, Rheinblickstrasse 24, Germany. ***Tel*** 010 49 (6121) 8208091; ***Telex*** 4186459.

German PGA (Deutscher Golflehrer Verband)
Albert Schweitzer Str. 13, 7290, Freudenstadt, W Germany. ***Tel*** 07441 81144.

Hellenic Golf Federation
Hon Sec, P Karamitsos, PO Box 70003, GR 16610, Glyfada, Athens, Greece. ***Tel*** 010 30 (1)894 6820 or 010 30 (1)360 2014; ***Telex*** 216586 222356 GR.

Iceland Golf Union (Golfsanband Islands)
Hon Sec, KR Bjarnason, Reykjavik 101, PO Box 1076, Iceland. ***Tel*** 010 354 (91)686686.

International Greenkeepers' Assoc
Hon Sec, Mrs B Harradine, Via Golf, CH6987, Caslano, Switzerland.

Italian Golf Federation (Federazione Italiana Golf)
Sec, Luigi Orlandini, 388 Via Flaminia 338-00196 Roma. ***Tel*** 101039 6394 641. ***Telex*** 613192 Golfed I.

Luxembourg Golf Club Grand Ducal
Sec, Miss J Schwartz, 1 Route de Treve 2633, Senningerberg, Luxembourg.

Netherlands Golf Federation
Gen Sec, JA van der Schraaf, Soestdijkerstraatweg 172, 1213XJ, Hilversum, Holland. ***Tel*** 010 3135-830565.

Netherlands Professional Golfers' Assoc
Sec, A Wessels, Karel De Grotelaan 190, Deventer.

Norwegian Golf Union (Norges Golfforbund)
Gen Sec, Anna Donnestrad, Hauger Skolevei 1, 1351 Rud, Norway. ***Tel*** 010 47 (02)13 42 90; ***Telex*** 18586 NIFN.

Portuguese Golf Federation (Federación Portuguesa de Golfe)
Sec, E Vieira, Rua Almeida Brandao 39, 1200 Lisbon, Portugal. ***Tel*** 010 351 (19)734 736.

Spanish Golf Association (Real Federación Espanola de Golf)
Capitan Haya, 9-5 Dcha, Madrid 28020, Spain. ***Tel*** 010 34 455 26 82/455 27 57.

Swedish Golf Federation (Svenska Golf Forbundet)
Sec Gen, Lars Granberg, PO Box 84, S-182 11 Danderyd, Sweden. ***Tel*** 010 46 08/753 02 65; ***Telex*** 16608.

Swedish PGA
Executive Director, Christer Lindberg, ***Chairman,*** John Cockin. PO Box 35, S-181 21 Lidingo, Sweden. ***Tel*** 08-767 83 23.

Swiss Golf Association (Association Suisse de Golf)
Sec, JC Storjohann, En Ballègue, Case Postale CH-1066, Epalinges-Lausanne. ***Tel*** 010 41 021 32 7701. ***Telex*** 24580.

Swiss Professional Golfers' Association
Hon Sec, Jakob Kressig, Perrelet 9, 2074 Marin, Switzerland. ***Tel*** (038) 33 23 79.

Yugoslavia Golf Federation
Vice president, Rudolf Leban, Autotehna, 6100 Ljubljana, Titova 36, Yugoslavia. ***Tel*** 061-319 877. ***Telex*** 31223 Yu Autena.

Middle East

Egyptian Golf Federation
c/o Gezira Sporting Club, Gezira, Cairo, Egypt. ***Tel*** 80 6000.

Israel Golf Union
Sec, Alon Ben-David, PO Box 1010, Caesarea 30660, Israel.

Libyan Golf Union
PO Box 879, Tripoli, Libya.

United Arab Emirates Golf Union
c/o Gazira Sporting Club, Gazira, Cairo. ***Tel*** 80 6000.

ENGLISH GOLF UNION

The English Golf Union was formed in February 1924, and is in fact the youngest Union of the Home Counties.

Originally 15 County Unions combined to form the Union, with a then membership of 459 affiliated clubs.

Today there are 34 County Unions with over 1300 affiliated clubs, which numerically exceeds the number of Clubs in Scotland, Ireland, Wales and the Continent of Europe added together. Overall these English Clubs have a male membership of approximately one and a half million golfers.

The objects of the Union have altered little since its inception. These are:

★ TO FURTHER THE INTERESTS OF AMATEUR GOLF IN ENGLAND.

★ TO ASSIST IN MAINTAINING A UNIFORM SYSTEM OF HANDICAPPING.

★ TO ARRANGE AN ENGLISH CHAMPIONSHIP; AN ENGLISH STROKE PLAY CHAMPIONSHIP; AN ENGLISH COUNTY CHAMPIONSHIP; INTERNATIONAL AND OTHER MATCHES AND COMPETITIONS.

★ TO CO-OPERATE WITH THE ROYAL AND ANCIENT GOLF CLUB OF ST. ANDREWS AND THE COUNCIL OF NATIONAL GOLF UNIONS.

★ TO CO-OPERATE WITH OTHER NATIONAL GOLF UNIONS AND ASSOCIATIONS IN SUCH MANNER AS MAY BE DECIDED.

The Union maintains continuous contact with the County Unions by means of the circulation of Committee Minutes and English Amateur Golf, the official journal of the Union which is published nine times a year. This magazine is sent free of charge to every affiliated golf club, and many more besides, and has an overall circulation exceeding 6000 copies.

Annually 'The Golfing Year' book is published by the E.G.U., which is primarily a record of all the E.G.U. golfing events, National and International Championships in which England teams have competed. The Committee structure of the E.G.U. is listed and each County Unions officials and affiliated clubs tabulated.

English Golf Union, 1-3 Upper King Street, Leicester LE1 6XF. Telephone: (0533) 553042.

Part IV
Courses and Clubs in the UK and Europe

Golf Clubs and Courses in Great Britain and Ireland

1. Geographical divisions

Golf Clubs are alphabetically listed in countries, sub-divided into areas, provinces and districts depending on the particular organization arrangements of the English, Irish, Scottish and Welsh Golf Unions. All clubs and courses are listed in the index at the back of the book.

Some clubs, usually on the border of two counties, are affiliated to a different county to that in which they are geographically situated. In most cases details of such clubs are listed in their affiliated county with mention of this in the geographical district.

In Scotland a distinction sometimes has to be made between a club and a course. In the main centres Edinburgh, Glasgow, Aberdeen, St Andrews, and those in Tayside, the courses, mainly municipal, and the clubs which play on them are listed separately.

Each club/course entry has a map reference given together with its course number to help in finding its location on the maps on pages 300-319.

2. Explanation of details given

a After the name of the club is the date when founded (where available) and a note saying whether the ***course*** on which the club plays is publicly or privately owned.

b The address is the postal address of each club or course. If the postal county is different from the one under which the club or course is listed, it will be shown in the address.

c The membership figure denotes the total number of members. The number of lady members (**L**), the number of juniors (**J**) and of five-day members (**5**) are sometimes shown separately.

d The general term of ***sec*** is used to cover secretary, honorary secretary, manager, general manager, administrator or proprietor. What it denotes is the name of the person to whom any queries on the club should be directed. If a club has no mail delivery point the secretary's home address is given.

e Telephone numbers for secretaries and professionals are shown if different from the club telephone number.

f V'trs: this shows what restrictions (if any) are in force for visitors:

(i) **WD**–Weekdays; **W/E**–Weekends; **BH**–Bank Holidays.
If no days stated, the particular restrictions apply at all times.

(ii) **U**–Unrestricted, ie casual visitors may play on the days stated unrestricted.
M–With a Member, ie casual visitors are not allowed. Only visitors playing with a Member are permitted on the days stated.
H–Handicap certificate required.
I–Introduction, ie visitors are permitted on the days stated if they have a letter of introduction from their own club, their own club's membership card, or a handicap certificate.
XL–No ladies allowed on the days stated.
NA–No visitors allowed.
SOC–Recognised Golfing Societies welcome if previous arrangements made with secretary.

g Fees: green fees are only quoted for visitors if they are permitted to play unaccompanied by a Member. The basic cost per round is shown first, then, in brackets, the cost of a weekend and/or Bank Holiday round where this is available to unaccompanied visitors. Green fees for visitors playing with a Member are not given. Weekly (W) monthly (M) and fortnightly (F) terms are shown where available.

Index of Counties

England: South-East (East)

Essex

1 Abridge
2 Basildon
3 Belfairs Park
4 Belhus Park Municipal
5 Bentley G & CC
6 Birch Grove
7 Boyce Hill
8 Braintree
9 Hartswood
10 Bunsay Downs
11 Burnham-on-Crouch
12 Canons Brook
13 Channels
14 Chelmsford
15 Chigwell
16 Chingford
17 Clacton
18 Colchester
19 Frinton
20 Hainault Forest
21 Harwich and Dovercourt
22 Havering
23 Ilford
24 Maldon
25 Manifold
26 Maylands
27 Orsett
28 Pipps Hill
29 Rochford Hundred
30 Romford
31 Royal Epping Forest
32 Skips
33 Theydon Bois
34 Thorndon Park
35 Thorpe Hall
36 Upminster
37 Wanstead
38 Warley Park
39 Warren
40 Three Rivers
41 West Essex
42 Woodford
43 Ballards Gore
44 Forrester Park
New entries 1987
45 Towerlands

Hertfordshire

1 Aldenham
2 Arkley
3 Ashridge
4 Batchwood Hall
5 Berkhamsted
6 Bishop's Stortford
7 Boxmoor
8 Brickendon Grange
9 Brookman's Park
10 Bushey
11 Bushey Hall
12 Chadwell Springs
13 Cheshunt Park
14 Chorleywood
15 Dyrham Park Country Club
16 East Herts
17 Hadley Wood
18 Harpenden
19 Harpenden Common
20 Hartsbourne Country Club
21 Knebworth
22 Letchworth
23 Little Hay
24 Mid Herts
25 Moor Park
26 Old Fold Manor
27 Panshanger
28 Hatfield London
29 Porters Park
30 Potters Bar
31 Redbourn
32 Rickmansworth
33 Sandy Lodge
34 South Herts
35 Stevenage
36 Verulam
37 Welwyn Garden City
38 West Herts
39 Whipsnade Park
40 Elstree

Kent

1 Aquarius
2 Ashford
3 Barnehurst
4 Bearsted
5 Beckenham Place Park
6 Bexley Heath
7 Broome Park
8 Canterbury
9 Cherry Lodge
10 Chestfield (Whitstable)
11 Chislehurst
12 Cray Valley
13 Cranbrook
14 Dartford
15 Deangate Ridge
16 Edenbridge
17 Eltham Warren
18 Faversham
19 Gillingham
20 Hawkhurst Golf
21 Herne Bay
22 High Elms
23 Hythe Imperial
24 Knole Park
25 Lamberhurst
26 Langley Park
27 Leeds Castle
28 Littlestone
29 Lullingstone Park
30 Magpie Hall Lane
31 Mid Kent
32 North Foreland
33 Poult Wood
34 Prince's
35 Rochester and Cobham Park
36 Royal Blackheath
37 Royal Cinque Ports
38 Royal St George's
39 Ruxley
40 St Augustines
41 Sene Valley Folkestone and Hythe
42 Sheerness
43 Shooter's Hill
44 Shortlands
45 Shoreham
46 Sidcup
47 Sittingbourne and Milton Regis
48 Sundridge Park
49 Tenterden
50 Tunbridge Wells
51 Walmer and Kingsdown
52 Westgate and Birchington
53 West Kent
54 West Malling
55 Whitstable and Seasalter
56 Wildernesse
57 Woodlands Manor
58 Wrotham Heath
59 Cobtree Manor Park

Middlesex

1 Ashford Manor
2 Brent Valley
3 Bush Hill Park
4 Crews Hill
5 Ealing
6 Enfield
7 Finchley
8 Fulwell
10 Grim's Dyke
11 Hampstead
12 Harefield Place
13 Harrow School
14 Haste Hill
15 Hendon
16 Highgate
17 Hillingdon
18 Holiday GC
19 Horsenden Hill
20 Hounslow Heath
21 Leaside
22 Mill Hill
23 Muswell Hill
24 North Middlesex
25 Northwood
26 Perivale Park
27 Picketts Lock
28 Pinner Hill
29 Ruislip
30 Stanmore
31 Strawberry Hill
32 Sudbury
33 Trent Park
34 Twickenham
35 West Middlesex
36 White Webbs
37 Wyke Green
New entries 1987
38 Airlinks
39 Lime Trees Park

Norfolk

1 Barnham Broom Hotel
2 Dereham
3 Eaton
4 Fakenham
5 Great Yarmouth and Caister
6 Hunstanton
7 King's Lynn
8 Links Country Park Hotel and Golf Club
9 Mundesley
10 Bawburgh
11 Royal Cromer
12 Royal Norwich
13 Royal West Norfolk
14 Ryston Park
15 Sheringham
16 Swaffham
17 Thetford
18 Feltwell
19 Sprowston Park
New entries 1987
20 Costessey Park
21 RAF Marham

Suffolk

1 Aldeburgh
2 Beccles
3 Bungay and Waveney Valley
4 Bury St Edmunds
5 Diss
6 Felixstowe Ferry
7 Flempton
8 Gorleston
9 Haverhill
10 Ipswich (Purdis Heath)
11 Fornham Park G & CC
12 Newton Green
13 Rookery Park
14 Royal Worlington and Newmarket
15 Rushmere
16 Southwold
17 Stoke by Nayland
18 Stowmarket
19 Thorpeness
20 Woodbridge
New entries 1987
21 Heath Farm

Public courses are set in italics.

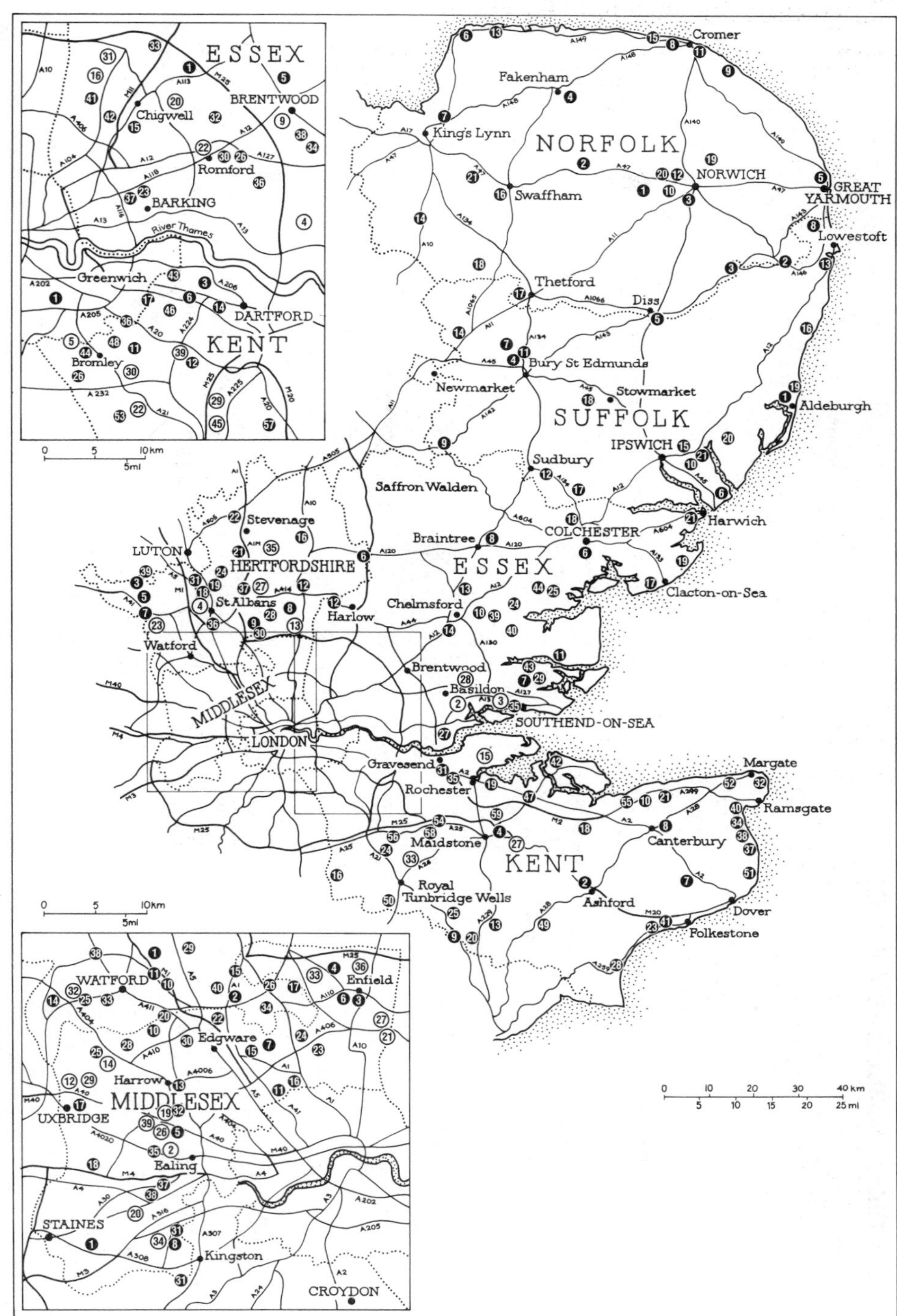
NORFOLK
SUFFOLK
ESSEX
HERTFORDSHIRE
MIDDLESEX
KENT
LONDON
Cromer
Fakenham
King's Lynn
NORWICH
GREAT YARMOUTH
Swaffham
Lowestoft
Thetford
Diss
Bury St Edmunds
Newmarket
Stowmarket
Aldeburgh
IPSWICH
Sudbury
Saffron Walden
Harwich
Stevenage
Braintree
COLCHESTER
LUTON
Clacton-on-Sea
St Albans
Harlow
Chelmsford
Watford
Brentwood
Basildon
SOUTHEND-ON-SEA
Gravesend
Rochester
Margate
Ramsgate
Maidstone
Canterbury
Royal Tunbridge Wells
Ashford
Dover
Folkestone
Chigwell
BRENTWOOD
Romford
BARKING
River Thames
Greenwich
DARTFORD
Bromley
WATFORD
Enfield
Edgware
Harrow
UXBRIDGE
Ealing
STAINES
Kingston
CROYDON
0 5 10km
5ml
0 10 20 30 40 km
5 10 15 20 25 ml

England: South-East (West)

Bedfordshire

1 Aspley Guise and Woburn Sands
2 Bedford and County
3 Bedfordshire
4 Cainhoe Wood G & CC
5 Dunstable Downs
6 John O'Gaunt
7 Leighton Buzzard
8 Mill Brook
9 Mowsbury
10 South Beds
11 Stockwood Park
12 Tilsworth
13 Wyboston Lakes
New entries 1987
14 Colworth

Bucks, Berks & Oxon

1 Abbey Hill
2 Badgemore Park
3 Beaconsfield
4 Bearwood
5 Berkshire
6 Bremhill Park
7 Buckingham
8 Burnham Beeches
9 Burford
10 Calcot Park
12 Chesham and Ley Hill
13 Chesterton
14 Chiltern Forest Golf Club
15 Chipping Norton
16 Datchet
17 Denham
18 Downshire
19 East Berkshire
20 Easthampstead
21 Ellesborough
22 Eton College
23 Farnham Park
24 Flackwell Heath
25 Frilford Heath
26 Gerrards Cross
27 Goring and Streatley
28 Harewood Downs
29 Henley
30 Huntercombe
31 Hurst
32 Ivinghoe
33 Lavender Park Golf Centre
34 Little Chalfont
35 Maidenhead
36 Newbury and Crookham
37 North Oxford
38 Reading
39 Royal Ascot
40 Sonning
41 Southfield
42 Stoke Poges
43 Swinley Forest
44 Tadmarton Heath
45 Temple
46 West Berkshire
47 Weston Turville
48 Wexham Park
49 Whiteleaf
50 Windmill Hill Golf Course
51 Winter Hill
52 Woburn
53 Iver
54 The Royal Household GC
55 RAF Benson
New entries 1987
56 Hazelmere
57 Stowe
58 Hawthorn Hill

Hampshire

1 Alresford
2 Alton
3 Ampfield Par Three
4 Andover
5 Army Golf Club
6 Barton-on-Sea
7 Basingstoke
8 Bishopswood
9 Blackmoor
10 Bramshaw
11 Bramshott Hill
12 Brokenhurst Manor
13 Burley
14 Corhampton
15 Dunwood Manor
16 Fleming Park
17 Gosport and Stokes Bay
18 Great Salterns
19 Hartley Wintney
20 Hayling
21 Hockley
22 Leckford and Longstock
23 Lee-on-the-Solent
24 Liphook
25 Old Thorns Golf Course and Hotel
26 Meon Valley
27 New Forest
28 North Hants
29 Petersfield
30 Portsmouth
31 Portsmouth
32 Queen's Park
33 Romsey
34 Rowlands Castle
35 Royal Winchester
36 Southampton
37 Southwick Park
38 Southwood
39 Stoneham
40 Tylney Park
41 Waterlooville
42 Basingstoke Hospitals

Isle of Wight

1 Cowes
2 Freshwater Bay
3 Newport IW
4 Osborne
5 Ryde
6 Shanklin and Sandown
7 Ventnor

Surrey

1 The Addington
2 Addington Court
3 Addington Palace
4 Banstead Downs
5 Barrow Hills
6 Betchworth Park
7 Bramley
8 Burhill
9 Camberley Heath
10 Chessington Golf Centre
11 Chipstead
12 Coombe Hill
13 Coombe Wood
14 Coulsdon Court
15 Croham Hurst
16 Cuddington
17 Dorking
18 Drift
19 Dulwich and Sydenham Hill
20 Effingham
21 Epsom
22 Farnham
23 Farnham Park
24 Foxhills
25 Gatton Manor Hotel and Golf Club
26 Goal Farm
27 Guildford
28 Hankley Common
29 Hindhead
30 Hoebridge Golf Centre
31 Home Park
32 Kingswood
33 Laleham
34 Leatherhead
35 Limpsfield Chart
36 Malden
37 Mitcham
38 Moore Place
39 New Zealand
40 North Downs
41 Oaks Sports Centre
42 Purley Downs
43 Puttenham
44 RAC Country Club
45 Redhill and Reigate
46 Reigate Heath
47 Richmond
48 Richmond Park
49 Roehampton
50 Royal Mid-Surrey
51 Royal Wimbledon
52 St George's Hill
53 Sandown Park
54 Selsdon Park Hotel
55 Shirley Park
56 Silvermere
57 Sunningdale
58 Surbiton
59 Tandridge
60 Thames Ditton and Esher
61 Tyrells Wood
62 Walton Heath
63 Wentworth
64 West Byfleet
65 West Hill
66 West Surrey
67 Wimbledon Common
68 Wimbledon Park
69 Windlemere
70 Woking
71 Woodcote Park
72 Worplesdon
73 Crondall Golf Course
74 Shillinglee Park
New entries 1987
75 Fernfell

Sussex

1 Ashdown Forest Hotel
2 Brighton and Hove
3 Bognor Regis
4 Cooden Beach
5 Copthorne
6 Cottesmore
7 Cowdray Park
8 Crowborough Beacon
9 Dale Hill
10 The Dyke
11 East Brighton
12 Eastbourne Downs
13 Effingham Park
14 Gatwick Manor
15 Goodwood
16 Ham Manor
17 Hastings
18 Haywards Heath
19 Highwoods (Bexhill)
20 Hollingbury Park (Brighton)
21 Holtye
22 Ifield
23 Lewes
24 Littlehampton
25 Mannings Heath
26 Nevill
27 Peacehaven
28 Piltdown
29 Pyecombe
30 Royal Ashdown Forest
31 Royal Eastbourne
32 Rye
33 Seaford GC and Dormy House
34 Seaford Head
35 Selsey
36 Waterhall
37 West Hove
38 West Sussex
39 Willingdon
40 Worthing
41 Hill Barn
42 Horam Park
43 Tilgate

Public courses are set in italics.

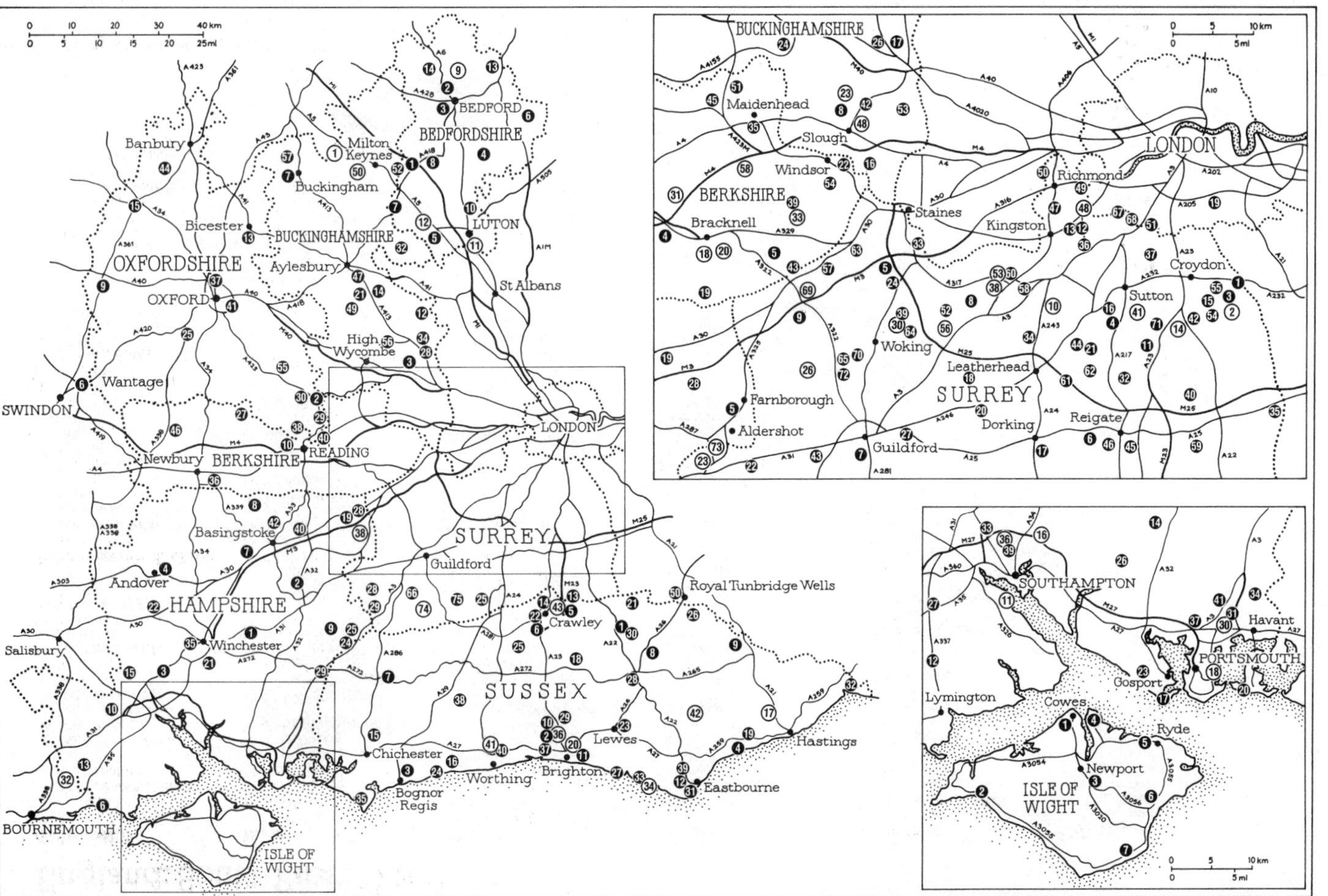
Banbury
Bicester
OXFORDSHIRE
OXFORD
Milton Keynes
Buckingham
BEDFORD
BEDFORDSHIRE
BUCKINGHAMSHIRE
LUTON
St Albans
Aylesbury
High Wycombe
Wantage
SWINDON
READING
Newbury
BERKSHIRE
LONDON
Basingstoke
SURREY
Guildford
Andover
HAMPSHIRE
Salisbury
Winchester
Crawley
Royal Tunbridge Wells
SUSSEX
Chichester
Bognor Regis
Worthing
Brighton
Lewes
Eastbourne
Hastings
BOURNEMOUTH
ISLE OF WIGHT
BUCKINGHAMSHIRE
Maidenhead
Slough
Windsor
BERKSHIRE
Bracknell
Staines
Richmond
LONDON
Kingston
Croydon
Sutton
Woking
Leatherhead
SURREY
Farnborough
Aldershot
Guildford
Dorking
Reigate
SOUTHAMPTON
Havant
PORTSMOUTH
Gosport
Lymington
Cowes
Ryde
Newport
ISLE OF WIGHT

England: South-West

Cornwall

1 Bude and North Cornwall
2 Budock Vean Hotel
3 Carlyon Bay
4 Culdrose
5 Falmouth
6 Isles of Scilly
7 Launceston
8 Looe Bin Down
9 Mullion
10 Newquay
11 Perranporth
12 Praa Sands
13 St Austell
14 St Enodoc
15 St Mellion
16 Tehidy Park
17 Trevose
18 Truro
19 West Cornwall
20 Whitsand Bay Hotel
New entries 1987
21 Tregenna Castle

Devon

1 Axe Cliff
2 Bigbury
3 Chulmleigh
4 Churston
5 Downes Crediton
6 East Devon
7 Elfordleigh Hotel C & GC
8 Exeter G & CC
9 Holsworthy
10 Honiton
11 Ilfracombe
12 Manor House Hotel
13 Newton Abbot (Stover)
14 Okehampton
15 Royal North Devon
16 Saunton
17 Sidmouth
18 Staddon Heights
19 Tavistock
20 Teignmouth
21 Thurlestone
22 Tiverton
23 Torquay
24 Torrington
25 Warren
26 Wrangaton (South Devon)
27 Yelverton

Dorset

1 Ashley Wood
2 Bridport and West Dorset
3 Broadstone
4 Came Down
5 Christchurch
6 Ferndown
7 Highcliffe Castle
8 Isle of Purbeck
9 Knighton Heath
10 Lakey Hill
11 Lyme Regis
12 Meyrick Park
13 Parkstone
14 Sherborne
15 Wareham
16 Weymouth
17 Yeovil

Gloucestershire

1 Bristol & Clifton
2 Broadway
3 Chipping Sodbury
4 Cirencester
5 Cleeve Cloud
6 Cleeve Hill
7 Coleford
8 Cotswold Hills
9 Filton
10 Gloucestershire Hotel and GC
11 Henbury
12 Knowle
13 Lansdown
14 Lilley Brook
15 Long Ashton
16 Lydney
17 Mangotsfield
18 Minchinhampton
19 Painswick
20 Ross-on-Wye
21 Shirehampton Park
22 Stinchcombe Hill
23 Tewkesbury Park Hotel
24 Tracy Park
25 Westonbirt
New entries 1987
26 Cotswold Edge

Somerset

1 Bath
2 Brean
3 Burnham and Berrow
4 Clevedon
5 Vivary Park Municipal
6 Enmore Park
7 Fosseway
8 Kingweston
9 Mendip
10 Minehead and West Somerset
11 Saltford
12 Taunton and Pickeridge
14 Wells
15 Weston-super-Mare
16 Windwhistle Golf Squash & Country Club
17 Worlebury
New entries 1987
18 Entry Hill

Wiltshire

1 Broome Manor
2 Chippenham
3 High Post
4 Kingsdown
5 Marlborough
6 North Wilts
7 RAF Upavon
8 Salisbury and South Wilts
9 Swindon
10 Tidworth Garrison
11 West Wilts
12 Brinkworth
13 RMCS Shrivenham

Public courses are set in italics.

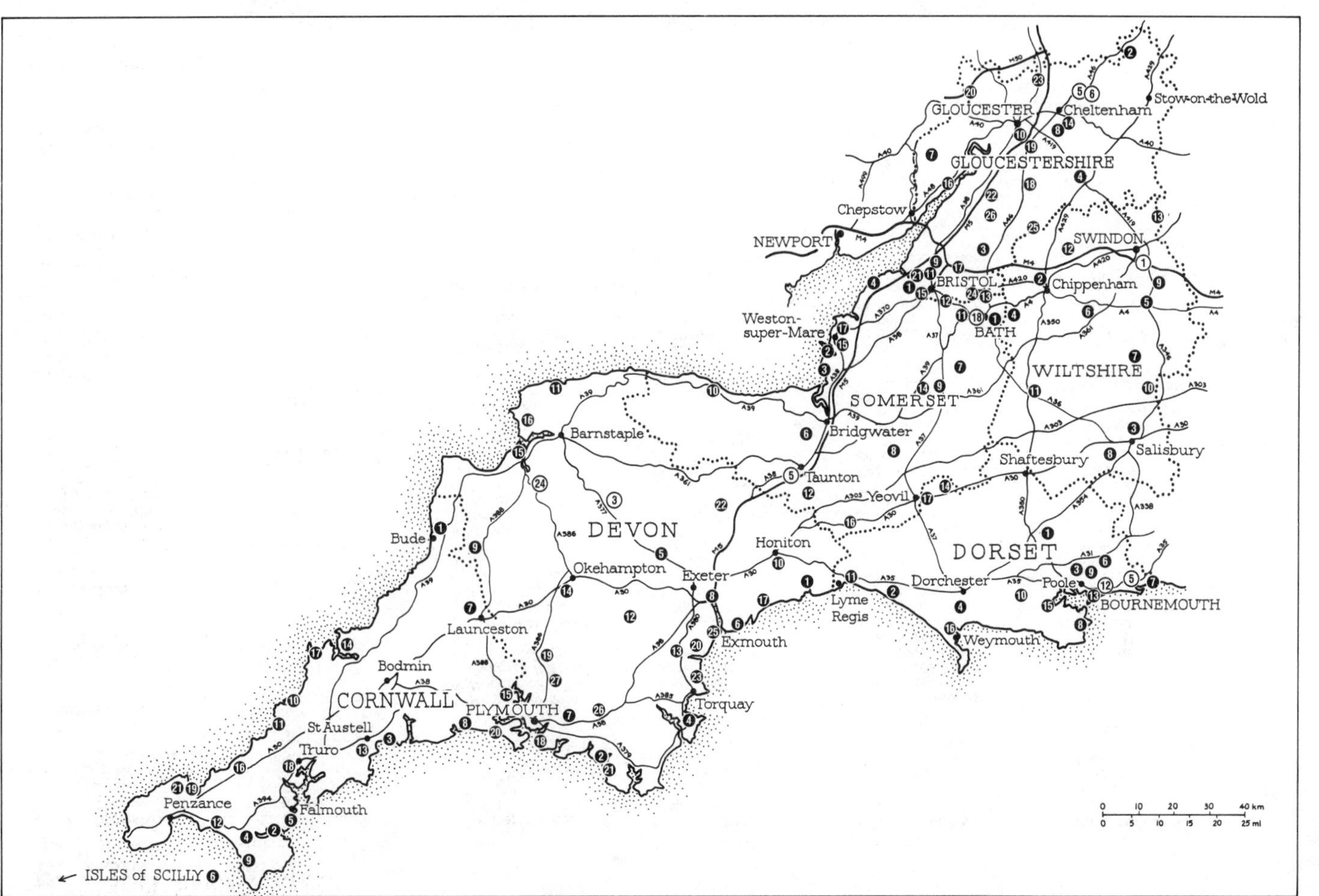
GLOUCESTER
Cheltenham
Stow-on-the-Wold
GLOUCESTERSHIRE
Chepstow
NEWPORT
SWINDON
BRISTOL
Chippenham
BATH
Weston-super-Mare
WILTSHIRE
SOMERSET
Barnstaple
Bridgwater
Salisbury
Shaftesbury
Taunton
Yeovil
DEVON
Bude
Honiton
DORSET
Okehampton
Exeter
Dorchester
Poole
BOURNEMOUTH
Lyme Regis
Launceston
Exmouth
Weymouth
Bodmin
CORNWALL
PLYMOUTH
Torquay
St Austell
Truro
Penzance
Falmouth
ISLES of SCILLY
0 10 20 30 40 km
0 5 10 15 20 25 ml

England: Midlands

Cambridgeshire
1 Cambridgeshire Moat House Hotel
2 Ely City Golf Course
3 Eynesbury Hardwicke
4 Girton
5 The Gog Magog
6 Links (Newmarket)
7 March
8 Ramsey
9 Royston
10 Saffron Walden
11 St Ives (Hunts)
12 St Neot's

Derbyshire
1 Alfreton
2 Allestree Park
3 Ashbourne
4 Bakewell
5 Breadsall Priory
6 Burton-on-Trent
7 Buxton and High Peak
8 Cavendish
9 Chapel-en-le-Frith
10 Chesterfield
11 Chesterfield Municipal
12 Chevin
13 Derby
14 Erewash Valley
15 Glossop and District
16 Ilkeston
17 Kedleston Park
18 Matlock
19 Mickleover
20 New Mills
21 Ormonde Fields
22 Pastures
23 Shirland
24 Stanedge
35 Craythorne Golf Centre
New entries 1987
26 Blue Circle

Leicestershire & Rutland
1 Birstall
2 Charnwood Forest
3 Cosby
4 Glen Gorse
5 Hinckley
6 Humberstone Heights
7 Kibworth
8 Kirby Muxloe
9 Leicestershire
10 Lingdale
11 Longcliffe
12 Luffenham Heath
13 Lutterworth
14 Market Harborough
15 Melton Mowbray
16 Oadby
17 RAF North Luffenham
18 Rothley Park
19 Scraptoft
20 Ullesthorpe Court
21 Western Park
22 Whetstone
23 Willesley Park
New entries 1987
24 Enderby

Lincolnshire
1 Belton Park
2 Blankney
3 Boston
4 Burghley Park
5 Carholme
6 Cleethorpes
7 Elsham
8 Grimsby
9 Holme Hall
10 Immingham GC
11 Kingsway
12 Lincoln
13 Louth
14 Market Rasen and District
15 Normanby Hall
16 North Shore
17 RAF Waddington
18 Sandilands
19 Scunthorpe
20 Seacroft
21 Sleaford
22 Southcliffe and Canwick
23 Spalding
24 Stoke Rochford
25 Sutton Bridge
26 Thonock
27 Woodhall Spa

Northamptonshire
1 Cold Ashby
2 Daventry and District
3 Delapre
4 Kettering
5 Kingsthorpe
6 Northampton
7 Northamptonshire County
8 Oundle
9 Peterborough Milton
10 Priors Hall
11 Rushden and District
12 Staverton Park
13 Thorpe Wood
14 Wellingborough
15 Woodlands
New entries 1987
16 Cherwell Edge

Nottinghamshire
1 Beeston Fields
2 Bulwell Forest
3 Chilwell Manor
4 Coxmoor
5 Kilton Forest
6 Mapperley
7 Newark
8 Nottingham City
9 Notts
10 Oxton
11 Radcliffe on Trent
12 Retford
13 Rushcliffe
14 Sherwood Forest
15 Stanton-on-the-Wolds
16 Wollaton Park
17 Woodhouse
18 Worksop
New entries 1987
19 Edwalton

Shropshire & Hereford
1 Belmont GC
2 Bridgnorth
3 Church Stretton
4 Hawkstone Park
5 Herefordshire
6 Hill Valley G & CC
7 Kington
8 Leominster
9 Lilleshall Hall
10 Llanymynech
11 Ludlow
12 Market Drayton
13 Meole Brace
14 Oswestry
15 Shifnal
16 Shrewsbury
17 Telford Hotel G & CC
18 Wrekin

Staffordshire
1 Beau Desert
2 Blackhill Wood
3 Bloxwich
4 Branston
5 Brocton Hall
6 Burslem
7 Calderfields
8 Dartmouth
9 Drayton Park
10 Druids Heath
11 Enville
12 Great Barr
13 Greenway Hall
14 Himley Hall
15 Ingestre Park
16 Lakeside (Barlaston)
17 Leek
18 Little Aston
19 Newcastle-under-Lyme
20 Newcastle Municipal
21 Onneley
22 Oxley Park
23 Patshull Park
24 Penn
25 Sandwell Park
26 South Staffordshire
27 Stafford Castle
28 Stone
29 Tamworth Municipal
30 Trentham Park
32 Uttoxeter
33 Walsall
34 Westwood
35 Whittington Barracks
36 Wolstanton
37 Alsager G & CC
New entries 1987
38 Golden Hill
39 Lakeside (Rugeley)

Warwickshire
1 Atherstone
2 The Belfry
3 Boldmere
4 City of Coventry (Brandon Wood)
5 Copt Heath
6 Coventry
7 Coventry Hearsall
8 Edgbaston
9 Forest of Arden
10 Grange
11 Handsworth
12 Harborne
13 Harborne Church Farm
14 Hatchford Brook
15 Hilltop Golf Club
17 Kenilworth
18 Ladbrook Park
19 Leamington and County
20 Maxstoke Park
21 Moor Hall
22 Newbold Comyn
23 North Warwickshire
24 Nuneaton
25 Olton
26 Purley Chase
27 Pype Hayes
28 Robin Hood
29 Rugby
30 Shirley
31 Sphinx
32 Stratford-on-Avon
33 Sutton Coldfield
34 Walmley (Wylde Green)
35 Warwick
36 Welcombe Hotel & GC

Worcestershire
1 Blackwell
2 Brand Hall
3 Churchill and Blakedown
4 Cocks Moor Woods
5 Droitwich
6 Dudley
7 Evesham
8 Fulford Heath
9 Gay Hill
10 Habberley
11 Hagley
12 Halesowen
13 Kidderminster
14 King's Norton
15 Lickey Hills
16 Little Lakes
17 Moseley
18 North Worcestershire
19 Pitcheroak
20 Redditch
21 Stourbridge
22 Tolladine
23 Warley
24 Worcester G & CC
25 Worcestershire

Public courses are set in italics.

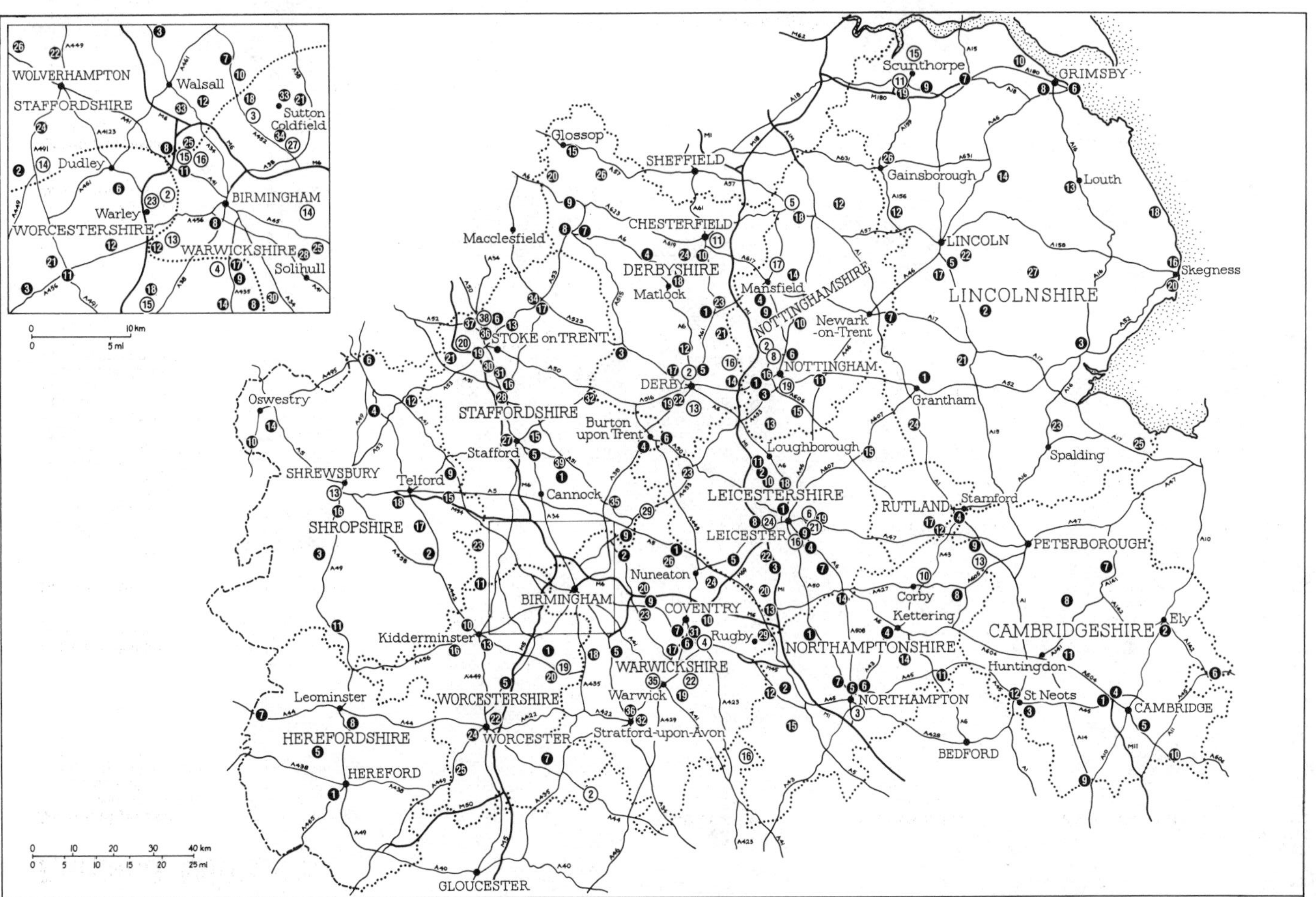
WOLVERHAMPTON
Walsall
STAFFORDSHIRE
Sutton Coldfield
Dudley
BIRMINGHAM
Warley
WORCESTERSHIRE
WARWICKSHIRE
Solihull
10 km
5 ml
Scunthorpe
GRIMSBY
Glossop
SHEFFIELD
Gainsborough
Louth
Macclesfield
CHESTERFIELD
LINCOLN
DERBYSHIRE
Skegness
Matlock
Mansfield
NOTTINGHAMSHIRE
LINCOLNSHIRE
Newark -on-Trent
STOKE on TRENT
NOTTINGHAM
DERBY
Grantham
Oswestry
STAFFORDSHIRE
Burton upon Trent
Loughborough
Stafford
Spalding
SHREWSBURY
Telford
Cannock
LEICESTERSHIRE
RUTLAND
Stamford
SHROPSHIRE
LEICESTER
PETERBOROUGH
Nuneaton
Corby
BIRMINGHAM
COVENTRY
Kettering
CAMBRIDGESHIRE
Ely
Kidderminster
Rugby
NORTHAMPTONSHIRE
Huntingdon
WARWICKSHIRE
Leominster
WORCESTERSHIRE
Warwick
St Neots
NORTHAMPTON
CAMBRIDGE
HEREFORDSHIRE
WORCESTER
Stratford-upon-Avon
BEDFORD
HEREFORD
GLOUCESTER
40 km
25 ml

England: North (East)

Durham

1 Barnard Castle
2 Beamish Park
3 Billingham
4 Birtley (Portobello)
5 Bishop Auckland
6 Blackwell Grange
7 Boldon
8 Brancepeth Castle
9 Castle Eden and Peterlee
10 Chester-le-Street
11 Consett and District
12 Crook
13 Darlington
14 Dinsdale Spa
15 Durham City
16 Eaglescliffe
17 Garesfield
18 Hartlepool
19 Heworth
20 Hobson Municipal
21 Houghton-le-Spring
22 Mount Oswald
23 Ravensworth
24 Woodham
25 Ryton
26 Seaham
27 Seaton Carew
28 South Moor
29 South Shields
30 Stressholme
31 Tyneside
32 Washington
33 Wearside
34 Whickham
35 Whitburn

New entries 1987

36 Aycliffe

Northumberland

1 Allendale
2 Alnmouth
3 Alnmouth Village
4 Alnwick
5 Arcot Hall
6 Backworth GC
7 Bamburgh Castle
8 Bedlingtonshire
9 Bellingham
10 Berwick-upon-Tweed
11 Blyth
12 City of Newcastle
13 Dunstanburgh Castle
14 Gosforth
15 Hexham
16 Magdalene Fields
17 Morpeth
18 Newbiggin-by-the-Sea
19 Newcastle United
20 Northumberland
21 Ponteland
22 Prudhoe
23 Rothbury
24 Seahouses
25 Stocksfield
26 Tynedale
27 Tynemouth
28 Wallsend
29 Warkworth
30 Westerhope GC
31 Whitley Bay
32 Gosforth Park Golf Centre

New entries 1987

33 Wooler

Yorkshire

1 Abbeydale
2 Alwoodley
3 Austerfield Park
4 Baildon
5 Barnsley
6 Beauchief Municipal
7 Bedale
8 Ben Rhydding
9 Beverley and East Riding
10 Bingley (St Ives)
11 Birley Wood
12 Boothferry (Spaldington)
13 Bradford
14 Bradford Moor
15 Bradley Park
16 Branshaw
17 Bridlington
18 Brough
19 Catterick Garrison
20 City of Wakefield
21 Clayton
22 Cleckheaton and District
23 Cleveland
24 Concord Park
25 Crimple Valley
26 Crookhill Park
27 Crosland Heath
28 Dewsbury District
29 Doncaster
30 Concaster Town Moor
31 Dore and Totley
32 Driffield
33 Easingwold
34 East Bierley
35 Elland
36 Filey
37 Flamborough Head
38 Fulford (York)
39 Fulneck
40 Ganstead Park
41 Ganton
42 Garforth
43 Ghyll
44 Gotts Park
45 Grange Park
46 Halifax
47 Halifax Bradley Hall
48 Halifax West End
49 Hallamshire
50 Hallowes
51 Hanging Heaton
52 Harrogate
53 Headingley
54 Headley
55 Hessle
56 Heworth
57 Hickleton
58 Hillsborough
59 Hornsea
60 Horsforth
61 Howley Hall
62 Huddersfield
63 Hull
64 Ilkley
65 Keighley
66 Kirkbymoorside
67 Knaresborough
68 Leeds
69 Lees Hall
70 Lightcliffe
71 Lindrick
72 Longley Park
73 Low Laithes
74 Malton and Norton
75 Marsden
76 Masham
77 Meltham
78 Middlesbrough
79 Middlesbrough Municipal
80 Middleton Park
81 Moor Allerton
82 Moortown
83 Mount Skip
84 Normanton
85 Northcliffe
86 Oakdale
87 Otley
88 Outlane
89 Painthorpe House
90 Pannal
91 Phoenix
92 Phoenix Park
93 Pike Hills
94 Pontefract and District
95 Pontefract Park
96 Queensbury
97 Rawdon
98 Renishaw Park
99 Richmond
100 Riddlesden
101 Ripon City
102 Rotherham
103 Roundhay
104 Ryburn
105 Saltburn
106 Sand Moor
107 Scarborough North Cliff
108 Scarborough South Cliff
109 Scarcroft
110 Selby
111 Serlby Park
112 Settle
113 Sheffield Transport Dept
114 Shipley
115 Sickleholme
116 Silkstone
117 Silsden
118 Sitwell Park
119 Skipton
120 South Bradford
121 South Leeds
122 Springhead Park
123 Stocksbridge and District
124 Sutton Park
125 Tankersley Park
126 Tees-side
127 Temple Newsam
128 Thirsk and Northallerton
129 Tinsley Park
130 Todmorden
131 Wakefield
132 Wath-upon-Dearne
133 West Bowling
134 West Bradford
135 Wetherby
136 Wheatley
137 Whitby
138 Wilton
139 Withernsea
140 Woodhall Hills
141 Woodsome Hall
142 Wortley
143 York
144 Aldwark Manor
145 Ampleforth College
146 Hainsworth Park

New entries 1987

147 Roundwood
148 Castlefields

Public courses are set in italics.

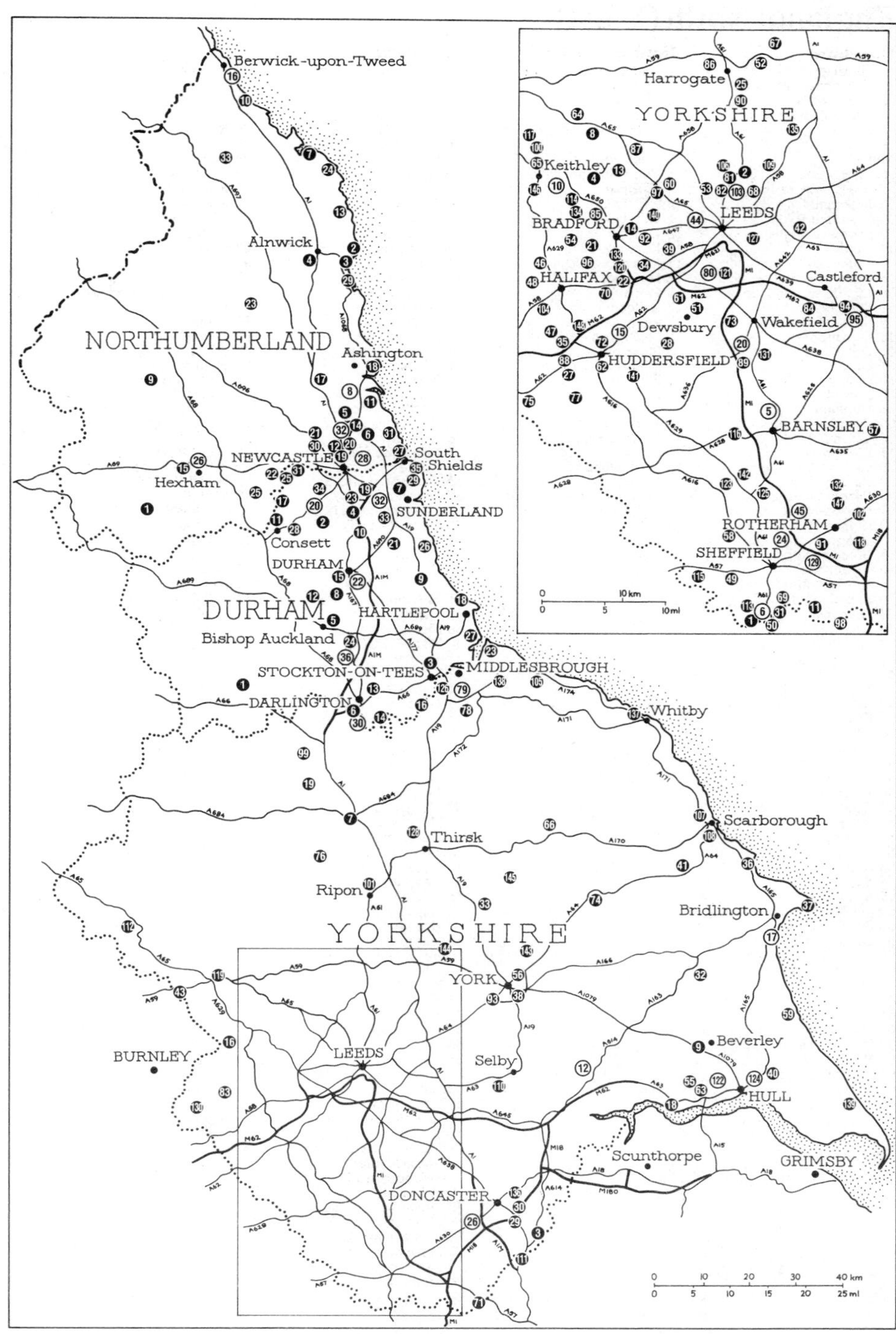
Berwick-upon-Tweed
Alnwick
NORTHUMBERLAND
Ashington
NEWCASTLE
South Shields
Hexham
SUNDERLAND
Consett
DURHAM
HARTLEPOOL
DURHAM
Bishop Auckland
STOCKTON-ON-TEES
MIDDLESBROUGH
DARLINGTON
Whitby
Scarborough
Thirsk
Ripon
Bridlington
YORKSHIRE
YORK
Beverley
BURNLEY
LEEDS
Selby
HULL
Scunthorpe
GRIMSBY
DONCASTER
Harrogate
YORKSHIRE
Keithley
BRADFORD
LEEDS
HALIFAX
Castleford
Dewsbury
Wakefield
HUDDERSFIELD
BARNSLEY
ROTHERHAM
SHEFFIELD
0 10 km
0 5 10 ml
0 10 20 30 40 km
0 5 10 15 20 25 ml

England: North (West)

Cheshire

1 Alderley Edge
2 Altrincham Municipal
3 Arrowe Park
4 Ashton-on-Mersey
5 Astbury
6 Avro
7 Bidston
8 Birchwood
9 Brackenwood
10 Bramhall
11 Bramhall Park
12 Bromborough
13 Caldy
14 Cheadle
15 Chester
16 Chorlton-cum-Hardy
17 Congleton
18 Crewe
19 Davenport
20 Delamere Forest
21 Didsbury
22 Disley
23 Dukinfield
24 Dunham Forest G & CC
25 Eastham Lodge
26 Eaton (Chester)
27 Ellesmere Port
28 Gatley
29 Hale
30 Hazel Grove
31 Heaton Moor
32 Helsby
33 Heswall
34 Houldsworth (Levenshulme)
35 Hoylake Municipal
36 Knutsford
37 Leasowe
38 Lymm
39 Macclesfield
40 Malkins Bank
41 Marple
42 Mellor and Townscliffe
43 Mere Golf and Country Club
44 Mirrlees
45 Northenden
46 Poulton Park
47 Prenton
48 Prestbury
49 Reddish Vale
50 Ringway
51 Romiley
52 Royal Liverpool
53 Runcorn
54 Sale
55 Sandbach
56 Sandiway
57 Stamford
58 Stockport
59 Upton-by-Chester
60 Vicars Cross
61 Wallasey
62 Warren
63 Walton Hall
64 Warrington
65 Werneth Low
66 Wilmslow
67 Wirral Ladies
68 Withington
69 Knights Grange

Cumbria

1 Alston Moor
2 Appleby
3 Barrow
4 Bentham
5 Brampton (Talkin Tarn)
6 Carlisle
7 Cockermouth
8 The Dunnerholme
9 Furness
10 Grange Fell
11 Grange-over-Sands
12 Kendal
13 Keswick
14 Kirkby Lonsdale
15 Maryport
16 Penrith
17 St Bees
18 Seascale
19 Sedbergh
20 Silecroft
21 Silloth-on-Solway
22 Silverdale
23 Stoneyholme
24 Ulverston
25 Windermere
26 Workington

Isle of Man

1 Castletown
2 Douglas
3 Douglas Municipal
4 Howstrake
5 Peel
6 Port St Mary
7 Ramsey
8 Rowany

Lancashire

1 Accrington & District
2 Allerton Park
3 Alt
4 Ashton and Lea
5 Ashton-in-Makerfield
6 Ashton-under-Lyne
7 Bacup
8 Baxenden and District
9 Beacon Park
10 Blackburn
11 Blackley
12 Blackpool North Shore
13 Blackpool Park
14 Bolton
15 Bolton Old Links
16 Bolton Municipal
17 Bootle
18 Bowring
19 Brackley Municipal
20 Breightmet
21 Brookdale
22 Burnley
23 Bury
24 Castle Hawk
25 Childwall
26 Chorley
27 Clitheroe
28 Colne
29 Crompton and Royton
30 Darwen
31 Davyhulme Park
32 Dean Wood
33 Deane
34 Denton
35 Dunscar
36 Duxbury Park
37 Ellesmere
38 Fairfield
39 Fairhaven
40 Fishwick Hall
41 Fleetwood
42 Flixton
43 Formby
44 Formby Ladies
45 Gathurst
46 Grange Park
47 Great Harwood
48 Great Lever and Farnworth
49 Green Haworth
50 Greenmount
51 Harwood
52 Haydock Park
53 Heaton Park
54 Hesketh
55 Heysham
56 Hillside
57 Hindley Hall
58 Horwich
59 Huyton and Prescot
60 Ingol Golf and Squash Club
61 Knott End
62 Lancaster G & CC
63 Lansil
64 Lee Park
65 Leigh
66 Leyland
67 Liverpool Municipal
68 Lobden
69 Longridge
70 Lowes Park
71 Lytham (Green Drive)
72 Manchester GC Ltd
73 Marsden Park
74 Morecambe
75 Nelson
76 North Manchester
77 Oldham
78 Ormskirk
79 Pennington
80 Penwortham
81 Pike Fold
82 Pleasington
83 Poulton-le-Fylde
84 Preston
85 Prestwich
86 Rishton
87 Rochdale
88 Rossendale
89 Royal Birkdale
90 Royal Lytham & St Annes
91 Saddleworth
92 St Annes Old Links
93 Shaw Hill G & CC
94 St Helens
95 Southport and Ainsdale
96 Southport Municipal Links
97 Southport Old Links
98 Springfield Park
99 Stand
100 Swinton Park
101 Towneley
102 Tunshill
103 Turton
104 Walmersley
105 Werneth
106 West Derby
107 The West Lancashire
108 Westhoughton
109 Whalley
110 Whitefield
111 Whittaker
112 Widnes
113 Widnes Municipal
114 Wigan
115 Haigh Hall
116 William Wroe
117 Wilpshire
118 Woolton
119 Worsley

Public courses are set in italics.

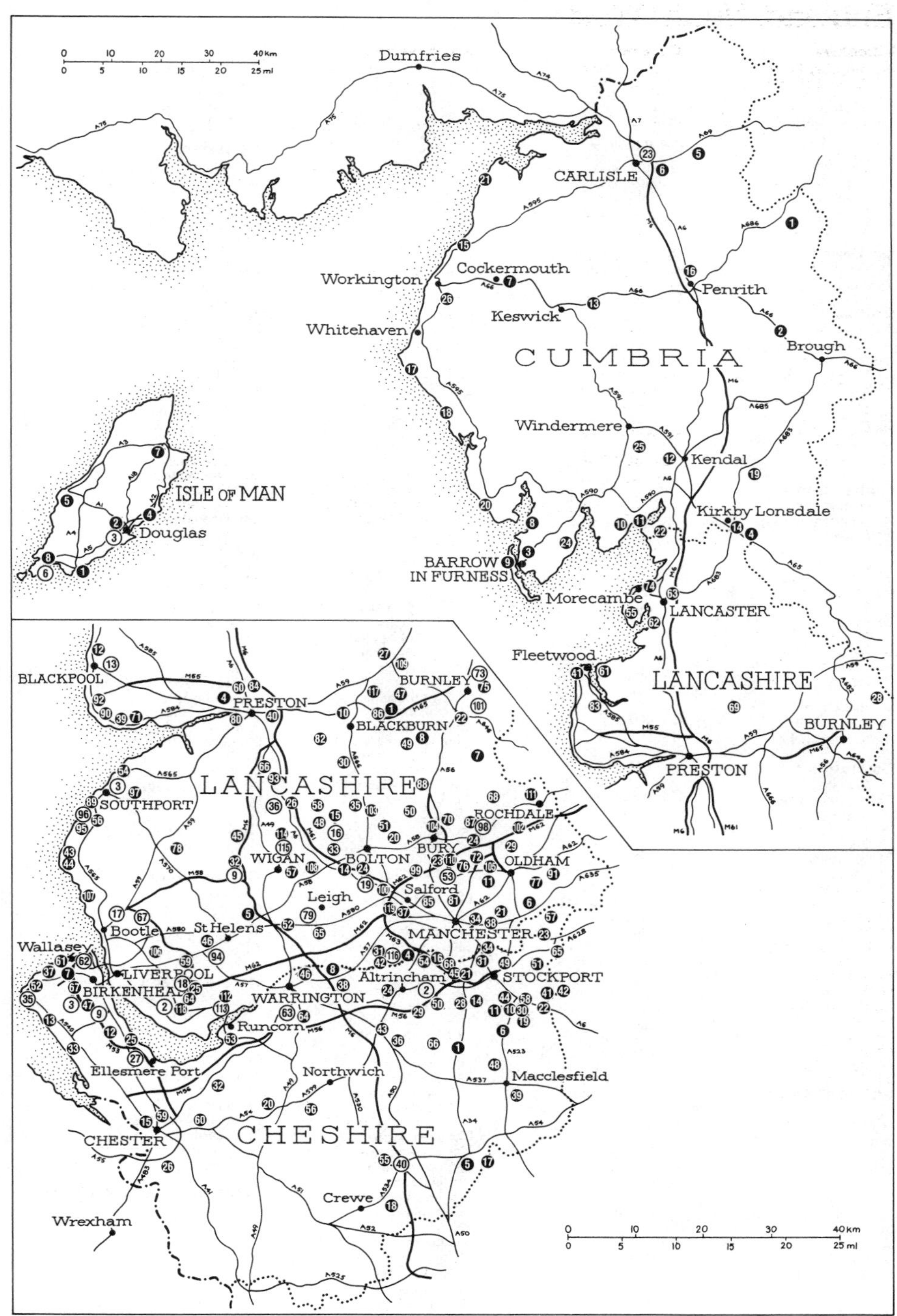
Dumfries
CARLISLE
Workington
Cockermouth
Keswick
Penrith
Whitehaven
CUMBRIA
Brough
Windermere
Kendal
ISLE OF MAN
Douglas
Kirkby Lonsdale
BARROW IN FURNESS
Morecambe
LANCASTER
Fleetwood
LANCASHIRE
BURNLEY
PRESTON
BLACKPOOL
BLACKBURN
LANCASHIRE
SOUTHPORT
ROCHDALE
WIGAN
BOLTON
BURY
OLDHAM
Leigh
Salford
Bootle
St Helens
MANCHESTER
Wallasey
LIVERPOOL
BIRKENHEAD
Altrincham
STOCKPORT
WARRINGTON
Runcorn
Ellesmere Port
Northwich
Macclesfield
CHESTER
CHESHIRE
Crewe
Wrexham

Ireland

Connacht

Co Galway
1 Athenry
2 Ballinasloe
3 Connemara
4 Galway
5 Gort
6 Loughrea
7 Mount Bellew
8 Oughterard
9 Portumna
10 Tuam

Co Leitrim
11 Ballinamore
12 Carrick-on-Shannon

Co Mayo
13 Achill Island
14 Ballina
15 Ballinrobe
16 Ballyhaunis
17 Belmullet
18 Castlebar
19 Claremorris
20 Mulrany
21 Swinford
22 Westport

Co Roscommon
23 Athlone
24 Ballaghaderreen
25 Boyle
26 Castlerea
27 Roscommon

Co Sligo
28 Ballymote
29 County Sligo
30 Enniscrone
31 Strandhill

Leinster

Co Carlow
1 Borris
2 Carlow

Co Dublin
3 Balbriggan
4 Ballinascorney
5 Beech Park
6 Corballis
7 Deer Park
8 Donabate
9 Dublin Sport
10 Dun Laoghaire
11 Forrest Little
12 Hermitage
13 The Island
14 Killiney
15 Lucan
16 Malahide
17 Newlands
18 Portmarnock
19 Rush
20 Skerries
21 Slade Valley
22 Woodbrook

Dublin City
23 Carrickmines
24 Castle
25 Clontarf
26 Edmondstown
27 Elm Park Golf and Sports Club
28 Foxrock
29 Grange
30 Howth
31 Milltown
32 Rathfarnham
33 Royal Dublin
34 St Anne's
25 Stackstown
36 Sutton

Co Kildare
37 Athy
38 Bodenstown
39 Cill Dara
40 Clongowes
41 Curragh
42 Naas
New entries 1987
80 Knockanally

Co Kilkenny
43 Callan
44 Castlecomer
45 Kilkenny

Co Laois
46 Abbey Leix
47 Heath (Portlaoise)
48 Mountrath
49 Portarlington
50 Rathdowney

Co Longford
51 Co Longford

Co Louth
52 Ardee
53 County Louth
54 Dundalk
55 Greenore

Co Meath
56 Gormanston College
57 Headfort
58 Laytown and Bettystown
59 Royal Tara
60 Trim

Co Offaly
61 Birr
62 Edenderry
63 Tullamore

Co Wexford
64 Courtown
65 Enniscorthy
66 New Ross
67 Rosslare
68 Wexford

Co Westmeath
69 Moate
70 Mullingar

Co Wicklow
71 Arklow
72 Baltinglass
73 Blainroe
74 Bray
75 Coollattin
76 Delgany
77 Greystones
78 Wicklow
79 Woodenbridge

Munster

Co Clare
1 Drumoland Castle
2 Ennis
3 Kilkee
4 Kilrush
5 Lahinch
6 Shannon
7 Spanish Point

Co Cork
8 Bandon
9 Bantry
10 Charleville
11 Cork
12 Doneraile
13 Douglas
14 Dunmore
15 East Cork
16 Fermoy
17 Glengarriff
18 Kanturk
19 Kinsale
20 Macroom
21 Mallow
22 Mitchelstown
23 Monkstown
24 Muskerry
25 Skibbereen
26 Youghal

Co Kerry
27 Ballybunion
28 Ceann Sibeal
29 Dooks and Caragh
30 Kenmare
31 Killarney Golf and Fishing Club
32 Parknasilla
33 Tralee
34 Waterville

Co Limerick
35 Adare Manor
36 Castletroy
37 Limerick
38 Newcastle West

Co Tipperary
39 Cahir Park
40 Carrick-on-Suir
41 Clonmel
42 Nenagh
43 Roscrea
44 Templemore
45 Thurles
46 Tipperary
New entries 1987
51 Rockwell College

Co Waterford
47 Dungarvan
48 Lismore
49 Tramore
50 Waterford

Ulster

Co Antrim
1 Ballycastle
2 Ballyclare
3 Ballymena
4 Bushfoot
5 Cairndhu
6 Carrickfergus
7 Cushendall
8 Dunmurry
9 Greenisland
10 Larne
11 Lisburn
12 Massereene
13 Royal Portrush
14 Whitehead

Co Armagh
15 County Armagh
16 Craigavon
17 Lurgan
18 Portadown
19 Tandragee

Belfast
20 Balmoral
21 Belvoir Park
22 Cliftonville
23 Fortwilliam
24 The Knock Golf Club
25 Malone
26 Ormeau
27 Shandon Park

Co Cavan
28 Belturbet
29 Blacklion
30 County Cavan
31 Virginia
New entries 1987
79 Cabra Castle

Co Donegal
32 Ballbofey and Stranorlar
33 Ballyliffin
34 Buncrana
35 Bundoran
36 Donegal
37 Dunfanaghy
38 Greencastle
39 Gweedone
40 Letterkenny
41 Nann and Portnoo
42 North West
43 Otway
44 Portsalon
45 Rosapenna
46 Tantallon

Co Down
47 Ardglass
48 Banbridge
49 Bangor
50 Carnalea
51 Clandeboye
52 Donaghadee
53 Downpatrick
54 Helen's Bay
55 Holywood
56 Kilkeel
57 Kirkistown Castle
58 Mahee Island
59 Royal Belfast
60 Royal County Down
61 Scrabo
62 The Spa
63 Warrenpoint
New entries 1987
80 Bright

Co Fermanagh
64 Enniskillen

Co Londonderry
65 Castlerock
66 City of Derry
67 Kilrea
68 Moyola Park
69 Portstewart

Co Monaghan
70 Clones
71 Nuremore
72 Rossmore

Co Tyrone
73 Dungannon
74 Fintona
75 Killymoon
76 Newtownstewart
77 Omagh
78 Strabane

Public courses are set in italics.

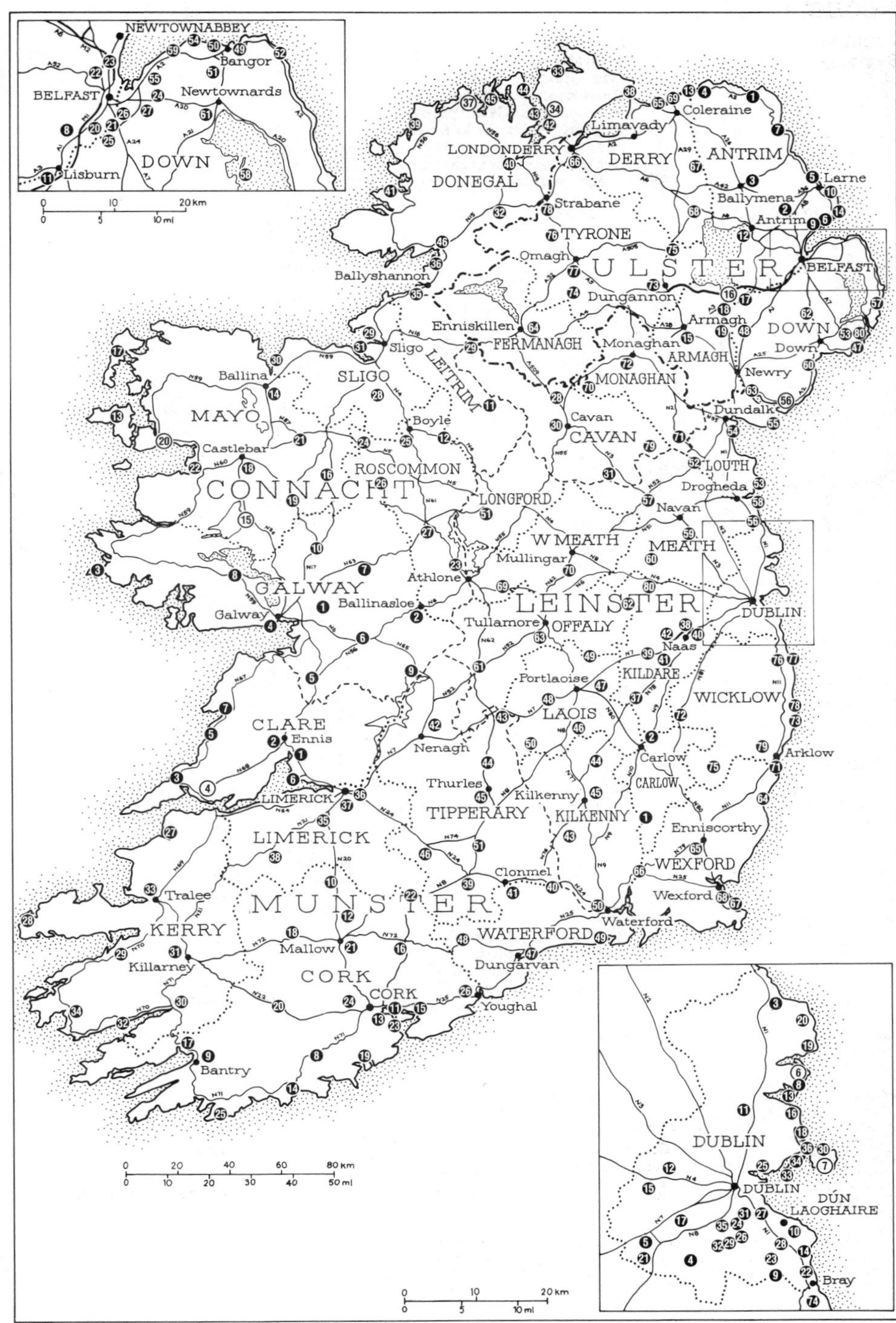
NEWTOWNABBEY
Bangor
BELFAST
Newtownards
DOWN
Lisburn
ULSTER
LEINSTER
CONNACHT
MUNSTER
DONEGAL
LONDONDERRY
DERRY
ANTRIM
Coleraine
Limavady
Larne
Ballymena
Antrim
Strabane
TYRONE
Omagh
Dungannon
Armagh
ARMAGH
Enniskillen
FERMANAGH
Monaghan
MONAGHAN
Newry
Down
Dundalk
Ballyshannon
Sligo
SLIGO
LEITRIM
Ballina
MAYO
Boyle
Castlebar
ROSCOMMON
Cavan
CAVAN
LOUTH
Drogheda
Navan
MEATH
LONGFORD
W MEATH
Mullingar
Athlone
GALWAY
Galway
Ballinasloe
Tullamore
OFFALY
DUBLIN
Naas
KILDARE
Portlaoise
LAOIS
WICKLOW
CLARE
Ennis
Nenagh
Carlow
CARLOW
Arklow
LIMERICK
Thurles
Kilkenny
TIPPERARY
KILKENNY
Enniscorthy
WEXFORD
Wexford
Clonmel
Tralee
KERRY
Waterford
WATERFORD
Mallow
Killarney
Dungarvan
CORK
Youghal
Bantry
DÚN LAOGHAIRE
Bray
0 10 20 km
0 5 10 ml
0 20 40 60 80 km
0 10 20 30 40 50 ml

Scotland: North

Angus (Tayside Region)

1 Arbroath
2 Brechin Golf and Squash Club

Carnoustie Courses
3 Carnoustie
4 Panmure

Dundee Courses
5 Caird Park
6 Caird Park
7 Camperdown
8 Downfield

9 Edzell
10 Forfar
11 Kirriemuir

Monifieth Courses
13 Monifieth Links

14 Montrose

Argyll and Bute (Strathclyde Region)

1 Blairmore and Strone
2 Bute
3 Carradale
4 Colonsay
5 Cowal
6 Craignure
7 Dunaverty
8 Glencruitten
9 Innellan
10 Islay
11 Kyles of Bute
12 Lochgilphead
13 Machrihanish
14 Millport
15 Port Bannatyne
16 Rothesay
17 Tarbert
18 Vaul
19 Western Isles

North (Highland Orkney & Shetland and Western Isles Regions including Caithness Inverness Morayshire (Grampian Region) Nairn Orkney & Shetland Ross & Cromarty Sutherland and Western Isles)

1 Abernethy
2 Alness
3 Askernish
4 Boat-of-Garten
5 Bonar-Bridge and Ardgay
6 Brora
7 Carrbridge
8 Elgin
9 Forres
10 Fort Augustus
11 Fortrose and Rosemarkie
12 Fort William
13 Gairloch
14 Garmouth and Kingston
15 Golspie
16 Grantown
17 Helmsdale
18 Hopeman
19 Invergordon
20 Inverness
21 Kingussie
22 Lochcarron
23 Lybster
24 Moray
25 Muir of Ord
26 Nairn
27 Nairn Dunbar
28 Newtonmore

Orkney & Shetland
29 Orkney
30 Scalloway
31 Shetland
32 Stromness
33 Westray

34 Reay
35 Royal Dornoch
36 Sconser
37 Stornoway
38 Strathpeffer Spa
39 Tain
40 Tarbat
41 Thurso
42 Torvean
43 Traigh
44 Wick

North East (Grampian Region including Aberdeen Banff and Kincardineshire)

1 Aboyne

Aberdeen Courses
2 Auchmill
3 Balnagask
4 Hazlehead
5 King's Links
6 Royal Aberdeen

7 Auchinblae
8 Ballater
9 Banchory
10 Braemar
11 Buckpool
12 Cruden Bay
13 Cullen
14 Deeside
15 Duff House Royal
16 Dufftown
17 Fraserburgh
18 Huntly
19 Insch
20 Inverallochy
21 Inverurie
22 Keith
23 Kemnay
24 Kintore
25 McDonald
26 Murcar
27 Newburgh-on-Ythan
28 Oldmeldrum
29 Peterhead
30 Royal Tarlair
31 Spey Bay
32 Stonehaven
33 Strathlene
34 Tarland
35 Torphins
36 Turriff
37 Westhill

Perthshire & Kinross (Tayside & Central Regions)

1 Aberfeldy
2 Alyth
3 Auchterarder
4 Bishopshire
5 Blair Atholl
6 Blairgowrie
7 Comrie
8 Craigie Hill
9 Crieff
10 Dalmunzie
11 Dunkeld and Birnam
12 Dunning
13 Glenalmond
14 Gleneagles Hotel Golf Courses
15 Green Hotel
16 Killin
17 King James VI
18 Milnathort
19 Muckhart
20 Murrayshall
21 Muthill
22 Pitlochry
23 Royal Perth Golfing Society and County and City Club
24 St Fillans
25 Strathtay
26 Taymouth Castle

Public courses are set in italics.

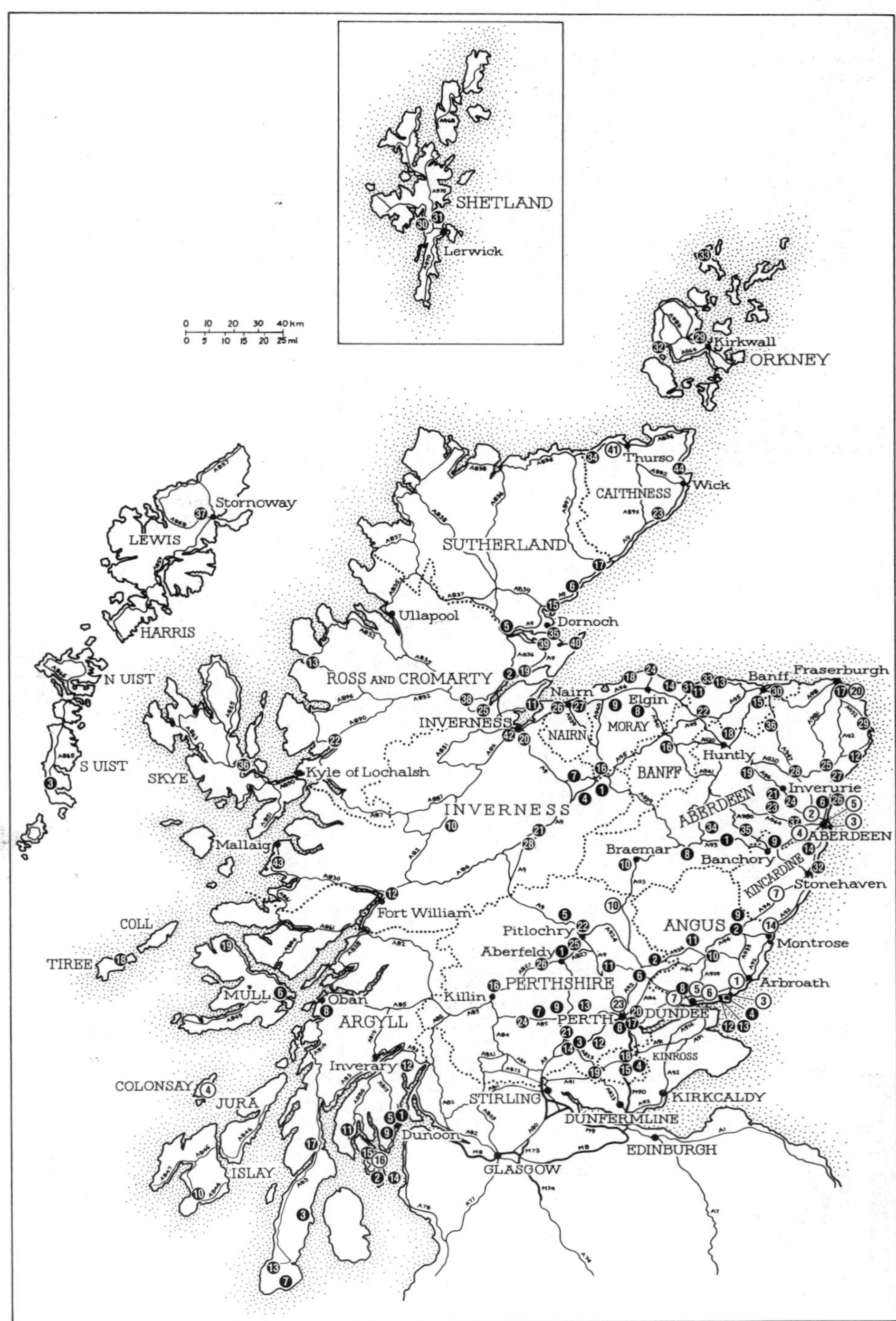
SHETLAND
Lerwick
ORKNEY
Kirkwall
Thurso
Wick
CAITHNESS
SUTHERLAND
Stornoway
LEWIS
HARRIS
N UIST
S UIST
SKYE
Ullapool
Dornoch
ROSS AND CROMARTY
INVERNESS
Nairn
NAIRN
Elgin
MORAY
Banff
Fraserburgh
Huntly
BANFF
Inverurie
ABERDEEN
Kyle of Lochalsh
Mallaig
Braemar
Banchory
KINCARDINE
Stonehaven
Fort William
COLL
TIREE
MULL
Oban
ARGYLL
Pitlochry
Aberfeldy
Killin
PERTHSHIRE
ANGUS
Montrose
Arbroath
DUNDEE
PERTH
KINROSS
Inverary
COLONSAY
JURA
ISLAY
STIRLING
DUNFERMLINE
KIRKCALDY
Dunoon
GLASGOW
EDINBURGH

Scotland: South

Ayrshire (including Isle of Arran (Strathclyde Region)

1 Annanhill
2 Ardeer

Ayr Courses
3 Auchenharvie
4 Belleisle/Seafield
5 Dalmilling

6 Ballochmyle
7 Beith
8 Caprington
9 Girvan
10 Glasgow Gailes
11 Irvine
12 Irvine Ravenspark

Isle of Arran Courses
13 Brodick
14 Corrie
15 Lamlash
16 Lochranza
17 Machrie Bay
18 Shiskine
19 Whiting Bay

20 Kilbirnie Place
21 Kilmarnock (Barassie)
22 Largs
23 Loudoun Gowf Club
24 Maybole
25 New Cumnock
26 Prestwick
27 Prestwick St Cuthbert
28 Prestwick St Nicholas
29 Routenburn
30 Skelmorlie

Troon Courses
31 Royal Troon
32 Troon Municipal

33 Turnberry Hotel
34 West Kilbride
35 Western Gailes

Borders (Berwickshire Peeblesshire Roxburghshire & Selkirkshire)

1 Duns
2 Eyemouth
3 Galashiels
4 Hawick
5 Innerleithen
6 Jedburgh
7 Kelso
8 Lauder
9 Langholm
10 Melrose
11 Minto
12 Peebles
13 St Boswells
14 Selkirk
15 The Hirsel
16 Torwoodlee

Clackmannanshire (Central Region)

1 Alloa
2 Alva
3 Braehead
4 Dollar
5 Tillicoultry
6 Tulliallan

Dunbartonshire (Strathclyde Region) and Glasgow (Strathclyde Region)

1 Balmore
2 Bearsden
3 Cardross
4 Clober
5 Clydebank and District
6 Clydebank Municipal
7 Cumbernauld
8 Dougalston
9 Douglas Park
10 Dullatur
11 Dumbarton
12 Hayston
13 Helensburgh
14 Hilton Park
15 Kirkintilloch
16 Lenzie
17 Milngavie
18 Vale of Leven
19 Windyhill

Glasgow Private Courses
20 Bishopbriggs
21 Cathcart Castle
22 Cathkin Braes
23 Cawder
24 Cowglen
25 Glasgow Killermont
26 Haggs Castle
27 Pollok
28 Ralston
29 Sandyhills
30 Williamwood

Glasgow Public Courses
31 Alexandra Park
32 Deaconsbank
33 King's Park
34 Knightswood
35 Lethamhill
36 Linn Park
37 Littlehill
38 Ruchill

Fife (Fife Region)

1 Aberdour
2 Anstruther
3 Auchterderran
4 Ballingry
5 Burntisland Golf House Club
6 Canmore
7 Crail Golfing Society
8 Cupar
9 Dunfermline
10 Dunnikier Park
11 Golf House Club
12 Glenrothes
13 Kinghorn
14 Kirkcaldy
15 Ladybank
16 Leslie (Fife)
17 Leven Links/Leven Municipal
18 Lochgelly
19 Lundin
20 Lundin Ladies
21 Pitreavie
22 St Andrews
23 Saline
24 Scotscraig
25 St Michael's
26 Thornton

Lanarkshire (Strathclyde Region)

1 Airdrie
2 Bellshill
3 Biggar
4 Blairbeth
5 Bothwell Castle
6 Calderbraes
7 Cambuslang
8 Carluke
9 Carnwath
10 Coatbridge
11 Colville Park
12 Crow Wood
13 Douglas Water
14 Drumpellier
15 East Kilbride
16 Easter Moffat
17 Hamilton
18 Strathclyde Park
19 Hollandbush
20 Kirkhill
21 Lanark
22 Larkhall
23 Leadhills
24 Mount Ellen
25 Shotts
26 Strathaven
27 Torrance House
28 Wishaw

The Lothians (East, Mid- and West Lothian)

2 Bathgate
3 Broomieknowe
4 Dalmahoy
5 Dunbar
6 Dundas Park

Edinburgh Public Courses
7 Braidhills No 1
7 Braidhills No 2
8 Carrick Knowe
9 Craigentinny
10 Portobello
11 Silverknowes

Edinburgh Private Courses
1 Baberton
12 Bruntsfield Links Golfing Society
13 Craigmillar Park
14 Duddingston
15 Kingsknowe
16 Liberton
17 Lothianburn
18 Merchants of Edinburgh
19 Mortonhall
20 Murrayfield
21 Prestonfield
22 Ratho Park
23 Ravelston
24 Royal Burgess Golfing Society of Edinburgh
25 Swanston
26 Torphin Hill
27 Gifford
28 Glencorse
29 Greenburn
30 Gullane
31 Haddington
32 Harburn
33 The Honorable Company of Edinburgh Golfers
34 Kilspindie
35 Linlithgow
36 Deer Park G & CC
37 Longniddry
38 Luffness New
39 Musselburgh
40 Newbattle

North Berwick Courses
41 Burgh Links
42 North Berwick

43 Polkemmet Country Park
44 Pumpherston
45 Royal Musselburgh
46 Turnhouse
47 Uphall
48 West Linton
49 West Lothian
50 Winterfield

Renfrewshire (Strathclyde Region)

1 Barshaw
2 Bonnyton
3 Caldwell
4 Cochrane Castle
5 East Renfrewshire
6 Eastwood
7 Elderslie
8 Erskine
9 Fereneze
10 Gleddoch
11 Gourock
12 Greenock
13 Kilmacolm
14 Lochwinnoch
15 Old Ranfurly
16 Paisley
17 Port Glasgow
18 Ranfurly Castle
19 Renfrew
20 Whinhill
21 Whitecraigs

South (Dumfriesshire & Galloway Regions Dumfriesshire Kirkcudbrightshire & Wigtownshire)

1 Castle Douglas
2 Colvend
3 Crichton Royal
4 Dalbeattie
5 Dumfries and County
6 Dumfries and Galloway
7 Gatehouse
8 Kirkcudbright
9 Lochmaben
10 Lockerbie
11 Moffat
12 New Galloway
13 Newton Stewart
14 Portpatrick Dunskey
15 Powfoot
16 Sanquhar
17 Southerness
18 St Medan
19 Stranraer
20 Thornhill
21 Wigtown and Bladnoch
22 Wigtownshire County

Stirlingshire (Strathclyde & Central Regions)

1 Aberfoyle
2 Bonnybridge
3 Bridge of Allan
4 Buchanan Castle
5 Callander
6 Campsie
7 Dunblane New
8 Falkirk
9 Falkirk Tryst
10 Glenbervie
11 Grangemouth
12 Kilsyth Lennox
13 Polmont
14 Stirling
15 Strathendrick

Public courses are set in italics.

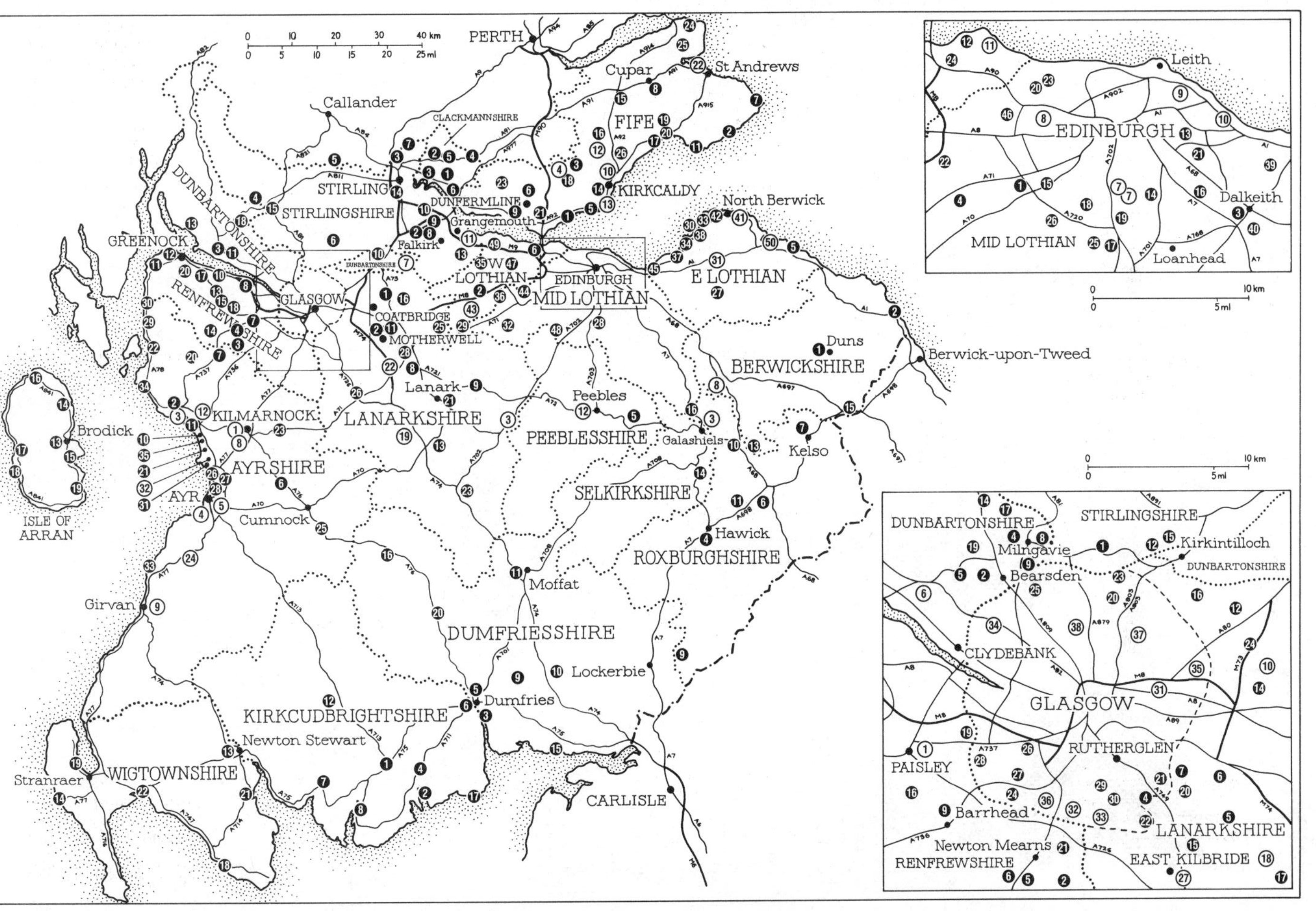
PERTH
Callander
CLACKMANNSHIRE
STIRLING
STIRLINGSHIRE
DUNBARTONSHIRE
GREENOCK
RENFREWSHIRE
GLASGOW
DUNFERMLINE
Grangemouth
Falkirk
W LOTHIAN
COATBRIDGE
MOTHERWELL
Lanark
LANARKSHIRE
KILMARNOCK
AYRSHIRE
AYR
Cumnock
Girvan
Brodick
ISLE OF ARRAN
Cupar
St Andrews
FIFE
KIRKCALDY
North Berwick
E LOTHIAN
EDINBURGH
MID LOTHIAN
BERWICKSHIRE
Duns
Berwick-upon-Tweed
Kelso
Galashiels
Peebles
PEEBLESSHIRE
SELKIRKSHIRE
ROXBURGHSHIRE
Hawick
Moffat
DUMFRIESSHIRE
Lockerbie
Dumfries
CARLISLE
KIRKCUDBRIGHTSHIRE
Newton Stewart
WIGTOWNSHIRE
Stranraer
Leith
EDINBURGH
MID LOTHIAN
Dalkeith
Loanhead
DUNBARTONSHIRE
STIRLINGSHIRE
Milngavie
Kirkintilloch
Bearsden
CLYDEBANK
GLASGOW
RUTHERGLEN
PAISLEY
Barrhead
LANARKSHIRE
Newton Mearns
RENFREWSHIRE
EAST KILBRIDE

Wales

Clwyd

1 Abergele and Pensarn
2 Bryn Morfydd
3 Denbigh
4 Flint
5 Hawarden
6 Holywell
7 Mold
8 Old Colwyn
9 Old Padeswood
10 Padeswood and Buckley
11 Prestatyn
12 Rhuddlan
13 Rhyl
14 Ruthin-Pwllglas
15 St Melyd
16 Vale of Llangollen
17 Wrexham

Dyfed

1 Aberystwyth
2 Ashburnham
3 Borth and Ynyslas
4 Cardigan
5 Carmarthen
6 Glynhir
7 Haverfordwest
8 Cilgwyn
9 Milford Haven
10 Newport (Pem)
11 St Davids City
12 South Pembrokeshire
13 Tenby

Gwent

1 Blackwood
2 Caerleon
3 Greenmeadow
4 Llanwern
5 Monmouth
6 Monmouthshire
7 Newport
8 Pontnewydd
9 Pontypool
10 The Rolls of Monmouth
11 St Mellons
12 St Pierre
13 Tredegar Park
14 Tredegar and Rhymney
15 West Monmouthshire

Gwynedd

1 Aberdovey
2 Abersoch
4 Bala
6 Betws-y-Coed
8 Caernarfon
9 Conwy (Caernarvonshire)
10 Criccieth
11 Dolgellau
12 Ffestiniog
14 Llandudno (Maesdu)
18 Llandudno (North Wales)
15 Llanfairfechan
17 Nefyn and District
19 Penmaenmawr
20 Portmadoc
21 Pwllheli
22 Rhos-on-Sea Residential
23 Royal St David's
24 St Deiniol

Isle of Anglesey

3 Anglesey
5 Baron Hill
7 Bull Bay
13 Holyhead
16 Llangefni

Mid Glamorgan

1 Aberdare
2 Bargoed
3 Bryn Meadows G & CC
4 Caerphilly
5 Llantrisant and Pontyclun
6 Maesteg
7 Merthyr Tydfil
8 Morlais Castle
9 Mountain Ash
10 Pontypridd
11 Pyle and Kenfig
12 Rhondda
13 Royal Porthcawl
14 Southerndown
15 Whitehall
16 Creigiau

Powys

1 Brecon
2 Builth Wells
3 Cradoc
4 Knighton
5 Llandrindod
6 Machynlleth
7 Newtown
8 Old Rectory Country Club
9 St Idloes
10 Welshpool

South Glamorgan

1 Brynhill
2 Cardiff
4 Dinas Powis
5 Glamorganshire
6 Llanishen
7 Radyr
8 RAF St Athan
9 Wenvoe Castle
10 Whitchurch (Cardiff)

West Glamorgan

1 Clyne
2 Fairwood Park G & CC
3 Glynneath
4 Inco
5 Langland Bay
6 Morriston
7 Neath
8 Palleg
9 Pennard
10 Pontardawe
11 Swansea Bay

Public courses are set in italics.

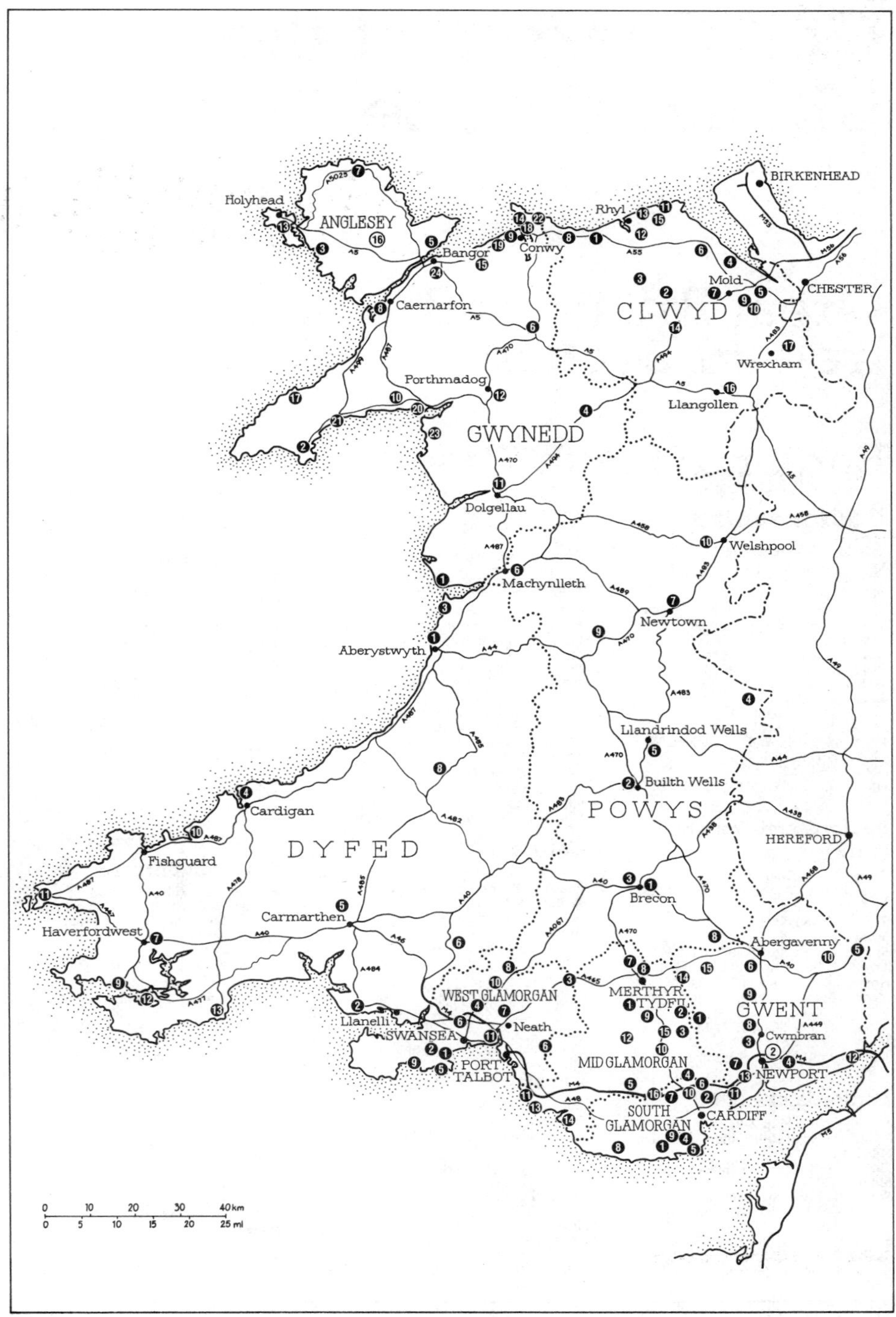

ANGLESEY
Holyhead
Bangor
Conwy
Rhyl
BIRKENHEAD
Mold
CHESTER
CLWYD
Caernarfon
Wrexham
Porthmadog
Llangollen
GWYNEDD
Dolgellau
Welshpool
Machynlleth
Newtown
Aberystwyth
Llandrindod Wells
Builth Wells
POWYS
Cardigan
HEREFORD
Fishguard
DYFED
Brecon
Carmarthen
Haverfordwest
Abergavenny
WEST GLAMORGAN
MERTHYR TYDFIL
GWENT
Llanelli
Neath
SWANSEA
Cwmbran
PORT TALBOT
MID GLAMORGAN
NEWPORT
SOUTH GLAMORGAN
CARDIFF
0 10 20 30 40 km
0 5 10 15 20 25 ml

Golf Courses of the UK and Europe

Great Britain and Ireland Section

England: South-East

Bedfordshire

Aspley Guise and Woburn Sands (1914)

Private (Map 2/1)
West Hill Aspley Guise Milton Keynes
Tel **Milton Keynes 582264**
Mem 500
Sec TE Simpson Tel MK 583596
Pro G McCarthy Tel MK 582974
Holes 18 L 6115 yds SSS 69
Recs Am–68 D Williams
N Abrahams
Pro–68 P Webster
V'trs WD–UH; W/E & BH–MH; Wed & Fri–SOC
Fees £8 D–£10
Loc 2 miles W of M1 junction 13

Bedford and County (1912)

Private (Map 2/2)
Green Lane Clapham Bedford MK41 6ET
Tel **(0234) 52617**
Mem 600
Sec AC Brinicombe Tel (0234) 52617
Pro E Bullock Tel (0234) 59189
Holes 18 L 6347 yds SSS 70
Recs Am–66 C Allen
Pro–66 M King
V'trs WD–U SOC; W/E–M
Fees £9 D–£11 (£8 D–£9)
Loc 2 miles NW of Bedford on A6

Bedfordshire (1891)

Private (Map 2/3)
Bromham Road Biddenham Bedford MK40 4AF
Tel **Bedford 53241 (Members)**
Mem 650
Sec Tel Bedford 61669
Pro Gary Buckle Tel Bedford 53653
Holes 18 L 6185 yds SSS 69
Recs Am–64 CM Beard
Pro–65 K Warren
V'trs WD–U (Phone first); WE–M before noon; SOC on WD
Fees £8 (£10)
Loc 1½m NW city boundary A428

Cainhoe Wood G & CC

Private (Map 2/4)
Beadlow Shefford Beds
Tel **Silsoe 60800**
Mem 700
Sec PV O'Connor Tel 60800
Pro PV O'Connor Tel 60800
Holes 18 L 6397 yds SSS 71
9 L 5918 yds SSS 68
Recs Am–71 I Goldman
Pro–66 PV O'Connor
V'trs U
Fees 18 hole £6 (£8); 9 hole £4.50 (£6)
Loc 2 miles W on A507
Mis Hotel, squash, restaurants

Colworth (1985)

Private (Map 2/14)
Unilever Research Sharnbrook Bedford MK44 1LQ
Tel **Bedford 222502**
Mem 180
Sec Dr W Kelly Tel Bedford 222502
Pro
Holes 9 L 2500 yds
Recs Am–
Pro–
V'trs NA
Loc 10 miles N of Bedford off A6

Dunstable Downs (1907)

Private (Map 2/5)
Whipsnade Road Dunstable
Tel **Dunstable 604472 (2 lines)**
Mem 550
Sec PJ Nightingale Tel Dunstable 604472
Pro M Weldon Tel Dunstable 62806
Holes 18 L 6184 yds SSS 70
Recs Am–65 RA Durrant
Pro–67 J Macdonald SL King
V'trs WD–U; W/E–M; SOC–Tue Thu Fri
Fees On application
Loc M1 Exit 11; Dunstable 2 miles

John O'Gaunt (1948)

Private (Map 2/6)
Sutton Park Sandy Biggleswade SG19 2LY
Tel **0767 260360**
Mem 1100
Sec DJ Wallace Tel 0767 260360
Pro P Round Tel 0767 260094
Holes John O'Gaunt 18 L 6505 yds SSS 71
Carthagena 18 L 5882 yds SSS 68
Recs Am–64 N Wharton
Pro–67 SC Evans
V'trs WD–U; W/E–H
Fees £14 (£20)
Loc 3 miles NE Biggleswade on B1040
Mis Advisable phone before visit

Leighton Buzzard (1925)

Private (Map 2/7)
Plantation Road Leighton Buzzard
Tel **Leighton Buzzard 373812**
Mem 510
Sec FJ Clements Tel LB 373525
Pro LJ Muncey Tel LB 372143
Holes 18 L 5366 yds SSS 68
Recs Am–65 D Horne
Pro–
V'trs WD exc Tue–U; W/E & BH–MH
Fees £9 (£11)
Loc 1 mile N of L Buzzard

Millbrook

Private (Map 2/8)
Millbrook Ampthill
Tel **(0525) 404683**
Mem 250
Sec CF Grimwood Tel (0525) 712001
Pro Terry Devine (0525) 402269
Holes 18 L 6966 yds SSS 73
Recs Am–65
Pro–
V'trs U; Ex Thu and W/E before 9.30 am

Fees £7 (£10) Jnrs half price
Loc Millbrook Village

Mowsbury (1975)

Public (Map 2/9)
Kimbolton Road Bedford
Tel **Bedford 771042**
Mem 375
Sec R Walpole
Pro S Allsop
Holes 18 L 6514 yds SSS 70
Recs Am–
Pro–66
V'trs U
Fees £3.25 (£5.60)
Loc 3 miles N of Bedford

South Beds (1894)

Private (Map 2/10)
Warden Hills Luton
Tel **Luton 55201**
Mem 750
Sec JJ Hackett Tel Luton 591500
Pro E Cogle Tel Luton 591209
Holes 18 L 6342 yds SSS 70
9 L 4954 yds SSS 64
Recs Am–
Pro–
V'trs W/E & BH–H; SOC; Ladies Day Tue
Fees 9 holes: £7; £4 with mem
18 holes: £7 D–£10; £4 D–£5 with mem (£12.50)
Loc 2 miles N of Luton on Bedford Road–A6

Stockwood Park (1973)

Public (Map 2/11)
London Road Luton
Tel **0582 413704**
Mem 550
Sec Tony White
Pro D Hunt Tel 0582 413704
Holes 18 L 5567 yds SSS 69
Recs Am–73 RM Harris
Pro–66 T Minshall
V'trs U
Fees £3.65 (£4.20)
Loc 1 mile S of centre on A6

Tilsworth

Public (Map 2/12)
Dunstable Road Tilsworth Dunstable
Tel **Leighton Buzzard 210721/2**
Mem 160
Sec
Pro Nick Webb Tel Leighton Buzzard 210721
Holes 9 L 2773 yds SSS 35
V'trs U
Fees £3 (£4) 18 holes
Loc 2 miles N of Dunstable on A5

Wyboston Lakes (1978)

Private (Map 2/13)
Wyboston
Tel **Huntingdon 219200**
Mem 70 Season ticket holders
Sec B Chinn Tel Huntingdon 219200
Pro P Ashwell Tel Huntingdon 212501
Holes 18 L 5688 metres SSS 69
Recs Am–
Pro–
V'trs SOC
Fees 18 holes £2.50 (W/E–£4 before noon. £3.50 after noon), 9 holes £1.50 (£2.50)
Loc S of St Neots off A1 and St Neots by-pass
Mis Pay and play

Woburn

(See Bucks, Berks & Oxon)

Bucks, Berks & Oxon

Abbey Hill (1975)

Public (Map 2/1)
Monks Way Two Ash Milton Keynes MK8 8AA
Tel **Milton Keynes 562408**
Mem 350
Sec Mrs SA Dimmock Tel MK 542513
Pro D Marcks Tel MK 563845
Holes 18 L 6193 yds SSS 69
Recs Am–67 T Mernagh
Pro–67 Hogan Stott
V'trs U
Fees On application
Loc 2 miles S of Stony Stratford

Badgemore Park (1972)

Private (Map 2/2)
Henley-on-Thames
Tel **0491 572206**
Mem 750
Sec LA Booker
Pro M Howell Tel 0491 574175
Holes 18 L 6112 yds SSS 69
Recs Am–67 SJ Mann
Pro–65 M Howell
V'trs WD–U; SOC; W/E–M
Fees £10–£14
Loc ¾ mile W of Henley-on-Thames on the B290 Henley to Rotherfield Greys/Peppard road

Beaconsfield (1914)

Private (Map 2/3)
Beaconsfield Bucks HP9 2UR
Tel **Beaconsfield 6545**
Mem 862
Sec MJR Hunter Tel Beaconsfield 6545
Pro M Brothers Tel Beaconsfield 6616
Holes 18 L 6469 yds SSS 71
Recs Am–69 ID Wheater
Pro–63 E Murray
V'trs WD–I; W/E–N/A
Fees £12
Loc 8 miles N of Slough

Bearwood (1986)

Private (Map 2/4)
Mole Road Sindlesham RG11 5DN
Tel **Aborfield Cross 760060**
Mem 570
Sec Major HD Burke
Pro Barry Tustin Tel Arborfield Cross 760060
Holes 9 L 2780 yds Par 35
Recs Am–
Pro–
V'trs M H SOC
Fees £1.75
Loc On B3030 to Arborfield M4 Junction 10 or 11
Mis 9 hole pitch and putt

Berkshire (1928)

Private (Map 2/5)
Ascot
Tel **Ascot 21495**
Mem 935
Sec Major PD Clarke Tel Ascot 21496
Pro KA Macdonald Tel Ascot 22351
Holes Red Course 18 L 6356 yds SSS 70
Blue Course 18 L 6258 yds SSS 70
Recs Red Course Am–None
Pro–None
Blue Course Am–None
Pro–None
V'trs WD–I; W/E and BH–M
Fees
Loc 3 miles Ascot on A332

Bremhill Park (1967)

Private (Map 2/6)
Shrivenham Swindon Wilts
Tel **782946**
Mem
Sec MJ Jefferies Tel Shrivenham 783202
Pro Andrew Cook Tel Shrivenham 782946
Holes 18 L 5889 yds SSS 70
Recs Am–68
Pro–67
V'trs U
Fees £5 (£8)
Loc 4 miles E of Swindon

Buckingham (1914)

Private (Map 2/7)
Tingewick Road Buckingham MK18 4AE
Tel **0280 813282**
Mem 600
Sec D Rolph Tel 0280 815566
Pro C Kaminski Tel 0280 815210
Holes 18 L 6082 yds SSS 69
Recs Am–71 RJ Gillam
Pro–
V'trs WD–U; W/E–M; SOC
Fees £10
Loc 1½ miles on Oxford Road

Burford (1936)

Private (Map 2/9)
Burford OX8 4JG
Tel **Burford 2149**
Mem 680
Sec R Cane Tel Burford 2583
Pro N Allen Tel Burford 2344
Holes 18 L 6405 yds SSS 71
Recs Am–67 DE Giles
Pro–67 H Weetman
V'trs WD–U; W/E & BH–M; H
Fees
Loc 19 miles W of Oxford on A40

Burnham Beeches (1891)

Private (Map 2/8)
Burnham Slough SL1 8EG
Tel **Burnham 61150**
Mem 670
Sec AJA Perkins Tel Burnham 61448
Pro Tony Buckner Tel Burnham 61661
Holes 18 L 6415 yds SSS 71
Recs Am–67 M Orris
Pro–66 John O'Leary
V'trs WD–I; W/E & BH–M
Fees £13 D–£15
Loc 4 miles W of Slough

Calcot Park (1930)

Private (Map 2/10)
Calcot nr Reading
Tel **Reading 427124**
Mem 700
Sec SD Chisholm
Pro Kim Brake Tel Reading 427797
Holes 18 L 6283 yds SSS 70
Recs Am–66 SA Scott
Pro–63 Craig Defoy
V'trs WD–U; W/E & BH–M
Fees £12
Loc 3 miles W of Reading on A4

Cherwell Edge
(see Northamptonshire)

Chesham and Ley Hill (1919)
Private (Map 2/12)
The Club House Ley Hill Chesham HP5 1UZ
Tel **0494 784541**
Mem 380
Sec RJ Carter Tel 0494 784541
Pro None
Holes 9 L 5158 yds SSS 65
Recs Am–67 GL Keen
Pro–69 TE Lebroge
V'trs Mon Wed Thu–U; Fri–U before 1 pm M after 1 pm; Tue–M after 3 pm; W/E–M; SOC Wed Thu
Fees £4.50
Loc 2 miles from Chesham
Mis Course closed Sun after 2 pm 1/4–30/9

Chesterton (1973)
Private (Map 2/13)
Chesterton nr Bicester Oxon OX6 8TE
Tel **Bicester 241204**
Mem 550
Sec BT Carter Tel Bic 241204
Pro Stephen Wynn Tel Bic 242023
Holes 18 L 6496 yds SSS 71
Recs Am–68
Pro–68
V'trs WD–U; W/E & BH–H SOC on WD
Fees —
Loc 2 miles SW Bicester

Chiltern Forest Golf Club (1921)
Private (Map 2/14)
Aston Hill Halton Aylesbury HP22 5NQ
Tel **Aylesbury 630899**
Mem 400
Man David G Smith Tel Aylesbury 631267
Pro G Skeet
Holes 9 L 5724 yds SSS 69
Recs Am–66 N Lucas D Evans
Pro–None
V'trs WD–U; W/E–M; SOC
Fees £7
Loc 5 miles SE of Aylesbury

Chipping Norton (1932)
Private (Map 2/15)
Southcombe Chipping Norton
Tel Chipping Norton 2383
Mem 290
Sec BA Hull Tel Long Compton 279
Pro Robert Gould Tel CN 3356
Holes 9 L 6137 yds SSS 69
Recs Am–67 A Perrie
Pro–
V'trs WD–U; W/E–M
Fees £8
Loc 1 mile E of town

Datchet (1890)
Private (Map 2/16)
Buccleuch Road Datchet
Tel **Slough 43887**
Mem 200 50 (L) 25 (J) 110 (5)
Sec Sqd Ldr WJ Brooks
Pro P Stanwick Tel Slough 42755
Holes 9 L 5978 yds SSS 69
Recs Am–66 R Blyfield
Pro–63 N Wood
V'trs WD–U before 3 pm only; after 3 pm and W/E–M
Fees £7 D–£10
Loc 2 miles Slough Windsor

Denham (1910)
Private (Map 2/17)
Tilehouse Lane Denham UB9 5DE
Tel **Denham 832022**
Mem 550
Sec Wing Commander D Graham Tel Denham 832022
Pro J Sheridan Tel Denham 832801
Holes 18L 6439 yds SSS 71
Recs Am–66 DMA Steel
Pro–68 J Sheridan
V'trs WD–Mon–Thu I H; WE–Fri–Sun+BH–M
Fees £11 D–£18
Loc 3 miles NW of Uxbridge

Downshire (1973)
Public (Map 2/18)
Easthampstead Park Wokingham
Tel **Bracknell 424066**
Mem 280
Sec Geoffrey Legouix
Pro Geoffrey Legouix
Holes 18 L 6382 yds SSS 70
Recs Am–67 T Smith
Pro–66 M King
V'trs U SOC
Fees summer £4.50; winter £3
Loc Off 9 Mile Road
Mis Easthampstead GC and Downshire GC play over this course

East Berkshire (1904)
Private (Map 2/19)
Ravenswood Ave Crowthorne
Tel **Crowthorne 772041**
Mem 700
Sec WH Short
Pro Arthur Roe Tel Crowthorne 774112
Holes 18 L 6315 yds SSS 70
Recs Am–65 J Davies
Pro–65 Neil Coles
V'trs I; W/E & BH–M SOC
Fees £15
Loc Near Crowthorne Station

Easthampstead (1973)
Public (Map 2/20)
Easthampstead Park, Wokingham
Tel **Bracknell 424066**
Mem
Sec
Pro Geoffrey Legouix Tel Bracknell 424066
Holes Play over Downshire

Ellesborough (1906)
Private (Map 2/21)
Butlers Cross nr Aylesbury HP17 OTZ
Tel **Wendover 622375**
Mem 780
Sec KM Ratcliff Tel Wendover 622114
Pro S Watkins Tel Wendover 623126
Holes 18 L 6207 yds SSS 70
Recs Am–66 N Lucas NM Allen P Stevens
Pro–68 G Will
V'trs WE+BH–I or H; SOC on WD
Fees £14
Loc 1 mile W of Wendover

Eton College (1973)
Private (Map 2/22)
Eton College Windsor
Tel **Windsor 66461**
Mem 500
Sec PTC Croker Tel Windsor 55299
Pro –
Holes 9 L 3560 yds SSS 58
Recs Am–55 DL Morkill
Pro–
V'trs None
Fees –
Loc –

Farnham Park (1974)
Public (Map 2/23)
Park Road Stoke Poges Slough
Tel **Farnham Common 3332**
Mem 448
Sec BJ Massingham Tel Burnham 61521
Pro Stuart Cannon
Holes 18 L 5847 yds SSS 68
Recs Am–69 N Harrison D Ivall
Pro–68 T Bowers
V'trs U
Fees £3.10 (£4.20) OAPs £2.50
Loc 2 miles N of Slough

Flackwell Heath (1920)
Private (Map 2/24)
High Wycombe HP10 9PE
Tel **Bourne End 20027**
Mem 685
Sec Major DJW Lampard Tel Bourne End 20929
Pro B Plucknett Tel Bourne End 23017
Holes 18 L 6150 yds SSS 69
Recs Am–67 AJ Finch
Pro–68 I Roberts
V'trs WD–I or H SOC; W/E–M
Fees £10
Loc Between High Wycombe & Beaconsfield off the A40 Turn-off 3 M40 from London

Frilford Heath (1908)
Private (Map 2/25)
Frilford Heath Abingdon OX13 5NW
Tel **Frilford Heath 390428**
Mem 750
Sec AH Greenwood
Pro DC Craik Tel FH 390887
Holes Red Course 18 L 6768 yds SSS 73
Green Course 18 L 6006 yds SSS 69
Recs Red Course Am–68 W Humphreys GG Benson
Pro–
Green Course Am–65 GRD Eyles KR Gough
Pro–
V'trs WD–U; W/E & BH–By arrangement
Fees £15 (£20)
Loc 3 miles W of Abingdon on A338 Oxford/Wantage road

Gerrards Cross (1934)
Private (Map 2/26)
Chalfont Park Gerrards Cross SL9 0QA
Tel **Gerrards Cross 883263**
Mem 780
Sec AM Granger-Brown
Pro AP Barr Tel Gerrards Cross 885300
Holes 18 L 6305 yds SSS 70
Recs Am–65 JB Berney
Pro–63 AP Barr
V'trs WD–H; W/E and BH–M
Fees £13 (£9 after 3 pm)
Loc 1 mile from station off A413

Goring and Streatley (1890)

Private (Map 2/27)
Streatley-on-Thames
Tel **Goring 872688**
Mem 740 110 (L) 80 (J) 120 (5)
Sec J Menzies Tel Goring 873229
Pro R Mason Tel Goring 873715
Holes 18 L 6232 yds SSS 70
Recs Am–65 DG Lane
Pro–65 C DeFoy
V'trs WD–U; W/E & BH–M SOC on WD
Fees £11.50
Loc 10 miles NW of Reading on A417

Harewood Downs (1908)

Private (Map 2/28)
Cokes Lane Chalfont St Giles
Tel **Little Chalfont 2308**
Mem 350
Sec RM Lennard Tel Little Chalfont 2184
Pro GC Morris Tel Little Chalfont 4102
Holes 18 L 5958 yds SSS 69
Recs Am–65 AL Parsons
Pro–65 JM Hume
V'trs WD–H; W/E and BH–M; SOC
Fees
Loc A413 to Amersham

Hawthorn Hill (1985)

Public (Map 2/58)
Drift Road Hawthorn Hill Maidenhead
Tel **Maidenhead (0628) 75588**
Mem
Sec Clive D Smith
Pro G Crisp, G Edmonds
Holes 18 L 6212 yds SSS 70
Recs Am–
Pro–
V'trs U
Fees £5.20 (£6.30) incl VAT
Loc 4 miles S of Maidenhead on A330
Mis 24 bay floodlit driving range; snooker; 90-seater restaurant; clubhouse and licensed bar

Hazlemere G & CC (1982)

Private (Map 2/56)
Penn Road Hazlemere High Wycombe Bucks HP15 7LR
Tel **High Wycombe 714722**
Mem 560
Sec DE Hudson Tel High Wycombe 714722
Pro Steve Morvell Tel High Wycombe 718098
Holes 18 L 5706 yds SSS 68
V'trs WD–U WE–booking necessary SOC on WD
Fees £10 (£14)
Loc 3 miles NE of High Wycombe on B474
Mis Buggies available for hire

Henley (1908)

Private (Map 2/29)
Harpsden Henley-on-Thames
Tel **Henley-on-Thames 573304**
Mem 720
Sec B Lovelock Tel Henley-on-Thames 575742
Pro J Cook Tel Henley-on-Thames 575710
Holes 18 L White 6329 yds SSS 70
yellow 6130 yds SSS 69
green 5902 yds SSS 68
Recs Am–68 M Orris, N Farmar
Pro–66 M Howell
V'trs WD–U; W/E–M
Fees WD–£12 (D–£12)
W/E–£15 (D–£15)
Loc 1 mile station

Huntercombe (1901)

Private (Map 2/30)
Nuffield, Henley-on-Thames RG9 5SL
***Tel* Nettlebed 641207 (V'trs 641472)**
Mem 630
Sec JP Bromley
Pro JB Draycott Tel 641241
Holes 18 L 6261 yds SSS 70
Recs Am–65 A Jackson
Pro–63 J Morris
V'trs U
Fees £12.50 (Sat/Sun £17.50 after 10.30 am) Four balls not allowed WE–3 balls not allowed
Loc 6 miles W Henley-on-Thames on A423

Hurst (1979)

Public (Map 2/31)
Dinton Pastures Davis Street Hurst Reading
Tel **Twyford 345143**
Mem
Sec
Pro G Legouix
Holes 9 L 3015 yds
Recs Am–
Pro–
V'trs U
Fees £1.60
Loc 5 miles Reading

Iver (1983)

Private (Map 2/53)
Hollow Hill Lane Iver Bucks SL0 0JJ
Tel **Iver 655615**
Mem 300
Man Terry Notley
Pro Terry Notley
Holes 9 L 6214 yds SSS 69
V'trs U SOC
Fees 18 holes £3 (£4)
Loc 1 mile to Langley station (nr Slough) off Langley Park Road

Ivinghoe (1967)

Private (Map 2/32)
Ivinghoe nr Leighton Buzzard
Tel **Cheddington 668696**
Mem 200
Sec AA Spencer
Pro PW Garrad Tel 668696
Holes 9 L 4508 yds SSS 62
Recs Am–61 J Dillon
Pro–60 R Garrad
V'trs U
Fees £3 (£3.50)
Loc Tring 3 miles Dunstable 2 miles

Lavender Park Golf Centre

Public (Map 2/33)
Swinley Road Ascot
Tel **Winkfield Row 884074**
Mem
Sec
Pro B Cutt
Holes 9 L 1104 SSS 27
Recs Am–
Pro–
V'trs U
Fees £1.20 (£1.40)
Loc
Mis Driving range

Little Chalfont (1981)

Private (Map 2/34)
Lodge Lane Little Chalfont nr Amersham Bucks
Tel **Little Chalfont 4877**
Mem 450
Sec JM Dunne
Pro Peter Gibbins
Holes 9 L 5852 yds SSS 68
Recs Am–76 D Brown
Pro–68 D Elliott
V'trs WD–U; W/EM
Fees £5 (£7)
Loc 1½ miles from station

Maidenhead (1898)

Private (Map 2/35)
Shoppenhangers Road Maidenhead
Tel **Maidenhead 20545**
Mem 450
Sec Brian Kirby Maidenhead 24693
Pro R Newman Tel Maidenhead 24067
Holes 18 L 6360 yds SSS 70
Recs Am–66 M Briggs
Pro–64, AN Walker
G Wolstenholme
V'trs WD–Before 4.30 by request After 4.30–M; W/E–M
Fees £11
Loc ½ mile Maidenhead station

Newbury and Crookham (1873)

Private (Map 2/36)
Bury's Bank Greenham Common Newbury
Tel **Newbury 40035**
Mem 626
Sec RF Church Tel Newbury 40035
Pro DW Harris Tel Newbury 31201
Holes 18 L 5880 yds SSS 68
Recs Am–63 D Rosier
Pro–61 M Howell
V'trs WD–U; W/E–M (Recognised Club Members) H
Fees £10
Loc 2 miles SE Newbury

North Oxford (1908)

Private (Map 2/37)
Banbury Road Oxford
Tel **(0865) 54415**
Mem 791
Sec W Forster Tel (0865) 54924
Pro P Lester Tel (0865) 53977
Holes 18 L 5805 yds SSS 67
Recs Am–65 S Donaghey
Pro–61 Max Faulkner
V'trs U
Fees £10 (£20)
Loc Between Oxford and Kidlington

Reading (1910)

Private (Map 2/38)
Kidmore End Road Emmer Green Reading RG4 8SG
Tel **Reading 472169**
Mem 688
Sec ANH Weekes Tel Reading 472909
Pro J Larrad Tel Reading 477359
Holes 18 L 6204 yds SSS 69
Recs Am–65, MG King
Pro–64 AP Morley
V'trs WD–U; W/E & BH–M
Fees £11
Loc 2 miles N of city off Peppard Road (B481)

RMCS Shrivenham

(See Wiltshire)

Royal Air Force Benson (1975)

Private **(Map 2/55)**
Royal Air Force Benson Oxon
Tel **(0491) 37766**
Mem 150
Sec
Holes 9 (18 Tees) L 4214 yds SSS 61
V'trs Visitors only by prior arrangement with Sec due to inherent access problems to course
Fees D–£2; no reductions for longer periods
Loc RAF Benson airfield: $3\frac{1}{2}$ miles NE of Wallingford

Royal Ascot (1887)

Private **(Map 2/39)**
Winkfield Road Ascot
Tel **Ascot 22923**
Mem 620
Sec Jim Young Tel Ascot 25175
Pro Clive Dell Tel Ascot 24656
Holes 18 L 5653 yds SSS 67
Recs Am–66 S Smith
Pro–
V'trs WD–U before 5 pm otherwise M
Fees £8 (£12) Soc/Parties 10 minimum £7 (£10)
Loc Bracknell 3 miles Windsor 4 miles

The Royal Household GC

Private **(Map 2/54)**
Buckingham Palace London SW1
Tel **01-930 4832**
Mem 200
Sec A Jarred
Holes 9 L 4524 yds SSS 62
V'trs Strictly by invitation and then only with a member
Loc The Home Park Private Windsor Castle

Sonning (1914)

Private **(Map 2/40)**
Sonning-on-Thames
Tel **Reading 693332**
Mem 500
Sec PF Williams
Pro RT McDougall Tel Readng 692910
Holes 18 L 6345 yds SSS 70
Recs Am–66 MT Rapley
Pro–65 B Lane
V'trs WD–U; W/E–M
Fees On application
Loc South side A4 nr Sonning

Southfield (1875)

Private **(Map 2/41)**
Hill Top Road Oxford OX4 1PF
Tel **Oxford 242158 and 242656**
Mem 500
Sec AG Hopcraft Tel Oxford 242158
Pro A Rees Tel Oxford 244258
Holes 18 L 6230 yds SSS 70
Recs Am–66 CM Barrett GL Morley
Pro–61 A Rees
V'trs WD–U; W/E & BH–M–H; SOC
Fees £11
Loc 2 miles E of city centre

Stoke Poges (1908)

Private **(Map 2/42)**
Park Road Stoke Poges SL2 4PG
Tel **Slough 26385**
Mem 700
Sec FA Tilley
Pro K Thomas Tel Slough 23609
Holes 18 L 6654 yds SSS 72
Recs Am–65 BA Price
Pro–65 J Hudson
V'trs WD–I or H; W/E & BH–M
Fees £14 (£8)
Loc 2 miles N of Slough

Stowe

Private **(Map 2/57)**
Stowe Buckingham Bucks MK18 5EH
Tel **(0280) 813650**
Mem 300
Sec Mrs SA Cross Tel (0280) 813684
Pro
Holes 9 L 4573 yds SSS 63
Recs Am–
Pro–
V'trs WD from dawn–1 pm and after 7 pm WE–as WD (no restrictions during school holidays) M SOC
Fees
Loc From Junction 16 M1–A5–A43–A413 4 miles from Buckingham on A413 to Brickley

Sunningdale

(See Surrey)

Swinley Forest (1909)

Private **(Map 2/43)**
Near Ascot
Tel **Ascot 20197**
Mem **250**
Sec **TW Ingham**
Pro **RC Parker**
Holes **18 L 6001 yds**
Recs **Am–64 EF Storey ER Sermon**
Pro–64 P Alliss
V'trs **M**
Fees **–**
Loc **S of Ascot**

Tadmarton Heath (1922)

Private **(Map 2/44)**
Wigginton Banbury OX15 5HL
Tel **0608 737649**
Mem 600
Sec RE Wackrill Tel 0608 737278
Pro Les Bond Tel 0608 730047
Holes 18 L 5917 yds SSS 69
Recs Am–68 J Fisher
Pro–65 P Cowen J Fowler
V'trs WD–UH; W/E–M or I
Fees £12
Loc 5 miles W of Banbury off B4035

Temple (1909)

Private **(Map 2/45)**
Henley Road Hurley Maidenhead
Tel **Littlewick Green 4248**
Mem **500**
Sec Capt RM Brounger Tel Littlewick Green 4795
Pro Alan Dobbins Tel Littlewick Green 4254
Holes 18 L 6206 yds SSS 70
Recs Am–67 R Berney
Pro–
V'trs WD–I SOC; W/E & BH–M
Fees £16
Loc Between Maidenhead and Henley A423

West Berkshire (1975)

Private **(Map 2/46)**
Chaddleworth Newbury
Tel **04882-574**
Mem 300
Sec Norman Edwards
Pro FS Boobyer
Holes 18 L 7053 yds SSS 74
Recs Am–74 J Pocock
Pro–69 M Howell B Laing
V'trs U SOC
Fees £6 (£7)
Loc M4 Junction 14 on 338 to Wantage

Weston Turville (1974)

Private **(Map 2/47)**
New Road Weston-Turville nr Aylesbury HP2 5QT
Tel **Aylesbury 24084**
Mem 350
Sec AK Holden
Pro Steve Harlock
Holes 13 L 6782 SSS 72
Recs Am–72 J Pursell
Pro–
V'trs U (Except Sun before 12 am)
Fees £5 (£7)
Loc $2\frac{1}{2}$ miles SE of Aylesbury

Wexham Park (1979)

Public **(Map 2/48)**
Wexham Street Wexham nr Slough Berkshire
Tel **Fulmer 3271**
Mem 450 50(L) 50(J) 50(5)
Sec JWE Mulley Tel Slough 24615
Pro D Morgan Tel Fulmer 3425
Holes Wexham 18 L 5836 yds SSS 68
Old Grange 9 L 2383 yds SSS 32
Recs Am–
Pro–
V'trs U SOC on WD
Fees 18 hole course £3.50 (£4.90)
9 hole course £2.40 (£3)
Loc 2 miles N of Slough

Whiteleaf (1904)

Private **(Map 2/49)**
Whiteleaf Aylesbury
Tel **Princes Risborough 3097**
Mem 250
Sec LS Edwards
Pro KS Ward Tel PR 5472
Holes 9 L 2756 yds SSS 66
Recs Am–64 M Copping
Pro–63, MM Caines
V'trs WD–U; W/E–M
Fees £9 (36 holes)
Loc Princes Risborough 2 miles

Windmill Hill (1972)

Public **(Map 2/50)**
Tattenhoe Lane Bletchley Milton Keynes Bucks MK3 7RB
Sec Colin Clingan Tel 0908 78623
Pro Colin Clingan
Recs Am–69 RJ Long
Pro–66 C Defoy
Holes 18 L 6773 yds SSS 72
V'trs U SOC
Fees £3.15 (£4.40)
Loc 4 miles M1 Exit 13, A421
Mis Floodlit driving range

Winter Hill (1976)

Private **(Map 2/51)**
Grange Lane Cookham Berkshire SL6 9RP
Tel **Bourne End 27613**

Mem 600
Sec GB Charters-Rowe
Pro P Hedges Tel Bourne End 27610
Holes 18 L 6432 yds SSS 71
Recs Am–70
Pro–
V'trs U; only after 12 noon W/E & BH
Fees £11 (£13)
Loc 3 miles from Maidenhead Centre

Woburn (1976)

Private (Map 2/52)
Bow Brickhill Milton Keynes
Tel **0908 70756**
Mem
Man Alex Hay
Pro Alex Hay Tel 0908 647987
Holes Duke's 18 L 6913 yds SSS 74
Duchess 18 L 6641 yds SSS 72
Recs Am–68 Duke's; 70 Duchess
Pro–Duke's 65 Robert Lee
V'trs WD–H (by prior arrangement); W/E–M
Fees By arrangement
Loc 4 miles W of M1 exit 13

Essex

Abridge G & CC (1964)

Private (Map 1/1)
Epping Lane Stapleford Tawney Essex RM4 1ST
Tel **Stapleford (04028) 388**
Mem 560
Sec PG Pelling Tel (04028) 396/7
Pro Bernard Cooke Tel (04028) 333
Holes 18 L 6703 yds SSS 72
Recs Am–68 NK Burch (Old Course)
Pro–68 David Feherty
V'trs WD–H; Sat–M; Sun–N/A; SOC
Fees £14
Loc Theydon Bois or Epping Station 3 miles
Mis Corporate membership available; no catering Fri

Ballards Gore (1980)

Private (Map 1/43)
Gore Road Canewdon Nr Rochford Essex
Tel **Canewdon 8917**
Mem 450+
Sec NG Patient Tel Canewdon 8917
Pro Mark Pierce Tel Canewdon 8924
Holes 18 L 7062 yds SSS 74
V'trs WD–U; WE–M after 12.30 pm summer, after 11.30 am winter; SOC
Fees WD £10
Loc 1½ miles NE of Rochford town centre

Basildon (1967)

Public (Map 1/2)
Kingswood Basildon
Tel **Basildon 3297**
Mem 250 30 (L) 30 (J)
Sec AM Burch Tel 0268 3849
Pro W Paterson Tel 0268 3532
Holes 18 L 6120 yds SSS 69
Recs Am–68 N Burch
Pro–63 W Longmuir
V'trs U SOC
Fees £1.95 (£4.30)
Loc Basildon

Belfairs Park (1926)

Public (Map 1/3)
Eastwood Road Leigh-on-Sea
Tel **Southend 525345**
Pro Roger Foreman
Holes 18 L 5857 yds SSS 68
Recs Am–68 I De'Ath
Pro–R Foreman
V'trs U
Fees £2.50 (£5)
Loc
Mis Southend-on-Sea and Belfairs clubs play here

Belfairs (1926)

Private (Map 1)
Eastwood Road Leigh-on-Sea Essex SS9 4LR
Tel **Southend 526911**
Mem 280
Sec RCP Hunter Tel 520322
Holes Play over Belfairs Park Municipal

Belhus Park Municipal (1972)

Public (Map 1/4)
South Ockendon
Tel **South Ockendon 854260**
Pro S Wimbleton
Holes 18 L 5701 SSS 68
Recs Am–67 M Jennings J Bearman
Pro–63 R Joyce
V'trs U
Fees £3 (£4)
Loc 1 mile N A13 London/Southend Road
Mis Thurrock club plays here

Bentley G & CC (1972)

Private (Map 1/5)
Ongar Road Brentwood
Tel **Brentwood 73179**
Mem 475
Sec JA Vivers Tel Brentwood 73179
Pro Keith Bridges Tel Brentwood 72933
Holes 18 L 6709 yds SSS 72
Recs Am–69
Pro–67
V'trs WD–U; W/E–M–afternoon; SOC on WD
Fees £8 D–£10
Loc 18 miles E of London

Birch Grove (1970)

Private (Map 1/6)
Layer Road Kingsford Colchester
Tel **Layer de la Haye 276**
Mem 230
Sec W Kerridge Tel 0206 240678 (Res)
Pro —
Holes 9 L 2828 yds SSS 54
Recs Am–55 S Short P Emerson
Pro–56
V'trs U WE–not before 1.30 pm Sun
Fees £3.50 (£4)
Loc 2 miles S of town

Boyce Hill (1921)

Private (Map 1/2)
Vicarage Hill Benfleet SS7 1PD
Tel **South Benfleet 3625**
Mem 500
Sec EJW Goodman Tel South Benfleet 3625
Pro G Burroughs Tel South Benfleet 52565
Holes 18 L 5882 yds SSS 68
Recs Am–65 RCD Gilbert
Pro–61 G Burroughs
V'trs W/E & BH–M–H; SOC Thu only; WD–U; H
Fees £10 PR; £10 PD
Loc 4 miles N of Southend

Braintree (1892)

Private (Map 1/8)
Kings Lane Stisted Braintree CM7 8DA
Tel **Braintree 24117**
Mem 600
Sec KW Reddall
Pro Tony Parcell Tel Braintree 43465
Holes 18 L 6026 yds SSS 69
Recs Am–65 M Hawes M Davis
Pro–
V'trs U (Sunday–M after noon); SOC
Fees £12 per day
Loc 1½ miles N of town

Bunsay Downs (1982)

Private (Map 1/10)
Little Baddow Road Woodham Walter nr Maldon Essex
Tel **Danbury 2648**
Man G Pike Tel Danbury 2369
Pro Gary Pike Tel Danbury 2648
Holes 9 L 2913 yds SSS 68
V'trs U BH & WE teeing-off times may be pre-booked up to 7 days in advance
Fees 9 holes £3.50; 18 holes £4.50
Loc 7 miles E of Chelmsford

Burnham-on-Crouch (1923)

Private (Map 1/11)
Creeksea Burnham-on-Crouch
Tel **Maldon 0621-782282**
Mem 450
Sec DG Morrison
Pro –
Holes 9 L 5866 yds SSS 68
Recs Am–66 D Clarke
Pro–64 FJ Winser
V'trs U (Not before noon W/E)
Fees £7 (£9)
Loc 1½ miles W of town

Canons Brook (1962)

Private (Map 1/12)
Elizabeth Way, Harlow
Tel **Harlow 21482**
Mem 650
Sec DF Moule
Pro D Scott Tel Harlow 444447
Holes 18 L 6745 yds SSS 73
Recs Am–68 H Cornick
Pro–65 G Burroughs
V'trs WD–U; W/E & BH–NA
Fees £9
Loc 25 miles N of London

Channels (1983)

Private (Map 1/13)
Belsteads Farm Lane, Little Waltham Chelmsford
Tel **Chelmsford 440005**
Mem 650
Sec SM Everitt Tel Chelmsford 440005
Pro IB Sinclair Tel Chelmsford 441056
Holes 18 L 6033 yds SSS 69
Recs
V'trs WD; SOC on WD
Fees £8.75
Loc 3 miles N of Chelmsford
Mis Pitch and putt course

Chelmsford (1892)

Private (Map 1/14)
Widford Chelmsford
Tel **Chelmsford 50555**
Mem 650
Sec Wg Cdr BA Templeman-Rooke Tel Chelmsford 56483
Pro GD Bailey Tel Chelmsford 57079
Holes 18 L 5912 yds SSS 68
Recs Am–67 G Turner
Pro–65 C Platts
V'trs WD–I; W/E & BH–M
Fees On application
Loc Off A12 at Widford roundabout

Chigwell (1925)

Private (Map 1/15)
High Road Chigwell IG7 5BH
Tel **01-500 2059**
Mem 650
Sec Mrs P King
Pro C Baker Tel 01-500 2384
Holes 18 L 6279 yds SSS 70
Recs Am–66 AM Ronald
Pro–66 H Flatman
V'trs WD–I; W/E & BH–M
Fees £9; D–£12
Loc 13½ miles NE of London A113

Chingford (1923)

Public (Map 1/16)
158 Station Road Chingford London E4
Tel **Silverthorne 529 2107**
Mem 350
Sec F Singleton Tel 01-527 6548
Pro LH and Robin Gowers Tel 01-529 5708
Holes 18 L 6136 yds SSS 70
Recs Am–65 Peter Barnes
Pro–65 Robin Gowers
V'trs U
Fees –
Loc
Mis Red coats must be worn

Clacton (1892)

Private (Map 1/17)
West Road Clacton-on-Sea CO15 1AJ
Tel **Clacton-on-Sea 424331**
Mem 475
Sec IM Simpson Tel Clacton 421919
Pro SJ Levermore Tel Clacton-on-Sea 426304
Holes 18 L 6217 yds SSS 70
Recs Am–67 A Hull
Pro–65 S Bryan
V'trs W/E and BH 1st tee not before 11 am, 10th tee not before 12.30 pm H; SOC
Fees D–£9 (D–£12)
Loc In town boundary on sea front

Colchester (1909)

Private (Map 1/18)
Braiswick Colchester CO4 5AU
Tel **Colchester 852946**
Mem 330 90(L) 70(J) 160(5)
Sec PM Warburton Tel 853396
Pro P Hodgson Tel 853920
Holes 18 L 6319 yds SSS 70
Recs Am–66 B Booth
Pro–68 A Parcell
V'trs WD–H W/E & BH–NA
Fees £8 (£12)
Loc ¾ mile NW of Colchester North station on road to West Bergholt

Forrester Park (1975)

Private (Map 1/44)
Beckingham Road Great Totham Maldon Essex
Tel **Maldon 891406**
Mem 270
Man T Forrester-Muir Tel Maldon 891406
Holes 9 L 2675 yds (5350 yds) SSS 66
V'trs U; SOC on WD
Fees £4 (£6)
Loc 3 miles from Maldon on Tiptree Road

Frinton (1896)

Private (Map 1/19)
1 The Esplanade Frinton-on-Sea Essex CO13 9EP
Tel **Frinton-on-Sea 4216**
Mem 700
Sec JR Dyer Tel Frinton-on-Sea 4618
Pro R Hall Tel 71618
Holes 18 L 6259 yds SSS 70; 9 L 2508 yds SSS 33
Recs Am–67 IA Quick
Pro–66 CS Denny
V'trs H SOC
Fees £10 D–£12; no green fees before 11.30 am WE & BH; 9 holes D–£4.50
Loc 18 miles E of Colchester
Mis Buggies for hire

Hainault Forest (1912)

Public (Map 1/20)
Chigwell Row Hainault Forest
Tel **01-500 2097**
Mem 500 60 (L) 50 (J)
Sec E Bayley Tel 01-590 0804
Pro AE Frost Tel 01-500 2131
Holes No 1 Course 18 L 5754 yds SSS 67
No 2 Course 18 L 6445 yds SSS 71
Recs No 1 Course Am–65 TG Patmore
Pro–65 A Frost
No 2 Course Am–66 K Saunders
Pro–68 AE Frost Jun
V'trs U
Fees £2.50 (£4.10)
Loc Hog Hill Redbridge

Hartswood (1967)

Public (Map 1/9)
King George's Playing Fields Brentwood
Tel 218714
Sec BL Farmer Tel Brentwood 218850
Pro J Stanion
Holes 18 L 6238 yds SSS 70
Recs Am–70 A Cornell
Pro–70 W Longmuir
V'trs U
Fees £2.70 (£4.20)
Loc Brentwood
Mis Hartswood club plays here. Societies welcome Tel Brentwood 218850

Harwich and Dovercourt (1906)

Private (Map 1/21)
Parkeston Road Harwich
Tel **Harwich 3616**
Mem 350
Sec BQ Dunham
Pro —
Holes 9 L 2931 yds SSS 68
Recs Am–
Pro–
V'trs WD–U; SOC
Fees On application
Loc A120 to roundabout to Parkeston Quay course entrance 20 yds on left

Havering

Public (Map 1/22)
Risebridge Chase Lower Bedfords Road Romford
Tel **0708 22942**
Mem
Sec/Pro P Jennings Tel 0708 41429
Holes 18 L 6252 yds SSS 70; 9 hole Par 3
Recs Am–
Pro–
V'trs WD–U; W/E–at certain times
Fees £2.95 (£4.50)
Loc 2 miles from Brentwood junction of M25–off A12
Mis Risebridge Club plays here

Ilford (1907)

Private (Map 1/23)
Wanstead Park Road Ilford Essex
Tel **01-554 5174**
Mem 579
Sec DGJ Hoare Tel 01-554 2930
Pro K Ashdown Tel 01-554 0094
Holes 18 L 5710 yds SSS 68
Recs Am–63 M Pinner
Pro–64 B Huggett A Campbell
V'trs U
Fees £6 (£9)
Loc

Maldon (1891)

Private (Map 1/24)
Beeleigh Langford Maldon CM9 7SS
Tel **Maldon 53212**
Mem 440
Sec JC Rigby Tel (0621) 53212
Pro —
Holes 9 L 5667 yds SSS 69
Recs Am–71 Byford
Pro–67 S Levermore
V'trs WD–U SOC; W/E–M
Fees £7 D–£9 (£8 D–£10)
Loc 3 miles NW Maldon on B1019

Manifold (1974)

Private (Map 1/25)
Colchester Road Tolleshunt D'Arcy nr Maldon
Tel **Maldon 860410**
Mem 350
Sec D Southgate
Pro J Phillips Tel Maldon 860576
Holes 18 L 6450 yds SSS 71
Recs Am–69 J Meakes
Pro–69 G Goldring
V'trs WD–U; W/E–M
Fees On application
Loc 8 miles S of Colchester off B1026

Maylands (1936)

Private (Map 1/26)
Harold Park Romford
Tel **Ingrebourne 42055**
Mem 600
Sec N/A Tel Ing 73080
Pro JS Hopkin Tel Ing 46466
Holes 18 L 6182 yds SSS 69
Recs Am–68 M Stokes
Pro–67 RA Knight
V'trs WD–I; W/E, BH–M

Fees £10
Loc 2 miles E of Romford 1 mile from Junction 28 on M25

Orsett (1898)

Private (Map 1/27)
Orsett
Tel **Grays Thurrock 891226**
Mem 800
Sec J Bissell Tel Grays Thurrock 891352
Pro G Roberts Tel Grays Thurrock 891302
Holes 18 L 6622 yds SSS 72
Recs Am–68 A Pollock I Quick
Pro–69 H Flatman
G Burroughs
V'trs WD–I; W/E & BH–NA
Fees £8 D–£10
Loc 2 miles from Grays

Pipps Hill

Private (Map 1/28)
Aquatels Recreation Centre Cranes Farm Road Basildon
Tel **Basildon 27278**
Mem
Sec
Pro
Holes 9 L 2829 yds SSS 67
Recs Am–
Pro–
V'trs WD–U; W/E–U
Fees On application
Loc Adjacent A127 London-Southend road

Risebridge (1973)

Public (Map 1/22)
Risebridge Chase Lower Bedford Road Havering Essex
Tel **(0708) 27376**
Mem
Sec Brian Wyles Tel (0708) 44581
Mis Play over Havering course

Rochford Hundred (1893)

Private (Map 1/29)
Rochford
Tel **Rochford 544302**
Mem 300 150(L) 60(J) 210(5)
Sec CB Wyatt
Pro GN Shipley
Holes 18 L 6256 yds SSS 70
Recs Am–65 DK Wood
Pro–69 FW Sutherland
V'trs WD–U; W/E–M
Fees On application
Loc 4 miles N of Southend-on-Sea

Romford (1894)

Private (Map 1/30)
Heath Drive Gidea Park Romford Essex RM2 5QB
Tel **Romford 40007 (Members)**
Mem 690
Sec W/Cdr J Hickox Tel 40986
Pro H Flatman Tel 49393
Holes 18 L 6377 yds SSS 70
Recs Am–67 A Bird
Pro–67 N Coles
V'trs WD–I SOC; W/E–NA
Fees £8 D–£12
Loc Gidea Park 1 mile E of Romford

Royal Epping Forest (1888)

Public (Map 1/31)
Forest Approach Station Road Chingford London E4
Tel **01-529 6407**
Mem 280 42 (L) 25 (J)
Sec To be appointed Tel 01-529 2195
Pro R Gowers Tel 01-529 2708
Holes 18 L 6620 yds SSS 70
Recs Am–68 A Johns
Pro–65 R Gowers
V'trs Booked times W/E. Must wear red garment
Fees £3.05 (£4.60)
Loc Bury Road London E4; 250 yds E of Chingford BR Stn
Mis Red coats or trousers compulsory

Saffron Walden

(See Cambridgeshire)

Skips (1973)

Private (Map 1/32)
Horsemanside Tysea Hill Stapleford Abbots RM4 1JU
Tel **Ingrebourne 48234**
Mem
Sec D Brautigan
Pro
Holes 18 L 6146 yds SSS 71
Recs Am–
Pro–
V'trs NA Season ticket holders only
Fees –
Loc 3 miles from Romford off B175

Southend-on-Sea (1953)

Public (Map 1/3)
Belfairs Park Southend-on-Sea
Tel **(0702) 524836**
Mem 80
Sec RL Steedon Tel (0702) 352925
Holes Play over Belfairs Municipal

Stoke by Nayland

(See Suffolk)

Theydon Bois (1897)

Private (Map 1/33)
Theydon Road Epping Essex CM16 4EH
Tel **Theydon Bois 2279**
Mem 600
Sec PP Shorter Tel Theydon Bois 3054
Pro D Edgar Tel Theydon Bois 2460
Holes 18 L 5472 yds SSS 68
Recs Am–67 SJ Allen
Pro–
V'trs Thu am restricted; WE–M
Fees £10 (£15)
Loc 1 mile S of Epping

Thorndon Park (1920)

Private (Map 1/34)
Ingrave Brentwood CM13 3RH
Tel **Brentwood 811666**
Mem 300 140(L) 60(J) 130(5)
Sec JE Leggitt Tel Brentwood 810345
Pro BV White Tel Brentwood 810736
Holes 18 L 6455 yds SSS 71
Recs Am–66 MES Davis
Pro–65 BJ Hunt B Waites
V'trs WD–I; W/E & BH–M
Fees £10
Loc 2 miles SE of Brentwood on A128

Thorpe Hall (1907)

Private (Map 1/35)
Thorpe Hall Avenue Thorpe Bay SS1 3AT
Tel **Southend 582050**
Mem 750
Sec RCP Hunter Tel Southend 582205
Pro Roger Smith Tel Southend 588195
Holes 18 L 6259 yds SSS 71
Recs Am–68 B Hillsden
Pro–67 L Platts
V'trs WD–H; WE & BH after 12 noon–H
Fees On application
Loc E of Southend-on-Sea

Three Rivers (1973)

Private (Map 1/40)
Stow Road Purleigh Nr Chelmsford Essex CM3 6RR
Tel **(0621) 828631**
Mem 600
Sec William S McGoff Tel (0621) 828631
Pro Lionel Platts Tel (0621) 828631
Holes 18 L 6609 yds SSS 72
9 L 1071 yds Par 3 course
Recs Am–
Pro–
V'trs WD–UI; W/E & BH–M; SOC Tue Thu mainly
Fees £10 R/D (WD)
Loc 5 miles S of Maldon
Mis Squash, tennis, swimming; catering and accommodation

Thurrock Belhus Park (1972)

(Map 1/4)
South Ockendon
Mem 302
Sec D Faust 11 Petworth Way Elm Park Hornchurch Essex Tel Hornchurch 46224
Holes Play over Belhus Park Course

Towerlands (1985)

Private (Map 1/45)
Panfield Road Braintree Essex CM7 5BJ
Tel **0376-26802**
Mem 290
Sec DJ Collar Tel 0376-26802
Pro
Holes 9 L 5406 yds SSS 66
Recs Am–
Pro–
V'trs WD–U WE–2 pm onwards SOC on WD
Fees 9 holes £3 18 holes £5 (£7)
Loc 1 mile NW of Braintree
Mis Indoor bowls; 3 squash courts; sports hall and equestrian

Upminster (1928)

Private (Map 1/36)
114 Hall Lane Upminster
Tel **Upminster 20249**
Mem 750
Sec Mrs J Wylie Tel Upminster 22788
Pro N Carr Tel Upminster 20000
Holes 18 L 5951 yds SSS 68

Recs Am–64 AT Bird
Pro–
V'trs WD–U; W/E & BH–NA
Fees £9
Loc ¾ mile from station

Wanstead (1893)

Private (Map 1/37)
Overton nr London E11
Tel **01-989 0604**
Mem 650
Sec BJ Preston Tel 01-989 3938; (01-989 0604 members)
Pro D Pugh Tel 01-989 9876
Holes 18 L 6262 yds SSS 70
Recs Am–64 BJ Hilsdon
Pro–66 CA Whitcombe
V'trs WD–I; W/E & BH–M
Fees £8
Loc Boundary with Epping Forest

Warley Park (1975)

Private (Map 1/38)
Magpie Lane Little Warley Brentwood
Tel **(0277) 224891**
Mem 600
Sec SP Greene
Pro F Sunderland Tel (0277) 212552
Holes 18 L 6261 yds SSS 70
9 L 3166 yds SSS 35
Recs Am–69 B Preston
V'trs WD–U; W/E–M
Fees £12
Loc 2 miles S of Brentwood

Warren (1932)

Private (Map 1/39)
Woodham Walter Maldon CM9 6RW
Tel **Dunbury 3198**
Mem 380 55(L) 70(J) 125(5)
Man WT Burke Tel Danbury 3258
Pro Mickey Walker Tel Danbury 4662
Holes 18 L 6211 yds SSS 69
Recs Am–66 C Laurence
Pro–66 H Flatman
V'trs WD–I; W/E–M
Fees £10 D–£12
Loc 7 miles E of Chelmsford

West Essex (1900)

Private (Map 1/41)
Sewardstonebury Chingford London E4 7QL
Tel **01-529 0928**
Mem 600
Sec Tel 01-529 7558
Pro C Cox Tel 01-529 4367
Holes White 18 L 6325 yds SSS 70
Yellow 18 L 5897 yds SSS 68
Recs Am–66 KG Budd
Pro–EE Whitcombe
V'trs WD–UH; W/E & BH–MH SOC (Mon/Wed/Fri)
Fees £10
Loc Bury Road, ¾ mile N Chingford Station

Woodford (1889)

Private (Map 1/42)
Sunset Avenue Woodford Green Essex
Tel **01-504 0553/01-504 4254**
Mem 400 64(L) 52(J) 80(5)
Sec IG Fowler Tel 01-504 3330
Pro Ashley Johns Tel 01-504 4254
Holes 9 L 5743 yds SSS 68
Recs Am–65 LW Burgess
Pro–
V'trs WD–U; W/E–M
Fees £4.50
Loc 11 miles NE of London

Hampshire

Alresford (1890)

Private (Map 2/1)
Cheriton Road Alresford SO24 0PN
Tel **Alresford 3153**
Mem 450
Sec Tel Alresford 3746
Pro M Scott Tel Alresford 3998
Holes 9 L 5923 yds SSS 68
Recs Am–
Pro–67 J Hay
V'trs U; W/E–after 11 am only
Fees £5 D–£6 (W/E & BH–£10)
Loc 1 mile S town centre

Alton (1908)

Private (Map 2/2)
Old Odiham Road Alton Hampshire GU34 4BU
Tel **Alton 82042**
Mem 335
Sec Ewart Barnett Tel Alton 82042/86485 (home)
Pro Martin Smith Tel 86518
Holes 9 L 5699 yds SSS 67
Recs Am–66 A Stevens
Pro–64 P Stanwick
V'trs U (exc comp days); SOC on WD
Fees £6 (£9) inc VAT
Loc 2 miles N Alton; 6 miles S Odiham; off A32

Ampfield Par Three (1963)

Private (Map 2/3)
Winchester Road Ampfield nr Romsey SO51 9BQ
Tel **Braishfield 68480**
Mem 500
Sec Mrs S Baker
Pro Ian Young Tel Braishfield 68750
Holes 18 L 2478 yds SSS 53
Recs Am–49 R Bailey
Pro–49 A Timms
V'trs WD–U; SOC–W/E Telephone first
Fees £3.60 (£6)
Loc On A31 Winchester to Romsey

Andover (1907)

Private (Map 2/4)
51 Winchester Road Andover Hants SP10 2EF
Tel **Andover 23980**
Mem 415 60 (L) 40 (J)
Sec DA Fairweather Tel Andover 58040
Pro A Timms Tel Andover 24151
Holes 9 L 5933 yds SSS 68
Recs Am–69 A Fairfoull
Pro–67 A Timms
V'trs WD–U SOC; W/E & BH–NA before noon
Fees £6 (£8)
Loc 1 mile S town centre

Army Golf Club (1883)

Private (Map 2/5)
Laffan's Road Aldershot GU11 2HF
Tel **Farnborough 541104**
Mem 600
Sec Michael Crouch Tel Farnborough 540638
Pro P Thompson Tel Farnborough 547232
Holes 18 L 6553 yds SSS 71
Recs Am–68 IL Pearce
Pro–69 I Young
V'trs WD–I; W/E–M
Fees £9 (special rates for Forces)
Loc Between Aldershot and Farnborough

Barton-on-Sea (1897)

Private (Map 2/6)
Marine Drive Barton-on-Sea BH25 7BY
Tel **New Milton 615308**
Mem 392 115(L) 35(J)
Sec CJ Wingfield
Pro Pat Coombs Tel New Milton 611210
Holes 18 L 5565 yds SSS 67
Recs Am–63 RM Tuddenham
Pro–66 P Alliss
V'trs H; WD–U; W/E & BH–NA before 11.15 am; SOC–Mon Wed Fri
Fees D/R £9 (£12)
Loc 1½ miles from New Milton Hants Junction 1 on M27

Basingstoke (1927)

Private (Map 2/7)
Kempshott Park Basingstoke RG23 7LL
Tel **Basingstoke 465990**
Mem 700
Sec PA Gill
Pro Ian Hayes Tel Bas 51332
Holes 18 L 6263 yds SSS 70
Recs Am–67 AJS Lowther
Pro–69 C de Bruin
V'trs WD–H; W/E–M; SOC–Wed Thu
Fees £9
Loc 3 miles W of Basingstoke on A30 M3 Exit 7

Basingstoke Hospitals

Private (Map 2/42)
Aldermaston Road Basingstoke Hants
Tel **0256 20347**
Mem 250
Man Tel 0256 20347
Holes 9 L 5480 yds SSS 67
V'trs WD–restricted play Wed after 4 pm; SOC
Fees £3.50 (£6)
Loc 1½ miles N of town centre

Bishopswood (1978)

Private (Map 2/8)
Bishopswood Lane Tadley Basingstone Hants
Tel **Tadley 5213**
Mem 350
Sec MW Phillips
Pro K Pickett
Holes 9 L 6494 SSS 71
Recs Am–71 MW Phillips
Pro–68 R Boxall
V'trs U
Fees £2.50 (£4)
Loc 6 miles N of Basingstoke off A340

Blackmoor (1913)

Private (Map 2/9)
Whitehill Bordon
Tel **04203 2775**
Mem 530 70(L) 60(J) 60(5)
Sec Major HRG Spiller
Pro Andrew Hall Tel 04203 2345
Holes 18 L 6213 yds SSS 70
Recs
V'trs I
Fees WD £8 (£14) WE £10 (£16.50)
Loc ½ mile W of Whitehill on A325

Bohunt Manor (1923)

(Map 2/24)
Liphook
Tel
Mem 60
Sec IR Baker 29 Headley Road Liphook
Holes Play over Liphook

Boscombe (1938)

Public (Map 2/32)
Queen's Park Bournemouth
Tel
Mem 350
Sec TI Williams Tel Ferndown 874843
Holes Play over Queen's Park course

Boscombe Ladies (1953)

Private (Map 2/32)
Queen's Park Pavilion Queen's Park West Drive Bournemouth
Tel **Bournemouth 36198**
Mem 90
Sec Mrs DM Read Tel Bournemouth 34170
Pro John Sharkey
Holes 18 L 5792 yds (ladies) SSS 73
V'trs SOC book with Corporation; last teeing-off times on Sun 11 am
Fees £5.25 Apr–Sep inc. Less in winter. 6-day season ticket Apr/86–£103
Loc 1½ miles NE town centre

Bournemouth (1890)

Public (Map 3/12)
Meyrick Park Bournemouth
Tel **Bournemouth 20307**
Mem 166
Sec KR Thorne
Holes Play over Meyrick Park course

Bramshaw (1880)

Public (Map 2/10)
Brook Lyndhurst
Tel **Southampton 813252**
Mem 900 116(L) 39(J) 195(5)
Sec FS Prince Tel Southampton 813433
Pro W Wiltshire Tel Southampton 813434
Holes Forest 18 L 5753 yds SSS 68
Manor 18 L 6257 yds SSS 70
Recs Forest Am–67 G Hill
Pro–66 W Wiltshire
Manor Am–67 G Lovelady
Pro–67 D Allen
V'trs U
Fees On application
Loc 10 miles from Southampton

Bramshott Hill (1974)

Public (Map 2/11)
Dibden Southampton
Tel **Hythe 845596**
Mem 300+
Sec WW Brown
Pro Alan Bridge
Holes 18 L 6223 yds SSS 71
Recs Am–
Pro–67 T Healey
V'trs U
Fees £3.20 (£4.50)
Loc 10 miles W of Southampton

Brokenhurst Manor (1919)

Private (Map 2/12)
Sway Road Brokenhurst Hants
Tel **Lymington 23332**
Mem 800
Sec CF Mackintosh Tel Lymington 23332
Pro Clive Bonner Tel Lymington 23092
Holes 18 L 6216 yds SSS 70
Recs Am–64 K Weeks (Ladies 65–H Wheeler)
Pro–66 D Haslam
V'trs WD–NA before 9.30 am; SOC; NA Tue (Ladies' Day); H
Fees £15 (£20) W–£80
Loc 1 mile from Brokenhurst
Mis Except for those using 19th Hole; cravats or tie required in clubhouse and jackets in dining room.

Burley (1905)

Private (Map 2/13)
Burley Ringwood BH24 4BB
Tel **Burley 2431**
Mem 470
Sec GR Kendall Tel Fordingbridge 53706
Pro —
Holes 9 L 3112 yds SSS 69
Recs Am–70 N Carpenter W Medd
Pro–
V'trs U
Fees £6 (£8) W–£25
Loc 4 miles SE Ringwood

Corhampton (1885)

Private (Map 2/14)
Sheeps Pond Lane Droxford Southampton SO3 1QZ
Tel **Droxford 877279**
Mem 600
Sec P Taylor Tel Droxford 877279
Pro J Harris Tel Droxford 877638
Holes 18 L 6088 yds SSS 69
Recs Am–67 M Keeling
Pro–66 B Lane
V'trs WD–U; W/E & BH–M; SOC–Mon, Thu
Fees £8 D–£10
Loc 9 miles S of Winchester

Dunwood Manor (1969)

Private (Map 2/15)
Shootash Hill Romsey SO5 10GF
Tel **Lockerley 40549**
Mem 850
Sec Bryan Foster Tel Lockerley 40549
Pro Gary Stubbington Tel Lockerley 40663
Holes 18 L 6004 yds SSS 69
Recs Am–71 A Devlin
Pro–69 G Stubbington
V'trs WD–SOC; W/E & BH–restricted
Fees £6 D–£8 (£10)
Loc 4 miles Romsey on A27

Fleming Park (1973)

Public (Map 2/16)
Fleming Park Eastleigh
Tel **Eastleigh 612797**
Mem 250
Sec C House
Pro D Miller
Holes 18 L 4436 yds SSS 62
Recs Am–J Butcher
Pro–D Miller
V'trs U
Fees £2.80 (£4) 9 holes after 2 pm
Loc 6 miles N of Southampton

Gosport and Stokes Bay (formerly United Service) (1885)

Private (Map 2/17)
Haslar Gosport
Tel **Gosport 581625**
Mem 170
Sec T Jopling Gosport 527941
Pro Peter Dawson
Holes 9 L 5668 yds SSS 69
Recs Am–
Pro–
V'trs U (except Sunday forenoon)
Fees D–£5
Loc S boundary Gosport

Great Salterns (1914)

Public (Map 2/18)
Portsmouth Golf Centre, Eastern Road Portsmouth PO3 6QB
Tel **0705 664549**
Pro T Healey 0705 664549
Holes 18 L 5970 yds SSS 68
V'trs U
Fees £3 (£4)
Loc 1 mile off M27, on A2030
Mis Southsea club plays here. Golf shop, driving range.

Hartley Wintney (1891)

Private (Map 2/19)
London Road Hartley Wintney nr Basingstoke
Tel **Hartley Wintney 2214**
Mem 410
Sec BD Powell Tel Hartley Wintney 4211
Pro T Barter Tel Hartley Wintney 3779
Holes 9 L 6096 yds SSS 69
Recs Am–70 M Wild
Pro–63 R Lewington
V'trs W/E & BH restricted; Wed–Ladies' Day; SOC
Fees £6 (£14)
Loc A30, London Road, Hartley Wintney between Camberley and Basingstoke

Hayling (1883)

Private (Map 2/20)
Ferry Road Hayling Island Hants PO11 0BX
Tel **Hayling Island 463712/463777**
Mem 900
Sec HR Jenkins Tel 464446
Pro Ray Gadd Tel 464491
Holes 18 L 6510 yds SSS 71
Recs Pro–66 F Gilbride
Am–66 D Harrison K Weeks
V'trs H; W/E & BH 10.30 am SOC
Fees
Loc 5 miles S of Havant on A3023

Hockley (1915)

Private (Map 2/21)
Twyford near Winchester
Tel **Twyford (Hants) 713461**
Mem 800
Sec Mrs JLL Sparkes Tel Twyford (Hants) 713165
Pro T Lane Tel Twyford (Hants) 713678
Holes 18 L 6260 yds SSS 70
Recs Am–67 PE Anthony CJ Hyde
Pro–66 P Dawson

V'trs WD–U; W/E & BH–M
Fees £10
Loc 2 miles Winchester Station on A333

Leckford and Longstock (1929)

Private (Map 2/22)
Leckford Stockbridge Hants SO20 65G
Tel **(0264) 810710**
Mem 200
Sec LG Lucas
Pro LG Lucas
Holes 9 L 3251 yds SSS 71
Recs Am–
Pro–
V'trs M
Loc 5 miles W Andover

Lee-on-the-Solent (1905)

Private (Map 2/23)
Brune Lane Lee-on-the-Solent
Tel **Lee 550207**
Mem 700
Sec Tel Lee 551170
Pro John Richardson Tel Lee 551181
Holes 18 L 5978 yds SSS 69
Recs Am–65 SJ Richardson
Pro–66 M Faulkner
V'trs WD–UH; W/E–MH; SOC on Thurs
Fees £6.50
Loc 3 miles S of Fareham

Liphook (1922)

Private (Map 2/24)
Liphook
Tel **Liphook 723271**
Mem 800
Sec Cdr J Ashton Tel 723785
Pro Ian Large Tel 723271
Holes 18 L 6207 yds SSS 70
Recs Am–70 R Tuddenham
M Wiggett
Pro–66 TR Pinner
V'trs IH (Max 24) W/E–NA before 1 pm Sunday
Fees £10 D–£16 (£15 D–£20) W–£40 M–£100
Loc 18 miles SW Guildford on A3
Mis Bohunt Manor Club also plays here

Meon Valley Hotel G & CC (1977)

Private (Map 2/26)
Sandy Lane Shedfield Southampton SO3 2HQ
Tel **(0329) 833455**
Mem 500
Sec CM Terry Tel (0329) 833455
Pro John Stirling Tel (0329) 833455
Holes 18 L 6519 yds SSS 71
Recs Am–69
Pro–
V'trs H SOC
Fees £12 (£14)
Loc 2 miles NW of Wickham N off A334

New Forest (1888)

Private (Map 2/27)
Lyndhurst
Tel **Lyndhurst 2450**
Mem 600
Sec MJ Tadgell
Pro K Gilhespy
Holes 18 L 5748 yds SSS 68
Recs Am–65 C White
Pro–67 S Clay R Brown

V'trs U (not am Sundays)
Fees £4 (£4)
Loc On Bournemouth to Southampton A35

North Hants (1904)

Private (Map 2/28)
Minley Road, Fleet
Tel **Fleet 616443**
Mem 650
Sec JM Gostling
Pro S Porter
Holes 18 L 6257 yds SSS 70
Recs Am–66 MC Hughesdon
Pro–67 B Hunt
V'trs WD–UH; W/E–MH
Fees £8.80
Loc 3 miles W of Farnborough

Old Thorns Golf Course and Hotel (1982)

Private (Map 2/25)
London Kosaido Company Ltd Longmoor Road Liphook Hampshire GU30 7PE
Tel **(0428) 724555**
Sec GM Jones
Pro Philip Loxley
Holes 18 L 6447 yds SSS 71
Recs Am–
Pro–69 I Aoki
V'trs U SOC
Fees £10 D–£15 Sat £13 D–£18 Sun £15 D–£20
Loc 1 mile off A3 from centre of Liphook on Longmoor Road
Mis 27 twin bedrooms plus country club facilities; 30 buggies for hire

Ordnance Survey (1934)

(Map 2/36)
Southampton Municipal GC Bassett Southampton
Tel **Southampton 768407**
Mem 85
Sec MB Swan 68A Wolseley Road Freemantle Southampton Tel Southampton 788393
Holes Play over Southampton Municipal

Petersfield (1881)

Private (Map 2/29)
Heath Road Petersfield Hants GU31 4EJ
Tel **Petersfield 63725**
Mem 314(M) 87(L) 85(J)
Sec RDJ Maxwell Tel Petersfield 62386
Pro S Clay Tel Petersfield 67732
Holes 18 L 5751 yds SSS 68
Recs Am–70 P Tupper
Pro–69 S Clay
V'trs U; W/E–NA before 10.30 am
Fees £6 (£8)
Loc ½ mile E of centre

Portsmouth (1926)

Public (Map 2/30)
Crookhorn Lane Widley Portsmouth
Tel **0705 372210**
Mem 450
Sec D Houlihan Tel 0705 318640
Pro W McHardy Tel 0705 372210
Holes 18 L 6259 yds SSS 70
V'trs U; SOC (arrangements with Pro)
Fees £3 (£4)
Loc 1 mile N of city on B2177

Queen's Park (1905 course; 1906 club)

Public (Map 2/32)
Queen's Park South Drive Bournemouth
Tel **Bournemouth 36198 course; 34900 club**
Mem 900
Sec JG Sharkey Tel Bournemouth 36817
Holes 18 L 6505 yds SSS 72
Recs Am–69 M Butcher
Pro–66 A Caygill H Boyle
V'trs U
Fees Oct-Apr £2.50; May-Sept £3
Loc 2 miles NE Bournemouth Sq
Mis Closed Sunday pm Boscombe club also plays here. Society bookings apply to Recreation Officer Town Hall Bournemouth

Romsey (1925)

Private (Map 2/33)
Nursling Southampton SO1 9XW
Tel **Soton 732218**
Mem 500
Sec FG Biles Tel Soton 734637
Pro SS Howard Tel Soton 736673
Holes 18 L 5752 yds SSS 68
Recs Am–66 NP Woodward
Pro–64 J Slade
V'trs WD–U; W/E & BH–M
Fees £6
Loc 4½ miles NW Southampton (A3057)

Rowlands Castle (1902)

Private (Map 2/34)
Links Lane Rowlands Castle PO9 6AE
Tel **Rowlands Castle 412216**
Mem 500 160(L) 60(J)
Sec Capt AW Aird Tel 412784
Pro P Klepacz Tel 412785
Holes 18 L 6627 yds SSS 72
Recs Am–70 N Cole C Anderson
Pro–66 M Gregson
V'trs U (Not before noon W/E); H; SOC Tue, Thu, Fri
Fees £9 (£11)
Loc 3 miles N of Havant

Royal Winchester (1888)

Private (Map 2/35)
Sarum Road Winchester SO22 5QE
Tel **Winchester 52462**
Mem 600
Sec RD Tingey Tel Winchester 52462; Winchester 65048 (Members)
Pro DP Williams Tel Winchester 62473
Holes 18 L 6218 yds SSS 70
Recs Am–67 R Elliot J Curren
Pro–68 P Dolton G Stubbinton (Revised course)
V'trs WD–UH W/E & BH–M; SOC on WD
Fees £10
Loc W of Winchester off A31

Southampton (1935)

Public (Map 2/36)
Bassett Southampton
Tel **(0703) 768407**
Mem 400
Sec KG Kennard
Pro J Cave Tel (0703) 768407
Holes 18 L 6218 yds SSS 70
9 L 2391 yds SSS 33
Recs 18 holes Am–64 P Dedman
Pro–62 SW Murray

V'trs U
Fees 18 holes £3.20 (£5); 9 holes £1.60 (£2.50)
Loc Turn left at footbridge off Bassett Avenue; approx 2 miles N of city centre

Southsea (1972)

Private **(Map 2/18)**
The Mansion Eastern Road Portsmouth
Tel **0705 664549**
Mem 470
Sec KP Parker Tel 0705 812435
Holes Play over Great Salterns public course.

Southwick Park (1977)

Private **(Map 2/37)**
Pinsley Drive Southwick PO17 6EL
Tel **0705 380131**
Mem 500 50(L)
Sec JG Griffiths Tel as club
Pro M Desmond Tel 0705 380442 (ext 545) or 350442
Holes 18 L 5970 yds SSS 68
Recs Am–67 Robert Edwards
Pro–64 Greg Hughes
V'trs Only before 11 am Monday to Friday unaccompanied; SOC Tue
Fees On application. Servicemen reduced rate
Loc ½ mile Southwick village

Southwood (1977)

Public **(Map 2/38)**
Ively Road Farnborough
Tel **Farnborough 548700**
Mem 350
Sec Bob Hammond
Pro Bob Hammond
Holes 9 L 2085 metres SSS 32
Recs Am–62
Pro–
V'trs U
Fees 9 holes £2.20 18 holes £3.80 (OAPs £1.20 and £1.80)
Loc 1 mile W of Farnborough off A 325

Stoneham (1908)

Private **(Map 2/39)**
Bassett Southampton SO2 3NE
Tel **0703 768151**
Mem 650
Sec Mrs AM Wilkinson Tel 0703 769272
Pro BAV Sparks Tel 0703 768397
Holes 18 L 6310 yds SSS 70
Recs Am–65 R Park
Pro–63 J Martin
V'trs U; SOC–Mon Thu Fri
Fees £10 (18 or 36) W/E–£12 per day
Loc 2 miles N of city

Tylney Park (1973)

Private **(Map 2/40)**
Rotherwick Basingstoke
Tel **Hook 2079**
Mem 460
Sec JC York
Pro C de Bruin
Holes 18 L 6108 yds SSS 69
Recs Am–
Pro–
V'trs WD–U; W/E–UH
Fees £8 (£10)
Loc 1 mile Hook, A30

Waterlooville (1907)

Private **(Map 2/41)**
Idsworth Road Cowplain Hants PO8 8BD
Tel **Waterlooville 252661**
Mem 600
Sec Mrs B Southwell Tel Waterlooville 263388
Pro J Hay Tel 256911
Holes 18 L 6647 yds SSS 72
Recs Am–70
Pro–
V'trs U (XL Sun am)
Fees £10 (R/D)
Loc On A3, 5 miles N of Portsmouth

Isle of Wight

Cowes (1908)

Private **(Map 2/1)**
Crossfield Avenue Cowes PO31 8HN
Tel **(0983) 292303**
Mem 250
Sec JW Lloyd Tel (0983) 292439
Pro
Holes 9 L 5880 yds SSS 68
Recs Am–69 I Graham
Pro–
V'trs I H Not before 4 pm Thu (Ladies Day), not before 12 noon Sunday, not after 5 pm Friday
Fees £6 W–£25
Loc Entry on Crossfield Ave (private road); opp end of playing field to Cowes High School

Freshwater Bay

Private **(Map 2/2)**
Afton Down Freshwater Isle of Wight
Tel **Freshwater 752955**
Mem 295
Sec JJ Pritchard
Pro –
Holes 18 L 5628 yds SSS 68
Recs Am–69 Smith
Pro–66 T Underwood
V'trs U SOC
Fees £7 (£8) W–£30
Loc 400 yds from Freshwater Bay off Military Road
Mis Snacks available

Newport IW (1896)

Private **(Map 2/3)**
St George's Down Near Shide
Tel **525076**
Mem 200
Sec WW Smallman
Pro
Holes 9 L 5704 yds SSS 68
Recs Am–
Pro–
V'trs U
Fees £6 (£8) W–£15
Loc 1 mile SE of Newport

Osborne (1903)

Private **(Map 2/4)**
Club House East Cowes
Tel **Cowes 29 5421**
Mem 260 90(L)
Sec Mrs Margaret Butler Tel Cowes 297758
Pro Mr Mark Wright Tel Cowes 295421
Holes 9 L 6286 yds SSS 70
Recs Am–
Pro–
V'trs SOC; U (The Ladies' Day Tees Res 11 am–2.30 pm and Sun after 11.30 am–NA)
Fees £7 (£8) 5 D–£20
Loc S of East Cowes in grounds of Osborne House

Ryde (1921)

Private **(Map 2/5)**
Ryde House Park Ryde
Tel **Ryde 614809**
Mem 450
Sec F Cockayne Tel Ryde 64388
Pro Steve Ward Tel 62088
Holes 9 L 5220 yds SSS 66
Recs Am–65 B Marshall D Chalon
Pro–64 T Underwood D Allen
V'trs U
Fees £6 (£7.50)
Loc On main Ryde/Newport Road

Shanklin and Sandown (1900)

Private **(Map 2/6)**
Fairway Lake Sandown IOW PO36 9PR Isle of Wight
Tel **IOW 403217**
Mem 700
Sec Flt Lt LV Edwards Tel IOW 403217
Pro RD Matthews Tel IOW 404424
Holes 18 L 6000 yds SSS 69
Recs Am–68 D McToldridge DJ Maidment
Pro–65 Bob Wynn
V'trs U; SOC–WD
Fees £9 (£11) 5 D–£35 W–£45 F–£80
Loc Sandown IOW

Ventnor (1892)

Private **(Map 2/7)**
Steephill Down Road Ventnor
Tel **Ventnor 0983-853326**
Mem 140
Sec W Clarkson Tel Ventnor 0983-853362
Pro
Holes 9 L 5772 yds SSS 68
Recs Am–73 IH Guy
Pro–
V'trs U
Fees £4 (£5)
Loc NW boundary, Ventnor

Channel Islands

Alderney (1969)

Private
Alderney
Tel **Alderney 2835**
Mem 150
Sec AAH Clark
Pro
Holes 9 L 2528 yds SSS 33
Recs Am–29 M Hugman
Pro–28 PL Cunningham
V'trs U
Fees D–£6 (£7)
Loc 1 mile E of St Anne

L'Ancresse

L'Ancresse Guernsey
Tel **0481 47408**
Mem 230
Sec BD Tullier Tel 0481 26375
Holes Share L'Ancresse course with Royal Guernsey

La Moye (1902)

Private
La Moye St Brelade
Tel **Central 42701**
Mem 1250
Sec D Lowton Tel Central 43401
Pro D Melville Tel Central 43130
Holes 18 L 6741 yds SSS 72
Recs Am–70 R Purdie J McGarragle
Pro–62 Gordon Brand Jr
V'trs IH; SOC after 9.30 am
Fees £14 (£16) W–£55 M–£125
Loc 6 miles W of St Helier

Royal Guernsey (1890)

L'Ancresse Guernsey
Tel **Guernsey 47022**
Mem 765
Sec GJ Nicolle Tel Guernsey 46523
Pro N Wood Tel Guernsey 45070
Holes 18 L 6206 yds SSS 70
Recs Am–64 R Eggo
Pro–64 P Cunningham
V'trs WD–U; W/E–M; H SOC
Fees £8 D–£10 W–£33 F–£50
Loc 5 miles N of St Peter Port

Royal Jersey (1878)

Private
Grouville Jersey
Tel **(0534) 51042**
Mem 1200
Sec RB Waymouth Tel (0534) 54416
Pro T Horton Tel (0534) 52234
Holes 18 L 6097 yds SSS 69
Recs Am–
Pro–
V'trs WD–H after 10 am; WE/BH–H after 2.30 pm (Winter 12.30 pm)
Fees £14 (£16) W–£70 F–£120
Loc Grouville

St Clements (1925)

Private
St Clements Jersey
Tel **Central 21938**
Mem 90
Sec D Leybourne Tel 54823
Pro R Marks
Holes 9 L 3972 yds SSS 61
Recs Am–61 T Gray B McCarthy
Pro–
V'trs U except Sunday am–NA
Fees £6
Loc 1 mile E St Helier
Mis Book by telephoning 21938

Western Golf Range

Public
The Mount Val de la Mare St Quens Jersey
Tel **(0534) 81947/82787**
Mem Open
Man J Le Bron Tel (0534) 82629
Holes 12 par 3 course, SSS 36
V'trs U
Fees 12 holes £2.25
Loc Five Mile Road St Quens Bay
Mis Open dawn till dusk. Driving range also available (30 Tee).

Hertfordshire

Aldenham G & CC (1975)

Private (Map 1/1)
Radlett Road Aldenham Nr Watford Herts
Tel **Radlett 7775**
Mem 475
Sec DW Phillips Tel Radlett 7775
Pro Alistair McKay Tel Radlett 7889
Holes 18 L 6500 yds SSS 71
Recs Am–
Pro–
V'trs U
Fees £8 D–£12 WE–£15
Loc

Arkley (1909)

Private (Map 1/2)
Rowley Green Road Barnet EN5 3HL
Tel **01-449 0394**
Mem 350
Sec JG Duncan Tel 01-449 0394
Pro M Ridge Tel 01-440 8473
Holes **9 L 6045 yds SSS 69**
Recs **Am–67 SN McWilliams**
Pro–63 LV Baker
V'trs WD–U; W/E–M; SOC on Wed Thu
Fees £6 D–£9
Loc 2 miles from Barnet station

Ashridge (1932)

Private (Map 1/3)
Little Gaddesden Berkhamsted Herts HP4 1LY
Tel **Little Gaddesden 2244**
Mem 650
Sec A Heron Tel Little Gaddesden 2244
Pro G Pook Tel Little Gaddesden 2307
Holes 18 L 6508 yds SSS 71
Recs Am–66 Sqd Ldr CI Skellern
Pro–66 JRM Jacobs
V'trs Ring Sec. for bookings
Fees On application
Loc 5 miles NW Berkhamsted

Batchwood Hall (1935)

Public (Map 1/4)
Batchwood Hall St Albans
Tel **St Albans 3349**
Mem 300
Sec M Waldron
Pro J Thomson
Holes 18 L 6465 yds SSS 71
Recs Am–67 M Cassidy
Pro–62 PP Wynne
V'trs U
Fees
Loc NW corner of town

Berkhamsted (1890)

Private (Map 1/5)
Berkhamsted HP4 2QB
Tel **Berkhamsted 3730**
Mem 280 113(L) 119(J) 150(5)
Sec PI Anderson Tel Berkhamsted 5832
Pro BJ Proudfoot Tel Berkhamsted 5851
Holes 18 L 6568 yds SSS 72
Recs Am–64 N Leconte
Pro–68 PP Wynne
V'trs U; H; SOC–Wed/Fri (W/E M before 11.30 am)
Fees On application
Loc 1½ miles E of town centre

Bishop's Stortford (1910)

Private (Map 1/6)
Dunmow Road Bishop's Stortford
Tel **Bishop's Stortford 54027**
Mem 425
Sec G Ditchfield Tel Bishop's Stortford 54715
Pro V Duncan Tel Bishop's Stortford 51324
Holes 18 L 6440 yds SSS 71
Recs Am–69 M Whitlock
Pro–66 J Bennett
V'trs WD–U SOC; W/E–M
Fees £9 D–£11
Loc 26 miles S of Cambridge
Mis Buggies for hire

Boxmoor (1890)

Private (Map 1/7)
18 Box Lane Hemel Hempstead
Tel **Hemel Hempstead 42434**
Mem 225
Sec E Duell Tel Hemel Hempstead 62427
Pro
Holes 9 L 4854 yds SSS 64
Recs Am–57 D Boyd A Reeves
Pro–
V'trs U–(Not Sundays)
Fees £3 (Sat £4)
Loc 1 mile W on A41

Brickendon Grange (1964)

Private (Map 1/8)
Brickendon nr Hertford
Tel **Bayford 228**
Mem 600
Sec PB Stokes Tel Bayford 258
Pro J Hamilton Tel Bayford 218
Holes 18 L 6325 yds SSS 70
Recs Am–70 J Paterson
M Passingham
Pro–67 S James K Robson
V'trs WD–U SOC; W/E & BH–M
Fees On application
Loc 3 miles S of Hertford

Brookman's Park (1930)

Private (Map 1/9)
Brookman's Park Hatfield AL9 7AT
Tel **Potters Bar 52487**
Sec JKA O'Brien Tel Potters Bar 52487
Pro MMR Plumbridge Tel Potters Bar 52468
Holes 18 L 5886 metres (6438 yds) SSS 71
Recs Am–67 N Jarman
Pro–66 GR Burroughs
V'trs WD–U; W/E & BH–M
Fees D–£12
Loc 3 miles S of Hatfield

Bushey (1980)

Private (Map 1/10)
The High Street Bushey Herts
Tel **01-960 2283**
Mem 550
Sec SG Pelham
Pro G Atkinson Tel 01-950 2215
Holes 9 L 3000 yds SSS 69
Recs Am—
Pro–
V'trs U
Fees £2.50 (£5)
Loc 2 miles S of Watford

Bushey Hall (1896)

Private (Map 1/11)
Bushey Watford WD2 2EP
Tel **Watford 25802**
Mem 450
Sec J Donnachie
Pro Kevin Hughes Tel Watford 22253
Holes 18 L 6071 yds SSS 69
Recs Am–65 G Kemble
Pro–
V'trs U; Suns & BH–M
Fees On application
Loc 1 mile SE Watford

Chadwell Springs (1974)

Private (Map 1/12)
Hertford Road Ware SG12 9LE
Tel **Ware 3647**
Mem 350
Sec DA Bussey Tel Ware 61447
Pro AN Shearn
Holes 9 L 3021 yds SSS 69
Recs Am–
Pro–
V'trs WD–U; W/E–M or I
Fees £4 (£6)
Loc Midway between Ware and Hertford on A119

Cheshunt Park (1976)

Public (Map 1/13)
The Club House Park Lane Cheshunt
Tel **Waltham Cross 24009**
Mem 350+
Sec MJ White Tel Waltham Cross 29777
Pro Chris Newton Tel Waltham Cross 24009
Holes 18 L 6608 yds SSS 71
Recs Am–
Pro–
V'trs Welcome by arrangement in person only
Fees £3.10 (£4.80)
Loc A10 London-Cambridge; turn off at College Road junction and proceed along Churchgate travelling W

Chorleywood (1890)

Private (Map 1/14)
Common Road Chorleywood Herts WD3 5LN
Tel **Chorleywood 2009**
Mem 150 45(L) 50(J)
Sec LW Turner
Pro
Holes 9 L 2838 yds SSS 67
Recs Am–65 SM McCready
Pro–64 H Bradshaw
V'trs WD–U (Ex Tues Thurs am); W/E–Sat pm only
Fees £5 (£6.50)
Loc Off A404 3 miles W of Rickmansworth

Dyrham Park Country Club (1964)

Private (Map 1/15)
Galley Lane Barnet Herts
Tel **01-440 3361**
Mem 300
Sec DU Prentice
Pro W Large Tel 01-440 3904
Holes 18 L 6369 yds SSS 70
Recs Am–
Pro–
V'trs M welcome WD SOC Wed
Fees
Loc 10 miles London, A1
Mis Guests must be accompanied by a member

East Herts (1898)

Private (Map 1/16)
Hamels Park Buntingford SG9 9NA
Tel **Ware 821923**
Mem 500
Sec JA Harper Tel Ware 821978
Pro James Hamilton Tel Ware 821922
Holes 18 L 6449 yds SSS 71
Recs Am–68 JA Watts
Pro–64 James Hamilton R Joyce
V'trs WD–H; W/E–M
Fees On application
Loc ¼ mile N of Puckeridge on A10

Elstree (1984)

Private (Map 1/40)
Watling Street Elstree Herts WD6 3AA
Tel **01-953 6115**
Mem 620
Sec P Stanton 01-953 6115
Pro J Lamble 01-207 5680
Holes 18 L 5245 yds SSS 66
V'trs U SOC
Fees £4 (£5.50)
Loc A5183, 1 mile N of Elstree
Mis Pay and play course; 15 bay floodlit driving range

Hadley Wood (1922)

Private (Map 1/17)
Beech Hill Hadley Wood Barnet Herts EN4 0JJ
Tel **01-449 4486**
Mem 584
Sec R Tolliday Tel 01-449 4328
Pro Alan McGinn Tel 01-449 3285
Holes 18 L 6473 yds SSS 71
Recs Am–67 CC Holton
Pro–67 PP Elson
V'trs WD–H or I; W/E & BH–M
Fees On application
Loc **10 miles N London off A111 between Potters Bar and** Cockfosters 2 miles S Junction 24, M25

Harpenden (1894)

Private (Map 1/18)
Hammonds End Harpenden
Tel **Harpenden 2580**
Mem 800
Sec S Halliwell Tel Harpenden 2580
Pro DH Smith Tel Harpenden 67124
Holes 18 L 6363 yds SSS 70
Recs Am–
Pro–
V'trs WD–U; SOC (exc Thu, Ladies Day); W/E & BH–M
Fees £8 D–£12
Loc 6 miles N of St Albans

Harpenden Common (1931)

Private (Map 1/19)
East Common Harpenden
Tel **Harpenden 2856**
Mem 700
Sec HC Uden Tel Harpenden 5959
Pro N Lawrence Tel Harpenden 4655
Holes 18 L 5613 yds SSS 67
Recs Am–
Pro–
V'trs WD–U; W/E–M
Fees £6
Loc 4 miles N of St Albans

Hartsbourne Country Club (1946)

Private (Map 1/20)
Bushey Heath WD2 1JW
Tel **01-950 1113**
Mem 400
Sec RJH Jourdan
Pro Geof Hunt Tel 01-950 2836
Holes 18 L 6305 yds SSS 70
9 L 5432 yds SSS 70
Recs 18 hole course Am–67 E Silver
Pro–62 P Oosterhuis 9 hole course Am–
Pro–
V'trs NA
Fees
Loc 5 miles SE of Watford

Hatfield London (1976)

Private (Map 1/28)
Bedwell Park Essendon Hatfield AL9 6JA
Tel **Potters Bar 42624**
Mem 100
Sec T Takisawa
Pro
Holes 18 L 6878 yds SSS 73
Recs Am–
Pro–
V'trs U
Fees £5 (£8.50)
Loc B158

Knebworth (1908)

Private (Map 1/21)
Knebworth SG3 6NL
Tel **Stevenage 812752**
Mem 800
Sec JC Wright
Pro MW Blainey Tel Stevenage 812757
Holes 18 L 6428 yds SSS 71
Recs Am–64 PR Robinson
Pro–66 J Hudson
V'trs WD–U SOC; WE–M
Fees £10 D–£13 (WD only)
Loc 1 mile S of Stevenage

Letchworth (1905)

Private (Map 1/22)
Letchworth SG6 3NQ
Tel **Letchworth 683203**
Mem 900
Sec BM Barber Tel Letchworth 683203
Pro SJ Mutimer Tel Letchworth 682713
Holes 18 L 6057 yds SSS 69
Recs Am–67 RF Croft
Pro–66 NC Coles
V'trs WD–U; W/E–M; SOC Wed Thu Fri
Fees £10
Loc Letchworth off A505

Little Hay (1977)

Public (Map 1/23)
Box Lane Bovingdon Hemel Hempstead
Tel **Hemel Hempstead 833798**
Mem
Sec
Pro D Johnson Tel Hemel Hempstead 833798
Holes 18 L 6610 yds SSS 72
Ladies–5432 yds SSS 71
Recs Am–
Pro–69
V'trs U
Fees £3.30 (£4.65)
Loc Off A41 at Box Lane

Mid Herts (1893)

Private (Map 1/24)
Gustard Wood Wheathampstead AL4 8RS
Tel **Wheathampstead 3118**
Mem 500(M) 125(L)
Sec Mr J Bowen Tel Wheathampstead 2242
Pro JL Fowler Tel 2788
Holes 18 L 6060 yds SSS 69
Recs Am–
Pro–67 C Platts
V'trs WD–U except Tues; W/E & BH–M; SOC
Fees £12 round or day
Loc 6 miles N of St Albans

Moor Park (1923)

Private (Map 1/25)
Rickmansworth
Tel **Rickmansworth 773146**
Mem 1950
Sec JE Linaker
Pro ER Whitehead
Holes High course 18 L6903 yds SSS 73
West course 18 L 5823 yds SSS 68
Recs High course
Am–69 RY Mitchell
Pro–67 M King
West course
Am–63 AJ Eisner
Pro–63 AD Locke A Lees EE Whitcombe
V'trs WD–I; W/E & BH–M
Fees On request
Loc Moor Park Station ¾ mile

Old Fold Manor (1910)

Private (Map 1/26)
Hadley Green Barnet Herts EN5 4QN
Tel **01-449 2266**
Mem 500
Sec P Bishop Tel 01-440 9185
Pro Peter Jones Tel 01-440 7488
Holes 18 L 6473 yds SSS 71
Recs Am–66 A Clark
Pro–68 SL King
V'trs WD–I/H; W/E–M
Fees £12
Loc 1 mile N of Barnet on A1000

Panshanger (1976)

Public (Map 1/27)
Panshanger Welwyn Garden City
Tel **Welwyn 33350**
Mem 300
Sec KP Wing Tel 0992 57496
Pro Alan Hall Tel Welwyn 33350
Holes 18 L 6035 metres SSS 70
Recs Am–70 S Lawrance
Pro–68 P Kilgour
V'trs U
Fees £3 (£4)
Loc 2 miles off A1, B1000 to Hertford

Porters Park (1899)

Private (Map 1/29)
Shenley Hill Radlett Herts WD7 7AZ
Tel **Radlett 6262**
Mem 760 (550 playing)
Sec MC Stamford Tel Radlett 4127
Pro JK Ramsden Tel Radlett 4366
Holes 18 L 6313 yds SSS 70
Recs Am–65 J Putt
Pro–64 P Townsend
V'trs WD–H; W/E & BH–M; SOC Wed Thu
Fees £10 D–£15
Loc ½ mile Radlett Station

Potters Bar (1923)

Private (Map 1/30)
Darkes Lane Potters Bar Herts EN6 1DE
Tel **(0707) 52020**
Mem 550
Sec F Ireland Tel (0707) 52020
Pro R Watkins Tel (0707) 52987
Holes 18 L 6273 yds SSS 70
Recs Am–66 RR Davis
Pro–65 D McClelland
V'trs WD–H; W/E–M; SOC Mon Tue Fri
Fees
Loc ½ mile Potters Bar Station Herts

Redbourn (1970)

Private (Map 1/31)
Kinsbourne Green Lane Redbourn nr St Albans
Tel **058285-3493**
Mem
Sec WM Dunn Tel Redbourn 2150
Pro Steve Baldwin Tel Redbourn 3493
Holes 18 L 6403 yds SSS 71
9 L 1361 yds SSS 27
Recs Am–
Pro–
V'trs WD–SOC (U 4.30 pm–6.30 pm); W/E–M
Fees 18-hole £5 (£6.50)
9-hole £3.50 (£3.50)
Loc 4 miles N of St Albans 4 miles S of Luton, 1 mile S of M1 Junction 9

Rickmansworth (1937)

Public (Map 1/32)
Moor Lane Rickmansworth
Tel **Rickmansworth 773163**
Mem 220
Sec LJ Miller Tel 01-958 3028
Pro I Duncan Tel Rickmansworth 775278
Holes 18 L 4412 yds SSS 62
Recs Am–62 L Silver
Pro–
V'trs U
Fees £3 (£4.30)
Loc SE of town

Royston

(See Cambridgeshire)

Sandy Lodge (1910)

Private (Map 1/33)
Northwood Middx
Tel **Northwood 25429**
Mem 500
Sec Major H Trim Tel Northwood 25429
Pro Alex Fox Tel Northwood 25321
Holes 18 L 6340 yds SSS 70
Recs Am–67 JM Brew IC Goode
Pro–64 A Jacklin
V'trs WD; W/E & BH–M
Fees £11
Loc Adjacent Moor Park Station Rickmansworth

South Herts (1899)

Private (Map 1/34)
Totteridge London N20
Tel **01-445 0117**
Mem 550
Sec RA Bond Tel 01-445 2035
Pro RS Livingston
Holes 18 L 6470 yds SSS 71
9 L 1581 yds SSS
Recs 18 holes Am–67 R Neil
Pro–66 D Thomas
9 holes Am–
Pro–
V'trs WD–I; W/E & BH–M
Fees D–£12
Loc 10 miles N of London Centre

Stevenage (1980)

Public (Map 1/35)
Aston Lane Stevenage Herts SG2 7EL
Tel **Shephall (0438 88) 424**
Mem 475
Sec ET Messent Tel (0438 88) 322
Pro DW Astill Tel Shephall 424
Holes 18 L 6451 yds SSS 71 Par 3
Recs Am–
Pro–71 R Mitchell
R Whitehead
V'trs U
Fees £3 (£4.35)
Loc Off A602 to Hertford
Mis Driving Range 9 hole Par 3

Verulam (1905)

Private (Map 1/36)
London Road St Albans
Tel **St Albans 53327**
Mem 600
Sec RJ McMillan
Pro S James Tel St Albans 61401
Holes 18 L 6432 yds SSS 71
Recs Am–72 DS Brodie
Pro–69 N Wichelow
V'trs WD–U; W/E & BH–NA
Fees £8; reduced Mon–£5
Loc

Welwyn Garden City (1922)

Private (Map 1/37)
Mannicotts High Oaks Road Welwyn Garden City AL8 7BP
Tel **Welwyn Garden City 322722**
Mem 600
Sec JL Carragher Tel Welwyn Garden City 325243
Pro H Arnott Tel Welwyn Garden City 325525
Holes 18 L 6200 yds SSS 69
Recs Am–65 I Fordyce
Pro–65 N Faldo
V'trs U (Sundays NA before noon; M after noon)
Fees £10 (£15)
Loc ¾ mile N of Hatfield; from A1 take B197 to Valley Road

West Herts (1890)

Private (Map 1/38)
Cassiobury Park Watford WD1 7SL
Tel **Watford 24264**
Mem 600
Sec RAS Gordon Tel Watford 36484
Pro CS Gough Tel Watford 20352
Holes 18 L 6488 yds SSS 71
Recs Am–68 SA Masson
Pro–67 R Whitehead
V'trs WD–I; W/E & BH–M; SOC–Wed Fri
Fees £10
Loc Between Watford and Rickmansworth off the A412

Whipsnade Park (1974)

Private (Map 1/39)
Studham Lane Dagnall Herts HP4 1RH
Tel **044284 2330**
Mem 400
Sec D Whalley
Pro M Lewendon
Holes 18 L 6812 yds SSS 72
Recs Am–71 A Calder
Pro–
V'trs WD–U; W/E–M; SOC–WD
Fees £8 (£15)
Loc S of Whipsnade Zoo between Dagnall and Studham

Kent

Aquarius (1913)

Private **(Map 1/1)**
Marmora Rd Honor Oak London SE22
Tel **01-693 1626**
Mem 350
Sec Mrs EB Grey
Pro F Private
Holes 9 L 5034 yds SSS 65
Recs Am–62 R Hare
Pro–63 F Private
V'trs M
Fees
Loc SE London

Ashford (1904)

Private **(Map 1/2)**
Sandyhurst Lane Ashford TN25 4NT
Tel **Ashford 20180**
Mem 600
Sec JP Thomas Tel Ashford 22655
Pro Hugh Sherman Tel Ashford 29644
Holes 18 L 6246 yds SSS 70
Recs Am–66 L Donovan
KC Elvin
Pro–63 RS Fidler
V'trs U (except Sat/Sun am–M)
Fees £9 (£12.50)
Loc Ashford 1½ miles (A20)

Barnehurst (1903)

Private **(Map 1/3)**
Mayplace Road East Barnehurst Kent DA7 6JU
Tel **Crayford 523746**
Mem 250
Sec GE Audsley Tel Crayford 54612
Pro Steve Barr Tel Cy 51205
Holes 9 L 5320 yds SSS 66
Recs Am–64
Pro–64
V'trs Mon, Wed, Fri–U; times restricted other days
Fees £3.50 (£5.70)
Loc Between Crayford and Bexley Heath
Mis Bar snacks; lunches arranged with stewardess

Bearsted (1898)

Private **(Map 1/4)**
Ware Street Bearsted nr Maidstone
Tel **Maidstone 38389**
Mem 548
Sec 0622 38198
Pro G Cowley Tel Maidstone 38024
Holes 18 L 6253 yds SSS 70
Recs Am–
Pro–
V'trs WD–U; W/E–HM Bona fide GC members only; SOC
Fees £7 D–£10
Loc 2½ miles Maidstone

Beckenham Place Park (1907)

Public **(Map 1/5)**
Beckenham Hill Road Beckenham Kent
Tel **01-650 2292**
Mem Approx 180
Sec Lee Snashfold Tel 01-650 0704
Pro Bill Woodman Tel 01-658 5374
Holes 18 L 5722 yds SSS 68
9 L–SSS
Recs Am–62 S Champion
Pro–65 T Cotton
V'trs U
Fees £3.50 (£5)
Loc 2 miles S of Catford SE6
Mis Course shared with Braeside GC

Bexley Heath (1907)

Private **(Map 1/6)**
Mount Road Bexley Heath Kent
Tel **01-303 4232**
Mem 350
Sec RJ Cawston Tel 01-303 6951
Pro C Phillips Tel 01-301 2929
Holes 9 L 5239 yds SSS 66
Recs Am–65 D Fillary
Pro–
V'trs H–up to 1.30 pm
Fees £7
Loc Station, 1 mile

Braeside (1947)

Public **(Map 1/5)**
The Mansion Beckenham Place Park Beckenham Kent
Tel 01-650 2292
Mem 150
Sec R Oliver
Pro **W Woodman Tel 01-658 5374**
Holes **18 L 5477 yds SSS 68**
Fees **WD £3 W/E £4.20**

Bromley (1948)

Public **(Map 1/30)**
Magpie Hall Lane Bromley Kent
Tel **01-462 8001**
Mem 100
Sec BJ Pratt Tel 01-310 5434
Pro Alan Hodgeson Tel 01-462 7014
Holes Play over Magpie Hall Lane Course

Broome Park (1981)

Private **(Map 1/7)**
Barham nr Canterbury
Tel **Barham 831701**
Mem
Sec Miss V Greatorex and D Lees Tel 831701
Pro T Britz Tel 831484
Holes 18 L 6006 yds SSS 70
Recs Am–70 G Brown
Pro–68 H Flatman
V'trs SOC
Fees £10 (£15)
Loc Off A2 at Folkestone A260 600 yds on RH side.

Canterbury (1927)

Private **(Map 1/8)**
Scotland Hills Canterbury CT1 1TW
Tel **Canterbury (0227) 463586**
Mem 600
Sec G Good Tel (0227) 453532
Pro Paul Everard (0227) 462865
Holes 18 L 6245 yds SSS 70
Recs Am–66 RJ Davies
Pro–64 K Redford
V'trs U exc before noon Sun; SOC Tue & Thu
Fees £9 D–£14
Loc 1 mile E of town centre on A257

Cherry Lodge (1969)

Private **(Map 1/9)**
Jail Lane Biggin Hill nr Westerham
Tel **Biggin Hill 72250**
Mem 840
Man J Bangs
Pro K Burns Tel 72989
Holes 18 L 6908 yds SSS 74
Short course: 6031 yds SSS 69
Recs Am–73 T Shannon
L Grindley
Pro–73 D Beattie
V'trs WD–U; W/E–M
Fees £10
Loc 15 miles SW London
Mis Buggies available; full catering

Chestfield (Whitstable) (1925)

Private **(Map 1/10)**
Chestfield Road Whitstable CT5 3LU
Tel **Chestfield 2243**
Mem 630
Sec D Kemp Tel Chestfield 2365
Pro John Brotherton
Holes 18 L 6068 yds SSS 69
Recs Am–67 RA Howard S Reid
Pro–64 Bob Cameron
V'trs WD–H; W/E–M
Fees On application
Loc East Kent

Chislehurst (1894)

Private **(Map 1/11)**
Camden Place Chislehurst Kent BR7 5HJ
Tel **01-467 3055**
Mem 740
Sec NE Pearson Tel 01-467 2782
Pro A Thompson Tel 01-467 6798
Holes 18 L 5128 yds SSS 65
Recs Am–63 DWR Rutnam
Pro–61 J Bennett
V'trs WD–Restricted; W/E–M
Fees D–£12
Loc 20 mins from Charing Cross

Cobtree Manor Park

Public **(Map 1/59)**
Chatham Road Boxley Maidstone Kent
Tel **(0622) 53276**
Mem 400
Sec PJ Rudd Tel (0622) 53276
Pro Martin Drew Tel (0622) 53276
Holes 18 L 5701 yds SSS 68
V'trs WD–U; W/E & BH–bookings only, to be made 7 days in advance; SOC on WD (bookings to be made with steward: Steve Wood Tel (0622) 53276
Fees £3.40 (£5)
Loc 3 miles from town centre, on A229 road to Chatham

Cranbrook (1969)

Private **(Map 1/13)**
Benenden Road Cranbrook
Tel **Cranbrook (0580) 712833/712934**
Mem 620
Sec HM Borissow Tel (0580) 712833
Pro Brian Impett Tel (0580) 712934
Holes 18 L 6128 yds SSS 70
Recs Am–70 D Southon
Pro–68 B Impett
V'trs WD–U SOC; W/E & BH–U (exc maj comp days)
Fees £6.50 (£9.50)
Loc 15 miles S of Maidstone

Cray Valley (1972)

Private **(Map 1/12)**
St Paul's Cray Orpington Kent
Tel **Orpington 37909**
Members–Orpington 31927
Mem
Sec JC Morgan
Pro P Smith
Holes 18 L 6338 yds SSS 70
Recs Am–
Pro–

V'trs U
Fees £3.50
Loc 14 miles S of London

Dartford (1897)

Private (Map 1/14)
Dartford Heath Dartford
Tel **Dartford 23616**
Mem 600
Sec MJF Meason Tel Dartford 26455
Pro A Blackburn Tel Dartford 26409
Holes 18 L 5914 yds SSS 68
Recs Am–66 G Wright
Pro–66 P Allis
V'trs WD–I; W/E–M H
Fees £11 (£5)
Loc

Deangate Ridge (1972)

Public (Map 1/15)
Hoo Rochester ME3 8RZ
Tel **Medway 251180**
Mem 800
Sec JA Penfold Tel Gravesend 52495
Pro Barry Aram Tel Medway 251180
Holes 18 L 6300 yds SSS 70
Recs Am–71 AJ Rossiter
Pro–
V'trs U
Fees £2.95 (£4.20)
Loc Hoo nr Isle of Grain

Edenbridge G & CC (1973)

Private (Map 1/16)
Crouch House Road Edenbridge
Tel **Edenbridge 865097**
Mem 700
Sec Mrs S Mitchell
Pro Brian Hemsley Tel 6732 865202
Holes 18 L 6635 yds SSS 72
Recs Am–72 I Martyr
Pro–
V'trs W/E & BH–U after 11.00 am; SOC on WD
Fees £6
Loc 15 miles S of London
Mis 16-bay floodlit driving range and 9-hole beginners' course mainly Par 3s

Eltham Warren (1890)

Private (Map 1/17)
Clubhouse Bexley Road Eltham London SE9 2PE
Tel **01-850 1166**
Mem 400
Sec P Standish Tel 01-850 4477
Pro J Cane Tel 01-859 7909
Holes 9 L 5840 yds SSS 68
Recs Am–68 D Gee
Pro–
V'trs WD–I; W/E & BH–M; SOC
Fees £7
Loc Eltham

Faversham (1910)

Private (Map 1/18)
Belmont Park Faversham
Tel **Eastling 251**
Mem 700
Sec DB Christie Tel Eastling 561
Pro GG Nixon Tel Eastling 275
Holes 18 L 5979 yds SSS 69
Recs Am–65 R Chapman
Pro–67 D Place
V'trs WD–I or H; W/E–M; SOC
Fees £9
Loc 2 miles from town and M2

Foxgrove

(Map 1/5)
Westgate Road Beckenham
Tel **01-650 1707**
Sec FG Wyatt
Holes Play over Beckenham Place Park

Gillingham (1908)

Private (Map 1/19)
Woodlands Road Gillingham
Tel **Medway 50999**
Mem 450 100(L) 40(J) 80(5)
Sec LP O'Grady Tel Gillingham 53017
Pro S Barrow Tel 55862
Holes 18 L 5911 yds SSS 68
Recs Am–65 T Williamson
Pro–64 P Clark
V'trs WD–U; W/E & BH–M
Fees £8 D£11
Loc A2/M2 2 miles

Hawkhurst Golf (1968)

Private (Map 1/20)
High Street Hawkhurst TN18 4JS
Tel **Hawkhurst 2396**
Mem 300
Sec AW Shipley
Pro T Collins Tel Hawkhurst 3600
Holes 9 L 5791 yds SSS 68
Recs Am–72
Pro–69
V'trs U
Fees £5 (£8)
Loc 14 miles S of Tunbridge Wells on A268

Herne Bay (1889)

Private (Map 1/21)
Eddington Herne Bay Kent
Tel **Herne Bay 4097**
Mem 360
Sec Bernard Warren Tel Herne Bay 373964
Pro Gary Peddir Tel Herne Bay 374727
Holes 18 L 5364 yds SSS 66
Recs Am–65 SJ Wood
Pro–65 Clive Clark
V'trs WD–U; W/E after 10.30 am; SOC
Fees £7 D–£9 (£8 D–£10.50)
Loc Herne Bay/Canterbury Road

High Elms (1969)

Public (Map 1/22)
High Elms Road Downe Orpington
Tel **Farnborough 58175**
Mem 230
Sec P Argent 01-462 2940
Pro A Hodgson 0689 58175
Holes 18 L 6210 yds SSS 70
Recs Am–68 I Farman
Pro–66 A Hodgson
V'trs U
Fees £4.50 (£6) special rates veterans and juniors
Loc Off A21 via Shire Lane

Holteye

(See Sussex)

Hythe Imperial (1950)

Private (Map 1/23)
Princes Parade Hythe Kent
Tel **Hythe 67441**
Mem 300
Sec PE Rosser Tel Hythe 67554
Pro David Gleeson Tel Hythe 67441
Holes 9 L 5583 yds SSS 67
Recs Am–63 PI Kaye
Pro–64 SH Sherman
V'trs H; U; SOC
Fees £6.50 (£9) W–£20
Loc On coast 4 miles W of Folkestone

Knole Park (1924)

Private (Map 1/24)
Seal Hollow Road Sevenoaks Kent TN15 0HT
Tel **0732 452709**
Mem 600
Sec DJL Hoppe Tel 0732 452150
Pro PE Gill Tel 0732 451740
Holes 18 L 6249 yds SSS 70
Recs Am–64 RW Seamer
Pro–
V'trs WD–Restricted; SOC; W/E & BH–M; H
Fees £12
Loc Seal Hollow Road

Lamberhurst (1892)

Private (Map 1/25)
Church Road Lamberhurst
Tel **Lamberhurst 890241**
Mem 659
Sec A Steward-Brooks Tel Lam 890591
Pro M Travers Tel Lam 890552
Holes 18 L 6249 yds SSS 70
Recs Am–
Pro–69 N Stott
V'trs WD–U; W/E (Before noon–NA)
Fees
Loc 5 miles SE Tunbridge Wells

Langley Park (1910)

Private (Map 1/26)
Barnfield Wood Road Beckenham BR3 2SZ
Tel **01-650 2090**
Mem 650
Sec PJ Macfarlane Tel 01-658 6849
Pro GT Ritchie Tel 01-650 1663
Holes 18 L 6488 yds SSS 71
Recs Am–66 T Trodd
Pro–67 George T Ritchie
V'trs WD–I; W/E–M; SOC on WD
Fees £12
Loc 1 mile Bromley South station

Leeds Castle (1928)

Public (Map 1/27)
Leeds Castle nr Maidstone
Tel **Hollingbourne 467**
Mem
Pro Chris Miller Tel Hollingbourne 467
Holes 9 L 6017 yds SSS 69
Recs Am–
Pro–66
V'trs U
Fees £4.50
Loc M20–A20 r Maidstone

Littlestone (1888)

Private (Map 1/28)
Littlestone New Romney TN28 8RB
Tel **New Romney 62310**
Mem 400
Sec JD Lewis Tel New Romney 63355
Pro Glynne Williams Tel New Romney 62231
Holes 18 L 6417 yds SSS 71
9 hole course 3996 yds Par 64

Recs Am–67 G Godmon
Pro–67 T Gale
V'trs WD–H; W/E by arrangement
Fees On application
Loc 15 miles S of Ashford

Lullingstone Park (1967)

Public (Map 1/29)
Park Gate Chelsfield nr Orpington
Tel **Badgers Mount 517**
Mem 400
Sec GS Childs
Pro Gilbert Lloyd Tel Badgers Mount 542
Holes 18 and 9
Recs Am–
Pro–
V'trs
Fees
Loc Off Orpington by-pass A224

Magpie Hall Lane (1948)

Public (Map 1/30)
Magpie Hall Lane Bromley
Tel **01-462 7014**
Pro A Hodgson
Holes 9 L 5538 yds SSS 66
Recs Am–66 HE Harding
KW Miles
Pro–
V'trs U
Fees 58p (£1)
Loc Off Bromley Common–A21
Mis Bromley Club plays here

Mid Kent (1909)

Private (Map 1/31)
Singlewell Road Gravesend
Tel **Gravesend 52387**
Mem 1050
Sec AF Reid Tel Gravesend 68035
Pro R Lee Tel Gravesend 332810
Holes 18 L 6206 yds SSS 70
V'trs WD–H; W/E–M
Fees £10
Loc 25 miles SE London

Nevill

(see Sussex)

North Foreland (1903)

Private (Map 1/32)
Kingsgate Broadstairs Thanet
Tel **Thanet 62140**
Mem 800
Sec LCR Hemmings
Pro Mike Lee Tel Thanet 69628
Holes 18 L 6374 yds SSS 70
Recs Am–66 P Walton
Pro–66 George Will
V'trs WD–H; W/E–NA–am H–pm
Fees Summer £9 (£12)
Winter £7 (£10)
Loc 1½ miles Broadstairs Station
Mis 18 holes Approach and Putt 1752 yds Bogey 54. Fees: £2.50 (£3.50)

Poult Wood (1974)

Public (Map 1/33)
Poult Wood Higham Lane Tonbridge
Tel **Tonbridge 364039**
Mem 500
Man A Hope Tel Tonbridge 366180
Pro K Adwick Tel Tonbridge 364039
Holes 18 L 5569 yds SSS 67
Recs Am–
Pro–
V'trs U; SOC on WD
Fees £3.25 (£5)
Loc 2 miles N of Tonbridge off A227

Prince's (1904)

Private (Map 1/34)
Sandwich Bay Sandwich
Tel **Sandwich 611118**
Mem 550
Sec B Hutchings Tel Sandwich 612000
Pro P Sparks Tel Sandwich 613797
Holes 27 hole Championship course 3×9 holes: Dunes/Himalayas/Shore. Combined courses vary 6238–6947 yds. Par varies 71–72 SSS varies 70–73
Recs Himalayas/Shore
Am–69 S Wood
Pro–69 M Mannelli
V'trs U; SOC incl W/E
Fees £12 (£14)
Loc Sandwich Bay

Rochester and Cobham Park (1891)

Private (Map 1/35)
Park Pale by Rochester
Tel **Shorne (047482) 3411**
Mem 680
Sec E Petch Tel Shorne 3411
Pro M Henderson Tel Shorne 3658
Holes 18 L 6467 yds SSS 71
Recs Am–67 MK Bills
Pro–67 M Henderson
V'trs WD–U; W/E–M before 5 pm H SOC Tues & Thurs
Fees £16 (£12)
Loc On A2, 3 miles E of Gravesend turn off

Royal Blackheath (1608)

Private (Map 1/36)
Court Road Eltham London SE9 5AF
Tel **01-850 1795**
Mem 600
Sec A Ross Tel 01-850 1795
Pro David Alton Tel 01-850 1763
Holes 18 L 6216 yds SSS 70
Recs Am–66 DM Woolmer
Pro–66 WC Thomas
V'trs U; SOC
Fees £16
Loc 20 mins Charing Cross Stat, Mottingham

Royal Cinque Ports (1892)

Private (Map 1/37)
Golf Road Deal
Tel **Deal 374328**
Mem 1015
Sec NS Phillips Tel Deal 374 007
Pro Andrew Reynolds Tel Deal 374170
Holes 18 L 6744 yds SSS 72
Recs Am–65 MF Bonallack
Pro–63 GD Manson
V'trs I
Fees
Loc Deal

Royal St George's (1887)

Private (Map 1/38)
Sandwich CT13 9PB
Tel **Sandwich 617308**
Mem 700
Sec Capt RJ Hitchen RN Tel Sandwich 613090
Pro Cyril Whiting Tel Sandwich 617380
Holes 18 L 6534 yds SSS 72
Recs Am–67 H Berwick
Pro–64 Christy O'Connor Jr
V'trs WD–I; W/E–M; SOC
Fees
Loc Sandwich 1 mile

Ruxley (1975)

Public (Map 1/39)
Sandy Lane St Paul's Cray Orpington Kent
Tel **Orpington 71490**
Mem 250
Sec D Simpson
Pro R Cornwell
Holes 18 L 5017 yds SSS 65
Recs Am–63 D Curtis
Pro–63 L Turner
V'trs WD–U; W/E & BH–before 11.30 am
Fees £6
Loc Off Ruxley roundabout on A20 at Sidcup

St Augustines (1907)

Private (Map 1/40)
Cottington Road Cliffsend Ramsgate CT12 5JN
Tel **(0843) 590 333**
Mem 300 80(L) 55(J) 120(5)
Sec R James Tel (0843) 590 333
Pro DB Scott Tel (0843) 590 222
Holes 18 L 5138 yds SSS 65
Recs Am–59 Dr S Hutton
Pro–61 Peter Mitchell
V'trs H; SOC–WE
Fees £10 (£12) W–£37.50 M–£85
Loc 2 miles S of Ramsgate Follow signs to St Augustines Cross

Sene Valley Folkestone and Hythe (1888)

Private (Map 1/41)
Sene Folkestone CT18 8BL
Mem 650
Sec RW Merry Tel Hythe 68513
Pro Trevor Dungate Tel Folkestone 68514
Holes 18 L 6320 yds SSS 70
Recs Am–69 G Moseley
Pro–69 G Will
V'trs U WD–I SOC
Fees £9 (£11)
Loc 2 miles N of Hythe on B2065

Sevenoaks Town (1927)

Private (Map 1/24)
Knole Park Seal Hollow Road Sevenoaks
Tel
Mem 45
Sec
Holes Play over Knole Park course

Sheerness (1906)

Private (Map 1/42)
Power Station Road Sheerness
Tel **Sheerness 662585**
Mem 350
Sec NO Larsen Tel Sheerness 662585
Pro Stephen Bryan Tel S'ness 662585
Holes 18 L 6500 yds SSS 71
Recs Am–68 J Simmance Jr
Pro–
V'trs WD–U; W/E & BH–By arrangement with Sec
Fees £8 (£12)
Loc 9 miles from Sittingbourne on A249

Shooter's Hill (1903)

Private (Map 1/43)
Lowood Eaglesfield Road London SE18 3DA
Tel **01-854 1216**
Mem 310 67(L) 43(J) 236(5)
Sec GD Sharp Tel 01-854 6388
Pro Robert Newberry Tel 01-854 0073
Holes 18 L 5718 yds SSS 68
Recs Am–63 M Holland
Pro–64 Neil Coles George Will Sydney Scott
V'trs WD–I; W/E & BH–M SOC Tues & Thurs only
Fees £11.50 D–£14.50
Loc 4 miles from Blackheath

Shoreham (1973)

Public (Map 1/45)
Darenth Valley Golf Course Station Road Shoreham
Tel **Otford 2922**
Mem 350
Sec AE Weller Tel Otford 2944
Pro P Edwards
Holes 18 L 6258 yds SSS 70
Recs Am–68 R Tempest
Pro–68 B Owens P Edwards
V'trs U
Fees £3.50 (£5.50)
Loc 3 miles from Sevenoaks

Shortlands (1897)

Private (Map 1/44)
Meadow Road Shortlands Bromley Kent
Tel **01-460 2471**
Mem 525
Sec Mrs L Burrows Tel 01-460 8828
Pro T Collingwood Tel 01-290 0304
Holes 9 L 5261 yds SSS 66
Recs Am–64 B Kent
Pro–61 David Pratt
V'trs M
Fees £5 (£7)
Loc Bromley Kent (or Greater London)

Sidcup (1891)

Private (Map 1/46)
Hurst Rd Sidcup Kent DA15 9AE
Tel **01-300 2864**
Mem 350
Sec KR Davison Tel 01-300 2150
Pro Ross Galgutt Tel 01-309 0679
Holes 9 L 5692 yds SSS 67
Recs Am–65 R Harris
Pro–66 WJ Lane
V'trs WD–U; W/E & BH–M
Fees £6
Loc Sidcup 2 miles from A2

Sittingbourne and Milton Regis (1929)

Private (Map 1/47)
Wormdale Newington Sittingbourne Kent ME9 7PX
Tel **Newington 842261**
Mem 325 100(L) 72(J) 175(5)
Sec HDG Wylie
Pro JR Hearn Tel Newington 842775
Holes 18 L 6121 yds SSS 69
Recs Am–67
Pro–62
V'trs WD–U; Sat–By arrangement; Sun–M SOC Tues & Thurs
Fees £9 (£12)
Loc 1 mile N of exit 5 M2 on A249

Sundridge Park (1901)

Private (Map 1/48)
Garden Lane Bromley Kent
Tel **01-460 8851 and 1822**
Mem 1167 99(L) 51(J) 189(5)
Sec P Holmes Tel 01-460 0278
Pro Bob Cameron Tel 01-460 5540
Holes East Course 18 L 6410 yds SSS 71
West Course 18 L 6027 yds SSS 69
Recs East Course Am–67
R Chapman R Seamer
Pro–64 R Cameron (revised course)
West Course Am–68
M Brosnan K Wilson
Pro–65 R Fidler
V'trs WD–SOC–I; W/E & BH–M
Fees On application
Loc 1 mile N of Bromley off Plaistow Lane opposite Sundridge Park station

Tenterden (1905)

Private (Map 1/49)
Woodchurch Road Tenterden
Tel **Tenterden 3987**
Mem 350
Sec MA North Tel Tenterden 3128
Pro Tony Collins
Holes 9 L 5119 yds SSS 65
Recs Am–
Pro–
V'trs U, except before noon Sun XL before noon Sunday
Fees On application
Loc 1 mile Tenterden

Tunbridge Wells (1889)

Private (Map 1/50)
Langton Road Tunbridge Wells TN4 8XH
Tel **T Wells 23034**
Mem 245 62(L) 35(J)
Sec EM Goulden Tel T Wells 36918
Pro RC Mudge Tel T Wells 41386
Holes 9 L 4684 yds SSS 62
Recs Am–59 EC Chapman
Pro–59 J Humphrey
V'trs WD–U; Tues pm, WE/BH–M
Fees 18 holes D–£7
Loc Tunbridge Wells; adjacent to Spa Hotel; behind Marchant's Garage

Walmer and Kingsdown (1909)

Private (Map 1/51)
Kingsdown nr Deal
Tel **Deal 373256**
Mem 550
Sec MJ Taylor
Pro T Hunt Tel 363017
Holes 18 L 6451 yds SSS 71
Recs Am–69 A Randall
Pro–70 MP Lee
V'trs WD–U; W/E–not before 10.30 am SOC
Fees D–£10 WE/BH–£12
W–£45 F–£70
Loc 2½ miles S of Deal

Westgate and Birchington (1893)

Private (Map 1/52)
Domneva Road Westgate-on-Sea
Tel **Thanet 31115**
Mem 325
Sec AJ Read
Pro Roger Game
Holes 18 L 4926 yds SSS 65
Recs Am–60 Miss W Morgan
Pro–60 J Hickman
V'trs WD–U; W/E & BH–NA before 10.30 am; H or I
Fees £5 (£6)
Loc Westgate Station ¼ mile

West Kent (1916)

Private (Map 1/53)
Downe
Tel **Farnborough 53737**
Mem 325
Sec AM Watt Tel Farn 51323
Pro RS Fidler Tel Farn 56863
Holes 18 L 6369 yds SSS 70
Recs Am–62 DC Smith
Pro–65 H Baiocchi
V'trs WD–I; W/E–M
Fees £12 D–£15
Loc Orpington 5 miles

West Malling (1974)

Private (Map 1/54)
Addington nr Maidstone
Tel **West Malling 844785**
Mem 550
Sec MR Ellis
Pro P Foston
Holes 18 L 6950 yds SSS 74
Recs Am–73 R Mitchell
Pro–68 N Job
V'trs WD–U; W/E–UH after 11.30 am
Fees D–£7.50 W/E–£9
Loc A20 London Road

Whitstable and Seasalter (1910)

Private (Map 1/55)
Collingwood Road Whitstable CT5 1EB
Tel **Whitstable 272020**
Mem 250
Sec Derek Spratt Tel Whitstable 273589
Pro
Holes 9 L 5284 yds SSS 63
Recs Am–
Pro–
V'trs WD–U; W/E–M
Fees £5
Loc Whitstable Station 1 mile

Wildernesse (1890)

Private (Map 1/56)
Seal Sevenoaks
Tel **Sevenoaks 61526**
Mem 800
Sec Major AS Furnival Tel Sev 61199
Pro Bill Dawson Tel Sev 61527
Holes 18 L 6478 yds SSS 72
Recs Am–66 P Benka M Pinner
Pro–65 I Grant
V'trs WD–I; W/E & BH–M
Fees £12 D–£16
Loc 2 miles E of Sevenoaks A25

Woodlands Manor (1928)

Private (Map 1/57)
Woodlands Sevenoaks TN15 6AB
Tel **Otford 3805**
Mem 650
Sec/ Owner Admin EF Newman Tel Otford 3806
Sec Joan Mills
Pro Nick Allen Tel Otford 4161
Holes 18 L 5858 yds SSS 68
Recs Am–
Pro–65 Neil Coles
V'trs U; W/E–H (NA before noon); WD–SOC

Fees £7 (£9)
Loc Between West Kinsdown and Otford; 2 miles S, off A20

Wrotham Heath (1906)

Private **(Map 1/58)**
Seven Mile Lane Comp Sevenoaks TN15 8QZ
Tel **Borough Green 884800**
Mem 200 70(L) 55(J) 50(5)
Sec JD Majendie Tel Borough Green 883099
Pro H Dearden Tel Borough Green 883854
Holes 9 L 5823 yds SSS 68
Recs Am–
Pro–
V'trs WD–H; W/E & BH–M; SOC (Fri only)
Fees £8.50 (£11.50)
Loc 8 miles W of Maidstone on B2106. 1 mile from M26/A20 junction

Middlesex

Airlinks

Private **(Map 1/38)**
Southall Lane Hounslow Middx TW5 9PE
Tel **01-561 1418**
Man J Shortland
Pro
Holes 18 L 5883 yds SSS 68
Fees
Loc

Ashford Manor (1898)

Private **(Map 1/1)**
Fordbridge Road Ashford Middx TW15 3RT
Tel **Ashford 252040**
Mem 800
Sec IR Goodliffe Tel Ashford 257687
Pro M Finney Tel Ashford 255940
Holes 18 L 6372 yds SSS 70
Recs Am–66 NM Curtis GA Homewood
Pro–64 David Talbot
V'trs I
Fees £12 (£14)
Loc Off A308 Ashford

Brent Valley (1938)

Public **(Map 1/2)**
Church Road Hanwell London W7
Tel **01-567 4230 (members)**
Mem 350
Sec AD Flett
Pro P Warner Tel 01-567 1411
Holes 18 L 5426 yds SSS 66
Recs Am–65 S Harper
Pro–63 A Bennett
V'trs U
Fees £2.80 (£4.40)
Loc Off Hanwell Broadway (Uxbridge Road) or A40 at Greenford

Bush Hill Park (1895)

Private **(Map 1/3)**
Bush Hill Winchmore Hill London N21 2BU
Tel **01-360 5738**
Mem 686
Sec JF Stocker Tel 01-360 5738
Pro George W Low Tel 01-360 4103
Holes 18 L 5809 yds SSS 68
Recs Am–65 T Sheaff
Pro–68 ST Murray
V'trs WD–U SOC; W/E–M
Fees D–£10
Loc 9 miles N of city centre

Crews Hill (1920)

Private **(Map 1/4)**
Cattlegate Road Crews Hill Enfield Middx EN2 8AZ
Tel **01-363 0787**
Mem 600
Sec/Man Tel 01-363 6674
Pro John Reynolds Tel 01-366 7422
Holes 18 L 6208 yds SSS 70
Recs Am–68 S Bishop
Pro–66 P Hunt
V'trs WD–UH SOC; W/E & BH–M
Fees On application
Loc 2½ miles N of Enfield

Ealing (1923)

Private **(Map 1/5)**
Perivale Lane Greenford Middx UB5 8SS
Tel **01-997 2595**
Mem 600
Pro A Stickley O Stickley Tel 01-997 3959
Holes 18 L 6216 yds SSS 70
Recs Am–67 R Latham
Pro–64 R Verwey (SA)
V'trs WD–U; W/E–M
Fees On application
Loc 6 miles Marble Arch on A40

Elstree

(see Hertfordshire)

Enfield (1893)

Private **(Map 1/6)**
Old Park Road South Windmill Hill Enfield EN2 7DA
Tel **01-363 0083 and 01-363 3921**
Mem 650
Sec AJ Hollis Tel 01-363 3970
Pro Ian Martin Tel 01-366 4492
Holes 18 L 6137 yds SSS 70
Recs Am–66 A Rogers
Pro–67 L Fickling
V'trs WD–I; W/E & BH–M; SOC on WD
Fees £10 D–£12
Loc 1 mile NE of Enfield

Finchley (1929)

Private **(Map 1/7)**
Nether Court Frith Lane London NW7
Tel **01-346 2436**
Mem 450
Sec JR Pearce 01-346 2436
Pro D Brown Tel 01-346 5086
Holes 18 L 6411 yds SSS 71
Recs Am–65 D Chatterton
Pro–67 T Moore
V'trs WD–U; SOC W/E–afternoon
Fees £11 (£16)
Loc 8 miles NW Charing Cross

Fulwell (1904)

Private **(Map 1/8)**
Hampton Hill Middlesex TW12 1JY
Tel **01-977 3188**
Mem 600
Sec GS East Tel 01-977 2733
Pro David Haslam Tel 01-977 3844
Holes 18 L 6490 yds SSS 71
Recs Am–68 KD Corcoran
SR Warrin
Pro–63 P Buchan
V'trs WD–I; W/E–M
Fees £15 (£20)
Loc Opp Fulwell Station

Grim's Dyke (1910)

Private **(Map 1/10)**
Oxhey Lane Hatch End Pinner Middlesex HA5 4AL
Tel **01-428 4093**
Mem 575
Sec T Ascough-Patterson Tel 01-428 4539
Pro N Macdonald Tel 01-428 7484
Holes 18 L 5600 yds SSS 67
Recs Am–66 S Kay
Pro–64 BJ Hunt
V'trs U; Sun–M; H; SOC
Fees £10
Loc 2 miles W of Harrow (A4008)

Hampstead (1894)

Private **(Map 1/11)**
Winnington Road London N2 0TU
Tel **01-455 0203**
Mem 526
Sec JEE Jones
Pro PJ Brown Tel 01-455 7089
Holes 9 L 5812 yds SSS 68
Recs Am–66 RDA Smith
Pro–62 GT Adams
V'trs I; H
Fees £10 D–£15 (£15 D–£20)
Loc Golders Green, 2 miles

Harefield Place (1947)

Public **(Map 1/12)**
The Drive Harefield Place Uxbridge Middx UB10 8PA
Tel **0895-31169**
Mem 490
Sec BL Russell Tel 01-561 6619
Pro P Howard Tel 0895-37287
Holes 18 L 5711 yds SSS 68
Recs Am–65 S Mylward
Pro–64 A Barr G Cullen
V'trs U
Fees £4.30
Loc 2 miles N of Uxbridge

Harrow School (1978)

Private **(Map 1/13)**
Harrow-on-the-Hill Middlesex
Tel
Mem 190 80(L) 30(J)
Sec DA Fothergill Tel 01-422 5237
Pro
Holes 9 L 1775 yds SSS 30
Recs Am–
Pro–
V'trs M
Fees
Loc Harrow School

Haste Hill (1933)

Public **(Map 1/14)**
The Drive Northwood Middx
Tel **Northwood 26485**
Mem 250
Sec ETA Rishton Tel 01-866 3175
Pro M Waldron
Holes 18 L 5794 yds SSS 68
Recs Am–68 J Joyce
Pro
V'trs U
Fees £3.50
Loc Northwood

Hendon (1900)

Private (Map 1/15)
off Sanders Lane Devonshire Road London NW7
Tel **01-346 7810**
Mem 530
Man KW Counsell Tel 01-346 6023
Pro S Murray Tel 01-346 8990
Holes 18 L 6241 yds SSS 70
Recs Am–68 AL MacLeod
Pro–66 SWT Murray
V'trs WD–U; W/E & BH–essential to book
Fees £10 D–£13 W–£16
Loc 10 miles from city centre

Highgate (1904)

Private (Map 1/16)
Denewood Road Highgate London N6 4AH
Tel **01-340 1906**
Mem 593
Sec JAS Luill
Pro R Turner Tel 01-340 5467
Holes 18 L 5964 yds SSS 69
Recs Am–66 D Kingsman P Bax
Pro–68 Peter Alliss
V'trs W/E & BH–M; WD–U SOC (Wed am reserved for ladies only)
Fees £11 (£18)
Loc London, 5 miles

Hillingdon (1892)

Private (Map 1/17)
18 Dorset Way Hillingdon Uxbridge Middx UB10 0JR
Tel **Uxbridge 39810**
Mem 375
Sec LAN Holland Tel Uxbridge 33956
Pro DJ McFadden Tel Uxbridge 51980
Holes 9 L 5459 yds (4989 metres) SSS 67
Recs Am–67 M Weir
Pro–69 P Cheyney
V'trs WD–U exc Thurs 12 am–4 pm (lady members only); W/E only afternoons when accompanied by a full member; SOC–Mon Tue Fri; H
Fees £4.50 with member; £9 18 holes; D–£9
Loc 1 mile E of Uxbridge Civic Centre, adjoining RAF Station, Uxbridge

Holiday GC (1975)

Private (Map 1/18)
Stockley Road West Drayton Middlesex
Tel
Mem 80
Man John O'Loughlin
Tel 0895 444232
Pro NC Coles
Holes 9 L 3800 yds SSS 32
Recs Am–
Pro–
V'trs U SOC
Fees 18 holes–£2 (£3)
Loc In grounds of Holiday Inn

Horsenden Hill (1935)

Public (Map 1/19)
Woodland Rise Greenford Middlesex
Tel **01-902 4555**
Mem 130
Sec V Le Picq Tel 01-903 3143
Pro T Martin Tel 01-902 4555
Holes 9 L 3060 yds SSS 54
Recs Am–
Pro–
V'trs U
Fees £1.65 (£2.30)
Loc Greenford

Hounslow Heath (1979)

Public (Map 1/20)
Staines Road Hounslow Middx TW4 5DS
Tel **01-570 5271**
Mem 304
Sec PJ Silvester
Pro Philip Cheyney
Holes 18 L 5820 yds Par 69 SSS 68
V'trs U Tee off times–booking weekends
Fees £3.25 (£4.15)
Loc Opp Green Lane, Staines Road, Hounslow

Leaside (1973)

Public (Map 1/21)
Picketts Lock Centre Edmonton London N9
Tel **01-803 3611**
Mem 140 12(L) 18(J)
Sec JK Husband Tel Billericay 53696
Pro R Gerken
Holes 9 L 2489 yds SSS 32
Recs Am–
Pro–
V'trs U
Fees £1.20 (£1.45)
Loc

Lime Trees Park (1984)

Public (Map 1/39)
Ruislip Road Northolt Middx UB5 6QZ
Tel **01-845 3180**
Mem 490
Sec AJ Besgrove Tel 01-845 3180
Pro Bill Mylward Tel 01-845 3180
Holes 9 L 5789 yds SSS 69
Recs Am–
Pro–
V'trs U SOC
Fees 9 holes £2.10 (£2.40) 18 holes £3.20 (£4.20)
Loc Off Western Avenue (A40) at Polish war memorial towards Yeading–$\frac{1}{4}$ mile

Mill Hill (1925)

Private (Map 1/22)
100 Barnet Way Mill Hill London NW7
Tel **01-959 2282**
Mem 450
Sec C Pole Tel 01-959 2339
Pro A Daniel Tel 01-959 7261
Holes 18 L 6309 yds SSS 70
Recs Am–65 H Aarons
Pro–67 J Hudson
V'trs WD–U; W/E & BH after 12 noon–U
Fees £11 (£16)
Loc Burnt Oak and Edgeware Stations

Muswell Hill (1893)

Private (Map 1/23)
Rhodes Ave Wood Green London N22 4UT
Tel **01-888 2044**
Mem 500
Sec JAB Connors Tel 01-888 1764
Pro IB Roberts Tel 01-888 8046
Holes 18 L 6470 yds SSS 71
Recs Am–68 BP Parker
Pro–65 H Weetman
V'trs WD–U; W/E & BH–M
Fees £10 D–£13 (£15 book with Pro)
Loc 1 mile Bounds Green Underground

North Middlesex (1928)

Private (Map 1/24)
The Manor House Friern Barnet Lane London N20 0NL
Tel **01-445 1732**
Mem 500
Sec D Dalingwater Tel 01-445 1604
Pro ASR Roberts Tel 01-445 3060
Holes 18 L 5611 yds SSS 67
Recs Am–65 M Cohen
Pro–64 S Levermore
V'trs WD–I; W/E & BH–at certain times
Fees £7.75 (£9.25)
Loc 10 miles Charing Cross

Northwood (1891)

Private (Map 1/25)
Northwood Middx
Tel **Northwood 25329**
Mem 420 240(L) 50(J) 111(5)
Sec CW Pipe Tel Northwood 21384
Pro CJ Holdsworth Tel Northwood 20112
Holes 18 L 6493 yds SSS 71
Recs Am–66 GS Lang
Pro–67 J Bland
V'trs WD–H SOC; W/E & BH–NA
Fees £10
Loc 3 miles E of Rickmansworth

Perivale Park (1932)

Public (Map 1/26)
Ruislip Road East Greenford Middlesex
Tel **01-578 1693**
Mem 200
Sec C Jonas Tel 01-578 1693
Pro P Bryant Tel 01-578 1693
Holes 9 L 5296 yds SSS 65
Recs Am–64
Pro–
V'trs U
Fees £3.60 (£4.40)
Loc 1 mile E of Greenford

Picketts Lock (1973)

Public (Map 1/27)
Picketts Lock Lane London N9 0AS
Tel **01-803 3611**
Mem
Sec JS Davie Tel 01-803 4756
Pro RG Gerken
Holes 9 L 2496 yds SSS 64
Recs Am–31 M Yates
Pro–30 JTB Rayner
V'trs U
Fees 40p (55p)
Loc Edmonton North London

Pinner Hill (1929)

Private (Map 1/28)
Pinner Hill Middlesex
Tel **01-866 0963**
Mem 500
Sec LHW Woodbridge
Pro J Rule Tel 01-866 2109
Holes 18 L 6293 yds SSS 70
Recs Am–63 SR Warrin
Pro–67 TH Cotton
G Player T Wilkes G Low
J Warren
V'trs WD–U; Sundays & BH–M
Fees On request
Loc 1 mile West Pinner Green

Potters Bar

(See Hertfordshire)

Ruislip (1936)

Public (Map 1/29)
Ickenham Road Ruislip Middx
Tel **Ruislip 32004/38081**
Mem 400
Man SMD Dunlop
Pro D Nash Tel Ruislip 38835
Holes 18 L 5235 yds SSS 67
Recs Am–66 T Burchell
Pro–59 P Glozier
V'trs U
Fees £3.10 (£4.90)
Loc W Ruislip–(BR and LTE Station)

Stanmore (1893)

Private (Map 1/30)
Gordon Ave Stanmore Middlesex HA7 2RL
Tel **01-954 4661**
Mem 500
Sec PF Wise Tel 01-954 2599
Pro VR Law Tel 01-954 2646
Holes 18 L 5925 yds SSS 68
Recs Am–66 H Preston
Pro–66 George Low
V'trs WD–H; W/E & BH–M SOC
Fees £8; Mon & Fri £3 (public days)
Loc E boundary of Harrow

Strawberry Hill (1900)

Private (Map 1/31)
Wellesley Road Twickenham Middx
Tel **01-894 1246**
Mem 350
Sec RC Meer Tel 01-894 0165
Pro P Buchan Tel 01-892 2082
Holes 9 L 2381 yds SSS 62
Recs Am–61 RE Heryet
Pro–59 H Fullicks
K Bousfield R Gerken
V'trs WD–U; W/E–M(XL)
Fees £6
Loc Strawberry Hill Station
Mis Course designed by JH Taylor 1910

Sudbury (1920)

Private (Map 1/32)
Bridgewater Road Wembley Middx HA0 1AL
Tel **01-902 0218**
Mem 550
Sec JA Smith Tel 01-902 3713
Pro Raymond Beard Tel 01-902 7910
Holes 18 L 6282 yds SSS 70
Recs Am–65 J Kirkham
Pro–65 J Gill
V'trs U; Sun & BH–M
Fees £11 (£16.50)
Loc Junction of A4005 and A4090

Trent Park (1973)

Public (Map 1/33)
Bramley Road Southgate London N14
Tel **01-366 7432**
Mem 500
Sec S Martin
Pro Craig Easton Tel 01-366 7432
Holes 18 L 6008 yds SSS 69
Recs Am–66 P Craig
Pro–64 V Law
V'trs U SOC
Fees £3.25 (£4.45)
Loc Opp Oakwood Tube (Piccadilly Line)

Twickenham (1976–Course; 1977–Club)

Public (Map 1/34)
Staines Road Twickenham Middx
Tel **01-979 6946**
Mem 232
Sec E Eldridge 01-892 5579
Pro PA Tickle Tel 01-979 0032
Holes 9 L 6014 yds SSS 69
Recs Am–
Pro–
V'trs U
Fees £2.40 (£4.20)
Loc 2 miles NW of Hampton Court

West Middlesex (1891)

Private (Map 1/35)
Greenford Road Southall Middx
Tel **01-574 3450**
Mem 900
Sec PJ Furness Tel 01-574 3450
Pro L Farmer Tel 01-574 1800
Holes 18 L 6242 yds SSS 70
Recs Am–65 J Walsh
Pro–64 L Farmer
V'trs WD–U; W/E–After 3 pm
Fees Mon, Wed–£4; Tues, Thur, Fri–£8 (£14)
Loc Junction Uxbridge Road and Greenford Road

White Webbs (1932)

Public (Map 1/36)
Enfield Municipal GC Whitewebbs Park Enfield Middx
Tel **01-363 4458**
Mem 475
Sec AC Cleves Tel Waltham Cross 23039
Pro D Lewis Tel 01-363 4454
Holes 18 L 5755 yds SSS 68
Recs Am–65 I Morley
Pro–68 D Lewis
V'trs U
Fees WD–£3; Sun–£4
Loc 1 mile N of Enfield Town

Wyke Green (1928)

Private (Map 1/37)
Syon Lane Isleworth Middlesex
Tel **01-560 8777**
Mem 618
Sec Maj WE Lyndon Moore TD Tel 01-560 8777
Pro A Fisher Tel 01-847 0685
Holes 18 L 6242 yds SSS 70
Recs Am–65 MR Johnson
Pro–64 C DeFoy
V'trs U
Fees £12 (£17)
Loc ½ mile from Gillettes Corner–A4

Norfolk

Barnham Broom Hotel (1977)

Private (Map 1/1)
Norwich NR9 4DD
Tel **060-545 393**
Mem 660
Sec Alan Long
Pro Peter Ballingall
Holes 18 L 6603 yds SSS 72
Recs Am–70 G Parkhill
Pro–69 D Vaughan, IR Porter
V'trs U
Fees On application
Loc 7 miles W of Norwich off A47

Bawburgh

Private (Map 1/10)
Long Lane Bawburgh
Tel **0603 746390**
Mem 300
Sec RJ Mapes
Pro Robert Waugh
Holes 9 L 5278 yds SSS 65
Rec Am–70 S Manser
Pro–72 T Simmonds
V'trs Restricted Sundays until 11 am; WD–SOC by arrangement
Fees 9-holes–£4; 18-holes–£6 £12.50
Loc S of A47. 1 mile from Norwich Ring road. Turn left at Round Well PH Rear of Royal Norfolk Showground

Costessey Park

Private (Map 1/20)
Costessey Park Costessey Norwich NR8 5AL
Tel
Mem 500
Sec Colin House Tel Norwich (0603) 746333
Pro Robert Foster Tel Norwich (0603) 747085
Holes 18 L 5633 yds SSS 67
Recs Am–
Pro–
V'trs U SOC on WD
Fees £6.90
Loc 3 miles W of Norwich; turn off A47 at Round Well pub

Dereham (1934)

Private (Map 1/2)
Quebec Road Dereham NR19 2DS
Tel **Dereham 3122**
Mem 560
Sec Noel Dodds Tel Dereham 5900
Pro Martin Elsworthy Tel Dereham 5631
Holes 9 L 6225 yds SSS 70
Recs Am–63 L Varney
Pro–65 M Elsworthy
V'trs H WE–M
Fees £6 (£7.50) W–£20 M–£50
Loc ½ mile town centre

Diss

(See Suffolk)

Eaton (1910)

Private (Map 1/3)
Newmarket Road Norwich NR4 6SF
Tel **Norwich (0603) 52881**
Mem 425 130(L) 70(J) 205(5)
Sec N Harrison OBE Tel Norwich (0603) 51686
Pro Frank Hill Tel Norwich (0603) 52478
Holes 18 L 6125 yds SSS 69
Recs Am–66
Pro–66
V'trs I; W/E–NA before noon
Fees £8 (£10)
Loc Norwich

Fakenham (1973)

Private (Map 1/4)
Fakenham
Tel **038-2867**
Mem 450
Sec G Cocker Tel Fakenham 55665
Pro J Westwood Tel Fakenham 3534
Holes 9

Recs Am–70 D Hood
Pro–70 M Leeder
V'trs WD–U; W/E–starting times alternate; Suns am
Fees £6 (£7.50)
Loc Racecourse

Feltwell (1976)

Private **(Map 1/18)**
Wilton Road Feltwell Norfolk
Mem 240
Sec Flt Lt KW Wright MBE DFM RAF(Ret) Tel Feltwell 828795
Holes 9 L 6260 yds (2 × 3 130) 5722 metres SSS 70
V'trs U
Fees £4 (£5)
Loc 1 mile S of Feltwell village on B1112
Mis Course laid out on former Feltwell aerodrome. Limited facilities, to be improved during 1986.

Gorleston

(See Suffolk)

Great Yarmouth and Caister (1882)

Private **(Map 1/5)**
Beach House Caister-on-Sea Gt Yarmouth
Tel **Gt Yarmouth 720421**
Mem 700
Sec MH Deere Tel Gt Yarmouth 728699
Pro Nick Catchpole Tel Gt Yarmouth 720421
Holes 18 L 6204 yds SSS 70
Recs Am–66 JW Nudds
Pro–67 A Jacklin
V'trs W/E–NA before noon; SOC
Fees £7.50 (£8.50)
Loc Caister-on-Sea

Hunstanton (1890)

Private **(Map 1/6)**
Hunstanton
Tel **Hunstanton 2811**
Mem 300 110(L) 65(J)
Sec GH Allen
Pro J Carter Tel Hunstanton 2751
Holes 18 L 6660 yds SSS 72
Recs Am–66 RDBM Shade
Pro–65 ME Gregson
V'trs U
Fees £12 (£17) W–£57
(Reduced in winter)
Loc ½ mile E of Hunstanton

King's Lynn (1923)

Private **(Map 1/7)**
Castle Rising King's Lynn PE31 6BD
Tel **Castle Rising 656**
Mem 905
Sec GJ Higgins Tel Castle Rising 654
Pro C Hanlon Tel Castle Rising 655
Holes 18 L 6552 yds SSS 71
Recs Am–69
Pro–72
V'trs WD–U H SOC; W/E & BH–NA unless booking accepted
Fees £11 (£15)
Loc 4 miles NE of King's Lynn

Links Country Park Hotel and Golf Club (1979)

Private **(Map 1/8)**
West Runton Cromer
Tel **West Runton 691**
Mem 220
Sec G Harvey
Pro G Harvey
Holes 9 L 4814 yds Par 66 SSS 64
Recs Am–68 R Rouse
Pro–65 R Mann
V'trs U
Fees £5 (£6)
Loc 2 miles E of Sheringham, in West Runton village
Mis Full snack, meal and accommodation facilities

Mundesley (1903)

Private **(Map 1/9)**
Links Road Mundesley Norfolk NR11 8HP
Tel **Mundesley 720279**
Mem 358
Sec BD Baxter Tel Mundesley 720095
Pro TG Symmons Tel Mundesley 720279
Holes 9 L 5410 yds SSS 66
Recs Am–
Pro–
V'trs U; Wed 12.00–3.00 pm–NA Sun until 11.30 am–NA
Fees 1 Nov–31 Mar £5.50 (£6.50)
1 Apr–31 Oct £6.50 (£8.50)
Loc 7 miles S of Cromer

RAF Marham (1974)

Private **(Map 1/21)**
RAF Marham Kings Lynn Norfolk PE33 9NP
Tel
Mem 190
Sec PC Ridge Tel Narborough 337261 ext 601/5
Pro
Holes 9 L 5280 yds SSS 66
Recs Am–
Pro–
V'trs By prior arrangement as course is situated on MOD land; WD–U WE–U except Sun am
Fees £4
Loc Near Narborough 11 miles SE of Kings Lynn
Mis Course may be closed without prior notice

Royal Cromer (1888)

Private **(Map 1/11)**
Overstrand Road Cromer NR27 0JH
Tel **Cromer 512884**
Mem 685
Sec TA King Tel Cromer 512884
Pro RJ Page Tel Cromer 512267
Holes 18 L 6508 yds SSS 71
Recs Am–69 MW Jubb
Pro–68 R Mann
V'trs H SOC on WD
Fees £10 (£12)
Loc 1 mile E of Cromer

Royal Norwich (1893)

Private **(Map 1/12)**
Drayton High Road Hellesdon Norwich
Tel **Norwich 45712**
Mem 780
Sec DF Cottier Tel Norwich 49928
Pro Barry Lockwood Tel Norwich 408459
Holes 18 L 6603 yds SSS 72
Recs Am–67 A Barker
Pro–66 HJ Boyle
V'trs Restricted W/E & BH; SOC
Fees £12 R/D ½ price with mem
Loc ½ mile E of Ring Road on Fakenham Road

Royal West Norfolk (1892)

Private **(Map 1/13)**
Brancaster King's Lynn PE31 8AX
Tel **Brancaster 210223**
Mem 530
Sec Major N Carrington Smith Tel Brancaster 210223
Pro RE Kimber Tel Brancaster 210616
Holes 18 L 6428 yds SSS 71
Recs Am–67 AH Perowne
Pro–
V'trs U; (W/E July, Aug, Sept–M)
Fees D–£11 W/E–£15
Loc 7 miles E of Hunstanton on A419

Ryston Park (1932)

Private **(Map 1/14)**
Ely Road Denver Downham Market
Tel **Downham 382133**
Mem 320
Sec AJ Wilson Tel Downham 383834
Pro
Holes 9 L 6292 yds SSS 70
Recs Am–JP Alflatt
Pro–
V'trs W/E–M
Fees £8
Loc 1 mile S of Downham Market on A10

Sheringham (1891)

Private **(Map 1/15)**
Sheringham
Tel **Sheringham 822038**
Mem 750
Sec MJ Garrett Tel Sheringham 823488
Pro MT Leeder Tel Sheringham 822980
Holes 18 L 6430 yds SSS 71
Recs Am–66 G Parkhill
Pro–67 B Waites, S Beckham
V'trs U; H; SOC
Fees £11 (£13)
Loc ½ mile W Town Centre

Sprowston Park (1980)

Private **(Map 1/19)**
Wroxham Road Sprowston Norwich NR7 8RP
Tel **Norwich 410657**
Mem 650
Sec DE Dowling Tel Norwich 410657
Pro Chris Potter Tel Norwich 415557
Holes 18 L 5985 yds SSS 69
V'trs H; W/E–U before 5 pm
Fees No green fees W/E
Loc 2 miles NE city centre

Swaffham (1922)

Private **(Map 1/16)**
Cley Road Swaffham
Tel **Swaffham 21611**
Mem 450
Sec HP Haverson
Pro CJ Norton Tel Gooderstone 284
Holes 9 L 6252 yds SSS 70

Recs Am–69 G Head
Pro–64 CJ Norton
V'trs WD–U; W/E–M (NA Sun am)
Fees £6
Loc 1½ miles from Swaffham

Thetford (1912)

Private (Map 1/17)
Brandon Road Thetford IP24 3ND
Tel **0842-2258**
Mem 650
Sec BC Moor Tel 0842-2169
Pro N Arthur Tel 0842-2662
Holes 18 L 6504 yds SSS 71
Recs Am–69 RE Clarke
Pro–69 B White
V'trs H SOC W/E by arrangement
Fees £12 (£15)
Loc Brandon Road (B1107) off A11

Suffolk

Aldeburgh (1884)

Private (Map 1/1)
Aldeburgh IP15 5PE
Tel **Aldeburgh 2408**
Mem 750
Sec RC Van de Velde Tel Aldeburgh 2890
Pro K Preston Tel Aldeburgh 3309
Holes 18 L 6330 yds SSS 71
9 L 2114 yds SSS 64
Recs Am–65 J Lloyd
Pro–67 JM Johnson
V'trs I
Fees On application
Loc 6 miles E of A12 midway between Ipswich and Lowestoft

Beccles (1899)

Private (Map 1/2)
The Common Beccles Suffolk
Tel **712244**
Mem 200
Sec Mrs LW Allen Tel 712479
Pro K Allen Tel 712244
Holes 9 L 2696 yds SSS 67
Recs Am–
Pro–64 K Allen
V'trs WD–U SOC; Sun–M
Fees £4.50 (W/E & BH £5.50)
Loc Lowestoft 10 miles Norwich 18 miles A146

Bungay and Waveney Valley (1889)

Private (Map 1/3)
Bungay
Tel **Bungay 2337**
Mem 600
Sec WJ Mann Tel Bungay 2329
Pro N Whyte Tel Bungay 2337
Holes 18 L 5944 yds SSS 68
Recs Am–67 R Kidd
Pro–64 T Spurgeon
V'trs WD–U SOC; W/E–M
Fees £8
Loc ½ mile town centre

Bury St Edmunds (1922)

Private (Map 1/4)
Tut Hill Bury St Edmunds
Tel **Bury St Edmunds 5979**
Mem 830 130(L) 34(J) 100(5) 80 (Squash)
Sec CD Preece Tel Bury St Edmunds 5979
Pro Mark Jillings Tel Bury St Edmunds 5978
Holes 18 L 6615 yds SSS 72
Recs Am–69 S Goodman A Currie
Pro–68 R Kemp
V'trs WD–U SOC; W/E–H NA before 10 am; BH–U
Fees D–£9 (D–£15)
Loc 2 miles West
Mis 2 squash courts

Diss (1903)

Private (Map 1/5)
Stuston Common Diss Norfolk
Tel **Diss 2847**
Mem 350
Sec J Bell Tel Diss 2679
Pro T Pennock Tel Diss 4399
Holes 9 L 5900 yds SSS 68
Recs Am–68 JE Doe
Pro–66 T Pennock
V'trs WD–not after 4 pm; W/E & BH– not before 4 pm; SOC
Fees £5 (£6)
Loc ½ mile Diss

Felixstowe Ferry (1880)

Private (Map 1/6)
Ferry Road Felixstowe IP4 9RY
Tel **Felixstowe 286834**
Mem 750
Sec GJ Stephens Tel Fel 286834
Pro I Macpherson Tel Felixstow 283975
Holes 18 L 6308 yds SSS 70
Recs Am–68 I Whinney
Pro–65 I Richardson
V'trs U; (W/E–M before 10.30 am); SOC
Fees £8 (£12)
Loc 2 miles NE of Felixstowe town centre
Mis Self-contained flats available

Flempton (1895)

Private (Map 1/7)
Bury St Edmunds
Tel **Culford 291**
Mem 250
Sec PH Nunn Tel Newmarket 750100
Pro M Jillings
Holes 9 L 6704 yds SSS 69
Recs Am–67 Lt J Reynolds
Pro–69 J Arbon
V'trs WD–U; W/E & BH–M
Fees £8 D–£10
Loc 5 miles NW of Bury St. Edmunds

Fornham Park G & CC (1974)

Private and Public (Map 1/11)
Fornham St Martin Bury St Edmunds
Tel **0284 63426**
Mem 692
Sec Mrs S Russell
Pro John Frew Tel 0284 63426
Holes 18 L 6212 yds SSS 72
Recs Am–75 A Mulinder
Pro–66 John Frew
V'trs U
Fees £5 (£10)
Loc From Cambridge first exit on A45; from Ipswich third exit on A45; 5 mins from A45

Gorleston (1926)

Private (Map 1/8)
Warren Road Gorleston Gt Yarmouth
Tel **Gt Yarmouth 661082**
Mem 830
Sec PG Rudd Tel Gt Yarmouth 661911
Pro RL Moffitt Tel Gt Yarmouth 662103
Holes 18 L 6279 yds SSS 70
Recs Am–68 J Maddock
Pro–
V'trs U H SOC
Fees £7 (£8.50) W–£25
Loc Gt Yarmouth

Haverhill (1974)

Private (Map 1/9)
Coupals Road Haverhill
Tel **61951**
Mem 236
Sec D Martin Tel Haverhill 61951
Pro Clive Cook Tel Haverhill 61951
Holes 9 L 5472 yds SSS 68
Recs Am–69 C Edwards
Pro–66 C Cook
V'trs U
Fees £7 (£9)
Loc Haverhill 1 mile off A604

Heath Farm (1983)

Private (Map 1/21)
Newborne Way Waldringfield
Woodbridge Suffolk IP12 4PT
Tel **0473-36768**
Mem 320
Sec LJ McWaye Tel 0473-36768 or 47569 (home)
Pro
Holes 9 L 4543 yds SSS 62
Recs Am–
Pro–
V'trs WD–U; WE/BH–M before noon, SOC on WD
Fees
Loc 3 miles N of Ipswich off A12

Ipswich (Purdis Heath) (1895)

Private (Map 1/10)
Purdis Heath Ipswich
Tel **(0473) 78941**
Mem 700
Sec AE Howell
Pro SJ Whymark Tel (0473) 74017
Holes 18 L 6405 yds SSS 71
9 L 1950 yds SSS 31
Recs 18 holes, Am–67 IP Whinney
Pro–67 RA Knight
9 holes, Am–
Pro
V'trs 18 hole–H or I. 9 hole–U; SOC
Fees 18 hole £8 (£10); 9 holes £5
Loc 3 miles E of Ipswich
Mis Steward (0473) 77474

Newton Green (1907)

Private (Map 1/12)
Newton Green Sudbury
Tel **Sudbury 77501**
Mem 400
Sec JR Steed Tel Sudbury 71254
Pro C Jervis
Holes 9 L 5442 yds SSS 66
Recs Am–64 (18 holes) J Humm
Pro–29 (9 holes) A Davey
V'trs WD–U; W/E–M
Fees £6
Loc 4 miles E of Sudbury

Rookery Park (1975)

Private (Map 1/13)
Carlton Colville Lowestoft NR33 8HJ
Tel **Lowestoft 4009/60380**
Mem 750
Sec Tel 60380
Pro S Beckham Tel 515103
Holes 18 L 6649 yds SSS 72
Recs Am–71 G Long
Pro–69 P Kent
V'trs WD–U; W/E & BH–Not before 11 am; SOC
Fees D–£9 (£11)
Loc West Lowestoft (A146)
Mis Par 3 Course in addition

Royal Worlington and Newmarket (1893)

Private (Map 1/14)
Worlington Bury St Edmunds
Tel **Mildenhall 712216**
Mem 358
Sec WN White MC MA
Pro AM Littlechild Tel Mildenhall 715224
Holes 9 L 6218 yds SSS 70
Recs Am–67 DJ Millensted
Pro–66 EE Beverley
V'trs U; W/E–NA
Fees £15
Loc Mildenhall 2 miles
Mis Prior warning essential

Rushmere (1895)

Private (Map 1/15)
Rushmere Heath Ipswich
Tel **Ipswich 77109**
Mem 750
Sec RW Whiting Tel Ipswich 75648
Pro NTJ McNeill Tel Ipswich 78076
Holes 18 L 6287 yds SSS 70
Recs Am–
Pro–69 J Johnson
V'trs U (ex before 10.30 W/E)
Fees On application
Loc Ipswich off Woodbridge Road (A12)

Southwold (1884)

Private (Map 1/16)
The Common Southwold Suffolk
Tel **0502 723234**
Mem 450
Sec IG Guy Tel 0502 723248
Pro Brian Allen Tel 0502 723790
Holes 9 L 6001 yds SSS 69
Recs Am–67 S Fitzgerald
Pro–65 Robin Mann
V'trs U subject to club fixtures
Fees £6 (W/E & BH £7) W–£25 F–£40 (subject to review)
Loc 35 miles N of Ipswich

Stoke by Nayland (1972)

Private (Map 1/17)
Keepers Lane Leavenheath Colchester Essex CO6 4PZ
Tel **Nayland 262836**
Mem 1047
Sec J Loshak Tel Nayland 262836
Pro K Lovelock Tel Nayland 262769
Holes 18 Gainsborough L 6471 yds SSS 71
18 Constable L 6498 yds SSS 71
Recs Am–66 (Gainsborough) RW Mann
Pro–69 (Gainsborough) PL Cowan
V'trs W/E & BH–H, NA before 10 am; WD–U, SOC
Fees £7 D–£10.50 (£9 D–£13) Weekly and monthly by arrangement
Loc Between Colchester and Sudbury on B1038

Stowmarket (1962)

Private (Map 1/18)
Lower Road Onehouse Stowmarket
Tel **Rattlesden 392**
Mem 600
Sec EJW Smith Tel Rattlesden 473
Pro C Aldred Tel Rattlesden 392
Holes 18 L 6119 yds SSS 69
Recs Am–67 I Oakes
Pro–66 H Flatman
V'trs H; SOC–Tue Thu Fri & Wed pm
Fees £7 D–£9 Sat/Sun–£10
Loc 2½ miles SW Stowmarket
Mis Buggies for hire

Thorpeness Golf Club Hotel

Private (Map 1/19)
Thorpeness
Tel **Aldeburgh 2176**
Mem 400
Sec NW Griffin
Pro R Mann Tel Aldeburgh 2524
Holes 18 L 6208 yds SSS 71
Recs Am–67 RJ Coombes
Pro–67 K McDonald
V'trs U
Fees £9 (£11)
Loc In village, 2 miles from Aldeburgh
Mis 20-bedroom hotel adjacent to course

Woodbridge (1893)

Private (Map 1/20)
Bromeswell Heath nr Woodbridge
Tel **Woodbridge 2038**
Mem 980
Sec JF Thom
Pro LA Jones Tel W'bdge 3213
Holes 18 L 6314 yds SSS 70
9 L 2243 yds SSS 31
18 L 5708 yds SSS 73 (Ladies)
9 L 2243 yds SSS 34 (Ladies)
Recs Am–64 JVT Marks
Pro–65 F Sunderland
V'trs H WE/BH–M
Fees £11 D–£15 (£15 D–£20) 1986 prices
Loc 2 miles E of Woodbridge; follow A12 towards Lowestoft; turn off Woodbridge by-pass at roundabout signposted towards Orford B1084

Surrey

The Addington (1913)

Private (Map 2/1)
Shirley Church Road Croydon Surrey CR0 5AB
Tel **01-777 1055**
Mem
Sec Mrs DJ Edwardes Tel 01-777 6057
Pro Ewan Campbell Tel 01-777 1701
Holes 18 L 6242 yds SSS 71
Recs Am–66 P Benka
Pro–68 F Robson
V'trs I
Fees On application
Loc 2½ miles from E Croydon

Addington Court (1931)

Public (Map 2/2)
Featherbed Lane Addington Croydon Surrey CR0 9AA
Tel **01-657 0281/2/3**
Mem
Sec Geoffrey Cotton
Pro Geoffrey Cotton
Holes Old Course 18 L 5577 yds SSS 67
New Course 18 L 5513 yds SSS 66
Lower Course 9 L 1812 yds SSS 62
18 hole Pitch and Putt course
Recs Pro–63 Chris Phillips
V'trs U
Fees Winter: Old £3.90; New £2.90; 9 hole £2.20 Summer: Old £4.90; New £3.80; 9 hole £2.80
Loc 3 miles E of Croydon

Addington Palace (1923)

Private (Map 2/3)
Gravel Hill Addington Croydon Surrey CR0 5BB
Tel **01-654 3061**
Mem 600
Sec Mrs S Palmer
Pro M Pilkington Tel 01-654 1786
Holes 18 L 6410 yds SSS 71
Recs Am–63 R Glading
Pro–65 AD Locke
V'trs WD–M or I; W/E & BH–M
Fees £13
Loc 2 miles E Croydon Station

Banstead Downs (1890)

Private (Map 2/4)
Burdon Lane Belmont Sutton Surrey SM2 7DD
Tel **01-642 2284**
Mem 650
Sec RS Barrett Tel 01-642 2284
Pro Ian Marr Tel 01-642 6884
Holes 18 L 6169 yds SSS 69
Recs Am–63 PJ Stone
Pro–MLA Perry
V'trs WD–I; W/E & BH–M
Fees £12; afternoon £7
Loc 1 mile S of Sutton

Barrow Hills (1970)

Private (Map 2/5)
Longcross Chertsey
Tel
Mem 190
Sec RW Routley Tel Weybridge 48117
Pro
Holes 18 L 3016 yds SSS 56
Recs Am–58 EJ Sewell
Pro–
V'trs M
Fees
Loc 4 miles W of Cherstey

Betchworth Park (1913)

Private (Map 2/6)
Reigate Road Dorking
Tel **0306 882052**
Mem 750
Sec DAS Bradney
Pro Alex King Tel 0306 884334
Holes 18 L 6266 yds SSS 70
Recs Am–68 CJ Copus
Pro–65 NC Coles
V'trs WD–U exc Tue & Wed am (NA); W/E by arrangement
Fees £11 (£15)
Loc 1 mile E of Dorking (A25)

Bramley (1913)

Private (Map 2/7)
Bramley nr Guildford GU5 0AL
Tel **Guildford 893042**
Mem 700
Sec Miss JM Martin Tel Guildford 892696
Pro VB Hood Tel Guildford 893685
Holes 18 L 5910 yds SSS 68
Recs Am–66 MI Farmer
Pro–63 PR Gill
V'trs WD–U; W/E–M SOC on WD
Fees £10 D–£12 (with mem £4 D–£5)
Loc 3 miles S of Guildford
Mis Buggies for hire

Burhill (1907)

Private (Map 2/8)
Walton-on-Thames Surrey KT12 4BL
Tel **Walton 227345**
Mem 1100
Sec AJ Acres
Pro Bryan Patterson Tel Walton 221729
Holes 18 L 6224 yds SSS 70
Recs Am–67 J Smith A Raitt
Pro–
V'trs WD–H; W/E & BH–M
Fees On application
Loc Between Walton-on-Thames and Cobham

Camberley Heath (1913)

Private (Map 2/9)
Golf Drive Camberley GU15 1JG
Tel **Camberley 23258**
Mem 725
Sec HW Hardy
Pro G Everett Tel Camberley 27905
Holes 18 L 6402 yds SSS 71
Recs Am–66 C Laurence
Pro–67 A Perry
V'trs WD–I; W/E–M
Fees £11 (£16)
Loc $1\frac{1}{4}$ miles S of Camberley on Old Portsmouth Road on A325

Centurion (1954)

Public (Map 2/48)
London
Tel **01-876 3205**
Mem 36
Sec DLR Aston Tel 01-870 4819
Pro
Holes Play over Richmond Park Golf Course

Chessington Golf Centre (1983)

Public (Map 2/10)
Garrison Lane Chessington Surrey KT9 2LW
Tel **01-391 0948**
Mem 300
Man Tony Maxted Tel 01-391 0948
Pro Patrick Tallack Tel 01-397 6502
Recs Am–60 N Murphy
Pro–54 R Hunter
V'trs WD–U W/E–NA before noon
Fees £2 (£2.50) per 9 holes
Loc Off A243 500 yards from Chessington Zoo, opposite Chessington South Station, Exit 9 M25

Chipstead (1906)

Private (Map 2/11)
Chipstead Coulsdon Surrey
Tel **Downland 51053**
Mem 550
Sec SLD Spencer-Skeen Tel Downland 55781
Pro N Child Tel Downland 54939
Holes 18 L 5450 yds SSS 67
Recs Am–64 ML Kirby
Pro–63 N Child
V'trs WD–U; W/E & BH–M
Fees £10; after 2 pm £7
Loc 200 yds Chipstead station

Coombe Hill (1911)

Private (Map 2/12)
Kingston Hill Surrey
Tel **01-942 2284**
Mem 437
Sec JA Davies
Pro Craig De Foy Tel 01-949 3713
Holes 18 L 6286 yds SSS 71
Recs Am–67 L Freedman
RL Glading
Pro–64 BJ Hunt
V'trs I or H; SOC
Fees £30 H By arrangment only
Loc 1 mile New Malden off Coombe Lane West

Coombe Wood (1904)

Private (Map 2/13)
George Road Kingston Hill Surrey KT2 7NS
Tel **01-942 3828**–Steward
Mem 620
Sec Mrs JF Salaman Tel 01-942 0388
Pro David Butler Tel 01-942 6764
Holes 18 L 5210 yds SSS 66
Recs Am–64 M Taylor
Pro–61 G Ritchie
V'trs WD–UH after 9 am; W/E & BH–M; SOC on WD
Fees £12
Loc 1 mile N of Kingston-upon-Thames off A3 at Robin Hood roundabout

Coulsdon Court (1937)

Public (Map 2/14)
Coulsdon Road Surrey CR3 2LL
Tel **01-660 0468**
Mem Membership available
Sec D Barnes Tel 01-660 0468
Pro C Staff Tel 01-660 6083
Holes 18 L 6030 yds SSS 70
Recs Am–
Pro–66 G Ralph
V'trs U
Fees £4 (£6.25)
Loc 5 miles S of Croydon on B2030
Mis Public course, now privately operated. Main house and course improved 1983.

Croham Hurst (1911)

Private (Map 2/15)
South Croydon Surrey
Tel **01-657 2075**
Mem 485 110(L) 75(J) 220(5)
Sec AH James Tel 01-657 2075
Pro Eric Stillwell Tel 01-657 7705
Holes 18 L 6274 yds SSS 70
Recs Am–64 SF Robson
Pro–66 B Firkins
V'trs WD–1; W/E & BH–M
Fees £14
Loc 1 mile from S Croydon

Crondall (1984)

Public (Map 2/73)
Oak Park Heath Lane Crondall Nr Farnham Surrey GU10 5PB
Tel **(0252) 850880**
Mem 350
Sec (0252) 850880
Pro Jim Graham Tel (0252) 850066
Holes 9 (18 tees) L 6370 yds SSS 71
V'trs U SOC
Fees 9 holes £3.50 (£4.50)
Loc Off A287 Farnham to Odiham Road
Mis Further 9 holes open Autumn 1987

Cuddington (1929)

Private (Map 2/16)
Banstead Road Banstead
Tel **01-393 0952**
Mem 900
Sec DM Scott
Pro R Gardner Tel 01-393 5850
Holes 18 L 6282 yds SSS 70
Recs Am–66 NJ Woods
Pro–64 J Pinsent
V'trs WD–I; W/E–M
Fees £16
Loc 200 yds Banstead station

Dorking (1897)

Private (Map 2/17)
Chart Park Dorking
Tel **Dorking 889786**
Mem 300
Sec RM Payne Tel 886917
Pro Paul Napier
Holes 9 L 5106 yds SSS 65
Recs Am–65 J Houston
Pro–62 Alex King
V'trs WD–U; W/E & BH–M; SOC on WD
Fees £7.50
Loc 1 mile S of Dorking on A24

Drift (1976)

Private (Map 2/18)
The Drift East Horsley
Tel **East Horsley 4641**
Mem 700
Sec Charles Rose
Pro Ken Norton Tel East Horsley 4772
Holes 18 L 6404 yds SSS 71 Par 72
Recs Am–72 J Scarfe
Pro–72 TM Powell
V'trs WD–U; SOC
Fees £13 before noon
£10 after noon
Loc 2 miles off A3, London 20 miles, 2 miles off M25

Dulwich and Sydenham Hill (1890)

Private (Map 2/19)
Grange Lane College Road London SE21
Tel **01-693 1221**
Mem 700
Sec EA Weber Tel 01-693 3961
Pro D Baillie Tel 01-693 8491
Holes 18 L 6051 yds SSS 69
Recs Am–62 T Bridle
Pro–63 LF Rowe
V'trs WD–I; W/E & BH–M
Fees £11
Loc Charing Cross 5 miles

Effingham (1927)

Private (Map 2/20)
Effingham
Tel **Bookham 52203/4**
Mem 1120
Sec AJB Norman
Pro Stephen Hoatson
Holes 18 L 6488 yds SSS 71

Recs Am–67 I Hawson
Pro–63 AD Locke
V'trs WD–I; W/E & BH–M
Fees £17
Loc 8 miles N of Guildford

Epsom (1889)

Private (Map 2/21)
Longdown Lane South Epsom Surrey KT17 4JR
Tel **Epsom 23363**
Mem 600
Sec KH Watson Tel Epsom 21666
Pro Bob Wynn Tel Epsom 41867
Holes 18 L 5725 yds SSS 68
Recs Am–68 R Goudie
Pro–68 R Wynn
V'trs WD–U; W/E & BH–U after 11 am
Fees £6 D–£8 (£6.50 D–£8)
Loc S Epsom Downs Rail Station

Farnham (1896)

Private (Map 2/22)
The Sands Farnham GU10 1PX
Tel **Runfold 3163**
Mem 700
Sec Capt (Retd) PV Dixon Tel Runfold 2109
Pro G Cowlishaw Tel Runfold 2198
Holes 18 L 6313 yds SSS 70
Recs Am–69 G Walmsley
Pro–
V'trs WD–H; W/E–M; SOC on WD (except Tues)
Fees £8.50 D–£11
Loc Signposted off A31 about 1 mile E of Farnham

Farnham Park (1966)

Public (Map 2/23)
Farnham Park Par 3 Golf Course Farnham Park Farnham GU9 0AU
Tel **(0252) 715216**
Mem
Sec Tel as above
Pro P Chapman Tel as above
Holes Par 3 course 9 holes L 1163 yds SSS 54
Recs Am–61 JA Pike
Pro–56 G Wheeler
V'trs U
Fees Adult £1.50 Jr/Sr £1.10 (Adult £1.75 Jr/Sr £1.25)
Loc Farnham Park by Farnham Castle

Fernfell G & CC (1985)

Private (Map 2/75)
Barhatch Lane Cranleigh Surrey GU6 7NG
Tel **Cranleigh (0483) 276626**
Mem 500
Man WM Lemon Tel (0483) 276626
Pro Ken Bennett Tel (0483) 277188
Holes 18 L 5780 yds SSS 68
Recs Am–
Pro–
V'trs WD–U WE/BH–M; SOC on WD only
Fees WD only £6
Loc Between Guildford and Horsham–1 mile N of A281; A3–8 miles; M25–11 miles
Mis Swimming, sauna, tennis, snooker

Foxhills (1975)

Private (Map 2/24)
Stonehill Road Ottershaw KT16 0EL
Tel **Ottershaw 2050**
Mem 647
Sec A Dupuy
Pro B Hunt Tel Ottershaw 3961
Holes 18 L 6880 yds SSS 73
18 L 6747 yds SSS 72
Recs Am–
Pro–65 P Dawson
V'trs U; SOC
Fees £16 (£25)
Loc 20 miles from London. 10 miles from Heathrow
Mis Buggies for hire

Gatton Manor Hotel and Golf Club (1969)

Private (Map 2/25)
Ockley nr Dorking Surrey RH5 5PQ
Tel **Oakwood Hill 555/6**
Mem 250
Sec DG Heath Tel as above
Pro R Sargent Tel Oakwood Hill 557
Holes 18 L 6903 yds SSS 72
Recs Am–75 T Braid
Pro–74 R Sargent
V'trs U (ex Sundays before noon–M)
Fees £7 (£8)
Loc 1½ miles SW Ockley off A29 M25 Exit 9

Goal Farm (1977)

Public (Map 2/26)
Pirbright Surrey GU24 OP2
Tel **Brookwood 3183/3205**
Mem 260
Sec J Church Tel as above
Pro
Holes Par 3 course 9 holes L 1273 yds SSS
Recs Am–27
Pro–
V'trs Sats reserved for club comps; WD–SOC
Fees 9 holes £1.40; 18 holes £2.60 (W/E & BH 9 holes £1.60; 18 holes £3)
Loc

Guildford (1886)

Private (Map 2/27)
High Path Road Merrow Guildford
Tel **Guildford 575243**
Mem 600
Sec HJ Warburton Tel Guildford 63941
Pro PG Hollington Tel Guildford 66765
Holes 18 L 6080 yds SSS 70
Recs Am–66 B White
Pro–68 E Sitwell
V'trs WD–U; W/E–M
Fees £7.50 (£11)
Loc 2 miles E of Guildford

Hankley Common (1895)

Private (Map 2/28)
Tilford Farnham GU10 2DD
Tel **Frensham 2493**
Mem 650
Sec DG Lee
Pro Will Brogden Tel Frensham 3761
Holes 18 L 6418 yds SSS 71
Recs Am–69 PJR Bathurst
PB Reynolds
Pro–64 H Muscroft
V'trs WD–I; W/E–At discretion of secretary
Fees £15 (£10 after 2 pm)
W/E £17 (£12 after 2 pm)
Loc 3 miles SE Farnham on Tilford Road

Hindhead (1905)

Private (Map 2/29)
Churt Road Hindhead Surrey GU26 6HX
Tel **Hindhead 4614**
Mem 450 106(L) 95(J) 124(S)
Sec ML Brown
Pro Neil Ogilvy Tel 4458
Holes 18 L 6357 yds SSS 70
Recs Am–65 W Rowland
Pro–65 DJ Rees
V'trs WD–U; HW/E & BH–NA before noon; SOC Wed & Thurs only
Fees £12 (£15)
Loc 4 miles N of Haslemere on A287

Hoebridge Golf Centre (1982)

Public (Map 2/30)
The Club House Old Woking Road Old Woking Surrey GU22 8JH
Tel Woking 22611
Mem 400
Sec TD Powell
Pro TD Powell
Holes 18 L 6587 yds SSS 71
Par 3 18 L 2298 yds
Recs Am–
Pro–
V'trs U
Fees £4.70; Par 3 £2.75
Loc Between Old Woking and West Byfleet, 2 miles off A3 on A247
Mis 25 bay floodlit driving range

Home Park (1895)

Private (Map 2/31)
Hampton Wick Kingston-upon-Thames Surrey
Tel **01-977 6645**
Mem 500
Sec CHH Gray Tel 01-977 2423
Pro Len Roberts Tel 01-977 2658
Holes 18 L 6519 yds SSS 71
Recs Am–
Pro–
V'trs U
Fees £7 (£11)
Loc 1 mile W of Kingston

Kingswood (1928)

Private (Map 2/32)
Sandy Lane Kingswood Tadworth
Tel **Mogador 832188**
Mem 700
Sec Edwin J Major
Pro David Ingram Tel Mogador 832334
Holes 18 L 6821 yds SSS 73
Recs Am–67 PR Cook
Pro–68 John O'Leary
V'trs U
Fees £15
Loc 5 miles S of Sutton

Laleham (1907)

Private (Map 2/33)
Laleham Reach Chertsey Surrey KT16 8RP
Tel **Chertsey 62188**
Mem 600
Sec/ Man P Fry Tel Chertsey 64211

Pro T Whitton Tel Chertsey 62877
Holes 18 L 6203 yds SSS 70
Recs Am–66 C Poulton
Pro–66 R Mandeville
J Hitchcock
V'trs WD–U before 4.30 pm; W/E–M; SOC Mon Tue Wed
Fees £8 D–£10
Loc 2 miles S of Staines

Leatherhead (1903)

Private (Map 2/34)
Kingston Road Leatherhead Surrey
Mem 490
Sec Bill Betts Tel Oxshott 3966
Holes 18 L 5701 yds SSS 68
Recs Am–68 PW Wynn
Pro–65 R Wynn
V'trs U SOC
Fees £10
Loc 1 mile off Leatherhead interchange of M25

Limpsfield Chart (1889)

Private (Map 2/35)
Limpsfield RH8 0SL
Tel **Limpsfield Chart 2106 & 3405**
Mem 395
Sec JC Woods Tel Westerham 63180
Pro Barrie A Finch
Holes 9 L 5718 yds SSS 68
Recs Am–67 N Simmons
Pro–64 B Huggett
V'trs WD Tues/Fri Wed pm
Fees On application
Loc 2 miles E of Oxted
Mis No play after 1 pm Sundays April/Sept incl

London Scottish (1865)

Private (Map 2/67)
Windmill Enclosure Wimbledon Common London SW19 5NQ
Tel **01-788 0135**
Mem 250
Sec R Allen Tel 01-789 7517
Pro Spencer Attwood Tel 01-788 0135
Holes 18 L 5486 yds SSS 67
Recs Am–64 A Glickberg
Pro–63 D Butler
V'trs WD–U; W/E (until 2 pm)–M; BH–NA
Fees £5 D–£8; with mem £3.50
Loc 2 miles Wimbledon Station
Mis This club has joint use of Wimbledon Common

Malden (1926)

Private (Map 2/36)
Traps Lane New Malden Surrey KT3 4RS
Tel **01-942 0654**
Mem 650
Sec Kathleen Pudner Tel 01-942 0654
Pro G Howard Tel 01-942 6009
Holes 18 L 6315 yds SSS 70
Recs Am–65 G Lashford
Pro–67 A Waters
V'trs WD–U; W/E–V'trs restricted; apply Sec; SOC–Wed Thu Fri
Fees £12 (£17)
Loc Close to A3 between Wimbledon and Kingston

Mitcham

Private (Map 2/37)
Carshalton Road Mitcham Junction CR4 4HN
Surrey
Tel **01-648 1508**
Mem 450
Sec CA McGahan Tel 01-648 4197
Pro JA Godfrey Tel 01-640 4280
Holes 18 L 5931 yds SSS 68
Recs Am–D Wilde
Pro–
V'trs U; W/E–NA 8 am–2 pm; SOC
Fees £5 (£6)
Loc 1 minute Mitcham Junction station

Mitcham Village (1907)

Public (Map 2/37)
Tel **01-648 1508**
Mem 240 10(J)
Sec HC Hinder Tel 01-542 5396
Pro JA Godfrey
Holes Play over Mitcham Golf Course

Moore Place (1926)

Public (Map 2/38)
Portsmouth Road Esher Surrey KT10 9LN
Tel **Esher 63533**
Mem 95
Sec J Darby Tel Walton-on-Thames 220575
Pro David Allen Tel Esher 63533
Holes 9 L 3512 yds SSS 58
Recs Am–29 W Cavanagh
Pro–25 Phil Loxley
V'trs U
Fees £2.25 (£2.85)
Loc Esher, Surrey

New Zealand (1895)

Private (Map 2/39)
Woodham Lane Woodham Weybridge Surrey KT15 3QD
Tel **Byfleet 45049**
Mem 300
Sec MJ Wood Tel Byfleet 42891
Pro VR Elvidge Tel Byfleet 49619
Holes 18 L 6012 yds SSS 69
Recs Am–66 P Cannings
Pro–72 Alex Herd
V'trs WD–not bank holidays
Fees On application
Loc Woking 4 miles. West Byfleet 1 mile

North Downs (1899)

Private (Map 2/40)
Northdown Road Woldingham
Tel **Woldingham 3298**
Mem 658
Sec SW Thomson Tel Woldingham 2057
Pro P Ellis Tel W'ham 3004
Holes 18 L 5787 SSS 68
Recs Am–68 AS Tait
Pro–64 P Ellis
V'trs WD–U; W/E–M; SOC Tue Wed
Fees £11 (1986 price)
Loc 3 miles E of Caterham

Oaks Sports Centre (1973)

Public (Map 2/41)
Woodmansterne Road Carshalton Surrey
Tel **01-643 8363**
Mem 500
Sec Tel 01-643 8363
Pro Geoff Horley Tel 01-643 8363
Holes 18 L 5873 yds SSS 68
9 L 1590 yds SSS 29
Recs Pro–66 J Woodroffe (18-hole)
Pro–27 J Woodroffe (9-hole)
V'trs U
Fees 18-hole £3.75 (£4.75)
9-hole £1.65 (£2)
Loc 2 miles from Sutton
Mis No Pitch and Putt any more; floodlit covered driving range open 9 am–10 pm 7 days a week

Purley Downs (1894)

Private (Map 2/42)
106 Purley Downs Road Purley Surrey CR2 0RB
Tel **01-657 1231**
Mem 600
Sec J Page Tel 01-657 8347
Pro G Wilson Tel 01-651 0819
Holes 18 L 6237 yds SSS 70
Recs Am–65 TB O'Neill
Pro–69 M Gregson
V'trs WD–I; W/E–M
Fees £12
Loc 3 miles S of Croydon

Puttenham (1895)

Private (Map 2/43)
Puttenham nr Guildford
Tel **Guildford 810498**
Mem 600
Sec M O'Bryan
Pro Gary Simmons Tel 810277
Recs Am–65 P Bivona
Pro–59 R Donald
V'trs WD–U; W/E & BH–M; SOC Wed and Thurs
Fees On application
Loc Midway between Guildford and Farnham on Hog's Back

RAC Country Club (1913)

Private (Map 2/44)
Woodcote Park Epsom KT18 7EW
Tel **Ashtead 76311**
Mem
Sec Major GV Simpson MBE Tel Ashtead 76311
Pro Peter Butler Tel Ashtead 76311
Holes 18 L 6672 yds SSS 72
18 L 5520 yds SS 67
Recs 18 L 6672 yds Am–
Pro–
18 L 5520 yds Am–
Pro–
V'trs I; SOC
Fees
Loc 1¾ miles Epsom station

Redhill and Reigate (1887)

Private (Map 2/45)
Clarence Lodge Pendleton Road Redhill Surrey RH1 6LB
Tel **Reigate 44626 and 44433**
Mem 300
Sec RH Hodder Tel Reigate 44626/40777
Pro Barry Davis Tel Reigate 44433
Holes 18 L 5193 yds SSS 65
Recs Am–65 M Gander CJ Weight
P Deighton R Donovan
Pro–63 GW Huggett
V'trs WD–U; W/E Restricted 10.30 am
Fees £5 (£7)
Loc 1 mile off Redhill on A23

Reigate Heath (1895)

Private (Map 2/46)
Reigate Heath
Tel **Reigate 42610**
Mem 250 90(L) 50(J)
Sec Mrs DM Howard Tel Reigate 45530
Pro WH Carter
Holes 9 L 5554 yds SSS 67
Recs Am–65 D Mahaney
Pro–65 P Loxley
V'trs U; Sun/BH–M; SOC–Wed & Thu
Fees On application
Loc W boundary

Richmond (1891)

Private (Map 2/47)
Sudbrook Park Richmond Surrey
Tel **01-940 1463**
Mem 500
Sec RD Tucker Tel 01-940 4351
Pro N Job Tel 01-940 7792
Holes 18 L 5965 yds SSS 69
Recs Am–63 J Lawson
Pro–62 AG King
V'trs WD–U; W/H & BH–10-12 noon
Fees £16 (£19)
Loc Between Richmond and Kingston-on-Thames

Richmond Park (1923)

Public (Map 2/48)
Richmond Park London SW15
Tel **Prospect 3205**
Pro Trevor Allen Tel 01-876 1795
Holes 18 L 5971 yds SSS 69
18 L 5925 yds SSS 69
Recs Am–
Pro–
V'trs U
Fees £1.70 (£2.50)
Loc

Roehampton (1901)

Private (Map 2/49)
Roehampton Lane London SW15 5LR
Tel **01-876 5505**
Mem 900
Sec RW Varley
Pro AL Scott Tel 01-876 3858
Holes 18 L 6057 yds SSS 69
Recs Am–67 AL Scott
Pro–63 SS Scott
V'trs WD–Introduced by member only; W/E–M
Fees
Loc nr Barnes

Royal Mid-Surrey (1892)

Private (Map 2/50)
Old Deer Park Richmond Surrey TW9 2SB
Tel **01-940 4847**
Mem 1100
Sec PH Covell Tel 01-940 1894
Pro D Talbot Tel 01-940 0459
Holes 18 (Outer) L 6331 yds SSS 70
18 (Inner) L 5446 yds LGU SSS 71
Recs (Outer) Am–66 GH Micklem
JC Davies D Gilford
Pro–64 Bob Charles
B Gallacher
(Inner) Am–
Pro–
V'trs WD–I or M, SOC; W/E & BH–with prior approval
Fees £17 (£25)
Loc Richmond Surrey

Royal Wimbledon (1865)

Private (Map 2/51)
29 Camp Road Wimbledon London SW19 4UW
Tel **01-946 2125**
Mem 800
Sec Major GE Jones
Pro Hugh Boyle Tel 01-946 4606
Holes 18 L 6300 yds SSS 70
Recs Am–66 JFM Connolly
Pro–71 R Burton
V'trs WD–I or M; W/E–M
Fees
Loc S of Wimbledon Common

St George's Hill (1912)

Private (Map 2/52)
Weybridge KT13 0NL
Tel **Weybridge 42406**
Mem 600
Sec Wg Cdr JR Marshall Tel Weybridge 47758
Pro AC Rattue Tel Weybridge 43523
Holes 18 L 6492 yds SSS 71
9 L 2360 yds SSS 35
Recs 18 holes Am–65 D Swanston
Pro–65 M Faulkner
9 holes Am–
Pro–
V'trs WD–I H; W/E & BH–NA; 9 hole–U
Fees Fees per day: £22.50 before 1.45 pm £15.75 after 1.45 pm; 9 hole: £6 before 1.45 pm £5 after 1.45 pm £4 after 4 pm
Loc ½ mile N of junction M25/A3 on A245 to Woking

Sandown Park (1970)

Public (Map 2/53)
More Lane Esher
Tel **Esher 63340**
Mem 250
Sec AG Wetherly Tel Esher 63340
Pro RJ Catley-Smith, P Stow
Holes 9 L 5658 yds SSS 67
Recs Am–69 P O'Halloran
Pro–
V'trs U
Fees £1.25 (£1.75)
Loc Esher

Sandown Park Golf Centre (1970)

Public **(Private members Sandown Park GC)** (Map 2/53)
More Lane Esher
Tel **Esher 63340**
Mem 250
Sec Michael Ford Tel Esher 63340
Pro RJ Catley-Smith, P Stow
Holes 9 L 5658 yds SSS 67
9 Par 3
V'trs U (Closed on race day until 30 mins after last race)
Fees 9 holes: £2.30 (£3.20)
Loc Sandown Park racecourse Esher
Mis 33-bay floodlit driving range

Selsdon Park Hotel (1929)

Private (Map 2/54)
Addington Road Sanderstead Surrey CR2 8YA
Tel **01-657 8811**
Pro Bill Mitchell Tel 01-657 4129
Holes 18 L 6402 yds SSS 71
Recs Am–68 B Stevenson
Pro–65 A Lacey J Hitchcock
V'trs U; HO–SOC (min 12 golfers)
Fees WD £10–18 holes £15–36 holes Sat £15–18 holes only Sun/BH £17.50–18 holes only. Starting times must be prebooked Tel 01-657 8811
Loc 3 miles S of Croydon on A2022 Purley–Addington road
Mis Course unsuitable for novice golfers

Shillinglee Park (1980)

Public (Map 2/74)
Chiddingfold Godalming Surrey
Tel **(0428) 53237**
Mem 350
Sec Roger Mace Tel (0428) 53237
Pro Roger Mace (0428) 53237
Holes 9 L 2400 yds Par 32
V'trs U SOC
Fees £3.25 D–£5.50; Jnrs OAPs £2.25 D–£3.75
Loc 2½ miles SE of Chiddingfold

Shirley Park (1914)

Private (Map 2/55)
Addiscombe Road Croydon Surrey
Tel **01-654 1143**
Mem 900
Sec A Baird
Pro H Stott Tel 01-654 8767
Holes 18 L 6210 yds SSS 70
Recs Am–68 N Durance
Pro–65 J Bennett
V'trs WD–U; W/E & BH–M
Fees £14
Loc 1 mile E of Croydon Station

Silvermere

Public (Map 2/56)
Redhill Road Cobham
Tel **Cobham 6007**
Mem 500
Sec Administration Tel Cobham 6007
Pro Tel Cobham 7275
Holes 18 L 6608 yds SSS 73
Recs Am–
Pro–71
V'trs U
Fees WD–£4; W/E & BH–£5
Loc Off Byfleet Road between Cobham and Byfleet

Sunningdale (1901)

Private (Map 2/57)
Sunningdale Berks SL5 9RW
Tel **Ascot 21681**
Mem 800
Sec Keith Almond
Pro Keith Maxwell Tel Ascot 20128
Holes Old Course 18 L 6341 yds SSS 70
New Course 18 L 6676 yds SSS 71
Recs Old Course Am–66
CHL Francis Pro–62 N Faldo
New Course Am–65 M Lunt
Pro–64 GJ Player
V'trs WD–I; W/E–M
Fees £35
Loc ¼ mile Sunningdale Station

Sunningdale Ladies (1902)

Private (Map 2/57)
Cross Road Sunningdale Berks
Tel **Ascot 20507**
Mem 400
Sec DPA Cox

Pro
Holes 18 L 3622 yds SSS 60
Recs Am–
V'trs WD/WE–By appt
Fees Ladies £8 (£10) Men £10 (£13)
Loc ¼ mile Sunningdale Station

Surbiton (1895)

Private **(Map 2/58)**
Woodstock Lane Chessington
Tel **01-398 3101**
Mem 670
Sec MO Wright
Pro P Milton Tel 01-398 6619
Holes 18 L 6211 yds SSS 70
Recs Am–64 DL Hyde
Pro–63 PE Gill
V'trs WD–U; W/E & BH–M
Fees £11
Loc 2 miles E of Esher

Tandridge (1925)

Private **(Map 2/59)**
Oxted
Tel **Oxted 2273/4**
Mem 450
Sec Air Marshal DCA Lloyd
Pro A Farquhar Tel Oxted 3701
Holes 18 L 6250 yds SSS 70
Recs Am–68 JC Robson
Pro–69 BGC Huggett
V'trs I (Mon-Wed-Thur only)
Fees £15
Loc Off A25, 5 miles E of Redhill

Thames Ditton and Esher (1892)

Private **(Map 2/60)**
Portsmouth Road Esher
Tel **01-398 1551**
Mem 300
Sec AC Gardner Tel 01-751 3076
Pro R Hutton
Holes 9 L 5415 yds SSS 65
Recs Am–61 T Petitt
Pro–64 R Hutton R Barr
V'trs WD–U WE–by arrangement
Fees £4.50
Loc Esher Surrey

Tyrrells Wood (1924)

Private **(Map 2/61)**
Leatherhead Surrey KT22 8QP
Tel **Leatherhead 376025 (2 lines)**
Mem 700
Sec BV Spencer Tel Leatherhead 376025
Pro P Taylor Tel Leatherhead 375200
Holes 18 L 6219 yds SSS 70
Recs Am–68 BK Hayes
Pro–68 C Phillips
V'trs WD–I; W/E & BH–I NA before noon
Loc Leatherhead 2 miles (off A24) nr Headley M25 Junction 9 1 mile

Walton Heath (1904)

Private **(Map 2/62)**
Tadworth
Tel **Tadworth 2060**
Mem 800
Sec Wg Cdr WE McCrea Tel Tadworth 2380
Pro K Macpherson Tel Tadworth 2152
Holes Old Course 18 L 6813 yds SSS 73
New Course 18 L 6659 yds SSS 72
Recs Old Course Am–68 R Revell
Pro–65 P Townsend
New Course Am–67 JK Tate
Pro–64 C Clark
V'trs WD–I; W/E & BH–M
Fees £20
Loc 3 miles S of Epsom

Wentworth (1924)

Private **(Map 2/63)**
Virginia Water Surrey GU25 4LS
Tel **Wentworth 2201**
Mem 1934
Sec DPC Beard
Pro B Gallacher Tel Wentworth 3353
Holes West Course 18 L 6945 yds SSS 74
East Course 18 L 6176 yds SSS 70
9 hole course L 1731 yds SSS 30
Recs West Am–72 P McEvoy
Pro–64 H Clarke
East Am–65
GB Wolstenholme
Pro–62 DN Sewell G Will
V'trs WD–H By prior arrangement
W/E–M; Tue Wed Thu–SOC
Fees D–£33
Loc 21 miles SW of London off A30 at Junction with A39

West Byfleet (1922)

Private **(Map 2/64)**
Sheerwater Road West Byfleet
Tel **Byfleet 45230**
Mem 550
Sec TR Walton Tel Byfleet 43433
Pro D Regan Tel Byfleet 46584
Holes 18 L 6211 yds SSS 70
Recs Am–66 W Calderwood
Pro–67 P Thomson
V'trs WD–I; W/E & BH–NA
Fees £13 R/D (No WE/BH)
Loc ½ mile from West Byfleet on A245

West Hill (1909)

Private **(Map 2/65)**
Brookwood nr Woking
Tel **Brookwood 2110 & 4365**
Mem 550
Sec WD Leighton MBE
Pro JA Clements Tel Brookwood 3172
Holes 18 L 6307 yds SSS 70
Recs Am–66 WA Murray
Pro–66 Vince Hood
V'trs WD–H; W/E–M; SOC
Fees £12 (£18)
Loc 5 miles W of Woking on A322

West Surrey (1909)

Private **(Map 2/66)**
Enton Green nr Godalming Surrey GU8 5AF
Tel **Godalming 21275**
Mem 743
Sec CNR Bateman OBE Tel Godalming 21275
Pro A Malcolm Tel Godalming 7278
Holes 18 L 6247 yds SSS 70
Recs Am–66 SD Cook
Pro–67 B Lane
V'trs H SOC on WD
Fees £14 (£16.50)
Loc ½ mile SE Milford Station

White Lodge (1923)

Public **(Map 2/48)**
Richmond Park London SW15
Tel **01-876 3205**
Mem 120
Sec MS McDonald Tel 01-876 5360
Holes Play over Richmond Park municipal courses

Wimbledon Common (1908)

Private **(Map 2/67)**
19 Camp Road Wimbledon Common London SW19
Tel 01-946 0294
Mem 250
Sec JE Miles Tel 01-946 7571
Pro JE Jukes
Holes 18 L 5486 yds SSS 67
Recs Am–65 T Mahon
Pro–64 JS Jukes
V'trs WD–U; W/E–M; BH–NA
Fees £6
Loc
Mis Pillarbox red outer garment (can be hired) must be worn. No play on Bank Holidays or Sunday pm London Scottish play here

Wimbledon Park (1889)

Private **(Map 2/68)**
Home Park Road London SW19
Tel **01-946 1002**
Mem 580
Sec MK Hale Tel 01-946 1250
Pro FC Lucas Tel 01-946 4053
Holes 18 L 5465 yds SSS 67
Recs Am–66 SJ Bennett
Pro–65 A Dixon
V'trs WD–U; W/E & BH–M; SOC
Fees £12 (£15)
Loc 8 miles central London

Windlemere (1978)

Public **(Map 2/69)**
Windlesham Road West End Woking
Tel **Chobham 8727**
Mem
Sec Clive D Smith
Pro Malcolm Hawkins, David Thomas
Holes 9 L 5346 yds SSS 66
Recs Am–
Pro–
V'trs U
Fees £2.70 (£3.40) incl VAT
Loc A319 at Lightwater
Mis 12-bay floodlit driving range; 9-hole full length public course adjacent; club house and licensed bar

Woking (1893)

Private **(Map 2/70)**
Pond Road Hook Heath Woking GU22 0JZ
Tel **Woking 60053**
Mem 350
Sec AW Riley
Pro J Thorne Tel Woking 69582
Holes 18 L 6322 yds SSS 70
Recs Am–65 PJ Benka
Pro–
V'trs WD–I; W/E–M
Fees £10
Loc 2½ miles W of Woking off Hollybank Road, just S of Road Bridge *over* Woking-Brookwood Rail

Woodcote Park (1912)

Private (Map 2/71)
Bridle Way Meadow Hill Coulsdon Surrey CR3 2QQ
Tel **01-660 0176**
Mem 750
Sec BP Nazer Tel 01-668 2788
Pro I Martin Tel 01-668 1843
Holes 18 L 6300 yds SSS 71
Recs Am–66 S Keppler
Pro–66 Clive Bonner
V'trs WD–U; W/E–M
Fees £12
Loc 2 miles Purley

Worplesdon (1908)

Private (Map 2/72)
Woking
Tel **Brookwood 2277**
Mem 500
Sec Lt Cdr Jon R Nightingale
Pro J Christine Tel Brookwood 3287
Holes 18 L 6422 yds SSS 71
Recs Am–65 M Johnson
Pro–62
V'trs WD–H; W/E–M SOC
Fees On application
Loc Woking

Sussex

Ashdown Forest Hotel

Private (Map 2/1)
Royal Ashdown Forest New Course Chapel Lane Forest Row
Tel **(034 282) 4866**
Mem 100
Dir AJ Riddick RL Pratt
Pro Hector Padgham Tel (034 282) 2247
Recs Am–
Pro–
V'trs U SOC
Fees £6 (£7)
Loc 4 miles S of East Grinstead. 12 miles W of Tunbridge Wells
Mis Hotel specialises in catering for golf breaks and golf society days. Full catering every day

Beauport Park

(Map 2/17)
Beauport Park St Leonards-on-Sea
Tel Hastings 52977
Mem 700
Sec PD Sitch
Holes Play over Hastings Public Course

Bognor Regis (1892)

Private (Map 2/3)
Downview Road Felpham Bognor Regis
Tel **Bognor Regis 865867**
Mem 570 173(L) (All categories)
Sec HWA Duck Tel Bognor Regis 821929
Pro Robin Day Tel Bognor Regis 865209
Holes 18 L 6238 yds SSS 70
Recs Am–67 LJ Cottrill
Pro–66 R Wynn
V'trs H; W/E Apr–Sep–M
Fees £10 (£14)
Loc 2 miles E of town

Brighton and Hove (1887)

Private (Map 2/2)
Dyke Road Brighton BN1 8YJ
Tel **Brighton 556482**
Mem 270
Sec SC Cawkwell Tel Brighton 556482
Pro
Holes 9 L 5722 yds SSS 68
Recs Am–67
Pro–
V'trs U SOC
Fees WD & Sat: £8 18 holes, £5 9 holes; BH & Sun: £10 18 holes, £6 9 holes
Loc 15 mins N of Brighton by car

Cooden Beach (1912)

Private (Map 2/4)
Cooden Beach nr Bexhill-on-Sea
Tel **Cooden 2040**
Mem 650
Sec Major PA Beacon
Pro K Benson Tel Cooden 3938
Holes 18/20 White Course L 6411 yds SSS 71
18/20 Yellow Course L 6099 yds SSS 70
Recs Am–67 G Burton Sir Henry Birkmyre CM Skinner
Pro–65 AG Harrison
V'trs By previous arrangement with Secretary at all times
Fees On application
Loc West boundary Bexhill

Copthorne (1892)

Private (Map 2/5)
Borers Arm Road Copthorne Crawley RH10 3LL
Tel **0342 712508**
Mem 565
Sec H Welfare
Pro Joe Burrell Tel 0342 712405
Holes 18 L 6205 yds SSS 71
Recs Am–64 HMR Deane
Pro–65 D Millensted
V'trs WD W/E & BH after 1.30 pm–U; H; SOC
Fees £10 (£12)
Loc Exit 10 M23, E on A264 1 mile to E Grinstead

Cottesmore (1974)

Private (Map 2/6)
Buchan Hill Crawley Sussex RH11 9AT
Tel **Crawley 28256**
Mem 1600
Sec MF Rogerson Tel Crawley 28256
Pro Paul Webster Tel Crawley 35399
Holes 36 L 6097 yds SSS 70 L 5321 yds SSS 68
Recs Am–69 I Geddes (old course)
Pro- 70 D Russel (old course)
V'trs U
Fees £10 (£10 new £15 old)
Loc 4 miles S of Crawley
Mis 3 squash courts. Overnight accommodation

Cowdray Park (1949)

Private (Map 2/7)
Midhurst Sussex GU29 0BB
Tel **Midhurst 2088**
Mem 650
Sec Captain P St Q Beadon Tel Midhurst 3599
Pro Stephen Hall Tel Midhurst 2091
Holes 18 L 6212 yds SSS 70
Recs Am–69 D Fay
Pro–68 G Ralph
V'trs U SOC on WD; v'trs must be members of recognised GC or introduced by a member
Fees £8 (£10)
Loc 1 mile E of Midhurst on A272

Crowborough Beacon (1895)

Private (Map 2/8)
Crowborough
Tel **Crowborough 4016**
Mem 600
Sec M Scargill Tel Crowborough 61511
Pro A Andrews Tel Crowborough 3877
Holes 18 L 6304 yds SSS 70
Recs Am–67 GCD Carter
SF Robson
Pro–67 K Ashdown
V'trs WD–I H; W/E & BH–After 12.30 pm
Fees £10 (£11)
Loc 7 miles S Tunbridge Wells (on A26)

Dale Hill (1973)

Private (Map 2/9)
Ticehurst nr Wadhurst E Sussex TN5 7DQ
Tel **Ticehurst 200112**
Mem 550
Sec SVC Nicholson Tel Ticehurst 200112
Pro A Collins Tel Ticehurst 200577
Holes 18 L 6035 yds SSS 69; 9 hole Par 3 course
Recs Am–71 A Briscoe
Pro–68 K Ashdown
A Forrester G Ralph
V'trs WD–U; W/E & BH–H after 10.30 am; SOC
Fees £8 (£9)
Loc B2087 off A21 at Flimwell

The Dyke (1908)

Private (Map 2/10)
Dyke Road Brighton BN1 8YJ
Tel **Poynings 296**
Mem 750
Sec D Cule Smith Tel Poynings 296
Pro P Longmore Tel Poynings 260
Holes 18 L 6519 yds SSS 71
Recs Am–68 N O'Byrne
Pro–65 C Jones
V'trs U ex NA before 12 noon Sunday
Fees £8 D–£10 (£12)
Loc 4 miles N of Brighton

Eastbourne Downs (1908)

Private (Map 2/12)
East Dean Road Eastbourne BN20 8ES
Tel **Eastbourne 20827**
Mem 600
Sec DJ Eldrett Tel Eastbourne 20827
Pro T Marshall Tel 32264
Holes 18 L 6635 yds SSS 72
Recs Am–71 R Arno
Pro–70 B Gallacher
V'trs U (Sun after 11 am)
Fees £5.50 (£6.75)
Loc 1 mile W of town on A259

East Brighton (1894)

Private (Map 2/11)
Roedean Brighton BN2 5RA
Tel **Brighton 603989**
Mem 540
Sec DG Pulford
Pro WH Street
Holes 18 L 6291 yds SSS 70
Recs Am–68 A Turner
Pro–63 S King
V'trs U
Fees £9
Loc N from Marina, Black Rock

Effingham Park (1980)

Private (Map 2/13)
nr Copthorne Sussex
Tel **0342 716528**
Mem 150
Man AJ Lecky Tel 0342 713011
Pro Ian Dryden Tel 0342 716528
Holes 9 L 1749 yds Par 30
Recs Am–29
Pro–26
V'trs WD–U; W/E–M before 10.30 am; U after 10.30 am
Fees £3.50 (£5)
Loc B2028/B2039

Gatwick Manor (1975)

Private (Map 2/14)
Crawley
Tel **Crawley 24470**
Mem No membership, green fees only
Sec C Hemsley
Pro BC Hemsley
Holes 9 L 1109 yds SSS 27 Holes redesigned
Recs Am–
Pro–
V'trs U
Fees 75p (£1)
Loc A23 to Crawley, 1 mile past Gatwick Airport

Goodwood (1892)

Private (Map 2/15)
Goodwood nr Chichester PO18 0PN
Tel **Chichester 785012**
Mem 867
Sec Major JK Fellowes MBE Tel Chi 774968
Pro K MacDonald Tel Chi 774994
Holes 18 L 6370 yds SSS 70
Recs Am–70 SD Thrower
Pro–69 K Dabson
V'trs WD–U, SOC; W/E–Not before 10 am
Fees £12 (£15)
Loc Chichester–3 miles

Ham Manor (1936)

Private (Map 2/16)
Angmering nr Littlehampton
Tel **Rustington 783288**
Mem 770
Sec/ Man Peter H Saubergue
Pro John Slinger Tel Rustington 783732
Holes 18 L 6216 yds SSS 70
Recs Am–67 CR Tregus JD Sloan
Pro–62 TA Horton
V'trs U
Fees On application
Loc Between Worthing and Littlehampton

Hastings (1973)

Public (Map 2/17)
Battle Road St Leonard-on-Sea
Tel **(0424) 52977**
Mem 250
Pro M Barton Tel (0424) 52981
Holes 18 L 6282 yds SSS 70
Recs Am–72
Pro–76
V'trs U
Fees £4.50 (£5)
Loc 3 miles N of Hastings
Mis Beauport Park Club plays here

Haywards Heath (1922)

Private (Map 2/18)
High Beech Lane Haywards Heath West Sussex RH16 1SL
Tel **Haywards Heath 414310**
Mem 625
Sec SW Cobbett Tel Haywards Heath 414457
Pro B Firkins Tel Haywards Heath 414866
Holes 18 L 6202 yds SSS 70
Recs Am–63 S Robson (Old course)
Pro–65 B Firkins (Old course)
V'trs H SOC Wed Thu WD/WE subject to competitions and tee reservation
Fees £9 (£12)
Loc 2 miles N of Haywards Heath

Highwoods (Bexhill) (1925)

Private (Map 2/19)
Ellerslie Lane Bexhill-on-Sea East Sussex TN39 4UJ
Tel **Bexhill 212625**
Mem 800
Sec DC Wright
Pro RJ McLean Tel Bexhill 212770
Holes 18 L 6218 yds SSS 70
Recs Am–67 AS Jenks
Pro–68 Clive Clark
V'trs WD and Sat–H; Sun am–M Sun pm–H
Fees £10 (£12)
Loc 2 miles N of Bexhill

Hill Barn (1935)

Public (Map 2/41)
Hill Barn Lane Worthing
Tel **(0903) 37301**
Pro P Higgins Tel (0903) 37301
Holes 18 L 6224 Par 70
Recs Am–66 H Francis B Roberts
Pro–63 J Kinsella
V'trs U
Fees £6 (£7)
Loc NE of A27 at Warren Road roundabout; clearly signposted

Hollingbury Park (Brighton) (1922)

Public (Map 2/20)
Ditching Road Brighton Sussex
Tel **0273 552010**
Mem 340
Sec AGJ Knight Tel 0273 552010
Pro P Brown Tel 0273 500086
Holes 18 L 6415 yds SSS 71
Recs Am–68 G Derkson
Pro–69 M Inglis
V'trs U; SOC
Fees £5 D–£7 (WE–£6.30)
Loc 1 mile from town centre

Holtye (1893)

Private (Map 2/21)
Holtye Cowden TN8 7ED Kent
Tel **Cowden 635**
Mem 440
Sec/ Man J Holmes Tel Cowden 576
Pro Mick Scarles
Holes 9 L 5259 yds SSS 66
Recs Am–66 P Scarles
Pro–64 S Frost
V'trs WD–U; W/E restricted am; SOC on WD
Fees £6.50 (£7)
Loc 4 miles E of Grinstead

Horam Park (1985)

Public (Map 2/42)
Chiddingly Road Horam East Sussex TN21 0JJ
Tel **(04353) 3477**
Mem 430
Sec W Arbon Tel (04353) 3477
Pro Alastair Neilson Tel (04353) 3477
Holes 9 L 2700 yds
V'trs U SOC
Fees 9 holes £3 D–£6
Loc ½ mile S of Horam on Chiddingly road
Mis Driving range, catering

Ifield (1927)

Private (Map 2/22)
Rusper Road Ifield Crawley RH11 0LW
Tel **0293 20222**
Mem 600
Sec DT Howe
Pro C Strathearn Tel 0293 23088
Holes 18 L 6289 yds SSS 70
Recs Am–67 M Jarvis
Pro–65 P Mitchell
G Cowlishaw
V'trs WD–H; W/E–M
Fees £10 D–£12
Loc nr Crawley

Lewes (1896)

Private (Map 2/23)
Chapel Hill Lewes
Tel **Lewes 473245**
Mem 350
Sec P Cattermole Tel Lewes 473074
Pro E Goldring
Holes 18 L 5951 yds SSS 69
Recs Am–70 R Brooks
Pro–66 E Goldring
V'trs U
Fees £6.50 (£8.50)
Loc Opp Junction Cliffe High/South Street

Littlehampton (1889)

Private (Map 2/24)
170 Rope Walk Littlehampton Sussex BN17 5DL
Tel **Littlehampton 717170**
Mem 650
Sec MV Bodilly Tel Littlehampton 717170
Pro CA Burgess Tel Littlehampton 716369
Holes 18 L 6072 yds SSS 69
Recs Am–67 S Graham
Pro–65 N Pook
V'trs SOC: W/E & BH–NA before noon; WD–U after 9.30 am
Fees £8 (£10)
Loc W bank River Arun Littlehampton

Mannings Heath (1908)

Private (Map 2/25)
Mannings Heath Horsham
Tel **Horsham 65224**
Mem 800
Sec JD Coutts Tel Horsham 66217
Pro M Denny Tel Horsham 63434
Holes 18 L 6402 yds SSS 71
Recs Am–66 PG Way
Pro–64 G Ralph
V'trs WD–H (M after 5 pm) SOC W/E–NA
Fees £10
Loc 3 miles SE of Horsham (A281)

Nevill (1914)

Private (Map 2/26)
Benhall Mill Road Tunbridge Wells Kent
Tel **T Wells 27820**
Mem 350 200(L) 120(J) 150(5)
Sec PD Mitchell Tel T Wells 25818
Pro Paul Huggett Tel T Wells 32941
Holes 18 L 6336 yds SSS 70
Recs Am–66 A Sykes
Pro–69 JS Spence
V'trs H; W/E & BH–M
Fees WD–£10
Loc Tunbridge Wells–1 mile

Peacehaven (1896)

Private (Map 2/27)
Brighton Road Newhaven BN9 9UH
Tel **Newhaven 514049**
Mem 270
Sec DT Jenkins Tel Newhaven 512571
Pro G Williams Tel Newhaven 512602
Holes 9 L 5235 yds SSS 66
Recs Am–67 D Balkham
Pro–
V'trs WD–U SOC; W/E & BH–after 11 am
Fees £5.50 (£7)
Loc 8 miles E of Brighton on A259

Piltdown (1904)

Private (Map 2/28)
Uckfield E Sussex TN22 3XB
Tel **Newick 2033**
Mem 350
Sec REH King
Pro John Amos Tel Newick 2389
Holes 18 L 6059 yds SSS 69
Recs Am–65 G Brown
Pro–69 S Frost P Lovesey
V'trs U; (Not Sun am)
Fees £12 Summer £9 Winter
Loc 2½ miles of Uckfield

Pyecombe (1894)

Private (Map 2/29)
Pyecombe Brighton BN4 7FF
Tel **Hassocks 4176**
Mem 550
Sec WM Wise MA Tel Hassocks 5372
Pro CR White Tel Hassocks 5398
Holes 18 L 6059 yds SSS 69
Recs Am–69 P Thorn
Pro–70 P Hammond C Giddins
V'trs U; (Except before 10 am Sat & 11 am Sun); SOC on WD except Tues
Fees £10 (£12)
Loc 6 miles N of Brighton on A272

Royal Ashdown Forest (1888)

Private (Map 2/30)
Chapel Lane Forest Row E Grinstead Sussex RH18 5LR
Tel **(034 282) 2018/3014**
Mem 450
Sec KPA Mathews Tel (034282) 2018/3014
Pro HA Padgham Tel (034282) 2247
Holes Old 18 L 6439 yds SSS 71
New 18 L 5572 yds SSS 69
Recs Am–67 G Evans
Pro–62 HA Padgham
V'trs On application; advisable to phone beforehand
Fees £12.50 (£15) 1986 rates
Loc 4 miles S of E Grinstead on B2110 Hartfield road M25 exit 6

Royal Eastbourne (1887)

Private (Map 2/31)
Paradise Drive Eastbourne BN20 8BP
Tel **0323 30412**
Mem 850
Sec HW Scallon OBE Tel 0323 29738
Pro Richard Wooller Tel 0323 36986
Holes 18 L 6084 yds SSS 69
9 L 2147 yds SSS 32
Recs Am–65 J Beland
Pro–66 JP Higgins
V'trs U; SOC
Fees 18 hole course £9.50 (£10.50)
9 hole course £6.75
Loc ½ mile from Town Hall

Rye (1894)

Private (Map 2/32)
Camber Rye TN31 7QS
Tel Rye 225241
Mem 820 140(L) 40(J)
Sec JM Bradley
Pro P Marsh Tel Rye 225218
Holes 18 L 6301 yds SSS 71
9 L 6625 yds SSS 72
Recs Am–67 GI Stradling
Pro–70 B Dawson
V'trs M
Fees
Loc 3 miles E of Rye

Seaford GC and Dormy House (1887)

Private (Map 2/33)
East Blatchington Seaford BN25 2JD
Tel **Seaford 892597**
Mem 410 135(L) 37(J) 65(5)
Sec MB Hichisson Tel Seaford 892442
Pro PT Brown Tel Seaford 894160
Holes 18 6241 yds SSS 70
Recs Am–66 EA Snow A Flygt
Pro–67 H Weetman
V'trs WD–U; W/E–U (after 1.00 pm)
Fees £14
Loc 1 mile N of Seaford town
Mis Dormy House accommodation

Seaford Head (1907)

Public (Map 2/34)
Southdown Road Seaford
Tel **Seaford 890139**
Mem 450
Sec AT Goodman Tel Seaford 894843
Pro AJ Lowles
Holes 18 L 5812 yds SSS 68
Recs Am–66 J Crawford
Pro–66 M Andrews
V'trs U
Fees £4.50 (£5.60)
Loc 8 miles W of Eastbourne and ¾ mile S of A259

Selsey (1906)

Private (Map 2/35)
Golf Links Lane Selsey West Sussex PO20 9DR
Tel **Selsey 602203**
Mem 300
Sec EC Rackstraw Tel Selsey 602029
Pro Peter Grindley Tel Selsey 602203
Holes 9 L 5932 yds SSS 68
Recs Am–66 A Kelly
Pro–
V'trs U
Fees £6 (£8)
Loc 7 miles S of Chichester

Shillinglee Park

(See Surrey)

Tilgate (1982)

Public (Map 2/43)
Titmus Drive Tilgate Crawley West Sussex
Tel **(0293) 30103**
Sec A Davidson Tel (0293) 30103
Pro H Spencer & D McClelland Tel (0293) 545411
Holes 18 L 6359 yds SSS 70
V'trs U
Fees £4.50 (£6.50)
Loc 1½ miles SE of Crawley town centre

Waterhall (1945)

Public (Map 2/36)
Patcham Brighton BN1 8YN
Tel **Brighton 508658**
Mem 400
Sec P Scarfield Tel Brighton 601939
Pro E Charman
Holes 18 L 5615 yds SSS 67
Recs Am–66 C Wilson
Pro–64 EF Goldring
V'trs U
Fees £4.00 (£5.00)
Loc Patcham Brighton

West Hove (1910)

Private (Map 2/37)
369 Old Shoreham Rd Hove BN3 7GD
Tel 0273 413411
Mem
Sec R Charman Tel 0273 419738
Pro Chris White Tel 0273 413494
Holes 18 L 6038 yds SSS 69
Recs Am–66 N O'Byrne
Pro–62 C Moody
V'trs WD–U; W/E–M
Fees £7 (£9)
Loc 300 yds N of Postslade & West Hove Station on A27

West Sussex (1930)

Private (Map 2/38)
Pulborough W Sussex RH20 2EN
Tel **Pulborough 2563**
Mem 800
Sec GR Martindale Tel Pul 2563
Pro G Gledhill Tel Pul 2426
Holes 18 L 6156 yds SSS 70
Recs Am–63 DJ Harrison
Pro–
V'trs I H Not before 9.30 am; Tue–M; SOC Wed Thu
Fees On application
Loc 2 miles from Pulborough A283

Willingdon (1898)

Private (Map 2/39)
Southdown Road Eastbourne BN20 9AA
Tel **Eastbourne 32383**
Mem 510
Sec RW Henley Tel Eastbourne 638728
Pro DJ Ashton Tel Eastbourne 31748
Holes 18 L 6049 yds SSS 69
Recs Am–65 J Hookway
Pro–64 C Defoy
V'trs WD–U; SOC–H; W/E–M H
Fees £8 D–£10 (£9 D–£11)
Loc ½ mile N of Eastbourne off A22 to London

Worthing (1905)

Private (Map 2/40)
Links Road Worthing BN14 9QZ
Tel **Worthing 60801**
Mem 1200
Sec Major RB Carroll
Pro Sean Geddes Worthing 60718
Holes Lower Course 18 L 6477 yds SSS 71
Upper Course 18 L 5243 yds SSS 66
Recs Lower Am–61 MV Jones
Pro–61 T Haliburton
V'trs WD–U; W/E–Confirm in advance with Secretary
Fees £10 (£14)
Loc 1½ miles from Central Station on A27

England: South-West

Cornwall

Bude and North Cornwall (1891)

Private (Map 3/1)
Burn View Bude Cornwall EX23 8DA
Tel **Bude 2006**
Mem 320 135(L) 60(J)
Sec
Pro Philip Sanders Tel Bude 3635
Holes 18 L 6202 yds SSS 70
Recs Am–67 D Cann
Pro–70 C Pennington
V'trs U; SOC
Fees £7.50 (£9.50) W–£30 F–£45
Loc Bude Town Centre

Budock Vean Hotel (1922)

Private (Map 3/2)
Falmouth
Tel **Falmouth 250288**
Mem 150
Sec FG Benney Tel Falmouth 250060
Pro
Holes 9 L 3100 yds SSS 66
Recs Am–72, NW Warner
Pro–64 David Short
V'trs U
Fees £5 (£7.50)
Loc 7 miles Falmouth

Carlyon Bay (1926)

Private (Map 3/3)
Carlyon Bay St Austell
Tel **Par 4250**
Mem 600
Sec CH Farmer
Pro NJ Sears Tel Par 4228
Holes 18 L 6510 yds SSS 71
Recs Am–69 M Boggia
Pro–65 N Coles
V'trs U
Fees £8.50 (£10) W–£40
Loc 2 miles E of town
Mis Buggies for hire

Culdrose

Private (Map 3/4)
Royal Naval Air Station Culdrose
Tel **Helston 4121 (Ext 7113)**
Mem 100
Sec D Ashman Tel Helston 4121 (Ext 7149)
Pro None
Holes 9 L 6412 yds SSS 71
V'trs M
Fees —

Falmouth (1928)

Private (Map 3/5)
Swanpool Road Falmouth
Tel **0326 311262**
Mem 600
Sec DJ de C Sizer Tel 0326 40525
Pro D Short Tel 0326 316229
Holes 18 L 5581 yds SSS 67
Recs Am–65 JL Gresson
Pro–65 Gordon Brand Jr
V'trs U; SOC
Fees £8 (£8) W–£40
Loc ½ mile W of Swanpool Beach

Isles of Scilly (1904)

Private (Map 3/6)
St Mary's Isles of Scilly TR21 0NF
Tel **(0720) 22692**
Mem 380
Sec PH Holway Tel (0720) 22050
Pro None
Holes 9 L 2987 yds SSS 69
Recs Am–69 M Twynham
Pro–
V'trs U (M–Sunday)
Fees £7 W–£15.50
Loc 1½ miles from Hughtown

Launceston (1928)

Private (Map 3/7)
St Stephen Launceston
Tel **Launceston 3442**
Mem 750
Sec KJ Lyon Tel Launceston 3442
Pro John Tozer
Holes 18 L 6454 yds SSS 71
Recs Am–67 H Reid
Pro–67 G Smith
V'trs U; SOC
Fees £7 (£6) W–£24
Loc 1 mile N of Launceston off Bude Road

Looe Bin Down (1933)

Private (Map 3/8)
Looe
Tel **Widegates 247**
Mem 345
Sec JG Rowe
Pro S Lloyd Tel Widegates 239
Holes 18 L 5875 yds SSS 68
Recs Am–67 AJK Rowe
Pro–66 R Stevenson
V'trs U SOC on WD
Fees £7
Loc 3 miles E of Looe

Mullion (1895)

Private (Map 3/9)
Cury Helston TR12 7BP
Tel **Mullion 240276**
Mem 716
Sec Derek Watts Tel Mullion 240685
Pro Mike Singleton Tel Mullion 240276
Holes 18 L 5610 yds SSS 67
Recs Am–66 PA Gilbert
Pro–68 BJ Hunt P Alliss
V'trs H; restricted comp days and open days; SOC on WD
Fees £7 W–£24 F–£35
Loc 6 miles S of Helston
Mis No dogs on course or in clubhouse

Newquay (1890)

Private (Map 3/10)
Tower Road Newquay TR7 1LT
Tel **Newquay 872091**
Mem 500
Sec G Binney Tel Newquay 874354
Pro P Muscroft Tel Newquay 874830
Holes 18 L 6140 yds SSS 69
Recs Am–65 I Veale
Pro–69 PJ Yeo
V'trs WD and Sat–H Sun–M
Fees £9 W–£36
Loc ½ mile from centre

Perranporth (1927)

Private (Map 3/11)
Budnick Hill Perranporth Cornwall TR6 0AB
Tel **(0872) 572454**
Mem 550
Sec VG Hill Tel (0872) 573701/572206 (day)
Pro DC Mitchell Tel (0872) 572317
Holes 18 L 6208 yds SSS 70
Recs Am–65
Pro–68
V'trs U SOC
Fees
Loc Budnick Hill, ½ mile NW town centre

Praa Sands (1971)

Private (Map 3/12)
Germoe Cross Penzance
Tel **0736-76 3445**
Mem 205
Sec AJ Hine
Pro John Elsey
Holes 9 L 4036 yds SSS 60
Recs Am–59 P Lorys
Pro–
V'trs U (Ex Sunday am)
Fees £4.50
Loc On A394 Penzance–Helston

St Austell (1912)

Private (Map 3/13)
Tregongeeves St Austell
Tel (0726) 74756
Mem 780
Sec SH Davey Tel (0726) 74756
Pro E Holland Tel (0726) 72649
Holes 18 L 5981 yds SSS 69
Recs Am–66 IG Jago
Pro–
V'trs SOC except competition days
Fees £7 W–£25
Loc 1½ miles W of St Austell

St Enodoc (1890)

Private (Map 3/14)
Rock
Tel **Trebetherick 3216**
Mem 950
Sec HE Watts
Pro NJ Williams Tel Trebetherick 2402
Holes Main course 18 L 6207 yds SSS 70
Short course 18 L 4151 yds SSS 61
Recs 18 holes Am–66 G Brand
Pro–67 Dai Rees
V'trs Short course–U; Main course–H 24 and under (ladies 36)
Fees Main course £12 W–£42
Short course £7 W–£28
Loc Wadebridge 6 miles

St Mellion (1976)

Private (Map 3/15)
St Mellion nr Saltash PL12 6SD
Tel **(0579) 50101**
Mem 700
Sec Lt Col C Hoatson
Pro PJ Yeo Tel (0579) 50724
Holes Resort Course 18 L 5927 yds SSS 68
Jack Nicklaus-designed Course 18 L 6626 yds SSS 72
Recs Am–
Pro–
V'trs H SOC
Fees
Loc Tamar Bridge
Mis Buggies for hire

Tehidy Park (1922)

Private (Map 3/16)
Camborne
Tel **Portreath 842208**
Mem 1000
Sec PM Green
Pro J Dumbreck Tel Portreath 842914
Holes 18 L 6222 yds SSS 70
Recs Am–65 S Hurley (Filton)
Pro–67 J Sharkey
V'trs H
Fees £8 (£12)
Loc 3 miles N of Camborne

Tregenna Castle Hotel (1982)

Private (Map 3/21)
St Ives Cornwall TR26 2DE
Tel **(0736) 795254**
Mem 127
Man David Houghton Tel (0736) 795254
Pro Leonard Knapp Tel (0736) 795254
Holes 18 L 3645 yds SSS 57
Recs Am–
Pro–
V'trs U SOC
Fees D–£6 Weekly rate available
Loc 1 mile from town centre

Trevose (1924)

Private (Map 3/17)
Constantine Bay Padstow
Tel **Padstow 520208**
Mem 625
Sec P Gammon J Duffy
Pro G Alliss Tel Pad 520261
Holes 18 L 6608 yds SSS 72
9 L 1367 yds SSS 29
Recs 18 holes Am–67 C Phillips
Pro–68 P Wilcox
V'trs H SOC 3 and 4 ball matches restricted
Fees On application
Loc 4 miles W of Padstow
Mis 3 and 4 balls restricted throughout the year. Phone for times

Truro (1937)

Private (Map 3/18)
Treliske Truro TR1 3LG
Tel **Truro 72640**
Mem 800
Sec BE Heggie Tel Truro 78684
Pro NK Bicknell Tel Truro 76595
Holes 18 L 5347 yds SSS 66
Recs Am–61 AJ Ring
Pro–63 M Hoyle
V'trs U; SOC
Fees £8 (£10) W–£30 M–£60
Loc 2 miles W of Truro on A390

West Cornwall (1889)

Private (Map 3/19)
Lelant St Ives TR26 3DZ
Tel **0736-753319**
Mem 825
Sec WS Richards Tel 0736-753401
Pro Paul Atherton Tel 0736-753177
Holes 18 L 6070 yds SSS 69
Recs Am–65 MC Edmunds
Pro–
V'trs I
Fees £7 (£8) W–£30
Loc 2 miles E of St Ives

Whitsand Bay Hotel (1909)

Private (Map 3/20)
Portwrinkle Torpoint
Tel **Hotel, St Germans 30276 Club 30470**
Mem 330
Sec GG Dyer Tel St Germans 30418
Pro Stephen Poole Tel St Germans 30778
Holes 18 L 5512 yds SSS 67
Recs Am–62 GG Dyer
Pro–63 M Faulkner
V'trs U
Fees £7.50
Loc 6 miles from Plymouth

Devon

Axe Cliff (1894)

Private (Map 3/1)
Seaton
Tel **Seaton 20499**
Mem ·380
Sec J Hankins Tel Seaton 20219
Pro
Holes 18 L 4998 yds SSS 64
Recs Am–65 P Crichard
Pro–
V'trs U
Fees £5.50 (£6)
Loc Seaton

Bigbury (1923)

Private (Map 3/2)
Bigbury-on-Sea Kingsbridge
Tel **Bigbury-on-Sea 810207**
Mem 790
Sec BJ Perry Tel Bigbury-on-Sea 810557
Pro Mike Rowett Tel Bigbury-on-Sea 810412
Holes 18 L 6076 yds SSS 69
Recs Am–66 K Dodd
Pro–67 S Lloyd
V'trs I; H; SOC
Fees £8.50 (£9.50)
Loc Plymouth 15 miles

Chulmleigh (1976)

Public (Map 3/3)
Leigh Road Chulmleigh North Devon EX18 7JL
Tel **(0769) 80519**
Mem 70
Sec PN Callow Tel (0769) 80519
Pro
Holes 18 L 1440 yds par 3
Recs Am–
Pro–48 D Franklin
V'trs U
Fees £2.75 D–£3.75
Loc 1 mile N A377 Exeter-Barnstaple road

Churston (1890)

Private (Map 3/4)
Churston Brixham
Tel **Churston 842218**
Mem 640
Sec DR Griffin Tel Churston 842751
Pro R Penfold Tel Churston 842894
Holes 18 L 6201 yds SSS 70
Recs Am–64 MWL Hampton
Pro–67 JM Green
V'trs U (members of recognised clubs only) No play on Tues am
Fees On application
Loc 5¼ miles Torquay, on main road

Downes Crediton (1976)

Private (Map 3/5)
Hookway Crediton
Tel **Crediton 3991**
Mem 550
Sec MJ Dunk Tel Crediton 3025
Pro P Millhouse Tel Crediton 4464
Holes 18 L 6003 yds SSS 69
V'trs U
Fees £6 (£8)
Loc Off A377 at entrance to Crediton

East Devon (1902)

Private (Map 3/6)
North View Road Budleigh Salterton EX9 6DQ
Tel **Budleigh Salterton 2018**
Mem 850
Sec RSB Luckman Tel Budleigh Salterton 3370
Pro Trevor Underwood Tel Budleigh Salterton 5195
Holes 18 L 6214 yds SSS 70
Recs Am–68 P Newcombe
Pro–69 Brian Huggett
V'trs H; SOC
Fees £10
Loc 12 miles SE of Exeter

Elfordleigh Hotel C & GC (1932)

Private (Map 3/7)
Elfordleigh Plympton Plymouth
Tel **(0752) 336428**
Mem 309
Sec A Dunstan Tel (0752) 703824
Pro Ian Marshall Tel (0752) 336428
Holes 9 L 5609 yds SSS 67
Recs Am–68 M Ellis
Pro–66 M Kemp
V'trs WD–U; W/E–phone first
Fees £7 (£8)
Loc 4 miles E of Plymouth
Mis 2nd 9 holes alternate tees

Exeter G & CC (1895)

Private (Map 3/8)
Countess Wear Exeter EX2 7AE
Tel **Topsham 4139**
Mem 896
Sec C Greetham Tel Topsham 4139
Pro Mike Rowett Tel Topsham 5028
Holes 18 L 6061 yds SSS 69
Recs Am–66 G Talman
Pro–64 G Laing
V'trs WD–U SOC W/E–I
Fees £10 (£10)
Loc Exeter

Holsworthy (1937)

Private (Map 3/9)
Kilatree Holsworthy
Tel **0409 253177**
Mem 250
Sec B Megson Tel 0409 253701 (Home)
Pro
Holes 18 L 5935 yds
Recs Am–66 A Ramsey
Pro–68 J Yeo
V'trs WD–U No play before 11 am on Sunday
Fees £6
Loc 1 mile west of town

Honiton (1896)

Private (Map 3/10)
Middlehills Honiton EX14 8TR
Tel **Honiton 3633**
Mem 726
Sec KT Melton Tel 44422
Pro J Mackie Tel 2943
Holes 18 L 5920 yds SSS 68
Recs Am–66 WT Collins
Pro–65 I Read
V'trs U (Recognised Club Member) SOC
Fees £7.50 (£9.50)
Loc 1 mile S Honiton

Ilfracombe (1892)

Private (Map 3/11)
Hele Bay Infracombe
Tel **Ilfracombe 62176**
Mem 420
Sec AG Pace
Pro David Hoare Tel Ilfracombe 63328
Holes 18 L 5857 yds SSS 68
Recs Am–67 RC Beer
Pro–
V'trs U SOC
Fees £8 5D–£24 10D–£40
Loc Between Ilfracombe and Combe Martin

Manor House Hotel (1976)

Private (Map 3/12)
Moretonhampstead
Tel **Moretonhampstead 40355**
Mem 104
Sec Dr P Howarth Tel Lustleigh 343
Pro R Lewis Tel Moretonhampstead 40355
Holes 18 L 6016 yds SSS 69
Recs Am–
Pro–66 N Sutton
V'trs U (Contact Course Manager A Egford)
Fees £9 (£9.50)
Loc 15 miles W of Exeter

Newton Abbot (Stover) (1930)

Private (Map 3/13)
Newton Abbot Devon TQ12 6QQ
Tel **Newton Abbot 52460**
Mem 861
Sec R Smith Tel Newton Abbot 52460
Pro M Craig Tel Newton Abbot 62078
Holes 18 L 5724 yds SSS 68
Recs Am–65 RH Knott JP Langmead
Pro–67 Brian Barnes
V'trs U; H; SOC on Thu
Fees £10 (£11)
Loc 3 miles N of Newton Abbot on A382

Okehampton (1913)

Private (Map 3/14)
Okehampton Devon EX20 1EF
Tel **(0837) 2113**
Mem 400
Sec DJ Fensom Tel (0837) 308
Pro Howard Finch Tel (0837) 2113
Holes 18 L 5300 yds SSS 67
Recs Am–67 MS Moore
Pro–H Finch
V'trs U SOC
Fees £7 (£8) W–£35
Loc S boundary of Okehampton, signposted from traffic lights

Royal North Devon (1864)

Private (Map 3/15)
Westward Ho!
Tel **Bideford 73824**
Mem 900
Sec EJ Davies Tel Bideford 73817
Pro G Johnston Tel Bideford 77598
Holes 18 L 6644 yds SSS 72
Recs Am–66 D Boughey
Pro–66 P Dawson KDG Nagle MF Foster
V'trs On request
Fees £9 (£10)
Loc 2 miles from Bideford

Saunton (1897)

Private (Map 3/16)
Saunton Nr Braunton N Devon
Tel **0271 812436**
Mem 900
Sec WE Geddes Tel 0271 812436
Pro JA McGhee Tel 0271 812013
Holes East 18 L 6703 yds SSS 73
West 18 L 6322 yds SSS 70
Recs East, Am–70 D Ray
Pro–70 D Talbot
West, Am–71 EJ Lewis
Pro–69 P Berry
V'trs U (telephone in advance)
Fees East: £12 (£14) W–£60
West: £10 (£10)
Loc 7 miles W of Barnstaple

Sidmouth (1889)

Private (Map 3/17)
Cotmaton Road Sidmouth EX10 8SX
Tel **Sidmouth 3023**
Mem 361 92(L) 39(J)
Sec DE Matthews Tel Sidmouth 3451
Pro M Kemp Tel 6407
Holes 18 L 5188 yds SSS 65
Recs Am–59 N Winchester
Pro–64 E Murray
V'trs U; SOC
Fees D–£8 (£8) W–£35
Loc ½ mile W of town centre 2 miles SE from Junction 30 M5

Staddon Heights (1895)

Private (Map 3/18)
Plymstock Plymouth PL9 9SP
Tel **Plymouth 42475**
Mem 550
Sec MG Holliday Tel Plymouth 42475
Pro Mark Grieve Tel Plymouth 492630
Holes 18 L 5861 yds SSS 68
Recs Am–64 R Clark D Roberts
Pro–62 GC Smale
V'trs W/E–H; SOC on WD
Fees £7 (£8) 5D–£22.50
Loc SE Plymouth

Tavistock (1891)

Private (Map 3/19)
Down Road Tavistock PL19 9AQ
Tel **Tavistock 2049**
Mem 650
Sec BG Steer Tel Tavistock 2344
Pro Tony Moore Tel Tavistock 2316
Holes 18 L 6250 yds SSS 70
Recs Am–66 MG Symons
Pro–69 S Chadwick N Bicknell
V'trs U; SOC on WD
Fees £7 (£9)
Loc Whitchurch Down

Teignmouth (1924)

Private (Map 3/20)
Teignmouth TQ14 9NY
Tel **Teignmouth 3614**
Mem 900
Sec D Holloway Tel Teignmouth 4194
Pro M Blackwell Tel Teignmouth 2894
Holes 18 L 6142 yds SSS 69
Recs Am–65 JH Laidler
Pro–69 S Torrance
V'trs H (recognised club member) SOC on WD
Fees £10 (£12)
Loc 2 miles N of Teignmouth

Thurlestone (1897)

Private (Map 3/21)
Thurlestone near Kingsbridge
Tel **Kingsbridge 560405/560221**
Mem 700
Sec Richard Marston Tel Kingsbridge 560405
Pro N Whitley Tel Kingsbridge 560715
Holes 18 L 6337 yds SSS 70
Recs Am–66 RP Knott
Pro–67 PJ Yeo

V'trs I or H
Fees £10 W–£45
Loc 5 miles Kingsbridge

Tiverton (1932)

Private (Map 3/22)
Post Hill Tiverton EX16 4NE
Tel **Tiverton (0884) 252187**
Mem 450 130(L) 55(J) 200(5)
Sec Maj DLJ Hicks
Pro SWR Adwick
Holes 18 L 6227 yds SSS 70
Recs Am–65 SC Waddington
Pro–70 A Moore
V'trs I H SOC
Fees £9 W–£40
Loc M5 Junct 27, 5 miles W; 1½ miles E of Tiverton on B3391

Torquay (1910)

Private (Map 3/23)
Petitor Road St Marychurch Torquay TQ1 4QF
Tel **Torquay 37471**
Mem 800
Sec AD Hunt Tel Torquay 37471
Pro Martin Ruth Tel Torquay 39113
Holes 18 L 6251 yds SSS 70
Recs Am–62 AR Copping
Pro–66 D Short
V'trs U (only members of recognised clubs); SOC
Fees £8 (£9) W–£38 M–£69
Loc Torquay

Torrington (1932)

Public (Map 3/24)
Weare Trees Torrington Devon EX38 7EZ
Tel **Bideford 72792**
Mem 411
Sec GSC Green Tel Bideford 72792
Pro None
Holes 9 L 4418 yds SSS 62
Recs Am–65 P Wheeler
Pro–
V'trs U (NA Sun am)
Fees £4
Loc 1 mile from Torrington on Weare Gifford Road

Warren (1892)

Private (Map 3/25)
Dawlish
Tel **Dawlish 862255**
Mem 550
Sec TE Allen
Pro G Wicks Tel Dawlish 864002
Holes 18 L 5968 yds SSS 69
Recs Am–68 T Aggett
Pro–None
V'trs U
Fees £7.50 W–£35
Loc 1½ miles E of Dawlish

Wrangaton (South Devon) (1895)

Private (Map 3/26)
Wrangaton, near South Brent
Tel **South Brent 3229**
Mem 300
Sec B Moores Tel Totnes 863688
Pro None
Holes 9 L 5790 yds SSS 68
Recs Am–67 MJ Sandry
Pro–67 FG Robins
V'trs U (except on comp days)
Fees £4 (£5)
Loc Dartmoor

Yelverton (1904)

Private (Map 3/27)
Yelverton nr Plymouth
Tel **Yelverton 853618**
Mem 650
Sec PW Holden Tel Yelverton 852824
Pro A Macdonald Tel Yelverton 853593
Recs Am–67
Pro–
V'trs U
Fees £7 (£9) W–£21
Loc 8 miles Plymouth on A386

Dorset

Ashley Wood (1983)

Private (Map 3/1)
Blandford
Tel **Blandford 52253**
Mem 500
Sec P Cherry
Pro
Holes 9 L 6227 yds SSS 70
Recs Am–
Pro–
V'trs U
Fees £6.50 (£10)
Loc 1½ miles from Blandford

Bridport and West Dorset (1891)

Private (Map 3/2)
East Cliff West Bay Bridport Dorset DT6 4EP
Tel **Bridport 22597**
Mem 500
Sec MG Loud Tel Bridport 22597
Pro JE Parish Tel Bridport 22597
Holes 18 L 5246 yds SSS 66
Recs Am–63 M Rees
Pro–66 S Bishop R Crockford
V'trs U
Fees £7 (£8)
Loc 1½ miles S of Bridport

Broadstone (1898)

Private (Map 3/3)
Wentworth Drive off Station Approach Broadstone Dorset BH18 8DQ
Tel **0202 693363**
Mem 750
Sec/Man JM Cowan Tel 0202 692595
Pro Nigel Tokely Tel 0202 692835
Holes 18 L 6129 yds SSS 70
Recs Am–66 KW Clarke GJ Butler
Pro–65 DN Sewell N Stainer
V'trs WD–after 9.30 am; W/E & BH–after 10 am summer (no visitors winter); H; SOC on WD
Fees £11 D–£14 (£13 D–£16)
Loc 4 miles N of Poole

Came Down (1905)

Private (Map 3/4)
Came Down Dorchester DT2 8NR
Tel **Upwey 2531**
Mem 700
Sec DR Foot Tel Upwey 3494
Pro R Preston Tel Upwey 2670
Holes 18 L 6121 yds SSS 70
Recs Am–69
Pro–
V'trs U (ex Sun am); SOC
Fees £8 (£10) W–£25
Loc 2 miles S of Dorchester

Christchurch (1977)

Public (Map 3/5)
Iford Bridge Barrack Road Christchurch
Tel **Christchurch 473817**
Mem 350
Sec BG Dodd Tel Ferndown 872818
Pro Peter Troth Tel Christchurch 473817
Holes 9 L 4824 yds SSS 64
Recs Am–65 D Pearcey
Pro–
V'trs U
Fees £2.85 (£3.30)
Loc Boundary of Bournemouth on Christchurch road
Mis Also golf range £1.15 (50 balls)

Ferndown (1926)

Private (Map 3/6)
119 Golf Links Road Ferndown BH22 8BU
Tel **0202-872022**
Mem 700
Sec CR Johnson Tel 0202-874602
Pro DN Sewell Tel 0202-873825
Holes 18 L 6442 yds SSS 71
9 L 5604 yds SSS 68
Recs Old Course, Am–66 JHA Leggett
Pro–68 DN Sewell
New course Am–68 A Pakes
Pro–68 DN Sewell
V'trs WD & W/E–I H not before 9.30 am; SOC Mon Wed Fri
Fees Old £16 New £7 WE–£20
Loc 6 miles N of Bournemouth

Highcliffe Castle (1913)

Private (Map 3/7)
107 Lymington Road Christchurch BH23 4LA
Tel **Highcliffe 72953**
Mem 350 100(L) 50(J)
Sec DW Blakeman Tel Highcliffe 72210
Pro R Crockford Tel Highcliffe 6640
Holes 18 L 4655 yds SSS 63
Recs Am–58 S Jenkins
Pro–60 D Sewell
V'trs I
Fees £8.50 (£10.50)
Loc Bournemouth 8 miles

Isle of Purbeck (1892)

Private (Map 3/8)
Studland BH19 3AB
Rel **Studland 361 (Members' tel 210)**
Mem 700
Sec Joan Robinson Tel Studland 361
Pro P Coombs Tel Studland 354
Holes 18 L 6283 yds SSS 71
9 L 2022 yds SSS 30
Recs Am–68 KJ Weeks
Pro–72 K Sparkes
V'trs U; SOC
Fees Purbeck £11 (£13)
Dene £6.50
Loc 2 miles from Swanage

Knighton Heath (1976)

Private (Map 3/9)
Francis Avenue West Howe Bournemouth
Tel **(0202) 572633**
Mem 700
Sec R Bestwick

Pro G Smith Tel (0202) 578275
Holes 18 L 6206 yds SSS 70
Recs Am–66 M McKenna
Pro–66 M Slater
V'trs H (not before 9.30 am)
Fees £12 (£14)
Loc 4 miles N of Bournemouth on A348

Lakey Hill (1978)

Private (Map 3/10)
Hyde Nr Wareham Dorset
Tel **Bere Regis 471776**
Mem 650
Sec Alan Stratford Tel Bere Regis 471776
Pro Graham Packer Tel Bere Regis 471574
Holes 18 L 6146 yds SSS 69
Recs Am–70 BT Kent
Pro–65 P Smith
V'trs WD–U; W/E–M; SOC on WD
Fees £8 (£10)
Loc Worgret Heath Wareham

Lyme Regis (1894)

Private (Map 3/11)
Timber Hill Lyme Regis
Tel **Lyme Regis 2043**
Mem 650
Sec YG Keep
Pro Andrew Black Tel Lyme Regis 3822
Holes 18 L 6262 yds SSS 70
Recs Am–67
Pro–71
V'trs U
Fees £8
Loc Between town and Charmouth off A35

Meyrick Park (1894 course; 1941 club)

Public (Map 3/12)
Bournemouth
Tel **Bournemouth 290871**
Mem 335
Sec Kevin Holmes Tel Bournemouth 577375
Pro Neil Jordan Tel Bournemouth 290862
Holes 18 L 5878 yds SSS 69
Recs Am–66 GG Burton
Pro–
V'trs U
Fees £6 (To be confirmed)
Loc ¼ mile Bournemouth sq.
Mis Closed Sunday pm
Bournemouth Club also plays here. Society bookings apply to Recreation Officer, Town Hall, Bournemouth

Parkstone (1910)

Private (Map 3/13)
Links Road Parkstone Poole BH14 9JU
Tel **Canford Cliffs 708025**
Mem 500 160(L) 50(J)
Sec DFC Thomas Tel Canford Cliffs 707138
Pro K Hockey Tel Canford Cliffs 708092
Holes 18 L 6250 yds SSS 70
Recs Am–65 RA Latham
Pro–63 Peter Alliss
V'trs H WD–Not before 9.30 am or between 12.30 and 2.10 pm
W/E–Not before 9.45 am or between 12.30 and 2.30 pm
Fees £13 (£17) W/E & BH–D–£18
Loc 3 miles W of Bournemouth off A35

Sherborne (1895)

Private (Map 3/14)
Clatcombe Sherborne DT9 4RN
Tel **Sherborne 812475**
Mem
Sec A Mouncer Tel Sherborne 814431
Pro JM Green Tel Sherborne 812274
Holes 18 L 5768 yds SSS 68
Recs Am–64 A Hodgson
Pro–63 Mark Thomas
V'trs H
Fees £9 (£12)
Loc 1 mile N of town

Wareham (1922)

Private (Map 3/15)
Sandford Road Wareham Dorset BH20 4DH
Tel **Wareham 54147**
Mem 300
Sec Mrs WM Coombes Tel Broadstone 690532
Pro Ashley Frampton
Holes 9 L 5196 yds SSS 65
Recs Am–64 CA Whitcombe
Pro–
V'trs WD–U; W/E–M; SOC
Fees £5
Loc On A351
Mis Extending to 18 holes

Weymouth (1909)

Private (Map 3/16)
Weymouth DT4 0PE
Tel **0305 784994**
Mem 620
Sec E Dickinson Tel 0305 773981
Pro John Irving Tel 0305 773997
Holes 18 L 5980 metres SSS 69
Recs Am–68 L Peters
Pro–65 D Bennett
V'trs WD–U SOC; W/E–H
Fees £7 (£9)
Loc 1 mile from town centre
Mis Course undergoing major re-organisation. SSS and course length will be increased July 1986

Yeovil (1919)

Private (Map 3/17)
Sherborne Road Yeovil Somerset
Tel **Yeovil 75949**
Mem 600 134(L) 70(J)
Sec J Riley Tel Yeovil 22965
Pro G Kite Tel Yeovil 73763
Holes 18 L 6139 yds SSS 69
Recs Am–67 A Watts D Watkins
Pro–66 E Stillwell
V'trs WD–U SOC; W/E–H (telephone Pro for starting time); BH–H
Fees £7.50 (£9)
Loc Yeovil 1 mile on A30 to Sherborne

Gloucestershire

Bristol & Clifton (1891)

Private (Map 3/1)
Beggar Bush Lane Failand nr Clifton Bristol BS8 3TH
Tel **Long Ashton 393117**
Mem 650
Sec Cdr PA Woolings RN Tel Long Ashton 393474
Pro P Mawson Tel Long Ashton 393031
Holes 18 L 6294 yds SSS 70
Recs Am–65 P Godsland
Pro–64 PA Oosterhuis
V'trs WD–U; W/E & BH–M
Fees On request
Loc 2 miles W of Suspension Bridge & 4 miles S of junction 19 M5

Broadway (1896)

Private (Map 3/2)
Willersey Hill Broadway Worcs WR12 7LG
Tel **Broadway 853561**
Mem 400 120(L) 70(J) 110(5)
Sec KS Lawrance Tel Broadway 853683
Pro John Freeman Tel Broadway 853275
Holes 18 L 6211 yds SSS 70
Recs Am–66 DM Fletcher
Pro–66 D Steele
V'trs H
Fees £10 (£12)
Loc 1½ miles E of Broadway (A44)

Chipping Sodbury (1954)

Private (Map 3/3)
Chipping Sodbury nr Bristol BS17 6PU
Tel **Chipping Sodbury 312024 (Mem)**
Mem 600
Sec RW Bland Tel CS 319042
Pro S Harris Tel CS 314087
Holes New course 18 L 6912 yds SSS 73
Old course 9 L 6194 yds SSS 69
Recs New course Am–68 JM Durbin
Am Durbin
Pro–
V'trs WD–U; W/E–pm Sundays only. XL–am Sat/Sun; SOC
Fees New Course £7 (£8) Jrs £3
Old course £2.50 Jrs £1
Loc M4 outlet 18–5 miles, M5 outlet 14–9½ miles. 12 miles NE of Bristol at C Sodbury
Mis Steward Tel CS 315822

Cirencester (1893)

Private (Map 3/4)
Cheltenham Road Bagendon Cirencester
Tel **Cirencester 3939**
Mem 600
Sec ND Jones Tel Cirencester 2465
Pro Mark Thomas Tel Cir 66124
Holes 18 L 6021 yds SSS 69
Recs Am–66 DJ Carroll
Pro–67 DJ Rees
V'trs BH; H; SOC on weekdays
Fees £8 (£10)
Loc 1½ miles N of Cirencester on A435

Cleeve Cloud (1976)

Public **(with private section) (Map 3/5)**
Cleeve Hill nr Cheltenham
Mem 290
Sec MJ Lee Tel Bishops Cleeve 2025 (Club) Bishops Cleeve 3733 (Home)
Pro Dave Finch Tel Bishops Cleeve 2592
Holes 18 L 6444 yds SSS 71
V'trs U (exc Sun am); SOC
Fees £3.50 (£4.50)

Cleeve Hill (1976)

Public (Map 3/6)
Cleeve Hill nr Prestbury Cheltenham
Tel **Bishops Cleeve 2025**
Pro M Steadman Tel Bishops Cleeve 2592
Holes 18 L 6169 yds SSS 70
Recs Am–
Pro–
V'trs U
Fees WD–£3, 10 holes–£2, OAP & Jnrs £1.20. W/E & B/H–£3.80
Loc 3 miles N of Cheltenham

Coleford (1974)

Private (Map 3/7)
Coalway Road Coleford Glos
Tel **Dean 33689**
Mem 450
Sec R Sanzen-Baker Tel Dean 33606
Pro John Nicol Tel Dean 33689
Holes 18 L 5519 yds SSS 67
Recs Am–
Pro–
V'trs U SOC
Fees £5 (£6)
Loc ½ mile on Parkend Road out of town.

Cotswold Edge (1980)

Private (Map 3/26)
Rushmire Wotton-under-Edge Glos GL12 7PT
Tel (0453) 84416
Mem 500
Man NJ Newman Tel (0453) 844167
Pro Ian Watts Tel (0453) 844398
Holes 18 L 5897 yds SSS 69
Recs Am–
Pro–
V'trs U SOC
Fees £6 (£7)
Loc 2 miles NE of Wotten-under-Edge on B4058 Tetbury road
Mis Full catering

Cotswold Hills (1902)

Private (Map 3/8)
Ullenwood nr Cheltenham
Tel **Cheltenham 522421**
Mem 700
Sec Lt Col PG Roberson Tel Cheltenham 515264
Pro N Boland Tel Cheltenham 515263
Holes 18 L 6716 yds SSS 72
Recs Am–68 R Day
Pro–
V'trs I (Members of recognised clubs)
Fees £6 (£9)
Loc 3 miles S of Cheltenham

Filton (1909)

Private (Map 3/9)
Golf Course Lane Bristol BS12 7QS
Tel **Bristol 692021**
Mem 600
Sec DF O'Leary Tel Bristol 694169
Pro JCN Lumb Tel Bristol 694158
Holes 18 L 6277 yds SSS 70
Recs Am–66 S Hurley
Pro–
V'trs WD–U; W/E & BH–M
Fees £7
Loc 4 miles N of Bristol

Gloucestershire Hotel and GC (1976)

Private (Map 3/10)
Matson Lane Gloucester
Tel **Glos 25653**
Mem 500
Sec R Jewell
Pro R Jewell P Darnell Tel Glos 411331
Holes 18 L 6127 yds SSS 69
9 L 1980 yds SSS 27
Recs Am–69 J Northam
Pro–65 P Darnell
V'trs U
Fees £6 (£8)
Loc 2 miles S of Gloucester off Painswick Road

Henbury (1891)

Private (Map 3/11)
Westbury-on-Trym Bristol BS10 7QB
Tel **0272 500660**
Mem 310 85(L) 68(J) 140(5)
Sec JW Estill Tel 0272 500044
Pro Bob Newton Tel 0272 502121
Holes 18 L 6039 yds SSS 70
Recs Am–63 R Tugwell
Pro–67 B Sandry
V'trs WD–H; W/E–M; SOC Tue Fri
Fees £9 (£10)
Loc N Bristol (centre 3 miles)

Knowle (1905)

Private (Map 3/12)
Fairway Brislington Bristol BS4 5DF
Tel **0272 776341**
Mem 700
Sec Mrs JD King Tel 0272 770660
Pro GM Brand Tel 0272 779193
Holes 18 L 6016 yds SSS 69
Recs Am–64 SD Hurley D Hares
Pro–64 S Brown
V'trs WD–U exc Thu H or I; W/E–U exc Sat pm & Sun am H or I; BH–U H I; SOC–Thu
Fees £8 (£10)
Loc 3 miles S of city centre right Brislington Hill; 800 yds from A4

Lansdown (1894)

Private (Map 3/13)
Lansdown Bath
Tel **Bath 25007**
Mem 600
Sec GHJ Spray Tel Bath 22138
Pro T Mercer Tel Bath 20242
Holes 18 L 6267 yds SSS 70
Recs Am–67 S Butler
Pro–67 J Yeo
V'trs SOC; WD–U; W/E restricted; H
Fees £8 (£9)
Loc Bath exit 18 M4

Lilley Brook (1922)

Private (Map 3/14)
Charlton Kings Cheltenham
Tel Cheltenham 526785
Mem 700
Sec K Skeen
Pro F Hadden Tel Cheltenham 525201
Holes 18 L 6226 yds SSS 70
Recs Am–68 D Evans
Pro–67 M Steadman
V'trs H or I (members of recognised clubs); SOC on WD
Fees £6 D–£7.50 (£10 D–£12.50)
Loc 3 miles S of Cheltenham

Long Ashton (1893)

Private (Map 3/15)
The Clubhouse Long Ashton Bristol BS18 9DW
Tel Long Ashton 392229
Mem 700
Sec RE Burniston Tel LA 392316
Pro DP Scanlan Tel LA 392265
Holes 18 L 6051 yds SSS 70
Recs Am–67 P Baker
Pro–65 D Snell
V'trs WD–U H; W/E & BH–IH; SOC–Wed
Fees £12.50 (£15)
Loc 3 miles S of Bristol on B3128

Lydney (1909)

Private (Map 3/16)
Lydney
Tel **(0594) 42614**
Mem 280
Sec DA Barnard Tel (0594) 43940
Pro None
Holes 9 L 5382 yds SSS 66
Recs Am–64 MA Barnard
Pro–68 F Goulding
V'trs WD–U; W/E–M; SOC
Fees £5 W–£15
Loc Off Lakeside Avenue

Mangotsfield (1975)

Private (Map 3/17)
Carsons Road Mangotsfield Bristol BS17 3LW
Tel **0272 565501**
Mem 450
Sec Ivor Chapman
Pro Mike Watts
Holes 18 L 5297 yds SSS 66
Recs Am–
Pro–
V'trs U
Fees £3.50 (£5)
Loc 3 miles city centre

Minchinhampton (1889)

Private (Map 3/18)
Minchinhampton Stroud Glos GL6 9BE
New Course
Tel **Nailsworth 2642 (old); 3866 (new)**
Mem 742
Sec GG Critchley Tel Nailsworth 3866
Pro C Steele Tel Nailsworth 3860
Holes Old course 18 L 6295 yds SSS 70
New course 18 L 6675 yds SSS 72
Recs Old course Am–67 PH Fisher AL Scott
New Course Am–69 RD Broad
Old course Pro–67 RA Brown
New course Pro–68 D Scanlon
V'trs U subject to availability of starting times; SOC
Fees Old course: £5 (£5.50)
New course: £8.50 (£10)
Loc New course 5 miles E of Stroud; Old course 3 miles E of Stroud

Painswick (1891)

Private (Map 3/19)
Painswick near Stroud Glos
Tel **(0452) 812180**
Mem 230
Sec IR Dudley Tel (0452) 812132
Pro
Holes 18 L 4780 yds SSS 64
Recs Am–61 J Woolley
Pro–

V'trs WD & Sat–U; Sun–NA; SOC
Fees £4 Sat–£5
Loc Painswick

Ross-on-Wye (1903)

Private (Map 3/20)
Two Park Gorsley Ross-on-Wye
Tel **Gorsley 267**
Mem 650
Sec GH Cason Tel Gorsley 267; Harewood End 650 (Home)
Pro Adrian Clifford Tel Gorsley 439
Holes 18 L 6500 yds SSS 73 Par 72
Recs Am–70 MG Lane
Pro–71 Gordon Brand Jr
V'trs U SOC (2 per week WD Wed Thu Fri) SOC tee reservation (20 or more) providing booking is made well in advance
Fees £9.50 (£10.50) ½ price with mem (subject to 1987 review)
Loc Adjacent junction 3, M50 Motorway

Shirehampton Park (1907)

Private (Map 3/21)
Park Hill Shirehampton Bristol BS11 0UL
Tel **0272 823059**
Mem 600
Sec D Stuckes Tel 0272 822083
Pro Kevin Spurgeon Tel 0272 822488
Holes 18 L 5486 yds SSS 67
Recs Am–64 MJ Bessell
Pro–63 M Steadman
V'trs WD–U; W/E–M
Fees £9
Loc 1½ miles from exit 18 on M5

Stinchcombe Hill (1889)

Private (Map 3/22)
Dursley Glos GL11 6AQ
Tel **(0453) 2015**
Mem 500
Sec GH Beetham Tel (0453) 2015
Pro Tony Valentine Tel (0453) 3878
Holes 18 L 5710 yds SSS 68
Recs Am–64 PC French
Pro–64 I Bolt
V'trs WD–U SOC; W/E & BH–NA before 10.30 am exc with mem
Fees £8 (£9) £6 with mem W–£24 F–£38 M–£60
Loc 1 mile Dursley town centre

Tewkesbury Park Hotel (1976)

Private (Map 3/23)
Lincoln Green Lane Tewkesbury GL20 7DN
Tel **(0684) 295405**
Mem 550
Sec Major JD McCarthy Tel (0684) 295405
Pro P Cane Tel (0684) 294892
Holes 18 L 6533 yds SSS 71
Recs Am–68 RN Roper
Pro–68 N Job
V'trs WD–UH SOC on WD
Fees £10 (£12)
Loc ½ mile S of town on A38; 3 miles Jct 9 M5
Mis Par 3, 6 holes. Fee £2 Buggy for hire

Tracy Park (1976)

Private (Map 3/24)
Tracy Park Bath Road Wick nr Bristol
Tel **(027582) 2251**
Mem 580
Sec Capt J Seymour-Williams Tel (027 582) 2251
Pro G Aitken Tel (027 582) 3521
Holes 27 holes Avon L 6834 yds SSS 73
Bristol L 6861 yds SSS 73
Cotswold L 6203 yds SSS 70
Recs Am–70 G Ryall
Pro–72 M Kedworth
V'trs WD–U; W/T-telephone; SOC welcome by arrangement inc W/E
Fees £8 (£10)
Loc 8 miles E of Bristol off A420 Bristol-Chippenham road and 5 miles N of Bath
Mis Squash, tennis, swimming, snooker, croquet, restaurant

Westonbirt (1971)

Private (Map 3/25)
Westonbirt Tetbury
Tel **066 88 242**
Mem 200
Sec Bursar Westonbirt School Tetbury Glos GL8 8QG
Pro C Steele Tel Nailsworth 3860
Holes 9 L 4504 yds SSS 61
Recs Am–62 S Dunlop
Pro–
V'trs U; WD–SOC
Fees WD–£3.20 per day
WE–£3.20 per round
Loc 3 miles S of Tetbury off A433

Somerset

Bath (1880)

Private (Map 3/1)
Sham Castle Bath BA2 6JG
Tel **Bath 25182**
Mem 650
Sec LW Pring Tel Bath 63834
Pro Tel Bath 66953
Holes 18 L 6369 yds SSS 70
Recs Am–67 M Bloxham
Pro–68 G Brand
V'trs Visitors with bona fide handicaps welcome SOC
Fees £7.50 (£9)
Loc 1½ miles SE of Bath city centre off A36

Brean (1973)

Private (Map 3/2)
Nr Burnham-on-Sea
Tel **Brean Down 467**
Mem 250
Man A Clark
Pro Keith Davis
Holes 18 L 5618 yds SSS 66
Recs Am–
Pro–
V'trs WD–U; W/E–NA before 10 am Sun, M 10 am-12 pm Sun, Sat–U
Fees £4 (£6)
Loc 3 miles N of Burnham-on-Sea

Burnham and Berrow (1890)

Private (Map 3/3)
St Christopher's Way Burnham-on-Sea Somerset TA8 2PE
Tel **(0278) 783137**
Mem 800
Sec Mrs EL Sloman Tel (0278) 785760
Pro NP Blake Tel (0278) 784545
Holes 18 L 6547 yds SSS 73
9 L 6550 yds SSS 72
Recs Am–68 Guy Thomas (Medal Course); 66 P Baker (C'ship Course)
Pro–
V'trs I SOC
Fees £12 (£14) W–£65 F–£100 9 hole £3
Loc 1 mile N of Burnham-on-Sea

Clevedon (1908)

Private (Map 3/4)
Castle Road Clevedon Avon BS21 7AA
Tel **Clevedon 873140**
Mem 690
Sec M Sullivan Tel Clevedon 874057
Pro CA Smith Tel Clevedon 874704
Holes 18 L 5835 yds SSS 68
Recs Am–65 B Reeves
Pro–66 D Scanlon
V'trs WD–H I; W/E & BH–H I NA before 11 am; SOC on Mon
Fees £9 (£12)
Loc Walton Clevedon overlooking Severn Junction 19 or 20 M5

Enmore Park (1932)

Private (Map 3/6)
Enmore Bridgwater
Tel **Spaxton 244**
Mem 670
Sec DB Spicer Tel Spaxton 481
Pro N Wixon Tel Spaxton 519
Holes 18 L 6443 yds SSS 71
Recs Am–67 CS Edwards
Pro–71 John Yeo
V'trs U; SOC on WD
Fees £8 (£10)
Loc 3 miles W of Bridgwater

Entry Hill

Public (Map 3/18)
Entry Hill Bath Avon BA2 5NA
Tel
Mem
Sec John Sercombe Tel 02756 68972
Pro Tim Tapley 0225 834248
Holes 9 L 4206 yds SSS 61

Fosseway (1970)

Private (Map 3/7)
Midsomer Norton nr Bath
Tel **Midsomer Norton 412214**
Mem
Sec EJ Jones
Pro
Holes 9 L 4148 yds SSS 61
Recs Am–
Pro–
V'trs U (Sunday NA–am)
Fees £3
Loc 10 miles SW of Bath

Kingweston (1983)

Private (Map 3/8)
Somerton Somerset
Tel **0458 72081**
Mem 180
Sec Mr P Mountain (all correspondence to 9 Behind Berry Somerton Somerset) Tel 0458 72081

Pro
Holes 9 L 4516 yds SSS 62
V'trs M Closed Wed and Sat 2 pm–5 pm
Fees No Green Fees permitted
Mis The club has been reformed from the old Millfield School, Kingweston Club. V'trs only with members, fee £1

Mendip (1908)

Private (Map 3/9)
Gurney Slade Bath Avon BA3 4UT
Tel **Oakhill 840570**
Mem 480 70(L) 50(J)
Sec MJ Lee Tel Oakhill 840570
Pro RF Lee Tel Oakhill 840793
Holes 18 L 5982 yds SSS 69
Recs Am–65 RH Flower
Pro–
V'trs WD–U; W/E–M or H
Fees £7.50 (£10)
Loc 3 miles N of Shepton Mallet (A37)

Minehead and West Somerset (1882)

Private (Map 3/10)
Warren Road Minehead
Tel **Minehead 2057**
Mem 473
Sec RA Lawrence
Pro I Read Tel Minehead 4378
Holes 18 L 6131 yds SSS 69
Recs Am–68 GE Vaulter
Pro–66 BJ Hunt
V'trs U
Fees £10 (£12.50) W–£36.50
Loc E end of sea front

Saltford (1904)

Private (Map 3/11)
Manor Road Saltford
Tel **02217 3220**
Mem 600
Sec RF Mann Tel 02217 3513
Pro D Millensted Tel 02217 2043
Recs Am–68 K Dobson
Pro–
V'trs U
Fees £7 (£9)
Loc Bath 6 miles, Bristol 7 miles

Taunton and Pickeridge (1892)

Private (Map 3/12)
Corfe Taunton TA3 7BY
Tel **Blagdon Hill 240**
Mem 550
Sec GW Sayers Tel Blagdon Hill 537
Pro Graham Glew Tel Blagdon Hill 790
Holes 18 L 5927 yds SSS 68
Recs Am–66 P Wathen
Pro–65 G Emerson
V'trs H
Fees £8.50 (£10)
Loc 5 miles S of Taunton on B3170

Vivary

(Map 3/5)
Taunton
Tel **0823 89274**
Mem 250
Sec D James Tel 0823 71494
Holes Play over Vivary Park Municipal Course

Vivary Park

Public (Map 3/5)
Taunton
Tel **Taunton 3875**
Mem 400 season ticket holders
Pro Ron Macrow
Holes 18 L 4620 yds SSS 63
V'trs Starting time required; book through Pro; U exc Wed evenings summer–M
Fees £4.50 (£4 off-peak)
Loc Town centre
Mis Vivary Club plays here

Wells (1900)

Private (Map 3/14)
East Horrington Road Wells Somerset
Tel **Wells 72868**
Mem 520
Sec PM Rhodes Tel Wells 75005
Pro Roy Clifton Tel Wells 72868
Holes 18 L 5288 yds SSS 66
Recs Am–66 RJ Coate
Pro–
V'trs U; H; SOC on WD
Fees £6 (£8)
Loc $1\frac{1}{2}$ miles from town centre off Radstock Road

Weston-super-Mare (1892)

Private (Map 3/15)
Uphill Road Weston-super-Mare
Tel **Weston-super-Mare 21360**
Mem 630
Sec RH White Tel Weston-super-Mare 26968
Pro T Murray Tel Weston-super-Mare 33360
Holes 18 L 6279 yds SSS 70
Recs Am–67 GD Robert
Pro–69 A Lees WJ Branch
V'trs U; SOC
Fees £8 (£10) W–£30
Loc Weston-super-Mare

Windwhistle Golf Squash & Country Club (1932)

Private (Map 3/16)
Cricket St Thomas Chard
Tel **Winsham 231**
Mem 300
Sec Ian Dodd Tel Winsham 231
Pro Neil Morris
Holes 12 L 6055 yds SSS 69
Recs Am–71 P Knight
Pro–70 D Colgan
V'trs U (W/E please phone)
Fees On application
Loc On A30, opposite Cricket St Thomas *To the Manor Born* TV series Wildlife Park. South Somerset

Worlebury (1909)

Private (Map 3/17)
Weston-super-Mare
Tel **0934 23214**
Mem 640
Sec RT Bagg Tel 0934 25789
Pro David Knight Tel 0934 418473
Holes 18 L 5967 yds SSS 69
Recs Am–65 N Roseff
Pro–68 S Hall
V'trs U; SOC on WD
Fees £7.50 (£12) W–£35
Loc 2 miles NE of town centre

Wiltshire

Brinkworth (1984)

Private (club) Public (course) (Map 3/12)
9 Callows Cross Brinkworth Nr Chippenham (Hon Sec)
Tel **Brinkworth 277**
Mem 106
Sec J Homersley Tel Brinkworth 392
Pro To be appointed
Holes 9 holes completed; 9 holes under construction 6086 yds SSS 69
V'trs U (but busy at W/E)
Fees £3 (£3.50) To be revised
Loc 2 miles from centre of village on Wootton Bassett–Malmesbury Road

Broome Manor (1976)

Public (Map 3/1)
Pipers Way Swindon Wilts SN3 1RG
Tel **Swindon 32403**
Mem 550
Man Tom Watt Tel Swindon 45761
Pro B Sandry Tel Swindon 32403
Holes 18 L 6359 yds SSS 70
9 L 2805 yds SSS 68
Recs Am–70 Bill Gleeson
Pro–71 Peter Green Alan Hemsley B Sandry
V'trs U
Fees 18 holes–£3.75 (£4.20); 9 holes £2.25 (£2.55)
Loc 2 miles from Swindon centre
Mis Driving Range (25 bay floodlit)

Chippenham (1896)

Private (Map 3/2)
Malmesbury Road Chippenham
Tel **Chippenham 652040**
Mem 475
Sec Victor J Carlisle Tel Chippenham 652040
Pro Bill Creamer Tel Chipp 655519
Holes 18 L 5540 yds SSS 67
Recs Am–62 M Darbyshire
Pro–64 B Sandry
V'trs U; SOC
Fees £7 (£9)
Loc 1 mile from town centre. Off Junction 17 of M4 motorway

High Post (1922)

Private (Map 3/3)
Great Durnford Salisbury
Tel **0722-73231**
Mem 600
Sec NP Lee Tel 0722-73356
Pro AJ Harman Tel 0722-73219
Holes 18 L 6267 yds SSS 70
Recs Am–64 K Weeks
Pro–65 P Alliss N Sutton
V'trs U after 9 am; SOC on WD
Loc Salisbury 4 miles

Kingsdown (1880)

Private (Map 3/4)
Kingsdown Corsham SN14 9BS
Tel **Box 742530**
Mem 480 97(L) 45(J)
Sec SH Phipps Tel Box 743472
Pro R Emery Tel Box 742634
Holes 18 L 6235 yds SSS 70
Recs Am–67 J Moody
Pro–66 I Bolt
V'trs WD–U (Competition days–M)
Fees £8 (£9.50)
Loc 5 miles E of Bath

Marlborough (1888)

Private (Map 3/5)
The Common Marlborough Wilts SN8 1DU
Tel **0672-52147**
Mem 710
Sec JD Belben
Pro L Ross Tel 0672-52493
Holes 18 L 6440 yds SSS 71
Recs Am–68 S Robertson
Pro–67 J Cook
V'trs U SOC on WD
Fees £7 (£8)
Loc 1 mile north of Marlborough A345

North Wilts (1890)

Private (Map 3/6)
Bishops' Cannings Devizes SN10 2LP
Tel **Cannings 257**
Mem 490 85(L) 27(J)
Sec Lt Cdr JBW McKelvie Tel Cannings 627
Pro Graham Laing Tel Cannings 330
Holes 18 L 5898 metres SSS 71
Recs Am–66 EAJ Pulleyblank
Pro–67 GJ Laing
V'trs U
Fees £7 (£8)
Loc 1 mile from A4 at Calne

RAF Upavon (1918)

Private (Map 3/7)
Upavon Pewsey Wilts SN9 6BE
Tel **(0980) 630787**
Mem 235
Sec Sqn Ldr AH Howard Tel (0980) 630351 ext 379
Pro
Holes 9 L 5597 yds SSS 67
Recs Am–66 Wg Cdr RB Duckett
Pro–
V'trs WD–U; W/E & Sun am–M
Fees £5
Loc 3 miles from Upavon on A342 towards Andover

RMCS Shrivenham (1953)

Private (Map 3/13)
RMCS Shrivenham Swindon Wilts SN6 8LA
Tel **0793 782551 ext 2355**
Mem 350
Sec GM Moss Tel 0793 782551 ext 2355
Holes 9 L 5206 yds SSS 66
V'trs M at any time; SOC
Loc In grounds of Royal Military College of Science adjacent to Shrivenham village. Entry to grounds must be arranged with Secretary.

Salisbury and South Wilts (1888)

Private (Map 3/8)
Netherhampton Salisbury
Tel **Salisbury 742131**
Mem 790
Sec Wg Cdr AW Pawson Tel Salisbury 742645
Pro N Blenkarne Tel Salisbury 742929
Holes 18 L 6189 yds SSS 70
9 L 2424 yds SSS 64
Recs Am–67 R Searle
Pro–62 N Blenkarne
V'trs U; SOC
Fees D–£7 (£8)
Loc 2 miles Salisbury/2 miles Wilton on A3094

Swindon (1907)

Private (Map 3/9)
Ogbourne St George Marlborough nr Swindon Wilts SN8 1TB
Tel **Ogbourne St George 217**
Mem 600
Sec GW Moore Tel Ogbourne St George 327
Pro I Bolt Tel Ogbourne St George 287
Holes 18 L 6226 yds SSS 70
Recs Am–67 BF McCallum
Pro–65 I Bolt
V'trs U; WD–SOC
Fees £6 (£10)
Loc On A345 5 miles S of Exit 15 M4

Tidworth Garrison (1908)

Private (Map 3/10)
Tidworth
Tel **(0980) 42321**
Mem 600
Sec Wg Cdr GF Clark Tel (0980) 42301
Pro T Gosden Tel (0980) 42393
Holes 18 L 5990 yds SSS 69
Recs Am–65 JN Flemming
Pro–
V'trs U; SOC on Tue Thu Fri
Fees £8 (£8)
Loc 1 mile from Tidworth on Bulford Road

West Wilts (1891)

Private (Map 3/11)
Elm Hill Warminster
Tel **Warminster 212702**
Mem 420 70(L) 55(J) 40(5)
Sec Maj LR Weaver Tel Warminster 213133
Pro Alan Harvey Tel Warminster 212110
Holes 18 L 5701 yds SSS 68
Recs Am–65 M Smith C Burton
Pro–64 R Emery
V'trs H; U
Fees £9.50 (£8)
Loc On A350

England: Midlands

Cambridgeshire

Cambridgeshire Moat House Hotel (1974)

Private (Map 4/1)
Bar Hill Cambridge CB3 8EU
Tel **Crafts Hill 80555**
Mem 200
Sec GW Huggett
Pro GW Huggett Tel Crafts Hill 80098
Holes 18 L 6734 yds SSS 72
Recs Am–68 P Way
Pro–68 P Townsend
V'trs U
Fees £9 (£13.50) Golf free to residents
Loc 5 miles NW Cambridge on A604
Mis Buggies for hire

Ely City Golf Course (1961)

Private (Map 4/2)
Cambridge Road Ely CB7 4HX
Tel **Ely 2751**
Mem 750
Sec GA Briggs
Pro F Rowden Tel Ely 3317
Touring Pro H Baiocchi
Holes 18 L 6686 yds SSS 72
Recs Am–69 P Oakey
Pro–66 L Trevino
V'trs WD–U; W/E–H; SOC Tue–Fri
Fees £8 (£12)
Loc 12 miles N of Cambridge

Eynesbury Hardwicke (1979)

Private (Map 4/3)
Eynesbury Hardwicke Club
Eynesbury-Hardwicke St Neots PE19 4XN
Tel **0480 215153**
Mem 500
Sec Colin Scott McDougall Tel Bedford 67193
Pro Trevor James Hill Tel Huntingdon 217591
Holes 18 L 6214 yds SSS 71
Recs Am–72 V Kyle
Pro–69 S Whymark
V'trs WD–U SOC; W/E–NA before 10 am
Fees £7 (£12)
Loc 2 miles SE St Neots (B1046)

Girton (1936)

Private (Map 4/4)
Dodford Lane Cambridge
Tel **Girton 276169**
Mem 615
Sec Mrs MA Cornwell
Pro J Sharkey
Holes 18 L 5810 SSS 68
Recs Am–66 J Clough
Pro–
V'trs WD–U SOC; W/E & BH–M
Fees D–£8 W–£25
Loc 3 miles N of Cambridge

The Gog Magog (1901)

Private (Map 4/5)
Shelford Bottom Cambridge CB2 4AB
Tel **(0223) 247626**
Mem 651 206(L) 130(J) 42(5)
Sec Tom Murphy Tel (0223) 247626
Pro Eddie Birchenough Tel (0223) 246058
Holes Old Course 18 L 6386 yds SSS 70
New Course 9 L 5833 yds SSS 68
Recs Am–Old Course 64 RW Guy
MT Seaton
Pro–64 G Wolstenholme
PJ Butler

V'trs WD–I; W/E & BH–M; SOC–Tue & Thu
Fees Old £15 New £10
Loc A604 2 miles S of Cambridge

Links (Newmarket) (1902)
Private (Map 4/6)
Cambridge Road Newmarket
Tel **Newmarket 662708**
Mem 685
Sec JJB Saul Tel Newmarket 663000
Pro DP Thomson Tel Newmarket 662395
Holes 18 L 6402 yds SSS 71
Recs Am–69 B Jackson
Pro–70 S Barlow
V'trs U; M before 11.30 am Sundays
Fees £12 (£16)
Loc 1 mile S of Newmarket

March (1922)
Private (Map 4/7)
Frogs Abbey Grange Rd Knights End March
Tel **March 52364**
Mem 300
Sec RA Philpott Tel March 54604
Pro Frank Kiddie
Holes 9 L 6278 yds SSS 70
Recs Am–68 JW Kisby
Pro–
V'trs H; W/E–M
Fees £7
Loc 18 miles E of Peterborough

Ramsey (1964)
Private (Map 4/8)
4 Abbey Terrace Ramsey Huntingdon Cambs PE17 1DD
Tel **Ramsey 813573**
Mem 530 100(L) 40(J) 55(5)
Sec R Muirhead Tel Ramsey 812600
Pro R Yates Tel Ramsey 813022
Holes 18 L 6136 yds SSS 70
Recs Am–68 T Seaton
Pro–69 S Turner
V'trs U
Fees £8 (£12)
Loc 12 miles SE of Peterborough

Royston (1893)
Private (Map 4/9)
Baldock Road Royston
Tel **Royston 42177 (Members)**
Mem 700
Sec Mrs S Morris Tel Royston 42696
Pro Mark Hatcher Tel Royston 43476
Holes 18 L 6032 yds SSS 69
Recs Am–65 T Moss
Pro–63 B Waites
V'trs U; SOC; WE by arrangement with Sec
Fees £7 (£9)
Loc Royston

Saffron Walden (1919)
Private (Map 4/10)
Windmill Hill Saffron Walden CB10 1BX
Tel **Saffron Walden 22689**
Mem 600
Sec E Reynolds Tel SW 22786
Pro Philip Davis Tel SW 27728
Holes 18 L 6608 yds SSS 72
Recs Am–69 KJB Hamilton
Pro–68 S Jackson
V'trs WD–U SOC; W/E–I or M
Fees £12
Loc On B184 at entry to town
Mis Buggies for hire

St Ives (Hunts) (1923)
Private (Map 4/11)
St Ives Huntingdon PE17 4RS
Tel **St Ives 64459**
Mem 320
Sec R Hill IPFA St Ives 68392
Pro A Headley Tel St Ives 66067
Holes 9 L 6052 yds SSS 69
Recs Am–67 Fl-Lt CJB Murdoch
Pro–61 P Alliss
V'trs U (After 11 am W/E)
Fees £7 (£9)
Loc 5 miles E of Huntingdon

St Neot's (1890)
Private (Map 4/12)
Crosshall Road St Neot's PE19 4AE
Tel **Huntingdon 74311**
Mem 596
Sec GA Walker Tel Hunt 72363
Pro G Bithrey Tel Huntington 76513
Holes 18 L 6005 yds SSS 69
Recs Am–65 JR Gray } new course
Pro–65 M Gallagher }
H Flatman
V'trs U
Fees £8 D–£10 (£10 D–£15)
Loc 1 mile W of St Neot's on A45

Derbyshire

Alfreton (1893)
Private (Map 4/1)
Oakerthorpe Alfreton
Tel **Alfreton 832070**
Mem 260
Sec Derek Tomlinson Tel Chesterfield 862661
Pro JR Turnbull Tel Alfreton 832070
Holes 9 L 5074 yds SSS 65
Recs Am–64 N Cluskey
Pro–65 J Smith
V'trs WD–except Mon; U before 4.30 pm M after 4.30; W/E & Mon–M
Fees £6 (£7.50)
Loc Alfreton

Allestree Park (1949)
Public (Map 4/2)
Allestree Hall Allestree Derby
Tel **Derby 550616**
Tel 250
Sec PWJ Bye Tel Derby 512099
Pro RG Brown Tel Derby 550616
Holes 18 L 5749 yds SSS 68
Recs Am–66 J McCann
Pro–
V'trs U (Book W/E) SOC
Fees £3 (£3.50)
Loc 2 miles N of Derby on A6

Ashbourne (1910)
Private (Map 4/3)
Clifton Ashbourne
Tel **Ashbourne 42078**
Mem 350
Sec NPA James Tel Ashbourne 42077
Pro None
Holes 9 L 5388 yds SSS 66
Recs Am–
Pro–
V'trs U; SOC
Fees £3 (£5)
Loc 2 miles W of Ashbourne

Bakewell (1899)
Private (Map 4/4)
Station Road Bakewell Derbys DE4 1GB
Tel **Bakewell 2307**
Mem 205 60(L) 40(J) 21(5)
Sec PS Newell Tel Bakewell 3229
Pro TE Jones
Holes 9 L 5240 yds SSS 66
Recs Am–64 MH Pigott
Pro–
V'trs U; SOC
Fees £6 (£10)
Loc Station Road, on valley side, ½ mile NE town centre

Blue Circle (1985)
Private (Map 4/26)
Cement Works Hope Derbyshire S30 2RP
Tel **(0433) 20317**
Mem 120
Sec DS Smith Tel (0433) 20317
Pro
Holes 9 L 5252 yds SSS 66
Recs Am–69 B Harper
Pro–
V'trs NA
Loc Hope Valley

Breadsall Priory (1976)
Private (Map 4/5)
Moor Road Morley Derby DE7 6DL
Tel **Derby 832235**
Mem 450
Pro Andrew Smith
Holes 18 L 6402 yds SSS 71
Recs Am–69 D Wigglesworth
Pro–68 D Steele
V'trs W/E–H
Fees £7.50 (£10)
Loc A61 Breadsall, left into Croft Lane, left into Rectory Lane, right on to Moor Road

Burton-on-Trent (1893)
Private (Map 4/6)
43 Ashby Road East Burton-on-Trent Staffs DE15 0PS
Tel **Burton-on-Trent 68708**
Mem 600
Sec A Maddock Tel Burton-on-Trent 44551
Pro JM Lower Tel Burton-on-Trent 62240
Holes 18 L 6555 yds SSS 71
Recs Am–69 JE Roberts
Pro–67 DA Stewart
V'trs I or M
Fees £7.50 (£10)
Loc 3 miles town centre

Buxton and High Peak (1887)
Private (Map 4/7)
Townend Buxton
Tel **Buxton 3453**
Mem 600
Sec D Poole Tel Buxton 6923
Pro RM Head Tel Buxton 3112
Holes 18 L 5954 yds SSS 69
Recs Am–66 MP Higgins D Moss
Pro–65 AJH Ellis
V'trs U
Fees £8 (£10)
Loc NE boundary of town on A6

Cavendish (1925)

Private (Map 4/8)
Gadley Lane Buxton SK17 6XD
Tel **Buxton 3494**
Mem 650
Sec DN Doyle-Davidson Tel Buxton 3256
Pro J Nolan Tel Buxton 5052
Holes 18 L 5833 yds SSS 68
Recs Am–65 J Slack
Pro–64 R Lambert
V'trs U; SOC (if previous arrangements made with Professional)
Fees £7 (£9)
Loc ¾ mile W of Buxton Station

Chapel-en-le-Frith (1905)

Private (Map 4/9)
Cockyard Chapel-en-le-Frith via Stockport
Tel **0298 812118**
Mem 500
Sec WG Carter Tel 0298 813943
Pro DA Stewart Tel 0298 812118
Holes 18 L 6048 yds SSS 69
Recs Am–70 F Fletcher
Pro–66 H Hunt
V'trs U
Fees £5.50 (£6.50)
Loc On A6 13 miles Stockport

Chesterfield (1909)

Private (Map 4/10)
Walton Chesterfield
Tel **Chesterfield 79256**
Mem 425
Sec CD Yates Tel Chesterfield 566032
Pro M McLean Tel Chesterfield 76297
Holes 18 L 6326 yds SSS 70
Recs Am–65 I Wyatt
Pro–66 Kel Nagle B Hutchison
V'trs WD–U; W/E–M; SOC
Fees £7.50
Loc 2 miles SW of Chesterfield

Chesterfield Municipal (1934)

Public (Map 4/11)
Murray House Crow Lane Chesterfield S41 0EQ
Tel **Chesterfield 73887**
Pro J Delany
Holes 18 L 6044 yds SSS 69
Recs Am–None
Pro–None
V'trs U
Fees £1.70 (£2.20)
Loc Chesterfield
Mis Tapton Park play here

Chevin (1894)

Private (Map 4/12)
Duffield Derby
Tel **Derby 841864**
Mem 500 66(L) 61(J) 8(5)
Sec JH Wales
Pro William Bird Tel Derby 841112
Holes 18 L 6057 yds SSS 69
Recs Am–66 Clive Radford
Pro–65 Gavin Christie
V'trs WD–U; W/E–M
Fees £8
Loc 5 miles N of Derby on A6

Craythorne Golf Centre (1972)

Public (Map 4/25)
Craythorne Road Stretton Burton on Trent DE13 0AZ
Mem 250
Prop C Johnson Tel Burton 64329
Pro Steve Hadfield Tel Burton 33745
Holes 18 L 5164 yds SSS 65
V'trs U SOC WD and WE
Fees £4 (£6)
Loc 1½ miles N Burton on Trent

Derby (1923)

Public (Map 4/13)
Shakespeare Street Sinfin Derby DE2 9HD
Tel **Derby 766323**
Mem 400
Sec P Davidson Tel Derby 764265
Pro Robert G Brown Tel Derby 766462
Holes 18 L 6183 yds SSS 69
Recs Am–65
Pro–
V'trs U
Fees £1.80 (£2.80)
Loc Shakespeare Street Derby

Erewash Valley (1905)

Private (Map 4/14)
Stanton-by-Dale nr Ilkeston Derbys
Tel **Ilkeston 323258**
Mem 400
Sec D Knowles Tel Ilkeston 322984
Pro MJ Ronan Tel Ilkeston 324667
Holes 18 L 6444 yds SSS 72
Recs Am–69 DL Clarke
Pro–68 MJ Ronan
V'trs W/E & BH–NA before noon; SOC on WD
Fees £8 (£10)
Loc Stanton-by-Dale midway Nottingham–Derby

Glossop and District (1894)

Private (Map 4/15)
Sheffield Road Glossop
Tel **Glossop 3117**
Mem 250
Sec J Dickson Tel Glossop 62713
Pro C Wadsworth
Holes 11 L 5716 yds SSS 68
Recs Am–66 DM Pike
Pro–68 S Sewgolum
V'trs U SOC
Fees £6 (£7)
Loc 1 mile E of town off A57

Ilkeston (1929)

Public (Map 4/16)
Peewit West End Drive Ilkeston
Tel
Mem 90
Sec SJ Rossington Tel Ilk 320304
Pro
Holes 9 L 4116 yds SSS 60
Recs Am–
Pro–
V'trs U
Fees On application
Loc ½ mile town centre

Kedleston Park (1947)

Private (Map 4/17)
Kedleston Derby
Tel **(0332) 840035**
Mem 900
Sec K Wilson Tel (0332) 840035
Pro Gavin Christie Tel (0332) 841685
Holes 18 L 6643 yds SSS 72
Recs Am–67 AF Simms
Pro–68 R Meek
V'trs U
Fees £10 (£12)
Loc 4 miles N of Derby

Matlock (1907)

Private (Map 4/18)
Chesterfield Road Matlock DE4 5LF
Tel **Matlock 2191**
Mem 325 57(L) 52(J) 90(5)
Sec Len Hooley
Pro Mike Deeley
Holes 18 L 5871 yds SSS 67
Recs Am–64 R Davenport A Hession
Pro–68 G Walker G Stevens
V'trs WD–U; W/E–M
Fees £9 W–£40 M–£70
Loc 1½ miles NE Matlock A632

Mickleover (1923)

Private (Map 4/19)
Uttoxeter Road Micleover
Tel **(0332) 513339 (Clubhouse)**
Mem 550
Sec D Rodgers Tel (0332) 512092 (home)
Pro G Stevens Tel (0332) 518662
Holes 18 L 5708 yds SSS 68
Recs Am–64 CRJ Ibbotson
Pro–63 Tony Skingle
V'trs U; SOC–Mon & Thu
Fees £9 (£15)
Loc 3 miles W of Derby on A516/B5020

New Mills (1907)

Private (Map 4/20)
Shaw Marsh New Mills Cheshire
Tel **New Mills 43485**
Mem 250
Sec W Hyde Tel New Mills 43816
Pro Garry Williams Tel New Mills 46161
Holes 9 L 5924 yds SSS 68
Recs Am–72 R Palmer S Hewson
Pro–67 A Ellis A Murray
V'trs WD–U; W/E–M
Fees D–£5
Loc
Mis SOC

Ormonde Fields

Private (Map 4/21)
Nottingham Road Codnor Ripley Derbys
Tel **Ripley 42987**
Mem 460
Sec RN Walters Tel Ripley 47301
Pro A Kelso Tel Ripley 42987
Holes 18 L 6007 yds SSS 69
Recs Am–67 S Clarke
Pro–67 C Jepson
V'trs U SOC
Fees £4 (£6)
Loc A610 Ripley to Nottm Road

Pastures (1969)

Private (Map 4/22)
Pastures Hospital Mickleover
Tel **513921 Extn 348**
Mem 320
Sec S McWilliams
Pro
Holes 9 L 5005 yds SSS 64
Recs Am–64 I Smith
Pro–

V'trs M SOC on WD
Fees
Loc 4 miles W of Derby

Renishaw Park

(See Yorkshire)

Shirland (1977)

Private (Map 4/23)
Lower Delves Shirland DE5 6AU
Tel **Alfreton 2515**
Mem 250
Sec RH Marsh Tel Mansfield 28500
Pro NB Hallam Tel Alfreton 4935
Holes 18 L 6137 yds SSS 69
Recs Am–
Pro–
V'trs U
Fees £2.90 (£3.75)
Loc 1 mile N of Alfreton off A61

Sickleholme

(See Yorkshire)

Stanedge (1934)

Private (Map 4/24)
Walton Hay Farm nr Chesterfield
Tel **(0246) 566156**
Mem 260
Sec J Hine Tel (0246) 34392
Pro None
Holes 9 L 4867 yds SSS 64
Recs Am–64
Pro–66
V'trs WD–U before 2 pm M after 2 pm Sat–M Sun–N/A
Fees £4 (Sat with member £4.50)
Loc 5 miles SW Chesterfield off B5057

Tapton Park (1934)

Public (Map 4/11)
Murray House Crow Lane Chesterfield S41 0EQ
Tel
Mem 450
Sec D Griffiths Tel Chesterfield 475260
Holes Play over Chesterfield Municipal

Leicestershire & Rutland

Birstall (1901)

Private (Map 4/1)
Station Road Birstall Leicester
Tel **Leicester 674450**
Mem 350 86(L) 57(J)
Sec Ms S Wells Tel Leicester 674322
Pro R Ball Tel Leicester 675245
Holes 18 L 6203 yds SSS 70
Recs Am–68 K Wells NH Abel D Hunter Walker
Pro–67 L Platts
V'trs Mon Wed Fri–I other days–M
Fees £10
Loc 3 miles N of town

Charnwood Forest (1890)

Private (Map 4/2)
Woodhouse Eaves Loughborough
Tel **Woodhouse Eaves 890259**
Mem 250
Sec BE Rees Tel Loughborough 231389
Pro –
Holes 9 L 6202 yds SSS 70
Recs Am–68 RJ Sallis
Pro–
V'trs H
Fees £6 (£8)
Loc Loughborough M1 Junction 23–3 miles

Cosby (1985)

Public (Map 4/3)
Chapel Lane Cosby nr Leicester
Tel **Leicester 864759**
Mem 520
Sec John D Horsburgh Tel Leicester 866197
Pro Tel Leicester 848275
Holes 18 L 6277 yds SSS 70
V'trs WD–U before 4 pm; W/E–M; SOC on WD H
Fees £7
Loc 7 miles S of Leicester

Enderby (1986)

Public (Map 4/24)
Mill Lane Enderby Leicester
Tel **Leicester 849388**
Mem 50
Sec LJ Speake Tel Leicester 841133
Pro C D'Araujo Tel Leicester 849388
Holes 9 L 4356 yds SSS 61
Recs Am–
Pro–
V'trs U
Fees £2 (£2.50)
Loc Enderby village 2 miles M1 exit 21 or M69 exit 1

Glen Gorse (1933)

Private (Map 4/4)
Glen Road Oadby Leicester LE2 4RF
Tel **Leicester 712226/714159**
Mem 358 96(L) 65(J)
Sec LA Hatton Tel Leicester 714159
Pro R Larratt Tel Leicester 713748
Holes 18 L 6641 yds SSS 72
Recs Am–68 IR Middleton P Toon
Pro–66 DT Steele
V'trs WD–U; W/E & BH–M; SOC on WD
Fees £10
Loc 3 miles S of Leicester on A6

Hinckley (1983)

Private (Map 4/5)
Leicester Road Hinckley LE10 3DR
Tel **Hinckley 615124**
Mem 500
Sec J Toon Tel Hinckley 30373
Pro Richard Jones Tel Hinckley 615014
Holes 18 L 6478 yds SSS 71; Championship course L 6578 yds SSS 71
Recs Am–
Pro–
V'trs WD–U; W/E–NA Sun after 12 noon; SOC
Fees £8 (BH £10)
Loc NE boundary Hinckley on A47

Humberstone Heights (1978)

Public (Map 4/6)
Gipsy Lane Leicester
Tel **Leicester 761905**
Mem 375
Sec BA Morris Tel Leicester 761905
Pro P Highfield Tel Leicester 764674
Holes 18 L 6444 yds SSS 71 Par 72
Recs Am–65
Pro–67
V'trs U
Fees
Loc 3 miles E of city centre off A47

Kibworth (1905)

Private (Map 4/7)
Weir Road Kibworth
Tel **Kibworth 2301**
Mem 550
Sec Mrs W Potter Tel Kibworth 2301 (Hon Sec JJ Gibbons)
Pro Peter Taggart Tel Kibworth 2283
Holes 18 L 6282 yds SSS 70
Recs Am–67 EE Feasey
Pro–67 J Briars
V'trs WD–U; W/E–M
Fees £7.50
Loc 9 miles SE of Leicester on A6

Kirby Muxloe (1910)

Private (Map 4/8)
Station Road Kirby Muxloe nr Leicester LE9 9EN
Tel **Leicester 393107**
Mem 425
Sec AJ Rabbitt Tel Leicester 393457
Pro RT Stephenson Tel Leicester 392813
Holes 18 L 6203 yds SSS 70
Recs Am–69 M Reay
Pro–65 Peter Thomson
V'trs WD–U before 3.45 pm, SOC; H; no restrictions with mem
Fees £8.50 (£10.50) W/E with captain's permission only
Loc 3 miles W of Leicester

Leicestershire (1890)

Private (Map 4/9)
Evington Lane Leicester LE5 6DT
Tel **Leicester 736035**
Mem 750
Sec Major DR Bettany Tel Leicester 738825
Pro K Dixon Pickup Tel Leicester 736730
Holes 18 L 6330 yds SSS 70
Recs Am–65 Alan Martinez
Pro–63 H Henning S Sherratt I Mosey
V'trs U
Fees £10 (£11)
Loc 2 miles E of Leicester

Lingdale (1967)

Private (Map 4/10)
Joe Moores Lane Woodhouse Eaves Loughborough
Tel **Woodhouse Eaves 890035**
Mem 450
Sec D Wardle Tel Woodhouse Eaves 890035
Pro P Highfield Tel Woodhouse 890684
Holes 9 L 6114 yds SSS 72
Recs Am–71 DS Cameron
Pro–
V'trs U SOC
Fees D–£6 (£8)
Loc Loughborough 6 miles; 4 miles exit 23 on M1

Longcliffe (1905)

Private (Map 4/11)
Nanpantan Loughborough
Tel **Loughborough 216321**
Mem 550
Sec Gordon Harle Tel Loughborough 239129
Pro I Bailey Tel Loughborough 231450
Holes 18 L 6551 yds SSS 71
Recs Am–67 S pepper D Hughes
Pro–71 K Barnes
V'trs WD–U; W/E–M
Fees £12
Loc 2½ miles Loughborough Exit 23 on M1

Luffenham Heath (1911)

Private (Map 4/12)
Ketton Stamford Lincs
Tel **Stamford 720205**
Mem 555
Sec Sq Ldr SA Lynch
Pro JA Lawrence Tel Stamford 720298
Holes 18 L 6254 yds SSS 70
Recs Am–66 RD Christian E Lloyd
Pro–67 PJ Butler RL Moffitt
V'trs U; WD–SOC
Fees On application
Loc 5 miles W of Stamford on A6121

Lutterworth (1904)

Private (Map 4/13)
Lutterworth Leicester
Tel **Lutterworth 2532**
Mem 310
Sec H Cooke Tel Lut 4631
Pro N Melvin
Holes 18 L 5570 yds SSS 67
Recs Am–67 M Moore
Pro–71 M Faulkner
V'trs WD–U SOC; W/E–M
Fees £6.50 (with mem £2.50)
Loc ½ mile centre ¼ mile M1 4 miles M6

Market Harborough (1898)

Private (Map 4/14)
Oxendon Road Market Harborough
Tel **Market Harborough 63684**
Mem 360
Sec JNT Lord Tel Kettering 761318
Pro N Gilks
Holes 9 L 6080 yds SSS 69
Recs Old course
Am–67 P Wood RC Gadd
Pro–67 H Granger
New course
Am–68 RC Gadd W Sneath
Pro–69 P Highfield R Adams
V'trs WD–U SOC
Fees £6
Loc 1 mile S of M Harborough

Melton Mowbray (1925)

Private (Map 4/15)
Waltham Rd Thorpe Arnold Melton Mowbray
Tel **0664 62118**
Mem 380
Sec Mrs TD Hudson Tel 066478 312
Pro
Holes 9 L 6168 yds SSS 69
Recs Am–65 N Street
Pro–66 W Hill
V'trs U
Fees £5 (£7)
Loc 2 miles NE of Melton Mowbray

Oadby (1974)

Public (Map 4/16)
Leicester Road Racecourse Oadby Leicester LE2 4AB
Tel **Leicester 700326/700215**
Mem 330 27(L) 42(J)
Sec C Chamberlain Tel Leics 889862
Pro Rick Adams Tel Leics 709052
Holes 18 L 6228 yds SSS 69
Recs Am–68 K Mould
Pro–73 C O'Connor Jnr
V'trs U; WD–Societies if pre-booked
Fees £2.50 (£3)
Loc 2 miles S of Leicester

RAF North Luffenham (1975)

Private (Map 4/17)
RAF North Luffenham Oakham LE15 8RL
Tel **Stamford 720041 ext 470**
Mem 104 26(L) 13(J)
Sec Brian Penrose Tel Stamford 720041 ext 300/Melton Mowbray 63212 (home)
Pro
Holes 9 L 5629 yds SSS 67
Recs Am–72 KP Hickman
Pro–
V'trs All visitors are to register at the main guardroom before proceeding to the golf club
Fees £3
Loc RAF N Luffenham ½ mile from south shore of Rutland Water

Rothley Park (1911)

Private (Map 4/18)
Westfield Lane Rothley Leicester LE7 7LH
Tel **Leicester 302019**
Mem 560
Sec MB Wheeler Tel Leicester 302809
Pro PJ Dolan Tel Leicester 303023
Holes 18 L 6487 yds SSS 71
Recs Am–67 EE Feasey
Pro–68 PJ Dolan
V'trs U
Fees £12 (£15)
Loc 6 miles N of Leicester W of A6

Scraptoft (1928)

Private (Map 4/19)
Beeby Road Scraptoft Leicester
Tel **Leicester 419000**
Mem 450
Sec JL Bates
Pro GER Papworth Tel Leicester 418863
Holes 18 L 6166 yds SSS 69
Recs Am–66 D Gibson
Pro–66 A Bownes
V'trs WD–U; W/E–M SOC on WD
Fees £8 (£10)
Loc 3 miles E of Leicester

Ullesthorpe Court (1976)

Private (Map 4/20)
Frolesworth Road Ullesthorpe
Tel **Leire 209021**
Mem 500
Sec DD Allderidge
Pro P Troop Tel Leire 209150
Holes 18 L 6300 yds SSS
Recs Am–70
Pro–68
V'trs U
Fees £4 (£4)
Loc 3 miles NW of Lutterworth

Western Park (1920)

Public (Map 4/21)
Scudamore Road Leicester
Tel **0533 872339 and 876158**
Mem 470 36(L) 31(J)
Sec AE Warren Tel 0533 874939
Pro SC Long Tel 0533 872339
Holes 18 L 6818 yds SSS 72
Recs Am–69 PJ Allen
Pro–68 H Boyle
V'trs U
Fees £2.05 (£2.80)
Loc 4 miles West Leicester

Whetstone (1965)

Private (Map 4/22)
Cambridge Road Whetstone Leicester
Tel Leicester 862399
Mem 50
Sec H Mitchell
Pro EL Callaway
Holes 9 L 3005 yds SSS 69
Recs Am–
Pro–
V'trs U
Fees 80p (£1.20)
Loc S boundary Leicester

Willesley Park (1921)

Private (Map 4/23)
Tamworth Road Ashby-de-la-Zouch
Tel **0530 414596**
Mem 550 99(L) 38(J)
Sec TR Hodgetts Tel 0530 414596
Pro C Hancock Tel 0530 414820
Holes 18 L 6310 yds SSS 70
Recs Am–64 PM Baxter
Pro–66 R Swain
V'trs I; SOC
Fees £8 D–£10
Loc A453 Ashby-de-la-Zouch

Lincolnshire

Belton Park (1892)

Private (Map 4/1)
Belton Lane Londonthorpe Road Grantham NG31 9SH
Tel **Grantham 3355**
Mem 750
Sec FC Ely Tel Grantham 67399
Pro K Saint Tel Grantham 63911
Holes 27 Brownlow L 6412 yds SSS 71
Ancaster L 6109 yds SSS 69
Belmont L 5857 yds SSS 68
Recs Am–69 DF Price
Pro–65 S Bennett
V'trs U
Fees £10 (£12)
Loc Grantham 2 miles

Blankney (1903)

Private (Map 4/2)
Blankney Lincoln
Tel **Metheringham 20263**
Mem 350 90(L) 60(J) 25(5)
Sec CE Woodcock Tel Lincoln 25272 (Day); Lincoln 791550 (Evening)
Pro Graham Bradley Tel Metheringham 20202
Holes 18 L 6232 yds SSS 70
Recs Am–65 SG Toyne
Pro–66 Ashley Carter
V'trs WD–U SOC; W/E–M
Fees £8
Loc 10 miles SE of Lincoln, B1188

Boston (1962)

Private (Map 4/3)
Cowbridge Horncastle Road Boston PE 22 7EL
Tel Boston 62306
Mem 650 110(L) 41(J)
Sec JM Mitchell Tel Boston 50589
Pro TR Squires
Holes 18 L 5795 yds SSS 68
Recs Am–67 SG Wood
Pro–64 G Cullen
V'trs U
Fees £7.50 (£8.50)
Loc 2 miles N of Boston on B1183

Burghley Park (1890)

Private (Map 4/4)
St Martin's Stamford PE9 3JX
Tel **(0780) 53789**
Mem 500 80(L) 80(J) 120(5)
Sec PH Mulligan Tel (0780) 53789
Pro Glenn Davies Tel (0780) 62100
Holes 18 L 6236 yds SSS 70
Recs Am–65 PG Barker
Pro–70 B Thompson
V'trs WD–U; (W/E after 3 pm May–Sept)
Fees £8 (£10)
Loc 1 mile S of Town. Turn off A1 at roundabout

Canwick Park (1893)

Private (Map 4/22)
Canwick Park Washingborough Road Lincoln
Tel **Lincoln 22166**
Mem 500
Sec PJ Richardson Tel Lincoln 694851
Pro S Williamson
Holes 18 L 6300 yds SSS 70
Recs Am–68 R Britt Robinson
Pro–
V'trs WD–U; W/E–M
Fees £5.50
Loc

Carholme (1906)

Private (Map 4/5)
Lincoln
Tel **Lincoln 23725**
Mem 420
Sec BW Robinson
Pro BA McKee Tel Lincoln 33263
Holes 18 L 6086 yds SSS 69
Recs Am–70 N Smith
Pro–
V'trs U (ex am Sundays)
Fees On application
Loc 1 mile from town centre

Cleethorpes (1896)

Private (Map 4/6)
Kings Road Cleethorpes DN35 0PN
Tel **814060**
Mem 750
Sec GB Standaloft
Pro E Sharp Tel Grimsby 812059
Holes 18 L 6015 yds SSS 69
Recs Am–67 DB Short
Pro–64 D Ramsey
V'trs WD–U (NA Wed pm); W/E–U(XL Sat pm Sun am)
Fees £6 (£8)
Loc Cleethorpes 1 mile

Elsham (1900)

Private (Map 4/7)
Barton Road Elsham nr Brigg
S Humberside DN20 0LS
Tel **0652 688 382**
Mem 600
Sec WH Horsfield Tel 0652 680 291
Pro R McKiernan Tel 0652 680432 (home) 0652 680235
Holes 18 L 6420 yds SSS 71
Recs Am–72 A Shepherd
Pro–69 MT Hoyle
V'trs WD–SOC; W/E–M
Fees £8
Loc nr Brigg

Grimsby (1923)

Private (Map 4/8)
Littlecoats Road Grimsby DN34 4LU
Tel Grimsby 42823
Mem 550 150(L) 70(J)
Sec RR Macintosh Tel Grimsby 42630
Pro S Houltby Tel Grimsby 56981
Holes 18 L 6058 yds SSS 69
Recs Am–66 M James
Pro–66 BJ Hunt
V'trs WD–U; W/E–XL Sat pm Sun am
Fees £7 (£9) W–£30
Loc 1 mile W centre

Holme Hall (1908)

Private (Map 4/9)
Holme Lane Bottesford Scunthorpe
S Humberside
Tel **Scunthorpe 840909** (Steward)
Mem 430 90(L) 66(J) 3(5)
Sec RR Loudon Tel Scun 862078
Pro K Highfield Tel Scun 851816
Holes 18 L 6475 yds SSS 71
Recs Am–67 S Steele A Thain
K Blow FW Wood
Pro–66 B Thompson
V'trs WD–U; W/E–M H SOC on WD
Fees £7 (£3 with mem)
Loc 2 miles SE of Scunthorpe M180 Junction 4

Immingham GC (1975)

Private and Public (Map 4/10)
Church Lane Immingham Grimsby
Tel **(0469) 75298**
Mem 350 60(L) 50(J)
Pro J Moffat Tel (0469) 75493
Holes 18 L 5809 yds SSS 68
Recs Am–67 J Lea C Robinson
Pro–
V'trs Sunday–NA before noon
Fees £5
Loc ½ miles from Immingham Civic Centre behind St Andrew's Church

Kingsway

Public (Map 4/11)
Kingsway Scunthorpe S Humberside DN15 7ER
Tel **Scunthorpe 840945**
Mem
Sec RD Highfield
Pro Chris Mann Tel Scunthorpe 840945
Holes 9 L 1915 yds SSS 59
Recs Am–
Pro–
V'trs U
Fees £1.10 Jnrs OAPs 50p (£1.40 Jnrs OAPs 65p)
Loc 300 yds from Berkeley Circle

Lincoln (1891)

Private (Map 4/12)
Lincoln
Tel **Torksey 210**
Mem 600
Sec D Boag Tel Torksey 721
Pro A Carter Tel Torksey 273
Holes 18 L 6400 yds SSS 70
Recs Am–66 A Thain P Taylor
Pro–65 Mark James
V'trs H; W/E–by appt
Fees £7 D–£10 (£10 D–£13.50)
Loc 12 miles W of Lincoln

Louth (1965)

Private (Map 4/13)
Crowtree Lane Louth LN11 9LJ
Tel **Louth 602554**
Mem 600
Sec RG Jackson Tel Louth 603681
Pro AJ Blundell Tel Louth 604648
Holes 18 L 6502 yds SSS 71
Recs Am–70 A Murray
Pro–A Cayhill
V'trs U; SOC on WD
Fees £7 D–£9 (£8 D–£10)
Loc ½ mile from town centre
Mis 3 squash courts

Market Rasen and District (1922)

Private (Map 4/14)
Legsby Road Market Rasen Lincs LN8 3DZ
Tel **(0673) 842416**
Mem 485
Sec A Vout Tel (0673) 842416
Pro AM Chester Tel (0673) 842416
Holes 18 L 6025 yds SSS 69
Recs Am–67 PJ Lacey
Pro–
V'trs WD–I; W/E–M
Fees £7
Loc 1 mile E of town

Normanby Hall (1978)

Public (Map 4/15)
Normanby Park Scunthorpe
S Humberside
Tel **Scunthorpe 720226**
Mem 566
Sec ID Reekie Tel Scunthorpe 862141 (Ext 300)
Pro Richard Highfield Tel Scunthorpe 720226
Holes 18 L 6548 yds SSS 71
V'trs U; SOC on WD
Fees £3.50 D–£5 (£5)
Loc Normanby Park 5 miles N of Scunthorpe

North Shore (1910)

Private (Map 4/16)
North Shore Road Skegness Lincs PE25 1DN
Tel **(0754) 3298**
Mem 650
Sec Maj E Coombes Tel (0754) 3298
Pro M Tongue Tel (0754) 4822
Holes 18 L 6124 yds SSS 69
Recs Am–72 M Myszczyszyn
Pro–
V'trs H SOC
Fees £7 (£8)
Loc 1 mile N of town centre
Mis Accommodation available

RAF Waddington

Private (Map 4/17)
Waddington Lincoln
Tel **0522 720271**
Mem 60
Sec Flt Lt Tull Tel Ext 407
Pro –
Holes 18 L 5223 yds SSS 66
Recs Am–73
Pro–
V'trs By prior arrangement
Fees £2
Loc A607 Lincoln–Grantham

Sandilands (1900)

Private (Map 4/18)
Roman Bank Sutton-on-Sea Mablethorpe LN12 2RJ
Tel **Sutton-on-Sea 41432**
Mem 500
Sec Dennis Mumby Tel Sutton-on-Sea 41617
Pro R Lawie Tel Sutton-on-Sea 41600
Holes 18 L 5995 yds SSS 69
Recs Am–66 JR Payne
Pro–63 FG Allott
V'trs U SOC
Fees £6 (£7) W–£25
Loc 1 mile S of Sutton-on-Sea off A52

Scunthorpe (1936)

Private (Map 4/19)
Ashby Decoy Scunthorpe
Tel **(0724) 842913/866561**
Mem 450 105(L) 50(J)
Sec EA Willsmore Tel (0724) 866561
Pro John Corden Tel (0724) 868972
Holes 18 L 6281 yds SSS 71
Recs Am–69 R Mortimer
Pro–
V'trs U SOC on WD
Fees £8 (£10–Sun NA)
Loc Burringham Road Ashby

Seacroft (1895)

Private (Map 4/20)
Seacroft Skegness PE25 3AU
Tel **Skegness 3020**
Mem 340 190(L) 90(J)
Sec JM Wattam
Pro J Cornelius
Holes 18 L 6478 yds SSS 71
Recs Am–64 TH Bowman
Pro–67 R James
V'trs U; W/E–XL before 11 am
Fees £7 (£9)
Loc Southern boundary Skegness

Sleaford (1905)

Private (Map 4/21)
South Rauceby Sleaford Lincs NG34 8PL
Tel **South Rauceby 273**
Mem 450 150(L) 50(J) 50(5)
Sec DBR Harris Tel Sleaford 303535
Pro T Hutton Tel South Rauceby 644
Holes 18 L 6443 yds SSS 71
Recs Am–67 K Blow
Pro–67 BJ Hunt
V'trs U; SOC on WD
Fees
Loc 1 mile W of Sleaford on A153

Spalding (1922)

Private (Map 4/23)
Surfleet Spalding Lincs PE11 4DG
Tel **Surfleet 234**
Mem
Sec WE Codling Tel Surfleet 386
Pro J Spencer Tel Surfleet 474
Holes 18 L 5847 yds SSS 68
Recs Am–65 G Palmer
Pro–65 J Spencer
V'trs U; H; Thu–SOC
Fees £6 (£8) W–£26
Loc 4 miles N of Spalding off A16

Stoke Rochford (1924)

Private (Map 4/24)
Great North Rd nr Grantham
Tel **Great Ponton 275**
Mem 500
Sec CE Leverett
Pro A Dow Tel Gt Ponton 218
Holes 18 L 6204 yds SSS 70
Recs Am–67 A Hare
Pro–66 A Carter
V'trs W/E–U after 10.30 am
Fees On application
Loc On A1 6 miles S Grantham entrance at service station

Sutton Bridge (1914)

Private (Map 4/25)
Sutton Bridge
Tel **Holbeach 350323**
Mem 330
Sec KC Buckle Tel Wisbech 870455
Pro K Short
Holes 9 L 5804 yds SSS 68
Rec Am–
Pro–62 CJ Norton
V'trs WD–U; W/E–NA
Fees £6
Loc Wisbech 8 miles

Thonock (Karsten (UK) Ltd) (1900)

Private (Map 4/26)
Thonock Gainsborough DN21 1PZ
Tel **(0427) 3088**
Mem 470
Sec/ Man A Knox Tel (0427) 616444
Pro G Stafford Tel (0427) 2278
Holes 18 L 5824 yds SSS 68
Recs Am–67
Pro–
V'trs U WE/BH–M SOC on WD
Fees £6 D–£8 (£10, with mem £5)
Loc Gainsborough

Woodhall Spa (1905)

Private (Map 4/27)
Woodhall Spa
Tel **Woodhall Spa 52511**
Mem 450
Sec SR Sharp
Pro P Fixter
Holes 18 L 6866 yds SSS 73
Recs Am–66 FW Wood
Pro–68 EB Williamson
V'trs U; booking essential SOC
Fees £10 (£12)
Loc 19 miles SE of Lincoln

Northamptonshire

Cherwell Edge (1980)

Public (Map 4/16)
Cherwell Chacombe nr Banbury North Oxford
Tel **Banbury 711591**
Man Richard Davies
Sec
Pro Richard Davies
Holes 18 L 5925 yds SSS 69
Recs Am–71
Pro–
V'trs U: WD–SOC
Fees £3 D–£5.50 (£4)
Loc 3 miles E of Banbury on B4525 (A422)

Cold Ashby (1974)

Private (Map 4/1)
Cold Ashby nr Northampton NN6 7EP
Tel **Northampton 740548**
Mem 500 40(L) 40(J)
Sec David Croxton
Pro Simon Ward Tel Northampton 740099
Holes 18 L 5946 yds SSS 69
Recs Am–68 David France
Pro–61 David Dunk
V'trs WD–U; W/E–U after 10.30 if booked
Fees £6 (£7.50)
Loc 5 miles J18 (Crick) M1

Daventry and District (1922)

Private (Map 4/2)
Norton Road Daventry
Tel **Daventry 702829**
Mem 300
Sec F Higham Tel Daventry 703204
Pro Michael Higgins
Holes 9 L 2871 yds SSS 67
Recs Am–
Pro–
V'trs WD–U; W/E–NA before 11 am Sun SOC
Fees £4.50 (£5.50)
Loc Norton Road

Delapre (1976)

Public (Map 4/3)
Eagle Drive Nene Valley Way Northampton
Tel **0604 64036/63957**
Mem 500
Sec JS Corby Tel 0604 63957
Pro John Corby Tel 0604 64036
Holes 18 L 6293 yds SSS 70
Recs Am–66 M McNally
Pro–
V'trs U; SOC
Fees £3.75 (W/E & BH £4.75)
Loc 3 miles from junction 15 on M1; A508
Mis Also two 9 hole par 3, 9 hole pitch and putt 36 open and 33 floodlit practice bays

Kettering (1891)

Private (Map 4/4)
Headlands Kettering
Tel **Kettering 512074**
Mem 370 100(L) 45(J) 50(5)
Sec T Cave Tel Kettering 511104
Pro K Theobald Tel Kettering 81014
Holes 18 L 6035 yds SSS 69
Recs Am–67 J Campbell
Pro–67 J Gallagher

V'trs WD–U; W/E & BH–M; SOC
Fees £9
Loc South boundary Kettering

Kingsthorpe (1908)

Private (Map 4/5)
Kingsley Road Northampton
Tel **0604 711173**
Mem 450
Sec NC Liddington Tel 0604 710610
Pro T Giles Tel 0604 719602
Holes 18 L 6006 yds SSS 69
Recs Am–63 S McDonald
Pro–64 B Larratt
V'trs WD–U; W/E & BH–M H SOC on WD
Fees £10 R–D
Loc Northampton

Northampton (1893)

Private (Map 4/6)
Kettering Road Northampton
Tel **0604 711054**
Mem 500 100(L) 70(J)
Sec TCA Knight Tel 0604 719453
Pro R Lovelady Tel 0604 714897
Holes 18 L 6002 yds SSS 69
Recs Am–67 M Poxon
Pro–66 M Gallagher
V'trs WD–U; W/E–M NA before 11.15 Sun
Fees £12 (£14)
Loc 2 miles E of town on A43

Northamptonshire County (1909)

Private (Map 4/7)
Church Brampton Northampton
Tel **Northampton 842170**
Mem 600
Sec GG Morley Tel Northampton 843025
Pro Stuart D Brown Tel Northampton 842226
Holes 18 L 6503 yds SSS 71
Recs Am–66 A Jackson
Pro–70 TJ Giles
V'trs WD–H; W/E–I H and XL before 4 pm Sat and 11.30 am Sun
Fees £10 (£12)
Loc 5 miles NW of Northampton off A50

Oundle (1894)

Private (Map 4/8)
Oundle
Tel **Oundle 73267**
Mem 500
Sec R Davis Tel Oundle 73267
Pro
Holes 18 L 5507 yds SSS 67
Recs Am–
Pro–
V'trs WD–U; W/E–M before 10.30 am; U after 10.30 am
Fees £6 (£8)
Loc Benefield Road

Peterborough Milton (1937)

Private (Map 4/9)
Milton Ferry Peterborough PE6 7AG
Tel **Castor 204**
Mem 700
Sec WA Fryer Tel Castor 489
Pro NS Bundy Tel Castor 793
Holes 18 L 6431 yds SSS 71 White Course 18 L 6150 yds SSS 69 Yellow Course
Recs Am–68 B Jackson
Pro–69 B Barnes G Will
V'trs WD–U SOC; W/E–M
Fees £11.50
Loc 4 miles W of Peterborough on A47

Priors Hall (1965)

Public (Map 4/10)
Stamford Road Weldon nr Corby
Tel **Corby 60756**
Mem 300
Sec M Evans Tel Corby 67546
Pro M Summers Tel Corby 60756
Holes 18 L 6677 yds SSS 72
Recs Am–75 R Beekie WF Kearney M Scott
Pro–70 RH Kemp
V'trs U
Fees £2.25 (£3.30)
Loc A43

Rushden (1919)

Private (Map 4/11)
Kimbolton Road Chelveston Wellingborough
Tel **0933 312581**
Mem 350
Sec Mr R Tomlin Tel 0933 312197
Pro –
Holes 9 L 6381 yds SSS 70
Recs Am–67
Pro–
V'trs WD–U exc Wed pm; W/E–M, XL Sat pm/Sun am; BH–U; SOC
Fees £7
Loc On A45 2 miles E of Higham Ferrers

Staverton Park (1977)

Private (Map 4/12)
Staverton nr Daventry NN11 6JJ
Tel **0327 705911**
Mem 480
Sec PJ Genasi
Pro B Mudge Tel 0327 705506
Holes 18 L 6634 yds SSS 72
Recs Am–67
Pro–64
V'trs U
Fees £8 (W/E & BH £10)
Loc 1 mile S of Daventry off A425

Thorpe Wood (1975)

Private (Map 4/13)
Nene Parkway Peterborough PE3 6SE
Tel **Peterborough 267701**
Mem 550
Sec K Boyer Tel Peterborough 264458
Pro D Fitton R Fitton
Holes 18 L 7086 yds SSS 74
Recs Am–74 N Brownlie JN Dodd
Pro–69 Roger Fitton
V'trs U
Fees £3 (£4.25)
Loc 3 miles W of town on A47

Wellingborough (1893)

Private (Map 4/14)
Harrowden Hall Great Harrowden Wellingborough
Tel **0933 673022**
Mem 697
Sec/Man MC Simpson Tel 0933 677234
Pro D Clifford Tel 0933 678752
Holes 18 L 6604 yds SSS 72
Recs Am–70 NG Grimmitt
Pro–69 D Clifford
V'trs WD–U (exc Tue pm) I; W/E–M SOC Wed/Thurs
Fees £9 D–£12
Loc 2 miles N of Wellingborough on A509 to Kettering

Woodlands (1974)

Private (Map 4/15)
Farthingstone nr Towcester
Tel **032-736 291**
Mem 500
Sec DC Donaldson
Pro M Gallagher Tel 032-736 291
Holes 18 L 6330 yds SSS 71
Rec Am–66 D Thorp
Pro–66 M Gallagher
V'trs U SOC
Fees £6 (£8)
Loc 6 miles W M1 Junction 16

Nottinghamshire

Beeston Fields (1923)

Private (Map 4/1)
Beeston Nottingham
Tel **0602 257062**
Mem 389 141(L) 85(J)
Sec DW Newbold Tel 0602 254280
Pro M Pashley Tel 0602 257503
Holes 18 L 6404 yds SSS 71
Recs Am–66 P Benson
Pro–
V'trs U; SOC
Fees £7.50 (£9)
Loc 4 miles W of Nottingham Exit 25 M1

Bulwell Forest (1902)

Public (Map 4/2)
Nottingham
Tel **Nottingham 278008**
Mem 500
Sec D Stubbs
Pro CD Hall Tel Nottm 763172
Holes 18 L 5746 yds SSS 68
Recs Am–62 DN Smedley J Dawes G Shepherd
Pro–64 D Snell
V'trs U
Fees £2.70
Loc 4 miles N of city centre

Chilwell Manor (1906)

Private (Map 4/3)
Meadow Lane Chilwell Nottingham NG9 5AE
Tel **Nottingham 257050**
Mem 620
Sec HL Morton Tel Nottingham 258958
Pro E McCausland Tel Nottingham 258993
Holes 18 L 6379 yds SSS 69
18 L 5438 yds SSS 67
Recs Am–67 C Gray
Pro–66 B Waites
V'trs U
Fees £7 (£9)
Loc 4 miles W of Nottingham

Coxmoor (1913)

Private (Map 4/4)
Coxmoor Road Sutton-in-Ashfield Notts NG17 5LF
Tel **(0623) 557359**
Mem 650
Sec R Allsop Tel (0623) 557359
Pro DJ Ridley Tel (0623) 559906
Holes 18 L 6501 yds SSS 72
Recs Am–67 M Nunn
Pro–65 B Waites
V'trs H; SOC (Ladies Day Tue)
Fees £10 (£15)
Loc $1\frac{1}{2}$ miles S of Mansfield

Edwalton (1982)

Public (Map 4/19)
Edwalton Nottingham
Tel **Nottingham 234775**
Sec
Pro Rod Wiseman Tel Nottingham 234775
Holes 9 L 3336 yds SSS 36
9 hole par 3 L 1592 yds SSS 27
Recs Am–
Pro–
V'trs U
Fees £1.80 (£2.20) Par 3 course £1.10 (£1.50)
Loc 2 miles S of Nottingham

Kilton Forest (1977)

Public (Map 4/5)
Blyth Road Worksop S81 0TL
Tel **0909 472488**
Mem 422
Sec EL James Tel 0909 477427
Pro PW Foster Tel 0909 486563
Holes 18 L 6569 yds SSS 72
Recs Am–71 S Pond
Pro–74 PH Hinton CR Jepson CH Ledbury
V'trs U
Fees £2.50 (£3.15)
Loc 1 mile NE of Worksop on B6045

Mapperley (1913)

Private (Map 4/6)
Central Avenue Plains Road Mapperley Nottingham NG3 5RH
Tel **(0602) 265611**
Mem 600
Sec JH Seddon Tel (0602) 265611
Pro R Daibell
Holes 18 L 6224 yds SSS 70
Recs Am–69 A Gray
Pro–72 D Snell
V'trs U; SOC
Fees £6.50 (£7.50)
Loc 3 miles NE of Nottingham centre

Newark (1901)

Private (Map 4/7)
Kelwick Coddington Newark
Tel **(0636 84) 241**
Mem 575
Sec JN Simpson Tel (0636 84) 282
Pro Tony Bennett (Tel (0636 84) 492
Holes 18 L 6486 yds SSS 71
Recs Am–72 RC Nicholson G Jones
Pro–69 CW Gray DJ Britten
V'trs I H
Fees £9 (£15)
Loc 4 miles E of Newark on A17

Nottingham City (1910)

Public (Map 4/8)
Lawton Drive Bulwell Nottingham NG6 8BL
Tel **0602 278021**
Mem 420
Sec DA Griffiths
Pro CR Jepson Tel 0602 272767
Holes 18 L 6218 yds SSS 70
Recs Am–67 T Payne A Scothern
Pro–67 R Daibell
V'trs WD–U; W/E–NA before noon SOC
Fees £3.30
Loc 3 miles M1 Junction 28

Notts (1887)

Private (Map 4/9)
Hollinwell Kirby-in-Ashfield NG17 7QR
Tel **Mansfield 753225 and 752042**
Mem 500
Sec JR Walker Tel Mansfield 753225
Pro BJ Waites Tel Mansfield 753087
Holes 18 L 7020 yds SSS 74
Recs Am–67 IT Simpson
Pro–64 John Bland
V'trs WD–H; Sats–M
Fees On application
Loc 4 miles S of Mansfield M1 Exit 27

Oxton (1974)

Private (Map 4/10)
Oaks Lane Oxton
Tel **(0602) 653545**
Mem 550
Man D Ridley Tel (0602) 653545
Pro D Ridley Tel (0602) 653545
Holes 18 L 6600 yds SSS 72
Recs Am–70 J Vaughan
Pro–68 D Dunk B Waites D Snell D Ridley
V'trs WD–SOC U; W/E & BH– arrange starting times with Man
Fees £4.75 D–£8 OAPs Jnrs £2.40 (£6 D–£10 OAPs Jnrs £4.75)
Loc 9 miles N of Nottingham on A614 to Doncaster

Radcliffe on Trent (1909)

Private (Map 4/11)
Radcliffe on Trent
Tel **Nottingham Radcliffe 3125**
Mem 650
Sec WJ Stewart Tel Radcliffe 3000
Pro P Hinton Tel Nott Radcliffe 2396
Holes 18 L 6423 yds SSS 71
Recs Am–
Pro–
V'trs U
Fees £9 (£12)
Loc 6 miles E of Nottingham off A52

Retford (1921)

Private (Map 412)
Brecks Road Ordsall Retford Notts DN22 7UA
Tel **Retford 703733**
Mem 300
Sec A Harrison Tel Retford 703733
Pro
Holes 9 L 6230 yds SSS 70
Recs Am–69 PM Edwards
Pro–
V'trs WD–U; W/E–M; SOC on WD
Fees £5 (£3)
Loc Ordsall

Rushcliffe (1910)

Private (Map 4/13)
East Leake nr Nottingham
Tel **East Leake 2209**
Mem 500
Sec MG Booth Tel East Leake 2959
Pro T Smart Tel East Leake 2701
Holes 18 L 6090 yds SSS 69
Recs Am–66 R Davenport D Kirkland
Pro–63 GL Hunt
V'trs U
Fees £6 (£8)
Loc 9 miles S of Nottingham

Sherwood Forest (1904)

Private (Map 4/14)
Eakring Road Mansfield Notts NG18 3EW
Tel **Mansfield 23327**
Mem 600
Sec Tel Mansfield 26689
Pro K Hall Tel Mansfield 27403
Holes 18 L 6710 yds SSS 73
Recs Am–65 PM Baxter
Pro–68 C Gray
V'trs U
Fees D–£12
Loc 2 miles N of Mansfield

Stanton-on-the-Wolds (1906)

Private (Map 4/15)
Stanton Lane Keyworth Notts
Tel **Plumtree 2044**
Mem 500 167(L) 100(J)
Sec HG Gray Tel Nottingham 787291
Pro KG Fear Tel Plumtree 2390
Holes 18 L 6437 yds SSS 71
Recs Am–
Pro–65 D Ridley
V'trs U; Sat Comp days–NA; The Ladies NA if comp on; SOC
Fees £8 (£11)
Loc 9 miles S of Nottingham

Wollaton Park (1927)

Private (Map 4/16)
Nottingham NG8 1BT
Tel **Nottingham 787574**
Mem 600
Sec B Morris BSc PhD Tel Nottingham 787574
Pro Roger Hastings Tel Nott 784834
Holes 18 L 6494 yds SSS 71
Recs Am–66 C Banks
Pro–65 H Weetman
V'trs U; SOC
Fees £8.50 (£11.50)
Loc 2 miles city centre

Woodhouse (1973)

Public (Privately owned)
Mansfield (Map 4/17)
Tel **Mansfield 23521**
Mem 250
Sec TG Shead Tel 641220
Pro –
Holes 9
Recs Am–67 S Fisher
Pro–
V'trs U
Fees £1.15
Loc 2 miles N of Mansfield

Worksop (1914)

Private (Map 4/18)
Windmill Lane Worksop S80 2SQ
Tel **Worksop 472696**
Mem 500
Sec PG Jordan Tel Worksop 477731
Pro John R King Tel Worksop 477732
Holes 18 L 6651 yds SSS 72
Recs Am–71 R Bardsley
Pro–71 C Snell
V'trs U
Fees £9 (£11)
Loc 1 mile SE of town off A6009 Approach from Worksop by-pass

Shropshire & Hereford

Belmont GC (1983)

Private (Map 4/1)
Belmont Hereford HR2 9SA
Tel **(0432) 277445**
Mem 370
Dir JP Boyd Tel (0432) 277445
Pro Mike Welsh Tel (0432) 277445
Holes 18 L 6400 yds SSS 71
Rec Am–79 J Price CB Jones
Pro–71 P Elson C Holmes
A Bownes
V'trs U SOC
Fees £10 (£15)
Loc $1\frac{1}{2}$ miles S of Hereford on A465

Bridgnorth (1889)

Private (Map 4/2)
Stanley Lane Bridgnorth
Tel **Bridgnorth 3315**
Mem 435
Sec EH Thomas Tel Bridgnorth 2400
Pro P Hinton Tel Bridgnorth 2045
Holes 18 L 6638 yds SSS 72
Recs Am–69 A Malcolm
Pro–
V'trs U
Fees £7
Loc 1 mile N of Bridgnorth

Church Stretton (1898)

Private (Map 4/3)
Trevor Hill Church Stretton Shropshire
Tel **0694 722281**
Mem 295
Sec R Broughton Tel 0694 722633
Pro
Holes 18 L 4579 yds SSS 65
Recs Am–65 BT Lewis RE Oakley
Pro–
V'trs U; SOC
Fees £5 (£7)
Loc Adjacent to town

Hawkstone Park (1921)

Private (Map 4/4)
Weston-under-Redcastle nr Shrewsbury SY4 5UY
Tel **Lee Brockhurst (093924) 611**
Mem 400
Dir of Golf Sandy Lyle
Man KL Brazier
Pro K Williams Tel Lee Brockhurst (093924) 209
Holes Hawkstone 18 L 6463 yds SSS 71
Weston 18 L 5368 yds SSS 66
Recs Am–67 AWB Lyle
Pro–
V'trs U after 10.35 am SOC
Fees Hawkestone £12.50 (£15)
Weston £6.50 (£7.50)
Loc 7 miles S of Whitchurch A49
14 miles N of Shrewbury on A49
Mis Buggies for hire
3 star golf hotel offers inclusive golf holidays

Herefordshire (1909)

Private (Map 4/5)
Raven's Causeway Wormsley nr Hereford HR4 8LY
Tel **0432 71219**
Mem 600 75(L) 85(J) 55(5)
Sec C Jones Tel 0432 760662
Pro D Hemming
Holes 18 L 6069 yds SSS 69
Recs Am–66 J Wilson
Pro–61 B Barnes
V'trs U
Fees £6 (£7) W–£20 M–£50
Loc 6 miles NW Hereford
Mis Buggy for hire

Hill Valley G & CC (1975)

Private (Map 4/6)
Terrick Road Whitchurch
Tel **0948 3584**
Mem 400
Sec RB Walker Tel 0948 3584
Pro AR Minshall Tel 0948 3032
Holes 18 L 6884 yds SSS 71
Recs Am–69 K Valentine
Pro–66 BJ Waites
V'trs U
Fees £7.50 (£9)
Loc 1 mile N of Whitchurch
Mis Buggies for hire

Kington (1926)

Private (Map 4/7)
Bradnor Hill Kington
Tel **Kington (230) 340**
Mem 420
Sec FH Bradley Tel Lyonshall 355
Pro WCL Griffiths
Holes 18 L 5786 yds SSS 68
Recs Am–68 A Marshmann AW Lyle
Pro–
V'trs U
Fees £5 (7)
Loc 1 mile N of Kington

Leominster (1967)

Private (Map 4/8)
Ford Bridge Leominster Herefordshire
Tel **(0568) 2863**
Mem 360
Sec JA Ashcroft Tel Sutton St Nicholas 493
Pro S Yates
Holes 9 L 2657 yds SSS 66
Recs Am–67 G Price
Pro–66
V'trs I or H
Fees £5 (£7.50)
Loc 3 miles S of Leominster on A49

Lilleshall Hall (1937)

Private (Map 4/9)
Lilleshall nr Newport TF10 9AS
Tel **Telford 603840**
Mem 600
Sec AP Thwaite Tel 604776
Pro NW Bramall Tel 604104
Holes 18 L 5861 yds SSS 68
Rec Am–65 P Baker
Pro–70 J Anderson
V'trs WD–U; W/E–M
Fees £8 (BH and following day £12)
Loc Abbey Road

Llanymynech (1933)

Private (Map 4/10)
Shropshire SY10 8LB Pant nr Oswestry Shropshire
Tel **Llanymynech 830542**
Mem 566
Sec NE Clews Tel 0691 830983
Pro A Griffiths Tel 0691 830879
Holes 18 L 6114 yds SSS 69
Recs Am–68 M Evans
Pro–65 I Woosnam
V'trs U
Fees £5.50 (£7.50)
Loc 5 miles S of Oswestry on A483
Mis No catering Mondays

Ludlow (1889)

Private (Map 4/11)
Bromfield nr Ludlow
Tel **Bromfield 285**
Mem 440
Sec RPJ Jones Tel Brimfield 334
Pro G Farr Tel Bromfield 366
Holes 18 L 6240 yds SSS 70
Recs Am–68 AT Adams
Pro–67 G Birch
V'trs U
Fees £7 (£9)
Loc A49 2 miles N of Ludlow

Market Drayton (1925)

Private (Map 4/12)
Sutton Market Drayton
Tel **0630 2266**
Mem 350
Sec JJ Moseley Tel 0630 3661 (Day)
Pro A Williams Tel 0630 2266
Holes 13 L 6240 yds SSS 70
Recs Am–
Pro–
V'trs WD Sat–U; Sun–NA
Fees £5 (£6)
Loc 1 mile S of Market Drayton

Meole Brace (1976)

Public (Map 4/13)
Meole Brace Shrewsbury
Tel **0743 64050**
Mem 250
Sec A Price Tel 0743 722733
Pro I Doran
Holes 9 L 2915 yds SSS 68
Recs Am–68 J Mansell
Pro–68 R Cockcroft
V'trs U
Fees 9 holes–£1.80 (£2.20)
18 holes–£2.55 (£3.20)
Loc Junction A5/A49 Meole Brace

Oswestry (1930)

Private (Map 4/14)
Aston Park Oswestry
Tel **Queens Head 221**
Mem 700
Sec Mrs PM Lindner Tel Queens Head 535
Pro D Skelton Tel Queens Head 448
Holes 18 L 6046 yds SSS 69
Recs Am–62 AL Strange
Pro–68 Jas W Walker
V'trs M or with official handicap; SOC on WD
Fees £8 (£10)
Loc $3\frac{1}{4}$ miles E of Oswestry

Shifnal (1929)

Private (Map 4/15)
Decker Hill Shifnal Shropshire
Tel **Telford 460467/460330**
Mem 550
Sec Joyce Bell Tel Telford 460330
Pro Steve Marr Tel Telford 460457
Holes 18 L 6422 yds SSS 71
Recs Am–66 R Howells
Pro–67 IN Doran
V'trs All visitors phone first W/E & BH–M

Fees D–£7.50
Loc 2 miles M54 Junction 4; 1 mile NE Shifnal

Shrewsbury (1891)

Private (Map 4/16)
Condover Shrewsbury
Tel **Bayston Hill 2976**
Mem 450 160(L) 75(J)
Sec JA Morrison Tel Bayston Hill 2977
Pro Tim Simpson Tel Bayston Hill 3751
Holes 18 L 6212 yds SSS 70
Recs Am–67 JR Burn
Pro–
V'trs SOC H
Fees £7 (£9)
Loc 4 miles SW of town

Telford Hotel G & CC (1981)

Private (Map 4/17)
Great Hay Sutton Hill Telford TF7 4DT
Tel **(0952) 585642**
Mem 500
Sec Major FE Snape Tel (0952) 585642
Pro Mike Woodbridge Tel (0952) 586052/585642
Holes 18 L 6742 yds SSS 72
Recs Am–71 G Moore
Pro–62 David Thorpe
V'trs U H SOC
Fees £8 (£12)
Loc Telford Sutton Hill off A442

Wrekin (1905)

Private (Map 4/18)
Wellington Telford Shropshire
Tel **Telford 44032**
Mem 500 85(L) 90(J) 30(5)
Sec S Leys
Pro K Housden
Holes 18 L 5657 yds SSS 67
Recs Am–65 GV Clayton R Jones P Baker
Pro–67 C Holmes
V'trs WD–U before 5 pm M after 5 pm; SOC
Fees £6.90 (£10)
Loc Wellington off A5

Staffordshire

Alsager G & CC (1977)

Private (Map 4/37)
Audley Road Alsager Stoke-on-Trent
Tel **09363 5700**
Mem 500
Sec AB Davies Tel 09363 5700
Pro David Poole Tel 09363 77432
Holes 18 L 6192 yds SSS 70
V'trs WD–U SOC; WE–NA before noon or M after noon
Fees £5.50 (£6.50); with mem £3.50 (£4.50)
Loc 2 miles E Junction 16 M6; 6 miles from Crewe, 7 from Stoke-on-Trent

Beau Desert (1921)

Private (Map 4/1)
Hazel Slade Cannock WS12 5PJ
Tel **(054 38) 2773**
Mem 500
Sec IE Williams Tel (0782) 2626
Pro B Stevens Tel (054 38) 2492
Holes 18 L 6279 yds SSS 71
Recs Am–68 WR Probert
Pro–64 T Minshall
V'trs WD–U SOC; BH–NA; W/E–phone in advance
Fees £11 (£14)
Loc 4 miles NE of Cannock

Blackhill Wood

Private (Map 4/2)
Bridgnorth Road Swindon nr Dudley
Tel **(0902) 892279**
Mem 600
Sec WIA Herrington Tel (0384) 37217
Pro K Bayliss Tel (0902) 895015
Holes 18 L 5474 metres SSS 69
Recs Am–68 B Cotterill
Pro–68 K Bayliss
V'trs WD–U SOC; W/E–M
Fees £6 (£9)
Loc 5 miles S of Wolverhampton
Mis Driving range–10 covered bays–floodlit Open 8 am–9 pm–7 days per week Professional tuition available Licensed Bar

Bloxwich (1924)

Private (Map 4/3)
Stafford Road Bloxwich
Tel **Bloxwich 405724**
Mem 475
Sec JC Minister
Pro B Janes Tel Bloxwich 76889
Holes 18 L 6277 yds SSS 70
Recs Am–67 JPG Windsor
Pro–65 J Rhodes
V'trs WD–U SOC; W/E–M
Fees £9
Loc On A34 N of Walsall

Branston (1975)

Private (Map 4/4)
Burton Road Branston Burton-on-Trent
Tel **Burton-on-Trent 43207**
Mem 300 23(L) 45(J)
Sec AM Allison
Pro S Warner
Holes 18 L 6458 yds SSS 71
Recs Am–71 F Allsop
Pro–67 P Kent
V'trs WD–U, W/E U (M before noon)
Fees £6.50 (£7.50) Winter £5 (£7.50)
Loc On A5121 ½ mile towards Burton-on-Trent from junction with A38
Mis Societies welcomed

Brocton Hall (1923)

Private (Map 4/5)
Brocton Stafford ST17 0TH
Tel (0785) 662627
Mem 500
Sec WR Lanyon Tel (0785) 661901
Pro R Johnson Tel (0785) 661485
Holes 18 L 6095 yds SSS 69
Recs Am–67 WB Taylor
Pro–
V'trs I
Fees £10 (£12)
Loc 4 miles SE Stafford

Burslem (1907)

Private (Map 4/6)
Wood Farm High Lane Stoke-on-Trent ST6 7JT
Tel **Stoke-on-Trent 87006**
Mem 250
Sec RJ Sutton Tel Stoke-on-Trent 87704
Pro
Holes 11 L 5527 yds SSS 67
Recs Am–68 S McNicholas
JE Hancock
Pro–66 T Williamson
V'trs M Sun–NA
Fees £6
Loc Burslem 2 miles

Burton-on-Trent

(see Derbyshire)

Calderfields

Private (Map 4/7)
Aldridge Road Walsall
Tel **Walsall 32243**
Mem
Sec
Pro
Holes 18 L 6026 yds SSS 69
Recs Am–67 E Dunne
Pro–69 Paul Dexter
V'trs U
Fees £3.50 (£4.50)
Loc 1 mile N of Walsall

Dartmouth (1910)

Private (Map 4/8)
Vale Street West Bromwich
Tel **021-588 2131**
Mem 250
Sec RH Smith
Pro J Flanagan Tel 021-588 2131
Holes 9 L 6060 yds SSS 69
Recs Am–68 P Griffiths
Pro–70 P Lester
V'trs WD–U; W/E–restricted
Fees £5.50 (£4 with mem)
Loc 1 mile centre at rear of Churchfields High School

Drayton Park (1897)

Private (Map 4/9)
Drayton Park Tamworth B78 3TN
Tel **Tamworth 251139**
Mem 450
Sec AO Rammell JP Tel Tamworth 251139
Pro MW Passmore Tel Tamworth 251478
Holes 18 L 6414 yds SSS 71
Recs Am–63 A Carman
Pro–65 A Stuart
V'trs WD–U; W/E–M after 10 am; SOC Tue Thu; BH–NA
Fees £9 D–£12
Loc 2 miles S of Tamworth (A4091)
Mis Wide wheel trolleys only

Druids Heath (1974)

Private (Map 4/10)
Stonnall Road Aldridge WS9 8JZ
Tel **Aldridge 55595**
Sec LE Swain
Mem 400 35(L) 35(J)
Pro John Pearsall Tel Aldridge 59523
Holes 18 L 6914 yds SSS 73
Recs Am–69 M Pearce
Pro–
V'trs WD–U; W/E–M
Fees £8
Loc 6 miles NW of Sutton Coldfield

Enville (1935)

Private (Map 4/11)
Highgate Common Enville nr Stourbridge DY7 5BN
Tel **0384 872551**
Mem 840
Sec/ Ron Davies Tel 0384 872074

Man
Pro RH Hinton Tel 0384 872585
Holes 18 Highgate L 6541 yds SSS 72
18 Lodge L 6207 yds SSS 70
Recs Am–68 A Stubbs } Highgate
Pro–66 PH Hinton }
V'trs WD–U; W/E & BH–M; H; SOC
Fees £12
Loc 6 miles W of Stourbridge
Mis Buggies for hire

Goldenhill (1983)

Public (Map 4/38)
Mobberley Road Goldenhill Stoke on Trent Staffordshire ST6 5SS
Tel
Mem
Sec
Pro Tony Clingan Tel Kidsgrove 4715
Holes 18 L 5933 yds Par 70
Recs Am–
Pro–
V'trs U
Fees £2.65 (£2.95)
Loc Between Tunstall and Kidsgrove off A50

Great Barr (1961)

Private (Map 4/12)
Chapel Lane Birmingham B43 7BA
Tel **021-357 1232**
Mem 427 74(L) 50(J) 53(5)
Sec K Pembridge Tel 021-358 4376
Pro JL Sutton Tel 021-357 5270
Holes 18 L 6545 yds SSS 72
Recs Am–69 AR Eden
Pro–71 J Higgins
V'trs WD–U; W/E–I (with max handicap 18)
Fees £9 (£12)
Loc 6 miles NW of Birmingham

Greenway Hall (1908)

Private (Map 4/13)
Stockton Brook Stoke-on-Trent
Tel **0782 503158**
Mem 390
Man EH Jones Tel 0782 503095
Pro
Holes 18 L 5676 yds SSS 67
Recs Am–65 A Bailey A Dathan
Pro–65 K Johnstone
V'trs Mon/Wed/Fri–H Tues/Thurs–M WE–M (Sun pm only)
Fees £8
Loc 5 miles N of Stoke

Himley Hall (1980)

Public (Map 4/14)
Himley Hall Park Dudley West Midlands
Tel **Wombourne 895207**
Mem 80
Sec DA Baker/WG Cox Tel Wombourne 895207
Pro
Holes 9 L 3090 yds SSS 34
Recs Am–
Pro–
V'trs U; W/E & BH restricted
Fees 9 holes £1.80 (£2.30)
18 holes £2.70 (£3.40)
Loc In grounds of Himley Hall Park nr Dudley. From A449 W'ton/Kidderminster turn into Himley Road, signposted Dudley

Ingestre Park (1977)

Private (Map 4/15)
Near Stafford
Tel **Weston 270061**
Mem 500
Sec R Ashton Tel Stafford 270845
Pro D Scullion Tel 270304
Holes 18 L 6367 yds SSS 70
Recs Am–69 S Smith N Jackson
Pro–68 D Scullion
V'trs WD–U; W/E & BH–M
Fees On application
Loc 5 miles E of Stafford

Lakeside (Barlaston) G & CC

Private (Map 4/16)
Meaford Road Barlaston Stone
Tel **Barlaston 3242**
Mem 400
Sec Tel Barlaston 3242
Pro None
Holes 18 L 5800 yds SSS 68
Recs Am–
Pro–
V'trs U
Fees £7 (£8)
Loc ¼ mile S of Barlaston; ¾ mile N of Stone

Lakeside (Rugeley) (1969)

Private (Map 4/39)
Rugeley Power Station Rugeley Staffs WS15 1PR
Tel **08894 3181**
Mem 150
Sec TA Yates Tel 08894 3181
0543 491435 (home)
Pro
Holes 9 L 4768 yds SSS 63
Recs Am–
Pro–
V'trs M only at all times
Loc Within grounds of Rugeley Power Station 2 miles SE of town centre on A513

Leek (1892)

Private (Map 4/17)
Big Birchall Leek
Tel **(0538) 385889**
Mem 400 90(L) 70(J) 100(5)
Sec F Cutts Tel (0538) 384779
Pro P Stubbs Tel (0538) 384767
Holes 18 L 6229 yds SSS 70
Recs Am–63 D Evans
Pro–66 CH Ward
V'trs U
Fees £9 (£12)
Loc Stone Road ½ mile from Leek

Little Aston (1908)

Private (Map 4/18)
Streetly Sutton Coldfield
Tel **021-353 2066**
Mem 250
Sec NH Russell Tel 021-353 2942
Pro J Anderson Tel 021-353 2942
Holes 18 L 6724 yds SSS 73
Recs Am–66
Pro–68
V'trs WD–U; W/E & BH–I (XL Sat and am Sun); SOC
Fees £15 Apr–Oct; £12 other months
Loc 4 miles NW Sutton Coldfield

Newcastle-under-Lyme (1908)

Private (Map 4/19)
Whitmore Road Newcastle-under-Lyme
Tel **Newcastle 616583**
Mem 575
Sec Robert B Irving Tel Newcastle 617006
Pro Paul Symonds Tel Newcastle 618526
Holes 18 L 6450 yds SSS 71
Recs Am–67 MC Hassall
Pro–66 AR Sadler
V'trs WD–U; W/E & BH–M
Fees £10
Loc Newcastle

Newcastle Municipal (1973)

Public (Map 4/20)
Keele Road Newcastle-under-Lyme
Tel **Newcastle 627596 (Professional)**
Mem 250
Sec RG Lane
Pro Colin Smith
Holes 18 L 5822 metres SSS 70
Recs Am–70 P Rowe
Pro–68 P Rowe
V'trs U
Fees £2.75 (£3.15)
Loc 2 miles NW on A525 opposite Keele University

Onneley (1968)

Private (Map 4/21)
Onneley nr Crewe Cheshire
Tel **0782 750577**
Mem 324
Sec WJ Paterson Tel 0270 624818
Pro
Holes 9 L 5584 yds SSS 67
Recs Am–68 D Gilford
Pro–
V'trs WD–U; Sats & BH–M; Sundays NA
Fees D–£4
Loc 1 mile from Woore off A51 to Newcastle

Oxley Park (1914)

Private (Map 4/22)
Stafford Road Bushbury Wolverhampton WV10 6DE
Tel **Wolverhampton 20506**
Mem 400
Sec FGE Hill Tel Wolverhampton 25892 (mornings)
Pro LA Burlison Tel Wolverhampton 25445
Holes 18 L 6153 yds SSS 69
Recs Am–64 CS White
Pro–65 D Thorp
V'trs U SOC
Fees £7.50 (£9)
Loc 1½ miles N of Wolverhampton

Patshull Park (1980)

Private (Map 4/23)
Pattingham Shropshire WV6 7HR
Tel **Pattingham 700100**
Mem 300
Sec Ann Taylor
Pro Ted Large
Holes 18 L 6460 yds SSS 71
Recs Am–69 D Evans
Pro–67 Richard Green
V'trs WD–U; W/E–U
Fees £7 (£8)
Loc 7 miles Wolverhampton

Penn (1908)

Private (Map 4/24)
Penn Common Wolverhampton
Tel **Wolverhampton 341142**
Mem 500
Sec PW Thorrington
Pro A Briscoe Tel Wolverhampton 330472
Holes 18 L 6449 yds SSS 71
Recs Am–68 RJ Green
Pro–70 J Rhodes R Cameron
V'trs WD–U; W/E–M; SOC
Fees £7
Loc 2 miles SW of Wolverhampton

Sandwell Park (1897)

Private (Map 4/25)
Birmingham Road West Bromwich B71 4JJ
Tel 021-553 0260
Mem 650
Sec CP Elliott Tel 021-553 4637
Pro AW Mutton Tel 021-553 4384
Holes 18 L 6470 yds SSS 72
Recs Am–67 B Charlton
Pro–67 J Rhodes
V'trs WD–U; W/E–M H; SOC on WD
Fees £8 (£10)
Loc West Bromwich/Birmingham boundary Junction 1 M5

South Staffordshire (1892)

Private (Map 4/26)
Danescourt Road Tettenhall Wolverhampton WV6 9BQ
Tel **Wolverhampton 751065**
Mem 600
Sec H Williams
Pro J Rhodes Tel Wolverhampton 754816
Holes 18 L 6538 yds SSS 71
Recs Am–67 D Gifford
Pro–66 A Sadler
V'trs WD–U; W/E & BH–M; SOC
Fees £10 D–£12
Loc 3 miles W of Wolverhampton

Stafford Castle (1907)

Private (Map 4/27)
Newport Road Stafford
Tel **Stafford 3821**
Mem 250
Sec S Cowburn
Pro
Holes 9 L 6462 yds SSS 71
Recs Am–74 P Duncan
Pro–
V'trs U; (W/E after 1 pm)
Fees £5 (£7)
Loc ½ mile W of town centre

Stone (1896)

Private (Map 4/28)
Filleybrooks Stone ST15 0NB
Mem 167 45(L) 38(J) 5(5)
Sec MG Pharaoh Tel Sandon 224
Pro D Brumpton Tel Stone 815520
Holes 9 L 6272 yds SSS 70
Recs Am–65 C Heard
Pro–
V'trs SOC on WD WD–U; W/E–BH–M
Fees £6
Loc ½ mile W on A34

Tamworth Municipal (1975)

Public (Map 4/29)
Eagle Drive Amington Tamworth
Tel **0827 53850**
Mem 380
Sec TW Joicey Tel 0827 57905
Pro Colin Christison Tel 0827 53850
Holes 18 L 6695 yds SSS 72
Recs Am–67 CJ Christison
Pro–70 C Christison
V'trs U
Fees £3
Loc 2½ miles E of Tamworth (B5000)

Trentham (1895)

Private (Map 4/30)
14 Barlaston Old Road Trentham Stoke-on-Trent ST4 8AB
Tel **Stoke-on-Trent 642347**
Mem 717
Sec IM Kirkwood Tel Stoke-on-Trent 658109
Pro D McDonald Tel Stoke-on-Trent 657309
Holes 18 L 6644 yds SSS 72
Recs Am–67 GC Marks
Pro–
V'trs WD–U; W/E–M (or enquire Sec); BH–enquire Sec; H; SOC on WD
Fees £12 (£15) 1986 rates
Loc 3 miles S of Newcastle (Staffs) off A34

Trentham Park (1936)

Private (Map 4/31)
Trentham Park Stoke-on-Trent ST4 8AE
Tel **0782 642245 (clubhouse)**
Mem 300 70(L) 70(J) 90(5) 84(Sen)
Sec CH Lindop Tel 0782 658800
Pro R Clarke Tel 0782 642125
Holes 18 L 6403 yds SSS 71
Recs Am–67 PG Nuthall
Pro–
V'trs U; SOC–Wed Fri
Fees D–£9 (D–£11)
Loc 4 miles S of Newcastle-under-Lyme on A34. 1 mile from junction 15 of M6

Uttoxeter (1975)

Private (Map 4/32)
Wood Lane Uttoxeter Staffs
Tel **Uttoxeter 4844**
Mem 330
Sec Mrs G Davies Tel Uttoxeter 4884
Pro
Holes 18 L 5460 yds SSS 67
Recs Am–73
Pro–
V'trs U except NA Sun am
Fees £5 (£7)
Loc ½ mile beyond Uttoxeter racecourse

Walsall (1907)

Private (Map 4/33)
Broadway Walsall
Tel **Walsall 22710**
Mem 800
Sec E Murray Tel Walsall 613512
Pro R Lambert Tel Walsall 26766
Holes 18 L 6232 yds SSS 70
Recs Am–66 RG Hiatt D Blakeman
Pro–66 N Brunyard
V'trs WD–U SOC; W/E–M
Fees £8.50
Loc 1 mile south

Westwood (1923)

Private (Map 4/34)
Newcastle Road Walbridge Leek
Tel **Leek 383060**
Mem 300
Sec AJ Lawton Tel Stoke-on-Trent 503780
Pro
Holes 9 L 5501 yds SSS 67
Recs Am–68 SD Spooner
Pro–
V'trs WD–U SOC; W/E–M; BH–NA
Fees £4
Loc W boundary of Leek on A53

Whittington Barracks (1886)

Private (Map 4/35)
Tamworth Road Lichfield WS14 9PW
Tel **Whittington 4332212**
Mem 670
Sec BA Cox Tel Whittington 432317
Pro Adrian R Sadler Tel Whittington 432 261
Holes 18 L 6457 yds SSS 71
Recs Am–65 CG Marks CG Poxon
Pro–67 AR Sadler
V'trs WD–U; SOC–Wed Thu; W/E & BH–M (day after BH–M)
Fees £12 R/D
Loc On A51 2½ miles from Lichfield on Tamworth road

Wolstanton (1904)

Private (Map 4/36)
Dimsdale Old Hall Newcastle Staffs ST5 9DR
Tel **(0782) 616995**
Mem 550
Sec KI Colderick Tel (0782) 622413
Pro LN Skelding Tel (0782) 622718
Holes 18 L 5807 yds SSS 68
Recs Am–65 P Sweetsur M Hassall R Maxfield
Pro–66 CH Ward
V'trs WD–I; W/E–M
Fees £6
Loc 1½ miles NW Newcastle-under-Lyme
Mis Golf shop Tel 622718

Warwickshire

Atherstone (1894)

Private (Map 4/1)
The Outwoods Atherstone
Tel **Atherstone 3110**
Mem 224 40(L) 36(J)
Sec AG Sarson Tel Atherstone 4579
Pro
Holes 18 L 6239 SSS 70
Recs Am–66 M Reay
Pro–65
V'trs WD (SOC) only
Fees D–£6
Loc ½ mile Atherstone

The Belfry (1977)

Public (Map 4/2)
Wishaw North Warks B76 9PR
Tel **Curdworth (0675) 70301**
Mem
Sec Sandra D Butler Tel Ext 280
Pro Peter McGovern Tel Ext 267
Holes Brabazon 18 L 6975 yds SSS 73
Derby 18 L 6082 yds SSS 70
Recs Am–
Pro–Brabazon 63 Eamonn Darcy (Eire)
Derby 69 Julie Brown (Leek)
V'trs U
Fees Brabazon £15 (£17)
Derby £8 (£10)
Loc 4 miles N of M6 (Exit 4)

Boldmere

Public (Map 4/3)
Monmouth Drive Birmingham
Tel **021-354 2324**
Pro Trevor Short
Holes 18 L 6078 yds SSS 69
Recs Am–66 R Kirkby
Pro–67 AW Ricketts
V'trs U
Fees £2 (£2)
Loc 8 miles NE city centre

City of Coventry (Brandon Wood) (1977)

Public (Map 4/4)
Brandon Lane Coventry
Tel **Wolston 3141**
Mem 550
Sec FJ Brannigan Tel Coventry 85032
Pro C Gledhill Tel Wolston 3141
Holes 18 L 6530 yds SSS 71
Recs Am–
Pro–68 AR Sadler
V'trs U
Fees £2.50, 90p OAP and Jrs
Loc SE 6 miles from city centre

Copt Heath (1910)

Private (Map 4/5)
1220 Warwick Road Knowle Solihull W Midlands B93 9LN
Tel **Knowle 2650**
Mem 700
Sec W Lenton
Pro BJ Barton
Holes 18 L 6504 yds SSS 71
Recs Am–66 P McEvoy
Pro–65 BJ Barton
V'trs WD–M or I; W/E & BH–M
Fees £14 incl VAT
Loc 2 miles S Solihull on A41

Coventry (1887)

Private (Map 4/6)
Finham Park Coventry CV3 6PJ
Tel **0203 411123**
Mem 750
Sec MSH Tott Tel 0203 414152
Pro P Weaver Tel 0203 411298
Holes 18 L 6613 yds SSS 72
Recs Am–66 P Downes
Pro–66 P Weaver
V'trs WD–U; W/E–M
Fees £12
Loc 2 miles S of Coventry on A444

Coventry Hearsall (1896)

Private (Map 4/7)
Beechwood Avenue Coventry CV5 6DF
Tel **0203 713470**
Mem 450
Sec WG Doughty
Pro Tim Rouse Tel 0203 713156
Holes 18 L 5951 yds SSS 69
Recs Am–66 JAC Farthing
Pro–66 B Hunt
V'trs WD–U; W/E–M
Fees £9
Loc $1\frac{1}{2}$ miles S of city centre

Edgbaston (1896)

Private (Map 4/8)
Church Road Birmingham B15 3TB
Tel **021-454 1736**
Mem 780
Sec Lt Col SB Matthews Tel 021-454 8445
Pro A Bownes Tel 021-454 3226
Holes 18 L 6118 yds SSS 69
Recs Am–68 P Skerrit
Pro–65 J Rhodes
V'trs U
Fees £10.50 (£17)
Loc 1 mile S of Birmingham city centre

Forest of Arden G & CC

Private (Map 4/9)
Maxstoke Lane Meriden Coventry CV7 7HR
Tel **Meriden (0676) 22118**
Sec GF Brown
Mem 650
Pro M Tarn M Kavanagh (0676) 22118
Holes 18 L 6900 Par 72
9 L 2500 Par 29
V'trs WD–U SOC; W/E–H M
Fees £10 D–£12.50
Loc Off A45 Birmingham to Coventry road; Birmingham Int Airport and Nat Exhibition Centre 3 miles
Mis Driving range 16 bays
Buggies for hire

Grange (1924)

Private (Map 4/10)
Copsewood Coventry CV3 1HS
Tel **Coventry 451465**
Mem 350
Sec E Soutar Tel Coventry 446324
Pro A Bowles
Holes 9 L 6002 yds SSS 69
Recs Am–
Pro–
V'trs WD–U before 2.30; Sat–NA; Sun–NA before noon
Fees £5 D–£7
Loc East Coventry

Handsworth (1895)

Private (Map 4/11)
Sunningdale Close Handsworth Wood Birmingham B20 1NP
Tel **021-554 0599**
Mem 720
Sec CE Clarke
Pro M Hicks Tel 021-523 3594
Holes 18 L 6297 yds SSS 70
Recs Am–67 AWB Lyle
Pro–71 HF Boyce
V'trs WD–U SOC; W/E & BH–M
Fees £10
Loc 3 miles NW of city centre

Harborne (1893)

Private (Map 4/12)
40 Tennal Road Harborne Birmingham B32 2JE
Tel **021-427 1728**
Mem 500
Sec RA Eddy Tel 021-427 3058
Pro A Quarterman Tel 021-427 3512
Holes 18 L 6240 yds SSS 70
Recs Am–65 JA Fisher R Ellis
Pro–65 E Cogle
V'trs WD–U SOC; W/E & BH–M
Fees £10 R/D
Loc 3 miles SW Birmingham centre

Harborne Church Farm

Public (Map 4/13)
Harborne Farm Golf Course Vicarage Road Harborne Birmingham B17 0SN
Tel **021-427 1204**
Mem 200
Sec P Johnston Tel 021-501 3001
Pro S Malin Tel 021-427 1204
Holes 9 L 4514 yds SSS 62
Recs Am–63 J Sankey
Pro–60 PR Rudge
V'trs U
Fees £1.25 9 holes
£2.50 18 holes
Loc 5 miles SW of city centre

Hatchford Brook (1969)

Public (Map 4/14)
Coventry Road Sheldon Birmingham B26 3PY
Tel **021-743 9821**
Mem 300
Sec D Williams Tel 0676 23383
Pro Paul Smith Tel 021-743
Holes 18 L 6164 yds SSS 69
Recs Am–70 P Williams
Pro–
V'trs U; no SOC
Fees £3.75
Loc City boundary, adjacent to airport

Hilltop Golf Club (1979)

Municipal (Map 4/15)
Park Lane Handsworth Birmingham West Mids B21 8LJ
Tel **Pro 021-554 4463**
Mem 021-551 3229
Sec DF Hiley
Pro BN Jones
Holes 18 L 6114 yds Par 71 SSS 69
Recs Am–66 H Ali
Pro–65 BN Jones
V'trs U
Fees £3.20 (£3.80)
Loc M5 West Brom opposite Hawthorns Football Ground

Kenilworth (1889)

Private (Map 4/17)
Crew Lane Kenilworth
Tel **Kenilworth 54296**
Mem 830
Sec BV Edwards Tel Kenilworth 58517
Pro Sid Mouland Tel Kenilworth 512732
Holes 18 L 6408 yds SSS 71
Recs Am–69 P Broadbent
Pro–
V'trs U
Fees £9.50 (£12.75)
Loc 5 miles S of Coventry lies to the right of A46 and B4115 roads and left off A429

Ladbrook Park (1908)

Private (Map 4/18)
Poolhead Lane Tanworth-in-Arden Solihull B94 5ED
Tel **056 44 2264**
Mem 708
Sec Mrs GP Taylor Tel 056 44 2264
Pro GR Taylor Tel 056 44 2581
Holes 18 L 6407 yds SSS 71
Recs Am–67 PJ Sant
Pro–65 RDS Livingston
V'trs WD–U H; W/E & BH–M
Fees £11 inc VAT W/E–NA
Loc 12 miles S of Birmingham

Leamington and County (1908)

Private (Map 4/19)
Golf Lane Whitnash Leamington Spa CV31 2QA
Tel **Leamington Spa 20298**
Mem 600
Sec GR Rees Tel Leamington Spa 25961
Pro J Gould Tel Leamington Spa 28014
Holes 18 L 6430 yds SSS 71
Recs Am–65 RG Hiatt
Pro–66 D Thomas
V'trs U
Fees £11
Loc 1½ miles S of Leamington Spa

Maxstoke Park (1896)

Private (Map 4/20)
Castle Lane Coleshill Birmingham B46 2RD
Tel **Coleshill 62158**
Mem 450
Sec HWA Evans
Pro RA Young Tel Coleshill 63479
Hole 18 L 6460 yds SSS 71
Recs Am–66 AM Allen
Pro–71 PJ Butler
V'trs WD–U; W/E–M
Fees £9
Loc 3 miles S of Coleshill

Moor Hall (1932)

Private (Map 4/21)
Four Oaks Sutton Coldfield
Tel **021-308 0103**
Mem 525
Sec JD Vale Tel 021-308 6130
Pro NR McDonald Tel 021-308 5106
Holes 18 L 6219 yds SSS 70
Recs Am–66 GW Tilbrook
Pro–67 NR McDonald
V'trs WD–U (Not before 12.30 pm Thur); W/E & BH–M
Fees £12
Loc 1 mile E of Sutton

Newbold Comyn (1973)

Public (Map 4/22)
Newbold Terrace East Leamington Spa
Tel **Leamington Spa 21157**
Mem 395
Sec A Pierce Tel Leamington Spa 22660
Pro Don Knight
Holes 18 L 6221 yds SSS 70
Recs Am–70 G Knight
Pro–69 S Hutchinson RDS Livingston
V'trs U
Fees £2.60 (W/E & BH £3.50)
Loc Central–Off Willes Road (B4099)
Mis Bar and Restaurant now open

North Warwickshire (1892)

Private (Map 4/23)
Hampton Lane Meriden Coventry CV7 7LL
Tel **Meriden 22259**
Mem 350
Sec EG Barnes Tel (office) Meriden 22915
Pro Peter Ball Tel Meriden 22259
Holes 9 L 6362 yds SSS 70
Recs Am–67 P Broadhurst
Pro–
V'trs WD–U SOC; W/E & BH–M
Fees £6 (£8)
Loc Coventry 6 miles Birmingham 13 miles

Nuneaton (1906)

Private (Map 4/24)
Golf Drive Whitestone Nuneaton
Tel **0203 347810**
Mem 650
Sec T Rosser Tel 0203 347810
Pro PF Kowalik Tel 0203 340201
Holes 18 L 6412 yds SSS 71
Recs Am–67 P Broadhurst
Pro–67 Chris Holmes
V'trs WD–UH; W/E–M
Fees £8 Special terms for societies
Loc 2 miles S Nuneaton
Mis Steward's Tel 344253

Olton (1893)

Private (Map 4/25)
Mirfield Road, Solihull B91 1JH
Tel **021-705 1083**
Mem 600
Sec MA Perry Tel 56-77953
Pro D Playdon Tel 021-705 7296
Holes 18 L 6229 yds SSS 71
Recs Am–65 T Allen
Pro–66 D Llewellyn
V'trs WD–U exc Wed am; W/E–M
Fees £11
Loc 7 miles South of Birmingham

Purley Chase (1980)

Private (Map 4/26)
Pipers Lane Ridge Lane Nuneaton Warwicks
Tel **Chapel End 393118**
Mem 600
Sec M Woodbine
Pro Mark Chamberlain Tel Chapel End 395348
Holes 18 L 6604 yds SSS 71
Recs Am–72 P Broadhurst
Pro–64 P Elson
V'trs WD–U SOC; W/E–U after 2.30 pm; BH–U
Fees With member £5 D–£8; without member £8 D–£12; Junior reduction WD £3 D–£5
Loc 4 miles WNW of Nuneaton on B414

Pype Hayes (1932)

Public (Map 4/27)
Eachelhurst Road Walmley Sutton Coldfield B76 8EP
Tel **021-351 1014**
Mem 400
Sec LJ Rose Tel 021-783 4920
Pro JF Bayliss
Holes 18 L 5811 yds SSS 68
Recs Am–62 L Jacks
Pro–59 J Cawsey
V'trs U
Fees £3.85
Loc 5 miles NE of Birmingham

Robin Hood (1893)

Private (Map 4/28)
St Bernards Road Solihull West Midlands B92 7DJ
Tel **021-706 0159**
Mem 650 120(L) 40(J) 85(5)
Sec KH Ellson MBE TD Tel 021-706 0061
Pro FE Miller Tel 021-706 0806
Holes 18 L 6609 yds SSS 72
Recs Am–69 B Worsley
Pro–68 A Miller
V'trs WD–U; W/E & BH–M; SOC on weekdays
Fees £10.50
Loc 7 miles S of Birmingham

Rugby (1891)

Private (Map 4/29)
Clifton Road Rugby CV22 3RD
Tel **Rugby 542306**
Mem 550
Sec HL Barker Tel Rugby 810933
Pro D Sutherland Tel Rugby 75134
Holes 18 L 5457 yds SSS 67
Recs Am–65 R Clynick
Pro–68 D Sutherland
V'trs WD–U; W/E & BH–M; SOC
Fees £6 £4 after 3 pm
Fees £7 £4.50 after 3 pm
Loc 1 mile N of Rugby South Warwicks on B5414

Shirley (1956)

Private (Map 4/30)
Stratford Road Solihull
Tel **021-744 6001**
Mem 300
Sec CA Pittaway
Pro C Wicketts
Holes 18 L 6411 yds SSS 71
Recs Am–68 M Payne
Pro–68
V'trs U
Fees £11 (£13)
Loc 8 miles S B'ham 400 yds city side of M42 Junction

Sphinx (1948)

Private (Map 4/31)
Siddeley Avenue Coventry
Tel **Coventry 458890**
Mem 400
Sec GE Brownbridge Tel Coventry 597731
Pro
Holes 9 L 4104 yds SSS 60
Recs Am–62 PR Thorpe
Pro–
V'trs U
Fees £3
Loc Coventry

Stratford-on-Avon (1894)

Private (Map 4/32)
Tiddington Road Stratford
Tel **Stratford-on-Avon 297296**
Mem 850
Sec JH Standbridge Tel Stratford-on-Avon 205749
Pro PA Elson Tel S-on-A 205677
Holes 18 L 6309 yds SSS 69
Recs Am–67 PB Rodgers NCF Dainton
Pro–65 J Whitehead
V'trs U
Fees On application
Loc Within town boundary

Sutton Coldfield (1889)

Private (Map 4/33)
Thornhill Road Sutton Coldfield
Tel **021-353 2014**
Mem 517
Sec DA Bashford (Admin M McClean Tel 021-353 9633)
Pro David Thorp Tel 021-353 9633
Holes 18 L 6541 yds SSS 71
Recs Am–65 L Jacks
Pro–64 PA Elson
V'trs U
Fees £10 (£12.50)
Loc 9 miles N of Birmingham

Walmley (Wylde Green) (1902)

Private (Map 4/34)
Brooks Road Wylde Green Sutton Coldfield B72 1HR
Tel **021-373 0029**
Mem 700
Sec Major DB Sullivan
Pro Michael J Skerritt Tel 021-373 7103
Holes 18 L 6277 yds SSS 70
Recs Am–67 Broadhurst
Pro–69 MJ Skerritt
V'trs WD–U; W/E–M
Fees £9.50
Loc N boundary Birmingham

Warwick (1971)

Public (Map 4/35)
Warwick Golf Centre Racecourse Warwick
Tel **Warwick 494316**
Mem 90
Sec Mrs R Dunkley Tel Warwick 494316
Pro S Baldwin Tel Warwick 491284
Holes 9 L 2612 yds SSS 66
Recs Am–64 S Hill
Pro–63 S Hutchinson
V'trs No play while racing in progress
Fees £1.40 (£1.70)
Loc Centre of Warwick Racecourse
Mis Driving range

Welcombe Hotel & GC

Private (Map 4/36)
Warwick Road Stratford-on-Avon CV37 0NR
Tel **0789 295252**
Golf Manager: PJ Day
Hotel Gen Manager: BAK Miller
Pro To be appointed
Holes 18 L 6202 yds SSS 70
Recs Am–67 R Fletcher
Pro–
V'trs Weekdays–U H preferred; W/E & BH–NA before noon U H afternoon
Fees £10 (£12)
Loc A46 1½ miles from Stratford

Worcestershire

Blackwell (1893)

Private (Map 4/1)
Blackwell nr Bromsgrove B60 1PY
Tel **021-445 1781**
Mem 300 100(L) 30(J)
Sec S Allen Tel 021-445 1994
Pro H MacDonald Tel 021-445 3113
Holes 18 L 6105 yds SSS 71
Recs Am–68 AJ Thomson
Pro–64 M Bembridge
V'trs WD–U; W/E & BH–M
Fees £12
Loc 3 miles E of Bromsgrove

Brand Hall (1946)

Public (Map 4/2)
Heron Road Oldbury Warley
Tel **021-552 7475 Pro Shop 021-552 2195**
Mem 250
Sec WH Rushton Tel 021-5446184
Pro B Bates Tel 021-552 2195
Holes 18 L 5813 yds SSS 68
Recs Am–66 M Curry
Pro–69 G Henderson
V'trs U (exc first two hours Sat/Sun)
Fees £2.30
Loc 6 miles NW of Birmingham 1½ miles off Junct 2 M5

Broadway

(see Gloucestershire)

Churchill and Blakedown (1926)

Private (Map 4/3)
Churchill Lane Blakedown nr Kidderminster
Tel **(0562) 700200**
Mem 334
Sec AJ Stanier Tel (0384) 73161
Pro S Price Tel (0562) 700358
Holes 9 L 5399 yds SSS 67
Recs Am–64 CMM Lea
Pro–61 R Livingston
V'trs WD–U; W/E–M
Fees D–£6
Loc On A453 3 miles N of Kidderminster

Cocks Moor Woods (1926)

Public (Map 4/4)
Alcester Road South King's Heath Birmingham BK1 6ER
Tel **021-444 2062**
Mem 250
Sec JW Black Tel 021-742 6317
Pro KF Dodsworth Tel 021–444 3584
Holes 18 L 5742 yds SSS 67
Recs Am–65 V Pailing
Pro–71 B Jones K Dodsworth
V'trs U
Fees £3.50 (£3.80)
Loc 6½ miles S of city centre
Mis Multi-purpose sports hall which includes squash, swimming, restaurant facilities open Spring 1987

Droitwich (1897)

Private (Map 4/5)
Ford Lane Droitwich WR9 0BQ
Tel **0905 770129**
Mem 728
Sec RJW Baldwin Tel 0905 774344
Pro CS Thompson Tel 0905 770207
Holes 18 L 6030 yds SSS 69
Recs Am–65 D Eddiford
Pro–
V'trs WD–U; W/E & BH–M; SOC–Wed Fri
Fees £9
Loc Junc 5 on M5; off A38 1 mile N of town

Dudley (1894)

Private (Map 4/6)
Turners Hill Rowley Regis Warley
Tel **Dudley 53719**
Mem 300
Sec RP Fortune Tel Dudley 233877
Pro JK Hayes Tel Dudley 54020
Holes 18 L 5715 yds SSS 67
Recs Am–66 AA Davies
Pro–63 R Livingstone
V'trs U except Sunday before 1 pm
Fees £7.50
Loc 2 miles S of Dudley

Evesham (1894)

Private (Map 4/7)
Craycombe Fladbury Pershore Worcs WR10 2QS
Tel **(0386) 860395**
Mem 300
Sec FG Vincent Tel (0386) 552373
Pro R Gray Tel (0386) 860395
Holes 9 L 6418 yds SSS 71 (played twice from different tees)
Recs Am–
Pro–
V'trs WD–M; SOC; H; NA on comp and match days
Fees £7
Loc 4 miles W Evesham (B4084) adjacent to Fladbury village

Fulford Heath (1934)

Private (Map 4/8)
Tanners Green Lane Wythall Birmingham
Tel **0564 822806 (clubhouse)**
0564 824758 (office)
Mem 675
Sec RG Bowen Tel 021-705 5480
Pro KA Hayward Tel 0564 822930
Holes 18 L 6256 yds SSS 70
Recs Am–66 KJ Miller
Pro–67 M James
V'trs WD–U; W/E & BH–M; SOC
Fees £9 D–£12
Loc 8 miles S of Birmingham

Gay Hill (1913)

Private (Map 4/9)
Alcester Road Hollywood Birmingham B47 5PP
Tel **021-430 6523/7077**
Mem 700
Sec Mrs EK Devitt Tel 021-430 8544
Pro D Dunk Tel 021-474 6001
Holes 18 L 6532 yds SSS 71
Recs Am–68 MJ Duggan
Pro–66 R Livingston
V'trs WD–U; W/E–M; SOC
Fees £10 inc VAT
Loc 7 miles S of city on A435

Habberley (1924)

Private (Map 4/10)
Trimpley Road Kidderminster
Tel **Kidderminster 745756**
Mem 400
Sec JM Pell Tel Kidderminster 3509
Pro
Holes 9 L 5440 yds SSS 67
Recs Am–68 D Beach
Pro–
V'trs WD–U SOC; W/E–M
Fees £6
Loc 3 miles NW of town

Hagley (1980)

Private (Map 4/11)
Nr Stourbridge
Tel **0562 883701**
Mem 360 & 50
Sec Vernon Lewis Tel 0562 883701
Pro Barry Wright Tel 0562 883852
Holes 18 L 6353 SSS 72
Recs Am–
Pro–
V'trs WD–U exc Wed before 1.30 pm; SOC W/E–M after 1 pm
Fees £8 (£10)
Loc Wassell Grove Hagley

Halesowen (1909)
Private (Map 4/12)
The Leasowes Halesowen West Mids B62 8QF
Tel **021-550 1041**
Mem 500
Sec IJ Hodgetts Tel 021-501 3606
Pro P Hancox Tel 021-503 0593
Holes 18 L 5673 yds SSS 68
Recs Am–66
Pro–66
V'trs WD–U; W/E & BH–M; SOC Mon Tue Thu Fri
Fees £8
Loc 2 miles from Junction 3, M5

Kidderminster (1909)
Private (Map 4/13)
Russell Road Kidderminster
Tel **(0562) 2303**
Mem 800
Sec John Sanders
Pro NP Underwood Tel (0562) 740090
Holes 18 L 6156 yds SSS 70
Recs
V'trs WD only
Fees £8.65 incl VAT
Loc 1 mile Kidderminster Rail Station

King's Norton (1892)
Private (Map 4/14)
Brockhill Lane Weatheroak nr Alvechurch
Tel **0564 826789**
Mem 950
Sec J Giles Tel 0564 826789
Pro C Haycock Tel 0564 822822
Holes 18 L 6754 yds SSS 72
9 L 3290 yds SSS 36
Recs Am–69 PR Swinburne
Pro–66 M Gregson
P Oosterhuis
V'trs WD–U SOC; W/E–M
Fees £9, 36 holes £10
Loc 8 miles S of Birmingham

Lickey Hills
Public (Map 4/15)
Rednal Birmingham
Tel **021-453 3159**
Pro MS March
Holes 18 L 6010 yds SSS 69
Recs Am–74 MSR Lunt
Pro–72 R Livingston
V'trs U
Fees £2 (£2)
Loc 10 miles SW city centre
Mis Rose Hill club plays here

Little Lakes (1975)
Private (Map 4/16)
Lye Head Bewdley
Tel **Bewdley 266385**
Mem 225 40 (L)
Sec PF Wright Tel Bewdley 403650
Pro M Laing
Holes 9 L 6247 yds SSS 72
Recs Am–
Pro–70 R Lane
V'trs WD–U; W/E–U
Fees £4 (£5)
Loc 2½ miles W of Bewdley off A456

Moseley (1982)
Private (Map 4/17)
Springfield Road King's Heath Birmingham B14 7DX
Tel **021-444 2115**
Mem 600
Sec PT Muddiman Tel 021-444 4957
Pro Gary Edge Tel 021-444 2063
Holes 18 L 6227 yds SSS 70
Recs Am–64 A Forrester
Pro–64 FE Miller
V'trs M or I
Fees £11
Loc S Birmingham

North Worcestershire (1907)
Private (Map 4/18)
Frankley Beeches Road Northfield Birmingham B31 5LP
Tel **021-475 1026**
Mem 550
Sec EJ Pearce Tel 021-475 1047
Pro K Jones Tel 021-475 5721
Holes 18 L 5907 yds SSS 69
Recs Am–64 DJ Russell
Pro–65 N Underwood
V'trs WD–U; W/E & BH–M
Fees £8 plus VAT
Loc 7 miles SW Birmingham

Pitcheroak (1973)
Public (Map 4/19)
Plymouth Road Redditch
Tel **Redditch 41054**
Mem 120
Sec A Sharp Tel Redditch 24594
Pro D Stewart
Holes 9 L 4584 yds SSS 63
Recs Am–
Pro–
V'trs U
Fees £2 (£2.80)
Loc Plymouth Road Redditch

Redditch (1913)
Private (Map 4/20)
Lower Grinsty Green Lane Callow Hill Ridditch B97 5PJ
Tel **(0527) 43309**
Mem 724
Sec C Holman Tel (0527) 43309
Pro F Powell Tel (0527) 46372
Holes 18 L 6671 yds SSS 72
Recs Am–
Pro–
V'trs WD–U; SOC
Fees £9 incl VAT
Loc 3 miles SW town centre; Heathfield Road off A441 or Callow Hill Lane off Windmill Drive

Rose Hill (1921)
Rednal Birmingham (Map 4/15)
Tel **021-453 3159**
Mem 275
Sec A Cushing Tel 021-453 2846
Holes Play over Lickey Hills Public Course

Stourbridge (1892)
Private (Map 4/21)
Worcester Lane Pedmore Stourbridge
Tel **Stourbridge 393062**
Mem 720
Sec FR McLachlan Tel Stourbridge 395566
Pro WH Firkins Tel Stourbridge 393129
Holes 18 L 6178 yds SSS 69
Recs Am–65 J Fisher
Pro–63 WH Firkins
V'trs WD–U; except Wed before 4 pm–M; W/E & BH–M
Fees £8.50
Loc

Tolladine (1895)
Private (Map 4/22)
The Fairway Tolladine Road Worcester WR4 9BA
Tel **(0905) 21074**
Mem 300
Sec Peter Coleman Tel (0905) 353760
Pro Tel (0905) 21074
Holes 9 L 5174 yds SSS 67
Recs Am–
Pro–
V'trs WD–U before 5 pm, W/E & BH–M
Fees £3.70 (£6)
Loc M5 Junct 6; Warndon (bearing left) 1 mile

Warley (1921)
Public (Map 4/23)
Lightwoods Hill Warley
Tel **021-429 2440**
Mem 116
Sec C Lowndes Tel 021-236 6943
Pro D Owen
Holes 9 L 2606 yds SSS 64
Recs Am–67 B Morris
Pro–58 B Fereday
V'trs U
Fees £3 for 18 holes
Loc 5 miles W of city centre

Worcester G & CC (1898)
Private (Map 4/24)
Boughton Park Worcester
Tel **Worcester 422555**
Mem 1100
Sec John M Kennedy
Pro C Colenso Tel Worcester 422044
Holes 18 L 5890 SSS 68
Recs Am–63 S Carpenter
Pro–66 BJ Hunt
V'trs WD–U; W/E–M
Fees £11
Loc 1¼ miles W of city

Worcestershire (1879)
Private (Map 4/25)
Wood Farm Malvern Wells WR14 4PP
Tel **Malvern 3905**
Mem 720
Sec GR Scott Tel Malvern 5992
Pro GM Harris Tel Malvern 64428
Holes 18 L 6449 yds SSS 71
Recs Am–69 NE Bolton
Pro–67 R Larratt
V'trs WD–U; W/E–after 10 am
Fees £9.50 (£11.50) W–£40
Loc 2 miles S of Gt Malvern off A449 and B4209

England: North

Cheshire

Alderley Edge (1907)

Private (Map 6/1)
Brook Lane Alderley Edge SK9 7RU
Tel **0625 585583**
Mem 212 80(L) 40(J) 40(5)
Sec RStD Heggs Tel 0625 528614
Pro M Stewart Tel 0625 584493
Holes 9 L 5836 yds SSS 68
Recs Am–65 FA Hardy DJ Austin
Pro–65 BR Boughey
V'trs M or H
Fees £8 (£10)
Loc 12 miles S of Manchester

Alsager

(see Staffordshire)

Altrincham Municipal

Public (Map 6/2)
Stockport Road, Timperley, Altrincham
Tel **061-928 0761**
Mem 335
Sec GRB McKinnell Tel 061-904 0333
Pro R West
Holes 18 L 6204 yds SSS 69
Recs Am–67
Pro–67
V'trs U
Fees £1.20 (£1.20)
Loc 9 miles SW of Manchester

Arrowe Park (1931)

Public (Map 6/3)
Arrowe Park Woodchurch Birkenhead Wirral
Tel **051-677 1527**
Mem 250
Sec K Finlay Tel 051-645 7602
Pro C Scanlon Tel 051-677 1527
Holes 18 L 6377 yds SSS 70
Recs Am–
Pro–
V'trs U
Fees £2.75
Loc 3 miles from Town Centre on A552 1 mile from Junction 3 M53

Ashton-on-Mersey (1898)

Private (Map 6/4)
Church Lane Sale Cheshire M33 5QQ
Tel **061-973 3220**
Mem 155 70(L) 40(J) 65(5)
Sec AH Marsland
Pro MJ Williams Tel 061-962 3727
Holes 9 L 3121 yds SSS 70
Recs Am–68 B Armitage M Gleave
Pro–67 R Williamson D Cooper
V'trs WD–U (except Tues after 5 pm and Wed before 5 pm); W/E–M
Fees £8
Loc 5 miles W of Manchester

Astbury (1922)

Private (Map 6/5)
Peel Lane Astbury nr Congleton CW12 4RE
Tel Congleton (0260) 272772
Mem 664
Sec J Moss Tel (0260) 272772
Pro SR Bassil Tel (0260) 272772
Holes 18 L 6269 yds SSS 70
Recs Am–65 AJA Hurst
Pro–69 I Mosey
V'trs WD & W/E–must be mem of recognised golf club unless with mem; SOC on Thu only Tee to be cleared by 4 pm
Fees £9
Loc 1 mile south of Congleton

Avro (1980)

Private (Map 6/6)
British Aerospace Woodford Cheshire
Tel **061-439 5050**
Mem 400
Sec E Ollerenshaw Tel 0625 875098
Pro None
Holes 9 L 5368 yds SSS 66
Recs Am– I Wyld
Pro–
V'trs M
Fees £3 (W/E & BH £5)
Loc Old Hall Lane Woodford

Bidston (1913)

Private (Map 6/7)
Scoresby Road, Leasowe Moreton L46 1QQ
Tel **051-638 3412**
Mem 500
Sec LA Kendrick Tel 051-638 8685
Pro JR Law Tel 051-630 6650
Holes 18 L 6207 yds SSS 70
Recs Am–67 P Whitehouse
Pro–68 JM Hume
V'trs WD–U; W/E–M; SOC
Fees £2.70 with mem, £5.50 without mem (£4.50 with mem, £9.36 without mem)
Loc Leasowe Wallasey

Birchwood (1979)

Private (Map 6/8)
Kelvin Close Birchwood Warrington
Tel **(0925) 818819**
Mem 500
Sec/ Man Alex Jackson Tel (0925) 818819
Pro D Cooper Tel (0925) 812876
Holes 18 L 6760 yds SSS 73
Recs Am–71 A Stokes
Pro–69 P Hunstone
V'trs U SOC Mon Wed Thurs
Fees £7 (£10)
Loc M62 Junction 11; 2 miles clubhouse

Brackenwood

Public (Map 6/9)
Bebington, Wirral
Tel
Mem
Sec
Pro
Holes 18
Rec Am–
Pro–
V'trs
Fees
Loc

Bramall Park (1894)

Private (Map 6/11)
20 Manor Road Bramall Stockport Cheshire SK7 6NW
Tel **061-485 3119**
Mem 720
Sec JH Spedding Tel 061-485 3119
Pro RL Johnson Tel 061-485 2205
Holes 18 L 6214 yds SSS 70
Recs Am–68 B Steele
Pro–
V'trs I
Fees £9 (W/E & BH–£11)
Loc 8 miles S of Manchester

Bramhall (1905)

Private (Map 6/10)
Ladythorn Road Bramhall Stockport SK7 2EY
Tel **061-439 4057**
Mem 290 175(L) 115(J) 100(5)
Sec F Chadfield Tel 061-439 4393
Pro B Nield Tel 061-439 1171
Holes 18 L 6300 yds SSS 70
Recs Am–68 K Moorhouse
Pro–67 M Slater D Wheeler
V'trs U exc Thu–SOC
Fees £9 (£11)
Loc Stockport

Bromborough (1904)

Private (Map 6/12)
Raby Hall Road, Bromborough
Tel **051-334 2155**
Mem 600
Sec LB Silvester Tel 051-334 2978
Pro Paul Andrew Tel 051-334 4499
Holes 18 L 6650 yds SSS 73
Recs Am–68 DP Jones
Pro–
V'trs U (Contact Pro in advance)
Fees £8.50 (£10)
Loc Mid Wirral

Caldy (1908)

Private (Map 6/13)
Links Hey Road Caldy Wirral Merseyside L48 1NB
Tel **051-625 5660**
Mem 800
Sec IS MacDonald Tel 051-625 5660
Pro K Jones Tel 051-625 1818
Holes 18 L 6665 yds SSS 73
Recs Am–66 PT Bailey J Greenough
Pro–68 G Harvey B McColl P Hoad
V'trs WD–SOC; 9 am–9.30 am–M 9.30 am–1.00 pm–U 1 pm–2 pm–M after 2 pm–U; W/E & BH–M all subject to previous reservations
Fees £11 After 2 pm £8
Loc 1½ miles S of West Kirby

Cheadle (1885)

Private (Map 6/14)
Shiers Drive Cheadle Cheshire SK8 1HW
Tel **061-428 2160**
Mem 350
Sec TA Eccles Tel 061-485 1233
Pro PA Devalle
Holes 9 L 5006 yds SSS 65
Recs Am–62 RP Bullock PR Shortt
Pro–63 F Memmott

V'trs H I M SOC
Fees £6 (Sun £8)
Loc 1 mile S of Cheadle village

Chester (1900)

Private (Map 6/15)
Curzon Park Chester CH4 8AR
Tel **Chester 675130**
Mem 750
Sec VFC Wood Tel Chester 677760
Pro G Parton Tel Chester 671185
Holes 18 L 6487 yds SSS 71
Recs Am–68 M Weetman
Pro–66 D Screeton
V'trs WD–U; W/E–U H; SOC
Fees £8 (£9)
Loc 1 mile from centre of Chester

Chorlton-Cum-Hardy (1902)

Private (Map 6/16)
Barlow Hall Manchester M21 2JJ
Tel **061-881 3139**
Mem 350
Sec FE Collis Tel 061-881 5830
Pro D Screeton Tel 061-881 9911
Holes 18 L 6003 metres SSS 69
Recs Am–63 JR Berry
Pro–65 FS Boobyer
V'trs U SOC
Fees £9 (£12)
Loc 4 miles S of Manchester

Congleton (1897)

Private (Map 6/17)
Biddulph Road Congleton CW12 3LZ
Tel (0260) 273540
Mem 380
Sec FT Pegg Tel (0260) 273540
Pro JA Colclough Tel (0260) 271083
Holes 9 L 5704 yds SSS 65
Recs Am–65 IR Hollinshead
Pro–59 N Coles
V'trs U
Fees On application
Loc 1½ miles from town on A527

Crewe (1911)

Private (Map 6/18)
Fields Road Haslington Crewe CW1 1TB
Tel Crewe 584099 (Steward Tel 584227)
Mem 604
Sec David G Elias BSc Tel Crewe 584099
Pro Ronald Rimmer Tel Crewe 585032
Holes 18 L 6277 yds SSS 70 (Par 71)
Recs Am–68 A Foster
Pro–68 A Thompson
V'trs W/E & BH–M; WD–U
Fees £10
Loc 2 miles NE Crewe Station
Mis Meals and snacks available

Davenport (1913)

Private (Map 6/19)
Middlewood Road Poynton Stockport
Tel **Poynton 877321**
Mem 600
Sec TD Swindells Tel Poynton 876951
Pro Wyn Harris Tel Poynton 877319
Holes 18 L 6006 yds SSS 69
Recs Am–65 I Muir
Pro–67 B Evans
V'trs U (Ex Sat–NA)
Fees £8 (Sun–£10)
Loc 5 miles S of Stockport

Delamere Forest (1910)

Private (Map 6/20)
Station Road Delamere Northwich CW8 2JE
Tel **Sandiway 882807**
Mem 400
Sec L Parkin
Pro D Comboy Tel Sandiway 883307
Holes 18 L 6287 yd SSS 70
Recs Am–66 B Stockdale
Pro–63 M Bembridge
V'trs U (2 balls only at weekends)
Fees £10 (£12)
Loc 10 miles E of Chester

Didsbury (1891)

Private (Map 6/21)
Ford Lane Northenden Manchester M22 4NQ
Tel 061-998 9278
Mem 525
Sec F Chinnery Tel 061-998 9278 (Home) 061-881 6518
Pro J Hammond Tel 061-998 2811
Holes 18 L 6230 yds SSS 70
Rec Am–65 RI Walker
Pro–
V'trs H WD–U SOC; W/E after 11 am–M
Fees £8 (£10) £6 (£8) after 4.30 pm
Loc 6 miles S of Manchester

Disley (1889)

Private (Map 6/22)
Stanley Hall Lane Disley Nr Stockport Cheshire
Tel **Disley 2071**
Mem 600
Sec BD Ainsbury
Pro AG Esplin Tel Disley 2884
Holes 18 L 5954 yds SSS 69
Recs Am–68 A Peck
Pro–63 B Charles
V'trs U
Fees £5 (£7)
Loc 6 miles S of Stockport

Dukinfield (1913)

Private (Map 6/23)
Yew Tree Lane Dukinfield Cheshire
Tel **061-338 2340**
Mem 170 80(L) 30(J)
Sec KP Parker Tel 061-338 2669
Pro
Holes 16 L 5544 yds SSS 67
Recs Am–69 Simon Woolley
Pro–
V'trs WD–U (except Wed); W/E–M
Fees £6
Loc 6 miles E of Manchester

Dunham Forest G & CC (1961)

Private (Map 6/24)
Oldfield Lane Altrincham Cheshire WA14 4TY
Tel **061-928 2605**
Mem 600
Sec E Rose Tel 061-928 2605
Pro I Wrigley Tel 061-928 2727
Holes 18 L 6636 yds SSS 72
Recs Am–
Pro–
V'trs WD–U SOC exc 12.45–13.45; W/E & BH–M
Fees £11 (£14)
Loc 1 mile SW of Altrincham

Eastham Lodge (1973)

Private (Map 6/25)
Ferry Road Eastham Wirral L62 0AP
Tel **051-327 1483**
Mem 400
Sec A Robertson Tel 051-327 3003
Pro I Jones Tel 051-327 3008
Holes 15 L 5826 yds SSS 68
Recs Am–64 EI Bradshaw
Pro–66 I Jones
V'trs WD–U; W/E & BH–M; SOC–Tue
Fees £7
Loc 6 miles from Birkenhead on A41

Eaton (Chester) (1965)

Private (Map 6/26)
Eccleston, Chester
Tel Chester 671420
Mem
Sec Major CL Hall Tel 680474
Pro Alex Mitchell Tel 680170
Holes 18 L 6446 yds SSS 71
Recs Am–
Pro–
V'trs I SOC on WD
Fees —
Loc 3 miles S of Chester

Ellesmere Port (1971)

Public (Map 6/27)
Chester Road Hooton South Wirral L66 1QH
Tel 051-339 7502
Mem 350
Sec DWG Hayward Tel 051-355 9759
Pro Robin Thompson Tel 051-339 7689
Holes 18 L 6432 yds Par 71 SSS 71
Rec Am–73 K Davies
Pro–67 B Evans A Caygill
V'trs SOC on WD; WE–by arrangement with Professional
Fees £2.30 (£2.90) OAPs 75p Concessions for unemployed
Loc 9 miles N of Chester on A41

Gatley (1911)

Private (Map 6/28)
Waterfall Farm Styal Road Heald Green Cheadle Cheshire SK8 3TW
Tel 061-437 2091
Mem 400
Sec CJ Rigby Tel 061-437 7961
Pro M Proffitt Tel 061-436 2830
Holes 9 L 5934 yds SSS 68
Recs Am–64 N Pattinson
Pro–63 C Timperley
V'trs W/E & Tue–NA; other days by prior arrangement with Sec
Fees £6
Loc 7 miles S of Manchester, 2 miles Manchester Airport

Hale (1903)

Private (Map 6/29)
Rappax Road Hale Cheshire
Tel **061-980 4225**
Mem 305
Sec JN Nichols
Pro
Holes 9 L 5734 yds SSS 68
Recs Am–66 JR Barlow
Pro–65 D Durnian
V'trs WD–U SOC Thu not before 5 pm, W/E&BH–M
Fees £8
Loc 2 miles S of Altrincham

Hazel Grove (1912)

Private (Map 6/30)
Club House Hazel Grove nr Stockport
Tel 061-483 3217
Mem 550
Sec A Burnett Tel 061-456 7037
Pro ME Hill Tel 061-483 7272
Holes 18 L 6300 yds SSS 70
Recs Am–67 A Hill
Pro–
V'trs U
Fees £10 (£13)
Loc 3 miles S of Stockport

Heaton Moor (1892)

Private (Map 6/31)
Heaton Mersey Stockport
Tel **061-432 2134**
Mem 350
Sec AA Gibbon Tel 061-432 6458
Pro CR Loydall Tel 061-432 0846
Holes 18 L 5876 yds SSS 68
Recs Am–67 RM Short
Pro–66 D Cooper
V'trs U
Fees £7.50 (£9)
Loc Greater Manchester

Helsby (1902)

Private (Map 6/32)
Tower's Lane Helsby Warrington WA6 0JB
Tel **09282 2021**
Mem 600
Sec Ian Wright Tel 09282 2021
Pro Ian Wright Tel 09282 2021
Holes 18 L 6260 yds SSS 70
Recs Am–69 F Wood JJ Spruce
Pro–68 I Wright
V'trs W/E–NA (no SOC)
Fees £8 D–£10
Loc Off A56 turn into Primrose Lane; first right Towers Lane

Heswall (1901)

Private (Map 6/33)
Cottage Lane Gayton Heswall Wirral Merseyside L60 8PB
Tel 051-342 2193
Mem 887
Sec/Man Peter Calvert Tel 051-342 1237
Pro AE Thompson Tel 051-342 7431
Holes 18 L 6472 yds SSS 72
Recs Am–67 J Butterworth
Pro–64 Kevin Jones
V'trs U; BH–NA SOC on Wed and Fri
Fees £10 (£13.50) with mem–£4; SOC £8 (not less than 25)
Loc 8 miles NW of Chester

Houldsworth (Levenshulme) (1910)

Private (Map /34)
Wingate House Higher Levenshulme Manchester M19 3JW
Tel 061-224 5055
Mem 300
Sec JB Hogg Tel 061-336 5044
Pro David Naylor Tel 061-224 4571
Holes 18 L 6078 yds SSS 69
Recs Am–67 R Arnold
Pro–63 D Vaughan
V'trs U SOC
Fees £5 (£7) inc VAT
Loc 4 miles S of Manchester

Hoylake Municipal

Public (Map 6/35)
Carr Lane Hoylake Wirral
Tel 051-632 2956
Mem 250
Sec Alan Peacock Tel 051-653 3164
Pro R Boobyer Tel 051-632 2956
Holes 18 L 6330 yds SSS 70
Recs Am–67 S Roberts
Pro–64 Tony Bennet
V'trs U (W/E–Phone in advance block booking times in operation) SOC
Fees £2.75
Loc 10 miles from Liverpool

Knights Grange (1983)

Public (Map 6/69)
Grange Lane Winsford Cheshire
Tel **06065 52780**
Mem 132
Sec Bert Peters Tel 06065 3521
Pro Steve McCarthy Tel 06065 52780
Holes 9 L 6240 yds (18) SSS 70
V'trs U SOC
Fees 9 holes £1.45 (£1.60)
18 holes £1.85 (£2.35)
Loc Signposted in the centre to Knights Grange Sports Complex

Knutsford (1891)

Private (Map 6/36)
Mereheath Lane Knutsford
Tel **Knutsford 3355**
Mem 135
Sec JH Curry Tel Bucklow Hill 830505
Pro A Wilson Tel Knutsford 3355
Holes 9 L 6288 yds SSS 70
Recs Am–65 B Stockdale
Pro–65 Derrick Cooper
V'trs I–No visitors Wed pm; SOC
Fees
Loc ½ mile from town

Leasowe (1891)

Private (Map 6/37)
Leasowe Road Moreton Wirral
Tel **051-677 5852**
Mem 450
Sec R Kerr Tel 051-677 5852
Pro Vic Harries Tel 051-677 5852
Holes 18 L 6204 yds SSS 70
Recs Old Course Am–66 L Winterburn
New Course Am–63 J Maddocks
V'trs U; Sunday–M
Fees £6 (£8)
Loc Moreton-Wirral

Leigh

(*See Lancashire*)

Lymm (1907)

Private (Map 6/38)
Whitbarrow Road Lymm Cheshire WA13 9AN
Tel Lymm 2177
Mem 400 110(L) 75(J) 75(5)
Sec JM Pearson Tel Lymm 5020
Pro RA Brown Tel Lymm 5054
Holes 18 L 6319 yds SSS 70
Recs Am–64 CN Brown
Pro–
V'trs U
Fees £8.50 (£10.50)
Loc 5 miles SE of Warrington

Macclesfield (1889)

Private (Map 6/39)
The Hollins Macclesfield
Tel **0625 23227**
Mem 400
Sec W Eastwood Tel 0625 615845
Pro T Taylor Tel 0625 616952
Holes 12 L 6184 yds SSS 69
Recs Am–69 RA Johnson
B Hodkinson
Pro–67 M Gregson
V'trs WD & BH–I; W/E–M
Fees £7
Loc 1 mile SE town centre

Malkins Bank

Public (Map 6/40)
Sandbach
Tel Crewe 765931
Mem
Sec
Pro D Wheeler Tel Crewe 765931
Holes 18 L 6178 yds SSS 69
Recs Am–
Pro–
V'trs
Fees £2.80 (£3.45)
Loc Junction 17 M6

Marple (1892)

Private (Map 6/41)
Hawk Green Marple Stockport Cheshire
Tel 061-427 2311
Mem 300 70(L) 60(J) 30(5)
Sec Terence Jackson Tel 061-427 6364
Pro R Tattersall (share with Stockport)
Holes 18 L 5506 yds SSS 67
Recs Am–
Pro–
V'trs WD–U (except Thurs); W/E and BH–M SOC
Fees £5
Loc 2 miles from High Lane North off A6

Mellor and Townscliffe (1895)

Private (Map 6/42)
Tarden Mellor nr Stockport Cheshire SK6 5NA
Tel **061-427 2208**
Mem 470
Sec JK Shaw
Pro
Holes 18 L 5939 yds SSS 69
Recs Am–67 CW Axon
Pro–64 MJ Slater
V'trs U
Fees £6 (£8)
Loc 7 miles SE of Stockport

Mere Golf and Country Club (1934)

Private (Map 6/43)
Mere Knutsford Cheshire WA16 6LJ
Tel 0565 830155
Mem 350 150(L) 100(J)
Sec AB Turner Tel 0565 830155
Pro EP Goodwin Tel 0565 830219
Holes 18 L 6788 yds SSS 72
Recs Am–68 CR Smethurst
Pro–69 N Faldo
V'trs W/E & BH Wed & Fri–NA; Mon Tue Thu–SOC; H
Fees £16
Loc 1 mile E junction 19 M6
Mis Buggies for hire

Mirrlees (1925)

Private (Map 6/44)
Hazel Grove Stockport Cheshire
Tel **061-483 1000**
Mem 230
Sec GS Robertshaw Tel 061-483 1000
Pro J Prest Tel 061-483 1000
Holes 9 L 6102 yds SSS 69
Recs Am–68 MH Travers
Pro–
V'trs M
Fees
Loc 2 miles S of Stockport off A6

New Mills

(*See Derbyshire*)

Northenden (1913)

Private (Map 6/45)
Palatine Road Manchester M22 4FR
Tel **061-998 2934**
Mem 600
Sec LG Massey Tel 061-998 4738
Pro D Durnian Tel 061-998 4079/945 3386
Holes 18 L 6435 yds SSS 71
Recs Am–67 JP O'Neill JS Cheetham
Pro–64 D Durnian
V'trs U SOC (check with Sec in advance)
Fees £8.50 (£11)
Loc 5 miles S of Manchester

Onneley

(*See Staffordshire*)

Poulton Park (1980)

Private (Map 6/46)
Dig Lane Cinnamon Brow
Tel **Warrington 812034**
Mem 360
Sec B Carr
Pro Ivan Norman Tel Warrington 825220
Holes 9 L 4937 metres SSS 66
Recs Am–72 S Bennett
Pro–
V'trs WD–U; Before 6 pm W/E–NA noon to 2.00 pm
Fees £6 (£7.50)
Loc Off Crabb Lane Fearnhead

Prenton (1905)

Private (Map 6/47)
Golf Links Road Prenton Birkenhead
Tel **051-608 1461/1053**
Mem 360 110(L) 38(J) 50(5)
Sec PE Manley Tel 051-608 1053
Pro N Hernon Tel 051-608 1636
Holes 18 L 6411 yds SSS 71
Recs Am–68 CJ Farey AJ Rainford WJ Beattie
Pro
V'trs U; SOC on WD
Fees £8 (£15) W–£30
Loc Outskirts of Birkenhead Junction 3 M53

Prestbury (1920)

Private (Map 6/48)
Prestbury near Macclesfield
Tel **0625 829388**
Mem 725
Sec/Man AWJ Wilkinson Tel 0625 828241
Pro PM Cheetham Tel 0625 828242
Holes 18 L 6359 yds SSS 71
Recs Am–66 R Foster JE Allen
Pro–68 Max Faulkner
V'trs WD I; W/E M
Fees £11
Loc 2 miles NW Macclesfield

Reddish Vale (1912)

Private (Map 6/49)
Southcliffe Reddish Stockport Cheshire SK5 7EE
Tel **061-480 2359**
Mem 400
Sec JL Blakey Tel 061-432 6544
Pro C Claridge Tel 061-480 3824
Holes 18 L 6086 yds SSS 69
Recs Am–64 KR Corton
Pro–67 R Williamson
V'trs WD U; W/E M
Fees £7.50
Loc 1 mile NNE of Stockport

Ringway (1909)

Private (Map 6/50)
Hale Mount Hale Barns Altrincham Cheshire WA15 8SW
Tel **061-980 4468**
Mem 352 165(L) 41(J) 25(5)
Sec D Wright Tel 061-980 2630
Pro N Ryan Tel 061-980 8432
Holes 18 L 6494 yds SSS 71
Recs Am–67 RE Preston
Pro–
V'trs Fri–M; Tue before 2 pm–M; Sun before 11 am–M
Fees £11.50 (£16)
Loc 8 miles S of Manchester off M56 Junction 6–A538

Romiley (1897)

Private (Map 6/51)
Goosehouse Green Romiley Stockport SK6 4LJ
Tel **061-430 2392**
Mem 750
Sec GM Beresford Tel 061-430 7257
Pro GS Ogden Tel 061-430 7122
Holes 18 L 6371 yds SSS 70
Recs Am–64 N Ryan
Pro–67 D Roberts
V'trs U SOC
Fees £9 (£12)
Loc ¾ mile station

Royal Liverpool (1869)

Private (Map 6/52)
Meols Drive Hoylake L47 4AL
Tel **Hoylake 051-632 3101/2**
Mem 650
Sec JR Davidson Tel 051-632 3101
Pro John Heggarty Tel 051-632 5868
Holes 18 L 6780 yds SSS 74
Recs Am–69 R Hayes
Pro–64 Brian Waites
V'trs I; SOC
Fees £16 (£18.50)
Loc 10 miles W of Liverpool

RLGC Village Play (1895)

(Map 6/52)
Hoylake Wirral
Tel
Mem 40
Sec J Chapman Tel 051-625 7013
Holes Play over Royal Liverpool

Runcorn (1909)

Private (Map 6/53)
Clifton Road Runcorn
Tel **Runcorn 72093 (Members) 74214 (Secretary)**
Mem 375 90(L) 100(J)
Sec GE Povey OBE JP Tel Runcorn 74214
Pro G Moore Tel Runcorn 64791
Holes 18 L 6012 yds SSS 69
Recs Am–66 D Staunton
Pro–
V'trs WD–U exc comp days; H; SOC
Fees £7.50 (£9)
Loc Runcorn

Sale (1913)

Private (Map 6/54)
Sale Lodge Golf Road Sale Cheshire M33 2LU
Tel **061-973 3404**
Mem 580
Sec E Tootill Tel 061-973 1638
Pro Martin Lake Tel 061-973 1730
Holes 18 L 6351 yds SSS 70
Recs Am–67 JR Barlow
Pro–
V'trs U SOC on WD
Fees £8.50 (£13)
Loc North boundary Sale

Sandbach (1925)

Private (Map 6/55)
Middlewich Road Sandbach CW11 9EA
Tel **Crewe 762117**
Mem 215 100(L) 50(J)
Sec G Knott
Pro –
Holes 9 L 5533 yds SSS 67
Recs Am–64 K Brooks
Pro–
V'trs WD–U; W/E & BH–M
Fees £7
Loc 1 mile Sandbach
Mis No catering Mon & Thu

Sandiway (1921)

Private (Map 6/56)
Sandiway CW8 2DJ
Tel **Sandiway 88 3247**
Mem 650
Sec WA Seaman
Pro RE Freeman Tel Sandiway 88 3180
Holes 18 L 6435 yds SSS 72
Recs Am–68 GD Wise
Pro–66 RC Vines
V'trs I
Fees £12 (£15)
Loc 15 miles from Chester on A556

Stamford (1900)

Private (Map 6/57)
Oakfield House Huddersfield Road Stalybridge Cheshire SK15 3PY
Tel **04575 2126**
Mem 504
Sec RH Makin Tel (home) 061-633 1985
Pro David Midgley (Golf shop; Brian Badger Tel 04575 4829)
Holes 18 L 5649 yds SSS 67
Recs Am–66 H Fletcher
Pro–
V'trs U SOC on WD (min 12 members £12 inc meals)
Fees £6 (£7.50)
Loc NE boundary Stalybridge, on B6175

Stockport (1906)

Private (Map 6/58)
Offerton Road Offerton Stockport Greater Manchester
Tel **061-427 2001**
Mem 495
Sec HE Bagshaw Tel 061-427 4425
Pro R Tattersall Tel 061-427 2421
Holes 18 L 6319 yds SSS 71
Recs Am–65 KR Gorton
Pro–66 E Lester
V'trs U
Fees £10 (£12)
Loc 1 mile along A626 from Hazel Grove to Marple

Upton-by-Chester (1934)

Private (Map 6/59)
Upton Lane Chester CH2 1EE
Tel **Chester 381183**
Mem 500
Sec/ Man TJ Harden
Pro PA Gardner Tel Chester 381333
Holes 18 L 5875 yds SSS 68
Recs Am–63 JD Norbury
Pro–66 A Perry
V'trs U SOC on WD
Fees £8 (£10)
Loc Off Liverpool Road nr 'Frog' PH
Mis Buggy available

Vicars Cross (1939)

Private (Map 6/60)
Vicars Cross Chester
Tel **Chester 335174**
Mem 650
Sec DC Chilton
Pro FA Nickells
Holes 18 L 5857 yds SSS 68
Recs Am–63 MK Jones
Pro–
V'trs U
Fees £7 (£9)
Loc 2 miles E of Chester

Wallasey (1891)

Private (Map 6/61)
Bayswater Road Wallasey L45 8LA
Tel **051-639 3630**
Mem 343 86(L) 63(J) 22(5)
Sec DF Haslehurst Tel 051-639 3700
Pro Mike Adams Tel 051-638 3888
Holes 18 L 6607 yds SSS 73
Recs Am–68 P Morgan
Pro–66 P Barber
V'trs U
Fees £10 (£12)
Loc Wallasey Grove Road Station

Walton Hall

Public (Map 6/63)
Warrington Road Higher Walton Warrington WA4 5LU
Tel **Warrington 66775**
Mem 400
Sec S Phillips Tel Warrington 64308
Pro MJ Slater Tel Warrington 63061
Holes 18 L 6647 yds SSS 72
Recs Am–
Pro–
V'trs U
Fees 50p (80p)
Loc 2 miles S of Warrington

Warren (1911)

Public (Map 6/62)
Grove Road Wallasey
Tel **051-639 5730**
Mem 100
Sec LRJ Lyon Tel 051-630 1907
Pro K Lamb
Holes 9 L 5914 yds SSS 68
Recs Am–66 J Hayes
Pro–66 JA MacLachlan
V'trs U
Fees £2.40
Loc Wallasey The Wirral

Warrington (1903)

Private (Map 6/64)
Hill Warren Appleton
Tel **Warrington 61620**
Mem 875
Sec P Brockehurst Tel Warrington 61775
Pro RJ Bridge Tel Warrington 65431
Holes 18 L 6305 yds SSS 70
Recs Am–66 JR Bennett
Pro–65 EG Lester
V'trs U; SOC Wed Thu
Fees £8.50 (W/E & BH–£12)
Loc 3 miles S of Warrington

Werneth Low (1912)

Private (Map 6/65)
Gee Cross Hyde Tameside
Tel **061-368 2503**
Mem 245 50(L) 60(J)
Sec H Howard Tel 061-366 0054
Pro Tony Bacchus Tel 061-336 6908
Holes 9 L 5734 yds SSS 68
Recs Am–67 ST Madden
Pro–57 D Cooper
V'trs U; Sun and BH–M
Fees £7.50 Sat–£11
Loc On Werneth Low-2 miles centre

West Hoyle

(Map 6/35)
Carr Lane Hoylake Wirral
Tel
Mem 170
Sec RG Jones Tel 051-632 2475
Holes 18 SSS 70 Play over Hoylake Municipal

Widnes

(*See Lancashire*)

Wilmslow (1889)

Private (Map 6/66)
Great Warford Mobberley Knutsford WA16 7AY
Tel **Mobberley 2579**
Mem 670
Sec CA Skelton Tel (Club) Mobberley 2148; (home) Chelford 861429
Pro J Nowicki Tel Mob 3620
Holes 18 L 6500 yds SSS 71
Recs Am–68 A O'Connor TB Taylor
Pro–64 J O'Leary
V'trs U (exc Wed NA before 2 pm)
Fees On application
Loc 3½ miles W Alderley Edge

Wirral Ladies (1894)

Private (Map 6/67)
93 Bidston Road Birkenhead
Tel **051-652 5797**
Mem 460
Sec Mrs DP Cranston-Miller Tel 051-652 1255
Pro Mark Jones Tel 051-652 2468
Holes 18 L 4966 yds (ladies) 5170 (men) SSS 70 (ladies) 66 (men)
Recs Am–71 Miss H Lyall
Pro–
V'trs U
Fees On application
Loc Birkenhead

Withington (1892)

Private (Map 6/68)
243 Palatine Road West Didsbury Manchester M20 8UD
Tel **061-445 3912**
Mem 340 97(L) 38(J) 30(5)
Sec A Larsen Tel 061-445 9544
Pro RJ Ling Tel 061-445 4861
Holes 18 L 6410 yds SSS 71
Recs Am–70 C Webb
Pro–
V'trs U H
Fees £7.50 (£9.50)
Loc 6 miles S of Manchester.

Cumbria

Alston Moor (1906)

Private (Map 6/1)
The Hermitage Alston Cumbria CA9 3DB
Tel **(0498) 81675**
Mem 250
Sec AR Frater Tel (0498) 81953
Pro
Holes 9 L 5380 yds SSS 64
Recs Am–67 A Rutherford
Pro–
V'trs U
Fees £4.50
Loc 2 miles from Alston on B6277

Appleby (1903)

Private (Map 6/2)
Appleby
Tel **Appleby 51432**
Mem 600
Sec B Waites
Pro
Holes 18 L 5914 yds SSS 68
Recs Am–63 K Bush
Pro–69 SS Scott
V'trs U
Fees £4.50 (£6)
Loc 2 miles S of Appleby

Barrow (1921)

Private (Map 6/3)
Rakesmoor Lane Hawcoat Barrow-in-Furness Cumbria
Tel Barrow-in-Furness 25444
Mem 370 115(L) 32(J)
Sec FG Leigh Tel B-in-F 24174
Pro B Oliver Tel B-in-F 32121
Holes 18 L 6209 yds SSS 70
Recs Am–66 NL Brooks
Pro–
V'trs U
Fees £5 (£5) W–£17.50
Loc Hawcoat

Bentham (1922)

Private (Map 6/4)
Robin Lane Bentham Lancaster
Tel **Bentham 61018**
Mem 250
Sec PS Shallcross Tel Bentham 61411
Pro
Holes 9 L 5752 yds SSS 69
Recs Am–
Pro–
V'trs U
Fees £4 (£5) W–£13.50
Loc B6480 NE of Lancaster towards Settle 13 miles E of junction 34 M6
Mis Meals available in clubhouse

Brampton (Talkin Tarn) (1907)

Private (Map 6/5)
Brampton
Tel **Brampton 2255**
Mem 750
Sec IJ Meldrum Tel Carlisle 23155
Pro S Harrison Tel Brampton 2000
Holes 18 L 6420 yds SSS 71
Recs Am–70 A McFee
Pro–70 W Laird
V'trs U
Fees £6 (£8) W–£20
Loc On B6413 1 mile SE of Brampton

Carlisle (1908)

Private (Map 6/6)
Aglionby Carlisle
Tel Scotby 303
Mem 870
Sec HE Potts C Baker
Pro JS More Tel Scotby 241
Holes 18 L 6278 yds SSS 70
Recs Am–66 PL Jack
Pro–65 D Llewellyn
V'trs WD after 9.30 am and 1.30 pm; W/E after 10 am and 2.30 pm; NA Tue pm and comp days; SOC Wed Fri
Fees £8.50 (£9.50) W–£30 M–£55
Loc 2 miles E of Carlisle

Cockermouth (1896)

Private (Map 6/7)
Embleton Cockermouth
Tel Bassenthwaite Lake 223
Mem 430
Sec RD Pollard Tel Cockermouth 822650
Pro
Holes 18 L 5496 yds SSS 67
Recs Am–65 S Gabb
Pro–
V'trs WD–U before 5 pm exc Wed; W/E–Sun NA before 11 am and 2 pm–2.30 pm; SOC
Fees £5 (£6)
Loc 4 miles East of town
Mis Meals by arrangement with stewardess

The Dunnerholme (1905)

Private (Map 6/8)
Askam-in-Furness
Tel 0229-62675
Mem 300
Sec JH Mutton 0229-62979
Pro
Holes 10 L 6101 yds SSS 69
Recs Am–68 H Bayliff
Pro–70 JB Ball
V'trs U
Fees £5 (£6)
Loc 6 miles N of Barrow on A595 Whitehaven–Workington road

Furness (1872)

Private (Map 6/9)
Walney Island Barrow-in-Furness
Tel Barrow 41232
Mem 600
Sec John Garnet
Pro K Bosward
Holes 18 L 6374 yds SSS 70
Recs Am–67 A miles
Pro–69 K Bosward
V'trs U
Fees £5 (£6)
Loc Walney Island, Barrow-in-Furness

Grange Fell (1952)

Private (Map 6/10)
Grange-over-Sands LA11 6HB
Tel **Grange 2536**
Mem 260
Sec JB Asplin Tel 044-84 2021
Pro
Holes 9 L 4826 metres SSS 66
Recs Am–68 GB Wolstenholme AI Bremner N Bremner D Airey G Park
Pro–66 F Robinson
V'trs U
Fees £4 (£6)
Loc Cartmel Road

Grange-over-Sands (1919)

Private (Map 6/11)
Meathop Road Grange-over-Sands LA11 6QX
Tel **Grange 3180**
Mem 300 150(L) 50(J)
Sec JR Green Tel Grange 2717
Pro J Brennand
Holes 18 L 5660 yds SSS 68
Recs Am–64 S McMillan
Pro–67 G Cuthbert
V'trs U
Fees £5 (£7)
Loc ½ mile Grange Station

Kendal (1903)

Private (Map 6/12)
The Heights, Kendal
Tel **0539-24079**
Mem 460
Sec EF Millar Tel 0539-20840
Pro D Bowring Tel 0539-23499
Holes 18 L 5550 yds SSS 67
Recs Am–63 J Brennand
Pro–63 P Tupling
GC Norton
V'trs U; H SOC
Fees £6 (£8)
Loc Kendal

Keswick (1978)

Private (Map 6/13)
Threlkeld Hall nr Keswick
Tel Threlkeld 324
Mem 410
Sec DS Cowen Tel Keswick (07687) 72147
Pro
Holes 18 L 6175 yds SSS 72
Recs Am–75 M Jordan BD Airey
Pro–69 Ian Clark
V'trs U; SOC
Fees £7
Loc 4 miles E of Keswick A66

Kirkby Lonsdale

Private (Map 6/14)
Casterton Road Kirkby Lonsdale
Tel **K Lonsdale 71483**
Mem 130 30(L) 20(J)
Sec Alan Gerrard Tel K Lonsdale 71483
Pro
Holes 9 L 4058 yds SSS 60
Recs Am–
Pro–
V'trs U
Fees £1.50 (£1.50)
Loc 1 mile on Sedbergh Road

Maryport (1905)

Private (Map 6/15)
Bankend Maryport
Tel Maryport 812605
Mem 400
Sec NHCook Tel Maryport 815652 (home) 815661 (office)
Pro
Holes 18 L 6272 yds SSS 71
Recs Am–70 JA Scott
Pro–
V'trs U
Fees £5
Loc 1 mile N of Maryport off B5300

Penrith (1890)

Private (Map 6/16)
Salkeld Road, Penrith CA11 8SG
Tel **Penrith 62217 & 65429**
Mem 850
Sec Sqn Ldr I Troughton RAF (Retd) Tel Penrith 62217
Pro C Brian Thomson Tel Penrith 62217
Holes 18 L 6026 yds SSS 69
Recs Am–64 JM Nutter
Pro–65 K Bousfield
V'trs W/E & BH–1006–1130 and after 1500 H
Fees £8 (£9.50)
Loc On Salkeld Road ½ mile E of Penrith
Mis No dogs on course or in club house

St Bees (1931)

Private (Map 6/17)
30 Main Street St Bees Cumbria CA27 0DE
Tel **822695**
Mem 275
Sec BG Cranston
Pro
Holes 9 L 5082 yds SSS 65
Recs Am–66 E Gulliksen
Pro–
V'trs U
Fees £3 (£4)
Loc 4 miles S of Whitehaven

Seascale (1893)

Private (Map 6/18)
The Banks Seascale Cumbria CA20 1QL
Tel **Seascale 28202 & 28800**
Mem 550
Sec C Taylor Tel Seascale 28662
Pro T Bacon Tel Seascale 28494
Holes 18 L 6396 yds SSS 70
Recs Am–67 D Weston
ID Stavert
Pro–68 EC Anderson
V'trs U SOC
Fees £7 (£8)
Loc 15 miles S of Whitehaven

Sedbergh (1896)

Private (Map 6/19)
The Riggs Sedbergh
Tel **None**
Mem 70
Sec AD Lord Tel 0587 20993
Pro

Holes 9 L 2067 yds SSS 61
Recs Am–64 S Gardner
Pro–
V'trs U
Fees £1 (£2)
Loc 1 mile S of Sedbergh at Millthrop

Silecroft (1903)

Private (Map 6/20)
Silecroft Millom LA18 4AG
Tel **0657 4250**
Mem 370
Sec M O'N Wilson JP Tel 0657 4160
Pro
Holes 9 L 5627 yds SSS 66
Recs Am–67 B Graham
Pro–
V'trs WD–U; W/E–often restricted until 5 pm; BH–until 5.30 pm
Fees £5
Loc 3 miles N of Millom through village towards shore

Silloth-on-Solway (1894)

Private (Map 6/21)
Silloth Nr Carlisle Cumbria CA5 4AD
Tel Silloth 31179
Mem 600
Sec J Todd Tel Silloth 31179
Pro D Forsythe Tel Silloth 31304
Holes 18 L 6343 yds SSS 70
Recs Am–66 C Wallace
Pro–
V'trs U H SOC
Fees D–£8 (D–£10) 5D–£30
Loc 24 miles W of Carlisle–adjacent Silloth town centre

Silverdale (1907)

Private (Map 6/22)
Silverdale
Tel 0524 701300
Mem 513
Sec EF Wright Tel 04482 3782
Pro
Holes 9 L 4996 yds SSS 67
Recs Am 66
Pro–
V'trs U
Fees £5 (£7.50)
Loc 3 miles NW of Carnforth

Stoneyholme (1974)

Public (Map 6/23)
Carlisle
Tel **0228 34856**
Mem 290
Sec DJ Scott Tel 0228 38098
Pro S Fox
Holes 18
Recs Am–69
Pro–
V'trs U
Fees £2.20
Loc 1 mile E of Carlisle

Ulverston (1894)

Private (Map 6/24)
Bardsea Park Ulverston
Tel **Ulverston 52824**
Mem 700
Sec DB Sharpe Tel Ulverston 53523
Pro MR Smith Tel Ulverston 52806
Holes 18 L 6092 yds SSS 69
Recs Am–67 D Weston
Pro–71 JA Raisbeck
V'trs U
Fees £8 (£9) W £30
Loc 3 miles from Ulverston B5087

Windermere (1892)

Private (Map 6/25)
Cleabarrow, Windermere LA23 3NB
Tel 096 62 3123
Mem 720
Sec P Hetherington
Pro WSM Rooke Tel 096 62 3550
Holes 18 L 5002 yds SSS 65
Recs Am–64 DN Smith
Pro–62 J Brennand
V'trs U
Fees £8 (£10)
Loc $1\frac{1}{2}$ miles E of Bowness-on-Windermere

Workington (1922)

Private (Map 6/26)
Branthwaite Road Workington
Tel **Workington 3460**
Mem 425 125(L) 110(J)
Sec JK Walker Tel Workington 5420
Pro J Forsythe
Holes 18 L 6252 yds SSS 70
Recs Am–65 A Drabble
Pro–
V'trs H SOC
Fees £7 (£9) W–£30
Loc 2 miles E of town

Durham

Aycliffe (1977)

Public (Map 5/36)
School Lane Newton Aycliffe Co Durham
Tel 0325 314334
Mem 60
Man S Hodgson Tel 0325 314334
Pro Tel 0325 310820
Holes 9 L 6054 yds SSS 69
Recs Am–
Pro–
V'trs U
Fees £1.25 (£2.50) Jrs/OAP $\frac{1}{2}$ price
Loc Sports complex on A6072 from A68 Station and town $1\frac{1}{2}$ miles

Barnard Castle (1898)

Private (Map 5/1)
Harmire Road Barnard Castle
Tel Teesdale 37237
Mem 600
Sec C Carling Tel Teesdale 38355
Pro J Harrison Tel Teesdale 31980
Holes 18 L 5838 yds SSS 68
Recs Am–65 M Porter
Pro–64 C Hamilton
V'trs U; SOC
Fees £6 (£8) 5D–£20
Loc N boundary Barnard Castle

Beamish Park (1950)

Private (Map 5/2)
Beamish Stanley Co Durham
Tel (0385) 701133
Mem 520
Sec A Curtis Tel (0385) 701133
Pro A Hartley Tel (0385) 701984
Holes 18 L 6205 yds SSS 70
Recs Am–67 A Stewart
Pro–
V'trs WD & Sat U before 4 pm; Sun–NA
Fees £6.50 (£8)
Loc Beamish nr Stanley

Billingham (1967)

Private (Map 5/3)
Sandy Lane Billingham
Tel **Stockton 554494 & 533816**
Mem 800
Sec J Taylor Tel Stockton 554587
Pro P Bradley Tel Stockton 557060
Holes 18 L 6430 yds SSS 71
Recs Am–66 M Duck
Pro–67 W Hector
V'trs WD–after 9 am only; W/E–NA
Fees D–£7
Loc W boundary Billingham adjacent to A19; E of Bypass
Mis No catering Mondays

Birtley (Portobello) (1922)

Private (Map 5/4)
Portobello Road Birtley
Tel **Birtley 402207**
Mem 200
Sec J Bainbridge Tel Birtley 402145
Pro
Holes 9 L 5580 yds SSS 67
Recs Am–64 G Hammond
Pro–
V'trs U
Fees £2 (£2.50)
Loc 6 miles S of Newcastle-upon-Tyne

Bishop Auckland (1893)

Private (Map 5/5)
High Plains Bishop Auckland
Tel **Bishop Auckland 602198**
Mem 680
Sec H Taylorson Tel Bishop Auckland 663648
Pro Bill Laird Tel Bishop Auckland 661618
Holes 18 L 6340 yds SSS 71
Recs Am–67 RL Aisbitt
Pro–65 BL Hunt
K Bousfield BJ Hunt
V'trs H Course closed Good Friday and Christmas Day
Fees £8 (£10)
Loc $\frac{1}{2}$ mile NE Bishop Auckland

Blackwell Grange (1930)

Private (Map 5/6)
Briar Close Blackwell Darlington DL3 8QX
Tel 0325-464464
Mem 600
Sec JMD Solly Tel 0325-464045
Pro Ralph Givens Tel 0325-462088
Holes 18 L 5587 yds SSS 67
Recs Am–64 HP Jolly S Santon
Pro–63 M Gregson
V'trs U SOC (NA Wed 11.30 am–2.30 pm; Sat: times must be booked; Sun: comps in progress)
Fees £8 (£9)
Loc 1 mile S of Darlington on A66

Boldon (1912)

Private (Map 5/7)
Dipe Lane East Boldon
Tel Wearside 5364182
Mem 500
Sec Tel Wearside 5365360
Pro Tel Wearside 5365835
Holes 18 L 6348 yds SSS 70
Recs Am–66 D Hunter
Pro–66 P Tupling
V'trs U
Fees £6 (£8)
Loc East Boldon

Brancepeth Castle (1924)

Private (Map 5/8)
Brancepeth Village Durham DH7 8EA
Tel Durham 780075
Mem 632 91(L) 81(J) 95(5)
Sec DC Carver
Pro D Howdon Tel Durham 780183
Holes 18 L 6300 yds SSS 70
Recs Am–66 S Hamer
Pro–70 H Spencer
V'trs WD–U; W/E–I; SOC
Fees £10 WD (reduced rates for societies)
Loc 4½ miles W of Durham City on A690

Castle Eden and Peterlee (1927)

Private (Map 5/9)
Castle Eden Hartlepool Cleveland
Tel **Castle Eden 836220**
Mem 650
Sec P Robinson
Pro T Jenkins Tel Castle Eden 836689
Holes 18 L 6297 yds SSS 70
Recs Am–66
Pro–
V'trs U
Fees £7 (£8)
Loc 2 miles S of Peterlee

Chester-Le-Street (1909)

Private (Map 5/10)
Lumley Park Chester-Le-Street Co Durham DH3 4NS
Tel **(0385) 883218**
Mem 400 130(L) 90(J)
Sec WB Dodds Tel (0385) 883218
Pro MA Strong Tel (0385) 890157
Holes 18 L 6269 yds SSS 70
Recs Am–69 CJ Garrity M Weetman
Pro–
V'trs WD–U; W/E–NA before 10.30 am and 12 noon–2 pm or by special arrangement
Fees £8 (£10)
Loc ¼ mile E of Chester-Le-Street

Consett and District (1911)

Private (Map 5/11)
Elmfield Road Consett DH8 5NN
Tel **Consett 502186**
Mem 650
Sec RW Spanton Tel Consett 505338
Pro
Holes 18 L 6001 yds SSS 69
Recs Am–65 H Ashby
Pro–
V'trs WD–U; SOC exc Sat
Fees £5 (£8)
Loc 12 miles NW Durham on A691 12 miles from Gateshead on A692

Crook (1919)

Private (Map 5/12)
Low Job's Hill Crook Co Durham
Tel **Bishop Auckland 762429**
Mem 450
Sec R King Tel Bishop Auckland 762429/746400 (home)
Pro
Holes 18 L 6075 yds SSS 69
Recs Am–66 N Tweddle
Pro–
V'trs U SOC
Fees £4 (£5)
Loc A690 ½ mile E of Crook town centre

Darlington (1908)

Private (Map 5/13)
Haughton Grange Darlington DL1 3JD
Tel **Darlington 463936**
Mem 410 87(L) 110(J) 70(5)
Sec NE Lomas Tel Darlington 484555
Pro I Todd Tel Darlington 462955
Holes 18 L 6272 yds SSS 70
Recs Am–64 H Teschner
Pro–67 M Gallacher
V'trs I
Fees £7.50 (£9) W–£40
Loc NE of Darlington

Dinsdale Spa (1909)

Private (Map 5/14)
Middleton St George Darlington DL2 1DW
Tel **Dinsdale 332222**
Mem 826
Sec N Sharp Tel Dinsdale 332297
Pro D Dodds Tel Dinsdale 332515
Holes 18 L 6078 yds SSS 69
Recs Am–64 PF Ward
Pro–69 DM Edwards
V'trs WD–U; W/E–M; BH–M SOC
Fees £7.50
Loc 5 miles SE of Darlington

Durham City (1887)

Private (Map 5/15)
Littleburn Langley Moor DH7 8HL
Tel Durham 780069
Mem 750
Sec JT Ross
Pro S Corbally Tel Durham 780029
Holes 18 L 6211 yds SSS 69
Recs Am–66 A Ramshaw K Cheseldine
Pro–
V'trs WD–U SOC: NA at W/E
Fees £6 (£8)
Loc 1½ miles W of Durham

Eaglescliffe (1914)

Private (Map 5/16)
Yarm Road Eaglescliffe Stockton-on-Tees
Tel 0642 780098
Mem 490
Sec R Tulip Tel 0642 780238
Pro J Munro Tel 0642 780588
Holes 18 L 6275 yds SSS 70
Recs Am–67 B Skipper
Pro–67 J Munro
V'trs H
Fees £8 (£10)
Loc 3 miles S of Stockton-on-Tees

Garesfield (1922)

Private (Map 5/17)
Chopwell NE17 7AP
Tel Ebchester 561278/561309
Mem 440
Sec GC Bennett
Pro Tel Ebchester 561309
Holes 18 L 6610 yds SSS 72
Recs Am–69 A McClure
Pro–70 David Dunk
V'trs U SOC
Fees £4.50 (£6)
Loc 7 miles SW of Newcastle between High Spen and Chopwell

Hartlepool (1906)

Private (Map 5/18)
Hart Warren Hartlepool
Tel **Hartlepool 74398**
Mem 600
Sec DB Walker Tel Hartlepool 67677
Pro ME Cole Tel Hartlepool 67473
Holes 18 L 5998 yds SSS 69
Recs Am–65 J Wrigley
Pro–65 A Bickerdyke
V'trs U
Fees £5 (£6) W–£20
Loc N boundary Hartlepool

Heworth (1912)

Private (Map 5/19)
Gingling Gate Heworth Gateshead Tyne & Wear
Tel Felling 4692137
Mem 600
Sec G Holbrow Tel Felling 4699832
Pro
Holes 18 L 6462 yds SSS 71
Recs Am–65 D Moralee
Pro–69 P Highmoor
V'trs WD–U; W/E after 12 noon
Fees £4 (£6.50)
Loc SE boundary Gateshead

Hobson Municipal (1978)

Public (Map 5/20)
Hobson nr Burnopfield Newcastle-upon-Tyne
Tel **Burnopfield 70941**
Mem 520
Sec JS Welch
Pro J Ord Tel Burnopfield 71605
Holes 18 L 6502 yds SSS 71
Recs Am–
Pro–
V'trs U; SOC
Fees £3.50 (W/E & BH £4.50)
Loc On A692 Gateshead–Consett

Houghton-le-Spring (1912)

Private (Map 5/21)
Copt Hill Links Houghton-le-Spring
Tel **Houghton 841198**
Mem 450
Sec FF Little Tel H-le-S 841198
Pro J Wright Tel H-le-S 847421
Holes 18 L 6248 yds SSS 70
Recs Am–70 J Hogg Jr
Pro–
V'trs U
Fees £4 (£5); Special terms for visiting parties
Loc 6 miles S of Sunderland

Mount Oswald

Public (Map 5/22)
South Road Durham City DH1 3TQ
Tel **Durham 67527**
Mem 106
Sec Gordon Clark Tel Durham 67527
Pro
Holes 18 L 6009 yds SSS 69
Recs Am–64
Pro–66 J Mathews
V'trs SOC
Fees £4 D–£6 (£5 D–£8)
Loc SW of Durham on South Road A1050

Ravensworth (1907)

Private (Map 5/23)
Mossheaps Wrekenton Gateshead NE9 7UU
Tel **Low Fell 876014 & 872843**
Mem 380
Sec JH Ford Tel Tyneside 487 6305
Pro Tim Wright Tel Tyneside 482 5715
Holes 18 L 5872 yds SSS 68
Recs Am–63 IR Hornsby
B Collingwood
Pro–64 T Horton
V'trs U
Fees £5 (£6)
Loc 3 miles S of Newcastle-upon-Tyne

Ryton (1891)

Private (Map 5/25)
Dr Stanners Clara Vale Tyne & Wear NE40 3TD
Tel **091-413 3737**
Mem 300
Sec B Swinbanks Tel 091-413 2459
Pro
Holes 18 L 6300 yds SSS 69
Recs Am–69 PR Brongham
Pro–
V'trs WD–U; W/E–U exc between 8–9.30 am and 12–1.30 pm; SOC
Fees £4 (£6)
Loc 7 miles W of Newcastle off A69

Seaham (1911)

Private (Map 5/26)
Dawdon Seaham Co Durham SR7 7RD
Tel **Seaham 5812354**
Mem 550
Sec GE Gustord Tel Hetton le Hole 5264044
Pro
Holes 18 L 5972 yds SSS 69
Recs Am–64 J Sanderson Jr
Pro–
Pro–
V'trs U; SOC
Fees £6 (£7)
Loc Dawdon

Seaton Carew (1874)

Private (Map 5/27)
Tees Road Hartlepool TS25 1DE Cleveland
Tel **(0429) 266249**
Mem 650
Sec T Waite Tel (0429) 267645
Pro W Hector Tel (0429) 266429
Holes Old Course 6604 yds SSS 72
Brabazon 6802 yds SSS 73
Recs Am–66 M Kelley
Pro–67 JW Johnson
V'trs U; SOC
Fees £9 (£11)
Loc Hartlepool 2 miles

South Moor (1925)

Private (Map 5/28)
The Middles Craghead Stanley Co Durham DH9 6AG
Tel **Stanley 232848**
Mem 482
Sec R Harrison Tel Durham 700515
Pro
Holes 18 L 6445 yds SSS 71
Recs Am–68 A Ainscough
Pro–65 A Webster
V'trs U
Fees On application
Loc 8 miles NW of Durham

South Shields (1893)

Private (Map 5/29)
Cleadon Hills South Shields Tyne & Wear
Tel **South Shields 4560475**
Mem 700
Sec WH Loades Tel South Shields 4568942
Pro David Race Tel South Shields 4560110
Holes 18 L 6264 yds SSS 70
Recs Am–67 J Dryden
Pro–64 M Gregson
V'trs U; SOC on WD
Fees £6 (£8) Jrs £5
Loc Cleadon Hills South Shields

Stressholme (1976)

Public (Map 5/30)
Snipe Lane Darlington
Tel **Darlington 53073**
Mem 550
Sec CR Thornton Tel Darlington 52783
Pro FC Thorpe Tel Darlington 461002
Holes 18 L 6511 yds SSS 71
Recs Am–68 M Wood
Pro–64 N Coles
V'trs U
Fees £3.50 (£4.50)
Loc 2 miles S of Darlington

Tyneside (1879)

Private (Map 5/31)
Westfield Lane Ryton NE40 3OE
Tel **(091) 413 2177**
Mem 500
Sec JR Watkin Tel (091) 413 2742
Pro M Gunn Tel (091) 413 3626
Holes 18 L 6055 yds SSS 69
Recs Am–66 J Surtees M Dunn
Pro–67 P Highmoor S Smith
V'trs U; SOC
Fees £7 (£10)
Loc 7 miles W of Newcastle-upon-Tyne

Washington (1979)

Public (Map 5/32)
Stone Cellar Road Washington
Tel **091-4172626**
Mem 310
Sec D Brown
Pro H Thomson
Holes 18 L 6528 yds SSS 71
Recs Am–72 DN Armstrong
Pro–
V'trs U
Fees £3.75 (£5.35)
Loc Washington District 12

Wearside (1892)

Private (Map 5/33)
Coxgreen Sunderland SR4 9JT
Tel **091 5342518**
Mem 650
Sec KD Wheldon Tel 091 5342518
Pro S Bradley Tel 091 5344269
Holes 18 L 6315 yds SSS 70
Recs Am–67 L Naisby D Curry
Pro–68 A Bickerdike
V'trs WD–H SOC; W/E–M H
Fees £6 (£9)
Loc 2 miles W of Sunderland off A183 ¼ mile W of A19

Whickham (1911)

Private (Map 5/34)
Hollinside Park Whickham
Tel **4887309**
Mem 500
Sec N Weightman Tel 4881576
Pro IF Lindsay Tel 4888591
Holes 18 L 6129 yds SSS 69
Recs Am–68
Pro–
V'trs U
Fees £5 (£7.50)
Loc 5 miles SW of Newcastle-upon-Tyne

Whitburn (1931)

Private (Map 5/35)
Lizard Lane South Shields Tyne & Wear
Tel **Whitburn 292144**
Mem 336 76(L) 34(J) 65(5)
Sec Dr R Blakey Tel Sunderland 674636
Pro D Stephenson Tel Whitburn 294210
Holes 18 L 6035 yds SSS 69
Recs Am–68 D Atkinson G Hills
I McConnell
Pro–70 M Gunn
V'trs U; SOC
Fees £5 (£6.50) W–£25
Loc 2 miles N Sunderland on coast road Bus route 539

Woodham (1983)

Private (Map 5/24)
Burnhill Way Newton Aycliffe DL5 4PM Co Durham
Tel **Aycliffe 320574**
Mem 100
Sec George Golightly
Pro
Holes 18 L 6767 yds SSS 72
Rec Am–
Pro–
V'trs U; SOC
Fees Pay as you play
Loc

Isle of Man

Castletown (1892)

Private (Map 6/1)
104 Ballycriy Park Colby Isle of Man
Tel **0624 834422**
Mem 300
Sec TH Dore Tel 0624 834422
Pro MC Crowe Tel 0624 822125
Holes 18 L 6716 yds SSS 72
Recs Am–68 WR Ennett
Pro–
V'trs U; SOC (arrangements with Pro)
Fees £7 (£8)
Loc 1¼ miles E of Castletown

Douglas (1937)

Private (Map 6/2)
Pullrose Road Douglas Isle of Man
Tel **0624 75952**
Mem 450
Sec WR Moore Tel 0624 25760
Pro B Devereau Tel 0624 5962
Holes 18 L 6080 yds SSS 69
V'trs U
Fees £4 D–£6 W–£20 (est for 1985)
Loc 1 mile from town centre on main road to Douglas Power Station

Douglas Municipal (1927)

Public (Map 6/3)
Pulrose Park Douglas
Tel **(0624) 5952**
Pro NR Devereau
Holes 18 L 6080 yds SSS 69
Recs Am–63
V'trs U
Fees £4
Loc 1 mile from Douglas Pier

Howstrake (1914)

Private (Map 6/4)
Groudle Road Onchan
Tel (0624) 20430
Mem 300
Sec JC Davies
Pro
Holes 18 L 5243 yds SSS 66
Recs Am–62 TP Kniveton
Pro–69
V'trs U
Fees £3.50
Loc Onchan 1 mile N of Douglas

Peel (1896)

Private (Map 6/5)
Rheast Lane Peel
Tel **Peel 2227**
Mem 500
Sec EH Drain Tel Peel 3456 (mornings)
Pro R Leach Tel Peel 3514
Holes 18 L 5914 yds SSS 68
Recs Am–64 J Sutton
Pro–
V'trs WD–U; W/E & BH not before 10.30 am
Fees £5 (£6)
Loc 10 miles W of Douglas

Port St Mary

Public (Map 6/6)
Port St Mary
Tel
Mem
Sec JM Keggen Tel (0624) 833133
Pro
Holes 9 L 2711 yds SSS 66
Recs Am–
Pro–
V'trs U
Fees £1 W–£4 M–£6
Loc Callow Road

Ramsey (1891)

Private (Map 6/7)
Brookfield Avenue Ramsey
Tel 0624 813365/812244
Mem 870
Sec SA Lockwood Tel 0624 812244
Pro Nick Summerfield Tel 0624 814736
Holes 18 L 6019 yds SSS 69
Recs Am–65 S Boyd
Pro–65 S Lyle
V'trs U SOC (arrangements with Sec); H for competitions
Fees £5 (D–£6) W & M tickets available
Loc W boundary Ramsey 12 miles N of Douglas

Rowany (1895)

Private (Map 6/8)
Port Erin
Tel 0624 834108
Mem 300
Sec GC Pipcock Tel 0624 832644
Pro
Holes 18 L 5840 yds SSS 69
Recs Am–68 A Cain
Pro–
V'trs U
Fees £4.50 (£6)
Loc South of island

Lancashire

Accrington and District (1893)

Private (Map 6/1)
West End Oswaldtwistle Accrington
Tel **Accrington 32734**
Mem 350
Sec JE Pilkington Tel Accrington 35070
Pro W Harling Tel Accrington 31091
Holes 18 L 5954 yds SSS 69
Recs Am–64 J Rothwell
Pro–
V'trs U; SOC on WD & W/E
Fees £5 (£6)
Loc

Acre Gate (1974)

Private (Map 6/116)
Pennybridge Lane Flixton Urmston Manchester
Tel **061-748 1226**
Mem 200
Sec J Stenstrom Tel 061-748 7721
Holes 6–Play over William Wroe Municipal; 18 L 4395 yds Par 64 SSS 61

Allerton Park (1934)

Public (Map 6/2)
Liverpool
Tel **051-428 1046**
Mem 300
Sec HG Drew Tel 051-427 4057
Pro J Large
Holes 18 L 5084 yds SSS 64
Recs Am–63 N McCormick
Pro–
V'trs U
Fees £1
Loc 5 miles S of city centre

Alt (1975)

Public (Map 6/3)
Park Road West Southport Lancs
Tel 0704 30435
Mem 68
Sec SD Ireland Tel 051-526 6914
Pro W Fletcher Tel 0704 35268
Holes 18 L 5939 yds SSS 69
Recs Am–
Pro–
V'trs U (Ring to book)
Fees £2.40 (£3)
Loc N of Marine Lake

Ashton and Lea (1913)

Private (Map 6/4)
Downtudor Ave off Blackpool Rd Lea nr Preston PR4 0XA
Tel 0772 726480
Mem 600
Sec JEJ Waters Tel 0772 729135 (home) 0772 735282 (club)
Pro Peter Laugher Tel 0772 7203743
Holes 18 L 6286 yds SSS 70
Recs Am–67 E Walsh
Pro–
V'trs U SOC
Fees £7 (£8)
Loc 3 miles W of Preston

Ashton-in-Makerfield (1902)

Private (Map 6/5)
Garswood Park Liverpool Road Ashton-in-Makerfield Merseyside
Tel **Ashton-in-Makerfield 727267**
Mem 500
Sec H Howard Elce Tel Ashton-in-Makerfield 727745
Pro Peter Allan Tel Ashton-in-Makerfield 724229
Holes 18 L 6120 yds SSS 69
Recs Am–67 GS Lacy
Pro–
V'trs WD–res Wed; W/E & BH–M; SOC
Fees £7 (with mem £3)
Loc 1 mile from town centre

Ashton-under-Lyne (1913)

Private (Map 6/6)
Gorsey Lane Hurst Ashton-under-Lyne Manchester (Greater)
Tel **061-330 1537**
Mem 450
Sec GE Spiby Tel 061-338 4265
Pro L Cain Tel 061-308 2095
Holes 18 L 6157 yds SSS 69
Recs Am–
Pro–
V'trs WD–U; W/E & BH–M; SOC
Fees £8
Loc 8 miles E of Manchester

Bacup (1912)

Private (Map 6/7)
Bankside Bacup
Tel Bacup 873170
Mem 395
Sec DR Gilligan Tel Bacup 873688
Pro
Holes 9 L 5656 yds SSS 67
Recs Am–65 M Butcher
Pro–67 H Higgins
V'trs U
Fees £6 (£7)
Loc Bankside Lane

Baxenden and District (1913)

Private (Map 6/8)
Top o' th' Meadow Baxenden nr Accrington
Tel **Accrington 34555**
Mem 250
Sec L Howard Tel Rossendale 213394
Pro
Holes 9 L 5740 yds SSS 68
Recs Am–67 JJ Walsh
Pro–66 C Tobin
V'trs U
Fees £4 (£5)
Loc 2 miles SE of Accrington

Beacon Park (1982)

Public (Map 6/9)
Beacon Lane Dalton Upholland Wigan WN8 7RU
Tel Upholland 622700
Mem 245
Sec JC McIlroy Tel Burscough 892930
Pro David Clarke Tel Upholland 622700
Holes 18 L 5927 yds SSS 69
Recs Am–68 D Parkin
Pro–
V'trs U
Fees £1.90 (£2.30)

Loc Signposted from Upholland and Parbold. Close to Ashurst Beacon and M58 and M6
Mis Private club playing over public course

Blackburn (1894)

Private (Map 6/10)
Beardwood Brow Blackburn BB2 7AX
Tel **Blackburn 51122**
Mem 440 110(L) 120(J)
Sec RB Smith
Pro G Bond Tel Blackburn 55942
Holes 18 L 6003 yds SSS 70
Recs Am–64 GH Readett
Pro–66 M Foster
V'trs U SOC on WD
Fees £7 (£8)
Loc In town

Blackley (1907)

Private (Map 6/11)
Victoria Avenue East Manchester M9 2HW
Tel **061-643 2980**
Mem 600
Sec CB Leggott Tel 061-643 4116
Pro M Barton Tel 061-643 3912
Holes 18 L 6235 yds SSS 70
Recs Am–65 D Royle
Pro–66 J Nixon
V'trs WD–U; W/E–M
Fees £8
Loc N Manchester area

Blackpool North Shore (1904)

Private (Map 6/12)
Devonshire Road Blackpool FY2 0RD
Tel **(0253) 51017**
Mem 820
Sec DS Walker Tel (0253) 52054
Pro B Ward Tel (0253) 54640
Holes 18 L 6440 yds SSS 71
Recs Am–66 CC Bowman
Pro–63 C O'Connor
V'trs U Special party rates but restricted W/E
Fees £10 (W/E & BH–£11)
Loc ½ mile behind North prom

Blackpool Park (1925)

Public (Map 6/13)
North Park Drive Blackpool
Tel **Blackpool 33960**
Mem 530
Sec Kenneth Shorrock Tel Blackpool 53382
Pro B Purdie Tel Blackpool 31004
Holes 18 L 6192 yds SSS 69
Recs Am–65 AV Moss
Pro–68 D Lewis
V'trs U
Fees £3 (£4)
Loc 1½ miles E of centre; adjacent to Stanley Park

Bolton (1912)

Private (Map 6/14)
Lostock Park Bolton BL6 4AJ
Tel **Bolton 43278**
Mem 600
Sec J Corner Tel Bolton 43067
Pro Bob Longworth Tel Bolton 43073
Holes 18 L 6215 yds SSS 70
Recs Am–66 JB Hope
DE Roocroft
Pro–67 WSM Rooke
V'trs U; SOC
Fees Mon Tue Thu Fri–£9; Wed Sat Sun & BH–£11
Loc 3½ miles W of town 1½ miles M61 exit Horwich

Bolton Municipal (1931)

Public (Map 6/16)
Links Road Lostock
Tel **Bolton 42336**
Pro A Holland
Holes 18 L 6012 yds SSS 69
Recs Am–67 PK Abbott
Pro–68 L Allamby
V'trs U
Fees £2 (£2.50)
Loc
Mis Regent Park Club plays here

Bolton Old Links (1898)

Private (Map 6/15)
Chorley Old Road Montserrat Bolton Lancs
Tel **Bolton 40050**
Mem 450
Sec H Cook Tel Bolton 42307
Pro P Horridge Tel Bolton 43089
Holes 18 L 6406 yds SSS 72
Recs Am–66 L Mooney
Pro–67 JR Harrison
V'trs U
Fees £9 (£12)
Loc 3 miles NW Bolton on B6226

Bootle (1934)

Public (Map 6/17)
Dunnings Bridge Road Bootle
Tel **051-928 6196**
Mem 300
Sec D Rankin Tel 051-526 9094
Pro S Sellers Tel 051-928 1371
Holes 18 L 6362 yds SSS 70
Recs Am–69 L Mooney
Pro–73 G Tomlinson
V'trs U
Fees £2 (£3)
Loc 5 miles N of Liverpool

Bowring (1914)

Public (Map 6/18)
Bowring Park Roby Road Huyton
Tel **051-489 1901**
Mem 80 (no lady members)
Sec P Bradshaw Tel 051-489 5985
Pro D Weston Tel 051-489 1901
Holes 9 L 5580 yds SSS 66
Recs Am–68 DJ Calligan
Pro–
V'trs U
Fees £1.95 (W/E & BH–£2.25)
Loc M62 motorway

Brackley Municipal (1977)

Public (Map 6/19)
Bullows Road Little Hulton
Tel **061-790 6076**
Mem 90
Sec RG Steel Tel 061-790 5072
Pro K Bates Tel 061-790 6076
Holes 9 L 3003 yds SSS 69
Recs Am–
Pro–
V'trs U
Fees £1.40 (£1.65)
Loc Off A6 2 miles from Walkden

Breightmet (1911)

Private (Map 6/20)
Red Bridge Ainsworth Nr Bolton
Tel **Bolton 27381**
Mem 200
Sec J Dawson
Pro
Holes 9 L 6448 yds SSS 71
Recs Am–
Pro–68 P Alliss
V'trs W/E–NA; SOC on WD
Fees £4 (£6)
Loc 3 miles Bury side

Brookdale (1905)

Private (Map 6/21)
Woodhouses Failsworth
Tel **061-681 4534**
Mem 650
Sec G Glass Tel 061-681 8996
Pro BJ Connor Tel 061-681 2655
Holes 18 L 6040 yds SSS 68
Recs Am–65 G Lever
Pro–
V'trs U SOC on WD
Fees £6.75 (£7.75)
Loc 5 miles N of Manchester

Burnley (1905)

Private (Map 6/22)
Glen View Burnley
Tel **Burnley 21045**
Mem 500
Sec PJ Searle Tel Burnley 22032
Pro RM Cade Tel Burnley 55266
Holes 18 L 5891 yds SSS 69
Recs Am–65 ID Gradwell L Samuels DA Brown
Pro–66 JS Steer
V'trs U
Fees £6 (£7.50)
Loc From centre via Manchester Road to Glenview Road

Bury (1891)

Private (Map 6/23)
Unsworth Hall Blackford Bridge Bury
Tel **061-766 2213**
Mem 410
Sec JP Meikle
Pro M Peel
Holes 18 L 5953 yds SSS 69
Recs Am–67 MN Seddon
Pro–PWT Evans
V'trs U; SOC
Fees £7 (£9)
Loc A56 5 miles N of Manchester

Castle Hawk (1975)

Private (Map 6/24)
Heywood Road Castleton Rochdale
Tel **0706 40841**
Mem 200
Sec G Hall
Pro D Harter Tel 0706 40841
Holes 18 L 3160 yds SSS 55
Recs Am–57 R Baker
Pro–56 G Bond
V'trs U SOC
Fees £3 (£4)
Loc 1 mile Castleton Station

Childwall (1913)

Private (Map 6/25)
Naylor's Road Gateacre Liverpool L27 2YB
Tel **051-487 0654**
Mem 650
Sec L Upton Tel 051-487 9871
Pro Nigel Parr Tel 051-487 9871

Holes 18 L 6425 yds SSS 71
Recs Am–66 M Gamble
Pro–
V'trs Restricted play W/E & BH, Tue
Fees £7.50 (£9 & £10)
Loc 2 miles from M62, M57 roundabout exit 6 or 7 miles E of Liverpool city centre

Chorley (1898)

Private (Map 6/26)
Hall o' th' Hill Heath Charnock nr Chorley PR6 9HX
Tel **Adlington 480263**
Mem 380
Sec GA Birtill Tel Chorley 63024
Pro Adrian Fryer Tel Adlington 481245
Holes 18 L 6277 yds SSS 70
Recs Am–65 WG Bromilow
Pro–66 Melvin Hughes
V'trs WD–I; W/E–by arrangement SOC
Fees On application
Loc 1 mile S of town

Clitheroe (1891)

Private (Map 6/27)
Whalley Road Clitheroe BB7 1PP
Tel **Clitheroe 22618**
Mem 750 122(L) 68(J)
Sec JB Kay Tel Clitheroe 22292
Pro P Geddes Tel Clitheroe 24242
Holes 18 L 6280 yds SSS 71
Recs Am–69 G Boardman S Holden P Marlow
Pro–
V'trs U
Fees £9 (£11)
Loc 2 miles S of town

Colne (1901)

Private (Map 6/28)
Law Farm Skipton Old Road Colne
Tel Colne 863391
Mem 294
Sec RG Knowles Tel Nelson 67158
Pro
Holes 9 L 5961 yds SSS 69
Recs Am–68 DP Murphy
Pro–
V'trs U (ex comp days)
Fees £6 (£7) W–£24
Loc 1½ miles N of town

Crompton and Royton (1913)

Private (Map 6/29)
High Barn Royton Oldham
Tel **061-624 2154**
Mem 620
Sec T Donovan Tel 061-624 0986
Pro DA Melling
Holes 18 L 6212 yds SSS 70
Recs Am–65 JA Osbaldeston
Pro–65 D Durnian
V'trs U; SOC on WD
Fees £6 (£8)
Loc Oldham 3 miles

Darwen (1893)

Private (Map 6/30)
Winter Hill Darwen
Tel **Darwen 71287**
Mem 360 70(L) 100(J) 40(5)
Sec J Kenyon Tel Darwen 75613
Pro Wayne Lennon Tel Darwen 776370
Holes 18 L 5752 yds SSS 68
Recs Am–66
Pro–65
V'trs U
Fees £4 (£5)
Loc 1½ miles of town centre

Davyhulme Park (1910)

Private (Map 6/31)
Gleneagles Road Davyhulme nr Manchester
Tel **061-748 2856**
Mem 600
Sec RF Streets Tel 061-748 2260
Pro Hugh Lewis Tel 061-748 3931
Holes 18 L 6237 yds SSS 70
Recs Am–67 TF Sharp
Pro–68 KG Geddes
Dai Rees
V'trs U; Competition days–M, after 3 pm only; SOC
Fees £7 (£9) W–£20
Loc 7 miles SW Manchester

Deane (1906)

Private (Map 6/33)
Off Junction Road Deane Bolton
Tel Bolton 61944
Mem 300
Sec J Bolton Tel Bolton 651808
Pro D Martindale
Holes 18 L 5511 yds SSS 67
Recs Am–62 N Hazzleton
Pro–
V'trs WD–U; W/E–Restricted
Fees £7
Loc 4 miles W of Bolton

Dean Wood (1922)

Private (Map 6/32)
Lafford Lane Up Holland Skelmersdale WN8 0QZ
Tel **Up Holland 622980**
Mem 850
Sec J Walls Tel Up Holland 622219
Pro AB (Tony) Coop Tel Upholland 622980
Holes 18 L 6097 yds SSS 70
Recs Am–66 D Dawber
JB Dickinson D Parkin
Pro–66 RA Morris
V'trs WD–U; W/E & BH–M
Fees £8.50 (£11.50)
Loc 4 miles W of Wigan (A577)

Denton (1909)

Private (Map 6/34)
Manchester Road Denton M34 2NU
Tel **061-336 3218**
Mem 520
Sec R Wickham
Pro Roger Vere Tel 061-336 2070
Holes 18 L 6290 yds SSS 70
Recs Am–
Pro–68 D Cooper S Scanlon
D Durnian
V'trs WD–U; W/E & BH–M; SOC on WD
Fees £7, with mem £3.50 (W/E & BH with mem £4)
Loc 5 miles SE of Manchester

Dunscar (1908)

Private (Map 6/35)
Longworth Lane Bromley Cross Bolton BL7 9QY
Tel **Bolton 53321**
Mem 410
Sec RL Smith Tel Bolton 54104
Pro K Parry Tel Bolton 592992
Holes 18 L 5968 yds SSS 69
Recs Am–66 M Wiggans
WR Whitehead W Vose
JW Smethurst
Pro–66 W Slater
V'trs U
Fees £6 (£7.50)
Loc 3 miles N of Bolton off A666

Duxbury Park (1975)

Public (Map 6/36)
Duxbury Hall Road Chorley
Tel **Chorley 77049**
Mem 200
Sec JP Roach Tel Leyland 432628
Pro Howard Bennett Tel Chorley 65380
Holes 18 L 6270 yds SSS 70
Recs Am–72 A Jones
Pro–74 H Bennett
V'trs U
Fees £3 (£4)
Loc 1½ miles S of Chorley off Wigan Lane

Ellesmere (1913)

Private (Map 6/37)
Old Clough Lane Worsley nr Manchester M28 5HZ
Tel **061-790 2122**
Mem 330 75(L) 60(J) 50(5)
Sec AC Kay Tel 061-790 7108
Pro John Pennington Tel 061-790 8591
Holes 18 L 5957 yds SSS 69
Recs Am–67 JA Pugh
Pro–66 G Weir
V'trs U (Members of recognised Clubs) Competitions excepted; WD–SOC (Check with Pro first)
Fees £7 (£8)
Loc 6 miles W of Manchester at junction of M62 and A580

Fairfield G & Sailing Club (1892)

Private (Map 6/38)
Booth Road Audenshaw Manchester M34 5GA
Tel **061-370 1641**
Mem 550
Sec BBJ Knowles
Pro CP Boyle Tel 061-370 2292
Holes 18 L 5664 yds SSS 68
Recs Am–65 PW Wrigley
ARS Pownell
Pro–
V'trs U; SOC on WD
Fees £7, with mem £4 (£9, with mem £5)
Loc East boundary A635

Fairhaven (1895)

Private (Map 6/39)
Lytham Hall Park Ansdell Lytham St Annes Lancs FY8 4JU
Tel Lytham 734787
Mem 800
Sec B Hartley Tel Lytham 736741
Pro WM Miller Tel Lytham 736976
Holes 18 L 6810 yds SSS 73
Recs Am–65 SG Birtwell
Pro–67 R Charles
V'trs U SOC on WD
Fees £10 (£13)
Loc 2 miles from Lytham and 2 miles St Annes

Fishwick Hall (1912)

Private (Map 6/40)
Glenluce Drive Farringdon Park Preston
Tel **Preston 798300**
Mem 300
Sec MG Gibbs
Pro H Smith Tel Preston 795870
Holes 18 L 6203 yds SSS 70
Recs Am–
Pro–

V'trs Apply to Secretary; SOC
Fees £6 (£8)
Loc 1 mile E town centre near junction of A59 and junction 31 of M6

Fleetwood (1932)

Private (Map 6/41)
Golf House Princes Way Fleetwood Lancs FY7 8AF
Tel 039 17 3114
Mem 548
Sec K Volter Tel 039 17 3661
Pro CT Burgess Tel 039 17 3661
Holes L 18 L 6723 yds SSS 72
S 18 L 6437 yds SSS 71
Recs L Am–69 JC Roberts
Pro–
S Am–64 JC Roberts
Pro–70 S Bennett
V'trs U; SOC
Fees £7 (W/E & BH £8)
Loc 1 mile W of town centre

Flixton (1893)

Private (Map 6/42)
Church Road Flixton Manchester
Tel **061-748 2116**
Mem 250
Sec JG Frankland Tel 061-747 0296
Pro P Reeves
Holes 9 L 6441 yds SSS 71
Recs Am–69 P O'Brien
Pro–65 P Reeves
V'trs U
Fees £4 (£6)
Loc 6 miles SW Manchester

Formby (1884)

Private (Map 6/43)
Golf Road Formby Liverpool L37 1LQ
Tel **Formby 74273**
Mem 600
Sec A Thirlwell Tel Formby 72164
Pro C Harrison Tel Formby 73090
Holes Red 18 L 6184 yds SSS 70 Par 71
Yellow 18 L 6643 yds SSS 73 Par 73
White 18 L 6871 yds SSS 74 Par 73
Recs White Am–67 DJ Eccleston
Pro–65 NC Coles
V'trs I
Fees £17 (£19)
Loc Adjacent to Freshfield Station

Formby Ladies' (1896)

Private (Map 6/44)
Formby Liverpool L37 1LQ
Tel **Formby 74127**
Mem
Sec Miss B Kettlewell Tel Formby 73493
Pro C Harrison Tel Formby 73090
Holes 18 L 5426 yds SSS 71
Recs Am–65 M Walls
Pro–
V'trs U
Fees £8 (£10)
Loc Near Southport

Gathurst (1913)

Private (Map 6/45)
Miles Lane Shevington nr Wigan WN6 8EW
Tel **Appley Bridge 2861**
Mem 300
Sec J Clarke Tel Appley Bridge 2432
Pro D Clarke Tel Appley Bridge 4909
Holes 9 L 6308 yds SSS 70
Recs Am–69 EF Smith
Pro–66 D Clarke
V'trs WD–U before 5 pm; W/E & BH, Wed–M; SOC on WD
Fees £6 & VAT (£6.90)
Loc 4 miles W of Wigan 1 mile S of junction 27 M6
Mis Wide-wheeled trolleys only

Grange Park (1891)

Private (Map 6/46)
Toll Bar Prescot Road St Helens WA10 3AD
Tel **St Helens 22980 (Members)**
Mem 700
Sec JE Jarman Tel St Helens 26318
Pro JE Jarman Tel St Helens 28785
Holes 18 L 6480 yds SSS 71
Recs Am–68 D Bullock
DAF Johnstone
Pro–
V'trs I
Fees £9 (W/E & BH–£12)
Loc 1½ miles W of St Helens centre on A58

Great Harwood (1895)

Private (Map 6/47)
Harwood Bar Great Harwood
Tel Great Harwood 884391
Mem 140 60(L) 30(J)
Sec A Garraway Tel GH 886802
Pro Alan Rodwell Tel GH 884535
Holes 9 L 6413 yds SSS 71
Recs Am–68 J Aspinall
Pro–64 AH Padgham
V'trs U
Fees £5 (£7)
Loc nr Blackburn

Great Lever and Farnworth

Private (Map 6/48)
Lever Edge Lane Bolton
Tel **Bolton 62582**
Mem 470
Sec Wm Ward Tel Bolton 651115
Pro C Parkinson Tel Bolton 656650
Holes 18 L 5859 yds SSS 69
Recs Am–68 J Dickinson
Pro–66 SC Evans
V'trs U
Fees £4 (£6)
Loc 1½ miles town centre

Green Haworth (1914)

Private (Map 6/49)
Green Haworth Accrington BB5 3SL
Tel **Accrington 37580**
Mem 200
Sec B Lawrence Tel Accrington 36097 (Home)
Pro
Holes 9 L 5470 yds SSS 67
Recs Am–66 Rod Peters
Pro–
V'trs WD–U; W/E–M; SOC; ladies only after 5 pm Wed
Fees £5 (W/E & BH–£6) Half price when playing with a member
Loc Willows Lane

Greenmount (1920)

Private (Map 6/50)
Greenmount nr Bury
Tel **Tottington 3712**
Mem 180
Sec HJ Billingham Tel Tottington 3401
Pro
Holes 9 L 4920 yds SSS 64
Recs Am–62 G Dalziel
Pro–
V'trs U–(Mon, Wed, Thurs, Fri); W/E–M
Fees £5 W–£12.50
Loc 3 miles N of Bury

Haigh Hall (1972)

Public (Map 6/115)
Haigh Hall Country Park Haigh Wigan
Tel Wigan 831107
Sec A Woodthorpe Tel Wigan 34399
Pro Ian Lee Tel Wigan 401107
Holes 18 L 6423 yds SSS 71
Recs Am–71 M Tomlinson
Pro–68 Noel Hunt
V'trs U
Fees £2.50 (£3.25)
Loc 3 miles NW of town

Harwood (1926)

Private (Map 6/51)
Springfield Roading Brook Road Bolton
Tel **Bolton 22878**
Mem 360
Sec JS Fairhurst Tel Bolton 28028
Pro MW Evans Tel Bolton 28360
Holes 9 L 5960 yds SSS 69
Recs Am–67 PM Lay N Stirling
Pro–
V'trs WD–U; W/E–M
Fees £7
Loc Harwood 4 miles NE of Bolton

Haydock Park (1877)

Private (Map 6/52)
Golborne Park Rob Lane Newton-le-Willows Merseyside WA12 0HX
Tel 092 52 4389
Mem 380 130(L)
Sec J Foy Tel 092 52 28525
Pro PE Kenwright Tel 092 52 6944
Holes 18 L 6014 yds SSS 69
Recs Am–64 D Pilkington
P Boydell
Pro–
V'trs M; SOC (WD except Tues)
Fees £10
Loc Rob Lane Newton-le-Willows M6 Exit 23
Mis Buggies for hire

Heaton Park (1912)

Public (Map 6/53)
Heaton Park Prestwich Manchester
Tel **061-798 0295**
Mem 150
Sec AF Roberts Tel 061-681 1476
Pro J Pennington Tel 061-798 0295
Holes 18 L 5849 yds SSS 68
Recs Am–66 J Griffiths
Pro–65 AP Thomson B Evans
I Collins M Gray
V'trs U
Fees £2.20 (£3)
Loc N Manchester
Mis Women's professional course record 66

Hesketh (1885)

Private (Map 6/54)
Cockle Dick's Lane off Cambridge Road Southport PR9 9QQ
Tel **Southport 30226**
Mem 580

Sec Norman Crewe Tel Southport 36897
Pro J Donoghue Tel Southport 30050
Holes 18 L 6478 yds SSS 72
Recs Am–66 G Brand
Pro–64 D Hayes
V'trs WD–U; W/E & BH limited; SOC
Fees £8.50 D–£11.50 (£10 D–£14)
Loc 1 mile N of town centre

Heysham (1910)

Private (Map 6/55)
Trumacar Park Middleton Road Heysham Morecambe LA3 3JH
Tel **Heysham 51011**
Mem 400
Sec A Hesketh
Pro R Williamson Tel Heysham 52000
Holes 18 L 6224 yds SSS 70
Recs Am–66 PW Coyle
Pro–64 H Clark
V'trs U
Fees £6.50 D–£9 (D–£12)
Loc 2 miles from Morecambe

Hillside (1911)

Private (Map 6/56)
Hastings Road Southport
Tel **Southport 69902**
Mem 800
Sec PW Ray Sec/Man Tel Southport 67169
Pro Brian Seddon Tel Southport 68360
Holes 18 L 6850 yds SSS 74
Recs Am–67 Paul Way
Pro–66 Mac O'Grady
Robert Craig
V'trs By arrangement with Sec/Man
Fees £14
Loc Southport

Hindley Hall (1905)

Private (Map 6/57)
Hall Lane Hindley Wigan WN2 2SQ
Tel **Wigan 55131**
Mem 430
Sec R Bell Tel Wigan 58356
Pro P Shepherd Tel Wigan 55991
Holes 18 L 5840 yds SSS 68
Recs Am–63 JB Dickinson
Pro–65
V'trs I SOC
Fees £7 (£9)
Loc 2½ miles S of Wigan

Horwich (1895)

Private (Map 6/58)
Victoria Road Horwich BL6 5PH
Tel **Horwich 696980**
Mem 180
Sec G Bates Tel Horwich 691124
Pro
Holes 9 L 5404 yds SSS 67
Recs Am–65 M Derbyshire
Pro–
V'trs M; SOC on WD
Fees
Loc 5 miles W of Bolton

Huyton and Prescot (1905)

Private (Map 6/59)
Hurst Park Huyton
Tel **051-489 1138**
Mem 700
Sec Mrs E Holmes Tel 051-489 3948
Pro J Edgar Tel 051-489 2022
Holes 18 L 5738 yds SSS 68
Recs Am–67
Pro–
V'trs U W/E M
Fees £7.25 D–£9.50
Loc 7 miles E of Liverpool

Ingol Golf and Squash Club (1983–4)

Private (Map 6/60)
Tanterton Hall Road Ingol Preston
Tel **(0772) 734556**
Mem 500
Man Harold Parker
Pro M Cartwright
Holes 18 L 6345 SSS 70
Recs Am–
Pro–
V'trs U; SOC
Fees £5 (£8)
Loc

Knott End (1911)

Private (Map 6/61)
Wyreside Knott End on Sea Blackpool FY6 0AA
Tel **Knott End 810254**
Mem 660
Sec C Desmond Tel Knott End 810576
Pro Chris Mawdsley Tel Knott End 811365
Holes 18 L 5351 metres SSS 68
Recs Am–66 DJ Martel
Pro–
V'trs WD–U; W/E & BH by arrangement SOC on WD
Fees £8 (£10) Special rate for 10 or more
Loc Over Wyre Knott End on Sea nr Blackpool

Lancaster G & CC (1932)

Private (Map 6/62)
Ashton Hall Ashton-with-Stodday nr Lancaster LA2 0AJ
Tel **Galgate 752090**
Mem 539 175(L) 141(J) 16(5)
Sec Mrs JM Ireland Tel 751247
Pro Robert Head Tel Galgate 751802
Holes 18 L 6422 yds SSS 71
Recs Am–67 R Whiteside
D Armistead
Pro–
V'trs H; arrange with Sec or Pro
Fees £11
Loc 2½ miles S of Lancaster on A588

Lansil (1947)

Private (Map 6/63)
Caton Road Lancaster LA1 3PD
Tel **Lancaster 39269**
Mem 310
Sec FM Parker Tel Lancaster 67143
Pro
Holes 9 L 5608 yds SSS 67
Recs Am–68 DC Whiteway
Pro–
V'trs WD–U; W/E–U after 1 pm
Fees £4 (£6)
Loc A683 2 miles E of centre

Lee Park (1954)

Private (Map 6/64)
Childwall Valley Road Gateacre Liverpool L27 3YA
Tel **051-487 9861 (Clubhouse)**
Mem 530
Sec Mrs Doris Barr Tel 051-487 3882
Pro Ian Bramall Tel 051-487 0268
Holes 18 L 6024 yds SSS 69
Recs Am–69 RA Knight
Pro–67 I Bramall
V'trs U
Fees On application
Loc 7 miles Liverpool city centre

Leigh (1906)

Private (Map 6/65)
Kenyon Hall Culcheth Warrington WA3 4BG
Tel **Culcheth 3130**
Mem 700
Sec J Stevenson Tel Culcheth 2943
Pro C Evans Tel Culcheth 2013
Holes 18 L 5853 vds SSS 68
Recs Am–64 J Critchely
Pro–67 D Coles
V'trs U
Fees £7.50 (£8.50)
Loc At Culcheth

Leyland (1924)

Private (Map 6/66)
Wigan Road Leyland
Tel **Leyland 421359**
Mem 400
Sec RE Wilkinson Tel Leyland 436457
Pro C Burgess Tel Leyland 23425
Holes 18 L 6105 yds SSS 69
Recs Am–66 G Norris
Pro–66 D Screeton
V'trs WD–U; W/E–M
Fees £7
Loc ¾ mile off M6

Liverpool Municipal (1967)

Public (Map 6/67)
Ingoe Lane Kirkby nr Liverpool
Tel **051-546 5435**
Mem 250
Sec
Pro Barry Large Tel 051-546 5435
Holes 18 L 6588 yds SSS 70
Recs Am–72
Pro–70
V'trs U
Fees £2 (£2) Jr/OAP £1 (£1)
Loc M57 motorway exit B5192
Mis Kirkby club plays here

Lobden (1888)

Private (Map 6/68)
Whitworth nr Rochdale
Tel **Whitworth 3228**
Mem 220
Sec A Taylor Tel Rochdale 49000
Pro
Holes 9 L 5770 yds SSS 68
Recs Am–67 C Turner
Pro–
V'trs U
Fees £4 (£5.50)
Loc 4 miles N of Rochdale

Longridge (1877)

Private (Map 6/69)
Fell Barn Jeffrey Hill Longridge nr Preston
Tel **(077 478) 3291**
Mem 400
Sec J Greenwood Tel (077 478) 2765
Pro NS James Tel (077 478) 3291
Holes 18 L 5678 yds SSS 68

Recs Am–68 RP Wood
Pro–
V'trs U
Fees £5 (£7)
Loc 8 miles NE of Preston off B6243

Lowes Park (1914)

Private (Map (Map 6/70)
Hill Top Walmersley Bury BL9 6SU
Tel **061-764 1231**
Mem 250
Sec E Brierley Tel 0706 67331
Pro
Holes 9 L 6043 yds SSS 69
Recs Am–
Pro–
V'trs WD–U; W/E–M; SOC Sun £4 by invitation only
Fees £5 inc VAT
Loc 2 miles NE town boundary off A56

Lytham (Green Drive) (1922)

Private (Map 6/71)
Ballam Road Lytham FY8 4LE
Tel **Lytham 734782**
Mem 700
Sec R Kershaw Tel Lytham 737390
Pro I Howieson Tel Lytham 737379
Holes 18 L 6013 yds SSS 69
Recs Am–64 NR Hughes
Pro–66 De Witt Weaver
V'trs U–H W/E–NA SOC on WD
Fees £10 (£12)
Loc Lytham St Annes

Manchester GC Ltd (1882)

Private (Map 6/72)
Hopwood Cottage Rochdale Road Middleton Manchester M24 2QP
Tel **061-643 2718**
Mem 500
Sec RE Tattersall Tel 061-643 3202
Pro John Nixon Tel 061-643 2638
Holes 18 L 6450 yds SSS 72
Recs Am–66 RE Tattersall
M Russell
Pro–65 I Mosey D Cooper
V'trs U (ex Sat)
Fees £8.50 (£10)
Loc N of city 7 miles (exit 19 M62)

Marsden Park (1969)

Public (Map 6/73)
Townhouse Road Nelson
Tel **Nelson 67525**
Mem 135
Sec D Manley Tel Nelson 63750
Pro N Brown
Holes 18 L 5806 yds SSS 68
Recs Am–66 MN Davies
Pro–74 T Gillett
V'trs U
Fees £2.50 (£3.50) 1985 rates
Loc Signposted Walton Lane Nelson

Morecambe (1904)

Private (Map 6/74)
Clubhouse Bare Morecambe LA4 6AJ
Tel **0524 418050**
Mem 923
Sec Maj BC Hodgson Tel 0524 412841
Pro Donald Helmn Tel 0524 415596
Holes 18 L 5766 yds SSS 68
Recs Am–64 J Swallow DP Carney
Pro–63 B Gallacher
P Oosterhuis
V'trs U; H; SOC; prior bookings
Fees £6.50 (£8.50)
Loc On sea front

Nelson (1902)

Private (Map 6/75)
Kings Causeway Brierfield Nelson
Tel **Nelson 64583**
Mem 500
Sec RW Baldwin
Pro R Geddes Tel Nelson 67000
Holes 18 L 5961 yds SSS 69
Recs Am–68 NJN Hawke M Davies
Pro–68 H Shoesmith
V'trs U
Fees £8 (£9)
Loc 2 miles N of Burnley

North Manchester (1894)

Private (Map 6/76)
Rhodes House Manchester Old Road Middleton Manchester M24 4PE
Tel **061-643 2941**
Mem 300 60(L) 38(J) 80(5)
Sec J Fallon Tel 061-643 9033
Pro M Vipond Tel 061-643 7094
Holes 18 L 6542 yds SSS 72
Recs Am–67 MJ Hyland
Pro–70 M Vipond
V'trs U
Fees £7 (£9)
Loc 5 miles N of Manchester (exit 18 M62)

Oldham (1891)

Private (Map 6/77)
Lees New Road Oldham
Tel **061-624 4986**
Mem 270 47(L) 32(J)
Sec DE Rees Tel 061-624 6380
Pro A Laverty Tel 061-626 8346
Holes 18 L 5045 yds SSS 65
Recs Am–63 A Squires
Pro–65 E Smith
V'trs U
Fees £4.50 (£5)
Loc 200 yds off Oldham–Stalybridge road

Old Manchester (1818)

Private (Map 6)
Mem 60
Sec PT Goodall 15 Pinfold Lane Whitefield Manchester M25 7NY Tel 061-766 4157
Holes Temporarily without a course

Ormskirk (1899)

Private (Map 6/78)
Cranes Lane Lathom Ormskirk L40 5UJ
Tel **Ormskirk 72112**
Mem 300
Sec PD Dromgoole Tel Ormskirk 72227
Pro AW Kirkby Tel Ormskirk 72074
Holes 18 L 6333 yds SSS 70
Recs Am–63 DJ Eccleston
Pro–68 R Green
V'trs I Sats–XL until 4 pm
Fees £11.50 (£14)
Loc 2 miles E of Ormskirk

Park (1915)

(Map 6/96)
Park Road Southport
Tel **Southport 30133**
Mem 250
Sec W Halsall
Holes Play over Southport Municipal Links

Pennington (1976)

Public (Map 6/79)
Wigan
Tel **672823**
Mem
Sec Director of Leisure
9/10 Bridgeman Terrace
Wigan
Pro
Holes 9
Recs Am–
Pro–
V'trs U
Fees £1 (£1.40)
Loc

Penwortham (1908)

Private (Map 6/80)
Blundell Lane Penwortham Preston
Tel 0772 743207
Mem 700
Sec J Parkinson Tel 0772 744630
Pro PA Wells Tel 0772 742345
Holes 18 L 5915 yds SSS 68
Recs Am–62 A Gillespie
Pro–66 Bill Fletcher
V'trs WD–U; W/E–no parties
Fees £8.50 (£10)
Loc Preston $1\frac{1}{2}$ miles W

Pike Fold (1909)

Private (Map 6/81)
Cooper Lane Victoria Avenue Blackley Manchester 9
Tel **061-740 1136**
Mem 200
Sec GVW Kendell Tel 061-766 6788
Pro
Holes 9 L 5789 yds SSS 68
Recs Am–68 M Hazelden
T Salmon C Neill
Pro–66 JE Wiggett
V'trs WD–U; W/E & BH–M
Fees £4
Loc 5 miles N of city

Pleasington (1891)

Private (Map 6/82)
Nr Blackburn BB2 5JF
Tel **Blackburn 21028**
Mem 442
Sec L Ingham Tel Blackburn 22177
Pro GJ Furey Tel Blackburn 21630
Holes 18 L 6445 yds SSS 71
Recs Am–64 SG Birtwell
Pro–
V'trs H
Fees £10 (£12)
Loc 3 miles W of Blackburn

Poulton-le-Fylde (1982)

Public and Private (Map 6/83)
Myrtle Farm Breck Road Poulton nr Blackpool
Tel **(0253) 892444**
Mem 250
Sec PB Webster Tel (0253) 893150
Pro John Wraith Tel (0253) 892444
Holes 9 L 2979 yds SSS 69
Recs Am–74 D Barker
Pro–70 J Wraith
V'trs U
Fees £1.80 (£3)
Loc 3 miles E of Blackpool
Mis Catering and teaching facilities 7 days; golf shop

Preston (1892)

Private (Map 6/84)
Fulwood Hall Lane Fulwood Preston
Tel 0772 794234 and 700436
Mem 700
Sec W Higginson Tel 0772 700011
Pro RJ Harris Tel 0772 700022
Holes 18 L 6249 yds SSS 70
Recs Am–65 MA Holmes
J Wright
Pro–66 JM Hulme
V'trs U
Fees £8 (£10)
Loc Near to exit 32 M6

Prestwich (1908)

Private (Map 6/85)
Hilton Lane Prestwich
Tel **061-773 2544**
Mem 363
Sec MT Thornton Tel 061-736 3084
Pro GP Coope
Holes 18 L 4522 yds SSS 63
Recs Am–61 M Garrod
Pro–
V'trs WD–U; Sun–M
Fees £5.50 (Sat–£7)
Loc 3 miles N of Manchester

Regent Park (1932)

(Map 6/16)
Links Road Lostock Bolton
Tel **44170**
Mem 280
Sec J Watson 8 Bee Fold Lane Atherton M29 0BL
Holes Play over Bolton Municipal Course

Rishton (1925)

Private (Map 6/86)
Eachill Links Rishton
Tel Gt Harwood 884442
Mem 250
Sec Mrs JD Banks
Pro
Holes 9 L 6199 yds SSS 69
Recs Am–71 John Catlow
Pro–
V'trs WD–U; W/E–M
Fees £4 (£2 with mem)
Loc 3 miles E of Blackburn

Rochdale (1888)

Private (Map 6/87)
Edenfield Road Bagslate Rochdale OL11 5YR
Tel **Rochdale 46024**
Mem 625
Sec
Pro FW Accleton Tel Rochdale 522104
Holes 18 L 5981 yds SSS 69
Recs Am–66 J Hawkard
R Kershaw
Pro–66 P Butler
P Cowan
V'trs U
Fees £8 (£9)
Loc 3 miles exit 20 M62 on A680

Rossendale (1903)

Private (Map 6/88)
Ewood Lane Head Haslingden Rossendale
Tel 0706 213056
Mem 427
Sec WP Whittaker Tel 0706 213056
Pro S Nicholls Tel 0706 213616
Holes 18 L 6262 yds SSS 70
Recs Am–69 I Lumb J Taylor Jr
Pro–
V'trs WD & Sun–U; Sat–M SOC
Fees £7 (£9)
Loc 7 miles N of Bury near end of M66 (Haslingden exit)

Royal Birkdale (1889)

Private (Map 6/89)
Waterloo Road Southport
Tel **Southport 69903 & 69928**
Mem
Sec MR Tapsell Tel Southport 67920
Pro RN Bradbeer Tel Southport 68857
Holes 18 L 6711 yds SSS 73
Recs Am–
Pro–64 C Stadler
V'trs I
Fees
Loc Southport

Royal Lytham and St Annes (1886)

Private (Map 6/90)
Links Gate Lytham St Annes FY8 3LQ
Tel **St Annes on Sea 724206/7**
Mem 600
Sec Lt Col TJ Hutchison (ret)
Pro M Chesters
Holes 18 L 6697 yds SSS 73
Recs Am–66 R Foster T Craddock
Pro–65 C O'Connor
BGC Huggett W Longmuir
S Ballesteros
V'trs I
Fees £14 (£19)
Loc 1 mile town centre

Saddleworth (1904)

Private (Map 6/91)
Uppermill nr Oldham Lancs
Tel Saddleworth 2059
Mem 1500
Sec IG Bennett
Pro ET Shard Tel Saddleworth 3653
Holes 18 L 5961 yds SSS 69
Recs Am–67 P Smethurst
Pro–69 M Melling A Gillies
V'trs U
Fees £6.50 (£8.50)
Loc 5 miles E of Oldham
Mis Buggy for hire

St Annes Old Links (1901)

Private (Map 6/92)
Highbury Road Lytham St Annes Lancashire FY8 2LD
Tel (0253) 723597 & 721826
Mem 975
Sec DJM Hemsted Tel (0253) 723597
Pro GG Hardiman Tel (0253) 722432
Holes 18 L 6616 yds SSS 72
Recs Am–66 RD Squire
Pro–66 AD Sowa
GL Parslow
V'trs WD–NA before 9.15 am and 12 pm–2 pm; W/E & BH–by arrangement with Sec; SOC
Fees £11 (£14) W (Mon–Fri) £40
Loc Midway between St Annes and Blackpool off A584

St Helens (1985)

Public **(Map 6/94)**
St Helens Lancs
Tel (0744) 813149
Mem 150
Sec MH Devenish Tel 0744 31955
Pro PR Parkinson Tel 0744 813149
Holes 18 L 5941 yds SSS 69
Recs Am–74 D Tierney M Venney
Pro–
V'trs U
Fees £2.10
Loc Sherdley Park 2 miles E of town on A570
Mis Sherdley Park club plays here

St Michael Jubilee

Public (Map 6/113)
Dundalk Road Widnes
Tel **051-424 0989**
Mem 130
Sec W Hughes
Holes Play over Widnes Municipal

Shaw Hill G & CC

Private (Map 6/93)
Whittle-le-Woods Chorley
Tel **Chorley 69221**
Mem 500
Sec RM Hodson
Pro Ian Evans Tel Chorley 69221 or direct 79222
Holes 18 L 6467 yds Par 72 SSS 71
Recs Am–68 A Squires
Pro–69 I Evans
V'trs WD–U; W/E–U
Fees £10 round or day
Loc On A6 1½ miles N of Chorley (exit 8 M61 exit 28 M6)

Silverdale

(See Cumbria)

Southport and Ainsdale (1907)

Private (Map 6/95)
Bradshaws Lane Ainsdale Southport PR8 3LG
Tel **Southport 78092**
Mem 340 100(L) 60(J) 130(5)
Sec DA Wood Tel Southport 78000
Pro M Houghton Tel Southport 77316
Holes 18 L 6603 yds SSS 73
Recs Am–67 JB Dickinson
JL Plaxton
Pro–67 DJ Russell
DI Vaughan
Pro (L)–69 B New M Walker K Ehrnlund
V'trs WD–SOC, I before 4 pm M after 4 pm; W/E & BH–M
Fees £10 (NA)
Loc 3 miles S of Southport

Southport Municipal Links

Public (Map 6/96)
Park Road Southport
Tel **Southport 35286**
Pro B & G Tomlinson
Holes 18 L 6253 yds SSS 69
Recs Am–
Pro–
V'trs U
Fees £1.80 (£2.40)
Loc
Mis Park Club plays here

Southport Old Links (1926)

Private (Map 6/97)
Moss Lane Southport
Tel 0704-24294 (Sec) 0704-28207 (Mem)
Mem 370
Sec N Boland Tel 0704-24294
Pro None
Holes 9 L 6486 yds SSS 71
Recs Am–68 J Robinson
Pro–
V'trs U; except weekend competition days BH–NA
Fees £5 (£7.50) Parties of 12 + £4.50 each
Loc Churchtown District

Springfield Park (1928)

Public (Map 6/98)
Marland Rochdale
Tel Rochdale 49801
Mem 170
Sec B Wynn Tel Rochdale 526064
Pro D Wills Tel Rochdale 49801
Holes 18 L 5209 yds SSS 66
Recs Am–68 B Walsh
Pro–67 ME Hill
V'trs U
Fees £2.30 (£2.60)
Loc West boundary of Rochdale

Stand (1904)

Private (Map 6/99)
The Dales Ashbourne Grove Whitefield Manchester M25 7NL
Tel **061-766 2388**
Mem 700
Sec AM Jenkins Tel 061-766 3197
Pro M Dance Tel 061-766 2214
Holes 18 L 6411 yds SSS 71
Recs Am–68 JE Cooke
Pro–69 N Hunt
V'trs U; SOC on WD
Fees £8 (£10)
Loc 5 miles N of Manchester

Swinton Park (1926)

Private (Map 6/100)
East Lancashire Road Swinton Manchester M27 1LX
Tel 061-794 1785
Mem 425 92(L) 50(J)
Sec J Stewart Tel 061-794 0861
Pro J Wilson Tel 061-793 8077
Holes 18 L 6628 yds SSS 72
Recs Am–
Pro–
V'trs WD–U; W/E–M SOC–Tues
Fees £8
Loc On A580 5 miles NW Manchester

Todmorden

(*See Yorkshire*)

Towneley (1932)

Public (Map 6/101)
Towneley Park Burnley
Tel 0282 38473
Mem 200
Sec D Rigby Tel 0282 29339
Pro D Whittaker Tel 0282 38473
Holes 18 L 5840 yds SSS 68
Recs Am–
Pro–
V'trs U
Fees £1.75 (£2)
Loc 1½ miles E of town

Tunshill (1901)

Private (Map 6/102)
Club House Kiln Lane Milnrow nr Rochdale
Tel **Rochdale 342095**
Mem 180
Sec AS Marston Tel Rochdale 342095
Pro Alec Bickerdike
Holes 9 L 5812 yds SSS 68
Recs Am–66 D Williams
Pro–
V'trs Sat comp days–NA Sun comp days NA 12–2 pm SOC
Fees £5 (£5.50)
Loc Milnrow 2 miles E Rochdale

Turton (1907)

Private (Map 6/103)
Woodend Farm Bromley Cross nr Bolton
Tel (0204) 852235
Mem 200 47(L) 31(J) 25(5)
Sec David Jackson Tel (0204) 594171
Pro
Holes 9 L 5805 yds SS 68
Recs Am–67 TD Bullough
Pro–
V'trs U; NA–comp days; Mon–M before 10 am Sun
Fees £6
Loc 3½ miles N of Bolton

Walmersley (1906)

Private (Map 6/104)
Garrett's Close Walmersley Bury
Tel **061-764 1429**
Mem 350
Sec HH Coles Tel 061-764 0018
Pro Tel 061-776 2213
Holes 9 L 5588 yds SSS 70
Recs Am–67 I Bamborough
Pro–
V'trs U exc Tue (Ladies Day), Sat (Men's Comp day); Sun–M; SOC–Wed Thu Fri
Fees £5
Loc 2 miles N of Bury, A56

Werneth (1909)

Private (Map 6/105)
Green Lane Garden Suburb Oldham OL8 3AZ
Tel 061-624 1190
Mem 350
Sec JH Barlow Tel 061-682 7378
Pro T Morley
Holes 18 L 5296 yds SSS 66
Recs Am–62 LA Lawton
Pro–
V'trs WD–U; W/E–M SOC
Fees £5 W–£18
Loc 2 miles S of town centre

West Derby (1896)

Private (Map 6/106)
Yew Tree Lane Liverpool L12 9HQ
Tel 051-228 1540
Mem 575
Sec A Winrow Tel 051-228 3420
Pro Iain Runcie Tel 051-220 5478
Holes 18 L 6322 yds SSS 70
Recs Am–66 M Gamble
Pro–67 AC Coop
V'trs U
Fees £7 (£10)
Loc East Liverpool

Westhoughton (1929)

Private (Map 6/108)
Long Island Westhoughton Bolton BL5 2BR
Tel **Westhoughton 811085**
Mem 225 50(L) 30(J)
Sec F Atkinson Tel Westhoughton 811085
Pro B Sharrock Tel Westhoughton 811085
Holes 9 L 5834 yds SSS 68
Recs Am–64 T Woodward
Pro–
V'trs WD–U; W/E & BH–M
Fees £4
Loc 4 miles SW of Bolton

The West Lancashire (1873)

Private (Map 6/107)
Blundellsands Crosby Liverpool L23 8SZ
Tel **051-924 4115**
Mem 700
Sec DE Bell Tel 051-924 1076
Pro D Lloyd Tel 051-924 5662
Holes 18 L 6756 yds SSS 73
Recs Am–69 G Boardman
Pro–66 Carl Mason
V'trs U SOC
Fees £12 (£15)
Loc Midway between Liverpool and Southport

Whalley (1912)

Private (Map 6/109)
Long Leese Barn Clerkhill Whalley nr Blackburn
Tel Whalley 2236
Mem 475
Sec PC Burt Tel Whalley 2367
Pro
Holes 9 L 5953 yds SSS 69
Recs Am–67 G Richards
Pro–
V'trs WD–U; W/E–U exc Sat Apr-Oct, BH–U; SOC
Fees £5 (£7)
Loc 7 miles E of Blackburn

Whitefield (1932)

Private (Map 6/110)
Higher Lane Whitefield Manchester M25 7EZ
Tel **061-766 2728**
Mem 500
Sec Mrs RL Vidler Tel 061-766 2904
Pro Richard Green Tel 061-766 3096
Holes 18 L 6041 yds SSS 69
18 L 5714 yds SSS 68
Recs Am–
Pro–
V'trs U; SOC on WD
Fees D–£7.95 inc VAT (D–£12.08 inc VAT)
Loc 4 miles N of Manchester

Whittaker (1906)

Private (Map 6/111)
Littleborough Lancs
Tel (0706) 78310
Mem 120
Sec GA Smith Tel (0484) 28546
Pro
Holes 9 L 5576 yds SSS 67
Recs Am–65 P Davies
Pro–65 MT Hoyle
V'trs NA Tue pm and Sun; SOC

Fees £3.50 (£5)
Loc 2½ miles N of Littleborough off A58

Widnes (1924)

Private (Map 6/112)
Highfield Road Widnes Cheshire WA8 7DT
Tel (051) 424 2440
Mem 630
Sec Margaret Cresswell Tel (051) 424 2995
Pro F Robinson Tel (051) 424 2995
Holes 18 L 5719 yds SSS 68
Recs Am–65 E Walsh L Wynne
Pro–64 A Murray
V'trs WD–U W/E–NA on comp days SOC on WD
Fees £6 (£8)
Loc ½ mile station

Widnes Municipal (1977)

Public (Map 6/113)
Dundalk Road Widnes
Tel **051-424 6230**
Mem 200
Sec R Doran
Pro Bob Bilton Tel 0295 65241
Holes 9 L 2991 yds SSS 69
Recs Am–73
Pro–
V'trs U
Fees 75p
Loc
Mis St Michael Jubilee Club plays here

Wigan (1898)

Private (Map 6/114)
Arley Hall Haigh Wigan WN1 2UH
Tel **Standish 421360**
Mem 250
Sec J Crompton Tel Wigan 41051
Pro
Holes 9 L 6058 yds SSS 69
Recs Am–68 RM Hodson
Pro–
V'trs U
Fees £5 (£7)
Loc 4 miles N of Wigan

William Wroe (1973)

Municipal (Map 6/116)
Pennybridge Lane Flixton Manchester
Tel **061-748 8680**
Pro R West
Holes 18 L 4395 yds SSS 60
Recs Am–45 FJ Barrow
Pro–48 GR Johnston
V'trs U; ring for details of booking system
Fees £2.50 Reductions Jrs OAPs (£3.75 All ages); season tickets available ¼
Loc 6 miles SW of Manchester close to M63
Mis Acre Gate Club plays here

Wilpshire (1889)

Private (Map 6/117)
72 Whalley Road Wilpshire Blackburn BB1 9LF
Tel Blackburn 48260/49691
Mem 650
Sec L McGuire Tel Blackburn 48276
Pro W Slaven Tel Blackburn 49558
Holes 18 L 5961 yds SSS 69
Recs Am–H Green MJ Savage
Pro–64 David Whelan
V'trs WD–U; W/E on request
Fees £7 (£8.50)
Loc 3 miles N of Blackburn

Woolton (1901)

Private (Map 6/118)
Doe Park Speke Road Woolton Liverpool L25 7TZ
Tel 051-486 1601
Mem 1540
Sec PB Seal Tel 051-486 2298
Pro
Holes 18 L 5706 yds SSS 68
Recs Am–64 AP Powell
Pro–66 DJ Rees
V'trs U (except competition days)
Fees £8 (£12)
Loc South Liverpool

Worlsley (1894)

Private (Map 6/119)
Stableford Avenue Monton Green Eccles Manchester
Tel **061-789 4202**
Mem 385
Sec B Dean Tel 061-789 4202
Pro Ceri Cousins Tel 061-789 4202
Holes 18 L 6217 yds SSS 70
Recs Am–66 B Dean
Pro–68 FS Boobyer
V'trs 1 (NA 9–10 am and noon–2 pm)
Fees £9
Loc 5 miles W of Manchester

Northumberland

Allendale (1923)

Private (Map 5/1)
Thornley Gate Allendale Hexham NE47 9LG
Tel
Mem 90 20(L) 9(J)
Sec JC Hall Tel (091) 2675875
Pro
Holes 9 L 4410 yds SSS 63
Recs Am–
Pro–
V'trs U; SOC
Fees £2.50 (£3.50); W–£12 Reduced fees after 5 pm
Loc 10 miles SW of Hexham

Alnmouth (1869)

Private (Map 5/2)
Foxton Hall Alnmouth
Tel Alnmouth 830231
Mem 600
Sec FK Marshall Tel Alnmouth 830368
Pro Not yet appointed
Holes 18 L 6414 yds SSS 71
Rec Am–65 P Deeble
Pro–
V'trs U; SOC Mon Thu
Fees £9 (£12)
Loc 5 miles SE of Alnwick
Mis Dormy House accommodation available

Alnmouth Village (1869)

Private (Map 5/3)
Marine Road Alnmouth
Tel **Alnmouth 830370**
Mem 340
Sec W Maclean Tel Alnwick 602096
Pro
Holes 9 L 6020 yds SSS 70
Recs Am–63 D Weddell
Pro–
V'trs U
Fees £4 (£6); W–£15
Loc Alnmouth

Alnwick (1907)

Private (Map 5/4)
Swansfield Park Alnwick
Tel **(0665) 602632**
Mem 400
Sec LE Stewart Tel Alnwick 602499
Pro
Holes 9 L 5379 yds SSS 66
Rec Am–65 Peter Deeble
Pro–
V'trs U
Fees £3 D–£3; W/E BH–£4
Loc Alnwick

Arcot Hall (1909)

Private (Map 5/5)
Dudley Cramlington NE23 7QP
Tel
Mem 540
Sec AG Bell Tel (091) 236 2794
Pro GM Cant Tel (091) 236 2147
Holes 18 L 6389 yds SSS 70
Recs Am–64 N McDonald
Pro–68 JW Ord
V'trs U
Fees £8 (£10)
Loc 7 miles N of Newcastle

Backworth GC (1937)

Private (Map 5/6)
The Hall Backworth Shiremoor Newcastle-upon-Tyne ME27 0AH
Tel **091-268 1048**
Mem 400
Sec Correspondence to Honorary Secretary
Pro
Holes 9 L 5930 yds SSS 69
Recs Am–66
Pro–
V'trs Mon, Fri–all day; Tues, Wed, Thurs–not after 5 pm unless with member. After 6 pm on competition Saturdays before 12.30 pm on non-competition Saturdays. Sundays after 12.30 pm
Fees £5 (£6.25)
Loc Off Tyne Tunnel link road Holystone round-about

Bamburgh Castle (1904)

Private (Map 5/7)
Bamburgh Northumberland NE69 7DE
Tel **Bamburgh 378**
Mem 620
Sec TC Osborne Tel Bamburgh 321
Pro
Holes 18 L 5465 yds SSS 67
Recs Am–63 RS Rutter
Pro–
V'trs U; SOC
Fees £5 (£9) D & R W–£25
Loc Bamburgh village; coast N Northumberland 7 miles E of A1 via B1341 or B1342
Mis Buggy for hire

Bedlingtonshire (1972)

Public (Map 5/8)
Acorn Bank Bedlington
Tel Bedlington 822457
Mem 652
Sec L Green
Pro J Mathews Tel Bedlington 822087
Holes 18 L 6224 metres SSS 73
Recs Am–68 D Gray
Pro–65 K Waters
V'trs No restriction
Fees £3.85 (£5)
Loc 12 miles N of Newcastle

Bellingham (1893)

Private (Map 5/9)
Bellingham Northumberland NE48 2DT
Tel **Bellingham 20530**
Mem 250 33(L) 28(J)
Sec H Walton
Pro
Holes 9 L 5226 yds SSS 66
Recs Am–63 I Wilson
Pro–
V'trs U (except on competition Sundays); SOC
Fees WD £3.50 Sat–£4 Sun–£5
Loc 15 miles N of Hexham

Berwick-upon-Tweed (1892)

Private (Map 5/10)
Goswick Beal Berwick-upon-Tweed TD15 2RW
Tel (0289) 87256
Mem 385
Sec Tel (0289) 87348
Pro M Leighton Tel (0829) 87380
Holes 18 L 6399 yds SSS 71
Recs Am–64 A Cotton
Pro–
V'trs WD–U SOC W/E 10-2.30 NA 1st tee
Fees £5.50 D–£7.50 (£8 D–£10) W–£23
Loc 5 miles S of town
Mis Buggies allowed but not for hire

Blyth (1905)

Private (Map 5/11)
New Delaval Blyth
Tel **Blyth 367728**
Mem 580 125(L) 120(J)
Sec K Steele Tel Blyth 367728
Pro K Phillips Tel Blyth 356514
Holes 18 L 5633 yds SSS 71
Recs Am–67 D Faulder
V'trs WD–U; W/E–M; BH–NA; SOC on WD
Fees £5
Loc West end of Plessey Road Blyth

City of Newcastle (1892)

Private (Map 5/12)
Three Mile Bridge Great North Road Gosforth Newcastle-upon-Tyne NE3 2DR
Tel **Tyneside 285 1775**
Mem 400 110(L) 60(J)
Sec AJ Matthew
Pro AJ Matthew Tel Tyneside 285 5481
Holes 18 L 6510 yds SSS 71
Recs Am–67 N Graham
Pro–64 T Horton
V'trs U
Fees £7 (£10)
Loc A1 three miles N of city

Dunstanburgh Castle (1907)

Private (Map 5/13)
Embleton NE 66 3XQ
Tel Embleton 562
Mem 100
Sec G Fettis
Pro
Holes 18 L 6357 yds SSS 70
Recs Am–69
Pro–
V'trs U
Fees
Loc Dunes

Gosforth (1906)

Private (Map 5/14)
Broadway East Gosforth Newcastle-upon-Tyne NE3 5ER
Tel 2856710
Mem 360 100(L) 80(J) 40(5)
Sec HV Smith Tel Newcastle 285 3495
Pro J Hetherington Tel Newcastle 285 0553
Holes 18 L 6030 yds SSS 69
Recs Am–64 J Hayes
Pro–
V'trs U
Fees £7 Sat/Sun–£9.50
Loc 3 miles N of Newcastle on A6125

Gosforth Park Golf Centre (1971)

Public (Map 5/32)
High Gosforth Park Newcastle 3
Tel 0632 364480/364867
Mem 450
Man/ Pros Grahame Garland
Andrew Mair
Holes 18 L 5807 yds SSS 68 Par 70
Recs Am–68 A Ingles
Pro–65 H Thomson
V'trs U
Fees £4 (£4.50) ½ price for 9 holes
Loc 5 miles N of Newcastle
Mis 9 hole pitch-putt course

Hexham (1906)

Private (Map 5/15)
Spital Park Hexham NE46 3RZ
Tel 0434 602067
Mem 700
Sec JC Oates Tel 0434 603072
Pro Ian Waugh Tel 0434 604904
Holes 18 L 6272 yds SSS 70
Recs Am–67 D Black JP Arnott M Nicholson G Gilhespy
Pro–67 I Waugh
V'trs U
Fees £5.50 (£6.50); W–£25; M–£50
Loc 21 miles W Newcastle-upon-Tyne

Magdalene Fields (1903)

Public (Map 5/16)
Berwick-upon-Tweed
Tel 0289 5109
Mem 160
Sec I Campbell Tel 0289 5380
Pro
Holes 18 L 6551 yds SSS 71
Recs Am–71 S Rutter
JA Hume
Pro–
V'trs U
Fees £1.50 W–£7
Loc 5 mins Berwick centre

Morpeth (1907)

Private (Map 5/17)
The Common Morpeth
Tel **0670 519980**
Mem 500
Sec T Weddell Tel 0670 55828
Pro MR Jackson Tel 0670 512065
Holes 18 L 5671 metres SSS 70
Recs Am–
Pro–
V'trs H
Fees £6.50 (£8)
Loc On A197 1 mile S of town

Newbiggin-by-the-Sea (1984)

Private (Map 5/18)
Newbiggin-by-the-Sea
Tel **Ashington 817344**
Mem 500
Sec WR Dent Tel Ashington 816078
Pro D Fletcher Tel Ashington 817833
Holes 18 L 6450 yds SSS 71
Recs Am–67 B Bennett
Pro–68 K Saint
V'trs U
Fees £4.50 W/E & BH–£6 W–£20
Loc Newbiggin Village, near Church Point

Newcastle United (1890)

Private (Map 5/19)
60 Ponteland Road Newcastle-upon-Tyne NE5 3JW
Tel **Newcastle 28 64693 shop 2713200**
Mem 500
Sec J Simpson
Pro
Holes 18 L 6484 yds SSS 71
Recs Am–69 J Simmonds
Pro–
V'trs WD–U; W/E–M; SOC
Fees £4.50
Loc Nuns Moor Cowgate

Northumberland (1898)

Private (Map 5/20)
High Gosforth Park Newcastle-upon-Tyne NE3 5HT
Tel **(091) 2362009**
Mem 500
Sec H Jones Tel (091) 2362498
Pro
Holes 18 L 6629 yds SSS 72
Recs Am–68 DP Davidson
PWS Bent DM Moffatt
Pro–65 A Jacklin
T Horton
V'trs WD–I; W/E & BH–M
Fees £15
Loc 4 miles N of Newcastle-upon-Tyne

Ponteland (1927)

Private (Map 5/21)
53 Bell Villas Ponteland Newcastle-upon-Tyne NE20 9BD
Tel **Ponteland 72844**
Mem 460 150(L) 95(J) 30(5)
Sec/ Man G Weetman
Pro I Clark Tel Ponteland 22689
Holes 18 L 6512 yds SSS 71
Recs Am–66 J Hayes
WMM Jenkins
Pro–66 Gaylord Burrows (USA)
V'trs WD–U; W/E & BH–M
Fees R–£7.50 D–£9
Loc 1 mile beyond Airport 6 miles NW of city on A696

Prudhoe (1930)

Private (Map 5/22)
Eastwood Park Prudhoe-on-Tyne Northumberland NE42 5DX
Tel **Prudhoe 32466**
Mem 400
Sec RA Lockey Tel Prudhoe 34134
Pro
Holes 18 L 5812 yds 68
Recs Am–65 DH Curry
Pro–65 A Crosby
V'trs WD–U; SOC W/E–M

Fees £4.50 (£6) D–£5.50
Loc A695 E approach
Mis 15 miles W of Newcastle-upon-Tyne

Rothbury (1890)

Private (Map 5/23)
On Race Course Rothbury
Tel **Rothbury 20718**
Mem 200
Sec WT Bathgate
Pro
Holes 9 L 5108 metres SSS 67
Recs Am–67 D Weddell
Pro–
V'trs U
Fees £1.75 (£3.50)
Loc 15 miles S of Morpeth

Seahouses (1916)

Private (Map 5/24)
Beadnell Road Seahouses Northumberland NE68 7XT
Tel 0665 720794
Mem 250
Sec Gordon Hogg Tel 0665 720091
Pro None
Holes 18 L 5399 yds SSS 66
Recs Am–64
Pro–
V'trs U SOC
Fees £4.50 (£6) W–£18
Loc 14 miles N of Alnwick (9 miles off A1)

Stocksfield (1913)

Private (Map 5/25)
New Ridley NE43 7RE
Tel (0661) 843041
Mem 341 79(L) 70 (J)
Sec DB Moon Tel 0661 842264
Pro Ken Driver Tel 0661 843041
Holes 18 L 6050 yds SSS 70
Recs Am–61 GED Bradley
Pro–66 P Harrison
V'trs U SOC
Fees £6 (£8)
Loc 3 miles E of A68 1 mile S A686

Tynedale (1908)

Public (Map 5/26)
Tyne Green Hexham
Tel
Mem 250
Sec K Peacock Tel Hexham 605701
Pro
Holes 9 L 5706 yds SSS 68
Recs Am–64 A Varty
Pro–
V'trs U (Ex Sun–Bookings only)
Fees £2 (£3) W–£6
Loc South side Hexham

Tynemouth (1913)

Private (Map 5/27)
Spital Dene Tynemouth North Shields NE30 2ER
Tel **091-574578**
Mem 854
Sec A Turnbull Tel 091-573381
Pro J McKenna Tel 091-580728
Holes 18 L 6351 yds SSS 70
Recs Am–66 CR Hinson
Pro–64 J Ord
V'trs WD–U SOC; Sat & Sun am–NA
Fees £6.50 (£8.50) W–£22 F–£40
Loc E of Newcastle-upon-Tyne

Wallsend (1973)

Public (Map 5/28)
Bigges Main Wallsend
Tel **Wallsend 2624231**
Mem 800
Sec John Heddon Tel Wallsend 2628478
Pro R Phipps
Holes 18 L 6459 yds SSS 72
Recs Am–
Pro–
V'trs U
Fees £3.20 (£4.05)
Loc Western boundary

Warkworth (1891)

Private (Map 5/29)
The Links Warkworth Northumberland
Tel **Warkworth 596**
Mem 400
Sec HE Slaughter Tel Morpeth 760270
Pro
Holes 9 L 5817 yds SSS 68
Recs Am–67 AR Barrett
Pro–
V'trs U
Fees £4 (£6)
Loc 15 miles NE of Morpeth

Westerhope GC

Private (Map 5/30)
Whorlton Grange Westerhope Newcastle-upon-Tyne NE5 1PP
Tel **Newcastle 2869125**
Mem 760
Sec D Rawlinson Tel Newcastle 2867636
Pro A Crosby Tel Newcastle 2860594
Holes 18 L 6407 yds SSS 71
Recs Am–66 A Morrison R Roper
Ladies Am–72 Miss C Hall
Pro–67 D Russell
V'trs U
Fees £6 (£7.50)
Loc 5 miles W of Newcastle

Whitley Bay (1890)

Private (Map 5/31)
Claremount Road Whitley Bay NE26 3UF
Tel **(091) 252 0180**
Mem 700
Sec A Bamber Tel (091) 252 0180
Pro WJ Light Tel (091) 252 5688
Holes 18 L 6614 yds SSS 72
Recs Am–68 Gordon J Clark
Pro–66 John Fourie
V'trs WD–U; W/E–M
Fees £6.50
Loc 10 miles E of Newcastle-upon Tyne

Wooler (1975)

Private (Map 5/33)
Doddington Wooler Northumberland
Tel
Mem 200
Sec RJ Macdonald Tel (0668) 81408
Pro
Holes 9 L 6327 yds SSS 71
Recs Am–
Pro–
V'trs U SOC
Fees D–£3 W–£10
Loc 2 miles NE of Wooler on Berwick road

Yorkshire

Abbeydale (1895)

Private (Map 5/1)
Twentywell Lane Dore nr Sheffield SL17 4QA
Tel Sheffield 360763
Mem 700
Sec Mrs KM Johnston
Pro S Cooper Tel Sheffield 365633
Holes 18 L 6419 yds SSS 71
Recs Am–
Pro–
V'trs U SOC Tue Fri by arrangement
Fees £10 (£12)
Loc 5 miles S of Sheffield

Aldwark Manor (1977)

Private (Map 5/144)
Aldwark Manor Aldwark Alne York YO6 2NF
Tel 03473 251
Mem 250
Man Brian C Horner Tel 03473 251
Holes 9 L 2612 yds (18 hole 5172) SSS 67
V'trs SOC
Fees WD with mem R–£3.50 (WE with mem R–£6.50) Jnrs £2 Hotel guests free use of course
Loc 5 miles SE of Boroughbridge off A1; 11½ miles NW of York off A19

Alwoodley (1908)

Private (Map 5/2)
Wigton Lane Alwoodley Leeds LS17 8SA
Tel **Leeds 681680**
Mem 450
Sec TG Turnbull
Pro Ian Duncan Tel Leeds 689603
Holes 18 L 6672 yds SSS 72
Recs Am–68 F Haughton
Pro–68 D Fitton
V'trs WD–U
Fees £12 (£15)
Loc 5 miles N of Leeds

Ampleforth College (1962)

Private (Map 5/145)
56 High Street Helmsley York YO6 5AE (Hon Sec–no clubhouse)
Mem 100
Sec JE Atkinson Tel Helmsley (0439) 70678
Holes 10 L 4018 yds SSS 63
V'trs U exc WD 2–4 pm; SOC on WD
Fees £2 (£4)
Loc Driveway to Gilling Castle in centre of Gilling East Village. 18 miles N of York on B1363
Mis Green fees payable at Fairfax Arms East Gilling

Austerfield Park (1974)

Private (Map 5/3)
Cross Lane Austerfield Bawtry nr Doncaster
Tel **(0302) 710841**
Mem 360 35(L) 40(J) 65(5)
Sec Alan Bradley Tel (0709) 540928
Pro Nick Newman (0302) 710850
Holes 18 L 6824 yds SSS 73
Recs Am–74 Malcolm Stubley
Pro–74 Ashley Carter

V'trs U
Fees £6 (£8)
Loc 2 miles NE Bawtry off A614
Mis 10-bay driving range

Baildon (1898)

Private (Map 5/4)
Moorgate Baildon Shipley BD17 5PP
Tel **Shipley 584266**
Mem 700
Sec D Farnsworth Tel Bradford 599215
Pro D Sutcliffe Tel Shipley 595162
Holes 18 L 6085 yds SSS 69
Recs Am–66 D Farnsworth
Pro–64 G Brand D Durnian
V'trs U
Fees £4 (£6.60)
Loc 5 miles NW of Bradford

Barnsley (1925)

Public (Map 5/5)
Staincross nr Barnsley
Tel **Barnsley 382856**
Mem 628
Sec Mrs K Southern
Pro M Melling Tel Barnsley 382954
Holes 18 L 6048 yds SSS 69
Recs Am–65 RI Shaw
T Chambers
Pro–69 M Melling
V'trs U
Fees £2.70 (£3.20)
Loc 4 miles N of Barnsley

Beauchief Municipal (1925)

Abbey Lane Sheffield
Tel **Sheffield 360648**
Mem 350
Sec P Rose Tel Retford 705018
Pro Brian English
Holes 18 L 5428 yds SSS 66
Recs Am–65 PW Hickinson
Pro–63 P Tupling
V'trs U
Fees £2.50 (£3)
Loc A621 Sheffield

Bedale (1896)

Private (Map 5/7)
Leyburn Road Bedale N Yorks DL8 1EZ
Tel **Bedale 22568**
Mem 390 90(L) 70(J)
Sec GA Shepherdson Tel Bedale 22451
Pro AD Johnson Tel Bedale 22443
Holes 18 L 5551 yds SSS 66
Recs Am–66 J Swain
Pro–64 John Hughes
V'trs U; SOC
Fees £6 (£7.50)
Loc North boundary Bedale

Ben Rhydding (1948)

Private (Map 5/8)
High Wood Ben Rhydding Ilkley
Tel **Ilkley 608759**
Mem 200 70(L) 35(J)
Sec JDB Watts
Pro
Holes 9 L 4711 yds SSS 64
Recs Am–65 AG Atkins
Pro–64 G Brand Senr
V'trs U
Fees £5 (£5)
Loc Ilkley

Beverley and East Riding (1889)

Private (Map 5/9)
The Westwood Beverley N Humberside HU17 8RG
Tel **(0482) 8671900**
Mem 460
Sec GE Fenn Tel (0482) 868757
Pro I Mackie Tel (0482) 869519
Holes 18 L 5937 yds SSS 68
Recs Am–64 I Woodhead
D Hannam
Pro–69 NS Bundy
V'trs U SOC on WD
Fees £4.50 (£6)
Loc Beverley Walkington Road

Bingley (St Ives) (1931)

Public (Map 5/10)
St Ives Estate Bingley
Tel **Bradford 562506**
Mem 650
Sec R Toothill Tel Bradford 564280
Pro R Firth Tel Bradford 562506
Holes 18 L 6466 yds SSS 71
Recs Am–70 WM Hopkinson
Pro–62 N Faldo
V'trs WD–U before 4.30 pm
Fees £4 (£7)
Loc 6 miles W of Bradford

Birley Wood (1974)

Private (Map 5/11)
Birley Lane Sheffield S12 3BP
Tel **Sheffield 390099**
Mem 400
Sec K Thompson Tel Sheffield 389198
Pro S Sherratt Tel Sheffield 390099
Holes 18 L 6275 yds SSS 70
Recs Am–
Pro–
V'trs U
Fees £3.50 (£5)
Loc 4 miles S of Sheffield on A616 to M1

Boothferry (Spaldington) (1981)

Public (Map 5/12)
Spaldington Lane Spaldington Howden Goole
Tel **Howden 30364**
Mem 900
Sec A Atkin Tel Goole 5141
Pro Stewart Wilkinson
Holes 18 L 6593 yds SSS 72
Recs Am–71 D Gisbourne
Pro–70 M Ingham
V'trs
Fees £4.20 (£6)
Loc From Howden N 3 miles on B1228

Bradford (1891)

Private (Map 5/13)
Hawksworth Lane Guiseley Leeds LS20 8NP
Tel **Guiseley 75570**
Mem 500
Sec GA Richardson Tel Guiseley 75570
Pro S Weldon Tel Guiseley 73719
Holes 18 L 6259 yds SSS 70
Recs Am–68 MJ Kelly
Pro–
V'trs WD–U W/E–not before noon SOC on WD
Fees
Loc 8 miles N of Bradford

Bradford Moor (1907)

Private (Map 5/14)
Scarr Hall Pollard Lane Bradford
Tel (0274) 638313
Mem 375
Sec IR Scaife
Pro RJ Hughes Tel (0274) 631163
Holes 9 L 5854 yds SSS 68
Recs Am–68 Ian Helliwell
Pro–69 H Waller
V'trs U
Fees £4.50 (£6.50)
Loc

Bradley Park (1978)

Public (Map 5/15)
Bradley Road Huddersfield W Yorks
Tel Huddersfield 539988
Mem 250 24(L) 12(J)
Sec G Hepworth Tel Huddersfield 538704
Pro P Reilly
Holes 18 L 6159 yds SSS 69
Recs Am–66 M Ingham
Pro–67 Mark James
V'trs U; SOC
Fees £2.75 (£4)
Loc 1½ miles from M62 exit 25

Branshaw (1912)

Private (Map 5/16)
Branshaw Moor Oakworth nr Keighley
Tel **Haworth 43235**
Mem 238 29(L) 45(J) 50(5)
Sec P Maddocks
Pro
Holes 18 L 5121 yds SSS 65
Recs Am–68 P Clayton
Pro–
V'trs U
Fees £3 (£5)
Loc 2½ miles W of Keighley

Bridlington (1905)

Private (Map 5/17)
Belvedere Road Bridlington YO15 3NA
Tel (0262) 672092
Mem 825
Sec GR Moody Tel (0262) 672561
Pro D Rands Tel (0262) 674721
Holes 18 L 6320 yds SSS 70
Recs Am–
Pro–
V'trs U Sun–Visitors from 11 am
Fees £5 D–£8 (£7 D–£10)
Loc 1½ miles Bridlington Station

Brough (1891)

Private (Map 5/18)
Brough HU15 1HB
Tel **Hull 667374**
Mem 550
Sec HJ Oldroyd Tel Hull 667291
Pro G Townhill Tel Hull 667483
Holes 18 L 6012 yds SSS 69
Recs Am–64 PWJ Greenhough
MJ Kelley
Pro–63 A Thompson
V'trs WD–U Weds after 2 pm
Fees £10
Loc 10 miles W of Hull on A63

Calverley (1984)

Private (Map 5/149)
Woodhall Lane Pudsey Yorks LS28 5JX
Tel (0532) 569244

Mem 300
Sec Alan Sheard
Pro
Holes 18 L 5516 yds SSS 67 9 hole course
Recs Am–71 M Hedley
Pro–
V'trs WD–U; WE–Sat and Sun pm only
Fees £3 per round
Loc 4 miles NE of Bradford

Castle Fields (1900)

Private (Map 5/148)
Rastrick Common Brighouse
Tel
Mem 140
Sec P Bentley Tel Brighouse 712108
Pro
Holes 6 L 2406 yds SSS 50
Recs Am–
Pro–
V'trs M at all times
Fees £1.50
Loc 1 mile S of Brighouse

Catterick Garrison (1930)

Private (Map 5/19)
Leyburn Road Catterick Garrison N Yorks DL9 3QE
Tel (0748) 833268
Mem 420
Sec Major CG Sandys Tel (0748) 833268
Pro Stephen McNally Tel (0748) 833671
Holes 18 L 6336 yds SSS 70
Recs Am–68 RM Roper
Pro–69 David Edwards
V'trs U
Fees £7 (£10)
Loc Catterick Garrison

City of Wakefield (1936)

Public (Map 5/20)
Lupset Park Horbury Road Wakefield WF2 8QS
Tel **Wakefield 374316**
Mem **500**
Sec **OS Ward Tel Wakefield 376214**
Pro **R Holland Tel Wakefield 360282**
Holes **18 L 6405 yds SSS 71**
Recs **Am–67 D Oxley**
G Andrews
Pro–68 M Ingham
V'trs **WD–U; W/E & BH–NA certain times: enquire Sec; SOC on weekdays**
Fees £2.94 (£4.60)
Loc **A642 2 miles W of Wakefield 2 miles E of M1 junctions 39 or 40**

Clayton (1906)

Private (Map 5/21)
Thornton View Road Clayton Bradford
Tel **Bradford 880047**
Mem 180 35(L) 35(J)
Sec FV Wood Tel Bradford 814628
Pro
Holes 9 L 5515 yds SSS 67
Recs Am–65 ND Hawkins
Pro–
V'trs WD–U; Sat–U Sun–NA before 4 pm
Fees £2.50 (£3.50)
Loc Clayton 2 miles W of city centre

Cleckheaton and District (1900)

Private (Map 5/22)
483 Bradford Road Cleckheaton
Tel 0274 874118
Mem 500
Sec Mrs P Bates Tel 0274 877851
Pro Michael Ingham Tel 0274 870707
Holes **18 L 5994 yds SSS 69**
Recs **Am–63 C Bloice**
Pro–
V'trs **U**
Fees **£7 (£9) Special party rates over 25**
Loc **Intersection 26 of M62 then A638 (Bradford) 200 yds**

Cleveland (1887)

Private (Map 5/23)
Queen Street Redcar TS10 1BT
Tel Redcar 483693
Mem 674
Sec GAE Toon Tel Redcar 471798
Pro Don Masey Tel Redcar 483462
Holes 18 L 6707 yds SSS 72
Recs Am–68 M Watson
NBJ Fick
Pro–70 B Hardcastle
V'trs WD–after 9.30 am Sun/BH no visiting parties; SOC on application
Fees £6.90 (£11.50) 50% reduction with member
Loc S bank River Tees mouth

Concord Park (1952)

Public (Map 5/24)
Shiregreen Lane Sheffield S5
Tel
Mem 147
Sec JA Bennett Tel (0742) 613605
Pro
Holes 18 L 4280 yds SSS 61
Recs Am–
Pro–
V'trs U
Fees £2 (£2.50)
Loc 1 mile junction 34 M1

Crimple Valley (1976)

Private (Map 5/25)
Hookstone Wood Road Harrogate
Tel 0423 883485
Mem 200
Sec J Lumb
Pro Robin A Lumb
Holes 9 L 2500 yds SSS 33
Recs Am–
Pro–
V'trs U
Fees £1.50
Loc Yorkshire Showground

Crookhill Park (1973)

Public (Map 5/26)
Conisbrough nr Doncaster
Tel 0709 862979
Mem 400
Sec DM Parry Tel 0709 863466
Pro
Holes 18 L 5846 yds SSS 68
Recs Am–67 R Jones
Pro–70
V'trs U
Fees £2 (£3)
Loc 3 miles W of Doncaster on A630

Crosland Heath (1914)

Private (Map 5/27)
Crosland Heath Huddersfield
Tel (0484) 653216
Mem 320
Sec D Walker Tel (0484) 653262
Pro S Kettlewell Tel (0484) 653877
Holes 18 L 5961 yds SSS 70
Recs Am–66 S Ellis
Pro–65 SW Dellar
V'trs U
Fees £6.50 (£8.50) SOC–£13 (£15) inc meals
Loc 3 miles W of Huddersfield

Dewsbury District (1891)

Private (Map 5/28)
The Pinnacle Mirfield W Yorks
Tel **(0924) 492399**
Mem 400
Sec P Bates Tel (0924) 492399/498673 (home)
Pro N Hirst Tel (0924) 496030
Holes **18 L 6256 yds SSS 70**
Recs **Am–68 M Colcombe**
Pro–69 G Townhill
V'trs **U SOC**
Fees **£5 (£7) £3.50 (£5.50) with mem**
Loc **West boundary Dewsbury**

Doncaster (1895)

Private (Map 5/29)
Bawtry Road Bessacarr nr Doncaster DN4 7PD
Tel **Doncaster 868316**
Mem **360**
Sec **F Colley Tel Doncaster 537815**
Pro **M Birkett Tel Doncaster 868404**
Holes **18 L 6230 yds SSS 70**
Recs **Am–66 H Green**
Pro–66 H Clark
V'trs **UH (not before 11 am W/E & BH) SOC on WD**
Fees **£7 (£9) incl VAT**
Loc **4½ miles S of Doncaster**

Doncaster Town Moor (1900)

Private (Map 5/30)
Neatherds House Bellevue Doncaster DN4 5HV
Tel Doncaster 535286
Mem 400
Sec JC Padley Tel Doncaster 535458
Pro G Bailey Tel Doncaster 535286
Holes 18 L 6103 yds SSS 69
Recs **Am–67 K Howarth**
Pro–69 D Snell
V'trs **U (none on Sun before 11.30 am)**
Fees **£5 (£6)**
Loc **Inside Racecourse**
Mis **Societies please contact Sec for tee reservations. No catering Mondays**

Dore and Totley (1913)

Private (Map 5/31)
Bradway Road Bradway nr Sheffield S17 4QR
Tel (0742) 360492
Mem 600
Sec KMC Stoneman Tel (0742) 369872
Pro **P Cowen Tel (0742) 366844**
Holes **18 L 6301 yds SSS 70**
Recs **Am–K Gozzard**
Pro–P Cowen
V'trs **WD–U; W/E & BH–M**
Fees £7.50
Loc 5 miles SW of town centre

Driffield (1938)

Private (Map 5/32)
Sunderlandwick Driffield
Tel **Driffield 43116**
Mem 350
Sec K Pickles Tel Driffield 44069
Pro
Holes 9 L 6227 yds SSS 70
Recs Am–
Pro–
V'trs U
Fees £6 (£9)
Loc 10 miles S of Bridlington

Easingwold (1930)

Private (Map 5/33)
Stillington Road Easingwold York YO6 3ET
Tel **Easingwold 21486**
Mem 560
Sec KC Hudson
Pro John Hughes Tel Easingwold 21964
Holes 18 L 6262 yds SSS 70
Recs Am–68 A Shepherd
Pro–67 D Padgett
V'trs U
Fees D–£9 (WE & BH–£12)
Loc 12 miles N of York on A19

East Bierley (1928)

Private (Map 5/34)
South View Road Bradford
Tel **Bradford 681023**
Mem 145 47(L) 38(J)
Sec JR Driscoll
Pro
Holes 9 L 4692 yds SSS 63
Recs Am–59 R Watts
Pro–62 B Hill
V'trs U
Fees £3.50 (£5.75)
Loc SE of Bradford 4 miles

Elland (1910)

Private (Map 5/35)
Hullen Edge Elland
Tel **Elland 72505**
Mem 350
Sec WH Pearson Tel Elland 73276
Pro Mr P Leach
Holes 9 L 2763 yds SSS 66
Recs Am–65 PS Cockroft
Pro–
V'trs U
Fees £3 (£5)
Loc ½ mile town centre

Filey (1897)

Private (Map 5/36)
South Cliff Filey
Tel **Scarborough 513293**
Sec John Winship Tel Scarborough 513293
Pro DW Currey Tel Scarborough 513134
Holes 18 L 6025 yds SSS 69
Recs Am–66 AS Roberts
Pro–64 AS Murray
V'trs H SOC
Fees £8 (£10)
Loc Filey

Flamborough Head (1932)

Private (Map 5/37)
Flamborough Head
Tel (0262) 850333
Mem 325
Sec DP Davison Tel (0262) 675897
Pro
Holes 18 L 5438 yds SSS 66
Recs Am–63 GR Allen
Pro–63 P Dawson
V'trs U SOC
Fees £5.50 (£7.50) W–£22
Loc 5 miles NE of Bridlington

Fulford (York) (1909)

Private (Map 5/38)
Heslington Lane York YO1 5DY
Tel York 413212
Mem 580
Sec JCA Gledhill Tel York 413579
Pro B Hessay Tel York 412882 (requests for visits)
Holes 18 L 6779 yds SSS 72
Recs Am–69 W Duston
Pro–62 I Woosnam
B Dassu
V'trs By prior arrangements
Fees £15 (£17)
Loc 2 miles S of York centre
Mis Venue for Benson and Hedges International Open

Fulneck (1892)

Private (Map 5/39)
Pudsey
Tel **Pudsey 565191**
Mem 230
Sec John Allan Tel Bradford 663349
Pro
Holes 9 L 5564 yds SSS 67
Recs Am–64 I Holdsworth
Pro–
V'trs WD–U SOC; W/E & BH–M
Fees £4 (£3)
Loc 5 miles W of Leeds

Ganstead Park (1976)

Private (Map 5/40)
Longdales Lane Coniston Hull North Humberside HU11 4LB
Tel (0482) 811280
Mem 350
Sec G Hague Tel (0482) 811280
Pro Mike Smee (0482) 811121
Holes 9 L 5769 yds SSS 68
Recs Am–68 C Gaines
Pro–67 Howard Clark
Mike Smee
V'trs U
Fees £5 (£9)
Loc E of Hull

Ganton (1891)

Private (Map 5/41)
Station Road Ganton Scarborough YO12 4PA
Tel (0944) 70329
Mem 600
Sec Air Vice Marshal RG Price CB
Pro Ian Bamborough Tel (0944) 70260
Holes 18 L 6693 yds SSS 73
Recs Am–67 Ian Caldwell
Pro–65 N Coles
V'trs By prior arrangement
Fees On application
Loc 9 miles from Scarborough on A64

Garforth (1913)

Private (Map 5/42)
Long Lane Garforth Leeds LS25 2DS
Tel Leeds 862021
Mem 550
Sec FA Readman Tel Leeds 863308
Pro K Findlater Tel Leeds 862063
Holes 18 L 6327 yds SSS 70
Recs Am–63 AR Gelsthorpe
Pro–
V'trs WD–UH; W/E & BH–M
Fees £10 (£12)
Loc 9 miles E of Leeds between Garforth and Barwick-in-Elmet

Ghyll (1907)

Private (Map 5/43)
Ghyll Brow Barnoldswick
Tel **Earby 842466**
Mem 225
Sec H Best Tel Skipton 2587
Pro
Holes 9 L 5706 yds SSS 68
Recs Am–67 M Davies
Pro–
V'trs U
Fees £4 (W/E & BH–£5)
Loc 1 mile Barnoldswick

Gotts Park (1934)

Public (Map 5/44)
Armley Ridge Road Armley Leeds 12
Tel **Leeds 638232**
Mem 250
Sec F Walker Tel Leeds 684865
Pro JK Simpson Tel Leeds 636600
Holes 18 L 4594 yds Par 65 SSS 62
V'trs U
Fees £2.75 (W/E & BH–£3)
Loc 2 miles W of city centre

Grange Park (1972)

Public (Map 5/45)
Upper Wortley Road Rotherham S61 2SJ
Tel (0709) 559497
Mem 486
Sec A Coultas Tel (0709) 540654
Pro E Clark Tel (0709) 559497
Holes 18 L 6461 yds SSS 71
Recs Am–68 J Beckitt
Pro–68 G Tickell
V'trs U
Fees £2.10 (£2.65)
Loc 2 miles W of town on A629

Hainsworth Park (1983)

Private (Map 5/146)
Brandesburton Driffield North Humberside
Mem 200
Prop Bryan Atkin Tel 0401 42362
Holes 9 L 5350 yds SSS 66
V'trs WD–U before 5 pm; WE–U after 4 pm; SOC on WD
Fees £3.50 (£5)
Loc A165, 8 miles N Beverley
Mis Parkland course; catering available

Halifax (1895)

Private (Map 5/46)
Ogden Halifax
Tel 0422 244171
Mem 450
Sec JB Kitchen Tel 0422 58178
Pro P Johnson Tel 0422 240047
Holes 18 L 6038 yds SSS 70
Recs Am–66 J Robinson
AMA Bagott
J Rushworth
Pro–65 PW Good
V'trs U; W/E–parties welcome; SOC
Fees £5 (£8) Special rates for parties
Loc 4 miles N town centre on A629

Halifax Bradley Hall (1907)

Private (Map 5/47)
Holywell Green Halifax
Tel Elland 74108
Mem 520
Sec AM Green Tel Huddersfield 646905
Pro P Wood Tel Elland 70231
Holes 18 L 6213 yds SSS 70
Recs Am–67 CD Doyle
Pro–
V'trs U
Fees £6 (£9)
Loc South of Halifax on A6112

Halifax West End (1913)

Private (Map 5/48)
Highroad Well Halifax
Tel Halifax 53608
Mem 350 135(L) 53(J)
Sec J Gill Tel Halifax 54803
Pro D Rishworth Tel Halifax 63293
Holes 18 L 6003 yds SSS 69
Recs Am–65 JR Crawshaw
Pro–64 AJ Bickerdike
V'trs U
Fees £6.50 (£8.50)
Loc 2 miles NW of Halifax

Hallamshire (1897)

Private (Map 5/49)
The Club House Sandygate Sheffield S10 4LA
Tel (0742) 302153
Mem 600
Sec R Burns Tel (0742) 302153
Pro G Tickell Tel (0742) 305222
Holes 18 L 6396 yds SSS 71
Recs Am–68 JA Howarth
Pro–63 JW Wilkinson
V'trs I
Fees £10 (£12)
Loc Western boundary Sheffield

Hallowes (1892)

Private (Map 5/50)
Dronfield Sheffield S18 6UA
Tel Dronfield 413149
Mem 600
Sec J Palmer Tel Dronfield 413734
Pro P Seal Tel Dronfield 411196
Holes 18 L 6366 yds SSS 71
Recs Am–67 JW Benson
Pro–67 R Ellis
V'trs U–W/E & BH–M; please telephone in advance
Fees £7 D–£9
Loc 6 miles S of Sheffield on A61 (not by-pass)

Hanging Heaton (1922)

Private (Map 5/51)
Whitecross Road Dewsbury WF12 7DT
Tel Dewsbury 461606
Mem 550
Sec SM Simpson Tel Dewsbury 461729
Pro R Jessop Tel Dewsbury 467077
Holes 9 L 2917 yds SSS 67
Recs Am–66 P Cockburn
Pro–AJ Bickerdyke
V'trs WD–U; W/E–restricted
Fees £5 (£7)
Loc A653 ¾ mile from town centre

Harrogate (1892)

Private (Map 5/52)
Forest Lane Head Starbeck Harrogate HG2 7TF
Tel Harrogate (0423) 863158
Mem 620
Sec RA Mayo Tel Harrogate (0423) 862999
Pro P Johnson Tel Harrogate (0423) 862547
Holes 18 L 6204 yds SSS 70
Recs Am–65 P Hall
Pro–64 D Durnian
V'trs WD–U; W/E & BH–enquiry necessary; SOC Mon–Thu
Fees £10.50 (£15)
Loc 2 miles Harrogate on Knaresborough Road (A59)

Headingley (1892)

Private (Map 5/53)
Adel Leeds LS16 8DW
Tel Leeds 673052
Mem 550
Sec WFD Elliott Tel Leeds 679573
Pro Chris W Green Tel Leeds 675100
Holes 18 L 6238 yds SSS 70
Recs Am–66 B Teasdale
Pro–67 GR Tickell
V'trs U
Fees £11 (W/E & BH R–£13 D–£15)
Loc 5 miles NW of city centre off A660 Leeds–Otley Road

Headley (1906)

Private (Map 5/54)
Lower Kipping Lane Thornton nr Bradford
Tel Bradford 833348
Mem 150
Sec JP Clark Tel Brad 814072
Pro
Holes 9 L 2457 yds SSS 64
Recs Am–62 A Cording
Pro–65 M Ingham
V'trs U (ex Sun)
Fees £2 (£4)
Loc Thornton 5 miles W of Bradford

Hessle (1906)

Private (Map 5/55)
Westfield Road Cottingham
Tel Hull 650171
Mem 600
Sec RL Dorsey Tel Hull 650171
Pro G Fieldsend Tel Hull 650190
Holes 18 L 6638 SSS 72 or 6290 SSS 70
Recs Am–68 A Wright
Pro–69 B Thompson
V'trs WD–U exc Tue 9.15 am–1 pm; W/E–M
Fees £6.50 (£9.50) W–£20 M–£40 Quarter–£70
Loc 3 miles SW of Cottingham

Heworth (1912)

Private (Map 5/56)
Muncaster House Muncastergate York YO3 9JX
Tel York 424618
Mem 245 80(L) 50(J) 60(5)
Sec KT Sawyers Tel York 490608 (home)
Pro SI Robinson Tel York 422389
Holes 11 L 6078 yds SSS 69
Recs Am–67 SJ Gledhill
Pro–72 D Durnian
V'trs U (Sundays not before noon) SOC on WD
Fees £6 (£7)
Loc NE boundary of York A64

Hickleton (1909)

Private (Map 5/57)
Hickleton nr Doncaster S Yorks
Tel Rotherham 892496
Mem 485
Sec R Jowett Tel Rotherham 893506
Pro K Bradley Tel Rotherham 895170
Holes 18 L 6373 yds SSS 70
Recs Am–68 A Bowkett
Pro–
V'trs WD Sat am and Sun pm–U; SOC
Fees Mon (exc BH) £4.50 £5.50 (£8)
Loc 6 miles W Doncaster; Hickleton village on A635 between Doncaster and Barnsley

Hillsborough (1920)

Private (Map 5/58)
Worrall Road Sheffield S6 4BE
Tel Sheffield 343608
Mem 713
Sec AW Platts Tel Sheffield 349151
Pro G Walker Tel Sheffield 332666
Holes 18 L 5672 metres SSS 70
Recs Am–
Pro–
V'trs U
Fees £7.50 (£9.50)
Loc Wadsley Sheffield

Hornsea (1908)

Private (Map 5/59)
Rolston Road Hornsea
Tel Hornsea 2020
Mem 550
Sec BW Kirton Tel Hornsea 2020
Pro B Thompson Tel Hornsea 4989
Holes 18 L 6461 yds SSS 71
Recs Am–65 P Binnington
Pro–67 B Thompson
V'trs WD–U; W/E-Restricted
Fees £7.50 (£10)
Loc Hornsea

Horsforth (1907)

Private (Map 5/60)
Layton Rise Layton Road Hornsforth Leeds LS18 5EX
Tel (0532) 586819
Mem 402 80(L) 74(J) 80(5)
Sec CB Carrington Tel (0532) 586819
Pro G Howard Tel (0532) 585200
Holes 18 L 6293 yds SSS 70
Recs Am–67 S Lax
Pro–67 HW Muscroft
V'trs U
Fees D–£8 (D–£10) W–£25 M–£40
Loc 6 miles NW of Leeds

Howley Hall (1900)

Private (Map 5/61)
Scotchman Lane Morley Leeds LS27 0NX
Tel Batley 472432
Mem 465
Sec Mrs A Pepper Tel Batley 478417
Pro SA Spinks Tel Batley 473852
Holes 18 L 6446 yds SSS 71
Recs Am–66 S Hamer
M Kelly
Pro–
V'trs U
Fees R–£7 D–£9 WE–£10
Loc 4 miles SW Leeds

Huddersfield (1891)

Private (Map 5/62)
Fixby Hall Huddersfield HD2 2EP
Tel **Huddersfield 20110**
Mem 630
Sec J Tracey Tel Huddersfield 26203
Pro RC Peters Tel Huddersfield 26463
Holes 18 L 6437 yds SSS 71
Recs Am–66 JR Crawshaw C Hartland
Pro–66 G Thornhill
V'trs I; (members of recognised clubs)
Fees £11 (£13)
Loc City limits

Hull (1904)

Private (Map 5/63)
The Hall 27 Packman Lane Kirk Ella nr Hull HU10 7TJ
Tel Hull 653026
Mem 610
Sec R Toothill Tel Hull 658919
Pro M Grantham Tel Hull 653074
Holes 18 L 6242 yds SSS 70
Recs Am–64 JD Dockar R Roper
Pro–66 D Dunk N Hunt S Smith D Jagger
V'trs U; W/E–NA
Fees £10
Loc 5 miles W Kingston-upon-Hull

Ilkley (1889)

Private (Map 5/64)
Myddleton Ilkley
Tel **Ilkley 607277**
Mem 530
Sec PS Leneghan Tel Ilkley 600214
Pro JL Hammond Tel Ilkley 607463
Holes 18 L 6249 yds SSS 70
Recs Am–66 A Squires B Thompson
Pro–64 B Hutchinson
V'trs U
Fees £10.50 (£13)
Loc 18 miles from Leeds

Keighley (1904)

Private (Map 5/65)
Howden Park Utley Keighley
Tel **Keighley 603179**
Mem 500
Sec J Scott Tel Keighley 604778
Pro CAC Smith Tel Keighley 65370
Holes 18 L 6134 yds SSS 70
Recs Am–65 RS Mitchell
Pro–65 J Holchaks
V'trs U
Fees £7.50 (£9.50)
Loc 1 mile W of Keighley

Kirkbymoorside (1951)

Private (Map 5/66)
Manor Vale Kirkbymoorside York YO6 6EG
Tel **31525**
Mem 400
Sec WK Ashford
Pro
Holes 18 L 5783 yds SSS 68
Recs Am–K Magson
Pro–
V'trs U
Fees £6 (£7) W–£20
Loc A170 between Helmsley and Pickering

Knaresborough (1919)

Private (Map 5/67)
Boroughbridge Road Knaresborough HG5 9XX
Tel (0423) 863219
Mem 662
Sec KB Hirst Tel (0423) 862690
Pro K Johnstone Tel (0423) 864865
Holes 18 L 6281 yds SSS 70
Recs Am–68 D Walker
Pro–65 J King
V'trs U
Fees £7.50 (£10.50)
Loc 1½ miles N of Knaresborough

Leeds (1896)

Private (Map 5/68)
Elmete Lane Roundhay Leeds LS8 2LJ
Tel **Leeds 658775**
Mem 480
Sec GW Backhouse Tel Leeds 659203
Pro D Johnson Tel 658786
Holes 18 L 6097 yds SSS 69
Recs Am–64 J Whiteley
Pro–64 AJ Bickerdike
V'trs WD–U; W/E–M
Fees £7.50 (£10.50)
Loc Off A58 4 miles NE of Leeds

Lees Hall (1909)

Private (Map 5/69)
Hemsworth Road Norton Sheffield S8 8LL
Tel Sheffield 554402
Mem 700
Sec NE Westworth Tel Sheffield 552900
Pro JR Wilkinson Tel Sheffield 554402
Holes 18 L 6137 yds SSS 69
Recs Am–65 AR Gelsthorpe
Pro–63 B Hutchinson
V'trs U
Fees £7 (£9)
Loc 3½ miles S centre

Lightcliffe (1907)

Private (Map 5/70)
Knowle Top Road Lightcliffe
Tel **Halifax 202459**
Mem 145 92(L) 87(J)
Sec SG Donaldson Tel Halifax 202532
Pro Bob Parry Tel Halifax 202459
Holes 9 L 5368 metres SSS 68
Recs Am–66 PH Wolfe NRA Denham
Pro–
V'trs U; except competitions days and Sundays before noon–M
Fees £7 (£9)
Loc 3 miles E of Halifax

Lindrick (1891)

Private (Map 5/71)
Lindrick Common nr Worksop Notts S81 8BH
Tel **Worksop 472120**
Mem 500
Sec Eric Taylor Tel Worksop 475282
Pro Tel Worksop 475820
Holes 18 L 6615 yds SSS 72
Recs Am–65 DF Livingston
Pro–65 G Bond J Morgan
V'trs U with prior arrangement; NA Tue am; SOC on WD
Fees £14 (£15) Winter £10 (£12)
Loc 4 miles W of Worksop on A57; Exit 31 from M1 then 4½ miles towards Worksop on A57

Longley Park (1911)

Private (Map 5/72)
Maple Street off Somerset Road Huddersfield HD5 9AX
Tel **Huddersfield 22304**
Mem 400
Sec KLW Ireland Tel Hudds 29826
Pro D Chapman
Holes 9 L 5324 yds SSS 65
Recs Am–64 JD Oxley
Pro–65 PW Booth
V'trs U
Fees £3 (£5)
Loc ½ mile town centre

Low Laithes (1925)

Private (Map 5/73)
Parkmill Lane Flushdyke Ossett
Tel **Wakefield 273275**
Mem 450
Sec Donald Walker Tel Wakefield 376553
Pro P Browning Tel Wakefield 274667
Holes 18 L 6440 yds SSS 71
Recs Am–
Pro–68
V'trs U no visiting parties W/E
Fees £6 (W/E & BH–£8.50)
Loc 2 miles N of Wakefield. Motorway Junction 40

Malton and Norton (1923)

Private (Map 5/74)
Welham Park Norton Malton YO17 9QE
Tel **Malton 2959**
Mem 500 120(L) 50(J)
Sec Sqn Ldr CJH Fox MBE Tel 0653 7912
Pro ML Henderson Tel Malton 3882
Holes 18 L Medal 6401 Club 6141 SSS 71/69
Recs Am–
Pro–
V'trs U
Fees £7 (£10)
Loc Off Welham Road Norton

Marsden (1921)

Private (Map 5/75)
Hemplow Marsden nr Huddersfield
Tel (0484) 844253
Mem 180 36(L) 30(J)
Sec GC Scott Tel (0484) 537634
Pro D Chapman
Holes 9 L 2860 yds SSS 68
Recs Am–63 AJ Bickerdike
Pro–A Bickerdike
V'trs U
Fees £3.50 (£5)
Loc 8 miles S of Huddersfield

Masham (1900)

Private (Map 5/76)
Swinton Road Masham nr Ripon
Tel **Ripon 89379**
Mem 280
Sec SA Blades Tel Ripon 89251
Pro
Holes 9 L 5142 yds SSS 65
Recs Am–
Pro–
V'trs WD–U before 5 pm; W/E–M; BH–NA
Fees £6
Loc 10 miles N of Ripon

Meltham (1908)

Private (Map 5/77)
Thick Hollins Hall Meltham Huddersfield HD7 3DQ
Tel **Huddersfield 850227**
Mem 450
Sec BF Precious Tel Holmfirth 682106
Pro S Kettlewell
Holes 18 L 6145 yds SSS 70
Recs Am–68 AT Garner
Pro–69 W Casper
V'trs U
Fees £7 (£9)
Loc 5 miles W of Huddersfield

Middlesbrough (1908)

Private (Map 5/78)
Brass Castle Lane Middlesbrough TS8 9EE
Tel **Middlesbrough 316430**
Mem 900
Sec Mr JM Jackson Tel Middlesbrough 311515
Pro DJ Jones Tel Middlesbrough 311766
Holes 18 L 5582 metres SSS 69
Recs Am–61 R Boxall
Pro–66 D Jagger
V'trs U
Fees £8 D–£10
Loc 3 miles S of town centre

Middlesbrough Municipal (1977)

Public (Map 5/79)
Ladgate Lane Middlesbrough TS5 7YZ
Tel **(0642) 315533**
Mem 510
Sec J Dilworth Tel (0642) 468893
Pro M Nutter Tel (0642) 315361
Holes 18 L 6314 yds SSS 70
Recs Am–70 NBJ Fick
Pro–67 B Gallagher
V'trs U
Fees £3.50 (£4.50)
Loc 3 miles S Middlesbrough centre on A174 Redcar Road
Mis Floodlit driving range

Middleton Park (1934)

Public (Map 5/80)
Ring Road Beeston Park Middleton Leeds 10
Tel **Leeds 700449**
Mem 250
Sec G Hepworth Tel Leeds 892321
Pro D Bulmer Tel Leeds 709506
Holes 18 L 5233 yds SSS 66
Recs Am–
Pro–
V'trs U
Fees £2.20 (£2.40)
Loc 3 miles S of city centre

Moor Allerton (1923)

Private (Map 5/81
Coal Road Leeds LS17 9NH
Tel **Leeds 661154**
Mem 1200
Sec Ian Teff
Pro Howard Clark and Peter Blaze
Holes 18 L 6542 SSS
9 L 3541 yds SSS
Recs 18 holes Am–68
Pro–65
9 holes Am–
Pro–
V'trs WD–U SOC; Sat–only 24 v'trs; Sun–NA
Fees £15 (W/E & BH–£17) Reduced rates after 4 pm summer and Nov–Mar
Loc 5½ miles N of Leeds

Moortown (1909)

Private (Map 5/82)
Harrogate Road Leeds LS17 7DB
Tel Leeds 686521
Mem 500
Sec KM Baldwin Tel Leeds 686521
Pro B Hutchinson Tel Leeds 683636
Holes 18 L 6606 yds SSS 72
Recs Am–65 Duncan Muscroft
Pro–64 Wayne Riley
V'trs WD–U; W/E & BH–M and I
Fees £15 D–£18 W/E–£20
Loc 5½ miles N of Leeds

Mount Skip (1955)

Private (Map 5/83)
Wadsworth Hebden Bridge
Tel **Hebden Bridge 842896**
Mem 365
Sec Dr RG Pogson Tel Hebden Bridge 843733
Pro
Holes 9 L 5114 yds SSS 66
Recs Am–63 IS Marsland
Pro–M Ingham
V'trs U
Fees £5
Loc 1 mile N of town

Normanton (1903)

Private (Map 5/84)
Snydale Road Normanton Wakefield
Tel **Wakefield 892943**
Mem 150
Sec J Watson
Pro
Holes 9 L 5284 yds SSS 66
Recs Am–
Pro–
V'trs U Sundays–NA
Fees £2.50 (£4)
Loc

Northcliffe (1921)

Private (Map 5/85)
Highbank Lane Moorhead Shipley BD18 4LJ
Tel **Bradford 584085**
Mem 600
Sec R Hodgkinson Tel Bradford 596731
Pro S Poot Tel Bradford 587193
Holes 18 L 6065 yds SSS 69
Recs Am–67 R Bell
Pro–67 M James
V'trs U SOC
Fees £7 (£9) 1986 prices
Loc 3 miles NW of Bradford

Oakdale (1914)

Private (Map 5/86)
Off Kent Road Harrogate
Tel Harrogate 502806
Mem 700
Sec DVJ Kendall Tel Harrogate 67162
Pro Nigel Sumner Tel Harrogate 60510
Holes 18 L 6456 yds SSS 71
Recs Am–70 C McAllister
Pro–68 M Ingham
V'trs U SOC
Fees £9 (£11) R/D
Loc ½ mile NE Royal Hall Harrogate

Otley (1906)

Private (Map 5/87)
West Busk Lane Otley W Yorks LS21 3NG
Tel **Otley 461015**
Mem 600
Sec AF Flowers Tel Otley 465329
Pro S Rolley Tel Otley 463403
Holes 18 L 6235 yds SSS 70
Recs Am–68 JC Rigg
Pro–63 C Gray
V'trs U SOC
Fees £10 (£12)
Loc Off Bradford Road Otley.

Outlane (1906)

Private (Map 5/88)
Slack Lane Outlane Huddersfield
Tel **Elland 74762**
Mem 300
Sec P Sykes
Pro Andrew Dyson
Holes 18 L 5590 yds SSS 67
Recs Am–62 G Crosland
Pro–62 W Garside
V'trs U
Fees £5 (£7)
Loc Nr M62 4 miles W of Huddersfield

Painthorpe House (1961)

Private (Map 5/89)
Painthorpe Lane Crigglestone nr Wakefield
Tel **Wakefield 255083**
Mem 120
Sec H Kershaw Tel Horbury 274527
Pro
Holes 9 L 4108 yds SSS 60
Recs Am–64 J Turner J Whitehouse
Pro–
V'trs U
Fees £2–Mon/Fri £3–Sat
Loc Nr junction 39 on M1

Pannal (1906)

Private (Map 5/90)
Follifoot Road Pannal Harrogate HG3 1ES
Tel **Harrogate 871641**
Mem 815
Sec G Kitchingman Tel Harrogate 872628
Pro M Burgess Tel Harrogate 872620
Holes 18 L 6594 yds SSS 71
Recs Am–65 NA Faldo
Pro–66 J Beattie
M James D Jones
V'trs H (WD) 9.30 am-12.00 and 1.30 pm onwards (W/E) after 10 am and after 2.30 pm
Fees R–£12 D–£14 W/E–£15
Loc 2½ miles S of Harrogate

Phoenix (1932)

Private (Map 5/91)
Brinsworth Rotherham
Tel **Rotherham 382624**
Mem 700
Sec J Burrows Tel Rotherham 370759
Pro A Limb
Holes 18 L 6170 yds SSS 69
Recs Am–
Pro–
V'trs WD–U; W/E–U
Fees D–£8 (D–£10)
Loc 2 miles Rotherham

Phoenix Park (1922)

Private (Map 5/92)
Phoenix Park Thornbury Bradford 3
Tel Bradford 667178
Mem 180
Sec G Dunn Tel Bradford 662369
Pro B Ferguson Tel Bradford 667178
Holes 9 L 4982 yds SSS 64
Recs Am–66 C Lally
Pro–
V'trs WD & BH–U; W/E–NA
Fees £3
Loc Thornbury Roundabout

Pike Hills (1920)

Private (Map 5/93)
Pike Hills Copmanthorpe York
Tel York 706566
Mem 800
Sec Geoffrey Wood Tel York 706566
Pro I Gradwell Tel York 708756
Holes 18 L 6048 yds SSS 69
Recs Am–
Pro–
V'trs WD–U before 4.30 pm, M–after 4.30 pm W/E & BH–M SOC
Fees £8 W–£20
Loc 3 miles W of York on Leeds Road. Parkland course around Nature Reserve

Pontefract and District (1900)

Private (Map 5/94)
Park Lane Pontefract
Tel **Pontefract 792241**
Mem 700 85(L) 92(J) 85(5)
Sec WT Smith Tel Pontefract 792115
Pro J Coleman Tel Pontefract 706806
Holes 18 L 6227 yds SSS 70
Recs Am–63 DC Rodice
Pro–67 GW Townhill
V'trs I SOC (Tues Thurs Fri)
Fees £7 (£8.50)
Loc Pontefract 1 mile

Pontefract Park (1973)

Public (Map 5/95)
Park Road Pontefract
Tel **Pontefract 702799**
Mem
Sec
Pro
Holes 18 L 4068 yds SSS 62
Recs Am–
Pro–
V'trs U
Fees 60p (75p)
Loc Between town and M62 roundabout

Queensbury (1923)

Private (Map 5/96)
Queensbury nr Bradford BD13 1QF
Tel **Bradford 882155**
Mem 200 45(L) 60(J) 25(5)
Sec
Pro J Holchaks
Holes 9 L 5102 yds SSS 65
Recs Am–64 S Rogers
H Wilkerson
Pro–63 P Cowan
V'trs U
Fees £3.50 (£6)
Loc Bradford 4 miles

Rawdon (1896)

Private (Map 5/97)
Buckstone Drive Micklefield Lane Rawdon LS19 6BD
Tel **Rawdon 506040**
Mem 250 50(L) 75(J) 100(5)
Sec Mrs S Poland
Pro David Walker Tel Rawdon 505017
Holes 9 L 5964 yds SSS 69
Recs Am–65 JM Clough
Pro–63 A Bickerdike
V'trs WD–U; W/E & BH–M
Fees £7.50 W–£25 M–£45
Loc 6 miles NW Leeds

Renishaw Park (1911)

Private (Map 5/98)
Renishaw nr Sheffield
Tel **Eckington 432044**
Mem 400
Sec DL Jones
Pro S Elliott Tel Eckington 435484
Holes 18 L 6253 yds SSS 70
Recs Am–65 AR Gersthorpe
Pro–66 D Dunk
R Emery J Rhodes
V'trs U
Fees £7.50 (£9)
Loc 7 miles from Sheffield

Richmond (1892)

Private (Map 5/99)
Bend Hagg Richmond
Tel **2457**
Mem 262 80(L) 48(J)
Sec Jim Mulvey Tel Richmond 2568
Pro David Edwards
Holes 18 L 5704 yds SSS 68
Recs Am–64 Gary Catt
Pro–64 P Tupling
V'trs U
Fees WD–£5 W/E & BH–£7.50
Loc 3 miles S Scotch Corner

Riddlesden (1927)

Private (Map 5/100)
Howden Rough Riddleston Keighley
Tel **Keighley 602148**
Mem 200
Sec Mrs KM Brooksbank Tel Keighley 607646
Pro
Holes 18 L 4150 yds SSS 61
Recs Am–65
Pro–62
V'trs U (exc before 10 am Sun)
Fees £3 (£4) £2 after 5 pm £1 Juniors if accompanied
Loc Keighley 3 miles

Ripon City (1905)

Private (Map 5/101)
Palace Road Ripon HG4 3HH
Tel **Ripon 3640**
Mem 280 50(L) 30(J) 70(5)
Sec E Bentley Tel Ripon 3991
Pro Tim Davis Tel Ripon 700411
Holes 9 L 5752 yds SSS 68
Recs Am–65 M Grant
Pro–66 B Hutchinson
V'trs U
Fees £5 (£7)
Loc 1 mile N on A6108

Rotherham (1903)

Private (Map 5/102)
Thybergh Park Rotherham
Tel Rotherham 850466 (Steward)
Mem 450
Sec GK Hulley Tel Rotherham 850812
Pro Brent Ellis Tel Rotherham 850480
Holes 18 L 6500 yds SSS 70
Recs Am–66 MJ Kelly
Pro–66 B Hutchison
V'trs U
Fees £10 (£12)
Loc Thrybergh Rotherham on A630

Roundhay (1923)

Public (Map 5/103)
Park Lane Leeds LS8 2EJ
Tel **(0532) 662695**
Mem 380 50(L) 55(J)
Sec RH McLauchlan Tel (0532) 492523
Pro Hedley Muscroft Tel (0532) 661686
Holes 9 L 5166 yds SSS 65
Recs Am–62 AR White
Pro–62 M Bembridge
V'trs U
Fees £2.75 (£3)
Loc 4 miles N of city centre

Roundwood (1976)

Private (Map 5/147)
Off Green Lane Rawmarsh Rotherham S62 6LA
Tel (0709) 523471
Mem 400
Sec T Barnfield Tel (0709) 541792
Pro
Holes 9 L 5646 yds SSS 67
Recs Am–
Pro–
V'trs W/E–not before 2.30 pm on comp days
Fees £2 (£4)
Loc 2 miles N of Rotherham on A633

Ryburn (1910)

Private (Map 5/104)
Norland Sowerby Bridge Halifax
Tel **Halifax 31355**
Mem 210
Sec HJ Singleton Tel Halifax 62484
Pro
Holes 9 L 4800 yds SSS 64
Recs Am–65 R Bickerdike
P Wolfe
Pro–
V'trs U
Fees £1.50 (£2)
Loc 3 miles S of Halifax

Saltburn (1894)

Private (Map 5/105)
Hob Hill Saltburn-by-the-Sea
Tel **Guisborough 22812**
Mem 800
Sec I Mackay Tel Guisborough 32768
Pro R Broadbent Tel Guisborough 24653
Holes 18 L 5803 yds SSS 68
Recs Am–
Pro–
V'trs U
Fees £7 (£9.20)
Loc NE coast

Sand Moor (1926)

Private (Map 5/106)
Alwoodley Lane Leeds LS17 7DJ
Tel Leeds 681685
Mem 560
Sec D Warboys Tel Leeds 685180

Pro J Foss Tel Leeds 683925
Holes 18 L 6423 yds SSS 71
Recs Am–67 R Muscroft JM Buxton
Pro–
V'trs H; SOC on WD; Tue after 11.30 am Thu after 11.30 am
Fees £12 D–£14 (£16 R/D)
Loc 5 miles N of Leeds off Harrogate Road

Scarborough North Cliff (1927)

Private (Map 5/107)
North Cliff Avenue Burniston Road Scarborough YO12 6PP
Tel **(0723) 360786**
Mem 700
Sec JR Freeman Tel (0723) 360786
Pro SN Deller Tel (0723) 365920
Holes 18 L 6425 yds SSS 71
Recs Am–66 MJ Kelly R Newton
Pro–
V'trs U exc Sun before 10 am
Fees £8.50 (£12)
Loc 2 miles N of town centre on coast road

Scarborough South Cliff (1903)

Private (Map 5/108)
Deepdale Avenue off Filey Road Scarborough
Tel **Scarborough 360522**
Mem 500
Sec CH Atkinson Tel Scarborough 374737
Pro DM Edwards Tel Scarborough 365150
Holes 18 L 6085 yds SSS 69
Recs Am–69 DR Kilburn
Pro–
V'trs U
Fees £8
Loc 1 mile S of centre

Scarcroft (1937)

Private (Map 5/109)
Syke Lane, Leeds LS14 3BQ
Tel **Leeds 892263**
Mem 500
Sec J Beetham Tel Leeds 892311
Pro M Ross Tel Leeds 892780
Holes 18 L 6426 yds SSS 71
Recs Am–67 E Shaw
Pro–65 D Dunk
V'trs WD–U; W/E & BH–M, or prior arrangements with secretary SOC
Fees £11 (£17)
Loc 7 miles N of Leeds

Selby (1907)

Private (Map 5/110)
Mill Lane Brayton Selby YO8 9LD
Tel **Gateforth 622**
Mem 691
Sec DE Cooper Tel Gateforth 622
Pro D Jagger Tel Gateforth 785
Holes 18 L 6246 yds SSS 70
Recs Am–65 L Walker
Pro–64 D Matthew
V'trs U; SOC Wed Thu Fri
Fees £9 (£11) 5D–£28
Loc 3 miles SW of Selby

Serlby Park (1905)

Private (Map 5/111)
Serlby Doncaster S Yorks DN10 6BA
Tel **Retford 818268**
Mem 270
Sec M Hunter Tel Doncaster 851349
Pro
Holes 9 L 5355 yds SSS 66
Recs Am–64 NL Pond
Pro–65 M Bembridge
V'trs M
Fees
Loc 12 miles S Doncaster

Settle (1892)

Private (Map 5/112)
Giggleswick Settle
Tel Settle 3912
Mem 250
Sec Les Whitaker Tel Settle 3912
Pro
Holes 9 L 2048 metres SSS 31
Recs Am–62 P Robinson
Pro–
V'trs U
Fees £2 (£4)
Loc 1 mile N of Settle on A65

Sheffield Transport Dept (1923)

Private (Map 5/113)
Meadow Head Sheffield
Tel **Sheffield 373216**
Mem 100
Sec P Clarricoates
Pro
Holes 18 L 3966 yds SSS 62
Recs Am–62 VR Hutton
Pro–
V'trs M
Fees 50p
Loc

Shipley (1896)

Private (Map 5/114)
Beckfoot Bingley
Tel **(0274) 563212**
Mem 550
Sec SL Holman Tel (0274) 568652
Pro D Sutcliffe Tel (0274) 563674
Holes 18 L 6203 yds SSS 70
Recs Am–66 GM Shaw
Pro–69 M Ingham
RH Emery
V'trs U, Ex Tues before 1.30 pm and Sat before 4 pm
Fees £9 (£12)
Loc Beckfoot Lane Cottingley Bridge Bingley. 6 miles N of Bradford on A650

Sickleholme (1895)

Private (Map 5/115)
Bamford Sheffield S30 2BH
Tel **Hope Valley 51306**
Mem 250 100(L) 72(J) 80(5)
Sec WT Scott
Pro PH Taylor
Holes 18 L 6064 yds SSS 69
Recs Am–63 IL Fletcher
Pro–65 AP Highfield
V'trs U (not Wed am)
Fees £9 (£11.50)
Loc Between Hathersage and Hope A625

Silkstone (1905)

Private (Map 5/116)
Field Head Silkstone nr Barnsley
Tel **Barnsley 790328**
Mem 450
Sec G Speight Tel Barnsley 244796
Pro Robert Lister Tel Barnsley 790128
Holes 18 L 6045 yds SSS 70
Recs Am–66 TG Garner
JG Clapham
Pro–
V'trs WD–U; W/E–M; SOC on WD
Fees £7
Loc 1 mile from M1

Silsden (1913)

Private (Map 5/117)
Brunthwaite Silsden nr Keighley
Tel **Steeton 52998**
Mem 300
Sec G Davey Tel Ilkley 601490
Pro
Holes 14 L 4870 SSS 64
Recs Am–61
Pro–
V'trs Weekend restricted–U Sun after 1 pm
Fees £4 (£6)
Loc 5 miles N of Keighley

Sitwell Park (1913)

Private (Map 5/118)
Shrogs Wood Road Rotherham
Tel 0709 541046
Mem 500
Sec MJ Hinchcliff Tel 0709 364780
Pro Richard Swaine
Holes 18 L 6250 yds SSS 70
Recs Am–67 RN Portas
Pro–
V'trs U
Fees £7 (£8)
Loc 2½ miles E of Rotherham

Skipton (1905)

Private (Map 5/119)
Off Grassington Road Skipton
Tel (0756) 3922
Mem 398
Sec G Cosway Tel (0756) 61167
Pro J Hammond Tel (0756) 3257
Holes 18 L 6191 yds SSS 70
Recs Am–70 WR Greenhalgh
Pro–69 N Brunyard
V'trs U
Fees £8 (£9) unlimited
Loc 1 mile from centre; access from bypass

South Bradford (1906)

Private (Map 5/120)
Pearson Road Odsal Bradford BD6 1BH
Tel Bradford 679195
Mem 220
Sec HH Kellett Tel Bradford 676911
Pro JA Taylor Tel Bradford 673346
Holes 9 L 6004 yds SSS 69
Recs Am–65 GM Yarnold
Pro–67 S Miguel A Caygill
V'trs WD–U; W/E–M
Fees On application
Loc 2 miles Bradford near Odsal Stadium

South Leeds (1914)

Private (Map 5/121)
Gipsy Lane Ring Road Beeston Leeds LS11 5TV
Tel **Leeds 700479**
Mem 500
Sec WG Ward Tel Leeds 771676
Pro JT Kerr Tel Leeds 702598
Holes 18 L 5835 yds SSS 68
Recs Am–66 M Guy
Pro–68 B Waites
V'trs WD–U; W/E–M; SOC
Fees £6 (£7)
Loc 4 miles S of Leeds off Dewsbury Road

Springhead Park (1903)

Public (Map 5/122)
Willerby Road Hull
Tel **Hull 656309**
Mem 449
Sec F Coggrave Tel Hull 656776
Pro B Herrington Tel Hull 659102
Holes 18 L 6439 yds SSS 71
Recs Am–69 AD Hill A Wright
Pro–65 S Rolley
V'trs U
Fees £2.10
Loc W boundary

Stocksbridge and District (1925)

Private (Map 5/123)
30 Royd Lane Townend, Deepcar nr Sheffield S30 5RZ
Tel **Sheffield 882003**
Mem 200
Sec S Lee Tel Sheffield 882408
Pro
Holes 15 L 5055 yds SSS 65
Recs Am–61 MR Prince
Pro–
V'trs U; SOC
Fees £5.50 (£6.50)
Loc 7 miles W of Sheffield

Sutton Park (1935)

Public (Map 5/124)
Salthouse Road Hull
Tel **(0482) 74242**
Mem 850
Sec RI Anson Tel (0482) 75452
Pro B Herrington Tel (0482) 796181
Holes 18 L 6251 yds SSS 70
Recs Am–69 GR Lamb
Pro–64 L Herrington
V'trs U
Fees £1.10
Loc 3 miles E of city centre

Tankersley Park (1907)

Private (Map 5/125)
High Green Sheffield S30 4LG
Tel **Sheffield 468247**
Mem 574
Sec S Jessop Tel Sheffield 468247
Pro V Scott Tel Sheffield 455583
Holes 18 L 6241 yds SSS 70
Recs Am–66 N Grice
Pro–69 W Atkinson
V'trs WD–U; W/E–M; SOC on WD
Fees £6 D–£8
Loc 7 miles N of Sheffield

Tees-side (1901)

Private (Map 5/126)
Acklam Road Thornaby Cleveland TS17 7JS
Tel **Stockton 676249**
Mem 600
Sec WA Hunter Tel Stockton 616516
Pro K Hall Tel Stockton 673822
Holes 18 L 6472 yds SSS 71
Recs Am–
Pro–
V'trs WD–before 4.30 pm; W/E–after 11 am; BH–after 11 am unless playing with a member; SOC
Fees D–£7.50, £4.50 with mem subject to review
Loc 2 miles S of Stockton

Temple Newsam (1923)

Public (Map 5/127)
Temple Newsam Road Halton Leeds 15
Tel Leeds 645624
Mem 600
Sec G Gower Tel Leeds 645624
Pro D Bulmer Tel Leeds 647362
Holes Lord Irwin 18 L 6448 yds SSS 71
Lady Dorothy Wood 18 L 6029 yds SSS 70
V'trs U SOC
Fees £2.50 (£3)
Loc 5 miles NE of town centre, off Selby Road

Thirsk and Northallerton (1914)

Private (Map 5/128)
Thornton-le-Street Thirsk N Yorks YO7 4AB
Tel **Thirsk 22170**
Mem 300
Sec PW McCarthy Tel Thirsk 23287
Pro Andrew Marshall (Touring Pro D Llewellyn)
Holes 9 L 6257 yds SSS 70
Recs Am–69 R Cable
Pro–69 P Blaze
V'trs WD–U SOC; Sun–M
Fees £6 (Sat & BH–£8)
Loc 2 miles N of Thirsk
Mis No catering Tue

Tinsley Park (1920)

Public (Map 5/129)
Darnall Sheffield
Tel **Sheffield 442237**
Mem 340
Sec J Booth Tel Sheffield 613168
Pro AP Highfield
Holes 18 L 6045 yds SSS 69
Recs Am–70 D Robbins
Pro–66 D Snell
V'trs U
Fees £4
Loc 1 mile from M1 exit 32

Todmorden (1895)

Private (Map 5/130)
Rive Rocks Cross Stone Todmorden Lancs
Tel **Todmorden 2986**
Mem 123 29(L) 19(J) 8(5)
Sec RA Ward
Pro
Holes 9 L 5818 yds SSS 68
Recs Am–68 RH Fielden
G Morgan
Pro–68 B Hunt
V'trs U; SOC
Fees £4 (£6)
Loc 2 miles N of Todmorden

Wakefield (1891)

Private (Map 5/131)
Woodthorpe Wakefield WF2 6JH
Tel Wakefield 255104
Mem 500
Sec DT Hall Tel Wakefield 250287
Pro IM Wright Tel Wakefield 255380
Holes 18 L 6626 yds SSS 72
Recs Am–65 T Margison
Pro–67 W Shoesmith
V'trs U; SOC
Fees £10
Loc 3 miles S of Wakefield

Wakefield Municipal

(See City of Wakefield)

Wath-upon-Dearne (1904)

Private (Map 5/132)
Abdy Rawmarsh Rotherham
Tel **Rotherham 872149**
Mem 235
Sec DL Steels Tel Rotherham 873260
Pro SC Poole Tel Rotherham 878677
Holes 9 L 5606 yds SSS 67
Recs Am–64 R Jones
Pro–65 D Jagger
V'trs WD–U; W/E–M
Fees £5
Loc Abdy Farm 1½ miles S of Wath-upon-Dearne
Mis Extension of course in construction in two phases. 1985/86–14 holes; 1988/89–18 holes

West Bowling (1898)

Private (Map 5/133)
Newall Hall Rooley Lane West Bowling Bradford BD5 8LB
Tel **Bradford 724449**
Mem 320 47(L) 40(J)
Sec JK Rasche Tel Bradford 393207
Pro AP Swaine Tel Bradford 728036
Holes 18 L 5756 yds SSS 68
Recs Am–66 TJ Wade
Pro–66 GA Caygill
V'trs U
Fees £6 (£8)
Loc Ring Road S Bradford

West Bradford (1900)

Private (Map 5/134)
Chellow Grange Haworth Road Bradford BD9 6NP
Tel Bradford 42767
Mem 450
Sec
Pro AJ Stephenson Tel Bradford 42102
Holes 18 L 5705 yds SSS 68
Recs Am–66
Pro–66
V'trs U
Fees £5.75 (£7.50) inc VAT
Loc Bradford 3 miles off Haworth Road

Wetherby (1910)

Private (Map 5/135)
Linton Lane Wetherby
Tel **Wetherby 62527**
Mem 500
Sec WF Gibb Tel Wetherby 63375
Pro D Padgett Tel Wetherby 63375
Holes 18 L 6224 yds SSS 70
Recs Am–66 JH Brook
Pro–64 H Muscroft
V'trs W/E–U after 10 am; SOC Wed Thu Fri
Fees £8.50 (£15)
Loc ¾ mile centre

Wheatley (1913)

Private (Map 5/136)
Armthorpe Road Doncaster DN2 5QB
Tel **Doncaster 831203**
Mem 385 100(L) 75(J) 5(5)
Sec KW Percival Tel Doncaster 66460

Pro Tel Doncaster 831655
Holes 18 L 6345 yds SSS 70
Recs Am–65 B Bremner
Pro–63 G Walker
V'trs U SOC on WD
Fees £7.50 (£10)
Loc 3 miles town centre E boundary

Whitby (1892)

Private (Map 5/137)
Low Straggleton Whitby
Tel Whitby 602768
Mem 500
Sec Alan Dyson Tel Whitby 600660
Pro M Haines Tel Whitby 602719
Holes 18 L 5710 yds SSS 67
Recs Am–67
Pro–68
V'trs U SOC
Fees £6.90 (£8) VAT inc
Loc E coast resort

Wilton (1949)

Private (Map 5/138)
Wilton Redcar
Tel Eston Grange 465265
Mem 700
Sec DW Lewis Tel Redcar 477570
Pro AL Maskell
Holes 18 L 6043 yds SSS 69
Recs Am–64 N Crapper
Pro–68 S Hunt
V'trs WD–U; Sat–NA; Sun & BH–U; SOC
Fees £7 (£8)
Loc 3 miles W of Redcar on A174

Withernsea (1909)

Private (Map 5/139)
Chestnut Avenue Withernsea HU19 2PG
Tel **(09642) 2258**
Mem 183 35(L) 68(J) 27(5)
Sec HD Mitchell Tel (09642) 2705
Pro
Holes 9 L 5112 yds SSS 64
Rec Am–62 SH Kellet
Pro– 63 Gordon Townhill
V'trs WD–U SOC; W/E–NA Sun am M Sun pm
Fees £3
Loc 17 miles E of Hull; south end of town

Woodhall Hills (1895)

Private (Map 5/140)
Calverley Pudsey LS28 5QY
Tel **(0532) 564771/554594**
Mem 315
Sec A Siddall
Pro MD Lord Tel (0532) 562857
Holes 18 L 6102 yds SSS 69
Recs Am–66 PA Crosby
Pro–66 M Ingham
V'trs U
Fees £6 (£9)
Loc 6 miles Leeds 4 miles Bradford

Woodsome Hall (1922)

Private (Map 5/141)
Woodsome Hall Fenay Bridge Huddersfield
Tel Huddersfield 602971
Mem 394 194(L) 103(J) 65(5)
Hon
Sec EV Hartley Tel Huddersfield 602739
Sec Mrs P Bates
Pro Karl B Scarr Tel Huddersfield 602034
Holes 18 L 6088 yds SSS 69
Recs Am–68 Edwin W Hirst
Pro–65 D Jagger
V'trs U except Tues–NA before 4 pm
Fees £11 (£14)
Loc 6 miles SE Huddersfield on Sheffield/Penistone Road A629

Wortley (1894)

Private (Map 5/142)
Hermit Hill Lane Wortley nr Sheffield S30 4DF
Tel **Sheffield 885294**
Mem 300
Sec JL Dalby Tel Sheffield 885294
Pro IA Kirk Tel Sheffield 886490
Holes 18 L 5983 yds SSS 69
Recs Am–68
Pro–66
V'trs U
Fees £8 (£10)
Loc 2 miles W of M1 junction 36 off A629

York (1890)

Private (Map 5/143)
Lords Moor Lane Strensall York YO3 5XF
Tel **(0904) 490304**
Mem 325 110(L) 75(J) 16(5)
Sec RF Harding
Pro A Mason
Holes 18 L 6275 yds SSS 70
Recs Am–64 S East
Pro–66 P Fowler
V'trs U SOC on WD and Sun
Fees £10 (£12)
Loc 6 miles NE of York

Ireland: Connacht

Co Galway

Athenry (1957)

Private (Map 7/1)
Derrydonnel Oranmore
Tel **091 84466**
Mem 150
Sec Patrick Burkitt Tel 091 94681
Pro
Holes 9 L 5448 yds SSS 67
Recs Am–69 Leo Gardner
Pro–
V'trs WD–U; Sun–M
Fees £3 (£4)
Loc 10 miles E of Galway City

Ballinasloe (1894)

Private (Map 7/2)
Ballinasloe Co Galway
Tel (0905) 42126
Mem 400
Sec C Oliver Tel (0905) 42593
Pro
Holes 18 L 5800 yds SSS 66 Par 68
Recs Am–64 M Lynch
Pro–66 C O'Connor
V'trs U SOC
Fees £5
Loc 2 miles from town centre

Connemara (1973)

Private (Map 7/3)
Aillebrack Ballyconneely nr Clifden
Tel **095-21153**
Mem 450
Sec H De-Lappé Tel 095-21153
Pro
Holes 18 Championship–6604 metres SSS 75
Medal–6186 metres SSS 73
Recs Am–
Pro–
V'trs U; H; SOC exc Sun and Open Weeks
Fees £8 W–£40 SOC (over 20) £5
Loc 8 miles SW of Clifden

Galway (1895)

Private (Map 7/4)
Blackrock Salthill Galway
Tel **Galway 21827**
Mem 950
Sec WC Caulfield Tel Galway 22169
Pro D Wallace Tel Galway 23038
Holes 18 L 6193 yds SSS 70
Recs Am–66 Billy Grealish
Pro–67 C Greene
V'trs Green fees restricted Tue and Sun
Fees £9
Loc 3 miles from city centre

Gort (1924)

Private (Map 7/5)
Laughtyshaughnessy Gort
Tel **(091) 31336**
Mem 117
Sec P Grealish Tel (091) 31375
Pro
Holes 9 L 5216 metres SSS 67
Recs Am–64 G Cooney
Pro–66 C O'Connor
V'trs U
Fees D–£4
Loc Tubber Road

Loughrea (1924)

Private (Map 7/6)
Loughrea
Tel **Loughrea 30**
Mem 165
Sec KF Hays Tel Loughrea 133
Pro
Holes 9 L 5,578 yds SSS 66
Recs Am–69
Pro–
V'trs U
Fees 50p W–£2.50 M–£5
Loc 20 miles E Galway

Mount Bellew (1929)

Private (Map 7/7)
Mount Bellew (Ballinasloe)
Tel **0905 9259**
Mem 104
Sec F Rushe
Pro
Holes 9 L 5564 yds SSS 67
Recs Am–67 B Hyland
Pro–
V'trs U
Fees £3 W–£15 M–£30
Loc

Oughterard (1973)

Private (Map 7/8)
Oughterard
Tel **(091) 82131**
Mem 300
Sec Jim Byrne
Pro M Ryan
Holes 18 L 6150 yds SSS 69
Recs Am–
Pro–
V'trs U
Fees £5 (£5)
Loc 15 miles W of Galway

Portumna (1907)

Private (Map 7/9)
Portumna
Tel **Portumna 59**
Mem 151
Sec Frank Kilkenny
Pro
Holes 9 L 5776 yds SSS 67
Recs Am–66 Michael Carty
Pro–63 H Bradshaw
V'trs U
Fees £3
Loc Portumna on road to Ennis

Tuam (1907)

Private (Map 7/10)
Barnacurragh Tuam
Tel **093 24354**
Mem 230
Sec Noel Mannion
Pro
Holes 18 L 6321 yds SSS 70
Recs Am–69 DJ McGrath
Pro–
V'trs NA on Sundays; WD–SOC
Fees £5 (1985) price
Loc 20 miles N of Galway

Co Leitrim

Ballinamore (1941)

Private (Map 7/11)
Ballinamore
Tel **(078) 44346**
Mem 86
Sec P Duigan (078) 44163
Pro
Holes 9 L 5680 yds SSS 67 Par 68
Recs Am–69 P Duigan
Pro–
V'trs U SOC
Fees £3 W–£15
Loc 1½ miles N of town

Carrick-on-Shannon (1910)

Private (Map 7/12)
Carrick-on-Shannon
Tel **C-on-S 157**
Mem 179
Sec TW Craig Tel 183
Pro
Holes 9 L 5922 yds SSS 67
Recs Am–68 S Flanagan
Pro–
V'trs U
Fees 40p (50p)
Loc

Co Mayo

Achill Island (1951)

Private (Map 7/13)
Keel Achill Island Co Mayo
Tel
Mem 16
Sec David Quinn Tel Keel (098) 43202
Pro
Holes 9 L 5240 yds SSS 65
Recs Am–
Pro–
V'trs U
Fees D–£2
Loc In Keel

Ballina (1910)

Private (Map 7/14)
Mosgrove Shanaghy Ballina
Tel **(096) 21050**
Mem 128 58(L)
Sec V Frawley Tel (096) 21795
Pro
Holes 9 L 5702 yds SSS 66
Recs Am–64 J Corcoran
Pro–66 C O'Connor
V'trs U
Fees £4 (£5) W–£15
Loc 1 mile E of town

Ballinrobe (1895)

Public (Map 7/15)
Ballinrobe Claremorris Co Mayo
Tel **092 41448**
Mem 180
Sec James Golden Tel 092 41234
Pro
Holes 9 L 5790 yds SSS 68
Recs Am–71 B Finlay
Pro–
V'trs U Sun–NA SOC
Fees £4 (£5 Sats) W–£15 M–£40
Loc Ballinrobe 1½ miles NW of town–Castlebar Road

Ballyhaunis (1929)

Private (Map 7/16)
Coolnaha Ballyhaunis
Tel **(0907) 30014**
Mem 162
Sec John Higgins Tel (0907) 30180
Pro
Holes 9 L 5887 yds SSS 68 Par 69
Recs Am–68 W Keane
Pro–70
V'trs U; SOC on WD
Fees £5
Loc 2 miles N of Ballyhaunis

Belmullet (1925)

Private (Map 7/17)
Belmullet Ballina
Tel **097 81093**
Mem 43
Sec
Pro
Holes 9 L 2829 yds SSS 67
Recs Am–
Pro–
V'trs U
Fees £3
Loc 3 miles W of Belmullet

Castlebar (1910)

Private (Map 7/18)
Rocklands Castlebar
Tel **094 21649**
Mem 211
Sec John Egan
Pro John Harnett
Holes 18 L 6109 yds SSS 69
Recs Am–67 Joe Langan
Pro–
V'trs U
Fees £5
Loc

Claremorris (1918)

Private (Map 7/19)
Claremorris
Tel **094 71527**
Mem 90
Sec G Conroy Tel Ballidine 84
Pro
Holes 9 L 5338 yds SSS 66
Recs Am–66 M Keane
Pro–63 C O'Connor
V'trs U
Fees £2 W–£10
Loc 2 miles S of Claremorris

Mulrany (1968)

Public (Map 7/20)
Mulrany Westport
Tel **098 36185**
Mem 35
Sec J O'Hara
Pro
Holes 9 L 6380 yds SSS 70
V'trs U SOC W/E
Fees D–£3 W–£15
Loc 9 miles E of Achill

Swinford (1922)

Private (Map 7/21)
Brabazon Park Swinford
Tel **094 51378**
Mem 103
Sec P Walsh
Pro
Holes 9 L 5230 yds SSS 65
Recs Am–68
Pro–
V'trs U
Fees D–£3 W–£15
Loc Off Dublin/Castlebar road

Westport (1926)

Private (Map 7/22)
Carrowholly Westport
Tel **Westport 547**
Mem 273
Sec S O'Malley Tel Westport 461
Pro
Holes 18 L 7012 yds SSS 73
Recs Am–73 Tony Joyce
Pro–
V'trs U
Fees £3 (£3)
Loc 2 miles from Westport

Co Roscommon

Athlone (1892)

Private (Map 7/23)
Hodson Bay Athlone
Tel **Athlone 2073**
Mem 540
Sec Tom Collins Tel (H) 0902-74796
Pro Martin Quinn Tel 0902-2073
Holes 18 L 6000 yds SSS 70
Recs Am–63 P Egan
Pro–70 M Quinn
V'trs U; SOC on WD
Fees £5 (£6)
Loc Shores of Lough Ree

Ballaghaderreen (1937)

Private (Map 7/24)
Ballaghaderreen
Tel
Mem 112
Sec JB Noonan P Hunt
Pro
Holes 9 L 5686 yds SSS 65
Recs Am–
Pro–
V'trs
Fees 50p W–£2
Loc 3 miles from town

Boyle (1911)

Private (Map 7/25)
Roscommon Road Boyle
Tel
Mem 80
Sec NG Scott
Pro
Holes 9 L 5728 yds SSS 65
Recs Am–68 S Young
Pro–
V'trs U
Fees 50p
Loc Roscommon Road

Castlerea (1905)

Private (Map 7/26)
Clonalis Castlerea
Tel **(0907) 20068**
Mem 145
Sec Brian Stenson Tel (0907) 20279
Pro
Holes 9 L 5466 yds SSS 66
Recs Am–63 Rupert de Lacy Staunton
Pro–
V'trs U
Fees £3 (£5)
Loc Town suburb Knock Road

Roscommon (1904)

Private (Map 7/27)
Mote Park Roscommon
Tel **0903 6382**
Mem 241
Sec J Halliday Tel 0903 6164
Pro
Holes 9 L 6215 yds SSS 68
Recs Am–68 D White
Pro–
V'trs U
Fees 75p W–£3 M–£6
Loc 1 mile E of town

Co Sligo

Ballymote (1940)

Private (Map 7/28)
Ballymote
Tel **Ballymote 3460**
Mem 42
Sec P Mullen
Pro
Holes 9 L 5032 yds SSS 63
Recs Am–67 P Mullen
Pro–
V'trs U
Fees £2
Loc Carrigans

County Sligo (1894)

Private (Map 7/29)
Rosses Point Co Sligo
Tel **071 77186**
Mem 762
Sec GA Eakins Tel 071 77134
Pro J McGonigle Tel 071 77171
Holes 18 L 6011 metres SSS 73
Recs Am–65 MD O'Brien
Pro–67 C O'Connor Sen
V'trs WD–U; W/E & BH–M 9 am–10.30 am and 1.30 pm–2.45 pm; SOC
Fees £10 (£12) M–£60
Loc 5 miles NW of Sligo

Enniscrone (1931)

Private (Map 7/30)
Enniscrone
Tel **096 36297**
Mem 271
Sec JM Fleming Tel 096 36297
Pro
Holes 18 L 6487 yds SSS 71
Recs Am–70 J. Corcoran M Canavan
Pro–71 C O'Connor Sen
J O'Leary
V'trs U
Fees D–£7 (£5 with member)
Loc On Ballina Road S of Enniscrone

Strandhill (1932)

Private (Map 7/31)
Strandhill
Tel **071 78188**
Mem 250
Sec F Carr Tel (071) 61776
Pro B Malone Tel (071) 68188/68213
Holes 18 L 5937 yds SSS 68
Recs Am–
Pro–
V'trs U/SOC W/E & BH Visitors allowed at certain times
Fees IR£7 (IR£8)
Loc 6 miles W of Sligo

Leinster

Co Carlow

Borris (1908)

Private (Map 7/1)
Deerpark Borris Co Carlow
Tel Borris (0503) 73143
Mem 250
Sec C Hughes Tel (0503) 75216
Pro
Holes 9 L 6026 yds SSS 69
Recs Am–67
Pro–
V'trs WD–U; Sun–M; SOC WD and Sat Apr–Sep
Fees £3 (£4)
Loc

Carlow (1899)

Private (Map 7/2)
Oak Park Carlow
Tel (0503) 31695
Mem 820
Sec Mrs A Moran Tel 0503 42599
Pro A Gilbert Tel 0503 31695
Holes 18 L 6347 yds SSS 70
Recs Am–65 P Mulcare RD Carr
Pro–68 C O'Connor
V'trs U
Fees £6 (£9)
Loc Carlow

Co Dublin

Balbriggan (1945)

Private (Map 7/3)
Blackhall Balbriggan
Tel Balbriggan 412173
Mem 500
Sec L Cashell Tel 412173 (club) 412229 (office)
Pro
Holes 18 L 5717 metres SSS 70
Recs Am–N Ennis GE Copeland
Pro–
V'trs WD–U; SOC; W/E–M
Fees £6 (£7)
Loc ¼ mile S of Balbriggan
Mis 9 new holes opened Sep 85

Ballinascorney (1971)

Private (Map 7/4)
Ballinascorney Tallaght
Tel (01) 512516
Mem 315
Sec M Walsh Tel 829030
Pro
Holes 9 L 5322 yds SSS 66
Recs Am–
Pro–
V'trs U
Fees
Loc

Beech Park (1973)

Private (Map 7/5)
Johnstown Rathcoole
Tel Dublin 580522/506887
Mem 375
Sec Gerald Cleary
Pro
Holes 18 SSS 67
Fees £4
Loc 1½ km from Rathcoole on Kilteel road

Corballis (1971)

Public (Map 7/6)
Donabate
Man Barry Langan Tel Dublin 450583
Holes 18 L 4971 yds SSS 64
Recs Am–
Pro–
V'trs U; SOC Mon–Sat (436583)
Fees D–£3.50 (£4.50); Yearly ticket–£120; Special rates unemployed and sen cits Mon–Fri £2

Deer Park (1974)

Private club; Public course (Map 7/7)
Howth
Tel 01 322624
Mem 250
Sec JJ Leonard
Pro
Holes 18 L 6647 yds 73 Par 72
Recs Am–72 N Hussey
Pro–
V'trs U
Fees £4.80 (£5.80)
Loc 8 miles NE of Dublin
Mis Par 3 and pitch and putt courses available

Donabate (1925)

Private (Map 7/8)
Balcarrick, Donabate
Tel 450335
Mem 501
Sec Mrs C Campion Tel 450346
Pro Hugh Jackson
Holes 18 L 6187 yds SSS 67
Recs Am–67 AJ Coughlan
Pro–65 M Murphy
V'trs W/E & BH–NA
Fees V'trs with mem £3.50 (£7)
Loc 8 miles from Dublin airport

Dublin and County (1972)

Public (Map 7)
Corballis Donabate
Tel 450583
Mem 352
Sec Michael McKenna
Holes Play over Corballis Public Course

Dublin Sport (1977)

Private (Map 7/9)
Kilternan Dublin
Tel 895418
Mem 255
Sec DJ Sullivan Tel 895418
Pro
Holes 18 L 5413 yds SSS 66
Recs Am–
Pro–
V'trs M
Fees
Loc 5 miles S of Dublin

Dun Laoghaire (1910)

Private (Map 7/10)
Dun Laoghaire Eglinton Park Dublin
Tel Dublin 801055
Mem 972
Sec T Stewart Tel 01 803916
Pro Owen Mulhall Tel 801694
Holes 18 L 5463 metres SSS 69
Recs Am–66 P McCormack
Pro–65 P Skerritt
V'trs WD–U exc 1–2 pm; W/E–M after 5 pm; SOC
Fees £10 (£12.50)
Loc 7 miles S of Dublin

Forrest Little (1972)

Private (Map 7/11)
Cloghran Co Dublin
Tel Dublin 401183/401763
Mem 900
Sec V Maslin
Pro T Murphy
Holes 18 L 5852 metres SSS 70
Recs Am–67
Pro–65
V'trs WD–U
Fees £8 (IRL)
Loc Adjacent Dublin Airport

Hermitage (1905)

Private (Map 7/12)
Lucan Co Dublin
Tel 01-264549
Mem 1152
Sec TE Griffin Tel 01-268072/268491
Pro David Daly Tel 268072/268491
Holes 18 L 6000 metres SSS 71
Recs Am–69 T Heverin
Pro–65 Rodger Davis
V'trs U
Fees £11 (W/E & BH–£16)
Loc 8 miles from city centre

The Island (1890)

Private (Map 7/13)
Corballis Donabate
Tel Dublin 436104
Mem 550
Sec/ Man LA O'Connor Tel 436205
Pro
Holes 18 L 6320 yds SSS 71
Recs Am–B Moore B Byrne
Pro–
V'trs U; W/E NA before noon
Fees £10 (£12)
Loc 14 miles N of Dublin

Killiney (1903)

Private (Map 7/14)
Killiney
Tel 01 851983
Mem 528
Sec JB Jordan
Pro P O'Boyle
Holes 9 L 6201 yds SSS 69
Recs Am–72 N Duke
Pro–65 H Bradshaw
V'trs U
Fees D–£10
Loc 8 miles S Dublin

Lucan (1897)

Private (Map 7/15)
Celbridge Road Lucan Co Dublin
Tel 01 280246
Mem 392
Sec/ Man 01 282106
Pro
Holes 9 L 6287 yds 5748 metres SSS 69
Recs Am–63 T Rogers
Pro–67 H Bradshaw
V'trs WD–U before 3 pm; W/E & BH–M; SOC Mon Tue Wed Fri
Fees £7
Loc 14 miles W of Dublin centre near village of Lucan

Malahide (1892)

Private (Map 7/16)
Coast Road Malahide Co Dublin
Tel Malahide 450248

Mem 250
Sec Brian Balger
Pro Cecil Connolly
Holes 9 L 5568 yds SSS 67
Recs Am–63 P Killeen
Pro–
V'trs U Restricted Sat & Sun
Fees £6; £2 with member
Loc 10 miles N of Dublin ½ mile from town centre

Newlands (1926)

Private (Map 7/17)
Clondalkin Dublin
Tel **Dublin 592903**
Mem 959
Sec S O'Donoghue Tel Dublin 593157
Pro G Brown
Holes 18 L 6184 yds SSS 69
Recs Am–66 R Burdon P Hanley Jun.
Pro–68 C O'Connor
V'trs U
Fees £4
Loc 6 miles from Dublin

Portmarnock (1894)

Private (Map 7/18)
Portmarnock Co Dublin
Tel **Dublin 323082**
Mem 971
Sec Wally Bornemann Tel Dublin 323082
Pro P Townsend Tel Dublin 325157
Holes 27 'A' Course L 7097 yds SSS 75
'B' Course L 7047 yds SSS 75
'C' Course L 6956 yds SSS 74
Recs Am–68 JB Carr
Pro–65 Gary Player
V'trs I; W/E–XL
Fees £20 (W/E & BH–£25) Ladies £5 WD only
Loc 8 miles NE of Dublin

Rush (1943)

Private (Map 7/19)
Rush Co Dublin
Tel **Dublin 437548**
Mem 302
Sec TJ Molloy Tel Dublin 437235
Pro Joseph O'Keeffe
Holes 9 L 5655 yds SSS 69
Recs Am–68 PJ Dolan
Pro–
V'trs WD–U; W/E–M
Fees £7
Loc 16 miles N of Dublin

Skerries (1906)

Private (Map 7/20)
Skerries
Tel **(01) 491204**
Mem 748
Sec AJB Taylor Tel (01) 491567
Pro J Kinsella
Holes 18 L 5852 metres SSS 70
V'trs U
Fees IR £8 (IR £12)
Loc 20 miles N of Dublin

Slade Valley (1970)

Private (Map 7/21)
Lynch Park Brittas
Tel **01 582207**
Mem 500
Sec P Maguire Tel 01 582183
Pro G Egan
Holes 18 L 5337 metres SSS 68
Recs Am–
Pro–64
V'trs
Fees D–£7 (£8)
Loc 8 miles W of Dublin off N4

Woodbrook (1921)

Private (Map 7/22)
Nr Bray
Tel **824799**
Mem 700
Sec Derek Smyth
Pro W Kinsella
Holes 18 L 6007 metres SSS 71
Recs Am–
Pro–
V'trs WD–U SOC; W/E–Call Secretary
Fees £13 (£16)
Loc Dublin 11 miles

Dublin City

Carrickmines (1900)

Private (Map 7/23)
Carrickmines
Tel **01-895 676**
Mem 371
Sec S Millington Tel 895931
Pro
Holes 9 L 6044 yds SSS 69
Recs Am–68
Pro–68
V'trs M
Fees £6 (£8 Sun only)
Loc 6 miles S of Dublin

Castle (1913)

Private (Map 7/24)
Woodside Drive Rathfarnham Dublin 14
Tel **Dublin 904207**
Mem 800
Sec LF Blackburne Tel 904207
Pro David Kinsella Tel 933444
Holes 18 L 6240 metres SSS 69
Recs Am–69 J Bourke
Pro–65 B Browne
V'trs WD–U; W/E&BH–M; SOC
Fees £11
Loc 5 miles S of city

Clontarf (1912)

Private (Map 7/25)
Donnycarney House Malahide Road Dublin 3
Tel **Dublin 332669**
Mem 960
Sec MG O'Brien Tel 01-315085
Pro J Craddock Tel 01-310016
Holes 18 L 5447 metres Medal 68
Recs Am–65 M O'Shea
Pro–64 H Bradshaw
V'trs WD–U; W/E–M SOC
Fees £10
Loc 2 miles from city centre

Edmondstown (1944)

Private (Map 7/26)
Rathfarnham Dublin 16
Tel **Dublin 907461**
Mem 448
Sec S Adams Tel Dublin 01 902082
Pro A Crofton Tel 01 941049
Holes 18 L 6177 yds SSS 69
Recs Am–
Pro–
V'trs U
Fees £6 (£7)
Loc

Elm Park Golf and Sports Club (1927)

Private (Map 7/27)
Nutley House Donnybrook Dublin 4
Tel **01 693438/693014**
Mem 1656
Sec/Man H Montag Tel 693014
Pro Seamus Green Tel Dublin 692650
Holes 18 L 5485 metres SSS 68
Recs Am–63 PF Hogan
Pro–63 Peter Townsend
V'trs U (phone in advance)
Fees £12 (£16) 5D–£40
Loc 3 miles S of city centre

Foxrock (1893)

Private (Map 7/28)
Foxrock Torquay Road Dublin 18
Tel **Foxrock 895668**
Mem 550
Sec J McReynolds Tel Foxrock 893992
Pro
Holes 9 L 5699 metres SSS 69
Recs Am–68 D Campbell
Pro–68 Hugh Jackson
V'trs WD BH & Sun–M; Tue & Sats–NA
Fees £10
Loc 5 miles S of Dublin city

Grange (1911)

Private (Map 7/29)
Whitechurch Rathfarnham Dublin 16
Tel **Dublin 932832**
Mem 1050 235(L) 210(J) 12(5)
Sec Comdt J Stewart Tel Dublin 932889
Pro WD Sullivan Tel Dublin 932299
Holes 18 L 5517 metres SSS 69
Recs Am–64 WB Buckley
Pro–62 Christy O'Connor Jun
V'trs WD–U; (Ex Tuesday and Wednesday afternoon–NA); W/E–M
Fees £8
Loc Nr Rathfarnham Dublin 16

Howth (1916)

Private (Map 7/30)
Carrickbrack Road Sutton Dublin 13
Tel **Dublin 323055**
Mem 1200
Sec Mrs A MacNiece Tel 323055
Pro JF McGuirk
Holes 18 L 5573 metres SSS 69
Recs Am–66 M Roe
Pro–71
V'trs WD–U exc Wed; W/E–M
Fees £8
Loc 9 miles NE of Dublin

Milltown (1907)

Private (Map 7/31)
Lower Churchtown Road Milltown Dublin 14
Tel **Dublin 977060**
Mem 1497
Sec B Cassidy Tel Dublin 973199/976090
Pro C Greene Tel Dublin 977072
Holes 18 L 5669 yds SSS 69

Recs Am–64 JB Carr
Pro–64 C Greene
V'trs U
Fees £5 (£12)
Loc 3 miles from city centre

Rathfarnham (1896)

Private (Map 7/32)
Newtown Dublin 16
Tel **931201/931561**
Mem 561
Sec VJ Coyle Tel Dublin 931201
Pro B O'Hara
Holes 9 L 5787 metres SSS 70
Recs Am–70 C O'Carrol N Hynes T O'Donnell
Pro–
V'trs WD–U (ex Tues); W/E–NA
Fees £9
Loc S Dublin 10 kilometres

Royal Dublin (1885)

Private (Map 7/33)
Dollymount Dublin 3
Tel Dublin 337153
Mem 780
Sec JA Lambe Tel Dublin 336346
Pro L Owens Tel Dublin 336477 (Tournament Pro C O'Connor)
Holes 18 L 6810 yds SSS 73
Recs Am–67 G O'Donovan
Pro–63 B Langer G Cullen
V'trs U (ex Sat)
Fees £16 (£20)
Loc 3¼ miles from city centre on coast road to Howth

St Anne's (1921)

Private (Map 7/34)
Bull Island Raheny Dublin 5
Tel **Dublin 332797**
Mem 411
Sec John T Kennedy Tel Dublin 336471
Pro P Skerritt Tel Dublin 332797
Holes 9 holes Medal L 5813 metres Par 71 SSS 70
Forward Course L 5424 metres Par 68 SSS 68
Recs Am–67 S Rodgers
Pro–64 P Skerritt
V'trs WD–am; W/E–none; BH–I; SOC
Fees £8 with mem £4
Loc 5 miles from Dublin city centre

Stackstown (1975)

(Map 7/35)
Kellystown Rathfarnham Dublin 14
Tel
Mem 438
Sec D Devine
Pro
Holes 18 L 5925 metres SSS 72
Recs Am–
Pro–
V'trs
Fees
Loc

Sutton (1890)

Private (Map 7/36)
Cush Point Burrow Road Sutton Dublin 13
Tel Sutton (01) 323013
Mem 198 162(L) 95(J) 53(5)
Sec Hugh Quirke
Pro N Lynch
Holes 9 L 5522 yds SSS 67
Recs Am–64 M Hanway
Pro–67 T Halpin
V'trs Tue–NA; Sat after 5.30 pm
Fees £8 (£10)
Loc 7 miles E of Dublin

Co Kildare

Athy (1906)

Private (Map 7/37)
Geraldine Athy
Tel Athy 0607 31729
Mem 250
Sec M Hannon Tel 0507 31171
Pro
Holes 9 L 6158 yds SSS 69
Recs Am–
Pro–
V'trs WD–U; W/E–M on Sats SOC on WD
Fees £4 (£6)
Loc Athy

Bodenstown (1983)

Bodenstown Sallins (Map 7/38)
Tel 045 97096
Mem 650
Sec Patrick Place
Pro T Halpin
Holes 18 L 7031 yds SSS 72
Recs Am–
Pro–
V'trs
Fees
Loc

Cill Dara (1920)

Private (Map 7/39)
Little Curragh Kildare Town
Tel 045 21433
Mem 200
Sec Pat Gill Tel 045 31946
Pro
Holes 9 L 5440 metres SSS 68
Recs Am–67 NP McAlinden
Pro–
V'trs U
Fees £4 (W/E & BH £6)
Loc 1 mile E of Kildare Town

Clongowes (1966)

Private (Map 7/40)
Clongowes Wood College Naas
Tel **Clongowes Wood 68202**
Mem 100
Sec A Pierce Tel as above
Pro
Holes 9 L 5374 yds SSS 65
Recs Am–67
Pro–
V'trs NA
Loc 2 miles from Clane

Curragh (1883)

Private (Map 7/41)
Curragh Co Kildare
Tel Curragh (045) 41238/41714
Mem 500 160(L)
Sec Eamon Quigley
Pro P Lawlor
Holes 18 L 6003 metres SSS 71 Par 72
Recs Am–67 S Conlon
Pro–69 A Whiston
V'trs U
Fees
Loc 3 miles S of Newbridge
Mis Golf played here since 1852 Oldest club in the Republic

Knockanally (1985)

Private (Map 7/80)
Donadea North Kildare
Tel 045 69322
Mem 100
Sec N Lyons
Pro Peter Hickey
Holes 18 L 6484 yds SSS 72
Recs Am–
Pro–70 J Purcell
V'trs U
Fees £6 (£10)
Loc 7 miles Maynooth 5 miles Kilcock 3 miles Enfield (Dublin/Galway road)

Naas (1896)

Private (Map 7/42)
Kerdiffstown Naas
Tel **Naas 7509**
Mem 514
Sec David J Carbery Tel 045-97509
Pro
Holes 9 L 6233 yds SSS 70
Recs Am–66
Pro–
V'trs U SOC
Fees £5 M–£30
Loc 2 miles N of Naas

Co Kilkenny

Callan (1930)

Private (Map 7/43)
Geraldine Callan
Tel **056 25136**
Mem 150
Sec S Rowan Tel 056 25176
Pro
Holes 9 L 5844 yds SSS 68
Recs Am–70 J Madden
Pro–71 M Kavanagh
V'trs U; SOC
Fees £3 W–£15
Loc 1 mile SE Callan Kilkenny 10 miles

Castlecomer (1935)

Private (Map 7/44)
Castlecomer
Tel 056 41139
Mem 120
Sec S Farrell Tel 056 41258
Pro
Holes 9 L 6985 yds SSS 71
Recs Am–70 M Curry
Pro–
V'trs U
Fees £4
Loc 11 miles N Kilkenny city

Kilkenny (1896)

Private (Map 7/45)
Glendine Kilkenny
Tel Kilkenny 22125
Mem 700
Sec S O'Neill
Pro M Kavanagh
Holes 18 L 6374 SSS 70
Recs Am–68 D White B Cashell
Pro–
V'trs U
Fees £6 (£7)
Loc 1 mile N of Kilkenny

Co Laois

Abbey Leix (1895)

Private (Map 7/46)
Abbey Leix Portlaoise
Tel
Mem 241
Sec E Thornton
Pro
Holes 9 L 5680 yds SSS 67
Recs Am–
Pro–
V'trs U
Fees £1 W–£4
Loc 60 miles SW Dublin on Cork Road

Heath (Portlaoise) (1930)

Private (Map 7/47)
Portlaoise
Tel **(0502) 26533**
Mem 375
Sec J McNamara Tel 0502 21327
Pro Danny Hutton
Holes 18 L 6247 yds SSS 70
Recs Am–67 Tom Tyrrell
Pro–
V'trs U
Fees £5
Loc 4 miles E of town

Mountrath (1929)

Private (Map 7/48)
Mountrath
Tel
Mem 74
Sec T O'Grady Tel 0502 32214
Pro
Holes 9 L 5492 yds SSS 65
Recs Am–64 C Carter T Brown
Pro–
V'trs U
Fees 75p
Loc 2 miles Mountrath

Portarlington (1909)

Private (Map 7/49)
Garryhinch Portarlington
Tel **Portarlington 23115**
Mem 198
Sec Don Cunningham Tel 0502 23482
Pro P Lawlor
Holes 9 L 5294 metres SSS 66
Recs Am–67 A Tynan
Pro–67 J Nangle
V'trs U
Fees £3 (£5)
Loc Halfway between Pontarlington and Mountmellick on L116

Rathdowney (1931)

Private (Map 7/50)
Rathdowney Portlaoise Eire
Tel 0505 46170
Mem 97
Sec Sean Bolger
Pro
Holes 9 L 5416 yds SSS 66
Recs Am–67 J O'Callaghan
Pro–69 P Mahon
V'trs U SOC
Fees £3
Loc 1 mile S of Rathdowney

Co Longford

Co Longford (1894)

Private (Map 7/51)
Dublin Road Longford
Tel **043-46310**
Mem 190 75(L) 50 (J)
Sec
Pro Joe Frawley
Holes 18 L 5912 yds SSS 68
Recs Am–71 P Duignan
Pro–69 D Carson
V'trs U
Fees £4
Loc ½ mile town centre

Co Louth

Ardee (1911)

Private (Map 7/52)
Ardee Townparks
Tel 041 53227
Mem 250
Sec Kevin Carrie
Pro
Holes 18 L 5833 yds SSS 68
Recs Am–74 John Higgins
Pro–71 C O'Connor Snr
V'trs U
Fees £5 (£6)
Loc ½ mile N of town

County Louth (1892)

(Residential)
Private (Map 7/53)
Baltray Drogheda
Tel 041 22327
Mem 350
Sec Michael Delany Tel 041 22329
Pro P McGuirk Tel 22444
Holes 18 L 6978 yds SSS 73
Recs Am–66 F Gannon
Pro–65 J Heggarty
V'trs U
Fees £11 (£15)
Loc 3 miles NE Drogheda

Dundalk (1905)

Private (Map 7/54)
Blackrock Dundalk
Tel (042) 21379
Mem 850
Sec P Moriarty Tel 042 21731
Pro J Cassidy Tel 042 22102
Holes 18 L 6067 metres SSS 72
Recs Am–
Pro–
V'trs U SOC
Fees £8 (£10)
Loc 3 miles S Dundalk

Greenore (1896)

Private (Map 7/55)
Greenore
Tel 042 73212
Mem 250 86 (Associates)
Sec Michael McCuninsky Tel 31650/35924 (home)
Pro
Holes 18 L 5614 metres SSS 69
Recs Am–67 S McParland
P McParland
Pro–67 C O'Connor Sen
V'trs WD–before 5 pm; W/E before noon; SOC
Fees £5 (W/E & BH £7)
Loc 15 miles N of Dundalk on main Greenore Road

Co Meath

Gormanston College (1961)

Private (Map 7/56)
Franciscan College Gormanston
Tel **01 412630**
Mem 140
Sec Fr Declan Timmons
Pro B Browne
Holes 9 L 3956 yds SSS 58
Recs Am–63 M Gannon
Pro–
V'trs M
Fees
Loc 22 miles N of Dublin

Headfort (1928)

Private (Map 7/57)
Kells
Tel (046) 40148
Mem 450
Sec H Flanagan
Pro Joe Purcell Tel (046) 40639
Holes 18 L 6350 yds SSS 69
Recs Am–67 D Snow
Pro–64 D Smyth
V'trs U
Fees £6 (£7)
Loc Kells ½ mile

Laytown and Bettystown (1909)

Private (Map 7/58)
Bettystown Drogheda
Tel **041 27534**
Mem 750
Sec/ Man JO Carr Tel 041 27170
Pro RJ Browne Tel Bettystown 27563 (Tournament Pro Des Smyth)
Holes 18 L 6254 yds SSS 69
Recs Am–
Pro–65 Ian Woosnam
V'trs U SOC on WD
Fees £7 (£10)
Loc 25 miles N of Dublin

Royal Tara (1923)

Private (Map 7/59)
Bellinter Park Navan
Tel 046 25244/25508
Mem 827
Sec Desmond Foley Tel 046 21098
Pro A Whiston
Holes 18 L 6343 yds SSS 70
Recs Am–70 D Leonard
Pro–
V'trs H
Fees £6 (£8)
Loc 24 miles N of Dublin

Trim (1970)

Private (Map 7/60)
Newtownmoynagh Trim
Tel 046 314463
Mem 250 (150 Associates)
Sec Peter J Darby Tel 046 31438
Pro
Holes 9 L 6266 yds SSS 70
Recs Am–69 P Rayfus
Pro–
V'trs WD–U (exc Ladies day); SOC exc Sun; W/E–restricted
Fees £5 (£6)
Loc 2½ miles SW of Trim

Co Offaly

Birr (1893)

Private (Map 7/61)
The Glenns Birr
Tel **0509-20082**
Mem 320
Sec P O'Gorman Tel 0509-20271
Pro
Holes 18 L 6216 yds SSS 70
Recs Am–66 JB Carr
Pro–68 RJ Browne
V'trs U; SOC exc Sun
Fees D–£6
Loc 2 miles from town of Birr

Edenderry (1910)

Private (Map 7/62)
Boherbree Edenderry
Tel (0405) 31072
Mem 230
Sec EA Moran Tel Edenderry (0405) 31342
Pro
Holes 9 L 5791 yds SSS 67
Recs Am–66 AJ McNally
Pro–

V'trs U
Fees £4 (£5)
Loc 1 mile E of Edenderry

Tullamore (1896)

Private (Map 7/63)
Brookfield Tullamore
Tel **0606-21439**
Mem 700
Sec William M Rossiter Tel 0506-21310
Pro JE Kelly Tel 0506-21439
Holes 18 L 6314 yds SSS 71
Recs Am–64 D White
Pro–68 H Boyle J Martin D Jones
V'trs WD–Tue Ladies Day; W/E–Sat members 12.30–3 pm, Sun–NA; SOC
Fees D–£6 (R–£8)
Loc 2½ miles S of Tullamore town
Mis Buggies for hire

Co Wexford

Courtown (1936)

Private (Map 7/64)
Courtown Harbour Gorey
Tel **Courtown 055 25166**
Mem 460
Sec J Sheehan Tel 055 21533
Pro
Holes 18 L 6398 yds SSS 70
Recs Am–67 T Keely
Pro–68 M Murphy
V'trs U SOC
Fees £5 (£7)
Loc 2½ miles S of Gorey

Enniscorthy (1908)

Private (Map 7/65)
Knockmarshal Enniscorthy
Tel **Enniscorthy 33191**
Mem 300
Sec J Whitney Tel 054-33670 (home)
Pro
Holes 9 L 6368 yds SSS 70
Recs Am–67 N Delaney
Pro–
V'trs U SOC exc Sun
Fees £4 (£5)
Loc 1 mile SW of town centre
Mis Full catering

New Ross (1917)

Private (Map 7/66)
Tinneranny New Ross
Tel **(051) 21433**
Mem 250
Sec/
Man (051) 21451
Pro
Holes 9 L 5578 metres SSS 69
Recs Am–66 M O'Brien
Pro–65 C O'Connor
V'trs U exc Sun; SOC
Fees £5
Loc 1 mile W

Rosslare (1908)

Private (Map 7/67)
Strand Rosslare
Tel **053 32113**
Mem 500
Sec Miss A O'Keefe Tel (053) 32203
Pro A Skerritt Tel Rosslare 32238
Holes 18 L 6502 yds SSS 70
Recs Am–65 D Noonan
V'trs U SOC
Fees £8 (£10)
Loc

Wexford (1966)

Private (Map 7/68)
Mulgannon Wexford
Tel (053) 42238
Mem 215
Sec Adrian Doyle Tel (053) 44720
Pro
Holes 18 L 6109 yds SSS 69
Recs Am–
Pro–
V'trs U SOC
Fees £5
Loc ½ mile Wexford town

Co Westmeath

Moate (1940)

Private (Map 7/69)
Moate
Tel **0902 31271**
Mem 176
Sec James Flynn
Pro
Holes 9 L 5348 yds SSS 65
Recs Am–68 T O'Brien
Pro–
V'trs U
Fees £1 (£1.50) W–£5
Loc 1 mile N of town

Mullingar (1896)

Private (Map 7/70)
Belvedere Mullingar
Tel **Mullingar 8366**
Mem 472
Sec A Lee
Pro J Burns
Holes 18 L 6370 yds SSS 70
Recs Am–64 R Carr
Pro–64 P Tupling
V'trs U
Fees £1.50 (£2)
Loc 3 miles S of Mullingar

Co Wicklow

Arklow (1927)

Private (Map 7/71)
Abbeylands Arklow
Tel **(0402) 32492**
Mem 310
Sec Brendan Timmons
Pro Kevin Daly
Holes 18 L 5770 yds SSS 68
Recs Am–66 T Dowling
Pro–66 T Halpin
V'trs WD–U; Sat–U after 5 pm; Sun–no green fees; SOC Mon–Sat
Fees £4 (£6)
Loc ½ mile from town centre

Baltinglass (1928)

Private (Map 7/72)
Baltinglass
Tel **Baltinglass 52**
Mem 350
Sec David Lord Tel (0508) 81350
Pro M Murphy
Holes 9 L 6070 yds SSS 68
Recs Am–66 D Kilcoyne Rev McDonnell
Pro–70 S Hunt
V'trs U SOC
Fees £4 (£6)
Loc 38 miles S of Dublin

Blainroe (1978)

Blainroe (Map 7/73)
Tel 0404 68168
Mem 600
Sec W O'Sullivan
Pro J McDonald
Holes 18 L 6681 yds SSS 72
Recs Am–
Pro–
V'trs U
Fees £7 (£10) W–£35 M–£75
Loc 3½ miles S of Wicklow on coast

Bray (1897)

Private (Map 7/74)
Ravenswell Road Bray
Tel **Bray 862484**
Mem 272 (151 Associates)
Sec EJ Crean
Pro M Walby
Holes 9 L 5230 metres SSS 70
Recs Am–
Pro–
V'trs U before 6 pm; SOC on WD
Fees £6
Loc Bray, 12 miles S of Dublin

Coollattin (1950)

Private (Map 7/75)
Coollattin Shillelagh Co Wicklow
Tel **055 29125**
Mem 240
Sec J O'Shea Tel 055 26290
Pro
Holes 9 L 6070 yds SSS 69
Recs Am–
Pro–
V'trs
Fees £3 (£4)
Loc

Delgany (1908)

Private (Map 7/76)
Delgany Co Wicklow
Tel **874645/874833**
Mem 800
Sec J Deally Tel 874536
Pro J Bradshaw Tel 874536
Holes 18 L 5249 yds SSS 69
Recs Am–63
Pro–
V'trs U exc comp days; SOC–Mon Thu Fri, or after 3.30 pm WD & W/E
Fees £8.50 (£9.50)
Loc 2 miles from Greystones

Greystones (1895)

Private (Map 7/77)
Greystones
Tel Dublin 876624
Mem 750
Sec O Walsh Tel Greystones 874136
Pro K Daly
Holes 18 L 5387 metres SSS 68
Recs Am–67
Pro–66
V'trs Mid-week
Fees £8 (£9)
Loc Greystones Co Wicklow

Wicklow (1904)

Private (Map 7/78)
Dunbur Road Wicklow
Tel **Wicklow 67379**
Mem 408
Sec J Kelly
Pro
Holes 9 L 5536 yds SSS 66
Recs Am–65 W Mitchell LJ Mooney
Pro–
V'trs I
Fees £5 (£6)
Loc

Woodenbridge (1884)

Private (Map 7/79)
Arklow Co Wicklow
Tel **Arklow 5202**
Mem 210
Sec TH Crummy
Pro
Holes 9 L 5790 yds SSS 66
Recs Am–63 Michael Holden
Pro–
V'trs U (ex Sat)
Fees £6 (£8)
Loc 45 miles S from Dublin and 4 miles W of Arklow

Munster

Co Clare

Drumoland Castle

Private (Map 7/1)
Newmarket-on-Fergus
Tel **(061) 71144**
Mem 150
Sec Michael Wright Ext 618
Pro
Holes 18 L 6089 yds SSS 70
Recs Am–
Pro–
V'trs U SOC
Fees D–£8 (D–£10)
Loc 18 miles NW of Limerick
Mis 9 new holes to be opened 1986

Ennis (1907)

Private (Map 7/2)
Drumbiggle Road Ennis
Tel **(065) 24074**
Men 521
Sec PE Dooley Tel (065) 24074
Pro Martin Ward
Holes 18 L 5358 metres SSS 68
Recs Am-64 G Roche
Pro-66 P Skerritt
V'trs U
Fees £6
Loc

Kilkee (1908)

Private (Map 7/3)
East End, Kilkee Co Clare
Tel **Kilkee 48**
Mem 343 160(L)
Sec TM Lillis Tel Kilkee 341
Pro
Holes 9 L 6185 yds SSS 69
Recs Am–68 D Nagle N Cotter
Pro–
V'trs U SOC (not mid-July to mid-August)
Fees £5.50 W–£22 M–£45
Loc E end Kilkee

Kilrush (1934)

Public (Map 7/4)
Parknamoney Kilrush
Tel **(065) 51138**
Mem 150
Sec Paul J Coady
Pro
Holes 9 L 2739 yds (×2 for 18) SSS 67
Recs 64 Gross
62 Nett DF Nagle
Pro
V'trs U; SOC
Fees W-£3
Loc Kerry-Clare route

Lahinch (1983)

Private (Map 7/5)
Lahinch
Tel **065 81003**
Mem 1255
Sec/Man Michael Murphy Tel 065 81003
Pro R McCavery Tel 065 81408
Holes Champ 18 L 6515 yds SSS 72
No 2 18 L 5450 yds SSS 67
Recs Medal Course Am–65 R Hennessy
Pro–67 C O'Connor
No 2 Course Am-None
Pro-W McCavery
V'trs WD–U; W/E–NA 9-10.30 and 1-2.00; SOC
Fees £12 (£15) £9 Castle Course
Loc 2 miles Ennistymon on T69

Shannon (1966)

Private (Map 7/6)
Shannon Airport
Tel **Shannon 61020**
Mem 403
Sec Maurice Sheehy Tel 61849
Pro Eugene O'Connor
Holes 18 L 6854 yds SSS 73
Recs Am–63 J Purcell
Pro–65 D Durnian
V'trs U
Fees £5 (£6)
Loc 300 yds Shannon Airport Terminal

Spanish Point (1915)

Private (Map 7/7)
Miltown Malbay Co Clare
Tel
Mem 100
Sec S Treacy J Logan
Pro
Holes 9 L 3124 yds SSS 54
Recs Am–28 PJ Leyden
Pro–23 P Skerritt
V'trs U
Fees £1.50 W–£5
Loc 2 miles from Milton Malby

Co Cork

Bandon (1910)

Private (Map 7/8)
Castlebernard Bandon
Tel **(023) 41111**
Mem 520
Sec B O'Neill Tel (023) 41998
Pro T O'Boyle Tel (023) 42224
Holes 18 L 5663 metres SSS 69
Recs Am–65 Donal O'Donovan
Pro–
V'trs U
Fees £5 (£4)
Loc Bandon 1½ miles

Bantry (1975)

(Map 7/9)
Donemark Bantry Co Cork
Tel **(027) 50132**
Mem 250
Sec Kevin O'Donovan Tel (027) 50132
Pro
Holes 9 L 6436 yds SSS 70
Recs Am–
Pro–66 C O'Connor Jr
V'trs U
Fees D–£5
Loc 1 mile from Bantry on Glengarriff Road

Charleville (1941)

Private (Map 7/10)
Charleville Co Cork
Tel **Charleville 257**
Mem 250
Sec T Murphy
Pro
Holes 18 L 6380 yds SSS 69
Recs Am–68 T Murphy
Pro–
V'trs U
Fees £6
Loc On main road between Cork and Limerick

Cork (1888)

Private (Map 7/11)
Little Island Co Cork
Tel **021-353263**
Mem 724
Sec JC Kennedy Tel (0) 353451 (home) 966432
Pro D Higgins Tel 353037
Holes 18 L 6065 metres SSS 72
Recs Am–66 AJ Heverin
Pro–
V'trs U W/D (except Thurs) W/E 10.30–12 and after 2.30 SOC £9 per player
Fees £10 (W/E & BH–£12)
Loc 5 miles E of Cork (½ mile off Cork-Cobh road)

Doneraile (1927)

Private (Map 7/12)
Doneraile
Tel **(022) 24137**
Mem 200
Sec Frank Carey
Pro
Holes 9 L 5528 yds SSS 67
Recs Am–
Pro–
V'trs U
Fees £3
Loc ½ mile from town

Douglas (1909)

Private (Map 7/13)
Douglas Co Cork
Tel **021 891086**
Mem 839
Sec GA Finn Tel 021 895297
Pro GS Nicholson Tel 021 932055
Holes 18 L 5651 metres SSS 69 Par 69
Recs Am–68 T Higgins
Pro–64 E Darcy
V'trs WD–U; W/E–NA before 11.30 am; SOC on WD
Fees IR£9 (IR£10)
Loc 3 miles from Cork

Dunmore (1968)

Private (Map 7/14)
Clonakilty Dunmore
Tel **023 33352**
Mem 92
Sec M Minihan
Pro
Holes 9 L 4180 yds SSS 60
Recs Am–65
Pro–62
V'trs U
Fees 75p
Loc

East Cork (1971)

Private (Map 7/15)
Gortacrue Midleton
Tel **021 631687**
Mem 175
Sec E Moloney
Pro
Holes 9 L 5602 yds SSS 72
Recs Am–
Pro–
V'trs
Fees 50p
Loc

Fermoy (1887)

Private (Map 7/16)
Corin Fermoy
Mem 200
Sec P McCarthy Tel (025) 31642 (home)
Holes 18 L 5399 metres SSS 68 Par 70
Recs Am–65 T Cleary
V'trs U SOC
Fees £5, £4 with mem
Loc 2 miles from Fermoy

Glengarriff (1936)

Private (Map 7/17)
Glengarriff
Tel **Glengarriff 150**
Mem **67**
Sec **Neill Clarke Tel Bantry 9**
Pro
Holes **9 L 4328 yds SSS 61**
Recs **Am–62 J O'Sullivan**
Pro–
V'trs **U**
Fees **£1 W–£4**
Loc **1 mile from Glengarriff**

Kanturk (1974)

Private (Map 7/18)
Fairy Hill Kanturk
Tel **029-50534**
Mem 148
Sec Richard O'Brien Tel 029-50181
Pro
Holes 9 L 5527 yds SSS 69
Recs Am–
Pro–
V'trs U
Fees D–£3 W–£10
Loc 1½ miles SW of town centre

Kinsale (1912)

Private (Map 7/19)
Ringenane Belgooly Kinsale
Tel 021 772197
Mem 310
Sec E O'Leary
Pro
Holes 9 L 5332 metres SSS 68
Recs Am–66 C Coughlan
Pro–
V'trs U; W/E–NA SOC
Fees £5
Loc 2 miles from Kinsale 16 miles from Cork

Macroom (1924)

Private (Map 7/20)
Lackaduve Macroom
Tel 026-41072
Mem 273
Sec JF Morris
Pro
Holes 9 L 5439 metres SSS 68
Recs Am–66 J Mills
Pro–
V'trs U; SOC
Fees D-IR £4
Loc ½ mile from Bus Depot

Mallow (1947)

Private (Map 7/21)
Balleyellis Mallow
Tel **Mallow (022) 21145**
Mem 1400
Sec Nick Redmond Tel (022) 21529
Pro Sean Conway Tel (022) 21145
Holes 18 L 6559 yds SSS 71
Recs Am–66 J Murphy
Pro–
V'trs U SOC
Fees £5 W–£20
Loc 1½ miles SE of Mallow Bridge
Mis Squash and tennis courts available; court fee £2

Mitchelstown (1908)

Private (Map 7/22)
Gurrane Mitchelstown
Tel **(025) 24072**
Mem **290**
Sec **Denis Keane**
Pro
Holes **9 L 5057 metres SSS 67**
Recs **Am-64 A Pierce**
Pro-
V'trs **U; SOC**
Fees **£4 (£5)**
Loc **30 miles N of Cork**

Monkstown (1908)

Private (Map 7/23)
Parkgarriffe Monkstown
Tel Cork 841225
Mem **600**
Sec **JP Curtin Tel Cork 841376**
Pro **B Murphy Tel 841686**
Holes **18 L 5534 mtrs SSS 68**
Recs **Am–66**
Pro–
V'trs **U**
Fees £8 (£9)
Loc 7 miles S of Cork

Muskerry (1897)

Private (Map 7/24)
Carrigrohane Co Cork
Tel **(021) 85297**
Mem 713
Sec JJ Moynihan Tel (021) 85297
Pro WM Lehane Tel (021) 85104
Holes 18 L 5786 metres SSS 70
Recs Am–66 J McHenry D O'Flynn
Pro–66 J Hegerty
V'trs WD–U exc 4.30 pm–6.30 pm; W/E–NA before 3.30 pm
Fees M £7 L £6; with mem M £4 L £3 (only one visitor per member on reduced rate)
Loc 6 miles W of Cork

Skibbereen (1931)

Private (Map 7/25)
Skibbereen
Tel 028 21227
Mem **240**
Sec **J Breen 028 21088**
Pro **None**
Holes **9 L 5774 yds SSS 68**
Recs **Am–65 B McDaid**
Pro–
V'trs **U**
Fees **£4 W–£20**
Loc **1 mile west**

Youghal (1940)

Private (Map 7/26)
Knockaverry Youghal
Tel Youghal 024 2787
Mem **130 63(L) 22(J)**
Sec **Wm White**
Pro **D Higgins**
Holes **18 L 6223 yds SSS 69**
Recs **Am–65 F Wright**
Pro–
V'trs **U**
Fees **IR £3.50**
Loc **30 miles E of Cork**

Co Kerry

Ballybunion (1896)

Private (Map 7/27)
Ballybunion
Tel (068) 27146
Mem 800
Sec S Walsh Tel (068) 27146
Pro Ted Higgins Tel (068) 27209
Holes Old Course 18 L 6542 yds
New Course 18 L 6477 yds
Recs Am–67 P Mulcare
Pro–
V'trs U; SOC
Fees D–£20 W–£70 M–£100
Loc

Ceann Sibeal (1924)

Private (Map 7/28)
Ballyferriter Tralee
Tel **066 56157**
Mem 102
Sec G Partington Tel 066 51657
Pro
Holes 9 L 6222 yds SSS 68
Recs **Am–69 P Slattery A Spring**
Pro–70 Liam Higgins
V'trs U SOC
Fees D–£6 W–£25
Loc Dingle Peninsula

Dooks and Caragh (1889)

Private (Map 7/29)
Glenbeigh Co Kerry
Tel 066 68205
Mem 298
Sec M Shanahan Tel 066 67370
Pro
Holes 18 L 5346 metres SSS 68
Recs Am–67 G Sullivan
Pro–
V'trs U; SOC
Fees D–£7 W–£30
Loc 3 miles N of Glenbeigh on Ring of Kenny

Kenmare (1903)

Private (Map 7/30)
Kenmare
Tel **(064) 41291**
Mem **150**
Sec **TA O'Shea**
Pro
Holes **9 L 4400 mtrs SSS 64**
Recs **Am–64 B Mulcahy**
Pro–
V'trs **U**
Fees **£4**
Loc **100m Kenmare Town**

Killarney Golf and Fishing Club (1891)

Private (Map 7/31)
Mahoney's Point Killarney
Tel 064 31034
Mem 734
Sec **Capt DD O'Connell Tel 064 31242**
Pro **T Coveney Tel 064 31615**
Holes **18 L 6677 yds SSS 70 (Mahoney's Point Course)**
18 L 6798 yds SSS 72 (Killeen Course)
Recs **Am–68 S Coyne (Mahoney's Point Course)**
Am–73 DF O'Sullivan (Killeen)
V'trs **U**
Fees £14
Loc 3 miles W of town

Parknasilla (1974)

Private (Map 7/32)
Parknasilla
Tel **(064) 45122**
Mem **20**
Sec **M Walsh Tel (064) 45233**
Pro **C McCarthy Tel (064) 45172**
Holes **9 4650 metres SSS 65**

Recs Am–28 J Bruen NE McCann
Pro–28 J McCarthy
V'trs U
Fees £5
Loc Great Southern Hotel

Tralee (1904)

Private (Map 7/33)
West Barrow Ardfert Co Kerry
Tel 066 36379
Mem 500
Man JW Kleynhans Tel 066 36379
Pro
Holes 18 L 6210 metres SSS 72
Recs Am–67 G O'Sullivan
Pro–
V'trs WD–U; W/E–U after noon; SOC on WD & Sat
Fees £10
Loc 8 miles W of Tralee centre
Mis First Arnold Palmer course in Europe

Waterville (1925)

Private (Map 7/34)
Waterville Lake Hotel
Tel **Waterville 79 81 56**
Mem 247
Sec Terry O'Kane Tel 0667-4102
Pro L. Higgins Tel 0667-4261
Holes 18 L 7146 yds SSS 74
Recs Am-
Pro-65 L Higgins
V'trs U; H; SOC
Fees £8
Loc Ring of Kerry

Co Limerick

Adare Manor (1900)

Private (Map 7/35)
Adare
Tel (061) 86204
Mem 350
Sec S Ryan Tel (061) 86204
Pro
Holes 9 L 5145 metres SSS 67
Recs Am–
Pro–
V'trs U; W/E–M
Fees D–£8
Loc 10 miles S of Limerick

Castletroy (1937)

Private (Map 7/36)
Castletroy Limerick
Tel 061 335261
Mem 984
Sec L Hayes Tel 061 335753
Pro N Cassidy Tel 061 338283
Holes 18 L 5927 metres SSS 71
Recs Am–66 B Begley
Pro–63 H Bradshaw
V'trs WD–U; W/E–U until 12 on Sats; M after noon and Suns; SOC–Mon Wed Fri
Fees £9 (£9)
Loc 2½ miles N of Limerick on Dublin Road

Limerick (1891)

Private (Map 7/37)
Ballyclough Limerick
Tel Limerick 061 44083
Mem 1070
Sec D McDonogh Tel 061 45146
Pro J Cassidy Tel 061 42492
Holes 18 L 5767 yds SSS 70
Recs Am–65 W Rice
Pro–67 F McGloin J Kinsella
V'trs WD–U before 5 pm exc Tues; W/E–M; SOC on WD
Fees £10
Loc 3 miles S of Limerick City

Newcastle West (1940)

Private (Map 7/38)
Newcastle West
Tel **Newcastle West 76**
Mem 345
Sec R Cussen Tel Newcastle West 20
Pro
Holes 9 L 5482 yds SSS 65
Recs Am–65 D Kennedy
Pro–
V'trs U
Fees £1
Loc ½ mile S of town

Co Tipperary

Cahir Park (1968)

Private (Map 7/39)
Kilcommon Cahir Co Tipperary
Tel Cahir 41474
Mem 187
Sec K Murphy Tel Cahir 062-52155 (Off)
Pro
Holes 9 L 6262 yds SSS 69
Recs Am–68
Pro–
V'trs U; SOC Mon to Sat
Fees £5 (£5)
Loc 1 mile S of Cahir

Carrick-on-Suir (1939)

Private (Map 7/40)
Garravoone Garrick-on-Suir
Tel (051) 40047
Mem 160
Sec Michael G Kelly Tel (051) 40300 (home)
Pro
Holes 9 L 5948 yds SSS 68
Recs Am–68 B Walsh
Pro–
V'trs U; SOC on WD & Sat
Fees £4
Loc 2 miles on Dungarvan Road

Clonmel (1911)

Private (Map 7/41)
Lyreanearla Clonmel
Tel Clonmel 052 21138
Mem 409
Sec T Darmody Tel 052 21138
Pro R Hayes
Holes 18 L 6330 yds SSS 70
Recs Am–65 S Wall
V'trs U
Fees £4 (£5)
Loc 3 miles SW of Clonmel

Nenagh (1929)

Private (Map 7/42)
Beechwood Nenagh
Tel **067 31476**
Mem 453
Sec Paul Malone
Pro
Holes 18 L 5911 yds SSS 67
Recs Am–
Pro–
V'trs U
Fees WD–£4 W/E–£5
Loc Nenagh 3 miles

Rockwell College (1964)

Private (Map 7/51)
Rockwell College Cashel
Tel
Mem 85
Sec John Ryan Tel 062 61444
Pro
Holes 9 L 4136 yds SSS 60
V'trs NA
Loc 3 miles S of Cashel on main Cork–Dublin road

Roscrea (1893)

Private (Map 7/43)
Roscrea
Tel Roscrea 21130
Mem 337
Sec MF Donnellan
Pro
Holes 9 L 6059 yds SSS 69
Recs Am–67 R Carr
Pro–
V'trs U
Fees £5
Loc 2 miles on Dublin Road

Templemore (1970)

Private (Map 7/44)
Manna South Templemore Co Tipperary
Tel Templemore 53
Mem 210
Sec John K Moloughney Tel 0504 31720
Pro
Holes 9 L 5442 yds SSS 66
Recs Am–
Pro–
V'trs U except Sun; SOC
Fees £4 (£5)
Loc ½ mile S of town

Thurles (1909)

Private (Map 7/45)
Turtula Thurles
Tel **Thurles 0504 21983**
Mem 555
Sec Benny Maher
Pro Sean Hunt
Holes 18 L 6230 yds SSS 70
Recs Am–66 DF O'Sullivan
Pro–70 H Bradshaw
V'trs U
Fees £7
Loc 1 mile S of Thurles

Tipperary (1879)

Private (Map 7/46)
Rathanny Tipperary
Tel **Tipperary (062) 51119**
Mem 200
Sec P O'Donogue St Michael Street
Pro
Holes 9 L 6074 yds SSS 69
Recs Am–65 AD Pierse
Pro–
V'trs U
Fees £3
Loc 1 mile Tipperary town

Co Waterford

Dungarvan (1924)

Private (Map 7/47)
Ballinacourty Dungarvan
Tel (058) 41605
Mem 489
Sec J Murphy
Pro
Holes 9 L 5721 mtrs SSS 69
Recs Am–67 ND O'Kennedy
Pro–
V'trs U
Fees £4 (£5)
Loc

Lismore (1965)

Private (Map 7/48)
Lismore Ballyin
Tel 058 54026
Mem 150
Sec M O'Shea Tel 058 54184

Pro T Maher Tel 058 54026
Holes 9 L 5127 metres SSS 67
Recs Am–66 R Ormonde
Pro–65 L Higgins
V'trs U; SOC exc Sun
Fees £4 W–£16
Loc 1 mile N

Tramore (1894)

Private (Map 7/49)
Tramore
Tel **(051) 86170 (office) (051) 81247 (public)**
Mem 550
Sec R Brennan Tel (H) 051 81616
Pro C Butler Tel 051 81000
Holes 18 L 5977 yds SSS 71
Recs Am–66 E Curran
Pro–66 H Boyle
V'trs U
Fees £10
Loc 7 miles S of Waterford

Waterford (1912)

Private (Map 7/50)
Newrath Waterford
Tel **Waterford 051 74182**
Mem 500
Sec PJ Burke Tel 051 32842
Pro J Condon Tel 051 76748
Holes 18 L 6232 metres SSS 70
Recs Am–66 P O'Rourke
Pro–70 C Kane
V'trs U
Fees £7 (£10)
Loc

Ulster

Co Antrim

Ballycastle (1891)

Private (Map 7/1)
Ballycastle BT54 6QP
Tel **Ballycastle 62536**
Mem 650
Sec TJ Sheehan Tel Ballycastle 62596
Pro AJ Hunter Tel Ballycastle 62506
Holes 18 L 5906 yds SSS 69
Recs Am–66 F Fleming J McAleese J McCoy
Pro–64 F Daly
V'trs U H SOC
Fees £4 (£6) W–£20 M–£45
Loc North Antrim coast midway between Portrush and Cushendall

Ballyclare (1923)

Private (Map 7/2)
25 Springvale Road Ballyclare
Tel **Ballyclare 22696**
Mem 400
Sec H McConnell Tel Ballyclare 22051
Pro
Holes 9 L 6708 yds SSS 71
Recs Am–69 J Foster
Pro–72 E Jones
V'trs U (except not before 6 pm Sat or noon Sunday)
Fees £3 (£6)
Loc 1½ miles N of Ballyclare 14 miles N of Belfast

Ballymena (1902)

Private (Map 7/3)
128 Raceview Road, Ballymena
Tel **Broughshane 861207**
Mem 893
Sec MDS Rainey Tel Ballymena 861487
Pro J Gallagher 861652
Holes 18 L 5168 yds SSS 67
Recs Am–62 D Cunning
V'trs WD & Sun-U; SOC: Sat-M
Fees £5 (£7.50 Sat)
Loc 2 miles E on A42

Bushfoot (1890)

Private (Map 7/4)
Portballintrae Bushmills
Tel **Bushmills 31317**
Mem 677
Sec JH McConnell
Pro
Holes 9 L 5572 yds SSS 67
Recs Am–57 W Smyth
Pro–
V'trs U; W/E–NA after noon Sat; SOC
Fees £4 (£5) W–£15 M–£30
Loc 1 mile N of Bushmills

Cairndhu (1928)

Private (Map 7/5)
192 Coast Road Ballygally Larne BT40 2QC
Tel **0547 83248**
Mem 800
Sec Mrs J Robinson Tel 0547 83324
Pro R Walker Tel 0547 83477
Holes 18 L 6112 yds SSS 69
Recs Am–64 B McMillen R Houston
Pro–64 D Jones P Townsend
V'trs U
Fees £4.70 (£7) W–£11 M–£22
Loc 4 miles N of Larne

Carrickfergus (1926)

Private (Map 7/6)
35 North Road, Carrickfergus, Co Antrim BT38 8LP
Tel **Carrickfergus 63713**
Mem 800
Sec ID Jardine Tel Carrickfergus 63713
Pro Ray Stevenson Tel Carrickfergus 65803
Holes 18 L 5769 yds SSS 68
Recs Am-64 Paul Vizard
Pro-64 Norman Drew
V'trs U
Fees £4.50 (£6) W–£18
Loc ½ mile Carrickfergus via Albert Road
Mis Buggies for hire

Cushendall (1937)

Private (Map 7/7)
21 Shore Road Cushendall
Tel **Cushendall 71318**
Mem 659
Sec DD Anderson Tel 71426
Pro
Holes 9 L 4678 yds SSS 63
Recs Am–61 B McCollam
Pro–
V'trs Restrictions W/E; SOC
Fees £5 (£6) M–£40
Loc In village 25 miles N of Larne

Dunmurry (1905)

Private (Map 7/8)
91 Dunmurry Lane Dunmurry Belfast BT17 9JS
Tel **Belfast 621402**
Mem 380 120(L) 50(J)
Sec WRN Blair Tel 610834
Pro G Bleakley Tel 620179
Holes 18 L 5333 metres SSS 68
Recs Am-68 A Young
Pro-70 V Bruce
V'trs NA after 5 pm Tue and Thurs
NA before 5 pm Sats
Fees £5 (£6); SOC £3.50 (£4.50)
Loc ½ mile from Dunmurry 5 miles from Belfast

Greenisland (1894)

Private (Map 7/9)
156 Upper Road Greenisland Carickfergus BT38 8RW
Tel **Whiteabbey 62236**
Mem 480
Sec J Wyness Tel Whiteabbey 64583
Pro
Holes 9 L 5434 metres SSS 68
Recs Am–66
Pro–
V'trs WD–U; W/E–NA Sat before 5 pm; SOC exc Sat
Fees £4 (£5)
Loc 9 miles NE of Belfast

Larne (1894)

Private (Map 7/10)
54 Ferris Bay Road Islandmagee Larne BT40 3RT
Tel **82228**
Mem 320
Sec JB Stewart Tel 09603 61217
Pro
Holes 9 L 6114 yds SSS 69
Recs Am–66 Ian A Nesbitt
Pro–68 Norman Drew
V'trs WD–U; W/E–M after 5 pm; SOC WD & Sun
Fees £2.50 (£5) M–£30
Loc 1 mile Larne Harbour (by sea) or 6 miles N of Whitehead on Browns Bay Road

Lisburn (1891)

Private (Map 7/11)
68 Eglantine Road Lisburn Co Antrim BT27 5RQ
Tel **Lisburn 2186**
Mem 1100
Sec TC McCullough Tel Lisburn 77216
Pro BR Campbell Tel Lisburn 77217
Holes 18 L 5708 metres SSS 72
Recs Am–68 J Boyd
Pro–
V'trs WD–U; W/E–M; SOC Mon Thu
Fees £6
Loc 3 miles S of Lisburn

Massereene (1895)

Private (Map 7/12)
51 Lough Road Antrim BT41 4DQ
Tel **(08494) 63293**
Mem 770
Sec Mrs M Agnew Tel (08494) 62096

Pro Jim Smyth Tel (08494) 64074
Holes 18 L 6614 metres SSS 73
Recs Am–
Pro–
V'trs U SOC
Fees £5 (W/E & BH–£7.50)
Loc ½ mile from Antrim

Rathmore (1947)

Bushmills Road, Portrush
Tel **Portrush 2285**
Mem 237
Sec RG McBride Tel 822996
Holes Play over Portrush

Royal Portrush (1888)

Private (Map 7/13)
Dunluce Road Portrush BT56 8JQ
Tel Portrush 822311
Mem 864 255(L)
Sec Miss Wilma Erskine
Tel Portrush 822311
Pro DA Stevenson Tel Portrush 823335
Holes Dunluce 18 L 6810 yds SSS 73
Valley 18 L 6259 yds SSS 70
9 holes L 1187 yds
Recs Dunluce Am–68 JB Carr
M Edwards
Pro–66 J Hargreaves
Valley Am–65 MJC Hoey
Pro–
9 holes Am–
Pro–
V'trs U; SOC
Fees Dunluce £8 (£12) W–£40
Valley £6 (£8) W–£30
9 holes 75p
Loc Coastal–½ mile Portrush

Whitehead (1904)

Private (Map 7/14)
McCrae's Brae Whitehead
Tel Whitehead 72792 and 78631
Mem 649
Sec/ Man J Niblock Tel Whitehead 78631
(Hon Sec DA Dinsmore)
Pro H Graham
Holes 18 L 6412 yds SSS 71
Recs Am–68 AB Armstrong
Pro–69 EC Brown
V'trs U exc Sat; SOC exc Sat
Fees M £4.50 (£6) L £4 (£5.50)
Loc ½ mile outside town off main road to Island Magee

Co Armagh

County Armagh (1893)

Private (Map 7/15)
Newry Road Armagh
Tel **Armagh 522501**
Mem 799
Sec I Dawson Tel Armagh 522914
Pro L Fisher
Holes 18 L 6184 yds SSS 69
Recs Am–68
Pro–65
V'trs U
Fees £3 (£5)
Loc 40 miles SW Belfast

Craigavon

Public (Map 7/16)
Golf/Ski Centre Turmoyra Lane
Silverwood Lurgan Craigavon
Tel **Lurgan (0762) 6606**
Mem
Sec SN McClelland
Pro D Paul
Holes 9 L 2932 yds Par 3 course
Recs
V'trs
Fees Season and daily tickets
Loc Lurgan 1½ miles
Mis 12-hole pitch & putt course
Floodlit driving range 20 bays (10 covered) Open weekdays 9 am-9.30 pm Sat/Sun 9 am-5 pm Professional tuition
Putting green

Lurgan (1893)

Private (Map 7/17)
The Demesne Lurgan
Tel Lurgan 22087 and 5306
Mem 617
Sec A Rae
Pro D Paul
Holes 18 L 5836 metres SSS 70
Recs Am–66 S Magee
Pro–66 R Carr
V'trs U; SOC
Fees £6 (£7)
Loc Town centre

Portadown (1906)

Private (Map 7/18)
Carrickblacker Portadown
Tel Portadown 332296
Mem 748
Sec/ Man Mrs ME Holloway
Tel Portadown 335356
Pro G Fairweather
Holes 18 L 6119 yds SSS 70
Recs Am–68
Pro–63
V'trs WD–U; W/E–M
Fees £5 (£6)
Loc 3 miles Portadown

Tandragee (1922)

Private (Map 7/19)
Market Hill Road Tandragee
Craigavon BT62 2EA
Tel 840727
Mem 650
Sec A Best Tel 841272
Pro John Black Tel 841761
Holes 18 L 6084 yds SSS 69
Recs Am–62 Paul Topley
Pro–
V'trs U; SOC
Fees £3.70 (£6.25)
Loc 10 miles Armagh city
8 miles Craigavon

Belfast

Balmoral (1914)

Private (Map 7/20)
Lisburn Road Belfast
Tel Belfast 668540
Mem 500
Sec Tel Belfast 668514
Pro John Fisher Tel Belfast 667747
Holes 18 L 5679 metres SSS 70
Recs Am–66 Martin Wilson
Pro–65 David Jones
V'trs U
Fees £6 (£9)
Loc Balmoral

Belvoir Park (1927)

Private (Map 7/21)
Newtown Breda Belfast BT8 4AN
Tel **Belfast 641159 and 692817**
Mem 970
Sec WI Davidson Tel Belfast 643693
Pro GM Kelly Tel 646714
Holes 18 L 6476 yds SSS 71
Recs Am–66 TS Anderson
Pro–66 P Alliss EC Brown
V'trs U (Sat–M)
Fees £8 (£10)
Loc 3 miles city centre

Cliftonville (1911)

Private (Map 7/22)
Westland Road Belfast
Tel **Belfast 744158**
Mem 429
Sec JM Henderson
Pro
Holes 9 L 4678 yds SSS 69
Recs Am–66 WRA Tennant
Pro–68 Fred Daly
V'trs U (ex Sats)
Fees On application
Loc Belfast

Fortwilliam (1894)

Private (Map 7/23)
Downview Avenue Belfast
Tel Belfast 771770
Mem 1050
Sec RJ Campbell Tel 771770
Pro Peter Hanna Tel Bel 770980
Holes 18 L 5642 yds SSS 67
Recs Am–63 G Glover
Pro–67 F Daly J Kinsella
V'trs U
Fees £5 (£7)
Loc 2 miles N of centre Belfast

The Knock Golf Club (1895)

Private (Map 7/24)
Summerfield Dundonald Belfast BT16 0QX
Tel **Dundonald 2249**
Mem 870
Sec B Jenkins OBE MBIM Tel Dundonald 3251
Pro K Revie Tel Dundonald 3825
Holes 18 L 5845 metres SSS 71
Recs Am–67 KH Graham
Pro–69 PR McGuirk
V'trs U; SOC Mon Thu
Fees £7.50 (£10)
Loc 5 miles E centre Belfast

Malone (1895)

Private (Map 7/25)
240 Upper Malone Road Dunmurry Belfast BT17 9LB
Tel **Belfast 612695**
Mem 759 379(L) 211(J) 29(5)
Sec RD Woods Tel Belfast 612758
Pro PM O'Hagan Tel Belfast 614917
Holes 18 L 6433 yds SSS 71
9 L 2895 yds SSS 34
Recs Am–
Pro–68 E Jones
V'trs NA Wed after 2 pm and Sat before 5 pm; SOC Mon and Thurs
Fees £9 (£12)
Loc 6 miles S of Belfast

Ormeau (1893)

Private (Map 7/26)
Ravenhill Road Belfast
Tel **Belfast 641069**
Mem 250 70(L) 20(J) 28(5)
Sec J Cooke Tel Belfast 59605
Pro
Holes 9 L 5308 yds SSS 64
V'trs U
Fees £3.50 (£4.50)
Loc South Belfast

Shandon Park (1926)

Private (Map 7/27)
73 Shandon Park Belfast BT5 6NY
Tel **Belfast 794856**
Mem 1060
Sec H Wallace Tel Belfast 794856
Pro P Posnett Tel Belfast 797859
Holes 18 L 5714 metres SSS 70
Recs Am–66 R Beaney
Pro–68 P Posnett
V'trs U
Fees £6 (£7)
Loc 3 miles city centre

Co Cavan

Belturbet (1950)

Private (Map 7/28)
Erne Hill Belturbet
Tel (049) 22287
Mem 140
Sec PF Coffey
Pro
Holes 9 L 5180 yds SSS 64
Recs Am–
Pro–
V'trs U
Fees £3
Loc

Blacklion (1962)

Private (Map 7/29)
Toam Blacklion via Sligo
Tel 0017 53024
Mem 120
Sec R Thompson
Pro
Holes 9 L 5544 metres SSS 69
Recs Am–66 P Cafferky
Pro–
V'trs U; SOC
Fees £3 (£4) W–£10
Loc 12 miles SW of Enniskillen on A4
10 miles E Manorhamilton

Cabra Castle (1978)

Private (Map 7/79)
Kingscourt Co Cavan
Tel
Mem 101
Sec D McCarthy Tel 042 67196
Pro
Holes 9 L 5308 metres SSS 68
V'trs U
Fees
Loc 2 miles E of Kingscourt

County Cavan (1894)

Private (Map 7/30)
Drumelis Cavan
Tel 049 31283
Mem 243 132(L) 40(J)
Sec W Harrington Tel 049 31321
Pro
Holes 18 L 6037 yds SSS 69
Recs Am–66 A Cafferty
Pro–
V'trs U
Fees £6
Loc 2 miles W of Cavan Town
Mis Full catering facilities

Virginia (1946)

Private (Map 7/31)
Virginia
Tel **Virginia 35**
Mem 199
Sec D Soden Tel Virginia 42
Pro
Holes 9 L 4520 yds SSS 61
Recs Am–PJ O'Reilly
Pro–
V'trs U
Fees 75p
Loc 50 miles NW Dublin

Co Donegal

Ballybofey and Stranorlar (1958)

Private (Map 7/32)
Ballybofey
Tel 074 31093
Mem 183 70(L) 32(J)
Sec Ivan Kee Tel Ballybofey 50
Pro
Holes 18 L 5913 yds SSS 68
Recs Am–64 J McMenamin
Pro–
V'trs U
Fees £5
Loc ¼ mile Stranorlar

Ballyliffin (1947)

Private (Map 7/33)
Ballyliffin Clonmany
Tel **Clonmany 19**
Mem 210
Sec K J O'Doherty Tel Clonmany 19
Pro
Holes 18 L 6611 yds SSS 71
Recs Am–67 G Doherty
Pro–
V'trs U; SOC (arrange with Sec)
Fees £3.50
Loc 12 miles N of Buncrana, within easy reach of Derry

Buncrana (1951)

Public (Map 7/34)
Buncrana
Tel **Buncrana 1**
Mem 69
Sec D Hegarty Tel Buncrana 116
Pro NS Doherty
Holes 9 L 2020 yds SSS 59
Recs Am–63 J McLaughlin
Pro–
V'trs U
Fees 15p
Loc

Bundoran (1894)

Private (Map 7/35)
Great Northern Hotel Bundoran
Tel Bundoran 41302
Mem 400
Sec JC Roarty Tel (072) 41360
Pro Leslie Robinson David Robinson Tel (072) 41302
Holes 18 L 6328 yds SSS 71
Recs Am–67 J Murray
Pro–66 E Darcy
V'trs U SOC (W/E busy)
Fees D–£7 (D–£8) W–£30
Loc East boundary Bundoran

Donegal (1962)

Private (Map 7/36)
Murvagh Donegal PO
Tel **Ballintra 54**
Mem 355
Sec MC Fox Tel 073 21262
Pro
Holes 18 L Champ 7271 yds Medal 6842 yds SSS 73 Par 73
Recs Am–68 Fr B McBride
Pro–
V'trs U
Fees £5; W/E–£6
Loc 7 miles S of town

Dunfanaghy (1903)

Public (Map 7/37)
Dunfanaghy Co Donegal
Tel **(074) 36238**
Mem 70
Sec K Ward Tel (074) 36238
Pro
Holes 18 L 4977 metres SSS 66
Recs Am–64 J Brogan
Pro–66 L Wallace
V'trs U
Fees £3.50 (£4.50)
Loc Dunfanaghy

Greencastle (1885)

Private (Map 7/38)
Via Lifford Greencastle
Tel **Greencastle 13**
Mem 300
Sec HM Morris Tel Moville 42
Pro
Holes 9 L 5290 yds SSS 66
Recs Am–62 C McCarroll
Pro–67 D Jones
V'trs Restricted W/E
Fees £2 (£3)
Loc Nr Mouille Co Donegal

Gweedone (1923)

Private (Map 7/39)
Derrybeg
Tel **Bunbeg 369**
Mem 150
Sec CP O'Flanagan
Pro
Holes 9 L 6234 yds SSS 69
Recs Am–64 S Murphy
Pro–
V'trs U
Fees £2.50; W–£15; M–£25
Loc West Donegal

Letterkenny (1913)

Private (Map 7/40)
Barnhill Letterkenny
Tel **Letterkenny 074 21150**
Mem 298
Sec B Ramsay
Pro
Holes 18 L 6299 yds SSS 71
Recs Am–67 P Shiels
Pro
V'trs U
Fees £5 (£5)
Loc 1 mile NE

Nairn and Portnoo (1931)

Private (Map 7/41)
Nairn Portnoo
Tel **Clooney 7**
Mem 400
Sec DT McBride Tel Ballybofey (31155) 074
Pro
Holes 18 L 5950 yds SSS 68 winter 67
Recs Am–64 B McBride
Pro–62 Robert Browne
V'trs WD–U; Sat restricted 1–2.30 pm; Sun restricted; H; SOC
Fees £5 W–£28
Loc 6 miles N of Ardara

North West (1887)

Private (Map 7/42)
Lisfannon Fahan
Tel **Buncrana 12**
Mem 348
Sec EF Murray Tel Derry 61287
Pro S McBriarty
Holes 18 L 5895 yds SSS 68

Recs Am–69 Neal Doherty
Pro–64 Michael Doherty
V'trs U
Fees £3
Loc 12 miles W of Londonderry

Otway (1893)

Private (Map 7/43)
Saltpans Rathmullen Letterkenny
Tel **(074) 58319**
Mem 110
Sec Hugh Gallagher Tel (074) 58210
Pro
Holes 9 L 4134 yds SSS 60
Recs Am–29 Friel
Pro–
V'trs U
Fees D–£3
Loc On Lough Swilly Co Donegal

Portsalon (1891)

Private (Map 7/44)
Portsalon Letterkenny
Tel **Portsalon 11**
Mem 81
Sec M Kerr
Pro
Holes 18 L 5844 yds SSS 68
Recs Am–68 J Brogan
Pro–71 J Henderson
V'trs U
Fees £4
Loc 20 miles N of Letterkenny

Rosapenna (1898)

Private (Map 7/45)
Rosapenna Golf Hotel
Tel **Downings 4**
Mem 89
Sec John J McBride
Pro
Holes 18 L 6254 yds SSS 70
Recs Am–M McGinley
Pro–68 F Daly
V'trs U
Fees £1.50 (£1.75)
Loc Via Letterkenny

Tantallon

Private (Map 7/46)
Mount Charles
Tel
Mem 70
Sec M O'Boyle
Pro P Wallace
Holes 9 L yds SSS
Recs Am–
Pro–
V'trs U
Fees 7p (10p)
Loc

Co Down

Ardglass (1896)

Private (Map 7/47)
Castle Place Ardglass
Tel **Ardglass 841219**
Mem 754
Sec Mrs P Rooney
Pro Hugh Duggan Tel Ardglass 841022
Holes 18 L 5985 metres SSS 68
Recs Am–67 P Trainor
Pro–69 H Jackson
V'trs U
Fees £1.50 (£3.75) plus VAT
Loc Downpatrick 7 miles

Banbridge (1913)

Private (Map 7/48)
Huntly Road Banbridge
Tel **Banbridge 22342**
Mem 400
Sec TF Fee Tel Banbridge 23831
Pro
Holes 12 L 5879 yds SSS 68
Recs Am–65 K Stevenson
Pro–
V'trs U; SOC
Fees £4 (£5)
Loc Banbridge 1 mile

Bangor (1903)

Private (Map 7/49)
Broadway Bangor
Tel **Bangor 465133**
Mem 1100
Sec EA Bolster Tel Bangor 473922
Pro N Drew Tel Bangor 462164
Holes 18 L 6450 yds SSS 71
Recs Am–68 E O'Connell
Pro–66 C O'Connor
V'trs U
Fees £7.50 (£10)
Loc Bangor

Bright (1979)

Private (Map 7/80)
14 Coniamstown Road Bright Downpatrick
Tel **Ardglass 841319**
Mem 40
Sec R Reid
Pro
Holes 18 L 6730 yds
V'trs U SOC
Fees £3 (£3.50)
Loc 5 miles from Downpatrick on Killough road
Mis Light catering only

Carnalea (1927)

Private (Map 7/50)
Station Road Bangor BT19 1EZ
Tel **Bangor 465004**
Mem 770
Sec JH Crozier Tel Bangor 461368
Pro M McGee Tel Bangor 466122
Holes 18 L 5564 yds SSS 67
Recs Am–65 A Robinson
Pro–
V'trs U SOC on WD
Fees £4.50 (£7.50)
Loc Adjoining Carnalea Station

Clandeboye (1933)

Private (Map 7/51)
Conlig Newtownards
Tel **Bangor (0247) 465767/473706**
Mem 1077
Secs TI Marks Tel Bangor 465767
Pro Peter Gregory Tel Bangor 460751
Holes 18 L 6072 metres SSS 73
18 L 5172 metres SSS 67
Recs Am–68 David Jackson
Pro–
V'trs WD–U W/E–M on Sats; M on Suns before 10 am and between 12.30 and 1.30 pm
Fees Long £7 (£10) Short £6 (£8) W–£30
Loc 2 miles from Bangor on Newtownards Road

Donaghadee (1899)

Private (Map 7/52)
Warren Road Donaghadee BT21 0PQ
Tel **Donaghadee 888697**
Mem 1250
Sec SG Managh Tel Donaghadee 883624
Pro W Hackworth Tel Donaghadee 882392
Holes 18 L 6099 metres Par 71
Recs Am–65 J Nelson
Pro–69 E Clarke
V'trs U
Fees £5.50 (£6.50)
Loc Belfast 18 miles

Downpatrick (1932)

Private (Map 7/53)
Saul Road Downpatrick
Tel **Downpatrick 2152**
Mem 600
Sec JP McCoubrey Tel Downpatrick 2693
Pro
Holes 18 L 3098 yds SSS 69
Recs Am–
Pro–
V'trs U
Fees £3
Loc

Helen's Bay (1896)

Private (Map 7/54)
Golf Road Helen's Bay Bangor BT19 1TL
Tel **Helen's Bay 852601**
Mem 693
Sec JH Ward Tel Helen's Bay 852815
Pro
Holes 9 L 5176 metres SSS 67
Recs Am–68 BW Lister
Pro–67 L Esdale
V'trs WD–U; Sat/BH–M; Sun–U
Fees On application
Loc 12 miles from Belfast

Holywood (1904)

Private (Map 7/55)
Nuns Walk Demesne Road Holywood
Tel **Holywood 2138**
Mem 800
Sec GR Magennis Tel Holywood 3135
Pro Michael Bannon Tel Holywood 5503
Holes 18 L 5885 yds SSS 68
Recs Am–61 J Watts
Pro–
V'trs WD–1.30 pm–2.15 pm; W/E–Sat after 5 pm
Fees £5.75 (£8.50)
Loc

Kilkeel (1948)

Public (Map 7/56)
Mourne Park Ballyardle Kilkeel
Tel **Kilkeel 62296**
Mem 400
Sec SW Rutherford Tel Kilkeel 62293
Pro
Holes 9 L 5623 metres SSS 69
Recs Am–65 F Reilly
Pro–
V'trs U
Fees £4 (W/E & BH–£5)
Loc 3 miles from Kilkeel on Newry Road

Kirkistown Castle (1902)

Private (Map 7/57)
142 Main Road Cloughey Newtownards
Tel **Portavogie 71233/71353**
Mem 800
Sec RC Vine NBEM M Inst AM Tel Portavogie 71233/71353

Pro J Peden Tel Portavogie 71233
Holes 18 L 5628 metres (6157 yds) SSS 70
Recs Am–68 Jas Brown
Pro–71 RJ Polley C O'Connor
V'trs WD–U SOC; WD & BH–1st tee reserved for members only 9.30 am–10.30 am and 12 noon–1.30 pm
Fees £5 (BH £7)
Loc 25 miles SE Belfast

Mahee Island (1930)

Private (Map 7/58)
Comber Belfast
Tel **Killinchy 541234**
Mem 400
Sec EP Trevorrow
Pro
Holes 9 L 2790 yds SSS 67
Recs Am–67 C Boyd
Pro–66 N Drew
V'trs U (Sat–NA before 4.30 pm); SOC WD exc Mon
Fees £3.50 (£5)
Loc 14 miles S of Belfast

Mourne (1946)

Private (Map 7)
36 Golf Links Road Newcastle BT33 0AX
Tel **Newcastle 23218**
Mem 330
Hon Sec S Keenan Tel Newcastle 23218
Sec PJ Rodgers Tel Newcastle 23889
Holes Play over Royal Co Down

Royal Belfast (1881)

Private (Map 7/59)
Holywood Craigavad
Tel **Holywood 2165**
Mem 1223
Sec Ian M Piggot
Pro D Carson
Holes 18 L 6205 yds SSS 70
Recs Am–65 RAD McMillan
Pro–67 C O'Connor
V'trs I; Sat NA before 4.30 pm
Fees £7 (£10)
Loc E of Belfast on A2

Royal County Down (1889)

Private (Map 7/60)
Newcastle (Co Down)
Tel **Newcastle 23314**
Mem 430
Sec RH Cotton Tel Newcastle 23314
Pro ET Jones Tel Newcastle 22419
Holes C'ship course 18 L 6968 yds SSS 74
No 2 course 18 L 4100 yds SSS 60
Recs C'ship course Am– 66 J Bruen JM Jamison
Pro–67 A Compston B Gadd
V'trs Contact Sec for information
Fees £12 (£15)
Loc 30 miles from Belfast

Scrabo (1907)

Private (Map 7/61)
233 Scrabo Road Newtownards BT23 4SL
Tel **Newtownards 812355**
Mem 750
Sec James D Porter Tel Newtownards 815048
Pro Billy Todd
Holes 18 L 5699 metres SSS 70
Recs Am–68 W Caughey
Pro–67 Hugh Jackson
V'trs WD–U SOC; W/E–after 5 pm
Fees £5 (W/E & BH £7)
Loc 2 miles W of Newtownards

The Spa (1907)

Private (Map 7/62)
20 Grove Road Ballynahinch BT24 8BR
Tel **Ballynahinch 562365**
Mem 350
Sec J McGlass Tel Belfast 812340
Pro
Holes 9 L 3155 yds SSS 70
Recs Am–67 R Wallace
Pro–
V'trs U exc Wed NA after 3 pm and NA Sat
Fees £4 (£5)
Loc

Warrenpoint (1893)

Private (Map 7/63)
Lr Dromore Rd Warrenpoint Co Down NI
Tel **Warrenpoint 72219**
Mem 1100
Sec John McMahon Tel 73695
Pro Nigel Shaw Tel 72371
Holes 18 L 5628 metres SSS 70
Rec Am–66 K Stevenson
Pro–68 D Feherty
V'trs U; SOC
Fees £5 (£7)
Loc 5 miles S of Newry

Co Fermanagh

Enniskillen (1896)

Private (Map 7/64)
Castlecoole Enniskillen
Tel (0365) 25250
Mem 560
Sec JT Prenter Tel (0365) 23213
Pro
Holes 9 L 5476 metres SSS 69
Recs Am–67 K Prenter
Pro–
V'trs U SOC
Fees D–£4
Loc 1 mile SE of Enniskillen in Castlecoole Estate

Co Londonderry

Castlerock (1900)

Private (Map 7/65)
Circular Road Castlerock
Tel **Castlerock 848314**
Mem 780
Sec D Smith Tel Castlerock 848314
Pro R Kelly
Holes 18 L 6694 SSS 72
Recs Am–68 TBC Hoey
Pro–
V'trs WD–U; SOC; W/E–SOC; M before 2.30 pm; U after 2.30 pm; Tue and Fri Ladies preference
Fees £5 (£7)
Loc 5 miles W Coleraine on coast on A2

City of Derry (1913)

Private (Map 7/66)
49 Victoria Road Londonderry
Tel (0504) 42610 & 46369
Mem 846
Sec Patrick J Doherty Tel Londonderry 46369(O) 41493(H)
Pro M Doherty Tel 46496
Holes 27: Prehen Course (18) L 6406 yds SSS 71; Dunhugh Course (9) L 4708 yds SSS 63
Recs 68 Des Ballentine
Pro–
V'trs WD–U before 4 pm; M after 4 pm; WE–U; SOC H
Fees Prehen £6 (£8); Dunhugh £2.50
Loc Londonderry–3 miles from E end of Craigavon Bridge

Kilrea (1920)

Private (Map 7/67)
Drumagarner Road Kilrea (All correspondence to Secretary: address below)
Tel **Rasharkin 397**
Mem 147
Sec WR McIlmoyle 125 Tamlaght Road Rasharkin; Tel Rasharkin 397
Pro
Holes 9 L 4326 yds SSS 62
Recs Am–61 R Rees
Pro–
V'trs U
Fees £3 (£4)
Loc ½ mile from Kilrea on Kilrea–Maghera Road

Moyola Park (1976)

(Map 7/68)
Shanemullagh Castledawson Magherafelt BT45 8DG
Tel **(0648) 68392/68468**
Mem 350
Sec Michael A Steele Tel (0648) 68392/68468
Pro
Holes 18 L 6517 yds SSS 71
Recs Am–71 T McNeill
Pro–70 Des Smyth
V'trs U
Fees £5 (£6); W–£15
Loc 40 miles N of Belfast by M2

Portstewart (1889)

Private (Map 7/69)
117 Strand Road Portstewart
Tel **Portstewart 2015**
Mem 1350 (500 full)
Sec M Moss BA Tel Portstewart 3839
Pro A Hunter Tel Portstewart 2601
Holes Strand 18 L 6784 yds SSS 72
Town 18 L 4733 yds SSS 62
Recs Strand Am–69 TBC Hoey D Ballentine
Pro–66 E Polland
Town Am–
Pro–
V'trs SOC by arrangement
Fees Strand: D–£7 with mem £4.50 (£10 with mem £6);
Town: £2.50 (£4) W–£15 M–£30
Loc W boundary town

Co Monaghan

Clones (1913)

Private (Map 7/70)
Hilton Park Scotshouse Clones
Tel **Scotshouse 17**
Mem 260
Sec Martin M Taylor Tel 049 52354
Pro None
Holes 9 L 5570 yds SSS 67
Recs Am–66 Dermot McGuigan
Pro–
V'trs U
Fees £3
Loc

Nuremore (1961)

Private (Map 7/71)
Nuremore Carrickmacross
Tel **Carrickmacross 61438**
Mem 107
Sec Fergus C Lane Tel 042 61450
Pro
Holes 9 L 6032 yds SSS 69
Recs Am–
Pro–
V'trs U
Fees £3 (£4.50)
Loc Hotel grounds

Rossmore (1906)

Private (Map 7/72)
Rossmore Park Monaghan
Tel **Monaghan 81316**
Mem 310
Sec Sean Kilroy Tel Monaghan 81316/87376
Pro
Holes 9 L 5859 yds SSS 68
Recs Am–64 R Berry
Pro–
V'trs WD–U SOC; W/E–U exc comp days; BH–U
Fees £3 (£4)
Loc 3 miles Monaghan/Cootehill Road

Co Tyrone

Dungannon (1890)

Private (Map 7/73)
Mullaghmore Dungannon
Tel **Dungannon 22098**
Mem 425
Sec L Campbell Tel Dungannon 23112
Pro
Holes 18 L 5914 yds SSS 68
Recs Am–64 P McAleer
Pro–
V'trs U
Fees £3 (£4)
Loc 1 mile W of Dungannon

Fintona (1896)

Private (Map 7/74)
Ecclesville Demesne Fintona
Tel **Fintona 841480**
Mem 250
Sec J Conway Tel Irvinestown 21484
Pro None
Holes 9 L 5716 yds SSS 70
Recs Am–68 E Donnell
Pro–69 L Higgins J Kinsilla L Robinson
V'trs U exc comp days; SOC on WD
Fees £3 (£5)
Loc 10 miles S of Omagh

Killymoon (1889)

Private (Map 7/75)
Killymoon Cookstown
Tel **Cookstown 63762 & 62254**
Mem 720
Sec TW Doonan Tel Cookstown 63700
Pro P Leonard
Holes 18 L 5498 metres SSS 69
Recs Am–64 A O'Neill
Pro–65 D Smyth
V'trs U
Fees £3 (£4)
Loc 1 mile S of Cookstown

Newtownstewart (1914)

Private (Map 7/76)
38 Golf Course Road Newtownstewart BT78 4HU
Tel **Newtownstewart 61466**
Mem 500
Sec RTA Farrow Tel Omagh 44262
Pro
Holes 18 L 5468 metres SSS 69
Recs Am–66 B Patton
Pro–66 John Fisher
V'trs U; SOC
Fees WD–£4 W–£13 M–£25; W/E & BH–£5
Loc 2 miles SW Newtownstewart on B84

Omagh (1910)

Private (Map 7/77)
Dublin Road Omagh BT78 1HQ
Tel **3160**
Mem 454
Sec CH Kerr Tel 3160
Pro
Holes 18 L 5298 metres SSS 67
Recs Am–63 H Johnston
Pro–
V'trs U
Fees £4 (£5) W–£15
Loc Omagh ½ mile

Strabane (1909)

Private (Map 7/78)
Ballycolman Strabane
Tel **Strabane 882271**
Mem 550
Sec JJ Harron Tel Strabane 883093
Pro
Holes 18 L 5458 metres SSS and Par 69
Recs Am–64 Chas Patton
Pro–69
V'trs U
Fees £4 (£5)
Loc Strabane ½ mile Fir Trees Hotel 400 yds

Scotland

Angus, Tayside Region

Arbroath (1877)

Public (Map 8/1)
Elliot by Arbroath
Tel **Arbroath 72272**
Mem 200
Sec AR Small Tel Arbroath 72666
Pro Lindsay Ewart Tel Arbroath 75837
Holes 18 L 6078 yds SSS 69
Recs Am–65 R Cargill
Pro–
V'trs U
Fees £3 (£4.50) W–£12 (Mon-Fri)
Loc 1 mile S of Arbroath

Arbroath Artisan (1904)

Public
Elliot by Arbroath
Tel **72069**
Mem 400
Pro Lindsay Ewart
Holes Play over Arbroath Golf Course

Brechin Golf and Squash Club (1893)

Private (Map 8/2)
Trinity Brechin Angus DD9 7PD
Tel **Brechin 2383**
Mem 617
Sec DA Milligan Tel Brechin 4969
Pro Brian Mason Tel Brechin 5270
Holes 18 L 5267 yds SSS 66
Recs Am–61 A Helmsley
Pro–
V'trs U except Wed SOC
Fees £4 D–£6 (£6 D–£8) W–£20 (Mon–Fri)
Loc 1 mile N of town on Aberdeen Road B966
Mis Buggies for hire

Carnoustie Courses

Carnoustie Courses: Details from Secretary Carnoustie Golf Links Management Committee Links Parade Carnoustie Tel 0241 53789

Buddon Links (1981)

Public (Map 8/3)
Carnoustie
Tel **0241 53249 (Starter's Box)**
Pro
Holes 18 L 6445 yds SSS 71
Recs Am–
Pro–
V'trs U
Fees £3 (1986 price)
Loc Carnoustie Links

Burnside

Public (Map 8/3)
Carnoustie
Tel **0241 53249 (Starter's Box)**
Pro
Holes 18 L 5935 yds SSS 69
Recs Am–
Pro–
V'trs U
Fees £6 (£7) W–£45 1986 prices
Loc Carnoustie Links

Carnoustie Championship

Public (Map 8/3)
Carnoustie
Tel **0241 53249 (Starter's Box)**
Pro
Holes 18 L 6931 yds SSS 74
Recs Am–
Pro–65 J Newton
V'trs U
Fees £12 (£14) W–£45 1986 prices
Loc Carnoustie Links

Carnoustie Clubs

Caledonia

Links Parade Carnoustie
Tel **0241 52115**
Mem 460

Sec DM Muir
Holes Play over Carnoustie courses

Carnoustie (1842)

Links Parade Carnoustie
Tel **0241 52480**
Mem 900
Sec DW Curtis
Holes Play over Carnoustie courses

Carnoustie Ladies (1873)

Links Parade Carnoustie
Tel Carnoustie (0241) 55252
Mem 103
Sec Mrs Edith Sullivan Tel Carnoustie 53159
Mis Play over Carnoustie Championship Burnside and Buddon Links

Dalhousie (1868)

Links Parade Carnoustie
Tel 0241 53208
Mem 262
Sec GW Ellis
Mis Play over Carnoustie courses

Mercantile (1896)

Private (Map 8)
Links Parade Carnoustie
Tel **0241 52525**
Mem 500
Sec MW Sullivan Tel 0241 53159
Holes Play over Carnoustie courses
V'trs U; bookings through Links Management office
Loc 11 miles N Dundee; ½ mile Carnoustie town centre

New Taymouth

Taymouth St Carnoustie
Tel **0241 52425**
Mem 450
Sec G Duncan
Holes Play over Carnoustie courses

Panmure (1845)

Private (Map 8/4)
Barry by Carnoustie
Tel **Carnoustie 53120**
Mem 480
Sec Captain JC Ray Tel Carnoustie 53120
Pro T Shiel Tel Carnoustie 53120
Holes 18 L 6302 yds SSS 70
Recs Am–68 S Macdonald DMA Steel RDBM Shade
Pro–65 R De Vicenzo R Cole D Webster
V'trs WD and Sun–U; Sat–NA
Fees £8 D–£12
Loc 2 miles W of Carnoustie

Dundee Courses

Caird Park (1926)

Public (Map 8/5)
Dundee
Tel Dundee 453606
Mem 413
Sec D Farquhar Jr Tel 457217
Pro J Black Tel 459438
Holes 18 L 6303 yds SS 70
Recs Am–
Pro–
V'trs U
Fees To be decided
Loc Off Kingsway bypass at Mains Loan
Mis Original 9-hole course extended to accommodate two 9-hole courses

Caird Park (1982)

Public (Map 8/6)
City of Dundee District Council Parks Dept 353 Clepington Road Dundee
Tel **Dundee 23141 ext 414 (For advance bookings phone 23141 ext 295)**
Pro Keith Todd
Holes Yellow Course 9 L 1626 yds SSS 29
Red Course 9 L 1983 yds SSS 29
V'trs Any time
Fees 50p Juniors 30p Off peak–adults juniors and OAP–25p
Loc Caird Park Dundee
Mis Original 9-hole course extended to accommodate two 9-hole courses in 1982

Camperdown (1960)

Public (Map 8/7)
Camperdown Park Dundee
Tel Dundee 623398
Mem 600
Sec JF Hart Tel 68340
Pro R Brown
Holes 18 L 6561 yds SSS 72
Recs Am–68 A Morgan
Pro–
V'trs U
Fees £2 (£3)
Loc 2 miles NW of Dundee

Downfield (1932)

Private (Map 8/8)
Turnberry Ave Dundee Angus DD2 3QP
Tel **Dundee 825595**
Mem 777
Sec JHC Herron Tel 0382 825595
Pro Colin Waddell Tel 89246
Holes 18 L 6899 yds SSS 73
Recs Am–67
Pro–67
V'trs WD–U 9 am–12 noon and 2 pm–4 pm; W/E–M
Fees On application
Loc North End Dundee off A923 (Timex Circle)

Edzell (1895)

Private (Map 8/9)
High St Edzell By Brechin Angus DD9 7TF
Tel **Edzell 235**
Mem 650
Sec JM Hutchison Tel (03564) 7283
Pro JB Webster Tel (03564) 462
Holes 18 L 6299 yds SSS 70
Recs Am–66 AJ Webster W Taylor
V'trs WD 5 pm–6.15 pm; W/E 8 am 9.30 am, 12 am–2 pm; SOC
Fees £6 D–£9 (£10 R/D, £6 after 4 pm) W–£30 M–£70
Loc 6 miles NW Brechin

Forfar (1871)

Private (Map 8/10)
Cunninghill Forfar DD8 2RL
Tel **(0307) 62120**
Mem 525 175(L) 150(J)
Sec/Man AIC Cameron Tel (0307) 63773
Pro Peter McNiven Tel (0307) 65683
Holes 18 L 5537 metres SSS 69
Recs Am–66 DM Chapman CC Sinclair
Pro–65 Eric Brown
V'trs U (Ex Sat)
Fees £8 (£10.50)
Loc 1½ miles E of Forfar

Kirriemuir (1908)

Private (Map 8/11)
Kirriemuir
Tel **(0575) 72144**
Mem 600
Sec Fox & Irvine Tel (0575) 72729
Pro Anthony Caira Tel (0575) 73317
Holes 18 L 5557 yds SSS 67
Recs Am–63 JL Adamson J Murray
Pro–
V'trs WD–U; W/E–M; SOC
Fees D–£7.50
Loc NE outskirts of town

Monifieth Courses

Monifieth Courses: Details from the Secretary, Monifieth Golf Links Committee of Management Ian F Baxter 45 Ferry Road Monifieth Dundee Tel 0382 533300

Monifieth Golf Links

Private (Map 8/13)
Princes Street Monifieth Dundee
Tel **Starter 0382 532767**
Mem
Sec Ian F Baxter Tel 0382 533300
Pro Ian McLeod Tel 0382 532945
Holes Medal Course 18 L 6650 yds SSS 72
Ashludie Course 18 L 5123 SSS 66
Recs Am–64 DG Greig
Pro–64 S Swelgolum
V'trs WD–U SOC NA–Sat Restricted–Sun
Fees £5 D–£7 (Sun–£6 D–£8) Reduced for juniors
Loc 6 miles E of Dundee
Mis Abertay, Broughty, Grange/Dundee and Monifieth clubs have playing rights over both courses

Montrose Courses

Montrose

Public (Map 8/14)
Starters Box Traill Drive Montrose DD10 8SW
Tel **0674 72634**
Sec Mrs M Stewart
Pro G Dornan
Holes **Medal Course 18 L 6451 yds SSS 71**
Broomfield 18 L 4815 yds SSS 63
Recs **Am–**
Pro–Medal 63 Gordon Cunningham David Huish
V'trs **U except no fourball Saturdays until 1500 hrs. April/September**
Fees Medal £5.75 (£6) reduced winter
Broomfield £3.50 (£4.30) reduced winter
(1986 prices)
Loc 1 mile off A92
Mis Royal Albert Caledonia and Mercantile clubs play here

Montrose Clubs

Mercantile (1897)

East Links Montrose Angus DD10 82W
Tel **0674 72408**
Mem 450
Sec Robert S West Tel 0674 75447
Holes 18 L 6451 yds Par 71
Loc 1½ miles E of town centre

Montrose Caledonia (1896)

Dorward Road Montrose
Tel 0674 72313
Mem
Sec G Hall Tel Montrose 5485
Holes Play over Montrose and Broomfield courses

Royal Albert (1810)

Dorward Road Montrose
Tel 0674 72376
Mem 309
Sec HHG Symes
Holes Play over Montrose and Broomfield courses

Victoria (1864)

Montrose
Tel 0674 72157
Sec KJ Clark Tel Montrose 4510
Holes Play over Montrose and Broomfield courses

Argyll and Bute, Strathclyde Region

Blairmore and Strone (1896)

Private (Map 8/1)
Strone-By-Dunoon Argyll
Tel **Kilmun 676**
Mem 160
Sec AB Horton Tel Kilmun 217
Pro
Holes 9 L 2112 yds SSS 62
Recs Am–67 T Armour
Pro–
V'trs NA Mon after 6 pm
NA Sat 12–4 pm
Fees £2 (£2) W–£8
Loc High Road at Strone N of Dunoon

Brodick

(see Ayrshire)

Bute

Private (Map 8/2)
Kingarth Kilchattan Bay
Tel
Mem 57
Sec J Connell Tel 0700 83242
Pro
Holes 9 L 2497 yds SSS 64
Recs Am–
Pro–
V'trs U
Fees £1 W–£5
Loc At Stravanan Bay

Carradale (1900)

Private (Map 8/3)
Carradale PA28 6QX
Tel Carradale 624
Mem 172
Sec J Taylor
Pro
Holes 9 L 2387 yds SSS 63
Recs Am–62 S Campbell
Pro–
V'trs U
Fees £2 for 9 holes D–£3
Loc Carradale

Colonsay

Public (Map 8/4)
Isle of Colonsay Argyll PA61 7YP
Tel 09512 316
Mem 100
Sec Kevin Byrne Tel 09512 316
Pro
Holes 18 L 4775 yds SSS 72
Recs Am–
Pro–
V'trs U
Fees Full membership £5 per family pa; no further fees
Loc Machrins

Corrie

(see Ayrshire)

Cowal (1890)

Private (Map 8/5)
Ardenslate Road Dunoon
Tel **Dunoon 2216**
Mem 512
Sec J Fletcher Tel Dunoon 5673
Pro RD Weir Tel Dunoon 2395
Holes 18 L 6251 yds SSS 70
Recs Am–64 Andrew Brodie
Pro–
V'trs U
Fees On application
Loc NE boundary Dunoon

Craignure

(Map 8/6)
Isle of Mull Hotel Mull
Tel Craignure 370/351
Mem 60
Sec Mrs Sheila Campbell Tel 06802 370
Pro
Holes 9 L 4908 yds SSS 64
Recs Am–
Pro–
V'trs U
Fees D–£2.50 W–£10
Loc 1 mile Craignure

Dunaverty (1889)

Private (Map 8/7)
Southend Argyll
Tel
Mem 220
Sec JE Sayers
Pro W McMillan
Holes 18 L 4597 yds SSS 63
Recs Am–61 S Campbell
Pro–65 EC Brown
V'trs U
Fees £1.10 W–£6.50
Loc 10 miles S of Campbeltown

Glencruitten (1905)

Private (Map 8/8)
Oban
Tel **0631 62868**
Mem 350 105(L) 115 (J)
Sec CM Jarvie Tel 0631 62308
Pro Iain Auld Tel 0631 64115
Holes 18 L 4452 yds SSS 63
Recs Am–65 JM Wilson
Pro–60 H Bannerman
G Cunningham
V'trs U
Fees £5.50 (£6.50)
Loc 1 mile town centre

Innellan (1895)

Private (Map 8/9)
Innellan Argyll
Tel **Dunoon 3546**
Mem 200
Sec C Clark Tel Innellan 446
Pro
Holes 9 L 4878 yds SSS 63
Recs Am–63
Pro–
V'trs U; SOC
Fees D–£3
Loc 4 miles S of Dunoon

Islay (1891)

Private (Map 8/10)
Tigh Rhaonastil Kildalton Isle of Islay
Tel **Port Ellen 2310**
Mem 202
Sec Donald F Stone Tel Port Ellen (0496) 2310
Pro
Holes 18 L 6226 yds SSS 70
Recs Am–67 SW Morrison
Pro–67 M Seymour
V'trs U
Fees £5 D–£9 W–£45 (half price with mem)
Mis Play over Machrie GC; clubhouse; catering at Machrie Hotel

Kyles of Bute (1907)

Private (Map 8/11)
Tighnabruaich Argyll
Tel **Tighnabruaich 811355**
Mem 160
Sec DW Gieve Tel Tighnabruaich 811355
Pro
Holes 9 L 2332 yds SSS 32
Recs Am–
Pro–
V'trs U
Fees D–£2.50 W–£10
Loc 26 miles W of Dunoon
Mis Changing room facilities

Lamlash

(see Ayrshire)

Lochgilphead (1963)

Private (Map 8/12)
Blarbuie Road Lochgilphead Argyll
Tel **Lochgilphead 2340**
Mem 170
Sec PW Tait Tel (0546) 2149
Pro
Holes 9 L 4484 yds SSS 63
Recs Am–63 Tommy Armour
Pro–
V'trs U SOC
Fees £3 (£5)
Loc ½ mile from town centre

Lochranza

(see Ayrshire)

Machrihanish (1876)

Private (Map 8/13)
Campbeltown Machrihanish
Tel **0586-81 213**
Mem 516 158(L) 125(J)

Sec Duncan M Macfarlane Tel 0586-52 313
Pro Arthur Thompson Tel 0586-81 277
Holes 18 L 6228 yds SSS 70 plus 9 hole course
Recs Am–66 Stuart J Campbell
Pro–65 R Walker
V'trs U
Fees £7.50 D–£9.25 (no round fees W/E)
Loc 5 miles W of Campbeltown

Machrie Bay

(see Ayrshire)

Millport (1888)

Private (Map 8/14)
Millport Isle of Cumbrae
Tel **Millport 530311**
Mem 267 97(L) 73(J)
Sec C Kerr Tel Millport 530485
Pro
Holes 18 L 5831 yds SSS 68
Recs Am–64 AD Harrington
Pro–
V'trs U
Fees £4.50 (£5) W–£20 F–£27.50 M–£40

Port Bannatyne (1968)

Private (Map 8/15)
Port Bannatyne Isle of Bute
Tel
Mem 131
Sec Iain L Macleod Tel 0700 2009
Pro
Holes 13 L 4654 yds SSS 63
Recs Am–61 J Ewing
Pro–64 W Watson
V'trs U
Fees £2 (£3) W–£10;
Jnrs £1 (£2) W–£5
Loc Bute

Rothesay (1892)

Public (Map 8/16)
Canada Hill Rothesay Isle of Bute
Tel **Rothesay 2244**
Mem 350
Sec D Shaw Tel Rothesay 2178
Pro G McKinlay Tel Rothesay 3554
Holes 18 L 5358 yds SSS 67
Recs Am–63 G Murray
Pro–72 RDBM Shade
V'trs U
Fees £4 (£6) W–£14 £70 per annum
Loc Bute, in town

Shiskine

(see Ayrshire)

Tarbert (1910)

Private (Map 8/17)
Kilberry Road Tarbert
Tel 565
Mem 91
Sec JB Sinclair Tel 676
Pro
Holes 9 L 4460 yds SSS 64
Recs Am–65 P Tait A Black
Pro–
V'trs U
Fees £3 D–£5 W–£20
Loc 1 mile W of Tarbert

Vaul

Private (Map 8/18)
Scarinish Isle of Tiree by Oban
Tel
Mem 100
Sec Mrs P Boyd Tel 087-92-344
Holes 9 L 3123 yds SSS 70
Recs Am–
Pro–
V'trs U (No Sunday play)
Fees £3 (WD)
Loc

Western Isles (1896)

Private (Map 8/19)
Tobermory Isle of Mull
Tel
Mem 95
Sec AD Brown Tel 2381
Pro
Holes 9 L 2460 yds SSS 64
Recs Am–
Pro–
V'trs U; Sundays all day
Fees D–£3 W–£12 M–£24
Loc Tobermory

Whiting Bay

(see Ayrshire)

Ayrshire, including Isle of Arran, Strathclyde Region

Annanhill (1957)

Public (Map 9/1)
Irvine Road Kilmarnock
Tel **Kilmarnock 21644**
Mem 280
Sec JA Murdoch
Pro Jim McLeod
Holes 18 L 6270 yds SSS 70
Recs Am–65 I McKenzie
Pro–65 Jim Farmer
V'trs WD–U W/E–NA Sat U Sun SOC–6 days NA Sat
Fees D–£3.50 (D–£6.60)
Loc 1 mile W of Kilmarnock

Ardeer (1880)

Private (Map 9/2)
Greenhead Stevenston
Tel **Stevenston 64542**
Mem 500
Sec WT Burnett Tel Saltcoats 64035
Pro
Holes 18 L 6630 yds SSS 72
Recs Am–67 NG Walker
Pro–68 A Brooks I Stanley R Walker
V'trs U exc Sat–NA
Fees £9 (Sun £11)
Loc ½ mile off A78 N of Stevenston

Ayr Courses

Ayr Public Courses Details from Director of Parks Ayr Tel Ayr 81511 (Ext 249)

Auchenharvie (1981)

Public (Map 9/3)
Moor Park Road West Brewery Park Saltcoats Ayrshire
Tel
Mem 100
Sec William J Thomson
Pro R Rodgers Tel 603103
Holes 9 L 5300 SSS 66
Recs Am–67 R Galloway J Murphy P Rodgers A Wylie
Pro–
V'trs U W/E–U after 9.30 am
Fees £2.40 (£3.60)
Loc Low road between Saltcoats and Stevenston

Belleisle (1927)

Public (Map 9/4)
Ayr
Tel **Alloway 41258**
Sec H Diamond Tel Alloway 41258
Pro J Easey Tel Alloway 41314
Holes 18 L 6540 yds SSS 71
Recs Am–63 K Gimson
Pro–65 D McLelland
J Farmer
V'trs U
Fees £4.30 D–£5.70 (£5.30 D–£8.60) (1986 prices)
Loc S boundary Ayr
Mis Belleisle club plays here

Dalmilling (1960)

Public (Map 9/5)
Westwood Avenue Whitletts Ayr
Tel **0292 263893**
Pro D Gemmell Tel Ayr 263893
Holes 18 L 5401 yds SSS 66
Recs Am–61 G McKay
Pro–
V'trs U
V'trs U
Fees £3.50 D–£4.40 (£4.30 D–£6.90) (1986 prices)
Loc NE boundary Ayr
Mis Dalmilling club plays here

Seafield (1930)

Public (Map 9/4)
Ayr
Tel **Alloway 41258**
Sec H Diamond Tel Alloway 41258
Pro John S Easey Tel Alloway 41314
Holes 18 L 5244 yds SSS 66
Recs Am–64 D Wilkie
Pro–
V'trs Any time
Fees £3 D–£3.90 (£3.60 D–£6) (1986 prices)
Loc S boundary Ayr in Belleisle Park
Mis Belleisle club plays here

Ayr Clubs

Belleisle (1928)

Private (Map 9)
Ayr
Tel **Alloway 41258**
Mem 250
Sec AF Wilson Tel Alloway 42136
Pro John S Easey Tel (0292) 41314
Holes Belleisle: 18 L 6540 yds SSS 71; Seafield: 18 L 5244 yds SSS 66
V'trs U SOC
Fees Belleisle: £4.30 D–£5.70 (£5.30 D–£8.60) W–£25.90
Loc 1½ miles SW of town centre
Mis Play over Belleisle and Seafield courses: Buggies for hire

Dalmilling (1960)

Public (Map 9)
Westwood Avenue Whitletts Ayr
Tel **0292 63893**
Mem 232

Sec CAH King 3 High Road Ayr Tel Ayr 268180
Holes Play over Ayr Dalmilling

Ballochmyle (1937)

Private (Map 9/6)
Ballochmyle Mauchline Ayrshire KA5 6RR
Tel (0290) 50469
Mem 860
Sec WD Ritchie Tel (0290) 20910
Pro
Holes 18 L 5952 yds SSS 69
Recs Am–66 NC Brown I Guthrie
Pro–
V'trs WD & W/E–U; BH–M
Fees D–£8.50 (£10) subject to review
Loc Adjoining A70 Kilmarnock/Dumfries Road 1 mile S of Mauchline
Mis Buggies available

Beith (1896)

Private (Map 9/7)
Bigholm Road Beith
Tel **Beith 3166**
Mem 240
Sec M Rattray Tel Beith 2011
Pro
Holes 9 L 5488 yds SSS 67
Recs Am–64 K Ross
Pro–
V'trs U (ex Sats Sun afternoon)
Fees £1.60 (£2.20)
Loc 1 mile E of Beith

Caprington

Municipal (Map 9/8)
Kilmarnock Municipal
Ayr Road Kilmarnock
Tel **21915**
Mem 400
Sec F McCulloch
Pro
Holes 18 L yds SSS 69
Recs Am–63 S Fraser
Pro–66 Eric Brown
V'trs U
Fees
Loc
Mis Also a 9-hole course

Girvan (1900)

Municipal (Map 9/9)
Golf Course Road Girvan
Tel Girvan (0465) 4272
Mem 180
Sec Mrs V. Connor Tel (0465) 2144
Pro
Holes 18 L 5075 yds SSS 65
Recs Am–61 J Cannon
Pro–61 K Stevely
V'trs U
Fees £3.50 (£4.30)
Loc N side town

Glasgow Gailes (1787)

Private (Map 9/10)
Gailes Ayrshire
Tel Irvine 311347
Mem 350
Sec WD Robertson Tel 041-942 2011
Pro Jack Steven Tel 041-942 8507
Holes 18 L 6447 yds SSS 71
Recs Am–62 CW Green
Pro–67 R Brownlie
V'trs WD–I; W/E–M
Fees On application
Loc 1 mile S of Irvine

Irvine (1887)

Private (Map 9/11)
Bogside Irvine
Tel Irvine 78139
Mem 450
Sec A MacPherson Tel Irvine 75979
Pro Keith Erskine Tel 75626
Holes 18 L 6454 yds SSS 71
Recs Am–65 DA Roxburgh
Pro–
V'trs SOC–Mon–Thurs incl
Fees £7.50 D–£10
Loc

Irvine Ravenspark (1907)

Public (Map 9/12)
Irvine
Tel **Irvine 79550**
Mem 400
Sec W McMahon
Pro Peter Bond Tel Irvine 76467
Holes 18 L 6496 yds SSS 71
Recs Am–66 F Moore
Pro–
V'trs U
Fees £1.60 (£3.70)
Loc

Isle of Arran Courses

Brodick (1897)

Private (Map 9/13)
Brodick Isle of Arran
Tel Brodick 2349
Mem 525
Sec GI Jameson Tel Brodick 2349
Pro David Pirie Tel Brodick 2513
Holes 18 L 4404 yds SSS 62
Recs Am–61 D Bell
Pro–
V'trs U
Fees D–£5
Loc 1 mile from pier

Corrie (1892)

Private (Map 9/14)
Corrie Isle of Arran
Tel **Corrie 223**
Mem 220
Sec J Long Tel Lochranza 678
Pro
Holes 9 L 1948 yds SSS 61
Recs Am–62 JC Reid
Pro–
V'trs U
Fees D–£3 W–£12 M–£20
Loc 6 miles N of Brodick

Lamlash (1892)

Private (Map 9/15)
Lamlash Isle of Arran
Tel **Lamlash 296**
Mem 400
Sec EDR Pointer Tel Lamlash 555
Pro
Holes 18 L 4681 yds SSS 63
Recs Am–62 B Morrison
Pro–64 R Burke
V'trs U
Fees D–£4 After 4 pm–£2.50 OAP–£3 W–£20 M–£45
Loc 4 miles from Brodick pier

Lochranza

Private (Map 9/16)
Lochranza Isle of Arran
Tel **Lochranza 273**
Mem 20
Sec Mrs R McAllister
Pro DJ McAllister
Holes 9 L 1700 yds SSS
Recs Am–26 GM Anserson
Pro–
V'trs U
Fees 25p W–£1 M–£2.50
Loc

Machrie Bay

Private (Map 9/17)
Machrie Bay Brodick Isle of Arran
Tel **258**
Mem 110
Sec JM Buchanan
Pro
Holes 9 L 2082 yds SSS 61
Recs Am–62 A Kelso
Pro–59 W Hagen
V'trs U
Fees D–£1 W–£4 M–£8
Loc W coast 9 miles from Brodick

Shiskine (1896)

Private (Map 9/18)
Blackwaterfoot Isle of Arran
Tel **Shiskine 226**
Mem 300 76(L) 22(J)
Sec Mrs Fiona Crawford
Pro
Holes 12 L 3000 yds SSS 41
Recs Am–39 J Melvin J Brown
Pro–36 DH McGillivray
V'trs U
Fees £1.75 (£1.75) W–£11.50 M–£20.70
Loc Blackwaterfoot

Whiting Bay (1895)

Private (Map 9/19)
Whiting Bay Isle of Arran
Tel **077 07 487**
Mem 290
Sec WA Jones Tel Whiting Bay 305
Pro
Holes 18 L 4405 yds SSS 63
Recs Am–63 JD Simpson D Burn
Pro–
V'trs U
Fees D–£4 W–£17 F–£25 M–£40
Loc Rear of village

Kilbirnie Place (1922)

Private (Map 9/20)
Largs Road Kilbirnie
Tel **Kilbirnie 683398**
Mem 300
Sec JF Galt
Pro
Holes 18 L 5411 yds SSS 67
Recs Am–64 G McLean
Pro–
V'trs U (ex Sats)
Fees £3.50 Sun–£5.50
Loc ½ mile W

Kilmarnock (Barassie) (1887)

Private (Map 9/21)
Hillhouse Road Barassie Troon KA10 6SY
Tel Troon 311077
Mem 430
Sec M Davis Tel (0292) 313920
Pro WR Lockie Tel (0292) 311322
Holes 18 L 6450 yds SSS 71
Recs Am–65 RL Crawford
Pro–66 D Swaelens R De Vicenzo B Yancey N Wood
V'trs W/E & Wed–NA; SOC Tues and Thurs
Fees On application
Loc Opposite Barassie Station
Mis Catering facilities

Largs (1891)

Private (Map 9/22)
Irvine Road Largs KA30 8EU
Tel **Largs (0475) 673594**
Mem 650
Sec Frank Gilmour Tel (0475) 672497
Pro Robbie Stewart Tel (0475) 686192
Holes 18 L 6257 yds SSS 70
Recs Am–AO Harrington
Pro–
V'trs U
Fees £7 D–£11
Loc 1 mile S of town centre

Loudoun Gowf Club (1909)

Private (Map 9/23)
Galston
Tel **Galston 820551**
Mem 475
Sec CA Bruce Tel Galston 821993
Pro
Holes 18 L 5854 metres SSS 68
Recs Pro–64 G Davidson
V'trs WD–U; W/E–M; SOC
Fees £5 D–£8 (1985)
Loc 5 miles E of Kilmarnock

Maybole

Public (Map 9/24)
Memorial Park Maybole
Tel
Mem 100
Sec A Hill Tel Maybole 82454
Pro
Holes 9 L 2635 yds SSS 65 (for 18)
Recs Am–64 WW McCulloch
Pro–
V'trs U
Fees £2.20 (£3)
Loc Off A77 Glasgow–Stranraer, S of Maybole

New Cumnock (1901)

Private (Map 9/25)
New Cumnock
Tel
Mem 125
Sec H Smith
Pro
Holes 9 L 2365 yds SSS 63
Recs Am–66 D Blackwood
Pro–
V'trs U
Fees 80p (£1.25) M—£15
Loc Cumnock Road

Prestwick (1851)

Private (Map 9/26)
Links Road Prestwick
Tel **Prestwick 77404**
Mem 425
Sec JA Reid
Pro Frank Rennie Tel 79483
Holes 18 L 6544 yds SSS 72
Recs Am–68 DF Wilkie
Pro–67 EC Brown
C O'Connor
V'trs I; WD–on application only
Fees On application
Loc 1 mile from Prestwick Airport nr Railway Station

Prestwick St Cuthbert (1899)

Private (Map 9/27)
East Road Prestwick KA9 25X
Tel **Prestwick 77101**
Mem 698
Sec RM Tonner Tel 0292 79120
Pro
Holes 18 L 6470 yds SSS 71
Recs Am–G Hogg
Pro–
V'trs WD&BH–U; W/E–M SOC on WD
Fees £7 D–£10 W–£30, L £20, Jnrs £10
Loc ½ miles E side of Prestwick

Prestwick St Nicholas (1851)

Private (Map 9/28)
Grangemuir Road Prestwick Ayrshire
Tel **Prestwick 77608**
Mem 600 125(L) 62(J)
Sec JC Wallace
Pro I Parker Tel Prestwick 79755
Holes 18 L 5809 yds SSS 68
Recs Am–64 JKB Thomson
Pro–65 I Stanley G Brand Jnr
V'trs WD–I: W/E&BH–NA
Fees On application
Loc Prestwick

Routenburn (1914)

Private (Map 9/29)
Largs
Tel **Largs 673230**
Mem 400
Sec JE Smeaton Tel Largs 674171
Pro R Torrance Tel Largs 674289
Holes 18 L 5650 yds SSS 67
Recs Am–65 AO Harrington
Pro–65 S Torrance
V'trs U; SOC on WD
Fees £3 (£5) W–£15
Loc Largs Ayrshire

Skelmorlie (1890)

Private (Map 9/30)
Skelmorlie PA 17 5ES
Tel **Wemyss Bay 520152**
Mem 300
Sec S Hay
Pro
Holes 13 L 5056 yds SSS 65
Recs Am–63 P Travers
JR Christie AM Napier
Pro–69 Jas Braid
George Duncan
V'trs U (ex Sats April–October)
Fees £4 (£6) Half price after 4 pm
Loc 1½ miles Wemyss Bay station

Troon Courses

Royal Troon (1878)

Private (Map 9/31)
Craigend Road Troon KA10 6EP Ayrshire
Tel **Troon 311555**
Mem 800
Sec JA Sword Tel Troon 311555
Pro RB Anderson Tel Troon 313281
Holes Old Course (Medal) 18 L 6641 yds SSS 73
Old Course (Championship) L 7067 yds SSS 74
Portland 18 L 6274 yds SSS 71
Recs Old Course C'ship Am–70
CW Green J Harkis
Pro–66 R Clampett S Lyle
T Purtzer
Portland Am–66 IR Harris
JH McKay
Pro–
V'trs I–H (W/E both courses–NA) Old course available for ladies on Mon Wed and Fri only; visitors advised to book in advance
Fees D–£25 Old & Portland D–£20 Portland only
Loc 3 miles from Prestwick Airport

Troon Municipal

Public (Map 9/32)
Harling Drive Troon
Tel **Troon 312464**
Pro G Cunningham
Holes Lochgreen 18 L 6687 yds SSS 72
Darley 18 L 6327 yds SSS 70
Fullarton 18 L 4784 yds SSS 63
Recs Lochgreen Am–66
R Milligan
Pro–65 J Chillas
Darley Am–66 M Rossi
Pro–66 J White
Fullarton Am–58 A McQueen
Pro–
V'trs U SOC except Sat
Fees Lochgreen and Darley £4.30 D–£5.70 (£5.30 D–£8.60)
Fullarton £3 D–£3.90 (£3.60 D–£6)
Loc 4 miles N of Prestwick at Station Brae

Troon Clubs

Troon Portland (1894)

Private (Map 9)
1 Crosbie Road Troon
Tel **Troon 311555**
Mem 120
Sec J Currie Tel Troon 311863
Holes 18 L 6274 yds SSS 71 (Play over Troon Portland of Troon GC)
V'trs Arrange with Royal Troon GC
Loc End of Bentinck Drive at Marine Hotel

Troon St Meddans (1907)

Harling Drive Troon KA10 6NF
Mem 150
Sec To be appointed
Holes Play over Troon Municipal courses Lochgreen SSS 72 Darley SSS 70

Turnberry Hotel (1906)

Private (Map 9/33)
Turnberry Ayrshire KA26 9LT
Tel **Turnberry (0655) 31000**
Gen Man CJ Rouse
Pro RS Jamieson
Holes Ailsa 18 L 6950 yds SSS 70
Arran 18 L 6276 yds SSS 69
Recs Ailsa Am–70 GK MacDonald
Pro–63 M Hayes (USA) G Norman (Aus)
Arran Am–66 AP Parkin
Pro–66 J McTear
V'trs H U after 12 noon (WD and W/E)
Fees On application
Loc 5 miles N of Girvan
Mis Dormy House Bar coffee shop

Turnberry (1903)

Private (Map 9)
Turnberry
Tel **Turnberry 202**
Mem 435
Sec Matthew Lawson
Holes Play over Turnberry Hotel golf courses

West Kilbride (1893)

Private (Map 9/34)
West Kilbride
Tel **West Kilbride 823128**
Mem 1,000
Sec John Mitchell Tel West Kilbride 823911 or 822498
Pro Gregor Howie Tel West Kilbride 823042
Holes 18 L 6348 yds SSS 70
Recs Am–63 BW Aitken
Pro–67 J Panton
V'trs WD–I; W/E–M; BH–NA; SOC
Fees On application
Loc West Kilbride

Western Gailes (1897)

Private (Map 9/35)
Gailes Irvine Ayrshire
Tel **0294 311649**
Mem 475
Sec James A Clement
Man Brian Cole ACFA
Holes 18 L 6614 yds SSS 72
Recs Am–68 Malcolm E Lewis
Pro–66 David J Russell
V'trs I
Fees £15 booked through Manager; £18 casual
Loc 3 miles N of Troon

Borders, Berwickshire, Peeblesshire, Roxburghshire & Selkirkshire

Duns (1898)

Private (Map 9/1)
Hardens Road Duns
Tel **Duns (0361) 83377**
Mem 200
Sec Frank Whyte Tel Duns (0361) 83377
Pro
Holes 9 L 5754 yds SSS 68
Recs Am–68 WV Paton
Pro–
V'trs U SOC
Fees £4 (£5) 50% reduction 1st November–15th March
Loc 1 mile W of Duns off A6105

Eyemouth (1880)

Private (Map 9/2)
Gunsgreen House Eyemouth
Tel **50551**
Mem 250
Sec JW Fleming
Pro C Maltman
Holes 9 L 5500 yds SSS 67
Recs Am–60 James Patterson
Pro–
V'trs U
Fees D–£3 W/E–£4

Galashiels (1884)

Public (Map 9/3)
Ladhope Recreation Ground Galashiels
Tel **Galashiels 3724**
Mem 250 60(J)
Sec WD Millar Tel Selkirk 21669
Pro
Holes 18 L 5309 yds SSS 67
Recs Am–63 P Gallagher
Pro–70 Jas Braid
V'trs U; SOC
Fees £3.70
Loc ¼ mile NE of town

Hawick (1877)

Private (Map 9/4)
Vertish Hill Hawick
Tel **Hawick 72293**
Mem 510
Sec JG Brown Tel 73183
Pro
Holes 18 L 5929 yds SSS 69
Recs Am–63 AJ Ballantyne
Pro–65 R McDonald
V'trs U
Fees £3 D–£5
Loc 1½ miles S of Hawick

Innerleithen (1886)

Private (Map 9/5)
Leithen Water Leithen Road
Tel **0896-830951**
Mem 175
Sec David Brunton Tel 0896-830540
Pro
Holes 9 L 5820 yds SSS 68
Recs Am–66 WN Smith
Pro–
V'trs U
Fees £3 (£4) W–£12
Loc Innerleithen 1½ miles on Heriot Road

Jedburgh (1892)

Private (Map 9/6)
Dunion Road Jedburgh
Tel **Jed 63587**
Mem 200
Sec N White Tel Jed 63770
Pro
Holes 9 L 5492 yds SSS 67
Recs Am–65
Pro–
V'trs U
Fees R/D £4 (R/D £5)
Loc 1 mile Jedburgh

Kelso (1887)

Private (Map 9/7)
Berrymoss Racecourse Road Kelso Roxburghshire
Tel **Kelso 23009**
Mem 350
Sec Andrew Walker Tel Kelso 23009
Pro
Holes 18 L 6066 yds SSS 69
Recs Am–64
Pro–
V'trs U SOC
Fees £4 (£6) WD; £5 (£8) W/E (subject to 1986 review)
Loc Inside Kelso racecourse 1 mile from town centre

Lauder (1896)

Public (Map 9/8)
Lauder
Tel **381**
Mem 70
Sec AW Baxter
Pro
Holes 9 L 6002 yds SSS 70
Recs Am–70 JFC Jeffries
Pro–
V'trs U
Fees £1.50 (Sun £2) Reduced for OAPs
Loc ½ mile W of Lauder

Langholm (1892)

Private (Map 9/9)
Langholm Dumfriesshire
Tel
Mem 150
Sec DI Beverley Tel 80061
Pro
Holes 9 L 2623 yds SSS 66
Recs Am–65 I Borthwick
Pro–
V'trs U
Fees £3 (£3)
Loc Within Burgh of Langholm

Magdalene Fields

(see Northumberland England)

Melrose (1880)

Private (Map 9/10)
Dingleton Melrose
Tel **Melrose 2855**
Mem 300
Sec LM Wallace Tel Earlston 617
Pro
Holes 9 L 5464 yds SSS 68
Recs Am–63 DF Campbell
Pro–
V'trs U
Fees £4 (£5)
Loc S boundary Melrose

Minto (1926)

Private (Map 9/11)
Denholm Hawick Roxburghshire
Tel **0450 87220**
Mem 300
Sec IR Welch Tel 0450 72267
Pro D Dunlop Tel 08356 2686
Holes 18 L 5460 yds SSS 68
Recs Am–64 I Oliver
Pro–
V'trs U SOC
Fees £5 (£6)
Loc 6 miles E of Hawick; ½ mile of Denholm

Peebles (1892)

Public (Map 9/12)
Kirkland Street Peebles
Tel **Peebles 20197**
Mem 600
Sec G Gardiner Tel Peebles 20153
Pro
Holes 18 L 6137 yds SSS 69
Recs Am–64 D Campbell
Pro–70 RDBM Shade
V'trs U
Fees £4.50–subject to review
Loc 22 miles S of Edinburgh

St Boswells (1899)

Private (Map 9/13)
St Boswells Roxburghshire
Tel **0835 22359**
Mem 210
Sec GB Ovens Tel 0835 22359
Pro
Holes 9 L 5054 yds SSS 65
Recs Am–61 CI Ovens
Pro–

V'trs U
Fees £2.50 (£3)
Loc On R Tweed ¼ mile off A68 at St Boswells Green

Selkirk (1883)

Private (Map 9/14)
Selkirk
Tel **Selkirk 20621**
Mem 380
Sec
Pro
Holes 9 L 5560 yds SSS 67
Recs Am–60 MD Cleghorn
Pro–
V'trs U
Fees
Loc 1 mile S of Selkirk

The Hirsel (1948)

Private (Map 9/15)
Coldstream
Tel **Coldstream 2678**
Mem 350
Sec RC Sturrock
Pro
Holes 9 L 5680 yds SSS 67
Recs Am–67 N Smith J McDonald
Pro–
V'trs U
Fees £3 (£4)
Loc ½ mile W of Coldstream

Torwoodlee (1895)

Private (Map 9/16)
Galashiels
Tel **Galashiels 2260**
Mem 280
Sec A Wilson Tel Galashiels 2260
Pro
Holes 9 L 5800 yds SSS 68
Recs Am–64 RV Rutherford
Pro–64 A Wilson
V'trs U exc Sat–NA; SOC
Fees £5
Loc 1 mile N Galashiels on A7
Mis Full catering arrangements provided Parties welcome by arrangement

West Linton

(see Lothians)

Clackmannanshire, Central Region

Alloa (1891)

Private (Map 9/1)
Schawpark Sauchie Alloa
Tel **(0259) 722745**
Mem 535 80(L) 130(J) 100(Seniors)
Sec Alan M Frame Tel (0259) 722 745
Pro Bill Bennett Tel (0259) 724476
Holes 18 L 6240 yds SSS 70
Recs Am–63 AJ Liddle
Pro–66 R Weir G Harvey
V'trs U; W/E–No parties
Fees £5 WD–£7 (W/E £8)
Loc Alloa

Alva

Private (Map 9/2)
Beauclerc Street Alva Clacks FK12 5LE
Tel **60431**
Mem 200
Sec D Davidson Tel Tillicoultry 51427
Pro
Holes 9 L 2407 yds SSS 64
Recs Am–63 R Lyon
Pro–
V'trs U
Fees £2 (£3)
Loc Back Road Alva

Braehead (1891)

Private (Map 9/3)
Cambus Alloa
Tel **Alloa 722078**
Mem 500
Sec June A Henderson Tel Alloa 722897
Pro
Holes 18 L 6013 yds SSS 69 Par 70
Recs Am–65 M Rust
Pro–
V'trs U
Fees £5 (£5 D–£7) W–£18
Loc 2 miles W of Alloa

Dollar (1896)

Private (Map 9/4)
Brewlands House Dollar
Tel **Dollar 2400**
Mem 300
Sec Alex Porteous Tel Dollar 2348
Pro
Holes 18 L 5144 yds SSS 66
Recs Am–
Pro–
V'trs U; SOC
Fees £3.50 D–£4.50 (£5.50)
Loc In town

Muckhart

(see Perth & Kinross)

Tillicoultry (1899)

Private (Map 9/5)
Tillicoultry
Tel **(50) 741**
Mem 180
Sec R Whitehead
Pro
Holes 9 L 2528 yds SSS 65
Recs Am–62 K Mitchell
Pro–
V'trs U
Fees £1.50 (£3)
Loc 9 miles E of Stirling

Tulliallan (1902)

Private (Map 9/6)
Kincardine by Alloa
Tel **Kincardine 30396**
Mem 525 53(L) 100(J) 19(5)
Sec JS McDowall Tel 0324 485420
Pro S Kelly Tel Kincardine 30798
Holes 18 L 5982 yds SSS 69
Recs Am–65 A Pickles D Johnson
Pro–70 D Huish S Walker G Gray
V'trs U (ex at competition times)
Fees £4 (£5)
Loc 5 miles E of Alloa

Dunbartonshire, Strathclyde Region

Balmore (1906)

Private (Map 9/1)
Balmore by Torrance
Tel **Balmore 2120240**
Mem 700
Sec GP Woolard Tel 041-332 0392
Pro
Holes 18 L 5735 yds SSS 67
Recs Am–63 Alan Brodie
Pro–
V'trs M; SOC
Fees £8 R/D
Loc 2 miles N of Glasgow

Bearsden (1892)

Private (Map 9/2)
Thorn Road Bearsden G61 4BE
Tel **Bearsden 2351**
Mem 730
Sec JD McArthur
Pro
Holes 9 L 5977 yds SSS 70
Recs Am–64 D MacLeod
Pro–
V'trs M
Fees
Loc 7 miles NW of Glasgow

Cardross (1895)

Private (Map 9/3)
Cardross Dumbarton G82 5LB
Tel **Cardross 841213**
Mem 800
Sec R Evans CA Tel Cardross 841754
Pro Niall Cameron Tel Cardross 841350
Recs 18 L 6466 yds SSS 71
Recs Am–65 JLS Kinloch
Pro–71 J Farmer W Lockie D Ross
V'trs WD–U; W/E–M; SOC
Fees £8.50 D–£12.50
Loc 4 miles W of town of Dumbarton

Clober (1951)

Private (Map 9/4)
Craigton Road Milngavie Glasgow G62 7HP
Tel **041-956 1685**
Mem 575
Sec WG Fairbrother Tel 041-956 3293
Pro G Lyle Tel 041-956 1685
Holes 18 L 5068 yds SSS 65
Recs Am–61 PW Smith J Graham Jr
Pro–
V'trs WD–U (Before 4.30 pm); SOC; W/E–M; BH–NA
Fees £4
Loc 7 miles NW of Glasgow

Clydebank and District (1905)

Private (Map 9/5)
Hardgate Clydebank
Tel **Duntocher 73289**
Mem 780
Sec JV Morrison Tel Duntocher 73488
Pro G Lennie
Holes 18 L 5815 yds SSS 68
Recs Am–64 D Galbraith
Pro–
V'trs D–£6 W–£20 M–£30
Fees £5 W–£20
Loc 2 miles N of Clydebank

Clydebank Municipal

Public (Map 9/6)
Overtoun Road Dalmuir Clydebank
Tel **041-952 6372**
Man Clydebank Dist Council Tel 041-941 1331
Pro R Bowman Tel 041-952 6372

Holes 18 L 5349 yds SSS 66
Recs Am–64 FG Jardine
Pro–64 R Bowman
V'trs U exc Sat 11.30 am–2.30 pm
Fees Mon-Sat–£2 Sun–£2.40
Loc 8 miles W of Glasgow

Clydebank Overtoun (1970)

Private
Tel **041-952 6372**
Mem 160
Sec D Turnbull Tel Duntocher 74065
Pro R Bowman Tel 041-952 6372
Recs Am–64 FG Jardine J Semple
Pro–64 R Bowman
V'trs U
Loc 8 miles W of Glasgow
Mis Play over Clydebank Municipal, Overtoun Rd, Dalmuir, Clydebank

Craigmaddie (1978)

Private
Dougalston Golf Course Milngavie Glasgow
Tel **041-956 5750**
Mem 500
Sec G More
Holes Play over Dougalston

Cumbernauld (1977)

Public **(Map 9/7)**
Cumbernauld Dunbartonshire
Tel **Cumbernauld 28138**
Mem
Holes 18 L 6412 yds SSS 71
Recs Am–73 A Buchanan
Pro–
V'trs U
Fees £2 (£3)
Mis Palacerigg GC plays here

Dougalston (1977)

(Map 9/8)
Milngavie Glasgow
Tel **041-956 5750**
Mem
Sec W McInnes
Pro W Murray Tel 041-956 5750
Holes 18 L 6673 yds SSS 72
Recs Am–70 D Carrick
Pro–73 B Barnes
V'trs U; SOC
Fees £4 (£5)
Loc 7 miles N of Glasgow on A81
Mis Craigmaddie Club plays here open to public WD & W/E

Douglas Park (1897)

Private **(Map 9/9)**
Hillfoot Bearsden
Tel **041-942 2220**
Mem 400 250(L) 100(J)
Sec J Rennie Thorburn Tel 041-331 1837
Pro David Scott Tel 041-942 1482
Holes 18 L 5957 yds SSS 69
Recs Am–65 DG Carrick
Pro–67 DB Wilson
V'trs M
Fees Parties arranged
Loc Bearsden at Hillfoot Station

Dullatur (1896)

Private **(Map 9/10)**
Dullatur Glasgow
Tel **Cumbernauld 23230**
Mem 420 60(L)
Sec W Laing Tel Cum 27847
Pro D Sinclair
Holes 18 L 6253 yds SSS 70
Recs Am–67 JM Moffat
Pro–68 J Farmer
V'trs WD–U; W/E–M
Fees £7.50
Loc 3 miles N of Cumbernauld

Dumbarton (1887)

Private **(Map 9/11)**
Broadmeadow Dumbarton
Tel **Dumbarton 32830**
Mem 500
Sec J Campbell Tel Dumbarton 63051
Pro
Holes 18 L 6157 yds SSS 69
Recs Am–64 C Green
Pro–
V'trs WD–U; W/E&BH–M
Fees £4
Loc ¾ mile N Dumbarton town centre

Hayston (1926)

Private **(Map 9/12)**
Campsie Road Kirkintilloch Glasgow G66 1RN
Tel **041-776 1244/041-776 1390**
Mem 445 70(L) 80(J)
Sec J Weir Tel 041-339 7176
Pro Richard Graham Tel 041-775 0882
Holes 18 L 6042 yds SSS 69
Recs Am–62 LS Mann
Pro–69 K Stables
V'trs WD–I before 4.30; M after 4.30; W/E–M; SOC
Fees £7
Loc 1 mile N of Kirkintilloch

Helensburgh (1893)

Private **(Map 9/13)**
25 East Abercromby Street Helensburgh
Tel **Helensburgh 4173**
Mem 825
Sec RC McKechnie Tel Helensburgh 4173
Pro Ian Laird Tel Helensburgh 5505
Holes 18 L 6058 yds SSS 69
Recs Am–64 A Scott
Pro–65 RT Drummond
D Chillas B Marchbank
V'trs WD–U; W/E–NA
Fees £8 D–£10
Loc 25 miles W of Glasgow

Hilton Park (1927)

Private **(Map 9/14)**
Auldmarroch Estate Stockiemuir Road Milngavie G62 7HB
Tel **041-956 5124 and 956 1215**
Mem 1200
Sec Mrs JA Dawson Tel 956 4657
Pro W McCondichie Tel 956 5125
Holes Hilton 18 L 6021 yds SSS 70
Allander 18 L 5409 yds SSS 67
Recs Hilton Am–66 A Cowie
Pro–64 AF Anderson
Allander Am–67 Andrew James
Pro–63 F Morris N Wood
V'trs W/D–U–before 5 pm W/E–M
Fees On application
Loc 8 miles N of Glasgow
Mis Dormy House available

Kirkintilloch (1894)

Private **(Map 9/15)**
Todhill Campsie Road Kirkintilloch G66 1RN
Tel **041-776 1256**
Mem 420 92(L) 104(J) 35(5)
Sec H Bannerman Tel 041-777 7971
Pro
Holes 18 L 5269 yds SSS 66
Recs Am–63 J Hay R Moir
Pro–68 R Weir
V'trs M
Fees
Loc 7 miles N of Glasgow

Lenzie (1889)

Private **(Map 9/16)**
19 Crosshill Road Lenzie G66 5DA
Tel **041-776 1535**
Mem 483 125(L) 125(J)
Sec AW Jones Tel 041-776 4377
Pro
Holes 18 L 5982 yds SSS 69
Recs Am–64 S Lindsay
Pro–
V'trs M SOC
Fees
Loc Glasgow 6 miles

Milngavie (1895)

Private **(Map 9/17)**
Laighpark Milngavie G62 8EP
Tel **Milngavie 1619**
Mem 390
Sec G Law Tel Duntocher 76286
Pro
Holes 18 L 5818 yds SSS 68
Recs Am–64 RGB McCallum
Pro–
V'trs M
Fees On application
Loc NW of Glasgow

Palacerigg

Cumbernauld
Tel **Cumbernauld 34969**
Mem 550
Sec L Peck
Holes Play over Cumbernauld Municipal

Vale of Leven (1907)

Private **(Map 9/18)**
Northfield Course Bonhill Alexandria
Tel **37 52351**
Mem 450
Sec JO Miller
Pro
Holes 18 L 5155 yds SSS 66
Recs Am–61 D Checkley
Pro–63 EC Brown
V'trs U (ex Sat from April-Sept)
Fees £3 (£8)
Loc Off A82 at Bonhill

Windyhill (1908)

Private **(Map 9/19)**
Windyhill Bearsden
Tel **041-942 2349**
Mem 650
Sec PO Bell Tel 041-956 4970
Pro Bob Collinson Tel 041-942 7157
Holes 18 L 6230 yds SSS 70
Recs Am–66 DJ Shaw
Pro–
V'trs WD–I; Sundays–M
Fees £7
Loc 8 miles NW of Glasgow

Fife, Fife Region

Aberdour (1904)

Private (Map 9/1)
Seaside Place Aberdour KY3 0TX
Tel **Aberdour 860688**
Mem 420 160(L)
Sec RM Walker Tel Aberdour 860352
Pro J Bennet Tel Aberdour 860256
Holes 18 L 5469 yds SSS 67
Recs Am–64 Derek Miller
Pro–
V'trs W/E–NA Sun and comp Sats
Fees £5 (£7)
Loc Aberdour
Mis Visitors may make tee reservations 1 day in advance with Pro

Anstruther (1890)

Private (Map 9/2)
Anstruther
Tel
Mem 500
Sec Tom Reid Tel Anstruther 310224
Pro
Holes 9 L 4504 yds SSS 63
Recs Am–63 R Wallace
T Anderson A Forrester
V'trs U SOC
Fees £3 (£4.50) subject to revision
Loc Outskirts of town

Auchterderran (1904)

Private (Map 9/3)
Woodend Road Cardenden
Tel **721547**
Mem 100
Sec SG Miller
Pro
Holes 9 L 5400 yds SSS 66
Recs Am–66 C McRae
Pro–
V'trs U
Fees £2 (£3.20) To be reviewed
Loc 1 mile N of town centre

Ballingry (1908)

Public (Map 9/4)
Lochore Meadows Country Park Crosshill Lochgelly Fife
Tel **0592-860086**
Mem 100
Sec James Mackie Tel 0592-860927
Pro
Holes 9 L 6244 yds SSS 71
Recs Am–70 T Easton AG Campbell D Walker
Pro–
V'trs U
Fees £2.25 (£3)
Loc Lochore Meadows Country Park

Burntisland GC (1797)

Private (Map 9)
Tel **Burntisland 873865**
Mem 120
Sec AD McPherson Tel Burntisland 873865
Pro
Holes Play over Dodhead Course, Burntisland

Burntisland Golf House Club (1898)

Private (Map 9/5)
Dodhead Burntisland
Tel **Burntisland (0592) 873247**
Mem 685
Sec AW Mann Tel 874093
Pro JC MacDonald
Holes 18 L 5871 yds SSS 68
Recs Am–66 DR Weir
Pro–69
V'trs U
Fees £4 D–£6 W/E–£9
Loc 1 mile E on B923

Canmore (1898)

Private (Map 9/6)
Venturefair Dunfermline
Tel **Dunfermline 724969**
Mem 480 60(L) 80(J)
Sec JC Duncan Tel Dunfermline 726098
Pro S Craig Tel Dunfermline 728416
Holes 18 L 5437 yds SSS 66
Recs Am–61 R Wallace
Pro–
V'trs WD–U
Fees £4 (£6.50)
Loc 1 mile N of Dunfermline on A823

Crail Golfing Society (1786)

Private (Map 9/7)
Balcomie Clubhouse Crail KY10 3XN
Tel **Crail 50278**
Mem 700 200(L)
Sec G Thomson Tel Crail 50686
Pro
Holes 18 L 5720 yds SSS 68
Recs Am–64 RW Malcolm
Pro–
V'trs U
Fees On application
Loc 11 miles SE of St Andrews

Cupar (1855)

Private (Map 9/8)
Hillarvitt Cupar Fife
Tel **Cupar 53549**
Mem 475
Sec IR Wilson Tel Cupar 53254
Pro
Holes 9 L 5074 yds SSS 65
Recs Am–62 J Fairfield
Pro–
V'trs SOC on WD & Sun; W/E–NA Sat
Fees £4 (£5)
Loc 10 miles W of St Andrews

Dunfermline (1887)

Private (Map 9/9)
Pitfirrane House Crossford by Dunfermline
Tel **Dunfermline 723534**
Mem 500
Sec JA Gillies
Pro D Symington
Holes 18 L 6271 yds SSS 72
Recs Am–65 AD Martin
Pro–66 J Farmer
V'trs I; SOC on WD
Fees £7.50 (R) on application WD
Loc 2 miles W of Dunfermline
Mis No catering Tue

Dunnikier Park (1963)

Public (Map 9/10)
Dunnikier Way Kirkcaldy KY1 3LP
Tel **Kirkcaldy 261599**
Mem 500 40(L) 75(J)
Sec DR Caird Tel 267462
Pro
Holes 18 L 6601 yds SSS 72
Recs Am–67 D Owler
Pro–
V'trs U; SOC
Fees £2.20 (£3.20)
Loc North boundary Kirkcaldy

Earlsferry Thistle (1875)

Melon Park Elie
Tel **Anstruther 310053**
Mem 60
Sec Jas Fyall Tel Anstruther 310053
Holes Play over Elie Golf House Club Course

Golf House Club (1875)

Private (Map 9/11)
Elie Leven KY9 1AS
Tel **Elie 330327**
Mem 450
Sec GA Forgie Tel 330301
Pro G Finlayson Tel 330955
Holes 18 L 6241 yds SSS 70
9 L 2277 yds SSS 32
Recs Am–63 AW Mathers
Pro–62 Kel Nagle
V'trs U (July, Aug, Sep ballot)
Fees £8 D–£12 (£10 D–£15) W–£40 F–£70
Loc 12 miles St Andrews

Glenrothes (1958)

Public (Map 9/12)
Golf Course Road Glenrothes KY6 2LA
Tel **Glenrothes 758686 and 758678**
Mem 600 35(L) 120(J)
Sec LD Dalrymple Tel Glenrothes 754561
Pro
Holes 18 L 6444 yds SSS 71
Recs Am–65 C Birrell
Pro–69 R Craig B Lawson
V'trs U
Fees £2.70 (£3.70)
Loc Glenrothes West

Kinghorn (1887)

Public (Map 9/13)
Macduff Cres Kinghorn
Tel **Kinghorn 890345**
Mem **195**
Sec D Mackenzie Tel Kinghorn 890157
Pro
Holes 18 L 5246 SSS 67
Recs Am–62 AJ McIntyre
Pro–
V'trs U
Fees £2.50 (£3)
Loc 5 minutes from station

Kinghorn Thistle

Kinghorn
Tel
Mem 60
Sec D Gordon
Holes Play over Kinghorn Municipal

Kinghorn Ladies (1905)

Private (Map 9)
Kinghorn
Tel **890345**
Mem 49
Sec Mrs M Craig Tel Kinghorn 890880
Holes Play over Kinghorn Municipal

Kirkcaldy (1904)

Private (Map 9/14)
Balwearie Road Kirkcaldy KY2 5LT
Tel **0592 260370**
Mem 450 80(L)
Sec Charles Taylor Tel Kirkcaldy 266597
Pro Brian Lawson Tel Kirkcaldy 203258
Holes 18 L 6007 yds SSS 70
Recs Am–69 TM Cochrane KG Stewart D Grimshaw M More
Pro–
V'trs U
Fees £4 D–£7 (£5 D–£8.50)
Loc SW end of town

Ladybank (1879)

Private (Map 9/15)
Annsmuir Ladybank
Tel **30320**
Mem 750
Sec D Downie Tel Ladybank 30814
Pro Martin J Gray Tel Ladybank 30725
Holes 18 L 6617 yds SSS 72
Recs Am–68 AG Campbell
Pro–69 S Walker
V'trs WD–9.15 am–5 pm U, M after 5 pm; Sat–NA; Sun 10.15 am–5 pm–SOC
Fees £8 D–£12 (£10 D–£15)
Loc 6 miles S of Cupar

Leslie (Fife) (1898)

Private (Map 9/16)
Leslie
Tel
Mem 300
Sec M Burns Tel 741449
Pro
Holes 9 L 4940 yds SSS 64
Recs Am–63 J Spital
Pro–64 J Chillas
V'trs U
Fees £2.50 (£3)
Loc Town boundary 11 miles M90 J5 or J7

Leven Golfing Society (1820)

Private (Map 9)
Links Road Leven KY8 4HS
Tel **Leven 26096**
Mem 500
Sec John Bennett Tel Leven 23898 (after 4 pm)
Pro
Holes 18 L 6434 yds SSS 71
V'trs SOC. Arrangements for parties must be made through Mr M Innes, Clydesdale Bank Buildings, Durie St, Leven, Fife.
Fees On application
Loc ½ mile E of town centre

Leven Links (1846)

Private (Map 9/17)
Leven
Tel
Mem 1000
Sec M Innes Tel 23509 (Links Joint Committee Leven Golfing Society and Leven Thistle)
Pro
Holes 18 L 6425 yds SSS 71
Recs Am–64 J Hawkesworth
Pro–63 Paul Hoad
V'trs U
Fees On application

Leven Municipal Course

Public (Map 9/17)
Leven
Tel
Pro J Simpson
Holes 18 L 5403 yds SSS 66
Recs Am–
Pro–
V'trs U
Fees 60p
Loc Adjoins Leven Links
Mis Scoonie Club plays here

Leven Thistle (1867)

Private (Map 9)
3 Balfour Street Leven
Tel **(0333) 26397**
Mem 400
Sec J Scott Tel (0333) 23798
Pro
Holes 18 L 6800 yds SSS 71
Fees £6 D–£9.50 (£7 D–£10.50) Reductions with mem, ladies; W–£25 F–£36
Loc On promenade

Lochgelly (1910)

Private (Map 9/18)
Cartmore Road Lochgelly
Tel **780174**
Mem 400
Sec RF Stuart Tel Cowdenbeath 512238
Pro
Holes 18 L 5429 yds SSS 67
Recs Am–65 J Stuart K Pettigrew
Pro–
V'trs U
Fees £3.50 (£4.75)
Loc NW boundary

Lundin (1869)

Private (Map 9/19)
Golf Road Lundin Links KY8 6BA
Tel **Lundin Links 320202**
Mem 700
Sec AC McBride
Pro DK Webster Tel 320051
Holes 18 L 6377 yds SSS 71
Recs Am–65 W Bergin (USA)
D Dunk (Austr)
P Brostedt (Swe)
Pro–
V'trs WD; Sats & BH–U; Sunds–M and temp members (minimum week)
Fees On application
Loc 3 miles E of Leven

Lundin Ladies (1910)

Private (Map 9/20)
Woodielea Road Lundin Links KY8 6AR
Tel **(0333) 320022**
Mem 214
Sec Mrs Maris MacCrossan Tel (0333) 320193
Pro
Holes 9 L 4730 yds SSS 67
Recs Am–68 Miss P Baxter
Pro–
V'trs U
Fees £2 (£2.80)
Loc 3 miles E of Leven

Methil (1892)

Private (Map 9)
Links House Links Road Leven Fife
Tel **Leven 25535**
Mem 50
Sec ATJ Traill
Holes Play over Leven Links

Pitreavie (1923)

Private (Map 9/21)
Queensferry Road Dunfermline KY11 5PR
Tel **(0383) 722591**
Mem 460
Sec WP Syme Tel (0383) 722591
Pro Alan D Hope Tel (0383) 723151
Holes 18 L 6086 yds SSS 69
V'trs U (telephone Pro in advance); SOC (Visiting parties restricted to 36 persons. Parties must be booked in advance)
Fees £4.50 D–£6.50 (D/R £10) with mem £1.50 (1986 prices)
Loc 2 miles off M90 Edinburgh/Perth, midway between Rosyth and Dunfermline

St Andrews Courses

Details from A Beveridge (Secretary) Links Management Committee of St Andrews Golf Place St Andrews KY16 9JA Tel 75757
A £35 weekly ticket allows unlimited play over the New, Eden and Jubilee courses for 7 days from date of purchase.

Balgove (1972)

Public (Map 9/22)
Tel
Holes 9 (Beginner's Course)
V'trs U
Fees £2 (18 holes)

Eden Course (1913)

Public (Map 9/22)
St Andrews
Tel **74296 (Starter)**
Holes 18 L 5971 yds SSS 69
Recs Am–65 RDBM Shade RD Park K Hastie
Pro–64 W McHardy
V'trs U SOC
Fees £7 3 day–£20 W–£40 available for unlimited play on Eden Course, Jubilee Course and New Course
Loc St Andrews Links

Jubilee Course (1899)

Public (Map 9/22)
St Andrews
Tel **73938 (Starter)**
Holes 18 L 6284 yds SSS 70
Recs Am–69 RJ Sturrock
Pro–
V'trs U SOC
Fees £5 3 day–£20 W–£40 (unlimited play over Jubilee, Eden and New Courses)
Loc St Andrews Links

New Course (1894)

Public (Map 9/22)
St Andrews
Tel **73938 (Starter)**
Holes 18 L 6604 yds SSS 72
Recs Am–67 GM Mitchell
Pro–63 F Jowie
V'trs U
Fees £7 3 day–£20 W–£40 (unlimited play over Jubilee, Eden and New courses)
Loc St Andrews Links

Old Course (15th Century)

Public (Map 9/22)
St Andrews
Tel **73393 (Starter)**
Holes 18 L 6566 yds SSS 72
Recs Am–67 Joe Carr
Pro–65 Neil Coles
Greg Norman
V'trs U; H; I; No Sunday play SOC
Fees £17
Loc St Andrews Links

St Andrews Clubs

New Golf Club (1902)

3-6 Gibson Place St Andrews Fife KY16 9JE
Tel **St Andrews 73426**
Mem 1600
Sec/ Treas Thomas Deas
Pro
Holes Play over St Andrews courses

Royal and Ancient (1754)

St Andrews
Tel **St Andrews 72112**
Mem 1800
Sec MF Bonallack OBE
Pro L Auchterlonie (Honorary)
Holes Play over St Andrews courses

St Andrews (1843)

Private (Map 9)
Links House The Links St Andrews
Tel **St Andrews 74637**
Mem 1800
Sec WS Simpson Tel St Andrews 73017
Holes Play over St Andrews courses
V'trs Rules in accordance with Links Management Committee, Golf Place, St Andrews

St Regulus Ladies' (1920)

9 Pilmour Links St Andrews KY16 9JG
Tel **St Andrews 74699**
Mem 170
Sec Mrs K Ferguson
Pro
Holes Play over St Andrews courses

St Rule Ladies' (1898)

Private (Map 9)
12 The Links St Andrews
Tel **0334 72988**
Mem 157
Sec Mrs R Hair Tel 0334 72988
Pro
Holes Play over St Andrews Courses
V'trs M
Loc Adjacent Old Course

Thistle (1817)

St Andrews
Tel
Mem 162
Sec Duncan L Joy Tel St Andrews 73749
Pro LB Ayton
Holes Play over St Andrews courses

Saline (1912)

Private (Map 9/23)
Kinneddar Hill Saline Fife
Tel New Oakley 591
Mem 300
Sec R Hutchison Tel (0383) 852344
Pro
Holes 9 L 5302 yds SSS 66
Recs Am–S Mellon
Pro–
V'trs U except medal Saturdays
Fees £3 (£4)
Loc 5 miles NW Dunfermline
Mis Catering by prior arrangement

Scoonie (1951)

Private (Map 9)
North Link Leven
Tel
Mem 180
Sec J Gilbert Tel Leven 24866
Pro
Holes 18 L 5400 yds SSS 66
V'trs U SOC
Tees £2.20 (£3.30)
Loc Within ½ mile of town centre
Mis Play over Leven Municipal

Scotscraig (1817)

Private (Map 9/24)
Golf Road Tayport Fife DD6 9DZ
Tel **Tayport (0382) 552515**
Mem 600
Sec
Pro
Holes 18 L 6477 yds SSS 71
Recs Am–65 M Milne Jr
Pro–66 J Berry
M Bembridge
V'trs WD–U; W/E–by prior arrangement; SOC
Fees £7 D–£11 (£8 D–£12.50)
Loc 10 miles N of St Andrews

St Michael's (1903)

Private (Map 9/25)
Leuchars
Tel **Leuchars 365**
Mem 350
Sec AJR MacKenzie Tel Balmullo 870421 (home) Cupar 54044 (work)
Pro
Holes 9 L 5510 yds SSS 67
Recs Am–
Pro–
V'trs NA Sun am March–October
Fees £3.50 (£4) D–£6 WD only; under 16 pay half
Loc 5 miles N of St Andrews on Dundee road

Thornton (1921)

Private (Map 9/26)
Station Road Thornton
Tel **Glenrothes 771111**
Mem 550
Sec M Moss Tel Glenrothes 754240
Pro
Holes 18 L 6175 yds SSS 69
Recs Am–65 R Malcolm
Pro–
V'trs U
Fees £4 (£6) WD–£6 W/E–£9 W–£18
Loc In Thornton 1 mile E A92

Glasgow, Strathclyde Region

Bishopbriggs (1906)

Private (Map 9/20)
Brackenbrae Road Bishopbriggs Glasgow G64
Tel **041-772 1810**
Mem 400
Sec RD Locke Tel 041-762 4828
Pro
Holes 18 L 6041 yds SSS 69
Recs Am–64 I Gillan AF Dunsmore
S Finlayson
Pro–63 M Miller
V'trs M or I
Fees £9
Loc 6 miles N of Glasgow

Bogside

(see Ayrshire Irvine)

Cathcart Castle (1895)

Private (Map 9/21)
Mearns Road Clarkston
Tel **041-638 0082**
Mem 700
Sec WG Buchan Tel 041-638 9449
Pro D Naylor Tel 041-638 3436
Holes 18 L 5832 yds SSS 68
Recs Am–62 S Black
Pro–64 A White
V'trs M
Fees
Loc 7 miles SW Glasgow

Cathkin Braes (1888)

Private (Map 9/22)
Cathkin Braes Rutherglen
Tel 041-634 4007
Mem 800
Sec GL Stevenson
Pro Stephen Bree Tel 041-634 0650
Holes 18 L 6266 yds SSS 71
Recs Am–J Graham
Pro–67 Jim Noon
V'trs I
Fees £8
Loc 5 miles S of Glasgow

Cawder (1933)

Private (Map 9/23)
Cadder Road Bishopbriggs Glasgow
Tel **041-772 7101**
Mem 1200
Sec GT Stoddart Tel 041-772 5167
Pro K Stevely Tel 041-772 7102
Holes Cawder Course 18 L 6244 yds SSS 71
Keir Course 18 L 5885 yds SSS 68
Recs Cawder Course Am–68 CW Green
Pro–65 R Weir
Keir Course Am–64 A Brodie J Hay
Pro–
V'trs WD only; SOC on WD
Fees £10
Loc 1¼ miles Bishopbriggs Station

Cowglen (1906)

Private (Map 9/24)
301 Barrhead Road Glasgow
Tel **041-632 0556**
Mem 450
Sec RJG Jamieson Tel Ayr 266600

Pro J McTear Tel 041-649 9401
Holes 18 L 6006 yds SSS 69
Recs Am–63 D Barclay Howard
Pro–63 S Torrance
V'trs M
Fees
Loc S side of Glasgow

Glasgow Killermont (1787)

Private **(Map 9/25)**
Killermont Glasgow
Tel **041-942 2340**
Mem 750
Sec WD Robertson Tel 041-942 2011
Pro J Steven Tel 041-942 8507
Holes 18 L 5968 yds SSS 69
Recs Am–63 JS Cochran
Pro–65 H Wheetman
V'trs M
Fees
Loc NW Glasgow

Haggs Castle (1910)

Private **(Map 9/26)**
70 Dumbreck Road Dumbreck Glasgow G41 4SN
Tel **041-427 0480**
Mem 1000
Sec ARC Alexander Tel 041-427 1157
Pro J McAlister
Holes 18 L 6464 yds SSS 71
Recs Am–67
Pro–63
V'trs M
Fees
Loc SW Glasgow

Pollok (1892)

Private **(Map 9/27)**
90 Barrhead Road Pollokshaws Glasgow G43 1BG
Tel **041-632 1080**
Mem 500
Sec A Mathison Boyd Tel 041-632 4361
Pro
Holes 18 L 6257 yds SSS 70
Recs Am–62 G Shaw
Pro–62 G Cunningham
V'trs I; XL W/E–NA SOC on WD
Fees £12 D–£18
Loc 3 miles SW Glasgow on B462

Ralston (1904)

Private **(Map 9/28)**
Ralston Paisley
Tel **041-882 1349**
Mem 440 165(L) 100(J)
Sec JW Horne Tel 041-883 7045
Pro
Holes 18 L 6100 yds SSS 69
Recs Am–63 J Armstrong
Pro–
V'trs M
Fees
Loc 2 miles E of Paisley

Sandyhills (1905)

Private **(Map 9/29)**
223 Sandyhills Road Glasgow G32 9NA
Tel **041-778 1179**
Mem 460
Sec G Muir CA Tel 0698 812203
Pro
Holes 18 L 6253 yds SSS 70
Recs Am–65 J Hay
Pro–
V'trs M
Fees
Loc 4 miles E city centre

Williamwood (1906)

Private **(Map 9/30)**
Clarkston Road Glasgow G44
Tel **041-637 1783**
Mem 680
Sec IJ Gilchrist Tel 041-226 4311
Pro J Gardner Tel 041-637 2715
Holes 18 L 5878 yds SSS 68
Recs Am–63 I Carslaw AA Nicol S Dixon
Pro–61 BJ Gallacher
V'trs M
Fees
Loc 5 miles S of Glasgow

Glasgow Public Courses

Alexandra Park

Public **(Map 9/31)**
Sannox Gardens Alexandra Parade Glasgow
Tel **041-556 3711**
Pro
Holes 9 L 1968 yds SSS 30
Recs Am–
Pro–
V'trs U
Fees 90p D–£1.50 (£1.20)
Loc ½ mile E city centre

Deaconsbank (1922)

Public **(Map 9/32)**
Glasgow
Tel
Pro
Holes 18 L 4800 yds SSS 63
Recs Am–
Pro–
V'trs U
Fees 60p (80p)
Loc 5 miles S of Glasgow nr Thornliebank

King's Park (1934)

Public **(Map 9/33)**
150A Croftpark Avenue Croftfoot Glasgow
Tel
Pro
Holes 9 L 2010 yds SSS 30
Recs Am–27 I Simpson
Pro–
V'trs U
Fees 90p D–£1.50 (£1.20)
Loc Croftfoot Glasgow GS4
3½ miles S of city centre

Knightswood (1929)

Public **(Map 9/34)**
Lincoln Avenue Glasgow G13
Tel **041-959 2131**
Mem 76
Sec Martin Kelly Tel 041-636 1225
Pro
Holes 9 L 2736 yds SSS 33
Recs Am–
Pro–
V'trs U
Fees 90p D–£1.50 (£1.20)
Loc 4 miles W of city centre

Lethamhill (1933)

Public **(Map 9/35)**
Cumbernauld Road Glasgow GE3
Tel **041-770 6220**
Pro
Holes 16 L 5946 yds SSS 68
Recs Am–70 R Harker
Pro–
V'trs U
Fees £1.80 D–£3 (£2.40)
Loc Glasgow GE3 3 miles E of city centre

Linn Park (1925)

Public **(Map 9/36)**
Simshill Road Glasgow G44
Tel **041-637 5871**
Mem 132
Sec Jim McLean 041-634 8991
Pro
Holes 18 L 4728 yds SSS 63
Recs Am–61 J McCann
Pro–
V'trs U
Fees £1.80 D–£3 (£2.40)
Loc 4 miles S city centre

Littlehill (1926)

Public **(Map 9/37)**
Auchinairn Road Bishopbriggs Glasgow
Tel **041-772 1916**
Pro
Holes 18 L 6199 yds SSS 69
Recs Am–66
Pro–
V'trs U
Fees £1.80 D–£3 (£2.40)
Loc 3 miles N of city centre

Ruchill (1928)

Public **(Map 9/38)**
Brassey Street Maryhill Glasgow G20
Tel
Mem 60
Sec DF Campbell Tel 041-946 7676
Pro
Holes 9 L 2240 yds SSS 31
Recs Am–62 (18 holes)
Pro–
V'trs U
Fees 90p D–£1.50 (£1.20)
Loc 2½ miles NW of city centre

Glasgow Gailes

(see Ayrshire)

Lanarkshire, Strathclyde Region

Airdrie (1877)

Private **(Map 9/1)**
Rochsoles Airdrie
Tel **Airdrie 62195**
Mem 457
Sec RP Kennedy Tel Airdrie 64864
Pro T Melville Tel Airdrie 54360
Holes 18 L 6004 yds SSS 69
Recs Am–64 G Russo R Marshall
Pro–
V'trs W/E & BH–NA; SOC
Fees Round £5.75 +VAT
Loc Airdrie 1 mile

Bellshill (1905)

Private **(Map 9/2)**
Orbiston Bellshill ML4 2RZ
Tel **745124**
Mem 400
Sec A Currie Tel 745124
Pro
Holes 18 L 6607 yds SSS 72

Recs Am–68 J Simpson A Megan M Brown
Pro–70 J McCallum
V'trs U exc WD 5 pm–6.30 pm
Fees £5 (£7)
Loc 10 miles S of Glasgow between Bellshill and Motherwell

Biggar (1895)

Public (Map 9/3)
Public Park Broughton Road Biggar Strathclyde ML12
Tel **Biggar 20618**
Mem 400
Sec WS Turnbull Tel (0899) 20566
Pro
Holes 18 L 5256 yds SSS 66
Recs Am–60 D Thorburn
Pro–65 W Murray
V'trs U
Fees £3.50 (£5.50) Special OAP terms October–March £3
Loc ½ mile Biggar town centre

Blairbeth (1910)

Private (Map 9/4)
Burnside Rutherglen
Tel **041-634 3355**
Mem 400
Sec FT Henderson Tel 041-632 0604
Pro
Holes 18 L 5448 yds SSS 67
Recs Am–60 DB Howard
Pro–69 WG Cunningham
V'trs M
Fees
Loc 1 mile S of Rutherglen

Bothwell Castle (1922)

Private (Map 9/5)
Blantyre Road Bothwell
Tel **853177**
Mem 548
Sec ADC Watson Tel 852395
Pro Wm A Walker
Holes 18 L 6456 yds SSS 71
Recs Am–64 Findlay Jardine
Pro–67 R Charles (NZ)
V'trs WD–U (8.30 am to 3.30 pm)
Fees £5
Loc 3 miles N of Hamilton

Calderbraes (1893)

Private (Map 9/6)
57 Roundknowe Road Uddingston
Tel **Uddingston 813425**
Mem 300
Sec S McGuigan Tel 02364-65286
Pro
Holes 9 L 5046 yds SSS 67
Recs Am–65 D Gilchrist
Pro–
V'trs M
Fees
Loc Start of M74

Cambuslang (1891)

Private (Map 9/7)
Westburn Drive Cambuslang G72 7AN
Tel **041-641 3130**
Mem 200 100(L) 75(J)
Sec W Lilly
Pro
Holes 9 L 6072 yds SSS 69
Recs Am–65 AM Grant
Pro–
V'trs I
Fees
Loc ¾ mile Cambuslang Station

Carluke (1894)

Private (Map 9/8)
Hallcraig Carluke
Tel **Carluke 71070**
Mem 460
Sec J Kyle Tel Carluke 70366
Pro A Brooks Tel Carluke 51053
Holes 18 L 5805 yds SSS 68
Recs Am–64 K Harrison
Pro–64 G Cunningham
R Davis W Milne
V'trs WD–before 4 pm; W/E–NA
Fees £6 D–£9
Loc Glasgow 20 miles

Carnwath (1907)

Private (Map 9/9)
Main Street Carnwath
Tel **Carnwath 840251**
Mem 380
Sec GP Pollock Tel Lanark 4359
Pro
Holes 18 L 5860 yds SSS 68
Recs Am–64 C Porteous
Pro–
V'trs U (Sats –NA)
Fees £6.50 (£8.50)
Loc 7 miles from Lanark

Coatbridge (1970)

Public (Map 9/10)
Townhead Road Coatbridge
Tel **28975**
Mem 370
Sec J McGlone 86 School St Coatbridge
Pro S Aird
Holes 18 L 5387 yds SSS 66
Recs Am–
Pro–
V'trs U
Fees 50p
Loc Townhead

Colville Park (1922)

Private (Map 9/11)
Jerviston Estate Motherwell
Tel **Motherwell 63017**
Mem 534 67(L) 143(J)
Sec E Wood Tel Motherwell 66045
Pro Golf Shop Tel Motherwell 65779
Holes 18 L 6208 yds SSS 70
Recs Am–66 J Johnston WS Bryson A Dunsmore
Pro–66 SD Brown
V'trs M Party bookings by arrangement WD only
Fees £7 inc VAT
Loc 1 mile Motherwell Station

Crow Wood (1925)

Private (Map 9/12)
Muirhead Chryston Glasgow
Tel **799 2011**
Mem 558
Sec Margt B Weir Tel 041-554 2391
Pro Tel 779 1943
Holes 18 L 6249 yds SSS 70
Recs Am–64 D Chalmers
Pro–66 John McTear
V'trs M
Fees
Loc 5 miles NE of Glasgow

Douglas Water (1922)

Private (Map 9/13)
Douglas Water Lanark
Tel **Douglas Water 460**
Mem 150
Sec R McMillan
Pro
Holes 9 L 2916 yds SSS 69
Recs Am–66 H Gold
Pro–
V'trs U
Fees £1.50 (£3)
Loc 7 miles SW Lanark

Drumpellier (1894)

Private (Map 9/14)
Langloan Coatbridge
Tel **Coatbridge 24139 or 28723**
Mem 450
Sec W Brownlie Tel Coatbridge 23065 or 28538
Pro I Collins Tel Coatbridge 32971
Holes 18 L 6227 yds SSS 70
Recs Am–65 AD Ferguson G Shanks ISS Russell
Pro–64 W Milne
V'trs I
Fees £7 D–£12
Loc 8 miles E of Glasgow

East Kilbride (1900)

Private (Map 9/15)
Chapelside Road Nerston East Kilbride G74 4PF
Tel **East Kilbride 20913**
Mem 700
Sec T McCracken Tel 47728
Pro J Taylor Tel 22192
Holes 18 L 6419 yds SSS 71
Recs Am–65 WF Bryce
Pro–64 David Ingram
V'trs M SOC
Fees £5 D–£8
Loc 8 miles S of Glasgow

Easter Moffat (1922)

Private (Map 9/16)
Plains by Airdrie
Tel **Caldercruix 842289/842878**
Mem 400
Sec John Reilly Tel Coatbridge 21864 (business)
Pro John Forsythe Tel Caldercruix 843015
Holes 18 L 6221 yds SSS 70
Recs Am–68
Pro–66 R Shade
V'trs Non introduced–WD only
Fees £4 D–£6
Loc 3 miles E of Airdrie

Hamilton (1892)

Private (Map 9/17)
Riccarton Ferniegair by Hamilton
Tel **Hamilton 282872**
Mem 480
Sec PE Soutter
Pro MJ Moir Tel Hamilton 282324
Holes 18 L 6255 yds SSS 70
Recs Am–62 G Hogg
Pro–
V'trs M or by arrangement
Fees £10 D–£12
Loc 1½ miles S of Hamilton

Hollandbush (1954)

Public (Map 9/19)
Acre Tophead Lesmahagow by Coalburn
Tel **Lesmahagow 893484**
Mem 500
Sec J Hamilton 260 Bellfield Road Coalburn Tel Coalburn 222
Pro I Rae Tel 893646
Holes 18 L 6110 yds SSS 70
Recs Am–63 G Brown
Pro–
V'trs U
Fees £4 (£6)
Loc Between Coalburn and Lesmahagow

Kirkhill (1910)

Private (Map 9/20)
Greenlees Road Cambuslang
Tel **041-641 3083 (clubhouse) 041-641 8499 (office)**
Mem 570
Sec CC Stanfield Tel 041-634 4276
Pro
Holes 18 L 5889 yds SSS 69
Recs Am–63 David Martin
Pro–68 Russel Weir (Cowal)
V'trs WD by prior arrangement; SOC welcome; N/A on BH or W/E
Fees £7 D–£10
Loc Cambuslang

Lanark (1851)

Private (Map 9/21)
The Moor Lanark
Tel **Lanark 3219**
Mem 500 130(L) 200(J)
Sec WW Law
Pro Ron Wallace Tel Lanark 61456
Holes 18 L 6426 yds SSS 71
9 L 1562 yds SSS 28
Recs 18 holes Am–64 CV McInally
Pro–64 AS Oldcorn
V'trs WD until 4 pm only–U; W/E–M (Small course–U)
Fees 18 hole course £8 D–£12
9 hole course £1.80 (all inclusive VAT)
Loc 30 miles S of Glasgow off A74

Larkhall

Public (Map 9/22)
Burnhead Road Larkhall
Tel **Larkhall 881113**
Mem 400
Sec Clifford Bruce 8 Caradale Gardens
Pro
Holes 9 L 6236 yds SSS 70
Recs Am–70 B Easton
Pro–
V'trs U (except Tues 5-8 pm and Sat 7 am-1 pm)
Fees 65p
Loc SW on B7019

Leadhills (1935)

Private (Map 9/23)
Leadhills Biggar Lanarkshire
Tel **Leadhills 222**
Mem 100
Sec H Shaw Tel Leadhills 222
Pro
Holes 9 L 2031 yds SSS
Recs Am–
Pro–
V'trs U
Fees D–£1.50 Jrs £1 (£2 adults)
Loc 6 miles off A74 at Abington, behind local hotel
Mis Highest golf course in Gt Britain; 1500 ft above sea level

Lenzie

(see Dunbartonshire)

Mount Ellen (1905)

Private (Map 9/24)
Gartcosh Glasgow
Tel **Glenboig 872277**
Mem 590
Sec WL Harvey Tel 041-776 0747
Pro
Holes 18 L 5525 yds SSS 68
Recs Am–63 J Brown
Pro–68 J Chillas
V'trs M/SOC
Fees
Loc 8 miles NE of Glasgow

Shotts (1895)

Private (Map 9/25)
Blairhead Shotts
Tel **Shotts 20431**
Mem 600
Sec J Hamilton Tel Shotts 21144
Pro J Forrester Tel Shotts 22658
Holes 18 L 6125 yds SSS 70
Recs Am–65 AJ Ferguson
Pro–65 B Gunson
V'trs WD–U W/E–NA before 4.30 Sat M until 4.30 Sun
Fees £6 (£7)
Loc Midway between Glasgow/Edinburgh 1½ miles off M8

Strathaven (1908)

Private (Map 9/26)
Strathaven ML10 6NL
Tel **Strathaven 20539**
Mem 430
Sec G Fleming Tel 20421
Pro M McCrorie Tel 21812
Holes 18 L 6226 yds SSS 70
Recs Am–66 RJC Milton
AW Wallace S Kirkland
Pro–63 D Huish
V'trs WD after 4.30 pm and W/E–NA; WD before 4.30 pm–I
Fees On request
Loc

Strathclyde Park

Public (Map 9/18)
Mote Hill Hamilton
Tel
Mem 170
Sec Alex Murray Tel Hamilton 458391
Pro
Holes 9 L 6294 yds SSS 70
Recs Am–69
Pro–
V'trs U exc medal days; phone to book Motherwell 60155
Fees £1.05
Loc Within Hamilton

Torrance House (1969)

Public (Map 9/27)
Strathaven Road East Kilbride
Tel **48638**
Mem 650
Sec Mrs J O'Brien Tel East Kilbride 49320
Pro J Dunlop Tel EK 33451
Holes 18 L 6403 yds SSS 71
Recs Am–67 A Pitt
Pro–66 I Collins
V'trs U
Fees £4.50
Loc East Kilbride boundary on Strathaven Road

Wishaw (1897)

Private (Map 9/28)
Cleland Road Wishaw
Tel **Wishaw 372869**
Mem 875
Sec A Connor
Pro JG Campbell Tel Wishaw 378247
Holes 18 L 6134 yds SSS 69
Recs Am–64 W Denholm
Pro–
V'trs U (N/A Sat and WD after 4 pm)
Fees £7 (£10)
Loc Centre of town

The Lothians,
East, Mid- and West Lothian

Aberlady

Aberlady
Mem 32
Sec Alan R Wood
Holes Play over Kilspindie course

Bathgate (1892)

Private (Map 9/2)
Edinburgh Road Bathgate EH48 1BA
Tel **Bathgate 52232**
Mem 460
Sec James Connor Tel 630505
Pro DRW Strachan Tel 630553
Holes 18 L 6326 yds SSS 70
Recs Am–64 J McLean
Pro–
V'trs U
Fees £5 (£7)
Loc 400 yds E of town centre

Broomieknowe (1906)

Private (Map 9/3)
36 Golf Course Road Bonnyrigg EH19 2HZ
Tel **031-663 9317**
Mem 500
Sec Ian Lawson Tel 031-663 9317
Pro Mark Patchett Tel 031-660 2035
Holes 18 L 6046 yds SSS 69
Recs Am–64 P Gallagher
Pro–64 J Hamilton A Horne
J Hume WB Murray
V'trs WD–U; W/E&BH–NA
Fees £6 (£7)
Loc 7 miles S of Edinburgh

Dalmahoy

Private (Map 9/4)
Dalmahoy Kirknewton Midlothian EH27 8EB
Tel **031-333 2055**
Mem
Sec Mrs I Auld Tel 031-333 2055
Pro Brian Anderson Tel 031-333 1436
Holes 18 L 6639 yds SSS 72 (East Course)
18 L 5212 yds SSS 66 (West Course)
Recs Am–69 G Russo (East Course)
Pro–62 B Barnes
Fees On application
Loc 7 miles W of Edinburgh on A71

Deer Park G&CC (1978)

Private (Map 9/36)
Carmondean Livingston EH54 9PG
Tel **Livingstone 38843 (Steward 37800)**
Mem 400
Man Bill Yule Tel 0506 38843
Pro Bill Yule
Holes 18 L 6636 yds SSS 72
Recs Am–72
Pro–
V'trs U
Fees £5 (£8.50)
Loc Bordering M8 N of Livingston New Town Knightsridge District

Dirleton Castle (1854)

Gullane
Tel **Gullane 0620 843496**
Mem 110
Sec RH Atkinson
Pro
Holes Play over Gullane courses

Dunbar (1794)

Private (Map 9/5)
East Links Dunbar EH42 1LP
Tel **Dunbar (0368) 62317**
Mem 650
Sec Arnold JR Poole Tel Dunbar 62317
Pro Derek Small Tel Dunbar 62086
Holes 18 L 6426 yds SSS 71
Recs Am–66 S Easingwood
Pro–65 DK Webster RA Doig
V'trs U SOC
Fees D–£8.50 (D–£11)
Loc ½ mile E of Dunbar

Dundas Park (1957)

Private (Map 9/6)
South Queensferry
Tel **031-331 3090**
Mem 370
Sec JC Simpson Tel 031-331 1902
Pro
Holes 9 L 5510 metres SSS 69
Recs Am–66 J McLaren
Pro–
V'trs M
Fees N/A
Loc Dundas Estate (Private)

Edinburgh Public Courses

Braidhills No 1 (1893)

Public (Map 9/7)
Edinburgh
Tel **031-447 6666**
Pro J Boath Tel 031-447 8205
Holes 18 L 5239 yds SSS 68
Recs Am–65
Pro–
V'trs U (No Sunday play)
Fees £2.20 (OAPs–35p Under-16s–40p)
Loc 3 miles S of Edinburgh Centre

Braidhills No 2 (1894)

Public (Map 9/7)
Edinburgh
Tel **031-447 6666**
Pro J Boath Tel 031-447 8205
Holes 18 L 4832 yds SSS 63
Recs Am–65
Pro–
V'trs U (No Sunday play)
Fees £2.20 (OAPs–35p Under-16s–40p)
Loc 3 miles S of Edinburgh Centre

Carrick Knowe (1930)

Public (Map 9/8)
Glendevon Park Edinburgh 12
Tel **031-337 1096**
Sec
Pro J Boath
Holes 18 L 6299 yds SSS 70
Recs Am–66
Pro–
V'trs U
Fees 44p
Loc 5 miles W of Edinburgh
Mis Carrickvale club plays here

Craigentinny (1891)

Public (Map 9/9)
Edinburgh
Tel **031-554 7501**
Pro J Boath 031-447 8205
Holes 18 L 5418 yds SSS 66
Recs Am–64
Pro–
V'trs U
Fees 60p
Loc 2½ miles E Edinburgh
Mis Lochend club plays here

Portobello (1853)

Public (Map 9/10)
Stanley Street Portobello Edinburgh
Tel **031-669 4361**
Mem 80
Sec FR Bain
Pro J Boath
Holes 9 L 2419 yds SSS 32
Recs Am–27
Pro–
V'trs U
Fees £1.20–9 holes
Loc 3½ miles NE Edinburgh

Silverknowes (1947)

Public (Map 9/11)
Silverknowes Parkway Edinburgh EH4 5ET
Tel **031-336 3843**
Mem 450
Sec J Munro Tel 031-336 5359
Pro
Holes 18 L 6210 yds SSS 70
Recs Am–66
Pro–
V'trs U
Fees £2
Loc 4 miles W Edinburgh

Edinburgh Clubs

Braids United (1897)

Public
Braid Hills Approach Edinburgh 10
Tel
Mem 150
Sec TG Mitchell Tel 031-447 5244
Holes Play over Braids 1 and 2 courses

Carrickvale

Carrick Knowe Municipal Glendevon Park Edinburgh EH12 5VZ
Tel **337 1932**
Mem 300
Sec Douglas Pagan
Pro J Boath
Holes Play over Carrick Knowe Municipal

Lochend

Craigentinny Course Edinburgh EH7 6RG
Tel **031-554 7960**
Mem 320
Sec DM Drysdale Tel 031-669 3134
Holes Play over Craigentinny Municipal Course, 4 miles NE town centre

Baberton (1893)

Private (Map 9/1)
Juniper Green Edinburgh EH14 5DU
Tel 031-453 3361
Mem 800
Sec DM McBain Tel 031-453 4911
Pro Kenneth Kelly
Holes 18 L 6140 yds SSS 69
Recs Am–65 HM Gilmour
D Beveridge Jr
Pro–62 B Barnes
V'trs M SOC on WD
Fees
Loc 5 miles W of Edinburgh

Bruntsfield Links Golfing Society (1761)

Private (Map 9/12)
32 Barnton Avenue Davidson's Mains Edinburgh EH4 6JH
Tel **031-336 2006**
Mem 1000
Sec MW Walton Tel 031-336 1479
Pro B Mackenzie Tel 031-336 4050
Holes 18 L 6407 yds SSS 71
Recs Am–69 AGG Miller
Pro–
V'trs I; WD–M before 5pm, H after 5pm; SOC
Fees On application
Loc 3 miles W of town centre

Craigmillar Park (1895)

Private (Map 9/13)
1 Observatory Road Edinburgh EH9 3HG
Tel **031-667 2837**
Mem 460 100(L) 70(J) 38(5)
Sec Mrs JH Smith Tel 031-667 0047
Pro Brian McGhee Tel 031-667 0047
Holes 18 L 5846 yds SSS 68
Recs Am–65 J Thomson
Pro–66 T Stangoe
V'trs WD–U before 3.30 pm W/E BH–NA
Fees On application
Loc Blackford Edinburgh

Duddingston (1897)

Private (Map 9/14)
Duddingston Edinburgh EH15 3QD
Tel **031-661 1005**
Mem 580
Sec Bruce P Underwood Tel 031-661 7688
Pro JC Farmer Tel 031-661 4301
Holes 18 L 6647 yds SSS 72
Recs Am–64 G Macgregor
Pro–65 S Torrance
V'trs Tues and Thurs only for Societies
Fees £6.90 (£9.20)
Loc Duddingston Road West Edinburgh EH15

Kingsknowe (1908)

Private (Map 9/15)
326 Lanark Road Edinburgh EH14 2JD
Tel 031-441 1144
Mem 701
Sec HH Hoddinott Tel 031-441 1145
Pro Willie Bauld Tel 031-441 4030
Holes 18 L 5966 yds SSS 69
Recs Am–63 JJ Little
Pro–64 WB Murray
V'trs WD–before 4.30 pm–U; W/E–M
Fees £4.50 D–£6.50
Loc SW Edinburgh

Liberton (1920)

Private (Map 9/16)
297 Gilmerton Road Edinburgh EH1 5UJ
Tel **031-664 8580**
Mem 815

Sec TJ Muirhead Tel 031-664 3009
Pro WV Wightman PJ Fielding Tel 031-664 1056
Holes 18 L 5299 yds SSS 66
Recs Am–61 RMF Jack
Pro–63 JL Brash
V'trs Mon Wed Fri v'trs must commence play before 5 pm; W/E & BH–No visiting clubs
Fees £6 (£8)
Loc S side of Edinburgh 3 miles from city centre

Lothianburn (1893)

Private (Map 9/17)
Biggar Road Edinburgh
Tel **031-445 2206**
Mem 430 75(L) 75(J) 50(5)
Sec AR Roxton Tel 031-663 8354
Pro B Mason Tel 031-445 2288
Holes 18 L 5750 yds SSS 69
Recs Am–63 PW Lamb
Pro–
V'trs WD–SOC; U before 5 pm; M after 5 pm; W/E–NA
Fees £5 D–£7 (£6.50 D–£9)
Loc S boundary Edinburgh

Merchants of Edinburgh (1907)

Private (Map 9/18)
Craighill Gardens Morningside Edinburgh EH10 5PY
Tel **031-447 1219**
Mem 400
Sec JB More Tel 031-443 1470
Pro Glynn Jenkins
Holes 18 L 4889 yds SSS 65
Recs Am–61 WJ Jeffrey Jr
Pro–
V'trs M or I SOC
Fees £6 D–£8
Loc Edinburgh; SW of city centre

Mortonhall (1892)

Private (Map 9/19)
231 Braid Road Edinburgh EH10 6PB
Tel **031-447 2411**
Mem 500
Sec PT Ricketts Tel 031-447 6974
Pro DB Horn Tel 031-447 5185
Holes 18 L 6557 yds SSS 71
Recs Am–67 G Macgregor
Pro–68 G Cunningham
V'trs I
Fees £12 (£15)
Loc Within the city

Murrayfield (1896)

Private (Map 9/20)
43 Murrayfield Road Edinburgh EH12 6EU
Tel **031-337 1009**
Mem 725
Sec JP Bullen Tel 031-337 3478
Pro J Fisher Tel 031-337 3479
Holes 18 L 5727 yds SSS 68
Recs Am–64 DED Neave
Pro–63 WB Murray
V'trs WD–I; W/E–M
Fees £7
Loc Edinburgh 2 miles W of city centre

Prestonfield (1920)

Private (Map 9/21)
6 Priestfield Road North Edinburgh EH16 5HS
Tel **031-667 1273**
Mem 700
Sec MDAG Dillon Tel 031-667 9665
Pro B Commins Tel 031-667 8597
Holes 18 L 6216 yds SSS 70
Recs Am–62 AM Dun
Pro–
V'trs Sat NA before 12.30 pm; Sun NA before 11.30 am; SOC
Fees £5 D–£7 (W/E & BH–£7 D–£9)
Loc 2 miles SE of city centre

Ratho Park (1928)

Private (Map 9/22)
Ratho Newbridge Midlothian
Tel **031-333 1252/1752**
Mem 500 98 (L) 65(J)
Sec Alex W McKinlay 031-333 1752
Pro Alan Pate Tel 031-333 1406
Holes 18 L 6028 yds SSS 69
Recs Am–64 CB Binnie
Pro–64 WG Stowe
V'trs U; SOC Tue Wed Thu
Fees £7 D–£9 W/E–£12
Loc 8 miles W of Edinburgh A71
Mis Practice area

Ravelston (1912)

Private (Map 9/23)
24 Ravelston Dykes Road Edinburgh EH4 5NZ
Tel **031-332 3486**
Mem 420 plus 120 5-day
Sec JMH Maxton Tel 031-332 4630
Pro
Holes 9 L 5332 yds SSS 66
Recs Am–
Pro–
V'trs M
Fees
Loc Off Queensferry Road (A90) by Barnton roundabout

Royal Burgess Golfing Society of Edinburgh (1735)

Private (Map 9/24)
181 Whitehouse Road Barnton Edinburgh EH4 6BY
Tel **031-339 2012**
Mem 620 50(J)
Sec JP Audis Tel 031-339 2075
Pro G Yuille Tel 031-339 6474
Holes 18 L 6604 yds SSS 72
Recs Am–64
Pro–63
V'trs I
Fees On request
Loc Queensferry Road

Swanston (1927)

Private (Map 9/25)
111 Swanston Road Fairmilehead Edinburgh 10
Tel **031-445 2239**
Mem 400
Sec J Allan
Pro Howard Ferguson Tel 031-445 4002
Holes 18 L 5024 yds SSS 65
Recs Am–64 J McLagan
Pro–
V'trs U; NA on comp days and after 1 pm Sat and Sun
Fees £3.45 D–£5.75
Loc W from city centre Biggar Road A702

Torphin Hill (1895)

Private (Map 9/25)
Torphin Road Edinburgh 13
Tel **031-441 1100**
Mem 450
Sec R Brannan Tel 031-334 6052
Pro
Holes 18 L 5025 yds SSS 66
Recs Am–62 G Wilkie AL Turner
Pro–
V'trs U
Fees £3 (£6)
Loc SW boundary Edinburgh

Gifford (1904)

Private (Map 9/27)
Gifford
Tel
Mem 419
Sec AC Harrison Tel Gifford 267
Pro
Holes 9 L 6138 yds SSS 69
Recs Am–
Pro–
V'trs NA noon Sun and Tue Wed after 4 pm
Fees D–£4 (18 holes)
Loc 4½ miles S of Haddington

Glencorse (1890)

Private (Map 9/28)
Milton Bridge Penicuik Midlothian EH26 0RD
Tel **Penicuik 77177**
Mem 400
Sec DA McNiven Tel Penicuik 77189
Pro Cliffe Jones Tel Penicuik 76481
Holes 18 L 5205 yds SSS 66
Recs Am–62 JH Moore
Pro–
V'trs WD before 4 pm SOC on WD
Fees £5 (£7)
Loc 8 miles S of Edinburgh

Greenburn (1953)

Private (Map 9/29)
Fauldhouse
Tel **Fauldhouse 70292**
Mem 450
Sec A Morrison Tel 70865
Pro
Holes 18 L 6223 yds SSS 70
Recs Am–68
Pro–
V'trs U
Fees £3.30 (£4.40)
Loc Fauldhouse

Gullane (1882)

Private (Map 9/30)
Gullane
Tel **Gullane 843115**
Mem 711 125(5) 50(J) 300(L)
Sec JS Kinnear Tel Gullane 842255
Pro Jimmy Hume Tel Gullane 843111
Holes No 1 Course 18 L 6491 yds SSS 71
No 2 Course 18 L 6127 yds SSS 69
No 3 Course 18 L 5035 yds SSS 64
9-hole course available for children
Recs No 1 Course Am–65 ME Lewis
Pro–64 RDBM Shade
No 2 Course Am–64 RCH Robertson
Pro–66 H Bannerman
No 3 Course Am–
Pro–
V'trs U
Fees No 1 Course £12 (£15) W–£70
No 2 Course £6 (£7) W–£35
No 3 Course £4 (£5) W–£25
Children's course free
Loc 18 miles E of Edinburgh

Haddington (1865)

Public (Map 9/31)
Amisfield Park Haddington E Lothian
Tel **Haddington 3627**
Mem 320
Sec T Shaw Tel 062 082 2584/3627
Pro J Muir 062 082 2727
Holes L 6280 yds SSS 70
Recs Am–65 S Stephens
Pro–
V'trs WD–U; W/E U 10 am–12 pm after 2 pm
Fees £4.50 D–£6.50 (£5.75 D–£8.50)
Loc 17 miles E Edinburgh on A1 ¾ mile E of Haddington

Harburn (1921)

Private (Map 9/32)
West Calder West Lothian EH55 8RS
Tel **West Calder 871256**
Mem 480 56(L) 76(J)
Sec GR Clark Tel West Calder 871131
Pro R Redpath Tel West Calder 871582
Holes 18 L 5843 yds SSS 68
Recs Am–62 M Kirk
Pro–
V'trs U
Fees £6 (£7.50)
Loc 2 miles S of West Calder

The Honourable Company of Edinburgh Golfers (1744)

Private (Map 9/33)
Muirfield Gullane EH31 2EG
Tel **Gullane (0620) 842123**
Mem 695
Sec Maj JG Vanreenen Tel as above
Pro
Holes 18 L 6601 yds (Championship 6941 yds) SSS 73
Recs Am–71 DED Neave
Pro–63 Isao Aoki (Japan)
V'trs WD–Tue, Thu, Fri am only; W/E & BH–NA; I; H; SOC
Fees £22 D–£33
Loc On NE outskirts of Gullane at far end of village if approaching from Edinburgh. The short access road is close to speed limit signs and opp sign for Greywalls Hotel on A198 E'burgh–N Berwick

Kilspindie (1867)

Private (Map 9/34)
Aberlady EH38 08D
Tel **Aberlady 216/358**
Mem 430 150(L) 50(J)
Sec J Thompson Tel Aberlady 358
Pro
Holes 18 L 4957 metres SSS 66
Recs Am–63 RJ Humble
Pro–62 F Coutts
V'trs U Advisable to ring Secretary, play subject to members' demands; SOC on WD
Fees On application
Loc Aberlady

Linlithgow (1913)

Private (Map 9/35)
Braehead Linlithgow
Tel **Linlithgow 842585**
Mem 450
Sec JT Menzies TD
Pro D Smith Tel 844356
Holes 18 L 5858 yds SSS 68
Recs Am–64 J Cuddihy
Pro–
V'trs U
Fees £7 (£9)
Loc SW of Linlithgow

Longniddry (1921)

Private (Map 9/37)
Links Road Longniddry East Lothian EH32 0NL
Tel **(0875) 52141**
Mem 875
Sec GC Dempster CA Tel (0875) 52141
Pro WJ Gray Tel Longniddry 52228
Holes 18 L 6210 yds SSS 70
Recs Am–65 JW Montgomery
Pro–64 K Nagle
V'trs U SOC Mon–Thu incl, starting from 9.18 am and 2 pm
Fees £10 D–£15 (£16 R/D)
Loc 15 miles E of Edinburgh
Mis Dining room closed Fri

Luffness New (1894)

Private (Map 9/38)
Aberlady EH32 0QA
Tel **Gullane 843114**
Mem 650
Sec JG Tedford Tel Gullane 843336
Pro
Holes 18 L 6100 yds SSS 69
Recs Am–67 I M Paterson
Pro–62 C O'Connor
V'trs M or by arrangement
Fees On application
Loc 1 mile from Gullane 4 miles from Longniddry

Musselburgh (1938)

Private (Map 9/39)
Monktonhall Musselburgh
Tel **031-665 2005**
Mem 500
Sec JR Brown
Pro T Stangoe Tel 031-665 7055
Holes 18 L 6623 yds SSS 72
Recs Am–65 RS Hall
Pro–67 EC Brown
G Cunningham A Jacklin
B Devlin
V'trs U
Fees £7 (£13)
Loc 1 mile S of Musselburgh

Newbattle (1934)

Private (Map 9/40)
Abbey Road Eskbank Dalkeith EH22 3AD
Tel **031-663 2123**
Mem 600
Sec DM Henderson Tel 031-663 4197
Pro J Henderson Tel 031-660 1631
Holes 18 L 6012 yds SSS 69
Recs Am–65 G Macgregor
P Hardwick J McLean
Pro–
V'trs WD–U before 4 pm; W/E–M
Fees £5 D–£7
Loc 6 miles S of Edinburgh on A7 and A68

North Berwick Courses

Burgh Links (1894)

Public (Map 9/41)
East Links North Berwick
Tel North Berwick 2726
Mem 300
Sec DR Montgomery Tel (0620) 2340
Pro
Holes 18 L 6079 yds SSS 69
Recs Am–65 D Drummond
Pro–
V'trs U
Fees On application
Loc North Berwick 23 miles Edinburgh
Mis Glen Club play here

North Berwick (1832)

Private (Map 9/42)
West Links Beach Road North Berwick
Tel **North Berwick 2135**
Mem 300
Sec R Russell
Pro D Huish Tel North Berwick 3233
Holes 18 L 6298 yds SSS 70
Recs Am–67 NJ Fisher
Pro–63 G Laing
V'trs U
Fees £7 D–£10 (£12 D–£16)
Loc 24 miles E of Edinburgh

North Berwick Clubs

Glen (1906)

East Links North Berwick
Tel **North Berwick 2221**
Mem 300
Sec
Recs Am–65 D Drummond
Pro–
Holes Play over East Links

Tantallon (1853)

Westgate North Berwick
Tel **North Berwick 2114**
Mem 286
Sec GA Milne
Holes Play over North Berwick West Links

Polkemmet Country Park (1981)

Public (Map 9/43)
By Whitburn West Lothian EH47 0AD
Tel **Whitburn 43905**
Mem
Sec
Pro
Holes 9 L 2967 metres SSS 37
Recs Am–
Pro–
V'trs U
Fees Adult £1.40 (£1.80) Jun/OAP/Unemployed 70p (£1)
Loc Between Whitburn and Harthill on B7066
Mis 15-bay driving range

Pumpherston (1910)

Private (Map 9/44)
Drumshoreland Road Pumpherston
Tel **(0506) 32869**
Mem 270 13(L) 82(J)
Sec JS Lamond Tel (0506) 32122
Pro
Holes 9 L 5142 yds SSS 65
Recs Am–61 Hugh Robertson
Pro–
V'trs M
Fees
Loc 14 miles W of Edinburgh

Royal Musselburgh (1774)

Private (Map 9/45)
Prestongrange House Prestonpans
Tel **Prestonpans 810276**
Mem 700
Sec DL Hewat
Pro Allan Minto Tel 810139
Holes 18 L 6237 yds SSS 70
Recs Am–66 A Roy
Pro–
V'trs WD–U; W/E–M
Fees £6.50 (£7.50) D–£11
Loc 8 miles SE Edinburgh on A198 North Berwick road

Thorntree

Private
Prestonpans
Tel
Mem 90
Sec J Hanratty
Holes Play over Royal Musselburgh course

Turnhouse (1909)

Private (Map 9/46)
154 Turnhouse Road Corstorphine Edinburgh
Tel **031-339 1014**
Mem 500
Sec AB Hay Tel 031-655 6119
Pro K Whitson Tel 031-339 7701
Holes 18 L 6171 yds SSS 69
Recs Am–65 various
Pro–64 D Huish
V'trs M or by arrangement
Fees –
Loc Edinburgh to Turnhouse Road (A9080)

Uphall

Private (Map 9/47)
Uphall
Tel **Broxburn 856404**
Mem 500
Sec Aidin Dobie
Pro
Holes 18 L 5567 yds SSS 67
Recs Am–
Pro–
V'trs U
Fees £5 (£8)
Loc 2 miles from Livingston

West Linton (1890)

Private (Map 9/48)
West Linton Peeblesshire
Tel **(0968) 60463**
Mem 605
Sec S Hunter OBE Tel (0968) 60373
Pro Douglas Stewart Tel (0968) 60256
Holes 18 L 5835 yds SSS 68
Recs Am–67 I Downie
Pro–71 B Gallacher
V'trs U
Fees £5.50 D–£7.50 (£6.50 D–£9)
Loc NW Peebles

West Lothian (1892)

Private (Map 9/49)
Airngath Hill Bo'ness West Lothian
Tel **Bo'ness 826030**
Mem 495
Sec DA Grant Tel Bo'ness 824405
Pro
Holes 18 L 6629 yds SSS 72
Recs Am–66 CK Cox
Pro–68 J Farmer
V'trs U
Fees £4 (£5)
Loc 1 mile S of Bo'ness

Winterfield

Public (Map 9/50)
Back Road Dunbar
Tel **0368 62280**
Mem 300
Sec M O'Donnell Tel 0368 62564
Pro John Sandilands
Holes 18 L 5053 yds SSS 65
Recs Am–61 R Walkinshaw
J Huggan
Pro–65 SWT Murray
V'trs U
Fees On application phone Pro shop Tel 0368 63562 Special *Golf and Meals Package* available
Loc W side of Dunbar
Mis W/E parties; all meals; apply Pro shop

North,

Highland, Orkney & Shetland and Western Isles Regions including Caithness, Inverness, Morayshire (Grampian Region), Nairn, Orkney & Shetland, Ross & Cromarty, Sutherland and Western Isles

Abernethy (1985)

Private (Map 8/1)
Nethy Bridge Inverness-shire
Tel **Nethy Bridge 305**
Mem 200
Sec Mrs A Burns Tel Grantown-on-Spey 2498
Pro
Holes 9 L 2484 yds SSS 66
Recs Am–61 I Murray
Pro–
V'trs U SOC
Fees D–£3.50 W–£17 Jrs £1.75 and £8.50
Loc 10 miles from Aviemore 5 miles from Grantown-on-Spey

Alness (1904)

Private (Map 8/2)
Ardross Rd Alness Ross-shire
Tel **Alness 883877**
Mem 300
Sec JD Ellis Tel 0349 882633
Pro
Holes 9 L 2436 yds SSS 63
Recs Am–62
Pro–
V'trs WD–SOC, U before 5 pm
Fees £2.50 (£4)
Loc ¼ mile N of Alness

Askernish (1981)

Private (Map 8/3)
Lochboisdale South Uist Western Isles
Tel
Mem 30
Sec N/A
Pro
Holes 9 (18 tees) L 5114 yds SSS 67
Recs Am–66
Pro–
V'trs U
Fees £2 (£2) W–£10
Loc 5 miles NW of Lochboisdale

Boat-of-Garten (1898)

Private (Map 8/4)
Boat-of-Garten Inverness-shire
Tel **Boat-of-Garten 282 (shop) 351 (clubhouse)**
Mem 396
Sec JR Ingram Tel B-of-G 684
Pro
Holes 18 L 5690 yds SSS 68
Recs Am–65 AP Thomson
Pro–70 GW McIntosh
V'trs U
Fees £5 (£6) 1985 prices
Loc 30 miles S of Inverness
Mis Starting Sheet at W/E

Bonar-Bridge and Ardgay (1904)

Private (Map 8/5)
Bonar-Bridge Sutherland
Mem 80
Secs Mrs J Gordon Tel Ardgay 577; Mr A Turner Tel Invershin 248
Pro
Holes 9 L 4616 yds SSS 63 LGU 66
Recs Am–70
Pro
V'trs U
Fees £2.50 W–£14
Loc ½ mile N of Bonar-Bridge village

Brora (1889)

Private (Map 8/6)
Golf Road Brora Sutherland KW9 62S
Tel **Brora 21417**
Mem 147
Sec RD Smith Tel Brora 21475
Pro
Holes 18 L 6110 yds SSS 69
Recs Am–61 J Miller
Pro–67 D Huish
V'trs SOC; U apart from tournament days; H for open tournaments
Fees £5 W–£20 F–£30 3W–£35 M–£40
Loc 75 miles N Inverness

Carrbridge (1980)

Private (Map 8/7)
Carrbridge Inverness-shire
Tel **Carrbridge 674**
Mem 132 inc 33(L) 18(J)
Sec EG Drayson Tel Carrbridge 674
Pro
Holes 9 L 2623 yds SSS 66
Recs Am–63
Pro–
V'trs U
Fees £3 W–£16 (J–£2) W/E £3.50 Subject to increase
Loc Carrbridge village

Elgin (1906)

Private (Map 8/8)
Hardhillock Birnie Road Elgin IV30 3SX Morayshire
Tel **Elgin 2338**
Mem 490 150(L) 150(J)
Sec W McKay
Pro Ian Rodger Tel Elgin 2884
Holes 18 L 6401 yds SSS 71
Recs Am–64 NS Grant
Pro–66 H Bannerman
R Jamieson
V'trs SOC; WD–U after 9.30 am; W/E–U after 10.30 am
Fees On application
Loc 1 mile S of Elgin

Forres (1889)

Private (Map 8/9)
Muiryshade Forres IV36 0RD Morayshire
Tel **0309-72949**
Mem 716 130(J)
Sec AW Buchanan Tel 0309 72959
Pro J Taylor Tel 0309 72250
Holes 18 L 6141 yds SSS 69
Recs Am–64 A Moir
Pro–
V'trs U SOC
Fees £4 (£4)
Loc 1 mile S town centre

Fort Augustus (1930)

Private (Map 8/10)
Fort Augustus Inverness-shire
Tel
Mem 100
Sec ID Aitchison Tel F Augustus 6460
Pro
Holes 9 L 5154 yds SSS 66
Recs Am–68 J Innes
Pro–
V'trs U
Fees D–£3
Loc W end village

Fortrose and Rosemarkie (1888)

Private (Map 8/11)
Ness Road East Fortrose Ross-shire
Tel **Fortrose 20529**
Mem 580
Sec Mrs M Collier Tel Fortrose 20529
Pro GA Hampton Tel Fortrose 20733
Holes 18 L 5973 yds SSS 69
Recs Am–64 G Paterson
Pro–
V'trs U; SOC
Fee £5.50 (£7) W–£22 After 3.30 pm–£4
Loc Black Isle 12 miles from Inverness

Fort William (1974)

Private (Map 8/12)
North Road Fort William Inverness-shire
Tel **0397 4464**
Mem 300
Sec J Allan
Pro
Holes 18 L 5686 metres SSS 71
Recs Am–
Pro–
V'trs U
Fees £4
Loc 3 miles N of town on A82

Gairloch (1898)

Private (Map 8/13)
Gairloch Ross-shire N21 2BQ
Tel **Gairloch 2407**
Mem 250
Sec WJ Pinnell An Gard Gairloch
Pro
Holes 9 L 1942 yds SSS 63
Recs Am–
Pro–
V'trs U (No Sunday golf)
Fees £3 D–£5 W–£15
Loc 60 miles W of Dingwall

Garmouth and Kingston (1932)

Private (Map 8/14)
Garmouth Fochabers Morayshire
Tel **Spey Bay 388**
Mem 400
Sec A Robertson
Pro
Holes 18 L 5637 yds SSS 67
Recs Am–66
Pro–70
V'trs U
Fees £4
Loc NE Elgin

Golspie (1889)

Private (Map 8/15)
Golspie Sutherland
Tel **Golspie 3266**
Mem 180 50(L) 40(J)
Sec A Mackintosh
Pro R Macrae
Holes 18 L 5900 yds SSS 68
Recs Am–65 J Miller
Pro–65 D Huish
V'trs U
Fees D–£4 W–£18
Loc 11 miles N of Dornoch

Grantown (1890)

Private (Map 8/16)
Grantown-on-Spey Morayshire
Tel **Grantown-on-Spey 2079**
Mem 200
Sec A McKenzie Tel Grantown-on-Spey 2749
Pro
Holes 18 L 5672 yds SSS 67
Recs Am–60 G Bain
Pro–62 D Webster
V'trs U
Fees £6
Loc East town boundary

Helmsdale

Private (Map 8/17)
Helmsdale Sutherland
Tel
Mem
Sec Mrs T Traill 18 Golf Road
Pro
Holes 9
Recs Am–
Pro–
V'trs U
Fees
Loc

Hopeman (1923)

Private (Map 8/18)
Hopeman Morayshire
Tel **Hopeman 830 578**
Mem 300
Sec Mrs V McPherson 27 Thom Street Tel 830444
Pro
Holes 18 L 5439 yds SSS 66
Recs Am–
Pro–
V'trs U SOC
Fees £3.50 (£4.50)
Loc 7 miles N Elgin

Invergordon (1954)

Private (Map 8/19)
Cromlet Drive Invergordon Ross & Cromarty
Tel **Invergordon 852116**
Mem 140 50(L) 60(J) (excluding 600 social)
Sec Keith L Hogg Tel Invergordon 853140
Pro
Holes 9 L 6028 yds SSS 69
Recs Am–65 D Ross
Pro–
V'trs U SOC
Fees £2.50 (£3)
Loc Invergordon
Mis Clubhouse on course; large social club in town

Inverness (1883)

Private (Map 8/20)
Inverness Inverness-shire
Tel **(0463) 233422**
Mem 1100
Sec CD Thew Tel 239882
Pro AP Thompson Tel 231989
Holes 18 L 6226 yds SSS 70
Recs Am–
Pro–63 J Farmer
V'trs Restricted play: W/E, BH; SOC
Fees £8 (£10) W–£20
Loc 1 mile S of town centre

Kingussie (1890)

Private (Map 8/21)
Kingussie Inverness-shire
Tel **Kingussie 374 (Clubhouse)**
Mem 227
Sec ND MacWilliam Tel Kingussie 600
Pro
Holes 18 L 5408 yds SSS 67
Recs Am–64 J Gunn
Pro–68 AG Havers
V'trs U
Fees £4 (£5)
Loc ½ mile from town shops off A9

Lochcarron

Private (Map 8/22)
Ross & Cromarty
Tel
Mem 36
Sec PCP Inglis Tel 311
Pro
Holes 9
Recs Am–
Pro–
V'trs U
Fees W–£1
Loc ½ mile E of village

Lybster

Private (Map 8/23)
Lybster by Wick Caithness
Tel
Mem 45
Sec E Sinclair Tel 359
Pro
Holes 9 L yds SSS 62
Recs Am–29 AG Doull
Pro–
V'trs U
Fees 25p M–£2
Loc

Moray (1889)

Private (Map 8/24)
Stotfield Road Lossiemouth Moray IV31 6QS
Tel **Lossiemouth 2018**
Mem 706 131(L) 89(J)
Sec
Pro A Thomson Tel Lossiemouth 3330
Holes Old 18 L 6643 yds SSS 72
New 18 L 6044 yds SSS 69
Recs Old course Am–68
A Thomson WF Thomson
HB Stuart
Pro–66 T Minshall
New course Am–
Pro–
V'trs U SOC
Fees Old course D–£7 (D–£10) W–£30
New course D–£5 (D–£7) W–£20
Loc 6 miles N of Elgin

Muir of Ord (1875)

Private (Map 8/25)
Great North Road Muir of Ord Ross and Cromarty IV6 7SX
Tel **(0463) 870825**
Mem 554
Sec Mrs C Moir
Pro Mr JT Hamilton Tel (0463) 870601
Holes 18 L 5129 yds SSS 65
Recs Am–63 S Ross C Gordon
Pro–
V'trs U
Fees D–£4 W/E–£5 W–£20 Jrs–£1
Loc 15 miles N of Inverness on A862; 12 miles N of Inverness on A9/A832

Nairn (1887)

Private (Map 8/26)
Seabank Road Nairn IV12 4HB
Tel **Nairn 52103**
Mem 830
Sec D Patrick Tel Nairn 53208
Pro Robin Fyfe Tel Nairn 52787
Holes 18 L 6540 yds SSS 71
9 L 1918 yds
Recs Am–Championship Tees 66
IC Hutcheon
Pro–Championship Tees 65
D Small
Am–Medal Tees 65 R Watson
Pro–
V'trs U SOC
Fees £9 (£10) W–£40
Loc Nairn West Shore

Nairn Dunbar (1899)

Private (Map 8/27)
Lochloy Road Nairn Nairnshire
Tel **Nairn 52741**
Mem 500
Sec Mrs SJ MacLennan Tel Nairn 52741
Pro Roy Phimister Tel Nairn 53964
Holes 18 L 6431 yds SSS 71
Recs Am–67 AP Thomson
Pro–
V'trs U
Fees £6 (£7) W–£28
Loc Nairn

Newtonmore (1890)

Private (Map 8/28)
Newtonmore Inverness-shire PH20 1AT
Tel **Newtonmore (05403) 328**
Mem 370
Sec GJ Fraser Tel (05403) 642
Pro
Holes 18 L 5890 yds SSS 68
Recs Am–64 I Barclay
Pro–
V'trs U
Fees D–£5.50 W–£22
Loc 46 miles S Inverness

Orkney & Shetland

Orkney (1889)

Private (Map 8/29)
Grainbank Kirkwall Orkney
Tel **2457**
Mem 140
Sec JR Sim Tel Kirkwall (0856) 2435
Pro
Holes 18 L 5406 yds SSS 68
Recs Am–65 KD Peace
Pro–71 I Smith
V'trs U
Fees £3 W–£10 2WK–£15 M–£20
Loc 1 mile W of town

Shetland (1894)

Private (Map 8/31)
PO Box 18 Lerwick
Tel **Gott 369**
Mem 264
Sec I Lindsay Tel Lerwick 3565
Pro
Holes 18 L 5971 yds SSS 71
Recs Am–
Pro–
V'trs U
Fees £3 (£4) W–£8 L and Jrs half price
Loc 3½ miles N of Lerwick

Stromness (1890)

Private (Map 8/32)
Ness Orkney
Tel **850772**
Mem 120
Sec FJ Groundwater Tel 850622
Pro
Holes 18 L 4665 yds SSS 64
Recs Am–62 CH Poke
Pro–66 R Macaskill
V'trs U
Fees £4 (£4)
Loc Stromness Orkney

Westray

Private (Map 8/33)
Westray Orkney
Tel **Westray 28**
Mem 12
Sec Louis Berstan Tel Westray 28
Pro
Holes 9 L yds SSS
Recs Am–36 Dr W Balfour
Pro–
V'trs U (No Sunday play)
Fees 10p
Loc

Reay (1893)

Private (Map 8/34)
Reay by Thurso
Tel **Reay 288**
Mem 116 35(L) 30(J)
Sec JA Marsh Tel Thurso 63035
Pro
Holes 18 L 5865 yds SSS 68
Recs Am–65 RS Taylor
Pro–
V'trs U except on competition days
Fees D–£4 W–£15 F–£20
Loc Thurso 11 miles
Mis The most northerly sea-side links on British mainland

Royal Dornoch (1877)

Private (Map 8/35)
Golf Road Dornoch IV25 3LW Sutherland
Tel **Dornoch Office 810219**
Public 810381
Mem 580 196(L) 28(J)
Sec KM Murray Tel 810219
Pro WE Skinner Tel 810219
Holes 18 L 6577 yds SSS 72
9 L 2485 yds SSS 32
Recs Am–65 J Miller
Pro–66 B Gallacher
V'trs U
Fees 9-hole: Apr–Oct D–£5 W–£17.50
Nov–Mar D–£2 W–£5
18-hole: Apr–Oct £15 (after 11 am £10) W–£50 F–£70 Nov–Mar D–£7.50 W–£25 Reduction for juniors
Loc 51 miles N of Inverness
Mis Airstrip adjacent

Sconser (1964)

Private (Map 8/36)
Between Broadford and Sligachan Skye
Tel
Mem 120
Sec MN Beaton Tel Portree 2277
Pro
Holes 9 L 4796 yds (4385 mtrs) SSS 63
Recs Am–65 JM Rodger
Pro–
V'trs U
Fees £3 D–£5 W–£10
Loc Midway Broadford–Portree

Spey Bay

(see North East)

Stornoway (1947)

Private (Map 8/37)
Lady Lever Park Stornoway Outer Hebrides
Tel **Stornoway (0851) 2240**
Mem 250
Sec DWM Duggie Tel (0851) 2570
Pro
Holes 18 L 5119 yds SSS 66
Recs Am–64 KW Galloway
Pro–65 JC Farmer
V'trs U No Sunday play
Fees £4 D–£6 W–£20 F–£30
Loc Stornoway

Strathpeffer Spa (1888)

Private (Map 8/38)
Strathpeffer Ross & Cromarty IV14 9AS
Tel **Strathpeffer 21219**
Mem 200 60(L) 80(J)
Sec N Roxburgh Tel Strathpeffer 21396
Pro
Holes 18 L 4813 yds SSS 65
Recs Am–60 D Krzyzanowski
Pro–66 Alex Herd
V'trs U SOC
Fees £4.50 (£4.50) 5D–£18
Loc ¼ mile N of village square (signposted)

Tain (1890)

Private (Map 8/39)
Tain Ross & Cromarty
Tel **Tain 2314**
Mem 400
Sec J Fraser
Pro Jock Lawson
Holes 18 L 6207 yds SSS 70
Recs Am–66 J Miller S Shaw K Berry
Pro–71 Norman Wood
V'trs U
Fees £6 (£8)
Loc Tain

Tarbat (1908)

Private (Map 8/40)
Portmahomack E Ross-shire
Tel **Portmahomack 519**
Mem 149
Sec JR Long OBE Tel 519
Pro
Holes 9 L 2328 yds SSS 63
Recs Am–63 D Mackay
Pro–
V'trs U (No Sunday play) H SOC
Fees D–£2 W–£8
Loc 6 miles SE of Tain

Thurso (1964)

Public (Map 8/41)
Newlands of Geise Thurso Caithness
Tel **Thurso 63807**
Mem 293
Sec Gordon Bailey Tel Thurso 63425
Pro
Holes 18 L 5818 yds SSS 69
Recs Am–65
Pro–
V'trs U
Fees £4(£5)
Loc 2 miles from railway station

Torvean

Private (Map 8/42)
Glenurquhart Road Inverness
Tel
Mem
Sec
Pro
Holes SSS 62
Recs Am–
Pro–
V'trs
Fees
Loc

Traigh

Private (Map 8/43)
5 Back of Keppoch Arisaig Inverness-shire
Tel **Arisaig (06875) 262**
Mem 20
Sec T McEachen
Pro
Holes 9 L 2100 yds SSS 68
Recs Am–
Pro–
V'trs U
Fees £1 W–£3
Loc Arisaig

Wick (1870)

Private (Map 8/44)
Reiss Wick Caithness KW1 4RW
Tel **Wick 2726**
Mem 210
Sec DR Sutherland Tel 0955 2101 or 2502
Pro
Holes 18 L 5945 yds SSS 69
Recs Am–65 R Klimas
Pro–68 Dai Rees
V'trs U
Fees D–£4
Loc 3 miles N Wick

North-East,
Grampian Region including Aberdeen, Banff and Kincardineshire

Aboyne (1883)

Private (Map 8/1)
Formaston Park Aboyne Aberdeenshire
Tel **Aboyne 2328**
Mem 650
Sec RD Gregson Tel Aboyne 2931
Pro I Wright Tel Aboyne 2469
Holes 18 L 5304 yds SSS 66
Recs Am–62 G Forbes
Pro–63 S Walker
V'trs U
Fees £5 (£8) W–£25
Loc E end of village

Aberdeen Courses

Aberdeen Public Courses Details from Director of Leisure and Recreation St Nicholas House Aberdeen

Auchmill (1975)

Public (Map 8/2)
Provost Rust Drive Aberdeen
Tel **714577**
Mem
Sec
Pro
Holes 9 L 2538 metres SSS
Recs Am–
Pro–
V'trs U
Fees £1.90
Loc 3 miles NW city centre

Balnagask

Public (Map 8/3)
Aberdeen
Tel **876407**
Pro Ian Smith
Holes 18 L 5468 metres SSS 69
Recs Am–
Pro–
V'trs U
Fees £3.90 Summer £2.60 Winter
Loc St Fitticks Road
Mis Nigg Bay club plays here

Hazlehead (1927)

Public (Map 8/4)
Hazlehead Aberdeen
Tel
Mem
Sec
Pro Ian Smith
Holes 18 L 5673 metres SSS 70
18 L 5303 metres SSS 68
Recs Am–67 J Fraser
Pro–67 P Oosterhuis
V'trs U
Fees £3.90 Summer £2.60 Winter
Loc Hazlehead
Mis 9 hole course available; Hazlehead GC play here

King's Links

Public (Map 8/5)
Aberdeen
Tel **632269**
Mem
Sec
Pro Ian Smith
Holes 18 L 5838 metres SSS 71
Recs Am–
Pro–
V'trs U
Fees £3.90 Summer £2.60 Winter
Loc Golf Road
Mis Bon-Accord Caledonian and Northern clubs play here

Aberdeen Clubs

Bon Accord (1872)

Public
19 Golf Road Aberdeen
Tel **Aberdeen 21464**
Mem 750
Sec GS Hunter
Holes Play over King's Links

Caledonian (1899)

Private
20 Golf Road Aberdeen AB2 1QB
Tel **Central 632443**
Mem 1141

Sec Nevile BC Smith Tel Central 632443
Holes Play over King's Links
V'trs U

Nigg Bay (1955)

Public
St Fitticks Road Balnagask
Tel **Aberdeen 871286**
Mem 850
Sec H Hendry
Holes 18 L 5984 yds 5468 metres SSS 69
V'trs U
Loc 2 miles SE town centre
Mis Play over Balnagask

Northern (1895)

King's Links Aberdeen
Tel **Aberdeen 21440**
Mem 900
Sec F Sutherland
Holes Play over King's Links

Royal Aberdeen (1780)

Private **(Map 8/6)**
Balgownie Bridge of Don
Tel **Aberdeen 702571**
Mem 350 117(J) 75(5/6)
Sec AW Baird Tel Aberdeen 648797
Pro R MacAskill Tel Aberdeen 702221
Holes 18 L 6372 yds SSS 71
18 L 4033 yds SSS 60
Recs Am–64 Fought
Pro–65 S McAllister
V'trs I
Fees £11 (£15)
Loc Aberdeen station–2 miles

Auchinblae (1984)

Public **(Map 8/7)**
Auchinblae Kincardineshire
Tel **Auchinblae 308**
Mem 54
Sec AI Robertson Tel Auchinblae 407
Pro
Holes 9 L 2174 yds SSS 30
Recs Am–60 C Whyte R Cattanach
Pro–
V'trs U (except competition nights Wed and Fri)
Fees £2.50 R/D (£3 R/D)
Loc 11 miles S of Stonehaven 5 miles N of Laurencekirk

Ballater (1892)

Private **(Map 8/8)**
Victoria Road Ballater AB3 5QX
Tel **Ballater 55567**
Mem 690
Sec Bert Ingram Tel Ballater 55567
Pro Fraser Mann Tel Ballater 55658
Holes 18 L 5704 yds SSS 67
Recs Am–64 J Crammond
Pro–68 R. Strachan
V'trs U
Fees D–£6 W/E–£7.50 W–£20.50
Loc 42 miles W of Aberdeen on A93

Banchory (1905)

Private **(Map 8/9)**
Kinneskie Banchory Kincardineshire
Tel **Banchory 2365**
Mem 650
Sec SAJ Adamson
Pro DW Smart Tel Banchory 2447
Holes 18 L 5284 yds SSS 66
Recs Am–61 JA Christie
Pro–61 A Thomson D Matthew
V'trs U
Fees £8 (£10) W–£30
Loc 18 miles W of Aberdeen

Braemar (1902)

Private **(Map 8/10)**
Braemar Aberdeenshire
Tel **Braemar 618**
Mem 219
Sec GA McIntosh
Tel Aberdeen 868535
Pro
Holes 18 L 5011 yds SSS 64
Recs Am–60 A Cruickshank
Pro–66 H. Bannerman
V'trs U SOC
Fees £3 D–£4 (£4.50 D–£7)
Loc ½ mile town centre

Buckpool (1933)

Private **(Map 8/11)**
Buckie Banffshire
Tel **Buckie 32236**
Mem 500
Sec F Macleod Tel Buckie 35368
Pro
Holes 18 L 6257 yds SSS 70
V'trs U
Fees £3 (£3 D–£5) W–£15
Loc W end of town ½ mile of A98

Cruden Bay (1791)

Private **(Map 8/12)**
Cruden Bay Aberdeenshire
Tel **(0779) 812285**
Mem 588
Sec IAD McPherson Tel (0779) 812285
Pro
Holes 18 L 6370 yds SSS 71
9 L 4710 yds SSS 62 (St Olaf Course)
Recs Am–67 SJ Bannerman S Davidson
Pro–
V'trs WD–U; W/E–H, not on competition days; SOC on WD
Fees £8 (£10)
Loc 22½ miles NE of Aberdeen

Cullen (1879)

Private **(Map 8/13)**
The Links Cullen Banffshire
Tel **Cullen 40685**
Mem 224
Sec John Douglas 103 Seatown Cullen AB5 2SN
Pro
Holes 18 L 4610 yds SSS 62
Recs Am–58 Bruce Main
Pro–
V'trs U
Fees £2.50 (£3) W–£16
Loc 200 yards W of Cullen

Deeside (1903)

Private **(Map 8/14)**
Bieldside Aberdeen
Tel **Aberdeen 869457**
Mem 500
Sec NM Scott Tel Aberdeen 867697
Pro D Thomson Tel Aberdeen 861041
Holes 18 L 5972 yds SSS 69
9 L 6632 yds SSS 72
Recs Am–64 AK Pirie
RH Wilcox
Pro–64 Sam Torrance
V'trs I
Fees £12 (£15)
Loc 4 miles W of Aberdeen

Duff House Royal (1909)

Private **(Map 8/15)**
The Barnyards Banff AB4 3SX
Tel **Banff 2062**
Mem 490 148(L) 110(J)
Sec M Pierog Tel Banff 2062
Pro RS Strachan Tel 2075
Holes 18 L 6161 yds SSS 69
Recs Am–64 G Webster
Pro
V'trs WD–U; W/E–NA 8.30-10.00, 12.00–2.00, 5–6.30 July/August
Fees £6.50 (£7.50)
Loc Moray Firth coast

Dufftown (1896)

Private **(Map 8/16)**
Dufftown Banffshire
Tel **(0340) 20325**
Mem 120
Sec Mrs M Swann
Pro
Holes 9 L 2265 yds SSS 63
Recs Am–61 GV Brand
Pro–63 P Smith
V'trs U
Fees £3 (£3)
Loc 1 mile Dufftown on Tomintoul Road

Fraserburgh (1881)

Private **(Map 8/17)**
Philorth Fraserburgh Aberdeenshire AB4 5TL
Tel **Fraserburgh 28287**
Mem 400 60(L) 110(J)
Sec CA Chalmers Tel 28921
Pro
Holes 18 L 6217 yds SSS 70
Recs Am–66 A Ritchie C McDonald A Ironside
Pro–67 I Smith
V'trs U SOC
Fees £5 (£7) W–£25
Loc 1 mile E of Fraserburgh

Huntly (1900)

Private **(Map 8/18)**
Huntly Aberdeenshire
Tel **0466 2643**
Mem 500
Sec G. Angus
Pro
Holes 18 L 5399 yds SSS 66
Recs Am–61 N Masson
Pro–
V'trs U
Fees £5 (£6) W–£20
Loc 38 miles NE of Aberdeen

Insch

Private **(Map 8/19)**
Golf Terrace Insch Aberdeenshire
Tel **04642 0363**
Mem 200
Sec George Miller Tel 0464 20252/0464 20243
Pro
Holes 9 L 5488 yds SSS 67
Recs Am–67 M McKenzie
Pro–
V'trs U
Fees £2.50 (£3.50) W–£10
Loc

Inverallochy

Public **(Map 8/20)**
Inverallochy nr Fraserburgh Aberdeenshire

Mem 150
Sec George M Young Tel Inverallochy 2324
Pro
Holes 18 L 5137 yds SSS 65
Recs Am–
Pro–
V'trs U
Fees D–£3
Loc $3\frac{1}{2}$ miles off A92 nr Fraserburgh
Mis Limited catering

Inverurie (1923)

Private **(Map 8/21)**
Blackhall Road Inverurie Aberdeenshire
Tel **(0467) 24080**
Mem 460 108(L)
Admin James Skinner Tel (0467) 24080
Pro
Holes 18 L 5703 yds SSS 68
Recs Am–66 K Hird
V'trs U SOC on WD
Fees D–£4.50 (£6.50)
Loc 16 miles N of Aberdeen; 1 mile W of town centre
Mis Buggies for hire at adjacent sports shop

Keith (1963)

Private **(Map 8/22)**
Fife Park Keith Banffshire
Tel **Keith 2469**
Mem 250
Sec A Stronach
Pro
Holes 18 L 5811 yds SSS 68
Recs Am–65
Pro–
V'trs U
Fees £3 (£4)
Loc Fife Park

Kemnay (1908)

Private **(Map 8/23)**
Kemnay Aberdeenshire
Tel
Mem 300
Sec A Findlater Tel Aberdeen 634684
Pro
Holes 9 L 1865 yds SSS 29
Recs Am–
Pro–
V'trs WD–U (ex after 5.30 Mon and Thur); Sun–M
Fees £1 (£1.50)
Loc Aberdeen 15 miles

Kintore (1911)

Private **(Map 8/24)**
Kintore Aberdeenshire
Tel **32631**
Mem 350 38(L) 60(J)
Sec Mrs C Lee
Pro
Holes 9 L 2688 yds SSS 66
Recs Am–64
Pro–
V'trs WD–U before 4.30 Mondays NA Weds 5–8 pm
Fees £4 (£6)
Loc

McDonald (1927)

Private **(Map 8/25)**
Ellon Aberdeenshire
Tel **Ellon 20576**
Mem 650
Sec G. Ironside
Pro R Urquhart Tel Ellon 22891
Holes 18 L 5986 yds SSS 69
Recs Am–68
Pro–69
V'trs U
Fees On application
Loc 15 miles N of Aberdeen

Murcar (1909)

Private **(Map 8/26)**
Bridge of Don Aberdeen AB2 8BD
Tel (0224) 704345
Mem 500
Sec DS Leighton Snr Tel (0224) 704354
Pro PA Smith Tel (0224) 704370
Holes 18 L 6226 yds SSS 70
Recs Am–65 R Grant J Savege
Pro–65 PA Smith
V'trs U
Fees Before noon £6 D–£10 (D–£12)
Loc 5 miles NE of Aberdeen
Mis 9-hole course available at Strabathie

Newburgh-on-Ythan (1888)

Private **(Map 8/27)**
Newburgh Aberdeenshire
Tel
Mem 180 25(L) 40(J)
Sec Rod Diack Tel Newburgh 298
Pro
Holes 9 L 3202 yds SSS 71
Recs Am–
Pro–
V'trs U (ex Tuesday after 3 pm)
Fees £5 (£6)
Loc 12 miles N of Aberdeen

Oldmeldrum (1885)

Private **(Map 8/28)**
Oldmeldrum Aberdeenshire
Tel
Mem 220
Sec GR Milton Tel 06512 2212
Pro
Holes 9 L 5252 yds
Recs Am–63 GJ Webster
Pro–
V'trs U
Fees £3 (£4)
Loc 17 miles NW of Aberdeen

Peterhead (1841)

Private **(Map 8/29)**
Craigewan Peterhead
Tel **Peterhead 2149**
Mem 525
Sec WG Noble
Pro –
Holes 18 L 6070 yds SSS 69
9 L 2600 yds SSS 32
Recs 18 Holes Am–66
Pro–
V'trs U
Fees £4 (£7.50)
Loc 34 miles N of Aberdeen on coast

Royal Tarlair (1926)

Private **(Map 8/30)**
Buchan Street Macduff Banffshire AB4 1TA
Tel **Macduff 32548/32897**
Mem 556
Sec Mrs Linda Edwards
Pro
Holes 18 L 5866 yds SSS 68
Recs Am–66 W Sim
Pro–
V'trs U
Fees £4 D–£6 (£5 D–£7)
Loc Macduff

Spey Bay (1907)

Private **(Map 8/31)**
Spey Bay Hotel Spey Bay Fochabers IV32 7PJ
Tel **(Hotel) Fochabers (0343) 820424 (Visitors)**
Mem 150 50(L) 50(J)
Sec Correspondence to: c/o Spey Bay Hotel; for playing and booking enquiries, ring the hotel manageress
Pro
Holes 18 L 6059 yds SSS 69
Recs Am–68 L Newlands
Pro–71 J Farmer
V'trs U
Fees £3 W–£14
Loc 5 miles off A96 at Fochabers
Mis Seaside Links

Stonehaven (1888)

Private **(Map 8/32)**
Cowie Stonehaven Kincardineshire
Tel **Stonehaven 62124**
Mem 430
Sec RM Murdoch
Pro
Holes 18 L 5128 yds SSS 65
Recs Am–62 AK Pirie
Pro–
V'trs Restricted play Sat to 3.45 pm, Sun to 10 am
Fees £5 (£6.50) W–£20
Loc 1 mile N of Stonehaven (past leisure centre and caravan site)

Strathlene (1877)

Private **(Map 8/33)**
Buckie Banffshire AB5 2DJ
Tel **Buckie 31798**
Mem 400
Sec F McKay Tel Buckie 31495
Pro
Holes 18 L 5957 yds SSS 69
Recs Am–65 JL Duthie
Pro–
V'trs U SOC
Fees £4 (£5) W–£20
Loc $\frac{1}{2}$ mile E of town

Tarland (1908)

Private **(Map 8/34)**
Tarland AB3 4YN Aberdeenshire
Tel **033 981 413**
Mem 240 +J
Sec J H Honeyman
Pro
Holes 9 L 5812 yds SSS 68
Recs Am–67 A Cruickshank
Pro–
V'trs U Enquiry advisable for W/E
Fees £4 (£6)
Loc 30 miles Aberdeen 5 miles Aboyne
Mis Full catering May–October

Torphins (1894)

Private **(Map 8/35)**
Torphins Aberdeenshire
Tel **Torphins 493**
Mem 250
Sec H Shepherd
Pro
Holes 9 L 2330 yds SSS 63
Recs Am–67 S Forbes K Leslie
Pro–
V'trs U SOC
Fees £3 (£4)
Loc Banchory 6 miles $\frac{1}{2}$ mile W of Torphins via Wester Beltie

Turriff (1985)

Private **(Map 8/36)**
Rosehall Turriff Aberdeenshire
Tel **0888 62745**
Mem 592
Sec Mrs Margaret Macrae Tel 0888 68789
Pro Alan Hemsley Tel 0888 63025
Holes 18 L 6105 yds SSS 69
Recs Am–65 J McManus G Malcolm Pro–67 R Strachan H Bannerman
V'trs U SOC
Fees £4.50 (£5.50)
Loc Turriff
Mis Buggies for hire

Westhill (1977)

Private **(Map 8/37)**
Westhill Skene Aberdeenshire
Tel **Aberdeen 740159**
Mem 500
Sec JL Webster
Pro P McCalla
Holes 18 L 5866 yds SSS 68
Recs Am–66 LR Fowler Pro–
V'trs WD–U before 4.30 pm and after 7 pm; 4.30-7 pm–M; W/E–Sat after 3.30 pm, Sun after 10 am
Fees £5 D–£7 (WE/BH £6 D–£9)
Loc 6 miles from Aberdeen on A944

Perthshire & Kinross,

Tayside & Central Regions

Aberfeldy (1895)

Private **(Map 8/1)**
Taybridge Road Aberfeldy PH15 2BH
Tel **Aberfeldy 20535**
Mem 260
Sec K Hamilton Tel Aberfeldy 20973
Pro
Holes 9 L 2733 yds SSS 67
Recs Am–67 D Douglas Pro–
V'trs U
Fees £4 D–£5 W–£16 F–£25
Loc Central Perthshire 10 miles off A9

Alyth (1894)

Private **(Map 8/2)**
Pitcrocknie Alyth
Tel **Alyth 2268**
Mem 850
Sec GB Crichton
Pro Brian Young Tel Alyth 2411
Holes 18 L 6226 yds SSS 70
Recs Am–67 E Lindsay JL Adamson Pro–64 I Young
V'trs U
Fees £6 D–£9 (£9 D–£12)
Loc 16 miles from Dundee

Auchterarder (1892)

Private **(Map 8/3)**
Orchil Road Auchterarder
Tel **Auchterarder 2804**
Mem 491
Sec JI Stewart Tel Auchterarder 3840
Pro
Holes 18 L 5737 yds SSS 68
Recs Am–67 RG Mailer
V'trs U SOC
Fees D–£6 (£7)
Loc 1 mile SW of town centre

Bishopshire (1903)

Private **(Map 8/4)**
Kinnesswood
Tel
Mem 170
Sec Andrew B Moffat Tel 860379
Pro
Holes 9 L 2180 yds SSS 63
Recs Am–63 J Morris Pro–
V'trs U
Fees £1 (£1.50)
Loc 3 miles E of Kinross off M90

Blair Atholl (1892)

Private **(Map 8/5)**
Blair Atholl Perthshire
Tel **407**
Mem 208
Sec JA McGregor Tel Blair Aitholl 274
Pro
Holes 9 L 2855 yds SSS 69
Recs Am–66 Pro–
V'trs U
Fees D–£4.50 W–£22
Loc Off A9 35 miles N of Perth
Mis Buggies for hire

Blairgowrie (1889)

Private **(Map 8/6)**
Rosemount Blairgowrie PH10 6LG
Tel **Blairgowrie (0250) 2594**
Mem 1200
Sec DW Kirkland Tel Blairgowrie 2622
Pro G Kinnoch Tel Blairgowrie 3116
Holes Rosemount 18 L 6581 yds SSS 72
Lansdowne 18 L 6865 yds SSS 73
Wee 9 L 4614 yds SSS 63
Recs Rosemount Am–66 ER Lindsay Pro–66 G Norman
Lansdowne Am–68 BRN Grieve Pro–69 J McAlister
V'trs U (W/E and Wed restricted)
Fees On application
Loc 15 miles NE of Perth off A93 16 miles NW of Dundee off A923
Mis Buggies for hire

Callander

(see Stirlingshire)

Comrie (1891)

Private **(Map 8/7)**
Comrie
Tel
Mem 150
Sec DG McGlashan Tel 70544
Pro H Donaldson
Holes 9 L 2983 yds SSS 69
Recs Am–69 D Donaldson Pro–
V'trs U
Fees £3 (£4)
Loc 7 miles W of Crieff

Craigie Hill (1911)

Private **(Map 8/8)**
Cherrybank Perth
Tel **Perth 24377**
Mem 700
Sec William A Miller Tel Perth 22644
Pro Frank Smith Tel Perth 22644
Holes 18 L 5379 yds SSS 66
Recs Am–63 A Wilson Pro–63 W Murray
V'trs U
Fees £5 (Sat/Sun–£8)
Loc W boundary Perth

Crieff (1891)

Private **(Map 8/9)**
Perth Road Crieff PH7 3LR
Tel **Crieff 2397/2909 (enquiries)**
Mem 550
Sec AH Smith Tel Crieff 2546
Pro JM Stark Tel Crieff 2909
Holes Ferntower 18 L 6419 yds SSS 71
Dornock 9 L 4772 yds SSS 63
Recs Ferntower Am–67 Pro–66
V'trs U (not from 12.30–2 pm or after 5 pm) SOC
Fees Ferntower £7 (£9)
Dornock £5 (£6)
Loc 17 miles W of Perth

Dalmunzie (1948)

Public **(Map 8/10)**
Glenshee Blairgowrie
Tel **Glenshee 025 085 226**
Mem 35
Sec Simon Winton
Pro
Holes 9 L 2035 yds SSS 62
V'trs U
Fees £5
Loc A93, 22 miles N of Blairgowrie (see Dalmunzie Hotel sign)

Dunblane New

(see Stirlingshire)

Dunkeld and Birnam (1910)

Private **(Map 8/11)**
Fungarth Dunkeld
Tel **524**

Mem 250
Sec Mrs FM Nunn Tel Dunkeld 673
Pro
Holes 9 L 4945 yds SSS 66
Recs Am–64 I Sinclair
Pro–
V'trs U
Fees £4 (£6)
Loc 1 mile Dunkeld off A923

Dunning (1953)

Private **(Map 8/12)**
Rollo Park Dunning
Tel
Mem
Sec J Lester
Pro
Holes 9 L 4836 yds SSS 64
Recs Am–
Pro–
V'trs WD–U; W/E–M (Sat after 4 pm only)
Fees £2 (£2.50)
Loc Perthshire (Tayside)

Glenalmond

Private **(Map 8/13)**
Trinity College Glenalmond
Tel
Mem
Sec JF Wainwright Tel Glenalmond 270
Pro
Holes 9 L 5812 yds SSS 68
Recs Am–70 CMW Robertson
Pro–72 M Dennis
V'trs M
Fees
Loc 10 miles NW of Perth

Gleneagles Hotel Golf Courses

Private **(Map 8/14)**
Gleneagles
Tel **Auchterarder 3543**
Sec IM Bulleid
Pro Ian Marchbank Tel Auchterarder 2231
Holes King's Course 18 L 6452 yds SSS 71
Queen's Course 18 L 5964 yds SSS 69
Prince's Course 18 L 4664 yds SSS 64
Glendevon Course 18 L 5719 yds SSS 68
Recs King's Course Am–65 GM Rutherford
Pro–63 B Barnes
Queen's Course Am–
Pro–63 Craig Stadler
Prince's Course–Am–
Pro–
V'trs WD & W/E K &Q Reserved until 10.30 am and between 1.30-2.30 for hotel guests and members Visitors must book in advance
Fees On application
Loc A9 from Perth 16 miles SW Bus meets train at Gleneagles station

Green Hotel (1900)

Private **(Map 8/15)**
Beeches Park Kinross
Tel **0577 63467**
Mem 400
Sec Mrs SM Stewart
Pro
Holes 18 L 6111 yds SSS 70
Recs Am–
Pro–
V'trs U
Fees £4.50 (£7)
Loc 17 miles S of Perth
Mis Kinross GC play on this course

Killin (1913)

Private **(Map 8/16)**
Killin Perthshire
Tel **Killin 312**
Mem 298
Sec J Blyth Tel Killin 234
Pro
Holes 9 L 2410 yds SSS 65
Recs Am–61 G Smith
Pro–
V'trs U; SOC–Apr May Sep
Fees £4 (£4)
Loc Killin village

King James VI (1858)

Private **(Map 8/17)**
Moncrieffe Island Perth
Tel **Perth 25170 (Starter Tel Perth 32460)**
Mem 600
Pro
Holes 18 L 6026 yds SSS 69
Recs Am–63 G Clark
Pro–
V'trs H (Ex Sat)
Fees £5 (£7; Sun £10.50)
Loc City centre Island in River Tay
Mis Special package for midweek parties

Kinross

Kinross
Tel **Kinross 62237**
Mem 505
Sec AR Malcolm
Holes Play over Green Hotel course

Milnathort (1910)

Private **(Map 8/18)**
South Street Milnathort
Tel Kinross 64069
Mem 300
Sec
Pro
Holes 9 L 2959 yds SSS 68
Recs Am–66 D Murphy
Pro–
V'trs U SOC
Fees £4 (£5)
Loc Between Dunfermline and Perth

Muckhart (1908)

Private **(Map 8/19)**
Muckhart by Dollar Clackmannanshire
Tel **Muckhart 423**
Mem 450 100(L) 100(J)
Sec A McBay
Pro Keith Salmoni Tel Muckhart 493
Holes 18 L 6112 yds SSS 70
Recs Am–66 E Carnegie
Pro–
V'trs U
Fees
Loc A91 3 miles E of Dollar turn right for Rumbling Bridge

Murrayshall (1981)

Private **(Map 8/20)**
Murrayshall New Scone Perth PH2 7PH
Tel **52784**
Mem 350
Sec
Pro Neil Mackintosh Tel 52784
Holes 18 L 6416 yds SSS 71
Recs Am–67 J McGraw
Pro–67 J Farmer
V'trs U SOC on WD and W/E
Fees £7.50 (£9)
Loc 2½ miles E of Perth off A94

Muthill (1935)

Private **(Map 8/21)**
Peat Road Muthill PH5 2AD
Tel
Mem 324
Sec WH Gordon Tel Crieff 3319
Pro
Holes 9 L 2371 yds SSS 63
Recs Am–65 E Campbell
Pro–68 RM Jamieson
W Milne
V'trs U
Fees £2.50 (£3)
Loc 3 miles S of Crieff on A822

Pitlochry (1909)

Private **(Map 8/22)**
Pitlochry
Tel **Pitlochry 2792**
Mem 350
Sec John Brydone Tel 2524
Pro J Wilson
Holes 18 L 5811 yds SSS 68
Recs Am–63 CP Christy
MM Niven
Pro–64
V'trs U
Fees £7 (£9)
Loc

Royal Perth Golfing Society and County and City Club

Public **(Map 8/23)**
1/2 Atholl Crescent Perth
Tel **Perth 22265**
Mem 250
Sec AG Dorward Tel Perth 37311
Pro
Holes 18 L 5141 yds SSS 64
Recs Am–
Pro–
V'trs U No Sunday play
Fees On application
Loc

St Fillans (1903)

Private **(Map 8/24)**
South Lochearn Rd St Fillans
Tel **St Fillans 312**
Mem 400
Sec R Adam Brown Tel St Fillans 302
Pro
Holes 9 L 2634 yds SSS (18 holes) 66
Recs Am–
Pro–
V'trs U SOC
Fees £3 D–£4 W–£15 (1986 prices)
Loc 12 miles Crieff

Strathtay (1909)

Private **(Map 8/25)**
Strathtay
Tel
Mem 100
Sec J Armstrong-Payne 08874-367
Pro
Holes 9 L 3880 yds SSS 63
Recs Am–61 AM Deboys
Pro–
V'trs U
Fees £4 (£5)
Loc 4 miles W of Ballinluig (A827)

Taymouth Castle (1923)

Private (Map 8/26)
Kenmore Tayside PH15 2NT
Tel **08873-228**
Mem 200
Sec
Pro A Marshall (Golf Director) Tel Kenmore 228
Holes 18 L 6066 yds SSS 69
Recs Am–63 MM Niven
Pro–
V'trs U SOC W/E booking essential
Fees £7 D–£10 (£9 D–£13) Jrs ½ price
Loc 6 miles W of Aberfeldy
Mis Buggies available for hire

Renfrewshire, Strathclyde Region

Barshaw

Public (Map 9/1)
Barshaw Park Paislay
Tel **041-889 2908**
Mem 68
Sec W Collins Tel 041-884 2533
Pro
Holes 18 L 5703 yds SSS 67
Recs Am–
Pro–
V'trs U
Fees £2
Loc 1 mile E of Paisley Cross off A737

Bonnyton (1957)

Private (Map 9/2)
Eaglesham Renfrewshire G76 0QA
Tel **035 53 2781**
Mem 850
Sec CJ Black Tel 035 53 2781
Pro
Holes 18 L 6252 yds SSS 71
Recs Am–67 Finlay Black
Pro–69 Norman Wood
V'trs I WD–SOC
Fees £8
Loc SW Eaglesham

Caldwell (1903)

Private (Map 9/3)
Caldwell Uplawmoor
Tel **Uplawmoor 329**
Mem 450
Sec DP MacLean Tel 041-221 8395
Pro Keith Baxter Tel Uplawmoor 616
Holes 18 L 6102 yds SSS 69
Recs Am–64 JM Sharp
Pro–
V'trs WD–Contact in advance before 4 pm, after 4 pm–M, SOC; W/E–M
Fees £6 D–£9
Loc 5 miles SW of Barrhead on A736 Glasgow–Irvine road

Cochrane Castle (1895)

Private (Map 9/4)
Craigston Johnstone PA5 0HF
Tel **Johnstone 20146**
Mem 400
Sec JC Cowan Tel Johnstone 20146
Pro TC Steele Tel Johnstone 28465
Holes 18 L 6226 yds SSS 70
Recs Am–66 D Abercrombie
Pro–71 S Kelly
V'trs WD–U; W/E–M
Fees £6 D–£9
Loc ½ mile S of A737

East Renfrewshire (1922)

Private (Map 9/5)
Pilmuir Newton Mearns G77 6RT
Tel **035 55 256**
Mem 450
Sec AL Gillespie CA Tel 041 226 4311
Pro Gordon D Clarke Tel 035 55 258
Holes 18 L 6097 yds SSS 70
Recs Am–64 A Dow
Pro–65 WR Lockie
V'trs By arrangement
Fees
Loc 2 miles SW Newton Mearns

Eastwood (1893)

Private (Map 9/6)
Muirshield Loganswell Newton Mearns Glasgow G77 6RX
Tel **035 55 261**
Mem 650
Sec Campbell Scouler Tel 035 55 280
Pro Kendal McWade Tel 035 55 285
Holes 18 L 5886 yds SSS 68
Recs Am–62 IA Carslaw
Pro–67 Peter Mills
V'trs M
Fees
Loc 9 miles SW of Glasgow

Elderslie (1908)

Private (Map 9/7)
Elderslie
Tel **Johnstone 23956**
Mem 400
Sec Wm Muirhead
Pro
Holes 18 L 6031 yds SSS 69
Recs Am–69 J Kyle B Clarkson
Pro–66 R Weir R Craig
V'trs M
Fees
Loc 2 miles from Paisley

Erskine (1904)

Private (Map 9/8)
Bishopton PA7 5PH
Tel **Bishopton 2302**
Mem 400 200(L)
Sec TA McKillop Tel Bishopton 862302
Pro Peter Thomson Tel Bishopton 862108
Holes 18 L 6287 yds SSS 70
Recs Am–66 IG Riddell
Pro–64 MC Douglas
V'trs WD–I; W/E–M
Fees £11 inc VAT
Loc 5 miles NW Paisley

Fereneze (1904)

Private (Map 9/9)
Barrhead G78 1HJ
Tel **041-881 1519**
Mem 501
Sec AD Gourley Tel 041-221 6394
Pro Alastair McLean Tel 041-880 7058
Holes 18 L 5821 yds SSS 68
Recs Am–64 EH McMillan
Pro–67 R Drummond D Huish J McTear R Weir
V'trs M
Fees
Loc 9 miles SW Glasgow

Gleddoch (1974)

Private (Map 9/10)
Langbank PA14 6YE
Tel **Langbank 304**
Mem 400
Sec
Pro Keith Campbell Tel 704
Holes 18 L 6200 yds SSS 71
Recs Am–69 DJ McDougall
Pro–67 J Chillas
V'trs WD–U; W/E–M
Fees £9
Loc 16 miles W of Glasgow by M8/A8

Gourock (1896)

Private (Map 9/11)
Cowal View Gourock
Tel **Largs 687222**
Mem 660 106(L) 112(J)
Sec JF MacLauchlan Tel Gourock 33696
Pro RM Collinson Tel Gourock 36834
Holes 18 L 6492 yds SSS 71
Recs Am–64 N Skinner
Pro–69 D Graham
V'trs WD–I; W/E–M; SOC
Fees On application
Loc 3 miles SW Gourock Station

Greenock (1890)

Private (Map 9/12)
Forsyth Street Greenock PA1 8RE
Tel **0475 20793**
Mem 478 149(L) 144(J)
Sec Eric J Black Tel 0475 26819
Pro Ken Murray Tel 0475 21435
Holes 18 L 5888 yds SSS 68
9 L 2149 yds SSS 32
Recs Am–65 RW Blackwood M J Sangster
Pro–66 H Thomson J Panton H Boyle
V'trs WD–U; W/E&BH–M
Fees £7 W–£18 M–£45
Loc 10 minutes from town centre

Kilmacolm (1891)

Private (Map 9/13)
Kilmacolm
Tel **Kilmacolm 2139**
Mem 623
Sec RF McDonald
Pro D Stewart Tel Kilmacolm 2695
Holes 18 L 5890 yds SSS 68
Recs Am–64 M Stevenson
Pro–66 EC Brown
V'trs WD–U; W/E–M
Fees
Loc 10 miles W of Paisley

Lochwinnoch (1897)

Private (Map 9/14)
Burnfoot Road Lochwinnoch
Tel **Lochwinnoch 842153**
Mem 500
Sec AH Booth Tel Lochwinnoch 842697
Pro
Holes 18 L 6223 yds SSS 70
Recs Am–67 IJ Gilmour
Pro–G Reilly
V'trs WD–U before 4.30 pm; W/E–M
Fees £5
Loc 9 miles S of Paisley
Mis Parties catered for

Old Ranfurly (1905)

Private **(Map 9/15)**
Bridge of Weir
Tel **Bridge of Weir 613612**
Mem 375
Sec R MacCallum
Pro
Holes 18 L 6283 yds SSS 70
Recs Am–65 DB Howard
Pro–66 Campbell Elliott
V'trs WD–I; W/E–M
Fees
Loc Bridge of Weir

Paisley (1895)

Private **(Map 9/16)**
Paisley
Tel **884 2292**
Mem 750
Sec WJ Cunningham Tel 884 3903
Pro
Holes 18 L 6424 yds SSS 71
Recs Am–64 DW Perrie
Pro–
V'trs W/E & BH–I SOC
Fees £6 D–£9
Loc Braehead Paisley

Port Glasgow (1895)

Private **(Map 9/17)**
Port Glasgow
Tel **Port Glasgow 704181**
Mem 375
Sec NL Mitchell Tel 706273
Pro
Holes 18 L 5712 yds SSS 68
Recs Am–63 John W McKechnie
Pro–
V'trs WD, until 3.55 pm only, U; all other times–I
Fees £5 D–£8
Loc 1 mile S of town centre

Ranfurly Castle (1889)

Private **(Map 9/18)**
Golf Road Bridge of Weir
Tel **Bridge of Weir 612609**
Mem 360 185(L) 100(J)
Sec Mrs TJ Gemmell
Pro Kevin Stables Tel Bridge of Weir 614795
Holes 18 L 6284 yds SSS 70
Recs Am–65 WMB Brown
Pro–66 B Watson
V'trs WD–I; W/E–M SOC on WD
Fees
Loc 7 miles W of Paisley

Renfrew (1894)

Private **(Map 9/19)**
Blythswood Estate Inchinnan Road Renfrew
Tel **041-886 6692**
Mem 450 110(L) 80(J)
Sec IG Park
Pro J. Mulgrew Tel 041-886 7477
Holes 18 L 6818 yds SSS 73
Recs Am–69 LR Pirie
DB Howard
Pro–70 J Chillas WB Milne
V'trs M
Fees
Loc 2 miles from Glasgow Airport

Whinhill (1911)

Private **(Map 9/20)**
Beith Road Greenock
Tel **0475 24694**
Mem 350
Sec A Polonis
Pro
Holes 18 L 5454 yds SSS 67
Recs Am–66 W Brewster
Pro–
V'trs U
Fees 40p (50p)
Loc 2 miles S of Greenock

Whitecraigs (1905)

Private **(Map 9/21)**
72 Ayr Road Giffnock Glasgow G46 6SW
Tel **041-639 1681**
Mem 500
Sec RW Miller Tel 041-639 4530
Pro W Watson Tel 041-639 2140
Holes 18 L 6230 yds SSS 70
Recs Am–65 GB Murray
Pro–
V'trs WD–I; W/E–M SOC on WD
Fees £12 D–£15
Loc 5 minutes from Whitecraigs Station

South,
Dumfriesshire & Galloway Regions, including Dumfriesshire, Kirkcudbrightshire & Wigtownshire

Castle Douglas (1905)

Private **(Map 9/1)**
Abercromby Road Castle Douglas Kirkcudbrightshire
Tel **2801**
Mem 450
Sec William G Coulthard
Pro
Holes 9 L 5400 yds SSS 66
Recs Am–62 W Blayney
Pro–
V'trs U
Fees £4 W–£15
Loc Near town centre

Colvend (1908)

Private **(Map 9/2)**
Sandyhills nr Dalbeattie Kirkcudbrightshire DG5 4PY
Tel **Rockcliffe (Kirkcudbright) 398**
Mem 350
Sec Duncan McNeil Tel Kippford 685
Pro
Holes 9 L 2104 yds SSS 61
Recs Am–
Pro–
V'trs U (exc Tue after 2 pm & Thu after 5 pm Apr–Nov)
Fees £3 (£3) Under 16s half price exc Sat/Sun
Loc 6 miles Dalbeattie on A710 Solway Coast Road

Crichton Royal (1884)

Private **(Map 9/3)**
Dumfries
Tel
Mem 400
Sec D Macfarlane
Pro
Holes 9 L 3084 yds SSS 69
Recs Am–67 RB Shearman
Pro–67 D Gemmell
V'trs M
Fees
Loc 1 mile from Dumfries on Bankend Road

Dalbeattie (1897)

Private **(Map 9/4)**
Dalbeattie Kirkcudbrightshire
Tel
Mem 220
Sec AK Scott
Pro
Holes 9 L 4200 yds SSS 61
Recs Am–
Pro–
V'trs U
Fees £2 (£3)
Loc

Dumfries and County (1912)

Private **(Map 9/5)**
Nunfield Edinburgh Road Dumfries DG1 1JX
Tel **Dumfries 53585**
Mem 600 150(L) 100(J)
Sec JK Wells Tel Dumfries 62045
Pro GD Gray Tel Dumfries 68918
Holes 18 L 5914 yds SSS 68
Recs Am–64 D James
Pro–63 A Thomson
J McAlister F Mann
V'trs U (ex competition days)
Fees £7 (£8.50) W–£25
Loc 1 mile NE town centre on A701

Dumfries and Galloway (1880)

Private **(Map 9/6)**
Laurieston Avenue Maxwelltown Dumfries
Tel **Dumfries 53582**
Mem 450
Sec Tel 63848
Pro J Fergusson Tel 56902
Holes 18 L 5782 yds SSS 68
Recs Am–64 R Shearman
Pro–63 K Baxter
V'trs U
Fees £6 (£8)
Loc In Dumfries

Gatehouse (1922)

Private (Map 9/7)
Gatehouse of Fleet Kirkcudbrightshire
Tel
Mem 200
Sec EJ Bryan Tel Gatehouse 654
Pro
Holes 9 L 2398 yds SSS 63
Recs Am–60 S Martin
Pro–
V'trs U
Fees £3.25 (£4) W–£10 2-week–£20
Loc ¾ mile N of town

Kirkcudbright (1895)

Private (Map 9/8)
Stirling Crescent Kirkcudbright
Tel
Mem 300
Sec A Gordon Tel Kirkcudbright 30542
Pro
Holes 18 L 5681 yds SSS 67
Recs Am–62 S Calladine
Pro–
V'trs U
Fees £5 W–£15 incl VAT
Loc Near town centre

Langholm

(see Borders)

Lochmaben (1925)

Private (Map 9/9)
Castlehill Gate Lochmaben
Tel **552**
Mem 210 75(L) 82(J) 41(5)
Sec G McN Dickson
Pro
Holes 9 L 5338 yds SSS 66
Recs Am–62 D Hutchison
Pro–64 G Gray
V'trs U–Up to 5 pm
Fees £3.50 (£5.25)
Loc 4 miles from Lockerbie 8 miles from Dumfries

Lockerbie (1889)

Private (Map 9/10)
Corrie Road Lockerbie
Tel **Lockerbie 3363**
Mem 360
Sec R Barclay Tel Lochmaben 274
Pro
Holes 18 L 5418 yds SSS 66
Recs Am–
Pro–
V'trs U
Fees £5 W–£20
Loc ½ mile town centre on Corrie Road

Moffat (1884)

Private (Map 9/11)
Coateshill Moffat DG10 9SB
Tel **Moffat 0683-20020**
Mem 400
Sec GW Kitt Tel Moffat 0683-20020
Pro
Holes 18 L 5218 yds SSS 66
Recs Am–60
Pro–
V'trs WD–Restricted play Tue 4.45 pm–6.30 pm, Wed 2 pm onwards, Thu 4.45 pm–5.45 pm; W/E–M before 9 am and 12.30 pm–1 pm; organised parties welcome
Fees £4 (£6) W–£7
Loc Leave A74 on A701 at Beattock; located 2 miles on left at top of hill

New Galloway (1902)

Private (Map 9/12)
New Galloway Kirkcudbrightshire
Mem 140
Sec DM Browning New Galloway 239
Pro
Holes 9 L 2509 yds SSS 65
Recs Am–
Pro–
V'trs U
Fees £4 (£4)
Loc In New Galloway

Newton Stewart

Private (Map 9/13)
Kirroughtree Avenue Minnigaff Newton Stewart Wigtownshire
Tel **0671 2172**
Mem 200
Sec DF Buchanan
Pro
Holes 9 L 5512 yds SSS 67
Recs Am–
Pro–
V'trs U
Fees WD–£3.50 W/E–£4.50 W–£16
Loc Edge of town

Portpatrick Dunskey (1930)

Private (Map 9/14)
Portpatrick
Tel **0776 81273**
Mem 298
Sec JA Horberry Tel 0776 83215
Pro
Holes 18 L 5644 yds and 9 L 1442 yds
Recs Am–65 A Cunningham
Pro–
V'trs U SOC
Fees D–£7 (£8) Reduced after 2.30 pm
£5.50 (£6.50) W–£25 W/E–£18
F–£35 (9 hole course D–£3)
Loc 8 miles SW of Stranraer
Mis No catering Mon
Buggies for hire

Powfoot (1903)

Private (Map 9/15)
Cummertrees Annan
Tel **Cummertrees 227**
Mem 820
Sec RG Anderson Tel Annan 2866
Pro Lee Johnson Tel Cummertrees 327
Holes 18 L 6283 yds SSS 70
Recs Am–66 DJ Warwick
Pro–67 J Stevens
V'trs WD–U, W/E–Limited
Fees Winter £4 (£5) 5 day £14
Summer £8 (£10) 5 day £32
Loc 4 miles W of Annan

Sanquhar (1894)

Private (Map 9/16)
Sanquhar
Tel **0659 50577**
Mem 110
Sec DA Hamilton Tel Kirkconnel 206
Pro
Holes 9 L 5630 yds SSS 68
Recs Am–66 Ian Brotherton John Copeland
Pro–
V'trs U SOC
Fees £5 (£8)
Loc Blackaddie Road Sanquhar

Southerness (1947)

Private (Map 9/17)
Southerness Dumfries DG2 8AZ
Tel **Kirkbean (038 788) 677**
Mem 530
Sec WT Train Tel Dumfries (0387) 53588
Pro
Holes 18 L 6551 yds SSS 72
Recs Am–68 RD Ireland I Milne
Pro–
V'trs U SOC
Fees On application
Loc 16 miles SW Dumfries

St Medan (1905)

Private (Map 9/18)
Port William Wigtownshire
Tel **Port William 358**
Mem 200
Sec D O'Neill Tel Whithorn 555
Pro
Holes 9 L 2277 yds SSS 62
Recs Am–
Pro–
V'trs U SOC
Fees £4 W–£20
Loc 3 miles S of Port William

Stranraer (1906)

Private (Map 9/19)
Creachmore Leswalt Stranraer Wigtownshire
Tel **0776 87245**
Mem 450
Sec WI Wilson CA Tel 0776 3539
Pro
Holes 18 L 6300 yds SSS 71
Recs Am–66 CG Findlay
Pro–72 J Panton
V'trs W/E–NA before 9.30 am and 12.30 pm–1.30 pm
Fees D–£6.75 W/E–£10
Loc 2 miles from town

Thornhill (1892)

Private (Map 9/20)
Thornhill Dumfriesshire
Tel **Thornhill 30546**
Mem 375 75(L) 45(J)
Sec JWD Wallace Tel (0387) 720401
Pro MC Douglas
Holes 18 L 5979 yds SSS 69
Recs Am–67 S Hiddleston
Pro–68 MC Douglas
V'trs U
Fees £5 (£7)
Loc 14 miles N of Dumfries

Wigtown and Bladnoch (1960)

Private (Map 9/21)
Wigtown
Tel **3354**
Mem 250
Sec D Heggie Tel Newton Stewart 2556
Pro
Holes 9 L 2712 yds SSS 67
Recs Am–64 R McGinn
DT McRae
V'trs U
Fees £3 (£4.50)
Loc 200 yds S town square

Wigtownshire County (1894)

Private (Map 9/22)
Glenluce
Tel **Glenluce 420**

Mem 180
Sec R McCubbin Tel Glenluce 277
Pro
Holes 18 L 5715 yds SSS 68
Recs Am–62 K Hardie
Pro–
V'trs U; Wed after 6 pm–NA
Fees £4.50 (£5)
Loc 8 miles E of Stranraer

Stirlingshire,
Strathclyde & Central Regions

Aberfoyle (1893)
Private **(Map 9/1)**
Aberfoyle
Tel **Aberfoyle 493**
Mem 200
Sec A Macdonald Tel Aberfoyle 441
Pro
Holes 18 L 5204 yds SSS 66
Recs Am–64–EJ Barnard
Pro–
V'trs U
Fees D–£6
Loc Braeval Aberfoyle

Balmore
(see Dunbartonshire)

Bonnybridge (1924)
Private **(Map 9/2)**
Larbert Road Bonnybridge
Tel **(0324) 812822**
Mem 425
Sec James J Keilt (0324) 812822
Pro
Holes 9 L 6058 yds SSS 69
Recs Am–66 D Riddell
Pro–66 J McTear
V'trs I
Fees By arrangement
Loc 3 miles W of Falkirk

Bridge of Allan (1895)
Private **(Map 9/3)**
Sunnylaw Bridge of Allan
Tel **Bridge of Allan 832332**
Mem 260
Sec G Cruickshank Tel 833087
Pro
Holes 9 L 4900 yds SSS 65
Recs Am–64 M Ferguson
Pro–
V'trs U (ex Sats)
Fees £3 (£4)
Loc Bridge of Allan

Buchanan Castle (1936)
Private **(Map 9/4)**
Nr Drymen
Tel **Drymen (0360) 60369**
Mem 830
Sec J Iain Hay Tel Drymen (0360) 60307
Pro Charles Cernie Tel Drymen (0360) 60330
Holes 18 L 6015 yds SSS 69
Recs Am–62 RGB McCallum
Pro–66 D Huish W Milne
V'trs M or by arrangement with secretary
Fees
Loc 18 miies NW of Glasgow

Callander (1890)
Private **(Map 9/5)**
Aveland Road Callander Perthshire FK17 8EN
Tel **Callander 30090**
Mem 520
Sec HG Slater Tel Callander 30931
Pro J McCallum Tel Callander 30975
Holes 18 L 5091 yds SSS 66
Recs Am–62 GK MacDonald
Pro–59 D Matthew
V'trs U SOC
Fees On application
Loc ½ mile off A84 E end of town
Mis Full catering facilities every day

Campsie (1895)
Private **(Map 9/6)**
Crow Road Lennoxtown
Tel **Lennoxtown 313099**
Mem 380
Sec JM Dolandson Tel Lenn 312249
Pro D Stevenson
Holes 18 L 5517 yds SSS 67
Recs Am–70 J Hope
Pro–73 K Stevely
V'trs WD–U before 4.30
Fees £3
Loc B822 Lennoxtown to Fintry Road

Dunblane New (1923)
Private **(Map 9/7)**
Dunblane Perthshire
Tel **Dunblane 822343**
Mem 600
Match
Sec AG Duncan Tel Dunblane 823822
Pro RM Jamieson Tel Dunblane 823711
Holes 18 L 5878 yds SSS 68
Recs Am–64 GK McDonald
Pro–64 RM Jamieson
V'trs WD–only Mon Tue Thu Fri (am); W/E–M; SOC
Fees £6 (£10)
Loc 6 miles N Stirling

Falkirk (1922)
Private **(Map 9/8)**
Stirling Road Camelon Falkirk
Tel **Falkirk 23457**
Mem 500
Sec A Bennie Tel Falkirk 21388
Pro
Holes 18 L 6201 yds SSS 70
Recs Am–
Pro–
V'trs WD–U until 4 pm
Parties Mon Tues Thurs by previous arrangement with Secretary; W/E–NA
Fees On application
Loc 1½ miles W of Falkirk town centre on A9

Falkirk Tryst (1885)
Private **(Map 9/9)**
86 Burnhead Road Larbert
Tel **Larbert (0324) 562415**
Mem 450
Sec JJ Weir Tel Larbert (0324) 562050
Pro D Slicer Tel Larbert (0324) 562091
Holes 18 L 6053 yds SSS 69
Recs Am–64 J Rankin
Pro–65 J Chillas
V'trs WD–U; Wed & W/E–M; SOC
Fees £5 (£7)
Loc 3 miles N of Falkirk

Glenbervie
Private **(Map 9/10)**
Stirling Road Larbert Stirlingshire FK5 4SJ
Tel **Larbert 562605**
Mem 600
Sec Mrs M Purves Tel Larbert 562605
Pro George McKay Tel Larbert 562725
Holes 18 L 6423 yds SSS 71
Recs Am–64 KW Goodwin
Pro–65 S Torrance
V'trs WD–I; W/E–M; SOC Tue Thu
Fees £9 D–£13
Loc Stirling Road 1 mile N of Larbert

Grangemouth (1973)
Public **(Map 9/11)**
Polmonthill Grangemouth Stirlingshire FK3 8TF
Tel **Polmont 711500**
Mem 680
Sec J Balfour Tel Polmont 711500
Pro SJ Campbell Tel Polmont 714355
Holes 18 L 6527 yds SSS 71
Recs Am–71
Pro–68 R Weir
V'trs U
Fees £3.50
Loc 3 miles E of Falkirk

Kilsyth Lennox (1900)
Private **(Map 9/12)**
Tak-Ma-Doon Road Kilsyth
Tel **Kilsyth 822190**
Mem 250
Sec AG Stevenson Tel Kilsyth 823213
Pro
Holes 9 L 5930 yds SSS 69
Recs Am–66 W Erskine G Walker
Pro–
V'trs WD–U before 5 pm, M after 5 pm; W/E–NA Sat before 4 pm, NA Sun before 2 pm; SOC on WD
Fees £4
Loc Glasgow 12 miles

Polmont (1901)
Private **(Map 9/13)**
Manuelrigg Maddiston Falkirk
Tel **Polmont 711277**
Mem 200
Sec P Lees Tel Polmont 713811
Pro
Holes 9 L 3044 yds SSS 69
Recs Am–71 W Shanks
Pro–
V'trs U (Sat after 1 pm)
Fees £2.50 Sat £3 Sun £3.50
Loc 4 miles S of Falkirk

Stirling (1869)
Private **(Map 9/14)**
Queen's Road Stirling
Tel **Stirling 73801**
Mem 1000
Asst
Sec Mrs LC Sayer
Tel Stirling 64098
Pro J Chillas Tel Stirling 71490
Holes 18 L 6409 yds SSS 71
Recs Am–64 R Gregan
Pro–65 J Chillas
V'trs WD–U SOC; W/E–NA
Fees £6.50 (£7.50)
Loc King's Park Stirling

Strathendrick (1901)

Private (Map 9/15)
By Drymen Stirlingshire
Tel
Mem 330
Sec H Munro Tel 041-942 3353
Pro
Holes 9 L 4962 yds SSS 65
Recs Am–62 P Heggarty
Pro–64 C Dernie
V'trs M
Fees
Loc Drymen, Stirlingshire

Wales

Clwyd

Abergele and Pensarn (1910)

Private (Map 10/1)
Tan-y-Goppa Road Abergele Clwyd LL22 8DS
Tel **Abergele 824034**
Mem 1150
Sec DR Rose Tel Abergele 824034
Pro Peter A Hopper Tel Abergele 823813
Holes 18 L 6086 yds SSS 69
Recs Am–64 J Buckley
Pro–68 BGC Huggett
V'trs U SOC
Fees £7 (£9)
Loc Abergele

Bryn Morfydd (1982)

(Map 10/2)
The Princess Course
Llanrhaeadr nr Denbigh Clwyd
Tel **(074 578) 313**
Mem 20
Sec W Lester
Pro
Holes 9 L 1190 yds SSS 27
V'trs
Fees £2.50 D–£5 (free if restaurant spend exceeds £5)

Denbigh (1922)

Private (Map 10/3)
Henllan Road Denbigh
Tel **074 571 4159**
Mem 350
Sec TH Aldrich
Pro M Carty
Holes 18 L 5650 yds SSS 67 (from Apr 1986)
Recs Am–62 H Parry
Pro–
V'trs U
Fees £5 (W/E & BH £7)
Loc B5382 2 miles W of Denbigh
Mis Catering facilities available: booking required

Flint (1966)

Private (Map 10/4)
Cornist Park Flint CH6 5HJ
Tel **Flint 2327**
Mem 265
Sec H Griffith Tel Flint 2186
Pro
Holes 9 L 5829 yds SSS 68
Recs Am–68 O O'Neil
Pro–
V'trs WD–U before 5 pm; W/E–M after noon; SOC on WD and Sats
Fees D–£3
Loc 1½ miles Railway Station; 1 mile town centre M56 8 miles

Hawarden (1911)

Private (Map 10/5)
Groomsdale La Hawarden Deeside Clwyd CH5 3EH
Tel **Hawarden 531447**
Mem 320 40 (5D)
Sec T Hinks-Edwards Tel Mold 57955
Pro M. Carty Tel Hawarden 531447
Holes 9 L 5729 yds SSS 68
Recs Am–65 DA Reidford
Pro–
V'trs M SOC
Fees £4 (with mem only)
Loc 6 miles W of Chester

Holywell (1906)

Private (Map 10/6)
Brynford Holywell
Tel **Holywell 710040**
Mem 300
Sec EH Jackson Tel Holywell 710693
Pro M Carty
Holes 9 L 3117 yds SSS 70
Recs Am–69 T Davies
Pro– N Jones
V'trs WD–U; W/E–M
Fees £4 (£5)
Loc 2 miles S Holywell

Mold (1909)

Private (Map 10/7)
Pantmywyn nr Mold
Tel **Mold 740318**
Mem 350 55(L) 110(J)
Sec A Newall
Pro Martin Carty
Holes 18 L 5521 yds SSS 67
Recs Am–65
Pro–64
V'trs U
Fees £6 (£7.50)
Loc 4 miles from Mold

Old Colwyn (1907)

Private (Map 10/8)
The Clubhouse Woodland Avenue Clwyd LL29 9NL
Tel **Colwyn Bay 515581**
Mem 350
Sec M Davies Tel Colwyn Bay 515581
Pro
Holes 9 L 5268 yds SSS 66
Recs Am–63 C Oldham JD Jones Roberts
Pro–67 DJ Rees
V'trs U
Fees £3 (£4)
Loc Colwyn Bay

Old Padeswood (1978)

Private (Map 10/9)
Station Road Padeswood nr Mold Clwyd
Tel **Buckley 547401**
Mem 425
Sec BV Hellen Tel Pontybodkin 770506
Pro Tony Davies Tel Buckley 547401
Holes 18 L 6728 yds SSS 72
Recs Am–70 L Lockett
Pro–72 P Dunn
V'trs U (exc comp days); SOC on WD
Fees £5 (£6)
Loc 2 miles from Mold on A5118

Padeswood and Buckley (1933)

Private (Map 10/10)
The Caia Station Lane Padeswood nr Mold Clwyd CH7 4JD
Tel **Buckley 542537**
Mem 592
Sec Tel Buckley 542537
Pro David Ashton Tel Buckley 543636
Holes 18 L 5746 yds SSS 68
Recs Am–66 RMA Morris
Pro–
V'trs WD–U 9 am–4 pm, M after 4 pm; W/E–Sat U, Sun NA exc with prior permission; SOC on WD from 9.30 am and 1.30 pm, not after 4 pm; Ladies day Wed
Fees £6 (£8)
Loc 8 miles W of Chester off A5118; 2nd golf club on right

Prestatyn (1905)

Private (Map 10/11)
Marine Road East Prestatyn LL19 7HS
Tel **Prestatyn 4320/88353**
Mem 550
Sec W Brown
Pro Tim Leah

Holes 18 L 6714 yds SSS 73
Recs Am–68 J Bamford
Pro–
V'trs U
Fees £6 (£8)
Loc Prestatyn 1 mile East

Rhuddlan (1930)
Private (Map 10/12)
Rhuddlan Rhyl LL18 6LB
Tel **Rhuddlan 590217**
Mem 435 135(L) 100(J)
Sec D Morris Tel Rhuddlan 590675 (home)
Pro Gerry Cox Tel Rhuddlan 590898
Holes 18 L 6038 yds SSS 69
Recs Am–63 P Jones
Pro–
V'trs H or L SOC on WD
Fees £7 (Sun–£9)
Loc 3 miles S of Rhyl

Rhyl (1890)
Private (Map 10/13)
Coast Road Rhyl Clwyd
Tel **Rhyl 53171**
Mem 240
Sec J Smith Tel Prestatyn 89450
Pro
Holes 9 L 6153 yds SSS 70
Recs Am–67 CH Rees
Pro–67 H Cotton N von Nida C Ward
V'trs U
Fees £3.50 (£4.50)
Loc Coast road between Rhyl and Prestatyn

Ruthin-Pwllglas (1920)
Private (Map 10/14)
Nr Ruthin Clwyd
Tel **Ruthin 2296**
Mem 360
Sec RD Roberts Tel Ruthin 4658
Pro
Holes 9 L 5306 yds SSS 66
Recs Am–64 MG Hughes
Pro–
V'trs U SOC
Fees £4 (£5) W–£15
Loc Pwllglas 2½ miles S of Ruthin

St Melyd (1922)
Private (Map 10/15)
The Paddock Meliden Road Prestatyn
Tel **Prestatyn 4405**
Mem 530
Sec DR Stewart Tel Prestatyn 4366
Pro NH Lloyd Tel Pres 88858
Holes 9 L 5857 yds SSS 68
Recs Am–67 Christopher Davies
Pro–68 N Hill
V'trs U SOC
Fees £5 (£6) Half price with mem
Loc On A547 between Prestatyn and Meliden

Vale of Llangollen (1908)
Private (Map 10/16)
Holyhead Road Llangollen Clwyd LL20 7PR
Tel **Llangollen 860050**
Mem 600
Sec TF Ellis Tel Llangollen 860040
Pro DI Vaughan Tel Llangollen 860040
Holes 18 L 6617 yds SSS 72
Recs Am–67
Pro–69
V'trs U
Fees £7.50 (£9)
Loc 1½ miles E of Llangollen on A5

Wrexham (1906)
Private (Map 10/17)
Holt Road Wrexham
Tel **Wrexham 364268/261033**
Mem 650
Sec KB Fisher
Pro David A Larvin Tel Wrexham 351476
Holes 18 L 6137 yds SSS 69
Recs Am–67 P Williams MS Chidley
Pro–
V'trs H SOC on WD
Fees On application
Loc 2 miles NE of Wrexham on A534

Dyfed

Aberystwyth (1911)
Private (Map 10/1)
Bryn-y-Mor Aberystwyth
Tel **0970-615104**
Mem 390 approx
Sec Wynn Hughes Tel 0970-3826
Pro Barry Thomas Tel 0970-615104
Holes 18 L 5868 yds SSS 68
Recs Am–66 Wyn Pugh
Pro–64 A Hodson
V'trs U SOC
Fees £5 (£6) W–£16
Loc ½ mile Aberystwyth

Ashburnham (1894)
Private (Map 10/2)
Cliffe Terrace Burry Port Dyfed SA16 0HN
Tel **Burry Port 2466**
Mem 800
Sec D Emrys Gravelle Tel Burry Port 2269
Pro RJ Playe Tel Burry Port 3846
Holes 18 L 7016 yds SSS 74
Recs Am–70 CI Morgan
Pro–67 M Cahill S Torrance P Townsend
V'trs H
Fees £7 (£5 with mem) D–£10 (£8 with mem)
WE/BH £12 (£10 with mem) D–£14 (£12 with mem)
Loc 5 miles W of Llanelli

Borth and Ynyslas (1885)
Private (Map 10/3)
Borth Dyfed
Tel **0970-81 (Borth) 202**
Mem 403
Sec JM Lewis and RB Mair
Pro JG Lewis Tel Borth 557
Holes 18 L 6094 yds SSS 70
Recs Am–70 W Pugh
Pro–68 JG Lewis
V'trs U SOC
Fees Minimum £6 (men); £5 (ladies), higher during summer
Loc Aberystwyth, 7 miles

Cardigan (1928)
Private (Map 10/4)
Gwbert-on-Sea Dyfed SA43 1PR
Tel **Cardigan 612035**
Mem 300
Sec J Owen Tel Cardigan 614595
Pro Colin Parsons
Holes White course 18 L 6207 yds SSS 70
Yellow course 18 L 5994 yds SSS 69
Recs Am–68 WEG James; Pro–69 L Mouland } 9-hole course
Am–69 Phil Daniel (18 hole course)

V'trs U
Fees D–£7 (W/E & BH–£8) W–£28 concessions for groups and in winter
Loc 2½ miles NW of town centre
Course playable throughout the year

Carmarthen (1907)
Private (Map 10/5)
Blaenycoed Road Carmarthen
Tel **Carmarthen 87214**
Mem 600
Sec Frank Coleman Tel Carmarthen 87588
Pro Pat Gillis
Holes 18 L 6212 yds SSS 71
Recs Am–69 BET Wheeler
Pro–69 B Barnes
V'trs U
Fees £5.50 (£6.50)
Loc 4 miles NW of Carmarthen

Cilgwyn (1977)
Private (Map 10/8)
Llangybi Lampeter Dyfed SA48 8NN
Tel **(0570-45) 286**
Mem 120
Sec JL Jones Tel (0570) 422375
Pro
Holes 9 L 5318 yds SSS 67
Recs Am–66 DG Evans
Pro–69 D Creamer
V'trs U SOC
Fees £5 (£6.50) W–£20
Loc 4 miles NE of Lampeter off A485 at Llangybi

Glynhir (1909)
Private (Map 10/6)
Glynhir Road Llandybie nr Ammanford SA18 2TF
Tel **0269 850472**
Mem 341
Sec JT Thomas Tel Llandybie 850571 EP Rees Tel Ammanford 2345
Pro Richard Playle
Holes 18 L 6090 yds SSS 70
Recs Am–67 Philip Child
Pro–
V'trs U SOC on WD
Fees £3 (£4) winter months; £6 (W/E & BH £7) summer months
Loc 3½ miles N of Ammanford

Haverfordwest (1904)
Private (Map 10/7)
Arnolds Down Haverfordwest
Tel **Haverfordwest 3585**
Mem 400
Sec MA Harding Tel Haverfordwest 3565
Pro Alex Pile Tel Haverfordwest 68409
Holes 18 L 5945 yds SSS 70
Recs Am–
Pro–
V'trs U
Fees £5.50 (£7) Mon-Sat–£28
Loc 1 mile Haverfordwest Carmarthen Road

Milford Haven (1913)
Private (Map 10/9)
Hubbertson Milford Haven
Tel **Milford Haven 2368**
Mem 189 47(L) 34(J)
Sec TA Elder Tel Milford Haven 2521 or 3424 (home)
Pro Alex Pile
Holes 18 L 6071 yds SSS 71

Recs Am–76
Pro–71 B Hugget
V'trs U SOC
Fees £6
Loc West boundary Milford Haven

Newport (Pembs) (1925)

Private **(Map 10/10)**
Newport Dyfed
Tel **(0239) 820244**
Mem 350
Sec Ron Dietrich
Pro
Holes 9 L 3089 yds SSS 69
Recs Am–
Pro–
V'trs U SOC
Fees £5.50 (£6.50) W–£22
Loc Newport Sands

St Davids City (1903)

Private **(Map 10/11)**
Whitesands St Davids Dyfed
Tel **St Davids 721620**
Mem 100 (including Country and Juniors)
Sec DR Thomas Tel St Davids 721620
Pro
Holes 9 L 5171 yds SSS 65
Recs Am–67 JC Evans
Pro–67 TRA Davies
V'trs U SOC on WDs
Fees £5, with mem £4
Loc w miles W of St Davids near Whitesands Beach

South Pembrokeshire (1970)

Private **(Map 10/12)**
Defensible Barracks Pembroke Dock
Tel **Pembroke 683817**
Mem 250
Sec GW Thomas Tel Pembroke 682035
Pro
Holes 9 (different tees back 9) L 2901 yds SSS 69
Recs Am–66 S Toy
Pro–
V'trs U (before 4.30 pm); SOC on WD
Fees £4 W–£10
Loc Pembroke Dock

Tenby (1888)

Private **(Map 10/13)**
The Burrows Tenby Dyfed
Tel **Tenby 2787**
Mem 500
Sec TR Arnold Tel Tenby 2978
Pro T Mountford Tel Tenby 4447
Holes 18 L 6450 yds SSS 71
Recs Am–66 G Clement
Pro–
V'trs U
Fees £8.50 (£10) W–£38.50 (Reduced in winter)
Loc Tenby

Gwent

Blackwood (1914)

Private **(Map 10/1)**
Cwmgelli Blackwood Gwent
Tel **Blackwood 223152**
Mem 300
Sec R Bennett Tel as above or Blackwood 223454 (home)
Pro
Holes 9 L 5304 yds SSS 66
Recs Am–65 DL Stevens
Pro–64 F Hill
V'trs I; SOC; U
Fees £4 (W/E & BH–£5)
Loc ¼ mile N of Blackwood

Caerleon (1974)

Public **(Map 10/2)**
Broadway Caerleon Gwent
Tel **Caerleon 420342**
Mem
Sec Leisure Services Dept Civic Centre Newport Gwent
Pro Alex Campbell
Holes 9 L 3092 yds SSS
Recs Am–
Pro–
V'trs U
Fees £1.60 (£2.20)
Loc 3 miles off M4 Junction 25

Greenmeadow (1980)

Private **(Map 10/3)**
Treherbert Road Cwmbran
Tel **Cwmbran 69321**
Mem 430
Sec PJ Richardson
Pro G Harding (06333) 62626
Holes 9 L 3109 yds SSS 70
Recs Am–
Pro–
V'trs W/D U W/E after 1 pm SOC
Fees £3 (£4.50)
Loc On B4042 4 miles from Newport

Llanwern (1928)

Private **(Map 10/4)**
Golf House Tennyson Ave Llanwern Gwent NP6 2DY
Tel Llanwern 412380
Mem 625
Sec D Baguley Tel Llanwern 412029
Pro S Price Tel Llanwern 415233
Holes 18 L 6139 yds SSS 69
9 L 5686 yds SSS 70
Recs Am–65 K Fitzgerald
Pro–68 P Alliss
V'trs WD–U; W/E–restricted; I H SOC
Fees D–£6
Loc 2 miles W town

Monmouth (1921)

Private **(Map 10/5)**
Leasebrook Lane Monmouth
Tel **Monmouth 2212**
Mem 350
Sec KA Prichard Tel Dean 33394
Pro
Holes 9 L 5454 yds SSS 66
Recs Am–65 DJ Wills
Pro–68 DR Hemming
V'trs U SOC
Fees £5 (£7)
Loc Signposted 1 mile along A40 (Monmouth-Ross)
Mis Catering every day exc Mon

Monmouthshire (1892)

Private **(Map 10/6)**
Llanfoist Abergavenny
Tel **0873 3171**
Mem 480 106(L) 90(J)
Sec GJ Swayne Tel 0873 2606
Pro P Worthing Tel 0873 2532
Holes 18 L 6045 yds SSS 69
Recs Am–64 WI Tucker
Pro–62 D Thomas
V'trs U H SOC
Fees £8 (£12)
Loc 2 miles Abergavenny Station

Newport (1903)

Private **(Map 10/7)**
Great Oak Rogerstone Newport NP1 6FX
Tel **892683/894496**
Mem 650
Sec Gordon Kay Tel 982643
Pro R Skuse Tel 893271
Holes 18 L 6370 yds SSS 71
Recs Am–67 G Davies
Pro–67 M Hughes
V'trs U; SOC on WD exc Tue; Sat 1 pm-4 pm–M
Fees £12 (£15)
Loc 3 miles Newport on B4591
1 mile M4 (Junc 27) on B4591

Pontnewydd (1875)

Private **(Map 10/8)**
Maesgwyn Farm West Pontnewydd Cwmbran
Tel **Cwmbran 2170**
Mem 235
Sec HR Gabe Tel Cwmbran 67185
Pro
Holes 10 L 5340 yds SSS 67
Recs Am–63 M Hayward
Pro–
V'trs WD–U SOC W/E–M
Fees £6
Loc Western outskirts of Cwmbran

Pontypool (1903)

Private **(Map 10/9)**
Trevethin Pontypool
Tel **Pontypool 3655**
Mem 402 81(L) 78(J)
Sec J Huckin Tel Pon 55802
Pro J Howard Tel Pon 55544
Holes 18 L 6070 yds SSS 69
Recs Am–64 M Hayward
Pro–67 I Richardson
V'trs U
Fees £7 (£8)
Loc 1 mile N of Pontypool

The Rolls of Monmouth (1982)

Private **(Map 10/10)**
The Hendre Monmouth
Mem 200
Sec JD Ross Tel 0600 5353
Pro
Holes 18 L 6723 yds SSS 72
Rec Am–71 D Wills
Pro–68 M Thomas
V'trs U
Fees £12.50
Loc 3½ miles W of Monmouth on B4233

St Mellons (1937)

Private **(Map 10/11)**
St Mellons Cardiff CF3 8XS
Tel **Castleton 680401**
Mem 544 93(L) 68(J) 27(5)
Sec F Newling Tel Castleton 680408
Pro E Foster Tel Castleton 680101
Holes 18 L 6225 yds SSS 70
Recs Am–68 N Hayward
Pro–66 E Foster
V'trs WD–U; W/E–M
Fees £10 WD
Loc 4 miles E of Cardiff on A48

St Pierre (1962)

Private **(Map 10/12)**
Chepstow Gwent NP6 6YA
Tel **(02912) 5261**

Mem
Man T Latty Tel (02912) 5261
Sec TJ Cleary Tel (02912) 5261
Pro Renton Doig Tel (02912) 5261
Holes 18 L 6700 yds SSS 73
18 L 5762 yds SSS 68
Recs Old: Am–69 AM Williams
Pro–63 H Henning
New: Am–63 M Bearcroft
V'trs H SOC on WD
Fees On application
Loc 2 miles W of Chepstow (A48)

Tredegar Park (1923)

Private **(Map 10/13)**
Bassaleg Road Newport
Tel **Newport 895219**
Mem 800
Sec AA Skinner DFM Tel Newport 894433
Pro Merfyn L Morgan Tel Newport 894517
Holes 18 L 6044 yds SSS 70
Recs Am–68 W Glyn Thomas
Pro–
V'trs I
Fees £8 (£10)
Loc Off Junction 27 M4

Tredegar and Rhymney (1921)

Private **(Map 10/14)**
Tredegar Rhymney
Tel **840743**
Mem 182
Sec Viv Davies Tel 6096
Pro
Holes 9 L 5564 yds SSS 67
Recs Am–34 CL Jones
Pro–33 WS Phillips
V'trs U
Fees £4, £2 with mem
Loc 1½ miles W of Tredegar

West Monmouthshire (1906)

Private **(Map 10/15)**
Nantyglo
Tel **Brynmawr 310233**
Mem 200
Sec CJ Lewis Tel 312746
Pro
Holes 18 L 6132 yds SSS 69
Recs Am–67 R Phillips
Pro–70 W Moses
V'trs U
Fees £4 (W/E & BH–£5)
Loc Nr Dunlop Semtex Brynmawr
Mis Highest tee in Wales, 14th, 1450 ft above sea level

Gwynedd

Aberdovey (1892)

Private **(Map 10/1)**
Aberdovey LL35 0RT
Tel **065 472 210**
Mem 800
Sec John M Griffiths Tel 065 472 493
Pro J Davies Tel 065 472 602
Holes 18 L 6445 yds SSS 71
Recs Am–69 PMS Low
Pro–67 J Smith
V'trs NA–8.25 am–9.30 am
11.45 am–12.45 pm
Fees £8.50 (£10)
Loc W end of Aberdovey

Abersoch (1907)

Private **(Map 10/2)**
Abersoch Gwynedd
Tel **Abersoch 2622**
Mem 600
Sec Peter Jones Tel Abersoch 2622
Pro
Holes 9 L 5800 yds SSS 68
Recs Am–
Pro–
V'trs U SOC
Fees On application
Loc Abersoch ½ mile S of village centre

Bala (1973)

Private **(Map 10/4)**
Penlan Bala Gwynedd LL23 7SW
Tel **0678 520 359**
Mem 250
Sec JR Jones Tel 0678 520 359
Pro
Holes 10 L 4934 yds SSS 64
Recs Am–64 DB Akroyd
Pro–
V'trs U SOC on WD
Fees £5 (£7) with mem half price
Loc ½ mile NW Bala

Betws-y-Coed

(Map 10/6)
Clubhouse Betws-y-Coed Gwynedd LL24
Tel **BYC 556**
Mem 250
Sec GB Archer Tel BYC 556
Pro J Waugh Tel BYC 556
Holes 9 L 2515 yds SSS 32
Recs Am–64 H Greenslade
Pro–
V'trs U SOC
Fees £5.50 (W/E & BH–£7.50)
Loc ½ mile off A5 in centre of village
Mis 18 holes different tee SSS 64

Caernarfon (1907)

Private **(Map 10/8)**
Llanfaglan Caernarfon LL54 5RP
Tel **3783**
Mem 300
Sec WT Matthews Tel Caernarfon 3555
Pro
Holes 18 L 5859 yds SSS 69
Recs Am–
Pro–66
V'trs U
Fees £6
Loc 2½ miles Caernarfon

Conwy (Caernarvonshire) (1890)

Private **(Map 10/9)**
Conway
Tel **Conway 3400**
Mem 700
Sec EC Roberts Tel Conway 2423
Pro JP Lees Tel Conway 3225
Holes 18 L 6901 yds SSS 73
Recs Am–
Pro–
V'trs W/E restricted; SOC
Fees £6.50 (£8)
Loc ½ mile W side of town walls

Criccieth (1905)

Private **(Map 10/10)**
Ednyfed Hill Criccieth
Tel **Criccieth 2154**
Mem 200
Sec DT Moores Tel Porthmadog (0766) 4137
Pro
Holes 18 L 5755 yds SSS 68
Recs Am–
Pro–
V'trs U
Fees £5 W–£25
Loc 18 miles S of Caernarfon, 4 miles W of Portmadoc. Within ½ mile of centre of Criccieth

Dolgellau (1911)

Private **(Map 10/11)**
Pencefn Road Dolgellau Gwynedd
Tel **(0341) 422603**
Mem 300
Sec PM Jones Tel (0341) 423116
Pro
Holes 9 L 4512 yds SSS 62
Recs Am–
Pro–
V'trs U SOC
Fees D–£5 W–£20
Loc ½ mile from town

Ffestiniog (1890)

Private **(Map 10/12)**
Ffestiniog
Tel **Ffestiniog (076676) 2612**
Mem 109
Sec A Pritchard
Pro
Holes 9 L 5032 metres SSS 66
Recs Am–
Pro–
V'trs U
Fees £3 (£2 with member) W–£10
Loc Bala Road, 1 mile from village

Llandudno (Maesdu) (1915)

Private **(Map 10/14)**
Hospital Road Llandudno Gwynedd LL30 1HU
Tel **Llandudno (0492) 76450**
Mem 875
Sec J Hallam Tel Llandudno 76450
Pro S Boulden Tel Llandudno 75195
Holes 18 L 6513 yds Par 73
Recs Am–67 G Jones CT Brown
Pro–66 PJ Butler
V'trs U; SOC; members of recognised GC welcome any day
Fees £7 (£8)
Loc 1 mile S Llandudno Station

Llandudno (North Wales) (1894)

Private **(Map 10/18**
72 Bryniau Road West Shore Llandudno Gwynedd LL30 2DZ
Tel **(0492) 75325**
Mem 550
Sec Mrs JC Window Tel (0492) 75325
Pro JF Waugh Tel (0492) 76878
Holes 18 L 6132 yds SSS 69
Recs Am–66 JHM Williams
Pro–63 WS Collins
V'trs U SOC (Ring Sec for restrictions)
Fees £7 (£8) W–£25
Loc ¾ mile from Llandudno town centre

Llanfairfechan (1971)

Private **(Map 10/15)**
Llannerch Road Llanfairfechan LL33 0EB
Tel **(0248) 680144**
Mem 330

Sec AC Williams
Pro
Holes 9 L 3119 yds SSS 57
Recs Am–
Pro–
V'trs U
Fees £3 (£4)
Loc Off A55 7 miles from Bangor

Nefyn and District (1907)
Private **(Map 10/17)**
Nefyn
Tel **Nefyn 720218**
Mem 700
Sec Lt Col RW Parry Tel Nefyn 720966
Pro JR Pilkington Tel Nefyn 720218
Holes 18 L 6346 yds SSS 71
Recs Am–68 TG Gruffydd
Pro–67 Ian Woosnam
V'trs U SOC
Fees £7.50 (£9.50)
Loc 1½ miles W of Nefyn

Penmaenmawr (1910)
Private **(Map 10/19)**
Conway Old Road Penmaenmawr Gwynedd LL34 6RD
Tel **(0492) 623330**
Mem 500
Sec Mrs JE Jones Tel (0492) 622085
Pro
Holes 9 L 5143 yds SSS 66
Recs Am–65 Mark Bellis
Pro–
V'trs U
Fees £4 (£6)
Loc 4 miles W of Conway

Portmadoc (1900)
Private **(Map 10/20)**
Morfa Bychan Porthmadog
Tel **0766 2037**
Mem 500
Sec Capt DG Thomas
Pro P Bright Tel 0766 3828
Holes 18 L 5838 yds SSS 68
Recs Am–63 J Morrow
Pro–
V'trs U welcome SOC
Fees £6 (£7) W–£25
Loc 2 miles West of town on road to Black Rock Sands

Pwllheli (1900)
Private **(Map 10/21)**
Pwllheli
Tel **(0758) 612520**
Mem 550
Sec R Eric Williams Tel (0758) 612520
Pro GD Verity
Holes 18 L 6110 yds SSS 69
Recs Am–68 Gwyndaf Jones P Morgan RT Jones
Pro–67 D Screeton
V'trs U
Fees On application
Loc ½ mile SW of town centre

Rhos-on-Sea Residential (1899)
Private **(Map 10/22)**
Penrhyn Bay Llandudno
Tel **Llandudno 49641**
Mem 500
Sec Trevor Frame (Dormy House)
Pro Michael Greenough
Holes 18 L 6064 yds SSS 69
Recs Am–64 J Roger Jones
Pro–
V'trs U
Fees On application
Loc On coast at Rhos-on-Sea

Royal St David's (1894)
Private **(Map 10/23)**
Harlech Gwynedd LL46 2UB
Tel **(0766) 780 203**
Mem 600
Sec/ Man HL Fairbrother Tel (0766) 780361
Pro John Barnett
Holes 18 L 6427 yds SSS 71
Recs Am–66 JL Morgan
Pro–66 JL Black
V'trs U SOC
Fees D–£9 (D–£12) incl VAT W–£38
Loc W of Harlech
Mis Buggies £10 per round

St Deiniol (1905)
Private **(Map 10/24)**
Bangor LL57 1PX
Tel **Bangor 353098**
Mem 330
Sec DW Fox
Pro P Lees
Holes 18 L 5036 metres SSS 67
Recs Am–
Pro–
V'trs U (Members of recognised clubs)
Fees £2 (£3)
Loc Off A5 eastern side of Bangor

Isle of Anglesey

Anglesey (1914)
Private **(Map 10/3)**
Rhosneigr
Tel **Rhosneigr 810219**
Mem 500
Sec RD Jones Tel Gwalchmai 720533
Pro Paul Roberts Tel Rhosneigr 810703
Holes 18 L 6204 yds SSS 70
Recs Am–68 GW Jones
D McLean
Pro–68 D Parsonage
V'trs U
Fees £5 W/E & BH–£6.50
Loc 8 miles from Holyhead

Baron Hill (1895)
Private **(Map 10/5)**
Beaumaris Anglesey LL58 8YW
Tel **(0248) 810231**
Mem 360
Sec Idris Owen Tel (0248) 810231 (club) (0248) 712333 (home)
Pro Peter Maton Tel (0248) 810231
Holes 9 L 5062 metres SSS 67
Recs Am–65 AW Jones
Pro–
V'trs U exc comp days; SOC on WD and Sat, apply Sec
Fees £5 (W/E & BH £6) W–£20
Loc 1 mile NW Beaumaris

Bull Bay (1913)
(Map 10/7)
Amlwch Anglesey Gwynedd
Tel **Amlwch 830960**
Mem 650
Sec BC Martyn Tel Amlwch 830960
Pro Stephen Tarrant Tel Amlwch 831188
Holes 18 L 6160 yds White Tees (5952 Yellow Tees) SSS 70
Recs Am–66 D McLean Aled Llyr
Pro–65 M Barton
V'trs U SOC
Fees £5 (£7); 1/11–31/3 £3 20% discount for 12 or more
Loc ½ mile Amlich

Holyhead (1912)
Private **(Map 10/13)**
Trearddur Bay Anglesey
Tel **Holyhead 3279**
Mem 484 225(L) 109(J)
Sec AJ Becker Tel Holyhead 3279
Pro P Capper Tel Holyhead 2022
Holes Am–64 D McLean
Pro–69 H Gould
V'trs H SOC
Fees On application
Loc 1 mile from Holyhead Station

Llangefni (1983)
Public **(Map 10/16)**
Llangefni Public Golf Course Llangefni Anglesey
Tel **Llangefni (0248) 722193**
Mem
Sec Paul Wiggins
Pro Paul Wiggins
Holes 9 L 1467 yds SSS
Recs Am–
Pro–
V'trs U
Fees £1.10 (£1.60); Jrs & OAPs 60p (80p)
Loc ½ mile from town centre on B5111

Mid Glamorgan

Aberdare (1921)
Private **(Map 10/1)**
Abernant Aberdare
Tel **Aberdare 871188**
Mem 500
Sec JL Jenkins Tel Aberdare 873387
Pro AW Palmer Tel 878735
Holes 18 L 5875 yds SSS 69
Recs Am–66 J Roger Jones
Pro–67 AW Palmer
V'trs U
Fees £6 (£7) W–£25
Loc ½ mile from town centre

Bargoed (1912)
Private **(Map 10/2)**
Heolddu Bargoed
Tel **Bargoed 830143**
Mem 385
Sec M Davies Tel Bargoed 830312
Pro W Clarke Tel Bargoed 830312
Holes 18 L 6012 yds SSS 69
Recs Am–64 T Holder
Pro–67 E Foster
V'trs WD–U; W/E–M
Fees £5
Loc NW boundary Bargoed

Bryn Meadows G & CC (1973)
Private **(Map 10/3)**
The Bryn Nr Hengoed
Tel **Blackwood 225590/227276**
Mem 440
Sec B Mayo
Pro Alex Campbell Tel (0495) 221905
Holes 18 L 6138 yds SSS 69
Recs Am–66 Glyn Davies
Pro–69 Stephen Price
V'trs U
Fees £5 (£7)
Loc 12 miles from Newport, Gwent

Caerphilly (1906)

Private (Map 10/4)
Mountain Road Caerphilly CF8 1HJ
Tel **0222 883481**
Mem 695
Sec JH Beynon Tel 0222 863441
Pro E McDonald Tel 0222 869104
Holes 14 L 6063 yds SSS 71
Recs Am–67 AW Norman
Pro–68 B Huggett
V'trs WD–U; W/E–M
Fees £7 W–£20 M–£50
Loc 7 miles N of Cardiff off A469 1 mile from railway and bus stations

Creigiau (1921)

Private (Map 10/16)
Creigiau Cardiff CF4 8NN
Tel **Pentyrch (0222) 890263**
Mem 472
Sec D Bryan Jones Tel (0222) 890263
Pro Andrew Kerr Smith Tel (0222) 891909
Holes 18 L 5715 yds SSS 68
Recs Am–69 D Samuel
Pro–
V'trs WD–U; W/E & BH–M; SOC on WD
Fees £7
Loc 5 miles NW of Cardiff

Llantrisant and Pontyclun (1927)

Private (Map 10/5)
Talbot Green Llantrisant
Tel **Llantrisant 222148**
Mem 500
Sec
Pro JJ Hastings
Holes 12 L 5712 yds SSS 68
Recs Am–66 DL Stevens
V'trs WD–U; W/E & BH–M
Fees £5
Loc 10 miles N of Cardiff

Maesteg (1912)

Private (Map 10/6)
Mount Pleasant Maesteg
Tel **Maesteg 732037**
Mem 390
Sec A Brace Tel Maesteg 733061
Pro WW Evans
Holes 18 L 5818 yds SSS 69
Recs Am–69 J James
Pro–
V'trs U
Fees £5 (£6)
Loc 1 mile W of Maesteg

Merthyr Tydfil (1908)

Private (Map 10/7)
Cilsanws Mountain Cefn Coed nr Merthyr Tydfil CF48 2HW
Tel **Merthyr Tydfil 3308**
Mem 148 54(L) 27(J)
Sec DN Davies Tel Merthyr 3063
Pro
Holes 9 L 5794 yds SSS 68
Recs Am–70 N Evans
Pro–70 J Howard
V'trs U
Fees £3 (£5)
Loc Off A470

Morlais Castle (1900)

Private (Map 10/8)
Pant Dowlais Merthyr Tydfil
Tel **Merthyr Tydfil 2822**
Mem 300
Sec Geoffrey Morgan Tel (0685) 2822
Pro
Holes 9 L 6258 yds SSS 71
Recs Am–
V'trs U exc 12 pm–4 pm Sat; SOC on WD
Fees £4; with mem £3 M–£25
Loc 3 miles N of Merthyr Tydfil

Mountain Ash (1907)

Private (Map 10/9)
Cefnpennar
Tel **Mountain Ash 472265**
Mem 555
Sec Geoffrey Matthews Tel Mountain Ash 474022
Pro J Sims Tel Aberdare 882835
Holes 18 L 5535 yds SSS 68
Recs Am–63 SJ Lewis
Pro–66 R Evans
V'trs U
Fees £6 (£8)
Loc 9 miles NW Pontypridd

Pontypridd (1905)

Private (Map 10/10)
Tygwyn Road Pontypridd
Tel **Pontypridd 402359**
Mem 500
Sec AM Thomas Tel Pontypridd 402469
Pro N Meatheringham Tel Pontypridd 491210
Holes 18 L 5650 yds SSS 68
Recs Am–
Pro–
V'trs U SOC on WDs
Fees £6 (£9)
Loc Pontypridd

Pyle and Kenfig (1922)

Private (Map 10/11)
Waun-y-Mer Kenfig CF33 4PU
Tel **Porthcawl 3093**
Mem 860
Sec RC Thomas Tel Porthcawl 3093
Pro Robert Evans Tel Porthcawl 772446
Holes 18 L 6655 yds SSS 73
Recs Am–70 S Cox S Curiel N Evans
Pro–68 D Matthew M Steadman C Gray
V'trs WD–U; W/E–M
Fees £9
Loc Porthcawl 2 miles

Rhondda (1910)

Private (Map 10/12)
Penrhys Pontygwaith Rhondda
Tel **Tonypandy 433204**
Mem 350
Sec CG Phillips
Pro
Holes 18 L 6428 yds SSS 71
Recs Am–K Thomas
Pro–
V'trs U
Fees £6 (£6)
Loc

Royal Porthcawl (1891)

Private (Map 10/13)
Porthcawl
Tel **Porthcawl 2251**
Mem 500 220(L) 85(J)
Sec Sqn Ldr DW Samuel
Pro Graham Poor Tel Porthcawl 6984
Holes 18 L 6605 yds SSS 74
Recs Am–70 JWH Mitchell
John Povall
Pro–65 Brian Barnes
V'trs I SOC
Fees £12 (£14)
Loc 14 miles E Swansea

Southerndown (1905)

Private (Map 10/14)
Ewenny Bridgend Mid Glam CF35 5BT
Tel **Southerndown 880326**
Mem 650
Sec C Roberts Tel S'down 880476
Pro DG McMonagle Tel S'down 880326
Holes 18 L 6705 yds SSS 73
Recs Am–66 Hogan Stott
Pro–64 Guy Hunt
V'trs WD & Sats–U; Sundays & BH–M; SOC Tue & Thu; H
Fees £8.50 (£12)
Loc Ewenny Ogmore-by-Sea Nr Ogmore Castle ruins

Whitehall (1922)

Private (Map 10/15)
The Pavilion Nelson Treharris
Tel **Abercynon 740245**
Mem 320
Sec EJ Whiteaker Tel 0443 740245
Pro Eddie Clark Tel 0222 614660
Holes 9 L 5750 yds SSS 68
Recs Am–66 M Heames
Pro–Old course 62 Ian Woosnam
New course 68 Simon Cox
V'trs WD–U; W/E–M
Fees £5 £3 with member
Loc 15 miles NW of Cardiff

Powys

Aberdovey

(see Gwynedd)

Brecon (1902)

Private (Map 10/1)
Llanfaes Brecon
Tel **Brecon 2004**
Mem 210
Sec GN Pugh Tel Brecon 3793
Pro
Holes 9 L 5218 yds SSS 66
Recs Am–61 R Dixon
Pro–66 WO Moses
V'trs U
Fees £3 (£4)
Loc ½ mile from town on A40

Builth Wells (1923)

Private (Map 10/2)
Golf Club Road Builth Wells Powys LD2 3NN
Tel **Builth Wells 553296**
Mem 250
Sec TE Turner Tel 553296
Pro A Forrester
Holes 9 L 5235 yds SSS 66
Recs Am–
Pro–
V'trs U SOC
Fees £5 (£7)
Loc Llandovery Road

Cradoc (1967)

Private (Map 10/3)
Penoyre Park Cradoc Brecon
Tel **Brecon 3658**

Mem 363
Sec BI Jones and JSW Davies
Pro John Staples
Holes 18 L 6234 yds SSS 71
Recs Am–65 DK Wood
Pro–
V'trs U SOC
Fees £6 (£9)
Loc 2 miles NW Brecon

Knighton (1913)

Private **(Map 10/4)**
Little Ffrydd Wood Knighton Powys
Tel **528646**
Mem 124
Sec PJ Isherwood Tel Knighton 528917
Pro
Holes 9 L 5320 yds SSS 66
Recs Am–66 M Caine
Pro–71 H Vardon
V'trs U SOC
Fees £3 (£5)
Loc ½ mile SW of Knighton

Llandrindod (1905)

Private **(Map 10/5)**
Llandrindod Wells
Tel **2010**
Mem 180 30(L) 50(J)
Sec MG Williams Tel 2059
Pro
Holes 18 L 5749 yds SSS 68
Recs Am–68 K Millican
Pro–
V'trs U
Fees £6 (£6)
Loc 1 mile E of Llandrindod Wells

Machynlleth (1905)

Private **(Map 10/6)**
Maes-y-Golen Machynlleth
Tel **Machynlleth 2000**
Mem 200
Sec WG and EA Evans Tel 2246 & 2969
Pro
Holes 9 L 5726 yds SSS 67
Recs Am–65
Pro–65
V'trs W/D–U; W/E–NA or M
Fees £4 (£4.50)
Loc Off A489, 1 mile E of town clock

Newtown (1919)

Private **(Map 10/7)**
Pool Road Newtown Powys
Tel **Newtown 25844**
Mem 320
Sec TL Dyke (0686) 25650
Pro DP Owen (0686) 25844
Holes 9 L 5864 yds SSS 68
Recs Am–64 AP Parkin
Pro–68 CB Jones
V'trs WD & BH–I; W/E–restricted
Fees £4 (W/E & BH & SOC–£5)
Loc ¾ mile E of town centre
Mis No steward exc Mon (Tel 27727)

Old Rectory Country Club (1968)

Private **(Map 10/8)**
Llangattock Crickhowell
Tel **Crickhowell 810373**
Mem 220
Sec RC Jones
Pro
Holes 9 L 1409 yds SSS 54
Recs Am–
Pro–
V'trs U (Ex competitions)
Fees £2.50 (£2.50)
Loc 8 miles W of Abergavenny

St Idloes

Private **(Map 10/9)**
Penrhalt Llanidloes
Tel **Llanidloes 2559**
Mem 120
Sec A Wynn Edwards Tel 2205
Pro
Holes 9 L 5210 yds SSS 66
Recs Am–63 J Davies
Pro–
V'trs U
Fees £3 (£4) W–£12
Loc ½ mile on Trefeglwys Road

Welshpool (1929)

Private **(Map 10/10)**
Golfa Hill Welshpool
Tel **Castle Caereinion 249**
Mem 250
Sec RGD Jones Tel Welshpool (0938) 3377
Pro
Holes 18 L 5708 yds SSS 69
Recs Am–65 DH Ryan
Pro–69 S Bowen
V'trs U
Fees £4 (£5)
Loc 4½ miles Welshpool on Dolgellau Road

South Glamorgan

Brynhill (1921)

Private **(Map 10/1)**
Port Road Colcot Barry
Tel **Barry 735061**
Mem 700
Sec DP Lloyd Tel Barry 720277
Pro P Fountain Tel Barry 733660
Holes 18 L 6000 yds SSS 69
Recs Am–68 P Cooper
Pro–
V'trs WD & Sat–U; Sun–M; SOC on WD
Fees £7.50 with mem £5 (Sat £10; with mem £7.50) SOC £5
Loc A4050 8 miles W of Cardiff

Cardiff (1921)

Private **(Map 10/2)**
Sherborne Avenue Cyncoed Cardiff
Tel **Cardiff 753067**
Mem 700
Sec R Morgan Tel 753320
Pro PD Johnson Tel 754772
Holes 18 L 6015 yds SSS 70
Recs Am–65 JL Toye
Pro– 65 D Ridley I Woosnam
V'trs WD–H; W/E–M
Fees £10
Loc 3 miles NE from centre of Cardiff 2 miles off Pentwyn exit of A48M

Dinas Powis (1914)

Private **(Map 10/4)**
Dinas Powis
Tel **Dinas Powis 512157**
Mem 650
Sec JD Hughes Tel 512727
Pro G Bennett
Holes 18 L 5377 yds SSS 66
Recs Am–67 Dr HD Maurice
Pro–67 P Fountain
V'trs U
Fees £7 (WD & BH–£9) Reduction if playing with member
Loc 3 miles W of Cardiff

Glamorganshire (1890)

Private **(Map 10/5)**
Lavernock Road Penarth CF6 2UP
Tel **(0222) 707048**
Mem
Sec GC Crimp Tel (0222) 701185
Pro A Kerr-Smith Tel (0222) 707401
Holes 18 L 6150 yds SSS 70
Recs Am–65 MG Mouland
Pro–65 A Jacklin
V'trs W/E & BH–M; WD–H SOC
Fees £8 (£10)
Loc 5 miles SW of Cardiff

Llanishen (1905)

Private **(Map 10/6)**
Cwm Lisvane nr Cardiff CF4 5UD
Tel **(0222) 752205**
Mem 800
Sec Elfed T Davies Tel (0222) 755078
Pro RA Jones Tel (0222) 755076
Holes 18 L 5296 yds SSS 66
Recs Am–64 MJG Strange
Pro–63 JT Taylor
V'trs WD–U; W/E–M; H; SOC
Fees £9
Loc 5 miles N Cardiff

Maesteg

(see Mid-Glamorgan)

Pyle & Kenfig

(see Mid-Glamorgan)

Radyr (1902)

Private **(Map 10/7)**
Radyr nr Cardiff CF4 8BS
Tel **Radyr 842442**
Mem 880
Sec Major MB Richards Tel 842408
Pro Steve Gough Tel 842476
Holes 18 L 6031 yds SSS 70
Recs Am–65 J Jermine
Pro–65 R Kemp
V'trs WD–U H; W/E–M SOC on Wed and Fri
Fees £9 (£12)
Loc 5 miles NW of Cardiff

RAF St Athan (1977)

Private **(Map 10/8)**
Barry, S Glamorgan CF6 9WA
Tel **St Athan 751043**
Mem 370
Sec PJ Power Tel Llantwit Major 6204
Pro
Holes 9 L 5957 yds SSS 69
Recs Am–
Pro–
V'trs U; Sun am–NA
Fees £5
Loc 2 miles E Llantwit Major

Royal Porthcawl

(see Mid-Glamorgan)

Southerndown

(see Mid-Glamorgan)

Wenvoe Castle (1936)

Private (Map 10/9)
Wenvoe nr Cardiff
Tel **Cardiff 591094**
Mem 500 90(L) 50(J)
Sec Mrs LM James Tel Cardiff 594371
Pro MA Pycroft Cardiff 593649
Holes 18 L 6422 yds SSS 71
Recs Am–65 R Jones
Pro–64 P Elson
V'trs I
Fees WD–£7
Loc 4 miles W of Cardiff

Whitchurch (Cardiff) (1915)

Private (Map 10/10)
Pantmawr Road Whitchurch Cardiff CF4 6XD
Tel **Cardiff 620125**
Mem 530 239(L) 59(J)
Sec Tel Cardiff 620985
Pro E Clark Tel 614660
Holes 18 L 6245 yds SSS 70
Recs Am–62 John Povall
Pro–62 Ian Woosnam
V'trs WD–H; W/E & BH–M
Fees £10
Loc 3 miles NW Cardiff on A470 2 of junction 32 M4

West Glamorgan

Clyne (1920)

Private (Map 10/1)
118, Owls Lodge Lane Mayals Swansea
Tel **Swansea 401989**
Mem 450
Sec Brian R Player
Pro ES Turner Tel Swansea 402094
Holes 18 L 6312 yds SSS 71
Recs Am–66 C Dickens
Pro–66 J Bland
V'trs U
Fees £7 (£8)
Loc Swansea

Fairwood Park (1970)

Private (Map 10/2)
Upper Killay Swansea
Tel **Swansea (0792) 203648**
Mem 300
Sec GH Edmond
Pro S Lloyd
Holes 18 L 6606 yds SSS 72
Recs Am–69
Pro–68
V'trs U SOC
Fees £7 £6 with mem (£10, £9 with mem)
Loc Swansea Airport $\frac{1}{4}$ mile

Glynneath (1931)

Private (Map 10/3)
Penygraig, Pontneathvaughan Neath
Tel **Glynneath 720452**
Mem 200
Sec RM Ellis Tel 720679
Pro
Holes 9 L 5472 yds SSS 68
Recs Am–66 JL Davies
Pro–
V'trs U
Fees £2.50 (£5)
Loc 10 miles N of Neath

Inco (1965)

Private (Map 10/4)
Clydach Swansea
Tel **Clydach 844216**
Mem 260
Sec DGS Murdoch Clydach 843336
Pro
Holes 13 L 5976 yds SSS 69
Recs Am–68 V Smith N O'Sullivan
Pro–
V'trs U
Fees £3 (£4)
Loc Swansea Valley

Langland Bay (1904)

Private (Map 10/5)
Langland Bay Swansea SA3 4QR
Tel **(0792) 66023**
Mem 620
Sec SO Campbell Tel (0792) 61721
Pro TJ Lynch Tel (0792) 66186
Holes 18 L 5812 yds SSS 69
Recs Am–65 H Evans
Pro–69 D Ridley
V'trs U SOC
Fees £8 (£9)
Loc 6 miles W of Swansea

Morriston (1919)

Private (Map 10/6)
160 Clasemont Road Morriston Swansea SA6 6AJ
Tel **Swansea 71079**
Mem 400
Sec Leonard T Lewis Tel Swansea 796528
Pro DA Rees Tel Swansea 72335
Holes 18 L 5734 yds SSS 68
Recs Am–65 DR Richards
Pro–64 DA Rees
V'trs H; SOC on WD; U
Fees £5 (£6)
Loc Swansea 4 miles

Neath (1934)

Private (Map 10/7)
Cadoxton Neath
Tel **Neath 3615**
Mem 654
Sec JR Evans Tel Neath 52759
Pro EM Bennett
Holes 18 L 6460 yds SSS 72
Recs Am–70 G Heath-Davies
Pro–66 F Hill
V'trs U
Fees WD–£4 W/E–£5
Loc 2 miles from Neath

Palleg (1932)

Private (Map 10/8)
Palleg Road Lowes Cwmtwrch Swansea SA9 1QT
Tel **Glantawe 842193**
Mem 250
Sec GH Thomas Tel Glantawe 842524
Pro
Holes 9 L 3209 yds SSS 72
Recs Am–71 C Williams
Pro–
V'trs U
Fees £4 (£5)
Loc Upper Swansea Valley (Ystalyfera 1 mile)

Pennard (1896)

Private (Map 10/9)
Southgate Road Southgate nr Swansea SA3 2BT
Tel **(044128) 3131**
Mem 571
Sec JD Eccles Tel Bishopton 3131 or 3170
Pro M Bennett Tel Bishopston 3451
Holes 18 L 6274 yds SSS 71
Recs Am–69 H Guest
Pro–69–WW Evans
V'trs U SOC
Fees £8 (£9) W–£25
Loc 8 miles W of Swansea

Pontardawe (1924)

Private (Map 10/10)
Cefn Llan Pontardawe Swansea
Tel **0792 863118**
Mem 320
Sec John Burrington Tel 0792 863118
Pro
Holes 18 L 6061 yds SSS 69
Races Am–66 B Fisher
Pro–71 D Thomas R Brook
V'trs U
Fees £5 (£7.50)
Loc 5 miles N junction 45 on M4 (A4067)

Swansea Bay (1894)

Private (Map 10/11)
Jersey Marine Neath
Tel **Skewen 812198/814153**
Mem 400
Sec Mrs G Thomas
Pro M Day
Holes 18 L 6417 yds SSS 71
Recs Am–67 A Evans
Pro–
V'trs U
Fees £5 (£6.50)
Loc Between Briton Ferry/Swansea nr A48

Driving Ranges in Great Britain and Ireland

Ascot

Lavender Park Golf Centre

Swinley Road, Ascot. *Tel* Winkfield Row 4074.
Open 9 am-10 pm Mon-Fri; 9 am-9 pm weekends. 55 balls for £1. 115 balls for £1.50. Floodlit. 9 hole course, par 28.

Belfast

Knockbracken Golf Centre

Ballymaconaghy Road, Belfast. *Tel* Belfast 643554.
Open 9 am-11 pm. Floodlit. Also putting, 18 hole course. Snooker and pool tables.

Blackpool

Phoenix Sporting and Leisure Centre

Fleetwood Road, Norbreck, Blackpool. *Tel* Cleveleys 854846.
Open 9 am-dusk 7 days. £1.20 per basket. Floodlit. 18 bays. Bunkers, par 3. Professional. Licensed bar. Refreshment kiosk.

Bolton

Kearsley Golf Range Ltd

Moss Lane, Kearsley, Bolton BL4 8SF, Lancs. *Tel* Farnworth 75726.
Open 11 am-10 pm weekdays; 11 am-5 pm weekends. Floodlit. Covered tees. Grass tees. Professional ER Warburton *Tel* Farnworth 75726. Shop. Licensed bar. Snacks. 9 hole pitch and putt.

Chatham

Chatham Golf Centre

Street-End Road, Chatham, Kent. *Tel* Medway 48925.
Open 7 days, 10 am-10 pm. Floodlit. Professional tuition. Licensed bar. Food.

Chingford

Chingford Golf Range

Waltham Way, Chingford E4 8AQ. *Tel* 01-529 2409
New purpose-built two-tier golf range. 18 covered floodlit bays. All-weather putting green. Professional Gordon Goldie PGA. Open 9.30 am-10.00 pm weekdays, 9.00 am-9.00 pm weekends. 40 balls £1.20, 60 balls £1.50, 100 balls £2.20. Clubs for hire 35p each. PGA approved. Golf shop. Club repair service. Tuition by appointment. Video lessons. 1 mile N of North Circular Road at Chingford turn-off. 2 miles S of M25 Junction 26.

Cobham

Fairmile Hotel

Portsmouth Road, Cobham, Surrey. *Tel* Cobham 64419
Open 10 am-10 pm WD; 9 am-9 pm WE. 24 covered tees. Floodlit. Bunkers. Professional. Licensed restaurant. Putting green.

Colchester

Ardleigh Golf Range

Crown Inn, Ipswick Road, Ardleigh, Colchester. *Tel* Colchester 230974.
Open 10 am-9 pm Mon-Fri. 10 am-5 pm Sat/Sun. 50 balls £1.20. 100 balls £2. Floodlit. Club hire. Bunkers. Putting.

Colnbrook (Bucks)

Colnbrook Golf Driving Range

Gallymead Road, Colnbrook, Slough SL3 0EN. *Tel* Slough 682670/685127.
Open 7 days, 9.30 am-10.30 pm. Floodlit. Professional. Restaurant. Licensed. 5 mins from Junction 5 M4 or Junction 14 M25.

Coventry

John Reay Golf Centre

Sandpits Lane, Keresley, Coventry. *Tel* (020) 333 3404 or 3920.
Professional shop.

Croydon

Croydon Golf Centre

175 Long Lane, Addiscombe, Surrey. *Tel* 01-656 8396.
Open Mon-Fri 9 am-10 pm; Sat/Sun 9 am-9 pm. 40 balls £1.25; 80 balls £2.50; 110 balls £3. 26 covered tees. Floodlit. Professional Sec/Pro SB Bookless *Tel* 6568396. Licensed. 3 miles E of Croydon.

Dublin

Leopardstown Golf Centre

Foxrock. *Tel* Dublin 895341/895671.
Manager William Hourihane. 9 holes golf course; 18 holes Par 3 course 2795 yds. Public course. Green fees: £4, W/E–£4.50 (18 holes); Par 3–£3. Special reductions Jrs and ladies.
Driving range: 36 indoor bays, 50 outdoor bays. Floodlit. £1.30-£2. Open WD 10 am-10 pm, W/E– 9 am-6 pm.

Ealing

Rowdell Road, Northolt, Middlesex. *Tel* 01-845 4967.
Open 10 am-10.30 pm, 7 days. 36 covered tees. Putting. 35p large or 25p small bucket. Professional. Licensed.

Edinburgh

Port Royal Golf Range

Ingliston (next to airport). *Tel* 031-333 4377.
Open all year, 10 am-11 pm. 24 bays. Floodlit. 9 hole par 3 course. Large putting green. Lounge and snack bar.

Finchley

High Road, Finchley, London, N12. *Tel* 01-445 0411.
Open 10 am-10 pm, 7 days. Bucket 90p. 32 floodlit bays. Putting. Professional. Cafe.

Gloucester

Gloucester Hotel & Country Club

Robinswood Hill, Gloucester. *Tel* Glos 25653.
Open 9 am-8.30 pm, 7 days. 12 bays. Floodlit. £1 for 50 balls. Squash. Skittles. Ski-slope. Full 18 hole course. 9 hole par 3. 75 bedrooms.

Hamilton

Strathclyde Park Golf Range

Mote Hill, Hamilton
24 bays. Floodlit. Cafeteria. Licensed bar. Open 9.30 am-9.30 pm. 9 hole golf course. Professional teaching (Ken Davidson). Route: A723 just off M74.

Horam

Easterfields Golf Complex

Chiddingly Road, Horam, Nr Heathfield, East Sussex. *Tel* (04353) 3355.
Open 9.30 am-10.30 pm all year round. Floodlit. 18 covered bays. Professional's shop with repair service. Tuition with video facilities. Clubhouse with private club facilities. Lounge bar and restaurant. Bucket of approx 60 balls: Members £1.10; Guests and non-members £1.40; Juniors 80p. Clubs and automatic teeing available for hire. Membership fees on application. 9 hole course available spring 1984.

Ilford

Fairlop Waters

Forest Road, Barkingside, Ilford, Essex. *Tel* 01-500 4426.
Open 9 am-10.30 pm. Floodlit. 36 covered bays. £1.10 for 40 balls. £1.75 for 90 balls. Golf shop. Bar.

Ipswich

Ipswich Golf Centre

Suffolk Show Ground, Bucklesham Road, Ipswich, Suffolk. *Tel* Ipswich 76821.
Open 8.30 am-dusk. Buckets of balls 90p and £1.40. 9 hole course £2. Professional JW Johnson *Tel* Ipswich 76821. Tuition at all times. Shop.

Jersey

Western Golf Range

St Ouen Bay, Jersey.
Open 10 am-dusk. 24 bays. Putting, crazy golf. 9 hole par 3. Professional.

Kingston-on-Hull

National Avenue, Hull, N Humberside. *Tel* Hull 492720.
24 covered tees. Open 9 am-9 pm, 7 days. Floodlit. £2 jumbo; £1.50 large; £1 small baskets. Pitch and putt. Professional. Licensed. Meals.

Leatherhead

Riverside Driving Range

River Lane, Fetcham, Leatherhead, Surrey. *Tel* Leatherhead 5713.

Leicester

Range Inn Golf Range

Melton Road, Leicester. *Tel* Leicester 664400.
Open 10 am-10 pm, 7 days. Floodlit. 20 covered tees. £1 for 85 balls. Licensed. 9 hole pitch and putt, 18 hole crazy golf.

Lightwater

Windlemere Golf Course

Windlesham Road, West End, Woking, Surrey. *Tel* Chobham (09905) 8727.
Open 8 am–10 pm, 7 days. Floodlit. 12 covered bays. 9-hole full-length public course. Two professionals. Large golf shop with repair services. Clubhouse–licensed bar with snooker/pool. Loc. A319 at Lightwater near Bagshot.

Maidenhead

Hawthorn Hill

Drift Road, Hawthorn Hill, Nr Maidenhead, Berks. *Tel* Maidenhead (0628) 75588.
24 bay floodlit driving range. Open 8.00 am-10.00 pm. Full 18 hole course. Snooker. 90-seater restaurant/steakhouse. Clubhouse and licensed bar. 4 miles S of Maidenhead on A330.

Milton Keynes

Windmill Hill Golf Complex

Tattenhoe Lane, Bletchley, Milton Keynes. *Tel* (0908) 78623
15 covered and 9 open bays. Floodlit. Open 9.00 am-9.00 pm Mon-Sat; 9.00 am-7.00 pm Sunday. Full 18 hole golf course. Putting greens. Golf shop. Bars and restaurant. 4 miles from Junction 13 M1 on A421.

Newcastle

Gosforth Park Golfing Complex

High Gosforth Park, Newcastle-Upon-Tyne. *Tel* 091-236 4480.
Open 8.00 am-10 pm, 7 days. Floodlit. 30 covered tees. Putting, pitching. Professional. Licensed. Restaurant. 9 hole pitch/putt and 18 hole putting green.

Newtownabbey

Ballyearl Leisure Centre

585 Doagh Road, Newtownabbey, *Tel* Glengormley 48287
Pro: Jim Robinson. 9 hole Par 3 course, 2362 yds. WD–Adults £1.75 Jnrs £1 OAPs 60p; W/E–Adults £2.50 Jnrs £1.50 OPAs £1. 2-tiered covered range, 15 tees (8 above, 7 below) with videoswing machine. Grass range, 3 tier, accommodates up to 35 people. 6 squash courts, snooker and pool. 2½ miles N of Glengormley. Public facility run by Newtownabbey Borough Council

Newtownards

Bradshaw's Brae Golf Centre Ltd

115 Belfast Road, Killarn, Newtownards, Co Down. *Tel* Newtownards 813484.

Northampton

Delapre Golf Complex

Eagle Drive, Nene Valley Way, Northampton.
36 open and 25 covered bays. Floodlit. Par 3, pitch and putt. Full 18 hole course. Golf shop. Full catering and bar facilities. 3 miles from junction 15 M1 on A508.

Norwich

Norwich Golf Centre

Long Lane, Bawburgh, Norwich, Norfolk.
9 hole course. Professional (Robert Waugh).

Nottingham

Carlton Forum Golf Target Range

Foxhill Road, Carlton, Nottingham.
Open 10 am-10 pm Mon-Fri; 10 am-5 pm Sat & Sun (last buckets of balls sold ½ hour prior to closing). 28 covered tees. Floodlit. Licensed bar and restaurant. *Tel* 0602 872333. Professional.

Old Woking

Hoebridge Golf Centre

Old Woking, Surrey. *Tel* Woking 22611/2.
25 bays, covered. Floodlit. 18 hole championship length course, 18 hole par 3 course. Lessons and hire equipment from Professional. Shop, bar and restaurant. 12 table snooker facility and large extension to clubhouse 1985. 5 mins from A3 on Woking/West Byfleet road.

Orpington

Ruxley Golf Centre

Sandy Lane, St Pauls Cray, Orpington, Kent. *Tel* Orpington 71490.
18 holes. L 5017 yards. SSS 65. WD–U. W/E and BH before 11.30 am. Soc on weekdays. £4 (£5). Off Ruxley roundabout on A20 at Sidcup. Floodlit driving range. 28 covered bays. Tuition. Club hire. Open 8 am-10:30 pm. Bar, restaurant, golfshop, tuition.

Pease Pottage

Fairway Golf Driving Range

Horsham Road, Pease Pottage, Sussex. *Tel* Crawley 33000.
Open 9 am-10.30 pm, 7 days. 60 balls for 60p. Floodlit. Professional. Licensed.

Portsmouth

Portsmouth Golf Centre

Eastern Road, Portsmouth, Hampshire. *Tel* 0705 664549.
Open 8 am-10 pm, 7 days. Floodlit. 30 covered bays. Professional. Shop. Tuition. Public house and restaurant.

Reading

Sindlesham Driving Range

Mole Road, Wokingham, Berks RG11 5DB. *Tel* Wokingham 788494.
Profession Paul Watson. Floodlit; 7 days a week, 14 hours a day; 20 bays; £1 machine operated.

Renfrew

Normandy Golf Range

Open 9.30 am-8.30 pm weekdays; 9.30 am-5.30 pm weekends. *Tel* 041-886 7477 (Monday-Friday). Video. Professional J Mulgrew. Floodlit. 50 balls for £1; £1.60 for 100.

Richmond

Richmond Driving Range

Richmond Athletic Sports Ground, Twickenham Road, Surrey (next door to Royal Mid-Surrey GC). *Tel* 01-940 5570.
Open 9 am-8.30 pm Mon-Fri; 9 am-5.30 pm Sat/Sun (Sep-Apr close at 12 noon Sat). 25 covered tees. £1.50 for 75 balls. Professional Sean Simpson.

St Neots

St Neots Leisure Centre

Eynesbury Hardwicke Golf Club, Eynesbury Hardwicke, St Neots, Cambridgeshire PE19 4XN. *Tel* Huntingdon 217951.
Open 8 am daily. Professional. 10 covered bays. Floodlit. Putting. Bunkers. £1 for 50 balls. Tuition. Shop. Licensed. Food.

Swindon

Broome Manor Driving Range

Broome Manor Golf Complex, Pipers Way, Swindon, Wilts SN3 1RG. *Tel* Swindon 32403.
Open 9.30 am-9.30 pm, 7 days (Mondays 12 noon-9.30 pm). 25 bays. Floodlit. £1.10 standard; £1.55 large bucket of balls. Hire of clubs 35p each. Professional Barry Sandry *Tel* Swindon 32403. Licensed. Food.

Tilsworth

Broad Range Golf and Leisure Centre

Dunstable Road, Tilsworth, Beds. *Tel* 0525 210721/2.
Open 10 am-9 pm, 7 days per week. 30 bays. 9 hole course open to public. Bar, licensed restaurant. Professionals' shop. Professional/Golf Manager—I Grant.

Uddingston

Clydeway Golf Centre

Blantye Farm Road, Uddingston, Lanarkshire. *Tel* 041-641 8899.
Open 10 am–9 pm weekdays; 10 am–6 pm weekends. 100 balls £1.60, 55 balls £1. Floodlit. Snack bar. Golf shop.

Warwick

Warwick Golf Centre

Racecourse, Warwick. *Tel* Warwick 494316.
Open 10 am-9 pm weekdays; 9 am 5 pm weekends. Small basket 60p; medium £1; large £1.20. 30 covered tees. Floodlit. Target. Putting. Professional. Shop. Licensed. 9 hole course, par 34.

Washington

George Washington Hotel

Stone Cellar Road, Washington, Tyne and Wear. *Tel* 091-417 2626.
Open 10 am-10 pm. 21 floodlit bays. Professional. Pitch and putt. 18 hole course. 10 table snooker club.

Watford

Watford Driving Range

Sheepcot Lane, Garston, Watford, Herts. *Tel* Garston 675560.
Open 10 am-10.30 pm, 7 days. 55 balls—£1. Floodlit. Covered tees. Professional. Licensed.

Welwyn Garden City

Welwyn Hatfield Sports Centre

Gosling Stadium Driving Range, Stanborough Road, Welwyn Garden City, Herts. *Tel* (0707) 331056.
Open 10 am daily. 9 bays. Floodlit. Large basket £1, small basket 50p. Cafeteria. Licensed bars. We are a Multi Sports Complex.

Wolverhampton

Three Hammers Golf Centre

Coven, nr Wolverhampton.
Open 9.30 am-10 pm weekdays; 9 am-5.30 pm weekends. Floodlit. 14 covered bays. 18 hole, par 3 course. Licensed.

Wokingham

Downshire GC

Easthampstead Park, Wokingham, Berks. *Tel* Bracknell 424066.
Open 8 am-dusk weekdays; 7 am-dusk weekends. Full 18 hole course. 9 hole pitch and putt. Driving range. Free house and restaurant. Professional.

Continental Section

Austria

Badgastein

Badgastein (1962)
5640 Badgastein PO Box 15
Tel **(0 64 34) 2775 or 2516**
Mem 150
Sec Francesco Carli
Holes 9 L 6012 metres SSS 71
Fees D–130 to 150s W–750 to 900s
Loc Badgastein 2 km

Bad Ischl

Salzkammergut (1932)
4820 Bad Ischl Postfach 145
Tel **(0 61 32) 6340**
Mem 300
Pro Ian Hay/Franz Laimer
Holes 9 L 5758 metres SSS 70 Par 70
Fees Low season: 190s (250s)
High season: Jul+Aug 250s
Loc Bad Ischl 6 km; Strobl 6 km

Bad Kleinkircheim

GC Bad Kleinkircheim-Reichenau (1984)
A-9546 Bad Kleinkircheim
Tel **04274-594**
Mem 100
Pro Gordon Manson
Holes 18 L 6127 metres SSS 72
Fees 240s
Loc 50 km NW of Klagenfurt

Enzesfeld

Enzesfeld (1970)
A-2551 Enzesfeld
Tel **(02256) 81272**
Mem 430
Pro Gary Purdue, Steve Jackson
Holes 18 L 6176 metres SSS 72
Fees 300s (450s)
V'trs H W/E only in July and August
Loc Enzesfeld 20 miles from Vienna

Graz

Murhof (1963)
A-8130 Frohnleiten
Tel **(03127) 210131**
Mem 330
Pro Keith Preston
Holes 18 L 6131 metres SSS 72
Fees 330s (220s hotel guests)
Loc Graz 20 km N; Vienna 150 km S
Mis Hotel on course; 4 star with Olympic size swimming pool

Hainburg/Donau

Hainburg/Donau (1977)
Auf der Heide 762 A-2410 Hainburg
Tel **(02165) 2628**
Mem 140
Pro John Dockray
Holes 9 L 5950 metres SSS 71 Par 70
Fees 130s (180s)
Loc
Mis Open March–November

Innsbruck

Innsbruck-Igls (1956)
A-6074 Rinn Postbox
Tel **(052 23) 8177**
Mem 450
Pro Jose Ruiz
Holes 18 L 5910 metres SSS 71
9 L 4709 metres SSS 66
Fees 220s (300s)
Loc Innsbruck–Rinn 10 km

Kitzbuhel

Kitzbuhel (1955)
6370 Kitzbuhel
Tel **(053 56) 30 07**
Mem 400
Pro Russell Maw
Holes 9 L 6085 metres SSS 72
Fees 200s (300s)
Loc Kitzbuhel 500 m

Klagenfurt

Kärntner (1927)
9082 Dellach 16 Maria Wörth
Tel **04273 2515**
Mem 250
Pro M. Brock P Memp
Holes 18 L 5740 metres SSS 70
Fees D–280s
Loc Velden 8 km

Liezen

Ennstal
PO Box 76 A-8940 Liezen
Tel **(03612) 22650**
Mem
Pro Paul Mackenzie
Holes 9 L 5550 metres SSS 70
Fees 200s (250s)
Loc

Schloss Pichlarn (1972)
A-8952 Irdning Ennstal Steiermark
Tel **(03682) 2841**
Mem 60
Pro Alan Mitchel
Holes 18 L 6123 metres SSS 72
Fees D–250s
Loc Irdning

Linz

Linz-St Florian (1960)
A-4490 St Florian Tillysburg 28
Tel **(07223) 2873**
Mem 520
Pro Paul Wright
Christopher Prasthofer
Holes 18 L 6131 metres SSS 72
Fees WD–300s
Loc 15 km from Linz 170 km from Vienna

Wels (1981)
4512 Weisskirchen Wels Weyerbach 37
Tel **07243 26455/07242 82947**
Mem 105
Pro Gordon D Manson and Asst
Holes 9 L 6330 metres SSS 73
Fees 180s (210s)
Loc 5 km from Salzburg–Vienna highway; 8 km from city centre
Mis Driving range, pitch and putt; pro-shop, restaurant

Pertisau/Achensee

Achensee (1934)
A-6213 Pertisau Postbox 3
Tel **(0 52 43) 5377**
Mem 180
Pro Isidor Schaffer
Holes 9 L 3916 metres SSS 62
Fees D–140s W–900s M–3500s
Loc Pertisau ½ km

Saalfelden

Brandlhof G & CC (1983)
A-5760 Saalfelden
Sporthotel Güt Brandlhof
Tel **06582 2176**
Mem 110
Pro Jonathan Crisp
Holes 18 L 5902 metres SSS 72
Fees 250s (300s)
Loc Sporthotel Güt Brandhof between Salzburg and Kitzbuhel 60 km from Salzburg
Mis Horse riding, tennis, squash, fishing, hunting, bowling, skiing, golf academy etc

Salzburg

Salzburg Klesheim (1955)
5071 Wals bei Salzburg
Tel **(0662) 850851**
Mem 390
Pro Tom Rogerson David Howard
Holes 9 L 5700 metres SSS 70
Fees 250s (300s)
Loc Salzburg 5 km

Schloss Fuschl (1964)
A-5322 Hof/Salzburg
Tel **(06229) 390**
Mem 200
Pro Franco Torrano
Holes 9 L 3054 metres Par 62 SSS 61
Fees 150s (200s) 1/7–20/9 200s
Loc Hotel Schloss Fuschl; Salzburg 12 km
Mis Driving range; bar & restaurant

Seefeld

Seefeld-Wildmoos (1968)
A-6100 Seefeld Postbox 22
Tel **(0 52 12) 3003**
Mem 238

Pro Mike Mawdsley
Holes 18 L 6135 metres SSS 72
Fees 280s (400s) W–1200s (Reduction for Golf Foundation Hotel Guests)
Loc 4 km W of Seefeld 115 km S of Munich 24 km W of Innsbruck

Steinakirchen Am Forst

Schloss Ernegg (1973)

A-3261 Steinakirchen am Forst NO
Tel **(74 88) 214 (May–October)**
Mem 70
Pro
Holes 9 L 2030 metres Par 32 SSS 63
Fees 150s (250s)
Loc 100 km W of Vienna, Autobahn exit Ybbs
Mis Castle Hotel Driving Range

Vienna

Wien (1901)

Freudenau 65a 1020 Wien
Tel **(02 22) 74 17 86**
Mem 650
Pro Ossi Gartenmaier Wade Walters Frank O'Connor
Holes 18 L 5790 metres SSS 70
Fees D–400s
Loc 10 mins from Vienna centre
Mis Open all year

Vienna Neustadt

Föhrenwald (1968)

Postfach 105 A-2700 Wr Neustadt
Tel **Wien 423396**
Mem 270
Pro G. Copeman
Holes 18 L 6080 metres SSS 72
Fees 150s (250s) W–1000s M–2500s
Loc Wiener Neustadt 5 km S on route 54

Semmering (1926)

2680 Semmering
Tel **(02664) 456**
Mem
Pro Adof Tonn
Holes 9 L 3860 metres SSS 60
Fees D–70s W–350s M–1000s
Loc Semmering 90 km S of Vienna
Mis Season May–October

Zell am See

GC Europasportregion (1983)

5700 Zell am See Kaprun
Tel **(06542) 6161**
Mem 400
Pro D Shaw S Brown M Richardson
Holes 18 L 6140 metres Par & SSS 72
Fees 300s (360s)
Loc 95 km from Salzburg
Mis Driving range, putting gree, pitching green, pro-shop; skiing, water-skiing, tennis, etc. Open May-October

Belgium

Antwerp

Rinkven G & CC (1980)

St Jobsesteenweg 54 2232 Schilde
Tel **03-3833341/03-383 4467**
Mem 915
Pro P Michielsen V Duyster
Holes 27 SSS 73
Fees 750fr (1000fr)
Loc 17 km NE of Antwerp; 5 km off E10 motorway
Mis Visitors welcome. Handicap certificate required.

Royal Antwerp (1888)

Georges Capiaulei 2, B-2080 Kapellen
Tel **03/666 84 56**
Mem 850
Pro H Stevens
Holes 18 L 6140 SSS 73; 9 L 2264 SSS 33
Fees 900fr (1300fr)
Loc Antwerp 20 km-Kapellen-Kalmthout

Ternesse

Uilenbaan 15 B-2220 Wommelgen
Tel **(03) 35302 92**
Mem 250
Pro S. Bouillon
Holes 18 L 5876 metres SSS 72
Fees D–750fr W/E–1050fr
Loc 5 mins from Antwerp on E-39

Brussels

Duisberg Militaire GC

Hertswegenstraat 39 1982 Duisburg
Tel **767 9752/767 3890 ext 388**
Mem
Pro
Holes 9 L 3630 metres SSS 60
Fees D–200fr W/E–300fr
Loc 13 km from Brussels

Golf Du Bercuit

Les Gottes 3 5980 Grez Doiceau
Tel **010-841501**
Mem 500
Pro Philippe Toussaint
Holes 18 L 5986 metres SSS 72
Fees D–800fr W/E–1500fr
Loc Brussels 27 km Highway Brussels–Namur Exit 8

Keerbergen

50 Vlieghavenlaan 2850 Keerbergen
Tel **015 234961**
Mem 556
Pro W Vanbegin W Mann Tel 015 234963
Holes 18 L 5530 metres SSS 69
Fees D–600fr W/E–900fr
Loc Brussels 18 miles

Golf de Rigenée (1981)

Rue de Chatelet 10a-6321 Villers-la-Ville
Tel **(071) 87 77 65**
Mem 510
Pro P Crepin Ch Ditlefsen
Holes 18 L 6150 metres SSS 69
Fees 600fr (1100fr)
Loc Between Charleroi Namur and Brussels

Royal Golf Club De Belgique (1906)

Chateau de Ravenstein 1980 Tervueren
Tel **(02) 7675801**
Mem 1150
Pro F Van Donck J Salmon D Aimé
Holes 18 & 9 L 6075 & 1960 metres SSS 62 (9-hole course Par 32)
Fees 1000fr (1200fr)
Loc Brussels 15 km
Mis Play on 18 hole course limited to h'caps 22 (men) 26 (ladies); official h'cap certificate must be produced. Always phone before visit

Royal Waterloo (1923)

Vieux Chemin de Wavre 1328 Ohain
Tel **(02) 6331850 50 (02) 6331597**
Mem 1300
Pro George Will John Gulesserian Joe Blair
Holes 45: 18 L 6260 metres SSS 73; 18 L 6440 SSS 72; 9 L 2143 metres SSS 33
Fees 950fr (2000fr)
Loc Brussels 22 km
Mis Handicap certificate required

Dinant

Club Du Chateau Royal D'Ardenne

5560 Hoyet Dinant
Tel **(082) 66 62 28**
Mem 350
Pro Fabrice Masson
Holes 18 L 5363 metres SSS 71
Fees 700fr (1000fr)
Loc On Rochefort road 9 km

Ghent

Royal Latem (1909)

B-9830 St Martens-Latem
Tel **(091) 82 54 11**
Mem 580
Pro Jan Verplancke
Holes 18 L 5767 metres SSS 70
Fees D–650fr W/E–900fr
Loc SW Ghent 10 km on route N14 Ghent–Deinze

Hasselt

Limburg (1966)

Golfstraat No 1 3530 Houthalen
Tel **011/383543**
Mem 550
Pro R Salmon
Holes 18 L 6044 metres SSS 72
Fees 650fr (1000fr)
Loc Hasselt 15 km

Knocke-Zoute

Royal Zoute

Berkenlaan 4 8300 Knokke-Heist Belgium
Tel **(050) 60 12 27/60 37 81**
Mem 1200
Pro A De Vulder
Holes 18 L 6172 metres SSS 72 18 L 3766 metres SSS 60
Fees D–900fr (1200fr) (July/Aug D–1100fr and 1500fr)
Loc Knocke 1 km

Liege

Royal GC Du Sart Tilman

541 Route du Condroz 4200 Ougree
Tel **041 362021**
Mem 500
Pro Rigo Braems
Holes 18 L 6002 metres SSS 71
Fees D–750fr W/E–850fr
Loc Ardennes; 10 km S of town centre on route 620 Liege–Marche

Mons

Royal GC Du Hainaut (1934)

Route d'Ath 7434 Erbisoeul
Tel **(065) 229610 22 94 74**
Mem 500
Pro F Lefever
Holes 18 L 6183 metres SSS 72
Fees D–250fr W/E–400fr
Loc Mons 6 km

Ostend

Koninklijke GC Ostend (1903)

2 Koninklijke 8420 De Haan
Tel **059/23 32 83**
Mem 450
Pro Trevor Bowden
Holes 18 L 5320 metres SSS 68
Fees 700–800fr (900–1050fr)
Loc Ostend 7 km

Oudenaarde

Oudenaarde GCC (1976)

Kasteel Petegem
Kortrykstraat 52 9790 Wortegem-Petegem
Tel **(055) 31 54 81**
Mem 650
Pro C Morton M Bradley
Holes 18 L 6039 metres SSS 73
Fees D–600fr W/E 1000fr
Loc 3 km SW from Oudenaarde

Spa

Royal GC Des Fagnes

Balmoral 4880 Spa
Tel **(087) 7716 13**
Mem 350
Pro WYS Robertson
Holes 18 L 5924 metres SSS 72
Fees D–600fr W/E–1200fr
Loc Spa 5 km Liege 35 km

Cyprus

Joint Services Golf Club Dhekelia

BFPO 58
Tel **Dhekelia 460**
Mem 180 50(L)
Pro
Holes 18 L 5886 metres SSS 69
Fees Summer £C2 Winter £C3
Loc 12 k E of Larnaca
Mis Non-patterned Shoes. No studs

Czechoslovakia

Brno

TJ Lokomotiva Brno

616 00 Brno Lučiní 30
Tel **Brno 41217**
Mem 65
Sec Bohumil Puchýř
Holes 9 L 5064 metres SSS 72
Fees 20Kcs (30Kcs)
Loc Brno 80 km Prague 100 km

Karlovy Vary

TJ Start VD–Golf (1970)

360 69 Karlovy Vary Manesova 3
Tel **27279**
Mem 84
Pres Edgar Sřebel
Holes 18 L 6087 metres SSS 72
Fees 100Kcs
Loc Prague 120 km Pilsen 90 km

Mariánské Lázně

GC Mariánské Lázně

353 01 Mariánské Lázně Fučíkova 435
Pres Dr Karel Horacek
Holes 18

Ostrava

TJ NHKG (1968)

Cingrova 10 701 Ostrava 1
Tel **(Clubhouse) Hlucin 449**
Mem 198
Holes 18 L 5773 metres SSS 72
Fees 80Kcs (100Kcs)
Loc Silherovice 15 km from Ostrava

Poděbrady

TJ Sklo Bohemia

280 00 Kolín II Ulci Družby 924
Pres Josef Puňochář
Holes 9

Prague

TJ Golf Praha (1969)

Na Morani 4 120 00 Praha 2
Tel **29 28 28**
Mem 220
Holes 9 L 2978 metres SSS 36
Fees 50Kcs (100Kcs)
Loc Prague direction Plzen

TJ Slavoj Praha

130 00 Praha 1 Přemyslovská 10
Pres Ivan Vávra
Holes 9

Semily

Golfovy Oddil TJ Semily (1971)

513 01 Semily
Tel
Mem 46
Holes 8 L 4002 metres SSS 64
Fees 20Kcs
Loc 2 km from Semily

Denmark

Jutland

Aalborg

Aalborg (1908)

Jargersprisvej, Restup Enge 9000 Aalborg
Tel **08 34 14 76**
Mem 850
Pro Howard Barton
Holes 18 L 5800 metres SSS 70
Fees D–100kr W/E–120kr
Loc Aalborg 7 km to SW

Bronderslev (1971)

PO Box 94 9700 Bronderslev
Tel **(08) 82 32 81**
Mem 300
Pro M Thven
Holes 18 L 5710 metres SSS 71
Fees 80kr
Loc 3 km W Bronderslev

Himmerlands GC

Centervej 1 Gatten 9670 Løgstør
Tel **(08) 66 16 00**
Mem 620
Pro Robert Kristensen
Holes 18 L 5277 metres SSS 68 9-hole Par 3 course
Fees WD & W/E–100kr Sat/Sun–200kr W–500 kr
Loc 35 km from Hobro on Hobro–Løgstør road. Course is signposted (W) from Gatten
Mis Clubhouse and restaurant open all year round

Aarhus

Aarhus (1931)

Ny Moesgaardvej 50 8270 Hojbjerg
Tel **06 27 63 22**
Mem 1100
Pro Neil Elston
Holes 18 L 5855 metres SSS 71 9 L 6093 metres SSS 72
Fees 60kr (100kr)
Loc Aarhus 6 km Route E3 North Aarhus 6 km Route 451 South

Abenraa

Sonderjyllands (1970)

Uge Hedegard 6360 Tinglev
Tel **(04) 68 75 25**
Mem 350
Pro Peter Dixon Tel (04) 687121
Holes 14 L 6427 yds SSS 70
Fees D–80kr
Loc 8 miles SW of Abenraa

Ebeltoft

Ebeltoft GC (1966)

Skelhojevej 6 DK–8400 Ebeltoft
Tel **45 6 344787**
Mem 307
Pro Svend Erik Hansen
Holes 18 L 5150 metres SSS 67
Fees D–60kr W–240kr
Loc Ebeltoft ½ km

Esbjerg

Esbjerg (1921)

Sonderhedevej Marbaek DK 6710 Esbjerg V
Tel **(05) 269219**
Mem 800
Pro A Tinning
Holes 18 L 5729 metres SSS 70
Fees 100kr
Loc 15 km N of Esbjerg

Fano Island (1900)

DK 6720 Nordby
Tel **(05) 16 32 82**
Mem 239
Pro N Aafeldt
Holes 18 L 4642 metres SSS 65
Fees D–80kr W–400 kr
Loc On Fano Island Ferry from Esbjerg

Grindsted

Gyttegard (1978)

PO Box 83 7200 Grindsted
Tel **05 335649**
Mem 175
Pro Frank Atkinson
Holes 9 L 5442 metres SSS 69
Fees WD/WE 75kr
Loc 10 km from Grindsted 6 km from Billund

Haderslev

Haderslev (1971)

c/o Klaus Bossen Birkevej 27 6100 Haderslev
Tel **(04) 528301**
Mem 350
Pro Carl Rota
Holes 14 L 4842 metres SSS 67
Fees D–60kr
Loc Egevej 22 1 mile NW of town centre

Herning

Herning (1964)

Silkeborgvej 7400 Herning
Tel **(07) 127521**
Mem 450
Pro Peter Dangerfield
Holes 18 L 5571 metres SSS 70
Fees D–70kr
Loc Herning 2 km E on route 15

Holstebro

Holstebro (1970)

Raasted 7570 Vemb
Tel **(07) 48 51 55**
Mem 421
Pro Roy Howett
Holes 18 L 6301 metres SSS 70
Fees D–80kr
Loc 8 miles W of Holstebro

Horsens

Horsens (1972)

Silkeborvej 8700 Horsens
Tel **(05) 615151**
Mem 400
Pro Graham Oakley
Holes 18+6 L 5905 metres SSS 72
Fees 100kr
Loc 1 km W of Horsens towards Silkeborg

Juelsminde Golf & Tennis Club (1973)

Bobroholtvej 9 7130 Juelsminde
Tel **05 69 34 92**
Mem 150
Pro Graham Oakley
Holes 9 L 5990 metres SSS 71
Fees D–60kr W–300kr
Loc 20 km S of Horsens on the coast
Mis 6 hole par 3 course opening Summer 1987

Kolding

Kolding (1933)

Emerholtsvej 6000 Kolding
Tel **(05) 52 3793**
Mem 500
Pro Frank Atkinson
Holes 18 L 5376 metres SSS 69
Fees 80kr
Loc 3 km from Kolding

Randers

Randers (1958)

Himmelbovej 9800 Randers
Tel **06 42 88 69**
Mem 400
Pro Graham Townhill
Holes 18
Fees 80kr W–380kr
Loc 5 km from city. Drive towards Silkeborg by Fladbrovej then follow signs 'Golfbane'.
Mis Beautiful surrounding countryside

Ribe

Ribe GC (1981)

Rønnehave Snepsgårdevej 14 6760 Ribe
Tel **(05) 44 12 30**
Mem 150
Pro Roy Howett
Holes 9 L 5092 SSS 67
Fees 60kr
Loc 5 miles SE Ribe; signposted on Hadeslev road

Silkeborg

Silkeborg (1966)

Resenbro 8600 Silkeborg
Tel **(06) 85 33 99**
Mem 675
Pro Mike Kelly
Holes 18 L 5956 metres SSS 72
Fees D–100kr W/E–100kr
Loc Silkeborg 5km

Skagen-Frederikshavn

Hvide Klit

Diget 9982 Albaek
Tel **(08) 48 84 26**
Mem 500
Pro Carl Poulsen Tel (08) 48 80 08
Holes 18 L 6470 yds SSS 72
Fees D–50kr W–400 kr
Loc 2 miles N of Albaek

Skjern

Dejbjerg GC (1968)

Public
Letagervej 1 Dejberg 6900 Skjern
Tel **(07) 35 09 59**
Mem 200
Pro Frank Atkinson
Holes 9 L 5066 metres SSS 67
Fees D–80kr
Loc 25 km from W coast on All Skjern-Rinkøbing 6 km from Skjern

Sonderborg

Alssund GK

Vestermark-Skydebanevej
Holes 6 L 4263 metres SSS 62

Thisted

Nordvestjysk (1971)

Nystrupvej 19 7700 Thisted
Tel **07-97 41 41**
Mem 265
Pro Svend Tinning
Holes 9 L 5599 metres SSS 70
Fees D–50kr W–60kr
Loc 13 km NW of Thisted

Vejle

Vejle (1970)

Faellessletgaard Ibaekvej 7100 Vejle
Tel **05-858 185**
Mem 730
Pro Jeffrey John
Holes 18 L 6042 yds SSS 71
Fees WD/WE 100kr
Loc 8 miles SE of Vejle
Mis Driving range. Par 3 course

Viborg

Skive

Resen 7800 Skive
Tel **(07) 524409**
Mem 200
Pro Richard Jackson
Holes 9
Fees D–30kr W/E–40kr
Loc 20 miles NW of Viborg

Viborg

Viborg 8800
Tel **06 61 11 19**
Mem 350
Pro Andrew Martin

Holes 13 L 5300 metres SSS 68
Fees 60kr
Loc Mollevei 26 Overlund 2 km E of Viborg

Funen

Glamsbjerg

Vestfyns GK

Ronnemosegaard Krengerupvej 27 5620 Glamsbjerg
Tel **(09) 72 21 24**
Holes 9 L 5680 metres SSS 71 Par 70
Loc 15 miles SW of Odense

Nyborg

SCT Knuds (1954)

Slipshavnsvej 16 DK 5800 Nyborg
Tel **09-311212**
Mem 572
Pro Herluf Hansen
Holes 18 L 5788 metres SSS 70
Fees 80kr (120kr) W/E-200kr
Loc Nyborg 3 km

Odense

Odense (1927)

Hestehaven 201 5220 Odense 50
Tel **(09) 95900**
Mem 1050
Pro Roger Brown
Holes 18 L 6156 metres SSS 71
9 L 4154 metres SSS 60
Fees 60kr (80kr)
Loc South-eastern outskirts of Odense

Svendborg

Svendborg (1970)

Tordengaardsvej Sorup 5700 Svendborg
Tel **(09) 22 40 77**
Mem 384
Pro Soren Jensen
Holes 9 L 5746 yds SSS 69
Fees 60kr (80kr)
Loc Svendborg 3 km

Bornholm Island

Ronne

Bornholms (1971)

Plantagavej 3700 Ronne
Tel (03) 95 68 54
Mem 260
Pro Stephen Judge
Holes 18 L 4511 metres SSS 65
Fees 80kr (100kr)
Loc 4 km E of Ronne

Zealand

Copenhagen

Furesø GC (1974)

Hestkøbvœenge 4 3460 Birkerød
Tel **02 817444**
Mem 950
Pro Colin Smith
Holes 18 L 5506 metres SSS 69
Fees WD-100kr W/E-140kr
Loc 25 km N of Copenhagen

Copenhagen (1898)

Dyrehaven 2 2800 KGS Lyngby
Tel **(01) 630483**
Mem 950
Pro H Kristensen H Aafeldt
Holes 18 L 5876 metres SSS 69
Fees WD-100kr W/E-130kr
Loc 8 miles N of city

Molleaens (1970)

Private
Stenbaekgard Bastrup DK 3540 Lynge
Tel **02 18 86 31**
Mem 729
Pro Richard Jackson
Holes 9 L 6015 metres SSS 71
Fees D-50kr W/E-80kr All WE-120kr
Loc 20 miles NW Copenhagen
Mis Driving range and 5 training holes. From September 1987 18 holes L 5555 metres SSS 69

Soelleroed (1972)

Overodvej 239 2840 Holte
Tel **(02) 801784**
Mem 1050
Pro Jorgen Korfitsen Tel (02) 801877
Holes 18 L 6069 metres SSS 73
Fees 100kr (130kr)
Loc 12 miles N of Copenhagen

Falster

Storstrommen (1969)

4863 Eskilstrup Falster
Tel **(03) 838080**
Mem 400
Pro Derek S Chadd Tel (03) 83 80 80
Holes 18 L 5945 metres SSS 72
Fees On application
Loc 15 km N of Nykobing Falster 5

Frederiksvaerk

Asserbo

Bodkergaardsvej 3300 Frederiksvaerk
Tel **(02) 12 03 29**
Mem 350
Pro L Middelboe
Holes 9 L 5187 metres SSS 69
Fees D-60kr W/E-80kr
Loc Frederiksvaerk 3 km

Gilleleje

Gilleleje Golf Klub

Bregnerodvej 35 3250 Gilleleje
Tel (02) 20 95 15
Mem 564
Pro Allan Jorgensen
Allan Kristensen
Holes 9 L 3270 yards SSS 71
Fees D-100kr (120kr)
Loc 38½ miles N of Copenhagen
Mis Free driving range Licensed restaurant

Helsingor

Helsingor

Gl Hellebaekvej 3000 Helsingor
Tel (02) 21 29 70
Mem 950
Pro Per Greve
Holes 18 L 5670 metres SSS 71
Fees D-110kr W/E-150kr
Loc Helsingor 1½ km

Hillerod

Hillerod (1966)

Private
Nysogard Ny Hammersholt 3400 Hillerod
Tel **Club (02) 265046**
Res (02) 267442
Mem 1000
Pro Mike Tulloch Tel (02) 25 40 30
Holes 18 L 5452 metres SSS 70
Fees 125kr (175kr)
Loc 3 km S of Hillerod

Holbaek

Holbaek

Kirsebaerholmen 4300 Holbaek
Tel **(03) 43 45 79**
Mem 320
Pro Mark Irwing
Holes 9 L 5158 metres SSS 67
Fees WD-50kr W/E-60kr
Loc Kirsebaerholmen

Kalundborg

Kalundborg GC (1974)

Kildekaergaard Rosnaesvej 225 4400 Kalundborg
Tel **(03) 50 13 85**
Mem 330
Pro Preben Jacobsen
Holes 9 L 5064 metres SSS 68
Fees WD-50kr W/E-70kr
Loc Rosnaes, appr 8 km W Kalundborg

Koge

Koge Golf Club

GL Hastrup 4600 Koge
Tel **03 65 10 00 & 03 65 64 00**
Mem 600
Pro Peter Taylor
Holes 18 L 5915 metres SSS 72
Fees D-60kr W/E-80kr
Loc 3 km S from Koge

Korsør

Korsør (1964)

Tarnborgparken 4220 Korsør
Tel **(03) 57 18 36**
Mem 600
Pro Mark Irving Tel (03) 574018
Holes 18 L 5998 metres SSS 72
Fees Tues/Fri 50kr Mon/Wed/Thurs 70kr Sat/Sun 80kr
Loc Korsor Bay

Naestved

Sydsjaellands GK

Borupgården Mogenstrup 4700 Naestved
Tel **(03) 76 15 03**
Holes 9 L 5700 metres SSS 70 Par 70
Loc 9 km SE of Naestved

Nykobing Sjaelland

Odsherred (1967)

4573 Hojby Sjaelland
Tel **(03) 42 20 76**
Mem 350
Pro Preben Jacobsen
Holes 12 L 5678 metres SSS 70
Fees D–40kr Sat/Sun–60kr
Loc SW of Nykobing 5 km

Roskilde

GK Hedeland

Staerkendevej 232 A 2640 Hedehusene
Tel **(02) 13 61 69**
Holes 9 L 5500 metres Par 70

Roskilde (1973)

Kongemarken 4000 Roskilde
Tel **(03) 370180**
Mem 487
Pro Tim Card
Holes 9 L 4853 metres SSS 69
Fees WD–80kr W/E–100kr
Loc 5 km W of Roskilde

Rungsted

Kokkedal (1971)

2980 Kokkedal Kokkedal Alle 9
Tel **4502 867647**
Mem 1023
Pro N Willett
Holes 18 L 6138 metres SSS 72
Fees WD–100kr W/E–150kr
Loc Hoersholm

Rungsted (1937)

DK 2960 Rungsted Kyst
Tel 02/86 3444 (Sec)
Mem 1050
Pro R Beattie
Holes 18 L 5893 metres SSS 72
Fees 160kr (200kr)
Loc Rungsted Copenhagen 30 km

Soro

Midtsjaellands GK

Tuelsovej 20 4180 Soro
Tel **(03) 63 27 75**
Holes 9 L 3670 metres Par 60
Loc Between Korsor and Ringsted

Finland

Hameenlinna

Aulangon (1959)

Hameenlinna
Tel **Hameenlinna 21271**
Mem 150
Pro
Holes 9 L 2450 metres SSS 67
Fees D–25 fmk
Loc Hameenlinna 5 km

Helsinki

Espoo Golfseura

Espoon Golfseura Box 26 02 781 Espoo
Tel **90-811212**
Mem 1100
Pro Juha Utter Ville Kalliala
Holes 18 L 6175 metres SSS 72
Fees 80fmk (100fmk)
Loc 24 km W from Helsinki centre

Helsingin Golfklubi (1932)

Talin Kartano SF-00350 Helsinki 35

Tel **550 235 & 557899**
Mem 1072
Pro Sigurd Nyström J Hämäläinen
Holes 18 L 5900 metres SSS 71
Fees WD–100fmk W/E 120fmk
Loc 7 km W of Helsinki centre

Suur-Helsingin (1965)

Franzeninkatu 3B 81 0050 Helsinki
Tel **85 86 87**
Mem 675
Pro Mrs Arja Sipronen
Holes 9 L 5970 metres SSS 72
Fees WD/WE–80fmk
Loc 20 km N of Helsinki
Mis Season May–Sept

Tuusulan GK

PL 135 04201 Kerava
Tel **(90) 251464**
Mem 560
Pro M Luukkonen
Holes 9 L 5860 SSS 71
Fees 80fmk (100fmk)
Loc 25 km N of Helsinki
Mis Hotel and restaurant

Karhula

Kymen

Ilmattarenkatu 16 48700 Kyminlinna
Tel
Mem
Pro
Holes 9
Fees
Loc Between Helsinki and Russian border

Kokkola

Kokkolan

Pitkansillankatu 31 Kokkola Gamakarleby
Tel **1 15 11**
Mem 50
Pro
Holes 9 L 5890 metres SSS 70
Fees No fees
Loc Kokkola 2 km

Lahti

Lahden Golf (1959)

15230 Lahti Takkula
Tel **918/841311**
Mem 342
Pro Veikko Kankkoner
Holes 9 L 6102 metres SSS 73 (Back Tee)
Fees D–60fmk W–300 fmk
Loc 6 km from Lahti

Lappeenranta

Viipurin Golf (1938)

54530 Luumaki
Tel **953 73812**
Mem 207
Pro
Holes 9 L 2450 metres SSS 66
Fees D–50fmk
Loc Near city centre, behind Etelà-Saimaa Hospital

Mariehamn

Alands GK

Haraldsby SF-22410 Godby
Holes 13 L 5350 metres Par 70 SSS 68

Mikkeli

Mikkelin

Kalervankatu 5 50130 Mikkeli
Tel
Mem
Pro
Holes 9
Fees
Loc 100 miles NW of Helsinki

Oulu

Oulu GC (1964)

Maakokantie 20 B7 90250 Oulu
Tel **981-571192**
Mem 250
Pro
Holes 9 5218 metres SSS 68
Fees 40fmk (50fmk)
Loc Kaukovainio 2 miles from city

Pori

Porin Golfkerho

Kalafornia 28100 Pori
Tel 415559
Mem 135
Pro P Makela
Holes 9 L 5650 metres SSS 70
Fees D–50fmk
Loc Pori 5 km

Tampere

Tammer Golf (1965)

Box 269 SF-33101 Tampere 10
Tel **931-611316**
Mem 450
Pro Juha Pentikainen
Holes 16 L 5801 metres SSS 71
Fees 90fmk
Loc Ruotula 5 km from city

Turku

Aura Golf

Ruissalo 85 Turku 10
Tel **921 306701/921 308667**
Mem 450

Pro
Holes 18 L 5689 metres SSS 72
Fees 80fmk (100fmk)
Loc 9 km to town centre

Vasa

Vaasan-Vasa (1969)

Sandog 3 C34 65100 Vasa 10 (office)
Tel **961-121 742 (sec) 269989 (clubhouse)**
Mem 206
Pro
Holes 9 L 2570 metres SSS 70
Fees 50fmk
Loc 6 km SE of town along route 717 at Kraklund
Mis Driving range

France

Agen

AS Golf Club d'Agen Bon-Encontre

Le Vigneau Passage d'Agen 47000 Agen
Pro P Navarro
Holes 9
Fees 50fr
Loc 5 km from Agen on N113 to Toulouse

Aix-les-Bains

Club D'Aix-les-Bains (1928)

Avenue du Golf 73100 Aix-les-Bains
Tel **61 23 35**
Mem 420
Pro C Chateauneuf P Blanc
Holes 18 L 5600 metres SSS 71
Fees WD–140fr W/E–210fr
Loc 2½ km from city limits

Amiens

Club d'Amiens (1951)

80115 Querrieu
Tel **22 91 02 04**
Mem 347
Pro Bruno Dachicourt
Holes 18 L 6110 metres SSS 72
Fees D–80fr Sun 110fr (1985 prices)
Loc 7 km NE of Amiens on route D929

Angers

Golf d'Angers

34 Rue De Brissac 49000 Angers
Tel **41 88 70 61/41 91 96 56**
Mem 230
Pro Thiery Lhommt
Holes 12 L 6042 metres SSS 70
Fees WD–74fr W/E–95fr W–137fr
Loc Angers 14 km

Angouleme

Club de L'Hirondelle

Chamfleuri 16-Angouleme
Tel **Angouleme 95 24 22**
Mem 72
Pro JM Duhalde
Holes 9 L 2500 mtres SSS 34
Fees D–30fr Sat/Sun 50fr W–160fr
Loc Angouleme 1 km

Annecy

Club du Lac d'Annecy (1953)

Echarvines Talloires
Tel **50 60 12 89 (Clubhouse) 50 60 03 16 (Restaurant)**
Mem 480
Pro Jean Noailly Denis Bonnaz
Holes 18 L 4770 metres SSS 69
Fees 150fr (180fr)
Loc Annecy 13 km

Antibes

Golf de la Bastide du Roy

06410 Biot
Tel **34 50 27**
Mem
Pro H Giraud L Casella Pettavino
Holes 18 L 5064 metres SSS 70
Fees D–30fr W–180fr M–550fr
Loc Antibes 5 km Nice 15 km

Arcachon

Club d'Arcachon (1955)

35 Bd d'Arcachon 33260 La Teste De Buch
Tel **56 54 44 00**
Mem 430
Pro P. Mendiburu
Holes 18 L 6150 metres SSS 71
Fees D–200fr 15 June–15 Sept D–135fr 16 Sept–14 June
Loc Bordeaux 60 km

Auray

Carnac Golf de St Laurent (1975)

Ploemel 56400 Auray
Tel **16 (97) 56 85 18**
Mem 250
Pro Kevin Condon
Holes 18 L 6025 metres SSS 72
3 L 302 metres SSS 9
Fees 90fr Summer–115fr
Loc Ploemel 10 miles off Carnac and Auray (well indicated)

Bar-Le-Duc

Golf Club de Combles

Combles-en-Barrois (Meuse 55000)
Tel **(29) 45 16 03**
Mem
Pro Maurice Vian
Holes 9 L 2700 metres
Fees D–60fr Sat/Sun–80fr W–140fr
Loc Bar Le Duc 70 km W of Nancy

Basel

Golf de Bale (1926)

Private
68220 Hagenthal-le-Bas Ht Rhin France
Tel **(89) 68 50 91**
Mem 630
Pro E Lagger A Perrone C Bisel
Holes 18 L 6255 metres SSS 74
Fees Open Apr–Oct; 150fr (220fr)
Loc Saint Louis 9 km Basel 15 km

La Baule

Golf de La Baule (1976)

Domaine de Saint-denac 44117 Saint-Andrew-Des-Eaux
Tel **(40) 60 46 18**
Mem 400
Pro Eric Mauger
Holes 18 L 6200 metres Par 72
Fees 100fr–270fr depending on time of year
Loc 3 miles from La Baule near Avrillac
Mis Swimming pool, driving range, restaurant & bar, Pro shop

Bayonne

Golf de Hossegor (1929)

40 150 Hossegor
Tel **58 435699**
Mem 470
Pro Y Hausseguy M Hausseguy
Holes 18 L 6004 metres SSS 71
Fees 200fr
Loc Bayonne 15 km

Besancon

Golf Club de Besancon

La Chevillote 25660 Saone

Tel **81 55 73 54**
Mem 340
Pro C Carle
Holes 18 L 6080 metres SSS 72
Fees D–140fr W/E–180fr
Loc Besancon 12 km Saone 3 km

Biarritz

Golf de Biarritz (1888)

Av Edith Cavell 64200 Biarritz
Tel **(59) 03 71 80**
Mem 570
Pro J Leglise Mlle S Fourment
Holes 18 L 5435 metres SSS 69
Fees Season 200fr WD–120fr W/E–125fr
Loc 2 mins city centre

Golf de Chiberta (1926)

Boulevard des Plages 64600 Anglet
Tel **Anglet (59) 63 83 20**
Mem 650
Pro P Dufourg H Brousson
Holes 18 L 5845 metres SSS 70
Fees Low Season 120fr (150fr) High Season 200fr
Loc 3 km Biarritz 5 km Bayonne Airport 5 km

Bourg-Saint-Maurice

Golf des Arcs

Arc 1800 73700
Bourg-Saint-Maurice
Tel **(79) 07 48 00**
Mem 700
Pro A Leclerq R Gollias J C Bard
Holes 18 L 4900 metres SSS 67
Fees D–105fr
Loc Les Arcs 90 km E of Chambery on N90
Mis Also 4 holes pitch and putt

Bordeaux

Golf Bordelais (1900)

Domaine de Kater Av d'Eysines 33200
Bordeaux Cauderan
Tel **(56) 28 56 04**
Mem 460
Pro Mme Monique Casella-Saubaber
Holes 18 L 4833 metres SSS 67
Fees 110fr (140fr)
Loc Bordeaux 3 km Course closed Monday
Mis Restaurant

Golf Municipal de Bordeaux

Avenue de Pernon 33300 Bordeaux
Tel **(56) 50 92 72**
Pro J Delgado
Holes 18 L 6083 metres SSS 72
Fees WD–60fr
Mis Closed Tue; airport Bordeaux-Merignac; restaurant

Sporting Club de Cameyrac (1972)

Saint-Sulpice 33450 Saint-Loubes
Tel **(56) 30 96 79**
Mem 250
Pro Jim Lynch
Holes 18 L 6082 metres SSS 72
Fees 100fr (160fr)
Loc 15 km from Bordeaux

Brehal

Club de Granville (1912)

Pavillon du Golf Breville 50290 Brehal
Tel **(33) 50 2306**
Mem 280
Pro R Artola
Holes 18 L 6010 metres SSS 72
Fees D–70fr W/E–125fr
Loc 5 km from Granville towards Coutances

Golf Municipal de Brehal (1964)

50290 Saint Martin de Brehal
Tel **(33) 50 58 88**
Mem 150
Pro
Holes 9 L 1975 metres Par 31
Fees D–70fr W/E–90fr Hol–100fr
Loc 10 km N of Granville along St Martin beach

La Bretesche

Golf de la Bretesche

44160-Missillac
Tel **(40) 88 30 03**
Mem 1600
Pro Thierry Mathon
Holes 2 × 18 L 6020 metres SSS 72 72
Fees 80fr–200fr depending on time of year
Loc Pontchateau 8 km Nantes 50 km Vannes 50 km

Brive

Association Correzienne de Golf Aubazine

Complexe Touristique du Coiroux
Aubazine 19190 Beynat
Tel **(55) 27 24 69**
Pro JF Encuentra
Holes 9 L 2851 metres SSS 35
Fees 70fr (80fr)
Loc 15 km E of Brive
Mis Closed Tue: airport Brive-Laroche; restaurant; camping & caravanning

Cabourg

Golf de Cabourg Lehome (1955)

14390 Cabourg Lehome Varaville, 38 Av President Rene Coty
Tel **31 21 25 56**
Mem 300
Pro Luc Allain
Holes 18 L 3890 metres SSS 61
Fees On application
Loc Cabourg 2 km

Golf du Clair Vallon

14510 Conneville
Tel **31 91 07 12**
Mem
Pro Jean Pol Chardonnet
Holes 18 L 5830 metres SSS 72
Fees D–45fr W/E–100fr
Loc On road to Conneville

Cannes

Golf Club Cannes (1891)

06210-Mandelieu-La Napoule
Tel **93 49 55 39**
Mem 300
Pro A Monge R Gorgerino R Damiano Carole Nunez
Holes 18 L 5871 metres SSS 71
9 L 2852 metres SSS 35
Fees 180fr (210fr)
Loc Mandelieu 7 km W of Cannes

Cannes Mougins Country Club

175 Route D'Antibes 06250 Mougins
Tel **(93) 75 79 13**
Mem 330 170(L) 50(J)
Pro Michel Damiano Lucien Autiero Patrick Lemaire
Holes 18 L 6300 metres SSS 72
Fees WD–200fr W/E–230fr
Loc Cannes 8 km

Golf CC Opio-Valbonne (1966)

06560 Valbonne
Tel **93 42 00 08**
Mem 350
Pro John Norsworthy Tel 93 42 05 29
Holes 18 L 5905 metres Par 72
Fees 150fr (200fr)
Loc 15 km from Cannes 20 km from Nice Airport

Chalon-sur-Saone

Golf Public de Chalon-sur-Saone

Zone de Sports et Loisirs de Saint-Nicolas Chatenoy-en-Bresse par 71380 Saint-Marcel
Tel **(85) 48 61 64**
Pro J Walter-Martin
Holes 18 L 6173 metres SSS 72
Fees 35fr
Loc SE of Chalon
Mis Practice green, pitch and putt

Chamonix

Club de Chamonix (1934)

BP 31 74402 Chamonix Cedex
Tel **50 53 06 28**
Mem 292
Pro Raymond Marro JC Bonnaz Gilbert Ravanel
Holes 18 L 6087 metres SSS 72
Fees 15 June–15 Sept–180fr; otherwise 150fr; 5 day pass 850fr
Loc Chamonix Centre 2 km on RN 506 Geneva 60 km

Chantilly (*see* Paris)

Chaource

Club de la Cordeliere

10210 Chateau de la Cordeliere
Tel **25 40 11 05**
Mem 250
Pro Maurice Vian
Holes 18 L 6033 metres SSS 72
Fees WD–100fr W/E–250fr
Loc NE of Chaource on N443 Troyes 30 km

Charleville

Golf des Ardennes

Les Poursaudes Villers-le-Tilleul
08430 Poix-Terron
Holes 6 L 1605 metres SSS 24
Fees 50fr
Loc 20 km SE of Charleville

Chaussy

Golf de Villarceaux

Chaussy 95710 Bray et Lu
Tel **467 70 25**
Mem
Pro Rene Alsuguren
Holes 18 L 6213 metres SSS
Fees D–25fr Sat/Sun–60fr
Loc 40 km NW of Paris

Cherbourg

Club de Cherbourg-La Glacerie (1973)

Domaine des Roches 50470-La Glacerie
Tel **(33) 44 45 48**
Mem 270
Pro J-F Lenoir

Holes 9 L 2842 metres SSS 36
Fees WD–90fr W/E–100fr
Loc 4 miles S of Cherbourg

Clermont Ferrand

Golf de Charade (1985)

Charade 631 30 Royat
Tel **(73) 35 73 09**
Mem 250
Pro R Picabea
Holes 9 L 2300 metres SSS 32
Fees D–70fr Sat/Sun–90fr
Loc Royat 3 km and 8 km W of Clermont Ferrand

Golf du Rigolet (1928)

6 Le Mont Dore
Tel **Mont Dore 73 (210079)**
Mem
Pro L Mencagli
Holes 9 L 4230 metres SSS 68
Fees D–30fr W–150fr
Loc Mont Dore $2\frac{1}{2}$ km and 35 km SW of Clermont Ferrand

Golf Club des Volcans (1984)

La Bruyère des Moines 63870 Orcines France
Tel **73621551**
Mem 350
Pro Lucien Roux Gilles Roux Odile Roux
Holes 18 L 1986 SSS 74
Fees 100fr (120fr)
Loc 12km W of Clermont Ferrand-RN 141

Compiegne

Compiegne

Avenue Royale 60 Compiegne
Tel **440 15 73**
Mem 300
Pro Christian Bonardi
Holes 18 L 5633 metres SSS 72
Fees D–20fr Sat/Sun–50fr
Loc Centre of town 70 km NE of Paris

Le Coudray-Montceaux (*see* Paris)

Coutances

Coutainville

Coutainville 50230
Tel **Agon 47 03 31**
Mem 150
Pro S Spencer
Holes 9 L 2700 metres SSS 70
Fees D-50fr W–400fr
Loc Coutainville 75 km S of Cherbourg

Deauville

New Golf Club (1929)

14 Saint Arnoult 14800 Deauville
Tel **31 88 20 53**
Mem 600
Pro C Hausseguy
Holes 18 & 9 L 5933 & 3033 metres SSS 71 & 72
Fees 130fr; 15 Jun–15 Sep 160fr (200fr; 15 Jun–15 Sep and hols 250fr)
Loc 3 km S of Deauville

Dieppe

Golf de Dieppe (1897)

76200 Dieppe
Tel **35 84 25 05**
Mem 430
Pro Sebastian Ortiz
Holes 18 L 5854 metres SSS 71
Fees 140fr (170fr 2D–260fr) July/August 150fr (180fr)
Loc Dieppe $1\frac{1}{2}$ km

Dijon

Golf de Bourgogne

Bois de Norges 21 Norges La Ville
Tel **(80) 357110**
Mem 350
Pro B Radcliffe
Holes 18 L 6164 metres SSS 72
9 hole pitch and putt
Fees WD–120fr W/E–180fr
Loc 10 km N Dijon towards Langres

Dinard

Golf de Dinard

35 Saint-Briach-sur-Mer
Tel **34 32 07**
Mem 150
Pro F Cavalo A Curely Miss Le Derff
Holes 18 L 5486 metres SSS 71
Fees D–$17\frac{1}{2}$fr Sat/Sun–26fr W–125fr
Loc Dinard 8 km

Divonne-les-Bains

Club de Divonne (1931)

01220 Divonne-les-Bains
Tel **(50) 20 07 19**
Mem 600
Pro R Guignet J Garaialde M Suhas
Holes 18 L 6055 metres SSS 72
Fees D–130fr (330fr)
Loc Divonne $\frac{1}{2}$ km Geneva 18 km

Douai

Association Sportive du Golf de Thumeries

Bois Lenglart 59239 Thumeries
Tel **(20) 86 58 98**
Mem 285
Pro B Tiradon
Holes 9 L 2923 metres SSS 36
Fees 55fr (75fr)
Loc 15 km S of Lille
Mis Practice-putting green; closed Tue; 18 holes planned

Epinal

GC des Images d'Epinal

Rue du Merle-Blanc 88001 Epinal
Tel **(29) 31 45 45**
Holes 9 L 2720 metres
Loc Epinal 70 km S of Nancy

Etretat

Golf Marin D'Etretat (1908)

PO Box 7 76790 Entretat
Tel **(35) 27 04 89 (office)/27 04 56 (clubhouse)**
Mem 320
Pro Jean Morea
Holes 18 L 5840 metres SSS 72
Fees 1 Apr–30 Sep: 150fr (220fr W/E–360fr)
1 Oct–30 Mar: 90fr (135fr W/E–225fr)
Loc $\frac{1}{2}$ km Etretat 28 km N of Le Havre

Evian

Royal Golf d'Evian (1905)

Rive Sud du lac de Geneve 74500-Evian
Tel **Evian 50 75 14 00**
Mem 220
Pro D Damevin F Anger
Holes 18 L 5973 metres SSS 70
Fees 130fr–220fr (depending on season)
Loc Evian 2 km Geneva Airport 40 km
Mis All-inclusive stay at Royal Club Evian–unlimited free access to golf

La Ferte Mace

Andaines Golf Club

61 Bagnoles de l'Orne Route de Domfront
Tel **(33) 37 81 42**
Mem
Pro Henri Dauge
Holes 9 L 2200 metres SSS 70
Fees D–40fr W/E–60fr W–180fr
Loc Bagnoles 80 km S of Caen

Flaine

Golf de Flaine-les-Carroz (1984)

74300 Flaine
Tel **50 90 85 44**
Mem 50
Pro Marc Malafosse
Holes 18 L 4180 metres Par 63
Fees 110fr
Loc Flaine 4 km Geneva Airport 60 km
Mis Practice greens; tennis, swimming, horse riding, etc.

Fontainebleau

Golf de Fontainebleau (1908)

Route d'Orleans Fontainebleau
Tel **422 22 95**
Mem 300
Pro JP Hirigoyen
Holes 18 L 6094 metres SSS 72
Fees D–130fr W/E–300fr
Loc City limits 2 km

Hardelot-Plage

Golf de Hardelot

62152 Avenue de Golf 62152 Neufchatel Hardelot
Tel **(21) 83 73 10**
Mem 400
Pro L Maisonnave
Holes 18 L 5951 metres SSS 73
Fees 125fr (170; 3D–360fr) (3 days) 330fr
Loc Boulogne 15 km

Havre

Golf du Havre (1933)

Octeville-sur-Mer Hameau St Supplix 76930
Tel 35 46 36 50/35 46 36 11
Mem 450
Pro Ian Lambie
Holes 18 L 5830 metres SSS 70
Fees WD–110fr W/E–200fr
Loc Le Havre 10 km
Mis Clubhouse closed Tuesday

Hyeres

Golf de Valcros

83 La Londe-les-Maures
Tel **66 81 02**
Mem
Pro M Berthet
Holes 18 L 5050 metres SSS 70
Fees
Loc Le Lavandou 16 km

Lacanau

Golf de L'Ardilouse (1980)

Domaine de l'Ardilouse 33680 Lacanau
Tel **56 03 25 60**
Mem 150
Pro P Delaville
Holes 18 L 6000 metres SSS 72
Fees High Season from 110–140fr Low Season from 90–110fr
Loc 45 km from Bordeaux

Landerneau

Golf de La Chambre de Commerce de Brest

Parc des Loisirs de Lann-Rohou 29220 Landerneau
Tel **(98) 85 16 17/85 19 39**
Pro Daniel Roumaud
Holes 18 L 6213 metres SSS 72
Fees 100fr
Loc 15 km E of Brest
Mis Closed Tue; airport Brest-Guipavas: restaurant

Lannion

Golf de Saint-Samson

Pleumeur-Bodou 22560
Tel **96 238734**
Mem
Pro Christian Arnut
Holes 18 L 5760 metres SSS 72
Fees WD–50fr W/E–90fr
Loc 7 km N of Lannion on Tregastel Road

Laval

Club de Laval

Le Jariel 53 Change-Les-Laval
Tel **(42) 20 18 70**
Mem
Pro
Holes 9 L 3050 metres SSS 36
Fees D–20fr Sat/Sun–30fr
Loc 7 km N of Laval

Le Mans

Club du Mans Mulsanne

72230 Arnage
Tel **(43) 27 00 36/42 00 36**
Mem 250
Pro M Dugue
Holes 18 L 5756 metres SSS 71
Fees WD–70fr W/E–110fr
Loc Mulsanne 12 km from Le Mans

Lille

Golf de Bondues

Chateau de la Vigne 59910 Bondues
Tel **(20) 23 20 62**
Mem 800
Pro Pierre Iturrioz Andre Vandamme Alan White
Holes 18 L 6223 metres SSS 73
9 L 3044 metres SSS 36
Fees 70fr (D–120fr W/E–170fr)
Loc Roubaix 10 km Tourcoing 5 km Lille 10 km

Golf de Brigode

36 Avenue de Golf 59650 Villeneuve
Tel **(20) 91 17 86**
Mem 600
Pro Roger Pollet
Holes 18 L 6182 metres SSS 72
Fees 85fr (140fr)
Loc Lille 8 km
Mis Closed Tues

Golf Club des Flandres

Bouleva Clemenceau
Tel **(20) 722074**
Mem 300
Pro Nicolas Fourrier and Bruno Tiradon
Holes 9 L 2339 metres SSS 33
Fees 60fr (100fr)
Loc 4 km from the centre of Lille, in the middle of Croisé Laroche racecourse

Club du Sart (1910)

5 Rue Jean Jaures 59650 Villeneuve D'Ascq
Tel **(20) 72 02 51**
Mem 510
Pro Robert Loth Freddy Swaefens
Holes 18 L 5750 metres SSS 71
Fees 80fr (140fr)
Loc Motorway Lille–Gent exit Wasquehal

Limoges

Golf Municipal de Limoges

Saint Lazere Avenue du Golf 87 Limoges
Tel **(55) 31 21 02**
Pro D Larretche
Holes 18 L 6218 metres SSS 72
Fees
Loc S of Limoges on N20
Mis Tennis, swimming

Loudun

Golf Loudun Saint-Hilaire

Roiffe 86120
Tel **(49) 987806**
Mem 320
Pro F Viau de Caumette
Holes 18 L 6310 metres Par 72
Fees 96fr (120fr)
Loc 15 km Loudun 20 km Saumur
Mis Pro-shop; practice green, putting greens

Luchon

Golf-Club Luchon (1908)

Route de Montauban 31110 Luchon
Tel **61 79 03 27**
Mem 200
Pro Tony Alcazar
Holes 9 L 2375 metres SSS 66
Fees 90fr (100fr)
Loc Luchon 90 km SE of Tarbes

Lyon

Club de Lyon (1964)

38280 Villette-d'Anthon
Tel **78 31 11 33**
Mem 750
Pro L Capoccia G Martin
Holes 27 L 6415 metres SSS 72
Fees D–130fr Sat/Sun–250fr
Loc Lyons 25 km

Golf de Lyon-Verger (1977)

69360 Saint-Symphorien D'Ozon
Tel **78 02 84 20**
Mem 460
Pro H Sauzet B Lacroix
Holes 18 L 5900 metres SSS 71
Fees 130fr (190fr)
Loc 14 km S of Lyon on A7 (exit Solaize) or RN7–2 km S of Feysin
Mis Closed Fri and first 3 weeks August

Macon

Golf de la Commanderie

Pres M Charles Piat Chateau de Bellevue 69910 Ville-Morgon Macon
Tel **(85) 33 40 24**
Mem 250
Pro Claude Soules
Holes 15 L 3283 yds SSS 71
Fees WD–70fr W/E–100fr
Loc Macon 5 km on Route to Bourg

Marseilles

Golf-Club Marseille-Aix (1935)

Private
Les Milles 13290
Tel **Sec 42 24 20 41/42 24 23 01; Rest 42 24 21 34**
Mem 550
Pro Roger Patrick and Bernard Cotton

Holes 18 L 6302 metres SSS 72
Fees 120fr (240fr) 1986 prices
Loc Aix en Provence 7 km; Marignane airport 15 km; Marseilles 20 km

Mazamet

Club de la Barouge (1956)

Association Sportive de la Barouge
81660 Pont de l'Arn
Tel **63 61 08 00**
Mem 260
Pro Jose-Maria Roca
Holes 18 L 5623 metres SSS 70
Fees 120fr (150fr)
Loc 2 km N of Mazamet 82 km E of Toulouse

Meaux (*see* Paris)

Megeve

Club du Mont-d'Arbois

74120 Megeve
Tel **(50) 21 29 79**
Mem 400
Pro M Alsuguren J-B Alsuguren G Parodi
Holes 18 L 6100 metres SSS 72
Fees 150–200fr
Loc Megeve 2 km
Mis Competitions every WE

Meribel

Association Sportive du Golf de Meribel-les-Allues

73550 Meribel Altiport
Tel **(79) 08 50 25 (Sec)**
Pro (July/Aug) G Watine G Martin
Holes 9 L 2433 metres SSS 67 (18 holes)
Fees 100fr
Loc 15 km S of Moutiers
Mis Tennis, swimming, horse riding, ice skating

Metz

Golf Club de Metz-Cherisey (1964)

Chateau de Cherisey 57240 Verney
Tel **(8) 777 70 18**
Mem 260
Pro P Brehier
Holes 9 L 5800 metres SSS 70
Fees 60fr (100fr)
Loc 13 km SE of Metz

Montbeliard

Golf de Pruneville (1930)

BP48 25600 Sochaux
Tel **81 98 11 77**
Mem 300
Pro R Le Souder
Holes 18 L 6281 metres SSS 73
Fees 110fr (120fr)
Loc 10km S Montbeliard; motorway exit 'Montbeliard Sud' and on to Besançon on D126 to Dampierre sur le Doubs
Mis Open 15/3–30/11. Bar and rest open every WD

Mont-de-Marsan

GC du Marsan

40090 Saint-Avit
Tel **(58) 75 63 05 (Sec)**
Pro P Navaro
Holes 9 L 2413 metres SSS 34
Fees 80fr
Loc 8 km from Mont-de-Marsan; 80 km N of Pau
Mis Covered practice range, putting green

Montebourg

Golf de Fontenay en Cotentin (1975)

Fontenay sur Mer 50301 Montebourg France
Tel **(33) 21 44 27**
Mem 70
Pro Monique Legarreres
Holes 9 L 2 × 3050 metres Par 2 × 36
Fees 80fr (100fr)
Loc 15 km SE of Valognes (station of turbo train Paris–Cherbourg); 32 km SE of Cherbourg by routes RN13 and D42

Monte Carlo

Monte Carlo (1910)

Mont Agel La Turbie
Tel **(93) 41 09 11**
Mem 420
Pro B Ducoulombier C Houtart R Halsall
Holes 18 L 5667 metres SSS 71
Fees 200fr (250fr)
Loc La Turbie 06320 Cap d'Ail
Mis Handicap certificate required

Mortefontaine (*see* Paris)

Montluçon

Golf du Val-de-Cher

Nassigny 03190 Vallon-en-Sully
Tel **(70) 06 71 15**
Mem 200
Pro JC Gassiat
Holes 18 L 5200 metres
Fees 100fr (120fr 2D–200fr)
Loc Nassigny N of Montlucon on N144
Mis Closed Tue; restaurant

Montreuil

Golf de Nampont-St-Martin (1978)

Chateau de Nampont-St-Martin
Nampont-St-Martin 80120
Tel **33 22 29 92 90 & 32 22 25 00 20**
Mem 200
Pro Mr Maisonnave Mr Kershaw
Holes 18 L 5505 metres SSS 72
Fees WD–80fr W/E–100fr Fri/Sat/Sun 200fr
Loc 12 km S Montreuil sur Mer on route N1 30 km SE of Le Touquet
Mis 200-metre water driving range

Mulhouse

Golf du Rhin (1969)

BP1152 F68053 Mulhouse Cedex
Tel **(89) 26 07 86**
Mem 450
Pro John Francis Halliwell
Holes 18 L 6200 metres SSS 72
Fees 120fr (180fr)
Loc Ile du Rhin–Chalampe 20 km E of Mulhouse

Nancy

Golf de Nancy-Aingeray

Aingeray 54460 Liverdun
Tel **(28) 25 76 46**
Mem 250
Pro P Delaville
Holes 18 L 5510 metres SSS 69
Fees D–35fr Sat/Sun–75fr
Loc Nancy 17 km

Nantes

Golf de Nantes

44360 Vigneux de Bretagne
Tel **40 63 25 82**
Mem 430
Pro N Gajan
Holes 18 L 5940 metres SSS 72
Fees D–130fr W/E–200fr
Loc Nantes 15 km

Nevers

Club du Nivernais

58400 Magny Cours
Tel **(86) 58 18 30**
Mem
Pro P Raguet
Holes 11 L 2500 metres SSS 34
Fees 40fr (80fr)
Loc Nevers 11 km on N7

Nimes

Club de Campagne

Route de Saint Gilles 30 Nimes
Tel **37 43 57**
Mem
Pro Martin Ado E Lassale
Holes 18 L 6200 metres SSS 72
Fees D–25fr W/E–50fr
Loc Nimes 9 km

Orleans

Golf d'Orleans

Donnery 45450 Pay aux Loges
Tel **65 75 48**
Mem
Pro Daniel Dugue
Holes 9 L 2940 metres SSS 72
Fees D–30fr W/E–40fr Sat/Sun–55fr
Loc 16 km E of Orleans

Golf de Sologne (1955)

Country Club des Olleries Route de Jouy le potier 45240 La Ferte St Aubin
Tel **38 76 57 33 or 38 76 68 79**
Pro Mark Vickery
Holes 18 L 7200 yds Par 72
9 L 2700 yds Par 35
Fees 90fr (140fr)
Loc 25 km S of Orleans on RN20
150 km from Paris

Paris

Golf de Chaumont en Vexin (1963)

60240 Chaumont en Vexin
Tel **16-1-44490081 or 44491476**
Mem 320
Pro Alain Gass
Holes 18 L 6190 metres Par 72
Fees D–100fr Sat/Sun–300fr
Loc Paris 60 km

Golf de Chantilly (1908)

60500 Chantilly Vineuil Saint Firmin
Tel **Chantilly 44-57-04-43**
Mem 450
Pro A Chardonnet P leglise
G Lamy
Holes 18 & 9 L 6250 & 2625 metres
SSS 71 & 35
Fees WD 200fr W/E–M
Loc 45 km from Paris

Golf Public de Chevry

91190 Gif-sur-Yvette
Tel **(6) 012 40 33/(1) 60 12 40 33**
Holes 9 L 2900 metres SSS 36; pitch and putt 9 holes 460 metres SSS 27

Golf de Coudray

91830 Le Coudray-Montceaux
Tel **64 93 81 76**
Mem 500
Pro JL Schneider M Lebrun
Holes 18 L 5530 metres SSS 70
9 L 1615 metres
Fees D–170fr W/E–360fr
Loc Paris 35 km

Golf de Domont

Route de Montmorency 85
Tel **991 07 50**
Mem
Pro R Changart G Gassiat
Holes 18 L 5616 metres SSS 71
Fees D–25fr Sat/Sun–60fr
Loc Paris 18 km

Club de Fourqueux (1963)

8 Rue St Nom (78112) Fourqueux
Tel **34 51 41 47**
Mem 520
Pro Hugues Gioux
Holes 18 and 9 L 6410 metres SSS 73
Fees 200 fr (300fr)
Loc St Germain en Laye 4 km
Mis 2 tennis courts; swimming pool, bridge club; nursery (4–12)

Golf de Grenouillere

Ile de la Grenouillere 78290 Croissy-sur-Seine
Tel **(1) 39 18 43 81**
Mem 400
Pro F Lefebvre A Alsuguren
Holes 9 L 2120 metres SSS 30
Fees 90fr (180fr)
Loc 25 km from Paris

International Club du Lys

Rond-Point du Grand Cerf 60260 Lamorlaye
Tel **(4) 421 26 00**
Mem
Pro F Saubaber
Holes 18 L 5986 metres SSS 71
18 L 4798 metres SSS 66
Fees 180fr (350fr) 1986 prices
Loc Chantilly 5 km

Golf d'Isabella (1969)

RN12 Sainte-Appoline 78370 Plaisir
Tel **(1) 3054 1062**
Mem 235
Pro
Holes 9 L 2454 metres SSS 34
Fees WD exc Tue 80fr (160fr)
Loc 28 km from Paris RN12 to Dreux

Golf de Meaux-Boutigny (1985)

Le Bordet Rue de Barrois 77470 Trilport
Tel **60256398**
Mem 450
Pro Alain Delannoy
Holes 18 L 6100 metres SSS 72; 9L 1600 metres SSS 30
Fees 120fr (200fr)
Loc 55 km E of Paris Highway 4

Golf de Morfontaine (1926)

Mortefontaine 60520 La Chapelle en Serval
Tel **44 54 68 27**
Mem 450
Pro S De Galard M Philippon
Holes 18 and 9 L 6063 and 2550 metres SSS 72 and 36
Fees 250fr (450fr) only with member
Loc Senlis 10 km

Golf d'Ormesson (1969)

94490 Ormesson s/Marne
Tel **45 76 20 71**
Mem 400
Pro G Minassian F Leclercq
Holes 18 L 6180 metres SSS 72
Fees WD–170fr W/E–350fr
Loc Paris 21 km

Golf Club d'Ozoir-la-Ferriere (1926)

Châteaux des Agneaux 77330 Ozoir la Ferriere
Tel **028 20 79**
Mem 450
Pro M Alsuguren G Henichard
Holes 18 and 9 L 6105 and 2235 metres SSS 72 and 33
Fees 18 holes 150fr (200fr)
9 holes 100fr (150fr)
Loc From Paris A4 (Sortie Val Maubuée)

Golf du Prieure

78440 Gargenville Sailly
Tel **476 70 12**
Mem 1200
Pro J Alsurguren M Lachaux
G Bourdy
Holes 2 x 18 L 6216 and 6317 metres SSS 72 and 72
Fees D–50fr W/E–140fr
Loc Meulan 9 km Mantes La Jolie, 10 km W of Paris

Racing Club de France

La Boulie 7800 Versailles
Tel **950 59 41**
Mem 950
Pro CH Bonardi F Castel
M Garaialde JP Quillo
Holes 2 x 18 and 9 L 6055 6206 and 1148 metres SSS 72
Fees D–160fr W/E–300fr
Loc Paris 15 km

Golf de Rochefort

78730 Rochefort-en-Yvelines
Tel **484 31 81**
Mem
Pro Eugene Demiautte
Holes 18 L 6020 metres SSS 73
Fees D–35fr Sat/Sun–85fr
Loc 35 km from Paris

St Aubin (1976)

91 St Aubin G 1190
Tel **941 25 19**
Mem
Pro C Chabrier B Antoine
Holes 18 L 6100 metres SSS 72
Fees WD–30fr W/E–36fr
Loc SW of Paris

Golf de Saint-Nom-La-Bretêche (1959)

78860 Saint Nom La Bretêche
Tel **(1) 34 62 54 00**
Mem 1600
Sec P Galitzine
Pro A Cadet R Golias A Ferran
P Rouquet G Leven
Holes 2 x 18 L 6685 and 6712 yds SSS 72 and 72
Fees WD only–250fr
Loc Paris 15 miles, A-13
Mis Handicap certificate required

Golf Public de Saint-Quentin en Yvelines

Base de Loisirs RN 12 78190 Trappes
Tel **(3) 050 86 40/(1) 30 50 86 40**
Holes 18 L 5900 metres SSS 71
Mis Swimming, tennis

Golf de Saint Cloud (1911)

60 Rue du 19 Janvier Garches 92380
Tel **47 01 01 85**
Mem 2000
Pro R Giraud F Berthet A Leclerc
Holes 2 x 18 L 6145 and 5135 metres SSS 72 and 68
Fees 200fr (360fr)
Loc Porte Dauphine Paris 9 km
Mis Handicap certificate required

Saint Germain en Laye (1922)

Private
Route de Poissy 78100 St Germain en Laye
Tel **451 75 90**
Men 800
Pro M Dallemagne O Saint-Hilaire
E Lafitte D Hausseguy

Holes 18 and 9 L 6115 and 2030 metres SSS 72 and 33
Fees WD–160fr W/E–250fr
Loc 20 km from Paris

St Pierre du Perray (1974)

St Pierre du Perray 91100 Corbeil
Tel **075 17 47**
Mem
Pro Bruno Antoine
Holes 18 L 6247 metres SSS 72
Fees D–40fr W/E–56 fr
Loc SE of Paris off N6

Club de Seraincourt

95 450 Vigny
Tel **475 45 70**
Mem 380
Pro Bard Legarres
Holes 18 L 5751 metres SSS 70
Fees D–30fr W/E–100fr
Loc 35 km from Paris

UCPA Base de Plein Air et de Loisirs (1985)

77590 Bois-le-Roi
Tel **(1) 60 69 72**
Holes 9; driving range 6; SSS 21
Loc SE of Paris

Golf Public de Villennes-sur-Seine

Route d'Orgeval 78670 Villennes-sur-Seine
Tel **(3) 975 30 00**
Holes 9 L 3000 metres SSS 36 (18 holes planned)
Loc W of Paris off N13
Mis Driving range; Pro-shop, restaurant

Pau

Pau GC (1856)

64-Billere Pau
Tel **Pau 22 73 33**
Mem 115
Pro Alfred Coussies
Holes 18 L 5330 metres SSS 70
Fees D–25fr Sun–25fr
Loc Pau 2 km

Perigueux

Golf Public de Périgueux (1980)

Domaine de Saltgourde 24430 Marsac
Tel **(53) 53 65 90**
Mem 300
Pro Crawford Campbell
Tel (53) 53 02 35
Holes 9 L 3030 metres SSS 71
Fees 80fr W–300fr M–600fr
Loc Angouleme to Riberac road 3 km from Perigueux
Mis 18 holes in preparation

Perpignan

St Cyprien (1974)

Le Mas D'Huston 66750 St Cyprien Plage
Tel **68 21 01 71**
Mem 550
Pro P Lacroix B Diagne E Boucau
Holes 18 L 6480 metres SSS 73 9 L 2724 metres SSS 35
Fees 130fr (150fr) clients staying in resort; 145fr (165fr) clients out side resort

Poitiers

Golf Club Poitevin

Terrain des Challons 86000
Tel **47 68 38**
Mem 100
Pro Roger Pollet
Holes 9 L 2660 metres SSS 35
Fees D–35fr W–200fr
Loc Poitiers 3 km

Pornic

Club de Pornic (1912)

49 bis Boulevard de l'Ocean Sainte Marie/Mer 44210 Pornic
Tel **(40) 82 06 69**
Mem 200
Pro O de Saint Hilaire
Holes 9 L 5120 metres Par 70 SSS 68
Fees D–90fr (15/6 to 15/9–150fr) W/E–160fr
Loc Pornic 1 km Nantes 45 km La Baule 35 km

Quimper

Golf de Cournouaille (1959)

29 S la Foret Fouesnant
Tel **(98) 56 97 09**
Mem 200
Pro H Ranieri
Holes 9 L 5641 metres SSS 69
Fees Season D–120fr W–545fr
Loc Quimper 15 km

Reims

Golf de Reims (1928)

Chateau des Dames de France 51390 Gueux
Tel **(26) 03 60 14**
Mem 460
Pro P Harrison
Holes 18 L 6026 metres SSS 72
Fees 100fr (130fr)
Loc Reims 10 km

Rennes

Golf de Rennes

Saint-Jacques-de-la-Lande 35000 Rennes
Tel **(99) 55 44 18**
Mem 131
Pro C Victor
Holes 9 L 2850 metres SSS 72
Fees D–30fr W/E–50fr
Loc Route de Redon 7 km Rennes

Rouen

Club de Rouen

Rue Boucicaut Mt St Aignan
Tel **Rouen 71 05 41**
Mem 250
Pro Henri Gassiat
Holes 18 L 5522 metres SSS 71
Fees D–20fr
Loc 3½ km from Rouen

Golf du Vaudreuil

27100 Le Vaudreuil
Tel **(16 32) 59 02 60**
Mem 350
Pro J Lecuellet
Holes 18 L 6411 metres SSS 73
Fees 100fr (200fr; W/E–350fr, group 550fr)
Loc Louviers 6 km; Rouen 25 km; Paris 100 km
Mis Lunch restaurant 15/3–6/11 (closed Tue)

Royan

Golf de la Cote de Beauté

Maine-Gaudin 17420 Saint-Palais
Tel **(46) 22 16 24**
Pro J-P Prieur
Holes 9 L 3170 metres SSS 72 (36)
Fees 100fr
Loc Saint-Palais 7 km W of Royan
Mis Closed Tue

Sables-d'Or-les-Pins

Club des Sables d'Or

22240 Sables-les-Pins
Tel **(96) 41 42 57**
Mem 140
Pro G Frangeu
Holes 9 L 5253 metres SSS 70
Fees D–140fr
Loc Dinard 30 km

Saint Brieuc

Golf Public des 'Ajoncs d'Or' (1976)

22410 Saint-Quay Portrieux
Tel **(96) 71 90 74**
Mem 300
Pro M Pouette
Holes 18 L 6230 metres SSS 72
Fees 100fr
Loc 18 km from Saint Brienc via Binic

St Cast

Golf de Pen Guen

22380 Saint Cast le Guildo 22380
Tel **(96) 419120**
Mem
Pro Didier Benet Laurent du Bouerie
Holes 9 L (18 Tees) 2580 metres SSS 70
Fees 15 Jun–15 Sep 100fr; winter 80fr
Loc Dinard 25 km

Saintes

Golf de Hautmont-Cognac

Chareutes-Poitou 17
Tel **(46) 93 04 35**
Mem 150
Pro Rene Poulliat
Holes 9 L 2687 metres SSS 71
Fees D–50fr Sat/Sun–100fr
Loc Saintes 3 km

St Jean de Luz

Club de Chantaco (1928)

64 Route d'Ascain
Tel **59 26 14 22 and 59 26 19 22**
Mem 400
Pro R Garaialde JC Harismendy
Holes 18 L 5690 metres SSS 70
Fees D–130fr (150fr) W–520fr July–mid September D–200fr W–760fr
Loc St Jean de Luz 2 km on Route d'Ascain

Nivelle (1907)

64500 Ciboure Place William Sharp
Tel **59471899/59471972**
Mem 400
Pro NJ Palli J Delgado
Holes 18 L 5594 metres SSS 70
Fees 180fr High season; 130fr Low season
Loc Saint Jean de Luz 1½ km
Mis No golf Thu low season. Jul & Aug creche (3–6 yrs)

Saint-Raphaël

Golf de Valescure (1896)

BP 451 83704 Saint Raphaël Cedex
Tel **(94) 52 16 58**
Mem 220
Pro E Cougourdan M Bromet
Holes 18 L 5233 metres Par 70
Fees 120fr (140fr)
Loc Saint Raphäel 5 km

St Tropez

Sporting Golf Club de Beauvallon

83120-Sainte Maxime
Tel **96 16 98**
Mem 320
Pro Pierre Delaville
Holes 9 L 2525 metres SSS 34
Fees D–80fr (July/Aug 100fr)
Loc Sainte Mazime 3 km Saint Tropez 10 km

Sens

Golf de Clairis (1974)

89150 Domaine de Clairis St Valerien
Tel **86 86 33 90**
Mem 180
Pro J Schilling
Holes 9
Fees 90fr (160fr)
Loc St Valerien 12 km W of Sens

Strasbourg

Golf Club de Strasbourg

Route du Rhin 67400 Illkirch-Graffenstaden
Tel **(88) 66 17 22**
Mem 600
Pro IP Tairraz N Madeuf
Holes 18 L 6115 metres SSS 72
Fees WD only–120fr
Loc 10 km from Strasbourg

Sully-sur-Loire

Club de Sully-sur-Loire

Viglain 45600 Sully-sur-Loire
Tel **(38) 01 02 35**
Mem 220
Pro P Antoine
Holes 18 L 6200 metres SSS 72
Fees D–20fr Sat/Sun–40fr
Loc Sully-sur-Loire 3 km

Tarbes

Golf Municipal de Laloubère

65310 Laloubère
Tel **(62) 96 06 22**
Pro M Uthurbide
Holes 9 L 3135 metres SSS 36–72
Fees 60fr (80fr)
Loc Tarbes
Mis Tennis, swimming, horse riding

Golf de Lannemezan et Capvern Les Bains

Demi-Lune Lannemezan 65300
Tel **(62) 98 01 01**
Mem
Pro Robert Lasserre
Holes 18 L 5945 metres SSS 71
Fees WD–70fr W/E–80fr
Loc 38 km from Tarbes

Tende

Golf de Vievola (1978)

06430 Tende (A.M.)
Tel **(93) 04 61 02**
Mem 40
Pro Nuccio Giordano
Holes 9 L 1780 metres SSS 30
Fees 85fr (110fr)
Loc 4 km from Italian border (Col di Tenda) on Route Nat 204
Mis Open 1/6–31/10

Tignes

Golf de Tignes

Club Sportif de Tignes Le Val Claret 73320 Tignes
Tel (79) 06 37 42
Pro JP Basurco
Holes 9 L 1820 metres
Fees 75fr
Mis Tennis, swimming, skiing, etc.

Toulouse

Club de Palmola

31 Buzet Sur Tarn
Tel **(61) 84 20 50**
Mem
Pro Dominique Barquez
Holes 18 L 6166 metres SSS 72
Fees WD–60fr Sat/Sun–90fr
Loc 20 km NE of Toulouse

Golf de Toulouse (1951)

Les Hts de Garonne Vielle Toulouse 31320-Castanet-Tolosan
Tel **61 73 45 48**
Mem 380
Pro Richard Olalainty
Holes 18 L 5400 metres SSS 69
Fees 100fr (120fr)
Loc 8 minutes from Toulouse

Le Touquet

Golf Club de Touquet (1904)

Ave du Golf 62520 Le Touquet
Tel **21 05 20 22 Telex 135 565 F**
Mem 550
Pro M Bembridge P Philippon
Holes 2 × 18 L 5612 and 5860 metres SSS 71 and 72
Fees 180fr (250fr)
Loc 2 km S of Le Touquet
Mis Man Dir Peter V Christensen

Tours

Golf de Touraine

Chateau de la Touche a Ballan Mire 37510 Joue les Tours
Tel **47 53 20 28**
Mem 348
Pro Marc Vol Phil Tabone
Dir Charly Decroix
Holes 18 L 5745 metres SSS 71
Fees 95fr (150fr)

Valenciennes

Golf de Valenciennes

59-Marly
Tel **46 30 10**
Mem 215
Pro Jean Roux
Holes 9 L 5190 metres SSS 66
Fees WD–25fr W/E–35fr
Loc Valenciennes 2 km

Vichy

Sporting Club de Vichy

Avenue de la République 03700 Bellerive sur Allier
Tel **(70) 32 29 11**
Mem 430
Pro Ch Roumand
Holes 18 L 5427 metres SSS 70
Fees D–155fr W/E–200fr (2D–340fr)
Loc In city limits

Vittel

Golf de Vittel

A Hodez Le Gros Buisson 88800 Vittel
Tel **(29) 081880**
Mem
Pro M Lachaux
Holes 18 L 6236 metres SSS 72
Fees D–105fr
Loc In city 70 km S of Nancy

Wimereux

Golf de Wimereux (1906)

Route d'Ambleteuse 62930 Wimereux
Tel **(21) 32 43 20**
Mem 300
Pro Jean-Marie Flory
Holes 18 L 6361 metres Par 62
Fees 110fr (135fr)
Loc 6 km N of Boulogne on D940 30 km N of Calais
Mis Bar/restaurant

Germany

Aachen

Aachener GC (1927)

Oligsbenden 20 5100 Aachen
Tel 0241 12501
Mem 520
Pro W Van Mock
Holes 18 L 6060 metres Par 72
Fees D–30dm (D–40dm)
Loc Aachen-Seffent, 5 km from centre

Ansbach

Ansbach GC

8800 Ansbach Neustadt 25
Tel 0981 5617 Wolfgantritsch
Mem
Pro John Speed
Holes 9 L 4200 metres Par 66
Fees WD–20dm W/E–25dm
Loc Colmberg 15 km from Ansbach

Aschaffenburger

Aschaffenburger GC (1977)

8750 Aschaffenburg Yorck-Str 28
Tel 06021-92271 or 06024-7222
Mem 450
Pro T Paterson
Holes 9 L 5184 metres SSS 67 (M) 68 (L)
Fees 30dm (40dm)
Loc Feldkahl (app 7 km E of Aschaffenburg am Main) Autobahn no 3 direction Würzburg/Nürnberg exit Hösbach

Augsburg

Augsburg GC (1959)

c/o Dresdner Bank Holbeinstr 2 8900 Augsburg
Tel 08234/5621
Mem 450
Pro Karl-Heinz Gögele
Holes 18 L SSS 70
Fees WD–30dm W/E–40dm

GC Eschenried (1983)

Kurfurstenweg 7 8066 Eschenried
Tel (08131) 32 38 (08131) 79655
Mem 35
Pro G Stewart A Parish
Holes 9 L 6194 metres (M) 5362 metres (L) SSS & Par 72
Fees 30dm (40dm)
Loc 8 km NW of Munich
Mis A la carte menu always available

Leitershofen (1980)

8902 Stadtbergen Deuringerstrasse
Tel 0821 434919
Mem 125
Pro Peter Garnier-Bradley
Holes 9 L 3090 metres SSS 72
Fees WD–25dm W/E–30dm
Loc 8901 Stadtbergen-Leitershofen

Baden-Baden

Baden-Baden GC (1901)

Baden-Baden Fremersbergstrade 127
Tel (07221) 2 35 79
Mem 400
Pro Erich Totzke Bob Kelland
Holes 18 L 4575 metres Par 64
Fees WD–30dm W/E–35dm W–110dm
Loc 1 km from town

Baden-Hills Golf- und Curling Club (1982)

Postfach 2191 7550 Rastatt
Tel (17221) 2 56 20 (Markus Fischer)
Holes 18 L 5672 metres Par 72 (G) 5190 metres Par 70

Golf-Club Bad Herrenalb-Bernbach

Golf-Club Bad Herrenalb-Bernbach
Tel 07083 8898
Mem 400
Pro Gordon Westen Dirk Randolf
Holes 9 L 5200 metres SSS 68
Fees 30dm (35dm)
Loc 1 km from centre

Bad Bramstedt

Bad Bramstedt (1975)

2357 Bad Bramstedt PO Box 1305 Ochsenweg 38
Tel (04192) 6376
Mem 150
Pro Stewart Butterworth
Holes 9 SSS 68
Fees WD–25dm W/E–30dm
Loc S Border of town next B4. 30 miles N of Hamburg on motorway A7

Bad Driburger

Bad Driburger GC (1977)

3490 Bad Driburg
Tel 05253 842349
Mem 200
Pro Ray Issitt
Holes 9 L 6106 metres SSS 72
Fees WD–25dm W/E–30dm W–150dm
Loc

Bad Ems

Mittelrheinischer GC (1930)

5427 Bad Ems Denzerheide
Tel 0 26 03 65 41
Mem
Pro Horst Goerke
Holes 18 L 6045 metres SSS 72
Fees W/E–75dm (Round 40dm)W–125dm (Round 30dm)
Loc Bad Ems 3 km Koblenz 15 km

Bad Harzburg

Harz GC (1972)

3388 Bad Harzburg 1 Am Breitenberg
Tel 05322 6737/1096
Mem 260
Pro Clive Westerman
Holes 9 L 5690 metres SSS 70
Fees 25dm (30dm)
Loc Centre of Bad Harzburg Braunschweig ¾ hr Hannover 1 hr

Bad Homburg

Homburger GC (1899)

Golfpark Röderwiesen Saalburgchaussee 2A 6380 Bad Homburg v.d. Höhe
Tel 06172/39919 and 38808
Mem 525
Pro F Tauber R Taylor
Holes 10 Par 70
Fees WD–30dm W/E–40dm
Loc On B456 to Usingen

Golf & Landclub Taunus (1979)

Kaiser-Friedrich-Promenare 6380 Bad Homburg
Tel (06172) 2 45 61
Holes 9 holes complete. 9 holes under construction

Bad Kissingen

Bad Kissingen GC (1911)

Euerdorfer Strasse 11 8730 Bad Kissingen PB 1443
Tel 09 71 36 08
Mem 530
Pro Jan Dibb
Holes 18 L 5464 metres SSS 69
Fees 32dm (40dm)
Loc Bad Kissingen 2 km

Bad Kreuznach

Nahetal (1970)

6550 Bad Kreuznach Postfach 1518
Tel 06708 2145
Mem 520
Pro F Schmaderer NB Morris T Goerke
Holes 18
Fees D–30dm (40dm)
Loc 6 km from Bad Kreuznach on 6550

Bad Mergentheim

Bad Mergentheim (1971)

6990 Bad Mergentheim Postfach 1304
Tel (07931) 7579
Mem
Pro Horst Rosenkranz
Holes 9 L 4230 metres Par 64
Fees WD–20dm W/E–30dm
Loc 40 km from Wurzburg

Bad Nauheim

Bad Nauheim GC

6350 Bad Nauheim Postfach 1524
Tel 0 60 32 2153
Mem 360
Pro B Raschke
Holes 9 L 5440 metres Par 68
Fees 25dm (35dm)
Loc Bad Nauheim 2 km; Frankfurt 40 km

Bad Neuenahr

GC Köhlerhof (1979)

D 5483 Bad Neuenahr-Ahrweiler
Tel **(Office) Simrockstr 14 5483 Bad Neuenahr-Ahrweiler 02641-4277; (Course) 02641-6693**
Mem 460
Pro Werner Rappenecker
Holes 18 L 6075 metres SSS 72
Fees 35dm (45dm) Special group arrangements possible
Loc From the north: Motorway A61 to exit Bad Neuenahr, direction Sinzig to end of Lohrsdorf, left, following sign Köhlerhof. From the South: Motorway A61 exit Sinzig, to end of Lohrsdorf, left, following sign Köhlerhof.

Bad Pyrmont

Pyrmonter GC

Postfach 10 08 28 3250 Hameln 1
Tel **05281 8196**
Mem 300
Pro Zvonko Vasovic
Holes 9 L 5720 metres SSS 70
Fees 30dm (35dm)
Loc Bad Pyrmont 4km 25 km Hameln

Bad Sackingen

GC Rickenbach (1980)

7884 Rickenbach Postfach 1041
Tel **07765 8880**
Mem 220
Pro Gary Gilligan
Holes 9 L 2749 metres Par 69
Fees 30dm (50dm)
Loc Bad Sackingen 30 km E of Basel

Bad Salzuflen

Ostwestfalen-Lippe GC

PO Box 225 4902 Bad Salzuflen
Tel **05222/10773**
Mem 400
Pro M Skeide
Holes 9 L 6040 metres Par 72
Fees D–25dm W/E–30dm
Loc Bad Salzuflen 3 km

Bad Soden-Salmünster

GC Spessart

Postfach 1102 6480 Wächtersbach 6483 Bad Soden-Salmünster
Tel 06056/3594
Mem 450
Pro Les Bolland
Holes 15 L 6127 metres (M) 5315 metres (L) Par 72 SSS 72
Fees 25dm (40dm)
Loc Bad Soden-Salmünster

Bad Toelz

Bad Toelz (1973)

Strass 124 8170 Wackersberg
Tel (0841) 9994
Mem 260
Pro Ian Lyons Stuart Allan
Holes 9 L 2492 metres SSS 71
Fees 30dm (40dm)
Loc 55 km S of Munich W of Bad Toelz

Bad Waldsee

GC Oberschwaben-Bad Waldsee

Postfach 1527 7967 Bad Waldsee 1
Tel **(07524) 5900**
Mem 365
Pro Wolfgang Jersombeck Peter B Phillips
Holes 18 L 6135 metres SSS 72
Fees 30dm (45dm)
Loc Furstl Hofgut Hopfenweiler

Bad Wiessee

Tegernseer GC Bad Wiessee (1958)

Robognerhof Postfach 56 8182 Bad Wiessee
Tel **08022 8769**
Mem 501
Pro B Pringle R Buschert
Holes 18 L 5483 metres (M) 5481 metres (L) SSS 69 Par 70
Fees 40dm (60dm)
Loc Bad Wiessee 1 km Munich 55 km

Bad Wildungen

Bad Wildungen GC (1930)

359 Bad Wildungen
Tel **05621 40 61**
Mem 100
Pro Alfred Stein
Holes 9 L 5670 metres Par 70
Fees D–8dm W–40dm
Loc Bad Wildungen 1½ km

Bad Wörishoffen

Bad Wörishoffen GC

8951 Rieden Schlingener Str 27
Tel **08246 777**
Mem 375
Pro M Seidel H Hœrenz
Holes 18 L 6318 metres SSS 71
Fees WD–28dm W/E–35dm
Loc

Badenweiler

Rhein Badenweiler (1971)

7847 Badenweiler
Tel 07632 5031
Mem 450
Pro JF Halliwell N Coles
Holes 18 L 6134 metres SSS 72
Fees WD–30dm W/E–50dm
Loc 16 km from Badenweiler

Bamberg

Bamberg

8600 PO Box 1525 Bamberg
Tel **0951 24631**
Mem
Pro
Holes 9 L SSS
Fees
Loc

Bayreuth

Oberfranken (1966)

8650 Kulmbach Postfach 1404
Tel **09221 4336 or 09228 319 (club house)**
Mem 400
Pro James Arnold
Holes 18 L 6152 metres (M) 5433 metres (L) SSS 72
Fees 30dm (50dm W/E–80dm)
Loc In Thurnau; 18 km NW Bayreuth, 14 km SW Kulmbach
Mis Restaurant; closed Mon

Berchtesgaden

Berchtesgaden GC (1955)

824 Berchtesgaden Schliessfach 346
Tel **08652-2100/3787**
Mem 230
Pro
Holes 9 L 5135 metres SSS 67
Fees 30dm (40dm)
Loc Berchtesgaden 3½ km 25 km from motorway

Berlin

Berlin G & CC

APO 19742 US Forces Europe
Tel **819 65 33**
Mem 600
Pro Larry Beem PGA
Holes 18 L 6350 yds Par 70
Fees WD–$10 W/E–$15
Loc Wannsee

Berlin-Wannsee GC (1895)

Am Stoepchenweg 1000 Berlin 39
Tel **805 50 75**
Mem 575
Pro U Tapperthofen J Galbraith
Holes 9 L 5690 metres SSS 70
Fees D–30dm Sat/Sun–40dm
Loc 17 km from city centre

British GC Gatow (1969)

BFPO 45 RAF Gatow
Tel **Berlin 3092670/365 7660**
Mem 400
Pro
Holes 9 L 5687 metres SSS 70
Fees British Forces and Families and British Passport holders–10dm Sat/Sun–20dm
Loc 16 km from city centre

Bielefeld

Bielefelder CG (1977)

Dornbergerstrasse 375, 4800 Bielefeld-Hoberge 1
Tel 0521 10 51 03
Mem 360
Pro Hans W Kahre Tel 0521 104450
Holes 9 L SSS 72
Fees
Loc

Blomberg

Lippischer GC Blomberg Cappel (1981)

Blomberg Ortsteil Cappel Huxoll
Tel **(05236) 4 59**
Holes 18 Par 72

Bochum

Bochumer GC (1982)

Im Mailand 125 4630 Bochum
Tel **(0234) 61 13 00**
Holes 9 Par 36

Bocholt

Wasserburg Anholt (1972)

4294 Isselburg Anholt
Tel **(02874) 2283**
Mem
Pro H Johannsen
Holes 9 L 5920 metres SSS 72
Fees D–17dm Sat/Sun–25dm
Loc Anholt Schloss 15 km from Bocholt

Bonn-Bad Godesberg

Bonn-Godesberg GC (1960)

Dechant-Heimbach Str 16
Tel **0228-34 40 03 (Clubhouse); 0228-31 74 94 (Sec)**
Mem 600
Pro K Riechart KP Vollrach
Holes 18 L 5900 metres Par 71
Fees D–25dm Sat/Sun–35dm
Loc Oberbachem 4 km from Bad Godesberg

Braunfels

Schloss Braunfels (1970)

6330 Wetzlar/Lahn Wertherstrasse 8
6333 Braunfels/Lahn
Tel **06442 5975**
Mem 500
Pro Derek McLellan Michael Laverman Tel 06442 5752
Holes 18 L 6288 metres SSS 72
Fees WD–30dm W/E–45dm
Loc

Braunschweig

Braunschweig GC (1926)

3300 Braunschweig
Tel **0531/691369**
Mem 570
Pro MA Emery
Holes 15 L 5893 metres SSS 71
Fees D–25dm Sat/Sun–30dm
Loc 5 km from city centre

Gifhorn (1982)

Postfach 1341 3170 Gifhorn
Tel **05371/16737**
Mem 111
Pro Ulrich Bruns
Holes 9 L 6160 metres SSS 72
Fees 20dm (30dm)

Bremen

Club zur Vahr (1905)

Bgm-Spitta-Allee 34 28 Bremen 41
Tel **0421 230041**
Mem 850
Pro H Weber KD Schneider J Seymour
Holes 18 and 9 L 6435 and 6060 metres SSS 75 and 72
Fees 18 holes: 30dm (40dm) 9 holes: 20dm (30dm)
Loc 9 hole Bremen Vahr 18 hole Garlstedt

Worpswede (1974)

IM Schluh 29 2862 Worpswede
Tel **04792/517; 04763/7313 (Clubhouse)**
Mem 314
Pro Rüdiger Prössel-Krnz (asst)
Holes 9 L 6200 metres SSS 72
Fees WD–15dm W/E–25dm
Loc Giehlermuhlen B74 Osterholz-Scharmbeck to Bremen

Bruggen

RAF Germany GC (1956)

RAF Bruggen BFPO 25
Tel **02163 881 Ext 463/5207**
Mem (Open to all UK Forces) 600
Sec RW Powell
Pro T Foster
Holes 18 L 6522 yds SSS 71
Fees 25dm
Loc On B230 1 km of Dutch/German border 25 km W of Mönchen Gladbach

Burgsteinfurt

Munsterland GC (1950)

Bagno D 4430 Steinfurt 1
Tel **02557 5178**
Mem 243
Pro Brian Whittle
Holes 9 L 4960 metres Par 66
Fees WD–25dm W/E & BH–30dm
Loc Burgsteinfurt 2 km
Mis Old parkland course

Chiemsee

Chiemsee GC

8210 Prien-Bauernberg
Tel **0 80 51 4820**
Mem
Pro Roman Krause
Holes 9 L 5960 metres SSS 71
Fees D–15dm Sat/Sun–25dm
Loc 3 km from Prien

GC im Chiemgau (1982)

Kötzing 1 8224 Chieming
Tel **(08669) 75 57**
Mem 350
Pro W Köhler
Holes 18 L 6200 metres SSS 73 9 holes Par 3
Fees 35dm (50dm)
Loc 20 km from Salzburg

Gut Kronberg (1977)

8201 Holswang Chiemgau
Tel **(08075) 7 14**
Mem
Pro Francesco Carli
Holes 9 L 6210 metres SSS
Fees WD–20dm W/E–25dm
Loc

Coburg

Golf-club Coburg Schloss Tambach

Tambach 8632 Weitramsdorf
Tel **09567/1212**
Mem 200
Pro Peter Spencer
Holes 9 L 6150 metres (M); 5410 metres (L) SSS 72
Fees D–25dm (D–30dm)
Loc Tambach 9 km west of Coburg

Cologne

Airport Golf (1984)

Flughafen Köln-Bonn
Holes 9. Par 36

Schloss Georghausen GC

5253 Lindlar-Hommerich
Tel **02207 4938**
Mem 570
Pro Günther Kessier Gerhard Baum
Holes 18 L 6045 metres SSS 72
Fees WD–30dm W/E–40dm
Loc Cologne 30 km

Köln G & LC

Golfplatz 2 5060 Bergisch Gladbach 1
Tel **02204 6 31 14/6 31 38**
Mem 630
Pro K Marx A Stein
Holes 18 L 6045 metres Par 72
Fees D–30dm Sat/Sun–40dm
Loc Köln centre 15 km

Köln-Marienburger GC (1949)

Schillingsrotter Weg
Tel **(0221) 38 47 93**
Holes 9. Par 36

Cuxhaven

Küstengolf-Club Hohe Klint (1979)

Rosenhof 25 2190 Cuxhaven
Tel **04721 48057 or 04723 2737 (clubhouse)**
Mem 700
Pro Andreas Hochgürtel
Holes 18 L 6150 metres SSS 72
Fees 30dm
Loc 10 km SW town centre on route 6 on right hand to village Oxstedt, Hohe Klint

Darmstadt

D Darmstadt Traisa

6109 Muehltal Dippelshof
Tel **06151 146543**
Mem 340
Pro Martin Rose
Holes 9 L 5150 metres SSS 68
Fees WD–20dm W/E–25dm
Loc Muehltal/Traisa Dippelshof

Deggendorf

Golf- und Land-Club Rusel (1981)

Postfach 1321 D-8360 Deggendorf
Tel **(991 resp 1991) 381-116 or 6687**
Mem 250
Pro Dietrich Gärtner Tel (0991) 32682, pro-shop; (09920) 1279
Holes 9 L 3035 metres/6070 metres (G); 2695 metres/5390 metres (L); Par+SSS 72

Fees (W/E & hols D–25dm) D–20dm
Loc 10 km from town centre on route 11 in the direction of Regen (town) Passau 45 km
Mis Driving ranges, pitch and putt greens, 4-holes pitch and putt for beginners

Donaueschingen

Land- & Golfclub Oeschberghof (1976)

Golfplatz 1 D-7710 Donaueschingen
Tel **771-841 (84525)**
Mem 470
Man Gerry Staehli
Pro T Gerhard B Birch
Holes 18 L 6175 metres SSS 72, 6570 metres SSS 74
Fees 45dm (70dm)
Mis Course only for members of a golf club & with handicap

Dortmund

Dortmunder GC (1956)

Reichsmarkstr 12 4600 Dortmund-Reichsmark 30
Tel **Dortmund 0231 774133/774609**
Mem 650
Pro G Goor J Weijers
Holes 18 L 6240 metres Par 73
Fees WD–35dm W/E–50dm
Loc 8 km Dortmund

Dortmund Garrison GC (1969)

Napier Barracks BFPO 20
Mem 400
Sec Military
Pro
Holes 18 L 5196 metres SSS 70
Fees 15dm (20dm)
Loc In Napier Barracks Dortmund Brackel
Mis Not open to public; visitors by prior arrangement only

Nordkirchen

Nordkirchen

4717 Nordkirchen Am Piekenbrock
Tel **(02596) 2495**
Mem 340
Pro Andreas Rossler
Holes 9 L 6200 metres SSS 72
Fees 25dm (30dm)
Loc Munster 30 km

Werl (1973)

Marianne-Heesestr 20 4760 Werl
Tel **02377-6307**
Mem 300
Pro A Stein
Holes 9 L 4640 metres SSS 66
Fees WD–15dm W/E–20dm
Loc

Duisberg

Niederrheinischer GC (1956)

Duisburg Grossenbaumer Allee 240
Tel **72 14 69**
Mem
Pro Udo Lechtermann
Holes 9 L 6082 metres SSS 72
Fees WD–30dm W/E–40dm
Loc Duisburg centre 8 km

Düren

Düren (1975)

Düren-Gürzenich Trierbachweg Katharinenstr 59 5160 Düren
Tel **02421 800112**
Mem 200
Pro H Ranft Tel 02421 41166
Holes 9 L 5706 metres SSS 70
Fees WD–30dm W/E–40dm
Loc Trierbachweg

Dusseldorf

GC Dusseldorfer/Hoesel

Grunerstrasse 13 4000 Dusseldorf 1
Tel **(0211) 6311 71 (02102) 68629**
Mem 550
Pro F Eckl M Pyatt
Holes 18 L 6160 metres SSS 72
Fees 25dm (35dm)
Loc Hoesel 15 km NE of Dusselforf

Dusseldorfer GC (1961)

Rommeljansweg 12 4030 Ratingen 1
Tel **Ratingen 81092**
Mem 750
Pro J Kupitz D Hollbach
Holes 18 L 5905 metres SSS 71
Fees 35dm (50dm)
Loc 11 km city centre

Hubbelrath (1961)

Private
Bergische Landstrasse 700 4000 Dusseldorf 12
Tel **Mettmann (02104) 72 178 and 71 848**
Mem 1250
Pro G Danz P Herbert S Hilton HP Ranft HP Thül R Noellé
Holes 18 L 6040 metres SSS 72 (East course)
18 L 4235 metres SSS 63 (West course)
Fees WD–35dm W/E–50dm
Loc Hubbelrath approx 13 km E of town centre on route B7

Eckernforde

Altenhof (1971)

2330 Altenhof bei Eckernforde
Tel **04351 41227**
Mem 410
Pro Nicholas Robinson
Holes 18 L 6071 metres SSS 72
Fees WD–25dm W/E–30dm
Loc 5 km Eckernforde
Mis 9 holes under construction

Erlangen

Erlangen (1977)

Postfach 1767 8520 Erlangen
Tel **09126 5040**
Mem 130
Pro Peter Zinterl
Holes 9 Par 64
Loc Am Schleinhof, 8524 Kleisendelbach
Mis Open only to members

Frankische Schweitz (1974)

D-8553 Ebermannstadt Postfach 11 10
Tel 0-91 94-92 28
Mem 230
Pro Konrad Messingschlager
Holes 9 L 2628 metres Par 68
Fees 25dm (35dm)
Loc 5 km E Ebermannstadt

Herzogenaurach GC (1967)

Altenburgerstr 36 8500 Nurnberg 80
Tel **(09132) 83628**
Mem 160+50 American members
Pro
Holes 9 L 6090 SSS 72
Fees 5+10dm (with members only)
Loc Next to Herzo base

Essen

Essener GC Haus Oefte (1959)

4300 Essen (Haus Oefte) Laupendahler Landstr
Tel **02054/83911**
Mem 650
Pro R Sommer Tel 02054 84722
Holes 18 L 6100 metres SSS 72
Loc 14 km from Essen city centre

Essen-Heidhausen (1970)

4300 Essen 16 Preutenborbeckstrasse 36
Tel **(0201) 404111**
Mem 670
Pro G Kothe T McGarva F Schefer
Holes 18 L 5702 metres SSS 70
Fees D–25dm Sat/Sun–40dm only with member
Loc 10 km from Essen city centre (on B224)

Golfriege des Etuf

Freiherr-vom-Stein Str 4300 Essen 1
Tel **0201 441426**
Mem 320
Pro U Knappmann
Holes 9 L 4580 metres SSS 64
Fees 25dm (30dm)
Loc 6 km S city centre

Feldafing

Feldafing (1926)

D-8133 Feldafing Tutzingerstr 15
Tel **08157 7005**
Mem 700
Pro Toni Flossmann Werner Herrmann Christoph Kilian
Holes 18 L 5865 metres SSS 70. Par 71
Fees 40dm (W/E & hol 60dm)
Loc 32 km S Munich
Mis Restaurant, bar, driving range, pitch & putt

Flensburg

Forde Glucksburg

Glucksburg
Tel
Mem
Pro
Holes 9 L SSS
Fees
Loc

Föhr Island

Föhr (1966)

2271 Nieblum auf Föhr
Tel **04681 3277**
Mem 301
Pro A Assmus
Holes 9 L 6100 metres SSS 72
Fees 30dm (35dm)
Loc 2 miles SW of Wyk

Frankfurt

Frankfurter GC (1913)

6000 Frankfurt/M 71 Golfstr 41
Tel **Frankfurt 666 23 18**
Mem 900
Pro H Struver W Wickham Cliff Potts
Holes 18 L 6455 yds Par 71
Fees D–35dm Sat/Sun–50dm
Loc 6 km from city 4 km from airport

Kronberg CG (1954)

6242 Kronberg Schloss Friedrichshof
Tel **06173 1426**
Mem 798
Pro A Schilling J Harder M Kessler W Mych I Thompson
Holes 18 L 5365 metres SSS 68
Fees 35dm (50dm)
Loc Frankfurt 15 km

Freiburg

Freiburger (1970)

7800 Freiburg/Br Post box 523
Tel **(07661) 5569**
Mem 400
Pro P Weggenmann
Holes 18 L 6100 metres SSS 72
Fees WD–30dm W/E–40dm
Loc Freiburg-Kappel/Kirchzarten; 7 km SE town centre on route L126b

Gutermann Gutach GC (1924)

7809 Gutach
Tel **07681**
Mem 300
Pro Ian M McK Stewart
Holes 9 L 5330 metres SSS 68
Fees D–25dm
Loc Freiburg 20 km

Freudenstadt

Freudenstadt (1929)

Golfplatz 7290 Freudenstadt
Tel **07441 3060**
Mem 300
Pro Gerold Fischer
Holes 9 L 5857 metres SSS 71
Fees 25dm (40dm)
Loc 1 km from centre
Mis Open Apr–Oct

Fulda

Rhoen (1971)

Am Golfplatz 6417 Hofbieber 1
Tel **06657 7077 or 1334**
Mem 420
Pro Nicholas Staples
Holes 18 L 5675 metres SSS 70
Fees 25dm (30dm)
Loc Hofbieber 11 km E of Fulda
Mis Hotel direct on golf course

Furth

GC Furth in Wald (1982)

Gutsverwaltung Voithenberg
8492 Furth in Wald
Tel **(09973) 1240**
Mem 90
Pro Simon Bates
Holes 9; SSS 71
Fees 15dm (20dm)
Loc 70 km NE of Regensburg
Mis New course constructed Summer 1986 Former 9-hole course obsolete

Garmisch-Partenkirchen

Garmisch-Partenkirchen GC (1928)

Postfach 1345 Garmisch-Partenkirchen
Tel **Oberau 08824 8344/1632**
Mem 450
Pro Andy Hagl
Holes 18 L 6200 metres SSS 72
Fees 40dm Sun–60dm
Loc Garmisch 9 km

Werdenfels (1973)

8100 Garmisch-Partenkirchen Schwaigwang
Tel **08821 750626**
Mem 200
Pro Billie Davidson
Holes 9 L 5896 metres SSS 71
Fees WD–40dm W/E–50dm
Loc 2 km S of Garmisch on B23 direction Farchant

Gmund

GC Margarethenhof am Tegernsee (1982)

8184 Gmund am Tegernsee
Tel **(08022) 73 66**

Goppingen

Hohenstauffen GC

732 Goppingen
Tel **27361**
Mem 160
Pro Wilhelm Hofmann
Holes 9 L 6540 yds SSS 72
Fees D–15dm Sat/Sun–20dm
Loc Donzdorf 15 km

Göttingen

Göttingen (1969)

Levershausen 3410 Northeim 1
Tel **05551 61915 & 7952**
Mem 390
Pro W Kreuzer P Dunn
Holes 18 L 6240 metres SSS 73
Fees 20dm (25dm)
Loc Between Göttingen and Northeim
Mis Clubhouse with pro-shop and restaurant

Günzburg

Schloss Klingenburg-Günzburg (1980)

Schloss Klingenbur 8876 Jettingen/Scheppach
Tel **08225 871**
Mem 320
Pro Hans Bessner
Holes 18 L 6089 metres SSS 72
Fees 30 dm (40 dm)
Loc 20 km from Günzburg

Gutersloh

RAF Gutersloh

RAF Gutersloh BFPO 47
Tel **05241 26021 Ext 426**
Mem 250
Pro
Holes 9 L 5761 yds SSS 68
Fees 10dm
Loc 5 km W Gutersloh

Westfaelischer Golf Club Guetersloh eV

4830 Guetersloh Postfach 3224
Tel **05244 2340**
Mem 600
Pro Manfred Schwichtenberg
Holes 18 L 6175 metres SSS 72
Fees D–20dm W/E–30dm
Loc 6 km from Guetersloh

Hachenburg

GC Westerwald (1979)

Dreifelden/Linden
Tel **(02662) 75 77**

Hagen

Märkischer GC Hagen (1964)

D-5800 Hagen Tiefendorfer Strasse 48
Tel **(02334) 51778**
Mem 400
Pro D Geise R Stehmans
Holes 9 L 6208 metres SSS 72
Fees WD–25dm W/E–70dm
Loc Hagen-Berchum
Mis Closed Mondays

Hamburg

GC An der Pinnau (1982)

Jebbenberg 32 2084 Rellingen
Tel **04101/28225**
Mem 510
Pro Martin Hughes Steve and Andrew Arrowsmith
Holes 18 L 6129 metres SSS 72
Fees 35dm (45dm)
Loc Motorway Hamburg Flousburg exit Quickborn
Mis Address of course is: Pinnebergerstr 81 2085 Quickborn

GC Auf der Wendlohe

2 Hamburg 61 Oldesiderstr 251
Tel **550 5014-5**
Mem 700
Pro Keith Vince David Entwhistle Liam Kelly
Holes 18 L 6060 metres SSS 72
Fees WD–35dm W/E–45dm
Loc 15 km city centre

Buxtehude GC (1982)

Zum Lehmfeld 1 2150 Buxtehude
Tel **04161/81333**
Mem 280
Pro John Dunford
Holes 18 L 6150 metres SSS 74
Fees 25dm (40dm) Juniors 10dm (15dm)
Loc 30 km SW of Hamburg on Route 73 from Harburg

GC Grossensee (1975)

An Der Hove 16 2077 Grossensee
Tel **(04154) 6261 or 6473**
Mem 200
Holes 9 L 6118 metres SSS 72
Fees 25dm (30dm)
Loc 30 km from Hamburg

Grossflottbeker THGC (1901)

Hamburg Otto-Ernst Strasse 32
Tel **Hamburg 82 72 08**
Mem 270
Pro Kenneth Storrier
Holes 9 L 4945 metres SSS 66
Fees D–25dm Sat/Sun–35dm
Loc 6 km from city centre

GC Gut Kaden (1984)

Kadenerstrasse 2081 Alveslohe
Tel **04193-1420**
Mem 155
Pro C Smailes G Clark
Holes 18 L 6220 metres SSS 73
Fees 30dm (45dm)
Loc Alveslohe 30km N of Hamburg

Gut Waldhof (1969)

2359 Kisdorferwohld Gut Waldhof
Tel **041 194 383**
Mem 720
Pro H Jersombeck D Geary
Holes 18 L 6073 metres (M) 5335 metres (L) Par 72
Fees 30dm (W/E & hols 40dm)
Loc 34 km N Hamburg centre via Autobahn A7 to Kaltenkirchen or via route B432
Mis Guests allowed unlimited WD; W/E only with members; W/E creche

Hamburger GC (1906)

In de Bargen 59 2000 Hamburg 55
Tel **040 812177**
Mem 1030
Pro A Mazza George Pilkington
Holes 18 L 5925 (men) 5276 (ladies) SSS 71
Fees 35dm (45dm) (only with a member)
Loc Blankenese 14 km Hamburg centre

Hamburg-Ahrensburg GC

Am Haidschlag 45 2070 Ahrensburg
Tel **04102 51309**
Mem 845
Pro H Heiser L Plesse C Kirchner
Holes 18 L 5782 metres SSS 71
Fees 35dm (45dm)
Loc 20 km from city centre

Hamburger GC In der Luneburger Heide (1957)

Private
2105 Seevetal 1
Tel **Hittfeld 0 41 05 23 31**
Mem 600
Pro J Struver
Holes 18 L 5865 metres SSS 71
Fees WD–25dm W/E–40dm
Loc Hamburg 25 km

Hamburg-Waldorfer (1960)

D 2071 Ammersbek 1 Scherenbarg
Tel **Hamburg 605 13 37**
Mem 850
Pro Klaus Sallman Gerry Bennett
Holes 18 L 6154 metres SSS 72 Par 73
Fees 30dm (40dm)
Loc 20 km N city centre
Mis Par-3 course; 9-hole pitch and putt; heated indoor swimming pool

GC Hoisdorf (1977)

Wentorfer Strasse 11 2050 Hamburg 80
Tel **(040) 7 21 68 68**
Holes 18 L 6010 metres (G) 5300 metres (L) Par 71

Wentorf-Reinbeker (1901)

Golfstrasse 2 2057 Wentorf
Tel **040 720 26 10**
Mem 321
Pro P Turner (PGA)
Holes 9 L 5675 metres SSS 70
Fees WD–25dm W/E–35dm
Loc 25 km city centre
Mis Co-Founder of German Golf Union 1907

Hanau

Hanau GC (1959)

6450 Hanau 1-Wilhelmsbad Wilhelmsbader Allee 32
Tel **06181 82071**
Mem 780
Pro G Koenig S Eckrodt A Payne
Holes 18 L 6227 metres Par 73
Fees D–35dm Sat/Sun 60dm
Loc 6 km NW of town centre on B8–40

Hanover

Burgdorfer (1970)

Waldstr 27 3167 Burgdorf-Ehlershausen
Tel **05085 7628/7144**
Mem 400
Pro Ludger Theeuwen
Holes 18 L 6460 metres SSS 74
Fees WD–25dm W/E–30dm
Loc Road B3 Burgdorf-Ehlershausen

Hanover GC (1923)

3008 Garbsen 1 Am Blauen See
Tel **Seelze 0 51 37 7 32 35**
Mem 600
Pro Horst Koch Bernd Schul
Holes 18 L 5855 metres SSS 71
Fees D–18dm W/E–25dm
Loc Hanover 20 km

Isernhagen (1983)

Auf Gut Lohne Haupstr 129 3004 Isernhagen
Tel **05139-87564**
Mem 450
Pro U Beuns J Beuns
Holes 18 L 6334 metres SSS 72
Fees 20dm (25dm)
Loc 12 km NE of Hanover

Hechingen

Hechingen-Hohenzollern (1955)

Golfplatz Hagelwasen Hechingen
Tel **Hechingen 07471 2600**
Mem 380
Pro Klaus Schieban Peter Eisenhut
Holes 9 SSS 70
Fees 20dm (W/E members only)
Loc Hechingen 2 km
Mis Closed Mon

Heidelberg

Heidelberg (US Army)

Oftersheim ECN 1851
Tel **06202 53767**
Mem 700
Pro Jay Sporl
Holes 18 L 6650 metres SSS 72
Fees 8 dollars (10 dollars)
Loc Heidelberg 10 km

Heidelberg-Lobenfeld (1968)

Postfach 102869 6900 Heidelberg *or* Biddersbacherhof 6921 Lobboch-Lobenfeld
Tel **06226-40490/41955**
Mem 600
Pro JP Godefroy
Holes 18 L 6240 metres SSS 73
Fees WD–25dm W/E–35dm
Loc 20 mins E of town

Rheintal

Schwetzingen
Tel
Mem
Pro
Holes 18 L SSS
Fees
Loc

Golf und Landclub Wiesloch-Hohenhardter Hof (1983)

Hohenhardter Hof 6908 Weisloch 4 Baiertal
Tel **(06222) 7 20 81**
Holes 18

Heidenheim

GC Hochstatt Härtsfeld-Ries (1981)

7086 Hochstatter Hof
Tel **(07326) 79 79**
Holes 9 Par 36

Heilbronn

Heilbronn-Hohenlohe

7111 Friedrichsruhe
Tel **07941-7886**
Mem 380
Pro Ben Amara
Holes 9 L 5890 metres SSS 71
Fees 25dm (35dm)
Loc Friedrichsruhe–Ohringen

Golf- und Landclub Schloss Liebenstein (1982)

Schlob Liebenstein 7129 Neckarwestheim
Tel **07133/16019**
Mem 600
Pro Wolfgang Kretschy (Asst: Rene Hartzheim)
Holes 18 L·5869 metres (G) 5178 metres (L) Par 72 SSS 71
Fees 40dm (W/E & hols 50dm)
Mis Hotel and restaurant

Hennef

Rhein Sieg (1971)

5202 Hennef Postfach 1224
Tel **02242 6501 or 1334**
Mem 280
Pro H Knopp D MacLauchlan
Holes 9 L 5790 metres Par 70
Fees D–25dm W/E–30dm
Loc Hennef 3 km
Mis 18 holes from 1987

Hildesheim

Bad Salzdetfurth-Hildesheim (1972)

Postfach 1445 3200 Hildesheim
Tel **(05063) 1516**
Mem
Pro L Theeuwen
Holes 9 L 6210 metres SSS 72
Fees WD–20dm W/E–25dm
Loc

GC Sieben-Berge

3211 Rheden
Tel **0 51 82 23 05**
Mem
Pro Artur Fiebing
Holes 9 L 6450 metres SSS 74
Fees D–12dm
Loc Rheden

Hillesheim-Berndorf

Eifel (1979)

Kölner Str 5533 Hillesheim-Berndorf
Tel **Sec 06593 1241, Pro-shop 8537, Rest. 8639**
Mem 260
Pro Colin Gess
Holes 9 L 6180 metres (M) 5442 metres (L) Par 72
Fees 25dm (40dm)
Loc Outside Hillesheim, direction Köln
Mis Course closed Tue

Hohne

British Army GC (Hohne) (1962)

Hohne BFPO 30
Tel **05051 4549**
Mem 250
Pro To be appointed
Holes 9 L 5682 metres SSS 71
Fees 20dm (25dm)
Loc 6 km S of Bergen Celle

Holzminden

GC Weserbergland (1982)

c/o W Bellmer Wallstrasse 13 3450 Holzminden
Tel **(15531) 1 00 33–35**
Pro Simon Fisher
Holes 9 SSS & Par 72

Ingoldstadt

Golf Und Landclub Ingoldstadt (1978)

Gerolfingerstrasse Spitzel Muehle 8070 Ingoldstadt
Tel **0841/85778**
Mem 225
Pro John Pugh
Holes 9 L 5500 metres SSS 69
Fees 20dm (30dm)
Loc 3km from town centre; direction of Gerolfing near hospital
Mis No catering Mon. Guests welcome. Dogs allowed

Issum

Issum-Niederrhein (1973)

4174 Issum Pauenweg 68
Tel **02835 3626**
Mem 550
Pro Simon Bates John Emery
Holes 18 L 6045 metres SSS 72
Fees 35dm (50 dm)
Loc 6 miles E of Geldern

Kassel

Kassel-Wilhelmhohe

Kassel
Tel
Mem
Pro
Holes 9 L SSS
Fees
Loc

Kiel

Kitzeberg GC (1902)

Sophienblatt 46 2300 Kiel 1
Tel **(0431) 630 48 Clubhouse (0431) 23404**
Mem 360
Pro Roger Denton
Holes 9 L 5700 metres Par 70
Fees D–25dm W/E–30dm
Loc Kiel 10 km

Kierspe

Varmert GC (1977)

5883 Kierspe-Varmert
Tel **(02269) 72 99**
Mem 220
Pro E Schreiber R Tanglmayer
Holes 9 L 6056 metres SSS 72
Fees WD–18dm W/E–25dm
Loc Near Gummersbach and Ludemscheid

Konstanz

Konstanz GC

D7753 Allensbach 3 Hofgut Kargegg
Tel **07533 5124**
Mem 450
Pro Manfred Bingger N Lancaster
Holes 18 L 6100 metres
Fees 30dm (W/E & hols 50dm)
Loc 15 km from Konstanz centre in direction of Bodman on route B219

Krefeld

Krefelder GC (1930)

Ind der Elt 2 4150 Krefeld 12
Tel **(02151) 570071/72**
Mem 600
Pro R Newsome N Brunyard
Holes 18 L 6070 metres SSS 72
Fees D–45dm W/E–60dm
Loc 7 km SE of Krefeld 16 km Dusseldorf
Mis Closed Monday

Laarbruch

Laarbruch GC RAF (1962)

Laarbruch BFPO 43
Tel **Weeze 89 5441**
Mem 200
Pro
Holes 9 L 4471 yds SSS 62
Fees D–10dm W/E–10dm
Loc Laarbruch 9 British Forces
Mis Access to course may be restricted

Lahr

GC Ortenau (1981)

7630 Lahr-Reichenbach Postfach 1469
Tel **(07821) 77217**
Mem 320
Pro PP Jarvis
Holes 9 L 5450 metres SSS 70
Fees 20dm (30dm)
Loc 35 km SE of Strasbourg 50 km N of Freiburg

Lichtenau

GC Lichtenau-Weickershof (1980)

Weickershof 1 8802 Lichtenau
Tel **(09827) 69 07**
Pro P Muller
Holes 9 L 6160 metres SSS 72
Fees 25dm (30dm)
Loc

Lindau

Bodensee (1969)

899 Lindau-Weissenberg
Hoyerbergstrasse 62
Tel **08382 6624**
Mem
Pro
Holes Under construction
Fees
Loc

Lindau-Bad Schachen GC (1954)

Kemptener Strasse 125 899 Lindau (Bodensee)
Tel **Lindau (083821) 69 88**
Mem 640
Pro Bob Richardson
Holes 18 L 5690 metres SSS 70
Fees 30dm (40dm)
Loc 1½ km Lindau centre
Mis Frequent open tournaments: v'trs welcome; accommodation nearby–bookings through club Sec

Lingen

Emstal (1977)

Postfach 1431 4450 Lingen
Tel **0591-612205 (Sec)**
0591-63837 (Course)
Mem 200
Pro David Bryan (4/86-)
Holes 9 L 5320 metres/4700 metres SSS 68
Fees 25dm
Loc 3 km N town centre, route B70 to Meppen

Lubeck

Lubeck-Travemunde GC

2407 Lubeck-Travemunde
Tel **04502 6017**
Mem
Pro Alan Varley
Holes 9 L 6100 metres SSS 72
Fees D–15dm W/E–20dm
Loc Travemunde centre

Maritim Timmendorfer Strand

2408 Timmendorfer Strand
Tel **04503 5152**
Mem 520
Pro R Hinz
Holes 18 L 6440 metres SSS 74
18 L 3720 metres SSS 60
Fees WD–30dm W/E–40dm
Loc Am Overdiek

Lüneberg

An Der Goehrde GC (1968)

3139 Zernien-Braasche
Tel **05836 556**
Mem 180
Pro H Johannsen
Holes 9 L 6200 metres SSS 72
Fees 15dm (20dm)
Loc 40 km E from Lüneburg
30 km E of Uelzen

St Dionys (1972)

2123 St Dionys
Tel **04133 6277**
Mem 565
Pro Karl Heinz Mahl
Holes 18 L 6225 metres SSS 73
Fees 30dm (45dm)
Loc Near Lüneberg

Mannheim

Mannheim-Viernheim

68 Mannheim P7, 10-15
Tel **169 332**
Men 475
Pro C Jenkins M Kagel
Holes 9 L 3125 metres SSS 72
Fees 25dm (50dm)
Loc Mannheim 10 km

Marburg

Oberhessischer GC Marburg (1973)

Postfach 1828 3550 Marburg/Lahn
Tel **06427 8558**
Mem 240
Pro R Pottage
Holes 9 L 6044 metres SSS 72
Fees 20dm (25dm)
Loc 5 miles N of Marburg off B3 (Bernsdorf) direction Reddehausen Maximilianenhof

Mönchengladbach

Schloss Myllendonk GC (1964)

Postfach 669 4050 Mönchengladbach 1
Tel **02161 641049**
Mem 420
Pro G Kerkman A Clark
Holes 18 L 6092 metres SSS 72
Fees 35dm (50dm)
Loc Korschenbroich, 5 km E of Mönchengladbach

Schmitzhof GC (1977)

Schmitzhof 5144 Wegberg
Tel **(02436) 4 79**
Mem
Pro E Theeuwen
Holes 9 L SSS 70
Fees
Loc

Mölln

GC Gut Grambek (1981)

2411 Grambek Schlosstrasse 21
Tel **(04542) 46 27**
Mem 285
Pro HJ Rumpf
Holes 18 L 6025 metres SSS 71
Fees 25dm (35dm)
Loc 30km S of Lubeck
50 km E of Hamburg

Munich

Erding-Grunbach (1973)

8058 Erding Aribostr 2
Tel **08122 6465**
Mem 350
Pro Gary Warner
Holes 9 L 6150 metres SSS 72
Fees D–30dm W/E–40dm
V'trs H
Loc 45 mins from Munich towards Vilsbiburg

Munchener GC (1910)

8021 Strasslach Golf Platz
Tel **08170 450**
Mem 1200
Pro H Fehring H Fluss E Junge H Bessner
Holes 18 and 9 L 6066 and 5056 metres SSS 72 and 67
Fees D–25dm W/E–40dm
Loc Thalkirchen and Strasslach

GC Olching (1981)

8037 Olchingz Feurtrasse 89
Tel **(08142) 15963**
Mem 550
Pro C Knauss D Cabus A Steinfurth
Holes 18 L 6021 metres SSS 72
Fees 40dm (60dm)
Loc 25 km from Munich Motorway A8 to Stuttgart–leave at Dachau exit on B471

Riverside Golf and Country Club US Forces (1947)

8060 Dachau An der Flosslaende 1
Tel **08131 10879**
Mem 250
Pro Chuck De Castro
Holes 9 L 2960 metres SSS 71
Fees D–35dm Sat/Sun–40dm
Loc 2 km E of Dachau on road to township of Herberthausener; Munich 17 km
Mis Guests welcome: tennis courts, trout fishing, camping, children's playground, picnic ground

Tutzing (1983)

8132 Tutzing-Deixlfurt
Tel **08158-3600**
Mem 530
Holes 18 L 6159 & 5438 metres SSS 72
Fees 40dm (60dm)
Loc Starnberger See off B2

Wörthsee (1982)

Gut Schluifeld 8031 Wörthsee
Tel **08153/2425**
Mem 500
Pro Jonathan Mills Peter Pemöller John Biddle
Holes 18 L 6270 metres SSS 71 Par 72
Fees 40dm (60dm)
Loc 25 km from Munich, direction Lindau; Autobahn B12
Mis Clubhouse closed Mon. 6-hole pitch and putt

Münster

Münster-Wilkinghege GC (1964)

Postfach 3212 D-4400
Tel **(0251) 211201**
Mem
Pro
Holes 18 SSS 71
Fees D–20dm W/E–40dm
Loc Münster 2 km Steinfurterstr. 448

Neheim-Husten

Sauerland GC (1958)

Zum Golfplatz 5760 Arnsberg 1 (Clubhouse); Werner Hille (Sec/Pres) Falkenhorst 15 5760 Arnsberg 1
Tel **02932 31546**
Mem 320
Pro V. Knörnschild
Holes 9 L 5874 metres (5166 metres) SSS 71 Par 70
Fees D–20dm W/E–25dm
Loc Nr village of Herdringen

Neumünster

Mittelholsteinischer Aukrug (1969)

2356 Aukrug-Bargfeld
Tel **04873 595**
Mem 280
Pro M Kimberly
Holes 18 L 6140 metres SSS 72
Fees WD–25dm W/E–30dm
Loc BAB exit Neumünster–Mitte; 10 km W of exit on route 430

Neunburg vorm Wald

Oberpfaelzer Wald GLC

Buchtalweg 7 D D-8472 Schwarzenfeld
Tel **09439 466**
Mem 260
Pro Joseph Anyon
Holes 9 L 6082 metres SSS 72
Fees 20dm (30dm)
Loc 10 km E of Schwarzenfeld on route to Neunburg

Neustadt

Pfalz (1971)

673 Neustadt Weinstrasse 22
Tel **06327 2973**
Mem 650
Pro G Hopp A Suchet W Linnenfelser
Holes 18 L 6180 metres SSS 72
Fees 30dm (WE+hols 40dm)
Loc At Geinsheim 15 km from Neustadt towards Speyer

Norderney Island

Norderney GC (1956)

2982 Norderney Box 1233
Tel **04932 680**
Mem 225
Pro R Bremer
Holes 9 L 4890 metres SSS 66
Fees WD–25dm W/E–30dm
Loc Norderney 7 km

Nurnberg

Club am Reichswald

85 Nurnberg-Kraftshof
Tel **0911 39 12 88**
Mem
Pro Joseph Gornert
Holes 18 L 6345 metres SSS 73
Fees D–15dm Sat/Sun–25dm
Loc Nurnberg 10 km

Oldenburg

Oldenburgischer GC (1964)

2900 Oldenburg Postbox 2928
Tel **04402 7240**
Mem 400
Pro A Gauld P Allen
Holes 18 L 6100 metres SSS 72
Fees WD–30dm W/E–40dm
Loc Rastede 3 km

Osnabrück

GC Dütetal (1983)

Werseneor Strasse 17 453L Lotte
Tel **(05404) 52 96**

Osnabrück GC (1955)

Karmannstrasse 1 4500 Osnabrück
Tel **Bissendorf 05402/636**
Mem 300
Pro Hans Theeuwen
Holes 18 L 5881 metres Par 71
Fees 30dm (40dm)
Loc Osnabrück 13 km

Velper G & CC (1973)

Heinrich Hensiek Str 4535 Westerkappeln-Velpe
Tel **(Pro-shop) 05456 287 (Clubhouse) 05456 419**
Mem 255
Pro Stephen L Walker
Holes 9 L 2891 metres (M) 2510 metres (L) SSS 70
Fees D–10dm
Loc 5 miles W of Osnabrück near highway crosspoint Osnabrück/Lotte. Follow sign to Industrial Velpe

Tecklenburger Land (1971)

Wallen-Lienen 1 4542 Tecklenburg
Tel **05455 1035**
Mem 260
Pro JP Laarmann
Holes 9 L 6160 metres SSS 72
Fees 30dm (40dm)
Loc $1\frac{1}{2}$ km W of Autobahn, exit Lengerich/Ibbenbueren, direction Ibbenbueren 20 km Osnabruck 35 km Munster

Ottobeuren

Algäuer Golf & Landclub (1984)

8942 Ottobeuren Höfgut Boschach
Tel (08332) 13 10
Mem 360
Pro KH Marx M Hocker
Holes 18 L 6215 metres SSS 72
Fees 30dm (40dm)
Loc Ottobeuren 2 km Kempten 20 km

Paderborn

GC Paderborner Land (1983)

Wilseder Weg 25 4790 Paderborn
Tel (05251) 4377
Holes 9 L 5670 metres SSS 70
Fees 20dm (30dm)
Loc Salzkotten/Thule between B-1 and B-64

Passau

Golf und Land Club Bayerwald (1970)

Dorn 39 8392 Waldkirchen
Tel **08581 1040**
Mem 390
Pro Nick Rayne
Holes 9 L 6080 metres SSS 72
Fees 25dm (35dm)
Loc Near Passau

Penzburg

GC Beuerberg (1982)

Gutsterz 1 8191 Beverberg
Tel **(08179) 6 71**
Holes 18 Par 74

St Eurach Land und GC (1973)

8127 Iffeldorf/OBB
Tel **08801 1332**
Mem 502
Pro J O'Flynn
Holes 18 L 6250 metres SSS 74
Fees D–40dm Sat/Sun–60dm
Loc 25 miles S of Munich

Pfarrkirchen

Rottaler (1972)

Rottaler Golf und Country Club Stadplatz 13–15 D-8340 Pfarrkirchen
Tel **08561/6487**
Mem 280
Pro Steve Tarrant
Holes 9 L 6100 metres SSS 72
Fees WD–£5 W/E–£6
Loc

Ramstein

Woodlawn GC

6792 Ramstein Flugplaz
Tel **06371-47-6240**
Mem Military GC Visitors limited
Pro Eric Sudy
Holes 18 L 6225 yds Par 70
Fees D–6 dollars W/E 8 dollars
Loc Ramstein 3 km

Recklinghausen

Vestischer GC Recklinghausen

Bockholter Str 475 Recklinghausen
Tel **02361 26520**
Mem 650
Pro S Vollrath E Schilling W Bollert
Holes 18 L SSS 72
Fees WD–20dm Sat/Sun–30dm
Loc Nr Loemuehle airport

Regensburg

Golf- und Landclub (1966)

8405 Donaustauf Thiergarten Schliessfach 45
Tel **09403/5 05**
Mem 500
Pro Peter Ries Bill Lloyd

Holes 18 L 5685 metres SSS 70
Fees WD–40dm W/E–60dm
Loc 14 km from Regensburg near Walhalla

Rendsburg

Lohersand GC (1958)

Sekretariat Vereins und Westbank AG Jungfernstieg 11-13 2370 Rendsburg
Tel **04331-599-100**
Mem 240
Pro Mike Fitton
Holes 9 L 6040 metres Par 72
Fees 25dm (30dm)
Loc Sorgbrück/B77

Saarbrücken

Saar-Pfalz Katharinenhof (1982)

c/o Treuarbeit AG Heinrich-Böckingstr 1 D-6600 Saarbrücken
Tel **(Sec) 0681 68094 (Clubhouse) 06843 8798**
Mem 325
Pro Wlater Baur Tel 06843 8878
Holes 9 L 6112 metres (M) 5378 metres (L) Par 72
Fees D–20dm (30dm W/E–50dm)
Loc 15 km S of Saarbrücken towards Blieskastel

Saarbrücken (1961)

Oberlimberger Weg 6634 Wallerfangen Gisingen
Tel **(06837) 401 and 841**
Mem
Pro Siegfried Mühlbauer Roswitha Heymanns Jody Morris
Holes 18 L SSS 73
Fees 30dm (40dm)
Loc

St Peter-Ording

St Peter-Ording (1971)

Hauke Haien-Weg 1 2252 St Peter-Ording
Tel **04863 1545/746**
Mem 150
Pro Tim Holroyd
Holes 9 L 5730 metres (men) 5100 metres (ladies) SSS 70 Par 72
Fees 30dm (35dm)
Loc St Peter-Bohl

Schmidmuhlen

Schmidmuhlen G & CC (1970)

8400 Regensberg Hochweg 70
Tel **09 41/2 20 41**
Mem 105
Pro Ludwig Perras
Holes 9 L 5328 metres SSS 68
Fees D–15dm
Loc Autobahn Nurn/Regensburg

Sennelager

Sennelager (British Army (1963)

Bad Lippspringe BFPO 16
Tel **Sennelager Mil (82) 2515**
Mem 405 82(L) 30(J)
Sec AG Bairstow
Pro
Holes 18 L 5964 metres SSS 72
Fees WD–18dm W/E–24dm (Forces) WD–24dm W/E–36dm (Civilians)
Loc 9 km from Paderborn off Route 1

Siegburg

GC Burg Overbach-Much (1984)

Postfach 1213 5203 Much
Tel **(02245) 5550**
Mem 550
Pro T Giedeon T Menne M Westphal
Holes 18 L 6056 metres SSS 72
Fees 30dm (40dm)
Loc Koln 45 km A4 from Koln towards Olpe

Siegen

Siegen-Olpe GC (1966)

D-5900 Siegen Bahnhofstr 4
Tel **0271 5831 or 02762 7589**
Mem 300
Pro Karl Hahn
Holes 9 L 5724 metres SSS 70
Fees D–25dm W/E–30dm
Loc Ottfigen 15 km from Siegen 80 km from Koln

Soest

Stahlerg Im Lippetal

Soest
Tel
Mem
Pro
Holes 9 L SSS
Fees
Loc

Soltau

Soltau (1982)

Golfplatz Hof Loh 3040 Soltau-Tetendorf
Tel **05191-14077**
Mem 420
Pro Andrew Horsman
Holes 18 L 6224 metres SSS 73 9 L 2340 metres SSS 54
Fees 25dm (30dm)

Sonthofen

Oberstdorf GC

Gebrgoibe 1 8980 Oberstdorf
Tel **08322 2895**
Mem 265
Pro Gordon Thomson
Holes 9 L 2795 metres Par 70
Fees WD–20dm W/E–25dm
Loc Oberstdorf 3 km

Sonnenalp (1976)

D-8972 Sonthofen Bavaria
Tel **08321-7276 (Sec) 08321-720 (Hotel)**
Mem 180
Pro Bernard Kennedy Andrew MacDonnald
Fees 55dm (65dm) Discount for hotel guests
Loc 4 km Sonthofen 3 km Fischen

Stuttgart

Neckartal (1974)

Gerokstrasse 64 7 Stuttgart
Tel **0711 233160**
Mem 250
Pro Ben Amara
Holes 18 L 6645 yds (men) 5475 yds (ladies) SSS 72 Par 73
Fees WD–$10 W/E–$12
Loc Kornwestheim-Aldingerstrasse

Stuttgarter GC Solitude (1927)

7251 Monsheim
Tel **07044 5852**
Mem 640
Pro F Becker F Lengsfeld
Holes 18 L 6040 metres SSS 72
Fees D–20dm Sat/Sun–25dm
Loc 25 km from Stuttgart

Sylt Island

Marine GC Westerland (1980)

2280 Westerland Marinefliegerhorst
Tel **(04651) 70 37**
Mem 250
Holes 6 L 4770 metres SSS 66
Fees 25dm (30dm)

Trier

GC Trier-Mosel (1977)

5559 Ensch-Birkenheck
Tel
Mem 200
Pro R Hickinbotham
Holes 9 L 6100 metres SSS 72
Fees 25dm (40dm)

Ulm

Ulm GC (1963)

Postfach 4068 D–7900 Ulm
Tel **0731 183214**
Mem 315
Pro Frank Piater
Holes 9 L 6170 metres Par 72
Fees D–25dm Sat/Sun–40dm
Loc 15 km S of Ulm between Illerkirchberg and Illerrieden

Waldsassen

GC Stiftland (1982)

Schloss Ernestgrün 8591 Neualbenreuth
Tel **(09638) 6 55**
Holes 9 Par 36

Walsrode

GC Tietlingen (1979)

3032 Fallingbostel Schüterberg 5
Tel **(05162) 30 36**
Holes 9 Par 36

Wiesbaden

GC Main-Taunus (1980)

Auf der Heide 6200 Wiesbaden-Delkenheim
Tel **06122/3251**
Mem 500
Pro G Jones S Bailey D Lewis
Holes 18 L 6088 metres SSS 72
Fees 30dm (40dm)
Loc Next to the US Air Force Base Wiesbaden-Erbenheim
Mis Clubhouse closed Mon; open 11am–10pm; driving range, fee 10dm, 20 balls 2dm

Rheinblick GC

62 Wiesbaden-Marchenland
Tel **Military 3889**
Mem US Forces (Guests limited)
Pro Peter Greenfield
Holes 18 L 6604 yds SSS 70
Fees D–$5 Sat/Sun–$10
Loc 2 km from centre

GC Rhein-Main (1977)

Steubenstrasse 9 6200 Wiesbaden
Tel **(06121) 37 30 14**
Holes 18 L 5966 metres SSS 71
Fees 12$ (18$)–only with member
Loc 6 km from Wiesbaden

Wiesbadener GC (1893)

6200 Wiesbaden-Chausseehaus
Tel **06121 460238**
Mem 470
Pro Martin Day Tim Robinson
Holes 9 L 5320 metres Par 68
Fees D–25dm Sat/Sun–35dm
Loc 8 km from city centre towards Schlangenbad

Wiesmoor

GC Ostfriesland (1980)

2964 Wiesmoor Postbox 1220
Tel **(04944) 801**
Mem 350
Pro Steven Parry
Holes 18 L 6265 SSS 73
Fees 30dm (40dm)
Loc Wilhelmshaven 25 km

Wiggensbach

GC Oberallgäu (1982)

Hof Waldegg (944m) 8961 Wiggensbach/Oberallgäu (857m)
Tel **(08370) 7 33**
Holes 18 Par 67

Wildenrath

Wildenrath

BFPO 42
Tel **02432 48 5440**
Mem 300 Service personnel only UK based civilians and dependants also
Pro
Holes 9 L 4335 yds SSS 61
Rec Am–62 J Ellis
Fees 10dm
Loc RAF Wildenrath

Wildeshausen

Wildeshausen (1978)

POB 1255 2870 Delmenhorst
Tel **04431/1232**
Mem 250
Pro Axel Greshake
Holes 9 L 6080 metres SSS 72
Fees 20dm (30dm)
Loc 3 km to Wildeshausen; road to Huntlosen

Wilhelmshaven

GC Wilhelmshaven (1980)

2940 Wilhelmshaven
Holes 9 Par 36

Windhagen

GC Waldbrunnen (1983)

Brunnenstrasse 7 5461 Windhagen/Rederscheid (Postal add)
Tel **(02645) 1 50**
Mem 233
Pro Julian Myerscough
Holes 9 L 6170 metres (G) 5430 (L) Par 72
Fees 20dm (25dm)
Loc Near Bad Honnef
Mis Golf Hotel facilities, swimming, riding, tennis

Winterberg

Winterberg GC

Postfach 1140 5788 Winterberg
Tel **0 29 81/1770**
Mem
Pro D Pugh
Holes 9 L 2945 metres Par 71
Fees 25dm (30dm)
Loc Winterberg 2 km

Wuppertal

Bergisch-Land eV

56 Wuppertal-Elberfeld Siebeneickerst 386
Tel **Neviges 02053 7177**
Mem
Pro Willy Kothe V Knornschild
Holes 18 L 5920 metres SSS 71
Fees
Loc 8 km from Wuppertal-Elberfeld

GC Juliana (1978)

Auf dem Golfgelände 5600 Wuppertal
Tel **(0202) 64 70 70**
Mem 650
Pro G Hillier J Walter G Problesch
Holes 18 L 6130 metres SSS 71
Fees 25dm (30dm)
Loc Dusseldorf 30 km

Würzburg

Würzburg-Kitzingen GC (1980)

Schwanenhof 3 8700 Wurzburg
Tel **(0931) 14043**
Mem 115
Pro F Dziwlewski
Holes 9 L 6020 metres SSS 72
Fees WD–7.50 dollars W/E–10 dollars
Loc 20 km Wurzburg

Gibraltar

Campamento GC

Capamento
Tel
Mem
Pro
Holes 9 L SSS 37
Fees D–2s W/E–4s

Greece

Athens

Glyfada GC (1963)

Glyfada Athens
Tel **8931 721**
Mem 1300
Pro Hector Thomson
Holes 18 L 6189 metres SSS 72
Fees D–800dra W/E–1300dra W–4200dra
Loc 12 km from Athens

Corfu

Corfu (1972)

Kerkyra PO Box 71 Ropa Valley Corfu
Tel **Corfu 94220/94221**
Mem 150
Pro David Crawley
Holes 18 L 6300 metres SSS 72
Fees D–2200dra W–8800dra
Loc Ermones Bay 15 km from Corfu town

Halkidiki

Porto Carras G & CC (1979)

Porto Carras Halkidiki
Tel **0375 71381/71221**
Telex **4124 96**
Mem
Pro Mrs P Andrade
Holes 18 L 6086 metres SSS 72
Fees D–2000dra W–10000dra
Loc Sithonia Peninsula 100 km from Thessaloniki

Rhodes

Afantou GC (1973)

Afantou Rhodes
Tel **(0241) 51255/51256**
Mem 96
Pro G Sotiropoulos
Holes 18 L 6060 metres SSS 72
Fees D–900dra W–5000dra

Holland

Alkmaar

De Noordhollandse GC (1982)

Sluispolderweg 6 1817 BM Alkmaar
Tel **Sec 072-156807; golfshop 072-156175**
Pro PG Ackerley P Horn
Holes 9 L 6171 metres (G) 5450 (L) SSS Par 72
Fees 19fl (W/E & hols 27fl)

Amsterdam

Amsterdam GC (1934)

Private
Zwarte Laantje 4 1099 CE Amsterdam
Tel **(31) (20) 94 36 50**
Mem 560 100(J)
Pro W Dorrestein Tel (31) (20) 94 7409
Holes 18 L 5510 metres SSS 69
Fees WD–30fl W/E–60fl
Loc Amsterdam 8 km

Olympus GC (1973)

Sportpark Overamstel Amsterdam
Tel **020 651863**
Mem 550
Pro P van Wijk
Holes 9 L 2236 metres SSS 64
Fees 10fl
Loc E of Amstel River nr junction with A1

Apeldoorn

Veluwse GC (1957)

Private
Hoog Soeren 57
Tel **05769 275**
Mem 400
Pro Cecil Brown
Holes 9 L 6264 yds SSS 70
Fees D–15fl Sat/Sun–17.50fl
Loc 5 km W of Apeldoorn

Arnhem

Edese GC (1979)

Levendaal 29 6715 KJ EDE
Tel **08306-1985**
Mem 440
Pro C Borst
Holes 9 L 3050 metres SSS 72
Fees WD–30fl (20fl mem) W/E 40fl (30fl mem)
Loc Sportcentre Papendal between Ede and Arnhem

Rosendaelsche GC (1895)

Private
Apeldoornsweg 450 6816 SN Arnhem
Tel **085 42 14 38**
Mem 800
Pro JGM Dorrestein P Coleman Tel 085 437 283
Holes 18 L 6037 metres SSS 72
Fees WD–30fl W/E–40fl
Loc 5 km N of town centre on route N50

Keppelse GC (1926)

Laag-Keppel
Tel **08348 1416**
Mem 150
Pro
Holes 9 L 3458 metres SSS 57
Fees D–20fl W/E–30fl
Loc Laag Keppel 1.5 km

Assen

Gelpenberg GC (1972)

De Gelpenberg Zweeloo
Tel **05917 1784**
Mem 375
Pro W Stevens Tel 05917 1525
Holes 9 L 5867 metres SSS 71
Fees 40fl (50fl) (Members of other clubs 50%)
Loc 10 miles W of Emmen

Breda

N-B Toxandria GC

Veenstraat 89 Molenschot
Tel 01611 1200
Mem 700
Pro C Renders
Holes 18 L 5936 metres SSS 71
Fees D–40fl Sat/Sun–50fl
Loc Breda 8 km
Mis Introduction necessary Please phone in advance

Wouwse Plantage (1973)

Zoomvlietweg 66 Wouwse Plantage
Tel **01657 593**
Mem 380
Pro F Nauta
Holes 9 L 3015 metres SSS 71
Fees WD–20fl W/E–30fl
Loc Wouwse Plantage (N 13)

Den Helder

Helderse GC (1981)

Post bus 63 1780 Den Helder
Tel 02230-14035 (sec)
Mem 190
Pro P Horn
Holes 9 (pitch and putt)
Mis General information Tel 02230-22987

Marine GC Nieuwediep (1958)

PO Box 932 1780AX Den Helder
Tel
Mem 250
Pro
Holes 9 L 4436 metres SSS 64
Fees 6fl
Loc Nieuwe Haven
Mis Situated on naval base; entry by permit or introduction only

Deventer

Sallandsche GC de Hoek (1934)

Private
PO Box 442 7400 AK Deventer
Tel **Diepenveen 05709 1214**
Mem 400
Pro J Balvert Tel 05709 2293
Holes 9 L 6122 yds SSS 69
Fees 40fl (50fl)
Loc 4 miles N of Deventer

Eindhoven

Eindhovensche GC (1930)

Eindhovensche Weg 300 5553 VB Valkenswaard
Tel **04902 14816**
Mem 500 250(L) 80(J)
Pro G Jeurissen J Renders
Holes 18 L 6106 metres SSS 71
Fees 50fl (70fl)
Loc 9 miles S of Eindhoven

Haviksoord GC (1976)

Private
Maarheezerweg Nrd 11 5595 XG **Leende (NB)**
Tel **04906 1818 also 040 813186**
Mem 330
Pro
Holes 9 L 5836 metres SSS 71
Fees 20fl (30fl)
Loc 10 km S of Eindhoven
Mis V'trs must have valid handicap card

GC De Schoot (1973)

Schootsedijk 18 5491 TD Sint Oedenrode
Tel 04138 73011
Sec 04990 71059
Mem 400
Pro J Ottevanger
Holes 9 L 2392 metres SSS 66
Fees 20fl (25fl)
Loc Eindhoven 20 km

Groningen

Noord Nederlandse G & CC (1950)

Private
Pollselaan 5 9756 CJ Glimmen
Tel **05906 1275**
Mem 550
Pro KC Visser K MacDonald
Holes 9 L 5400 metres SSS 70
Fees 40fl (50fl)
Loc On route A28, junction Eelde, direction Glimmen; after 1½ km direction Zuidlaren; signposted after 1 km
Mis Another 9 holes under construction–ready September 1987

The Hague

Haagsche GC (1893)

Private
Groot Haesebroekseweg 22 2242 EC Wassenaar
Tel **01751 79607**
Mem 1400
Pro Alex Loesberg SJ van den Berg
Holes 18 L (men) 5674 metres SSS 71 (ladies) 5056 metres SSS 71
Fees Intro only D–50fl Sat/Sun–70fl
Loc Den Haag 6 km

Haarlem

Spaarnwoude GC (1977)

Antillenstraat 9 2071 VL Santpoort
Tel **023 378669/382708**
Mem 1500
Sec J van der Zee
Pro AC Wessels

Holes 18 L 5469 metres SSS 69
Fees 17fl (24fl)
Loc 9 miles W of Amsterdam

Kennemer G & CC (1910)

78-80 Kennemerweg PO Box 85
2042 XT Zandvoort
Tel **02507 12836**
Mem 840
Pro J Buchanan
Holes 18 L 5860 metres SSS 72
9 L 2901 metres
Fees WD–50fl W/E–70fl
Loc Haarlem 6 km

Hengelo

Twentsche GC (1930)

Enschedesestraat 381
Tel **074 912773**
Mem 400
Pro Joost Poppe
Holes 9 L 5444 metres SSS 69
Fees 20fl (25fl)
Loc Hengelo 3 km
Mis Secretary: Wilgenkampweg 75 7547 R2 Enschede. Tel 05428–1523. Admission only for union members and guests

Herrenveen

Lauswolt G & CC (1964)

Harinxmaweg 8A 9244 CJ
Beetsterzwaag
Tel **05126 2594**
Mem 450
Pro John Too
Holes 9 L 5993 metres SSS 71
Fees 40fl (50fl)
Loc Beesterzwaag 5 km S of Drachten

Hertogenbosch

De Dommel GC

Zegenwerp St Michielsgestel
Tel **04105 23 16**
Mem 430
Pro M Groenendaal
Holes 12 L 5565 metres SSS 69
Fees D–20fl Sat/Sun–30fl
Loc Hertogenbosch 10 km

Hilversum

Hilversum GC (1910)

Private
172 Soestdijkerstraatweg 1213 XJ
Hilversum
Tel **035 857060**
Mem 950
Pro Donald Armour Roy Cattell
Holes 18 L 6458 yds SSS 71
Fees 50fl (70fl)
Loc Hilversum 3 km on road to Baarn

Leiden

Noordwijkse GC (1922)

Private
Randweg 25 PO Box 70 2200
AB-Noordwijk
Tel **02523 73761**
Mem 910
Pro T O'Mahoney P Horn
Holes 18 L 5910 metres SSS 72
Fees D–50fl Sat/Sun–70fl
Loc 5 km N of Noordwyk
Mis Restaurant

Maastricht

Wittem GC

Dal-Bissenweg 22 Wittem
Tel **04455 1397**
Mem 500
Pro AV Pinxten WV Mook
Holes 9 L 6350 yds SSS 72
Fees 25fl (30fl)
Loc Gulpen 5 km

Middelburg

Domburgsche GC (1913)

Private
Domburg Walcheren
Tel **01188 1573**
Mem 320
Pro Brian Gee
Holes 9 L 5032 metres SSS 67
Fees D–20fl Sat/Sun–25fl
Loc Middelburg 15 km

Rotterdam

Openbare GC Kralingen (1933)

Kralingseweg 200
Tel **010-522 283**
Mem 300
Pro R Heykant C Kuysters
Holes 9 L 5277 yds SSS 66
Fees D–16fl W/E 25fl
Loc 5 km from Rotterdam centre

Oude Maas GC (1975)

Public
Nieuwe Polder Veerweg Rhoon
Tel **01890 18058**
Mem
Pro Rinus Goor
Holes 9 L 5876 metres SSS 71 9 hole Par 3
Fees 15fl (25fl)
Loc 10 km S of Rotterdam

Schiedam

Public Course Kleiburg (1974)

Krabbeweg 9 3231 NB Brielle
Pro W Koudijs
Holes 18 L 5534 metres SSS 69
Fees 19fl
Loc 3 km W from N57 Rotterdam–Hellevoetsluis

Utrecht

Utrechtse GC 'De Pan' (1984)

Amersfoortseweg 1 3735 L J Bosch en Duin
Tel **03404 55223 (Sec), 56427 (Shop), 56225 (Clubhouse)**
Mem 800
Pro C Dorresteijn
Holes 18 L 6088 metres SSS 70
Fees 50fl (70fl)
Loc Utrecht 10 km on A28 Utrecht–Amersfoort
Mis Advisable to ring first

De Haar (1974)

PO Box 104 Parkweg 5
3450 AC Vleuten
Tel **03407 2860**
Mem 450
Pro Allan Saddington
Holes 9 L 6650 yds SSS 71
Fees 25fl (35fl)
Loc 10 km NW of Utrecht

Venlo

Geysteren G & GC (1974)

Het Spekt 2 Geysteren (L) 5862 AZ
Lel **04784 1809**
Mem 700
Pro LG van Mook W van Mook
Holes 18 L 5984 metres SSS 71
Fees 50fl (60fl)
Loc Road N271 Venlo–Nymegan at Well; cross river, through village of Wanssum
Mis 18 holes SSS 72

Vlaardingen

Golfclub Broekpolder (1981)

Watersportweg 100 31 38 HD
Vlaardingen
Tel **010 475011/478142/4748140**
Mem 840
Pro J Stoop H Kuysters J Hage
Holes 18 L 6101 metres SSS 72
Fees 30/45fl (50/70fl)
Loc 15 km from Rotterdam A20 Rotterdam–Hoek van Holland. Turn right Vlaardingen

Zwolle

Hattemse G & CC (1930)

Veenwal 11 8051 AS Hattem
Tel **05206 41909**
Mem 385
Pro AR Donald
Holes 9 L 5808 yds SSS 68
Fees 40fl (50fl)
Loc Off the Zwolle-Apeldoorn road
Mis Sec: MM Jansen-van Angeren Tel 03412-53900

Iceland

Akranes

Leynir GC (1965)

Akranes PO Box 9
Tel **93 2711**
Mem 80
Pro
Holes 9 L 2640 metres SSS 69
Fees 100kr
Loc Akranes

Akureyri

Akureyri (1935)

PO Box 896 602 Akureyri
Tel **22974**
Mem 500
Pro David G Barnwell

Holes 18 L 5851 metres SSS 72
Fees 600 Ikr
Loc North Innland
Mis World's most Northern 18-hole golf course

Borgarnesi

Borgarness GC (1973)

Haniri 310 Borganes PO Box 112
Tel **(95) 7663**
Mem 60
Pro
Holes 18 L 5260 metres SSS 69
9 holes L 2630 metres SSS 69
Fees 300kr
Loc 5 km from centre of Borgarnes

Eskifjördur

Eskifjardar GC (1976)

Byggdarholt, 735 Eskifjördur
Tel
Mem 56
Pro
Holes 9 L 2206 metres SSS 65
Fees D–300kr
Loc 3km W of town

Grindavik

GK Grindavikur (1980)

Húsatóftavöllur
Tel **92-8720**
Holes 9 Par 35

Hafnarfjordur

Keilir GC (1967)

Hvaleyri Hafnarfjordur
Tel **53360**
Mem 300
Pro Thorvaldur Asgeirsson
Holes 18 L 5090 metres SSS 68
Fees 500 IKr
Loc S side of town 10 km from Reykjavik

Hornafirdi

Hornafjardar GC

Hornafirdi
Tel **97-8030**
Mem 44
Pro
Holes 9 L 3610 metres SSS 63
Fees 200 IKr
Loc Hofn

Huolsvelli

Hellu GC (1974)

Austurveg 1 2 Huolsvelli
Tel **8166**
Mem 74
Pro
Holes 9 L 3886 metres SSS 61
Fees 100 kr
Loc South Innland

Husavik

Husavikur GC (1967)

640 Húsavik
Private
Húsavik
Tel **41499/41101**
Mem 75
Pro
Holes 18 L 5232 metres SSS 68
Fees 250 Icelandic kr
Loc 2 km from Húsavik

Isafjordur

Isafjordur GC (1978)

Tel **(Chairman) 94-3035**
Mem 75
Pro
Holes 9 L 4860 metres SSS 67
Fees 250 IKr
Loc 3 km W of town
Mis Course mostly closed WE for competitions

Keflavik

Sudurnesja GC (1964)

Keflavik
Tel **2908**
Mem 165
Pro
Holes 12 L 5961 metres SSS 71
Fees
Loc
Mis Links course

Olafsjordur

Olafsfjardar GC (1967)

Olafsfjordur
Tel
Mem 25
Pro
Holes 9 L 4652 metres SSS 65
Fees
Loc

Olafsvik

Jokull GC (1973)

Olafsvik
Tel
Mem 38
Pro
Holes 9 L 4800 metres SSS 65
Fees
Loc 5 km SE of town

Reykjavik

Kjolur GC (1980)

Mosfellssueit
Tel
Mem
Pro
Holes 9
Fees
Loc

Ness GC (1964)

PO Box 66 172 Seltjarnesi
Tel **611930**
Mem 170
Pro TH Asgeirsson
Holes 9 L 4986 metres SSS 68
Fees 500 IKr
Loc 3 km W from city

Reykjavikur GC (1934)

Box 4071 Reykjavik
Tel **84735 82815**
Mem 706
Pro John Nolan
Holes 18 L 6030 metres SSS 70
Fees 200kr
Loc

Saudarkrokur

Saudarkroks GC (1970)

Saudarkrokur
Tel **95-5075**
Mem 50
Pro
Holes 9 L 5708 metres SSS 71
Fees 150kr
Loc 1½km W of town

Selfoss

Selfoss GC (1971)

Selfoss
Tel
Mem 48
Pro
Holes 9 L 5070 metres SSS 69
Fees
Loc Innland South

Siglufjordur

Siglufjardar GC (1970)

Siglufjordur
Tel
Mem 35
Pro
Holes 9 L 4950 metres SSS 66
Fees
Loc

Vestmannaeyjar

Vestmannaeyja GC (1938)

Tel **2363**
Mem 132
Pro
Holes 9 L 2881 metres SSS 70 (18 holes)
Fees 300 IKr
Loc 2 km W of town centre
Large island on S coast–20 minute flight from Reykjavik

Italy

Alassio

Garlenda GC (1965)

17030 Garlenda (Savona)
Tel **0182 580012**
Mem 600 130(L) 85(J)
Pro F Zanini F Picco
Holes 18 L 5740 metres SSS 70
Fees 35000L (50000L)
5D–140000L
Loc 15 km from Alassio–Liguria West

Alessandria

Margara (1975)

15043 Fubini Alessandria
Tel **0131 772377**
Mem 170
Pro A Reale
Holes 18 L 6218 metres SSS 72
Fees WD–10000L W/E–15000L
Loc 15 km from Alessandria

La Serra

15048 Valenza (Alessandria)
Tel **0131 93425**
Mem
Pro M Avanzino
Holes 9 L 2850 metres SSS 70
Fees
Loc 4 km from Valenza

Bergamo

Bergamo L'Albenza (1960)

Via Longoni 12
24030 Almenno San Bartolomeo
Tel **035 640028-640707**
Mem 480
Pro S Locatelli M Rendina F Ripamonti C Rocca
Holes 18 L 5980 metres SSS 71/6222 metres SSS 73
Fees 25000L (40000L)
Loc 13 km from Bergamo 45 km from Milan
Mis closed Mon

Bergamo La Rossera

24060 Chiuno Bergamo
Tel **035 830600 and 035 244251**
Mem
Pro F Maestroni
Holes 9 L 2510 metres
Fees
Loc 18 km from Bergamo

Biella

Biella *Le Betulle* GC (1958)

Magnano Vercelli
Tel **679151**
Mem 250
Pro Maurizio Guerisoli Agostino Reale
Holes 18 L 6100 metres SSS 72
Fees 30000L (50000L)
Loc 17 km from Biella

Bologna

Bologna GC (1959)

40050 Chiesa Nuova di Monte San Pietro
Tel **051 756154**
Mem 280
Pro Bruno Chezzo
Holes 18 L 5860 metres SSS 71
Fees D–4000L Sat/Sun–5000L
Loc 17 km from Bologna

Brescia

Bogliaco GC (1952)

25080 Bogliaco Lago di Garda Brescia
Tel **0365 641406**
Mem 150
Pro Franco Zanini
Holes 9 L 2700 metres SSS 70
Fees Limited D–1500L Sat/Sun–3000L

Gardagolf CC (1985)

Località Le Posteghe 25080 Soiano Del Lago Brescia
Tel **0365/674116**
Mem 220
Pro Franco Maestroni
Holes 18 & 9 L 6465 & 1985 SSS 72
Loc Near Lake Garda, North Italy
Mis In May 1986 the first 18 holes will be open. In May 1987 the complete course (last 9 holes) will be open.

Catanzaro Lido

Porto D'Orra (1977)

CP 102 88063 Catanzaro Lido
Tel **0961 964245**
Mem
Pro P Venanzi
Holes 9 L 3030 metres SSS
Fees
Loc SW corner Italy

Cervinia

Cervino GC (1955)

Cervinia-Breuil 11021
Tel **9 41 31**
Mem 150
Pro F Luzzi M Avanzini
Holes 9 L 2592 metres SSS 67
Fees D–10000L
Loc 5 minutes from town

Como

Carimate GC (1962)

Via Airoldi 22060 Carimate
Tel **(031) 790226**
Mem 500
Pro E Songia M Brigerio B Molteni
Holes 18 L 5982 metres SSS 71
Fees 25000 L (50000 L)
Loc Como 15 km Milano 27 km

Lanzo Intelvi GC (1962)

22024 Lanzo-Intelvi Como
Tel **84 01 69**
Mem 188
Pro G Frigerio
Holes 9 L 2438 metres SSS 66
Fees WD–20000L W/E–30000L
Loc 32 km Lugano (CH) 10 km Campione d' Italia

Menaggio and Cadenabbia GC (1907)

Via Golf 12 22010 Grandola E Uniti (Como)
Tel **0344 32103**
Mem 260
Pro G Delfino
Holes 18 L 5327 metres SSS 69
Fees WD–30000L W/E–50000L
Loc 5 km from Menaggio 27 km from Lugano 80 km from Milano

Monticello (1975)

22070 Cassina Rizzardi Como
Tel **031 928055**
Mem 800
Pro A Croce V Damonte E Bianchi A Schiroli M Barzan
Holes 18 L 6413 metres SSS 72
18 L 6056 metres SSS 72
Fees WD–30000L W/E–60000L
Loc 10 km from Como

La Pinetina Di Carbonate (1971)

22070 Appiano Gentile
Tel **031 930931**
Mem 321
Pro Angelo Croce
Holes 18 L 6001 metres SSS 71
Fees D–8000 L Sat/Sun–14000L
Loc Como 12 km

Royal Sant'Anna (1978)

22040 Annone di Brianza Como
Tel **0341 577551**
Mem
Pro G Locatelli E Della Torre
Holes 9 L 5370 metres SSS 69
Fees 25000L (35000L)
Loc 15 km from Como 40 km from Milano

Villa D'Este GC (1926)

Via Cantà 13 22030 Montorfano (Como)
Tel **031 200200**
Mem 400
Pro GC Frigerio P Molteni G Ciprandi
Holes 18 L 5750 metres SSS 70
Fees 35000L (Sat & hols 60000L)
Loc At Montorfano 7 km from Como
Mis Restaurant (closed Mon), driving range, pro-shop

Courmayeur

Courmayeur & Grandes Jorasses

Courmayeur 11013
Tel **8 91 03**
Mem
Pro F Venier E Ros
Holes 9 L 2650 metres SSS 67
Fees D–4000L
Loc Courmayeur 5 km

Elba

Elba Dell'Acquabona

57037-Portoferraio Elba
Tel **0565 940066**
Mem 220
Pro Cesidio Croce
Holes 9 L 2671 metres Par 34
Fees WD–10000L W/E–16000L
Loc Portoferraio 5 km Portoazzurro 4 km

Fiuggi Fonte

Fiuggi GC (1926)

Superstrada Anlicolana 1 03015 Fiuggi Fonte (Frosinone)
Tel **0775 55250**
Mem 200
Pro Zito Angelo
Holes 9 L 5697 metres SSS 70
Fees 20000L (25000L)
Loc City limits
Mis Pro-shop, driving range, swimming pool, restaurant, bar, tennis

Florence

Ugolino GC

Strada Chaintigiana 3 50015 Grassina
Tel **055 205 1009**
Mem 700
Pro F Rosi R Campagnoli C Poletti
Holes 18 L 5785 metres SSS 70
Fees D–40000L W/E–60000L
Loc 12 km from Florence

Genoa

Arenzano Della Pineta

Pineta-Arenzano 16011
Tel **912 7296**
Mem 672
Pro S Gori A Mori V Mori
Holes 9 L 5540 metres SSS 70
Fees 25000L (Sat & hols 40000L)
Loc Genoa 25 km

Grosseto

GC Punta Ala (1964)

58040 Punta Ala
Tel **0564/92 21 21 (Secretary)**
0564/92 26 43 (Restaurant)
Mem 310
Pro M Mulas P Manca F Rosi
Holes 18 L 6190 metres SSS 72 Par 72
Fees Low season 25000L
High season 45000L
Loc 43 km W of Grosseto 145 km from Pisa 150 km from Florence

Madonna Di Campiglio

Campo Carlo Magno GC (1922)

38084 Madonna di Campiglio (Trento)
Tel **0465 41003 Telex Carupi 400882 Golf**
Mem 45
Pro A Silva
Holes 9 L 4992 metres SSS 68
Fees D–8000L
Loc 1 km from Madonna di Campiglio

Milan

Barlassina Country Club (1952)

Via Privata Golf, 42
20030 Birago di Camnago (MI)
Tel **0362 560621/560622/560623**
Mem 300
Pro N Rendina S Betti
Holes 18 L 5929 (M) 5210 (L) metres
Fees Limited 40000L (50000L)
Loc Milan 22 km Como 22 km

Milano GC (1928)

Parco di Monza 20052
Tel **039 303081/303082**
Mem 1050
Pro G Grappasonni
Holes 18 L 6077 metres SSS 72
9 L 2998 metres SSS 36
Fees D–30000L W/E–40000L
Loc 17 km from Milan

Molinetto CC

SS Padana Superiore 11 20063 Cernusco sul Naviglio (M1)
Tel **(02) 92 38 500/92 49 373**
Pro Fernando Perino Romolo Nappoleoni
Holes 18 L 6010 metres Par 72
Mis Driving range, restaurant, swimming pool, tennis courts

Golf Pubblico Le Rovedine

Via C Marx 20090 Noverasco di Opera (M1)
Tel **(02) 524 27 30**
Pro R Benassi L Marsala
L Ghirardo G Veronelli
Holes 9 L 3024 metres Par 36
Loc 4 km from Milan centre

GC Zoate

20067 Zoate di Tribiano (M1)
Tel **(02) 90 60 015/90 60 036**
Pro L Grappasonni S Zerega
Holes 18 L 6116 metres Par 72
Loc 17 km from Milan
Mis Swimming, tennis; restaurant

Montecatini

Montecatini Golf (1985)

Via Dei Brogi Loc Pievaccia 51005 Monsummano Terme
Tel **0572-62218**
Mem 184
Pro M Ravinetto
Holes 9 L 3072 metres SSS 72
Fees 20000L (25000L)
Loc 40 km NW of Florence on A11
Mis Further 9 holes opening 1987

Naples

Circolo Golf Napoli

c/o Afsouth GC via Campiglione 11
80072 Arco Felice (NA)
Tel **(081) 867 42 96**
Holes 9 L 4776 metres Par 70
Loc Pozzuoli 10 km W of Naples
Mis Putting green; restaurant

Novara

GC Castelconturbia (1985)

Via Suno-28010 Agrate Conturbia (Novara)
Tel **0322 801070/802093**
Holes 27
Pro A Angelini A Feraloni
D Lovato M Bianco
Loc 18 km from Novara; 60 km from Milan
Mis Driving range, putting greens restaurant, swimming, tennis

GC Santa Martretta Vigevano (1974)

Via Chitola 49 27029 Vigevano
Tel **0381 76872**
Mem 174
Pro A Zito R Russo
Holes 9 L 5880 metres Par 72
Fees 20000L (35000L)
Loc Novara 25 km Milano 35 km Pavia 35 km

Padua

Padova GC (1966)

35030 Valsanzibio di Galzigano
Tel **049 9130078**
Mem 600
Pro A Lionello P Bernardini
Holes 18 L 6053 metres SSS 72
Fees 40000L (45000L)
Loc 20 km from Padova

Parma

Golf Club La Rocca (1985)

Via Campi 8 43038 Sala Baganza (Parma)
Tel **0521-834037**
Mem 300
Pro R Bolognesi P Taricone
Holes 9 L 2891 metres Par 35 SSS 70
Fees £10 (£14)
Loc 8 km from Parma

Perugia

Perugia GC (1970)

Ellera 06074 Perugia
Tel **(075) 79704**
Mem 220
Pro R Paris
Holes 9 L 2890 metres SSS 35
Fees 20000L
Loc 6 km NW of Perugia

Piacenza

Croara CC (1977)

29010 Croara di Gazzola (Piacenza)
Tel **0523 977105**
Mem 230
Pro G Turrini R Vaira
Holes 18 L 6040 metres SSS 72
Fees 20000L (30000L)
Loc 80 km Milan
Mis Restaurant, tennis, swimming pool

Pisa

Tirrenia GC (1968)

Viale San Guido 56018 Tirrenia (Pisa)
Tel **050 37518**
Mem 320
Pro M Ravinetto
Holes 9 L 3065 metres SSS 72
Fees WD–20000L W/E–25000L
Loc Halfway between Pisa and Livorno

Rapallo

Rapallo GC (1930)

Via Mameli 377 16035 Rapallo (Genova)
Tel **0185-50210/57187**
Mem 769
Pro M Canessa M Erbisti C Costa
A Brizzolari M Avanzino
A Schiaffino
Holes 18 L 5694 metres SSS 70
Fees 30000L (Sat 50000L)
Loc Inside city limits open all year round
Mis Tennis courts

Rome

GC Fioranello

Casella Postale 96 00040 Santa Maria delle Mole (Rome)
Tel **(06) 608 291/608 058**
Mem 250
Pro R Croce A Pelliccioni
Holes 9 L 5276 metres SSS 68
Fees 20000L (25000L)
Loc 17 km from Rome
Mis Pro shop, putting green, restaurent, swimming pool, driving range

Olgiata Golf Club (1961)

Largo Olgiata 15
Tel **3789141**
Mem 800
Pro U Grappasonni
Holes 18 and 9 L 6230 and 2833 metres SSS 72 and 71
Fees D–25000L W/E–35000L
Loc On Via Cassia 19 km from Rome
Mis Restaurant, bar, swimming pool (open air), pro-shop, driving range

Circolo Del Golf Di Roma (1903)

Via Appia Nuova 716 Acquasanta Rome
Tel **783 407**
Mem 1300
Pro P Manca C Croce M Peri
Holes 18 L 5707 metres SSS 70
Fees D–5000L Sat/Sun–8000L
Loc 7½ km from city centre

Rovigo

Albarella (1975)

45010 Isola de Albarella Rosolina Rovigo
Tel **0426 67077**
Mem
Pro F Ghezzo
Holes 18 L 6222 metres SSS
Fees D–14000L
Loc 65 km from Venice

San Remo

Degli Ulivi GC (1932)

Strada Campo Golf 59 18038 San Remo
Tel **0184 67093/71945**
Mem 360
Pro M Bianco G Ammirati G Gandelli G de Andreis
Holes 18 L 5230 metres SSS 67
Fees 30000L (45000L)
Loc 5 km from city centre

Sardinia

Is Molas (1975)

S Margherita Di Pula
Tel **070 9209007**
Mem 300
Pro L Cau
Holes 18 L 6992 yrds SSS 72
Fees D–20000L W–100000L
Loc

Pevero GC Costa Smeralda (1972)

Private
1-07020 Porto Cervo Sardegna Italy
Tel **Italy 0789 96072/96210/96211**
Mem 279
Pro David Bryan Mills
Holes 18 L 6186 metres SSS 72
Fees D–43000L
Loc Costa Smeralda

Sestriere

Sestriere GC (1932)

10058 Sestriere near Turin
Tel **0122 76 276/76 888**
Mem 400
Pro M Vinzi S Bertaina
Holes 18 L 4598 metres SSS 65
Fees 35000L (45000L)
Loc Centre of Sestriere
Mis Highest course in Europe Open June–September

La Spezia

GC Marigola

Via Biagina 5 19032 Lerici (La Spezia)
Tel **0187-970193**
Mem 60
Pro Carlos Aceto Le Chevallier
Holes 6 L 2346 metres
Loc 65 km Pisa

Stresa

Golf Alpino Di Stresa (1925)

28040 Vezzo (Novara)
Tel **(0323) 20101 20642**
Mem 280
Pro Pasquali Giacono
Holes 9 L 5359 metres Par 69 SSS 67
Fees 20000L (30000L)
Loc Stresa 7 km

Piandisole GC (1964)

Via Pineta 1 28057 Premeno
Tel **0323 47100**
Mem 150
Pro Valentino Vier
Holes 9 L 2830 metres SSS 67 Par 68
Fees 20000L–30000L
Loc Verbania 13 km

Taranto

Riva Dei Tessali (1971)

74025 Marina di Ginosa Riva dei Tessali
Tel **099 643071**
Mem 120
Pro B Cosenza
Holes 18 L 6016 metres SSS 71
Fees D–5000L Sat/Sun–7000L
Loc Taranto 34 km

Tarquinia

Marina Velca GC

01016 Tarquinia Viterbo
Tel **0766 812109**
Mem 150
Pro R Napoleoni
Holes 9 L 2604 metres SSS 50
Fees D–5000L (Closed Wed)
Loc Pian Di Spille

Trieste

Trieste GC (1954)

Casella Postale 283 34100 Trieste
Tel **040/226159**
Mem 200
Pro E Pavan
Holes 9 L 2725 metres SSS 69
Fees 20000L (22000L)
Loc 7 km from city centre
Mis Tennis. Restaurant. Closed Tuesdays

Turin

Le Chioccole GC

Loc Fraschetta casc Roma 12062 Cherasco (CN)
Tel **(0172) 43772 (Sec)/48759 (Rest)**
Pro A Fiammengo V Pelle
Holes 9 L 3050 metres Par 35

Claviere GC (1927)

10050 Claviere Torino
Tel **0122 878917**
Sec Corso Novara 59-10154 Torino Tel 011 23981
Pro Merlino Lucio Giacotto Franco
Holes 9 holes (18 tees) L 4390 metres SSS 63 Par 66
Mis Restaurant, bar, practice course

Le Fronde

Via Sant' Agostino 68 10051 Avigliana (Torino)
Tel **011/938053 6 930540**
Mem 310
Pro Michele Rolando
Holes 18 L 6081 metres SSS 72
Fees 20000L (30000L)
Loc 15 km from Turin
Mis Restaurant, swimming pool

I Roveri

La Mandria 10070 Fiano
Tel **011 9235683**
Mem
Pro M Vinzi
Holes 18 L 6549 metres SSS 72 9 L 2930 metres SSS 35
Fees
Loc 16 km from Turin

Stupinigi GC (1972)

10135 Torino
Tel **011/34 39 75**
Mem
Pro D Canonica F Luzi
Holes 9 L 1975 metres SSS 60
Fees
Loc Turin

Torino GC(1924)

Via Grange 137/10070 Fiano Torinese
Tel **(011) 9235440/9235670/ 9235448**
Mem 800
Pro O Bolognesi L Merlino S Bertaina
Holes Course 1–18 L 6291 metres SSS 72
Course 2–18 L 6208 metres SSS 72
Fees 50000L
Loc 23 km from Turin centre

Udine

Udine GC (1971)

33034 Fagagna-Villaverde (Udine)
Tel **0432 800418**
Mem 210
Pro L Paolillo L Tavarini
Holes 9 L 2944 metres SSS 71
Fees D–25000L W/E–30000L
Loc 15 km from Udine

Varese

Varese GC (1934)

21020 Luvinate (Varese)
Tel **0332 227394/229302**
Mem 622
Pro S Abbiati M Ballarin V Viero
Holes 18 L 5936 metres SSS 72
Fees 25000L (40000L) (Closed Monday)
Loc Varese 5 km
Mis Sec: A Gervasini Pres: E Zucchi

Venice

Lido Di Venezia GC (1928)

CP 30011 Alberoni Lido-Venezia
Tel **041 731015**
Mem 430
Pro Tuilio Scarso R Pavan R Trentin
Holes 18 L 6138 metres SSS 72
Fees D–40000L W/E–50000L
Loc 10 km from Lido of Venice

Villa Condulmer Golf Club

31021 Mogliano Veneto (Treviso)
Tel **041 457062**
Mem 350
Pro Scafa Ugo
Holes 18 L 5880 metres SSS 71
Fees D–18000L Sun–20000L
Loc Venice 17 km

Verona

Verona GC (1963)

Sommacampagna VR CAP 37066
Tel **045 510060**
Mem 430
Pro E Ridolfi M Bolognesi
Holes 18 L 6037 metres SSS 72
Fees 40000L (W/E & Hols–50000L)
Loc 16 km from Verona

Vicenza

Asiago GC (1967)

36012 Asiago Vicenza
Tel **62 721**
Mem 200
Pro Renzo Trentin
Holes 9 L 2873 metres SSS 70
Fees D–5000 L Sat/Sun–6000L
Loc Asiago 3 km

Vittorio Veneto

Cansiglio GC (1950)

Cansiglio CP 32010 Spert d'Alpago
Tel **0438 585 398**
Mem 180
Pro U Scafa
Holes 9 L 5666 metres SSS 69
Fees 28000L (35000L)
Loc 21 km from Vittorio Veneto

Luxembourg

CC Grand-Ducal De Luxembourg (1936)

Senningerberg
Tel **Luxembourg 340 90**
Mem 1100
Pro R Badella E Saquet
Holes 18 L 5765 metres SSS 71
Fees 700fr (1000fr)
Loc 7 km from Luxembourg

Malta

Marsa Sports Club (1888)

Private
The Marsa
Tel **603809 624251**
Mem 350
Pro Bob Josie
Holes 18 L 5800 yds SSS 67
Fees D–£M4 (including temporary day membership of club)
Mis Club facilities include tennis courts, squash courts, mini-golf course, open-air swimming pool, gym/health and leisure centre, billiards room. Full catering facilities

Norway

Bergen

Bergen GC

PO Box 470 5001 Bergen
Tel **18 20 77**
Mem 250
Pro Steve Norris
Holes 9 L 4461 SSS 33
Fees D–100kr
Loc 8 km from Bergen

Drammen

Kjekstad GC (1976)

PO Box 201 3440 Royken
Tel **02 855850**
Mem 650
Pro Douglas Craig
Holes 9 L 5100 SSS 68
Fees 90kr
Loc 40 km SW of Oslo and 12 km SE of Drammen on route 282
Mis Under construction to 18 hole

Hamar

Hedmark Golfklubb

PO Box 1131 2301 Hamar
Tel **065 39617**
Mem 35
Pro
Holes 9 (Par 3) L 1413 metres SSS 27
Fees D–20kr

Kristiansand

Kristiansand (1973)

PO Box 31 N-4601 Kristiansand
Tel **042 45863**
Mem 300
Pro DR Clark
Holes 9 L 2485 metres SSS 70
Fees 80kr
Loc 5 miles E of K'sand off E18

Oslo

Oslo GC (1924)

Private
Bogstad 0757 Oslo 7
Tel **02 504402**
Mem 2742
Pro Stephen Newey Tel 02 50 54 92
Holes 18 L 6574 yds SSS 72
Fees 130kr (200kr)
Loc 8 km NW of Oslo centre; follow road signs to 'Bogstad Camping'

Oustoen CC

PO Box 1166–Sentrum 6107 Oslo 1
Tel **53 52 95/48 65 63 (Sec)**
Mem 360
Pro
Holes 11
Fees 100kr
Loc On small island in Oslo fjord–W of Oslo
Mis Private club. V'trs must be accompanied by a member

Sarpsborg

Borregaard GC (1927)

PO Box 348 1701 Sarpsborg
Tel **031 57401**
Mem 300
Pro Fraser Mudie
Holes 9 L 2300 metres SSS 33
Fees D–60kr
Loc 1 km N of town centre, in Opsund

Skien

Grenland GC (1983)

GGK PO Box 433 3701 Skien
Tel
Mem 127
Pro Peter Congreve
Holes 6 SSS 57
Fees 50kr
Loc Jarseng Sporstve

Stavanger

Stavanger GC (1956)

Longebakken 45 N 4040 Madla
Tel **55 54 31**
Mem 850
Pro Raymond Lees
Holes 18 L 5090 metres SSS 68
Fees 100kr

Tonsberg

Vestfold GC (1958)

PO Box 64 3101 Tonsberg
Tel **033 65105**
Mem 900
Pro George Beal
Holes 18 L 5824 metres SSS 72
Fees D–75kr Sat/Sun–100kr
Loc Tonsberg 8 km Sandefjord 10 km

Trondheim

Trondheim GC (1950)

PO Box 169 7001 Trondheim
Tel **53 18 85**
Mem 330
Pro Lars Nilsson
Holes 9 L 5632 metres SSS 72
Fees 100kr
Loc Trondheim 3 km

Portugal

Algarve

Palmares

Palmares Lagos Algarve
Tel **62961/62953 Tlx 57434**
Mem 100
Pro Luis Espadinha
Holes 18 L 5961 metres SSS 72
Fees D–3500esc
Loc 5 km Lagos

Penina GC (1966)

PO Box 146 Penina Portimao 8502 Algarve
Tel **82 22051/58 Telex 57307P**
Sec Ralph Gregan
Mem 220
Pro Robin Liddle J Lourenco
Holes 18 L 6889 yds SSS 73
9 L 3500 yds SSS 36
9 L 2278 yds SSS 33
Fees D–4500esc
Loc Portimao 5 km
Mis Henry Cotton Resident Consultant

Quinta Do Lago

Quinta Do Lago Almancil 8100 Loule Algarve
Tel **089-94 782/94 529**
Mem 300
Pro DG Silva
Holes 3 x 9 holes
A + B L 6310 metres Par 72
B + C L 6430 metres Par 72
C + A L 6320 metres Par 72
Fees 4700esc
Loc 20 km from Faro
Mis Driving range

Vale Do Lobo GC

Vale Do Lobo Almancil Algarve
Tel **Faro 94145**
Sec Mrs J Walker
Mem 250
Pro P McGuinness
Holes Green 9 L 2813 metres SSS 35
Orange 9 L 2975 metres SSS 36
Yellow 9 L 3036 metres SSS 36
Fees D–4800esc (Hotel guests 3600esc)
Loc 19 km from Faro Airport
Mis Also par-3 course; 30-bay driving range; discounts available

Vilamoura GC (1969)

Vilamoura 8125 Quarteira Algarve
Tel **Quarteira (089) 33652 Telex 56914**
Mem 200
Pro Joaquim Catarino (& 3 assistants)
Holes Old course (Vilamoura 1) 18 L 6331 metres SSS 72; New Course (Vilamoura 2) 18 L 6183 metres SSS 72
Fees Old course 4000esc (Vilamoura guests 3200esc)
New course 3500esc (Vilamoura guests 2800esc)
Loc 25 km W of Faro Airport
Mis New course was originally Dom Pedro golf course

The Azores

São Miguel GC

PO Box 55 9501 Ponta Delgada Azores
Tel **31925/54341**
Holes 9 (18 tees) L 5492 metres SSS 71 Par 72
Loc São Miguel Island
Mis Driving range; further 9 holes to be added to course

Terceira Island GC (1954)

9760 Praia da Victória Azores
Tel **25847**
Mem 680
Pro Eduardo Mendes Correia
Holes 18 L 6173 yds SSS 69
Fees D–4.50 US $ (W/E & hols D–7.50 US $)
Loc 13 km from Angra do Heroismo and Praia da Victória and international airport of Lajes Azores

Estoril

Estoril GC (1945)

Avenida Republica 2765 Estoril
Tel **2680176**
Mem 800
Pro J Rodrigues H Paulino
Holes 18 and 9 L 5210 and 2350 metres SSS 68 and 65
Fees 2540esc (3040esc)
Loc 2 km from Estoril station

Estoril Sol (1976)

Linho 2710 Sintra
Tel **923 24 61**
Mem 65
Pro D Moita
Holes 9 L 4228 metres Par 66
Fees WD–1250esc Sat/Sun–2000esc
Loc 7 km N of Estoril 35 km from Lisbon

Quinta da Marinha G & CC (1984)

Quinta da Marinha 2750 Cascais
Tel **28 90 08/28 93 88**
Pro António Dantas
Holes 18 L 6600 yds Par 71
Loc 20 miles W of Lisbon
Mis Driving range, restaurant, etc

Lisbon

Campo De Lisboa

Fonte da Telha 2825 Monte da Caparica
Tel **226 3244**
Mem
Pro A Paulino
Holes 18 L 6171 metres SSS 73
Fees 3000esc
Loc 17 km S of Lisbon

Lisbon Sports Club (1922)

Casal da Carragueira Belas 2475 Queluz
Tel **4310077**
Mem 900
Pro J Baltazar
Holes 14 + 4 L5866 metres SSS 68
Fees D–3000esc
Loc Belas-Queluz 5 km 20 km E of Lisbon

Madeira

Santo Da Serra GC (1967)

Sto Antonio da Serra 9100 Santa Cruz Madeira
Tel **55139**
Mem 130
Pro J de Sousa
Holes 9 L 2622 yds SSS 67
Fees 1500esc
Loc 6 km from airport 22 km E of Funchal

Porto

Oporto GC (1890)

Sisto-Paramos 4500 Espinho
Tel **722008**
Mem 300
Pro CA Agostinho E Maganinho
Holes 18 L 3002 metres SSS 71
Fees 2000esc
Loc City limits of Espinho 15 km from Porto

Miramar GC (1934)

Praia de Miramar-4405 Valadares
Tel **7622067**
Mem 500
Pro Manuel Ribeiro
Holes 9 L 2477 metres SSS 66
Fees D–2000esc
Loc Porto 12 km
Mis Bar, restaurant, beach, swimming pool

Setubal

Troia Golf

Torralta Troia 2900 Setubal
Tel **(065) 44151/44236**
Mem
Pro Fernando Pina
Holes 18 L 6338 metres SSS 74
Fees D–2750esc
Loc 30 miles from Lisbon

Torres Vedras

Vimeiro GC

Termas do Vimeiro Praia do Porto Novo 2560 Torres Vedras
Tel **061-98157**
Pro
Holes 9 L 5900 yds Par 70
Fees D–500esc (Hotel guests 350esc)
Loc Torres Vedras 20 km Lisbon 65 km

Vidago

Vidago GC

Pavilhao Golfe–5425 Vidago
Tel **97512 or 97356**
Mem 400

Pro M Carneiro
Holes 9 L 2256 metres SSS 64
Fees D–750esc
Loc 130 km NE of Porto 45 km from Vila Real

Romania

Bucharest

Diplomatic Club

Aleia Dr Minovici 1 Sect 1
Tel **183525 184990**
Mem 900
Pro P Tomita
Holes 9
Fees 50 Lei
Loc Bucharest 3 miles

Spain

Algeciras

Sotogrande GC (1964)

Apartado 1 Sotogrande (Cadiz)
Tel **(956) 792050**
Mem 300
Pro T Gonzalez
Holes 18 L 5885 metres SSS 72
18 L 6263 metres SSS 72
9 L 1299 metres SSS 29
Fees D–1000P W–2500P M–6000P
Loc San Roque Gibraltar 18 km

Valderrama (1985)

Sotogrande Cadiz
Tel **(56) 792775**
Mem 112
Pro Juan Zumaquero
Holes 18 L 6326 metres SSS 72
Fees D–7000P
Loc 30 km from Gibraltar

Alicante Region

Don Cayo (1974)

Conde de Altea 49 Altea (Alicante)
Tel **965/84 07 16**
Mem
Pro Gregorio Sanz
Holes 9 L 6044 metres SSS 72
Fees D–600P
Loc 4 km from Altea

Ifach (1974)

Carretera Moraira-Calpe Benisa
Tel
Mem
Pro
Holes 9 L 3290 metres SSS 60
Fees D–500P
Loc

Javea (1981)

Carretera Benitachell, Km4
Tel **965 792584**
Mem 500
Pro Gregorio Sanz Lazaro Jose A Mogano Correderas
Holes 9 L (twice) 6070 metres (5330 metres for ladies) SSS 72
Fees Day–1300P (Summer and Christmas–1600P) Book of 10 tickets–1100P
Loc On Costa Blanca between Valencia and Alicante

Villa Martin (1972)

Apartado 35 Torrevieja (Alicante)
Tel **(965) 32 03 50 54 58**
Mem
Pro E Pareja
Holes 18 L 5899 metres SSS 72
Fees D–500P W/E–600P
Loc Torrevieja

Almeria

Golf Almerimar (1976)

Urb Almerimar El Ejido Almeria
Tel **51-480950**
Mem 60
Pro Juan Parron
Holes 18 L 5928 metres Par 72
Fees 3200P W–16000P
Mis Course designed by Gary Player; next to yacht marine with +1000 moorings. Golf hotel
Loc Almeria 36 km

Cortijo Grande (1976)

Turre Almeria
Tel **Turre 99**
Mem 72
Pro Santiago Sota
Holes 18 L 5545 metres SSS 70
Fees D–1000P W–4000P
Loc 2 miles W of Turre

Playa Serena (1977)

Playa Serena Roquetas de Mer Almeria
Tel **(951) 32 20 55**
Mem 300
Pro F Parron
Holes 18 L 5905 metres SSS 72
Fees 2200–2500P
Loc 20 km from Almeria

Barcelona Region

Golf Llavaneras (1945)

Camino del Golf San Andrés de Llavaneras
Tel **(93) 792 60 50**
Mem 595
Pro Franciscon Gonzalez Joaquim Bertrán Juan Gonzalez
Holes 9 L 4298 metres (18) SSS 63
Fees Jan–June, Oct–Dec 1500P; July–Sep & hols 2900P
Loc Barcelona 32 km on N-11

El Prat GC (1956)

8820 Prat de Llobregat Barcelona
Tel **(93) 379 02 78**
Mem 2200
Pro P Marin M Rodriguez
Holes 18 and 9 L 5800 metres SSS 72
Fees D–3360P Sat/Sun–6720P
Loc El Prat Airport 3 km Barcelona 15 km

Sant Cugat GC (1914)

Sant Cugat del Valles
Tel **(93) 674 39 08 58**
Mem 130
Pro A Demelo A Diaz
Holes 18 L 5085 metres SSS 67
Fees D–3000P Sat/Sun–5600P
Loc 20 km from Barcelona

Vallromanas (1969)

Apt 43 Montornes del Valles
Tel **(93) 568 03 62/568 01 58**
Mem 1230
Pro J Gallardo
Holes 18 L 6038 metres SSS 72
Fees D–2240P W/E–5600P
Loc Vallromanas 23 km from Barcelona A-17 Exit 13 A-19 Exit 5

Bilbao

La Bilbaina (1976)

Laucariz Munguia (Vizcaya)
Tel **(94) 674 08 58/674 04 62**
Mem
Pro FG Perez S Larrazabal
Holes 18 L 6112 metres SSS 72
Fees D–700P
Loc

Golf De Neguri (1911)

1.911 Apartado Correos no 9 Algorta
Tel **(94) 4690200 04 08**
Mem 2500
Pro C Celles L Losada JM Fuente JR Larrazabal
Holes 18 L 6319 metres SSS 72
Fees D–4000P
Loc Bilbao 20 km

Canary Islands

Costa Teguise (1978)

Lanzarote
Tel **(928) 81 35 12**
Mem
Pro NG Perez
Holes 18 L 6082 metres SSS 71
9 L 1455 metres SSS 28
Fees D–1000P
Loc 7 km N of Arrecife

Club De Golf Las Palmas (1891)

POB 183 35000 Las Palmas
Tel **35 10 50/35 01 04**
Mem 750
Pro F Santana E Perera S Sanchez
Holes 18 L 5690 metres SSS 70
Fees 3500P
Loc Bandana 14 km Las Palmas
Mis Driving range, pitch & putt greens, swimming pool, sauna & solarium, video, tennis & table tennis. Guests at Bandana Golf Hotel: fees included in hotel charges

Maspalomas GC (1968)

Paseo de Chil 282 Las Palmas
Tel **(928) 24 60 43**
Sec G Baker
Pro Bartolome Jimenez
Holes 18 L 5834 metres SSS 70
18 L 5678 metres SSS 70
Fees D–750P
Loc Maspalomas

Tenerife GC (1932)

Apartado 125 La Laguna Tenerif
Tel **(922) 25 02 40**
Mem 540
Pro G Gonzales
Holes 18 L 5100 metres SSS 68

Fees March to Oct and Dec–900P
April and Sept–600P
Loc Airport 2 km

Cadiz

Vista Hermosa (1975)

Apartado 77 Puerto de Santa Maria Cadiz
Tel **(956) 85 00 11**
Mem
Pro M Velasco
Holes 9 L 5680 metres SSS 70
Fees 1000P
Loc On bay of Cadiz

Cartagena

La Manga (1971)

Los Belones Cartagena (Murcia)
Tel **(968) 569111**
Mem 500
Pro Severiano and Manuel Ballesteros
Holes North 18 L 5573 metres SSS 70
South 18 L 5925 metres SSS 72
Fees D–1500P (residents)
Loc 20 km from Cartagena

Castellon de la Plana

Costa De Azahar GC (1960)

Carretera de Benicasim Grao Castellon
Tel **(964) 22 70 64**
Mem 300
Pro AM Zorrilla
Holes 9 L 5820 metres SSS 70
Fees D–750P
Loc Castellon de la Plana 6 km

Mediterraneo (1978)

La Coma Borriol Castellón
Tel **(964) 321227**
Mem 1300
Pro V Garcia
Holes 18 L 6038 metres SSS 72
Fees Winter–1910P Summer–2580P
Loc La Coma Castellon

Cordoba

Pozoblanco (1984)

San Gregorio 2 Pozoblanco Cordoba
Tel **(975) 100805**
Holes 9
Loc 3 km from Pozoblanco

Los Villares (1976)

Avda del Generalisimo 1-2° PO Box 463 Cordoba
Tel **(957) 22 58 22**
Mem
Pro AG Trujillo
Holes 18 L 6087 metres SSS 72
Fees D–600P
Loc Between Cordoba and Obejo

La Coruna

La Coruna (1962)

Apartado 737 La Coruna
Tel **(981) 28 5200**
Mem 1356
Pro J Santiago JL Naya JA Salgado
Holes 18 L 5782 metres SSS 72
Fees 2000P
Loc 7 km from La Coruna

Gerona

Costa Brava GC (1962)

Santa Cristina de Aro Gerona
Tel **(972) 83 71 50**
Mem 530 170(L) 70(J)
Pro Miguel Gil
Holes 18 L 5556 metres Par 70
Fees D–3000P (Summer 4000P)
Sun–3500P (Summer 4000P)
Loc Playo de Aro 5 km Barcelona 100 km

Golf De Pals GC

Pals Gerona
Tel **(972) 63 60 06**
Mem 750
Pro J Anglada M Ramos J Riera
Holes 18 L 6222 metres SSS 72
Fees July–Sept D–4500P Oct–June D–2300P W/E–4000P
Loc 10 km from Bagur

Huelva

Bellavista (1976)

Carretera Huelva-Aljaraque (Huelva)
Tel **(955) 31 80 83**
Mem 800
Pro M Sanchez
Holes 9 L 6300 metres SSS 72
Fees 500P
Loc 7 km Carretera Huelva-Punta Umbria

Ibiza

Roca Llisa (1971)

Apartado 200 Ibiza (Baleares)
Tel **(971) 30 20 00**
Mem
Pro G Castillo
Holes 9 L 5902 metres SSS 71
Fees 1000P
Loc

Madrid Region

Centro Deportivo Barberan (1967)

Apartado 46263 Cuatro Vientos (Madrid)
Tel **(91) 218 85 05**
Mem
Pro J Hernandez
Holes 9 L 6048 metres SSS 72
Fees D–250P Sat/Sun–600P
Loc 10 km from Madrid

Las Encinas de Boadilla (1984)

Boadilla del Monte (Madrid)
Tel **(91) 6331100**
Pro P Maestro
Holes 9 L 1464 metres SSS 52

Herreria (1966)

San Lorenzo de El Escorial (Madrid)
Tel 8 90 51 11
Mem 3450
Pro 2
Holes 18 L 6015 metres White
5108 metres Red SSS 72
Fees 1000P–1500P (1250P–2000P)
Loc 50 km from Madrid

Club de Campo Villa de Madrid (1984)

Carretera Castilla 28040 Madrid
Tel **(91) 2070395/2070629**
Mem 3500
Pro M Morcillo
Holes 27 L 6118 metres SSS 73
Fees 1800P (3600P)
Loc Madrid 4 km
Mis Municipal club from 1984. (Course built 1932.) Tennis, hockey, swimming pools, shooting

La Moraleja (1976)

Maruquesa Viuda de Aldama La Moraleja-Alcobendas Madrid
Tel **(91) 6500 700**
Mem 600
Pro V Barrios M Montes
Holes 18 L 5617 metres SSS 69
Fees D–750P W/E–3000P
Loc

Real Club Deportivo Las Lomas-El Bosque (1973)

Urbanizacion has homas Boadilla Del Morte Madrid
Tel **(91) 464 32 15**
Mem 1000
Pro M Roman
Holes 27 L 6075 metres SSS 72
Fees D–650P W/E–1350P
Loc 18 km Madrid

Nuevo De Madrid (1972)

Las Matas (Madrid)
Tel **(91) 630 08 20**
Mem
Pro J Marimon
Holes 18 L 6037 metres SSS 72
Fees D–700P W/E–1000P
Loc 18 km from Madrid

Puerta de Hierro (1904)

Madrid 8035
Tel **(91) 216 17 45**
Mem 1442
Pro Jose Gallardo Jaime Benito
Holes 36 L 6347 and 5273 SSS 73 and 67
Fees 2000P (3000P)
Loc 4 km N town centre on route VI
Mis V'trs must be accompanied by a member

Real Automovil Club de España (1903)

c/o José Abascal no 3 28010-Madrid
Tel **(91) 447 32 00 or 652 26 00**
Mem 300
Pro F Alvarez J Alvarez F Valera R del Castillo
Holes 18 SSS 72; +9
Fees 1500P (W/E & hols 2200P)
Loc 28 km from Madrid

Somosaguas (1971)

Somosaguas Madrid 11-1
Tel **(91) 212 16 47**
Mem
Pro M Cabrera A Garrido
Holes 9 L 5621 metres SSS 69
Fees D–650P Sun–750P
Loc Somosaguas

Valdelaguila (1975)

Villalbilla (Madrid)
Tel **255 23 37**
Mem
Pro V Gutierrez
Holes 9 L 5714 metres SSS 70
Fees D–400P W/E–500P
Loc 8 km Alcala de Henares

Majorca

Pollensa (1984)

Predio Son Porquer Ctra Palma-Pollensa Majorca
Tel **53 32 65/16**
Mem 200
Pro
Holes 9 L 3025 metres SSS 72
Fees 3500P (4000P)
Loc Pollensa 3 km Palma 51 km
Mis 18 holes due in 1987

Poniente Magaluf (1978)

Magaluf/Calvia Mallorca
Tel **(971) 22 36 15**
Mem
Pro
Holes 18 L 6100 metres SSS 72
Fees
Loc 16 km from Palma

Golf Santa Ponsa (1976)

Santa Ponsa Mallorca
Tel **(71) 690211 1690800**
Mem 350
Pro Sebastian Bruna
Holes 18 L 6520 metres SSS 74
Fees 4100 (Feb–Mar–Apr 3500P)
Loc 18 km from Palma; motorway Andraitx
Mis Hotel guests 50% discount on green fees

Son Servera GC (1967)

Private
Costa de Los Pinos/Son Servera (Mallorca)
Tel **Son Servera (971) 56 78 02**
Mem 250
Pro Santiago Sota
Holes 9 L 5840 metres SSS 72
Fees D–2750P
Loc 70 km from Palma via Manacor

Son Vida GC (1964)

Son Vida 07013 Palma de Mallorca
Tel **(971) 23 76 20**
Mem 500
Pro Florencio Fuentes
Holes 18 L 5414 metres SSS 68
Fees 4000P
Loc 5 km NW from Palma

Malaga Region

Club De Golf El Candado (1965)

Urbanizacion el Candado El Palo
Tel **(952) 294666**
Mem
Pro Manuel Lucas
Holes 9 L 4508 metres SSS 65
Fees D–1250P
Loc Malaga 5 km route N340

Mijas (1976) (Los Lagos and Los Olivos)

Apartado 138 Fuengirola Malaga
Tel **(34-52) 476843**
Pro Juan Rosa
Holes Los Lagos 18 L 6348 metres SSS 73 Los Olivos (new course): 18 L 5896 metres SSS 71
Fees D–3500P
Loc 4 km from Fuengirola
Mis Public course Handicap certificate required

Nerja

Nerja G & CC
PO Box 154 Nerja Malaga
Tel **(952) 52 02 08**
Pro Mr Angel Carsin
Holes 9 L 3000 metres SSS 59
Fees 1500P
Loc 1 km E of Nerja on motorway Málaga–Almeria
Mis Swimming pool; restaurant/bar; accommodation

Parador Nacional Torremolinos (1925)

Apartado 324 Malaga
Tel **52-381255**
Mem
Pro J Sanchez
Holes 18 L 6042 metres SSS 71
Fees 2900P
Loc 9 km from Malaga 3 km from Torremolinos
Mis Parador residents 50% green fee reduction

Torrequebrada (1977)

PO Box 67 Carretera de Cadiz KM 226 Benalmadena Costa
Tel **(52) 44 27 42**
Mem 200
Pro Juan Jimenez
Holes 18 L 5860 metres SSS 72
Fees 4500P (High season); 3400P (Low season)
Loc In front of Casino Torrequebrada
Mis Tennis, squash, swimming pool, sauna, bar, restaurant

Marbella

Aloha (1975)

Urbanizacion Aloha Marbella
Tel **78-2389**
Mem 1500
Pro J Mangas A Jimenez
Holes 18 L 6261 metres SSS 72
Fees 5000P+12%
Loc 8 km from Marbella
Mis 9 hole short course, swimming pool

Atalaya Park G & CC (1968)

Carretera Benhavis Estepona Marbella
Tel **(952) 781894**
Mem 150
Pro Derek Strachan
Holes 18 L 6272 SSS 73
Fees 4000P
Loc Between Marbella and Estepona; 4 km from Puerto Banus; 68 km from Malaga; 45 mins from Gibraltar

Club De Golf Las Brisas (1968)

Apartado 147 URB: Nueva Anadalucia (Malaga) Spain
Tel **785544/787747**
Mem 1250
Pro Sebastian Miguel
Holes 18 L 6198 metres SSS 73
Fees 5600P
Loc Nueva Andalucia opposite Puerto Banus 8 km S of Marbella

Guadalmina GC (1959)

Golf Hotel San Pedro de Alcántara Marbella (Malaga)
Tel **(952) 78 13 17**
Mem 600
Pro A Hernandez F Hernandez
Holes 18 L 6060 metres SSS 72
18 L 6200 metres SSS 72
Fees 2500P
Loc 68 km Malaga airport; 70 km Gibraltar airport
Mis Swimming pool, putting green, driving range, restaurant

Nueva Andalucia (Los Naranjos)

Apartado 2 Nueva Andalucia Marbella
Tel **(952) 78 72 00/78 03 00**
Mem 420
Pro M Escudero
Holes 18 L 6484 metres SSS 72
Fees
Loc Marbella 8 km

El Paraiso (1974)

Estepona Malaga
Tel **(952) 81 28 40**
Mem 50
Pro T Bellido
Holes 18 L 5690 metres SSS 70
Fees WD–700P
Loc Marbella 14 km

Golf Rio Real (1965)

Apartado 82 Marbella
Tel **(952) 77 17 00 Ext 3086**
Mem
Pro A Miguel
Holes 18 L 6130 metres SSS 72
Fees D–4000P (Free for Hotel Los Monteros and Inconsol)
Loc Marbella 5 km

Minorca

Real Club De Golf De Menorca (1976)

Apartado 97 Mahon Menorca
Tel **(971) 36 39 00**
Mem 350
Pro Juan Tollegrosa
Holes 9 L 5724 metres SSS 70
Fees D–500P
Loc 7 km N of Mahon

Son Parc (1977)

Plaza Bastion 11 Mahon Menorca
Tel **(971) 35 22 50**
Mem
Pro
Holes 9 L 2775 metres SSS 69
Fees 500P
Loc Mercadel 18 km from Mahon

Motril

Playa Granada (1974)

Apartado 139 Motril Granada
Tel **(958) 60 04 12**
Mem
Pro
Holes 9 L 5702 metres SSS 70
Fees
Loc

Oviedo

Club Deportivo la Barganiza (1982)

Apartado 277–33080 Oviedo
Pro Don Victor Garcia de la Cruz
Holes 9 Par 72 SSS 70
Loc 12 km from Oviedo

Castiello GC (1958)

Apartado de Correos 161 Gijon
Tel **(985) 36 63 13**
Mem 450
Pro J Hernandez
Holes 9 L 4817 metres SSS 67
Fees D–2000P
Loc Gijon 4 km

Pamplona

Ulzama (1965)

Guerendiain (Navarra)
Tel **(948) 31 31 62**
Mem
Pro R Echeverria
Holes 9 L 5984 metres SSS 71
Fees Summer D–500P
Winter D–400P
Loc 21 km N of Pamplona

Pontevedra

Golf La Toja (1970)

Isla de La Toja El Grove (Pontevedra)
Tel **(986) 73 08 18**
Mem 200
Pro P Medrano
Holes 9 L 6046 metres SSS 72
Fees D–2500P W/E–3500P
Loc Isla de La Toja
Vigo 60 km Santiago 70 km

Puigcerda

Real Club de Golf de Cerdaña (1929)

Apartado de Correos 63 Puigcerdá Gerona
Tel **(972) 880 862/881 338**
Mem 300
Pro S Diaz
Holes 18 L 5735 metres SSS 70
Fees 2000P (2500P) Nov–Apr 1500P
Loc 2 km Puigcerdá on route C-1313; 50 km Andorra
Mis Hotel Chalet de Golf on course. Tel (972) 880 970

San Sebastian

Real San Sebastian (1910)

Apartado 6 Fuenterrabia Guipuzcoa
Tel **(943) 61 68 45**
Mem
Pro M Arruti
Holes 18 L 5461 metres SSS 69
Fees D–1000P
Loc Lasarte Village Valley

Real Zarauz GC (1916)

Apartado 82 Zarauz Guipuzcoa
Tel **(943) 830145**
Mem 1100
Pro N Belartieta
Holes 9 L 4882 metres SSS 67
Fees D–2000P (Winter) 1000P
Loc Zarauz 1 km

Santander

Pedrena GC (1928)

Apartado 233 Santander
Tel **(942) 500001/500266**
Mem 1050
Pro Ramon Sota
Holes 18 L 5721 metres SSS 70
Fees D–300P–5000P
Loc Santander 20 km

Santiago

Aero Club De Santiago (1976)

General Pardinas 34 Santiago de Compostela
Tel **(981) 592400**
Mem
Pro J Ybarra
Holes 9 L 5422 metres SSS 68
Fees 500P
Loc 9 km from Santiago

Seville

Pineda De Sevilla GC (1939)

Apartado 796 Seville
Tel **6 11400**
Mem
Pro F Martin
Holes 9 L 5684 metres SSS 71
Fees Limited D–300P W/E–400P
Loc Sevilla 3 km

Sitges

Terramar GC (1922)

Apartado 6 08870 Sitges Barcelona
Tel **894 05 80 or 894 20 43**
Mem 930
Pro A Hernandez S Perez
J Hernandez
Holes 18 L 5578 metres SSS 70
Fees 2800P Hols–4500P
Loc Barcelona 40 km

Tarragona

Club de Golf Costa Dorada

Apartado 600 Tarragona
Tel **(977) 655416**
Pro F Jimenez J Cruz T Sanchez
Holes 9 L 3155 metres Par 72
Fees 1500P (2000P)

Valencia Region

El Bosque (1972)

En Chiva Valencia
Tel **3 26 3800**
Mem
Pro
Holes 18 L 6040 metres SSS 72
Fees
Loc

Escorpion (1975)

Apartado 1 Torre en Conill Betera Valencia
Tel **1601211**
Mem 1200
Pro J Rodriguez
Holes 18 L 6345 metres SSS 73
Fees WD–2400P; W/E–3000P
Loc Betera 20 km from Valencia

Club De Golf De Manises (1954)

Apartado 22.029 Valencia
Tel **25 63 90**
Mem 110
Pro J Bernardino P Contreras
Holes 9 L 2607 metres Par 72
Fees D–50P Sat/Sun–100P
Loc Valencia 12 km

El Saler (1968)

Parador Luis Vives El Saler Valencia
Tel **Campo 32 36850**
Mem 400
Pro JA Cabo J Navarro
Holes 18 L 6485 metres SSS 75
Fees D–1400P; 7 days–9200P; 30 days–27000P
Loc 18 km from Valencia
Mis Golf hotel; tennis; football

Vigo

RAC De Vigo (1951)

Reconquista Vigo (Pontevedra)
Tel **(986) 22 11 60 and 27 24 93**
Mem
Pro DS Roman
Holes 9 L 4384 metres SSS 63
Fees 500P
Loc Beside Peinador Airport

Zaragoza

Aero Club De Zaragoza (1966)

Coso 34 Zaragoza
Tel **(976) 21 43 78**
Mem
Pro
Holes 9 L 4953 metres SSS 66
Fees D–1000P (Not Tuesday) W/E–2000P
Loc 12 km from capital

La Penaza (1973)

Apartado 3039 Zaragoza
Tel **(976) 34 28 00**
Mem 700
Pro V Tapia del Valle
Holes 18 L 6161 metres SSS 72
Fees D–2000P W/E–3000P
Loc 15 km from Zaragoza on Madrid road

Sweden

Almhults

Almhults GC (1975)

Box 152 343 00 Almhult
Tel **0476 141 35**
Mem 117 63(L) 96(J)
Pro
Holes 9 L 5350 metres SSS 69
Fees D–50kr
Loc Askya Almhult

Amal

Billerud GC

661 00 Saffle
Tel **0555 91054 and 91313**
Mem 520
Pro Farouk Badri
Holes 18 L 5874 metres SSS 72
Fees D–40kr Sat/Sun–40kr
Loc Saffle Valnas 15 km

Forsbacka (1969)

Box 136 662 00 Amal
Tel **0532 43055**
Mem 550
Pro Mohamed El Sayed
Holes 18 L 5860 metres SSS 72
Fees WD–40kr W/E–45kr
Loc 4 miles W on Road 164

Angelholm

Angelholms GC (1973)

Box 1117 26201 Angelholm
Tel **0431-30260**
Mem 1050
Pro Y Mahmoud
Holes 18 L 5760 metres SSS 72
Fees 65–100kr (85–100kr)
Loc 10 km E of town centre on Route 114

Molle GC (1943)

Private
260 42 Molle
Tel **042 47012, 47520**
Mem 1000
Pro Johanna Pyk
Holes 18 L 5640 metres SSS 70
Fees Jun–Aug 125kr (low season cheaper)
Loc Molle 3 km

Arvika

Arvika

Box 33 671 01 Arvika 1
Tel **0570 54133**
Pro Anders Söderqvist
Holes 9 L 5815 metres SSS 71
Fees D–15kr
Loc 11 km E Arvika road 61

Askersund

Askersunds GC (1980)

S-6903 Ammeberg, Sweden
Tel **0583-34440**
Mem 380
Pro Lars Johansson
Holes 9 L 5650 metres SSS 72
Fees 50kr
Loc 10km SE of Askersund. In Askersund follow road to Ammeberg (9km). Club is 1 km on road to Kärra

Avesta

Avesta GC (1963)

Box 2145 77400 Avesta
Tel **0226 10866**
Mem 475
Pro Gordon Long
Holes 9 L 5860 metres SSS 71
Fees WD–40kr W/E–50kr
Loc Avesta 4 km

Fagersta GC (1970)

Box 2051 77302 Fagersta
Tel **0223 54060**
Mem 425
Pro
Holes 9 L 5775 metres SSS 72
Fees 40kr (40 kr)
Loc 7 km W of town centre on route 65

Bastad

Bastad GC (1929)

Box 1037 26901 Bastad
Tel **0431-73136**
Mem 1050
Pro Per Hansson
Holes 18 L 5760 metres SSS 71
Fees 60kr (140kr)
Loc 4 km W of town on route 115

Torekovs GC (1924)

Box 81 26093 Torekov
Tel **0431/63572**
Mem 1050
Pro Gösta Hall
Holes 18 L 5775 metres SSS 72
Fees 80 kr (20/6–17/8 120kr)
Loc 3 km N Torekov

Bollnäs

Bollnäs GC

Box 72 82101 Bollnäs
Tel **0278 50920/50540**
Mem 500
Pro Karl Hagström
Holes 14 L 5870 metres Par 72
Fees 50kr
Loc 15 km S of Bollnäs on route 83

Boras

Boras GC (1933)

Ostra VIK Krakered 50590 Borås
Tel **033 50142**
Mem 1100
Pro Lars Prick
Holes 18 L 5815 metres SSS 72
Fees 75kr
Loc 6 km S of town centre on route 41 towards Varberg
Mis Season April to October

Marks GC (1962)

PO Box 127 Kinna 511 01
Tel **0320 11275**
Mem 480
Pro L Dahlstrom
Holes 18 L 5310 metres SSS 69
Fees D–30kr
Loc Centre of Kinna

Borlänge

Falun-Borlänge GC (1956)

Box 40 S-791 21 Falun
Tel **023 310 15**
Mem 620
Pro A Ryberg
Holes 18 L 6085 metres SSS 72
Fees 60kr; Jnrs 30kr
Loc At Aspeboda between Falun 13 km and Borlange 8 km; 15 km Dala Airport

Eksjo

Eksjo GC (1938)

Hasslav 6 57500 Eksjo
Tel **0381 135 25**
Mem 550
Pro David Nicholson
Holes 18 L 5930 metres SSS 72
Fees D–50kr
Loc Road to Nassjo

Emmaboda

Emmaboda GK

36060 Vissefjard
Tel **0471 20505 or 20540**
Holes 9 L 5165 metres SSS 68
Loc 12 km from Emmaboda

Enkoping

Enkoping GC (1970)

Box 206 19902 Enkoping
Tel **0171 20830**
Mem 630
Pro Lennart Andersson
Holes 9 L 5820 metres SSS 72
Fees WD–60kr W/E–80kr
Loc 3 km E of town off E18
Mis 18 holes from June 1987 Restaurant (limited)

Eskilstuna

Eskilstuna GC (1951)

Box 238 631 03 Eskilstuna 1
Tel **016 142629**
Mem 830
Pro Alastair Robinson
Holes 18 L 5610 metres SSS 70
Fees WD–60kr W/E–100kr
Loc Strangnasvagen Eskilstuna

Nyby Bruks GC (1960)

c/o Tavemark Morellv 6 63353 Eskilstuna
Tel **016 356782**
Mem 350
Pro
Holes 9 L 6013 metres SSS 72
Fees D–35kr Sat/Sun–45kr
Loc Torshalla 1 km

Eslöv

Eslöv GC (1966)

Box 150 241 00 Eslöv
Tel **0413/18610 or 13494**
Mem 927
Pro PO Johanssen Tel 0413 16213
Holes 18 L 5670 metres SSS 71
Fees 70kr (199kr)
Loc 4 km S of town centre on route 113

Falkenberg

Falkenberg GC (1949)

Golfvagen 311 00 Felkenberg
Tel **0346 50287**
Mem 1100
Pro SA Parson
Holes 27 L 5650–5770 metres SSS 72
Fees 70–100kr (90–120kr)
Loc 5 km S town centre

Falkoping

Falkopings

Box 81 521 01 Falkoping 1
Tel **0515 312 70**
Mem 600
Pro Gunnar Johansson
Holes 18 L 5915 metres SSS 72
Fees D–40kr
Loc Road 46 7 km E Falkoping towards Skovde

Falsterbo

Falsterbo GC (1909)

PO Box 71 Fyrvagen 230 11 Falsterbo
Tel **Malmo 04047 00 78**
Mem 1049
Pro P Chamberlain
Holes 18 L 6400 yards SSS 72
Fees D–80kr–140kr
Loc Malmo 35 km south

Flommens GC (1935)

Falsterbo 230 11
Tel **040 470568**
Mem 1000
Pro B Kristofferson
Holes 18 L 5610 metres SSS 72
Fees 100kr (130kr)
Loc Malmo 35 km

Ljunghusens GC (1932)

Kinellsvag Ljunghusen S-236 00 Höllviken
Tel **040 450384**
Mem 1231
Pro G Sandegard
Holes 1-18 L 5895 metres SSS 73
10-27 L 5670 SSS 71
19-9 L 5455 SSS 70
Fees 1/5–31/10: 100kr (130kr)
1/11–30/4: 70kr (90kr)
Loc Falster Bo Peninsula 25 km from Malmo
Mis Open all year round

Filipstad

Saxå GC (1964)

Asphyttegatan 24 68200 Filipstad
Tel **0590 24070**
Mem 550
Pro Robin Bailey
Holes 9 L 5860 metres Par 72 SSS 73
Fees 50kr
Loc 15 km E Filipstad on route 63

Fjallbacka

Fjallbacka (1965)

450 71 Fjallbacka
Tel **0525/3 11 50**
Mem 750
Pro Jim Kennedy
Holes 18 L 5775 metres SSS 71
Fees D–70kr June–Aug D–100kr
Loc 1 km from town NW coast of Sweden

Gallivare

Gallivare-Malmbergets GC (1973)

Box 52 972 00 Gallivare
Tel **0970 139 52**
Mem 165
Pro
Holes 6 L 5310 metres SSS 70
Fees D–10kr
Loc Behind the airport

Gavle

Gavle GC (1949)

Brannarebacken 3 803 59 Gavle
Tel **026 113163**
Mem 650
Pro G Sandegard
Holes 18 L 5705 yds SSS 71
Fees D–30kr W/E–50kr
Loc Gavie 3 km

Högbo GC (1962)

Daniel Tilas Väg 4 81192 Sandviken
Tel **026 45015**
Mem 1000
Pro Gunnar Sandegård
Holes 18 L 5680 metres SSS 71
Fees D–70kr
Loc N Sandviken 6 km (route 22)
Mis Bungalows to rent beside the course

Gislaved-Anderstorp-Gnosjö

Isaberg GC (1968)

Private
Box 40 33200 Gislaved
Tel **0370 36330**
Mem 750
Pro Stephen Carpenter
Holes 18 L 5983 metres SSS 72
Fees 100kr (120kr)
Loc 15 km N of Anderstorp and Gislaved and 10 km W of Gnosjö; 110 km E of Gothenburg

Gothenburg

Albatross (1973)

Lillhagsvagen 422 50 Hisings-Backa
Tel **031 55 19 01**
Mem 950
Pro Alan Anderton
Holes 18 L 6020 metres SSS 72
Fees 100kr
Loc 6 miles N of Gothenburg on Hising Island

Delsjö GC (1962)

Kallebäck 412 76 Gothenburg
Tel **031 40 69 59**
Mem 900
Pro J Anderson
Holes 18 L 5785 metres SSS 71
Fees 90kr (100kr)
Loc 5 km E of town centre on route 40
Mis Driving range, practice ground, restaurtant

Gothenburg GC (1902)

430 80 Hovas
Tel **031 28 24 44**
Mem 950
Pro Michael Kennedy
Holes 18 L 5935 yds SSS 69
Fees 100kr (120 kr)
Loc 11 km S of Gothenburg RD158

Gullbringa GC (1967)

442 90 Kungalv
Tel **0303 27872 27161**
Mem 500
Pro R Bayliss
Holes 18 L 5775 metres Par 72
Fees D–60kr Sat/Sun–80kr
Loc
Mis 14 km W of Kungalv on road to Marstrand

Hulta GC (1972)

Box 54 517 01 Bollebygd
Tel **033 88180**
Mem 900
Pro Bill Byard
Holes 18 L 6000 metres SSS 72
Fees 90kr (120kr)
Loc Near Gothenburg

Kungsbacka GC (1971)

Box 98 434 01 Kungsbacka 1
Tel **031 706277**
Mem 915
Pro Gösta Ignell
Holes 13 L 5855 metres SSS 72
Fees 90kr (120kr)
Loc 7 km W on road 158

Lysegardens GC (1966)

Vetegangen 8 442 39 Kungalv
Tel **0303 23426**
Mem 420
Pro PO Johansson
Holes 18 L 5700 metres SSS 71
Fees D–20kr Sat/Sun–30kr
Loc Kungalv 10 km

Oijared GC (1958)

Pl 1082 448 00 Floda
Tel **0302 30604**
Mem 1542
Pro Eric Dawson
Holes 2 × 18 L 5875 metres and 5655 metres SSS 71 and 71
Fees 70kr (110kr)
Loc 24 km from Alingsas; 35 km from Gothenburg

Partille GC (1971)

Box 234 433 24 Partille
Tel **031-987004/987114**
Mem 850
Pro Dan Olsson
Holes 18 L 5330 metres SSS 70
Fees 100kr
Loc 1 km outside Gothenburg in Öjersjö, Partille
Mis 9 holes opened 1986; 18 holes open June 1987

Saro GC (1899)

Box 74 43040 Saro
Tel **031-936317**
Mem 750
Pro Jan Rosell
Holes 9 short holes Par 27
Fees 60kr (80kr)
Loc On route 158 Gothenburg 18 km Kungsback 10 km
Mis 9 long holes to be built in 1987

Stora Lundby GC (1983)

Pl 4035 440 06 Grabo
Tel **0302 44150, 44125, 44156**
Mem 632
Pro L Svensson Göran Larsson
Holes 18 L 6040 metres Par 72; 9 hole course Par 27
Fees 60kr (100kr)
Loc 20 min drive centre Gothenburg on Swedish W coast
Mis Championship course; fully licensed restaurant

Hagfors

Uddeholms GC

683 03 Rada
Tel **Hagfors 0563 60335/60025**
Mem 550
Pro Tord Palm
Holes 18 L 6200 metres SSS 73
Fees D–60kr
Loc 80 km N Karlstad RD62 at Lake Rada

Halmstad

Backavattnets GC (1977)

Box 173 30103 Halmstad
Tel **035 442 71**
Mem 900
Pro Stanley Grant
Holes 9 L 5770 metres SSS 73
Fees 85kr
Loc 13 km E of Halmstad on RD25

Halmstad GC (1930)

302 70 Halmstad
Tel **Halmstad 035 30077**
Mem 2047
Pro Bruce Grafton Mikael Sorling Bo Gostaffson
Holes 18 and 18 L 5980 and 5720 metres SSS 73 and 72
Fees 100kr June–Aug 150kr W/E 150kr in May and September
Loc Halmstad 9 km

Härnösand

Härnösand GC

Box 52 Härnösand 871 01
Tel **0611 66027**
Mem 449
Pro To be appointed
Holes 10 L 5510 metres SSS 70
Fees 50kr Jnrs 25kr
Loc Vängnön 12 km N from Härnösand

Hassleholm

Hassleholm GC

Box 114 S-282 00 Tyringe
Tel **(0) 451 53266 (Pro)**
(0) 451 53268 (Sec)
Mem 530
Pro Peter Hamblett
Holes 18 L 5830 metres SSS 72
Fees WD–60kr W/E–80kr
Loc At Lake of Finja, nr Manor of Skyrup; 6 km S Finja Church

Wittsjo GC

Wittsjo 280 22
Tel **0451 22635**
Mem 600
Pro Billy Falk
Holes 18 L 5366 metres SSS 70
Fees 60kr (80kr)
Loc Wittsjo 2 km

Helsingborg

Helsingborg GC (1924)

26040 Viken
Tel **042 236147**
Mem 450
Pro
Holes 9 L 4578 metres SSS 65
Fees 40kr (50kr)
Loc 15 km N of Helsingborg

Rya GC (1934)

Rya 5500 225 90 Helsingborg
Tel **042 22 10 82**
Mem 900
Pro Jimmy Grant
Holes 18 L 5775 metres SSS 71
Fees 100kr (120kr)
Loc 10 km S of town

Soderasens (1966)

Box 41 260 50 Billesholm
Tel **Billesholm 042 733 37**
Mem 850
Pro Tony Lidholm
Holes 18 and 9 L 6110 and 1600 metres SSS 74 and 27
Fees D–80kr
Loc Helsingborg 20 km

Vasatorps GC (1973)

255 90 Helsingborg
Tel **042 235058**
Mem 1400
Pro James Suckling Tel 042 235045
Holes 27 5875 & 2940 metres SSS 72
Fees 90–100kr
Loc 5 miles E of town

Hjo

Hokensas GC (1962)

PO Box 116 S 54400 Hjo
Tel **0503 16059**
Mem 630
Pro Gunnar Nyberg
Holes 18 L 5540 metres SSS 71
Fees 75kr (100kr)
Loc 8 km S of town Hjo centre, on route 195

Hofors

Hofors GC (1965)

Box 117 813 00 Hofors
Tel **0290 85125**
Mem 370
Pro Olle Hedblom
Holes 12 L 5930 metres SSS 72
Fees 30kr (40kr)
Loc 5 km SE Hofors
Mis 18 holes Aug 86

Hoor

Bosjokloster (1974)

243 00 Hoor
Tel **0413 25858**
Mem 750
Pro K Davies
Holes 18 L 6200 metres SSS 72
Fees 80kr (120kr)
Loc 7 km S of Hoor 40 km NE of Malmo

Hudiksvall

Hudiksvall GC (1964)

AB Iggesunds Bruk 825 00 Iggesund
Tel **0650 15930**
Mem 250
Pro K Finmo
Holes 14 L 5690 metres SSS 70
Fees D–20kr Sat/Sun–30kr
Loc Hudiksvall 5 km

Jönköping

Hooks GC (1942)

560 13 Hok
Tel **Vaggeryd 0393 21080/21420**
Mem 620
Pro Alan Steen
Holes 18 L 5748 metres SSS 72
Fees 80kr (100kr)
Loc Vaggeryd 13 km

Jönköping GC (1936)

Kettilstorp S-552 67 Jönköping
Tel **036 76567**
Mem 950
Pro Allan Turnbull
Holes 18 L 6370 yds SSS 70
Fees 70kr (90kr)
Loc 3 km S of city

Kalmar

Kalmar GC (1947)

Kalmar
Tel **0480 72111**
Mem 972
Pro Hans Weinhofer
Holes 18 L 5950 metres SSS 72
Fees WD–80kr W/E–100kr
Loc Kalmar 9 km N

Nybro GC (1971)

Box 235 382 00 Nybro
Tel **0480 550 44**
Mem 350
Pro
Holes 9 L 5452 metres SSS 70
Fees
Loc 10 km from Nybro
Mis 18 holes from 1988

Karlsborg

F6 (1959)

(Sec) Box 3056 54601 Karlsborg
Tel **0505 40155**
Mem 260
Pro
Holes 9
Fees Members only
Loc Vastgola Air Base

Karlshamn

Karlshamns GC (1962)

Karlshamn 292 00
Tel **0454 50085**
Mem 720
Pro Bo Fredriksson
Holes 18 L 5861 metres SSS 72
Fees WD–75kr W/E–100kr
Loc Morrum

Karlskoga

Karlskoga GC (1975)

Bricketorp 647 S69194 Karlskoga
Tel **46 586 28597 or 28663**
Mem 850
Pro Per Glimaker
Holes 18 L 5705 metres Par 72
Fees D–60kr
Loc 6 km E town centre on route E18–Valasen

Orebro GC (1939)

Private
Vreta Lannabruk 710 15 Vintrosa
Tel **019 91065**
Mem 950
Pro Eric Ericson
Holes 18 L 5865 metres Par 71 SSS 72
Fees 110kr
Loc 20 km W of Orebro on route E18
Mis Golf hotel and restaurant Championship course

Karlskrona

Carlskrona GC (1949)

PO Almo S-370 24 Nättraby
Tel **0455 35102**
Mem 700
Pro A Malmberg
Holes 18 L 5525 metres Par 70
Fees D–60kr
Loc Karlskrona 15 km

Ronneby GC (1964)

Box 26 S-37200 Ronneby
Tel **0457 13212**
Mem 400
Pro Sola Ohlsson
Holes 15 L 5390 metres SSS 70
Fees D–40kr W–150kr
Loc Ronneby 2 km

Karlstad

Karlstad GC (1957)

PO Box 294 651 09 Karlstad
Tel **054 36353**
Mem 1000
Pro H Eriksson
Holes 18 L 5900 metres SSS 72
Fees 80kr
Loc 12 km E of town centre on route 63

Katrineholm

Katrineholms GC (1959)

Box 74 641 21 Katrineholm
Tel **0150 39012 and 39011**
Mem 953
Pro H Skogfeldt
Holes 18 L 5860 metres SSS 72
Fees 70kr (80kr)
Loc Katrineholm 7 km

Köping

Korslöts GC (1963)

Box 125 73123 Köping
Tel **46221 81090**
Mem 520
Pro Bengt Malmquist
Holes 18 L 5636 metres SSS 71
Fees 60kr (70kr)
Loc 5km N of Köping. Route 250 for 3 km until sign 'Golfbana

Kopparberg

Stjernfors GC (1973)

c/o Nyberg Laxbrog 24 71400 Kopparberg
Tel **0580 410 48**
Mem 325
Pro David McLean
Holes 10 L 5400 metres SSS 70
Fees WD–25kr
Loc

Kristianstad

Kristianstads GC (1924)

Box 41 296 00 Ahus
Tel **044 2406 56**
Mem 1350
Pro David Green
Holes 18 L 5848 metres SSS 72
9 L 2841 metres SSS 36
Fees 80kr (100krs)
Loc 18 km SW of Kristianstad 20 km from airport
Mis Club restaurant and hotel; tennis, swimming

Ostra Goinge GC (1981)

28900 Knislinge
Tel **044-61197**
Mem 338
Holes 9 L 5450 metres Par 70
Fees 40kr
Loc 20 km from Kristianstad

Skepparslovs GK (1984)

Varpagatan 17 29165 Kristianstad
Tel **044 229031**
Mem 850
Pro C Claesson
Holes 18 L 5900 metres SSS 72
Tees 60kr Jnrs 40kr
Loc 7 km W of town

Kristinehamn

Kristinehamns GC (1974)

Box 3037 681 03 Kristinehamn
Tel **0550 823 10**
Mem 450
Pro E Richter
Holes 9 L 5730 metres SSS 71
Fees 40kr
Loc 3 km N Kristinehamn

Laholm

Laholm GC (1964)

Box 101 31200 Laholm
Tel **0430 301 71**
Mem 883
Pro Claes Eklund
Holes 18 L 5430 metres SSS 70
Fees 85 kr
Loc 5 miles E of Laholm, Way 24

Landskrona

Barseback

Box 214 S-24022 Loddekopinge
Tel **046/77 58 00**
Mem 1135
Pro Ingemar Christersson
Holes 18 L 5900 metres SSS 72
9 L 2840 metres SSS 36
Fees 110kr
Loc Malmo 35 km

Landskrona GC (1960)

Holmgatan 7 S-261 61 Landskrona
Tel **0418 19528**
Mem 382 211(L) 217(J)
Pro Anders Olsson
Holes 18 L 5700 metres SSS 71
Fees D–40kr W/E–55kr
Loc North Landskrona 4 km

St Ibb (1972)

Ulf Ohrvik Victoriagatan 7c S-261 35 Landskrona
Tel **0418 72363**
Mem 175
Pro Nils Knutsson
Holes 9 L 5180 metres SSS 68
Fees 60kr
Loc Island of Hven
Mis Ferry from Landskrona (30 min) Open all year

Lidkoping

Lidkopings (1967)

Box 2029 531 02 Lidkoping
Tel **05 10 46122**
Mem 615
Pro T Lundahl
Holes 18 L 5725 metres SSS 71
Fees D–60kr
Loc 3 miles E of town

Linkoping

Atvidaberg GC (1954)

59700 Atvidaberg
Tel **0120 11425/14614**
Mem 700
Pro B Nygren Tel 0120 12510
Holes 18 L 6010 metres SSS 72
Fees D–75kr
Loc Linkoping 30 km

Linkoping GC (1945)

Box 10054 580 10 Linkoping
Tel **013120646**
Mem 900
Pro Bertil Lemke Bill Patterson
Holes 18 L 5675 metres SSS 71
Fees 80kr
Loc Linkoping 1 km

Ljungby

Lagans GC (1966)

Box 63 34014 Lagan
Tel **0372 30450**
Mem 450
Pro Inger Lindh
Holes 18 L 5600 metres SSS 71
Fees D–70kr; couple–120kr
Loc 1 mile SW (6 miles) N of Ljungby in Lagan
Mis New clubhouse with restaurant

Ljungbyhed

F5

c/o H Pommer Myrstigen 3 264 00 Klippan
Tel **0435 41467**
Mem 440
Pro
Holes 9 L 5675 metres SSS 71
Fees D-25kr
Loc On the airfield

Ljungskile

Lyckorna Golfklubb (1967)

Box 66 45900 Ljungskile
Tel **0522 20 176**
Mem 850
Pro Bobby Heyman
Holes 18 L 5845 metres SSS 72
Fees 80kr
Loc 20 km from Uddevalla

Ljusdal

Ljusdals Golfklubb (1973)

Box 151 S-82700 Ljusdal
Tel **0651 14366**
Mem 300
Pro
Holes 9 L 5920 metres SSS 72
Fees 40kr
Loc 1 mile E of town

Ljusnedal

Harjedalsfjallens

820 95 Funasdalen
Tel **0684 21240**
Mem 230
Pro Veijo Agardh
Holes 9 L 5300 metres Par 70
Fees D–20kr
Loc Wardshuset Gyllene Bocken Ljusnedal

Ludvika-Smedjebacken

Hagge

Hagge 771 00 Ludvika
Tel **0240 28087**
Mem 504
Pro U Sandberg
Holes 9 L 5680 metres SS 71
Fees D–40kr Sat/Sun–50kr
Loc Hagge 2 km Ludvika 6 km

Lulea

Bodens GC (1946)

Box 110 96121 Boden
Tel **0921 61071**
Mem 355
Pro Jörgen Gidlund
Holes 9 L 5796 metres Par 72 SSS 73
Fees D–15kr W/E–20kr W–60kr
Loc Boden 17 km

Lulea GC (1955)

Box 314 95125 Lulea
Tel **0920 560 91/56174**
Mem 560
Pro Leslie Stewart
Holes 9 L 5950 metres SSS 72
Fees 50kr
Loc Rutvik 12 km E of Lulea
Mis 18 holes from 1988

Pitea GC (1960)

Nötön S-94190 Pitea
Tel **0911 14990**
Mem 370
Pro Alan Gillard
Holes 9 L 5950 metres SSS 73
Fees 40kr
Loc 2 km NE of town centre
Mis Cottages to rent; restaurant. Midnight sun golf Jun-Jul

Lysekil

Skafto (1963)

Private
450 34 Fiskebackskil
Tel **0523 22544**
Mem 380
Pro B Malmqvist
Holes 9 L 5310 metres SSS 69
Fees D–35kr
Loc

Malmo

Bokskogens GC (1963)

Box 30 230 40 Bara I
Tel **040 481004**
Mem 1200
Pro Jan Larsson
Holes 18 and 9 L 6050 and 5490 metres SSS 73 and 70
Fees D–80kr Sat/Sun–100kr
Loc Malmo 15 km

Hylliekrokens (1983)

Box 5230 20072 Malmo
Tel **040-683 20 040-16 09 00**
Holes 6 Par 54
Fees 3pkr (40kr)
Loc SW of Malmo

Lunds Akademiska GC (1936)

Kungsmarken 225 90 Lund
Tel **046 99005**
Mem 1080
Pro Van MacDougall
Holes 18 L 5780 metres SSS 72
Fees D–80kr Sat/Sun–120kr
Loc 5 km E of Lund

Malmö GC

Segesvängen Box 21068 S-20021 Malmö
Tel **040-292535**
Mem 800
Pro Hans Bergdahl
Holes 12 L 5410 metres SSS 69
Fees 60kr (70kr W/E & hols)
Loc NE Malmö, next to motorway from Gothenburg
Mis 18 Holes 1986/7, Golfshop, driving range, practice greens, restaurant

Mariestad

Mariestads GC (1975)

PO Box 299 542 01 Mariestad
Tel **0501 17383**
Mem 670
Pro Richard Hutton
Holes 18 L 5885 metres SSS 72
Fees Single–60kr; couple–100kr; junior–30kr; family–120kr
Loc 3 miles W of town at Lake Vänern

Mjolby

Mjolby Golfklubb (1983)

Box 171 S-595 00 Mjolby
Tel **0142-125 70**
Mem 465
Pro
Holes 9 L 2800 metres SSS 72
Fees 50kr (70kr) juniors 30kr (50kr)
Loc 35 km WSW of Linkoping on E4 between Stockholm and Gothenburg

Motala

Motala GC (1956)

PO Box 264 S-59123 Motala
Tel **0141-50856 (Clubhouse); 0141-50865 (Restaurant); 0141-50834 (Shop)**
Mem 700
Pro O Asplund Tel 0141 50834/0141 50592
Holes 18 L 5855 metres SSS 72
Fees 70kr W–200kr
Loc 3 km S of Motala

Vadstena GC (1956)

Vadstena 592 00
Tel **0143 12743**
Mem 339
Pro
Holes 9 L 5486 metres SSS 70
Fees D–40kr
Loc Vadstena 2½ km

Munkedal

Torreby GC (1961)

Postlada Torreby 450 50 Munkedal
Tel **0524 21109**
Mem 400
Pro H Nimark
Holes 18 L 5885 metres SSS 72
Fees D–25kr
Loc Munkedal 6 km

Norrkoping

Finspangs GC

Viberga Gard 61200 Finspang
Tel **0122 16574**
Mem 450
Pro Conny Wikstrom
Holes 9 L 5935 metres Par 72
Fees D-50kr
Loc 3 km E town centre on route 51

Norrkoping GC (1928)

Klinga 605 90 Norrkoping 2
Tel **011 35234**
Mem 830
Pro Pierre Karstrom
Holes 18 L 5860 metres SSS 72
Fees D–100kr W/E–120kr
Loc Klinga 2 km S of Norrkoping on E4

Söderköpings GC (1983)

c/o Mats Beijer-Olsen Blamesstigen 3 S-61400 Söderköping
Tel **011-700 39**
Mem 450
Pro Lars Cernald
Holes 18 L 4770–6135 metres SSS 73
Fees To be decided
Loc 9 km W of Söderköping. In Västra Husby turn on to road leading to Norrköping. 500m to club

Norrtalje

Almunge GK (1983)

Stavhults Gard 74010 Almunge
Tel **0174/25005**
Holes 6
Fees 30kr (50kr)
Loc Between Uppsala and Norrtalje

Roslagens GC

Norrtalje 761 00
Tel **0176 37137**
Mem 400
Pro G Dickinson
Holes 18 L 5725 metres SSS 71
Fees D–70kr W/E–100kr
Loc Norrtalje 7 km

Nyköping-Oxelosund

Arila GC (1951)

PL 6027B 61190 Nyköping
Tel **0155 14967**
Mem 1050
Pro Olle Jansson
Holes 18 L 5735 metres SSS 72
Fees 100kr (1986 price)
Loc Nyköping 5 km

Nynashamns

Nynashamns GC (1977)

Box 4 148 00 Osmo
Tel **0752 386 66**
Mem 600
Pro Carl Johan Bernce
Holes 9 L 5720 metres SSS 71
Fees D–70kr (90kr)
Loc Near Nynashamn

Öland

Ölands GC (1983)

c/o Molin Glomminge
387 00 Borgholm
Tel **1485 11161**
Mem 200
Holes 9
Fees WD–50kr W/E–60kr
Loc 35 km of Borgholm

Ornskoldsvik

Oviks GC-Puttom (1966)

Box 216 89101 Ornskoldsvik
Tel **0660/6 40 70 64080 64091**
Mem 700
Pro Tomas Mogren
Holes 18 L 5795 metres SSS 72
Fees D–70kr
Loc 15 km N of Ornskoldsvik on E4
Mis Season June–September

Orust

Orust Golfclub (1981)

Box 108 440 90 Henan
Tel **0304053170/030453171**
Mem 360
Pro Einar Richter
Holes 9 (18 1986) L 5860 metres Par 72
Fees 40kr; Jnrs 20kr (60kr, Jnrs 30kr)
Loc 80 km N Gothenburg

Oskarshamn

Oskarshamns GC (1972)

Box 148 572 01 Oskarshamn
Tel **0491 940 22**
Mem 550
Pro Ian Hult
Holes 18 L 5545 metres SSS 72
Fees 50kr (60kr)
Loc 10 km S on route E66 towards Fliseryd

Ostersund

Ostersund-Froso GC (1947)

Box 40 S-83201 Froson
Tel **Nat–063–43001**
Inter–46 634 3001
Mem 1000
Pro Goran Knutsson
Holes 18 L 6000 metres SSS 73
Fees D–50kr W–200kr
Loc Island of Froso
Mis Play May–Sep; golf shop, restaurant

Perstorp

Perstorp GC (1964)

PO Box 87 284 00 Perstorp
Tel **0435 35411**
Mem 700
Pro Jim Kennedy
Holes 18 L 5668 metres SSS 71
Fees 75kr (125kr)
Loc 30 miles inland from Helsingborg; 1 km from centre of Perstorp
Mis 6 hole short course Apartments to let

Rattvik

Leksands GC (1977)

Box 25 793 01 Leksand
Tel **0247/14204 (Office)**
0247/10922 (Rest)
Mem 410
Pro Anders Israelsson
Holes 18 5681 metres SSS 72
Fees 60kr
Loc 2 km N of Leksand

Mora GK (1980)

Box 264 79201 Mora
Tel **0250 10182**
Mem 310
Holes 18 L 5600 metres Par 72
Fees 70kr
Loc 40 km NW of Rattvik

Rattvik GC (1954)

Private
Box 29 795 00 Rattvik
Tel **0248 10773**
Mem 510
Pro Peter Michols
Holes 18 L 5321 metres SSS 69
Fees 60kr
Loc 2 km from Rattvik
Mis 15 × 4-bed houses for rent near clubhouse

Sala

Sala (1970)

Box 16 733 00 Sala
Tel **0224 53077**
Mem 500
Pro John Long
Holes 9 L 2943 metres SSS 71
Fees 40kr
Loc Fallet Sala; 8km E from Sala, against Uppsala, route 67/72
Mis 18 holes September 1987

Simrishamn

Osterlens GC (1945)

Lilla Vik Simrishamn 272 00
Tel **0414 24230**
Mem 575
Pro Gunnar Mueller
Holes 18 L 5855 metres SSS 72
Fees 80kr
Loc Vik 8 km N of Simrishamn
Mis Sauna, pool, restaurant

Skelleftea

Skelleftea GC (1967)

Box 152 S-93122 Skelleftea
Tel **0910 15604 79333**
Mem 689
Pro Nigel Fosker
Holes 18 L 6135 metres SSS 73
Fees 60kr (70kr)
Loc 5 km from town
Mis Most northerly 18-hole course in the world

Skovde

Billingens GC

Billingens GC Box 290 54017 Lerdala
Tel **0511 80291**
Mem 600
Pro H Damstoft
Holes 18 L 5605 metres Par 71
Fees D–70kr
Loc Between Skara and Skövde

Soderhamns

Soderhamns GC (1961)

Trumslagareg 24 826 00 Soderhamns
Tel **0270 51000**
Mem 425
Pro M Anderson
Holes 18 L 5940 metres SSS 72
Fees D–40kr Sat/Sun–40kr

Sodertalje

Sodertalje GC (1952)

Sodertalje 151 21
Tel **0755 38240**
Mem 1100
Pro B Tomlinson
Holes 18 L 5875 metres SSS 72
Fees 80kr (100kr)
Loc 4 km W of town centre

Trosa-Vagnharads GC (1972)

150 13 Trosa
Tel **0156 22211**
Mem 415
Pro Colin Rose
Holes 9 L 5860 metres SSS 72
Fees D–40kr W/E–50kr
Loc 5 km from Trosa toward Uttervik

Solleftea

Solleftea-Langsele (1970)

Box 213 881 01 Solleftea
Tel **0620 214 77**
Mem 347
Pro
Holes 18 L 5890 metres SSS 72
Fees WD–20kr W/E–30kr
Loc Osterforse

Stockholm

Agesta GC (1958)

Agesta 12352 Farsta
Tel **0864 5641**
Mem 1367
Pro R Tomlinson
Holes 18 L 5705 metres SSS 72
9 L 3660 metres SSS 59
Fees WD–100kr W/E–120kr
Loc At Farsta

Björkhagens

Box 430 12104 Johanneshov 4
Tel **08 7730431**
Mem 500
Pro Kenneth Johnson
Holes 9 L 4600 metres SSS 66
Fees WD–25kr W/E–40kr
Loc 7 miles S of Stockholm

Bro-Balsta GC (1978)

Box 2510 S-196 02 Kungsangen
Tel **758 413 00**
Mem 500
Pro Anders Sjohagen
Holes 18
Fees D–60kr
Loc Thoresta 30 min NW of Stockholm

Djursholms GC (1931)

Hagbardsvägen 1 18263 Djursholm
Tel **08 755 1477**
Mem 1603
Pro George Deverell
Holes 18 and 9 L 5595 and 4400 metres SSS 71 and 64
Fees 140kr (165kr)
Loc 12 km N of Stockholm

Drottningholms GC (1956)

Drottningholm 170 11
Tel **08 759 03 00**
Mem 765
Pro Ake Bergkvist
Holes 18 L 5820 metres SSS 72
Fees 110kr (140kr)
Loc Stockholm 10 km

Haninge GC (1983)

Arsta slott Box S-136 90 Handen
Tel **0750/322 40**
Mem 1100
Pro Björn Deilert
Holes 18 L 5930 metres Par 73 SSS 73
Fees 100kr (120kr) W/E–2 days 200kr
Loc Motorway from Stockholm towards Nynäsham. After Handen turn left towards Dalarö.
Follow the signs 'Arsta havsbad'
Mis The course is located around a seventeenth-century castle. One of the wings of the castle is our clubhouse, restaurant and pub

Ingaro GC (1962)

Fogelvik S-130 35 Ingaro
Tel **0766 28244**
Mem 675
Pro Mike Lord
Holes 18 L 5565 metres SSS 71
Fees D–50kr W/E–80kr
Loc 32 km E of Stockholm

Lidingo GC (1933)

Box 1035 S-181 21 Lidingo
Tel **08 7657911**
Mem 1260
Pro P Hansson D Johnston
Holes 18 L 5770 metres SSS 71
Fees D–120kr W/E–150kr
Loc Stockholm 6 km

Lindo GC (1978)

Box 1043 18600 Vallentuna
Tel **0762 72260**
Mem 350
Pro 2
Holes 27 (3 × 9 L 2850 metres) SSS 72
Fees WD–90kr W/E–110kr
Loc Vallentura 20 km N of Stockholm
Mis Lindo GC is part of the Bjorn Borg Sports Club

Saltsjöbadens GC (1929)

Box 51 13300 Saltsjöbadens
Tel **08 7173319**
Mem 1200
Pro John Cockin Tel 08 7171035
Holes 18 L 5685 metres SSS 72
9 L 3640 metres SSS 60
Fees 18 holes: D–90kr (110kr)
9 holes: D–50kr (70kr)
Loc 15 km E of town centre

SAS GC (1954)

161 87 Stockholm-Bromma
Tel **08 7801000**
Mem 154
Holes 6
Fees
Loc Bromma Airport, Stockholm S-16187

Sollentuna GC (1967)

Box 6026 191 06 Sollentuna
Tel **08 754 3625**
Mem 650
Pro Knut Ekberg
Holes 18 L 5910 metres SSS 72
Fees D–100kr W/E–130kr
Loc 12 miles N of Stockholm
½ mile W of E4 (Rotebro)
Mis Driving range Handicap card required

Stockholm GC (1904)

182 31 Danderyd
Tel **08 755 00 31**
Mem 1020
Pro Mike Sheard
Holes 18 L 5525 metres SSS 71
Fees 120kr (150kr)
Loc Stockholm NE 7 km

Täby GC (1968)

Skålhamra 18343 Täby
Tl **0762 23261**
Mem 1100
Pro T Holmström
Holes 18 L 5776 metres SSS 73
Fees 80–100kr
Loc 2 miles N Stockholm

Ullna GC (1981)

Box 166 S-18400 Åkersberga
Tel **0762 26075**
Mem 580
Pro Neil Fossett
Holes 18 L back tee 6265 metres; club tee 5770 metres SSS 72
Fees 125kr (150kr)
Loc 20 km N of Stockholm on road E3
Mis Season Apr–Oct, driving range; golf shop; restaurant

Viksjo Golfklubb (1969)

Fjallen Gard 175 90 Jarfalla
Tel **0758 16600**
Mem 1140
Pro Sayed El Cherif
Holes 18 L 6075 metres SSS 73
Fees 75kr (100kr)
Loc 18 km Stockholm

Wermdö G & CC (1966)

Torpa 139 00 Värmdö
Tel **0766 20849**
Mem 700
Pro M Jansson
Holes 18 L 5705 metres SSS 72
Fees 120kr (170kr)
Loc 25 km E Stockholm on route 222
Mis Tennis court, swimming pool, marina, restaurant

Strangnas

Strangnas GC (1968)

Box 21 15201 Strangnas
Tel **0152 14731**
Mem 520
Pro L Hellsten
Holes 18 L 5780 SSS 72
Fees D–50kr
Loc 2 miles S of Strangnas

Stromstad

Stromstad GC (1967)

Box 129 452 00 Stromstad 1
Tel **0526 11788**
Mem 600
Pro T Hunter
Holes 9 L 5490 metres SSS 70
Fees D–70kr W–350kr
Loc 4 miles N of town
Mis 18 holes ready in 1987

Sundsvalls

Sundsvalls GC (1952)

Segelv 14 852 54 Sundsvalls
Tel **060 561020**
Mem 800
Pro T Bjornsson
Holes 18 L 5885 metres SSS 72
Fees D–50kr Sat/Sun–60kr
Loc Near Skottsund

Sunne

Sunne GC (1970)

Box 108 68600 Sunne
Tel **0565 60300**
Mem 340
Pro Tord Palm
Holes 9 L 2845 metres SSS 71
Fees 50kr
Loc Road 234 to Rottneros

Töreboda

Töreboda GC (1965)

Box 18 S-54500 Töreboda
Tel **0506 123 05**
Mem 350

Pro Inge Johansson
Holes 9 L 5390 metres SSS 70
Fees 40kr
Loc 7 miles E of town
Mis Restaurant open every day

Tranas

Tranas GC (1952)

N Storgatan 130 573 00 Tranas
Tel **0140 11661 or 12281**
Mem 700
Pro Erik Oster
Holes 9 L 5830 metres SSS 72
Fees 70kr
Loc Svartan 2 km N of Tranas

Trelleborg

Bedinge GC (1931)

Vag 52 23021 Beddingestrand
Tel **04 10 25514**
Mem 500
Pro Ivan Persson
Holes 18 L 4500 metres SSS 68
Fees D–50kr W–200kr
Loc Trelleborg 20 km

Trelleborgs GC (1963)

Private
Pl 3307A 23100 Trelleborg
Tel **0410 30460**
Mem 850
Pro M Malmstrom
Holes 18 L 5320 metres SSS 69
Fees 70kr (90kr)
Loc 5 km W of Trelleborg

Trollhattan

Ekarna Grastorp (1970)

Balders Väg 12 S-46700 Grästorp
Tel **0514 11450**
Mem 2309
Pro
Holes 9 L 4480 metres SSS 64
Fees 25kr
Loc 30 km from Trollhätten, 35 km from Lidköping

Onsjö GC (1974)

Box 100 462 00 Vänersborg
Tel **0521 64149**
Mem 750
Pro Neil Goodison
Holes 18 L 5730 metres SSS 72
Fees D–60kr
Loc 8 km drive N of Gothenburg (Road 45) 4 km S of Vanersborg

Trollhattans GC (1963)

Private
Box 254 461 26 Trollhattan
Tel **0520 41000**
Mem 700
Pro Graham Clark
Holes 18 L 6200 metres SSS 73
Fees D–50kr
Loc Trollhattan 21 km

Ulricehamn

Ulricehamns GC (1947)

Box 87 52300 Ulricehamn
Tel **0321 10021**
Mem 415
Pro John Byard
Holes 18 L 5370 metres SSS 69
Fees D–30kr
Loc Backasen 2 km E

Umea

Umea GC (1954)

Vinterg 18 902 54 Umea
Tel **090 41071**
Mem 690
Pro Jim Anderson
Holes 18 L 5900 metres SSS 72
Fees 50kr
Loc Umea 16 km

Uppsala

Sigtunabygdens GC (1961)

Box 89 19300 Sigtuna
Tel **0760/540 12**
Mem 675
Pro Bill Youngman
Holes 18 L 5850 metres SSS 72
Fees D–50kr W/E–100kr
Loc 51 km N of Stockholm

Uppsala GC (1937)

Box 12015 S-750 12 Uppsala
Tel **018 461270 or 018 461241 (shop)**
Mem 1350
Pro Mike Lord
Holes 27 L 6310 SSS 75
Fees D–70kr Sat/Sun–110kr
Loc Uppsala 8 km
Mis Shop, restaurant

Varberg

Varbergs GC (1950)

Box 39 432 01 Varberg
Tel **0340/37470**
Mem 875
Pro F Englund
Holes 18 L 5797 metres SSS 73
Fees 90kr
Loc 15 km E Varberg

Värnamo

Värnamo GC (1962)

Private
Box 146 S–33101 Värnamo
Tel **46-370-23123**
Mem 625
Pro Tony Marshall
Holes 18 L 6253 metres SSS 72
Fees 60kr (70kr)
Loc 8 km E of town on route 127
Mis Driving range, restaurant

Vasterås

Ångsö Golfclub (1979)

Skultunavägen 7 722 17 Västerås
Tel **0171-410 12**
Mem 560
Pro David Mclean
Holes 18 SSS 72
Fees 60kr (70kr) 1985 prices
Loc 15 km from Västerås

Västerås GC (1931)

Bjärby 72481 Västerås
Tel **021 35754 3**
Mem 1025
Pro
Holes 18 L 5380 metres SSS 69
Fees WD–60kr W/E–80kr
Loc Västerås 2 km N

Vastervik

Vasterviks GC (1959)

Box 62 Vastervik 593 01
Tel **0490 315 21**
Mem 400
Pro Mats Andersson
Holes 9 L 5720 metres SSS 71
Fees D–50kr
Loc Vastervik 2 km

Vaxjo

Vaxjo GC (1959)

Box 227 351 05 Vaxjo
Tel **0470 21539/14004**
Mem 875
Pro L Ibsonius Tel 0470 14004
Holes 18 L 5860 metres SSS 72
Fees WD–70kr W/E–90kr
Loc Vaxjo 3 km

Venberod

Romeleasens GC (1969)

Kvarnbrodda 240 14 Venberod
Tel **046 82012/82090**
Mem 900
Pro H Bergdahl
Holes 18 L 5900 metres SSS 72
Fees D–40kr Sat/Sun–70kr
Loc Venberod/Doerroed 20 miles E of Malmo

Vetlanda

Vetlanda GC (1983)

c/o Lennart Aspengreen Rosenv 3 E-sjön S 57400 Vetlanda
Tel **0383-18310**
Mem 485
Pro Staffan Petersson
Holes 10 Par 71 SSS 71
Fees Sen 50kr, Jrs 30kr, Couple 70kr
Loc Östana 3km from Vetlanda centre

Vimmerby

Tobo GC (1971)

Tobo Gard 598 00 Vimmerby
Tel **0492 30005**
Mem
Pro Lars Wiberg
Holes 9 L 5950 metres SSS 72
Fees D–15kr
Loc

Visby

Visby GC

Visby 621 56
Tel **0498 45058**
Mem 965
Pro Jack Wenman
Holes 18 L 5855 metres SSS 72
Fees D–80kr W–400kr
Loc Visby 25 km

Ystad

Ystad GC (1930)

Box 162 27100 Ystad
Tel **0411 50350**
Mem 700
Pro Bernard Jones
Holes 18 L 5800 metres SSS 72
Fees D–60kr (1/6–31/8 80kr)
Loc E Ystad 7 km on way to Simrishamn
Mis 9 additional holes planned

Switzerland

Arosa

Arosa GC (1947)

CH-7050 Arosa
Tel **312215**
Mem 200
Pro AM Platz
Holes 9 L 4435 metres SSS 63
Fees D–25kr
Loc Arosa 1 km

Bad Ragaz

Bad Ragaz GC (1956)

Hans Albrechtstrasse 7310 Bad Ragaz
Tel **085 91556**
Mem 686
Pro C Gaud Th Villiger M Caligari
Holes 18 L 5766 metres SSS 70
Fees D–40fr W/E–50fr
Loc Chur 20 km Zurich 100 km
Mis Handicap certificate required

Basel

Basel (1928)

68220 Hagenthal-le-Bas (See under France)

Bern/Fribourg

Blumisberg (1959)

3184 Wunnewil
Tel **037 361380**
Mem 400
Pro F Schiroli B Marx
Holes 18 L 6048 metres SSS 73
Fees 35 fr (50fr)
Loc Fribourg 14 km Berne 16 km

Brig

GC Riederalp (1986)

CH-3981 Riederalp
Tel **028/27 14 63 (Kruger Sport)**
Mem 100
Pro T Cordoba
Holes 9 L 3016 metres SSS 57
Fees 25fr
Loc 10 km from Brig
Mis Season June–October

Brugg

Schinznach–Bad GC (1929)

5116 Schinznach–Bad
Tel **056 431226**
Mem 205
Pro H Zimmermann
Holes 9 L 6036 metres Par 72
Fees D–30fr Sat/Sun–50fr
Loc Brugg 6 km

Crans-sur-Sierre

GC Crans-sur-Sierre (1927)

3963 Crans-sur-Sierre
Tel **0271 41 21 68 (Telex 473805)**
Mem 780
Pro J Bonvin J Bagnoud RJ Barras J-M Barras B Cordonier B Mittaz M Bonvin A Rey A Jeanquartier LJ Valera
Holes 18 and 9 L 6260 and 2575 metres SSS 72 and 34
Fees D–48fr and 38fr Reduced out of season
Loc At Crans-sur-Sierre

Davos

Davos GC (1929)

Mattastrasse 25 CH-7270 Davos Platz
Tel **083 5 56 34**
Mem 400
Pro HJ Hörenz
Holes 18 L 5715 yds SSS 67
Fees 30fr (40fr)
Loc 1 km outside Davos
Mis Closed 15/10–1/5

Geneva

Club de Bonmont (1983)

Château de Bonmont 1261 Cheserex
Tel **022 69 23 45**
Mem 600
Pro F Boillat G Kaye Y Radal
Holes 18 L 6160 metres Par 71
Fees D–45fr
Loc Nyon 10 mins, Geneva 25 mins, Lausanne 35 mins

G & CC Bossey

F-74160 St-Julien-en-Genevois
Pres Robert Banner
Pro JP Charpenel Eliane Berthet Bill Reid
Holes 18 L 6145 metres Par 71
Loc 6 km from Geneva
Mis Driving range, tennis, squash, swimming

Golf de Geneva (1923)

70 Route de la Capite 1223 Cologny
Tel **022 35 75 40**
Mem 1000
Pro JM Larretche PM Borgeat Pat Bagnoud J Berthet
Holes 18 L 6250 metres Par 72
Fees WD–60fr W/E–M
Loc Geneva 4 km

Gstaad

Gstaad GC (1962)

CH 3780 Saanenland Gstaad
Tel **030 42636**
Mem 196
Pro Bruno Herrmann
Holes 9 L 2870 metres Par 71
Fees WD–25fr W/E–30fr
Loc Gstaad 15 km

Interlaken

Interlaken-Unterseen (1964)

3800 Interlaken
Tel **036 226022**
Mem 350
Pro F Macchi B Chenaux
Holes 18 L 5980 metres SSS 72
Fees 42fr
Loc Interlaken centre 3 km
Mis Reduction of 5fr for Interlaken hotel guests

Lausanne

Lausanne GC (1921)

Le Chalet a Gobet 1000 Lausanne 25
Tel **916316**
Mem 700
Pro G Grisoni A Gallardo M Gallardo C Duran
Holes 18 L 6165 metres Par 72
Fees 40fr (60fr)
Loc Lausanne 7 km

Lenzerheide

Lenzerheide Valbella GC (1950)

Public
7078 Lenzerheide
Tel **081 3415 88/081 341316**
Mem 450
Pro H Schumacher R Blaesi +guest Pro
Holes 18 L 5269 metres Par 69
Fees 40fr
Loc Lenzerheide 2½ km

Locarno

Patriziale Ascona GC (1928)

Public
Via al Lido 81 6612 Ascona
Tel **093 35 21 32**
Mem 350 250(L) 50(J)
Pro V Caccia F Codiga F Salmina
Holes 18 L 5893 metres SSS 71
Fees 40fr
Loc Ascona 1 km Locarno 5 km

Lucerne

Burgenstock GC (1928)

6366 Burgenstock
Tel **041 641474**
Mem
Pro Grahame Denny
Holes 9 L 2300 yds Par 64
Fees D–20fr
Loc Burgenstock

Lucerne GC (1903)

Dietschiberg CH 6006
Tel **041 369787**
Mem 300
Pro L Mudry B Lagger
Holes 18 L 5700 metres SSS 71
Fees WD–40fr W/E–50fr
Loc Lucerne 2 km

Mis Only v'trs with a valid handicap certificate are permitted on course

Lugano

Lugano GC (1923)

6983 Magliaso
Tel **091 71 1557**
Mem 800
Pro D Maina O Schopfer G Parisi I Tremolada
Holes 18 L 5740 metres SSS 71
Fees WD–40fr W/E–50fr
Loc Lugano 8 km direction Ponte Tresa

Montreux

Golf Club de Montreux (1900)

(Case Post 187 1820 Montreux) 1860 Aigle
Tel **025 26 46 16 (Dir/Sec)**
Mem 491
Pro P Bagnoud J Bagnoud J-L Chable
Holes 18 L 6205 SSS 72
Fees WD–30fr W/E–40fr
Loc Montreux 15 km

Neuchatel

Neuchatel GC (1928)

Voens/St Blaise
Tel **038 335550**
Mem 300
Pro Jakob Kressig
Holes 18 L 5840 metres SSS 70
Fees D–30fr Sat/Sun–40fr
Loc Neuchatel 5 km

St Gallen

Ostschweizischer GC (1948)

9246 Niederburen
Tel **071 811856**
Mem 340
Pro CB Craig
Holes 18 L 5920 metres SSS 71
Fees D–40fr Sat/Sun–50fr
Loc St Gallen 25 km

St Moritz

Engadine GC (1898)

CH 7503 Samedan
Tel **082 6 52 26**
Mem 310
Pro A Casera A Chiogna I Tremolada
Holes 18 L 6105 metres SSS 72
Fees 40fr (45fr)
Loc Samedan/St Moritz

Verbier

Verbier (1969)

1936 Verbier Vs
Tel **026 7 49 95 (Nov-May: 026 7 45 66)**
Mem 140
Pro
Holes 18 (par 3) L 2195 metres SSS 54
Fees D–15fr Sat/Sun–20fr Ticket for whole summer–220fr (individual); 300fr (family)
Loc Centre of resort; 10 km from intern. road to St Bernard
Mis Open June to October

Villars

Villars GC (1922)

Case Postale 152 1884 Villars
Tel **025 35 35 98**
Mem 300
Pro JL & G Chable
Holes 18 L 4093 metres SSS 61
Fees 35fr (50fr)
Loc City centre 7 km

Vulpera

Vulpera GC (1923)

Vulpera Spa CH 7552
Tel **084 9 96 88**
Mem 184
Pro P Jones
Holes 9 L 2021 metres SSS 62
Fees D–30fr W–175fr M–550fr
Loc Centre of town 60 km from St Moritz in lower Engadin

Zurich

GC Breitenloo (1964)

Nr Bassersdorf
61 Bassersdorf CH 8303 Oberwil
Tel **01 836 64 86**
Mem 350
Pro Keith Marriott
Holes 18 L 6100 metres SSS 72
Fees Limited 40fr (60fr)
Loc 8 km from Zurich Airport

Dolder GC (1907)

Kuthausstrasse 66 8032 Zurich
Tel **01 47 50 45**
Mem 295
Pro Dolf Dieter Carlo Brazerol
Holes 9 L 1825 metres SSS 58 (18 holes)
Fees WD–40fr W/E–Members only (and guests of Hotel Waldhaus Dolder & Grand Hotel Dolder
Mis Golfclub and Club restaurant open 1/4–15/11

Hittnau-Zurich GC (1964)

PO Box 8700 Kuesnacht
Tel **01 950 24 42**
Mem 450
Pro Ernst Bauer Danilo Parini
Holes 18 L 5980 metres Par 72
Fees 50fr W/E–Closed for non-members
Loc 30 km from Zurich

Schöenenberg G & CC (1969)

8821 Schöenenberg
Tel **01 788 16 24**
Mem 400
Pro T Charpié J Wallwork PL Freeman
Holes 18 L 6340 metres SSS 74
Fees D-50fr
Loc 20 km centre of Zurich

Zurich-Zumikon GC (1931)

Private
8126 Zumikon ZH
Tel **01 918 00 50**
Mem 700
Pro R Lanz G Denny T Huyton
Holes 18 L 6360 metres SSS 74
Fees D–60ft Sat/Sun–No visitors
Loc Zurich 10 km
Mis Visitors introduced

Yugoslavia

Bled

GC Bled (1974)

YU-64260 Bled C Svobode 13
Tel **Sec 064-78282 Off 064-77932**
Mem 350
Pro Jurman Dŭsan
Holes 18 L 6320 metres SSS 73 Par 73
Fees 10.50 Lstg W–63 Lstg
Loc 3 km W of Bled

Part V

Who's Who in Golf

British Players

Explanation of abbreviations used

Add Present Address
Cls Club Membership
Opn Open and US Open Championships
Tls Overseas Opens
Chp British and National Union Amateur Championships
Maj European Tours and Major Amateur Tournaments
Ove Overseas Championships (other than Opens) and Tournaments
Oth Other British Tournaments
Reg Regional and County Championships
Int International Appearances
Am Amateur Record
Jun Junior Titles
Mis Miscellaneous
WPGA Women's PGA Tour

Adams, Michael Phillip Darwin
Born Grantham, Lincs on 31st January, 1944

Add 166 Cathedral Road, Cardiff
Cls Llantrisant and Pontyclun, Porthcawl
Chp Welsh Close 1970. Welsh Amateur 1976
Int Wales (Home Int) 1969-70-71-72-75-76-77; (Eur Team Ch) 1971

Aitken, Miss Wilma
See Mrs W Leburn

Alliss, Peter
Born Berlin on 28th February, 1931. Turned Professional 1946

Tls Spanish Open 1956-58. Italian Open 1958. Portuguese Open 1958. Brazilian Open 1961
Maj Daks 1954-63 (tied). Dunlop 1955-59. PGA Close 1957-62-65. Sprite 1960 (tied). Swallow-Penfold 1964. Esso Golden 1964. Jeyes 1965. Martini 1966 (tied). Rediffusion 1966. Agfa-Gevaert 1967. Piccadilly 1969
Oth West of England Open Professional 1956-58-62-66. Sunningdale Foursomes 1958-61. Wentworth Pro-Am Foursomes 1959. British Assistants 1952
Int Ryder Cup 1953-57-59-61-63-65-67-69. England in World Cup 1954-55-57 58-59-61-62-64-66-67. Home International 1967 (capt). UK v Europe 1954-55-56
Amr Boy International 1946
Mis PGA Captain 1962, 1987. Harry Vardon Trophy 1964-66. Author. TV commentator

Anderson, Miss Jessie
See Mrs G Valentine

Anstey, Miss Veronica
See Mrs V Beharrell

Armitage, Miss Susan
See Mrs S Langridge

Attenborough, Michael F
Born Britford, nr Salisbury in October, 1939

Add 17 Parkgate, Blackheath, London SE3
Cls Chislehurst, Royal St George's, Royal and Ancient
Maj Hampshire Hog 1960. County Champion of Champions 1964. Duncan Putter 1966. Prince of Wales Challenge Cup 1969
Oth President's Putter 1962-66
Reg Kent Amateur 1963-64-65
Ove Scandinavian Amateur 1965
Jun Boy International 1957
Int Walker Cup 1967. GB v Europe 1966-68. England (Home Int) 1964-66-67-68; (Eur Team Ch) 1967

Bailey, Mrs D (formerly Mrs D Frearson, *née* Robb)
Born Wolverhampton in 1943

Add Durlin, Abinger Common, Dorking, Surrey
Cls Enville (Hon), Reigate Heath, Betchworth Park
Chp Runner-up British Ladies 1961
Maj Avia Foursomes 1972. Worplesdon Mixed Foursomes 1971
Reg Lincolnshire Ladies 1966-67. Staffordshire Ladies 1961. Midland Ladies 1966
Jun British Girls 1961. Scottish Girls Open Stroke Play 1959-61. English Girls International 1957 to 61
Int Curtis Cup 1962-72. Vagliano Trophy 1961, 1983 (captain), 1985 (captain). World Team Chp 1968. England (Home Int) 1961-62-71. Captain Curtis Cup 1984.
Mis Surrey Ladies County Captain 1981-82. British Ladies Commonwealth Team 1983 (captain).

Baker, Peter

Born 7th October, 1967. Turned Professional 1986

Chp English Open Amateur Stroke Play 1985 (shared)
Oth Carris Trophy 1983-85
Int Walker Cup 1985. GB v Europe 1986

Banks, Charles

Born

Chp English Open Amateur Stroke Play 1983

Bannerman, Harry

Born Aberdeen on 5th March, 1942. Turned Professional 1965

Oth Scottish Professional 1967-72. Northern Scottish Open 1967-69-72. East of Scotland PGA Match Play 1969. Scottish Coca Cola 1976
Int Ryder Cup 1971. Scotland in World Cup 1967-72. Scotland in Double Diamond 1972-74
Amr Boy International 1959. North East Scotland Stroke Play 1963-64-65. North of Scotland Stroke Play 1962
Mis Frank Moran Trophy 1972

Barber, Mrs DN (*née* Sally Bonallack)

Born Chigwell, Essex on 9th April, 1938

Add III, Wyatts Drive, Thorpe Bay, Essex
Cls Thorpe Hall, Thorndon Park, Hunstanton (Hon), Killarney (Hon)
Chp English Ladies 1968, runner-up 1970-71
Maj Astor Salver 1972. Avia Foursomes 1976. London Foursomes 1984
Reg Essex Ladies 1958-59-60-61-62-63-66-67-70-71
Ove German Ladies 1958
Int Curtis Cup 1962. Vagliano Trophy 1961-69. England (Home Int) 1960-61-62-63-68-70-72-77 (capt), (non-playing captain 1978); (Eu Team Ch) 1969-71
Mis Turned professional March 1979. Reinstated as amateur 1982

Barnes, Brian

Born Addington, Surrey on 3rd June, 1945. Turned Professional 1964

Tls Dutch Open 1974. French Open 1975. Spanish Open 1978. Second in New Zealand Open 1978. Italian Open 1979. Portuguese Open 1979. Zambian Open 1979-81. Kenya Open 1981. TPC 1981. Scottish Professional Champion 1981-82
Maj Agfacolor 1969. Martini International 1972. Sun Alliance PGA Match Play 1976. Greater Manchester Open 1978
Ove Australian Masters 1970. Flame Lily (Rhodesia) 1967
Oth Coca-Cola Young Professionals 1969. East of Scotland Professional 1975. Northern Scottish Open 1978
Int Ryder Cup 1969-71-73-75-77-79. Scotland in Double Diamond 1972-73-74-75-76-77. Scotland in World Cup 1974-75-76-77. GB v Europe 1974-76-78-80; v South Africa 1976
Amr British Youths' 1964. Somerset Amateur 1964. South Western Counties Amateur 1964
Mis Finished 4th in inaugural Alcan Golfer of the Year 1967. Third in Doral Open 1970. European American Express 1975

Bayman, Mrs Linda (*née* Denison-Pender)

Born 10th June, 1948

Chp English Ladies 1983
Maj Avia Foursomes 1969-71-73-79-80. Worplesdon Mixed Foursomes 1980-84. Astor Salver 1983-84. Critchley Salver 1984
Reg Kent Champion 1968-72-73-78
Jun Kent Girls 1966
Int England (Home Int) 1971-72-73. Vagliano Trophy 1971-73. European Team Championship 1983

Beck, Mrs JB (*née* Pim)

Born Cantibeely, Co Dublin on 1st July, 1901

Add Felder Lodge, Worth, Deal, Kent
Cls Royal Portrush, The Berkshire, Prince's
Chp Irish Ladies 1938, runner-up 1949
Oth Ladies Veteran 1952-55-56-59
Reg Middlesex Ladies 1937
Int Ireland (Home Int) 1926 to 1950-56
Mis Curtis Cup non-playing captain 1954. Captain of LGU team to tour South Africa 1951. Irish hockey internationalist 1920

Behan, Miss Lillian

Born

Chp British Ladies 1985
Int Vagliano Trophy 1985. Curtis Cup 1986. Ireland (Home Int) 1986

Beharrell, John Charles

Born Solihull, Warwickshire on 2nd May, 1938

Add Tracery, Little Aston, Park Road, Streetly, Sutton Coldfield, Warwickshire
Cls Royal and Ancient, Edgbaston, Aldeburgh. Hon member of Little Aston, Blackwell, Handworth
Chp Amateur Champion 1956
Maj Antlers Royal Mid-Surrey 1960. Central England Mixed Foursomes 1956-57-75
Jun English Boy International 1955
Int GB v Europe 1956; v Professionals 1956. England (Home Int) 1956
Mis EGU selector 1972 to 1974. Member of R & A Championship Committee 1976-77 and Rules of Golf Committee 1979

Beharrell, Mrs Veronica (*née* Anstey)

Born Birmingham on 14th January, 1935

Add Tracery, Little Aston, Park Road, Streetly, Sutton Coldfield, Warwickshire
Cls Edgbaston (Hon), Little Aston
Maj Central England Mixed Foursomes 1957-75
Reg Warwickshire Ladies 1955-56-57-58-60-71-72-75
Ove Australian Ladies 1955. New Zealand Ladies 1955. Victoria (Australia) Ladies Open 1955
Jun Girl International 1953
Int Curtis Cup 1956. England (Home Int) 1955-56-58 (non-playing captain 1961)

Bembridge, Maurice

Born Worksop on 21st February, 1945. Turned Professional 1960

Opn Leading British Player in Open Championship 1968 (5th)
Tls Kenya Open 1968-69-79. Second New Zealand Open 1971-72. German Open 1975
Maj PGA Match Play 1969. Sumrie 1969. Dunlop Masters 1971. Martini 1973. Piccadilly Medal 1974. Viyella PGA 1974. Double Diamond Individual 1974. Benson and Hedges International 1979
Ove Caltex (New Zealand) 1970. Lusaka Open 1972
Oth British Assistants 1967
Int Ryder Cup 1969-71-73-75. GB v South Africa 1976. England in Double Diamond 1973-74-75. England in World Cup 1974-75
Mis His 63 in the qualifying round for the 1967 Open Championship equals the lowest recorded. Second in Order of Merit 1973. Scored 64 in last round 1974 US Masters equalling record; his inward half of 30 also equalled the record

Benka, Peter

Born London on 18th September, 1946

Add Manaries, Newdigate, Surrey
Cls Addington, West Sussex
Chp Second in Scottish Open Amateur Stroke Play 1969
Maj County Champion of Champions 1967. Sunningdale Foursomes 1969. St George's Challenge Cup 1969. St George's Hill Trophy 1971-75. Mullingar Trophy 1970
Reg Surrey Amateur 1967-68
Ove Dutch Amateur 1972
Jun British Youths 1967-68. Boy International 1964. Youth International 1966-67-68
Int Walker Cup 1969. GB v Europe 1970. England (Home Int) 1967-68-69-70; (Eur Team Ch) 1969
Mis Leading Amateur Open Championship 1967

Bennett, Stephen

Born Cleethorpes on 23rd April, 1959. Turned Professional 1979

Tls Tunisian Open 1985. Zimbabwe Open 1986
Reg Lincolnshire Open 1979. Lincolnshire Amateur 1977-78

Bentley, Arnold Lewis

Born Southport on 11th June, 1911

Add 24 Sandringham Court, Lord Street, Southport, Lancs
Cls Royal and Ancient, Hesketh (Hon), Royal Birkdale
Chp English Amateur 1939
Jun Boy International 1928
Int England (Home Int) 1936-37; v France 1937-39
Mis Played for British Seniors 1969

Bentley, Harry Geoffrey

Born Manchester on 13th October, 1907

Add Bentley's House, Avenue Francois Godin, Le Touquet, Pas-de-Calais. Tel (21) 051865; and Bentley's House, 133 Guadalmina, Baja, Marbella, Andalucia, Spain
Cls Royal and Ancient, Hesketh (Hon), Le Touquet
Chp English Amateur 1936, runner-up 1954. Runner-up Irish Amateur Open 1934
Maj Royal St George's Challenge Cup 1932. Prince of Wales Cup 1935
Reg Lancashire Amateur 1931-32-39
Ove French Amateur 1931-32. German Amateur 1933-37-38-39. Italian Amateur 1954
Int Walker Cup 1934-36-38. GB v Professionals 1930-31-32-34-35. England (Home Int) 1931-32-33-34-35-36-37-38-47; v France 1934-36-37-38-39 (capt) 54
Mis Chairman Walker Cup Selectors 1953. Captain British Seniors 1967. Leading Amateur French, Belgian, German, Czechoslovakian Opens 1935

Bisgood, Miss Jeanne, CBE

Born Richmond, Surrey on 11th August, 1923

Add 12 Water's Edge, Brudenell Road, Poole, Dorset BH13 7NN
Cls Parkstone (Hon)
Chp English Ladies 1951-53-57
Maj Astor Salver 1951-52-53. Roehampton Gold Cup 1951-52-53. Daily Graphic 1945-51
Reg South Eastern Ladies 1950-52. Surrey Ladies 1951-53-69
Ove Norwegian Ladies 1955. Swedish Ladies 1952. Italian Ladies 1953. German Ladies 1953. Portuguese Ladies 1954
Int Curtis Cup 1950-52-54 (non-playing captain 1970). England (Home Int) 1949-50-51-52-53-54-56-58

Blakeman, David

Born 10th June, 1960

Chp English Amateur 1981

Bloice, Cecil

Born 30th July, 1954

Int Walker Cup 1985. Scotland (Home Int) 1986

Bolton, Mrs SM (*née* Zara Davis)

Born London on 16th March, 1914

Add Strandmore House, Portrush, Co Antrim
Cls Hon Member of Royal Portrush, Bishop's Stortford, Maccauvlei, County Down, Castlerock, Ballycastle
Chp Runner-up English Ladies 1948
Reg Herts Ladies 1935. Kent Ladies 1948. Ulster Scratch Cup 1947-48-49-50-56-60
Int Curtis Cup 1948 (non-playing captain 1956-66-68). GB v France 1948. England (Home Int) 1939-49-50-51-55 (capt)-56
Mis Non-playing captain of British Commonwealth Team 1967. Member of LGU team to tour South Africa 1951

Bonallack, Michael Francis, OBE

Born Chigwell on 31st December, 1934

Add Clatto Lodge, Blebo Craigs, Cupar, Fife
Cls Thorpe Hall, Pine Valley, Elie. Hon member of Thorndon Park, Orsett, Royal Lytham, Royal Blackheath, The Warren, Boyce Hill, Woodhall Spa, Burnham and Berrow, Royal Porthcawl, Spalding, Clitheroe, The Berkshire, Sunningdale, Rochford and others
Chp Amateur Champion 1961-65-68-69-70. English Open Amateur Stroke Play 1964-68-69 (tied)-71, second 1959-66-67. English Amateur 1962-63-65-67-68, runner-up 1959
Maj Berkshire Trophy 1957-61-65-68-70-71 (tied). Hampshire Hog 1957-79. Lytham Trophy 1965 (tied) -72. Golf Illustrated Gold Vase 1961 (tied)-67 (tied)-68-69 (tied)-71-75. Royal St George's Challenge Cup 1965-68-81. Prince of Wales Challenge Cup 1967. Scrutton Jug 1961-64-66-68-70-71. Antlers Royal Mid-Surrey 1964. Sunningdale Foursomes 1959. Worplesdon Mixed Foursomes 1958
Reg Essex Amateur 1954-57-59-60-61-63-64-68-69-70-72. Essex Open 1969. East Anglian Open 1973
Jun British Boys 1952
Int Walker Cup 1957-59-61-63-65-67-69 (capt)-71 (capt)-73. GB Commonwealth Team 1959-63-67-71 (captain 1967-71, non-playing captain 1975). Eisenhower Trophy 1960-62-64-66-68-70-72 (captain 1968-70-72). GB v Professionals 1957-58-59-60; v Europe 1958-60-62-64-66-68-70-72. England (Home Int) 1957-58-59-60-61-62-63-64-65-66-67-68-69-70-71-72-74 (captain 1962-63-64-65-66-67); (Eur Team Ch) 1959-61-63-65-67-69-71
Mis Leading Amateur Open Championship 1968-71. Golf Writers Trophy 1968. Bobby Jones Award 1972. Best equal individual score Eisenhower Trophy 1968. EGU selector 1974. Chairman Royal and Ancient Selection Committee 1975 to 1979 and Amateur Status Committee 1976 to 1979. PGA Chairman 1976. Chairman Golf Foundation 1977. Member of Royal and Ancient Rules of Golf Committee 1979-80. President English Golf Union 1982. Secretary Royal and Ancient GC 1983

Bonallack, Mrs Angela (*née* Ward)

Born Birchington on 7th April, 1937

Add Clatto Lodge, Blebo Craigs, Cupar, Fife
Cls Prince's, Thorpe Hall, St Rule
Chp English Ladies 1958-63, runner-up 1960-62-72. Runner-up British Ladies 1962-74
Maj Astor Salver 1957-58-60-61-66. Worplesdon Mixed Foursomes 1958. Kayser-Bondor Foursomes 1958 (tied). Astor Prince's 1968. Avia Foursomes 1976. Roehampton Gold Gup 1980
Reg Essex Ladies 1968-69-73-74-76-77-78-82. South East Ladies 1957-65. Kent Ladies 1955-56-58
Ove Swedish Ladies 1955. German Ladies 1955. Scandinavian Ladies 1956. Portuguese Ladies 1957
Jun British Girls 1955

Int	Curtis Cup 1956-58-60-62-64-66. Vagliano Trophy 1959-61-63. England (Home Int) 1956-57-58-59-60-61-62-63-64-66-72
Mis	Selected for 1974 Curtis Cup but could not be available for whole tour, so did not accept. Leading amateur Colgate European Ladies' Open 1975-76

Bonallack, Miss Sally

See Mrs DN Barber

Boomer, Aubrey Basil

Born Grouville, Jersey on 1st November, 1897. Turned Professional 1919

Opn	Second in Open Championship 1927
Tls	French Open 1921-22-26-29-31. Belgian Open 1922-26. Dutch Open 1924-25-26. Italian Open 1932
Maj	Daily Mail 1926
Ove	French International PGA 1928-29
Int	Ryder Cup 1926-27-29. GB v France 1929

Bousfield, Kenneth

Born Marston Moor on 2nd October, 1919. Turned Professional 1938

Tls	German Open 1955-59. Swiss Open 1958. Belgian Open 1958. Portuguese Open 1960-61
Maj	News Chronicle 1951. PGA Match Play 1955. PGA Close 1955. Yorkshire Evening News 1956 (tied). Dunlop 1957. Sprite 1959. Irish Hospitals 1960 (tied). Swallow-Penfold 1961
Oth	Gleneagles Pro-Am 1964. Southern England Professional 1951-57-74. Pringle Seniors 1972
Int	Ryder Cup 1949-51-55-57-59-61. England in World Cup 1956-57

Bradshaw, Harry

Born Delgany, Co Wicklow on 9th October, 1913. Turned Professional 1934

Opn	Tied for Open Championship 1949, lost play-off
Tls	Irish Open 1947-49
Maj	Dunlop Masters 1953-55. PGA Close 1958. Penfold-Swallow 1958 (tied)
Oth	Irish Professional 1941-42-43-44-47-50-51-53-54-57. Irish Dunlop 1950
Int	Ryder Cup 1953-55-57. Ireland in World Cup 1954-55-56-57-58 (winning team)-59
Mis	Second Individual section World Cup 1958

Brand, Gordon Jr

Born Burntisland, Fife on 19th August, 1958. Turned Professional 1981

Add	Knowle Golf Club, Brislington, Bristol BS4
Cls	Hon member of Woodhall Spa, Knowle
Chp	English Open Amateur Stroke Play 1978. Scottish Open Amateur Stroke Play 1980
Maj	Golf Illustrated Vase 1980. Sunningdale Foursomes 1981. Coral Classic 1982. Bob Hope British Classic 1982. Celtic International 1984. European Open 1984
Reg	South Western Counties Amateur 1977-78. Gloucestershire Amateur 1977
Ove	Swedish Open Amateur Stroke Play 1979. Ivory Coast Open 1981
Jun	British Youths 1979. Scottish Youths 1980. Youth International 1977-78-79
Int	Walker Cup 1979. Eisenhower Trophy 1978-80. GB v Europe 1978-80. Scotland (Home Int) 1978-80; (Eur Team Ch) 1979; v England 1979; v Italy 1979; v Belgium 1980; v France 1980; in Fiat Trophy 1980. Scotland in World Cup 1984-85; in Dunhill Cup 1985-86. Nissan Cup 1985
Mis	Rookie of the Year 1982

Brand, Gordon, Sr

Born Cambridge on August, 1955. Turned Professional 1976

Tls	Nigerian Open 1983-86. Ivory Coast Open 1981-86
Ove	Ivory Coast Cup 1981. Nigerian Open 1983
Int	Ryder Cup 1983. England in World Cup 1983. Dunhill Cup 1986. Nissan Cup 1986
Mis	Former English Amateur Internationalist. Won Tooting Bec Cup 1981

Branigan, Declan

Born Drogheda, Ireland on 22nd July, 1948

Add	Queensboro, Drogheda, Co Louth, Ireland
Cls	Laytown and Bettystown
Chp	Irish Amateur 1976-81
Maj	West of Ireland Open Amateur 1976-81. East of Ireland Open Amateur 1981
Jun	Irish Youths 1969
Int	Ireland (Home Int) 1975-76-77-80-86; (Eur Team Ch) 1977-81; v France, West Germany and Sweden 1976

Briggs, Mrs Audrey (*née* Brown)

Born Kent on 31st January, 1945

Add	Manor Farm, Old Village, West Kirby, Merseyside
Cls	Royal Liverpool, Rye
Chp	Welsh Ladies 1970-71-73-74, runner-up 1978-79-80-81
Reg	Sussex Ladies 1969. Cheshire Ladies 1971-73-76-80-81. North of England Ladies 1976
Int	Vagliano Trophy 1971-73. Wales (Home Int) 1969-70-71-72-73-74-75-76-77-78-79-80-81-82-83-84, (Eur Team Ch) 1969-71-73-75-77-79-81-83; in Fiat Trophy 1978-79-80
Mis	Captain of Wales 1981-83

Brodie, Allan

Born Glasgow on 25th September, 1947

Add	102 Main Street, Torrance, by Glasgow
Cls	Balmore (Hon), Glasgow
Chp	Scottish Amateur 1977, runner-up 1973. Second in Scottish Open Amateur Stroke Play 1970
Maj	Tennant Cup 1972-80. West of Scotland Open Amateur 1974. Golf Illustrated Gold Vase 1976
Reg	Dunbartonshire Amateur Stroke Play 1975-76
Jun	Youth International 1966-67
Int	Walker Cup 1977-79. GB v Europe 1974-76-78-80. Eisenhower Trophy 1978. Scotland (Home Int) 1970-72-73-74-75-76-77-78-80; (Eur Team Ch) 1973-77-79; v Belgium 1977; v Spain 1977; v France 1978; v England 1979; v Italy 1979

Brooks, A

Born 22nd December, 1946

Jun	Boy International 1964. Youth International 1965-66-67-68
Int	Walker Cup 1969. Scotland (Home Int) 1968-69; (Eur Team Ch) 1969
Mis	Turned Professional 1969. Represented Scotland in Double Diamond Internationals 1971. Won Skol Tournament with 4-round aggregate of 259

Brooks, Colin

Born 14th July 1965

Chp	Scottish Amateur 1986
Maj	Tennant Cup 1985. Gran Primo 1986. West of Scotland Open Amateur Stroke Play 1986
Int	GB v Europe 1986

Brown, Miss Audrey

See Mrs A Briggs

Brown, Miss Julie

Born 26th December, 1963. Turned Professional 1985

Reg	Staffordshire Champion 1982-83
Int	Vilmorin Trophy 1984. England (Home Int) 1984
WPGA	LBS Ladies German Open 1985

Brown, Kenneth

Born Harpenden, Herts on 9th January, 1957. Turned Professional 1975

Tls Dutch Open 1983. Kenya Open 1983
Maj Carrolls Irish Open 1978. Glasgow Classic 1984. Four Stars National 1985
Int Ryder Cup 1977-79-83-85. GB v Europe 1978. Scotland in Double Diamond 1977. Scotland in World Cup 1977-78-79-83. Hennessy-Cognac Cup 1984
Amr Boy International 1974. Carris Trophy 1974. Herts Open 1975

Buckley, James A

Born Ontario, Canada on 14th September, 1950

Add 3 Moor Park, Abergele, Clwyd, N Wales
Cls Abergele, Killarney (Hon)
Chp Welsh Amateur 1968. Welsh Amateur Stroke Play 1968-77, second 1978. Welsh Close 1969
Reg Denbighshire Amateur 1967-68-76-78. North Wales Professional (as Amateur) 1976
Jun Welsh Boys 1966-67-68
Int Walker Cup 1979. Wales (Home Int) 1967-68-69-76-77-78; (Eur Team Ch) 1967-69; v Denmark 1976-77
Mis In 1969 held Boys' Close (open to Amateur and Professional), Amateur and Amateur Stroke Play Welsh titles. Turned Professional 1969 and won Welsh Professional 1971-72. Reinstated as Amateur in 1976

Burke, Miss Ita

See Mrs E Butler

Bussell, Alan Francis

Born Glasgow on 25th February, 1937

Add Bennamie, Kirkham Lane, Fritchley, Derbyshire
Cls Whitecraigs (Hon), Coxmoor (Hon), Chevin
Maj Antlers Royal Mid-Surrey 1956. Golf Illustrated Gold Vase 1959
Reg Nottinghamshire Amateur 1959-60-62-63-64-68-69. Nottinghamshire Open 1960-62. Nottinghamshire Match Play 1960-62. Renfrewshire Amateur 1955
Jun British Boys 1954. Boy International 1954. British Youths 1956. Youth International 1954-55-56
Int Walker Cup 1957. GB v Europe 1956-62; v Professionals 1956-57-59. Scotland (Home Int) 1956-57-58-61; v Scandinavia 1956-60

Butler, Mrs E (*née* Ita Burke)

Born Nenagh, Co Tipperary

Add Kilbride, Torquay Road, Foxrock, Co Dublin
Cls Hon member of Elm Park, Killarney, Woodbrook, Nenagh
Chp Runner-up Irish Ladies 1972-78
Reg Leinster Ladies three times. Munster and Midland Ladies twice
Int Curtis Cup 1966. World Team Championship 1966. Vagliano Trophy 1965. Ireland (World Cup) 1964; (Home Int) 1962-63-64-65-66-68-71-72-73-76-77-78-79; (Eur Team Ch) 1967; in Fiat Trophy 1978

Butler, Peter J

Born Birmingham on 25th March, 1932. Turned Professional 1948

Tls French Open 1968. Colombian Open 1975
Maj Swallow-Penfold 1959. Yorkshire Evening News 1962. PGA Close 1963. Bowmaker 1963-67. Cox Moore 1964. PGA Match Play runner-up 1964-75. Martini 1965. Piccadilly 1965-67. Penfold 1968. Wills 1968. RTV 1969. Classic International 1971. Sumrie 1974
Ove Evian International 1963. Grand Bahama Invitation Open 1971-72
Oth Midland Open 1956-58-60-65-69. Midland Professional 1961. Gleneagles Pro-Am 1963. Sunningdale Foursomes 1974
Int Ryder Cup 1965-69-71-73. England in World Cup 1969-70-73. England in Double Diamond 1971-72-76. GB v Europe 1976
Mis Equal lowest round in British events of 61. Second in Order of Merit 1968. PGA Captain 1972

Cadden, Miss Suzanne

See Mrs J McMahon

Caldwell, Ian

Born Streatham on 17th May, 1930

Add 51 Campden Hill Towers, London W11
Cls Royal and Ancient, Sunningdale, Walton Heath
Chp English Amateur 1961
Maj Prince of Wales Challenge Cup 1950-51-52
Oth Boyd Quaich 1954. Carris Trophy 1947-48
Reg Surrey Amateur 1961
Int Walker Cup 1951-55. GB Commonwealth Team 1954. GB v Europe 1955. England (Home Int) 1950-51-52-53-54-55-56-57-61

Caldwell, Mrs Ian (*née* Carole Redford)

Born Kingston, Surrey on 23rd April, 1949

Add 51 Campden Hill Towers, London W11
Cls Canterbury (Hon), Sunningdale
Maj Newmark-Avia International 1973. Roehampton Gold Cup 1973-75-78. Hampshire Rose 1973, 1984. Avia Foursomes 1974. Critchley Salver 1974. London Foursomes 1984
Reg South Eastern Ladies 1973-78. Kent Ladies 1970-75-77. Berkshire Ladies 1982
Ove Canadian Ladies Foursomes 1978. Portuguese Ladies 1980
Int Vagliano Trophy 1973. Curtis Cup 1978-80. England (Home Int) 1973-78-79-80
Mis Playing captain of LGU under-23 team to tour Canada 1973. Lost at 27th hole in first round of American Ladies Amateur 1978

Carr, Joseph B

Born Dublin on 18th February, 1922

Add Suncroft, Sutton, Dublin
Cls Hon member of Sutton, Portmarnock, Milltown, Dublin, Killarney, Lahinch, Royal Portrush, Macroom, Malone, Howth, Newlands, Youghal, Douglas, The Island, Malahide, Moate, Lucan, Tramore, County Cork, Dun Laoghaire, Skerries, Warrenpoint, Delgany, Ballina, Mullingar, Rosslare, Ballycastle, Portumna, Royal Lytham, Augusta, Pine Valley
Chp Amateur Champion 1953-58-60, runner-up 1968. Irish Amateur 1954-57-63-64-65-67, runner-up 1951-59. Irish Open Amateur 1946-50-54-56, runner-up 1947-48-51
Maj South of Ireland Open Amateur 1948-66-69. East of Ireland Open Amateur 1941-43-45-46-48-56-57-58-60-61-64-69. West of Ireland Open Amateur 1946-47-48-51-53-54-56-58-60-61-62-66. Gleneagles Saxone 1955. Golf Illustrated Gold Vase 1951. Berkshire Trophy 1959. Formby Hare 1962. Mullingar Trophy 1963. Antlers Royal Mid-Surrey 1970
Int Walker Cup 1947-49-51-53-55-57-59-61-63 (capt)-67 (non-playing captain 1965). GB v Europe 1954-56-64 (capt)-66 (capt)-68. Eisenhower Trophy 1958-60 (non-playing captain 1964-66). Ireland (Home Int) 1947-48-49-50-51-52-53-54-55-56-57-58-59-60-61-62-63-64-65-66-67-68-69; (Eur Team Ch) 1965-67-69
Mis Semi-finalist American Amateur 1961. Leading Amateur Open Championship 1956-58. Golf Writers Trophy 1953. Bobby Jones Award 1961. Walter Hagen Award 1967

Carr, Roderick J

Born 27th October, 1950. Turned Professional 1971. Reinstated Amateur 1983

Add Suncroft, Sutton, Dublin
Maj Antlers Royal Mid-Surrey 1970. East of Ireland Open Amateur 1970. West of Ireland Open Amateur 1971. Turnberry Pro-Am 1970

Jun Youth International 1970-71
Int Walker Cup 1971. Ireland (Home Int) 1970-71; (Eur Team Ch) 1971
Mis Leading Amateur South African Open 1971.

Carrick, David
Born 28th January, 1957

Chp Scottish Amateur 1985
Maj Scottish Champion of Champions 1983. Glasgow Amateur 1980-81
Reg Dunbartonshire Amateur 1979-80-82-83
Int Walker Cup 1983. GB v Europe 1986. Scotland (Home Int) 1981-82-83-84-85-86

Carslaw, Iain Alexander
Born Glasgow on 4th October, 1949

Add 4 Woodvale Avenue, Giffnock, Glasgow
Cls Williamwood (Hon), Walton Heath
Chp Scottish Amateur 1978
Maj Tennant Cup 1978. Golf Illustrated Gold Vase 1982
Reg Glasgow County Match Play 1977-78-79-80. Glasgow Amateur 1978
Jun Boy International 1967. Youth International 1971
Int Walker Cup 1979. GB v Europe 1978. Scotland (Home Int) 1976-77-78-80-81; (Eur Team Ch) 1977-79; v Spain 1977; v Belgium 1978; v France 1978-83; in Fiat Trophy 1978; v Italy 1979; v England 1979; in Moroccan International 1979

Cater, John Robert
Born Edinburgh in 1919

Add Avernish, Elie, Fife
Cls Williamwood (Hon), Royal and Ancient, Elie
Maj Gleneagles Silver Tassie 1952
Reg West of Scotland Amateur 1951-55. Glasgow County 1957
Int Walker Cup 1955. Scotland (Home Int) 1952-53-54-55-56; v South Africa 1954; v Scandinavia 1956
Mis Captain of Royal and Ancient 1986-87

Chadwick, Miss Elizabeth
See Mrs AD Pook

Chapman, Roger
Born in Nakuru, Kenya on 1st May, 1959. Turned Professional 1981

Chp English Amateur 1979
Maj Duncan Putter 1981 (shared). Lytham Trophy 1981
Reg Kent Open 1977
Int Walker Cup 1981. GB v Europe 1980. England (Home Int) 1980-81; (Eur Team Ch) 1981
Mis Sunningdale Open Foursomes 1979-86

Christison, Diane
Born 30th June, 1962

Chp English Ladies Amateur 1981
Reg Staffordshire Ladies 1983
Int (Eur Team Ch) 1981

Christmas, Martin J
Born 1939

Add Dean Cottage, Dean, nr Bishops Waltham, Hants
Cls West Sussex, Addington
Chp Runner-up English Amateur 1960. Second in English Open Amateur Stroke Play 1960
Maj Gleneagles Pro-Am 1961. Wentworth Pro-Am Foursomes 1962
Reg Sussex Amateur 1962
Ove Belgian Open Amateur 1976
Int Walker Cup 1961-63. Eisenhower Trophy 1962. GB v Europe 1960-62-64. England (Home Int) 1960-61-62-63-64

Chugg, Mrs Pamela Mary (*née* Light)
Born Cardiff on 10th May, 1955

Add 22 Lon Robin Coch, Glenfield, Caerphilly, Mid Glamorgan
Cls Whitechurch, St Pierre (attached)
Chp Welsh Ladies 1978. Welsh Ladies Open Stroke Play 1976
Reg South Western Ladies 1975-78
Jun Welsh Girls 1971. Girl International 1970-71-72-73
Int Wales (Home Int) 1973-74-75-76-77-78; (Eur Team Ch) 1973-75-77
Mis Turned Professional February 1979

Clark, Clive Anthony
Born Winchester, Hants on 27th June, 1945. Turned Professional 1965

Opn Third in Open Championship 1967 (leading British player)
Tls Danish Open 1966
Chp Runner-up Amateur Championship 1965. Runner-up English Amateur 1965. English Open Amateur Stroke Play 1965 (tied)
Maj Lytham Trophy 1965 (tied). Golf Illustrated Gold Vase 1965. Scrutton Jug 1965. Bowmaker 1968. Agfa-Gevaert 1968. John Player Trophy 1970. Sumrie 1974
Oth Sunningdale Foursomes 1974-76
Int Walker Cup 1965. GB v Europe 1964. England (Home Int) 1964-65. Ryder Cup 1978
Mis Lost play-off for 1972 French Open. TV commentator

Clark, Gordon James
Born Newcastle-upon-Tyne on 15th April, 1933

Chp Amateur Champion 1964. Runner-up English Amateur 1961. Scottish Open Amateur Stroke Play 1973 (tied)
Reg Northumberland Amateur 1956-71. Northumberland Amateur Stroke Play 1967-71
Ove Portuguese Amateur 1974
Jun English Boy International 1950
Int Walker Cup 1965. GB v Europe 1964-66. England (Home Int) 1961-64-65-66-67-68-71; (Eur Team Ch) 1961-65
Mis Turned Professional 1974. Reinstated Amateur 1983

Clark, Howard K
Born Leeds on 26th August, 1954. Turned Professional October 1973

Tls Portuguese Open 1978
Maj Madrid Open 1978-84-86. PGA Championship 1984. Jersey Open 1985. Glasgow Open 1985
Oth Under-25 TPD 1976. Greater Manchester Open 1975
Reg Yorkshire Amateur 1973
Int Ryder Cup 1977-81-85. Walker Cup 1973. England (Home Int) 1973. GB v Europe 1978. England in World Cup 1978-84-85. Hennessy-Cognac Cup 1978-84. Individual World Cup Champion 1985. Dunhill Cup 1985-86. Nissan Cup 1986
Jun British Boys 1971. Boy International 1969-71. Youth International 1971-72-73

Coles, Neil
Born London on 26th September, 1934. Turned Professional 1950

Opn Third in Open Championship 1961; second in 1973; leading British player 1975 (7th)
Tls German Open 1971. Spanish Open 1973

Maj Ballantine 1961. Senior Service 1962. Daks 1963 (tied)-64-70-71 (tied). Martini 1963 (tied). Bowmaker 1964-70. PGA Match Play 1964-65-73, runner-up 1966-72-78. Carrolls 1965-71. Pringle 1966. Dunlop Masters 1966. Sumrie 1970-73. Penfold 1971. Sunbeam 1972. Wills 1974. Penfold PGA 1976. Tournament Players' Championship 1977. Sanyo Open 1982
Ove Engadine Open 1963. Shell BP Italy 1970. Walworth Aloyco Italy 1970
Oth British Assistants 1956. Sunningdale Foursomes 1962-67-80. Wentworth Pro-Am Foursomes 1963-70. Southern England Professionals 1970
Int Ryder Cup 1961-63-65-67-69-71-73-77. England in World Cup 1963-68. England in Double Diamond 1971-73-75-76-77. GB v Europe 1974-76-78-80
Mis Harry Vardon Trophy 1963-70. Second in Order of Merit 1971

Connachan, Miss Jane
Born Haddington, East Lothian on 25th February, 1964
Turned Professional 1984

Add 33 Grange Crescent East, Prestonpans, East Lothian
Cls Royal Musselburgh (Hon)
Chp Scottish Ladies 1982. British Ladies Stroke Play 1982
Jun Australian Junior Championship 1982. European Junior Ladies Team 1983
Maj Helen Holm Trophy 1983
Reg East Lothian Ladies 1978-79
Jun Scottish Girls 1978-79-80. Scottish Girls Open Stroke Play 1978-80. British Girls 1980-81. Australian Girls 1982. Girl International 1976-77-78-79-80. British Girls Open 1981. Second British Ladies Stroke Open 1981-83
Int Curtis Cup 1980-82. World Team Championship 1980-82. Scotland (Home Int) 1979-80-82-83. World Invitational, Scots Girls International, Scots Ladies International 1981. Vagliano Trophy 1981-83. World Team 1982. European Ladies Team 1983. Commonwealth Team 1983
Mis Avia Golfer of the Year 1982. British Olivetti 1985. 415 Match-Play 1985

Corlett, Miss Elsie
Born Lytham on 2nd September, 1902

Add 16A East Beach, Lytham, Lancs
Cls Royal Lytham and St Annes (Hon)
Chp Runner-up British Ladies 1938. English Ladies 1938, runner-up 1926-35
Oth Veteran Ladies 1954
Reg Lancashire Ladies 1927-29
Int Curtis Cup 1932-38 (non-playing captain 1964). GB v France 1931-36-37-38-39. England (Home Int) 1927-29-30-31-32-33-35-36-37-38-39
Mis President Lancashire Ladies Golf Association 1970-71-72. President Lancashire Veteran Ladies Golf Association 1979-80-81-82. Non-playing captain England in European Team Championship 1965

Corridan, T
Born

Chp Irish Amateur
Int Ireland (Home Int) 1983-84

Cosh, Gordon B
Born Glasgow on 26th March, 1939

Add 8 Bute Court, Dirleton Drive, Glasgow
Cls Troon, Royal Aberdeen, Bruntsfield Links. Hon member of Cowglen, Killarney
Chp Scottish Amateur 1968, runner-up 1965. Second in Scottish Open Amateur Stroke Play 1968
Maj Newlands Trophy 1980
Reg West of Scotland Amateur 1961-64-65-66. Glasgow County Match Play 1965-66. Glasgow Amateur 1969. Glasgow County Stroke Play 1972-74
Jun Youth International 1959-60
Int Walker Cup 1965. Eisenhower Trophy 1966-68. GB Commonwealth Team 1967. GB v Europe 1966-68. Scotland (Home Int) 1964-65-66-67-68-69; (Eur Team Ch) 1965-69 (capt)

Cotton, Thomas Henry, MBE
Born Holmes Chapel, Cheshire on 26th January, 1907. Turned Professional 1924

Opn Open Champion 1934-37-48, third 1933-38-46. Joint leading British player (4th) Open Championship 1946
Tls Belgian Open 1930-34-38. Italian Open 1936. German Open 1937-38-39. Czechoslovakian Open 1937-38. French Open 1946-47
Maj PGA Match Play 1932-40-46, runner-up 1928-30-49. Dunlop Southport 1931-32. Yorkshire Evening News 1935-47 (tied). Silver King 1937. Dunlop-Metropolitan 1936. Daily Mail 1939. Penfold League 1939 (tied). News Chronicle 1945. Star 1946. Spalding 1947. Dunlop 1953. Penfold 1954
Ove White Sulphur Springs Invitation 1948. Mar Del Plata Open (Argentina) 1930
Int Ryder Cup 1929-37-47 (capt)-1953 (non-playing captain). GB v France 1929
Mis Hon member of the Royal and Ancient. Member of PGA Committee from 1934-54. Captain PGA 1934-48. Founder member of the Golf Foundation. Holder of many records for low scoring in the Open Championship and other events. (See relevant Section of the Handbook.) Had 17 holes-in-one up to 1976. Harry Vardon Trophy 1938. Author of many Golf Books. Golf Course Architect. Walter Hagen Award 1979

Craddock, Tom
Born Malahide on 16th December, 1931

Add Seamount Road, The Hill, Malahide, Co Dublin
Cls Malahide, Donabate, Sutton, The Island Malahide, Malone, Woodbrook, Mullingar, Carlow, Howth, Tara, Killarney
Chp Irish Amateur 1959, runner-up 1965. Irish Open Amateur 1958
Maj East of Ireland Open Amateur 1959-65-66. Lytham Trophy 1969
Int Walker Cup 1967-69. Ireland (Home Int) 1955-56-57-58-59-60-65-66-67-69; (Eur Team Ch) 1967-71

Critchley, Bruce
Born 9th December, 1942

Add Doone, Ridgemount Road, Sunningdale, Berks
Cls Sunningdale, Killarney (Hon)
Maj Worplesdon Mixed Foursomes 1961. Sunningdale Foursomes 1964. Hampshire Hog 1969. Antlers Royal Mid-Surrey 1974
Reg Surrey Amateur 1969
Int Walker Cup 1969. GB v Europe 1970. England (Home Int) 1962-69-70; (Eur Team Ch) 1969
Mis TV commentator.

Critchley, Mrs AC (*née* Diana Lesley Fishwick)
Born London 12th April, 1911

Add Doone, Ridgemount Road, Sunningdale, Berks
Cls North Foreland, Bramley, Canterbury, Sunningdale, Sunningdale Ladies
Chp British Ladies 1930. English Ladies 1932-49, runner-up 1929
Maj Sunningdale Foursomes 1934
Reg Kent Ladies 1934. Surrey Ladies 1936-46
Ove French Ladies 1932. German Ladies 1936-38. Belgian Ladies 1938. Dutch Ladies 1946. Florida (USA) West Coast 1933
Int Curtis Cup 1932-34 (non-playing captain 1950). GB v France 1931-32-33-34 (non-playing captain 1948); v Canada 1934-50. England (Home Int) 1930-31-32-33-35-36-47
Jun British Girls 1927-28
Mis Chairman of ELGA Selection Committee 1967-68-69-70. LGU International Selector 1970-71-72-73. Member LGU Team to tour South Africa 1933

Crowcroft, Sue
Born 6th September, 1954. Turned Professional 1980

Chp Welsh Ladies Open Amateur Stroke Play 1979

Curry, David H
Born

Chp Amateur Champion 1986
Maj Selbourne Salver 1984
Int England (Home Int) 1984-86. GB v Europe 1986

Dalgleish, Colin R
Born Glasgow 24th September, 1960

Add 21 East Abercromby Street, Helensburgh
Cls Helensburgh (Hon), Millstone Mills (Hon)
Chp Scottish Amateur 1981
Maj Tennant Cup 1983
Ove East of India Amateur 1981. Indian Amateur runner-up 1981. Lake Macquarie International Stroke-Play Champion (Australia) 1983
Oth Scottish Universities Champion 1983
Jun International Junior Masters 1977. Belgian Junior Championship 1980. Runner-up British Boys 1977. Runner-up British Youths 1979-82. Boy International 1976-77-78. Youth International 1979-80-81-82
Int Walker Cup 1981. Scotland (Home Int) 1981-82-83; v France 1982; (Eur Team Ch) 1981-83. GB v Europe 1982. Europe v South America 1982

Daly, Fred
Born Portrush on 11th October, 1911

Opn Open Champion 1947, runner-up 1948, joint third 1950, third 1952
Tls Irish Open 1946
Maj PGA Match Play 1947-48-52. Dunlop Southport 1948. Penfold 1948. Lotus 1950. Daks 1952
Oth Ulster Professional 1936-40-41-42-43-46-51-55-56-57-58. Irish Professional 1940-46-52. Irish Dunlop 1946-52
Int Ryder Cup 1947-49-51-53. Ireland 1936-37-38. World Cup 1954-55

Darcy, Eamonn
Born 7th August, 1952. Turned Professional 1969

Tls Spanish Open 1983
Maj Sumrie 1976-78. Greater Manchester Open 1977
Ove Air New Zealand Open 1980. Cock o' the North Open 1981. Kenya Open 1982. Mufulira Open 1984
Oth Irish Dunlop 1976. Cacharel World Under-25 1976. Irish Match Play 1981
Int Ryder Cup 1975-77-81. Ireland in Double Diamond 1975-76-77. Ireland in World Cup 1976-77-84-85. GB v Europe 1976; v South Africa 1976. Hennessy-Cognac Cup 1984
Mis Second in Order of Merit 1976

Davies, G
Born

Chp Welsh Amateur Stroke Play 1983
Int Wales (Home Int) 1981-82-83

Davies, John C
Born London on 14th February, 1948

Add April Cottage, Coronation Road, Ascot, Berks
Cls Mid-Surrey, Sunningdale, Royal Cinque Ports, Killarney
Chp Runner-up Amateur Championship 1976. Runner-up English Amateur 1971-76. Second in English Open Amateur Stroke Play 1977
Maj Berkshire Trophy 1969-71 (tied). Royal St George's Challenge Cup 1972-73-74-75-76-77. Sunningdale Foursomes 1968-72. Antlers Royal Mid-Surrey 1969-75-77. Golf Illustrated Gold Vase 1973-77. Prince of Wales Cup 1975. Berkhamsted Trophy 1976-78-79
Reg Surrey Amateur 1971-72-77
Ove Second equal in South African Open Amateur Stroke Play 1974
Int Walker Cup 1973-75-77-79. Eisenhower Trophy 1974-76 (winning team). GB v Europe 1972-74-76-78; England (Home Int) 1969-70-71-72-73-74-78; (Eur Team Ch) 1973-75-77
Mis Member of European Team to tour South Africa 1974

Davies, Karen L
Born 19th June, 1965

Jun Welsh Girls 1980-82
Oth Florida State Tournament 1985. South-Eastern USA Championship 1985
Int Curtis Cup 1986. Wales (Home Int) 1981-82-83 (Eur Ladies Under-22) 1981-82-83-84-85-86

Davies, Miss Laura
Born 5th October, 1963. Turned Professional 1985

Maj London Foursomes 1981. Welsh Open Stroke-Play 1984. English Intermediate 1983
Reg South-Eastern Champion 1983-84
Jun Surrey Girls 1982
Int England (Home Int) 1983-84. Vilmorin Trophy 1984. Curtis Cup 1984.
WPGA Belgian Ladies Open 1985. Order of Merit 1985. McEwan's Lager Classic 1986. Greater Manchester Tournament 1986

Davies, Miss Pamela
See Mrs Large

Davies, Miss Zara
See Mrs SM Bolton

Davis, Mark
Born 4th July, 1964

Chp English Open Amateur Stroke Play 1984
Maj Golf Illustrated Gold Vase 1985. Prince of Wales Cup 1983. Lagonda Trophy 1984
Reg Essex Amateur 1983
Int England (Home Int) 1984-85

Dawson, Peter
Born Doncaster on 9th May, 1950. Turned Professional 1970

Maj Double Diamond Individual 1975
Int Ryder Cup 1977. England in World Cup 1977. England in Double Diamond 1977
Amr Runner-up English Amateur 1969. England in Home International 1969. Carris Trophy 1968. Youth International 1969-70. Boy International 1967
Mis Plays left-handed

De Bendern, Count John (John de Forest)
Born 1907

Add Villa Roveray, 1602 La Croix/Lutry, Vaud-1602, Switzerland
Cls Royal and Ancient, Sunningdale, Addington, Lausanne
Chp Amateur Champion 1932, runner-up 1931
Reg Surrey Amateur 1931-49
Ove Austrian Amateur 1937. Czechoslovakian Amateur 1937
Int Walker Cup 1932. England (Home Int) 1931

Deeble, Peter George
Born Alnwick on 27th February, 1954

Add 19 The Maltings, Alnwick, Northumberland
Cls Alnmouth, Alnwick, Ponteland (Hon), Hexham (Hon), Rothbury (Hon), Washington (Hon), Tynedale (Hon)
Chp English Amateur 1976-80

Maj Antlers Royal Mid-Surrey 1976. Lytham Trophy 1977. Berkhamsted Trophy 1975. EGUC of C Tour 1982. County Champion of Champions 1982
Reg Northumberland Amateur 1975-82-83. Northumberland Stroke Play 1973-75-77-78-79. Northumberland and Durham Open 1976
Jun Boy International 1970-71. Youth International 1973-75-76
Int Walker Cup 1977-81. GB v Europe 1978. Europe v South America 1980. GB in Colombian International 1978. England (Home Int) 1975-76-77-78-80-81-83; (Eur Team Ch) 1979-81; v Scotland 1979; v France 1982. England in Fiat Trophy 1980

Deighton, Dr FWG

Born Glasgow on 21st May, 1927

Add 4 Hatfield Drive, Glasgow W2
Cls Royal and Ancient, Western Gailes, Elie, Glasgow, Hilton Park (Hon), North Hants
Chp Scottish Amateur 1956-59
Maj Edward Trophy 1954. Gleneagles Silver Tassie 1956. Tennant Cup 1958-60-64
Oth Boyd Quaich 1947 (tied). Royal and Ancient Silver Cross 1953-60-63-70-73. Royal Medal 1956-59-61-63-66-73. Glennie Medal 1956-58-59-60-66-70-73
Reg West of Scotland Amateur 1959. Dunbartonshire Amateur 1949-50-53-54. Glasgow Amateur 1951-55
Int Walker Cup 1951-57. GB Commonwealth Team 1954-59. GB v Professionals 1956-57. Scotland (Home Int) 1950-52-53-56-58-59-60; v South Africa 1954; v New Zealand 1954; v Scandinavia 1956
Mis Member of British Touring Team to South Africa 1952

Douglas, Miss Katrina

Born 6th September, 1960. Turned Professional 1984

Chp British Ladies 1982
Maj Critchley Salver 1983
Ove Portuguese Champion 1983
Reg Gloucestershire Champion 1980-81-82-83-84
Jun Scottish Girls Stroke-Play 1981
Int England (Home Int) 1981-82. Curtis Cup 1982. European Team Championship 1983. Vagliano Trophy 1983
WPGA For Classic 1984. Swedish Ladies Open 1984. Rookie of the Year 1984

Dowling, Miss Deborah

Born 26th July, 1962. Turned Professional 1981

Reg Surrey Champion 1980
Int England in European Team Championship 1981
WPGA Jersey Open, Woodhall Hills 1983. Portuguese Ladies Open 1985

Downes, Paul

Born Coventry on 27th September, 1959

Add 105 Mantilla Drive, Styvechale Grange, Coventry CV3 6LJ
Cls Coventry (Hon)
Chp English Amateur 1978. English Amateur Stroke Play 1982
Maj Berkshire Trophy 1980
Reg Midland Open Amateur Stroke Play 1976-77-80. Warwickshire Match Play 1977-82. Warwickshire Open 1982
Ove Leading Amateur Malaysian Dunlop Masters 1977. Leading Amateur Singapore Open Championship 1978
Jun Boy International 1974-75-76-77. Youth International 1976-77-78-79-80-81
Int England (Home Int) 1976-77-78-80-81-82; (Eur Team Ch) 1977-79-81. GB v Europe 1980

Draper, Mrs Marjorie Lilian (formerly Mrs Peel, *née* Thomas)

Born Edinburgh on 18th June, 1905

Add Broadbury, Gullane, East Lothian
Cls Gullane
Chp Scottish Ladies 1954, runner-up 1952-62
Maj Worplesdon Mixed Foursomes 1952
Reg East of Scotland Ladies 1951-52-54-55-56-57-61. East Lothian Ladies 1950
Int Curtis Cup 1954. GB v France and Belgium 1955. Scotland (Home Int) 1929-34-37-49-50-51-52-53-54-55-56-57-58-62 (non-playing captain 1961-63-65)
Mis Non-playing captain Vagliano Trophy Team 1963. President Scottish Ladies Golfing Association 1973-75

Drew, Norman Vico

Born Belfast on 25th May, 1932

Chp Irish Open Amateur 1952-53
Maj North of Ireland Open Amateur 1950-52. East of Ireland Open Amateur 1952
Int Walker Cup 1953. Ireland (Home Int) 1952-53. Ryder Cup 1959. Ireland in World Cup 1960-61
Mis Turned Professional 1958
Maj Yorkshire Evening News 1959
Oth Irish Professional 1959. Irish Dunlop 1959. Ulster Professional 1966-72

Duncan, Colonel Anthony Arthur, OBE

Born Cardiff on 10th December, 1914

Add Steepways Corner, Churt Road, Hindhead, Surrey
Cls Royal and Ancient, Southerndown, Hindhead, Porthcawl
Chp Runner-up Amateur Championship 1939. Welsh Amateur 1938-48-52-54, runner-up 1933
Maj Worplesdon Mixed Foursomes 1946-47. Hampshire Hog 1959
Oth President's Putter 1948-58
Int Wales (Home Int) 1933-34-36-38-47-48-49 (capt)-50-51-52-53-54-55-56-57-58 (capt)-59
Mis Walker Cup 1953 (capt). Chairman Walker Cup Selection Committee 1954-55. Won all six matches in 1956 Home Internationals. President Oxford and Cambridge Golfing Society 1979-83

Evans, Albert David

Born Newton, Brecon, South Wales on 28th August, 1911

Add Newton House, Kilcot, Newent, Glos
Cls Royal and Ancient, Royal Porthcawl. Hon member of Brecon, Ross-on-Wye, Hereford, Worcestershire, Builth Wells, Pennard, Monmouth, Killarney
Chp Welsh Amateur 1949-61
Reg Herefordshire Amateur 1938-46-49-51-53-54-55-59-60-61-62. Breconshire Amateur 1929-31-32-33-34-37
Int Wales (Home Int) 1931-32-33-34-35-38-39-47-48-49-50-51-52-53-54-55-56, capt 1960-61-62-63-64-65; v Australia 1954
Misc Walker Cup Selector 1964-75

Evans, Duncan

Born Crewe on 23rd January, 1959

Add 9 Lancaster Avenue, Leek, Staffs ST13 8AX
Cls Leek (Hon), Conway (Hon), Holyhead (Hon), Royal Porthcawl (Hon), Westwood (Hon)
Chp Amateur Champion 1980. Second in Welsh Amateur Stroke Play 1980. Welsh Amateur Stroke Play Championship 1981
Reg Staffordshire Amateur 1979. Aberconwy Trophy 1981
Jun Youth International 1980
Int GB v Europe. Europe v South America 1980. Wales (Home Int) 1978-80; v Ireland 1979; in Fiat Trophy 1980. Walker Cup 1981; (Eur Team Ch) 1981

Evans, HJ
Born

Chp Welsh Amateur Stroke Play 1978
Maj Duncan Putter 1979
Int Wales (Home Int) 1976-77-78-80-81-84-85; (Eur Team Ch) 1979-81

Everard, Miss D Mary
See Mrs Laupheimer

Faldo, Nicholas Alexander
Born Welwyn Garden City on 18th July, 1957. Turned Professional 1976

Chp English Amateur 1975
Maj Berkshire Trophy 1975. Scrutton Jug 1975. County Champion of Champions 1975
Reg Hertfordshire Amateur 1975
Ove South African Golf Union Special Stroke Championship 1975
Jun British Youths 1975. Boy International 1974. Youth International 1975
Int GB Commonwealth Team 1975. England (Home Int) 1975
Tls French Open 1983. Swiss Open 1983
Maj Skol Lager 1977. Colgate PGA 1978. Sun Alliance PGA 1980-81. Tour Players Championship 1982. Martini International 1983. Lawrence Batley International 1983. Car Care International 1983-4
Ove ICL International (SA) 1979. Heritage Classic (USA) 1984
Int Ryder Cup 1977-79-81-83-85. GB v Europe 1978-80. England in World Cup 1977. England in Double Diamond 1977. Hennessy-Cognac Cup 1984. Dunhill Cup 1985-86. Nissan Cup 1986
Mis Rookie of the Year 1977. Harry Vardon Trophy 1983

Fallon, John
Born at Lanark on 29th April, 1913

Opn Second in Open Championship 1955. Third in Open Championship 1939
Maj PGA Match Play runner-up 1954. Stuart C Goodwin 5000 Guineas 1956 (tied)
Oth Leeds Challenge Cup 1937-49. Northern England Professional 1950-53-56
Int Ryder Cup 1955. Non-playing captain 1963. Scotland 1936-37-38

Faulkner, Max
Born Bexhill, Sussex on 29th July, 1916. Turned Professional June 1933

Opn Open Championship 1951
Tls Spanish Open 1952-53-57. Portuguese Open 1968
Maj Dunlop Southport 1946. Dunlop 1949-52. Penfold Foursomes 1949. Lotus 1949. Dunlop Masters 1951. PGA Match Play 1953. Irish Hospitals 1959
Oth West of England Open Professional 1947. Sunningdale Foursomes 1950. Southern England Professional 1964. Pringle Seniors 1968-70
Int Ryder Cup 1947-49-51-53-57

Feherty, David
Born in Bangor, NI on 13th August, 1958. Turned Professional 1976

Tls Italian Open 1986
Maj Scottish Open 1986
Oth ICL International, SA
Int Ireland; Dunhill Cup 1986

Ferguson, Mrs AJR (*née* Marjory Fowler)
Born North Berwick on 15th May, 1937

Add Clova, Westgate, North Berwick
Cls North Berwick, Gullane, Killarney (Hon)
Chp Runner-up Scottish Ladies 1966-71
Reg East of Scotland Ladies 1959-60-62-75. East Lothian Ladies 1957-58-59-60-61-62-63-64-66-67-69-74-81
Ove Portuguese Ladies 1960
Int Curtis Cup 1966. Vagliano Trophy 1965. Scotland (Home Int) 1959-62-63-64-65-66-67-69-70; (Eur Team Ch) 1965-67-71

Fiddian, Eric Westwood
Born Stourbridge on 28th March, 1910

Add Jasmine, Hanbury, Redditch, Worcs
Cls Stourbridge, Handsworth, Lindrick
Chp Runner-up Amateur Championship 1932. English Amateur 1932, runner-up 1935. Runner-up Irish Open Amateur 1933
Reg Worcestershire Amateur 1928-30-50. Midland Counties 1931
Jun Boys Champion 1927. England Boy International 1926-27
Int Walker Cup 1932-34. England (Home Int) 1929-30-31-32-33-34-35
Mis Had two holes-in-one in the Final of 1933 Irish Open Amateur

Fishwick, Miss Diana L
See Mrs AC Critchley

Foster, Rodney
Born Shipley, Yorkshire on 13th October, 1941

Add 5 Cliffestone Drive, Morton, Keighley, Yorkshire
Cls Royal and Ancient Hon member of Bradford, Halifax, Leeds, West Bowling, Ilkley, East Bierley
Chp Runner-up English Amateur 1964. English Open Amateur Stroke Play 1969 (tied)-70, second 1965
Maj Berkshire Trophy 1964. Lytham Trophy 1967-68. County Champion of Champions 1963 (tied)
Reg Yorkshire Amateur 1963-64-65-67-70
Jun Boy International 1958. Youth International 1959
Int Walker Cup 1965-67-69-71-73 (non-playing captain 1979). GB v Europe 1964-66-68-70 (non-playing captain 1980). Eisenhower Trophy 1964-70 (non-playing captain 1980). GB Commonwealth Team 1967-71. England (Home Int) 1963-64-66-67-68-69-70-71-72 (non-playing captain 1976-77-78); (Eur Team Ch) 1963-65-67-69-71-73 (non-playing captain 1977)

Fowler, Miss Marjory
See Mrs AJR Ferguson

Francis, Craig
Born London on 18th March, 1950

Add Bird Cay, PO Box N626, Nassau, Bahamas
Cls Sunningdale, Lyford Cay, Geneva, Lausanne
Maj Third in Golf Illustrated Gold Vase 1973. Runner-up Berkshire Trophy 1974
Ove Luxembourg Amateur 1972-75-82. Swiss Amateur 1973-74-77. Swiss Amateur Stroke Play 1982. Belgian Amateur 1975. Italian Amateur 1982, runner-up 1972-81. Runner-up Dutch Amateur 1976

Frearson, Mrs Diane (*née* Robb)
See Mrs Bailey

Gallacher, Bernard
Born Bathgate on 9th February, 1949

Chp Scottish Open Amateur Stroke Play 1967
Maj Tennant Cup 1967
Reg Lothians Amateur 1967
Jun Boy International 1965-66

Int Scotland (Home Int) 1967
Mis Turned Professional end of 1967
Tls Spanish Open 1977. French Open 1979
Maj Schweppes 1969. Wills 1969. Martini International 1971-82. Carrolls International 1974. Dunlop Masters 1974-75. Tournament Players' Championship 1980. Greater Manchester Open 1981. Jersey Open 1982-84
Ove Zambia Eagle Open 1969. Zambia Cock o' the North 1969. Mufulira Open 1970
Oth Scottish Professional 1971-73-74-77. Coca-Cola Young Professionals 1973
Int Ryder Cup 1969-71-73-75-77-79-81-83. Scotland in World Cup 1969-71-74-82-83. Scotland in Double Diamond 1971-72-73-74-75-76-77. GB v Europe 1974-78-82; v South Africa 1976. Hennessy-Cognac Cup 1984
Mis Harry Vardon Trophy 1969 (then youngest ever winner). Scottish Sportsman of the Year 1969. Frank Moran Trophy 1973. Rookie of the Year 1968.

Gannon, Mark Andrew
Born Drogheda, Ireland on 15th July, 1952

Add 39 Broadmeadows, Swords, Co Dublin
Cls Co Louth (Hon)
Chp Irish Amateur 1977, runner-up 1974-79
Maj South of Ireland Open Amateur 1973. Mullingar Trophy 1973. West of Ireland Open Amateur 1974. East of Ireland Open Amateur 1978
Jun Irish Boys 1968. Irish Youths 1971-72. Youth International 1971
Int GB v Europe 1974-78. Ireland (Home Int) 1973-74-77-78-80; (Eur Team Ch) 1979; v France, West Germany and Sweden 1978-80; in Fiat Trophy 1979; (Eur Team Ch) 1981

Garner, Mrs Maureen (*née* Madill)
Born 1st February, 1958
Born Coleraine, Co Derry on 1st February, 1958

Add 8 Larkhill Road, Portstewart, Co Derry, N Ireland
Cls Hon member of Portstewart, Royal Portrush, Milltown, Co Down, Brancepeth Castle, Delamere Forest
Chp British Ladies 1979. British Ladies Open Amateur Stroke Play 1980. Irish Foursomes 1980.
Maj Avia Foursomes 1980-85. Ulster Champion 1983
Reg North-West Scratch Cup 1978. Ulster Ladies 1980
Jun Girl International 1972-73-74-75-76
Int Vagliano Trophy 1979-81. GB Commonwealth Team 1979. Curtis Cup 1980. World Team Championship 1980. Ireland (Home Int) 1978-79-80-81-82-83; (Eur Team Ch) 1979-81-83

Garrett, Mrs Maureen (*née* Ruttle)
Born 22nd August, 1922

Chp French Ladies 1964
Int Curtis Cup 1960 (Captain). England (Home Int) 1960 (Captain). Vagliano Trophy 1960 (Captain)
Mis LGU President 1982-85. Bobby Jones Award 1983

Garvey, Miss Philomena K
Born Drogheda, Co Louth

Add 11 Whitehorn Road, Clonskeagh, Dublin
Cls Co Down, Co Lough, Portrush, Milltown
Chp British Ladies 1957, runner-up 1946-53-60-63. Irish Ladies 1946-47-48-50-51-53-54-55-57-58-59-60-62-63-70
Maj Worplesdon Mixed Foursomes 1955
Reg Munster Ladies 1951
Int Curtis Cup 1948-50-52-54-56-60. GB v France 1949-51-53-55; v Belgium 1951-53. Vagliano Trophy 1959-63. Ireland (Home Int) 1947-48-49-50-51-52-53-54-55-56-59-60-61-62-63-69; v Australia 1950
Mis Quarter-finalist US Ladies 1950. Turned Professional 1964, subsequently reinstated

Gemmill, Miss Alison
Born 13th September, 1958

Chp Scottish Ladies 1981-85
Reg Ayrshire Champion 1980-81-82-83-84
Int European Team Championship 1981. Scotland (Home Int) 1984
Jun Scottish Girl Stroke-play 1979

Gibbs, Mrs Roderick (*née* Carol Le Feuvre)
Born Jersey on 18th October, 1951

Add Les Arches, 14 Brackenborough, Brixworth, Northampton
Cls Jersey, Lee-on-the-Solent
Chp Runner-up English Ladies 1973
Maj Avia Foursomes 1974
Reg Jersey Ladies 1966-67-68. Hampshire Ladies 1970-71-72-73-74-76. South-Eastern Ladies 1974
Ove Dutch Ladies 1972
Jun English Girls 1969-70. British Girls 1970. Girl International 1968-69-70
Int Curtis Cup 1974. Vagliano Trophy 1973. England (Home Int) 1971-72-73-74; (Eur Team Ch) 1973
Mis Member of LGU Team to tour Australia 1973, and Under-25 team to tour Canada 1973

Gilford, David
Born 14th September, 1965. Turned Professional 1986

Chp English Amateur 1984
Maj Lagonda Trophy 1986
Jun British Youths 1986
Oth Carris Trophy 1981
Int Walker Cup 1985. GB v Europe 1986. England (Home Int) 1983-84-85

Glover, John
Born Belfast on 3rd March, 1933

Add Braetrees, 96A Hepburn Gardens, St Andrews, Fife KY16 9LN
Cls Killarney (Hon), New Club, St Andrews
Maj Formby Hare 1963
Chp Carris Trophy 1950. British Universities 1954-55
Reg Lancashire Amateur 1970
Jun Boy Champion 1950
Int Ireland (Home Int) 1951-52-53-55-59-60-62-70.
Mis Secretary Royal and Ancient Rules of Golf Committee

Godwin, Geoffrey Frank
Born Wanstead on 28th July, 1950

Add 2 Wyses Cottage, Wyses Road, Highwood Quarter, Chelmsford, Essex
Cls Thorndon Park
Maj Royal St George's Challenge Cup 1979. Prince of Wales Challenge Cup 1979. Hampshire Hog 1978
Reg Essex Amateur 1978-80
Int Walker Cup 1979-81. Europe v South America 1978. England (Home Int) 1976-77-78-80-81; (Eur Team Ch) 1979-81; v Scotland 1979; v France 1982

Gorry, Miss Mary Philomena
Born Baltinglass, Co Wicklow on 11th June, 1952

Add Main Street, Baltinglass, Co Wicklow
Cls Baltinglass (Hon), Grange (Hon)
Chp Irish Ladies 1975-78
Maj Hermitage Scratch Cup 1978
Reg South of Ireland Scratch Cup 1975-78-80. Irish Midland Ladies 1974-79. Leinster Ladies 1977-79. Ulster Ladies 1979. Connaught Ladies 1979
Jun Girl International 1970
Int Vagliano Trophy 1977. Ireland (Home Int) 1971-72-73-74-75-76-77-78-79-80; (Eur Team Ch) 1971-73-75-77-79; in Fiat Trophy 1978
Mis Irish Lady Golfer of the Year 1977-78. Non-playing captain of Irish team for European Ladies' Junior Championship 1983

Gourlay, Miss Mary Perceval (Molly), OBE

Born Kempshott Park, Basingstoke, 1898

Add Queries, 51 Brackendale Road, Camberley, Surrey Tel Camberley 23315
Cls Hon member of Camberley Heath, Temple, Basingstoke, Dorset, Sunningdale Ladies, Beaconsfield, Winchester, Maccauvlei, Bastad
Chp English Ladies 1926-29, runner-up 1931
Maj Worplesdon Mixed Foursomes 1929-30-34
Oth Veteran Ladies 1962
Reg Surrey Ladies 1923-26-27-31-33-34-38
Ove French Ladies 1923-28-29. Belgian Ladies 1925-26. Swedish Ladies 1932-36-39
Int Curtis Cup 1932-34. GB v Canada 1934; v France 1931-32-33-39. England (Home Int) 1923-24-27-28-29-31-32-33-34
Mis Member LGU team to tour South Africa 1933. Non-playing captain English Ladies 1957. Chairman LGU 1957-58-59. President ELGA 1963-65. Retired from playing aged 73 when handicap was 4

Green, Charles Wilson

Born Dumbarton on 2nd August, 1932

Add 51 Napier Avenue, Cardross, Dunbartonshire
Cls Dumbarton, Cardross, Helensburgh
Chp Scottish Amateur 1970-82-83, runner-up 1971-80. Scottish Open Amateur Stroke Play 1975, 1984, second 1967-83
Maj Lytham Trophy 1970 (tied)-74. Eden Tournament 1959. Tennant Cup 1968-70-75. Edward Trophy 1968-73-74-75
Reg West of Scotland Amateur 1962-70-79. Dunbartonshire Amateur 1960-67-68-73-77. Dunbartonshire Match Play 1965-67-69-71-74. Glasgow Amateur 1979
Int Walker Cup 1963-69-71-73-75 (non-playing captain 1983-85). GB v Scandinavia 1962; v Europe 1962-66-68-70-72-74-76. Eisenhower Trophy 1970-72. GB Commonwealth Team 1971. Scotland (Home Int) 1961-62-63-64-65-67-68-69-70-71-72-73-74-75-76-77-78 (non-playing captain 1980); v Australia 1964; (Eur Team Ch) 1965-67-69-71-73-75-77-79; v Belgium 1973-75-77-78; v Spain 1977; v Italy 1979; v England 1979
Mis Leading Amateur Open Championship 1962. Frank Moran Trophy 1974. British Selector 1980. Scottish Sports Photographer Award 1983

Greenhalgh, Miss Julia

Born Bolton on 6th January, 1941

Add Woodliving, Under Billinge Lane, Blackburn BB2 6RL
Cls Hon member of Pleasington, Killarney, Ganton, Hermitage
Chp British Ladies Stroke Play 1974-75. Runner-up British Ladies Open Amateur 1978. English Ladies 1966-79. Welsh Ladies Open Amateur Stroke Play 1977
Maj Astor Salver 1969-79. Hermitage Cup 1977. Hampshire Rose 1977. Sunningdale Foursomes 1978
Reg Lancashire Ladies 1961-62-66-68-73-75-76-77-78. Northern Ladies 1961-62
Ove New Zealand Ladies 1963
Jun Scottish Girls Open Stroke Play 1960. Girl International 1957-58-59
Int Curtis Cup 1964-70-74-76-78. Vagliano Trophy 1961-65-75-77. GB Commonwealth Team 1963-75. World Team 1970 (capt)-74 (capt)-78. England (Home Int) 1960-61-63-66-69-70-71-76-77-78; (Eur Team Ch) 1971-75-77-79
Mis Leading Amateur (4th) in Australian Wills Ladies Open Stroke Play 1974. Daks Woman Golfer of the Year 1974. Selected for 1966 Curtis Cup and 1979 Vagliano Trophy but withdrew due to wrist injury

Gregson, Malcolm Edward

Born Leicester on 15th August, 1943. Turned Professional 1961

Maj Schweppes 1967. RTV 1967. Daks 1967-68. Martini 1967 (tied). Sumrie 1972
Ove Zambia Cock o' the North 1974. Gambian Open 1981
Oth Pannal Foursomes 1964. British Assistants 1964
Int Ryder Cup 1967. England in World Cup 1967. England 1967. GB v France 1966. England in Double Diamond 1975
Amr Boy International 1959-60
Mis Harry Vardon Trophy 1967

Greig, David G

Born Broughty Ferry on 24th January, 1950

Add 12 Church Street, Carnoustie, Angus
Cls Carnoustie (Hon), Caledonia
Chp Scottish Amateur 1975
Reg Angus Stroke Play 1978. Angus Match Play 1978. Scottish Counties Champion of Champions 1978. East of Scotland Open Amateur 1980
Oth Boyd Quaich 1972. British Universities Stroke Play 1969
Jun Scottish Boys 1967. Boy International 1967. Youth International 1969-71
Int GB Commonwealth Team 1975. Scotland (Home Int) 1972-73-75

Grice-Whittaker, Mrs Peggy

Born 11th October, 1964. Turned Professional 1985

Chp English Intermediate Champion 1984. English Stroke-Play 1984
Reg Yorkshire Champion 1981-82-83. Northern Foursomes 1984
Jun English Girls 1983
Int England (Home Int) 1983-84. European Team Championship 1983. Curtis Cup 1984. Vilmorin Trophy 1984. Espirito Santo 1984
WPGA Belgian Open 1986

Hargreaves, Jack

Born Fleetwood on 12th February, 1914. Turned Professional 1930

Opn Third in Open Championship 1948
Maj Spalding 1951. Swallow-Harrogate 1953. Goodwin Foursomes 1953
Oth Midland Professional 1952-60
Int Ryder Cup 1951
Mis Secretary Midland PGA. Captain PGA 1977

Harrington, J

Born

Chp Irish Amateur 1979
Int Ireland (Home Int) 1960-61-74-75-76 (Eur Team Ch) 1975

Harris, Mrs Marley (formerly Mrs Spearman)

Born in 1928

Add Broom Cottage, Exmouth Road, Budleigh Salterton, East Devon
Cls Sudbury
Chp British Ladies 1961-62. English Ladies 1964
Maj Sunningdale Foursomes 1965. Kayser-Bondor Foursomes 1958 (tied). Casa Pupo Foursomes 1965. Worplesdon Mixed Foursomes runner-up 1956-64. Roehampton Gold Cup 1965. Astor Salver 1964-65. Astor Princes' Trophy 1964-65. Hovis Ladies 1965. Spalding Ladies 1956. London Ladies Foursomes 1960
Reg Middlesex Ladies 1955-56-57-58-59-61-64-65. South-East Ladies 1956-58-61
Ove New Zealand Ladies Stroke Play 1963
Int Curtis Cup 1960-62-64. Vagliano Trophy 1959-61. GB Commonwealth Team 1959-63. England (Home Int) 1955-56-57-58-59-60-61-62-63-64-65
Mis Golf Writers' Trophy 1962. Non-playing captain English Team European Team Championship 1971

Harrold, Miss J Lynne
Born London on 9th November, 1956

Cls Gerrards Cross (Hon), Wentworth
Chp English Ladies 1976, runner-up 1975
Maj Roehampton Gold Cup 1974
Reg South-Eastern Ladies 1976. Bucks Ladies 1974-75-76-77
Jun Girl International 1973-74-75
Int GB in Colombian International 1977. England (Home Int) 1974-75-76; (Eur Team Ch) 1975
Mis Turned Professional summer 1977

Hastings, Miss Joan
See Mrs J Rennie

Hastings, Mrs JL (*née* Dorothea Sommerville)
Born Glasgow on 21st June, 1934

Add 13 Calside Avenue, Paisley, Renfrewshire
Cls Haggs Castle (Hon), Troon Ladies (Hon), Erskine
Chp Scottish Ladies 1958, runner-up 1960
Reg West of Scotland Ladies 1961. Renfrewshire Ladies 1956-57-58-59-61-63-83
Jun Junior International 1953. Junior Tour of Australasia 1955
Int Curtis Cup 1958. Vagliano Trophy 1963. Scotland (Home Int) 1955-56-57-58-59-60-61-62-63

Hawksworth, John
Born 27th March, 1961

Maj Berkhamsted Trophy 1983. Hampshire Hog 1984. Lytham Trophy 1984
Int Walker Cup 1985. England (Home Int) 1984-85

Heathcoat-Amory, Lady (*née* Joyce Wethered)
Born 17th November, 1901

Add Knightshayes House, Tiverton, Devon. Tel (08842) 2438
Cls Worplesdon
Chp British Ladies 1922-24-25-29, runner-up 1921. English Ladies 1920-21-22-23-24
Maj Worplesdon Mixed Foursomes 1922-23-27-28-31-32-33-36. Sunningdale Foursomes 1935-36
Reg Surrey Ladies 1921-22-24-29-32
Int Curtis Cup 1932. GB v France 1931. England (Home Int) 1921-22-23-24-25-29
Mis Forfeited Amateur status and toured USA in 1935. Reinstated as Amateur after the war

Hedges, Peter J
Born 30th March, 1947

Add 21 The Rise, Sevenoaks, Kent
Cls Langley Park (Hon), Royal Cinque Ports, Addington, Wildernesse, Royal and Ancient
Chp English Open Amateur Stroke Play 1976
May Royal St George's Challenge Cup 1970. Prince of Wales Challenge Cup 1972-73-74-77. Berkshire Trophy 1973-76-78. Golf Illustrated Gold Vase 1974. Scrutton Jug 1976
Reg Kent Amateur 1968-71-79. Kent Open 1970-74
Jun Youth International 1968
Int Walker Cup 1973-75. GB v Europe 1974-76. Eisenhower Trophy 1974. England (Home Int) 1970-73-74-75-76-77-78-82; (Eur Team Ch) 1973-75-77
Mis Member of European Team to tour South Africa 1974

Hedges, Mrs Susan Claire (*née* Whitlock)
Born Beckenham, Kent on 8th May, 1947

Add 8 Stuart Close, Maidstone, Kent
Cls Wrotham Heath (Hon), Royal Cinque Ports, Langley Park
Chp Welsh Ladies Open Amateur Stroke Play 1978. Runner-up English Ladies 1979
Maj Central England Mixed Foursomes 1977-81; Hoylake Mixed Foursomes 1982
Reg Kent Ladies 1976-79
Ove Belgian Ladies 1974. Luxembourg Ladies 1976-77. Zaire Ladies 1980
Int Vagliano Trophy 1979. GB Commonwealth Team 1979. England (Home Int) 1979; (Eur Team Ch) 1979
Mis Leading Amateur (3rd) British Ladies Open 1979

Henson, Mrs Dinah (*née* Oxley)
Born Dorking on 17th October, 1948

Add No 12, The Birches, Heathside Road, Woking, Surrey
Cls West Byfleet (Hon), Killarney (Hon), Fairfield, US (Hon)
Chp British Ladies 1970. English Ladies 1970-71, runner-up 1968. Second in British Ladies Stroke Play 1969
Maj Wills Ladies 1969-70-71. Worplesdon Mixed Foursomes 1968-77. Newmark International 1975 (tied)-77
Reg Surrey Ladies 1967-70-71-76
Jun British Girls 1963. English Girls 1965. French Girls 1969. Girl International 1964-65-66
Int Curtis Cup 1968-70-72-76. Vagliano Trophy 1967-69-71. World Team 1970. GB Commonwealth Team 1967-71. England (Home Int) 1967-68-69-70-75-76-77-78; (Eur Team Ch) 1971-77
Mis Daks Woman Golfer of the Year 1970. Leading Amateur Colgate European Ladies Open 1974

Hetherington, Mrs GW (*née* McClure)
See Mrs Jean Holmes

Hill, George Alec, DSO
Born Northwood, Middlesex in 1908

Add Two Trees, Bowling Street, Sandwich, Kent
Cls Royal and Ancient, Royal St George's, Hon Company of Edinburgh Golfers, Sandy Lodge
Jun Boy International 1926
Int Walker Cup 1936, non-playing captain 1955. England (Home Int) 1936-37
Mis Chairman R and A Championship Committee 1955. Chairman Rules of Golf Committee 1958-59. Captain Royal and Ancient 1964-65

Hoey, TBC
Born

Chp Irish Amateur 1984

Holmes, Mrs Jean (formerly Mrs GW Hetherington, *née* McClure)
Born Wanstead, Essex on 17th August, 1923

Add Elder House, 25 Mill Lane, Wateringbury, Kent ME18 5SP
Cls Wanstead, Hunstanton, Thorndon Park
Chp British Ladies 1946, runner-up 1958. English Ladies 1966
Reg Nottinghamshire Ladies 1949-50-51. Essex Ladies 1956-57
Int England (Home Int) 1957-66 (non-playing captain 1967)

Homer, Trevor Walter Brian
Born Bloxwich on 8th September, 1943

Chp Amateur Champion 1972-74
Maj Leicestershire Fox 1972. Harlech Gold Cross 1970
Int Walker Cup 1973. Eisenhower Trophy 1972. GB v Europe 1972. England (Home Int) 1972-73; (Eur Team Ch) 1973
Mis Turned Professional July 1974. Reinstated as Amateur in 1978

Hope, Miss Lesley Alexandra
Born Gullane, East Lothian on 22nd May, 1955

Add 16 Muirfield Drive, Gullane, East Lothian
Cls Gullane Ladies, Catterick
Chp Scottish Ladies Amateur 1975, runner-up 1979
Reg East of Scotland Ladies 1977-78
Int Scotland (Home Int) 1975-76-80; (Eur Team Ch) 1975-77-79; in Fiat Trophy 1979

Horton, Tommy
Born St Helens, Lancs on 16th June, 1941. Turned Professional 1957

Opn Joint leading British player in Open Championship 1976 (5th)-1977 (9th)
Tls South African Open 1970. Nigerian Open 1973. Zambian Open 1977
Maj Carrolls 1956-67. RTV 1968. PGA Match Play 1970. Gallaher Ulster 1971. Piccadilly 1972. Penfold 1974. Uniroyal International 1976. Dunlop Masters 1978
Ove Tobago Open 1975. Gambian Open 1975
Int Ryder Cup 1975-77. GB v France 1966. England in World Cup 1976. England in Double Diamond 1971-74-75-76-77. GB v Europe 1974-76
Mis Second in Order of Merit 1967. PGA Captain 1978

Hourihane, Miss Claire
Born 18th February, 1958

Chp Irish Ladies 1983-84-85
Reg South Ireland Cup 1977. Leinster Ladies 1980
Maj Hampshire Rose 1986
Ove South Atlantic (USA) 1983
Int Ireland (Home Int) 1979-80-82-84. Vagliano Trophy 1981. European Team Championship 1981-83. Curtis Cup 1984

Howard, Mrs Ann (*née* Phillips)
Born Prestwich on 22nd October, 1934

Add 4 Homefield Park, Ballasalla, Isle of Man
Cls Whitefield (Hon), Royal Birkdale, Castletown
Reg Lancashire Ladies 1957. Manx Ladies 1977-78
Ove Danish Ladies 1955
Jun British Girls 1952
Int Curtis Cup 1956-68. GB v France and Belgium 1955-57. England (Home Int) 1953-54-55-56 (non-playing captain 1979-80). Non-playing captain Senior European 1981

Huggett, Brian George Charles, MBE
Born Porthcawl on 18th November, 1936. Turned Professional 1951

Opn Second in Open Championship 1965. Third in 1962
Tls Dutch Open 1962. German Open 1963 Portuguese Open 1974
Maj Cox-Moore 1963. Smart-Weston 1965. Sumrie 1968-72. PGA Close 1967. Martini 1967 (tied)-68. Shell Winter Tournament 1967-68. PGA Match Play 1968, runner-up 1977. Daks 1969-71 (tied). Bowmaker 1969 (tied). Carrolls 1970. Dunlop Masters 1970. British Airways-Avis 1978
Ove Singapore International 1962. Algarve Open 1970
Oth Sunningdale Foursomes 1957. British Assistants 1958. Gleneagles Pro-Am 1961-65. East Anglian Open 1962-67. Turnberry Pro-Am 1968. Welsh Professional 1978
Int Ryder Cup 1963-67-69-71-73-75 (non-playing captain 1977). Wales in World Cup 1963-64-65-68-69-70-71-76-79. Wales in Double Diamond 1971-72-73-74-75-76-77. GB v Europe 1974-78 (capt)
Mis Vardon Trophy 1968. European American Express 1972

Hughes, Miss Ann
See Mrs JS Johnson

Huke, Miss Beverly Joan Mary
Born Great Yarmouth on 10th May, 1951. Turned Professional 1978

Add 302 Brook Street, Broughty Ferry, Dundee
Cls Cotswold Hills (Hon), Windmill Hill (Hon), Leighton Buzzard, Panmure Barry
Chp Runner-up British Ladies 1971. English Ladies 1975
Maj Roehampton Gold Cup 1971. Renfrew Rose Bowl 1976-77-78. Helen Holm Trophy 1977
Reg Gloucestershire Ladies 1972. Angus Ladies 1976
Jun Scottish Girls Open Stroke Play 1970-71. Girl International 1966-67-68
Int Curtis Cup 1972. Vagliano Trophy 1971-75. England (Home Int) 1971-72-75-76-77; (Eur Team Ch) 1975-77
WPGA Carlsberg (Ballater) 1979. Carlsberg (Rosemount) 1980. NABS Pro-Am 1st Pro Individual 1981. Winner Brickendon Grange and Stourbridge Pro-Am 1983; co-winner Lark Valley Classic 1983; Winner White Horse Whisky Challenge Trophy 1983. Trusthouse Forte Classic 1985. German Ladies Open 1984. Wester Volkswagen Classic 1986

Humphreys, Warren
Born Kingston, Surrey on 1st April, 1952

Chp English Amateur 1971
Maj Sunningdale Foursomes 1968. Antlers Royal Mid-Surrey 1969. Duncan Putter 1971. Lytham Trophy 1971
Jun Boy International 1967-68-69 (capt). Youth International 1969-70-71
Int Walker Cup 1971. GB v Europe 1970. England (Home Int) 1970-71; (Eur Team Ch) 1971
Mis Turned Professional Autumn 1971. Accles and Pollock Award 1972. Portuguese Open 1985

Hunt, Bernard John, MBE
Born Atherstone on 2nd February, 1930. Turned Professional 1946

Opn Third in Open Championship 1960. Leading British player (4th) 1964
Tls Egyptian Open 1956. Belgian Open 1957. German Open 1961. Brazilian Open 1962. French Open 1967
Maj Spalding 1953-57. Goodwin Foursomes 1953-54. PGA Match Play runner-up 1958. Bowmaker 1958 (tied). Martini 1961. Daks 1961. Carrolls 1963. Swallow-Penfold 1963. Smart-Weston 1963. Gevacolor 1963. Dunlop Masters 1963-65. Gallaher Ulster 1965-67. Rediffusion 1964. Piccadilly 1966. Penfold 1970. Sumrie 1970-73. Agfacolor 1970. Wills 1971
Ove Algarve Open 1969. BP Italy 1969
Oth British Assistants 1953. Gleneagles-Saxone 1953. Southern England Professional 1959-60-62-67. West of England Open Professional 1960-61
Int Ryder Cup 1953-57-59-61-63-65-67-69, non-playing captain 1973-75. England in World Cup 1958-59-60-62-63-64-68. England in Double Diamond 1971-72-73
Mis In Spalding Tournament 1953 scored 28 for first nine holes in second round. Harry Vardon Trophy 1958-60-65. Second (equal) in Order of Merit 1964

Hutcheon, Ian C
Born Monifieth, Angus on 22nd February, 1942

Add 10 Laird Street, Monifieth, Angus
Cls Monifieth (Hon), Grange and Dundee (Hon)
Chp Scottish Amateur 1973. Scottish Open Amateur Stroke Play 1971-74-79
Maj Tennant Cup 1976. Lytham Trophy 1980. Scottish Champion of Champions 1980-81-86
Reg Scottish Central District Amateur 1972. Angus Match Play 1965-70-72. Angus Stroke Play 1968-71-72-74. North of Scotland District Amateur Stroke Play 1975-76-82
Ove North of Spain Stroke Play 1972

Int GB v Europe 1974-76. Eisenhower Trophy 1974-76 (winning team and joint winning individual)-80. Scotland (Home Int) 1971-72-73-74-75-76-77-78-80; (Eur Team Ch) 1973-75-77-79-81; v Spain 1972-77; v Belgium 1973-75-77-78-80; v France 1978-80-81; v Italy 1979; in Fiat Trophy 1979. GB in Dominican International 1973. Walker Cup 1975-77-79-81. GB in Colombian International 1975. GB Commonwealth Team 1975
Mis Frank Moran Trophy 1976

Irvin, Miss Ann Lesley
Born 11th April, 1943

Add 177 Victoria Road, Thornton, Lancs
Cls Lytham (Hon), Lytham Green Drive (Hon)
Chp British Ladies 1973, runner-up 1969. English Ladies 1967-74. British Ladies Stroke Play 1969. Second British Girls Championship 1961
Maj Roehampton Gold Cup 1967-68-69-72-76. Hovis Ladies 1966-68-70. Avia Foursomes 1968
Reg Northern Ladies 1963-64. Lancashire Ladies 1965-67-69-71-72-74. Northern Foursomes Championship 1973
Jun French Girls 1963. Girl International 1960-61
Int Curtis Cup 1962-68-70-76. Vagliano Trophy 1961-63-65-67-69-71-73-75. GB Commonwealth Team 1967-75. England (Home Int) 1962-63-65-67-68-69-70-71-72-73-75; (Eur Team Ch) 1965-67-69-71-73-75
Mis Daks Woman Golfer of the Year 1968-69. Captain of British Team to tour Australia 1973. Selected for 1974 Curtis Cup but withdrew through injury. Lancashire County Captain 1979. England Junior Captain 1981-82. International Selector 1981-82. England Selector 1981-82. County Selector and Junior Organiser

Jack, Robert Reid
Born Cumbernauld on 17th January, 1924

Add The Stell, Muirton, Drem, North Berwick EH39 5LW
Cls Hon Company of Edinburgh Golfers. Gullane. Hon member of Buchanan Castle, Dullatur, Bearsden
Chp Amateur Champion 1957. Scottish Amateur 1955
Maj Edward Trophy 1959. Tennant Cup 1961
Oth Royal and Ancient Royal Medal 1965-67. Silver Cross 1956-66. Glennie Medal 1965
Reg Glasgow Amateur 1953-54-58. Dunbartonshire Match Play 1949
Int Walker Cup 1957-59. Eisenhower Trophy 1958. GB Commonwealth Team 1959. GB v Europe 1956. Scotland (Home Int) 1950-51-54-55-56-57-58-59-61; v Scandinavia 1956-58
Mis Leading Amateur Open Championship 1959

Jacklin, Tony, OBE
Born Scunthorpe on 7th July, 1944. Turned Professional 1962

Opn Open Champion 1969. Third 1971-72. Leading British player 1970 (5th). U.S. Open Champion 1970
Tls Italian Open 1973. German Open 1979
Maj Blaxnit 1966. Pringle 1967. Dunlop Masters 1967-73. Wills 1970. Benson & Hedges Festival 1971. Viyella PGA Close 1972. Kerrygold International Classic 1976. Jersey Open 1981. Sun Alliance PGA 1982
Ove Forest Products, New Zealand 1967. Kimberley (SA) 1966 (tied), New Zealand PGA 1967. Greater Jacksonville Open, USA 1968-72. Lancome Trophy 1970. Dunlop International Australia 1972. Los Lagartos Open 1973-74. Scandinavian Enterprises Open 1974. Venezuelan Open 1979
Oth British Assistants 1965. English Professional 1977
Int Ryder Cup 1967-69-71-73-75-77-79-83 (Captain) 1985 (Captain). GB v Europe 1976. England in World Cup 1966-70-71-72. England in Double Diamond 1972-73-74-76-77
Amr Lincolnshire Open 1961
Mis Became the first British player since Harry Vardon to hold the Open and US Open titles simultaneously and the first British player to hold the US Open since Ted Ray in 1920. Hon Life President PGA. Rookie of the Year 1963

Jackson, Miss Barbara Amy Bridget
Born Birmingham on 10th July, 1936

Add 15 Kesteven Close, Edgbaston, Birmingham B15 2UT
Cls Royal St David's Edgbaston. Hon member of Handsworth, Hunstanton, Killarney
Chp Runner-up British Ladies 1964. English Ladies 1956, runner-up 1958
Maj Fairway and Hazard Foursomes 1954. Kayser Bondor Foursomes 1962. Avia Foursomes 1967. Worplesdon Mixed Foursomes 1960. Astor Prince's 1963
Reg Midland Ladies 1954-56-57-58-59-60-69. Staffordshire Ladies 1954-56-57-58-59-63-64-66-67-68-69-76
Ove German Ladies 1956. Canadian Ladies 1967
Jun British Girls 1954
Int Curtis Cup 1958-64-68. Vagliano Trophy 1959-63-65-67 (non-playing captain 1973-75). GB Commonwealth Team 1959-67. GB v Belgium 1957; v France 1957. World Team Championship 1964. England (Home Int) 1955-56-57-58-59-63-64-65-66 (non-playing captain 1973-74); (Eur Team Ch) 1975 (non-playing captain); v France 1964-66
Mis LGU International Selector 1983. English Selector 1983

Jacobs, John Robert Maurice
Born Lindrick, Yorkshire on 14th March, 1925. Turned Professional 1947

Tls Dutch Open 1957
Ove South African Match Play 1957
Int Ryder Cup 1955 (non-playing captain 1979-81). GB v Continent 1954-55-58
Mis Former PGA Tournament Director-General. TV commentator

James, Mark H
Born Manchester on 28th October, 1953. Turned Professional 1975

Chp English Amateur 1974. Runner-up Amateur Championship 1975
Reg Lincs Match Play 1972. Lincs Amateur 1975
Jun Boy International 1971. Youth International 1974-75
Opn Leading British player 1976 (tied 5th)-79 (4th)
Tls Italian Open 1982
Maj Leicestershire Fox 1974. PGA Match Play 1978. Carrolls Irish Open 1979-80. Welsh Classic 1979. GSI Open 1985. Benson & Hedges 1986
Ove Lusaka Open 1977. Tunisian Open 1983
Int England (Home Int) 1974-75; (Eur Team Ch) 1975. Walker Cup 1975. Ryder Cup 1977-79-81. GB v Europe 1978-80. England in World Cup 1978-79-82-84. Hennessy-Cognac Cup 1984
Mis Rookie of the Year 1976

Jamieson, Donald
Born

Chp Scottish Amateur 1980
Int Scotland (Home Int) 1980

Johnson, Mrs JS (*née* Ann Hughes)
Born Llandudno, Gwynedd on 18th October, 1946

Add 36 Churchill Road, Church Stretton, Salop
Cls Ludlow, Killarney (Hon)
Chp Welsh Ladies 1966-72-75, runner-up 1969-76
Reg Caernarvonshire and Anglesey Ladies 1964-68-69-72-78
Jun Welsh Girls 1960-63-64-65. Girl International 1965
Int Wales (Home Int) 1964-66-67-68-69-70-71-72-73-74-75-76-78-79; (Eur Team Ch) 1965-67-69-71-75-79

Johnson, Miss Patricia
Born 17th January, 1966

Chp English Ladies 1985. English Ladies Stroke-Play 1985
Maj Roehampton Gold Cup 1986
Reg South-Western Ladies 1984
Jun Devon Girls 1982
Int England (Home Int) 1984-85

Jones, E

Born

Chp Welsh Amateur 1985
Int Wales (Home Int) 1983-85-86

Jones, John Roger

Born Old Colwyn, Denbighshire on 14th June, 1944

Add 8 Northway Court, Bishopton, Swansea, West Glam
Cls Langland Bay (Hon)
Chp Welsh Amateur Stroke Play 1972-73-82, runner-up 1983. Welsh Amateur Championship 1983
Maj Harlech Gold Cross 1976
Reg Denbighshire Amateur 1969-71. Caernarvonshire and Anglesey Amateur 1970 (tied)-72-74-75. Glamorgan Amateur 1977-79. North Wales Amateur 1976. Carmarthenshire Amateur 1979-80. Landsdowne Trophy (Channel League) Stroke-Play 1979-80-83
Int Wales (Home Int) 1970-72-73-77-78-80-81-82-83; (Eur Team Ch) 1973-79-81-83; v Denmark 1976-80; v Ireland 1979; v Switzerland 1980; v Spain 1980; in Asian Team Championship 1979

Jones, SP

Born

Chp Welsh Amateur 1981
Int Wales (Home Int) 1981-82-83-84-85

Kelley, Michael John

Born Scarborough on 6th February, 1945

Add Red Gates, 108 Stepney Road, Scarborough
Cls Ganton, Hon member of Scarborough North Cliff, Bridlington, Bradford
Maj Lytham Trophy 1976. Antlers Royal Mid-Surrey 1972
Reg Yorkshire Amateur 1969-74-81. Yorkshire Open 1969-75. Champion of Champions 1981
Jun Boy International 1962. Youth International 1965-66
Int Walker Cup 1977-79. Eisenhower Trophy 1976 (winning team). GB v Europe 1976-78-82; GB in Colombian International 1978. England (Home Int) 1974-75-76-77-78-80-81-82; (Eur Team Ch) 1977-79; v France 1982

Keppler, Steven D

Born 17th February, 1961

Maj Berkshire Trophy 1982. Golf Illustrated Gold Vase 1983
Reg Surrey Amateur 1981
Int Walker Cup 1983. England (Home Int) 1982-83

King, Michael

Born 15th February, 1950. Turned Professional 1974

Maj St George's Hill Trophy 1970. County Champion of Champions 1970. Sunningdale Foursomes 1972. Lytham Trophy 1973 (tied). Tournament Players Championship 1979
Reg Berks, Bucks and Oxon Amateur 1968-69-70-73-74. Berks, Bucks and Oxon Open 1968-73
Int Walker Cup 1969-73. GB Commonwealth Team 1971. GB v Europe 1972. England (Home Int) 1971-72-73; (Eur Team Ch) 1971-73. Ryder Cup 1979. England in World Cup 1979

King, Samuel Leonard

Born Godden Green, Sevenoaks, Kent on 27th March, 1911

Opn Third in Open Championship 1939
Maj Daily Mail 1937. Yorkshire Evening News 1944-49
Oth British Assistants 1933. Dunlop-Southern 1936-37. Sunningdale Foursomes 1948. Teachers Senior 1961-62
Int Ryder Cup 1937-47-49. England 1934-36-37-38

Kyle, Alexander Thomson

Born Hawick on 16th April, 1907

Add 15 Burnbridge, Harrogate
Cls Royal and Ancient, Easingwold, Sandmoor, Moortown, Harrogate, Knaresborough, Peebles, Fulford (Hon)
Chp Amateur Champion 1939. Runner-up Irish Open Amateur 1946. Second in English Open Amateur Stroke Play 1952
Maj Newlands Trophy 1930
Reg Borders Amateur 1929-30. Yorkshire Amateur 1935-36
Int Walker Cup 1938-47-51. GB v South Africa 1952. Scotland (Home Int) 1938-47-49-50-51-52-53
Mis Played for British Seniors 1969-75

Langley, John DA

Born Northwood, Middlesex on 25th April, 1918

Add c/o Lloyds Bank Ltd, Law Courts Branch, 222 Strand, London WC2
Cls Sunningdale, Burnham (Hon), Swinley Forest, Fulwell (Hon), Metropolitan (Aus)
Chp English Amateur 1950, runner-up 1936
Maj Golf Illustrated Gold Vase 1952-53. St George's Hill Trophy 1952
Oth Carris Trophy 1936
Jun British Boys 1935. Boy International 1932-33-34-35
Int Walker Cup 1936-51-53. England (Home Int) 1950-51-52-53; v France 1950-52
Mis Chairman Royal and Ancient Selection Committee 1967 to 1969

Langmead, Jonathan

Born 3rd November, 1967

Chp English Amateur 1986
Int England (Home Int) 1986

Langridge, Mrs Susan (*née* Armitage)

Born Huddersfield on 5th April, 1943

Add Johannesburg, South Africa
Cls Walsall, Whittington Barracks (Hon)
Reg Midland Ladies 1961-65
Jun Scottish Girls Open Stroke Play 1962
Int Curtis Cup 1964-66. Vagliano Trophy 1963-65-67. England (Home Int) 1963-64-65-66-67

Large, Mrs (*née* Pamela Davies)

Born Coventry on 12th April, 1930

Add Springfield, Crackley Lane, Kenilworth, Warwickshire
Cls Coventry (Hon)
Chp English Ladies 1952, runner-up 1950
Reg Midland Ladies 1952. Warwickshire Ladies 1952
Jun British Girls 1949
Int England (Home Int) 1950-51-52; v Australia 1950
Mis Captain English Ladies (Home Int) Team 1981-82

Laupheimer, Mrs D Mary (*née* Everard)

Born Sheffield on 8th October, 1942

Add 45 Hallam Grange Close, Sheffield S10 4BN and 54 Greensward Lane, Sugar Land, Texas 77478, USA
Cls Hallamshire (Hon), Woodhall Spa (Hon), Kilton Forest (Hon), Lindrick, Somerset Hills (USA), Merion (USA)
Chp Runner-up British Ladies Amateur 1967. British Ladies Amateur Stroke Play 1970, second 1971-73. Second in British Ladies Open 1977. English Ladies 1972, runner-up 1964-77
Maj Astor Salver 1967-68-78. Hovis Ladies 1967. Roehampton Gold Cup 1970. Sunningdale Foursomes 1973. Hoylake Mixed Foursomes 1965-67-71-76. Avia Foursomes 1978

Reg North of England Ladies 1972. Yorkshire Ladies 1964-67-72-73-77
Int Curtis Cup 1970-72-74-78. Vagliano Trophy 1967-69-71-73. GB Commonwealth Team 1971. World Team Championship 1968-72 (capt)-78. England (Home Int) 1964-67-70-72-73-77-78; (Eur Team Ch) 1967-71-73-77
Mis Member of British team to tour Australia 1973. Captain English team to tour Kenya 1973

Laurence, Craig

Born 3rd August, 1963

Chp English Amateur 1983
Int England (Home Int) 1983-84-85

Lawrence, Miss Joan B

Born Kinghorn, Fife on 20th April, 1930

Add 36 Venturefair Avenue, Dunfermline, Fife
Cls Hon member Dunfermline, Aberdour, Killarney
Chp Scottish Ladies 1962-63-64, runner-up 1965. Scottish Veteran Ladies Champion 1982
Reg East of Scotland Ladies 1971-72. Fife Ladies 1953-57-58-59-60-61-62-63-64-65-67-68-69
Jun Girl International 1949
Int Curtis Cup 1964. World Team Champion 1964. GB Commonwealth Team 1971 (capt). Vagliano Trophy 1963-65. Scotland (Home Int) 1959-60-61-62-63-64-65-66-67-68-69-70 (non-playing captain 1977); (Eur Team Ch) 1965-67-69 (capt)-71 (non-playing captain 1977)
Mis LGU International Selector 1973-74-75-76-80-81-82-83. Treasurer Scottish Ladies Golfing Association from 1980

Leburn, Mrs Wilma (*née* Aitken)

Born 24th January, 1959

Chp British Girls 1977. Helen Holm Trophy 1978-80-82.
Maj Helen Holm Trophy 1978-80-82. Avia Foursomes 1982
Reg West of Scotland 1978-80-81. Renfrewshire Champion 1978-79-80-81-82
Jun Scottish Girls 1975-77. West of Scotland Girls 1977. Scottish International 1975-77-78
Int Scotland (Home Int) 1978-79-80-81-82-83. Vilmorin Cup 1979. European Team Championship 1979-81-83. Curtis Cup 1982. Vagliano Trophy 1981-83

Lee, Robert

Born in London on 12th October, 1961. Turned Professional 1982

Tls Brazilian Open 1985
Maj Cannes Open 1985

Lee Smith, Miss Jennifer

Born Newcastle-upon-Tyne on 2nd December, 1948. Turned Professional 1977

Add 41 Kirkbride Place, Eastfield Dale, Cramlington NE23 9XH
Cls Gosforth (Hon), Ponteland (Hon), Wideopen (Hon), Ganton (Hon), Hexham (Hon), Dunstanburgh Castle
Chp British Ladies Open Stroke Play 1976
Maj Wills Match Play 1974. Newmark 1976
Oth Hoylake Mixed Foursomes 1969
Reg Northumberland Ladies 1972-73-74
Int Curtis Cup 1974-76. England (Home Int) 1973-74-75-76; (Eur Team Ch) 1975. GB in Colombian International 1975. World Team Championship 1976. GB Commonwealth Team 1975
Mis Daks Woman Golfer of the Year 1976 (joint)
WPGA Carlsberg (Arcot Hall) 1979. Volvo Swedish Invitational 1980. Carlsberg (Shifnal), Robert Winsor, Manchester Evening News Classic. Sports Space 1981. McEwans Lager Welsh Classic 1981. Lambert and Butler Match Play 1982. Ford Classic 1982. Hambro Life Order of Merit winner 1981-82. British Open 1984

Lees, Arthur

Born Sheffield on 21st February, 1908

Tls Irish Open 1939
Maj Dunlop Masters 1947. Penfold 1951-53
Oth Midland Professional 1948-49. Southern England Professional 1956. Wentworth Pro-Am Foursomes 1957. Teachers Seniors 1959
Int Ryder Cup 1947-49-51-55. England 1938

Le Feuvre, Miss Carol

See Mrs R Gibbs

Lewis, Malcolm

Born 8th January, 1959

Maj Dutch International Amateur 1982. India Amateur 1981. Prince of Wales Cup 1983
Oth Boyd Quaich 1980-82. British Universities 1980-81

Light, Miss Pamela Mary

See Mrs PM Chugg

Llewellyn, David

Born at Dover on 18th November, 1951. Turned Professional 1968

Tls Ivory Coast Open 1985. Kenya Open 1972
Int Wales in World Cup 1974-85. Dunhill Cup 1985
Mis Rookie of the Year 1971

Long, David Charles

Born Belfast on 13th October, 1952

Add 4A Kensington Park, Belfast 5
Cls Shandon Park
Chp English Open Amateur Stroke Play 1979
Maj South of Ireland Open Amateur 1974. West of Ireland Open Amateur 1979. North of Ireland Open Amateur 1981-82
Int Europe v South America 1979. Ireland (Home Int) 1973-74-80-81-82-83; (Eur Team Ch) 1979; v Wales 1979

Longmuir, Bill

Born Essex on 10th June, 1953. Turned Professional 1968

Tls Nigerian Open 1976-80-85. Ivory Coast Open 1983
Mis Tooting Bec Cup 1979

Lucas, Percy Belgrave, CBE, DSO, DFC

Born Sandwich Bay, Kent on 2nd September, 1915

Add 11 Onslow Square, London SW7 3NJ
Cls Sandy Lodge, Walton Heath, Prince's, Royal West Norfolk
Maj Berkshire Trophy 1947-49. Royal St George's Challenge Cup 1947. Prince of Wales Challenge Cup 1947
Oth President's Putter 1949
Reg Herts Amateur 1946-47
Jun British Boys 1933. Boy International 1930-31-32-33
Int Walker Cup 1936-47 (non-playing captain 1949). GB v Professionals 1935. England (Home Int) 1936-48-49 (capt); v France 1936-47
Mis President Golf Foundation 1963 to 1966. President National Golf Clubs Advisory Association 1963 to 1969. President Association of Golf Club Secretaries 1968 to 1974. Member UK Sports Council 1971 to 1983

Lugton, Miss Constance J, MVO
Born Edinburgh on 17th November, 1936

Add Crabtree Cottage, 45 Hopetoun Terrace, Gullane, East Lothian
Cls Gullane Ladies, Musselburgh
Chp Scottish Ladies Amateur 1977, runner-up 1972
Reg East of Scotland Ladies 1974. East Lothian Ladies 1965-68-70-71-72-73-76-77-80
Jun Girl International 1955
Int Scotland (Home Int) 1965-68-72-73-77-78-80 (non-playing captain 1975-76); (Eur Team Ch) 1977

Lumb, Mrs JCN (*née* Kathryn Phillips)
Born Bradford on 24th February, 1952

Cls Hon member of Bradford, West Bowling, Killarney, Filton
Maj Central England Mixed Foursomes 1966-70
Reg Yorkshire Ladies 1968-69
Jun English Girls 1968. Scottish Girls Open Stroke Play 1968-69. French Girls 1970. Girl International 1967-68-69
Int Curtis Cup 1970-72. Vagliano Trophy 1969-71. England (Home Int) 1968-69-70-71; (Eur Team Ch) 1969

Lunt, Michael Stanley Randle
Born Birmingham on 20th May, 1935

Add Smugglers Wood, Sandy Lane, Kingswood, Surrey
Cls Royal and Ancient, Walton Heath, St Enodoc. Hon member of Blackwell, Royal St David's, Moseley, Edgbaston, Stourbridge, Willesley Park, Kibworth, Handsworth, King's Norton, Dudley
Chp Amateur Champion 1963, runner-up 1964. English Amateur 1966, runner-up 1962. Second in English Open Amateur Stroke Play 1961
Maj Golf Illustrated Gold Vase 1958. Harlech Gold Cross 1959-61-64-65-66-67. Leicestershire Fox 1966
Reg Midland Counties Amateur 1960-62
Jun Boy International 1949-50-51-52
Int Walker Cup 1959-61-63-65. Eisenhower Trophy 1964. GB Commonwealth Team 1963. England (Home Int) 1956-57-58-59-60-62-63-64-66 (non-playing captain 1972-73-74-75). Non-playing captain in Eur Team Ch 1973-75
Mis Golf Writers' Trophy 1963. President Midland Counties Golf Association 1978 to 1980

Lunt, Stanley
Born Moseley, Birmingham on 14th November, 1900

Add Love Lyne Farm, Hunt End, nr Redditch, Worcestershire
Cls Royal and Ancient. Hon member of Stourbridge, Moseley, Handsworth, Edgbaston, Barnehurst, Shifnal, Killarney, Aberdovey, Blackwell
Chp English Amateur 1934
Maj Harlech Gold Cross 1953
Reg Midland Counties Amateur 1934. Worcestershire Amateur 1925-36
Int British Amateurs v Professionals 1932-35. England (Home Int) 1932-33-34-35 (capt), (non-playing captain 1952-53); v France 1934-35-39
Mis President English Golf Union 1960. Senior Golfers Society v USA and Canada 1957-59-61-63-65. Captain Senior Golfers' Society 1964

Lyle, Alexander Walter Barr
Born Shrewsbury on 9th February, 1958. Turned Professional 1977

Chp Open Champion 1985. English Open Amateur Stroke Play 1975-77
Maj County Champion of Champions 1974. Hampshire Hog 1977. Berkshire Trophy 1977. Scrutton Jug 1977. Berkhamsted Trophy 1977
Oth Carris Trophy 1975
Reg Midland Amateur 1974. Midland Open 1975. Shropshire and Herefordshire Amateur 1974-76
Jun British Youths 1977. Boy International 1972-73-74-75. Youth International 1975-76-77
Int Walker Cup 1977. GB Commonwealth Team 1975. GB v Europe 1976. England (Home Int) 1975-76-77; (Eur Team Ch) 1977
Tls Nigerian Open 1978. French Open 1981. Italian Open 1984
Maj British Airways-Avis 1979. European Open 1979. Welsh Classic 1980. Lawrence Batley 1981-82. Madrid Open 1983. Hennessy-Cognac Cup Individual 1984. Lancôme Trophy 1984. Benson & Hedges International 1985
Ove Scandinavian Enterprises Open 1979. Kapulua International 1984. Casio World Open 1984. Greater Greenboro Open 1986
Oth Scottish Professional 1979
Int Ryder Cup 1979-81-83. Scotland in World Cup 1979-80. GB v Europe 1980. Hennessy-Cognac Cup 1984. Dunhill Cup 1985-86. Nissan Cup 1985-86
Mis In 1975 represented England at boy, youth and full international level. Turned Professional September, 1977. Rookie of the Year 1978. Vardon Trophy 1979-80-85. Frank Moran Trophy 1979. Individual World Cup Winner 1980. Benson & Hedges Golfer's Handbook Golfer of the Year 1985

Macara, MA
Born

Chp Welsh Amateur Stroke Play 1985

McCann, Mrs PG (*née* Catherine Syme)
Born Clonmel, Co Tipperary in 1922

Add Colbert House, O'Moore Street, Tullamore, Offaly, Eire
Cls Tullamore
Chp British Ladies 1951. Irish Ladies 1949-61, runner-up 1947-52-57-60
Reg Munster Ladies 1958, Irish Midland Ladies 1952-57-58
Int Curtis Cup 1952. Ireland (Home Int) 1947-48-49-50-51-52-53-54-56-57-58-60-61-62; v New Zealand 1953; v Canada 1953

McClure, Miss Jean
See Mrs J Holmes

McCorkindale, Miss Isabella
See Mrs IC Robertson

Macdonald, JS
Born St Andrews on 9th July, 1944

Add 109 Duncan Drive, Elgin, Moray IV30 2NH
Cls Elgin, Baberton, Killarney (Hon), Frigate Bay (Hon)
Chp Scottish Amateur Open Stroke Play 1969. Second in English Open Amateur Stroke Play 1970-71. Kuwait Open Champion 1977
Oth Boyd Quaich 1963-65. British Universities 1965
Reg South East Scotland Amateur 1969-71
Jun Boy International 1961. Youth International 1962-64-65
Int Walker Cup 1971. GB v Europe 1970. Scotland (Home Int) 1969-70-71-72; (Eur Team Ch) 1971; v Belgium 1973

McEvoy, Peter
Born London on 22nd March, 1953

Add 12 Kensington Avenue, Cheltenham, Glos
Cls Copt Heath (Hon), Handsworth (Hon), City of Derry (Hon), St Annes (Hon), Chantilly (Hon), L'Ancresse (Hon), Cotswold Hills
Chp Amateur Champion 1977-78. English Open Amateur Stroke Play 1980 (tied), second 1978. Runner-up English Amateur 1980
Maj Duncan Putter 1978-80. Scrutton Jug 1978-80. Lytham Trophy 1979. Selborne Salver 1979-80. Leics Fox 1976. Lagonda Trophy 1980. Berkshire Trophy 1985. County Champion of Champions 1984 (shared)

Oth British Universities Stroke Play 1973
Reg Warwickshire Match Play 1973-75-81. Warwickshire Amateur 1974-76-77-80. Warwickshire Open 1973-74. West of England Open Amateur Stroke Play 1977-80-83. Midland Open Amateur Stroke Play 1978
Jun Youth International 1974
Int Walker Cup 1977-79-81-85. Eisenhower Trophy 1978-80. GB v Europe 1978-80. England (Home Int) 1976-77-78-80-81-83-84-85-86; (Eur Team Ch) 1977-79-81-83; v Scotland 1979; in Fiat Trophy 1980. England v France 1983
Mis Leading amateur Open Championship 1978-79. First British amateur to complete 72 holes in US Masters (1978). Golf Writers' Trophy 1978

McGimpsey, Garth

Born

Chp Amateur Champion 1985
Maj North of Ireland Open Amateur 1984
Int Walker Cup 1985. GB v Europe 1986. Ireland (Home Int) 1978-80-81-82-83-84-85-86

Macgregor, George

Born Edinburgh on 19th August, 1944

Add Esklea, Milton Bridge, Penicuik, Midlothian
Cls Glencorse, Killarney (Hon), West Linton (Hon)
Chp Scottish Open Amateur Stroke Play 1982. Runner-up 1975-79-80
Maj Lytham Trophy 1975
Reg Lothians Amateur 1968. South-East Scotland Amateur 1972-75-79-80-81. East of Scotland Open Amateur 1979-82
Jun Youth International 1964-65-66
Int Walker Cup 1971-75-83-85. GB v Europe 1970-74. GB Commonwealth Team 1971-75. Scotland (Home Int) 1969-70-71-72-73-74-75-76-80-81-82-83-84-85-86; (Eur Team Ch) 1971-73-75-81-83; v Belgium 1973-75-80; v England 1979; v France 1981-82; Scotland v Sweden 1983
Mis Leading Amateur Wills PGA Open 1970-71

McHenry, John

Born

Chp Irish Amateur 1986
Int Ireland (Home Int) 1985-86

Macintosh, Keith William

Born Cardross, Dunbartonshire on 21st June, 1949

Add 106A Sinclair Street, Helensburgh G84 9QE
Cls Cardross (Hon), Glasgow
Chp Scottish Amateur 1979. Second in Scottish Open Amateur Stroke Play 1978 (tied)
Oth Scottish Universities 1969. Cameron Corbett Vase 1979, Cadzow Cup 1968
Reg Glasgow District Amateur 1973. Dunbartonshire Match Play 1980
Ove Belgian Open Amateur 1980
Jun Youth International 1969
Int GB v Europe 1980. Scotland (Home Int) 1980; v England 1979; v France 1980; v Belgium 1980; in Fiat Trophy 1980. Moroccan Amateur Team Champion 1980. Simon Bolivar Trophy 1979

McKellar, Paul James

Born Clarkston, Glasgow on 6th April, 1956

Cls East Renfrewshire (Hon)
Chp Runner-up Amateur Championship 1978. Scottish Open Amateur Stroke Play 1977. Runner-up Scottish Amateur 1977-79
Reg West of Scotland Close 1980
Jun Youth International 1974-75-76-77
Int Walker Cup 1977. GB v Europe 1978. Europe v South America 1979. Scotland (Home Int) 1976-77-78; v Belgium 1978; v France 1978; v England 1979; in Caracas International 1979
Mis Non-playing captain Scottish Youths Team 1978-79

McKenna, Miss Mary A

Born Dublin on 29th April, 1949

Add Moyola, Cloghran, Co Dublin
Cls Donabate, Hermitage, Woodbrook, Killarney (Hon), Milltown, Moseley, Clontarf, Fairfield (USA) (Hon)
Chp British Ladies Open Amateur Stroke Play 1979, second 1976. Irish Ladies 1969-72-74-77-79-81-82, runner-up 1968-73-76. Irish Women's Close Championship 1981
Maj Dorothy Grey Stroke Play 1970-71-73. Players No 6 Cup 1971-72-74. Avia Foursomes 1977-84-86. Hermitage Scratch Cup 1975-79
Reg South of Ireland Scratch Cup 1973-74-76-79
Int Curtis Cup 1970-72-74-76-78-80-82-84. Vagliano Trophy 1969-71-73-75-77-79. World Team Championship 1970-74-76 (selected 1980 but injury caused withdrawal). Ireland (Home Int) 1968-69-70-71-72-73-74-75-76-77-78-79-80; (Eur Team Ch) 1969-71-73-75-77-79-81-82-83; in Fiat Trophy 1979
Mis Semi-finalist US Women's Western 1972, Broadmoor Tournament 1972 and US Women's Amateur 1980. Captain of LGU Touring Team to South Africa 1974. Leading Amateur Colgate European LPGA 1977 (tied)-79. Daks Woman Golfer of the Year 1979

McLean, David

Born Holyhead on 30th January, 1947

Add Gleneagles, Four Mile Bridge, Valley Anglesey
Cls Holyhead, Baron Hill, Killarney
Chp Welsh Amateur 1973-78. Welsh Amateur Stroke Play 1975-79
Maj Duncan Putter 1982
Reg North Wales Amateur 1971-75-77-81. Caernarvonshire Amateur 1966-68-69-70 (tied)-77-79-81-82. Anglesey Amateur 1965-67-68-69-70-72-73-74-76-78-79-80-81-82
Int Wales (Home Int) 1968-69-70-71-72-73-74-75-76-77-78-80-81-82-83-85-86; (Eur Team Ch) 1975-77-79-81-83; v France 1975-76; v Denmark 1976-80-82; v Ireland 1979; v Spain 1980: v Austria 1982; v Switzerland 1980-82; in Fiat Trophy 1978-79; in Asian Team Championship 1979

McMahon, Mrs J (*née* Suzanne Cadden)

Born Old Kilpatrick, Dunbartonshire on 8th October, 1957

Add 340 Dumbarton Road, Dalmuir, Glasgow G81
Cls Troon
Chp Runner-up British Ladies 1975. Second in British Ladies Stroke Play 1975
Maj Scottish Ladies Foursomes 1972
Reg Dunbartonshire Ladies 1976-77-79
Ove World Junior Championship 1973
Jun Scottish Girls 1974-76. Scottish Girls Open Stroke Play 1976-77. British Girls 1975. Girl International 1972-73-74-75-76
Int Curtis Cup 1976. Vagliano Trophy 1975. Scotland (Home Int) 1974-75-76-77-79; (Eur Team Ch) 1975
Mis Daks Woman Golfer of the Year 1975

Madill, Miss Maureen

See Mrs Garner

Maher, Mrs S (*née* Sheila Vaughan)

Born Whiston, Liverpool in 1942

Add 25 Knowsley Road, Rainhill, Merseyside L35 0PA
Cls Huyton and Prescot
Reg Lancashire Ladies 1958-63-64
Jun British Girls 1959. England Girl International 1956-57-58-59
Int Curtis Cup 1962-64. Vagliano Trophy 1961-65. GB Commonwealth Team 1963. England (Home Int) 1960-61-62-63-64
Mis In 1963 on tour of Australasia as member of GB Commonwealth Team, tied first in Australian Ladies Foursomes, won New Zealand Ladies Foursomes and won New Zealand Junior Stroke Play

Mann, Lindsay S
Born 28th February, 1962

Maj Tennant Cup 1982
Int Walker Cup 1983. Scotland (Home Int) 1982-83

Marchbank, Brian
Born Perth on 20th April, 1958. Turned Professional 1979

Add Rosemount, Tulibardine Crescent, Auchterarder, Perthshire
Cls Auchterarder (Hon)
Chp Second equal in English Open Amateur Stroke Play 1979
Maj Lytham Trophy 1978. Scottish Champion of Champions 1979
Jun British Boys 1975. Scottish Boys 1976. British Youths 1978. Boy International 1973-74-75. Youth International 1976-77-78-79
Int Walker Cup 1979. GB v Europe 1976-78. Eisenhower Trophy 1978. Scotland (Home Int) 1978; (Eur Team Ch) 1979; v Italy 1979

Marks, GC
Born Hanley, Stoke-on-Trent, in November, 1938

Add Bar Hill House, Madeley, nr Crewe, Cheshire
Cls Hon member of Trentham, Trentham Park, Greenway Hall, Killarney, Walsall, Newcastle, Trevose, Stone. Royal and Ancient
Chp Second in English Open Amateur Stroke Play 1973-75
Maj Scrutton Jug 1967. Prince of Wales Challenge Cup 1968. Leicestershire Fox 1968. Lytham Trophy 1970 (tied). Harlech Gold Cup 1974. Homer Salver 1977
Reg Midland Amateur 1967. Staffordshire Amateur 1959-60-63-66-67-68-69-73
Jun Boy International 1955-56. Youth International 1957-58-59-60
Int Walker Cup 1969-71. Eisenhower Trophy 1970. GB v Europe 1968-70. England (Home Int) 1963-67-68-69-70-71-74-75 (non-playing captain 1980-81-82-83); (Eur Team Ch) 1967-69-71-75. GB Commonwealth Team 1975. GB in Colombian International 1975
Mis England Selector 1980-81-82-83 (chairman)

Marsh, Dr David Max
Born Southport on 29th April, 1934

Add 26 Blundell Drive, Southport, Lancashire
Cls Royal and Ancient. Hon member of Southport and Ainsdale, Ormskirk, West Lancashire, Worlington and Newmarket, Hillside, Clitheroe, Whalley
Chp English Amateur 1964-70
Maj Antlers Royal Mid-Surrey 1964-66. Formby Hare 1968
Oth Boyd Quaich 1957
Jun Boy International 1951
Int Walker Cup 1959-71 (non-playing captain 1973-75); GB v Europe 1958 (non-playing captain 1972-74). GB v Professionals 1959. England (Hone Int) 1956-57-58-59-60-64-65-66-68-69-70-71-72 (captain 1968-69-70-71); (Eur Team Ch) 1971
Mis EGU Selector 1974. British Selector 1975. Chairman Royal and Ancient Selection Committee 1979-83. President EGU 1987

Martin, Steve W
Born Dundee on 21st December, 1955

Chp Scottish Open Amateur Stroke Play 1976
Maj East of Scotland Open Amateur Stroke Play 1976. Tennant Cup 1977
Reg Central District Amateur 1973. Angus Amateur 1973
Jun Scottish Boys Stroke Play 1972-73. Boy International 1972-73. Youth International 1973-75-76-77
Int Walker Cup 1977. Eisenhower Trophy 1976 (winning team). GB v Europe 1976. Scotland (Home Int) 1975-76-77; (Eur Team Ch) 1977; v Belgium 1977; v Spain 1977
Mis Turned Professional September 1977. Represented Scotland in World Cup 1980

Marvin, Miss Vanessa Price
Born Cosford on 30th December, 1954

Add 24 Bradford Road, Otley, West Yorks, LS21 3EQ
Cls Easingwold (Hon)
Chp English Ladies Amateur 1977-78. Runner-up British Ladies Amateur 1977
Maj Hampshire Rose 1975-78 (tied). Roehampton Gold Cup 1976. Newmark-Avia 1978
Reg Yorkshire Ladies 1975-78. North of England Ladies 1975
Int Curtis Cup 1978. Vagliano Trophy 1977. England (Home Int) 1977-78; (Eur Team Ch) 1977; in Fiat Trophy 1978
Mis Leading amateur Colgate European LPGA 1977. Daks Woman Golfer of the Year 1978. Turned professional October, 1978

Mayo, Paul
Born

Reg Gwent Amateur 1982
Int Walker Cup 1985. GB v Europe 1986. Wales (Home Int) 1982

Melia, Terry J
Born Wrexham on 7th July, 1955

Add 39 Hampton Crescent, West Cyncoed, Cardiff
Cls Cardiff
Reg Glamorgan County 1981-82
Chp Welsh Amateur 1979. Welsh Amateur Stroke Play 1980
Int Wales (Home Int) 1976-77-78-80-81-82; (Eur Team Ch) 1977-79; v Denmark 1976-80; v Ireland 1979; v Switzerland 1980; v Spain 1980; v S America 1979

Melville, Miss Janet
Born Barrow-in-Furness on 16th March, 1958

Add 9, Orchard Road, Bardsea, Ulverston, Cumbria
Cls Furness, Royal Birkdale, Grewash Valley
Chp British Ladies Open and Amateur Stroke Play (played concurrently) 1978. Highland Open 1978. Lancashire Champion 1983
Maj Worplesdon Mixed Foursomes 1979. Northern Foursomes 1977-78. Mary McCalley Trophy 1980
Jun Girl International 1976
Int Vagliano Trophy 1979. England (Home Int) 1978-79-81; (Eur Team Ch) 1979. English Girls (non-playing captain) 1981
Mis Varsity Athlete in golf at Florida International University 1980-81

Micklem, Gerald Hugh, CBE
Born Burgh Heath, Surrey on 14th August, 1911

Add Titlarks Hill House, Sunningdale, Berks
Cls Royal and Ancient, Royal Liverpool, Royal St George's, Rye, Sunningdale
Chp English Amateur 1947-53. Second in English Open Amateur Stroke Play 1948
Maj Royal St George's Challenge Cup 1952. Berkshire Trophy 1955
Oth President's Putter 1953
Int Walker Cup 1947-49-53-55 (non-playing captain 1957-59). England (Home Int) 1947-48-49-50-51-52-53-54-55 (non-playing captain 1956-57-58); v France 1947-48-54 (non-playing captain 1956)
Mis Non-playing captain GB v Europe 1956-58. Amateurs v Professional 1956-57-58 and Eisenhower Trophy Team 1958. Chairman Rules of Golf Committee 1960 to 1963. Chairman R & A Selection Committee 1959 to 1963. Chairman R & A Championship Committee 1963 to 1966. Captain Royal and Ancient 1968-69. President English Golf Union 1965-66. President European Golf Association 1967 to 1969. Bobby Jones Award 1969

Milne, William TG
Born Perth on 13th July, 1951

Maj Newlands Trophy 1972
Reg North of Scotland Stroke Play 1971. Perthshire Stroke Play 1973
Jun Scotland Youth International 1970-71-72
Int Walker Cup 1973. Scotland (Home Int) 1972-73; (Eur Team Ch) 1973, v Belgium 1973
Mis Turned Professional October, 1973. Won Lusaka Eagle Open 1974 and Northern Scottish Open 1974-75

Milton, Mrs John C (*née* Moira Paterson)
Born 18th December, 1923

Add White Willows, Theale, Wedmore, Somerset, BS28 4SR
Cls Turnhouse. Hon Member of Gullane, Lenzie, Maccauvlei
Chp British Ladies 1952. Runner-up Scottish Ladies 1951
Reg Dunbartonshire Ladies 1949. Midlothian Ladies 1962
Int Curtis Cup 1952. GB v France 1949-50; v Belgium1950. Scotland (Home Int) 1949-50-51-52; v Australia 1951; v South Africa 1951
Mis Member of LGU Team to South Africa 1951. Non-playing captain Scotland in Eur Team Championship 1973

Moir, Angus
Born 1st May, 1963

Chp Scottish Amateur 1984
Int Scotland (Home Int) 1983-84

Montgomerie, Colin S
Born 23rd June, 1963

Chp Scottish Open Amateur Stroke Play 1985
Int Walker Cup 1985. GB v Europe 1986. Scotland (Home Int) 1984-85-86

Montgomerie, John Speir
Born Cambuslang on 7th August, 1913

Add 6, Cavendish Drive, Newton Mearns, Glasgow
Cls Royal and Ancient, Cambuslang, Kilmarnock (Barassie), Pollok
Chp Scottish Amateur 1957
Reg Lanarkshire Amateur 1951-54
Int Scotland (Home Int) 1957, (non-playing captain) 1962-63; v Scandinavia 1958
Mis Non-playing captain Scottish Team (Eur Team Ch) 1965. Walker Cup Selector 1957 to 1965. President Scottish Golf Union 1965-66

Moore, Miss Linda
See Mrs L Simpson

Morgan, John
Born Oxford on 3rd September, 1943. Turned Professional 1968

Tls Nigerian Open 1979. Ivory Coast 1982
Maj Lusaka Open 1979. Jersey Open 1986

Morgan, John Llewellyn
Born Llandrindod Wells on 23rd June, 1918

Add 2 Kinver Crescent, Aldridge, Staffs
Cls Llandrindod Wells, Sutton Coldfield, Builth Wells, Little Aston, Aberystwyth, Killarney, St Deiniol, Ashburnham
Chp Welsh Amateur 1950-51, runner-up 1952
Maj Berkshire Trophy 1953. Duncan Putter 1968. Harlech Gold Cross 1951-55
Oth British Seniors 1974
Reg Midlands Amateur 1949-50-52. Midlands Open 1950. Warwickshire Amateur 1951
Int Walker Cup 1951-53-55. Wales (Home Int) 1948-49-50-51-52-53-54-56-57-58-59-60-61-62-63-64-66-67; (Eur Team Ch) 1965
Mis Professional for 4 years subsequently re-instated as Amateur

Morgan, Miss Wanda
Born Lymm, Cheshire on 22nd March, 1910

Add 67 Russell Drive, Swalecliffe, Whitstable, Kent CT5 2RG. Tel Chestfield 2319
Cls Canterbury, Westgate, St Enodoc, Herne Bay, Belmont, Chestfield, Rochester and Cobham Park, Cooden Beach, Littlestone, Prince's, Seasalter, Barnehurst, Hon Life member of *ALL* clubs listed
Chp British Ladies 1935, runner-up 1931. English Ladies 1931-36-37
Maj Sunningdale Foursomes 1948. Worplesdon Mixed Foursomes 1948. Fairway and Hazard Foursomes 1956. Daily Graphic 1941-42
Reg Kent Ladies 1930-31-33-35-36-37-53
Int Curtis Cup 1932-34-36. GB v France 1932-33-34-35-36-37; v Canada 1934. England (Home Int) 1931-32-33-34-35-36-37-53

Morris, MF
Born

Chp Irish Amateur 1978
Int Ireland (Home Int) 1978-80-82-83-84 (Eur Team Ch) 1979

Mosey, Ian
Born Keighley on 29th August, 1951. Turned Professional 1972

Maj Monte Carlo Open 1984
Oth Merseyside International 1980. Kalahari Classic 1980. Holiday Inns, SA 1981

Mouland, Mark
Born 23rd April, 1961. Turned Professional 1981

Maj Car Care Plan International 1986
Int Wales: in Dunhill Cup 1986

Mulcare, Pat
Born Ballybunion, 1945

Add 35 Beech Lawn, Dundrum, Dublin 14
Cls Woodbrook (Hon), Dublin (Hon)
Maj East of Ireland Open Amateur 1971-72-73. South of Ireland Open Amateur 1971
Int Walker Cup 1975. Ireland (Home Int) 1968-69-70-71-72-73-74-78-80; (Eur Team Ch) 1975-79; v France, West Germany and Sweden 1978-80

Murray, Gordon H
Born Paisley on 19th December, 1936

Add 78 Braeside Drive, Barrhead, Renfrewshire
Cls Fereneze (Hon)
Chp Scottish Amateur 1974-76, runner-up 1975
Maj West of Scotland Open Amateur 1973-76-78. Scottish Stroke Play 1983
Reg West of Scotland Amateur 1971
Int Walker Cup 1977. GB v Europe 1978. Scotland (Home Int) 1973-74-75-76-77-78-83; (Eur Team Ch) 1975-77; v.Spain 1974-77; v Belgium 1975-77

Murray, Stuart WT
Born Paisley on 10th November, 1933

Chp Scottish Amateur 1962, runner-up 1961
Maj Tennant Cup 1963. Edward Trophy 1960-61
Reg West of Scotland Amateur 1958. Renfrewshire Amateur 1958-59. Glasgow Amateur 1960. Hampshire Amateur 1963
Int Walker Cup 1963. GB Commonwealth Team 1963 GB v Europe 1958-62. Scotland (Home Int) 1959-60-61-62-63; v Scandinavia 1960
Mis Turned professional 1963 and won Midland Professional 1964-67-68 and Middlesex Open 1973

Needham, Miss Sandra Claire
See Mrs Roy

Nesbitt, Miss Claire
See Mrs C Robinson

New, Miss Beverley Jayne
Born Bristol on 30th July, 1960. Turned Professional 1984

Add 3 Willow Close, Wick, Bristol
Cls Lansdown (Hon)
Oth Martin Bowl 1983. Runner-up Keighley Trophy 1983
Chp English Ladies 1980. Second in Welsh Ladies Open Stroke Play 1979
Maj Hampshire Rose 1980. Runner-up Roehampton Gold Cup 1981-82. Winner Roehampton Gold Cup 1983. WPGA United Friendly Insurance Tour 1982. Worplesdon Mixed Foursomes 1982-83
Reg Somerset Ladies 1979-80-82-83; Somerset Ladies Champion 1981-83. Runner-up South West Ladies Championship 1981-82-83. Bristol and District Open 1983
Jun England Under 22 International 1979-80-81. South West Under 21 Champion 1980, runner-up Under 23 English Championship 1982
Int (Home Int) 1980-81-82-83; in Fiat Trophy 1980. England (Eur Team Ch) 1981-83. Vagliano Team 1983. Curtis Cup 1984.

Nichol, Miss Margaret
See Mrs A Pickard

Nicholas, Miss Alison
Born 6th March, 1962. Turned Professional 1984

Chp British Ladies Stroke-Play 1983
Reg Northern Foursomes 1983. Yorkshire Ladies 1984
Jun Northern Girls 1982-83

O'Connor, Christy
Born Galloway on 21st December, 1924

Opn Second in Open Championship 1965, third in 1961. Leading British player 1963 (6th)
Maj Swallow-Penfold 1955. Dunlop Masters 1956-59. Spalding 1956 (tied). PGA Match Play 1957. Daks 1959. Ballantine 1960. Irish Hospitals 1960-62. Carling-Caledonian 1961. Martini 1963 (tied)-64. Jeyes 1964. Carrolls 1964-66-67-72. Senior Service 1965. Gallaher Ulster 1966-68-69. Alcan International 1968 (tied). Bowmaker 1970. John Player Classic 1970. PGA Seniors 1981-82
Oth Ulster Professional 1953-54. Irish Professional 1958-60-61-62-63-65-66-71-75-77. Irish Dunlop 1962-65-66-67. Gleneagles Pro-Am 1962. Southern Ireland Professional 1969-76. Sean Connery Pro-Am 1970. PGA Seniors 1976-77-79. World Seniors 1976-77
Int Ryder Cup 1955-57-59-61-63-65-67-69-71-73. GB v Commonwealth 1956. Ireland in World Cup 1956-57-58 (winning team)-59-60-61-62-63-64-66-67-68-69-71-75. Ireland in Double Diamond 1971-72-73-74-75-76-77
Mis Harry Vardon Trophy 1961-62. Second in order of Merit 1964 (equal)-65-66-69-70. Represented Great Britain and Ireland in the Ryder Cup ten times. Golf Writers Trophy 1977

O'Connor, Christy, Jr
Born Galway on 19th August, 1948. Turned Professional 1965

Opn Joint leading British player (5th) in Open Championship 1976. 3rd in Open 1985
Maj Martini 1975 (tied). Carrolls Irish Open 1975. Sumrie 1976-78
Tls Zambian Open 1974
Oth Irish Dunlop 1974. Carrolls Irish Match Play 1975-77
Int Ireland in Double Diamond 1974-75-76-77. Ireland in World Cup 1974-75-78-85. GB v Europe 1974. Ryder Cup 1975. GB v South Africa 1976. Dunhill Cup 1985

Oldcorn, Andrew
Born Bolton on 31st March, 1960. Turned Professional 1983

Chp English Amateur 1982
Int Walker Cup 1983. England (Home Int) 1982-83

O'Leary, John E
Born Dublin on 19th August, 1949. Turned Professional 1970

Maj Sumrie 1975. Greater Manchester Open 1976. Carrolls Irish Open 1982
Ove Holiday Inns (Swaziland) 1975
Oth Irish Dunlop 1972
Int Ryder Cup 1975. Ireland in World Cup 1972-80-82. Ireland In Double Diamond 1972-73-74-75-76-77. GB v Europe 1976-78
Amr South of Ireland Amateur 1970. Youth Int 1970. Ireland (Home Int) 1969-70; (Eur Team Ch) 1969

O'Reilly, Mrs Therese (*née* Moran)
Born 29th January, 1954

Chp Irish Ladies Amateur 1986
Reg Leinster Ladies 1975-78. Irish Midland Ladies 1974
Int Ireland (Home Int) 1986

O'Sullivan, D
Born

Chp Irish Amateur 1985
Int Ireland (Home Int) 1985

O'Sullivan, Dr William M
Born Killarney on 13th March, 1911

Add Inch House, Killarney, Co Kerry, Ireland
Cls Killarney (Hon), Dooks (Hon), Tralee (Hon), Muskerry (Hon), Cork (Hon), Ballybunion (Hon), Waterville
Chp Irish Open Amateur 1949, runner-up 1936-53. Runner-up Irish Amateur 1940
Int Ireland (Home Int) 1934-35-36-37-38-47-48-49-50-51-53-54. President Golfing Union of Ireland 1959-60

Oosterhuis, Peter A
Born London on 3rd May, 1948

Maj Berkshire Trophy 1966. Agfacolor 1971. Sunbeam Pro-Am 1971. Piccadilly 1971-73. Penfold 1972. Viyella PGA 1973
Jun British Youths 1966. Youth Int 1966-67-68. Boy Int 1964-65
Int Walker Cup 1967. Eisenhower Trophy 1968. England (Home Int) 1966-67-68. Ryder Cup 1971-73-75-77-79-81. England in World Cup 1971-73. England in Double Diamond 1973-74. GB v Europe 1974
Mis Turned professional November, 1968.
Opn Second in Open Championship 1974. Leading British player 1975(7th)-78(6th)-82(third)
Tls French Open 1973-74. Italian Open 1974. Canadian Open 1981

Oth Sunningdale Foursomes 1969. Under 23's PGA 1970. Coca Cola Young Professionals 1970-72. Southern England Professional 1971
Ove General Motors, South Africa 1970. Transvaal Open 1971. Schoeman Park 1971. Rhodesian Dunlop Masters 1971. Glen Anil Classic (SA) 1972. Rothmans Match Play (SA) 1973. Maracaibo Open 1973. El Paraiso Open 1974. Canadian Open 1981
Mis Vardon Trophy 1971-72-73-74. Third in US Masters in 1973, the best achieved by any British player. Golf Writers Trophy 1973-74. In addition to three victories on 1974 British-European circuit, was second five times (Open included) and lost play-off in 1974 US Tournament–Monsanto Open. European American Express 1974. Qualified for USPGA tour November 1974. Finished second in the 1975 New Orleans Open. 28th on US Tour Money List 1981

Oxley, Miss Dinah
See Mrs D Henson

Panton, Miss Catherine Rita
Born Bridge of Allan, Stirlingshire on 14th June, 1955. Turned Professional 1978

Add 116C Nether Street, West Finchley, London N12
Cls Glenbervie (Hon), Pitlochry (Hon), Silloth (Hon), South Herts
Chp British Ladies 1976
Reg East of Scotland Ladies 1976
Jun Scottish Girls 1969. Girl Int 1969-70-71-72-73
Int World Team Championship 1976. Vagliano Trophy 1977. Scotland (Home Int) 1972-73-76-77-78; (Eur Team Ch) 1973-77
Mis Scottish Sportswoman of the Year 1976. Member of LGU under-25 team to tour Canada 1973
WPGA Carlsberg Tournament 1979. State Express Ladies Championship 1979 and headed WPGA Order of Merit. In 1980 won Elizabeth Ann Classic. European Ladies Champion 1981, also won two WPGA events. Moben Kitchens Classic 1982. Qualified for USLPGA Tour, January 1983. Won Smirnoff Irish Classic 1983. UBM Northern Classic 1983, Dunham Forest Pro-Am 1983. McEwans Wirral Caldy Classic 1985. Delsjö Open 1985. Portuguese Open 1986

Panton, John MBE
Born Pitlochry, Perthshire on 9th October, 1916. Turned Professional 1935

Opn Leading British player in 1956 Open Championship (5th)
Maj Silver King 1950. Daks 1951. North-British-Harrogate 1952. Goodwin Foursomes 1952. Yorkshire Evening News 1954. PGA Match Play 1956, runner-up 1968
Ove Woodlawn Invitation Open (Germany) 1958-59-60
Oth West of Scotland Professional 1947-48-52-54-55-61-63. Scottish Professional 1948-49-50-51-54-55-59-66 (tied). Northern Open 1948-51-52-56-59-60-62. West of Scotland PGA Match Play 1954-55-56-64. Goodwin Foursomes 1952. Gleneagles-Saxone 1956. Pringle Seniors 1967-69. World Seniors 1967
Int Ryder Cup 1951-53-61. Scotland in World Cup 1955-56-57-58-59-60-62-63-64-65-66-68
Mis Harry Vardon Trophy 1951. Golf Writers Trophy 1967

Parkin, Philip
Born Doncaster on 12th December, 1961. Turned Professional 1984

Chp Amateur Champion 1983
Jun British Youths 1982
Int Walker Cup 1983. Wales (Home Int) 1980-81-82. Wales in World Cup 1984. Dunhill Cup 1985-86

Paterson, Miss Moira
See Mrs JC Milton

Peel, Mrs M
See Mrs M Draper

Perkins, Miss Tegwen
See Mrs Thomas

Perowne, Arthur Herbert
Born Norwich on 21st February, 1930

Add Bawburgh Villa, Bawburgh, Norwich
Cls Royal Norwich, Hunstanton, West Norfolk
Chp English Open Amateur Stroke Play 1958
Maj Berkshire Trophy 1958 (tied)
Oth Carris Trophy 1946
Reg East Anglia Open 1952. Norfolk Amateur 1948-51-52-53-54-55-56-57-58-60-61. Norfolk Open 1964
Ove Swedish Amateur 1974
Jun Boy International 1946
Int Walker Cup 1949-53-59. Eisenhower Trophy 1958. GB v Denmark 1955; v Professionals 1956-58. England (Home Int) 1947-48-49-50-51-53-54-55-57; v France 1950-54-56-59; v Sweden 1947; v Denmark 1947

Peters, Gordon Buchanan
Born Barrhead, Renfrewshire on 9th August, 1910

Add 25 Corrour Road, Newlands, Glasgow
Cls Royal and Ancient, Fenereze, Buchanan Castle, Pollock
Maj Tennant Cup 1939
Reg Glasgow Amateur 1934
Int Walker Cup 1936-38. Scotland (Home Int) 1934-35-36-37-38 (non-playing captain 1950)

Phillips, Miss Ann
See Mrs A Howard

Phillips, Miss Kathryn
See Mrs JCN Lumb

Pickard, Mrs A (*née* Margaret Nichol)
Born on 25th April, 1938

Add East Farm, Eshott, Felton, Morpeth, Northumberland
Cls Hexham (Hon), Alnmouth (Hon), Gullane
Chp English Ladies 1960, runner-up 1957-67
Reg Northern Ladies 1957-58. Northumberland Ladies 1956-57-58-61-62-64-65-66-67-69-70-71-76-77-82
Int Curtis Cup 1968-70. Vagliano Trophy 1959-61-67. England (Home Int) 1957-58-59-60-61-67-69, non-playing captain 1983. European Team Championship 1983 (non-playing captain)

Pierse, Arthur D
Born

Maj West of Ireland Open Amateur 1980-82
Int Walker Cup 1983, GB v Europe 1980. Ireland (Home Int) 1976-77-78-80-81-82-83-84-85; (Eur Team Ch) 1981

Pirie, Alex Kemp
Born Aberdeen on 21st June, 1942

Add The Golf Inn, Montrose, Angus
Cls Hazelhead (Hon), Cruden Bay
Chp Runner-up Scottish Amateur 1972-74
Maj Eden Tournament 1963. Northern Scottish Open 1970. West of Scotland Open Amateur 1972. East of Scotland Open Amateur Stroke Play 1975
Reg North East Scotland Match Play 1964-66-67-68-71-73. Aberdeenshire Stroke Play 1966-68
Int Walker Cup 1967. GB v Europe 1970. Scotland (Home Int) 1966-67-68-69-70-71-72-73-74-75; (Eur Team Ch) 1967-69; v Belgium 1973-75; v Spain 1974

Polland, Eddie
Born Newcastle, Co Down on 10th June, 1947. Turned Professional 1967

Tls Spanish Open 1976-80
Maj Penfold 1973. Sun Alliance PGA Match Play 1975
Oth Irish Dunlop 1973-75. Irish Professional 1974. Carrolls Irish Match Play 1974. Ulster Professional 1976
Int Ryder Cup 1973. Ireland in World Cup 1973-74-76-77-78-79. Ireland in Double Diamond 1972-73-74-75-76-77. GB v Europe 1974-76-78-80; v South Africa 1976

Pook, Mrs Antony D (*née* Elizabeth Chadwick)
Born Inverness on 4th April, 1943

Add 9 Manor Gardens, Buckden, Huntingdon, Cambs. Tel Huntingdon 810922
Cls Hon member of Bramall Park (Home Club), Alderley Edge, Stockport, Anglesey
Chp British Ladies 1966-67. Runner-up English Ladies 1963
Maj Central England Mixed Foursomes 1962-63-64
Reg North of England Ladies 1965-66-67. Cheshire Ladies 1963-64-65-66-67
Jun Girl International 1961
Int Curtis Cup 1966. GB Commonwealth 1967. GB v Europe 1963. England (Home Int) 1963-65-66-67; (Eur Team Ch) 1967; v France 1965
Mis Retired from competitive golf in 1968

Porter, Miss Ruth
See Mrs Slark

Price Fisher, Mrs Elizabeth
Born London on 17th January, 1923

Add Flat 1, Keep House, Castle Street, Farnham, Surrey GU9 7JB
Cls Hankley Common, Farnham, Berkshire
Chp British Ladies 1959, runner-up 1954-58. Runner-up English Ladies 1947-54-55
Maj Spalding Ladies 1955-59. Astor Salver 1955-56-59. Fairway and Hazard Foursomes 1954-60. Kayser Bondor Foursomes 1958 (tied). Roehampton Gold Cup 1960. Central England Mixed Foursomes 1971-76-82
Reg South Eastern Ladies 1955-59-60-69. Surrey Ladies 1954-55-56-57-58-59-60
Ove Danish Ladies 1952. Portuguese Ladies 1964
Int Curtis Cup 1950-52-54-56-58-60. Vagliano Trophy 1959. GB v Canada 1950-54-58; v France 1953-55-57; v Belgium 1953-55-57. GB Commonwealth Team 1955-59. England (Home Int) 1948-51-52-53-54-55-56-57-58-59-60
Mis Golf Writers Trophy 1952. Turned Professional 1968, re-instated as an Amateur 1971

Rafferty, Ronan
Born 13th January, 1964. Turned Professional 1981

Add 5 Burren Road, Warrenpoint, Co Down, N Ireland
Cls Warrenpoint (Hon), Ardglass
Chp Irish Amateur 1980. English Open Amateur Stroke Play 1980 (tied)
Jun British Boys 1979. Irish Youths 1979. Ulster Youths 1979. Boy International 1978-79. Youth International 1979-80
Int Eisenhower Trophy 1980. GB v Europe 1980. Ireland (Home Int) 1980; v Wales 1979; v France, Germany, Sweden 1980; in Fiat Trophy 1980. (Eur Team Ch) 1981. Walker Cup 1981. Ireland in World Cup 1983-84. Dunhill Cup 1986. Hennessy-Cognac Cup 1984
Mis Youngest player ever to play in Walker Cup

Rawlings, Miss Mandy
Born Bargoed, Glamorganshire on 15th June, 1964

Add 53 John Street, Bargoed, Mid Glam
Cls Bargoed, Whitchurch, Radyr (Hon)
Chp Welsh Ladies 1980-81
Jun Welsh Girls 1979-81. Girl International 1976-77-78-79-80. De Beers Ch 1980
Int Wales (Home Int) 1978-79-80; in Fiat Trophy 1980. Girls International 1981. Senior International 1981-83-84. Vagliano 1981

Rawlings, Miss Vicki
See Mrs V Thomas

Reddan, Mrs M (*née* Clarrie Tiernan)
Born Drogheda on 3rd July, 1916

Add Baltry, Drogheda, Co Louth
Cls Co Louth
Chp Irish Ladies 1936, runner-up 1946-48. Runner-up British Ladies 1949
Ove New Jersey State Ladies 1937. Runner-up Canadian Ladies 1938
Int Curtis Cup 1938-48. GB v Canada 1938. Ireland (Home Int) 1935-36-37-38-39-47-48-49

Redford, Miss Carole
See Mrs I Caldwell

Rees, Christopher
Born

Chp Welsh Amateur 1986
Int Wales (Home Int) 1986

Reid, Miss Dale
Born 20th March, 1959. Turned Professional 1979

Jun Fife Girls 1973-75. Scottish Girls International 1974-75-76-77
Int Scotland (Home Int) 1978
WPGA Carlsberg (Coventry) 1980. Carlsberg (Gleneagles) 1981. Moben Kitchens 1981. Guernsey Open 1982. United Friendly 1983. International Classic 1983. Caldy Classic 1983. UBM Classic 1984. JS Bloor Classic 1984. Ulster Volkswagen Classic 1985. Brend Hotels International 1985. Order of Merit 1984. British Olivetti 1986

Rennie, Mrs Joan Kerr (*née* Hastings)
Born Troon on 29th May, 1941

Add 334 Queens Road, Aberdeen
Cls Aberdeen Ladies, Hon member of Troon Bentinck, Kilmarnock (Barassie), Troon Municipal
Chp Scottish Ladies 1967, runner-up 1968
Reg Ayrshire Ladies 1960-61-63-64-66-67. Aberdeenshire Ladies 1980
Jun Scottish Girls 1960. Girl International 1957-58-59
Int Curtis Cup 1966. Vagliano Trophy 1961-67. Scotland (Home Int) 1961-65-66-67-71-72; (Eur Team Ch) 1973

Richmond, Mrs Maureen (*née* Walker)
Born Kilmacolm on 22nd April, 1955

Add 8 Greenbank Place, Morningside, Edinburgh
Cls Kilmacolm (Hon), Troon, Shiskine (Hon)
Jun British Girls 1972. Scottish Girls 1970-71-73. Girl International 1969-70-71-72-73
Int Curtis Cup 1974. Vagliano Trophy 1975. Scotland (Home Int) 1972-73-74-75-77-78; (Eur Team Ch) 1973-75
Mis Member of LGU Under-25 Team to tour Canada 1973. Selected for World Team Championship 1974 but declined due to studies

Robb, Miss Diane
See Mrs D Bailey

Roberts, Sharon
Born 8th June, 1964

Chp Welsh Ladies Amateur 1984
Int Wales (Home Int) 1986

Robertson, Mrs IC, MBE (*née* Isabella McCorkindale)
Born Southend, Argyll, on 11th April, 1936

Add 15 Buchanan Drive, Bearsden, Glasgow G61 2EW
Cls Hon member of Dunaverty, Troon, Machrihanish, Carradale, Hermitage, Trophil Hill, Silloth-on-Solway, Fairfield CC (USA), Caernarvonshire, Trevose
Chp British Ladies Stroke Play 1971-72-85. Runner-up British Ladies 1959-65-70. Scottish Ladies 1965-66-71-72-78-80, runner-up 1959-63-70. Second in British Ladies Open 1980 (also top Amateur). 2nd in British Ladies Open 1981 (also top Amateur). British Ladies Open Amateur 1981
Maj Sunningdale Foursomes 1960. Avia Foursomes 1972-81-84-86. Helen Holm Trophy 1973-79-86. Player's No 6 Cup 1973-76. Roehampton Gold Cup 1978 (tied)-79-81-82
Reg West of Scotland Ladies 1957-64-66-69. Dunbartonshire Ladies 1958-59-60-61-62-63-65-66-68-69-78
Ove New Zealand Ladies Match Play 1971
Int Curtis Cup 1960-66-68-70-72-82-86 (non-playing captain 1974-76). Vagliano Trophy 1959-63-65-69-71-81. World Team Championship (for Scotland) 1964, (for GB) 1966-68 (capt)-72-80-82. GB Commonwealth Team 1971, (non-playing captain 1975). Scotland (Home Int) 1958-59-60-61-62-63-64-65-66-69-72-73-78-80-81-82; (Eur Team Ch) 1965-67 (capt)-69-71-73-81-83; in Fiat Trophy 1978-80
Mis Daks Woman Golfer of the Year 1971-81. Frank Moran Trophy 1971. Leading qualifier in US Ladies Amateur 1978. Scottish Sportswoman of the Year 1968-71-78-81. Avia Golfer of the Year 1985

Robertson, Miss Janette
See Mrs I Wright

Robinson, Mrs C (*née* Nesbitt)
Born 7th March, 1953

Chp Irish Ladies Amateur 1976-80
Reg Ulster Ladies 1976-78
Int Curtis Cup 1980. Eur Team Ch 1975-77-79. Vagliano Trophy 1979

Roderick, Neil
Born

Chp Welsh Amateur Stroke Play 1984
Int Wales (Home Int) 1983-84-85-86

Roper, Roger
Born 15th April, 1962

Chp English Open Amateur Stroke Play 1985 (shared)
Int England (Home Int) 1984-85-86

Roy, Mrs Sandra Clair (*née* Needham)
Born Bishopton, Renfrewshire on 8th March, 1946

Add 4 Carron Crescent, Lenzie, Glasgow G66 5PJ
Cls Cawder (Hon), Machrihanish (Hon), Troon
Chp Scottish Ladies 1976
Maj Helen Holm Trophy 1974
Reg West of Scotland Ladies 1967-71-72-73-75. Lanarkshire Ladies 1969-72-73-77-83-84
Int Vagliano Trophy 1973-75, Scotland (Home Int) 1969-71-72-73-74-75-76-83; (Eur Team Ch) 1969-75-77
Mis Member of LGU team to tour South Africa 1974

Russell, David J
Born Birmingham on 2nd May, 1954. Turned Professional 1973

Maj Car Care Plan International 1985

Saddler, AC
Born Forfar, Angus on 11th August, 1935

Add Little Vantage, Forfar, Angus
Cls Forfar, Carnoustie
Chp Runner-up Scottish Amateur 1960
Maj Berkshire Trophy 1962
Int Walker Cup 1963-65-67 (non-playing captain 1977). Eisenhower Trophy 1962 (non-playing captain 1976) (winning team)-78. GB Commonwealth Team 1959-63-67; v Europe 1960-62-66 (non-playing captain 1976-78); v Professionals 1959-61. Scotland (Home Int) 1959-60-61-62-63-65 (non-playing captain 1974-75-76-77); (Eur Team Ch) (non-playing captain 1975-77)

Saunders, Miss Vivien Inez
Born Sutton on 24th November, 1946

Add Hunters Moon, Spicers Field, Oxshott, Surrey KT22 0UT. Tel Oxshott 2389
Cls Tyrrells Wood, Fulwell
Chp British Ladies Open 1977. Runner-up British Ladies Amateur 1966
Maj Avia Foursomes 1967-78. Keighley Trophy 1981. In 1980 won British Car Auctions
Jun Girl International 1964-65-66-67
Int Curtis Cup 1968. Vagliano Trophy 1967. GB Commonwealth Team 1967. England (Home Int) 1967-68; (Eur Team Ch) 1967; v France 1966-67
Mis Turned Professional 1st January, 1969. Qualified for USLPGA tour 1969, the first European to do so. Won Schweppes-Tarax Open (Australia) 1973 and Chrysler Open (Australia) 1973. Founder WPGA and Chairman 1978-79

Sewell, Douglas
Born Woking on 19th November, 1929. Turned Professional 1960

Chp English Amateur 1958-60. English Open Amateur Stroke Play 1957-59
Maj Sunningdale Foursomes 1959. Golf Illustrated Gold Vase 1960. Scrutton Jug 1959. Martini International 1970 (tied)
Reg Surrey Amateur 1954-56-58
Int Walker Cup 1957-59. Eisenhower Trophy 1960. GB Commonwealth Team 1959. England (Home Int) 1956-57-58-59-60
Oth Wentworth Pro-Am Foursomes 1968. West of England Open Professional 1968-70

Shapcott, Miss Susan
Born 2nd November, 1969

Chp English Women's Stroke Play 1986
Int England (Home Int) 1986

Sharp, Mrs Christine (*née* Holroyd)
Born 21st January, 1954. Turned Professional 1978

Jun Essex Girls 1971-72
WPGA Billingham South Staffs 1980. Clandeboye Classic 1983. JS Bloor Eastleigh Classic 1985

Sheahan, Dr David B
Born Southsea, England on 25th February, 1940

Add 57 Terenure Road East, Dublin 6. Tel Dublin 908204
Cls Grange
Chp Irish Amateur 1961-66-70
Maj Jeyes Professional 1962 (as an Amateur)
Oth Boyd Quaich 1962
Int Walker Cup 1963. GB v Europe 1962-64. Ireland (Home Int) 1961-62-63-64-65-66-67-70; (Eur Team Ch) 1965-67 (winning team on both occasions)

Shepperson, AE
Born Sutton-in-Ashfield on 8th April, 1936

Add Orchard House, High Oakham Road, Mansfield, Notts
Cls Coxmoor (Hon), Notts
Chp Second in English Open Amateur Stroke Play 1958-62
Oth President's Putter 1957
Reg Nottinghamshire Amateur 1955-58-61-65. Nottinghamshire Open 1955-58
Jun British Boys 1953
Int Walker Cup 1957-59. England (Home Int) 1956-57-58-59-60-62

Shingler, Terence Robert
Born Kearsley, Lancs on 9th August, 1935

Add Westways, 55 Sandhills Lane, Barnt Green, nr Birmingham B45 8NU
Cls Blackwell (Hon), Handsworth (Hon)
Chp English Amateur 1977. Worcestershire Amateur 1983
Maj Homer Salver 1972. Formby Hare 1974
Reg Leicester & Rutland Amateur 1962-63-64. Leicester & Rutland Open 1965-66. Worcestershire Amateur 1972-73. Worcestershire Open 1970-74. Worcestershire Amateur Match Play 1975-76-79
Int England (Home Int) 1977

Simpson, Mrs Linda (*née* Moore)
Born 7th October, 1961

Reg Cornwall Ladies 1979-80-81. South-West Ladies 1981
Int Curtis Cup 1980. Eur Team Ch 1981

Sinclair, Alexander
Born West Kilbride, Ayrshire on 6th July, 1920

Add 17 Blairston Avenue, Bothwell, Glasgow
Cls Royal and Ancient, West Kilbride (Hon), Drumpellier (Hon), Bothwell Castle (Hon), Royal Troon (Hon)
Maj Newlands Trophy 1950
Oth Royal and Ancient Silver Cross 1972. Royal Medal 1977. Scottish Open Amateur Seniors 1979
Reg West of Scotland Amateur 1950. Lanarkshire Amateur 1952-59-61. Glasgow Amateur 1961
Int Scotland (Home Int) 1950, (non-playing captain 1966-67). Non-playing captain Eur Team Ch 1967
Mis Chairman R & A Selection Committee from 1969 to 1975. Leading Amateur (joint second) in Northern Open 1948. President Scottish Golf Union 1976-78. Frank Moran Trophy 1978. Chairman R and A Amateur Status Committee 1979-81. President European Golf Association 1981-82-83

Slark, Mrs WA (*née* Ruth Porter)
Born Chesterfield on 6th May, 1939

Add 2 Shagbrook, Reigate Heath, Reigate, Surrey
Cls Long Ashton (Hon), Bath, Burnham and Berrow, Reigate Heath, Walton Heath
Chp English Ladies 1959-61-65, runner-up 1978
Maj Astor Prince's 1961. Fairway and Hazard Foursomes 1958. Roehampton Gold Cup 1963. Astor Salver 1962-63. Hovis Ladies 1966 (tied). Avia Foursomes 1968
Reg South Western Ladies 1956-57-60-61-62-64-65-66-67-69-72-77-79. Gloucestershire Ladies 1957-59-61-62-63-64-66-67-69-73-74-75-76-77
Ove Australian Ladies runner-up 1963
Jun British Girls 1956. Scottish Girls Open Stroke Play 1958. Girls International 1955-56-57
Int Curtis Cup 1960-62-64. Vagliano Trophy 1959-61-65. GB Commonwealth Team 1963. World Team Ch 1964-66. England (Home Int) 1959-60-61-62-64-65-66-68-75-78; (Eur Team Ch) 1965

Smith, Mrs Anne (formerly Stant, *née* Willard)
Born Calcutta, India on 23rd May, 1950

Add 19 Broadway, Walsall, West Midlands
Cls Walsall, Hon member of Gorleston, Purdis Heath (Ipswich), Ganton, Beau Desert
Chp British Ladies Stroke Play 1973
Maj Sunningdale Foursomes 1970. Central England Mixed Foursomes 1968. Hoylake Mixed Foursomes 1978
Reg Suffolk Ladies 1967-69-70-71. Midland Ladies 1973-75. Staffordshire Ladies 1975-78-79, runner-up 1977
Jun British Girls 1965. English Girls 1967. Girl International 1965-66-67-68
Int England (Home Int) 1974-75-76; (Eur Team Ch) 1975. Vagliano Trophy 1975. GB Commonwealth Team 1975. Curtis Cup 1976
Mis Member of LGU Touring Team to South Africa 1974

Smith, William Dickson
Born Glasgow on 2nd February, 1918

Add 12 Douglas Court, Beach Road, Troon
Cls Prestwick (Hon), Royal and Ancient, Royal Troon. Selkirk (Hon), Southerness, Gullane
Chp Scottish Amateur 1958. Scottish Senior Open Amateur 1983
Maj Worplesdon Mixed Foursomes 1957
Oth Royal and Ancient Royal Medal 1971
Reg Border Amateur 1949-51-57-63. Dumfriesshire Amateur 1956
Ove Indian Open Amateur 1945. Portuguese Open Amateur 1967-70
Int Walker Cup 1959. GB v Europe 1958. Scotland (Home Int) 1957-58-59-60-63 (non-playing captain 1983); v Scandinavia 1958-60
Mis Leading Amateur (5th) Open Championship 1957

Smye, Miss Catherine
See Mrs PG McCann

Smyth, Des
Born 12th February, 1953. Turned Professional 1973

Maj PGA Match Play 1979. Newcastle Brown 900 1980. Greater Manchester Open 1980. Coral Classic 1981. Sanyo Open 1983
Oth Irish Professional 1979. Carrolls Irish Match Play 1980. Irish Dunlop 1980
Int Ryder Cup 1979-81. GB v Europe 1980. Ireland in World Cup 1979-80-82-83. Hennessy-Cognac Cup 1984. Dunhill Cup 1985-86
Amr Ireland (Home Int) 1972-73; (Eur Team Ch) 1973

Sommerville, Miss Dorothea
See Mrs JL Hastings

Soulsby, Janet
Born 25th December, 1964. Turned Professional 1985

Reg Northumberland Ladies 1983
Chp Ladies British Stroke Play 1981
Int Curtis Cup 1982

Spearman, Mrs Marley
See Mrs M Harris

Squirrell, Hew Crawford
Born Cardiff on 15th August, 1932

Add The Nut House, 8 Hill Rise, Rickmansworth, Herts
Cls Hon member of Cardiff, Moseley, Killarney
Chp Welsh Amateur 1958-59-60-64-65, runner-up 1962-71
Maj Antlers Royal Mid-Surrey 1959-61. Hampshire Hog 1961. Berkhamsted Trophy 1960-63
Oth Boyd Quaich 1955
Reg Glamorgan Amateur 1959-65. Herts Amateur 1963-73
Int Wales (Home Int) 1955-56-57-58-59-60-61-62-63-64-65-66-67-68-69-70-71 (captain 1969-70-71)-73-74-75; (Eur Team Ch) 1965-67-69-71-75; v France 1975
Mis Deputy-Director Golf Foundation

Stant, Mrs Anne
See Mrs A Smith

Stephen, Alexander R (Sandy)
Born St Andrews on 8th January, 1954. Turned Professional 1985

Add 51 Station Park, Lower Largo, Fife
Cls Lundin (Hon), Muckhart (Hon), Broomieknowe
Chp Scottish Amateur 1971
Maj East of Scotland Open Amateur 1974-77-83-84. West of Scotland Open Amateur 1975
Reg North of Scotland Open Amateur 1972-77. Fife Amateur 1973. Lothians Amateur 1978
Jun Scottish Boys 1970. Boy International 1970-71. Youth International 1972-73-74-75
Int GB v Europe 1972. Scotland (Home Int) 1971-72-73-74-75-76-77-84-85; (Eur Team Ch) 1975; v Spain 1974; v Belgium 1975-77-78. Walker Cup 1985
Mis Finished third in World Boys International Trophy (USA) 1970

Stevens, David Llewellyn
Born Church Village, Glamorgan on 14th April, 1950

Add Nant-y-Garth, Gwaelod-y-Garth, Taffs Well, Cardiff
Cls Llantrisant and Pontyclun, Southerndown, Killarney (Hon)
Chp Welsh Amateur Stroke Play 1969. Welsh Amateur 1977-80
Reg Glamorgan Amateur 1974-76-80
Int Wales (Home Int) 1968-69-70-74-75-76-78-80-82; (Eur Team Ch) 1969-77; v France 1976; v Denmark 1977; in Fiat Trophy 1980

Stewart, Miss Gillian
Born Inverness on 21st October, 1958. Turned Professional 1985

Add 14 Annfield Road, Inverness
Cls Inverness (Hon), Nairn
Chp Scottish Ladies 1979-83-84. British Ladies Match Play runner-up 1982. IBM European Open 1984 (as Amateur)
Maj Helen Holm Trophy 1981-84
Reg Northern Counties Ladies 1976-78-82. North of Scotland Ladies 1975-78-80-82-83
Jun British Girls 1976. Girl International 1975-76-77. Scottish Under-19 Stroke Play Champion 1975
Int GB Commonwealth Team 1979-83. Vagliano Trophy 1979-81-83. Curtis Cup 1980-82. Scotland (Home Int) 1979-80-81-82-83-84; (Eur Team Ch) 1979-81-83. World Cup 1982-84
Mis Member of Scottish team which won the 1980 European Junior Team Championship. Avia Golfer of the Year 1984. Ford Ladies Classic 1985

Storey, Eustace Francis
Born Lancaster on 30th August, 1901

Add Flat 4, Larchwood Lodge, Larch Avenue, Sunninghill, Berks
Cls Swinley Forest
Chp Runner-up Amateur Championship 1924
Maj Worplesdon Mixed Foursomes 1938-48
Oth President's Putter 1926 (tied)
Int Walker Cup 1924-26-28. England (Home Int) 1924-25-26-27-28-30-36; v France 1936
Mis Leading Amateur in Open Championship 1938

Stowe, Charles
Born Sandyfields, Sedgley on 11th January, 1909

Add 46 Butts Road, Penn, Wolverhampton
Cls Penn, Brocton Hall, Beau Desert, Shifnal
Chp Runner-up Amateur Championship 1948. English Open Amateur Stroke Play 1948-53. Runner-up English Amateur 1947-49
Maj Prince of Wales Challenge Cup 1937-49
Reg Midland Counties Amateur 1935-48-59-63. Staffordshire Amateur 1934-39-46-48-53-54-57-64. Staffordshire Open 1948
Int Walker Cup 1938-47. England (Home Int) 1935-36-37-38-46-49; v France 1938-39
Mis Played for British Seniors 1967

Stuart, Hugh Bannerman
Born Forres on 27th June, 1942

Add 33 Loirston Manor, Cove, Aberdeen
Cls Forres (Hon), Murcar (Hon)
Chp Scottish Amateur 1972, runner-up 1970-76
Reg North of Scotland Amateur 1967-74. Moray Amateur 1960. Nairnshire Amateur 1966
Jun Scottish Boys 1959. Boy International 1959
Int Walker Cup 1971-73-75. GB Commonwealth Team 1971. Eisenhower Trophy 1972. GB v Europe 1968-72-74. Scotland (Home Int) 1967-68-70-71-72-73-74-76; (Eur Team Ch) 1969-71-73-75; v Belgium 1973-75
Mis Won all his matches in 1971 Walker Cup. Member of European Team to tour South Africa 1974

Swallow, Carole
Born 9th August, 1967

Chp Welsh Ladies Open Amateur Stroke Play 1985
Int (Eur Team Ch) 1984

Taylor, Alastair Ramsey
Born Lanarkshire on 21st May, 1959

Add 35 Abbotsford Brae, East Mains, East Kilbride, Lanarkshire
Cls East Kilbride
Chp Scottish Open Amateur Stroke Play 1978
Jun Boy International 1976. Youth International 1977-78-79-80
Int Scotland in Fiat Trophy 1978; v England 1979

Thirlwell, Alan
Born 8th August, 1928

Add 19 Birch Green, Formby, Merseyside L37 1NG
Cls Gosforth, Formby
Chp Runner-up Amateur Championship 1958-72. English Amateur 1954-55, runner-up 1963. Second in English Open Amateur Stroke Play 1964
Maj County Champion of Champions 1962. Wentworth Pro-Am Foursomes 1960-61-68
Reg Northumberland Amateur 1952-55-62-64. Northumberland and Durham Open 1960
Int Walker Cup 1957. GB Commonwealth Team 1954-63. GB v Europe 1956-58; v Denmark 1955; v Professionals 1963. England (Home Int) 1951-52-54-55-56-57-58-59-63-64; v France 1954-56-59
Mis Semi-finalist Canadian Amateur 1957. EGU Selector 1974 to 1977. Secretary CONGU

Thom, Kenneth Gordon
Born 1st March, 1922

Add 305 London Road, Westcliffe-on-Sea
Cls Hendon
Chp Runner-up English Amateur 1946
Reg Middlesex Amateur 1947-48
Jun Boy International 1939
Int Walker Cup 1949. England (Home Int) 1947-48-49-53

Thomas, David C
Born Newcastle-upon-Tyne on 16th August, 1934. Turned Professional 1949

Opn Second in Open Championship 1958 (lost play-off for title). Second 1966
Tls Belgian Open 1955. Dutch Open 1958. French Open 1959

Maj Esso Golden 1961 (tied)-62-66. PGA Match Play 1963. Silentnight 1965 (tied). Penfold-Swallow 1966. Jeyes 1966. Penfold 1968 (tied). Graham Textiles 1969. Pains-Wessex 1969
Ove Caltex (NZ) 1958-59. Olgiata Trophy (Rome) 1963
Oth British Assistants 1955. Wentworth Pro-Am Foursomes 1960-61
Int Ryder Cup 1959-63-65-67. Wales in World Cup 1957-58-59-60-61-62-63-66-67-69-70. Wales in Double Diamond 1972-73
Mis Won qualifying competition for US Open 1964

Thomas, Mrs Tegwen (*née* Perkins)

Born Cardiff on 2nd October, 1955

Add 35 Headland Road, Bishopston, Swansea SA3 3DH
Cls Wenvoe Castle, Porthcawl, Pennard
Chp Welsh Ladies Amateur 1976-77. Welsh Ladies Open Amateur Stroke Play 1980. Second in British Ladies Amateur Stroke Play 1974
Maj Wills Match Play 1973. Avia Foursomes 1977. Worplesdon Mixed Foursomes 1973-78
Reg South-Western Ladies 1973-74-76. Glamorganshire Ladies 1972-74-75-77-78-80-81-83
Jun Welsh Girls 1970. Girl International 1970-71-72-73
Int Curtis Cup 1974-76-78-80. Vagliano Trophy 1973-75-77-79. World Team Championship 1974. Wales (Home Int) 1972-73-74-75-76-77-78-79-80-81-82-83-84; (Eur Team Ch) 1975-77-79-81-83; in Fiat Trophy 1978. GB Commonwealth Team 1975-79. GB in Colombian International 1977-79
Mis Member of LGU Team to tour South Africa 1974. First Welsh player in Curtis Cup Team. In 1976 became first Welsh woman player to win all matches in Home Internationals. Daks Woman Golfer of the Year 1976 (joint)

Thomas, Mrs Vicki (*née* Rawlings)

Born Northampton on 27th October, 1954

Add 9 South Close, Bishopston, Swansea
Cls Bargoed, Pennard
Chp Welsh Ladies Amateur 1979-82-83-85. Second in British Ladies Amateur Stroke Play 1979. Welsh Ladies Open Stroke Play 1981-82, runner-up 1980
Maj Roehampton Gold Cup 1983-85. Cotswold Gold Vase 1983. Keithley Trophy 1983
Reg Glamorganshire Ladies 1970-71-79
Jun Welsh Girls 1973. Girl International 1969-70-71-72-73
Int GB Commonwealth Team 1979-83. Vagliano Trophy 1979-83. Wales (Home Int) 1971-72-73-74-75-76-77-78-79-80-81-82-83-84; (Eur Team Ch) 1973-75-77-79-81-83. Curtis Cup 1982-84

Thompson, Martyn S

Born 27th January, 1964

Chp Amateur Champion 1982
Int Walker Cup 1983. England (Home Int) 1982

Thomson, Hector

Born Machrihanish, Argyll on 21st November, 1913. Turned Professional 1940

Chp Amateur Champion 1936. Scottish Amateur 1935, runner-up 1939. Irish Open Amateur 1934-35
Maj Tennant Cup 1933. Edward Trophy 1934
Reg Glasgow Amateur 1935
Jun British Boys 1931. Boy International 1931
Int Walker Cup 1936-38. Scotland (Home Int) 1934-35-36-37-38
Oth West of Scotland PGA Match Play 1949-53. West of Scotland Professional 1950. Scottish Professional 1953
Mis Joint leading overseas player in Tam o' Shanter World 1953

Thomson, Miss Muriel

Born Aberdeen on 12th December, 1954. Turned Professional 1979

Add
Cls Murcar (Hon)
Chp Runner-up Scottish Ladies 1977
Maj Helen Holm Trophy 1975-76. Winner of Elizabeth Ann Classic 1981
Reg North of Scotland Ladies 1973-74. Aberdeenshire Ladies 1977
Ove Canadian Ladies Foursomes 1978
Jun Girl International 1970-71-72-73
Int Curtis Cup 1978. Vagliano Trophy 1977. World Team Championship 1978. GB in Colombian International 1979. Scotland (Home Int) 1974-75-76-77-78; (Eur Team Ch) 1975-77
WPGA Carlsberg (Tyrrells Wood) 1980. Viscount Double Glazing 1980. Barnham Broom 1980. Headed Carlsberg and Hambro Life Order of Merit 1980. Winner of Frank Moran Trophy 1981. Winner of Elizabeth Ann Classic 1981. Order of Merit 1983. Guernsey Open 1984. Sands International 1984. Laing Ladies Classic 1985

Thornhill, Mrs Jill

Born 18th August, 1942

Add 10 Wallace Fields, Epsom, Surrey
Cls Walton Heath, Silloth-on-Solway
Chp Runner-up English Ladies 1974. British Ladies' Amateur 1983
Maj Avia Foursomes 1970-83. Astor Salver 1972-75. Newmark International 1974. Worplesdon Mixed Foursomes 1975. Hampshire Rose 1982
Reg South Eastern Ladies 1963-64-85. Surrey Ladies 1962-64-65-73-74-77-78-81-82-83-84
Ove Belgian Ladies 1967
Int Vagliano Trophy 1965. England (Home Int) 1964-65-74-82-83. Commonwealth Team Ch 1983; (Eur Team Ch) 1983. Curtis Cup 1984-86. Avia Golfer of the Year 1983

Tiernan, Miss Clarrie

See Mrs Reddan

Torrance, Sam

Born Largs, Ayrshire on 24th August, 1953

Tis Zambian Open 1975. Colombian Open 1979. Spanish Open 1982. Portuguese Open 1982-83. Scandinavian Open 1983. Tunisian Open 1984
Maj Piccadilly Medal 1976. Martini 1976. Benson & Hedges International Open 1984. Sanyo Open 1984. Monte Carlo Open 1985
Ove Australian PGA 1980
Oth Lord Derby's Under-25 1972. Scottish Uniroyal 1975. Scottish Professional 1978-80
Int GB v Europe 1976-78-80. Scotland in World Cup 1976-78-82-84-85. Scotland in Double Diamond 1973-76-77. Ryder Cup 1983-85. Hennessy-Cognac Cup 1982-84. Dunhill Cup 1985-86
Amr Boy International 1970
Mis Rookie of the Year 1982

Townsend, Peter Michael Paul

Born Cambridge on 16th September, 1946. Turned Professional 1966

Chp English Open Amateur Stroke Play 1966
Maj Duncan Putter 1965. Mullingar Trophy 1965-66. Lytham Trophy 1966. Golf Illustrated Gold Vase 1966. Prince of Wales Challenge Cup 1966. Royal St George's Challenge Cup 1966. Berkhamsted Trophy 1966. PGA Close 1968
Reg Herts Amateur 1964
Jun British Boys 1962-64. British Youths 1965
Int Walker Cup 1965. GB v Europe 1966. Eisenhower

Trophy 1966. England (Home Int) 1965-66. Ryder Cup 1969-71. England in World Cup 1969-74. England in Double Diamond 1971-72-74. GB v Europe 1974

Tls Dutch Open 1967. Swiss Open 1971. Zambian Open 1978

Ove Chesterfield (USA) 1968. Western Australia Open 1968. Walworth Aloyco 1971. Los Lagaratos Open 1972-78. Caracas Open 1969. ICL International (SA) 1975. Moroccan Grand Prix 1978. Caribbean Open 1978. Laurent Perrier 1981

Oth Carris Trophy 1964. Coca-Cola Young Professionals 1968. Carrolls Irish Match Play 1971-76. Irish Dunlop 1977

Mis Equalled British PGA record of 7 consecutive birdies in 1974 Viyella PGA Championship. Captain PGA 1984

Tucker, William Iestyn

Born Nantyglo, Monmouth on 9th December, 1926

Add Nant Morlais, Caeracca Villas, Pant, Merthyr Tydfil

Cls Monmouthshire, Brecon, Killarney, Morlais Castle, Tredegar and Rhymney, Pontynewydd, Llantrisant, Radyr, Whitehall

Chp Welsh Amateur 1963-66, runner-up 1951-56-64-67-75-76. Welsh Amateur Stroke Play 1976

Maj Duncan Putter 1960-61 (tied)-63-69-76

Reg Monmouthshire Amateur 1949-52-53-54-55-56-57-58-59-60-61-62-63-67-69-74. Gwent Amateur 1976

Int Wales (Home Int) 1949-50-51-52-53-54-55-56-57-58-59-60-61-62-63-64-65-66-67-68-69-70-71-72-74-75; (Eur Team Ch) 1965-67-69-75; v Australia 1953; v France 1975. Captain Welsh Team 1966-67-68

Mis Record number of consecutive international appearances for Wales–from 1949-72. On 25th October, 1972 completed a Medal round at Cardiff GC (SSS 68) in 59 strokes. Holed in one 12 times

Uzielli, Mrs WJ (*née* Angela Carrick)

Born Swanton Morley, Norfolk on 1st February, 1940

Add Buckhurst Park Cottage, Buckhurst Road, Cheapside, Ascot, Berks

Cls Hon member of Berkshire, Denham, Trevose, Hunstanton

Chp British Ladies Open Amateur 1977. Runner-up English Ladies Amateur 1976

Maj Astor Salver 1971-73 (tied)-77-81. Roehampton Gold Cup 1977. Avia Foursomes 1982. Hampshire Rose 1985

Reg Berkshire Ladies 1976-77-78-79-80-81-83

Int Curtis Cup 1978. Vagliano Trophy 1977. England (Home Int) 1976-77-78; (Eur Team Ch) 1977

Mis Daks Woman Golfer of the Year 1977

Valentine, Mrs George, MBE (*née* Jessie Anderson)

Born Perth on 18th March, 1915

Add Daintree, 11 Brompton Terrace, Perth

Cls Hon member of Craigie Hill, St Rule, Hunstanton, Blairgowrie, Murrayshall

Chp British Ladies 1937-55-58, runner-up 1950-57. Scottish Ladies 1938-39-51-53-55-56, runner-up 1934-54

Maj Spalding Ladies 1957. Kayser Bondor Foursomes 1959-61. Worplesdon Mixed Foursomes 1963-64-65

Reg East of Scotland Ladies 1936-38-39-50

Ove New Zealand Ladies 1935. French Ladies 1936

Jun British Girls 1933

Int Curtis Cup 1936-38-50-52-54-56-58. GB v France 1935-36-38-39-47-49-51-55; v Belgium 1949-51-54-55; v Canada 1938-50. GB Commonwealth Team 1953-55 (non-playing captain 1959). Scotland (Home Int) 1934-35-36-37-38-39-47-49-50-51-52-53-54-55-56-57-58

Mis Semi-finalist Canadian Ladies 1938. Member of LGU Team to Australia and New Zealand 1935. Turned Professional 1960. Frank Moran Trophy 1967

Vaughan, Miss Sheila

See Mrs S Maher

Wadsworth, Helen

Born 7th April, 1964

Chp Welsh Ladies Open Amateur Stroke Play 1986

Maj Astor Salver 1985

Oth South-East Girls 1981

Int (Eur Team Ch) 1985

Waite, Miss Claire

Born 4th November, 1964. Turned Professional 1985

Chp British Girls 1982. English Ladies 1984. British Ladies Stroke-Play 1984

Reg Wiltshire Ladies 1980-81-83

Ove Australian Stroke-Play Team 1982. South Atlantic (USA) 1984. Trans National (USA) 1984

Jun English Girl International 1981-82. English Girls 1982

Int England (Home Int) 1981-82-83. European Team Championship 1983. Commonwealth Tournament 1983. Vagliano Trophy 1983. Curtis Cup 1984. Espirito Santo 1984

Mis Avia Golfer of the Year 1984.

Waites, Brian J

Born Bolton on 1st March, 1940. Turned Professional 1957

Tls Kenya Open 1980

Maj Tournament Players' Championship 1978. Car Care Plan International 1982

Ove Mufulira Open (Zambia) 1980-82. Cock of North (Zambia) Open 1985

Oth Midland Open 1971-76-81. Midland Professional Stroke Play 1972-77-78-79. Midland Professional Match Play 1972-73-74. Hennessy-Cognac Cup 1984

Int GB v Europe 1980. England in World Cup 1980-82-83

Walker, James

Born Bartonholm, by Irvine, on 11th February, 1921

Add 17 Greenbank Road, Irvine, Ayrshire

Cls Irvine Bogside

Chp Scottish Amateur 1961. Runner-up Amateur Championship 1961

Reg West of Scotland Amateur 1954. Ayrshire Amateur 1956 (tied)

Int Walker Cup 1961, selected 1959. GB v Europe 1958-60; v Professionals 1958-60. Scotland (Home Int) 1954-55-57-58-60-61-62-63

Walker, Mrs JB, MBE

Born Ireland on 21st June, 1896

Cls Gosforth. Hon member of Troon, Island, Malahide, Alnmouth, Foxton Hall

Chp Irish Ladies 1930, runner-up 1934

Reg Ayrshire Ladies 1934-37-38

Ove Australian Ladies 1935. Runner-up New Zealand Ladies 1935

Int Curtis Cup 1934-36-38. GB v France 1935-38-39; v Canada 1938. Ireland (Home Int) 1928-29-30-31-32-33-34-35-36-37-38-48

Mis Two holes-in-one in the same week

Walker, Kenneth

Born 1st December, 1966

Chp Scottish Open Amateur Stroke Play 1986

Maj Edward Trophy 1984

Oth Scottish Universities Individual 1985

Int Scotland (Home Int) 1986

Walker, Carol Michelle

Born Alwoodley, nr Leeds on 17th December, 1952. Turned Professional 1973

Add 127 Victoria Road, New Barnet, Herts EN4 9PE

Chp British Ladies 1971-72, runner-up 1973. Second in British Ladies Stroke Play 1972. English Ladies 1973. Second in British Ladies Open 1979

Maj Hovis Ladies 1972. Sunningdale Foursomes 1982
Reg Kent Ladies 1971
Ove Portuguese Ladies 1972. US Trans-Mississippi 1972. Spanish Ladies 1973
Jun Girl International 1969-70-71. French Girls Under-22 Open 1971
Int Curtis Cup 1972. GB Commonwealth Team 1971. World Team Championship 1972. Vagliano Trophy 1971. England (Home Int) 1970-72; (Eur Team Ch) 1971-73
Mis Golf Writers Trophy 1972. Undefeated in 1972 Curtis Cup. First British woman to win a major US event for 36 years. Daks Woman Golfer of the Year 1972
WPGA Awarded USLPGA card 1974, then on having to re-qualify in 1975 school, led qualifiers. Tied first in Jerry Lewis Classic 1976 but lost play-off. In 1979 won Carlsberg (Strensall), won Carlsberg (St Pierre) 1981; In 1980 won Lambert and Butler Match Play. Sunningdale Foursomes 1982. Sands International 1983. Baume & Mercier Classic, Lorne Stewart Match Play 1984. Chairman WPGA 1981-82-83-84

Walker, Miss Maureen
See Mrs Richmond

Walter, Julie
Born 4th December, 1952

Chp English Ladies Amateur 1982
Reg Midland Ladies 1980

Walton, Philip
Born Dublin on 28th March, 1962. Turned Professional 1983

Chp Irish Amateur 1982
Maj Scottish Open Amateur Stroke Play 1981
Int Walker Cup 1981-83. Ireland (Home Int) 1980-81; (Eur Team Ch) 1981

Ward, Miss Angela
See Mrs A Bonallack

Ward, Charles Harold
Born Birmingham on 16th September, 1911

Opn Third in Open Championship 1948-51, leading British player (4th) 1946
Maj Daily Mail Victory 1945. Silver King 1948 (tied). Yorkshire Evening News 1948. Spalding 1949. North British-Harrogate 1949. Dunlop Masters 1949. Daily Mail 1950. Dunlop 1951. Lotus 1951. PGA Close 1956
Oth West of England Open Professional 1937. Daily Telegraph Pro-Am 1947-48. Midland Professional 1933-34-50-53-55-63. Midland Open 1949-51-52-54-57
Int Ryder Cup 1947-49-51
Mis Vardon Trophy 1948-49

Way, Paul
Born 12th March, 1963. Turned Professional 1981

Tls KLM Dutch Open 1982. Whyte & McKay PGA 1985
Int Ryder Cup 1983-85. England in World Cup 1985. Dunhill Cup 1985
Amr Walker Cup 1981. English Open Amateur Stroke Play Champion 1981
Mis Second Lawrence Batley International 1983. Second St Mellion Time Share Tournament 1983

Wethered, Miss Joyce
See Lady Heathcoat-Amory

White, Ronald James
Born Wallasey on 9th April, 1921

Add Lark Rise, 11 Oldfield Drive, Heswall, Wirral, Merseyside
Cls Hon member of Royal Birkdale, Woolton, Buxton and High Peak, Killarney
Chp English Amateur 1949, runner-up 1953. English Open Amateur Stroke Play 1950-51
Maj Golf Illustrated Gold Vase 1949. Daily Telegraph Pro-Am 1947-49
Oth Carris Trophy 1937. British Seniors Open Amateur 1978-79
Reg Lancashire Amateur 1948
Jun Boy International 1936-37-38
Int Walker Cup 1947-49-51-53-55. England (Home Int) 1947-48-49-53; France 1947-48

Whitlock, Miss SC
See Mrs Susan Hedges

Willard, Miss A
See Mrs A Smith

Wilson, Miss Enid
Born Stonebroom, nr Alfreton, Derbyshire on 15th March, 1910

Add The Oast, Redbridge Farm, Redbridge Lane, Crowborough, East Sussex TN6 3SR
Cls Hon member of Notts, Sherwood Forest, Chesterfield, Bramley, Sandy Lodge, Knole Park, North Hants, Crowborough
Chp British Ladies 1931-32-33. English Ladies 1928-30, runner-up 1927
Maj Roehampton Gold Cup 1930
Reg Midland Ladies 1926-28-29-30. Derbyshire Ladies 1925-26. Cheshire Ladies 1933
Jun British Girls 1925
Int Curtis Cup 1932. England (Home Int) 1928-29-30
Mis Semi-finalist US Ladies Amateur 1931-33

Winchester, Roger
Born 28th March, 1967

Chp English Amateur 1985
Int England (Home Int) 1985

Wood, David K
Born

Chp Welsh Amateur 1982
Int Wales (Home Int) 1982-83-84-85-86

Woosnam, Ian
Born 2nd March, 1958. Turned Professional 1976

Tls Swiss Open 1982. Scandinavian Open 1984. Zambian Open 1985. Kenya Open 1986
Maj News of the World Under-23 Match Play 1982. Swiss Open 1982. Cacharel Under-25 1982. Silk Cut Masters 1983. Lawrence Batley TPC 1986
Int GB and Ireland Team Hennessy Cognac Cup 1982. European Team Ryder Cup 1983-85. Represented Wales in World Cup 1980-82-83-84-85. Hennessy-Cognac Cup 1984. Dunhill Cup 1985-86. Nissan Cup 1986
Mis Second Spanish Open 1982. Second Nigerian Open 1982. Italian Open 1982. Benson and Hedges International 1982

Wright, Mrs Innes (*née* Janette Robertson)

Born Glasgow on 7th January, 1935

Add Glenelg, Aboyne, Aberdeenshire
Cls Hon member of Lenzie, Troon, Cruden Bay, Aboyne, St Rule
Chp Scottish Ladies 1959-60-61-73, runner-up 1958
Maj Kayser Bondor Foursomes 1958 (tied)-61. Worplesdon Mixed Foursomes 1959
Reg North of Scotland Ladies 1970. Lanarkshire Ladies 1954-55-56-57-58-59. West of Scotland Ladies 1956-58-59
Jun British Girls 1950. Girl International 1950-51-52-53
Int Curtis Cup 1954-56-58-60. Vagliano Trophy 1959-61. GB v France 1957; v Belgium 1957; v Canada 1954. GB Commonwealth Team 1959. Scotland (Home Int) 1952-53-54-55-56-57-58-59-60-61-63-65-66-67-73 (non-playing captain 1978-79-80); (Eur Team Ch) 1965-73 (non-playing captain 1979)
Mis British Team to Australasia 1955
Reg Caernarvonshire District Ladies 17 times. Caernarvonshire and Angelesey Ladies 8 times
Int World Team Championship 1964. Wales (Home Int) 1938-47-48-49-51-52-53-54-56-57-58-59-60-62-63-64-66-68-71-73 (capt)

Wright, Miss Pamela

Born 24th January, 1964

Jun North of Scotland Girls 1979. Scottish Girls International 1979-80. British Under-18 1980
Int Vilmorin Trophy 1980. European Team Championship 1981-83. Vagliano Trophy 1981. Scotland (Home Int) 1982-83-84
Reg Aberdeenshire Ladies 1982-85

Overseas Players

Explanation of abbreviations used

Bri Victories (also second place in a few top events) in British events
Nat Victories (also second place in a few top events) in major events in native country
For Victories (also second place in a few top events) in important foreign events excluding British and Native country
USC Number of victories on US circuit excluding US Open, Masters and USPGA which are shown separately
Oth Victories in less important events in native country or overseas
Sen Senior Tour Events
Int International appearances
Mis Miscellaneous

Aaron, Tommy

Born Gainesville, Georgia, USA on 22nd February, 1937. Turned Professional 1961

Nat Runner-up US Amateur 1958. US Masters 1973. USPGA second 1972
For Canadian Open 1969
USC 1970–one
Oth Lancome Trophy 1972
Int Walker Cup 1959. Ryder Cup 1969-73
Mis Was nine times second before winning his first event

Alcott, Amy

Born Turned Professional

Nat US Women's Open 1980
USC 1985–three, 1986–two

Aoki, Isao

Born Abiko, Chiba, Japan on 31st August, 1942. Turned Professional 1964

Eur World Match Play Championship 1978. European Open 1983
Nat Japan Open 1983. Japan Professional 1973-81
For Hawaiian Open 1983
Int Japan v US 1982-83-84. Nissan Cup 1985. Dunhill Cup 1985

Baiocchi, Hugh

Born Johannesburg on 17th August, 1946. Turned Professional 1971

Bri PGA Match Play 1977
Nat South African Amateur 1970. South African Open 1978. South African PGA 1980
For Brazilian Amateur 1968. Swiss Open 1973-79. Dutch Open 1975. Scandinavian Enterprises Open 1976. Zimbabwe Open 1980
Oth Glen Anil Classic 1972. Western Province Open 1973. General Motors International Classic (SA) 1973. Transvaal Open 1973-76. ICL International (SA) 1976. Holiday Inns (Swaziland) 1976. Rhodesian Masters 1976. State Express Classic 1983
Int South Africa seven times as an amateur. South Africa in World Cup 1973-77
Mis European American Express 1973. Second in Order of Merit 1977. Captain South African PGA 1978

Baker, K

Born . Turned Professional

Nat US Women's Open 1985
Int Curtis Cup 1982

Baker-Finch, Ian

Born Nambour, Australia on 24th October, 1960. Turned Professional 1979

For Scandinavian Open 1985. New Zealand Open 1983
Nat West Australian Open 1984. NSW Open 1984. Queensland PGA 1984. Victoria Open 1985
Int Nissan Cup 1986

Ballesteros, Severiano

Born Spain on 9th April, 1957

Bri Open Champion 1979-84; second 1976. Uniroyal International 1977. Martini 1978-80. English Classic 1979. Suntory 1981-82-84-85. Sun Alliance PGA 1983-84. Carrolls Irish Open 1983-85-86. Timex Open 1983-85. Sanyo Open 1985. Dunhill Masters 1986
Nat Madrid Open 1980-82. Spanish Open 1985
For Dutch Open 1976-80-86. French Open 1977-82-85-86. Swiss Open 1977-78-85. Japan Open 1977-78. Scandinavian Enterprises Open 1978. Kenya Open 1978. German Open 1978. US Masters 1980-83. Australian PGA 1981. Monte Carlo Open 1986
USC 1978-one. 1983-one. 1985-one
Oth Lancôme Trophy 1976-83-86 (shared). Dunlop Phoenix (Japan) 1977. Otago Classic (NZ) 1977
Int Europe v GB 1976-78-80. Spain in World Cup 1975-76 (winning team)-77 (winning team). Ryder Cup 1979-83-85. Dunhill Cup 1985-86
Mis Vardon Trophy 1976-77-78. European American Express 1976. Second in Order of Merit 1979. Golf Writers Trophy 1979

Barber, Miller

Born Shreveport, Louisiana, USA on 31st March, 1931. Turned Professional 1958

USC 1964–one. 1967–one. 1968–one. 1969–one. 1970–one. 1971–one. 1972–one. 1973–one (World Open when it was the world's richest tournament) 1974–one. 1977–one. 1978–one
Sen US Seniors PGA 1981 US Seniors Open 1982
Int Ryder Cup 1969-71

Bean, Andy

Born Lafayette, GA on 13th March, 1953. Turned Professional 1975

USC 1977–one. 1978–three. 1979–one. 1980–one. 1981–one. 1982–one. 1984–one. 1986–three
Int Ryder Cup 1979

Beman, Deane R

Born Washington, DC, USA on 22nd April, 1938. Turned Professional 1967

Bri Amateur Champion 1959
Nat US Amateur 1960-63. Second in US Open 1969
USC 1969–one. 1970–one. 1972–one. 1973–one
Oth Eastern Amateur 1960-61-63-64
Int Walker Cup 1959-61-63-65. Eisenhower Trophy 1960-62-64-66
Mis Became USPGA Tour Commissioner 1974

Berg, Miss Patricia Jane

Born Minneapolis, USA on 13th February, 1918. Turned Professional 1940

Nat US Ladies Amateur 1938. US Women's Open 1946, second 1957
USC 41 tournament victories
Oth Western Amateur 1938
Int Curtis Cup 1936-38
Mis US leading money winner 1954-55-57. Bobby Jones Award 1963. First President of USLPGA Ben Hogan Award 1975

Bland, John

Born Johannesburg on 22nd April, 1945. Turned Professional 1968

Bri Benson & Hedges International 1983
Nat South African PGA 1977. Nine SAf circuit wins
For Cannes Open 1968
Int World Cup 1975

Boros, Julius

Born Fairfield, Connecticut on 3rd March, 1920. Turned Professional 1950

Nat US Open Champion 1952-63. USPGA 1968
USC 1952–one. 1954–two. 1955–one. 1958–two. 1959–one. 1960–one. 1963–two. 1964–one. 1967–three. 1968–one. USPGA Seniors 1971-77. Legends of Golf 1979
Int Ryder Cup 1959-63-65-67. USA in World Cup 1953-68
Mis US leading money winner 1952-55. USPGA Player of the Year 1952-63

Bradley, Pat

Born .Turned Professional

Nat US Women's Open 1981
USL 1985–three 1986–five

Burke, Jack, Jr

Born Fort Worth, Texas, USA in January, 1923. Turned Professional 1940

Nat US Masters 1956, second 1952. USPGA 1956
USC 1950–three. 1952–five. 1953–one. 1956–two. 1958–one. 1959–one. 1961–one. 1963–one
Int Ryder Cup 1951-53-55-57 (capt.)-59, non-playing captain 1973
Mis USPGA Player of the Year 1956

Campbell, William Cammack

Born West Virginia, USA on 5th May, 1923

Bri Amateur Championship runner-up 1954
Nat US Amateur Champion 1964
For Mexican Amateur 1956. Canadian Amateur runner-up 1952-54-65
Oth North and South Amateur 1950-53-57-67. Tam O'Shanter World Amateur 1948-49. Ontario Amateur 1967. USGA Seniors 1979-80
Int Walker Cup 1951-53-55 (capt.)-57-65-67-71-75. Eisenhower Trophy 1964, non-playing captain 1968
Mis Bobby Jones Award 1956. Member of the USGA Committee 1962 to 1965. Uniform Ball Committee 1970. President USGA 1983.

Canizares, Jose-Maria

Born Madrid on 18th February, 1947. Turned Professional 1967

Bri Avis-Jersey Open 1980. Bob Hope British Classic 1980-83
Oth Lancia D'Oro 1972. Italian Open 1981. Kenya Open 1984
Int Europe v GB 1974-76-78-80. Spain in World Cup 1974-80-82-83-84. Ryder Cup 1983. Hennessy-Cognac Cup 1984. Dunhill Cup 1985.
Mis Lowest 9-hole aggregate of 27 on Europe PGA circuit in 1978 Swiss Open

Caponi, Miss Donna

Born Detroit, Michigan, USA on 29th January, 1945. Turned Professional 1965

Nat US Women's Open 1969, 1970. USLPGA 1979
USC 19 tournament wins
Mis LA Times Women Golfer of the Year 1970

Carner, Mrs Don R (*née* Jo Anne Gunderson)

Born Kirkland, Washington, USA on 4th April, 1939. Turned Professional 1970

Nat US Girls 1956. US Ladies Amateur 1957-60-62-66-68; runner-up 1956-64. US Women's Open 1971-76; second 75(tied)-78(tied)
For Australian Ladies Open 1975
USC 40 Victories on USLPGA circuit up to end of 1980
Oth Western Ladies Open 1959
Int Represented US in Curtis Cup four times
Mis Rookie of the Year 1970. Leading US money winner 1974. US Ladies Player of the Year 1974. Bob Jones Award 1981

Casper, Bill

Born in San Diego, USA on 24th June, 1931. Turned Professional 1954

Nat US Open Champion 1959-66. US Masters 1970; second 1969. USPGA second 1958-65-71
For Canadian Open 1967. Italian Open 1975
USC 1956–one. 1957–two. 1958–four. 1959–three. 1960–five. 1961–one. 1962–one. 1963–two. 1964–four. 1965–four. 1966–three. 1967–one. 1968–six. 1969–three (includes Alcan Golfer of the Year). 1970–three. 1971–one. 1973–two. 1975–one.
Oth Lancome Trophy 1974. Moroccan Grand Prix 1973-75. Lancia D'Oro 1974. Mexican Open 1977
Int Ryder Cup 1961-63-65-67-69-71-73-75 (non-playing captain 1979)
Mis Vardon Trophy 1960-63-65-66-68. US leading money winner 1966-68; second 1958-70. USPGA Player of the Year 1966-70. Byron Nelson Award 1966-68-70. Second player to win over one million dollars in prize money.

Charles, Robert J

Born Carterton, New Zealand on 14th March, 1936. Turned Professional 1960

Bri Open Champion 1963; second 1968-69. Bowmaker 1961. Daks 1962(tied). Piccadilly World Match Play 1969. John Player Classic 1972. Dunlop Masters 1972

Nat New Zealand Open 1954 (as amateur)-66-70-73; second 1974. New Zealand Professional 1961-79-80
For Swiss Open 1962-74. Canadian Open 1968. Second USPGA 1968. South African Open 1973. Scandinavian Open 1973
USC 1963–one. 1965–one. 1967–one. 1974–one
Oth Caltex (NZ) 1961-62-67(tied)-68-71. Engadine Open 1962. Watties Open (NZ) 1963-66-67-68. Forest Products (NZ) 1966. Metalcraft (NZ) 1966. Wills Masters (NZ) 1967. Spalding Masters (NZ) 1968-72. Otago Classic (NZ) 1972. Auckland Classic (NZ) 1973. New Zealand Classic 1978
Int Eisenhower Trophy 1960. New Zealand in World Cup 1962-63-64-65-66-67-68-71-72. Dunhill Cup 1985-86.
Mis First New Zealander and first left-handed golfer to win the Open

Coe, Charles R
Born Oklahoma City, USA on 26th October, 1923

Bri Amateur Champion runner-up 1951
Nat US Amateur Champion 1949-58; runner-up 1959. Second in US Masters 1961
Oth Western Amateur 1950
Int Walker Cup 1949-51-53-59-61-63. Eisenhower Trophy 1960
Mis Bobby Jones Award 1964

Cole, Robert
Born Springs, South Africa on 11th May, 1948. Turned Professional 1966

Bri Amateur Champion 1966. Second in English Amateur Stroke Play 1966
Nat South African Open 1974-80. Dunlop Masters (SA) 1969
For Rhodesian Masters 1972
USC 1977–one
Oth Natal Open 1969-70-72. Cape Classic 1970. Transvaal Open 1972. Vavasseur (SA) 1974
Int Eisenhower Trophy 1966. Winning team World Cup 1974, individual winner 1974. South Africa in World Cup 1969-74-76
Mis Won Amateur Championship at age of 18

Crenshaw, Ben
Born Austin, Texas, USA on 11th January, 1952. Turned Professional 1973

Bri Second in Open Championship 1978(tied)-79(tied). Carrolls Irish Open 1976
Nat US Masters 1984. Second US Masters 1976-83. Second USPGA 1979
For Second in Australia Open 1978. Mexican Open 1982
USC 1973–one. 1976–three. 1977–one. 1979–one. 1980–one. 1983-one. 1986-one
Int Eisenhower Trophy winning team 1972. Ryder Cup 1983
Mis Won the first tournament he played in after turning professional, the 1973 San Antonio Open. Rookie of the Year 1974. US second money winner 1976. Byron Nelson Award 1976

Crosby, Nathaniel
Born Los Angeles on 29th October, 1961. Turned Professional 1984

Nat US Amateur 1981
Int Walker Cup 1983

Daniel, Miss Beth
Born S Carolina, USA on 14th October, 1956. Turned Professional October, 1978

Nat US Women's Amateur 1975-77
For World Ladies Championship (Japan) 1979
USC 1979–one. 1980–four. 1982–five. 1983–one. 1985–one
Int Curtis Cup 1976–78
Mis USLPGA Rookie of the Year 1979. USLPGA leading money winner 1980. USLPGA Player of the Year 1980

Davies, RD
Born USA on 29th October, 1930

Bri Amateur Champion 1962
Int Walker Cup 1963
Mis Leading Amateur US Open 1963

Davis, Rodger
Born Sydney, New South Wales, Australia on 18th May, 1951. Turned Professional 1974

Bri State Express Classic 1981. Whyte & Mackay PGA 1986
For Lost play-off for German Open 1986
Nat South Australia Open 1978. Victoria Open 1979-85. Australian Open 1986
Int World Cup 1985. Dunhill Cup 1986 (winning team). Nissan Cup 1986

Dickson, Robert B
Born McAlester, Oklahoma, USA on 25th January, 1944. Turned Professional 1968

Bri Amateur Champion 1967
Nat US Amateur 1967
USC 1968–one. 1973–one
Int Walker Cup 1967
Mis Joined select few to win British and US Amateur titles in the same year. Bobby Jones Award 1968

Fernandez, Vicente
Born Corrientes, Argentina on 5th April, 1946. Turned Professional 1964

Bri Benson & Hedges 1975. Colgate PGA 1979
For Dutch Open 1970. Brazil Open 1983-84
Nat Argentine Open 1968-69-81
Int World Cup 1970-72-78-84-85. Dunhill Cup 1986

Finsterwald, Dow
Born Athens, Ohio, USA on 6th September, 1929. Turned Professional 1951

Nat USPGA Champion 1958; runner-up 1957
For Canadian Open 1956
USC 1955–two. 1956–one. 1957–one. 1958–one. 1959–three. 1960–two. 1963–one
Int Ryder Cup 1957-59-61-63 (non-playing captain 1977)
Mis USPGA Player of the Year 1958

Floyd, Ray
Born Fort Bragg, North Carolina, USA on 4th September, 1942. Turned Professional 1961

Bri Second in Open Championship 1978(tied)
Nat USPGA Champion 1969-82; second 1976. US Masters 1976. US Open 1986
For Brazilian Open 1978
USC 1963–one. 1965–one. 1969–two. 1975–one. 1976–one. 1977-two. 1979-one. 1980-one. 1981-four. 1982-three. 1985-one. 1986-one.
Int Ryder Cup 1969-75-77-83 Dunhill Cup 1985-86
Mis Rookie of the year 1963.

Ford, Doug
Born West Haven, Connecticut, USA on 6th August, 1922. Turned Professional 1949

Nat US Masters 1957; second 1958. USPGA Champion 1955
For Canadian Open 1959-63
USC 1952–one. 1953–three. 1954–two. 1955–two. 1957–two. 1958–one. 1960–one. 1961–one. 1962–two
Int Ryder Cup 1955-57-59-61
Mis USPGA Player of the Year 1955

Garrido, Antonio

Born Madrid on 2nd February, 1944. Turned Professional 1961

Bri Benson and Hedges International 1977. Standard Four Stars National 1986
Nat Madrid Open 1973-77. Spanish Open 1972
For Tunisian Open 1982
Int Europe v GB 1976-78-80. Spain in World Cup 1977 (winning team)-78-79. Ryder Cup 1979. Hennessy-Cognac Cup 1976-78-80-82-84

Giles, Marvin

Bri Amateur Champion 1975
Nat US Amateur Champion 1972, second 1967-68-69
Int Walker Cup 1969-71-73-75. Eisenhower Trophy winning team 1968-70-72
Mis Leading Amateur US Open 1973

Goldschmid, Mrs Isa (*née* Bevione)

Born Italy

Bri Kayser Bondor 1963
Nat Italian Ladies' Close 1947-51-53-54-55-56-57-58-59-60-61-62-63-64-65-66-67-69-71-73-74. Italian Ladies' Open 1952-57-58-60-61-63-64-67-68-69
For Spanish Ladies 1952. French Ladies 1975
Int Vagliano Trophy 1959-61-63-65-67-69-71-73 (non-playing captain 1977). Eur v United States 1968. Italy in World Team Championship 1964-66-68-70-72

Graham, David

Born Windsor, Tasmania on 23rd May, 1946. Turned Professional 1962

Bri Piccadilly World Match Play 1976
Nat Australian Open 1977; second 1972. Australian Wills Masters 1975
For French Open 1970. Thailand Open 1970. USPGA 1979. US Open 1981. Lancome Trophy 1982
USC 1972–one. 1976–two. 1980–one. 1983–one
Oth Victoria Open 1970. Tasmanian Open 1970. Yomiuri Open 1970. Caracas Open 1971. Japanese Airlines 1971. Chunichi Crowns (Japan) 1976. West Lakes Classic (Aust.) 1979. Air New Zealand Open 1979
Int Australia in World Cup 1970 (winning team)-71. Dunhill Cup 1985 (winning team) 1986 (winning team). Nissan Cup 1986
Mis Australian *Sportsman of the Year* 1979

Graham, Lou

Born Nashville, Tennessee, USA on 7th January, 1938. Turned Professional 1962

Nat US Open 1975; second 1977
USC 1967–one. 1972–one. 1979–three
Int Ryder Cup 1973-75-77. Winning team World Cup 1975

Green, Hubert

Born Birmingham, Alabama, USA on 18th December, 1946. Turned Professional 1970

Bri Carrolls Irish Open 1977
Nat US Open 1977. Second in US Masters 1978 (tied). USPGA 1985
USC 1971–one. 1973–two. 1974–four. 1975–one. 1976–three. 1978–two. 1979–two. 1984–one
Oth Dunlop Phoenix (Japan) 1975
Int Ryder Cup 1977-79-85. USA in World Cup 1977
Mis Rookie of the Year 1971

Guldahl, Ralph

Born Dallas, Texas, USA on 22nd November, 1912. Turned Professional 1928

Nat US Open Champion 1937-38; second 1933. US Masters 1939; runner-up 1937-38
USC 1932–one. 1936–three. 1937–two. 1938–one. 1939–two. 1940–two
Int Ryder Cup 1937
Mis Hall of Fame 1981

Gunderson, Miss Jo Anne

See Mrs DR Carner

Harper, Chandler

Born Portsmouth, Virginia, USA on 10th March, 1914. Turned Professional 1934

Nat USPGA 1950
USC Won over 20 tournaments. Ten times Virginia Open Champion. USPGA Seniors 1968. National Seniors 1965
Oth World Senior Professional 1968
Int Ryder Cup 1955
Mis Elected to USPGA Hall of Fame 1969. Holder of USPGA 54- and 36-hole records (see *Record Scoring*). In 1941 scored round of 58 (29-29) on 6,100 yards, Portsmouth, Virginia

Hayes, Dale

Born Pretoria, South Africa on 1st July, 1952. Turned Professional 1970

Bri English Open Amateur Stroke Play second 1969. Scottish Open Amateur Stroke Play 1970. Coca-Cola Young Professionals 1974. PGA Under-25's 1975
Nat South African Amateur Stroke Play 1969-70. Leading Amateur South African Open 1969. South African PGA 1974-75-76. South African Open 1976
For German Amateur 1969. Brazilian Open 1970. Spanish Open 1971-79. World Junior Champion 1969. Dunlop Masters (Rhod.) 1973. Swiss Open 1975. Italian Open 1978. French Open 1978
Oth Transvaal Amateur 1969. Western Province Amateur 1970. Transvaal Open 1970. Bert Hagerman (SA) 1971. Schoeman Park (SA) 1973. Rolux Open (SA) 1973. Holiday Inns (SA) 1973-75-76. Corlett Drive Classic 1973. Royal Swaziland International 1974. ICL International (SA) 1978. Cape Open 1978. Bogota Open 1979
Int South Africa Eisenhower Trophy 1970 (runner-up Individual Section). South Africa in World Cup 1974 (winning team)-76
Mis Accles and Pollock Award 1973. Second in Order of Merit 1974-78. Vardon Trophy 1975

Henning, Harold

Born Johannesburg, South Africa on 3rd October, 1934. Turned Professional 1953

Bri Third in Open Championship 1960-70. Daks 1958 (tied). Yorkshire Evening News 1958 (tied). Spalding 1959 (tied). Sprite 1960. Pringle 1964
Nat South African Open 1957-62. South African PGA 1965-66-67-72
For Italian Open 1957. Swiss Open 1960-64. Danish Open 1960-64-65. German Open 1965. Malaysian Open 1966
USC 1966–one. 1970–one
Oth Transvaal Open 1957. Natal Open 1957. Western Province Open 1957-59. Cock o' the North 1959. Engadine Open 1966. South African International Classic 1972. ICL International (SA) 1980
Int South Africa in World Cup 1957-58-59-61-65 (winning team)-66-67-69-70-71

Hogan, Ben W

Born Dublin, Texas, USA on 13th August, 1912. Turned Professional 1929

Bri Open Champion 1953
Nat US Open Champion 1948-50-51-53; second 1955-56. USPGA Champion 1946-48. US Masters 1951-53; runner-up 1942-46-54-55
USC 1938–one. 1940–four. 1941–five. 1942–six. 1945–five. 1946–twelve. 1947–seven. 1948–eight. 1949–two. 1950–one. 1951–one. 1952–one. 1953–three. 1959–one
Int Ryder Cup 1947 (capt.)-49 (capt.)-51, non-playing captain 1967. World Cup 1956 (winning team and individual winner)-58

Mis USPGA Player of the Year 1948-50-51-53. US leading money winner 1940-41-42-46-48. Sportsman of the Decade Award 1946-56. Had a serious car crash in 1949 which seemed likely to prevent him playing golf again but returned to win more major victories. In 1965 was named the greatest professional of all time by US golf writers. Bobby Jones Award 1976

Hyndman, William III

Born on 25th December 1915

Bri Amateur Championship runner-up 1959-69-70
Nat US Amateur runner-up 1955
Oth US Seniors 1973
Int Walker Cup 1957-59-61-71. Eisenhower Trophy 1958-60 (capt.)

Inkster, Julie

Born Turned Professional

Nat US Ladies Amateur 1980-81-82
Int Curtis Cup 1982
USL 1985–one. 1986–four

Irwin, Hale

Born Joplin, Montana, USA on 3rd June, 1945. Turned Professional 1968

Bri Piccadilly World Match Play 1974-75. Second Open 1983
Nat US Open 1974-79
For Australian PGA 1978. South African PGA 1978. Bridestone 1981
USC 1971–one. 1973–one. 1975–two. 1976–two. 1977–three. 1981–two. 1982–one. 1983–one. 1984–one. 1985–one. 1986–one
Int Ryder Cup 1975-77-79-81. USA in World Cup 1974-79 (winning teams and individual winner)

January, Don

Born Plainview, Texas, USA on 20th November, 1929. Turned Professional 1955

Nat USPGA Champion 1967; second 1961-76
USC 1956–two. 1959–one. 1960–one. 1961–one. 1963–one. 1966–one. 1968–one. 1970–one. 1975–one. 1976–one
Int Ryder Cup 1965-77
Mis In 1961 won 50,000 dollars for a hole-in-one

Kennedy, Edwina

Born

Nat Ladies Amateur 1978

King, Betsy

Born .Turned Professional

Nat Ladies Open 1986
USL 1985–two. 1986–two

Kite, Tom

Born Austin, Texas, USA on 9th December, 1949. Turned Professional 1972

Bri Second in Open Championship 1978 (tied). European Open 1980
Nat Second in US Amateur 1970
USC 1976–one. 1978–one. 1981–one. 1982–one. 1983–one. 1984–one. 1985–one. 1986–one
Oth Auckland Classic (NZ) 1974
Int Eisenhower Trophy winning team 1970. Walker Cup 1971. Ryder Cup 1979-81-83-85
Mis US Rookie of the Year 1973. Bobby Jones Award 1979. Vardon Trophy 1981. Leading US money winner 1981. Golf Writers Player of the Year 1981

Knight, Mrs Nancy

See Miss Nancy Lopez

Kuramoto, M

Born . Turned Professional

Nat Japan Amateur 1975-77-80. Japan Professional 1982
Jap 1983–two. 1984–two. 1985–two. 1986–two

Langer, Bernhard

Born Anhousen, Germany on 27th August, 1957. Turned Professional 1972

Chp US Masters 1985
Bri Dunlop Masters 1980, 2nd in Open 1981-84. Irish Open 1984
Nat German Open 1981-82-85-86. German Professional 1979
For Colombian Open 1980. Italian Open 1983. French Open 1984. Dutch Open 1984. Spanish Open 1984. European Open 1985. US Masters 1985. Sea Pines Heritage Classic 1985. Australian Masters 1985
Oth German Professional in 1979. Cacharel Under-25 1979. Dunlop Masters 1980. Bob Hope Classic 1981. Glasgow Classic 1983. St Mellion Time-share 1983. Lancome Trophy 1986 (shared)
Int Europe v GB 1976-78-80-82. Germany in World Cup 1976-77-78-79-80. Ryder Cup 1981-83-85. Nissan Cup 1986
Mis Leader of South American Order of Merit 1979. Leader of the European Order of Merit 1981-84

Littler, Gene

Born San Diego, California, USA on 21st July, 1930. Turned Professional 1954

Nat US Amateur 1953. US Open 1961; second 1954. Second US Masters 1970. Second USPGA 1977
For Canadian Open 1965. Taiheiyo Pacific Masters 1974-75. Australian Masters 1980
USC 1954–one (as amateur). 1955–four. 1956–three. 1957–one. 1959–five. 1960–two. 1962–two. 1969–two. 1971–two. 1973–one. 1975–three. 1977–one. World Series 1966
Oth Yellow Pages (SA) 1977
Int Ryder Cup 1961-63-65-67-69-71-75
Mis USPGA second money winner 1959-62. Bobby Jones Award 1973. Ben Hogan Award 1973. Byron Nelson Award 1959

Locke, Arthur D'Arcy (Bobby)

Born Germiston, Transvaal, SA on 20th November, 1917. Turned Professional 1938

Bri Open Champion 1949-50-52-57; second 1946-54. Leading Amateur 1936-37. Irish Open 1938. Dunlop Masters 1946 (tied)-54. Yorkshire Evening News 1946. Dunlop 1950-54. Spalding 1950. North British Harrogate 1950. Lotus 1952. Daks 1957. Bowmaker 1957 (tied)-59.
Nat South African Boys 1931. South African Amateur 1935-37. South African Open 1935-37 (as amateur)-1938-39-40-46-50-51. South African Professional 1938-39-40-46-50-51
For New Zealand Open 1938. Canadian Open 1947 French Open 1952-53. German Open 1954. Swiss Open 1954. Egyptian Open 1954
USC 1947–five. 1948–two. 1949–three. 1950–one
Oth Natal Amateur 1935-36. Natal Open 1935-36 (as amateur). Transvaal Amateur 1935-37. Orange Free State Amateur 1937. Transvaal Open 1938-39
Int South Africa in World Cup 1953-54-56-60
Mis Third in US Open 1949-51. Second money winner in US 1947. Harry Vardon Trophy 1946-50-54. Has had 15 holes-in-one. Made an honorary member of the Royal and Ancient GC 1976

Lopez, Miss Nancy

Born California, USA on 6th January, 1957. Turned Professional July, 1977

Bri Colgate European 1978-79
Nat US Girls 1972-74. Second in US Ladies' Open 1975 (as amateur)-77. USLPGA Championship 1978
USC 1978–six. 1979–seven. 1980–three. 1984–one. 1985–five

For Colgate Far East 1978
Int Curtis Cup 1976. World Amateur Team 1976
Mis USLPGA leading money winner 1978-79. USLPGA Rookie of the Year 1977. USLPGA Player of the Year 1978-79. US Sportswoman of the Year 1978. In 1978, in first full year as a professional, won nine tournaments and a then record total of 189,813 dollars.

McGuire, Marnie
Born New Zealand

Nat Ladies Amateur 1986

McIntire, Miss Barbara

Bri British Ladies 1960
Nat US Ladies Amateur 1959-64. Second in US Women's Open 1956
Int Curtis Cup 1958-60-62-64-66-72

McNulty, Mark
Born Zimbabwe on 25th October, 1953. Turned Professional 1977

For German Open 1980. Malay Open 1980. Portuguese Open 1986
Nat SA Amateur Stroke Play 1977. SA Masters 1981-82
Oth Greater Manchester Open 1979

Mahaffey, John Drayton
Born Kerrville, Texas, USA on 9th May, 1948. Turned Professional 1971

Nat USPGA 1978
USC 1973–one. 1978–two. 1979–one. 1980–one. 1984–one. 1985–one. 1986–one
Int Ryder Cup 1979. US in World Cup 1978-79. Nissan Cup 1986
Mis NCAA Champion 1970

Marsh, Graham, MBE
Born Kalgoorlie, Australia on 14th January, 1944

Bri Sunbeam Electric 1973. Benson & Hedges International 1976-80. Colgate World Match Play 1977. Dunlop Masters 1979. European Open 1981. Lawrence Batley 1985
Nat Runner-up Australian Amateur 1967. Australian PGA 1982.
USC 1977–one
For Swiss Open 1970-72. Indian Open 1971-73. German Open 1972. Thailand Open 1973. Malaysian Open 1974-75. Dutch Open 1979-85
Oth Watties Open (NZ) 1970. Spalding Masters (NZ) 1971. Lancôme 1977. Western Australian Open 1976. On Japanese circuit 1972–one victory. 1973–one victory. 1974–four victories (three in successive weeks). 1975–two victories. 1976–four victories. 1977–two victories. 1979–one victory. 1981–two victories.
Int Dunhill Cup 1985 (winning team). Nissan Cup 1986
Mis US Rookie of the Year 1977. Australian *Sportsman of the Year* 1977. Awarded MBE in 1982

Melnyk, Steven Nicholas
Born Brunswick, Georgia, USA on 26th February, 1947. Turned Professional 1971

Bri Amateur Champion 1971. Leading Amateur Open Championship 1970
Nat US Amateur Champion 1969. Leading Amateur US Masters 1970
Oth Western Amateur 1969. Eastern Amateur 1971
Int Walker Cup 1969-71
Mis US Amateur Golfer of the Year 1969

Middlecoff, Cary
Born Halls, Tennessee, USA on 6th January, 1921. Turned Professional 1947

Nat US Open Champion 1949-56; second 1957. US Masters 1955, runner-up 1948. USPGA runner-up 1955
USC 1947–one. 1948–two. 1949–four. 1950–three. 1951–six. 1952–four. 1953–three. 1954–one. 1955–five. 1956–two. 1958–one. 1959–one. 1961–one
Int Ryder Cup 1953-55-59. USA in World Cup 1959
Mis Byron Nelson Award 1955

Miller, Alice
Born . Turned Professional

USL 1985–four

Miller, Johnny Lawrence
Born San Francisco, USA on 29th April, 1947. Turned Professional 1969

Bri Open Championship 1976; second 1973
Nat US Open 1973. Second in US Masters 1971-75 (tied)-81 (tied)
For Dunlop Phoenix International (Japan) 1974
USC 1971–one. 1972–one. 1974–eight. 1975–four. 1976–two. 1980–one. 1982–one. 1983–one. 1984–one
Oth Otago Classic (NZ) 1972. Lancome Trophy 1973-79
Int USA in World Cup 1973 (winning team)-75 (winning team)-80; individual winner 1973-75. Ryder Cup 1975.
Mis Lowest round (63) in US Open in 1973. USPGA Player of the Year 1974. US leading money winner 1974; second 1975. Byron Nelson Award 1974

Nagle, Kelvin DG
Born North Sydney, Australia on 21st December, 1920. Turned Professional 1946

Bri Open Champion 1960; second 1962. Irish Hospitals 1961. Dunlop 1961. Bowmaker 1962-65. Esso Golden 1963-67. British Seniors 1971-73-75
Nat Australian Open 1959. Australian Professional 1949-54-58-59-65-68
For Second in US Open 1965. Canadian Open 1964. French Open 1961. New Zealand Professional 1957-58-60-70-73-74-75. New Zealand Open 1957-58-62-64-67-68-69. World Senior 1971-75
Oth In New Zealand: BP 1968, Caltex 1969, Garden City 1969, Otago Charity Classic 1970-76. Stars Travel 1970. In Australia: West End 1968-72-74, New South Wales Open 1968, Victoria Open 1969, NBN Newcastle 1970, New South Wales Professional 1971, South Coast Open 1975, Western Australia PGA 1977
Int Australia in World Cup 1954 (winning team)-55-58-59-(winning team)-60-61-62-65-66
Mis His score of 260 in Irish Hospitals event in 1961 established a new low scoring record with rounds of 64-65-66-65

Nakajima, Tsuneyuki
Born Turned Professional

Nat Japan Amateur 1973. Japan Open 1985-86. Japan PGA 1983-84-86
Jap 1984–one. 1985–five. 1986–five
Oth Nissan Cup (individual) 1986
Int Dunhill Cup 1986. Nissan Cup 1986

Nelson, Byron
Born Fort Worth, Texas, USA on 4th February, 1912. Turned Professional 1932

Nat US Open Champion 1939; second 1946. USPGA Champion 1940-45; second 1939-41-44. US Masters 1937-42; second 1941-47
For Canadian Open 1945. Canadian PGA 1945. French Open 1955
USC 1935–one. 1936–one. 1937–two. 1938–two. 1939–three. 1940–two. 1941–three. 1942–three. 1944–six. 1945–fifteen. 1946–five.
Int Ryder Cup 1937-47
Mis Won eleven consecutive tournaments in period March to August 1945 and his total was eighteen for the year. US leading money winner 1944-45. Bobby Jones Award 1974

Nelson, Larry Gene

Born Fort Payne, Alabama, USA on 10th September, 1947. Turned Professional 1971

Nat US Open 1983. USPGA 1981
USC 1979–one. 1980–one
Int Ryder Cup 1979-81
Mis Is undeafeted in Ryder Cup matches

Newton, Jack

Born Sydney, Australia on 30th January, 1950. Turned Professional 1969

Bri Benson & Hedges Festival 1972. Benson & Hedges PGA Match Play 1974. Second in Open Championship 1975. Sumrie 1975
Nat Australian Open 1979
For Dutch Open 1972. Nigerian Open 1974. Second equal in New Zealand Open 1974. Second equal in US Masters 1980
USC 1978–one
Oth City of Auckland Classic (NZ) 1972. Amoco Forbes (Aust) 1972. Cock o' the North (Zambia) 1976. Mufulira Open 1976. New South Wales Open 1976-79
Mis Seriously injured on tarmac by aeroplane propeller accident 1983

Nicklaus, Jack William

Born Columbus, Ohio, USA on 21st January, 1940. Turned Professional 1961

Bri Open Champion 1966-70-78; second 1964-67-68-72-76-77-79. Piccadilly Match Play 1970. Royal St George's Challenge Cup 1959
Nat US Amateur 1959-61. US Open 1962-67-72-80; second 1960-68-82. US Masters 1963-65-66-72-75-86; second 1964-71-77-81. USPGA 1963-71-73-75-80; second 1964-65-74-83
For Australian Open 1964-68-71-75-76-78. Second in Canadian Open 1965-68-75-76
USC 1962–two. 1963–three. 1964–four. 1965–four. 1966–two. 1967–four. 1968–two. 1969–three. 1970–two. 1971–four. 1972–five. 1973–six. 1974–two. 1975–three. 1976–two. 1977–three. 1978–three. 1982–one. 1984–one. World Series 1962-63-67-70-76
Oth Dunlop International (Aust) 1971
Int Ryder Cup 1969-71-73-75-77-81-Captain 1983. Walker Cup 1959-61. USA in World Cup 1963-64-65 (winning team-63-64-66-67-71-73; individual winner 1963-64-71). Eisenhower Trophy winning team 1960; individual winner 1960
Mis Rookie of the Year 1962. US leading money winner 1964-65-67-71-72-73-75-76; second 1963-66-68-74-77. USPGA Player of the Year 1967-72-73-75-76. Byron Nelson Award 1964-65-67-72-73. Bobby Jones Award 1975. By 1973 had won over two million dollars in prize money and by 1977 over three million dollars. First person to win over 300,000 dollars in one year (1972). World record of 19 major titles. US Sportsman of the Year 1978. Athlete of Decade 1970's. Walter Hagen Award 1980

Norman, Greg

Born Mt Asa, Queensland, Australia on 10th Feburary, 1955. Turned Professional 1976

Bri Open Champion 1986. Martini 1977-79-81. World Match Play 1980-83-86. Dunlop Masters 1981-82. Benson & Hedges International Open 1982. State Express Classic 1982
Nat Australian Open 1980. Australian Masters 1984. Australian PGA 1984–85
For Hong Kong Open 1979. Scandinavian Enterprises Open 1980. French Open 1980. Canadian Open 1984. Eur 1986.
USC 1986–two
Oth West Lakes Classic (Aust) 1976. South Seas Classic (Fiji) 1978. NSW Open 1978-83-86. Japanese circuit: 1977–one. US circuit: 1984–two. Victorian Open 1984. Queensland Open 1986
Int Australia in World Cup 1976-78. Dunhill Cup 1985 (winning team) -86 (winning team). Nissan Cup 1986
Mis Second in Order of Merit 1980

North, Andy

Born Thorp, Wisconsin, USA on 9th March, 1950. Turned Professional 1972

Nat US Open 1978, 1985
USC 1977–one. 1978–one
Int US in World Cup 1978

Okamoto, Ayako

Born .Turned Professional

Nat Ladies Open 1984
USL 1986–two

Olazabal, Jose-Maria

Born Spain on 5th February, 1966. Turned Professional 1984

Chp Amateur Champion 1984
Nat Spanish Open Amateur 1983
Oth Italian Open Amateur 1983. British Youths 1985
For Sanyo Open 1986. Swiss Open 1986
Int Dunhill Cup 1986

O'Meara, Mark

Born Goldsboro, North Carolina, USA on 13th January, 1957. Turned Professional 1980

Chp US Amateur 1979
USC 1984–one. 1985–two
Int Ryder Cup 1985. Nissan Cup 1985. Dunhill Cup 1985-86

Palmer, Arnold

Born Latrobe, Pennsylvania, USA on 10th September, 1929. Turned Professional 1954

Bri Open Champion 1961-62; second 1960. Piccadilly World Match Play 1964-67. Penfold PGA 1975
Nat US Amateur Champion 1954. US Open 1960; second 1962-63-66-67. US Masters 1958-60-62-64; second 1961-65. USPGA second 1964-68-70
For Canadian Open 1955. Australian Open 1966. Spanish Open 1975. Canadian PGA 1980
USC 1956–four. 1957–four. 1958–two. 1959–three. 1960–six. 1961–five. 1962–six. 1963–seven. 1964–one. 1965–one. 1966–four. 1967–four. 1968–two. 1969–two. 1970–one. 1971–four. 1973–one
Oth Lancome Trophy 1971
Int Ryder Cup 1961-63-65-67-71-73, non-playing captain 1975. USA in World Cup 1960-62-63-64-66-67 (winning team each time; individual winner 1967)
Mis USPGA Player of the Year 1960-62. US leading money winner 1958-60-62-63; second 1961-64-67. First player ever to earn 100,000 dollars in one year (1963). US Athlete of the Year 1960. Bobby Jones Award 1971. Byron Nelson Award 1957-60-61-62-63. Made an honorary member of the Royal and Ancient GC in 1979. Athlete of Decade 1960's. Walter Hagen Award 1981

Pate, Jerry

Born Macon, Georgia, USA on 16th September, 1953. Turned Professional 1975

Nat US Amateur 1974. US Open 1976; second 79 (tied). Second in USPGA 1978
For Canadian Open 1976. Taiheiyo Pacific Masters 1976. Brazilian Open 1980
USC 1977–two. 1978–one. 1982–one
Int Eisenhower Trophy winning team 1974, joint individual winner 1974. Walker Cup 1975. USA in World Cup 1976
Mis Rookie of the Year 1976 with then record first year prize money of 153,000 dollars on US circuit. Youngest player to make 1 million dollars on US tour

Pavin, Corey

Born Oxnard, California, USA on 16th November, 1959. Turned Professional 1981

USC 1984–one. 1985–one. 1986–two
For German Open 1983. SA PGA 1983
Int Walker Cup 1981. Nissan Cup 1985

Peete, Calvin

Born Detroit, USA on 18th July 1943. Turned Professional 1971

USC 1979–one. 1982–four. 1983–two. 1984–one. 1985–two. 1986–two
Int Ryder Cup 1983-85. Nissan Cup 1985-86
Oth Vardon Trophy 1984

Pinero, Manuel

Born Puebla de la Calzada, Spain on 1st September, 1952. Turned Professional 1968

Bri Penfold PGA 1977. English Classic 1980. European Open 1982
Nat Madrid Open 1974-81-85
For Swiss Open 1976. Italian Open 1985
Oth Spanish Professional 1972-73
Int Spain in World Cup 1974-76 (winning team)-78-79-80-82 (individual and team winner)-83-85. Europe v GB 1974-76-78-80. Ryder Cup 1985

Player, Gary

Born Johannesburg, South Africa on 1st November, 1935. Turned Professional 1953

Bri Open Champion 1959-68-74. Dunlop 1956. Piccadilly World Match Play 1965-66-68-71-73
Nat South Africa Open 1956-60-65-66-67-68-69-72-75-76-77-79-81. South African Masters 1959-60-64-67-71-72-73-74-76-76-(held twice)-79. South African PGA 1968-79-81
For US Open Champion 1965, second 1958-79 (tied). US Masters 1961-74-78, second 1962-65. USPGA 1962-72, second 1969. Australian Open 1958-62-63-65-69-70-74. Australian PGA 1957. Brazilian Open 1972-74. Ibergolf European Champions 1974. Chile Open 1980
USC 1958–one. 1961–two. 1962–one. 1963–one. 1964–one. 1969–one. 1970–one. 1971–two. 1972–one. 1973–one. 1974–one. 1978–two. US World Series 1965-68-72
Oth Transvaal Open 1959-60-62-66. Natal Open 1958-60-66-68. Western Province Open (SA) 1968-71-72. Wills Masters (Aust) 1968. Dunlop International (Aust) 1970. Rothmans Match Play (SA) 1973. Japan Airlines Open 1972. International Classic (SA) 1974. Lancome 1975. General Motors (SA) 1971-75-76. ICL International (SA) 1977. Johannesburg International 1979. Sun City Classic (SA) 1979. Ivory Coast Open 1980
Int South Africa in World Cup 1956-57-58-59-60-62-63-64-65 (winning team and individual winner)-66-67-68-71-72-73-77 (individual winner)
Mis First overseas player to win the US Open for 45 years. Third man in history to win all four Major World Professional titles. US leading money winner 1961. In 1974 recorded his 100th win as a professional. In 1974 Brazilian Open scored 59 in second round. This was the first time 60 had been broken in a national championship. Bobby Jones Award 1966. In 1976 became the first player to be made an honorary member of the USPGA. Captain South African PGA 1977. President South African PGA 1978. Became the oldest player to win the US Masters aged 42 in 1978, in which his last round 64 and inward half of 30 equalled the record.

Ploujoux, P

Born

Chp Amateur Champion 1981
Nat French Amateur Close 1982

Prado, Señora J de (*née* Catherine Lacoste)

Born Paris on 27th June, 1945

Bri British Ladies 1969. Astor Prince's 1966. Worplesdon Foursomes 1967. Hovis 1969
Nat French Ladies' Open 1967-69-70-72. French Ladies' Close 1968-69
For US Ladies' Open 1967. US Ladies' Amateur 1969. Western Ladies' Amateur (US) 1968. Spanish Ladies 1969-72-76
Int World Team Championship winning team 1964; winner individual section 1964-68
Mis Was first amateur, first non-American and youngest player at the time she won the US Ladies' Open in 1967

Price, N

Born *Turned Professional*

Nat SA Masters 1980
For Swiss Open 1980
Oth Lancome Trophy 1985

Randolph S

Born

Chp US Amateur 1985
Int Walker Cup 1985

Rivero, Jose

Born Spain on 20th September, 1955. Turned Professional 1973

Bri Lawrence Batley International 1984
Int Ryder Cup 1985. World Cup 1984 (winner). Dunhill Cup 1986

Rogers, William Charles

Born Waco, Texas, USA on 10th September, 1951. Turned Professional 1974

Bri Open 1981. Suntory World Match Play 1980
For Suntory Open 1980. Australian Open 1981
USC 1978–one. 1981–three. 1983–one
Oth Pacific Masters 1977
Int Ryder Cup 1981

Rosenthal, J

Born

Chp Ladies Amateur 1984
Int Curtis Cup 1984

Sander, A

Born

Chp Ladies Open 1980
Int Curtis Cup 1974-84

Sarazen, Gene

Born Harrison, New York, USA on 27th February, 1902. Turned Professional 1920

Bri Open Champion 1932; second 1928. North of England Professional 1923
Nat US Open Champion 1922-32; second 1934-40. USPGA 1922-23-33; second 1930. US Masters 1935
For Australian Open 1936
USC 1922–one. 1925–one. 1927–two. 1928–two. 1930–two. 1935–one. 1936–one. 1937–two. 1938–one. 1939–one. 1941–one. USPGA Seniors 1954-58
Int Ryder Cup 1927-29-31-33-35-37
Mis One of the few to win the Open and the US Open in the same year. Honorary member of the Royal and Ancient

Segard, Mme Patrick (formerly Vcmtsse De St Sauveur *née* Lally Vagliano)

Bri British Ladies 1950. Worplesdon Foursomes 1962. British Girls 1937. Avia Foursomes 1966. Kayser-Bondor Foursomes 1960
Nat French Ladies' Open 1948-50-51-52. French Ladies' Close 1939-46-49-50-51-54
For Swiss Ladies 1949-65. Luxembourg Ladies 1949. Italian Ladies 1949-51. Spanish Ladies 1951
Int France 1937-38-39-47-48-49-50-51-52-53-54-55-56-57-58-59-60-61-62-63-64-65-70. Vagliano Trophy 1959 (capt)-61 (capt)-63-65, non-playing captain 1975
Mis Chairman of The Women's Committee of World Amateur Golf Council 1964 to 1972

Semple, Miss Carol

Bri British Ladies 1974. Newmark International 1975 (tied)
Nat US Ladies' Amateur 1973
Int Curtis Cup 1974-76-80. World Team Championship 1974 (winning team)-80 (winning team)

Sheehan, Patty

Born Turned Professional

USL 1985–two. 1986–three
Int Curtis Cup 1980

Siderowf, R

Bri Amateur Champion 1973-76
For Canadian Amateur 1971
Int Walker Cup 1969-73-75-77 (non-playing captain 1979). Eisenhower Trophy 1968-76

Sigel, J

Born

Chp Amateur Champion 1979
Nat US Amateur 1982-83
Int Walker Cup 1977-79-81-83 (captain)-85

Snead, Samuel Jackson

Born Hot Springs, Virginia, USA on 27th May, 1912. Turned Professional 1934

Bri Open Champion 1946
Nat US Masters 1949-52-54; second 1939-57. USPGA Champion 1942-49-51; second 1938-40. Second in US Open 1937-47-49-53
For Canadian Open 1938-40-41
USC 1936–one. 1937–four. 1938–six. 1939–four. 1940–two. 1941–four. 1942–two. 1944–two. 1945–six. 1946–five. 1948–one. 1949–four. 1950–ten. 1951–one. 1952–five. 1953–three. 1954–one. 1955–four. 1956–one. 1957–one. 1958–one. 1959–one. 1960–two. 1961–two. 1964–one. 1965–one. USPGA Seniors 1964-65-67-70-72-73
Oth World Senior Professional 1964-65-70-72-73
Int Ryder Cup 1937-47-49-51 (capt)-53-55-59 (capt); non-playing captain 1969. USA in World Cup 1954-56-57-58-59-60-61-62; (winning team 56-60-61-62; individual winner 1961)
Mis US leading money winner 1938-49-50. USPGA Player of the Year 1949. Oldest professional to win a major tournament 1965. Unofficially credited with 164 victories (including 84 official USPGA tournaments) in his long career of which full details are not available. Finished 2nd equal in a 1974 USPGA tournament aged 61 and 3rd equal in 1974 USPGA Championship aged 62. 24 holes-in-one

Somerville, Charles Ross

Born London, Ontario, Canada on 4th May, 1903

Nat Canadian Amateur 1926-28-30-31-35-37; runner-up 1924-25-34-38
For US Amateur Champion 1932
Oth Ontario Amateur 1927-28-29-37. Manitoba Amateur 1926. Canadian Seniors 1960-61 (tied)-65-66 (tied).
Mis President Royal Canadian Golf Association 1957

Stacy, Miss Hollis

Born Savannah, Georgia, USA on 16th March, 1954. Turned Professional 1974

Nat US Ladies Open 1977-78-84. US Girls 1969-70-71
USC 1977–two. 1978–one. 1979–one. 1980–one. 1982–three. 1983–three. 1984–two. 1985–one

Stadler, Craig

Born San Diego, California, USA on 2nd June, 1953. Turned Professional 1975

Nat US Amateur 1973
Int Walker Cup 1975
Chp US Masters 1982
USC 1980–two. 1981–one. 1982–three. 1984–one
Int Ryder Cup 1983-85

Stephenson, J

Born . Turned Professional

Chp US Women's Open 1983
Nat Australian Ladies Open 1977
USL 1985–one

Stewart, Payne

Born Springfield, Missouri, USA on 30th January, 1957. Turned Professional 1979

Bri 2nd in Open 1985
USC 1982–two. 1983–one
For Indian Open 1981. Indonesian Open 1981
Int Nissan Cup 1986

Stockton, Davie

Born San Bernardino, California, USA on 2nd November, 1941. Turned Professional 1964

Nat USPGA Champion 1970-76. Second equal in US Masters 1974. Second in US Open 1978 (tied)
USC 1967–two. 1968–two. 1971–one. 1973–one. 1974–three
Int Ryder Cup 1971-77. USA in World Cup 1970-76

Stranahan, Frank R

Born Toledo, Ohio, USA on 5th August, 1922. Turned Professional 1954

Bri Amateur Champion 1948-50; runner-up 1952. Second in Open Championship 1947-53; leading Amateur 1947-49-50-51-53
Nat Second in US Amateur 1950
For Canadian Amateur 1947-48
USC 1955–one. 1958–one
Oth North and South Amateur 1946-49-52. Western Amateur 1946-49-51-53. Mexican Amateur 1946-48-51. Tam O'Shanter All American Amateur 1948-49-50-51-52-53. Tam O'Shanter World Amateur 1950-51-52-53-54
Int Walker Cup 1947-49-51

Strange, Curtis

Born Norfolk, Virginia, USA on 20th January, 1955. Turned Professional 1976

Int Eisenhower Trophy 1974. Walker Cup 1975
For Canadian Open 1985
USC 1979–one. 1980–two. 1983–two. 1984–one. 1985–three. 1986–one
Int Ryder Cup 1983–85. Dunhill Cup 1985. Nissan Cup 1985

Streit, Mrs Marlene Stewart

Born Cereal, Alberta, Canada on 9th March, 1934

Bri British Ladies 1953
Nat Canadian Ladies' Open 1951-54-55-56-58-59-63-68-72-73. Canadian Ladies' Close 1951-52-53-54-55-56-57-63-68
For US Ladies 1956; runner-up 1966. Australian Ladies 1963
Oth Ontario Provincial 1951-56-57-58. US North and South Ladies 1956
Int Canadian Commonwealth Team 1959-63-79 (capt)
Mis Canadian Athlete of the Year 1951-53-56. Canadian Woman Athlete of the Year 1951-53-56-60-63

Suggs, Miss Louise

Born Atlanta, Georgia, USA on 7th September, 1923. Turned Professional 1948

Bri British Ladies 1948
Nat US Ladies' Amateur 1947. US Ladies' Open 1949-52; second 1951-55 (tied)-58-59-63 (tied). USLPGA–1957
USC 50 victories on USLPGA circuit up to end of 1979
Int Curtis Cup 1948
Mis Leading US money winner 1953-60

Sutton, Hal

Born Shreveport, Louisiana, USA on 28th April, 1958. Turned Professional 1981

Nat US Amateur 1980
Int Walker Cup 1979-81
Chp US PGA 1983
USC 1982–one. 1983–one. 1985–two. 1986–two
Int Ryder Cup 1985. Nissan Cup 1986

Sweetser, Jess W

Born St Louis, Missouri, USA on 18th April, 1902

Bri Amateur Champion 1926
Nat US Amateur Champion 1922; runner-up 1923
Int Walker Cup 1922-23-24-26-28-32; non-playing captain 1967-73. World Amateur Cup non-playing captain 1966

Thomson, Peter W CBE

Born Melbourne, Australia on 23rd August, 1929. Turned Professional 1949

Bri Open Champion 1954-55-56-58-65; second 1952-53-57. PGA Match Play 1954-61-66-67. Yorkshire Evening News 1957-60-61. Dunlop 1958. Daks 1958 (tied)-60-65. Dunlop Masters 1961-68. Bowmaker 1960. Esso Golden 1961 (tied). Martini International 1962-70 (tied). Piccadilly 1962. Alcan International 1967. Wills 1972
Nat Australian Open 1951-67-72; second 1950. Australian Professional 1967. Leading Amateur Australian Open 1948
For New Zealand Open 1950-51-53-55-59-60-61-65-71. New Zealand Professional 1953. Italian Open 1959. Spanish Open 1959. Hong Kong Open 1960-65-67. German Open 1960. India Open 1963-76. Philippines Open 1964. On Japanese circuit: 1972–two. 1976–one
USC 1956–one. 1957–one
Oth New Zealand Caltex 1967. Victorian Open 1973
Int Australia in World Cup 1953-54 (winning team)-55-56-57-59 (winning team)-60-61-62-65-69
Mis His five victories in the Open Championship, including three in succession, were unequalled until Tom Watson's 1983 victory Honorary member of the Royal and Ancient

Trevino, Lee

Born Dallas, Texas, USA on 1st December, 1939. Turned Professional 1961

Bri Open Champion 1971-72; second 1980. Benson & Hedges International 1978. Dunhill British Masters 1985
Nat US Open Champion 1968-71. USPGA Champion 1974-84
For Canadian Open 1971-77-79. Canadian PGA 1979-83
USC 1968–one. 1969–one. 1970–two. 1971–three. 1972–three. 1973–two. 1974–one. 1975–one. 1976–one. 1978–one. 1980–three. 1981–one. World Series 1974
Int **Ryder Cup 1969-71-73-75-79-81-85 (captain). USA in World Cup 1968-69 (winning team and individual winner)-70-71 (winning team)-74**
Oth Chrysler Classic (Aust) 1973. Mexican Open 1975. Moroccan Grand Prix 1977. Lancome 1978-80
Mis Rookie of the Year 1967. Won three major Open titles–US Open, Canadian Open, Open–in four weeks. US leading money winner 1970; second 1971-72-80. USPGA Player of the Year 1971. Byron Nelson Award 1971. Ben Hogan Award 1979. Vardon Trophy Winner five times. Inducted into American Golf Hall of Fame 1979. World Golf Hall of Fame **1981. Benson & Hedges Golfer's Handbook Golfer of the Year 1984**

Tway, Bob

Born Oklahoma City, USA on 4th May, 1959. Turned Professional 1981

Chp US PGA 1986
USC 1986–three
Int Nissan Cup 1986

Van Donck, Flory

Born Tervueren, Brussels, Belgium on 23rd June, 1912

Bri Second in Open Championship 1956-59. PGA Match Play runner-up 1947-52. Silver King 1951-53. North British-Harrogate 1951. South of England Professional 1952. Yorkshire Evening News 1953
Nat Belgian Open 1939-46-47-53-56; second 1935-51. Belgian Professional 1935-38-49-52-53-54-55-56-57-59-60-63-64-65-66-68
For Dutch Open 1936-37-46-51-53. Italian Open 1938-47-53-55. Swiss Open 1953-55. French Open 1954-57-58. German Open 1953-56. Uruguay Open 1954. Portuguese Open 1955. Danish Open 1959. Venezuelan Open 1957
Int Belgium in World Cup 1954 to 1970-72-79, individual winner 1960. Europe v GB 1954-55-56-58
Mis Harry Vardon Trophy 1953

Varangot, Mlle Brigitte

Born Biarritz, France on 1st May, 1940

Bri British Ladies 1963-65-68. Kayser Bondor Foursomes 1960-63. British Girls 1957. Casa Pupo Foursomes 1965. Avia Foursomes 1966-73
Nat French Ladies' Open 1961-62-64-65-66-73; runner-up 1960-63-67-70. French Ladies' Close 1959-61-63-70. French Girls 1959-60-61
For Italian Ladies 1970
Int France, 1956 to 1973. Vagliano Trophy 1959-61-63-65-69-71. World Team Championship 1964 (winning team)-66-68-70-72-74

Vare, Mrs Edwin H (*née* Glenna Collett)

Born New Haven, Connecticut, USA on 20th June 1903

Bri British Ladies runner-up 1929-30
Nat US Ladies' Amateur 1922-25-28-29-30-35; runner-up 1931-32
For Canadian Ladies 1923-24
Oth North and South Ladies 1922-23-24-27-29-30. Eastern Ladies 7 times
Int Curtis Cup 1932-36-38-48 (capt); non-playing captain 1950
Mis Bobby Jones Award 1965

Verplank, Scott

Born Dallas, Texas, USA on 9th July, 1964

Nat US Amateur 1984
Int Walker Cup 1985
USC 1985–one (as amateur)

Vicenzo, Roberto De

Born Buenos Aires on 14th April, 1923. Turned Professional 1938

Bri Open Champion 1967; second 1950; third 1948-49-56-60-64-69. North British-Harrogate 1948
Nat Argentine Open 1944-49-51-52-58-65-67-70-74. Argentine Professional 1944-45-47-48-49-51-52
For Chile Open 1946. Colombia Open 1947. Uruguay Open 1949. Belgian Open 1950. Dutch Open 1950. French Open 1950-60-64. Mexican Open 1951-53. Panama Open 1952-73-74. Jamaican Open 1956-57. Brazilian Open 1957-60-63-64-73. Caracas Open 1973. German Open 1964. Spanish Open 1966. US Masters second 1968. Bogota Open 1969
USC 1951–two. 1953–one. 1957–two. 1966–one
Oth USPGA Seniors 1974. World Senior Professional 1974. Legends of Golf 1979. US Senior Open 1980
Int Argentina in World Cup 1953 (winning team)-54-55-62 (individual winner)-63-64-65-66-68-69-70 (individual winner)-71-72-73-74; Mexico in World Cup 1956-59-60-61
Mis Credited with 240 victories world wide including 40 National Championships. In the last round of the 1968 US Masters signed his card for a four at a hole at which he took three and so forfeited the right to playoff for the title. Became the oldest winner of the Open Championship (Cup) in 1967 at the age of 44 years and 93 days. Bobby Jones Award 1970. Made an honorary member of the Royal and Ancient GC 1976. Walter Hagen Award 1979

Wadkins, Lanny

Born Richmond, Virginia, USA on 5th December, 1949. Turned Professional 1971

Nat US Amateur 1970. USPGA 1977
For Canadian PGA 1978
USC 1972–one. 1973–two. 1979–two. 1982–two. 1983–two. 1985–three. World Series 1977
Oth Victorian PGA (Aust) 1978
Int Eisenhower Trophy winning team 1970. Walker Cup 1969-71. Ryder Cup 1977-79-83-85. USA in World Cup 1977. Dunhill Cup 1986.
Mis Rookie of the Year 1972 winning 116,616 dollars. Runner-up 1971 Heritage Classic as amateur

Ward, Harvie

Born 1926. Turned Professional 1973

Bri Amateur Champion 1952; runner-up 1953
Nat US Amateur Champion 1955-56
For Canadian Amateur 1954
Oth North and South Amateur 1948
Int Walker Cup 1953-55-59

Watson, Tom

Born Kansas City, Montana, USA on 4th September, 1949. Turned Professional 1971

Bri Open Champion 1975-77-80-82-83
Nat US Masters 1977-81, second 1978 (tied)-79 (tied). Second USPGA 1978 (tied). US Open 1982; second 1983
USC 1974–one. 1975–one. 1977–three. 1978–five. 1979–five. 1980–five. 1981–four. 1982–two. 1984–three. World Series 1975-80
Oth Phoenix Open (Japan) 1980
Int Ryder Cup 1977-81-83
Mis Byron Nelson Award 1977-78-79. US leading money winner 1977-78-79-80. His 1980 winnings of 530,808 dollars is the largest in one year. USPGA Player of the Year 1977-78-79-80. Bobby Jones Award 1986

Weiskopf, Tom

Born Ohio, USA on 9th November, 1942. Turned Professional 1964

Bri Open Champion 1973. Piccadilly World Match Play 1972
Nat Second US Master 1969-72-74 (equal)-75- (equal). Second in US Open 1976 (equal)
For Canadian Open 1973-75. South African PGA 1973. Argentine Open 1979
USC 1968–two. 1971–two. 1972–one. 1973–three. 1975–one. 1977–one. 1978–one. 1982–one. World Series 1973
Int Ryder Cup 1973-75. USA in World Cup 1972

Whitworth, Miss Kathy

Born New Mexico, USA on 27th September, 1939. Turned Professional 1959

Nat Second in US Women's Open 1971
USC 86 victories to end of 1984 including LPGA Championship 1967-71-75 and 10 victories in 1968
Mis US Ladies' Player of the Year 1966-67-68-69-71-72-73. Leading US money winner 1965-66-67-68-70-71-72-73; second in 1969. All-time leading money winner. Woman Athlete of the Year 1965-66

Wright, Miss Mary Kathryn (Mickey)

Born San Diego, California, USA in 1935. Turned Professional 1954

Nat US Girls 1952. US Ladies' Amateur runner-up 1954. US Ladies' Open 1958-59-61-64, second 1968. USLPGA 1958-60-61-63
USC In 1973 recorded her 82nd win in all tournaments with her Colgate-Dinah Shore victory
Mis Woman Athlete of the Year 1963-64. Leading US money winner 1961-62-63-64. Won 13 tournaments in 1963

Yates, Charles Richardson

Born Atlanta, Georgia, USA on 9th September, 1913

Bri Amateur Champion 1938
Oth Western Amateur 1935. Leading Amateur Masters 1934-39-40
Int Walker Cup 1936-38; non-playing captain 1953
Mis Bobby Jones Award 1980

Zoeller, Frank Urban

Born New Albany, Indiana, USA on 11th November, 1951. Turned Professional 1973

Nat US Open 1984. US Masters 1979; second 1981
USC 1979–two. 1983–two. 1985–one. 1986–three
Int Ryder Cup 1983-85
Mis Won US Masters at first attempt

The British Association of Golf Course Architects

Members

Full

J Hamilton Stutt	Hamilton Stutt and Co., 12 Bingham Avenue, Poole, Dorset BW14 8NE *Tel* 0202 708406
Donald Harradine	CH 6987 Caslano, Switzerland *Tel* 091 711561
Fred and Martin Hawtree	Hawtree and Son, 5 Oxford Street, Woodstock, Oxford OX7 1TQ *Tel* 0993 811976
Donald Steel	Cotton, Pennink Steel and Partners Ltd, Miller House, Corporation Street, Rugby CV21 2DW *Tel* 0788 77191
Tom McAuley	38 Moira Drive, Bangor, Co. Down, N. Ireland BT20 4RW *Tel* 0247 465953
Peter Harradine	PO Box 1165, Sharja, United Arab Emirates *Tel* 009716 356446

Provisional

Alistair Rae	26 Tannoch Road, Uplawmoor Road, Glasgow G78 4AD *Tel* 050-585 371
Cameron Sinclair	Cotton, Pennink Steel and Partners Ltd, Miller House, Corporation Street, Rugby CV21 2DW *Tel* 0788 77191
Simon Gidman	Hawtree and Son, 5 Oxford Street, Woodstock, Oxford OX7 1TQ *Tel* 0993 811976

Overseas (Full)

Eddie Hackett	28 Ailesbury Drive, Dublin 4, Eire *Tel* Dublin 691592
Joan Dudok Van Heel	Benkenlaan 4, 1640 St Genesius, Rode, Nr Brussels, Belgium *Tel* 358 5518
Piero Mancinelli	21 Via Achille Papa 00195, Rome, Italy *Tel* 06-36036 35
Jan Sederholm	S–252 34 Helsinborg, K Kristoffersg, 3A, Sweden *Tel* 042-371 84

Overseas (Provisional)

Kurt Rossknecht	Dennenmoos 5a, 8990 Lindau-Bad, Schachen, West Germany *Tel* 08382-230 05
Robert Berthet	57–59 Rue Llomond, 75005, Paris, France *Tel* (1) 336-77 50

Senior

Fraser Middelton	15 Kilmaron Crescent, Cupar, Fife KY15 4DS *Tel* 0334 54904

Association of Golf Writers

Andrew, Harry H	39 Moorburn Avenue, Orchard Park, Giffnock, Renfrewshire
(L) Baker, John E	3 Cissbury Drive, Findon Valley, Worthing, West Sussex BN14 0DT
Ballantine, John	Brick Hill Cottage, Hook Norton, Banbury, Oxon
Blackstock, Dixon	*Sunday Mail,* Anderston Quay, Glasgow
Blighton, Bill	Exchange Telegraph, Extel House, East Harding Street, London EC4
Blomquist, Jan	Swedish News Agency (TT), Kungsholmstorg 5, 10512 Stockholm, Sweden
Bolze, Gerd A	D2 Hamburg 73, Immensweg 11D, West Germany
Booth, Alan	21 Westminster Court, St Albans, Hertfordshire AL1 2DU
Bowden, Ken	56 Hermit Lane, PO Box 573, Westport, Connecticut 06881, USA
Britten, Mike	Exchange Telegraph, Extel House, East Harding Street, London EC4
(H) Butler, Frank	Robin Hill, Chislehurst Road, Orpington, Kent
Caird, Douglas	*Fairway and Hazard,* Gunners, Windlesham, Surrey
Callander, Colin	*Golf Monthly,* 1 Park Circus, Glasgow G3 6AP
Campbell, John G	*The Daily Telegraph,* 9 Woodend Drive, Glasgow G3 6AP
Chapman, Jeremy	*The Sporting Life,* Alexander House, 81-89 Farringdon Road, London EC1M 3LH
Clark, Bill	*Sunday Mirror,* Mark Royal House, Donegall Street, Belfast
Clough, Frank	*The Sun,* News International, 1 Virginia Street, London E1 9XP
Coffman, Ron	*Golf World,* PO Box 2000, Southern Pines, North Carolina, USA
(L) Cousins, Geoffrey	Hunts End, St Mary's Road, East Hendred, Wantage, Oxfordshire OX12 8JA
Davies, David	*The Guardian,* 119 Farringdon Road, London EC1R 3ER
Dobereiner, Peter	*The Observer,* St Andrews Hill, London EC4
Dodd, Richard	*The Yorkshire Post,* Wellington Street, Leeds 1
Donald, Peter	*Daily Mail* (*Scotland*), 7 House o'Hill Grove, Edinburgh EH4 5DW

Ebbinge, Jan B	President Kennedylaan 86, 1079 NH Amsterdam, Holland
(L) Edwards, Leslie	26 Beachcroft Road, Meols, Cheshire
Elliott, Bill	4 Fairway Close, Glossop, Derbyshire SK13 9QN
Ellison, Stanley	*Turf Management,* 3 Twelve Acre Close, Great Bookham, Surrey
Elsey, Neil	*Golf World,* Advance House, Mill Harbour, Isle of Dogs, London E14 9TX
Farquharson, Colin	*Press and Journal,* Lang Stracht, Mastrick, Aberdeen AB9 8AF
(H) Fenton, John	17 Macadam Street, Enfield, Middlesex
Ferrier, Bob	*World of Sport Ltd,* Aveland House, 91 East Princes Street, Helensburgh G84 7DG
Fraser, Alan	*Dundee Courier,* Bank Street, Dundee
Frederick, Adrian	*The Sunday Star,* 47 Sauer Street, Johannesburg, South Africa
Garrod, Mark	Press Association, 85 Fleet Street, London EC4
Gibbon, Sidney	26 Mowlem Court, Swanage, Dorset
Gilleece, Dermot	*The Irish Times,* D'Olier Street, Dublin 2
Goodner, Ross	*Golf Digest,* 495 Westport Avenue, Norwalk, Connecticut, USA
Green, Bob	The Associated Press, 50 Rockefeller Plaza, New York, NY 10020, USA
Green, Robert	*London Daily Post,* Mirror Building, Holborn Circus, London EC1
Grimsley, Will	The Associated Press, 50 Rockefeller Plaza, New York, NY 10020
Hamilton, David	*Golf Illustrated,* 47 Dartford Road, Sevenoaks, Kent TN13 3TE
Hamilton, Eddie	Netherton Court, Ayr Road, Newton Mearns, Glasgow G77 6EN
Haslam, Peter	*Golf World,* Advance House, 37 Mill Harbour, Isle of Dogs, London E14 9TX
(L) Hart, Maurice	11 Ivymount Road, London SE27
Hedley, Alan	*The Journal,* Groat Market, Newcastle-upon-Tyne
Hennessy, John	*The Times,* PO Box 481, Virginia Street, London E1 9BD
Herron, Allan	*Sunday Mail,* Anderston Quay, Glasgow G3 8DA
Higgs, Peter	*Mail on Sunday,* Northcliffe House, Tudor Street, London EC4Y 0JA
Hopkins, John	*The Sunday Times,* News International, 1 Virginia Street, London E1 9XP
Horne, Cyril	22 Lochmaddy Avenue, Braehead, Glasgow G44 3NU
(L) Huggins, Percy	43 Beechlands Drive, Clarkston, Nr Glasgow G76 7UZ
Ingham, John	Alfred Dunhill Ltd, 30 Duke Street, St James's, London SW1Y 6DL
Jacobs, Raymond	*Glasgow Herald,* 195 Albion Street, Glasgow G1 1QP
Jenkins, Bob	*Sunday Post* and *Golf Monthly,* Glasgow

Jenkins, Dan	*Golf Digest*, 495 Westport Avenue, Norwalk, Ct 06856, USA
Johnson, Bill	*Bolton Evening News*, Mealhouse Lane, Bolton, Lancashire
Kahn, Elizabeth	The Chase, Hadley Common, Barnet, Hertfordshire
Lafaurie, André-Jean	*Golf Européan*, 19 Rue de Prony, 75017 Paris, France
Laidlaw, Renton	*The London Standard*, Fleet Street, London EC4
Lawrenson, Derek J	*Birmingham Post and Mail*, Colmore Circus, Birmingham B4 6AX
Lincoln, Stanley	206 Park Avenue, Bushey, Hertfordshire
McDonnell, Michael	*Daily Mail*, Tudor Street, London EC4
Mackie, Keith	Dundrennan House, 12 Woodburn Terrace, St Andrews, Fife, Scotland
(H) McKinlay, SL	92 Killermont Road, Bearsden, Glasgow
Macniven, Ian	*Edinburgh Evening News*, North Bridge, Edinburgh
MacVicar, Jock	*Scottish Daily Express*, Park House, 2–4 Park Circus Place, Glasgow G3 6AF
Magowan, Jack	*Belfast Telegraph*, Belfast
Mair, Norman	*The Scotsman*, North Bridge, Edinburgh
Mair, Lewine	15 Dreghorn Loan, Colinton, Edinburgh 13
Maitland, Bobby	*Scottish Daily Express*, Park House, 2-4 Park Circus Place, Glasgow G3 6AF
Mancinelli, Piero	*La Gazzetta dello Sport*, 36 Via Solferino, 20121 Milan, Italy
Mearing, Paddy	Exchange Telegraph Co Ltd., Extel House, East Harding Street, London EC4
Moody, John	Tryfan, Danybryn Avenue, Radyr, Nr Cardiff
Morgan, John	Dray Lodge, Dray Corner, Headcorn, Kent TN27 9PA
Moseley, Ron	Press Association, 85 Fleet Street, London EC4
Mulqueen, Charles	*Cork Examiner*, 95 Patrick Street, Cork, Ireland
(H) Neale, Bert	Action Photos, Unit 6, 21 Wren Street, London WC1X 0HB
Nicol, Alister	*Daily Record*, 90A George Street, Edinburgh
Oakley, John	10 Cairn Close, Camberley, Surrey
Ortega, Jesus Ruiz	*Golf*, Basilica 15, 8°A, 28020 Madrid, Spain
Ostermann, Ted	*Golf Vertrieb*, Hamburgstrasse 3-11/3, D 2000 Hamburg 76, West Germany
Pargeter, John	26 Princes Road, Brunton Park, Newcastle-upon-Tyne NE3 5AL
Pastor, Nuria	*La Vanguardia*, Pelayo 28, Barcelona, Spain
(H) Place, Tom	USPGA Tour, 100 Nina Court, Ponte Vedra Beach, Florida 32082, USA
Platts, Mitchell	*The Times*, News International, 1 Virginia Street, London E1 9BD
Plumridge, Chris	*The Illustrated London News*, 4 Bloomsbury Square, London WC1A 2RL

Price-Fisher, Elizabeth	*The Daily Telegraph,* Fleet Street, London EC4
Radosta, John	37 Washington Square, New York NY 10011, USA
Ramsey, Tom	News Limited, Australia, PO Box 1349, North Sydney 2060, New South Wales, Australia
Rea, Chris	Victoria House, Uffington, Nr Stamford, Lincs PE9 4SN
Redmond, John	*Irish Press,* Burgh Quay, Dublin 2
Reece, John K	Hailstones, Broadfield Down, Redhill, Nr Bristol BS18 7TL
Richardson, Gordon	Tress, Post Office Lane, Hyde, Nr Fordingbridge, Hampshire
Roberts, Steve	7 Marsham Lodge, East Common, Gerrards Cross, Buckinghamshire SL9 7AB
Robertson, Bill	*Golf Illustrated,* 47 Dartford Road, Sevenoaks, Kent TN13 3TE
Robertson, Jack	*Evening Times,* 195 Albion Street, Glasgow G1 1QP
Rodrigo, Robert (Bob Rodney)	Woodlands, 1 Elm Close, Dullingham, Newmarket, Suffolk
Ross, John M	19 Riverfield Drive, Weston, Ct., 06883, USA
Ruddy, Pat	*Golfer's Companion,* PO Box 14, Dun Laoire, County Dublin
Ryde, Peter	4 Phene Street, Chelsea, London SW3
Scatchard, Charles	2 Manor Cottages, Follifoot, Harrogate HG3 1DT
Seitz, Nick	*Golf Digest,* 495 Westport Avenue, Norwalk, Ct., 06856, USA
Severino, Dick	Golf Features Service, 10081 Mesa Madera Drive, San Diego, California 92131, USA
Simms, George	10 Melsted Road, Hemel Hempstead, Hertfordshire HP1 1SX
Simpson, Gordon	Press Association, 96 Warroch Street, Glasgow G3 8DB
Skelton, Ronald	*Dundee Courier,* Bank Street, Dundee
Smith, Colm	Independent Newspapers, 91 Middle Abbey Street, Dublin 1
Sommers, Robert	United States Golf Association, Far Hills, New Jersey 07931, USA
Spander, Art	*San Francisco Examiner,* 110 5th Street, San Francisco, California 94103, USA
Steel, Donald	*Sunday Telegraph,* 135 Fleet Street, London EC4
Stobbs, John	*General Golf and Greenkeeping,* 73 Vicarage Road, Marsworth, Nr Tring, Hertfordshire
Taylor, Dick	*Golf World,* Box 2000, Southern Pines, North Carolina 28387, USA
Taylor, Frankie	*Sunday People,* Orbit House, 9 New Fetter Lane, London EC4
(H) Thornberry, Henry W	*New York Times,* News Service, 229 W 43rd Street, New York, NY 10036, USA

(H) Ullyett, Roy	*Daily Express,* Fleet Street, London EC4P 4JT
Van Esbeck, Edmund	*The Irish Times,* 31 Westmorland Street, Dublin
Ward, Barry E	*Holiday Golf International,* 16 Georgia Avenua, Worthing, West Sussex BN14 8AZ
Whitbread, John S	Surrey Herald Newspapers, Windsor Street, Chertsey
White, Gordon S	*New York Times,* 229 West 43rd Street, New York, NY 10036, USA
Wills, Ron	*Daily Mirror,* Holborn Circus, London EC1
Williams, Michael	*The Daily Telegraph,* Fleet Street, London EC4
(L) Wilson, Enid	The Oast, Redbridge Farm, Redbridge Lane, Crowborough, East Sussex TN6 3SR
Wilson, Mark	PGA European Tour, Wentworth, Virginia Water, Surrey
Wind, Herbert Warren	*The New Yorker,* 25 W 43rd Street, New York, NY 21, USA
Wright, Ben	116 Midland Drive, Asheville, North Carolina 28804, USA

GOLF WORLD
EUROPE'S BEST SELLING GOLF MAGAZINE
Find success with our 8 keys to consistency
GOLF WORLD
Europe's Best Golf Magazine
May 1985
£1.00
THE RISE AND RISE OF SEVE BALLESTEROS
— an in-depth profile
Learn to drive with confidence
Juniors' dilemma — top names speak out
Win a Saab 900 car or a set of Taylor Made irons
THERE'S A WORLD OF DIFFERENCE

Part VI
The Records

The Championships

The Open Championship

The Belt

Year	Winner	Score	Venue	Entrants
1860	W Park, Musselburgh	174	Prestwick	8
1861	Tom Morris, sen, Prestwick	163	Prestwick	12
1862	Tom Morris, sen, Prestwick	163	Prestwick	6
1863	W Park, Musselburgh	168	Prestwick	14
1864	Tom Morris, sen, Prestwick	167	Prestwick	6
1865	A Strath, St Andrews	162	Prestwick	10
1866	W Park, Musselburgh	169	Prestwick	12
1867	Tom Morris, sen, St Andrews	170	Prestwick	10
1868	Tom Morris, jun, St Andrews	157	Prestwick	10
1869	Tom Morris, jun, St Andrews	154	Prestwick	8
1870	Tom Morris, jun, St. Andrews	149	Prestwick	17

The Belt having been won thrice in succession by young Tom Morris, it became his property, and the Championship remained in abeyance for one year, when the present cup was offered for yearly competition, to be held by the leading club in the district in which the winner resided.

The Cup

Year	Winner	Score	Venue	Entrants
1872	Tom Morris, jun, St Andrews	166	Prestwick	8
1873	Tom Kidd, St Andrews	179	St Andrews	26
1874	Mungo Park, Musselburgh	159	Musselburgh	32
1875	Willie Park, Musselburgh	166	Prestwick	18
1876	Bob Martin, St Andrews	176	St Andrews	34
(David Strath tied but refused to play off)				
1877	Jamie Anderson, St Andrews	160	Musselburgh	24
1878	Jamie Anderson, St Andrews	157	Prestwick	26
1879	Jamie Anderson, St Andrews	169	St Andrews	46
1880	Bob Ferguson, Musselburgh	162	Musselburgh	30
1881	Bob Ferguson, Musselburgh	170	Prestwick	22
1882	Bob Ferguson, Musselburgh	171	St Andrews	40
1883	W. Fernie, Dumfries	159	Musselburgh	41
After a tie with Bob Ferguson, Musselburgh				
1884	Jack Simpson, Carnoustie	160	Prestwick	30
1885	Bob Martin, St Andrews	171	St Andrews	51
1886	D Brown, Musselburgh	157	Musselburgh	46
1887	W. Park, jun, Musselburgh	161	Prestwick	36
1888	Jack Burns, Warwick	171	St Andrews	53
1889	W. Park, jun, Musselburgh	155	Musselburgh	42
After a tie with Andrew Kirkcaldy				
1890	John Ball, Royal Liverpool (Am)	164	Prestwick	40
1891	Hugh Kirkaldy, St Andrews	166	St Andrews	82
After 1891 the competition was extended to 72 holes and for the first time entry money was imposed				
1892	HH Hilton, Royal Liverpool (Am)	305	Muirfield	66
1893	W. Auchterlonie, St Andrews	322	Prestwick	72
1894	JH Taylor, Winchester	326	Sandwich	94
1895	JH Taylor, Winchester	322	St Andrews	73
1896	H Vardon, Ganton	316	Muirfield	64
After a tie with JH Taylor. Replay scores for 36 holes: H Vardon, 157; Taylor, 161				

The Open Championship
continued

Year	Winner	Score	Venue	Ents
1897	HH Hilton, Royal Liverpool (Am)	314	Hoylake	86
1898	H Vardon, Ganton	307	Prestwick	78
1899	H Vardon, Ganton	310	Sandwich	98
1900	JH Taylor, Mid-Surrey	309	St Andrews	81
1901	James Braid, Romford	309	Muirfield	101
1902	Alex Herd, Huddersfield	307	Hoylake	112
1903	H. Vardon, Totteridge	300	Prestwick	127
1904	Jack White, Sunningdale	296	Sandwich	144
1905	James Braid, Walton Heath	318	St Andrews	152
1906	James Braid, Walton Heath	300	Muirfield	183
1907	Arnaud Massy, La Boulie	312	Hoylake	193

Year	Winner	Score	Venue	Qual	Ents
1908	James Braid, Walton Heath	291	Prestwick	180	
1909	JH Taylor, Mid-Surrey	295	Deal	204	
1910	James Braid, Walton Heath	299	St Andrews	210	
1911	Harry Vardon, Totteridge	303	Sandwich	226	
After a tie with Arnaud Massy. The tie was over 36 holes, but Massy picked up at the 35th hole before holing out. He had taken 148 for 34 holes, and when Vardon holed out at the 35th hole his score was 143.					
1912	E Ray, Oxhey	295	Muirfield	215	
1913	JH Taylor, Mid-Surrey	304	Hoylake	269	
1914	Harry Vardon, Totteridge	306	Prestwick	194	
1915–19	No Championship owing to the Great War				
1920	George Duncan, Hanger Hill	303	Deal	81	190
1921	Jock Hutchison, Glenview, Chicago	296	St Andrews	85	158
After a tie with RH Wethered (Am), Royal and Ancient–Replay scores: Jock Hutchison 150; RH Wethered 159.					
1922	Walter Hagen, Detroit, USA	300	Sandwich	80	225
1923	AG Havers, Coombe Hill	295	Troon	88	222
1924	Walter Hagen, Detroit, USA	301	Hoylake	86	277
1925	Jim Barnes, USA	300	Prestwick	83	200
1926	RT Jones, USA (Am)	291	Lytham and St Annes	117	293
1927	RT Jones, USA (Am)	285	St Andrews	108	207
1928	Walter Hagen, USA	292	Sandwich	113	271
1929	Walter Hagen, USA	292	Muirfield	109	242
1930	RT Jones, USA (Am)	291	Hoylake	112	296
1931	TD Armour, USA	296	Carnoustie	109	215
1932	G Sarazen, USA	283	Prince's, Sandwich	110	224
1933	D Shute, USA	292	St Andrews	117	287
After a tie with Craig Wood, USA–Replay scores: D Shute 149; Craig Wood 154.					
1934	TH Cotton, Waterloo, Belgium	283	Sandwich	101	312
1935	A Perry, Leatherhead	283	Muirfield	109	264
1936	AH Padgham, Sundridge Park	287	Hoylake	107	286
1937	TH Cotton, Ashridge	290	Carnoustie	141	258
1938	RA Whitcombe, Parkstone	295	Sandwich	120	268
1939	R. Burton, Sale	290	St Andrews	129	254
1940–45	*No Championship owing to World War*				
1946	S Snead, USA	290	St Andrews	100	225
1947	Fred Daly, Balmoral	293	Hoylake	100	263
1948	TH Cotton, Royal Mid-Surrey	284	Muirfield	97	272
1949	AD Locke, South Africa	283	Sandwich	96	224
After a tie with Harry Bradshaw, Kilcroney–Replay scores: Locke 135; Bradshaw 147.					
1950	AD Locke, South Africa	279	Troon	93	262
1951	M. Faulkner, Unattached	285	Portrush	98	180
1952	AD Locke, South Africa	287	Lytham and St Annes	96	275
1953	Ben Hogan, USA	282	Carnoustie	91	196
1954	PW Thomson, Australia	283	Birkdale	97	349
1955	PW Thomson, Australia	281	St Andrews	94	301
1956	PW Thomson, Australia	286	Hoylake	96	360
1957	AD Locke, South Africa	279	St Andrews	96	282
1958	PW Thomson, Australia	278	Lytham and St Annes	96	362
After a tie with DC Thomas, Sudbury–Replay scores: Thomson 139; Thomas 143.					
1959	GJ Player, South Africa	284	Muirfield	90	285
1960	KDG Nagle, Australia	278	St Andrews	74	410
1961	Arnold Palmer, USA	284	Birkdale	101	364
1962	Arnold Palmer, USA	276	Troon	119	379
1963	RJ Charles, New Zealand	277	Lytham and St Annes	119	261
After a tie with Phil Rodgers, USA–Replay scores: Charles 140; Rodgers 148.					
1964	Tony Lema, USA	279	St Andrews	119	327
1965	PW Thomson, Australia	285	Birkdale	130	372
1966	J Nicklaus, USA	282	Muirfield	130	310
1967	R De Vicenzo, Argentine	278	Hoylake	130	326
1968	G Player, South Africa	289	Carnoustie	130	309

The Open Championship *continued*

Year	Winner	Score	Venue	Qual	Ents
1969	A Jacklin, Potters Bar	280	Lytham and St Annes	129	424
1970	J Nicklaus, USA	283	St Andrews	134	468
After a tie with Doug Sanders, USA–Replay scores: Nicklaus 72; Sanders 73.					
1971	L Trevino, USA	278	Birkdale	150	528
1972	L Trevino, USA	278	Muirfield	150	570
1973	T Weiskopf, USA	276	Troon	150	569
1974	G Player, South Africa	282	Lytham and St Annes	150	679
1975	T Watson, USA	279	Carnoustie	150	629
After a tie with J Newton, Australia–Replay scores: Watson 71; Newton 72.					
1976	J Miller, USA	279	Birkdale	150	719
1977	T Watson, USA	268	Turnberry	150	730
1978	J Nicklaus, USA	281	St Andrews	150	788
1979	S Ballesteros, Spain	283	Lytham and St Annes	150	885
1980	T Watson, USA	271	Muirfield	151	994
1981	B Rogers, USA	276	Sandwich	153	971
1982	T Watson, USA	284	Troon	176	1,121
1983	T Watson, USA	275	Birkdale	151	1,107
1984	S Ballesteros, Spain	276	St Andrews		1,413
1985	A Lyle	282	Sandwich	149	1,361
1986	G Norman	280	Turnberry	152	1,347

1946 at St Andrews

Entries 225. Qualified 100 (Professionals 91, Amateurs 9). Qualifying aggregate 159. Finally qualified for last 36 holes, 38 (33 Professionals, 5 Amateurs). Final qualifying aggregate 155.

Name	Score
S. Snead (USA)	71, 70, 74, 75–290
AD Locke (South Africa)	69, 74, 75, 76–294
J. Bulla (USA)	71, 72, 72, 79–294
CH Ward (Little Aston)	73, 73, 73, 76–295
TH Cotton (Royal Mid-Surrey)	70, 70, 76, 79–295
DJ Rees (Hindhead)	75, 67, 73, 80–295
N von Nida (Australia)	70, 76, 74, 75–295
F Daly (Balmoral)	77, 71, 76, 74–298
J Kirkwood (USA)	71, 75, 78, 74–298
L Little (USA)	78, 75, 72, 74–299
H Bradshaw (Kilcroney)	76, 75, 76, 73–300

1947 at Hoylake

Entries 263. Qualified 100 (92 Professionals, 8 Amateurs). Qualifying aggregate 155. Finally qualified for last 36 holes, 40 (38 Professionals, 2 Amateurs). Final qualifying aggregate 156.

Name	Score
F Daly (Balmoral)	73, 70, 78, 72–293
RW Horne (Hendon)	77, 74, 72, 71–294
FR Stranahan (USA) (Am)	71, 79, 72, 72–294
W Shankland (Templenewsam)	76, 74, 75, 70–295
R Burton (Coombe Hill)	77, 71, 77, 71–296
CH Ward (Little Aston)	76, 73, 76, 72–297
SL King (Wildernesse)	75, 72, 77, 73–297
A Lees (Dore and Totley)	75, 74, 72, 76–297
J Bulla (USA)	80, 72, 74, 71–297
TH Cotton (Royal Mid-Surrey)	69, 78, 74, 76–297
N von Nida (Australia)	74, 76, 71, 76–297

1948 at Muirfield

Entries 272. Qualified 97. Qualifying aggregate 152. Qualified for last 36 holes, 36 (33 Professionals, 3 Amateurs). Final qualifying aggregate 148.

Name	Score
TH Cotton (Royal Mid-Surrey)	71, 66, 75, 72–284
FJ Daly (Balmoral)	72, 71, 73, 73–289
NG von Nida (Australia)	71, 72, 76, 71–290
R De Vicenzo (Argentina)	70, 73, 72, 75–290
J Hargreaves (Sutton Coldfield)	76, 68, 73, 73–290
CH Ward (Little Aston)	69, 72, 75, 74–290
SL King (Knole Park)	69, 72, 74, 76–291
J Bulla (USA)	74, 72, 73, 72–291
F Van Donck (Waterloo, Belgium)	69, 73, 73, 76–291
AH Padgham (Sundridge Park)	73, 70, 71, 77–291
Capt EC Kingsley (USA) (Am)	77, 69, 77, 70–293
Mario Gonzalez (Brazil) (Am)	76, 72, 70, 75–293
A Lees (Dore and Totley)	73, 69, 73, 78–293
A Waters (Stand)	75, 71, 70, 77–293

The Open Championship
continued

1949 at Sandwich

Entries 224. Qualified 96. Qualifying aggregate 154. Qualified for last 36 holes, 31 (29 Professionals, 2 Amateurs). Final qualifying aggregate 147.

Name	Score
AD Locke (S Africa)	69, 76, 68, 70–283
H Bradshaw (Kilcroney)	68, 77, 68, 70–283
R De Vicenzo (Argentina)	68, 75, 73, 69–285
SL King (Knole Park)	71, 69, 74, 72–286
CH Ward (Little Aston)	73, 71, 70, 72–286
A Lees (Dore and Totley)	74, 70, 72, 71–287
M Faulkner (Mid-Surrey)	71, 71, 71, 74–287
J Adams (Wentworth)	67, 77, 72, 72–288
W Smithers (Long Ashton)	72, 75, 70, 71–288
J Fallon (Huddersfield)	69, 75, 72, 72–288
W Shankland (Templenewsam)	69, 73, 74, 73–289
K Bousfield (Coombe Hill)	69, 77, 76, 67–289

1950 at Troon

Entries 262. Qualified 93 (81 Professionals, 12 Amateurs). Qualifying aggregate 153. Qualified for final 36 holes, 35 (31 Professionals, 4 Amateurs). Final qualifying aggregate 148.

Name	Score
AD Locke (S. Africa)	69, 72, 70, 68–279
R De Vicenzo (Argentina)	72, 71, 68, 70–281
F Daly (Balmoral)	75, 72, 69, 66–282
DJ Rees (South Herts)	71, 68, 72, 71–282
E Moore (South Africa)	74, 68, 73, 68–283
M Faulkner (Mid-Surrey)	72, 70, 70, 71–283
A Lees (Sunningdale)	68, 76, 68, 72–284
F Bullock (Lytham and St Annes)	71, 71, 71, 71–284
F van Donck (Waterloo, Belgium)	73, 71, 72, 70–286
FR Stranahan (USA) (Am)	77, 70, 73, 66–286
SL King (Knole Park)	70, 75, 68, 73–286

1951 at Portrush

Entries 180. Qualified 98 (85 Professionals, 13 Amateurs). Qualifying aggregate 155. Qualified for final 36 holes, 46 (42 Professionals, 4 Amateurs). Final qualifying aggregate 154.

Name	Score
M Faulkner (unattached)	71, 70, 70, 74–285
A Cerda (Argentina)	74, 72, 71, 70–287
CH Ward (Little Aston)	75, 73, 74, 68–290
F Daly (Balmoral)	74, 70, 75, 73–292
J Adams (Wentworth)	68, 77, 75, 72–292
AD Locke (South Africa)	71, 74, 74, 74–293
W Shankland (Templenewsam)	73, 76, 72, 72–293
N Sutton (Leigh)	73, 70, 74, 76–293
H Weetman (Croham Hurst)	73, 71, 75, 74–293
PW Thomson (Australia)	70, 75, 73, 75–293
J Panton (Glenbervie)	73, 72, 74, 75–294
DJ Rees (South Herts)	70, 77, 76, 72–295
R Burton (Coombe Hill)	74, 77, 71, 73–295
FR Stranahan (USA) (Am)	75, 75, 72, 73–295

1952 at Lytham and St Annes

Entries 275. Qualified 96 (87 Professionals, 9 Amateurs). Qualifying aggregate 152. Qualified for final 36 holes, 46 (41 Professionals, 5 Amateurs). Final qualifying aggregate 152.

Name	Score
AD Locke (South Africa)	69, 71, 74, 73–287
PW Thomson (Australia)	68, 73, 77, 70–288
F Daly (Balmoral)	67, 69, 77, 76–289
TH Cotton (Royal Mid-Surrey)	75, 74, 74, 71–294
A Cerda (Argentina)	73, 73, 76, 73–295
SL King (Knole Park)	71, 74, 74, 76–295
F van Donck (Belgium)	74, 75, 71, 76–296
F Bullock (Glasgow)	76, 72, 72, 77–296
SS Scott (Carlisle City)	75, 69, 76, 78–298
H Bradshaw (Portmarnock)	70, 74, 75, 79–298
A Lees (Sunningdale)	76, 72, 76, 74–298
NG von Nida (Australia)	77, 70, 74, 77–298
EC Brown (Sandy Lodge)	71, 72, 78, 77–298
W Goggin (USA)	71, 74, 75, 78–298
J Panton (Glenbervie)	72, 72, 78, 77–299
H Weetman (Croham Hurst)	74, 77, 71, 77–299

1953 at Carnoustie

Entries 196. Qualified 91 (82 Professionals, 9 Amateurs). Qualifying aggregate 154. Qualified for final 36 holes, 49 (48 Professionals, 1 Amateur). Final qualifying aggregate 154.

Name	Score
Ben Hogan (USA)	73, 71, 70, 68–282
FR Stranahan (USA) (Am)	70, 74, 73, 69–286
DJ Rees (South Herts)	72, 70, 73, 71–286
P Thomson (Australia)	72, 72, 71, 71–286
A Cerda (Argentina)	75, 71, 69, 71–286
R De Vicenzo (Argentina)	72, 71, 71, 73–287
SL King (Knole Park)	74, 73, 72, 71–290
AD Locke (S Africa)	72, 73, 74, 72–291
P Allis (Ferndown)	75, 72, 74, 71–292
EC Brown (unattached)	71, 71, 75, 75–292
F Daly (Balmoral)	73, 75, 71, 75–294
M Faulkner (St George's Hill)	74, 71, 73, 77–295
A Lees (Sunningdale)	76, 76, 72, 72–296
H Weetman (Croham Hurst)	80, 73, 72, 72–297
JRM Jacobs (Sandy Lodge)	79, 74, 71, 73–297
THT Fairbairn (Reddish Vale)	74, 71, 73, 79–297
H Hassanein (Egypt)	78, 71, 73, 76–298
E Lester (Bristol and Clifton)	83, 70, 72, 73–298
CH Ward (Little Aston)	78, 71, 76, 73–298
RW Horne (Hendon)	76, 74, 75, 74–299
F van Donck (Belgium)	77, 71, 78, 73–299
SS Scott (Carlisle City)	74, 74, 78, 74–300
H Thomson (unattached)	76, 74, 74, 76–300

1954 at Birkdale

Entries 349. Qualified 97 (85 Professionals, 12 Amateurs). Qualifying aggregate 151. Qualified for final 36 holes, 50 (48 Professionals, 2 Amateurs). Final qualifying aggregate 151.

Name	Score
PW Thomson (Australia)	72, 71, 69, 71–283
SS Scott (Carlisle City)	76, 67, 69, 72–284
DJ Rees (South Herts)	72, 71, 69, 72–284
AD Locke (S Africa)	74, 71, 69, 70–284
J Adams (Mid-Surrey)	73, 75, 69, 69–286
A Cerda (Argentina)	71, 71, 73, 71–286
J. Turnesa (USA)	72, 72, 71, 71–286
P. Alliss (Ferndown)	72, 74, 71, 70–287
SL King (Knole Park)	69, 74, 74, 70–287
J Demaret (USA)	73, 71, 74, 71–289
F van Donck (Belgium)	77, 71, 70, 71–289
H Bradshaw (Portmarnock)	72, 72, 73, 73–290
TW Spence (Dartford)	69, 72, 74, 75–290
A Angelini (Italy)	76, 70, 73, 71–290
R Halsall (Birkdale)	72, 73, 73, 73–291
P Toogood (Tasmania) (Am)	72, 75, 73, 71–291
C Kane (Dublin)	74, 72, 74, 72–292
G Sarazen (USA)	75, 74, 73, 70–292
U Grappasonni (Italy)	72, 75, 74, 71–292

1955 at St Andrews

Entries 301. Qualified 94 (86 Professionals, 8 Amateurs). Qualifying aggregate 148. Qualified for final 36 holes, 49 (46 Professionals, 3 Amateurs). Final qualifying aggregate 148.

Name	Score
PW Thomson (Australia)	71, 68, 70, 72–281
J Fallon (Huddersfield)	73, 67, 73, 70–283
F Jowle (Edgbaston)	70, 71, 69, 74–284
AD Locke (S Africa)	74, 69, 70, 72–285
A Cerda (Argentina)	73, 71, 71, 71–286
K Bousfield (Coombe Hill)	71, 75, 70, 70–286
H Weetman (Croham Hurst)	71, 71, 70, 74–286
BJ Hunt (Hartsbourne CC)	70, 71, 74, 71–286
F van Donck (Belgium)	71, 72, 71, 72–286
R Barbieri (Argentina)	71, 71, 73, 72–287
C O'Connor (Bundoran)	71, 75, 70, 71–287
EC Brown (Buchanan Castle)	69, 70, 73, 76–288
F Daly (Balmoral)	75, 72, 70, 71–288
JRM Jacobs (Sandy Lodge)	71, 70, 71, 76–288
WJ Henderson (Troon)	74, 71, 72, 72–289
JS Anderson (Bruntsfield Links)	71, 72, 77, 69–289
DF Smalldon (Cardiff)	70, 69, 78, 73–290
A Soto (Argentina)	72, 73, 72, 73–290
E Furgol (USA)	71, 76, 72, 73–292
K Nagle (Australia)	72, 72, 74, 74–292
SS Scott (Carlisle City)	69, 77, 73, 73–292

The Open Championship *continued*

1956 at Hoylake

Entries 360. Qualified 96 (89 Professionals, 7 Amateurs). Qualifying aggregate 152. Qualified for final 36 holes, 48 (47 Professionals, 1 Amateur). Final qualifying aggregate 153.

Name	Score	Name	Score
PW Thomson (Australia)	70, 70, 72, 74–286	F Stranahan (USA) (Am)	72, 76, 72, 76–296
F van Donck (Belgium)	71, 74, 70, 74–289	DJ Rees (South Herts)	75, 74, 75, 73–297
R De Vicenzo (Argentina)	71, 70, 79, 70–290	A Miguel (Spain)	71, 74, 75, 77–297
G Player (South Africa)	71, 76, 73, 71–291	B Crampton (Australia)	76, 77, 72, 72–297
J Panton (Glenbervie)	74, 76, 72, 70–292	JRM Jacobs (Sandy Lodge)	73, 77, 76, 72–298
TH Cotton (Temple)	72, 76, 71, 74–293	DC Thomas (Sudbury)	70, 78, 77, 75–300
E Bertolino (Argentina)	69, 72, 76, 76–293	R Rossi (Argentina)	75, 77, 72, 76–300
A Cerda (Argentina)	72, 81, 68, 73–294	A Balding (Canada)	70, 81, 76, 73–300
M Souchak (USA)	74, 74, 74, 72–294	CH Ward (Little Aston)	73, 75, 78, 74–300
C O'Connor (Bundoran)	73, 78, 74, 70–295	J Hargreaves (Sutton Coldfield)	72, 80, 75, 73–300
H Weetman (Croham Hurst)	72, 76, 75, 72–295		

1957 at St Andrews

Entries 282. Qualified 96 (83 Professionals, 13 Amateurs). Qualified for final 36 holes, 46 (44 Professionals, 2 Amateurs). Final qualifying aggregate 148.

Name	Score	Name	Score
AD Locke (S Africa)	69, 72, 68, 70–279	P Allis (Parkstone)	72, 74, 74, 68–288
PW Thomson (Australia)	73, 69, 70, 70–282	H Weetman (Croham Hurst)	75, 71, 71, 71–288
EC Brown (Buchanan Castle)	67, 72, 73, 71–283	C Middlecoff (USA)	72, 71, 74, 72–289
A Miguel (Spain)	72, 72, 69, 72–285	EG Lester (Hazel Grove)	71, 76, 70, 73–290
DC Thomas (Sudbury)	72, 74, 70, 70–286	S Miguel (Spain)	71, 75, 76, 68–290
TB Haliburton (Wentworth)	72, 73, 68, 73–286	N Drew (Knock)	70, 75, 71, 74–290
WD Smith (Prestwick) (Am)	71, 72, 72, 71–286	J Panton (Glenbervie)	71, 72, 74, 73–290
F van Donck (Belgium)	72, 68, 74, 72–286	H Bradshaw (Portmarnock)	73, 74, 69, 75–291
TH Cotton (Temple)	74, 72, 69, 72–287	C O'Connor (Bundoran)	77, 69, 72, 73–291
M Faulkner (Selsey)	74, 70, 71, 72–287	FR Stranahan (USA)	74, 71, 74, 72–291
A Cerda (Argentina)	71, 71, 72, 73–287	J Fallon (Huddersfield)	75, 67. 73, 76–291

1958 at Lytham and St Annes

Entries 362. Qualified 96 (87 Professionals, 9 Amateurs). Qualifying aggregate 148. Qualified for final 36 holes, 40 (39 Professionals, 1 Amateur). Final qualifying aggregate 147.

Name	Score	Name	Score
PW Thomson (Australia)	66, 72, 67, 73–278	P Alliss (Parkstone)	72, 70, 70, 73–285
DC Thomas (Sudbury)	70, 68, 69, 71–278	D Swaelens (Belgium)	74, 67, 74, 70–285
EC Brown (Buchanan Castle)	73, 70, 65, 71–279	HR Henning (S Africa)	70, 71, 72, 73–286
C O'Connor (Killarney)	67, 68, 73, 71–279	DJ Rees (South Herts)	77, 69, 71, 70–287
F van Donck (Belgium)	70, 70, 67, 74–281	J Garaialde (France)	69, 74, 72, 72–287
L Ruiz (Argentina)	71, 65, 72, 73–281	AD Locke (S Africa)	76, 70, 72, 70–288
GJ Player (S Africa)	68, 74, 70, 71–283	G Sarazen (USA)	73, 73, 70, 72–288
TH Cotton (Temple)	68, 75, 69, 72–284	E Moore (S Africa)	72, 72, 70, 74–288
H Weetman (Selsdon Park)	73, 67, 73, 71–284	M Faulkner (Selsey)	68, 71, 71, 78–288
EG Lester (Hazel Grove)	73, 66, 71, 74–284	C Greene (Milltown)	75, 71, 72, 72–290
		F Daly (Balmoral)	71, 74, 72, 73–290
		NV Drew (Knock)	69, 72, 75, 74–290
		AB Coop (Dean Wood)	69, 71, 75, 75–290

Play-off Scores:

PW Thomson (Australia) 68, 71–139
DC Thomas (Sudbury) 69, 74–143

The Open Championship
continued

1959 at Muirfield

Entries 285. Qualified 90 (80 Professionals, 10 Amateurs). Qualifying aggregate 147. Qualified for final 36 holes, 48 (44 Professionals, 4 Amateurs). Final qualifying aggregate 148.

Name	Score	Name	Score
GJ Player (S Africa)	75, 71, 70, 68–284	K Bousfield (Coombe Hill)	73, 73, 71, 73–290
F van Donck (Belgium)	70, 70, 73, 73–286	J Hitchcock (Ashford Manor)	75, 68, 70, 77–290
F Bullock (Prestwick St Nicholas)	68, 70, 74, 74–286	AF Stickley (Ealing)	68, 74, 77, 71–290
SS Scott (Roehampton)	73, 70, 73, 71–287	MF Bonallack (Thorpe Hall) (Am)	70, 72, 72, 76–290
C O'Connor (Royal Dublin)	73, 74, 72, 69–288	GB Wolstenholme (Kirby Muxloe) (Am)	78, 70, 73, 70–291
RR Jack (Dullatur) (Am)	71, 75, 68, 74–288	P Alliss (Parkstone)	76, 72, 76, 67–291
SL King (Knole Park)	70, 74, 68, 76–288	H Bradshaw (Portmarnock)	71, 76, 72, 72–291
J Panton (Glenbervie)	72, 72, 71, 73–288	H Weetman (Selsdon Park Hotel)	72, 73, 76, 70–291
DJ Rees (South Herts)	73, 73, 69, 74–289	A Cerda (Argentina)	69, 74, 73, 75–291
L Ruiz (Argentina)	72, 74, 69, 74–289		
BJ Hunt (Hartsbourne CC)	73, 75, 71, 71–290		

1960 at St Andrews

Centenary Championship. Entries 410. Qualified 74 (61 Professionals, 13 Amateurs). Qualifying aggregate 147. Qualified for final 36 holes, 47 (38 Professionals, 9 Amateurs). Final qualifying aggregate 149.

Name	Score	Name	Score
KDG Nagle (Australia)	69, 67, 71, 71–278	DJ Rees (South Herts)	73, 71, 73, 69–286
A Palmer (USA)	70, 71, 70, 68–279	Maj DA Blair (R & A) (Am)	70, 73, 71, 72–286
BJ Hunt (Hartsbourne CC)	72, 73, 71, 66–282	EC Brown (Buchanan Castle)	75, 68, 72, 71–286
HR Henning (S Africa)	72, 72, 69, 69–282	PW Thomson (Australia)	72, 69, 75, 70–286
R De Vicenzo (Argentina)	67, 67, 75, 73–282	R Sota (Spain)	74, 72, 71, 70–287
GB Wolstenholme (Sunningdale) (Am)	74, 70, 71, 68–283	A Miguel (Spain)	72, 73, 72, 71–288
GJ Player (S Africa)	72, 71, 72, 69–284	RR Jack (Dullatur) (Am)	74, 71, 70, 73–288
JB Carr (Sutton) (Am)	72, 73, 67, 73–285	J Smith (Hesketh)	74, 70, 73, 71–288
H Weetman (Selsdon Park)	74, 70, 71, 71–286	F de Luca (Argentina)	69, 73, 75, 71–288
SS Scott (Roehampton)	73, 71, 67, 75–286		

1961 at Birkdale

Entries 364. Qualified 108 (101 Professionals, 7 Amateurs). Qualifying aggregate 148. Qualified for final 36 holes, 48 (46 Professionals, 2 Amateurs). Final qualifying aggregate 153.

Name	Score	Name	Score
A Palmer (USA)	70, 73, 69, 72–284	P Alliss (Parkstone)	73, 75, 72, 71–291
DJ Rees (S Herts)	68, 74, 71, 72–285	SS Scott (Roehampton)	76, 75, 71, 71–293
C O'Connor (Dublin)	71, 77, 67, 73–288	HR Henning (S Africa)	68, 74, 75, 76–293
NC Coles (Coombe Hill)	70, 77, 69, 72–288	R Sota (Spain)	71, 76, 72, 76–295
EC Brown (unattached)	73, 76, 70, 70–289	A Coop (Dean Wood)	71, 79, 73, 74–297
KDG Nagle (Australia)	68, 75, 75, 71–289	RA Knight (Wanstead)	71, 80, 73, 74–298
PW Thomson (Australia)	75, 72, 70, 73–290	N Johnson (Haydock Park)	69, 80, 70, 79–298
K Bousfield (Coombe Hill)	71, 77, 75, 68–291	S Miguel (Spain)	71, 80, 70, 77–298
		A Miguel (Spain)	73, 79, 74, 72–298

1962 at Troon

Entries 379. Qualified 119 (103 Professionals, 16 Amateurs). Qualifying aggregate 154. Qualified for final 36 holes, 39 (38 Professionals, 1 Amateur). Final qualifying aggregate 152.

Name	Score	Name	Score
A Palmer (USA)	71, 69, 67, 69–276	B Huggett (Romford)	75, 71, 74, 69–289
KDG Nagle (Australia)	71, 71, 70, 70–282	P Rodgers (USA)	75, 70, 72, 72–289

The Open Championship
continued

Name	Score
R Charles (NZ)	75, 70, 70, 75–290
S Snead (USA)	76, 73, 72, 71–292
PW Thomson (Australia)	70, 77, 75, 70–292
D Thomas (Sunningdale)	77, 70, 71, 75–293
P Alliss (Parkstone)	77, 69, 74, 73–293
SS Scott (Roehampton)	77, 74, 75, 68–294
R Moffitt (Coventry Hearsall)	75, 70, 74, 76–295
S Miguel (Spain)	72, 79, 73, 72–296
R Whitehead (Banstead Downs)	74, 75, 72, 75–296
J Garaialde (France)	76, 73, 76, 71–296
H Weetman (Selsdon Park)	75, 73, 73, 75–296
C O'Connor (Dublin)	74, 78, 73, 72–297
D Hutchinson (S Africa)	78, 73, 76, 70–297
R Foreman (Belfairs)	77, 73, 72, 75–297
BJ Hunt (Hartsbourne)	74, 75, 75, 73–297
J Panton (Glenbervie)	74, 73, 79, 71–297
J Martin (Edmondstown)	73, 72, 76, 76–297

1963 at Lytham and St Annes

Entries 261. Qualified 119 (111 Professionals, 8 Amateurs). Qualifying aggregate 148. Qualified for final 36 holes, 47 (all Professionals). Final qualifying aggregate 149.

Name	Score
RJ Charles (NZ)	68, 72, 66, 71–277
P Rodgers (USA)	67, 68, 73, 69–277
J Nicklaus (USA)	71, 67, 70, 70–278
KDG Nagle (Australia)	69, 70, 73, 71–283
PW Thomson (Australia)	67, 69, 71, 78–285
C O'Connor (Royal Dublin)	74, 68, 76, 68–286
G Player (S Africa)	75, 70, 72, 70–287
R Sota (Spain)	69, 73, 73, 72–287
S Miguel (Spain)	73, 69, 73, 73–288
J Garaialde (France)	72, 69, 72, 75–288
AG King (Ganton)	71, 73, 73, 72–289
BJ Hunt (Hartsbourne)	72, 71, 73, 73–289
S Sewgolum (S Africa)	71, 74, 73, 72–290
H Lewis (Altrincham)	71, 77, 69, 74–291
BGC Huggett (Romford)	73, 74, 70, 74–291
B Allen (Denton)	75, 71, 71, 74–291
ID MacDonald (Farnham)	71, 71, 74, 75–291
P Alliss (Parkstone)	74, 71, 77, 70–292
F Philips (Australia)	70, 73, 75, 74–292

Play-off Scores:

RJ Charles (NZ) 69, 71–140
P Rodgers (USA) 72, 76–148

1964 at St Andrews

Entries 327. Qualified 119 (111 Professionals, 8 Amateurs). Qualifying aggregate 149. Qualified for final 36 holes, 45 (all Professionals). Final qualifying aggregate 153.

Name	Score
A Lema (USA)	73, 68, 68, 70–279
J Nicklaus (USA)	76, 74, 66, 68–284
R De Vicenzo (Argentina)	76, 72, 70, 67–285
BJ Hunt (Hartsbourne)	73, 74, 70, 70–287
B Devlin (Australia)	72, 72, 73, 73–290
C O'Connor (Royal Dublin)	71, 73, 74, 73–291
H Weetman (Selsdon Park)	72, 71, 75, 73–291
HR Henning (S Africa)	78, 73, 71, 70–292
G Player (S Africa)	78, 71, 73, 70–292
A Miguel (Spain)	73, 76, 72, 71–292
D Sanders (USA)	78, 73, 74, 68–293
F Philips (Australia)	77, 75, 72, 70–294
C Greene (Milltown)	74, 76, 73, 73–296
DC Thomas (Sunningdale)	75, 74, 75, 72–296
RL Moffitt (Coventry Hearsall)	76, 72, 74, 74–296
J Garaialde (France)	71, 74, 79, 72–296
GA Caygill (Pannal)	77, 74, 71, 75–297
RJ Charles (NZ)	79, 71, 69, 78–297

1965 at Birkdale, Southport

Entries 372. Qualifying aggregate (over Hillside and Southport and Ainsdale), 151. Qualified for final 36 holes (over Birkdale) 50 (47 Professionals, 3 Amateurs). Final qualifying aggregate 149.

Name	Score
PW Thomson (Australia)	74, 68, 72, 71–285
C O'Connor (Royal Dublin)	69, 73, 74, 71–287
BGC Hugget (Romford)	73, 68, 76, 70–287
R De Vicenzo (Argentina)	74, 69, 73, 72–288
KDG Nagle (Australia)	74, 70, 73, 72–289
A Lema (USA)	68, 72, 75, 74–289
BJ Hunt (Hartsbourne)	74, 74, 70, 71–289
S Miguel (Spain)	72, 73, 72, 73–290
BJ Devlin (Australia)	71, 69, 75, 75–290
J Panton (Glenbervie)	74, 74, 75, 70–293
M Faulkner (Selsey)	74, 72, 74, 73–293

Name	Score	Name	Score
NC Coles (Coombe Hill)	73, 74, 77, 70–294	T Horton (Ham Manor)	75, 73, 76, 72–296
JW Nicklaus (USA)	73, 71, 77, 73–294	GB Wolstenholme (St George's Hill)	72, 75, 77, 72–296
L Platts (Wanstead)	72, 72, 73, 77–294	EC Brown (Cruden Bay)	72, 70, 77, 77–296
HT Boyle (unattached)	73, 69, 76, 76–294		
A Palmer (USA)	70, 71, 75, 79–295		
C Legrange (S Africa)	76, 73, 75, 72–296		

1966 at Muirfield

Entries 310. Qualifying aggregate (over Luffness and Gullane) 145. Qualified for final 36 holes (over Muirfield) 64 (60 Professionals, 4 Amateurs). Final qualifying aggregate 150. Prize Money increased by 20 per cent from £12,500 to £15,000.

Name	Score	Name	Score
J Nicklaus (USA)	70, 67, 75, 70–282	HR Henning (S Africa)	71, 69, 75, 76–291
D Thomas (Dunham Forest)	72, 73, 69, 69–283	J Boros (USA)	73, 71, 76, 72–292
D Sanders (USA)	71, 70, 72, 70–283	J Hitchcock (Croham Hurst)	70, 77, 74, 72–293
G Player (S Africa)	72, 74, 71, 69–286	PJ Butler (Harborne)	73, 65, 80, 75–293
B Devlin (Australia)	73, 69, 74, 70–286	GA Caygill (Cleckheaton)	72, 71, 73, 77–293
K Nagle (Australia)	72, 68, 76, 70–286	RDBM Shade (Duddingston) (Am)	71, 70, 75, 77–293
P Rodgers (USA)	74, 66, 70, 76–286	P Alliss (Parkstone)	74, 72, 75, 73–294
D Marr (USA)	73, 76, 69, 70–288	DN Sewell (Wentworth)	76, 69, 74, 75–294
PW Thomson (Australia)	73, 75, 69, 71–288	R De Vicenzo (Argentina)	74, 72, 71, 77–294
S Miguel (Spain)	74, 72, 70, 72–288		
A Palmer (USA)	73, 72, 69, 74–288		
RH Sikes (USA)	73, 72, 73, 72–290		
C O'Connor (Royal Dublin)	73, 72, 74, 72–291		

1967 at Hoylake

Entries 326. Qualifying aggregate 149 Delamere Forest, 150 Sandiway. Qualified for final 36 holes (over Hoylake) 58 (all Professionals). Final qualifying aggregate 149.

Name	Score	Name	Score
R De Vicenzo (Argentina)	70, 71, 67, 70–278	L Platts (Pannal)	68, 73, 72, 76–289
J Nicklaus (USA)	71, 69, 71, 69–280	BJ Coxon (Australia)	73, 76, 71, 70–290
CA Clark (Sunningdale)	70, 73, 69, 72–284	D Sanders (USA)	71, 73, 73, 73–290
G Player (S Africa)	72, 71, 67, 74–284	HW Muscroft (Moor Allerton)	72, 73, 72, 73–290
A Jacklin (Potters Bar)	73, 69, 73, 70–285	C O'Connor (Royal Dublin)	70, 74, 71, 76–291
S Miguel (Spain)	72, 74, 68, 72–286	RP Mills (High Post)	72, 75, 73, 72–292
H Henning (S Africa)	74, 70, 71, 71–286	D Hutchinson (S Africa)	73, 72, 71, 76–292
B Devlin (Australia)	70, 70, 72, 75–287	K Nagle (Australia)	70, 74, 69, 79–292
A Balding (Canada)	74, 71, 69, 73–287	RRW Davenport (N Hants)	76, 69, 75, 73–293
T Horton (Ham Manor)	74, 74, 69, 70–287	BW Barnes (Burnham and Berrow)	71, 75, 74, 73–293
PW Thomson (Australia)	71, 74, 70, 72–287	B Franklin (S Africa)	70, 74, 73, 76–293
HF Boyle (Jacobs Golf Centre)	74, 74, 71, 68–287	BGC Huggett (Warren)	73, 75, 72, 73–293
GB Wolstenholme (St George's Hill)	74, 71, 73, 71–289	FS Boobyer (Whitefield)	70, 71, 74, 79–294
S Peach (Australia)	71, 75, 73, 70–289	JM Hume (Formby)	69, 72, 73, 80–294
M Hoyle (Castle Inn)	74, 75, 69, 71–289		
D Beman (USA)	72, 76, 68, 73–289		

1968 at Carnoustie

Entries 309. Qualifying aggregate 148 Monifieth, 146 Panmure. Qualified for final 18 holes (over Carnoustie) 45 (44 Professionals, 1 Amateur). Final qualifying aggregate 228.

Name	Score	Name	Score
G Player (S Africa)	74, 71, 71, 73–289	M Bembridge (Little Aston)	71, 75, 73, 74–293
J Nicklaus (USA)	76, 69, 73, 73–291	B Barnes (Burnham and Berrow)	70, 74, 80, 71–295
RJ Charles (NZ)	72, 72, 71, 76–291		
W Casper (USA)	72, 68, 74, 78–292		

The Open Championship
continued

Name	Score
NC Coles (Coombe Hill)	75, 76, 71, 73–295
G Brewer (USA)	74, 73, 72, 76–295
A Balding (Canada)	74, 76, 74, 72–296
R De Vicenzo (Argentina)	77, 72, 74, 74–297
B Devlin (Australia)	77, 73, 72, 75–297
A Palmer (USA)	77, 71, 72, 77–297
T Horton (Ham Manor)	77, 74, 73, 74–298
K Nagle (Australia)	74, 75, 75, 74–298
P Alliss (Parkstone)	73, 78, 72, 75–298
R Cole (S Africa)	75, 76, 72, 75–298
BGC Huggett (Betchworth Park)	76, 71, 75, 76–298
EC Brown (Cruden Bay)	76, 76, 74, 73–299
P Skerritt (St Annes, Dublin)	72, 73, 77, 77–299
A Jacklin (Potters Bar)	72, 72, 75, 80–299
DL Webster (Lundin)	77, 71, 78, 74–300
S Miguel (Spain)	73, 75, 76, 76–300
MF Bonallack (Thorpe Hall) (Am)	70, 77, 74, 79–300
GA Caygill (Cleckheaton)	79, 76, 71, 75–301
PW Thomson (Australia)	77, 71, 78, 75–301
KA MacDonald (Hankley Common)	80, 71, 73, 77–301
S Wilson (Selby)	73, 81, 74, 74–302
M Gregson (Dyrham Park)	77, 75, 76, 74–302
RJ Shaw (Australia)	75, 76, 73, 78–302
DC Thomas (Dunham Forest)	75, 71, 78, 78–302

Chief Money Prize-Winners:

G. Player (South Africa), £3,000; J. Nicklaus (USA); RJ Charles (New Zealand), £1,737 10s each; W Casper (USA), £1,225; M Bembridge (Little Aston), £1,000; B Barnes (Burnham and Berrow), NC Coles (Coombe Hill), G Brewer (USA), £658 each; A Balding (Canada), £475; R De Vicenzo (Argentina), B Devlin (Australia), A Palmer (USA), £401 10s each; T Horton (Ham Manor), K Nagle (Australia), P Alliss (Parkstone), R Cole (South Africa), BGC Huggett (Betchworth Park), £321 each.

Other Totals

J. Gallardo (Spain), D. Huish (North Berwick), H. Bannerman (Royal Aberdeen), 303; D Sanders (USA), 304; M Murphy (Dublin), J Martin (Rush), G. Cunningham (Troon Municipal), 305; H Habjan (USA), 306; C Greene (Milltown), A Grubb (Coombe Hill), M Said Moussa (UAR), 307; B Yancey (USA), BJ Coxon (Australia), P Mills (High Post), 311; H. Weetman (Selsdon Park), 313.

1969 at Lytham and St Annes

Entries 424. Qualifying aggregate 151 Lytham and St Annes, 150 Fairhaven. Qualified for final 18 holes, 46 (44 Professionals, 2 Amateurs). Final qualifying aggregate 222.

Name	Score
A Jacklin (Potters Bar)	68, 70, 70, 72–280
RJ Charles (NZ)	66, 69, 75, 72–282
PW Thomson (Australia)	71, 70, 70, 72–283
R De Vicenzo (Argentina)	72, 73, 66, 72–283
C O'Connor (Dublin)	71, 65, 74, 74–284
J Nicklaus (USA)	75, 70, 68, 72–285
DM Love, Jr (USA)	70, 73, 71, 71–285
P Alliss (Parkstone)	73, 74, 73, 66–286
K Nagle (Australia)	74, 71, 72, 70–287
M Barber (USA)	69, 75, 75, 69–288
NC Coles (Coombe Hill)	75, 76, 70, 68–289
C Le Grange (S Africa)	79, 70, 71, 69–289
G Wolstenholme (Australia)	70, 71, 76, 72–289
T Horton (Ham Manor)	71, 76, 70, 72–289
G Brewer (USA)	76, 71, 68, 75–290
H Henning (S Africa)	72, 71, 75, 73–291
B Devlin (Australia)	71, 73, 75, 72–291
PMP Townsend (Porters Park)	73, 70, 76, 72–291
EC Brown (Braid Hills)	73, 76, 69, 73–291
O Moody (USA)	70, 71, 74, 76–291
B Yancey (USA)	72, 71, 71, 77–291
BGC Huggett (Betchworth Park)	72, 72, 69, 78–291
BJ Hunt (Hartsbourne)	73, 71, 75, 73–292
G Player (S Africa)	74, 68, 76, 74–292
FS Boobyer (Whitefield)	74, 70, 76, 73–293
GA Caygill (Cleckheaton and District)	71, 67, 79, 76–293
W Casper (USA)	70, 70, 75, 78–293
LP Tupling (Tankersley Park) (Am)	73, 71, 78, 72–294
HW Muscroft (Moor Allerton)	68, 77, 73, 76–294

Chief Money Prize-Winners:

A Jacklin (Potters Bar), £4,250; RJ Charles (New Zealand), £3,000; PW Thomson (Australia), R De Vicenzo (Argentina), £2,125 each; C O'Connor (Dublin), £1,750; J Nicklaus (USA), DM Love, Jr (USA), £1,375 each; P Alliss (Parkstone), £1,100; K Nagle (Australia), £1,000; M Barber (USA), £900; NC Coles (Coombe Hill), C Le Grange (S Africa), G Wolstenholme (Australia), T Horton (Ham Manor), £657 each; G Brewer (USA), £480.

Other Totals

J Garaialde (France), M Faulkner (Ifield), D Swaelens (Belgium), MB Ingham (Moor Allerton), 295; BJ Waites (Notts), R Floyd (USA), L Trevino (USA), JR Garner (unattached), G Cunningham (Troon Municipal), VB Hood (Bramley), 296; BW Barnes (West Sussex), J Hitchcock (Croydon Driving Range), 297; PH Wilcock (Warren), A Gallardo (Spain), MF Bonallack (Thorpe Hall) (Am), 298; J Panton (Glenbervie), 300; H Jackson (Knockbracken), 301.

1970 at St Andrews

Entries 468. Qualifying aggregate 145 Panmure, 149 Carnoustie, 145 Monifieth. Qualified for final 36 holes, 80 (75 Professionals, 5 Amateurs) with score of 149. Qualified for final 18 holes, 57 (55 Professionals, 2 Amateurs) with score of 223.

Name	Score
J Nicklaus (USA)	68, 69, 73, 73–283
D Sanders (USA)	68, 71, 71, 73–283
(Play-off: Nicklaus 72; Sanders 73)	
H Henning (S Africa)	67, 72, 73, 73–285
L Trevino (USA)	68, 68, 72, 77–285
A Jacklin (Potters Bar)	67, 70, 73, 76–286
NC Coles (Coombe Hill)	65, 74, 72, 76–287
PA Oosterhuis (Dulwich)	73, 69, 69, 76–287
H Jackson (Knockbracken)	69, 72, 73, 74–288
J Panton (Glenbervie)	72, 73, 73, 71–289
PW Thomson (Australia)	68, 74, 73, 74–289
T Horton (Ham Manor)	66, 73, 75, 75–289
A Palmer (USA)	68, 72, 76, 74–290
M Bembridge (Little Aston)	67, 74, 75, 76–292
J Richardson (Lee-on-the-Solent)	67, 72, 76, 77–292
B Yancey (USA)	71, 71, 73, 77–292
R Charles (NZ)	72, 73, 73, 74–292
R Bernardini (Italy)	75, 69, 74, 75–293
W Casper (USA)	71, 74, 73, 75–293
R De Vicenzo (Argentina)	71, 76, 71, 75–293
C Clark (Sunningdale)	69, 70, 77, 77–293
C O'Connor (Royal Dublin)	72, 68, 74, 79–293
G Wolstenholme (Australia)	68, 77, 72, 77–294
T Weiskopf (USA)	70, 74, 72, 78–294
W Godfrey (NZ)	71, 75, 74, 74–294
B Devlin (Australia)	72, 76, 72, 75–295
G Marsh (Australia)	75, 72, 74, 74–295
R Shade (Duddingston)	72, 75, 69, 79–295
T Shaw (USA)	73, 71, 73, 79–296
S Brown (Hallamshire)	73, 73, 71, 79–296
B Huggett (Betchworth Park)	68, 78, 73, 77–296
R Cole (S Africa)	71, 76, 71, 78–296

Chief Money Prize-Winners:

J Nicklaus, £5,250; D Sanders, £3,750; H Henning, £2,750; L Trevino, £2,750; A Jacklin, £2,200; NC Coles, £1,750; PA Oosterhuis, £1,750; H Jackson, £1,400; J Panton, £1,200; PW Thomson, £1,200; T Horton, £1,200; A Palmer, £1,000; M Bembridge, £750; J Richardson, £750; B Yancey, £750; R Charles, £750.

Other Totals

P Alliss (Parkstone), F Molina (Argentina), D Douglass (USA), EC Brown (unattached), D Thomas (Dunham Forest), B Barnes (West Sussex), D Graham (Australia), K Nagle (Australia), G Brewer (USA), 297; GA Caygill (Cleckheaton and District), S Melnyck (USA) (Am), D Marr (USA), A Grubb (Laleham), 298; J Hume (Formby), G Will (Sundridge Park), P Townsend (Portmarnock), 299; G Hunt (Wentworth), J Martin (unattached), 300; N Wood (Turnberry), W Humphreys (Mid-Surrey) (Am), T Aaron (USA), T Lopez (Spain), 301; D Small (Dunnikier Park), 302; D Love (USA), 303; R Livingston (Churchill and Blakedown), 304; S Walker (Cupar), 307.

1971 at Birkdale

Entries 528. Qualifying aggregates 144 Southport and Ainsdale, 146 Hesketh, 148 Hillside. Qualified for final 36 holes, 82 competitors (80 Professionals, 2 Amateurs) with a score of 151. Qualified for final 18 holes, 64 competitors (62 Professionals, 2 Amateurs) with a score of 224.

Name	Score
L Trevino (USA)	69, 70, 69, 70–278
Liang Huan Lu (Formosa)	70, 70, 69, 70–279
A Jacklin (Potters Bar)	69, 70, 70, 71–280
C DeFoy (Coombe Hill)	72, 72, 68, 69–281
JW Nicklaus (USA)	71, 71, 72, 69–283
C Coody (USA)	74, 71, 70, 68–283
WJ Casper (USA)	70, 72, 75, 67–284
G Player (S Africa)	71, 70, 71, 72–284
D Sanders (USA)	73, 71, 74, 67–285
PW Thomson (Australia)	70, 73, 73, 69–285
K Nagle (Australia)	70, 75, 73, 69–287
D Stockton (USA)	74, 74, 68, 71–287
H Bannerman (Banchory)	73, 71, 72, 71–287
B Yancey (USA)	75, 70, 71, 71–287
R Sota (Spain)	72, 72, 70, 73–287
R De Vicenzo (Argentina)	71, 70, 72, 74–287
D Hayes (S Africa)	71, 72, 70, 75–288

The Open Championship
continued

Name	Score	Name	Score
R Charles (NZ)	77, 71, 71, 70–289	V Fernandez (Argentina)	69, 79, 73, 71–292
P Oosterhuis (Dulwich and Sydenham Hill and Fiji)	76, 71, 66, 76–289	W Large (Dyrham Park)	73, 75, 73, 71–292
B Hunt (Hartsbourne)	74, 73, 73, 70–290	D Sewell (Ferndown)	73, 74, 74, 71–292
H Johnson (USA)	69, 76, 72, 73–290	B Huggett (Betchworth Park)	73, 73, 74, 72–292
N Coles (Coombe Hill)	76, 72, 72, 71–291	J Lister (NZ)	74, 71, 74, 73–292
M Bonallack (Thorpe Hall) (Am)	71, 72, 75, 73–291	R Vines (Australia)	75, 71, 73, 73–292
H Jackson (Knockbracken)	71, 73, 72, 75–291	P Butler (Harborne)	73, 73, 73, 73–292
		M Gregson (W Sussex)	71, 71, 73, 77–292

Chief Money Prize-Winners:
L Trevino, £5,500; Liang Huan Lu £4,000; A Jacklin, £3,250; C DeFoy, £2,750; J Nicklaus, £2,300; C Coody, £2,300; W Casper, £1,775; G Player, £1,775; D Sanders, £1,550; P Thomson, £1,550; K Nagle, £1,150; D Stockton, £1,150; H Bannerman, £1,150; B Yancey, £1,150; R Sota, £1,150; R De Vicenzo, £1,150; D Hayes, £800.

Other Totals
Min Nan Hseih (Formosa), G Wolstenholme (Australia), 293; C O'Connor (Dublin), J Garner (Moor Park), 294; B Gallacher (Wentworth), B Devlin (Australia), T Horton (Ham Manor), 295; L Platts (Pannal), P. Townsend (Portmarnock), W Godfrey (Australia), J Kinsella (Castle), T. Weiskopf (USA), J O'Leary (Foxrock), E Brown (Dunbar), 296; P Alliss (Moor Allerton), J Miller (USA), 297; S Melnyk (USA) (Am), T Britz (South Africa), V Barrios (Spain), J. Wilkshire (St Annes Old Links), A Locke (South Africa), J Newton (Australia), J Sharkey (Queens Park), D Swaelens (Belgium), 298; G Marsh (Australia), 299; D Snell (Worksop), B Waites (Notts), 300; M Bembridge (Little Aston), M Barber (USA), R Manning (Rhodesia), 301; D Talbot (Mid-Surrey), 302; B Barnes (West Sussex), 303.

1972 at Muirfield
Entries 570. Qualifying aggregates 143 Gullane No. 1, 140 Gullane No. 2, 140 Luffness, 143 North Berwick. Qualified for final 36 holes, 88 competitors (84 Professionals, 4 Amateurs) with score of 152 and below. Qualified for final 18 holes, 64 competitors (all Professionals) with score of 225 and below.

Name	Score	Name	Score
L Trevino (USA)	71, 70, 66, 71–278	J Miller (USA)	76, 66, 72, 75–289
JW Nicklaus (USA)	70, 72, 71, 66–279	H Bannerman (Banchory)	77, 73, 73, 67–290
A Jacklin (Potters Bar)	69, 72, 67, 72–280	M Bembridge (Little Aston)	73, 71, 75, 71–290
D Sanders (USA)	71, 71, 69, 70–281	F Beard (USA)	70, 76, 74, 70–290
BW Barnes (Fairway DR)	71, 72, 69, 71–283	B Yancey (USA)	73, 72, 72, 73–290
G Player (S Africa)	71, 71, 76, 67–285	C O'Connor (Royal Dublin)	73, 74, 73, 71–291
DI Vaughan (N Wales)	74, 73, 70, 69–286	D McClelland (Hartsbourne)	73, 74, 72, 72–291
T Weiskopf (USA)	73, 74, 70, 69–286	C DeFoy (Coombe Hill)	70, 75, 71, 75–291
AD Palmer (USA)	73, 73, 69, 71–286	BGC Huggett (Cambs Hotel)	73, 72, 79, 68–292
GL Hunt (Wentworth)	75, 72, 67, 72–286	B Devlin (Australia)	75, 70, 77, 70–292
C Clark (Sunningdale)	72, 71, 73, 71–287	P Oosterhuis (Fiji)	75, 75, 73, 70–293
D Marr (USA)	70, 74, 71, 72–287	J Heard (USA)	75, 75, 71, 72–293
R Bernardini (Italy)	73, 71, 76, 68–288	JR Garner (Hartsbourne)	71, 71, 76, 75–293
P Townsend (Portmarnock)	70, 72, 76, 70–288		
RJ Charles (NZ)	75, 70, 74, 70–289		
PJ Butler (Harborne)	72, 75, 73, 69–289		
JGM Dorrestein (Holland)	74, 71, 72, 72–289		

Chief Money Prize-Winners:
L Trevino, £5,500; JW Nicklaus, £4,000; A Jacklin, £3,250; D Sanders, £2,750; BW Barnes, £2,450; G Player, £2,150; DI Vaughan, £1,650; T Weiskopf, £1,650; AD Palmer, £1,650; GL. Hunt, £1,650; C Clark, £1,350; D Marr, £1,350; R Bernardini, £1,150; P Townsend, £1,150.

Other Totals
P Alliss (Moor Allerton), K Nagle (Australia), V Fernandez (Argentina), Min Nan Hsieh (Taiwan), B Thomson (Belton Park), WG Cunningham (Troon Municipal), D Stockton (USA), RA Shearer (Australia), PW Thomson (Australia), 294; CH Kuo (Taiwan), VB Hood (Bramley), T Horton (Ham Manor), LH Lu (Taiwan), J Newton (Australia), WJ Casper (USA), 295; S Torrance (Routenburn), D Oakley (USA), E Jones (Bangor), LP Tupling (Phoenix), 296; GV Marsh (Australia), D Sewell (Ferndown), D Talbot (Mid-Surrey), N Wood (Turnberry Hotel), A Brooks (Lanark), B Hutchinson (Moortown), 298; JE O'Leary (Oppermans), D Llewellyn (Olton), 299; RT Walker (Downfield), 300; A Garrido (Spain), T Britz (S Africa), JM Hume (Formby), 301; G Baleson (S Africa), 302; JL Fowler (Thames Ditton and Esher), 304; SD Brown (Hallamshire), 305.

1973 at Troon

Entries 569. Qualifying aggregates 146 Barassie, 145 Glasgow Gailes, 149 Troon Lochgreen; 147 Western Gailes. Qualified for final 36 holes, 84 competitors (80 Professionals, 4 Amateurs) with a score of 152 and below. Qualified for final 18 holes, 60 competitors (59 Professionals, 1 Amateur) with score of 224 and below.

Name	Score
T Weiskopf (USA)	68, 67, 71, 70–276
J Miller (USA)	70, 68, 69, 72–279
NC Coles (Holiday Inns)	71, 72, 70, 66–279
J Nicklaus (USA)	69, 70, 76, 65–280
B Yancey (USA)	69, 69, 73, 70–281
PJ Butler (Peter Butler Golf Domes)	71, 72, 74, 69–286
C O'Connor (Dublin)	73, 68, 74, 73–288
L Wadkins (USA)	71, 73, 70, 74–288
RJ Charles (NZ)	73, 71, 73, 71–288
L Trevino (USA)	75, 73, 73, 68–289
G Brewer (USA)	76, 71, 72, 70–289
H Henning (S Africa)	73, 73, 73, 70–289
B Barnes (Fairway DR)	76, 67, 70, 76–289
A Palmer (USA)	72, 76, 70, 72–290
G Player (S Africa)	76, 69, 76, 69–290
A Jacklin (Potters Bar)	75, 73, 72, 70–290
D McClelland (Hartsbourne)	76, 71, 69, 74–290
B Gallacher (Wentworth)	73, 69, 75, 75–292
DJ Good (unattached)	75, 74, 73, 70–292
D Hill (USA)	75, 74, 74, 69–292
BW Devlin (Australia)	72, 78, 71, 71–292
B Crampton (Australia)	71, 76, 73, 72–292
E Polland (Balmoral)	74, 73, 73, 72–292
P Oosterhuis (Fiji)	80, 71, 69, 72–292
PH Wilcock (Warren)	71, 76, 72, 73–292
H Boyle (Effingham)	75, 75, 69, 73–292
H Baiocchi (S Africa)	75, 74, 69, 74–292
D Sanders (USA)	79, 72, 72, 70–293
R De Vicenzo (Argentina)	72, 75, 74, 72–293
JA Rodriguez (Puerto Rico)	72, 73, 73, 75–293

Chief Money Prize-Winners:

T Weiskopf, £5,500; J Miller, £3,625; NC Coles, £3,625; JW Nicklaus, £2,750; B Yancey, £2,450; PJ Butler, £2,150; C O'Connor, £1,716; L Wadkins, £1,716; R Charles, £1,716; L Trevino, £1,350; G Brewer, £1,350; H Henning, £1,350; B Barnes, £1,350.

Other Totals

E Murray (Walton Heath), GV Marsh (Australia), R Wynn (Leatherhead), C DeFoy (Coombe Hill), P Thomson (Australia), T Horton (Ham Manor), 294; V Baker (S Africa), D Vaughan (Liverpool), 295; G Wolstenholme (Australia), K Nagle (Australia), D Hayes (South Africa), P Elson (Portugal), B Dassu (Italy), D Gammon (Rhodesia), D Edwards (USA) (Am), 296; H Bannerman (Banchory), MJ Moir (Hamilton), DK Webster (Lundin), 297; J Fourie (S Africa), BJ Hunt (Hartsbourne), 298; P Alliss (Moor Allerton), R Shade (Duddingston), D Jagger (Abbeydale), J McTear (Cathkin Braes), 299; P Townsend (Portmarnock), 300; D Huish (North Berwick), R Lambert (Chevin), WB Murray (Downfield), 301; D Dunk (Beauchief), 303; G Mueller (Sweden), 305.

1974 at Lytham and St Annes

Entries 679. Qualifying aggregates 154 St Annes Old, 155 Fairhaven, 148 Blackpool North Shore, 148 Lytham Green Drive. Qualified for final 36 holes, 81 competitors (79 Professionals, 2 Amateurs) with score of 156 and below. Qualified for final 18 holes, 60 competitors (all Professionals) with score of 231 and below.

Name	Score
G Player (S Africa)	69, 68, 75, 70–282
PA Oosterhuis (Fiji)	71, 71, 73, 71–286
J Nicklaus (USA)	74, 72, 70, 71–287
H Green (USA)	71, 74, 72, 71–288
D Edwards (USA)	70, 73, 76, 73–292
LH Lu (Taiwan)	72, 72, 75, 73–292
R Cole (S Africa)	70, 72, 76, 75–293
D Swaelens (Belgium)	77, 73, 74, 69–293
T Weiskopf (USA)	72, 72, 74, 75–293
J Miller (USA)	72, 75, 73, 74–294
J Garner (Hartsbourne)	75, 78, 73, 69–295
D Graham (Australia)	76, 74, 76, 69–295
NC Coles (Holiday Inns)	72, 75, 75, 74–296
A Geiberger (USA)	76, 70, 76, 74–296
J Morgan (Stoneham)	69, 75, 76, 76–296
A Tapie (USA)	73, 77, 73, 73–296
P Townsend (Portmarnock)	79, 76, 72, 69–296
P Dawson (Filey)	74, 74, 73, 76–297
A Jacklin (Potters Bar)	74, 77, 71, 75–297
G Littler (USA)	77, 76, 70, 74–297
D Weaver (USA)	73, 80, 70, 74–297
RD Shade (Duddingston)	78, 75, 73, 72–298
L Wadkins (USA)	78, 71, 75, 74–298
C O'Connor, Jun (Carlow)	78, 76, 72, 73–299
B Gallacher (Wentworth)	76, 72, 76, 75–299
A Gallardo (Spain)	74, 77, 75, 73–299
H Irwin (USA)	76, 73, 79, 71–299
B Crenshaw (USA)	74, 80, 76, 70–300
D Jagger (Tobago)	80, 71, 76, 73–300
D McClelland (Hartsbourne)	75, 79, 73, 73–300

Chief Money Prize-Winners:

G Player, £5,500; PA Oosterhuis, £4,000; J Nicklaus, £3,250; H Green, £2,750; D Edwards, £2,300; LH Lu, £2,300; R Cole, £1,717; D Swaelens, £1,717; T Weiskopf, £1,717; J Miller, £1,500; J Garner, £1,350; D Graham, £1,350; NC Coles, £1,000; A Geiberger, £1,000; J Morgan, £1,000; A Tapie, £1,000; P Townsend, £1,000.

Other Totals

PJ Butler (Golf Domes), AO Cerda (Mexico), D Chillas (Turnberry Hotel), T Horton (Ham Manor), H Jackson (Holme Hall), L Trevino (USA), 301; G Brewer (USA), V Fernandez (Argentina), 302; J Cook (Brickendon Grange), B Devlin (Australia), G Hunt (unattached), 303; BJ Hunt (Hartsbourne), D Small (Barbados), 304; B Barnes (Copthorne Hotel), M Bembridge (Little Aston), N Hunt (Fairfield), J O'Leary (unattached), JD Mahaffey (USA), G Marsh (Australia), 305; SJ Levermore (Hadley Wood), 306; M Gregson (Almaina Park), R De Vicenzo (Argentina), BJ Waites (Notts), 307; MJ Slater (Walton Hall), N Wood (Turnberry Hotel), 308; C O'Connor (Dublin), J Panton (Glenbervie), IE Stanley (Australia), 309; J Fourie (South Africa), RA Shearer (Australia), 310.

1975 at Carnoustie

Entries 629. Qualifying aggregates 151 St Andrews Old, 145 St Andrews New, 146 Panmure, 145 Monifieth. Qualified for final 36 holes, 86 competitors (83 Professionals, 3 Amateurs) with a score of 149 and below. Qualified for final 18 holes, 63 competitors (all Professionals) with score of 221 and below.

Name	Score
T Watson (USA)	71, 67, 69, 72–279
J Newton (Australia)	69, 71, 65, 74–279
(Play-off: Watson 71; Newton 72)	
R Cole (S Africa)	72, 66, 66, 76–280
J Nicklaus (USA)	69, 71, 68, 72–280
J Miller (USA)	71, 69, 66, 74–280
GV Marsh (Australia)	72, 67, 71, 71–281
P Oosterhuis (Fiji)	68, 70, 71, 73–282
N Coles (Holiday Inns)	72, 69, 67, 74–282
H Irwin (USA)	69, 70, 69, 75–283
G Burns (USA)	71, 73, 69, 71–284
J Mahaffey (USA)	71, 68, 69, 76–284
P Leonard (Co Down)	70, 69, 73, 74–286
RJ Charles (NZ)	74, 73, 70, 69–286
A Oosthuizen (S Africa)	69, 69, 70, 78–286
T Weiskopf (USA)	73, 72, 70, 72–287
A Palmer (USA)	74, 72, 69, 73–288
M Bembridge (Little Aston)	75, 73, 67, 73–288
A Tapie (USA)	70, 72, 67, 79–288
S Torrance (Routenburn)	72, 74, 71, 72–289
R Hinkle (USA)	76, 72, 69, 72–289
BJ Gallacher (Wentworth)	72, 67, 72, 78–289
T Horton (Royal Jersey)	72, 71, 71, 75–289
R Floyd (USA)	71, 72, 76, 71–290
M Foster (Clayton)	72, 74, 73, 71–290
H Baiocchi (S Africa)	72, 72, 73, 73–290
B Barnes (Cluny Hills)	71, 74, 72, 73–290
D Edwards (USA)	70, 74, 71, 75–290
D Graham (Australia)	74, 70, 72, 75–291
GL Hunt (Southampton Municipal)	73, 68, 76, 74–291
R De Vicenzo (Argentina)	71, 74, 72, 74–291
SFN Hobday (Rhodesia)	70, 70, 76, 75–291

Chief Money Prize-Winners:

T Watson, £7.500; J Newton, £6,000; R Coles, £3,866; J Nicklaus, £3,866; J Miller, £3,866; GV Marsh, £3,000; P Oosterhuis, £2,700; N Coles, £2,700; H Irwin, £2,400; G Burns, £2,125; J Mahaffey, £2,125; P Leonard, £1,750; RJ Charles, £1,750; A Oosthuizen, £1,750; T Weiskopf, £1,450; A Palmer, £1,150; M Bembridge, £1,150; A Tapie, £1,150.

Other Totals

D Huish (North Berwick), P Dawson (Hartsbourne), G Player (South Africa), M Cahill (Australia), H Green (USA), D Hayes (South Africa), T Britz (South Africa), R Shearer (Australia), 292; R Gilder (USA), ND Wood (Turnberry Hotel), BGC Huggett (Cambridgshire Hotel), L Trevino (USA), KDG Nagle (Australia) BJ Waites (Notts), 293; IE Stanley (Australia), 294; B Brask (USA), C O'Connor, Jun (Carlow), L Graham (USA), B Garrett (USA), PH Wilcock (Trevose), 295; EL Pearce (USA), 296; DI Vaughan (Hill Valley), LH Lu (Taiwan), V Fernandez (Argentina), JA Jacobs (USA), 297; T Le Brocq (Hampstead), PMP Townsend (Portmarnock), D Clark (New Zealand), 298; H Hansen (Denmark), 299; J Dorrestein (Holland), 300; SC Mason (Goring and Streatley), 301; R Carr (Sutton), 302.

1976 at Birkdale

Entries 719. Qualifying aggregates: 150 Formby; 146 Hesketh; 148 Hillside; 146 Southport and Ainsdale; 148 West Lancashire. Qualified for final 36 holes, 83 competitors (all Professionals) with score of 152 and below. Qualified for final 18 holes, 66 competitors with score of 226 and below.

Name	Score
J Miller (USA)	72, 68, 73, 66–279
JW Nicklaus (USA)	74, 70, 72, 69–285
S Ballesteros (Spain)	69, 69, 73, 74–285
R Floyd (USA)	76, 67, 73, 70–286
M James (Burghley Park)	76, 72, 74, 66–288
H Green (USA)	72, 70, 78, 68–288
C O'Connor, Jun (Shannon)	69, 73, 75, 71–288
T Kite (USA)	70, 74, 73, 71–288
TA Horton (Jersey)	74, 69, 72, 73–288
N Suzuki (Japan)	69, 75, 75, 70–289
G Burns (USA)	75, 69, 75, 70–289
V Fernandez (Argentina)	79, 71, 69, 70–289
PJ Butler (unattached)	74, 72, 73, 70–289
BW Barnes (Caledonian Hotel)	70, 73, 75, 72–290
J Fourie (S Africa)	71, 74, 75, 71–291
E Darcy (Erewash Valley)	78, 71, 71, 71–291
T Weiskopf (USA)	73, 72, 76, 71–292
J Newton (Australia)	70, 74, 76, 72–292
GB Wolstenholme (Australia)	76, 72, 71, 73–292
GV Marsh (Australia)	71, 73, 72, 76–292
S Hobday (Rhodesia)	79, 71, 75, 68–293
R Shearer (Australia)	76, 73, 75, 69–293
D Graham (Australia)	77, 70, 75, 71–293
S Ginn (Australia)	78, 72, 72, 71–293
A Tapie (USA)	74, 72, 75, 72–293
CS Hsu (Taiwan)	81, 69, 71, 72–293
D Huish (North Berwick)	73, 74, 72, 74–293
N Faldo (Welwyn Garden City)	78, 71, 76, 69–294
GJ Player (S Africa)	72, 72, 79, 71–294
D Sanders (USA)	77, 73, 73, 71–294
NC Coles (Holiday Inns)	74, 77, 70, 73–294

Chief Money Prize-Winners:

J Miller, £7,500; S Ballesteros, £5,250; J Nicklaus, £5,250; R Floyd, £3,800; C O'Connor, Jun, £2,820; T Kite, £2,820; T Horton, £2,820; H Green, £2,820; G Burns, £1,975; N Suzuki, £1,975; P Butler, £1,975; V Fernandez, £1,975; B Barnes, £1,600; E Darcy, £1,375; J Fourie, £1,375.

Other Totals

R De Vicenzo (Argentina), P McGuirk (County Louth), H Irwin (USA), G Littler (USA), G Hunt (Southampton Municipal), RE Cole (South Africa) 296; D Jagger (Tobago), V Hood (Bramley), M Foster (Clayton), I Mosey (Denton) 297; A Jacklin (Sardinia), PA Oosterhuis (Dulwich and Sydenham Hill), B Burgess (Australia), P Dawson (Hartsbourne), M Gregson (unattached), W Humphreys (Mid-Surrey) 298; B Garrett (USA), C Higgins (USA), R Murphy (USA), D McClelland (Hartsbourne), S Adwick (Tiverton), P Berry (Tewkesbury Park), D Hayes (South Africa) 299; A O'Connor (Hazel Grove), A Oosthuizen (South Africa), A Palmer (USA), J Hammond (Filey), D Talbot (Mid-Surrey) 300; D Edwards (USA), R Wynn (Leatherhead), BJ Gallacher (Wentworth) 301; GA Caygill (France), L Higgins (Waterville), WR Lockie (Barassie), LP Tupling (Watford DR) 301.

1977 at Turnberry

Entries 730. Qualifying aggregates: 145 Barassie; 147 Glasgow Gailes; 149 Western Gailes. Qualified for final 36 holes, 87 competitors (all Professional) with score of 150 and below. Qualified for final 18 holes, 64 competitors with score of 221 and below.

Name	Score
T Watson (USA)	68, 70, 65, 65–268
J Nicklaus (USA)	68, 70, 65, 66–269
H Green (USA)	72, 66, 74, 67–279
L Trevino (USA)	68, 70, 72, 70–280
B Crenshaw (USA)	71, 69, 66, 75–281
G Burns (USA)	70, 70, 72, 69–281
A Palmer (USA)	73, 73, 67, 69–282
R Floyd (USA)	70, 73, 68, 72–283
T Horton (Jersey)	70, 74, 65, 75–284
J Miller (USA)	69, 74, 67, 74–284
J Schroeder (USA)	66, 74, 73, 71–284
M Hayes (USA)	76, 63, 72, 73–284
PW Thomson (Australia)	74, 72, 67, 73–286
HK Clark (Moor Allerton)	72, 68, 72, 74–286
GL Hunt (Gloucester Hotel)	73, 71, 71, 72–287
R Cole (S Africa)	72, 71, 71, 73–287
PJ Butler (RAC)	71, 68, 75, 73–287
J Pate (USA)	74, 70, 70, 73–287
S Ballesteros (Spain)	69, 71, 73, 74–287
GV Marsh (Australia)	73, 69, 71, 74–287
R Shearer (Australia)	72, 69, 72, 74–287
T Weiskopf (USA)	74, 71, 71, 72–288
GJ Player (S Africa)	71, 74, 74, 69–288
P Dawson (Hartsbourne)	74, 68, 73, 73–288
J Fourie (S Africa)	74, 69, 70, 75–288
G Burrows (USA)	69, 72, 68, 80–289
R Maltbie (USA)	71, 66, 72, 80–289
R Massengale (USA)	73, 71, 74, 71–289
D Ingram (Dalmahoy)	73, 74, 70, 72–289
MF Foster (Clayton)	67, 74, 75, 73–289
A Gallardo (Spain)	78, 65, 72, 74–289
J O'Leary (Hill Valley)	74, 73, 68, 74–289
N Suzuki (Japan)	74, 71, 69, 75–289

Chief Money Prize-Winners

T Watson, £10,000; J Nicklaus, £8,000; H Green, £6,000; L Trevino, £5,000; B Crenshaw, £4,250; G Burns, £4,250; A Palmer, £3,750; R Floyd, £3,500; T Horton, £2,875; J Miller, £2,875; J Schroeder, £2,875; M Hayes £2,875; PW Thomson, £2,200; HK Clark, £2,200.

Other Totals

E Darcy (Erewash Valley), KJ Brown (Ridge Engineering) 290; BW Barns (Caledonian Hotel), M-N Hsieh (Taiwan), M Pinero (Spain), B Dassu (Italy), J Morgan (Liverpool) 291; NC Coles (Holiday Inns), DI Vaughan 292; J Gonzalez (Brazil), A Jacklin (Tracy Park), RJ Charles (New Zealand) 293; S Ginn (Australia), H Irwin (USA) 294; R De Vicenzo (Argentina), V Fernandez (Argentina), BGC Huggett (Cambridgeshire Hotel), MG King (Heath International) 295; C O'Connor Jun (Shannon), JC Farmer (Drumpellier), R Davis (Australia), BJ Waites (Notts) 296; M Bembridge (The Belfry), V Tshabalala (South Africa) 297; I Mosey (Denton), D Jones (Bangor), C-S Hsu (Taiwan), GD Jacobson (USA) 298; NA Faldo (Welwyn Garden City), S Locatelli (Italy), V Baker (South Africa) 299.

The Open Championship

continued

1978 at St Andrews

Entries 788. Qualifying aggregates 148 Ladybank; 147 Leven; 147 Lundin. Qualified for final 36 holes, 80 competitors (76 Professionals, 4 Amateurs) with score of 148 and below. Qualified for final 18 holes, 64 competitors (60 Professionals, 4 Amateurs) with score of 222 and below.

Name	Score
J Nicklaus (USA)	71, 72, 69, 69–281
B Crenshaw (USA)	70, 69, 73, 71–283
R Floyd (USA)	69, 75, 71, 68–283
T Kite (USA)	72, 69, 72, 70–283
S Owen (NZ)	70, 75, 67, 71–283
P Oosterhuis (GB)	72, 70, 69, 73–284
I Aoki (Japan)	68, 71, 73, 73–285
N Faldo (unattached)	71, 72, 70, 72–285
J Schroeder (USA)	74, 69, 70, 72–285
R Shearer (Australia)	71, 69, 74, 71–285
M Cahill (Australia)	71, 72, 75, 68–286
D Hayes (S Africa)	74, 70, 71, 71–286
O Moody (USA)	73, 69, 74, 70–286
M Hayes (USA)	70, 75, 75, 67–287
M Ozaki (Japan)	72, 69, 75, 71–287
T Watson (USA)	73, 68, 70, 76–287
S Ballesteros (Spain)	69, 70, 76, 73–288
B Byman (USA)	72, 69, 74, 73–288
G Hunt (unattached)	71, 73, 71, 73–288
T Nakajima (Japan)	70, 71, 76, 71–288
T Weiskopf (USA)	69, 72, 72, 75–288
B Gallacher (Wentworth)	72, 71, 76, 70–289
N Job (Coombe Hill)	73, 75, 68, 73–289
A Garrido (Spain)	73, 71, 76, 70–290
H Irwin (USA)	75, 71, 76, 68–290
C Mason (St Pierre)	70, 74, 72, 74–290
J Newton (Australia)	69, 76, 71, 74–290
P Thomson (Australia)	72, 70, 72, 76–290
T Britz (S Africa)	73, 74, 72, 72–291
H Green (USA)	78, 70, 67, 76–291
J Morgan (Royal Liverpool)	74, 68, 77, 72–291
G Norman (Australia)	72, 73, 74, 72–291
L Trevino (USA)	75, 72, 73, 71–291

Chief Money Prize-Winners

J Nicklaus, £12,500; B Crenshaw, £7,312; R Floyd, £7,312; T Kite, £7,312; S Owen, £7,312; P Oosterhuis, £5,000; I Aoki, £3,937; N Faldo, £3,937; J Schroeder, £3,937; R Shearer, £3,937; M Cahill, £3,016; D Hayes, £3,016; O Moody,£3,016; M Hayes, £2,400; M Ozaki, £2,400; T Watson, £2,400.

Other Totals

B Barnes (unattached), K Brown (unattached), G Cullen (Stoke Poges), A Palmer (USA), G Player (South Africa) 292; D Graham (Australia), M Krantz (USA), P McEvoy (Copt Heath) (Am), N Price (South Africa), G Wolstenholme (Australia) 293; F Abreu (Spain), M Ballesteros (Spain), H Clark (Moor Allerton), M Miller (Cawder) (Am) 294; A Bean (USA); Allan Brodie (Balmore) (Am), R Charles (New Zealand), N Coles (unattached) 295; J Bland (South Africa), R Davis (Australia), D Good (Australia), S Hobday (Rhodesia), W Longmuir (unattached), V Somers (Australia), R Thompson (USA) 296; P Butler (RAC) 297; G Godwin (Thorndon Park) (Am), R Wynn (Leatherhead) 298; P Dawson (Holiday Inns) 299; E Murray (Walton Heath) 300; J Pate (USA) withdrew, injured.

1979 at Lytham and St Annes

Entries 885. Qualifying aggregates: 150 Fairhaven; 141 Lytham Green Drive; 146 St Annes Old. Qualified for final 36 holes, 82 competitors (80 Professionals, 2 Amateurs) with score of 152 and below. Qualified for final 18 holes, 61 competitors (60 Professionals, 1 Amateur) with score of 227 and below.

Name	Score
S Ballesteros (Spain)	73, 65, 75, 70–283
J Nicklaus (USA)	72, 69, 73, 72–286
B Crenshaw (USA)	72, 71, 72, 71–286
M James (Burghley Park)	76, 69, 69, 73–287
R Davis (Australia)	75, 70, 70, 73–288
H Irwin (USA)	68, 68, 75, 78–289
G Marsh (Australia)	74, 68, 75, 74–291
I Aoki (Japan)	70, 74, 72, 75–291
R Byman (USA)	73, 70, 72, 76–291

Name	Score	Name	Score
R Charles (NZ)	78, 72, 70, 72–292	P Toussaint (Belgium)	76, 75, 74, 70–295
M Ozaki (Japan)	75, 69, 75, 73–292	O Moody (USA)	71, 74, 76, 74–295
G Norman (Australia)	73, 71, 72, 76–292	G Player (S Africa)	77, 74, 69, 75–295
S Owen (NZ)	75, 76, 74, 68–293	K Brown (GB)	72, 71, 75, 77–295
W Armstrong (USA)	74, 74, 73, 72–293	A Jacklin (GB)	73, 74, 76, 73–296
J O'Leary (Ireland)	73, 73, 74, 73–293	T Nakamura (Japan)	77, 75, 67, 77–296
T Gale (Australia)	71, 74, 75, 73–293	P Thomson (Australia)	76, 75, 72, 74–297
L Trevino (USA)	71, 73, 74, 76–294	E Sneed (USA)	76, 75, 70, 76–297
P McEvoy (Copt Heath) (Am)	71, 74, 72, 77–294	J Pate (USA)	69, 74, 76, 78–297
N Faldo (GB)	74, 74, 78, 69–295	T Watson (USA)	76, 68, 76, 81–297
A Lyle (Hawkstone Park)	74, 76, 75, 70–295		

Chief Money Prize-Winners

S Ballesteros, £15,000; J Nicklaus, £11,250; B Crenshaw, £11,250; M James, £7,500; R Davis, £6,500; H Irwin, £6,000, G Marsh, £5,000; I Aoki, £5,000; R Byman, £5,000; R Charles, £4,000; M Ozaki, £4,000; G Norman, £4,000; S Owen, £3,125; W Armstrong, £3,125; J O'Leary, £3,125; T Gale, £3,125; L Trevino, £2,500.

Other Totals

M Hayes (USA), R Verwey (South Africa), A Saavedra (Argentina), T Kite (USA), S Hobday (Zimbabwe-Rhodesia), W Longmuir (GB), 298; L Elder (USA), P Cowen (GB), C O'Connor (Ireland), R Floyd (USA), M King (GB) 299; M Foster (GB), N Ratcliffe (Australia), H Baiocchi (South Africa), P Oosterhuis (GB), D Watson (South Africa), H Green (USA), J Schroeder (USA), D Clark (New Zealand) 300; B Barnes (GB), C Mason (GB), D Weaver (USA), G Cullen (GB) 301; G Parslow (Australia), I Richardson (Worcestershire), K Shimada (Japan) 302; J Newton (Australia), Y Yamamoto (Japan), J Miller (USA), G Wolstenholme (Australia) 303; R Fyfe (Largs) 307.

1980 at Muirfield

Entries 994. Qualifying aggregates: 144 Luffness New; 146 Gullane No 1; 143 Gullane No 2. Qualified for final 36 holes, 87 competitors (86 Professionals, 1 Amateur) with scores of 149 and below. Qualified for final 18 holes, 65 competitors (64 Professionals, 1 Amateur) with scores of 219 and below.

Name	Score	Name	Score
T Watson (USA)	68, 70, 64, 69–271	J Bland (S Africa)	73, 70, 70, 72–285
L Trevino (USA)	68, 67, 71, 69–275	J Pate (USA)	71, 67, 74, 73–285
B Crenshaw (USA)	70, 70, 68, 69–277	B Rogers (USA)	76, 73, 68, 69–286
J Nicklaus (USA)	73, 67, 71, 69–280	B Lietzke (USA)	74, 69, 73, 70–286
C Mason (GB)	72, 69, 70, 69–280	N Suzuki (Japan)	74, 68, 72, 72–286
C Stadler (USA)	72, 70, 69, 71–282	S Ballesteros (Spain)	72, 68, 72, 74–286
A Bean (USA)	71, 69, 70, 72–282	P Oosterhuis (GB)	72, 71, 75, 69–287
H Green (USA)	77, 69, 64, 72–282	M McNulty (S Africa)	71, 73, 72, 71–287
K Brown (GB)	70, 68, 68, 76–282	WJ McColl (GB)	73, 73, 68, 71–287
J Newton (Australia)	69, 71, 73, 70–283	GA Cullen (GB)	72, 72, 69, 74–287
G Morgan (USA)	70, 70, 71, 72–283	T Kite (USA)	72, 72, 74, 70–288
N Faldo (GB)	69, 74, 71, 70–284	N Price (Zimbabwe)	72, 71, 71, 74–288
L Nelson (USA)	72, 70, 71, 71–284	N Coles (GB)	75, 69, 69, 76–289
S Lyle (GB)	70, 71, 70, 73–284	H Baiocchi (S Africa)	76, 67, 69, 77–289
I Aoki (Japan)	74, 74, 63, 73–284	D Graham (Australia)	73, 71, 68, 77–289
T Weiskopf (USA)	72, 72, 71, 70–285		

Chief Money Prize-Winners

T Watson, £25,000; L Trevino, £17,500; B Crenshaw, £13,500; J Nicklaus, £9,250, C Mason, £9,250; C Stadler, £7,250; A Bean, £7,250; H Green, £7,250; K Brown, £7,250; J Newton, £5,750; G Morgan, £5,750; N Faldo, £4,250; L Nelson, £4,250; S Lyle, £4,250; I Aoki, £4,250; T Weiskopf, £2,900; J Bland, £2,900; J Pate, £2,900.

Other Totals

M Hayes (USA), T Horton (GB), A Jacklin (GB), J Mahaffey (USA), B Waites (GB), HK Clark (GB) 290; J Sigel (USA) (Am), S Torrance (GB), R Davis (Australia), S Ginn (Australia), T Nakamura (Japan), B Brask Jun (USA), D Hayes (South Africa) 291; A North (USA), W Armstrong (USA), G Marsh (Australia), M James (GB), E Darcy (Ireland), V Fernandez (Argentina) 292; A Garrido (Spain), B Gilder (USA), S Hobday (Zimbabwe), B Langer (West Germany), B Shearer (Australia), H Henning (South Africa), DA Cooper (GB) 293; M Pinero (Spain), B Barnes (GB) 294; R Charles (New Zealand), D Jagger (GB), M Ozaki (Japan) 295; P Tupling (GB) 296; S Owen (New Zealand) 297; D Bies (USA) 298.

The Open Championship
continued

1981 at Sandwich

Entries 972. Qualifying aggregates: 146 Littlestone; 146 North Foreland; 148 Princes; 144 Deal. Qualified for final 36 holes, 82 competitors (75 Professionals, 7 Amateurs) with score of 150 and below. Qualified for final 18 holes, 61 competitors (59 Professionals, 2 Amateurs) with scores of 222 and below.

Name	Score	Name	Score
B Rogers (USA)	72, 66, 67, 71–276	N Job (GB)	70, 69, 75, 74–288
B Langer (W Germany)	73, 67, 70, 70–280	G Marsh (Australia)	75, 71, 72, 71–289
R Floyd (USA)	74, 70, 69, 70–283	G Brand (GB)	78, 65, 74, 72–289
M James (GB)	72, 70, 68, 73–283	P Townsend (GB)	73, 70, 73, 73–289
S Torrance (GB)	72, 69, 73, 70–284	J Pate (USA)	73, 73, 69, 74–289
B Lietzke (USA)	76, 69, 71, 69–285	M McNulty (S Africa)	74, 74, 74, 68–290
M Pinero (Spain)	73, 74, 68, 70–285	N Price (Zimbabwe)	77, 68, 76, 69–290
H Clark (GB)	72, 76, 70, 68–286	H Green (USA)	75, 72, 74, 69–290
B Crenshaw (USA)	72, 67, 76, 71–286	J Nicklaus (USA)	83, 66, 71, 70–290
B Jones (GB)	73, 76, 66, 71–286	A Palmer (USA)	72, 74, 73, 71–290
L Trevino (USA)	77, 67, 70, 73–286	T Watson (USA)	73, 69, 75, 73–290
N Faldo (GB)	77, 68, 69, 73–287	A Jacklin (GB)	71, 71, 73, 75–290
I Aoki (Japan)	71, 73, 69, 74–287	S Owen (NZ)	71, 74, 70, 75–290
E Darcy (Ireland)	79, 69, 70, 70–288	J Morgan (GB)	77, 72, 73, 69–291
A Lyle (GB)	73, 73, 71, 71–288	G Norman (Australia)	72, 75, 72, 72–291
D Graham (Australia)	71, 71, 74, 72–288	D Smyth (Ireland)	77, 67, 73, 74–291
B Barnes (GB)	76, 70, 70, 72–288	T Powell (GB)	75, 68, 73, 75–291

Chief Money Prize-Winners

B Rogers, £25,000; B Langer, £17,500; R Floyd, £11,750; M James, £11,750; S Torrance, £8,500; B Lietzke, £7,750; M Pinero, £7,750; H Clark, £6,500; B Crenshaw, £6,500; B Jones, £6,500; L Trevino, £5,000; N Faldo, £5,000; I Aoki, £5,000; E Darcy, £3,240; S Lyle, £3,240; D Graham, £3,240; B Barnes, £3,240; N Job, £3,240; G Marsh, £2,013; G Brand, £2,013; P Townsend, £2,013; J Pate, £2,013.

Other Totals

T Horton (GB), EW Dunk (Australia), B Charles (New Zealand), M Ozaki (Japan) 292; S Ballesteros (Spain), F Molina (Argentina), N Coles (GB), R Davis (Australia), J Miller (USA) 293; K Brown (GB), R Streck (USA), T Gale (Australia) 294; J Gonzales (Brazil), M O'Meara (USA), H Sutton (USA) (Am) 295; D Jones (GB), D Thorpe (GB), B Waites (GB) 296; E Polland (Ireland), G Cullen (GB), M Ferguson (GB) 297; N Hunt (GB), W Humphreys (GB) 298; J O'Leary (Ireland), D Stewart (GB), G Godwin (GB) (Am) 299; D McLean (USA) 300.

1982 at Troon

Entries 1,121. Qualifying aggregates: 144 Glasgow Gailes; 143 Kilmarnock (Barassie); 140 Prestwick St Nicholas; 145 Western Gailes. Qualified for final 36 holes, 90 competitors (89 Professionals, 1 Amateur) with scores of 152 and below. Qualified for final 18 holes, 60 competitors (59 Professionals, 1 Amateur) with scores of 226 and below.

Name	Score	Name	Score
T Watson (USA)	69, 71, 74, 70–284	D Watson (GB)	75, 69, 73, 74–291
P Oosterhuis (GB)	74, 67, 74, 70–285	K Brown (GB)	70, 71, 79, 72–292
N Price (S Africa)	69, 69, 74, 73–285	T Nakamura (Japan)	77, 68, 77, 71–293
T Purtzer (USA)	76, 66, 75, 69–286	I Aoki (Japan)	75, 69, 75, 74–293
N Faldo (GB)	73, 73, 71, 69–286	J-M Canizares (Spain)	71, 72, 79, 72–294
M Kuramoto (Japan)	71, 73, 71, 71–286	J Miller (USA)	71, 76, 75, 72–294
D Smyth (Ireland)	70, 69, 74, 73–286	B Rogers (USA)	73, 70, 76, 75–294
F Zoeller (USA)	73, 71, 73, 70–287	G Marsh (Australia)	76, 76, 72, 71–295
A Lyle (GB)	74, 66, 73, 74–287	B Gallacher (GB)	75, 71, 74, 75–295
J Nicklaus (USA)	77, 70, 72, 69–288	J Haas (USA)	78, 72, 75, 71–296
B Clampett (USA)	67, 66, 78, 77–288	G Norman (Australia)	73, 75, 76, 72–296
S Torrance (GB)	73, 72, 73, 71–289	A Palmer (USA)	71, 73, 78, 74–296
S Ballesteros (Spain)	71, 75, 73, 71–290	L Trevino (USA)	78, 72, 71, 75–296
B Langer (W Germany)	70, 69, 78, 73–290	D Graham (USA)	73, 70, 76, 77–296
C Strange (USA)	72, 73, 76, 70–291	L Nelson (USA)	77, 69, 77, 74–297
B Crenshaw (USA)	74, 75, 72, 70–291	M Thomas (GB)	72, 74, 75, 76–297

Chief Money Prize-Winners

T Watson, £32,000; P Oosterhuis, £19,300; N Price, £19,300; T Purtzer, £11,000; N Faldo, £11,000; M Kuramoto, £11,000; D Smyth, £11,000; F Zoeller, £8,750; A Lyle, £8,750; J Nicklaus, £7,350; B Clampett, £7,350; S Torrance, £6,300; S Ballesteros, £5,400; B Langer, £5,400; R Floyd, £3,900; C Strange, £3,900; B Crenshaw, £3,900; D Watson, £3,900; K Brown, £2,900; T Nakamura, £2,500; I Aoki, £2,500; J-M Canizares, £2,200; J Miller, £2,200; B Rogers, £2,200.

Other Totals

E Darcy (Ireland), J Ferenz (USA), P Way (GB), C Stadler (USA), B Barnes (GB), D Russell (GB), 298; H Henning (South Africa) 299; B Shearer (New Zealand), M Lewis (GB) (Am), G Player (South Africa), T Gale (Australia), N Coles (GB) 300; B Longmuir (GB), T Britz (USA), R Chapman (GB), B Waites (GB) 301; M James (GB), Hsu Sheng-San (Taiwan), M Pinero (Spain) 302; M McNulty (S Africa), P Townsend (GB), M Poxton (GB), K Waters (GB) 303; P Harrison (GB) 304; M King (GB) 305; M Cahill (Australia) 306.

1983 at Birkdale

Entries 1,107. Qualifying aggregates: 143 Hesketh; 145 Southport and Ainsdale; 147 Hillside; 148 Wast Lancs. Qualified for final 36 holes, 83 competitors (all Professionals) with scores of 146 and below. Qualified for final 18 holes, 63 competitors with scores of 217 and below.

Name	Score	Name	Score
T Watson (USA)	67, 68, 70, 70–275	G Koch (USA)	75, 71, 66, 70–282
H Irwin (USA)	69, 68, 72, 67–276	F Zoeller (USA)	71, 71, 67, 73–282
A Bean (USA)	70, 69, 70, 67–276	R Floyd (USA)	72, 66, 69, 75–282
G Marsh (Australia)	69, 70, 74, 64–277	D Graham (Australia)	71, 69, 67, 75–282
L Trevino (USA)	69, 66, 73, 70–278	G Norman (Australia)	75, 71, 70, 67–283
S Ballesteros (Spain)	71, 71, 69, 68–279	H Green (USA)	69, 74, 72, 68–283
H Henning (S Africa)	71, 69, 70, 69–279	T Britz (S Africa)	71, 74, 69, 69–283
D Durnian (GB)	73, 66, 74, 67–280	B Waites (GB)	70, 70, 73, 70–283
C O'Connor, Jr (Ireland)	72, 69, 71, 68–280	B Gallacher (GB)	72, 71, 70, 70–283
		S Hobday (S Africa)	70, 73, 70, 70–283
B Rogers (USA)	67, 71, 73, 69–280	J Haas (USA)	73, 72, 68, 70–283
N Faldo (GB)	68, 68, 71, 73–280	E Darcy (Ireland)	69, 72, 74, 69–284
P Jacobsen (USA)	72, 69, 70, 70–281	H Clark (GB)	71, 72, 69, 72–284
C Stadler (USA)	64, 70, 72, 75–281	R Davis (Australia)	70, 71, 70, 73–284
M Sullivan (USA)	72, 68, 74, 68–282		

Chief Money Prize-Winners

T Watson, £40,000; H Irwin, £23,000; A Bean, £23,000; G Marsh, £15,000; L Trevino, £13,600; S Ballesteros, £12,500; H Henning, £12,250; D Durnian, £9,625; C O'Connor, Jr, £9,625; B Rogers, £9,625; N Faldo, £9,625; P Jacobsen, £7,250; C Stadler, £7,250; M Sullivan, £5,040; G Koch, £5,040; F Zoeller, £5,040; R Floyd, £5,040; D Graham, £5,040; G Norman, £2,957; H Green, £2,957; T Britz, £2,957; B Waites, £2,957; B Gallacher, £2,957; S Hobday, £2,957; J Haas, £2,957; E Darcy, £2,150; H Clark, £2,150; R Davis, £2,150.

Other Totals

C-S Lu (Taiwan), L Wadkins (USA), J Nicklaus (USA), T Kite (USA), M McCullough (USA), H Sutton (USA), M James (GB), T Nakamura (Japan), C Strange (USA), T Gale (Australia) 285; A Jacklin (GB), K Arai (Japan), B Gilder (USA), V Fernandez (Argentina), C Moody (GB), I Collins (GB) 286; C Tucker (GB), M Muramoto (Japan), M Pinero (Spain), G Burroughs (GB), T Weiskopf (USA), V Somers (Australia), T Simpson (USA), M McNulty (South Africa) 287; B Clampett (USA), L Nelson (USA), S Torrance (GB) 288; B Langer (West Germany), A Palmer (USA), M Johnson (GB), 289; M Calero (Spain), J O'Leary (Ireland) 290; R Rafferty (Ireland) 291; M Ingham (GB) 292; Y-S Hsieh (Taiwan) 295.

1984 at St Andrews

Entries 1,413. Regional qualifying courses: Glenbervie, Pleasington, Lindrick, Little Aston, Porters Park, Camberley Heath. Final qualifying courses: Ladybank, Leven, Lundin, Scotscraig. Qualified for final 36 holes: 94 competitors (92 Professionals, 2 Amateurs) with scores of 148 and below. Qualified for final 18 holes: 63 competitors with scores of 219 and below.

Name	Score	Name	Score
S Ballesteros (Spain)	69, 68, 70, 69–276	A Bean (USA)	72, 69, 75, 69–285
B Langer (W Germany)	71, 68, 68, 71–278	F Zoeller (USA)	71, 72, 71, 71–285
T Watson (USA)	71, 68, 66, 73–278	P Senior (Australia)	74, 70, 70, 71–285
F Couples (USA)	70, 69, 74, 68–281	W Bergin (USA)	75, 73, 66, 71–285
L Wadkins (USA)	70, 69, 73, 69–281	H Irwin (USA)	75, 68, 70, 72–285
N Faldo (GB)	69, 68, 76, 69–282	L Trevino (USA)	70, 67, 75, 73–285
G Norman (Australia)	67, 74, 74, 67–282	C Pavin (USA)	71, 74, 72, 69–286
M McCumber (USA)	74, 67, 72, 70–283	B Crenshaw (USA)	72, 75, 70, 69–286
G Marsh (Australia)	70, 74, 73, 67–284	T Kite (USA)	69, 71, 74, 72–286
S Torrance (GB)	74, 74, 66, 70–284	P Way (GB)	73, 72, 69, 72–286
R Rafferty (Ireland)	74, 72, 67, 71–284	P Jacobsen (USA)	67, 73, 73, 73–286
H Baiocchi (S Africa)	72, 70, 70, 72–284	G Morgan (USA)	71, 71, 71, 73–286
I Baker-Finch (Australia)	68, 66, 71, 79–284	T Gale (Australia)	71, 74, 72, 70–287
		J Gonzales (Brazil)	69, 71, 76, 71–287
A Lyle (GB)	75, 71, 72, 67–285	C Stadler (USA)	75, 70, 70, 72–287
K Brown (GB)	74, 71, 72, 68–285		

The Open Championship
continued

Chief Money Prize-Winners

S. Ballesteros £55,000; B Langer, T Watson £31,900; F Couples, L Wadkins £19,800; G Norman, N. Faldo £16,390; M McCumber £14,300; G. Marsh, S. Torrance, R. Rafferty, H Baiocchi, I Baker-Finch £11,264; A Lyle, K Brown, A Bean, F Zoeller, P Senior, W Bergin, H Irwin, L Trevino £6,751; C Pavin, B Crenshaw, T Kite, P Way, P Jacobsen, G Morgan £3,850; T Gale, J Gonzales, C Stadler £2,970.

Other Totals

P Parkin (GB), R Drummond (GB), B Gallacher (GB), J Miller (USA), J Nicklaus (USA) 288; M Pinero (Spain), J Haas (USA), G Levenson (S Africa), J Heggarty (GB), E Murray (GB), D Dunk (GB), T Nakajima (Japan), JM Canizares (Spain) 289; N Price (S Africa), M Poxon (GB), M James (GB) 290; M Calero (Spain), I Aoki (Japan), D Frost (S Africa), R Charles (New Zealand), R Chapman (GB) 291; H Clark (GB), J Chillas (GB), R Boxall (GB) 292; M Mackenzie (GB), D Russell (GB), W Longmuir (GB), E Rodriguez (Spain) 293; S Fujiki (Japan) 294; J Garner (GB), G Koch (USA), R Hartman (USA), N Ozaki (Japan) 295.

1985 at St Georges

Entries 1,361. Regional qualifying courses: Camberley Heath, Glenbervie, Lindrick, Little Aston, Pleasington, Porters Park, Wildernesse. Final qualifying courses: Royal Cinque Ports Deal, Littlestone, North Foreland. Qualified for final 36 holes: 85 (83 Professionals, 2 Amateurs) with scores of 149 and below. Qualified for final 18 holes: 60 (59 Professionals, 1 Amateur) with scores of 221 and below.

Name	Score
A Lyle (GB)	68, 71, 73, 70–282
P Stewart (USA)	70, 75, 70, 68–283
J Rivero (Spain)	74, 72, 70, 68–284
C O'Connor Jr (Ireland)	64, 76, 72, 72–284
M O'Meara (USA)	70, 72, 70, 72–284
D Graham (Australia)	68, 71, 70, 75–284
B Langer (W Germany)	72, 69, 68, 75–284
A Forsbrand (Sweden)	70, 76, 69, 70–285
DA Weibring (USA)	69, 71, 74, 71–285
T Kite (USA)	73, 73, 67, 72–285
E Darcy (Ireland)	76, 68, 74, 68–286
G Koch (USA)	75, 72, 70, 69–286
J-M Canizares (Spain)	72, 75, 70, 69–286
F Zoeller (USA)	69, 76, 70, 71–286
P Jacobsen (USA)	71, 74, 68, 73–286
S Bishop (GB)	71, 75, 72, 69–287
S Torrance (GB)	74, 74, 69, 70–287
G Norman (Australia)	71, 72, 71, 73–287
I Woosnam (GB)	70, 71, 71, 75–287
I Baker-Finch (Australia)	71, 73, 74, 70–288
J Gonzales (Brazil)	72, 72, 73, 71–288
L Trevino (USA)	73, 76, 68, 71–288
G Marsh (Australia)	71, 75, 69, 73–288
M James (GB)	71, 78, 66, 73–288
P Parkin (GB)	68, 76, 77, 68–289
K Moe (USA)	70, 76, 73, 70–289
J-M Olazabal (Spain) (Am)	72, 76, 71, 70–289
M Cahill (Australia)	72, 74, 71, 72–289
D Frost (South Africa)	70, 74, 73, 72–289
G Brand Sr (GB)	73, 72, 72, 72–289
M Pinero (Spain)	71, 73, 72, 73–289
R Lee (GB)	68, 73, 74, 74–289

Chief Money Prize-Winners

A Lyle £65,000; P Stewart £40,000; J Rivero, C O'Connor Jr, M O'Meara, D Graham B Langer £23,600; A Forsbrand, DA Weibring, T Kite £15,566; E Darcy, G Koch, J-M Canizares, F Zoeller, P Jacobsen £11,400; S Bishop, S Torrance, G Norman, I Woosnam £7,900; I Baker-Finch, J Gonzales, L Trevino, G Marsh, M James £5,260; P Parkin, K Moe, M Cahill, D Frost, G Brand Sr, M Pinero, R Lee £3,742

Other Totals

O Sellberg (Sweden), W Riley (Australia) 290, H Baiocchi (South Africa), B Crenshaw (USA), A Bean (USA), R Shearer (Australia) 291; A Johnstone (Zimbabwe), M Parsson (Sweden), J Pinsent (GB), S Ballesteros (Spain), C Pavin (USA) 292; P Senior (Australia), R Rafferty (N Ireland), D Russell (GB) 293; D Watson (South Africa), M Mouland (GB), G Brand, Jr (GB), B Gallacher (GB), H Clark (GB), T Watson (USA) 294; N Faldo (GB), E Rodriquez (Spain) 295; L Nelson (USA), P Fowler (Australia) 296; D Whelan (GB) 298; D Williams (GB) 300; V Somers (Australia) 301; R Charles (New Zealand) retired.

1986 at Turnberry

Entries 1,347. Regional qualifying courses: Glenbervie, Haggs Castle, Hankley Common, Langley Park, Lindrick, Little Aston, Ormskirk, Porters Park. Final qualifying courses: Glasgow Gailes, Kilmarnock (Barassie), Prestwick St Nicholas, Western Gailes. Qualified for final 36 holes: 77 Professionals. Non-qualifiers after 36 holes: 74 (71 Professionals, 3 Amateurs) with scores of 152 and above.

Name	Score	Name	Score
G Norman (Australia)	74, 63, 74, 69–280	A Forsbrand (Sweden)	71, 73, 77, 71–292
GJ Brand Jr (GB)	71, 68, 75, 71–285	J-M Olazabal (Spain)	78, 69, 72, 73–292
B Langer (W Germany)	72, 70, 76, 68–286	R Floyd (USA)	78, 67, 73, 74–292
I Woosnam (GB)	70, 74, 70, 72–286	R Charles (New Zealand)	76, 72, 73, 72–293
N Faldo (GB)	71, 70, 76, 70–287	M Pinero (Spain)	78, 71, 70, 74–293
S Ballesteros (Spain)	76, 75, 73, 64–288	R Rafferty (N Ireland)	75, 74, 75, 70–294
G Koch (USA)	73, 72, 72, 71–288	D Cooper (GB)	72, 79, 72, 71–294
F Zoeller (USA)	75, 73, 72, 69–289	V Somers (Australia)	73, 77, 72, 72–294
B Marchbank (GB)	78, 70, 72, 69–289	B Crenshaw (USA)	77, 69, 75, 73–294
T Nakajima (Japan)	74, 67, 71, 77–289	R Lee (GB)	71, 75, 75, 73–294
C O'Connor Jr (Ireland)	75, 71, 75, 69–290	P Parkin (GB)	78, 70, 72, 74–294
D Graham (Australia)	75, 73, 70, 72–290	D Edwards (USA)	77, 73, 70, 74–294
J-M Canizares (Spain)	76, 68, 73, 73–290	V Fernandez (Argentina)	78, 70, 71, 75–294
C Strange (USA)	79, 69, 74, 69–291	S Torrance (GB)	78, 69, 71, 76–294
A Bean (USA)	74, 73, 73, 71–291		

Chief Money Prize-Winners

G Norman £70,000; GJ Brand Jr £50,000; B Langer, I Woosnam £35,000; N Faldo £25,000; S Ballesteros, G Koch £22,000; F Zoeller, B Marchbank, T Nakajima £17,333; C O'Connor Jr, D Graham, J-M Canizares £14,000; C Strange, A Bean £11.500; A Forsbrand, J-M Olazabel, R Floyd £9,000; R Charles, M Pinero £7,250; R Rafferty, D Cooper, V Somers, B Crenshaw, R Lee, P Parkin, D Edwards, V Fernandez, S Torrance £5,022.

Other Totals

I Stanley (Australia), J Mahaffey (USA), M Karamoto (Japan), DA Weibring (USA), A Lyle (Scotland) 295; T Watson (USA), R Chapman (England), A Brooks (Scotland), R Commans (USA), M James (England), P Stewart (USA), G Player (South Africa), G Turner (New Zealand) 296; R Maltbie (USA), M O'Meara (USA), HM Chung (Taiwan) 297; J Nicklaus (USA), M O'Grady (USA), T Charnley (England), F Couples (USA), M Clayton (Australia), L Mize (USA), J Hawkes (South Africa), LS Chuen (Taiwan), R Tway (USA), T Armour III (USA) 298; S Randolph (USA), G Marsh (Australia), C Mason (England) 300; M McNulty (South Africa), M Mackenzie (England), L Trevino (USA), E Darcy (Ireland), T Lamore (USA), F Nobilo (New Zealand) 301; A Chandler (England), J Heggarty (N Ireland), M Gray (Scotland), D Hammond (USA), S Simpson (USA) 302; O Moore (Australia), P Fowler (Australia) 303; D Jones (N Ireland), R Drummond (Scotland) 305; T Horton (Scotland) 306; G Weir (Scotland) 307; K Moe (USA) 314; H Green (USA) retired.

Amateur Championship

Year	Winner	Runner-up	Venue	By	Ent
1885	AF MacFie	HG Hutchinson	Hoylake	7 and 6	44
1886	HG Hutchinson	Henry Lamb	St Andrews	7 and 6	42
1887	HG Hutchinson	John Ball	Hoylake	1 hole	33
1888	John Ball	JE Laidlay	Prestwick	5 and 4	38
1889	JE Laidlay	LMB Melville	St Andrews	2 and 1	40
1890	John Ball	JE Laidlay	Hoylake	4 and 3	44
1891	JE Laidlay	HH Hilton	St Andrews	20th hole	50
1892	John Ball	HH Hilton	Sandwich	3 and 1	45
1893	Peter Anderson	JE Laidlay	Prestwick	1 hole	44
1894	John Ball	SM Fergusson	Hoylake	1 hole	64
1895	LMB Melville	John Ball	St Andrews	19th hole	68
1896*	FG Tait	HH Hilton	Sandwich	8 and 7	64
**36 holes played on and after this date.*					
1897	AJT Allan	James Robb	Muirfield	4 and 2	74
1898	FG Tait	SM Fergusson	Hoylake	7 and 5	77
1899	John Ball	FG Tait	Prestwick	37th hole	101
1900	HH Hilton	James Robb	Sandwich	8 and 7	68
1901	HH Hilton	JL Low	St Andrews	1 hole	116
1902	C Hutchings	SH Fry	Hoylake	1 hole	114
1903	R Maxwell	HG Hutchinson	Muirfield	7 and 5	142
1904	WJ Travis (USA)	Edward Blackwell	Sandwich	4 and 3	104
1905	AG Barry	Hon O Scott	Prestwick	3 and 2	148

Amateur Championship

continued

Year	Winner	Runner-up	Venue	By	Ent
1906	James Robb	CC Lingen	Hoylake	4 and 3	166
1907	John Ball	CA Palmer	St Andrews	6 and 4	200
1908	EA Lassen	HE Taylor	Sandwich	7 and 6	197
1909	R Maxwell	Capt CK Hutchison	Muirfield	1 hole	170
1910	John Ball	C Aylmer	Hoylake	10 and 9	160
1911	HH Hilton	EA Lassen	Prestwick	4 and 3	146
1912	John Ball	Abe Mitchell	Westward Ho!	38th hole	134
1913	HH Hilton	R Harris	St Andrews	6 and 5	198
1914	JLC Jenkins	CO Hezlet	Sandwich	3 and 2	232
1915-19	*No Championship owing to the Great War*				
1920	CJH Tolley	RA Gardner (USA)	Muirfield	37th hole	165
1921	WI Hunter	AJ Graham	Hoylake	12 and 11	223
1922	EWW Holderness	J Caven	Prestwick	1 hole	252
1923	RH Wethered	R Harris	Deal	7 and 6	209
1924	EWE Holderness	EF Storey	St Andrews	3 and 2	201
1925	Robert Harris	KF Fradgley	Westward Ho!	13 and 12	151
1926	Jesse Sweetser (USA)	AF Simpson	Muirfield	6 and 5	216
1927	Dr W Tweddell	DE Landale	Hoylake	7 and 6	197
1928	TP Perkins	RH Wethered	Prestwick	6 and 4	220
1929	CJH Tolley	JN Smith	Sandwich	4 and 3	253
1930	RT Jones (USA)	RH Wethered	St Andrews	7 and 6	271
1931	Eric Martin Smith	J De Forest	Westward Ho!	1 hole	171
1932	J De Forest	EW Fiddian	Muirfield	3 and 1	235
1933	Hon M Scott	TA Bourn	Hoylake	4 and 3	269
1934	W Lawson Little (USA)	J Wallace	Prestwick	14 and 13	225
1935	W Lawson Little (USA)	Dr W Tweddell	Lytham St Annes	1 hole	232
1936	H Thomson	J Ferrier (Australia)	St Andrews	2 holes	283
1937	R Sweeny, Jun (USA)	LO Munn	Sandwich	3 and 2	223
1938	CR Yates (USA)	RC Ewing	Troon	3 and 2	241
1939	AT Kyle	AA Duncan	Hoylake	2 and 1	167
1940-45	*Suspended during war*				
1946	J Bruen	R Sweeny (USA)	Birkdale	4 and 3	263
1947	WP Turnesa (USA)	RD Chapman (USA)	Carnoustie	3 and 2	200
1948	FR Stranahan (USA)	C Stowe	Sandwich	5 and 4	168
1949	SM McCready	WP Turnesa (USA)	Portmarnock	2 and 1	204
1950	FR Stranahan (USA)	RD Chapman (USA)	St Andrews	8 and 6	324
1951	RD Chapman (USA)	CR Coe (USA)	Porthcawl	5 and 4	192
1952	EH Ward (USA)	FR Stranahan (USA)	Prestwick	6 and 5	286
1953	JB Carr	E Harvie Ward (USA)	Hoylake	2 holes	279
1954	DW Bachli (Australia)	WC Campbell (USA)	Muirfield	2 and 1	286
1955	JW Conrad (USA)	A Slater	Lytham St Annes	3 and 2	240
1956*	JC Beharrell	LG Taylor	Troon	5 and 4	200
1957*	R Reid Jack	HB Ridgley (USA)	Formby	2 and 1	200
**In 1956 and 1957 the Quarter Finals, Semi-Finals and Final were played over 36 holes*					
1958*	JB Carr	A Thirlwell	St Andrews	3 and 2	488
**In 1958, Semi-Finals and Final only were played over 36 holes*					
1959	DR Beman (USA)	W Hyndman (USA)	Sandwich	3 and 2	362
1960	JB Carr	R Cochran (USA)	Portrush	8 and 7	183
1961	MF Bonallack	J Walker	Turnberry	6 and 4	250
1962	RD Davies (USA)	J Povall	Hoylake	1 hole	256
1963	MSR Lunt	JG Blackwell	St Andrews	2 and 1	256
1964	Gordon J Clark	MSR Lunt	Ganton	39th hole	220
1965	MF Bonallack	CA Clark	Porthcawl	2 and 1	176
1966	RE Cole (S Africa)	RDBM Shade	Carnoustie (18 holes)	3 and 2	206
1967	RB Dickson (USA)	RJ Cerrudo (USA)	Formby	2 and 1	
1968	MF Bonallack	JB Carr	Troon	7 and 6	249
1969	MF Bonallack	W Hyndman (USA)	Hoylake	3 and 2	245
1970	MF Bonallack	W Hyndman (USA)	Newcastle C Down	8 and 7	256
1971	S Melnyk (USA)	J Simons (USA)	Carnoustie	3 and 2	256
1972	T Homer	A Thirlwell	Sandwich	4 and 3	253
1973	R Siderowf (USA)	PH Moody	Porthcawl	5 and 3	222
1974	T Homer	J Gabrielsen (USA)	Muirfield	2 holes	330
1975	MM Giles (USA)	MH James	Hoylake	8 and 7	206
1976	R Siderowf (USA)	JC Davies	St Andrews	37th hole	289
1977	P McEvoy	HM Campbell	Ganton	5 and 4	235
1978	P McEvoy	PJ McKellar	Troon	4 and 3	353
1979	J Sigel (USA)	S Hoch (USA)	Hillside	3 and 2	285
1980	D Evans	D Suddards (SA)	Porthcawl	4 and 3	265
1981	P Ploujoux (France)	J Hirsch (USA)	St Andrews	4 and 2	256
1982	M Thompson	A Stubbs	Deal	4 and 3	245
1983	AP Parkin	J Holtgrieve (USA)	Turnberry	5 and 4	288
1984	JM Olazabal (Spain)	C Montgomerie	Formby	5 and 4	291
1985	G McGimpsey	G Homewood	Dornoch	8 and 7	
1986	D Curry	G Birtwell	Lytham St Annes	11 and 9	

Ladies' British Open Amateur Championship

Year	Winner	Runner-up	Venue	By
1893	Lady Margaret Scott	Miss Isette Pearson	St Annes	7 and 5
1894	Lady Margaret Scott	Miss Isette Pearson	Littlestone	3 and 2
1895	Lady Margaret Scott	Miss E Lythgoe	Portrush	5 and 4
1896	Miss Pascoe	Miss L Thomson	Hoylake	3 and 2
1897	Miss EC Orr	Miss Orr	Gullane	4 and 2
1898	Miss L Thomson	Miss EC Neville	Yarmouth	7 and 5
1899	Miss M Hezlet	Miss Magill	Newcastle Co Down	2 and 1
1900	Miss Adair	Miss Neville	Westward Ho!	6 and 5
1901	Miss Graham	Miss Adair	Aberdovey	3 and 1
1902	Miss M Hezlet	Miss E Neville	Deal	19th hole
1903	Miss Adair	Mss F Walker-Leigh	Portrush	4 and 3
1904	Miss L Dod	Miss M Hezlet	Troon	1 hole
1905	Miss B Thompson	Mss ME Stuart	Cromer	3 and 2
1906	Mrs Kennion	Miss B Thompson	Burnham	4 and 3
1907	Miss M Hezlet	Miss F Hezlet	Newcastle Co Down	2 and 1
1908	Miss M Titterton	Miss D Campbell	St Andrews	19th hole
1909	Miss D Campbell	Miss F Hezlet	Birkdale	4 and 3
1910	Miss Grant Suttie	Miss L Moore	Westward Ho!	6 and 4
1911	Miss D Campbell	Miss V Hezlet	Portrush	3 and 2
1912	Miss G Ravenscroft	Miss S Temple	Turnberry	3 and 2
(Final played over 36 holes after 1912)				
1913	Miss M Dodd	Miss Chubb	St Annes	8 and 6
1914	Miss C Leitch	Miss G Ravenscroft	Hunstanton	2 and 1
1915-18	*No Championship owing to Great War*			
1919	*Should have been played at Burnham in October, but abandoned owing to Railway Strike*			
1920	Miss C Leitch	Miss Molly Griffiths	Newcastle Co Down	7 and 6
1921	Miss C Leitch	Miss J Wethered	Turnberry	4 and 3
1922	Miss J Wethered	Miss C Leitch	Prince's, Sandwich	9 and 7
1923	Miss D Chambers	Miss A Macbeth	Burnham, Somerset	2 holes
1924	Miss J Wethered	Mrs Cautley	Portrush	7 and 6
1925	Miss J Wethered	Miss C Leitch	Troon	37th hole
1926	Miss C Leitch	Mrs Garon	Harlech	8 and 7
1927	Miss Thion de la Chaume (France)	Miss Pearson	Newcastle Co Down	5 and 4
1928	Miss Nanette Le Blan (France)	Miss S Marshall	Hunstanton	3 and 2
1929	Miss J Wethered	Miss G Collett (USA)	St Andrews	3 and 1
1930	Miss D Fishwick	Miss G Collett (USA)	Formby	4 and 3
1931	Miss E Wilson	Miss W Morgan	Portmarnock	7 and 6
1932	Miss E Wilson	Miss CPR Montgomery	Saunton	7 and 6
1933	Miss E Wilson	Miss D Plumpton	Gleneagles	5 and 4
1934	Mrs AM Holm	Miss P Barton	Porthcawl	6 and 5
1935	Miss W Morgan	Miss P Barton	Newcastle Co Down	3 and 2
1936	Miss P Barton	Miss B Newell	Southport and Ainsdale	5 and 3
1937	Miss J Anderson	Miss D Park	Turnberry	6 and 4
1938	Mrs AM Holm	Miss E Corlett	Burnham	4 and 3
1939	Miss P Barton	Mrs T Marks	Portrush	2 and 1
1946	Mrs GW Hetherington	Miss P Garvey	Hunstanton	1 hole
1947	Mrs George Zaharias (USA)	Miss J Gordon	Gullane	5 and 4
1948	Miss Louise Suggs (USA)	Miss J Donald	Lytham St Annes	1 hole
1949	Miss Frances Stephens	Mrs Val Reddan	Harlech	5 and 4
1950	Vicomtesse de Saint Sauveur (France)	Mrs G Valentine	Newcastle Co Down	3 and 2
1951	Mrs PG MacCann	Miss Frances Stephens	Broadstone	4 and 3
1952	Miss Moira Paterson	Miss Frances Stephens	Troon	39th hole
1953	Miss Marlene Stewart (Canada)	Miss P Garvey	Porthcawl	7 and 6
1954	Miss Frances Stephens	Miss E Price	Ganton	4 and 3
1955	Mrs G Valentine	Miss B Romack (USA)	Portrush	7 and 6
1956	Miss Margaret Smith (USA)	Miss Mary P Janssen (USA)	Sunningdale	8 and 7
1957	Miss P Garvey	Mrs G Valentine	Gleneagles	4 and 3
1958	Mrs G Valentine	Miss E Price	Hunstanton	1 hole
1959	Miss E Price	Miss B McCorkindale	Ascot	37th hole
1960	Miss B McIntyre (USA)	Miss P Garvey	Harlech	4 and 2
1961	Mrs AD Spearman	Miss DJ Robb	Carnoustie	7 and 6
1962	Mrs AD Spearman	Mrs MF Bonallack	Birkdale	1 hole
1963	Miss B Varangot (France)	Miss P Garvey	Newcastle Co Down	3 and 1

Ladies' British Open Amateur Championship

continued

Year	Winner	Runner-up	Venue	By
1964	Miss C Sorenson (USA)	Miss BAB Jackson	Prince's Sandwich	37th hole
1965	Miss B Varangot (France)	Mrs I Robertson	St Andrews	4 and 3
1966	Miss E Chadwick	Miss V Saunders	Ganton	3 and 2
1967	Miss E Chadwick	Miss M Everard	Harlech	1 hole
1968	Miss B Varangot (France)	Mrs C Rubin (France)	Walton Heath	20th hole
1969	Miss C Lacoste (France)	Miss A Irvin	Portrush	1 hole
1970	Miss D Oxley	Mrs IC Robertson	Gullane	1 hole
1971	Miss Michelle Walker	Miss B Huke	Alwoodley	3 and 1
1972	Miss Michelle Walker	Mrs C Rubin (France)	Hunstanton	2 holes
1973	Miss A Irvin	Miss Michelle Walker	Carnoustie	3 and 2
1974	Miss C Semple (USA)	Mrs A Bonallack	Porthcawl	2 and 1
1975	Mrs N Syms (USA)	Miss S Cadden	St Andrews	3 and 2
1976	Miss C Panton	Miss A Sheard	Silloth	1 hole
1977	Mrs A Uzielli	Miss V Marvin	Hillside	6 and 5
1978	Miss E Kennedy (Australia)	Miss J Greenhalgh	Notts	1 hole
1979	Miss M Madill	Miss J Lock (Australia)	Nairn	2 and 1
1980	Mrs A Sander (USA)	Mrs L Wollin (Sweden)	Woodhall Spa	3 and 1
1981	Mrs IC Robertson	Miss W Aitken	Conway	20th hole
1982	Miss K Douglas	Miss G Stewart	Walton Heath	4 and 2
1983	Mrs J Thornhill	Miss R Lautens (Switzerland)	Silloth	4 and 2
1984	Miss J Rosenthal (USA)	J Brown	Royal Troon	4 and 3
1985	Miss L Beman (Eire)	C Waite	Ganton	1 hole
1986	Miss McGuire (NZ)	L Briars (Australia)	West Sussex	2 and 1

Ladies' British Open Amateur Stroke Play Championship

Year	Winner	Club	Venue	Score
1969	Miss A Irvin	Lytham St Annes	Gosforth Park	295
1970	Miss M Everard	Hallamshire	Birkdale	313
1971	Mrs IC Robertson	Dunaverty	Ayr Belleisle	302
1972	Mrs IC Robertson	Dunaverty	Silloth	296
1973	Mrs A Stant	Beau Desert	Purdis Heath	298
1974	Miss J Greenhalgh	Pleasington	Seaton Carew	302
1975	Miss J Greenhalgh	Pleasington	Gosforth Park	298
1976*	Miss J Lee Smith	Gosforth Park	Fulford	299
1977*	Miss M Everard	Hallamshire	Lindrick	306
1978*	Miss J Melville	Furness	Foxhills	310
1979	Miss M McKenna	Donabate	Moseley	305
1980	Miss M Madill	Portstewart	Brancepeth Castle	304
(After a tie with Miss P Wright)				
1981	Miss J Soulsby	Prudhoe	Norwich	300
1982	Miss J Connachan	Musselburgh	Downfield	294
1983	Miss A. Nicholas		Moortown	292
1984	Miss C Waite	Swindon	Caernarvonshire	295
1985	Mrs IC Robertson	Dunaverty	Formby	300
1986	Miss C Hourihane†		Blairgowrie	291

**Played concurrently with Ladies' British Open Championship*
†After a tie with Miss P Johnson

Senior Ladies' British Open Amateur Stroke Play Championship

Instituted 1981

Year	Winner	Club	Venue	Score
1981	Mrs BM King	Pleasington	Formby	159
1982	Mrs P Riddiford	Royal Ashdown Forest	Ilkley	161
1983	Mrs M Birtwistle		Troon Portland	167
1984	Mme O Semelaigne	France	Woodbridge	152
1985	Dr G Costello		Prestatyn	158
1986	Mrs P Riddiford	Royal Ashdown Forest	Longniddry	154

Ladies' British Open Championship

Instituted 1976

Year	Winner	Club/Country	Venue	Score
1976	Miss J Lee Smith	Gosforth Park	Fulford	299
1977	Miss V Saunders	Tyrrells Wood	Lindrick	306
1978	Miss J Melville	Furness	Foxhills	310
1979	Miss A Sheard	South Africa	Southport and Ainsdale	301
1980	Mss D Massey	USA	Wentworth (East)	294
1981	Miss D Massey	USA	Northumberland	295
1982	M Figueras-Dotti	Spain	Birkdale	296
1983	*Not played*			
1984	A Okamoto	Japan	Woburn	289
1985	Mrs B King	USA	Moor Park	300
1986	Miss L Davies	GB		

Boys' Amateur Championship

Year	Winner	Runner-up	Venue	By
1921	ADD Mathieson	GH Lintott	Ascot	37th hole
1922	HS Mitchell	W Greenfield	Ascot	4 and 2
1923	ADD Mathieson	HS Mitchell	Dunbar	3 and 2
1924	RW Peattie	Pierre Manuevrier	Coombe Hill	2 holes
1925	RW Peattie	A McNair	Barnton	4 and 3
1926	EA McRuvie	CW Timmis	Coombe Hill	1 hole
1927	EW Fiddian	K Forbes	Barnton	4 and 2
1928	S Scheftel	A Dobbie	Formby	6 and 5
1929	J Lindsay	J Scott-Riddell	Barnton	6 and 4
1930	J Lindsay	J Todd	Fulwell	9 and 8
1931	H Thomson	F McGloin	Killermont	5 and 4
1932	IS MacDonald	LA Hardie	Lytham St Annes	2 and 1
1933	PB Lucas	W McLachlan	Carnoustie	3 and 2
1934	RS Burles	FB Allpass	Moortown	12 and 10
1935	JDA Langley	R Norris	Balgownie, Ab'deen	6 and 5
1936	J Bruen	W Innes	Birkdale	11 and 9
1937	IM Roberts	J Stewart	Bruntsfield	8 and 7
1938	W Smeaton	T Snowball	Moor Park	3 and 2
1939	SB Williamson	KG Thom	Carnoustie	4 and 2
1940-45	*Suspended during War*			
1946	AFD MacGregor	DF Dunstan	Bruntsfield	7 and 5
1947	James Armour	Ian Caldwell	Hoylake	5 and 4
1948	John D Pritchett	DH Reid	Barassie	37th hole
1949	Harry MacAnespie	NV Drew	St Andrews	3 and 2
1950	John Glover	Ian Young	Lytham St Annes	2 and 1
1951	Neville Dunn	MSR Lunt	Prestwick	6 and 5
1952	Michael Bonallack	AE Shepperson	Formby	37th hole
1953	AE Shepperson	AT Booth	Dunbar	6 and 4
1954	AF Bussell	Keith Warren	Hoylake	38th hole
1955	SC Wilson	BJK Aitken	Barassie	39th hole
1956	John F Ferguson	Clive W Cole	Sunningdale	2 and 1
1957	David Ball	John Wilson	Carnoustie	2 and 1

Boys' Amateur Championship

continued

Year	Winner	Runner-up	Venue	By
1958	R Braddon	IM Stungo	Moortown	4 and 3
1959	AR Murphy	EM Shamash	Pollok	3 and 1
1960	P Cros	PO Green	Olton	5 and 3
1961	FS Morris	C Clark	Dalmahoy	3 and 2
1962	PM Townsend	DC Penman	Mid-Surrey	1 hole
1963	AHC Soutar	DI Rigby	Prestwick	2 and 1
1964	PM Townsend	RD Gray	Formby	9 and 8
1965	GR Milne	DK Midgley	Gullane	4 and 2
1966	A Phillips	A Muller	Moortown	12 and 11
1967	LP Tupling	SC Evans	Western Gailes	4 and 2
1968	SC Evans	K Dabson	St Annes Old Links	3 and 2
1969	M Foster	M Gray	Dunbar	37th hole
1970	ID Gradwell	JE Murray	Hillside	1 hole
1971	H Clark	G Harvey	Barassie	6 and 5
1972	G Harvey	R Newsome	Moortown	7 and 5
1973	DM Robertson	S Betti	Blairgowrie	5 and 3
1974	TR Shannon	AWB Lyle	Hoylake	10 and 9
1975	B Marchbank	AWB Lyle	Bruntsfield	1 hole
1976	M Mouland	G Hargreaves	Sunningdale	6 and 5
1977	I Ford	CR Dalgleish	Downfield	1 hole
1978	S Keppler	M Stokes	Seaton Carew	3 and 2
1979	R Rafferty	D Ray	Barassie	6 and 5
1980	D Muscroft	A Llyr	Formby	7 and 6
1981	J Lopez	R Weedon	Gullane	4 and 3
1982	M Grieve	G Hickman	Burnham and Berrow	37th hole
1983	J Olazabal	M Pendaries	Glenbervie	6 and 5
1984	L Vannett	A Mednick	Royal Porthcawl	2 and 1
1985	J Cook	W Henry	Barnton	5 and 4
1986	L Walker	G King	Seaton Carew	5 and 4

Girls' British Open Amateur Championship

Year	Winner	Runner-up	Venue	By
1924	Miss Thion de la Chaume	Miss D Pearson	Stoke Poges	4 and 2
1925	Miss Enid Wilson	Miss KM Nicholls	Stoke Poges	5 and 3
1926	Miss Diana Esmond	Miss M Ramsden	Stoke Poges	6 and 5
1927	Miss Diana Fishwick	Miss Irene Taylor	Stoke Poges	7 and 6
1928	Miss Diana Fishwick	Miss M Jolly	Stoke Poges	3 and 2
1929	Miss Nan Baird	Miss S Bailey	Stoke Poges	4 and 3
1930	Miss Pauline Doran	Miss D Wilkins	Stoke Poges	19th hole
1931	Miss Pauline Doran	Miss D Wilkins	Stoke Poges	2 and 1
1932	Miss Pauline Doran	Miss A de Gunzbourg	Stoke Poges	19th hole
1933	Miss J Anderson	Miss EM Pears	Stoke Poges	5 and 3
1934	Miss N Jupp	Miss J Mountford	Stoke Poges	3 and 1
1935	Miss P Faulkner	Miss J Pemberton	Stoke Poges	1 hole
1936	Miss P Edwards	Miss J Gordon	Stoke Poges	3 and 2
1937	Miss L Vagliano	Miss P Edwards	Stoke Poges	5 and 4
1938	Miss S Stroyan	Miss J Pemberton	Stoke Poges	4 and 3
1949	Miss Pamela Davies	Miss Arlette Jacquet	Beaconsfield	1 hole
1950	Miss J Robertson	Miss A Phillips	Formby	5 and 4
1951	Miss J Redgate	Miss J Robertson	Gullane	19th hole
1952	Miss A Phillips	Miss S Marbrook	Stoke Poges	7 and 6
1953	Miss Susan Hill	Miss Angela Ward	Woodhall Spa	3 and 2
1954	Miss B Jackson	Miss D Winsor	West Kilbride	20th hole
1955	Miss Angela Ward	Miss Alison Gardner	Beaconsfield	5 and 4
1956	Miss Ruth Porter	Miss Annette Nicholson	Seaton Carew	5 and 4
1957	Miss B Varangot	Miss Ruth Porter	North Berwick	3 and 2
1958	Miss T Ross-Steen	Miss Varangot	Cotswold Hills	2 and 1
1959	Miss SM Vaughan	Miss JA Greenhalgh	Nottingham	1 hole
1960	Miss S Clarke	Miss AL Irvin	Barassie	2 and 1
1961	Miss D Robb	Miss J Roberts	Beaconsfield	3 and 2
1962	Miss S McLaren-Smith	Miss A Murphy	Foxton Hall	2 and 1
1963	Miss D Oxley	Miss B Whitehead	Gullane	2 and 1
1964	Miss P Tredinnick	Miss K Cumming	Camberley Heath	2 and 1
1965	Miss A Willard	Miss A Ward	Formby	3 and 2
1966	Miss J Hutton	Miss D Oxley	Troon Portland	20th hole
1967	Miss P Burrows	Miss J Hutton	Liphook	2 and 1
1968	Miss C Wallace	Miss C Reybroeck	Leven	4 and 3
1969	Miss J de Witt Puyt	Miss C Reybroeck	Ilkley	2 and 1
1970	Miss C Le Feuvre	Miss Michelle Walker	North Wales	2 and 1
1971	Miss J Mark	Miss Maureen Walker	North Berwick	4 and 3
1972	Miss Maureen Walker	Miss S Cadden	Norwich	2 and 1
1973	Miss AM Palli	Miss N Jeanson	Northamptonshire	2 and 1
1974	Miss R Barry	Miss T Perkins	Dunbar	1 hole

Girls' British Open Amateur Championship
continued

Year	Winner	Runner-up	Venue	By
1975	Miss S Cadden	Miss L Isherwood	Henbury	4 and 3
1976	Miss G Stewart	Miss S Rowlands	Pyle and Kenfig	5 and 4
1977	Miss W Aitken	Miss S Bamford	Formby Ladies	2 and 1
1978	Miss M De Lorenzi	Miss D Glenn	Largs	2 and 1
1979	Miss S Lapaire	Miss P Smillie	Edgbaston	19th hole
1980	Miss J Connachan	Miss L Bolton	Wrexham	2 holes
1981	Miss J Connachan	Miss P Grice	Woodbridge	20th hole
1982	Miss C Waite	Miss M Mackie	Edzell	6 and 5
1983	Miss E Orley	Miss A Walters	Leeds	7 and 6
1984	Miss C Swallow	Miss E Farquharson	Maesdu	1 hole
1985	Miss S Shapcott	Miss E Farquharson	Hesketh	3 and 1
1986	Miss S Croce	Miss S Bennett	West Kilbride	5 and 4

Senior Open Amateur Championship

Year	Winner	Venue	Score
1969	R Pattison	Formby	154
1970	K Bamber	Prestwick	150
1971	GH Pickard	Deal	150
1972	TC Hartley	St Andrews	147
1973	JT Jones	Hoylake	142
1974	MA Ivor-Jones	Moortown	149
1975	HJ Roberts	Turnberry	138
1976	WM Crichton	Berkshire	149
1977	Dr TE Donaldson	Panmure	228
1978	RJ White	Formby	225
1979	RJ White	Harlech	226
1980	JM Cannon	Prestwick St Nicholas	218
1981	T Branton	Hoylake	227
1982	RL Glading	Blairgowrie	218
1983	AJ Swann (USA)	Walton Heath	222
1984	JC Owens (USA)	Western Gailes	222
1985	D Morey (USA)	Hesketh	223
1986	AN Sturrock	Panmure	229

British Youths' Open Amateur Championship

Year	Winner	Club	Venue	Score
1954	JS More	Swanston, Edinburgh	Erskine	287
1955	B Stockdale	Royal Lytham St Annes	Pannal	297
1956	AF Bussell	Coxmoor	Barnton	287
1957	G Will	St Andrews	Pannal	290
1958	RH Kemp	Glamorganshire	Dumfries and County	281
1959	RA Jowle	Moseley	Pannal	286
1960	GA Caygill	Sunningdale	Pannal	279
1961	JS Martin	Kilbirnie Place	Bruntsfield	284
1962	GA Caygill	Sunningdale	Pannal	287
1963	AJ Low	St Andrews University	Pollok	283
1964	BW Barnes	Burnham and Berrow	Pannal	290
1965	PM Townsend	Porters Park	Gosforth Park	281
1966	PA Oosterhuis	Dulwich and Sydenham	Dalmahoy (54 holes)	219
1967	PJ Benka	Addington	Copt Heath	278
1968	PJ Benka	Addington	Ayr Belleisle	281
1969	JH Cook	Calcot Park	Lindrick	289
1970	B Dassu	Italy	Barnton	276
1971	P Elson	Coventry	Northamptonshire	277
1972	AH Chandler	Regent Park	Glasgow Gailes	281
1973	SC Mason	Goring and Streatley	Southport and Ainsdale	284
1974	DM Robertson	Dunbar	Downfield	284
1975	NA Faldo	Welwyn Garden City	Pannal	278
1976	ME Lewis	Henbury	Gullane	277

British Youths' Open Amateur Championship

continued

Year	Winner	Club	Venue	Score
1977	AWB Lyle	Hawkstone Park	Moor Park	285
1978	B Marchbank	Auchterarder	East Renfrewshire	278
1979	G Brand	Knowle	Woodhall Spa	291
1980	G Hay	Hilton Park	Troon	303
1981	T Antevik	Sweden	Gullane	290
1982	AP Parkin	Newtown	St Andrews New	280
1983	P Mayo	Newport	Sunningdale	290
1984	R Morris	Padeswick and Buckley	Blairgowrie	281
1985	J-M Olazabal	Spain	Ganton	281
1986	D Gilford	GB	Carnoustie	283

English Amateur Championship

Year	Winner	Runner-up	Venue	By
1925	TF Ellison	S Robinson	Hoylake	1 hole
1926	TF Ellison	Sq Ldr CH Hayward	Walton Heath	6 and 4
1927	TP Perkins	JB Beddard	Little Aston	2 and 1
1928	JA Stout	TP Perkins	Lytham St Annes	3 and 2
1929	W Sutton	EB Tipping	Northumberland	3 and 2
1930	TA Bourn	CE Hardman	Burnham	3 and 2
1931	LG Crawley	W Sutton	Hunstanton	1 hole
1932	EW Fiddian	AS Bradshaw	Sandwich	1 hole
1933	J Woollam	TA Bourn	Ganton	4 and 3
1934	S Lunt	LG Crawley	Formby	37th hole
1935	J Woollam	EW Fiddian	Hollinwell	2 and 1
1936	HG Bentley	JDA Langley	Deal	5 and 4
1937	JJ Pennink	LG Crawley	Saunton	6 and 5
1938	JJ Pennink	SE Banks	Moortown	2 and 1
1939	AL Bentley	W Sutton	Birkdale	5 and 4
1946	IR Patey	K Thom	Mid-Surrey	5 and 4
1947	GH Micklem	C Stow	Ganton	1 hole
1948	AGB Helm	HJR Roberts	Little Aston	2 and 1
1949	RJ White	C Stowe	Formby	5 and 4
1950	JDA Langley	IR Patey	Deal	1 hole
1951	GP Roberts	H Bennett	Hunstanton	39th hole
1952	E Millward	TJ Shorrock	Burnham and Berrow	2 holes
1953	GH Micklem	RJ White	Birkdale	2 and 1
1954	A Thirlwell	HG Bentley	Sandwich	2 and 1
1955	A Thirlwell	M Burgess	Ganton	7 and 6
1956	GB Wolstenholme	H Bennett	Lytham St Annes	1 hole
1957	A Walker	G Whitehead	Hoylake	4 and 3
1958	DN Sewell	DA Procter	Walton Heath	8 and 7
1959	GB Wolstenholme	MF Bonallack	Formby	1 hole
1960	DN Sewell	MJ Christmas	Hunstanton	41st hole
1961	Ian Caldwell	GJ Clark	Wentworth	37th hole
1962	MF Bonallack	MSR Lunt	Moortown	2 and 1
1963	MF Bonallack	A Thirlwell	Burnham and Berrow	4 and 3
1964	Dr D Marsh	R Foster	Hollinwell	1 hole
1965	MF Bonallack	CA Clark	Berkshire	3 and 2
1966	MSR Lunt	DJ Millensted	Lytham St Annes	3 and 2
1967	MF Bonallack	GE Hyde	Woodhall Spa	4 and 2
1968	MF Bonallack	PD Kelley	Ganton	12 and 11
1969	JH Cook	P Dawson	Sandwich	6 and 4
1970	Dr D Marsh	SG Birtwell	Birkdale	6 and 4
1971	W Humphreys	JC Davies	Burnham and Berrow	9 and 8
1972	H Ashby	R Revell	Northumberland	5 and 4
1973	H Ashby	SC Mason	Formby	5 and 4
1974	M James	JA Watts	Woodhall Spa	6 and 5
1975	N Faldo	D Eccleston	Lytham St Annes	6 and 4
1976	P Deeble	JC Davies	Ganton	3 and 1
1977	TR Shingler	J Mayell	Walton Heath	4 and 3
1978	P Downes	P Hoad	Birkdale	1 hole
1979	R Chapman	A Carman	Sandwich	6 and 5
1980	P Deeble	P McEvoy	Moortown	4 and 3
1981	D Blakeman	A Stubbs	Burnham and Berrow	3 and 1
1982	A Oldcorn	I Bradshaw	Hoylake	4 and 3
1983	G Laurence	A Brewer	Wentworth	7 and 6
1984	D Gilford	M Gerrard	Woodhall Spa	4 and 3
1985	R Winchester	P Robinson	Little Aston	1 hole
1986	J Langmead	B White	Hillside	2 and 1

English Ladies' Amateur Championship

Year	Winner	Runner-up	Venue	By
1912	Miss M Gardner	Mrs Cautley	Prince's, Sandwich	20th hole
1913	Mrs FW Brown	Mrs McNair	Nottingham	1 hole
(The 1912 and 1913 Championships were run by the National Golf Alliance)				
1914	Miss Cecil Leitch	Miss Bastin	Walton Heath	2 and 1
1915-18	*No Championship owing to the Great War*			
1919	Miss Cecil Leitch	Mrs Temple Dobell	St Annes	10 and 8
1920	Miss J Wethered	Miss Cecil Leitch	Sheringham	2 and 1
1921	Miss J Wethered	Mrs Mudford	St Annes	12 and 11
1922	Miss J Wethered	Miss J Stocker	Hunstanton	7 and 6
1923	Miss J Wethered	Mrs TA Lodge	Ganton	8 and 7
1924	Miss J Wethered	Miss DR Fowler	Cooden Beach	8 and 7
1925	Miss DR Fowler	Miss Joy Winn	Westward Ho!	9 and 7
1926	Miss M Gourlay	Miss E Corlett	Woodhall Spa	6 and 4
1927	Mrs Guedalla	Miss E Wilson	Pannal	1 hole
1928	Miss E Wilson	Miss D Pearson	Walton Heath	9 and 8
1929	Miss M Gourlay	Miss D Fishwick	Broadstone	6 and 5
1930	Miss E Wilson	Mrs RO Porter	Aldeburgh	12 and 11
1931	Miss W Morgan	Miss M Gourlay	Ganton	3 and 1
1932	Miss D Fishwick	Miss B Brown	Ashdown Forest	5 and 4
1933	Miss D Pearson	Miss M Johnson	Westward Ho!	5 and 3
1934	Miss P Wade	Miss M Johnson	Seacroft	4 and 3
1935	Mrs M Garon	Miss E Corlett	Birkdale	38th hole
1936	Miss W Morgan	Miss P Wade	Hayling	2 and 1
1937	Miss W Morgan	Miss M Fyshe	St Enodoc	4 and 2
1938	Miss E Corlett	Miss J Winn	Aldeburgh	2 and 1
1947	Miss M Wallis	Miss E Price	Ganton	3 and 1
1948	Miss Frances Stephens	Mrs Zara Bolton	Hayling	1 hole
1949	Mrs AC Critchley	The Lady Katherine Cairns	Burnham	3 and 2
1950	Hon Mrs A Gee	Miss Pamela Davies	Sheringham	8 and 6
1951	Miss J Bisgood	Mrs A Keiller	St Annes Old Links	2 and 1
1952	Miss Pamela Davies	Miss Jacqueline Gordon	Westward Ho!	6 and 5
1953	Miss J Bisgood	Miss J McIntyre	Prince's, Sandwich	6 and 5
1954	Miss Frances Stephens	Miss Elizabeth Price	Woodhall Spa	1 hole
1955	Mrs F Smith	Miss E Price	Moortown	4 and 3
1956	Miss Bridget Jackson	Mrs Ruth Ferguson	Hunstanton	2 and 1
1957	Miss J Bisgood	Miss M Nichol	Bournemouth	10 and 8
1958	Mrs MF Bonallack	Miss Bridget Jackson	Formby	3 and 2
1959	Miss R Porter	Mrs F Smith	Aldeburgh	5 and 4
1960	Miss M Nichol	Mrs MF Bonallack	Burnham	3 and 1
1961	Miss R Porter	Mrs P Reece	Littlestone	2 holes
1962	Miss J Roberts	Mrs MF Bonallack	Woodhall Spa	3 and 1
1963	Mrs MF Bonallack	Miss E Chadwick	Liphook	7 and 6
1964	Mrs AD Spearman	Miss M Everard	Lytham St Annes	6 and 5
1965	Miss R Porter	Miss G Cheetham	Whittington Barracks	6 and 5
1966	Miss J Greenhalgh	Mrs JC Holmes	Hayling Island	3 and 1
1967	Miss A Irvin	Mrs A Pickard	Alwoodley	3 and 2
1968	Mrs S Barber	Miss D Oxley	Hunstanton	5 and 4
1969	Miss B Dixon	Miss M Wenyon	Burnham and Berrow	6 and 4
1970	Miss D Oxley	Mrs S Barber	Rye	3 and 2
1971	Miss D Oxley	Mrs S Barber	Hoylake	5 and 4
1972	Miss M Everard	Mrs MF Bonallack	Woodhall Spa	2 and 1
1973	Miss M Walker	Miss C Le Feuvre	Broadstone	6 and 5
1974	Miss A Irvin	Mrs J Thornhill	Sunningdale	1 hole
1975	Miss B Huke	Miss L Harrold	Birkdale	2 and 1
1976	Miss L Harrold	Mrs A Uzielli	Hollinwell	3 and 2
1977	Miss V Marvin	Miss M Everard	Burnham and Berrow	1 hole
1978	Miss V Marvin	Miss R Porter	West Sussex	2 and 1
1979	Miss J Greenhalgh	Mrs S Hedges	Hoylake	2 and 1
1980	Miss B New	Miss J Walter	Aldeburgh	3 and 2
1981	Miss D Christison	Miss S Cohen	Cotswold Hills	2 holes
1982	Miss J Walter	Miss C Nelson	Brancepeth Castle	4 and 3
1983	Mrs L Bayman	Miss C Mackintosh	Hayling Island	4 and 3
1984	Miss C Waite	Mrs L Bayman	Hunstanton	3 and 2
1985	Miss P Johnson	Mrs L Bayman	Ferndown	1 hole
1986	Mrs J Thornhill	Miss S Shapcott	Princes	3 and 1

English Ladies' Under-23 Championship

Instituted 1978

Year	Winner	Venue	Score
1978	Miss S Bamford	Caldy	228
1979	Miss B Cooper	Coxmoor	223
1980	Miss B Cooper	Porters Park	226
1981	Miss J Soulsby	Willesley Park	220
1982	Miss M Gallagher	Highpost	221
1983	Miss P Grice	Hallamshire	219
1984	Miss P Johnson	Moor Park	300
1985			
1986	Miss S Shapcott		

English Open Amateur Stroke Play Championship

(formerly Brabazon Trophy)

Year	Winner	Club	Venue	Score
1947	DMG Sutherland			306
1948	Chas Stowe			299
1949	PB Hine			287
1950	RJ White			294
1951	RJ White			293
1952	PF Scrutton			290
1953	Chas Stowe			283
1954	PF Scrutton			302
1955	PF Scrutton			283
1956	Stanley Fox			292
For later years see English Open Amateur Stroke Play Championship				
1957	D Sewell	Hook Heath	Moortown	287
1958	AH Perowne	Norwich	Birkdale	289
1959	D Sewell	Hook Heath	Hollinwell	300
1960	GB Wolstenholme	Sunningdale	Ganton	286
1961	RDBM Shade	Duddingston	Hoylake	284
1962	A Slater	Wakefield	Woodhall Spa	209
1963	RDBM Shade	Duddingston	Birkdale	306
1964	MF Bonallack	Thorpe Hall	Deal	290
1965	CA Clark DJ Millensted MJ Burgess	Ganton Wentworth West Sussex } tie	Formby	289
1966	PM Townsend	Porters Park	Hunstanton	282
1967	RDBM Shade	Duddingston	Saunton	299
1968	MF Bonallack	Thorpe Hall	Walton Heath	210
1969	R Foster MF Bonallack	Bradford Thorpe Hall } tie	Moortown	290
1970	R Foster	Bradford	Little Aston	287
1971	MF Bonallack	Thorpe Hall	Hillside	294
1972	PH Moody	Notts	Hoylake	296
1973	R Revell	Farnham	Hunstanton	294
1974	N Sundelson	South Africa	Moortown	291
1975	AW Lyle	Hawkstone Park	Hollinwell	298
1976	P Hedges	Langley Park	Saunton	294
1977	AWB Lyle	Hawkstone Park	Hoylake	293
1978	G Brand	Knowle	Woodhall Spa	289
1979	D Long	Shandon Park	Little Aston	291
1980	R Rafferty P McEvoy	Warrenpoint Copt Heath } tie	Hunstanton	293
1981	P Way	Neville	Hillside	292
1982	P Downes	Coventry	Woburn	299
1983	C Banks	Notts	Hollinwell	294
1983	C Banks	Stanton-on-the-Wolds	Hollinwell	294
1984	M Davis	Thorndon Park	Royal Cinque Ports	286
1985	R Roper P Baker	Catterick Garrison Lillieshall Park } tie	Seaton Carew	296
1986	R Kaplan	South Africa	Sunningdale	286

English County Championship (Men)

Year	Winner	Year	Winner	Year	Winner
1928	Warwickshire	1953	Yorkshire	1971	Staffordshire
1929	Lancashire	1954	Cheshire	1972	Berks, Bucks, Oxon
1930	Lancashire	1955	Yorkshire	1973	Yorkshire
1931	Yorkhire	1956	Staffordshire	1974	Lincolnshire
1932	Surrey	1957	Surrey	1975	Staffordshire
1933	Yorkshire	1958	Surrey	1976	Warwickshire
1934	Worcestershire	1959	Yorkshire	1977	Warwickshire
1935	Worcestershire	1960	Northumberland	1978	Kent
1936	Surrey	1961	Lancashire	1979	Gloucestershire
1937	Lancashire	1962	Northumberland	1980	Surrey
1938	Staffordshire	1963	Yorkshire	1981	Surrey
1939	Worcestershire	1964	Northumberland	1982	Yorkshire
1947	Staffordshire	1965	Northumberland	1983	Berks, Bucks, Oxon
1948	Staffordshire	1966	Surrey	1984	Yorkshire
1949	Lancashire	1967	Lancashire	1985	Devon Hertfordshire
1950	*Not played*	1968	Surrey	1986	Hertfordshire
1951	Lancashire	1969	Berks, Bucks, Oxon		
1952	Yorkshire	1970	Gloucestershire		

English Girls' Championship

Year	Winner	Runner-up	Venue	By
1964	Miss S Ward	Miss P Tredinnick	Wollaton Park	2 and 1
1965	Miss D Oxley	Miss A Payne	Edgbaston	2 holes
1966	Miss B Whitehead	Miss D Oxley	Woodbridge	1 hole
1967	Miss A Willard	Miss G Holloway	Burhill	1 hole
1968	Miss K Phillips	Miss C le Feuvre	Harrogate	6 and 5
1969	Miss C le Feuvre	Miss K Phillips	Hawkstone Park	2 and 1
1970	Miss C le Feuvre	Miss M Walker	High Post	2 and 1
1971	Miss C Eckersley	Miss J Stevens	Liphook	4 and 3
1972	Miss C Barker	Miss R Kelly	Trentham	4 and 3
1973	Miss S Parker	Miss S Thurston	Lincoln	19th hole
1974	Miss C Langford	Miss L Harrold	Knowle	2 and 1
1975	Miss M Burton	Miss R Barry	Formby	6 and 5
1976	Miss H Latham	Miss D Park	Moseley	3 and 2
1977	Miss S Bamford	Miss S Jolly	Chelmsford	21st hole
1978	Miss P Smillie	Miss J Smith	Willesley Park	3 and 2
1979	Miss L Moore	Miss P Barry	Cirencester	1 hole
1980	Miss P Smillie	Miss J Soulsby	Kedleston Park	3 and 2
1981	Miss J Soulsby	Miss C Waite	Worksop	7 and 5
1982	Miss C Waite	Miss P Grice	Wilmslow	3 and 2
1983	Miss P Grice	Miss K Mitchell	West Surrey	2 and 1
1984	Miss C Swallow	Miss S Duhig	Bath	3 and 1
1985	Miss L Fairclough	Miss K Mitchell	Coventry	6 and 5
1986	Miss S Shapcott	Miss N Way	Huddersfield	7 and 6

England and Wales (Ladies') County Finals

Year	Winner	Year	Winner	Year	Winner
1908	Lancashire	1926	Surrey	1938	Lancashire
1909	Surrey	1927	Yorkshire	1947	Surrey
1910	Cheshire	1928	Cheshire	1948	Yorkshire
1911	Cheshire	1929	Yorkshire	1949	Surrey
1912	Cheshire	1930	Surrey	1950	Yorkshire
1913	Surrey	1931	Middlesex	1951	Lancashire
1920	Middlesex	1932	Cheshire	1952	Lancashire
1921	Surrey	1933	Yorkshire	1953	Surrey
1922	Surrey	1934	Surrey	1954	Warwickshire
1923	Surrey	1935	Essex	1955	Surrey
1924	Surrey	1936	Surrey	1956	Kent
1925	Surrey	1937	Surrey	1957	Middlesex

England and Wales (Ladies') County Finals

continued

Year	Winner	Year	Winner	Year	Winner
1958	Lancashire	1968	Surrey	1978	Glamorgan
1959	Middlesex	1969	Lancashire	1979	Essex
1960	Lancashire	1970	Yorkshire	1980	Lancashire
1961	Middlesex	1971	Kent	1981	Glamorgan
1962	Staffordshire	1972	Kent	1982	Surrey
1963	Warwickshire	1973	Northumberland	1983	Surrey
1964	Lancashire	1974	Surrey	1984	Surrey/Yorkshire
1965	Staffordshire	1975	Glamorgan	1985	
1966	Lancashire	1976	Staffordshire	1986	
1967	Lancashire	1977	Essex		

Irish Open Championship

Year	Winner	Club/Country	Venue	Score
1927	George Duncan	Wentworth	Portmarnock	312
1928	ER Whitcombe	Meyrick Park	Newcastle	288
1929	Abe Mitchell	Unattached	Portmarnock	309
1930	CA Whitcombe	Crews Hill	Portrush	289
1931	EW Kenyon	West Lancs	Dollymount	291
1932	AH Padgham	Royal Ashdown Forest	Cork	283
1933	EW Kenyon	West Lancs	Malone	286
1934	S Easterbrook	Knowle	Portmarnock	284
1935	ER Whitcombe	Meyrick Park	Newcastle	292
1936	RA Whitcombe	Parkstone	Dollymount	281
1937	B Gadd	West Cheshire	Portrush	284
1938	AD Locke	South Africa	Portmarnock	292
1939	A Lees	Dore and Totley	Newcastle	287
1946	F Daly	Belfast	Portmarnock	288
1947	H Bradshaw	Kilcroney	Portrush	290
1948	DJ Rees	South Herts	Portmarnock	295
1949	H Bradshaw	Kilcroney	Belvoir Park, Belfast	286
1950	HO Pickworth	Australia	Dollymount	287
1951-52	*No Championship*			
1953	EC Brown	Unattached	Belvoir Park, Belfast	272

Discontinued until 1975 when renewed with Carrolls sponsoring. *See under Major Professional Sponsored Tournaments–Carrolls Irish Open*

Irish Amateur Championship

Instituted 1893

Year	Winner	Runner-up	Venue	By
1931	J Burke	FP McConnell	Rosses Point	6 and 4
1932	J Burke	M Crowley	Portrush	6 and 5
1933	J Burke	GT McMullan	Cork	3 and 2
1934	JC Brown	Roy McConnell	Rosslare	6 and 5
1935	Roy McConnell	J Burke	Galway	2 and 1
1936	J Burke	Roy McConnell	Castlerock	7 and 6
1937	J Bruen, Jun	J Burke	Ballybunion	3 and 2
1938	J Bruen, Jun	R Simcox	Rathfarnham Castle	3 and 2
1939	GH Owens	Roy McConnell	Rosses Point	6 and 5
1940	J Burke	WM O'Sullivan	Dollymount	4 and 3
1946	J Burke	RC Ewing	Dollymount	2 and 1
1947	J Burke	J Fitzsimmons	Lahinch	2 holes
1948	RC Ewing	BJ Scannell	Portrush	3 and 2
1949	J Carroll	Pat Murphy	Galway	4 and 3
1950	B Herlihy	BC McManus	Baltray	4 and 3
1951	M Power	JB Carr	Cork	3 and 2
1952	TW Egan	JC Brown	Holywood, Belfast	41st hole
1953	J Malone	M Power	Rosses Point	2 and 1
1954	JB Carr	J Forsythe	Carlow	4 and 3
1955	Dr James Mahon	George Crosbie	Lahinch	3 and 2
1956	Garry Love	George Crosbie	Malone	37th hole
1957	JB Carr	George Crosbie	Galway	2 holes
1958	RC Ewing	GA Young	Ballybunion	5 and 3
1959	T Craddock	JB Carr	Portmarnock	38th hole
1960	M Edwards	N Fogarty	Portstewart	6 and 5
1961	D Sheahan	J Brown	Rosses Point	5 and 4
1962	M Edwards	J Harrington	Baltray	42nd hole
1963	JB Carr	EC O'Brien	Killarney	2 and 1
1964	JB Carr	A McDade	Co Down	6 and 5
1965	JB Carr	T Craddock	Rosses Point	3 and 2

Irish Amateur Championship

continued

Year	Winner	Runner-up	Venue	By
1966	D Sheahan	J Faith	Dollymount	3 and 2
1967	JB Carr	PD Flaherty	Lahinch	1 hole
1968	M O'Brien	F McCarroll	Portrush	2 and 1
1969	V Nevin	J O'Leary	Co Sligo	1 hole
1970	DB Sheahan	M Bloom	Grange	2 holes
1971	R Kane	M O'Brien	Ballybunion	3 and 2
1972	K Stevenson	B Hoey	Co Down	2 and 1
1973	RKM Pollin	RM Staunton	Rosses Point	1 hole
1974	R Kane	M Gannon	Portmarnock	5 and 4
1975	MD O'Brien	JA Bryan	Cork	5 and 4
1976	D Brannigan	D O'Sullivan	Portrush	2 holes
1977	M Gannon	A Hayes	Westport	19th hole
1978	M Morris	T Cleary	Carlow	1 hole
1979	J Harrington	MA Gannon	Ballybunion	2 and 1
1980	R Rafferty	MJ Bannon	Co Down	8 and 7
1981	D Brannigan	E McMenamin	Co Sligo	19th hole
1982	P Walton	V Smyth	Woodbrook	7 and 6
1983	T Corridan	E Power	Killarney	2 holes
1984	CB Hoey	L McNamara	Malone	20th hole
1985	D O'Sullivan	D Branigan	Westport	1 hole
1986	J McHenry	P Rayfus	Dublin	4 and 3

Irish National Professional Championship

Instituted 1907

Year	Winner	Club	Venue	Score
1931	J McCartney	Ormeau	Portstewart	273
1932	H McNeill	Portrush	Dollymount	304
1933	J Adams	Co Down	Castlerock	291
1934	W Nolan	Portmarnock	Kingstown	282
1935	S Fairweather	Malone	Belfast	293
1936	J McCartney	Holywood	Galway	281
1937	PJ Mahon	Royal Dublin	Portmarnock	298
1938	PJ Mahon	Royal Dublin	Portrush	291
1939	PJ Mahon	Royal Dublin	Bundoran	290
1940	F Daly	City of Derry	Little Island	305
1941	H Bradshaw	Kilcroney	Rosses Point	293
1942	H Bradshaw	Kilcroney	Hermitage	285
1943	H Bradshaw	Kilcroney	Dun Laoghaire	277
1944	H Bradshaw	Kilcroney	Hermitage	291
1945	C McKendrick	Douglas (Cork)	Kilkee	283
1946	F Daly	Balmoral	Clandeboye	285
1947	H Bradshaw	Kilcroney	Baltray	291
1948	J McKenna	Douglas (Cork)	Galway	285
1949	Christopher Kane	Royal Dublin	Portrush	301
1950	H Bradshaw	Portmarnock	Grange	277
1951	H Bradshaw	Portmarnock	Balmoral	280
1952	F Daly	Balmoral	West Meath	284
1953	H Bradshaw	Portmarnock	Dundalk	272
1954	H Bradshaw	Portmarnock	Newcastle	300
1955	E Jones	Carlow	Castletroy	276
1956	C Greene	Mill Town	Clandeboye	281
1957	H Bradshaw	Portmarnock	Ballybunion	286
1958	C O'Connor	Killarney	Belfast	279
1959	NV Drew	Knock	Mullingar	282
1960	C O'Connor	Royal Dublin	Warrenpoint	271
1961	C O'Connor	Royal Dublin	Lahinch	280
1962	C O'Connor	Royal Dublin	Bangor	264
1963	C O'Connor	Royal Dublin	Little Island	271
1964	E Jones	Bangor	Knock	279
1965	C O'Connor	Royal Dublin	Mullingar	283
1966	C O'Connor	Royal Dublin	Warrenpoint	269
1967	H Boyle	Jacobs Golf Centre	Tullamore (3 rounds)	214
1968	C Greene	Mill Town	Knock	282
1969	J Martin	Unattached	Dundalk	268
1970	H Jackson	Knockbracken	Massereene	283
1971	C O'Connor	Royal Dublin	Galway	278
1972	J Kinsella	Castle	Bundoran	289
1973	J Kinsella	Castle	Limerick	284
1974	E Polland	Balmoral	Portstewart	277
1975	C O'Connor	Royal Dublin	Carlow	275
1976	P McGuirk	Co Louth	Waterville	291

From 1977 sponsored by Rank Xerox

Irish National Professional Championship
continued

Year	Winner	Club	Venue	Score
1977	P Skerritt	St Annes	Woodbrook	281
1978	C O'Connor	Royal Dublin	Dollymount	286
1979	D Smyth	Bettystown	Dollymount (54 holes)	215
1980	D Feherty	Balmoral	Dollymount	283
1981	D Jones	Bangor	Woodbrook	283
1982	D Feherty	Balmoral	Woodbrook	287
1983	L Higgins	Waterville	Woodbrook	275
1984	M Sludds		Skerries	277
1985	DJ Smyth		Co Louth	204
(Played over 54 holes due to bad weather)				
1986	DJ Smyth		Waterville	282

Irish Girls' Championship

Year	Winner	Runner-up	Venue	By
1951	Miss Jocelyn Davies	Miss Irene Hurst	Milltown	3 and 2
1952	Miss Jane Redgate	Miss Ann B Phillips	Grange	22nd hole
1953	Miss Jane Redgate	Miss Irene Hurst	Grange	4 and 3
1954-60	*Suspended*			
1961	Miss M Coburn	Miss C McAuley	Portrush	6 and 5
1962	Miss Pearl Boyd	Miss Patricia Atkinson	Elm Park	4 and 3
1963	Miss P Atkinson	Miss C Scarlett	Donaghadee	8 and 7
1964	Miss C Scarlett	Miss A Maher	Milltown	6 and 5
1965	Miss V Singleton	Miss P McKenzie	Ballycastle	7 and 6
1966	Miss M McConnell	Miss D Hulme	Dun Laoghaire	3 and 2
1967	Miss M McConnell	Miss C Wallace	Portrush	6 and 5
1968	Miss C Wallace	Miss A McCoy	Louth	3 and 1
1969	Miss EA McGregor	Miss M Sheenan	Knock	6 and 5
1970	Miss EA McGregor	Miss J Mark	Greystones	3 and 2
1971	Miss J Mark	Miss C Nesbitt	Belfast	3 and 2
1972	Miss P Smyth	Miss M Governey	Elm Park	1 hole
1973	Miss M Governey	Miss R Hegarty	Mullingar	3 and 1
1974	Miss R Hegarty	Miss M Irvine	Castletroy	2 holes
1975	Miss M Irvine	Miss P Wickham	Carlow	2 and 1
1976	Miss P Wickham	Miss R Hegarty	Castle	5 and 3
1977	Miss A Ferguson	Miss R Walsh	Birr	3 and 2
1978	Miss C Wickham	Miss B Gleeson	Killarney	1 hole
1979	Miss L Bolton	Miss B Gleeson	Milltown	3 and 2
1980	Miss B Gleeson	Miss L Bolton	Kilkenny	5 and 3
1981	Miss B Gleeson	Miss E Lynn	Donegal	1 hole
1982	Miss D Langan	Miss S Lynn	Headfort	5 and 4
1983	Miss E McDaid	Miss S Lynn	Ennis	20th hole
1984	Miss S Sheehan	Miss L Tormey	Thurles	6 and 4
1985	Miss S Sheehan	Miss D Hanna	Laytown/Bettystown	5 and 4
1986	Miss D Mahon	Miss T Eakin	Mallow	

Irish Ladies' Amateur Championship

Instituted 1894

Year	Winner	Runner-up	Venue	By
1930	Mrs JB Walker	Mrs JF Jameson	Portmarnock	2 and 1
1931	Miss Pentony	Mrs JH Todd	Rosses Point	2 and 1
1932	Miss B Latchford	Miss D Ferguson	Ballybunion	7 and 5
1933	Miss Pentony	Miss F Blacke	Newcastle	3 and 2
1934	Mrs P Sherlock Fletcher	Mrs JB Walker	Portmarnock	3 and 2
1935	Miss D Ferguson	Miss Ellis	Rosapenna	2 and 1
1936	Miss C Tiernan	Miss S Moore	Ballybunion	7 and 6
1937	Mrs HV Glendinning	Mrs EL Kidd	Portrush	37th hole
1938	Mrs J Beck	Miss B Jackson	Portmarnock	5 and 4
1939	Miss C MacGeagh	Miss E Gildea	Bundoran	1 hole
1946	Miss P Garvey	Mrs V Reddan	Lahinch	39th hole
1947	Miss P Garvey	Miss C Syme	Portrush	5 and 4
1948	Miss P Garvey	Mrs Val Reddan	Rosslare	9 and 7
1949	Miss C Syme	Mrs J Beck	Baltray	9 and 7
1950	Miss P Garvey	Mrs T Marks	Rosses Point	6 and 4
1951	Miss P Garvey	Miss D Forster	Ballybunion	12 and 10
1952	Miss DM Forster	Mrs PG McCann	Newcastle	3 and 2
1953	Miss P Garvey	Mrs Hegarty	Rosslare	8 and 7

Irish Ladies' Amateur Championship *continued*

Year	Winner	Runner-up	Venue	By
1954	Miss P Garvey	Mrs HV Glendinning	Portmarnock	13 and 12
1955	Miss P Garvey	Miss A O'Donohoe	Rosses Point	10 and 9
1956	Miss P O'Sullivan	Mrs JF Hegarty	Killarney	14 and 12
1957	Miss P Garvey	Mrs K McCann	Portrush	3 and 2
1958	Miss P Garvey	Mrs Z Fallon	Carlow	7 and 6
1959	Miss P Garvey	Miss H Colhoun	Lahinch	12 and 10
1960	Miss P Garvey	Mrs PG McCann	Cork	5 and 3
1961	Mrs K McCann	Miss A Sweeney	Newcastle	5 and 3
1962	Miss P Garvey	Mrs M Earner	Baltray	7 and 6
1963	Miss P Garvey	Miss E Barnett	Killarney	9 and 7
1964	Mrs Z Fallon	Miss P O'Sullivan	Portrush	37th hole
1965	Miss E Purcell	Miss P O'Sullivan	Mullingar	3 and 2
1966	Miss E Bradshaw	Miss P O'Sullivan	Rosslare	3 and 2
1967	Mrs G Brandom	Miss P O'Sullivan	Castlerock	3 and 2
1968	Miss E Bradshaw	Miss M McKenna	Lahinch	4 and 3
1969	Miss M McKenna	Mrs C Hickey	Ballybunion	3 and 2
1970	Miss P Garvey	Miss M Earner	Portrush	2 and 1
1971	Miss E Bradshaw	Miss M Mooney	Baltray	3 and 1
1972	Miss M McKenna	Mrs I Butler	Killarney	5 and 4
1973	Miss M Mooney	Miss M McKenna	Bundoran	2 and 1
1974	Miss M McKenna	Miss V Singleton	Lahinch	3 and 2
1975	Miss M Gorry	Miss E Bradshaw	Tramore	1 hole
1976	Miss C Nesbitt	Miss M McKenna	Rosses Point	20th hole
1977	Miss M McKenna	Miss R Hegarty	Ballybunion	2 holes
1978	Miss M Gorry	Mrs I Butler	Grange	4 and 3
1979	Miss M McKenna	Miss C Nesbitt	Donegal	6 and 5
1980	Miss C Nesbitt	Miss C Hourihane	Lahinch	1 hole
1981	Miss M McKenna	Miss M Kenny	Laytown & Bettystown	1 hole
1982	Miss M McKenna	Miss M Madill	Portrush	2 and 1
1983	Miss C Hourihane	Mrs V Hassett	Cork	6 and 4
1984	Miss C Hourihane	Miss M Madill	Rosses Point	19th hole
1985	Miss C Hourihane	Miss M McKenna	Waterville	4 and 3
1986	Mrs T O'Reilly	Miss E Higgins	Castlerock	4 and 3

Irish Seniors' Open Amateur Championship

Year	Winner	Venue	Score
1970	C Ewing	Lahinch	153
1971	J O'Sullivan	Rosslare	159
1972	B Scannell	Co Sligo	152
1973	JW Hulme	Warrenpoint	147
1974	Rev P Walsh	Roscrea	155
1975	SA O'Connor	Athy	152
1976	BJ Scannell	Woodbrook	150
1977	DB Somers	Warrenpoint	150
1978	DP Herlihy	Limerick	150
1979	P Kelly	Tara	156
1980	GN Fogarty	Galway	144
1981	GN Fogarty	Bundoran	149
1982	J Murray	Douglas	141
1983	F Sharpe	Courtown	153
1984	J Boston	Connemara	147
1985	J Boston	Newcastle	155
1986			

Irish Youths' Open Amateur Championship

Year	Winner	Venue	Score
1969	D Brannigan	Delgany	142
1970	LA Owens	Tullamore	286
1971	M Gannon	Athlone	277
1972	M Gannon	Mullingar	291
1973	J Purcell	Tullamore	289
1974	A Dunlop	Athlone	293
1975	P McNally	Edenderry	287
1976	R McCormack	Warrenpoint	294

Irish Youths' Open Amateur Championship

continued

Year	Winner	Venue	Score
1977	B McDaid	Athlone	290
1978	T Corridan	Thurles	279
1979	R Rafferty	Tullamore	293
1980	J McHenry	Clandeboye	296
1981	J McHenry	Westport	303
1982	K O'Donnell	Mullingar	286
1983	P Murphy	Cork	287
1984	J Morris	Bangor	292
1985	J McHenry	Co Sligo	287
1986			

Scottish Amateur Championship

Year	Winner	Runner-up	Venue	By
1922	J Wilson	E Blackwell	St Andrews	19th hole
1923	TM Burrell	Dr AR M'Callum	Troon	1 hole
1924	WW Mackenzie	W Tulloch	Aberdeen	3 and 2
1925	JT Dobson	WW Mackenzie	Muirfield	3 and 2
1926	WJ Guild	SO Shepherd	Leven	2 and 1
1927	A Jamieson, Jr	Rev DS Rutherford	Gailes	22nd hole
1928	WW Mackenzie	WE Dodds	Muirfield	5 and 3
1929	JT Bookless	JE Dawson	Aberdeen	5 and 4
1930	K Greig	T Wallace	Carnoustie	9 and 8
1931	J Wilson	A Jamieson, Jr	Prestwick	2 and 1
1932	J McLean	K Greig	Dunbar	5 and 4
1933	J McLean	KC Forbes	Aberdeen	6 and 4
1934	J McLean	W Campbell	Western Gailes	3 and 1
1935	H Thomson	J McLean	St Andrews	2 and 1
1936	ED Hamilton	R Neill	Carnoustie	1 hole
1937	H McInally	KG Patrick	Barassie	6 and 5
1938	ED Hamilton	R Rutherford	Muirfield	4 and 2
1939	H McInally	H Thomson	Prestwick	6 and 5
1946	EC Brown	R Rutherford	Carnoustie	3 and 2
1947	H McInally	J Pressley	Glasgow Gailes	10 and 8
1948	AS Flockhart	GN Taylor	Balgownie, Aberdeen	7 and 6
1949	R Wright	H McInally	Muirfield	1 hole
1950	WC Gibson	DA Blair	Prestwick	2 and 1
1951	JM Dykes	JC Wilson	St Andrews	4 and 2
1952	FG Dewar	JC Wilson	Carnoustie	4 and 3
1953	DA Blair	JW McKay	Western Gailes	3 and 1
1954	JW Draper	WGH Gray	Nairn	4 and 3
1955	RR Jack	AC Miller	Muirfield	2 and 1
1956	Dr FWG Deighton	A MacGregor	Troon	8 and 7
1957	JS Montgomerie	J Burnside	Balgownie	2 and 1
1958	WD Smith	IR Harris	Prestwick	6 and 5
1959	Dr FWG Deighton	RMK Murray	St Andrews	6 and 5
1960	JR Young	S Saddler	Carnoustie	5 and 3
1961	J Walker	SWT Murray	Western Gailes	4 and 3
1962	SWT Murray	RDBM Shade	Muirfield	2 and 1
1963	RDBM Shade	N Henderson	Troon	4 and 3
1964	RDBM Shade	J McBeath	Nairn	8 and 7
1965	RDBM Shade	GB Cosh	St Andrews	4 and 2
1966	RDBM Shade	CJL Strachan	Western Gailes	9 and 8
1967	RDBM Shade	A Murphy	Carnoustie	5 and 4
1968	GB Cosh	RL Renfrew	Muirfield	4 and 3
1969	JM Cannon	AH Hall	Troon	6 and 4
1970	CW Green	HB Stuart	Balgownie, Aberdeen	1 hole
1971	S Stephen	CW Green	St Andrews	3 and 2
1972	HB Stuart	AK Pirie	Prestwick	3 and 1
1973	IC Hutcheon	Allan Brodie	Carnoustie	3 and 2
1974	GH Murray	AK Pirie	Western Gailes	2 and 1
1975	D Greig	GH Murray	Montrose	7 and 6
1976	GH Murray	HB Stuart	St Andrews	6 and 5
1977	Allan Brodie	PJ McKellar	Troon	1 hole
1978	IA Carslaw	J Cuddihy	Downfield	7 and 6
1979	K Macintosh	PJ McKellar	Prestwick	5 and 4
1980	D Jamieson	CW Green	Balgownie, Aberdeen (18 holes)	2 and 1
1981	C Dalgleish	A Thomson	Western Gailes	7 and 6
1982	CW Green	G Macgregor	Carnoustie	1 hole
1983	CW Green	J Huggan	Gullane	1 hole
1984	A Moir	K Buchan	Renfrew	3 and 3
1985	D Carrick	D James	Southerness	4 and 2
1986	C Brooks	A Thomson	Monifieth	3 and 2

Scottish Open Amateur Stroke Play Championship

Year	Winner	Club	Venue	Score
1967	BJ Gallacher	Bathgate	Muirfield and Gullane	291
1968	RDBM Shade	Duddingston	Prestwick and Prestwick St Nicholas	282
1969	JS Macdonald	Dalmahoy	Carnoustie and Monifieth	288
1970	D Hayes	South Africa	Glasgow Gailes and Barassie	275
1971	IC Hutcheon	Monifieth	Leven and Lundin Links	277
1972	BN Nicholson	Nairn	Dalmahoy and Ratho Park	290
1973	DM Robertson GJ Clark	Dunbar Whitley Bay } tie	Dunbar and North Berwick	284
1974	IC Hutcheon	Monifieth	Blairgowrie and Alyth	283
1975	CW Green	Dumbarton	Nairn and Nairn Dunbar	295
1976	S Martin	Downfield	Monifieth and Carnoustie	283
1977	PJ McKellar	East Renfrewshire	Muirfield and Gullane	299
1978	AR Taylor	East Kilbride	Keir and Cawder	281
1979	IC Hutcheon	Monifieth	Lansdowne and Rosemount	296
1980	G Brand	Knowle	Musselburgh and R Musselburgh (54 holes)	207
1981	P Walton	Malahide	Erskine and Renfrew	287
1982	G Macgregor	Glencorse	Downfield and Camperdown	287
1983	G Murray	Fereneze	Irvine	291
1984	CW Green	Dumbarton	Blairgowrie	287
1985	C Montgomerie		Dunbar	274
1986	KH Walker		Carnoustie	289

Scottish Boys' Championship

Year	Winner	Runner-up	Venue	By
1935	D Blair	AG Lowe	North Berwick	5 and 3
1936	R Stewart	AH Nesbit	North Berwick	8 and 6
1937	RG Inglis	J Sibbald	North Berwick	1 hole
1938	RG Inglis	W Smeaton	North Berwick	1 hole
1939	KW Walker	JM Steel	North Berwick	9 and 8
1947	J Brydone	DH Reid	North Berwick	38th hole
1948	Ronald Nicol	DH Reid	North Berwick	3 and 1
1949	DH Reid	Ronald Nicol	North Berwick	5 and 4
1950	A Miller	R Brotherston	North Berwick	3 and 1
1951	I Young	DS Blair	North Berwick	12 and 10
1952	CB Thomson	IPA Rodger	North Berwick	38th hole
1953	Ronald Aitken	J Carter	North Berwick	5 and 4
1954	Maurice J Moir	Hamish McCrae	North Berwick	8 and 6
1955	George Will	James B Neish	North Berwick	8 and 6
1956	RDBM Shade	AJ Hanley	North Berwick	7 and 6
1957	JR Young	Ian Leitch	North Berwick	8 and 7
1958	J Grant	HC Brownlee	North Berwick	4 and 2
1959	HB Stuart	RT Walker	North Berwick	3 and 2
1960	L Carver	S Wilson	North Berwick	6 and 5
1961	Kelvin Thomson	G Wilson	North Berwick	10 and 8
1962	HF Urquhart	S MacDonald	North Berwick	3 and 2
1963	Finlay S Morris	Iain Clark	North Berwick	9 and 8
1964	WR Lockie	MD Cleghorn	North Berwick	1 hole
1965	RL Penman	J Wood	North Berwick	9 and 8
1966	J McTear	DG Greig	North Berwick	4 and 3
1967	DG Greig	I Cannon	North Berwick	2 and 1
1968	RD Weir	M Grubb	North Berwick	6 and 4
1969	RP Fyfe	IF Doig	North Berwick	4 and 2
1970	S Stephen	M Henry	North Berwick	38th hole
1971	JE Murray	AA Mackay	North Berwick	4 and 3
1972	DM Robertson	G Cairns	North Berwick	9 and 8
1973	R Watson	H Alexander	North Berwick	8 and 7

Scottish Boys' Championship
continued

Year	Winner	Runner-up	Venue	By
1974	DM Robertson	J Cuddihy	North Berwick	6 and 5
1975	A Brown	J Cuddihy	North Berwick	6 and 4
1976	B Marchbank	J Cuddihy	Dunbar	2 and 1
1977	JS Taylor	GJ Webster	Dunbar	3 and 2
1978	J Huggan	KW Stables	Dunbar	2 and 1
1979	DR Weir	S Morrison	West Kilbride	5 and 3
1980	R Gregan	AJ Currie	Dunbar	2 and 1
1981	C Stewart	G Mellon	Dunbar	3 and 2
1982	A Smith	J White	Dunbar	39th hole
1983	C Gillies	C Innes	Dunbar	38th hole
1984	K Buchan	L Vannet	Dunbar	2 and 1
1985	AD McQueen	FJ McCulloch	Dunbar	1 hole
1986	AG Tait	EA McIntosh	Dunbar	6 and 5

Scottish Boys' Open Amateur Stroke Play Championship

Year	Winner	Club	Venue	Score
1970	D Chillas	R Aberdeen	Carnoustie	298
1971	JE Murray	Baberton	Lanark	274
1972	S Martin	Downfield	Montrose	280
1973	S Martin	Carnoustie	Barnton	284
1974	PW Gallacher	Peebles	Lundin	290
1975	A Webster	Edzell	Kilmarnock Barassie	286
1976	A Webster	Edzell	Forfar	292
1977	J Huggan, L Mann (tie)	Winterfield	Renfrew	303
1978	R Fraser	Hilton Park	Arbroath	283
1979	L Mann	Carnoustie	Stirling	289
1980	ASK Glen	Ormesson (France)	Forfar	288
1981	J Gullen	Tillicoultry	Bellshill	296
1982	D Purdie	Turriff	Monifieth	296
1983	L Vannet	Carnoustie	Barassie	286
1984	K Walker		Carnoustie	280
1985	G Matthew	Melrose	Baberton	297
1986	C Cassells		Edzell	294

Scottish Girls' Amateur Championship

Year	Winner	Runner-up	Venue	By
1960	Miss J Hastings	Miss A Lurie	Kilmacolm	6 and 4
1961	Miss I Wylie	Miss W Clark	Murrayfield	3 and 1
1962	Miss I Wylie	Miss U Burnet	West Kilbride	3 and 1
1963	Miss M Norval	Miss S MacDonald	Carnoustie	6 and 4
1964	Miss JW Smith	Miss C Workman	West Kilbride	2 and 1
1965	Miss JW Smith	Miss I Walker	Leven	7 and 5
1966	Miss Jillian Hutton	Miss F Jamieson	Arbroath	2 holes
1967	Miss Jillian Hutton	Miss K Lackie	West Kilbride	4 and 2
1968	Miss M Dewar	Miss J Crawford	Dalmahoy	2 holes
1969	Miss C Panton	Miss A Coutts	Edzell	23rd hole
1970	Miss M Walker	Miss L Bennett	Largs	3 and 2
1971	Miss M Walker	Miss S Kennedy	Edzell	1 hole
1972	Miss G Cadden	Miss C Panton	Stirling	3 and 2
1973	Miss M Walker	Miss M Thomson	Cowal, Dunoon	1 hole
1974	Miss S Cadden	Miss D Reid	Arbroath	3 and 1
1975	Miss W Aitken	Miss S Cadden	Leven	1 hole
1976	Miss S Cadden	Miss D Mitchell	Dumfries and County	4 and 2
1977	Miss W Aitken	Miss G Wilson	West Kilbride	2 holes
1978	Miss J Connachan	Miss D Mitchell	Stirling	7 and 5
1979	Miss J Connachan	Miss G Wilson	Dunbar	3 and 1
1980	Miss J Connachan	Miss P Wright	Dumfries and County	21st hole
1981	Miss D Thomson	Miss P Wright	Barassie	2 and 1
1982	Miss S Lawson	Miss D Thomson	Montrose	1 hole
1983	Miss K Imrie	Miss D Martin	Leven	2 and 1
1984	Miss T Craik	Miss D Jackson	Peebles	3 and 2
1985	Miss E Farquharson	Miss E Moffat	West Kilbride	2 holes
1986	Miss C Lambert			

Scottish Girls' Open Stroke Play Championship

Year	Winner	Venue
1955	Miss M Fowler	Erskine
1956	Miss B McCorkindale	Erskine
1957	Miss M Fowler	Kilmacolm
1958	Miss R Porter	Ranfurly Castle
1959	Miss D Robb	Helensburgh
1960	Miss J Greenhalgh	Ranfurly Castle
1961	Miss D Robb	Whitecraigs
1962	Miss S Armitage	Dalmahoy
1963	Miss A Irvin	Dumfries
1964	Miss M Nuttall	Dalmahoy
1965	Miss I Wylie	Carnoustie
1966	Miss J Smith	Douglas Park
1967	Miss J Bourassa	Dunbar
1968	Miss K Phillips	Dumfries
1969	Miss K Phillips	Prestonfield
1970	Miss B Huke	Leven
1971	Miss B Huke	Dalmahoy
1972	Miss L Hope	Troon, Portland
1973	Miss G Cadden	Edzell
1974	Miss S Lambie	Stranraer
1975	Miss S Cadden	Lanark
1976	Miss S Cadden	Prestonfield
1977	Miss S Cadden	Edzell
1978	Miss J Connachan	Peebles
1979	Miss A Gemmill	Troon, Portland
1980	Miss J Connachan	Kirkcaldy
1981	Miss K Douglas	Downfield
1982	Miss J Rhodes	Dumfries & Galloway
1983	Miss S Lawson	Largs
1984	Miss S Lawson	Dunbar
1985	Miss K Imrie	Ballater
1986	Miss K Imrie	Dumfries & County

Scottish Ladies' Amateur Championship

Instituted 1903

Year	Winner	Runner-up	Venue	By
1905	Miss D Campbell	Miss MA Graham	North Berwick	19th hole
1906	Miss D Campbell	Miss AM Glover	Cruden Bay	3 and 1
1907	Miss F Teacher	Miss D Campbell	Troon	21st hole
1908	Miss D Campbell	Miss MA Cairns	Gullane	7 and 6
1909	Miss EL Kyle	Miss D Campbell	Machrihanish	3 and 1
1910	Miss EL Kyle	Miss AM Glover	Nairn	4 and 3
1911	Miss E Grant-Suttie	Miss IL Kyle	St Andrews	1 hole
1912	Miss DM Jenkins	Miss M Neil Fraser	Lossiemouth	4 and 2
1913	Miss JW McCulloch	Miss R MacKintosh	Machrihanish	4 and 3
1914	Miss ER Anderson	Miss FS Teacher	Muirfield	20th hole
1915-19	*War period*			
1920	Mrs JB Watson	Miss L Scroggie	Cruden Bay	5 and 3
1921	Mrs JB Watson	Mrs M Martin	Machrihanish	1 hole
1922	Mrs JB Watson	Miss A Kyle	St Andrews	2 and 1
1923	Mrs WH Nicholson	Mrs JB Watson	Lossiemouth	2 and 1
1924	Miss C Purvis-Russell-Montgomery	Miss H Cameron	Turnberry	5 and 4
1925	Miss J Percy	Miss E Grant-Suttie	Gullane	2 holes
1926	Miss MJ Wood	Mrs J Cochrane	Cruden Bay	2 and 1
1927	Miss B Inglis	Miss H Cameron	Machrihanish	1 hole
1928	Miss J McCulloch	Miss P Ramsay	St Andrews	3 and 1
1929	Mrs JB Watson	Miss D Park	Nairn	3 and 1
1930	Mrs AM Holm	Miss Doris Park	Turnberry	1 hole
1931	Miss J McCulloch	Miss Doris Park	Gullane	19th hole
1932	Mrs AM Holm	Mrs G Coates	Cruden Bay	23rd hole
1933	Miss MJ Couper	Mrs AM Holm	Turnberry	22nd hole
1934	Miss N Baird	Miss J Anderson	North Berwick	1 hole
1935	Miss M Robertson-Durham	Miss N Baird	Lossiemouth	20th hole
1936	Miss D Park	Miss CPR Montgomery	Turnberry	19th hole
1937	Mrs AM Holm	Mrs I Bowhill	Gleneagles	3 and 2

Scottish Ladies' Amateur Championship

continued

Year	Winner	Runner-up	Venue	By
1938	Miss J Anderson	Mrs AM Holm	Nairn	2 holes
1939	Miss J Anderson	Miss CM Park	Turnberry	19th hole
1947	Miss J Donald	Miss J Kerr	Elie	5 and 3
1948	Mrs AM Holm	Mrs Falconer	Gleneagles	5 and 4
1949	Miss J Donald	Mrs AM Holm	Troon	6 and 4
1950	Mrs AM Holm	Mrs EC Beddows	St Andrews	6 and 5
1951	Mrs G Valentine	Miss MC Paterson	Nairn	3 and 2
1952	Miss J Donald	Mrs RT Peel	Gullane	13 and 11
1953	Mrs G Valentine	Miss J Donald	Carnoustie	8 and 7
1954	Mrs RT Peel	Mrs G Valentine	Turnberry	7 and 6
1955	Mrs G Valentine	Miss N Couper	North Berwick	8 and 6
1956	Mrs G Valentine	Mrs AM Holm	Dornoch	8 and 7
1957	Miss M Speir	Mrs AM Holm	Troon	7 and 5
1958	Miss DT Sommerville	Miss JS Robertson	Elie	1 hole
1959	Miss JS Robertson	Miss B McCorkindale	Nairn	6 and 5
1960	Miss JS Robertson	Miss DT Sommerville	Turnberry	2 and 1
1961	Mrs I Wright (Miss Robertson)	Miss AM Lurie	St Andrews	1 hole
1962	Miss JB Lawrence	Mrs C Draper	Dornoch	5 and 4
1963	Miss JB Lawrence	Mrs IC Robertson	Troon	2 and 1
1964	Miss JB Lawrence	Mrs SM Reid	Gullane	5 and 3
1965	Mrs IC Robertson	Miss JB Lawrence	Nairn	5 and 4
1966	Mrs IC Robertson	Miss M Fowler	Machrihanish	2 and 1
1967	Miss J Hastings	Miss A Laing	North Berwick	5 and 3
1968	Miss Joan Smith	Mrs J Rennie	Carnoustie	10 and 9
1969	Mrs JH Anderson	Miss K Lackie	West Kilbride	5 and 4
1970	Miss A Laing	Mrs IC Robertson	Dunbar	1 hole
1971	Mrs IC Robertson	Mrs A Ferguson	Dornoch	3 and 2
1972	Mrs IC Robertson	Miss CJ Lugton	Machrihanish	5 and 3
1973	Mrs I Wright	Dr AJ Wilson	St Andrews	2 holes
1974	Dr AJ Wilson	Miss K Lackie	Nairn	22nd hole
1975	Miss LA Hope	Miss JW Smith	Elie	1 hole
1976	Miss S Needham	Miss T Walker	Machrihanish	3 and 2
1977	Miss CJ Lugton	Miss M Thomson	Dornoch	1 hole
1978	Mrs IC Robertson	Miss JW Smith	Prestwick	2 holes
1979	Miss G Stewart	Miss LA Hope	Gullane	2 and 1
1980	Mrs IC Robertson	Miss F Anderson	Carnoustie	1 hole
1981	Miss A Gemmill	Miss W Aitken	Stranraer	2 and 1
1982	Miss J Connachan	Miss P Wright	Troon	19th hole
1983	Miss G Stewart	Miss F Anderson	North Berwick	3 and 1
1984	Miss G Stewart	Miss A Gemmill	Dornoch	3 and 2
1985	Miss A Gemmill	Miss D Thomson	Barassie	2 and 1
1986	Mrs IC Robertson	Miss L Hope	St Andrews	3 and 2

Scottish Professional Championship

Instituted 1907

Year	Winner	Club	Venue	Score
1936	J Forrester	Cruden Bay	Lossiemouth	287
1937	WM Hastings	Kilmarnock	Barassie	305
1938	JH Ballingall	Balmore	Lundin Links	284
1939	W Davis	Dumfries and County	Inverness	295
1946	W Anderson	Murcar	Nairn	296
1947	J McCondichie	Hilton Park	Luffness	287
1948	J Panton	Glenbervie	Prestwick	299
1949	J Panton	Glenbervie	Nairn	282
1950	J Panton	Glenbervie	Longniddry	276
1951	J Panton	Glenbervie	Ayr, Belleisle	290
1952	J Campbell	Aberdeen	Lossiemouth	292
1953	H Thomson	Unattached	Gullane	283
1954	J Panton	Glenbervie	Turnberry	283
1955	J Panton	Glenbervie	Elie	272
1956	EC Brown	Buchanan Castle	Nairn	281
1957	EC Brown	Buchanan Castle	Barassie	284
1958	EC Brown	Buchanan Castle	Dornoch	286
1959	J Panton	Glenbervie	Turnberry	282
1960	EC Brown	Buchanan Castle	West Kilbride	278
1961	RT Walker	Downfield, Dundee	Forres	271
1962	EC Brown	Unattached	Dunbar	283
1963	WM Miller	Cardross	Crieff	284
1964	RT Walker	Downfield, Dundee	Machrihanish	277
1965	EC Brown	Cruden Bay	Forfar	271
1966	EC Brown J Panton	Cruden Bay Glenbervie } tie	Cruden Bay (36 holes)	137
1967	H Bannerman	Aberdeen	Montrose	279

Scottish Professional Championship

continued

Year	Winner	Club	Venue	Score
1968	EC Brown	Cruden Bay	Monktonhall	286
1969	G Cunningham	Troon Municipal	Machrihanish	284
1970	RDBM Shade	Duddingston	Montrose	276
1971	BJ Gallacher	Wentworth	Lundin	282
1972	H Bannerman	Banchory	Strathaven	268
1973	BJ Gallacher	Wentworth	Kings Links, Aberdeen	275
1974	BJ Gallacher	Wentworth	Drumpellier	276
1975	D Huish	North Berwick	Duddingston	279
1976	J Chillas	Crow Wood	Haggs Castle	286
1977	BJ Gallacher	Wentworth	Barnton	282
1978	S Torrance	Caledonian Hotel	Strathaven	269
1979	AWB Lyle	Hawkstone Park	Glasgow Gailes	274
1980	S Torrance	Caledonian Hotel	East Kilbride	273
1981	B Barnes	Caledonian Hotel	Dalmahoy	275
1982	B Barnes	Caledonian Hotel	Dalmahoy	286
1983	B Gallacher	Wentworth	Dalmahoy	276
(After play-off)				
1984	I Young		Dalmahoy	276
1985	S Torrance		Dalmahoy	277
1986	R Drummond		Glenbervie	270

Scottish Open Amateur Seniors' Championship

Instituted 1978

Year	Winner
1978	JM Cannon / GR Carmichael tie
1979	A Sinclair
1980	JM Cannon
1981	IR Harris / AN Sturrock / JL Hastings tie
1982	JM Cannon / J Niven tie
1983	WD Smith
1984	A Sinclair
1985	AN Sturrock
1986	R Glading

Scottish Youths' Open Amateur Stroke Play Championship

Instituted 1979

Year	Winner	Club	Venue	Score
1979	A Oldcorn	Ratho Park	Dalmahoy	217
1980	G Brand	Knowle	Monifieth and Ashludie	281
1981	S Campbell	Cawder	Cawder and Keir	279
1982	LS Mann	Carnoustie	Leven and Scoonie	270
1983	A Moir	McDonald	Mortonhall	284
1984	B Shields	Bathgate	Eastwood, Renfrew	
1985	H Kemp	Cawder	East Kilbride	282
1986	A Mednick	Sweden		

Welsh Amateur Championship

Instituted 1895

Year	Winner	Runner-up	Venue	By
1934	SB Roberts	GS Noon	Prestatyn	4 and 3
1935	R Chapman	GS Noon	Tenby	1 hole
1936	RM de Lloyd	G Wallis	Aberdovey	1 hole
1937	DH Lewis	R Glossop	Porthcawl	2 holes
1938	AA Duncan	SB Roberts	Rhyl	2 and 1
1946	JV Moody	A Marshman	Porthcawl	9 and 8
1947	SB Roberts	G Breen Turner	Harlech	8 and 7
1948	AA Duncan	SB Roberts	Porthcawl	2 and 1
1949	AD Evans	Mervyn A Jones	Aberdovey	2 and 1
1950	JL Morgan	DJ Bonnell	Southerndown	9 and 7
1951	JL Morgan	WI Tucker	Harlech	3 and 2
1952	AA Duncan	JL Morgan	Ashburnham	4 and 3
1953	SB Roberts	D Pearson	Prestatyn	5 and 3
1954	AA Duncan	K Thomas	Tenby	6 and 5
1955	TJ Davies	P Dunn	Harlech	38th hole
1956	A Lockley	WI Tucker	Southerndown	2 and 1
1957	ES Mills	H Griffiths	Harlech	2 and 1
1958	HC Squirrell	AD Lake	Conway	4 and 3
1959	HC Squirrell	N Rees	Porthcawl	8 and 7
1960	HC Squirrell	P Richards	Aberdovey	2 and 1
1961	AD Evans	J Toye	Ashburnham	3 and 2
1962	J Povall	HC Squirrell	Harlech	3 and 2
1963	WI Tucker	J Povall	Southerndown	4 and 3
1964	HC Squirrell	WI Tucker	Harlech	1 hole
1965	HC Squirrell	G Clay	Porthcawl	6 and 4
1966	WI Tucker	EN Davies	Aberdovey	6 and 5
1967	JK Povall	WI Tucker	Ashburnham	3 and 2
1968	J Buckley	J Povall	Conway	8 and 7
1969	JL Toye	EN Davies	Porthcawl	1 hole
1970	EN Davies	J Povall	Harlech	1 hole
1971	CT Brown	HC Squirrell	Southerndown	6 and 5
1972	EN Davies	JL Toye	Prestatyn	40th hole
1973	D McLean	T Holder	Ashburnham	6 and 4
1974	S Cox	EN Davies	Caernarvonshire	3 and 2
1975	JL Toye	WI Tucker	Porthcawl	5 and 4
1976	MPD Adams	WI Tucker	Harlech	6 and 5
1977	D Stevens	JKD Povall	Southerndown	3 and 2
1978	D McLean	A Ingram	Caernarvonshire	11 and 10
1979	TJ Melia	MS Roper	Ashburnham	5 and 4
1980	DL Stevens	G Clement	Prestatyn	10 and 9
1981	S Jones	G Davies	Porthcawl	5 and 3
1982	D Wood	G Davies	Harlech	8 and 7
1983	JR Jones	AP Parkin	Southerndown	2 holes
1984	JR Jones	A Llyr	Prestatyn	1 hole
1985	ED Jones	MA Macara	Ashburnham	2 and 1
1986	C Rees	B Knight	Conwy	1 hole

Welsh Amateur Stroke Play Championship

Year	Winner	Club	Venue	Score
1967	EN Davies	Llantrisant	Harlech	295
1968	JA Buckley	Rhos-on-Sea	Harlech	294
1969	DL Stevens	Llantrisant	Tenby	288
1970	JK Povall	Whitchurch	Newport	292
1971	EN Davies JL Toye	Llantrisant Radyr } tie	Harlech	296
1972	JR Jones	Wrexham	Pyle and Kenfig	299
1973	JR Jones	Caernarvonshire	Llandudno (Maesdu)	300
1974	JL Toye	Radyr	Tenby	307
1975	D McLean	Holyhead	Wrexham	288
1976	WI Tucker	Monmouthshire	Newport	282
1977	JA Buckley	Abergele and Pensarn	Prestatyn	302
1978	HJ Evans	Langland Bay	Pyle and Kenfig	300
1979	D McLean	Holyhead	Holyhead	289
1980	TJ Melia	Cardiff	Tenby	291
1981	D Evans	Leek	Wrexham	270
1982	JR Jones	Langland Bay	Cradoc	287
1983	G Davies	Pontypool	Aberdovey	287
1984	N Roderick	Portardawe	Newport	292
1985	MA Macara	Llandudno	Harlech	291
1986	M Calvert	Aberystwyth	Pyle and Kenfig	299

Welsh Boys' Championship

Year	Winner	Runner-up	Venue	By
1954	JWH Mitchell	DA Rees	Llandrindod Wells	8 and 6
1955	EW Griffith	DA Rees	Llandrindod Wells	3 and 2
1956	DA Rees	JP Hales	Llandrindod Wells	2 and 1
1957	P Waddilove	JG Jones	Llandrindod Wells	2 and 1
1958	P Waddilove	J Williams	Llandrindod Wells	1 hole
1959	C Gilford	JG Jones	Llandrindod Wells	6 and 4
1960	C Gilford	JL Toye	Llandrindod Wells	5 and 4
1961	AR Porter	JL Toye	Llandrindod Wells	3 and 2
1962	RC Waddilove	W Wadrup	Harlech	20th hole
1963	G Matthews	R Witchell	Penarth	6 and 5
1964	D Lloyd	M Walters	Conway	2 and 1
1965	G Matthews	DG Lloyd	Wenvoe Castle	7 and 6
1966	J Buckley	DP Owen	Holyhead	4 and 2
1967	J Buckley	DL Stevens	Glamorganshire	2 and 1
1968	J Buckley	C Brown	Maesdu	1 hole
1969	K Dabson	P Light	Glamorganshire	5 and 3
1970	P Tadman	A Morgan	Conway	2 and 1
1971	R Jenkins	T Melia	Ashburnham	3 and 2
1972	MG Chugg	RM Jones	Wrexham	3 and 2
1973	R Tate	N Duncan	Penarth	2 and 1
1974	D Williams	S Lewis	Llandudno	5 and 4
1975	G Davies	PG Garrett	Glamorganshire	20th hole
1976	JM Morrow	MG Mouland	Caernarvonshire	1 hole
1977	JM Morrow	MG Mouland	Glamorganshire	2 and 1
1978	JM Morrow	A Laking	Harlech	2 and 1
1979	P Mayo	M Hayward	Penarth	24th hole
1980	A Llyr	DK Wood	Llandudno (Maesdu)	2 and 1
1981	M Evans	P Webborn	Pontypool	5 and 4
1982	CM Rees	KH Williams	Prestatyn	2 holes
1983	MA Macara	RN Roderick	Radyr	1 hole
1984	GA Macara	D Bagg	Llandudno	1 hole
1985	B Macfarlane	R Herbert	Cardiff	1 hole
1986	C O'Carroll	GA Macara	Rhuddlan	1 hole

Welsh Close Championship

Year	Winner	Club	Venue	Score
1961	J Povall (Am)	Whitchurch	Southerndown	281
1962	S Mouland	Glamorganshire	Porthcawl	302
1963	H Gould	Southerndown	Wrexham	291
1964	B Bielby	Portmadoc	Tenby	297
1965	S Mouland	Glamorganshire	Penarth	281
1966	S Mouland	Glamorganshire	Conway	279
1967	S Mouland	Glamorganshire	Pyle and Kenfig (54 holes, fog)	219
1968	RJ Davies	South Herts	Southerndown	292
1969	JA Buckley (Am)	Rhos-on-Sea	Llandudno	274
1970	MPD Adams (Am)	Llantrisant	Tredegar Park	288
1971	*Discontinued*			

Welsh Professional Championship

Instituted 1904

Year	Winner	Club	Venue	Score
1930	H Palferman	Nantffranoon	Wrexham	302
1931	R Watts	Pennard	Newport	290
1932	WG Smalldon	Cardiff	Porthcawl	294
1933	F Collins	Llandudno	Rhyl	305
1934	CA Pickett	Creigiau	Swansea Bay	296
1935	F Hill	Llanwern	Penarth	281
1936	F Lloyd	Rhos-on-Sea	Prestatyn	291
1937	F Hill	St Mellons	Clyne	298
1938	WS Collins	North Wales	St Mellons	295
1939	C Grabham	Llandrindod Wells	Harlech	299
1946	H Gould	Royal Porthcawl	Porthcawl	308
1947	K Williams	Radyr	Llandrindod	280
1948	H Gould	Royal Porthcawl	Aberdovey	291

Welsh Professional Championship
continued

Year	Winner	Club	Venue	Score
1949	H Gould	Royal Porthcawl	Radyr	275
1950	G James	Newport (Mon)	Newport	303
1951	H Gould	Southerndown	Llandudno	305
1952	WS Collins	North Wales	Southerndown	301
1956	D Smalldon	Cardiff	Porthcawl	300
1957	J Black	Royal St David's	Llandudno (36 holes)	144
1958	RH Kemp, jun	Glamorganshire	Radyr	275
1959	D Smalldon	Cardiff	Newport	288
1960	RH Kemp, jun	Unattached	Llandudno	288
1961	S Mouland	Glamorganshire	Southerndown	286
1962	S Mouland	Glamorganshire	Porthcawl	302
1963	H Gould	Southerndown	Wrexham	291
1964	B Bielby	Portmadoc	Tenby	297
1965	S Mouland	Glamorganshire	Penarth	281
1966	S Mouland	Glamorganshire	Conway	279
1967	S Mouland	Glamorganshire	Pyle and Kenfig (54 holes, fog)	219
1968	RJ Davies	South Herts	Southerndown	292
1969	S Mouland	Glamorganshire	Llandudno	277
1970	W Evans	Pennard	Tredegar Park	289
1971	J Buckley	North Wales	St Pierre	291
1972	J Buckley	Rhos-on-Sea	Porthcawl	298
1973	A Griffiths	Wrexham	Newport	289
1974	M Hughes	Aberystwyth	Cardiff	284
1975	C DeFoy	Bryn Meadows	Whitchurch	285
1976	S Cox	Wenvoe Castle	Radyr	284
From 1977 sponsored by Rank Xerox				
1977	C DeFoy	Calcot Park	Glamorganshire	135
1978	BGC Huggett	Cambridgeshire Hotel	Whitchurch	145
1979	*Cancelled*			
1980	A Griffiths	Llanymynech	Cardiff	139
1981	C DeFoy	Coombe Hill	Cardiff	139
1982	C DeFoy	Coombe Hill	Cardiff	137
1983	S Cox	Wenvoe Castle	Cardiff	136
1984	K Jones	Caldy	Cardiff	135
1985	D Llewellyn		Whitchurch	132
1986	P Parkin		Whitchurch	142

Welsh Girls' Amateur Championship

Year	Winner	Runner-up	Venue	By
1957	Miss A Coulman	Miss S Wynn-Jones	Newport (Mon)	1 hole
1958	Miss S Wynn-Jones	Miss A Coulman	Conway	3 and 1
1959	Miss C Mason	Miss T Williams	Glamorgan	3 and 2
1960	Miss A Hughes	Miss D Wilson	Llandrindod Wells	6 and 4
1961	Miss Jill Morris	Miss S Kelly	North Wales	3 and 2
1962	Miss Jill Morris	Miss Peta Morgan	Southerndown	4 and 3
1963	Miss A Hughes	Miss A Brown	Conway	8 and 7
1964	Miss A Hughes	Miss M Leigh	Holyhead	5 and 3
1965	Miss A Hughes	Miss A Reardon-Hughes	Swansea Bay	19th hole
1966	Miss S Hales	Miss J Rogers	Prestatyn	1 hole
1967	Miss E Wilkie	Miss L Humphreys	Pyle and Kenfig	1 hole
1968	Miss L Morris	Miss J Rogers	Portmadoc	1 hole
1969	Miss L Morris	Miss L Humphreys	Wenvoe Castle	5 and 3
1970	Miss T Perkins	Miss P Light	Rhuddlan	2 and 1
1971	Miss P Light	Miss P Whitley	Glamorganshire	4 and 3
1972	Miss P Whitley	Miss P Light	Llandudno (Maesdu)	2 and 1
1973	Miss V Rawlings	Miss T Perkins	Whitchurch	19th hole
1974	Miss L Isherwood	Miss S Rowlands	Wrexham	4 and 3
1975	Miss L Isherwood	Miss S Rowlands	Swansea Bay	1 hole
1976	Miss K Rawlings	Miss C Parry	Rhuddlan	5 and 4
1977	Miss S Rowlands	Miss D Taylor	Clyne	7 and 5
1978	Miss S Rowlands	Miss G Rees	Abergele	3 and 2
1979	Miss M Rawlings	Miss J Richards	St Mellons	19th hole
1980	Miss K Davies	Miss M Rawlings	Vale of Llangollen	19th hole
1981	Miss M Rawlings	Miss F Connor	Radyr	4 and 3
1982	Miss K Davies	Miss K Beckett	Wrexham	6 and 5
1983	Miss N Wesley	Miss J Foster	Whitchurch	4 and 2
1984	Miss J Foster	Miss J Evans		6 and 5
1985	Miss J Foster	Miss S Caley	Langland Bay	6 and 5
1986	Miss J Foster			

Welsh Ladies' Amateur Championship

Instituted 1905

Year	Winner	Runner-up	Venue	By
1930	Miss MJ Jeffreys	Mrs Rieben	Llandudno	2 holes
1931	Miss M Jeffreys	Miss B Pyman	Southerndown	4 and 3
1932	Mrs I Rieben	Miss MJ Jeffreys	Aberdovey	2 and 1
1933	Miss M Jeffreys	Mrs Bridge	Porthcawl	2 and 1
1934	Miss I Rieben	Miss MJ Jeffreys	Harlech	3 and 2
1935	*Owing to snowstorm play had to be abandoned in third round–Venue Tenby*			
1936	Mrs Rieben	Miss M Thompson	Prestatyn	2 and 1
1937	Mrs GS Emery	Dr P Whitaker	Porthcawl	10 and 9
1938	Miss B Pyman	Mrs GS Emery	Llandudno	1 hole
1939	Mrs B Burrell	Miss H Reynolds	Swansea	2 and 1
1947	Miss M Barron	Miss E Jones	Prestatyn	1 hole
1948	Mrs N Seely	Miss M Barron	Prestatyn	12 and 11
1949	Miss S Bryan-Smith	Mrs ED Brown	Newport	3 and 2
1950	Dr Garfield Evans	Miss N Cook	Porthcawl	2 and 1
1951	Mrs E Bromley-Davenport	Miss N Cook	Harlech	1 hole
1952	Miss E Lever	Miss P Roberts	Southerndown	6 and 5
1953	Miss Nancy Cook	Miss Elsie Lever	Llandudno	3 and 2
1954	Miss Nancy Cook	Mrs ED Brown	Tenby	1 hole
1955	Miss Nancy Cook	Miss P Roberts	Holyhead	2 holes
1956	Miss P Roberts	Miss Barron	Porthcawl	2 and 1
1957	Miss M Barron	Miss P Roberts	Harlech	6 and 4
1958	Mrs M Wright (*née* Cook)	Miss P Roberts	Newport	1 hole
1959	Miss P Roberts	Miss A Gwyther	Conway	6 and 4
1960	Miss M Barron	Mrs E Brown	Tenby	8 and 6
1961	Mrs M Oliver	Miss N Seddon	Aberdovey	5 and 4
1962	Mrs M Oliver	Miss P Roberts	Radyr	4 and 2
1963	Miss P Roberts	Miss N Sneddon	Harlech	7 and 5
1964	Mrs M Oliver	Mrs M Wright	Southerndown	1 hole
1965	Mrs M Wright	Mrs E Brown	Prestatyn	3 and 2
1966	Miss A Hughes	Miss P Roberts	Ashburnham	5 and 4
1967	Mrs M Wright	Miss C Phipps	Harlech	21st hole
1968	Miss S Hales	Mrs M Wright	Porthcawl	3 and 2
1969	Miss P Roberts	Miss A Hughes	Caernarvonshire	3 and 2
1970	Mrs A Briggs	Miss J Morris	Newport	19th hole
1971	Mrs A Briggs	Mrs EN Davies	Harlech	2 and 1
1972	Miss A Hughes	Miss J Rogers	Tenby	3 and 2
1973	Mrs A Briggs	Mrs J John	Holyhead	3 and 2
1974	Mrs A Briggs	Dr H Lyall	Ashburnham	3 and 2
1975	Mrs A Johnson (*née* Hughes)	Miss K Rawlings	Prestatyn	1 hole
1976	Miss T Perkins	Mrs A Johnson	Porthcawl	4 and 2
1977	Miss T Perkins	Miss P Whitley	Aberdovey	5 and 4
1978	Miss P Light	Mrs A Briggs	Newport	2 and 1
1979	Miss V Rawlings	Mrs A Briggs	Caernarvonshire	2 holes
1980	Miss M Rawlings	Mrs A Briggs	Tenby	2 and 1
1981	Miss M Rawlings	Mrs A Briggs	Harlech	5 and 3
1982	Mrs V Thomas (*née* Rawlings)	Miss M Rawlings	Ashburnham	7 and 6
1983	Mrs V Thomas	Mrs T Thomas (*née* Perkins)	Llandudno	1 hole
1984	Miss S Roberts	K Davies	Newport	5 and 4
1985	Mrs V Thomas	S Jump	Prestatyn	1 hole
1986	Mrs V Thomas	L Isherwood	Porthcawl	7 and 6

Welsh Ladies' Open Amateur Stroke Play Championship

Instituted 1976

Year	Winner	Club	Venue	Score
1976	Miss P Light	Whitchurch	Aberdovey	227
1977	Miss J Greenhalgh	Pleasington	Aberdovey	239
1978	Mrs S Hedges	Wrotham Heath	Aberdovey (49 holes, fog)	209
1979	Miss S Crowcroft	Blackwell	Aberdovey	228
1980	Mrs T Thomas (*née* Perkins)	Wenvoe Castle	Aberdovey	223
1981	Mrs V Thomas	Pennard	Aberdovey	224
1982	Mrs V Thomas	Pennard	Aberdovey	225
1983	Mrs J Thornhill		Aberdovey	239
1984	Miss L Davies	West Byfleet	Aberdovey	230
1985	Miss C Swallow		Aberdovey	219
1986	Miss H Wadsworth		Aberdovey	223

Welsh Seniors' Amateur Championship

Instituted 1975

Year	Winner	Club	Score
1975	A Marshaman	Brecon	77 (18 holes)
1976	AD Evans	Ross on Wye	156
1977	AE Lockley	Swansea Bay	154
1978	AE Lockley	Swansea Bay	75 (18 holes)
1979	CR Morgan	Monmouthshire	158
1980	ES Mills	Llandudno Maesdu	152
1981	T Branton	Newport	153
1982	WI Tucker	Monmouthshire	147
1983	WS Gronow	East Berks	153
1984			
1985			
1986	E Mills	Aberdovey	154

Overseas National Championships

American Amateur Championship

Year	Winner	Runner-up	Venue	By
(Prior to organisation of USGA)				
1893	WG Lawrence	CB Macdonald	Newport RI	4 and 3
1894	LB Stoddart	CB Macdonald	St Andrews	5 and 4
(Under the auspices of USGA)				
1895	CB Macdonald	C Sands	Newport RI	12 and 11
1896	HJ Whigham	JG Thorp	Shinnecock	8 and 7
1897	HJ Whigham	WR Betts	Wheaton, Ill	8 and 6
1898	Finlay S Douglas	WB Smith	Morris County	5 and 3
1899	HM Harriman	FS Douglas	Onwentsia	3 and 2
1900	WJ Travis	FS Douglas	Garden City	2 holes
1901	WJ Travis	WE Egan	Atlantic City	5 and 4
1902	Louis N James	EM Byers	Glen View	4 and 3
1903	WJ Travis	EM Byers	Nassau	4 and 3
1904	H Chandler Egan	F Herreschoff	Baltusrol	8 and 6
1905	H Chandler Egan	DE Sawyer	Wheaton, Ill	6 and 5
1906	EM Byers	Geo S Lyon	Englewood	2 holes
1907	Jerome D Travers	Arch Graham	Cleveland	6 and 5
1908	Jerome D Travers	Max H Behr	Midlothian, Ill	8 and 7
1909	R Gardner	HC Egan	Wheaton, Ill	4 and 3
1910	WC Fownes, jun	WK Wood	Brookline	4 and 3
1911	HH Hilton	F Herreschoff	Apawamis	37th hole
1912	Jerome D Travers	Charles Evans	Wheaton, Ill	7 and 6
1913	Jerome D Travers	JG Anderson	Garden City	5 and 4
1914	F Ouimet	JD Travers	Ekwanok	6 and 5
1915	RA Gardner	JG Anderson	Detroit	5 and 4
1916	Chas Evans	RA Gardner	Merion	4 and 3
1919	D Heron	RT Jones, jun	Oakmont	5 and 4
1920	C Evans	F Ouimet	Engineers Club	5 and 4
1921	J Guildford	Robert Gardner	St Louis, Mo	7 and 6
1922	J Sweetser	Chas Evans	Brookline	3 and 2
1923	Max Marston	Jesse Sweetser	Flossmoor	38th hole
1924	RT Jones, jun	G von Elm	Merion	9 and 8
1925	RT Jones, jun	W Gunn	Oakmont	8 and 7
1926	Geo von Elm	RT Jones, jun	Baltusrol	2 and 1
1927	RT Jones, jun	C Evans	Minikahda	8 and 7
1928	RT Jones, jun	TP Perkins	Brae Burn	10 and 9
1929	HR Johnston	Dr OF Willing	Del Monte	4 and 3
1930	RT Jones, jun	EV Homans	Merion	8 and 7
On and after 1931 Sectional Qualifying Competitions over 36 holes medal play were inaugurated				
1931	F Ouimet	J Westland	Beverley	6 and 5
1932	CR Somerville (Canada)	J Goodman	Baltimore	2 and 1
1933	GT Dunlap	MR Marston	Kenwood	6 and 5
1934	W Lawson Little	D Goldman	Brookline	8 and 7
1935	W Lawson Little	W Emery	Cleveland	4 and 2
1936	J Fischer	J McLean (GB)	Garden City	37th hole
1937	J Goodman	R Billows	Portland	2 holes
1938	WP Turnesa	BP Abbott	Oakmont	8 and 7
1939	MH Ward	R Billows	Glenview	7 and 5
1940	RD Chapman	WB McCullough	Winged Foot	11 and 9
1941	MH Ward	BP Abbott	Omaha	4 and 3
1942-45	*No Championship*			
1946	SE Bishop	S Quick	Baltusrol	37th hole
1947	RH Riegel	J Dawson	Pebble Beach	2 and 1
1948	WP Turnesa	R Billows	Memphis	2 and 1
1949	CR Coe	Rufus King	Rochester	11 and 10
1950	S Urzetta	FR Stranahan	Minneapolis	39th hole

American Amateur Championship
continued

Year	Winner	Runner-up	Venue	By
1951	WJ Maxwell	J Cagliardi	Saucon Valley, Pa	4 and 3
1952	J Westland	A Mengert	Seattle	3 and 2
1953	G Littler	D Morey	Oklahoma City	1 hole
1954	A Palmer	R Sweeney	Detroit	1 hole
1955	E Harvie Ward	W Hyndman	Richmond, Va	9 and 8
1956	E Harvie Ward	C Kocsis	Lake Forest, Ill	5 and 4
1957	H Robbins	Dr F Taylor	Brookline	5 and 4
1958	C Coe	T Aaron	San Francisco	5 and 4
1959	JW Nicklaus	CR Coe	Broadmoor	1 hole
1960	DR Beman	R Gardner	St Louis, Mo	6 and 4
1961	JW Nicklaus	D Wysong	Pebble Beach	8 and 6
1962	LE Harris, jun	D Gray	Pinehurst	1 hole
1963	DR Beman	D Sikes	Des Moines	2 and 1
1964	W Campbell	E Tutwiler	Canterbury, Ohio	1 hole
Changed to stroke play				
1965	R Murphy	USA	Tulsa, Okla	291
1966	G Cowan	Canada	Ardmore, Penn	285
1967	R Dickson	USA	Colorado	285
1968	B Fleisher	USA	Columbus	284
1969	S Melnyk	USA	Oakmont	286
1970	L Wadkins	USA	Portland	280
1971	G Cowan	Canada	Wilmington	280
1972	M Giles	USA	Charlotte, NC	285
Reverted to match play				
1973	C Stadler	D Strawn	Inverness, Toledo, Ohio	6 and 5
1974	J Pate	J Grace	Ridgewood, NJ	2 and 1
1975	F Ridley	K Fergus	Richmond, Va	2 holes
1976	B Sander	P Moore	Bel-Air	8 and 6
1977	J Fought	D Fischesser	Aronimink, Pa	9 and 8
1978	J Cook	S Hoch	Plainfield, NJ	5 and 4
1979	M O'Meara	J Cook	Canterbury, Ohio	8 and 7
1980	H Sutton	B Lewis	North Carolina	9 and 8
1981	N Crosby	B Lyndley	San Francisco	37th hole
1982	J Sigel	D Tolley	The Country Club, Brookline	8 and 7
1983	J Sigel	C Perry	North Shore, Chicago	8 and 7
1984	S Verplank		Oak Tree	
1985	S Randolph	P Persons	Montclair, NJ	1 hole
1986	S Alexander	C Kite	Shoal Creek	5 and 3

American Open Championship

Year	Winner	Runner-up	Venue	By
1894	Willie Dunn	W Campbell	St Andrews, NY	2 holes

After 1894 decided by medal play

Year	Winner	Country	Venue	Score
1895	HJ Rawlins	USA	Newport	173
1896	J Foulis	USA	Southampton	152
1897	J Lloyd	USA	Wheaton, Ill	162
1898	F Herd	USA	Shinnecock Hills	328
72 holes played from 1898				
1899	W Smith	USA	Baltimore	315
1900	H Vardon	England	Wheaton, Ill	313
1901	W Anderson	USA	Myopia, Mass	315
1902	L Auchterlonie	USA	Garden City	305
1903	W Anderson	USA	Baltusrol	307
1904	W Anderson	USA	Glenview	304
1905	W Anderson	USA	Myopia	335
1906	A Smith	USA	Onwentsia	291
1907	A Ross	USA	Chestnut Hill, Pa	302
1908	F McLeod	USA	Myopia, Mass	322
1909	G Sargent	USA	Englewood, NJ	290
1910	A Smith	USA	Philadelphia	289
(After a tie with JJ McDermott and Macdonald Smith)				
1911	JJ McDermott	USA	Wheaton, Ill	307
1912	JJ McDermott	USA	Buffalo, NY	294
1913	F Ouimet (Am)	USA	Brookline, Mass	304
(After a tie with H Vardon and E Ray)				
1914	W Hagen	USA	Midlothian	297
1915	JD Travers (Am)	USA	Baltusrol	290
1916	C Evans (Am)	USA	Minneapolis	286
1919	W Hagen	USA	Braeburn	301
1920	E Ray	England	Inverness	295
1921	J Barnes	USA	Washington	289
1922	G Sarazen	USA	Glencoe	288

American Open Championship

continued

Year	Winner	Runner-up	Venue	Score
1923	RT Jones, jun (Am)	USA	Inwood, LI	295
(After a tie with RA Cruikshank. Play-off: 76; Cruikshank 78)				
1924	C Walker	USA	Oakland Hills	297
1925	W MacFarlane	USA	Worcester	291
1926	RT Jones, jun (Am)	USA	Scioto	293
1927	TD Armour	USA	Oakmont	301
(After a tie with H Cooper. Play-off: Armour 76; Cooper 79)				
1928	J Farrell	USA	Olympia Fields	294
(After a tie with RT Jones, jun. Play-off: Farrell 143; Jones 144)				
1929	RT Jones, jun (Am)	USA	Winged Foot, NY	294
(After a tie with A Espinosa. Play-off: Jones 141; Espinosa 164)				
1930	RT Jones, jun (Am)	USA	Interlachen	287
1931	B Burke	USA	Inverness	292
(After a tie with G von Elm. Play-off: Burke 149, 148; von Elm 149, 149)				
1932	G Sarazen	USA	Fresh Meadow	286
1933	J Goodman (Am)	USA	North Shore	287
1934	O Dutra	USA	Merion	293
1935	S Parks	USA	Oakmont	299
1936	T Manero	USA	Springfield	282
1937	R Guldahl	USA	Oakland Hills	281
1938	R Guldahl	USA	Cherry Hills	284
1939	Byron Nelson	USA	Philadelphia	284
(After a tie with Craig Wood and D Shute)				
1940	W Lawson Little	USA	Canterbury, Ohio	287
(After a tie with G Sarazen. Tie scores: Little 70; Sarazen 73)				
1941	Craig Wood	USA	Fort Worth, Texas	284
1946	Lloyd Mangrum	USA	Canterbury	284
(After a tie with Byron Nelson and Vic Ghezzie)				
1947	Lew Worsham	USA	St Louis	282
(After a tie with Sam Snead. Replay scores: Worsham 69; Snead 70)				
1948	Ben Hogan	USA	Los Angeles	276
1949	Dr Cary Middlecoff	USA	Medinah, Ill	286
1950	Ben Hogan	USA	Merion, Pa	287
(After a tie with Lloyd Mangrum and George Fazio. Replay scores: Hogan 69; Mangrum 73; Fazio 75)				
1951	Ben Hogan	USA	Oakland Hills, Mich	287
1952	Julius Boros	USA	Dallas, Texas	281
1953	Ben Hogan	USA	Oakmont	283
1954	Ed Furgol	USA	Baltusrol	284
1955	J Fleck	USA	San Francisco	287
(After a tie with Ben Hogan. Replay scores: Fleck 69; Hogan 72)				
1956	Dr Cary Middlecoff	USA	Rochester	281
1957	Dick Mayer	USA	Inverness	282
(After a tie with Dr Cary Middlecoff. Tie scores: Mayer 72; Middlecoff 79)				
1958	Tommy Bolt	USA	Tulsa, Okla	283
1959	W Casper	USA	Winged Foot, NY	282
1960	Arnold Palmer	USA	Denver, Col	280
1961	Gene Littler	USA	Birmingham, Mich	281
1962	JW Nicklaus	USA	Oakmont	283
(After a tie with Arnold Palmer: Nicklaus 71; Palmer 74)				
1963	Julius Boros	USA	Brookline, Mass	293
(After a tie. Play-off: J Boros, 70; Jack Cupit 73; Arnold Palmer 76)				
1964	Ken Venturi	USA	Washington	278
1965	Gary Player	South Africa	St Louis, Mo	282
(After a tie with KDG Nagle, Australia. Replay scores: Player 71; Nagle 74)				
1966	W Casper	USA	San Francisco	278
(After a tie with Arnold Palmer. Replay scores: Casper 69; Palmer 73)				
1967	JW Nicklaus	USA	Baltusrol	275
1968	Lee Trevino	USA	Rochester	275
1969	Orville Moody	USA	Houston, Texas	281
1970	A Jacklin	England	Chaska, Minn	281
1971	L Trevino	USA	Merion, Pa	280
(After a tie with J Nicklaus. Play-off: Trevino 68; Nicklaus 71)				
1972	JW Nicklaus	USA	Pebble Beach	290
1973	J Miller	USA	Oakmont, Pa	279
1974	H Irwin	USA	Winged Foot, NY	287
1975	L Graham	USA	Medinah, Ill	287
(After a tie with Mahaffey. Play-off: Graham 71; Mahaffey 73)				
1976	J Pate	USA	Atlanta, Georgia	277
1977	H Green	USA	Southern Hills, Tulsa	278
1978	A North	USA	Cherry Hills	285
1979	H Irwin	USA	Inverness, Ohio	284
1980	JW Nicklaus	USA	Baltusrol	272
1981	D Graham	Australia	Merion, Pa	273
1982	T Watson	USA	Pebble Beach	282
1983	L Nelson	USA	Oakmont, Pa	280
1984	F Zoeller	USA	Winged Foot	276
(After tie with G Norman, Australia. Play-off: Zoeller 67; Norman 75)				
1985	A North	USA	Oakland Hills, Mich	279
1986	R Floyd	USA	Shinnecock Hills, NY	279

American Ladies' Amateur Championship

Instituted 1895

Year	Winner	Runner-up	Venue	By
1930	Miss Glenna Collett	Miss V Van Wie	Los Angeles	2 and 1
1931	Miss H Hicks	Mrs GC Vare	Buffalo	2 and 1
1932	Miss V Van Wie	Mrs GC Vare	Peabody	10 and 8
1933	Miss V Van Wie	Miss H Hicks	Exmoor	4 and 3
1934	Miss V Van Wie	Miss T Traung	Whitemarsh Valley	2 and 1
1935	Mrs GC Vare (Collett)	Miss P. Berg	Interlachen	3 and 2
1936	Miss Pam Barton (GB)	Mrs MO Crews	Canoe Brook	4 and 3
1937	Mrs JA Page	Miss P Berg	Memphis City	7 and 6
1938	Miss P Berg	Mrs JA Page	Westmoreland	6 and 5
1939	Miss B Jameson	Miss D Kirby	Wee Burn	3 and 2
1940	Miss B Jameson	Miss J Cochran	Pebble Beach	6 and 5
1941	Mrs H Newell	Miss H Sigel	Brookline	5 and 3
1942-45	*No Championship*			
1946	Mrs G Zaharias	Mrs C Sherman	Southern Hills, Tulsa	11 and 9
1947	Miss L Suggs	Miss D Kirby	Detroit	2 holes
1948	Miss Grace Lenczyk	Miss Helen Sigel	Pebble Beach	4 and 3
1949	Mrs Mark A Porter	Miss D Kielty	Merion	3 and 2
1950	Miss Beverley Hanson	Miss Mae Murray	Atlanta	6 and 4
1951	Miss Dorothy Kirby	Miss Claire Doran	St Paul, Minn.	2 and 1
1952	Mrs J Pung	Miss S McFedters	Long Beach, Calif'	2 and 1
1953	Miss ML Faulk	Miss P Riley	Rhode Island	3 and 2
1954	Miss B Romack	Miss M Wright	Pittsburgh	4 and 2
1955	Miss Pat Lesser	Miss J Nelson	Charlotte	7 and 6
1956	Miss Marlene Stewart	Miss J Gunderson	Indianapolis	2 and 1
1957	Miss J Gunderson	Mrs AC Johnstone	Del Paso	8 and 6
1958	Miss A Quast	Miss B Romack	Wee Burn, Darien	3 and 2
1959	Miss B McIntyre	Miss J Goodwin	Washington	4 and 3
1960	Miss J Gunderson	Miss J Ashley	Tulsa, Oklahoma	6 and 5
1961	Mrs A Decker	Miss P Preuss	Tacoma	14 and 13
1962	Miss J Gunderson	Miss A Baker	Rochester, NY	9 and 8
1963	Mrs Anne Welts (Quast)	Miss P Conley	Williamstown	2 and 1
1964	Miss B McIntyre	Miss J Gunderson	Prairie Dunes, Kansas	3 and 2
1965	Miss J Ashley	Mrs Anne Welts	Denver	5 and 4
1966	Mrs D Carner (Miss Gunderson)	Mrs JD Streit	Pittsburgh	41st hole
1967	Miss L Dill	Miss J Ashley	Annandale, Pasadena	5 and 4
1968	Mrs JA Carner	Mrs A Welts	Birmingham, Mich	5 and 4
1969	Miss C Lacoste (France)	Miss S Hamlin	Las Colinas, Texas	3 and 2
1970	Miss M Wilkinson	Miss Cynthia Hill	Darien, Conn	3 and 2
1971	Miss L Baugh	Miss B Barry	Atlanta	1 hole
1972	Miss M Budke	Miss Cynthia Hill	St Louis, Mo	5 and 4
1973	Miss C Semple	Mrs A Sander (Welts)	Montclair, NJ	1 hole
1974	Miss Cynthia Hill	Miss C Semple	Broadmoor, Seattle	5 and 4
1975	Miss Beth Daniel	Miss D Horton	Brae Burn, Mass	3 and 2
1976	Miss D Horton	Mrs M Bretton	Del Paso, California	2 and 1
1977	Miss Beth Daniel	Mrs C Sherk	Cincinnati	3 and 1
1978	Mrs C Sherk	Mrs J Oliver	Sunnybrook, Pa	4 and 3
1979	Miss Carolyn Hill	Miss P Sheehan	Memphis	7 and 6
1980	Mrs J Inkster	Miss P Rizzo	Prairie Dunes, Kansas	2 holes
1981	Mrs J Inkster	Mrs L Goggin (Aus)	Portland, Oregon	1 hole
1982	Mrs J Inkster	Miss C Hanlon	Colorado Springs	4 and 3
1983	Miss J Pacillo	Miss S Quinlan	Canoe Brook, NJ	2 and 1
1984	Miss D Richard	Miss K Williams	Broadmoor, Seattle	37th hole
1985	Miss M Hattori (Japan)			
1986	Miss K Cockerill	Miss K McCarthy	Pasatiempo, California	9 and 7

American Women's Open Championship

(American unless stated)

Year	Winner	Venue	By
1946	Miss P Berg	Spokane	5 and 4

Changed to stroke play

Year	Winner	Venue	Score
1947	Miss B Jameson	Greensboro	300
1948	Mrs G Zaharias	Atlantic City	300
1949	Miss Louise Suggs	Maryland	291
1950	Mrs G Zaharias	Wichita	291
1951	Miss B Rawls	Atlanta	294
1952	Miss L Suggs	Bala, Philadelphia	284
1953	Miss B Rawls	Rochester, NY	302
(After a tie with Mrs J Pung)			
1954	Mrs G Zaharias	Peabody, Mass	291
1955	Miss F Crocker	Wichita	299
1956	Mrs K Cornelius	Duluth	302
(After a tie with Miss B McIntire)			
1957	Miss B Rawls	Mamaroneck	299
1958	Miss M Wright	Bloomfield Hills, Mich	290
1959	Miss M Wright	Pittsburgh, Pa	287
1960	Miss B Rawls	Worcester, Mass	292
1961	Miss M Wright	Springfield, NJ	293
1962	Mrs M Lindstrom	Myrtle Beach	301
1963	Miss M Mills	Kenwood	289
1964	Miss M Wright	San Diego	290
(After a tie with Miss Ruth Jessen, Seattle)			
1965	Miss C Mann	Northfield, NJ	290
1966	Miss S Spuzich	Hazeltine National GC, Minn	297
1967	Miss C Lacoste (France)	Hot Springs, Virginia	294
1968	Mrs SM Berning	Moselem Springs, Pa	289
1969	Miss Donna Caponi	Scenic-Hills	294
1970	Miss Donna Caponi	Muskogee, Oklahoma	287
1971	Mrs J Gunderson-Carner	Erie, Pennsylvania	288
1972	Mrs SM Berning	Mamaroneck, NY	299
1973	Mrs SM Berning	Rochester, NY	290
1974	Miss S Haynie	La Grange, Illinois	295
1975	Miss S Palmer	Northfield, NJ	295
1976	Mrs J Carner	Springfield, Pa	292
(After a tie with Miss S Palmer)			
1977	Miss H Stacy	Hazeltine, Minn	292
1978	Miss H Stacy	Indianapolis	289
1979	Miss J Britz	Brooklawn, Conn	284
1980	Miss A Alcott	Richland, Tenn	280
1981	Miss P Bradley	La Grange, Illinois	279
1982	Mrs J Alex	Del Paso, Sacramento	283
1983	Miss J Stephenson (Aus)	Broken Arrow, Oklahoma	290
1984	Miss H Stacy	Salem, Mass	290
1985	Miss K Baker	Baltusrol, NJ	280
1986	Miss J Geddes	NCR	287

American Masters' Championship

Venue–Augusta National Golf Course, Augusta, Georgia

Year	Winner	Score	Year	Winner	Score
1934	Horton Smith	284	1948	Claude Harmon	279
1935	Gene Sarazen	282	1949	Sam Snead	283
1936	Horton Smith	285	1950	Jimmy Demaret	282
1937	Byron Nelson	283	1951	Ben Hogan	280
1938	Henry Picard	285	1952	Sam Snead	286
1939	Ralph Guldahl	279	1953	Ben Hogan	274
1940	Jimmy Demaret	280	1954	Sam Snead	289
1941	Craig Wood	280	1955	Cary Middlecoff	279
1942	Byron Nelson	280	1956	Jackie Burke	289
1946	Herman Keiser	282	1957	Doug Ford	283
1947	Jimmy Demaret	281	1958	Arnold Palmer	284

American Masters' Championship
continued

Year	Winner	Score	Year	Winner	Score
1959	A Wall	284	1973	T Aaron	283
1960	Arnold Palmer	282	1974	GJ Player (SA)	278
1961	GJ Player (SA)	280	1975	JW Nicklaus	276
1962	Arnold Palmer	280	1976	R Floyd	271
1963	JW Nicklaus	286	1977	T Watson	276
1964	Arnold Palmer	276	1978	GJ Player (SA)	277
1965	JW Nicklaus	271	1979	F Zoeller	280
1966	JW Nicklaus	288	1980	S Ballasteros (Sp)	275
1967	G Brewer	280	1981	T Watson	280
1968	R Goalby	277	1982	C Stadler	284
1969	G Archer	281	1983	S. Ballesteros (Sp)	280
1970	W Casper	279	1984	B Crenshaw	277
1971	C Coody	279	1985	B Langer	282
1972	JW Nicklaus	286	1986	JW Nicklaus	279

Leading Scores 1986

J Nicklaus	74-71-69-65	279	T Watson	70-74-68-71	283
T Kite	70-74-68-68	280	J Haas	76-69-71-67	283
G Norman	70-72-68-70	280	P Stewart	75-71-69-69	284
S Ballesteros	71-68-72-70	281	B Tway	70-73-71-70	284
N Price	79-69-63-71	282	T Nakajima	70-71-71-72	284

American PGA Championship

Year	Winner	Runner-up	Venue	By
1916	Jim Barnes	Jock Hutchison	Siwanoy	1 hole
1919	Jim Barnes	Fred McLeod	Engineers' Club	6 and 5
1920	Jock Hutchison	Douglas Edgar	Flossmoor	1 hole
1921	Walter Hagen	Jim Barnes	Inwood Club	3 and 2
1922	Gene Sarazen	Emmet French	Oakmont	4 and 3
1923	Gene Sarazen	Walter Hagen	Pelham	38th hole
1924	Walter Hagen	Jim Barnes	French Lick	2 holes
1925	Walter Hagen	WE Mehlhorn	Olympic Fields	6 and 4
1926	Walter Hagen	Leo Diegel	Salisbury	4 and 3
1927	Walter Hagen	Joe Turnesa	Dallas, Texas	1 hole
1928	Leo Diegel	Al Espinosa	Five Farms	6 and 5
1929	Leo Diegel	J Farrell	Hill Crest	6 and 4
1930	TD Armour	G Sarazen	Fresh Meadow	1 hole
1931	T Creavy	D Shute	Wannamoisett	2 and 1
1932	O Dutra	F Walsh	St Paul, Minnesota	4 and 3
1933	G Sarazen	W Goggin	Milwaukee	5 and 4
1934	P Runyan	Craig Wood	Buffalo	38th hole
1935	J Revolta	TD Armour	Oklahoma	5 and 4
1936	D Shute	J Thomson	Pinehurst	3 and 2
1937	D Shute	H McSpaden	Pittsburgh	37th hole
1938	P Runyan	S Snead	Shawnee	8 and 7
1939	H Picard	B Nelson	Pomonok	37th hole
1940	Byron Nelson	Sam Snead	Hershey, Pa	1 hole
1941	Vic Ghezzie	Byron Nelson	Denver, Colo	38th hole
1942	Sam Snead	Jim Turnesa	Atlantic City	2 and 1
1943	*No Championship*			
1944	Bob Hamilton	Byron Nelson	Spokane, Wash	1 hole
1945	Byron Nelson	Sam Byrd	Dayton, Ohio	4 and 3
1946	Ben Hogan	Ed Oliver	Portland	6 and 4
1947	Jim Ferrier	Chick Harbert	Detroit	2 and 1
1948	Ben Hogan	Mike Turnesa	Norwood Hills	7 and 6
1949	Sam Snead	Johnny Palmer	Richmond, Va	3 and 2
1950	Chandler Harper	Henry Williams	Scioto, Ohio	4 and 3
1951	Sam Snead	Walter Burkemo	Oakmont, Pa	7 and 6
1952	Jim Turnesa	Chick Harbert	Big Spring, Louisville	1 hole
1953	Walter Burkemo	Felice Lorza	Birmingham, Michigan	2 and 1
1954	Chick Harbert	Walter Burkemo	St Paul, Minnesota	4 and 3
1955	D Ford	C Middlecoff	Detroit	4 and 3
1956	J Burke	T Kroll	Boston	3 and 2
1957	L Hebert	D Finsterwald	Miami Valley, Dayton	3 and 1

Changed to Stroke Play

Year	Winner	Score	Year	Winner	Score
1958	D Finsterwald	276	1963	JW Nicklaus	279
1959	Bob Rosburg	277	1964	Bobby Nichols	271
1960	Jay Hebert	281	1965	D Marr	280
1961	Jerry Barber*	277	1966	Al Geiberger	280
1962	GJ Player	278	1967	Don January*	281

American PGA Championship

continued

Year	Winner	Score	Year	Winner	Score
1968	Julius Boros	281	1978	J Mahaffey*	276
1969	Ray Floyd	276	1979	D Graham*	272
1970	Dave Stockton	279	1980	JW Nicklaus	274
1971	JW Nicklaus	281	1981	L Nelson	273
1972	GJ Player	281	1982	R Floyd	272
1973	JW Nicklaus	277	1983	H Sutton	274
1974	L Trevino	276	1984	L Trevino	273
1975	JW Nicklaus	276	1985	H Green	278
1976	D Stockton	281	1986	R Tway	276
1977	L Wadkins*	287	(*After a tie)		

Argentine Open Championship

Instituted 1905

Year	Winner	Year	Winner	Year	Winner
1931	J Jurado	1949	R De Vicenzo	1967	R De Vicenzo
1932	A Perez	1950	M Pose	1968	V Fernandez
1933	M Pose	1951	R De Vicenzo	1969	V Fernandez
1934	M Churio	1952	R De Vicenzo	1970	R De Vicenzo
1935	JI Cruickshank	1953	M Gonzalez	1971	F Molina
1936	JI Cruickshank	1954	F de Luca	1972	F de Luca
1937	H Picard	1955	E Bertolino	1973	F Molina
1938	P Runyan	1956	A Cerda	1974	R De Vicenzo
1939	M Pose	1957	L Ruiz	1975	F Molina
1940	M Gonzalez (Am)	1958	R De Vicenzo	1976	F Molina
1941	Jimmy Demaret	1959	L Ruiz	1977	F Molina
1942	M Martin	1960	F de Luca	1978	A Sowa
1943	M Churio	1961	F de Luca	1979	T Weiskopf
1944	R De Vicenzo	1962	A Miguel (Spain)	1980	G Hallberg
1945	Not played	1963	J Ledesma (Am)	1981	V Fernandez
1946	Lloyd Mangrum	1964	Elcido Nari	1982	J Soto
1947	E Bertolino	1965	R De Vicenzo	1983	*Not available*
1948	A Cerda	1966	Juan Castillo	1984	*Not available*

Argentine Amateur Championship

Instituted 1895

Year	Winner	Year	Winner	Year	Winner
1931	H Wesley Smith	1949	AE Texier	1968	E Maglione (b)
1932	AM Moffat	1950	JB Segura	1969	AE Texier
1933	AM de Zuberhuhler	1951	JA Barbera	1970	Jorge M Ocampo
		1952	JB Segura	1971	RH Monguzzi
1934	AL Zuberhuhler	1953	H O'Farrell	1972	H Carbonetti
1935	GO Dunsmore	1954	H Nicora	1973	AE Texier
1936	I Lopez Naguil	1955	H Nicora	1974	JC Devoto
1937	AM de Anchorena	1956	H Nicora	1975	H Carbonetti
1938	EN de Anchorena	1957	C Bracht	1976	R Monguzzi
1939	LM Gonzalez	1958	H Fernandez	1977	H Carbonetti
1940	M Gonzalez	1959	JC Ledesma	1978	JC Devoto
1941	JE de Anchorena	1960	R Travieso	1979	MA Prado
1942	LA de Herrera	1961	OE Cella	1980	MA Prado
1943	EN de Anchorena	1962	R Travieso	1981	JC Devoto
1944	M Gonzalez	1963	T Travieso	1982	D Vizzolini
1945	Not played	1964	R Travieso	1983	*Not available*
1946	AE Texier	1965	OE Cella	1984	*Not available*
1947	AE Texier	1966	JC Ledesma		
1948	AE Texier	1967	JC Ledesma		

Argentine Ladies' Championship

Instituted 1904

Year	Winner
1931	Mrs AG Nicholson
1932	Miss F Crocker
1933	Mrs AG Nicholson
1934	Miss F Crocker
1935	Miss F Crocker
1936	Mrs MM de Maglione
1937	Miss F Crocker
1938	Miss L Labourette
1939	Mrs MM de Maglione
1940	Miss F Crocker
1941	Mrs MM de Maglione
1942	Miss F Crocker
1943	Miss F Crocker
1944	Miss F Crocker
1945	Not played
1946	Miss F Crocker
1947	Miss F Crocker
1948	Miss F Crocker
1949	Miss F Crocker
1950	Mrs JB de Arnold
1951	Miss F Crocker
1952	Mrs MM de Maglione
1953	Miss F Crocker
1954	Miss S Garcia
1955	Mrs MM de Maglione
1956	Mrs MM de Maglione
1957	Mrs MM de Maglione
1958	Miss MM Chavarria
1959	Mrs CBC de Conen
1960	Miss Carola Zappa
1961	Miss S Patrizi
1962	Miss C Brandes
1963	Mrs CBC de Conen
1964	MJ Caserta
1965	MJ Caserta
1966	MS Valiente
1967	B Rossello
1968	Carmen Baca Castex de Conen
1969	B Rosello
1970	Carmen Baca Castex de Conen
1971	MJC de Aftalion
1972	S Bertolaccini
1973	MJC de Aftalion
1974	CB de Mollnari
1975	B Rossello
1976	MJC de Aftalion
1977	BG Rossello
1978	BG Rossello
1979	ME Cossio de Teran
1980	A Scarafia de Felizia
1981	Susana Garmendia
1982	Susana Garmendia
1983	*Not available*
1984	*Not available*

Australian Open Championship

Year	Winner	Score
1904	Hon Michael Scott (Am)	324
1905	D Soutar	330
1906	Carnegie Clark	322
1907	Hon Michael Scott (Am)	318
1908	Clyde Pearce (Am)	311
1909	C Felstead (Am)	316
1910	Carnegie Clark	311
1911	Carnegie Clark	321
1912	Ivo Whitton (Am)	321
1913	Ivo Whitton (Am)	302
1920	JH Kirkwood	290
1921	A Le Fevre	295
1922	C Campbell	307
1923	TE Howard	301
1924	A Russell (Am)	303
1925	F Popplewell	299
1926	Ivo Whitton (Am)	297
1927	R Stewart	297
1928	F Popplewell	295
1929	Ivo Whitton (Am)	309
1930	FP Eyre	306
1931	Ivo Whitton (Am)	301
1932	MJ Ryan (Am)	296
1933	ML Kelly	302
1934	WJ Bolger	283
1935	FM Mahon	293
1936	G Sarazen	282
1937	G Naismith	299
1938	J Ferrier (Am)	283
1939	J Ferrier (Am)	285
1946	HO Pickworth	289
1947	HO Pickworth	285
1948	HO Pickworth	289
1949	E Cremin	287
1950	NG Von Nida	286
1951	PW Thomson	283
1952	NG Von Nida	278
1953	NG Von Nida	278
1954	HO Pickworth	280
1955	AD Locke	290
1956	B Crampton	289
1957	F Phillips	287
1958	G Player	271
1959	K Nagle	284
1960	Bruce Devlin (Am)	282
1961	F Phillips	275
1962	Gary Player	281
1963	Gary Player	278
1964	JW Nicklaus	287
1965	Gary Player	264
1966	Arnold Palmer	276
1967	PW Thomson	281
1968	JW Nicklaus	270
1969	Gary Player	288
1970	Gary Player	280
1971	JW Nicklaus	269
1972	PW Thomson	281
1973	JC Snead	280
1974	Gary Player	277
1975	JW Nicklaus	279
1976	JW Nicklaus	286
1977	D Graham	284
1978	JW Nicklaus	284
1979	J Newton	288
1980	G Norman	284
1981	B Rogers	282
1982	R Shearer	287
1983	P Fowler	285
1984	T Watson	281
1985	G Norman	212
(54 holes only–rain)		
1986	R Davis	278

Australian Ladies' Open

Year	Winner	Country	Venue	Score
1974	Mrs Chako Higuchi	Japan	Victoria, Melbourne	219
1975	Mrs J Carner	USA	Australian, Sydney	228
1976	Mrs D Young	USA	Victoria, Melbourne	206
1977	Miss J Stephenson	Australia	Manly, Sydney	145
1978	Miss D Austin	USA	Manly, Sydney	213
1979-86	*Not played*			

Australian Amateur Championship

Year	Winner	Year	Winner	Year	Winner
1906	EA Gill	1936	J Ferrier	1964	B Baker
1907	Hon Michael Scott	1937	HL Williams	1965	K Donohoe
1908	Clyde Pearce	1938	J Ferrier	1966	W Britte
1909	Hon Michael Scott	1939	J Ferrier	1967	J Muller
1910	Hon Michael Scott	1946	AN Waterson	1968	R Stott
1911	JD Howden	1947	HW Hattersley	1969	RA Shearer
1912	Hector Morrison	1948	D Bachli	1970	PA Bennett
1913	AR Lempriere	1949	WD Ackland-Horman	1971	GR Hicks
1920	EL Apperley			1972	CR Kaye
1921	CL Winser	1950	H Berwick	1973	RJ Jenner
1922	Ivo Whitton	1951	Peter Heard	1974	TR Gale
1923	Ivo Whitton	1952	R Stevens	1975	C Bonython
1924	H Sinclair	1953	Peter Heard	1976	P Sweeney
1925	H Sinclair	1954	P Toogood	1977	AY Gresham
1926	Len Nettlefold	1955	J Rayner	1978	MA Clayton
1927	WS Nankivell	1956	H Berwick	1979	J Kelly
1928	Len Nettlefold	1957	BH Warren	1980	R Mackay
1929	MJ Ryan	1958	K Hartley	1981	O Moore
1930	HW Hattersley	1959	BW Devlin	1982	E Couper
1931	HL William	1960	Ted Ball	1983	W Smith
1932	Dr RH Bettington	1961	T Crow	1984	
1933	WL Hope	1962	D Bachli	1985	S Ruangit
1934	TS McKay	1963	J Hayes	1986	D Ecob
1935	J Ferrier				

Australian Professional Championship

Year	Winner	Year	Winner	Year	Winner
1924	TE Howard	1950	NG Von Nida	1969	B Devlin
1925	TE Howard	1951	NG Von Nida	1970	B Devlin
1926	F Eyre	1952	W Holder	1971	W Dunk
1927-28	*Not decided*	1953	H Pickworth	1972	R Vines
1929	R Stewart	1954	K Nagle	1973	R Vines
1930	J Robertson	1955	H Pickworth	1974	W Dunk
1931	JD Spence	1956	L Wilson	1975	W Dunk
1932	F McMahon	1957	G Player	1976	W Dunk
1933	VS Richardson	1958	K Nagle	1977	M Cahill
1934	ML Kelly	1959	K Nagle	1978	H Irwin
1935	VS Richardson	1960	J Sullivan	1979	S Ginn
1936	WJ Clifford	1961	A Murray	1980	S Torrance
1937	E Cremin	1962	Bill Dunk	1981	S Ballesteros
1938	E Cremin	1963	C Johnson	1982	G Marsh
1939	E Naismith	1964	C Johnson	1983	B Shearer
1946	NG Von Nida	1965	K Nagle	1984	G Norman
1947	H Pickworth	1966	W Dunk	1985	G Norman
1948	NG Von Nida	1967	PW Thomson	1986	G Norman
1949	K Nagle	1968	K Nagle		

Australian Ladies' Amateur Championship

Instituted 1894

Year	Winner	Year	Winner	Year	Winner
1911	Miss N Parbury	1939	Miss J Lewis	1967	Mrs Judy Perkins
1912	Miss V Binnie	1947	Mrs JD Fisher	1968	Miss B Dalgleish
1913	Mrs Harrison	1948	Miss Pat Borthwick	1969	Miss Marea Hickey
1920	Mrs Guy Williams	1949	Miss Pat Borthwick	1970	Mrs G Perkins
1921	Miss M. Macleod	1950	Miss J Wellard	1971	Mrs CN Coggin
1922	Miss G Hay	1951	Miss M Bishop	1972	Mrs I McCaw
1923	Miss Gordon	1952	Mrs JD Fisher	1973	Miss M Mooney
1924	Mrs Newton Lees	1953	Miss Pat Borthwick	1974	Mrs I McCaw
1925	Mrs J Gatehouse	1954	Miss J Percy	1975	Miss Jane Lock
1926	Miss M Macleod	1955	Miss Veronica Anstey (GB)	1976	Miss Jane Lock
1927	Miss M Macleod	1956	Miss P Borthwick	1977	Mrs CN Coggin
1928	Mrs J Gatehouse	1957	Miss B Chevney	1978	Miss K Permezel
1929	Miss L Wray	1958	Miss M Masters	1979	Miss J Lock
1930	Miss S Tolhurst	1959	Mrs E Dawson	1980	Mrs CN Coggin
1931	Miss S Tolhurst	1960	Miss J Percy	1981	Miss C Dibnah
1932	Miss M Macleod	1961	Miss B Hayley	1982	Miss R Lautens (Switzerland)
1933	Miss O Kay	1962	Miss J Percy	1983	Mrs S McCaw
1934	Mrs C Robinson (Ireland)	1963	Mrs M Streit (Canada)	1984	
1935	Mrs JB Walker	1964	Miss Marea Hickey	1985	
1936	Miss O Kay	1965	Miss Gail Corry	1986	Mrs E Kennedy
1937	Miss B Kernot	1966	Miss Gail Corry		
1938	Miss B Kernot				

Austrian Amateur Open Championship

Instituted 1909

Year	Winner	Year	Winner	Year	Winner
1930	Ingenieur Fritz Gross	1957	Hermann Tissies	1975	G Wattine (France)
1931	Donald Grant	1958	OF Dillier	1976	JR Sale (USA)
1932	Graf Otto Salm	1959	AJ Cullinane	1977	JR Sale (USA)
1933	Viscount Newport	1960	Alex Maculan	1978	Hsi-Chuen Lu (Taiwan)
1934	IP Brick	1961	Klaus Nierlich	1979	Tse-Chung Chen (Taiwan)
1935	G Wadsworth	1962	Robert E Smith	1980	Max Lamberg
1936	F Gutmann	1963	Alex Maculan	1981	C Kilian (Germany)
1937	Count J Bendern	1964	Alex Maculan	1982	Ching-Chi Yuan (Taiwan)
1938-46	*No Championship*	1965	W McCrea	1983	Ching-Chi Yuan (Taiwan)
1947	John K Evans	1966	G Koenig	1984	Chin-Han Yu (Taiwan)
1948	Robert Baird	1967	J Penrose (USA)	1985	Chin-Sheng Hsieh (Taiwan)
1949	Hermann Tissies	1968	Gerhard Koenig	1986	
1950	S Sgt James Munro	1969	J Penrose (USA)		
1951	Robert Baird	1970	K Nierlich		
1952	Hermann Tissies	1971	A Maculan		
1953	Robert Baird	1972	H Giesen (Germany)		
1954	Hermann Tissies	1973	K Nierlich		
1955	Robert Baird	1974	K Nierlich		
1956	WE Cagle				

Austrian Ladies' Open Championship

Year	Winner	Year	Winner	Year	Winner
1925	Grafin Ella Festetics	1927	Frau Erzsebet von Szlavy	1929	Frau Erzsebet von Szlavy
1926	Frl Madeleine von Kuh	1928	Frau Erzsebet von Szlavy	1930	Frl Madeleine von Kuh

Austrian Ladies' Open Championship

continued

Year	Winner	Year	Winner	Year	Winner
1931	Frl Madeleine von	1956	Miss W Rosa	1975	H Hueber
	Kuh	1957	Frl Sylvia Lorenz	1976	G Box
1932	Frl Rega von	1958	Mrs BC Alexander	1977	M Chang (China)
	Pollak-Parnau	1959	Frl Monika Moller	1978	Miss K Ehrnlund
1933	Frl A Weyhausen	1960	Luisa Abrahams		(Sweden)
1934	Frau M Gross	1961	Mrs BC Alexander	1979	Miss Bie-Shyuen
1935	Frau M Gross	1962	Frau Ruth Richter		Huang (Taiwan)
1936	Frau E von Szlavy	1963	Mrs BC Alexander	1980	Miss Bie-Shyuen
1937	Mme M de Moss	1964	Frau L Strenger		Huang (Taiwan)
1938-46	*No Championship*	1965	Marion Petersen	1981	Miss N Le Roux
1947	Frau Ruth Richter	1966	Marion Petersen		(SA)
1948	Frau Ruth Richter	1967	M Steegmann	1982	Miss J Orley
1949	Frau Lieselotte	1968	Brigitte Mahl		(Switzerland)
	Strenger	1969	Jeanette Edye	1983	Miss Yueh-Ying
1950	Frau Lilian Fischer	1970	S Rutkowski		Chen (Taiwan)
1951	Frau Ruth Richter	1971	MC Hueber	1984	Miss Mei-Chi
1952	Frau Ruth Richter	1972	S Rutkowski		Cheng
1953	Frau Mimi Strauss	1973	U Fichler		(Taiwan)
1954	Frau Ruth Richter		(Germany)	1985	Frl P Peter
1955	Frau V Lorenz	1974	A Reichel		

Belgian Open Amateur Championship

Instituted 1919

Year	Winner	Year	Winner	Year	Winner
1930	RW Ripley	1952	J Mortelmaus	1969	J Moerman
1931	L Munn	1953	H de Lamaze	1970	J Moerman
1932	L Munn	1954	J Mortelmaus	1971	JW Wilson
1933	B Thompson	1955	J Moerman	1972	J Sousa E Melo
1934	F Ricardo	1956	JC Murray	1973	J Moerman
1935	J de Arana	1957	E Tavernier	1974	J Miller
1936	HL Archibald	1958	R Taylor	1975	CL Francis
1937	J Cavrois	1959	W Kawakami	1976	MJ Christmas (GB)
1938	Brig-Gen AC	1960	J Moerman	1977	G Turner (GB)
	Critchley	1961	GA Bielke	1978	C Staedler
1939	JM Baillieu	1962	Fr Rodesch		(Germany)
1946	G Huet	1963	E Carbonnelle	1979	T Goossens
1947	W-Cdr CH	1964	J Moerman	1980	K Mackintosh (GB)
	Beamish	1965	J Moerman	1981	J Moerman
1948	J Leglise	1966	Van de Weeghe	1982	Th Goossens
1949	J Charles	1967	J Moerman	1983	E Rombouts
1950	F Ricardo	1968	Sutherland-Pilch	1984	O Buysse
1951	W-Cdr CH				
	Beamish				

Belgian Women's Open Championship

Year	Winner	Year	Winner	Year	Winner
1967	Mrs JR Thornhill	1975	Mrs L van den	1981	Miss D Pelzer
1968	Mlle C Reybroeck		Berghe	1982	Miss R Lautens
1969	Mlle C Reybroeck	1976	Miss M Toussaint		(Switzerland)
1970	Mme O Garaialde	1977	Mrs B Collette	1983	Miss L Maritz (SA)
1971	Miss J De Witt Puyt	1978	Miss I Declercq	1984	
1972	Miss J De Witt Puyt	1979	Miss C Bromet (Fr)		
1973	J Heyster	1980	Miss J Crafter		
1974	Mrs S Hedges		(Aust)		

Brazilian Open Championship

Year	Winner	Year	Winner	Year	Winner
1945	M Pose	1959	Billy Casper	1974	G Player
1946	Mario Gonzalez	1960	R De Vicenzo	1975	JPG Diniz (Am)
1947	*Not played*	1961	P Alliss	1976	J Quinteros
1948	Mario Gonzalez	1962	BJ Hunt	1977	V Fernandez
1949	Mario Gonzalez	1963	R De Vicenzo	1978	R Floyd
1950	Mario Gonzalez	1964	R De Vicenzo	1979	F de Luca
1951	Mario Gonzalez	1965	Ramon Sota	1980	J Pate
1952	Sam Snead	1966	Rex Baxter	1981	T Sieckmann
1953	Mario Gonzalez	1968	Takaaki Kono	1982	H Irwin
1954	R De Vicenzo	1969	Mario Gonzalez	1983	V Fernandez
1955	Mario Gonzalez	1970	B Greene	1984	R Lee
1956	Fidel de Luca	1971	B Fleischer	1985	R Lee
1957	R De Vicenzo	1972	G Player		
1958	Billy Casper	1973	R De Vicenzo		

Brazilian Amateur Championship

Year	Winner	Year	Winner	Year	Winner
1951	R Hume	1962	C Sozio	1975	JPG Diniz
1952	R Hume	1963	FC Barcellos	1976	J Gonzalez
1953	J Gonzalez	1964	H de Almeida	1977	R Rossi
1954	J Gonzalez	1968	H Baiocchi	1978	R Rossi
1955	J Gonzalez	1969	J Gonzalez	1979	E Macedo
1956	J Gonzalez	1970	JJ Barboa	1980	*No information*
1957	F Chaves Barcellos	1971	J Gonzalez	1981	R Gomez
1958	R Benito	1972	J Gonzalez	1982	*No information*
1959	R Falkenburg	1973	R Rossi	1983	*No information*
1960	R Falkenburg	1974	JP Diniz	1984	*No information*
1961	R Falkenburg			1985	*No information*

Canadian Amateur Championship

Year	Winner	Year	Winner	Year	Winner
1895	TH Harley	1927	DD Carrick	1960	RK Alexander
1896	JS Gillespie	1928	CR Somerville	1961	G Cowan
1897	WAH Kerr	1929	E Held	1962	R Taylor
1898	GS Lyon	1930	CR Somerville	1963	N Weslock
1899	Vere C Brown	1931	CR Somerville	1964	N Weslock
1900	GS Lyon	1932	GB Taylor	1965	G Henry
1901	WAH Kerr	1933	A Campbell	1966	N Weslock
1902	FR Martin	1934	A Campbell	1967	S Jones
1903	GS Lyon	1935	CR Somerville	1968	J Doyle
1904	J Percy Taylor	1936	F Haas, jun	1969	Wayne McDonald
1905	GS Lyon	1937	CR Somerville	1970	A Miller
1906	GS Lyon	1938	T Adams	1971	R Siderowf
1907	GS Lyon	1939	K Black	1972	D Roxburgh
1908	Alex Wilson	1946	H Martell	1973	G Burns
1909	E Legge	1947	FR Stranahan	1974	D Roxburgh
1910	F Martin	1948	FR Stranahan	1975	J Nelford
1911	GH Hutton	1949	RD Chapman	1976	J Nelford
1912	GS Lyon	1950	W Mawhinney	1977	R Spittle
1913	GH Turpin	1951	W McElroy	1978	R Spittle
1914	GS Lyon	1952	L Bouchey	1979	R Alarcon
1919	W M'Luckie	1953	D Cherry	1980	G Olson
1920	CB Grier	1954	E Harvie Ward	1981	R Zokol
1921	F Thompson	1955	M Norman	1982	D Roxburgh
1922	CC Fraser	1956	M Norman	1983	D Mijovic
1923	WJ Thompson	1957	N Weslock	1984	
1924	F Thomson	1958	B Castator	1985	
1925	DD Carrick	1959	J Johnston		
1926	CR Somerville				

Canadian Ladies' Open Amateur Championship

Instituted 1901

Year	Winner	Year	Winner	Year	Winner
1931	Miss M Orcutt	1955	Miss Marlene Stewart	1971	Miss J Bourassa
1932	Miss M Kirkham	1956	Miss Marlene Stewart	1972	Mrs M Stewart-Streit
1933	Miss Ada Mackenzie	1957	Miss B Stanhope	1973	Mrs M Stewart-Streit
1934	Mrs Alex S Fraser	1958	Mrs MS Streit (*nee* Stewart)	1974	Miss D Massey
1935	Miss Ada Mackenzie	1959	Mrs MS Streit	1975	Miss D Massey
1936	Mrs AB Darling	1960	Miss J Darling	1976	Miss D Massey
1937	Mrs JA Rogers	1961	Miss J Darling	1977	Mrs C Sherk
1938	Mrs FJ Mulqueen	1962	Miss G Hitchens	1978	Mrs C Sherk
1947	Miss Grace Lenczyk	1963	Mrs MS Streit	1979	Miss Stacey West
1948	Miss Grace Lenczyk	1964	Miss M Masters	1980	Miss E Kennedy (Aust)
1949	Miss DeMoss	1965	Miss J Bourassa	1981	Miss J Lock
1950	Miss D Kielty	1966	Miss H Gagnon	1982	Miss C Pleger
1951	Miss Marlene Stewart	1967	Miss B Jackson	1983	Miss D Coe
1952	Miss Edean Anderson	1968	Mrs M Stewart-Streit	1984	
1953	Miss Romack	1969	Mrs M Stewart-Streit	1985	
1954	Miss Marlene Stewart	1970	Mrs G Harvey Moore		

Canadian Open Championship

Year	Winner	Year	Winner	Year	Winner
1904	JH Oke	1934	TD Armour	1962	E Kroll
1905	George Cumming	1935	G Kunes	1963	D Ford
1906	Charles R Murray	1936	W Lawson Little	1964	KDG Nagle
Inc to 72 holes from 1907		1937	H Cooper	1965	Gene Littler
1907	Percy Barrett	1938	S Snead	1966	Don Massengale
1908	Albert Murray	1939	H McSpaden	1967	W Casper
1909	Karl Keffer	1940	S Snead	1968	RJ Charles
1910	D Kenny	1941	S Snead	1969	T Aaron
1911	CR Murray	1942	Craig Wood	1970	K Zarley
1912	George Sargent	1943-44	*No Championship*	1971	L Trevino
1913	Albert Murray	1945	Byron Nelson	1972	G Brewer
1914	Karl Keffer	1946	G Fazio	1973	T Weiskopf
1919	J Douglas Edgar	1947	AD Locke	1974	B Nichols
1920	J Douglas Edgar	1948	C Congdon	1975	T Weiskopf
1921	William Trovinger	1949	EJ Harrison	1976	J Pate
1922	A Watrous	1950	J Ferrier	1977	L Trevino
1923	Clarence Hackney	1951	J Ferrier	1978	B Lietzke
1924	Leo Diegel	1952	J Palmer	1979	L Trevino
1925	Leo Diegel	1953	D Douglas	1980	B Gilder
1926	Macdonald Smith	1954	Pat Fletcher	1981	P Oosterhuis
1927	TD Armour	1955	A Palmer	1982	B Leitzke
1928	Leo Diegel	1956	D Sanders	1983	J Cook
1929	Leo Diegel	1957	G Bayer	1984	G Norman
1930	TD Armour	1958	Wes Ellis, jun	1985	C Strange
1931	Walter Hagen	1959	D Ford	1986	B Murphy
1932	H Cooper	1960	Art Wall		
1933	Joe Kirkwood	1961	Jack Cupit		

Canadian Professional Golfers' Association Championship

Instituted 1912

Year	Winner	Score	Year	Winner	Score
1963	Al Balding	202	1975	Bill Tape	275
1964	G Knudson	199	1976	G Knudson	275
1965	Wilf Homenuik	215	1977	G Knudson	277
1966	M Norman	204	1978	L Wadkins	270
1967	G Knudson	134	1979	L Trevino	285
1968	G Knudson	268	1980	A Palmer	271
1969	Bob Cox, jun	280	1981	R Floyd	277
1970	Al Balding	282	1982	J Thorpe	
1971	Wilf Homenuik	273	1983	L Trevino	271
1972	Bob Panasiuk	279	1984		
1973	Bob Panasiuk	272	1985		
1974	M Norman	271	1986	D Halldorson	277

Colombian Open Championship

Year	Winner	Year	Winner	Year	Winner
1945	G Felice	1959	P Cooper	1974	H Valenzuela
1946	R Posse	1960	B Watson	1975	Peter Butler (GB)
1947	P Valdi	1961	R De Vicenzo	1976	R Gonzalez
1948	P Valdi	1962	M Sala	1977	J Shroeder (USA)
1949	A Serra	1963	Chi Chi Rodriguez	1978	A Rivadeneira
1950	R Posse	1964	*Not played*	1979	S Torrance (GB)
1951	R Posse	1965	*Not played*	1980	B Langer (Ger)
1952	A Besselink	1966	P Garcia	1981	J Pate (USA)
1953	MJ Sala	1967	R Gonzalez	1982	J Pate (USA)
1954	P Molina	1968	R Gonzalez	1983	*No information*
1955	E Sorolla	1969	R Gonzalez	1984	*No information*
1956	A Palmer	1970	A Rivadeneira	1985	*No information*
1957	D Sanders	1971	B Greene		
1958	L Ruiz	1972	D Correa (Am)		

Cyprus Open Amateur Championship

Year	Winner	Year	Winner	Year	Winner
1979	I Christie	1982	M Galpin	1985	
1980	R Gornall	1983	M Hague		
1981	A Marshall	1984	B Turnbull		

Danish Amateur Close Championship

Year	Winner	Year	Winner	Year	Winner
1933	F Hegel	1951	Erik Staerk	1969	K Friche
1934	F Hegel	1952	N Thygesen	1970	J Jacobsen
1935	N Ammentorp	1953	N Thygesen	1971	K Friche
1936	PW Jorgensen	1954	N Thygesen	1972	S Steffensen
1937	E Schnack	1955	H Lund	1973	K Hove
1938	J Schnack	1956	H Lund	1974	J Thomasen
1939	PW Jorgensen	1957	Erik Staerk	1975	J Lindberg
1940	J Schnack	1958	N Thygesen	1976	L Jacobsen
1941	J Schnack	1959	M Kirkegaard	1977	HP Jacobsen
1942	CC Thomsen	1960	Erik Staerk	1978	J Jacobsen
1943	*Not played*	1961	H Hansen	1979	J Lindberg
1944	G Lockey	1962	H Hansen	1980	C Pein
1945	Peter Frigast	1963	F Pfingstl	1981	A Sorensen
1946	J Schnack	1964	N Thygesen	1982	J Rasmussen
1947	J de Coninck Smith	1965	OW Jorgensen	1983	S Tinning
1948	Peter Frigast	1966	H Stenderup	1984	
1949	J de Coninck Smith	1967	Nils Elsoe Jensen	1985	
1950	Erik Staerk	1968	H Knudsen		

Danish Ladies' Close Championship

Year	Winner	Year	Winner
1933	Mrs W Anderson	1960	Mrs Tove Geertz
1934	Mrs H Kier	1961	Mrs Tove Geertz
1935	Mrs G Preisler	1962	Mrs Tove Geertz
1936	Mrs H Kier	1963	Mrs Bjoerg Dam
1937	Mrs H Kier	1964	Mrs IB Bay Nielsen
1938	Mrs H Kier	1965	Miss V Knudsen
1939	Mrs G Preisler	1966	Miss V Knudsen
1940	Mrs G Preisler	1967	Vibeke Morgan
1941	Miss V Malm	1968	K Siegumfeldt
1942	Mrs H Kier	1969	K Siegumfeldt
1943	*Not played*	1970	K Siegumfeldt
1944	Mrs E Jac Olsen	1971	B Holm-Petersen
1945	Miss V Malm	1972	V Morgan
1946	Miss V Malm	1973	K Birch
1947	Miss V Malm	1974	M Meiland
1948	Mrs Tove Bredfeldt	1975	A Hagdrup
1949	Mrs Tove Palsby	1976	M Meiland
1950	Mrs Tove Palsby	1977	M Meiland
1951	Mrs Tove Palsby	1978	L Schmidt
1952	Mrs Tove Palsby	1979	T Pors
1953	Mrs Tove Palsby	1980	A Peitersen
1954	Mrs Tove Palsby	1981	A Peitersen
1955	Mrs Tove Palsby	1982	M Meiland
1956	Mrs Tove Palsby	1983	T Pors
1957	Mrs Tove Palsby	1984	
1958	Mrs Tove Palsby	1985	
1959	Mrs Tove Palsby		

Danish Amateur Stroke Play Championship

Instituted 1981

Year	Winner	Venue	Score
1981	IG Andersen	Holstebro	291
1982	A Sorensen	Rungsted	304
1983	T Morsbol	Silkeborg	300
1984			
1985			

Danish Ladies' Stroke Play Championship

Instituted 1981

Year	Winner	Venue	Score
1981	A Peitersen	Holstebro	291
1982	L Eliasen	Rungsted	316
1983	M Meiland	Silkeborg	313
1984			
1985			

Dutch International Amateur Championship

Instituted 1921

Year	Winner	Year	Winner
1935	F Francis	1965	D Montagu
1936	F Francis	1966	WE McCrea
1937	Count A de Bendern	1967	J van Neck
1938	Brig-Gen AC Critchley	1968	R Falkenburg
1939	Brig-Gen AC Critchley	1969	HG Green
1946	Dr WR Hope	1970	R Falkenburg
1947	O van Zinnicq Bergmann	1971	J de Sousa E Melo
1948	Major H Davies	1972	P Benka
1949	Lt LJ Ranells	1973	G Van Reede
1950	J Spinks	1974	N Burch
1951	EH Potter	1975	CA Braun
1952	JF Dudok van Heel	1976	U Nievert
1953	JF Dudok van Heel	1977	U Nievert
1954	GR Guy	1978	U Schulte
1955	JF Dudok van Heel	1979	I Gray
1956	WJ Giradet	1980	M Clayton (Aust)
1957	DW Frame	1981	B Van Dam
1958	DW Frame	1982	M Lewis (GB)
1959	DW Frame	1983	
1963	CC Bowman	1984	
1964	DW Frame	1985	

Dutch Open Championship

Instituted 1912

Year	Winner	Year	Winner	Year	Winner
1919	D Oosterveer	1939	AD Locke	1967	P Townsend
1920	H Burrows	1948	Cecil Denny	1968	J Cockin
1921	H Burrows	1949	J Adams	1969	G Wolstenholme
1922	Geo Pannell	1950	R De Vicenzo	1970	V Fernandez
1923	H Burrows	1951	F van Donck	1971	R Sota
1924	A Boomer	1952	Cecil Denny	1972	J Newton
1925	A Boomer	1953	F van Donck	1973	D McClelland
1926	A Boomer	1954	Ugo Grappasonni	1974	B Barnes
1927	P Boomer	1955	A Angelini	1975	H Baiocchi
1928	ER Whitcombe	1956	A Cerda	1976	S Ballesteros
1929	JJ Taylor	1957	J Jacobs	1977	B Byman
1930	J Oosterveer	1958	D Thomas	1978	B Byman
1931	F Dyer	1959	S Sewgolum	1979	G Marsh
1932	A Boyer	1960	S Sewgolum	1980	S Ballesteros
1933	M Dallemagne	1961	BBS Wilkes	1981	H Henning
1934	SF Brews	1962	Brian Huggett	1982	P Way
1935	SF Brews	1963	R Waltman	1983	K Brown
1936	F van Donck	1964	S Sewgolum	1984	B Langer
1937	F van Donck	1965	A Miguel	1985	G Marsh
1938	AH Padgham	1966	R Sota	1986	S Ballesteros

Dutch International Ladies' Championship

Instituted 1921

Year	Winner	Year	Winner
1921	Miss M Van Heukelon	1950	Mme J Abbeloos
1922	Mrs Th Van den W Bake	1951	Mme J Abbeloos
1923	Miss B Van Tienhoven	1952	Mrs N Van Riemsdijk
1924	Miss B Van Tienhoven	1966	Miss A Van Riemsdijk
1925	Mrs Sellschopf	1967	Mrs GD de Groot
1926	Miss B Van Tienhoven	1968	Miss A Janmaat
1927	Miss A Van Tienhoven	1969	Mrs GD de Groot
1928	Miss Phyllis Lobbett	1970	Miss A Janmaat
1929	Miss D Fowler	1971	Miss M Petersen
1930	Mrs Buma	1972	Miss C Le Feuvre
1931	Mrs Buma	1973	Miss A Janmaat
1932	Mrs Buma	1974	Miss A Janmaat
1933	Mrs Buma	1975	Miss M Swane
1934	Mrs F Low	1976	Miss A Janmaat
1935	Mlle de T de Bossiere	1977	Miss A Janmaat
1936	Mrs Buma	1978	Miss N Spits
1937	Miss S Stroyan	1979	Mrs J Heyster
1938	Miss S Stroyan	1980	Mrs J Heyster
1939	Miss S Stroyan	1981	Mrs E Koopman
1946	Mrs AC Critchley	1982	Miss A Janmaat
1947	Miss R Woodward	1983	
1948	Mme J Abbeloos	1984	
1949	Mme J Abbeloos	1985	

French Open Amateur Championship

Year	Winner	Year	Winner	Year	Winner
1904	HG Beeche	1934	J Arana	1965	G Mourgue d'Algue
1905	AH Crosfield	1935	G de Ybarra		
1906	RG Graham	1936	M Carlhian	1966	G Mourgue d'Algue
1907	SJ Chesterton	1937	J Leglise		
1908	WG Pringle	1938	R Dunkelberger	1967	A Godillot
1909	Francoise de Bellet	1939	RD Chapman	1968	*No Competition*
1910	Rev P Gannon	1946	M Carlhian	1969	A Godillot
1911	Charles Evans, jun	1947	H de Lamaze	1970	R Taylor
1912	Hon M Scott	1948	H de Lamaze	1971	JC Desbordes
1913	Lord Charles Hope	1949	H de Lamaze	1972	R Lagarde
1914	F Ouimet	1950	H de Lamaze	1973	H Frayssineau
1920	TD Armour	1951	RW Knowles	1974	A Godillot
1921	CS Lipscomb	1952	RD Chapman	1975	T Planchin
1922	Hon Michael Scott	1953	R La Garde	1976	T Planchin
1923	Lt-Col GD Hannay	1954	H de Lamaze	1977	T Planchin
1924	JG Anderson	1955	H de Lamaze	1978	G Levenson
1925	AM Vagliano	1956	H de Lamaze	1979	A Godillot
1926	JG Anderson	1957	H de Lamaze	1980	AY Gresham (Aust)
1927	JE Mellor	1958	H de Lamaze		
1928	TA Bourn	1959	H de Lamaze	1981	F Illouz
1929	J Westland	1960	H de Lamaze	1982	F Illouz
1930	G von Elm	1961	J Moerman	1983	A Godillot
1931	HG Bentley	1962	G Mourgue d'Algue	1984	
1932	HG Bentley			1985	
1933	Brig-Gen AC Critchley	1963	P Cros		
		1964	JP Bostwick (USA)		

French Amateur Close Championship

Year	Winner	Year	Winner	Year	Winner
1930	AM Vagliano	1953	H de Lamaze	1969	A Godillot
1931	AM Vagliano	1954	M Cavrois	1970	A Godillot
1932	M Carlhian	1955	H de Lamaze	1971	H de Lamaze
1933	Y de Quellec	1956	H de Lamaze	1972	R Lagarde
1934	M Carlhian	1957	H de Lamaze	1973	P Cotton
1935	M Carlhian	1958	H de Lamaze	1974	A Godillot
1936	M Carlhian	1959	JP Cros	1975	G Leven
1937	J Leglise	1960	M Bardana	1976	G Leven
1938	M Carlhian	1961	H de Lamaze	1977	P Ploujoux
1939	JP Boucheron	1962	H de Lamaze	1978	A Godillot
1945	H Alibaux	1963	Patrick Cros	1979	A Godillot
1946	Ph Boulart	1964	Patrick Cros	1980	A Godillot
1947	H de Lamaze	1965	Patrick Cros	1981	T Planchin
1948	H de Lamaze	1966	H de Lamaze	1982	A Godillot
1949	H de Lamaze	1967	G Mourgue d'Algue	1983	
1950	H de Lamaze			1984	
1951	H de Lamaze	1968	G Mourgue d'Algue	1985	
1952	M Bardana				

French Open Championship

Year	Winner	Score	Year	Winner	Score
1906	A Massy	292	1953	AD Locke	276
1907	A Massy	298	1954	F van Donck	275
1908	JH Taylor	300	1955	Byron Nelson	271
1909	JH Taylor	293	1956	A Miguel	277
1910	James Braid	298	1957	F van Donck	266
1911	Arnaud Massy	284	1958	F van Donck	276
1912	Jean Gassiat	289	1959	DC Thomas	276
1913	George Duncan	304	1960	R De Vicenzo	275
1914	J Douglas Edgar	288	1961	KDG Nagle	271
1920	Walter Hagen	298	1962	A Murray	274
1921	A Boomer	284	1963	B Devlin	273
1922	A Boomer	286	1964	R De Vicenzo	272
1923	Jas Ockenden	288	1965	R Sota	268
1924	CJH Tolley (Am)	290	1966	DJ Hutchinson	274
1925	A Massy	291	1967	BJ Hunt	271
1926	A Boomer	280	1968	PJ Butler	272
1927	George Duncan	299	1969	J Garaialde	277
1928	CJH Tolley (Am)	283	1970	D Graham	268
1929	A Boomer	283	1971	Liang Huan Lu	262
1930	ER Whitcombe	282	1972	B Jaeckel	265
1931	A Boomer	291	1973	P Oosterhuis	280
1932	AJ Lacey	295	1974	P Oosterhuis	284
1933	B Gadd	283	1975	B Barnes	281
1934	SF Brews	284	1976	V Tshabalala	272
1935	SF Brews	293	1977	S Ballesteros	282
1936	M Dallemagne	277	1978	D Hayes	269
1937	M Dallemagne	278	1979	B Gallacher	284
1938	M Dallemagne	282	1980	G Norman	268
1939	M Pose	285	1981	AWB Lyle	270
1946	TH Cotton	269	1982	S Ballesteros	278
1947	TH Cotton	285	1983	N Faldo	277
1948	F Cavalo	287	*(After Play-Off with J-M Canizares and DJ Russell)*		
1949	U Grappasonni	275			
1950	R De Vicenzo	279	1984	B Langer	270
1951	H Hassanein	278	1985	S Ballesteros	263
1952	AD Locke	268	1986	S Ballesteros	269

French Ladies' Open Championship

Instituted 1909

Year	Winner	Year	Winner
1930	Miss Thion de la Chaume	1962	Miss B Varangot
1931	Mrs P Munier	1963	Miss M Gajan
1932	Miss D Fishwick	1964	Miss B Varangot
1933	Miss K Garnham	1965	Miss B Varangot
1934	Miss P Barton	1966	Miss B Varangot
1935	Mrs R Lacoste	1967	Miss C Lacoste
1936	Miss J Anderson	1968	Miss C Cros Rubin
1937	Miss K Garnham	1969	Miss C Lacoste
1938	Mrs R Lacoste	1970	Miss C Lacoste
1939	Mrs R Lacoste	1971	Mrs O Garaialde
1946	Miss M Ruttle	1972	Mrs C Lacoste de Prado
1947	Miss J Donald	1973	Miss B Varangot
1948	Vicomtesse de Saint Sauveur	1974	Mrs L Bayman
1949	Miss Frances Stephens	1975	Mrs I Goldschmid
1950	Vicomtesse de Saint Sauveur	1976	Miss C Maestre
1951	Vicomtesse de Saint Sauveur	1977	Miss A-M Palli
1952	Vicomtesse de Saint Sauveur	1978	Mrs C Mourgue d'Algue
1953	Miss M Caillol	1979	M Figueras-Dotti
1954	Miss O Semelaigne	1980	ML de Lorenzi
1955	Miss O Semelaigne	1981	Mrs C Mourgue D'Algue
1956	Miss M Smith	1982	ML de Lorenzi
1957	Miss M Paul	1983	Miss R Lautens
1958	Mrs Bergamo	1984	Miss LA Chen
1959	Miss O Semelaigne	1985	
1960	Miss C Cros		
1961	Miss B Varangot		

French Ladies' Close Championship

Instituted 1908

Year	Winner	Year	Winner
1934	Miss A de Gunzbourg	1964	Miss C Cros
1935	Miss F Tollon	1965	Miss C Cros
1936	Mrs R Lacoste	1966	Miss B Varangot
1937	Mrs R Lacoste	1967	Miss J Garaialde
1938	Mrs R Lacoste	1968	Miss C Lacoste
1939	Miss L Vagliano	1969	Miss C Lacoste
1946	Vicomtesse de Saint Sauveur	1970	Miss B Varangot
1947	Mrs Binoche	1971	Mrs O Garaialde
1948	Mrs Y de Quellec	1972	Miss A-M Palli
1949	Vicomtesse de Saint Sauveur	1973	Miss A-M Palli
1950	Vicomtesse de Saint Sauveur	1974	Miss A-M Palli
1951	Vicomtesse de Saint Sauveur	1975	Miss M Giraud
1952	Miss M Caillol	1976	Miss A-M Palli
1953	Miss M Caillol	1977	Miss A Lanrezac
1954	Vicomtesse de Saint Sauveur	1978	Miss N Jeanson
1955	Miss O Semelaigne	1979	Miss M-C Ubald-Bocquet
1956	Miss M Paul	1980	E Berthet
1957	Comtesse des Courtil	1981	C Soules
1958	Miss O Semelaigne	1982	E Berthet
1959	Miss B Varangot	1983	Mrs ML de Lorenzi de Taya
1960	Mrs M Mahe		
1961	Miss B Varangot	1984	
1962	Miss B Varangot	1985	
1963	Miss B Varangot		

German Open Championship

Year	Winner	Score	Year	Winner	Score
1912	JH Taylor	277	1962	R Verwey	276
1913-25	*No Competition*		1963	BGC Huggett	278
1926	P Alliss	284	1964	R De Vicenzo	275
1927	P Alliss	288	1965	HR Henning	274
1928	P Alliss	280	1966	R Stanton	274
1929	P Alliss	285	1967	D Swaelens	273
1930	A Boyer	266	1968	B Franklin	285
1931	R Golias	298	1969	J Garaialde	272
1932	A Boyer	282	1970	J Garaialde	276
1933	P Alliss	284	1971	NC Coles	279
1934	AH Padgham	285	1972	G Marsh	271
1935	A Boyer	280	1973	F Abreu	276
1936	A Boyer	291	1974	S Owen	276
1937	TH Cotton	274	1975	M Bembridge	285
1938	TH Cotton	285	1976	S Hobday	266
1939	TH Cotton	280	1977	T Britz	275
1951	A Cerda	286	1978	*For the Braun Trophy*	
1952	A Cerda	283	1978	S Ballesteros	268
1953	F van Donck	271	1979	A Jacklin	277
1954	AD Locke	279	1980	M McNulty	280
1955	K Bousfield	279	1981	B Langer	272
1956	F van Donck	277	1982	B Langer	279
1957	H Weetman	279	1983	C Pavin	275
1958	F de Luca	275	1984	W Grady	268
1959	K Bousfield	271	1985	B Langer	183
1960	PW Thomson	281	*(54 holes only–rain)*		
1961	BJ Hunt	272	1986	B Langer	273

German Open Amateur Championship

Instituted 1913

Year	Winner	Year	Winner	Year	Winner
1950	E Sellschopp	1963	J Hood	1976	H Hedjersson
1951	J Case	1964	KR Bez	1977	J Rube
1952	E Sellschopp	1965	O Wiberg	1978	C Strenger
1953	AT Gonzalez	1966	F Janssen	1979	T Hubner
1954	J Plant	1967	JG Muller	1980	J Rube
1955	K Venturi	1968	R Hunter	1981	K Flint
1956	G Wolstenholme	1969	D Hayes	1982	F Schlig
1957	HB Ridgley	1970	JG Muller	1983	C Stadler
1958	R Taylor	1971	K Nierlich	1984	T Hübner
1959	GA Bielke	1972	V Swane	1985	R Thielemann
1960	Ed Brantley	1973	A Verster	1986	
1961	M Holliday	1974	J Kilian		
1962	P Moller	1975	R Stewart		

German Ladies' Open Championship

Year	Winner
1984	B Huke
1985	J Brown
1986	

German Ladies' Open Amateur Championship

Instituted 1927

Year	Winner	Year	Winner	Year	Winner
1936	Miss D Fishwick	1960	Miss S Lorenz	1974	Dr B Bohm
1937	Miss GE Rudgard	1961	Miss C Cros	1975	Mrs M Gutermann
1938	Miss D Fishwick	1962	Miss M Moller	1976	Miss S Schultz
1939	Miss D Oury	1963	Miss M Steegman	1977	Miss N Eicke
1950	Mrs L Strenger	1964	Mrs M Gutermann	1978	K Ehrnlund
1951	Mrs I Groos	1965	Miss M Petersen	1979	Miss S Blecher
1952	Mrs L Strenger	1966	Miss S Ward	1980	Miss S Blecher
1953	Miss J Bisgood	1967	Miss M Petersen	1981	Miss S Blecher
1954	Mrs L Strenger	1968	Miss M Petersen	1982	Miss S Knodler
1955	Miss A Ward	1969	Mrs O Garaialde	1983	Miss I Bockelmann
1956	Miss B Jackson	1970	Mrs M Gutermann	1984	Mrs S Lampert
1957	Mrs L Strenger	1971	Miss J de Witt Puyt	1985	Mrs M Koch
1958	Miss S Bonallack	1972	Mrs J Weghmann	1986	
1959	Miss S Clifford	1973	Mrs M Gutermann		

German Close Amateur Championship

Instituted 1938

Year	Winner	Year	Winner	Year	Winner
1939	F Boslau	1961	E Sellschopp	1974	V Pagel
1949	H Tissies	1962	P Moller	1975	U Nievert
1950	E Sellschopp	1963	J Burghartz	1976	H-G Heinrigs
1951	E Sellschopp	1964	D Gaertner	1977	T Hubner
1952	E Sellschopp	1965	W Bruhne	1978	V Pagel
1953	E Sellschopp	1966	W Bruhne	1979	C Stadler
1954	A Pemoller	1967	G Koenig	1980	HG Reiter
1955	E Sellschopp	1968	C Strenger	1981	U Schulte
1956	E Sellschopp	1969	J Weghmann	1982	F Schlig
1957	W Goetz	1970	P Jochums	1983	C Domin
1958	H Lampert	1971	P Jochums	1984	A Stamm
1959	H Lampert	1972	JG Muller	1985	F Schlig
1960	G Bruns	1973	P Jochums	1986	

German Ladies' Close Championship

Instituted 1938

Year	Winner	Year	Winner	Year	Winner
1939	Miss M Reuter	1961	Mrs L Strenger	1974	Mrs M Gutermann
1949	Mrs L Strenger	1962	Miss M Steegmann	1975	Mrs M Gutermann
1950	Mrs I Groos	1963	Mrs M Gutermann	1976	Mrs M Gutermann
1951	Mrs L Strenger	1964	Miss M Moller	1977	Dr B Bohm
1952	Mrs L Strenger	1965	Mrs M Gutermann	1978	Mrs M Gutermann
1953	Mrs V Moller	1966	Miss B Bohm	1979	N Eicke-Huth
1954	Mrs L Strenger	1967	Mrs Zintl	1980	Dr B Bohm
1955	Mrs E Buckup	1968	Miss M Moller	1981	Dr B Bohm
1956	Miss M Burghartz	1969	Miss M Petersen	1982	Miss E Peter
1957	Mrs E Buckup	1970	Miss M Steegman	1983	Miss S Knodler
1958	Mrs M Gutermann	1971	Miss M Petersen	1984	Mrs M Koch
1959	Mrs M Gutermann	1972	Miss M Petersen	1985	Mrs R Ruland
1960	Miss M Moller	1973	Mrs M Gutermann	1986	

German Close Professional Championship

Instituted 1927

Year	Winner	Year	Winner	Year	Winner
1930	R Murray	1954	Georg Bessner	1971	S Muehlbauer
1931	Franz Bessner	1955	Georg Bessner	1972	T Kugelmuller
1932	J Kerr	1956	Georg Bessner	1973	S Vollrath
1933	Gerh Muller	1957	Friedel Becker	1974	G Koenig
1934	B Jersombeck	1958	Willy Jersombeck	1975	S Vollrath
1935	D McEwan	1959	K Marx	1976	K-H Goegele
1936	Hans Gonert	1960	Hans Bessner	1977	R Krause
1937	H Kruger	1961	F Schmaderer	1978	K-H Maehl
1938	Gerh Muller	1962	F Schmaderer	1979	B Langer
1939-46	*No Championship*	1963	KH Kleinhenz	1980	H Heiser
1947	B Jersombeck	1964	HJ Hoerenz	1981	M Kessler
1948	Georg Bessner	1965	J Ammer	1982	Heinz-P Thul
1949	Georg Bessner	1966	T Kugelmuller	1983	T Gledeon
1950	Hans Gornert	1967	T Kugelmuller	1984	H-J Kupitz
1951	Georg Bessner	1968	T Kugelmuller	1985	Heinz-P Thul
1952	Georg Bessner	1969	Hans Heiser	1986	
1953	Hans Gornert	1970	T Kugelmuller		

Ghana Championship

Year	Winner	Year	Winner	Year	Winner
1946	AC Russell	1960	P McGonagle	1973	J Doe
1947	PR Marriott	1961	JJ Goggin	1974	CS Ferry
1948	JE Stewart	1962	JJ Goggin	1975	SK Appiah
1949	JE Stewart	1963	S Appiah	1976	P Tetteh
1950	JE Stewart	1964	P McGonagle	1977	J Doe
1951	JE Stewart	1965	GW Davey	1978	Y Kwashie
1952	PR Marriott	1966	EF Munn	1979	J Dey
1953	D McTurk	1967	Fl-Lt CJB Murdock	1980	JK Quarshie
1954	JK Dougal			1981	S Gruter
1955	Dr AM Boyd	1968	EF Munn	1982	*No information*
1956	Dr AM Boyd	1969	EF Munn	1983	*No information*
1957	DA Lane	1970	D Ragni	1984	*No information*
1958	R Leonard	1971	D Abaloo	1985	*No information*
1959	JJ Goggin	1972	SK Appiah	1986	*No information*

Hong Kong Open Championship

Instituted 1959

Year	Winner	Year	Winner	Year	Winner
1959	Lu Liang Huan	1969	T Sugihara	1979	G Norman
1960	Peter Thomson	1970	I Katsumata	1980	Kuo Chi-Hsiung
1961	Kel Nagle	1971	O Moody	1981	Chen Tse Ming
1962	Len Woodward	1972	W Godfrey	1982	Kurt Cox
1963	Hsieh Yung Yo	1973	F Phillips	1983	G Norman
1964	Hsieh Yung Ho	1974	Liang Huan Lu	1984	B Brask
1965	PW Thomson	1975	Hsieh Yung Ho	1985	M Aebli
1966	F Phillips	1976	Ming-Chung Ho	1986	S Kanai
1967	PW Thomson	1977	Hsieh Min Nan		
1968	R Vines	1978	Hsieh Yung Yo		

Iceland Amateur Championship

Year	Winner	Year	Winner	Year	Winner
1942	G Olafsson	1948	JG Helgason	1954	Ol Ag Olaffson
1943	G Olafsson	1949	J Egilson	1955	H Ingmarsson
1944	G Olafsson	1950	Th Asgeirsson	1956	Ol Ag Olafsson
1945	Th Asgeirsson	1951	Th Asgeirsson	1957	Sv Arsælsson
1946	S Júhusson	1952	B Sigurosson	1958	Ma Gudmundson
1947	E Berndsen	1953	E Berndsen	1959	Sv Arsælsson

Iceland Amateur Championship *continued*

Year	Winner	Year	Winner	Year	Winner
1960	J Eyjólfsson	1969	P Kjærbo	1978	H Eyvindsson
1961	G Sólnes	1970	P Kjærbo	1979	H Eyvindsson
1962	O Yngvason	1971	B Thorsteinsson	1980	H Eyvindsson
1963	M Gudmundsson	1972	L Olafsson	1981	R Olafsson
1964	M Gudmundsson	1973	B Thorsteinsson	1982	P Sigurdur
1965	M Gudmundsson	1974	B Thorsteinsson	1983	G Kristinnsson
1966	M Gudmundsson	1975	B Thorsteinsson	1984	S Pétursson
1967	G Sólnes	1976	B Thorsteinsson	1985	S Pétursson
1968	P Kjærbo	1977	B Thorsteinsson	1986	V Jonsson

Iceland Ladies' Championship

Instituted 1967

Year	Winner	Year	Winner
1967	G Sigurthorsdottir	1977	J Ingolfsdottir
1968	G Sigurthorsdottir	1978	J Ingolfsdottir
1969	E Moeller	1979	J Ingolfsdottir
1970	J Gudlaugsdottir	1980	S Thorsteinsdottir
1971	G Sigurthorsdottir	1981	Thorsteinsdóttir So'lveig
1972	J Gudlaugsdottir	1982	Thorsteinsdóttir So'lveig
1973	J Gudlaugsdottir	1983	A Sverrisdottir
1974	J Gudlaugsdottir	1984	A Sverrisdóttir
1975	K Pálsdottir	1985	R Sigurdardóttir
1976	K Pálsdottir	1986	S Saemundsdottir

India Open Championship

Year	Winner	Year	Winner	Year	Winner
1963	PW Thomson	1973	G Marsh	1981	P Stewart
1965	PG Sethi (Am)	1974	Chie-Hsiung Kuo	1982	Hsu Sheng San
1966	PW Thomson	1975	T Ball	1983	J Takahashi (after play-off)
1968	K Hosoishi	1976	PW Thomson	1984	R Alarcon
1969	B Arda	1977	B Jones	1985	A Grimes
1970	C Chung Chen	1978	B Brask	1986	S Saemundsdottir
1971	G Marsh	1979	G Burrows		
1972	B Jones	1980	K Cox		

India Amateur Championship

Instituted 1892

Year	Winner	Year	Winner	Year	Winner
1945	Capt WD Smith	1959	Capt Sethi	1973	RK Pitamber
1946	Col WHH Aitken	1960	AS Malik	1974	V Singh
1947	Brig WHH Aitken	1961	Capt PG Sethi	1975	A Singh
1948	JL Esplen	1962	Capt PG Sethi	1976	A Singh
1949	Mohinder Bal	1963	AS Malik	1977	V Singh
1950	IS Malik	1964	R Pandey	1978	L Singh
1951	JRB Kean	1965	AGG Miller	1979	V Singh
1952	WP Fernando	1966	RK Pitamber	1980	R Mohta
1953	Mohinder Bal	1967	Ashok Malik	1981	M Lewis
1954	WP Fernando	1968	V Singh	1982	L Singh
1955	IS Malik	1969	A Malik	1983	
1956	IS Malik	1970	Maj PG Sethi	1984	
1957	JRB Kean	1971	V Singh	1985	
1958	IS Malik	1972	PG Sethi		

India Ladies' Championship

Year	Winner	Year	Winner
1951	Mrs FC Kidd	1955	Mrs GW Ribbins
1952	Mrs RL de Chaza	1956	Mrs RC Taggart
1953	Mrs RA Wood	1957	Mrs GW Ribbins
1954	Mrs E Lyne	1958	Mrs GW Ribbins

India Ladies' Championship
continued

Year	Winner	Year	Winner
1959	Mrs GW Ribbins	1973	Miss T Fernando (Ceylon)
1960	Mrs CA Buxton	1974	Miss T Fernando (Ceylon)
1961	Mrs GW Ribbins	1975	Miss T Fernando (Sri Lanka)
1962	Mrs HC Brown	1976	Mrs S Rawlley
1963	Mrs GW Ribbins	1977	Mrs S Rawlley
1964	Mrs GW Ribbins	1978	Mrs S Rawlley
1965	Mrs Duncan Smith	1979	Mrs V Tripathi
1966	Mrs Duncan Smith	1980	Miss T Fernando
1967	Mrs Duncan Smith	1981	Ms Maureen Wallis
1968	Mrs Duncan Smith	1982	Mrs R Grewal
1969	Mrs C Wallis	1983	Mrs K Kanwar
1970	Mrs N Desai	1984	
1971	Mrs A Desai	1985	
1972	Mrs B Zemla		

Italian Open Amateur Championship

Instituted 1906

Year	Winner	Year	Winner
1931	Count A di Carpegna	1963	A Schiaffino
1932	JE Dewiel	1964	Min-Nam Hsieh
1933	P Charlton	1965	A Croce
1934	F Malaspina	1966	L Silva
1935	T Fraschini	1967	G Hyde
1936	F Boulart	1968	J Jacobsen
1937	L Luzzatto	1969	P Toussaint
1938	R Schill	1970	G Moerman
1947	L Corti	1971	L Silva
1948	A Barras	1972	D Lovato
1949	HD Dillier	1973	A Schiaffino
1950	J Haslewood	1974	E de la Riva
1951	R Terrat	1975	A Lionello
1952	F Bevione	1976	S Betti
1953	E Bergamo	1977	L Silva
1954	H Bentley	1978	R Taya
1955	H de Lamaze	1979	M Lamberg
1956	F Bevione	1980	A Canessa
1957	F Bevione	1981	M Durante
1958	H de Lamaze	1982	C Francis
1959	M Bardana	1983	JM Olazabal
1960	Richard Chapman	1984	M Luzzi
1961	M Bardana	1985	JM Olazabal
1962	A Croce	1986	A Binaghi

Italian Ladies' Open Championship

Year	Winner	Year	Winner
1931	Mrs Maxwell	1958	Mrs I Goldschmid
1932	Mrs Rivolta	1959	Mrs V Bohus Rosa
1933	*No competition*	1960	Mrs I Goldschmid
1934	Mrs O Mundy	1961	Mrs I Goldschmid
1935	Mrs S Uzielli	1962	Mrs A Engel Jacquet
1936	*No competition*	1963	Mrs I Goldschmid
1937	Miss AR de Orchi	1964	Mrs I Goldschmid
1938	Miss L Fummi	1965	Mrs V Bohus Rosa
1948	Psse Liliane de Rethi	1966	Miss A van Lanshot
1949	Vicomtesse de Saint Sauveur	1967	Mrs I Goldschmid
1950	Mrs Bergamo	1968	Mrs I Goldschmid
1951	Vicomtesse de Saint Sauveur	1969	Mrs I Goldschmid
1952	I Goldschmid-Bevione	1970	Miss B Varangot
1953	Miss J Bisgood	1971	Miss C Reybroeck
1954	Mrs M Dommers	1972	M Ciaffi Ragher
1955	Miss A Jacquet	1973	M Ciaffi Ragher
1956	Mrs J Prion	1974	E Garcia Ogara
1957	Mrs I Goldschmid	1975	C de Artasona

Italian Ladies' Open Championship *continued*

Year	Winner	Year	Winner
1976	F Dassu	1982	M Figueras Dotti
1977	C Mourgue d'Algue	1983	Miss C Maestre
1978	M Ragher	1984	Miss R Lautens
1979	M Figueras Dotti	1985	Miss R Lautens
1980	E Braito	1986	Miss S Shapcott
1981	E Berthet		

Italian Close Amateur Championship

Instituted 1930

Year	Winner	Year	Winner	Year	Winner
1946	F Bevione	1961	F Bevione	1976	A Lionello
1947	F Bevione	1962	A Croce	1977	F Gigliarelli
1948	L Corti	1963	C Cobianchi	1978	L Silva
1949	F Bevione	1964	L Silva	1979	S Grappasonni
1950	F Bevione	1965	L Silva	1980	F Ghirardi
1951	E Bergamo	1966	A Croce	1981	A Canessa
1952	A Lang	1967	F Bevione	1982	L Silva
1953	F Bevione	1968	F Bevione	1983	S Grappasonni
1954	F Bevione	1969	A Schiaffino	1984	S Prati
1955	F Bevione	1970	F Camilotti	1985	E Nistri
1956	F Bevione	1971	F Bevione	1986	A Binaghi
1957	E Bergamo	1972	S Esente		
1958	A Croce	1973	L Silva		
1959	F Bevione	1974	M Mannelli		
1960	F Bevione	1975	A Croce		

Italian Professional Championship

Year	Winner	Year	Winner	Year	Winner
1936	L Prette	1956	A Casera	1972	D Canonica
1937	G Zuppini	1957	U Grappasonni	1973	R Bernardini
1938	U Grelli	1958	A Angelini	1974	B Dassu
1939	G Zuppini	1959	A Angelini	1975	R Bernardini
1940	P Manca	1960	A Croce (Am)	1976	B Dassu
1941	U Grappasonni	1961	A Angelini	1977	B Dassu
1942	P Travaini	1962	A Angelini	1978	R Campagnoli
1947	A Angelini	1963	O Bolognesi	1979	D Lovato
1948	A Casera	1964	A Angelini	1980	R Campagnoli
1949	A Casera	1965	A Angelini	1981	M Mannelli
1950	*Not played*	1966	D Canonica	1982	D Lovato
1951	A Angelini	1967	R Bernardini	1983	S Locatelli
1952	A Angelini	1968	R Bernardini	1984	C Rocca
1953	A Angelini	1969	A Angelini	1985	G Coli
1954	U Grappasonni	1970	M Canessa	1986	M Mannelli
1955	U Grappasonni	1971	M Canessa		

Italian Open Championship

Year	Winner	Score	Year	Winner	Score
1927	P Alliss	145	1937	M Dallemagne	276
1928	A Boyer	145	1938	F van Donck	276
1929	R Golias	143	1947	F van Donck	263
1930	A Boyer	140	1948	A Casera	267
1931	A Boyer	141	1949	H Hassanein	263
1932	A Boomer	143	1950	U Grappasonni	281
1933	*No competition*		1951	J Adams	289
1934	N Nutley	132	1952	EC Brown	273
1935	P Alliss	262	1953	F van Donck	267
1936	TH Cotton	268	1954	U Grappasonni	272

Italian Open Championship

continued

Year	Winner	Score	Year	Winner	Score
1955	F van Donck	287	1977	A Gallardo	286
1956	A Cerda		1978	D Hayes	293
1957	H Henning	273	1979	B Barnes	281
1958	P Alliss	282	1980	M Mannelli	276
1959	PW Thomson	269	1981	JM Canizares	280
1960	BBS Wilkes	285	1982	M James	280
1961-70	*No competition*		1983	B Langer	271
1971	R Sota	282	*(After Play-Off with K Brown and S Ballesteros)*		
1972	N Wood	271	1984	AWB Lyle	277
1973	A Jacklin	284	1985	M Pinero	267
1974	PA Oosterhuis	249	1986	D Feherty	270
1975	W Casper	286	*(After Play-Off with R Rafferty)*		
1976	B Dassu	280			

Jamaica Open Championship

Year	Winner	Year	Winner	Year	Winner
1953	WL Ward	1965	H Urquhart, snr	1977	S Rose
1954	R Posse	1966	W Urquhart	1978	R Bassett
1955	A Cerda	1967	J Markland	1979	N Marsh
1956	R De Vicenzo	1968	W Ward, jun	1980	R Blake
1957	R De Vicenzo	1969	L Yearwood	1981	D Markham
1958	R Toski	1970	A Cunningham	1982	Seymour Rose
1959	Ed Oliver	1971	S Maharaj (3 rds)	1983	B Lane
1960	P Cooper	1972	M Higuera	1984	
1961	J Ferree	1973	N Wood	1985	
1962	H Williams, jun	1974	M Higuera		
1963	John Barnum	1975	Bob Shaw		
1964	J Markland (3 rds)	1976	M Higuera		

Japan Amateur Championship

Year	Winner	Year	Winner	Year	Winner
1930	R Akahoshi	1954	N Miyoshi	1971	T Irie
1931	K Nitta	1955	N Miyoshi	1972	T Irie
1932	K Narumiya	1956	H Chock	1973	T Nakajima
1933	N Nabeshima	1957	A Small	1974	G Nakabe
1934	N Nabeshima	1958	K Ishimoto	1975	M Kuramoto
1935	N Nabeshima	1959	I Nakabe	1976	M Mori
1936	AG Satoh	1960	M Tanaka	1977	M Kuramoto
1937	AG Satoh	1961	K Ishimoto	1978	G Nakabe
1938	AG Satoh	1962	G Nakabe	1979	N Yuhara
1939	M Harada	1963	H Morimoto	1980	M Kuramoto
1941	AG Satoh	1964	G Nakabe	1981	M Naito
1942	K Narumiya	1965	S Morikawa	1982	I Kanamoto
1943-49	*No championship*	1966	G Nakabe	1983	
1950	K Tsukimoto	1967	G Nakabe	1985	
1951	PE Abraham	1968	K Okawa	1986	Y Ito
1952	J Shibamoto	1969	K Yamada		
1953	N Miyoshi	1970	K Yamada		

Japan Open Championship

Year	Winner	Score	Year	Winner	Score
1927	R Akahoshi	309	1941	En Toku Shun	290
1928	R Asami	301	1942-49	*No championship*	
1929	T Miyamoto	298	1950	Y Hayashi	288
1930	T Miyamoto	287	1951	Son Shi Kin	284
1931	R Asami	281	1952	T Nakamura	278
1932	T Miyamoto	298	1953	Son Shi Kin	299
1933	K Nakamura	294	1954	Y Hayashi	291
1934	*No championship*		1955	K Ono	293
1935	T Miyamoto	293	1956	T Nakamura	281
1936	T Miyamoto	296	1957	H Kobari	285
1937	Chin Sei Sui	284	1958	T Nakamura	288
1938	RM Fuku	294	1959	Chen Ching-Po	298
1939	T Toda	287	1960	H Kobari	296
1940	T Miyamoto	285	1961	K Hosoishi	289

Japan Open Championship

continued

Year	Winner	Score	Year	Winner	Score
1962	T Sugihara	287	1975	T Murakami	278
1963	T Toda	283	1976	K Shimada	288
1964	H Sugimoto	288	1977	S Ballesteros	284
1965	T Kitta	284	1978	S Ballesteros	281
1966	S Sato	285	1979	Kuo Chie-Hsiung	285
1967	T Kitta	282	1980	S Kikuchi	296
1968	T Kono	284	1981	Y Hagawa	280
1969	H Sugimoto	284	1982	A Yabe	277
1970	M Kitta	282	1983	Barry Lane	
1971	Y Fujii	282	1984	K Uehara	283
1972	H Chang Sang	278	1985	T Nakajima	285
1973	B Arda	278	1986	T Nakajima	284
1974	M Ozaki	279			

Japan Professional Championship

Year	Winner	Year	Winner	Year	Winner
1931	R Asami	1955	K Ono	1971	M Ozaki
1932	L Montes	1956	Y Hayashi	1972	S Kanai
1933	L Montes	1957	T Nakamura	1973	I Aoki
1934	T Miyamoto	1958	T Nakamura	1974	M Ozaki
1935	T Toda	1959	T Nakamura	1975	T Murakami
1936	T Miyamoto	1960	R Tanaami	1976	S Kanai
1937	I Uekata	1961	Y Hayashi	1977	T Nakajima
1938	T Toda	1962	T Nakamura	1978	F Kobayashi
1939	T Toda	1963	T Kitta	1979	Hsieh Min-Nan
1940	T Toda	1964	T Kitta	1980	Y Yamamoto
1941-49	*No championship*	1965	M Kono	1981	I Aoki
1950	Y Hayashi	1966	M Kono	1982	M Kuramoto
1951	T Ishii	1967	S Miyamoto	1983	
1952	S Inoue	1968	K Shimada	1984	T Nakajima
1953	Chin Sei Sui	1969	H Ishii	1985	T Ozaki
1954	S Ishif	1970	S Sato	1986	I Aoki

Kenya Open Championship

Year	Winner	Year	Winner	Year	Winner
1967	G Wolstenholme	1974	D Jagger	1981	B Barnes
1968	M Bembridge	1975	G Smith	1982	E Darcy
1969	M Bembridge	1976	*Cancelled*	1983	K Brown
1970	J Dorrestein	1977	L Higgins	1984	J Canizares
1971	E Jones	1978	S Ballesteros	1985	G Harvey
1972	D Llewellyn	1979	M Bembridge	1986	I Woosnam
1973	J Dorrestein	1980	B Waites		

Korea Open Championship

Year	Winner	Year	Winner	Year	Winner
1979	Shen Chung Shyan	1982	Choi Yoon Soo	1985	Chen Tze-Chung
1980	Chen Tze Ming	1983	*Not available*	1986	C-T Tsao
1981	Chen Tze Ming	1984	M Clayton		

Korea Professional Championship

Year	Winner	Year	Winner	Year	Winner
1979	Kang Cheon Lee	1982	Sang Ho Choi	1985	
1980	Seun Hak Kim	1983	Jin Han Lim		
1981	Jung Woong Park	1984	*Not available*		

Korea Amateur Championship

Year	Winner	Year	Winner	Year	Winner
1979	Byung Hoon Kim	1982	Yoo Hyun Kwak	1985	
1980	Byung Hoon Kim	1983	Suk Jong Kim		
1981	Nam Hyun Kim	1984	*Not available*		

Malaysian Open Championship

Year	Winner	Year	Winner	Year	Winner
1963	Billy Dunk	1971	T Kono	1979	Hsi-Chuen Lu
1964	T Ishii	1972	T Murakami	1980	M McNulty
1965	T Ishii	1973	Hideyo Sugimoto	1981	Hsi-Chuen Lu
1966	HR Henning	1974	G Marsh	1982	D Hepler
1967	I Legaspi	1975	G Marsh	1983	T Gale
1968	K Hosoishi	1976	Hsu Sheng-San	1984	L Chien-Soon
1969	T Kono	1977	S Ginn	1985	T Gale
1970	B Arda	1978	B Jones	1986	S Ginn

New Zealand Amateur Championship

Instituted 1893

Year	Winner	Year	Winner	Year	Winner
1930	HA Black	1953	DL Woon	1970	EJ McDougall
1931	R Wagg	1954	DL Woon	1971	SG Jones
1932	R Wagg	1955	SG Jones	1972	RC Murray
1933	BV Wright	1956	PA Toogood	1973	MN Nicholson
1934	BM Silk	1957	EJ McDougall	1974	RM Barltrop
1935	JP Hornabrook	1958	WJ Godfrey	1975	SF Reese
1936	JP Hornabrook	1959	SG Jones	1976	TR Pulman
1937	BM Silk	1960	R Newdick	1977	TR Pulman
1938	PGF Smith	1961	SG Jones	1978	F Nobilo
1939	JP Hornabrook	1962	SG Jones	1979	J Durry
1946	WG Horne	1963	J Durry	1980	PE Harlstone
1947	BM Silk	1964	SG Jones	1981	T Cochrane
1948	A Gibbs	1965	J Durry	1982	I Peters
1949	J Holden	1966	SG Jones	1983	
1950	DL Woon	1967	J Durry	1984	
1951	DL Woon	1968	BA Stevens	1985	
1952	H Berwick	1969	G Stevenson		

New Zealand Open Championship

Year	Winner	Year	Winner	Year	Winner
1907	ADS Duncan (Am)	1935	A Murray	1965	PW Thomson
1908	JA Clements	1936	AJ Shaw	1966	R Charles
1909	JA Clements	1937	JP Hornabrook	1967	KDG Nagle
1910	ADS Duncan (Am)	1938	AD Locke	1968	KDG Nagle
1911	ADS Duncan (Am)	1939	JP Hornabrook	1969	KDG Nagle
1912	JA Clements	1946	RH Glading (Am)	1970	RJ Charles
1913	ES Douglas	1947	RH Glading (Am)	1971	P Thomson
1914	ES Douglas	1948	A Murray	1972	EW Dunk
1919	ES Douglas	1949	James Galloway	1973	RJ Charles
1920	JH Kirkwood	1950	PW Thomson	1974	R Gilder
1921	ES Douglas	1951	PW Thomson	1975	EW Dunk
1922	A Brooks	1952	A Murray	1976	S Owen
1923	A Brooks	1953	PW Thomson	1977	B Byman
1924	EJ Moss	1954	RJ Charles	1978	R Shearer
1925	EM Macfarlane (Am)	1955	PW Thomson	1979	S Ginn
1926	AJ Shaw	1956	NW Berwick	1980	B Allin
1927	EJ Moss	1957	K Nagle	1981	R Shearer
1928	S Morpeth (Am)	1958	K Nagle	1982	T Gale
1929	AJ Shaw	1959	PW Thomson	1983	I Baker-Finch
1930	AJ Shaw	1960	PW Thomson	1984	B Devlin
1931	AJ Shaw	1961	PW Thomson	1985	DA Weilbring
1932	AJ Shaw	1962	K Nagle	1986	C Pavin
1933	EJ Moss	1963	BW Devlin		
1934	AJ Shaw	1964	KDG Nagle		

New Zealand Ladies' Open Championship

Instituted 1893

Year	Winner	Year	Winner
1930	Miss O Kay	1962	Miss P Harrison
1931	Miss B Gainsford	1963	Miss J Greenhalgh (GB)
1932	Mrs JC Templer	1964	Miss M Hickey
1933	Miss O Kay	1965	Miss G Taylor
1934	Miss B Gainsford	1966	Miss N White
1935	Miss J Anderson (GB)	1967	Mrs DA Whitehead
1936	Miss E White Parsons	1968	Mrs J Perkins
1937	Mrs GW Hollis	1969	Miss U Wickham
1938	Miss S Collins	1970	Mrs ND Cullen
1946	Miss J Horwell	1971	Mrs IC Robertson (GB)
1947	Miss E Wilkinson	1972	Mrs H Gosse
1948	Mrs J Ball (*née* J Horwell)	1973	Mrs DA Whitehead
1949	Miss Z Hudson	1974	Miss C Sullivan
1950	Miss Z Hudson	1975	Miss R Low
1951	Miss M Bishop	1976	Mrs WR Douglas
1952	Miss M Hughes	1977	Miss K Maxwell
1953	Miss M Bishop	1978	Miss J Crafter
1954	Miss A Nash	1979	Miss S Tonkin
1955	Miss V Anstey (GB)	1980	Mrs B Rhodes
1956	Miss M Masters	1981	Mrs B Rhodes
1957	Miss S Grigg	1982	Miss J Arnold
1958	Miss N Campbell	1983	Miss C Dibnah
1959	Miss Una Wickham	1984	
1960	Miss N Campbell	1985	
1961	Miss N Campbell	1986	Miss A Kita

New Zealand Professional Championship

Year	Winner	Year	Winner	Year	Winner
1920	JH Kirkwood	1947	A Murray	1967	R Shaw
1921	ES Douglas	1948	A Murray	1968	R Shaw
1922	A Ham	1949	BH Glading	1969	T Kendall
1923	EJ Moss	1950	EA Southernden	1970	KDG Nagle
1924	EJ Moss	1951	RA Jackson	1971	J Lister
1925	EJ Moss	1952	GE Hudson	1972	M Ozaki
1926	J McIntosh	1953	PW Thomson	1973	KDG Nagle
1927	J McIntosh	1954	B Crampton	1974	KDG Nagle
1928	AJ Shaw	1955	F Phillips	1975	KDG Nagle
1929	AJ Shaw	1956	J Kelly	1976	J Lister
1930	F Rutter	1957	KDG Nagle	1977	J Lister
1931	AJ Shaw	1958	KDG Nagle	1978	S Owen
1932	AJ Shaw	1959	EA Southernden	1979	R Charles
1933	AJ Shaw	1960	KDG Nagle	1980	R Charles
1934	AJ Shaw	1961	Bob Charles	1981	T Gale
1935	A Murray	1962	EA Southernden	1982	S Reese
1936	CC Clement	1963	R Tuohy	1983	
1937	ES Douglas	1964	*Not played*	1984	
1938	NH Fuller	1965	BJ Coxon	1985	
1939	A Murray	1966	R Newdick		

Nigerian Open Championship

Year	Winner	Year	Winner	Year	Winner
1969	MC Douglas	1975	D Jagger	1981	P Tupling
1970	J Cook	1976	W Longmuir	1982	D Jagger
1971	L Elder	1977	D Jagger	1983	G Brand
1972	*Not played*	1978	AWB Lyle	1984	E Murray
1973	T Horton	1979	J Morgan	1985	W Longmuir
1974	J Newton	1980	W Longmuir	1986	G Brand

Pakistan Amateur Championship

Year	Winner	Year	Winner
1961	JG Downie	1974	T Hassan
1962	Ibrahim Musa	1975	T Hassan
1963	MM Hashim Khan	1976	T Hassan
1964	J Fischer	1977	T Hassan
1965	MM Hashim Khan	1978	T Hassan
1966	Mohammad Ali Shah	1979	T Hassan
1967	Mahmood Hussian	1980	T Hassan
1968	Asad Anis Ansari	1981	T Hassan
1969	MM Hashim Khan	1982	I Ahmed
1970	Murtaza Qasim	1983	
1971	Taimur Hassan	1984	
1972	T Hassan	1985	
1973	T Hassan		

Pakistan Ladies' Championship

Year	Winner	Year	Winner
1961	Mrs Hastings	1967	Miss Ghazala Ansari
1962	Miss S Allum	1968	Miss Yasmeen Waheed
1963	Miss S Allum	1969	Miss Nizhat Shahban
1964	Miss Ghazala Ansari	1970	Miss Nizhat Shahban
1965	Miss Ghazala Ansari	1971	Mrs Ghazala Sattar
1966	Miss Ghazala Ansari	1972	*Not played*

Pakistan Ladies' Championship *continued*

Year	Winner	Year	Winner
1973	Mrs T Shah	1980	Miss S Wali
1974	Mrs S Nazir	1981	Miss T Butt
1975	Mrs T Shah	1982	Miss A Aftab
1976	Miss S Wali	1983	
1977	Miss G Ansari	1984	
1978	Mrs N Afridi	1985	
1979	*Not played*		

Pakistan Open Championship

Year	Winner	Year	Winner
1967	Aameen Taqi Butt (Am)	1977	M Ejaz Malik
1968	Mehmood Hussain	1978	M Ejaz Malik
1969	Mehmood Hussain	1979	Taimur Hassan (Am)
1970	Mehmood Hussain	1980	Abdul Rashid
1971	Mehmood Hussain	1981	*Not played*
1972	Mohammad Ejaz Malik	1982	Gaulam Nabi
1973	Mehmood Hassain	1983	
1974	Mohammad Shafique	1984	
1975	M Angoor Khan	1985	
1976	Taimur Hassan (Am)		

Philippines Open Championship

Year	Winner	Year	Winner
1962	C Tugot	1975	Kuo Chie Hsiong
1963	B Arda	1976	Q Mancao
1964	PW Thomson	1977	Hsieh Yung Yo
1965	Liang Huan Lu	1978	Liang Huan Lu
1966	L Silverio (Am)	1979	B Arda
1967	Hsu-Sheng San	1980	Hsi-Chuen Lu
1968	Hsu Chi San	1981	Tom Sieckmann
1969	Haruo Yasuda	1982	Min-Nan Hsieh
1970	Hsieh Yung Yo	1983	Hsi-Chuen Lu
1971	C Chien Chung	1984	R Lavares
1972	H Sugimoto	1985	
1973	King Seung Hack		
1974	Liang Huan Lu		

Portuguese Open Amateur Championship

Year	Winner	Year	Winner
1936	John Delaforce	1954	Carlos de Vilhena
1937	Francis Ricardo	1955	Ivan Maura
1938	TC Irving	1956	JG Murray, jun
1939	NG de Brito e Cunha	1957	MTW Easby
1940	Javier Araña	1958	MTW Easby
1941	Marquês de Sobroso	1959	M de Brito e Cunha
1942	Visconde P Machado	1960	D Chapman
1943	Visconde P Machado	1961	J de Figueirado
1944	TC Irving	1962	NA de Brito e Cunha
1945	Luis Ignácio Araña	1963	NA de Brito e Cunha
1946	Luis Ignácio Araña	1964	Duque de Fernan Nunez
1947	Visconde P Machado	1965	F Pinto Coelho
1948	Visconde P Machado	1966	F Pinto Coelho
1949	Enrique F-Villaverde	1967	WD Smith
1950	Enrique F-Villaverde	1968	John M Leach
1951	Peter E Dawson	1969	KG Drage
1952	Henri de Lamaze	1970	WD Smith
1953	Fernando Pinto Coelho	1971	J Lara Sousa e Melo

Portuguese Open Amateur Championship

continued

Year	Winner	Year	Winner
1972	J Lara Sousa e Melo	1980	J Sousa e Melo
1973	A Pearce	1981	G Brand
1974	G Clark	1982	M Higgins
1975	P Caupers	1983	U Schulte
1976	J Lara Sousa e Melo	1984	
1977	U Nievert	1985	
1978	J Sousa e Melo		
1979	N Brito e Cunha, jun		

Portuguese Ladies' Open Amateur Championship

Year	Winner	Year	Winner
1940	Miss Dawson	1963	Bárbara de Brito e Cunha
1941	Mrs Shervington	1964	Miss E Fisher
1942	Mrs R Woodward	1965	Vanda Bohus
1943	Núria Soler	1966	Vanda Bohus
1944	Helena Perez	1967	Miss L Forsell
1945	Colette Hanley	1968	Mrs B Green
1946	Colette Hanley	1969	Vera Lennox
1947	Colette Hanley	1970	P Tredinnick
1948	Katya d'Andrade	1971	Vera Lennox
1949	Vera Espirito Santo Silva	1972	Miss Michelle Walker
1950	Colette Hanley	1973	Miss A Gale
1951	Princesa Chirinsky-Chihmatoff	1974	Miss C Mackintosh
1952	Bárbara de Brito e Cunha	1975	C Marcusson
1953	M Améliade Sousa Lara	1976	E Braito
1954	Miss Jeanne Bisgood	1977	A Gale
1955	Vanda Rosa	1978	A Gale
1956	Vanda Rosa	1979	A Gale
1957	Miss Angela Ward	1980	Mrs C Caldwell
1958	Vanda Rosa	1981	V Dulout
1959	Bárbara de Brito e Cunha	1982	Miss S Blecher
1960	Marjory A Fowler	1983	Miss K Douglas
1961	Bárbara de Brito e Cunha	1984	
1962	Ana Maria Marfull	1985	

Portuguese Close Amateur Championship

Year	Winner	Year	Winner
1938	NG de Brito e Cunha	1963	Manuel Leao
1939	NG de Brito e Cunha	1964	Fernando Pinto Coelho
1940	NG de Brito e Cunha	1965	NA de Brito e Cunho
1941	NG de Brito e Cunha	1966	Jorge de Figueredo
1942	Visconde P Machado	1967	Manuel Leao
1943	Visconde P Machado	1968	F Pinto Coelho
1944	Visconde P Machado	1969	JL de Sousa e Melo
1945	Luis de Sousa Lara	1970	JL de Sousa e Melo
1946	Antonió Casanovas	1971	JL de Sousa e Melo
1947	Manuel de Brito e Cunha	1972	JL de Sousa e Melo
1948	José Posser de Andrade	1973	JL de Sousa e Melo
1949	Luis de Meyrelles	1974	A Carmona Santos
1950	Nuno de Castro Pereira	1975	J Caupers
1951	Nuno de Castro Pereira	1976	JL de Sousa e Melo
1952	Visconde P Machado	1977	R Bivar
1953	Carlos de Vilhena	1978	JL de Sousa e Melo
1954	Fernando Pinto Coelho	1979	JL de Sousa e Melo
1955	Visconde P Machado	1980	NA de Brito e Cunha
1956	Fran Posser de Andrade	1981	Antonio Dantas
1957	Jose de Sousa e Melo	1982	J Silva Bento
1958	D Espirito Santo Silva	1983	Antonio Guerreiro
1959	D Espirito Santo Silva	1984	
1960	NA de Brito e Cunha	1985	
1961	JFC de Oliveira		
1962	DE Santo Silva		

Portuguese Open Championship

Year	Winner	Score	Year	Winner	Score
1953	EC Brown	260	1970	R Sota	274
1954	A Miguel	263	1971	L Platts	277
1955	F van Donck	267	1972	G Garrido	196
1956	A Miguel	268	1973	J Benito	294
1957	*Not played*		1974	BGC Huggett	272
1958	P Alliss	264	1975	H Underwood	292
1959	Sebastian Miguel	265	1976	S Balbuena	283
1960	Ken Bousfield	268	1977	M Ramos	287
1961	Ken Bousfield	263	1978	HK Clark	291
1962	Alfonso Angelini	269	1979	B Barnes	287
1963	R Sota	204	1980	*Not played*	
1964	A Miguel	279	1981	*Not played*	
1965	*Not played*		1982	S Torrance	207
1966	Alfonso Angelini	273	1983	S Torrance	286
1967	Angel Gallardo	214	1984	T Johnstone	274
1968	M Faulkner	273	1985	W Humphreys	279
1969	R Sota	270	1986	M McNulty	270

Scandinavian Ladies' Open Amateur Championship

Year	Winner	Year	Winner
1956	Miss A Ward	1971	Liv Forsell
1957	Mrs B Mattsson	1972	Liv Wollin
1958	Miss M Moller	1973	M Anderson
1959	Mrs B Mattsson	1974	A Skanse
1960	Miss M Moller	1975	E Gedervall
1961	Miss S Lorentz	1976	A Skanse
1962	Miss MV Riemsdijk	1977	E Wahlquist
1963	Miss L Forsell	1978	V Hoff
1964	Miss L Forsell	1979	G Linner
1965	Miss L Forsell	*Played every second year*	
1966	Miss A van Lanschot	1981	H Morse
1967	Miss Liv Forsell	1983	Miss A Peitersen
1968	Nina Rehnqvist	1984	T Pors
1969	S Bjorge	1985	
1970	Liv Forsell		

Scandinavian Men's Open Amateur Championship

Year	Winner	Year	Winner
1956	GA Bielke	1971	G Mueller
1957	L Leinborn	1972	C Johncke
1958	G Carlander	1973	J Horn
1959	Franco Bevione	1974	H Hedjersson
1960	L Leinborn	1975	O Dahlgren
1961	Maj DA Blair	1976	M Sorling
1962	A le Page	1977	M Sorling
1963	L Leinborn	1978	M Sorling
1964	P Heidenreich	1979	T Eriksen
1965	M Attenborough	*Played every second year*	
1966	RR Unger	1981	M Hennberg
1967	Claes Johncke	1983	S Hylen
1968	Nils E Jensen	1984	S Tinning
1969	Claes Johncke	1985	
1970	Sven Tumba		

Sierra Leone Open Championship

Instituted 1932

Year	Winner	Year	Winner	Year	Winner
1970	P Urwin	1976	RD Shade	1982	M Miller
1971	J Brown	1977	DL Ingram	1983	
1972	RG Leonard	1978	E Murray	1984	
1973	RG Leonard	1979	E Murray	1985	
1974	J Brown	1980	*Not played*		
1975	J Brown	1981	M Miller		

Singapore Open Championship

Year	Winner	Year	Winner
1957	H Knaggs	1973	B Arda
1958	DW McMullen	1974	E Nival
1959	RCW Stokes	1975	Y Suzuki
1961	F Phillips	1976	K Uchida
1962	Brian Wilkes	1977	Chi-San Hsu
1963	A Brookes	1978	T Gale
1964	T Ball	1979	Hsi Cheun Lu
1965	F Phillips	1980	K Cox
1966	R Newdick	1981	M Aye
1967	B Arda	1982	Hsu Cheng San
1968	Hsieh Yung Yo	1983	Chien-Soon Lu
1969	T Kamata	(*After Play-Off with B Brask*)	
1970	Hsieh Yung Yo	1984	T Sieckmann
1971	H Yasuda	1985	Chen Tze Ming
1972	T Kono	1986	G Turner

Singapore Open Amateur Championship

Year	Winner	Year	Winner
1957	H Knaggs	1972	JW Stewart
1958	DW McMullen	1973	W Bosley
1959	RCW Stokes	1974	T Manotoc
1960	NA Harvey	1975	JW Stewart
1961	S du Plessis	1976	Bill Bosley
1962	S du Plessis	1977	AS Malik
1963	S du Plessis	1978	E Tjahjana
1964	NA Harvey	1979	Sumarno
1965	A Murdoch	1980	G Suwirjo
1966	HMV de Lacy Staunton	1981	J Stewart
1967	Luis Silverio	1982	
1968	Phus Thin Kiay	1983	
1969	JC Halliday	1984	
1970	JC Halliday	1985	
1971	JT Clifford		

South African Amateur Championship

Year	Winner	Year	Winner	Year	Winner
1935	AD Locke	1938	B Wynne	1946	JR Boyd
1936	CE Olander	1939	O Haynes	1947	C de G Watermeyer
1937	AD Locke	1940	HEP Watermeyer	1948	RR Ryan

South African Amateur Championship

continued

Year	Winner	Year	Winner	Year	Winner
1949	RW Glennie	1962	J Hayes	1975	P Vorster
1950	EA Dalton	1963	D Symons	1976	R Kotzen
1951	ES Irwin	1964	JR Langridge	1977	EA Webber
1952	M Janks	1965	P Vorster	1978	EA Webber
1953	R Brews	1966	Comrie du Toit	1979	L Norval
1954	A Jackson	1967	Derek Kemp	1980	E Groenewald
1955	B Keyter	1968	R Williams	1981	D Suddards
1956	RC Taylor	1969	D Thornton	1982	N James
1957	A Stewart	1970	H Baiocchi	1983	G-C Yuan
1958	JR Boyd	1971	C Dreyer	1984	M Wiltshire
1959	A Walker	1972	N Sundelson	1985	N Clarke
1960	WM Grinrod	1973	A Oosthuizen		
1961	JG Le Roux	1974	T Lagerwey		

South African Amateur Stroke Play Championship

Instituted 1969

Year	Winner	Year	Winner	Year	Winner
1969	D Hayes	1975	G Levenson	1981	CC Yuan
1970	D Hayes	1976	G Harvey	1982	WS Li
1971	K Suddards	1977	MW McNulty	1983	P van der Riet
1972	P Dunne	1978	D Suddards	1984	D James
1973	G Harvey	1979	D Suddards	1985	D van Staden
1974	N Sundelson	1980	E Groenewald		

South African Open Championship

Year	Winner	Score	Year	Winner	Score
1930	SF Brews	297	1962	HR Henning	285
1931	SF Brews	302	1963	R Waltman	281
1932	C McIlvenny	304	1964	A Henning	278
1933	SF Brews	297	1965	Gary Player	273
1934	SF Brews	319	1966	Gary Player	274
1935	AD Locke (Am)	296	1967	Gary Player	279
1936	CE Olander (Am)	297	1968	Gary Player	278
1937	AD Locke (Am)	288	1969	Gary Player	273
1938	AD Locke	279	1970	T Horton	285
1939	AD Locke	279	1971	S Hobday	276
1940	AD Locke	293	1972	Gary Player	274
1946	AD Locke	285	1973	RJ Charles	282
1947	RW Glennie (Am)	293	1974	R Cole	272
1948	M Janks (Am)	298	1975	Gary Player	278
1949	SF Brews	291	1976	D Hayes	287
1950	AD Locke	287	1976	Gary Player	280
1951	AD Locke	275	1977	Gary Player	273
1952	SF Brews	300	1978	H Baiocchi	285
1953	JR Boyd (Am)	302	1979	Gary Player	279
1954	RC Taylor (Am)	289	1980	R Cole	279
1955	AD Locke	283	1981	Gary Player	272
1956	Gary Player	286	1982	*Not played*	
1957	H Henning	289	1983	C Bolling	278
1958	AA Stewart (Am)	281	1984	A Johnstone	274
1959	D Hutchinson (Am)	282	1985	G Levenson	280
1960	Gary Player	288	1986	D Frost	275
1961	R Waltman	289			

South African Masters

Year	Winner	Year	Winner	Year	Winner
1960	GJ Player	1969	RE Cole	1978	*Not played*
1961	DJ Hutchinson	1970	J Fourie (Am)	1979	GJ Player
1962	DJ Hutchinson	1971	GJ Player	1980	Nick Price
1963	B Keyter	1972	GJ Player	1981	M McNulty
1964	GJ Player	1973	GJ Player	1982	M McNulty
1965	DJ Hutchinson	1974	GJ Player	1983	*Not played*
1966	C Amm	1975	J Fourie (Am)	1984	A Johnstone
1967	G Player	1976	GJ Player	1985	
1968	C Legrange	1977	GJ Player	1986	M McNulty

South African PGA Championship

Year	Winner	Year	Winner	Year	Winner
1965	H Henning	1973	T Weiskopf (Am)	1981	*Not played*
1966	H Henning	1974	D Hayes	1982	G Player
1967	H Henning	1975	D Hayes	1983	C Pavin (USA)
1968	G Player	1976	D Hayes	1984	G Levenson
1969	D Hutchinson	1977	J Bland	1985	C Williams
1970	T Britz	1978	H Irwin (USA)		
1971	T Britz	1979	G Player		
1972	H Henning	1980	H Baiocchi		

South African Ladies' Championship

Year	Winner	Year	Winner
1947	Mrs R Green	1967	Mrs Jeanette Burd
1948	Miss Jacqueline Smith	1968	Mrs Rita Easton
1949	Mrs B Peltz	1969	Miss Marea Hickey
1950	Miss R Levetan	1970	Mrs Jeanette Burd
1951	Miss R Levetan	1971	Miss Sally Little
1952	Mrs R Green	1972	Mrs J Nellmapius
1953	Mrs P Easton (*née* R Levetan)	1973	Miss J Bruce
1954	Mrs R Green	1974	Mrs J Mercer
1955	Mrs P Easton	1975	Miss J Bruce
1956	Miss I Kay	1976	Miss A Sheard
1957	Miss M Masters	1977	Miss A Sheard
1958	Mrs P Easton	1978	Miss A Sheard
1959	Mrs Blumberg	1979	Mrs J Mercer
1960	Mrs Rita Easton	1980	Ms V Farrell
1961	Mrs Jean Tindal	1981	Ms ML de Lorenzi
1962	Miss M Clemence	1982	Ms R Hast
1963	Mrs J Mercer	1983	Miss L Copeman
1964	Mrs Jeanette Burd	1984	Miss S Whitfield
1965	Miss M Palliser	1985	Miss W Warrington
1966	Miss Judy Angel		

Spanish Open Amateur Championship

Instituted 1911

Year	Winner	Year	Winner
1944	Marquis de Sobroso	1966	F Sanchiz
1945	Augusto Battlo	1967	T Howard
1946	William L Shea	1968	J Gancedo
1947	Luis I Arana	1969	J Gancedo
1948	Vic de Llanteno	1970	E de Lariva Casanueva
1949	Luis I Arana	1971	E de la Riva
1950	Henri de Lamaze	1972	Mr Bonham
1951	Henri de Lamaze	1973	H Hedjerson (Sweden)
1952	Henri de Lamaze	1974	H Hedjerson (Sweden)
1953	Marques de Cabrinana	1975	S Boinet
1954	Ivan Maura	1976	G Leven
1955	Duque de Fernan-Nunez	1977	S Fernandez
1956	Ivan Maura	1978	N Sagardia
1957	Jacques Moernan	1979	R Taya
1958	Luis Rezola	1980	F Illouz
1959	Ivan Maura	1981	P Walton (Ireland)
1960	Ivan Maura	1982	D Williams
1961	Duque de Fernan-Nunez	1983	JM Olazabal
1962	Alvaro Muro	1984	JM Olazabal
1963	F Sanchiz	1985	B Quippe de Llano
1964	Dru Montagu		
1965	LA Bohorques		

Spanish Open Championship

Instituted 1912

Year	Winner	Year	Winner	Year	Winner
1945	C Celles	1959	PW Thomson	1973	NC Coles
1946	M Morcillo	1960	S Miguel	1974	J Heard
1947	Don M Gonzalez	1961	A Miguel	1975	Arnold Palmer
1948	M Morcillo	1962	*Not played*	1976	E Polland
1949	M Morcillo	1963	R Sota	1977	B Gallacher
1950	A Cerda	1964	A Miguel	1978	B Barnes
1951	M Provencio	1965	*Not played*	1979	D Hayes
1952	M Faulkner	1966	R De Vicenzo	1980	E Polland
1953	M Faulkner	1967	S Miguel	1981	S Ballesteros
1954	Sebastian Miguel	1968	R Shaw	1982	S Torrance
1955	H de Lamaze	1969	J Garaialde	1983	S Lyle
1956	Peter Alliss	1970	A Gallardo	1984	B Langer
1957	M Faulkner	1971	D Hayes	1985	S Ballesteros
1958	Peter Alliss	1972	A Garrido	1986	H Clark

Spanish Ladies' Open Amateur Championship

Instituted 1911

Year	Winner	Year	Winner
1944	Srta A Ma Perogordo	1956	Rosanna Bergamo
1945	Dona Concha Rauet	1957	Ma EC de Gibernau
1946	Marquesa de Sobroso	1958	Sofia P Tordesillas
1947	Marquesa de Sobroso	1959	Sandra Clifford
1948	Marquesa de Sobroso	1960	Martine Gajan
1949	*Not played*	1961	Miss Van der Berghe
1950	Marquesa de Movella	1962	M Etchart de Artach
1951	Vicomtesse de St Sauveur	1963	Anna Maria Marfull
1952	Isa Goldschmid-Bevione	1964	Sra de Lepori
1953	Elvira Lamazabal	1965	Cristina Marsans
1954	Elvira Lamazabal	1966	Marta Balet
1955	*Not played*	1967	Marta Balet

Spanish Ladies' Open Amateur Championship

continued

Year	Winner	Year	Winner
1968	Miss A Higgott	1978	Miss ML Lorenzi
1969	Mlle C Lacoste	1979	Marquesa de Artasona
1970	Miss E Corominas	1980	Miss ML de Lorenzi
1971	V Pertierra	1981	Marquesa de Artasona
1972	Mrs C Lacoste De Prado	1982	Cecile Mourgue D'Algue
1973	Michelle Walker	1983	M Laure de Lorenzi
1974	Miss A-M Palli (France)	1984	M Carmen Navrro
1975	Miss N Jeansson (France)	1985	Corine Espinasse
1976	Mrs C Lacoste De Prado	1986	M Lautens
1977	Marquesa de Artasona		

Swedish Close Men's Championship

Instituted 1904 (before 1984: Close Amateur)

Year	Winner	Year	Winner	Year	Winner
1961	L Leinborn	1970	H Hedjerson	1979	H Svedin
1962	PO Johansson	1971	H Hedjerson	1980	G Knutsson
1963	G Goransson	1972	C Johncke	1981	G Knutsson
1964	L Leinborn	1973	M Lindberg	1982	B Svedin
1965	J Johncke	1974	J Rube	1983	K-G Drotz
1966	T Holmstrom	1975	G Lundqvist	1984	M Lanner
1967	J Johncke	1976	B Haggstrom	1985	Nillso
1968	J Rosell	1977	M Sorling		
1969	J Rosell	1978	M Sorling		

Swedish Ladies' Close Championship

Instituted 1911

Year	Winner	Year	Winner	Year	Winner
1961	A-K Svensson	1970	B Forssman	1979	H Hagstrom
1962	A-M Brynolf	1971	L Wingard	1980	L Wollin
1963	L Wollin	1972	L Wollin	1981	M Wennersten
1964	L Wollin	1973	L Wollin	1982	M Wennersten
1965	C Perslow	1974	M Anderson	1983	G Linner
1966	L Wollin	1975	E Cedervall	1984	L Neumann
1967	L Wollin	1976	L Wollin	1985	S Gronberg
1968	L Wollin	1977	K Ehrnlund		
1969	L Wollin	1978	K Ehrnlund		

Swedish Open International Stroke Play Championship

Instituted 1964 (before 1984: Amateur)

Year	Winner	Year	Winner	Year	Winner
1964	C Johncke	1972	M Lindberg	1980	J Rube
1965	C Johncke	1973	S Mannerstrom	1981	D Carrick
1966	C Johncke	1974	Y Hofstetter (Swit)	1982	D Carrick
1967	C Johncke	1975	H Hedjerson	1983	M Hogberg
1968	C Johncke	1976	J Rube	1984	A Forsbrand
1969	C Johncke	1977	M Sorling	1985	Y Nilson
1970	H Hedjerson	1978	B Svedin		
1971	G Ignell	1979	G Brand (GB)		

Swedish Ladies' International Open Stroke Play Championship

Instituted 1971 (before 1984: Amateur)

Year	Winner	Year	Winner	Year	Winner
1971	L Wollin	1977	L Wollin	1983	A Oxenstierna
1972	L Wollin	1978	K Ehrnlund	1984	C Montgomery
1973	H Hagstrom	1979	L Wollin	1985	
1974	M Anderson	1980	MC de Werra (Swit)		
1975	M Wennersten	1981	L Neumann		
1976	H Hagstrom	1982	L Neumann		

Swedish Professional Championship

Instituted 1976

Year	Winner	Year	Winner	Year	Winner
1976	John Cockin	1980	Peter Lindvall	1984	P Brostedt
1977	Hans Hedjerson	1981	Gunnar Mueller	1985	
1978	Gunnar Mueller	1982	Anders Forsbrand		
1979	Gunnar Mueller	1983	Mats Lanner		

Swiss Open Amateur Championship

Instituted 1907

Year	Winner	Year	Winner	Year	Winner
1924	DEB Soulby	1950	E Sellschopp	1969	C Strenger
1925	Capt TD Richardson	1951	E Sellschopp	1970	F Andina
1926	P Feraldo	1952	S Bernolfo	1971	K Nierlich
1927	EW Hayley	1953	Otto Dillier	1972	M Kessler
1928	D Welch	1954	J Anderson	1973	C Francis
1929	Capt TD Richardson	1955	C Dunphy	1974	C Francis
1930	Capt B White	1956	F Bevione	1975	T Fortmann
1931	H Schweizer, jun	1957	P Gütermann	1976	M Rey
1932	F Parodi	1958	Francis Francis	1977	C Francis
1933	J Woollam	1959	N Berruti	1978	M Frank
1934	J Hudson	1960	Francis Francis	1979	JW Schuchmann
1935	L de Arana	1961	MJ Cannon-Brookes	1980	JW Schuchmann
1936	L Luzzatto	1962	R Falkenburg	1981	C Staedler
1937	HS Hudson	1963	O Barras	1982	F Illouz
1938	H Schweizer, jun	1964	P Gütermann	1983	J Lamberg
1946	Antoine Barras	1965	P Gütermann	1984	F Illouz
1947	John Plant	1966	R Johnson	1985	T Hubner
1948	G Corti	1967	K Nierlich	1986	
1949	G Payot	1968	T Brugger		

Swiss Ladies' Open Amateur Championship

Instituted 1907

Year	Winner	Year	Winner
1946	Miss J White	1967	Mme A Berglund
1947	Mrs Peltz (Johannesburg)	1968	Mlle J Stuckie
1948	Mrs Style	1969	Mme M Gütermann
1949	Vicomtesse de Saint Sauveur	1970	Miss A Beck
1950	Mrs J Hodgkin	1971	Mme J Stevens
1951	Miss J White	1972	Miss A Beck
1952	Miss J White	1973	Miss M de Werra
1953	Mrs J Hodgkin	1974	Miss M de Werra
1954	Mrs Dommers	1975	Miss K Dilthey
1955	Miss E Stergiou	1976	Mrs B Bohm
1956	Miss Van den Berghe	1977	Miss E Berthet
1957	Mlle A Jacquet	1978	Miss C Charbonnier
1958	Mlle Steegmann	1979	Miss MC de Werra
1959	Miss S Lorenz	1980	M Franz
1960	Mrs P Leysin	1981	Miss R Lautens
1961	Miss M Moller	1982	Miss MC de Werra
1962	*No championship*	1983	Miss E Berthet
1963	Mrs R Sauter	1984	E Girardi
1964	Mrs G Gutermann	1985	Mrs M Koch
1965	Vicomtesse de Saint Sauveur	1986	
1966	Mlle Peterssen		

Swiss Ladies' Close Amateur Championship

Year	Winner	Year	Winner	Year	Winner
1958	Mlle J Stucki	1968	Mlle J Stucki	1978	Mrs V Salvisberg
1959	Mlle J Stucki	1969	Mme L Zeerleder	1979	Miss MC de Werra
1960	Mrs Clews	1970	Miss A Beck	1980	Miss MC de Werra
1961	Mrs J Bordier	1971	Miss A Beck	1981	A Hadorn
1962	Mrs J Bordier	1972	Miss A Beck	1982	Miss R Lautens
1963	Mrs H Von Tobel	1973	Miss M de Werra	1983	Miss R Lautens
1964	Mrs J Bordier	1974	Miss M de Werra	1984	Miss R Lautens
1965	Mrs J Bordier	1975	Mrs V Salvisberg	1985	Miss E Orley
1966	Mrs L Clews	1976	Miss MC de Werra		
1967	Mme Zeerleder	1977	Miss R Lautens		

Swiss Open Championship

Year	Winner	Year	Winner	Year	Winner
1923	Alex Ross	1952	U Grappasonni	1971	PM Townsend
1924	Percy Boomer	1953	F van Donck	1972	G Marsh
1925	Alex Ross	1954	AD Locke	1973	H Baiocchi
1926	Alex Ross	1955	F van Donck	1974	RJ Charles
1927-28	*No championship*	1956	DJ Rees	1975	D Hayes
1929	A Wilson	1957	A Angelini	1976	M Pinero
1930	A Boyer	1958	K Bousfield	1977	S Ballesteros
1931	M Dallemagne	1959	DJ Rees	1978	S Ballesteros
1932-33	*No championship*	1960	H Henning	1979	H Baiocchi
1934	A Boyer	1961	KDG Nagle	1980	N Price
1935	A Boyer	1962	RJ Charles	1981	M Pinero (*After Play-Off*)
1936	Mr F Francis	1963	DJ Rees		
1937	M Dallemagne	1964	HR Henning	1982	I Woosnam (*After Play-Off*)
1938	J Saubaber	1965	HR Henning		
1939	F Cavalo	1966	A Angelini	1983	N Faldo (*After Play-Off*)
1948	U Grappasonni	1967	R Vines		
1949	M Dallemagne	1968	R Bernardini	1984	J Anderson
1950	A Casera	1969	R Bernardini	1985	C Stadler
1951	EC Brown	1970	G Marsh	1986	JM Olazabal

Swiss Close Amateur Championship

Year	Winner	Year	Winner	Year	Winner
1946	G Payot	1960	O Barras	1974	J Storjohann
1947	H Schweizer, jun	1961	O Barras	1975	J Storjohann
1948	H Schweizer, jun	1962	O Barras	1976	R Kessler
1949	G Payot	1963	P Gütermann	1977	M Rey
1950	O Barras	1964	O Barras	1978	J Storjohann
1951	O Barras	1965	P Gütermann	1979	M Frank
1952	André Barras	1966	Rudy Muller	1980	Y Courturier
1953	P Gütermann	1967	M Lamm	1981	J Storjohann
1954	Olivier Barras	1968	T Matti	1982	C Rampone
1955	André Barras	1969	P Gütermann	1983	P Jaquet
1956	O Barras	1970	P Gütermann	1984	M Buchter
1957	P Gütermann	1971	T Fortmann	1985	M Gottstein
1958	O Barras	1972	U Lamm		
1959	O Dillier	1973	P Gütermann		

Trinidad and Tobago Open Amateur

Instituted 1907

Year	Winner	Year	Winner	Year	Winner
1946	CM MacIntyre	1960	EH Mariott	1974	C Hinds
1947	W Hill	1961	JD Sellier	1975	E Grell
1948	GM Wilson	1962	JD Sellier	1976	C Hinds
1949	CM MacIntyre	1963	R Grell	1977	C Harries
1950	WS Fulton	1964	B Grell	1978	A Mew
1951	WS Fulton	1965	P Arrindell	1979	R Grell
1952	GK Nichols	1966	R Grell	1980	C Ammon
1953	GC Scott	1967	P Arrindell	1981	S Rose
1954	JD Sellier	1968	R Grell	1982	B Ferdinand
1955	AMC Johnston	1969	A Mew	1983	R Charlett
1956	GM Wilson	1970	C Hinds	1984	
1957	JD Sellier	1971	C Harries	1985	
1958	WS Fulton	1972	R Grell		
1959	JD Sellier	1973	E Grell		

Trinidad and Tobago Open

Instituted 1972

Year	Winner	Year	Winner	Year	Winner
1972	G Phillips	1977	C Harries (Am)	1982	K Murray (Canada)
1973	G Phillips	1978	R Bassett	1983	I Richardson
1974	L Yearwood	1979	S Rose	1984	
1975	R Bassett	1980	G Brand (GB)	1985	J Bennett (GB)
1976	C Hinds (Am)	1981	C Ammon		

Zambian Open Championship

Instituted 1972

Year	Winner	Year	Winner	Year	Winner
1972	C DeFoy	1978	P Townsend	1983	B Calfee
1973	C DeFoy	1979	B Barnes		(*After Play-Off with E Darcy*)
1974	C O'Connor, jun	1980	E Murray	1984	C Mason
1975	S Torrance	1981	B Barnes	1985	I Woosnam
1976	P Cowen	1982	B Waites	1986	G Cullen
1977	T Horton				

Professional Tournaments and Matches

British Isles and Europe

Benson and Hedges International

Year	Winner	Venue	Score
1971	A Jacklin, Britain	Fulford	279
1972	J Newton, Australia	Fulford	281
1973	V Baker, South Africa	Fulford	276
1974	P Toussaint, Belgium	Fulford	276
1975	V Fernandez, Argentina	Fulford	266
1976	G Marsh, Australia	Fulford	272
1977	A Garrido, Spain	Fulford	280
1978	L Trevino, USA	Fulford	274
1979	M Bembridge, Britain	St Mellion	272
1980	G Marsh, Australia	Fulford	272
1981	T Weiskopf, USA	Fulford	272
1982	G Norman, Australia	Fulford	283
1983	J Bland, South Africa	Fulford	273
1984	S Torrance, Britain	Fulford	270
1985	S Lyle	Fulford	274
1986	M James	Fulford	274

Car Care Plan International

Year	Winner	Country	Venue	Score
1982	B Waites	England	Moor Allerton	276
1983	N Faldo	England	Sand Moor	272
1984	N Faldo	England	Moortown	276
1985	DJ Russell	England	Moortown	277
1986	M Mouland	England	Moortown	272

Carrolls Irish Open

Formerly Carrolls International

Year	Winner	Club	Venue	Score
1963	BJ Hunt	Hartsbourne	Woodbrook	270
1964	C O'Connor	Royal Dublin	Woodbrook	268
1965	NC Coles	Coombe Hill	Little Island, Cork	269
1966	C O'Connor	Royal Dublin	Dublin	272
1967	C O'Connor	Royal Dublin	Woodbrook	277
1968	J Martin	Rush	Woodbrook	281
1969	RDBM Shade	Duddingston	Woodbrook	289
1970	BGC Huggett	Betchworth Park	Woodbrook	279

Carrolls Irish Open

continued

Year	Winner	Club	Venue	Score
1971	NC Coles	Coombe Hill	Woodbrook	276
1972	C O'Connor	Royal Dublin	Woodbrook	284
1973	P McGuirk	Co Louth	Woodbrook	277
1974	B Gallacher	Wentworth	Woodbrook	279
1975	C O'Connor, jun	Carlow	Woodbrook	275
1976	B Crenshaw	USA	Portmarnock	284
1977	H Green	USA	Portmarnock	283
1978	K Brown	GB	Portmarnock	281
1979	M James	Burghley Park	Portmarnock	282
1980	M James	Burghley Park	Portmarnock	284
1981	Sam Torrance	GB	Portmarnock	276
1982	J O'Leary	Unattached	Portmarnock	287
1983	S Ballesteros	Spain	Dublin	271
1984	B Langer	Germany	Dublin	267
1985	S Ballesteros	Spain	Dublin	278
1986	S Ballesteros	Spain	Portmarnock	285

Dunhill Masters' Tournament

Formerly sponsored by Dunlop, 1946–62 (1963–8: Silk Cut)

Year	Winner	Club/Country	Venue	Score
1946	AD Locke J Adams	South Africa Beaconsfield tie	Stoneham	286
1947	A Lees	Dore and Totley	Little Aston	286
1948	N Von Nida	Australia	Sunningdale	272
1949	CH Ward	Little Aston	St Andrews	290
1950	DJ Rees	South Herts	Hoylake	281
1951	M Faulkner	Unattached	Wentworth	281
1952	H Weetman	Croham Hurst	Mere	281
1953	H Bradshaw	Portmarnock	Sunningdale	272
1954	AD Locke	South Africa	Prince's, Sandwich	291
1955	H Bradshaw	Portmarnock	Little Aston	277
1956	C O'Connor	Bundoran	Prestwick	277
1957	EC Brown	Buchanan Castle	Hollinwell	275
1958	H Weetman	Selsdon Park	Little Aston	276
1959	C O'Connor	Royal Dublin	Portmarnock	276
1960	J Hitchcock	Ashford Manor	Sunningdale	275
1961	PW Thomson	Australia	Porthcawl	284
1962	DJ Rees	South Herts	Wentworth	278
1963	BJ Hunt	Hartsbourne	Little Aston	282
1964	C Legrange	South Africa	Birkdale	288
1965	BJ Hunt	Hartsbourne	Portmarnock	283
1966	NC Coles	Coombe Hill	Lindrick	278
1967	A Jacklin	Potters Bar	St George's	274
1968	PW Thomson	Australia	Sunningdale	274
1969	C Legrange	South Africa	Little Aston	281
1970	BGC Huggett	Betchworth Park	Lytham, St Annes	293
1971	M Bembridge	Little Aston	St Pierre	273
1972	R Charles	New Zealand	Northumberland	277
1973	A Jacklin	Potters Bar	St Pierre	272
1974	B Gallacher	Wentworth	St Pierre	282
1975	B Gallacher	Wentworth	Ganton	289
1976	B Dassu	Italy	St Pierre	271
1977	GL Hunt	Gloucester Hotel	Lindrick	291
1978	TA Horton	Royal Jersey	St Pierre	279
1979	G Marsh	Australia	Woburn (Dukes Course)	283
1980	B Langer	West Germany	St Pierre	270
1981	G Norman	Australia	Woburn	273
1982	G Norman	Australia	St Pierre	267
1983	I Woosnam	Wales	St Pierre	269
1984	*Not played*			
1985	L Trevino	USA	Woburn	278
1986	S Ballesteros	Spain	Woburn	275

Epson Match-Play

Instituted 1986

Year	Winner	Venue	Score
1986	O Sellberg (Sweden)	St Pierre	

Bell's Scottish Open

Formerly Glasgow Classic, 1983-85

Year	Winner	Venue	Score
1983	B Langer	Haggs Castle	274
1984	K Brown	Haggs Castle	266
1985	H Clark	Haggs Castle	274
1986	D Feherty	Haggs Castle	270

Jersey Open

Formerly British Airways-Avis Tournament and Billy Butlin Open

Year	Winner	Venue	Score
1978	BGC Huggett	La Moye	271
1979	AWB Lyle	La Moye	271
1980	JM Canizares, Spain	La Moye	281
1981	T Jacklin	La Moye	279
1982	B Gallacher	La Moye	273
1983	J Hall	La Moye	278
1984	B Gallacher	La Moye	274
1985	H Clark	La Moye	279
1986	J Morgan	La Moye	275

Lancôme Trophy

Year	Winner	Venue	Score
1970	A Jacklin (GB)	St Nom de la Breteche (54 holes)	206
1971	A Palmer (USA)	St Nom de la Breteche (54 holes)	202
1972	T Aaron (USA)	St Nom de la Breteche	279
1973	J Miller (USA)	St Nom de la Breteche	277
1974	W Casper (USA)	St Nom de la Breteche	283
1975	G Player (South Africa)	St Nom de la Breteche	278
1976	S Ballesteros (Spain)	St Nom de la Breteche	283
1977	G Marsh (Australia)	St Nom de la Breteche	273
1978	L Trevino (USA)	St Nom de la Breteche	272
1979	J Miller (USA)	St Nom de la Breteche	281
1980	L Trevino (USA)	St Nom de la Breteche	280
1981	D Graham (Australia)	St Nom de la Breteche	280
1982	D Graham (Australia)	St Nom de la Breteche	276
1983	S Ballesteros (Spain)	St Nom de la Breteche	269
1984	S Lyle (GB)	St Nom de la Breteche	278
(After tie with S Ballesteros (Spain))			
1985	N Price	St Nom de la Breteche	275
1986	S Ballesteros (Spain)	St Nom de la Breteche	274

Lawrence Batley International

Year	Winner	Country	Venue	Score
1981	AWB Lyle	Great Britain	Bingley St Ives	280
1982	AWB Lyle	Great Britain	Bingley St Ives	269
1983	N Faldo	Great Britain	Bingley St Ives	266
1984	J Rivero	Spain	The Belfry	280
1985	G Marsh	Australia	The Belfry	283
1986	I Woosnam	Great Britain	The Belfry	277

Madrid Open Championship

Year	Winner	Venue	Score
1968	G Garrido (Spain)	Madrid	279
1969	R Sota (Spain)	Madrid	278
1970	M Cabrera (Spain)	Madrid	286
1971	V Barrios (Spain)	Puerto de Hierro	285
1972	J Kinsella (Ireland)	Puerto de Hierro	283
1973	G Garrido (Spain)	RAC Madrid	287
1974	M Pinero (Spain)	Puerto de Hierro	283
1975	R Shearer (Australia)	Lomas Bosque *(36 holes, rain)*	135
1976	F Abreu (Spain)	Puerto de Hierro	275
1977	A Garrido (Spain)	Club de Campo	278
1978	HK Clark (GB)	Puerto de Hierro	282
1979	S Hobday (Rhodesia)	Puerto de Hierro	285
1980	S Ballesteros (Spain)	Puerto de Hierro	270
1981	M Pinero (Spain)	Puerto de Hierro	279
1982	S Ballesteros (Spain)	Puerto de Hierro	273
1983	S Lyle (Scotland)	Puerto de Hierro	285
1984	H Clark (GB)	Puerto de Hierro	274
1985	M Pinero (Spain)	Puerto de Hierro	278
1986	H Clark (GB)	Puerto de Hierro	274

Panasonic European Open

Year	Winner	Country	Venue	Score
1978	RL Wadkins	USA	Walton Heath	283
1979	AWB Lyle	GB	Turnberry	275
1980	T Kite	USA	Walton Heath	284
1981	G Marsh	Australia	Liverpool	275
1982	M Pinero	Spain	Sunningdale	266
1983	I Aoki	Japan	Sunningdale	274
1984	G Brand	GB	Sunningdale	270
1985	B Langer	Germany	Sunningdale	269
1986	G Norman	Australia	Sunningdale	269

PGA Championship

Formerly PGA Close Championship

Year	Sponsor	Winner	Club	Venue	Score
1955		K Bousfield	Coombe Hill	Pannal	277
1956		CH Ward	Little Aston	Maesdu	282
1957		Peter Alliss	Parkstone	Maesdu	286
1958		H Bradshaw	Portmarnock	Llandudno	287
1959		DJ Rees	South Herts	Ashburnham	283
1960		AF Stickley	Ealing	Coventry *(63 holes)*	247
1961	Schweppes	BJ Bamford	Wentworth	Mid-Surrey	266
1962	Schweppes	Peter Alliss	Parkstone	Little Aston	287
1963	Schweppes	PJ Butler	Harborne	Birkdale	306
1964	Schweppes	AG Grubb (Asst)	Coombe Hill	Western Gailes	287
1965	Schweppes	Peter Alliss	Parkstone	Prince's	286
1966	Schweppes	GB Wostenholme	St George's Hill	Saunton	278
1967	PGA Vice-Presidents	BCG Huggett	Betchworth Park	Thorndon Park	271
1968	Piccadilly	PM Townsend	Porter's Park	Mid-Surrey	275
1969-71	*Not played*				
1972	Viyella	A Jacklin		Wentworth	279
1973	Viyella	P Oosterhuis		Wentworth	280
1974	Viyella	M Bembridge		Wentworth	278
1975	Penfold	A Palmer	USA	Sandwich	285
1976	Penfold	NC Coles	Great Britain	Sandwich	280
1977	Penfold	M Pinero	Spain	Sandwich	283
1978	Colgate	N Faldo	Great Britain	Birkdale	278
1979	Colgate	V Fernandez	Argentina	St Andrews	288
1980	Sun Alliance	N Faldo	Great Britain	Sandwich	283
1981	Sun Alliance	N Faldo	Great Britain	Ganton	274

Year	Sponsor	Winner	Club	Venue	Score
1982	Sun Alliance	A Jacklin	Great Britain	Hillside	284
1983	Sun Alliance	S Ballesteros	Spain	Sandwich	278
1984	Whyte & McKay	H Clark	Great Britain	Wentworth	204
	(3 rounds only due to weather)				
1985	Whyte & McKay	P Way	Great Britain	Wentworth	282
1986	Whyte & McKay	R Davis	Australia	Wentworth	281

Scandinavian Enterprises Open

Year	Winner	Country	Venue	Score
1973	RJ Charles	New Zealand	Drottningholm	278
1974	A Jacklin	Britain	Bokskogen	279
1975	George Burns	USA	Malmo	279
1976	H Baiocchi	South Africa	Drottningholm	271
1977	B Byman	USA	Drottningholm	275
1978	S Ballesteros	Spain	Helsingborg	279
1979	AWB Lyle	Britain	Helsingborg	276
1980	G Norman	Australia	Helsingborg	276
1981	S Ballesteros	Spain	Linkoping	273
1982	B Byman	USA	Linkoping	275
1983	S Torrance	Scotland	Stockholm	280
1984	I Woosnam	Britain	Stockholm	280
1985	I Baker-Finch	Australia	Stockholm	274
1986	G Turner	New Zealand	Stockholm	270

Sanyo Open

Year	Winner	Country	Venue	Score
1982	NC Coles	Britain	San Cugat, Spain	266
1983	D Smyth	Ireland	Real Club de Golf, El Prat	279
1984	S Torrance	Scotland	El Prat	281
(After play-off with D Smyth (Ireland))				
1985	S Ballesteros	Spain	El Prat	272
1986	J-M Olazabal	Spain	El Prat	273

Suntory World Match Play Championship

Sponsored by Piccadilly until 1976 and by Colgate 1977 and 1978

Year	Winner	Runner-up	Venue	By
1964	Arnold Palmer	NC Coles	Wentworth	2 and 1
1965	Gary Player	PW Thomson	Wentworth	3 and 2
1966	Gary Player	JW Nicklaus	Wentworth	6 and 4
1967	Arnold Palmer	PW Thomson	Wentworth	1 hole
1968	Gary Player	R Charles	Wentworth	1 hole
1969	R Charles	G Littler	Wentworth	37th hole
1970	JW Nicklaus	L Trevino	Wentworth	2 and 1
1971	Gary Player	JW Nicklaus	Wentworth	5 and 4
1972	T Weiskopf	L Trevino	Wentworth	4 and 3
1973	Gary Player	G Marsh	Wentworth	40th hole
1974	H Irwin	Gary Player	Wentworth	3 and 1
1975	H Irwin	A Geiberger	Wentworth	4 and 2
1976	D Graham	H Irwin	Wentworth	38th hole

Year	Winner	Club	Venue	Score
1977	G Marsh	R Floyd	Wentworth	5 and 3
1978	I Aoki	S Owen	Wentworth	3 and 2
1979	W Rogers	I Aoki	Wentworth	1 hole
1980	G Norman	AWB Lyle	Wentworth	1 hole
1981	S Ballesteros	B Crenshaw	Wentworth	1 hole
1982	S Ballesteros	AWB Lyle	Wentworth	37th hole
1983	G Norman	N Faldo	Wentworth	3 and 2
1984	S Ballesteros	B Langer	Wentworth	2 and 1
1985	S Ballesteros	B Langer	Wentworth	6 and 5
1986	G Norman	AWB Lyle	Wentworth	2 and 1

PGA Close Events
Assistants' Championship

Formerly PGA Under-23 Match Play

Year	Winner	Runner-up	Venue	By
1978	T Rastall	W McAdams	The Belfry	2 holes
1979	I Woosnam	J Hay	Scarborough SC	4 and 3
1980	K Waters	S Deller	Royal Eastbourne	2 and 1
Renamed the Dorset Foods PGA Assistants' Match Play Championship				
1981	I Grant	G Walker	Henbury	3 and 1
1982	H Stott	M Wiggins	Henbury	4 and 3
Re-named Foot Joy PGA Assistants' Championship				
1983	Barry Lane		Coombe Hill	287
1984	Gary Weir		Coombe Hill	286
1985	Gary Coles		Coombe Hill	284
Sponsored by Peugeot-Talbot				
1986	J Brennand		Sand Moor	280

Club Professionals' Championship

Year	Winner	Club	Venue	Score
1973	DN Sewell	Ferndown	Calcot Park	276
1974	WB Murray	Coombe Wood	Calcot Park	275
1975	DN Sewell	Ferndown	Calcot Park	276
1976	WJ Ferguson	Ilkley	Moortown	283
1977	D Huish	North Berwick	Notts	284
1978	D Jones	Bangor	Pannal	281
1979	D Jones	Bangor	Pannal	278
1980	D Jagger	Selby	Turnberry	286
1981	M Steadman	Cleeve Hill Mun	Woburn	289
1982	D Durnian	Northenden	Hill Valley	285
Sponsored by Wilson				
1983	J Farmer		Heaton Park	270
1984	D Durnian		Bolton Old Links	278
1985	R Mann	Thorpeness	The Belfry	291
1986	D Huish	North Berwick	Birkdale	278

Senior Professional Tournament

From 1957 to 1968 sponsored by Teachers; from 1969 to 1974 sponsored by Pringle; from 1975 sponsored by Ben Sayers and Allied Hotels; from 1977 by Cambridgeshire Hotel; from 1983 by Trust House Forte

Year	Winner	Club/Country	Venue	Score
1957	John Burton	Hillside	Fulwell *(54 holes)*	213
1958	N Sutton	Exeter	Copt Heath	214
1959	A Lees	Sunningdale	Mid-Surrey	204
1960	RW Horne	Hendon	Mere	213
1961	SL King	Knole Park	Hill Barn	208
1962	SL King	Knole Park	Harrogate	214
1963	G Evans	Roehampton	Weston-Super-Mare	222
1964	SS Scott	Roehampton	Gosforth Park	213
1965	CH Ward	Little Aston	Ashford Manor	210
1966	DJ Rees	South Herts	Coventry	215
1967	John Panton	Glenbervie	Ayr Belleisle *(72 holes)*	282
1968	M Faulkner	Unattached	Aldeburgh	283
1969	J Panton	Glenbervie	West Kilbride	281
1970	M Faulkner	Ifield	Longniddry	288
1971	KDG Nagle	Australia	Elie	269
1972	K Bousfield	Coombe Hill	Longniddry	291
1973	KDG Nagle	Australia	Elie	270
1974	E Lester	Astbury	Lundin	282
1975	KDG Nagle	Australia	Longniddry	268
1976	C O'Connor	Royal Dublin	Cambridgeshire Hotel	284
1977	C O'Connor	Royal Dublin	Cambridgeshire Hotel	288
1978	P Skerritt	St Annes, Dublin	Cambridgeshire Hotel	288
1979	C O'Connor	Royal Dublin	Cambridgeshire Hotel	280
1980	P Skerritt	St Annes, Dublin	Gleneagles Hotel	286
1981	C O'Connor	Royal Dublin	North Berwick	287
1982	C O'Connor	Royal Dublin	Longniddry	285
1983	C O'Connor	Royal Dublin	Burnham and Berrow	277
1984	E Jones	Royal Co Down	Stratford-upon-Avon	280
1985	N Coles	Expotel	Pannal, Harrogate	284
1986	N Coles	Expotel	Mere, Cheshire	276

Events Previously Played but Now Discontinued

Agfa Gevaert

Year	Winner	Club	Venue	Score
1965	J Hitchcock	Croham Hurst	Stoke Poges	267
1966	A Miguel	Spain	Stoke Poges	275
1967	P Alliss	Parkstone	Stoke Poges	270
1968	CA Clark	Sunningdale	Stoke Poges	288
1969	BW Barnes	West Sussex	Stoke Poges	277
1970	BJ Hunt	Pacific Harbour	Stoke Poges	277
1971	P Oosterhuis	Hartsbourne	Stoke Poges	276

Alcan Golfer of the Year Championship

Year	Winner	Venue	Score
1967	G Brewer, USA	St Andrews	283
1968	G Brewer, USA	Birkdale	283
1969	W Casper, USA	Portland, Oregon	274
1970	B Devlin, Australia	Portmarnock	278

Alcan International Championship

Year	Winner	Venue	Score
1967	PW Thomson, Australia	St Andrews	281
1968	C O'Connor, Royal Dublin, tied with W Large, Dyrham Park	Birkdale	288
1969	*Not played*		
1970	P Skerritt, St Annes, Dublin	Portmarnock	286

Algarve International Open Championship

Year	Winner	Venue	Score
1969	BJ Hunt, Britain	Penina	292
1970	BGC Huggett, Britain	Vilamoura	293
1971	R Sota, Spain	Vale do Lobo	290
1972	V Barrios, Spain	Penina	287

Amalgamated with Portuguese Open

Bob Hope British Classic

Year	Winner	Country	Venue	Score
1980	J-M Canizares	Spain	RAC	269
1981	B Langer	Germany	Moor Park	200
	(54 holes only, due to heavy rain)			
1982	G Brand, jun	GB	Moor Park	272
1983	J-M Canizares	Spain	Moor Park	269

Bowmaker Amateur-Professional Tournament

Year	Winner	Club/Country		Venue	Score
1957	AD Locke	South Africa	tie	Berkshire	135
	F Jowle	Edgbaston			
1958	RP Mills	Pinner Hill	tie	Sunningdale	129
	BJ Hunt	Hartsbourne			
1959	AD Locke	South Africa		Sunningdale	132
1960	PW Thomson	Australia		Sunningdale	132
1961	RJ Charles	New Zealand		Sunningdale	132
1962	KDG Nagle	Australia		Sunningdale	133
1963	PJ Butler	Harborne		Sunningdale	132
1964	NC Coles	Coombe Hill		Sunningdale	136
1965	KDG Nagle	Australia		Sunningdale	133
1966	FS Boobyer	Whitefield		Sunningdale	135
1967	PJ Butler	Harborne		Sunningdale	131
1968	CA Clark	Sunningdale		Sunningdale	136
1969	BGC Huggett	Betchworth Park	tie	Sunningdale	135
	AG Grubb	Coombe Hill			
1970	NC Coles	Coombe Hill		Mid-Surrey	132
In 1971 taken over by Sunbeam Electric					
1971	P Oosterhuis	Dulwich Sydenham Hill		Mid-Surrey	132

Cacharel World Open Under-25

Year	Winner	Venue	Score
1976	E Darcy	Evian	274
1977	*Not played*		
1978	J Nelford, Canada	Nimes	280
1979	B Langer, Germany	Nimes	274
1980	J Renner, USA	Nimes	292
1981	T Simpson, USA	Nimes	287
1982	I Woosnam, Wales	Nimes	290
1983	M McLean	Nimes	285

Classic International Tournament

Year	Winner	Club	Venue	Score
1970	H Muscroft	Moor Allerton	Copt Heath	282
1971	PJ Butler	Harborne	Copt Heath	277

Coca-Cola Young Professionals

Year	Winner	Club	Venue	Score
1968	P Townsend	Porters Park	Coventry	270
1969	BW Barnes	West Sussex	Bristol and Clifton	280
1970	P Oosterhuis	Dulwich and Sydenham	Morecambe and Heysham	274
1971	JR Garner	Moor Park	Southampton	273
1972	PA Oosterhuis	Pacific Harbour, Fiji	Long Ashton	278
1973	B Gallacher	Wentworth	Bristol and Clifton	277
1974	D Hayes	South Africa	Long Ashton	274
Taken over by Tournament Players' Section of PGA				
1975	D Hayes	South Africa	Worthing Hill Barn	266
1976	HK Clark	Moor Allerton	Westcliff	281

Colgate European WPGA Championship

Year	Winner	Country	Venue	Score
1974	Mrs J Rankin	USA	Sunningdale	218
1975	Mrs D Young	USA	Sunningdale	283
1976	Mrs C Higuchi	Japan	Sunningdale	284
1977	Mrs J Rankin	USA	Sunningdale	281
1978	Miss N Lopez	USA	Sunningdale	289
1979	Miss N Lopez	USA	Sunningdale	282

Coral Classic

Year	Winner	Country	Venue	Score
1979	M James	Britain	Wenvoe Castle	278
1980	AWB Lyle	Britain	Porthcawl	277
1981	D Smyth	Britain	Porthcawl	282
1982	G Brand, jun	Britain	Porthcawl	273

Daks Tournament

Year	Winner	Club/Country	Venue	Score
1950	N Sutton	Leigh	Mid-Surrey	272
1951	J Panton	Glenbervie	Sunningdale	282
1952	F Daly	Balmoral	Wentworth	280
1953	DJ Rees	South Herts	Wentworth	280
1954	Peter Alliss	Ferndown	Little Aston	279
1955	JD Pritchett	Sunningdale	Sunningdale	275
1956	Trevor Wilkes	South Africa	Wentworth	276
1957	AD Locke	South Africa	Wentworth	281
1958	PW Thomson HR Henning	Australia South Africa } tie	Wentworth	275
1959	C O'Connor	Royal Dublin	Wentworth	274
1960	PW Thomson	Australia	Wentworth	279
1961	BJ Hunt	Hartsbourne	Wentworth	279
1962	DJ Rees RJ Charles	South Herts New Zealand } tie	Wentworth	278
1963	Peter Alliss NC Coles	Parkstone Coombe Hill } tie	Wentworth	280
1964	NC Coles	Coombe Hill	Wentworth	282
1965	PW Thomson	Australia	Wentworth	275
1966	Hugh Boyle	Jacobs GC	Wentworth	286
1967	ME Gregson	Dyrham Park	Wentworth	279
1968	ME Gregson	Dyrham Park	Wentworth	284
1969	BGC Huggett	Betchworth Park	Wentworth	289
1970	NC Coles	Coombe Hill	Wentworth	281
1971	BGC Huggett NC Coles	Betchworth Park Coombe Hill } tie	South Herts	284

Double Diamond World of Golf Classic

Year	Winner	Venue	Year	Winner	Venue
1971	England	South Staffordshire	1975	The Americas	Turnberry
1972	England	Pannal	1976	England	Gleneagles
1973	Scotland	Prince's, Sandwich	1977	USA	Gleneagles
1974	England	Gleneagles			

Esso Golden Tournament

Year	Winner	Club/Country	Venue	Points
1961	PW Thomson DC Thomas	Australia Sunningdale tie	Moor Park	21
1962	DC Thomas	Sunningdale	Moor Park	19
1963	KDG Nagle	Australia	Moor Park	23
1964	P Alliss	Parkstone	Moor Park	25
1965	George Will	Sundridge Park	Moor Park	24
1966	DC Thomas	Dunham Forest	Moor Park	23
1967	K Nagle	Australia	Moor Park	20

Gallaher (Ulster) Open Championship

Year	Winner	Club/Country	Venue	Score
1965	BJ Hunt	Hartsbourne	Shandon Park, Belfast	273
1966	C O'Connor	Royal Dublin	Shandon Park	268
1967	BJ Hunt	Hartsbourne	Shandon Park	267
1968	C O'Connor	Royal Dublin	Shandon Park	267
1969	C O'Connor	Royal Dublin	Shandon Park	271
1970	J Lister	New Zealand	Shandon Park	264
1971	T Horton	Ham Manor	Malone	274

Greater Manchester Open

Year	Winner	Club/Country	Venue	Score
1976	J O'Leary	Unattached	Wilmslow	276
1977	E Darcy	Erewash Valley	Wilmslow	269
1978	B Barnes	G.B.	Wilmslow	275
1979	M McNulty	South Africa	Wilmslow	267
1980	D Smyth	Ireland	Wilmslow	273
1981	B Gallacher	Wentworth	Wilmslow	264

Irish Dunlop Tournament

Year	Winner	Club	Venue	Score
1957	J Henderson W Gaffney	Warrenpoint Killiney tie	Dun Laoghaire	283
1962	C O'Connor	Royal Dublin	Elm Park	276
1964	C Greene	Milltown	—	276
1965	C O'Connor	RoyalDublin	Carlow	288
1966	C O'Connor	Royal Dublin	Bettystown	265
1967	C O'Connor	Royal Dublin	Tramore	275
1968	H Jackson	Knockbracken Golf Centre	Limerick	279
1969	M Murphy	Royal Dublin	Bundoran	284
1970	H Boyle	Sandown Park DR	Tullamore	277
1971	J Kinsella	Castle	Douglas	279
1972	J O'Leary	Oppermans	Kilkenny	280
1973	E Polland	Balmoral	Headfort	283
1974	C O'Connor, jun	Carlow	Hermitage	284
1975	E Polland	Balmoral	Bundoran	275
1976	E Darcy	Erewash Valley	Hermitage	275
1977	P Townsend	Cortijo Grande	Douglas	276
1978	D Jones	Bangor	Hermitage	279
1979	D Jones	Bangor	Tramore	284
1980	D Smyth	Laytown and Bettystown	Headfort	261

Kerrygold International Classic

Year	Winner	Club/Country	Venue	Score
1974	L Higgins	Waterville	Waterville (63 holes)	256
1975	G Burns	USA	Waterville	294
1976	A Jacklin	Is Molas	Waterville	290
1977	L Higgins	Waterville	Waterville	287

Lord Derby's Under-25

From 1968 to 1971 was sponsored by PGA for under-23s

Year	Winner	Venue	Score
1968	GL Hunt	Hillside *(72 holes)*	288
1969	C DeFoy	Hesketh *(54 holes)*	214
1970	P Oosterhuis	St Annes Old	218
1971	D Vaughan	Lytham St Annes	218

From 1972 changed to Match Play

Year	Winner	Runner-up	Venue	By
1972	S Torrance	D McClelland	Birkdale	5 and 4
1973	B Thompson	J McTear	Morecambe	2 holes
1974	R Jewell	P Herbert	West Lancashire	6 and 5

Martini International Tournament

Year	Winner	Club/Country	Venue	Score
1961	BJ Hunt	Hartsbourne	Sundridge Park	270
1962	PW Thomson	Australia	St Andrews	275
1963	NC Coles C O'Connor	Coombe Hill Royal Dublin } tie	Hoylake	298
1964	C O'Connor	Royal Dublin	Wentworth	286
1965	PJ Butler	Harborne	Little Aston	275
1966	P Alliss W Large	Parkstone Unattached } tie	Long Ashton	275
1967	ME Gregson BGC Huggett	Dyrham Park Warren } tie	Fulford	279
1968	BGC Huggett	Betchworth Park	Southerndown	278
1969	G Henning GA Caygill	South Africa Cleckheaton & District } tie	Bournemouth	282
1970	P Thomson D Sewell	Australia Ferndown } tie	Conway	268
1971	BJ Gallacher	Wentworth	Norwich	282
1972	BW Barnes	Fairway DR	Abridge	277
1973	M Bembridge	Little Aston	Barnton	279
1974	S Ginn	Australia	Pannal	286
1975	IE Stanley C O'Connor, jun	Australia Carlow } tie	North Devon	279
1976	S Torrance	Routenburn	Ashburnham	280
1977	G Norman	Australia	Blairgowrie	277
1978	S Ballesteros	Spain	RAC	270
1979	G Norman	Australia	Wentworth	288
1980	S Ballesteros	Spain	Wentworth	286
1981	G Norman	Australia	Wentworth	287
1982	B Gallacher	Wentworth	Lindrick	277
1983	N Faldo After Play-Off with J-M Canizares	G.B.	Wilmslow	268

Newcastle Brown 900 Tournament

Year	Winner	Venue	Score
1980	D Smyth	Northumberland	276

PGA Match Play Tournament

Sponsored 1903–1969 by **The News of the World**

Year	Winner	Runner-up	Semi-finalists		Venue
1903	J Braid	E Ray	JH Taylor	G Coburn	Sunningdale
1904	JH Taylor	A Toogood	J Hepburn	A Herd	Mid-Surrey
1905	J Braid	T Vardon	R Jones	A Mitchell	Walton Heath
1906	A Herd	C Mayo	G Duncan	R Jones	Hollinwell
1907	J Braid	JH Taylor	E Ray	H Vardon	Sunningdale
1908	JH Taylor	F Robson	C Mayo	JG Sherlock	Mid-Surrey
1909	T Ball	A Herd	H Vardon	J Hepburn	Walton Heath
1910	JG Sherlock	G Duncan	E Bannister	C Hughes	Sunningdale
1911	J Braid	E Ray	T Williamson	H Vardon	Walton Heath
1912	H Vardon	E Ray	RG Wilson	H Cawsey	Sunningdale
1913	G Duncan	J Braid	RG Wilson	W Watt	Walton Heath
1919	A Mitchell	G Duncan	P Rainford	F Robson	Walton Heath
1920	A Mitchell	Josh Taylor	B Seymour	L Holland	Mid-Surrey
1921	B Seymour	J Gaudin	E Ray	C Wingate	Oxhey
1922	G Gadd	F Leach	ER Whitcombe	C Johns	Sunningdale
1923	RG Wilson	T Renouf	A Mitchell	T Williamson	Walton Heath
1924	ER Whitcombe	G Gadd	A Herd	T Barber	St George's Hill
1925	A Compston	G Gadd	G Duncan	L Holland	Moor Park
1926	A Herd	J Bloxham	RG Wilson	WH Ball	Mid-Surrey
1927	A Compston	J Braid	T Williamson	ER Whitcombe	Walton Heath
1928	CA Whitcombe	TH Cotton	JJ Taylor	HC Jolly	Stoke Poges
1929	A Mitchell	P Rodgers	A Compston	A Beck	Wentworth
1930	CA Whitcombe	TH Cotton	A Mitchell	S Easterbrook	Oxhey
1931	AH Padgham	M Seymour	CH Ward	CW Thomson	Mid-Surrey
1932	TH Cotton	A Perry	AJ Lacey	JH Jolly	Moor Park
1933	P Alliss	M Seymour	ER Whitcombe	A Compston	Purley Downs
1934	JJ Busson	CA Whitcombe	A Chevalier	RA Whitcombe	Walton Heath
1935	AH Padgham	P Alliss	R Burton	RA Whitcombe	Mid-Surrey
1936	DJ Rees	ER Whitcombe	P Alliss	JJ Taylor	Oxhey
1937	P Alliss	J Adams	D Curtis	CA Whitcombe	Stoke Poges
1938	DJ Rees	EE Whitcombe	AG Havers	L Ayton, jun	Walton Heath
1940	TH Cotton	AH Padgham	RG French	AJ Lacey	Mid-Surrey
1945	RW Horne	P Alliss	RA Knight	TE Odams	Walton Heath
1946	TH Cotton	J Adams	AD Locke	R Burton	Hoylake
1947	F Daly	F Van Donck	CH Ward	TH Cotton	St Annes
1948	F Daly	L Ayton	SL King	CH Ward	Birkdale
1949	DJ Rees	TH Cotton	SL King	L Mangrum	Walton Heath
1950	DJ Rees	F Jowle	K Bousfield	TH Cotton	Carnoustie
1951	H Weetman	J Adams	AS Waters	SL King	Hoylake
1952	F Daly	F Van Donck	J Panton	G Johnson	Walton Heath
1953	M Faulkner	DJ Rees	JRM Jacobs	F Daly	Ganton
1954	P Thomson	J Fallon	F Jowle	N Sutton	St Andrews
1955	K Bousfield	EC Brown	A Lees	F Jowle	Walton Heath
1956	J Panton	H Weetman	K Bousfield	RP Mills	Hoylake
1957	C O'Connor	TB Haliburton	H Bradshaw	EC Brown	Turnberry
1958	H Weetman	BJ Hunt	C O'Connor	AM Fox	Walton Heath
1959	D Snell	H Weetman	N Sutton	DC Thomas	Birkdale
1960	EC Brown	H Weetman	TB Haliburton	DC Thomas	Turnberry
1961	PW Thomson	RL Moffitt	NC Coles	BJ Hunt	Walton Heath
1962	EC Brown	E Whitehead	DC Thomas	TA Fisher	Walton Heath
1963	DC Thomas	J MacDonald	G Will	I Wright	Turnberry
1964	NC Coles	PJ Butler	M Faulkner	HW Muscroft	Walton Heath
1965	NC Coles	L Platts	C Greene	A Jacklin	Walton Heath
1966	PW Thomson	NC Coles	A King	P Alliss	Walton Heath
1967	PW Thomson	DJ Rees	M Faulkner	NC Coles	Walton Heath
1968	BGC Huggett	J Panton	NC Coles	J Martin	Walton Heath
1969	M Bembridge	DJ Rees	BGC Huggett	D Talbot	Walton Heath
Sponsored by Long John Scotch Whisky					
1970	TA Horton	RD Shade	RT Walker	R Bernardini	Moor Park
1971	*Not played*				

PGA Match Play Tournament *continued*

Year	Winner	Runner-up	Semi-finalists		Venue
Sponsored by Benson and Hedges					
1972	JR Garner	NC Coles	RDBM Shade	D Stockton	Moor Park
1973	NC Coles	D McClelland	P Wilcock	H Muscroft	Hillside
1974	J Newton	C Sanudo	NC Coles	D Jagger	Downfield
Sponsored by Sun Alliance					
1975	E Polland	PJ Butler	D Hayes	RD Shade	Lindrick
1976	BW Barnes	CB DeFoy	J O'Leary	SF Hobday	King's Norton
1977	H Baiocchi	BGC Huggett	NC Coles	C O'Connor, jun	Stoke Poges
1978	M James	NC Coles	S Torrance	M Pinero	Dalmahoy
In 1978 the latter stages involved a round robin					
1979	D Smyth	N Price	A Garrido	C Mason	Fulford

Penfold Tournament

Year	Winner	Club/Country	Venue	Score
1932	P Alliss	Beaconsfield	Porthcawl	278
1933	J Burton	Hillside	Porthcawl	292
1934	RA Whitcombe	Parkstone	Fairhaven	284
1935	P Alliss	Beaconsfield	Gleneagles	273
1936	J Adams	Romford	Ayr Belleisle	287
1946	N Sutton	Leigh	Sutton Coldfield	283
1947	DJ Rees RA Whitcombe N Von Nida	South Herts Parkstone } tie Australia	Stoke Poges	270
1948	Fred Daly	Balmoral	Gleneagles	273
1949	Max Faulkner and John Burton	F Van Donck and Dick Burton	Totteridge	1 hole
1950	Mrs A Gee and N Sutton	Miss A Barnett and SL King	Sutton Coldfield	1 hole
1951	A Lees	Sunningdale	Bournemouth	278
In 1952 qualifying over 36 holes by stroke play and lowest 32 played off by match play				
1952	E Brown	L Ayton	Maesdu	6 and 5
1953	A Lees	K Bousfield	Maesdu	2 holes
1954	TH Cotton	JRM Jacobs	Maesdu	5 and 4
From 1955-1966 jointly sponsored with Swallow Ltd and known as Swallow-Penfold Tournament				
1955	C O'Connor	Bundoran	Southport and Ainsdale	292
1956	EG Lester	Hazel Grove	Burgess	275
1957	H Weetman	Croham Hurst	Killermont	270
1958	H Weetman	Selsdon Park	Prestwick	289
1959	PJ Butler	Harborne	Barnton	280
1960	H Weetman	Selsdon Park	Copt Heath	271
1961	K Bousfield	Coombe Hill	Stoneham	266
1962	H Weetman	Selsdon Park	Llandudno	280
1963	BJ Hunt	Hartsbourne	Ayr Belleisle	272
1964	P Alliss	Parkstone	Llandudno	293
1965	A Miguel	Spain	Pannal	287
1966	DC Thomas	Dunham Forest	Little Aston	281
From 1967 sponsored by Penfold alone				
1967	J Cockin	Unattached	Blackpool North Shore	275
1968	PJ Butler	Harborne	Maesdu	281
1969	GA Caygill	Cleckheaton and District	Worthing Hill Barn	278
1970	BJ Hunt	Hartsbourne	Worthing Hill Barn	271
1971	NC Coles	Coombe Hill	Bournemouth	284
1972	PA Oosterhuis	Pacific Harbour	Bournemouth	285
1973	E Polland	Balmoral	Bournemouth	281
1974	T Horton	Ham Manor	Worthing Hill Barn	272

Piccadilly Tournament

From 1962-67 a 72-hole stroke event. In 1968 a four-ball match play event. In 1969, under title of Piccadilly Medal, a match play event decided on strokes then in 1976 returned to 72-hole stroke play

Year	Winner	Runner-up	Venue	Score
1962	PW Thomson	C O'Connor	Southport	283
1963	*No competition*			
1964	J Martin	BJ Hunt	Wentworth	268
1965	PJ Butler	DJ Rees	Wentworth	267
1966	BJ Hunt	PO Green	Wentworth	262
1967	PJ Butler	BGC Huggett	Wentworth	263
1968	H Jackson and RH Emery	NC Coles and B Hutchison	Wentworth	2 and 1
1969	P Alliss (149)	G Will (149)	Prince's	37th hole
1970	J Lister (134)	TA Horton (137)	Southerndown	—
1971	P Oosterhuis (75, 56)	EC Brown (73, 62, ret)	Southerndown	—
1972	TA Horton (80, 77)	GL Hunt (80, 78)	Hillside	—
1973	P Oosterhuis (67)	T Westbrook (73)	Finham Park	—
1974	M Bembridge (65)	P Oosterhuis (70)	Finham Park	—
1975	RA Shearer (70)	A Oosthuizen (70)	Finham Park	19th hole
1976	S Torrance	Britain	Finham Park	277

John Player Classic

Year	Winner	Country	Venue	Score
1970	C O'Connor	Ireland	Notts	286
1971	*Not played*			
1972	RJ Charles	New Zealand	Turnberry	285
1973	C Coody	USA	Turnberry	289

John Player Trophy

Year	Winner	Club	Venue	Score
1970	CA Clark	Sunningdale	Notts	141
1971	*Not played*			
1972	R Whitehead	Moor Park	Bognor Regis	286

Schweppes Championship

Year	Winner	Club	Venue	Score
1967	ME Gregson	Dyrham Park	Hunstanton	275
1968	D Talbot	Nottinghamshire	Dunbar	276
1969	BJ Gallacher	Ilfield	Ashburnham	291

State Express English Classic

Year	Winner	Country	Venue	Score
1979	S Ballesteros	Spain	The Belfry	286
1980	M Pinero	Spain	The Belfry	286
1981	R Davis	Australia	The Belfry	284
1982	G Norman	Australia	The Belfry	279
1983	H Baiocchi	South Africa	The Belfry	279

Sumrie Better-Ball Tournament

Year	Winners	Venue	Score
1969	M Bembridge and A Gallardo	Pannal	263
1970	NC Coles and BJ Hunt	Pannal	257
1971	*Not played*		
1972	BGC Huggett and ME Gregson	Blairgowrie	264
1973	NC Coles and BJ Hunt	Blairgowrie	265
1974	C Clark and PJ Butler	Queens Park, Bournemouth	267
1975	J Newton and J O'Leary	Queens Park, Bournemouth	256
1976	E Darcy and C O'Connor, jun	Queens Park, Bournemouth	260
1977	*Not played*		
1978	E Darcy and C O'Connor, jun	Queens Park, Bournemouth	255

Sunbeam Electric Scottish Open Championship

Year	Winner	Club/Country	Venue	Score
1972	NC Coles	Coombe Hill	Downfield	283
1973	G Marsh	Australia	St Andrews	286

Timeshare Tournament Players' Championship

Year	Winner	Venue	Score
1977	NC Coles	Foxhills	288
1978	BJ Waites	Foxhills	286
1979 sponsored by SOS Talisman			
1979	M King	Moor Park	281
1980-82 sponsored by Haig			
1980	BJ Gallacher	Moortown	268
1981	B Barnes	Dalmahoy	276
After play-off			
1982	N Faldo	Notts	270
1983	B Langer	St Mellion	269
1984	J Gonzalez	St Mellion	265

Timex Open

Instituted 1983

Year	Winner	Venue	Score
1983	S Ballesteros	Biarritz	262
1984	M Clayton	Biarritz	260

Uniroyal International

Year	Winner	Club/Country	Venue	Score
1976	TA Horton	Royal Jersey	Moor Park	277
1977	S Ballesteros	Spain	Moor Park	276

WD & HO Wills Tournament

Year	Winner	Club/Country	Venue	Score
1968	Peter Butler	Harborne & St Cloud	Pannal	281
1969	Bernard Gallacher	Wentworth	Moor Park	275
1970	Tony Jacklin	Potters Bar	Dalmahoy	267
1971	Bernard Hunt	Hartsbourne	Dalmahoy	276
1972	PW Thomson	Australia	Dalmahoy	270
1973	C Coody	USA	Kings Norton	281
1974	NC Coles	Holiday Inns	Kings Norton	283

World Senior Professional Championship

Year	Winner	Runner-up	Venue	By
1961	Paul Runyan	SL King	Fairhaven	3 and 1
1962	Paul Runyan	SL King	Prestwick	2 and 1
1963	H Barron	G Evans	St Annes	3 and 2
1964	Sam Snead	SS Scott	Wentworth	7 and 6
1965	Sam Snead	CH Ward	Formby	37th hole
1966	Fred Haas	Dai Rees	Dalmahoy	3 and 2
1967	J Panton	S Snead	Wallasey	3 and 2
1968	Chandler Harper	M Faulkner	Downfield	2 holes
1969	T Bolt	J Panton	Portsmouth, Va	39th hole
1970	S Snead	M Faulkner	Portsmouth, Va	3 and 2
1971	K Nagle	J Boros	Portsmouth, Va	4 and 3
1972	S Snead	K Bousfield	Longniddry	3 and 2
1973	S Snead	K Nagle	Portsmouth, Va	41st hole
1974	R De Vicenzo	E Lester	Lundin	5 and 4
1975	KDG Nagle	C Sifford	Portsmouth, Va	1 hole
1976	C O'Connor	P Cooper	Whitecraigs	2 and 1
1977	C O'Connor	J Boros	Portsmouth, Va	6 and 5
1978	J Jiminez	P Skerritt	Whitecraigs	5 and 4

Professional Internationals

Great Britain *v* USA

Year	Great Britain			USA			Venue
1921 (June 6)	Foursomes Singles	4 6½	10½	Foursomes Singles	1 3½	4½	Gleneagles
1926 (June 4-5)	Foursomes Singles	5 8½	13½	Foursomes Singles	0 1½	1½	Wentworth

The Ryder Cup

(Instituted 1927)

Year	Great Britain			USA			Venue
1927 (June 3-4)	Foursomes Singles	1 1½	2½	Foursomes Singles	3 6½	9½	Worcester, Mass
1929 (May 26-27)	Foursomes Singles	1½ 5½	7	Foursomes Singles	2½ 2½	5	Moortown
1931 (June 26-27)	Foursomes Singles	1 2	3	Foursomes Singles	3 6	9	Scioto, Ohio
1933 (June 26-27)	Foursomes Singles	2½ 4	6½	Foursomes Singles	1½ 4	5½	Southport and Ainsdale
1935 (Sept 28-29)	Foursomes Singles	1 2	3	Foursomes Singles	3 6	9	Ridgewood, NJ
1937 (June 29-30)	Foursomes Singles	1½ 2½	4	Foursomes Singles	2½ 5½	8	Southport and Ainsdale
1947 (Nov 1-2)	Foursomes Singles	0 1	1	Foursomes Singles	4 11	15	Portland, Oregon
1949 (Sept 16-17)	Foursomes Singles	3 2	5	Foursomes Singles	1 6	7	Ganton
1951 (Nov 2 and 4)	Foursomes Singles	1 1½	2½	Foursomes Singles	3 6½	9½	Pinehurst, N Carolina
1953 (Oct 2-3)	Foursomes Singles	1 4½	5½	Foursomes Singles	3 3½	6½	Wentworth
1955 (Nov 5-6)	Foursomes Singles	1 3	4	Foursomes Singles	3 5	8	Thunderbird, Calif
1957 (Oct 4-5)	Foursomes Singles	1 6½	7½	Foursomes Singles	3 1½	4½	Lindrick
1959 (Nov 6-7)	Foursomes Singles	1½ 2	3½	Foursomes Singles	2½ 6	8½	Eldorado, Calif

At Lytham and St Annes, 13th and 14th October, 1961

From 1961 all matches played over 18 holes

Foursomes

Morning

Great Britain	Matches	USA	Matches
C O'Connor and P Alliss (4 and 3)	1	G Littler and D Ford	0
J Panton and BJ Hunt	0	A Wall and J Hebert (4 and 3)	1
DJ Reés and K Bousfield	0	W Casper and A Palmer (2 and 1)	1
TB Haliburton and NC Coles	0	M Souchak and W Collins (1 hole)	1

Ryder Cup

continued

Foursomes

Afternoon

Great Britain	Matches	USA	Matches
C O'Connor and P Alliss	0	A Wall and J Hebert (1 hole)	1
J Panton and BJ Hunt	0	W Casper and A Palmer (5 and 4)	1
DJ Rees and K Bousfield (4 and 2)	1	M Souchak and W Collins	0
TB Haliburton and NC Coles	0	J Barber and D Finsterwald (1 hole)	1
	2		6

Singles

Morning

Great Britain	Matches	USA	Matches
H Weetman	0	D Ford (1 hole)	1
RL Moffitt	0	M Souchak (5 and 4)	1
P Alliss (halved)	0	A Palmer (halved)	0
K Bousfield	0	W Casper (5 and 3)	1
DJ Rees (2 and 1)	1	J Hebert	0
NC Coles (halved)	0	G Littler (halved)	0
BJ Hunt (5 and 4)	1	J Barber	0
C O'Connor	0	D Finsterwald (2 and 1)	1

Afternoon

Great Britain	Matches	USA	Matches
H Weetman	0	A Wall (1 hole)	1
P Alliss (3 and 2)	1	W Collins	0
BJ Hunt	0	M Souchak (2 and 1)	1
TB Haliburton	0	A Palmer (2 and 1)	1
DJ Rees (4 and 3)	1	D Ford	0
K Bousfield (1 hole)	1	J Barber	0
NC Coles (1 hole)	1	D Finsterwald	0
C O'Connor (halved)	0	G Littler (halved)	0
	6		7

Grand Aggregate: Great Britain 8; USA 13; 3 matches halved.
Captains–DJ Rees, Great Britain, and Jerry Barber, USA.

At Atlanta, Georgia, 11th, 12th and 13th October, 1963

Foursomes

Morning

USA	Matches	Great Britain	Matches
A Palmer and J Pott	0	BGC Huggett and G Will (3 and 2)	1
W Casper and D Ragan (1 hole)	1	P Alliss and C O'Connor	0
J Boros and A Lema (halved)	0	NC Coles and BJ Hunt (halved)	0
E Littler and D Finsterwald (halved)	0	DC Thomas and H Weetman (halved)	0

Afternoon

USA	Matches	Great Britain	Matches
W Maxwell and R Goalby (4 and 3)	1	DC Thomas and H Weetman	0
A Palmer and W Casper (5 and 4)	1	BGC Huggett and G Will	0
E Littler and D Finsterwald (2 and 1)	1	NC Coles and GM Hunt	0
J Boros and A Lema (1 hole)	1	TB Haliburton and BJ Hunt	0
	5		1

Totals: USA 5; Great Britain 1; 2 halved.

Four-Ball

Morning

USA		Great Britain	
A Palmer and D Finsterwald (5 and 4)	1	BGC Huggett and DC Thomas	0
E Littler and J Boros (halved)	0	P Alliss and BJ Hunt (halved)	0
W Casper and W Maxwell (3 and 2)	1	H Weetman and G Will	0
R Goalby and D Ragan	0	NC Coles and C O'Connor (1 hole)	1
	2		1

Afternoon

USA		Great Britain	
A Palmer and D Finsterwald (3 and 2)	1	NC Coles and C O'Connor	0
A Lema and J Pott (1 hole)	1	P Alliss and BJ Hunt	0
W Casper and W Maxwell (2 and 1)	1	TB Haliburton and GM Hunt	0
R Goalby and D Ragan (halved)	0	BGC Huggett and DC Thomas (halved)	0
	3		0

Totals: USA 5; Great Britain 1; 2 halved.

Singles

Morning

USA	Matches	Great Britain	Matches
A Lema (5 and 3)	1	GM Hunt	0
J Pott	0	BGC Huggett (3 and 1)	1
A Palmer	0	P Alliss (1 hole)	1
W Casper (halved)	0	NC Coles (halved)	0
R Goalby (3 and 2)	1	DC Thomas	0
E Littler (1 hole)	1	C O'Connor	0
J Boros	0	H Weetman (1 hole)	1
D Finsterwald	0	BJ Hunt (2 holes)	1
	3		4

Afternoon

USA	Matches	Great Britain	Matches
A Palmer (3 and 2)	1	G Will	0
D Ragan (2 and 1)	1	NC Coles	0
A Lema (halved)	0	P Alliss (halved)	0
E Littler (6 and 5)	1	TB Haliburton	0
J Boros (2 and 1)	1	H Weetman	0
W Maxwell (2 and 1)	1	C O'Connor	0
D Finsterwald (4 and 3)	1	DC Thomas	0
R Goalby (2 and 1)	1	BJ Hunt	0
	7		0

Totals: USA 10; Great Britain 4; 2 halved.
Grand Aggregate: USA 20; Great Britain 6; 6 halved.
Captains–A Palmer, USA; J Fallon (non-playing), Great Britain.

At Birkdale, 7th, 8th and 9th October, 1965

Foursomes

Morning

Great Britain	Matches	USA	Matches
DC Thomas and G Will (6 and 5)	1	D Marr and A Palmer	0
C O'Connor and P Alliss (5 and 4)	1	K Venturi and D January	0
L Platts and PJ Butler	0	J Boros and A Lema (1 hole)	1
BJ Hunt and NC Coles	0	W Casper and G Littler (2 and 1)	1

Afternoon

Great Britain	Matches	USA	Matches
DC Thomas and G Will	0	D Marr and A Palmer (6 and 5)	1
J Martin and J Hitchock	0	J Boros and A Lema (5 and 4)	1
C O'Connor and P Alliss (2 and 1)	1	W Casper and G Littler	0
BJ Hunt and NC Coles (3 and 2)	1	K Venturi and D January	0
	4		4

Totals: Great Britain 4; USA 4.

Four-Ball

Morning

Great Britain		USA	
DC Thomas and G Will	0	D January and T Jacobs (1 hole)	1
L Platts and PJ Butler (halved)	0	W Casper and G Littler (halved)	0
P Alliss and C O'Connor	0	D Marr and A Palmer (5 and 4)	1
NC Coles and BJ Hunt (1 hole)	1	J Boros and A Lema	0

Afternoon

Great Britain		USA	
P Alliss and C O'Connor (1 hole)	1	D Marr and A Palmer	0
DC Thomas and G Will	0	D January and T Jacobs (1 hole)	1
L Platts and PJ Butler (halved)	0	W Casper and G Littler (halved)	0
NC Coles and BJ Hunt	0	A Lema and K Venturi (1 hole)	1
	2		4

Totals: Great Britain 6; USA 8; 2 halved.

Ryder Cup

continued

Singles

Morning

Great Britain	Matches	USA	Matches
J Hitchcock	0	A Palmer (3 and 2)	1
L Platts	0	J Boros (4 and 2)	1
PJ Butler	0	A Lema (1 hole)	1
NC Coles	0	D Marr (2 holes)	1
BJ Hunt (2 holes)	1	G Littler	0
P Alliss (1 hole)	1	W Casper	0
DC Thomas	0	T Jacobs (2 and 1)	1
G Will (halved)	0	D January (halved)	0
Afternoon			
PJ Butler	0	A Palmer (2 holes)	1
J Hitchcock	0	J Boros (2 and 1)	1
C O'Connor	0	A Lema (6 and 4)	1
P Alliss (3 and 1)	1	K Venturi	0
BJ Hunt	0	D Marr (1 hole)	1
NC Coles (3 and 2)	1	W Casper	0
G Will	0	G Littler (2 and 1)	1
L Platts (1 hole)	1	T Jacobs	0
	5		10

Grand Aggregate: Great Britain 11; USA 18; 3 halved.
Non-playing Captains: H Weetman, Great Britain; Byron Nelson, USA.

At Houston, Texas, 20th, 21st and 22nd October, 1967

Foursomes

Morning

USA	Matches	Great Britain	Matches
W Casper and J Boros (halved)	0	BGC Huggett and G Will (halved)	0
A Palmer and G Dickinson (2 and 1)	1	P Alliss and C O'Connor	0
D Sanders and G Brewer	0	A Jacklin and DC Thomas (4 and 3)	1
B Nichols and J Pott (6 and 5)	1	BJ Hunt and NC Coles	0
Afternoon			
J Boros and W Casper (1 hole)	1	BGC Huggett and G Will	0
G Dickinson and A Palmer (5 and 4)	1	M Gregson and HF Boyle	0
G Littler and A Geiberger	0	A Jacklin and DC Thomas (3 and 2)	1
B Nichols and J Pott (2 and 1)	1	P Alliss and C O'Connor	0
	5		2

Totals: USA 5; Great Britain 2; 1 halved.

Four-Ball

Morning

USA		Great Britain	
W Casper and G Brewer (3 and 2)	1	P Alliss and C O'Connor	0
B Nichols and J Pott (1 hole)	1	BJ Hunt and NC Coles	0
G Littler and A Geiberger (1 hole)	1	A Jacklin and DC Thomas	0
G Dickinson and D Sanders (3 and 2)	1	BGC Huggett and G Will	0
Afternoon			
W Casper and G Brewer (5 and 3)	1	BJ Hunt and NC Coles	0
G Dickinson and D Sanders (3 and 2)	1	P Alliss and M Gregson	0
A Palmer and J Boros (1 hole)	1	G Will and HF Boyle	0
G Littler and A Geiberger (halved)	0	A Jacklin and DC Thomas (halved)	0
	7		0

Totals: USA 12; Great Britain 2; 2 halved.

Singles

Morning

USA	Matches	Great Britain	Matches
G Brewer (4 and 3)	1	HF Boyle	0
W Casper (2 and 1)	1	P Alliss	0
A Palmer (3 and 2)	1	A Jacklin	0
J Boros	0	BGC Huggett (1 hole)	1
D Sanders	0	NC Coles (2 and 1)	1
A Geiberger (4 and 2)	1	M Gregson	0
G Littler (halved)	0	DC Thomas (halved)	0
B Nichols (halved)	0	BJ Hunt (halved)	0
Afternoon			
A Palmer (5 and 3)	1	BGC Huggett	0
G Brewer	0	P Alliss (2 and 1)	1
G Dickinson (3 and 2)	1	A Jacklin	0
B Nichols (3 and 2)	1	C O'Connor	0
J Potts (3 and 1)	1	G Will	0
A Geiberger (2 and 1)	1	M Gregson	0
J Boros (halved)	0	BJ Hunt (halved)	0
D Sanders	0	NC Coles (2 and 1)	1
	9		4

Grand Aggregate: USA 21; Great Britain 6; 5 halved.
Non-playing Captains: B Hogan, USA; DJ Rees, Great Britain.

At Birkdale, 18th, 19th and 20th September, 1969

Foursomes

Morning

Great Britain	Matches	USA	Matches
NC Coles and BGC Huggett (3 and 2)	1	M Barber and R Floyd	0
B Gallacher and M Bembridge (2 and 1)	1	L Trevino and K Still	0
A Jacklin and P Townsend (3 and 1)	1	D Hill and T Aaron	0
C O'Connor and P Alliss (halved)	0	W Casper and F Beard (halved)	0
Afternoon			
NC Coles and BGC Huggett	0	D Hill and T Aaron (1 hole)	1
B Gallacher and M Bembridge	0	L Trevino and G Littler (2 holes)	1
A Jacklin and P Townsend (1 hole)	1	W Casper and F Beard	0
BJ Hunt and PJ Butler	0	J Nicklaus and D Sikes (1 hole)	1
	4		3

Foursomes Totals: Great Britain 4; USA 3; 1 halved.

Four-Ball

Morning

Great Britain		USA	
C O'Connor and P Townsend (1 hole)	1	D Hill and D Douglass	0
BGC Huggett and GA Caygill (halved)	0	R Floyd and M Barber (halved)	0
B Barnes and P Alliss	0	L Trevino and G Littler (1 hole)	1
A Jacklin and NC Coles (1 hole)	1	J Nicklaus and D Sikes	0
Afternoon			
P Townsend and PJ Butler	0	W Casper and F Beard (2 holes)	1
BGC Huggett and B Gallacher	0	D Hill and K Still (2 and 1)	1
M Bembridge and BJ Hunt (halved)	0	T Aaron and R Floyd (halved)	0
A Jacklin and NC Coles (halved)	0	L Trevino and M Barber (halved)	0
	2		3

Four-Ball Totals: Great Britain 2; USA 3; 3 halved.

Ryder Cup

continued

Singles

Morning

Great Britain	Matches	USA	Matches
P Alliss	0	L Trevino (2 and 1)	1
P Townsend	0	D Hill (5 and 4)	1
NC Coles (1 hole)	1	T Aaron	0
B Barnes	0	W Casper (1 hole)	1
C O'Connor (5 and 4)	1	F Beard	0
M Bembridge (1 hole)	1	K Still	0
PJ Butler (1 hole)	1	R Floyd	0
A Jacklin (4 and 3)	1	J Nicklaus	0
Afternoon			
B Barnes	0	D Hill (4 and 2)	1
B Gallacher (4 and 3)	1	L Trevino	0
M Bembridge	0	M Barber (7 and 6)	1
PJ Butler (3 and 2)	1	D Douglass	0
C O'Connor	0	G Littler (2 and 1)	1
BGC Huggett (halved)	0	W Casper (halved)	0
NC Coles	0	D Sikes (4 and 3)	1
A Jacklin (halved)	0	J Nicklaus (halved)	0
	7		7

Singles Totals: Great Britain 7; USA 7; 2 halved.
Grand Aggregate: Great Britain 13; USA 13; 6 halved.
Non-playing Captains: EC Brown, Great Britain; S Snead, USA

At St Louis, Missouri, 16th, 17th and 18th September, 1971

Foursomes

Morning

USA	Matches	Great Britain	Matches
WJ Casper and M Barber	0	NC Coles and C O'Connor (2 and 1)	1
A Palmer and G Dickinson (2 holes)	1	PMP Townsend and PA Oosterhuis	0
JW Nicklaus and D Stockton	0	BGC Huggett and A Jacklin (3 and 2)	1
C Coody and F Beard	0	ME Bembridge and PJ Butler (1 hole)	1
Afternoon			
WJ Casper and M Barber	0	H Bannerman and BJ Gallacher (2 and 1)	1
A Palmer and G Dickinson (1 hole)	1	PMP Townsend and PA Oosterhuis	0
L Trevino and M Rudolph (halved)	0	BGC Huggett and A Jacklin (halved)	0
JW Nicklaus and JC Snead (5 and 3)	1	ME Bembridge and PJ Butler	0
	3		4

Foursomes Totals: USA 3; Great Britain 4; 1 halved.

Four-Ball

Morning

USA		Great Britain	
L Trevino and M Rudolph (2 and 1)	1	C O'Connor and BW Barnes	0
F Beard and JC Snead (2 and 1)	1	NC Coles and J Garner	0
A Palmer and G Dickinson (5 and 4)	1	PA Oosterhuis and BJ Gallacher	0
JW Nicklaus and G Littler (2 and 1)	1	PMP Townsend and H Bannerman	0
Afternoon			
L Trevino and WJ Casper	0	BJ Gallacher and PA Oosterhuis (1 hole)	1
G Littler and JC Snead (2 and 1)	1	A Jacklin and BGC Huggett	0
A Palmer and JW Nicklaus (1 hole)	1	PMP Townsend and H Bannerman	0
C Coody and F Beard (halved)	0	NC Coles and C O'Connor (halved)	0
	6		1

Four-Ball Totals: USA 6; Great Britain 1; 1 halved.

Ryder Cup
continued

Singles

Morning

	Matches		Matches
L Trevino (1 hole)	1	A Jacklin	0
D Stockton (halved)	0	BJ Gallacher (halved)	0
M Rudolph	0	BW Barnes (1 hole)	1
G Littler	0	PA Oosterhuis (4 and 3)	1
JW Nicklaus (3 and 2)	1	PMP Townsend	0
G Dickinson (5 and 4)	1	C O'Connor	0
A Palmer (halved)	0	H Bannerman (halved)	0
F Beard (halved)	0	NC Coles (halved)	0

Afternoon

L Trevino (7 and 6)	1	BGC Huggett	0
JC Snead (1 hole)	1	A Jacklin	0
M Barber	0	BW Barnes (2 and 1)	1
D Stockton (1 hole)	1	PMP Townsend	0
C Coody	0	BJ Gallacher (2 and 1)	1
JW Nicklaus (5 and 3)	1	NC Coles	0
A Palmer	0	PA Oosterhuis (3 and 2)	1
G Dickinson	0	H Bannerman (2 and 1)	1
	7		6

Singles Totals: USA 7; Great Britain 6; 3 halved.
Grand Aggregate: USA 16; Great Britain 11; 5 halved.
Non-playing Captains: Jay Herbert, USA; EC Brown, Great Britain.

At Muirfield, 20th, 21st and 22nd September, 1973

First Day–Foursomes

GB and Ireland	Matches	USA	Matches
BW Barnes and BJ Gallacher (1 hole)	1	L Trevino and WJ Casper	0
C O'Connor and NC Coles (3 and 2)	1	T Weiskopf and JC Snead	0
A Jacklin and PA Oosterhuis (halved)	0	J Rodriguez and L Graham (halved)	0
ME Bembridge and E Polland	0	JW Nicklaus and A Palmer (6 and 5)	1

Four-Ball

BW Barnes and BJ Gallacher (5 and 4)	1	T Aaron and G Brewer	0
ME Bembridge and BGC Huggett (3 and 1)	1	A Palmer and JW Nicklaus	0
A Jacklin and PA Oosterhuis (3 and 1)	1	T Weiskopf and WJ Casper	0
C O'Connor and NC Coles	0	L Trevino and H Blancas (2 and 1)	1

First Day Totals: Great Britain and Ireland 5; USA 2; 1 halved.

Second Day–Foursomes

GB and Ireland	Matches	USA	Matches
BW Barnes and PJ Butler	0	JW Nicklaus and T Weiskopf (1 hole)	1
PA Oosterhuis and A Jacklin (2 holes)	1	A Palmer and D Hill	0
ME Bembridge and BGC Huggett (5 and 4)	1	J Rodriguez and L Graham	0
NC Coles and C O'Connor	0	L Trevino and WJ Casper (2 and 1)	1

Four-Ball

BW Barnes and PJ Butler	0	JC Snead and A Palmer (2 holes)	1
A Jacklin and P Oosterhuis	0	G Brewer and WJ Casper (3 and 2)	1
C Clark and E Polland	0	JW Nicklaus and T Weiskopf (3 and 2)	1
ME Bembridge and BGC Huggett (halved)	0	L Trevino and H Blancas (halved)	0

Second Day Totals: Great Britain and Ireland 2; USA 5; 1 halved.

Third Day–Singles

Morning

BW Barnes	0	WJ Casper (2 and 1)	1
BJ Gallacher	0	T Weiskopf (3 and 1)	1
PJ Butler	0	H Blancas (5 and 4)	1
A Jacklin (3 and 1)	1	T Aaron	0
NC Coles (halved)	0	G Brewer (halved)	0
C O'Connor	0	JC Snead (1 hole)	1
ME Bembridge (halved)	0	JW Nicklaus (halved)	0
PA Oosterhuis (halved)	0	L Trevino (halved)	0

Ryder Cup

continued

Afternoon

	Matches		Matches
BGC Huggett (4 and 2)	1	H Blancas	0
BW Barnes	0	JC Snead (3 and 1)	1
BJ Gallacher	0	G Brewer (6 and 5)	1
A Jacklin	0	WJ Casper (2 and 1)	1
NC Coles	0	L Trevino (6 and 5)	1
C O'Connor (halved)	0	T Weiskopf (halved)	0
ME Bembridge	0	JW Nicklaus (2 holes)	1
PA Oosterhuis (4 and 2)	1	A Palmer	0

Singles Totals: Great Britain and Ireland 3; USA 9; 4 halved.
Grand Aggregate: Great Britain and Ireland 10; USA 16; 6 halved.
Non-playing Captains: BJ Hunt, Great Britain and Ireland; J Burke, USA.

At Laurel Valley, Pennsylvania, 19th, 20th and 21st September, 1975

First Day–Foursomes

USA	Matches	GB and Ireland	Matches
JW Nicklaus and T Weiskopf (5 and 4)	1	BW Barnes and BJ Gallacher	0
G Littler and H Irwin (4 and 3)	1	N Wood and M Bembridge	0
A Geiberger and J Miller (3 and 1)	1	A Jacklin and P Oosterhuis	0
L Trevino and JC Snead (2 and 1)	1	T Horton and J O'Leary	0

Four-Ball

WJ Casper and R Floyd	0	P Oosterhuis and A Jacklin (2 and 1)	1
T Weiskopf and L Graham (3 and 2)	1	E Darcy and C O'Connor, Jr	0
JW Nicklaus and R Murphy (halved)	0	BW Barnes and BW Gallacher (halved)	0
L Trevino and H Irwin (2 and 1)	1	T Horton and J O'Leary	0

First Day Totals: USA 6; Great Britain and Ireland 1; 1 halved.

Second Day–Four-Ball

WJ Casper and J Miller (halved)	0	P Oosterhuis and A Jacklin (halved)	0
JW Nicklaus and JC Snead (4 and 2)	1	T Horton and N Wood	0
G Littler and L Graham (5 and 3)	1	BW Barnes and BJ Gallacher	0
A Geiberger and R Floyd (halved)	0	E Darcy and GL Hunt (halved)	0

Foursomes

L Trevino and R Murphy	0	A Jacklin and BW Barnes (3 and 2)	1
T Weiskopf and J Miller (5 and 3)	1	C O'Connor, Jr and J O'Leary	0
H Irwin and WJ Casper (3 and 2)	1	P Oosterhuis and M Bembridge	0
A Geiberger and L Graham (3 and 2)	1	E Darcy and GL Hunt	0

Second Day Totals: USA 5; Great Britain and Ireland 1; 2 halved.

Third Day–Singles

Morning

R Murphy (2 and 1)	1	A Jacklin	0
J Miller	0	P Oosterhuis (2 holes)	1
L Trevino (halved)	0	BJ Gallacher (halved)	0
H Irwin (halved)	0	T Horton (halved)	0
G Littler (4 and 2)	1	BGC Huggett	0
WJ Casper (3 and 2)	1	E Darcy	0
T Weiskopf (5 and 3)	1	GL Hunt	0
JW Nicklaus	0	BW Barnes (4 and 2)	1

Afternoon

R Floyd (1 hole)	1	A Jacklin	0
JC Snead	0	P Oosterhuis (3 and 2)	1
A Geiberger (halved)	0	BJ Gallacher (halved)	0
L Graham	0	T Horton (2 and 1)	1
H Irwin (2 and 1)	1	J O'Leary	0
R Murphy (2 and 1)	1	M Bembridge	0
L Trevino	0	N Wood (2 and 1)	1
JW Nicklaus	0	BW Barnes (2 and 1)	1

Third Day Totals: USA 7; Great Britain and Ireland 6; 3 halved.
Grand Aggregate: USA 18; Great Britain and Ireland 8; 6 halved.
Non-playing Captains: A Palmer, USA; BJ Hunt, Great Britain and Ireland.

At Lytham and St Annes, 15th, 16th and 17th September, 1977

Ryder Cup
continued

First Day–Foursomes

GB and Ireland	Matches	USA	Matches
BJ Gallacher and BW Barnes	0	L Wadkins and H Irwin (3 and 1)	1
NC Coles and P Dawson	0	D Stockton and J McGee (1 hole)	1
N Faldo and P Oosterhuis (2 and 1)	1	R Floyd and L Graham	0
E Darcy and A Jacklin (halved)	0	E Sneed and D January (halved)	0
T Horton and M James	0	JW Nicklaus and T Watson (5 and 4)	1
	1		3

Second Day–Four-Ball

BW Barnes and T Horton	0	T Watson and H Green (5 and 4)	1
NC Coles and P Dawson	0	E Sneed and L Wadkins (5 and 3)	1
N Faldo and P Oosterhuis (3 and 1)	1	JW Nicklaus and R Floyd	0
A Jacklin and E Darcy	0	D Hill and D Stockton (5 and 3)	1
M James and K Brown	0	H Irwin and L Graham (1 hole)	1
	1		4

Third Day–Singles

H Clark	0	L Wadkins (4 and 3)	1
NC Coles	0	L Graham (5 and 3)	1
P Dawson (5 and 4)	1	D January	0
BW Barnes (1 hole)	1	H Irwin	0
T Horton	0	D Hill (5 and 4)	1
BJ Gallacher (1 hole)	1	JW Nicklaus	0
E Darcy	0	H Green (1 hole)	1
M James	0	R Floyd (2 and 1)	1
N Faldo (1 hole)	1	T Watson	0
P Oosterhuis (2 holes)	1	J McGhee	0
	5		5

Match Aggregate: Great Britain and Ireland 7; USA 12; 1 halved.
Non-playing Captains: BGC Huggett, Great Britain and Ireland; D Finsterwald, USA.

At Greenbrier, West Virginia, on 14th, 15th and 16th September, 1979

From 1979 players from Europe became available for selection in addition to those from Great Britain and Ireland.

First Day–Four-Ball

USA	Matches	GB and Europe	Matches
L Wadkins and L Nelson (2 and 1)	1	A Garrido and S Ballesteros	0
L Trevino and F Zoeller (3 and 2)	1	K Brown and M James	0
A Bean and L Elder (2 and 1)	1	P Oosterhuis and N Faldo	0
H Irwin and J Mahaffey	0	B Gallacher and B Barnes (2 and 1)	1
	3		1

Foursomes

H Irwin and T Kite (7 and 6)	1	K Brown and D Smyth	0
F Zoeller and H Green	0	S Ballesteros and A Garrido (3 and 2)	1
L Trevino and G Morgan (halved)	0	A Lyle and A Jacklin (halved)	0
L Wadkins and L Nelson (4 and 3)	1	B Gallacher and B Barnes	0
	2		1

Second Day–Foursomes

L Elder and J Mahaffey	0	A Jacklin and A Lyle (5 and 4)	1
A Bean and T Kite	0	N Faldo and P Oosterhuis (6 and 5)	1
F Zoeller and M Hayes	0	B Gallacher and B Barnes (2 and 1)	1
L Wadkins and L Nelson (3 and 2)	1	S Ballesteros and A Garrido	0
	1		3

Ryder Cup
continued

Four-Ball

	Matches		Matches
L Wadkins and L Nelson (5 and 4)	1	S Ballesteros and A Garrido	0
H Irwin and T Kite (1 hole)	1	A Jacklin and A Lyle	0
L Trevino and F Zoeller	0	B Gallacher and B Barnes (3 and 2)	1
L Elder and M Hayes	0	N Faldo and P Oosterhuis (1 hole)	1
	2		2

Third Day–Singles

L Wadkins	0	B Gallacher (3 and 2)	1
L Nelson (3 and 2)	1	S Ballesteros	0
T Kite (1 hole)	1	A Jacklin	0
M Hayes (1 hole)	1	A Garrido	0
A Bean (4 and 3)	1	M King	0
J Mahaffey (1 hole)	1	B Barnes	0
L Elder	0	N Faldo (3 and 2)	1
H Irwin (5 and 3)	1	D Smyth	0
H Green (2 holes)	1	P Oosterhuis	0
F Zoeller	0	K Brown (1 hole)	1
L Trevino (2 and 1)	1	A Lyle	0
G Morgan (halved, match not played)	0	M James (halved, match not played, injured)	0
	8		3

Match Aggregate: USA 16; Great Britain and Europe 10; 2 halved.
Non-playing Captains: W Casper, USA; J Jacobs, Great Britain and Europe.

At Walton Heath, 18th, 19th and 20th September, 1981

First Day–Foursomes

GB and Europe	Matches	USA	Matches
A Lyle and M James (2 and 1)	1	W Rogers and B Lietzke	0
B Langer and M Pinero	0	L Trevino and L Nelson (1 hole)	1
B Gallacher and D Smyth (3 and 2)	1	H Irwin and R Floyd	0
P Oosterhuis and N Faldo	0	T Watson and J Nicklaus (4 and 3)	1
	2		2

Four-Ball

D Smyth and J Canizares (6 and 5)	1	W Rogers and B Lietzke	0
A Lyle and M James (3 and 2)	1	B Crenshaw and J Pate	0
S Torrance and H Clark (halved)	0	T Kite and J Miller (halved)	0
B Gallacher and E Darcy	0	H Irwin and R Floyd (2 and 1)	1
	2		1

Second Day–Foursomes

P Oosterhuis and S Torrance	0	L Trevino and J Pate (2 and 1)	1
A Lyle and M James	0	W Rogers and R Floyd (3 and 2)	1
B Langer and M Pinero	0	J Nicklaus and T Watson (3 and 2)	1
D Smyth and B Gallacher	0	T Kite and L Nelson (3 and 2)	1
	0		4

Four-Ball

N Faldo and S Torrance	0	L Trevino and J Pate (7 and 5)	1
A Lyle and M James	0	L Nelson and T Kite (1 hole)	1
B Langer and M Pinero (2 and 1)	1	R Floyd and H Irwin	0
J Canizares and D Smyth	0	J Nicklaus and T Watson (3 and 2)	1
	1		3

Third Day–Singles

	Matches		Matches
S Torrance	0	L Trevino (5 and 3)	1
A Lyle	0	T Kite (3 and 2)	1
D Smyth	0	B Crenshaw (6 and 4)	1
B Gallacher (halved)	0	W Rogers (halved)	0
M James	0	L Nelson (2 holes)	1
M Pinero (4 and 2)	1	J Pate	0
B Langer (halved)	0	B Lietzke (halved)	0
N Faldo (2 and 1)	1	J Miller	0
H Clark (4 and 3)	1	T Watson	0
J Canizares	0	H Irwin (1 hole)	1
E Darcy	0	J Nicklaus (5 and 3)	1
P Oosterhuis	0	R Floyd (2 holes)	1
	3		7

Match Aggregate: Great Britain and Europe 8; USA 17; 3 halved.

At PGA National, Florida, 14th, 15th and 16th October, 1983

First Day–Foursomes

USA	Matches	GB and Europe	Matches
T Watson and B Crenshaw (4 and 2)	1	B Gallacher and A Lyle	0
L Wadkins and C Stadler	0	N Faldo and B Langer (4 and 2)	1
T Kite and C Peete (2 and 1)	1	S Ballesteros and P Way	0
R Floyd and B Gilder	0	J-M Canizares and S Torrance (4 and 3)	1
	2		2

Four-Ball

G Morgan and F Zoeller	0	B Waites and K Brown (2 and 1)	1
T Watson and J Haas (2 and 1)	1	N Faldo and B Langer	0
R Floyd and C Strange	0	S Ballesteros and P Way (1 hole)	1
B Crenshaw and C Peete	0	S Torrance and I Woosnam	0
	1		2

Second Day–Foursomes

R Floyd and T Kite	0	N Faldo and B Langer (3 and 2)	1
J Haas and C Strange (3 and 1)	1	K Brown and B Waites	0
L Wadkins and G Morgan (7 and 5)	1	S Torrance and J-M Canizares	0
B Gilder and T Watson	0	S Ballesteros and P Way (2 and 1)	1
	2		2

Four-Ball

C Stadler and L Wadkins (1 hole)	1	K Brown and B Waites	0
C Peete and B Crenshaw	0	N Faldo and B Langer (2 and 1)	1
G Morgan and J Haas	0	S Ballesteros and P Way	0
T Watson and B Gilder (5 and 4)	1	S Torrance and I Woosnam	0
	2		1

Third Day–Singles

F Zoeller	0	S Ballesteros	0
J Haas	0	N Faldo (2 and 1)	1
G Morgan	0	B Langer (2 holes)	1
B Gilder (2 holes)	1	G Brand	0
B Crenshaw (3 and 1)	1	A Lyle	0
C Peete (1 hole)	1	B Waites	0
C Strange	0	P Way (2 and 1)	1
C Stadler (3 and 2)	1	I Woosnam	0
T Kite	0	S Torrance	0
L Wadkins	0	J-M Canizares	0
R. Floyd	0	K Brown (4 and 3)	1
T Watson (2 and 1)	1	B Gallacher	0
	5		4

Match Aggregate: USA 12; Great Britain and Europe 11; 5 halved.
Non-playing Captains: J Nicklaus, USA; T Jacklin, Great Britain and Europe.

For 1985 match details, see Ryder Cup report in Part I, pp. 63–66.

At The Belfry, Sutton Coldfield, 13th, 14th and 15th September, 1985

First Day–Foursomes

Europe	Matches	USA	Matches
S Ballesteros and M Pinero (2 and 1)	1	C Strange and M O'Meara	0
B Langer and N Faldo	0	C Peete and T Kite (3 and 2)	1
A Lyle and K Brown	0	L Wadkins and R Floyd (4 and 3)	1
H Clark and S Torrance	0	C Stadler and H Sutton (3 and 2)	1
	1		3

Four-ball

P Way and I Woosnam (1 hole)	1	F Zoeller and H Green	0
S Ballesteros and M Pinero (2 and 1)	1	A North and P Jacobsen	0
B Langer and J-M Canizares (halved)	0	C Stadler and H Sutton (halved)	0
S Torrance and H Clark	0	R Floyd and L Wadkins (1 hole)	1
	2		1

Second Day–Four-ball

S Torrance and H Clark (2 and 1)	1	T Kite and A North	0
P Way and I Woosnam (4 and 3)	1	H Green and F Zoeller	0
S Ballesteros and M Pinero	0	M O'Meara and L Wadkins (3 and 2)	1
B Langer and A Lyle (halved)	0	C Stadler and C Strange (halved)	0
	2		1

Foursomes

J-M Canizares and J Rivero (7 and 5)	1	T Kite and C Peete	0
S Ballesteros and M Pinero (5 and 4)	1	C Stadler and H Sutton	0
P Way and I Woosnam	0	C Strange and P Jacobsen (4 and 2)	1
B Langer and K Brown (3 and 2)	1	R Floyd and L Wadkins	0
	3		1

Third Day–Singles

M Pinero (3 and 1)	1	L Wadkins	0
I Woosnam	0	C Stadler (2 and 1)	1
P Way (2 holes)	1	R Floyd	0
S Ballesteros (halved)	0	T Kite (halved)	0
A Lyle (3 and 2)	1	P Jacobsen	0
B Langer (5 and 4)	1	H Sutton	0
S Torrance (1 hole)	1	A North	0
H Clark (1 hole)	1	M O'Meara	0
N Faldo	0	H Green (3 and 1)	1
J Rivero	0	C Peete (1 hole)	1
J-M Canizares (2 holes)	1	F Zoeller	0
K Brown	0	C Strange (4 and 2)	1
	7		4

Match Aggregate: Europe 15; USA 10; 3 halved.
Non-playing Captains: T Jacklin, Europe; L Trevino, USA.

Individual Records

Ryder Cup

continued

(Matches were contested as Great Britain v USA from 1927-71; as Great Britain and Ireland from 1973-7; and as Europe v USA from 1979.)

Europe

Name	Year	Played	Won	Lost	Halved
Jimmy Adams	*1939-47-49-51-53	7	2	5	0
Percy Alliss	1929-31-33-35-37	6	3	2	1
Peter Allis	1953-57-59-61-63-65-67-69	30	10	15	5
Laurie Ayton	1949	0	0	0	0
Severiano Ballesteros	1979-83-85	15	6	6	3
Harry Bannerman	1971	5	2	2	1
Brian Barnes	1969-71-73-75-77-79	26	11	14	1
Maurice Bembridge	1969-71-73-75	16	5	8	3
Aubrey Boomer	1927-29	4	2	2	0
Ken Bousfield	1949-51-55-57-59-61	10	5	5	0
Hugh Boyle	1967	3	0	3	0
Harry Bradshaw	1953-55-57	5	2	2	1
Gordon Brand, Snr	1983	1	0	1	0
Eric Brown	1953-55-57-59	8	4	4	0
Ken Brown	1977-79-83-85	11	4	7	0
Stewart Burns	1929	0	0	0	0
Dick Burton	1935-37-*39-49	5	2	3	0
Jack Busson	1935	2	0	2	0
Peter Butler	1965-69-71-73	14	3	9	2
Jose-Maria Canizares	1981-83-85	9	4	3	2
Alex Caygill	1969	1	0	0	1
Clive Clark	1973	1	0	1	0
Howard Clark	1977-81-85	7	3	3	1
Neil Coles	1961-63-65-67-69-71-73-77	40	12	21	7
Archie Compston	1927-29-31	6	1	4	1
Henry Cotton	1929-37-*39-47	6	2	4	0
Bill Cox	1935-37	3	0	2	1
Allan Dailey	1933	0	0	0	0
Fred Daly	1947-49-51-53	8	3	4	1
Eamonn Darcy	1975-77-81	9	0	7	2
William Davies	1931-33	4	2	2	0
Peter Dawson	1977	3	1	2	0
Norman Drew	1959	1	0	0	1
George Duncan	1927-29-31	5	2	3	0
Syd Easterbrook	1931-33	3	2	1	0
Nick Faldo	1977-79-81-83-85	17	11	6	0
John Fallon	1955	1	1	0	0
Max Faulkner	1947-49-51-53-57	8	1	7	0
George Gadd	1927	0	0	0	0
Bernard Gallacher	1969-71-73-75-77-79-81-83	31	13	13	5
John Garner	1971-73	1	0	1	0
Antonio Garrido	1979	5	1	4	0
Eric Green	1947	0	0	0	0
Malcolm Gregson	1967	4	0	4	0
Tom Haliburton	1961-63	6	0	6	0
Jack Hargreaves	1951	0	0	0	0
Arthur Havers	1927-31-33	6	3	3	0
Jimmy Hitchcock	1965	3	0	3	0
Bert Hodson	1931	1	0	1	0
Reg Horne	1947	0	0	0	0
Tommy Horton	1975-77	8	1	6	1
Brian Huggett	1963-67-69-71-73-75	24	8	10	6
Bernard Hunt	1953-57-59-61-63-65-67-69	28	6	16	6
Geoffrey Hunt	1963	3	0	3	0
Guy Hunt	1975	3	0	2	1
Tony Jacklin	1967-69-71-73-75-77-79	35	13	14	8
John Jacobs	1955	2	2	0	0
Mark James	1977-79-81	10	2	7	1
Edward Jarman	1935	1	0	1	0
Herbert Jolly	1927	2	0	2	0
Michael King	1979	1	0	1	0
Sam King	1937-*39-47-49	5	1	3	1
Arthur Lacey	1933-37	3	0	3	0
Bernhard Langer	1981-83-85	14	7	4	3
Arthur Lees	1947-49-51-55	8	4	4	0
Sandy Lyle	1979-81-83-85	14	4	8	2
Jimmy Martin	1965	1	0	1	0
Peter Mills	1957	1	1	0	0
Abe Mitchell	1929-31-33	6	4	2	0
Ralph Moffitt	1961	1	0	1	0
Christy O'Connor, Jnr	1975	2	0	2	0
Christy O'Connor, Snr	1955-57-59-61-63-65-67-69-71-73	35	11	20	4
John O'Leary	1975	4	0	4	0
Peter Oosterhuis	1971-73-75-77-79-81	28	14	11	3
Alf Padgham	1933-35-37-*39	6	0	6	0
John Panton	1951-53-61	5	0	5	0
Alf Perry	1933-35-37	4	0	3	1

Ryder Cup
continued

Name	Year	Played	Won	Lost	Halved
Manuel Pinero	1981-85	9	6	3	0
Lionel Platts	1965	5	1	2	2
Eddie Polland	1973	2	0	2	0
Ted Ray	1927	2	0	2	0
Dai Rees	1937-*39-47-49-51-53-55-57-59-61	18	7	10	1
Jose Rivero	1985	2	1	1	0
Fred Robson	1927-29-31	6	2	4	0
Syd Scott	1955	2	0	2	0
Des Smyth	1979-81	7	2	5	0
Dave Thomas	1959-63-65-67	18	3	10	5
Sam Torrance	1981-83-85	13	3	7	3
Peter Townsend	1969-71	11	3	8	0
Brian Waites	1983	4	1	3	0
Charlie Ward	1947-49-51	6	1	5	0
Paul Way	1983-85	9	6	2	1
Harry Weetman	1951-53-55-57-59-61-63	15	2	11	2
Charles Whitcombe	1927-29-31-33-35-37-*39	9	3	2	4
Ernest Whitcombe	1929-31-35	6	1	4	1
Reg Whitcombe	1935-*39	1	0	1	0
George Will	1963-65-67	15	2	11	2
Norman Wood	1975	3	1	2	0
Ian Woosnam	1983-85	7	2	4	1

(Great Britain named eight members of their 1939 side, but the match was not played because of the Second World War.)

United States of America

Name	Year	Played	Won	Lost	Halved
Tommy Aaron	1969-73	6	1	4	1
Skip Alexander	1949-51	2	1	1	0
Jerry Barber	1955-61	5	1	4	0
Miller Barber	1969-71	7	1	4	2
Herman Barron	1947	1	1	0	0
Andy Bean	1979	3	2	1	0
Frank Beard	1969-71	8	2	3	3
Homero Blancas	1973	4	2	1	1
Tommy Bolt	1955-57	4	3	1	0
Julius Boros	1959-63-65-67	16	9	3	4
Gay Brewer	1967-73	9	5	3	1
Billy Burke	1931-33	3	3	0	0
Jack Burke	1951-53-55-57-59	8	7	1	0
Walter Burkemo	1953	1	0	1	0
Billy Casper	1961-63-65-67-69-71-73-75	37	20	10	7
Bill Collins	1961	3	1	2	0
Charles Coody	1971	3	0	2	1
Wilfred Cox	1931	2	2	0	0
Ben Crenshaw	1981-83	6	3	2	1
Jimmy Demaret	**1941-47-49-51	6	6	0	0
Gardner Dickinson	1967-71	10	9	1	0
Leo Diegel	1927-29-31-33	6	3	3	0
Dale Douglas	1969	2	0	2	0
Dave Douglas	1953	2	1	0	1
Ed Dudley	1929-33-37	4	3	1	0
Olin Dutra	1933-35	4	1	3	0
Lee Elder	1979	4	1	3	0
Al Espinosa	1927-29-31	4	2	1	1
Johnny Farrell	1927-29-31	6	3	2	1
Dow Finsterwald	1957-59-61-63	13	9	3	1
Ray Floyd	1969-75-77-81-83-85	23	7	13	3
Doug Ford	1955-57-59-61	9	4	4	1
Ed Furgol	1957	1	0	1	0
Marty Furgol	1955	1	0	1	0
Al Geiberger	1967-75	9	5	1	3
Vic Ghezzi	*1939-**41	0	0	0	0
Bob Gilder	1983	4	2	2	0
Bob Goalby	1963	5	3	1	1
Johnny Golden	1927-29	3	3	0	0
Lou Graham	1973-75-77	9	5	3	1
Hubert Green	1977-79-85	7	4	3	0
Ralph Guldahl	1937-*39	2	2	0	0
Fred Haas, Jnr	1953	1	0	1	0
Jay Haas	1983	4	2	1	1
Walter Hagen	1927-29-31-33-35	9	7	1	1
Bob Hamilton	1949	2	0	2	0
Chick Harbert	1949-55	2	2	0	0
Chandler Harper	1955	1	0	1	0
Dutch (EJ) Harrison	1947-49-51	3	2	1	0
Fred Hawkins	1957	2	1	1	0
Mark Hayes	1979	3	1	2	0

Ryder Cup
continued

Name	Year	Played	Won	Lost	Halved
Clayton Heafner	1949-51	4	3	0	1
Jay Hebert	1959-61	4	2	1	1
Lionel Hebert	1957	1	0	1	0
Dave Hill	1969-73-77	9	6	3	0
Jimmy Hines	*1939	0	0	0	0
Ben Hogan	**1941-47-51	3	3	0	0
Hale Irwin	1975-77-79-81	16	11	4	1
Tommy Jacobs	1965	4	3	1	0
Peter Jacobsen	1985	3	1	2	0
Don January	1965-77	7	2	3	2
Herman Keiser	1947	1	0	1	0
Tom Kite	1979-81-83-85	15	8	4	3
Ted Kroll	1953-55-57	4	3	1	0
Ky Laffoon	1935	1	0	1	0
Tony Lema	1963-65	11	8	1	2
Bruce Lietzke	1981	3	0	2	1
Gene Littler	1961-63-65-67-69-71-75	27	14	5	8
John Mahaffey	1979	3	1	2	0
Harold McSpaden	*1939-**41	0	0	0	0
Jerry McGee	1977	2	1	1	0
Tony Manero	1937	2	1	1	0
Lloyd Mangrum	**1941-47-49-51-53	8	6	2	0
Dave Marr	1965	6	4	2	0
Billy Maxwell	1963	4	4	0	0
Dick Mayer	1957	2	1	0	1
Bill Mehlhorn	1927	2	1	1	0
Dick Metz	*1939	0	0	0	0
Cary Middlecoff	1953-55-59	6	2	3	1
Johnny Miller	1975-81	6	2	2	2
Gil Morgan	1979-83	6	1	2	3
Bob Murphy	1975	4	2	1	1
Byron Nelson	1937-*39-**41-47	4	3	1	0
Larry Nelson	1979-81	9	9	0	0
Bobby Nichols	1967	5	4	0	1
Jack Nicklaus	1969-71-73-75-77-81	28	17	8	3
Andy North	1985	3	0	3	0
Ed Oliver	1947-51-53	5	3	2	0
Mark O'Meara	1985	3	1	2	0
Arnold Palmer	1961-63-65-67-71-73	32	22	8	2
Johnny Palmer	1949	2	0	2	0
Sam Parks	1935	1	0	0	1
Jerry Pate	1981	4	2	2	0
Calvin Peete	1983-85	7	4	2	1
Henry Picard	1935-37-*39	4	3	1	0
Johnny Pott	1963-65-67	7	5	2	0
Dave Ragan	1963	4	2	1	1
Henry Ransom	1951	1	0	1	0
Johnny Revolta	1935-37	3	2	1	0
Chi Chi Rodriguez	1973	2	0	1	1
Bill Rogers	1981	4	1	2	1
Bob Rosburg	1959	2	2	0	0
Mason Rudolph	1971	3	1	1	1
Paul Runyan	1933-35-*39	4	2	2	0
Doug Sanders	1967	5	2	3	0
Gene Sarazen	1927-29-31-33-35-37-**41	12	7	2	3
Densmore Shute	1931-33-37	6	2	2	2
Dan Sikes	1969	3	2	1	0
Horton Smith	1929-31-33-35-37-*39-**41	4	3	0	1
JC Snead	1971-73-75	11	9	2	0
Sam Snead	1937-*39-**41-47-49-51-53-55-59	13	10	2	1
Ed Sneed	1977	2	1	0	1
Mike Souchak	1959-61	6	5	1	0
Craig Stadler	1983-85	8	4	2	2
Ken Still	1969	3	1	2	0
Dave Stockton	1971-77	5	3	1	1
Curtis Strange	1983-85	7	3	3	1
Hal Sutton	1985	4	1	2	1
Lee Trevino	1969-71-73-75-79-81	30	17	7	6
Jim Turnesa	1953	1	1	0	0
Joe Turnesa	1927-29	4	1	2	1
Ken Venturi	1965	4	1	3	0
Lanny Wadkins	1977-79-83-85	17	12	4	1
Art Wall, Jnr	1957-59-61	6	4	2	0
Al Watrous	1927-29	3	2	1	0
Tom Watson	1977-81-83	12	9	3	0
Tom Weiskopf	1973-75	10	7	2	1
Craig Wood	1931-33-35-**41	4	1	3	0
Lew Worsham	1947	2	2	0	0
Fuzzy Zoeller	1979-83-85	10	1	8	1

(US teams were selected in 1939(*) and 1941(**), but the matches were not played because of the Second World War.)

Great Britain *v* Continent of Europe (Hennessy Cup)

Match instituted 1974
Cup presented 1976
Format changed 1982 and 1984

Year	Winner	Venue	Result
1974	Great Britain	Sotogrande	31-25
1976	Great Britain	Bondues, Lille	20-10
1978	Great Britain	The Belfry	17½-14½
1980	Great Britain	Sunningdale	16½-13½
1982	Great Britain–106, Rest of World–86, Europe–67, at Ferndown		
1984	Scotland	Ferndown	394

Nissan Cup

Year	Winner	Venue	Result
1985	USPGA	Kapalua, Hawaii	10-2
1986	Japan PGA	Yomiuri, Tokyo	7-5

World Cup

Until 1966, called Canada Cup

Year	Winners	Runners-up	Venue	Score
1953	Argentina (A Cerda and R De Vicenzo)	Canada (S Leonard and B Kerr)	Montreal	287
(Individual: A Cerda, Argentina, 140)				
1954	Australia (P Thomson and K Nagle)	Argentina (A Cerda and R De Vicenzo)	Laval-Sur-Lac	556
1955	United States (C Harbert and Ed Furgol)	Australia (P Thomson and K Nagle)	Washington	560
(Individual: E Furgol, US, after a play-off with P Thomson and F van Donck, 279)				
1956	United States (Ben Hogan and Sam Snead)	South Africa (AD Locke and Gary Player)	Wentworth	567
(Individual: B Hogan, USA, 277)				
1957	Japan (Torakichi Nakamura and Koichi Ono)	United States (Sam Snead and Jimmy Demaret)	Tokio	557
(Individual: T Nakamura, Japan, 274)				
1958	Ireland (H Bradshaw and C O'Connor)	Spain (A Miguel and S Miguel)	Mexico City	579
(Individual: A Miguel, Spain, after a play-off with H Bradshaw, 286)				
1959	Australia (PW Thomson and K Nagle)	United States (Sam Snead) and C Middlecoff)	Melbourne	563
(Individual: Stan Leonard, Canada, 275, after a tie with P Thomson, Australia)				
1960	United States (Sam Snead and A Palmer)	England (H Weetman and BJ Hunt)	Portmarnock	565
(Individual: Flory van Donck, Belgium, 279)				
1961	United States (Sam Snead and J Demaret)	Australia (PW Thomson and KDG Nagle)	Puerto Rico	560
(Individual: Sam Snead, USA, 272)				
1962	United States (Sam Snead and A Palmer)	Argentina (F de Luca and R De Vicenzo)	Buenos Aires	557
(Individual: R De Vicenzo, Argentina, 276)				
1963	United States (A Palmer and JW Nicklaus)	Spain (S Miguel and R Sota)	St Nom-La-Breteche	482
(Individual: JW Nicklaus, USA, 237 [63 holes])				
1964	United States (A Palmer and JW Nicklaus)	Argentina (R De Vicenzo and L Ruiz)	Maui, Hawaii	554
(Individual: JW Nicklaus, USA, 276)				

World Cup
continued

Year	Winners	Runners-up	Venue	Score
1965	South Africa (G Player and HR Henning)	Spain (A Miguel and R Sota)	Madrid	571
(Individual: G Player, South Africa, 281)				
1966	United States (JW Nicklaus and A Palmer)	South Africa (GJ Player and HR Henning)	Tokio	548
(Individual: G Knudson, Canada, and H Sugimoto, Japan, each 272; Knudson won play-off)				
1967	United States (JW Nicklaus and A Palmer)	New Zealand (RJ Charles and W Godfrey)	Mexico City	557
(Individual: A Palmer, USA, 276)				
1968	Canada (Al Balding and G Knudson)	United States (J Boros and L Trevino)	Olgiata, Rome	569
(Individual: Al Balding, Canada, 274)				
1969	United States (O Moody and L Trevino)	Japan (T Kono and H Yasuda)	Singapore	552
(Individual: L Trevino, USA, 275)				
1970	Australia (B Devlin and D Graham)	Argentina (R De Vicenzo and V Fernandez)	Buenos Aires	545
(Individual: R De Vicenzo, Argentina, 269)				
1971	United States (J Nicklaus and L Trevino)	South Africa (H Henning and G Player)	Palm Beach, Florida	555
(Individual: J Nicklaus, USA, 271)				
1972	Taiwan (Hsieh Min Nan and Lu Liang Huan)	Japan (Takaaki Kono and Takashi Murakami)	Melbourne	438
(Individual: Hsieh Min Nan, Taiwan, 217 [3 rounds only])				
1973	United States (J Nicklaus and J Miller)	South Africa (G Player and H Baiocchi)	Marbella, Spain	558
(Individual: J Miller, USA, 277)				
1974	South Africa (R Cole and D Hayes)	Japan (I Aoki and M Ozaki)	Caracas	554
(Individual: R Cole, South Africa, 271)				
1975	United States (J Miller and L Graham)	Taiwan (Hsieh Min-Nan and Kuo Chie Hsiung)	Bangkok	554
(Individual: J Miller, USA, 275)				
1976	Spain (S Ballesteros and M Pinero)	United States (J Pate and D Stockton)	Palm Springs, USA	574
(Individual: EP Acosta, Mexico, 282)				
1977	Spain (S Ballesteros and A Garrido)	Philippines (R Lavares and B Arda)	Manilla, Philippines	591
(Individual: G Player, South Africa, 289)				
1978	United States (J Mahaffey and A North)	Australia (G Norman and W Grady)	Hawaii	564
(Individual: J Mahaffey, USA, 281)				
1979	United States (J Mahaffey and H Irwin)	Scotland (AWB Lyle and K Brown)	Glyfada, Greece	575
(Individual: H Irwin, USA, 285)				
1980	Canada (D Halldorson and J Nelford)	Scotland (AWB Lyle and S Martin)	Bogota	572
(Individual: AWB Lyle, Scotland, 282)				
1981	Not played			
1982	Spain (M Pinero and J Canizares)	United States (B Gilder and B Clampett)	Acapulco	563
(Individual: M Pinero, Spain, 281)				
1983	United States (R Caldwell and J Cook)	Canada (D Barr and J Anderson)	Pondok Inah, Jakarta	565
(Individual: D Barr, Canada, 276)				
1984	Spain (J-M Canizares and J Rivero)	Scotland (S Torrance and G Brand Jun)	Olgiata, Rome	414
(Individual: J-M Canizares, Spain, 205. Played over 54 holes due to storm.)				
1985	Canada (D Halidorson and D Barr)	England (H Clark and P Way)	La Quinta, Calif, USA	559
(Individual: H Clark, England 272)				
1986	Discontinued			

PGA Cup

Instituted 1973

Year	Winner	Venue	Result
1973	USA	Pinehurst, USA	13-3
1974	USA	Pinehurst, USA	11½-4½
1975	USA	Hillside	9½-6½
1976	USA	Moortown	9½-6½
1977	Halved	Miss Hills, USA	8½-8½
1978	GB	St Mellion	10½-6½
From 1979 sponsored by Britannia Financial Services			
1979	GB	Castletown	12½-4½
1980	USA	Oak Tree	15-6
1981	Halved	Turnberry, Isle	10½-10½
1982	USA	Knoxville, Tennessee	13-7
From 1983 sponsored by Bell's Scotch Whisky			
1983	GB & I	Muirfield	14½-6½
1984	GB & I	Turnberry	12½-8½
To be played alternate years. To take place in USA in 1986			
1986	USA	Knollwood	16-9

British International Players, Professional

Adams, J
(Scotland): v England 1932 -33 -34 -35 -36 -37 -38; v Wales 1937 -38; v Ireland 1937 -38. (GB): v America 1947 -49 -51 -53

Ainslie, T
(Scotland): v Ireland 1936

Alliss, Percy
(England): v Scotland 1932 -33 -34 -35 -36 -37; v Ireland 1932 -38; v Wales 1938. (GB): v France 1929; v America 1929 -31 -33 -35 -37

Alliss, Peter
(England): in Canada Cup 1954 -55 -57 -58 -59 -61 -62 -64 -66; in World Cup 1967. (GB): v America 1953 -57 -59 -61 -63 -65 -67 -69

Anderson, Joe
(Scotland): v Ireland 1932

Anderson, W
(Scotland): v Ireland 1936; v England 1937; v Wales 1937

Ayton, LB
(Scotland): v England 1910 -12 -13 -33 -34

Ayton, LB, jr
(Scotland): v England 1937. (GB): v America 1949

Ballantine, J
(Scotland): v England 1932 -36

Ballingall, J
(Scotland): v England 1938; v Ireland 1938; v Wales 1938

Bamford, BJ
(England): in Canada Cup 1961

Bannerman, H
(Scotland): in World Cup 1967 -72. (GB): v America 1971

Barber, T
(England): v Ireland 1932 -33

Barnes, BW
(Scotland): in World Cup 1974 -75 -76 -77. (GB): v America 1969 -71 -73 -75 -77 -79; v Europe 1974 -76 -78 -80; v South Africa 1976

Batley, JB
(England): v Scotland 1912

Beck, AG
(England): v Wales 1938; v Ireland 1938

Bembridge, M
(England): in World Cup 1974 -75. (GB): v America 1969 -71 -73 -75; v South Africa 1976

Boomer, A
(England): (GB): v America 1926 -27 -29

Bousfield,K
(England): in Canada Cup 1956 -57. (GB): v America 1949 -51 -55 -57 -59 -61

Boyle, HF
(Ireland): in World Cup 1967. (GB): v America 1967

Bradshaw, H
(Ireland): in Canada Cup 1954 -55 -56 -57 -58 -59; v Scotland 1937 -38; v Wales 1937; v England 1938. (GB): v America 1953 -55 -57

Braid, J
(Scotland): v England 1903 -04 -05 -06 -07 -09 -10 -12. (GB): v America 1921

Branch, WJ
(England): v Scotland 1936

Brand, G, jr
(Scotland): in World Cup 1984-85; in Dunhill Cup 1985 -86; (Eur): in Nissan Cup 1985

Brand, G, sr
(England): in World Cup 1983; in Dunhill Cup 1986. (GB): v America 1983

Brown, EC
(Scotland): in Canada Cup 1954 -55 -56 -57 -58 -59 -60 -61 -62 -65 -66; in World Cup 1967 -68. (GB): v America 1953 -55 -57 -59

Brown, K
(Scotland): in World Cup 1977 -78 -79 -83. (GB): v America 1977 -79 -83 -85; v Europe 1978

Burns, S
(Scotland): v England 1932. (GB): v America 1929

Burton, J
(England): v Ireland 1933

Burton, R
(England): v Scotland 1935 -36 -37 -38; v Ireland 1938: v Wales 1938. (GB): v America 1935 -37 -49

Busson, JH
(England): v Scotland 1938

Busson, JJ
(England): v Scotland 1934 -35 -36 -37. (GB): v America 1935

Butler, PJ
(England): in World Cup 1969 -70 -73. (GB): v America 1965 -69 -71 -73; v Europe 1976

Callum, WS
(Scotland): v Ireland 1935

Campbell, J
(Scotland): v Ireland 1936

Carrol, LJ
(Ireland): v Scotland 1937 -38; v Wales 1937; v England 1938

Cassidy, J
(Ireland): v England 1933; v Scotland 1934 -35

Cassidy, D
(Ireland): v Scotland 1936 -37; v Wales 1937

Cawsey, GH
(England): v Scotland 1906 -07

Caygill, GA
(England): (GB): v America 1969

Clark, C
(England): (GB): v America 1973

Clark, HK
(England): in World Cup 1978 -84 -85; in Dunhill Cup 1985 -86. (GB): v America 1977 -81 -85; v Europe 1978 -84. (Eur): in Nissan Cup 1985

Coles, NC
(England): in Canada Cup 1963; in World Cup 1968. (GB): v America 1961 -63 -65 -67 -69 -71 -73 -77; v Europe 1974 -76 -78 -80

Collinge, T
(England): v Scotland 1937

Collins, JF
(England): v Scotland 1903 -04

Coltart, F
(Scotland): v England 1909

Compston, A
(England): v Scotland 1932 -35; v Ireland 1932. (GB): v America 1926 -27 -29 -31; v France 1929

Cotton, TH
(England): (GB): v America 1929 -37 -47; v France 1929

Cox, S
(Wales): in World Cup 1975

Cox, WJ
(England): v Scotland 1935 -36 -37. (GB): v America 1935 -37

Curtis, D
(England): v Scotland 1934 -38; v Ireland 1938; v Wales 1938

Dabson, K
(Wales): in World Cup 1972

Dailey, A
(Scotland): v England 1932 -33 -34 -35 -36 -38; v Ireland 1938; v Wales 1938. (GB): v America 1933

Daly, F
(Ireland): v Scotland 1936 -37 -38; v England 1938; v Wales 1937; in Canada Cup 1954 -55. (GB): v America 1947 -49 -51 -53

Darcy, E
(Ireland): in World Cup 1976 -77 -83 -84 -85. (GB): v America 1975 -77 -81; v Europe 1976 -84; v South Africa 1976

Davies, R
(Wales): in World Cup 1968

Davies, WH
(England): v Scotland 1932 -33; v Ireland 1932 -33. (GB): v America 1931 -33

Davis, W
(Scotland): v Ireland 1933 -34 -35 -36 -37 -38; v England 1937 -38; v Wales 1937 -38

Dawson, P
(England): in World Cup 1977. (GB): v America 1977

De Foy, CB
(Wales): in World Cup 1971 -73 -74 -75 -76 -77 -78

Denny, CS
(England): v Scotland 1936

Dobson, T
(Scotland): v England 1932 -33 -34 -35 -36 -37; v Ireland 1932 -33 -34 -35 -36 -37 -38; v Wales 1937 -38

Don, W
(Scotland): v Ireland 1935 -36

Donaldson, J
(Scotland): v England 1932 -35 -38; v Ireland 1937; v Wales 1937

Dornan, R
(Scotland): v Ireland 1932

Drew, NV
(Ireland): in Canada Cup 1960 -61. (GB): v America 1959

Duncan, G
(Scotland): v England 1906 -07 -09 -10 -12 -13 -32 -34 -35 -36 -37. (GB): v America 1921 -26 -27 -29 -31

Durward, JG
(Scotland): v Ireland 1934; v England 1937

Easterbrook, S
(England): v Scotland 1932 -33 -34 -35 -38; v Ireland 1933. (GB): v America 1931 -33

Edgar, J
(Ireland): v Scotland 1938

Fairweather, S
(Ireland): v England 1932; v Scotland 1933. (Scotland): v England 1933 -35 -36; v Ireland 1938; v Wales 1938

Faldo, NA
(England): in World Cup 1977; in Dunhill Cup 1985 -86. (GB): v America 1977 -79 -81 -83 -85; v Europe 1978 -80 -82 -84; v Rest of World 1982

Fallon, J
(Scotland): v England 1936 -37 -38; v Ireland 1937 -38; v Wales 1937 -38. (GB): v America 1955

Faulkner, M
(England): (GB): v America 1947 -49 -51 -53 -57

Feherty, D
(Ireland): in Dunhill Cup 1985 -86

Fenton, WB
(Scotland): v England 1932; v Ireland 1932 -33

Fernie, TR
(Scotland): v England 1910 -12 -13 -33

Foster, M
(England): in World Cup 1976. (GB): v Europe 1976

Gadd, B
(England): v Scotland 1933 -35 -38; v Ireland 1933 -38; v Wales 1938

Gadd, G
(England): (GB): v America 1926 -27

Gallacher, BJ
(Scotland): in World Cup 1969 -71 -74 -82 -83. (GB): v America 1969 -71 -73 -75 -77 -79 -81 -83; v Europe 1974 -78 -82 -84; v South Africa 1976; v Rest of World 1982

Garner, JR
(England): (GB): v America 1971 -73

Gaudin, PJ
(England): v Scotland 1905 -06 -07 -09 -12 -13

Good, G
(Scotland): v England 1934 -36

Gould, H
(Wales): in Canada Cup 1954 -55

Gow, A
(Scotland): v England 1912

Grabham, C
(Wales): v England 1938; v Scotland 1938

Grant, T
(Scotland): v England 1913

Gray, E
(England): v Scotland 1904 -05 -07

Green, E
(England): (GB): v America 1947

Green, T
(England): v Scotland 1935. (Wales): v Scotland 1937 -38; v Ireland 1937; v England 1938

Greene, C
(Ireland): in Canada Cup 1965

Gregson, M
(England): in World Cup 1967. (GB): v America 1967

Haliburton, TB
(Scotland): v Ireland 1935 -36 -38; v England 1938; v Wales 1938; in Canada Cup 1954. (GB): v America 1961 -63

Hamill, J
(Ireland): v Scotland 1933 -34 -35; v England 1932 -33

Hargreaves, J
(England): (GB): v America 1951

Hastings, W
(Scotland): v England 1937 -38; v Wales 1937 -38; v Ireland 1937 -38

Havers, AG
(England): v Scotland 1932 -33 -34; v Ireland 1932 -33. (GB) v America 1921 -26 -27 -31 -33; v France 1929

Healing, SF
(Wales): v Scotland 1938

Hepburn, J
(Scotland): v England 1903 -05 -06 -07 -09 -10 -12 -13

Herd, A
(Scotland): v England 1903 -04 -05 -06 -09 -10 -12 -13 -32

Hill, EF
(Wales): v Scotland 1937 -38; v Ireland 1937; v England 1938

Hitchcock, J
(England): (GB): v America 1965

Hodson, B
(England): v Ireland 1933. (Wales): v Scotland 1937 -38; v Ireland 1937; v England 1938. (GB): v America 1931

Holley, W
(Ireland): v Scotland 1933 -34 -35 -36 -38; v England 1932 -33 -38

Horne, R
(England): (GB): v America 1947

Horton, T
(England): in World Cup 1976. (GB): v Europe 1974 -76; v America 1975 -77

Houston, D
(Scotland): v Ireland 1934

Huggett, BGC
(Wales): in Canada Cup 1963 -64 -65; in World Cup 1968 -69 -70 -71 -76 -79. (GB): v America 1963 -67 -69 -71 -73 -75; v Europe 1974 -78

Huish, D
(Scotland): in World Cup 1973

Hunt, BJ
(England): in Canada Cup 1958 -59 -60 -62 -63 -64; in World Cup 1968. (GB): v America 1953 -57 -59 -61 -63 -65 -67 -69

Hunt, GL
(England): in World Cup 1972 -75. (GB): v Europe 1974; v America 1975

Hunt, Geoffrey M
(England): (GB): v America 1963

Hunter, W
(Scotland): v England 1906 -07 -09 -10

Hutton, GC
(Scotland): v Ireland 1936 -37; v England 1937 -38; v Wales 1937

Ingram, D
(Scotland): in World Cup 1973

Jacklin, A
(England): in Canada Cup 1966; in World Cup 1970 -71 -72. (GB): v America 1967 -69 -71 -73 -75 -77 -79; v Europe 1976 -82; v Rest of World 1982

Jackson, H
(Ireland): in World Cup 1970 -71

Jacobs, JRM
(England): (GB): v America 1955

Jagger, D
(England): (GB): v Europe 1976

James, G
(Wales): v Scotland 1937; v Ireland 1937

James, MH
(England): in World Cup 1978 -79 -82 -84. (GB): v America 1977 -79 -81; v Europe 1978 -80 -82; v Rest of World 1982

Jarman, EW
(England): v Scotland 1935. (GB): v America 1935

Job, N
(England): (GB): v Europe 1980

Jolly, HC
(England): (GB): v America 1926 -27; v France 1929

Jones, DC
(Wales): v Scotland 1937 -38; v Ireland 1937; v England 1938

Jones, E
(Ireland): in Canada Cup 1965

Jones, R
(England): v Scotland 1903 -04 -05 -06 -07 -09 -10 -12 -13

Jones, T
(Wales): v Scotland 1936; v Ireland 1937; v England 1938

Kenyon, EWH
(England): v Scotland 1932; v Ireland 392

King, M
(England): in World Cup 1979. (GB): v America 1979

King, SL
(England): v Scotland 1934 -36 -37 -38; v Wales 1938; v Ireland 1938. (GB): v America 1937 -47 -49

Kinsella,J
(Ireland): in World Cup 1968 -69 -72 -73

Kinsella, W
(Ireland): v Scotland 1937 -38; v England 1938

Knight, G
(Scotland): v England 1937

Lacey, AJ
(England): v Scotland 1932 -33 -34 -36 -37 -38; v Ireland 1932 -33 -38; v Wales 1938. (GB): v America 1933 -37

Laidlaw, W
(Scotland): v England 1935 -36 -38; v Ireland 1937; v Wales 1937

Lees, A
(England): v Scotland 1938; v Wales 1938; v Ireland 1938. (GB): v America 1947 -49 -51 -55

Llewellyn, D
(Wales): in World Cup 1974 -85; in Dunhill Cup 1985. (GB): v Europe 1984

Lloyd, F
(Wales): v Scotland 1937 -38; v Ireland 1937; v England 1938

Lockhart, G
(Scotland): v Ireland 1934 -35

Lyle, AWB
(Scotland): in World Cup 1979 -80; in Dunhill Cup 1985 -86. (GB): v America 1979 -81 -83 -85; v Europe 1980 -82 -84; v Rest of World 1982. (Eur): in Nissan Cup 1985

McCartney, J
(Ireland): v Scotland 1932 -33 -34 -35 -36 -37 -38; v England 1932 -33 -38; v Wales 1937

McCulloch, D
(Scotland): v England 1932 -33 -34 -35 -36 -37; v Ireland 1932 -33 -34 -35

McDermott, M
(Ireland): v England 1932; v Scotland 1932

McDowall, J
(Scotland): v England 1932 -33 -34 -35 -36; v Ireland 1933 -34 -35 -36

McEwan, P
(Scotland): v England 1907

McIntosh, G
(Scotland): v England 1938; v Ireland 1938; v Wales 1938

McKenna, J
(Ireland): v Scotland 1936 -37 -38; v Wales 1937 -38; v England 1938

McKenna, R
(Ireland): v Scotland 1933 -35; v England 1933

McMillan, J
(Scotland): v England 1933 -34 -35; v Ireland 1933 -34

McMinn, W
(Scotland): v England 1932 -33 -34

McNeill, H
(Ireland): v England 1932

Mahon, PJ
(Ireland): v Scotland 1932 -33 -34 -35 -36 -37 -38; v Wales 1937 -38; v England 1932 -33 -38

Martin, J
(Ireland): in Canada Cup 1962 -63 -64 -66; in World Cup 1970. (GB): v America 1965

Martin, S
(Scotland): in World Cup 1980

Mason, SC
(England): in World Cup 1980. (GB): v Europe 1980

Mayo, CH
(England): v Scotland 1907 -09 -10 -12 -13

Mills, RP
(England): (GB): v America 1957

Mitchell, A
(England): v Scotland 1932 -33 -34. (GB): v America 1921 -26 -29 -31 -33

Moffitt, R
(England): (GB): v America 1961

Mouland, M
(Wales): in Dunhill Cup 1986

Mouland, S
(Wales): in Canada Cup 1965 -66; in World Cup 1967

O'Brien, W
(Ireland): v Scotland 1934 -36 -37; v Wales 1937

Ockenden, J
(England): (GB): v America 1921

O'Connor, C
(Ireland): in Canada Cup 1956 -57 -58 -59 -60 -61 -62 -63 -64 -66; in World Cup 1967 -68 -69 -71 -73. (GB): v America 1955 -57 -59 -61 -63 -65 -67 -69 -71 -73

O'Connor, C, jr
(Ireland): in World Cup 1974 -75 -78 -85; in Dunhill Cup 1985. (GB): v Europe 1974 -84; v America 1975; v South Africa 1976

O'Connor, P
(Ireland): v Scotland 1932 -33 -34 -35 -36; v England 1932 -33

Oke, WG
(England): v Scotland 1932

O'Leary, JE
(Ireland): in World Cup 1972 -80 -82. (GB): v America 1975; v Europe 1976 -78 -82; v Rest of World 1982

O'Neill, J
(Ireland): v England 1933

O'Neill, M
(Ireland): v Scotland 1933 -34; v England 1933

Oosterhuis, PA
(England): in World Cup 1971. (GB): v America 1971 -73 -75 -77 -79 -81; v Europe 1974

Padgham, AH
(England): v Scotland 1932 -33 -34 -35 -36 -37 -38; v Ireland 1932 -33 -38; v Wales 1938. (GB): v America 1933 -35 -37

Panton, J
(Scotland): in Canada Cup 1955 -56 -57 -58 -59 -60 -61 -62 -63 -64 -65 -66; in World Cup 1968. (GB): v America 1951 -53 -61

Park, J
(Scotland): v England 1909

Parkin, P
(Wales): in World Cup 1984; in Dunhill Cup 1985 -86. (GB): v Europe 1984

Patterson, E
(Ireland): v Scotland 1933 -34 -35 -36; v England 1933; v Wales 1937

Perry, A
(England); v Ireland 1932; v Scotland 1933 -36 -38. (GB): v America 1933 -35 -37

Pickett, C
(Wales): v Scotland 1937 -38; v Ireland 1937; v England 1938

Platts, L
(Wales): (GB): v America 1965

Polland, E
(Ireland): in World Cup 1973 -74 -76 -77 -78 -79. (GB): v America 1973; v Europe 1974 -76 -78 -80; v South America 1976

Pope, CW
(Ireland): v England 1932; v Scotland 1932

Rafferty, R
(Ireland): in World Cup 1983 -84; in Dunhill Cup 1986. (GB): v Europe 1984

Rainford, P
(England): v Scotland 1903 -07

Ray, E
(England): v Scotland 1903 -04 -05 -06 -07 -09 -10 -12 -13. (GB): v America 1921 -26 -27

Rees, DJ
(Wales): v Scotland 1937 -38; v Ireland 1937; England 1938; in Canada Cup 1954 -56 -57 -58 -59 -60 -61 -62 -64. (GB): v America 1937 -47 -49 -51 -53 -55 -57 -59 -61

Reid, W
(England): v Scotland 1906 -07

Renouf, TG
(England): v Scotland 1903 -04 -05 -10 -13

Ritchie, WL
(Scotland): v England 1913

Robertson, F
(Scotland): v Ireland 1933; v England 1938

Robertson, P
(Scotland): v England 1932; v Ireland 1932 -34

Robson, F
(England): v Scotland 1909 -10. (GB): v America 1926 -27 -29 -31

Rowe, AJ
(England): v Scotland 1903 -06 -07

Sayers, B, jr
(Scotland): v England 1906 -07 -09

Scott, SS
(England): (GB): v America 1955

Seymour, M
(England): v Scotland 1932 -33; v Ireland 1932 -33. (Scotland): v Ireland 1932

Shade, RDBM
(Scotland): in World Cup 1970 -71 -72
Sherlock, JG
(England): v Scotland 1903 -04 -05 -06 -07 -09 -10 -12 -13. (GB): v America 1921
Simpson, A
(Scotland): v England 1904
Smalldon, D
(Wales): in Canada Cup 1955 -56
Smith, CR
(Scotland): v England 1903 -04 -07 -09 -13
Smith, GE
(Scotland): v Ireland 1932
Smyth, D
(Ireland): in World Cup 1979 -80 -82 -83; in Dunhill Cup 1985 -86. (GB): v America 1979 -81; v Europe 1980 -82 -84; v Rest of World 1982
Snell, D
(England): in Canada Cup 1965
Spark, W
(Scotland): v Ireland 1933 -35 -37; v England 1935; v Wales 1937
Stevenson, P
(Ireland): v Scotland 1933 -34 -35 -36 -38; v England 1933 -38
Sutton, M
(England): in Canada Cup 1955

Taylor, JH
(England): v Scotland 1903 -04 -05 -06 -07 -09 -10 -12 -13. (GB): v America 1921
Taylor, JJ
(England): v Scotland 1937
Taylor, Josh
(England): v Scotland 1913. (GB): v America 1921
Thomas, DC
(Wales): in Canada Cup 1957 -58 -59 -60 -61 -62 -63 -66; in World Cup 1967 -69 -70. (GB): v America 1959 -63 -65 -67
Thompson, R
(Scotland): v England 1903 -04 -05 -06 -07 -09 -10 -12
Tingey, A
(England): v Scotland 1903 -05
Torrance, S
(Scotland): in World Cup 1976 -78 -82 -84 -85; in Dunhill Cup 1985 -86. (GB): v Europe 1976 -78 -80 -82 -84; v America 1981 -83 -85; v Rest of World 1982. (Eur): in Nissan Cup 1985
Townsend, P
(England): in World Cup 1969 -74. (GB): v America 1969 -71; v Europe 1974
Twine, WT
(England): v Ireland 1932

Vardon, H
(England): (GB): v America 1921
Vaughan, DI
(Wales): in World Cup 1972 -73 -77 -78 -79 -80

Waites, BJ
(England): in World Cup 1980 -82 -83. (GB): v Europe 1980 -82 -84; v Rest of World 1982; v America 1983
Walker, RT
(Scotland): in Canada Cup 1964
Wallace, L
(Ireland): v England 1932; v Scotland 1932
Ward, CH
(England): v Ireland 1932. (GB): v America 1947 -49 -51
Watt, T
(Scotland): v England 1907
Watt, W
(Scotland): v England 1912 -13
Way, P
(England): in Dunhill Cup 1985; in World Cup 1985. (GB): v America 1983 -85
Weetman, H
(England): in Canada Cup 1954 -56 -60. (GB): v America 1951 -53 -55 -57 -59 -61 -63
Whitcombe, CA
(England): v Scotland 1932 -33 -34 -35 -36 -37 -38; v Ireland 1933. (GB): v America 1927 -29 -31 -33 -35 -37; v France 1929
Whitcombe, EE
(England): v Scotland 1938; v Wales 1938; v Ireland 1938
Whitcombe, ER
(England): v Scotland 1932; v Ireland 1933. (GB): v America 1926 -29 -31 -35; v France 1929
Whitcombe, RA
(England): v Scotland 1933 -34 -35 -36 -37 -38. (GB): v America 1935
White, J
(Scotland): v England 1903 -04 -05 -06 -07 -09 -12 -13
Wilcock, P
(England): in World Cup 1973
Will, G
(Scotland): in Canada Cup 1963; in World Cup 1969 -70. (GB): v America 1963 -65 -67
Williams, K
(Wales): v Scotland 1937 -38; v Ireland 1937; v England 1938
Williamson, T
(England): v Scotland 1904 -05 -06 -07 -09 -10 -12 -13
Wilson, RG
(England): v Scotland 1913
Wilson, T
(Scotland): v England 1933 -34; v Ireland 1932 -33 -34
Wolstenholme, GB
(England): in Canada Cup 1965
Wood, N
(Scotland): in World Cup 1975. (GB): v America 1975
Woosnam, I
(Wales): in World Cup 1980 -82 -83 -84 -85; in Dunhill Cup 1985 -86. (GB): v Europe 1982 -84; v Rest of World 1982; v America 1983 -85. (Eur): in Nissan Cup 1985

Amateur International Tournaments and Matches

United States *v* Great Britain (Walker Cup Matches)

Unofficial

Year	Great Britain			USA			Venue
1921 (May 21)	Foursomes Singles	0 3	3	Foursomes Singles	4 5	9	Hoylake

The Walker Cup

(Instituted 1922)

Year	Great Britain			USA			Venue
1922 (Aug 29)	Foursomes Singles	1 3	4	Foursomes Singles	3 5	8	Long Island, NY
1923 (May 18-19)	Foursomes Singles	3 2½	5½	Foursomes Singles	1 5½	6½	St Andrews
1924 (Sept 12-13)	Foursomes Singles	1 2	3	Foursomes Singles	3 6	9	Garden City, NY
1926 (June 2-3)	Foursomes Singles	1 4½	5½	Foursomes Singles	3 3½	6½	St Andrews
1928 (Aug 30-31)	Foursomes Singles	0 1	1	Foursomes Singles	4 7	11	Chicago
1930 (May 15-16)	Foursomes Singles	1 1	2	Foursomes Singles	3 7	10	Sandwich
1932 (Sept 1-2)	Foursomes Singles	0 2½	2½	Foursomes Singles	4 5½	9½	Brookline, Mass
1934 (May 11-12)	Foursomes Singles	1 1½	2½	Foursomes Singles	3 6½	9½	St Andrews
1936 (Sept 2-3)	Foursomes Singles	1 0½	1½	Foursomes Singles	3 7½	10½	Pine Valley, NJ
1938 (June 3-4)	Foursomes Singles	2½ 5	7½	Foursomes Singles	1½ 3	4½	St Andrews
1947 (May 16-17)	Foursomes Singles	2 2	4	Foursomes Singles	2 6	8	St Andrews
1949 (Aug 19-20)	Foursomes Singles	1 1	2	Foursomes Singles	3 7	10	Winged Foot, NY
1951 (May 11-12)	Foursomes Singles	1 3½	4½	Foursomes Singles	3 4½	7½	Royal Birkdale
1953 (Sept 4-5)	Foursomes Singles	1 2	3	Foursomes Singles	3 6	9	Kittansett, Mass
1955 (May 20-21)	Foursomes Singles	0 2	2	Foursomes Singles	4 6	10	St Andrews
1957 (Sept 1-2)	Foursomes Singles	1½ 2	3½	Foursomes Singles	2½ 6	8½	Minikahda
1959 (May 15-16)	Foursomes Singles	0 3	3	Foursomes Singles	4 5	9	Muirfield

United States v Great Britain (Walker Cup Matches)

continued

At Seattle, 1st and 2nd September, 1961

Foursomes

USA	Matches	Great Britain	Matches
J Nicklaus and DR Beman (6 and 5)	1	J Walker and BHG Chapman	0
CR Coe and D Cherry (1 hole)	1	DA Blair and MJ Christmas	0
W Hyndman and R Gardner (4 and 3)	1	JB Carr and G Huddy	0
R Cochran and E Andrews (4 and 3)	1	MF Bonallack and RDBM Shade	0
	4		0

Singles

USA	Matches	Great Britain	Matches
DR Beman (3 and 2)	1	MF Bonallack	0
CR Coe (5 and 4)	1	MSR Lunt	0
F Taylor (3 and 2)	1	J Walker	0
W Hyndman (7 and 6)	1	DW Frame	0
J Nicklaus (6 and 4)	1	JB Carr	0
C Smith	0	MJ Christmas (3 and 2)	1
R Gardner (1 hole)	1	RDBM Shade	0
D Cherry (5 and 4)	1	DA Blair	0
	7		1

Grand Aggregates: USA, 11; Great Britain, 1.

At Turnberry, 24th and 25th May, 1963

First Day–Foursomes

Great Britain	Matches	USA	Matches
MF Bonallack and SWT Murray (4 and 3)	1	WJ Patton and RH Sikes	0
JB Carr and CW Green	0	AD Gray and LE Harris (2 holes)	1
MSR Lunt and DB Sheahan	0	DR Beman and CR Coe (5 and 3)	1
JFD Madeley and RDBM Shade (halved)	0	RW Gardner and ER Updegraff (halved)	0
	1		2

Singles

Great Britain	Matches	USA	Matches
SWT Murray (3 and 1)	1	DR Beman	0
MJ Christmas	0	WJ Patton (3 and 2)	1
JB Carr (7 and 5)	1	RH Sikes	0
DB Sheahan (1 hole)	1	LE Harris	0
MF Bonallack (1 hole)	1	RD Davies	0
S Saddler (halved)	0	CR Coe (halved)	0
RDBM Shade (4 and 3)	1	AD Gray	0
MSR Lunt (halved)	0	CB Smith (halved)	0
	5		1

First day's aggregate: Great Britain, 6; USA, 3; 3 matches halved.

Second Day–Foursomes

Great Britain	Matches	USA	Matches
MF Bonallack and SWT Murray	0	WJ Patton and RH Sikes (1 hole)	1
MSR Lunt and DB Sheahan	0	AD Gray and LE Harris (3 and 2)	1
CW Green and S Saddler	0	RW Gardner and ER Updegraff (3 and 1)	1
JFD Madeley and RDBM Shade	0	DR Beman and CR Coe (3 and 2)	1
	0		4

United States v Great Britain (Walker Cup Matches)

continued

Singles

Great Britain	Matches	USA	Matches
SWT Murray	0	WJ Patton (3 and 2)	1
DB Sheahan (1 hole)	1	RD Davies	0
JB Carr	0	ER Updegraff (4 and 3)	1
MF Bonallack	0	LE Harris (3 and 2)	1
MSR Lunt	0	RW Gardner (3 and 2)	1
S Saddler (halved)	0	DR Beman (halved)	0
RDBM Shade (2 and 1)	1	AD Gray	0
CW Green	0	CR Coe (4 and 3)	1
	2		5

Second day's aggregate: Great Britain, 2; USA, 9; 1 match halved.
Grand Match aggregate: Great Britain, 8; USA, 12; 4 matches halved.

At Baltimore, USA, 3rd and 4th September, 1965

First Day–Foursomes

USA	Matches	Great Britain	Matches
W Campbell and D Gray	0	MSR Lunt and GB Cosh (1 hole)	1
DR Beman and D Allan (halved)	0	MF Bonallack and CA Clark (halved)	0
BJ Patton and E Tutwiler (5 and 4)	1	R Foster and GJ Clark	0
JM Hopkins and D Eichelberger	0	PM Townsend and RDBM Shade (2 and 1)	1
	1		2

Singles

USA	Matches	Great Britain	Matches
W Campbell (6 and 5)	1	MF Bonallack	0
DR Beman (2 holes)	1	R Foster	0
D Gray	0	RDBM Shade (3 and 1)	1
JM Hopkins	0	CA Clark (5 and 3)	1
BJ Patton	0	PM Townsend (3 and 2)	1
D Morey	0	AC Saddler (2 and 1)	1
D Allen	0	GB Cosh (2 holes)	1
ER Updegraff	0	MSR Lunt (3 and 1)	1
	2		6

First day's aggregate: USA, 3; Great Britain, 8; 1 match halved.

Second Day–Foursomes

USA	Matches	Great Britain	Matches
W Campbell and D Gray (4 and 3)	1	AC Saddler and R Foster	0
DR Beman and D Eichelberger	0	RDBM Shade and PM Townsend (2 and 1)	1
E Tutwiler and BJ Patton (2 and 1)	1	GB Cosh and MSR Lunt	0
D Allen and D Morey	0	CA Clark and MF Bonallack (2 and 1)	1
	2		2

Singles

USA	Matches	Great Britain	Matches
E Tutwiler (5 and 3)	1	RDBM Shade	0
W Campbell (3 and 2)	1	R Foster	0
D Allen	0	GB Cosh (4 and 3)	1
DR Beman (1 hole)	1	AC Saddler	0
D Eichelberger (5 and 3)	1	MF Bonallack	0
D Gray (1 hole)	1	PM Townsend	0
JM Hopkins (halved)	0	CA Clark (halved)	0
BJ Patton (4 and 2)	1	MSR Lunt	0
	6		1

Second day's aggregate: USA, 8; Great Britain, 3; 1 match halved.
Grand Match aggregate: USA, 11; Great Britain, 11; 2 matches halved.
USA, as holders, retain the Walker Cup.

United States v Great Britain (Walker Cup Matches)

continued

At St George's, Sandwich, 19th and 20th May, 1967

First Day–Foursomes

USA	Matches	Great Britain	Matches
RJ Murphy and RJ Cerrudo (halved)	0	RDBM Shade and PA Oosterhuis (halved)	0
AD Gray and EM Tutwiler (4 and 2)	1	MF Bonallack and MF Attenborough	0
WC Campbell and JW Lewis (1 hole)	1	R Foster and AC Saddler	0
R Dickson and JA Grant (3 and 1)	1	JB Carr and TC Craddock	0
	3		0

Singles

USA	Matches	Great Britain	Matches
RJ Cerrudo (4 and 3)	1	MF Attenborough	0
WC Campbell (2 and 1)	1	RDBM Shade	0
R Dickson (6 and 4)	1	PA Oosterhuis	0
RJ Murphy (2 and 1)	1	R Foster	0
AD Gray (halved)	0	MF Bonallack (halved)	0
M Fleckman	0	AC Saddler (3 and 2)	1
JW Lewis (2 and 1)	1	T Craddock	0
DC Allen (halved)	0	AK Pirie (halved)	0
	5		1

First day's aggregate: USA, 8; Great Britain, 1; 3 matches halved.

Second Day–Foursomes

USA	Matches	Great Britain	Matches
RJ Murphy and RJ Cerrudo	0	T Craddock and MF Bonallack (2 holes)	1
AD Gray and EM Tutwiler	0	RDBM Shade and PA Oosterhuis (3 and 1)	1
WC Campbell and JW Lewis (1 hole)	1	AC Saddler and AK Pirie	0
DC Allen and M Fleckman	0	R Foster and DJ Millensted (2 and 1)	1
	1		3

Singles

USA	Matches	Great Britain	Matches
WC Campbell (3 and 2)	1	RDBM Shade	0
RJ Murphy	0	MF Bonallack (4 and 2)	1
JW Lewis	0	T Craddock (5 and 4)	1
AD Gray	0	AC Saddler (3 and 2)	1
R Dickson (4 and 3)	1	AK Pirie	0
RJ Cerrudo (halved)	0	R Foster (halved)	0
EM Tutwiler (3 and 1)	1	DJ Millensted	0
JA Grant (1 hole)	1	PA Oosterhuis	0
	4		3

Second day's aggregate: USA, 5; Great Britain, 6; 1 match halved.
Grand Match aggregate: USA, 13; Great Britain, 7; 4 matches halved.

At Milwaukee, USA, on 22nd and 23rd August, 1969

First Day–Foursomes

USA	Matches	Great Britain	Matches
M Giles and S Melnyk (3 and 2)	1	MF Bonallack and T Craddock	0
L Wadkins and R Siderowf	0	CW Green and A Brooks (3 and 2)	1
B Fleisher and AL Miller (halved)	0	PJ Benka and B Critchley (halved)	0
W Hyndman and J Inman (2 and 1)	1	R Foster and GC Marks	0
	2		1

United States v Great Britain (Walker Cup Matches)

continued

Singles

USA	Matches	Great Britain	Matches
B Fleisher (halved)	0	MF Bonallack (halved)	0
M Giles (1 hole)	1	CW Green	0
R Siderowf (6 and 5)	1	P Tupling	0
S Melnyk	0	PJ Benka (3 and 1)	1
L Wadkins	0	GC Marks (1 hole)	1
AL Miller (1 hole)	1	B Critchley	0
J Bohmann (2 and 1)	1	MG King	0
E Updegraff (6 and 5)	1	R Foster	0
	5		2

First day's aggregate: USA, 7; Great Britain, 3; 2 matches halved.

Second Day–Foursomes

USA	Matches	Great Britain	Matches
M Giles and S Melnyk (halved)	0	CW Green and A Brooks (halved)	0
B Fleisher and AL Miller	0	PJ Benka and B Critchley (2 and 1)	1
R Siderowf and L Wadkins (6 and 5)	1	R Foster and MG King	0
E Updegraff and J Bohmann	0	MF Bonallack and P Tupling (4 and 3)	1
	1		2

Singles

USA	Matches	Great Britain	Matches
B Fleisher	0	MF Bonallack (5 and 4)	1
R Siderowf (halved)	0	B Critchley (halved)	0
AL Miller (1 hole)	1	MG King	0
M Giles (halved)	0	T Craddock (halved)	0
J Inman (2 and 1)	1	PJ Benka	0
J Bohmann	0	A Brooks (4 and 3)	0
E Updegraff	0	GC Marks (3 and 2)	1
W Hyndman (halved)	0	CW Green (halved)	0
	2		3

Second day's aggregate: USA, 3; Great Britain, 5; 4 matches halved.
Grand Match aggregate: USA, 10; Great Britain, 8; 6 matches halved.

At St Andrews, 26th and 27th May, 1971

First Day–Foursomes

Great Britain	Matches	USA	Matches
MF Bonallack and W Humphreys (1 hole)	1	JL Wadkins and JB Simons	0
CW Green and R Carr (1 hole)	1	SN Melnyk and M Giles	0
DM Marsh and G Macgregor (2 and 1)	1	AL Miller and J Farquhar	0
JS Macdonald and R Foster (2 and 1)	1	WC Campbell and T Kite	0
	4		0

Singles

Great Britain	Matches	USA	Matches
CW Green	0	JL Wadkins (1 hole)	1
MF Bonallack	0	M Giles (1 hole)	1
GC Marks	0	AL Miller (1 hole)	1
JS Macdonald	0	SN Melnyk (3 and 2)	1
R Carr (halved)	½	W Hyndman (halved)	½
W Humphreys	0	JR Gabrielsen (1 hole)	1
HB Stuart (3 and 2)	1	J Farquhar	0
R Foster	0	T Kite (3 and 2)	1
	1½		6½

First day's aggregate: Great Britain, 5½; USA, 6½.

United States v Great Britain (Walker Cup Matches)
continued

Second Day–Foursomes

Great Britain	Matches	USA	Matches
GC Marks and CW Green	0	SN Melnyk and M Giles (1 hole)	1
HB Stuart and R Carr (1 hole)	1	JL Wadkins and JR Gabrielsen	0
DM Marsh and MF Bonallack	0	AL Miller and J Farquhar (5 and 4)	1
JS Macdonald and R Foster (halved)	½	WC Campbell and T Kite (halved)	½
	1½		2½

Singles

Great Britain	Matches	USA	Matches
MF Bonallack	0	JL Wadkins (3 and 1)	1
HB Stuart (2 and 1)	1	M Giles	0
W Humphreys (2 and 1)	1	SN Melnyk	0
CW Green (1 hole)	1	AL Miller	0
R Carr (2 holes)	1	J Simons	0
G Macgregor (1 hole)	1	JR Gabrielsen	0
DM Marsh (1 hole)	1	W Hyndman	0
GC Marks	0	T Kite (3 and 2)	1
	6		2

Second day's aggregate: Great Britain, 7½; USA, 4½.
Grand Match aggregate: Great Britain, 13; USA, 11.

At Brookline, Massachusetts, USA, on 24th and 25th August, 1973

First Day–Foursomes

USA	Matches	Great Britain	Matches
M Giles and G Koch (halved)	½	M King and P Hedges (halved)	½
R Siderowf and M Pfeil (5 and 4)	1	H Stuart and J Davies	0
D Edwards and J Ellis (2 and 1)	1	C Green and WT Milne	0
M West and D Ballenger (2 and 1)	1	R Foster and T Homer	0
	3½		½

Singles

USA	Matches	Great Britain	Matches
M Giles (5 and 4)	1	H Stuart	0
R Siderowf (4 and 2)	1	M Bonallack	0
G Koch	0	J Davies (1 hole)	1
M West	0	H Clark (2 and 1)	1
D Edwards (2 holes)	1	R Foster	0
M Killian	0	M King (1 hole)	1
W Rodgers	0	C Green (1 hole)	1
M Pfeil	0	WT Milne (4 and 3)	1
	3		5

First day's aggregate: USA, 6½; Great Britain, 5½.

Second Day–Foursomes

USA	Matches	Great Britain	Matches
M Giles and G Koch (7 and 5)	1	T Homer and R Foster	0
R Siderowf and M Pfeil (halved)	½	H Clark and J Davies (halved)	½
D Edwards and J Ellis (2 and 1)	1	P Hedges and M King	0
W Rodgers and M Killian (1 hole)	1	H Stuart and WT Milne	0
	3½		½

United States v Great Britain (Walker Cup Matches)

continued

Singles

USA

	Matches
J Ellis	0
R Siderowf	0
D Edwards (2 and 1)	1
M Giles (halved)	½
M West (1 hole)	1
M Killian	0
G Koch (halved)	½
M Pfeil (1 hole)	1
	4

Great Britain

	Matches
H Stuart (5 and 4)	1
J Davies (3 and 2)	1
T Homer	0
C Green (halved)	½
M King	0
WT Milne (2 and 1)	1
P Hedges (halved)	½
H Clark	0
	4

Second day's aggregate: USA, 7½; Great Britain, 4½.
Grand Match aggregate: USA, 14; Great Britain, 10.

At St Andrews, 28th and 29th May, 1975

First Day–Foursomes

Great Britain

	Matches
M James and GRD Eyles (1 hole)	1
JC Davies and MA Poxon	0
CW Green and H B Stuart	0
G Macgregor and IC Hutcheon	0
	1

USA

	Matches
J Pate and RL Siderowf	0
GF Burns and C Stadler (5 and 4)	1
J Haas and C Strange (2 and 1)	1
MM Giles and G Koch (5 and 4)	1
	3

Singles

Great Britain

	Matches
M James (2 and 1)	1
JC Davies (halved)	½
P Mulcare (1 hole)	1
HB Stuart	0
MA Poxon	0
IC Hutcheon (halved)	½
GRD Eyles	0
G Macgregor	0
	3

USA

	Matches
J Pate	0
C Strange (halved)	½
RL Siderowf	0
G Koch (3 and 2)	1
J Grace (3 and 1)	1
W Campbell (halved)	½
J Haas (2 and 1)	1
MM Giles (3 and 2)	1
	5

First day's aggregate: Great Britain, 4; USA, 8.

Second Day–Foursomes

Great Britain

	Matches
P Mulcare and IC Hutcheon (1 hole)	1
CW Green and HB Stuart	0
M James and GRD Eyles (5 and 3)	1
P. Hedges and JC Davies	0
	2

USA

	Matches
J Pate and RL Siderowf	0
GF Burns and C Stadler (1 hole)	1
WC Campbell and J Grace	0
J Haas and C Strange (3 and 2)	1
	2

Singles

Great Britain

	Matches
IC Hutcheon (3 and 2)	1
P Mulcare	0
M James	0
JC Davies (2 and 1)	1
CW Green	0
G MacGregor	0
GRD Eyles	0
P Hedges (halved)	½
	2½

USA

	Matches
J Pate	0
C Strange (4 and 3)	1
G Koch (5 and 4)	1
GF Burns	0
J Grace (2 and 1)	1
C Stadler (3 and 2)	1
WC Campbell (2 and 1)	1
MM Giles (halved)	½
	5½

Second day's aggregate: Great Britain, 4½; USA, 7½.
Grand Match aggregate: Great Britain, 8½; USA, 15½.

United States v Great Britain (Walker Cup Matches)

continued

At Shinnecock Hills, New York, 26th and 27th August, 1977

First Day—Foursomes

USA	Matches	Great Britain	Matches
J Fought and V Heafner (4 and 3)	1	P McEvoy and AWB Lyle	0
S Simpson and L Miller (5 and 4)	1	JC Davies and MJ Kelley	0
R Siderowf and G Hallberg	0	IC Hutcheon and P Deeble (1 hole)	1
J Sigel and M Brannan (1 hole)	1	A Brodie and S Martin	0
	3		1

Singles

USA	Matches	Great Britain	Matches
L Miller (2 holes)	1	P McEvoy	0
J Fought (4 and 3)	1	IC Hutcheon	0
S Simpson (7 and 6)	1	GH Murray	0
V Heafner (4 and 3)	1	JC Davies	0
B Sander	0	A Brodie (4 and 3)	1
G Hallberg	0	S Martin (3 and 2)	1
F Ridley (2 holes)	1	AWB Lyle	0
J Sigel (5 and 3)	1	P McKellar	0
	6		2

First day's aggregate: USA, 9; Great Britain, 3.

Second Day–Foursomes

USA	Matches	Great Britain	Matches
J Fought and V Heafner (4 and 3)	1	IC Hutcheon and P Deeble	0
L Miller and S Simpson (2 holes)	1	P McEvoy and JC Davies	0
R Siderowf and B Sander	0	A Brodie and S Martin (6 and 4)	1
F Ridley and M Brannan	0	GH Murray and MJ Kelley (4 and 3)	1
	2		2

Singles

USA	Matches	Great Britain	Matches
L Miller (1 hole)	1	S Martin	0
J Fought (2 and 1)	1	JC Davies	0
B Sander	0	A Brodie (2 and 1)	1
G Hallberg (4 and 3)	1	P McEvoy	0
R Siderowf	0	MJ Kelley (2 and 1)	1
M Brannan	0	IC Hutcheon (2 holes)	1
F Ridley (5 and 3)	1	AWB Lyle	0
J Sigel (1 hole)	1	P Deeble	0
	5		3

Second day's aggregate: USA, 7; Great Britain, 5.
Grand Match aggregate: USA, 16; Great Britain, 8.

At Muirfield, 30th and 31st May, 1979

First Day–Foursomes

Great Britain	Matches	USA	Matches
P McEvoy and B Marchbank	0	S Hoch and J Sigel (1 hole)	1
G Godwin and IC Hutcheon (2 holes)	1	M West and H Sutton	0
G Brand and MJ Kelley	0	D Fischesser and J Holtgrieve (1 hole)	1
A Brodie and I Carslaw (2 and 1)	1	G Moody and M Gove	0
	2		2

United States *v* Great Britain (Walker Cup Matches)

continued

Singles

Great Britain	Matches	USA	Matches
P McEvoy (halved)	½	J Sigel (halved)	½
JC Davies	0	D Clark (8 and 7)	1
IC Hutcheon	0	J Holtgrieve (6 and 4)	1
J Buckley	0	S Hoch (9 and 7)	1
B Marchbank (1 hole)	1	M Peck	0
G Godwin (3 and 2)	1	G Moody	0
MJ Kelley (3 and 2)	1	D Fischesser	0
A Brodie	0	M Gove (3 and 2)	1
	3½		4½

First day's aggregate: Great Britain, 5½; USA, 6½.

Second Day–Foursomes

USA	Matches	Great Britain	Matches
G Godwin and G Brand	0	S Hoch and J Sigel (4 and 3)	1
P McEvoy and B Marchbank (2 and 1)	1	D Fischesser and J Holtgrieve	0
MJ Kelley and IC Hutcheon (halved)	½	M West and H Sutton (halved)	½
I Carslaw and A Brodie (halved)	½	D Clarke and M Peck (halved)	½
	2		2

Singles

USA	Matches	Great Britain	Matches
P McEvoy	0	S Hoch (3 and 1)	1
G Brand	0	D Clarke (2 and 1)	1
G. Godwin	0	M Gove (3 and 2)	1
IC Hutcheon	0	M Peck (2 and 1)	1
A Brodie (3 and 2)	1	M West	0
MJ Kelley	0	G Moody (3 and 2)	1
B Marchbank	0	H Sutton (3 and 1)	1
I Carslaw	0	J Sigel (2 and 1)	1
	1		7

Second day's aggregate: Great Britain, 3; USA, 9.
Grand Match aggregate: Great Britain, 8½; USA, 15½.

At Cypress Point, 28th and 29th August, 1981

First Day–Foursomes

USA	Matches	Great Britain and Ireland	Matches
H Sutton and J Sigel	0	P Walton and R Rafferty (4 and 2)	1
J Holtgrieve and F Fuhrer (1 hole)	1	R Chapman and P McEvoy	0
B Lewis and D von Tacky (2 and 1)	1	P Deeble and T Hutcheon	0
R Commans and C Pavin (5 and 4)	1	D Evans and P Way	0
	3		1

Singles

USA	Matches	Great Britain and Ireland	Matches
H Sutton (3 and 1)	1	R Rafferty	0
J Rassett (1 hole)	1	C Dalgleish	0
R Commans	0	P Walton (1 hole)	1
B Lewis	0	R Chapman (2 and 1)	1
C Pavin (4 and 3)	1	T Hutcheon	0
J Mudd (1 hole)	1	J Godwin	0
D von Tacky	0	P Way (3 and 1)	1
J Sigel (4 and 2)	1	P McEvoy	0
	5		3

First day's aggregate: USA. 8; Great Britain and Ireland, 4.

Second Day–Foursomes

USA	Matches	Great Britain and Ireland	Matches
H Sutton and J Sigel	0	R Chapman and P Way (1 hole)	1
J Holtgrieve and F Fuhrer	0	P Walton and R Rafferty (6 and 4)	1
B Lewis and D von Tacky	0	D Evans and C Dalgleish (3 and 2)	1
J Rassett and J Mudd (5 and 4)	1	T Hutcheon and J Godwin	0
	1		3

United States v Great Britain (Walker Cup Matches)

continued

Singles

USA	Matches	Great Britain and Ireland	Matches
H Sutton	0	R Chapman (1 hole)	1
J Holtgrieve (2 and 1)	1	R Rafferty	0
F Fuhrer (4 and 2)	1	P Walton	0
J Sigel (6 and 5)	1	P Way	0
J Mudd (7 and 5)	1	C Dalgleish	0
R Commans (halved)	½	J Godwin (halved)	½
J Rassett (4 and 3)	1	P Deeble	0
C Pavin (halved)	½	D Evans (halved)	½
	6		2

Second day's aggregate: USA, 7; Great Britain and Ireland, 5.
Grand Match aggregate USA, 15; Great Britain and Ireland, 9.

At Hoylake, 25th and 26th May, 1983

First Day–Foursomes

Great Britain and Ireland	Matches	USA	Matches
M Lewis and M Thompson	0	B Lewis and J Holtgrieve (7 and 6)	1
G MacGregor and P Walton (3 and 1)	1	J Sigel and R Fehr	0
L Mann and A Oldcorn (5 and 4)	1	W Hoffer and D Tentis	0
S Keppler and A Pierse	0	W Wood and B Faxon (3 and 1)	1
	2		2

Singles

Great Britain and Ireland	Matches	USA	Matches
P Parkin (6 and 4)	1	N Crosby	0
L Mann	0	J Holtgrieve (6 and 5)	1
A Oldcorn (4 and 3)	1	B Tuten	0
P Walton (1 hole)	1	J Sigel	0
S Keppler	0	R Fehr (1 hole)	1
D Carrick	0	B Faxon (3 and 1)	1
G Macgregor (halved)	½	W Wood (halved)	½
A Pierse	0	B Lewis (3 and 1)	1
	3½		4½

First day's aggregate: Great Britain and Ireland, 5½; USA, 6½.

Second Day–Foursomes

Great Britain and Ireland	Matches	USA	Matches
G Macgregor and P Walton	0	N Crosby and W Hoffer (2 holes)	1
P Parkin and M Thompson (1 hole)	1	B Faxon and W Wood	0
L Mann and A Oldcorn (1 hole)	1	B Lewis and J Holtgrieve	0
S Keppler and A Pierse (halved)	½	J Sigel and R Fehr	½
	2½		1½

Singles

Great Britain and Ireland	Matches	USA	Matches
P Walton (2 and 1)	1	W Wood	0
P Parkin	0	B Faxon (3 and 2)	1
G Macgregor	0	R Fehr (2 and 1)	1
M Thompson	0	B Tuten (3 and 2)	1
L Mann (halved)	½	D Tentis (halved)	½
S Keppler	0	B Lewis (6 and 5)	1
A Oldcorn (3 and 2)	1	J Holtgrieve	0
D Carrick	0	J Sigel (3 and 1)	1
	2½		5½

Second day's aggregate: Great Britain and Ireland, 5; USA, 7.
Grand Match aggregate: Great Britain and Ireland, 10½; USA, 13½.

At Pine Valley, New Jersey, 21st and 22nd August, 1985

United States v Great Britain (Walker Cup Matches)

continued

First Day-Foursomes

Great Britain and Ireland	Matches	USA	Matches
C Montgomerie and G Macgregor	0	S Verplank and J Sigal (1 hole)	1
J Hawksworth and G McGimpsey (4 and 3)	1	D Waldorf and S Randolph	0
P Baker and P McEvoy (6 and 5)	1	R Sonnier and J Haas	0
C Bloice and S Stephen	½	M Podolak and D Love	½
	2½		1½

Singles

Great Britain and Ireland	Matches	USA	Matches
G McGimpsey	0	S Verplank (2 and 1)	1
P Mayo	0	S Randolph (5 and 4)	1
J Hawksworth	½	R Sonnier	½
C Montgomerie	0	J Sigal (5 and 4)	1
P McEvoy (2 and 1)	1	B Lewis	0
G Macgregor (2 holes)	1	C Burroughs	0
D Gilford	0	D Waldorf (4 and 2)	1
S Stephen (2 and 1)	1	J Haas	0
	3½		4½

First-day's aggregate: Great Britain and Ireland 6; USA 6.

Second Day-Foursomes

Great Britain and Ireland	Matches	USA	Matches
P Mayo and C Montgomerie	½	S Verplank and J Sigal	½
J Hawksworth and G McGimpsey	0	S Randolph and J Haas (3 and 2)	1
P Baker and P McEvoy	0	B Lewis and C Burroughs (2 and 1)	1
C Bloice and S Stephen	0	M Podolak and D Love (3 and 2)	1
	½		3½

Singles

Great Britain and Ireland	Matches	USA	Matches
G McGimpsey	½	S Randolph	½
C Montgomerie	0	S Verplank (1 hole)	1
J Hawksworth (4 and 3)	1	J Sigal	0
P McEvoy	0	D Love (5 and 3)	1
P Baker (5 and 4)	1	R Sonnier	0
G Macgregor 3 and 2	1	C Burroughs	0
C Bloice	0	B Lewis (4 and 3)	1
S Stephen (2 and 1)	1	D Waldorf	0
	4½		3½

Second-day's aggregate: Great Britain and Ireland 5; USA 7.
Grand Match aggregate: Great Britain and Ireland 11; USA 13.

Individual Records

Great Britain and Ireland

United States v Great Britain (Walker Cup Matches)

continued

Name		Year	Played	Won	Lost	Halved
MF Attenborough	Eng	1967	2	0	2	0
CC Aylmer	Eng	1922	2	1	1	0
P Baker	Eng	1985	3	2	1	0
JB Beck	Eng	1928-**(38)**-**(47)**	1	0	1	0
PJ Benka	Eng	1969	4	2	1	1
HG Bentley	Eng	1934-36-38	4	0	2	2
DA Blair	Scot	1955-61	4	1	3	0
C Bloice	Scot	1985	3	0	2	1
MF Bonallack	Eng	(1957)-59-61-63-65-67 -**69**-**71**-73	25	8	14	3
G Brand	Scot	1979	3	0	3	0
OC Bristowe	Eng	(1923)-24	1	0	1	0
A Brodie	Scot	1977-79	8	5	2	1
A Brooks	Scot	1969	3	2	0	1
Hon WGE Brownlow	Eng	1926	2	0	2	0
J Bruen	Ire	1938-49-51	5	0	4	1
JA Buckley	Wales	1979	1	0	1	0
J Burke	Ire	1932	2	0	1	1
AF Bussell	Scot	1957	2	1	1	0
I Caldwell	Eng	1951-55	4	1	2	1
W Campbell	Scot	1930	2	0	2	0
JB Carr	Ire	1947-49-51-53-55-57 -59-61-63-**(65)**-**67**	20	5	14	1
RJ Carr	Ire	1971	4	3	0	1
DG Carrick	Scot	1983	2	0	2	0
IA Carslaw	Scot	1979	3	1	1	1
JR Cater	Scot	1955	1	0	1	0
J Caven	Scot	1922	2	0	2	0
BHG Chapman	Eng	1961	1	0	1	0
R Chapman	Eng	1981	4	3	1	0
MJ Christmas	Eng	1961-63	3	1	2	0
*CA Clark	Eng	1965	4	2	0	2
GJ Clark	Eng	1965	1	0	1	0
*HK Clark	Eng	1973	3	1	1	1
GB Cosh	Scot	1965	4	3	1	0
T Craddock	Ire	1967-69	6	2	3	1
LG Crawley	Eng	1932-34-38-47	6	3	3	0
B Critchley	Eng	1969	4	1	1	2
CR Dalgleish	Scot	1981	3	1	2	0
B Darwin	Eng	1922	2	1	1	0
JC Davies	Eng	1973-75-77-79	13	3	8	2
P Deeble	Eng	1977-81	5	1	4	0
FWG Deighton	Scot	(1951)-57	2	0	2	0
*NV Drew	Ire	1953	1	0	1	0
AA Duncan	Wales	**(1953)**	0	0	0	0
JM Dykes	Scot	1936	2	0	1	1
D Evans	Wales	1981	3	1	1	1
RC Ewing	Ire	1936-38-47-49-51-55	10	1	7	2
GRD Eyles	Eng	1975	4	2	2	0
EW Fiddian	Eng	1932-34	4	0	4	0
J de Forest	Eng	1932	1	0	1	0
R Foster	Eng	1965-67-69-71-73-**(79)** -**(81)**	17	2	13	2
DW Frame	Eng	1961	1	0	1	0
D Gilford	Eng	1985	1	0	1	0
G Godwin	Eng	1979-81	7	2	4	1
CW Green	Scot	1963-69-71-73-75-**(83)**	17	4	10	3
RH Hardman	Eng	1928	1	0	1	0
R Harris	Scot	**(1922)**-**23**-**26**	4	1	3	0
RW Hartley	Eng	1930-32	4	0	4	0
WL Hartley	Eng	1932	2	0	2	0
J Hawksworth	Eng	1985	4	2	1	1
P Hedges	Eng	1973-75	5	0	2	3
CO Hezlet	Ire	1924-26-28	6	0	5	1
GA Hill	Eng	1936-**(55)**	2	0	1	1
Sir EWE Holderness	Eng	1923-26-30	6	2	4	0
TWB Homer	Eng	1973	3	0	3	0
CVL Hooman	Eng	1922-23	3	1**	2	0**
WL Hope	Scot	1923-24-28	5	1	4	0
G Huddy	Eng	1961	1	0	1	0
W Humphreys	Eng	1971	3	2	1	0
IC Hutcheon	Scot	1975-77-79-81	15	5	8	2
RR Jack	Scot	1957-59	4	2	2	0
*M James	Eng	1975	4	3	1	0
A Jamieson, jr	Scot	1926	2	1	1	0
MJ Kelley	Eng	1977-79	7	3	3	1
SD Keppler	Eng	1983	4	0	3	1
*MG King	Eng	1969-73	7	1	5	1
AT Kyle	Scot	1938-47-51	5	2	3	0
DH Kyle	Scot	1924	1	0	1	0

United States *v* Great Britain (Walker Cup Matches)
continued

Name		Year	Played	Won	Lost	Halved
JA Lang	Scot	(1930)	0	0	0	0
JDA Langley	Eng	1936-51-53	6	0	5	1
CD Lawrie	Scot	**(1961)**-**(63)**	0	0	0	0
ME Lewis	Eng	1983	1	0	1	0
PB Lucas	Eng	(1936)-47-**(49)**	2	1	1	0
MSR Lunt	Eng	1959-61-63-65	11	2	8	1
*AWB Lyle	Scot	1977	3	0	3	0
AR McCallum	Scot	1928	1	0	1	0
SM McCready	Ire	1949-51	3	0	3	0
JS Macdonald	Scot	1971	3	1	1	1
P McEvoy	Eng	1977-79-81-85	14	3	10	1
G McGimpsey	Ire	1985	4	1	2	1
G Macgregor	Scot	1971-75-83-85	12	5	6	1
RC MacGregor	Scot	1953	2	0	2	0
P McKellar	Scot	1977	1	0	1	0
WW Mackenzie	Scot	1922-23	3	1	2	0
SL McKinlay	Scot	1934	2	0	2	0
J McLean	Scot	1934-36	4	1	3	0
EA McRuvie	Scot	1932-34	4	1	2	1
JFD Madeley	Ire	1963	2	0	1	1
LS Mann	Scot	1983	4	2	1	1
B Marchbank	Scot	1979	4	2	2	0
GC Marks	Eng	1969-71	6	2	4	0
DM Marsh	Eng	(1959)-71-**(73)**-**(75)**	3	2	1	0
GNC Martin	Ire	1928	1	0	1	0
S Martin	Scot	1977	4	2	2	0
P Mayo	Wales	1985	2	0	1	1
GH Micklem	Eng	1947-49-53-55-**(57)**-**(59)**	6	1	5	0
DJ Millensted	Eng	1967	2	1	1	0
EB Millward	Eng	(1949)-55	2	0	2	0
WTG Milne	Scot	1973	4	2	2	0
CS Montgomerie	Scot	1985	4	0	3	1
JL Morgan	Wales	1951-53-55	6	2	4	0
P Mulcare	Ire	1975	3	2	1	0
GH Murray	Scot	1977	2	1	1	0
SWT Murray	Scot	1963	4	2	2	0
WA Murray	Scot	1923-24-(26)	4	1	3	0
A Oldcorn	Eng	1983	4	4	0	0
*PA Oosterhuis	Eng	1967	4	1	2	1
R Oppenheimer	Eng	**(1951)**	0	0	0	0
P Parkin	Wales	1983	3	2	1	0
JJF Pennink	Eng	1938	2	1	1	0
TP Perkins	Eng	1928	2	0	2	0
AH Perowne	Eng	1949-53-59	4	0	4	0
GB Peters	Scot	1936-38	4	2	1	1
AD Pierse	Ire	1983	3	0	2	1
AK Pirie	Scot	1967	3	0	2	1
MA Poxon	Eng	1975	2	0	2	0
R Rafferty	Ire	1981	4	2	2	0
AC Saddler	Scot	1963-65-67-**(77)**	10	3	5	2
Hon M Scott	Eng	1924-**34**	4	2	2	0
R Scott, jr	Scot	1924	1	1	0	0
PF Scrutton	Eng	1955-57	3	0	3	0
DN Sewell	Eng	1957-59	4	1	3	0
RDBM Shade	Scot	1961-63-65-67	14	6	6	2
DB Sheahan	Ire	1963	4	2	2	0
AE Shepperson	Eng	1957-59	3	1	1	1
AF Simpson	Scot	(1926)	0	0	0	0
JN Smith	Scot	1930	2	0	2	0
WD Smith	Scot	1959	1	0	1	0
AR Stephen	Scot	1985	4	2	1	1
EF Storey	Eng	1924-26-28	6	1	5	0
JA Stout	Eng	1930-32	4	0	3	1
C Stowe	Eng	1938-47	4	2	2	0
HB Stuart	Scot	1971-73-75	10	4	6	0
A Thirlwell	Eng	1957	1	0	1	0
KG Thom	Eng	1949	2	0	2	0
MS Thompson	Eng	1983	3	1	2	0
H Thomson	Scot	1936-38	4	2	2	0
CJH Tolley	Eng	1922-23-**24**-26-30-34	12	4	8	0
TA Torrance	Scot	1924-28-30-**32**-34	9	3	5	1
WB Torrance	Scot	1922	2	0	2	0
*PM Townsend	Eng	1965	4	3	1	0
LP Tupling	Eng	1969	2	1	1	0
W Tweddell	Eng	**1928**-**(36)**	2	0	2	0
J Walker	Scot	1961	2	0	2	0
P Walton	Ire	1981-83	8	6	2	0
*P Way	Eng	1981	4	2	2	0
RH Wethered	Eng	1922-23-26-**30**-34	9	5	3	1
RJ White	Eng	1947-49-51-53-55	10	6	3	1
J Wilson	Scot	1923	2	2	0	0

United States *v* Great Britain (Walker Cup Matches) *continued*

Name		Year	Played	Won	Lost	Halved
JC Wilson	Scot	1947-53	4	0	4	0
GB Wolstenholme	Eng	1957-59	4	1	2	1

Notes: Bold type indicates captain; in brackets, did not play.
*Players who have also played in the Ryder Cup.
**CVL Hooman and J Sweetser in 1922 were all square after 36 holes; instructions to the contrary not being readily available, they played on and Hooman won at the 37th. On all other occasions halved matches have counted as such.

United States of America

Name	Year	Played	Won	Lost	Halved
*TD Aaron	1959	2	1	1	0
DC Allen	1965-67	6	0	4	2
ES Andrews	1961	1	1	0	0
D Ballenger	1973	1	1	0	0
R Baxter, jr	1957	2	2	0	0
DR Beman	1959-61-63-65	11	7	2	2
RE Billows	1938-49	4	2	2	0
SE Bishop	1947-49	3	2	1	0
AS Blum	1957	1	0	1	0
J Bohmann	1969	3	1	2	0
M Brannan	1977	3	1	2	0
GF Burns	1975	3	2	1	0
C Burroughs	1985	3	1	2	0
AE Campbell	1936	2	2	0	0
JE Campbell	1957	1	0	1	0
WC Campbell	1951-53-**(55)**-57-65-67-71-75	18	11	4	3
RJ Cerrudo	1967	4	1	1	2
RD Chapman	1947-51-53	5	3	2	0
D Cherry	1953-55-61	5	5	0	0
D Clarke	1979	3	2	0	1
RE Cochran	1961	1	1	0	0
CR Coe	1949-51-53-**(57)**-**59**-61-63	13	7	4	2
R Commans	1981	3	1	1	1
JW Conrad	1955	2	1	1	0
N Crosby	1983	2	1	1	0
BH Cudd	1955	2	2	0	0
RD Davies	1963	2	0	2	0
JW Dawson	1949	2	2	0	0
RB Dickson	1967	3	3	0	0
GT Dunlap, jr	1932-34-36	5	3	1	1
D Edwards	1973	4	4	0	0
HC Egan	1934	1	1	0	0
D Eichelberger	1965	3	1	2	0
J Ellis	1973	3	2	1	0
W Emery	1936	2	1	0	1
C Evans, jr	1922-24-28	5	3	2	0
J Farquhar	1971	3	1	2	0
B Faxon	1983	4	3	1	0
R Fehr	1983	4	2	1	1
JW Fischer	1934-36-38-**(65)**	4	3	0	1
D Fischesser	1979	3	1	2	0
MA Fleckman	1967	2	0	2	0
B Fleisher	1969	4	0	2	2
J Fought	1977	4	4	0	0
WC Fownes, jr	**1922**-24	3	1	2	0
F Fuhrer	1981	3	2	1	0
JR Gabrielsen	1977-**(81)**	3	1	2	0
RA Gardner	1922-**23-24-26**	8	6	2	0
RW Gardner	1961-63	5	4	0	1
M Giles	1969-71-73-75	15	8	2	5
HL Givan	1936	1	0	0	1
JG Goodman	1934-36-38	6	4	2	0
M Gove	1979	3	2	1	0
J Grace	1975	3	2	1	0
JA Grant	1967	2	2	0	0
AD Gray, jr	1963-65-67	12	5	6	1
JP Guilford	1922-24-26	6	4	2	0
W Gunn	1926-28	4	4	0	0
*F Haas Jr	1938	2	0	2	0
*J Haas	1975	3	3	0	0
J Haas	1985	3	1	2	0

United States *v* Great Britain (Walker Cup Matches)

continued

Name	Year	Played	Won	Lost	Halved
G Hallberg	1977	3	1	2	0
GS Hamer, jr	(1947)	0	0	0	0
LE Harris, jr	1963	4	3	1	0
V Heafner	1977	3	3	0	0
SD Herron	1923	2	0	2	0
S Hoch	1979	4	4	0	0
W Hoffer	1983	2	1	1	0
J Holtgrieve	1979-81-83	10	6	4	0
JM Hopkins	1965	3	0	2	1
W Howell	1932	1	1	0	0
W Hyndman	1957-59-61-69-71	9	6	1	2
J Inman	1969	2	2	0	0
JG Jackson	1953-55	3	3	0	0
HR Johnston	1923-24-28-30	6	5	1	0
RT Jones, jr	1922-24-26-**28-30**	10	9	1	0
AF Kammer	1947	2	1	1	0
M Killian	1973	3	1	2	0
*TO Kite	1971	4	2	1	1
RE Knepper	(1922)	0	0	0	0
RW Knowles	1951	1	1	0	0
G Koch	1973-75	7	4	1	2
CR Kocsis	1938-49-57	5	2	2	1
B Lewis, jr	1981-83-85	10	6	4	0
JW Lewis	1967	4	3	1	0
WL Little, jr	1934	2	2	0	0
*GA Littler	1953	2	2	0	0
D Love	1985	3	2	0	1
MJ McCarthy, jr	(1928)-32	1	1	0	0
BN McCormick	1949	1	1	0	0
JB McHale	1949-51	3	2	0	1
RR Mackenzie	1926-28-30	6	5	1	0
MR Marston	1922-23-24-34	8	5	3	0
SN Melnyk	1969-71	7	3	3	1
AL Miller	1969-71	8	4	3	1
L Miller	1977	4	4	0	0
DK Moe	1930-32	3	3	0	0
G Moody	1979	3	1	2	0
GT Moreland	1932-34	4	4	0	0
D Morey	1955-65	4	1	3	0
J Mudd	1981	3	3	0	0
*RJ Murphy	1967	4	1	2	1
JF Neville	1923	1	0	1	0
*JW Nicklaus	1959-61	4	4	0	0
LW Oehmig	**(1977)**	0	0	0	0
FD Ouimet	1922-23-24-26-30-**32** **-34-(36)-(38)-(47)-(49)**	16	9	5	2
HD Paddock, jr	1951	1	0	0	1
*J Pate	1975	4	0	4	0
WJ Patton	1955-57-59-63-65-**(69)**	14	11	3	0
C Pavin	1981	3	2	0	1
M Peck	1979	3	1	1	1
M Pfeil	1973	4	2	1	1
M Podolak	1985	2	1	0	1
SL Quick	1947	2	1	1	0
S Randolph	1985	4	2	1	1
J Rassett	1981	3	3	0	0
F Ridley	1977	3	2	1	0
RH Riegel	1947-49	4	4	0	0
H Robbins, jr	1957	2	0	1	1
W Rodgers	1973	2	1	1	0
GV Rotan	1923	2	1	1	0
*EM Rudolph	1957	2	1	0	1
B Sander	1977	3	0	3	0
CH Seaver	1932	2	2	0	0
RL Siderowf	1969-73-75-77-**(79)**	14	4	8	2
J Sigel	1977-79-81-**83**-85	19	11	5	3
RH Sikes	1963	3	1	2	0
JB Simons	1971	2	0	2	0
S Simpson	1977	3	3	0	0
CB Smith	1961-63	2	0	1	1
R Smith	1936-38	4	2	2	0
R Sonnier	1985	3	0	2	1
*C Stadler	1975	3	3	0	0
FR Stranahan	1947-49-51	6	3	2	1
*C Strange	1975	4	3	0	1
*H Sutton	1979-81	7	2	4	1
JW Sweetser	1922-23-24-26-28-32 **-(67)-(73)**	12	7	4**	1**
FM Taylor	1957-59-61	4	4	0	0
D Tentis	1983	2	0	1	1
RS Tufts	**(1963)**	0	0	0	0
WP Turnesa	1947-49-**51**	6	3	3	0

United States v Great Britain (Walker Cup Matches)

continued

Name	Year	Played	Won	Lost	Halved
B Tuten	1983	2	1	1	0
EM Tutweiler	1965-67	6	5	1	0
ER Updegraff	1963-65-69-**(75)**	7	3	3	1
S Urzetta	1951-53	4	4	0	0
K Venturi	1953	2	2	0	0
S Verplank	1985	4	3	0	1
GJ Voigt	1930-32-36	5	2	2	1
G Von Elm	1926-28-30	6	4	1	1
D von Tacky	1981	3	1	2	0
*JL Wadkins	1969-71	7	3	4	0
D Waldorf	1985	3	1	2	0
EH Ward	1953-55-59	6	6	0	0
MH Ward	1938-47	4	2	2	0
M West	1973-79	6	2	3	1
J Westland	1932-34-53-**(61)**	5	3	0	2
HW Wettlaufer	1959	2	2	0	0
E White	1936	2	2	0	0
OF Willing	1923-24-30	4	4	0	0
JM Winters, jr	**(1971)**	0	0	0	0
W Wood	1983	4	1	2	1
FJ Wright	1923	1	1	0	0
CR Yates	1936-38-**(53)**	4	3	0	1
RL Yost	1955	2	2	0	0

Notes: Bold type indicates captain: in brackets, did not play.
*Players who have also played in the Ryder Cup.
**CVL Hooman and J Sweetser in 1922 were all square after 36 holes; instructions to the contrary not being readily available, they played on and Hooman won at the 37th. On all other occasions halved matches have counted as such.

Eisenhower Trophy (World Cup)

Instituted 1958

Year	Winners	Runners-up	Venue	Score
1958	Australia (B Devlin, P Toogood, RF Stevens, D Bachli)	United States (C Coe, WJ Patton, Dr F Taylor, W Hyndman)	St Andrews	918
After a tie, Australia won the play-off by two strokes. Australia 222; United States 224. (Best individual score (unofficial), B Devlin, W Hyndman, RR Jack, 301).				
1960	United States (DR Beman, RW Gardner, W Hyndman, J Nicklaus)	Australia (E Ball, J Coogan, BW Devlin, EG Routley)	Ardmore, USA	834
(Best individual score, J Nicklaus, 269)				
1962	United States (DR Beman, WJ Patton, R Silkes, L Harris)	Canada (G Cowan, B Wakeham, N Weslock, R. Wylie)	Kawana, Japan	854
(Best individual score, G Cowan, 280)				
1964	Great Britain and Ireland (RDBM Shade, R Foster, MSR Lunt MF Bonallack)	Canada (N Weslock, D Silverberg RK Alexander)	Olgiata, Rome	895
(Best individual score, Min Nan Hsieh, Formosa, 294)				
1966	Australia (KW Hartley, PK Billings, W Berwick, KK Donohoe)	United States (DR Beman, RJ Murphy RJ Cerrudo, D Gray)	Mexico City	877
(Best individual score, RDBM Shade, Great Britain, 281)				
1968	United States (M Giles, B Fleisher, J Lewis Jr, R Siderowf)	Great Britain and Ireland (MF Bonallack, PA Oosterhuis, RDBM Shade, GB Cosh)	Melbourne	868
(Best individual score, MF Bonallack and M Giles, 286)				
1970	United States (M Giles, T Kite, A Miller, L Wadkins)	New Zealand (G. Clarke, S Jones, T McDougall, R Murray)	Madrid	857
(Best individual score, V Regalado, Mexico, 280)				
1972	United States (B Crenshaw, M Giles, M Hayes, M West)	Australia (M Cahill, T Gale, A Gresham N Ratcliffe	Buenos Aires	865
(Best individual score, A Gresham, Australia, 285)				
1974	United States (G Burns, G Koch, J Pate, C Strange)	Japan (G Nakabe, T Irie, T Sakata, S Yamazaki)	Dominican Republic	888
(Best individual score, J Pate, USA, and J Gonzalez, Brazil, 294)				
1976	Great Britain (J Davies, I Hutcheon, M Kelley S Martin)	Japan (M Kuramoto, M Mori, G Nakabe, T Sakata)	Penina, Portugal	892
(Best individual score, I Hutcheon, Great Britain, and TM Chen, Taiwan, 293)				
1978	United States (R Clampett, J Cook, S Hoch, J Sigel)	Canada (G Cowan, D Mick, D Roxburgh, Y Tremblay	Fiji	873
(Best individual score, R Clampett, USA, 287)				
1980	United States (H Sutton, J Holtgrieve, B Tway, J Sigel)	South Africa (D Suddards, E Groenwald, W Player, D Lindsay-Smith)	Pinehurst, USA	848
(Best individual score, H Sutton, USA, 276)				
1982	United States (N Crosby, B Lewis, J Holtgrieve, J Sigel)	Sweden (K Kinell, O Sellberg, M Persson, P Andersson)	Lausanne	859
(Best individual score, L Carbonetti, Argentine, 284)				
1984	Japan	United States	Hong Kong	870
1986	Canada	United States	Caracas, Venezuela	860

Commonwealth Tournament

At St Andrews, 1954

Australia beat South Africa
Australia beat New Zealand
Australia beat Canada
Australia halved with Great Britain
Canada beat Great Britain
Canada beat New Zealand
Great Britain beat New Zealand
Great Britain halved with South Africa
South Africa beat Canada
New Zealand beat South Africa

At Johannesburg, 1959

South Africa beat Great Britain
South Africa beat Canada
South Africa beat New Zealand
Australia beat South Africa
Australia beat Canada
New Zealand beat Australia
New Zealand beat Great Britain
Great Britain beat Australia
Great Britain beat Canada
Canada beat New Zealand

At Sydney, 1963

Australia beat Great Britain
Australia beat New Zealand
Australia tied with South Africa
Australia tied with Canada
Great Britain beat New Zealand
Great Britain beats South Africa
Great Britain beat Canada
Canada beat New Zealand
South Africa beat Canada
New Zealand beat South Africa

At Victoria, Canada, 1967

New Zealand beat South Africa
New Zealand beat Australia
New Zealand tied with Great Britain
Great Britain beat Canada
Great Britain beat Australia
South Africa beat Great Britain
South Africa beat Australia
Canada beat New Zealand
Canada beat South Africa
Australia beat Canada

At Auckland, 1971

Canada beat Australia
Canada beat Great Britain
Canada beat New Zealand
Australia beat Great Britain
Australia beat New Zealand
Great Britain beat New Zealand

At Durban, 1975

Canada lost to South Africa
Canada beat Great Britain
Canada beat New Zealand
Great Britain beat New Zealand
Great Britain beat South Africa
South Africa lost to New Zealand

St Andrews Trophy (Great Britain *v* Europe)

Match instituted 1956
Trophy presented 1962

Year	Winner	Venue	Result
1956	Great Britain	Wentworth	12½-2½
1958	Great Britain	St Cloud, France	10-5
1960	Great Britain	Walton Heath	13-5
1962	Great Britain	Halmstead, Sweden	18-12
1964	Great Britain	Muirfield	23-7
1966	Great Britain	Bilbao, Spain	19½-10½
1968	Great Britain	Portmarnock	20-10
1970	Great Britain	La Zoute, Belgium	17½-12½
1972	Great Britain	Berkshire	19½-10½
1974	Europe	Punta Ala, Italy	16-14
1976	Great Britain	St Andrews	18½-11½
1978	Great Britain	Bremen, Germany	20½-9½
1980	Great Britain	St George's	19½-10½
1982	Europe	Rosendaelsche, Netherlands	14-10
1984	Great Britain	Taunton, Devon	13-11
1986	Great Britain	Halmstead, Sweden	14½–9½

European Amateur Team Championship

Year	Winner	Second	Venue
1959	Sweden		
1961	Sweden	England	Brussels, Belgium
1963	England	Sweden	Falsterbo, Sweden
1965	Ireland	Scotland	St George's, England
1967	Ireland	France	Turin, Italy
1969	England	W Germany	Hamburg, W Germany
1971	England	Scotland	Lausanne, Switzerland
1973	England	Scotland	Penina, Portugal
1975	Scotland	Italy	Killarney, Ireland
1977	Scotland	Sweden	The Haagsche, Holland
1979	England	Wales	Esbjerg, Denmark
1981	England	Scotland	St Andrews, Scotland
1983	Ireland	Spain	Chantilly, France
1985	Scotland	Sweden	Halmstad, Sweden

Home International Results

The Amateur Internationals

1902 Scotland . . . 32 holes . . . England, 25 holes, at Hoylake. From 1902 to 1911, matches were 36-hole Singles. In 1912, Foursomes, five couples a-side, played. The match of 1902 was only semi-official.

Home Internationals

From 1932 the International matches between the four countries of Great Britain came under the control of the Golf Unions, and the "Walker Cup" which had been presented for the England-Scotland match was abandoned. Prior to that year an International between England and Scotland, inaugurated in 1902, was arranged by the Royal and Ancient Golf Club.

1932–At Troon

Scotland beat England	8 matches to 7
Scotland beat Ireland	11½ matches to 4½
Scotland beat Wales	9 matches to 6
England beat Ireland	12 matches to 3
England beat Wales	11½ matches to 3½
Ireland beat Wales	9½ matches to 5½

1933–At Newcastle, Co Down

Scotland beat England	9½ matches to 5½
Scotland beat Ireland	9 matches to 6
Scotland beat Wales	11 matches to 4
England beat Ireland	9½ matches to 5½
England beat Wales	9 matches to 6
Ireland beat Wales	11 matches to 4

1934–At Porthcawl

Scotland beat England	10 matches to 5
Scotland beat Ireland	10½ matches to 4½
Scotland beat Wales	9½ matches to 5½
Ireland beat Wales	10 matches to 5
Ireland beat England	12 matches to 3
England beat Wales	10 matches to 5

1935–At Lytham St Annes

Scotland beat Wales	10½ matches to 4½
Scotland beat England	12½ matches to 2½
England beat Ireland	8½ matches to 6½
England beat Wales	10½ matches to 4½
Ireland beat Scotland	9 matches to 6
Ireland beat Wales	10½ matches to 4½

1936–At Prestwick

Scotland beat Wales	9½ matches to 5½
Scotland beat Ireland	8 matches to 7
Scotland beat England	8 matches to 7
England beat Ireland	13 matches to 2
England beat Wales	12 matches to 3
Ireland beat Wales	11 matches to 4

1937–At Portmarnock

Scotland beat Ireland	9½ matches to 5½
Scotland beat England	9 matches to 6
Scotland halved with Wales	7½ matches each
England beat Ireland	8 matches to 7
England beat Wales	8½ matches to 6½
Ireland beat Wales	9 matches to 6

1938–At Porthcawl

England beat Ireland	10 matches to 5
England beat Wales	10½ matches to 4½
England beat Scotland	8½ matches to 6½
Scotland beat Wales	8½ matches to 6½
Scotland beat Ireland	9½ matches to 5½
Ireland beat Wales	9 matches to 6

1947–At Hoylake

England beat Wales	14 matches to 1
England beat Ireland	9 matches to 6
England beat Scotland	8 matches to 7
Scotland beat Ireland	10 matches to 5
Scotland beat Wales	11 matches to 4
Ireland beat Wales	12 matches to 3

Home International Results *continued*

1948–At Muirfield

England beat Scotland	10½ matches to 4½
England beat Wales	8½ matches to 6½
England beat Ireland	8 matches to 7
Ireland beat Scotland	10½ matches to 4½
Ireland beat Wales	12½ matches to 2½
Scotland beat Wales	11 matches to 4

1949–At Portmarnock

England beat Ireland	8 matches to 7
England beat Wales	10 matches to 5
England beat Scotland	10 matches to 5
Ireland beat Wales	10½ matches to 4½
Ireland beat Scotland	10½ matches to 4½
Wales beat Scotland	8½ matches to 6½

1950–At Harlech

Ireland beat Wales	10 matches to 5
Ireland halved with Scotland	7½ matches each
Ireland beat England	8½ matches to 6½
Scotland beat England	9 matches to 6
Scotland halved with Wales	7½ matches each
England beat Wales	10 matches to 5

1951–At Lytham St Annes

Ireland beat Scotland	8½ matches to 6½
Ireland beat England	8 matches to 7
Scotland beat Wales	8 matches to 7
Scotland beat England	8 matches to 7
Wales beat Ireland	9½ matches to 5½
England beat Wales	10 matches to 5

1952–At Troon
(for Raymond Trophy presented 1952)

Scotland beat Wales	10 matches to 5
Scotland beat England	9 matches to 6
Scotland beat Ireland	9½ matches to 5½
England beat Wales	9 matches to 6
Ireland halved with England	7½ matches each
Ireland halved with Wales	7½ matches each

1953–At Killarney

Scotland beat Wales	10 matches to 5
Scotland beat England	8½ matches to 6½
Scotland halved with Ireland	7½ matches each
Ireland beat England	9 matches to 6
England beat Wales	9 matches to 6
Wales beat Ireland	8½ matches to 6½

1954–At Porthcawl

England beat Wales	12 matches to 3
England beat Scotland	9 matches to 6
England beat Ireland	8½ matches to 6½
Ireland beat Scotland	9 matches to 6
Scotland beat Wales	9 matches to 6
Wales beat Ireland	8 matches to 7

1955–At Southport

Ireland beat Scotland	9 matches to 6
Ireland beat Wales	9 matches to 6
Ireland halved with England	7½ matches each
Scotland beat Wales	8 matches to 7
Scotland beat England	8 matches to 7
England beat Wales	9½ matches to 5½

1956–At Muirfield

Scotland beat Wales	10½ matches to 4½
Scotland beat Ireland	8 matches to 7
Scotland beat England	9½ matches to 5½
England beat Ireland	11 matches to 4
England beat Wales	10½ matches to 4½
Wales beat Ireland	9 matches to 6

1957–At Newcastle, Co Down

England beat Scotland	12 matches to 3
England beat Wales	9 matches to 6
England beat Ireland	10½ matches to 4½
Scotland beat Ireland	13 matches to 2
Scotland beat Wales	10 matches to 5
Wales beat Ireland	8½ matches to 6½

1958–At Porthcawl

England beat Ireland	9 matches to 6
England beat Wales	11½ matches to 3½
England beat Scotland	8 matches to 7
Scotland beat Ireland	8½ matches to 6½
Scotland beat Wales	10½ matches to 4½
Wales beat Ireland	8 matches to 7

1959–At Lytham St Annes

England beat Scotland	10 matches to 5
Ireland beat Wales	8 matches to 7
Scotland beat Wales	10 matches to 5
Ireland beat England	8½ matches to 6½
Scotland beat Ireland	8½ matches to 6½
England beat Wales	11½ matches to 3½

1960–At Turnberry

Scotland halved with England	7½ matches each
Scotland beat Wales	9 matches to 6
England beat Ireland	8 matches to 7
England beat Wales	11½ matches to 3½
Ireland beat Wales	12 matches to 3
Ireland beat Scotland	8 matches to 7

1961–At Portmarnock

Scotland beat England	12½ matches to 2½
Scotland beat Ireland	11½ matches to 3½
Scotland beat Wales	8 matches to 7
Ireland beat Wales	11 matches to 4
Ireland beat England	8 matches to 7
Wales beat England	12 matches to 3

Home International Results

continued

1962–At Porthcawl

Scotland beat England	9 matches to 6
Scotland beat Wales	9 matches to 6
England beat Ireland	8½ matches to 6½
England beat Wales	11½ matches to 3½
Ireland beat Scotland	8 matches to 7
Ireland beat Wales	10½ matches to 4½

1963–At Lytham St Annes

Scotland beat England	10½ matches to 4½
Scotland beat Wales	10½ matches to 4½
England beat Ireland	8½ matches to 6½
England beat Wales	9 matches to 6
Ireland beat Scotland	10 matches to 5
Ireland beat Wales	11 matches to 4

1964–At Carnoustie

England beat Wales	12½ matches to 2½
England beat Ireland	8½ matches to 6½
England beat Scotland	8 matches to 7
Ireland beat Scotland	8 matches to 7
Ireland beat Wales	10 matches to 5
Scotland beat Wales	12½ matches to 2½

1965–At Portrush

England beat Wales	8 matches to 7
England beat Scotland	11½ matches to 3½
England beat Ireland	8½ matches to 6½
Ireland beat Wales	10½ matches to 4½
Ireland beat Scotland	9½ matches to 5½
Scotland beat Wales	9 matches to 6

1966–At Porthcawl

England beat Scotland	8 matches to 7
England beat Ireland	12½ matches to 2½
England beat Wales	8 matches to 7
Ireland beat Scotland	10½ matches to 4½
Ireland beat Wales	9 matches to 6
Scotland beat Wales	8 matches to 7

1967–At Ganton

Scotland beat England	8 matches to 7
Scotland beat Ireland	8½ matches to 6½
Scotland beat Wales	8 matches to 7
England beat Ireland	10½ matches to 4½
England beat Wales	10½ matches to 4½
Ireland beat Wales	8½ matches to 6½

1968–At Gullane

England beat Scotland	9½ matches to 5½
England beat Ireland	12 matches to 3
England beat Wales	11 matches to 4
Scotland beat Ireland	8 matches to 7
Scotland beat Wales	9 matches to 6
Ireland beat Wales	9 matches to 6

1969–At Killarney

England beat Scotland	10½ matches to 4½
England halved with Ireland	7½ matches each
England beat Wales	11 matches to 4
Scotland beat Ireland	9½ matches to 5½
Wales beat Scotland	8 matches to 7
Ireland beat Wales	8 matches to 7

1970–At Porthcawl

Scotland beat Ireland	10 matches to 5
Scotland beat Wales	10 matches to 5
Scotland beat England	9½ matches to 4½
Ireland beat Wales	8 matches to 7
Ireland halved with England	7½ matches each
Wales beat England	8½ matches to 6½

1971–At Formby

Scotland beat England	8 matches to 7
Scotland beat Ireland	8½ matches to 6½
Scotland beat Wales	12 matches to 3
England beat Ireland	12 matches to 3
England beat Wales	8½ matches to 6½
Ireland beat Wales	9½ matches to 5½

1972–At Troon

Scotland halved with England	7½ matches each
Scotland beat Ireland	8½ matches to 6½
Scotland beat Wales	10½ matches to 4½
England beat Ireland	8 matches to 7
England beat Wales	10½ matches to 4½
Ireland beat Wales	12 matches to 3

1973–At Lytham St Annes

England beat Scotland	9 matches to 6
England beat Ireland	10½ matches to 4½
England beat Wales	9½ matches to 5½
Scotland beat Ireland	9½ matches to 5½
Scotland halved with Wales	7½ matches each
Ireland beat Wales	10½ matches to 4½

1974–At Harlech

England beat Scotland	10½ matches to 4½
England beat Ireland	11 matches to 4
England halved with Wales	7½ matches each
Scotland beat Ireland	9 matches to 6
Scotland beat Wales	9 matches to 6
Ireland beat Wales	8 matches to 7

1975–At Portmarnock

Scotland beat England	9½ matches to 5½
Scotland beat Ireland	10½ matches to 4½
Scotland beat Wales	13 matches to 2
England beat Ireland	10½ matches to 4½
England beat Wales	11 matches to 4
Ireland beat Wales	9 matches to 6

1976–At Muirfield

Scotland beat England	10 matches to 5
Scotland beat Ireland	10 matches to 5
Scotland beat Wales	9 matches to 6
England beat Ireland	10½ matches to 4½
England beat Wales	10 matches to 5
Ireland beat Wales	8 matches to 7

1977–At Hillside

England beat Scotland	8 matches to 7
England beat Wales	9 matches to 6
England beat Ireland	8½ matches to 6½
Scotland beat Wales	10 matches to 5
Scotland beat Ireland	11½ matches to 3½
Wales beat Ireland	9 matches to 6

Home International Results

continued

1978–At Ashburnham

England beat Wales	8½ matches to 6½
England beat Scotland	9 matches to 6
England beat Ireland	8½ matches to 6½
Wales beat Scotland	8 matches to 7
Scotland beat Ireland	9 matches to 6
Ireland beat Wales	8 matches to 7

1979–*Cancelled*

In place of the Home International Matches
Scotland beat England 17-13 at Troon, and Wales beat Ireland 17-15 at Porthcawl

1980–At Dornoch

England halved with Ireland	7½ matches each
England beat Wales	10 matches to 5
England beat Scotland	11 matches to 4
Ireland halved with Wales	7½ matches each
Ireland beat Scotland	9 matches to 6
Wales halved with Scotland	7½ matches each

1981–At Woodhall Spa

Scotland beat Ireland	9 matches to 6
Scotland beat England	11½ matches to 3½
Scotland beat Wales	9½ matches to 5½
Ireland beat England	8 matches to 7
Ireland beat Wales	10½ matches to 4½
Wales halved with England	7½ matches each

1982–At Porthcawl

Scotland beat England	8 matches to 7
Scotland beat Wales	9½ matches to 5½
England beat Ireland	8½ matches to 6½
England beat Wales	8 matches to 7
Ireland beat Scotland	8 matches to 7
Ireland halved with Wales	7½ matches each

1983–At Portmarnock

Ireland beat Scotland	9½ matches to 5½
Ireland halved with England	7½ matches each
Ireland beat Wales	10 matches to 5
Scotland beat England	8½ matches to 6½
Scotland beat Wales	8 matches to 7
England beat Wales	9 matches to 6

1984–At Troon

Ireland halved with Wales	7½ matches each
England beat Scotland	8 matches to 7
Scotland beat Ireland	10 matches to 5
England beat Wales	12½ matches to 2½
Scotland beat Wales	7 matches to 3
Ireland beat England	6 matches to 4

(*Foursomes of third series of matches cancelled due to torrential rain.*)

1985–At Formby

England beat Wales	11 matches to 4
England beat Scotland	8 matches to 7
England beat Ireland	8½ matches to 6½
Wales beat Scotland	8 matches to 7
Wales beat Ireland	9½ matches to 5½
Ireland beat Scotland	11½ matches to 3½

1986–At Harlech

Scotland beat England	9½ matches to 5½
Scotland beat Ireland	10½ matches to 4½
Scotland beat Wales	10 matches to 5
England beat Wales	9 matches to 6
Ireland beat England	8 matches to 7
Wales halved with Ireland	7½ matches each

Boys' International England *v* Scotland

Instituted 1928

Year	Winner	Result	Venue
1923	Scotland	7½-4½	Dunbar
1924	Scotland	7-5	Coombe Hill
1925	England	7-5	Burgess
1926	England	6½-5½	Coombe Hill
1927	Scotland	7-5	Burgess
1928	England	6½-5½	Formby
1929	Scotland	9½-2½	Burgess
1930	Scotland	8-4	Fulwell
1931	Scotland	7½-4½	Killermont
1932	Scotland	8-4	Lytham St Annes
1933	Scotland	7-5	Carnoustie
1934	England	9-3	Moortown
1935	Halved	6-6	Aberdeen
1936	Scotland	8½-3½	Birkdale
1937	Scotland	9½-2½	Bruntsfield
1938	Scotland	7½-4½	Moor Park
1939	Scotland	7-5	Carnoustie
1940-45	*Not played*		
1946	England	8½-3½	Bruntsfield
1947	England	7-5	Hoylake
1948	England	9-3	Barassie
1949	Scotland	8-4	St Andrews
1950	Scotland	8½-3½	Lytham St Annes
1951	England	7-5	Prestwick
1952	England	6½-5½	Formby
1953	Scotland	7-5	Dunbar
1954	England	6½-5½	Hoylake
1955	Scotland	9-3	Barassie
1956	England	7½-4½	Sunningdale
1957	Scotland	7½-4½	Carnoustie
1958	England	7-5	Moortown
1959	England	8½-3½	Pollok
1960	England	10-2	Olton
1961	Scotland	7-5	Dalmahoy
1962	England	6½-5½	Mid-Surrey
1963	Scotland	9-3	Prestwick
1964	England	9-3	Formby
1965	England	10-5	Gullane
1966	England	12-3	Moortown
1967	Scotland	8-7	Western Gailes
1968	England	10-5	St Annes Old Links
1969	England	12-3	Dunbar
1970	England	12-3	Hillside
1971	Halved	7½-7½	Barassie
1972	England	13½-1½	Moortown
1973	England	9-6	Blairgowrie
1974	England	11-4	Liverpool
1975	England	9½-5½	Bruntsfield
1976	Scotland	8-7	Sunningdale
1977	England	8-7	Downfield
1978	Scotland	8½-6½	Seaton Carew
1979	England	11-4	Barassie
1980	England	9-6	Formby
1981	Halved	7½-7½	Gullane
1982	England	8-7	Burnham & Berrow
1983	England	8-7	Glenbervie
1984	England	9½-5½	Porthcawl
1985	England	10-5	Barnton
1986	Scotland	8½-6½	Seaton Carew

Wales *v* Ireland

Instituted 1972

Year	Winner	Result	Venue
1972	Ireland	5-4	Moortown
1973	Ireland	5½-3½	Blairgowrie
1974	Wales	5-4	Hoylake
1975	Wales	6½-2½	Bruntsfield
1976	Wales	7½-1½	Sunningdale
1977	Ireland	6½-5½	Downfield
1978	Wales	8-4	Seaton Carew
1979	Ireland	9½-2½	Barassie
1980	Wales	6½-5½	Formby
1981	Ireland	8-4	Gullane
1982	Wales	9-3	Burnham & Berrow
1983	Ireland	7-5	Glenbervie
1984	Wales	6½-5½	Porthcawl
1985	Ireland	11½-3½	Barnton
1986	Ireland	8½–6½	Seaton Carew

Great Britain *v* Europe

Instituted 1958

Year	Winner	Result	Venue
1958	Great Britain	11½-½	Moortown
1959	Great Britain	7-2	Pollok
1960	Great Britain	8-7	Olton
1961	Great Britain	11-4	Dalmahoy
1962	Great Britain	11-4	Mid-Surrey
1963	Great Britain	12-3	Prestwick
1964	Great Britain	12-1	Formby
1965	Great Britain	12-1	Gullane
1966	Great Britain	10-2	Moortown
1967-76	*Not played*		
1977	Europe	7-6	Downfield
1978	Europe	7-6	Seaton Carew
1979	Great Britain	9½-2½	Barassie
1980	Great Britain	7-5	Formby
1981	Great Britain	8-4	Gullane
1982	Great Britain	11-1	Burnham & Berrow
1983	Great Britain & Ireland	6½-5½	Glenbervie
1984			
1985	Great Britain & Ireland	7½-4½	Barnton
1986	Europe	8½–3½	Seaton Carew

Youths' Internationals England *v* Scotland

Instituted 1955

Year	Winner	Result	Venue
1955	England	13-5	Pannal
1956	Scotland	+17 holes	Burgess
1957	*Not played*		
1958	England	+4 holes	Dumfries & County
1959	Scotland	12-6	Pannal
1960	Scotland	11½-6½	Pannal
1961	England	11½-6½	Bruntsfield
1962	England	9½-8½	Pannal
1963	Scotland	9-6	Pollok
1964	Scotland	9-6	Pannal
1965	Scotland	10½-3½	Northumberland
1966	England	9½-5½	Dalmahoy
1967	Halved	7½-7½	Copt Heath

Youths' International England v Scotland

continued

Year	Winner	Result	Venue
1968	Scotland	8½-6½	Ayr Belleisle
1969	England	8½-6½	Lindrick
1970	Scotland	8½-6½	Barnton
1971	England	11-4	Northampton County
1972	England	11-4	Glasgow Gailes
1973	England	10-5	Southport & Ainsdale
1974	England	9-6	Downfield
1975	Scotland	11-4	Pannal
1976	England	8½-6½	Gullane
1977	Scotland	9½-5½	Moor Park
1978	Scotland	8½-6½	East Renfrewshire
1979	Halved	7½-7½	Woodhall Spa
1980	Scotland	9-6	Troon
1981	Scotland	8-7	West Lancs
1982	Halved	7½-7½	St Andrews New
1983	Scotland	8½-6½	Sunningdale
1984	Scotland	9-6	Blairgowrie
1985	Halved	7½-7½	Ganton
1986			

Great Britain v Europe

Instituted 1967

Year	Winner	Result	Venue
1967	Great Britain	8-7	Copt Heath
1968	Great Britain	11-4	Ayr Belleisle
1969	Great Britain	13½-1½	Lindrick
1970	Great Britain	10½-4½	Barnton
1971	Great Britain	10-5	Northampton County
1972	Great Britain	11½-3½	Glasgow Gailes
1973	Great Britain	10-5	Southport & Ainsdale
1974	Great Britain	10-5	Downfield
1975	Great Britain	9-6	Pannal
1976	Great Britain	17-13	Chantilly
1977	Great Britain	11½-3½	Moor Park
1978	Great Britain	12½-2½	East Renfrewshire
1979	Great Britain	12-3	Woodhall Spa
1980	Europe	13-11	Lunds Akademiska
1981	Great Britain	7½-4½	West Lancs
	(Singles curtailed owing to weather)		
1982	Great Britain	7½-4½	St Andrews New
1983	Great Britain	11-13	Punta Ala, Italy
1984	Halved	6-6	Blairgowrie
1985	Great Britain & Ireland	8-4	Ganton
1986			

British International Players, Amateur

Abbreviations:

(GB) played for Great Britain;
Com Tnmt Commonwealth Tournament;
Eur T Ch played in European Team Championship for home country;
Home Int played in Home International matches

Adams, MPD
(Wales): Home Int 1969 -70 -71 -72 -75 -76 -77; Eur T Ch 1971

Aitken, AR
(Scotland): v England 1906 -07 -08

Alexander, DW
(Scotland): Home Int 1958; v Scandinavia 1958

Allison, A
(Ireland): v England 1928; v Scotland 1929

Anderson, N
(Ireland): Home Int 1985 -86

Anderson, RB
(Scotland): v Scandinavia 1960 -62; Home Int 1962 -63

Andrew, R
(Scotland): v England 1905 -06 -07 -08 -09 -10

Armour, A
(Scotland): v England 1922

Armour, TD
(GB): v America 1921

Ashby, H
(England): Home Int 1972 -73 -74. (GB): in Dominican Int 1973. (GB): v Europe 1974

Atkinson, HN
(Wales): v Ireland 1913

Attenborough, M
(England): Home Int 1964 -66 -67 -68; Eur T Ch 1967. (GB): v Europe 1966 -68; v America 1967

Aylmer, CC
(England): v Scotland 1911 -22 -23 -24. (GB): v America 1921 -22

Babington, A
(Ireland): v Wales 1913

Baker, P
(England): Home Int 1985. (GB): v America 1985; v Europe 1986

Baker, RN
(Ireland): Home Int 1975

Ball, J
(England): v Scotland 1902 -03 -04 -05 -06 -07 -08 -09 -10 -11 -12

Bamford, JL
(Ireland): Home Int 1954 -56

Banks, C
(England): Home Int 1983

Banks, SE
(England): Home Int 1934 -38

Barker, HH
(England): v Scotland 1907

Barrie, GC
(Scotland): Home Int 1981 -83

Barry, AG
(England): v Scotland 1906 -07

Bayliss, RP
(England): v Ireland 1929; Home Int 1933 -34

Bayne, PWGA
(West): Home Int 1949

Beamish, CH
(Ireland): Home Int 1950 -51 -53 -56

Beck, JB
(England): v Scotland 1926 -30; Home Int 1933. (GB): v America 1928 -38 (Captain) -47 (Captain)

Beddard, JB
(England): v Wales/Ireland 1925; v Ireland 1929; v Scotland 1927 -28 -29

Beharrell, JC
(England): Home Int 1956

Bell, HE
(Ireland): v Wales 1930; Home Int 1932

Bell, RK
(England): Home Int 1947

Benka, PJ
(England): Home Int 1967 -68 -69 -70: Eur T Ch 1969. (GB): v America 1969; v Europe 1970

Bennett, H
(England): Home Int 1948 -49 -51

Bennett, S
(England): v Scotland 1979

Bentley, AL
(England): Home Int 1936 -37; v France 1937 -39

Bentley, HG
(England): v Ireland 1931; v Scotland 1931. Home Int 1932 -33 -34 -35 -36 -37 -38 -47; v France 1934 -35 -36 -37 -39 -54. (GB): v America 1934 -36 -38

Berry, P
(England): Home Int 1972. (GB): v Europe 1972

Bevan, RJ
(Wales): Home Int 1964 -65 -66 -67 -73 -74

Beveridge, HW
(Scotland): v England 1908

Birtwell, SG
(England): Home Int 1968 -70 -73

Black, D
(Scotland): Home Int 1966 -67

Black, FC
(Scotland): Home Int 1962 -64 -65 -66 -68; v Scandinavia 1962; Eur T Ch 1965 -67. (GB): v Europe 1966

Black, GT
(Scotland): Home Int 1952 -53; v South Africa 1954

Black, JL
(Wales): Home Int 1932 -33 -34 -35 -36

Black, WC
(Scotland): Home Int 1964 -65

Blackwell, EBH
(Scotland): v England 1902 -04 -05 -06 -07 -09 -10 -12 -23 -24 -25

Blair, DA
(Scotland): Home Int 1948 -49 -51 -52 -53 -55 -56 -57; v Scandinavia 1956 -58 -62. (GB): v America 1955 -61; in Com Tnmt 1954

Blakeman, D
(England): Home Int 1981; v France 1982

Bloice, C
(Scotland): Home Int 1985 -86. (GB): v America 1985

Bloxham, JA
(England): Home Int 1966

Blyth, AD
(Scotland): v England 1904

Bonallack, MF
(England): Home Int 1957 -58 -59 -60 -61 -62 -63 -64 -65 -66 -67 -68 -69 -70 -71 -72 -73 -74; Eur T Ch 1969 -71. (GB): v America 1957 -59 -61 -63 -65 -67 -69 (Captain) -71 (Captain) -73; v Europe 1958 -62 -64 -66 -68 -70 -72; in Com Tnmt 1959 -63 -67 -71; in World Team Ch 1960 -62 -64 -66 -68 -70 -72

Bonnell, DJ
(Wales): Home Int 1949 -50 -51

Bookless, JT
(Scotland): v England 1930 -31; v Ireland 1930; v Wales 1931

Bottomley, S
(England): Home Int 1986

Bourn, TA
(England): v Ireland 1928; v Scotland 1930; Home Int 1933 -34; v France 1934. (GB): v Australia 1934

Bowen, J
(Ireland): Home Int 1961

Bowman, TH
(England): Home Int 1932

Boxall, R
(England): Home Int 1980 -81 -82; v France 1982

Boyd, HA
(Ireland): v Wales 1913 -23

Bradshaw, AS
(England): Home Int 1932

Bradshaw, EI
(England): v Scotland 1979; Eur T Ch 1979

Braid, H
(Scotland): v England 1922 -23

Bramston, JAT
(England): v Scotland 1902

Brand, G
(England): Home Int 1976. (GB) v Europe 1976

Brand, G
(Scotland): Home Int 1978 -80; v England 1979; Eur T Ch 1979; v Italy 1979; v Belgium 1980; v France 1980. (GB): v Europe 1978 -80; in World Team Ch 1978 -80; v America 1979; v France 1981

Branigan, D
(Ireland): Home Int 1975 -76 -77 -80 -81 -82 -86; Eur T Ch 1977 -81; v West Germany, France, Sweden 1976

Bretherton, CF
(England): v Scotland 1922 -23 -24 -25; v Wales/Ireland 1925

Briscoe, A
(Ireland): v England 1928 -29 -30 -31; v Scotland 1929 -30 -31; v Wales 1929 -30 -31; Home Int 1932 -33 -38

Bristowe, OC
(GB): v America 1923 -24

Broad, RD
(Wales): v Ireland 1979; Home Int 1980 -81 -82 -84; Eur T Ch 1981

Broadhurst, P
(England): Home Int 1986

Brock, J
(Scotland) v Ireland 1929; Home Int 1932

Brodie, Allan
(Scotland): Home Int 1970 -72 -73 -74 -75 -76 -77 -78 -80; Eur T Ch 1973 -77 -79; v England 1979; v Italy 1979; v Belgium 1977; v Spain 1977; v France 1978. (GB): v America 1977 -79; v Europe 1974 -76 -78 -80; in World Team Ch 1978

Brodie, Andrew
(Scotland): Home Int 1968 -69; v Spain 1974

Bromley-Davenport, E
(England): Home Int 1938 -51

Brooks, A
(Scotland): Home Int 1968 -69; Eur T Ch 1969. (GB): v America 1969

Brooks, CJ
(Scotland): Home Int 1984 -85. (GB): v Europe 1986

Brotherton, IR
(Scotland): Home Int 1984 -85

Brough, S
(England): Home Int 1952 -55 -59 -60; v France 1952 -60. (GB): v Europe 1960

Brown, CT
(Wales): Home Int 1970 -71 -72 -73 -74 -75 -77 -78 -80; Eur T Ch 1973; v Denmark 1977 -80; v Ireland 1979; v Switzerland, Spain 1980

Brown, D
(Wales): v Ireland 1923 -30 -31; v England 1925; v Scotland 1931

Brown, JC
(Ireland): Home Int 1933 -34 -35 -36 -37 -38 -48 -52 -53

Brownlow, Hon WGE
(GB): v America 1926

Bruen, J
(Ireland): Home Int 1937 -38 -49 -50. (GB): v America 1938 -49 -51

Bucher, AM
(Scotland): Home Int 1954 -55 -56; v Scandinavia 1956

Buckley, JA
(Wales): Home Int 1967 -68 -69 -76 -77 -78; Eur T Ch 1967 -69; v Denmark 1976 -77. (GB): v America 1979

Burch, N
(England): Home Int 1974

Burgess, MJ
(England): Home Int 1963 -64 -67; Eur T Ch 1967

Burke, J
(Ireland): v England 1929 -30 -31; v Wales 1929 -30 -31; v Scotland 1930 -31; Home Int 1932 -33 -34 -35 -36 -37 -38 -47 -48 -49. (GB): v America 1932

Burns, M
(Ireland): Home Int 1973 -75 -83

Burnside, J
(Scotland): Home Int 1956 -57

Burrell, TM
(Scotland): v England 1924

Bussell, AF
(Scotland): Home Int 1956 -57 -58 -61; v Scandinavia 1956 -60. (GB): v America 1957; v Europe 1956 -62

Butterworth, JR
(England): v France 1954

Cairnes, HM
(Ireland): v Wales 1913 -25; v England 1904; v Scotland 1904 -27

Caldwell, I
(England): Home Int 1950 -51 -52 -53 -54 -55 -56 -57 -58 -59 -61; v France 1950. (GB): v America 1951 -55

Calvert, M
(Wales): Home Int 1983 -84 -86

Cameron, D
(Scotland): Home Int 1938 -51

Campbell, Bart, Sir Guy C
(Scotland): v England 1909 -10 -11

Campbell, HM
(Scotland): Home Int 1962 -64 -68; v Scandinavia 1962; v Australia 1964; Eur T Ch 1965. (GB): v Europe 1964

Campbell, JGS
(Scotland): Home Int 1947 -48

Campbell, W
(Scotland): v Ireland 1927 -28 -29 -30 -31; v England 1928 -29 -30 -31; v Wales 1931; Home Int 1933 -34 -35 -36. (GB): v America 1930

Cannon, JHS
(England): v Ireland/Wales 1925

Cannon, JM
(Scotland): Home Int 1969; v Spain 1974

Carman, A
(England): v Scotland 1979; Home Int 1980

Carr, FC
(England): v Scotland 1911

Carr, JB
(Ireland): Home Int 1947 -48 -49 -50 -51 -52 -53 -54 -55 -56 -57 -58 -59 -60 -61 -62 -63 -64 -65 -66 -67 -68 -69; Eur T Ch 1965 -67 -69. (GB): v America 1947 -49 -51 -53 -55 -57 -59 -61 -63 -65 (Captain) -67 (Captain); v Europe 1954 -56 -64 -66 -68; in World Team Ch 1958 -60

Carr, JJ
(Ireland): Home Int 1981 -82 -83

Carr, JP
(Wales): v Ireland 1913

Carr, JR
(Ireland): v Wales 1930 -31; v England 1931; Home Int 193

Carr, R
(Ireland): Home Int 1970 -71; Eur T Ch 1971. (GB): v America 1971

Carrgill, PM
(England): Home Int 1978

Carrick, DG
(Scotland): Home Int 1981 -82 -83 -84 -85 -86. (GB): v America 1983; v Europe 1986

Carroll, CA
(Ireland): v Wales 1924

Carroll, JP
(Ireland): Home Int 1948 -49 -50 -51 -62

Carroll, W
(Ireland): v Wales 1913 -23 -24 -25; v England 1925; v Scotland 1929; Home Int 1932

Carslaw, IA
(Scotland): Home Int 1976 -77 -78 -80 -81; Eur T Ch 1977 -79; v England 1979; v Italy 1979; v Spain 1977; v Belgium 1978; v France 1978. (GB): v Europe 1978; v America 1979

Cashell, BG
(Ireland): Home Int 1978; v France, West Germany, Sweden 1978

Castle, H
(England): v Scotland 1903 -04

Cater, JR
(Scotland): Home Int 1952 -53 -54 -55 -56. (GB): v America 1955

Caul, P
(Ireland): Home Int 1968 -69 -71 -72 -73 -74 -75

Caven, J
(Scotland): v England 1926. (GB): v America 1922

Chapman, BHG
(England): Home Int 1961 -62. (GB): v America 1961; v Europe 1962

Chapman, JA
(Wales): v Ireland 1923 -29 -30 -31; v Scotland 1931; v England 1925

Chapman, R
(Wales): v Ireland 1929; Home Int 1932 -34 -35 -36

Chapman, R
(England): v Scotland 1979; Home Int 1980 -81; Eur T Ch 1981. (GB): v Europe 1980; v America 1981

Charles, WB
(Wales): v Ireland 1924

Chillas, D
(Scotland): Home Int 1971

Christmas, MJ
(England): Home Int 1960 -61 -62 -63 -64. (GB): v America 1961 -63; v Europe 1962 -64; in World Team Ch 1962

Clark, CA
(England): Home Int 1964. (GB): v Europe 1964; v America 1965

Clark, GJ
(England): Home Int 1961 -64 -66 -67 -68 -71. (GB): v Europe 1964 -66; v America 1965

Clark, HK
(England): Home Int 1973. (GB): v America 1973

Clark, MD
(Wales): v Ireland 1947

Clay, G
(Wales): Home Int 1962

Cleary, T
(Ireland): Home Int 1976 -77 -78 -82 -83 -84 -85 -86; v Wales 1979; v France, West Germany, Sweden 1976

Clement, G
(Wales): v Ireland 1980

Cochran, JS
(Scotland): Home Int 1966

Colt, HS
(England): v Scotland 1908

Cook, JH
(England): Home Int 1969

Corridan, T
(Ireland): Home Int 1983 -84

Corcoran, DK
(Ireland): Home Int 1972 -73; Eur T Ch 1973

Cosh, GB
(Scotland): Home Int 1964 -65 -66 -67 -68 -69; Eur T Ch 1965 -69. (GB): v America 1965; v Europe 1966 -68; in Com Tnmt 1967; in World Team Ch 1966 -68

Coulter, JG
(Wales): Home Int 1951 -52

Coutts, FJ
(Scotland): Home Int 1980 -81 -82; Eur T Ch 1981; v France 1981 -82

Cox, S
(Wales): Home Int 1970 -71 -72 -73 -74; Eur T Ch 1971 -73

Crabbe, JL
(Ireland): v Wales 1925; v Scotland 1927 -28

Craddock, T
(Ireland): Home Int 1955 -56 -57 -58 -59 -60 -67 -68 -69 -70; Eur T Ch 1971. (GB): v America 1967 -69

Craigan, RM
(Ireland): Home Int 1963 -64

Crawley, LG
(England): v Ireland 1931; v Scotland 1931; Home Int 1932 -33 -34 -36 -37 -38 -47 -48 -49 -54 -55; v France 1936 -37 -38 -49. (GB): v America 1932 -34 -38 -47

Critchley, B
(England): Home Int 1962 -69 -70; Eur T Ch 1969. (GB): v America 1969; v Europe 1970

Crosbie, GF
(Ireland): Home Int 1953 -55 -56 -57

Crowley, M
(Ireland): v England 1928 -29 -30 -31; v Wales 1929 -31; v Scotland 1929 -30 -31; Home Int 1932

Cuddihy, J
(Scotland): Home Int 1977

Curry, DH
(England): Home Int 1984 -86. (GB): v Europe 1986

Dalgleish, CR
(Scotland): Home Int 1981 -82 -83; v France 1982; Eur T Ch 1981. (GB): v America 1981

Darwin, B
(England): v Scotland 1902 -04 -05 -08 -09 -10 -23 -24. (GB): v America 1922

Davies, EN
(Wales): Home Int 1959 -60 -61 -62 -63 -64 -65 -66 -67 -68 -69 -70 -71 -72 -73 -74; Eur T Ch 1969 -71 -73

Davies, JC
(England): Home Int 1969 -71 -72 -73 -74 -78; Eur T Ch 1973 -75 -77. (GB): v Europe 1972 -74 -76 -78; v America 1973 -75 -77 -79; in World Team Ch 1974 -76

Davies, FE
(Ireland): v Wales 1923

Davies, G
(Wales): v Denmark 1977; Home Int 1981 -82 -83

Davies, HE
(Wales): Home Int 1933 -34 -36

Davies, M
(England): Home Int 1984 -85

Davies, TJ
(Wales): Home Int 1954 -55 -56 -57 -58 -59 -60

Dawson, JE
(Scotland): v Ireland 1927 -29 -30 -31; v England 1930 -31; v Wales 1931; Home Int 1932 -33 -34 -37

Dawson, M
(Scotland): Home Int 1963 -65 -66

Dawson, P
(England): Home Int 1969

Deboys, A
(Scotland): Home Int 1956 -59 -60; v Scandinavia 1960

Deeble, P
(England): Home Int 1975 -76 -77 -78 -80 -81 -83 -84; v Scotland 1979; Eur T Ch 1979 -81. (GB): v America 1977 -81; v Europe 1978; v France 1982; in Colombian Int 1978

Deighton, FWG
(Scotland): Home Int 1950 -52 -53 -56 -57 -58 -59 -60. (GB): v America 1951 -57; v South Africa 1952; in Com Tnmt 1954 -59

Denholm, RB
(Scotland): v Ireland 1929 -31; v Wales 1931; v England 1931; Home Int 1932 -33 -34 -35

Dewar, FG
(Scotland): Home Int 1952 -53 -55

Dick, CE
(Scotland): v England 1902 -03 -04 -05 -09 -12

Dickson, HM
(Scotland): v Ireland 1929 -31

Dickson, JR
(Ireland): Eur T Ch 1977; Home Int 1980

Disley, A
(Wales): Home Int 1976 -77 -78; v Denmark 1977; v Ireland 1979

Dodd, SC
(Wales): Home Int 1985

Donellan, B
(Ireland): Home Int 1952

Dowie, A
(Scotland): Home Int 1949

Downes, P
(England): Home Int 1976 -77 -78 -80 -81 -82; Eur T Ch 1977 -79 -81. (GB): v Europe 1980

Downie, JJ
(England): Home Int 1974

Draper, JW
(Scotland): Home Int 1954

Drew, NV
(Ireland): Home Int 1952 -53. (GB): v America 1953

Duffy, I
(Wales): Home Int 1975

Duncan, AA
(Wales): Home Int 1933 -34 -36 -38 -47 -48 -49 -50 -51 -52 -53 -54 -55 -56 -57 -58 -59. (GB): v America (Captain) 1953

Duncan, GT
(Wales): Home Int 1952 -53 -54 -55 -56 -57 -58

Duncan, J, Jr
(Wales): v Ireland 1913

Duncan, J
(Ireland): Home Int 1959 -60 -61

Dunn, NW
(England): v Ireland 1928

Dunn, P
(Wales): Home Int 1957 -58 -59 -60 -61 -62 -63 -65 -66

Dunne, E
(Ireland): Home Int 1973 -74 -76 -77; v Wales 1979; Eur T Ch 1975

Durrant, RA
(England): Home Int 1967; Eur T Ch 1967

Dykes, JM
(Scotland): Home Int 1934 -35 -36 -48 -49 -51. (GB): v America 1936

Easingwood, S
(Scotland): Home Int 1986

Eaves, CH
(Wales): Home Int 1935-36 -38 -47 -48 -49

Edwards, B
(Ireland): Home Int 1961 -62 -64 -65 -66 -67 -68 -69 -73

Edwards, M
(Ireland): Home Int 1956 -57 -58 -60 -61 -62

Edwards, TH
(Wales): Home Int 1947

Egan, TW
(Ireland): Home Int 1952 -53 -59 -60 -62 -67 -68; Eur T Ch 1967 -69

Eggo, R
(England): Home Int 1986

Elliott, C
(Scotland): Home Int 1982

Elliott, IA
(Ireland): Home Int 1975 -77 -78; Eur T Ch 1975; v France, West Germany, Sweden 1978

Ellis, HC
(England): v Scotland 1902 -12

Ellison, TF
(England): v Scotland 1922 -25 -26 -27

Emerson, T
(Wales): Home Int 1932

Emery, G
(Wales): v Ireland 1925; Home Int 1933 -36 -38

Evans, AD
(Wales): v Scotland 1931 -35; v Ireland 1931; Home Int 1932 -33 -34 -35 -38 -47 -49 -50 -51 -52 -53 -54 -55 -56 -61

Evans, Duncan
(Wales): Home Int 1978 -80 -81; v Ireland 1979; Eur T Ch 1981. (GB): v Europe 1980; v America 1981

Evans, G
(England): Home Int 1961

Evans, HJ
(Wales): Home Int 1976 -77 -78 -80 -81 -84 -85; v France 1976; v Denmark 1977 -80; v Ireland 1979; Eur T Ch 1979 -81; v Switzerland, Spain 1980

Evans, M Gear
(Wales): v Ireland 1930 -31; v Scotland 1931

Ewing, RC
(Ireland): Home Int 1934 -35 -36 -37 -38 -47 -48 -49 -50 -51 -53 -54 -55 -56 -57 -58. (GB): v America 1936 -38 -47 -49 -51 -55

Eyles, GR
(England): Home Int 1974 -75; Eur T Ch 1975. (GB): v America 1975; v Europe 1974; in World Team Ch 1974

Flockhart, AS
(Scotland): Home Int 1948 -49

Fogarty, GN
(Ireland): Home Int 1956 -58 -63 -64 -67

Fogg, HN
(England): Home Int 1933

Forest, J de (now Count J de Bendern)
(England): v Ireland 1931; v Scotland 1931. (GB): v America 1932

Foster, MF
(England): Home Int 1973

Foster, R
(England): Home Int 1963 -64 -66 -67 -68 -69 -70 -71 -72; Eur T Ch 1967 -69 -71 -73. (GB): v Europe 1964 -66 -68 -70; v America 1965 -67 -69 -71 -73 -79 (Captain) -81 (Captain); in Com Tnmt 1967 -71; in World Team Ch 1964 -70

Fowler, WH
(England): v Scotland 1903 -04 -05

Fox, SJ
(England): Home Int 1956 -57 -58

Frame, DW
(England): Home Int 1958 -59 -60 -61 -62 -63. (GB): v America 1961

Francis, F
(England): Home Int 1936; v France 1935 -36

Frazier, K
(England): Home Int 1938

Froggatt, P
(Ireland): Home Int 1957

Fry, SH
(England): v Scotland 1902 -03 -04 -05 -06 -07 -09

Fairchild, CEL
(Wales): v Ireland 1923; v England 1925

Fairchild, LJ
(Wales): v Ireland 1924

Fairlie, WE
(Scotland): v England 1912

Faldo, N
(England): Home Int 1975. (GB): in Com Tnmt 1975

Farmer, JC
(Scotland): Home Int 1970

Ferguson, M
(Ireland): Home Int 1952

Ferguson, WJ
(Ireland): Home Int 1952 -54 -55 -58 -59 -61

Fergusson, S Mure
(Scotland): v England 1902 -03 -04

Ffrench, WF
(Ireland): v Scotland 1929; Home Int 1932

Fiddian, EW
(England): v Scotland 1929 -30 -31; v Ireland 1929 -30 -31; Home Int 1932 -33 -34 -35; v France 1934. (GB): v America 1932 -34

Fitzgibbon, JF
(Ireland): Home Int 1955 -56 -57

Fitzsimmons, J
(Ireland): Home Int 1938 -47 -48

Flaherty, JA
(Ireland): Home Int 1934 -35 -36 -37

Flaherty, PD
(Ireland): Home Int 1967; Eur T Ch 1967 -69

Fleury, RA
(Ireland): Home Int 1974

Gairdner, JR
(Scotland): v England 1902

Gallacher, BJ
(Scotland): Home Int 1967

Galloway, RF
(Scotland): Home Int 1957 -58 -59; v Scandinavia 1958

Gannon, M
(Ireland): Home Int 1973 -74 -77 -78 -80 -81 -83 -84; v France, West Germany, Sweden 1978 -80; Eur T Ch 1979 -81. (GB): v Europe 1974 -78

Garner, PF
(England): Home Int 1977 -78 -80; v Scotland 1979

Garnet, LG
(England): v France 1934. (GB): v Australia 1934

Garson, R
(Scotland): v Ireland 1928 -29

Gent, J
(England): v Ireland 1930; Home Int 1938

Gibb, C
(Scotland): v England 1927; v Ireland 1928

Gibson, WC
(Scotland): Home Int 1950 -51

Gilford, CF
(Wales): Home Int 1963 -64 -65 -66 -67

Gilford, D
(England): Home Int 1983 -84 -85. (GB): v America 1985; v Europe 1986

Gill, WJ
(Ireland): v Wales 1931; Home Int 1932 -33 -34 -35 -36 -37

Gillies, HD
(England): v Scotland 1908 -25 -26 -27

Girvan, P
(Scotland): Home Int 1986

Glossop, R
(Wales): Home Int 1937 -38 -47; v Scotland 1935
Glover, J
(Ireland): Home Int 1951 -52 -53 -55 -59 -60 -70
Godwin, G
(England): Home Int 1976 -77 -78 -80 -81; v Scotland 1979; v France 1982; Eur T Ch 1979 -81. (GB): v America 1979 -81
Graham, AJ
(Scotland): v England 1925
Graham, J
(Scotland): v England 1902 -03 -04 -05 -06 -07 -08 -09 -10 -11
Graham, JSS
(Ireland): Home Int 1938 -50 -51
Gray, CD
(England): Home Int 1932
Green, CW
(Scotland): Home Int 1961 -62 -63 -64 -65 -67 -68 -69 -70 -71 -72 -73 -74 -75 -76 -77 -78; Eur T Ch 1965 -67 -69 -71 -73 -75 -77 -79; v Scandinavia 1962; v Belgium 1973 -75 -77 -78; v Spain 1977; v Italy 1979; v England 1979. (GB): v Europe 1962 -66 -68 -70 -72 -74 -76; v America 1963 -69 -71 -73 -75 -83 (Captain); in Com Tnmt 1971; in World Team Ch 1970 -72
Green, HB
(England): v Scotland 1979
Green, PO
(England): Home Int 1961 -62 -63. (GB): in Com Tnmt 1963
Greene, R
(Ireland): Home Int 1933
Greig, DG
(Scotland): Home Int 1972 -73 -75. (GB): in Com Tnmt 1975
Greig, K
(Scotland): Home Int 1933
Griffiths, HGB
(Wales): v Ireland 1923 -24 -25
Griffiths, HS
(Wales) v England 1958
Griffiths, JA
(Wales): Home Int 1933
Guild, WJ
(Scotland): v England 1925 -27 -28; v Ireland 1927 -28

Hales, JP
(Wales): v Scotland 1963
Hall, AH
(Scotland): Home Int 1962 -66 -69
Hall, D
(Wales): Home Int 1932 -37
Hall, K
(Wales): Home Int 1955 -59
Hambro, AV
(England): v Scotland 1905 -08 -09 -10 -22
Hamilton, CJ
(Wales): v Ireland 1913
Hamilton, ED
(Scotland): Home Int 1936 -37 -38
Hamer, S
(England): Home Int 1983 -84
Hanway, M
(Ireland): Home Int 1971 -74
Hardman, RH
(England): v Scotland 1927 -28. (GB): v America 1928
Hare, WCD
(Scotland): Home Int 1953
Harrington, J
(Ireland): Home Int 1960 -61 -74 -75 -76; Eur T Ch 1975; v Wales 1979
Harris, IR
(Scotland): Home Int 1955 -56 -58 -59
Harris, R
(Scotland): v England 1905 -08 -10 -11 -12 -22 -23 -24 -25 -26 -27 -28. (GB): v America 1922 (Captain) -23 (Captain) -26 (Captain)
Harrison, JW
Home Int 1937 -50
Hartley, RW
(England): v Scotland 1926 -27 -28 -29 -30 -31; v Ireland 1928 -29 -30 -31; Home Int 1933 -34 -35. (GB): v America 1930 -32
Hartley, WL
(England): v Ireland/Wales 1925; v Scotland 1927 -31; v Ireland 1928 -31; Home Int 1932 -33; v France 1935. (GB): v America 1932
Hassall, JE
(England): v Scotland 1923; v Ireland/Wales 1925
Hastings, JL
(Scotland): Home Int 1957 -58; v Scandinavia 1958
Hawksworth, J
(England): Home Int 1984 -85. (GB): v America 1985
Hay, G
(Scotland): v England 1979; Home Int 1980; v Belgium 1980; v France 1980. (GB): v Europe 1980
Hay, J
(Scotland): Home Int 1972
Hayes, JA
(Ireland): Home Int 1977
Hayward, CH
(England): v Scotland 1925; v Ireland 1928
Healy, TM
(Ireland): v Scotland 1931; v England 1931
Heather, D
(Ireland): Home Int 1976; v France, West Germany, Sweden 1976
Hedges, PJ
(England): Home Int 1970 -73 -74 -75 -76 -77 -78 -82 -83; Eur T Ch 1973 -75 -77. (GB): v America 1973 -75; v Europe 1974 -76; in World Team Ch 1974
Hegarty, J
(Ireland): Home Int 1975
Hegarty, TD
(Ireland): Home Int 1957
Helm, AGB
(England): Home Int 1948
Henderson, J
(Ireland): v Wales 1923
Henderson, N
(Scotland): Home Int 1963 -64
Henriques, GLQ
(England): v Ireland 1930
Herlihy, B
(Ireland): Home Int 1950
Herne, KTC
(Wales): v Ireland 1913
Heverin, AJ
(Ireland): Home Int 1978; v France, West Germany, Sweden 1978
Hezlet, CO
(Ireland): v Wales 1923 -25 -27 -29 -31; v Scotland 1927 -28 -29 -30 -31; v England 1929 -30 -31. (GB): v America 1924 -26 -28; v South Africa 1927
Higgins, L
(Ireland): Home Int 1968 -70 -71
Hill, GA
(England): Home Int 1936 -37. (GB): v America 1936 -55 (Captain)

Hilton, HH
(England): v Scotland 1902 -03 -04 -05 -06 -07 -09 -10 -11 -12

Hoad, PGJ
(England): Home Int 1978; v Scotland 1979

Hodgson, C
(England): v Scotland 1924

Hoey, TBC
(Ireland): Home Int 1970 -71 -72 -73 -77 -84; Eur T Ch 1971 -77

Hogan, P
(Ireland): Home Int 1985 -86

Holderness, Sir EWE
(England): v Scotland 1922 -23 -24 -25 -26 -28. (GB): v America 1921 -23 -26 -30

Holmes, AW
(England): Home Int 1962

Homer, TWB
(England): Home Int 1972 -73; Eur T Ch 1973. (GB): v America 1973; v Europe 1972; in World Team Ch 1972

Homewood, G
(England): Home Int 1985

Hooman, CVL
(England): v Scotland 1910 -22. (GB): v America 1922 -23

Hope, WL
(Scotland): v England 1923 -25 -26 -27 -28 -29. (GB): v America 1923 -24 -28

Horne, A
(Scotland): Home Int 1971

Hosie, JR
(Scotland): Home Int 1936

Howard, DB
(Scotland) : v England 1979; Home Int 1980 -81 -82 -83; v Belgium 1980; v France 1980 -81; Eur T Ch 1981. (GB): v Europe 1980

Howell, HR
(Wales): v Ireland 1923 -24 -25 -29 -30 -31; v England 1925; v Scotland 1931; Home Int 1932 -34 -35 -36 -37 -38 -47

Howell, H Logan
(Wales): v Ireland 1925

Huddy, G
(England): Home Int 1960 -61 -62. (GB): v America 1961

Huggan, J
(Scotland): Home Int 1981 -82 -83 -84; v France 1982; Eur T Ch 1981

Hughes, I
(Wales): Home Int 1954 -55 -56

Hulme, WJ
(Ireland): Home Int 1955 -56 -57

Humphrey, JG
(Wales): v Ireland 1925

Humphreys, AR
(Ireland): v England 1957

Humphreys, DI
(Wales): Home Int 1972

Humphreys, W
(England): Home Int 1970 -71; Eur T Ch 1971. (GB): v Europe 1970; v America 1971

Hunter, NM
(Scotland): v England 1903 -12

Hunter, WI
(Scotland): v England 1922

Hutcheon, I
(Scotland): Home Int 1971 -72 -73 -74 -75 -76 -77 -78 -80; v Belgium 1973 -75 -77 -78 -80; v Spain 1977; v France 1978 -80 -81; v Italy 1979; Eur T Ch 1973 -75 -77 -79 -81. (GB): v Europe 1974 -76; v America 1975 -77 -79 -81; in World Team Ch 1974 -76 -80; in Com Tnmt 1975; in Dominican Int 1973; in Colombian Int 1975

Hutchings, C
(England): v Scotland 1902

Hutchinson, HG
(England): v Scotland 1902 -03 -04 -06 -07 -09

Hutchison, CK
(Scotland): v England 1904 -05 -06 -07 -08 -09 -10 -11 -12

Hyde, GE
(England): Home Int 1967 -68

Illingworth, G
(England): v Scotland 1929; v France 1937

Inglis, MJ
(England): Home Int 1977

Isitt, GH
(Wales): v Ireland 1923

Jack, RR
(Scotland): Home Int 1950 -51 -54 -55 -56 -57 -58 -59 -61; v Scandinavia 1958. (GB): v America 1957 -59; v Europe 1956; in World Team Ch 1958; in Com Tnmt 1959

Jack, WS
(Scotland): Home Int 1955

Jacob, NE
(Wales): Home Int 1932 -33 -34 -35 -36

James, D
(Scotland): Home Int 1985

James, M
(England): Home Int 1974 -75; Eur T Ch 1975 (GB): v America 1975

James, RD
(England): Home Int 1974 -75

Jameson, JF
(Ireland): v Wales 1913 -24

Jamieson, A, Jr
(Scotland): v England 1927 -28 -31; v Ireland 1928 -31; v Wales 1931; Home Int 1932 -33 -36 -37. (GB): v America 1926

Jamieson, D
(Scotland): Home Int 1980

Jenkins, JLC
(Scotland): v England 1908 -12 -22 -24 -26 -28; v Ireland 1928. (GB): v America 1921

Jermine, JG
(Wales): Home Int 1972 -73 -74 -75 -76 -82; Eur T Ch 1975 -77; v France 1975

Jobson, RH
(England): v Ireland 1928

Johnson TWG
(Ireland): v England 1929

Johnston, JW
(Scotland): Home Int 1970 -71

Jones, DK
(Wales): Home Int 1973

Jones, EO
(Wales): Home Int 1983 -85 -86

Jones, JG Parry
(Wales): Home Int 1959 -60

Jones, JL
(Wales): Home Int 1933 -34 -36

Jones, JR
(Wales): Home Int 1970 -72 -73 -77 -78 -80 -81 -82 -83 -84 -85; Eur T Ch 1973 -79 -81; v Denmark 1976 -80; v Ireland 1979; v Switzerland, Spain 1980; v Ireland 1979

Jones, JW
(England): Home Int 1948 -49 -50 -51 -52 -54 -55

Jones, MA
(Wales): Home Int 1947 -48 -49 -50 -51 -53 -54 -57

Jones, Malcolm F
(Wales): Home Int 1933

Jones, SP
(Wales): Home Int 1981 -82 -83 -84 -85 -86

Kane, RM
(Ireland): Home Int 1967 -68 -71 -72 -74 -78; Eur T Ch 1971 -79; v Wales 1979. (GB): v Europe 1974

Kelleher, WA
(Ireland): Home Int 1962

Kelley, MJ
(England): Home Int 1974 -75 -76 -77 -78 -80 -81 -82; v France 1982; Eur T Ch 1977 -79. (GB): v America 1977 -79; v Europe 1976 -78; in World Team Ch 1976; in Colombian Int 1978

Kelley, PD
(England): Home Int 1965 -66 -68

Kelly, NS
(Ireland): Home Int 1966

Keppler, SD
(England): Home Int 1982 -83; v France 1982. (GB): v America 1983

Kilduff, AJ
(Ireland): v Scotland 1928

Killey, GC
(Scotland): v Ireland 1928

King, M
(England): Home Int 1969 -70 -71 -72 -73; Eur T Ch 1971 -73. (GB): v America 1969 -73; v Europe 1970 -72; in Com Tnmt 1971

Kissock, B
(Ireland): Home Int 1961 -62 -74 -76; v France, West Germany, Sweden 1978

Kitchin, JE
(England): v France 1949

Knight, B
(Wales): Home Int 1986

Knipe, RG
(Wales): Home Int 1953 -54 -55 -56

Knowles, WR
(Wales): v England 1948

Kyle, AT
(Scotland): Home Int 1938 -47 -49 -50 -51 -52 -53. (GB): v America 1938 -47 -51; v South Africa 1952

Kyle, D
(Scotland): v England 1924 -30. (GB): v America 1924

Kyle, EP
(Scotland): v England 1925

Laidlay, JE
(Scotland): v England 1902 -03 -04 -05 -06 -07 -08 -09 -10 -11

Lake, AD
(Wales): Home Int 1958

Lang, JA
(Scotland): v England 1929 -31; v Ireland 1929 -30 -31; v Wales 1931. (GB): v America 1930

Langley, JDA
(England): Home Int 1950 -51 -52 -53; v France 1950. (GB): v America 1936 -51 -53

Langmead, J
(England): Home Int 1986

Lassen, EA
(England): v Scotland 1909 -10 -11 -12

Last, CN
(Wales): Home Int 1975

Laurence, C
(England): Home Int 1983 -84 -85

Lawrie, CD
(Scotland): Home Int 1949 -50 -55 -56 -57 -58; v Scandinavia 1958. (GB): v South Africa 1952; v America 1961 (Captain) -63 (Captain)

Layton, EN
(England): v Scotland 1922 -23 -26; v Ireland/Wales 1925

Lee, IGF
(Scotland): Home Int 1958 -59 -60 -61 -62; v Scandinavia 1960

Lee, M
(England): Home Int 1950

Lee, MG
(England): Home Int 1965

Lehane, N
(Ireland): Home Int 1976; v France, West Germany, Sweden 1976

Lewis, DR
(Wales): v Ireland 1925 -29 -30 -31; v Scotland; Home Int 1932 -34

Lewis, DH
(Wales): Home Int 1935 -36 -37 -38

Lewis, ME
(England): Home Int 1980 -81 -82; v France 1982. (GB): v America 1983

Lewis, R Cofe
(Wales): v Ireland 1925

Leyden, PJ
(Ireland): Home Int 1953 -55 -56 -57 -59

Lincoln, AC
(England): v Scotland 1907

Lindsay, J
(Scotland): Home Int 1933 -34 -35 -36

Lloyd, HM
(Wales): v Ireland 1913

Lloyd, RM de
(Wales): v Scotland 1931; v Ireland 1931; Home Int 1932 -33 -34 -35 -36 -37 -38 -47 -48

Llyr, A
(Wales): Home Int 1984 -85

Lockhart, G
(Scotland): v England 1911 -12

Lockley, AE
(Wales): Home Int 1956 -57 -58 -62

Logan, GW
(England): Home Int 1973

Long, D
(Ireland): Home Int 1973 -74 -80 -81 -82 -83 -84; v Wales 1979; Eur T Ch 1979

Low, AJ
(Scotland): Home Int 1964 -65; Eur T Ch 1965

Low, JL
(Scotland): v England 1904

Lowe, A
(Ireland): v Wales 1924; v England 1925 -28; v Scotland 1927 -28

Lucas, PB
(England): Home Int 1936 -48 -49; v France 1936. (GB): v America 1936 -47 -49 (Captain)

Lunt, MSR
(England): Home Int 1956 -57 -58 -59 -60 -62 -63 -64 -66. (GB): v America 1959 -61 -63 -65; v Europe 1964; in Com Tnmt 1963; in World Team Ch 1964

Lunt, S
(England): Home Int 1932 -33 -34 -35; v France 1934 -35 -39

Lygate, M
(Scotland): Home Int 1970 -75; Eur T Ch 1971

Lyle, AWB
(England): Home Int 1975 -76 -77; Eur T Ch 1977. (GB): v America 1977; in Com Tnmt 1975; v Europe 1976

Lyon, JS
(England): Home Int 1937 -38

Lyons, P
(Ireland): Home Int 1986

McAllister, SD
(Scotland): Home Int 1983

Macara, MA
(Wales): Home Int 1983-84-85

McArthur, W
(Scotland): Home Int 1952 -54

McBeath, J
(Scotland): Home Int 1964

McBride, D
(Scotland): Home Int 1932

McCallum, AR
(Scotland): v England 1929. (GB): v America 1928

McCarrol, F
(Ireland): Home Int 1968 -69

McCart, DM
(Scotland): Home Int 1977; v Belgium 1978.

McCarthy, L
(Ireland): Home Int 1953 -54 -55 -56

McConnell, FP
(Ireland): v Wales 1929 -30 -31; v England 1929 -30 -31; v Scotland 1930 -31; Home Int 1934

McConnell, RM
(Ireland): v Wales 1924 -25 -29 -30 -31; v England 1925 -28 -29 -30 -31; v Scotland 1927 -28 -29 -31; Home Int 1934 -35 -36 -37

McConnell, WG
(Ireland): v England 1925

McCormack, JD
(Ireland): v Wales 1913 -24; v England 1928; Home Int 1932 -33 -34 -35 -36 -37

McCrea, WE
(Ireland): Home Int 1965 -66 -67; Eur T Ch 1965

McCready, SM
(Ireland): Home Int 1947 -49 -50 -52 -54. (GB): v America 1949 -51

McDaid, B
(Ireland): v Wales 1979

MacDonald, GK
(Scotland): Home Int 1978 -81 -82; v England 1979; v France 1981 -82

McDonald, H
(Scotland): Home Int 1970

Macdonald, JS
(Scotland): Home Int 1969 -70 -71 -72; v Belgium 1973; Eur T Ch 1971. (GB): v Europe 1970; v America 1971

McEvoy, P
(England): Home Int 1976 -77 -78 -80 -81 -83 -84 -85 -86; v Scotland 1979; v France 1982; Eur T Ch 1977 -79 -81. (GB): v America 1977 -79 -81 -85; v Europe 1978 -80 -86; in World Team Ch 1978 -80

Macfarlane, CB
(Scotland): v England 1912

McGimpsey, G
(Ireland): Home Int 1978 -80 -81 -82 -83 -84 -85 -86; v Wales 1979; Eur T Ch 1981. (GB): v America 1985; v Europe 1986

Macgregor, A
(Scotland): v Scandinavia 1956

Macgregor, G
(Scotland): Home Int 1969 -70 -71 -72 -73 -74 -75 -76 -80 -81 -82 -83 -84 -85 -86; v Belgium 1973 -75 -80; v England 1979; Eur T Ch 1971 -73 -75 -81. (GB): v Europe 1970 -74; v America 1971 -75 -83 -85; in Com Tnmt 1971 -75; v France 1981 -82

MacGregor, RC
(Scotland): Home Int 1951 -52 -53 -54. (GB): v America 1953

McHenry, J
(Ireland): Home Int 1985 -86

McInally, H
(Scotland): Home Int 1937 -47 -48

McInally, RH
(Ireland): Home Int 1949 -51

Macintosh, KW
(Scotland): v England 1979; Home Int 1980; v France 1980; v Belgium 1980. (GB): v Europe 1980

McKay, G
(Scotland): Home Int 1969

McKay, JR
(Scotland): Home Int 1950 -51 -52 -54

McKellar, PJ
(Scotland): Home Int 1976 -77 -78; v Belgium 1978; v France 1978; v England 1979. (GB): v America 1977; v Europe 1978

Mackenzie, F
(Scotland): v England 1902 -03

Mackenzie, WW
(Scotland): v England 1923 -26 -27 -29; v Ireland 1930. (GB): v America 1922 -23

Mackeown, HN
(Ireland): Home Int 1973; Eur T Ch 1973

Mackie, GW
(Scotland): Home Int 1948 -50

McKinna, RA
(Scotland): Home Int 1938

McKinlay, SL
(Scotland): v England 1929 -30 -31; v Ireland 1930; v Wales 1931; Home Int 1932 -33 -35 -37 -47. (GB): v America 1934

McKinnon, A
(Scotland): Home Int 1947 -52

McLean, D
(Wales): Home Int 1968 -69 -70 -71 -72 -73 -74 -75 -76 -77 -78 -80 -81 -82 -83 -85 -86; Eur T Ch 1975 -77 -79 -81; v France 1975 -76; v Denmark 1976 -80; v Ireland 1979; v Switzerland, Spain 1980

McLean, J
(Scotland): Home Int 1932 -33 -34 -35 -36. (GB): v America 1934 -36; v Australia 1934

McLeod, AE
(Scotland): Home Int 1937 -38

McLeod, WS
(Scotland): Home Int 1935 -37 -38 -47 -48 -49 -50 -51

McMenamin, E
(Ireland): Home Int 1981

McMullan, C
(Ireland): Home Int 1933 -34 -35

McNair, AA
(Scotland): v Ireland 1929

McNamara, L
(Ireland): Home Int 1977 -83 -84 -85 -86; Eur T Ch 1977

McRuvie, EA
(Scotland): v England 1929 -30 -31; v Ireland 1930 -31; v Wales 1931; Home Int 1932 -33 -34 -35 -36. (GB): v America 1932 -34

McTear, J
(Scotland): Home Int 1971

Madeley, JFD
(Ireland): Home Int 1959 -60 -61 -62 -63 -64. (GB): v Europe 1962; v America 1963

Mahon, RJ
(Ireland): Home Int 1938 -52 -54 -55

Maliphant, FR
(Wales): Home Int 1932

Malone, B
(Ireland): Home Int 1959 -64 -69 -71 -75; Eur T Ch 1971 -75

Manford, GC
(Scotland): v England 1922 -23

Manley, N
(Ireland): v Wales 1924; v England 1928; v Scotland 1927 -28

Mann, LS
(Scotland): Home Int 1982 -83. (GB): v America 1983

Marchbank, B
(Scotland): Home Int 1978; v Italy 1979; Eur T Ch 1979. (GB): v Europe 1976 -78; in World Team Ch 1978; v America 1979

Marks, GC
(England): Home Int 1963 -67 -68 -69 -70 -71 -74 -75 -82; Eur T Ch 1967 -69 -71 -75. (GB): v Europe 1968 -70; v America 1969 -71; in World Team Ch 1970; in Com Tnmt 1975; in Colombian Int 1975. Non playing capt v France 1982

Marren, JM
(Ireland): v Wales 1925

Marsh, DM
(England): Home Int 1956 -57 -58 -59 -60 -64 -66 -68 -69 -70 -71 -72; Eur T Ch 1971. (GB): v Europe 1958; v America 1959 -71 -73 (Captain) -75 (Captain)

Marshman, A
(Wales): Home Int 1952

Marston, CC
(Wales): v Ireland 1929 -30 -31; v Scotland 1931

Martin, DHR
(England): Home Int 1938; v France 1934 -49

Martin, GNC
(Ireland): v Wales 1923 -29; v Scotland 1928 -29 -30; v England 1929 -30. (GB): v America 1928

Martin, S
(Scotland): Home Int 1975 -76 -77; Eur T Ch 1977; v Belgium 1977; v Spain 1977. (GB): v America 1977; v Europe 1976; in World Team Ch 1976

Mason, SC
(England): Home Int 1973

Mathias-Thomas, FEL
(Wales): v Ireland 1924 -25

Matthews, RL
(Wales): Home Int 1935 -37

Maxwell, R
(Scotland): v England 1902 -03 -04 -05 -06 -07 -09 -10

Mayo, PM
(Wales): Home Int 1982. (GB): v America 1985

Meharg, W
(Ireland): Home Int 1957

Melia, TJ
(Wales): Home Int 1976 -77 -78 -80 -81 -82; v Ireland 1979; Eur T Ch 1977 -79; v Denmark 1976 -80; v Switzerland, Spain 1980

Mellin, GL
(England): v Scotland 1922

Melville, LM Balfour
(Scotland): v England 1902 -03

Melville, TE
(Scotland): Home Int 1974

Menzies, A
(Scotland): v England 1925

Micklem, GH
(England): Home Int 1947 -48 -49 -50 -51 -52 -53 -54 -55. (GB): v America 1947 -49 -53 -55 -57 (Captain) -59 (Captain); in World Team Ch 1958

Mill, JW
(Scotland): Home Int 1953 -54

Millensted, DJ
(England): Home Int 1966; Eur T Ch 1967. (GB): v America 1967; in Com Tnmt 1967

Miller, AC
(Scotland): Home Int 1954 -55

Miller, MJ
(Scotland): Home Int 1974 -75 -77 -78; v Belgium 1978; v France 1978

Milligan, J
(Scotland): Home Int 1986

Mills, ES
(Wales): Home Int 1957

Millward, EB
(England): Home Int 1950 -52 -53 -54 -55. (GB): v America 1949 -55

Milne, WTG
(Scotland): Home Int 1972 -73; Eur T Ch 1973; v Belgium 1973. (GB): v America 1973

Mitchell, A
(England): v Scotland 1910 -11 -12

Mitchell, CS
(England): Home Int 1975 -76 -78

Mitchell, FH
(England): v Scotland 1906 -07 -08

Mitchell, JWH
(Wales): Home Int 1964 -65 -66

Moffat, DM
(England): Home Int 1961 -63 -67; v France 1959 -60

Moir, A
(Scotland): Home Int 1983 -84

Montgomerie, CS
(Scotland): Home Int 1984 -85 -86. (GB): v America 1985; v Europe 1986

Montgomerie, JS
(Scotland): Home Int 1957; v Scandinavia 1958

Montmorency, RH de
(England): v Scotland 1908; v Wales/Ireland 1925; v South Africa 1927. (GB): v America 1921

Moody, JV
(West): Home Int 1947 -48 -49 -51 -56 -58 -59 -60 -61

Moody, PH
(England): Home Int 1971 -72. (GB): v Europe 1972

Moore, GJ
(Ireland): v England 1928; v Wales 1929

Morgan, JL
(Wales): 1948 -49 -50 -51 -52 -53 -54 -55 -56 -57 -58 -59 -60 -61 -62 -64 -68. (GB): v America 1951 -53 -55

Morris, FS
(Scotland): Home Int 1963

Morris, MF
(Ireland): Home Int 1978 -80 -82 -83 -84; v Wales 1979; Eur T Ch 1979; v France, West Germany, Sweden 1980

Morris, R
(Wales): Home Int 1983 -86

Morris, TS
(Wales): v Ireland 1924 -29 -30

Morrison, JH
(Scotland): v Scandinavia 1960

Morrison, JSF
(England): v Ireland 1930

Morrow, AJC
(Ireland): Home Int 1975 -83

Morrow, JM
(Wales): v Ireland 1979; Home Int 1980 -81; Eur T Ch 1979 -81; v Denmark, Switzerland, Spain 1980

Mosey, IJ
(England): Home Int 1971

Moss, AV
(Wales): Home Int 1965 -66 -68

Mouland, MG
(Wales): Home Int 1978 -81; v Ireland 1979; Eur T Ch 1979

Moxon, GA
(Wales): v Ireland 1929 -30

Mulcare, P
(Ireland): Home Int. 1968 -69 -70 -71 -72 -74 -78 -80; v France, West Germany, Sweden 1978 -80; Eur T Ch 1975 -79. (GB): v Europe 1972; v America 1975

Munn, E
(Ireland): v Wales 1913 -23 -24; v Scotland 1927

Munn, L
(Ireland): v Wales 1913 -23 -24; Home Int 1936 -37

Munro, RAG
(Scotland): Home Int 1960

Murdoch, D
(Scotland): Home Int 1964

Murphy, AR
(Scotland): Home Int 1961 -65 -67

Murphy, P
(Ireland): Home Int 1985 -86

Murray, GH
(Scotland): Home Int 1973 -74 -75 -76 -77 -78 -83; v Spain 1974 -77; v Belgium 1975 -77; Eur T Ch 1975 -77. (GB): v America 1977; v Europe 1978

Murray, SWT
(Scotland): Home Int 1959 -60 -61 -62 -63; v Scandinavia 1960. (GB): v Europe 1958 -62; v America 1963

Murray, WA
(Scotland): v England 1923 -24 -25 -26 -27. (GB): v America 1923 -24

Murray, WB
(Scotland): Home Int 1967 -68 -69; Eur T Ch 1969

Muscroft, R
(England): Home Int 1986

Neech, DG
(England): Home Int 1961

Neill, JM
(Ireland): Home Int 1938 -47 -48 -49

Neill, R
(Scotland): Home Int 1936

Nestor, JM
(Ireland): Home Int 1962 -63 -64

Nevin, V
(Ireland): Home Int 1960 -63 -65 -67 -69 -72; Eur T Ch 1967 -69 -73

Newey, AS
(England): Home Int 1932

Newman, JE
(Wales): Home Int 1932

Newton, H
(Wales): v Ireland 1929

Nicholson, J
(Ireland): Home Int 1932

Noon, GS
(Wales): Home Int 1935 -36 -37

O'Boyle, P
(Ireland): Eur T Ch 1977

O'Brien, MD
(Ireland): Home Int 1968 -69 -70 -71 -72 -75 -76 -77; Eur T Ch 1971; v France, West Germany, Sweden 1976

O'Connell, E
(Ireland): Home Int 1985

O'Connor, A
(Ireland): Home Int 1967 -70 -71 -72

O'Leary, JE
(Ireland): Home Int 1969 -70; Eur T Ch 1969

O'Neill, JJ
(Ireland): Home Int 1968

Oldcorn, A
(England): Home Int 1982 -83. (GB): v America 1983

Oosterhuis, PA
(England): Home Int 1966 -67 -68. (GB): v America 1967; v Europe 1968; in World Team Ch 1968

Oppenheimer, RH
(England): v Ireland 1928 -29 -30; v Scotland 1930. (GB): v America 1957 (Captain)

O'Rourke, P
(Ireland): Home Int 1980 -81 -82 -84 -85

O'Sullivan, D
(Ireland): Home Int 1985 -86

O'Sullivan, DF
(Ireland): Home Int 1976; Eur T Ch 1977

O'Sullivan, WM
(Ireland): Home Int 1934 -35 -36 -37 -38 -47 -48 -49 -50 -51 -53 -54

Osgood, TH
(Scotland): v England 1925

Owen, JB
(Wales): Home Int 1971

Owens, GF
(Wales): Home Int 1960 -61

Ownes, GH
(Ireland): Home Int 1935 -37 -38 -47

Palferman, H
(Wales): Home Int 1950 -53

Palmer, DJ
(England): Home Int 1962 -63

Parfitt, RWM
(Wales): v Ireland 1924

Parkin, AP
(Wales): Home Int 1980 -81 -82. (GB): v America 1983

Parry, JR
(Wales): Home Int 1966 -75 -76 -77; v France 1976

Patterson, AH
(Ireland): v Wales 1913

Patey, IR
(England): Home Int 1952; v France 1948 -49 -50

Patrick, KG
(Scotland): Home Int 1937

Pattinson, R
(England): Home Int 1949

Payne, J
(England): Home Int 1950 -51

Pearson, AG
(GB): v South Africa 1927

Pearson, MJ
(England): Home Int 1951 -52

Pease, JWB (*later* Lord Wardington)
(England): v Scotland 1903 -04 -05 -06

Pennink, JJF
(England): Home Int 1937 -38 -47; v France 1937 -38 -39. (GB): v America 1938

Perkins, TP
(England): v Scotland 1927 -28 -29. (GB): v America 1928

Perowne, AH
(England): Home Int 1947 -48 -49 -50 -51 -53 -54 -55 -57. (GB): v America 1949 -53 -59; in World Team Ch 1958

Peters, GB
(Scotland): Home Int 1934 -35 -36 -37 -38. (GB): v America 1936 -38

Phillips, LA
(Wales): v Ireland 1913

Pierse, AD
(Ireland): Home Int 1976 -77 -78 -80 -81 -82 -83 -84 -85; v Wales 1979; v France, West Germany, Sweden 1980; Eur T Ch 1981. (GB): v Europe 1980; v America 1983

Pinch, AG
(Wales): Home Int 1969

Pirie, AK
(Scotland): Home Int 1966 -67 -68 -69 -70 -71 -72 -73 -74 -75; Eur T Ch 1967 -69; v Belgium 1973 -75; v Spain 1974. (GB): v America 1967; v Europe 1970

Plaxton, J
(England): Home Int 1983 -84

Pollin, RKM
(Ireland): Home Int 1971; Eur T Ch 1973

Pollock, VA
(England): v Scotland 1908

Povall, J
(Wales): Home Int 1960 -61 -62 -63 -65 -66 -67 -68 -69 -70 -71 -72 -73 -74 -75 -76 -77; Eur T Ch 1967 -69 -71 -73 -75 -77; v France 1975 -76; v Denmark 1976. (GB): v Europe 1962

Powell, WA
(England): v Scotland 1923 -24; v Wales/Ireland 1925

Power, M
(Ireland): Home Int 1947 -48 -49 -50 -51 -52 -54

Poxon, MA
(England): Home Int 1975 -76; Eur T Ch 1975. (GB): v America 1975

Pressdee, RNG
(Wales): Home Int 1958 -59 -60 -61 -62

Pressley, J
(Scotland): Home Int 1947 -48 -49

Price, P
(Wales): Home Int 1986

Pugh, RS
(Wales): v Ireland 1923 -24 -29

Purcell, J
(Ireland): Home Int 1973

Raeside, A
(Scotland): v Ireland 1929

Rafferty, R
(Ireland): v Wales 1979; Home Int 1980 -81; v France, West Germany, Sweden 1980; Eur T Ch 1981. (GB): v Europe 1980; in World Team Ch 1980; v America 1981

Rainey, WHE
(Ireland): Home Int 1962

Rawlinson, D
(England): Home Int 1949 -50 -52 -53

Ray, D
(England): Home Int 1982; v France 1982

Rayfus, P
(Ireland): Home Int 1986

Reade, HE
(Ireland): v Wales 1913

Rees, C
(Wales): Home Int 1986

Rees, DA
(Wales): Home Int 1961 -62 -63 -64

Renfrew, RL
(Scotland): Home Int 1964

Renwick, G, Jr
(Wales): v Ireland 1923

Revell, RP
(England): Home Int 1972 -73; Eur T Ch 1973

Ricardo, W
(Wales): v Ireland 1930 -31; v Scotland 1931

Rice, JH
(Ireland): Home Int 1947 -52

Rice-Jones, L
(Wales): v Ireland 1924

Richards, PM
(Wales): Home Int 1960 -61 -62 -63 -71

Richardson, S
(England): Home Int 1986

Risdon, PWL
(England): Home Int 1935 -36

Robb, J, Jr
(Scotland): v England 1902 -03 -05 -06 -07

Robb, WM
(Scotland): Home Int 1935

Roberts, AT
(Scotland): v Ireland 1931

Roberts, G
(Scotland): Home Int 1937 -38

Roberts, GP
(England): Home Int 1951 -53; v France 1949

Roberts, HJ
(England): Home Int 1947 -48 -53

Roberts, J
(Wales): Home Int 1937

Roberts, SB
(Wales): Home Int 1932 -33 -34 -35 -37 -38 -47 -48 -49 -50 -51 -52 -53 -54

Roberts, WJ
(Wales): Home Int 1948 -49 -50 -51 -52 -53 -54

Robertson, A
(England): Home Int 1986

Robertson, CW
(Ireland): v Wales 1930; v Scotland 1930

Robertson, DM
(Scotland): Home Int 1973 -74; v Spain 1974

Robertson-Durham, JA
(Scotland): v England 1911

Robinson, J
(England): v Ireland 1928

Robinson, J
(England): Home Int 1986

Robinson, S
(England): v Scotland 1925; v Ireland 1928 -29 -30

Roderick, RN
(Wales): Home Int 1983 -84 -85 -86

Rolfe, B
(Wales): Home Int 1963 -65

Roobottom, EL
(Wales): Home Int 1967

Roper, HS
(England): v Ireland 1931; v Scotland 1931

Roper, MS
(Wales): v Ireland 1979

Roper, R
(England): Home Int 1984 -85 -86

Rothwell, J
(England): Home Int 1947 -48

Rutherford, DS
(Scotland): v Ireland 1929

Rutherford, R
(Scotland): Home Int 1938 -47

Saddler, AC
(Scotland): Home Int 1959 -60 -61 -62 -63 -64 -66; Eur T Ch 1965 -67. (GB): v Europe 1960 -62 -64 -66; v America 1963 -65 -67 -77 (Captain); in Com Tnmt 1959 -63 -67; in World Team Ch 1962

Scannel, BJ
(Ireland): Home Int 1947 -48 -49 -50 -51 -53 -54

Scott, KB
(England): Home Int 1937 -38; v France 1938

Scott, Hon M
(England): v Scotland 1911 -12 -23 -24 -25- 26. (GB): v America 1924 -34 (Captain); v Australia 1934

Scott, Hon O
(England): v Scotland 1902 -05 -06

Scott, R, Jr
(Scotland): v England 1924 -28. (GB): v America 1924

Scratton, EWHB
(England): v Scotland 1912

Scroggie, FH
(Scotland): v England 1910

Scrutton, PF
(England): Home Int 1950 -55. (GB): v America 1955 -57

Sewell, D
(England): Home Int 1956 -57 -58 -59 -60. (GB): v America 1957 -59; in Com Tnmt 1959; in World Team Ch 1960

Shade, RDBM
(Scotland): Home Int 1957 -60 -61 -62 -63 -64 -65 -66 -67 -68; v Scandinavia 1960 -62; Eur T Ch 1965 -67. (GB): v America 1961 -63 -65 -67; v Europe 1962 -64 -66 -68; in World Team Ch 1962 -64 -66 -68; in Com Tnmt 1963 -67

Shaw, G
(Scotland): Home Int 1984 -86

Sheals, HS
(Ireland): v Wales 1929; v England 1929 -30 -31; v Scotland 1930; Home Int 1932 -33

Sheahan, D
(Ireland): Home Int 1961 -62 -63 -64 -65 -66 -67 -70. (GB): v Europe 1962 -64 -67; v America 1963

Shepperson, AE
(England): Home Int 1956 -57 -58 -59 -60 -62. (GB): v America 1957 -59

Sherborne, A
(England): Home Int 1982 -83 -84

Shields, B
(Scotland): Home Int 1986

Shingler, TR
(England): Home Int 1977

Shorrock, TJ
(England): v France 1952

Simcox, R
(Ireland): v Wales 1930 -31; v Scotland 1930 -31; v England 1931; Home Int 1932 -33 -34 -35 -36 -38

Simpson, AF
(Scotland): v Ireland 1928; v England 1927

Simpson, JG
(Scotland): v England 1906 -07 -08 -09 -11 -12 -22 -24 -26. (GB): v America 1921

Sinclair, A
(Scotland): Home Int 1950

Slark, WA
(England): Home Int 1957

Slater, A
(England): Home Int 1955 -62

Slattery, B
(Ireland): Home Int 1947 -48

Sludds, MF
(Ireland): Home Int 1982

Smith, Eric M
(England): v Ireland 1931; v Scotland 1931

Smith, Everard
(England): v Scotland 1908 -09 -10 -12

Smith, GF
(England): v Scotland 1902 -03

Smith, JN
(Scotland): v Ireland 1928 -30 -31; v England 1929 -30 -31; v Wales 1931; Home Int 1932 -33 -34. (GB): v America 1930

Smith, JR
(England): Home Int 1932

Smith, LOM
(England): Home Int 1963

Smith, VH
(Wales): v Ireland 1924 -25

Smith, W
(England): Home Int 1972. (GB): v Europe 1972

Smith, WD
(Scotland): Home Int 1957 -58 -59 -60 -63; v Scandinavia 1958 -60. (GB): v Europe 1958; v America 1959

Smyth, D
(Ireland): Home Int 1972 -73; Eur T Ch 1973

Smyth, DW
(Ireland): v Wales 1923 -30; v England 1930; v Scotland 1931; Home Int 1933

Smyth, HB
(Ireland): Home Int 1974 -75 -76 -78; Eur T Ch 1975 -79; v France, West Germany, Sweden 1976. (GB): v Europe 1976

Smyth, V
(Ireland): Home Int 1981 -82

Snowdon, J
(England): Home Int 1934

Soulby, DEB
(Ireland): v Wales 1929 -30; v England 1929 -30; v Scotland 1929 -30

Spiller, EF
(Ireland): v Wales 1924; v England 1928; v Scotland 1928 -29

Squirrell, HC
(Wales): Home Int 1955 -56 -57 -58 -59 -60 -61 -62 -63 -64 -65 -66 -67 -68 -69 -70 -71 -73 -74 -75; Eur T Ch 1967 -69 -71 -75; v France 1975

Staunton, R
(Ireland): Home Int 1964 -65 -72; Eur T Ch 1973

Steel, DMA
(England): Home Int 1970

Stephen, AR
(Scotland): Home Int 1971 -72 -73 -74 -75 -76 -77 -84 -85; Eur T Ch 1975; v Spain 1974; v Belgium 1975 -77 -78. (GB): v Europe 1972; v America 1985

Stevens, DI
(Wales): Home Int 1968 -69 -70 -74 -75 -76 -77 -78 -80 -82; Eur T Ch 1969 -77; v France 1976; v Denmark 1977

Stevens, LB
(England): v Scotland 1912

Stevenson, A
(Scotland): Home Int 1949

Stevenson, JB
(Scotland): v Ireland 1931; Home Int 1932 -38 -47 -49 -50 -51

Stevenson, JF
(Ireland): v Wales 1923 -24; v England 1925

Stevenson, K
(Ireland): Home Int 1972

Stockdale, B
(England): Home Int 1964 -65

Stoker, K
(Wales): v Ireland 1923 -24

Stokoe, GC
(Wales): v England 1925; v Ireland 1929 -30

Storey, EF
(England): v Scotland 1924 -25 -26 -27 -28 -30; Home Int 1936; v France 1936. (GB): v America 1924 -26 -28

Stott, HAN
(England): Home Int 1976 -77

Stout, JA
(England): v Scotland 1928 -29 -30 -31; v Ireland 1929 -31. (GB): v America 1930 -32

Stowe, C
(England): Home Int 1935 -36 -37 -38 -47 -48 -49 -54; v France 1938 -39 -49. (GB): v America 1938 -47

Strachan, CJL
(Scotland): Home Int 1965 -66 -67; Eur T Ch 1967

Straker, R
(England): Home Int 1932

Stuart, HB
(Scotland): Home Int 1967 -68 -70 -71 -72 -73 -74 -76; Eur T Ch 1969 -71 -73 -75; v Belgium 1973 -75. (GB): v Europe 1968 -72 -74; v America 1971 -73 -75; in Com Tnmt 1971; in World Team Ch 1972

Stuart, JE
(Scotland): Home Int 1959

Stubbs, AK
(England): Home Int 1982

Sutherland, DMG
(England): Home Int 1947

Sutton, W
(England): v Scotland 1929 -31; v Ireland 1929 -30 -31

Symonds, A
(Wales): v Ireland 1925

Taggart, J
(Ireland): Home Int 1953

Tate, JK
(England): Home Int 1954 -55 -56

Taylor, GN
(Scotland): Home Int 1948

Taylor, HE
(England): v Scotland 1911

Taylor, JS
(Scotland): v England 1979; Home Int 1980; v Belgium 1980; v France 1980

Taylor, LG
(Scotland): Home Int 1955 -56

Taylor, TPD
(Wales): Home Int 1963

Thirlwell, A
(England): Home Int 1951 -52 -54 -55 -56 -57 -58 -63 -64. (GB): v Europe 1956 -58 -64; v America 1957; in Com Tnmt 1953 -64

Thirsk, TJ
(England): v Ireland 1929; Home Int 1933 -34 -35 -36 -37 -38; v France 1935 -36 -37 -38 -39

Thom, KG
(England): Home Int 1947 -48 -49 -53. (GB): v America 1949

Thomas, I
(England): Home Int 1933

Thomas, KR
(Wales): Home Int 1951 -52

Thompson, ASG
(England): Home Int 1935 -37

Thompson, MS
(England): Home Int 1982. (GB): v America 1983

Thomson, AP
(Scotland): Home Int 1970; Eur T Ch 1971

Thomson, H
(Scotland): Home Int 1934 -35 -36 -37 -38. (GB): v America 1936 -38

Thomson, JA
(Scotland): Home Int 1981 -82 -83 -84 -85 -86

Thorburn, K
(Scotland): v England 1928; v Ireland 1927

Timbey, JC
(Ireland): v Scotland 1928 -31; v Wales 1931

Timmis, CW
(England): v Ireland 1930; Home Int. 1936 -37

Tipping, EB
(England): v Ireland 1930

Tipple, ER
(England): v Ireland 1928 -29; Home Int 1932

Tolley, CJH
(England): v Scotland 1922 -23 -24 -25 -26 -27 -28 -29 -30; Home Int 1936 -37 -38; v Ireland/Wales 1925; v France 1938. (GB): v America 1921 -22 -23 -24 (Captain) -26 -30 -34; v South Africa 1927

Tooth, EA
(Wales): v Ireland 1913

Torrance, TA
(Scotland): v England 1922 -23 -25 -26 -28 -29 -30; Home Int 1933. (GB): v America 1924 -28 -30 -32 (Captain) -34

Torrance, WB
(Scotland): v England 1922 -23 -24 -26 -27 -28 -30; v Ireland 1928 -29 -30. (GB): v America 1922

Townsend, PM
(England): Home Int 1965 -66. (GB): v America 1965; v Europe 1966; in World Team Ch 1966

Toye, JL
(Wales): Home Int 1963 -64 -65 -66 -67 -69 -70 -71 -72 -73 -74 -76 -78; Eur T Ch 1971 -73 -75 -77; v France 1975

Tredinnick, SV
(England): Home Int 1950

Tucker, WI
(Wales): Home Int 1949 -50 -51 -52 -53 -54 -55 -56 -57 -58 -59 -60 -61 -62 -63 -64 -65 -66 -67 -68 -69 -70 -71 -72 -74 -75; Eur T Ch 1967 -69 -75; v France 1975

Tulloch, W
(Scotland): v England 1929 -30 -31; v Ireland 1930 -31; v Wales 1931; Home Int 1932

Tupling, LP
(England): Home Int 1969; Eur T Ch 1969. (GB): v America 1969

Turnbull, CH
(Wales): v Ireland 1913 -25

Turner, A
(England): Home Int 1952

Turner, GB
(Wales): Home Int 1947 -48 -49 -50 -51 -52 -55 -56

Tweddell, W
(England): v Scotland 1928 -29 -30; Home Int 1935. (GB): v America 1928 (Captain) -36 (Captain)

Vannet, L
(Scotland): Home Int 1984

Waddell, G
(Ireland): v Wales 1925

Walker, J
(Scotland): Home Int 1954 -55 -57 -58 -60 -61 -62 -63; v Scandinavia 1958 -62. (GB): v Europe 1958 -60; v America 1961

Walker, KH
(Scotland): Home Int 1985 -86

Walker, MS
(England): v Ireland/Wales 1925

Walker, RS
(Scotland): Home Int 1935 -36

Wallis, G
(Wales): Home Int 1934-36-37-38

Walls, MPD
(England): Home Int 1980 -81 -85

Walters, EM
(Wales): Home Int 1967 -68 -69; Eur T Ch 1969

Walton, AR
(England): Home Int 1934 -35

Walton, P
(Ireland): v Wales 1979; Home Int 1980 -81; v France, Germany, Sweden 1980; Eur T Ch 1981. (GB): v America 1981 -83

Warren, KT
(England): Home Int 1962

Way, P
(England): Home Int 1981; Eur T Ch 1981. (GB): v America 1981

Webster, A
(Scotland): Home Int 1978

Webster, F
(Ireland): Home Int 1949

Welch, L
(Ireland): Home Int 1936

Wemyss, DS
(Scotland): Home Int 1937

Werner, LE
(Ireland): v Wales 1925

West, CH
(Ireland): v England 1928; Home Int 1932

Wethered, RH
(England): v Scotland 1922 -23 -24 -25 -26- 27 -28 -29 -30. (GB): v America 1921 -22 -23 -26 -30 (Captain) -34

White, RJ
(England): Home Int 1947 -48 -49 -53 -54. (GB): v America 1947 -49 -51 -53 -55

Whyte, AW
(Scotland): Home Int 1934

Wilkie, D
(Scotland): Home Int 1962 -63 -65 -67 -68

Wilkie, G
(Scotland): v England 1911

Wilkie, GT
(Wales): Home Int 1938

Willcox, FS
(Wales): v Scotland 1931; v Ireland 1931

Williams, DF
(England): v Scotland 1979

Williams, JH
(Wales): Home Int 1985

Williams, KH
(Wales): Home Int 1983 -84 -86

Williams, PG
(Wales): v Ireland 1925

Williamson, SB
(Scotland): Home Int 1947 -48 -49 -51 -52

Wilson, F
(Scotland): Home Int 1985

Wilson, J
(Scotland): v England 1922 -23 -24 -26. (GB): v America 1923

Wilson, JC
(Scotland): Home Int 1947 -48 -49 -51 -52 -53. (GB): v America 1947 -53; v South Africa 1952; in Com Tnmt 1954

Wilson, P
(Scotland): Home Int 1976; v Belgium 1977

Winchester, R
(England): Home Int 1985

Winfield, HB
(Wales): v Ireland 1913

Wise, WS
(England): Home Int 1947

Wolstenholme, G
(England): Home Int 1953 -55 -56 -57 -58 -59 -60. (GB): v America 1957 -59; in World Team Ch 1958 -60; in Com Tnmt 1959

Wood, DK
(Wales): Home Int 1982 -83 -84 -85 -86

Woollam, J
(England): Home Int 1933 -34 -35; v France 1935

Woolley, FA
(England): v Scotland 1910 -11 -12

Woosnam, IA
(Wales): v France 1976

Worthington, JS
(England): v Scotland 1905

Wright, I
(Scotland): Home Int 1958 -59 -60 -61; v Scandinavia 1960

Yeo, J
(England): Home Int 1971

Young, D
(Ireland): Home Int 1969 -70 -77

Young, ID
(Scotland): Home Int 1981 -82; v France 1982

Young, JR
(Scotland): Home Int 1960 -61 -65; v Scandinavia 1960. (GB): v Europe 1960

Zacharias, JP
(England): Home Int 1935

Zoete, HW de
(England): v Scotland 1903 -04 -06 -07

Women's Amateur International Competitions

British Isles *v* USA (Ladies) Curtis Cup

Instituted 1932

	British Isles			USA			Venue
1932	Foursomes	0	3½	Foursomes	3	5½	Wentworth
	Singles	3½		Singles	2½		
1934	Foursomes	1½	2½	Foursomes	1½	6½	Chevy Chase
	Singles	1		Singles	5		
1936	Foursomes	1½	4½	Foursomes	1½	4½	Gleneagles
	Singles	3		Singles	3		
1938	Foursomes	2½	3½	Foursomes	½	5½	Essex County Club
	Singles	1		Singles	5		
1948	Foursomes	1	2½	Foursomes	2	6½	Birkdale
	Singles	1½		Singles	4½		
1950	Foursomes	1	1½	Foursomes	2	7½	Buffalo
	Singles	½		Singles	5½		
1952	Foursomes	2	5	Foursomes	1	4	Muirfield
	Singles	3		Singles	3		
1954	Foursomes	0	3	Foursomes	3	6	Merion
	Singles	3		Singles	3		
1956	Foursomes	1	5	Foursomes	2	4	Prince's, Sandwich
	Singles	4		Singles	2		
1958	Foursomes	2	4½	Foursomes	1	4½	Brae Burn GC
	Singles	2½		Singles	3½		
1960	Foursomes	1	2½	Foursomes	2	6½	Lindrick
	Singles	1½		Singles	4½		
1962	Foursomes	0	1	Foursomes	3	8	Colorado Springs
	Singles	1		Singles	5		
1964	Foursomes	3½	7½	Foursomes	2½	10½	Porthcawl
	Singles	4		Singles	8		
1966	Foursomes	1½	5	Foursomes	4½	13	Hot Springs
	Singles	3½		Singles	8½		

At Newcastle, Co Down, 14th and 15th June, 1968

First Day—Foursomes

Great Britain & Ireland		United States	
Mrs IC Robertson and Miss A Irvin (6 and 5)	1	Miss S Hamlin and Mrs A Welts	0
Mrs A Pickard and Miss V Saunders (3 and 2)	1	Miss L Dill and Miss P Conley	0
Mrs A Howard and Miss P Tredinnick	0	Miss P Preuss and Miss J Ashley (1 hole)	1
	2		1

Singles

Great Britain & Ireland		United States	
Miss A Irvin (3 and 2)	1	Mrs A Welts	0
Miss V Saunders	0	Miss S Hamlin (1 hole)	1
Mrs IC Robertson	0	Miss R Albers (1 hole)	1
Miss BAB Jackson	½	Miss P Conley	½
Miss D Oxley	½	Miss P Preuss	½
Mrs A Pickard (2 holes)	1	Miss J Ashley	0
	3		3

British Isles v USA (Ladies) Curtis Cup

continued

Second Day—Foursomes

Great Britain & Ireland		United States	
Miss P Tredinnick and Miss D Oxley	0	Miss P Preuss and Miss J Ashley (5 and 4)	1
Mrs IC Robertson and Miss A Irvin	½	Miss L Dill and Miss P Conley	½
Mrs A Pickard and Miss V Saunders	0	Miss S Hamlin and Mrs A Welts (2 and 1)	1
	½		2½

Singles

Great Britain & Ireland		United States	
Miss A Irvin (3 and 2)	1	Miss S Hamlin	0
Mrs IC Robertson	½	Mrs A Welts	½
Miss V Saunders	½	Miss H Albers	½
Mrs A Howard	0	Miss L Dill (4 and 2)	1
Mrs A Pickard	0	Miss P Conley (1 hole)	1
Miss BAB Jackson	0	Miss P Preuss (2 and 1)	1
	2		4

Aggregate: United States 10½; Great Britain and Ireland 7½

At Brae Burn, USA, 7th and 8th August, 1970

First Day—Foursomes

Great Britain & Ireland		United States	
Miss P Oxley and Miss M KcKenna (4 and 2)	0	Miss S Hamlin and Miss J Bastanchury (5 and 3)	0
Mrs IC Robertson and Miss A Irvin	0	Miss T Preuss and Miss M Wilkinson (4 and 3)	1
Miss M Everard and Miss J Greenhalgh (5 and 3)	1	Miss C Hill and Miss J Fassinger	0
	2		1

Singles

Great Britain & Ireland		United States	
Miss D Oxley	0	Miss J Bastanchury (5 and 3)	1
Miss A Irvin	0	Miss M Wilkinson (1 hole)	1
Mrs IC Robertson	½	Miss S Hamlin	½
Miss M McKenna (4 and 2)	1	Miss T Preuss	0
Mrs M Pickard	0	Miss N Hager (5 and 4)	1
Miss J Greenhalgh	0	Mrs P Dye (1 hole)	1
	1½		4½

Second Day—Foursomes

Great Britain & Ireland		United States	
Miss D Oxley and Miss M McKenna	0	Miss T Preuss and Miss M Wilkinson (6 and 4)	1
Miss M Everard and Miss J Greenhalgh	½	Miss C Hill and Mrs P Dye	½
Mrs IC Robertson and Miss A Irvin	0	Miss S Hamlin and Miss J Bastanchury (1 hole)	1
	½		2½

Singles

Great Britain & Ireland		United States	
Miss A Irvin	0	Miss J Bastanchury (4 and 3)	1
Miss D Oxley	½	Miss S Hamlin	½
Mrs IC Robertson	0	Miss T Preuss (1 hole)	1
Miss J Greenhalgh (6 and 4)	1	Miss M. Wilkinson	0
Miss M Everard (4 and 3)	1	Miss N Hager	0
Miss M McKenna	0	Miss C Hill (2 and 1)	1
	2½		3½

Aggregate: United States 11½: Great Britain and Ireland 6½

British Isles v USA (Ladies) Curtis Cup

continued

At Western Gailes, 9th and 10th June 1972

First Day—Foursomes

Great Britain & Ireland		United States	
Miss M Everard and Miss B Huke	0	Miss L Baugh and Mrs M Kirouac (2 and 1)	1
Mrs IC Robertson and Mrs D Frearson (2 and 1)	1	Mrs J Booth and Miss B McIntire	0
Miss M Walker and Miss M McKenna (1 hole)	1	Miss B Barry and Miss H Stacy	0
	2		1

Singles

Great Britain & Ireland		United States	
Miss M Walker	½	Miss L Baugh	½
Mrs IC Robertson	0	Mrs J Booth (3 and 1)	1
Miss M Everard	0	Mrs M Kirouac (4 and 3)	1
Miss D Oxley	0	Miss B McIntire (4 and 3)	1
Miss K Phillips (2 holes)	1	Miss L Smith	0
Miss M McKenna	0	Miss B Barry (2 and 1)	1
	1½		4½

Second Day—Foursomes

Great Britain & Ireland		United States	
Miss M Walker and Miss M McKenna (3 and 2)	1	Miss L Baugh and Mrs M Kirouac	0
Miss M Everard and Miss B Huke	0	Mrs J Booth and Miss B McIntire (5 and 4)	1
Mrs IC Robertson and Mrs D Frearson	½	Miss B Barry and Miss H Stacy	½
	1½		1½

Singles

Great Britain & Ireland		United States	
Mrs IC Robertson	0	Miss L Baugh (6 and 5)	1
Miss M Everard (6 and 5)	1	Miss B McIntire	0
Miss M Walker (1 hole)	1	Mrs J Booth	0
Miss M McKenna (3 and 1)	1	Mrs M Kirouac	0
Mrs D Fearson	0	Miss L Smith (3 and 1)	1
Miss K Phillips	0	Miss B Barry (3 and 1)	1
	3		3

Aggregate: United States 10; Great Britain and Ireland 8

At San Francisco, USA, on 2nd and 3rd August, 1974

First Day—Foursomes

Great Britain & Ireland		United States	
Miss M. McKenna and Miss J. Greenhalgh	½	Miss C Semple and Miss C Hill	½
Miss J Lee-Smith and Miss C Le Feuvre	0	Mrs A Sander and Mrs J Booth (6 and 5)	1
Miss M Walker and Miss M Everard (5 and 4)	1	Miss M Budke and Miss B Lauer	0
	1½		1½

Singles

Great Britain & Ireland		United States	
Miss M Walker (2 and 1)	1	Miss C Semple	0
Miss M McKenna	0	Mrs J Booth (5 and 3)	1
Miss M Everard	0	Miss D Massey (1 hole)	1
Miss J Lee-Smith	0	Miss B Lauer (6 and 4)	1
Miss J Greenhalgh	0	Miss B Barry (1 hole)	1
Miss T Perkins	½	Miss C Hill	½
	1½		4½

British Isles v USA (Ladies) Curtis Cup
continued

Second Day—Foursomes

Great Britain & Ireland		United States	
Miss M McKenna and Miss M Walker	0	Mrs A Sander and Mrs J Booth (5 and 4)	1
Miss M. Everard and Miss C. Le Feuvre	0	Miss M Budke and Miss B Lauer (5 and 3)	1
Miss J Greenhalgh and Miss T Perkins (3 and 2)	1	Miss C Semple and Miss C Hill	0
	1		2

Singles

Great Britain & Ireland		United States	
Miss M Everard	0	Mrs A Sander (4 and 3)	1
Miss J Greenhalgh	0	Mrs J Booth (7 and 5)	1
Miss C Le Feuvre	0	Miss D Massey (6 and 5)	1
Miss M Walker	0	Miss C Semple (2 and 1)	1
Miss T Perkins	0	Miss M Budke (5 and 4)	1
Miss M McKenna (2 and 1)	1	Miss B Lauer	0
	1		5

Aggregate: United States 13; Great Britain and Ireland 5

At Lytham and St Annes, 11th and 12th June, 1976

First Day—Foursomes

Great Britain & Ireland		United States	
Miss M McKenna and Miss J Greenhalgh	0	Miss B Daniel and Miss C Hill (3 and 2)	1
Mrs D Henson and Miss S Cadden	0	Miss D Massey and Miss D Horton (6 and 5)	1
Miss A Irvin and Miss T Perkins (3 and 2)	1	Mrs N Syms and Miss C Semple	0
	1		2

Singles

Great Britain & Ireland		United States	
Miss A Irvin	0	Miss B Daniel (4 and 3)	1
Mrs D Henson (1 hole)	1	Miss C Hill	0
Miss S Cadden	0	Miss N Lopez (3 and 1)	1
Miss M McKenna	0	Mrs N Syms (1 hole)	1
Miss T Perkins	0	Miss D Massey (1 hole)	1
Miss J Greenhalgh	½	Miss B Barrow	½
	1½		4½

Second Day–Foursomes

Great Britain & Ireland		United States	
Miss A Irvin and Miss S Cadden	0	Miss B Daniel and Miss C Hill (4 and 3)	1
Mrs D Henson and Miss T Perkins (2 and 1)	1	Miss C Semple and Mrs N Syms	1
Miss M McKenna and Mrs A Stant	0	Miss N Lopez and Miss B Barrow (4 and 2)	1
	1		2

Singles

Great Britain & Ireland		United States	
Mrs D Henson	0	Miss B Daniel (3 and 2)	1
Miss J Greenhalgh (2 and 1)	1	Mrs N Syms	0
Miss S Cadden	0	Miss D Horton (6 and 5)	1
Miss J Lee-Smith	0	Miss D Massey (3 and 2)	1
Miss T Perkins (1 hole)	1	Miss C Hill	0
Miss M McKenna (1 hole)	1	Miss C Semple	0
	3		3

Aggregate: United States 11½; Great Britain and Ireland 6½

British Isles v USA (Ladies) Curtis Cup

continued

At Apawamis, New York, USA, 4th and 5th August, 1978

First Day–Foursomes

Great Britain & Ireland		United States	
Miss J Greenhalgh and Miss V Marvin (3 and 2)	1	Miss B Daniel and Miss B Goldsmith	0
Miss M Everard and Miss M Thomson (2 and 1)	1	Miss Cynthia Hill and Miss L Smith	0
Miss T Perkins and Miss M McKenna	½	Miss P Cornett and Miss Carolyn Hill	½
	2½		½

Singles

Great Britain & Ireland		United States	
Miss V Marvin	0	Miss B Daniel (5 and 4)	1
Miss M Everard (7 and 6)	1	Mrs N Uihlein	0
Mrs A Uzielli	0	Miss L Smith (4 and 3)	1
Miss J Greenhalgh	0	Miss Cynthia Hill (2 and 1)	1
Mrs C Caldwell	½	Miss Carolyn Hill	½
Miss T Perkins	0	Mrs J Oliver (2 and 1)	1
	1½		4½

Second Day–Foursomes

Great Britain & Ireland		United States	
Miss M Everard and Miss M Thomson	0	Miss Cynthia Hill and Miss L Smith (1 hole)	1
Miss T Perkins and Miss M McKenna	0	Miss B Goldsmith and Miss B Daniel (1 hole)	1
Miss J Greenhalgh and Miss V Marvin	0	Mrs N Uihlein and Mrs J Oliver (4 and 3)	1
	0		3

Singles

Great Britain & Ireland		United States	
Miss M McKenna	0	Miss B Daniel (2 and 1)	1
Mrs C Caldwell	0	Miss P Cornett (3 and 2)	1
Miss M Thomson (2 and 1)	1	Miss Cynthia Hill	0
Miss T Perkins	0	Miss L Smith (2 holes)	1
Miss J Greenhalgh	½	Mrs J Oliver	½
Miss M Everard	½	Mrs N Uihlein	½
	2		4

Aggregate: United States 12; Great Britain and Ireland 6

At St Pierre, 6th and 7th June, 1980

First Day–Foursomes

Great Britain & Ireland		United States	
Miss M McKenna and Miss C Nesbitt	½	Miss L Smith and Miss T. Moody	½
Mrs T Thomas and Miss G Stewart	0	Miss P Sheehan and Miss L Castillo (5 and 3)	1
Miss M Madill and Mrs C Caldwell	½	Mrs J Oliver and Miss C Semple	½
	1		2

Singles

Great Britain & Ireland		United States	
Miss M McKenna	0	Miss P Sheehan (3 and 2)	1
Miss C Nesbitt	½	Miss L Smith	½
Miss J Connachan	0	Miss B Goldsmith (2 holes)	1
Miss M Madill	0	Miss C Semple (4 and 3)	1
Miss L Moore	½	Miss M Hafeman	½
Mrs C Caldwell	0	Mrs J Oliver (1 hole)	1
	1		5

British Isles v USA (Ladies) Curtis Cup

continued

Second Day–Foursomes

Great Britain & Ireland		United States	
Mrs C Caldwell and Miss M Madill	0	Miss P. Sheehan and Miss L Castillo (3 and 2)	1
Miss C Nesbitt and Miss M McKenna	0	Miss L Smith and Miss T Moody (6 and 5)	1
Mrs T Thomas and Miss L Moore	0	Mrs J Oliver and Miss C Semple (1 hole)	1
	0		3

Singles

Great Britain & Ireland		United States	
Miss M Madill	0	Miss P Sheehan (5 and 4)	1
Miss M McKenna (5 and 4)	1	Miss L Castillo	0
Miss J Connachan	0	Miss M Hafeman (6 and 5)	1
Miss G Stewart (5 and 4)	1	Miss L Smith	0
Miss L Moore (1 hole)	1	Miss B Goldsmith	0
Mrs T Thomas	0	Miss C Semple (4 and 3)	1
	3		3

Aggregate: United States 13; Great Britain and Ireland 5

At Denver, Colorado, USA, on 5th and 6th August, 1982

First Day–Foursomes

Great Britain & Ireland		United States	
Mrs IC Robertson and Miss M McKenna	0	Mrs J Inkster and Miss C Semple (5 and 4)	1
Miss K Douglas and Miss J Soulsby	½	Miss K Baker and Miss L Smith	½
Miss G Stewart and Miss J Connachan	0	Miss A Benz and Miss C Hanlon (2 and 1)	1
	½		2½

Singles

Great Britain & Ireland		United States	
Miss M McKenna	0	Miss A Benz (2 and 1)	1
Miss J Connachan	0	Miss C Hanlon (5 and 4)	1
Miss W Aitken	0	Mrs M McDougall (2 holes)	1
Mrs. IC Robertson	0	Miss K Baker (7 and 6)	1
Miss J Soulsby (2 holes)	1	Mrs J Oliver	0
Miss K Douglas	0	Mrs J Inkster (7 and 6)	1
	1		5

Second Day–Foursomes

Great Britain & Ireland		United States	
Miss J Connachan and Miss W Aitken	0	Mrs J Inkster and Miss C Semple (3 and 2)	1
Miss K Douglas and Miss J Soulsby	0	Miss K Baker and Miss L Smith (1 hole)	1
Miss M McKenna and Mrs IC Robertson (1 hole)	1	Miss A Benz and Miss C Hanlon	0
	1		2

Singles

Great Britain & Ireland		United States	
Miss K Douglas	0	Mrs J Inkster (7 and 6)	1
Miss G Stewart	0	Miss K Baker (4 and 3)	1
Mrs V Thomas	0	Mrs J Oliver (5 and 4)	1
Miss J Soulsby	0	Mrs M McDougall (2 and 1)	1
Miss M McKenna	0	Miss C Semple (1 hole)	1
Mrs IC Robertson (5 and 3)	1	Miss L Smith	0
	1		5

Aggregate: United States 14½; Great Britain and Ireland 3½

British Isles v USA (Ladies) Curtis Cup

continued

At Muirfield on 8th and 9th June, 1984

First Day–Foursomes

Great Britain & Ireland		United States	
C Waite and B New (2 holes)	1	J Pacillo and A Sander	0
J Thornhill and P Grice	½	L Smith and J Rosenthal	½
M McKenna and L Davies	0	M Widman and H Farr (1 hole)	1
	1½		1½

Singles

Great Britain & Ireland		United States	
J Thornhill	½	J Pacillo	½
C Waite	0	P Hammel (4 and 2)	1
C Hourihane	0	J Rosenthal (3 and 1)	1
V Thomas (2 and 1)	1	D Howe	0
P Grice (2 holes)	1	A Sander	0
B New	0	M Widman (4 and 3)	1
	2½		3½

Second Day–Foursomes

Great Britain & Ireland		United States	
C Waite and B New	0	L Smith and J Rosenthal (3 and 1)	1
J Thornhill and P Grice (2 and 1)	1	M Widman and H Farr	0
V Thomas and C Hourihane	½	D Howe and P Hammel	½
	1½		1½

Singles

Great Britain & Ireland		United States	
J Thornhill	0	J Pacillo (3 and 2)	1
L Davies (1 hole)	1	A Sander	0
C Waite (5 and 4)	1	L Smith	0
P Grice	0	D Howe (2 holes)	1
B New	0	H Farr (6 and 5)	1
C Hourihane (2 and 1)	1	P Hammel	0
	3		3

Aggregate: Great Britain and Ireland 8½; United States 9½

At Prairie Dunes, Kansas, USA on 1st and 2nd August, 1986

First Day–Foursomes

Great Britain & Ireland		United States	
L Behan and J Thornhill (7 and 6)	1	K Kessler and C. Schreyer	0
P Johnson and K Davies (2 and 1)	1	D Ammaccapane and D Mochrie	0
B Robertson and M McKenna (1 hole)	1	K Gardner and K McCarthy	0
	3		0

Singles

Great Britain & Ireland		United States	
P Johnson (1 hole)	1	L Shannon	0
J Thornhill (4 and 3)	1	K Williams	0
L Behan (4 and 3)	1	D Ammaccapane	0
V Thomas	0	K Kessler (3 and 2)	1
K Davies	½	D Mochrie	½
C Hourihane	0	C Schreyer (2 and 1)	1
	3½		2½

British Isles *v* USA (Ladies) Curtis Cup

continued

Second Day–Foursomes

Great Britain & Ireland		United States	
P Johnson and K Davies (1 hole)	1	D Ammaccapane and D Mochrie	0
L Behan and J Thornhill (5 and 3)	1	L Shannon and K Williams	0
B Robertson and M McKenna	½	K Gardner and K McCarthy	½
	2½		½

Singles

Great Britain & Ireland		United States	
J Thornhill	½	L Shannon	½
P Johnson (5 and 3)	1	K McCarthy	0
L Behan	0	K Gardner (1 hole)	1
V Thomas (4 and 3)	1	K Williams	0
K Davies	½	K Kessler	½
C Hourihane (5 and 3)	1	C Schreyer	0
	4		2

Aggregate: Great Britain and Ireland 13; United States 5

Vagliano Trophy–Great Britain & Ireland *v* Europe (Ladies)

Played for biennially between teams of women amateur golfers representing the British Isles and Europe. (From 1947 to 1957 was between the British Isles and France.)

Year	Winner	Result	Venue	Year	Winner	Result	Venue
1959	GB	12-3	Wentworth	1973	GB	20-10	Eindhoven
1961	GB	8-7	Villa d'Este	1975	GB	13½–10½	Muirfield
1963	GB	20-10	Muirfield	1977	GB	15½–8½	Malmo
1965	Europe	17-13	Cologne	1979	Halved	12-12	R Porthcawl
1967	Europe	15½–14½	Lytham	1981	Europe	14-10	P. de Hierro
1969	Europe	16-14	Chantilly	1983	GB	14-10	Woodhall Spa
1971	GB	17½–12½	Worplesdon	1985	GB	14–10	Hamburg

Commonwealth Tournament (Ladies)

At St Andrews, 2nd to 6th June, 1959

Australia beat New Zealand	4 matches to 2
Canada beat South Africa	4 matches to 2
Great Britain beat Australia	4 matches to 2
Canada beat New Zealand	4½ matches to 1½
Great Britain beat New Zealand	6 matches to 0
South Africa beat Australia	4½ matches to 1½
Great Britain beat Canada	5 matches to 1
South Africa beat New Zealand	4 matches to 2
Australia drew with Canada	3 matches each
Great Britain beat South Africa	4 matches to 2

Great Britain 4 pts; Canada 2½ pts; South Africa 2 pts; Australia 1½ pts; New Zealand 0 pts.

At Melbourne, Australia, August, 1963

Great Britain beat Canada	5 matches to 0 (1 halved)
Great Britain beat Australia	4 matches to 2
Great Britain beat New Zealand	6 matches to 0
Australia beat Canada	3 matches to 2 (1 halved)
Australia beat New Zealand	4 matches to 2
Canada beat New Zealand	5 matches to 0 (1 halved)

Great Britain 3 pts; Australia 2 pts; Canada 1 pt; New Zealand 0 pts.

Commonwealth Tournament (Ladies)

continued

At Ancaster, Ontario, August, 1967

Great Britain beat New Zealand	4 matches to 2
Great Britain beat Australia	3 matches to 2 (1 halved)
Great Britain beat Canada	3 matches to 2 (1 halved)
Canada beat Australia	6 matches to 0
Canada halved with New Zealand	3 matches to 3
Australia beat New Zealand	5 matches to 1

Great Britain 3 pts; Canada 1½ pts; Australia 1 pt; New Zealand ½ pt.

At Hamilton, New Zealand, September, 1971

Great Britain beat Canada	4 matches to 1 (1 halved)
Great Britain beat New Zealand	4 matches to 1 (1 halved)
Great Britain beat Australia	5 matches to 0 (1 halved)
Canada halved with New Zealand	3 matches each
Canada beat Australia	3 matches to 2 (1 halved)
New Zealand halved with Australia	3 matches each

Great Britain 3 pts; Canada 1½ pts; New Zealand 1 pt; Australia ½ pt

At Ganton, England, June, 1975

Great Britain beat Australia	4 matches to 2
Great Britain beat New Zealand	4½ matches to 1½
Great Britain beat Canada	4 matches to 2
Australia beat New Zealand	3½ matches to 1½
Australia beat Canada	6 matches to 0
New Zealand beat Canada	4 matches to 2

Great Britain 3 pts; Australia 2 pts; New Zealand 1 pt; Canada 0 pts

At Lake Karrinyup, Australia, September, 1979

Canada beat Australia	4 matches to 2
Canada beat Great Britain	4½ matches to 1½
Canada beat New Zealand	4 matches to 2
Australia beat Great Britain	5½ matches to ½
Australia beat New Zealand	5 matches to 1
Great Britain beat New Zealand	3½ matches to 2½

Canada 3 pts; Australia 2 pts; Great Britain 1 pt; New Zealand 0 pts

Women's World Amateur Team Championship (Espirito Santo Trophy)

Year	Winners	Runners-up	Venue	Score
1964	France (C Lacoste, B Varangot, C Cros)	United States	St Germain	588
1966	United States (S Hamlin, B Boddie, A Welts)	Canada	Mexico	580
1968	United States (A Welts, J Bastanchury, S Hamlin)	Australia	Melbourne	616
1970	United States (C Hill, J Bastanchury, M Wilkinson)	France	Madrid	598
1972	United States (L Baugh, J Bastanchury Booth, M Budke)	France	Buenos Aires	583
1974	United States (C Hill, D Massey, C Semple)	Great Britain South Africa	Dominican Republic	620
1976	United States (N Lopez, D Horton, D Massey)	France	Vilamoura Portugal	605
1978	Australia (L Goggin, E Kennedy, J Lock)	Canada	Fiji	596
1980	United States (J Inkster, P Rizzo, C Semple)	Australia	Pinehurst, USA	588
1982	United States (J Inkster, K Baker, A Benz)	New Zealand	Geneva, Switzerland	579
1984	United States	France	Hong Kong	585
1986	Spain	France	Caracas	580

European Ladies' Amateur Team Championship

Year	Winner	Second	Venue
1967	England	France	Penina, Portugal
1969	France	England	Tylosand, Sweden
1971	England	France	Ganton, England
1973	England	France	Brussels, Belgium
1975	France	Spain	Paris, France
1977	England	Spain	Sotogrande, Spain
1979	Ireland	Germany	Hermitage, Ireland
1981	Sweden	France	Troia, Portugal
1983	Ireland	England	Waterloo, Belgium
1985	England	Italy	Stavanger, Norway

Women's Home Internationals

At Lytham and St Annes, 1948

England beat Scotland	5 matches to 4
England beat Ireland	7 matches to 2
England beat Wales	8 matches to 1
Scotland beat Ireland	7 matches to 2
Scotland beat Wales	7 matches to 2
Ireland beat Wales	6 matches to 3

At Harlech, 1949

England beat Scotland	5 matches to 4
England beat Ireland	7 matches to 2
England beat Wales	8 matches to 1
Scotland beat Ireland	8 matches to 1
Scotland beat Wales	8 matches to 1
Ireland beat Wales	8 matches to 1

At Newcastle, Co Down, 12th and 13th May, 1950

Scotland beat England	6 matches to 3
Scotland beat Ireland	6 matches to 3
Scotland beat Wales	8 matches to 1
England beat Ireland	6 matches to 3
England beat Wales	8 matches to 1
Ireland beat Wales	6 matches to 3

At Broadstone, Dorset, 31st May and 1st June, 1951

Scotland beat England	9 matches to 0
Scotland beat Ireland	5 matches to 4
Scotland beat Wales	6 matches to 3
England beat Ireland	6 matches to 3
England beat Wales	9 matches to 0
Ireland beat Wales	6 matches to 3

At Troon, 12th and 13th June, 1952

Scotland beat England	6 matches to 3
Scotland beat Ireland	5 matches to 4
Scotland beat Wales	6 matches to 3
England beat Wales	9 matches to 0
Ireland beat England	6 matches to 3
Ireland beat Wales	7 matches to 2

At Porthcawl, 18th and 19th June, 1953

England beat Ireland	6 matches to 3
England beat Scotland	5 matches to 4
England beat Wales	7 matches to 2
Scotland beat Ireland	6 matches to 3
Scotland beat Wales	8 matches to 1
Ireland beat Wales	7 matches to 2

At Ganton, 24th and 25th June, 1954

England beat Ireland	5 matches to 4
England beat Scotland	$7\frac{1}{2}$ matches to $1\frac{1}{2}$
England beat Wales	9 matches to 0
Scotland beat Ireland	5 matches to 4
Scotland beat Wales	9 matches to 0
Ireland beat Wales	7 matches to 2

At Portrush, 12th and 13th May, 1955

Scotland Halved with England	$4\frac{1}{2}$ matches each
Scotland beat Wales	9 matches to 0
Scotland beat Ireland	6 matches to 3
England beat Wales	$6\frac{1}{2}$ matches to $2\frac{1}{2}$
England beat Ireland	$6\frac{1}{2}$ matches to $2\frac{1}{2}$
Ireland beat Wales	$6\frac{1}{2}$ matches to $2\frac{1}{2}$

Women's Home Internationals

continued

At Sunningdale, 2nd and 3rd July, 1956

Scotland beat England	5 matches to 4
Scotland beat Ireland	8 matches to 1
Scotland beat Wales	$7\frac{1}{2}$ matches to $1\frac{1}{2}$
England beat Wales	$8\frac{1}{2}$ matches to $\frac{1}{2}$
England halved with Ireland	$4\frac{1}{2}$ matches each
Ireland beat Wales	7 matches to 2

At Troon, 21st and 22nd June, 1957

Scotland beat England	4 matches to 3
Scotland beat Ireland	5 matches to 2
Scotland beat Wales	7 matches to 0
England beat Ireland	5 matches to 2
England beat Wales	5 matches to 2
Ireland beat Wales	5 matches to 2

At Hunstanton, 20th and 21st June, 1958

England beat Wales	6 matches to 1
Ireland beat Scotland	4 matches to 3
Ireland beat Wales	5 matches to 2
England beat Scotland	6 matches to 1
England beat Ireland	5 matches to 3
Scotland beat Wales	6 matches to 1

At Hoylake, 30th September and 1st October, 1959

Scotland beat Wales	9 matches to 0
England beat Ireland	6 matches to 3
England beat Scotland	6 matches to 3
Ireland beat Wales	8 matches to 1
England beat Wales	9 matches to 0
Scotland beat Ireland	$5\frac{1}{2}$ matches to $3\frac{1}{2}$

At Gullane, 5th to 7th October, 1960

England beat Scotland	7 matches to 2
England beat Ireland	$8\frac{1}{2}$ matches to $\frac{1}{2}$
England beat Wales	7 matches to 2
Scotland beat Wales	7 matches to 2
Scotland beat Ireland	7 matches to 2
Ireland beat Wales	4 matches to 3

At Portmarnock, 4th to 6th October, 1961

Scotland beat Wales	8 matches to 0
Scotland beat Ireland	8 matches to 1
Scotland beat England	4 matches to 2
England beat Ireland	5 matches to 4
England beat Wales	9 matches to 0
Ireland beat Wales	7 matches to 1

At Porthcawl, 27th to 29th June, 1962

Scotland beat England	4 matches to 3
Scotland beat Ireland	6 matches to 3
Scotland beat Wales	6 matches to 1
England beat Ireland	8 matches to 0
England beat Wales	9 matches to 0
Ireland beat Wales	7 matches to 1

At Formby, 26th to 28th June, 1963

England beat Scotland	5 matches to 3
England beat Ireland	6 matches to 2
England beat Wales	8 matches to 1
Scotland beat Ireland	5 matches to 2
Scotland beat Wales	9 matches to 0
Ireland beat Wales	6 matches to 2

At Troon, 10 to 12th June, 1964

England beat Scotland	7 matches to 1
England beat Wales	7 matches to 1
England beat Ireland	7 matches to 2
Scotland beat Ireland	6 matches to 1
Scotland beat Wales	6 matches to 3
Ireland tied with Wales	4 matches each

At Portrush, 16th to 18th June, 1965

England beat Ireland	7 matches to 0
England beat Scotland	5 matches to 3
England beat Wales	7 matches to 2
Scotland beat Ireland	5 matches to 4
Scotland beat Wales	9 matches to 0
Ireland beat Wales	7 matches to 2

At Woodhall Spa, 8th to 10th June, 1966

England beat Ireland	6 matches to 2
England beat Scotland	5 matches to 3
England beat Wales	9 matches to 0
Scotland beat Wales	7 matches to 1
Scotland beat Ireland	7 matches to 1
Ireland halved with Wales	4 matches each

At Sunningdale, 20th to 22nd June, 1967

England halved with Scotland	4 matches each
England beat Wales	8 matches to 1
England beat Ireland	6 matches to 2
Scotland beat Ireland	6 matches to 2
Scotland beat Wales	7 matches to 0
Ireland halved with Wales	4 matches each

Women's Home Internationals
continued

At Porthcawl, 25th to 27th September, 1968

England halved with Scotland	4 matches each
England beat Ireland	4 matches to 3
England beat Wales	7 matches to 2
Scotland beat Ireland	5 matches to 4
Scotland beat Wales	6 matches to 3
Ireland beat Wales	5 matches to 3

At Western Gailes, 17th to 19th September, 1969

scotland beat Ireland	8 matches to 0
Scotland beat Ireland	7 matches to 2
England beat Scotland	4 matches to 2
England beat Wales	8 matches to 0
Ireland beat England	5 matches to 4
Ireland halved with Wales	4 matches each

At Killarney, 14th to 16th September, 1970

England beat Ireland	7 matches to 1
England beat Scotland	8 matches to 0
England beat Wales	6 matches to 2
Ireland beat Scotland	5 matches to 3
Ireland beat Wales	8 matches to 1
Scotland beat Wales	7 matches to 1

At Longniddry, 8th to 10th September, 1971

England beat Scotland	6 matches to 3
England beat Ireland	6½ matches to 2½
England beat Wales	8 matches to 1
Scotland beat Ireland	8 matches to 1
Scotland beat Wales	7 matches to 2
Ireland beat Wales	5½ matches to 3½

At Lytham, 20th to 22nd September, 1972

England beat Scotland	5½ matches to 3½
England beat Ireland	9 matches to 0
England beat Wales	8 matches to 1
Scotland halved with Ireland	4½ matches each
Scotland beat Wales	8 matches to 1
Ireland beat Wales	5 matches to 4

At St David's, 12th to 14th September, 1973

England beat Scotland	5½ matches to 3½
England beat Wales	7 matches to 2
England beat Ireland	8 matches to 1
Scotland halved with Wales	4½ matches each
Scotland beat Ireland	5 matches to 4
Wales beat Ireland	5 matches to 4

At Prince's, 18th to 20th September, 1974

Scotland beat Ireland	7 matches to 2
Scotland beat Wales	7½ matches to 1½
England beat Scotland	5½ matches to 3½
England beat Wales	5½ matches to 3½
Ireland beat England	5 matches to 4
Ireland beat Wales	5 matches to 4

At Newport, 17th to 19th September, 1975

England beat Wales	5½ matches to 3½
England beat Ireland	6 matches to 3
England beat Scotland	6 matches to 3
Wales beat Ireland	7 matches to 2
Ireland beat Scotland	6 matches to 3
Scotland beat Wales	5 matches to 4

At Troon, 15th to 17th September, 1976

England halved with Wales	4½ matches each
England beat Ireland	7½ matches to 1½
England beat Scotland	5 matches to 4
Wales halved with Ireland	4½ matches each
Wales halved with Scotland	
Ireland beat Scotland	5 matches to 4

At Cork, 14th to 16th September, 1977

England beat Ireland	5½ matches to 3½
England beat Scotland	6 matches to 3
England beat Wales	7½ matches to 1½
Ireland beat Scotland	7½ matches to 1½
Ireland beat Wales	7 matches to 2
Scotland beat Wales	8 matches to 1

At Moortown, 13th to 15th September, 1978

England beat Ireland	5½ matches to 3½
England beat Scotland	5 matches to 4
England beat Wales	5½ matches to 3½
Ireland beat Scotland	5½ matches to 3½
Ireland beat Wales	6½ matches to 2½
Scotland beat Wales	6½ matches to 2½

At St Davids, 12th to 14th September, 1979

Scotland beat Wales	5 matches to 4
Scotland beat England	7 matches to 2
Ireland beat Scotland	5½ matches to 3½
Ireland beat England	5 matches to 4
Wales beat Ireland	5½ matches to 3½
England beat Wales	6 matches to 3

Women's Home Internationals

continued

At Cruden Bay, 10th to 12th September, 1980

Ireland beat Scotland	6½ matches to 2½
Ireland beat England	5 matches to 4
Ireland beat Wales	8½ matches to 1½
Scotland beat England	5½ matches to 3½
Scotland beat Wales	5 matches to 4
England halved with Wales	4½ matches each

At Portmarnock, 16th to 18th September, 1981

Scotland beat England	5½ matches to 3½
Scotland beat Ireland	6 matches to 3
Scotland beat Wales	81½ matches to 1½
England beat Ireland	5½ matches to 3½
England halved with Wales	4½ matches each
Ireland beat Wales	7 matches to 2

At Burnham and Berrow, 22nd to 24th September, 1982

England beat Scotland	5 matches to 4
England halved with Ireland	4½ matches each
England beat Wales	7 matches to 2
Scotland beat Ireland	5½ matches to 3½
Scotland beat Wales	6½ matches to 2½
Ireland beat Wales	7 matches to 2

At Gullane, 9th to 14th September, 1984

England beat Wales	6½ matches to 2½
Scotland beat Ireland	7½ matches to 1½
Ireland beat Wales	9 matches to 0
England beat Scotland	5½ matches to 3½
Scotland beat Wales	5½ matches to 3½
England beat Ireland	7 matches to 2

At Waterville, Co Kerry 1985

England beat Scotland	7 matches to 2
England beat Wales	6½ matches to 2½
Ireland beat England	5½ matches to 3½
Ireland beat Wales	6 matches to 3
Scotland beat Ireland	5 matches to 4
Scotland beat Wales	6 matches to 3

At Whittington Barracks, Staffs 1986

England halved with Scotland	4½ matches each
England beat Wales	7½ matches to 1½
Wales beat Ireland	5 matches to 4
Ireland beat Scotland	6½ matches to 2½
Ireland beat England	5 matches to 4
Scotland beat Wales	6 matches to 3

Girls' Internationals

England *v* Scotland

Year	Winner	Result	Venue
1938	Scotland	4-3	Stoke Poges
1939-48	*No contest*		
1949	England	4-1	Beaconsfield
1950	England	3-2	Formby
1951	England	6-1	Gullane
1952	England	4-3	Stoke Poges
1953	England	4-3	Woodhall Spa
1954	England	8-1	West Kilbride
1955	England	7-1	Beaconsfield
1956	England	9-0	Seaton Carew
1957	England	8-1	North Berwick
1958	England	7-2	Cotswold Hills
1959	England	7-3	Nottingham
1960	Draw	6-6	Barassie
1961	England	9-3	Beaconsfield
1962	England	9-3	Foxton Hall
1963	England	9-3	Gullane
1964	England	9½-2½	Formby
1965	Draw	4½-4½	Formby
1966	Scotland	5½-3½	Troon, Portland
1967	England	7-2	Liphook
1968	Draw	4-4	Leven

From 1969 became included in Home Internationals.

Ireland *v* Wales

Year	Winner	Result	Venue
1967	Ireland	7-2	Liphook
1968	Ireland	6½-2½	Leven

From 1969 became included in Home Internationals.

Girls' Home Internationals

1969 at Ilkley

England beat Scotland 5½-1½
England beat Ireland 5-2
England beat Wales 7-0
Scotland beat Ireland 5-2
Scotland beat Wales 5-2
Ireland beat Wales 6-1

1970 at North Wales

England beat Scotland 4-3
England beat Ireland 5-2
England beat Wales 6-1
Scotland beat Ireland 4½-2½
Scotland beat Wales 6-1
Ireland beat Wales 6½-½

1971 at North Berwick

England beat Scotland 4½-2½
England beat Ireland 5-2
England beat Wales 5-2
Scotland beat Ireland 4½-2½
Scotland beat Wales 5½-1½
Ireland beat Wales 4-3

1972 at Royal Norwich

Scotland beat England 5-2
Scotland beat Wales 5½-1½
Scotland beat Ireland 6½-½
England beat Wales 5-2
England beat Ireland 6½-½
Wales beat Ireland 4-3

1973 at Northamptonshire

Scotland beat England 5-2
Scotland beat Ireland 6-1
Scotland beat Wales 5-2
England beat Ireland 4½-2½
England beat Wales 4-3
Ireland beat Wales 6½-½

1974 at Dunbar

England beat Scotland 5-2
England beat Ireland 5½-1½
England beat Wales 4-3
Scotland beat Ireland 6½-½
Scotland beat Wales 5-2
Ireland beat Wales 5-2

1975 at Henbury

England halved with Scotland
England beat Ireland 6½-½
England beat Wales 6-1
Scotland beat Ireland 5-2
Scotland beat Wales 5-2
Ireland beat Wales 5-2

1976 at Pyle and Kenfig

Scotland beat England 4½-2½
Scotland beat Wales 5-2
Scotland beat Ireland 4-3
England beat Wales 6-1
England beat Ireland 6½-½
Wales beat Ireland 4-3

1977 at Formby

England halved with Scotland
England beat Wales 7-0
England beat Ireland 6-1
Scotland beat Wales 5-2
Scotland beat Ireland 7-0
Wales beat Ireland 5-2

1978 at Largs

England beat Scotland 5-2
England beat Wales 6-1
England beat Ireland 7-0
Scotland beat Wales 6-1
Scotland beat Ireland 4½-2½
Wales beat Ireland 5-2

1979 at Edgbaston

England halved with Wales
England beat Ireland 7-0
England beat Scotland 5½-1½
Wales beat Ireland 4½-2½
Wales beat Scotland 4½-2½
Ireland beat Scotland 4-3

1980 at Wrexham

England beat Scotland 5½-1½
England halved with Ireland
England beat Wales 5½-1½
Scotland beat Ireland 4-3
Scotland beat Wales 6-1
Ireland beat Wales 4½-2½

1981 at Woodbridge

England beat Scotland 4½-2½
England beat Ireland 5½-1½
England beat Wales 6½-½
Scotland halved with Ireland
Scotland beat Wales 5-2
Ireland beat Wales 5-2

1982 at Edzell

England beat Ireland 7-0
England beat Scotland 5-2
England beat Wales 6-1
Ireland beat Scotland 4-3
Ireland beat Wales 4½-2½
Scotland beat Wales 6-1

1983 at Alwoodley

England beat Ireland 4½-2½
England beat Scotland 4-3
England beat Wales 7-0
Ireland beat Scotland 4-3
Ireland beat Wales 6-1
Scotland beat Wales 5½-1½

1985 at Hesketh

England beat Scotland 5-2
England beat Ireland 5½-1½
England beat Wales 6-1
Ireland beat Scotland 4-3
Ireland beat Wales 4-3
Scotland beat Wales 6½-½

1986 at West Kilbride

England beat Scotland 4-3
England beat Wales 4½-2½
England beat Ireland 5-2
Scotland beat Wales 5-2
Scotland beat Ireland 5-2
Wales beat Ireland 5-2

Girls' Home Internationals *continued*

County and District Championships

Aberdeenshire Ladies' Championship

Year	Winner	Year	Winner	Year	Winner
1976	Miss CA Stewart	1980	Miss JB Rennie	1984	Miss J Self
1977	Miss M Thomson	1981	Miss CA Stewart	1985	Miss P Wright
1978	Miss AV Laing	1982	Miss P Wright	1986	Miss E Farquharson
1979	Miss J Self	1983	Miss E Farquharson		

Angus Ladies' Championship

Instituted pre 1935

Year	Winner	Year	Winner	Year	Winner
1958	Miss M Walker	1968	Miss S Chalmers	1978	Miss JW Smith
1959	Mrs AG Duncan	1969	Miss I Taylor	1979	Miss JW Smith
1960	Miss S Cushnie	1970	Miss J Smith	1980	Miss N Duncan
1961	Miss E Allan	1971	Miss K Lackie	1981	Miss K Sutherland
1962	Mrs A Beattie	1972	Miss K Lackie	1982	Miss K Imrie
1963	Miss E Allan	1973	Miss K Lackie	1983	Miss K Imrie
1964	Miss J Smith	1974	Miss N Duncan	1984	Miss K Imrie
1965	Miss N Duncan	1975	Miss JW Smith	1985	M Mackie
1966	Miss K Lackie	1976	Miss B Huke	1986	Miss E Farquharson
1967	Miss J Smith	1977	Miss JW Smith		

Argyll and Bute Amateur Championship

Year	Winner	Year	Winner	Year	Winner
1979	AK Gallacher	1982	J Ewing	1984	D MacIntyre
1980	GJ Tyre	1983	G Tyre	1985	
1981	M Cannon	1984	D MacIntyre	1986	

Astor Salver

Instituted 1951

Venue: The Berkshire

Year	Winner	Score	Year	Winner	Score
1951	Miss J Bisgood	146	1957	Miss A Ward	148
1952	Miss J Bisgood	147	1958	Mrs MF Bonallack	145
1953	Miss J Bisgood	147	1959	Miss E. Price	149
1954	Miss J Donald	151	1960	Mrs MF Bonallack	144
1955	Miss E Price	148	1961	Mrs MF Bonallack	145
1956	Mrs J Barton, Miss E Price	151	1962	Miss R Porter	150
			1963	Miss R Porter	151

Astor Salver
continued

Year	Winner		Year	Winner	
1964	Mrs M Spearman	148	1975	Mrs JR Thornhill	150
1965	Mrs M Spearman	145	1976	Miss HD Clifford	151
1966	Mrs MF Bonallack	145	1977	Mrs WJ Uzielli	142
1967	Miss DM Everard	150	1978	Miss DM Everard	143
1968	Miss DM Everard	152	1979	Miss J Greenhalgh	144
1969	Miss J Greenhalgh	148	1980	Miss J Lock (Aust)	141
1970	Miss B Whitehead	148	1981	Mrs WJ Uzielli	148
1971	Mrs WJ Uzielli	149	1982	*Abandoned after one round due to weather*	
1972	Mrs JR Thornhill	152			
1973	Miss L Denison-Pender, Mrs WJ Uzielli	155	1983	Mrs L Bayman	148
			1984	Mrs L Bayman	142
			1985	Miss H Wadsworth	138
1974	Mrs C Barclay	147	1986	Miss C Pierce	144

Avia Ladies' International Tournament

Venue: The Berkshire

Year	Winners	Year	Winners
1966	Vicomtesse de St Sauveur and Mlle B Varangot (France)	1977	Miss T Perkins (Wenvoe Castle) and Miss M McKenna (Donabate)
1967	Miss BAB Jackson (Handsworth) and Miss V Saunders (Kingswood)	1978	Miss M Everard (Hallamshire) and Miss V Saunders (Tyrrells Wood)
1968	Miss R Porter (Long Ashton) and Miss A Irvin (Lytham and St Anne's)	1979	Mrs A Sander (Sunningdale) and Mrs L Bayman (The Berkshire)
1969	Miss C Reybroeck (Belgium) and Miss L Denison-Pender (Prince's)	1980	Mrs L Bayman (The Berkshire) and Miss M Madill (Portstewart)
1970	Miss G Cheetham (Crompton and Royton) and Mrs J Thornhill (Walton Heath)	1981	Mrs IC Robertson (Dunaverty) and Mrs W Wooldridge (Wentworth)
1971	Miss C Reybroeck (Belgium) and Miss L Denison-Pender (Prince's)	1982	Mrs A Uzielli (The Berkshire) and Miss W Aitken (Old Ranfurly)
1972	Mrs D Frearson (Tandridge) and Mrs IC Robertson (Dunaverty)	1983	Mrs J Thornhill (Walton Heath) and Mrs J Nicholson (Worplesdon)
1973	Miss Michelle Walker (Faversham) and Miss L Denison-Pender (Prince's) Miss B Varangot (France) and Miss AM Palli (France)	1984	Miss M McKenna (Donabate) and Mrs IC Robertson (Dunaverty)
1974	Miss C Redford (Canterbury) and Miss C le Feuvre (Jersey)	1985	Mrs L Bayman and Miss M Madill
1975	*Cancelled due to snow*	1986	Mrs IC Robertson and Miss M McKenna
1976	Mrs MF Bonallack and Mrs S Barber (Thorpe Hall)		

Ayrshire Amateur Championship

Year	Winner	Year	Winner	Year	Winner
1950	A Stevenson	1962	RR Davidson	1975	L Crawford
1951	HC Maclaine	1963	S Anderson	1976	JT Moffat
1952	J Armour	1964	D Murdoch	1977	B Stevely
1953	JM Cannon	1965	CJL Strachan	1978	A Thomson
1954	JR McKay	1966	JA Morrison	1979	JT Moffat
1955	M Alexander	1967	M Lygate	1980	J Bunting
1956	J McKay / J Walker	1968	WR Lockie	1981	D Murdoch
		1969	A Cruickshanks	1982	C Evans
1957	JH Morrison	1970	JM Cannon	1983	L Crawford
1958	JM Cannon	1971	JT Moffat	1984	J Milligan
1959	JH Morrison	1972	AMB Sym	1985	P Girvan
1960	A MacGregor	1973	JM Cannon	1986	
1961	JH Morrison	1974	M Rae		

Ayrshire Ladies' Championship

Instituted 1923

Year	Winner	Year	Winner	Year	Winner
1936	Mrs AM Holm	1958	Mrs B Singleton	1973	Miss I Wylie
1937	Mrs JB Walker	1959	Mrs B Singleton	1974	Mrs JM Sharp
1938	Mrs JB Walker	1960	Miss J Hastings	1975	Miss S Lambie
1939	Miss B Henderson	1961	Miss J Hastings	1976	Miss S Lambie
1947	Mrs AM Holm	1962	Mrs B Singleton	1977	Miss T Walker
1948	Mrs AM Holm	1963	Miss J Hastings	1978	Miss S Lambie
1949	Mrs Q McCall	1964	Miss J Hastings	1979	Miss S Lambie
1950	Mrs AM Holm	1965	Mrs ID Hamilton	1980	Miss A Gemmill
1951	Mrs AM Holm	1966	Miss J Hastings	1981	Miss A Gemmill
1952	Mrs M Park	1967	Miss J Hastings	1982	Miss A Gemmill
1953	Mrs B Singleton	1968	Mrs ID Hamilton	1983	Miss A Gemmill
1954	Mrs PH Wylie	1969	Miss I Wylie	1984	Miss A Gemmill
1955	Mrs A McCall	1970	Miss I Wylie	1985	Miss J Leishman
1956	Mrs B Singleton	1971	Miss I Wylie	1986	Miss A Gemmill
1957	Mrs B Singleton	1972	Miss I Wylie		

Bedfordshire Amateur Championship

Instituted 1923

Year	Winner	Year	Winner	Year	Winner
1936	LG Randall	1957	AL Day	1972	N Wharton
1937	RG Field	1958	AL Day	1973	R Coogan
1938	WG Groves	1959	AL Day	1974	R Coogan
1939	WG Groves	1960	AL Day	1975	S Evans
1946	LG Randall	1961	AL Day	1976	S Evans
1947	AL Day	1962	E Woodward	1977	R Drew
1948	LG Randall	1963	AJ Southam	1978	A Rose
1949	LG Randall	1964	AL Day	1979	P Wharton
1950	LG Randall	1965	CW Day	1980	D Ellis
1951	I Anderson	1966	R Sharp	1981	C Beard
1952	LG Randall	1967	RA Durrant	1982	A Rose
1953	I Anderson	1968	RA Durrant	1983	A Rose
1954	LG Randall	1969	F Rowden	1984	MA Stokes
1955	AL Day	1970	RA Durrant	1985	R Harris
1956	LG Randall	1971	R Coogan	1986	

Bedfordshire Ladies' Championship

Instituted 1926

Year	Winner	Year	Winner	Year	Winner
1930	Mrs Antliff	1953	Mrs Crew	1971	Mrs S Kempster
1931	Miss Dalton	1954	Mrs CJ Allen	1972	Mrs P Deman
1932	Miss Dalton	1955	Mrs Arnold	1973	Mrs J Hawkins
1933	Miss R Payne	1956	Mrs Greer	1974	Mrs S Kempster
1934	Miss M Dalton	1957	Mrs Greer	1975	Mrs P Deman
1935	Mrs Hedges	1958	Mrs FW Wood	1976	Mrs S Kempster
1936	Miss B Gorrell	1959	Mrs L Cook	1977	Mrs P Deman
1937	Miss N Sanderson	1960	Mrs Turner	1978	Mrs P Deman
1938	Mrs Crew	1963	Mrs Murray	1979	Mrs J Latch
1939	Mrs Crew	1964	Mrs Greer	1980	Miss S Kiddle
1947	Mrs Oakins	1965	Mrs G Brandom	1981	Miss S Kiddle
1948	Miss Walsh	1966	Mrs G Brandom	1982	Miss S Kiddle
1949	Miss Walsh	1967	Mrs G Brandom	1983	Mrs S White
1950	Mrs Seale	1968	Mrs S Kempster	1984	Mrs S White
1951	Mrs Crew	1969	Mrs S Kempster	1985	Mrs S White
1952	Mrs Crew	1970	Mrs B Hawkins	1986	Mrs C Westgate

Berkhamsted Trophy

Year	Winner	Score	Year	Winner	Score
1960	HC Squirrell	150	1975	P Deeble	147
1961	DW Frame	147	1976	J Davies	144
1962	DG Neech	149	1977	AWB Lyle	144
1963	HC Squirrell	149	1978	JC Davies	146
1964	PD Flaherty	149	1979	JC Davies	147
1965	LF Millar	153	1980	R Knott	143
1966	PM Townsend	150	1981	P Dennett	146
1967	DJ Millensted	150	1982	DG Lane	148
1968	PD Flaherty	144	1983	J Hawksworth	146
1969	MM Niven	149	1984	R Willison	139
1970	R Hunter	145	1985	F George	144
1971	A Millar	144	1986	P McEvoy	144
1972	C Cieslewicz	148			
1973	SC Mason	141			
1974	P Fisher	144			

Berkshire Trophy

Year	Winner	Score	Year	Winner	Score
1946	R Sweeney JB Beck	148	1967	DJ Millensted	283
1947	PB Lucas	298	1968	MF Bonallack	273
1948	LG Crawley	301	1969	J Davies	278
1949	PB Lucas	300	1970	MF Bonallack	274
1950	PF Scrutton	296	1971	MF Bonallack J Davies	277
1951	PF Scrutton	301	1972	DP Davidson	280
1952	PF Scrutton	286	1973	P Hedges	278
1953	JL Morgan	289	1974	J Downie	280
1954	E Bromley-Davenport Fl Lt K Hall	303	1975	N Faldo	281
1955	GH Micklem	282	1976	P Hedges	284
1956	G Wolstenholme	285	1977	AWB Lyle	279
1957	MF Bonallack	291	1978	P Hedges	281
1958	G Wolstenholme AH Perowne	284	1979	D Williams	274
1959	JB Carr	279	1980	P Downes	280
1960	G Wolstenholme	276	1981	D Blakeman	280
1961	MF Bonallack	275	1982	S Keppler	278
1962	SC Saddler	279	1983	S Hamer	288
1963	DW Frame	289	1984	JL Plaxton	276
1964	R Foster	281	1985	P McEvoy	279
1965	MF Bonallack	278	1986	R Muscroft	280
1966	P Oosterhuis	287			

Berkshire Ladies' Championship

Instituted 1925

Year	Winner	Year	Winner	Year	Winner
1950	Mrs Tegner	1964	Mrs AC Marks	1976	Mrs A Uzielli
1951	Miss Bryant	1965	Mrs Garnett	1977	Mrs A Uzielli
1952	Mrs Simmons	1966	Mrs D O'Brien	1978	Mrs A Uzielli
1954	Miss Bryant	1967	Mrs W Henney	1979	Mrs A Uzielli
1955	Mrs Van Oss	1968	Mrs MK Garnett	1980	Mrs A Uzielli
1956	Miss Bryant	1969	Mrs D Hanbury	1981	Mrs A Uzielli
1958	Miss I Clifton	1970	Mrs M Garnett	1982	Mrs C Caldwell
1959	Mrs E Simmons	1971	Mrs D Hanbury	1983	Mrs A Uzielli
1960	Mrs M Garnett	1972	Mrs D Hanbury	1984	Mrs A Uzielli
1961	Mrs D Buchanan	1973	Mrs P Cardy	1985	Mrs A Uzielli
1962	Miss E Clifton	1974	Mrs Leatham	1986	Mrs A Uzielli
1963	Mrs AC Marks	1975	Miss S Jolly		

Berks, Bucks and Oxfordshire Amateur Championship

Instituted 1924

Year	Winner	Year	Winner	Year	Winner
1930	CB Booth	1953	IR Harris	1970	MG King
1931	D Provan	1954	RK Pitamber	1971	K Borrett
1932	R Fortescue	1955	RSG Scott	1972	JA Putt
1933	GR Girdlestone	1956	JJ MacBeth	1973	MG King
1934	JO Greenly	1957	NJ Niven	1974	MG King
1935	CW Moie	1958	FB Reed	1975	A Parsons
1936	EH Chambers	1959	JK Tullis	1976	WS Gronow
1937	A Keith	1960	WOT Cocker	1977	MD Owers
1938	CB Booth	1961	J Lawrence	1978	A Parsons
1939	HC Stone	1962	J Lawrence	1979	A Miller
1946	R Sweeny	1963	J Coomber	1980	DG Lane
1947	R Sweeny	1964	J Lawrence	1981	M Rapley
1948	AR Strong	1965	J Coomber	1982	DG Lane
1949	JE Kitchin	1966	J Lawrence	1983	M Orris
1950	BW Parmenter	1967	RWT Addey	1984	NG Webber
1951	NRM Philcox	1968	MG King	1985	M Rapley
1952	Dr GMF Bisset	1969	MG King	1986	

Border Counties Ladies' Championship

Year	Winner	Year	Winner	Year	Winner
1980	Miss S Gallacher	1983	Mrs E White	1986	Miss S Gallacher
1981	Miss A Hunter	1984	Miss S Gallacher		
1982	Mrs S Simpson	1985	Miss S Gallacher		

Border Golfers' Association Amateur Championship

Instituted 1893

Year	Winner	Year	Winner	Year	Winner
1930	AT Kyle	1954	WW Cowe	1971	WD Simpson
1931	T Sanderson	1955	CW Telfer	1972	AR Potts
1932	T Sanderson	1956	CW Telfer	1973	K Allan
1933	T Sanderson	1957	WD Smith	1974	JK Wells
1934	AT Cleghorn	1958	TT Sanderson	1975	MD Cleghorn
1935	JC Conn	1959	JA Brown	1976	DF Campbell
1936	T Sanderson	1960	TT Sanderson	1977	J Hume
1937	JA Brown	1961	Ian Turnbull	1978	PWJ Gallagher
1938	JA Brown	1962	TT Sanderson	1979	PWJ Gallagher
1939	JW Gladstone	1963	WD Smith	1980	PWJ Gallagher
1947	T Sanderson	1964	TT Sanderson	1981	PWJ Gallagher
1948	TA Fairbairn	1965	JF Thomas	1982	DF Campbell
1949	WD Smith	1966	JK Wells	1983	B Reid
1950	TW Fraser	1967	R McAllan	(After play-off)	
1951	WD Smith	1968	JF Thomas	1984	A Turnbull
1952	WW Cowe	1969	JK Wells	1985	
1953	R Livingstone	1970	JK Wells	1986	D Ballantyne

Boyd Quaich Tournament

Year	Winner	Year	Winner	Year	Winner
1946	AS Mayer	1959-61	*Not played*	1975	S Dunlop
1947	Harry Brews / Frank Deighton	1962	DB Sheahan	1976	R Watson
1948	JL Lindsay	1963	S MacDonald	1977	R Watson
1949	FD Tatum	1964	AJ Low	1978	R Watson
1950	GP Roberts	1965	S MacDonald	1979	D McLeary
1951	H Dooley	1966	FE McCarroll	1980	ME Lewis
1952	G Parker	1967	B Nicholson	1981	P Gallagher
1953	JL Bamford	1968	JW Johnston	1982	ME Lewis
1954	Ian Caldwell	1969	PH Moody	1983	R Risan
1955	HC Squirrell	1970	JT Moffatt	1984	J Huggan
1956	JL Bamford	1971	JW Johnston	1985	S Elgie
1957	DM Marsh	1972	D Greig	1986	
1958	R Mummery	1973	J Rube		
		1974	G Cairns		

British Universities Championship (Men)

Year	Winner	Year	Winner	Year	Winner
1957	J Price	1968	WD Raymond	1978	S Potter
1958	AHH Campbell	1969	J Johnston	1979	A Wilmot
1960	RG Aitken	1970	PH Moody	1980	M Lewis
1961	JA Mather	1971	A Harrington	1981	M Lewis
1962	WT Easson	1972	I Bamborough	1982	K McCall
1963	AJ Low	1973	J Whiteley	1983	A Glenn
1964	Fraser Hall	1974	I Gillan	1984	
1965	S MacDonald	1975	J Savage	1985	
1966	DS Cameron	1976	I Gillan	1986	
1967	R Radway	1977	P Craigon		

Bucks Ladies' Championship

Instituted 1924

Year	Winner	Year	Winner
1931	Mrs Gold	1963	Mrs AWH Baucher
1932	Mrs Gold	1964	Miss A Mobbs
1933	Mrs Greenly	1965	Mrs B Dutton
1934	Mrs Gold	1966	Miss A Mobbs
1935	Mrs O Jones	1967	Miss A Mobbs
1936	Mrs Gold	1968	Mrs RB Parton
1937	Mrs Gold	1969	Mrs P Newman
1938	Mrs A Scott	1970	Mrs A Baucher
1939	Mrs Barnes	1971	Mrs M Baxter
1947	Mrs Gold	1972	Mrs J Marshall
1948	Mrs Whitworth Jones	1973	Mrs G Gordon
1949	Mrs Whitworth Jones	1974	Miss L Harrold
1950	Mrs Gold	1975	Miss L Harrold
1951	Mrs Gold	1976	Miss L Harrold
1952	Mrs Braddon	1977	Miss L Harrold
1953	Miss DM Speir	1978	Mrs M Purdy
1954	Mrs WM Paul	1979	Miss J Lee
1955	Mrs CW Stothert	1980	Mrs K Copley
1956	Mrs AWH Baucher	1981	Miss J Warren
1957	Mrs AWH Baucher	1982	Miss J Warren
1958	Mrs M Baxter	1983	Miss G Bonallack
1959	Miss A Mobbs	1984	Miss J Warren
1960	Miss A Mobbs	1985	Miss E Franklin
1961	Mrs E Braithwaite	1986	Miss A Tyreman
1962	Mrs AWH Baucher		

Caernarvonshire Amateur Championship

Instituted 1922

Year	Winner	Year	Winner	Year	Winner
1930	J Morris	1953	W Vale	1971	WG Jones
1931	JL Black	1954	H Palferman	1972	J Roger Jones
1932	JL Black	1955	H Palferman	1973	C Brown
1933	JL Black	1956	W Vale	1974	J Roger Jones
1934	JL Black	1957	P Mills	1975	J Roger Jones
1935	JL Black	1958	ES Mills	1976	GW Jones
1936	SB Roberts	1959	EC Roberts	1977	D McLean
1937	SB Roberts	1960	WJ Hobson	1978	C Brown
1938	AH Wright	1961	A Moss	1979	D McLean
1939	GE Roberts	1962	C Hobley Eaves	1980	A Llyr
1940	James Roberts	1963	W Vale	1981	WG Jones
1946	Mervyn Jones	1964	WJ Hobson	1982	D McLean
1947	AM Goodwin	1965	WJ Roberts	1983	JR Parry / WG Jones
1948	AM Goodwin	1966	D McLean	1984	
1949	JB Wilson	1967	E Mills	1985	
1950	CG Guy	1968	D McLean	1986	
1951	WW Prytherch	1969	D McLean		
1952	H Palferman	1970	D McLean / J Roger Jones		

Caernarvonshire and Anglesey Ladies' Championship

Instituted 1924

Year	Winner	Year	Winner
1947	Miss A Stockton	1967	Mrs JH Brown
1948	Miss N Cook	1968	Miss A Hughes
1949	Miss EHA Lever	1969	Miss A Hughes
1950	Miss EHA Lever	1970	Mrs Marcus Wright
1951	Miss EHA Lever	1971	Mrs JH Brown
1952	Miss EHA Lever	1972	Miss A Hughes
1953	Miss N Cook	1973	Mrs JH Brown
1954	Mrs JH Brown	1974	Miss VJ Brammer
1955	Miss EHA Lever	1975	Mrs R Ferguson
1956	Miss EHA Lever	1976	Mrs M Wright
1957	Miss N Seddon	1977	Miss A Thomas
1958	Miss N Seddon	1978	Mrs A Johnson
1959	Mrs DV Ingham	1979	Miss A Thomas
1960	Mrs BJ Jenkin	1980	Miss A Thomas
1961	Mrs Marcus Wright	1981	Miss S Jump
1962	Mrs DV Ingham	1982	Miss F Connor
1963	Miss N Seddon	1983	Miss SL Roberts
1964	Miss A Hughes	1984	Miss S Jump
1965	Mrs Marcus Wright	1985	Miss A Lewis
1966	Mrs JH Brown	1986	Mrs S Turner

Cambridge Area GU Amateur Championship

Year	Winner	Year	Winner	Year	Winner
1950	IN Reynolds	1954	GG Kerr	1958	J Goddard
1951	GH Duncan	1955	A Peck	1959	Flt-Lt AJA Heyns
1952	LW Wheeler	1956	WB Dunn	1960	J Goddard
1953	WB Dunn	1957	G Rand	1961	J Goddard

Cambridge Area GU Amateur Championship

continued

Year	Winner	Year	Winner	Year	Winner
1962	FG Rand	1971	A Garner	1980	MT Seaton
1963	KA Cameron	1972	G Powell	1981	MT Seaton
1964	RJ Brown	1973	RW Guy	1982	RW Guy
1965	FG Rand	1974	MT Seaton	1983	JR Gray
1966	CP Harrison	1975	S Derbyshire	1984	NK Hughes
1967	B McCulloch	1976	BJ McCulloch	1985	DWG Wood
1968	RAC Blows	1977	RW Guy	1986	
1969	WS Harrison	1978	MT Seaton		
1970	RW Guy	1979	RW Guy		

Cambridgeshire and Hunts Ladies' Championship

Year	Winner	Year	Winner
1947	Mrs Holland	1967	Mrs VJ Mackenzie
1948	Mrs Baker	1968	Mrs VJ Mackenzie
1949	Mrs A Newport	1969	Mrs J Honey
1950	Mrs Holland	1970	Mrs M Gray
1951	Mrs Baker	1971	Mrs S Stephenson
1952	Mrs Holland	1972	Mrs M Gray
1953	Mrs Holland	1973	Mrs D Baker
1954	Mrs Hill	1974	Miss J Walter
1955	Mrs Croxton	1975	Miss M. Maddocks
1956	Mrs Baker	1976	Miss J Walter
1957	Mrs Baker	1977	Miss J Walter
1958	Mrs Baker	1978	Miss J Walter
1959	Mrs Baker	1979	Miss J Walter
1960	Mrs Thomas	1980	Miss J Richards
1961	Mrs Croxton	1981	Miss J Walter
1962	Mrs Baker	1982	Miss J Walter
1963	Mrs Nan Richmond	1983	Miss J Walter
1964	Miss Janet Peck	1984	Miss J Walter
1965	Mrs J Sedgwick	1985	Miss J Walter
1966	Mrs VJ Mackenzie	1986	Miss J Walter

Carris Trophy

Venue: Moor Park

Year	Winner	Score	Year	Winner	Score
1935	R. Upex	75	1964	PM Townsend	148
1936	JDA Langley	152	1965	G McKay	145
1937	RJ White	149	1966	A Black	151
1938	IP Garrow	147	1967	RF Brown	147
1939	CW Warren	149	1968	P Dawson	149
1946	AH Perowne	158	1969	ID Gradwell	150
1947	I Caldwell	159	1970	MF Foster	146
1948	I Caldwell	152	1971	RJ Evans	146
1949	PB Hine	148	1972	L Donovan	143
1950	J Glover	144	1973	S Hadfield	148
1951	I Young	154	1974	KJ Brown	304
1952	N Thygesen	150	1975	AWB Lyle	270
1953	N Johnson	148	1976	H Stott	285
1954	K Warren	149	1977	R Mugglestone	293
1955	ID Wheater	151	1978	J Plaxton	144
1956	G Maisey	141	1979	P Hammond	288
1957	G Maisey	145	1980	MP McLean	290
1958	J Hamilton	149	1981	D Gilford	290
1959	RT Walker	152	1982	M Jarvis	298
1960	PM Baxter	150	1983	P Baker	288
1961	DJ Miller	143	1984	I Coe	283
1962	FS Morris	145	1985	P Baker	286
1963	EJ Threlfall	147	1986	G Evans	292

Channel Islands Amateur Championship

Instituted 1927

Year	Winner	Year	Winner
1952	JS Heaume	1970	G Binding
1953	D Lowe	1971	CWF Wagner
1954	DF Ashton	1972	DJ Warr
1955	JS Heaume	1973	DJ Warr
1956	JS Heaume	1974	R Mahy
1957	AJ Monamy	1975	RV De La Haye
1958	AJ Monamy	1976	TF Tanner
1959	AJ Monamy	1977	R Mahy
1960	R Mahy	1978	R Laffoley
1961	DF Ashton	1979	PF James
1962	C Farnham	1980	P Wilcox
1963	R Mahy	1981	D Warr
1964	G Binding	1982	D Warr
1965	RF Mahy	1983	F Weeks
1966	RE Osborne-Smith	1984	R Eggo
1967	A Baker	1985	
1968	G Binding	1986	
1969	CP Dobin		

Channel Islands Ladies' Championship

Year	Winner	Year	Winner
1937	Mrs JP Ross	1967	Mrs A Lindsay
1938	Mrs HM de la Rue	1968	Mrs A Lindsay
1939	Mrs JP Ross	1969	Mrs A Lindsay
1949	Mrs NB Grant	1970	Mrs A Lindsay
1950	Mrs JA McDade	1971	Mrs A Lindsay
1951	Mrs WF Mauger	1972	Mrs A Lindsay
1952	Mrs DWM Randell	1973	Mrs A Lindsay
1953	Mrs JA McDade	1974	Mrs P Haley
1954	Mrs DWM Randell	1975	Miss M Darbyshire
1955	Mrs D Porter	1976	Miss M Darbyshire
1956	Mrs JA McDade	1977	Miss M Darbyshire
1957	Mrs JA McDade	1978	Mrs E Roberts
1958	Mrs JA McDade	1979	Mrs J Bunbury
1959	Hon Mrs Siddeley	1980	Mrs E Roberts
1960	Miss P Stacey	1981	Miss L Cummins
1961	Mrs D Porter	1982	Miss V Bougourd
1962	Miss P Stacey	1983	Mrs D Heaton
1963	Mrs JA McDade	1984	Mrs E Roberts
1964	Mrs A Lindsay	1985	Miss L Cummins
1965	Mrs A Lindsay	1986	Miss V Bougourd
1966	Mrs A Lindsay		

Cheshire Amateur Championship

Instituted 1921

Year	Winner	Year	Winner
1932	HD Porter	1963	MJ Pearson
1933	HMN Fogg	1964	A O'Connor
1934	CW Timmis	1965	MJ Pearson
1935	J Abraham	1966	GM Edwards
1936	W Sutton	1967	AP O'Connor
1937	HE Walker	1968	NB Moir
1938	E Bromley-Davenport	1969	D Jones
1939	MW Budd	1970	B Stockdale
1946	CW Timmis	1971	TD Frost
1947	P Clark	1972	DK Jones
1948	CW Timmis	1973	GM Edwards
1949	S Mettam	1974	PH Dennett
1950	HC Humphreys	1975	EI Bradshaw
1951	HC Humphreys	1976	R Biggs
1952	DHL Shone	1977	EI Bradshaw
1953	S Mettam	1978	CR Smethurst
1954	MJ Pearson	1979	P Bailey
1955	E Crimes	1980	EI Bradshaw
1956	AE Billington	1981	C Harrison
1957	P Clark	1982	CR Smethurst
1958	S Ball	1983	CR Smethurst
1959	JT Jones	1984	I Spencer
1960	JT Jones	1985	C Harrison
1961	JT Jones	1986	
1962	GM Edwards		

Cheshire Ladies' Championship

Instituted 1912

Year	Winner	Year	Winner
1932	Mrs Alan Macbeth	1964	Miss E Chadwick
1933	Miss E Wilson	1965	Miss E Chadwick
1934	Mrs Clement	1966	Miss E Chadwick
1935	Mrs Alan Macbeth	1967	Miss E Chadwick
1936	Mrs Hartley	1968	Mrs C Comboy
1937	Mrs Alan Macbeth	1969	Mrs C Comboy
1938	Mrs Whitfield	1970	Mrs C Comboy
1939	Mrs JB Hartley	1971	Mrs A Briggs
1947	Miss J Pemberton	1972	Dr H Lyall
1948	Miss J Pemberton	1973	Mrs A Briggs
1949	Mrs Cowper	1974	Mrs S Graveley
1950	Mrs Horabin	1975	Mrs E Wilson
1951	Miss Lloyd	1976	Mrs A Briggs
1952	Mrs Horabin	1977	Miss H Latham
1953	Mrs M Appleby	1978	Mrs J Hughes
1954	Miss A. Christian-Jones	1979	Miss H Latham
1955	Miss B Lloyd	1980	Mrs A Briggs
1956	Miss M Wolff	1981	Mrs A Briggs
1958	Miss S McNicoll	1982	Miss H Latham
1959	Mrs C Grott	1983	Miss H Latham
1960	Mrs T Briggs	1984	Miss J Hill
1961	Mrs C Comboy	1985	Miss L Percival
1962	Mrs C Comboy	1986	Miss J Hill
1963	Miss E Chadwick		

Cornwall Amateur Championship

Instituted 1896

Year	Winner	Year	Winner
1935	Com Bannerman	1964	GN Bicknell
1936	RM Jewson	1965	PJ Yeo
1937	AD Stocks	1966	PJ Yeo
1938	AI Roberts	1967	PJ Yeo
1939	Col GL Tyringham	1968	JV Brown
1946	H Hutchinson	1969	HG Champion
1947	AJ Billing	1970	PJ Yeo
1948	PC Vardon	1971	PJC Ward
1949	H Hutchinson	1972	G Medlyn
1950	E Bennett	1973	RE Libby
1951	E Bennett	1974	CS Carveth
1952	E Bennett	1975	P Hasson
1953	H Hutchinson	1976	JW Bradley
1954	H Hutchinson	1977	JW Bradley
1955	H Hutchinson	1978	AJK Rowe
1956	H Hutchinson	1979	PA Gilbert
1957	G Medlyn	1980	M Boggia
1958	DM Payne	1981	JR Hirst
1959	GN Bicknell	1982	MC Edmunds
1960	GN Bicknell	1983	MC Edmunds
1961	DM Payne	1984	RJ Simmons
1962	E Holland	1985	CD Phillips
1963	RGW Sanders	1986	

Cornwall Ladies' Championship

Instituted 1896

Year	Winner	Year	Winner
1935	Miss E Ratcliffe	1965	Miss M Roskrow
1936	Miss M Ratcliffe	1966	Miss M Roskrow
1937	Miss M Roskrow	1967	Miss E Luxon
1938	Miss M Roskrow	1968	Mrs MC Rowe
1939	Miss M Roskrow	1969	Miss S Mitchell
1947	Miss M Roskrow	1970	Mrs D Luxon
1948	Miss M Roskrow	1971	Mrs D Luxon
1949	Mrs Wills	1972	Miss S Mitchell
1950	Miss M Roskrow	1973	Mrs J Clowes
1951	Miss H Trant	1974	Miss J Dodd
1952	Miss M Roskrow	1975	Miss E Luxon
1953	Miss M Roskrow	1976	Miss J Ryder
1954	Miss B Soper	1977	Miss J Ryder
1955	Miss M Roskrow	1978	Miss S Cann
1956	Miss M Roskrow	1979	Miss L Moore
1957	Miss M Roskrow	1980	Miss L Moore
1958	Miss M Roskrow	1981	Miss L Moore
1959	Miss M Roskrow	1982	Miss S Cann
1960	Mrs J Rodgers	1983	Miss J Ryder
1961	Miss M Roskrow	1984	Miss J Fernleigh
1962	Miss M Roskrow	1985	Miss J Fern
1963	Miss M Roskrow	1986	Miss J Ryder
1964	Mrs WA Tomlinson		

County Champions' Tournament (England)

For President's Bowl

Year	Winner	Year	Winner
1962	GM Edwards, Cheshire A Thirwell, Northumberland	1974	GE Hyde, Sussex AWB Lyle, Shrops & Hereford
1963	MJ Burgess, Sussex R Foster, Yorkshire	1975	NA Faldo, Herts
		1976	RPF Brown, Devon
1964	MF Attenborough, Kent	1977	M Walls, Cumbria
1965	MG Lees, Lincs	1978	IT Simpson, Nottinghamshire
1966	RP Stephenson, Middx	1979	N Burch, Essex
1967	PJ Benka, Surrey	1980	D Lane, Berks, Bucks and Oxon
1968	GE Hyde, Sussex	1981	M Kelly, Yorkshire
1969	AW Holmes, Herts	1982	P Deeble, Northumberland
1970	MG King, Berks, Bucks and Oxon	1983	N Chesses, Warwickshire
1971	M Lee, Yorkshire	1984	N Briggs, Hertfordshire P McEvoy, Warwickshire
1972	P Berry, Glos		
1973	AH Chandler, Lancs	1985	P Robinson
		1986	A Gelsthorpe

Cumberland and Westmorland Amateur Championship

Instituted 1910

Year	Winner	Year	Winner	Year	Winner
1935	A Grieve	1954	A Grieve	1966	JB Carr
1936	A Grieve	1955	WD Longcake	1967	WD Longcake
1937	A Grieve	1956	WD Longcake	1968	J Terris
1938	TS Hartley	1957	WA Anderson	1969	JH French
1939	L Steele	1958	WR Sharp	1970	ID Stavert
1947	F Todd	1959	WD Longcake	1971	ID Stavert
1948	F Todd	1960	WR Sharp	1972	M Walls
1949	F Todd	1961	W Anderson	1973	JDM Dodds
1950	F Todd	1962	A Grieve		
1951	F Todd	1963	WD Longcake		
1952	RS Furness	1964	WR Sharp		
1953	IE Kilshaw	1965	JB Carr		

In 1974 became Cumbria Amateur Championship

Cumbria Amateur Championship

Formerly Cumberland and Westmorland Amateur Championship

Year	Winner	Year	Winner	Year	Winner
1974	M Walls	1979	AJ Payne	1984	M Lowe
1975	M Walls	1980	AR Morrison	1985	J Longcake
1976	E Gulliksen	1981	J Kirkpatrick	1986	
1977	M Walls	1982	E Gulliksen		
1978	M Barrand	1983	A Drabble		

Cumbria Ladies' Championship

Year	Winner	Year	Winner	Year	Winner
1928	Miss M Howe	1953	Miss LB Clark	1971	Miss P Brough
1929	Miss E Hartlet	1954	Mrs PE Gillman	1972	Miss M Stavert
1930	Miss M Howe	1955	Miss LB Clark	1973	Miss M Stavert
1931	Miss M Howe	1956	Miss LB Clark	1974	Miss H Long
1932	Mrs RD Burgess	1957	Mrs JH French	1975	Miss J Allison
1933	Miss DJ Jordan	1958	Miss LB Clark	1976	Miss J Allison
1934	Miss M Howe	1959	Miss LB Clark	1977	Miss H Long
1935	Miss H Howe	1960	Mrs J Stafford	1978	Miss N Pieri
1936	Miss LB Clark	1961	Miss LB Clark	1979	Miss D Thomson
1937	Miss LB Clark	1962	Miss LB Clark	1980	Miss D Thomson
1938	Miss LB Clark	1963	Mrs J Stafford	1981	Miss D Thomson
1939	Miss LB Clark	1964	Miss MA Peile	1982	Miss D Thomson
1947	Miss H Scott	1965	Mrs WJ Ward	1983	Miss P Brumwell
1948	Miss H Scott	1966	Miss P Brough	1984	Miss D Thomson
1949	Miss JI Johnstone	1967	Miss P Brough	1985	Miss J Currie
1950	Miss LB Clark	1968	Miss P Brough	1986	Mrs H Porter
1951	Miss LB Clark	1969	Miss N Peile		
1952	Miss LB Clark	1970	Miss P Brough		

Denbighshire Championship

Year	Winner	Year	Winner	Year	Winner
1952	ER Gors	1964	JT Williams	1976	J Buckley
1953	ER Gors	1965	AE Walker	1977	Clive Wright
1954	Dr AM Millar	1966	L Roobottom	1978	J Buckley
1955	WW Prytherch	1967	J Buckley	1979	G Pattison
1956	WW Prytherch	1968	J Buckley	1980	Clive Wright
1957	ER Jackson	1969	John R Jones	1981	*No information*
1958	Dr AM Millar	1970	P Riley	1982	
1959	Brian Thornton	1971	JR Jones	1983	
1960	J Williams	1972	P Riley	1984	
1961	PH Davies	1973	Clive Wright	1985	
1962	PH Davies	1974	Clive Wright	1986	
1963	AE Walker	1975	Clive Wright		

Denbighshire Ladies' Championship

Year	Winner	Year	Winner	Year	Winner
1960	Mrs M Hartley	1969	Miss M Lea	1978	Miss P Whitley
1961	Mrs M Hartley	1970	Mrs B Jones	1979	Miss P Whitley
1962	Mrs HM Bellis	1971	Mrs B Jones	1980	Miss K Davies
1963	Mrs M Hartley	1972	Miss P Whitley	1981	Mrs E Higgs
1964	Mrs OW Jones	1973	Miss P Whitley	1982	Miss K Davies
1965	Mrs OW Jones	1974	Miss P Whitley	1983	Miss E Davies
1966	Mrs OW Jones	1975	Mrs L Hayes	1984	Mrs C Ellis
1967	Mrs JK Bellis	1976	Mrs E Davies	1985	Miss E Davies
1968	Miss M Lea	1977	Miss P Whitley	1986	

Derbyshire Amateur Championship

Instituted 1913

Year	Winner	Year	Winner	Year	Winner
1946	J Armitt	1960	H Bennett	1974	D Mason
1947	R Pattinson	1961	H Bennett	1975	JK Lawton
1948	R Pattinson	1962	R Pattinson	1976	R Davenport
1949	R Pattinson	1963	JM Booth	1977	JE Roberts
1950	J Armitt	1964	R. Pattinson	1978	PM Baxter
1951	R Pattinson	1965	DP Cross	1979	R Davenport
1952	H Bennett	1966	WT Easson	1980	JC Thomas
1953	H Bennett	1967	JC Thomas	1981	RJ Hall
1954	H Bennett	1968	JE Beddington	1982	R Davenport
1955	H Bennett	1969	PM Baxter	1983	R Davenport
1956	H Bennett	1970	TJ Hanson	1984	G Shaw
1957	H Bennett	1971	JC Thomas	1985	R Davenport
1958	R Pattinson	1972	N Rogers	1986	J Feeney
1959	D Mason	1973	PM Baxter		

Derbyshire Ladies' Championship

Instituted 1921

Year	Winner	Year	Winner
1947	Mrs A Gee (*née* J Hives)	1967	Miss M Wenyon
1948	Mrs A Gee	1968	Hon Mrs J Gee
1949	Mrs A Gee	1969	Miss M Wenyon
1950	Mrs A Gee	1970	Miss D Rose
1951	Mrs A Gee	1971	Mrs EMJ Wenyon
1952	Mrs A Gee	1972	Miss M Mason
1953	Hon Mrs J Gee	1973	Miss E Clark
1954	Mrs EM Jones	1974	Miss E Colledge
1955	Mrs K Dickie, jun	1975	Mrs A Bemrose
1956	Hon Mrs J Gee	1976	Mrs M Close
1957	Mrs ESC Pedley	1977	Mrs M Close
1958	Hon Mrs J Gee	1978	Mrs M Close
1959	Mrs R Gascoyne	1979	Mrs M Close
1960	Mrs JH Gibbs	1980	Miss A Howe
1961	Hon Mrs J Gee	1981	Miss A Howe
1962	Mrs Jean Burns	1982	Miss V McWilliams
1963	Hon Mrs J Gee	1983	Miss J Williams
1964	Hon Mrs J Gee	1984	Miss J Williams
1965	Miss M Grey	1985	Miss L Holmes
1966	Hon Mrs J Gee	1986	Miss E Robinson

Derbyshire Match-Play Championship

Instituted 1971

Year	Winner	Year	Winner
1971	JC Thomas	1980	CRJ Ibbotson
1972	PM Baxter	1981	N Rowland
1973	PM Baxter	1982	MP Higgins
1974	PM Baxter	1983	G Shaw
1975	AT Bird	1984	G Shaw
1976	PM Baxter	1985	CRJ Ibbotson
1977	PM Baxter	1986	J Feeney
1978	CRJ Ibbotson		
1979	N Rowland		

Derbyshire Open Championship

Year	Winner	Year	Winner
1930	T Barber	1962	LJ Feeney (Am)
1931	J Fallon	1963	LJ Feeney (Am)
1932	J Armitt (Am)	1964	RI Tickle (Am)
1933	J Armitt (Am)	1965	AF Simms (Am)
1934	C Thorpe (Am.)	1966	D Mason (Am)
1935	A Norton	1967	JC Thomas (Am)
1936	J Armitt (Am)	1968	H Lester
1937	F Jowie	1969	CRJ Ibbotson (Am)
1938	A Norton	1970	JB Flanders (Am)
1939	A Norton	1971	R Lambert
1946	C Thorpe (Am)	1972	E Darcy
1947	J Armitt (Am)	1973	E Darcy
1948	E Lester	1974	MJ Ronan
1949	*No championship*	1975	A Ellis (Am)
1950	W Walker	1976	MC Orme (Am)
1951	H Lester	1977	R Davenport (Am)
1952	H Bennett (Am)	1978	RH Lambert
1953	SM McCready (Am)	1979	R Davenport (Am)
1954	WW Walker	1980	I Gretton (Am)
1955	WW Walker	1981	RRW Davenport (Am)
1956	H Bennett (Am)	1982	RRW Davenport (Am)
1957	W Walker	1983	C Radford (Am)
1958	H Lester	1984	J Feeney (Am)
1959	D Ferguson (Am)	1985	M McLean
1960	LJ Feeney (Am)	1986	N Furniss (Am)
1961	LJ Feeney (Am)		

Derbyshire Professional Championship

Instituted 1921

Year	Winner	Year	Winner	Year	Winner
1935	TB Robertson	1956	H Lester	1973	E Darcy
1936	A Norton	1957	W Walker	1974	E Darcy
1937	A Norton	1959	H Lester	1975	RH Lambert
1938	A Norton	1960	W Walker	1976	C Jepson
1939	A Norton	1961	H Lester	1977	E Darcy
1947	W Walker	1962	H Lester	1978	P Seal
1948	E Lester	1963	H Lester	1979	D Russell
1949	W Walker	1964	H Lester	1980	P Taylor
1950	W Walker	1967	H Lester	1981	J Lower
1951	EB Williamson	1968	LJ Feeney	1982	A Wardle
1952	JE Wiggett	1969	KD Pickup	1983	PK Seal
1953	W Walker	1970	DT Parsonage	1984	W Bird
1954	H Lester	1971	K Oliver	1985	J Turnbull
1955	H Lester	1972	C Jepson	1986	J Lower

Devon Amateur Championship

Instituted 1912

Year	Winner	Year	Winner	Year	Winner
1936	AG Skinner	1958	CH Scott	1973	MW Hampton
1937	LC Lake	1959	ED Trapnell	1974	RPF Brown
1938	LC Lake	1960	RPF Brown	1975	AP Vivary
1939	AGT Rees	1961	TDW Slater	1976	RPF Brown
1947	Dr RM Munro	1962	RPF Brown	1977	R Knott
1948	JP Phillips	1963	RB Redfern	1978	M Jewell
1949	Dr RM Munro	1964	RB Redfern	1979	MWL Hampton
1950	ED Trapnell	1965	BG Steer	1980	MG Symons
1951	R Thairlwall	1966	RB Redfern	1981	M Jewell
1952	Dr DI Stirk	1967	TB Jones, jun	1982	MG Symons
1953	ED Trapnell	1968	BG Steer	1983	A Richards
1954	LC Lake	1969	RM Leach	1985	J Lansmead
1955	AD Inglis	1970	D Lang	1986	P Newcombe
1956	ED Trapnell	1971	RW Holmes		
1957	LC Lake	1972	RB Williams		

Devon Ladies' Championship

Instituted 1922

Year	Winner	Year	Winner	Year	Winner
1930	Miss Radford	1954	Mrs Anstey	1971	Mrs J Dymond
1931	Miss L Foster	1955	Miss P Morris	1972	Mrs B Salz
1932	Miss B Radford	1956	Miss P Morris	1973	Mrs R Coleman
1933	Miss P Williams	1957	Miss A Nicholson	1974	Mrs J Lawson
1934	Miss B Radford	1958	Mrs B Ord	1975	Mrs J Mason
1935	Miss P Williams	1959	Mrs K Sharp	1976	Miss M Wardrop
1936	Miss P Williams	1960	Mrs Anstey	1977	Mrs J Mason
1937	Miss Dent	1961	Mrs Greenwood	1978	Mrs D Baxter
1938	Miss Dent	1962	Mrs R Emerson	1979	Miss S Tyler
1939	Miss M Foster	1963	Mrs TW Slater	1980	Mrs J Mason
1947	Mrs Ord	1964	Miss J Buswell	1981	Miss C Stephens
1948	Miss Pyman	1965	Mrs Anstey	1982	Miss J Hurley
1949	Miss M Taylor	1966	Mrs P Anstey	1983	Miss J Hurley
1950	Mrs Anstey	1967	Mrs Fox	1984	Miss J Hurley
1951	Miss M Taylor	1968	Mrs J Mason	1985	Miss L Lines
1952	Mrs Anstey	1969	Mrs J Mason	1986	Miss J Hurley
1953	Mrs Anstey	1970	Mrs J Mason		

Devon Open Championship

Instituted 1923

Year	Winner	Year	Winner	Year	Winner
1935	E Hooker	1958	S Taggart	1974	RB Williams (Am)
1936	W Ivory	1959	JJ Spencer (Am)	1975	J Green
1937	E Hooker	1960	N Sutton	1976	J Green
1938	CH Ward	1961	N Sutton	1977	A Valentine
1947	KJ Hooker	1963	B Bamford	1978	BG Steer (Am)
1948	KJ Hooker	1964	DI Stirk (Am)	1979	M Jewell (Am)
1949	KJ Hooker	1965	B Bamford	1980	M Kemp
1950	KJ Hooker	1966	AM MacDonald	1981	D Sheppard
1951	KJ Hooker	1967	B Jolly	1982	M Jewell (Am)
1952	N Sutton	1968	TB Jones, jun (Am)	1983	M Symons (Am)
1953	A Easterbrook	1969	N Sutton	1984	
1954	N Sutton	1970	N Sutton	1985	
1955	N Sutton	1971	R Radway (Am)	1986	
1956	N Sutton	1972	DI Stirk (Am)		
1957	N Sutton	1973	K Whitfield (Am)		

Dorset Amateur Championship

Instituted 1924

Year	Winner	Year	Winner	Year	Winner
1935	A Dore	1956	K Longmore	1972	G Butler
1936	HE Botting	1957	K Longmore	1973	AK Jones
1937	RM Chadwick	1958	P Saunders	1974	J Lawrence
1938	EJ Nicholl	1959	G Butler	1975	G Butler
1939	C Glass Hooper	1960	K Longmore	1976	G Butler
1946	KJ Longmore	1961	G Butler	1977	D Scholes
1947	O Austreng	1962	AJ Richmond	1978	G Butler
1948	EB Millward	1963	G Butler	1979	M Farley
1949	J Santall	1964	AJ Richmond	1980	J Nash
1950	EB Millward	1965	GJ Butler	1981	R Hearn
1951	RE Garselt	1967	GJ Butler	1982	R Miles
1952	EB Millward	1968	RG Peach	1983	R Miles
1953	K Clarke	1969	LG Butler	1984	JD Gordon
1954	RE Garrett	1970	R Lawford	1985	J Bloxham
1955	R Lawford	1971	EJS Garrett	1986	A Lawrence

Dorset Ladies' Championship

Instituted 1923

Year	Winner	Year	Winner	Year	Winner
1947	Miss Bannister	1961	Mrs PM Crow	1975	Mrs J Sugden
1948	Mrs Stuart Smith	1962	Mrs PM Crow	1976	Mrs J Sugden
1949	Mrs McPherson	1963	Mrs PM Crow	1977	Mrs W Russell
1950	Mrs McPherson	1964	Mrs J Sugden	1978	Mrs W Russell
1951	Mrs Stuart Smith	1965	Mrs S Smith	1979	Miss S Reeks
1952	Mrs PM Crow	1966	Miss B Dixon	1980	Mrs C Stirling
1953	Dr E Kyle	1967	Mrs P Crow	1981	Mrs R Page
1954	Mrs PM Crow	1968	Miss B Dixon	1982	Mrs B Langley
1955	Mrs PM Crow	1969	Mrs A Humphreys	1983	Mrs J Sugden
1956	Mrs PM Crow	1970	Miss B Dixon	1984	Miss S Lowe
1957	Miss J Alexander	1971	Mrs P Crow	1985	Miss S Lowe
1958	Mrs S Smith	1972	Miss D Chalkley	1986	Miss H Delew
1959	Mrs J Cooper	1973	Mrs P Crow		
1960	Mrs J Cooper	1974	Mrs W Russell		

Dumfriesshire Ladies' Championship

Year	Winner	Year	Winner	Year	Winner
1980	Mrs G Barclay	1983	Miss DM Hill	1986	Mrs M McKerrow
1981	Mrs E Hill	1984	Miss DM Hill		
1982	Mrs BW Hill	1985	Mrs R Morrison		

Dunbartonshire Amateur Championship

Year	Winner	Year	Winner	Year	Winner
1949	FWG Deighton	1952	D Cameron	1955	J Wallace
1950	FWG Deighton	1953	FWG Deighton	1956	J Munro
1951	JG Campbell	1954	FWG Deighton	1957	RI Ross

Dunbartonshire Amateur Championship

continued

Year	Winner	Year	Winner	Year	Winner
1958	MN Ferguson	1968	CW Green	1978	I Hulme
1959	MN Ferguson	1969	JS Cochrane	1979	DG Carrick
1960	CW Green	1970	D Black	1980	DG Carrick
1961	J Wallace	1971	CJ Smith	1981	J Graham
1962	GD Gray	1972	JMJ McMahon	1982	DG Carrick
1963	AH Hill	1973	CW Green	1983	DG Carrick
1964	AM Grant	1974	D Weir	1984	T Eckford
1965	RM Douglas	1975	Allan Brodie	1985	
1966	DC Penman	1976	Allan Brodie	1986	
1967	CW Green	1977	CW Green		

Dunbartonshire and Argyll Ladies' Championship

Year	Winner	Year	Winner
1949	Miss M Paterson	1968	Mrs IC Robertson
1950	Mrs TS Currie	1969	Mrs IC Robertson
1951	Mrs S Cochran	1970	Miss V McAlister
1952	Miss M Bell	1971	Miss F Jamieson
1953	Miss I Keywood	1972	Miss V McAlister
1954	Miss I Keywood	1973	Miss V McAlister
1955	Mrs TS Currie	1974	Miss V McAlister
1956	Miss B Geekie	1975	Miss V McAlister
1957	Miss I Keywood	1976	Miss S Cadden
1958	Miss B McCorkindale	1977	Miss S Cadden
1959	Miss B McCorkindale	1978	Mrs IC Robertson
1960	Miss B McCorkindale	1979	Mrs S McMahon
1961	Mrs IC Robertson (*née* B McCorkindale)	1980	Mrs MP Grant
		1981	Miss V McAlister
1962	Mrs IC Robertson	1982	Miss V McAlister
1963	Mrs IC Robertson	1983	Miss V McAlister
1964	Miss I Keywood	1984	Miss V McAlister
1965	Mrs IC Robertson	1985	Miss V McAlister
1966	Mrs IC Robertson	1986	Miss M Wright
1967	Miss E Low		

Duncan Putter

Year	Winner	Score	Year	Winner	Score
1959	G Huddy	301	1973	JKD Povall	299
1960	WI Tucker	289	1974	S Cox	302
1961	WI Tucker / G Huddy	295	1975	JG Jermine	295
1962	EN Davies	297	1976	W Tucker / H Stott	286
1963	WI Tucker	296	1977	H Stott	295
1964	J Toye	293	1978	P McEvoy	295
1965	P Townsend	305	1979	HJ Evans	292
1966	MF Attenborough	291	1980	P McEvoy	296
1967	D Millensted	297	1981	R Chapman / PG Way	294
1968	JL Morgan	299	1982	D McLean	283
1969	WI Tucker	304	1983	JG Jermine	297
1970	JL Toye	305	1984	JP Price	297
1971	W Humphreys	295	1985	P McEvoy	299
1972	P Berry (3 rds, fog)	230	1986	D Wood	300

Durham Amateur Championship

Instituted 1908

Year	Winner	Year	Winner	Year	Winner
1930	A Harrison	1953	W Moffitt	1970	R Clark
1931	A Harrison	1954	G Pickering	1971	R Green
1932	A Harrison	1955	WR Thomson	1972	RW Renaut
1933	JV Todd	1956	TE Jones	1973	H Ashby
1934	JV Todd	1957	D Hunter	1974	JW Ord
1935	JV Todd	1958	IR Hornsby	1975	A Doxford
1936	JV Todd	1959	KT Thomson	1976	D Oghton
1937	RR Dodd	1960	R Clark	1977	J Naisby
1938	Dr RR Dodd	1961	R Clark	1978	AJ McLure
1939	C Crosthwaite	1962	JA Sanderson	1979	J Naisby
1946	W Irvine	1963	H Ashby	1980	AJ McLure
1947	C Moffitt	1964	IR Hornsby	1981	D Hawkins
1948	JV Todd	1965	J Wrigley	1982	JE Ellwood
1949	Col. WHH Aitken	1966	G Hedley	1983	M Ure
1950	Brig WHH Aitken	1967	RW Green	1984	M Ure
1951	TH Tooley	1968	J Ord	1985	A Robertson
1952	W Moffitt	1969	DW McClelland	1986	H Ashby

Durham Ladies' Championship

Instituted 1923

Year	Winner	Year	Winner	Year	Winner
1931	Miss Walker	1957	Mrs Riddell	1975	Mrs A Biggs
1932	Miss Sardler	1958	Mrs Riddell	1976	Miss R Kelly
1933	Mrs Waugh	1959	Mrs Riddell	1977	Miss C Barker
1934	Mrs Waugh	1960	Mrs J Kinsella	1978	Miss C Barker
1935	Mrs Waugh	1961	Mrs Riddell	1979	Miss P Hunt
1936	Mrs Waugh	1962	Miss E Reed	1980	Mrs L Still
1937	Mrs Richardson	1963	Mrs J Riddell	1981	Miss C Barker
1938	Miss Curry	1964	Mrs Riddell	1982	Miss P Hunt
1939	Miss Bell	1965	Mrs Bennett	1983	Miss P Hunt
1948	Miss Curry	1966	Miss P Dinning	1984	Miss B Mansfield
1949	Mrs JH Carter	1967	Mrs M Whitehead	1985	Miss M Scullan
1950	Mrs Birbeck	1968	Mrs P Twinn	1986	Miss L Chesterton
1951	Mrs JH Carter	1969	Mrs D Harrison		
1952	Mrs Butler	1970	Miss L Hope		
1953	Mrs JH Carter	1971	Mrs M Thompson		
1954	Mrs C Wright	1972	Miss R Kelly		
1955	Mrs Birbeck	1973	Miss C Barker		
1956	Miss Paton	1974	Mrs C Bowerbank		

East Anglian Ladies' Championship

Year	Winner
1986	Miss J Walter

East Anglian Open Championship

Year	Winner	Year	Winner	Year	Winner
1951	RA Knight	1963	L Platts	1975	F Flatman
1952	AH Perowne	1964	EE Whitcombe	1976	G Schader
1953	EE Whitcombe	1965	R Foreman	1977	W Longmuir
1954	LB Ayton	1966	H Flatman	1978	G Schader
1955	K Budd	1967	B Huggett	1979	N Burch
1956	EE Whitcombe	1968	M Leeder	1980	S Levermore
1957	A Poulton	1969	A Ibberson	1981	F Hill
1958	R Foreman	1970	H Flatman	1982	RW Mann
1959	RA Knight	1971	G Burroughs	1983	RW Mann
1960	PJ Shanks	1972	J Frew	1984	
1961	MT Leeder	1973	MF Bonallack	1985	
1962	BG Huggett	1974	H Flatman	1986	

East Lothian Ladies' Championship

Year	Winner	Year	Winner
1934	Miss MJ Couper	1965	Miss CJ Lugton
1935	Miss MJ Couper	1966	Miss M Fowler
1936	Miss MM Robertson	1967	Miss M Fowler
1937	Mrs IH Bowhill	1968	Miss CJ Lugton
1938	Miss MJ Couper	1969	Mrs AJR Ferguson
1939	Mrs EC Mackean	1970	Miss CJ Lugton
1948	Miss J Donald	1971	Miss CJ Lugton
1949	Miss J Donald	1972	Miss CJ Lugton
1950	Mrs RT Peel	1973	Miss CJ Lugton
1951	Miss J Donald	1974	Mrs AJR Ferguson
1952	Miss J Donald	1975	Mrs D McIntosh
1953	Miss J Donald	1976	Miss CJ Lugton
1954	Mrs E Woodcock	1977	Miss CJ Lugton
1955	Mrs E Woodcock	1978	Miss J Connachan
1956	Mrs Paton	1979	Miss J Connachan
1957	Miss M Fowler	1980	Miss CJ Lugton
1958	Miss M Fowler	1981	Mrs AJR Ferguson
1959	Miss M Fowler	1982	*Null and void*
1960	Miss M Fowler	1983	Mrs M Thomson
1961	Miss M Fowler	1984	Miss M Ferguson
1962	Miss M Fowler	1985	Miss M Ferguson
1963	Miss M Fowler	1986	Miss J Kinloch
1964	Miss M Fowler		

East of Ireland Open Amateur Championship

Year	Winner	Score	Year	Winner	Score
1948	JB Carr	298	1968	P Caul	289
1949	M Ferguson	305	1969	JB Carr	292
1950	J Carroll	311	1970	R Carr	291
1951	M Power	297	1971	P Mulcare	292
1952	NV Drew	306	1972	P Mulcare	292
1953	JP Carroll	303	1973	P Mulcare	291
1954	BJ Scannell	298	1974	H Smyth	295
1955	BJ Scannell	298	1975	A Morrow	300
1956	JB Carr	300	1976	D White	295
1957	JB Carr	287	1977	T Cleary	299
1958	JB Carr	288	1978	M Gannon	295
1959	T Craddock	294	1979	AD Pierse	288
1960	JB Carr	290	1980	P Caul	292
1961	JB Carr	291	1981	D Branigan	292
1962	TW Egan	290	1982	MF Sludds	285
1963	N Fogarty	296	1983	AJC Morrow	291
1964	JB Carr	292	1984	BUM Reddan	293
1965	T Craddock	291	1985	F Ronan	286
1966	T Craddock	288	1986	P Hogan	
1967	GN Fogarty	293			

Eastern Division Ladies' Championship (Scotland)

Year	Winner	Year	Winner
1936	Miss J Anderson	1966	Miss A Laing
1937	Miss CPR Montgomery	1967	Mrs A McIntosh
1938	Miss J Anderson	1968	Miss N Duncan
1939	Miss J Anderson	1969	Miss Jillian Hutton
1947	Miss J Donald	1970	Miss J Hutton
1948	Miss J Donald	1971	Miss J Lawrence
1949	Miss J Donald	1972	Miss J Lawrence
1950	Mrs G Valentine	1973	Miss J Bald
1951	Mrs RT Peel	1974	Miss C Lugton
1952	Mrs RT Peel	1975	Mrs AJR Ferguson
1953	Miss J Donald	1976	Miss C Panton
1954	Mrs RT Peel	1977	Miss L Hope
1955	Mrs RT Peel	1978	Miss L Hope
1956	Mrs RT Peel	1979	Miss M Stavert
1957	Mrs RT Peel	1980	Mrs J Marshall
1958	Mrs J Aitken	1981	Miss E Kimmen
1959	Miss M Fowler	1982	Miss J Bald
1960	Miss M Fowler	1983	Mrs J Marshall
1961	Mrs C Draper	1984	Miss L Hope
1962	Miss M Fowler	1985	Miss L Bennett
1964	Miss B Crichton	1986	Miss J Harrison
1965	Miss J Bald		

East of Scotland Open Amateur Stroke Play

Year	Winner	Year	Winner	Year	Winner
1974	S Stephen	1979	G Macgregor	1984	S Stephen
1975	AK Pirie	1980	D Greig	1985	A McQueen
1976	S Martin	1981	K Gray	1986	S Knowles
1977	S Stephen	1982	G Macgregor		
1978	GK MacDonald	1983	S Stephen		

Edward Trophy

Instituted 1892

Year	Winner	Year	Winner	Year	Winner
1949	JC Wilson	1962	JE Stuart	1975	CW Green
1950	J McKay	1963	Finlay S Morris	1976	DM McCart
1951	JC Wilson	1964	HM Campbell	1977	R Blackwood
1952	D Cameron	1965	W Thornton	1978	R Blackwood
1953	RDR Walker	1966	JM Cannon	1979	J Cuddihy
1954	Dr F Deighton	1967	M Alexander	1980	D Murdoch
1955	LG Taylor	1968	CW Green	1981	A Liddle
1956	JC Wilson	1969	WR Lockie	1982	F Dunsmore
1957	WS Jack	1970	J Johnston	1983	S Morrison
1958	Dr JL Hastings	1971	IH Ritchie	1984	K Walker
1959	RR Jack	1972	B Nicholson	1985	GK MacDonald
1960	SWT Murray	1973	CW Green	1986	J Noon
1961	SWT Murray	1974	CW Green		

Essex Ladies' Championship

Year	Winner	Year	Winner
1947	Mrs Kenneth Hawes	1968	Mrs A Bonallack
1948	Mrs Munro	1969	Mrs A Bonallack
1949	Miss MA McKenny	1970	Mrs S Barber
1950	Mrs S Munro	1971	Mrs S Barber
1951	Miss A Barrett	1972	Mrs B Lewis
1952	Mrs MR Garon	1973	Mrs A Bonallack
1954	Mrs Hanson-Abbott	1974	Mrs A Bonallack
1955	Mrs J Willis	1975	*Cancelled*
1956	Mrs G Hetherington	1976	Mrs A Bonallack
1957	Mrs G Hetherington	1977	Mrs A Bonallack
1958	Miss S Bonallack	1978	Mrs A Bonallack
1959	Miss S Bonallack	1979	Miss B Cooper
1960	Miss S Bonallack	1980	Mrs E Boatman
1961	Miss S Bonallack	1981	Mrs P Jackson
1962	Miss S Bonallack	1982	Mrs A Bonallack
1963	Mrs S Barber (*née* Bonallack)	1983	Mrs E Boatman
1964	Miss E Collis	1984	Mrs S Barber
1966	Mrs S Barber	1985	Mrs S Barber
1967	Mrs S Barber	1986	Miss S Moorcroft

Essex Amateur Championship

Year	Winner	Year	Winner	Year	Winner
1935	KS Duncan	1957	MF Bonallack	1973	N Burch
1936	JH Rogers	1958	P O'Connor	1974	H Weber
1937	KS Duncan	1959	MF Bonallack	1975	G Turner
1938	WH Ferns	1960	MF Bonallack	1976	J Darling
1946	AW McClure	1961	MF Bonallack	1977	G Turner
1947	KS Duncan	1962	E Bullman	1978	G Godwin
1948	CD Cocks	1963	MF Bonallack	1979	N Burch
1949	Major NA Gray	1964	MF Bonallack	1980	G Godwin
1950	W Kennedy	1965	CK Jones	1981	C Davies
1951	KG Budd	1966	J Thorogood	1982	C Laurence
1952	HM Clarke	1968	MF Bonallack	1983	M Davis
1953	KG Budd	1969	MF Bonallack	1984	M Stokes
1954	MF Bonallack	1970	MF Bonallack	1985	D Wood
1955	KG Budd	1971	A Budd	1986	
1956	KG Budd	1972	MF Bonallack		

Essex Open Championship

Year	Winner	Year	Winner	Year	Winner
1935	B Hodson	1956	RA Knight	1970	A Parcell
1936	J Adams	1957	R Foreman	1971	G Gledhill
1937	JR Steel	1958	RA Knight	1972	F Hill
1938	CS Denny	1959	RA Knight	1973	EE Whitcombe
1946	B Hodson	1960	EE Whitcombe	1974	R Smith
1947	H Adams	1961	B Huggett	1975	H Flatman
1948	CS Denny	1962	L Platts	1976	L Platts
1949	AM Dailey	1963	L Platts	1977	G Burroughs
1950	CS Denny	1964	L Platts D Gledhill	1978	G Burroughs
1951	RA Knight			1979	G Burroughs
1952	RA Knight	1965	B Huggett	1980	S Jackson
1953	RA Knight	1966	R Foreman	1981	M Stokes
1954	RA Knight	1968	P Lee	1982	B Longmuir (Am)
1955	EE Whitcombe	1969	MF Bonallack (Am)		

Fife Amateur Championship

Instituted 1925

Year	Winner	Year	Winner	Year	Winner
1930	GE Hutton	1954	JT Pearson	1971	GT Russell
1931	EA McRuvie	1955	Ian Reid	1972	WA Thomson
1932	CL Muir	1956	AS Melville	1973	S Stephen
1933	EA McRuvie	1957	G Will	1974	TE Melville
1934	JE Ballingall	1958	JF Ferguson	1975	JA McIntyre
1935	DM Stewart	1959	J Clark	1976	T Cochrane
1936	JN Smith	1960	A Reid	1977	ST Reith
1937	W Murray	1961	A Cunningham	1978	TM Cochrane
1938	JH Mathieson	1962	W Moyes	1979	DJ Gray
1939	A Dowie	1963	W Moyes	1980	JW Noble
1947	R Easson	1964	Ian Clark	1981	D Ross
1948	HG Rodger	1965	A Drysdale	1982	D Weir
1949	D Foulis	1966	WMO Petrie	1983	T Cochrane
1950	A Dowie	1967	AN Wilson	1984	
1951	WRM Foulis	1968	GT Russell	1985	
1952	George W Low	1969	J Farmer		
1953	A Dowie	1970	G Milne		

Fife County Ladies' Championship

Year	Winner	Year	Winner
1935	Miss Alison Hopwood	1965	Miss Joan B Lawrence
1936	Miss Madeline Everard	1966	Miss J Bald
1937	Miss N Orr	1967	Miss Joan B Lawrence
1938	Miss N Orr	1968	Miss Joan B Lawrence
1939	Miss N Orr	1969	Miss Joan B Lawrence
1947	Mrs FL Dornan	1970	Miss J Bald
1948	Mrs EAD Thomson	1971	Miss J Bald
1949	Mrs Lockhart-Cowan	1972	Miss J MacNeill
1950	Mrs Lockhart-Cowan	1973	Miss J Bald
1951	Mrs TM Burton	1974	Miss J McNeill
1952	Mrs TM Burton	1975	Miss M Speir
1953	Miss Joan B Lawrence	1976	Mrs J Louden (*née* McNeill)
1954	Mrs TM Burton	1977	Mrs J Louden
1955	Mrs Frances L Dornan	1978	Miss D Mitchell
1956	Mrs Ethel AD Thomson	1979	Miss J Bald
1957	Miss Joan B Lawrence	1980	Mrs J Louden
1958	Miss Joan B Lawrence	1981	Miss J Bald
1959	Miss Joan B Lawrence	1982	Miss J Bald
1960	Miss Joan B Lawrence	1983	Mrs R Scott
1961	Miss Joan B Lawrence	1984	Miss E Hunter
1962	Miss Joan B Lawrence	1985	Miss L Bennett
1963	Miss Joan B Lawrence	1986	Miss P Lees
1964	Miss Joan B Lawrence		

Flintshire Ladies' Championship

Year	Winner	Year	Winner
1960	Mrs M Davies	1974	Miss F Ellard
1961	Mrs R Johnson	1975	Mrs P Davies
1962	Miss P Griffiths	1976	Miss S Rowlands
1963	Mrs P Rogers	1977	Mrs P Davies
1964	Mrs P Rogers	1978	Mrs P Davies
1965	Miss P Griffiths	1979	Miss P Strange
1966	Mrs J Hughes	1980	Mrs P Davies
1967	Mrs M Lloyd-Jones	1981	Mrs P Griffiths
1968	Mrs J Hughes	1982	Mrs P Davies
1969	Mrs P Davies	1983	Mrs S Thomas (*née* Rowlands)
1970	Mrs J Hughes	1984	Mrs S Thomas
1971	Mrs J Hughes	1985	Mrs S Thomas
1972	Miss L Hughes	1986	Mrs S Thomas
1973	Miss L Hughes		

Galloway Ladies' Championship

Year	Winner	Year	Winner	Year	Winner
1980	Miss FM Rennie	1983	Miss S McDonald	1986	Miss M Wright
1981	Miss M Clements	1984	Miss S McDonald		
1982	Miss M Clements	1985	Miss M Wright		

Glamorgan Amateur Championship

Year	Winner	Year	Winner	Year	Winner
1935	Norman Jacob	1957	G Knipe	1972	PE Light
1936	GS Emery	1958	RJ Pressdee	1973	JG Jermine
1937	HR Howell	1959	H Squirrell	1974	DL Stevens
1938	J Lyndon Jones	1960	JKD Povall	1975	CN Last
1939	GS Emery	1961	Gordon Clay	1976	DL Stevens
1947	HR Howell	1962	AE Lockley	1977	JR Jones
1948	RM de Lloyd	1963	JKD Povall	1978	HJ Evans
1949	AD Lake	1964	Gordon Clay	1979	JR Jones
1950	AE Lockley	1965	HC Squirrell	1980	DL Stevens
1951	RM de Lloyd	1966	JL Toye	1981	T Melia
1952	AE Lockley	1967	JKD Povall	1982	T Melia
1953	RM de Lloyd	1968	JHM Jones	1983	P Bloomfield
1954	G Knipe	1969	JKD Povall	1984	
1955	G Knipe	1970	JG Jermine	1985	R Brown
1956	AE Lockley	1971	CT Brown	1986	LP Price

Glamorgan County Ladies' Championship

Instituted 1927

Year	Winner	Year	Winner	Year	Winner
1935	Miss J Jeffreys	1959	Miss E Owen	1974	Miss T Perkins
1936	Mrs GS Emery	1960	Mrs J Treharne	1975	Miss T Perkins
1937	Mrs GS Emery	1961	Mrs M Fisher	1976	Miss L Isherwood
1938	Mrs GS Emery	1962	Miss E Owen	1977	Miss T Perkins
1939	Miss M Thompson	1963	Mrs J Treharne	1978	Miss T Perkins
1948	Mrs RB Roberts	1964	Mrs J Treharne	1979	Miss M Rawlings
1949	Mrs RB Roberts	1965	Mrs J Treharne	1980	Mrs T Thomas (*née* Perkins)
1950	Miss E Owen	1966	Miss Jill Morris		
1951	Mrs RB Roberts	1967	Miss C Phipps	1981	Mrs T Thomas
1952	Mrs H Jenkins	1968	Miss Jill Morris	1982	Miss M Rawlings
1953	Mrs H Jenkins	1969	Miss C Phipps	1983	Mrs T Thomas
1954	Mrs RB Roberts	1970	Miss V Rawlings	1984	Miss J Foster
1955	Mrs RB Roberts	1971	Miss V Rawlings	1985	Miss P Johnson
1956	Miss H Wakelin	1972	Miss T Perkins	1986	Miss P Johnson
1958	Mrs C Robinson	1973	Miss C Phipps		

Glasgow Amateur Championship

Instituted 1897
Winners since 1925

Year	Winner	Year	Winner	Year	Winner
1925	A Jamieson, jun	1929	W Tulloch	1933	J McLean
1926	W Campbell	1930	JA Lang	1934	G Peters
1927	JA Lang	1931	J McLean	1935	H Thomson
1928	W Campbell	1932	W Campbell	1936	SL McKinlay

Glasgow Amateur Championship

continued

Year	Winner	Year	Winner	Year	Winner
1937	JC More	1959	WS Jack	1974	I Gillan
1938	SL McKinlay	1960	SWT Murray	1975	EW Hammond
1939	D Cameron	1961	A Sinclair	1976	I Gillan
1947	ED Hamilton	1962	AD Gray	1977	JT Moffat
1948	WS McLeod	1963	WS Jack	1978	I Carslaw
1949	D Cameron	1964	CJL Strachan	1979	CW Green
1950	SL McKinlay	1965	JE Stuart	1980	D Carrick
1951	FWG Deighton	1966	AH Hall	1981	D Carrick
1952	D Cameron	1967	EW Hammond	1982	B Pearson
1953	RR Jack	1968	JS Cochran	1983	B Pearson
1954	RR Jack	1969	GB Cosh	1984	I Carslaw
1955	FWG Deighton	1970	EW Hammond	1985	S Savage
1956	MN Ferguson	1971	J McTear	1986	G Shaw
1957	JE Stuart	1972	Andrew Brodie		
1958	RR Jack	1973	K MacIntosh		

Glasgow GU Championship

Year	Winner	Year	Winner	Year	Winner
1955	WS Jack	1966	JW Campbell	1977	M Miller
1956	ED Hamilton	1967	JR Young	1978	M Miller
1957	JR Cater	1968	EW Hammond	1979	J Cubbage
1958	WS Jack	1969	G Hewitt	1980	WC Black
1959	JR Young	1970	EW Hammond	1981	BA Pearson
1960	W Norris	1971	WC Black	1982	R Gregory
1961	WS Jack	1972	GB Cosh	1983	IA Carslaw
1962	A Cribbes	1973	S Barclay	1984	IA Carslaw
1963	RL Renfrew	1974	GB Cosh	1985	
1964	WC Black	1975	D McCart	1986	
1965	JW Campbell	1976	D McCart		

Gloucestershire Amateur Championship

Instituted 1906

Year	Winner	Year	Winner	Year	Winner
1930	HP Bazeley	1953	Dr WG Hunt	1970	AG Clay
1931	GC Brooks	1954	GE Randel	1971	P Berry
1932	GC Brooks	1955	Dr DS Maunsell	1972	P Berry
1933	HG Pruett	1956	CG Griffith	1973	JA Bloxham
1934	GC Killey	1957	G Jackson	1974	D Carroll
1935	WS Watson	1958	WS Wise	1975	C Mitchell
1936	GC Brooks	1959	RJ Gardiner	1976	S Dunlop
1937	GC Brooks	1960	Max Clarke	1977	G Brand, jun.
1938	GC Brooks	1961	Max Clarke	1978	CS Mitchell
1939	DM Anderson	1962	RJ Gardiner	1979	R Broad
1946	WSJ Watson	1963	JN Littler	1980	M Lewis
1947	WSJ Watson	1964	RW Clarke	1981	J Durbin
1948	WSJ Watson	1965	GM Brand	1982	D Ray
1949	WSJ Watson	1966	RF Brown	1983	D Rollo
1950	WS Wise	1967	RJ Gardiner	1984	C Robinson
1951	LF Brown	1968	JK Graveney	1985	D Carroll
1952	RE Strange	1969	G Brand	1986	

Gloucestershire Ladies' Championship

Instituted 1923

Year	Winner	Year	Winner	Year	Winner
1930	Miss V Bramwell	1935	Mrs Whitley	1947	Mrs Dickinson
1931	Miss V Bramwell	1936	Miss V Bramwell	1948	Mrs Whitley
1932	Miss W Williams	1937	Miss V Bramwell	1950	Mrs Whitley
1933	Miss V Bramwell	1938	Mrs Whitley	1951	Mrs SL Dickinson
1934	Miss V Bramwell	1939	Mrs Collier	1952	Mrs J Reece

Gloucestershire Ladies' Championship

continued

Year	Winner	Year	Winner	Year	Winner
1953	Mrs J Reece	1965	Mrs P Reece	1976	Miss R Porter
1954	Mrs J Reece	1966	Miss Ruth Porter	1977	Miss R Porter
1956	Mrs J Reece	1967	Miss Ruth Porter	1978	Miss D Park
1957	Miss Ruth Porter	1968	Mrs P Reece	1979	Mrs P Reece
1958	Mrs B Popplestone	1969	Miss Ruth Porter	1980	Miss K Douglas
1959	Miss Ruth Porter	1970	Mrs P Reece	1981	Miss K Douglas
1960	Mrs Peggy Reece	1971	Mrs P Reece	1982	Miss K Douglas
1961	Miss Ruth Porter	1972	Miss B Huke	1983	Miss K Douglas
1962	Miss Ruth Porter	1973	Miss R Porter	1984	Miss K Douglas
1963	Miss Ruth Porter	1974	Miss R Porter	1985	Miss C Griffiths
1964	Miss Ruth Porter	1975	Miss R Porter	1986	Miss S Shapcott

Golf Illustrated Gold Vase

Instituted 1909

Year	Winner	Year	Winner	Year	Winner
1930	RT Jones	1956	Major DA Blair	1971	MF Bonallack
1931	WA Murray	1957	G Wolstenholme	1972	H Ashby
1932	RW Hartley	1958	M Lunt	1972	DP Davidson / R Hunter
1933	RW Hartley	1959	A Bussell		
1934	WL Hartley	1960	D Sewell	1973	J Davies
1935	I Thomas	1961	DJ Harrison / MF Bonallack	1974	P Hedges
1936	J Ferrier			1975	MF Bonallack
1937	R Sweeney, jr	1962	BHG Chapman	1976	Allan Brodie
1938	CJ Anderson	1963	RH Mummery	1977	J Davies
1939	SB Roberts	1964	D Moffat	1978	P Thomas
1948	RD Chapman	1965	C Clark	1979	KJ Miller
1949	RJ White	1966	PM Townsend	1980	G Brand
1950	AW Whyte	1967	RA Durrant / MF Bonallack	1981	P Garner
1951	JB Carr			1982	I Carslaw
1952	JDA Langley	1968	MF Bonallack	1983	S Keppler
1953	JDA Langley	1969	MF Bonallack / J Hayes	1984	JV Marks
1954	H Ridgeley			1985	M Davis
1955	Major DA Blair	1970	D Harrison	1986	R Eggo

Grafton Morrish Trophy

Public Schools Old Boys' Golf Association

Year	Winner	Year	Winner	Year	Winner
1963	Tonbridge	1971	Dulwich	1979	Harrow
1964	Tonbridge	1972	Sedbergh	1980	Charterhouse
1965	Charterhouse	1973	Pangbourne	1981	Charterhouse
1966	Charterhouse	1974	Millfield	1982	Marlborough
1967	Charterhouse	1975	Oundle	1983	Wellington
1968	Wellington	1976	Charterhouse	1984	Sedbergh
1969	Sedbergh	1977	Haileybury	1985	Warwick
1970	Sedbergh	1978	Charterhouse	1986	Tonbridge

Gwent Amateur Championship

Formerly Monmouthshire Amateur Championship

Year	Winner	Year	Winner	Year	Winner
1975	T Branton	1980	A Disley	1984	P Hughes
1976	WI Tucker	1981	A Disley	1985	M Brimble
1977	AB Morgan	1982	P Mayo	1986	G Hughes
1979	A Jones	1983	NR Davies		

Halford-Hewitt Challenge Cup

Public Schools Old Boys' Tournament
Instituted 1924

Played at Deal

Year	Winner	Year	Winner	Year	Winner
1935	Charterhouse	1958	Harrow	1974	Charterhouse
1936	Charterhouse	1959	Wellington	1975	Harrow
1937	Charterhouse	1960	Rossall	1976	Merchiston
1938	Marlborough	1961	Rossall	1977	Watsons
1939	Charterhouse	1962	Oundle	1978	Harrow
1947	Harrow	1963	Repton	1979	Stowe
1948	Winchester	1964	Fettes	1980	Shrewsbury
1949	Charterhouse	1965	Rugby	1981	Watsons
1950	Rugby	1966	Charterhouse	1982	Charterhouse
1951	Rugby	1967	Eton	1983	Charterhouse
1952	Harrow	1968	Eton	1984	Charterhouse
1953	Harrow	1969	Eton	1985	Harrow
1954	Rugby	1970	Merchiston	1986	Repton
1955	Eton	1971	Charterhouse		
1956	Eton	1972	Marlborough		
1957	Watsons	1973	Rossall		

Hampshire, Isle of Wight and Channel Islands Open Championship

Instituted 1967

Year	Winner	Year	Winner
1967	W McHardy	1977	TR Pinner
1968	W Woodman	1978	TR Pinner
1969	D Miller	1979	I Young
1970	I MacDonald	1980	RA Doig
1971	J Stirling	1981	BJ Winteridge (Am)
1972	D Miller	1982	J Hay
1973	A Bridge	1983	J Hay
1974	J Morgan	1984	
1975	D Miller	1985	R Alker
1976	BJ Winteridge (Am)	1986	I Young

Hampshire, Isle of Wight, and Channel Islands Amateur Championship

Instituted 1894

Year	Winner	Year	Winner
1930	AE Phillips	1951	S Cole
1931	Com HE Raymond	1952	S Cole
1932	AP Sharpe	1953	JF Cripps
1933	WL Barnett	1954	HP Lock
1934	IR Patey	1955	SJ Fox
1935	IR Patey	1956	SJ Fox
1936	IR Patey	1957	AA Sutcliffe
1937	IR Patey	1958	C Burke
1938	EW St George Spencer	1959	EH James
1939	JE Mellor	1960	JE Rish
1946	AP Sharpe	1961	CW Cole
1947	D Lewcock	1962	RJ Mahy
1948	IR Patey	1963	SWT Murray
1949	PB Hine	1964	CW Cole
1950	J Earl	1965	DJ Harrison

Year	Winner	Year	Winner
1966	JB Airth	1977	BJ Winteridge
1967	JB Airth	1978	K Weeks
1968	T Koch de Gooreynd	1979	T Whittaker
1969	DJ Harrison	1980	RW Johnson
1970	DJ Harrison	1981	BJ Winteridge
1971	G Foden	1982	BJ Winteridge
1972	G Binding	1983	KJ Weeks
1973	DJ Harrison	1984	R Eggo
1974	DJ Harrison	1985	RA Alker
1975	BJ Winteridge	1986	
1976	DJ Harrison		

Hampshire, Isle of Wight and Channel Islands Amateur Championship

continued

Hampshire Ladies' Championship

Instituted 1924

Year	Winner	Year	Winner
1937	Miss P Wade	1966	Mrs B Bavin
1938	Miss P Wade	1967	Miss H Clifford
1939	Miss RS Morgan	1968	Miss P Shepherd
1947	Miss M Walls	1969	Miss H Clifford
1948	Mrs Bavin	1970	Miss C Le Feuvre
1949	Mrs Bavin	1971	Miss C Le Feuvre
1950	Mrs JSF Morrison	1972	Miss C Le Feuvre
1951	Mrs JSF Morrison	1973	Miss C Le Feuvre
1952	Mrs F Allan	1974	Miss C Le Feuvre
1953	Miss B Lowe	1975	Miss S Thurston
1954	Mrs Bavin	1976	Mrs C Gibbs (*née* Le Feuvre)
1955	Mrs Bavin	1977	Miss C Mackintosh
1956	Miss B Lowe	1978	Miss C Mackintosh
1957	Mrs B Green	1979	Miss C Mackintosh
1958	Mrs Bavin	1980	Miss C Mackintosh
1959	Mrs B Green	1981	Mrs S Pickles
1960	Mrs B Green	1982	Miss A Wells
1961	Mrs B Green	1983	Miss C Hayllar
1962	Mrs J Morrison	1984	Miss C Mackintosh
1963	Mrs B Green	1985	Miss C Stirling
1964	Mrs B Bavin	1986	Miss C Hayllar
1965	Mrs B Bavin		

Hampshire Professional Championship

Year	Winner	Year	Winner	Year	Winner
1950	JE Watt	1963	D Miller	1977	A Bridge
1951	G West	1964	J Stirling	1978	J Hay
1952	BW Spanner	1967	R Davenport	1979	C Bonner
1953	WH Wiltshire	1968	Alan White	1980	T Pinner
1954	G West	1969	JC Richardson	1981	J Grant
1955	A Freemantle	1970	J Sharkey	1982	J Garner
1956	DA Nash	1971	I Macdonald	1983	T Pinner
1957	CL Cargill	1972	J Sharkey	1984	
1958	CL Cargill	1973	D Miller	1985	
1959	D Miller	1974	J Sharkey		
1961	D Miller	1975	D Miller		
1962	D Miller	1976	C Bonner		

Hampshire Hog

Played annually at North Hants GC

Year	Winner	Score	Year	Winner	Score
1957	MF Bonallack	142	1961	HC Squirrell	144
1958	PF Scrutton	146	1962	FD Physick	150
1959	Lt Col AA Duncan	145	1963	Sq Ldr WE McCrea	146
1960	MF Attenborough	140	1964	DF Wilkie	145

Hampshire Hog
continued

Year	Winner	Score	Year	Winner	Score
1965	T Koch de Gooreynd	142	1978	GF Godwin	141
1966	Major DA Blair	145	1979	MF Bonallack	141
1967	Major DA Blair	141	1980	RA Durrant	140
1968	MJ Burgess	137	1981	G Brand (Only 1 round due to snowfall)	68
1969	B Critchley	142	1982	A Sherborne	143
1970	Major DA Blair	139	1983	I Gray	140
1971	WD Frame	142	1984	J Hawkesworth	140
1972	R Revell	138	1985	A Clapp	137
1973	C Mason	142	1986	R Eggo	142
1974	T Giles	141			
1975	H Stott	141			
1976	M Hughesdon	141			
1977	AWB Lyle	140			

Hampshire Rose

Instituted 1973

Played annually at North Hants GC

Year	Winner	Year	Winner	Year	Winner
1973	Miss C Redford	1978	Miss V Marvin / Mrs H Glynn-Jones	1983	Miss J Pool
1974	Mrs P Riddiford	1979	Mrs C Larkin	1984	Mrs C Caldwell
1975	Miss V Marvin	1980	Miss B New	1985	Mrs A Uzielli
1976	Miss H Clifford / Miss W Pithers	1981	Mrs J Nicolson	1986	Miss C Hourihane
1977	Miss J Greenhalgh	1982	Mrs J Thornhill		

Helen Holm Trophy

Instituted 1973

Year	Winner	Year	Winner	Year	Winner
1973	Mrs IC Robertson	1978	Miss W Aitken	1983	Miss J Connachan
1974	Miss SC Needham	1979	Mrs IC Robertson	1984	Miss G Stewart
1975	Miss MN Thomson	1980	Miss W Aitken	1985	Miss P Wright
1976	Miss MN Thomson	1981	Miss G Stewart	1986	Mrs IC Robertson
1977	Miss B Huke	1982	Miss W Aitken		

Herts Amateur Championship

Year	Winner	Year	Winner	Year	Winner
1935	J McKay	1957	TS Waddell	1973	H Squirrell
1936	J McKay	1958	GAD Dailey	1974	R Durrant
1937	MGS Fox	1959	GH Dudley	1975	N Faldo
1938	WC Gronow	1960	WJ Glenny	1976	R Durrant
1939	CW Measor	1961	SN Perry	1977	R Durrant
1946	PB Lucas	1962	BHG Chapman	1977	C Allen
1947	PB Lucas	1963	H Squirrell	1978	R Durrant
1948	K Leslie Smith	1964	Peter Townsend	1979	DF Williams
1949	GA Hill	1965	BHG Chapman	1980	JE Ambridge
1950	EH Holt	1966	Chris Allen	1981	RY Mitchell
1951	BM Atkinson	1967	A Holmes	1982	JE Ambridge
1952	ER Anscombe	1968	PN Wingfield	1983	C McKay
1953	E Holt	1969	A Holmes	1984	N Briggs
1954	CG Ostler	1970	M Hastings	1985	PR Robinson
1955	E Holt	1971	A Holmes		
1956	BHG Chapman	1972	D Woolmer		

Herts Open Championship

Year	Winner	Year	Winner	Year	Winner
1935	E Ray	1958	BJ Hunt	1973	R Whitehead
1936	PP Wynne	1959	BJ Hunt	1974	A Phillips
1937	A Mitchell	1960	RM Mandeville	1975	K Brown
1938	AG Havers	1961	BJ Hunt	1976	D Matthew
1946	AG Havers	1962	BJ Hunt	1977	ER Whitehead
1947	EE Whitcombe	1963	DJ Rees	1978	S Bishop
1948	H Weetman (Asst)	1964	GM Hunt	1979	T Powell
1949	WJ Branch	1965	DJ Rees	1980	T Parker
1950	DJ Rees	1966	D Lewis	1981	T Price
1952	AJ Harman	1967	AW Holmes (Am)	1982	K Robson
1953	EC Brown	1968	W Large	1983	B Puttick
1954	DJ Rees	1969	G Hunt	1984	
1955	N Coles	1970	W Large	1985	
1956	DJ Rees	1971	R Whitehead	1986	
1957	BJ Hunt	1972	DJ Rees		

Herts Ladies' Championship

Instituted 1924

Year	Winner	Year	Winner	Year	Winner
1947	Mrs Mawson	1962	Mrs R Oliver	1976	Mrs R Turnbull
1948	Mrs KM Clerke	1963	Mrs R Oliver	1977	Miss J Smith
1949	Miss E Dixon	1964	Mrs R Oliver	1978	Miss J Smith
1950	Mrs Davies	1965	Mrs M Cuneen	1979	Miss S Latham
1951	Mrs Oliver	1966	Miss M Paton	1980	Mrs H Kaye
1952	Mrs Davies	1967	Mrs P Rumble	1981	Mrs V Pearson
1954	Mrs HJ Davies	1968	Mrs R Oliver	1982	Miss N McCormack
1955	Mrs R Oliver	1969	Mrs R Oliver	1983	Mrs E Provan
1956	Mrs E Beck	1970	Mrs B Smith	1984	Miss K Hurley
1957	Miss A Gardiner	1971	Mrs J Kaye	1985	Mrs H Kaye
1958	Mrs R Oliver	1972	Mrs R Turnbull	1986	Miss T Jeaty
1959	Miss P Lane	1973	Miss S Parker		
1960	Miss P Lane	1974	Mrs R Turnbull		
1961	Mrs R Oliver	1975	Mrs M Rumble		

Isle of Wight Amateur Championship

Instituted 1924

Year	Winner	Year	Winner
1935	JE Mellor	1964	A Pemberton
1936	JE Mellor	1965	C Haworth
1937	FH Hayward	1966	MV Lyon
1938	Capt. AC Newnham	1967	C Haworth
1939	JE Mellor	1968	WA Close
1946	IR Patey	1969	K Johnston
1947	FH Hayward	1970	C Haworth
1948	C Haworth	1971	S Trueman
1949	C Haworth	1972	P Nuttall
1950	C Haworth	1973	P Cridland
1951	GT White	1974	P Nuttall
1952	K Chiverton	1975	RA Lock
1953	GT White	1976	BA Claridge
1954	C Haworth	1977	T Underwood
1955	C Haworth	1978	D Green
1956	GT White	1979	H Brownsdon
1957	HD Robinson	1980	RJ Beach
1958	S Trueman	1981	DJ Maidment
1959	EA Young	1982	B Lewis
1960	JT Shiel	1983	JKM Sutton
1961	C Haworth	1984	DJ Maidment
1962	L Scovell	1985	DJ Maidment
1963	H Minchin	1986	

Isle of Wight Ladies' Championship

Instituted 1923

Year	Winner	Year	Winner
1930	Mrs P Snelling	1965	Miss H Day
1931	Mrs FHT Buchanan	1966	Mrs CG Dinham
1932	Miss L Storr	1967	Mrs AB Oliveira
1933	Miss L Storr	1968	Miss H Day
1934	Miss R Storr	1969	Miss S Baker
1935	Miss L Storr	1970	Mrs AB Oliveira
1936	Miss L Storr	1971	Mrs P Oliveira
1937	Miss L Storr	1972	Mrs P Matthews
1938	Mrs M White	1973	Mrs P Matthews
1939	Miss L Storr	1974	Miss G Wright
1953	Mrs WM Driver	1975	Mrs P Matthews
1954	Mrs WJ Bennett	1976	Miss G Wright
1955	Mrs WJ Bennett	1977	Mrs P Oliveira
1956	Miss H Day	1978	Mrs P Matthews
1957	Mrs D Boyd	1979	Mrs M Butler
1958	Miss H Day	1980	Miss G Wright
1959	Mrs K Webb	1981	Miss G Wright
1960	Miss H Day	1982	Miss G Wright
1961	Mrs K Webb	1983	Miss G Wright
1962	Miss H Day	1984	
1963	Mrs K Webb	1985	
1964	Miss H Day	1986	

Kayser-Bondor Women's Foursomes

Year	Winners
1958	Miss E Price and Mrs AD Spearman, Miss J Robertson and Mrs M Bonallack
1959	Mrs G Valentine and Mrs J Anderson
1960	V'tesse de St Sauveur and Miss B Varangot
1961	Mrs G Valentine and Mrs I Wright
1962	Mrs J Anderson and Miss B Jackson
1963	Miss B Varangot and Mrs I Goldschmid

In 1964 became the Casa Pupo Women's Foursomes. From 1966 onwards see under Avia Ladies' International Tournament.

Kent Amateur Championship

Instituted 1925

Year	Winner	Year	Winner	Year	Winner
1930	ER Tipple	1953	TA Torrance	1970	RH Mummery
1931	MCV Moberley	1954	JD Lyons	1971	PJ Hedges
1932	F McGloin	1955	SM McCready	1972	J Ryan
1933	HS Mitchell	1956	SM McCready	1973	G Brown
1934	O Austreng	1957	G Darlington	1974	RH Mummery
1935	F McGloin	1958	JD Lyons	1975	J Powell
1936	O Austreng	1959	MF Wisher	1976	P Hoad
1937	O Austreng	1960	JR Langridge	1977	P Hoad
1938	AT Wilson	1961	A LePage	1978	P Hoad
1939	Dr JA Flaherty	1962	RA Hogg	1979	PJ Hedges
1946	TD Page	1963	M Attenborough	1980	M McLean
1947	Dr MG Heugh	1964	M Attenborough	1981	M McLean
1948	AGS Penman	1965	M Attenborough	1982	S Baldwin
1949	AGS Penman	1966	Peter Gracey	1983	M Lawrence
1950	AGS Penman	1967	M Bills	1984	M Lawrence
1951	AGS Penman	1968	PJ Hedges	1985	J Simmance
1952	MD Asprey	1969	RJ Redsull	1986	

Kent Ladies' Championship

Instituted 1920

Year	Winner	Year	Winner
1930	Miss W Morgan	1963	Mrs M Richards
1931	Miss W Morgan	1964	Miss Shirley Ward
1932	Miss I Doxford	1965	Mrs D Neech
1933	Miss W Morgan	1966	Mrs D Neech
1934	Miss D Fishwick	1967	Miss Shirley Ward
1935	Miss W Morgan	1968	Miss L Denison-Pender
1936	Miss W Morgan	1969	Miss S German
1937	Miss W Morgan	1970	Miss C Redford
1938	Miss B Mackenzie	1971	Miss M Walker
1939	Miss Jackson	1972	Miss L Denison-Pender
1948	Mrs Z Bolton	1973	Miss L Denison-Pender
1949	Mrs M Richards	1974	Miss A Langford
1950	Miss B Jackson	1975	Miss C Redford
1951	Miss B Jackson	1976	Mrs S Hedges
1952	Miss B Jackson	1977	Mrs C Caldwell (*née*) Redford)
1953	Miss W Morgan	1978	Mrs L Bayman (*née* Denison-Pender)
1954	Mrs C Falconer		
1955	Miss A Ward	1979	Mrs S Hedges
1956	Miss A Ward	1980	Mrs A Robinson
1957	Miss SB Smith	1981	Miss J Guntrip
1958	Mrs M Bonallack (née Ward)	1982	Mrs S Hedges
1959	Mrs C Falconer	1983	Miss J Guntrip
1960	Miss E Hearn	1984	Mrs S Kitchen
1961	Mrs R Brown	1985	Mrs L Bayman
1962	Mrs R Brown	1986	Mrs C Caldwell

Kent Open Championship

Year	Winner	Year	Winner	Year	Winner
1962	R Fidler	1971	B Sandry	1980	I Grant
1964	R Fidler	1972	G Will	1981	G Potter
1965	C Whiting	1973	N Job	1982	P Mitchell
1966	SL King M Henderson	1974 1975	PJ Hedges (Am) G Will	1983 1984	G Potter N Terry
1967	R Fidler	1976	P Gill	1985	J Bennett
1968	G Will	1977	R Chapman (Am)	1986	P Mitchell
1969	G Will	1978	R Cameron (Am)		
1970	PJ Hedges (Am)	1979	PGJ Hoad		

Kent Professional Championship

Instituted 1912

Year	Winner	Year	Winner	Year	Winner
1946	SL King	1959	C Whiting	1975	G Will
1947	SL King	1960	SL King	1976	G Will
1948	SL King	1961	N Quigley	1977	K Ashdown
1949	SL King	1962	W Dawson	1978	G Will
1950	SL King	1966	RS Fidler	1979	R Fidler
1951	SL King	1967	D Bonthron	1980	R Fidler
1952	F Taylor	1968	R Game	1981	D Russell
1953	L Roberts	1969	N Job	1982	R Watkins
1954	AH Padgham	1970	RS Fidler	1983	G Potter
1955	SL King	1971	G Norton	1984	R Cameron
1956	W West	1972	G Will	1985	G Will
1957	N Quigley	1973	R Fidler	1986	J Bennett
1958	FL Roberts	1974	G Will		

The Lagonda Trophy

Instituted 1975

Venue: Camberley Heath
From 1982 played over 72 holes

Year	Winner	Score	Year	Winner	Score
1975	WJ Reid	143	1982	A Sherborne	290
1976	JC Davies	142	1983	I Sparkes (3 rounds)	216
1977	WS Gronow	145			
1978	JC Davies	135	1984	M Davis	289
1979	JG Bennett	142	1985	J Robinson	283
1980	P McEvoy	139	1986	D Gilford	282
1981	N Mitchell	138			

Lanarkshire Amateur Championship

Year	Winner	Year	Winner	Year	Winner
1950	G Parker	1963	AV Baxter	1976	J Johnston
1951	JS Montgomerie	1964	A Neil	1977	W Paterson
1952	A Sinclair, jun	1965	DB Mackie	1978	H Milligan
1953	GR Morgan	1966	I Frame	1979	R Smith
1954	JS Montgomerie	1967	W Redpath	1980	H Miller
1955	JW Gardner	1968	J McTear	1981	G Banks
1956	I Young	1969	TB Main	1982	G Jones
1957	RJ Jameson	1970	J Howieson	1983	R Lynch
1958	DA Walkinshaw	1971	J McTear	1984	WS Bryson
1959	A Sinclair	1972	W Smeaton	1985	
1960	JF Milligan	1973	DC Longmuir	1986	
1961	A Sinclair	1974	DC Longmuir		
1962	J Abernethy	1975	EAE Quinn		

Lanarkshire Match Play Championship

Year	Winner	Year	Winner	Year	Winner
1964	JF Milligan	1972	D Longmuir	1980	J Simpson
1965	AA McLarty	1973	A Grant	1981	Bert Lynch
1966	J Nielan	1974	A Orr	1982	K Ross
1967	DB Mackie	1975	D Martin	1983	S Taylor
1968	J McTear	1976	G Russo	1984	WS Bryson
1969	R McTavish	1977	N Good	1985	
1970	J Thomson	1978	HS Milligan	1986	
1971	G O'Keane	1979	G Sinclair		

Lanarkshire Ladies' County Championship

Instituted 1928

Year	Winner	Year	Winner
1935	Miss N Forest	1952	Miss H Murdoch
1936	Miss W Morrison	1953	Miss J Cadzow
1937	Mrs Ballantine	1954	Miss J Robertson
1938	Miss W Morrison	1955	Miss J Robertson
1939	Mrs AW Ballantine	1956	Miss J Robertson
1947	Miss J Hill	1957	Miss J Robertson
1948	Miss J Hill	1958	Miss J Robertson
1949	Miss S Conacher	1959	Miss J Robertson
1950	Miss G Galbraith	1960	Miss H Murdoch
1951	Miss H Murdoch	1961	Miss H Murdoch

Lanarkshire Ladies' County Championship
continued

Year	Winner	Year	Winner
1962	Miss H Murdoch	1975	Mrs W Norris
1963	Miss B McCormack	1976	Mrs A Burden
1964	Miss J Smith	1977	Miss S Needham
1965	Miss M Park	1978	Miss B McCormack
1966	Mrs W Norris	1979	Mrs W Norris
1967	Miss B McCormack	1980	Mrs JC Scott
1968	Mrs W Norris	1981	Miss E Dunn
1969	Miss S Needham	1982	Mrs W Norris
1970	Mrs W Norris	1983	Mrs S Roy (*née* Needham)
1971	Mrs W Norris	1984	Mrs S Roy
1972	Miss S Needham	1985	Miss P Hutton
1973	Miss S Needham	1986	Mrs JC Scott
1974	Mrs W Norris		

Lancashire Amateur Championship

Instituted 1910

Year	Winner	Year	Winner	Year	Winner
1935	E Halliwell	1957	D Anderson	1973	AH Chandler
1936	DS Coates	1958	EJ Riley	1974	JB Dickinson
1937	IW Calder	1959	EJ Riley	1975	A Squires
1938	IW Calder	1960	D Rawlinson	1976	MJ Reece
1939	HG Bentley	1961	MJ Reece	1977	JB Dickinson
1946	RK Bell	1962	AB Kidd	1978	HAN Stott
1947	WK Hargreaves	1963	GP Roberts	1979	MPD Walls
1948	RJ White	1964	EJ Threlfall	1980	A Squires
1949	JW Jones	1965	RH Tupling	1981	MJ Wild
1950	JW Calder	1966	AV Moss	1982	A Squires
1951	JR Wroe	1967	SG Birtwell	1983	MPD Wallis
1952	DT Stevenson	1968	SG Birtwell	1984	SG Birtwell
1953	GP Roberts	1969	PH Evans	1985	RA Bardsley
1954	JW Jones	1970	J Glover	1986	
1955	D Anderson	1971	MJ Reece		
1956	D Rawlinson	1972	SG Birtwell		

Lancashire Ladies' Championship

Instituted 1912

Year	Winner	Year	Winner	Year	Winner
1936	Miss WM Berry	1958	Miss S Vaughan	1974	Miss A Irvin
1937	Miss JD Firth	1959	Mrs F Smith	1975	Miss J Greenhalgh
1938	Miss Robinson	1960	Mrs F Smith	1976	Miss J Greenhalgh
1939	Miss P Edwards	1961	Miss J Greenhalgh	1977	Miss J Greenhalgh
1947	Miss P Edwards	1962	Miss J Greenhalgh	1978	Miss J Greenhalgh
1948	Miss F Stephens	1963	Miss S Vaughan	1979	Miss A Norman
1949	Miss F Stephens	1964	Miss S Vaughan	1980	Miss A Brown
1950	Miss F Stephens	1965	Miss A Irvin	1981	Miss A Brown
1951	Miss F Stephens	1966	Miss J Greenhalgh	1982	Mrs C Costello
1952	Miss F Stephens	1967	Miss A Irvin	1983	Miss J Melville
1953	Miss F Stephens	1968	Miss J Greenhalgh	1984	Mrs A Goucher
1954	Miss F Stephens	1969	Miss A Irvin	1985	Mrs A Bromilow
1955	Mrs Roy Smith (née Stephens)	1970	Miss P Burrows	1986	Mrs J Collingham (*née* Melville)
		1971	Miss A Irvin		
1956	Miss S Stewart	1972	Miss A Irvin		
1957	Mrs D Howard	1973	Miss J Greenhalgh		

Lancashire Open Championship

Instituted 1973

Year	Winner	Year	Winner	Year	Winner
1973	GA Caygill	1978	IJ Mosey	1983	S Hammer (Am)
1974	IJ Mosey	1979	IJ Mosey	1984	
1975	K Hornby (Am)	1980	D Clarke	1985	R Longworth
1976	AH Chandler	1981	D Durnian	1986	R Green
1977	F Till (Am)	1982	S Hadfield		

Leicestershire and Rutland Amateur Championship

Instituted 1925

Year	Winner	Year	Winner	Year	Winner
1935	RB Weston Webb	1957	GB Wolstenholme	1973	J Hayles
1936	DB May	1958	EF Bayden	1974	P Haddon
1937	ST Matthews	1959	EF Bayden	1975	R Taylor
1938	ST Matthews	1960	ES Blackadder	1976	E Hammond
1939	ST Matthews	1961	RD Christian	1977	M Dayus
1946	ST Matthews	1962	TR Shingler	1978	IR Middleton
1947	ST Matthews	1963	TR Shingler	1979	IR Middleton
1948	CM Warren	1964	TR Shingler	1980	A Harrison
1949	ST Matthews	1965	W Ridgeway	1981	EW Hammond
1950	ST Matthews	1966	RD Christian	1982	C Gotla
1951	ST Matthews	1967	W Ridgeway	1983	T Stephens
1952	EF Bayden	1968	JR Riley	1984	A Martinez
1953	GB Wolstenholme	1969	RR Campbell	1985	E Hammond
1954	Peter Wood	1970	RJ Taylor	1986	IR Middleton
1955	GB Wolstenholme	1971	RA Campbell		
1956	GB Wolstenholme	1972	P Wood		

Leicestershire and Rutland Open Championship

Year	Winner	Year	Winner	Year	Winner
1963	BN Davies	1972	KD Pickup	1981	SH Adams (Am)
1964	P Wood (Am)	1973	D Kirkland	1982	I Middleton
1965	TR Shingler (Am)	1974	RD Christian (Am)	1983	EE Feasey (Am)
1966	TR Shingler (Am)	1975	*Cancelled*	1984	R Larratt
1967	RD Christian (Am)	1976	*No championship*	1985	R Adams
1968	E Martin	1977	K Barnes	1986	
1969	BJ Bates	1978	B Edmundson		
1970	P Wood (Am)	1979	R Swaine		
1971	JD Morgan	1980	EW Hammond		

Leicestershire and Rutland Ladies' Championship

Year	Winner	Year	Winner	Year	Winner
1950	Mrs A Kerslake	1953	Mrs A Kerslake	1956	Miss F Brunton
1951	Miss F Brunton	1954	Mrs A Kerslake	1957	Miss F Brunton
1952	Mrs A Kerslake	1955	Miss F Brunton	1958	Miss F Brunton

Leicestershire and Rutland Ladies' Championship

continued

Year	Winner	Year	Winner	Year	Winner
1959	Mrs W Howard	1969	Mrs H McKay	1979	Mrs A Mansfield
1960	Mrs A Kerslake	1970	Mrs P Martin	1980	Miss J Roberts
1961	Mrs JF Walton	1971	Miss J Stevens	1981	Mrs Rosemary Reed
1962	Mrs JF Walton	1972	Miss J Stevens	1982	Miss P Gray
1963	Mrs A Marrion	1973	Miss J Stevens	1983	Mrs R Reed
1964	Mrs GA Wheatley	1974	Mrs O Sturton	1984	Mrs P Martin
1965	Mrs GA Wheatley	1975	Mrs J Chapman	1985	Miss A Waters
1966	Miss M Howard	1976	Mrs J Chapman	1986	Mrs V Davis
1967	Mrs R Reed	1977	Mrs J Chapman		
1968	Mrs AM Reed	1978	Mrs R Reed		

Lincolnshire Amateur Championship

Instituted 1925

Year	Winner	Year	Winner	Year	Winner
1946	JW Ellmore	1960	JW Ellmore	1974	PG Shillington
1947	CH Caswell	1961	MG Lee	1975	M James
1948	Dr L Jones	1962	Flt-Lt RD Shrivell	1976	K Waters
1949	DJ Baxter	1963	JC Baggott	1977	S Bennett
1950	AM Tew	1964	KP Allan	1978	S Bennett
1951	CH Beamish	1965	MG Lee	1979	PK Allen
1952	TA Saul	1966	F Wood	1980	A Thain
1953	JW Ellmore	1967	F Wood	1981	L Brumpton
1954	Dr L Jones	1968	RJ Barrell	1982	S Graves
1955	PJ Butler	1969	RJ Nix	1983	P Stenton
1956	Dr L Jones	1970	RJ Barrell	1984	JA Purdy
1957	PJ Butler	1971	A Thain	1985	AGS Robinson
1958	DJ Baxter	1972	RJ Barrell	1986	
1959	S Kennedy	1973	F Woods		

Lincolnshire Ladies' Championship

Year	Winner	Year	Winner	Year	Winner
1947	Miss D Taylor	1961	Miss R Gale	1975	Mrs P Harvey
1948	Miss J Johnson	1962	Mrs B Watson	1976	Mrs P West
1949	Miss FE Kearney	1963	Mrs B Watson	1977	Mrs B Hix
1950	Mrs C Jones	1964	Mrs B Watson	1978	Mrs P West
1951	Mrs C Jones	1965	Mrs R Winn	1979	Mrs B Hix
1952	Mrs P Powell	1966	Mrs D Frearson	1980	Mrs E Annison
1953	Miss J Johnson	1967	Mrs D Frearson	1981	Miss R Broughton
1954	Mrs C Jones	1968	Mrs B Watson	1982	Mrs B Hicks
1955	Miss J Johnson	1969	Mrs B Dawson	1983	Mrs B Hix
1956	Mrs P Powell	1970	Mrs B Watson	1984	Mrs A Burtt
1957	Mrs C Jones	1971	Mrs E Annison	1985	Miss H Dobson
1958	Mrs L Jones	1972	Mrs P Chatterton	1986	Miss A Johns
1959	Miss R Gale	1973	Mrs P Harvey		
1960	Miss R Gale	1974	Mrs B Watson		

Lincolnshire Open Championship

Year	Winner	Year	Winner	Year	Winner
1947	A Fixter	1952	A Fixter	1957	J Wiggett
1948	DJ Baxter	1953	JH Ellis	1958	J Wiggett
1949	A Fixter	1954	PJ Butler	1959	CJ Norton
1950	A Fixter	1955	Dr L Jones	1960	JW Elmore
1951	A Fixter	1956	J Wiggett	1961	A Jacklin

Lincolnshire Open Championship *continued*

Year	Winner	Year	Winner	Year	Winner
1962	RD Shrivell (Am)	1970	TR Squires	1979	S Bennett
1963	T Squires	1971	B Simpson	1980	K Daubney (Am)
1964	IH Stackhouse (Am)	1972	B Thompson	1981	P Davies
		1973	TR Squires	1982	TR Squires
1965	R Issitt	1974	B Thompson	1983	S Dickinson (Am)
1966	TR Squires	1975	H Jackson	1984	
1967	T Squires	1976	J Wraith	1985	
1968	B Thompson	1977	K Waters (Am)	1986	A Carter
1969	P Leslie	1978	M James		

Lothians Amateur Championship

Year	Winner	Year	Winner	Year	Winner
1947	AS Flockhart	1961	HC Brownlee	1975	RE Muir
1948	RM Lees	1962	HM Campbell	1976	N Fisher
1949	CM Meek	1963	A Lourie	1977	ID Stavert
1950	Ian Macniven	1964	RDBM Shade	1978	S Stephen
1951	AB Taylor	1965	AJ Low	1979	CP Dhristy
1952	WCD Hare	1966	GE Robertson	1980	ST Knowles
1953	WCD Hare	1967	B Gallacher	1981	B Dunlop
1954	S Smith	1968	G McGregor, jun	1982	R Bradley
1955	AMM Bucher	1969	DF Campbell	1983	A Roy
1956	PR Bryce	1970	C McCulloch	1984	PJ Smith
1957	DW Alexander	1971	AGG Miller	1985	
1958	JR Kyle	1972	P Bucher	1986	
1959	AHH Campbell	1973	W Davidson		
1960	DW Alexander	1974	L Morton		

The Lytham Trophy

Venue: Lytham and St Annes

Year	Winner	Score	Year	Winner	Score
1965	MF Bonallack CA Clark	295	1974	CW Green	291
			1975	G Macgregor	299
1966	PM Townsend	290	1976	MJ Kelley	292
1967	R Foster	296	1977	P Deeble	296
1968	R Foster	286	1978	B Marchbank	288
1969	T Craddock	290	1979	P McEvoy	279
1970	SG Birtwell JC Farmer CW Green GC Marks	296	1980	IC Hutcheon	293
			1981	R Chapman	221
			1982	MF Sludds	306
			1983	S McAllister	299
1971	W Humphreys	292	1984	J Hawksworth	289
1972	MF Bonallack	281	1985	L Macnamara	144
1973	MG King SG Birtwell	292	1986	S McKenna	297

Manx Amateur Championship

Instituted 1926

Year	Winner	Year	Winner	Year	Winner
1946	WA Kirkpatrick	1960	R Ennett	1974	MJ Kewley
1947	WA Kirkpatrick	1961	B Jones	1975	SJ Boyd
1948	CH Cain	1962	M Anderson	1976	SJ Boyd
1949	CW Jackson	1963	WE Ashworth	1977	WR Ennett
1950	WA Kirkpatrick	1964	WE Ashworth	1978	G Wilson
1951	WA Kirkpatrick	1965	WA Stead	1979	G Wilson
1952	WCA Stead	1966	A Copley	1980	SJ Boyd
1953	WA Kirkpatrick	1967	D Jones	1981	G Kelley
1954	D Jones	1968	R Moore	1982	J Sutton
1955	WA Kirkpatrick	1969	A Copley	1983	J Sutton
1956	David Ball	1970	W Stead	1984	J Sutton
1957	SA Ashworth	1971	J Sutton	1985	J Sutton
1958	NC Corlett	1972	J Sutton	1986	
1959	KJ Skillicorn	1973	J Sutton		

Middlesex Amateur Championship

Instituted 1925

Year	Winner	Year	Winner	Year	Winner
1935	LA Wilson	1957	AB Simmonds	1973	M Devetta
1936	CJ Anderson	1958	GT Mills	1974	R Kane
1937	CJ Anderson	1959	N Frazer	1975	R Kane
1938	Dr LF Clarke	1960	Keith Warren	1976	IM Stungo
1939	LA Wilson	1961	AB Simmonds	1977	SR Warrin
1946	WH Macdonald	1962	N Brown	1978	IM Stungo
1947	KG Thom	1963	JA Ransome	1979	IM Stungo
1948	KG Thom	1964	JA Ransome	1980	NM Curtis
1949	E Gibbs	1965	JA Ransome	1981	GA Homewood
1950	CE Hetherington	1966	RP Stephenson	1982	ML Weir
1951	DJ Scott	1967	S Warrin	1983	GA Homewood
1952	JRB Johnstone	1968	T Lane	1984	RB Willison
1953	DJ Scott	1969	S Warrin	1985	RB Willison
1954	JA Ransome	1970	M Whelan	1986	
1955	DJ Scott	1971	S Warrin		
1956	J Kirkham	1972	I Buchan		

Middlesex Ladies' Championship

Instituted 1923

Year	Winner	Year	Winner
1935	Miss R Harris	1965	Mrs M Spearman
1936	Miss B Taylor	1966	Mrs A Denny
1937	Mrs JB Beck	1967	Miss B Hayhurst
1938	Mrs C Eberstein	1968	Mrs B Jones
1939	Miss M Ruttle	1969	Miss S Hills
1947	Miss J Gordon	1970	Mrs M Barton
1948	Miss J Gordon	1971	Miss S Hills
1949	Mrs CR Eberstein	1972	Miss C Mackintosh
1950	Miss J Gordon	1973	Mrs RE Garrett
1951	Mrs Bromley-Davenport	1974	Miss A Daniel
1952	Miss J Gordon	1975	Miss A Daniel
1953	Mrs RE Garrett (*née* Ruttle)	1976	Miss J Boulter
1954	Miss J Gordon	1977	Miss A Daniel
1955	Mrs M Spearman	1978	Mrs A Gems
1956	Mrs M Spearman	1979	Mrs C Turnbull
1957	Mrs M Spearman	1980	Mrs C Turnbull
1958	Mrs M Spearman	1981	Mrs A Gems
1959	Mrs M Spearman	1982	Mrs A Gems
1960	Mrs M Barton	1983	Miss C McGillivray
1961	Mrs M Spearman	1984	Miss C Nelson
1962	Mrs M Barton	1985	Miss C Nelson
1963	Miss P Moore	1986	Mrs A Gems
1964	Mrs M Spearman		

Middlesex Open Championship

Year	Winner	Year	Winner	Year	Winner
1966	R Emery	1973	S Murray	1980	P Buchan
1967	JK Ramsden	1974	A Toner (Am)	1981	P Glozier
1968	K Warren	1975	JN Paramor (Am)	1982	L Farmer
1969	J Hudson	1976	J Hamilton	1983	
1970	GW Low	1977	SJ Levermore	1984	
1971	T Lane	1978	J Reynolds	1985	
1972	S Murray	1979	J Reynolds	1986	

Midland Counties Amateur Stroke Play Championship

Instituted 1895

Year	Winner	Year	Winner	Year	Winner
1931	EW Fiddian	1952	JL Morgan	1966	MA Payne
1932	ST Matthews	1953	WM Robb	1967	GC Marks
1933	Dr AR McCallum	1954	P Skerritt	1968	RD James
1934	S Lunt	1955	D Dailey	1969	RD Christian
1935	C Stowe	1956	H Roberts	1970	PD Kelley
1936	DM Sutherland	1957	E Walton	1971	J Fisher
1937	Dr W Anderson	1958	HJ Roberts	1972	RD James
1938	JS Mitchley	1959	C Stowe	1973	DJ Russell
1939	Dr WM Robb	1960	MSR Lunt	1974	A Lyle
1947	JH Roberts	1961	RA Jowle	1975	M Poxon
1948	C Stowe	1962	MSR Lunt	*From 1976 played*	
1949	JL Morgan	1963	C Stowe	*concurrently with the*	
1950	JL Morgan	1964	NA Newbitt	*Midland Open Amateur*	
1951	JM Urry	1965	PD Kelley	*Stroke Play Championship.*	

Midland Open Amateur Stroke Play Championship

Year	Winner	Year	Winner	Year	Winner
1976	P Downes	1980	P Downes	1984	K Valentine
1977	P Downes	1981	P Baxter	1985	M Hassall
1978	P McEvoy	1982	NJ Chesses	1986	
1979	M Tomlinson	1983	CA Banks		

Midland Ladies' Championship

Instituted 1897

Year	Winner	Year	Winner	Year	Winner
1936	Miss B Newell	1958	Miss B Jackson	1973	Mrs A Stant
1937	Miss E Pears	1959	Miss B Jackson	1974	Mrs B Bargh
1938	Miss E Pears	1960	Miss B Jackson	1975	Mrs A Stant
1939	Mrs Jackson	1961	Miss S Armitage	1976	Mrs J Chapman
1947	Mrs Sheppard	1962	Miss A Higgott	1977	Mrs S Westall
1948	Miss M Hampson	1963	Miss A Higgott	1978	Mrs S Westall
1949	Mrs Sheppard	1964	Miss A Coxill	1979	Mrs M Carr
1950	Mrs Gaskell	1965	Miss S Armitage	1980	Miss J Walter
1951	Mrs Denham	1966	Mrs D Frearson	1981	Miss J Walter
1952	Miss P Davie	1967	Mrs R Tomlinson	1982	Miss S Kiddle
1953	Hon Mrs Jean Gee	1968	Mrs J Roles	1983	Miss T Hammond
1954	Miss B Jackson	1969	Miss B Jackson	1984	Miss L Waring
1955	Mrs Beeson	1970	Miss J Blaymire	1985	Miss L Waring
1956	Miss B Jackson	1971	Miss J Stant	1986	Mrs J Collingham
1957	Miss B Jackson	1972	Miss J Blaymire		

Midland Open Championship

Year	Winner	Year	Winner	Year	Winner
1947	W Lees	1962	GR Maisey	1977	J Anderson
1948	EB Williamson	1963	A Rees	1978	AP Griffiths
1949	CH Ward	1964	RL Moffitt	1979	DJ Ridley
1950	JL Morgan (Am)	1965	PJ Butler	1980	AP Griffiths
1951	CH Ward	1966	D Snell	1981	B Waites
1952	CH Ward	1967	TM Collinge	*From 1982 renamed Midland*	
1953	F Miller	1968	L Thompson	*All-Star Championship*	
1954	CH Ward	1969	PJ Butler	1982	AR Minshall
1955	F Jowle	1970	R Moffitt	1983	DJ Russell
1956	PJ Butler	1971	BJ Waites	1984	P Elson
1957	CH Ward	1972	RDS Livingstone	1985	*Not played*
1958	PJ Butler	1973	K Hodgkinson (Am)	1986	*Not played*
1959	D Snell	1974	J Rhodes		
1960	PJ Butler	1975	AWB Lyle (Am)		
1961	RL Moffitt	1976	BJ Waites		

Midland Professional Stroke Play Championship

Instituted 1897

Year	Winner	Year	Winner	Year	Winner
1935	WR Firkins	1956	RL Hastelow	1972	BJ Waites
1936	WJ Branch	1957	D Snell	1973	RDS Livingston
1937	AG Beck	1958	JH Cawsey	1974	M Gallacher
1938	HR Manton	1959	GA Maisey	1975	HFJ Boyle
1939	WJ Martin	1960	J Hargreaves	1976	PR Herbert
1940-45	*No competition*	1961	PJ Butler	1977	BJ Waites
1946	W Lees	1962	A Rees	1978	BJ Waites
1947	KWC Adwick	1963	CH Ward	1979	BJ Waites
1948	A Lees	1964	SWT Murray	1980	DI Vaughan
1949	A Lees	1965	SA Hunt	1981	D Stewart
1950	CH Ward	1966	J Anderson	1982	P Elson
1951	JR Moses	1967	SWT Murray	1983	AR Minshall
1952	J Hargreaves	1968	SWT Murray	1984	M Mouland
1953	CH Ward	1969	TR Squires	1985	K Hayward
1954	A Cunningham	1970	D Llewellyn	1986	A Skingle
1955	CH Ward	1971	RA Beattie		

Midland Professional Match Play Championship

Instituted 1899

Year	Winner	Year	Winner	Year	Winner
1972	BJ Waites	1977	J Rhodes	1982	P Elson
1973	BJ Waites	1978	DT Steele	1983	PG Ackerley
1974	BJ Waites	1979	RDS Livingstone	1984	P Elson
1975	PJ Weaver	1980	RDS Livingston	1985	D Ridley
1976	M Gallagher	1981	P Elson	1986	J Higgins

Midlothian Ladies' Championship

Instituted 1924

Year	Winner	Year	Winner	Year	Winner
1935	Miss CM Park	1958	Mrs CH Ritchie	1974	Dr M Norval
1936	Miss CM Park	1959	Miss E Philip	1975	Miss J More
1937	Miss M Nicoll	1960	Miss P Dunn	1976	Miss M Stavert
1938	Miss CM Park	1961	Miss E Philip	1977	Miss M Stavert
1939	Mrs SH Morton	1962	Mrs J Milton	1978	Miss M Stavert
1947	Miss CM Park	1963	Mrs M Duthie	1979	Miss M Stavert
1948	Miss CM Park	1964	Mrs D Antonio	1980	Mrs BM Marshall
1949	Mrs J Scott	1965	Miss F Miller	1981	Miss MF Allen
1950	Miss E McLarty	1966	Miss E Philip	1982	Miss S Little
1951	Mrs WC Ritchie	1967	Miss M Norval	1983	Mrs J Marshall
1952	Miss JL Dunbar	1968	Mrs E Jack	1984	Mrs F de Vries
1953	Mrs WC Ritchie	1969	Miss M Norval	1985	Mrs F de Vries
1954	Mrs JJG Thomson	1970	Miss S MacDonalc	1986	Mrs J Marshall
1955	Mrs JB Cormack	1971	Mrs J Marshall		
1956	Mrs WC Ritchie	1972	Miss C Hardwick		
1957	Mrs JB Cormack	1973	Miss C Hardwick		

Monmouthshire Amateur Championship

Instituted 1920

Year	Winner	Year	Winner	Year	Winner
1935	JA Chapman	1954	WI Tucker	1966	W Windsor
1936	RB Bennett	1955	WI Tucker	1967	WI Tucker
1937	LJ Rowlands	1956	WI Tucker	1968	K Dabson
1938	K Llewellyn	1957	WI Tucker	1969	WI Tucker
1939	RB Bennett	1958	WI Tucker	1970	W Dwyer
1947	H Lloyd	1959	WI Tucker	1971	A Morgan
1948	HW Wright	1960	WI Tucker	1972	G Pinch
1949	WI Tucker	1961	WI Tucker	1973	A Disley
1950	H Phillips	1962	WI Tucker	1974	WI Tucker
1951	P Dunn	1963	WI Tucker	*For later years see under*	
1952	WI Tucker	1964	C Gilford	*Gwent Amateur*	
1953	WI Tucker	1965	C Gilford	*Championship*	

Monmouthshire Ladies' Championship

Instituted 1920

Year	Winner	Year	Winner	Year	Winner
1935	Dr P Whittaker	1956	Miss P Roberts	1972	Miss P Roberts
1936	Miss M Williams	1957	Miss P Roberts	1973	Miss E Davies
1937	Mrs JG Meredith	1958	Mrs P Inglis	1974	Miss E Davies
1938	Mrs G Evans	1959	Miss P Roberts	1975	Mrs B Chambers
1939	Miss H Reynolds	1960	Mrs R Hartley	1976	Miss E Davies
1947	Miss MP Roberts	1961	Mrs R Hartley	1977	Miss C Parry
1948	Mrs Garfield	1962	Miss P Roberts	1978	Miss E Davies
	Evans	1963	Miss P Roberts	1979	Miss E Davies
1949	Miss MP Roberts	1964	Miss P Roberts	1980	Miss M Davis
1950	Miss MP Roberts	1965	Miss P Roberts	1981	Miss K Beckett
1951	Mrs Garfield	1966	Miss P Roberts	1982	Miss M Davis
	Evans	1967	Mrs G Galliers	1983	Miss K Beckett
1952	Miss P Roberts	1968	Miss P Roberts	1984	Miss J Lapthorne
1953	Miss P Roberts	1969	Mrs B Chambers	1985	Miss P Lord
1954	Miss P Roberts	1970	Miss P Roberts	1986	Miss H Buckley
1955	Miss P Roberts	1971	Dr M Smith		

Norfolk Amateur Championship

Instituted 1921

Year	Winner	Year	Winner	Year	Winner
1935	WD Robinson	1958	AH Perowne	1974	BJ Ashton
1936	WD Robinson	1959	JPA Clymer	1975	J-D Crawford
1937	GP Burroughes	1960	AH Perowne	1976	DC Hatton
1938	WD Robinson	1961	AH Perowne	1977	MJF Bell
1939	JH Thompson	1962	DW Rains	1978	DJ Hood
1947	JPA Clymer	1963	Archie Cook	1979	JG Parkhill
1948	AH Perowne	1964	J Nudds	1980	JG Parkhill
1949	JA Floyd	1965	RJ Trower	1981	MR Few
1950	FA Brett	1966	RJ Trower	1982	DW Rains
1951	AH Perowne	1967	G Williams	1983	MN Sperrin
1952	AH Perowne	1968	RJ Trower	1984	T Hurrell
1953	AH Perowne	1969	J Nudds	1985	CJ Lamb
1954	AH Perowne	1970	PR Johnston	1986	
1955	AH Perowne	1971	S Cranmer		
1956	AH Perowne	1972	S Cranmer		
1957	AH Perowne	1973	MM Orr		

Norfolk Ladies' Championship

Instituted 1912

Year	Winner	Year	Winner	Year	Winner
1935	Mrs VM Cross	1958	Mrs BTF Carrick	1973	Mrs N Rains
1936	Miss G Watts	1959	Miss H Smith	1974	Mrs M Davies
1937	Mrs Jackson	1960	Miss H Smith	1975	Mrs M Davies
1938	Miss P Bullard	1961	Mrs BTF Carrick	1976	Mrs N Rains
1939	Mrs Carrick	1962	Miss AM Rust	1977	Mrs P Carrick
1947	Mrs Carrick	1963	Miss VE Cooper	1978	Mrs M Davies
1948	Mrs Richardson	1964	Miss AM Rust	1979	Mrs D Sutton
1949	Mrs Carrick	1965	Mrs B Carrick	1980	Miss VE Cooper
1950	Mrs JH Martin	1966	Mrs M Leeder	1981	Mrs AM Davies
1951	Miss J Cowell	1967	Mrs H Leeder	1982	Miss VE Cooper
1952	Mrs Carrick	1968	Mrs M Leeder	1983	Mrs M Davies
1953	Miss JM Harrison	1969	Mrs N Rains	1984	Mrs L Elliott
1954	Mrs BTF Carrick	1970	Mrs N Rains	1985	Mrs M Whybrow
1955	Miss JM Harrison	1971	Miss VE Cooper	1986	Mrs N Clarke
1956	Mrs BTF Carrick	1972	Mrs N Rains		

Norfolk Professional Championship

Instituted 1921

Year	Winner	Year	Winner	Year	Winner
1935	R Donald	1959	M Leeder	1974	MT Leeder
1936	J Mackie	1960	M Leeder	1975	N Catchpole
1937	J Mackie	1961	Alan Poulton	1976	MT Leeder
1938	BR Kelly	1962	MT Leeder	1977	MT Leeder
1948	BR Kelly	1963	MT Leeder	1978	MT Leeder
1949	L Ball	1964	MT Leeder	1979	MT Leeder
1950	BR Kelly	1965	J Carter	1980	MT Leeder
1951	J Mackie	1966	J Carter	1981	SLH Beckham
1952	M Leeder	1967	J Carter	1982	RJ Page
1953	M Leeder	1968	J Carter	1983	RG Foster
1954	BR Kelly	1969	MT Leeder	1984	MJ Elsworthy
1955	BR Kelly	1970	TG Symmons	1985	M Spooler
1956	Alan Poulton	1971	MT Leeder	1986	M Spooler
1957	L Ball	1972	MT Leeder		
1958	L Ball	1973	MT Leeder		

Norfolk Open Championship

Year	Winner	Year	Winner	Year	Winner
1963	MT Leeder	1971	MT Leeder	1979	MT Leeder
1964	AH Perowne (Am)	1972	MT Leeder	1980	MT Leeder
1965	J Carter	1973	MT Leeder	1981	JG Parkhill
1966	J Carter	1974	MT Leeder	1982	RJ Page
1967	J Carter	1975	N Catchpole	1983	RG Foster
1968	J Carter	1976	DC Hatton	1984	
1969	MT Leeder	1977	MT Leeder	1985	T Hurrell
1970	JW Nudds	1978	R Clarke	1986	

North-East and North-West Professional Championship

(Prior to 1974 was Northumberland and Durham Professional Championship)

Year	Winner	Year	Winner	Year	Winner
1974	R Webster	1978	PS Highmoor	1982	R Webster
1975	I Lambie	1979	K Saint	1983	
1976	P Harrison	1980	P Tupling	1984	
1977	IS Lambie	1981	P Harrison	1985	

Northamptonshire Amateur Championship

Instituted 1927

Year	Winner	Year	Winner	Year	Winner
1936	RW Kilsby	1958	CS Catlow	1974	JC Hodgson
1937	CS Catlow	1959	RG Halliday	1975	CR Cieslewicz
1938	CS Catlow	1960	CS Catlow	1976	TJ Giles
1939	CS Catlow	1961	EJ Kingdon	1977	RG Aitken
1946	M Gear Evans	1962	RG Aitken	1978	CJ Cieslewicz
1947	CS Catlow	1963	RG Aitken	1979	CR Cieslewicz
1948	CS Catlow	1964	RG Aitken	1980	C Cieslewicz
1949	FC Roe	1965	JE Saxby	1981	MJ Haddon
1950	CS Catlow	1966	RG Aitken	1982	S McDonald
1951	AJ Harrison	1967	JM Pettigrew	1983	DJJ Warren
1952	FG Roe	1968	RG Aitken	1984	M Scott
1953	MJ Worley	1969	RG Aitken	1985	M McNally
1954	RL Mobbs	1970	RG Aitken	1986	M Scott
1955	CS Catlow	1971	RS Larratt		
1956	CS Catlow	1972	RJ Gray		
1957	CF Clarke	1973	CR Cieslewicz		

Northamptonshire Ladies' Championship

Year	Winner	Year	Winner
1932	Mrs RT Phipps	1963	Mrs L Everard
1933	Miss DR Wooding	1964	Mrs L Everard
1934	Mrs C Everard	1965	Mrs N Paton
1935	Mrs WT Phipps	1966	Mrs S Stephenson
1936	Mrs RE Dazeley	1967	Mrs S Stephenson
1937	Miss GT Swannell	1968	Mrs J Sugden
1938	Mrs RT Phipps	1969	Mrs M Stephenson
1939	Mrs WT Swannell	1970	Mrs K Lock
1946	Mrs WT Swannell	1971	Mrs J Blezard
1947	Mrs AM Troup	1972	Mrs A Duck
1948	Mrs WT Swannell	1973	Mrs J Sugden
1949	Miss AM Troup	1974	Miss J Dicks
1950	Mrs W Taylor	1975	Miss J Lee
1951	Mrs R Larratt	1976	Miss J Lee
1952	Mrs K Lock	1977	Miss J Lee
1953	Marchioness Northampton	1978	Miss J Dicks
1954	Marchioness Northampton	1979	Miss VJ Dicks
1955	Miss Spencer	1980	Mrs M Hutheson
1956	Marchioness Northampton	1981	Miss J Dicks
1957	Mrs L Everard	1982	Mrs P Coles
1958	Mrs WT Swannell	1983	Miss J Dicks
1959	Mrs L Everard	1984	Mrs A Duck
1960	Mrs L Everard	1985	Mrs A Duck
1962	Mrs G Hollingsworth	1986	Mrs P Le Vai

Northamptonshire Professional Championship

Year	Winner	Year	Winner	Year	Winner
1947	J Holland	1961	W Allen	1975	R Kemp
1948	TP Cheal	1962	A Lovelady	1976	R Larratt
1949	G Gledhill	1963	A Lovelady	1977	M Gallagher
1950	T Burrell	1964	SWT Murray	1978	T Giles
1951	G Gledhill	1965	R Hamer	1979	TJ Giles
1952	T. Burrell	1966	SWT Murray	1980	A Charnley
1953	GF Weston	1967	R Kemp	1981	M Gallagher
1954	GF Weston	1968	R Kemp	1982	S Ward
1955	GF Weston	1969	SWT Murray	1983	SP Ward
1956	GF Weston	1970	R Kemp	1984	
1957	GF Weston	1971	SWT Murray	1985	
1958	A Walker	1972	M Gallagher	1986	
1959	W Cann	1973	M Gallagher		
1960	R Hamer	1974	M Gallagher		

Northern (England) Professional Championship

Instituted 1920

Year	Winner	Year	Winner	Year	Winner
1946	N Sutton	1960	E Large	1974	GA Caygill
1947	E Green	1961	JW Wilkshire	1975	D Dunk
1948	A Perry	1962	IG Smith	1976	W Ferguson
1949	N Quigley	1963	GA Caygill	1977	B Hutchinson
1950	J Fallon	1964	HW Muscroft	1978–79	*No championship*
1951	N Sutton	1965	J Wilkshire	1980	G Townhill
1952	HW Myers	1966	M Hoyle	1981	B Evans
1953	J Fallon	1967	G Parton	1982	H Muscroft
1954	J Burton	1968	AC Gillies	1983	
1955	DA Lewis	1969	HB Allen	1984	
1956	J Fallon	1970	L Platts	1985	A Murray
1957	F Bullock	1971	L Platts	1986	D Stirling
1958	A Coop	1972	W Ferguson		
1959	E Green	1973	D Jagger		

Northern Counties (Scotland) Ladies' Championship

Year	Winner	Year	Winner	Year	Winner
1967	Mrs B Drakard	1974	Mrs I McIntosh	1981	Miss S Ross
1968	Miss J Cumming	1975	Mrs I McIntosh	1982	Miss G Stewart
1969	Mrs I McIntosh	1976	Miss G Stewart	1983	Miss L Anderson
1970	Mrs I McIntosh	1977	Miss S Ross	1984	Miss J Buist
1971	Miss M Kirk	1978	Miss G Stewart	1985	Miss A Shannon
1972	Miss J Cumming	1979	Mrs I McIntosh	1986	Miss F McKay
1973	Mrs I McIntosh	1980	Mrs I McIntosh		

North of Ireland Open Amateur Championship

Year	Winner	Year	Winner	Year	Winner
1950	NV Drew	1952	NV Drew	1954	JL Bamford
1951	Dr W Meharg	1953	C Knox	1955	R Fleury

North of Ireland Open Amateur Championship

continued

Year	Winner	Year	Winner	Year	Winner
1956	M Edwards	1967	WR Tennant	1978	G McGimpsey
1957	M Edwards	1968	M Hoey	1979	TBC Hoey
1958	T Dijon	1969	M Hoey	1980	MJ Malone
1959	J Duncan	1970	J Faith	1981	D Long
1960	WHE Rainey	1971	R Pollin	1982	D Long
1961	J Duncan	1972	JL Bamford	1983	TBC Hoey
1962	JFD Madeley	1973	B Edwards	1984	G McGimpsey
1963	JFD Madeley	1974	BJS Kissock	1985	I Elliott
1964	FA McCorry	1975	J Heggarty	1986	D Ballantine
1965	WHE Rainey	1976	B Kissock		
1966	B Edwards	1977	DJF Young		

Northern Scottish Open Championship

Instituted 1931

Year	Winner	Year	Winner
1935	RS Walker (Am)	1966	R Liddle (Asst)
1936	RS Walker (Am)	1967	H Bannerman (Asst)
1937	J McLean	1968	AK Pirie
1938	TB Haliburton	1969	H Bannerman (Asst)
1939	J McLean	1970	DK Webster
1946	WS Forrester	1971	F Rennie
1947	JH Ballingall	1972	H Bannerman
1948	J Panton	1973	D Huish
1949	JH Ballingall		*From 1974 sponsored by*
1950	EC Brown		*Clydesdale Bank*
1951	J Panton	1974	W Milne
1952	J Panton	1975	W Milne
1953	EC Brown	1976	D Chillas
1954	EC Brown	1977	JE Murray
1955	EC Brown	1978	BW Barnes
1956	J Panton	1979	JC Farmer
1957	EC Brown	1980	D Huish
1958	G Will	1981	A Thomson
1959	J Panton	1982	T Minshall
1960	J Panton	1983	D Cooper
1961	H Weetman	1984	JS Macdonald
1962	J Panton	1984	D Huish
1963	G Will (Asst)	1985	BW Barnes
1964	LR Taylor (Asst)	1986	R Weir
1965	JT Brown		

Northern Women's Championship

Year	Winner	Year	Winner	Year	Winner
1957	Miss M Nichol	1968	Mrs E Brown	1978	Miss L Ghent
1959	Mrs SM Wood	1969	Miss P Burrows	1979	Miss H Wilson
1960	Mrs FW Ferguson	1970	Mrs F Smith	1980	Miss C Barker
1961	Miss J Greenhalgh	1971	Mrs V Stone	1981	Miss A Brown
1962	Miss J Greenhalgh	1972	Miss M Everard	1982	Miss C Swallow
1963	Miss Ann Irvin	1973	Mrs V Stone	1983	Miss C Hall
1964	Miss Ann Irvin	1974	Mrs C Comboy	1984	Miss C Hall
1965	Miss E Chadwick	1975	Miss V Marvin	1985	Miss C Hall
1966	Miss E Chadwick	1976	Mrs A Briggs	1986	Miss L Fairclough
1967	Miss E Chadwick	1977	Miss C Barker		

Northumberland Amateur Championship

Instituted 1907

Year	Winner	Year	Winner	Year	Winner
1946	RE Gray	1960	N Dunn	1974	JK Tate
1947	RJ Rutherford	1961	D Moffat	1975	P Deeble
1948	DL Couves	1962	A Thirwell	1976	J Hayes
1949	GRB Fairbairn	1963	JE Hayes	1977	J Hayes
1950	WB Blake	1964	A Thirwell	1978	D Faulder
1951	W Embleton	1965	JE Hayes	1979	S Elliott
1952	A Thirwell	1966	J Hayes	1980	S Smith
1953	JK Tate	1967	D Moffat	1981	D George
1954	JK Tate	1968	DP Davidson	1982	P Deeble
1955	A Thirwell	1969	D Moffat	1983	P Deeble
1956	G Clark	1970	J Hayes	1984	J Straker
1957	J Hayes	1971	G Clark	1985	D Faulder
1958	D Moffat	1972	DP Davidson	1986	
1959	D Moffat	1973	DP Davidson		

Northumberland Ladies' Championship

Instituted 1921

Year	Winner	Year	Winner
1935	Mrs H Percy	1965	Miss M Nichol
1936	Miss M Hodgson	1966	Miss M Nichol
1937	Mrs H Percy	1967	Mrs M Pickard
1938	Mrs H Percy	1968	Miss A Mortimer
1939	Miss M Hodgson	1969	Mrs M Pickard
1947	Mrs A Dodds	1970	Mrs M Pickard
1948	Mrs G Moore	1971	Mrs M Pickard
1949	Mrs AMH Wardlaw	1972	Miss J Lee-Smith
1950	Mrs Storey	1973	Miss J Lee-Smith
1951	Mrs Storey	1974	Miss J Lee-Smith
1952	Mrs AMH Wardlaw	1975	Mrs E Elliot
1953	Mrs AMH Wardlaw	1976	Mrs M Pickard
1955	Mrs Thatcher	1977	Mrs M Pickard
1956	Miss M Nichol	1978	Mrs E Elliot
1957	Miss M Nichol	1979	Miss H Wilson
1958	Miss M Nichol	1980	Miss D Glenn
1959	Mrs G Kennedy	1981	Mrs E Elliot
1960	Mrs G Kennedy	1982	Mrs M Pickard
1961	Miss M Nichol	1983	Miss J Soulsby
1962	Miss M Nichol	1984	Miss CM Hall
1963	Mrs G Kennedy	1985	Miss CM Hall
1964	Miss M Nichol	1986	Miss CM Hall

North Wales Amateur Championship

Instituted 1925

Year	Winner	Year	Winner	Year	Winner
1935	G Wallis	1957	HS Griffiths	1972	EN Davies
1936	JL Black	1958	HS Griffiths	1973	D Chidley
1937	SB Roberts	1959	CL Lacey	1974	CT Brown
1938	CC Marston	1960	MA Jones	1975	D McLean
1939	SB Roberts	1961	MA Jones	1976	JR Jones
1947	Mervyn Jones	1962	ES Mills	1977	D McLean
1948	C Hobley Eaves	1963	ES Mills	1978	KD Bostock
1949	WJ Roberts	1964	EN Davies	1979	P Williams
1950	SB Roberts	1965	ES Mills	1980	*No championship*
1951	C Hobley Eaves	1966	EW Griffith	1981	D McLean
1952	M Jones	1967	L Roobottom	1982	P Jones
1953	M Jones	1968	EN Davies	1983	
1954	W Vale	1969	EN Davies	1984	
1955	Percy Mills	1970	EN Davies	1985	D McLean
1956	Percy Mills	1971	D McLean	1986	RM Morris

Northern Division Ladies' Championship (Scotland)

Year	Winner	Year	Winner	Year	Winner
1970	Mrs I Wright	1976	Miss AV Laing	1982	Miss G Stewart
1971	Mrs I McIntosh	1977	Miss F Anderson	1983	Miss G Stewart
1972	Miss AV Laing	1978	Miss G Stewart	1984	Miss P Wright
1973	Miss M Thomson	1979	Mrs J Self	1985	
1974	Miss M Thomson	1980	Miss G Stewart	1986	Miss C Middleton
1975	Miss G Stewart	1981	Miss F McNab		

North of Scotland Open Amateur Stroke Play Championship

Instituted 1970

Year	Winner	Year	Winner	Year	Winner
1970	WTG Milne	1976	IC Hutcheon	1982	I Hutcheon
1971	RM Grant	1977	S Stephen	1983	D Kryzanowski
1972	S Stephen	1978	NS Grant	1984	JS Macdonald
1973	BM Nicholson	1979	ID Grant	1985	JS MacDonald
1974	HB Stuart	1980	BC Milne	1986	S Cruickshank
1975	IC Hutcheon	1981	NS Grant		

Nottinghamshire Amateur Championship

Instituted 1924

Year	Winner	Year	Winner	Year	Winner
1946	AP Burgass	1960	AF Bussell	1974	AWP White
1947	WAC Glennie	1961	AE Shepperson	1975	I Simpson
1948	Dr J Angus	1962	AF Bussell	1976	RP Naylor
1949	CHV Elliott	1963	AF Bussell	1977	P Shaw
1950	CHV Elliott	1964	AF Bussell	1978	I Simpson
1951	HS Johnson	1965	AE Shepperson	1979	PM Baxter
1952	Dr J Angus	1966	AD McLuckie	1980	T Leigh
1953	DC Gardner	1967	FK Shaw	1981	CA Banks
1954	DC Gardner	1968	AF Bussell	1982	CA Banks
1955	AE Shepperson	1969	AF Bussell	1983	TM Estrop
1956	DC Gardner	1970	GAL Coleman	1984	G Krause
1957	V Kregel	1971	JD Hall	1985	M Scothern
1958	AE Shepperson	1972	P Shaw	1986	G Krause
1959	AF Bussell	1973	P Shaw		

Nottinghamshire Ladies' Championship

Instituted 1925

Year	Winner	Year	Winner
1935	Mrs AS Bright	1965	Miss A Payne
1936	Mrs Elliott	1966	Mrs B Brewer
1937	Mrs Elliott	1967	Mrs B Brewer
1938	Mrs AH Bloomer	1968	Mrs G Marshall
1939	Mrs AS Bright	1969	Miss K Horberry
1947	Mrs RH Taylor	1970	Mrs B Brewer
1948	Miss Lowe	1971	Miss V O'Sullivan
1949	Mrs GW Hetherington	1972	Miss RM Clay
1950	Mrs GW Hetherington	1973	Mrs B Brewer
1951	Mrs GW Hetherington	1974	Miss K Horberry
1952	Mrs CHV Elliott	1975	Miss K Horberry
1953	Miss J Redgate	1976	Miss K Horberry
1954	Miss J McIntyre	1977	Miss K Horberry
1955	Mrs B Baker	1978	Mrs J Brewer
1956	Mrs J McIntyre	1979	Miss M Elswood
1957	Mrs GR Needham	1980	Miss M Elswood
1958	Mrs B Baker	1981	Miss KM Horberry
1959	Mrs B Baker	1982	Miss KM Horberry
1960	Miss J Redgate	1983	Miss M Elswood
1961	Miss J Redgate	1984	Miss M Elswood
1962	Mrs B Brewer (*née* Redgate)	1985	Miss KM Horberry
1963	Mrs B Brewer	1986	CG Palmer
1964	Mrs B Brewer		

Nottinghamshire Open Championship

Year	Winner	Year	Winner
1933	T Williamson	1964	S Hunt
1934	AG Beck	1965	D Talbot
1935	AG Beck	1966	AD McLuckie
1936	AG Beck	1967	D Talbot
1937	AG Beck	1968	D Snell
1938	G Johnson	1969	B Waites
1939	G Johnson	1970	P Bottell
1947	G Johnson	1971	B Waites
1948	George Thomson	1972	GM White
1949	G Johnson	1973	BJ Waites
1950	EB Williamson	1974	BJ Waites
1951	W Hill	1975	G Tickell
1952	CA Winks	1976	RP Naylor (Am)
1953	DC Gardner (Am)	1977	P Shaw (Am)
1954	D Gardner (Am)	1978	BJ Waites
1955	AE Shepperson (Am)	1979	DJ Ridley
1956	GM White	1980	C Banks (Am)
1957	MW Youngs	1981	C Banks (Am)
1958	AE Shepperson (Am)	1983	B Waites
1959	D Snell	1983	C Banks (Am)
1960	AF Bussell (Am)	1984	
1961	GM White	1985	C Jepson
1962	AF Bussell (Am)	1986	
1963	D Smart		

One-Armed Championship

Year	Winner	Year	Winner
1934	FW Berridge	1964	RP Reid
1935	R McKarell	1965	DR Lawrie
1936	FW Berridge	1966	RG Sandler (USA)
1937	A Hanson	1967	A Wilmott
1938	A Burns	1968	DR Lawrie
1939	A Burns	1969	S Eggo
1940	J Sharples	1970	T Atkinson
1946	R McKarell	1971	A Wilmott
1947	J Buckley	1972	G Kerr (USA)
1948	JE Lithgo	1973	DC Fightmaster (USA)
1949	George Jackson	1974	A Wilmott
1950	J Buckley	1975	DC Fightmaster (USA)
1951	R Graham	1976	DR Lawrie
1952	H Nicolson	1977	A Wilmott
1953	AH Barclay	1978	A Wilmott
1954	RP Reid	1969	A Robinson
1955	R McKarell	1980	RP Reid
1956	RP Reid	1981	A Robinson
1957	JE Lithgo	1982	MJ O'Grady
1958	A Wilmott	1983	A Robinson
1959	CW Gardner	1984	ASL Robinson
1960	JE Watt	1985	ASL Robinson
1961	R Sandler	1986	MJ O'Grady
1962	A Wilmott		
1963	RP Reid		

Oxford *v* Cambridge

Instituted 1878

Year	Winners	Venue
1930	Oxford	Hoylake
1931	Oxford	Prince's, Sandwich
1932	Oxford	Lytham and St Annes
1933	Cambridge	Prince's, Sandwich
1934	Oxford	Formby
1935	Cambridge	Burnham-on-Sea

Oxford v Cambridge
continued

Year	Winners	Venue
1936	Cambridge	Hoylake
1937	Cambridge	Prince's, Sandwich
1938	Cambridge	Westward Ho!
1939	Cambridge	Sandwich
1946	Cambridge	Lytham and St Annes
1947	Oxford	Rye
1948	Oxford	Sandwich
1949	Cambridge	Hoylake
1950	Oxford	Lytham and St Annes
1951	Cambridge	Rye
1952	Cambridge	Rye
1953	Cambridge	Rye
1954	Cambridge	Rye
1955	Cambridge	Rye
1956	Oxford	Formby
1957	Oxford	Sandwich
1958	Cambridge	Rye
1959	Cambridge	Burnham and Berrow
1960	Cambridge	Lytham and St Annes
1961	Oxford	Sandwich
1962	Halved	Hunstanton
1963	Cambridge	Birkdale
1964	Oxford	Rye
1965	Cambridge	Sandwich
1966	Cambridge	Hunstanton
1967	Cambridge	Rye
1968	Cambridge	Porthcawl
1969	Cambridge	Formby
1970	Halved	Sandwich
1971	Oxford	Rye
1972	Cambridge	Formby
1973	Oxford	Saunton
1974	Cambridge	Ganton
1975	Cambridge	Hoylake
1976	Cambridge	Woodhall Spa
1977	Cambridge	Porthcawl
1978	Oxford	Rye
1979	Oxford	Harlech
1980	Oxford	Hoylake
1981	Cambridge	Formby
1982	Cambridge	Hunstanton
1983	Cambridge	Royal St Georges
1984	Cambridge	Sunningdale
1985	Oxford	Rye
1986	Oxford	Ganton

Played 97; Cambridge won 54; Oxford 38; halved 5

Oxford and Cambridge Golfing Society's "President's" Putter

Instituted 1920

Venue: Rye

Year	Winner	Year	Winner
1947	LG Crawley	1967	JR Midgley
1948	Major AA Duncan	1968	AWJ Holmes
1949	PB Lucas	1969	P Moody
1950	DHR Martin	1970	DMA Steel
1951	LG Crawley	1971	GT Duncan
1952	LG Crawley	1972	P Moody
1953	GH Micklem	1973	AD Swanston
1954	G Huddy	1974	R Biggs
1955	G Huddy	1975	CJ Weight
1956	GT Duncan	1976	MJ Reece
1957	AE Shepperson	1977	AWJ Holmes
1958	Lt-Col AA Duncan	1978	MJ Reece
1959	ID Wheater	1979	*Cancelled due to snow*
1960	JME Anderson	1980	S Melville
1961	ID Wheater	1981	AWJ Holmes
1962	MF Attenborough	1982	DMA Steel
1963	JG Blackwell	1983	ER Dexter
1964	DMA Steel	1984	A Edmond
1965	WI Uzielli	1985	ER Dexter
1966	MF Attenborough	1986	J Caplan

Oxfordshire Ladies' Championship

Year	Winner	Year	Winner	Year	Winner
1948	Mrs Trepte	1962	Mrs L Abrahams	1976	Mrs L Davies
1949	Mrs Halban	1963	Mrs J Grandison	1977	Mrs L Davies
1950	Mrs W Bamberger	1964	Mrs L Abrahams	1978	Mrs L Davies
1951	Mrs Richards	1965	Mrs G Hanks	1979	Mrs L Davies
1952	Mrs L Abrahams	1966	Miss 'T' Ross Stein	1980	Mrs L Davies
1953	Mrs L Abrahams	1967	Mrs J Glennie	1981	Miss N Sparks
1954	Mrs L Abrahams	1968	Mrs A Delany	1982	Mrs M Glennie
1955	Mrs L Abrahams	1969	Mrs L Davies	1983	Mrs M Glennie
1956	Mrs Nightingale	1970	Mrs A Delany	1984	Miss T Craik
1957	Mrs L Abrahams	1971	Mrs L Davies	1985	Miss N Sparks
1958	Mrs L Abrahams	1972	Mrs L Davies	1986	Miss T Craik
1959	Mrs L Abrahams	1973	Miss N Sparks		
1960	Miss V Morris	1974	Mrs L Davies		
1961	Mrs L Abrahams	1975	Mrs L Davies		

Parliamentary Handicap

Instituted 1891

Year	Winner	Year	Winner	Year	Winner
1956	Cyril Osborne MP	1968	Sir Robert Speed	1979	Lord Windlesham
1957	ARW Low MP	1969	HRM Farmer	1980	GR Russell
1958	Cyril Osborne MP	1970	Lord Campball of Eskan	1981	Rodney Foster
1959	PB Lucas MP	1971	DS Gordon	1982	Stanley Clinton Davis MP
1960	Sir Toby Low MP	1972	Graham Cawthorne	1983	Stanley Clinton Davis MP
1961	HRM Farmer	1973	Lord Aldington	1984	Stanley Clinton Davis
1962	KA Bradshaw	1974	PA Rawstorne	1985	Michael Morris MP
1963	JR Rose	1975	John Osborn MP	1986	Sir Anthony Grant MP
1964	John Osborn MP	1976	WSI Whitelaw MP		
1965	Lord Allerton	1977	Lord Allerton		
1966	Lord Allerton DS Gordon	1978	Lord Allerton		
1967	HRM Farmer				

Perth and Kinross Ladies' Championship

Year	Winner	Year	Winner	Year	Winner
1960	Mrs Gibb	1969	Mrs Norwell	1978	Miss F Anderson
1961	Mrs Norwell	1970	Mrs Norwell	1979	Miss F Anderson
1962	Mrs Aitken	1971	Mrs Aitken	1980	Mrs J Aitken
1963	Mrs Hay	1972	Mrs Aitken	1981	Mrs J Aitken
1964	Mrs Norwell	1973	Mrs W Hay	1982	Mrs J Aitken
1965	Mrs Hay	1974	Mrs W Hay	1983	Miss F Anderson
1966	Mrs Gibb	1975	Miss F Anderson	1984	Miss E Aitken
1967	Mrs Norwell	1976	Mrs J Hay	1985	Miss A Guthrie
1968	Mrs Norwell	1977	Miss F Anderson	1986	Mrs I Shannon

Perth and Kinross Amateur Stroke Play Championship

Instituted 1930

Year	Winner	Year	Winner	Year	Winner
1946	KT Thomson	1949	J Wilson	1952	RL Haggart
1947	J Wilson	1950	JT Smith	1953	TL Jackson
1948	RL Haggart	1951	E Tanser	1954	E Tanser

Perth and Kinross Amateur Stroke Play Championship

continued

Year	Winner	Year	Winner	Year	Winner
1955	K Doig	1966	J Freeman	1977	BRN Grieve
1956	AG Robertson	1967	DA Steven	1978	A Munro
1957	JG Moir	1968	JL Leith	1979	CP Christy
1958	JPG Windsor	1969	DJ Donaldson	1980	GT Russell
1959	WR Brown	1970	DA Steven	1981	AG Campbell
1960	KS Thomson	1971	G Simpson	1982	M Niven
1961	WI MacDonald	1972	JBT Douglas	1983	ER Lindsay
1962	GR Sinclair	1973	W Milne	1984	G Lowson
1963	J Freeman	1974	G Simpson	1985	
1964	GR Sinclair	1975	CP Christy	1986	
1965	HC Miller	1976	JBT Douglas		

HRH Prince of Wales Challenge Cup

Instituted 1927

Venue: Deal

Year	Winner	Score	Year	Winner	Score
1933	John B Nash	147	1964	NA Paul	153
1934	ASG Thompson	154	1965	NA Paul and VE Barton (tied)	150
1935	PWL Risdon	154	1966	Peter Townsend	150
1936	ASG Thompson	148	1967	MF Bonallack	141
1937	C Stowe	148	1968	GC Marks and N Paul (tied)	144
1938	*No competition*		1969	M Attenborough	152
1939	GH Micklem	150	1970	J Butterworth	153
1940–46	*No competition*		1971	VE Barton	147
1947	PB Lucas	154	1972	P Hedges	162
1948	Capt. DA Blair	151	1973	P Hedges	138
1949	C Stowe	142	1974	P Hedges	146
1950	I Caldwell	151	1975	JC Davies	140
1951	I Caldwell	151	1976	MJ Inglis	162
1952	I Caldwell	150	1977	PJ Hedges	154
1953	JG Blackwell	159	1978	ER Dexter	145
1954	DLW Woon	143	1979	GF Godwin	148
1955	C Taylor and GT Duncan (tied)	153	1980	GM Dunsire and B Nicholson (tied)	149
1956	PF Scrutton	151	1981	JM Baldwin	146
1957	*No competition*		1982	G Homewood	145
1958	KR Mackenzie and BAF Pelmore (tied)	158	1983	M Davis	141
1959	D Johnstone	149	1984	DH Niven and F Wood (tied)	146
1960	CG Moore	162	1985		
1961	RH Bazell	151	1986		
1962	Dr J Pittar	154			
1963	Sq. Ldr WE McCrae	155			

Queen Elizabeth Coronation Schools' Trophy

Venue: Royal Burgess Golfing Society, Barnton, Edinburgh

Year	Winners	Year	Winners
1953	Watsonians	1970	Dollar Academicals
1954	Daniel Stewart's College FP	1971	Merchistonians
1955	Watsonians	1972	Merchistonians
1956	Watsonians	1973	Merchistonians
1957	Hillhead High School FP	1974	Old Carthusians
1958	Watsonians	1975	Old Lorettonians
1959	Glasgow High School FP	1976	Watsonians
1960	Glasgow High School FP	1977	Glasgow High School FP
1961	Watsonians	1978	Old Lorettonians
1962	Glasgow High School FP	1979	Gordonians
1963	Glasgow High School FP	1980	George Heriots FP
1964	Dollar Academicals	1981	Ayr Academicals
1965	Old Lorettonians	1982	George Heriots FP
1966	Merchistonians	1983	Perth Academy FP
1967	Merchistonians	1984	Glasgow High School FP
1968	Glasgow Hillhead High School FP	1985	Glasgow High School FP
1969	Kelvinside Academicals	1986	Watsonians

Renfrewshire Amateur Championship

Year	Winner	Year	Winner	Year	Winner
1950	WS McLeod	1964	FC Black	1976	I Bell
1951	JC Russell	1965	FC Black	1977	R Blackwood
1952	J Winning	1966	IL Rae	1978	DB Howard
1953	WA Stewart	1967	FC Black	1979	R Blackwood
1954	JC Russell	1968	FC Black	1980	N Skinner
1955	AF Russell	1969	FC Black	1981	DB Howard
1956	J Fulton	1970	J Armstrong	1982	A Hunter
1957	WB McIntyre	1971	AD Sutherland	1983	G Thomson
1960	LG Taylor	1972	TC Houston	1984	DB Howard
1961	DD Cameron	1973	N Douglas	1985	
1962	J Gardner	1974	SG Cairns	1986	
1963	DD Cameron	1975	JA Jones		

Renfrewshire County Ladies' Championship

Instituted 1927

Year	Winner	Year	Winner
1935	Miss J McLintock	1966	Mrs JH Anderson
1936	Miss M Pearcy	1967	Mrs JH Anderson
1937	Mrs CM Falconer	1968	Mrs JH Anderson
1938	Miss J McLintock	1969	Miss E Gibb
1939	Mrs Fleming	1970	Mrs JH Anderson
1949	Mrs Drummond	1971	Mrs JH Anderson
1950	Mrs Drummond	1972	Mrs JH Anderson
1951	Mrs Drummond	1973	Mrs JH Anderson
1952	Mrs AR Gray	1974	Dr AJ Wilson
1953	Miss M Pearcy	1975	Miss L Bennett
1954	Mrs J Drummond	1976	Dr AJ Wilson
1955	Miss N Menzies	1977	Miss L Bennett
1956	Miss D Sommerville	1978	Miss W Aitken
1957	Miss D Sommerville	1979	Miss W Aitken
1958	Miss D Sommerville	1980	Miss W Aitken
1959	Miss D Sommerville	1981	Miss W Aitken
1960	Mrs J Anderson	1982	Miss W Aitken
1961	Miss D Sommerville	1983	Mrs JL Hastings (*née* Sommerville)
1962	Miss J Lethem		
1963	Miss D Sommerville	1984	Dr A Wilson
1964	Mrs JH Anderson	1985	Miss S Lawson
1965	Miss E Gibb	1986	Miss S Lawson

Roseberry Challenge Cup

Venue: Ashridge

Year	Winner	Year	Winner
1933	GA Hill	1958	JT Anderson
1934	JS Rowell	1959	RW Acton
1935	PB Lucas	1960	EJ Wiggs
1936	LG Crawley	1961	KT Warren
1937	JO Levinson	1962	PR Johnston
1938	AS Anderson	1963	CA Murray
1939	AS Anderson	1964	A Millar
1949	AA McNair	1965	EJ Wiggs
1950	RAR Black	1966	Alex Holmes
1951	JW Taylor	1967	Alex Holmes
1952	R Pattinson	1968	Alex Holmes
1953	R Pattinson	1969	Alex Holmes
1954	C Ostler	1970	PW Bent
1955	D Gray	1971	AW Holmes
1956	W/Cdr CH Beamish	1972	AW Holmes
1957	GH Foster	1973	AJ Mason

Roseberry Challenge Cup

continued

Year	Winner	Year	Winner
1974	G Stradling	1981	RY Mitchell JB Berney RY Mitchell won play-off
1975	JA Watts	1982	DS Lane
1976	G Stradling	1983	N Briggs
1977	J Ambridge	1984	DG Lane
1978	R Bevan	1985	P Wharton
1979	JB Berney	1986	JE Ambridge
1980	JA Watts		

St David's Gold Cross

Instituted 1930

Venue: Royal St David's, Harlech

Year	Winner	Year	Winner	Year	Winner
1946	SB Roberts	1960	LJ Ranells	1974	GC Marks
1947	G Mills	1961	MSR Lunt	1975	CP Hodgkinson
1948	CH Eaves	1962	PD Kelley	1976	JR Jones
1949	SB Roberts	1963	JKD Povall	1977	JA Fagan
1950	DMG Sutherland	1964	MSR Lunt	1978	S Wild
1951	JL Morgan	1965	MSR Lunt	1979	MA Smith
1952	SB Roberts	1966	MSR Lunt	1980	CP Hodgkinson
1953	S Lunt	1967	MSR Lunt	1981	G Broadbent
1954	GB Turner	1968	AW Holmes	1982	MW Calvert
1955	JL Morgan	1969	AJ Thomson	1983	RD James
1956	CH Beamish	1970	AJ Thomson	1984	RJ Green
1957	CD Lawrie	1971	A Smith	1985	KH Williams
1958	GB Turner	1972	EN Davies	1986	
1959	MSR Lunt	1973	RD James		

St George's Challenge Cup

Instituted 1888

Venue: Royal St George's, Sandwich

Year	Winner	Year	Winner
1947	PB Lucas	1968	MF Bonallack
1948	Mario Gonzale	1969	PJ Benka
1949	PF Scrutton	1970	P Hedges
1950	E Bromley-Davenport	1971	A Garrett
1951	PF Scrutton	1972	J Davies
1952	GH Micklem	1973	JC Davies
1953	Major DA Blair	1974	JC Davies
1954	Harry Berwick	1975	JC Davies
1955	PF Scrutton	1976	JC Davies
1956	DAC Marr	1977	JC Davies
1957	PF Scrutton	1978	C Phillips
1958	PF Scrutton	1979	GF Godwin
1959	J Nicklaus	1980	J Simmance
1960	JG Blackwell	1981	MF Bonallack
1961	Sq-Ldr WE McCrea	1982	S Wood, G Broadbent, N Taylor (Wood won play-off)
1962	Sq-Ldr WE McCrea		
1963	Sq-Ldr WE McCrae		
1964	Major DA Blair	1983	R Willison
1965	MF Bonallack	1984	SJ Wood
1966	Peter Townsend	1985	SJ Wood
1967	Major DA Blair	1986	

Scottish Area Team Championship

Instituted 1977

Year	Winner	Year	Winner	Year	Winner
1977	North of Scotland	1981	Stirlingshire	1985	Lothians
1978	Lothians	1982	Renfrewshire	1986	Ayrshire
1979	North East	1983	Lothians		
1980	Dunbartonshire	1984	Glasgow.		

Scottish Champion of Champions

Instituted 1970

Year	Winner	Year	Winner	Year	Winner
1970	A Horne	1976	A Brodie	1982	G Macgregor
1971	D Black	1977	V Reid	1983	DG Carrick
1972	RS Strachan	1978	DG Greig	1984	S Stephen
1973	*Not held*	1979	B Machbank	1985	IR Brotherston
1974	MM Niven	1980	IC Hutcheon	1986	IC Hutcheon
1975	A Brodie	1981	I Hutcheon		

Scottish Foursome Tournament–*Glasgow Evening Times* Trophy

Instituted 1891

Year	Winner	Year	Winner
1936	Ayr Academy	1966	Bathgate
1937	Ayr Academy	1967	Prestonfield
1938	Western Gailes	1968	Troon St Medans
1946	New Club (St Andrews)	1969	Irvine
1947	Western Gailes	1970	Cardross
1948	Melville College	1971	Airdrie
1949	Troon Portland	1972	Sco Building Contractors
1950	'36 Club	1973	Glasgow Insurance
1951	Troon Portland	1974	Baberton
1952	Western Gailes	1975	Prestwick St Cuthbert
1953	Irvine	1976	Wishaw
1954	Glasgow University	1977	Stirlingshire JYS
1955	Haggs Castle	1978	Helensburgh
1956	Prestonfield	1979	Helensburgh
1957	Falkirk Tryst	1980	Helensburgh
1958	Troon St Meddans	1981	Duddingston
1959	Cambuslang	1982	Haggs Castle
1960	Irvine	1983	Haggs Castle
1961	Falkirk Tryst	1984	Royal Musselburgh
1962	Irvine	1985	East Renfrewshire
1963	Clydebank & District	1986	Hamilton
1964	Sco Building Contractors		
1965	Falkirk Tryst		

Scottish Ladies' County Championship

Instituted 1909

Year	Winner	Year	Winner
1935	Midlothian	1965	Fife
1936	East Lothian	1966	Fife
1937	Ayrshire	1967	Fife
1938	Ayrshire	1968	Ayrshire
1947	East Lothian	1969	Dunbartonshire and Argyll
1948	Ayrshire	1970	Ayrshire
1949	East Lothian	1971	Aberdeenshire
1950	East Lothian	1972	Aberdeenshire
1951	Perth and Kinross	1973	Dunbartonshire and Argyll
1952	Perth and Kinross	1974	Fife
1953	Perth and Kinross	1975	Lanarkshire
1954	Renfrewshire	1976	Lanarkshire
1955	Ayrshire	1977	Lanarkshire
1956	Renfrewshire	1978	East Lothian
1957	Renfrewshire	1979	Dunbartonshire and Argyll
1958	Fife	1980	Northern Counties
1959	Renfrewshire	1981	Northern Counties
1960	Renfrewshire	1982	Renfrewshire
1961	Renfrewshire	1983	Lanarkshire
1962	Ayrshire	1984	Lanarkshire
1963	Dunbartonshire and Argyll	1985	East Lothian
1964	Ayrshire	1986	Aberdeenshire

Scottish Ladies' Foursomes

Year	Winner	Year	Winner
1958	Falkirk	1973	Troon
1959	Gullane	1974	Edinburgh University
1960	Caldwell	1975	Aberdour
1961	Elie and Earlsferry	1976	Panmure, Barry
1962	Milngavie	1977	Gullane
1963	Caldwell	1978	Dumfries and County
1964	Gullane	1979	Craigie Hill
1965	Troon	1980	Dumfries and County
1966	Gullane	1981	Baberton
1967	Haggs Castle	1982	Aberdour
1968	Gullane	1983	Hamilton
1969	Dumfries and County	1984	Gullane
1970	Hamilton	1985	No Championship
1971	Gullane	1986	
1972	W of Scotland Girls' Ass		

Scottish Universities' Championship

Instituted 1923

Year	Winner	Year	Winner	Year	Winner
1945	St Andrews	1956	Glasgow	1966	Glasgow
1946	Glasgow	1957	Glasgow	1967	Glasgow
1947	Glasgow	1958	Glasgow	1968	Edinburgh
1948	Glasgow	1959	Glasgow	1969	Edinburgh
1949	St Andrews	1960	Glasgow	1970	Edinburgh
1950	Glasgow	1961	Edinburgh	1971	Edinburgh
1951	Glasgow	1962	Glasgow	1972	Aberdeen
1952	Glasgow	1963	Edinburgh	1973	Heriot-Watt
1953	Glasgow	1964	Glasgow &	1974	Aberdeen
1954	Aberdeen		St Andrews (tie)	1975	Glasgow
1955	Edinburgh	1965	Glasgow	1976	Aberdeen

The 1976 championship at Carnoustie was abandoned due to snow, and played coincidentally with the British event later in the year

Year	Winner	Year	Winner	Year	Winner
1977	Aberdeen	1981	Edinburgh	1985	Edinburgh
1978	Aberdeen	1982	Edinburgh	1986	Stirling
1979	Edinburgh	1983	Aberdeen		
1980	St Andrews	1984	Edinburgh		

Scottish Universities' Individual Championship

Instituted 1931

Year	Winner	Year	Winner	Year	Winner
1945	AS Mayer	1961	CC Bird	1975	W Pretswell
1947	H McLean	1962	AJ Low	1976	R Dick
1948	TM McCulloch	1963	D Murdoch		AJ Robertson
	RA Black	1964	AJ Low	1977	W Pretswell
1949	RR Jack	1965	AR Murphy		S Hall
	FWG Deighton	1966	AM Fleming	1978	B Bell
1950	JL Lindsay	1967	G Hogg	1979	D Smyth
1951	H Munro	1968	WR Lockie		D McLeary
1952	GR Parker	1969	DG Greig	1980	D Livesey
1953	AC Miller		KW Mackintosh	1981	C Armour
1954	GR Parker	1970	JA McIntyre	1982	D Beveridge
1955	A Brodie	1971	G Hogg	1983	C Dalgleish
	J Macdonald		HS Milligan	1984	J Huggan
1956	AC Miller	1972	JT Moffat	1985	K Walker
1958	CJ Macleod	1973	GC Cairns	1986	I Menzies
1959	DA Walkinshaw		A Stephen		
1960	RO Aitken	1974	RG Cairns		

Selborne–Salver

Venue: Blackmoor GC, Hampshire

Year	Winner	Year	Winner	Year	Winner
1976	A Miller	1980	P McEvoy	1984	D Curry
1977	CS Mitchell	1981	A Sherborne	1985	SM Bottomley
1978	G Brand	1982	I Gray	1986	TE Clarke
1979	P McEvoy	1983	D Lane		

Shropshire and Herefordshire Amateur Championship

Year	Winner	Year	Winner	Year	Winner
1956	RP Yates	1967	DI Humphreys	1978	JR Burn
1957	CG Griffith	1968	R Issitt	1979	MA Smith
1958	CG Griffith	1969	DI Humphreys	1980	MA Smith
1959	CG Griffith	1970	J Black	1981	JA Wilson
1960	CG Griffith	1971	GH Roberts	1982	NS Kelly
1961	D Mercer	1972	DI Humphreys	1983	PA Baker
1962	RP Yates	1973	MA Smith	1984	PA Baker
1963	RP Yates	1974	AWB Lyle	1985	PA Baker
1964	A Parsonage	1975	IH Woosnam	1986	
1965	CG Griffith	1976	AWB Lyle		
1966	RP Yates	1977	MA Smith		

Shropshire Ladies' Championship

Instituted 1923

Year	Winner	Year	Winner
1935	Miss M Black	1965	Mrs M Wynne-Thomas
1936	Mrs Wycherley	1966	Mrs M Wynne-Thomas
1937	Miss M Black	1967	Mrs G Geddes
1938	Miss M Black	1968	Mrs G Geddes
1939	Mrs AR Blockley	1969	Mrs G Geddes
1948	Mrs V Jones	1970	Mrs J Shrimpton
1949	Mrs Argles	1971	Mrs G Geddes
1950	Miss M Loy	1972	Miss J Foster
1951	Mrs Argles	1973	Mrs D Watkin
1952	Mrs Argles	1974	Mrs G Geddes
1953	Mrs Beetham	1975	Mrs G Geddes
1954	Mrs Beetham	1976	Miss S McLachlin
1955	Mrs Argles	1977	Mrs J Shrimpton
1956	Miss M Loy	1978	Miss J Dingley
1957	Mrs AM Argles	1979	Mrs S Pidgeon
1958	Miss M Loy	1980	Mrs S Pidgeon
1959	Mrs GM Argles	1981	Mrs S Pidgeon
1960	Mrs M Wynne-Thomas	1982	Mrs S Pidgeon
1961	Mrs J Shrimpton	1983	Miss C Gauge
1962	Mrs M Scott	1984	Mrs A Johnson
1963	Mrs M Wynne-Thomas	1985	Mrs A Johnson
1964	Mrs M Wynne-Thomas	1986	Mrs S Pidgeon

Somerset Amateur Championship

Instituted 1911

Year	Winner	Year	Winner	Year	Winner
1930	H Grey	1947	RN Jutsum	1957	RN Jutsum
1931	SHR Hornby	1948	RN Jutsum	1958	RN Jutsum
1932	HD Grey	1949	RN Jutsum	1959	RC Champion
1933	P MacAlister	1950	J Payne	1960	GT Irlam
1934	Dr G Cook	1951	JWR Swayne	1961	GT Irlam
1935	EJ Poole, jun	1952	J Payne	1962	PO Green
1936	BR Beaver	1953	GT Irlam	1963	RN Jutsum
1937	EJ Poole, jun	1954	RC Champion	1964	BW Barnes
1938	RN Jutsum	1955	A Cook	1965	RN Jutsum
1939	EP Tomkinson	1956	RN Jutsum	1966	DE Jones

Somerset Amateur Championship

continued

Year	Winner	Year	Winner	Year	Winner
1967	GK Baker	1974	TW Jones	1981	J Clifford
1968	DJ Jacobs	1975	TE Knott	1982	BJ Reeves
1969	RN Jutsum	1976	AJ Hill	1983	DJ Huxtable
1970	WR Hartree	1977	PC Emery	1984	CS Edwards
1971	LF Millar	1978	NJ Roseff	1985	PR Hare
1972	WP Hucker	1979	D Meredith	1986	CS Edwards
1973	NJ Roseff	1980	LF Millar		

Somerset Ladies' Championship

Instituted 1913

Year	Winner	Year	Winner
1935	Miss DR Fowler	1965	Mrs C Walpole
1936	Miss DR Fowler	1966	Miss A Alford
1937	Miss M Wall	1967	Mrs P Watford
1938	Lady K Cairns	1968	Miss K Counsell
1939	Lady K Cairns	1969	Mrs C Walpole
1947	Mrs B Popplestone	1970	Mrs M Perriam
1948	Mrs B Popplestone	1971	Mrs S Chambers
1949	Mrs B Popplestone	1972	Mrs S Chambers
1950	Lady K Cairns	1973	Mrs S Chambers
1951	Mrs G Lovell	1974	Mrs S Chambers
1952	Mrs G Lovell	1975	Miss C Hammond
1953	Lady K Cairns	1976	Mrs M Perriam
1954	Lady K Cairns	1977	Miss C Trew
1955	Mrs S Jones	1978	Miss C Trew
1956	Mrs G Lovell	1979	Miss B New
1957	Mrs G Lovell	1980	Miss B New
1958	Mrs P Watford	1981	Miss B New
1959	Mrs FR Brown	1982	Miss B New
1960	Mrs FR Brown	1983	Miss B New
1961	Mrs R Watford	1984	Mrs M Perriam
1962	Mrs FR Brown	1985	Miss K Nicholls
1963	Mrs R Watford	1986	Miss K Nicholls
1964	Miss J Jurgens		

South-Eastern Ladies' Championship

Year	Winner	Year	Winner
1950	Miss J Bisgood	1969	Mrs E Fisher (*née* Price)
1951	Lady Katheraine Cairns	1970	Mrs A Warren
1952	Miss J Bisgood	1971	Miss H Clifford
1953	Miss Beryl Lowe	1972	Miss H Clifford
1954	Miss B Jackson	1973	Miss C Redford
1955	Miss E Price	1974	Miss C Le Feuvre
1956	Mrs Marley Spearman	1975	Miss W Pithers
1957	Miss Angela Ward	1976	Miss L Harrold
1958	Mrs A Spearman	1977	Miss S Bamford
1959	Miss E Price	1978	Mrs C Caldwell (*née* Redford)
1960	Miss E Price	1979	Miss B Cooper
1961	Mrs A Spearman	1980	Miss J Rumsey
1962	Mrs B Green	1981	Mrs C Caldwell
1963	Mrs J Thornhill	1982	Mrs J Nicolson
1964	Mrs J Thornhill	1983	Miss L Davies
1965	Mrs M Bonallack	1984	Miss L Davies
1966	Miss H Clifford	1985	Mrs J Thornhill
1967	Mrs J Baucher	1986	Miss S Moorcroft
1968	Miss E Collis		

Southern (England) Professional Championship

Year	Winner	Year	Winner	Year	Winner
1952	F van Donck	1961	GB Wolstenholme	1970	NC Coles
1953	TE Oldhams	1962	BJ Hunt	1971	P Oosterhuis
1954	DJ Rees	1963	H Weetman	1972	JH Cook
1955	J Adams	1964	Max Faulkner	1973	N Job
1956	A Lees	1965	I Macdonald	1974	K Bousfield
1957	K Bousfield	1966	DJ Rees	1975	DJ Rees
1958	H Weetman	1967	BJ Hunt	1976	R Jewell
1959	BJ Hunt	1968	GL Hunt	1977	GR Burroughs
1960	BJ Hunt	1969	T Grubb		

From 1978 became

South Region PGA

Year	Winner	Year	Winner	Year	Winner
1978	VB Hood	1981	Paul Milton	1984	M McLean
1979	Not played	1982	D McClelland	1985	C Mason
1980	PR Mitchell	1983	M McLean	1986	

South of Ireland Open Amateur Championship

Instituted 1895

Venue: Lahinch (Co Clare)

Year	Winner	Year	Winner	Year	Winner
1940	Dr P Murray	1956	PJ Leyden	1973	M Gannon
1941	J Burke	1957	PJ Leyden	1974	D Long
1942	J Burke	1958	J Brown	1975	B Malone
1943	J Burke	1959	G Roberts	1976	V Nevin
1944	J Burke	1961	M Guerin	1977	L McNamara
1945	J Burke	1962	M Guerin	1978	V Nevin
1946	J Burke	1963	M Guerin	1979	P O'Rourke
1947	B Slattery	1964	WA Kelleher	1980	M Burns
1948	JB Carr	1965	R de L Staunton	1981	P O'Rourke
1949	J Carroll	1966	JB Carr	1982	M Maurice
1950	M Power	1967	N Fogarty	1983	AJC Morrow
1951	G Gilligan	1968	JD Smyth	1984	N Anderson
1952	M Power	1969	JB Carr	1985	P O'Rourke
1953	PJ Leyden	1970	J O'Leary	1986	J McHenry
1954	P Bugler	1971	P Mulcare		
1955	PJ Leyden	1972	R Staunton		

South of Scotland Championship

Instituted 1932

Year	Winner	Year	Winner	Year	Winner
1933	TB Manson	1939	S Hastings	1952	A Hall
1934	TB Manson	1947	JC Carver	1953	MH Forrest
1935	R Murray	1948	R Murray	1954	D Maxwell
1936	TB Manson	1949	R Anderson	1955	D Maxwell
1937	JH Hill	1950	R Murray	1956	Dr JB Cochran
1938	RH Stevenson	1951	S Hastings	1957	R Anderson

South of Scotland Championship *continued*

Year	Winner	Year	Winner	Year	Winner
1958	MC Douglas	1969	E Shamash	1978	I Brotherston
1959	MC Douglas	1970	J Miller	1979	I Brotherston
1960	MC Douglas	1971	W Jackson	1980	A Clark
1961	RB Anderson	1972	R Nairn	1981	D James
1963	Brian Anderson	1973	D MacRae	1982	I Brotherston
1965	R Murray	1974	W Jackson	1983	I Brotherston
1966	Robert Smith	1975	B Wilson	1984	D Ireland
1967	E Shamash	1976	I Brotherston	1985	I Brotherston
1968	E Shamash	1977	D Ireland	1986	I Semple

Southern Division Ladies' Championship (Scotland)

Year	Winner	Year	Winner	Year	Winner
1976	Mrs S Simpson	1980	Miss DM Hill	1984	Miss FM Rennie
1977	Mrs A Barclay	1981	Miss A Gallagher	1985	Mrs S Simpson
1978	Miss S Gallagher	1982	Miss A Hunter	1986	Miss M Wright
1979	Miss S Gallagher	1983	Miss S McDonald		

South of Scotland Ladies' Championship

Year	Winner	Year	Winner	Year	Winner
1976	Mrs A Barclay	1980	Miss Elma Hill	1984	Miss M Wright
1977	Mrs A Barclay	1981	Mrs A Barclay	1985	Miss FM Rennie
1978	Mrs A Barclay	1982	Miss DM Hill	1986	Miss FM Rennie
1979	Mrs Elma Hill	1983	Miss S McDonald		

South-Western Ladies' Championship

Year	Winner	Year	Winner
1935	Miss MJ Jeffreys	1965	Miss R Porter
1936	Mrs G Emery (*née* Jeffreys)	1966	Miss R Porter
1937	Mrs G Emery	1967	Miss R Porter
1938	Mrs C Beard	1968	Mrs P Reece
1939	Mrs V Bramwell	1969	Miss R Porter
1947	Miss M Roskrow	1970	Mrs S Chambers
1948	Mrs B Wills	1971	Mrs P Reece
1949	Miss M Roskrow	1972	Miss R Porter
1950	Miss Roberts	1973	Miss T Perkins
1951	Miss P Roberts	1974	Miss T Perkins
1952	Mrs PJE Reece	1975	Miss P Light
1953	Lady Katharine Cairns	1976	Miss T Perkins
1954	Mrs PM Crow	1977	Miss R Porter
1955	Mrs PM Crow	1978	Miss P Light
1956	Miss R Porter	1979	Mrs WA Slark (*née* Porter)
1957	Miss R Porter	1980	Miss L Isherwood
1958	Miss T Ross Steen	1981	Miss L Moore
1959	Mrs PJE Reece	1982	Miss L Moore
1960	Miss R Porter	1983	Miss P Johnson
1961	Miss R Porter	1984	Miss P Johnson
1962	Miss R Porter	1985	Miss S Shapcott
1963	Mrs P Reece	1986	Miss K Nicholls
1964	Miss R Porter		

South-Western Counties Amateur Championship

Instituted 1924

Year	Winner	Year	Winner	Year	Winner
1935	SHR Hornby	1957	ED Trapnell	1972	JH Davis
1936	GE Newton	1958	RC Champion	1973	RW Tugwell
1937	EJ Poole	1959	G Butler	1974	CS Mitchell
1938	LC Lake	1960	ED Trapnell	1975	R Abbott
1939	EJ Poole	1961	RN Jutsum	1976	GT Irlam
1947	LF Brown	1962	GN Bicknell	1977	G Brand
1948	EB Millward	1963	RN Jutsum	1978	G Brand
1949	J Payne	1964	Brian W Barnes	1979	S Davidson
1950	J Payne	1965	JA Bloxham	1980	CS Mitchell
1951	EB Millward	1966	R Lawford	1981	P Newcombe
1952	EB Millward	1967	PJ Yeo	1982	D Ray
1953	ED Trapnell	1968	BG Steer	1983	C Edwards
1954	EB Millward	1969	DJ Carroll	1984	M Blaber
1955	R Lawford	1970	PJ Yeo	1985	C Phillips
1956	RG Peach	1971	JA Bloxham	1986	C Phillips

Staffordshire Amateur Championship

Instituted 1924

Year	Winner	Year	Winner
1935	TR Deighton	1964	C Stowe
1936	TR Deighton	1965	RD James
1937	KW Chaundy	1966	GC Marks
1938	G Mills	1967	GC Marks
1939	C Stowe	1968	GC Marks
1946	C Stowe	1969	GC Marks
1947	E Perry	1970	K Hodgkinson
1948	C Stowe	1971	A Dathan
1949	P Squire	1972	PH Minton
1950	MB Morgan	1973	GC Marks
1951	SM Sangster	1974	K Hodgkinson
1952	J Beales	1975	AN Dathan
1953	C Stowe	1976	MA Payne
1954	C Stowe	1977	D Blakeman
1955	RB Bayliss	1978	D Blakeman
1956	RB Bayliss	1979	D Evans
1957	C Stowe	1980	AR Eden
1958	Gp Capt CH Beamish	1981	M Hassall
1959	GC Marks	1982	A Stubbs
1960	GC Marks	1983	M Hassall
1961	JPG Windsor	1984	M Hassall
1962	Gp Capt CH Beamish	1985	M Hassall
1963	GC Marks	1986	M Scarrett

Staffordshire Ladies' Championship

Instituted 1926

Year	Winner	Year	Winner	Year	Winner
1934	Miss Birkett	1957	Miss B Jackson	1973	Miss M Hood
1935	Miss Dobson	1958	Miss B Jackson	1974	Mrs B Bargh
1936	Miss Dobson	1959	Miss B Jackson	1975	Mrs A Stant
1937	Miss M Evershed	1960	Miss A Higgott	1976	Miss BAB Jackson
1938	Miss Dobson	1961	Miss D Robb	1977	Mrs A Booth
1939	Mrs AE Parkes	1962	Miss A Higgott	1978	Mrs A Stant
1947	Miss M Evershed	1963	Miss B Jackson	1979	Mrs A Smith
1948	Miss M Evershed	1964	Miss B Jackson		(formerly Mrs Stant)
1949	Mrs G Parrott	1965	Miss A Coxhill	1980	Mrs A Booth
1950	Mrs H Pritchards	1966	Miss B Jackson	1981	Miss J Brown
1951	Mrs F King	1967	Miss B Jackson	1982	Miss J Brown
1952	Mrs A Denham	1968	Miss B Jackson	1983	Miss D Christison
1953	Miss M Evershed	1969	Miss B Jackson	1984	Miss D Boyd
1954	Miss B Jackson	1970	Mrs A Booth	1985	Miss L Hackney
1955	Mrs A Denham	1971	Mrs A Booth	1986	Mrs A Booth
1956	Miss B Jackson	1972	Mrs A Booth		

Staffordshire Open Championship

Year	Winner	Year	Winner	Year	Winner
1948	C Stowe (Am)	1961	G Johnson	1974	A Sadler
1949	CH Ward	1962	JR Moses	1975	J Rhodes
1950	CH Ward	1963	RD James (Am)	1976	MA Poxon (Am)
1951	CH Ward	1964	E Large	1977	J Anderson
1952	CH Ward	1965	A Smith (Am)	1978	J Anderson
1953	G Johnson	1966	Roger James	1979	J Anderson
1954	CH Ward	1967	E Large	1980	P Robinson (Am)
1955	CH Ward	1968	M Bembridge	1981	J Rhodes
1956	JR Moses	1969	A Smith (Am)	1982	A Stubbs (Am)
1957	CH Ward	1970	B Janes	1983	C Poxon (Am)
1958	RL Hastelow	1971	H Jones (Am)	1984	
1959	J Sharkey	1972	P Hinton (Am)	1985	
1960	G Johnson	1973	J Rhodes	1986	

Staffordshire and Shropshire Professional Championship

Year	Winner	Year	Winner	Year	Winner
1947	CH Ward	1961	CH Ward	1974	J Rhodes
1948	CH Ward	1962	CH Ward	1975	J Rhodes
1949	CA Winks	1963	CH Ward		A Sadler
1950	CH Ward	1964	CH Ward	1976	P McGarry
1951	CH Ward		E Large	1977	H Boyle
1952	CH Ward	1965	D Fitton	1978	A Sadler
1953	CH Ward	1966	E Large	1979	J Rhodes
1954	CH Ward	1967	M Bembridge	1980	A Sadler
1955	CH Ward	1968	CH Ward	1981	A Griffiths
1956	CH Ward	1969	J Rhodes	1982	A Griffiths
1957	CH Ward	1970	AR Sadler	1983	CM Holmes
1958	JR Moses	1971	AR Sadler	1984	
1959	CH Ward	1972	RDS Livingstone	1985	
1960	CH Ward	1973	A Sadler	1986	J Annable

Stirlingshire Amateur Championship

Year	Winner	Year	Winner	Year	Winner
1947	KG Patrick	1961	IA MacMillan	1975	DJ Smith
1948	J Lindsay	1962	DF Wilkie	1976	AY Wilson
1949	GN Taylor	1963	HM Campbell	1977	GK MacDonald
1950	TD Wilson	1964	WJ Dalling	1978	AC MacLaren
1951	KG Patrick	1965	M Murray	1979	AJ Liddle
1952	KT Thomson	1966	C McLachlan	1980	DF Wilkie
1953	DW Anderson	1967	EC Gibson	1981	A Liddle
1954	J Lindsay	1968	AJ Macnaught	1982	A Liddle
1955	DW Anderson	1969	R Thomas	1983	C Gillies
1956	T Harrower	1970	HM Campbell	1984	G Barrie
1957	HM Campbell	1971	HM Campbell	1985	
1958	J Nimmo	1972	WJ Dalling	1986	
1959	AM Grant	1973	WJ Dalling		
1960	D Mackintosh	1974	JAS Zuill		

Stirling and Clackmannan County Ladies' Championship

Year	Winner	Year	Winner	Year	Winner
1969	Mrs D Smith	1975	Miss E Miskimmin	1981	Miss E Miskimmin
1970	Mrs GE Mitchell	1976	Mrs R Frame	1982	*Null and void*
1971	Mrs D Smith	1977	Mrs D Smith	1983	Miss J Harrison
1972	Mrs GE Mitchell	1978	Mrs J MacCallum	1984	Mrs W McCallum
1973	Mrs D Smith	1979	Mrs J MacCallum	1985	Miss S Michie
1974	Mrs GE Mitchell	1980	Miss E Miskimmin	1986	Miss S Michie

Suffolk Amateur Championship

Instituted 1924

Year	Winner	Year	Winner	Year	Winner
1936	RB Beare	1958	HW Howlett	1973	JC Broad
1937	ASG Thompson	1959	Flt Lt AD Mencer	1974	J Marks
1938	ED Keeble	1960	RF Long	1975	P Saggers
1939	Dr KW Mackenzie	1961	RF Long	1976	J Doe
1947	RM Fell	1962	RJ Taylor	1977	S Block
1948	HW Howlett	1963	HW Howlett	1978	R Taylor
1949	HW Howlett	1964	RR Sparrow	1979	J Cook
1950	Dr SJS Pitts	1965	DC Whinney	1980	I Whinney
1951	WJ Brooks	1966	PJ Parsons	1981	P Buckle
1952	J Newson	1967	DC Whinney	1982	CJC Lloyd
1953	P Rush	1968	DC Whinney	1983	M Turner
1954	C Branch	1969	DC Whinney	1984	S Goodman
1955	H Ridgley	1970	RF Long	1985	R Barrell
1956	RJ Taylor	1971	IL Pearce		
1957	HW Howlett	1972	RW Mann		

Suffolk Ladies' Championship

Instituted 1926

Year	Winner	Year	Winner	Year	Winner
1935	Miss Winn	1959	Mrs Openshaw	1974	Miss S Dawson
1936	Miss Winn	1960	Mrs Gaskell	1975	Miss S Dawson
1937	Lady Eddis	1961	Mrs M Openshaw	1976	Mrs V Cullen
1938	Mrs A Eddis	1962	Miss S Dawson	1977	Miss S Dawson
1939	Lady Eddis	1963	Mrs M Openshaw	1978	Miss S Field
1947	Lady Eddis	1964	Mrs AM Eddis	1979	Miss S Dawson
1948	Miss P Marsh	1965	Miss S Dawson	1980	Miss S Field
1949	Mrs Evans	1966	Mrs AM Eddis	1981	Miss D Marriott
1950	Mrs Gaskell	1967	Miss Ann Willard	1982	Miss D Marriott
1951	Mrs Gaskell	1968	Mrs RDR Biggar	1983	Miss D Marriott
1952	Mrs Wilkins	1969	Miss A Willard	1984	Dr J Gibson
1953	Lady Eddis	1970	Miss A Willard	1985	Dr J Gibson
1954	Mrs A Smith	1971	Miss A Willard	1986	J Wade
1956	Miss J Winn	1972	Mrs A Eddis		
1958	Mrs Wilkins	1973	Mrs J Biggar		

Suffolk Open Championship

Year	Winner	Year	Winner	Year	Winner
1936	SG Rush	1958	LB Ayton	1973	SJ Whymark
1937	JD Freeman	1959	JW Johnson	1974	RG Webb
1938	Dr KW Mackenzie	1960	LA Jones	1975	J Cook (Am)
1947	AD Stewart (Am)	1961	BJ Proudfoot	1976	T Bird (Am)
	EE Beverley	1962	LB Ayton	1977	JW Johnson
1948	EE Beverley	1963	LB Ayton	1978	R Knight
1949	FJ Davis	1964	AD Levermore	1979	C Jervis
1950	RA Knight	1965	DC Whinney (Am)	1980	SJ Whymark
1951	FJ Davis	1966	J Frew	1981	P Buckle (Am)
1952	HB Ridgley (Am)	1967	JW Johnson	1982	RW Mann
1953	HB Ridgley (Am)	1968	TE Sutton	1983	SJ Whymark
1954	DA Levermore	1969	DC Whinney (Am)	1984	
1955	LB Ayton	1970	C Aldred	1985	K Preston
1956	LB Ayton	1971	J Frew	1986	
1957	LB Ayton	1972	S Wymark		

Suffolk Professional Championship

Instituted 1927

Year	Winner	Year	Winner	Year	Winner
1935	SG Rush	1958	LB Ayton	1973	JW Johnson
1936	RA Knight	1959	JW Johnson	1974	RW Mann
1937	RA Knight	1960	LA Jones	1975	J Frew
1938	E Gray	1961	BJ Proudfoot	1976	J Frew
1948	EE Beverley	1963	LB Ayton	1977	R Mann
1949	FJ Davis	1964	LA Jones	1978	R Mann
1950	RA Knight	1965	C Aldred	1979	R Webb
1951	FJ Davis	1966	J Frew	1980	T Pennock
1952	J Proudfoot	1967	AA Butcher	1981	M Elsworthy
1953	FT Davies	1968	SJ Whymark	1982	M Elsworthy
1954	DA Levermore	1969	JW Johnson	1983	RW Mann
1955	LB Ayton	1970	J Frew	1984	RW Mann
1956	LB Ayton	1971	JW Johnson	1985	S Beckhoon
1957	LB Ayton	1972	J Frew	1986	RW Mann

Sunningdale Open Foursomes

Year	Winners
1934	Miss D Fishwick (Wentworth) and EN Layton (Walton Heath) beat Miss M Gourlay (Camberley Heath) and Capt GE Hawkins (Sunningdale), 2 and 1
1935	Miss J Wethered (Worplesdon) and JS Morrison (Sunningdale) beat Miss P Barton (Mid-Surrey) and LG Garrett (Addington), 3 and 2
1936	Miss J Wethered (Worplesdon) and JSF Morrison (Sunningdale) beat DH Kyle (Sunningdale) and Maj WHH Aitken (West Hill), 5 and 4
1937	AS Anderson (Hindhead) and Dai Rees (Asst Pro, Surbiton) beat GD Hanney (Woking) and RG French (Asst Pro Berkshire), 5 and 4
1938	Miss P Barton (Mid-Surrey) and Alf Padgham (Pro, Sundridge Park) beat LG Crawley (Sunningdale) and Francis Francis (Sunningdale), 19th hole
1939	C Rissik (Beaconsfield) and EWH Kenyon (Pro, Beaconsfield) beat CM Bell (Thorpe Bay) and C Denny (Pro, Thorpe Bay), 19th hole
1948	Miss Wanda Morgan and Sam King (Pro) beat Peter Risdon and Dick Burton (Pro)
1949	RG French (Pro) and SS Field (Pro), beat Miss Jacqueline Gordon and J Knipe (Pro)
1950	M Faulkner (Pro) and J Knipe (Asst Pro, Mid-Surrey) beat F Francis and A Lees (Pro, Sunningdale), 6 and 5
1951	Miss J Donald and TB Haliburton (Pro), beat RG French (Pro) and AE Poulton (Pro), 3 and 2
1952	Mr P Scrutton and Alan Waters (Pro), beat AE Poulton (Pro) and RG French (Pro), 2 and 1
1953	Miss J Donald (North Berwick) and TB Haliburton (Pro, Wentworth), beat G Knipe (Southerndown) and D Smalldon (Asst Pro, Cardiff), 3 and 2
1954	Mr P Scrutton (Addington) and Alan Waters (Pro, Worplesdon) beat P Mills (Asst Pro, Wentworth) and T Harman (Asst Pro, Berkshire), 4 and 3
1955	Mr W Sharp (Penrich) and SS Scott (Pro, Carlisle City) beat RG French (Pro, West Surrey) and E Ward (Pro, Tyrrells Wood), 2 and 1
1956	G Knipe (Southerndown) and DG Smalldon (Asst Pro, Cardiff) beat Mr LG Crawley (Rye) and GH Foster (Oxford Univ), 3 and 2
1957	B Huggett (Asst Pro, West Sussex) and R Whitehead (Asst Pro, Walton Heath) beat Mr R Galloway (Broomieknowe) and S Robertson (Asst Pro, Mid-Surrey), 2 holes
1958	Miss J Donald (Gullane) and P Alliss (Parkstone) beat DMP Beard (RAC) and B Bamford (West Hill), 1 hole
1959	MF Bonallack (Thorpe Hall) and D Sewell (Hook Heath) beat WA Slark (Walton Heath) and PE Gill (Addington), 5 and 3
1960	Miss B McCorkindale (Dunaverty) and MJ Moir (Asst Pro, Sunningdale) beat HC Squirrell (Cardiff) and SD Mouland (Knowle) at 19th
1961	Mrs J Anderson (Gullane) and P Alliss (Parkstone) beat W Dubabney and A Grubb (Coombe Hill), 2 and 1
1962	ER Whitehead (Asst Pro, Walton Heath) and NC Coles (Pro, Coombe Hill) beat MJ Christmas and MJ Burgess (West Sussex), 3 and 2
1963	L Platts (Pro, Thorndon Park) and D Snell (Pro, Worksop) beat KA MacDonald (Pro, Hankley Common) and ID MacDonald (Pro, Farnham), 1 hole
1964	B Critchley and R Hunter (Sunningdale) beat MJ Burgess (West Sussex) and PO Green (Asst Pro, Knowle), 2 and 1
1965	Mrs AD Spearman and T Fisher (Sudbury) beat MJ Burgess (West Sussex) and PO Green (Knowle Park), 1 hole
1966	RRW Davenport (Asst, N Hants) and A Walker (Asst, Wimbledon) beat G Burroughs (Asst, Boyce Hill) and F Sunderland (Asst, Abridge), 4 and 3
1967	NC Coles (Coombe Hill) and K Warren (Finchley Range) beat Mlle B Varangot (France) and CA Clark (Sunningdale) at 19th
1968	JC Davies (Mid-Surrey) and W Humphreys (Mid-Surrey) beat M Faulkner (unattached) and B Barnes (Burnham and Berrow), 6 and 4
1969	P Oosterhuis (Dulwich and Sydenham) and PJ Benka (Addington) beat Jean-Michel Larretche (France) and Mlle. C Lacoste (France), 3 and 2
1970	R Barrell (Woodhall Spa) and Miss A Willard (Gorleston) beat R Hunter (Sunningdale) and Miss M Everard (Hallamshire), 2 and 1
1971	A Bird (Romford) and H Flatman (Romford) beat J Putt (Frilford Heath) and Miss K Phillips (Bradford), 3 and 2
1972	JC Davies and MG King (Sunningdale) beat JK Tullis and AJ Howard (Sunningdale), 6 and 5
1973	JA Putt (Frilford Heath) and Miss M Everard (Hallamshire) beat H Clark (Cobble Hall) and SC Mason (Goring and Streatley), 6 and 5
1974	PJ Butler (Golf Domes) and C Clark (Sunningdale) beat HK Clark (Moortown) and DN Brunyard (Pontefract and District), 1 hole
1975	*Cancelled due to snow*
1976	C Clark and M Hughesdon (Sunningdale) beat BJ Hunt (Foxhills) and IM Stungo (Sunningdale), 2 and 1
1977	GN Hunt and D Matthew (Hartsbourne) beat D Huish and G Logan (North Berwick), 3 and 2
1978	GA Caygill (Crimple Valley) and Miss J Greenhalgh (Pleasington) beat A Stickley (Ealing) and Mrs C Caldwell (Sunningdale), 5 and 4
1979	G Will (Sundridge Park) and R Chapman (Langley Park) beat NC Coles (Dunlop Sports) and D McClelland (Laleham), 3 and 2
1980	NC Coles (GB) and D McClelland (Laleham) beat SC Mason (Goring and Streatley) and J O'Leary (Ireland), 2 and 1

Sunningdale Open Foursomes
continued

Year	Winners
1981	A Lyddon (Knowle) and G Brand (Knowle) beat MG King (Sunningdale) and MH Dixon (Sunningdale), 1 hole
1982	Miss MA McKenna and Miss M Madill beat Miss C Langford and Miss M Walker, 1 hole
1983	J Davies and M Devetta beat M Hughesdon and Mrs L Bayman, 4 and 3
1984	Miss M McKenna and Miss M Madill beat Miss M Walker and Miss C Langford
1985	J O'Leary and S Torrance beat B Gallacher and P Garner at 25th
1986	R Rafferty and R Chapman beat Mrs M Garner and Miss M McKenna, 1 hole

Surrey Amateur Championship

Instituted 1924

Year	Winner	Year	Winner
1936	F Francis	1965	D Millensted
1937	WA Stevenson	1966	Ken Thom
1938	Brig-Gen AC Critchley	1967	PJ Benka
1939	C Gray	1968	PJ Benka
1946	Capt F Francis	1969	B Critchley
1947	A McNair	1970	R Glading
1948	WA Slark	1971	J Davies
1949	Count John de Bendern	1972	J Davies
1950	EM Pollitt	1973	RP Revell
1951	PF Scrutton	1974	PD Flaherty
1952	RH Miller	1975	PD Flaherty
1953	WA Slark	1976	Dr HUS McMichen
1954	D Sewell	1977	JC Davies
1955	JR Thornhill	1978	PF Garner
1956	D Sewell	1979	M Devetta
1958	D Sewell	1980	JG Bennet
1959	D Frame	1981	SD Keppler
1960	JL McClue	1982	R Boxall
1961	Ian Caldwell	1983	C Lashford
1962	Robin Hunter	1984	PM Talbot
1963	RH Miller	1985	G Walmsley
1964	PD Flaherty	1986	B White

Surrey Open Championship

Instituted 1926

Year	Winner	Year	Winner	Year	Winner
1930	G Faulkner	1954	M Faulkner	1972	KA MacDonald
1931	A Perry	1955	J Adams	1973	D Talbot
1932	F Robson	1956	J Adams	1974	EP Stilwell
1933	A Perry	1957	T Haliburton	1975	K Bousfield
1934	A Perry	1958	D Miller	1976	W Humphreys
1935	W Laidlaw	1959	EW Ward	1977	D Talbot
1936	D Rees	1960	N Coles	1978	RE Wynn
1937	WJ Cox	1961	K MacDonald	1979	W Humphreys
1938	A Perry	1962	P Lee	1980	W Humphreys
1946	R Burton	1963	TB Haliburton	1981	D Talbot
1947	A Compston	1965	J Sharkey	1982	P Milton
1948	F French	1966	Nigel Paul (Am)	1983	D Ingram
1949	J Adams	1967	P Gill	1984	
1950	A Perry	1968	AG Grubb	1985	A MacKenzie
1951	K Bousfield	1969	NC Coles	1986	
1952	AJ Harman	1970	H Boyle		
1953	R Burton	1971	J Fowler		

Surrey Ladies' Championship

Instituted 1921

Year	Winner	Year	Winner
1931	Miss M Gourlay	1964	Mrs J Thornhill
1932	Miss Wethered	1965	Mrs J Thornhill
1933	Miss M Gourlay	1966	Miss C Denneny
1934	Miss M Gourlay	1967	Miss D Oxley
1935	Miss P Barton	1968	Mrs R Sutherland-Pitch
1936	Miss D Fishwick	1969	Miss J Bisgood
1937	Miss J Hamilton	1970	Miss D Oxley
1938	Miss M Gourlay	1971	Miss D Oxley
1939	Miss J Kerr	1972	Mrs S Birley
1946	Mrs Critchley (*née* Fishwick)	1973	Mrs J Thornhill
1950	Mrs Style	1974	Mrs J Thornhill
1951	Miss J Bisgood	1975	Miss D Strickland
1952	Mrs CA Barclay	1976	Mrs D Henson (*née* Oxley)
1953	Miss J Bisgood	1977	Mrs J Thornhill
1954	Miss E Price	1978	Mrs J Thornhill
1955	Miss E Price	1979	Miss S Peters
1956	Miss E Price	1980	Miss D Dowling
1957	Miss E Price	1981	Mrs J Thornhill
1958	Miss E Price	1982	Mrs J Thornhill
1959	Miss E Price	1983	Mrs J Thornhill
1960	Miss E Price	1984	Mrs J Thornhill
1961	Mrs CA Barclay	1985	J Nicolson
1962	Mrs J Thornhill	1986	Miss S Prosser
1963	Miss A Rampton		

Sussex Amateur Championship

Instituted 1899

Year	Winner	Year	Winner	Year	Winner
1930	RVK Finlay	1954	DD Grant White	1971	G Hyde
1931	EB Topping	1955	WG Pierce	1972	C King
1932	D Watson	1956	WG Pierce	1973	GE Hyde
1933	CJH Tolley	1957	WG Pierce	1974	G Hyde
1934	D Watson	1958	WG Pierce	1975	MV Jones
1935	FG Mirfield	1959	WG Pierce	1976	MIR Ross
1936	DD Grant White	1960	MJ Burgess	1977	SC Illingworth
1937	RA Howell	1961	RB Carroll	1978	AW Schofield
1938	L Green	1962	GE Hyde	1979	AP Higgins
1939	RK Furneaux	1963	MJ Burgess	1980	N Mitchell
1947	A Heasman	1964	MJ Burgess	1981	N Mitchell
1948	HG Francis	1965	I Shepherd	1982	DJ Sewell
1949	JH Langmead	1966	AG Clay	1983	P Scarles
1950	A Warnett	1967	T Frost	1984	JS Spence
1951	J McKay	1968	G Hyde	1985	MS Jarvis
1952	JJF Pennink	1969	P Royle	1986	AW Schofield
1953	WG Pierce	1970	G Hyde		

Sussex Ladies' Championship

Instituted 1923 (After 1936 Final over 36 holes)

Year	Winner	Year	Winner	Year	Winner
1935	Miss VG Davies	1957	Miss B Strange	1972	Mrs P Riddiford
1936	Mrs G White	1958	Miss B Strange	1973	Mrs P Riddiford
1937	Miss B Norris	1959	Mrs J Hayter	1974	Mrs P Riddiford
1938	Miss B Norris	1960	Miss B Strange	1975	Mrs S Tredinnick
1939	Miss R Powell	1961	Mrs P Riddiford	1976	Mrs C Larkin
1947	Mrs Dennier	1962	Mrs P Riddiford	1977	Miss S Bamford
1948	Mrs Cleary	1963	Miss P Tredinnick	1978	Mrs J Tate
1949	Mrs Jerdein	1964	Mrs P Riddiford	1979	Mrs S Sutton
1950	Mrs Jerdein	1965	Mrs M Tredinnick	1980	Miss C Pierce
1951	Mrs Dennier	1966	Mrs P Riddiford	1981	Mrs C Larkin
1952	Mrs Dennier	1967	Mrs P Riddiford	1982	Mrs C Larkin
1953	Mrs P Riddiford	1968	Mrs P Riddiford	1983	Miss M Gallagher
1954	Mrs M Groom	1969	Miss A Brown	1984	Miss C Rolph
1955	Mrs Grant-White	1970	Miss P Tredinnick	1985	Miss N Way
1956	Miss J Yuille	1971	Miss E Mountain	1986	Miss M Cornelius

Sussex Open Championship

Year	Winner	Year	Winner	Year	Winner
1946	Jack McLean	1960	MJ Burgess (Am)	1975	GE Hyde (Am)
1947	LB Ayton	1961	*Cancelled*	1976	RM Jewell
1948	W Anderson	1962	M Christmas (Am)	1977	CR Jones (Am)
1949	AG Harrison	1963	RJ McLean	1978	JC Burrell
1950	AG Harrison	1965	HA Padgham	1979	JC Burrell
1951	AG Harrison	1966	B Bamford	1980	JC Burrell
1952	K Beckett	1967	B Bamford	1981	J Pinset (Am)
1953	LB Ayton	1968	JR Hollands (Am)	1982	C Jones
1954	W Anderson	1969	Paul Huggett	1983	C Giddins
1955	AH Harrison	1970	SR Bassil	1984	J Dodds (Am)
1956	WG Pierce (Am)	1971	B Firkins	1985	JS Spence (Am)
1957	W Anderson	1972	B Morrison	1986	C Giddins
1958	JT Baker	1973	AJ Lowles		
1959	HA Padgham	1974	AJ Lowles		

Tennant Cup

This trophy was presented by Sir Charles Tennant to the Glasgow Club in 1880. It is the oldest open amateur stroke play competition in the world

Year	Winner	Year	Winner
1932	SL McKinlay	1963	SWT Murray
1933	Hector Thomson	1964	Dr FWG Deighton
1934	James Lindsay, jun	1965	J Scott Cochran
1935	JM Dykes, jun	1966	AH Hall
1936	JNW Dall	1967	BJ Gallacher
1937	WS McLeod	1968	CW Green
1938	A Jamieson, jun	1969	J Scott Cochran
1939	GB Peters	1970	CW Green
1946	JB Stevenson	1971	Andrew Brodie
1947	JC Wilson	1972	Allan Brodie
1948	J Wallace	1973	PJ Smith
1949	W Irvine	1974	D McCart
1950	JW Mill	1975	CW Green
1951	WS McLeod		*From 1976, 72 holes*
1952	GT Black	1976	IC Hutcheon
1953	AD Gray	1977	S Martin
1954	H McInally	1978	IA Carslaw
1955	LG Taylor	1979	G Hay
1956	JM Dykes	1980	Allan Brodie
1957	LG Taylor	1981	G MacDonald
1958	Dr FWG Deighton	1982	LS Mann
1959	JF Milligan	1983	C Dalgleish
1960	Dr FWG Deighton	1984	E Wilson
1961	R Reid Jack	1985	CJ Brooks
1962	WS Jack	1986	

Ulster Youths' Open Amateur Championship

Year	Winner	Year	Winner	Year	Winner
1969	J O'Leary	1975	J Hegarty	1981	M Windebank
1970	P Malone	1976	P O'Hagan	1982	G Hamill
1971	P Malone	1977	P O'Hara	1983	M Froggatt
1972	M Patterson	1978	P Leckey	1984	G Clarke
1973	J Hegarty	1979	R Rafferty	1985	J Carvill
1974	J Hegarty	1980	J Jones	1986	DA Mulholland

Ulster Professional Championship

Instituted 1924 (decided by stroke play 1938–39)

Year	Winner	Year	Winner	Year	Winner
1935	S Fairweather	1955	F Daly	1973	D Carson
1936	F Daly	1956	F Daly	1974	E Jones
1937	S Fairweather	1957	F Daly	1975	D Jones
1938	S Fairweather	1958	F Daly	*Changed to Stroke Play*	
1939	S Fairweather	1959	H Middleton	1976	E Polland
1942	C McCluskey	1960	J Henderson	1977	B Brennan
1943	F Daly	1961	John Hunter	*Reverted to Match Play*	
1944	*No championship*	1962	J Henderson	1978	P Leonard
1945	S Fairweather	1963	Hugh Jackson	1979	P Leonard
1946	F Daly	1964	E Jones	1980	P Leonard
1947	J McCartney	1965	H Jackson	1981	P Leonard
1948	S Fairweather	1966	NV Drew	1982	P Leonard
1949	S Black	1967	J Henderson	1983	RB Campbell
1950	J Henderson	1968	H Jackson	1984	D Carson
1951	F Daly	1969	H Jackson	1985	D Jones
1952	WJ Clarke	1970	H Jackson	1986	W Todd
1953	C O'Connor	1971	H Jackson		
1954	C O'Connor	1972	NV Drew		

Warwickshire Ladies' Championship

Instituted 1923

Year	Winner	Year	Winner	Year	Winner
1936	Miss E Pears	1958	Miss V Anstey	1973	Mrs S Westall
1937	Miss E Pears	1959	Miss S Armstrong	1974	Mrs S Westall
1938	Mrs Peppercorn	1960	Miss V Anstey	1975	Mrs V Beharrell
1939	Miss M Frysche	1961	Mrs J Roles	1976	Mrs MF Roles
1947	Mrs EM Sheppard	1962	Miss J Roberts	1977	Miss A Middleton
1948	Mrs EM Sheppard	1963	Miss J Roberts	1978	Mrs S Westall
1949	Mrs EM Sheppard	1964	Miss J Roberts	1979	Mrs S Nicolson
1950	Mrs EM Sheppard	1965	Miss J Roberts	1980	Miss T Hammond
1951	Mrs EM Sheppard	1966	Mrs J Roles	1981	Mrs J Evans
1952	Miss P Davies	1967	Mrs J Tomlinson	1982	Miss T Hammond
1953	Mrs M Peppercorn	1968	Mrs J Tomlinson	1983	Miss T Hammond
1954	Mrs EM Sheppard	1969	Miss J Roberts	1984	Miss M Stevens
1955	Miss V Anstey	1970	Mrs J Roles	1985	Mrs S Seville
1956	Miss V Anstey	1971	Mrs V Beharrell	1986	Miss T Hammond
1957	Miss V Anstey	1972	Mrs V Beharrell		

Warwickshire Amateur Championship

Instituted 1906

Year	Winner	Year	Winner	Year	Winner
1930	WA Stockwin	1953	E Walton	1970	J Mayell
1931	H Hall	1954	JM Urry	1971	JA Fisher
1932	SA Dark	1955	T Mannion	1972	JA Fisher
1933	SA Dark	1956	P Skerritt	1973	JMH Mayell
1934	V Gerstenberg	1957	RJ Nauen	1974	P McEvoy
1935	KR Frazier	1958	P Skerritt	1975	R Pritchard
1936	KR Frazier	1959	JL Whitworth	1976	P McEvoy
1937	KR Frazier	1960	PG Jones	1977	P McEvoy
1938	DM Sutherland	1961	AW Pullar	1978	T Allen
1939	RJ Nauen	1962	AW Holmes	1979	M Biddle
1946	JM Urry	1963	P Skerritt	1980	P McEvoy
1947	BJ Newey	1964	GW Barton	1981	B Wilkes
1948	AW Pullar	1965	P Skerritt	1982	A Roach
1949	AW Pullar	1966	RG Hiatt	1983	NM Chesses
1950	WL Smart	1967	CC Black	1984	P McEvoy
1951	JL Morgan	1968	JM Lower	1985	C Suneson
1952	T Mannion	1969	JA Fisher	1986	P Downes

Warwickshire Professional Championship

Year	Winner	Year	Winner	Year	Winner
1937	WJ Martin	1959	F Jowle	1974	RDS Livingston
1938	HR Manton	1960	T Collinge	1975	PR Herbert
1939	GA Maisey	1961	GA Maisey	1976	BJ Barton
1947	J Cawsey	1962	NR McDonald	1977	J Higgins
1948	T Hassall	1963	GA Maisey	1978	AFC Miller
1949	J Hargreaves	1964	RL Moffitt	1979	RDS Livingston
1950	J Hargreaves	1965	PJ Butler	1980	D Steele
1951	J Hargreaves	1966	PJ Butler	1981	P Weaver
1952	J Hargreaves	1967	PJ Butler	1982	N Selwyn-Smith
1953	BJ Hunt	1968	M Reece	1983	PJ Weaver
1954	GA Maisey	1969	RL Moffitt	1984	A Bownes
1955	F Jowle	1970	J Byard	1985	
1956	F Jowle	1971	J Byard	1986	P Elson
1957	F Jowle	1972	P Butler		
1958	P Butler	1973	PJ Weaver		

Warwickshire Open Championship

Year	Winner	Year	Winner	Year	Winner
1946	GA Maisey	1960	F Jowle	1974	P McEvoy (Am)
1947	GA Maisey	1961	PJ Butler	1975	PJ Weaver
1948	J Hargreaves	1962	PJ Butler	1976	PJ Weaver
1949	JH Cawsey	1963	PJ Butler	1977	N Selwyn-Smith
1950	GA Maisey	1964	PJ Butler	1978	J Higgins
1951	J Hargreaves	1965	PJ Butler	1979	R Livingston
1952	GA Maisey	1966	PJ Butler	1980	D Steele
1953	GA Maisey	1967	RL Moffitt	1981	T Allen (Am)
1954	J Hargreaves	1968	TM Collinge	1982	T Allen (Am) P Downes (Am)
1955	PJ Butler	1969	RL Moffitt		
1956	J Hargreaves	1970	RL Moffitt	1983	PJ Weaver
1957	GR Maisey	1971	JM Lower	1984	
1958	F Jowle	1972	P Weaver	1985	J Gould
1959	PJ Butler	1973	P McEvoy (Am)	1986	PJ Weaver

Welsh Cup Championship

Instituted 1895

Year	Winner	Year	Winner	Year	Winner
1947	Brecon	1961	Ashburnham	1974	Whitchurch
1948	Rhyl	1962	St David's	1975	Caernarvonshire
1949	Llandudno	1963	Cardiff	1976	Caernarvonshire
1950	Southerndown	1964	St David's	1977	Wenvoe
1951	St David's	1965	St David's	1978	Pontypool
1952	Prestatyn	1966	Whitchurch	1979	Pontypool
1953	Llandudno	1967	Whitchurch	1980	Radyr
1954	Aberystwyth	1968	Holyhead	1981	Radyr
1955	Rhyl	1969	Whitchurch	1982	Newport
1956	Southerndown	1970	Porthcawl	1983	Pontypridd
1957	Ashburnham	1971	St Pierre	1984	
1959	St David's	1972	Whitchurch	1985	
1960	Newport	1973	Caernarvonshire	1986	Pontnewydd

Welsh Ladies' Team Championship

Instituted 1905

Year	Winner	Year	Winner
1947	Radyr	1969	Prestatyn
1948	North Wales (Llandudno)	1970	Newport
1949	North Wales	1971	Prestatyn
1950	North Wales	1972	Tenby
1951	North Wales	1973	Porthcawl
1952	Porthcawl	1974	St David's
1953	North Wales	1975	Porthcawl
1956	Radyr	1976	Whitchurch
1958	Monmouthshire	1977	Whitchurch
1959	Radyr	1978	Whitchurch
1960	Tenby	1979	Bargoed
1961	St David's	1980	Monmouthshire
1962	Radyr	1981	Porthcawl
1963	St David's	1982	St David's
1964	Newport (Mon)	1983	Llandudno (Maesdu)
1965	St David's	1984	Monmouthshire
1966	St David's	1985	Llandudno (Maesdu)
1967	North Wales	1986	Porthcawl
1968	Prestatyn		

West of England Open Amateur Championship

Instituted 1912

(Venue: Burnham-on-Sea)

Year	Winner	Year	Winner	Year	Winner
1935	JJ Pennink	1958	AJN Young	1974	CS Mitchell
1936	PH White	1959	DM Woolmer	1975	MR Lovett
1937	O Austreng	1960	AW Holmes	1976	*Cancelled because*
1938	HJ Roberts	1961	JM Leach		*of damage to*
1946	JH Neal	1962	Sq-Ldr W McCrea		*course by drought*
1947	WF Wise	1963	KT Warren	1977	AR Dunlop
1948	WF Wise	1964	DC Allen	1978	R Broad
1949	J Payne	1965	DE Jones	1979	N Burch
1950	EB Millward	1966	A Forrester	1980	JM Durbin
1951	J Payne	1967	A Forrester	1981	M Mouland
1952	EB Millward	1968	SR Warrin	1982	M Higgins
1953	F Griffin	1969	SR Warrin	1983	C Peacock
1954	EB Millward	1970	C Ball	1984	GB Hickman
1955	SJ Fox	1971	G Irlam	1985	AC Nash
1956	SJ Fox	1972	JA Bloxham	1986	J Bennett
1957	D Gardner	1973	SC Mason		

West of England Open Amateur Stroke Play Championship

Instituted 1968

Year	Winner	Year	Winner	Year	Winner
1968	PJ Yeo	1975	BG Steer	1982	MP Higgins
1969	A Forrester	1976	R Abbott	1983	P McEvoy
1970	PJ Yeo	1977	P McEvoy	1984	A Sherborne
1971	P Berry	1978	J Bennett	1985	P McEvoy
1972	P Berry	1979	R Kane	1986	P Baker
1973	SC Mason	1980	P McEvoy		
1974	R Abbott	1981	N Taee		

West of England Professional Championship

Instituted 1922

Year	Winner	Year	Winner	Year	Winner
1935	A Easterbrook	1954	WD Smithers	1967	T Lebrocq
1936	A Perry	1955	H Weetman	1968	D Sewell
1937	CH Ward	1956	Peter Alliss	1969	S Peach
1938	RA Whitcombe	1957	H Weetman	1970	D Sewell
1939	S Easterbrook	1958	Peter Alliss	1971	RM Anderson
1946	TB Haliburton	1959	WD Smithers	1972	P Green
1947	M Faulkner	1960	BJ Hunt	1973	T Pinner
1948	RA Whitcombe	1961	BJ Hunt	1974	FS Boobyer
1949	WD Smithers	1962	Peter Alliss	1975	A MacDonald
1950	RA Whitcombe	1963	EG Lester	1976	J Yeo
1951	WD Smithers	1964	FS Boobyer	*From 1977 became:*	
1952	WD Smithers	1965	J McAlister	*West Region PGA*	
1953	E Lester	1966	Peter Aliss	*Championship*	

West Region PGA Championship

Year	Winner	Year	Winner	Year	Winner
1977	G Smith	1981	T Horton	1985	D Sheppard
1978	G Smith	1982	G Smith	1986	
1979	S Brown	1983			
1980	P Ward	1984			

West of Ireland Open Amateur Championship

Instituted 1923

Venue: Rosses Point

Year	Winner	Year	Winner	Year	Winner
1936	J Burke	1953	JB Carr	1970	J McTear
1937	JF McLoughlin	1954	JB Carr	1971	R Carr
1938	J Burke	1955	Dr I Forsythe	1972	V Nevin
1939	Cecil Ewing	1956	JB Carr	1973	D Smyth
1940	J Burke	1957	JA Mahon	1974	M Gannon
1941	Cecil Ewing	1958	JB Carr	1975	I Elliott
1942	Cecil Ewing	1959	W Ferguson	1976	D Branigan
1943	Cecil Ewing	1960	JB Carr	1977	B Hoey
1944	J Burke	1961	JB Carr	1978	B Reddan
1945	Cecil Ewing	1962	JB Carr	1979	D Long
1946	JB Carr	1963	RM Craigan	1980	A Pierse
1947	JB Carr	1964	Brian Malone	1981	D Branigan
1948	JB Carr	1965	RM Craigan	1982	A Pierse
1949	Cecil Ewing	1966	JB Carr	1983	C Glasgow
1950	Cecil Ewing	1967	RK Pollin	1984	G McGimpsey
1951	JB Carr	1968	DM Nelson	1985	J Feeney
1952	JC Brown	1969	R Pollin	1986	

West of Scotland Amateur Championship

Year	Winner	Year	Winner	Year	Winner
1950	A Sinclair	1963	FS Morris	1974	Allan Brodie
1951	JR Cater	1964	GB Cosh	1975	S Stephen
1952	J Campbell	1965	GB Cosh	1976	GH Murray
1953	J Mill	1966	GB Cosh	1977	MJ Miller
1954	J Walker	1967	CL Strachan	1978	GH Murray
1955	JR Cater	1968	AM Grant	1979	CW Green
1956	HVS Thomson	1969	W Smeaton	1980	DB Howard
1957	Dr JL Hastings	1970	CW Green	1981	H McMorran
1958	SWT Murray	1971	GH Murray	1982	G MacDonald
1959	Dr FWG Deighton	*From 1972 became open*		1983	G Barrie
1960	IGF Lee	*event*		1984	G Shaw
1961	GB Cosh	1972	AK Pirie	1985	JA Thomson
1962	CW Green	1973	GH Murray	1986	C Brooks

West of Scotland Close Amateur Championship

Instituted 1977

Year	Winner	Year	Winner	Year	Winner
1977	R Blackwood	1981	DB Howard	1985	S Savage
1978	AP McDonald	1982	G Shaw	1986	S Savage
1979	N Skinner	1983	D Murdoch		
1980	PJ McKellar	1984			

Western Division Ladies' Championship (Scotland)

Year	Winner	Year	Winner
1936	Mrs AM Holm	1966	Mrs IC Robertson
1937	Mrs AM Holm	1967	Miss S Needham
1938	Miss B Henderson	1968	Mrs W Norris
1947	Miss J McCulloch	1969	Mrs IC Robertson
1948	Mrs AM Holm	1970	Miss F Jamieson
1949	Mrs AM Holm	1971	Miss S Needham
1950	Mrs AM Holm	1972	Miss S Needham
1951	Mrs B Singleton	1973	Miss S Needham
1952	Miss K McNeil	1974	Miss G Cadden
1953	Mrs B Singleton	1975	Miss S Needham
1954	Mrs J Drummond	1976	Miss S Lambie
1955	Miss B Geakie	1977	Miss S Lambie
1956	Miss J Robertson	1978	Miss W Aitken
1957	Miss B McCorkindale	1979	Miss S Lambie
1958	Miss J Robertson	1980	Miss W Aitken
1959	Miss J Robertson	1981	Miss W Aitken
1960	Mrs B Singleton	1982	Miss S Lawson
1961	Miss DT Sommerville	1983	Miss S Lawson
1962	Miss S McKinven	1984	Dr A Wilson
1963	Mrs B Singleton	1985	Mrs IC Robertson
1964	Mrs. IC Robertson	1986	Miss S Lawson
1965	Mrs ID Hamilton		

West of Scotland Girls' Championship

Year	Winner	Year	Winner	Year	Winner
1960	Miss A Lurie	1969	Miss M Walker	1978	Miss A Hammond
1961	Miss I Wylie	1970	Miss M Walker	1979	Miss A Hammond
1962	Miss I Wylie	1971	Miss G Cadden	1980	Miss S Lawson
1963	Miss F Griffiths	1972	Miss G Cadden	1981	Miss S Lawson
1964	Miss F Griffiths	1973	Miss G Cadden	1982	Miss S Lawson
1965	Miss D Reid	1974	Miss S Cadden	1983	Miss A Johnson
1966	Miss D Reid	1975	Miss W Aitken	1984	Miss D Jackson
1967	Miss A Buchanan	1976	Miss S Cadden	1985	Miss K Fitzgerald
1968	Miss J Crawford	1977	Miss W Aitken	1986	Miss L Lundie

West of Scotland Boys' Championship

Year	Winner	Year	Winner	Year	Winner
1964	G McKay	1972	I Gillan	1980	J Milligan
1965	WR Lockie	1973	P McNiven	1981	S Thompson
1966	RA Bennett	1974	D Carrick	1982	P Girvan
1967	IA Carslaw	1975	A Taylor	1983	G Collinson
1968	PY Reed	1976	A Taylor	1984	G Orr
1969	M Gray	1977	G Haugh	1985	
1970	S Torrance	1978	J Queen	1986	G King
1971	D Stratton	1979	T Reid		

Wigtownshire Championship

Instituted 1936

Year	Winner	Year	Winner	Year	Winner
1946	RHU Stevenson	1960	CG Findlay	1975	M Gibson
1947	MH Forrest	1961	A Simpson	1976	K Russell
1948	MH Forrest	1963	R Murray	1977	M Gibson
1949	R Murray	1964	R Murray	1978	AV Plant
1950	R Murray	1965	R McGinn	1979	M Gibson
1951	R Murray	1966	Alan Johnstone	1980	Dr RNC Douglas
1952	R Murray	1967	CG Findlay	1981	J Young
1953	T Stangoe	1968	CG Findlay	1982	Dr RNC Douglas
1954	R Murray	1969	M Gibson	1983	K Hardie
1955	JS Boyd	1970	R McGinn	1984	A Burns
1956	GM Cook	1971	M Gibson	1985	
1957	R Murray	1972	K Wallace	1986	
1958	R Murray	1973	M Gibson		
1959	A Simpson	1974	R McGinn		

Wiltshire Amateur Championship

Instituted 1924

Year	Winner	Year	Winner	Year	Winner
1946	RP Bowie	1959	DL Pugsley	1974	B Townsend
1947	RP Bowie CF Macpherson	1960 1961	Major RG Kelley DL Pugsley	1975 1976	RE Searle BM Townsend
1948	DL Pugsley	1962	PE Edgington	1977	B Townsend
1949	EI Hobden	1963	PE Edgington	1978	RE Searle
1950	Major R Davenport	1964	RB Robertson	1979	KA Clark
1951	MC Swift	1965	P Edgington	1980	RE Searle
1952	AS Mayer	1966	SML Morgan	1981	JN Fleming
1953	AS Mayer	1967	P Edgington	1982	BF McCallum
1954	DL Pugsley	1968	RE Searle	1983	D Kingsman
1955	DL Pugsley MC Swift	1969 1970	RE Searle RB Robertson	1984 1985	NC Garfoot S Amor
1956	H Watson	1971	RE Searle	1986	
1957	AS Mayer	1972	M Lovett		
1958	EN Davis	1973	BF McCallum		

Wiltshire Ladies' Championship

Year	Winner	Year	Winner	Year	Winner
1936	Mrs Hart	1958	Mrs Taunton	1973	Mrs P Bucher
1937	Mrs Potts	1959	Mrs Taunton	1974	Mrs V Morgan
1938	Miss Pywell	1960	Mrs J Taunton	1975	Mrs J Lawrence
1939	Miss Pywell	1961	Mrs J Taunton	1976	Mrs V Morgan
1947	Mrs Evans	1962	Mrs M Strong	1977	Mrs J Lawrence
1948	Mrs Potts	1963	Mrs M Morris	1978	Mrs P Millar
1949	Mrs Kennard	1964	Mrs C Jones	1979	Mrs P Board
1950	Mrs Greenland	1965	Mrs Taunton	1980	Miss C Waite
1951	Mrs Greenland	1966	Mrs RJA Morris	1981	Miss C Waite
1952	Mrs Glendinning	1967	Miss A Mackenzie	1982	Miss F Dawson
1953	Mrs Glendinning	1968	Mrs A Bucher	1983	Miss C Waite
1954	Mrs Greenland	1969	Miss P Lord	1984	Mrs V Morgan
1955	Mrs Curnick	1970	Miss P Lord	1985	Miss C Waite
1956	Mrs Curnick	1971	Mrs V Morgan	1986	Miss S Marks
1957	Mrs Taunton	1972	Mrs P Board		

Wiltshire Professional Championship

Instituted 1925
Now known as the "Hills" Wiltshire Pro Champ

Year	Winner	Year	Winner	Year	Winner
1930	J Webb	1953	J Powell	1971	P Coombs
1931	J Webb	1954	SEG Slocombe	1972	P Coombs
1932	J Webb	1955	SEG Slocombe	1973	G Pickup
1933	C Easterbrook	1956	SEG Slocombe	1971	A Harman
1934	J Webb	1957	D Haslam	1975	B Sandry
1935	J Webb	1958	D Haslam	1976	B Sandry
1936	RV Redmond	1959	Tony Harman	1977	L Bowen
1937	C Easterbrook	1960	D Haslam	1978	G Smith
1938	AW Edmonds	1961	D Haslam	1979	B Sandry
1939	J Webb	1962	AJ Harman	1980	B Sandry
1946	A Illingworth RA Brown	1963	D Haslam	1981	Gary Smith
		1964	AJ Harman	1982	R Emery
1947	RV Redmond	1965	AJ Harman	1983	I Bolt
1948	J Webb	1966	AJ Harman	1984	G Laing
1949	AS Illingworth	1967	P Coombs	1985	G Laing
1950	RA Brown	1968	P Coombs	1986	B Sandry
1951	RA Brown	1969	D Haslam		
1952	SEG Slocombe	1970	P Coombs		

Worcestershire Amateur Championship

Instituted 1906

Year	Winner	Year	Winner	Year	Winner
1936	Stanley Lunt	1957	HJ Roberts	1972	TR Shingler
1937	Dr WM Robb	1958	HJ Roberts	1973	TR Shingler
1938	Dr W Tweddell	1959	HJ Roberts	1974	R Langridge
1939	Dr W Anderson	1960	RW Sandilands	1975	D Turner
1946	Dr WM Robb	1961	RA Jowle	1976	R Hobbis
1947	HJ Roberts	1962	JR Butterworth	1977	SJ Pimley
1948	SL Elliott	1963	HJ Roberts	1978	M Curry
1949	Dr WM Robb	1964	R Hobbis	1979	PD Kelley
1950	EW Fiddian	1965	PD Kelley	1980	PR Swinburne
1951	JS Mitchley	1966	A Forrester	1981	MC Reynard
1952	NA Seers	1967	MWL Hampton	1982	DJ Eddiford
1953	JR Butterworth	1968	A Thomson	1983	TR Shingler
1954	JR Butterworth	1969	A Forrester	1984	T Martin
1955	JR Butterworth	1970	J Toddington	1985	SJ Pimley
1956	FL Wilkinson	1971	J Toddington	1986	DJ Eddiford

Worcestershire Ladies' Championship

Instituted 1924

Year	Winner	Year	Winner	Year	Winner
1935	Mrs E Fiddian	1951	Mrs Challen	1960	Miss M Hampson
1936	Mrs Brinton	1952	Miss M Fyshe	1961	Miss M Hampson
1937	Mrs E Fiddian	1953	Miss M Hampson	1962	Mrs G Strang
1938	Mrs Challen	1954	Miss M Fyshe	1963	Mrs Joan Odell
1939	Miss M Hampson	1955	Miss M Hampson	1964	Mrs RL Brinton
1947	Miss M Hampson	1956	Miss M Hampson	1965	Mrs C Banner
1948	Miss M Hampson	1957	Miss M Hampson	1966	Mrs C Banner
1949	Miss M Hampson	1958	Mrs M Downing	1967	Miss J Blaymire
1950	Miss M Hampson	1959	Miss A Cawsey	1968	Mrs M Hayes

Worcestershire Ladies' Championship *continued*

Year	Winner	Year	Winner	Year	Winner
1969	Miss J Blaymire	1975	Miss J Blaymire	1981	Miss J Blaymire
1970	Miss J Blaymire	1976	Miss J Blaymire	1982	Miss J Blaymire
1971	Miss J Blaymire	1977	Miss J Blaymire	1983	Miss S Nicklin
1972	Miss J Blaymire	1978	Miss S Crowcroft	1984	Miss S Nicklin
1973	Miss J Blaymire	1979	Miss J Blaymire	1985	Miss L Waring
1974	Mrs V Cotterill	1980	Mrs R West	1986	Miss K Cheetham

Worcestershire Open Championship

Year	Winner	Year	Winner	Year	Winner
1949	JS Mitchley (Am)	1962	HJ Roberts (Am)	1975	I Richardson
1950	WR Firkins	1963	FE Miller	1976	R Hobbis
1951	Dr WM Robb	1964	FE Miller	1977	SJ Carpenter (Am)
1952	FE Miller	1965	JE Wiggett	1978	RA Jowle (Am)
1953	FE Miller	1966	JE Wiggett	1979	I Richardson
1954	FE Miller	1967	FE Miller	1980	RA Jowle (Am)
1955	HJ Roberts (Am)	1968	PD Kelley (Am)	1981	W Firkins
1956	HJ Roberts (Am)	1969	H Macdonald	1982	MC Reynard (Am)
1957	GF Reynolds	1970	T Shingler (Am)	1983	AJ Hill
1958	FE Miller	1971	PD Kelley (Am)	1984	K Hayward
1959	SS Seymour (Am)	1972	K Bayliss	1985	DJ Eddiford
1960	WH Firkins	1973	H Macdonald	1986	
1961	RA Jowle (Am)	1974	TR Shingler (Am)		

Worcestershire Professional Championship

Year	Winner	Year	Winner	Year	Winner
1947	L Cliffe	1961	WE Booy	1975	DJ Russell
1948	WR Firkins	1962	JE Wiggett	1976	I Richardson
1949	HE Lewis	1963	JE Wiggett	1977	I Richardson
1950	WR Firkins	1964	RDS Livingston	1978	I Richardson
1951	WE Booy	1965	JR Moses	1979	I Richardson
1952	WR Firkins	1966	FE Miller	1980	WH Firkins
1953	FT Sumner	1967	S Fogarty	1981	R Livingston
1954	WR Firkins	1968	JR Moses	1982	WH Firkins
1955	FE Miller	1969	S Fogarty	1983	KA Hayward
1956	FE Miller	1970	JR Moses	1984	
1957	WR Firkins	1971	WH Firkins	1985	KA Hayward
1958	FE Miller	1972	S Fogarty	1986	D Dunk
1959	JE Wiggett	1973	N Underwood		
1960	JE Wiggett	1974	I Richardson		

Worplesdon Mixed Foursomes

Instituted 1921

Year	Winners
1946	Miss J Gordon (Stanmore) and AA Duncan (Southerndown) beat Miss J Pemberton (Prestwick) and H Longhurst (Bedfordshire) 4 and 3
1947	Miss J Gordon (Stanmore) and AA Duncan (Southerndown) beat Mrs Beck and John B Beck (Coombe Wood) 8 and 7
1948	Miss W Morgan (Rochester and Cobham) and EF Storey (Sunningdale) beat Lady Heathcoat-Amory (Worplesdon) and Sir John Heathcoat-Amory (Tiverton) 5 and 4
1949	Miss F Stephens (Birkdale) and LG Crawley (Rye) beat Mrs AC Critchley (Wentworth) and CJH Tolley (Royal and Ancient) 4 and 3
1950	Miss F Stephens (Birkdale) and LG Crawley (Rye) beat Miss E Johnston (West Hill) and Peter MacDonald (Mid-Surrey) 6 and 5

Worplesdon Mixed Foursomes

continued

Year	Winners
1951	Mrs AC Barclay and G Evans (Hook Heath) beat Mrs RT Peel and GW Mackie (Gullane) by 1 hole
1952	Mrs RT Peel and GW Mackie (Gullane) beat Miss Frances Stephens (Birkdale) and WA Slark (Walton Heath) 3 and 2
1953	Miss J Gordon (Stanmore) and G Knipe (Southerndown) beat Mrs M Spearman and JCE Atkins (Sudbury) 1 hole
1954	Miss F Stephens (Birkdale) and WA Slark (Walton Heath) beat Miss J McIntyre (Lindrick) and PF Scrutton (Addington) 2 holes
1955	Miss P Garvey (Co Louth) and PF Scrutton (Sunningdale) beat Mrs A van Oss (Berks) and G Duncan (Porthcawl) 2 and 1
1956	Mrs L Abrahams (Sunningdale) and Major WD Henderson (Sunningdale) beat Mlle. O Semelaigne (France) and GH Micklem (Sunningdale) 3 and 1
1957	Mrs B Singleton and WD Smith (Prestwick) beat Miss J Gordon (Sunningdale) and HB Ridgeley (Sandy Lodge) 5 and 4
1958	Mr and Mrs M Bonallack (Thorpe Hall) beat Mrs B Singleton and WD Smith (Prestwick) 4 and 3
1959	Miss J Robertson and I Wright beat Signora Goldschmid and Tudor Davies, 4 and 3
1960	Miss B Jackson (Handsworth) and MJ Burgess (West Sussex) beat Mr and Mrs JC Beharrel (Little Aston) 2 and 1
1961	Mrs R Smith (Birkdale) and B Critchley (Sunningdale) beat Miss J Woodside (Purley Downs) and J Thornhill (Walton Heath) 3 and 2
1962	Viscomtesse de Saint Sauveur (France) and DW Frame (Worplesdon) beat Miss W Clark (Walton Heath) and KT Warren (Coombe Hill) 5 and 3
1963	Mrs G Valentine (Craigie Hill) and JE Behrend (Liverpool) beat Signora I Goldschmid (Italy) and MJ Burgess (West Sussex) 4 and 3
1964	Mrs G Valentine (Craigie Hill) and JE Behrend (Liverpool) beat Mrs AD Spearman (Sudbury) and A Thirwell (Gosforth) 3 and 2
1965	Mrs G Valentine (Craigie Hill) and JE Behrend (Worplesdon) beat Mrs J Anderson (Gullane) and CA Clark (Ganton) 1 hole
1966	Mrs C Barclay (West Hill) and DJ Miller (Addington) beat Miss E Mountain (Crowborough Beacon) and P Benka (Addington) at 19th
1967	JF Gancedo (Spain) and Miss C Lacoste (France) beat DJ Miller (Mid-Surrey) and Mrs C Barclay (West Hill) 1 hole
1968	JD van Heel (Holland) and Miss Dinah Oxley (West Byfleet) beat RPF Brown (Worplesdon) and Mrs Jessie Valentine (Craigie Hill) 2 and 1
1969	Mrs R Ferguson (Manchester) and Alistair Wilson (Turnberry) beat Miss P Tredinnick (Worthing) and B Critchley (Sunningdale) 4 and 3
1970	Miss R Roberts and RL Glading (Addington Place) beat Mrs J Roberts (St George's Hill) and Sir George Cole (Woking) 2 and 1
1971	Mrs D Frearson (Tandridge) and A Smith (Walsall) beat Miss J de Witt Puyt (Holland) and J Ward (West Wilts) 3 and 2
1972	Miss B Le Garreres (France) and CA Strang (St George's Hill) beat Mrs CA Barclay (West Hill) and P Garner (Wentworth) 1 hole
1973	Miss T Perkins (Wenvoe Castle) and RJ Evans (Woodbridge) beat Mrs WJ Uzielli (Berkshire) and WJ Uzielli (Denham) 3 and 2
1974	Mrs S Birley and RL Glading (Addington Palace) beat Mr and Mrs JR Thornhill (Walton Heath) 4 and 3
1975	Mr and Mrs J Thornhill (Walton Heath) beat Mrs S Birley and R Glading (Addington Palace) at 20th
1976	Mrs B Lewis (Rochford Hundred) and J Caplan (Worplesdon) beat Miss T Perkins and R Jones (Wenvoe Castle) 1 hole
1977	Mrs D Henson (Cirencester) and J Caplan (Worplesdon) beat Miss P Light and M Chugg (Whitchurch) 4 and 3
1978	Miss T Perkins (Wenvoe Castle) and R Thomas (Pennard) beat Mrs C Caldwell (Sunningdale) and JC Davies (Mid-Surrey) 2 and 1
1979	Miss J Melville and A Melville (Furness) beat Miss G Gunby and D Robson (Chigwell) 2 and 1
1980	Mrs L Bayman and I Boyd (Berkshire) beat Mrs L Davies (Berkshire) and R Hurst (Woking) 1 hole
1981	Mrs J Nicholsen and MN Stern (Worplesdon) beat Mrs S Birley (Tandridge) and RL Glading (Addington Palace) 2 and 1
1982	Miss B New and K Dobson (Lansdown) beat Miss S Cohen and J Tarbuck (Coombe Hill), 2 and 1
1983	Miss B New and K Dobson (Lansdown) beat Miss N McCormack (Porters Park) and N Briggs (Berkhamsted) at 19th
1984	Mrs L Bayman and MC Hughesdon (Sunningdale) beat Miss N McCormack (Porters Park) and N Briggs (Berkhamsted) 5 and 4
1985	Mrs H Kaye (Harpenden) and D Longmuir (Verulam) beat Mrs J Collingham (Royal Birkdale) and GS Melville (Brockenhurst Manor)
1986	Miss P Johnson and RN Roderick (Ponterdawe) beat Miss C Duffy and L Hawkins (Maidenhead), 2 and 1

Yorkshire Amateur Championship

Instituted 1894

Year	Winner	Year	Winner	Year	Winner
1946	WV Hembry	1960	Geo Ash	1974	M Kelley
1947	JE Gent	1961	Bernard Meldrum	1975	R Mitchell
1948	Dr JR Acfield	1962	John Greenwood	1976	G Brand
1949	Malcolm Lee	1963	R Foster	1977	I Mackenzie
1950	Malcolm Lee	1964	R Foster	1978	P Carrigill
1951	R Arend	1965	R Foster	1979	KJ Miller
1952	Malcolm Lee	1966	C Bland	1980	MI Mackenzie
1953	Alan Turner	1967	R Foster	1981	M Kelley
1954	DF Livingston	1968	P Tupling	1982	S East
1955	Sam J Brough	1969	M Kelley	1983	JL Plaxton
1956	Malcolm Lee	1970	R Foster	1984	J Whiteley
1957	Sam Brough	1971	M Lee	1985	G Field
1958	Sam Brough	1972	M Holliday	1986	AR Gelsthorpe
1959	Sam Brough	1973	HK Clark		

Yorkshire Open Championship

Instituted 1927

Year	Winner	Year	Winner	Year	Winner
1936	P Alliss	1957	E Large	1972	B Hutchinson
1937	P Alliss	1958	J Fallon	1973	R Emery
1938	H Crapper	1959	G Weston	1974	N Melvin
1939	A Lees	1960	B Hutchinson	1975	M Kelley (Am)
1946	A Lees	1961	CE Hughes	1976	R Hardcastle
1947	J Fallon	1962	B Hutchinson	1977	RS Mitchell (Am)
1948	JD Henderson	1963	B Hutchinson	1978	M Ingham
1949	F Jowie	1964	B Hutchinson	1979	A Bickerdike
1950	J Shanks	1965	HW Muscroft	1980	D Jagger
1951	J Fallon	1966	Brian Waites	1981	D Jagger
1952	J Wade	1967	H Muscroft	1982	B Thompson
1953	B Shelton	1968	L Platts	1983	H Muscroft
1954	J Fallon	1969	M Kelley (Am)	1984	D Jagger
1955	SJ Brough (Am)	1970	S Evans	1985	D Jagger
1956	W Lees	1971	GA Caygill	1986	*Not played*

Yorkshire Ladies' Championship

Instituted 1896

Year	Winner	Year	Winner	Year	Winner
1947	Miss J McIntyre	1961	Mrs P Foster	1975	Miss V Marvin
1948	Mrs Kyle	1962	Miss G Coldwell	1976	Miss P Wrightson
1949	Mrs Kyle	1963	Miss G Hickson	1977	Miss M Everard
1950	Mrs Hartley	1964	Miss M Everard	1978	Miss V Marvin
1951	Miss G Rudgard	1965	Mrs TJ Briggs	1979	Miss J Rhodes
1952	Miss A Scargill	1966	Miss C Bell	1980	Miss L Batty
1953	Mrs E Hartley	1967	Miss M Everard	1981	Miss P Grice
1954	Miss J Mitton	1968	Miss K Phillips	1982	Miss P Grice
1955	Mrs E Hartley	1969	Miss K Phillips	1983	Miss P Grice
1956	Mrs E Hartley	1970	Mrs J Hunter	1984	Miss A Nicholas
1957	Miss P Bagley	1971	Miss G Ringstead	1985	Miss A Farmery
1958	Mrs E Hartley	1972	Miss M Everard	1986	Miss P Smillie
1959	Mrs E Hartley	1973	Miss M Everard		
1960	Mrs E Hartley	1974	Mrs B Allison		

Yorkshire Professional Championship

Instituted 1921

Year	Winner	Year	Winner	Year	Winner
1946	F Jowle	1960	WJ Branch	1974	P Cowen
1947	WH Green	1961	GA Caygill	1975	M Ingham
1948	J Fallon	1962	B Hutchinson	1976	RH Emery
1949	A Lees	1963	B Hutchinson	1977	P Cowen
1950	F Jowle	1964	GA Caygill	1978	A Swaine
1951	JA Jacobs	1965	B Hutchinson	1979	G Manson
1952	WJ Branch	1966	GA Caygill	1980	M Ingham
1953	J Fallon	1967	H Muscroft	1981	G Townhill
1954	S Stenhouse	1968	L Platts	1982	M Mackenzie
1955	WJ Branch	1969	H Muscroft	1983	P Cowen
1956	J Fallon	1970	B Hutchinson	1984	
1957	WJ Branch	1971	H Muscroft	1985	
1958	M Law	1972	W Ferguson	1986	M Ingham
1959	WJ Branch	1973	S Rolley		

Royal and Ancient Tournaments

Royal and Ancient Club of St Andrews

Captain 1985-86 HC Maclaine

Medal and Cup Winners

Royal Medal

presented by His Majesty King William the Fourth (First prize at Autumn Meeting)

Instituted 1837

Year		Strokes	Year		Strokes
1930	JN Nock	77	1961	Dr FWG Deighton	69
1931	WL Hartley	75	1962	Major DW Nisbet	71
1932	Brig Gen AC Critchley	73	1963	Dr FWG Deighton	72
1933	HE Taylor	73	1964	G Alex Hill (Captain)	72
1934	CGB Stevens	83	1965	R Reid Jack	71
1935	Major WHH Aitken	73	1966	Dr FWG Deighton	71
1936	LG Crawley	71	1967	RR Jack	70
1937	RH Wethered	73	1968	TC Schuller	70
1939	LG Crawley	72	1969	HC Maclaine	73
1939-45	*No competition owing to the War*		1970	JG Salvesen	73
1946	Dr JC Lawrie	78	1971	WD Smith	73
1947	JM Dykes	80	1972	Dr D Greenhough	71
1948	Col WHH Aitken	71	1973	Dr FWG Deighton	69
1949	GH Micklem	73	1974	HC Maclaine	73
1950	GH Micklem	74	1975	P Davidson	73
1951	JG Blackwell	73	1976	BJ Ingham	73
1952	JM Dykes	74	1977	A Sinclair	73
1953	KG Patrick	72	1978	M Lee	73
1954	HJ Ballingall	71	1979	DP Davidson	73
1955	Major DA Blair	69	1980	F Illouz	72
1956	Dr FWG Deighton	70	1981	R Foster	72
1957	HJ Ballingall	73	1982	H Campbell	72
1958	DW Nisbet	74	1983	AJ Low	72
1959	Dr FWG Deighton	71	1984	C McLachlan	75
1960	Robin Galloway	73	1985	GJ Cotla	70
			1986	P Greenhough	70

Gold Medal

presented by the Club

From 1806 to 1836, the Gold Medal was awarded to the winner of the Autumn Meeting. From 1837 the Gold Medal became the second prize at the Autumn Meeting.

Silver Cross

presented by Colonel J Murray Belshes, of Buttergask (First prize at Spring Meeting)

Instituted 1836

Year		Strokes	Year		Strokes
1928	WA Sievwright	76	1960	Dr FWG Deighton	70
1929	CJH Tolley	73	1961	JG Salvesen	73
1930	RK Blair	77	1962	GW Mackie	73
1931	WB Torrance	74	1963	Dr FWG Deighton	74
1932	EM Prain	78	1964	G Robertson-Durham	75
1933	R Harris	77	1965	WS McLeod	75
1934	DH Kyle	72	1966	R Reid Jack	74
1935	LG Crawley	77	1967	CD Lawrie	71
1936	RH Oppenheimer	75	1968	DA Blair	71
1937	CGB Stevens	74	1969	RHJ Mackie	71
1938	LG Crawley	73	1970	Dr FWG Deighton	72
1939	LG Crawley	75	1971	RHJ Mackie	74
1940-45	*No competition owing to the War*		1972	A Sinclair	73
1946	GW Mackie	75	1973	Dr FWG Deighton	71
1947	Donald Cameron	74	1974	DA Blair	74
1948	GH Micklem	71	1975	M Lee	75
1949	RH Oppenheimer	74	1976	D Montagu	73
1950	TA Torrance	75	1977	EJ Threlfall	72
1951	Donald Cameron	72	1978	DP Davidson	71
1952	JC Wilson	72	1979	PD Kelley	73
1953	Dr FWG Deighton	74	1980	C McLachlan	75
1954	JC Wilson	68	1981	C McLachlan	66
1955	DA Blair	70	1982	P Bucher	73
1956	R Reid Jack	71	1983	GM Simmers	74
1957	AMM Bucher	70	1984	HM Campbell	72
1958	GH Micklem	70	1985	Dr DM Lawrie	69
1959	DA Blair	74	1986	MJ Reece	73

The George Glennie Medal

presented by the Royal Blackheath Golf Club (lowest aggregate score at Spring and Autumn Meetings)

Instituted 1882

Year		Strokes	Year		Strokes
1930	JH Nock	159	1962	M Tweddell	150
1931	J Gordon Simpson	154	1963	Dr FWS Deighton	159
1932	WB Torrance	160	1964	WR Alexander	150
1933	J Gordon Simpson	155	1965	R Reid Jack	147
1934	DH Kyle	150	1966	Dr FWG Deighton	148
1935	LG Crawley	154	1967	CD Lawrie	148
1936	LG Crawley	148	1968	CD Lawrie	149
1937	CGB Stevens	149	1969	WF Callander, Jr	148
1938	LG Crawley	145	1970	Dr FWG Deighton	149
1939-45	*No Competition owing to the War*		1971	WMS Ironside	149
1946	GW Mackie	155	1972	M Lee	146
1947	Dondald Cameron	152	1973	Dr FWG Deighton	140
1948	CJH Tolley	148	1974	PBM Bucher	155
1949	CJH Tolley	148	1975	A Sinclair	150
1950	Dr CRD Leeds	155	1976	PBM Bucher	150
1951	Donald Cameron	146	1977	C McLachlan	149
1952	JM Dykes	148	1978	DP Davidson	145
1953	KG Patrick	150	1979	PD Kelley	150
1954	JC Wilson	140	1980	RD Muckart, Jr	152
1955	Major DA Blair	139	1981	C MacLachlan	139
1956	Dr FWG Deighton	145	1982	H Campbell	147
1957	DW Nisbet	147	1983	AJ Low	147
1958	GH Micklem	144	1984	HM Campbell	150
1959	Dr FWG Deighton	149	1985	Dr DM Lawrie	148
1960	Dr FWG Deighton	145	1986	DW Frame	146
		143			

Part VII
Interesting Facts and Record Scoring

Interesting Facts and Unusual Incidents

Royal Golf Clubs

● The right to the designation *Royal* is bestowed by the favour of the Sovereign or a member of the Royal House. In most cases the title is granted along with the bestowal of royal patronage on the club. The Perth Golfing Society was the first to receive the designation *Royal*. That was accorded in June 1833. King William IV bestowed the honour on the Royal and Ancient Club in 1834.

Royal and Presidential Golfers

● In the long history of the Royal and Ancient game no reigning British monarch has played in an open competition. The Duke of Windsor, when Prince of Wales in 1922, competed in the Royal and Ancient Autumn Medal at St Andrews. He also took part in competitions at Mid-Surrey, Sunningdale, Royal St George's and in the Parliamentary Handicap. He also occasionally competed in American events, sometimes partnered by a professional, and on a private visit to London in 1952 he competed in the Autumn competition of Royal St George's at Sandwich scoring 97.

● King George VI (when Duke of York) in 1930 and the Duke of Kent in 1937 also competed in the Autumn Meeting of the Royal and Ancient, these occasions being after they had formally played themselves into the Captaincy of the Club and each returned his card in the medal round.

● King Leopold of Belgium played in the Belgian Amateur Championship at Le Zoute, the only reigning monarch ever to have played in a national championship. The Belgian King played in many competitions subsequent to his abdication. In 1949 he reached the quarter-finals of the French Amateur Championship at St Cloud, playing as Count de Rethy.

● King Baudouin of Belgium in 1958 played in the triangular match Belgium-France-Holland and won his match against a Dutch player. He also took part in the Gleneagles Hotel tournament (playing as Mr B de Rethy), partnered by Dai Rees in 1959.

● HRH Prince Claus of the Netherlands played in the American-Express Pro-Am preceding the 1971 Dutch Open. His handicap was 18. Partnered by Peter Oosterhuis, he won the same event in 1974 with a score of 62.

● US President Gerald Ford played in the pro-am before the 1975 Jackie Gleason Classic in a group which included Jack Nicklaus. Following his defeat in the 1977 presidential election, he became a fairly frequent competitor at pro-am tournaments and succeeded in holing in one (his first ever) during the 1977 Memphis Classic.

● The King of Morocco is an enthusiastic golfer and plays frequently with top professionals, in particular Billy Casper.

● Exiled King Constantine of Greece is also a keen golfer. Since 1973 he has played in several pro-am tournaments.

● President Kaunda of Zambia is a keen supporter and player of the game. There is a 9-hole course in the grounds of the Presidential Palace at Lusaka where he plays regularly.

First Lady Golfer

● Mary Queen of Scots, who was beheaded on 8th February, 1587, was probably the first lady golfer so mentioned by name. As evidence of her indifference to the fate of Darnley, her husband who was murdered at Kirk o' Field, Edinburgh, she was charged at her trial with having played at golf in the fields beside Seton a few days after his death.

Record Championship Victories

● In the Amateur Championship at Muirfield, 1920, Captain Carter, an Irish golfer, defeated an American entrant by 10 and 8. This is the only known instance where a player has won every hole in an Amateur Championship tie.

● In the final of the Canadian Ladies Championship at Rivermead, Ottawa, 1921, Cecil Leitch defeated Mollie McBride by 17 and 15. Miss Leitch only lost 1 hole in the match, the ninth. She was 14 up at the end of the first round, and only 3 holes were necessary in the second round, Miss Leitch winning them all. She won 18 holes out of 21 played, lost 1, and halved 2.

● In the final of the French Ladies' Open Championship at Le Touquet in 1927, Mlle de la Chaume (St Cloud) defeated Mrs Alex Johnston (Moor Park) by 15 and 14, the largest victory in a European golf championship.

● At Prestwick in 1934, W Lawson Little, Presidio, San Francisco, defeated James Wallace, Troon Portland, by 14 and 13 in the final of the Amateur Championship, the record victory in the Amateur Championship. Wallace failed to win a single hole.

● The largest victory in the Walker Cup in 18-hole matches was in 1979 when American Scott Hoch beat Jim Buckley by 9 and 7. Buckley had a back injury.

Outstanding Records in Championships, International Matches and on the Professional Circuit

● The record number of victories in the Open Championship is six, held by Harry Vardon who won in 1896-98-99-1903-11-14.

● Five-time winners of the Championship are JH Taylor in 1894-95-1900-09-13; James Braid in 1901-05-06-08-10; Peter Thomson in 1954-55-56-58-65 and Tom Watson in 1975-77-80-82-83. Thomson's 1965 win was achieved when the Championship had become a truly international event. In 1957 he finished second behind Bobby Locke. By winning again in 1958 Thomson was prevented only by Bobby Locke from winning five consecutive Open Championships.

● Four successive victories in the Open by *Young* Tom Morris is a record so far never equalled. He won in 1868-69-70-72. (The Championship was not played in 1871.) Other four-time winners are Bobby Locke in 1949-50-52-57, Walter Hagen in 1922-24-28-29, Willie Park 1860-63-66-75, and *Old* Tom Morris 1861-62-64-67.

● Since the Championship began in 1860, players who have won three times in succession are Jamie Anderson, Bob Ferguson, and Peter Thomson.

● Robert Tyre Jones won the Open three times in 1926-27-30; the Amateur in 1930; the American Open in 1923-26-29-30; and the American Amateur in 1924-25-27-28-30. In winning the four major golf titles of the world in one year (1930) he achieved a feat unlikely ever to be equalled. Jones retired from competitive golf after winning the 1930 American Open, the last of these Championships, at the age of 28.

● Jack Nicklaus has had the most wins (six) in the US Masters Tournament, followed by Arnold Palmer with four.

● In modern times there are four championships generally regarded as standing above all others–the Open, US Open, US Masters, and USPGA. Four players have held all these titles, Gene Sarazen, Ben Hogan, Gary Player, and Jack Nicklaus, who in 1978 became the first player to have held each of them at least three times. His record in these events is–Open 1966-70-78; US Open 1962-67-72-80; US Masters 1963-65-66-72-75-86; USPGA 1963-71-73-75-80. His total of major championships is now 18.

The nearest approach to achieving the Grand Slam of the Open, US Open, US Masters and USPGA in one year was by Ben Hogan in 1953 when he won the first three and could not compete in the USPGA as it then overlapped with the Open Championship.

● In 1975 Jack Nicklaus came very near to winning the Grand Slam, winning the Masters and the USPGA and finishing only two shots and one shot behind the winning scores in the US Open and the Open Championship respectively.

● The record number of victories in the US Open is four, held by W Anderson, Bobby Jones, Ben Hogan and Jack Nicklaus.

● Bobby Jones (amateur), Gene Sarazen, Ben Hogan, Lee Trevino and Tom Watson are the only players to have won the Open and US Open Championships in the same year.

● John Ball holds the record number of victories in the Amateur Championship, which he won eight times. Next comes Michael Bonallack with five wins.

● In winning the Amateur Championship in 1970 Michael Bonallack became the first player to win in three consecutive years.

● Cecil Leitch and Joyce Wethered each won the British Ladies' title four times.

● The English Amateur record number of victories is held by Michael Bonallack, who has won the title five times.

● The Scottish Amateur record is held by Ronnie Shade, who won five titles in successive years–1963-64-65-66-67. His long reign as Champion ended when he was beaten in the fourth round of the 1968 Championship after winning 44 consecutive matches.

● Joyce Wethered established an unbeaten record by winning the English Ladies' in five successive years from 1920 to 1924 inclusive.

● In winning the Amateur Championships of Britain and America in 1934 and 1935 Lawson Little won 31 consecutive matches. Other dual winners of these championships in the same year are RT Jones (1930) and

Bob Dickson (1967).

● Gary Player won the South African Open for the 13th time in 1981. He has also won the Australian Open seven times.

● Peter Thomson's victory in the 1971 New Zealand Open Championship was his ninth in that championship.

● In a four week spell in 1971, Lee Trevino won in succession the US Open, the Canadian Open and the Open Championships.

● The finalists in the 1970 Amateur Championship, MF Bonallack and W Hyndman, were the same as in 1969. This was the first time the same two players reached the final in successive years.

● Seve Ballesteros holds the record for most wins in one year on the European Tour, 6 in 1986; this followed his record equalling number in 1985. The best British players have been Bernard Hunt in 1963 and Nick Faldo in 1983, both with 5 victories.

● On the US professional circuit the greatest number of consecutive victories is 11, achieved by Byron Nelson in 1945. Nelson also holds the record for most victories in one calendar year, again in 1945 when he won a total of 18 tournaments.

● Jack Nicklaus and the late Walter Hagen have had five wins each in the USPGA Championship. All Hagen's wins were in successive years and at match play; all Nicklaus's at stroke play.

● In 1953 Flori van Donck of Belgium had seven major victories in Europe, including the Open Championships of Switzerland, Italy, Holland, Germany and Belgium.

● In 1947 Norman von Nida (Australia) had seven major tournament victories in England.

● Mrs Anne Sander won four major amateur titles each under a different name. She won the US Ladies' in 1958 as Miss Quast, in 1961 as Mrs Decker, in 1963 as Mrs Welts and the British Ladies' in 1980 as Mrs Sander.

● The highest number of appearances in the Ryder Cup matches is held by Christy O'Connor who made his tenth appearance in 1973.

● The greatest number of appearances in the Walker Cup matches is held by Irishman Joe Carr who made his tenth appearance in 1967.

● In the Curtis Cup Mary McKenna made her ninth consecutive appearance in 1986.

● Players who have represented their country in both Walker and Ryder Cup matches are Fred Haas, Ken Venturi, Gene Littler, Jack Nicklaus, Tommy Aaron, Mason Rudolph, Bob Murphy, Lanny Wadkins, Tom Kite, Jerry Pate, Craig Stadler, Jay Haas and Bill Rodgers (US), and Norman Drew, Peter Townsend, Peter Oosterhuis, Clive Clark, Howard Clark, Mark James, Michael King, Paul Way and Sandy Lyle (British Isles).

Remarkable Recoveries in Match Play

● There have been two remarkable recoveries in the Walker Cup Matches. In 1930 at Sandwich, JA Stout, Great Britain, round in 68, was 4 up at the end of the first round against Donald Moe. Stout started in the second round, 3, 3, 3, and was 7 up. He was still 7 up with 13 to play. Moe, who went round in 67, won back the 7 holes to draw level at the 17th green. At the 18th or 36th of the match, Moe, after a long drive placed his iron shot within three feet of the hole and won the match by 1 hole.

● In 1936 at Pine Valley, George Voigt and Harry Girvan for America were 7 up with 11 to play against Alec Hill and Cecil Ewing. The British pair drew equal at the 17th hole, or the 35th of the match, and the last hole was halved.

● In the 1965 Piccadilly Match-Play Championship Gary Player beat Tony Lema after being 7 down with 17 to play.

● Bobby Cruickshank, the old Edinburgh player, had an extraordinary recovery in a 36-hole match in a USPGA Championship for he defeated Al Watrous after being 11 down with 12 to play.

● In a match at the Army GC, Aldershot, on 5th July, 1974, for the Gradoville Bowl, MC Smart was eight down with eight to play against Mike Cook. Smart succeeded in winning all the remaining holes and the 19th for victory.

Oldest Champions

Open Championship

Belt: 46 years. Tom Morris sen in 1867.

Cup: 44 years 93 days. Roberto De Vicenzo in 1967.
44 years 42 days. Harry Vardon in 1914.
42 years 97 days. JH Taylor in 1913.

Amateur Championship: Hon Michael Scott, 54 years, Hoylake 1933.

British Ladies Amateur: Mrs Jessie Valentine, 43 years, Hunstanton 1958.

Scottish Amateur: JM Cannon, 53 years, Troon 1969.

English Amateur: Terry Shingler, 41 years 11 months, Walton Heath 1977. Gerald Micklem, 41 years 8 months, Royal Birkdale 1947.

UK Professional: Dai Rees, 60 years, equal second Martini International, Barnton 1973.

US Open: Ted Ray (GB), 43 years, Inverness Ohio 1920.

US Amateur: Jack Westland, 47 years, Seattle 1952. Westland was defeated in the 1931 final, 21 years previously, by Francis Ouimet at Beverley, Chicago, Illinois.

US Masters: Jack Nicklaus, 46 years, in 1986.

USPGA; Julius Boros, 48 years, in 1968. Lee Trevino, 43 years, in 1984.

USPGA Tour: Sam Snead, 52 years, Greensborough Open in 1965. Julius Boros lost play-off in Westchester Classic 1975. Sam Snead, 61 years, equal second in Glen Campbell Open 1974.

Youngest Champions

Open Championship

Belt: 17 years 5 months. Tom Morris, jun in 1868.

Cup: 21 years 25 days. Willie Auchterlonie in 1893.

21 years 5 months. Tom Morris, jun in 1872.

22 years 103 days. Severiano Ballesteros in 1979.

Amateur Championship: JC Beharrell, 18 years 1 month, Troon 1956. R Cole (S Africa) 18 years 1 month, Carnoustie 1966.

British Ladies Amateur: May Hezlett, 17 years, Newcastle Co Down 1899. Michelle Walker, 18 years, Alwoodley 1971.

English Amateur: Nick Faldo, 18 years, Lytham St Annes 1975. Paul Downes, 18 years, Birkdale 1978.

English Amateur Stroke Play: Ronan Rafferty, 16 years, Hunstanton 1980.

British Ladies Open Stroke Play: Janet Melville, 20 years, Foxhills 1978.

Disqualifications

Disqualifications are now numerous, usually for some irregularity over signing a scorecard or for late arrival at the first tee. We therefore show here only incidents in major events involving famous players or players who were in a winning position or, alternatively, incidents which were in themselves unusual.

● JJ McDermott, the American Open Champion 1911-12, arrived for the Open Championship at Prestwick in 1914 to discover that he had made a mistake of a week in the date the championship began. The American could not play as the qualifying rounds were completed on the day he arrived.

● An amusing case was that of a competitor in the Amateur Championship at Prestwick in 1922. He boarded the train at Ayr thinking it stopped at Prestwick, but it did not halt until Troon some miles further on. The railway runs alongside the first hole at Prestwick and the player frantically yelled from the train that he would be back as soon as he could, but that was of no avail.

● The Hon Michael Scott was disqualified in the third round of the 1910 Amateur Championship for not being on the tee in time. He was also disqualified in the 1924 championship when the starting times owing to slowness on the course were nearly 40 minutes late. Scott calculated that his starting time would be at least half an hour late, but he failed to observe that there was an interval of forty-five minutes in the times for starting, and consequently starting had resumed at times given on the programme.

● In the Amateur Championship at Sandwich in 1937, Brigadier-General Critchley, arriving on the *Queen Mary*, which had been delayed by fog, at Southampton from New York, flew by specially chartered aeroplane to Sandwich. He circled over the clubhouse, so that the officials knew he was nearly there, but he arrived six minutes late, and his name had been struck out. At the same championship a player, entered from Burma, who had travelled across the Pacific and the American Continent, and also was on the *Queen Mary*, travelled from Southampton by motor car and arrived four hours after his starting time to find after journeying more than halfway round the world he was *struck out*.

● Archie Compston was disqualified in the American Open Championship, 1932, for being late, and in the 1941 Championship Johnny Bulla was disqualified for starting *before* his time.

● An unprecedented disqualification was that of A Murray in the New Zealand Open Championship, 1937. Murray, who was New Zealand Champion in 1935, was playing with JP Hornabrook, New Zealand Amateur Champion, and at the 8th hole in the last round, while waiting for his partner to putt, Murray dropped a ball on the edge of the green and made a practice putt along the edge. Murray returned the lowest score in the championship, but he was disqualified for taking the practice putt.

● At the Open Championship at St Andrews in 1946, John Panton, Glenbervie, in the evening practised putting on a green on the New Course, which was one of the qualifying courses. He himself reported his inadvertence to the Royal and Ancient and he was disqualified.

● At the Open Championship, Sandwich, 1949, C Rotar, an American, qualified by four strokes to compete in the championship but he was disqualified because he had used a putter which did not conform to the accepted form and make of a golf club, the socket being bent over the centre of the club head. This is the only case where a player has been disqualified in the Open Championship for using an illegal club.

● In the 1957 American Women's Open Championship, Mrs Jackie Pung had the lowest score, 298 over four rounds, but lost the championship. The card she signed for the final round read *five* at the 4th hole instead of the correct *six*. Her total of 72 was correct but the error, under rigid rules, resulted in her disqualification. Betty Jameson, who partnered Mrs Pung and also returned a wrong score, was also disqualified.

Longest Match

● WR Chamberlain, a retired farmer, and George New, a postmaster at Chilton Foliat, on 1st August, 1922, met at Littlecote, the 9-hole course of Sir Ernest Wills, and they agreed to play every Thursday afternoon over the course. This they did until New's sudden death on 13th January, 1938. An accurate record of the matches was kept giving details of each round including wind direction and playing conditions. In the elaborate system nearly two million facts were recorded. They played 814 rounds, and aggregated 86,397 strokes, of which Chamberlain took 44,008 and New 42,371. New, therefore, was 1,637 strokes up. The last round of all was halved, a suitable end to such an unusual contest.

Longest Ties

● The longest known ties in 18-hole match play rounds in major events were in an early round of the News of the World Match Play Championship at Turnberry in 1960, when WS Collins beat WJ Branch at the 31st hole and in the third round of the same tournament at Walton Heath in 1961 when Harold Henning beat Peter Alliss also at the 31st hole.

● In the 1970 Scottish Amateur Championship at Balgownie, Aberdeen, E Hammond beat J McIvor at the 29th hole in their second round tie.

● CA Palmer beat Lionel Munn at the 28th hole at Sandwich in 1908. This is the record tie of the British Amateur Championship. Munn has also been engaged in two other extended ties in the Amateur Championship. At Muirfield, in 1932, in the semi-final, he was defeated by John de Forest, the ultimate winner, at the 26th hole, and at St Andrews, in 1936, in the second round he was defeated by JL Mitchell, again at the 26th hole.

The following examples of long ties are in a different category for they occurred in competitions, either stroke play or match play, where the conditions stipulated that in the event of a tie a further stated number of holes had to be played–in some cases 36 holes, but mostly 18. With this method a vast number of extra holes was sometimes necessary to settle ties.

● The longest known was between two American women in a tournament at Peterson (New Jersey) when 88 extra holes were required before Mrs Edwin Labaugh emerged as winner.

● In a match on the Queensland course, Australia, in October, 1933, HB Bonney and Col HCH Robertson versus BJ Canniffe and Dr Wallis Hoare required to play a further four 18-hole matches after being level at the end of the original 18 holes. In the fourth replay Hoare and Caniffe won by 3 and 2 which meant that 70 extra holes had been necessary to decide the tie.

● After finishing all square in the final of the Dudley GC's foursomes competition in 1950, FW Mannell and AG Walker played a further three 18-hole replays against T Poole and E Jones, each time finishing all square. A further 9 holes were then arranged when Mannell and Walker won by 3 and 2 making a total of 61 extra holes to decide the tie.

● RA Whitcombe and Mark Seymour tied for first prize in the Penfold £750 Tournament at St Annes-on-Sea, in 1934. They had to play off over 36 holes and tied again. They were then required to play another 9 holes when Whitcombe won with 34 against 36. The tournament was over 72 holes. The first tie added 36 holes and the extra 9 holes made an aggregate of 117 holes to decide the winner. This is a record in first-class British golf but in no way compares with other long ties as it involved only two replays–one of 36 holes and one of 9.

● In the American Open Championship at Toledo, Ohio, in 1931, G Von Elm and Billy Burke tied for the title. Each returned aggregates of 292. On the first replay both finished in 149 for 36 holes but on the second replay Burke won with a score of 148 against 149. This is a record tie in a national open championship.

● Paul Downes was beaten by Robin Davenport at the 9th extra hole in the 4th round of the 1981 English Amateur Championship. A record marathon match for the championship.

● Severiano Ballesteros was beaten by Johnny Miller at the 9th extra hole of a sudden-death play-off at the 1982 million dollar Sun City Challenge, a record for any 72 hole professional event.

● In the semi-finals of the Wentworth Mixed Foursomes at Aldeburgh GC on 28th August, 1983, John Raison and Jackie Sheffield beat Andrew Mangeot and June Mangeot (the holders) at the 9th extra hole (the 27th).

Long Drives

It is impossible to state with any certainty what is the longest ever drive. Many long drives have never been measured and many others have most likely never been brought to our attention. Then there are several outside factors which can produce freakishly long drives, such as a strong following wind, downhill terrain or bonehard ground. Where all three of these favourable conditions prevail outstandingly long drives can be achieved. Another consideration is that a long drive made during a tournament is a different proposition from one made for length alone, either on the practice ground, a long driving competition or in a game of no consequence. All this should be borne in mind when considering the long drives shown here.

● Tommie Campbell of Portmarnock is regarded as having hit the longest drive without any favourable conditions prevailing with a drive of 392 yards at Dun Laoghaire GC in July 1964.

● Playing in Australia, American George Bayer is reported to have driven to within chipping distance of a 589 yards hole. *It was certainly a drive of over 500 yards,* said Bayer acknowledging the strong following wind, sharp downslope where his ball landed and the bonehard ground.

● American senior professional Mike Austin, playing in the US National Seniors' Open at Las Vegas in 1974, amazingly drove his ball many yards through the 5th green at Winterwood GC, a hole measuring 450 yards. The total length of his downwind drive, which struck hard ground, was given at 515 yards.

● In September, 1934, over the East Devon course, THV Haydon, Wimbledon, drove to the edge of the 9th green which was a hole of 465 yards, giving a drive of not less than 450 yards. The hole was downhill and presumably other favourable conditions were also present. Haydon is also reported to have nearly driven the 15th hole (420 yards) at Royal Wimbledon in October, 1929. The ball finished just short of the green on a hole which was slightly uphill all the way and when the following wind was described as only a breeze.

● EC Bliss drove 445 yards at Herne Bay in August, 1913. The drive was measured by a Government Surveyor who also measured the drop in height from tee to resting place of the ball at 57 feet.

● Craig Wood of America in the play-off for the 1933 Open Championship at St Andrews drove into the bunkers in the face of the hill short of the 5th green. This was estimated at 430 yards. There was a considerable following wind and the ground was parched dry.

● At Sitwell Park, Rotherham, in 1935, W Smithson, the home professional, drove the 2nd green, a distance of 416 yards. Smithson's ball carried a dyke which ran across the hole at a distance of 380 yards from the tee. The remaining distance was a steep uphill approach to the green where his ball finished pin-high. A strong following wind was present.

● George Johnson in 1972, with the assistance of a following wind, drove a ball 413 yards at the 8th hole at Delamere Forest.

● The longest recorded drive on the US tournament circuit is 426 yards by George Bayer in the 1955 Tucson Open. It is assumed that he was assisted by some favourable conditions but this is not established.

Long Carries

● At Sitwell Park, Rotherham, in 1935, W Smithson, the home professional, drove a ball which carried a dyke at 380 yards from the 2nd tee.

● George Bell, of Penrith GC, New South Wales, Australia, using a number 2 wood drove across the Nepean River, a certified carry of 309 yards in a driving contest in 1964.

● After the 1986 Irish Professional Championship at Waterville, Co. Kerry, four long-hitting professionals tried for the longest-carry record over water, across a lake in the Waterville Hotel grounds. Liam Higgins, the local professional, carried 310 yards and Paul Leonard 311, beating the previous record by 2 yards.

● In the 1972 Algarve Open at Penina, Henry Cotton vouched for a carry of 305 yards over a ditch at the 18th hole by long-hitting Spanish professional Francisco Abreu. There was virtually no wind assistance.

● At the Home International matches at Portmarnock in 1949 a driving competition was held in which all the players in the English, Scottish, Welsh and Irish teams competed. The actual carry was measured. The longest was 280 yards by Jimmy Bruen.

● When Walter Hagen was in Britain for the Open Championship in 1928, he drove a ball from the roof of the Savoy Hotel to the other side of the Thames.

● On 6th April, 1976, Tony Jacklin hit a number of balls into Vancouver harbour, Canada, from the 495-foot high roof of a new building complex. The longest carry was measured at 389 yards.

Long Hitting

There have been numerous long hits, not on

golf courses, where an outside agency has assisted the length of the shot. Such an example was a 'drive' by Liam Higgins in 1986, on the Airport runway at Baldonal, near Dublin, of 632 yards.

Longest Albatrosses

● The longest-known albatrosses (three under par) recorded at par 5 holes are:

● 609 yards–15th hole at Mahaka Inn West Course, Hawaii, by John Eakin of California on 12th November, 1972.

● 602 yards–16th hole at Whiting Field Golf Course, Milton, Florida, by 27-year-old Bill Graham with a drive and a 3-wood, aided by a 25 mph tail wind.

● The longest-known albatrosses in Open Championships are:

580 yards–14th hole at Crans-sur-Sierre, by American Billy Casper in the 1971 Swiss Open.

558 yards–5th hole at Muirfield by American Johnny Miller in the 1972 Open Championship.

Eagles (Multiple and Consecutive)

● Wilf Jones scored three consecutive eagles at the first three holes at Moor Hall GC when playing in a competition there on August Bank Holiday Monday 1968. He scored 3, 1, 2 at holes measuring 529 yards, 176 yards and 302 yards.

● In a round of the 1980 Jubilee Cup, a mixed foursomes match play event of Colchester GC, Mrs Nora Booth and her son Brendan scored three consecutive gross eagles of 1, 3, 2 at the 8th, 9th and 10th holes.

● In the Wisconsin (USA) Oil Dealers' annual 18-hole tournament, Bernard Antisdel scored an eagle 2 at the same 285-yards hole in four consecutive years, from 1960 to 1963.

● Three players in a four-ball match at Kington GC, Herefordshire, on 22nd July, 1948, all had eagle 2s at the 18th hole (272 yards). They were RN Bird, R Morgan and V Timson.

● Four Americans from Wisconsin on holiday at Gleneagles in 1977 scored three eagles and a birdie at the 300-yard par-4 14th hole on the King's course. The birdie was by Dr Kim Lulloff and the eagles by Dr Gordon Meiklejohn, Richard Johnson and Jack Kubitz.

● In an open competition at Glen Innes GC, Australia on 13th November, 1977, three players in a four-ball scored eagle 3s at the 9th hole (442 metres). They were Terry Marshall, Roy McHarg and Jack Rohleder.

Speed of Golf Ball and Club Head and Effect of Wind and Temperature

● In *The Search for the Perfect Swing*, a scientific study of the golf swing, a first class golfer is said to have the club head travelling at 100 mph at impact. This will cause the ball to leave the club at 135 mph. An outstandingly long hitter might manage to have the club head travelling at 130 mph which would produce a ball send-off speed of 175 mph. The resultant shot would carry 280 yards.

● According to Thomas Hardman, Wilson's director of research and development, wind will reduce or increase the flight of a golf ball by approximately 1½ yards for every mile per hour of wind. Every two degrees of temperature will make a yard difference in a ball's flight.

Highest Golf Courses

● The highest golf course in the world is thought to be the Tuctu GC in Peru which is 14,335 feet above sea-level. High courses are also found in Bolivia with the La Paz GC being about 13,500 feet. In the Himalayas, near the border with Tibet, a 9-hole course at 12,800 feet has been laid out by keen golfers in the Indian Army.

● The highest known course in Europe is at Sestriere in the Italian Alps, 6,500 feet above sea-level.

● The highest courses in Great Britain are Leadhills in Scotland at 1,500 feet, Tredegar in Wales rising to 1,300 feet and Church Stretton in England at 1,250 feet.

● Although no course exists at the place, Captain FES Adair tells of playing shots on a suitable piece of grassy ground over 16,000 feet when crossing a pass into Tibet.

Lowest Courses

● The lowest known course in the world was at Kallia, south of Jericho. No longer in existence, this 9-hole course, running along the shore of the Dead Sea, lay 1,250 feet below normal sea-level.

Coldest Courses

● Golf courses are to be found in every climate. A Scot founded the Polar Bear Club in the Arctic. Eskimos became members.

● A group of golfers at Thule air base held a competition in 1975 at the top of Mount Dundas in Greenland, some 800 miles from the North Pole. The golfers carried their own piece of carpet which served as teeing grounds and greens.

● Missionary Dave Freeman in 1975 founded the High Country Club, a 9-hole course with sand greens off the shores of the Beaufort Sea in Northern Canada, 400 miles inside the Arctic Circle. Membership is over 700. Another keen golfer in this area, Bill Josh, the base manager of the local airline at Victoria Island, each winter stakes out 9 holes on the Beaufort Sea when it freezes over. The temperature is said to fall to below minus 40 degrees.

● Although shut in for three years amid the eternal snow and ice of the Antarctic, Arbroath golfer Munro Sievwright did not neglect his practice with club and ball. His luggage included three clubs and a dozen red painted golf balls. In the light of the midnight sun he hit adventurous shots along the white wasteland on *fairways* of hard-packed snow. Munro, a physicist at the Antarctic Survey Base at Halley Bay, won the Carnoustie Craw's Nest Tassie in 1962, and was in the Edinburgh team which won the Scottish Universities' Championship in 1963.

● In September, 1956, Major Gus Watson, chief scientific officer of the British Antarctic Expedition's advance party, radioed the following account of life at the explorer's base camp: *Summer has come to the Antarctic–and with it the golfing season. Our two carpenters brought their clubs with them and now they spend much of their spare time driving, chipping and putting in the area around the hut.*

Longest Courses

● The longest course in the world is Dub's Dread GC, Piper, Kansas, USA measuring 8,101 yards (par 78).

● The longest course for the Open Championship was 7,252 yards at Carnoustie in 1968.

Longest Holes

● The longest hole in the world, as far as is known, is the 6th hole measuring 782 metres (860 yards) at Koolan Island GC, Western Australia. The par of the hole is 7. There are several holes over 700 yards throughout the world. At Teyateyaneng, South Africa, one hole measures 619 yards and another 37 yards.

● The longest hole for the Open Championship was 577 yards (6th hole) at Troon in 1973.

Longest Tournaments

● The longest tournament held was over 144 holes in the World Open at Pinehurst, N Carolina, USA, first held in 1973. Play was over two weeks with a cut imposed at the halfway mark.

● An annual tournament is played in Germany on the longest day of the year, comprising 100 holes' medal play. We are told that the players usually lose several pounds in weight during the tournament. The best return, in 1968, was 417 strokes.

Largest Entries

The Open–1413, St Andrews, 1984
The Amateur–488, St Andrews, 1958.
British Youths'–244, Woodhall Spa, 1979.
The Boys'–247, Formby, 1980.
Ladies' British Open Amateur–157, St Andrews, 1975.
British Ladies Stroke Play–120, Formby, 1985.
British Girls'–94, Hesketh, 1985.
English Amateur–370, Moortown, 1980, also Woodhall Spa, 1984.
English Open Amateur Stroke Play–313, Royal Cinque Ports, Deal 1984.
Irish Amateur–302, Portmarnock, 1974.
Scottish Amateur–244, Gullane, 1983.
Scottish Open Amateur Stroke Play–249, Dunbar, North Berwick, 1985.
Scottish Boys'–354, North Berwick, 1973.
Welsh Amateur–108, Prestatyn, 1980.
Welsh Boys'–112, Glamorganshire, 1975.

● The largest entry for a PGA ETPD event was 398 for the 1978 Colgate PGA Championship. Since 1985, when the all-exempt ruling was introduced, all PGA tournaments have had 144 competitors, slightly more or less.

● The 1976 Daily Mirror Amateur Tournament, which is a competition requiring a personal entry as opposed to a club entry on behalf of its members, drew an entry of 6,176 competitors.

● In 1952, Bobby Locke, the Open Champion, played a round at Wentworth, against any golfer in Britain. Cards costing 2s. 6d. each (12½p), were taken out by 24,000 golfers. The challenge was to beat the local par by more than Locke beat the par at Wentworth; 1,641 competitors, including women, succeeded in *beating* the Champion and each received a certificate signed by him. As a result of this challenge the British Golf Foundation benefited to the extent of £3,026, the proceeds from the sale of cards. A similar tournament was held in the United States and Canada when 87,094 golfers participated; 14,667 players bettered Ben Hogan's score under handicap. The fund benefited by $80,024.

Largest Prize Money

● The largest prize money for an event in Britain was £839,000 in the Dunhill Nations Cup at St Andrews in October 1985.

● In 1985 the total prize money at the Open at Royal St George's was £530,000, with a first prize of £65,000. In 1986 at Turnberry, these sums will be increased to £600,000 and £70,000 respectively.

● The Machrie Tournament of 1901 was the first tournament with a first prize of £100. It was won by JH Taylor, then Open Champion, who beat James Braid in the final.

● The world's richest tournament is the annual Million Dollar Sun City Challenge, held at the Gary Player Country Club in Bophuthatswana, first played in 1982 with a first prize of $500,000.

● For the Glasgow Herald Tournament at Gleneagles and the Daily Mail Tournament in 1921, the prize money for each event was 1,000 guineas, the first golf meetings where the prize-money was over £1,000. The Daily Mail Tournament was restored in 1936 with total prize money of £2,000 and the first prize, £500. This was the first tournament in Europe where £2,000 was the prize fund. In 1951 the Penfold-Bournemouth Festival of Britain Golf Tournament had a prize fund of £3,000 which was the largest then offered for a professional tournament in the British Isles. The winner received £650. A first prize of £1,000 was first played for in the Swallow-Penfold Tournament in 1955.

● (For prize money in the Open Championship see under Conditions and History of Open Championship.)

Attendance and Gate Money

Open Championship

Year	Attendance	Gate Money £
1962	37,098	15,207
1963	24,585	14,173
1964	35,954	14,704
1965	32,927	21,214
1966	40,182	23,075
1967	29,880	20,180
1968	51,819	31,907
1969	46,001	46,188
1970	81,593	62,744
1971	70,076	90,052
1972	84,746	98,925
1973	78,810	115,000
1974	92,796	158,729
1975	85,258	176,012
1976	92,021	243,793
1977	87,615	249,073
1978	125,271	421,474
1979	134,501	467,924
1980	131,610	538,288
1981	114,522	599,100
1982	133,299	665,000
1983	142,894	794,000
1984	193,126	1,050,000
1985	141,619	988,725
1986	133,130	

Holing-in-One

Holing-in-One–Odds Against

● At the Wanderers Club, Johannesburg in January, 1951, forty-nine amateurs and professionals each played three balls at a hole 146 yards long. Of the 147 balls hit, the nearest was by Koos de Beer, professional at Reading Country Club, which finished 10½ inches from the hole. Harry Bradshaw, the Irish professional who was touring with the British team in South Africa, touched the pin with his second shot, but the ball rolled on and stopped 3 feet 2 inches from the cup.

● A competition on similar lines was held in 1951 in New York when 1,409 players who had done a hole-in-one held a competition over several days at short holes on three New York golf courses. Each player was allowed a total of five shots, giving an aggregate of 7,045 shots. No player holed-in-one, and the nearest ball finished 3½ inches from the hole.

● A further illustration of the element of luck in holing-in-one is derived from an effort by Harry Gonder, an American professional, who in 1940 stood for 16 hours 25 minutes and hit 1,817 balls trying to do a 160 yard hole-in-one. He had two official witnesses and caddies to tee and retrieve the balls and count the strokes. His 1,756th shot struck the hole but stopped an inch from the hole. This was his nearest effort.

● Cyril Wagner, another American professional, got a hole-in-one in 805 shots.

● From this and other similar information an estimate of the odds against holing-in-one at any particular hole within the range of one shot was made at somewhere between 1,500 and 2,000 to 1 by a proficient player. Subsequently, however, statistical analysis in America has come up with the following odds: a male professional or top amateur 3,708 to 1; a female professional or top amateur 4,648 to 1; an average golfer 42,952 to 1.

Hole-in-One First Recorded

● Earliest recorded hole-in-one was in 1868 at the Open Championship when Tommy Morris (Young Tom) did the 8th hole 145 yards Prestwick in one stroke. This was the first of four Open Championships won successively by Young Tom.

● The first hole-in-one recorded with the 1.66 in ball was in 1972 by John G Salvesen, a member of the R & A Championship Committee. At the time this size of ball was only experimental. Salvesen used a 7-iron for his historical feat at the 11th hole on the Old Course, St Andrews.

Holing-in-One in Important Events

● **Since the day of the first known hole-in-one by Tom Morris jun, at the 8th hole (145 yards) at Prestwick in the 1868 Open Championship, holes-in-one, even in championships, have become too numerous for each to be recorded. Only where other unusual or interesting circumstances prevailed are the instances shown here.**

● 1878–Jamie Anderson, competing in the Open Championship at Prestwick, holed the 17th hole in one. Anderson was playing the next to last hole, and though it seemed then that he was winning easily, it turned out afterwards that if he had not taken this hole in one stroke he would very likely have lost. Anderson was just about to make his tee shot when Andy Stuart (winner of the first Irish Open Championship in 1892), who was acting as marker to Anderson, remarked he was standing outside the teeing ground, and that if he played the stroke from there he would be disqualified. Anderson picked up his ball and teed it in a proper place. Then he holed-in-one. He won the Championship by one stroke.

● 1885–AF Macfie in the fourth round of the initial competition at Hoylake for the Amateur Championship, holed the 14th or *Rushes* hole in one. Since then this particular hole at Hoylake has strangely enough been the scene of several holes-in-one in major championships–in 1898 by S Winkley Smith, West Middlesex, in the Amateur Championship; in 1902 by Daniel Brown, Musselburgh, in the Open Championship; and in 1925 by GNP Humphries, Stourbridge, in the English Amateur Championship.

● 1889–In the Open Championship at Musselburgh an amateur, who partnered Andrew Kirkaldy, holed the last hole in one. It was almost dark when the championship finished and when the player hit his cleek shot the green could scarcely be made out from the tee.

● 1906–R Johnston, North Berwick, competing in the Open Championship, did the 14th hole at Muirfield in one. Johnston played with only one club throughout–an adiustable head club.

● 1925–JH Taylor, in his second round in the Open Championship at Prestwick, did the 2nd hole in one stroke. In contrast, Murdoch (Troon Municipal), who played with Taylor, took 14 at the 1st hole.

● 1930–Maurice McCarthy, jun, in the qualifying stroke competition of the United States Amateur Championship at Merion did a hole-in-one. McCarthy tied for the last place and qualified for the Championship on the *play off.*

● 1933–In the final round of the Irish Open Championship over 36 holes at Newcastle, Co Down, on 23rd September, 1933, Eric Fiddian, Stourbridge, who was boy champion in 1927 and English champion in 1932, was opposed to Jack McLean. In the first round Fiddian did the 7th hole, 128 yards, in one stroke, and in the second round he did the 14th hole, 205 yards, also in one stroke. These remarkable strokes did not carry Fiddian to victory for he was defeated by 3 and 2.

● 1959–The first hole-in-one in the US Women's Open Championship was recorded. It was by Patty Berg on the 7th hole (170 yards) at Churchill Valley CC, Pittsburgh.

● 1962–On 6th April, playing in the second round of the Schweppes Close Championship at Little Aston, H Middleton of Shandon Park, Belfast, holed his tee shot at the 159 yards 5th hole, winning a prize of £1,000. Ten minutes later, playing two matches ahead of Middleton, RA Jowle, son of the professional, Frank Jowle, holed his tee shot at the 179 yards 9th hole. As an amateur he was rewarded by the sponsors with a £30 voucher.

● 1962–Dick Mayer, US professional, won £17,857 for scoring a hole-in-one in the Palm Springs tournament. This was the third successive year the feat had been performed in this tournament. The sponsors insured against *aces* with Lloyds of London.

● 1963–By holing out in one stroke at the 18th hole (156 yards) at Moor Park on the first day of the Esso Golden round-robin tournament, HR Henning, South Africa, won the £10,000 prize offered for this feat.

● 1967–Tony Jacklin in winning the Masters tournament at St George's, Sandwich, did the 16th hole in one. His ace has an exceptional place in the records for it was seen by millions on TV, the ball in view in its flight till it went into the hole in his final round of 64.

● 1971–John Hudson, 25-year-old professional at Hendon, achieved a near miracle when he holed two consecutive holes-in-one in the Martini Tournament at Norwich. They were at the 11th and 12th holes (195 yards and 311 yards respectively) in the second round. (See also section entitled *Holing Successive Holes-in-One.*).

● 1971–In the Open Championship at Birkdale, Lionel Platts holed-in-one at the 212-yard 4th hole in the second round. This was the first instance of an Open Championship hole-in-one being recorded by television. It was incidentally Platts' seventh ace of his career.

● 1972–Two holes-in-one were recorded at the 180-yard 5th hole at Pebble Beach in the US Open. They were achieved by Jerry

McGee in the third round and Bobby Mitchell in the final round.

● 1973–Peter Butler achieved what is thought to be the first hole-in-one in the Ryder Cup when he holed out at the 16th hole at Muirfield in the 1973 match.

● 1973–In the 1973 Open Championship at Troon, two holes-in-one were recorded, both at the 8th hole, known as the Postage Stamp, in the first round. They were achieved by Gene Sarazen and amateur David Russell, who were by coincidence respectively the oldest and youngest competitors.

● Mrs Argea Tissies, whose husband Hermann took 15 at Royal Troon's Postage Stamp 8th hole in the 1950 Open, scored a hole-in-one at the 2nd hole at Punta Ala in the second round of the Italian Ladies Senior Open of 1978. Exactly 5 years later on the same date, at the same time of day, in the same round of the same tournament at the same hole, she did it again with the same club.

Holing-in-One–Longest Holes

● Bob Mitera, when a 21-year-old American student, standing 5 feet 6 inches and weighing under 12 stones, claimed the world record for the longest hole-in-one. Playing over the appropriately named Miracle Hill course at Omaha, on 7th October, 1965, Bob holed his drive at the 10th hole, 447 yards long. The ground sloped sharply downhill. He was further aided by a strong following wind and (he admits) a lot of luck.

● Two longer holes-in-one have been achieved, but because they were at dog-leg holes they are not generally accepted as being the longest holes-in-one. They were 480 yards (5th hole, Hope CC, Arkansas) by L Bruce on 15th November, 1962 and 477 yards (14th hole, Martin County CC, Stuart, Florida) by Billy Newman on 13th August, 1972. The estimated length by cutting the corner was around 360 yards.

● In March, 1961, Lou Kretlow holed his tee shot at the 427 yards 16th hole at Lake Hefner course, Oklahoma City, USA.

● Another very long hole accomplished in one was the 9th hole at Hillcrest Golf Club, Winston-Salem, North Carolina, USA, by Mr Cardwell. The hole (425 yards) is a par four. The authenticity of this feat was vouched for by Ken C Abels, the Manager of the Hillcrest Golf Club.

● A ball driven by a driving machine holed out in one at the 435-yard 1st hole at Hermitage Country Club, Richmond, Virginia, USA.

● The longest known hole-in-one in Great Britain was the 393-yard 7th hole at West Lancashire GC, where in 1972 the assistant professional Peter Parkinson holed his tee shot.

● Other long holes-in-one recorded in Great Britain have been 380 yards (5th hole at Tankersley Park) by David Hulley in 1961; 380 yards (12th hole at White Webbs) by Danny Dunne on 30th July, 1976; 370 yards (17th hole at Chilwell Manor, distance from the forward tee) by Ray Newton in 1977; 365 yards (10th hole at Harewood Downs) by K Saunders in 1965; 365 yards (7th hole at Catterick Garrison GC) by Leslie Bruckner on 18th July, 1980.

● The longest-recorded hole-in-one by a woman was that accomplished in September, 1949 by Marie Robie–the 393-yard hole at Furnace Brook course, Wollaston, Mass, USA.

Holing-in-One–Greatest Number by One Person

47–Amateur Norman Manley of Long Beach, California.

42–US professional Art Wall between 1936 and April 1979.

35–Mancil Davis, professional at the Trophy Club, Forth Worth, Texas. Davis achieved his last in 1979 at the age of 25.

31–British professional CT le Chevalier who died in 1973.

17–British amateur, Jim Hay of Kirkintilloch GC.

10–Mrs Olga Penman, formerly of Harewood Downs GC.

At One Hole

10–Joe Vitullo at 16th hole of Hubbard GC, Ohio.

5–Left-hander, the late Fred Francis at 7th (now 16th) hole of Cardigan GC.

Holing-in-One–Greatest Frequency

● The greatest number of holes-in-one in a calendar year is 11, by JO Boydstone of California in 1962.

● John Putt of Frilford Heath GC had six holes-in-one in 1970, followed by three in 1971.

● Douglas Porteous, of Ruchill GC, Glasgow, achieved seven holes-in-one in the space of eight months. Four of them were scored in a five-day period from 26th to 30th September, 1974, in three consecutive rounds of golf. The first two were achieved at Ruchill GC in one round, the third in his next round there two days later, and the fourth at Clydebank and District GC in the next round another two days later. The following May, Porteous had another three holes-in-one, the first at Linn Park GC incredibly followed by two more in the one round at Clober GC. All the courses except Clydebank and District and Clober are municipal ones in and around Glasgow. (See also *Holing-in-One Twice in One Round.*)

● Mrs Kathleen Hetherington of West Essex has holed-in-one five times, four being at the 15th hole at West Essex. Four of her five aces were within seven months in 1966.

● Miss Dorothy Hill of Dumfries and Galloway GC holed-in-one three times in 11 days in 1977.

Holing Successive Holes-in-One

● Successive holes-in-one are rare; successive par 4 holes-in-one may be classed as near miracles. NL Manley performed the most incredible feat in September, 1964, at Del Valle Country Club, Saugus, California, USA. The par 4 7th (330 yards) and 8th (290 yards) are both slightly downhill, dog-leg holes. Manley had *aces* at both, en route to a course record of 61 (par 71).

● The first recorded example in Britain of a player holing-in-one stroke at each of two successive holes was achieved on 6th February, 1964, at the Walmer and Kingsdown course, Kent. The young assistant professional at that club, Roger Game (aged 17) holed out with a No. 4 wood at the 244-yard 7th hole, and repeated the feat at the 256-yard 8th hole, using a No. 5 iron.

● The first occasion of holing-in-one at consecutive holes in a major professional event occurred when John Hudson, 25-year-old professional at Hendon, holed-in-one at the 11th and 12th holes at Norwich during the second round of the 1971 Martini tournament. Hudson used a 4-iron at the 195-yard 11th and a driver at the 311-yard downhill 12th hole.

● Assistant professional Tom Doty (23 years), playing in a friendly match on a course near Chicago in October, 1971 had a remarkable four hole score which included two consecutive holes-in-one, sandwiched either side by an albatross and an eagle: 4th hole (500 yards)–2; 5th hole (360 yards dog-leg)–1; 6th hole (175 yards)–1; 7th hole (375 yards)–2. Thus he was 10 under par for four consecutive holes.

Holing-in-One Twice (or more) in Same Round by Same Person

(See also Successive Holes-in-One)

What might be thought to be a very rare feat indeed–that of holing-in-one twice in the same round–has in fact happened on many occasions as the following instances show. It is, nevertheless, compared to the number of golfers in the world, still something of an outstanding achievement. The first occasion known to us was in 1907 when J Ireland playing in a three-ball match at Worlington holed the 5th and 18th holes in one stroke and two years later in 1909 HC Josecelyne holed the 3rd (175 yards) and the 14th (115 yards) at Acton on 24th November.

● The Rev Harold Snider, aged 75, scored his first hole-in-one on 9th June, 1976 at the 8th hole of the Ironwood course, near Pheonix. By the end of his round he had scored three holes-in-one, the other two being at the 13th (110 yards) and 14th (135 yards). Ironwood is a par-3 course, giving more opportunity of scoring holes-in-one, but, nevertheless, three holes-in-one in one round on any type of course is an outstanding achievement.

● The first mention of two holes-in-one in a round by a woman is of special note in that it was followed later by a similar feat by another lady at the same club. On 19th May, 1942, Mrs W. Driver, of Balgowlah Golf Club, New South Wales, holed out in one at the 3rd and 8th holes in the same round, while on 29th July, 1948, Mrs F Burke at the same club holed out in one at the 2nd and 8th holes.

● The youngest-known person to have had two holes-in-one in one round was a 14-year-old American, Peter Townsend.

● The youngest British player was Ian Robertson in June, 1972, at Torphin Hill GC, Edinburgh, when 15 years old. The holes were the 252-yard 9th and 210-yard 14th.

● The youngest woman to have performed the feat was a 17-year-old, Marjorie Merchant, playing at the Lomas Athletic GC, Argentina, at the 4th (170 yards) and 8th (130 yards) holes.

Two Holes-in-One at Same Hole in Same Game

First in World

● George Stewart and Fred Spellmeyer at the 18th hole, Forest Hills, New Jersey, USA in October 1919.

First in Great Britain

● Miss G Clutterbuck and Mrs HM Robinson at the 15th hole (120 yards), St Augustine GC, Ramsgate, on 8th May, 1925.

Holing-in-One and Holing a Full Shot to Win a Championship or Match

Ending a match by holing-in-one or with a full shot is infrequent enough to be worthy of placing on record individually here.

● The most lucrative holing of a full shot to win occurred in the *Tam O'Shanter* World Championship at Chicago in 1953. Chandler

Harper appeared to have victory and the first prize of $25,000 in the bag when Lew Worsham holed a full wedge shot of some 135 yards for a 2 at the 410-yard last hole of the tournament to win by one stroke.

● In the first round of the Oxford and Cambridge Society's President's Putter at Rye, January, 1937, between PHF White, the West of England Championship, 1936, and Leonard Crawley, Crawley was two up and six to play. White won the next three to take the lead and then holed the 17th–230 yards–with his tee shot to win by 2 and 1.

● Willie Park, in 1898, at Troon in the second half of his match for £200 against Willie Fernie, holed a full brassie shot at the 7th hole–the 61st of the match–to win, the most dramatic ending to a first class professional match.

● When FE McCarroll (Queen's University), Belfast, won the Boyd Quaich at St Andrews in 1966, his 291st and last shot, played with a sand wedge, finished in the hole for an eagle 2.

● MG Milton completed a match in the Moray and Nairn league on 22nd May, 1972, at Nairn Dunbar GC by holing-in-one at the 174-yard 15th to win by 5 and 3.

● In the 1973 Welsh Amateur at Ashburnham, Ted Davies, defending champion, ended one of his matches by holing-in-one at the 13th hole.

● In the 1974 Home International matches at the Royal St David's GC, against Ireland in the top foursomes match, Sandy Pirie of Scotland holed-in-one at the last hole giving Scotland a one-hole victory.

● Two Australian golfers, John Wise and Glen Hutton, influenced by the fact that two tennis players had signed a contract for a 100 match series, agreed to play a similar golf series limited to ten matches per year. In 1967 Hutton won the 99th match to lead in the series by one match. In the 100th match Wise holed-in-one at the last hole to win the hole, the game and end the series all square.

● In the Assistants' Championship at Worsley, 1950, Harry Weetman (Hartsbourne Golf Club), who won the Championship for the second year in succession, holed his tee shot at the 172-yard 18th hole in the final round–the 72nd hole of the championship. Weetman, however, had had several strokes in hand for victory.

Holing-in-One–Miscellaneous Incidents

(See also Holing-in-One in the Championships)

● The late Harry Vardon, who scored the greatest number of victories in the Open Championship, only once did a hole-in-one. That was in 1903 at Mundesley, Norfolk, where Vardon was convalescing from a long illness.

● Walter Hagen, one of the greatest and most colourful golfers of all time, in his long career also did only one hole-in-one–at the 6th hole at Worcester, Mass, in 1925. It was the first shot played with a new ball, he used a No 1 iron and it was the first of July.

● In April 1984 Joseph McCaffrey and his son, Gordon, each holed in one in the Spring Medal at the 164 yard 12th hole at Vale of Leven Club, Dunbartonshire.

● Having watched Paul Hahn play a trick shot from a kneeling position, 16-year-old Jim Hadderer, of Elgin, Illinois, USA, tried the same *gag* at a 190-yard hole at the Wing Park course in 1965. He improved on Hahn's performance by popping the ball into the hole in one.

● Identical twins, John and Desmond Rosser scored holes-in-one in consecutive rounds at Auckland GC, New Zealand. Playing in a medal competition on Saturday 15th March, 1975 with his twin and two other members, John, the elder twin, holed-in-one at the 10th hole with his wedge. In their next game, the following Wednesday, the twins were again playing in a four-ball with two other members when Desmond holed-in-one at the 13th hole using his driver.

● In 1977, 14-year-old Gillian Field after a series of lessons holed-in-one at the 10th hole at Moor Place GC in her first round of golf.

● Having taken some golf lessons in Britain, Mrs Joan Birtley of Flamstead, Herts., accompanied her husband on a business trip to America in 1977. At Doral CC, Miami, Mrs Birtley hired some clubs and played her first-ever round of golf. At the 4th hole (116 yards) she holed-in-one.

● Mrs Fred Reeves (71) of Midland, Michigan, watched golf on television and thought it looked easy. So she borrowed a few clubs, went out to a little 9-hole course, and shot the 3rd hole (90 yards) in one stroke. She completed the 9 holes in 48–or 21 over par.

● By holing-in-one at the 2nd hole in a match against D Graham in the 1979 Suntory World Match Play at Wentworth, Japanese professional Isao Aoki won himself a Bovis home at Gleneagles worth, inclusive of furnishings, £55,000.

● In the 1979 French Open, Willie Milne appeared to have won a Mercedes car when he holed-in-one. However the organisers later declared the prize had been withdrawn. Threatening to sue, Milne was subsequently presented with a Mercedes.

● When he holed-in-one at the 105-yard 14th hole at Tahoe Paradise course, USA, in the Harrah Invitational Tournament in 1965,

Dick Kolbus, from Oakland, California, won an $18,500 Rolls-Royce car.

● One hour before he retired as Captain of the Guernsey Golf Club, Channel Islands, RJ Mahy (handicap 1) holed out in one at the 18th hole, while playing in a medal competition on 12th March, 1964. This was his first hole-in-one and a fitting climax to his year as captain.

● Playing a holiday round on Rotorua course, New Zealand, on 25th July, 1964, Dr AW Reid of Taumaranui, holed his tee shot at the 110-yard 6th hole. While approaching the next hole he was hit on the head by a ball driven from the eighth tee, and knocked unconscious. Recovering, he completed the round, and duly paid a double penalty–once for holing-in-one, and once for being still alive!

● JoAnn Washam twice holed-in-one in the 1979 Kemper Open, a USLPGA Tournament.

● R Buckell, a member of Pinner Hill GC and W Dunbar, playing together in a society outing over Pinner Hill on 30th August, 1968, each holed-in-one at the 17th hole (225 yards).

● On 30th November, 1975, her last day of office as lady captain of Alderley Edge GC, Mrs Gertrude Wright holed-in-one at the 4th hole (115 yards).

● Veteran American, Earl Hooker, of Paris, Texas, holed-in-one in the month of July in four consecutive years, 1968 to 1971.

● Golfers in three consecutive groups at Blowing Rock CC, North Carolina, one day in 1979 each holed-in-one at the 156-yard 7th hole. They were Charles Wood, Harold Beal and Wallace Brawley.

● Russell Dewald, Ray Newman and Hal Martin, players in three consecutive games, holed-in-one on 23rd January, 1980 at the 14th hole (120 yards) at Lakewood CC, Florida.

● On the morning after being elected captain for 1973 of the Norwich GC, JS Murray hit his first shot as captain straight into the hole at the 169 yards first hole.

● Bob Dellow and John Watt, of Millicent Golf Club in South Australia, playing with another two members in a competition on 24th July, 1970, each holed-in-one at the 153-yard 13th hole. The following day, one of the other members of the four, Greg Nitschke, holed-in-one at the same hole.

● Using the same club and ball, 11-handicap left-hander Christopher Smyth holed-in-one at the 2nd hole (170 yards) in two consecutive medal competitions at Headfort GC, Co Meath, in January, 1976.

● Two members of Middlesbrough GC both holed the 103-yard 10th hole in one twice in 1976. They were LA Dilcock and GT Crombie.

● In the space of one month during 1976, Mr and Mrs Carl Sexton and Mr and Mrs Bob Cook all achieved holes-in-one at Soboba Springs CC, San Jacinto, California.

● In a knock-out competition at Ely, Cambridgeshire, on 13th October, 1962, Mr Challis drove to within four feet of the 1st hole (170 yards). His opponent, Mr Delwage, pitched his second shot; his ball struck that of Mr Challis, knocking it into the hole and giving him the hole-in-one.

● Dr Tucker, New Orleans, Louisiana, 1936, put his name down for a hole-in-one golf tournament. After doing so he walked out to the contest hole–160 yards–and hit the ball with an iron. The ball trickled into the hole. Elated, Dr Tucker rushed back to the clubhouse, only to find that the competition was not due to begin until two weeks later.

● The late Miss Gertrude Lawrence, a distinguished actress, when playing golf for the first time, holed-in-one with her first tee shot.

● In an RAF outing in 1973 at Peterborough Milton GC two holes-in-one were made with the same ball but not by the same person. The first was in the morning singles by Des Tuson at the 142-yard 11th hole. Then in the afternoon, playing in a greensome competition, his partner, Keith Schofield, holed-in-one at the 174-yard 2nd hole. The ball was then carefully put away.

● General Eisenhower, early in 1968, holed the 13th at Seven Lakes Country Club in one. It was his first ace and *13* was not an unlucky number.

● Joe Kirkwood holed-in-one on 11 occasions including one when doing a Newsreel Movie at the 5th (168 yards), Sea Island, Georgia, and another when he was performing trick shots off the face of a watch at the 1st (268 yards), Cedar Rapids, Iowa.

● A one-armed golfer, Andrew Harrison, has had three holes-in-one. The latest was achieved at the 16th hole (160 yards) at West Lothian GC in 1971.

● Another one-armed golfer, Don Reid of Ravensworth GC, has twice holed-in-one at his club's 8th hole, once in 1977 and again in 1979.

● A Wilmott, who had been the One-Armed Champion on several occasions, holed-in-one at the 3rd hole which measured 230 yards during a round of the 1979 club championship at Downfield GC.

● A woman who has only her right arm, Mrs Frank Andreucci, of Florida, holed-in-one at the 136-yard 13th hole at Crystal Lake CC in 1971.

● At Royal Hong Kong Golf Club, Susan Tonroe, aged 16, and her brother, aged 11, each did the 7th hole in one in junior competitions in the same week.

● Playing over Rickmansworth course at Easter, 1960, Mrs AE (Paddy) Martin achieved a remarkable sequence of *aces*. On Good Friday she sank her tee shot at the third hole (125 yards). The next day, using the same ball and the same No. 8 iron, at the same hole, she scored another *one*. And on the Monday (same ball, same club, same hole) she again holed out from the tee. (See also *Holing-in-One in Successive Rounds*).

● Joan Jankins, aged 12, achieved a hole-in-one at the 240-yard 3rd hole at Abersoch, Gwynedd, in October 1984.

●In January 1985 Otto Bucher of Switzerland, aged 99, holed in one at the 130-yard 12th hole at the La Manga Championship South course in Spain.

Bookmakers and Golf

(See also Wagers, Curious and Large)

● Wagering on a heavy scale has been associated with golf from its earliest days, but the first time a bookmaker appeared at a golf tournament and shouted the odds was in 1898 in a professional tournament at Carnoustie. In 1927, at the Open Championship at St Andrews, a Glasgow bookmaker and two assistants mixed among the crowds following the players and shouting the odds. In the Open Championship at Portrush, 1951, a bookmaker set up his stand during the qualifying rounds and shouted the odds. In 1934 various bookmakers' lists were promiscuously issued and publicly advertised, giving odds for the Amateur and Open Championships, and representatives of different commission agents attended the two championships and touted for bets, but this was carried out individually and odds were not publicly shouted. Since 1934 reputable bookmakers in London and the Provinces annually bet to any sum on the Amateur and Open Championships.

● At the John Player Classic Tournament at Turnberry in 1971 a firm of bookmakers had a stand in the tented village. A lot of bets were placed including several by competitors. There was much talk of the possibilities of malpractice this could lead to, and as a result, the authorities decided to ban on-course betting in British tournaments. Then in 1980 the PGA gave permission to the Coral Leisure Group for a mobile betting office to be situated on the course at several major tournaments but no head to head bets were allowed to be offered.

Challenge Matches

Before the days of large prize-money from sponsored tournaments professional golfers had little opportunity to augment their meagre regular income except by taking part in challenge matches. Sometimes wealthy sponsors would put up cash, but frequently the players staked their own money on a winner-take-all basis. This naturally meant a great deal of tension for the competitors and the matches created a great deal of interest in rival groups of supporters.

As will be seen from the following record of the more important of these challenge matches, the sums of money involved were very considerable for the times.

● 1843–Allan Robertson, St Andrews, beat Willie Dunn, Musselburgh, in a match of 20 rounds, 360 holes, by 2 rounds and 1 to play.

● 1849–Allan Robertson and Tom Morris, of St Andrews, beat the brothers Dunn, of Musselburgh, over Musselburgh, St Andrews, and North Berwick, for a stake of £400. The Dunns won at Musselburgh by 13 and 12; but Robertson and Morris got even at St Andrews. The match, therefore, reverted to North Berwick. The Dunns were 4 up and 8 to play. Odds of 20 to 1 were laid on the Dunns at this point but Robertson and Morris won by one hole.

● 1852–Tom Morris and Allan Robertson defeated Sir Robert Hay and Willie Dunn by 6 and 5 over two rounds at St Andrews. Morris and Robertson staked £100 to £50 on the issue.

● 1853–Willie Park, sen, twice defeated Tom Morris, sen, in £100 matches. Allan Robertson was repeatedly challenged by Park, but refused to play.

● 1854–Tom Morris and Bob Anderson beat Allan Robertson and Willie Dunn for £200 by one hole, in an 18 hole match at St Andrews.

● 1854-5–Willie Park and Tom Morris played six £100 matches, and honours were about evenly divided. In the fifth match at Musselburgh the spectators interfered with Morris's ball repeatedly, and the referee stopped play. Morris and the referee, Bob Chambers, an Edinburgh publisher, retired to a nearby public house. Park waited for some time and then sent a message to Chambers and Morris that if they did not come out to play to a finish he would play the remaining holes alone and claim the stakes. Morris and Chambers remained in the public house and Park, completing the round, was subsequently awarded the stakes.

● 1857–Allan Robertson and Andrew Strath beat Tom Morris and Willie Park for £100 by six holes in two rounds.

● 1859–Willie Park, sen, beat Willie Dunn at Prestwick for £100.

● 1868–Lord Kennedy and Mr Cruikshank, of Langley Park, played a match of three holes for £500 a hole at St Andrews. Play started at 10 pm, and the only light was given by lamps stuck on the flag pins of the three holes. It is not known who won this extraordinary match.

● 1868-9–Old Tom and Bob Ferguson played six matches over Luffness and Musselburgh, and Ferguson won them all.

● 1869–Young Tom beat Bob Ferguson at Musselburgh by one hole.

● 1875–Old and Young Tom beat Willie Park and Mungo Park for £50 at North Berwick by one hole.

● This was the last big money match Young Tom played. A telegram had been received in North Berwick before the end of the match intimating that Young Tom's wife had died. The news was kept from him until he boarded John Lewis's yacht which took the St Andrews party across the Forth. Young Tom never recovered from the shock and died on Christmas Day of the same year, aged 24.

● 1876–In October, 1875, John Ball, sen, father of John Ball, the eight times amateur champion, with David Strath, challenged any amateur and professional AH Molesworth and John Allan, Westward Ho! accepted. The match was played at Hoylake over four rounds for a stake of £100 a side. Ball and Strath won by 7 and 5.

● 1883–Douglas Rolland (who afterwards turned professional) beat John Ball, jun, in a home and away match over Earlsferry and Hoylake. Over the two rounds at Elie, Rolland finished nine holes up. On the first round at Hoylake, Ball reduced the lead by one hole, but Rolland finally won by 11 and 10. A fresh match of two rounds was played the following day, and this Rolland also won.

● 1894–Douglas Rolland beat Willie Park, jun, in a 36-hole match at Sandwich by 3 and 2 for £100. Park had challenged the world.

● 1895–Andrew Kirkaldy defeated JH Taylor by one hole over 36 holes at St Andrews for £50 a side. Taylor, reigning Open Champion, had never played over St Andrews when he issued his challenge. The match was played prior to the Open Championship, 1895, which Taylor retained.

● 1896–Willie Park defeated JH Taylor in a 72-hole match over Musselburgh and Sudbrook Park. The match was notable for the rowdyism of the spectators at Musselburgh, and there was so much local partisanship that three years later Harry Vardon refused to include Musselburgh as Park's home course in their great match, and Park had to take North Berwick.

● 1899–Harry Vardon, in a 72-hole match (36 holes over North Berwick and 36 holes over Ganton), defeated Willie Park, jun, by 11 and 10 for £100 a side. At the end of 36 holes at North Berwick Vardon was two holes up. The first ten holes were halved. At the 11th hole, Park had the honour and Vardon's drive pitched on Park's ball and rebounded two feet. Vardon duffed his next shot and lost the hole–the first change in the match. The spectators at North Berwick numbered over 10,000, and represented an unprecedented attendance for an individual match up to that time and for many years afterwards.

● 1899–John Ball and Harry Vardon beat FG Tait and Willie Park at Ganton by 5 and 4 in a 36-hole match.

● 1904–The brothers Harry and Tom Vardon defeated James Braid and Jack White at Sunningdale in a 36-hole match by 3 and 1. They also won the last hole.

● 1905–JH Taylor and Harry Vardon, representing England, defeated James Braid and Alex Herd, representing Scotland, by 13 and 12 over four courses, for £200 a side. Results: St Andrews–Scotland 2 up; Troon–England 12 up; St Annes–England 7 up; Deal–England won by 13 and 12. At Troon the attendance equalled the great crowd at North Berwick for the Vardon–Park match.

● 1906–Harry Vardon and James Braid beat George Duncan and Charles Mayo, in a 72-hole match for £100, by 9 and 8. Results: Walton Heath–Vardon and Braid, 4 up. Timperley–Vardon and Braid, 9 and 8.

● 1926–Walter Hagen beat Abe Mitchell in a 72-hole match over Wentworth and St George's Hill by 2 and 1 for a stake of £1,000 (£500 a-side). At the end of 36 holes Mitchell was 4 up.

● 1926–Walter Hagen beat Bobby Jones in a 72-hole match at St Petersburg and Sarasota Bay by 11 and 10. Hagen was paid $5,000 for the St Petersburg half and received all the gate money at $3 per ticket at Sarasota. The gate money was $3,500. Hagen's combined fee of $8,500 was the largest ever received by a professional golfer for a challenge match. Hagen presented Jones with a set of shirt studs and cuff links.

● 1928–Archie Compston, on 27th and 28th April, at Moor Park, London, defeated Walter Hagen in a 72-hole match by 18 and 17. At the end of the 36 holes, Compston was 14 holes up. This is the greatest margin of victory ever recorded in a first class professional match. Stake £500. Hagen proceeded to Sandwich where he won for the third time the Open Championship.

● 1937–Henry Cotton, Open Champion, beat Densmore Shute, American professional champion, over 72 holes at Walton Heath. At the end of 18 holes they were all square; after 36 holes Cotton was two up; 54 holes (end third round) Cotton was five up and he won by 6 and 5. The match followed immediately after the Open Championship at Carnoustie. A sum of £500 was put up to be won outright, but the donor, when the winning cheque was handed to Cotton, also presented Shute with £100.

● 1938–Reginald Whitcombe, Open Champion of the year, and Henry Cotton accepted a challenge by AD Locke and Sid Brews, South Africa, for a 72-hole four-ball match, for £500 a side. The match was played at Walton Heath. At the end of the first round the Englishmen were one up, after two rounds two down, then two up again after three rounds, finally winning by 2 and 1.

● 1938–AD Locke, South African Champion, defeated Alf Padgham, Sunridge Park, by 2 holes in a 36-hole challenge match for £100 at Selsdon Park, Croydon. Locke did the last nine holes in 32–6 under bogey–and did not lead until the 35th hole.

● 1939–AD Locke (South Africa) in a 72-hole match for £500 a side at Coombe Hill, on 1st and 2nd June, beat Reginald Whitcombe, Parkstone, the Open Champion of 1938, by 6 and 5.

● 1939–AD Locke (South Africa) beat Richard Burton (Sale), the Open Champion, 1939, by 10 and 9 over 72 holes for £250 a side at Mere Country Club on 19th-20th July.

● 1939–Alfred Perry, Leatherhead, partnered by HJG Hare, six handicap, beat AD Locke, South Africa, and his backer, LH Oates, 10 handicap, by 4 and 2. Perry and Hare won £125; £25 on the first nine holes; £25 on the second; £50 on the match and £25 on the bye. On a rain-soaked course Perry had an individual score of 63.

● 1951–AD Locke (South Africa) beat Norman Von Nida (Australia) by 11 and 9 over 144 holes. 36 holes were played at Cape Town, 36 at Durban and 72 at Johannesburg. The match was for £1,500. Locke received £1,000 and Von Nida, £500.

● 1952–Henry Cotton and Fred Daly defeated AD Locke and Eric Brown, 8 and 7, over 36 holes at Walton Heath. The winners each received £250 and the losers each £100.

Curious and Large Wagers

(See also bets recorded under* Cross-Country Matches, *and in* Challenge Matches*)

● In the Royal and Ancient Club minutes an entry on 3rd November, 1870 was made in the following terms: *Sir David Moncreiffe, Bart, of Moncrieffe, backs his life against the life of John Whyte-Melville, Esq, of Strathkinnes, for a new silver club as a present to the St Andrews Golf Club, the price of the club to be paid by the survivor and the arms of the parties to be engraved on the club, and the present bet inscribed on it. No balls to be attached to it. In testimony of which this bet is subscribed by the parties thereto.* Thirteen years later, Mr Whyte-Melville, in a feeling and appropriate speech, expressed his deep regret at the lamented death of Sir Robert Moncrieffe, one of the most distinguished and zealous supporters of the club. Whyte-Melville, while lamenting the cause that led to it, had pleasure in fulfilling the duty imposed upon him by the bet, and accordingly delivered to the captain the silver putter. Whyte-Melville in 1883 was elected captain of the club a second time; he died in his eighty-sixth year in July, 1883, before he could take office and the captaincy remained vacant for a year. His portrait hangs in the Royal and Ancient clubhouse and is one of the finest and most distinguished pictures in the smoking-room.

● In 1766, the Honourable Company of Edinburgh Golfers who then played at Leith Links passed a resolution that *no match should be played for more than 100 merks on the day's play, or a guinea the round.* A merk was worth approximately 6p and the limit of 100 merks would be approximately £5.60 in present-day money.

● Heavy wagering is frequently associated with private or golfing society matches, in which rich men are engaged and rounds on which £1,000 depended are not unknown. Amateurs playing for £100 a round are not out of the way.

● Bobby Jones won the four major championships in 1930 (the Amateur, the Open, the American Amateur and the American Open). Long odds had been laid against such a result by bookmakers, and extensive sums were paid out.

● In 1914 Francis Ouimet, who in the previous autumn had won the American Open Championship after a triangular tie with Harry Vardon and Ted Ray, came to Great Britain with Jerome D Travers, the holder of the American amateur title, to compete in the British Amateur Championship at Sandwich. An American syndicate took a bet of £30,000 to £10,000 that one or other of the two United States champions would be the winner. It only took two rounds to decide the bet against the Americans. Ouimet was beaten by a then quite unknown player, HS Tubbs, while Travers was defeated by Charles Palmer, who was fifty-six years of age at the time.

● 1907 John Ball for a wager undertook to go round Hoylake during a dense fog in under 90, in not more than two and a quarter hours and without losing a ball. Ball played with a black ball, went round in 81, and also beat the time.

● The late Ben Sayers, for a wager, played the eighteen holes of the Burgess Society course scoring a four at every hole. Sayers was about to start against an American, when his opponent asked him what he could do the course in. *Fours* replied Sayers, meaning 72, or an average of 4s for the round. A bet was made and the American then added, *Remember a three or a five is not a four.* There were eight bogey 5s and two 3s on the Burgess course at the time Old Ben achieved his feat.

● After a hole had been halved in one at Forest Hills, New Jersey, one of the players offered to bet $10,000 to $1 that the occurrence would not be repeated at the hole during his lifetime.

● Cross-country and freak matches, embraced on another page, have been fruitful of many wagers, and matches have been played between distinguished golfers using only a putting cleek against players carrying all their clubs. At Hoylake a match was fixed between a scratch golfer and a handicap 6 player. They played level, the handicap player having the right to say *Boo* three times on the round. He said *Boo* at the 13th hole and won the match easily with two *Boos* in hand, the scratch player, of course, being affected by always anticipating the *Boo*.

● A match was arranged on a south of England course for a considerable bet between a scratch player and a long-handicap man, playing level, the scratch man to drink a whisky-and-soda on each tee. On the 16th tee the scratch man, who had a hole lead, collapsed, and was not very well for some time afterwards.

● In June, 1950, Bryan Field, vice-president of the Delaware Park racecourse, USA, who had not played golf for several years, accepted a wager that, without practice, he would not go round Pine Valley, rated one of the hardest courses in the world, in less than 300 shots. With borrowed clubs, he set off at 8 am planning to finish in time for lunch. He started 7, 9, 4, 11, and when he got a 10 at the 5th, one of the most testing on the course, after putting three tee shots into the lake, it was obvious that he was well on the way to winning the bet. With an 11 at the 8th, another difficult hole he reached the turn in 73. Coming home in 75, Mr Field holed the course in 148 and won his wager with 152 strokes in hand. He took two hours, fifty minutes to complete the round.

Feats of Endurance

Although golf is not a game where endurance, in the ordinary sense in which the term is employed in sport, is required, there are several instances of feats on the links which demanded great physical exertion.

● In 1971 during a 24-hour period from 6 pm on November 27 until 5.15 pm on 28th November, Ian Colston completed 401 holes over the 6,061 yards Bendigo course, Victoria, Australia. Colston was a top marathon athlete but was not a golfer. However prior to his golfing marathon he took some lessons and became adept with a 6-iron, the only club he used throughout the 401 holes. The only assistance Colston had was a team of harriers to carry his 6-iron and look for his ball, and a band of motor cyclists who provided light during the night. This is, as far as is known, the greatest number of holes played in 24 hours on foot on a full-size course.

● In 1934 Col Bill Farnham played 376 holes in 24 hours 10 minutes at the Guildford Lake Course, Guildford, Connecticut, using only a mashie and a putter.

● To raise funds for extending the Skipton GC course from 12 to 18 holes, the club professional, 24-year-old Graham Webster, played 277 holes in the hours of daylight on Monday 20th June, 1977. Playing with nothing longer than a 5-iron he averaged 81 per 18-hole round. Included in his marathon was a hole-in-one.

● Michael Moore, a 7 handicap 26-year-old member of Okehampton GC, completed on foot 15 rounds 6 holes (276 holes) there on Sunday, 25th June, 1972, in the hours of daylight. He started at 4.15 am and stopped at 9.15 pm. The distance covered was estimated at 56 miles. Nine brief stoppages for salty soup were made. His time for 6 rounds was 6 hours 2 minutes; for 12 rounds, 12 hours 58 minutes.

● On 21st June, 1976, 5-handicapper Sandy Small played 15 rounds (270 holes) over his home course Cosby GC, length 6,128 yards, to raise money for the Society of Physically Handicapped Children. Using only a 5-iron, 9-iron and putter, Small started at 4.10 am and completed his 270th hole at 10.39 pm with the aid of car headlights. His fastest round was his first (40 minutes) and slowest his last (82 minutes). His best round of 76 was achieved in the second round.

● In 1957, Bert L Scoggins, a US serviceman, played 260 holes in one day on the American golf course at Berlin. He started out at 2.30 am, and played continuously for 18 hours, walking 56 miles in the course of his marathon feat. His lowest single round score was 84.

● Bill Falkingham, jun, of Amstel GC, Victoria, Australia, played 257 holes between 12.30 am and 6.15 pm on 14th December, 1968. The first three holes were played in darkness. He was accompanied by his brother and a friend who held a torch to assist direction. Ten balls were lost but the first ball lasted eight rounds. His best round was 90 over a course measuring 6,673 yards, par 73, over which a gale force wind blew all day, in a temperature of 90 degrees. During the morning he trod on a snake but did not stop to kill it. He was sustained by only sandwiches and soft drinks and although completely exhausted when he finished he had completely recovered next morning and went out for another round.

● During the weekend of 20th-21st June, 1970, Peter Chambers of Yorkshire completed over 14 rounds of golf over the Scarborough South Cliff course. In a non-stop marathon lasting just under 24 hours, Chambers played 257 holes in 1,168 strokes, an average of 84.4 strokes per round.

● Stan Gard, a member of North Brighton Golf Club, New South Wales, in 1938 completed fourteen rounds and four holes on his home course. Gard started his marathon performance at 12.55 am, and finished with the aid of car lights at 9.30 pm. He played consistent golf, his best being 78 in the tenth round, and his worst 92 in the second round.

● Bruce Sutherland, on the Craiglockhart Links, Edinburgh, started at 8.15 pm on 21st June, 1927, and played almost continuously until 7.30 pm on 22nd June, 1927. During the night four caddies with acetylene lamps lit the way, and lost balls were reduced to a minimum. He completed fourteen rounds. Mr Sutherland, who was a physical culture teacher, never recovered from the physical strain and died a few years later.

● Sidney Gleave, motor cycle racer, and Ernest Smith, golf professional, Davyhulme Club, Manchester, on 12th June, 1939, played five rounds of golf in five different countries–Scotland, Ireland, Isle of Man, England and Wales. Smith had to play the five rounds under 80 in one day to win the £100 wager. They travelled by plane, and the following was their programme with time taken and Smith's score:

Start–Prestwick St Nicholas (Scotland), 3.40 am. Score 70. Time taken, 1 hour 35 minutes. 2nd Course–Bangor (Ireland), 7.15 am. Score 76. Time taken, 1 hour 30 minutes. 3rd Course–Castletown (Isle of Man), 10.15 am. Score 76. Time taken, 1 hour 40 minutes. 4th Course–Blackpool, Stanley Park (England), 1.30 pm. Score 72. Time taken, 1 hour 55 minutes. 5th Course–Hawarden (Wales), 6 pm. Score 68 (record). Time taken, 2 hours 15 minutes.

● On Wednesday, 3rd July, 1974, ES Wilson, Whitehead, Co Antrim, and Dr GW Donaldson, Newry, Co Down, played a nine-hole match in each of seven countries in the one day. The first 9 holes was at La Moye (Channel Islands) followed by Hawarden (Wales), Chester (England), Turnberry (Scotland), Castletown (Isle of Man), Dundalk (Eire) and Warrenpoint (N Ireland). They started their first round at 4.25 am and their last round at 9.25 pm. Wilson piloted his own plane throughout.

● Rick Garcia and Don Tanner from Gallup, New Mexico, played 18 holes, selected from seven States, in one day in 1976 to raise money for muscular dystrophy. The States concerned were Texas, New Mexico, Colorado, Utah, Arizona, California and Nevada. A distance of over 2,000 miles was covered by private plane.

● In June 1986 to raise money for the upkeep of his medieval church, the Rector of Mark with Allerton, Somerset, the Revd Michael Pavey, played a sponsored 18 holes on 18 different courses in the Bath & Wells Diocese. With his partner, the well-known broadcaster on music, Antony Hopkins, they played the 1st at Minehead at 5.55 am and finished playing the 18th at Burnham and Berrow at 6.05 pm. They covered 240 miles in the 'round' including the distances to reach the correct tee for the 'next' hole on each course. Par for the 'round' was 70. Together the pair raised £10,500 for the church.

Fastest Rounds

● Dick Kimbrough (aged 41) completed a round on foot on 8th August, 1972, at North Platte CC, Nebraska (6,068 yards) in 30 minutes 10 seconds. He carried only a 3-iron. Earlier the same year Kimbrough played 364 holes in 24 hours.

● At Mowbray Course, Cape Town, November 1931, Len Richardson, who had represented South Africa in the Olympic Games, played a round which measured 6,248 yards in 31 minutes 22 seconds.

● The women's all-time record for a round played on a course of at least 5,250 yards is held by Dianne Taylor, 37, Jacksonville, Florida. She played the 5,692 yards University GC at Jacksonville in 55 minutes 54 seconds on 7th April, 1980.

● Faster rounds have been recorded, but they have not been done on foot. The fastest of these was achieved by 3 handicap Ken Wildey at Calcot Park GC on 20th July, 1980. Wildey, riding in a motorised cart, completed the 6,010 yards course in 24 minutes 3 seconds.

The sole purpose in each of the above instances was speed. The following are examples of fast rounds in a match or competition.

● In 14th June, 1922, Jock Hutchison and Joe Kirkwood (Australia) played round the Old Course at St Andrews in 1 hour 20 minutes. Hutchison, out in 37, led by three holes at the ninth and won by 4 and 3.

● In April, 1934, after attending a wedding in Bournemouth, Hants, Captain Gerald Moxom hurried to his club, West Hill in Surrey, to play in the captain's prize competition. With daylight fading and still dressed in his morning suit, he went round in 65 minutes and won the competition with a net 71 into the bargain.

● Fastest rounds can also take another form–the time taken for a ball to be propelled round 18 holes. The fastest known round of this type is 8 minutes 53.8 seconds on 25th August, 1979 by 42 members at Ridgemount CC Rochester, New York, a course measuring 6,161 yards. The Rules of Golf were observed but a ball was available on the following tee to be driven off the instant the ball had been holed at the preceding hole.

Slow Play

Standards have changed dramatically over the years as to what constitutes slow play as the following statement, which first appeared in the 1949 Golfer's Handbook, shows: *Slow motion golf has marred many championships, and notorious tortoises have been known to take three-and-a-half hours in a championship tie.*

Nowadays a round taking three-and-a-half hours is commonplace, but for the sake of history we record here examples of what was considered very slow play up to 1950.

● When Henry Cotton and RA Whitcombe played Bobby Locke and Sid Brews at Walton Heath, 1938, for a stake of £500 a side, the match made headlines with the slowness of play. Locke, who was engaging in his first important professional match in Great Britain, was ultra-careful, and the marshalling of the crowd–there were 5,000 spectators present during the second round–caused many delays, sometimes as much as 10 minutes being required for the players to leave one green and play off the next tee. The first round took three hours 40 minutes and the second round four hours 15 minutes. Cotton and Whitcombe won by 2 and 1. Locke, although on the defeated side, played phenomenal golf. He went round in 63. Walton Heath tees were far extended and it was a cruel test.

● In the Scottish Amateur Championship, 1922, at St Andrews, a competitor was deplorably slow and in one tie his opponent, in the hope of shaming the sloth into quickening his play brought to the links a camp bed, which was carried round by others who had been playing in the championship. The camp bed was placed at the side of each green, and while the tortoise crawled about studying the line of the putt, his opponent reclined on the bed and nonchalantly observed the antics of his rival. The attempt to secure a speed-up was unsuccessful and the tortoise was even more deliberate in his play.

● The Amateur Championship, St Andrews, 1950, was remarkable for slowness of play and the inordinate time taken by some players to play their shots. The main cause of the slowness was the time taken to study putts. In some cases five minutes were spent over a stroke on the greens, although the record entry of 324 and the huge double greens of the Championship Course were also contributory to the sluggish pace. Many matches took four hours to complete and five couples waited at some tees. A record for the championship was made on the third day when play in the third and fourth rounds occupied 14 hours. The first ball was struck at 8 am and the last match finished on the 17th green in the lamplit dusk shortly before 10 pm. In the final between FR Stranahan and RD Chapman the first nine holes of the morning round took an hour and 50 minutes to play. A field telephone message was sent to the referee, Colonel CO Hezlet, Portrush, to warn the players that the second round would start at the scheduled time. This increased the pace slightly and the round was finished in three hours 40 minutes, the slowest round in the final of the championship at that time.

Curious Scoring

● Three threes, four fours, five fives and six sixes is one of only two progressive combinations that can work out for 18 holes. A player in a South African competition had this sequence and noticed the curiosity in scoring. The other combination is five fives, six sixes and seven sevens.

● RH Corbett, playing in the semi-final of the Tangye Cup at Mullim in 1916, did a score of 27. The remarkable part of Corbett's score was that it was made up of nine successive 3s, bogey being 5, 3, 4, 4, 5, 3, 4, 4, 3.

● At Little Chalfont in June 1985 Adrian Donkersley played six successive holes in 6, 5, 4, 3, 2, 1 from the 9th to the 14th holes against a par of 4, 4, 3, 4, 3, 3.

● On 2nd September, 1920, playing over Torphin, near Edinburgh, William Ingle did the first five holes in 1, 2, 3, 4, 5.

● In the summer of 1970, Keith McMillan, on holiday at Cullen, had a remarkable series of 1, 2, 3, 4, 5 at the 11th to 15th holes.

● Playing at Addington Palace, July, 1934, Ronald Jones, a member of Hendon Club, holed five consecutive holes in 5, 4, 3, 2, 1.

● Harry Dunderdale of Lincoln GC scored 5, 4, 3, 2, 1 in five consecutive holes during the first round of his club championship in 1978. The hole-in-one was the 7th, measuring 294 yards.

● At Westerhope near Newcastle in January 1986 Alan Crosby, the Club professional, played the first four holes in 4, 3, 2, 1 against the par of 4, 4, 3, 4.

● Playing in his club medal competition at Hindley Hall GC on 25th August, 1974, H

Rowlance had every digit from 1 to 8 on his card. His 1 was at the 6th hole (156 yards).

● In a club competition Mr A Mitchell had every digit from 1 to 8 on his card.

● At Nairn in August 1985 Brian Crowther of Swinton Park and Andrew Watson of Kelso, each 12 handicap, completed 18 holes without halving a hole. Crowther won at the 19th.

● PC Chase and John North finished all square in their regular weekly match at Woking GC on 30th October, 1972, without having halved a single hole. An actuarial calculation put the odds against this at 1,413,398-1.

● Another instance of this occurred in a first round foursomes match in the Halford-Hewitt Cup at Deal in 1979 when a Hurstpierpoint pair beat St Bee's at the 19th hole, without any hole being halved. The first ten holes were exchanged, St Bee's winning the next four and Hurstpierpoint the following five.

● At the Open Amateur Tournament of the Royal Ashdown Forest in 1936 Bobby Locke in his morning round had a score of 72, accomplishing every hole in 4.

● Severiano Ballesteros in winning the 1978 Swiss Open scored four rounds of 68.

● In a four-ball match in 1936, Richard Chapman partnered by Joe Ezar, the *Clown* prince of golf, against the Hon Michael Scott and Bobby Locke, then 18 years old, were four down and five to play. Ezar asked Scott if he had ever seen five birdies in a row. Scott replied that he could not recall that happening and so Ezar made a bet on the same and pulled the match out 1 up by shooting five birdies to win the match.

● Henry Cotton tells of one of the most extraordinary scoring feats ever. With some other professionals he was at Sestrieres in the thirties for the Italian Open Championship and Joe Ezar, a colourful character in those days on both sides of the Atlantic, accepted a wager from a club official–1,000 lira for a 66 to break the course record; 2,000 for a 65; and 4,000 for a 64. *I'll do 64*, said Ezar, and proceeded to jot down the hole-by-hole score figures he would do next day for that total. With the exception of the ninth and tenth holes where his predicted score was 3, 4 and the actual score was 4, 3, he accomplished this amazing feat exactly as nominated.

High Scores

● In the qualifying competition at Formby for the 1976 Open Championship, Maurice Flitcroft, a 46-year-old crane driver from Barrow-in-Furness, took 121 strokes for the first round and then withdrew saying, *I have no chance of qualifying*. Flitcroft entered as a professional but had never before played 18 holes. He had taken the game up 18 months previously but, as he was not a member of a club, had been limited to practising on a local beach. His round was made up thus: 7, 5, 6, 6, 6, 6, 12, 6, 7–61; 11, 5, 6, 8, 4, 9, 5, 7, 5–60, total 121. After his round Flitcroft said, *I've made a lot of progress in the last few months and I'm sorry I did not do better. I was trying too hard at the beginning but began to put things together at the end of the round.* R and A officials who were not amused by the bogus professional's efforts, refunded the £30 entry money to Flitcroft's two fellow-competitors.

● Playing in the qualifying rounds of the 1965 Open Championship at Southport, an American self-styled professional entrant from Milwaukee, Walter Danecki, achieved the inglorious feat of scoring a total of 221 strokes for 36 holes, 81 over par. His first round over the Hillside course was 108, followed by a second round of 113. Walter, who afterwards admitted he felt *a little discouraged and sad,* declared that he entered because he was *after the money.*

● The highest individual scoring ever known in the rounds connected with the Open Championship occurred at Muirfield, 1935, when a Scottish professional started 7, 10, 5, 10, and took 65 to reach the 9th hole. Another 10 came at the 11th and the player decided to retire at the 12th hole. There he was in a bunker, and after playing four shots he had not regained the fairway.

● In 1883 in the Open Championship at Musselburgh, Willie Fernie, the winner, had a 10, the only time double figures appeared on the card of the Open Champion of the year. Fernie won after a tie with Bob Ferguson, and his score for the last hole in the tie was 2. He holed from just off the green to win by one stroke.

● In the first Open Championship at Prestwick in 1860 a competitor took 21, the highest score for one hole ever recorded in this event. The record is preserved in the archives of the Prestwick Golf Club, where the championship was founded.

● In 1938, in the final two rounds of the Open Championship, the players who had qualified for this stage had to contend with a hurricane during the greater part of the day. So fierce was the wind that the players had difficulty in keeping their stance during their swing. Scores of nine for individual holes were numerous; there were many 10's and one player had 14, the equal third highest score ever recorded for a single hole in the Open Championship.

● In the first round of the 1980 US Masters, Tom Weiskopf hit his ball into the water hazard in front of the par-3 12th hole five times and scored 13 for the hole.

● American Ben Crenshaw took 11 shots at the 16th hole at Firestone CC in the third round of the 1976 World Series. He hit three consecutive wedge shots into the lake in front of the green.

● In the French Open at St Cloud, in 1968, Brian Barnes took 15 for the short 8th hole in the second round. After missing putts at which he hurriedly snatched while the ball was moving he penalised himself further by standing astride the line of a putt. The amazing result was that he actually took 12 strokes from about three feet from the hole.

● US professional Dave Hill 6-putted the fifth green at Oakmont in the 1962 US Open Championship.

● In the 1973 Transvaal Open at Germiston GC, Canadian professional Ken Trowbridge took 16 putts on the last green in a deliberate move to protest over the condition of the greens.

● Many high scores have been made at the Road Hole at St Andrews. Davie Ayton, on one occasion, was coming in a certain winner of the Open Championship when he got on the road and took 11. In 1921, at the Open Championship, one professional took 13. In 1923, competing for the Autumn Medal of the Royal and Ancient, JB Anderson required a five and a four to win the second award, but he took 13 at the Road Hole. Anderson was close to the green in two, was twice in the bunkers in the face of the green, and once on the road. In 1935, RH Oppenheimer tied for the Royal Medal (the first award) in the Autumn Meeting of the Royal and Ancient. On the play-off he was one stroke behind Captain Aitken when they stood on the 17th tee. Oppenheimer drove three balls out of bounds and eventually took 11 to the Road Hole.

● In the English Amateur at Hunstanton in 1931, a competitor pitched five times into a ditch before giving up the hole.

● In the 1974 Tallahassee Open, Mike Reasor, a regular PGA tour competitor, qualified for the final 36 holes in which he then scored 123 and 114. After making the halfway cut, Reasor injured his left shoulder in a riding accident, but because of the automatic entry into the next tournament given to all who completed the current one, he decided to play on using only his right arm for the last two rounds.

● British professional Mark James scored 111 in the second round of the 1978 Italian Open. He played the closing holes with only his right hand due to an injury to his left hand.

● In the 1927 Shawnee Open, Tommy Armour took 23 strokes to the 17th hole. Armour had won the American Open Championship a week earlier. In an effort to play the hole in a particular way, Armour hooked ball after ball out of bounds and finished with a 21 on the card. There was some doubt about the accuracy of this figure and on reaching the clubhouse Armour stated that it should be 23. This is the highest score by a professional in a tournament.

Freak Matches

● In 1912, the late Harry Dearth, an eminent vocalist, attired in a complete suit of heavy armour, played a match at Bushey Hall. He was beaten 2 and 1.

● In 1914, at the start of the First World War, JN Farrar, a native of Hoylake, was stationed at Royston, Herts. A bet was made of 10-1 that he would not go round Royston under 100 strokes, equipped in full infantry marching order, water bottle, full field kit and haversack. Farrar went round in 94. At the camp were several golfers, including professionals, who tried the same feat but failed.

● Captain Pennington, who was killed in an air crash in 1933, took part in a match *from the air* against AJ Young, the professional at Sonning. Captain Pennington, with 80 golf balls in the locker of his machine, had to find the Sonning greens by dropping the balls as he circled over the course The balls were covered in white cloth to ensure that they did not bounce once they struck the ground. The airman completed the course in 40 minutes, taking 29 *strokes*, while Young occupied two hours for his round of 68.

● In April 1924, at Littlehampton, Harry Rowntree, an amateur golfer, played the better ball of Edward Ray and George Duncan, receiving an allowance of 150 yards to use as he required during the round. Rowntree won by 6 and 5 and had used only 50 yards 2 feet of his handicap. At one hole Duncan had a two–Rowntree, who was 25 yards from the hole, took this distance from his handicap and won the hole in one. Ray (died 1945) afterwards declared that, conceded a handicap of one yard per round, he could win every championship in the world. And he might, when reckoning is taken of the number of times a putt just stops an inch or two or how much difference to a shot three inches will make for the lie of the ball, either in a bunker or on the fairway. Many single matches on the same system have been played. An 18 handicap player opposed to a scratch player should make a close match with an allowance of 50 yards.

● The first known instance of a golf match by telephone occurred in 1957, when the Cotswold Hills Golf Club, Cheltenham, England, won a golf tournament against the Cheltenham Golf Club, Melbourne,

Australia, by six strokes. A large crowd assembled at the English club to wait for the 12,000 miles telephone call from Australia. The match had been played at the suggestion of a former member of the Cotswold Hills Club, Harry Davies, and was open to every member of the two clubs. The result of the match was decided on the aggregate of the eight best scores on each side and the English club won by 564 strokes to 570.

Golf Matches Against Other Sports

● HH Hilton and Percy Ashworth, many times racket champion, contested a driving match, the former driving a golf ball with a driver, and the latter a racket ball with a racket. Best distances: Against breeze–Golfer 182 yards; Racket player 125 yards. Down wind–Golfer 230 yards; Racket player 140 yards. Afterwards Ashworth hit a golf ball with the racket and got a greater distance than with the racket ball, but was still a long way behind the ball driven by Hilton.

● In 1913, at Wellington, Shropshire, a match between a golfer and a fisherman casting a 2½ oz weight was played. The golfer, Rupert May, took 87; the fisherman JJD Mackinlay, required 102. The fisherman's difficulty was in his short casts. His longest cast, 105 yards, was within 12 yards of the world record at the time, held by a French angler, Decautelle. When within a rod's length of a hole he ran the weight to the rod end and dropped into the hole. Five times he broke his line, and was allowed another shot without penalty.

● In December, 1913, FMA Webster, of the London Athletic Club, and Dora Roberts, with javelins, played a match with the late Harry Vardon and Mrs Gordon Robertson, who used the regulation clubs and golf balls. The golfers conceded two-thirds in the matter of distance, and they won by 5 up and 4 to play in a contest of 18 holes. The javelin throwers had a mark of two feet square in which to *hole out* while the golfers had to get their ball into the ordinary golf hole. Mr Webster's best throw was one of 160 feet.

● Several matches have taken place between a golfer on the one side and an archer on the other. The wielder of the bow and arrow has nearly always proved the victor. In 1953 at Kirkhill Golf Course, Lanarkshire, five archers beat six golfers by two games to one. There were two special rules for the match; when an archer's arrow landed six feet from the hole or the golfer's ball three feet from the hole, they were counted as holed. When the arrows landed in bunkers or in the rough, archers lifted their arrow and added a stroke. The sixth archer in this match called off and one archer shot two arrows from each of the 18 tees.

● In 1954, at the Southbroom Club, South Africa, a match over 9 holes was played between an archer and a fisherman against two golfers. The participants were all champions of their own sphere and consisted of Vernon Adams (archer), Dennis Burd (fisherman), Jeanette Wahl (champion of Southbroom and Port Shepstone), and Ron Burd (professional at Southbroom). The conditions were that the archer had holed out when his arrows struck a small leather bag placed on the green beside the hole and in the event of his placing his approach shot within a bow's length of the pin he was deemed to have 1-putted. The fisherman, to achieve a 1-putt, had to land his sinker within a rod's length of the pin. The two golfers were ahead for brief spells, but it was the opposition who led at the deciding 9th hole where *Robin Hood* played a perfect approach for a birdie.

● An *Across England* combined match was begun on 11th October, 1965, by four golfers and two archers from Crowborough Beacon Golf Club, Sussex, accompanied by *Penny*, a white Alsatian dog, whose duty it was to find lost balls. They teed *off* from Carlisle Castle via Hadrian's Wall, the Pennine Way, finally holing out in the 18th hole at Newcastle United Golf Club in 612 teed shots. Casualties included 110 lost golf balls and 19 lost or broken arrows. The match took five-and-a-half days, and the distance travelled was about 60 miles. The golfers were Miss P Ward, K Meaney, K Ashdown and CA Macey; the archers were WH Hulme and T Scott. The first arrow was fired from the battlements of Carlisle Castle, a distance of nearly 300 yards, by Cumberland champion R Willis, who also fired the second arrow right across the River Eden. R Clough, president of Newcastle United GC, holed the last two putts. The match was in aid of *Guide Dogs for the Blind* and *Friends of Crowborough Hospital*.

Cross-country Matches

● Taking 1 year, 114 days, Floyd Rood golfed his way from coast to coast across the United States. He took 114,737 shots including 3,511 penalty shots for the 3,397 mile *course*.

● Two Californian teenagers, Bob Aube (17) and Phil Marrone (18) went on a golfing safari in 1974 from San Francisco to Los Angeles, a trip of over 500 miles lasting 16 days. The first six days they played alongside motorways. Over 1,000 balls were used.

● In 1830, the Gold Medal winner of the Royal and Ancient backed himself for 10 sovereigns to drive from the 1st hole at St Andrews to the toll bar at Cupar, distance nine miles, in 200 teed shots. He won easily.

● In 1848, two Edinburgh golfers played a match from Bruntsfield Links to the top of Arthur's Seat–an eminence overlooking the Scottish capital, 822 feet above sea level.

● On a winter's day in 1898, Freddie Tait backed himself to play a gutta ball in 40 teed shots from Royal St George's Clubhouse, Sandwich, to the Cinque Ports Club, Deal. He was to hole out by hitting any part of the Deal Clubhouse. The distance as the crow flies was three miles. The redoubtable Tait holed out with his 32nd shot, so effectively that the ball went through a window.

● On 3rd December, 1920, P Rupert Phillips and W Raymond Thomas teed up on the first tee of the Radyr Golf Club and played to the last hole at Southerndown. The distance as the crow flies was 15½ miles, but circumventing swamps, woods, and plough, they covered, approximately, 20 miles. The wager was that they would not do the *hole* in 1,000 strokes, but they holed out at their 608th stroke two days later. They carried large ordnance maps.

● In 1900 three members of the Hackensack (NJ) Club played a game of four-and-a-half hours over an extemporised course six miles long, which stretched from Hackensack to Paterson. Despite rain, cornfields, and wide streams, the three golfers–JW Hauleebeek, Dr ER Pfaare, and Eugene Crassons–completed the round, the first and the last named taking 305 strokes each, and Dr Pfaare 327 strokes. The players used only two clubs, the mashie and the cleek.

● On 12th March, 1921, A Stanley Turner, Macclesfield, played from his house to the Cat and Fiddle Inn, five miles distance, in 64 strokes. The route was broken and hilly with a rise of nearly 1,000 feet. Turner was allowed to tee up within two club lengths after each shot and the wagering was 6-4 against his doing the distance in 170 strokes.

● In 1919, a golfer drove a ball from Piccadilly Circus and, proceeding via the Strand, Fleet Street and Ludgate Hill, *holed out* at the Royal Exchange, London. The player drove off at 8 am on a Sunday, a time when the usually thronged thoroughfares were deserted.

● On 23rd April, 1939, Richard Sutton, a London stockbroker, played from Tower Bridge, London, to White's Club, St James's Street, in 142 strokes. The bet was he would not do *the course* in under 200 shots. Sutton used a putter, crossed the Thames at Southwark Bridge, and hit the ball short distances to keep out of trouble.

● Golfers produced the most original event in Ireland's three-week national festival of An Tostal, 1953–a cross-country competition with an advertised £1,000,000 for the man who could hole out in one. The 150 golfers drove off from the first tee at Kildare Club to hole out eventually on the 18th green, five miles away, on the nearby Curragh course, a distance of 8,800 yards. The unusual hazards to be negotiated included the main Dublin-Cork railway line and highway, the Curragh Racecourse, hoofprints left by Irish thoroughbred racehorses out exercising on the plains from nearby stables, army tank tracks and about 150 telephone lines. The Golden Ball Trophy, which is played for annually–a standard size golf ball in gold, mounted on a black marble pillar beside the silver figure of a golfer on a green marble base, designed by Captain Maurice Cogan, Army GHQ, Dublin–was for the best gross. And it went to one of the longest hitters in international golf–Amateur Champion, Irish internationalist and British Walker Cup player Joe Carr, with the remarkable score of 52.

● Four Aberdeen University students (as a 1961 Charities Week stunt) set out to golf their way up Ben Nevis (4,406 feet). After losing 63 balls and expending 659 strokes, the quartet, about halfway up, conceded victory to Britain's highest mountain.

Long-lived Golfers

● The oldest golfer who ever lived we believe was Arthur Thompson of British Columbia, Canada. He equalled his age when 103 at Uplands GC, a course of over 6,000 yards. He died two years later aged 105 but it is not known whether he played after the age of 103. Mr Thompson also features in the section *Low Scoring Veterans*.

● Nathaniel Vickers celebrated his 103rd birthday on Sunday, 9th October, 1949, and died the following day. He was the oldest member of the United States Senior Golf Association and until 1942 he competed regularly in their events and won many trophies in the various age divisions. When 100 years old, he apologised for being able to play only 9 holes a day. Vickers predicted he would live until 103 and he died a few hours after he had celebrated his birthday.

● American George Miller, who died in 1979 aged 102, played regularly when 100 years old.

● In his 93rd year, the Rev Harcourt Just had a daily round of six to 10 holes at St Andrews. In 1950, the Town Council gave him the *Courtesy of the Course,* which excused the venerable minister paying the yearly charge.

● George Swanwick, a member of Wallasey, celebrated his 90th birthday with a luncheon at the club on 1st April, 1971. He played golf several times a week, carrying his own clubs and had holed-in-one at the ages of 75 and 85. His ambition was to complete the sequence aged 95 . . . but he died in 1973 aged 92.

● The 10th Earl of Wemyss played a round on his 92nd birthday, in 1910, at Craigielaw. When 87 the Earl was partnered by Harry Vardon in a match at Kilspindie, the golf course on his East Lothian estate at Gosford. The venerable earl, after playing his ball, mounted a pony and rode to the next shot. He died on 30th June, 1914, in his 96th year.

● FL Callender, aged 78, in September 1932, played nine consecutive rounds in the Jubilee Vase, St Andrews. He was defeated in the ninth, the final round, by 4 and 2. Callender's handicap was 12. This is the best known achievement of a septuagenarian in golf.

Playing in the Dark

On numerous occasions it has been necessary to hold lamps, lighted candles, or torches at holes in order that players might finish a competition. Large entries, slow play, early darkness and an eclipse of the sun have all been causes of playing in darkness.

● At the Open Championship in Musselburgh in November 1889 many players finished when the light had so far gone that the adjacent street lamps were lit. The cards were checked by candlelight. Several players who had no chance of the championship were paid small sums to withdraw in order to permit others who had a chance to finish in daylight. This was the last championship at Musselburgh.

● At the Southern Section of the PGA tournament on 25th September, 1907, at Burnham Beeches, several players concluded the round by the aid of torch lights placed near the holes.

● In the Irish Open Championship at Portmarnock in September, 1907, a tie in the third round between WC Pickeman and A Jeffcott was postponed owing to darkness, at the 22nd hole. Pickeman on the following morning won at the 24th.

● The qualifying round of the American Amateur Championship in 1910 could not be finished in one day, and several competitors had to stop their round on account of darkness, and complete it early in the morning of the following day.

● On 10th January, 1926, in the final of the President's Putter, at Rye, EF Storey and RH Wethered were all square at the 24th hole. It was then 5 pm and so dark that, although a fair crowd was present, the balls could not be followed, and the tie was abandoned and the Putter held jointly for the year. The winner of the Putter each year affixes the ball he played; for 1926 there are two balls, respectively engraved with the names of the finalists.

● In the 1932 Walker Cup contest at Brooklyn, a total eclipse of the sun occurred.

● At Perth, on 14th September, 1932, a competition was in progress under good clear evening light, and a full bright moon. The moon rose at 7.10 and an hour later came under eclipse to the earth's surface. The light then became so bad that on the last three greens competitors holed out by the aid of the light from matches.

● At Carnoustie, 1932, in the competition for the *Craw's Nest* the large entry necessitated competitors being sent off in 3-ball matches. The late players had to be assisted by electric torches flashed on the greens.

● In February, 1950, Max Faulkner and his partner, R Dolman, in a Guildford Alliance event finished their round in complete darkness. A photographer's flash bulbs were used at the last hole to direct Faulkner's approach. Several others of more than 100 competitors also finished in the darkness. At the last hole they had only the light from the clubhouse to aim at and one played his approach so boldly that he put his ball through the hall doorway and almost into the dressing room.

● On the second day of the 1969 Ryder Cup contest, the last 4-ball match ended in near total darkness on the 18th green at Birkdale. With the help of the clubhouse lights the two American players, Lee Trevino and Miller Barber, and Tony Jacklin for Britain each faced putts of around five feet to win their match. All missed and their game was halved.

● The occasions mentioned above all occurred in competitions where it was not intended to play in the dark. There are, however, numerous instances where players set out to play in the dark either for bets or for novelty.

● On 29th November, 1878, RW Brown backed himself to go round the Hoylake links in 150 strokes, starting at 11 pm. The conditions of the match were that Mr Brown was only to be penalised *loss of distance* for a lost ball, and that no one was to help him to find it. He went round in 147 strokes, and won his bet by the narrow margin of three strokes.

● In 1876 David Strath backed himself to go round St Andrews under 100, in moonlight. He took 95, and did not lose a ball.

● In September 1928, at St Andrews, the first and last holes were illuminated by lanterns, and at 11 pm four members of the Royal and Ancient set out to play a foursome over the 2 holes. Electric lights, lanterns, and rockets were used to brighten the fairway, and the headlights of motor cars parked on Links Place formed a helpful battery. The 1st hole was won in four, and each side got a five at the 18th. About 1,000 spectators followed the freak match, which was played to celebrate the appointment of Angus Hambro to the captaincy of the club.

● In 1931, Rufus Stewart, professional, Kooyonga Club, South Australia, and former Australian Open Champion, played 18 holes of exhibition golf at night without losing a single ball over the Kooyonga course, and completed the round in 77.

● At Ashley Wood Golf Club, Blandford, Dorset, a night-time golf tournament is arranged annually with up to 180 golfers taking part over four nights. Over £6000 has been raised in four years for the Muscular Dystrophy Charity.

● At Pannal, 3rd July, 1937, RH Locke, playing in bright moonlight, holed his tee shot at the 15th hole, distance 220 yards, the only known case of holing-in-one under such conditions.

● In August, 1970, a group of Canadians held a stroke competition at the Summit Golf and Country Club, Ontario, in total darkness. Organised by Peter Kennedy, seven competitors took part, starting at midnight. Special rules drawn up included only a 1-stroke penalty for a lost ball, but if 12 balls were lost the competitor had to retire. The best score was 84 by Lief Pettersen.

Fatal and Other Accidents on the Links

The history of golf is, unfortunately, marred by a great number of fatal accidents on or near the course. In the vast majority of such cases they have been caused either by careless swinging of the club or by an uncontrolled shot when the ball has struck a spectator or bystander. In addition to the fatal accidents there is even larger number on record which have resulted in serious injury or blindness. We do not propose to list these accidents, which have hitherto been recorded in the Golfer's Handbook, except where they have some unusual feature. We would remind all golfers of the tragic consequences which have so often been caused by momentary carelessness. The fatal accidents which follow have an unusual cause and other accidents given may have their humorous aspect.

● In July, 1971, 43-year-old Rudolph Roy was killed at a Montreal course when, in playing out of woods, the shaft of his club snapped, rebounded off a tree and the jagged edge plunged into his body.

● Harold Wallace, aged 75, playing at Lundin Links with two friends in 1950, was crossing the railway line which separates the fifth green and sixth tee, when a light engine knocked him down and he was killed instantly.

● Edward M Harrison, November, 1951, while playing alone on the Inglewood Country Club, Seattle, apparently broke the shaft of his driver and the split shaft pierced his groin. He tried to reach the clubhouse, but collapsed and bled to death 100 yards from the ninth tee where the accident happened.

● In the summer of 1963, Harold Kalles, of Toronto, Canada, died six days after his throat had been cut by a golf club shaft, which broke against a tree as he was trying to play out of a bunker.

● At Jacksonville, Florida, on 18th March, 1952, two women golfers were instantly killed when hit simultaneously by the whirling propeller of a navy fighter plane. They were playing together when the plane with a dead engine and coming in against the wind, out of control, hit them from behind. The pilot, who had been making a test flight from the Navy Air Station which adjoins the golf course, stepped out of the burning plane and did not know for some seconds that the plane had killed the women.

● In September, 1956, Myrl G Hanmore, aged 50, died from an accident at the Riviera Country Club, Los Angeles, apparently caused when he lost control of a golf car on a steep incline and was crushed between the vehicle he was driving and one he was towing from the first tee to a storage barn.

● On a Welsh course a player had played a shot out of a bunker and jumped up to see the result, when he was hit on the head by a ball driven from behind. He felt no ill effects at the moment, except a slight smarting of the eyes, but within a week he was totally blind.

● At Knott End Golf Club, on 20th June, 1953, Charles Langley, playing in a competition for the Captain's Prize, hit his tee shot from the 10th and struck the cone-shaped wood marker at the ladies' tee, which was approximately nine feet from where Mr Langley had teed his ball. The ball rebounded at lightning speed striking and destroying Mr Langley's left eye.

● Gary Player was accidentally pushed into a lake beside the 18th hole at Congressional CC by young spectators seeking his autograph as he came off the green after a practice round for the 1976 Championship.

● The ambulance crew responded in minutes to a call from the Point Grey Golf and CC in Vancouver, British Columbia, reporting a golfer had suffered a heart attack. But the supposed *victim* definitely was not suffering. Justice JM Coody, 95, a retired member of British Columbia's supreme court had been spotted resting in a golf car. A passing golfer asked what the problem was and he thought the judge replied, *Heart failure*. He didn't. Justice Coody's car was stalled. He'd actually said *Cart failure*.

Lightning on the Links

There have been a considerable number of fatal and serious accidents through players and caddies having been struck by lightning on the course. The Royal and Ancient and the USGA have, since 1952, provided for discontinuance of play during lightning storms under the Rules of Golf (Rule 37, 6) and the United States Golf Association have given the following guide for personal safety during thunderstorms:

(a) Do not go out of doors or remain out during thunderstorms unless it is necessary. Stay inside of a building where it is dry, preferably away from fireplaces, stoves, and other metal objects.

(b) If there is any choice of shelter, choose in the following order:

1. Large metal or metal-frame buildings.
2. Dwellings or other buildings which are protected against lightning.
3. Large unprotected buildings.
4. Small unprotected buildings.

(c) If remaining out of doors is unavoidable, keep away from:

1. Small sheds and shelters if in an exposed location.
2. Isolated trees.
3. Wire fences.
4. Hilltops and wide open spaces.

(d) Seek shelter in:

1. A cave.
2. A depression in the ground.
3. A deep valley or canyon.
4. The foot of a steep or overhanging cliff.
5. Dense woods.
6. A grove of trees.

Note–Raising golf clubs or umbrellas above the head is dangerous.

● A serious incident with lightning involving well-known golfers was at the 1975 Western Open in Chicago when Lee Trevino, Jerry Heard and Bobby Nichols were all struck and had to be taken to hospital. At the same time Tony Jacklin had a club thrown 15 feet out of his hands.

● Two well-known competitors were struck by lightning in European events in 1977. They were Mark James of Britain in the Swiss Open and Severiano Ballesteros of Spain in the Scandinavian Open. Fortunately neither appeared to be badly injured.

Spectators Interfering with Balls

● Deliberate interference by spectators with balls in play during important money matches was not unknown in the old days when there was intense rivalry between the *schools* of Musselburgh, St Andrews, and North Berwick, and disputes arose in stake matches caused by the action of spectators in kicking the ball into either a favourable or an unfavourable position.

● Tom Morris, in his last match with Willie Park at Musselburgh, refused to go on because of interference by the spectators, and in the match on the same course about 40 years later, in 1895, between Willie Park junior and JH Taylor, the barracking of the crowd and interference with play was so bad that when the Park–Vardon match came to be arranged in 1899, Vardon refused to accept Musselburgh as a venue.

● Even in modern times spectators have been known to interfere deliberately with players' balls, though it is usually by children. In the 1972 Penfold Tournament at Queen's Park, Bournemouth, Christy O'Connor jun had his ball stolen by a young boy, but not being told of this at the time had to take the penalty for a lost ball. O'Connor finished in a tie for first place, but lost the play-off.

● In 1912 in the last round of the final of the Amateur Championship at Westward Ho! between Abe Mitchell and John Ball, the drive of the former to the short 14th hit an open umbrella held by a lady protecting her from the heavy rain, and instead of landing on the green the ball was diverted into a bunker. Mitchell, who was leading at the time by 2 holes, lost the hole and Ball won the Championship at the 38th hole.

● In the match between the professionals of Great Britain and America at Southport in 1937 a dense crowd collected round the 15th green waiting for the Sarazen–Alliss match. The American's ball landed in the lap of a woman, who picked it up and threw it so close to the hole that Sarazen got a two against Alliss' three.

● In a memorable tie between Bobby Jones and Cyril Tolley in the 1930 Amateur Championship at St Andrews, Jones' approach to the 17th green struck spectators massed at the left end of the green and led to controversy as to whether it would otherwise have gone on to the famous road. Jones himself had deliberately played for that part of the green and had requested stewards to get the crowd back. Had the ball gone on to the road, the historic Jones Quadrilateral of the year–the Open and Amateur Championships of Britain and the United States–might not have gone into the records.

● Now that golf has become such a widely enjoyed spectator sport with vast crowds lining the fairways, instances of a ball being deflected by spectators are no longer unusual, but are accepted as an almost normal occurrence in major events. In general it is thought that this is usually in favour of the player, as the ball is often destined for bad or even unplayable positions when it is stopped by impact with an onlooker. It is also to the advantage of a player that a ball is seldom lost, as its position is nearly always pin-pointed by a spectator in the area.

● In the 1983 Suntory World Match-play Championship at Wentworth Nick Faldo hit his second shot over the green at the 16th hole into a group of spectators. To everyone's astonishment and discomforture the ball reappeared on the green about 30 ft from the hole, propelled there by a thoroughly misguided and anonymous spectator. The referee ruled that Faldo play the ball where it lay on the green. Faldo's opponent, Graham Marsh, understandably upset by the incident, took three putts against Faldo's two, thus losing a hole he might well otherwise have won. Faldo won the match 2 and 1, but lost in the final to Marsh's fellow Australian Greg Norman by 3 and 2.

Golf Balls Killing Animals and Fish, and Incidents with Animals

● An astounding fatality to an animal through being hit by a golf ball occurred at St Margaret's-at-Cliffe Golf Club, Kent on 13th June, 1934, when WJ Robinson, the professional, killed a cow with his tee shot to the 18th hole. The cow was standing in the fairway about 100 yards from the tee, and the ball struck her on the back of the head. She fell like a log, but staggered to her feet and walked about 50 yards before dropping again. When the players reached her she was dead.

● JW Perret, of Ystrad Mynach, playing with Chas R Halliday, of Ralston, in the qualifying rounds of the Society of One Armed Golfers' Championship over the Darley course, Troon, on 27th August, 1935, killed two gulls at successive holes with his second shots. The *deadly* shots were at the 1st and 2nd holes.

● On the first day of grouse shooting of the 1975 season (12th August), 11-year-old schoolboy, Willie Fraser, of Kingussie, beat all the guns when he killed a grouse with his tee shot on the local course.

● On 10th June, 1904, while playing in the Edinburgh High Constables' Competition at Kilspindie, Captain Ferguson sent a long ball into the rough at the Target hole, and on searching for it found that it had struck and killed a young hare.

● Playing in a mixed open tournament at the Waimairi Beach Golf Club in Christchurch, New Zealand, in the summer of 1961, Mrs RT Challis found her ball in fairly long spongy grass where a placing rule applied. She picked up, placed the ball and played her stroke. A young hare leaped into the air and fell dead at her feet. She had placed the ball on the leveret without seeing it and without disturbing it.

● In 1906 in the Border Championship at Hawick, a gull and a weasel were killed by balls during the afternoon's play.

● A golfer at Newark, in May, 1907, drove his ball into the river. The ball struck a trout 2lb in weight and killed it.

● On 24th April, 1975, at Scunthorpe GC, Jim Tollan's drive at the 14th hole, called *The Mallard*, struck and killed a female mallard duck in flight. The duck was stuffed and is displayed in the Scunthorpe Clubhouse.

● Playing over the Killarney Course, June, 1957, a golfer sliced his ball into one of the lakes and knocked out a trout rising to catch a fly. His friend waded into the water to get the ball–and the trout.

● A Samuel, Melbourne Club, at Sandringham, was driving with an iron club from the 17th tee, when a kitten, which had been playing in the long grass, sprang suddenly at the ball. Kitten and club arrived at the objective simultaneously, with the result that the kitten took an unexpected flight through the air, landing some 20 yards away.

● As Susan Rowlands was lining up a vital putt in the closing stages of the final of the 1978 Welsh Girls' Championship at Abergele, a tiny mouse scampered up her trouser leg. After holing the putt, the mouse ran down again. Susan, who won the final admitted that she fortunately had not known it was there.

● While on tour with British professionals, 1936-37, in South Africa, Abe Mitchell, at the first hole on the Hill course at Port Elizabeth, noticed that his club struck something hard when he played his second shot from the edge of the rough. Taking another swing he *unearthed* a tortoise upon which his ball had perched from the tee shot.

Interference by Birds and Animals

● Crows, ravens, hawks and seagulls frequently carry off golf balls, sometimes dropping the ball actually on the green, and it is a common incident for a cow to swallow a golf ball. A plague of crows on the Liverpool course at Hoylake are addicted to golf balls–they stole 26 in one day–selecting only new balls. It was suggested that members should carry shotguns as a 15th club!

● A match was approaching a hole in a rather low-lying course, when one of the players made a crisp chip from about 30 yards from the hole. The ball trickled slowly across the green and eventually disappeared into the hole. After a momentary pause, the ball was suddenly ejected on to the green, and out jumped a large frog.

● In Massachusetts a goose, having been hit rather hard by a golf ball which then came to rest by the side of a water hazard, took revenge by waddling over to the ball and kicking it into the water.

● A large black crow named Jasper which frequented the Lithgow GC in New South Wales, Australia, stole 30 golf balls in the club's 1972 Easter Tournament.

● As Mrs Molly Whitaker played from a bunker at Beachwood course, Natal, South Africa, a large monkey leaped from a bush and clutched her round the neck. A caddie drove it off by clipping it with an iron club.

● Jimmy Stewart playing in the 1982 Singapore Open at the Bukit course approached his ball for his second shot at the 3rd hole and found a 10 foot cobra also making for his ball. He killed the snake only to see another emerge from the dead snake's mouth. This too was killed.

● In 1921, on the course at Kirkfield, Ontario, P McGregor and H Dowie were all square going to the home hole in the final, and when they reached the green McGregor needed to hole a long putt to win the match. It seemed to have stopped on the lip of the hole when a large grasshopper landed squarely on the ball and caused it to drop into the hole and decide the match in favour of McGregor.

● In the summer of 1963, SC King had a good drive to the 10th hole at the Guernsey Club. His partner, RW Clark, was in the rough, and King helped him to search. Returning to his ball, he found a cow eating it. Next day, at the same hole, the positions were reversed, and King was in the rough. Clark placed his woollen hat over his ball, remarking, *I'll make sure the cow doesn't eat mine*. On his return he found the cow thoroughly enjoying his hat; nothing was left but the pom-pom.

Armless, One-armed, Legless and Ambidextrous Players

● In September, 1933, at Burgess Golfing Society of Edinburgh, the first championship for one-armed golfers was held. There were 43 entries and 37 of the competitors had lost an arm in the 1914-18 war. Play was over two rounds and the championship was won by WE Thomson, Eastwood, Glasgow, with a score of 169 (82 and 87) for two rounds. The Burgess course was 6,300 yards long. Thomson drove the last green, 260 yards. The championship and an international match are played annually.

● In the Boys' Amateur Championship, 1923, at Dunbar and 1949 at St Andrews, there were competitors each with one arm. The competitor in 1949, RP Reid, Cupar, Fife, who lost his arm working a machine in a butcher's shop, got through to the third round.

● There have been cases of persons with no arms playing golf. One, Thomas McAuliffe, who held the club between his right shoulder and cheek, once went round Buffalo CC, USA, in 108.

● Group Captain Bader, who lost both legs in a flying accident prior to the World War 1939-45, took part in golf competitions and reached a single-figure handicap in spite of his disability.

● In 1909, Scott of Silloth, and John Haskins of Hoylake, both one-armed golfers, played a home and away match for £20 a side. Scott finished five up at Silloth. He was seven up and 14 to play at Hoylake but Haskins played so well that Scott eventually only won by 3 and 1. This was the first match between one-armed golfers. Haskins in 1919 was challenged by Mr Mycock, of Buxton, another one-armed player. The match was 36 holes, home and away. The first half was played over the Buxton and High Peak Links, and the latter half over the Liverpool Links, and resulted in a win for Haskins by 11 and 10. Later in the same year Haskins received another challenge to play against Alexander Smart of Aberdeen. The match was 18 holes over the Balgownie Course, and ended in favour of Haskins.

● In a match, November, 1926, between the Geduld and Sub Nigel Clubs–two golf clubs connected with the South African gold mines of the same names–each club had two players minus an arm. The natural consequence was that the quartet were matched. The players were–AWP Charteris and E Mitchell, Sub Nigel; and EP Coles and J Kirby, Geduld. This is the first record of four one-armed players in a foursome.

● At Joliet Country Club, USA, a one-armed golfer named DR Anderson drove a ball 300 yards.

● Left-handedness, but playing golf right-handed, is prevalent and for a man to throw with his left hand and play golf right-handed is considered an advantage, for Bobby Jones, Jesse Sweetser, Walter Hagen, Jim Barnes, Joe Kirkwood and more recently Johnny Miller were eminent golfers who were left-handed and ambidextrous.

● In a practice round for the Open Championship in July, 1927, at St Andrews, Len Nettlefold and Joe Kirkwood changed sets of clubs at the 9th hole. Nettlefold was a left-handed golfer and Kirkwood right-handed. They played the last nine, Kirkwood with the left-handed clubs and Nettlefold with the right-handed clubs.

● The late Harry Vardon, when he was at Ganton, got tired of giving impossible odds to his members and beating them, so he collected a set of left-handed clubs, and rating himself at scratch, conceded the handicap odds to them. Vardon won with the same monotonous regularity.

● Ernest Jones, who was professional at the Chislehurst Club, was badly wounded in the war in France in 1916 and his right leg had to be amputated below the knee. He persevered with the game, and before the end of the year he went round the Clacton course balanced on his one leg in 72. Jones later settled in the United States where he built fame and fortune as a golf teacher.

● Major Alexander McDonald Fraser of Edinburgh had the distinction of holding two handicaps simultaneously in the same club—one when he played left-handed and the other for his right-handed play. In medal competitions he had to state before teeing up which method he would use.

● Former England test cricketer Brian Close once held a handicap of 2 playing right-handed, but after retiring from cricket in 1977 decided to apply himself as a left-handed player. His left-handed handicap at the time of his retirement was 7. Close had the distinction of once beating Ted Dexter, another distinguished test cricketer and noted golfer twice in the one day, playing right-handed in the morning and left-handed in the afternoon.

Blind and Blindfolded Golf

● Major Towse, VC, whose eyes were shot out during the South African War, 1899, was probably the first blind man to play golf. His only stipulations when playing were that he should be allowed to touch the ball with his hands to ascertain its position, and that his caddie could ring a small bell to indicate the position of the hole. Major Towse, who played with considerable skill, was also an expert oarsman and bridge player. He died in 1945, aged 81.

● The United States Blind Golfers' Association in 1946 promoted an Invitational Golf Tournament for the blind at Country Club, Inglewood, California. This competition is held annually and in 1953 there were 24 competitors and 11 players completed the two rounds of 36 holes. The winner was Charley Boswell who lost his eyesight leading a tank unit in Germany in 1944.

● In July, 1954, at Lambton Golf and Country Club, Toronto, the first international championship for the blind was held. It resulted in a win for Joe Lazaro, of Waltham, Mass, with a score of 220 for the two rounds. He drove the 215-yard 16th hole and just missed an ace, his ball stopping 18 inches from the hole. Charley Boswell, who won the United States Blind Golfers' Association Tournament in 1953, was second. The same Charles Boswell, of Birmingham, Alabama holed the 141-yard 14th hole at the Vestavia CC in one in October, 1970.

● Another blind person to have holed-in-one was American Ben Thomas while on holiday in South Carolina in 1978.

● Rick Sorenson undertook a bet in which, playing 18 holes blindfolded at Meadowbrook Course, Minneapolis, on 25th May, 1973, he was to pay $10 for every hole over par and receive $100 for every hole in par or better. He went round in 86 losing $70 on the deal.

● Alfred Toogood played in a match at Sunningdale in 1912 blindfolded. His opponent was Tindal Atkinson, and Toogood was beaten 8 and 7. I Millar, Newcastle-upon-Tyne, played a match, blindfolded, against AT Broughton, Birkdale, at Newcastle, County Down, in 1908. Putting matches while blindfolded have been frequently played.

● Wing-Commander *Laddie* Lucas, DSO, DFC, MP, played over Sandy Lodge golf course in Hertfordshire on 7th August, 1954, completely blindfolded and had a score of 87.

Trick Shots

● Joe Kirkwood, Australia, specialised in public exhibitions of trick and fancy shots. He played all kinds of strokes after nominating them, and among his ordinary strokes nothing was more impressive than those hit for low flight. He played a full drive from the face of a wristlet watch, and the toe of a spectator's shoe, full strokes at a suspended ball, and played for slice and pull at will, and exhibited his ambidexterity by playing left-handed strokes with right-handed clubs. Holing six balls, stymieing, a full shot at a ball catching it as it descended, and hitting 12 full shots in rapid succession, with his face turned away from the ball, were shots among his repertoire. In playing the last named Kirkwood placed the balls in a row, about six inches apart, and moved quickly along the line. Kirkwood, who was born in Australia lived for many years in America. He died in November, 1970 aged 73.

● Joe Ezar, an American professional, who specialised in trick shots, included in his show a number of clowning acts with balls.

● On 2nd April, 1894, a 3-ball match was played over Musselburgh course between Messrs Grant, Bowden, and Waggot, the clubmaker, the latter teeing on the face of a watch at each tee. He finished the round in 41 the watch being undamaged in any way.

● At Westbrook, USA, in 1901, ET Knapp drove a ball off the top of a hen's egg. The egg was slightly dented on one end to afford a hold for the ball.

● At Esher, 23rd November, 1931, George Ashdown, the club professional, in a match played his tee shot for each of the 18 holes from a rubber tee strapped to the forehead of Miss Ena Shaw.

● EA Forrest, a South African professional in a music hall turn of trick golf shots, played blindfolded shots, one being from the ball teed on the chin of his recumbent partner.

● The late Paul Hahn, an American trick specialist could hit four balls with two clubs. Holding a club in each hand he hit two balls, hooking one and slicing the other with the same swing. Hahn had a repertoire of 30 trick shots. In 1955 he flew completely round the world, exhibiting in 14 countries and on all five continents.

Balls Colliding and Touching

● Competing in the 1980 Corfu International Championship, Sharon Peachey drove from one tee and her ball collided in mid-air with one from a competitor playing another hole. Her ball ended in a pond.

● Playing in the Cornish team championship in 1973 at West Cornwall GC Tom Scott-Brown, of West Cornwall GC, and Paddy Bradley, of Tehidy GC, saw their drives from the fourth and eighth tees collide in mid-air.

● Playing in a 4-ball match at Guernsey Club in June, 1966, all four players were near the 13th green from the tee. Two of them–DG Hare and S Machin–chipped up simultaneously; the balls collided in mid-air; Machin's ball hit the green, then the flagstick, and dropped into the hole for a birdie 2.

● Playing to the 13th hole on Carnoustie course on 6th October, 1911, the Rev AR Taylor's ball met in the air the ball of another player, who had struck off from the 14th tee. The balls met so square–if one can use such an expression–that they rebounded a long distance straight back towards the players who hit them.

● In May, 1926, during the meeting of the Army Golfing Society at St Andrews, Colonel Howard and Lieutenant-Colonel Buchanan Dunlop, while playing in the foursomes against J Rodger and J Mackie, hit full iron shots for the seconds to the 16th green. Each thought he had to play his ball first, and hidden by a bunker the players struck their balls simultaneously. The balls, going towards the hole about 20 yards from the pin and five feet in the air, met with great force and dropped either side of the hole five yards apart.

● In 1972, before a luncheon celebrating the centenary of the Ladies' Section of Royal Wimbledon GC, a 12-hole competition was held during which two competitors, Mrs L. Champion and Mrs A McKendrick, driving from the eighth and ninth tees respectively, saw their balls collide in mid-air.

● In 1928, at Wentworth Falls, Australia, Dr Alcorn and EA Avery, of the Leura Club, were playing with the professional, E Barnes. The tee shots of Avery and Barnes at the 9th hole finished on opposite sides of the fairway. Unknown to each other, both players hit their seconds (chip shots) at the same time. Dr Alcorn, standing at the pin, suddenly saw two balls approaching the hole from different angles. They met in the air and then dropped into the hole.

● At Rugby, 1931, playing in a 4-ball match, H Fraser pulled his drive from the 10th tee in the direction of the ninth tee. Simultaneously a club member, driving from the ninth tee, pulled his drive. The tees were about 350 yards apart. The two balls collided in mid-air.

● Two golf balls, being played in opposite directions, collided in flight over Longniddry Golf Course on 27th June, 1953. Immediately after Stewart Elder, of Longniddry, had driven from the third tee, another ball, which had been pulled off line from the second fairway, which runs alongside the third, struck his ball about 20 feet above the ground. SJ Fleming, of Tranent, who was playing with Elder, heard a loud crack and thought Elder's ball had exploded. The balls were found undamaged about 70 yards apart.

Three and Two Balls Dislodged by One Shot

● In 1934 on the short 3rd hole (now the 13th) of Olton Course, Warwickshire, JR Horden, a scratch golfer of the club, sent his tee shot into long wet grass a few feet over the back of the green. When he played an *explosion* shot three balls dropped on to the putting green, his own and two others.

● AM Chevalier, playing at Hale, Cheshire, March, 1935, drove his ball into a grass bunker, and when he reached it there was only part of it showing. He played the shot with a niblick and to his amazement not one but three balls shot into the air. They all dropped back into the bunker and came to rest within a foot of each other. Then came another surprise. One of the *finds* was of the same manufacture and bore the same number as the ball he was playing with.

● Playing to the 9th hole, at Osborne House Club, Isle of Wight, George A Sherman lost his ball which had sunk out of sight on the sodden fairway. A few weeks later, playing from the same tee, his ball again was plugged, only the top showing. Under a local rule he lifted his ball to place it, and exactly under it lay the ball he had lost previously.

Balls in Strange Places

● Playing at the John o' Gaunt Club, Sutton, near Biggleswade (Bedfordshire), a member drove a ball which did not touch the ground until it reached London–over 40 miles away. The ball landed in a vegetable lorry which was passing the golf course and fell out of a package of cabbages when they were unloaded at Covent Garden, London.

● In the English Open Amateur Stroke Play at Moortown in 1974, Nigel Denham, a Yorkshire County player, in the first round saw his overhit second shot to the 18th green bounce up some steps into the clubhouse. His ball went through an open door, ricochetted off a wall and came to rest in the men's bar, 20 feet from the windows. As the clubhouse was not out of bounds Denham decided to play the shot back to the green and opened a window 4 feet by 2 feet through which he pitched his ball to 12 feet from the flag. (Several weeks later the R&A declared that Denham should have been penalised two shots for opening the window. The clubhouse was an immovable obstruction and no part of it should have been moved.)

● In the Open Championship at Sandwich, 1949, Harry Bradshaw, Kilcroney, Dublin, at the 5th hole in his second round, drove into the rough and found his ball inside a beer bottle with the neck and shoulder broken off and four sharp points sticking up. Bradshaw, if he had treated the ball as in an unplayable lie might have been involved in a disqualification, so he decided to play it where it lay. With his blaster he smashed the bottle and sent the ball about 30 yards. The hole, a par 4, cost him 6.

● Kevin Sharman of Woodbridge GC hit a low, very straight drive at the club's 8th hole in 1979. After some minutes' searching, his ball was found embedded in a plastic sphere on top of the direction post.

● On the Dublin Course, 16th July, 1936, in the Irish Open Championship, AD Locke, the South African, played his tee shot at the 100-yard 12th hole, but the ball could not be found on arrival on the green. The marker removed the pin and it was discovered that the ball had been entangled in the flag. It dropped near the edge of the hole and Locke holed the short putt for a *birdie* two.

● On a London course a player found his ball inside a derelict boot.

● While playing a round on the Geelong Golf Club Course, Australia, Easter, 1923, Captain Charteris topped his tee shot to the short 2nd hole, which lies over a creek with deep and steep clay banks. His ball came to rest on the near slope of the creek bank. He elected to play the ball as it lay, and took his niblick. After the shot, the ball was nowhere to be seen. It was afterwards found embedded in a mass of gluey clay stuck fast to the face of the niblick. It could not be shaken off. Charteris did what was afterwards approved by the R&A, cleaned the ball and dropped it behind without penalty.

● In October, 1929, at Blackmoor Golf Club, Bordon, Hants, a player driving from the first tee holed out his ball in the chimney of a house some 120 yards distant and some 40 yards out of bounds on the right. The owner and his wife were sitting in front of the fire when they heard a rattle in the chimney and were astonished to see a golf ball drop into the fire.

● A similar incident occurred in an inter-club match between Musselburgh and Lothianburn at Prestongrange in 1938 when a member of the former team hooked his ball at the 2nd hole and gave it up for lost. To his amazement a woman emerged from one of the houses adjacent to this part of the course and handed back the ball which she said had come down the chimney and landed on a pot which was on the fire.

● In July, 1955, J Lowrie, starter at the Eden Course, St Andrews, witnessed a freak shot. A visitor drove from the first tee just as a north-bound train was passing. He sliced the shot and the ball disappeared through an open window of a passenger compartment. Almost immediately the ball emerged again, having been thrown back on to the fairway by a man in the compartment, who waved a greeting which presumably indicated that no one was hurt.

● Many balls have been hit into the pockets of spectators, stewards, other competitors and even the players' own pockets. They have also been found in trouser turn-ups and in the folds of sweaters and waterproofs.

● At Coombe Wood Golf Club a player hit a ball towards the 16th green where it landed in the vertical exhaust of a tractor which was mowing the fairway. The greenkeeper was somewhat surprised to find a temporary loss of power in the tractor. When sufficient compression had built up in the exhaust system, the ball was forced out with tremendous velocity, hit the roof of a house nearby, bounced off and landed some three feet from the pin on the green.

● There have been many occasions when misdirected shots have finished in strange places after an unusual line of flight and bounce. At Ashford, Middlesex, John Miller, aged 69, hit his tee shot out of bounds at the 12th hole (237 yards). It struck a parked car, passed through a copse, hit more cars, jumped a canopy, flew through the clubhouse kitchen window, finishing in a cooking stock-pot, without once touching the ground. Mr Miller had previously done the hole-in-one on four occasions.

Balls Hit to and from Great Heights

● In 1798 two Edinburgh golfers undertook to drive a ball over the spire of St Giles' Cathedral, Edinburgh, for a wager. Mr Sceales, of Leith, and Mr Smellie, a printer, were each allowed six shots and succeeded in sending the balls well over the weather-cock, a height of more than 160 feet from the ground.

● Some years later Donald McLean, an Edinburgh lawyer, won a substantial bet by driving a ball over the Melville Monument in St Andrew Square, Edinburgh–height, 154 feet.

● Tom Morris in 1860, at the famous bridge of Ballochmyle, stood in the quarry beneath and, from a stick elevated horizontally, attempted to send golf balls over the bridge. He could raise them only to the pathway, 400 feet high, which was in itself a great feat with the gutta ball.

● Captain Ernest Carter, on 28th September, 1922, drove a ball from the roadway at the 1st tee on Harlech Links against the wall of Harlech Castle. The embattlements are 200 feet over the level of the roadway, and the point where the ball struck the embattlements was 180 yards from the point where the ball was teed. Captain Carter, who was laid odds of £100 to £1, used a baffy.

● In 1896 Freddie Tait, then a subaltern in the Black Watch, drove a ball from the Rookery, the highest building on Edinburgh Castle, in a match against a brother officer to hole out in the fountain in Princes Street Gardens 350 feet below and about 300 yards distant.

● Prior to the 1977 Lâncome Tournament in Paris, Arnold Palmer hit three balls from the second stage of the Eiffel Tower, over 300 feet above ground. The longest was measured at 403 yards. One ball was hooked and hit a bus but no serious damage was done as all traffic had been stopped for safety reasons.

● Long drives have been made from mountain peaks, across the gorge at Victoria Falls, from the Pyramids, high buildings in New York, and from many other similar places. As an illustration of such freakish *drives* a member of the New York Rangers' Hockey Team from the top of Mount Edith Cavell, 11,033 feet high, drove a ball which struck the Ghost Glacier 5,000 feet below and bounced off the rocky ledge another 1,000 feet–a total drop of 2,000 yards. Later, in June, 1968, from Pikes Peak, Colorado (14,110 feet), Arthur Lynskey hit a ball which travelled 200 yards horizontally but 2 miles vertically.

Remarkable Shots

● Remarkable shots are to be numbered as the grains of sand; around every 19th hole, legends are recalled of astounding shots. One shot is commemorated by a memorial tablet at the 17th hole at the Lytham and St Annes Club. It was made by Bobby Jones in the final round of the Open Championship in 1926. He was partnered by Al Watrous, another American player. They had been running neck and neck and at the end of the third round, Watrous was just leading Jones with 215 against 217. At the 16th Jones drew level then on the 17th he drove into a sandy lie in broken ground. Watrous reached the green with his second. Jones took a mashie-iron (the equivalent to a No. 4 iron today) and hit a magnificent shot to the green to get his 4. This remarkable recovery unnerved Watrous, who 3-putted, and Jones, getting another 4 at the last hole against 5, won his first Open Championship with 291 against Watrous' 293. The tablet is near the spot where Jones played his second shot.

● Arnold Palmer (USA), playing in the second round of the Australian Wills Masters tournament at Melbourne, in October, 1964, hooked his second shot at the 9th hole high into the fork of a gum tree. Climbing 20 feet up the tree, Palmer, with the head of his No. 1 iron reversed, played a *hammer* stroke and knocked the ball some 30 yards forward, followed by a brilliant chip to the green and a putt.

● In the foursome during the Ryder Cup at Moortown in 1929, Joe Turnesa hooked the American side's second shot at the last hole behind the marquee adjoining the clubhouse. Johnny Farrel then pitched the ball over the marquee on to the green only feet away from the pin and Turnesa holed out for a 4.

● In 1922, Peter Robertson, Braid Hills, Edinburgh, holed the Road Hole, St Andrews (17th, Old Course) in two shots, a drive and a brassie.
● Lew Worsham, in the *World's Championship* at Tam O'Shanter, 9th August, 1953, at the last hole from a distance of 135 yards, holed a wedge shot for a two at the 410-yard hole. This incredible shot made him the winner by one stroke and gave him the greatest jackpot in golf at that time, $25,000. The difference between the first and third prizes was equivalent to £5,000.

Miscellaneous Incidents and Strange Golfing Facts

● Gary Player of South Africa was honoured by his country by having his portrait on new postage stamps which were issued on 12th December, 1976. It was the first time a specific golfer had ever been depicted on any country's postage stamps. In 1981 the US Postal Service introduced stamps featuring Bobby Jones and Babe Zaharias. They are the first golfers to be thus honoured by the United States.
● Prior to the 1976 Curtis Cup Match, members of the British Isles and United States teams were presented to the Queen at Buckingham Palace, the first occasion this has occurred.
● In February, 1971, the first ever golf shots on the moon's surface were played by Captain Alan Shepard, commander of the Apollo 14 spacecraft. Captain Shepard hit two balls with an iron head attached to a makeshift shaft. With a one-handed swing he claimed he hit the first ball 200 yards aided by the reduced force of gravity on the moon. Subsequent findings put this distance in doubt. The second was a shank. Acknowledging the occasion the R&A sent Captain Shepard the following telegram: *Warmest congratulations to all of you on your great achievement and safe return. Please refer to Rules of Golf section on etiquette, paragraph 6, quote–before leaving a bunker a player should carefully fill up all holes made by him therein, unquote.* Shepard presented the club to the USGA Museum in 1974.
● Charles (Chick) Evans competed in every US Amateur Championship held between 1907 and 1962 by which time he was 72 years old. This amounted to 50 consecutive occasions discounting the six years of the two World Wars when the championship was not held.
● In the winning the 1977 US Open at Southern Hills CC, Tulsa, Oklahoma, Hubert Green had to contend with a death threat. Coming off the 14th green in the final round, he was advised by USGA officials that a phone call had been received saying that he would be killed. Green decided that play should continue and happily he went on to win, unharmed.
● It was discovered at the 1977 USPGA Championship that the clubs with which Tom Watson had won the Open Championship and the US Masters earlier in the year were illegal, having grooves which exceeded the permitted specifications. The set he used in winning the 1975 Open Championship were then flown out to him and they too were found to be illegal. No retrospective action was taken.
● Mrs Fred Daly, wife of the former Open champion, saved the clubhouse of Balmoral GC, Belfast, from destruction when three men entered the professionals' shop on 5th August, 1976 and left a bag containing a bomb outside the shop beside the clubhouse when refused money. Mrs Daly carried the bag over to a hedge some distance away where the bomb exploded 15 minutes later. The only damage was broken windows. On the same day several hours afterwards, Dungannon GC in Co Tyrone suffered extensive damage to the clubhouse from terrorist bombs. Co Down GC, proposed venue of the 1979 home international matches suffered bomb damage in May that year and through fear for the safety of team members the 1979 matches were cancelled.
● A small plane crash-landed on the 18th fairway during the pro-am preceding the 1978 Hawaiian Open, coming to rest about 50 yards short of the 18th green where American professional Jim Simons and his amateur partners were putting.
● The Army Golfing Society and St Andrews on 21st April, 1934, played a match 200-a-side, the largest golf match ever played. Play was by foursomes. The Army won 58, St Andrews 31 and 11 were halved.
● In an issue of the PGA Official Journal in 1976, it was stated *Ladies will now be permitted full privileges of membership including sectional and national voting at Annual Meetings; be eligible for election to committees and be permitted to play in section events off the back tees with the men.*
● The government of Fiji, where the 1978 men's and women's world amateur team championships were held in 1978, refused to allow teams from South Africa to compete because of South Africa's apartheid policy.
● On the eve of the 1979 World Cup in Greece, Dale Hayes and Hugh Baiocchi, representing South Africa, were compelled to withdraw when the Greek government, on a demand from the anti-apartheid committee of the United Nations, refused

permission for them to compete.

● John Cook, professional at Brickendon Grange, and former English Amateur champion, narrowly escaped death during an attempted coup against King Hassan of Morocco in July 1971. Cook had been playing in a tournament arranged by King Hassan, a keen golfer, and was at the King's birthday party in Rabat when rebels broke into the party demanding that the king give up his throne. Cooke and many others present were taken hostage. Over 200 people were killed before King Hassan surrendered minutes before the group which included Cook was due for the firing squad.

● When playing from the 9th tee at Lossiemouth golf course in June, 1971, Martin Robertson struck a Royal Navy jet aircraft which was coming in to land at the nearby airfield. The plane was not damaged.

● In November, 1983, as John Gallacher (39), a 9-handicap player, was driving off at the 9th hole at Machrihanish in a winter league 4-ball tie, a Hercules transport plane from Germany coming in to land at the adjoining RAF airfield passed overhead, and was struck by Gallacher's ball. A mark that could have been caused by a golf ball was subsequently found on the aircraft's fuselage, but Gallacher's ball was never found.

● In view of the increasing number of people crossing the road (known as Granny Clark's Wynd) which runs across the first and 18th fairways of the Old Course, St Andrews, as a right of way, the St Andrews Links committee decided in 1969 to control the flow by erecting traffic lights, with appropriate green for go, yellow for caution and red for stop. The lights are controlled from the starter's box on the first tee. Golfers on the first tee must wait until the lights turn to green before driving off and a notice has been erected at the Wynd warning pedestrians not to cross at yellow or stop.

● A traffic light for golfers was also installed in 1971 on one of Japan's most congested courses. After putting on the uphill 9th hole of the Fukuoka course in Southern Japan, players have to switch on a go-ahead signal for following golfers waiting to play their shots to the green.

● A 22-year-old professional at Brett Essex GC, Brentwood, David Moore, who was playing in the Mufulira Open in Zambia in 1976, was shot dead it is alleged by the man with whom he was staying for the duration of the tournament. It appeared his host then shot himself.

● The first round of the Amateur Championship in 1887 and again in 1953, both strangely enough at Hoylake, consisted of only one tie, all the other competitors receiving byes. The first round of the English Ladies' in 1924 and the Scottish Amateur in 1932 also consisted of only one tie.

● Patricia Shepherd won the ladies' club championship at Turriff GC in 1980 for the 22nd consecutive time.

● Mrs Jackie Mercer won the South African Ladies' Championship in 1979, 31 years after her first victory in the event as Miss Jacqueline Smith.

● At Geelong course, near Melbourne, Australia, while FD Walter was driving off, the strap of his wrist watch broke. The watch fell on top of the ball at the exact moment of impact. The player picked up the watch unbroken 40 yards down the fairway.

● Lee Trevino, a few days after winning the 1972 Open Championship, thereby thwarting Jack Nicklaus' attempt to win all four major championships in the one year, was knocked down and kicked during an exhibition match at Scioto CC, Ohio. Ohio is the state in which Nicklaus was born and where he used to live.

● After playing a tee shot at Heworth, County Durham, in 1968, Mrs Helen Paterson found her ball impaled on the peg tee.

● During the Royal and Ancient medal meeting on 25th September, 1907, a member of the Royal and Ancient drove a ball which struck the sharp point of a hatpin in the hat of a lady who was crossing the course. The ball was so firmly impaled that it remained in position. The lady was not hurt.

● At the Northwest Park course, Washington, USA in 1975, fighting broke out between the members of two 4-ball games. One group claimed the other was holding them back and the other group claimed the group behind had driven into them. Clubs were used as weapons resulting in serious injuries including a fractured skull. Police had to be called.

● At a court in Inglewood, California, in 1978, Jim Brown was convicted of beating and choking an opponent during a dispute over where a ball should have been placed on the green.

● FG Tait, at St Andrews, drove a ball through a man's hat and had to pay the owner 5/- (25p) to purchase a new one. At the end of the round he was grumbling to old Tom Morris about the cost of this particular shot, when the sage of St Andrews interrupted him: *Eh, Mr Tait, you ought to be glad it was only a new hat you had to buy, and not an oak coffin.*

● During the Northern Ireland troubles a home-made hand grenade was found in a bunker at Dungannon GC, Co Tyrone, on

Sunday, 12th September, 1976.

● At Rhymney and Tredegar, South Wales, on 10th September, 1934, the hard felt hat of a pedestrian who was crossing the fairway was hit by the drive of a golfer. The man fell, but his head was only slightly grazed. The ball had gone right through the hat and was found 20 yards farther on.

● To mark the centenary of the Jersey Golf Club in 1978, the Jersey Post Office issued a set of four special stamps featuring Jersey's most famous golfer, Harry Vardon. The background of the 13p stamp was a brief biography of Vardon's career reproduced from the Golfer's Handbook.

● In 1977, William Collings tried to hit his ball over a grapefruit tree at Eldorado CC, Palm Desert, California. He hit the shot thin and the ball became embedded in a grapefruit.

● Three boys who searched a pond at Buchanan Castle GC, near Glasgow, one day in 1975, found 604 old balls which were valued at £8. However, they were charged and found guilty of stealing the balls and fined £10, £20 and £30 in court.

● Driving from the 11th tee at the Belfairs Golf Course, Leigh, on 4th September, 1935, the player heard a startled exclamation. Hurrying to investigate, he discovered that his shot, at 160 yards distance, had smashed the pipe of a man taking a stroll over the course. The ball had cut the pipe clean out of the man's mouth without hurting him.

● At the international between British and American women golfers for the Curtis Cup at Chevy Chase, Washington, USA, on 27th September, 1934, a number of State policemen stood around the first tee. They were in their shirt-sleeves, with revolvers and cartridges in their ammunition belts and handcuffs dangling from their hips.

● Forty-one-year-old John Mosley went for a round of golf at Delaware Park GC, Buffalo, New York, in July, 1972. He stepped on to the first tee and was challenged over a green fee by an official guard. A scuffle developed, a shot was fired and Mosley, a bullet in his chest, died on the way to hospital. His wife was awarded $131,250 in an action against the City of Buffalo and the guard. The guard was sentenced to 7½ years for second-degree manslaughter.

● When three competitors in a pro-am event in 1968 in Pennsylvania were about to drive from the 16th tee, two bandits (one with pistol) suddenly emerged from the bushes, struck one of the players and robbed them of wrist watches and $300.

● A 5-hole miniature course has been built on top of a seven-storey garage at Pompano Beach, Florida.

● In the 1932 Walker Cup match at Brooklyn, Leonard Crawley succeeded in denting the cup. An errant iron shot to the 18th green hit the cup, which was on display outside the clubhouse.

● A mayor in an English Midland town at the opening ceremony of a new course had to putt on the 18th green. The unfortunate man missed the ball completely.

● There has rarely been a man who played better golf that the late Harry Vardon played in 1898 and 1899. All the same, at Wheaton, Illinois, in the American Open Championship, in 1900, which he won, he made the humiliating mistake of regarding a six-inch putt with such indifference that, in trying to knock it gaily into the hole, he missed the ball entirely, and struck his club into the ground, thus counting a stroke.

● Three golf officials appeared in court in Johannesburg, South Africa, accused of violating a 75-year-old Sunday Observance Law by staging the final round of the South African PGA championship on Sunday, 28th February, 1971. The championship should have been completed on the Saturday but heavy rain prevented any play.

● At the 11th hole at Troon in the 1962 Open Championship, Max Faulkner carelessly tapped the ball against his foot, and the hole ultimately cost him 11 strokes.

● In the Open Championship of 1876, at St Andrews, Bob Martin and David Strath tied at 176. A protest was lodged against Strath alleging he played his approach to the 17th green and struck a spectator. The Royal and Ancient ordered the replay, but Strath refused to play off the tie until a decision had been given on the protest. No decision was given and Bob Martin was declared the Champion.

● At Rose Bay, New South Wales, on 11th July, 1931, DJ Bayly MacArthur, on stepping into a bunker, began to sink. MacArthur, who weighed 14 stone, shouted for help. He was rescued when up to the armpits. He had stepped on a patch of quicksand, aggravated by excess of moisture.

● The late Bobby Cruickshank was the victim of his own jubilation in the 1934 US Open at Merion. In the 4th round while in with a chance of winning he half-topped his second shot at the 11th hole. The ball was heading for a pond in front of the green but instead of ending up in the water it hit a rock and bounced on to the green. In his delight Cruickshank threw his club into the air only to receive a resounding blow on the head as it returned to earth.

● A dog with an infallible nose for finding lost golf balls was, in 1971, given honorary membership of the Waihi GC, Hamilton, New Zealand. The dog, called Chico, was trained to search for lost balls, to be sold back to the members, the money being put into the club funds.

● By 1980 Waddy, an 11-year-old beagle

belonging to Bob Inglis, the secretary of Brokenhurst Manor GC, had found over 35,000 golf balls.

● On 6th July, 1938, N Bathie, playing on Downfield, Dundee, was about to hit an iron shot when the ball was suddenly whisked away. Then the player was spun completely round. He had been caught in the fringe of a whirlwind. The whirlwind lifted a wooden shelter 60 feet into the air and burst it into smithereens over the 11th green. A haystack was uprooted and a tree razed.

● In a match over Queen's Park, Bournemouth, Archie Compston, finding that his ball had finished in the branches of a tree, played a shot with his club at the full stretch of his arms, above his head. The result was a wonderful shot which almost reached the green.

● Donald Grant, a competitor in the Dornoch Open Amateur Tournament in 1939, cycled from London and tied for second place in the first round of the competition with 74.

● Herbert M Hepworth, Headingley, Leeds, Lord Mayor of Leeds in 1906, scored one thousand holes in 2, a feat which took him 30 years to accomplish. It was celebrated by a dinner in 1931 at the Leeds club. The first 2 of all was scored on 12th June, 1901, at Cobble Hall Course, Leeds, and the 1,000th in 1931 at Alwoodley, Leeds. Hepworth died in November, 1942.

● Mrs Joy Traill of Kloof CC, South Africa, holed from off the green six times in a round there on 20th October, 1977 at the age of 70.

● Nineteen-year-old Ron Stutesman holed chips at five consecutive holes in a round at Orchard Hills CC, Washougal, USA in January, 1978.

● On Saturday, 12th July, 1975, 16-year-old, 3-handicap Colin Smith, of Cowal GC broke his handicap on three different courses. Playing in the Glasgow Youths' Championship at Cawder he scored 73 over the Cawder Course (SSS 71) and 70 over the Keir Course (SSS 68). Then in the evening in the Poseidon Trophy at his home club he scored 70 (SSS 70).

● At Carnoustie in the first qualifying round for the 1952 Scottish Amateur Championship a competitor drove three balls in succession out of bounds at the 1st hole and thereupon withdrew.

Strange Local Rules

● The Duke of Windsor, who played on an extraordinary variety of the world's courses, once took advantage of a local rule at Jinja in Uganda and lifted his ball from a hippo's footprint without penalty.

● Another local rule in Uganda read: *If a ball comes to rest in dangerous proximity to a crocodile, another ball may be dropped.*

● At the Glen Canyon course in Arizona a local rule provides that *If your ball lands within a club length of a rattlesnake you are allowed to move the ball.* It would be no surprise if players under these circumstances just gladly opted for the *unplayable ball* rule.

● Signs that have been seen in Africa intimate that *Elephants have right of way* and warn *You are in wild animal country*.

● The 6th hole at Koolan Island GC, Western Australia also serves as a local air strip and a local rule reads *Aircraft and vehicular traffic have right of way at all times.*

● A local rule at the RAF Waddington GC reads *When teeing off from the 2nd, right of way must be given to taxi-ing aircraft.*

Record Scoring

Open Championship

Lowest 72 Hole Aggregate
268 by Tom Watson at Turnberry in 1977.

Lowest 72 Holes

Birkdale	275	Tom Watson in 1983
Carnoustie	279	Tom Watson and Jack Newton in 1975
Hoylake	278	Roberto De Vicenzo in 1967
Lytham	277	Bob Charles and Phil Rodgers in 1963
Muirfield	271	Tom Watson in 1980
Prince's	283	Gene Sarazen in 1932
St Andrews	276	Sevariano Bellesteros in 1984
Sandwich	276	B Rogers in 1981
Troon	276	Arnold Palmer in 1962 and Tom Weiskopf in 1973
Turnberry	268	Tom Watson in 1977

Lowest 18 Holes
63 by Mark Hayes at Turnberry in 1977, by Isao Aoki at Muirfield in 1980 and Greg Norman at Turnberry in 1986.

Scores of 64

Horacio Carbonetti, Muirfield	1980
Hubert Green, Muirfield	1980
Tom Watson, Muirfield	1980
Craig Stadler, Birkdale	1983
Graham Marsh, Birkdale	1983
Christy O'Connor Jr, Sandwich	1985
Seve Ballesteros, Turnberry	1986

Scores of 65

Henry Cotton, Sandwich	1934
Eric Brown, Lytham	1958
Leopoldo Ruiz, Lytham	1958
Peter Butler, Muirfield	1966
Christy O'Connor, Lytham	1969
Neil Coles, St Andrews	1970
Jack Nicklaus, Troon	1973
Jack Newton, Carnoustie	1975
Angel Gallardo, Turnberry	1977
Tom Watson, Turnberry (twice)	1977
Jack Nicklaus, Turnberry	1977
Tommy Horton, Turnberry	1977
Bill Longmuir, Lytham	1979
Severiano Ballesteros, Lytham	1979
Gordon Brand, Sandwich	1981

Lowest 18 Holes

Birkdale	64	Craig Stadler and Graham Marsh in 1983
Carnoustie	65	Jack Newton in 1975
Hoylake	67	Roberto De Vicenzo and Gary Player in 1967
Lytham	65	Eric Brown and Leopoldo Ruiz in 1958; Christy O'Connor in 1969; Bill Longmuir and Severiano Ballesteros in 1979
Muirfield	63	Isao Aoki in 1980
Prince's	68	Arthur Havers in 1932
St Andrews	65	Neil Coles in 1970
Sandwich	64	Christy O'Connor Jr in 1985
Troon	65	Jack Nicklaus in 1973
Turnberry	63	Mark Hayes in 1977 Greg Norman in 1986

Lowest 9 Holes
28 by Denis Durnian at Birkdale (outward half of second round) in 1983.

29 by Tom Haliburton and Peter Thomson at Lytham (outward half) in 1963; by Tony Jacklin at St Andrews (outward half) in 1970; and by Bill Longmuir at Lytham (outward half) in 1979.

Scores of 30

Eric Brown, St Andrews (outward half)	1957
Eric Brown, Lytham (inward half)	1958
Leopoldo Ruiz, Lytham (outward half)	1958
Phil Rodgers, Muirfield (inward half)	1966
Jimmy Kinsella, Birkdale (outward half)	1971
Lee Trevino, Muirfield (inward half)	1972
Harry Bannerman, Muirfield (outward half)	1972
Bert Yancey, Troon (outward half)	1973
Christy O'Connor, jun, Birkdale (outward half)	1976
Arnold Palmer, Turnberry (inward half)	1977
Jack Nicklaus, Lytham (outward half)	1979
Denis Watson, Muirfield (inward half)	1980
Tom Watson, Muirfield (inward half)	1980
Lee Trevino, Birkdale (outward half)	1983
Sam Torrance, St Andrews (outward half)	1984

Christy O'Connor, Sandwich (outward half) 1985
Tsuneyuki Nakajima, Turnberry (inward half) 1986

Lowest First 36 Holes
132 by Henry Cotton at St George's in 1934.

Lowest Final 36 Holes
130 by Tom Watson at Turnberry in 1977.

Lowest 18 Holes by an Amateur
66 by Frank Stranahan at Troon in 1950.

Lowest Score in Qualifying Rounds
63 by Frank Jowle at St Andrews in 1955; by Peter Thomson at Lytham in 1958; by Maurice Bembridge at Delamere Forest in 1967; and by Malcolm Gunn at Gullane No 2 in 1972.

Lowest Qualifying Round by an Amateur
65 by Ronnie Shade at St Andrews in 1964.

Other Outstanding Scoring
In the Southern Section Qualifying competition for the Open Championship in 1926 played at Sunningdale, Bobby Jones had rounds of 68 and 66. His round of 66 (six under par) was regarded as an almost perfect round. Never over par, he missed only one green in regulation or better figures–the short 13th where he was a few yards short but achieved par with a single putt. His round consisted of 33 out, 33 in. He had 33 putts and 33 other shots, which shows the high quality of his golf through the green.

Dale Hayes of South Africa had rounds of 68 and 64 over Hesketh in the qualifying rounds for the 1971 Open Championship. Hayes at the time was aged 19 years and one week and had been a professional for only eight months.

European PGA Tour

Lowest 72 Hole Aggregate
260 by Kel Nagle (Australia) in the Irish Hospital Tournament at Woodbrook in 1961.

Lowest 18 Holes
61 by Tom Haliburton in the first round of a professional tournament at Worthing in 1952; by Tony Coop and Hugh Boyle in the Senior Service tournament at Dalmahoy East in 1965; and by Peter Butler in the Bowmaker tournament at Sunningdale in 1967.

Lowest 9 Holes
27 by Jose Canizares of Spain for the first 9 holes in the third round of the 1978 Swiss Open at Crans sur Sierre.

Lowest 36 holes
126 by Tom Haliburton in the Spalding tournament at Worthing in 1952.

Lowest 54 Holes
194 by John Lister (New Zealand) in the Gallaher Ulster Open at Shandon Park in 1970 and by Vicente Fernandez (Argentina) in the Benson and Hedges Festival at Fulford in 1975.

Largest Winning Margin
17 strokes by Bernhard Langer in the 1979 Cacharel Under-25s' Championship.

Miscellaneous British

Andrew Brooks recorded a 72-hole aggregate of 259 in winning the Skol (Scotland) tournament at Williamwood in 1974.

Playing on the ladies' course (4,020 yards) at Sunningdale on 26th September, 1961, Arthur Lees, the professional there, went round in 52, 10 under par. He went out in 26 (2, 3, 3, 4, 3, 3, 3, 3, 2) and came back in 26 (2, 3, 3, 3, 2, 3, 4, 3, 3).

AE Smith, the Woolacombe Bay professional, recorded a score of 55 in a game there with a club member on 1st January, 1936. The course measured 4,248 yards. Smith went out in 29 and came back in 26 finishing with a hole in one at the 18th hole.

Other low scores recorded in Britain are by CC Aylmer, an English International who went round Ranelagh in 56; George Duncan, Axenfels in 56; Harry Bannerman, Banchory in 56 in 1971; Ian Connelly, Welwyn Garden City in 56 in 1972; James Braid, Hedderwick near Dunbar in 57; H Hardman, Wirral in 58; Norman Quigley, Windermere in 58 in 1937; Robert Webster, Eaglescliffe in 58, in 1970.

Harry Weetman scored 58 in a round at Croham Hurst on 30th January, 1956. The course measured 6,171 yards.

D Sewell had a round of 60 in an Alliance Meeting at Ferndown, Bournemouth, a full-size course. He scored 30 for each half and had a total of 26 putts.

In September 1986, Jeffrey Burn, handicap 1 of Shrewsbury GC scored 60 in a club competition, made up of 8 birdies, an eagle and 9 pars. He was 30 out and 30 home and no 5 on his card.

Andrew Sherborne, a 20-year-old amateur, went round Cirencester in 60 strokes.

Dennis Gray completed a round at Broome Manor, Swindon (6,906 yards, SSS 73) in the summer of 1976 in 60 (28 out, 32 in).

Playing over Aberdour on 13th June, 1936, Hector Thomson, British Amateur champion, 1936, and Jack McLean, former Scottish Amateur champion, each did 61 in the second round of an exhibition. McLean in his first round had a 63, which gave him an aggregate 124 for 36 holes.

Steve Tredinnick in a friendly match against business tycoon Joe Hyman scored a 61 over West Sussex (6,211 yards) in 1970. It included a hole in one at the 12th (198 yards) and a 2 at the 17th (445 yards).

Another round of 61 on a full-size course was achieved by 18-year-old Michael Jones on his home course, Worthing GC (6,274 yards) in the first round of the President's Cup in May, 1974.

In the Second City Pro-Am tournament in 1970, at Handsworth, Simon Fogarty did the second 9 holes in 27 against the par of 36.

In the second round of a 36-hole open amateur competition at Sandyhills GC on 10th September, 1978, Barclay Howard completed the last 9 holes in 27.

RH Corbett, in 1916, in the semi-final of the Tangye Cup at Mullim did 9 holes in 27 as did Dr James Stothers of Ralston over the 2,056 yards 9-hole course at Carradale, Argyll, during the summer of 1971. In each case the total was made up of nine 3s.

US Open

Lowest 72 Hole Aggregate
272 by Jack Nicklaus at Baltusrol in 1980.

Lowest 18 Holes
63 by Johnny Miller at Oakmont in 1973 in the final round and by Jack Nicklaus and Tom Weiskopf at Baltusrol in 1980, both in the first round.

Lowest 9 Holes
30 by Jimmy McHale in 1947, Arnold Palmer in 1960, Ken Venturi in 1964, Bob Charles and Tom Shaw in 1971, and Raymond Floyd in 1980.

Lowest 36 Holes
134 by Jack Nicklaus at Baltusrol in 1980.

Lowest 54 Holes
204 by Jack Nicklaus and Isao Aoki at Baltusrol in 1980.

US Professional events

Lowest 72 Hole Aggregate
257 (60, 68, 64, 65) by Mike Souchak in the 1955 Texas Open.

Lowest 18 Holes
59 by Sam Snead in the third round of the Greenbrier Open (Sam Snead Festival) at White Sulphur Springs, West Virginia in 1959 and by Al Geiberger in the second round of the 1977 Danny Thomas Memphis Classic at Colonial CC when preferred lies were in operation.

Lowest 9 Holes
27 by Mike Souchak in the 1955 Texas Open and by Andy North in the 1975 BC Open.

Lowest First 36 Holes
126 by Tommy Bolt in 1954. (On the US mini-tour a 36-hole score of 123 was achieved by Bob Risch in the 1978 Mesa Centennial Open.)

Lowest Final 36 Holes
122 by Sam Snead in the Greenbrier Open (Sam Snead Festival) in 1959. On the USPGA Tour it is 125 by Ron Streck in the 1978 Texas Open.

Lowest 54 Holes
189 by Chandler Harper in the 1954 Texas Open (last three rounds).

192 by Bob Gilder in the 1982 Westchester Classic (first three rounds).

Largest Winning Margin
16 strokes by J Douglas Edgar in the 1919 Canadian Open Championship and by Bobby Locke in the 1948 Chicago Victory National Championship.

Miscellaneous USA

The lowest scores recorded for 18 holes in America are 55 by EF Staugaard in 1935 over the 6,419 yards Montebello Park, California, and 55 by Homero Blancas in 1962 over the 5,002 yards Premier course in Longview, Texas. Staugaard in his round had 2 eagles, 13 birdies and 3 pars.

Equally outstanding is a round of 58 (13 under par) achieved by a 13-year-old boy, Douglas Beecher, on 6th July, 1976 at Pitman CC, New Jersey. The course measured 6,180 yards from the back tees, and the middle tees, off which Douglas played, were estimated by the club professional to reduce the yardage by under 180 yards.

In 1941 at a course in Portsmouth, Virginia, measuring 6,100 yards, Chandler Harper scored 58.

Jack Nicklaus in an exhibition match at Breakers Club, Palm Beach, California, in 1973 scored 59 over the 6,200 yards course.

Ben Hogan, practising on a 7,006-yard course at Palm Beach, Florida, went round in 61–11 under par.

The lowest 9-hole score in America is 25, held jointly by Bill Burke over the second half of the 6,384 yards Normandie CC, St Louis in May, 1970 at the age of 29; by Daniel Cavin who had seven 3s and two 2s on the par 36 Bill Brewer Course, Texas in September, 1959; and by Douglas Beecher over the second half of Pitman CC, New Jersey on 6th July, 1976 at the amazingly young age of 13. The back 9 holes of the Pitman course measured 3,150 yards (par 35) from the back tees, but even though Douglas played off the middle tees, the yardage was still over 3,000 yards for the 9 holes. He scored 8 birdies and 1 eagle.

Horton Smith scored 119 for two consecutive rounds in winning the Catalina Open in California in December, 1928. The course, however, measured only 4,700 yards.

National Opens—excluding Europe and USA

Lowest 72 Hole Aggregate
255 by Peter Tupling in the Nigerian Open at Lagos, 1981.

Lowest 36 Hole Aggregate
124 (18 under par) by Sandy Lyle in the 1978 Nigerian Open at Ikoyi GC, Lagos. (Lyle was in his first year as a professional.)

Lowest 18 Holes
59 by Gary Player in the second round of the 1974 Brazilian Open at Gavea GC (6,185 yards), Rio de Janeiro.

Professional Events—excluding GB and USA

Lowest 72 Hole Aggregate
260 (66, 62, 69, 63) by Bob Charles in the Spalding Masters at Tauranga, New Zealand, in 1969.

Lowest 18 Hole Aggregate
60 by Australian Billy Dunk at Merewether, NSW in November, 1970.

Lowest 9 Hole Aggregate
27 by American Bill Brask at Tauranga in the New Zealand PGA in 1976.

Miscellaneous—excluding GB and USA

Tony Jacklin won the 1973 Los Lagartos Open with an aggregate of 261, 27 under par.

Henry Cotton in 1950 had a round of 56 at Monte Carlo (29 out, 27 in).

In a Pro-Am tournament prior to the 1973 Nigerian Open, British professional David Jagger went round in 59.

Max Banbury recorded a 9-hole score of 26 at Woodstock, Ontario, playing in a competition in 1952.

Women

The lowest score recorded on a full-size course by a woman is 62 by Mary (Mickey) Wright of Dallas, Texas. This was achieved on the Hogan Park course (6,286 yards) at Midland, Texas, in November, 1964. It was equalled by 16-year-old Rae Rothfelder on 9th July, 1978 at Diamond Oak G&CC, Fort Worth, Texas, a course measuring 6,124 yards.

The lowest 72-hole score on the US Ladies' PGA circuit is 271 by Hollis Stacy in the 1977 Rail Muscular Dystrophy.

The lowest 9-hole score on the US Ladies' PGA circuit is 29, first achieved by Marlene Bauer Hagge in 1971 and equalled by Carol Mann (1975), Pat Bradley (1978 and again in 1979), Alexandra Reinhardt (1978), and Silvia Bertolaccini (1979).

The lowest score for 36 holes on the USLPGA circuit is 131 achieved by Kathy Martin in the 1976 Birmingham Classic and by Silvia Bertolaccini in the 1977 Lady Keystone Open.

The lowest 9-hole score on the WPGA circuit is 30 by Susan Moon at Valbonne in 1979.

In the Women's World Team Championship in Mexico in 1966, Mrs Belle Robertson, playing for the British team, was the only player to break 70. She scored 69 in the third round.

At Westgate-on-Sea GC (measuring 5,002 yards), Wanda Morgan scored 60 in an open tournament in 1929.

Since scores cannot properly be taken in match play no stroke records can be made in match play events. Nevertheless we record here two outstanding examples of low scoring in the finals of national championships. Mrs Catherine Lacoste de Prado is credited with a score of 62 in the first round of the 36-hole final of the 1972 French Ladies' Open Championship at Morfontaine. She went out in 29 and came back in 33 on a course measuring 5,933 yards.

In the final of the English Ladies' Championship at Woodhall Spa in 1954, Frances Stephens (later Mrs Smith) did the first nine holes against Elizabeth Price (later Mrs Fisher) in 30. It included a hole-in-one at the 5th. The nine holes measured 3,280 yards.

Amateur National Championships

The following examples of low scoring cannot be regarded as genuine stroke play records since they took place in match play.

Nevertheless they are recorded here as being worthy of note.

Michael Bonallack in beating D Kelley in the final of the English championship in 1968 at Ganton did the first 18 holes in 61 with only one putt under two feet conceded. He was out in 32 and home in 29. The par of the course was 71.

Charles McFarlane, playing in the fourth round of the Amateur Championship at Sandwich in 1914 against Charles Evans did the first nine holes in 31, winning by 6 and 5.

This score of 31 at Sandwich was equalled on several occasions in later years there. Then, in 1948, Richard Chapman of America went out in 29 in the fourth round eventually beating Hamilton McInally, Scottish Champion in 1937, 1939 and 1947, by 9 and 7.

In the fourth round of the Amateur Championship at Hoylake in 1953, Harvie Ward, the holder, did the first nine holes against Frank Stranahan in 32. The total yardage for the holes was 3,474 yards and included one hole of 527 yards and five holes over 400 yards. Ward won by one hole.

Francis Ouimet in the first round of the American Amateur Championship in 1932 against George Voigt did the first nine holes in 30. Ouimet won by 6 and 5.

Low scores by Amateurs in Open competitions

The 1970 South African Dunlop Masters Tournament was won by an amateur, John Fourie, with a score of 266, 14 under par. He led from start to finish with rounds of 65, 68, 65, 68, finally winning by six shots from Gary Player.

Jim Ferrier, Manly, won the New South Wales championship at Sydney in 1935 with 266. His rounds were: 67, 65, 70, 64, giving an aggregate 16 strokes better than that of the runner-up. At the time he did this amazing score Ferrier was 20 years old and an amateur.

Most holes below par

EF Staugaard in a round of 55 over the 6,419 yards Montbello Park, California, in 1935, had 2 eagles, 13 birdies and 3 pars.

American Jim Clouette scored 14 birdies in a round at Longhills GC, Arkansas, in 1974. The course measured 6,257 yards.

Jimmy Martin in his round of 63 in the Swallow-Penfold at Stoneham in 1961 had 1 eagle and 11 birdies.

In the Ricarton Rose Bowl at Hamilton, Scotland, in August, 1981, Wilma Aitken, a women's amateur internationalist, had 11 birdies in a round of 64, including 9 consecutive birdies from the 3rd to the 11th.

Mrs Donna Young scored 9 birdies and 1 eagle in one round in the 1975 Colgate European Women's Open.

Consecutive holes below par

Lionel Platts had 10 consecutive birdies from the 8th to 17th holes at Blairgowrie GC during a practice round for the 1973 Sumrie Better-Ball tournament.

Roberto De Vicenzo in the Argentine Centre of the Republic Championship in April, 1974 at the Cordoba GC, Villa Allende, broke par at each of the first 9 holes. (By starting his round at the 10th hole they were in fact the second 9 holes played by Vicenzo.) He had 1 eagle (at the 7th hole) and 8 birdies. The par for the 3,602 yards half was 37, completed by Vicenzo in 27.

Nine consecutive holes under par have been recorded by Claude Harmon in a friendly match over Winged Foot GC, Mamaroneck, NY, in 1931; by Les Hardie at Eastern GC, Melbourne, in April, 1934; by Jimmy Smith at McCabe GC, Nashville, Tenn, in 1969; by Jim DeForest on a 9-hole sand-green course at New Salem, North Dakota, in August, 1974; by 13-year-old Douglas Beecher, in 1976, at Pitman CC, New Jersey; and by Rick Sigda at Greenfield CC, Mass, in 1979.

TW Egan in winning the East of Ireland Championship in 1962 at Baltray had 8 consecutive birdies (2nd to 9th) in the third round.

On the USPGA circuit 8 consecutive holes below par have been achieved twice–by Bob Goalby in the 1961 St Petersburg Open, and by Fuzzy Zoeller in the 1976 Quad Cities Open.

Seven successive birdies have been recorded by Peter Thomson at Wentworth in the 1958 Dunlop; by Bernard Hunt at Wentworth in the 1958 Daks; by Angel Miguel at Wentworth (East) in the 1960 Daks; by Peter Butler at Fulford in the 1971 Benson and Hedges; by Peter Townsend at Wentworth in 1974 Viyella PGA; and by Brian Waites at the RAC in the 1980 Bob Hope Classic.

The United States Ladies' PGA record is 7 consecutive holes below par achieved by Carol Mann in the Borden Classic at Columbus, Ohio in 1975.

Miss Wilma Aitken recorded 9 successive birdies (from the 3rd to the 11th) in the 1981 Ricarton Rosebowl.

Low scoring rarities

In the qualifying rounds of the 1956 Dunlop Tournament at Sunningdale, Arthur Lees, the resident professional, played 27 consecutive holes without taking more than a 4 at any hole. His first round was 65 and his second 69.

At Standerton GC, South Africa, in May, 1937, FF Bennett, playing for Standerton against Witwatersrand University, did the 2nd hole, 110 yards, in three 2s and a 1. Standerton is a 9-hole course, and in the match Bennett had to play four rounds.

In 1973 in the 36-hole Club Championship at Mufulira GC, Zambia, Amateur HG McQuillan, completed two rounds in 65 and 66 for a winning score of 131.

In 1957 a four-ball comprising HJ Marr, E Stevenson, C Bennett and WS May completed the 2nd hole (160 yards) in the grand total of 6 strokes. Marr and Stevenson both holed in 1 while Bennett and May both made 2.

The old Meadow Brook Club of Long Island, USA, had five par 3 holes and George Low in a round there in the 1950s scored 2 at each of them.

In a friendly march on a course near Chicago in 1971, assistant professional Tom Doty (23 years) had a remarkable low run over four consecutive holes: 4th (500 yards) 2; 5th (360 yards, dogleg) 1; 6th (175 yards) 1; 7th (375 yards) 2.

RW Bishop, playing in the Oxley Park, July medal competition in 1966, scored three consecutive 2s. They occurred at the 12th, 13th and 14th holes which measured 151, 500 and 136 yards respectively.

In the 1959 PGA Close Championship at Ashburnham, Bob Boobyer score five 2s in one of the rounds.

American Art Wall scored three consecutive 2s in the first round of the US Masters in 1974. They were at the 4th, 5th and 6th holes, the par of which was 3, 4 and 3.

Nine consecutive 3s have been recorded by RH Corbett in 1916 in the semi-final of the Tangye Cup; by Dr James Stothers of Ralston GC over the 2,056 yards 9-hole course at Carradale, Argyll during the summer of 1971; by Irish internationalist Brian Kissock in the Homebright Open at Carnalea GC, Bangor in June, 1975; and by American club professional Ben Toski.

The most consecutive 3s in a British PGA event is seven by Eric Brown in the Dunlop at Gleneagles (Queen's Course) in 1960.

Hubert Green scored eight consecutive 3s in a round in the 1980 US Open.

The greatest number of 3s in one round in a British PGA event is 11 by Brian Barnes in the 1977 Skol Lager tournament at Gleneagles.

Fewest putts

The lowest known number of putts in one round is 14, achieved by Colin Collen-Smith in a round at Betchworth Park, Dorking in June, 1947. He single-putted 14 greens and chipped into the hole on four occasions. Professional Richard Stanwood in a round at Riverside GC, Pocatello, Idaho on 17th May, 1976 took 15 putts, chipping into the hole on 5 occasions. Several instances of 16 putts in one round have been recorded in friendly games.

For 9 holes, the fewest putts is 5 by Ron Stutesman for the first 9 holes at Orchard Hills G&CC, Washington, USA in 1978.

Walter Hagen in nine consecutive holes on one occasion took only seven putts. He holed long putts on seven greens and chips at the other two holes.

In competitive stroke rounds in Britain and Ireland, the lowest known number of putts in one round is 18, in a medal round at Portpatrick Dunskey GC, Wilmslow GC professional Fred Taggart is reported to have taken 20 putts in one round of the 1934 Open Championship. Padraigh Hogan (Elm Park), when competing in the Junior Scratch Cup at Carlow in 1976, took only 20 putts in a round of 67.

The fewest putts in a British PGA event is believed to be 22 by Bill Large in a qualifying round over Moor Park High Course for the 1972 Benson and Hedges Match Play.

Overseas, outside the United States of America, the fewest putts is 19 achieved by Robert Wynn (GB) in a round in the 1973 Nigerian Open and by Mary Bohen (US) in the final round of the 1977 South Australian Open at Adelaide.

The USPGA record for fewest putts in one round is 18, held by Sam Trahan in the 4th round of the 1979 Philadelphia Classic. For 9 holes the USPGA record is 8, by Jim Colbert in the 1967 Greater Jacksonville Open.

The fewest putts recorded for a 72-hole USPGA tournament is 94 by George Archer in the 1980 Heritage Classic.

The fewest putts recorded by a woman is 17, by Joan Joyce in the Lady Michelob tournament, Georgia in May, 1982.

Index

Advertisers' Index